Thomas Hardy: *The Poetic Structure*

Novelists and Their World

General Editor: Graham Hough
Professor of English at the University of Cambridge

Thomas Hardy

The Poetic Structure

Jean R. Brooks

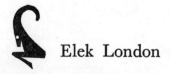 Elek London

© 1971 Jean R. Brooks

ISBN 0 236 15416 8

Published in Great Britain by
ELEK BOOKS LIMITED
2 All Saints Street London N 1

Printed in Great Britain by
W & J Mackay & Co Ltd
Chatham

Contents

I   Introduction: The Heart and Inner Meaning   7

II   'Life offers—to Deny': The Philosophical Poems   25

III   'The Homeliest of Heart-Stirrings': Shorter Lyrics   49

IV   The Elegies: *Poems of 1912–13*   81

V   Dramatic and Narrative Lyrics   105

VI   Poetry and Narrative: Minor Fiction   137

VII   *Far from the Madding Crowd:* A Pastoral Novel   158

VIII   *The Return of the Native:* A Novel of Environment   177

IX   *The Mayor of Casterbridge:* A Novel of Character and Environment   196

X   *The Woodlanders:* A Novel of Assimilation   216

XI   *Tess of the d'Urbervilles:* A Novel of Assertion   233

XII   *Jude the Obscure:* A Novel of Affirmation   254

XIII   *The Dynasts:* An Epic-Drama of Evolution   276

XIV   Afterwards   302

       Bibliography   319

       Index   328

Acknowledgements

Quotations from Hardy's published works are made by kind permissions of The Trustees of the Hardy Estate and Macmillan London Ltd., and the Macmillan Company of New York.

My thanks are due to the staff of the Dorset County Museum, the British Museum, the Fitzwilliam Museum, Cambridge, the Bodleian Library, Oxford, and the Birmingham City Museum and Art Gallery, for permission to examine manuscripts.

My inexpressible thanks go to the help and encouragement of my family and friends; especially to the constructive criticism of my husband, Professor Harold F. Brooks, to fellow Hardeians Dr C. J. P. Beatty of the University of Oslo and Mr R. F. Dalton, former Curator of the Dorset County Museum; and to the students of Rose Bruford College, whose lively discussions and appreciation of Hardy from the viewpoint of drama students contributed to my chapter on *The Dynasts* and the final assessment of Hardy's place in the modern world.

Jean R. Brooks
Welwyn Garden City
April 1971

I

Introduction: The Heart and Inner Meaning

Hardy scholarship is a flourishing industry. The reader may question the need for yet another book of criticism. But for an author whose place in literature has always been controversial, constant reassessment is essential to keep the balance between modern and historical perspective. The strong disagreements about what is 'good' or 'bad' in Hardy's work prove only the relativity of judgement and the vitality of the author. Time has revealed Hardy's anti-realistic devices to be imaginative truths about cosmic Absurdity rather than the author's incompetence. Modern depth psychology has vindicated his profound intuition of character in terms of irrational drives. A. J. Guérard rightly draws attention to features which modern preoccupations have taught the reader to appreciate:

'We are in fact attracted by much that made the post-Victorian realist uneasy: the inventiveness and improbability, the symbolic use of reappearance and coincidence, the wanderings of a macabre imagination, the suggestions of supernatural agency; the frank acknowledgement that love is basically sexual and marriage usually unhappy; the demons of plot, irony and myth.'

(Thomas Hardy: The Novels and Stories)

But Guérard, like many other modern critics, assumes a too inclusive scepticism of values which the modern failure of nerve can ignore, but cannot displace.

'And we are repelled or left indifferent by what charmed that earlier generation: the regionalist's ear for dialect, the botanist's eye for the minutiae of field and tree, the architect's eye for ancient mansions, and the farmer's eye for sheepshearings; the pretentious meditation on Egdon Heath; the discernible architecture of the novels and the paraphrasable metaphysic; the Franciscan tenderness and sympathy—and, I'm afraid, the finally unqualified faith in the goodness of a humanity more sinned against than sinning.'

One must respect the values of Hardy both as an individual and as a product of his age to avoid the temptation to assess his work according to twentieth-century obsessions. In the Overworld perspective of *The Dynasts*, these will stand as local cults. An age which suspects Henchard's strong affection for Farfrae, which can define Giles Winterborne's sacrifice for Grace's reputation as 'close to absurd' and the selfless self-control of Oak, Winterborne and Venn as an 'immature refusal to accept life and enjoy it', reveals its own limitations rather than Hardy's. The things which Guérard finds repellent, in fact, constitute Hardy's intense celebration of life in all its physical manifestations and metaphysical mystery in face of the full look at the worst advocated in 'In Tenebris II'—less repellent than the modern trend to reduce plain goodness to perverted ulterior motive. Recent biographical conjecture stemming from Lois Deacon's unproved contention in *Providence and Mr Hardy* that Hardy's relationship with his cousin Tryphena was incestuous and produced a son, distorts both the man and his work by attributing to this cloudy episode both his lifelong—and constitutional—tragic vision and much of the material in his works.* To substitute biography, conjectural or otherwise, for imaginative truth is to replace the profound mystery of the suffering artist's creative indictment of the cosmos with a cause small and personal enough for unawakened minds to grasp.

The critic's first concern at this point of time (1971) is to stress once more Hardy's power—the poetic power—to make real those great commonplaces of heroic, though doomed, human nature which the modern Iago thinks he has seen through because, if they exist, their beauty makes him ugly. The reader will find them given weight by critics of an earlier generation: Lascelles Abercrombie, Edmund Blunden, David Cecil, H. C. Duffin, Lionel Johnson, Arthur McDowall. Other critics, in the light of modern social and psychological theory, have profitably explored certain aspects of Hardy's complex richness. W. R. Rutland and H. C. Webster set him in the context of nineteenth-century thought. Evolution through natural selection, the origin of man, the long stretch of geological time behind him, the displacement of a transcendent personal Deity by immanent process without mind or purpose, the

*Research done on the photographers responsible for the two portraits alleged to be of Hardy's son (*Providence and Mr. Hardy*; Lois Deacon, *Tryphena's Portrait Album*, Toucan Press, 1967) seems to prove that both had gone out of business at the address on the reverse of the portraits long before the alleged son could have reached the age of the subjects portrayed. See R. F. Dalton, 'Thomas Hardy's Alleged Son', *Notes and Queries*, ccxiii, July 1968, and C. J. P. Beatty, *Notes and Queries*, Vol. 17, No. ix, Sept. 1970.

'Higher Criticism' of sacred texts, Herbert Spencer's philosophy of the Unknowable, John Stuart Mill's essays on the religious and social liberty of the individual—all left their mark on Hardy's vision of man's place in nature. Douglas Brown stresses the destructive effect on a stable peasant culture of the revolution in industry that joined with the revolution in thought to define man as product and victim of a soulless mechanism. The insecurity of a displaced peasantry contributes to several of the tragedies, notably *The Woodlanders, Tess of the d'Urbervilles* and *Jude the Obscure*. A. J. Guérard and Richard Carpenter have rescued the grotesque, anti-realistic elements from derision and shown them to be powerful expressionistic images of existential absurdity and the irrationality of subconscious drives. R. C. R. Morrell has corrected the view that Hardy weights the scales unfairly against his characters, by drawing attention to the recurrent rhythm of reprieves and second chances, and the responsibility of the human will to direct fate at those neutral moments 'when the mighty necessitating forces . . . happen to be in equilibrium'.

The poetry has received less critical attention than the novels, though the balance has recently been redressed by Samuel Hynes's *The Pattern of Hardy's Poetry* and Kenneth Marsden's *The Poems of Thomas Hardy: A Critical Introduction*. Both have useful chapters on Hardy's revisions, and the kind of 'development' to be expected in a poet whose eight volumes of verse, most of them containing work widely separated in date of composition, were published in the last thirty years of a very long creative life. Hynes devotes his study to a demonstration of a common (but not invariable) principle of order in Hardy's poetry—'the eternal conflict between irreconcilables'. Like J. G. Southworth's earlier study, and many recent articles and chapters on the poetry, Hynes's book leaves a general impression of Hardy's weaknesses rather than his strengths. Marsden's introduction, however, is a model of balanced judgement in this respect as in others, clarifying clichés and misconceptions about Hardy's poetic method, philosophy, and reputation.

Hardy's flaws as poet, novelist, and dramatist have attracted enough attention. The present study concentrates on a body of successful work which is large enough to give him the status of major artist: a fair proportion of the poems, a few short stories, six major novels, and *The Dynasts*, in the definitive published form in which Hardy left them to the public.

The critic who follows a host of capable predecessors wonders at times whether anything new can be said. One can only reiterate that in a new encounter with Hardy the light falls differently from of old. When the obvious has been repeated, a need has been felt to stress the basic qualities that may have been pushed aside in the excitement of following a specialized trail. When the obvious has been passed over, other critics have explored it thoroughly and space is limited.

What are the basic qualities of Hardy's creative power to give new beauty to old commonplaces? They are an amalgam of traditional moulds and personal vision, harmonized by poetic associative structures and a deeply-felt poetic emotion that affirms and links subjective experience to the universal commonplaces of the race—birth, death, love, suffering, work.

'Nobody can deny Hardy's power—the true novelist's power—to make us believe that his characters are fellow-beings driven by their own passions and idiosyncrasies, while they have—and this is the poet's gift—something symbolical about them which is common to us all.
(Virginia Woolf, 'The Novels of Thomas Hardy',
The Common Reader, Second Series)

The poet's gift has not gone unremarked, but what it means to Hardy's art has not been explored in great detail in the light of modern poetic structure. One could, without much profit, compare some of Hardy's poems with their prosed counterparts to discover the link between poet and poetic novelist. Different kinds of poetry—philosophical, lyrical, elegiac, narrative/dramatic—isolate microscopically various ingredients which unite in the novels to produce the true Hardeian flavour. They crystallize a certain mood or moment of vision which are emotional arias in the novels. 'Beyond the Last Lamp', 'Tess's Lament', 'Proud Songsters', and 'A Light Snow-fall after Frost' (*Tess of the d'Urbervilles*); 'The Pine Planters' and 'In a Wood' (*The Woodlanders*); 'Childhood among the Ferns' and 'Midnight on the Great Western' (*Jude the Obscure*) are fine poems in their own right, because Hardy has added or subtracted features which re-create them in terms of lyric. Usually, however, the prosed poems are more successful in the novels, where they are an organic part of narrative structure and emotional accumulation of detail. To compare 'The Puzzled Game-Birds' with the end of Chapter XLI of *Tess* proves the futility of computer exercises.

The poetic strain is more complex. It is a way of looking at and ordering experience. It includes the ballad qualities of Hardy's narrative, poetic presentation of event and character, his poetic sense of place and history in the re-creation of Wessex, his imaginative blending of new Victorian science and old folk superstition, and the Gothic strangeness of his vision and style. It includes a sensuous apprehension of daily life that embraces the contemplative and metaphysical. Virginia Woolf reminds us ('Impassioned Prose', *Granite and Rainbow*) that the novelist has his hands full of the facts of daily living, so 'how can we ask [him] . . . to modulate beautifully off into rhapsodies about Time and Death . . .?' Hardy's achievement of this difficult transition vindicates him as a poetic novelist.

The poetic impulse, expressing the basic but multiple faces of experience, defines the Hardeian quality. He thought of himself as 'an English poet who had written some stories in prose', and in prose tried to preserve the poetry.

'He had mostly aimed at keeping his narratives close to natural life and as near to poetry in their subject as the conditions would allow, and had often regretted that those conditions would not let him keep them nearer still.'

(*Life*)

It reconciles all the seeming contradictions of Hardy's subject, style, and philosophy by giving them equal weight but no synthesis. Hardy anticipates the modern anguish of unresolved tensions in the stylized forms which contain the undirected chaos of life; the traditional character types who reveal Freudian subtleties of psychology; grand gestures punctured by absurd and vulgar intrusions; the dichotomies of common and uncommon, simple and complex, protest and acquiescence. Yeats's definition of the double face of poetry is appropriate to the powerful tensions that constitute the Hardy vision:

'The passion . . . comes from the fact that the speakers are holding down violence or madness—'down Hysterica passio'. All depends on the completeness of the holding down, on the stirring of the beast underneath . . . Without this conflict we have no passion only sentiment and thought.'

(Letter to Dorothy Wellesley, Aug. 5, 1936)

The multiple perspective of poetry is more often a strength than a weakness. It gives simultaneously the personal and formal vision; the subjective feel of experience falling on 'all that side of the mind

11

which is exposed in solitude' (Virginia Woolf, op. cit., *Granite and Rainbow*) and the bold epic relief of those characters who 'stand up like lightning conductors to attract the force of the elements' (op. cit., *The Common Reader*) in their mythopoeic relation to time, death, and fate, both enhanced and diminished by the time-marked Wessex scene that rings their actions. It is the source of Hardy's distinctive ironic tone and structure, his tragi-comedy, his blend of fatalism and belief in the power of chance, and his profound sense of tragedy.

Hardy's ironic mode is the reverse face of his compassion. The pattern of what is runs in tension with the pattern of what ought to be according to human values. Mismatings, mistimings and undesired substitutions for an intended effect point to the 'if only' structure of Hardeian irony. If only Newson had entered the tent a few minutes earlier or later; if only Angel had danced with Tess on the green; if only Tess had not been 'doomed to be seen and coveted that day by the wrong man' instead of by the 'missing counterpart' who 'wandered independently about the earth waiting in crass obtuseness till the late time came'. Hardy's notorious use of coincidence to demonstrate cosmic absurdity is shadowed by its traditional function as an agent of cosmic design. As Barbara Hardy points out in *The Appropriate Form*, the use of coincidence in *Jane Eyre* is directed by Charlotte Brontë's belief in Providence; in *Jude the Obscure* by Hardy's belief in the absence of Providence. In Victorian melodrama the 'heroine' of *Tess of the d'Urbervilles* would have been rescued providentially by the 'hero' from the 'villain'. Hardy has neither hero, villain, nor Providence, and the alternative reasons he suggests for Tess's seduction point to the impenetrable mystery of the cosmic scheme.

When passionate personal emotion counterpoints the control of a traditional form, the ironic double vision thus obtained questions the unthinking acceptance of cosmic and social arrangements implied by the patterns Hardy took over from popular narrative and drama. Received morality is shaken and measured by the morality of compassion; poetic and Divine justice by the honesty that allows Arabella and Fitzpiers to flourish while Jude and Winterborne suffer unjustly and die, in a world where personal worth does not decide the issue. The internal tensions between the betrayed-maid archetype of balladry and the fallen woman of Victorian moral literature, set against the intense subjective world of Tess, provoke a complex reaction to her story. The psychological study of a frustrated woman strains against the breathless action of the sensa-tion novel in *Desperate Remedies*. The Golden-Age pastoral exposes the cosmic dissonances of *Far from the Madding Crowd* and *The Wood-landers*. The expected end of the story in marriage or death takes on a bitter irony in *Jude the Obscure*, where the marriage of Sue is more tragic than the death of Jude. The hymn metres behind some of Hardy's poetic questionings of the First Cause; the ballad of revenge behind his ballads of generous action; the popular con-ception of romantic love behind the cruel, blind, sexual force that sweeps his characters to ecstasy, madness, suffering, and death, make the ironic mode of double vision inseparable from style. The puzzled game-birds in the poem of that name sing their bewilder-ment at man's inconsistent cruelty in a graceful triolet. 'The Voice' sets Hardy's grief for his wife's death to the gay tune of a remem-bered dance. The harsh physical facts of death deflate the pattern of the consolation poem in which 'Transformations' is written. Marsden points out that the beautiful patterns made on the page by 'The Pedigree' bring out the subtle variations and irregularities of structure which enact personal defiance of the realization of heredity to which the poem moves—'I am merest mimicker and counterfeit!—'

Hardy's multiple vision of experience brings him close to the modern Absurdist form of tragi-comedy or comi-tragedy.

'If you look beneath the surface of any farce you see a tragedy; and, on the contrary, if you blind yourself to the deeper issues of a tragedy you see a farce.'

(*Life*)

The comic court-room scene of *The Mayor of Casterbridge* in which the furmity hag works Henchard's downfall, the comic constables who take the foreground while Lucetta lies dying from the shock of the skimmity ride their incompetence has been unable to prevent; the rustics who discuss, at length, folklore remedies as Mrs Yeo-bright lies mortally wounded from snakebite; the two lovers who quarrel about their precedence in Elfride's affections when they have travelled unknowingly with her dead body; the farcical con-junctions of Ethelberta's three lovers; the love-sick de Stancy's un-dignified eavesdropping on Paula's gymnastic exercises in pink flannel; the Kafka-like distortions of figure or scene, stress the ironic deflation of romance, heroism, and tragedy by the objective incursion of absurdity; without, however, denigrating the value of romance, heroism, and suffering. 'All tragedy is grotesque—if you allow yourself to see it as such' (*Life*).

In all his work Hardy's personal voice, with its humane values, its Gothic irregularities, its human contradictions and rough edges, its commonness and uncommonness, strains against the rigidities of traditional patterns and expectations. The first two paragraphs of *The Mayor of Casterbridge*, for example, can provide the mixture to be found in all the other novels, *The Dynasts*, and most of the poems—the amalgam of homely simplicity, awkward periphrasis, triteness, and sharp sensuous vision that invests an ordinary scene with the significance of myth and Sophoclean grandeur. The dissonance of the multiple vision dramatically enacts Hardy's metaphysic of man's predicament as a striving, sensitive, imperfect individual in a rigid, non-sentient, absurd cosmos, which rewards him only with eternal death.

The predicament is tragic. A poetic ambiguity of perspective is inherent in the nature of tragedy. It is part of the texture of human hope.

'The end of tragedy . . . is to show the dignity of man for all his helpless littleness in face of the universe, for all his nullity under the blotting hand of time.'

(Bonamy Dobrée, *The Lamp and the Lute*)

In Hardy's tragedy one finds the tragic protagonist, defined for his role by a tragic greatness (not in high estate, as in Sophocles and Shakespeare, but in character alone) that intensifies the sense of life, and flawed by a tragic vulnerability that unfits him for the particular tragic situation he has to face. Jude's sexual and self-degrading impulses are disastrous in view of the obstacles to higher education for working men. Henchard's rash and inflexible temper cannot ride the agricultural changes that overtake Casterbridge. In the tragic universe human errors become tragic errors which co-operate with Fate (those circumstances within and without, which man did not make and cannot unmake, incarnated as natural forces, the clockwork laws of cause and effect, the workings of chance, coincidence, and time, irrational impulses, man-made conventions, and the search for happiness) to bring evil out of his goodness and good intentions, and to bring down on him, and innocent people connected with him, tragic suffering and catastrophe out of all proportion to its cause. The irresponsible sending of a valentine, the concealment of a seduction until the day of the wedding to another man, the careless sealing of love letters and choice of an untrustworthy messenger, release forces of death and destruction which inspire tragic terror at the contemplation of the painful mystery of the workings of inexorable law. Tragic pity is aroused, as Dobrée points out, 'not because someone suffers, but because something fine is bruised and broken'—something too sensitively organized for an insentient world of defect.

But the sense of tragic waste is tempered by tragic joy, because in the tragic confrontation with futility and absurdity Hardy affirms some of the highest values men and women can achieve.

'The great writer of tragedy manages to convey that though this be the truth, it is well that men should behave thus and thus; that in spite of all the seeming cruelty and futility of existence, one way of life is better than another; that Orestes is right and Clytemnestra wrong, that Othello is fairer than Iago. Not that fault is to be imputed to the wrongdoer; he also is a pebble of fate, destined to play his part in the eternal drama of good and evil.'

(Dobrée: op. cit.)

These values remain unchanged when the people who embodied them are destroyed, and whether the gods are alive or dead. Giles Winterborne's death may contain a criticism of his former backwardness and of Victorian sexual hypocrisy, but in its essence it celebrates the selfless love that can see further than temporary satisfaction of physical desire to the preservation of Grace's image untarnished to posterity. Modern permissiveness cannot change his nobility or the value of his suffering. Giles, Clym, Henchard, Tess, Jude, and Sue are not fulfilled in the eyes of the world. But their tragedy asserts the values for which they suffered (even Eustacia, whose selfishness limits our sympathy, asserts the value of self-assertion), stripped of all recommendations of success.

Hardy's tragic figures, rooted in an unconscious life-process more deterministic than their own, try to mould their lives according to human values, personal will, feeling, and aspiration. Though their self-assertion is overcome by the impersonality of the cosmos, including those instinctive drives they share with the natural world, their endeavour to stamp a humane personal design on cosmic indifference makes them nobler than what destroys them. Hardy had no time for Nietzsche. 'To model our conduct on Nature's apparent conduct, as Nietzsche would have taught, can only bring disaster to humanity' (*Life*). His characters' close and conscious relationship to unconscious nature defines the hope that is contained in the tragic suffering. Hardy's greatest novels are tragic actions which demonstrate the incomplete evolutionary state of man, a throb of the universal pulse, suffering as the pioneer of a more compassionate cosmic awareness—the hope towards which the whole of *The Dynasts* moves. His poems are the cries of tragic love, tragic error, tragic injustice, tragic waste, and tragic awareness with which tragic poets and dramatists from Aeschylus to Beckett have defined the sense of life.

> HAMM: What's he doing? . . .
> CLOV: He's crying . . .
> HAMM: Then he's living.
>
> (Samuel Beckett: *Endgame*)

That Hardy's voice still has the authentic tragic note defines his importance to the modern world. Recent assertions (as in George Steiner's *The Death of Tragedy*) that tragedy died with the gods and an ordered system of Hellenic or Christian values shared by artist and audience, which gave reasons for the suffering and struggle, can hardly stand against the tragic experience of Hardy's work. Hardeian man, sustained only by his own qualities as a human being, defies the chaotic void as Hellenic and Shakespearean man, placed in reference to cosmic myth, defied powers which were, if cruel and unknowable, at least *there* to be defied.

> Then would I bear it, clench myself, and die,
> Steeled by the sense of ire unmerited;
> Half-eased in that a Powerfuller than I
> Had willed and meted me the tears I shed.
> ('Hap')

A strong plot, 'exceptional enough to justify its telling', explicit in the novels and implicit in many poems, was Hardy's formal correlative for the tragic vision of man confronting his destiny. As Bonamy Dobrée points out, plot ('this is how things happen') is a more important symbol for tragedy than character ('this is what people are like'), 'since the tragic writer is concerned with the littleness of man (even though his greatness in his littleness) in the face of unescapable odds'. The hammer strokes of a clockwork universe on human sensitivity are enacted in a pattern as rigid as scientific law, likened by Lascelles Abercrombie to a process of chemistry, in which the elements

'are irresistibly moved to work towards one another by strong affinity;
and the human molecules in which they are ingredients are dragged
along with them, until the elemental affinity is satisfied, in a sudden
flashing moment of disintegration and re-compounding.'

(Thomas Hardy)

There is no inconsistency between Hardy's determinism and the
important role in his works of chance and coincidence. Chance is
direction which we cannot see; but it is the direction of a blind,
groping force, unrelated to anything we can conceive as conscious
purpose. Once more the double perspective of chaos and determinism conjures up a richly complex poetic response to the fate of
living creatures subject to inhuman cause and effect.

The symmetry and intensity of Hardy's plots, with every link in
the chain of cause and effect made clear, join with his poetic vision
of natural rhythms, and traditional devices of dramatic development, in a disproportioning of reality to bring out the pattern of
the larger forces driving the cosmos and its creatures. Sensational
events, disastrous coincidences, untimely reappearances, overheard
or revealed secrets, present a universe where every action is a host-
age to a predetermined and hidden fate. The supernatural detail,
the rural superstitition and folk belief, stand in for the missing
Providential direction. Without Providence, everything contributes to the longing for significance. Besides giving the poetic
frisson at inexplicable mysteries, Hardy's use of superstition is integral to the characters' relation to fate. The tragedy of *The Woodlanders* is touched off by old John South's anthropological involvement with a tree. The primitive emotion conjured up by the events
at the Midsummer Eve 'larries' lays the foundation of Grace's
marriage, her separation, and Mrs Charmond's death. As J. O.
Bailey demonstrates in 'Hardy's Visions of the Self' (*Studies in
Philology*, LVI, 1959) the Hardeian 'ghost' (a waking vision, a
dream, a real sight suggesting guilt, or a mental image presented
to the reader) plays the part of a directing Nemesis in revealing to
the character his own inner nature, causing him to accept responsibility for disasters he had blamed on circumstances, and to
take the action that brings the novel to a conclusion.

The characters too have a simple epic and tragic strength. They
are types, though not without individuality. All the subtleties of
psychology and sociology that might obscure the pattern of their
ritual interaction with Fate are stripped away. Life is reduced to
its basic elements: birth, mating, death, the weather, man's pain

and helplessness in an indifferent universe; the passions and conflicts that spring from an enclosed rural community with its roots
in an ancient past and an ancient countryside, its pagan fatalism
and ballad values and personal loyalties, being gradually invaded
by modern urban restlessness and alienation. The catastrophic
passions of the main characters are set off by a peasant chorus
quietly enduring the realistic slow trivialities of daily living, which
shape human fate by steady accumulation. They are as slow to
change as the natural rhythms they are part of. Hardy creates a
fundamental persistence from the tension between the two kinds of
stability; the eternal recurrence of the natural cycle and the recurrent finiteness of men.

'They compose a pool of common wisdom, of common humour, a
fund of perpetual life. They comment upon the actions of the hero and
heroine, but while Troy or Oak or Fanny or Bathsheba come in and out
and pass away, Jan Coggan and Henry [sic] Fray and Joseph Poorgrass
remain. They drink by night and they plough the fields by day. They
are eternal. We meet them over and over again in the novels, and they
always have something typical about them, more of the character that
marks a race than of the features which belong to an individual. The
peasants are the great sanctuary of sanity, the country the last strong-
hold of happiness. When they disappear, there is no hope for the race.'
(Virginia Woolf, op. cit., *The Common Reader*)

They are equivalent to Camus's nostalgia for a lost paradisal homeland of harmony with things as they are.

The human emotional force of the characters counterpoints the
regularity of plot and scientific process; a process which they both
obey and defy. Hardy's double vision of man's greatness in values
and littleness in the cosmic scheme keeps the tragic balance between fate—the impersonal nature of things—and personal responsibility. When Henchard disregards his wife's last wishes and
reads the letter in which she discloses that Elizabeth-Jane is not his
child,

'he could not help thinking that the concatenation of events this evening
had produced was the scheme of some sinister intelligence bent on
punishing him. Yet they had developed naturally. If he had not
revealed his past history to Elizabeth he would not have searched the
drawer for papers, and so on.'

The doubt reflects the painful ambiguity and inscrutability of
things; a poetic asset. While it is true that Hardy's poetic pattern

stresses the action of fate, it does so to stress too the human responsibility to deflect fate from its path before it is too late. Misery, which teaches Henchard 'nothing more than a defiant endurance of it', teaches Clym to limit his ambitions and Oak to keep one step ahead of an infuriated universe. The adaptive resourcefulness of Farfrae, the loving-kindness of Viviette which triumphs over her sexual passion for Swithin, the determination of Paula to follow her lover through Europe regardless of etiquette, modify a fate that seemed predetermined. Their conscious purpose redefines the concept of fate as what must be *only if no resistance is made*.

In the complexity of things resistance itself has a double edge. The greatest value ephemeral man can find to stand against the threat of meaninglessness is love. It promises to satisfy the thirst for happiness and harmony with cosmic purposes. Hardy's definition of love is unfashionably wide. It includes, as well as the physiological fact and frank relationship between the sexes which he wanted to show his Victorian readers, Viviette's sublimated maternal love for her young lover Swithin, Mr Melbury's for his daughter and Mrs Yeobright's for her son, Henchard's for Farfrae and the girl who is not his daughter, Charley's idealized love for his mistress Eustacia, Clym's for suffering mankind, and the life-loyalties of the interrelated Hintock community. But because its roots are in the impersonal sexual impulses that drive the natural world, love contributes to the tragedy of human consciousness. Respect for the real being of the beloved is lost in illusory wish-projections which cause suffering when they clash with reality. Angel's image of Tess as an inhumanly pure woman, Clym's vision of Eustacia as a school matron and Eustacia's of Clym as a gay Parisian escort, Bathsheba's defence of Troy as a regular church-goer, Jude's intermittent treatment of Sue as the 'average' woman, are nature's devices, working on the human tendency to idealization, to accomplish the mating process. The projection causes pain when it moves from lover to lover; love rarely ceases for both at the same moment. But though agony is the inevitable corollary of ecstasy, the pain affirms the life-enhancing quality of love. The caprice it inspires in women—a type of the cosmic caprice of fate—is also a measure of their vitality and truth to life. The will to enjoy, inseparably bound up with the opposing will to suffer (part of 'the circumstantial will against enjoyment'); the instinctive zest for existence modified by the modern view of life as a thing to be put up with, can bring maturity and even happiness. Bathsheba attains maturity and a realistic appraisal of Oak's controlled fidelity. Even Tess is only robbed of the purely human Paradise promised in Talbothays by the inhumanity of man.

Virginia Woolf accepts the great emotional crises as part of Hardy's poetic pattern.

'In all the books love is one of the great facts that mould human life. But it is a catastrophe; it happens suddenly and overwhelmingly, and there is little to be said about it.'

(op. cit., *The Common Reader*)

T. S. Eliot, on the other hand, attacks the 'emotional paroxysms' which seem to him a 'symptom of decadence' expressing

'a powerful personality uncurbed by any institutional attachment or by submission to any objective beliefs . . . He seems to me to have written as nearly for the sake of "self-expression" as a man well can; and the self which he had to express does not strike me as a particularly wholesome or edifying matter of communication . . .'

(*After Strange Gods*)

His criticism suggests the distrust of someone who feels the meaning of orthodox allegiances threatened by the affirmation of a life without God or ultimate purpose. But in a world where Eliot's own poetry has revealed the dehumanization of hollow men living in an emotionless waste land, the intense emotion of Hardy's characters and Hardy's personal voice affirm the response of living passion to the human predicament. 'The function of the artist is to justify life by feeling it intensely' (J. E. Barton, 'The Poetry of Thomas Hardy'). Far from robbing the characters of their human individuality, as Eliot claims, heightened emotion stresses both their basic humanness and the resistance of the unique personality to the habit of despair which Camus found worse than despair itself ('None of us was capable any longer of an exalted emotion; all had trite, monotonous feelings'—*The Plague*), and which Matthew Arnold had defined in a letter to Clough (14 December 1852) as 'the modern situation in its true *blankness* and *barrenness*, and *unpoetrylessness*'.

Hardy's poetic persona is untouched by the modern taboo on tenderness and top notes, though the understatement of deep feeling also forms part of his vision. His emotional scenes are operatic rather than melodramatic; arias which reveal the inner quality of life, with all its dissonant primary passions reconciled in the musico-poetic form, while the outer action is suspended. The effect of Boldwood's final gesture, with its poignant return of his old courtesy, 'Then he broke from Samway, crossed the room to Bathsheba, and kissed her hand', in the context of his murder of Troy, can only be compared with the return of the love leitmotif at the end of Verdi's *Otello*. (The *Life* proves that Verdi was a composer with whom Hardy felt some affinity.) As the emotional persuasiveness of music suspends disbelief in what would be absurd in spoken drama, Hardy's poetic heightening carries him through operatic implausibilities of action and clumsinesses of style. The unrealistic 'libretto' of the quarrel between Clym and Eustacia, reminiscent of the quarrel of Brachiano and Vittoria in *The White Devil*, directs attention away from the technicalities of expression to the white-hot emotion underneath that compels the jerky speech rhythms, the trembling of Eustacia's hands, and the agony of a man still in love with the wife he is rejecting on principle, who while he ties her bonnet strings for her, 'turned his eyes aside, that he might not be tempted to softness'.

It is the emotion of Hardy's work which one remembers. It expresses the whole of his many-sided personality, spilling over the barriers of artistic form to make his work an experience which is musical and artistic as well as literary. Virginia Woolf's definition of the special quality of Hardy's characters—

'We recall their passions. We remember how deeply they have loved each other and often with what tragic results . . . But we do not remember how they have loved. We do not remember how they talked and changed and got to know each other, finely, gradually, from step to step and from stage to stage . . .'

(op. cit., *The Common Reader*)

—places his work with those sister arts (in which Hardy was a competent practitioner) which create a universal image of the essence of things to transcend the personal and local details that gave it birth. As W. H. Auden remarked about his experience of writing opera libretti (the T. S. Eliot Memorial lectures given at the University of Kent at Canterbury, 1967): 'Music can, I believe, express the equivalent of *I love*, but it is incapable of saying whom or what I love, you, God, or the decimal system.' In the extraordinary states of violent emotion that distinguish the operatic mode, all differences in social standing, sex, and age are abolished, so that even in a foreign language one can tell the emotion that is being expressed.

Hardy's equivalent for the operatic state often takes a form that is both musical and pictorial. Dance and song are linked with ritual survivals of fertility rites that are an 'irresistible attack upon . . . social order', as in the village gipsying on Egdon and the dance that inspires the change of marriage partners in 'The History of the Hardcomes'. The folk or church music that was part of Hardy's heritage often moves a sexual or compassionate emotion that precipitates a definite step in the story. The step is not always disastrous. The sound of children's voices singing 'Lead kindly Light' re-establishes Bathsheba's relationship with Oak after her tragedy; Farfrae's song stops Henchard from killing him in the loft. Boldwood feels encouraged to consider himself as good as engaged to Bathsheba after their exhibition of harmony at the shearing supper. Wildeve feels that there is nothing else to do but marry Tamsin after they have been celebrated by Grandfer's crew as a married couple. Farfrae's modest dance with Elizabeth-Jane at his entertainment precipitates a half-declaration of love. Tess's interest in Angel's music rivets his attention on this unusual milkmaid, whose 'fluty' tones had interrupted his meditations on a music score. The hymn tune of the Wessex composer, which made Sue and Jude clasp hands by an 'unpremeditated instinct', gives rise to her confession of an 'incomplete' marriage with Phillotson, and points to her search for spiritual harmony with Jude. Even Melbury's irritation at Cawtree's low ballad, which contributes to his rejection of Giles as a suitable mate for his daughter, is a refusal to recognize the primitive side of Grace's nature which is in harmony with the sentiments of the song and the simple woodland company who sang it. The effect of ritual music becomes a correlative for the operations of the Immanent Will, moving people through their emotions to obey its own inscrutable purposes.

Ritual itself is, in modern terms, total theatre. The ritual character of Hardy's operatic scenes—the village gipsying, the skimmity ride, the Egdon bonfires, the arrest at Stonehenge—is stressed by his balletic groupings and his description of scene and characters in terms of the strong contrast of light and shade. This pictorial treatment abstracts personality from the actors and leaves their faces mask-like, with no 'permanent moral expression'. The silhouette, employed most frequently in descriptions of the rustic chorus, expresses a communal emotion rather than indi-

22

vidual idiosyncrasy. The figure defined in sharp relief against a dun background, like Clym against the settle or Mrs Yeobright against the heath, or suddenly illuminated, Rembrandt-fashion, in a long shaft of light (Marty at the window, Eustacia in the light from Susan Nunsuch's cottage), suddenly fixes the moving characters through the distancing of pictorial art as eternal tableaux of the littleness of conscious human experience in the surrounding darkness. (Alastair Smart, 'Pictorial Imagery in the Novels of Thomas Hardy', *Review of English Studies*, XII, 1961.) As Cytherea's father falls to his death from the tower, shafts of light falling across the room become for her an objective correlative of tragedy. The essential nature of Arabella and of her opposite Sue Bridehead is caught in the framed picture of Delilah and the comparison of Sue to a Parthenon frieze. When the heart and inner meaning has thus been established in a frozen image, it dissolves once more into the drama of people in motion acting out that reality, leaving the reader with a new perspective of their place in the cosmic scheme. This technique provides a major principle of dramatic development in *The Dynasts*.

Hardy's emotionally charged poetic pattern integrates all his personal interests into a new artistic unity. Different forms of art—architecture, sculpture, painting—and different schools add to the complex richness of his multiple perspective. The Impressionist view of Marty's hair, as it strikes the barber; of Grace through the Romantic vision of Fitzpiers, 'a sylph-like greenish-white creature, as toned by the sunlight and leafage'; of landscape, weather and people toned to the mood of the observer, opposes subjective reality to the homely detail of a Dutch painting, seen to perfection in *Under the Greenwood Tree* and 'The Homecoming'—the unheroic objective reality to which the human spirit must adjust. Even the unartistic facets contribute to the artistic whole. Hardy's much-criticized philosophical incursions and 'heavy lumps of social reform' are essential to the emotional texture of the work. The long passage on rural migration to the towns that begins Chapter LI of *Tess* falls into place as a re-creation in social terms of the central poetic image of purposeless mechanical process driving units of life in an unnatural direction. If one places the modern cult of the disappearance of the author into proper perspective as only one form of literature among many equally valid, the expansive scope of the novel can afford the author's compassionate voice pointing to the scheme of things that motivates his action. In the smaller compass of a poem, the charge that Hardy's philosophy was intrusive may carry more weight. But in his successful work the 'sentiment and thought' (in Yeats's phrase) is carried by the passion of Hardy's total portrayal of the cosmic predicament. The totality is the achievement of the poetic vision.

'Life offers—to Deny':
The Philosophical Poems

> It says that Life would signify
> A thwarted purposing:
> That we come to live, and are called to die.
> Yes, that's the thing
> In fall, in spring,
> That Yell'ham says:—
> "Life offers—to deny!"

The tragic paradox expressed in 'Yell'ham-Wood's Story' is the recurring theme of several poems that put forward a philosophic view of the universe. Hardy disclaimed the title of systematic philosopher: repeatedly his Prefaces insist that 'no harmonious philosophy is attempted in these pages' (*Winter Words*); that his poems are 'unadjusted impressions' . . . 'written down in widely differing moods and circumstances' (*Poems of the Past and the Present*); mere '"questionings" in the exploration of reality' (*Late Lyrics and Earlier*). As an explorer of reality he is, like every other serious artist who has a controlling vision of man's relation to the cosmos, a man with a personal slant on reality that can be called a philosophy. Hardy's tragic vision of the 'thwarted purposing' evident in the conflict between the fine potentialities of conscious man and the indifference of the unconscious universe which had produced him, informs the bulk of the *Collected Poems*. There are many poems which seem designed to give prominent expression to Hardy's philosophical concepts: 'The Bedridden Peasant', 'The Lacking Sense', 'The Mother Mourns', 'The Convergence of the Twain', 'God-Forgotten', 'The Subalterns', 'Hap', 'Agnosto Theo', 'Nature's Questioning', 'A Dream Question', 'Before Life and After', spring immediately to mind. And among these are some overtly philosophical poems in which the poet uses some of the tools of the professional philosopher—direct statement, logical argument, analysis, abstract concepts placed in the foreground as

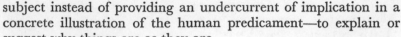

subject instead of providing an undercurrent of implication in a concrete illustration of the human predicament—to explain or suggest why things are as they are.

While the poems which state philosophical beliefs are obviously the product of careful thought on man's predicament, their speculations are diverse enough to justify Hardy's denial of the charge that he tried to build up a system of organized philosophy. His personification of the ultimate Cause of things moves from God ('God-Forgotten', 'A Dream Question', 'By the Earth's Corpse') to Nature ('The Mother Mourns', 'The Sleep-Worker', 'The Lacking Sense') to the 'Willer masked and dumb' of 'Agnosto Theo' and the neuter 'It' of 'A Philosophical Fantasy' and 'The Absolute Explains'. In some poems two or more manifestations of the ultimate Cause share responsibility; Doom and Nature in 'Doom and She'; in 'Hap', Time and Chance; the elements and all the ills of the flesh, driven by Necessity, in 'The Subalterns'. His tentative conclusions on the origin of human suffering range from the traditional theological view of 'severance, self-entailed' from God in 'God-Forgotten' and 'The Bedridden Peasant', the indifference of an unknowing and unknowable God in 'A Dream Question' and 'A Philosophical Fantasy', to the more charitable impressions of the purposeless workings 'by vacant rote' of a blind necessitating force, liable to make mistakes ('The Sleep-Worker', 'The Mother Mourns', 'The Lacking Sense', 'Nature's Questioning'). Nevertheless, it is a force which may one day grow sensitive to the sufferings of its creatures ('Agnosto Theo') and either restore a state of universal unconsciousness ('Before Life and After') or 'patiently adjust, amend, and heal' ('The Sleep-Worker').

The variety of Hardy's 'mood-dictated' impressions does not conceal his belief that presentation of a world-view or views is as proper a function for the poet as for the novelist, and may make for easier reception by the public. A note written in 1896 after the shocked public reaction to his arraignment of the universe in *Tess of the d'Urbervilles* and *Jude the Obscure* leaves no doubt that he intended to continue the 'application of ideas to life' in poetry:

'Perhaps I can express more fully in verse ideas and emotions which run counter to the inert crystallized opinion—hard as a rock—which the vast body of men have vested interests in supporting. To cry out in a passionate poem that (for instance) the Supreme Mover or Movers, the Prime Force or Forces, must be either limited in power, unknowing, or cruel—which is obvious enough, and has been for centuries—will cause

26

them merely a shake of the head; but to put it in argumentative prose will make them sneer, or foam, and set all the literary contortionists jumping upon me, a harmless agnostic, as if I were a clamorous atheist, which in their crass illiteracy they seem to think is the same thing. . . .

The proposition that 'the Prime Force or Forces must be either limited in power, unknowing, or cruel' does not always produce a passionate poem.

> I asked the Lord: "Sire, is this true
> Which hosts of theologians hold,
> That when we creatures censure you
> For shaping griefs and ails untold
> (Deeming them punishments undue)
> You rage, as Moses wrote of old?
>
> When we exclaim: 'Beneficent
> He is not, for he orders pain,
> Or, if so, not omnipotent:
> To a mere child the thing is plain!'
> Those who profess to represent
> You, cry out: 'Impious and profane!'"
>
> He: "Save me from my friends, who deem
> That I care what my creatures say!
> Mouth as you list: sneer, rail, blaspheme,
> O manikin, the livelong day,
> Not one grief-groan or pleasure-gleam
> Will you increase or take away.
>
> "Why things are thus, whoso derides,
> May well remain my secret still. . . . .
> A fourth dimension, say the guides,
> To matter is conceivable.
> Think some such mystery resides
> Within the ethic of my will."
>
> ('A Dream Question')

The answer to the dreamer's question—that there is no answer to the riddle of pain—has elsewhere produced the true poetic thrill of awe at the mystery of things. But here there is no resonance beyond the unemotive question and statement. Both speakers are too dispassionate for the poem to take fire in a reader's mind. Shadowy

Causes 'vacant of feeling', 'labouring all-unknowingly', which can
ask:

> "World-weaver! what *is* Grief?
> And what are Right, and Wrong,
> And Feeling, that belong
> To creatures all who owe thee fief?
> Why is Weak worse than Strong?"
> ('Doom and She')

are not the most fitting mouthpieces to express or respond to the
passionate human indictment of creation, since 'nor joy nor pain/
It lies in [them] to recognize'. The 'incensed Deity' of Milton has
no parallel in the indifferent First Cause of Hardy. Where such a
metaphysical mouthpiece does spring to passionate life it is, significantly, as the fantasy of a primitive 'vengeful god' conceived and
communicated in personal terms by the human mind of the
'suffering thing'—one of the 'infallible estimators' of pain:

> If but some vengeful god would call to me
> From up the sky, and laugh: "Thou suffering thing,
> Know that thy sorrow is my ecstasy,
> That thy love's loss is my hate's profiting!"
>
> Then would I bear it, clench myself, and die,
> Steeled by the sense of ire unmerited;
> Half-eased in that a Powerfuller than I
> Had willed and meted me the tears I shed.
>
> But not so. How arrives it joy lies slain
> And why unblooms the best hope ever sown?
> —Crass Casualty obstructs the sun and rain,
> And dicing Time for gladness casts a moan. . . .
> These purblind Doomsters had as readily strown
> Blisses about my pilgrimage as pain.
> ('Hap')

Here, crass Casualty and dicing Time do not exceed their function
as abstract concepts of the blind and dumb arbiters of man's fate,
conceived as such by the same ordering human mind which created
the illusion of cosmic design in the first eight lines of the sonnet.
The philosophical idea develops, not in bare statement or debate,
but in a human context of moral and dramatic confrontation which
compels an immediate shock of recognition. To rejoice in the

downfall of one's enemy acknowledges his importance. To bear pain with resignation, 'half-eased in that a Powerfuller than I/Had willed and meted me the tears I shed', suggests acknowledgement of the importance of the divine antagonist's design. The clash of two meaningful opposites—Captain Ahab and the white whale, Hemingway's Old Man and the big fish, Job and his God—is easier to realize in a concrete poetic image than an encounter between a puzzled representative 'manikin' and an unmoral, loveless and hateless force which cannot realize passion.

'But not so'. The honest colloquial shrug at the turn of the sonnet rejects the comforting illusion of a personal God to whom human suffering is meaningful for the less flattering truth of an impersonal absurdity. A cosmos operated by impersonal abstractions is delicate ground for a poet whose interests in philosophical concepts lies predominantly in their bearing on human life. But the precise dramatic image of one man's confrontation of fate, enriched by the poet's emotional response to this aspect of human experience, has generated enough poetic feeling to impregnate the abstractions of the sestet. The world of abstract concepts is held in constant and fruitful tension, fundamental to Hardy's best poetry, with specific images from the world of sense experience, felt on the pulses of an individual human being.

'Hap' is shaped by the basic conflict implied in much of Hardy's poetry; usually a variation of Yell'ham-wood's theme song "Life offers—to deny". It grows out of the tensions between human and inhuman, personal and impersonal, concrete and abstract, feeling and thought. The knotted strength of the poem comes from the simultaneous presence of the opposing worlds, maintaining the powerful unresolved balance of two wrestlers sculptured in granite. The human mind of the protagonist, within which both terms of the opposition are conceived, creates the poetic emotion from his simultaneous acceptance of the truth of the nineteenth-century scientific view of man's unimportance to the cosmic scheme, and his desire to go on believing in the traditional significance of individual man. The divided allegiance to harsh absurd truth and meaningful fantasy is acknowledged by the reader as authentic, because it is communicated as a deeply-felt cry—the whole poem—from a sensitive and tormented individual experiencing as a human being 'the inherent will to enjoy, and the circumstantial will against enjoyment'.

Life and its denial, the tensions inherent in personal experience of the impersonal cosmos, are presented in a pattern of thought and emotion, structure, diction and word-music, balance and disturbance of rhythm, that is peculiarly Hardy's own, where his quirks of style are major assets inseparable from the thought. When 'Crass Casualty obstructs' the sun and rain, the obstruction to the smoothly-singing monosyllables from the world of simple sense experience is caused by the overwhelming polysyllabic sonority of the Latin abstraction with its hard alliterative consonants. The concept of a fundamental disharmony inheres in the wrestle of words taken from every level of language, which combine and strain against each other. The archaic 'Doomsters' (judges) exists in ironic tension with the unusual but still extant 'purblind'. Judges are not expected to be blind, obtuse, or dull; Fate is, and because the root of 'Doomsters' evokes Fate a musical discord is set up between the worlds of human and inhuman values. The outmoded, but Biblical, second person singular invests the dramatic scene with the emotional resonance that belongs to every mythical confrontation of a heroic human being with a primitive god made in man's tribal image. The coinage 'unblooms', in its characteristic Hardeian use of the negative particle, which has been happily defined by Viola Meynell as 'the *un* that summons in order that it may banish, and keeps the living word present to hear sentence and denial', is concrete and precise in its evocation of the reversal of an expected natural process. The question in which the word occurs realizes imaginatively the denial of the meaning of life, growth, and sense experience which is mirrored in the answer. The negating 'unblooms' is linked to the abstract causes of denial, not only by the sound echo in 'Doomsters', but also by their parallel positions of stress in the line.

Hardy's concern with stress and rhythm, which has caused so much bafflement to readers and critics with other than Hardeian expectations, constitutes a major contribution to the poetry of tension and paradox. His fascination with the technical problems of scansion, and impatience with critics who could not see that 'those oft are Stratagems which Errors seem', is demonstrated by the many notes on rhythm and metre found among his papers:

'Years earlier he had decided that too regular a beat was bad art . . . He knew that in architecture cunning irregularity is of enormous worth, and it is obvious that he carried on into his verse, perhaps in part unconsciously, the Gothic art-principle in which he had been trained—the principle of spontaneity, found in mouldings, tracery, and such-like—resulting in the 'unforeseen' (as it has been called) character of his metres and stanzas, that of stress rather than syllable, poetic texture rather than poetic veneer . . . He shaped his poetry accordingly, introducing metrical pauses, and reversed beats; and found for his trouble that some particular line of a poem exemplifying this principle was greeted with a would-be jocular remark that such a line "did not make for immortality."'

(*The Life of Thomas Hardy*)

In 'Hap', the reader who respects the metrical stress of the normal iambic pentameter of the sonnet form will get into difficulties, for example, with the fourth line, where natural emphasis in the speaking voice demands three consecutive heavy stresses on the opposing phrases 'thy love's loss' and 'my hate's profiting'. But a reader sensitive to the authentic speech rhythms of an idiosyncratic human voice in the grip of a deeply-felt emotion, responding painfully, precisely, to the affirmations and denials of life, will re-create the heroic confrontation that is forced on his senses by the balancing stresses on 'My . . . thy' and 'Crass Casualty . . . sun and rain.'

The speaking voice realizing in its own personal music the double face of the universe is a varied instrument. Hardy reproduces it faithfully, warts and all, in all its human contrariness—its smoothness and roughness, simplicities and complexities of expression, colloquialisms and bookish clichés, clipped phrases and prosinesses, sublime harmonies and harsh dissonances, pauses, passions, and meditations, broken rhythms, quickenings and retardings of pace. But the human voice alone, however faithfully reproduced, is not enough to make poetry. Hardy, like Camus, was too honest and too aware of human dignity to leave out of his formal structure the mechanical insentient universe against which conscious man shatters himself.

'Negating one of the terms of the opposition on which he lives amounts to escaping it . . . To impoverish that reality whose inhumanity constitutes man's majesty is tantamount to impoverishing him himself.'

(Camus: *The Myth of Sisyphus*)

The individual speaking voice responding fully to experience runs in counterpoint against the rigidity of an expected metrical structure; often, as in 'Hap', of a conventional poetic form such as the sonnet, sometimes obeying the underlying structure, sometimes straining against it. The resulting tension creates a striking re-enactment of a conscious human being painfully striving to impose order and significance on the mechanical insentience of the universe, 'that reality whose inhumanity constitutes man's majesty', by the very qualities of unmechanical imperfection that constitute his humanness.

The characteristic tension of Hardy's verse is most noticeable in short poems. Concentration of form often seems to produce concentration of thought, emotion, mood, and image. The borrowed philosophy of constant change as the ultimate stable reality can hardly have been summed up in a more succinct paradox than '"According to the Mighty Working"':

> When moiling seems at cease
> > In the vague void of night-time,
> > And heaven's wide roomage stormless
> > Between the dusk and light-time,
> > And fear at last is formless,
> We call the allurement Peace.
>
> Peace, this hid riot, Change,
> > This revel of quick-cued mumming,
> > This never truly being,
> > This evermore becoming,
> > This spinner's wheel onfleeing
> Outside perception's range.

Here, though Hardy denies himself the aid of a specific human context to give dramatic realization to his philosophic concepts, the poetry is not unbalanced by the philosophy. The poetic emotion, often created by some personal pressure of suffering, is here implied in the title, taken from the Burial Service, which had both a personal and universal relevance for many of Hardy's readers in 1917. Though the speaking voice in this poem is less personal than representative of all those for whom the war was a symbol of the ceaseless elemental hostilities of the cosmos, the Hardeian tensions are still present in the very structure of the poem, framed as it is between the key-words of the paradox inherent in existence—cease-Peace, Change-range. Peace is reduced to its opposite Change in the space of one economical six-syllable line by the pivotal 'hid riot' implied in the 'moiling' of the first stanza. Hardy's idiosyncratic word-music of dissonance is captured in the tensions between abstract idea and vivid specific image ('mumming' is a favourite Hardeian metaphor for the automatic processes of the cosmos); between a resonant mixture of unusual diction ('moiling', 'roomage', 'onfleeing') and plain words, often juxtaposed in evocative combinations ('light-time', 'quick-cued'). The long open vowels of the first stanza, which bring to the ear vast formless reaches of space and time in a state of seeming suspension, are set in opposition to the short rapid vowels of the second, which presents the eternal 'onfleeing' in a whirl of accelerating activity that returns over and over again to the fixed point of assonance in 'revel . . . never . . . evermore'. The diction of each stanza is carefully chosen and combined to give to each its appropriate rhythm and movement, as a comparison, for example, of the second line of each stanza makes clear. The slow monosyllables of 'In the vague void of night-time', which retard the swift Swinburnian metre, also retard the speaking voice, while the sound as well as the sense of 'This revel of quick-cued mumming' calls for accelerated reading. One can hardly read the poem aloud without becoming conscious of the paradox at the heart of existence being enacted in every detail of the structure.

'"According to the Mighty Working"' succeeds as poetry because Hardy has resisted the temptation to explain the workings of the contradictory mysteries of life. He leaves them as a presented image of unresolved tension. The speculative definitions of the Peace-Change paradox in the second stanza, reminiscent of Vaughan's metaphysical 'Son-Days', draw no conclusions that are beyond the limits of human knowledge. The same reticence operates, in spite of reference to the Immanent Will and the Spinner of the Years, in 'The Convergence of the Twain' to make this longer poem a successful poetic image of 'thwarted purposing' in its unexplained juxtaposition of human purpose—the 'smart ship' —and its denial, the 'sinister mate' of ice that was to be the agent of its destruction. The sexual terms in which the disaster is seen makes the final 'consummation', in which the separately-developing 'twin halves of one august event' come together for the first time, when Time and Chance coincide, a symbol of cosmic mismarriage that is central to Hardy's universe. In such a mismarriage, as Hynes points out in *The Pattern of Hardy's Poetry*, there can be no resolution of discord, only honest recognition of its unreconciled ironies. The question of the sea's natural inhabitants,

"What does this vaingloriousness down here?"

receives no answer from the accident that jarred two hemispheres, for there is no answer known to humankind to the mystery of suffering. The possible absurdity of the universe is presented by letting the inexplicable contraries of the event speak for themselves in the various 'mismarriages' of idea and structure. The bare, direct language of dignified abstraction that clothes the philosophy of predestination in the second half of the poem ('A Shape of Ice, for the time far and dissociate', 'In shadowy silent distance') is ironically mismated to the rich, grotesque, sensuous diction and evocative imagery of the first half, the specific context of 'vain-gloriousness' which the experience of the second half is predestined to contradict. The two short lines of each stanza are contrasted with the long final lines, which in the first half coil in and out of the poem with the inevitability of the fatal sea. In stanzas VI to XI, however, the rhythm of these final lines is changed by simpler, smoother diction into a movement that is colder, more inhuman. That the contrasts and juxtapositions have no meaning to 'mortal eye' is the meaning of this poem, and many others. Human lack of knowledge, man's inability to impose rational order on the incongruities of life, is powerfully suggested by what Hardy does *not* say. As G. K. Chesterton points out in his book on Browning, 'there is a certain poetic value . . . in this sense of having missed the full meaning of things. There is beauty, not only in wisdom, but in this dazed and dramatic ignorance.'

When Hardy rejects the poetic value of the human individual's 'dazed and dramatic ignorance' for discursive argument with and through vague non-human mouthpieces, the poetic impact is often blunted by an overweight of philosophic content that disperses the instigating passion. The cry of passion, by its very nature, cannot be long sustained. The presentation of the same idea— for example, the idea of Nature's unreflecting blindness—is more effective in the concentrated sonnet 'The Sleep-Worker'* than in the long argument of 'The Lacking Sense'. The sonnet begins with a direct cry of passionate protest from the human sufferer to the Cause of his suffering:

> When wilt thou wake, O Mother, wake and see . . .?

Her nature and mode of operation are implied only through simile and metaphor—the usual bridge between the known of the physi-

*The diversity of critical viewpoint can be illustrated by referring to Hynes's judgement of 'The Sleep-Worker' as a failure.

cal world and the metaphysical unknown. No explanation is demanded; relief from pain is of more immediate concern to the sufferer than explanation of its cause. The mystery of life's dissonances is simply presented, and left unsolved. The poem ends, as it begins, with a question—a natural human speculation on the wished-for development of cosmic awareness which has grown inevitably out of the original cry of protest. The personal cry from an individual who has felt in his 'palpitating tissues' the effects of Nature's faulty workmanship is more powerful than the questioning and explanation of 'the Mother's moody look' in 'The Lacking Sense'. The direct expression of pain is curiously distanced both by the concern of the human questioner for the Mother's moody look rather than for his own suffering, and by the third-party intervention of Time. Hardy's Time, except possibly in the *Dynasts*, which is a deliberate attempt to create a new mythology in the temper of the modern age, is too shadowy to have the traditional reverberations of the scythe-and-hour-glass figure familiar to readers of George Herbert's dialogue-poem 'Time'. And even with his reliance on the seventeenth-century conditioned response to the partly humanized figure, Herbert gives most of the argument to his controlling human character, whereas four out of the six stanzas of 'The Lacking Sense' are spoken by Hardy's specification of a Time whose nature, to the nineteenth and twentieth centuries, is unknown. Distancing of emotion has its effect on the language too. Abstractions and literary clichés replace the vivid visual and aural dissonances of 'The Sleep-Worker'. The general language of statement and explanation—

Into her would-be perfect motions, modes, effects, and features
Admitting cramps, black humours, wan decay, and baleful blights,
        Distress into delights

—has no reverberation beyond itself. But the emotional response to 'Strange orchestras of victim-shriek and song' takes on a rich complexity when one reflects on the directly-experienced discords combined in the same line with an evocation of the harmony of individual instruments working together in an orchestra. The language of poetry, as opposed to the language of prosaic statement, requires an emotional and imaginative contribution from the reader to blossom into full meaning.

Hardy's humanizing compassion for all things groaning together in creation gives distinction to some poems whose ingredients would seem to invite complete failure. 'The Subalterns' has a higher measure of success than some other poems in which non-human mouthpieces speak because man's antagonists Sickness, Death, and the elements are imbued with his own compassion. Human and non-human manifestations alike are driven by the force of necessity, which is allowed to remain outside the poem, potent in its unknowable mystery. Its 'subalterns' make no attempt to explain or justify the mystery of necessity; the poem is a simple concrete presentation of the effects of their orders from 'laws in force on high' on the body of an individual human being, with a disclaimer of responsibility which turns these former antagonists into fellow-victims. 'Nature's Questioning', though less successful than 'The Subalterns' in its use of inanimate poetic mouthpieces, owes its memorable quality to Hardy's feeling that human and non-human nature alike are fellow-sufferers from the First Cause. Both human and non-human manifestations appear in the first stanza in a sympathetic relationship; the First Cause does not appear except as speculations of 'pool, field, flock, and lonely tree', though its effects are felt, as in 'The Subalterns', throughout the poem. The alternative guesses at an explanation of the faulty cosmic scheme are among Hardy's most striking realizations of the metaphysical in terms that bring it within the range of human comprehension but do not rob it of all mystery by too concrete an image. His characteristic mixture of the physical with the metaphysical, the high poetic style with the colloquial, as in

Or are we live remains
Of Godhead dying downwards, brain and eye now gone?

the abstract Miltonic majesty of 'some Vast Imbecility', the hymn-like dignity of the metre with its unexpected long final line (an Alexandrine) breaking the pattern to focus attention on the effects of the First Cause on its manifestations, all work together to give these three verses a high rank in philosophical poetry. But when they are placed in the context of the whole poem, one wonders whether language worthy of a Miltonic angel could be the 'lippings mere' of cowed inanimate things, still less of the 'chastened children sitting silent in a school' to which they are compared almost before their identity as inanimate things has been established. The metaphors in this poem are perhaps too strong for the realities they represent, and the poet's philosophy too strong for the metaphors. The dramatization of the First Cause as a schoolmaster humanizes it into something very close to the personal God of primitive myth, which injures its presentation as a nonhuman force. The poem is pulled in two directions by the poet's fellow-feeling for 'things around': the tension is not tight enough to be fully creative. Nevertheless, a kind of unity operates through the consciousness of the poet as passive observer, registering through his imaginative fantasy the universal questioning of the mystery written on the face of all nature:

> . . . . No answerer I . . .
> Meanwhile the winds, and rains,
> And Earth's old glooms and pains
> Are still the same, and Life and Death are neighbours nigh.

The sense of impenetrable mystery informing the human being's relationship to the laws of the cosmos produces the most authentic poetic emotion when it is left as a question mark:

> Why joys they've found I cannot find,
> Abides a mystery.
>> ('The Impercipient')

> Wilt thou destroy, in one wild shock of shame,
> Thy whole high heaving firmamental frame,
> Or patiently adjust, amend, and heal?
>> ('The Sleep-Worker')

> Ere nescience shall be reaffirmed
> How long, how long?
>> ('Before Life and After')

> Perhaps Thy ancient rote-restricted ways
> Thy ripening rule transcends;
>> ('Agnosto Theo')

Human knowledge of the unknowable cannot go beyond a speculative 'perhaps' or 'how much' or 'as if':

> How much of consciousness informs Thy will,
> Thy biddings, as if blind,
> Of death-inducing kind,
> Nought shows to us ephemeral ones who fill
> But moments in thy mind.
>> ('Agnosto Theo')

But human ignorance can allow the human heart to hope; and the hope of growing awareness in the unconscious cosmos at the end of 'Agnosto Theo' is all the more powerful for the honest admission at the beginning of ignorance of the unknown and unknowable:

> Long have I framed weak phantasies of Thee,
> O Willer masked and dumb!

While the Willer remains masked and dumb, a mere fantasy of human speculation, its lack of definition can arouse the proper poetic awe and terror at the unknowable. A God made in man's image, like the vengeful god of 'Hap' and even Milton's rather unorthodox deity, has enough traditional authority to give him credibility when he opens his mouth to argue, justify, or explain. But in a transitional age when, as Leslie Stephen said in a note quoted by Hardy in the *Life*, 'the old ideals have become obsolete, and the new are not yet constructed', it is difficult to respond to a Prime Force which is neither one thing nor the other. The question which Hardy so often asks of the universe:

"And how explains thy Ancient Mind her crimes upon her creatures?"

postulates a being which has enough mind to reason—a humanized conception which neighbours uneasily with the mindless mechanical Causes of nineteenth-century science that Hardy's integrity compelled him to present. Insensitive mindless mouthpieces which have no recognizable reverberations from tradition are not qualified to justify the cosmic scheme, to explain or withhold explanation, to mourn 'man's mountings of mindsight' ('The Mother Mourns', 'New Year's Eve', 'God's Education'), to be schoolmaster to natural phenomena ('Nature's Questioning') when, as God remarks in 'God's Education':

> "Forsooth, though I men's master be,
> Theirs is the teaching mind!"

or to give moral advice on man's function in the cosmos ('The Lacking Sense', 'A Plaint to Man'). Moral speculation on man's possible relationship to cosmic laws as conscious 'pioneer' of Nature's growth of awareness comes more naturally as a personal response of the maker of 'weak phantasies' to the unknowable:

Part is mine of the general Will,
Cannot my share in the sum of sources
Bend a digit the poise of forces,
And a fair desire fulfil?

('He Wonders About Himself')

Only suffering man is qualified to mourn, hope, make moral resolutions, admit shortcomings, or entertain contradictory speculations on the nature and power of the First Cause, since, as the 'phasm' of God admits in 'A Plaint to Man',

My virtue, power, utility,
Within my maker must all abide,
Since none in myself can ever be.

Only he can choose to absolve God from his crimes and keep up the fantasy of a merciful deity while facing the harsh truth of his neglect, as in the fine lyric 'The Bedridden Peasant'.

'Human beings, in their generous endeavour to construct a hypothesis that shall not degrade a First Cause, have always hesitated to conceive a dominant power of lower moral quality than their own; and even while they sit down and weep by the waters of Babylon, invent excuses for the oppression which prompts their tears.'

(*The Return of the Native*)

The vivid dramatization of this idea in the archetypal figure of the bedridden peasant makes this poem superior in poetic quality to 'God-Forgotten', which appears on the previous page in *Poems of the Past and the Present*: poems which are close neighbours often show different attempts to work out the same thought. The idea common to both 'God-Forgotten' and 'The Bedridden Peasant' is God's neglect of the human race. 'God-Forgotten' is written in the form of a dialogue between a God who does most of the talking and a respectful but dogged representative of humankind, 'Sent thither by the sons of Earth, to win/Some answer to their cry.' The poem develops logically and straightforwardly from the first encounter, when the supercilious and absent-minded deity is prodded into vague remembrance of creating 'Some tiny sphere I built long back (Mid millions of such shapes of mine)'; into admission of lost interest at the time of Earth's 'severance, self-entailed'; into self-justification of his continuing neglect—

"Thou shouldst have learnt that *Not to Mend*
For Me could mean but *Not to Know*:"

and finally into a plan to 'straightway put an end/To what men undergo'. In spite of the admirable persistence of the human representative, the dialogue is too distanced from the specific human context to rouse much emotion. It pales before the direct prayer of the suffering peasant to an unknowing God, who does not have to state his ignorance like the God of 'God-Forgotten', for he is conspicuous by his absence throughout the poem. The absence of what ought to be there, ironically pointed up by the simple prayer form and hymn metre of 'O God Our Help in Ages Past', creates a fruitful tension with what *is* there—the nobility of a human individual who hesitates to conceive a dominant power of lower moral quality than his own, and so is prepared to give his absent God the benefit of the doubt. The self-revelation of the God of 'God-Forgotten' does not reveal so much of the contrast between man and God as the endeavour of the forgotten victim to protect the good name of his Maker. Shut in by the 'dead wall' of the physical world, that is the physical wall of his bedridden confinement as well as the metaphysical wall of his alienation from God and meaning, he can only reason from his limited human experience; and when the actions of God are judged by the moral standards of men, God is seen by the reader to be the inferior being:

> For, say one puts a child to nurse,
> He eyes it now and then
> To know if better it is, or worse,
> And if it mourn, and when.

But his conception of the God made in man's image remains stubbornly charitable. It is hard to conceive of a deity who would allow meaningless pain when no human being would, 'For Thou art mild of heart'. The very limitations of the peasant's philosophical point of view, which we all recognize when faced with the mystery of pain, creates the poetic emotion. If it was difficult to sympathize with an all-powerful deity which is so inhuman that it has to be prodded into remembrance of earthly pain, it is not difficult to thrill to the human nobility and compassion of the powerless peasant who makes a deliberate choice to stand by his fantasy of what God ought to be, in face of the truth of what God is—unknowing and unknowable.

> Then, since thou mak'st not these things be,
> But these things dost not know,

40

> I'll praise Thee as were shown to me
> The mercies Thou wouldst show!

The great strength of a poem like 'The Bedridden Peasant' with its sublime human response to the unknowable couched in the simple, direct, often Biblical language of the sufferer, is a strength of tension between the poet's intellectual allegiance to scientific truth and his emotional nostalgia for the Christian God and the Christian myth. The emotion of poignant regret for the loss of traditional belief while accepting the harsh truth of a meaningless world motivates and permeates such fine short lyrics as 'The Impercipient', 'The Oxen', and 'A Drizzling Easter Morning'. In these poems, the tension is first of all objectified in the poet's physical situation—among the gravestones on a wet Easter morning, 'By the embers in hearthside ease' on Christmas Eve, hovering on the outskirts of a Cathedral service—the archetypal alien from the harmony of a God-directed universe. He both observes and suffers the assaults of a physical world that has lost hope of Christian salvation, while his mind reaches back to the lost belief that would give meaning to suffering. The physical presence of the poet throughout, experiencing the divided allegiances of his time, gives emotional resonance to the simple but traditional details without which a poem like 'A Drizzling Easter Morning' would hardly rise above the factual observation of a wet day. His observation of the eternally heavy-laden as he stands amid the eternally at rest makes an ironic comment on the meaning of the Resurrection referred to in the first line: 'And is he risen? Well, be it so', which modifies the tone of the repetition in the last:

> And toilers with their aches are fain
> For endless rest—though risen is he.

The poet's figure within the poem, at once both a private individual and universal representative, throwing his mood of regret for lost faith over the whole poem, can make a success of a longer work such as 'God's Funeral', whereas 'A Plaint to Man', which presents the same idea—the growth and decay of man's conception of the deity—is less happy in its point of view. The dead God of 'A Plaint to Man'—one 'thin as a phasm on a lantern-slide'—can hardly transmit the powerful personal pressure of human nostalgia for a lost value that resides in the traditional associations of a funeral procession seen through the eyes of a stricken mourner.

> I saw a slowly-stepping train—
> Lined on the brows, scoop-eyed and bent and hoar—
> Following in files across a twilit plain
> A strange and mystic form the foremost bore.

The visual scene, with its vivid details of death and sorrow in the second line and its evocation of crowds engaged in some strange symbolic action, is reminiscent of Dante. So is the sad observing figure of the poet, whose sympathy with the figures of his vision sustains and unifies a poem of seventeen stanzas. The sympathy with this image of human sorrow, as yet unexplained, is established in the second stanza by 'contagious throbs of thought', and followed in stanzas III and IV by a changing image of what the dead shape had meant in all its 'phantasmal variousness' to the poet. Only when his personal response and mood has been clarified does he draw 'towards the moving columns without a word'. From stanzas VI to XII his personal response becomes involved with the general lament, which he overhears, of the human race for its 'man-projected Figure, of late/Imaged as we'. The explanation in these stanzas is not the emotionless explanation of cosmic operations given by a deity or Cause, but of the vision of human sorrow we have just seen, suffused with the grief of the observer. The growth of man's conception of God, and his grief at the loss of his comforting fantasy, is more comprehensible to the human mind than explanations of the cause of pain, which is inexplicable. The question 'And who or what shall fill his place?' returns the poem in stanza XIII to the personal response of the poet.

> I could not buoy their faith: and yet
> Many I had known: with all I sympathized;
> And though struck speechless, I did not forget
> That what was mourned for, I, too, long had prized.
>
> xv
> Still, how to bear such loss I deemed
> The insistent question for each animate mind . . .

Standing in the cold light of a godless day, without belief in a man-made God, or in a God that has survived the 'requiem' of his false man-made mockery, the insistent question of how to live in a meaningless absurdity is faced by the human individual with courage and integrity. Characteristically, Hardy does not place too much reliance on the small gleam of hope on the horizon,

42

perhaps a new God still to make himself manifest, but ends in the dazed and dramatic ignorance of the human being, isolated from his ordering fantasy, accepting the inexplicable mystery of a dissonant godless world:

> Thus dazed and puzzled 'twixt the gleam and gloom
> Mechanically I followed with the rest.

God is dead: all we can know of him is the value of his image to the human mind that created him. That value is developed in the poem through Hardy's dramatic use of the human consciousness, with its capacity for emotion, vision, fantasy, and truth, shaping the structure of the poem itself.

The importance of a tenable philosophy in a poem like 'God's Funeral' pales before the strength of the poet's feeling of regret for the passing of one which had imposed order on chaos. The strain of living without a comforting fantasy gives rise in countless shorter poems to the bewildered cry of personal pain that lifts poems like 'Hap' and 'Before Life and After' into the rank of major poetry. But the directionless bewilderment can also succeed at lower tension when it takes an ironic or humorous turn, as in 'The Respectable Burgher on "The Higher Criticism" ' and 'Drinking Song'. A characteristic tone of humorous and resigned regret can be found in the chorus of 'Drinking Song'—

> Fill full your cups: feel no distress;
> 'Tis only one great thought the less!

—which punctuates the roll-call of man's diminishing importance as reflected in the history of Western philosophy, from Thales' conjecture that 'everything was made for man' to Darwin's 'We are all one with creeping things'. The encompassing image of bewildered man, facing the dark with cheering cup in hand and an unshakeable faith in the one value he is left with, the value of human action ('We'll do a good deed nevertheless!'), to set against the loss of all sustaining philosophies, has more power to move than all the explanations of the Absolute. The colloquial language, such as the homely dialect word 'rathe' in the middle of Einstein relativity, and the awkward syntax that clothes the Copernican theory—

> We trod, he told,
> A globe that rolled
> Around a sun it warmed it at. . . .

present a vivid impression of the muddled human mind stutteringly trying to formulate incomprehensible abstractions in down-to-earth concrete terms. Einstein's 'notion' of relativity ('just a sort of bending-ocean') is more effective, by reason of the honest admission with which it begins, that it is

> Not yet quite clear
> To many here—

than its long scientific analysis in 'The Absolute Explains'.

To laugh at the absurdity of his tragic predicament in the universe is man's prerogative. God's attempts at grim humour in 'A Philosophical Fantasy' are not successful, any more than his attempts at thinking and feeling in other poems where he is the mouthpiece for Hardy's ideas. In spite of the wry rejection of man-centred philosophies in 'Drinking Song', the human being, with his capacity to feel, was always the centre of Hardy's universe. When the human cry is submerged in argumentative verse of direct statement or analysis, the poem is liable to fall flat. But when the cry of protest at 'the intolerable antilogy/Of making figments feel' is passionate enough to shape substance and style from the philosophy, a major poem is born.

> A time there was—as one may guess
> And as, indeed, earth's testimonies tell—
> Before the birth of consciousness,
> When all went well.
>
> None suffered sickness, love, or loss,
> None knew regret, starved hope, or heart-burnings;
> None cared whatever crash or cross
> Brought wrack to things.
>
> If something ceased, no tongue bewailed,
> If something winced and waned, no heart was wrung;
> If brightness dimmed, and dark prevailed,
> No sense was stung.
>
> But the disease of feeling germed,
> And primal rightness took the tint of wrong;
> Ere nescience shall be reaffirmed
> How long, how long?
> ('Before Life and After')

Here, the whole poem moves towards the passionate cry of human suffering in the last line. The germinal idea is one expressed by Hardy many times—'that the human race is too extremely developed for its corporeal conditions, the nerves being evolved to an activity abnormal in such an environment . . . This planet does not supply the materials for happiness to higher existences.' (*Life*)

Much of Hardy's overt philosophical poetry, in which the idea takes precedence over unadjusted impression of life, differs little in its presentation from such a prose statement, and at times descends to doggerel:

> But seeing indications
> That thou read'st my limitations,
> And since my lack of forethought
> Aggrieves thy more and more thought . . .
>> ('A Philosophical Fantasy')

But in 'Before Life and After', the concept is a consequence of the immediate experience—the instigating cry of agony at the insensitivity of the cosmos. The idea of dissonance is modified by the poet's personal emotion, which imposes a complex pattern of structure, rhythm, and diction on the prose facts of the world he is reacting to. Poetry is, for Hardy, 'emotion put into measure', and 'the Poet takes note of nothing that he cannot feel emotively'. The poet's job is to order his materials in such a way that the reader is infected with his own feeling about the experience that inspired the poem. In this poem, the simple objective statement of primal harmony in the world, with its economical but evocative glance at the long sweep of evolutionary history ('earth's testimonies') is framed between two mood-inducing echoes of earlier poetry. 'A time there was' smuggles in a memory of Wordsworth's 'Ode on the Intimations of Immortality', which begins likewise in a mood of regret for a lost sense of harmony. But the resonance is ironic. Wordsworth's nostalgia is for the loss of a child's heightened awareness, Hardy's for a time 'before the birth of consciousness', since heightened awareness is so often awareness of suffering. The slow, dignified movement of the four monosyllables 'When all went well', which one can hardly speak without placing a major stress on each word, catches the deathly calm of Keats' 'And no birds sing', and so enriches by association the sense of a landscape without life. The complex ironies contained in these reverberations, added to

45

the prose sense of the words, have already established the tension between conscious man and the unconscious universe which produces both poem and poetic emotion.

The tensions, strains, stresses and hesitations which characterize human life make themselves felt in the very different movement and music of the second stanza. The 'nescience' of things before life, implied in the negation of the pronoun 'one', is combined significantly with active verbs that affirm the moral values which developed with human consciousness. These three phrases, placed in parallel positions of emphasis at the beginning of the line, hold balance in the stanza with general definitions of the ills that flesh is heir to, which *then* were unfelt. The 'now' which in a Hardy poem is set in inevitable opposition to the 'then', is expressed in the various pains of a conscious world fighting strenuously against the expected beat of the line, which has been set in a fairly smooth-running pattern by the first stanza. The reader's uncertainties on the placing of speech stress may be art rather than incompetence—a required imaginative contribution to the sense of the difficulties of emergent human consciousness struggling with the intractable denseness of matter. Does one, for example, place heavy stresses on both components of 'starved hope' and both root-syllables of 'heart-burnings'? Or even on all three syllables (as Benjamin Britten has done in his musical setting of the poem), which is suggested by the rhyme-word 'things', and would be a practice in keeping with the medieval ballad level of diction which Hardy drew on for this particular compound? Does one stress both subject and verb of 'None suffered . . . none knew . . . none cared'? To do so is to retard the movement of the second line at least with heavy stresses, but the very weight of the line, added to the increased alliteration of the whole stanza, points up the straining tensions between life and no-life which make the reader's perplexities part of the poem's creative process.

The third stanza reverses the placings of negative and positive elements. The negative of the person, 'none', is replaced at the beginning of the line by the positive abstractions 'something' and 'brightness', while the negative connotations move over to the verbs—'ceased', 'winced and waned', 'dimmed'. The human pain evoked by these verbs is brought nearer home by the diction of this stanza—'tongue' and 'heart' are parts of the human body traditionally associated with the expression of feeling.

Hardy's emotional manipulation of negation is masterly. The

response of consciousness *after* the appearance of life is continually implied in his vision of the world *before* life by denial of the responses we have come to recognize as human. 'None suffered . . . None knew . . . none cared . . . no tongue bewailed . . . no heart was wrung . . . no sense was stung.' The last stanza brings to birth the cry of human pain that has been implicit through its denial in the first three stanzas. The passion behind it inspires that imaginative, evocative use of words and word-music that turns what could have been an emotionless scientific analysis of the relationship between man and his environment into a poetic experience of the highest quality. In the context of a longing for 'nescience' the word 'dis-ease' evokes its original meaning of discomfort and disharmony, as well as the more usual sense of illness, which in turn requires a double response to 'germed' in its suggestions of springing and decaying life, and to the rare poetic 'tinct' with its connotations of moral taint as well as impregnated colour. The preciseness with which Hardy invests the words taken from every level of language can be felt in the unpretentious 'if something winced'. Wincing is defined as an *involuntary* shrinking, therefore a movement that is appropriate to the state of unconsciousness that existed before human knowledge of pain.

Simplicity and something which is almost the opposite of simplicity—terms in which Leonard Woolf described the man Hardy—can be seen in rich tension in 'Before Life and After', as in all Hardy's best poetry. The simple phrases, the sonorous dignity of the abstractions 'consciousness', 'nescience', 'rightness', 'wrong', set against the concrete vision of human suffering; the echoes of Biblical and traditional literature with its ready-made emotional associations—'If brightness dimmed, and dark prevailed'; the subtle vowel progressions and assonances in the key-words 'burnings—things—wrung—stung—wrong—long': all work together to produce a poem which has the idiosyncratic simplicity and complexity of the man, and yet achieves universality and objectivity through the very depth of his personal reaction to the universe.

In his philosophical poetry, Hardy sometimes succumbs to the temptation to attempt an explanation of the inexplicable dissonances of life. They cannot be explained by unrepresentable Forces; they can only be felt in the power of their mystery on the pulses of a human being. The vividly communicated personal pain of 'How long, how long?' would make Hardy rather less than the perfect artist of T. S. Eliot's ideal in 'Tradition and the Individual

Talent': 'the more perfect the artist, the more completely separate in him will be the man who suffers and the mind which creates'. But perfection is not a human quality. As Hardy remarks in a note (*Life*) 'It is the incompleteness that is loved, when love is sterling and true'.

'Hardy . . . put everything he felt, everything he noticed, everything he was, into his poetry. As a result he wrote a great many bad poems—far more than Mr Eliot will ever have written: but also, because what he gave so unreservedly was the impressions of a magnanimous heart, the thoughts of a mind closely engaged in the problems of its own time and possessed of a strong historical sense, the experience of a man thoroughly versed in human suffering, his poetry has that breadth of matter and manner which only a major poet can compass.'

(C. Day Lewis, 'The Lyrical Poetry of Thomas Hardy', *Proceedings of the British Academy XXXVII*, 1951)

It is the note of personal suffering which makes Hardy speak truly to those human beings who think humbly, deeply, and in jagged personal rhythms about their relationship to the mysteries of the cosmos.

'The Homeliest of Heart-Stirrings':
Shorter Lyrics

'I believe few persons have read *Faust* without disappointment . . . A masterpiece excites no sudden enthusiasm; it must be studied much and long, before it is fully comprehended; we must grow up to it, for it will not descend to us. Its influence is less sudden, more lasting. Its emphasis grows with familiarity. We never become disenchanted; we grow more and more awestruck at its infinite wealth. We discover no trick, for there is none to discover. Homer, Shakespeare, Raphael, Beethoven, Mozart, never storm the judgment; but, once fairly in possession, they retain it with increasing influence . . . With *Faust* my first feeling was disappointment. Not understanding the real nature of the work, I thought Goethe had missed his aim, because he did not fulfil my conceptions. It is the arrogance of criticism to demand that the artist, who never thought of us, should work in the direction of our thoughts.'
(G. H. Lewes: *The Life and Works of Goethe*)

Lewes' experience with *Faust* mirrors the road which many readers of Hardy's non-dramatic lyrics must travel, Whereas the best of his philosophical poetry is shaped by passionate personal feeling, the cry of unadulterated joy or sorrow which certain theories of poetry regard as indispensible to lyric form seems to be missing, or to exist at low tension, in many of Hardy's successful lyrics. Nor can one find the subtleties and ambiguities on which the modern reader of Eliot or Empson has been trained to exercise his talent for the elucidation of mysteries. It is perhaps difficult not to feel a sense of disappointment on first reading, for example, 'Life and Death at Sunrise':

> The hills uncap their tops
> Of woodland, pasture, copse,
> And look on the layers of mist
> At their foot that still persist:
> They are like awakened sleepers on one elbow lifted,
> Who gaze around to learn if things during night have shifted.

A waggon creaks up from the fog
With a laboured leisurely jog;
Then a horseman from off the hill-tip
Comes clapping down into the dip;
While woodlarks, finches, sparrows, try to entune at one time,
And cocks and hens and cows and bulls take up the chime.

With a shouldered basket and flagon
A man meets the one with the waggon,
And both the men halt of long use.
"Well," the waggoner says, "What's the news?"
"—'Tis a boy this time. You've just met the doctor trotting back.
She's doing very well. And we think we shall call him 'Jack.'

"And what have you got covered there?"
He nods to the waggon and mare.
"Oh, a coffin for old John Thinn:
We are just going to put him in."
"—So he's gone at last. He always had a good constitution."
"—He was ninety-odd. He could call up the French Revolution."

There are no tricks to discover here. It is difficult for the most
ardent student of ambiguity to make the poem carry a meaning
other than the one intended by the poet. Hardy has ventured so
near the prosaic in matter and manner that one is tempted to think
that he set out to prove to himself how much 'poetry' he could do
without. Yet, like Wordsworth's deceptively simple 'A Slumber
Did My Spirit Seal', the poem grows in depth and richness until
one realizes that its centrality of theme has subtly changed one's
awareness of life.

The observation of a chance encounter between two country-
men, and their fragment of completely natural conversation, seems
at first sight too trivial to carry much significance. Yet the prosaic
conjunction of two men is made poetic by the conjunction of life
and death embodied in their meeting. Quiet acceptance of the
eternal rhythms of human life is reflected in their brief unemotional
exchange of news. The baby, taking the name of the dead man
whose memory reaches so far back into the past, promises for the
future the only kind of continuity the human race can hope to
attain. Hardy's hawk-like vision, which so often in his poetry and
novels sets tiny individual figures in a landscape, gradually extends
to link his two speakers, through the old man and baby and the
distant figure of the doctor, mediator of life and death, not only to

their local social context but also to the whole of human history. Finally these ephemeral human lives are set firmly in the larger rhythms of nature. Their conjunction takes place to the dawn chorus of wild birds and farm livestock. Hardy's affectionate and slow-moving enumeration by species suggests the eternal recurrence of natural things, and with them, of leisurely funeral waggons eternally meeting and passing the hurry of new life. These things go onward the same though Dynasties pass. And the whole of sentient life—birds, farm animals, human beings—is set in the vast timeless context of the insentient universe in which they live and die—the landscape of hill, wood, pasture, copse, and morning mist.

Like so many of Hardy's lyrics, 'Life and Death at Sunrise' (subtitled 'Near Dogbury Gate, 1867') begins with a precise evocation of time and place. The details of the moment when 'the hills uncap their tops' to reveal their reality while human figures emerge from and disappear into the fogs that 'still persist' at the foot, show a naturalist's exact observation of phenomena, yet they are emotionally charged with the imponderable mystery of life and death. Natural features of the landscape, night, and mist arouse deep traditional responses which turn the hills into watchers from an Overworld of unobscured reality, and the foggy lowland into the darkling plain of blinkered human action. Apart from the one simile of the hills as 'awakened sleepers', which brings overtones of resurrection into this poem of life and death, and the personalizing metaphors of 'uncap' and 'look', the details of the poem are not of the kind to satisfy the image-hunter. Hardy seems to depend more on factual statement than suggestion; yet the steady piling up of observed detail of this moment of sunrise manages to suggest more than the content of the statements. When the scene has been set, human action appears in the second stanza. The movement of sentient life counterpoints the stability of the insentient landscape with another kind of stability—the perpetual recurrence of the life cycle. Things have not shifted during night; only the individual actors in the drama are likely to be different. The last two stanzas focus on the two individual figures—the most important features of Hardy's landscape—to bring the dramatic immediacy of homely colloquial speech into the descriptive but as yet non-dramatic scene. At this pivotal point of time and space evoked by the details of the first two stanzas, no extraneous comment from the poet is needed to realize the conjunction of light and dark inherent in the exchange of words.

The effect of the poem springs from the reality of a normal everyday experience honestly recorded and felt; the moment of insight into our relationship to the rhythms of the universe from the unflinching response of Hardy's senses to all facets of the objective world. Lyric ecstasy gives way to loving fidelity to what he sees and hears; yet this very devotion to fact produces lyric emotion.

> 'The only way of expressing emotion in the form of art is by finding an "objective correlative"; in other words, a set of objects, a situation, a chain of events which shall be the formula of that *particular* emotion; such that when the external facts, which must terminate in sensory experience, are given, the emotion is immediately evoked.'
>
> (T. S. Eliot: *Selected Essays*)

In this homely Wessex scene Hardy has found an objective correlative for his intuitions about life and death. In the simple but precise diction, the natural speech rhythms straining against metrical rigidity, in the verse form itself, he has found the means to infect his readers with those intuitions. While all four stanzas keep roughly to the metrical pattern of three stresses in the first four lines and six in the last two, the wide variations in speech stress and number of syllables to the stress make the movement of each stanza very different. Syllabic and speech stress do not pull too far apart in the first stanza. As the stability of the landscape gives way, however, to the eccentricites of human and animal life, the tension between regular metre and irregular speech stress becomes more elastic: a crisp six-syllable line of alternating stress and unstress, such as 'The hills uncap their tops', has grown to nine syllables of completely natural speech rhythm in

"Well," the waggoner says, "What's the news?"

as human speech and movement gradually dominate the insentient natural scene. The 'closeness of phrase to his vision' which Hardy admired in his fellow Dorset poet William Barnes has been achieved here.

The unpretentious nature of both phrase and vision may call for a redefinition of lyrical quality. Hardy himself, in his Preface to *Select Poems of William Barnes*, objected to too severe a classification that would exclude much of the finest English poetry as well as his own characteristic mixture of lyrical, dramatic, narrative, and contemplative elements in the same poem.

'. . . many fine poems that have lyric moments are not entirely lyrical; many largely narrative poems are not entirely narrative; many personal reflections or meditations in verse hover across the frontiers of lyricism . . . the same lines may be lyrical to one temperament and meditative to another; nay, lyrical and not lyrical to the same reader at different times, according to his mood and circumstance . . .

'One might, to be sure, as a smart impromptu, narrow down the definition of lyric to the safe boundary of poetry that has all its nouns in the vocative case, and so settle the question by the simple touchstone of the grammar-book, adducing the *Benedicite* as a shining example. But this qualification would be disconcerting in its stringency, and cause a fluttering of the leaves of many an accepted anthology.'

Other 'impromptu' definitions are just as wide of the mark. The gnarled and knotted nature of much of Hardy's thought and diction does not accord with the singing quality once thought to be essential to a lyric, though the technical challenge they present to musicians has produced several successful settings, notably Benjamin Britten's 'Winter Words'. There are some exceptions: few people would disagree with Hardy's estimate that 'When I Set Out for Lyonnesse' has 'the song-ecstasy that a lyric should have', but in general he found 'So little cause for carolings/Of such ecstatic sound' that his poetic impulse took other directions. And though much of that impulse is personal, it is difficult to make 'Life and Death at Sunrise', 'An Unkindly May', or 'The Sheep-Boy' fit exactly the definition of Ruskin: 'Lyrical poetry is the expression by the poet of his own feelings'. There is too much fact within the feeling for most of his poetry to exist as simple cries of joy or sorrow; too much contemplation for the complete merging of poet and subject that takes place in 'pure' lyric, though 'Weathers' approaches this rare purity. But the isolated details of experience that he selects to relate in the significant pattern of a poem imply his subjective response where it is not explicit, and the complex of objective reality and subjective response add up to a poetic unity (not invalidated by the contrasts of mood and experience which may be contained within a single poem) that can be called lyrical, however mixed the genres within the poem may be.

Hardy's best lyrics are moments of vision that have found their objective correlative in something close to common experience which yet evokes the underlying deeper reality that he admired in Turner's late paintings. All the unremarkable and usually unremarked aspects of routine life are brought into consciousness by

Hardy's penetrating vision in a search for the attainable significance that does not aspire beyond the world of here and now. He finds it in the burning of an old photograph, a car 'whanging' down a country road, a thrush singing in the gloom of a death-marked landscape at the turn of the century, an old woman raking up leaves, a girl who 'passed foot-faint with averted head' the scene of her former love, a boy at midnight on the Great Western,

> Bewrapt past knowing to what he was going,
> Or whence he came,

a mysterious couple promenading beyond the last lamp on Tooting Common, whose human quality of sadness immortalizes the scene in the poet's memory, 'the mould of a musical bird long passed from light' in a museum, the loss of a drinking glass, a broken appointment, a moment of indecision whether to meet or not, the memory of imperfections in a face or in social graces, the scene of youthful pleasures, old furniture, a dream of the loved one in old age, a map on the wall, a family pedigree which mocks illusions of individual free will and significance, a glance in the mirror, a visit to his first school, the death of a cat, a superstition that 'this candle-wax is shaping to a shroud', a flash of sunlight reflected from the coffin of a fellow-poet and friend. Poems like 'After the Last Breath' and 'The Announcement' catch the imperceptible moment when the death of a person makes an undefinable difference to routine rhythms:

> They came, the brothers, and took two chairs
>   In their usual quiet way;
> And for a time we did not think
>   They had much to say.
>
> And they began and talked awhile
>   Of ordinary things,
> Till spread that silence in the room
>   A pent thought brings.
>
> And then they said: "The end has come.
>   Yes: it has come at last."
> And we looked down, and knew that day
>   A spirit had passed.
>   ('The Announcement')

Our awareness of the moment when things have changed their look and quality is enlarged by the quiet prosaic observation of habitual actions that sustain life, the suggestion of regular recurrence in the repetition of 'And', the sudden tightening of natural speech rhythms to end the second stanza on three stressed monosyllables which bring expectation of change; the dramatization of that change, as in 'Life and Death at Sunrise', in colloquial speech; the respectful embarrassed gesture 'And we looked down' in the presence of the reluctantly-voiced mystery which has brought the larger rhythms of the cosmos into intersection with the ordinariness of the daily round.

Often in Hardy's world, as in Samuel Beckett's, 'nothing happens, nobody comes, nobody goes', as a glance at some of his titles may indicate—'A Commonplace Day', 'A Broken Appointment', 'Nobody Comes', 'She did not Turn', 'You were the Sort that Men Forget'. Yet, like Beckett, Hardy extracts significance from the insignificant. The moment of awareness can be projected as strongly from what does not happen as from a dramatic conjunction of persons, time, and place, as in 'A Commonplace Day':

> Wanly upon the panes
> The rain slides, as have slid since morn my colourless thoughts; and yet
> Here, while Day's presence wanes,
> And over him the sepulchre-lid is slowly lowered and set,
> He wakens my regret.

The poet's attempt to define the quality of an uneventful day begins, characteristically, at the twilight hour, which in many poems ('Nobody Comes', 'At Day-Close in November', 'Birds at Winter Nightfall', 'The Darkling Thrush', and others) carries a traditional emotional charge of loneliness, sadness, loss and regret. The striking metaphor 'turning ghost' gives the lead to 'the pale corpse-like birth . . . bearing blanks in all its rays', and the images of colourlessness which define the insubstantiality of the day. The colloquial 'scuttles' suggests the undignified character of its insignificance in a precise concrete verb which, in true Hardy fashion, is immediately swallowed up like the day itself in the abstract Latinate grandeur of 'the anonymous host/Of those that throng oblivion' and the formal 'ceding his place, maybe,/To one of like degree'. But the cautious colloquial 'maybe' which punctuates the formal phrase and the personification of the day cast doubt on the poet's complete assent to its insignificance.

When the time of day has been precisely set, stanza II brings place and person into conjunction with it. The fireside seems to be a favourite spot for contemplation, as poems like 'The Photograph', 'Logs on the Hearth', and 'Surview' bear additional witness. The poet's physical presence in the poem by a physical fireside gives authenticity to an experience that can only be made significant by the human capacity to feel and think. His precise, orderly actions reinforce the 'end-of-the-day' atmosphere, which closes in again with the dragging extent of the fourth line, unpunctuated by the pauses that characterize the human action of the previous lines, and the overwhelming alliterative weight of 'beamless black'. In stanza III his meditating mind brings human values into fruitful tension with the uneventfulness of the day through pondering on what he has *not* done to make it significant—a characteristic Hardeian affirmation through negation. His relationship as a human being to 'this diurnal unit' is suggested by the compound of cancelling opposites in 'corpse-like birth' and the 'blanks' in its 'rays', for only conscious human action can realize the dormant potentialities that each day is born with. The preponderance of cloddish 'u's and heavy alliterating 'b's and 'd's end the stanza with the brutish thump of the cosmic insignificance which the conscious human mind has to face and transform.

Stanza IV develops the link between the poet's human consciousness and the dull world he inhabits by the simile of colourless thoughts; outer and inner environments slide, with the long vowels and repetitions of 'n', to one dead level of insignificance, until the positive turn 'and yet'. The humanized image of Day as a dead person returns, in a context which stresses the actualities of place—'Here'—and time—'while Day's presence wanes'—and these antidotes to insubstantiality are joined by the most powerful positive of all—human emotion. Stanza V moves in closer to the poet's meditating mind to turn over the irrational feeling of regret.

The idiosyncratic rhythm of the overheard voice is now in full swing, with all the stops and starts, slow hesitations, and eccentricities of thought in process, so the stanza can carry such Hardeian medievalisms as 'that I wot of' and 'toward'—which gives a better sense of forward motion than a commoner word. Hardy's unflinching look at the worst in this stanza—the commonplaceness of the day, unmarked by any significant human action that he knows of—is immediately and characteristically balanced in stanza VI by his tendency to hope for the best and believe that there was some extra-sensory reason for his emotion. The scrupulous hesitancy of 'Yet, maybe'—for he will not pretend to absolute conviction—serves to emphasize the outward swing from the personal to 'the wide world' which began in stanza v and is carried on in 'some soul,/In some spot undiscerned on sea or land', and the unpunctuated rush of the 'enkindling ardency' which brings the imagined positive impulse to a soaring conclusion in the last three lines. The fire of matter and manner in this penultimate stanza balances the dying embers of the second; the prefix of the unusual compound 'upstole' gives a lift to the 'waning' imagery that predominated in the first half of the poem. The final stanza does not lose the impetus of the upward lift, though Hardy's respect for truth qualifies the hope of the noble intent by making it potential rather than actual; 'benumbed at birth/By momentary chance or wile'—a misfire. Yet the human emotion of regret for the 'thwarted purposing' of the day which created his moment of vision remains valid, as the most important thing in the poem, and ends it with an affirmation of waking awareness that balances all its corpses. The feeling cannot be explained by reason, but the irrational and supernatural which Hardy's respect for scientific truth rejected intellectually persists in powerful emotional tension with that scrupulously presented truth in the 'undervoicings' of the poem.

'A Commonplace Day', like many of Hardy's successful lyrics, has a quietness that comes of contemplating the values of life from the standpoint of their denial. The poetic significance to him of what does not happen can be gauged from the number of fine poems in which negative statements occupy a key position. They may begin a poem:

Breathe not, hid Heart: cease silently . . .

For Life I had never cared greatly . . .

You did not come . . .

Not a line of her writing have I,
Not a thread of her hair . . .

Her laugh was not in the middle of her face quite . . .

You were the sort that men forget;
Though I—not yet!—

They may bring the poem to a close:

"He hears it not now, but used to notice such things".

. . . And nobody pulls up there.

O never I turned, but let, alack,
    These less things hold my gaze!

    As we seemed we were not
      That day afar,
    And now we seem not what
      We aching are . . .

                . . . But none replies:
    No warnings loom, nor whisperings
    To open out my limitings,
    And Nescience mutely muses: When a man falls he lies.

A negative statement in the body of the poem often points to the contrast between the potentialities of life and their denial:

    Alas, I knew not much of her,
    And lost all sight and touch of her!

Now no Christmas brings in neighbours,
    And the New Year comes unlit;
Where we sang the mole now labours,
    And spiders knit.

A pattern of denial running through all the stanzas of a poem can act as a refrain which is a powerful instrument of the irony contained in two contrasted states. The harsh denying present is brought into violent juxtaposition with pleasant memories of the past in 'During Wind and Rain' by the repeated refrain of the years; and in 'Molly Gone' by the first line pattern of each stanza, 'No more summer [planting, jauntings, singing] for Molly and me', and by the memory-denying actions that begin each stanza of 'Shut out that Moon'. The sinister denial of evidence of the senses in the first three stanzas of "Who's in the Next Room?" prepares the way inevitably for the affirmation of negation—death's world of no-sense—in the final stanza. What is not seen or heard or said or done or known can create a more potent mood of dread than the most explicit statements of positive knowledge. The repeated

determination in each stanza of 'He Resolves to Say No More' to
'keep the rest unknown' says all that Hardy wished to say about
the harsh conditions within which value and meaning must be
achieved. But other, tenderer moods can be evoked too by his
negative refrains and repetitions. The comments of the animal,
human and stellar world which end each stanza of "I Am the One"
paint an affirming picture of 'one for whom Nobody cares' enough
to interrupt their normal rhythms; a gentle, unassuming character
whose reticence is not due to any lack of interest or observation,
but to a genuine humility about his place in nature and a feeling
of kinship with all its parts, which provides the final affirmative:
'He is one with us/Beginning and end.' On the other hand, the
refrain-like repetitions in 'The Fallow Deer at the Lonely House'
of 'One without looks in tonight' and 'We do not discern those
eyes' intensify the central opposition between the natural bleakness without and the unnatural bleakness within. Hardy often
uses an animal to crystallize a human attitude to life: here, the
cold landscape is given affirmative significance by the movements
of body and mind that characterize a living creature—on tiptoe,
wondering, watching, 'aglow' with the dynamic fire that is missing from the silent unobservant couple nursing the fireside, who
shelter in their passive ('lit') comfort from the pain of a full
response to life. 'The Reminder' shows that Hardy knew the
penalty of a full response, as he sits in a similarly cheerful Christmas blaze:

> Why, O starving bird, when I
> One day's joy would justify,
> And put misery out of view,
> Do you make me notice you!

A poem like 'The Photograph' dramatizes a painful affirmation of
living warmth in the very act of negating it. The woman's photograph is burned 'in a casual clearance of life's arrears', but as the
flame moves over her pictured sexual attractions

> . . . I vented a cry of hurt, and averted my eyes;
> The spectacle was one that I could not bear,
> To my deep and sad surprise.

Hardy himself was no life-denier. Poems such as 'Let Me Enjoy'
and 'Great Things' bear direct witness to his pleasure in the simple

sensuous joys of the world as it is. Even "For Life I had never Cared Greatly" denies the initial denial by admitting the ebb and flow of life's appeal, 'till evasions gave in to its song'. Only a man who loved life in every fibre of his being could feel so keenly the betrayal of its potentialities in the sight of a starving thrush, a blinded bird, or an unwanted pauper child. His inability to put misery out of view is a direct corollary of the intense wish to justify life and joy, and the interaction of these two emotions a major source of his resonant power. Only a man who upheld the value of life and the individual human being is capable of the compassion that begins 'To an Unborn Pauper Child' with

> Breathe not, hid Heart: cease silently,

and consistently negates the negating injunction by the living personal rhythms of his own voice affirming painfully, honestly, against the rigid metrical pattern, the value of human emotion—'unreasoning, sanguine, visionary'—which

> can hope
> Health, love, friends, scope
> In full for thee; can dream thou'lt find
> Joys seldom yet attained by humankind!

The affirmation is all the more impressive for refusing to deny the life-denying realities of travails, teens, and Time-wraiths their power and place in human experience. The manuscript shows Hardy's indecision between 'seldom' and 'never' in the last line. His final choice of 'seldom' is more accurate; but the hope of joys remains a hope rather than a conviction. However, its truth is accepted without question because it has been hardly won through a struggle with life's denials. Where the tension between what is and what ought to be is missing in thought and structure, the result is a lesser poem. 'To C.F.H. on Her Christening Day' and 'The Unborn' make the same indictment of birth, but without the sense of painful personal involvement that springs from Hardy's conflicting allegiances to scientific truth and human aspiration. The beginning of 'To C.F.H.':

> Fair Caroline, I wonder what
> You think of earth as a dwelling-spot,
> And if you'd rather have come, or not?

pales before the immediate dramatic power of an injunction to stop breathing. The equivalent question to the pauper child, 'Wilt thou take Life so?' comes, not as a desultory speculation to start a poem, but as a fitting climax to the failure of life's illusions set out in the previous stanza, and it gains resonance from the poet's knowledge, which he never allows us to forget as he voices his desires for the child, that it is *not* free 'To cease, or be', but 'Must come and bide'. The prayer for 'good things with glad' in the last stanza of 'To C.F.H.' is less effective than the scrupulously cautious hope that ends 'To an Unborn Pauper Child' because it does not rise out of the travails and teens that invariably balance good things and glad. The sense of painful personal struggle towards affirmation of life is less effective in 'The Unborn', where it is left distanced and un-dramatic. The tension in 'the news that pity would not break/Nor truth leave unaverred' does not come to life in the verse form, the clichés, the abstractions, the generalized vagueness of 'crowding shapes'. But it can be felt in the anguished hesitations and broken personal rhythms of a man experienced in life's travails and teens addressing a potential human being who comes to stand for the human predicament.

In 'To An Unborn Pauper Child' the Hardeian idiosyncrasies of rhythm and diction enact what it means to be human, with illusions of freedom, against the predestination of the verse pattern. It means dignity and tenderness: Hardy has managed to suggest both by using the second person singular throughout, hallowed by Biblical and traditional associations and the intimacy of its con-tinuing usage in dialect. It means sublimity and simplicity: the rolling Latinate grandeur of 'unreasoning, sanguine, visionary' and 'Ere their terrestrial chart unrolls' is followed immediately by short monosyllabic statements. The Revelations image of cosmic power in Stanza IV leads to a stanza on man's weakness in which only one of the Anglo-Saxon words is not a monosyllable. It means losing the concrete joys of life—'songsingings'—to ghostly abstrac-tions in the march of Time, and human aspirations to the process of physical decay:

> Hark, how the peoples surge and sigh,
> And laughters fail, and greetings die:
>   Hopes dwindle; yea,
>   Faiths waste away,
> Affections and enthusiasms numb;
> Thou canst not mend these things if thou dost come.

It means being part of the cosmic rhythm of suffering as an individual, and as a member of the human race; and it means companionship in suffering, helplessness, and loss of illusion. It means accepting fully the human being's inability to change the nature of things: the dream of doing so as a 'vain vow'—but nevertheless a positive contribution to the value of life, as the hammer-blows on 'Health, love, friends, scope' indicate. It means, finally, feeling the complex emotion that inspired the poem: the love-hate relationship with life; the compassion and reverence for the human individual subjected to its ills; the irrepressible desire to hope for the best while believing that it cannot be, which affirms the significance of life denied to it by the cosmic scheme.

Only a rare reverence for the phenomena and potentialities of life could rebel so passionately at the injustice of finding them meaningless. Hardy loved them well enough not to see eternity in a grain of sand. In 'A Sign-Seeker', the poetic emotion is generated from the tension between his desire to believe that the beauty, sublimity and horror of the physical world, including man, are part of a cosmic design which will justify their existence, and his reluctant conviction that they are not. The poet's usual position as observer within the poem becomes a symbol of man's predicament in the physical universe, helpless to alter its course, able only to endure the effects of its phenomena on his senses while remaining in ignorance of their ultimate cause and meaning. 'I mark . . . I see . . . And hear . . . have felt . . . And trodden . . . I learn . . . I witness . . .' but he cannot say 'I understand'. Yet the full response to the physical world as the only world that exists, by the whole man—human being, lover and hater of life, scholar, philosopher, observer—in the idiosyncratic Hardy voice, paradoxically evokes 'undervoicings' from the details of natural phenomena which deny portents of meaning. The characteristic mixture of simplicity and complexity, prosaic and rare, archaic, dialect, and literary expression, unusual forms and coinages, awkward constructions, and jagged personal rhythms fights against the simple verse form with its enclosed rhyme scheme and long last line that hammers home with alliteration and assonance the denseness of matter and passage of time which mock at man's search for significance—

And hear the monotonous hours clang negligently by.

Hardy's choice of words sets up reverberations that extend far beyond a mere record of the physical world. The 'eyeless countenance of the mist' juxtaposes the blank face of nature with the groping 'view' of its human observer, conscious but hardly less blind in his search for meaning. The accuracy of the rare Latinate 'subtrude' evokes the traditional and appropriate associations of night, and night as the image of death, *thrusting* its presence *stealthily* on the human being, as Hardy's first thought in the manuscript, 'I know the Nod of Night subdued', did not. And no other word but the coined 'outbreathing' could express so succinctly the desire that dead matter should give out a sign of continued existence to the living world. 'Eccentric' attached to 'orbs' revives its original astronomical meaning which, in conjunction with its more usual modern sense of caprice in human behaviour, points to the lack of a fixed centre of reference which would justify all things as part of an intelligent design. 'Moils' invests the human activity of work with the additional connotation of turmoil and confusion, which also mean 'a world alive'. The unusual form of 'solve' for 'dissolve' carries undertones of the solution of life's mysteries that is only to be found in dissolution.

The meaning of a search for meaning in a physical world that denies it is gradually revealed through the shifts in the seeker's viewpoint. Close observation of the familiar rhythms of hours, days, seasons, and weathers changes to observation of the extraordinary rhythms of nature at extremes, which distance and diminish the observer. Then the angle of vision suddenly soars to an Overworld view of humanity as a rhythmic, conglomerate mass of impulses involuntarily obeying the same fundamental force that powers 'the earthquake's lifting arm' and 'the leaping star':

> I witness fellow earth-men surge and strive;
> Assemblies meet, and throb, and part;
> Death's sudden finger, sorrow's smart;
> —All the vast various moils that mean a world alive.

When mass movement has abstracted all significance from the human individual, the viewpoint sweeps back to earth again, to the personal search for meaning among the last physical traces of a close human relationship, 'in graveyard green, where his pale dust lies pent'. Only the physical world exists for Hardy; only a physical sign would appease his hunger for justification—a voice from the grave, a 'print to prove her spirit-kisses real' from a dead Love's lips, 'one plume as pledge that Heaven inscrolls the wrong' to witness that earthly injustice is part of heavenly design. The honest admission of the faith of others emphasizes the final return to Hardy's sole surety—the existence of the physical world, meaningless as it is. The denseness of unresponsive matter is present in the weight of monosyllables in

> I have lain in dead men's beds, have walked
> The tombs of those with whom I had talked . . .

and also in the simple finality of 'When a man falls he lies'—the inescapable physical fact that makes a mockery of man's search for metaphysical meaning. Yet the wide-ranging movements of the conscious human mind in its deep hunger for metaphysical truth and its refusal to deny the physical world its own truth, 'even if despair', relates all things within the poem to invest it with the design that is missing from the cosmic process.

In the absence of cosmic significance, affirmation of life is wrested out of those things which seem to deny it value. The large and small phenomena of the physical world have no small value to a man who can hardly bear to attribute them to the void, and they take their place with the less tangible values of life and love, friendship and justice, in a Hardeian pattern of poetry where denial infers the value of the things denied. The call in 'Shut out that Moon' to deny the joys of the senses leaves no doubt of what they had meant to Hardy

> When living seemed a laugh, and love
> All it was said to be.

The vivid factual details of the natural world in 'Afterwards', the fleeting actions of small creatures which the poet tries to fix against the flux of time and relate to the exact moment of his own fixity in death, suggest how much they mean in themselves, without metaphysical justification, to 'a man who used to notice such things'. And the attraction that natural phenomena held for him adds a rich complexity to the mood of regret that ends 'Overlooking the River Stour':

> And never I turned my head, alack,
>   While these things met my gaze
>   Through the pane's drop-drenched glaze,
> To see the more behind my back . . .
> O never I turned, but let, alack,
>   These less things hold my gaze!

The details of the riverside scene fix by repetition his immersion in a sense of the present moment; the obvious attraction for him of 'these less things' comments on and enhances the value of 'the more behind my back'—the human relationship with his wife that his position at the window denies.

Hardy's fidelity to factual presentation of the physical world needs no intimation of hidden signs and portents to stir delight in recognition of its truth. He brings the naturalist's ultra-sensitive eye and ear to the sights, sounds, and processes of nature in poems like "I Watched a Blackbird", 'Throwing a Tree', 'On Sturminster Footbridge', and 'Snow in the Suburbs'; an artist's eye for colour, shape, line, and contrast, and a musician's ear for evocative sounds. Yet the unflinching integrity of his response to the physical world, along with a poet's command of language and rhythm, provides him with one of the most powerful weapons of poetry to replace metaphysical significance—a sense of wonder at the mysteries of the cosmos. 'I feel that Nature is played out as a Beauty, but not as a Mystery' he wrote in a note of 1887. There are strange conjunctions in the natural world—as of poet, longlegs, moth, dumbledore, and 'sleepy fly, that rubs its hands' in 'An August Midnight'—

> Thus meet we five, in this still place,
> At this point of time, at this point in space

—which bring, not the expected elucidation of their significance, but a sense of humility and awe at the mystery of things:

> "God's humblest, they!" I muse. Yet why?
> They know Earth-secrets that know not I.

In 'The Darkling Thrush' the defiant bird-song speaks to him, cautiously, of 'some blessed Hope, whereof he knew/And I was unaware': but more often, not even a tentative conclusion is allowed to creep into his wonder at the mysterious rhythms contained in physical phenomena. In 'The Year's Awakening', the repeated question 'How do you know?' to the 'vespering bird' and the hidden crocus sufficiently points up the mystery of their instinctive knowledge of the vast movements of the Zodiac and transformation of light which are part of an intricate process that adds up to the miracle of Spring. Poems such as 'A Backward Spring', 'An Unkindly May', and 'The Sheep-Boy' do not even ask a question: the sense of wonder is generated from accurate report of the physical facts. The bees' foreknowledge of a change in the weather in 'The Sheep-Boy' is left without comment on their action except the contrasting ignorance of the human figure: 'Awhile he waits, and wonders what they mean'. Their sudden flight before the mist simply adds one more external detail to the process which describes the mystery, none the less a mystery for being so full of physical facts, of one of nature's sudden transformations. The vivid pictorial quality brings undertones of the greater mystery of the final blotting out of all human life and landscape, 'folded into those creeping scrolls of white'. The transformation is given ironical point by one of Hardy's rare similes, of the mist 'like the moving pillar of cloud raised by the Israelite', because the Biblical cloud was a meaningful sign from God. Even a poem so unemotively factual as 'Throwing a Tree' culminates in

The tree crashes downward: it shakes all its neighbours throughout,
And two hundred years' steady growth has been ended in less than two
    hours

which hints at the mysteries contained in the transformations of Time. Such mysteries are treated variously: in a straightforward manner, as the continuance of human life in vegetable form, in 'Transformations'; humorously and ironically, in the appropriateness and inappropriateness of the transformations, in 'Voices from Things Growing in a Churchyard'. The best of these lyrics have in common an exact attention to the physical fact of the present moment, which, in poems like 'Proud Songsters' and 'At Day-Close in November', combines with a negation in the last stanza to invite us to wonder at the mystery of growth and transformation from one state to another. Twelve months ago the different species whose song is dwelt on so carefully 'no finches were, nor nightingales'; the tall trees which had been set 'in my June time' have become a permanent feature of the landscape to children who

Conceive that there never has been
A time when no tall trees grew here . . .

Time and transience are the great negations which deny meaning to the physical world. Hardy's constant concern, like Proust's, was to find credible values which could stand against the flux. Many of his nature poems are successful in catching and fixing the actual moment of transformation from one state to another by observation of the small physical detail that would have escaped the eye of anyone but a devoted naturalist, as, for example, in stanzas II and IV of 'A Light Snow-fall after Frost':

> The frost is on the wane,
> And cobwebs hanging close outside the pane
> Pose as festoons of thick white worsted there,
> Of their pale presence no eye being aware
> Till the rime made them plain.
>
> The snow-feathers so gently swoop that though
> But half an hour ago
> The road was brown, and now is starkly white,
> A watcher would have failed defining quite
> When it transformed it so.

But not Hardy; for 'he was a man who used to notice such things'. Only a poet who was also a countryman to his bones could have indicated the moment when an almost imperceptible change of temperature gives cobwebs the look of 'thick white worsted' because the snow and frost that covers them is wet. The mystery of the physical change remains unexplained; only the poignant significance of the transient moment can be felt through the careful accumulation of details that catch the moment and the scene—colour or lack of it, outline, movement, and most important of all for Hardy, the presence of central human figures.

'The method of Boldini . . . of Hobbema, in his view of a road with formal lopped trees and flat tame scenery—is that of infusing emotion into the baldest external objects either by the presence of a human figure among them, or by mark of some human connection with them.'

(*Life*)

Stanzas I and III are devoted to human figures whose connection with the elemental world of snow and frost provides the relevant emotion.

> On the flat road a man at last appears:
> How much his whitening hairs
> Owe to the settling snow's mute anchorage,
> And how much to a life's rough pilgrimage,
> One cannot certify.

A second man comes by;
His ruddy beard brings fire to the pallid scene:
His coat is faded green;
Hence seems it that his mien
Wears something of the dye
Of the berried holm-trees that he passes nigh.

Any emotional reverberation there may be in the first man's 'whitening hairs' is cautiously qualified and distanced by the observer's disclaimer of exact knowledge. The detail serves mainly to unite him to the landscape in a monotone of white. The details of the second man's colouring—the contrasting 'life' colours of red and green, which he shares with the evergreen holly—indicate that he has not travelled so far along 'life's rough pilgrimage' as the first man. But the physical transformation of snow and frost from one state to another in the intervening stanza, and the overwhelming of the brown road (related by colour to the ruddiness of the second man) by the lack of colour which characterizes the first man, gives intimations that the effects of time and transience are not confined to the landscape. At some undefinable moment the fire of the ruddy beard will be transformed by whitening hairs in one of the small undramatic defeats of life which Hardy knows so well how to suggest. The mood of regret for such transformations, and wonder at their mystery, is built up almost entirely by observation and selection of details from the world experienced by the senses—the only kind of truth available to the agnostic. Yet, as Hemingway said of the naturalistic details in his own *The Old Man and the Sea*:

'I tried to make a real old man, a real boy, a real sea and a real fish and real sharks. But if I made them good and true enough they would mean many things.'

The poems which are concerned to fix the transient moment bear a close relationship to the poems of regret at failing to catch its importance, and the solidity of the physical world takes a prominent place in both kinds. As in 'Overlooking the River Stour' it can prove to be a rival attraction that overwhelms the moment: or it can in itself present potentialities of significant moments which are overlooked in one's dreams of future happiness, as in 'The Temporary the All', "Known Had I", 'The Musical Box', and 'Before and After Summer':

When went by their pleasure, then?
I, alas, perceived not when.

The truth and stability of the physical environment turn nostalgia, which could be an enervating emotion, into something that is both more complex and more bracing. Hardy is above all a poet of memory, which dramatizes subjective isolation, and meditation. Memory of the relationship of a vividly-realized landscape with a human figure and human emotion can affirm the quality of a past moment in the teeth of a harsh denying present. 'Under the Waterfall' not only recaptures a moment of happiness in Hardy's courtship by a Proustian physical sensation—

> "Whenever I plunge my arm, like this,
> In a basin of water, I never miss
> The sweet sharp sense of a fugitive day
> Fetched back from its thickening shroud of gray"

—but also, through the details of the idyllic scene and loss of the glass which contains the memory of their love, 'intact' and purified by the waterfall, becomes an objective correlative of 'a real love-rhyme'. The value of the moment is also affirmed, more strikingly, through what may seem to deny it meaning—the death of love, or the death of the loved person—by the same fidelity to the Wordsworthian dictum that 'the passions of men are incorporated with the beautiful and permanent forms of nature'. Hardy's forms of nature are not always beautiful; but they have the beauty of truth which enables them to become part of the permanent emotional inner landscape of a painful love experience.

There are some lyrics scattered through the *Collected Poems* which re-create in memory the bitter end of a youthful passion. Most of them have the ring of personal experience, and some of the details are left obscure by the poet, but recent attempts to cast light on them by biographical speculation only respond 'to the desire of a good many readers that poetry should be explained to them in terms of something else' (T. S. Eliot, *On Poetry and Poets*). As Eliot asks apropos of conflicting views about Wordsworth's love affairs:

'. . . does it matter? does this account help me to understand the Lucy poems any better than I did before? For myself, I can only say that a knowledge of the springs which released a poem is not necessarily a help towards understanding the poem: too much information about the origins of the poem may even break my contact with it.'

All that matters in this group of poems is that Hardy or his poetic persona went through a common experience of 'misprized love' which seemed to deny the meaning of all that life offers, but out of the intensity of his pain re-created a sense of the abiding value of love itself that enabled him to fall in love again. The titles of many of these poems—'At Rushy-Pond', 'The Mound', 'The Place on the Map', 'On a Heath', 'In the Vaulted Way'—indicate a new and mature awareness of the human being's relationship to environment which had been burnt into him by the death of the passion that flourished in these places. The present sight of the mound, the pond, the place on the map, where 'she' told him something that would bring the affair to an end

> re-creates therewith our unforeboded troublous case
>   All distinctly to my sight,
> And her tension, and the aspect of her face:

the reflected moon in Rushy-Pond becomes 'corkscrewed' with the human agony that is displaced from the end of the love affair and transferred to the natural scene. The most complete objective correlative of the emotion felt at the end of an affair comes, in this group of poems, in the desolate winter landscape of 'Neutral Tones'. The lovers' quarrel is integrated so fully with details of landscape in a potent image of the death of love that all future experience of love's pain comes to mean this particular landscape, person and mood:

> Since then, keen lessons that love deceives,
>   And wrings with wrong, have shaped to me
> Your face, and the God-curst sun, and a tree,
>   And a pond edged with grayish leaves.

Hardy is too honest to admit to any consolation for what has been taken from him: nevertheless, the stability of scene and objects associated with the lost person fixes the value of love, which includes pain at its loss, as a positive quality against the flux of time. 'Just here it was' he says of the painful experience at the Mound, and many of his poems start with such a definite statement of place. 'Here is the ancient floor', 'Here we broached the Christmas barrel', 'Where once we danced, where once we sang'. But it is not long before a memory of human activity appears to give the scene value:

Here was the former door
Where the dead feet walked in.
'(The Self-Unseeing')

Old furniture, a broken-down garden seat, a little creaking table, are valued for the time-defeating memories they bring of loved people associated with them. The stability of the scene enshrines the memory, but even when time and transience have taken the figure from the scene, the scene takes its significance from the figure:

Yet her rainy form is the Genius still of the spot,
    Immutable, yea,
Though the place now knows her no more, and has known her not
    Ever since that day.
                                ('The Figure in the Scene')

'Curious quizzings' may see in his rain-blotted drawing of the figure, 'only her outline shown', the *lacrimae rerum* that takes away the solidity of the loved human being and leaves only the cragged slope and the rain. But the relationship of figure and environment has created something 'immutable, yea'—an affirmation out of life's denial.

Death, the greatest negation of all, affirms the life and love it denies through the strength of Hardy's feeling for the value of purposeful human activity in relation to the natural rhythms of death and seasonal renewal. In poems of elegiac memory, such as 'Molly Gone', 'During Wind and Rain', and 'The Five Students', work and play, energy and stillness, alternate. The diminishing number of students of life 'beating by' on their 'urgent way', now in harmony with the unexpected strenuous violence of spring that 'boils the dew to smoke by the paddock-path', now in discord with the summer heat and cold visual and aural deadness of the winter scene that mocks human aspiration with the icicles that 'tag the church-aisle leads' and the meaningless ghostly gibbering of the flag-rope, celebrate the human endeavour to make order in the absurdity of the physical world. Memory responds to the absence of human activity in its meaningful rhythm of work and play in 'During Wind and Rain' and 'Molly Gone': that there is no more 'making the pathways neat/And the garden gay,' planting, 'training the clambering rose', singing, 'jauntings' to well-loved places whose roll-call of names is a pledge of their stability, sets up the characteristic fruitful dissonance between their value and the refrains of mortality and loss that restrain uninhibited indulgence in the past. The significance of the individuals exhumed in the vivid accuracy of the details of their relationship with scene is qualified in 'During Wind and Rain' by archetypal symbols of the anonymity of death —the 'sick leaves reel down in throngs', rain obliterates the names carved on their gravestones. The beginning of 'Molly Gone' and the end of 'During Wind and Rain' and 'The Five Students' present us with the harsh denying reality—'The Five Students' in a typical pattern of elimination that is repeated in many poems, for example, 'Looking Across' and "Ah, are you Digging on my Grave?" But in the best elegiac poems, we are also left with the stability of the landscape and the eternal rhythms of nature inseparable from the order-making activities of human beings linked by 'life-loyalties' and enshrined in the memory of the poet shuttling between past and present to make his own significant order in the pattern of the poem.

Hardy's achievement has been to make meaningful poetry out of experience that has no inherent meaning. For those sign-seekers 'who aspired beyond and above the human individual towards something they could not even imagine, there had been no answer' (Camus: *The Plague*). But, to quote Camus again, 'if there is one thing one can always yearn for, and sometimes attain, it is human love'. In Hardy's poetry the yearning may be more obvious than the attainment, but it is a yearning of memory that infers a high moral value in love and life-loyalties. Men are frail, and Fate indifferent to human values. An image of 'thwarted purposing' is implicit in the negations, silences, Pinteresque inadequacies and failures to connect, the missed opportunities while 'we were looking away', the unwanted substitutions, ironical mismeetings, mismatings, and mistimings when

> . . . the face,
> And the eyes,
> And the place,
> And the sighs,
> Were not, alas, the right ones—the ones meet for him—
> ('Mismet').

But though Hardy's vision gives full weight to the dissonances brought about by Time and Chance, it is important not to underestimate the emphasis he places on human responsibility to affirm human values against the negation of death and denial of meaning.

The darkling thrush in the death-marked landscape, made ironically resonant by echoes of poetic identification with the immortal ecstasy of Keats' nightingale and Shelley's skylark, points to a more acceptable identification with age, frailty, and endurance of mortality in the bird's irrational defiance. 'O never I turned my head, alack' suggests some culpability for missing 'the more behind my back'. In 'Thoughts at Midnight' Hardy calls Mankind to task for

> Acting like puppets
> Under Time's buffets.

'The Blinded Bird', with its strong three-beat pulse of throbbing indignation, its intimate and respectful use of the second person singular, as in 'To an Unborn Pauper Child', and its bold application of St Paul's words to one of the humbler species, is a passionate indictment of man's as well as God's consent to the bird's needless pain and indignity. In 'Nobody Comes', intoning telegraph wires and a car hint at the possibilities of human communication, yet the car 'has nothing to do with me/And whangs along in a world of its own,/ . . . And nobody pulls up there.' The great negation of death, which ends all human striving, makes the vacillating lover's indecision whether 'To Meet, or Otherwise' understandable. But the brilliant use of negative particles reverses the negation, and leaves no doubt about the value Hardy placed on human effort to make relationship:

> By briefest meeting something sure is won;
> It will have been:
> Nor God nor Demon can undo the done,
> Unsight the seen,
> Make muted music be as unbegun,
> Though things terrene
> Groan in their bondage till oblivion supervene.
>
> So, to the one long-sweeping symphony
> From times remote
> Till now, of human tenderness, shall we
> Supply one note,
> Small and untraced, yet that will ever be
> Somewhere afloat
> Amid the spheres, as part of sick Life's antidote.

In both 'To Meet, or Otherwise' and 'Nobody Comes' (the telegraph wires like a 'spectral lyre') communication is presented in terms of music as something that can impose harmony on life's discords. The pity of missing an opportunity to supply that one note of human tenderness runs through much of Hardy's poetry of small occasions. It strikes the keynote of the emotion in 'A Broken Appointment' and provides the positive value that is both inferred and framed by its denial in the repetitions of 'You did not come' and 'You love not me'.

> You did not come,
> And marching Time drew on, and wore me numb.—
> Yet less for loss of your dear presence there
> Than that I thus found lacking in your make
> That high compassion which can overbear
> Reluctance for pure lovingkindness' sake
> Grieved I, when, as the hope-hour stroked its sum,
> You did not come.

> You love not me,
> And love alone can lend you loyalty;
> —I know and knew it. But, unto the store
> Of human deeds divine in all but name,
> Was it not worth a little hour or more
> To add yet this: Once you, a woman, came
> To soothe a time-torn man; even though it be
> You love not me?

The importance Hardy gives to 'that high compassion' which missed fire is suggested by the characteristic inversion of the long-awaited main verb and subject. The rhythmic build-up of the long periodic sentence, logically, painfully and precisely forming the poet's feelings as he contemplates them, comes to rest, not on the individual sufferer 'I' but on the grief that is common to all. The personal pain of Thomas Hardy takes on the impersonal quality of great poetry: the failure of 'a woman' to respond to 'a time-torn man' becomes a universal loss to 'the store/Of human deeds divine in all but name'. But it is great personal poetry too: the impersonality flowers from a depth of personal feeling that will not deny even the negative aspects of human experience. Those negative aspects are presented physically as the destructive actuality of Time—the only visual image in a poem developed through pure statement, though the sound as well as the cancellations contained in 'the hope-hour stroked its sum' brings to the sense of hearing all the heaviness of human endurance of Time without hope. The failure implied in 'You love not me' (another significant inversion), stated simply and honestly in a personal rhythm of thought that is jerky and abrupt as each unit of the analysis is accepted and drops painfully into place, exists in tension with the understanding compassion for individual human frailty that tempers the dignified reproach and develops the main statement of the first line of the final stanza into the concessive clause of the last lines, which places the importance of this failure in 'lovingkindness' once and for all.

Hardy was no mean poet of great occasions as well as small, as 'The Convergence of the Twain' can demonstrate, and war stirred him as the most obvious expression of cosmic futility and missed opportunities for lovingkindness. Other poets have written better songs for the men who march away and the girls they leave behind them, and his heart was not in a call to National Service. But few have integrated more successfully an Overworld philosophy of war as an image of tragic cosmic absurdity with the microscopic details of its physical impact on human beings and lesser creatures; as in the impressive "And there was a Great Calm", written to celebrate the Armistice of 1918.

> Aye; all was hushed. The about-to-fire fired not,
> The aimed-at moved away in trance-lipped song.
> One checkless regiment slung a clinching shot
> And turned. The Spirit of Irony smirked out, "What?
> Spoil peradventures woven of Rage and Wrong?"
>
> Thenceforth no flying fires inflamed the gray,
> No hurtlings shook the dewdrop from the thorn,
> No moan perplexed the mute bird on the spray;
> Worn horses mused: "We are not whipped today";
> No weft-winged engines blurred the moon's thin horn.

He is nearer to Owen in 'The Man He Killed', where he emphasizes by the very limitations of the speaker's viewpoint the sinister distortion of communication that abstracts humanity from the ordinary kindly individual. But the internal rhyming and repetition, the hesitations of speech that recapture the perplexity of the common soldier as he tries to rationalize the absurdity of war which turns friend into 'foe' when they are 'ranged as infantry' on opposite sides, are pure Hardy. In this poem and "And there was a Great Calm", Hardy comments on the significance simple words may be made to carry. They can be destructive of communication, but he also finds in 'many an ancient word/Of local lineage like "Thu bist", "Er war" ', a more constructive significance in their similarity to the language that

> they speak who in this month's moon gird
> At England's very loins . . .
>> ('The Pity of It')

Hardy's view of patriotism was unfashionably catholic.

> Then said I, "What is there to bound
> My denizenship? It seems I have found
> Its scope to be world-wide."
>> ('His Country')

But it makes a poem like 'Drummer Hodge' more representative of the universal Unknown Soldier than Rupert Brooke's 'The Soldier'. Brooke's soldier is narrowly centripetal: his death means only 'that there's some corner of a foreign field/That is for ever England'. Drummer Hodge dies for a cause and in a country he does not understand, beneath foreign stars he cannot name,

> Yet portion of that unknown plain
> Will Hodge for ever be;
> His homely Northern breast and brain
> Grow to some Southern tree,
> And strange-eyed constellations reign
> His stars eternally.

Hardy's characteristic unsentimental response to a dead man's physical relationship to environment, creative and centrifugal, which is reported with a dignified simplicity and restraint that is indicative of deep feeling, gives the local lad from Wessex the importance of a citizen of the world and the cosmos that Brooke's 'richer dust' and 'pulse in the eternal mind' cannot compass.

The significance of death in war lies less in the 'glory and war-mightiness' than in 'the long-ago commonplace facts/Of our lives' ('The Souls of the Slain') enshrined in the memory of the living by death's very power to deny. This is the long-awaited revelation whose Pentecostal imagery and elemental setting at Portland Bill, where 'contrary tides meet', as Hardy's note tells us, provide 'undervoicings' of the intersection of the timeless with time that make 'The Souls of the Slain' a memorable war poem, in spite of the 'senior soul-flame' in incongruous military command of impalpable 'sprites without mould'. In time of the breaking of nations, significance resides in the individual human being asserting the eternal rhythms of life against the abstract negation of death—the transformed body of Drummer Hodge contributing to the true meaning of patriotism; the common soldier puzzling out in his own slow, country way why he killed another common soldier called 'the foe'; 'a maid and her wight' indulging in a passion older than the Anglo-Saxon words, and a man and an old horse engaged in the eternal occupation of taming the earth from which they grew.

Hardy's intensely personal yet universal affirmations of life against the negations of old age and death can perhaps be justly assessed by comparing them with the equally valid but very different affirmations of another poet who wrote some of his finest poetry in and about old age, W. B. Yeats. The insistent question of mortality is raised both in Yeats' 'Among School Children' and Hardy's 'He Revisits his First School' by the discrepancy between the youth of the children and their elderly visitor. In contrast to the detailed realism of the children in their schoolroom that begins Yeats' poem, Hardy's poem gives more prominence to the unwished-for physical presence of the poet, 'standing solidly there as when fresh', than to the children, who exist only as an undefined 'they' of the future in the third stanza. The whole poem develops from the half-humorous, half-apologetic deprecation of his intrusive physical body, unbecoming in its old age, to a fanciful superstition of his return as a ghost.

> Yes; wrong was the way;
> But yet, let me say,
> I may right it—some day.

The ghostly image, 'beglimpsed through the quaint quarried glass/ Of green moonlight, by me greener made', is more acceptable and more in harmony with place and children than the reality, but in spite of its whimsical treatment, Hardy can admit no transformation of the reality except through death.

To Yeats too the harsh reality of 'a sixty-year-old smiling public man' in the midst of children is one that cannot be denied. Yet 'Both nuns and mothers worship images'; the changeless conceptions of love-blinded eyes defeat the physical negation of 'Old clothes upon old sticks to scare a bird'. The poem, more complex than Hardy's single lyrical mood, develops from the realism of the encounter with children and nuns through a reverie on the poet's beloved Maud Gonne as a child and as an elderly woman, to an extended statement of his personal philosophy that ends in a symbolic image of tree and dancer which reconciles the mortality of the individual with the recurring cycle of life to whose changeless image the individual contributes her changing body.

> O chestnut-tree, great-rooted blossomer,
> Are you the leaf, the blossom or the bole?
> O body swayed to music, O brightening glance,
> How can we know the dancer from the dance?

Hardy makes the point more simply, and more physically, in 'Heredity':

> I am the family face;
> Flesh perishes, I live on,

and many of his lyrics (for example, 'At Waking', 'Thoughts of Phena', 'He Abjures Love'), realizing the bleakness of life without illusions, clearly recognize the value of images to worship.

There can be sad acceptance, but no reconciliation to perishing of the flesh in Hardy. Grief is the one note that suffuses 'I Look into My Glass', which presents the dissonance between passions still strong and the ageing physical body. There is none of the rage that batters the language and rhythm of Yeats' 'The Tower':

> What shall I do with this absurdity—
> O heart, O troubled heart—this caricature,
> Decrepit age that has been tied to me
> As to a dog's tail?
>   Never had I more
> Excited, passionate, fantastical
> Imagination, nor an ear and eye
> That more expected the impossible—

The passion of imagination that is so strong in Yeats is able to call up 'images and memories' of those who had peopled his environment, and of his own literary creations; and to leave to 'young upstanding men' those qualities which had affirmed him as a man —his full acceptance of both body and soul, his pride, and faith that 'Death and life were not/Till man made up the whole'

78

And further add to that
That, being dead, we rise,
Dream and so create
Translunar Paradise.

The strongest passion in Hardy is of human affection, as the second stanza of 'I Look into My Glass' bears witness. No triumph of imagination or compulsion on his soul to 'study/In a learned school' (Yeats) could make the distress of 'hearts grown cold to me' (Hardy) 'seem but the clouds of the sky' (Yeats). Yet the value of his passion is affirmed just as strongly through his sadness at its loss as Yeats' through his more complex assertion.

Hardy had no faith in a translunar Paradise to leave to anyone. Like Camus, he can leave no more than the experience of having known plague (by which Camus here means death) and remembering it,

'of having known friendship and remembering it, of knowing affection and being destined one day to remember it. So all a man could win in the conflict between plague and life was knowledge and memories . . . how hard it must be to live only with what one knows and what one remembers, cut off from what one hopes for!'

(Camus: *The Plague*)

Hardy has achieved this miracle of integrity by accepting Camus' definition of the double face of knowledge: 'Knowing meant that: a living warmth, and a picture of death'. His ability to touch the two chords simultaneously puts him in the front rank of elegiac poets. His first wife's death in 1912 released his full poetic power in the elegiac vein; but the death of a lesser creature suffices to bring out Hardy's idiosyncratic affirmation of living warmth through a vivid picture of its negation by death. 'Dead "Wessex" the Dog to the Household' misses fire, like some of his philosophical poems, because the mouthpiece—Wessex himself—is beyond the suffering his death causes, the verse form is rather too jaunty for its subject, and there are few concrete details about the dog or his relationship to Max Gate to give the quality of the loss. But in 'Last Words to a Dumb Friend', the tenderness of immediate memory recreates through tightly-controlled couplets and directly-felt observations the dead cat's relationship to his human family and environment. The natural first reaction of any pet-lover, never to have another, followed by factual details of the impossibility of blotting out his memory by blotting out 'each mark he made', rises to a deeply personal, creative meditation on the relationship of any living creature to the negation of death:

> Strange it is this speechless thing. . . .
> Should—by crossing at a breath
> Into safe and shielded death,
> By the merely taking hence
> Of his insignificance—
> Loom as largened to the sense,
> Shape as part, above man's will,
> Of the Imperturbable.

The negation inevitably calls up the affirmation of the value of life; the empty scene speaks of the importance of the missing figure.

> And this home, which scarcely took
> Impress from his little look,
> By his faring to the Dim,
> Grows all eloquent of him.

We are left with the harsh reality of knowledge, and the inextricably-linked pain and triumph of human memory and emotion that enshrine the significance of life in its relation to the physical fact of death:

> Housemate, I can think you still
> Bounding to the window-sill,
> Over which I vaguely see
> Your small mound beneath the tree,
> Showing in the autumn shade
> That you moulder where you played.

But Hardy, perhaps, like Camus' Tarrou, would have called that winning the match.

The Elegies: *Poems of 1912–13*

Thy voice is on the rolling air;
   I hear thee where the waters run;
   Thou standest in the rising sun,
And in the setting thou art fair.
           (Tennyson: '*In Memoriam*', cxxix)

Then through the great town's harsh, heart-wearying roar,
   Let in thy voice a whisper often come,
   To chase fatigue and fear:
Why faintest thou? I wander'd till I died.
   Roam on! the light we sought is shining still.
   Dost thou ask proof? Our Tree yet crowns the hill,
Our Scholar travels yet the loved hillside.
           (Matthew Arnold: 'Thyrsis')

Woman much missed, how you call to me, call to me,
Saying that now you are not as you were
When you had changed from the one who was all to me,
But as at first, when our day was fair.
           (Hardy: 'The Voice')

The difference in tone between these three voices of the dead is a measure of the difference Hardy has made to the elegy. Tennyson's friend Hallam, 'mixed with God and Nature', has attained a lofty metaphysical existence that consoles the poet for his physical death. Arnold's agnosticism makes Clough's voice less of a certainty, and less sublime as a Wordsworthian voice that rolls through all things; but it is nevertheless a stern Victorian voice of moral precept which gives metaphysical consolation by linking the temporal search for truth which he and Arnold pursued to the eternal symbol of the tree. Both voices—Clough's 'whisper' notwithstanding—are public voices, speaking through poets who have made the death of a close friend the occasion for a general meditation on Man's relationship to Death.

    Emma Hardy's voice is just loud enough to be overheard. Hardy's elegy speaks in the intimate personal rhythms of twentieth century conversation of a private relationship between husband and wife, thrown into painful relief by Emma's death. The relationship was more troubled than Tennyson's and Arnold's to their dead friends; but there is no grasping at metaphysical consolation. The world of nature does not contain for Hardy the 'diffusive power' of the dead person that Tennyson felt: it is the harsh physical reality the poet is left with as Emma's phantom voice recedes:

> Can it be you that I hear? Let me view you, then,
> Standing as when I drew near to the town
> Where you would wait for me: yes, as I knew you then,
> Even to the original air-blue gown!
>
> Or is it only the breeze, in its listlessness
> Travelling across the wet mead to me here,
> You being ever dissolved to wan wistlessness,
> Heard no more again far or near?
>
> Thus I; faltering forward,
> Leaves around me falling,
> Wind oozing thin through the thorn from norward,
> And the woman calling.

'The Voice', which reaches a low water mark of desolation in the sequence of elegies published as 'Poems of 1912–13' in *Satires of Circumstance* after Emma's death, shows 'how hard it must be to live only with what one knows and what one remembers, cut off from what one hopes for'. Tennyson had to add faith to the inadequacies of knowledge ('for knowledge is of things we see'); without belief in a life after death, earth would, for him, be 'darkness at the core,/ And dust and ashes all that is'. Hardy, cut off from faith and the hope of ever being able to repair the errors of this life in another one, unable to believe in any far-off divine event that would justify pain and loss, accepts the darkness at the core but affirms through knowledge and memories alone the human value of the relationship with his wife, imperfect and incomplete as it was. The human quality of Clough and Hallam in their friendship with their elegists is not the primary concern of 'Thyrsis' and '*In Memoriam*'. The elegiac conventions distance the relationship too much to re-create the give and take between two people that we recognize as human. In 'The Voice', the complex nuances of such a relationship between two living people are projected into the tensions and uncertainties of thought and rhythm which mirror the grief-stricken response of the living survivor to the death of his partner. His mood of utter desolation, mingled with remorse and regret that the chance to perfect an imperfect relationship has been irrevocably lost, projects him wishfully into the past, 'when our day was fair', on the unexpected but brilliantly appropriate rhythm of a triple-time dance tune that carries the insubstantial voice of the 'woman much missed'. We know that music was a shared interest of the Hardys' courtship and marriage; it may be more than coincidence that the rhythmic pattern of 'The Voice' fits that of 'Haste to the Wedding', one of the traditional dance tunes notated in the Hardy family's music manuscript book. Our response to this metrical reminder of their early happiness counterpointing the poet's present desolation is rich and complex. Tune and voice rush inseparably on his musing memory: the personal loss is related to and ordered by the experience of the race in the lilting folk rhythm and curiously formal but deeply moving 'Woman much missed' and 'the woman calling' which frame the personal bereavement.

As the poem develops the rhythm of the dance begins to falter. The regular, distancing folk-beat gives way to the irregularity of the distressed human mind trying to grasp and clarify its vision of time past, with all the broken speech rhythms, hesitations and abrupt changes of emotional tempo that re-create the painful struggle towards affirmation as the aural appeal of the insubstantial voice turns to visual realization of the past in the second stanza. One cannot read

> Can it be you that I hear? Let me view you, then,

without placing heavy stress on the internal rhyme 'view' and the first 'you', which points up Hardy's uncertainty about the truth of the phantom voice: he is the same man who would only be satisfied by a physical manifestation of meaning in 'A Sign-Seeker'. The sense of the third line asks for a heavy stress on the final 'then'. Hardy's vision of Emma

> Standing as when I drew near to the town
> Where you would wait for me:

has been recaptured and held for a moment in perfect clarity; but in its very affirmation, as the rhythm gathers certainty—'yes, as I knew you *then*' (my italics) the vision has been doubted by the

83

counterpointing speech stress that suggests the irrevocable pastness of time past. The clinching detail of the visual re-creation, 'Even to the original air-blue gown', draws attention to itself as an authentic groping after precise definition of the past by the poly-syllabic awkwardness of 'original' after two stanzas consisting almost entirely of monosyllables.

The moment of clear vision in the second stanza comes within and yet extends the scope of the usual elegiac convention. It corresponds to Arnold's sudden, almost involuntary, sight of the tree he had been vainly searching for, which leads to his final affirmation, and Tennyson's trance in which he holds mystic communion with Hallam and 'the deep pulsations of the world'. Hardy's memory of Emma does not move into the metaphysical dimension. There is no communication between living and dead: the phantom voice, a wish-fantasy born of the wind and mental confusion, makes no physical manifestation as a presence, though it intensifies an absence.

In Stanza III the idiosyncratic irregularity of the musing human voice becomes unsure of the truth of the vision. No longer in command of its pulsations, it responds to the drift of the listless breeze as the power of the vision recedes before the harsh encroaching reality of the physical world in which the poet is discovered 'faltering'. The dissolution that overtakes both vision and physical body is enacted in diction. The subjective 'you' who was so clearly defined in the previous stanza is swallowed up in the impersonal dragging indefiniteness of that strange but exact coinage from Anglo-Saxon, 'wistlessness'. 'Dissolved to wan wistlessness' (i.e. to a state of being without knowing) is a more precise evocation in sound and sense than the vague 'consigned to existlessness' of the manuscript: it negates the crisp firmness of 'as I *knew* you then' (my italics) of Stanza II. The active finite verbs 'hear', 'view', 'would wait', 'knew', which defined the human relationship between two people in the recaptured moment of time past, are replaced in Stanzas III and IV by past and present participles that cannot be modified by a subject. The unalterable presentness of present reality is felt in the present participles which contain the action of the fourth stanza. But they exist in tension with the human subject that lacks a verb to modify—'Thus I'—the lonely human figure now shown in dramatic close-up faltering through the desolation of an autumn landscape to a clipped faltering metre that has changed utterly from the dancing tune which had resurrected the past vision. Only the third line brings a suggestion of the old rhythm, and the difficulty of forcing vowels through the proliferating 'th' sounds halts the lilt sufficiently to place the phantom voice as an illusion projected on to the sound of the wind.

If, as Leslie Stephen remarked in a note that Hardy took down, 'the ultimate aim of the poet should be to touch our hearts by showing his own', then Hardy has achieved the ultimate aim in these sad tributes to his marriage. Never before had the elegy sounded such a note of purely personal grief. Yet they become representative of the universal experience of bereavement by the intensity of that grief, the integrity of Hardy's response and refusal to deny any part of the experience, and his truth to the feeling of remorse, justified or unjustified, which overtakes the survivor when the opportunities to improve a relationship are denied for ever by death. This most painful of common human emotions had not before complicated the simple sense of loss in the elegy, which usually meant eulogy. If tensions existed between Arnold and Clough, Tennyson and Hallam, they are kept hidden. Both the elegist and the elegized emerge as serene figures untroubled by the stresses and strains of an intimacy of thirty-eight years—the period of Hardy's marriage. A realistic literary treatment of marital incompatibility was made difficult by Victorian insistence on the sanctity of marriage, which ensured a horrified public reception of Ibsen's plays, Hardy's own *Jude the Obscure*, and Meredith's *Modern Love*. It is to *Modern Love*, not to an elegy, that one must turn for a courageous attempt to present in a series of poems the breakdown of a marriage. Meredith's wife was still living when he wrote them, so he was not forced, like Hardy, to a painful reappraisal of the relationship by his wife's death; but perhaps the form of Hardy's elegies would not have been quite the same if *Modern Love* had not broken new ground in the poetical treatment of marriage. Hardy's excellence and originality as an elegist lies in his individual blend of the elegy with the love lyric and the honest treatment of stress in marriage, for which *Modern Love* provided contemporary precedent, to produce one of the most intense artistic expressions of inseparably linked love and death since Wagner's *Tristan und Isolde*.

Modern Love, though considered very avant-garde for its period, lacks the unforced personal note that places Hardy's poems in the modern world. Meredith's work is a serious attempt to convey in a linked series of fifty poems the range of complex emotions that attend the breaking-point of a marriage; and the stresses, cruelties and deceits of keeping up appearances. The point of view switches from the subjective first person to an attempted detachment expressed in the third person, but it is always the poet who speaks, interprets, remembers and relates. There is no attempt to re-create the experience through the eyes of his wife, though there are moments of real sympathy for her predicament:

> Yet it was plain she struggled, and that salt
> Of righteous feeling made her pitiful.
> Poor twisting worm, so queenly beautiful!
> Where came the cleft between us? Whose the fault?

A woman who is only known through the interpretation of a prejudiced observer is inevitably more distanced in the role she played in the break-up than even the ghost of the dead Emma, who is given her say in three poems out of twenty-one, and a stanza of 'Your Last Drive'.

> When I could answer he did not say them [words]:
> > When I could let him know
> How I would like to join in his journeys
> > Seldom he wished to go.
> > > ('The Haunter')

The pathos of the married couple's failure to communicate in life and death touches the quick more directly in the simplicity of speech that was apparently characteristic of Emma than the satirical tone of Meredith's dramatized account:

> Madam would speak with me. So, now it comes:
> The Deluge or else Fire! She's well; she thanks
> My husbandship. Our chain on silence clanks.
> Time leers between, above his twiddling thumbs.
> Am I quite well? Most excellent in health!
> The journals, too, I diligently peruse.
> Vesuvius is expected to give news:
> Niagara is no noisier. By stealth
> Our eyes dart scrutinizing snakes.

In spite of an attempt to reproduce the authentic rhythm of false give and take in defensive non-communication, Meredith's external view of his wife places emphasis on the persona of the poet himself. He is insufficiently distanced from his ironic exhibition of egotism, and so it is difficult not to take away from *Modern Love* an impression of the poet striking a melodramatic attitude appropriate to the role of Injured Husband, which inevitably places his co-star in the role of Erring Wife. The violent language and heavy sarcasm are further aids to the distancing of pain.

Self-dramatization is not necessarily a fault in poetry: in Yeats, for example, it is an essential virtue. In conventional elegiac poetry, when the poet is using the death of an individual as a springboard to generalizations about man's relation to death, a suitable persona is necessary. As Tennyson remarked of *In Memoriam*, ' "I" is not always the author speaking of himself, but the voice of the human race speaking through him.' Tennyson deliberately assumes the dignified mantle of Man and Poet. He suffers the expected grief and makes the expected recovery, in noble and serene diction and rhythm that are fitting to the voice of the human race. Hardy would never have dreamed of speaking for the human race, though in the event he did so by speaking as an individual. His elegies are quite innocent of self-dramatization: they are 'feeling confessing itself to itself' (John Stuart Mill). To him the individual was more important than the species: the loss of a particular woman to a particular man was an injustice that no grand vision of the future of the species could make up for. Though we are conscious all the time of the complexity of his relationship with Emma, 'Poems of 1912–13' stands as the finest tribute a wife could have, for she occupies the centre of a cosmos from which her husband has effaced all that makes up his persona except the quality of his naked grief.

The twenty-one poems which Hardy chose to make up the sequence, and others scattered through subsequent volumes of poetry, are devoted to a vivid imaginative re-creation of Emma in all her humanness—including her human imperfection—which gives her a second life, though one which must inevitably include the pain of remorse and of her physical absence. 'One looked back through the years, and saw some pictures; a loss like that just makes one's old brain vocal!' Hardy told A. C. Benson in 1913. We see her as 'a little girl of grace' in Plymouth; we see her in the early days of courtship in Cornwall, as a charming companion, ready like Desdemona to fall in love with the teller of a romantic tale ('of sunk Lyonnesse'); a practitioner of the arts that were 'great things' to Hardy too—painting and music—and sharer of his ideals: a woman of quick sympathy with animals, plants, and

87

landscape. We see her independent and characteristic qualities; as a fearless rider and ardent walker; her child-like pleasure in simple things—flowers, parties, pretty clothes. We come to know her physical appearance—her fragility, 'her delicate head', her

> nut-coloured hair,
> And gray eyes, and rose-flush coming and going . . .

and the familiar habits that characterize her death as well as her life:

> It was your way, my dear,
> To vanish without a word
> When callers, friends, or kin
> Had left . . .

We see her simultaneously in three tenses, as in 'The Walk'. The remote past of 'earlier days', the recent past of her weakness when she could not take her usual walk, and her absence at the present moment combine in the poet's memory and emotion to give a sense, through the contrasting moods of his two walks, of the durable quality of their relationship, whatever its stresses. 'The look of a room on returning thence' after Emma's death has intimations of the significance of the lacking figure. Death was needed to 'couch' his eyes 'of the mis-vision that blurred me' ('The Spell of the Rose'). It puts a different perspective on the tensions that marred their marriage, which was denied to Meredith writing while still involved. Hardy is free of the temptation to blame Emma, and the even greater temptation to indulge in futile remorse and excessive self-accusation, though he accepts the burden of a certain amount of culpability:

> Well, well! All's past amend,
> Unchangeable. It must go.

Quietly he accepts that to give and receive pain is part of the human condition, and to remember is part of the pain that matures. 'The dark space wherein I have lacked you' affirms what was true and real in his relationship to Emma's life.

> Primaeval rocks form the road's steep border,
>   And much have they faced there, first and last,
> Of the transitory in Earth's long order;
>   But what they record in colour and cast
> Is—that we two passed.

And to me, though Time's unflinching rigour,
  In mindless rote, has ruled from sight
The substance now, one phantom figure
  Remains on the slope, as when that night
Saw us alight.

The figure in the scene, as always, gives significance to the scene when it knows her no more.

The traditional elegy has always given scope for expression of the profound link between human life and the natural world with its recurring rhythms and promise of new life to come out of death. Hardy's predecessors Arnold and Tennyson had managed to adapt the old pastoral conventions of the elegy to a personal vision nurtured by the spiritual unrest of the nineteenth century. Proserpine, who brought new life out of death, had trod the Sicilian fields in classical myth,

        But ah, of our poor Thames she never heard!
        Her foot the Cumnor cowslips never stirr'd!
      And we should tease her with our plaint in vain.

In the absence of gods of death and renewal we are left with the Cumnor cowslips of the here and now, and the garden of Somersby Rectory—real features of real English landscapes, where the weather can be as uncomfortable as in the realistic-pastoral Forest of Arden. But the bones of pastoral elegy show through, as in the recurring seasonal poems of *In Memoriam* which define the poet's progress in recovery from his bereavement, for their application to Hallam is the traditional link of 'life re-orient out of dust.' The value of such 'a friendship as had master'd Time' depends on the feeling that death is not the end. If 'Man dies: nor is there hope in dust', the effort to cherish love as a thing meaningful only in itself would be lost in

        The moanings of the homeless sea,
          The sound of streams that swift or slow
          Draw down Æonian hills, and sow
        The dust of continents to be.

For Hardy, the passage of chronological time towards death cannot alter the quality of love. In 'At Castle Boterel' he faces it squarely in the primaeval rocks that form the background to Emma's phantom figure, and in the loss that is remembered simultaneously with the joy of recaptured experience. But time's 'mindless rote' imaged in Hardy's hills is controlled by his projection against their insentient infinity of the moment of value contained in a human relationship: a moment measured not by time but by intensity.

> It filled but a minute. But was there ever
> A time of such quality, since or before,
> In that hill's story? To one mind never . . .

Daily life is full of the time-sense, and something else, as E. M. Forster reminds us in *Aspects of the Novel*:

'We think one event occurs after or before another, the thought is often in our minds, and much of our talk and action proceeds on the assumption. Much of our talk and action, but not all; there seems something else in life besides time, something which may conveniently be called "value," something which is measured not by minutes or hours, but by intensity, so that when we look at our past it does not stretch back evenly but piles up into a few notable pinnacles, and when we look at the future it seems sometimes a wall, sometimes a cloud, sometimes a sun,but never a chronological chart. Neither memory nor anticipation is much interested in Father Time, and all dreamers, artists and lovers are partially delivered from his tyranny; he can kill them, but he cannot secure their attention, and at the very moment of doom, when the clock collected in the tower its strength and struck, they may be looking the other way. So daily life, whatever it may be really, is practically composed of two lives—the life in time and the life by values—and our conduct reveals a double allegiance. "I only saw her for five minutes but it was worth it." There you have both allegiances in a single sentence.'

'At Castle Boterel' indicates from the first that Hardy's moment of value is independent of time and local conditions. The place is the same, and the month is again March, but these constants only serve to highlight the difference between the present of the poet's reverie and the past scene that forms its subject. It was a March day of 1913, when he revisited the Cornish scenes of his courtship, which called into being his vision of a previous March of forty years ago, and the time of day was light enough for him to see the slope of the fading byway 'now glistening wet'. Yet what he sees in vision on the slope is

> Myself and a girlish form benighted
> In dry March weather.

The contrast between past and present is further pointed by the solitude of the musing man as he *drives* in a waggonette, remembering the compassionate gesture that his younger self shared with Emma in *walking*

> Beside a chaise. We had just alighted
> To ease the sturdy pony's load
> When he sighed and slowed.

A direct vision is built up by each apparently trivial detail of setting and action, recalled in short, precisely-punctuated statements that move jerkily with the recollecting emotion across a metrical pattern of long and short lines which expand and contract in his memory with the two kinds of time. The minutely realized particulars of a chronological action—getting out of a chaise and climbing a hill—pile up into what Forster would call a notable pinnacle. It expands in his memory over forty years and the dark space wherein he has lacked his partner of the scene, to become an honest and joyous affirmation of the timeless quality contained in those apparently unimportant particulars of the daily life of time:

> What we did as we climbed, and what we talked of
> Matters not much, nor to what it led . . .

Their marriage, with its pain of misunderstanding, death and remorse marking the chronological chart, is accepted and enfolded into the life by values. But Hardy's integrity and fidelity to the world of here and now will not let him leave the last word entirely with the life by values. The timeless moment of value, in which a quality in life is discerned, gains strength from being placed in perspective at the peak of the poem against the hard primaeval rocks that image 'Time's unflinching rigour'. The double vision that can see the human relationship both as part of 'the transitory in Earth's long order' and as a triumph of human consciousness which can record on the rocks their importance to human emotional history—'that we two passed'—produces a poetic tension rich in complexity. The poem ends in absolute honesty, with Hardy's vision and the expansion of time it afforded now 'shrinking, shrinking', separated from him by time and distance as his waggonette drives forward into the future and away from the physical scene. As the harsh rain-washed reality of the time-ruled present breaks into, but does not destroy, the timeless quality of his recaptured vision, the natural movement of musing colloquial speech settles down into quiet acceptance of the daily life of time which must be lived through.

> I look and see it there, shrinking, shrinking,
>   I look back at it amid the rain
> For the very last time; for my sand is sinking,
>   And I shall traverse old love's domain
>   Never again.

The figure is inseparable from the landscape in Hardy's search for value after his loss. A comparison of the relationship between figure and landscape in Hardy's elegies and Arnold's 'Thyrsis' shows how personal to himself was each poet's use of the elegiac pastoral convention in this respect. Arnold's search, like Hardy's, is localized first of all in a world of nature familiar to the dead and the survivor. The natural scene calls up both pain at the loss of the missing figure and memory of a shared past there; and at Arnold's moment of deepest despair, it becomes the measure of his grief, for the cuckoo will return next year, while Clough-Thyrsis will not. But it also provides his moment of affirmation in the signal-elm—a symbol of the continuity of the search for truth which he had shared with Clough, only intermittently manifested to the disordered nineteenth century, but still there. The Cumnor world of cowslips, brambles, and garden flowers has been realized with a vivid detail that makes the world of here and now seem to be the most actual thing in the poem: it pushes Clough into the background. Yet it shows so many signs of time and change to the visitor that he wonders whether it is illusory, just as Hardy asks, in 'A Dream or No', 'Does there even a place like Saint-Juliot exist?' because the death of the woman who gave meaning to the place casts doubt on the permanence of things. Death, to the Victorian agnostic, invalidated the traditional pastoral convention of a death-less and timeless order of existence mirrored in the calm seclusion of a rural retreat where gods of life's renewal were part of the props. The shadow of the mythic world of elegiac tradition that is felt behind the real Oxfordshire countryside connected with Arnold's bereavement produces a complex vision. It points the distance between the modern world of uncertainty and the ideal mythic order which the agnostic can no longer accept unmodified, but it also lifts the personal temporal experience of Clough's death into the universal timeless order represented by the pastoral elegy.

The shadow of the timeless world of myth hovers also behind Hardy's personal tragedy, for the Cornish landscape of Emma's home was also the setting for the tragic death-marked love of Tristram and Iseult. Though Hardy makes no specific reference to their story in 'Poems of 1912–13', it was heavily marked in his copy of Malory, and a visit to Tintagel in 1916 with his second wife elicited the comment, in a letter to Sir Sydney Cockerell, 'I visited the place 44 years ago with an Iseult of my own, and of course she was mixed in the vision of the other.' His 'Iseult', described in terms that could have come straight out of a ballad-version of the legend—'Fair-eyed and white-shouldered, broad-browed and brown-tressed'—and placed in intimate connection with the scene that had witnessed the archetypal love-death relationship, acquires a significance that extends beyond the personal aspect of a marriage gone wrong and ended by death. Though Emma was a woman of thirty when he met her, Hardy stresses in many poems her child-like capacity to live with her whole undivided being—'Lament', 'Rain on a Grave', 'Places', 'Beeny Cliff', 'The Phantom Horse-woman'. One of his most recurring memories of Emma is of

> A ghost-girl-rider. And though, toil-tried,
> > He withers daily,
> > Time touches her not,
> > But still she rides gaily
> > In his rapt thought
> > On the shagged and shaly
> > Atlantic spot,
> And as when first eyed
> Draws rein and sings to the swing of the tide.

There is an essential freedom in her harmonious relationship to this elemental scene of sea and primaeval rock which reminds one of the first Cathy's relationship to the moors in *Wuthering Heights*. There is also the same isolation from everyday concerns of someone in contact with absolutes.

> > There lonely I found her,
> > The sea-birds around her,
> And other than nigh things uncaring to know.

Emma's sea-birds and the shot lapwing of Cathy's delirium call up the limitless, timeless world of absolutes from which marriage has exiled them. Marriage brings maturity, compromise, complexity, and alienation from the child and folklore world of elemental harmony where past and present, near and far, natural and supernatural, love and death, are one. The world of absolute oneness which time cannot touch can only be regained, as in Wagner's version of the Tristram legend, through death.

> Yet her shade, maybe,
> Will creep underground
> Till it catch the sound
> Of that western sea
> As it swells and sobs
> Where she once domiciled,
> And joy in its throbs
> With the heart of a child.

In poems such as this one, "I Found Her out There", there is a feeling that it had been a betrayal of Emma's essential being to bring her 'here' and lay her to rest

> In a noiseless nest
> No sea beats near

when 'out there' she was vividly alive, in harmony with the violence of the Atlantic gales which she joyed in 'with the heart of a child'. The form of the poem, in its subtle interplay of speech stress and metre, dramatically enacts the woman's intimate association with the elements. The quiet, controlled two-beat line of the first two stanzas rises in the next two to an urgent pounding throb in which two or three syllables crushed to the beat are varied with lines in which almost every word demands a major stress:

> As a wind-tugged tress
> Flapped her cheek like a flail

as Emma's harmony with elemental violence reaches a peak of intensity. But the speech stress fighting strenuously against the inexorable throb of the sea suggests that it is a humanly-controlled harmony which does not allow the human identity to be submerged. Emma's association with the stormy scene which imbues her with its own ambiguous vital energy dramatically revalues the initial threat of the 'hurricane [which] shakes/The solid land' in the first stanza, and by implication, the meaning of violence and death in the universe. Through the outrage of Emma's death

Hardy has regained an intensified sense of their lost love at a time and place when Emma was most alive, most herself. These scenes of time past

> Have a savour that scenes in being lack,
> And a presence more than the actual brings . . .
>   ('Places')

As in *Wuthering Heights* country, there is a very thin line dividing natural and supernatural in what Hardy describes as the 'region of dream and mystery', where a ghostly voice calls out to him from forty years ago. Nevertheless, Emily Bronte's sense of the supernatural is not Hardy's: his feet are always firmly on the ground even in his moments of greatest confusion and distress, and he never doubts for a second that Emma has no life as a spirit beyond the grave. The Cornish scene, with its ambivalent destructive and creative energies, speaks strongly of the missing figure: Hardy's elegies are not original in this respect. It implies the contrast or contrasts on which his poems are so often constructed: between a happy companiable past and a harsh desolate present; between Emma's affection for the landscape when living and its indifference to her death; between the sensitivity of the living woman to the elements and her insensitivity when dead; between ignorance of the significance of a certain spot in the scene or a certain moment in human relationships and the importance they gain in retrospect from Emma's death and burial. Death is the moment that alters all: the event that gives retrospective meaning to the individual life in all its varied settings.

Hardy's search for the meaning of Emma's life in relation to his own returns constantly to the Cornish landscape around St Juliot, for 'much of my life claims the spot as its key'. But their married life at Max Gate forms part of the pattern too, and the first eleven poems of the sequence set Emma firmly, alive or dead, in Dorset. In these poems which centre on Max Gate or Stinsford (the place of her burial), written before Hardy's journey into Cornwall in March 1913, the fact of Emma's death is paramount. The general mood is one of unreconciled desolation: the key of Hardy's life, like the key that illustrates the manuscript of 'Nature's Questioning' in *Wessex Poems*, is broken and meaningless. The twelfth poem, 'A Dream or No', though written a month before his Cornish revisitation, begins in memory and recollected emotion the search for 'that time's renewal' in the places connected with Emma's youth and love. Slowly the shattered key starts to knit together and turn again as Emma's recaptured vitality brings a sense of time by values into the passage of chronological time that had robbed him of her presence.

The movement of the whole sequence develops according to the poetic and musical logic of a song cycle. Hardy's theme, of the mysterious relationship between love and death and the affirmative possibility of time's renewal through memory of past love, is a common theme of song cycles: Schubert's 'Winterreise' and Tippett's 'The Heart's Assurance' come to mind. 'Poems of 1912–13' has the unity of theme and mood that belongs to a song cycle, with its internal variations of feeling, tempo, and aspect, its peaks and troughs. As the 'cycle' stands now, it is constructed on the peaks of six major poems which form stages in the poet's acceptance of Emma's death: 'The Going', "I Found Her out There", 'The Voice', 'After a Journey', 'At Castle Boterel', and 'Where the Picnic Was'. The interspersed poems are generally of a lower tension and less complex in metre and form. Many of them use the strong two-beat line which by its descent from traditional folk rhythms serves to stylize and distance the poet's personal grief and so link it with the *lacrimae rerum* of the human race which lives and loves under the shadow of death.

'The Going' opens the sequence with Hardy's naked reaction to Emma's death. The abrupt mid-conversational opening which is so characteristic of Hardy (and which he shares with Browning, Pope, Donne, and Juvenal) takes the feel of the very moment of bereavement in its spontaneous cry of pain, surprise, remorse, and desolation. The poem is worthy of its position as the first poem in the cycle: it establishes straightaway the love/death theme. The suffering that must be faced in loneliness and remorse, the consciousness that death has given their alienation a finality which must be reckoned with in the survivor's reintegration into normal life, is present in this first poem. But so is the possibility of 'that time's renewal' to be sought in later poems through memory of the missing figure linked to the two landscapes of Dorset and Cornwall which are introduced in 'The Going' as symbols of the recent past of illusion and the remote past of reality; and the final sober reconciliation with what is 'past amend'. Above all, 'The Going' introduces the search for the source of Emma's true identity, which Hardy had lost not only through her death but through the change that overtook their relationship in their married life. Here, the rapid rush of recollection of the circumstances of her death, so typical in its non-communication of what their relationship had become, settles into two contrasting pictures of Emma's persona. The first, in stanza III, is of the married woman at Max Gate, exercising the power of the recently dead (in contrast to her quiet leavetaking of life) to create an illusion of her presence.

> Why do you make me leave the house
> And think for a breath it is you I see
> At the end of the alley of bending boughs
> Where so often you used to be . . .

Married woman

But the vision is not a true recapture of time past; the hard consonants and varied 'a' sounds of 'darkening dankness' and 'yawning blankness', like the earlier 'Saw morning harden upon the wall', pull the stanza back to the unwelcome emptiness and heaviness of the physical world without Emma, unrelieved by any momentary flash of insight. A hint that the true hiding-place of her personality is to be found in the past is contained in the past tense—'You were she'—of stanza IV, which presents her in her Cornish setting, already linked with vital symbols of pulsing life— but a life related to death because it is transfixed in the primaeval rocks:

> You were she who abode
> By those red-veined rocks far West,
> You were the swan-necked one who rode
> Along the beetling Beeny Crest . . .

Long past

The next stanza holds to this vision as the true essence of Emma when it returns to painful questioning of their shattered marriage:

> Why, then, latterly did we not speak,
> Did we not think of those days long dead,
> And ere your vanishing strive to seek
> That time's renewal? We might have said,
> > "In this bright spring weather
> > We'll visit together
> Those places that once we visited."

The last stanza is typical of many poems in the sequence in that it swings back from illusion and regret for what might have been to the harsh denying reality the poet must live with.

> Well, well! All's past amend,
> Unchangeable. It must go.
> I seem but a dead man held on end
> To sink down soon . . .

The rhythm and sentence-structure that had the uninterrupted swing of folk-song suddenly collapses into the dry, jerky movement of an individual human voice controlling the emotion of a personal grief. Then, brilliantly, the counterswing from stoic soliloquy to passionate address affirms in broken, awkward phrases that could belong to no-one but Hardy, the intensity and quality of the sorrow from which the whole cycle springs:

> . . . O you could not know
> That such swift fleeing
> No soul foreseeing—
> Not even I—would undo me so!

This is not a man talking about his grief, but the essence of grief as a quality displaying itself through the unselfconscious motions of a passionate and deep-feeling human mind.

"I Found Her out There", flanked on either side by three poems concerning Emma's life and death in Dorset, sees what her marriage entailed, the breaking of her harmony with the violent Cornish scene, as a betrayal of her essential being, and a symbol of the human adult's alienation from meaning in the world. This poem holds a focal position in the cycle. It corresponds to those songs in which a change of key or an unexpected harmonic colouring presents the dual face of experience simultaneously. Though "I Found Her out There" is still concerned with Emma's death and burial, her vital relationship with the violence of the elements points to this equivocal natural energy as an essential part of the woman Hardy loved. Love and death are related in a harmony of dissonance. 'The Voice', coming between two dramatizations of Emma as a sad but solicitous ghost, swings to the depth of desolation without reconciliation in setting her illusory presence against her real absence in the physical world. Yet the unexpected ground-base of a dance tune, steadying the confused uncertainty of the poet's speech-rhythms, again brings love into a vital harmonic tension with death, though at this stage the juxtaposition does not find any ultimate meaning in Emma's death. 'The Voice' is the last of the peak poems in the sequence to be controlled by the past.

98

'A Dream or No', a musical bridge to the poems that follow, develops the undervoiced change of harmonies in facing honestly the difficulty of distinguishing between fact and fiction, when 'nought of that maid from Saint-Juliot I see;/Can she ever have been here . . .?' The confusion of past and present is finally thrashed out, and both are valued and placed, in the next poem, the climactic 'After a Journey'.

Hardy did well to change the rather formal first line, 'Hereto I come to interview a ghost' to 'Hereto I come to view a voiceless ghost' in subsequent editions. 'View' introduces the major theme of clear vision that can at last accept and so penetrate the darkness to distinguish between illusion and reality: 'voiceless' characterizes the ghost as something different from the illusion of 'the woman calling' in 'The Voice'. The alliteration stresses the link between clear vision and departure of illusion. The only voice in the poem, of 'the cave just under', with

> a voice still so hollow
> That it seems to call out to me from forty years ago,
> When you were all aglow,
> And not the thin ghost that I now fraily follow!

is placed firmly, in its hollowness, in the perspective of the past, and with it, Emma in the illusion of her living presence. The heavy stresses on the 'then fair hour' and the 'then fair weather' point up the poet's clear recognition of the past for what it is, and his realization that he cannot return to 'then'. He comes through finally in this poem to a liberation from his lively and tantalizing ghost, but only because he does not refuse the experience of disorientation. The shifting perspectives of time and vision that cloud his memory—

> Where you will next be there's no knowing,
> Facing round about me everywhere . . .

affect sense, rhythm, structure, and sound. The flitting movement of his vividly-defined ghost, with her 'rose-flush coming and going', is mirrored in the jerky uncertainty of Hardy's own coming and going in pursuit—'Up the cliff, down, till I'm lonely, lost'; and the opening and closing vowels of 'the unseen waters' ejaculations awe me'. The clumsiness of this line has caused some protest; but it is a deliberate change from the first edition's 'unseen waters' soliloquies', and there is no doubt that its particular arrangement of

99

reverberating vowels and clashing consonants helps to create the 'coming and going' of the ghost, of the throbbing sea which is a groundbase controlling all the other kinds of movement in the poem, of the different dimensions of time, of the waves of reality and illusion, of the poet's recollecting consciousness, and the urgent, intimate speech rhythm of a man gradually coming to terms with the onrush of his grief. Life offers—to deny: the rhythm of ebb and flow controls the lines, stretching out the voice from death to life to issue finally in the affirmative simplicity of

> I am just the same as when
> Our days were a joy, and our paths through flowers.

The nuances of uncertainty in the second stanza contribute towards a final honest reckoning with guilt for the past, for it is set clearly in its proper dimension of time. 'Through the years, through the dead scenes I have tracked you'. 'Your olden haunts' may be a common figure of poetic speech, but its semantic relationship to 'dead scenes' in the next line suggests that the ghost which has trespassed over its proper boundary of time is about to be laid. Time dominates the poem, and especially in the diction of this stanza.

> What have you now found to say of our past—
> > Scanned across the dark space wherein I have lacked you?
> Summer gave us sweets, but autumn wrought division?
> > Things were not lastly as firstly well
> > > With us twain, you tell?
> But all's closed now, despite Time's derision.

The hollow mockery of time, which mingled past and present, no longer has power to confuse Hardy's definition of reality. His eyes are wide open and his vision unblurred: 'I see what you are doing: you are leading me on . . .' She leads him on from the 'dead scenes' into a fully-accepted present that balances two realities, equally valid: the reality of the present moment of dawn after physical and spiritual darkness, that is defined through the acute response of his senses to the eternal affirmations of waking animal life; and the reality of his vision, no longer the ghost tantalizing him with her physical absence, but a presence enshrined in his memory as the deepest truth he had known. He knows that the exchange of illusion for daylight reality brings pain, but his decision is firm:

100

> Soon you will have, Dear, to vanish from me,
>   For the stars close their shutters and the dawn
>   whitens hazily.

He does not need the deceptions of memory now; living through them has brought him to a quiet acceptance of what memory can give: a sense of 'that time's renewal' in perpetuating the most valued experience of his past, untouched by time's slow stain, into the present. Now he can say, with that simple tenderness which is one of Hardy's deepest notes,

> Trust me, I mind not, though Life lours,
>   The bringing me here; nay, bring me here again!

for he can trust himself to keep a positive hold on life.

The note of quiet but positive contemplation is held in the next two poems, which ponder on the scene's indifference to Emma's death and its comparative immortality, with the steady vision of 'the woman whom I loved so, and who loyally loved me' placed in the past and holding its own against the physical bulk of Beeny Cliff. These two comparatively muted poems lead to the intense affirmation of that time's quality against the record of chronological time in 'At Castle Boterel'. The poet's steady look at physical reality in the last stanza, with his vision 'shrinking, shrinking', provides a diminuendo that leads to the less passionate tone of the next two poems, though the vision of Emma in all her youth and vitality, always balanced against the pain of her absence from the scenes that knew her, stays with him all the time. The second of these two poems, 'The Phantom Horsewoman', originally formed the last poem of the sequence. While in many ways it makes a fitting conclusion with its reiteration of the theme of the power of memory to perpetuate the poet's vision of the essential Emma, the three poems which follow in subsequent editions add something more to the cycle. The ballad form of 'The Spell of the Rose', which retells the story of their love-death romance with the appurtenances of romantic allegory, links their personal tragedy to the universal folk-experience of the human race. 'St. Launce's Revisited' moves tersely from allegory to the blunt reality he has to live with: the wish 'Slip back, Time!' is almost immediately denied by the strange faces of the servants, and the denial clinched by the final wry comment:

101

> Why waste thought,
> When I know them vanished
> Under earth; yea, banished
> Ever into nought!

Its tone prepares the way for the final peak of the sequence, 'Where the Picnic Was'. There is no ecstasy, and no affirmation; these are stages past. There is only retracing of the external act of human communion that a picnic represents, noting of the external signs of human occupation, by the 'last relic of the band/Who came that day'; and quiet acceptance of his isolation in the continuing scene. 'Yes, I am here': Hardy has survived an overwhelming grief, and has learned not to deflect its natural course, not to refuse those memories which give value and meaning to the broken relationship of love at the same time as they revive the pain of death that is the other deepest truth about life.

The life that is affirmed by 'Poems of 1912–13' and Hardy's other elegies is not one of inflated operatic grandeur. It moves us precisely because it is an ordinary unpretentious life of doing and suffering, often empty and commonplace, full of human imperfections. It is a life of prose quality such as most people live: W. H. Auden, who describes Hardy as his poetic father, has paid tribute to Hardy's peculiar power of investing the most prosaic of colloquial statements with the light that never was, to express the 'poetry in what is left [in life] after all the false romance has been abstracted' (*Life*).

> "There was a frost
> Last night," she said,
> "And the stove was forgot
> When we went to bed . . ."

> I see what you are doing: you are leading me on . . .

First lines in particular introduce and make memorable the prosaic quality of the little unremembered acts that constituted life at Max Gate or St Juliot: 'You did not walk with me', 'It was your way, my dear', 'How she would have loved/A party today!' 'It never looks like summer'—the last a poem made out of a chance remark of Emma's, which is pencilled on one of Hardy's sketches of the Cornish scene.

Sometimes the prosaic quality and stumbling awkwardness that expresses an inarticulate grief almost too great for expression, which make a poem like 'After a Journey' so powerful, do not produce poetry of the first rank. 'A Circular', with its predictable ending in a shroud, hardly goes beyond the form of the Fashion catalogue that inspired it. 'The Prospect', which starts promisingly with one of Hardy's vivid silhouettes of trees against a winter sky and develops through simile and metaphor an image of the season linked to old age, finishes its first stanza with a picture of Emma 'greeting a gathered band/Of the urban and the bland', in which the diction seems chosen more for the needs of rhyme than for precision of poetic statements. There is not here the intensity of feeling which inspires concise expression even in some of the 'variation' poems of the main cycle, such as 'Rain on a Grave', 'Your Last Drive', and 'Lament'. In the last, what might have been a routine description in the familiar before-and-after pattern of trivial social occasions at Max Gate, is exalted by the controlled passion of the ballad-like refrain, 'She is shut, she is shut', with its variations from stanza to stanza and its sudden tightening of rhythm and diction. In general, Hardy's fidelity to the truth of feeling, phrasing and syntax, diction and stress of common speech, and the rhythms of the ordinary human mind recollecting some great emotion, makes great poetry out of the elegiac experience mortal men must undergo. His achievement gives the lie to the view expressed in Joseph Wood Krutch's *The Modern Temper* and George Steiner's *The Death of Tragedy* that tragedy and other human values are not possible to modern man. Hardy brings the values of tragedy within the scope of the ordinary human individual. Tennyson's 'stars in their courses blindly run'; Hardy's 'stars close their shutters' in a homely image of human experience that is as undignified as the words 'flop' and 'flitting' in the same stanza. Yet 'After a Journey', which never leaves the world of common human experience, is one of the finest expressions of tragic values in any language.

The values by which an ordinary human being may live in a death-marked life can be traced in the hundred or so poems inspired directly by Hardy's relationship with Emma. Though sadness and regret for the waste recur in his deep self-questioning—('An Upbraiding', 'We Sat at the Window', 'Best Times', 'Known Had I', 'Overlooking the River Stour', 'Near Lanivet')—there is a high proportion of poems devoted to happiness in this most tragic of poets. It is strongly implied by its negation in poems of the before-and-after type ('A Riddle', "It Never Looks like Summer", 'On the Doorstep', "The Curtains now are Drawn"); and such lyrics as "When I Set Out for Lyonnesse", 'The Wind's Prophecy', 'A Two Years' Idyll', 'At the Piano', 'She Opened the Door', and 'Once at Swanage' say Yea unequivocally to their love. In "The Curtains now are Drawn", he still hears the notes of her song, 'And death may come, but loving is divine'. The value of the dream as well as the reality is given its place too, when it can be clearly distinguished from illusion, as it can in 'The Shadow on the Stone', where Hardy determines not to 'unvision' the shape though he knows it cannot be 'her I long had learned to lack'.

Respect for what is due to any human being places high among Hardy's values love, tenderness, tolerance, a forgiveness that he extends to himself, and a fidelity that survives death while recognizing that death may render it futile:

> True: never you'll know. And you will not mind.
> But shall I then slight you because of such?
> Dear ghost, in the past did you ever find
> The thought, "What profit," move me much?

Posthumous existence in the memory of the living is the only kind of immortality Hardy can recognize. There, the essential truth of a person that has survived years of misunderstanding can be recaptured from death. The essential Emma lies not in the worn, dead body that 'looked quite other than theretofore,/As if it could not *be* you' ('Days to Recollect') but in the preceding memory of her, young and vital, collecting on her petticoat winged thistle seeds that 'sailed on the breeze in a nebulous stream/Like a comet's tail behind you'. Her immortality is here, in an intense moment of vision which burnt into the poet's mind vivid details of her relationship to the natural world that trembles with an inscrutable significance. This is how he remembers Emma; vital, human, imperfect. 'He Prefers Her Earthly' is the elegist's ultimate tribute to the ordinary individual that was Emma Hardy. He firmly rejects the kind of immortality that would rob her of her human qualities and change her 'mortal mould'

> to a firmament-riding earthless essence
> From what you were of old:

> All too unlike the fond and fragile creature
> Then known to me . . . Well, shall I say it plain?
> I would not have you thus and there,
> But still would grieve on, missing you, still feature
> You as the one you were.

V

Dramatic and Narrative Lyrics

01 877755.

Hardy is a poet who resists rigid classification. In the *Life* he quotes with approval a sentence from the *Edinburgh Review*

'which I might have written myself: "The division [of poems] into separate groups [ballad, lyrical, narrative &c.] is frequently a question of the preponderance, not of the exclusive possession, of certain aesthetic elements."'

So the poems to be considered as dramatic or narrative have merely a preponderance of story and dramatic expression. Dramatic conjunctions of people, time and circumstance do not preclude lyrical elements which would be equally at home in the 1912–13 poems. The lyrical emotion that sets the tone of 'The Peasant's Confession' —a first-person narrative of war-time action—

> I hid him deep in nodding rye and oat—
> His shroud green stalks and loam;
> His requiem the corn-blade's husky note—
> And then I hastened home . . .

is not vastly different from

> His crypt the cloudy canopy,
> The wind his death-lament

of 'The Darkling Thrush', though the narrative modifies, and is modified by, the lyrical feeling. Nor have dramatic and narrative elements been excluded from reflective lyrics. Within the framework of his own poetic persona recollecting, Hardy re-creates in the 1912–13 poems the story of his marriage. A situation conceived in dramatic terms of action, figure, scene, and often dialogue provides an objective correlative to personal emotions. The strange couple eternally promenading in 'Beyond the Last Lamp' possibly dramatizes the unhappiness of his marriage: the travelling boy in

'Midnight on the Great Western' gives dramatic embodiment to Hardy's tragic vision of the unknown region into which man's birth thrusts him.

Hardy's Prefaces insist on the dramatic nature of his verse, 'even that which is in other than narrative form—much is dramatic or impersonative even where not explicitly so' (*Poems of the Past and the Present*). Even 'those lyrics penned in the first person . . . are to be regarded, in the main, as dramatic monologues by different characters' (*Time's Laughingstocks*). His insistence can be defended if one regards his poetic persona as a dramatic instrument in itself, recording the inner and outer conflicts of human experience. Intensity of lyrical feeling and personal reflection does not rob poems like 'The Going' and 'To an Unborn Pauper Child' of dramatic immediacy:

> Why did you give no hint that night
> That quickly after the morrow's dawn,
> And calmly, as if indifferent quite,
> You would close your term here, up and be gone
> Where I could not follow . . .

> Breathe not, hid Heart: cease silently,
> And though thy birth-hour beckons thee,
> Sleep the long sleep . . .

However, Hardy's dramatic monologues do not re-create the excitement of immediate experience as Browning's re-create Fra Lippo Lippi's escapade or the exposure of Mr Sludge the medium. More often, they are either past situations recollected by a speaker in present equilibrium, or they are heavy with nostalgia engendered by 'the long drip of human tears' behind the specific situation.

Even poems such as 'The Curate's Kindness', 'The Chapel-Organist', and 'At Shag's Heath', which appear to be related while the old man is actually being conveyed to the workhouse, the organist giving her last performance, and the guilt-haunted wife on her way to drown herself, are really completed actions. Past events condition the immediate situation. Though 'The Chapel-Organist' is in the form of a monologue being thought or spoken in a present action, a glance at Browning's 'Abt Vogler' or 'Master Hugues of Saxe-Gotha' will show how much Hardy's poem depends on a narration of past conflict. The organist's thoughts as she plays grow from the conflict of body and soul which her whole life-story expresses, and not from her present performance, which is rather the final consequence of that story. Abt Vogler's reflections on music as an expression of the Absolute are a direct result of 'the palace of music I reared' while extemporizing at the organ. The vision of the organist in 'Master Hugues of Saxe-Gotha' of life as 'God's gold . . . Palled beneath man's usurpature' develops spontaneously from his struggle to find meaning under the dusty fugue structures of an obscure composer as he plays them in the organ loft whose unusual perspective shows him both the cobweb-covered gold of the ceiling and the usurping human activities of the sacristan below sweeping the church. Neither a philosophy of life, the quality of the music, nor the character of the organist is re-created in Hardy's poem by the organist's present activity. She and her playing exist simply as a fundamental image of the cosmic disharmony between what is and what might be, shown in her story.

Browning's 'interest's on the dangerous edge of things' in character and motive: his situations merely contributory. Hardy, in spite of a fascination with the grotesque and melodramatic aspects of experience which he shares with Browning, has no revelation of complexity in his speakers to compare with the Bishop who orders his tomb, Fra Lippo Lippi, Andrea del Sarto, Porphyria's lover, or the protagonists of 'The Laboratory' and 'My Last Duchess'. In the form of monologue favoured by Browning and Tennyson, the objective events and other characters concerned in the situation are filtered through the subjective screen of a speaker whose self-knowledge is limited by the presentness of his perspective. Caliban's natural theology owes its physical concreteness and moral short-sightedness to the bottom of the swamp on which he is reclining; St Simeon Stylites' lofty distortion of the world below and clear vision of the angel, to his perch on top of a pillar. The organist's definition of meaning in Master Hugues' 'mountainous fugues' as gold hidden under a mass of cobwebs is inspired both by his unusual position in the organ loft and the physical attack of his fingers on the spidery texture of the old fugue. The speaker so committed to a present situation reveals more than he understands. Tennyson's old maid in 'The Spinster's Sweet'arts' avows her independence of men while fondling the cats she has named after her rejected lovers: the reader is left to complete her self-revelation by judging the extent of her substitution of manageable cats for unmanageable men. Similarly, it is the reader who comprehends and passes judgement on the Duke's insolent monomania as he talks about the failings of his last duchess to the official who is arranging the marriage to his next; and on the extent of Karshish's belief in the miracle he tries to explain by rational means. The dramatic effect of a double perspective, of reader and speaker, is lost when the subject of the monologue is a past action, unless its retelling is conditioned by the speaker's present situation, as it is in Andrea del Sarto's attempts to impress Lucrezia with his past achievements and Karshish's endeavour to pierce the scientific scepticism of his superior. Though a few poems like 'Rake-hell Muses' and 'The Pink Frock' gain some dramatic effect from the moral blinkers of their speakers, Hardy usually sacrifices the psychological subtlety that results from Browning's double perspective to a stress on the situation itself, which came nearer to expressing the quality of his personal vision. Whereas Browning's double viewpoint on the lover who steals his friend's mistress in 'A Light Woman' leads the reader to understand the lover's moral and emotional ambiguities better than he does himself, Hardy's emphasis in 'The Face at the Casement' falls on the lover's 'deed of hell' and the chance—'why I turned I know not'—that dictated it.

> It was done before I knew it;
> What devil made me do it
> I cannot tell!
>
> Yes, while he gazed above,
> I put my arm about her
> That he might see, nor doubt her
> My plighted Love.

There is no excuse or pretence of motive for the inexplicable. The deed is morally evaluated within the poem by a first-person narrator whose perspective is identical with the reader's. The complex emotions of 'Porphyria's Lover' are replaced by a simple archetype of the guilt-haunted man, and a final reflection which shows the speaker standing outside his own situation, understanding something at least about the quality of contradictory passions:

> Love is long-suffering, brave,
> Sweet, prompt, precious as a jewel;
> But jealousy is cruel,
> Cruel as the grave!

Complexity or development of persona would be out of place in Hardy's vision of man's predicament. It is the quirks of time and chance, best seen through a completed action which is necessary to the ironic perspective from which he reflects on the madness of circumstance, rather than quirks of character, which form Hardy's climaxes. 'The Slow Nature' is less a study of the motions of a shocked psyche than a study of the quixotic action of time, which a fortnight after her husband's death strikes the woman with grief, while the unwontedly grave messenger

> amazed that a wife struck to widowhood
> Thought first of her unkempt room

is restored to his usual humour. It is therefore no great matter whether the narrator is an actor in the story or a persona who views it objectively, since his perspective does not require a contribution from the reader to complete the total meaning of the poem.

In Browning's account of the medical experiences of 'Karshish, the Arab Physician' and Hardy's 'Panthera' and 'The Wood Fire', both poets employ the convention of the neutral narrator on the periphery of a great event—the story of Lazarus in Browning's poem, and the Crucifixion in Hardy's. 'Panthera', in addition, insets the narration of Christ's supposed father, who might be presumed to have a personal interest in the Crucifixion, inside the narration of an uncommitted character. But Panthera's calm account of the Crucifixion at which he recognized Mary as his former mistress and Christ as their son might have yielded Browning more psychological tension than

> "Though I betrayed some qualms, she marked me not;
> And I was scarce of mood to comrade her
> And close the silence of so wide a time
> To claim a malefactor as my son—"

The effect of the Crucifixion on the human mind is not Hardy's primary business. Browning's emphasis, however, is placed on the effect of Lazarus' experience, and 'how he takes up the after-life', on the uneasy paganism of Karshish, the physician who examined him. The full force of Karshish's revaluation of the scientific attitude, depending as it does on a non-rational feeling of 'peculiar interest/And awe indeed this man has touched me with', can only strike us because his character as a responsible citizen of the world and sober scientific witness, trusting in physical 'things of price'

like 'blue-flowering borage . . . very nitrous' that can be botani-
cally and chemically defined, has been established from the beginning. But his interest in Lazarus carries the meaning of the poem
beyond what he actually says; beyond his anxiety to define the
case to a sceptical superior in physical and rational terms as 'a
case of mania—subinduced/By epilepsy'. The end of the poem—
a contemplation on the 'madman's' idea of the 'All-Great' as 'the
All-Loving too'—implicitly denies Karshish's protestations that he
has been writing 'of trivial matters'.

Hardy's neutral narrators, like Browning's, distance the strangeness of events. We cannot give full assent to the story of Panthera
when the narrator warns

> That the said woman did not recognize
> Her lover's face, is matter for surprise.
> However, there's his tale, fantasy or otherwise.

Nevertheless, it is the strangeness of circumstance which is stressed
by the lack of psychological subtlety in the narrators. We see in
Panthera only one of Time's laughingstocks, like the soldier of
'San Sebastian' whose daughter supernaturally inherits the eyes of
'the maiden I wronged in Peninsular days'; the elderly returned
lover of 'The Revisitation' who learns from the sight of the lady in
full daylight that 'Love is lame at fifty years'; the mother of 'A
Sunday Morning Tragedy' whose procuring of an abortion for her
daughter kills the girl on the day her tardy lover had published
the banns. Neither the personal character of narrators, nor the
effect of the Crucifixion on them, is functional in Hardy's poems.
What is significant, in fact, is the *lack* of effect, which has its
dramatic function in eliciting the reader's response to the Crucifixion. What should have been a 'day of wont' to Panthera, when
'some three or four were stript, transfixed, and nailed,/And no
great stir occurred' has only an economical importance to the
Christopher Coney of Calvary in 'The Wood Fire'; he buys
the crosses 'bargain-cheap of the executioners' and commends the
piece that Christ was on for its cheery blaze in a bleak spring:
"And it's worthless for much else, what with cuts and stains
thereon." Poor people and Roman soldiers alike are more conscious
of the ever-present enmity of nature and the physical world, of
aches and wounds occasioned by active service and duties in damp
outposts, than the implications of the Crucifixion. The physical
struggle for survival leaves little room for speculation on the

miraculous. Browning, in contrast, gives little space to the *events* of Lazarus' 'death'. Hardy's concern with the fate of the human being —to be eternally active but ignorant of final causes—places stress inevitably on event rather than its effect on character.

Hardy's vision is expressed most succinctly through the bare statement of event that composes 'Satires of Circumstance in Fifteen Glimpses'. Here, the quintessence of a situation of human delusion is presented at a moment of crisis, the culmination of an implied drama, which reveals the situation for what it is. The means used are dramatic and narrative. The poet-narrator observes gesture, dialogue, tone, appearance, and allows them to speak for themselves. The danger that the effect of a shock revelation may stale on re-reading is largely avoided by variety of presentation. The series does not depend exclusively on the mechanical reversal of viewpoint from the apparent situation in the first stanza to the real situation in the second, by means of which the irony is shown, though this method can be seen at its best in 'At Tea', 'In the Nuptial Chamber', 'In Church', and 'In the Cemetery'. The ironic form is varied, for example, in 'In the Study', where it is present only in the narrator's compassionate piercing of the lady's nonchalant façade, by her hesitant speech rhythms as she offers her father's books for sale, by clauses of manner: 'as if necessity were unknown', 'as if to sell were a mere gay whim'; and details of appearance and gesture that show her poverty. 'In the Restaurant' is less an ironic reversal of attitude than a study of two different points of view—the man's and the woman's—towards marital deceit and the expected child of their illicit union. In 'At the Draper's' the incident which caused a double revelation to husband and wife—the wife's precipitate ordering of fashionable widow's weeds, observed by her still-living husband—is placed in the past, and the poem consists almost entirely of the husband's words as his knowledge of the incident strips her vanity bare. 'In the Moonlight' expresses its sense of life's grim irony in the question-and-answer form reminiscent of certain traditional ballads, which eliminates from the initial question—why the lonely workman stands staring at a grave—all its possible answers until the final stanza reveals the truth:

> "Ah—she was the one you loved, no doubt,
> Through good and evil, through rain and drought,
> And when she passed, all your sun went out?"

> "Nay: she was the woman I did not love,
> Whom all the others were ranked above,
> Whom during her life I thought nothing of."

'In the Room of the Bride-Elect' provides the shock at the beginning, in the bride's revelation that she would have married the man of her parents' choice with a little more parental pressure. The poem moves towards a bitter image of resignation to her self-imposed fate:

> "Ah! here he comes with his button-hole rose.
> Good God—I must marry him I suppose!"

Even in those poems which make use of the usual ironic antithesis there is normally enough variation to exempt them from the charge of overwhelming the human experience with a mechanical formula. They ring the changes on the ignorance or knowledge which a revelation of the reality under the appearance leaves with the actors. 'At Tea', 'At a Watering-Place' and 'In the Cemetery' leave the victims of duplicity or circumstance in blissful ignorance. 'In Church', 'Outside the Window', 'At the Altar-Rail' and 'In the Nuptial Chamber' depend for their irony on the presence of someone within the poem who has beheld a soul undraped. The victims in 'By her Aunt's Grave' and 'Over the Coffin' are dead: their dead presence is the touchstone which shows up the disloyalty of the girl who spends her aunt's headstone money on a dance (though the tone here is not unqualified by a suggestion of Christopher Coney's philosophy, "Why should death rob life o' fourpence?") and the narrow conventions of the eternal triangle that hinged on the man now in his coffin.

> "But now I am older, and tell you true,
> For life is little, and dead lies he;
> I would I had let alone you two!"

The effect of irony is also subtly varied according to the viewpoint and commitment of the narrator. The poet-narrator who observes the undercurrents which stir action, gesture, scene, dialogue, and tone in 'At Tea' distances the irony of ignorance as the actor-narrator of 'At a Watering-Place' does not. Whereas the apparent harmony of 'At Tea' is not destroyed by the observer-narrator pointing out the ironic cross-currents of wife, husband and mistress, the peaceful tone and scene of 'At a Watering-Place' is

112

violently disrupted in the second stanza by the ex-lover's passionate details of his love-making to the girl who is to be married to another:

> ". . . How little he thinks
> That dozens of days and nights on end
> I have stroked her neck, unhooked the links
> Of her sleeve to get at her upper arm. . . ."

A more compassionate, even humorous irony appears in the narration of 'the man of the cemetery' who, like the Overworld of *The Dynasts*, has knowledge denied to mothers squabbling over the empty graves of their children.

> "And then the main drain had to cross,
> And we moved the lot some nights ago,
> And packed them away in the general foss
> With hundreds more. But their folks don't know,
> And as well cry over a new-laid drain
> As anything else, to ease your pain!"

Occasionally, as in 'On the Death-bed', Hardy tries to pack too much incident into a form which makes its effect through stark statement of a dramatic situation stripped bare of all but the culminating crisis implying the steps that led up to it. But the best of these situations, told in the language of bare simplicity and natural cadences of the human voice in strong but controlled emotion, stand as memorable images of some essential quality of life. Even the titles have dramatic relevance as scene-setting and agents in the action. The restaurant carries an aura of snatched guilty meetings. The altar-rail, the room of the bride-elect, and the nuptial chamber are places which reveal the frailty of the eternal Eve: the grave and the coffin measure the importance of human actions: the draper's exposes their vanity, and the church their false professions. 'In Church', 'In the Cemetery', and 'Over the Coffin' crystallize that essential quality of life which is bounded by place and time. Every word contributes economically to the meaning. The connotations of falsehood as original sin are felt in the alliterating 'glide,' 'gloss or guile' of 'In Church', with its smooth flowing rhythm: the man of the cemetery's image of the dead children as 'sprats in a tin' implies their unimportance as human individuals to the First Cause. But the essence lies primarily in the vividly-sketched situations: the child's accidental sight of her adored minister's re-enactment in the vestry mirror 'in deft dumb-show' of the pulpit gestures that had so moved the congregation in the first stanza, before she had been initiated into the evil of false-seeming; the mothers' futile quarrelling over their children's graves; the confrontation, 'the coffin between', of 'his wife of old, and his wife of late' in a dramatic image that is reminiscent of the final scene of *John Gabriel Borkman*, when their struggles for the dead man have been valued by the timeless state into which he has disappeared:

> And the dead man whose they both had been
> Seems listening aloof, as to things past date.

All are really deft dumb-shows, manipulated by the narrator to illustrate the absurdity of active, passionate life. They look back to the Dumb Shows of *The Dynasts* and in some respects forward to Camus' image of the telephone booth in *The Myth of Sisyphus*:

'At certain moments of lucidity, the mechanical aspect of their gestures, their meaningless pantomime, make silly everything that surrounds them. A man is talking on the telephone behind a glass partition; you cannot hear him but you see his incomprehensible dumb-show: you wonder why he is alive.'

Hardy's vision needed anonymous voices speaking out of the human predicament, both as sufferers and reflective commentators on its absurdity and tragedy. The dramatic form alone does not suit his particular genius, as a glance at 'Aristodemus the Messenian' and the rather better 'At Wynyard's Gap' will show. His unsureness with dialogue crushed into stylized form, and (in 'Aristodemus') the overbalance of melodrama tell against him when the dramatic situation is not made poetic and reflective (a function supplied by the extended stage directions and the presence of the Overworld in *The Dynasts*). The ironies of 'cynic circumstance' need the perspective of a narrator. The strange behaviour of Mad Judy at weddings and christenings could not be seen in its true light as a criticism of life without the narrator's refrain, 'Judy was insane, we knew.' The delusion of the father scrubbing the Statue of Liberty until 'her shape looms pure as snow' would not be shown for what it is without the comment of the sculptor in the last stanza: 'His child, my model, held so saintly. . . ./In the dens of vice had died.' In 'At the Railway Station, Upway' the 'pitying child', the 'grimful glee' of the convict who sings to the boy's violin

> "This life so free
> Is the thing for me!"

and the constable's tolerant smile, stand in for the Spirits of Pity and Irony who in *The Dynasts* comment on the dissonant forces of human life thus harmonized for a moment. The comment is of more significance than the narrator.

With stress falling so markedly on the ironies of action, it is not surprising that Hardy's personae do not create so strong an impression in their own right as Browning's. They take their life from the dramatic situation. The simple archetypal features of lover, wronged woman, returned soldier, tragic mother, guilt-haunted wrongdoer and victims of circumstance generally which Hardy's characters display, enable them to comment without unfitness in their creator's voice on the action which expresses his quarrel with the cosmic scheme. The chapel-organist, a kind of musical Tess, answers criticism of a 'bosom too full for her age; in her lips too voluptuous a dye' as Tess might have done when speaking in Hardy's voice: ('It may be. But who put it there? Assuredly it was not I.') The girl of 'Her Dilemma', forced into a false declaration of love out of pity for a dying man, reflects:

> But the sad need thereof, his nearing death,
> So mocked humanity that she shamed to prize
> A world conditioned thus, or care for breath
> Where Nature such dilemmas could devise.

If Hardeian reflections on life run the risk of destroying both dramatic illusion and the impersonal tone of ballad narration, one could answer that a modern poet cannot revive the original climate that produced traditional country ballads. Since then,

> Souls have grown seers, and thought outbrings
> The mournful many-sidedness of things.
> ('The Sick Battle-God')

If it is the business of a poet to express 'the emotion of all the ages and the thought of his own' (*Life*) an impersonal blow-for-blow account of a battle will not express the mournful many-sidedness of things so accurately for the war-sated nineteenth and twentieth centuries as the narrator's interpolation of the thoughts of the old folk at the battle of Leipzig:

> 'O,' the old folks said, 'ye Preachers stern!
> O so-called Christian time!
> When will men's swords to ploughshares turn?
> When comes the promised prime?'

Hardy's dual interest as a modern poet in action and emotion gives a resonance beyond bare statement of situation in concentrated dramatic lyrics like 'The Woman in the Rye' and 'The Whitewashed Wall'. They make their effect in simple diction and rhythms hardly different from those of prosaic speech, but their placing of stress, pause, and repetition invests ordinary speech with 'the emotion of all the ages':

> But she knows he's there. And when she yearns
> For him, deep in the labouring night,
> She sees him as close at hand, and turns
> To him under his sheet of white.
>
> ('The Whitewashed Wall')

> "I told him I wished him dead," said she.
>
> "Yea, cried it in my haste to one
> Whom I had loved, whom I well loved still;
> And die he did. And I hate the sun,
> And stand here lonely, aching, chill;
>
> "Stand waiting, waiting under skies
> That blow reproach, the while I see
> The rooks sheer off to where he lies
> Wrapt in a peace withheld from me!"
>
> ('The Woman in the Rye')

The situation is unfolded in spare, economical statement in answer to a leading question posed by an anonymous listener—usually the only function of Hardy's listeners—about an oddity of human behaviour, which elicits the tale of its cause. The mother's 'raptured rite' of kissing the blank wall of her cottage and the girl's stance in the dripping rye, 'cold-lipped, unconscious, wet to the knee', are explained by the answers received, but a great deal is left to the imagination. No reason is given for the girl's wish,

116

though a passionate quarrel is implied: nor for the son's absence from home, though the date when the poem appeared—November 1918—suggests absence on military service, if not death. The tone of 'The Whitewashed Wall' does not seem correlative with an actual death; but the vivid details of the 'sheet of white' under which the shadow-drawn image lies, the whitener whose activity symbols the inevitable on-going of the world—

> The whitener came to cleanse the nook,
> And covered the face from view. . . .

> ". . . When you have to whiten old cots and brighten,
> What else can you do, I wonder?"

—and the drawing of the 'lifelike semblance' of the boy on the flame-lit cottage wall, evoke a complex response to the power of mothers to worship images in the Plato-cave of shadows when the substance shall be hidden under the final annihilating sheet of white.

In the swift telling of bare essentials in 'The Woman in the Rye' there is the same sense of inexplicable human action, and inexplicable fatal catastrophe, that one finds in 'Lord Randal' or 'The Three Ravens'. Ballad-like, the poem focuses on action and physical detail rather than meaning and motive. The solitary human figure standing against a dark backdrop of cosmic indifference expressed for Hardy, in many poems and novels, the plight of human consciousness and feeling waiting in an insentient universe for a lost harmony that can only be regained by death. The indifference of the elements to human significance conjures up the authentic ballad note, but the impersonality of

> Oer his white banes, when they are bare,
> The wind sall blaw for evermair

is very different from the emotive effect of Hardy's living, feeling woman making of the universe a vast reproach. The subjective emotion of the sufferer is essential here to answer the objective viewpoint of the observer; 'unconscious' is the one thing she is not. Her situation and her response to it crystallize sharply in a haunting visual image the high moral quality of a being who takes onto her own shoulders the guilt of a cosmic bad joke and, like the ballad protagonists of 'Edward', 'Mary Hamilton' and 'Bonnie

Annie', decrees her own punishment. The self-decreed death of the traditional ballad protagonists would have been easier: the death-wish is truer to modern psychology. It is objectified in the woman's hatred of the sun, her deliberate courting of nature's hostility, and her sight of the rooks which, in common with other black death-linked birds of folklore, know a harmony with cosmic purposes denied to alienated man.

Bare factual statement of situation and dialogue which is so effective in these two poems does not succeed without careful choice of evocative image and diction—'deep in the *labouring* night', 'waiting, waiting under skies/That blow reproach'; the woman in the wet rye watching the rooks fly to her dead lover, the haunting figure of the whitener and his annihilating sheet of white—to give cosmic significance to the specific situation. Some poems carry the elements of a good dramatic narrative without unifying their traditional features and modern sensibility. 'In Sherborne Abbey' begins with a fugitive couple flying the vengeance of kin, like so many ballad lovers, surrounded as they rest in a church by the forms of looming effigies, 'recumbent like their own,/Yet differing; for they are chiselled in frigid stone'. This striking visual image, full of dramatic and poetic potentiality to a century haunted by transience, leads in rather forced fashion to a revelation of the lovers' position, in uninspired dialogue:

> ". . . We two are not marble yet."
> "And, worse," said she; "not husband and wife!"

The final twist to the story—

> "Why did you make me ride in your front?" says she.
> "To outwit the law. That was my strategy.
>   As I was borne off on the pillion behind you,
>   Th' abductor was you, Dearest, let me remind you"

is a bit of irrelevant legal quibbling too trivial to carry the expectations aroused by the initial contrast between human passion and the stone passivity of the dead against which all departure from convention must be measured. Here, Hardy has allowed his love of a strange situation to run away with his artistic sense of unity. As Edmund Blunden remarks, in his book *Thomas Hardy*:

'so greatly did Hardy feel the incidents of life which had anything of the unexpected or peculiar in them, that he believed they would tell very well in some sort of ballad form, without much accompaniment of reflection or choice of phrase.'

'The Children and Sir Nameless', on the other hand, is successful in fusing the evocative possibilities of a stone effigy with the situation and story portrayed. In simple statement that hardly strays from common usage, yet is irradiated by the unifying concept behind the poem, it tells of the proud Sir Nameless' irritation with children, which leads him to seek 'green remembrance' not in offspring, but in a huge alabaster effigy.

> Three hundred years hied; Church-restorers came,
> And, no one of his lineage being traced,
> They thought an effigy so large in frame
> Best fitted for the floor. There it was placed,
> Under the seats for schoolchildren. And they
> Kicked out his name, and hobnailed off his nose;
> And, as they yawn through sermon-time, they say,
> "Who was this old stone man beneath our toes?"

The simply told story, and the vivid physical details, culminating in the attack by other people's posterity upon the effigy that was to be the proud man's 'green remembrance', becomes a striking objective correlative for the ironic operations of Hubris, Time, and Chance. The comment of 'green' on the lifeless whiteness of alabaster and the lively children who carry the seeds of human immortality shows a care for evocative language that characterizes Hardy at his best.

Hardy learned much about dramatic and narrative art from traditional ballad and folksong, which was the most common way of telling or hearing a story in nineteenth-century rural Dorset. One can point to his concern with a strong, often melodramatic, situation; with the staple food of village gossip which at its best expressed from the perspective of a shared and settled peasant culture the timeless truths of human life—the focal points of birth, love, death, and the primitive social code of human conduct centred on these points. In the ballad world the values in face of sudden death that was always round the corner are simple and self-supporting, based on the life-loyalties important to the survival of the rural community: courage, love, friendship, loyalty to friends and kin, swift vengeance on traitors and enemies, pride in human achievement wrested out of a mechanical universe that makes 'The

Old Workman' akin to 'John Henry'. Transgression of natural and social taboos brings guilt and self-punishment that is not resented:

> My punishment I cannot bear,
> But pray God *not* to pity me

cries the tragic mother of Pydel Vale in 'A Sunday Morning Tragedy', in the spirit of Michael Henchard. The action is primal and violent and ruled by an inexplicable fatality indifferent to man. It takes place in a metaphysical and social void which is filled instead with the tangible importance of physical things. The jilted lover of 'Rose-Ann', like Farmer Boldwood, objectifies his feeling in the goods he was putting by for the wedding:

> Down home I was raising a flock of stock ewes,
>   Cocks and hens, and wee chickens by scores,
> And lavendered linen all ready to use,
>   A-dreaming that they would be yours.

Circumstances and action are given barely: the tale tells itself in dramatic or semi-dramatic form. Dialogue and gesture objectify obliquely much of the action, situation, essential information, motivation, meaning, result, character, feeling, and mood; with much more left to the imagination. We are often introduced to the drama only in the fifth act, or even the epilogue, when a final conjunction of people, time and place illuminates the meaning of a past story inferred, Ibsen-like, through the present crisis.

Hardy's debt to balladry can be seen in tone and certain aspects of structure, adapted for modern consumption. 'Satires of Circumstance in Fifteen Glimpses' show what he could do with a strong situation and a drama that discloses itself only when it has reached the fifth act. In his concentrated lyrics generally he was able to draw on those ballad techniques of implication through economical speech and gesture which told a story as much through what was missed out as through what was put in. The mother-in-law situation which is so common in ballads, and which Hardy made good use of in *The Return of the Native*, is implied succinctly in 'The Nettles' through the mother's first words:

> This, then, is the grave of my son,
>   Whose heart she won! And nettles grow
> Upon his mound; and she lives just below.

The 'strange phantasmal sight' of the lady dancing when she has heard of her husband's death ('Seen by the Waits'), seen as a mirror reflection by the waits who provocatively refuse to comment, speaks eloquently of her married life. 'The Dark-eyed Gentleman', like *Tess of the d'Urbervilles*, leaps over the act that produced 'a fine lissom lad' in the third stanza, though it is implied in the refrain lines by the gentleman's concern for the lady's garter and the lady's mixed emotions that she allowed him to tie it. 'A Practical Woman' —a poem in the common four-three ballad metre—likewise leaps over the means which the woman found to produce a healthy son after enumerating the defects of her seven (folklore magic number) sickly legitimate children. It has a ring of 'Sir Patrick Spens' in the abrupt beginning—"O who'll get me a healthy child"—the swift resolve, and the economical statement of action and result:

> She went away. She disappeared,
>   Years, years. Then back she came:
> In her hand was a blooming boy
>   Mentally and in frame.

In 'John and Jane', the incremental repetition of balladry, with a variation which advances the story in each repetition, implies the disillusionment that has taken place between the four stages of human life crystallized in the four stanzas. John sees the world as a boisterous place, 'Does John', comments the refrain line, implying his single state. 'They' find the world a pleasant place, 'Do John and Jane'. They see their cottage as a palace, containing a pearl, 'Do John and Jane with a baby-child.' They rate the world as a gruesome place, 'Do John and Jane with their worthless son.' The question-and-answer technique reveals the situation of 'The Ruined Maid' as very different from the Victorian conception of ruin, with the questioner pointing the contrast between the hardness of the village girl's lot and the refinements displayed by 'Melia, and the refrain-line answer varying the theme of 'ruined'.

Yet ballad technique alone would not account for the peculiar flavour of Hardy's narratives. His most original successes rely on our conditioned response to ballad and folksong, which contain the emotion of all the ages, counterpointing those touches of modern sensibility which mark the thought of our own. The intensity of lyrical feeling which comes from a modern and idiosyncratic outlook on human destiny is controlled by the impersonality which belongs to ballad technique. A complexity of response is added to

'The Dark-eyed Gentleman', 'A Practical Woman' and 'The Ruined Maid' when one recalls the tragedy, not infrequently the death of the lovers at the hands of husband or kin, that often attended a sexual slip in balladry. The positive attitude of the practical woman and the mother of the fine lissom lad, and the un-guilt-laden prosperity of the ruined maid, question traditional sexual codes. The husband's view, in the poem of that name—

> "And what with our serious need
> Of sons for soldiering,
> That accident, indeed,
> To maids, is a useful thing!"

criticizes not only the intolerance of sexual morality, but the morals of a modern society that needs sons for soldiering. There are several poems, including 'The Burghers', 'A Wife and Another', 'Her Death and After', which gain their effect from the ghost of the old ballad of vengeance walking behind the modern narrative in which the deceived husband or wife or lover acts nobly. The passionate treatment of love in balladry receives a sharp check from the progress of disillusionment briefly set out in 'John and Jane' in a form which more usually records the stages of passionate action.

The pattern of false assumption and elimination through question and answer—the pattern of 'Edward'—lies behind such poems as 'The Statue of Liberty', "Ah, are you Digging on my Grave?" 'Heiress and Architect', 'A Sound in the Night', and 'The Work-box', but Hardy does not use it merely as a mechanical formula. The initial situation which is stripped of the values implied in it in "Ah, are You Digging on my Grave?"—the idea of immortality through the memory of the living—gains added ironic point from fusion with the 'Unquiet Grave' convention of dialogue between the dead and the lover who will not let her sleep. For the dog, her last hope, has only disturbed the grave to bury a bone in it. In 'Heiress and Architect' the rigidity of this ballad form gives physical check, like the 'arch-designer', to the soaring line of the heiress' romantic notions of a dwelling place, which are ruthlessly whittled down to the bare denying reality of the heavily-stressed

> ". . . Give space (since life ends unawares)
> To hale a coffined corpse adown the stairs;
> For you will die."

The question-and-denial form which inevitably advances the story of 'A Sound in the Night' towards solution of a mystery at the same time as it eliminates all possible answers except murder is a manifestation (as in 'Edward') of the woman's dominant will, which during the course of the poem drives the farmer to kill his former mistress as it had driven him to marry her supplanter. In 'The Workbox' the discipline of this particular ballad form uncovers the deceit in the relationship of the married pair, through the wife's evasions of the true reason why she shrinks from her husband's gift of a workbox which had been made out of the coffin wood supplied for a lad from her home town. The eloquent gesture of the final stanza—

> Yet still her lips were limp and wan,
>   Her face still held aside,
> As if she had known not only John,
>   But known of what he died.

—implies the answer she does not give. 'In the Servants' Quarters' —Hardy's version of St. Peter's betrayal of Christ—gives a double twist to the form. It begins with the truth everyone knows— imaginatively presented, through recognition of Peter's dialect as akin to the 'criminal's'—and moves through Peter's denying answers to the counterdenial of the cock.

The importance of physical things in balladry is adapted variously to Hardy's vision of the importance of the physical world. The traditional roll-call of familiar names and places, which implies a certain security in an unpredictable world, is extended to include dance tunes in 'The Dance at the Phoenix' and inns in 'A Trampwoman's Tragedy'. The role of the physical in determining human fate is suggested by the part played by physical objects as agents of action, or as the measure of value and reality. The workbox which becomes a powerful image of the wife's relationship to the dead man and her unsuspecting husband—a relationship which is itself inextricably bound up with the proximity of life and love to death—

> "The shingled pattern that seems to cease
>   Against your box's rim
> Continues right on in the piece
>   That's underground with him"

—has dramatic importance as the cause of the wife's agony. In 'The Satin Shoes', the delicate shoes which unhinged the bride's mind when rain prevented her wearing them for her wedding, enact a sinister marriage with her when they persuade her to enter the un-fairytale coach which takes her to the madhouse. The gay trinkets in which ballad heroines usually deck themselves motivate the lover to rob a church in 'The Sacrilege', and ruthlessly show Jenny's age as she 'rose, arrayed, and decked her head/Where the bleached hairs grew thin' to go to the dance at the Phoenix. The 'raiment rare' which the wife in 'The Burghers' had heaped up to pay for her elopement, and the luxuries rejected by the wife who meets her lover 'On Martock Moor'—

> I'd feather-beds and couches,
> And carpets for the floor,
> Yet brighter to me was, at eves,
> The bareness of the moor

—value the superior wealth of love. In 'The Homecoming', which bears some resemblance to 'My Boy Billy', the vivid particulars of

> . . . great black beams for ceiling, and a floor o' wretched stone,
> And nasty pewter platters, horrid forks of steel and bone

and 'a skimmer-cake for supper, peckled onions, and some pears' provide a humorous objective correlative for the child-wife's disillusion and her elderly husband's crude but kindly comfort.

Hardy's use of refrains, too, shows a fusion of traditional and modern features which is both original and idiosyncratic. They range in kind from the repeated half-line of 'A Trampwoman's Tragedy' and 'A Sunday Morning Tragedy' to the detailed mood-and-landscape painting of 'The Homecoming' and 'The Sacrilege'. The balance between expectation and surprise is skilfully managed. Hardly ever does Hardy use a rigidly unvarying refrain. The keening 'alas for me' that ends the second line of most stanzas—not all—of 'A Sunday Morning Tragedy' adds a sense of obsessive grief and guilt to the effect of stifling enclosure caused by the thirty-two end rhymes in 'e'. And the guilt fixation caused by the recurrence of Monmouth's name in the last line of each stanza of 'At Shag's Heath' gives a literal truth to the end of the poem, which anticipates his betrayer's suicide:

> When comes the waterman, he'll say,
> "Who's done her thuswise?"—'Twill be, yea,
> Sweet, slain King Monmouth—he!

One has only to compare this poem with Browning's 'The Confessional', on a similar theme, to see the difference made to mood by the obsessive refrain. The half-line repetition of 'A Trampwoman's Tragedy' embodies the weariness of the travellers in the blazing sun, which played its part in encouraging the 'wanton idleness' that sets off the tragedy. Variations and word-stresses are important. One notes the added ironic affirmative, the emphasis on number that was soon to be decreased by a murder, a hanging, and a natural death, and a repetition of the emotive 'alone':

> For months we had padded side by side,
>> Ay, side by side . . .

> Inside the settle all a-row—
>> All four a-row . . .

> Thereaft I walked the world alone,
>> Alone, alone!

The alternative refrains of 'A Military Appointment'—'That soldier/lover of yours/mine'—advances the story to the inevitable point where the alternatives fuse for a moment, then neatly change partners in the sexual dance:

> "—Nell, him I have chanced so much to see,
> That—he has grown the lover of me!—
>> That lover of yours—
> And it's here our meeting is planned to be."

'The Sacrilege' and 'The Homecoming' make use of local landscape in the refrain in a way that recalls *The Return of the Native* though obviously in a much smaller compass. The wind that blows through 'The Homecoming' as a refrain is an active agent in the child-wife's adjustment to the reality of marriage. The basic refrain—

> *Gruffly growled the wind on Toller downland broad and bare,*
> *And lonesome was the house, and dark; and few came there*

embodies both the reality she must now face, very different from the farmer's 'pretty song of lovely flowers and bees,/And happy lovers taking walks within a grove o' trees', and her mood of desolation. Its variations are integrated into the story. The wind makes practical trial of the bride's discovery of 'a monstrous crock in chimney.' The sorely tried husband's threat to consign his wife to the mercy of the elements, "And leave 'ee to go barefoot to your d—d daddee!" is preceded by a hint of the wind's rough treatment of objects in its path:

> *Straight from Whit'sheet Hill to Benvill Lane the blusters pass,*
> *Hitting hedges, milestones, handposts, trees, and tufts of grass*

and followed by its diminuendo '*away down Crimmercrock's long lane*' as the wife capitulates. The last appearance of the refrain returns to its basic form: man has passed the trial of the elements, and they have no further power over him. In 'The Sacrilege', though the landscape of Exon and Dunkery Tor appears only in the second line of each stanza, it has something of the complex effect of Egdon Heath in evoking both the indifference of nature to human passions, and the close link between natural and human moods. The link gives birth to the style, for the landscape is integrated into the structure of the human sentence:

> "I said: 'I am one who has gathered gear
> From Marlbury Downs to Dunkery Tor . . .'"

> And all could see she clave to him
> As cleaves a cloud to Dunkery Tor . . .

Some narrative poems give the impression of being either too long or too short—a sign that Hardy was experiencing difficulties in adapting a traditional narrative form to modern sensibilities. They dissipate the concentrated drama that can be packed into a single moment of crisis, and miss the lyrical mood which needs room to expand, reflect, and connect the emotions and incidents to the natural world in which they happen. 'The Moth-Signal', for example, suffers from the lack of a lyrical mood which in 'The Sacrilege' was developed through landscape-refrain. The poetic conception of 'The Moth-Signal' needed for its fulfilment more than the situation itself, expressed in snatches of conversation and a statement of the lovers' meeting. Comparison with a similar incident in *The Return of the Native* shows how much it gains in the novel from the slow build-up of fire as a creative-destructive symbol to which Eustacia and Wildeve, like the moth Wildeve has released to Eustacia, are irresistibly attracted. And the grinning Ancient Briton of the poem who pops up from the tumulus in the last stanza to comment on the sameness of human destiny through time is no substitute for the presence of Egdon Heath that broods over the novel from beginning to end. When Hardy does manage to integrate the lyrical mood that comes out of his vision of nature with the ballad-swing of a good story, he produces a new and modern kind of ballad, such as 'A Sound in the Night' and 'Her Death and After'. The sounds of disturbed nature in 'A Sound in the Night', repeated though not formalized into a refrain, evoke not only mood and the farmer's guilty knowledge that the strange sound is human—

> "It may be a tree, bride, that rubs his arms acrosswise,
> If it is not the eaves-drip upon the lower slopes,
> Or the river at the bend, where it whirls about the hatches
>   Like a creature that sighs and mopes"

—but also the situation gradually revealed by their absence:

> "Nay, husband, you perplex me; for if the noise I heard here,
> Awaking me from sleep so, were but as you avow,
> The rain-fall, and the wind, and the tree-bough, and the river,
> Why is it silent now?"

'My Cicely' has received attention from many critics as a failure; it has been cited as an example of 'the most incredible and unnatural mish-mash of language.' The diction seems to reflect a fundamental disunity in imaginative concept. The poem falls uneasily between the two stools of ballad narrative and dramatic lyric, without fusion. Concentration on stark statement of the moment of revelation might have produced a poem like 'The Newcomer's Wife', in which an overheard conversation reveals to the newcomer that he has married 'the Hack of the Parade'. The splash in the fifth and final stanza, and the grim statement

> They searched, and at the deepest place
> Found him with crabs upon his face

say all that is necessary about his response to the news. But a similar technique in 'My Cicely' would have ignored the ironic relevance of the lover's spiritual and physical journey through ancient Wessex landmarks—the poem's lyrical element—to his wish to reverse Time. Its slow development as an image overbalances the dramatic moment of swift double revelation from a stranger that *his* Cicely is not the dead woman of the same name, and that he had failed to recognize his Cicely in the coarse barmaid at the Three Lions.

Comparison with another poem which has for its theme the same wish to reverse Time, 'The Revisitation', suggests why the latter is more successful in its fusion of traditional narrative and dramatic ballad tone with modern lyric personal intensity. In this long poem all the details of landscape—barrows, 'dateless' Sarsen stone, flint-tipt arrows trampled by living cattle, the wailing of peewits that

> Seemed the voicings of the self-same throats I had heard
> when life was green,
> Though since that day uncounted frail forgotten generations
> Of their kind had flecked the scene

—build up a vivid objective correlative to the emotion of a man 'living long and longer/In a past that lived no more.' The elusive and illusive flitting quality of life, which he forgets, is caught in the flashing of the 'spry white scuts of conies', the past peewits who had 'flecked' the scene and their present descendants who revealed 'their pale pinions like a fitful phosphorescence/Up against the cope of cloud', and 'the open drouthy downland thinly grassed' where 'an arid wind went past.' When the narrative of the lover's sentimental journey and his state of mind have been built up in this fashion, 'a figure broke the skyline—first in vague contour, then stronger', and as we move into his illusion that time has slipped back we move, rightly, into drama, the direct medium of illusion, with the immediacy of speech and gesture. The immediacy of drama has power to balance the poetic significance of landscape, as the stranger's report of Cicely's fortunes had not. Though there are some Hardeian clumsinesses in the dialogue—surely no-one ever started a sentence with the colloquial "Dear, I could not sleep for thinking" to end it with "of our trystings when twin-hearted"? —the hesitations and inflexions are true to the rhythms of emotion. Lyric narrative takes over again at the end of the scene, when the 'red upedging sun' that glorifies natural features, 'flinging tall thin tapering shadows from the meanest mound and molehill' cruelly lights up the daylight reality of 'Time's transforming chisel' on the lady's human features. An exit which is the dramatic reversal of her entrance—

> And I saw her form descend the slopes, and smaller grow and smaller,
>   Till I caught its course no more. . . .

leads to the narrator's quiet impersonal reflection, authentic because it springs from the direct personal experience just dramatized, that 'Love is lame at fifty years.'

The strange conjunctions which appealed to Hardy's narrative and dramatic sense are operatic in nature, and like opera libretti, incomplete without a lyrical element to preserve the drama from degenerating into either melodrama or prosaic short stories in rhyme. Browning's objective viewpoint supplies the place of music in his dramatic monologues. One could imagine what Browning might have done in his own convention with the calm tale, in 'Her Second Husband Hears her Story', of the lady who sewed up her drunken first husband in a sheet, and the second husband's equally phlegmatic response, "Well, it sounds strange—told here and now to me". A more lyrical approach to such melodramatic material would not, in Hardy's hands, produce the psychological subtleties of 'The Confessional' or 'The Laboratory' or 'My Last Duchess', but it did produce, when he allowed himself to expand beyond the bare telling, 'A Trampwoman's Tragedy', 'The Revisitation', and 'Her Death and After'. The subjective exploration of emotion, or complexity of mood, provided by the music of an operatic aria finds its Hardeian equivalent so often in lyric touches, dramatic in function as well as lyrical, which express his vision of man in relation to nature. In 'The Burghers', 'the Froom's mild hiss' which can be heard 'from Pummery-Tout to where the Gibbet is' suggests the complexity of the husband's emotions which can hold both charity and thoughts of murder: these are the sounds his state of mind selects to listen to. In 'Her Death and After', the change of mood after the dying woman's confession of love is shown clearly by the change from a death-marked landscape presented in slow-moving monosyllables—'And the trees shed on me their rime and hoar'—to a new dynamic conception of life and landscape that affects diction and rhythm:

> —When I had left, and the swinging trees
>   Rang above me, as lauding her candid say,
>   Another was I.

His decision to 'insert a deed back in Time' by claiming the unwanted child of his rival and the woman he loved subtly alters our response to the Roman Amphitheatre, the 'Ring' of *The Mayor of*

Casterbridge, where it takes place. Henchard continues to feel the power of man's primitive past of which the Ring is a grim reminder: the lover of the poem neutralizes it through his disinterested kindness.

Lyric emotion inheres by nature in bare but well-chosen statement of a dramatic event; but when Hardy leaves the concentrated lyric of crisis for more leisurely narration of Wessex events his achievement is variable. Without the distancing effect that ballad form and cadence places on a strange story, and the evocative phrase that makes traditional form speak to the modern age, village gossip tends to remain the untransmuted trivia that it often is. The rural relish for scandal and a strange story can be seen too faithfully recorded in 'The Dame of Athelhall', 'The Flirt's Tragedy', 'In the Days of Crinoline', 'The Two Wives', 'The Whipper-in', 'One who Married above Him', 'Her Second Husband Hears her Story', 'The Moth-Signal', 'On the Death-bed', 'In Sherborne Abbey'. 'A Poor Man and a Lady', 'The Mock Wife', 'The Elopement', 'The Contretemps', 'The Duel', 'A Woman's Fancy', 'The Turnip-Hoer', 'The Noble Lady's Tale', and others, whose truth in local tradition was too often for Hardy the only excuse for writing them.

However, when the village gossip concerns either the supernatural or the great events of military history, he can make a firm success of local tradition in straight narrative of events. His skill can be judged first of all from the group of Napoleonic war poems which are perhaps relics of his first conception of *The Dynasts* as a ballad sequence. They are distanced by memory, and helped by the existing tradition of ballad-making on some memorable battle. Ironically, this war-hater succeeds in conveying the excitement of a military action, the ebb and flow of personal fortunes, the physical sight and sound and smell of carnage, often in traditional ballad metres, with traditional ballad features—the varying refrain line, the honourable roll-call of fighters and place-names, the narrator recounting events he knew by experience or hearsay. Heroic action there is in plenty, but the uncomplex glory of war in traditional balladry is qualified by the lyrical touches that relieve the stark telling of the action with personal emotion. Even the emotive adjective or simile—'And harmless townsfolk fell to die', 'when the Allies/Burst on her home like flame'—would be out of place in 'The Battle of Otterburn' or 'Andrew Barton'. The fine description of the blowing of Bridge Lindenau in 'Leipzig'—

When there surged on the sky an earthen wave,
        And stones, and men, as though
    Some rebel churchyard crew updrave
        Their sepulchres from below

places the carnage of war as a cosmic death-wish of some nether
tidal force which destroys men as indifferently as stones. The
touches of natural description in these war ballads not only brings
to mind the use of nature in traditional balladry, which sets human
passions against the indifferent on-going of the world—

    He's killed this may, and he's laid her by,
        Eh vow bonnie
    For to bear the red rose company
        On the bonnie bank o' Fordie
            ('Babylon')

    "We've fetched en back to quick from dead,
    But never more on earth while rose is red
        Will drum rouse Corpel!" Doctor said
            O' me at Valencieën.
                ('Valenciennes')

but also sets against the destructive interruptions of war the eternal
values of human relationships linked closely to the cycle of life.
The precise evocation of time and place that begins 'The Alarm'
presents the most tempting of the soldier's alternative choices—to
return to his pregnant wife, or to march on and meet the invader.
One can forgive Hardeian unevennesses in this poem, such as the
unlikely peasant dialogue—"And if our July hope should ante-
date", "Why courting misadventure shoreward roam?" for the
genuine fusion of traditional ballad qualities (in an untraditional
stanza form) with personal lyricism. No-one but Hardy could
have saved the ballad 'prop' of the guiding bird-omen from the
suspicion of synthetic tone by the acutely and compassionately
observed incident of its release by the soldier from the river
vegetation:

    While he stood thinking,
        A little bird, perched drinking
    Among the crowfoot tufts the river bore,
Was tangled in their stringy arms and fluttered, almost sinking
        Near him, upon the moor.

The reality of the bird, its stringy trap and the compassionate act of the soldier that releases its power as an agent of fate together with its trapped body, and the events that follow from its release, become a reverberating image of the longing of the human heart which guides it back through a roundabout route of military duty to the homestead in the ferny byway of Wessex. The lyric emotion that inheres for Hardy in the natural cycle is skilfully and movingly integrated with the military event in 'Valenciennes':

> I never hear the zummer hums
> O' bees; and don' know when the cuckoo comes;
> But night and day I hear the bombs
> We threw at Valencieën. . . .

The traditional 'props' of spring and summer—the sounds of nature which should be a human birthright—revalue the unnatural sounds of military 'humming' in the first stanza, when stanza IX reveals that the narrator is a soldier for whom time stopped revolving when he was deafened by the shells of Valenciennes. His personal reflections, unemotional as they are (for his deafness shuts him off from passion) add the many-sidedness of modern thought to the extravert war ballad.

> 'Twas said that we'd no business there
> A-topperèn the French for disagreeèn;
> However, that's not my affair—
> We were at Valencieën.

'We were at Valencieën'. The common soldier's part is to experience and suffer, to take part in the eternal human predicament of acting without understanding. His dialect and touches of fumbling inarticulacy contribute to the sense of eternal human values—courage, fairness, resignation, pride—which war cannot extinguish.

It is perhaps to be expected that Hardy, with his profound and tragic response to death, should show some of his most successful fusions of ballad mode and modern sensibility in those narratives which rely on a sense of the supernatural. Narratives which are not otherwise remarkable suddenly spring to life for a moment when the supernatural touches human life with a mysterious finger. The poetic conception contained in stanza VI of 'The Bird-catcher's Boy'—a poem constantly threatened by inept diction and sentimentality—

> Through the long passage, where
> Hang the caged choirs:
> Harp-like his fingers there
> Sweep on the wires

—lifts the poem momentarily onto another plane when its repetition-with-a-difference coincides with the boy's death at sea. The child's supernatural knowledge that 'My false father/Has murdered my true' turns the strangely-worded melodrama of 'The Flirt's Tragedy' into opera for a moment, and the archetypal demon lover of 'Burning the Holly' adds a shiver to a tale of seduction. The Unquiet Grave theme, when the dead begin to speak, lurks behind several poems—'Her Immortality', 'The Harvest Supper', "Ah, are you Digging on my Grave?", and 'The Dead and the Living One', for example. But Hardy appeals to his own century in the tension that exists between the familiar framework and the subject of the dead person's reproaches to the living. When primitive familiarity with the Otherworld has given way to belief in everlasting death,

> 'Oh who sits weeping on my grave
> And will not let me sleep?'

is replaced by the ghosts pleading, not for repose, but remembrance:

> 'A Shade but in its mindful ones
> Has immortality.'

Hardy told William Archer that he would give ten years of his life to see an authenticated ghost. His failure to do so is reflected in the insubstantiality of his revenants. Though Hardy's peasants show as little surprise as their primitive forebears at encountering a ghost, his revenants do not normally bring all the attributes of the physical corpse from the grave as ballad ghosts do. "My old love rises from the worms" in 'The Harvest Supper' has some echo of the realistic physical details of grave-life found in 'The Unquiet Grave', 'The Wife of Usher's Well', and 'Sweet William's Ghost': the tardy lover of 'The Second Night' does not recognize that the girls he meets is a ghost, though a sense of strangeness inheres in her mysterious relationship to the 'mad star' that 'crossed the sky to the sea':

> The sparks of the star in her pupils gleamed,
> She was vague as a vapour now . . .

But these are exceptions to Hardy's general rule. His revenants are more often incorporeal, dreams, or hallucinations. The 'Cruel Mother' of folk tradition does not recognize the 'twa pretty babes playing at the ba'' as ghosts of her murdered children: the girl who procures an abortion in Hardy's 'Reluctant Confession' sees 'in hell-dark dreams' . . . 'a newborn child in the clothes I set to make'. Guilt takes a subjective form in 'A Sound in the Night', 'The Catching Ballet of the Wedding Clothes', and 'The Sacrilege'. Modern dream psychology backs up the folk-motif of a physical feature inherited not from the natural parents but from a projection of desire, which Hardy used both in 'San Sebastian' and the short story 'An Imaginative Woman', and Ibsen in 'The Lady from the Sea'. The supernatural manifestations are left unexplained, but the state of mind of the narrators places them as hallucinations correlative to guilt or suspicion, as in 'At Shag's Heath' and 'A Trampwoman's Tragedy'. The motifs are traditional; the temper which ascribes them to natural rather than supernatural causes is modern.

The neutral or plural narrator is another favourite Hardeian device for disclaiming responsibility for the truth of a ghost story. The Mellstock quire, and personages from it, take responsibility for 'The Paphian Ball' and 'The Choirmaster's Burial', distanced from the reader by time and memory:

> Such the tenor man told
> When he had grown old.

In 'The Lost Pyx', 'some say the spot is banned', but 'the ancient Vale-folk tell' a different story. Hardy does not vouch for either.

But though the manifestation of ghosts may be insubstantial and doubtful, their environment is not. Hardy's strong sense of the physical and local life of Wessex gives validity to expressions of the metaphysical. The 'viewless quire' of Mellstock follows a well-trodden path,

> Dogged by the living; till it reached
> The bottom of Church Lane.

The traditional storm of romantic balladry sweeps over Wessex landmarks in 'The Lost Pyx', and the miracle of the found Pyx is vividly incarnated in the local nature of its animal guardians,

> Of Blackmore's hairy throng,
> Whereof were oxen, sheep, and does,
> And hares from the brakes among . . .

God's heavy humour and the Last Judgment vision of the dead sitting upright in their coffins in 'Channel Firing' are earthed by the particular detail:

> The mouse let fall the altar-crumb,
> The worms drew back into the mounds.

The melodrama and bathos that threatens the ghostly apparition of Monmouth in 'At Shag's Heath' is boldly turned aside by the sudden descent to a homely dialect word:

> "I love you still, would kiss you now,
> But blood would stain your nighty-rail!"

The memories of the 'local hearts and heads' who speak from the grave in 'Friends Beyond' are intimate and local. Mutability and the values of a particular Wessex community speak through William Dewey's old bass viol, Farmer Ledlow's favourite heifer, and the concern implied by farmer, squire, squire's lady, and peasants for the proper upkeep of land and property. The supernatural event, fused with the sharply accurate local detail, expresses that sense of local continuity and community in which narrative and dramatic art have their roots.

The supernatural mode of balladry, when it controls the telling of the tale as tautly as it does in 'The Dead and the Living One', catches perfectly the essence of the human life, pausing beside a grave, trapped in a network of ironic convergences that impinge on it from the Overworld and the Underworld:

> The dead woman lay in her first night's grave,
> And twilight fell from the clouds' concave,
> And those she had asked to forgive forgave.

The cosmic irony that mocks the living woman's gratitude for her rival's death in the form of 'a martial phantom of gory dye' which provides the surprise twist in the Unquiet Grave theme, weights the supernatural ballad mode with the emotion of nineteen disillusive centuries. The result of the fusion is an intense impersonality that could only be achieved through a deep personal response to the human predicament.

> There was a cry by the white-flowered mound,
> There was a laugh from underground,
> There was a deeper gloom around.

The cry is the cry of all humanity caught in the situations of violence (the poem was written in 1915) that have inspired narrative and dramatic art from *The Iliad* to *The Royal Hunt of the Sun*. The laugh is with the dead, for the ironies that attend the passions of the living cannot touch them. The gloom that is deeper than the cloud's concave expresses the compassion of the poet who sees in the drama of events the enduring values and sorrows of Everyman, working out his destiny in the shadow of the darkness which forms the backdrop to authentic balladry ancient and modern.

VI

Poetry and Narrative: Minor Fiction

It is commonly accepted that Hardy wrote a number of great novels and some others with flashes of greatness. The number placed in each category varies with the reader. However, *Far from the Madding Crowd*, *The Return of the Native*, *The Mayor of Casterbridge*, *The Woodlanders*, *Tess of the d'Urbervilles*, and *Jude the Obscure* are frequently assessed as pillars of his achievement, with *Under the Greenwood Tree* and *The Trumpet Major* as notable minor supports. It is not easy to define precisely what is missing from the rest of his fiction. However, one may usefully adapt T. S. Eliot's distinction between poetic and prose drama to suggest that the lacking quality is a consistent poetic 'underpattern' which produces 'a kind of doubleness in the action, as if it took place on two planes at once.'

The poetic impulse is never absent from Hardy's fiction. But in the minor works it appears in isolated flashes and pulls against the narrative and dramatic impulses instead of creating a fruitful tension with them 'to intensify the expression of things . . . so that the heart and inner meaning is made vividly visible' (*Life*). The great novels are memorable not only for plot but for the poetic-dramatic scenes that carry the inner meaning of the plot. In *The Return of the Native*, the gambling scene by glow-worm light on Egdon Heath, besides being crucial to plot development, is also a unit in the organic conflict of light and darkness, chance and control.

Reading one of the successful novels inspires poetic emotion. It has become a cliché of criticism to say that Hardy's novels are 'poetic'. The word needs closer definition to establish the factors which give Hardy's novels this quality, and to distinguish the poetry of a Hardy novel from the poetry of *Wuthering Heights* or *The Waves*. As David Cecil points out in *Hardy the Novelist*, 'the English literary genius is, most characteristically, a poetic genius', which shows itself in other forms besides poetry. Cecil has made a study of the poetic aspects of Hardy's imagination. He defines the poetic imagination as 'of a type that more often chooses verse as its mode of expression'. Hardy was inspired by those aspects of experience which required the emotional and imaginative intensity of lyric, ballad and poetic drama. His vision of life was not primarily of man's relation to man, but of man's relation to the forces of ultimate reality. His characters live most fully not in the social encounters of Jane Austen's Bath or George Eliot's Middlemarch, but in the great emotional crises that express their heroic resistance to fate, the conflict of reason and instinct, or their harmonies and disharmonies with the natural world.

Hardy's revelations of meaning through surface action are made through the weapons of a poet. It has often been noticed how close to balladry is Hardy's vision of basic passions and strong highlights. Donald Davidson ('The Traditional Basis of Hardy's Fiction', *Southern Review*, 1940) measures his success in terms of his debt to balladry and folklore; his failures are 'attempts to be a fully modern and literary novelist'. This view does not account for the power of Hardy's most 'modern' novel, *Jude the Obscure*, where the ballad echoes are fainter than the modern climate of opinion. But in general it is true to say that plot, situation, character and setting of the major fiction have a unity of tone that owes much to ballad ancestry, while the better moments of the minor fiction elicit an emotional response that has been conditioned by folklore archetypes: the demonic element in Miss Aldclyffe, Aeneas Manston, and William Dare; the sinister prophetic dream of Cytherea Graye and Ethelberta's Kafkaesque view of Neigh's estate; the tower that reaches from the world of nature to the stellar universe; the Cliff without a Name that faces Knight with his littleness; and the series of ironic conjunctions and parallel motifs in *A Pair of Blue Eyes*, for example, that call up the incremental repetition of ballad stanzas.

Fundamental ballad types abound: patient Griseldas of both sexes, inconstant lovers, often with a streak of the supernatural demon lover; the dashing soldier and the sailor returned from the sea to claim his kin; forlorn milkmaids; girls driven by a wild impulse to reject the true and love the false; lords and ladies of high degree; and the lowly man who, like Gabriel Oak, rises by hard work and, like Henchard, falls again. The furmity hag, the mysterious reddleman who emanates from the heath, old John South, whose life is linked to a tree—these are folklore symbols of a reality beyond man. Perhaps Little Father Time owes as much to them as to Ibsen's anti-naturalistic dramatic symbols, which are equally rooted in folklore. The plots are as tightly-knit, in the major fiction, as 'Edward' or 'Chevy Chase', They develop, stanza-like, through encounters with human and fatal forces. Event dominates motive. Situations and characters balanced usually for tragic resolution, repeat the staple material of balladry. The triangle of man or woman poised between constant and inconstant lover is a frequent motif, varied as in *Far from the Madding Crowd* by another lover from the dramatis personae of balladry, the rich squire, or linked, as in *The Mayor of Casterbridge*, with another theme, of rise and fall.

The situations that produce tragedy are ballad situations: family tensions, the clash of irreconcilable passions, the inconvenient return and the long-kept secret, social barriers, unpredictable accidents. The dramatic highlights objectify the clash of fatal forces which dominate the ballad world. Eustacia's romantic meeting in boy's disguise with Clym, Mrs Yeobright's death by snakebite on the indifferent heath, the simultaneous drowning of two fleeing lovers in stormy darkness to weird incantations over a wax image, the fight between Henchard and Farfrae in the loft, the macabre scene by Fanny's coffin, Grace Melbury's capture in a mantrap, like Mollie Vaughan in the ballad of that name, the wife-sale that begins *The Mayor of Casterbridge*, the sleep-walking and final scenes of *Tess*—these and countless other episodes carry the resonances of myth and folklore. Ritual, omens, the workings of chance and coincidence which replace ballad expressions of supernatural agency, the grotesque distortions of reality which objectify the workings of the cosmic will; the moral comment which acts like ballad tags; the irony revealed by stylized pattern; the choral interludes, the importance of physical things, and the involvement of human action with the natural world, place Hardy's major fiction securely in the ballad world made inherently poetic by its stark delineation of man's tragic predicament.

However, the fact remains that Hardy's novels are novels and his ballads ballads. 'The Revisitation' and 'A Sunday Morning Tragedy' are genuine ballad poetry, stripped to the essence of character, situation, and scene. In Hardy's novels, ballad techniques and overtones combine with a full-length picture of human lives in developing relationships to men, environment, and fate to present a vision that speaks to the complex modern spirit. In this combination, Hardy resembles Emily Brontë. Both need the distorted reality of the sensational ballad incident—heroic, romantic, wild, irregular, grotesque, mysterious, sublime—pitched in a high emotional key, to point through superficial naturalism to the deeper reality of their vision. Both need more space than a ballad can give to show the effect of time and to accumulate the mass of observed fact, rooted in common experience, that suspends disbelief in their unprosaic metaphors of reality. That Hardy's canvas is fuller than Emily Brontë's is due to the difference in their vision. Because Emily Brontë's vision of the ultimate resolution of elemental disharmonies is mystical, she can keep closer to the balladist's familiarity with the supernatural. In Darwin's scientific universe, Hardy had to deny himself the aid of the supernatural in persuading his readers to accept strange events. Hence the meticulous evocation of Wessex in all its aspects, for which *Wuthering Heights* offers no comparison.

Nature, the visible world as pointer to the invisible, has long been a poetic symbol to English lyric writers. We know Hardy's Wessex in all its moods and seasons, in the intimate detail of heath, pasture, arable, woodland, and water; its vegetable, animal and human outgrowths; its occupations; and its past of earthworks, barrows, extinct species, flints, and geological strata—its record of the eternal processes of time. As Cecil points out, Hardy's vision of nature combines breadth and intimacy. The ever-widening perspective from the familiar natural detail of grass-bent or heath-bell to the unfamiliar stellar reaches makes of the local scene a poet's metaphor of the unknowable, without departing from the objective fact.

It is appropriate to Hardy's post-Darwinian vision that nature dominates the scene, as in *Wuthering Heights* it does not, though the changing face of the Yorkshire moor, like Hardy's Wessex, reflects the conflict of elemental forces which move the passions of men. Often a Hardy novel begins with a powerful evocation of the natural scene before a tiny human being appears to give it meaning. Emily Brontë's Yorkshire moor appears piecemeal throughout the novel, as actual scene and as psychic image. Lockwood, after the strange events at Wuthering Heights that blur the limits of normal human experience, sees 'dark night coming down prematurely, and sky and hills mingled in one bitter whirl of wind and suffocating snow.' In Chapter xi of *Far from the Madding Crowd*, the sheer physical weight of Hardy's description of the snowy scene makes Fanny Robin an image of human unimportance to the cosmos. The evocation includes not only the present objective scene,

140

but also the subjective mood called up by the rhythmic melancholy associations of past seasonal changes:

'the retreat of the snakes, the transformation of the ferns, the filling of the pools, a rising of fogs, the embrowning by frost, the collapse of the fungi, and an obliteration by snow.'

Exact physical details are massed and placed in relation to time and space to conjure up the mood of Fanny's isolation. We are given both the fact, and its significance to the imagination. It is a poet's way of working, familiar to readers of Hardy's verse. And always in his vision, the metaphysical perspective never loses sight of the physical fact in which it is rooted. The apocalyptic birds which universalize Tess's situation in a chaotic universe are also starving creatures who watch the girls disturbing the earth for signs of food. The rabbit in the trap whose long and useless sufferings adumbrate Jude's own becomes a correlative for the human condition through the grim physical sound of the trap dragged about in its writhings.

Any meaning in Hardy's vision must rise from his truth to the physical world. But its beauty and terror blend with the romantic poet's subjective presentation of nature as a symbol of the inner life, transforming and transformed by the angle of vision. Clym's despair at obstructive cross-purposes both rises from and is embodied by the uncompromising flatness of Egdon heath. Boldwood's unbalanced state of mind is not analysed in terms of complexes and obsessions, but sensuously felt in his view of the brittle frozen grass and birds' footprints, and the unnatural reversed light of the snow.

This is the poet's way. As Cecil points out, Hardy's greatest poetic asset is the power to make us see—and, coming not very far behind, to make us hear and feel the different qualities of sound and texture in the physical world. To cut out the appeal to the senses in Hardy's novels would rob the libretto of the music that makes it meaningful. His stories are a series of scenes, not photographic, but lyric, dramatic, sometimes distorted in Kafkaesque fashion to show the deeper reality underlying the scenic. The unstable effect of firelight, picking out 'shadowy eye-sockets, deep as those of a death's head', stresses the burden of mortality carried by the dancers round the bonfire in *The Return of the Native*. Words, gestures, movement, setting, are lit up with the tragic sense—which is the poet's sense—of the pain and glory of life.

However, Hardy is not blind to that other kind of poetry that lies in the trivial round, as his poems show. Truth to fact saves his presentation of the countryman's working relationship to nature—another poetic device as old as Virgil—from being sentimental Marty is blue with cold as she plants pines, and Tess finds reed-drawing and threshing a severe trial of strength. The rustic chorus has a realistic share of untrustworthy members; but their collective function is poetic through their concern with daily bread and the rituals that mark human and natural seasons. Commonplace life is heightened by their eternal actions and their ruminating Wessex speech, with its delight in word-play that suddenly charges the basic rhythms of living with a new perspective. There is a Shakespearian poetry of incongruity in their juxtaposition of comic and tragic—their discussion on folklore remedies for snake-bite while Mrs Yeobright lies dying; their 'tendency to talk on principle which is characteristic of the barley-corn' in the *Buck's Head* while Fanny's coffin with its explosive secret lies outside.

Hardy's poetic power lies in the detail of style that expresses subject. The evocative word, phrase, or figure of speech; the emotive verb that gives anthropomorphic force to nature; the comparisons from nature and art which illuminate both terms of the comparison; the grotesque or unusual angle or light that exposes a fundamental relationship to reality; the hint of myth below the surface—'He looked and smelt like Autumn's very brother' the simple statement that holds the weight of *lacrimae rerum* or the ecstasy of love—'Winterborne was gone, and the copses seemed to show the want of him', 'There was hardly a touch of earth in her love for Clare'; the rhythms of speech and narrative cadence which precisely express the emotion or movement of a scene: all these weapons amalgamate the disparate experiences of life into a new whole compounded of complexity and simplicity.

The poetic detail is rarely superfluous. In Chapter XXII of *Far from the Madding Crowd*, the sharply realized shape and colour of the 'fern-sprouts like bishops' croziers' and the 'odd cuckoo-pint,—like an apoplectic saint in a niche of malachite' equate the force of nature with the deity in the preceding sentence, 'God was palpably present in the country, and the devil had gone with the world to town,' and prepare for the natural conception of religion in the long description of the Shearing Barn, where 'the defence and salvation of the body by daily bread is still a study, a religion, and desire'. In *Tess*, where contrast between reality and image is central frequent references to religious works of art underline the theme. The returned Angel as 'Crivelli's dead *Christus*', the two girls in the swede field as 'some early Italian conception of the two Marys', Angel and 'Liza-Lu as Giotto's 'Two Apostles' at Tess's death, are sharply described, universalized, and contrasted in their living reality by the fixed images of art. The prospect of Wintoncester as 'an isometric drawing', to which Lionel Johnson objected because the architectural term spoilt the emotional tone of Tess's death, can also be justified by the theme. Stonehenge carried the crisis of emotion: the architect's abstract of the city distances the emotion to stress the inhuman blueprint of reality to which Tess is sacrificed.

Such attention to detail as part of the total conception looks forward to Virginia Woolf's poetic organization of the novel. However, one must distinguish the poetic method of Virginia Woolf or James Joyce from the poetic method of Hardy or Emily Brontë. In the modern writers, associative structure of themes largely replaces the narrative of a succession of events in time as the pattern of meaning. Hardy and Emily Brontë include the narrative line as part of a contrapuntal symphony of images and scenes that have the power of images. Cecil points out that 'Hardy's strain of poetry shows itself not just in atmosphere but in the actual turn of the action, not in the scenery but in the play'. The narrative provides action in time. The poetic underpattern, with its accumulation of echoes, parallels, and contrasts, shows the significance of that action.

The result of lack of space to develop the delicate counterpoint between narrative and poetic impulses can be seen in many of Hardy's tales.

'They give us, in varying forms and manners, his characteristic vision of life; what we miss in them is the subtle declaration of what that vision profoundly *means* to his inmost emotion.'

(Lascelles Abercrombie: *Thomas Hardy*)

Many tales suffer from an overbalance of one or the other. Sometimes it is an excess of poetic feeling. 'A Tryst at an Ancient Earthwork' builds up a powerful mood picture of Maiden Castle that recalls Egdon heath in *The Return of the Native*. But its 'obtrusive personality' overpowers the slight incident of the scholar's discovery, and probable theft, of a Roman statuette. On the other hand, the slow-paced evocation of night, storm and pastoral setting that begins 'The Three Strangers' contributes to its meaning. The ironic but unlikely conjunction of life and death embodied in the meeting of hangman and intended victim gains imaginative belief from the echoes of Christian ritual—the shepherd's cottage at the cross-roads, the christening, the three strangers, the three knocks, the victim's drink at the door, the ritual withdrawal in a 'remote circle' from the *cinder*-gray stranger, 'whom some of them seemed to take for the Prince of Darkness himself'—blended with the sharp details of the pastoral world that is at once part of the myth and a guarantee of authenticity in the world of sense experience; 'the tails of little birds trying to roost on some scraggy thorn were blown inside-out like umbrellas', and the earthy Wessex humour of the guests. The swift telling of the tale, with its skilful use of primary narrative effects of suspense, surprise, expectation, ritual repetition, false inference, and true conclusion, all converging on a single dramatic crisis, makes a satisfactory poetic image of life such as one finds in poems of situation like 'Life and Death at Sunrise', 'At the Railway Station, Upway', and the title poems of *Satires of Circumstance*.

The most obvious lack of balance comes in those tales where plot dominates. The power of events and the effects of time are among Hardy's major themes. An extended form, almost a skeleton novel, is used to develop the consequences of missed chances, possibilities of rechoice, the righting or consolidation of old wrongs, the maturing of ambition, revenge, compassion, or indifference, and the quirks of fate that complete a design in an unexpected manner. But the sensational happenings and coincidences that embody Hardy's sense of the cosmic Absurd become less credible in a crowded synopsis unprepared for by poetic atmosphere. The sudden deaths of Mrs Downes and Mrs Barnet, Helena Hall, Selina's Dragoon lover, Baptista's newly-wed husband, the village youth who married the Marchioness of Stonehenge, and the Duchess of Hamptonshire, are little more than improbable plot devices to set in motion the endeavour 'to rectify early deviations of the heart by harking back to the old point'.

Hardy's art is descriptive, not impressionistic in the Chekhov or Hemingway tradition. But when he gives credence to the irrational events from the shadow side which disrupt normal living, by a blend of strong shaping action, overtones of folklore, descriptive evocation of the world of sense, and a pervading poetic symbol, the tales have a consistent poetic force which carries their meaning beyond the limited human action. The blasting but involuntary jealousy of Rhoda Brook (the rejected Bonnie Annie figure of 'The Withered Arm') based on a distorted image of her supplanter, and objectified in the nightmare incubus and her beautiful rival's growing deformity, is surrounded by the rhythms of a simple agricultural community, where belief in sympathetic magic is not abnormal. Sleepy Stickleford, the Great Exhibition, and the sights and sounds of Farmer Tucker's dairy accompany the strange manifestations of the death-yearning for the absolute state which assail the robust Margery Tucker of 'The Romantic Adventures of a Milkmaid' as well as the sensitive Car'line Aspent in 'The Fiddler of the Reels', in the traditional form of a demon lover. Mop Ollamoor's irresistible 'chromatic subtleties', which force Car'line, Hardy's Fair Janet, to dance a sexual dance against her will, his sudden appearances and disappearances, and mirror reflection, are demonic properties. Baron von Xanten, first revealed significantly contemplating suicide in a wooden structure which shelters its occupant from the seasonal weathers of an imperfect world, who shows Margery all the kingdoms of the world, is a more complex demonic symbol than the fiddler. His efforts to return Margery to her normal sphere, with truelove Jim's help, give him the ambivalence of a modern shadow symbol like Michael Tippett's King Fisher; the provocative force which initiates a needed transformation process. Margery's translation from milkmaid to fairy princess fit to go to a ball is accomplished by evocative description that keeps us in the natural world among the birds and hares of Chillington wood, while at the same time suggesting archetypal symbols of translation to a dangerously abnormal sphere of inflated possession. Margery's imprisonment in her airy creation inside the tree where she had found it—'huge, hollow, distorted, and headless, with a rift in its side' until the Baron 'tore away pieces of the wooden shell which enshrouded Margery and all her loveliness', sounds the note of birth into death that is repeated in her inverted vision of the ballroom 'floored with black ice; the figures of the dancers appearing upon it upside down'.

The central symbol in 'Barbara of the House of Grebe', the statue of Edmund Willowes, evoking echoes of Pygmalion and Beauty and the Beast, controls a network of images taken from art and the theatre. This image cluster defines, against various 'masks' of appearance, the heroic worth of Edmund's character ('beauty . . . was the least of his recommendations') and Barbara's maladjustment to the changing reality of the world of time that would ultimately have turned her handsome husband into the 'thing of the charnel-house' hidden by the face mask. The burning of the theatre, from which Edmund emerges physically disfigured but morally a hero, offers Barbara a chance to destroy *her* world of masquerade. Her failure to do so leads to her puppet submission to the diabolic stage-management of Uplandtowers, whose resolve to win her at all costs started the story with a hint of the Immanent Will controlling his actions. The stage-shrine which he sets up in her bedroom, with 'a wax-candle burning on each side of it to throw the [statue's] cropped and distorted features into relief', faces her with a foreshortened image of reality which is really appearance. The end of the tale, telling of Barbara's strange revenge in depriving Uplandtowers of a male image of the only kind of nobility he believes in, and the final discovery of the broken statue, which was considered to be either 'a mutilated Roman satyr; or, if not, an allegorical figure of Death', gains resonance from the powerful poetic underpattern of fixed image and fluid reality that controls its metaphysic.

The inner meaning of 'On the Western Circuit' is pointed immediately by the powerful image of the 'pleasure-machine' which is going to whirl Charles Raye, Anna and her mistress into a merry-go-round of cross-purposes and passions as arbitrary as the decision of the 'inexorable stoker, grimly lurking behind the glittering rococo-work' (brother to the engineer in *Tess*) that 'this set of riders had had their pennyworth'.

'A smoky glare, of the complexion of brass-filings, ascended from the fiery tongues of innumerable naphtha lamps affixed to booths, stalls and other temporary erections which crowded the spacious market square. In front of this irradiation scores of human figures, more or less in profile, were darting athwart and across, up, down, and around, like gnats against a sunset.'

The details of light, shape, and texture point to the infernal (i.e. meaningless) nature of the mechanical process, and the diminution of human importance, counterpointing Anna's illusion of being a fixed point in an 'undulating, dazzling, lurid universe' moving and 'countermoving in the revolving mirrors.'

There are poetic elements, of course, even in the less successful tales, which stand out in the memory. The active power of wha is absent is conveyed through symbols—Joseph Halcomb's walking stick flowering in the sedge after his drowning, the re-donned wedding dress and mummied cake of 'Enter a Dragoon', the photograph of the poet Ella had never seen, immortalized, like the Stranger in Ibsen's *Lady from the Sea*, in the eyes of the baby son whose birth fulfilled her death-wish. The power of actions which do not remain passive in the past, but start up to drive the process to its appointed end, is embodied in people and things: the gown intended for Sally Hall's wedding but worn by her lover's old flame Helena, so that 'he seemed to feel that fate had impishly changed his *vis-à-vis* in the lover's jig he was about to foot'; the long-lost Bellston's clothes, delivered to his wife on the eve of her marriage to her old lover, which stops the marriage even when Bellston has been found dead; the corpse of Baptista's first husband lying in the next room on her honeymoon with her second; the sea-sickness that reveals the relationship of Millborne and his daughter by investing their features with 'the spectral presence of entombed and forgotten ancestors'; the snobbish son of 'The Son's Veto' set against the 'green bastions of cabbages' journeying to Covent Garden, which remind his uprooted mother of the lost securities of her country home. Ghosts do not appear in Hardy's fiction, but the power of a past image assumes control of the action. 'The insistent shadow of that unconscious one', the dead hero Maumbry, prevents his widow's second marriage. Mrs Petrick's fantasy about her son's noble birth influences his real father's treatment of the boy; and Milly's refusal to relinquish the role of widow with child foisted on to her to save the reputation of the Marchioness of Stonehenge contributes to the noble lady's death.

Most of the tales recall balladry. Some, such as 'The Lady Penelope' and 'What the Shepherd Saw', would have gained intensity and credibility in the stripped ballad form suggested by their stanzaic shape and incremental repetition. The theme of missed and second chances is emphasized by the ballad device of repetition, and resolved tragically or ironically, in 'The Son's Veto', 'For Conscience' Sake', 'Fellow-Townsmen', 'Interlopers at the Knap', 'The Marchioness of Stonehenge', 'The Duchess of Hamptonshire', 'The Lady Icenway', 'The Waiting Supper', 'Alicia's Diary', and 'Enter a Dragoon'. The balladist's irony blends with the modern poet's sense of the ambiguity of things to question the rightness of certain choices: Millborne's belated impulse to marry the lady he wronged twenty years ago; the rising solicitor's marriage to the 'unlettered peasant' who was to bear his child; the curate's refusal to elope with the Duchess of Hampton-shire, whom he later unwittingly buried at sea; Alicia's unselfish encouragement of her lover's marriage to her sister; the conversion of the dashing Sergeant Maumbry to a dull parson; Barnet's decision to save, and the brothers Halcombe's decision not to save, the life of their obstructive relation; and the ballad ethic of *crime passionel* which kills innocent people in 'What the Shepherd Saw' and 'Master John Horseleigh, Knight'. But there is also the poet's feeling for simple human values and loyalties, and humour, and the ability to snatch limited victories from boredom and despair, in the lively smuggling story 'The Distracted Preacher'; in Bap-tista Trewthen's growing love for her four dull stepdaughters; the happiness of Betty Countess of Wessex with the husband, 'old enough to be compassionate', who had passed the challenge—of kissing her with the smallpox—failed by her lover; and the deter-mination of Sally Hall to retain her unmarried independence.

The problem of striking the right balance between poetry and narrative makes the tales unequal in quality. However, there are two collections, *A Group of Noble Dames* and *A Few Crusted Characters*, in which the total effect is greater than the sum of its parts. Hardy has borrowed the method of Chaucer's *Canterbury Tales* to create a group mood. It is compounded of the social occasion, the inter-linked stories of local hearts and heads, the spirit of place, and the characteristics of the orally-descended tale which is Hardy's medium rather than the written short story—its personal flourishes and digressions, changes of pace and rhythm, and consciousness of a shared tradition between narrator and audience. The occasion of *A Group of Noble Dames* is a weather-bound meeting of the Wessex Field and Antiquarian Club. The Museum fossils, and the tales told by the members, of women (naturally, in a male gathering) whose sexual desires, image of the impersonal cosmic will, cannot be bounded by facile formulae or paper pedigrees, measure with compassionate irony the blindness of these comfortable types who 'still praise the Lord with one voice for His best of all possible worlds.' The return of a native by carrier's van provides the occasion of *A Few Crusted Characters*. The reminiscences of his fellow-passengers about the village characters he knew in his youth—humorous sketches, anecdotal, fabliau-like, ballad-like tales with folklore never very far behind and fundamental human values stressed with warmth and sanity, rich in Wessex idiom and rhythm—build up a mood of nostalgia for the vigorous life that has passed, which finds its climax in the traveller's realization that the roots he was searching for are in the churchyard.

The unresolved tension between poetic and narrative impulses robs the minor novels, except in flashes, of universal meaning. *Two on a Tower* and *The Well-Beloved*, as Cecil points out, lean towards the poetic impulse. After the first thrill in *Two on a Tower* at the central contrast between the inhuman stellar universe and human passions, which informs the lyrics 'In Vision I Roamed' and 'At a Lunar Eclipse', the uninhabited sky proves to be an unresponsive partner in the conflict between man and the nature of things. In *The Return of the Native* or *The Woodlanders*, the conflict grows from the nature of Egdon or the Hintocks. The poor man and the lady theme, and the unlikely intrigue-plot that fills up the rest of the novel with a caricatured bishop, a brother who is invariably where he is least wanted, and a shoal of coincidences and chances missed by a minute, could have developed without the stars.

The beginning promises well, with the sunlit tower, isolated like the two chief characters, rising unimpeded into the sky from a sunless, sobbing forest rooted in palaeolithic dead men and rocking 'in seconds, like inverted pendulums', to evoke the deeper reality of absolute aspiration rooted in human pain, darkness, and time. The romantic tragi-comedy of Swithin's descent from his 'primitive Eden of unconsciousness' on the tower to the lower world of passions, Viviette's mature control over natural instincts to release her young lover, and their defeat by time, has some relevance to the scene. The Wessex chorus has a fine comic choir practice, but is forgotten for long periods. Swithin's sudden appearance in Sir Blount's clothes foreshortens in an anti-realistic image the legal resurrection of the husband and Swithin's usurpation of his place. But these scattered poetic evocations do not coalesce into an underpattern of meaning that pervades the whole novel, though the tower as an imaginative symbol acts as focus to concentrate the plot and draw all the characters into its magnetic field, and gives ballast to the mind adrift on change.

In *The Well-Beloved*, the poetry of place proves too rocky to carry the fantasy of the sculptor's pursuit of his ideal love through three generations of one family. The theme of the immortal face in perishable flesh has been treated adequately in Hardy's poetry; notably 'Heredity' and 'The Pedigree'. The contrast between fixed image and living individuality found lyrical expression in several poems, and a fable to incarnate it in fiction in 'Barbara of the House of Grebe' and *Tess*. The powerful evocation in time and space of 'the peninsula carved by Time out of a single stone'; of unity made out of diversity, as in Deadman's Bay, 'a presence—an imaginary shape or essence from the human multitude lying below', demands the strength of Tess's personality and tragedy to oppose it. The scene is stronger than the repetitive, conventional narrative and the characters. A prophetic example of the film 'fade-in' which dissolves the human faces at a fashionable dinner into the rocky features of the Isle is symbolic of Hardy's failure, apart from Pierston's realistic choice of the aging Marcia, to bring the narrative into unity with the overpowering factual poetry of the scene.

A Pair of Blue Eyes is, as Coventry Patmore told Hardy, 'not a conception for prose', but he succeeds intermittently in uniting poetic and narrative strains to suggest underlying causes. Its lyrical Cornish setting, romantic heroine, anti-realistic symbols and stylized form (an overplus of ironic coincidences, sensational and macabre episodes, repeated situations with cast changes, and characters whose force depends on situation rather than depth of personality) ask for ballad treatment. Mrs Jethway's unmotivated appearances would be less improbable in ballad form; in prose, she is a less credible symbol of the fatal past than the furmity hag of *The Mayor of Casterbridge*, whose appearance in a court of law sometime was quite probable. The effort to fill out a poetic conception of young love with event leads to disunited impulses in the narrative itself. The tone varies from romantic comedy and social comedy to tragi-comedy, melodrama and ironic tragedy. The comic parson and Stephen's robust Wessex parents hardly seem to inhabit the world of the last scenes and the Cliff without a Name, which as a presence of cosmic indifference is worthy to stand beside Egdon Heath. However, juxtaposition of comic and tragic can sometimes have a complex poetic effect that recalls Shakespeare or Ibsen. Hardy scratches the surface of a tragedy to find a comedy in Knight's rescue from the cliff by Elfride's underwear, the Hamlet-like gravediggers and Knight's pompous lecture on mortality in the vault while Elfride and Stephen suffer agonies of emotion, the absurd self-esteem of the two lovers quarrelling over their precedence in the dead Elfride's affections, and Knight's catechism of Elfride on Jethway's tomb:

' "Did you say you were sitting on that tomb?" he asked moodily.
"Yes; and it was true."
"Then how, in the name of Heaven, can a man sit upon his own tomb?"
"That was another man. Forgive me, Harry, won't you?"
"What, a lover in the tomb and a lover on it?" '

The Cornish scene is not linked to Elfride's character as it is to Emma's in *Poems of 1912–13*, where it gives universal dimension to the personal tragedy. However, the scene does yield elements of a poetic underpattern in one prominent image: the recurring skeletons, real and metaphorical, which warn of the dangers of indecision. The leaf-skeletons in the pool where Elfride, like its primitive insect life, lets chance choose her course, are recalled in the 'dancing leaf-shadows', awakened gnats and earthworms, and 'the horizontal bars of woodwork, which crossed their forms like the ribs of a skeleton' when Stephen sees Elfride with Knight in the summer-house; in the Luxellian vault and Jethway's tomb; in the final irony when Elfride's two lovers unknowingly travel on the same train as her coffin to ask her hand; and, most impressively of all, in the anatomical structure of the Cliff without a Name and the fossil trilobite which shows Knight, hanging over the cliff, not only their common insignificance to space and time, but also the difference that can be made to their fate by human intelligence and forethought and, on this occasion, Elfride's unaccustomed decision and resourcefulness. Dr C. J. P. Beatty, in his London Ph.D. thesis *The Part played by Architecture in the Life and Works of Thomas Hardy*, points out that the evocation of chaos circumscribed by shape in Hardy's description of cliff and sea adumbrates the theme of man's efforts at construction; and the problem of reconciling nature's fixed forms with individual ephemera is mirrored in the rigid Knight's relationship to the mercurial Elfride. But these traces of poetic pattern demonstrate the lack of a shaping action or characters of tragic stature, which in *Tess of the d'Urbervilles* turns the intolerance of Angel and the suffering of Tess into great tragic myth.

In *The Hand of Ethelberta*, where the impulses to poetry, romance, comedy of manners, farce, and social satire cannot reconcile their differences, the narrative of Ethelberta's manoeuvres to climb into high society cannot compete with Hardy's powerful poetic evocation of the corruption at its heart which her conscious aim will not admit. On Neigh's estate, on the site 'where, by every law of manorial topography, the mansion would be situate', Ethelberta sees

'numerous horses in the last stage of decrepitude, the animals being such mere skeletons that at first Ethelberta hardly recognized them to be horses at all; they seemed rather to be specimens of some attenuated heraldic animal, scarcely thick enough through the body to throw a shadow . . .'

The cumbrous formality of the language describing her walk down the drive, the heraldic associations of the de-natured and two-dimensional creatures, flesh and blood reduced by Neigh's ambition to an ironic travesty of pedigree, the 'chronological sequel' of rotting horseflesh hung on trees which have been lopped to a distorted parody of life for the purpose, mock Ethelberta's expectations with the life-denying qualities of the upper classes. The context of the lopped trees makes the emotional tone very different from that created in the Talbothays idyll (*Tess*, xxvii):

'At the door the wood-hooped pails, sodden and bleached by infinite scrubbings, hung like hats on a stand upon the forked and peeled limb of an oak fixed there for that purpose; all of them ready and dry for the evening milking.'

As a warning of evil from what Jung and Eliot would recognize as Ethelberta's 'Guardians', this expressionistic scene indicates a three-dimensional humanity in her and sets overtones vibrating which disrupt the unemotional comedy of situation in which she moves.

A Laodicean and *Desperate Remedies* suffer in different ways from too much plot. The scenes that begin *A Laodicean*—Somerset copying transitional architecture against a sunset that irradiates ephemeral insects, Paula's rejection of total immersion, and the conjunction of ancient castle with modern telegraph—introduce the poetic contrast of new and old. But the limited interest of Paula's Laodicean tactics is padded out with inorganic incidents. Somerset's fall down the turret staircase, unlike Knight's down the Cliff without a Name, leads nowhere in plot or poetic vision. The sudden return of Uncle Abner, and his equally unexpected revolutionary past, revealed by Dare in a melodramatic scene where they face each other across the vestry table with revolvers and mutual blackmail, are motivated only by the need to provide opposition to

Somerset's romance. There are poetic symptoms, however, of another story under the one Hardy actually wrote, which lights up at rare moments the daemonic energies that disturb the surface of modern life. The 'appearance, as from the tomb, of this wintry man' (Abner) is marked by his connection with non-human elements: his face has been 'the plaything of strange fires or pestilences'. De Stancy's Protean gift of assuming the features of his ancestral portraits aligns him with the impersonal past. Both have a negative quality that links them to the grotesque figure from which the book derives most of its energy, though the link remains seminal. The demonic Dare is not an impossible figure: Rimbaud could provide a contemporary parallel. He is, however, closer to folklore and the nihilistic medievalism of Thomas Mann's devil in *Dr Faustus*. His presentation as 'a being of no age, no nationality and no behaviour' . . . 'a complete negative'; a photographer who distorts Paula's romantic image of her lover; a student and taker of chances; a diabolic showman of the human absurdity that allows him to manipulate people and events (a view that modifies Cecil's objection to 'a romance . . . inspired by the sight of physical jerks in pink flannel'); makes him a symbol of impersonal destructive cosmic chaos, which is turned aside by the human determination of Paula in the last scenes and the unselfishness of Charlotte.

Desperate Remedies, unlike *A Laodicean*, does not flag in the telling. Its complicated plot would provide material for several different novels—a romantic comedy, a detective novel, a sensation novel, an expressionistic novel, a Wessex pastoral, a psychological study of a frustrated woman, even, as D. H. Lawrence observed, a morality play. These different impulses do not, as in the major novels, blend into a unity of poetic effect. But they show flashes of poetic energy which brand this first novel with Hardy's mark. The most impressive character, Miss Aldclyffe, lives through suggestive details that present her as a tragic, tormented figure motivated by daemonic sources that contradict her will and the virago-type of Mrs Henry Wood which she outwardly resembles. The relationship between her and Manston reaches beyond the mother-and-son actuality through the elemental imagery that surrounds them both. Cytherea's first sight of Miss Aldclyffe, in a crimson room lit by a late sun, of a woman 'like a tall black figure standing in the midst of fire', is duplicated in her first encounter with Manston, an unnaturally tall silhouette against a gathering thunderstorm, who proves to have the devil's power of staring open-eyed at lightning and, like the demonic Fiddler of the Reels, of sexually fascinating an impressionable girl by his music. The death-wish implicit in contact with daemonic sources is suggested by the recurring sound of the waterfall that accompanies the death of Miss Aldclyffe's father, Cytherea's meeting with Manston, and the typically Hardeian conjunction of watchers depending on the chain that starts with Manston burying his wife's corpse; and in Cytherea's masochistic nightmare on her wedding eve, expressive of guilt in the conflict between instinct and reason, that she was being whipped by a masked Manston 'with dry bones suspended on strings, which rattled at every blow like those of a malefactor on a gibbet'. Nature is used variously, but always poetically; as objective fact, to mirror and affect human emotions, to measure human conduct and reflect the cosmos. The happy and ephemeral creatures in the rain-butt inspire Manston to follow nature; the slow, minutely described fire of couch-grass, which grew out of hand only because of human casualness, shows the consequences of doing so. The 'sensuous natures of the vegetable world' encourage Manston's animal passions; the 'helpless flatness of the landscape' takes away Cytherea's impulse to resist. The sinister mandrakes and weeds flourish in a garden where there is no Gardener. The tragic elements of the underpattern pull against the comic trend of the sensation novel whose tidy development implies the cosmic order missing from Hardy's universe.

The Trumpet Major and *Under the Greenwood Tree* are the best of the minor novels because their poetic elements are not inconsistent with the other impulses. Both narrative and poetry are at ease in the rustic community Hardy knew well. His lesser novels suffer from his unease with 'high life', and lack of a rustic chorus, or at best one which appears infrequently. These two novels miss the Hardeian tragic intensity, but give more scope to the rich humour of caricature, character, situation and Wessex idiom which contribute to a poetic meditation on the importance of the small eternal things of life that go on in time of the breaking of nations and ancient traditions. The vacillations of Anne Garland and Fancy Day, the domestic comedy and country humour, are none the worse for an honourable descent from balladry and folklore, the traditional guardians of basic values. The grotesque scenes and sensational events of the major novels would destroy the quiet unity of tone that encloses one novel with the cycle of the seasons and the other with the coming and going of the dragoons. The coincidences, such as John's recognition of Matilda and Maybold's meeting with Dick just after he has written to accept a living in Yorkshire for himself and Dick's fiancée, do not strain credulity.

In *The Trumpet Major* the war itself is kept in the background. The foreground is occupied by the physical and emotional realities of daily life which oppose their values to its impersonal power. Food and drink and gay gatherings are lovingly detailed. The mill becomes a poetic symbol of the eternal struggle for daily bread that touches everyone: Mrs Garland does not mind the noise or the flour on her furniture, 'being as it was, not nasty dirt, but the blessed staff of life'. The 'genial and historical value' of its human associations is inferred by the description of the spring-cleaning process which removes 'the tawny smudges of bygone shoulders in the passage' and other visible marks and ancient smells of long human occupation (one can compare the description of Geoffrey Day's cottage, in which every object has a human association or interest); and the paving stones worn by the ebb and flow of feet since Tudor times.

Descriptive detail accumulates to a total vision that reaches beyond the logical meaning of the words, and beyond the close-up of ordinary life in a particular period. The processes of nature frame wars and human passions. The sun rises, as usual, on the unusual scene of the King's review, giving the resplendent trumpet major a lilac shadow (the colour of death) and the transitory significance of 'a very god of war'. Hardy reminds us that the connection of the characters with nature is deeper than their involvement in war. Anne, whose vacillations are an outgrowth of impersonal cosmic movement, inspires natural imagery: her yellow boots 'looked like a pair of yellow-hammers flitting under her dress'. The miller's weather-vane, metamorphosed from soldier to sailor, and the intensely poetic conception of the Aeolian harp, whose 'strange mixed music of water, wind, and strings' is an objective correlative of Anne's emotional relationship to John, become symbolic of human emotion played on by irrational elemental forces which bring love to the less worthy and death to the better man.

The total effect of the novel depends on the mood of muted elegy that has been built up through details of ordinary living, with all their emotional association, and an interplay between recollection and the present moment that recalls the structure of many poems. At moments when the viewpoint moves back to reveal

155

the action, the war itself, and the future death of the actors in battles that are now the facts of history, as episodes in a long perspective of time, it reveals that the objective play is controlled by the subjective mood and personal voice of the poet; which selects 'through the mists of the seventy or eighty years that inter-vene between then and now' the details that conjure up the spirit and colour of the time. The candles, brilliant uniforms, and heads outlined against a dark background of his evocation are a recurring image which returns and is distanced, in the final paragraph, to hold in solution noble but transient human qualities and the long but meaningless stretch of time that dims the light and silences the assertive trumpet in the darkness.

All the elements of *Under the Greenwood Tree* evoke a poetic mood compounded of nostalgia for old rural ways and hope for the resil-ience of life in the new order. Fancy Day, educated above her station, is the structural pivot, both in her vacillation between the rustic virtues of Dick Dewy and the refinements of the innovating parson, and in her ability to play the organ which displaces the Mellstock quire. The scenes that show the rustics in communal action, working, feasting, dancing, celebrating the seasons of the natural and Christian calendar, measuring all the small repetitive events that give their lives significance in the rich Wessex speech and gesture that shows respect for self and others, build up a solid image of the sustaining ritual of a community that gives the dis-persal of an obscure band of musicians more than local significance. The quiet pathos of their appearance in church on the day of Fancy's installation, scattered among the congregation, 'awkward, out of place, abashed, and inconvenienced by their hands', points to the loss of communal involvement in religion that deepens in the later novels to a tragic alienation from the stabilities of religious and natural harmony.

But the sustaining power of ritual close to nature has not yet left Mellstock. The ritual processions, feasts and dances which frame the story between Christmas and Fancy's summer wedding realize the controlling image of permanence in transience. Out of the dark wood whose individual voices evoke a whole range of emotions, Dick and the quire evolve, first of all as merely another quality of sound, and then as two-dimensional black profiles against the sky, 'which suggested some processional design on Greek or Etruscan pottery'. It recurs in Grandfather William's 'Titanic shadow at least thirty feet in length', which stretches to infinity as the natural world knows it, 'his head finally terminating upon the trunk of a grand old oak-tree': and in the ancient greenwood tree outside Keeper Day's cottage, that for generations has nurtured the great continuous movement of mating, birth, and supersession.

Nature pervades the novel to contribute, in Hardy's distinctive manner, to a poetic underpattern of resonances. The overflow of human emotions into external phenomena gives the story deeper significance. Stable tree trunks 'writhed like miserable men' in the rain to mirror the feelings of Dick and Fancy at her father's opposition, and the compelling power of the witch's 'charm' that removes it. The fertile promise of their wedding day is mirrored in the noisy activity of birds and bees and the fullness of blossom. There are times, too, when man's juxtaposition with nature defines cosmic absurdity and disharmony. The honey-taking, with its unimpassioned working rhythm, shows up the absurd rivalry of Dick and Shiner to fetch hartshorn for Fancy's sting. The desolate stillness that marks Dick's unsuccessful attempt to ask Geoffrey Day for Fancy's hand is intensified and disturbed by

some small bird that was being killed by an owl in the adjoining wood, whose cry passed into the silence without mingling with it.'

But this note is rare in the poetic texture of this early novel that celebrates the continuance of life through all its changes.

The poetic strain in Hardy is too complex to yield to labels. What is clear is that the novelist could not exist without the poet. It is the poet's eye for the ultimates of the human situation, for the metaphysic in the physical fact, for the truth in distortion, and for the underpattern of symphonic connections running parallel with surface cause and effect, which gives Hardy's major novels their tragic greatness.

VII

Far from the Madding Crowd:
A Pastoral Novel

Far from the Madding Crowd is the first of Hardy's novels to rise to tragic stature through interplay between surface narrative and poetic underpattern. The calm of *Under the Greenwood Tree* and *The Trumpet Major* is scarcely rippled by Fancy's deviation from Dick, Mr Maybold's rejection, Anne's vacillation, rumours of invasion, or John Loveday's muted death far away in time and space on the battlefields of Spain. But Troy's sexual charm, Bathsheba's caprice, and Boldwood's madness—the fatal consequence of both—provide not only incidents in the plot but also intimations of an archetypal pattern of behaviour tragically asserting itself against conscious human purpose.

The means by which Hardy probes under the surface of events are poetic. The plot itself, a dramatic metaphor that touches the mystery of things with its scenes of heightened passion, lyrical feeling and celebration of seasonal rites that link man to nature reveals the stylized shape and basic characteristics of balladry.

'There are the neat, rounded, and intertwining groups of events, the simple and decisive balancing of characters . . . There is the narrative method whereby encounter (whether of person with person, or person with Fate) is the life of the tale.'

(Douglas Brown: *Thomas Hardy*

Fanny Robin is the betrayed maiden, Oak the faithful lover tested by his lady, Troy the inconstant soldier whose conquest by 'winning tongue' is ironically foretold in the ballad of Allan Water that Bathsheba sings at the shearing supper. Qualities of character are taken for granted. Much is revealed through dialogue, tone, movement and gesture. The shepherd's rise from rags to riches to marry his lady of high degree, and Boldwood's crime of passion and swift self-punishment are in true ballad tradition. The story has the simplicity of a ballad plot that pushes the characters into tragic relationships which converge on a climax of love, passion and death.

The action in the eleven serial instalments (Chapters I–V, VI–VIII, IX–XIV, XV–XIX, XX–XXIV, XXV–XXIX, XXX–XXXIII, XXXIV–XXXVIII, XXXIX–XLII, XLIII–XLVII, XLVIII–LVII) advances the story by definite stages like the stanzas of a ballad. Each section strongly concludes a certain stage in the fortunes of the characters and hints at future developments which may change the emotional current. In the first instalment, for example, Gabriel's rejection by Bathsheba and loss of his sheep require a response in the following instalment. The central part (Chapters XXV–XXIX) destroys Boldwood's rising hopes when Bathsheba capitulates to Troy, and ends with Gabriel's attempt to warn her against him. The penultimate instalment prepares for Troy's return, and the last chapters move swiftly to the final tragic consequence of Troy's infidelity to Fanny and Bathsheba's infatuation.

The poetic qualities of the novel could not be felt without the clearly-defined plot. It provides the melody to Hardy's poetic counterpoint in the texture, and focuses on the central chapters—Bathsheba's fatal attraction to Troy—to suggest that poetic 'doubleness in the action' which

'should remove the surface of things, expose the underneath, or the inside, of the natural surface appearance. It may allow the characters to behave inconsistently, but only with respect to a deeper consistency. It may use any device to show their real feelings and volitions, instead of just what, in actual life, they would normally profess or be conscious of; it must reveal, underneath the vacillating or infirm character, the indomitable unconscious will; and underneath the resolute purpose of the planning animal, the victim of circumstance and the doomed or sanctified being.'

(T. S. Eliot: Introduction to S. L. Bethell, *Shakespeare and the Popular Dramatic Tradition*)

The 'deeper consistency' of a poetic reading troubles readers who are looking for the novel Hardy did not write. Its most obvious manifestation, perhaps, is in the Hardeian stress on chance and coincidence. A naturalistic appraisal of the novel might consider Gabriel Oak exceptionally unlucky to lose his sheep before they were insured, and exceptionally lucky to get a lift to Weatherbury in Bathsheba's waggon, to be at hand when fire breaks out on her farm, and to be recalled so soon after his dismissal to cure blasted

159

sheep. It is unfortunate that Boldwood is the one man who would take a valentine seriously, or that Troy should invade Weatherbury twice as 'the impersonator of Heaven's persistent irony towards him'. The *deus ex machina* which rescues Troy from drowning or the favourable conjunction of events that enables him to snatch Penny-ways' note from Bathsheba's hand may come too pat on their cue. The mockery of the weather and the gurgoyle, the fog coinciding with the journey of the most fearful of the rustics, Bathsheba's decision to be guided by the position of the tossed Bible instead of her reason, Fanny's mistake in the church: the workings of chance and coincidence add up rapidly to a poetic vision of the 'silent workings of an invisible hand', irrational and unknowable, direct-ing the buried life away from merely human purposes to fulfil the 'indomitable unconscious will'. For all its wealth of agricultural detail, *Far from the Madding Crowd* is a non-naturalistic novel that exposes the underneath of surface appearance.

A poetic talent is at home in stylization. Though specific chapters do not tally with the rigidity of an architectural blueprint, there is a careful placing of parallel scenes in a before-and-after relationship to the central chapters that invites the comparisons and contrasts of a poetic reading. They show how the central action of human choice releases a fatal force which reverses the current of all fortunes except Gabriel Oak's. Gabriel proposes twice, and Boldwood three times. Boldwood's rise in Bathsheba's favour from his first proposal (rejected) to his second (half ac-cepted) is offset on the other side of the central episode by his second rejection, so much more terrible in Chapter xxxi because it is accompanied by a loss of control that hints at a tragic outcome to his obsession. There is a shearing feast and a wedding feast, linked thematically by Troy's harvest/wedding revel that profanes both. Time and chance jeer twice at Troy, through their grotesque embodiment in clockwork and stone in All Saints and Weatherbury Churches. The second occasion, when Fanny is past his help, points up with tragic irony his failure to persist after the first mockery. Troy takes two locks of hair, and abandons both women; Bathsheba's discovery of the colour of Fanny's hair precipitates her own crisis. The effect of Bathsheba's valentine—serious but not yet tragic—on Boldwood's temperament is set off by his intensified agony in Chapter xxxvii. On both occasions Oak meets his soli-tary figure at daybreak. In the later meeting, Boldwood's inco-herent grief and evidence of diminished responsbility recall the earlier Boldwood, who felt 'twinges of shame and regret at having so far exposed his mood by those fevered questions to a stranger', and had discussed Fanny's elopement with intelligent responsibility. The complete isolation of Fanny Robin in an indifferent landscape, helped only by a dog, in Chapter XL comments on Chapters VII and XI, when her lonely figure at least had Oak's practical sympathy and the uncertain support of Troy's promise. The comfortable Wessex ritual of drinking in Warren's Malthouse (VIII) has its less pleasant counterpart in the Buck's Head, where Gabriel Oak, who had been received as 'one of us' in the earlier ritual, takes charge of the muddle caused by Joseph Poorgrass's multiplying eye. At Warren's, news was heard of Fanny's disappearance: the delay at the Buck's Head is the cause of her dramatic reappearance to direct events from her coffin, and the disappearance of Troy, which in its turn forges another link in the tragic chain of cause and effect when *he* reappears. At the farthest points of radiation from the centre, the novel begins and ends with the fortunes of Gabriel Oak who, as his name suggests, watches and endures throughout.

There is hardly a scene, a character, or an image which has not its reflections on either side of the central crisis. It is characteristic of Hardy that their poetic force is carried by the relationship of characters to their environment. Nature dominates an agricultural community: 'Weatherbury' is well named. The adjustment or maladjustment of the characters to its seasonal rituals and emergencies—that is, to the reality of life—controls the deeper meaning of the story.

Hardy knows Nature too well to limit its presentation to the pathetic fallacy. There are scenes where Nature seems to be in sympathy with the human actors. Incidents in the story of human love run a diurnal and seasonal course. Oak is rejected in January, the intense passion of Bathsheba and Troy reaches its peak in high summer, Fanny dies at the onset of winter, Troy at Christmas, and hope begins to revive for Bathsheba and Oak in the new year. Dawn initiates action, reveals, and challenges: Bathsheba's spirit is revealed to Oak in her early morning ride in Chapter III, Oak discovers the loss of his flock in V, the effect of the valentine on Boldwood in XIV, and in Chapter XXXVIII the depth of the farmer's unbalance in neglecting his farm. In Chapter IX Boldwood pays his first visit to Bathsheba, and in XLIV and XL the dawn reveals Bathsheba's and Fanny's plight and their efforts to control it. Evenings often darken in storm and passion (XXXI, XXXIV, XXXVI, LXIV). When the distracted Bathsheba faces the stormy sunset after Boldwood's passionate reproaches in Chapter XXXI, 'the unresting world wheeled her round to a contrasting prospect eastward, in the shape of indecisive and palpitating stars'. But the subjective view of nature is corrected by the objective. As Boldwood walks across the meadow after he has received the valentine, 'the ground was melodious with ripples, and the sky with larks', but nature ruins his crops and Troy's romantic repentance, snows on an unprotected Fanny, and kills Gabriel's sheep.

Subjective and objective are fused when Nature becomes a correlative for those impulses which, because of their complexity or the character's failure in 'mapping out my mind upon my tongue', or ignorance of true motives, or Victorian taboos, cannot be expressed directly. The pool which 'glittered like a dead man's eye' is a vivid expression of Oak's unspoken impulse to suicide after the accident to his flock. The morning breeze which blew, 'shaking and elongating the reflection of the [skeleton] moon without breaking it' as he rejects the impulse conveys a basic concept of his resilient character.

Gabriel Oak's vital relationship to the natural world provides a touchstone by which the other characters are measured, a central leitmotif that links scenes, incidents and characters symphonically, and a powerful example of the poetic force of Hardy's Wessex. While Hardy takes some licence with his environment—the gurgoyles on Weatherbury (Puddletown) Church, for example, have probably been imported from the church of Sydling St Nicholas and 'the heroine's fine old Jacobean house [Waterston Manor] would be found in the story to have taken a witch's ride of a mile or more from its actual position'—it has the physical solidity of actual place. In Chapter II Norcombe Hill, 'not far from lonely Toller-Down', is given an identity that distinguishes it from any other hill by its minutely detailed features. The 'desolating wind which creates different sound responses from the differing textures of wood, leaves, grasses, and hedgerows; the decaying plantation of beeches, 'whose upper verge formed a line over the crest, fringing its arched curve against the sky, like a mane', bring Norcombe Hill sharply to the senses in its varying shapes, textures, and qualities of sound, as one of the ultimates of the human situation an active agent of fate with a will and effective power of its own

As in the poetry, Hardy's truth to physical detail adds a meta physical dimension: Norcombe Hill is also 'a mysterious sheet of fathomless shade'. The poet's power of leaping from the known to the unknown resides first of all in the evocative exactness of his vocabulary. The 'sound' words, 'smote', 'floundered', 'grumbling', 'gushed', 'weakened moan', 'simmered', 'boiled', 'rattled', 'rubbing', 'raking', 'brushing', evoke familiar human emotions and moods in tension with the non-human processes of time, wind and weather bending every digit to their unalterable course. Sound combines with sense, stress, sentence and paragraph structure, rhythm and control of tempo to make 'the roll of the world eastward . . . almost a palpable movement' to the reader. Short objective statements of time and place give way in the second paragraph to a Latinate weight of rhythm and vocabulary appropriate to Hardy's definition of Norcombe Hill as 'a shape approaching the indestructible as nearly as any to be found on earth,' and to the more personal rhythms and subjective evocations of the two paragraphs following. The cosmic pulse established rhythmically in the first two paragraphs sweeps with cumulative force through complex sentences and balanced clauses which place speech stress on the 'sound' qualities of Norcombe Hill, until the carefully built-up mood dies away, after the last sound climax of 'hurrying gust', on the soft consonants and open vowels of 'plunged into the south, to be heard no more'. The change of rhythm and tempo is typical of the whole novel. Sentences, paragraphs and chapters are juxtaposed as artistically as the fast and slow movements of a symphony.

Many of the poems can parallel in miniature the swing back from the heightened sense of awe at the sweep of mysterious natural forces to the sharp objective detail that anchors Hardy's Nature to the physical world. The adjectives which define the colour of the stars above Norcombe Hill—'a steely glitter', 'a fiery red'—stress with their non-human extremes 'the complete abstraction from all its compass of the sights and sounds of man'. Norcombe Hill, despite the emotional music of its wind cadences and poetry of motion, is a place without consciousness, and therefore without significance to Hardy except as reflected sensation 'derived from a tiny human frame'. The unordered motions of nature are suddenly jolted into perspective by the crowning climax of Farmer Oak's flute, whose notes 'had a clearness which was to be found nowhere in the wind, and a sequence which was to be found nowhere in nature'.

The focus now moves to Gabriel Oak. It is perhaps not accidental that Hardy's extended character studies of Oak, Boldwood, Troy and Bathsheba in Chapters I, XVIII, XXV and XXIX are juxtaposed with episodes in which their relationship to nature defines and judges their attitude to physical reality. Oak is linked vitally to the natural world in the novel's first sentence: his smile wrinkles his face 'like the rays in a rudimentary sketch of the rising sun'. His practical dress, unromantic capacity to wear well, the unassuming movements that suggest his conviction that 'he had no great claim on the world's room', and his special 'static' power, give him a likeness in certain respects to the indestructible 'featureless convexity' of Norcombe Hill going on its 'stately progress through the stars.' He appreciates the sky as 'a useful instrument' more reliable than his man-made timepiece, and as 'a work of art superlatively beautiful'. But his human capacity to make order, morality and beauty in the spinning universe isolates the movement of his life, in spite of its adjustment to seasonal rhythms, from the throb of the impersonal pulse with which it is counterpointed. Norcombe Hill now appears transformed by Oak's human purpose. The 'wild slope' is dotted with protective hurdles and the lambing hut, whose practical contents challenge the unordered natural furnishings of the hillside.

The introduction of Gabriel Oak on Norcombe Hill shows that his relationship to nature is one of open-eyed reality. After the lapses of attention that cost him his consciousness in an unventilated hut and his precious flock, he never relaxes his watch against nature's indifference. He knows how far he can utilize its resources to control the chaos of a spinning universe. The poetic texture throughout the novel shows Oak true to his role of creating order out of chaos. Hardy's description of the fire in Chapter VI and the storm in Chapters XXXVI and XXXVII stress the 'remarkable confusion of purpose' that invades both men and macrocosm. The men's 'shadows danced merrily up and down, timed by the jigging of the flames, and not at all by their owners' movements': flames of all shapes, sizes and noises consume the rick haphazardly in all directions. The factual details modulate into a poetic truth, linked to the grotesque mechanism of the All Saints jackaclock and the Weatherbury gurgoyle,

'Individual straws in the foreground were consumed in a creeping movement of ruddy heat, as if they were knots of red worms, and above shone imaginary fiery faces, tongues hanging from lips, glaring eyes, and other impish forms, from which at intervals sparks flew in clusters like birds from a nest . . .'

to reveal the world of strange chaotic forces to which Gabriel must oppose his intelligence and moral order. Characteristically, there is a swing back to the physical reality of the fire through the 'nest' simile that carries the mind back to the straw rick. In the storm Gabriel opposes an infuriated universe, strengthened by Troy's irresponsibility, with his experienced reading of the weather-lore of lower creatures, his improvised lightning conductor, endurance and devotion. The details of animal behaviour, transformation of landscape by light and shade, and *unfulfilled* warnings of the 'dance of death', throw into sharp relief the triumph of human contrivance against time and chance, and when Bathsheba joins him, the harmonious bond of mutual responsibility to life that is more enduring than the sexual attraction between Bathsheba and Troy. The lightning which brings them close to death reveals blinding truths in vivid image about their relationship to reality: Bathsheba's figure, running to join the solitary Oak; her confession of irrational impulse to marry Troy, which accords with the wild confusion of the storm raging about them; and an enlarged shadow-image of 'two human shapes, black as jet', that compels comparison with the mangled shadows of Troy and Bathsheba in the fir plantation (xxiv) as archetypes of her relationship to the two men.

Bathsheba's entry into the story implies the dominance of impulse over reason and intelligence which allows nature to assert its power. Her showy red jacket, a dissonant note in the 'featureless convexity' where survival depends on adjustment to the unexciting daily round, links her on the poetic level with the alien red coat Troy, who wins her by the dazzle of passion, and the tragic one-sidedness of Boldwood, which leads to bloodshed. (In Chapter L the colour leitmotif and her raised position in the tent, 'enthroned alone in this place of honour, against a scarlet background', suggests how far her infatuation for Troy has isolated her from her natural background.) Her irrational impulse to admire her image on Norcombe Hill is a visual metaphor of the blindness to reality which links the three in a tragic trio. All three mistake a projection of their own desires for love, and are too sensitive to the mockery of men and nature. Oak's sensible clothes and purposeful movements throw into relief Bathsheba's longing to escape the demands of life. She would like to be a bride at a wedding, 'if I could be one without having a husband'. 'That's a terrible wooden story' says Oak.

Hardy's moral judgement of Bathsheba is made in the chapter that follows her capitulation to Troy in the hollow in the ferns. Chapter XXVIII, when examined with XLIV, suggests by poetic means the nature of her blindness, and her recovery from it, in terms that would hardly have been acceptable to the Victorian reader in straight statement. To readers of the surface story, and to Bathsheba herself, she was captured by a soldier's 'winning tongue'. But the poetic texture makes it clear that she was won as a woman by the phallic sword. The sword exercise is a correlative in action of the appeal of danger, death, and the dominant male.

Hardy's setting is essential to the meaning of both chapters. The film of *Far from the Madding Crowd* (1968) set the scene in grim, angular Maiden Castle. But Hardy's sensuous description of the lush ferns, 'their soft, feathery arms caressing her up to her shoulders', the thick, flossy, yielding carpet of moss and grass, make clear Bathsheba's inarticulate sexual desires. We are prepared for her to make a response to Troy that is emotional, not rational, by the shape of the pit, 'shallow enough to allow the sunshine to reach their heads'. The shadow in which their bodies stand looks back to the intimate sexual darkness of the fir plantation in which she becomes so dramatically 'entangled' with Troy. His sudden appearance in the hollow is like the suddenness of the 'fairy transformation' revealed by Bathsheba's dark lantern, and as diabolically 'magic' as his mastery of the sword and scarlet garb. The transformation is into something below the human level. If one views the sword exercise as a dazzling courtship ritual, Bathsheba's rejection of the less glamorous Oak and Boldwood becomes clear.

The complexity of the attraction is evoked by the swift action and evocative power of the words. An accumulation of active verbs and words of rapid hissing movement build up a powerful impression of Troy's slipperiness and Bathsheba's fascinated response to the fatal attraction of the sword. Troy's role as bringer of death is defined at the end of the chapter in an image that brings back, with a difference, Gabriel's rejection of suicide:

'He was altogether too much for her, and Bathsheba seemed as one who, facing a reviving wind, finds it blow so strongly that it stops the breath.'

166

Bathsheba submits: Gabriel resists, and the reviving breeze distorts the moon's reflection without breaking it.

Reminders of the earlier scene in Chapter xliv stress the difference. The scene of Troy's mating display is now a refuge from him. The summer 'ferns with their feathery arms' are now 'yellowing' in the winter: the 'blades' of 'a peculiar species of flag' which 'glistened in the emerging sun, like scythes' recall Troy's explanation of his cuts in terms of sowing and harvesting. Bathsheba's advice to Liddy—really to herself—'Stand your ground, and be cut to pieces' recalls her danger, and the courage she has transferred from that romantic situation to the present hard reality. The fungi, 'marked with great splotches, red as arterial blood', remind of Troy's appearance on the natural scene as 'a dim spot of artificial red' and his role as bringer of death. Even the language in Chapter xxviii, full of hissing and explosive consonants, has changed to an evocation in sound and sense of oozing and rotting. The difference lies in Bathsheba's new assessment of reality after Fanny's revelation. Her eyes are now open to the presence of evil. The beautiful flossy carpet has hidden a malignant swamp.

But she does not allow the evil to distort her vision. It is from here, her Slough of Despond, that the dawn reveals to her the rebirth of natural life, the comforting ritual of the daily round—the schoolboy learning his collect—in contrast to the dazzling mating ritual which had 'well-nigh shut out earth and heaven', and her own choice to endure, which aligns her with Gabriel Oak. Her poetic link to her surroundings shows the distorted perception of her youth giving way to the clear sight of maturity. The reflected image of her solitary self at the beginning of the novel, which blinded her to the consequences of toying with the affections of the reserved farmer who did not bow down to her image, is replaced at the end by a contrasting picture of Bathseba in harmony with man and nature. Her wedding to Oak is marked by practical plainness; clogs, cloak and umbrella acknowledging the weather and the Weatherbury band acknowledging renewed harmony with rustic tradition. The whole novel, with its picture of Bathsheba presiding over the minutely described affairs of household and farm, is a great evocation of that 'mass of hard prosaic reality' which she accepts as the basis of marriage in marrying Oak, after the failure of high romance.

Troy's relationship to his environment is marked from beginning to end by distortion. He makes his entry in Chapter xi

167

as a voice 'so much a part of the building, that one would have said the wall was holding a conversation with the snow.' The implied inflexibility marks his attitude at All Saints, where he 'stood still with the abnormal rigidity of the old pillars around.'

The stone rigidity of what should be humanly flexible is balanced in Chapter XLVI by the grotesque Walpurgis-night writhing of flowers which should be rooted in Fanny's grave. The resulting chaos enacts visibly the 'element of absurdity' in his belated repentance. His acceptance of chaos as his element is pointed by his response to the mockery of the gurgoyle, and Bathsheba's contrasting attempt to restore order in the churchyard, though it means acknowledgment of her own unimportance: 'she wiped the mud spots from the tomb as if she rather liked its words than otherwise, and went home again.' Troy, unlike Bathsheba, never realizes that independence involves responsibility and order.

The laughter of an absurd universe which constantly opposes Troy's self-importance is realized in a cluster of images that defines his attitude to reality. It is heard first in Chapter XI, 'hardly distinguishable from the tiny whirlpools outside', and realized finally in the grotesque gurgoyle that creates another whirlpool on Fanny's grave. The chuckling of the two 'bowed and toothless old almsmen' in All Saints modulates into the cosmic mockery of the gurgoyle, whose 'lower row of teeth was quite washed away'. Time itself is distorted: visibly, in the grotesque shapes of the clockwork mannikin and gurgoyle which embody time's revenge on Troy's illusion that past errors can be retrieved, and warn him, in vain, not to let time and chance direct his actions; and aurally, in the very movement of the prose. The coarse directness of 'The gurgoyle spat' develops into a rhythmic spate, and in Chapter XI Troy's suspense, and the reader's, is sustained by recounting in detail the mechanism of the striking of the hours, halves, and quarters in language that is heavy with consonants and monosyllables.

Troy's first encounter with Bathsheba is seen as a grotesque distortion of surface reality. One has only to compare Chapter XXIV with the first meeting of Dorothea and Casaubon in George Eliot's *Middlemarch* to notice how Hardy has changed the appearance of the world of common experience to bring out the deeper reality, the 'real feelings and volitions' of Bathsheba's relation to Troy. Dorothea meets her future husband at dinner with her uncle. Her false estimate of Casaubon arises out of trivial table talk about home and political economy. Her practical sister's comment on his looks and lack of social graces fixes him in George Eliot's world of prosaic reality and measures the extent of Dorothea's illusion. Bathsheba's walk round the farm begins in the familiar world of cows that can be identified in the darkness by mundane sounds, friendly contact, visual memory of features, and individual names. The fir plantation through which she then passes, a 'vast, low, naturally formed hall' with a 'plumy ceiling' and yielding carpet of 'dead spikelets and mildewed cones' takes her gradually on a Jungian night journey from the familiar world of everyday experience to a grotesque, irrational, Kafkaesque expression of subconscious motives and warnings. Her first encounter with Troy is of touch. Its violence, which 'nearly threw Bathsheba off her balance', is sexual. The phallic spur caught in the soft tissues of her dress (which, as Hardy has remarked earlier, is part of a woman's personality) define Bathsheba's attraction to Troy as a wish for domination by the virile male 'cockbird' rather than its rationalization as 'It was a fatal omission of Boldwood's that he had never once told her she was beautiful.' The dialogue which rises out of the darkness expresses the primal recognition of sex between Man and Woman.

> ' "We have got hitched together somehow, I think."
> "Yes."
> "Are you a woman?"
> "Yes."
> "A lady, I should have said."
> "It doesn't matter."
> "I am a man." '

Finally, the flamboyant scarlet figure revealed by the lantern, which 'had upon her the effect of a fairy transformation', joins with the dazzled Bathsheba in a Gothic dance of shadows that warns of the suffering in store if they persist in a relationship that breeds distorted vision. The lantern

'radiated upwards into their faces, and sent over half the plantation gigantic shadows of both man and woman, each dusky shape becoming distorted and mangled upon the tree-trunks till it wasted to nothing.'

Hardy constantly draws attention to Troy's military dress as a visible symbol of his relationship to nature. In its realistic aspect of army uniform, it opposes the rootlessness of the soldier to a way of life rooted in seasonal ritual. The red coat, alien to the landscape with which Oak's working clothes harmonize, carries traditional charges of danger, death, pride, and passion. It also carries diabolic overtones. Troy has touches of the resistless demon lover, the devil's sudden appearances and disguises (soldier, civilian, haymaker, Dick Turpin), the devil's luck and the devil's trickery in his cruel teasing of Boldwood in Chapter xxxiv. The grotesque pictorial composition that meets Oak's gaze in the barn, focused on the Mephistophelian figure of Troy,

'. . . the wretched persons of all the work-folk, the hair of their heads at such low levels being suggestive of mops and brooms. In the midst of these shone red and distinct the figure of Sergeant Troy, leaning back in a chair . . .'

suggests the devil's power to distort human dignity. It is a striking contrast to the previous picture of genuine though precarious harmony at the Shearing feast, where Bathsheba and Boldwood at the peak of their relationship are framed by the window, with Oak accompanying them, outside, on his flute. The soldier is death to the farm. The 'Soldier's Joy' with which he profanes the harvest home, enforcing it with threats of dismissal, violates traditional customs and responsibilities and the spontaneity of rustic music, seen in its true function both at the shearing feast and Bathsheba's wedding to Oak. His sword as an instrument of deception and destruction carries an implied contrast with Gabriel's lance—borrowed, significantly, from Boldwood—which heals the stricken sheep and saves the economy of the farm. It places him as a human agent of cosmic dissonance. The 'deathy' cuts of the sword exercise are recalled in Chapter xxxvii by the 'dance of death' of an infuriated universe, described in terms of mailed armies and military manoeuvres. The distortion he has created by his drunken revel has entered the cosmos. 'The night had a haggard look, like a sick thing.'

Boldwood's tragic distortion of reality compels comparison with Troy's. He too enters the story as a voice, but a voice sharply distinguished from the outside world, not reproaching Fanny, but asking kindly for news of her. His first appearance at the Corn Exchange picks out his Roman features and erect carriage as components of his pre-eminent trait, dignity. He is a more worthy man than Troy, yet his kind of inflexibility leads to a self-absorbed concern with his own image that links him to the playboy. His mirror reflection in Chapter xiv (compare Bathsheba's colourful image) is 'wan in expression, and insubstantial in form'. Together with his various settings, it defines his defective vision of physical reality as an inversion of life. As the valentine rests on 'a time-piece, surmounted by a spread eagle'—suggestive not only of Roman dignity but also of 'the symmetry of his existence' which he felt 'to be slowly getting distorted in the direction of an ideal passion', the reflected moonlight

'had that reversed direction which snow gives, coming upward and lighting up his ceiling in an unnatural way, casting shadows in strange places, and putting lights where shadows had used to be'.

His vision is blocked prophetically by a correlative of blind and death-marked passion. 'The large red seal became as a blot of blood on the retina of his eye.' It fixes the natural features of the snowy landscape in a frozen 'glaze'. 'Withered grass-bents, encased in icicles, bristled through the smooth wan coverlet in the twisted and curved shapes of old Venetian glass'. The brittle rigidity of old Venetian glass, not of stone pillars, suggests the fragility of Boldwood's mental balance. But a brilliant modulation of the unnatural 'rayless' sun (which recalls by contrast Gabriel's smiling face) 'like a red and flameless fire shining over a white hearthstone', introduces the reality against which Boldwood's inversion is measured. 'On the ridge, up against the blazing sky, a figure . . . like the black snuff in the midst of a candle-flame', the eternal shepherd Gabriel Oak, creates order as the snuff vitalizes and controls the candle-flame, and directs the chapter to the life-giving warmth of 'the scarlet and orange glow' inside Warren's.

Boldwood's interest—good for the serial—as a man on the dangerous edge of things is heightened emotionally by Hardy's presentation of his solitary figure against dawns and sunsets of unpredictable weather. As chaos is Troy's element, extremity is Boldwood's. Chapter xviii, which shows him in his element, suggests the nature of the subconscious disturbance that is to overthrow his fine 'balance of enormous antagonistic forces.' His round of the stables recalls Bathsheba's round of the cowsheds before her ill-fated liaison. But thoroughbred horses are more delicately balanced than cows: their contented munching is varied by 'the restless and shadowy figure of a colt' who mirrors 'the celibate' restlessly pacing 'his almonry and cloister'. The religious image, the traditional association of horses with the extremes of sexual and imaginative power, the poles of stillness and restlessness that constitute the atmosphere, define Boldwood's tragic flaw as similar to

Angel Clare's—a devotion to the absolute ideal at the expense of suppression of the flesh. His wild happiness at the prospect of 'six years of intangible ethereal courtship' and the psychotic clothes fetishism are correlative to his desire to worship Bathsheba's image in place of the flesh and blood woman.

Outside his cloister, in the social or natural world, he is ill at ease. When all nature is bursting with new life, 'Boldwood went *meditating* down the slopes with his eyes on his boots, which the yellow pollen from the buttercups had bronzed in artistic gradations.' (My italics.) Scenes of social ineptness stress his unfitness for the world of human concerns. He is forced to ask whether Bathsheba is considered handsome, and whether any late tie-knot is in fashion. Even Troy in Chapter XXXIV shows up his scheme to bargain with human counters.

' "Bad as I am, I am not such a villain as to make the marriage or misery of any woman a matter of huckster and sale . . . You say you love Bathsheba; yet on the merest apparent evidence you instantly believe in her dishonour. A fig for such love!" '

His self-consuming passion abstracts dignity from the man and responsibility from the farmer. The tragic picture in XXXVIII of the solitary self-alienated man in the rain that has ruined his crops through his neglect of husbandry, is an effective comment on Boldwood's unbalanced view of reality.

Fanny Robin's relationship to nature is marked by assimilation. Always alone, usually anonymous—she is described as 'a form', 'the shape', 'the blurred spot', 'a mere shade upon the earth', 'the woman', 'the wayfarer', 'the pedestrian', 'a shapeless heap', 'the panting heap of clothes'—slight and colourless against a colourless indifferent expanse of earth, she inherits the common burden of journeying, death, dissolution into the elements, and transformation. She melts into the shade of a tree and evolves out of the snowy landscape as imperceptibly as a snowflake. Chapter XI consists largely of mood-painting details that build up to a general poetic impression of the basic human predicament. The natural transformations that mark the changes of the seasons, ending inevitably in 'an obliteration by snow', the null snow-covered moor—'its irregularities were forms without features; suggestive of anything, proclaiming nothing'; the flatness of the river, the vertical mass of wall that is part of Troy's unresponsiveness; the muffled bell, the darkness and drabness, make up an oppressive image of the negation of human significance by the density of physical matter, against which Fanny's weak aim at her lover's window is inadequate.

Yet Chapter XL defines the anonymous woman as a significant human being by virtue of her ability to make use of nature. The only action of the chapter is that a dying pregnant woman covers two miles of highway to the workhouse. But interest is sustained by constant tension between the 'blind obtuseness of inanimate things' and the Oak-like ingenuity of the girl to direct nature. The crust of cloud shuts out 'every speck of heaven': no superhuman help will guide her to the earthly 'haven of rest' marked by the Casterbridge aurora. Contrasts between light and darkness, silence and sound—the attenuated clock striking one, the dull boom of the morning wind over the flats, the funereal note of the fox's bark, her own voice encouraging herself and the dog—stress her isolation in a non-human world. Her actions are described in short direct statements from the outside, with Brechtian alienation. As she selects sticks for crutches, she begins to control her environment by 'feeling with her hands.' The phrase links her to Gabriel Oak, who worked entirely by feeling with his hands, an image of human ignorance and intelligence, in the darkness of the storm, to repair another consequence of Troy's carelessness. The link with Oak, Hardy's measure of man's adjustment to nature, implies criticism of Fanny's earlier compliance. Her heroic efforts to save herself and her baby—too late—suggest that arriving at the right church should not have been beyond her capacity.

When her physical aids fail, Fanny demonstrates the power of mind over matter. When 'the faculty of contrivance was worn out', help appears from nature. Hardy's dog, as might be expected, is a real dog, 'as homeless as she', and frantic with distress when Fanny falters. His fate at the end of the chapter comments on man's inhumanity and ignorance of the potentialities of lower nature directed by human intelligence. But Hardy's double vision endows a suffering fellow-creature with mythical overtones. Like Fanny, he is anonymous, 'being thus assignable to no breed'. He is 'a portion of shade' which detaches itself from 'the stripe of shadow' on the bridge. 'Night, in its sad, solemn, and benevolent aspect, apart from its stealthy and cruel side, was personified in this form.' Jungians would recognize him as a projection of the subconscious reserves of power that rise from stress and despair to order a transformation of personality. The dog in Egyptian mythology is the divine helper and sacred animal of death. This mysterious helper from the lower world leads Fanny towards the death that transforms her scarcely perceptible life into an instrument of dramatic power.

Fanny's 'resurrection' as a power from the grave is stressed ritually by the association of her death with flowers. They are the sign of Troy's repentance, and Bathsheba's atonement to the dead girl in Chapter XLII: and Bathsheba gives orders, reminiscent of Ophelia's death, that the new spring waggon, washed very clean, which carries her body should be covered in hardy flowers and various evergreens. The result of Fanny's power is to make the other characters realize their unimportance in the cosmic scheme. Her first victim is Joseph Poorgrass. His 'pale companion' joins with the monotonous enveloping fog—a typically Fanny Robin scene—to rob him of his sense of identity. Its restoration at the Buck's Head leads to the discovery that inspires Bathsheba's wild, egoistic bid for Troy's attention by the open coffin, Troy's departure and return, and Boldwood's final act of madness.

Fanny Robin and Oak, while involved with the fortunes of the tragic trio of unadjusted lovers, are also part of that aspect of Wessex evoked by Hardy's chorus of rustics. Fanny belongs to their class, and when she moves out of it to follow Troy and initiate the tragedy Hardy stresses her isolation by juxtaposing Chapters VII, XI, XVI, XL–XLII with scenes that portray the communal life of rural Wessex. Gabriel Oak, on the other hand, is to be found taking an active part in these choric scenes of rural gossip, work, play, and ritual. He is accepted as an equal and part of the traditional scene because the old maltster, symbol of natural continuance with 'his frosty white hair and beard overgrowing his gnarled figure like the grey moss and lichen upon a leafless apple tree', 'knowed yer grandfather for years and years!' and the features of the local landscape which are a shared heritage. He shares with them the sheep-washing, shearing and other seasonal ritual that control the rhythms and crises of the story, and as 'a clever man in talents' takes charge of their confused fire-fighting and the muddle caused by Joseph's multiplying eye.

The functions of Hardy's rustic chorus have often been appreciated, and its loss felt in *Tess of the d'Urbervilles* and *Jude the Obscure* as a loss of humour and balance. It has a poetic function. The lyrical and meditative poetry of the countryman's close involvement with nature and the basic realities presents the ultimates of immutability in the human situation, to set off the passionate search for personal stability through love that moves the more sensitive characters to strange and momentous actions. The rustics are a natural outgrowth of the 'functional continuity' of the medieval shearing barn, for both 'embodied practices which had suffered no mutilation at the hands of time'—the long perspective of birth, marriage, death, ritual, superstition, and custom that make up the Wessex past, so changeless that the rooting of an apple-tree and the pulling down of a wooden cider-house are taken as evidence of 'stirring times'. Occasionally they commit or fail to commit an action that changes the tenor of the story. Joseph's weakness at the Buck's Head and Liddy's encouragement of Bathsheba's whim to send the valentine are trivial actions that enliven the monotonous daily round but have tragic consequences. (Liddy, as Bathsheba's confidante, has a multiple function. Her shallowness and dependence on Bathsheba's favour make her an unsafe guide for superior minds to follow, as in the valentine episode. Her attempts to keep on the right side of her mistress while passing the judgement of common humanity on her behaviour, as in Chapter xxx; her symbolic negotiation of the swamp in ignorance of its existence in Chapter xliv, and her parody of her mistress' airs in Chapters x, make her an effective foil to Bathsheba's wise and foolish actions.)

Hardy has no illusions that his rustics live in a golden age. Their confusion does nothing to fight fire or storm, and wastes precious minutes while the sheep are in the clover and Troy is on his way to Boldwood's party. But their chief function is not to act, but to be. Their conversation, full of a pithy humour and proverbial wisdom that is Shakespearean as well as Hardeian, builds up a poetic texture of simple eternal values to live by that make limited opportunities endurable. It ranges widely through birth and death, love and marriage, the strange behaviour of their superiors and Providence, religion of church and chapel and the more pagan religion evinced by a wealth of superstition and ritual, the wonders of the city of Bath transformed by their miraculous expectations, to the local hero-myths—Joseph's encounter with the owl, Pa'son Thirdly's charity, Farmer Everdene's ruse to keep himself faithful—which build up a sense of man's significance. Their kindly if sometimes exaggerated appreciation of rustic talent—Gabriel's learning and performance on the flute, Joseph's efforts at ballad-singing, even Pennyways' unwonted honesty at the shearing supper—shows a respect for the 'otherness' of people which Troy and Boldwood never learn. Their insistence on marks of individuality—(which Hardy presents, as he presents the jackaclock and gurgoyle, with a relish for the strange manifestation) the maltster's age, Joseph's shyness, Jacob's milestone-like tooth, Henery Fray's eccentric spelling and intimations of wasted genius—are the marks of self-sufficiency which constitute their defiance of darkness; a self-sufficiency which the modern habit of taking too much thought has undermined.

The story of *Far from the Madding Crowd* plots the tragic cross-purposes of five people fighting for happiness through love. The poetic aspects of the underpattern 'intensify the expression of things . . . so that the heart and inner meaning is made vividly visible'. The vivid visibility of what the action *means* is achieved through the organization of the novel like a poem through interconnecting ideas, images, and phrases; through the vitality of figure, metaphor, and simile taken from nature and art; through intensely dramatic and sometimes grotesque scenes charged with inherent emotion and the mystery of subconscious impulses leaping theatrically to the surface, set against a running river of quiet lyric meditation on old ways and changeless things; through moments of spiritual revelation rising out of sense experience of the physical world. It is backed up aurally by personal rhythms of speech and gesture (worth noting are Boldwood's gradual disintegration from the solemnity of his first proposal to his disjointed outpourings and feverish search for reassurance in the later part of the novel; and Bathsheba's varying speech patterns in her talk to Liddy and the rustics, her skittish play with Oak changing to mature respect, and the verbal love-fencing with Troy that ends in confused submission) counterpointing the larger rhythms of seasonal ebb and flow punctuated by crises of human emotion that temporarily impose a different rhythm, as in Chapters XI and XXXIV. Hardy's stern moral comment on the failure of all but Oak to control reality underlines the insignificance of their struggles to an indifferent universe. But the poetic relation to environment of these ephemeral creatures living and suffering in a remote part of Wessex lifts their story onto the cosmic plane of archetypal conflict of great ultimates—chaos and order, adjustment and non-adjustment, suffering and peace, tragedy and comedy, good and evil, and life and death.

VIII

The Return of the Native:
A Novel of Environment

The Return of the Native strikes a harsher note than *Far from the Madding Crowd*. Egdon Heath, the resistant matter of the cosmos on which the action takes place, bears, shapes, nourishes, and kills conscious organisms possessed of its striving will without its unconsciousness of suffering. The six main characters take their key from Egdon. They all feel its pull through some affinity of temperament. Clym, Mrs Yeobright and Diggory Venn share its look of isolation; Thomasin, Clym and Venn its endurance; Eustacia and Wildeve, though they hate it, share its primal vitality and indifference to others. The rustics, too, take a more subdued tone from the heath. The accent of their talk falls on time passing, change and decay. Their environment is one in which change and chance, death and darkness, prevail, and 'the overpowering of the fervid by the inanimate' is a recognized conclusion to human effort.

It is fashionable in this denigrating age to decry Hardy's description of the heath in Chapter 1 as pretentious. An earlier critic was nearer the mark in likening it to the entry of the Gods in Wagner. Large orchestras are not out of place in making the power of cosmic forces felt on the pulse. Egdon is presented as a visual correlative of space and time and the modern view of life 'as a thing to be put up with'. It is characteristic of Hardy's poetic style to begin with the specific—'A Saturday afternoon in November'— and widen the local view gradually to a philosophic vision of cosmic processes which the heath has power to affect:

'The face of the heath by its mere complexion added half an hour to evening; it could in like manner retard the dawn, sadden noon, anticipate the frowning of storms scarcely generated, and intensify the opacity of a moonless midnight to a cause of shaking and dread.'

The description of the heath in terms of a face, 'a face on which time makes but little impression', which will later be recalled by the face (Clym's) on which time has recorded disillusive experience, introduces the theme of shape that opposes the chaos of Egdon's primal matter. But in this first chapter the details emphasize storm and darkness. Jungians will recognize in Hardy's hint of the tragic climax the subconscious hinterland of elemental myth that presents man's painful predicament in relation to a demonic landscape of barren earth, isolating wind, stormy water, and creative/destructive fire.

'The storm was its lover, and the wind its friend. Then it became the home of strange phantoms; and it was found to be the hitherto unrecognized original of those wild regions of obscurity which are vaguely felt to be compassing us about in midnight dreams of flight and disaster, and are never thought of after the dream till revived by scenes like this.'

Its 'Titanic form' widens the perspective still further to invest the heath with heroic echoes of classical myth; particularly the Prometheus myth of rebellion against darkness. There is a swing back again, characteristic of Hardy's poetic method, from these long philosophical perspectives to 'intelligible facts regarding landscape', its emotional and practical connection with man and his efforts to civilize it. The evocation ends with another swing from localized human vision to a vista of geological aeons. The Latinate dignity of the language, the balanced pauses, the unhurried rhythm, the slow build-up of paragraph structure, enact a persistent hammering at intractable physical substance which is part of the character and theme of Egdon.

'The great inviolate place had an ancient permanence which the sea cannot claim. Who can say of a particular sea that it is old? Distilled by the sun, kneaded by the moon, it is renewed in a year, in a day, or in an hour. The sea changed, the fields changed, the rivers, the villages, and the people changed, yet Egdon remained. Those surfaces were neither so steep as to be destructible by weather, nor so flat as to be the victims of floods and deposits. With the exception of an aged highway, and a still more aged barrow . . . themselves almost crystallized to natural products by long continuance—even the trifling irregularities were not caused by pickaxe, plough, or spade, but remained as the very finger-touches of the last geological change.'

The Return of the Native is concerned with the Promethean struggle of conscious life against the unconscious 'rayless' universe from which it sprang. <u>The poetic-dramatic structure of the first chapters initiates the underlying metaphor of the novel, the ancient conflict of light and darkness.</u> The white man-made road that crosses the brown heath, the red glow of bonfires, the 'blood-coloured' figure of Diggory Venn, challenge the dark drabness of the earth.

'To light a fire is the instinctive and resistant act of man when, at the winter ingress, the curfew is sounded throughout Nature. It indicates a spontaneous, Promethean rebelliousness against the fiat that this recurrent season shall bring foul times, cold darkness, misery and death. Black chaos comes, and the fettered gods of the earth say, Let there be light.'

The almost supernatural figure of Diggory Venn modulates between the heath and the human beings whose desire for joy and purpose troubles the scene. He is dyed into an identification of the heath and its products. Yet his conspicuous fiery colour suggests a character that will master reality through involvement with it.

Chapter II begins with one of Hardy's familiar images of the human condition, the meeting of two lonely figures on a deserted road. One wonders about the meaning of the two walking figures and the woman concealed in the van. The chapter ends with another anonymous figure rising from the central point of Rainbarrow as the apex of plain, hill, and tumulus. Between the two scenes of human interest stands the modulating chord of the heath. Hardy is careful to plant his descriptions of scene where they will direct emotion. The reader's eye is forced to follow the reddleman's musing survey upwards from the 'speck on the road' that defines the vanishing Captain to the protuberance of the barrow and the ambiguous potential of the crowning figure to make or mar human significance.

The shifting perspective, that enlarges and diminishes the human figure ('a spike from a helmet', 'the only obvious justification of [the hills'] outline', 'it descended . . . with the glide of a water-drop down a bud'), and transforms the barrow itself from 'a wart on an Atlantean brow' to 'the pole and axis of this heathery world', leaves in suspension the comparative significance of scene and human actors. The figure of unknown potential has been associated with the Celts who built the barrow as a bulwark of order against chaos; but what it marks is a place of death. It gives a perfect aesthetic finish to the mass; yet the Greek ideal of perfect beauty has been defined in Chapter I as an anachronism. As it disappears, the surprise of the movement where all seemed fixity stresses the function of human consciousness on the natural scene. It can change and be changed.

Change is the keynote of the distanced 'sky-backed pantomime of silhouettes' which replaces the composition of barrow and lonely figure. In Chapter III the focus shifts from the permanent mass of the heath, with solitary wanderers crawling like ants over its surface and the still figure on its central point, to a firelit impression of movement and evanescence.

'All was unstable; quivering as leaves, evanescent as lightning. Shadowy eye-sockets, deep as those of a death's head, suddenly turned into pits of lustre: a lantern-jaw was cavernous, then it was shining; wrinkles were emphasized to ravines, or obliterated entirely by a changed ray.'

Stillness gives way to motion; the solitary figure reaching for the sky to several 'burdened figures' bowed down under the furze they carry, playing out the next stage of human development. The pyramid-shaped bonfire they build to top the barrow enacts a wordless ritual of human function to shape and control. The heath, detached from them by the radiant circle of light they have created, becomes the 'vast abyss' of Milton's, Dante's and Homer's hell. By implication, the distorted human features evoke tormented souls acting out a timeless doom.

Hardy modulates from ritual to the human plane by bringing the fragmented Grandfer Cantle gradually forward from the composition to speak and act as a mortal limited by time and the need for warmth and self-assertion. The elemental ritual of light and darkness recedes as the kindly rustic voices gather strength. But it remains in the imagination to colour the talk of local human concerns with its larger rhythms. The conflict of wills that emerges from the gossip about Mrs Yeobright forbidding the banns, Tamsin's rash choice of Wildeve, Wildeve's character and attainments, the criticism of Eustacia's non-communal bonfire, the anticipation of Clym's Promethean role—'What a dog he used to be for bonfires!'—the nostalgia for youth and quiet acceptance of death as part of the seasonal cycle: all are marked with the preceding evocation of the limitations of the earth and the desire to tránscend them; the fire of life and passion and the distortion of reality it brings with its comfort; the double vision of man's speck-

180

like insignificance on the face of the heath and the poetic light that gives his ephemeral features the eternal grandeur of ravines and caverns.

The human drama evolves, as it were, from the scene and its implications. The character of Egdon encourages resistance and determines the kind of action that can take place within its bounds. Isolation fosters Eustacia's attraction to Clym and to a man of inferior calibre, the misunderstanding between Clym and his mother, the misapprehension about Mrs Yeobright's guineas. The openness of the country enables bonfire signals to be seen for miles; and kills Mrs Yeobright after her exhausting walk from one isolated cottage to another. Much of the action consists of solitary journeys across the heath to keep up communications or assignations, to spy out the land, or pursue erring mortals who have lost their way literally and figuratively on the dark criss-crossing paths that become symbolic of their antagonistic purposes. The presence of the vast passionless heath puts the human movements into perspective as the scurrying of ephemeral ants.

The plot resembles *Far from the Madding Crowd* in the tragic chain of love relationships and the situation of Wildeve, the gay man vacillating between the innocent girl he is engaged to and the woman of greater passion and complexity. The pattern is again complicated by an idealist with an obsession, though Clym Yeobright's ambition, unlike Boldwood's, is unconnected with the irrational force of sexual love. Mrs Yeobright adds another colour to the figure in the carpet in the conflict between generations and their ideals of progress. As usual, the poetic stylization contributes to meaning. Douglas Brown (op. cit.) notes that

'the very grouping of the protagonists tells much. On one far side is Thomasin ("All similes concerning her began and ended with birds") and on the other, Wildeve, the ineffectual engineer, invading the country to become a publican. Clym (the native home from exile) and Eustacia (seeking exile, and confusing that with home) stand between them. At the centre, between Clym and Eustacia, Mrs Yeobright is subtly placed, a countrywoman upholding urban attitudes whose true nature and effect she cannot perceive.'

R. W. Stallman, in his ingenious article 'Hardy's Hour-Glass Novel' (*Sewanee Review*, LV, 1947) sees in the novel a chain of seven 'hour-glass' plots, in which Fate keeps turning the hour-glass over to reverse events, situations, and partners.

The tragic action was designed originally to lead to the double death in the weir, involving the earlier tragedy of Mrs. Yeobright's death. The original five-part structure, the strict regard for unities of place, time (the year and a day of folklore quest) and action, may recall Shakespearean and Classical drama. The two signal fires are the novel's poles of time and action, and Rainbarrow its axis in space. But such stylization is part of Hardy's normal poetic technique. The five parts clearly graph the stages in the inter-related love affairs, and the disillusionment which reality brings to Eustacia's romantic dreams of happiness and Clym's dreams of finding a purpose.

Book First introduces the three women whose relationship to the two men is to promote a tragic antagonism of ideals. The wedding complications of Tamsin and Wildeve introduce the blind obstructiveness of things (the marriage licence, and the subconscious reluctance of Wildeve that allowed the mistake to happen; Mrs Yeobright's 'Such things don't happen for nothing' anticipates the psychology of Freudian error), and the countermoves of human intelligence (Mrs Yeobright's unscrupulous use of Venn as a rival lover to bring Wildeve to heel, and Venn's active determination to look after Tamsin's interests). Book Second, 'The Arrival', resolves the marriage complications and changes the emotional current by the return of Clym Yeobright. Interest is sustained by the potential of conflict and attraction between a man who has rejected the worldly vanity of Paris and a woman for whom he represents an avenue of escape to its delights. Book Third, 'The Fascination', charts the blind sexual attraction between Clym and Eustacia, each a distorted projection of fulfilment to the other, and the serious division it causes between Clym and his mother. Mrs Yeobright's attempt to heal the breach by her gift of money to Tamsin and Clym sows the seeds of the catastrophe by a combination of carelessness (she entrusts the money to the weak-witted Christian Cantle), blind chance (Wildeve wins the guineas from Cantle), and ignorance (Venn does not know that half the money he wins back from Wildeve was destined for Clym).

Book Fourth, 'The Closed Door', shows more than one door closing on human possibilities. Clym's blindness limits his ambitions to knowledge of a few square feet of furze. Simultaneously it dashes Eustacia's hopes of escaping Egdon through Clym, and sends her back to Wildeve. Wildeve's presence in the cottage with Eustacia when Mrs Yeobright calls keeps the door closed against her, and Clym's heavy sleep is another closed door. Hope of reconciliation is closed for ever by Mrs Yeobright's lonely death on the heath. But Johnny Nunsuch's dramatic restatement of Mrs Yeobright's words, 'she said I was to say that I had seed her, and she was a broken-hearted woman and cast off by her son' opens the door to Clym's painful discovery in Book Fifth of the circumstances of her death and Eustacia's part in it. 'The Discovery' charts the steps Clym takes to find out the truth, and the Oedipus-like irony that each step he takes drives him deeper into a hell of remorse, self-knowledge, and division from the other woman he loves. The final step drives Eustacia from his anger to seek escape through Wildeve, and to a despairing death with him in storm and darkness.

Hardy gave way to editorial necessity and common probability to add Book Sixth, which presents 'the inevitable movement onward' that restores order after tragic catastrophe. Tamsin and Diggory Venn find happiness in marriage, and Clym partial fulfilment as an itinerant preacher, to the accompaniment of the rituals of May Day and the waxing of a feather bed for the married pair, which involve them all in the seasonal rite of fertility and regeneration.

One can point to the usual incidents in the working out of plot which compel comparisons vital to structure. The different purposes, selfish and altruistic, which motivate the characters to seek conflicting manifestations of fulfilment; which animate the various figures who crown Rainbarrow, and inspire the lonely journeys taken across the heath, are worth close study. The different attitudes to Egdon and its limitations and traditions are embodied, as Dr Beatty has shown, in Hardy's descriptions of Mistover Knap and Blooms-End. Captain Vye's house at Mistover Knap has 'the appearance of a fortification'. Blooms-End is separated from the heath only by a row of white palings and a little garden (which orders nature by control, not defence). The traditional mummers find a warm welcome at Blooms-End, the family home of the Yeobrights; while 'for mummers and mumming Eustacia had the greatest contempt'. At Blooms-End, the loft over the fuel-house 'was lighted by a semicircular hole, through which the pigeons crept to their lodgings in the same high quarters of the premises', and the sun irradiated Tamsin as she selected apples from their natural packing of fern, with 'pigeons . . . flying about her head with the greatest unconcern'. At the fuel-house of Mistover Knap, the outsider Eustacia looks in from the darkness at the mummers' rehearsal to relieve her boredom, through 'a small rough hole in the mud wall, originally made for pigeons', but now disused, and the building is lit from the inside.

What the contrasts reveal is that all the stylizations draw their meaning from the underpattern of conflicting light and dark. This central opposition moves the conflict between Clym and Eustacia, to which all the other characters stand in dramatic relationship. Their association with the elemental forces in conflict is defined by the fire and light images which identify them with the Promethean myth, and the images of darkness and death that endow Eustacia additionally with some of the attributes of Persephone Queen of the Shades.

The different manifestations of light and fire which define the characters also define their responses to the leitmotif question 'What is doing well?' Wildeve has the 'curse of inflammability'; Eustacia is a smouldering subterranean fire reaching by blind instinct for the sun; they snatch at the heat of momentary passion in a rebellion that speaks to the twentieth-century rebellion against the permanence of things. Clym's way of opposing the gods of darkness is to bring light rather than fire to mankind. (The name 'Yeobright' is significant in both its parts.) Tamsin is marked by the image of benevolent sunshine. Mrs Yeobright, who has ignored the primitive power of the cosmos in her 'civilized' desires for Clym's advancement, meets death by fire in a parched waste land with a poisonous serpent and a sun that foreshadows the hostile antagonist of Camus' *The Outsider.* Diggory Venn is permeated with the colour of fire, and shares the craft and symbolic ambiguity of the early fire-god Loki. Fire as an answer to darkness can be creative or destructive; an instrument of mastery or chaos. The scenes that carry the underpattern show the characters acting out their ritual roles as bringers of light or darkness to the pattern of human fate.

Clym Yeobright plays the double role of Promethean hero and ironic parody of primitive heroic attitudes. There is no doubt about his altruistic Promethean aspirations. 'The deity that lies ignominiously chained within an ephemeral human carcase shone out of him like a ray'. His absence has taught him that Egdon realities are realities the world over. Yet the context in which we first see Clym at close quarters (Book Second, VI) qualifies our approval of his aim to teach the Egdon eremites 'how to breast the misery they are born to'. At the Blooms-End Christmas party the snug picture framed by the settle does not show much evidence of misery.

'At the other side of the chimney stood the settle, which is the necessary supplement to a fire so open that nothing less than a strong breeze will carry up the smoke. It is, to the hearths of old-fashioned cavernous fireplaces, what the east belt of trees is to the exposed country estate, or the north wall to the garden. Outside the settle candles gutter, locks of hair wave, young women shiver, and old men sneeze. Inside is Paradise. Not a symptom of a draught disturbs the air; the sitters' backs are as warm as their faces, and songs and old tales are drawn from the occupants by the comfortable heat, like fruit from melon-plants in a frame.'

Hardy's selection of concrete detail to build up poetic mood and sequence takes us from the physical effects of the coldness outside to the simple statement that sums up human yearning for fulfilment, 'Inside was Paradise'. The simile of melon-plants in a frame clinches the natural sequence of comfort and growth that order this earthly Paradise—which Clym would jump in his ascetic plans for higher development.

'To argue upon the possibility of culture before luxury to the bucolic world may be to argue truly, but it is an attempt to disturb a sequence to which humanity has been long accustomed.'

Outside the ordered frame of unreflective comfort are Clym, who has passed beyond it, and Eustacia, who has not yet reached it. The conjunction of traditional scene of conviviality, blind animal will to enjoy that has motivated Eustacia's presence, and Clym's 'typical countenance of the future' marked by consciousness of man's tragic predicament in an uncaring universe, questions whether modern perceptiveness may be an unmixed blessing to men untouched by the disillusive centuries and adapted to the world they live in.

Clym's troubles spring from his failure to respect the laws of physical reality. His blindness is both a natural consequence of ignoring physical strain on his eyes, a simplification of the modern complexity of life which denies him 'any more perfect insight into the conditions of existence', and a complex poetic symbol of the figurative blindness displayed by this representative of 'modern perceptiveness' who 'loved his kind', to the needs of the individuals closest to him, and to the nature of his illusions. He is blind to the reality which is in the heath, himself, his mother, Eustacia, and the 'Egdon eremites' he had come to teach how to bear it. He meets its obstructiveness in the common resistance to the kind of progress that jumps the stage of social advance, in the irrational demands of sexual love, in the reality of Eustacia's primitive nature that runs counter to his projected image of her (a fault that makes him brother to Angel Clare and Knight). His sense of affinity with the dead and virgin moonscape (Book Third, IV), and the appearance of the 'cloaked figure' of Eustacia, who is repeatedly associated with night, death, and the moon, at the base of Rainbarrow simultaneously with the eclipse ('for the remote celestial phenomenon had been pressed into sublunary service as a lover's signal') are correlative to his destructive and self-destructive attachment to Absolute Reality.

The failure of Clym's Promethean aim leads one to consider his role as an ironic reversal of the traditional hero-myth. R. Carpenter, in *Thomas Hardy*, sees the heroic archetype in Clym's quest for meaning. His originality is recognized at an early age, he serves his apprenticeship in a foreign land guarding treasure, and becomes possessed of deeper knowledge which he wishes to pass on to his people. His temporary withdrawal from the world suggests the initiation of a sun-god-hero into a religious cult. He returns to his birthplace, a dark and fallen world (Tartarus, the prison of the exiled Titans) but is not really recognized. He is diverted from his quest by a dark and beautiful enchantress against the wishes of his goddess mother, undergoes a period of spiritual trial and is symbolically blinded, like Oedipus and Milton's Samson, so that he may achieve true insight. The counterpointing strain of the hero who triumphs over obstacles to shape destiny, questions the validity, to the modern mind aware of 'the obstructive coil of things', of simple heroic resistance. To Louis Crompton ('The Sunburnt God: Ritual and Tragic Myth in *The Return of the Native*', *Boston University Studies in English*, IV, 1960) Clym is a compound of the free hero of romance, the hero of classical tragedy, subject to fate and moral judgement, whose *hubris* leads to his downfall, and the diminished hero of modern realism, subject to biological and economic laws which limit human responsibility. But the wry comment on ancient heroic standards should not hide the genuine heroism achieved by a man who must painfully scale down his notions of progress to the limitations that condition the slow rate of evolutionary change. ('This was not the repose of actual stagnation, but the apparent repose of incredible slowness.')

The new concept of heroic action redefines Clym's quest as the quest of fallen man to re-establish harmony with nature. Clym takes his first steps towards Paradise regained when he accepts his primitive roots, puts on his old brown clothes, and becomes of no more account than a parasitic insect fretting the surface of the heath. Knowledge is redefined, in a poetic passage that emphasizes each unit of the physical scene with a major stress and pause, as 'having no knowledge of anything in the world but fern, furze, heath, lichens, and moss'. His movements over the heath, feeling, sensing through the dark, bring an intense regenerative contact with the physical world that is a source of strength in misery, even though conscious man can never achieve complete harmony. Hardy's description of Clym working among the small heath creatures, with its details of colour and movement, its varying rhythms of natural activity, its acceptance of the sun's meaning as simple warmth and beauty for the earth's creatures, its delight in vitality, and its superbly simple climax, celebrates like his poetry an enlargement of the horizon within those limited areas where man can still find certainty.

'His daily life was of a curious microscopic sort, his whole world being limited to a circuit of a few feet from his person. His familiars were creeping and winged things, and they seemed to enrol him in their band. Bees hummed around his ears with an intimate air, and tugged at the heath and furze-flowers at his side in such numbers as to weigh them down to the sod. The strange amber-coloured butterflies which Egdon produced, and which were never seen elsewhere, quivered in the breath of his lips, alighted upon his bowed back, and sported with the glittering point of his hook as he flourished it up and down. Tribes of emerald-green grasshoppers leaped over his feet, falling awkwardly on their backs, heads, or hips, like unskilful acrobats, as chance might rule; or engaged themselves in noisy flirtations under the fern-fronds with silent ones of homely hue. Huge flies, ignorant of larders and wire-netting, and quite in a savage state, buzzed about him without knowing that he was a man. In and out of the fern-dells snakes glided in their most brilliant blue and yellow guise, it being the season immediately following the shedding of their old skins, when their colours are brightest. Litters of young rabbits came out from their forms to sun themselves upon hillocks, the hot beams blazing through the delicate tissue of each thin-fleshed ear, and firing it to a blood-red transparency in which the veins could be seen. None of them feared him.'

Clym has recently been demoted from protagonist, and Eustacia promoted, on the grounds that she has the heroic force which he lacks. But it is surely intentional that a character possessing the animal vitality of a more primitive era should make a greater sensuous impact than the new heroic type, 'slighted and enduring', distinguished by contemplative rather than active heroism. The two characters are perfectly balanced in their vital opposition to carry the meaning of the story.

Eustacia's delineation as 'Queen of Night' indicates her function as a reverse parallel to Clym. Her first and last appearance is on the barrow, house of the dead. She shares, while she suffers from, the heath's darkness, 'Tartarean dignity', indifference, and slumbrous vitality. But her relation to Clym is not a simple opposition of darkness to light. It is also the antagonism of illumination at different stages of development.

The first sentence of Chapter vii, Book First, where she is defined as Queen of Night, stresses the two qualities that associate her on one side with the heath and on the other with the Promethean Clym. 'Eustacia Vye was the raw material of a divinity.' Her animal nature, unreflecting and unpurposive ('she would let events fall out as they might sooner than wrestle to direct them') partakes of the blind chaos of the heath's raw material, which has not yet reached Promethean forethought. The many Classical and Romantic metaphors and the 'geometric precision' of her perfect beauty define Eustacia as an anachronistic reincarnation of the Hellenic age whose 'old-fashioned revelling in the general situation' is being replaced by the record of disillusive time (destroyer of beauty) that scars the other faces, of Clym and the heath. But the subterranean fire of divinity is there, chained to an ideal of fulfilment antagonistic to Clym's and out of tune with the haggard times.

Her poetic context in vi defines the sun she seeks for her soul. The cumulative evocation of the wind over the heath, that begins in distinguishing the special notes of the 'infinitesimal vegetable causes' which harmonize to produce 'the linguistic peculiarity of the heath', and rises to a philosophical contemplation of Infinity as it is made sensuously manifest in the sound of the combined multitudes of mummied heath-bells scoured by the wind, is a rich image that evokes simultaneously the timelessness of nonhuman time that diminishes human importance, against which Eustacia rebels, and the absolute loneliness that is the price of her god-like rejection of human compromise. Her challenge to the forces that render beauty ephemeral is 'a blaze of love, and extinction, . . . better than a lantern glimmer . . . which should last long years', and a too thorough identification, suggested by hour-glass and telescope, with the metaphysic of transience.

Eustacia's will to enjoy in the present moment is the universal thrust of life to grow out of the primal stage of blind, self-absorbed groping towards the sun to a state of being where light, form and meaning are imposed on matter. But she is false to her humanity by acquiescing in the lower state, as Clym is false to his by wanting to jump the intermediate stage of evolution to reach the higher. Consequently her environment controls her as it controls the ear of corn in the ground. The two movements down from and up beyond the human norm meet in a god-like desire for absolute reality, which Hardy's poetic transformations of light into darkness define as a form of the death-wish.

Eustacia's dream (Book Second, III) is the first of a series of related ritual enactments of her subconscious drive to self-destruction. A comparison with her mumming adventure (Book Second, V, VI), the Egdon gipsying (Book Fourth, III) and her death (Book Fifth, VII–IX) reveals the fantastic action of the dream ironically transformed and realized in a complex love/death sequence. The shining knight with whom she dances and plunges into the water is transformed from her Paradisal Clym to the commonplace Wildeve. The visor that hides his face turns into the mummers' ribbons that hide hers, as their true natures are concealed by their projected roles. The ecstatic dance becomes a Dionysiac revel that replaces a 'sense of social order' with the self-destructive sexual impulse. The expected consummation under the pool is revealed first as her ritual death at the hands of the Christian Knight in the mummers' play, and finally as the real embrace of death with Wildeve in the weir, for which her ideal knight is partly responsible. The woman who feels she is in Paradise becomes the woman who is excluded, with Clym, from the earthly Paradise inside the settle. The brilliant rainbow light modulates to the moonlight of the mumming and the gipsying, the familiar illusory moonlight existence of Eustacia's imagination, which stresses the fantastic, trance-like ritual aspect of movement and mask-like features. It resolves finally into the hellish red glow from Susan Nunsuch's cottage that reveals the 'splendid woman' who arraigns the Prince of the World as a mere waxen image of pride and vanity, and reconciles Eustacia's death by water to the death by fire consuming her in effigy. The heath that is only dimly felt in the dream looms larger and blacker in the following scenes to block her desire for absolute heroic existence. The shining knight who falls into fragments as the dreamer's translation of 'the cracking . . . of the window-shutter downstairs, which the maid-servant was opening to let in the day', foreshadows the disintegration of her ideal world in face of the obstructive reality of Clym's nature and the world's daylight triviality. Her death sets her in her only 'artistically happy background', where her conflicting drives to darkness and sunlight are reconciled. 'Pallor did not include all the quality of her complexion, which seemed more than whiteness; it was almost light.'

Clym and Eustacia each have a partial truth that bears on the question of how to live. Mrs Yeobright provides another. Her conception of doing well is coloured by Egdon, which she neither loves nor hates, but tries to ignore in her desire to civilize the wilderness. She is one of T. S. Eliot's women of Canterbury, fearful of the 'disturbance of the quiet seasons' and human order from the ultimate powers of the cosmos which Clym and Eustacia know as light and heat and darkness.

Mrs Yeobright is related poetically to the heath and to the elemental struggle of light and darkness by Hardy's visual presentation. When she steps forward into the light of the bonfire in Book First, III, 'her face, encompassed by the blackness of the receding heath, showed whitely, and without half-lights, like a cameo.' The profile etched distinctly on a dark ground, repeated in our first sight of Clym's face (Book Second, VI) and Eustacia's (Book First, VI) suggests inflexible resistance to cosmic darkness.

Her journey across the heath to her death builds up a complex poetic image of her confrontation by the ultimate reality of the cosmos which civilization does not cope with. Its absurdity and hostility to human purpose are demonstrated in the action of the closed door. Poetically, they are embodied in the merciless sun and the parched obstructive earth she has to cross; major symbols of the elemental conflict between Clym and Eustacia which destroys her in its working out. Every image, every word, is selected for sound and sense to evoke a harsh waste land on fire with the blazing sun that 'had branded the whole heath with his mark': the scorched and flagging plants, the air 'like that of a kiln', the 'incineration' of the quartz sand, the 'metallic mirrors' of smooth-fleshed leaves, the moan of lightning-blasted trees. Echoes of Lear and his Fool on the stormy heath in Johnny Nunsuch's innocent questions and statements of fact and Mrs Yeobright's answers charged with experience of human misery, heighten the poetic emotion. But it is controlled by the changing perspective that measures Mrs Yeobright's human effort objectively against the lowly species of the heath 'busy in all the fulness of life' and indifferent to her prostration.

'Independent worlds of ephemerons were passing their time in mad carousal, some in the air, some on the hot ground and vegetation, some in the tepid and stringy water of a nearly dried pool. All the shallower ponds had decreased to a vaporous mud amid which the maggoty shapes of innumerable obscure creatures could be indistinctly seen, heaving and wallowing with enjoyment.'

Human isolation from primal harmony is complete. The 'vaporous mud' and 'maggoty shapes . . . heaving and wallowing' evoke a preconscious world in which human emotion and purpose are anachronisms. If these lowly creatures recall Eustacia's preconscious will to enjoy, the gleaming wet heron who flies towards the sun recalls the unworldly aspirations of Clym, equally antagonistic to Mrs Yeobright's desire for civilization. The ants who share with her the shepherd's-thyme where she lies dying, 'where they toiled a never-ending and heavy-laden throng' in a miniature city street, define the futile bustle of her 'doing well' in face of the sun, which 'stood directly in her face, like some merciless incendiary, brand in hand, waiting to consume her.'

Wildeve's relationship to Egdon and the Promethean light that rebels against it denotes a man who is not great enough to become a force of nature instead of a helpless instrument. Even his vices are petty; his little meannesses about Tamsin's allowance, his trumpery schemes of revenge. Our first sight of him through the window of the Quiet Woman is not of a sharp profile, but an indeterminate 'vast shadow, in which could be dimly traced portions of a masculine contour'. His tendency 'to care for the remote, to dislike the near' recalls Eustacia's and Clym's dissatisfaction with human limitations. But Wildeve cannot initiate rebellion. He can only respond to Eustacia's fire, and be consumed in her flame, like the moth-signal he releases to her.

Tamsin Yeobright and Diggory Venn are grouped together to reflect the passive and active principle of acquiescence in the human condition that is Egdon. Tamsin, the gentle point of rest between the major antagonists, has no awkward ideas about doing well to thrust her out of her environment. Doing simply means marrying for Tamsin, and her firmness on this point helps to retrieve the error of the unfulfilled wedding that begins the novel. The sun-lighted ritual of braiding her hair on the wedding day stresses her adherence to the traditional ordering of birth, marriage, children, and death—one of the few ambitions that tally with the Egdon rate of progress. The images of light and music which introduce her (Book First, IV) imply a relationship to the earth that has not yet become discordant. Benevolent sunshine is her natural form of light, but even on the night of storm and chaos which is a perfect complement to the chaos within Eustacia, Tamsin's sense of proportion and lack of that pride which demands a personal antagonist preserves her from harm.

'To her there were not, as to Eustacia, demons in the air, and malice in every bush and bough. The drops which lashed her face were not scorpions, but prosy rain; Egdon in the mass was no monster whatever, but impersonal open ground. Her fears of the place were rational, her dislikes of its worst moods reasonable.'

Diggory Venn, acquiescing in human limitations while working at the same time, like Oak, with the grain of his environment, has a link with darkness and fire that is ambiguous. When action depends on intimate knowledge of the heath—when he uses the camouflage of turves to eavesdrop on the plans of Eustacia and Wildeve, or when his familiarity with Shadwater Weir enables him to devise a plan of rescue—his triumph is due to the light of human intelligence controlling events. But his sudden appearances and disappearances, his colour, his devil's luck in gambling, his tricksy pranks with their unpredictable outcome, invest him with the poetry of a supernatural folkore character; not so much a 'Mephistophilian visitant' of the Christian era as a primitive fire daemon capable of good or evil. John Hagan points out ('A Note on the Significance of Diggory Venn', *Nineteenth Century Fiction*, XVI, 1961–2) that his well-intentioned interventions solve immediate problems, but initiate unwittingly the long-range tragedy of cosmic cross-purposes: Eustacia's decision to abandon Wildeve for Clym, and the events connected with the closed door.

Hardy's extended description of the reddleman stresses the ambiguity in his character which mirrors the ambiguity of the cosmos. The domestic picture (Book First, VIII) of a peaceful red man smoking a red pipe and darning a red stocking, kindly binding Johnny's wounds with a red bandage, gives way in IX to an evocation of his shadow side. His link with the heath is stressed in the 'blood-coloured figure' which is, like Egdon in storm, 'a sublimation of all the horrid dreams' of the human race. 'Blood-coloured', an alteration from the simple 'red' of the manuscript, takes up the theme of guilt suggested in 'the mark of Cain' simile which defines the effects of reddle, and amplified in the evocation of the reddleman as an isolated 'Ishmaelitish' character (the same adjective describes both the heath and the reddleman) who had taken to the trade as a lifelong penance for criminal deeds. The imaginative details of a legendary inheritance of guilt superimposed on the good and well-balanced human character of Diggory Venn suggest, paradoxically, a harmony with what Egdon means through acceptance of isolation and the guilt inherent in existence. After Clym's agonized self-reproach at Eustacia's death, it is Venn who puts it into perspective.

' "But you can't charge yourself with crimes in that way," said Venn. "You may as well say that the parents be the cause of a murder by the child, for without the parents the child would never have been begot." '

The heightened poetic tone of Chapter VIII, Book Third, where Venn wins back the Yeobright guineas, defines his ambiguous relation to light and darkness in a brilliant sensuous correlative. The overpowering darkness of the heath at night is fitfully broken by various forms of light which illuminate the flat stone, reminiscent of the flatness of the heath, and human participation in a game of chance, which becomes an image of the human predicament. It is natural that Venn's familiarity with the heath should give him an advantage over the excitable Wildeve, who is disturbed by the humbler heath-dwellers. Wildeve's confused actions and Venn's calmness, chance and direction, range themselves with the antagonisms of darkness and light that motivate the novel. The visual presentation of Venn as a 'red automaton' raises him to the plane of a supernatural agent of fate. But his human lack of knowledge that half the guineas were destined for Clym qualifies his control of the situation.

The ritual patterns in the scene intensify its effect as a glimpse of destiny working itself out on another plane. In the heightened poetic tension, Venn's ballad-like incantation of the incremental phrases of Wildeve's gambling stories as the money coils in in reverse direction; the night moths which circle the lantern twice; the heath-croppers who encircle the gamblers twice, 'their heads being all towards the players, at whom they gazed intently'; the thirteen glow-worms placed in a circle round the dice, take on the aspect of mechanical functions of fate controlled by the 'red automaton'. The moths attracted to the light and the death's-head moth which extinguishes the lantern to the accompaniment of 'a mournful whining from the herons which were nesting lower down the vale', foreshadow in symbol and detail the deaths of Wildeve and Mrs Yeobright.

The transformation of a folklore character into a mundane dairy farmer with a bank balance in Book Sixth worries some critics. While Hardy's note to Chapter III indicates that his 'austere artistic code' did not originally plan such a transformation, Venn's change tallies with the laws that condition Egdon's rate of progress. The cycle of aeons as well as the cycle of seasons directs his evolution from a 'nearly perished link between obsolete forms of life and those which generally prevail'. It is part of the movement of the novel from primitive darkness to conscious understanding appropriate to the modern era.

The poetic development of the novel is completed by a return to the visual image of 'a motionless figure standing on the top of the tumulus, just as Eustacia had stood on that lonely summit some two years and a half before'. But the transformation of Eustacia into Clym has replaced the dark winter night with summer afternoon, isolation with relationship to man and the lower species, and the self-absorbed unconscious drives of nature with hope of redemption through man's consciousness of the roots from which he sprang. Clym's suffering has taught him that love of place or woman is not enough without understanding, and that in order to move forward on Egdon one must move back.

To know Egdon is to know the great forces that move the world. It is not isolated from the rest of space, and time. Vapours from other continents arrive upon the wind, and rare migrants as well as native species watch the alien movements of man in a setting that 'seemed to belong to the ancient carboniferous period'. Egdon contains all the elements of the world before the Fall, including a secluded Paradise and a serpent. All its Promethean characters are seeking a place where they will feel at home after the development of isolating consciousness. Their survival depends on their reassessment of the place where they are. Hardy's sensuous evocation o the heath and its effect on human fate makes its physical presence impossible to ignore. At moments of crisis its 'oppressive horizontality' gives Clym, and others, 'a sense of bare equality with, and no superiority to, a single living thing under the sun'. There is no special place in nature for man. But from the heath's dark negation springs that affirmation of its raw vitality and that yearning for the light which combine to enable conscious man, as part of the general Will, to

> Bend a digit the poise of forces,
> And a fair desire fulfil.
>> ('He Wonders about Himself')

IX

The Mayor of Casterbridge:
A Novel of Character and Environment

The Mayor of Casterbridge, like *The Return of the Native*, is primarily a novel of environment in relation to character. But instead of the almost changeless face of Egdon heath, with its few scattered inhabitants, the factor that controls the action is the evolving social organism of Casterbridge the county town. The novel reflects the changes that were taking place in Casterbridge, and beyond, in the nineteenth century: the increasing mastery over environment, the advance of mechanization, the development of new business methods to keep pace, the importance of education for a rapidly changing world, the breaking down of social barriers, the spread of co-operative and humanitarian principles. The concept of a static world in which changes are only superficial was being replaced by the evolutionary concept of change as ultimate reality.

The plot, with its epic hero representing a whole culture and way of life, the characters, situations, and rhythms of narrative movement, are subtly balanced in relation to the Casterbridgean environment of space, time, and society, to form a poetic correlative of the inevitable on-going of the world. The two chief characters, Michael Henchard and Donald Farfrae, are engaged in a commercial struggle that brings in the new order to supersede the old.

'The break between Henchard and Farfrae is not so much between personalities as between methods, the capacities of different generations to meet changing needs. For Henchard's muscle, Farfrae substitutes brain, for energy system, for antiquated drudgery the efficiency of the machine. Thus Henchard's downfall is more than personal; like the downfall of the archetypal tragic hero it signifies the passing of an era, of ways which have outlived their purpose. By the end of the novel Henchard is one with the patriarchal shepherd who appears briefly in the market place to survey an alien world that has no use for him.'
(D. A. Dike: 'A Modern Oedipus: *The Mayor of Casterbridge*'
Essays in Criticism II, 1952)

The movement of the plot, divided clearly into a prologue and six acts, or the stanzaic steps of a ballad, is one of reversal that recalls Greek tragedy. It climbs upward through intensifying conflict and complication to a peak point—Henchard's bankruptcy, and the hag's disclosure—from which he falls and Farfrae rises. The movement is repeated, fugue-like, a little later in the fall of Lucetta and the rise of Elizabeth-Jane. The Prologue tells, in the simple rhythms of fable, of Henchard's sale of wife and daughter, the act to which all subsequent action looks back. The rest of the story plots his double pursuit of the affection he has sold to his ambition, and of the self-destruction he unconsciously invites to punish the guilt of self-assertion against the limitations of the human condition.

The twenty-year gap between prologue and the drama proper stresses the link between crime and punishment. The first act shows his wilful violation of human relationship apparently bearing fruit. He is rich, successful, and the Mayor of Casterbridge. But the seeds of his destruction are already there; in the corruption of bread, for which his ignorance is responsible (which, as a spoiling of nature, recalls the furmity hag's corruption of wholesome furmity and its consequences); in the return of Susan and her daughter, hand in hand—a detail that compels comparison with the isolation of Henchard from his wife at the beginning of the story—and in his appointment of the astute Farfrae as his manager. But the re-marriage of Susan and Henchard brings the act to a close on a note of apparent retrieval of past error.

The second act robs Henchard of affection—friend and manager Farfrae, wife, and child. Farfrae is lost to him through the possibilities of division that are present, together with the possibilities of creative partnership, in the new ideas of the man 'frae far'. Susan is lost through death, and Elizabeth-Jane through his disregard of Susan's instructions not to open, until the girl's wedding day, the letter which discloses that she is Newson's daughter. The irony of reversal operates again when Elizabeth-Jane's removal to the house of Lucetta, the lady whom Henchard 'ought' to marry for conventional reasons, and Henchard's withdrawal of his objection to Farfrae's courtship of Elizabeth-Jane, results in Farfrae's attraction to Lucetta.

The third act graphs the competition in business and love between Henchard and Farfrae, and Henchard's failure in the ambition which he substituted for affection. In the conflict between old

197

and progressive ideas, in the foresight and judgement needed to safeguard Casterbridge crops and Casterbridge entertainment from uncertain weather, Farfrae gains ground and Henchard's wrongheaded impulsiveness leads to bankruptcy. His social status receives 'a startling fillip downwards' by the furmity hag's disclosure in court of his sale of Susan, which robs him of the moral right to lead the flourishing town. Reversal of roles with his rival is complete when Farfrae buys his house and business, employs him as workman, marries the woman he was going to marry and eventually Henchard's stepdaughter, and becomes Mayor of Casterbridge.

Act four charts the degradation and increasing isolation of the former Mayor. The close of his period of teetotalism marks violations of human dignity that recall the beginning of the novel; the anathema on Farfrae, the fight in the loft, the self-humiliation at the Royal visit. Twenty-four hours sees violent reversals. The pomp of the Royal visit is parodied by the grotesque skimmity in the evening; Lucetta is dead in the dawn after her triumph; Henchard's murderous attack on Farfrae in the morning is balanced by his desperate attempt to warn Farfrae of Lucetta's illness in the evening. Finally, his new hope of affection from Elizabeth-Jane is qualified by the return of Newson, who brings with him, like Farfrae in act two, possibilities for good or ill, and is sent away with a lie.

The fifth stage is a period of regeneration for Henchard; of renewed contact with love through Elizabeth-Jane, and with the natural world untouched by big business through his little seed-shop. He schools himself to accept Elizabeth-Jane's growing love for Farfrae, but the uneasy interval comes to an end with Newson's second return and Henchard's departure from Casterbridge, outwardly the hay-trusser who had entered it twenty years ago. The final act brings him to full stature as the tragic, isolated, self-alienated scapegoat, whose impulse to self-destruction sends him to die like an animal on the heath after Elizabeth-Jane's rebuff and his refusal 'to endeavour strenuously to hold his own in her love'.

Hardy's poetic readings of life, the stylized ironies of reversal and substitution, are evident in a mere recital of the events. Hardy was conscious of the packed incidents.

'It was a story which Hardy fancied he had damaged more recklessly as an artistic whole, in the interest of the newspaper in which it appeared serially, than perhaps any other of his novels, his aiming to get an incident into almost every week's part causing him in his own judgment to add events to the narrative somewhat too freely . . . though it must be said in favour of the plot, as he admitted later, that it was quite coherent and organic, in spite of its complication.'

(Life)

The incidents that affect Henchard's life are like violent hammer blows set in motion by his first violent act. A chain of eventful arrivals which substitutes something else for the thing desired—Farfrae's friendship for wife and child, Susan and Elizabeth-Jane for Farfrae, Lucetta for the daughter lost in Elizabeth-Jane, and Farfrae for Henchard in Lucetta's affections—leads the mind back inevitably to the first link in the chain, the substitution of ambition for love. The crises are brought about by revelation of hidden acts: the sale of wife and child, Henchard's association with Lucetta, the secret of Elizabeth-Jane's birth. Accidents and coincidences add their effect to acts of human wilfulness. Some can hardly be called accidents; Henchard's impulse to self-punishment places him in the way of bad luck. Nothing else can account for his entrusting Lucetta's letters to his enemy Jopp, or his rashness in acting on the long-range forecast of the weather-prophet without waiting for the oracle's full development. The return of Susan, Newson, Lucetta, and the furmity hag (who appears in court on the one day when Henchard is sitting as substitute magistrate): the appearance of Farfrae at the very moment when Henchard needs his knowledge to get out of a difficulty; the bad weather that intensifies his failure by the failure of others involved in his speculations—stress the long arm of coincidence. But not all the coincidences are disastrous—Henchard's sight of his substitute self, the effigy, in the water saves him from suicide—and the poetic mood created by the stylized plot makes them credible as correlatives of the past and its claim to atonement.

The plot owes some of its emotional force to the feeling that it is archetypal. The myth of human responsibility and rebellion against the human condition is deep-seated. Henchard is overtly or implicitly compared with Achilles, Ajax, Oedipus, Orestes pursued by the Furies, Cain, Saul, Samson working in the mill of the Philistines after his fall, Job, Coriolanus, King Lear, and Faust. Farfrae can be regarded as the Creon to his Oedipus and David to his Saul; Elizabeth-Jane as the Cordelia to his Lear. The Abel to his Cain, and Fool to his Lear, is provided by Abel Whittle, who represents, at Henchard's first clash of principle with Farfrae (xv) and at Henchard's death, the brotherhood which the self-alienated man had rejected and finally embraced. His self-alienation and impulse to self-destruction recall more modern heroes: Emily Brontë's Heathcliff, Melville's Captain Ahab, Conrad's Lord Jim and Razumov, the ambiguous heroes of Gide and Dostoievsky, Camus' Meursault. Older than any literary manifestation is the seasonal rite of the corn-king supplanted, after ritual combat and supernatural agency (furmity hag and weather-prophet) by his adopted 'son' in his role as virile leader of an agricultural community. The ancient myth of the scapegoat-king meets the modern saga of the nineteenth-century self-made man deposed by the new order of big business, in a penetrating study of the alienation from self and natural harmony that follows the guilt of wilfully imposing conscious desires on the human condition.

The alienation suffered by Henchard and his feminine counterpart, Lucetta (who suffers in a pathetic, not tragic, capacity) is expressed through scenes that function as dramatic metaphor. The scenes of civic ritual point to the gulf between appearance and reality that is a vital theme of the story. The bow window that separates the banqueters at the King's Arms from the 'plainer fellows [that] bain't invited' also puts a stage-frame round the feast. The disharmony within, the distorted shapes of the diners, the straight-backed figure in the Mayoral chair, distance the scene to a mock representation of Mayoral responsibility. Elizabeth-Jane's relationship to the public image—'the natural elation she felt at discovering herself akin to a coach'—is later balanced by the bankrupt Henchard's sight, through the same window, of the reality of the love he has missed in Elizabeth-Jane. It is the public image which Henchard wishes to preserve. When he is superseded in his civic role, he crumbles to the nothingness implied by his will.

The high drama of the police court faces his public image with the reality of the past action his appearance has denied. The furmity hag is part of his past, and so part of the self he cannot escape. The power of that other self is one of the notes that creates the rich resonance of Chapter XLI, where Henchard gazes at his effigy-self in Ten Hatches Weir. The savage ritual of the skimmity which placed effigies of himself and Lucetta in positions of inverted honour, recalls the past of that other self and points to his future fate as scapegoat outcast for the sins of existence. Yet at this juncture the sense of a magical substitution saves the life of the man who cannot escape from himself. The phenomenon has a natural cause, yet the theatrical, hallucinatory effect of the scene becomes symbolic of a Dostoievskian ultimate reality of the divided self.

The skimmity ride is a caricature of the Royal visit, whose pomp has already been parodied within itself by the drunken Henchard, drawing down on his grotesque image of Mayoralty the degradation imposed by the real Mayor Farfrae. The maid's description of the effigies' dress—an effective adaptation of the Greek messenger technique—dramatically diminishes the civic importance of Henchard and Lucetta to a puppet show of hollow pomp and poses covering an inharmonious past.

' "The man has got on a blue coat and kerseymere leggings; he has black whiskers, and a reddish face. 'Tis a stuffed figure, with a falseface. . . . Her neck is uncovered, and her hair in bands, and her back-comb in place; she's got on a puce silk, and white stockings, and coloured shoes." '

The market place, where many of the important scenes of the novel are enacted, takes on the character of a commercial stage. 'The *carrefour* was like the regulation Open Place in spectacular dramas, where the incidents that occur always happen to bear on the lives of the adjoining residents.' There, men assume the roles and 'market-faces' required by buying and selling. Seen from Lucetta's window, they take on distortions ('men of extensive stomachs, sloping like mountain sides; men whose heads in walking swayed as the trees in November gales') that compel comparison with the dehumanizations of the banqueters: gigantic inflations caused by the ready money they represent to Casterbridge, which misshapes reality. Lucetta, who believes that she can remain in the wings as a mere spectator ('I look as at a picture merely') is forced onto the stage because her house is part of the *carrefour*. High Place Hall has a market face of Palladian reasonableness, counterpointed by the distorted mask, recalling the grotesque theatrical masks that hang over the proscenium arch, that marks a past of intrigue and violence. It is significant that Henchard chooses this entrance to make his renewed contact with Lucetta.

The commercial stage, viewed through Lucetta's window, defines her relationship with Farfrae. Their common sympathy for the predicament of the old shepherd and the courting couple, whose relationship is threatened by the commercial standards of the hiring fair, and its resolution by Farfrae's compassion, draw hem together. The old shepherd remains in the memory as a poetic symbol of the human cost of the new market techniques introduced in the next scene. Lucetta is linked to the seed-drill by the assumption of a role that foreshadows, through the leitmotif of colour, both her triumph and tragedy. Her decision to be 'the cherry-coloured person at all hazards' links her to the red machine, to the future of Farfrae and the commercial values of Casterbridge, and to the 'puce silk' of her effigy that comments on the hollowness of her role. The artificial brightness of her appearance is suddenly placed by the reality of the sun, which is in harmonious relationship with the drill.

'The sun fell so flat on the houses and pavement opposite Lucetta's residence that they poured their brightness into her rooms. Suddenly, after a rumbling of wheels, there were added to this steady light a fantastic series of circling irradiations upon the ceiling, and the companions turned to the window. Immediately opposite a vehicle of strange description had come to a standstill, as if it had been placed there for exhibition.'

The metaphor of the stage, in fact, is one which pervades the novel. The action grows out of dramatic conflict, and life is seen as a vast arena where the battle for survival takes place. The Ring has always been an arena for violent and tragic spectacle. Its ghosts and skeletons are a memorial to the military power of the Romans. Reverberations of gladiatorial combat, the law of force, add pathos to Henchard's furtive meetings there with Susan and Lucetta. As Henchard leaves Casterbridge, the metaphor sums up his experience. 'He had no wish to make an arena a second time of a world that had become a mere painted scene to him.' It recalls, with compassionate irony, Elizabeth-Jane's hopeful entry into Casterbridge, which was to her a romantic sunset backdrop of 'towers, gables, chimneys, and casements'—romantic, but not insubstantial—and the earlier sunset backdrop that defines Henchard's act of human violation as part of a great cosmic drama.

'The sun had recently set, and the west heaven was hung with rosy cloud, which seemed permanent, yet slowly changed. To watch it was like looking at some grand feat of stagery from a darkened auditorium. In presence of this scene after the other there was a natural instinct to abjure man as the blot on an otherwise kindly universe; till it was remembered that all terrestrial conditions were intermittent, and that

202

mankind might some night be innocently sleeping when these quiet objects were raging loud.'

The prologue concentrates into a dramatic scene, which has the starkness of a ballad, the themes that operate in the wider world of Casterbridge to drive Michael Henchard to destruction. He enters the novel anonymously, as the 'skilled countryman' defined by his clothes, his tools, and 'measured, springless walk'. The atmosphere of 'stale familiarity' that surrounds him and Susan identifies him with the universal drabness of the human condition, embodied in the long dusty road,

'neither straight nor crooked, neither level nor hilly, bordered by hedges, trees, and other vegetation, which had entered the blackened-green stage of colour that the doomed leaves pass through on their way to dingy, and yellow, and red.'

The 'noises off' of Weydon Fair counterpoint the drabness with the search for gaiety that is another familiar Hardy image. Henchard's sale of his wife, to the background noises of 'the sale by auction of a few inferior animals, that could not otherwise be disposed of', in a blaze of narrative intensity, challenges human limitation with a self-assertive act that violates the deepest human, natural and moral instincts.

The swallow, seeking escape from the mercenary perversion of nature inside the tent, provides a moment of equilibrium, always present in Hardy's work, when human choice could give fate a different turn; and looks forward to the caged goldfinch of XLV, which symbolizes the consequences of the act that made Henchard unfree. But Henchard assumes his role and his destiny. The result is to turn a stage play into reality, with 'the demand and response of real cash' which is to become a symbol of power in Casterbridge.

'The sight of real money in full amount, in answer to a challenge for the same till then deemed slightly hypothetical, had a great effect upon the spectators. Their eyes became riveted upon the faces of the chief actors, and then upon the notes as they lay, weighted by the shillings, on the table.'

The meaning of the scene—Henchard's obsessive desire to sacrifice human relationships to the power of money—is pointed by the similarity of Susan's warning, 'If you touch that money, I and this

203

girl go with the man. Mind, it is a joke no longer', to Farfrae's, when he clashes with Henchard over respect for Abel Whittle.

' "I say this joke has been carried far enough."
"And I say it hasn't! Get up in the waggon, Whittle."
"Not if I am manager," said Farfrae. "He either goes home, or I march out of this yard for good." '

The prologue ends with a return of leitmotifs. The morning after, the drabness of the cosmos is accentuated by the buzzing fly and the barking dog; Henchard's isolation by routine family matters proceeding at all levels: 'He went on in silent thought, unheeding the yellowhammers which flitted about the hedges with straws in their bills'. But the movement from lurid candlelight through darkness to the newly risen sun, from the temporary man-made structure of the tent and its man-made commercial atmosphere to the fresh September morning on the uplands 'dotted with barrows, and trenched with the remains of prehistoric forts', to the church where Michael Henchard is defined for the first time by name and the conscious purpose of his oath, stresses the rhythm of defeat and regeneration, degradation and redefinition, that marks the life of Michael Henchard in Casterbridge. The whole movement, with its foreshadowing in stark dramatic terms of the delicate balance between human dignity and vaulting ambition, its market ethics, and its denial of nature and responsibilities formed in the past, ends with a widening out from the claustrophobic tent to the social world where the balance will be worked out.

'Next day he started, journeying south-westward, and did not pause, except for nights' lodgings, till he reached the town of Casterbridge, in a far distant part of Wessex.'

The solidity of Hardy's evocation of Casterbridge, both concrete and poetic, vouches for its effect on the characters. The plane of myth and fable in the prologue modulates to the plane of physical reality as Elizabeth-Jane moves from the fairy-tale transformation of Henchard to the local voices and local issues of bad bread which prove the fairy-tale Mayor vulnerable. But continuity with the prologue is there, in the evocation of Casterbridge as a town in vital contact with the forces which Henchard's act had denied or embraced—nature, the past, and the values of the market.

The environment that changes lives is itself in a continuous process of change, without which there is no progress. The passing of time finds its correlative in the clocks, chimes, and curfews; the seasonal character of the shop-window display; references to Casterbridge features no longer in existence. And while Casterbridge is growing in stature by virtue of its size and favourable position, the three visits to Weydon stress that 'pulling down is more the nater of Weydon', where 'the new periodical great markets of neighbouring towns were beginning to interfere seriously with the trade carried on here for centuries.' These cyclic rhythms of rise and fall, seen and heard through the observant senses of Elizabeth-Jane as she approaches the town, prepare us for their re-enactment in the career of the man they are seeking. The square-ness she notes in Casterbridge is repeated in the descriptions of the Mayor, its representative citizen; its conservative distrust, 'huddled all together', in his inflexible attitude to new inventions.

The approach of the two women, downhill towards the town, is sensuously realized in a description that moves from the archi-ect's plan ('to birds of the more soaring kind') to an elevation drawn in increasing detail as its features are encountered by 'the level eye of humanity'. Yet it is not a blueprint. The details are elected to form an impressionist picture of an interlocking 'mosaic-work of subdued reds, browns, greys, and crystals' in vital pattern-elation to the 'rectangular frame of deep green' and the 'miles of rotund down and concave field' that held the individual pieces in shape. The architect's eye and the poet's selective detail provide a comment on the relationship of Casterbridge individuals to their surroundings. The weather- and time-nibbled church, the indivi-dual voices of curfew and clocks, add the dimension of time to Hardy's evocation of Casterbridge in space. The cumulative poetic effect is to make the entry of the two unassuming women into the boxed-in 'snugness and comfort' of the town through the dark avenue of trees, an image of the tragic solitary human condition. Then, the individual sounds modulate into the communal brass band, and the still-life picture begins to move with the rhythms of vigorous natural life.

The physical position of Casterbridge, 'a place deposited in the block upon a corn-field', without transitional mixture of town and down, is essential to its growth as a living organism. It retains a vital link with nature, which Henchard corrupts and Farfrae res-pects, in his treatment of the corrupted grain, his purchase of the seed-drill that takes the chance out of sowing, his creative use of the tree-lined walk for his entertainment, and his respect for human dignity.

'Casterbridge was the complement of the rural life around; not its urban opposite. Bees and butterflies in the cornfields at the top of the town, who desired to get to the meads at the bottom, took no circuitous course, but flew straight down High Street without any apparent consciousness that they were traversing strange latitudes. And in autumn airy spheres of thistledown floated into the same street, lodged upon the shop fronts, blew into drains; and innumerable tawny and yellow leaves skimmed along the pavement, and stole through people's doorways into their passages with a hesitating scratch on the floor, like the skirts of timid visitors.'

The poet's sensitive ear for sound quality—'circuitous', 'innumerable', 'skimmed', 'stole', 'a hesitating scratch', soft feminine consonants and singing vowel progressions, realizes the insidious creep of nature into the lives of Casterbridge citizens. The simile that ends the paragraph prepares for the timid visitors who are about to remind Henchard of his offence against natural law.

Dr Beatty (op. cit.) has made a fruitful comparison of Hardy's Casterbridge with Dickens' Coketown (*Hard Times*, 1, Chapter x) which is what Casterbridge was not—one of the 'many manufacturing towns which are as foreign bodies set down, like boulders on a plain, in a green world with which they have nothing in common.

'In the hardest working part of Coketown, in the innermost fortifications of that ugly citadel, where Nature was as strongly bricked out a killing airs and gases were bricked in, at the heart of the labyrinth of narrow courts upon courts, and close streets upon streets, which had come into existence piecemeal, every piece in a violent hurry for some one man's purpose, and the whole an unnatural family, shouldering and trampling, and pressing one another to death; in the last close nook of this great exhausted receiver, where the chimneys, for want of air to make a draught, were built in an immense variety of stunted and crooked shapes, as though every house put out a sign of the kind of people who might be expected to be born in it; among the multitude of Coketown, generically called "the hands"—a race who would have found more favour with some people, if Providence had seen fit to make them only hands, or, like the lower creatures of the seashore, only hands and stomachs—lived a certain Stephen Blackpool, forty years of age.'

Nature is bricked out: consequently Coketown reflects denial of life in its piecemeal shapelessness, deformity, and embrace of death

The individuals and buildings of Casterbridge 'which spoke so cheerfully of individual unrestraint as to boundaries' reflect the penetrating forces of life and growth (which can, however, be destructively distorted by the power of money). Casterbridge is not an 'exhausted receiver', but 'the pole, focus, or nerve-knot of the surrounding country life'. Coketown depends on utilitarian 'hands' minus the creative brain to direct them. The 'unnatural family' of Coketown, put there for the sole purpose of making money, compels contrast with the interrelationship of all the Casterbridge people, from the Mayor to the labourers, with the staff of life that grows in the surrounding cornfields.

Differences of style in Dickens and Hardy stress the difference between the two towns. The complex sentence that takes up most of the page mirrors the piecemeal labyrinthine construction of Coketown. The subject, closing the sentence, suggests the neglect of the human being who should provide meaning to the heaped-up phrases. The picture of Casterbridge in Chapter XIV as 'the complement of the rural life around; not its urban opposite', is built up by an accumulation of complementary details—farmer's boy/town clerk, judge/sheep-stealer, barns/main thoroughfare.

'Here lived burgesses who daily walked the fallow; shepherds in an intra-mural squeeze. A street of farmers' homesteads—a street ruled by a mayor and corporation, yet echoing with the thump of the flail, the flutter of the winnowing-fan, and the purr of the milk into the pails—a street which had nothing urban in it whatever . . .'

The synthesis of incongruities, the rhythmic cadences, and the onomatapoeic diction of the final sentence, evoke the sensuous vitality of Casterbridge as only a poet can.

The reality of the evocation gives authenticity to the mythical aspects of the story. The diminished perspective, through Elizabeth-Jane's eyes, of Farfrae and Henchard 'ascending to the upper end of the long street till they were small as two grains of corn' is an image natural to the evocation of man linked with nature, but it remains in the memory to qualify, a moment later, the correlative of Henchard's importance, the five loaded waggons of hay marked with his name. The shifting perspective of the link established here returns as leitmotif in XXVII, to invest the collision of Henchard's loaded waggon and Farfrae's with the mythic significance of ritual combat between corn-king and successor.

The link with nature in Casterbridge is often integrated with evidence of past layers of Casterbridge life. The wall of Henchard's house 'was studded with rusty nails speaking of generations of fruit-trees that had been trained there', and the open doors of the houses passed by Elizabeth-Jane reveal a floral blaze 'backed by crusted grey stone-work remaining from a yet remoter Casterbridge than the venerable one visible in the street'.

The 'past-marked prospect' of Casterbridge, dotted with tumuli, earth-forts, Roman remains, and evidence of violent blood sports and man's continuing inhumanity to man, is a physical reminder of the barbarity of a ruthless competitive battle for survival, still present (as in Mixen Lane) under the civilized front. Henchard is placed in a setting that speaks of the primitive past (II, XI, XXXV, etc.), which both diminishes and enhances his ephemeral dignity, whenever he tries to disown his own past. Significantly, it is from the massive prehistoric fort of Mai-Dun that he sees the past he tried to deny catching up on the present, in the figure of Newson striding relentlessly along 'the original track laid out by the legions of the Empire', to claim his daughter.

Casterbridge as a market town has symbolic value. The market, as D. A. Dike points out, organizes the values and desires of the citizens. The perennial problem of a market town is to preserve respect for the individuality of human beings who are cogs in a machine for making money. Henchard and Lucetta, who buy and sell human relationships, fail to keep the balance. Lucetta's offer of money to pay Henchard's debts on the day she had broken faith with him to marry his rival; Henchard's gift to her sent 'as plaster to the wound'; the annuity he settles on Elizabeth-Jane to rid himself of her presence when the discovery of her parentage makes her worthless stock in his eyes; his gift of five guineas to buy Susan back again; his free entertainment; his reaction to Farfrae's disinterested help, 'What shall I pay you for this knowledge?'; his insult to the self-respect of Jopp and Whittle when business cannot wait for their tardy arrival; all are repetitions of the original violation of love by measuring it in the commercial terms of the market place. Farfrae, on the other hand, manages to keep the delicate balance between humanity and business. It is in the market place, appropriately, that he shows respect for the family unit of the old shepherd as well as for the revolutionary seed-drill. Abel Whittle, another man who has cause to thank Farfrae's respect for human dignity, sums up the meaning of the change from Henchard's ownership of the corn business to Farfrae's.

' "Yaas, Miss Henchet,' he said, 'Mr. Farfrae have bought the concern and all of we work-folk with it; and 'tis better for us than 'twas—though I shouldn't say that to you as a daughter-law. We work harder, but we bain't made afeard now. It was fear made my few poor hairs so thin! No busting out, no slamming of doors, no meddling with yer eternal soul and all that; and though 'tis a shilling a week less I'm the richer man; for what's all the world if yer mind is always in a larry, Miss Henchet?" '

Casterbridge is a more complex Egdon heath, in that it represents the given conditions of life which the characters variously adjust to or defy. Their responses to the values of nature, the past, and the market control the curves of their lives. Henchard's career, after the bid for freedom that enslaves his life and liberates his awareness, is a hard-won progress through rejection of market ethics to integration with the past and the family he had cast off, and finally to the realization that he can love what is beyond market price and not his own, in Elizabeth-Jane.

The primitive past and primitive nature operate in Michael Henchard's instinctive impulses, usually disastrous in a modern civilization that must progress morally. The elemental and animal imagery that defines him ('moving like a great tree in a wind', 'leonine', 'tigerish', 'a bull breaking fence'); his energy and inarticulacy, his retrogression to brutal loneliness after his defiance of the moral order; his recourse to rivalry for love, territory, and possessions; his admiration for ruthless business methods in and out of the market; the touchstone of brute strength in all things which makes him despise Farfrae's slight physique while admiring his brains, and give himself a handicap before he fights Farfrae in the loft—are all traits that link Henchard to the pre-human world. The instructions he leaves for his burial are appropriate for an animal—one whose conscious self-assertion against nothingness has failed. When, stripped of everything that built up his public image as man and Mayor, he accepts the nothingness under the robes of office; a nothingness that is physically present in the mud hovel where he dies, scarcely distinguishable from the ancient natural world of Egdon Heath, and advances to the unselfish love which alone can make him significant, Henchard has risen, paradoxically, from the status of a magnificent animal to the nobility of man.

In Casterbridge Farfrae is faced with the same chances and conditions of success or failure. But his character and the needs of the time are on his side. In a social organism where further progress depends as much on co-operation as competition, Farfrae is the man whose chariot they will follow to the Capitol. No-one could be less of a gloomy being who had quitted the ways of vulgar men. While Henchard believes that superiority can only be maintained by standing aloof, Farfrae can be found dancing reels at his co-operative entertainment and singing songs at the Three Mariners, where, we remember, Henchard violated the social ritual of music by forcing the choir to sing an anathema on his rival. He has no past to hide, and no market face required by a role that is different from his reality. He provides the education, method, intelligence, foresight, drive, judgment, sympathy and respect for others, and swift adaptation to conditions of environment, which is lacking in Henchard's 'introspective inflexibility.' The reign of chance and rule of thumb comes to an end under Farfrae's leadership. The new seed drill is symbolic of man's increasing mastery of his environment: 'Each grain will go straight to its intended place, and nowhere else whatever!' His ability to live with honour and dignity within human limitations balances the other great value of Henchard's defiance.

The relation of Henchard's other rival, Newson, to the market ethics of the place where he is an alien passing through (as his name suggests) is double-edged. He holds the rights of property, by which Henchard has lived, and which deal the last blow to his hopes of Elizabeth-Jane. His unpossessiveness is an effective foil to Henchard's possessiveness, yet it is a bitter irony that soon after the wedding he leaves his daughter. Henchard is not capable of the abnegation of identity by which Newson drops out of Susan's life, until the terrible negation of his Will. Yet Newson's too facile acceptance of another man's wife and contribution to the skimmity suggest that the character he negates is not deep. However, he is more socially acceptable to Casterbridge than the deeper-souled Henchard, because he never attempts to disguise his real character, slight as it is. Hence his closeness to the ballad stereotype of the genial, open-handed sailor is a merit rather than a defect in characterization.

Newson shares with Susan Henchard, that other lightly-sketched but convincing ghost from the past, a fidelity to the basic human loyalties expressed for her by the simple moral code of the unlettered peasant. It is founded on acceptance of cosmic injustices and the cyclic movement of lives and seasons. Market ethics is something Susan suffers from, as a woman dependent on a man,

210

but does not subscribe to in her individual values. Her momentary flash of independence at Weydon Fair has the fatalistic assumption of property rights behind it—

' "Will anybody buy her?" said the man.
' "I wish somebody would," said she firmly. "Her present owner is not at all to her liking!" '

—but her feeling for the continuity of past with present (it is fitting that she should be buried in the old Roman burial ground) and present with future, in her desire for a wider horizon for her daughter, liberates her from Lucetta's need to snatch feverishly at evanescent present pleasures.

Lucetta and Elizabeth-Jane compel comparison in their response to Casterbridge. The values of the market impel Lucetta's emotions and actions.

' "I was so desperate—so afraid of being forced to anything else—so afraid of revelations that would quench his love for me, that I resolved to do it off-hand, come what might, and purchase a week of happiness at any cost!" '

The commercial terms in which her confession of marriage to Farfrae is worded, her assessment and use of her ephemeral beauty as an asset of marketable worth, her treatment of Elizabeth-Jane as a counter in her pursuit of a man, now as bait for Henchard, now as 'a watch-dog to keep her father off' when 'a new man she liked better' appears, her concern for external appearance, suggest how thoroughly Lucetta has embraced market ethics. She has tried to repudiate her past in the change of environment from Jersey to Casterbridge, and the change of name from Le Sueur to Templeman 'as a means of escape from mine, and its wrongs.' She has also rejected the role she could have taken in Casterbridge. Ostensibly she is the stranger, like Farfrae, who brings new ideas into the town. Her furniture, contrasting with Henchard's old-fashioned, pretentious Spanish mahogany, is fifty years ahead of the Casterbridge times. Her ability to distinguish between true culture and false in Elizabeth-Jane, as Henchard cannot (' "What, not necessary to write ladies'-hand?" cried the joyous Elizabeth') provides an ironic comment on the gulf she makes in her own life between appearance and reality, past and present. What might have been remains in the mind as the external image she has built up crumbles under the skimmity ride's rude revelation of what lies underneath. It kills her, but keeps Henchard alive, because his will to defy circumstances makes him more than the puppet of his role.

It is fitting that Hardy draws Lucetta from the outside, while Elizabeth-Jane's thoughts and feelings guide the reader's emotions. She is trustworthy and balanced, because she does not admit any gulf between appearance and reality, past and present, nature and civilization. Consequently the values of the market cannot touch her. She can see nothing wrong in waiting on at the Three Mariners to pay her board, speaking dialect, or picking up coals for the servant—all 'social catastrophes' to Henchard. She refuses to be treated as a chattel either by Henchard or Lucetta. The confusions that surround her name do not affect the intrinsic worth of her character, which Henchard comes to value. The social forms of a simple moral code are not artificial conventions to which she pays only lip-service, but expressive of her deepest convictions. However, there is a final appeal from them to the basic instinctive loyalties she inherits from her parents. It is the same woman who shares the adversity of the man she believes to be her father, and who would 'root out his image as that of an arch-deceiver' to return to a still deeper loyalty of the past, even though by current social standards recognition of Newson's paternity makes her illegitimate. The mood built up by Hardy's picture of Casterbridge in its natural setting, in Chapter xɪv, leads to the poetic suggestion of her affinity with that world, when the wheat-husks on her clothes make the instinctive contact with Farfrae that her mother had desired. Her vision of the past as continuous with the present is reflected in her 'study of Latin, incited by the Roman characteristics of the town she lived in', in contrast to Lucetta's irreverent attitude. Though she balances the enterprise of Farfrae by keeping 'in the rear of opportunity', her desire for knowledge, to make the furnishings of her mind match the furnishings of her beauty, faces her towards a future of complex change—the future of Tess and Jude—where the simple unquestioning values of the older generation will prove inadequate to human experience.

The meaning of those values, expressed through characters and action, is assessed by the Casterbridge people, who both suffer from change and have the elective power to bring it about. The Hardeian chorus is divided into one main and two subsidiary groups, whose social and moral status is marked by their inns. At the top and bottom of the social scale, the King's Arms and Peter's Finger groups are both deceived by appearances. The King's Arms, where Henchard is seen in his success, tests his worth by his actions. But the story reveals that the truth about the curse sung on Farfrae, the hag's disclosure, and Henchard's failure to preserve correspondence between bulk and sample, is more complex than their simple definitions of hatred, immorality, and dishonesty.

If the vision of the King's Arms is distorted by wealth and the power of the civic image, the grotesque effigy of vice created by Mixen Lane is just as far from the truth. Mixen Lane is a negative place, doomed to extinction. The negative way of life is threatened by the vitality of Henchard's bid to achieve meaning. (One can compare the situation in John Whiting's play, *The Devils*.) Reality for them is measured by the failings, not the virtues, of the more vital characters. Hardy's presentation of Mixen Lane makes it less of a place than a human problem correlative to the unlocalized guilt of godless man. Physical description is limited, but a selection of details—the white aprons covering vice, the swivelling eye at a man's footfall, the concealed plank that significantly connects the cancerous tissue with the body of Casterbridge, the dampness, the ruined Priory, the patched structure of Jopp's cottage that conceals the broken lives within, and the symbols of crime—gaol, hangman's cottage, gallows—poetically evoke the misery and guilt that operate, in Henchard and Lucetta, to provide the 'missing feature' needed to complete the design of the gallows—'the corpse of a man' (xix). Their sense of guilt accepts the judgment of Mixen Lane too seriously. One must wait for Jude Fawley to find a man capable of bearing personal and inherited guilt alone.

The 'philosophic party' of rustics who frequent the friendly, unpretentious Three Mariners provide the most realistic judgement on Casterbridge affairs. Their concern with the essentials of labouring and victualling, bringing up their children, and burying their dead leaves them little time to be influenced by appearances. The two-dimensional inn sign of traditional worthies symbolizes the values of their traditional community. There are no barriers at the Three Mariners. Even the horses stabled at the back mingle with the guests coming and going, and the inn has given hospitality to the Mayor and to members of the Peter's Finger group. The ale lives up to its promise, and no one sings out of tune until Henchard chooses the Three Mariners to break his vow and their traditional Sunday custom. Though they do not put too fine a point on honour ('why *should* death rob life of fourpence? I say there was no treason in it') they take a kindly interest in the careers of Farfrae and Elizabeth-Jane, and their judgement of Elizabeth-Jane (XXXVII and XLIII) severs her intrinsic worth from accidents of family connection and environment. Their response to Farfrae's mixture of commonsense and idealism (which does not preclude criticism of his musical sentiment, 'What did ye come away from yer own country for, young maister, if ye be so wownded about it?') places the promise of the new age firmly in the commonalty of the Three Mariners.

Yet it is through the workfolk of Casterbridge that Hardy sounds the deep elegiac note for the passing of the old order, in the deaths of Susan and Michael Henchard. Direct death-bed scenes do not attract Hardy, for the meaning of a life that defies death is to be found in its effect on the survivors. The biblical and Shakespearean cadences of Mrs Cuxsom's elegy on Susan join with homely Wessex idiom, and the refusal to be overawed by sentiment in contemplation of Coney's theft of the penny weights, to celebrate her patience and endurance, her closeness to the facts of the earth, and the necessity for preserving human dignity in death, 'that 'a minded every little thing that wanted tending.'

The sublime tragic simplicity of Whittle's elegy on Henchard, with its physical details of his last hours offset by the bond of compassionate love (' "What, Whittle," he said, "And can ye really be such a poor fond fool as to care for such a wretch as I!" ') which has become Henchard's ultimate value, defines the meaning of his life with a fierce affirmation of love and pain that makes the negations of his Will positive. The Biblical rhythms of deep emotion in the elegiac Wessex voice are the pervading rhythms of Hardy's poetic images of the human condition; of a lonely heroic man, outside the traditional rituals that celebrate the human dignity which his Will refuses, creating his own moral order and meaning.

'Then Henchard shaved for the first time during many days, and put on clean linen, and combed his hair; and was as a man resuscitated thenceforward.'

(XLI)

' ". . . God is my witness that no man ever loved another as I did thee at one time. . . . And now—though I came here to kill 'ee, I cannot hurt thee!" '

(XXXVIII)

214

' "If I had only got her with me—if I only had!" he said. "Hard work would be nothing to me then! But that was not to be. I—Cain—go alone as I deserve—an outcast and a vagabond. But my punishment is *not* greater than I can bear!"

He sternly subdued his anguish, shouldered his basket, and went on.'

(XLIII)

Henchard's tragic plight is threefold: cosmic (representative of man's predicament in an uncaring universe), social (showing the plight of a rural community when old methods are swept away by new) and personal. But it is intense poetic response to the personal tragedy that makes *The Mayor of Casterbridge* cosmic tragedy that will stand comparison with the Greeks and Shakespeare.

X

The Woodlanders:
A Novel of Assimilation

'On taking up *The Woodlanders* and reading it after many years I think I like it, *as a story*, the best of all. Perhaps that is owing to the locality and scenery of the action, a part I am very fond of.'

(Life)

Hardy's explanation of his preference for *The Woodlanders* '*as a story*' by 'the locality and scenery' implies a close organic connection between plot and the poetry of place. The story hinges on Melbury's struggles to lift his daughter above the levelling processes of life. The larger rhythms of woodland and orchard counterpoint the assertion of his will with intimations of 'how the whitey-brown creeps out of the earth over us' to assimilate the personal movement of human life to the impersonal drive of nature. The tension between the two movements, expressed with a poet's sensitivity to language and rhythm, generates an emotion of lyrical force. It could not, however, have been expressed in a lyric. The insidious creep of time towards absorption into the earth demands the extended action of a novel.

The plot is a metaphor of the Unfulfilled Intention that pervades the natural world with manifestations of frustrated desire. Social status, a weapon of sexual selection in the human species, is integral to the tragedy. The emotional relationship which combines a group in chain formation where each character loves the one who is a step higher in social grade, leads to frustration for everyone. The permutations of the group are changed, as Hardy so often changes them, by intervention from another environment; the aristocrats Fitzpiers and Felice Charmond, who disturb the simple workable moralities of the woodlanders, rooted in nature and tried by tradition, with their urban values and complex psychology. 'In the simple life he [Melbury] had led it had scarcely occurred to him that after marriage a man might be faithless.' Melbury's misplaced trust in civil law, foreign to the unwritten 'household laws' that kept Hintock stability, gives a blow to Winterborne's revived hopes which weakens him and leads, with other apparently trivial causes, to the most tragic unfulfilment of all—his death and assimilation into the woods.

In no other novel perhaps, does the natural environment permeate human life so thoroughly. Egdon Heath dominates by its physical mass: the atmosphere of the Hintocks, composed of myriads of frail individual lives of many species struggling for survival, creeps into the very bones and minds of the woodlanders. Egdon concentrates: the woodland disperses the characters in a confusion of purposes that recalls Shakespeare's dark wood near Athens, and Matthew Arnold's darkling plain. Its character-limitations, scene, climate, crafts, traditions, and folklore determine the kind of action that takes place there.

'It was one of those sequestered spots outside the gates of the world where may usually be found more meditation than action, and more listlessness than meditation; where reasoning proceeds on narrow premisses, and results in inferences wildly imaginative; yet where, from time to time, dramas of a grandeur and unity truly Sophoclean are enacted in the real, by virtue of the concentrated passions and closely-knit interdependence of the lives therein.'

The woodlanders are involved closely in the battle of natural selection that links all species in a mystery of suffering. Trees, woodland creatures and human beings alike sound the dominant note of pain at the disharmony of natural things interrelated in 'one great network or tissue which quivers in every part when one point is shaken, like a spider's web if touched' (*Life*); a disharmony made poignant so often by the human character given through imagery to vegetation:

'They went noiselessly over mats of starry moss, rustled through interspersed tracts of leaves, skirted trunks with spreading roots whose mossed rinds made them like hands wearing green gloves; elbowed old elms and ashes with great forks, in which stood pools of water that overflowed on rainy days, and ran down their stems in green cascades. On older trees still than these huge lobes of fungi grew like lungs. Here, as everywhere, the Unfulfilled Intention, which makes life what it is, was as obvious as it could be among the depraved crowds of a city slum. The leaf was deformed, the curve was crippled, the taper was interrupted; the lichen ate the vigour of the stalk, and the ivy slowly strangled to death the promising sapling.'

Trees rub each other into wounds; dripping hedges ruin garden plots; Giles sets traps to catch the rabbits who eat his winter-greens; the cramps of Melbury's old age are the long credits of time and nature, 'the net product of the divers sprains and over-exertions that had been required of him in handling trees and timber when a young man': the creeping damps and heavy rains kill Giles when he is too weak to fence them off. The sombre isola-tion of the woodland drives the two aliens, Fitzpiers and Felice Charmond, to seek interest and human assertion in each other. The enclosed situation of Hintock House, built 'when shelter from the boisterous was all that men thought of in choosing a dwelling place, the insidious being beneath their notice', is 'a stimulus to vegetation' and 'prejudicial to humanity'.

The action takes colour from the meditative spirit of the Hin-tocks and the insidious nature of evolutionary change. There are some traces of the more sensational Hardy: in Fitzpiers' bloody head at Mrs Charmond's window, in the stereotyped picture of the *femme fatale* which Mrs Charmond presents to Fitzpiers' eyes, and in the passionate lover from South Carolina whose sole function is to shoot Mrs Charmond. But they do not destroy the unity of tone imposed by the woodland context. Fitzpiers' bloody head is expressionistic of the pain and guilt of an affair which the appari-tion prevents from being broken off. It is not necessary for Mrs Charmond to be more than another subjective reflection of 'joy accompanied by an idea' which promises Fitzpiers escape from the levelling influence of the Hintocks. The lover from South Caro-lina, in his one physical appearance, can be defended as part of the symbolic context. His incongruous appearance in evening dress at the ancient Midsummer rites, his theatrical aspect, his definition as 'Satan pursuing us with his hour-glass', his rout of girls and animals which drives both Grace and Suke Damson into Fitzpiers' arms, mark him as an expressionistic dramatic symbol of modern values and the irrational power of time and circumstance imping-ing grotesquely on the woodland world; not inappropriate to an evening that begins in divination and ends in the ritual of nature's larger purposes (Fitzpiers' sexual pursuit of a village girl in the moonlit hayfield). But in general, the plot is developed less through sensational coincidences and catastrophic events than through an accumulation of small acts and isolated purposes rubbing each other into wounds through the close interdepen-dence of Hintock lives. Grace's early arrival at Sherton, and Melbury's at Winterborne's party, cutting across his unhurried country rhythm; the slug well-boiled in its natural home which somehow came upon Grace's plate; Mrs Charmond's decision to go abroad without Grace, which Melbury erroneously attributed to the ill-fated party held just before; the coincidence of Grace's flight with Winterborne's illness and the Autumn rains, and of Fitzpiers' accident with Mrs Charmond's determination to fly from him—these seemingly trivial concurrences are signs of cosmic cross-purposes as surely as the struggling species in the woodland scene. Marty's letter, 'the tiny instrument of a cause deep in nature', produces a mixed bag of delayed consequences that she could scarcely have wished, since they included two violent deaths as well as the desired object of returning Fitzpiers to his wife. The battle for right of way in a narrow lane between Mrs Charmond's carriage and Winterborne's loaded timber waggon, resulting in her refusal to disturb 'the natural course of things' by renewing the lease of his house, dooms her affair with Fitzpiers as well as Winterborne's romance with Grace, and undermines his health by the loss of his shelter. The houses themselves, doomed to be absorbed into an estate Mrs Charmond did not want, hung on a group of lives, at last attenuated to 'the one fragile life—that had been used as a measuring-tape of time by law'. And old South's life, the measuring-tape of time, depended on the life of a tree.

The poetic underpattern of *The Woodlanders* is appropriately a close network of interrelated images which make it the despair and delight of the critic. Every scene and every character triggers off a wealth of thematic reflection and cross-reflection that develop under the human action the stylized ritual of nature's larger purposes working themselves out through character and event. Sometimes Hardy's voice makes comparison explicit. When Grace tends the dying Winterborne, Hardy reminds us of Mrs Charmond's care of the wounded Fitzpiers: 'Outwardly like as it had been, it was yet infinite in spiritual difference; though a woman's devotion had been common to both.' Sometimes a simple juxtaposition points forward to an implied contrast. 'The lights in the village went out, house after house, till there only remained two in the darkness.' One comes from the house of 'the young medical gentleman in league with the devil', the other lights Marty South in league with nature at her woodland work. The force of the juxtaposition comes home a few pages later. The rapidly changing colour of Fitzpiers' light does not augur well for the adjustment to

Marty's woodland world of a doctor reputed to be in league with the powers of chaos.

> 'Almost every diurnal and nocturnal effect in that woodland place had hitherto been the direct result of the regular terrestrial roll which produced the season's changes; but here was something dissociated from these normal sequences, and foreign to local knowledge.'

The literal situation may imply a comparison that is metaphorical. Mrs Charmond lost in the woods is matched by Melbury, out of his depth in the laws and deceptions of a complex civilization. Different actors placed in the same situation comment on both actors and situation. The party given by Giles, where the Melburys are ill at ease, adds resonance to and gains from the supper given by Mrs Melbury where Fitzpiers is the outsider. Hardy is adept at setting up tensions between different social classes and different levels of sensitivity by the small thing that jars—oil on the chair, a slug in the wintergreens, Creedle's rough and ready method of serving, the desire of the woodland community to welcome Fitzpiers as one of themselves when he wants to preserve his identity by keeping aloof.

As an artist, Hardy knew the value of a 'frame' which concentrates attention on a pictorial or dramatic composition, and points to vital comparisons by altering a few details when the image recurs. We get our first view of Marty South through the window of her cottage, in a shaft of light, hard at work. The scene, to Barber Percomb,

> 'composed itself into an impression-picture of extremest type, wherein the girl's hair alone, as the focus of observation, was depicted with intensity and distinctness, while her face, shoulders, hands, and figure in general were a blurred mass of unimportant detail lost in haze and obscurity'.

Marty's hair, thus picked out as the central feature in a framed composition, links the scene to two more portraits framed by the window. In the second, Grace sees her writing what proves to be the fatal letter to Fitzpiers about Mrs Charmond's borrowed attraction. In the third, Fitzpiers, returning repentant to the Hintocks after the death of Mrs Charmond, sees Marty, hard at work again, polishing the dead Winterborne's tools. 'His glance fell upon the girl's rare-coloured hair, which had grown again.' His reference to the cause of his regeneration, and his help in buying Winterborne's cider-making equipment so that Marty can continue his seasonal work, stresses the cumulative force of Marty's hair as a fertility talisman. Its 'rape' in the first chapters (likened to the rape of Sif's hair in Norse fertility myth by Loki, the capricious and deceiving god who bears some resemblance to Mrs Charmond) has been retrieved, at the cost of suffering and death, by the continuance of natural growth.

Grace's meetings with Fitzpiers, contrasted with her fruitful association with Giles, are framed and reflected in images whose details invest her choice between two men and two worlds with the significance of a choice between the forces of life and death, appearance and reality. Her first sight of Fitzpiers, asleep, inspires a simile of death—'a recumbent figure within some canopied mural tomb of the fifteenth century'—which looks forward to the sparse ruins of the Oakbury Fitzpiers property, melancholy evidence of the near-extinction of the doctor's ancient family. (The man of modern scientific notions springing out of primitive medievalism is an interesting forerunner of Thomas Mann's definition of the daemonic death wish, combining progression and regression, in *Dr Faustus*.) Their significant experience of each other at his meeting is of reflections in the mirror. It is a warning from the subconscious powers of the dangers of Fitzpiers' platonic idealism—'Nature has at last recovered her lost union with the Idea!'—and wish-projection of 'joy accompanied by an idea which we project against any suitable object in the line of our vision', which Giles bluntly defines as 'what we call being in love down in these parts, whether or no.' Grace's mysterious compulsion by the reflected image, which differs from the reality in having its eyes open, recalls 'The Fiddler of the Reels' and folklore of demonic possession through the reflected image. Her hurried exit and return to the house so that Fitzpiers sees her coming instead of going, out of the natural order of things; the imagery taken from theatrical speech and gesture, the overtones of deception to come, add to the dream-like quality of the scene, and invest it with the importance of a compressed subconscious drama of the action that depends on Grace's choice. The scene ends with a reminder of Fitzpiers' association with death and dissection, in the view of John South's brain reflected under a microscope. It throws the mind back to the true woodlander's living link with trees, and the very different first meeting of Grace and Giles under the apple tree,

221

indubitably real and muddy but symbolic of future bloom and growth.

Fitzpiers' reflected world of reality recurs in action and scene, contrasted with the physical world as it is, in Chapter xix. He surveys the woodland scene, and makes his approach to Grace on the strength of his impression, from the sentimental viewpoint of an observer, reading his book inside the shelter while the physical process of bark-ripping, its sights, sounds, smells, textures, surrounds him with the reality at the heart of the sylvan scene. The reality includes 'great undertakings on the part of vegetable nature' which he is too indolent to copy, ancient timber stories and traditions which his lack of association with place and people present and past cannot make meaningful, and the economic facts of woodland life which are inextricably involved with the display of Marty's superior skill. Her position 'encaged amid the mass of twigs and buds like a great bird' in branches which had 'caught the earlier rays of the sun and moon while the lower part of the forest was still in darkness' may tinge her with the light of a tree-spirit but the poetic fact depends on the economic fact. ''Tis only that they've less patience with the twigs, because their time is worth more than mine.' As Grace and her father leave the magic firelit circle which has shaped a new stage in the relationship of Grace and Fitzpiers, and they spare a thought for the distanced Giles contemplating his apple bloom while their carriage wheels crush the minute forms of life underneath, the feeling built up by the interplay of narrative, scene, and memory of that first meeting with Fitzpiers charges their departure with the force of a rejection of Winterborne's world of life and growth and reality.

Hardy's dramatic and pictorial composition of scenes where human relationships are interwoven with the seasonal movements of woodland work, from planting to felling, gives the poetic under-pattern the resonance of myth where human beings ritually act out their archetypal roles. The shrouding and felling of the tree to which John South's life is mysteriously linked is one of the inter-related generative images of the poetic network which sharply focuses the theme of man's connection with the natural world. It involves all the main characters, to whose fortunes the tree, a kind of Hintock Yggdrasil, is central, in a compressed symbolic drama, but never loses sight of the modern facts that carry the ancient ritual. While South's belief in his link with the tree reflects the sympathetic magic that expressed primitive man's sense of kinship with nature, there is a rational explanation of his 'terrifying illusion' in the action of the wind. The disaster that overtakes him and his kin when the tree is felled, attested by primitive belief in the tree-soul, has its modern cause in the lifehold conditions attached to South's cottages. Much of the scene's evocative power lies in the poetic interplay between mystery and fact, rational and irrational, different expressions of the same thing—a close natural interdependence that can only be broken at great risk.

It is broken, symbolically by Mrs Charmond, to whom the tree belongs and the cottages revert at South's death, and actually by Fitzpiers, whose rational remedy does not allow for the strength of old forest faiths (reinforced by Grammar Oliver's reversion to type). These two aliens drive a destructive wedge between the kinship loyalties, sacred to the woodland code, that arose out of the mutual interdependence imaged in the world of nature. Giles Winterborne, forced to operate on the tree by Fitzpiers' orders, seals the loss of his houses and his own death as well as South's. His ascent up the tree, 'cutting away his perches as he went', gathers layer upon layer of meaning. It dramatizes the destructive power of modern thought and codes, which cut away the stability of man's roots in nature and the past. As he works higher up the tree in darkness and mist which is likened to Niflheim, the Norse region of cold and death, 'cutting himself off more and more from all intercourse with the sublunary world', the distancing becomes more than physical. Grace's snub moves him fatally out of the everyday world of human concerns. 'He could only just be discerned as a dark grey spot on the light grey zenith', as the sound of boughs falling and the stroke of his billhook, and, when he descends, by a shiver and sigh from the tree that expresses his emotion. His identification with tree and sky, his distance from the human world on the ground, the loneliness and shade of the woodland reflected in his position and gesture, invest him with the impersonal role of wood-god climbing towards the otherworld doomed to death and absorption into his non-human environment. The ritual aspect comes out in his contact with Grace, which places her share of responsibility for destroying the fruitful connection between man and nature. He calls her twice; twice she passes by. On the third passing, she calls twice to him. His decision to move higher up after her snub, which pushes him out of his merely human into his archetypal role, may also carry an implied criticism of his acquiescence in his fate.

'Had Giles, instead of remaining still, immediately come down from the tree to her . . . the probabilities are that something might have been done . . .'

The episode gains retrospective ritual force from later episodes, which gather richness from it in turn. Giles Winterborne's call to Grace from the heights of South's tree—'Thinking that she might not see him, he cried, "Miss Melbury, here I am" '—presents Grace with a vital appeal to recognize his, and her, identity with the natural world. The cost of her failure to do so recalls this scene when she sits luxuriously in the 'Earl of Wessex', the poor little rich girl of folklore, figuring as a fine lady on the balcony above, separated from Giles cider-making in the yard by the window, the height, and the nature of the choice she made under South's tree. The appeal is ritually reversed. Twice she calls down to him to recognize her superiority to the workaday world. He recognizes her finally by a stern rebuke for her choice of separation, which has contributed to his misery. And Winterborne's last illness gains accumulated resonance from these two scenes by the repetition of his separation from Grace, though both are now at ground level, by a window. Through the window of his hut she gives him his meals, calls but fails to make him hear, and knows him only through a handclasp in the darkness. His isolation from human contact and her separation from the organic world are complete.

The deeper meaning that accumulates into myth and the factual, sensuous descriptions of Giles at his seasonal work are inseparable. Grace's desire to escape from the levelling processes of the Hintocks embodies the modern alienation from physical conditions, including the march of time, that is treated more fully in *Tess* and *Jude*. Her meetings with Giles, actively engaged in his seasonal work, at points of crisis and conflict between her two worlds, surround her with the mud, the whitey-brown, the natural transformations which are inescapable. Winterborne's control of the physical world through working with its produce imposes a pattern of meaning on the physical chaos that is sombre but satisfying. It is the pattern of fertility ritual, which involves Grace, like all the heroes and heroines of the major novels, in a process of regeneration through contact with her roots in the earth, and deepens the social theme with anthropological significance.

The pervading sight and smell of apples, which characterizes the

Hintocks to Barber Percomb in the first chapter, becomes a recurring metaphor for the regenerative process. Winterborne's first meeting with Grace, fresh from her expensive education, 'looking glorified and refined to much above her former level', occurs under the boughs of the specimen apple tree he is trying to sell in Sherton market place.

'Winterborne, being fixed to the spot by his apple-tree, could not advance to meet her: he held out his spare hand with his hat in it, and with some embarrassment beheld her coming on tip-toe through the mud to the middle of the square where he stood.'

The distance between their worlds is already implied by the mud, the embarrassed gestures, the identification of Winterborne with his tree, 'being fixed to the spot' by it like a local tree-god; and re-iterated later by Grace's inability to distinguish between bitter-sweets and John-apples. The pictorial composition of the cider-making at the 'Earl of Wessex' recalls her earlier reluctance in the same town to cross the mud to more abundant life. 'She had felt superior to him then, and she felt superior to him now.' The named varieties of apples quivering in the hopper, the rich colours, the stress on verbs of energetic action, the poet's sensitivity to rhythm and diction, bring the physical process to our senses, and recall the vitality of a link with nature that Grace has rejected. But the ritual movements, and the appearance of Giles, coated with apple-rind and pips like a primitive fruit-god, bring to the surface an intuitive response to her need. When Fitzpiers defines himself as a different species to the workers in the yard, Grace replies, 'And from me, too, then. For my blood is no better than theirs.'

Grace's recognition of identity prepares for the regenerative process that starts with her third meeting with Giles in his ritual aspect, in the rich Autumn landscape that places him as 'Autumn's very brother', as she returns from watching Fitzpiers ride away to his new love on the gentle horse that was Winterborne's gift to Grace. Every detail of colour, movement, gesture, and speech in the chapter contributes to a pattern of association that opposes the vitality of a controlled relationship with nature's fertility to its abuse in Fitzpiers' infatuation. The scene begins with a memory of Chapter XIX, that links the spring promise of that scene to its Autumn fulfilment in human and natural life. Fitzpiers, looking towards Mrs Charmond's residence, leans over the gate on High

Stoy Hill where in the earlier scene, fresh from a romantic encounter with Fitzpiers, Melbury and Grace had noticed the rejected Giles contemplating his apple blossom. The recapitulation points the ironical difference from the original: the emotional disturbances experienced between the two scenes have changed the underlying harmonies to re-direct the story. A transitional minor harmony has been supplied by the memory that High Stoy Hill was also the spot from which Melbury pointed out the decayed Fitzpiers property, now significantly used by a local farmer for his young stock. The rustic opinion that Darling has been 'hag-rid' after her long journey to Middleton Abbey points to the irrational 'black magic' character of Fitzpiers' infatuation, later opposed by the 'white magic' of the horse's natural instinct (embodying Winterborne's natural wisdom) which brought her unconscious rider safely home—a scene that has some of the resonance of the sleepwalking episode in *Tess*. Her pale colour, which defines her rider clearly against the background—'the sky behind him being deep violet she could still see white Darling in relief upon it'—looks back to Winterborne's identification with the grey sky surrounding South's tree, and forward to his blending with the Autumn landscape.

As Fitzpiers moves away from her, Grace accepts the evil that is part of nature's carefully detailed natural bounty. 'In all this proud show some kernels were unsound as her own situation.' It is the turning point of her recovery. Fitzpiers' movement *away* from her is answered ritually by Giles and Creedle 'moving up the valley towards her', defined as god-like symbols of fertility and regeneration by the reflected sunlight on their tools and the sensuous perceptions.

'He looked and smelt like Autumn's very brother, his face being sunburnt to wheat-colour, his eyes blue as corn-flowers, his sleeves and leggings dyed with fruit-stains, his hands clammy with the sweet juice of apples, his hat sprinkled with pips, and everywhere about him that atmosphere of cider which at its first return each season has such an indescribable fascination for those who have been born and bred among the orchards. Her heart rose from its late sadness like a released bough; her senses revelled in the sudden lapse back to Nature unadorned.'

The dance-like figure which replaces the destructive Fitzpiers with the regenerative Giles who 'had arisen out of the earth ready to her hand'; the vital sensuousness of his description in terms of autumn's colour, texture, smell, produce, and process; the rhythm, that rises to little climaxes of stress on nature's seasonal products, and leads to a relaxation in sound and sense, 'Her heart rose from its late sadness like a released bough', vividly embody Grace's return to a living relationship with nature through love for a human being. Their shared experience of the sunset, a correlative of 'her abandonment to the seductive hour' and the natural passion ritually expressed in Giles' caress of the flower at her breast, compels comparison with the sunset that defines Fitzpiers' caprice when he refuses the Budmouth practice to stay near Mrs Charmond. 'His motive was fantastic, glowing, shapeless as the fiery scenery about the western sky.' The passion of Giles and Grace has its surrogate climax in complete identification with the 'bottomless medium of soft green fire', but it is anything but shapeless. Its development is controlled by the creative art of nature.

'They passed so far round the hill that the whole west sky was revealed. Between the broken clouds they could see far into the recesses of heaven . . . the eye journeying on under a species of golden arcades, and past fiery obstructions, fancied cairns, logan-stones, stalactites and stalagmite of topaz. Deeper than this their gaze passed thin flakes of incandescence, till it plunged into a bottomless medium of soft green fire.'

The regenerative power of Giles acting out his deeper purposes sustains Grace while she waits for news of a divorce. His ritual death completes for her the meaning of his role as Autumn's brother. 'Autumn, this year, was coming in with rains', which kill as well as fertilize. The vital colour of the earlier Autumn figure is recalled by the absence of colour in the dark wood and the destructive violence of the storm that is 'only an invisible colourless thing'. The living sunlight that defined the scene is shut out by lush foliage. The darkness and images of death remind us that much of Autumn's colour and fertility is provided by decaying vegetation. Hardy gets every ounce of emotive value out of the traditional elegiac associations of rain, darkness, and decay, which invest the objective world of the woodland with Grace's state of mind and the reader's expectation of tragedy.

'The plantations were always weird at this hour of eve—more spectral far than in the leafless season, when there were fewer masses and more minute lineality. The smooth surfaces of glossy plants came out like weak, lidless eyes: there were strange faces and figures from expiring lights that had somehow wandered into the canopied obscurity; while now and then low peeps of the sky between the trunks were like sheeted shapes, and on the tips of boughs sat faint cloven tongues.'

The absence of definition by colour and 'lineality' robs the human being, isolated in a wood full of decaying vegetable presences, of personal identity. Grace 'seemed almost to be apart from herself—a vacuous duplicate only. The recent self of physical animation and clear intentions was not there.' Giles' gentle slide towards death mirrors the absorption of all human, animal and vegetable purposes into the whitey-brown of the earth, that is the obverse side of Autumn fertility. The man who was 'fixed to the spot' by his apple-tree, house and local ties is gradually pushed out of the social structure of the Hintocks till he is revealed as essentially continuous with nature. After the loss of his houses he 'retired into the background of human life and action thereabout' to become a wanderer, like Tess and Jude. From a shadow of his former self he dissolves into the wood by imperceptible degrees. As Grace's isolation from him increases—the isolation of the conscious human being in a non-human universe—she and the reader are overwhelmed by woodland sights, sounds, and textures. 'The stopping of the clock for want of winding' places her in a world of non-human time. The eft that rustles out to bask in the last sun-rays, the lower species investigating Winterborne's hut with a view to winter quarters, the thrush who steals his untouched food; the evocation in sound and sense of decaying vegetation whose individual struggles for fulfilment are backed by evidence of past defeats by time, 'Dead boughs were scattered about like ichthyosauri in a museum', and linked inextricably to human life and death in the image of 'rotting stumps of those of the group that had been vanquished long ago, rising from their mossy setting like black teeth from green gums'; all add up to an overpowering sense of transience and trespass. As Giles moves down the evolutionary scale, distinguished at first by a cough that sounds like a squirrel or a bird, then as a 'voice . . . floating upon the weather as though a part of it', and finally indistinguishable, as 'an endless monologue, like that we sometimes hear from inanimate nature in deep secret places where water flows, or where ivy leaves flap against stones', the meaning of identity with the natural world, so often sounded as his keynote, comes home with tragic force to the modern reader, developed beyond the primitive, hardly conscious needs answered once by fertility ritual.

The three elegies that mark Winterborne's death bring together the natural, social and cosmic themes which make his life and death an inevitable poetic outgrowth of the woodland evocation that began the novel. The first is the lament of nature (recalling the lament for Baldur the Beautiful) for the loss of his controlling power.

> 'The whole wood seemed to be a house of death, pervaded by loss to its uttermost length and breadth. Winterborne was gone, and the copses seemed to show the want of him; those young trees, so many of which he had planted, and of which he had spoken so truly when he said that he should fall before they fell, were at that very moment sending out their roots in the direction that he had given them with his subtle hand.'

The simplicity, the poetic precision that infuses the fact with deep elegiac emotion, is achieved through the run of the sentences—the first cut off abruptly with short vowels and hard consonants; the second, after a check at 'want of him', gathering strength as it expresses the continuity of life in which Winterborne was involved, with stress falling on the words that develop the regenerative process from death to new growth. It casts the mind back to Giles in the fullness of his life planting firs with Marty, and harmonizes the two deep notes sounded then that immortalize his quality both as a natural genius (in both senses of the word) and as a man; his 'marvellous power of making things grow', and Marty's perception of universal *lacrimae rerum* in the sighing of the young pines. It stresses the regenerative power of his life and death, which functions even as he lies dying while Grace runs for help: 'The spirit of Winterborne seemed to keep her company and banish all sense of darkness', the same rain that killed him lighting the path with phosphorescent gleams; and looks forward to the muted regeneration of Grace and a more considerate Fitzpiers, whose gift to Marty of Giles' cider-making equipment ensures the continuation of his memory, genius and work. It sounds again the dominant keynote of the novel, sounded at the beginning, where the descriptive details (the trees which make the 'wayside hedges ragged by their drip and shade', the leaves which *bury* the track, the *tomb-like stillness*, the melancholy associations called up by emotion and scene of past charioteers now *perished*, the 'blistered soles that have trodden [the highway] and the tears that have wetted it') introduce the novel with overtones of pain and death, loss, transience, vanished generations in the agelessness of natural process, assimilation to the earth, human isolation, and the insignificance to the larger movements of nature of the human figure who stands on the deserted road uncertain of his way: overtones which are now fulfilled.

The elegy of Robert Creedle mourns the loss of Winterborne to a community. Spoken in the simple, rhythmic idiom of Wessex workfolk whose contact with concrete things and the earth evokes the loss of a physical human presence, it laments the practical agricultural worker, the end of a local family, and the goodness that makes Giles a mainstay of Hintock tradition.

' "Forgive me, but I can't rule my mourning nohow as a man should, Mr Melbury," he said. "I ha'nt seen him since Thursday se'night, and have wondered for days and days where he's been keeping. There was I expecting him to come and tell me to wash out the cider-barrels against the making, and here was he . . . Well, I've knowed him from table-high; I knowed his father—used to bide about upon two sticks in the sun afore he died!—and now I've seen the end of the family, which we can ill afford to lose, wi' such a scanty lot of good folk in Hintock as we've got. And now Robert Creedle will be nailed up in parish boards 'a b'lieve; and nobody will glutch down a sigh for he!" '

Creedle speaks for the rustic chorus (less comic, less prominent and more integrated into tone and movement than in the previous major novels) whose communal memory holds the codes and traditions of the locality. They measure character and action by their adjustment to the Hintock world. Mrs Charmond is 'the wrong sort of woman for Hintock, hardly knowing a beech from a woak'. Fitzpiers is censured for his roving eye, and Grace for making workfolk traipse seven miles needlessly in search of her at the end of the novel. Melbury deplores Grace's equivocal status, neither married nor single, because it 'will always be remembered against us in Hintock'. Though Hintock law cannot provide the last word on modern problems of a complex civilization, the rustics dramatize the ability to make limited opportunities endurable through fixed responses hallowed by local tradition; lack of ambition; a way of life that remains close to nature while improving on its morality by control, mutual loyalties, respect for others and the sacredness of life; respect for truth; and a long memory that enshrines the transient life in the hero-myths of Hintock. It is the

Hintock memory that inspires Winterborne's sacrifice for Grace's reputation, which some modern critics find absurd or proof of impotence—a view not shared by Hardy. Creedle's elegy ensures a place for Giles as a local hero.

The last elegiac voice in the novel is Marty South's, sounding the simultaneous chords of love, pain, life and death that combine in the elegies to Emma Hardy. It combines personal sorrow with remembrance of the immortal good in Winterborne's way of life as a woodland worker and human being. While intensifying the elegiac tone of the opening chapters to shape the novel to a harmonious close, Marty's elegy stresses the loss of moral fineness in the human consciousness that makes the fall of a man so much more tragic than the fall of a leaf. 'You was a good man, and did good things.' It is appropriate that Marty—Winterborne's counterpart as the spirit of the woods in its purity, versed like him in the language of the woods and now his living heir—should begin and end the novel by pointing the difference between the purposes of man and the purposes of nature. In the first chapters she evolves out of the poetic evocation of natural selection and assimilation as an image of human involvement in the process. Her hair, symbol of the vitality of life close to nature, is destined to follow the downward trend of assimilation into an impersonal movement, evidenced by the coffin stool in her cottage, Mr Melbury's house, Winterborne's cottages, the vanished charioteers, and the fallen leaves. Her final elegy is enriched by her consciousness of the cost of involvement to human sensitivity in pain and unfulfilment. Pain is the dominant emotion of the novel. Marty, more sensitive even than Giles to the pain of all living things, brings it poetically to the reader's senses. Her sense of unfulfilment when she overhears Mr Melbury's plans for Giles to marry Grace enters the cosmos in a physical metaphor charged with emotional force: 'The bleared white visage of a sunless winter day emerged like a dead-born child.' It is Marty who hears the pines sigh, envies the pheasants whose lack of human consciousness gives them nothing more than the weather to think of, and comments on the symbolism of the two quarrelling pigeons who fall into the ashes of the fire by which Fitzpiers declared his feelings: 'That's the end of what is called love.' It is Marty who comes to share with Grace the pain of Giles' death, with a dignity and truth that compels comparison with the tragi-comedy of Grace's treatment of Fitzpiers' two other 'wives' when they come for news of his accident.

' "He belongs to neither of us now, and your beauty is no more powerful with him than my plainness. I have come to help you, ma'am. He never cared for me, and he cared much for you; but he cares for us both alike now." '

Quietly she accepts the truth of pain as part of the great impersonal movement of nature without accepting the morality of nature uncontrolled by man. Her elegy restores the poetic keynote after the deliberately commonplace slackening of tension which marks Grace's reunion with Fitzpiers, and which, far from being a fault, enacts the gradual reassertion of life, including Grace's response to Fitzpiers' sexuality, after the numbness caused by Winterborne's death. It stresses Marty's function as Giles Winterborne's heir in a scene where woodland and orchard speak of nature unrestrained and nature held in check—to keep the tools that control and direct in good order. It distances Winterborne's death by opening up a long perspective of man's fruitful and continuing contact with the perpetual renewal of the earth. Her lonely figure, sexless, colourless, hardly distinguishable from the misty landscape, speaks the sublime simple words that affirm both the good of the individual human life rooted in but not controlled by nature (as South was controlled by his tree) and the pain that defines its value. It is a lament for all human beings who deserve the name, and for a simple way of life whose passing creates the complex problems of *Tess of the d'Urbervilles* and *Jude the Obscure*.

' "Now, my own, own love,' she whispered, 'you are mine, and only mine; for she has forgot 'ee at last, although for her you died! But I—whenever I get up I'll think of 'ee, and whenever I lie down I'll think of 'ee again. Whenever I plant the young larches I'll think that none can plant as you planted; and whenever I split a gad, and whenever I turn the cider wring, I'll say none could do it like you. If ever I forget your name let me forget home and heaven! . . . But no, no, my love, I never can forget 'ee; for you was a good man, and did good things!" '

XI

Tess of the d'Urbervilles:
A Novel of Assertion

' ". . . what's the use of learning that I am one of a long row only—finding out that there is set down in some old book somebody just like me, and to know that I shall only act her part; making me sad, that's all. The best is not to remember that your nature and your past doings have been just like thousands' and thousands', and that your coming life and doings 'll be like thousands' and thousands'." '

(Tess of the d'Urbervilles)

Tess of the d'Urbervilles is not about a pure woman betrayed by man, morality, and the President of the Immortals; her fight for re-acceptance and happiness; 'the incessant penalty paid by the innocent for the guilty' (*Academy* review) or the decay of the peasantry. All these aspects are there, but all are contributory to the major conflict suggested by the two parts of the title. ' "Call me Tess," she would say askance' when Angel Clare 'called her Artemis, Demeter, and other fanciful names half teasingly', and it is as the dairymaid Tess, an individual human being, that she 'had set herself to stand or fall by her qualities'. But she is also Tess 'of the d'Urbervilles', and the novel is shaped by the tension between the personal and impersonal parts of her being. The right to be human is not easy to assert against the laws of nature, heredity, society and economy which abstract from people 'the differences which distinguished them as individuals'.

The surface story of Tess narrates the events that defeat her struggle for personal happiness. But the poetic underpattern reveals 'underneath the resolute purpose of the planning animal, the victim of circumstance and the doomed or sanctified being' —a more archetypal direction to her life, hostile to personal claims.

The plot is simple and unoriginal. Its familiarity springs from two sources. The eternal triangle, the wronged woman who cannot escape her past, 'the woman pays', the double standard of morality

233

for men and women, were themes known to Victorian literature. Balladry can produce Patient Griselda, the highborn lady in disguise, the seduced milkmaid, the murder of a betrayer, and retribution on the gallows. Hardy's poetic power lies first of all in crossing and challenging the Victorian moral tale with the ethic of folk tradition. The Victorian assumption that the fallen woman did not rise again is questioned by the timeless values of the ballad world, closer to natural law.

> 'Though a knave hath by me leyne,
> Yet am I noder dede nor slowe;
> I trust to recouer my harte agayne,
> And Crystes curse goo wyth yow!'
> ('Crow and Pie')

The ballad mode, non-naturalistic and poetic, also lends belief to those unlikely incidents which disturb a naturalistic view of the novel but fall into place as manifestations of 'the indomitable unconscious will' that directs the underpattern. Angel's sleepwalking, Alec's conversion and his blood soaking through the ceiling, the gift of an empty mansion in the New Forest; the impish operations of time, chance, coincidence and cross-purpose, mock the resolute purpose of the planning animal with intimations of her archetypal destiny. Such are the collision of the mailcart with the Durbeyfield waggon, the coincidence of Chaseborough Fair with the market, the drunken revel and Tess's fatigue; the mistiming that dooms Tess 'to be seen and coveted that day by the wrong man', and Angel to dance with the wrong girl and return from Brazil too late; the events which frustrate her attempts to confess and seek aid from Angel's parents; the tenant-farmer of the 'starve-acre' farm turning out to be the Trantridge man who owed her a grudge; Angel's chance glimpse of the d'Urberville portraits as he hesitates outside Tess's bedroom; the build-up of her family's misfortunes just after she has refused Alec's help; and the omens—all add up to an impressive vision of the workings of a Fate familiar to folklore, irrational and unknowable, ordering the affairs of men to a non-human rhythm.

The plot is organized round the seven 'phases' of Tess's personal story to give pointers to the direction in which her impersonal life is moving. Her first phase as 'The Maiden' ends when Alec seduces her.

'An immeasurable social chasm was to divide our heroine's personality thereafter from that previous self of hers who stepped from her mother's door to try her fortune at Trantridge poultry farm.'

The second phase follows Tess's return home with the consciousness of original sin on her—'she looked upon herself as a figure of Guilt intruding into the haunts of Innocence'—to the birth and death of her baby, and her reintegration into country ritual. 'The past was past; whatever it had been was no more at hand.'

'On one point she was resolved: there should be no more d'Urberville air-castles in the dreams and deeds of her new life. She would be the dairymaid Tess, and nothing more.'

In Phase the Third, 'The Rally', the experience and personality of the dairymaid Tess are enlarged at Talbothays by Angel Clare. The unpremeditated kiss that ends this phase means that 'something had occurred which changed the pivot of the universe for their two natures'. That 'something', in the next phase, is that Tess hands over part of her self to the impersonal force of love. This phase follows the maturing natural relationship of two lovers 'converging, under an irresistible law, as surely as two streams in one vale,' until Tess's fatal confession on her wedding night. In Phase the Fifth, 'The Woman Pays', the personal Tess is gradually depersonalized, first of all by the abstract ideal of purity which Angel prefers to her real human self, and secondly, when he has abandoned her, by the increasingly automatic mode of her life.

'There was something of the habitude of the wild animal in the unreflecting instinct with which she rambled on—disconnecting herself by littles from her eventful past at every step, obliterating her identity.'

Now seeking not happiness, but mere survival, she has a second recovery through endurance of winter weather and rough work at Flintcombe Ash. This time it is halted on her return from Emminster, when a meeting with Alec gives her 'an almost physical sense of an implacable past which still engirdled her'.

The closing in of her implacable past to submerge her personal identity occupies the sixth phase. She makes her last helpless gesture as an independent woman in the d'Urberville vaults, where her homeless family have camped for the night. 'Why am I on the wrong side of this door!' In the last phase, the 'coarse pattern' that had been traced 'upon this beautiful feminine tissue, sensitive as gossamer', is fulfilled at Stonehenge, a place of religious sacrifice, and Wintoncester, ancient social capital of Wessex. Alec's murder and Tess's execution identify the personal Tess with the d'Urberville family type, the scapegoat victim of fertility rites, and those innate and external pressures which level down the human being into something less than human—'her breathing now was quick and small, like that of a lesser creature than a woman.'

The pivotal points in Tess's fight to be herself show fundamental parallels that compel comparisons and contrasts. These draw the lines of the 'coarse pattern' for us. Tess has three 'deaths' and three rebirths: the first at Talbothays into the fullness of human and natural existence; the second at Flintcombe Ash into a lower plane of animal survival; the third in a metaphysical sense, when she hands over the meaning of her life to 'Liza-Lu and Angel standing, significantly, in the position of Giotto's 'Two Apostles'. Her two violations, physical and spiritual, invite comparison as well as contrast between Alec d'Urberville and Angel Clare. Both deny Tess the right to be human, Alec in obedience to the sub-human impulse of sex, Angel to the superhuman power of the image that substitutes essence for existence. Both are incompletely characterized when compared with the rounded humanness of Tess, but this is surely stratagem rather than error. Alec's resemblance to the Victorian stage villain and the morality Vice, and Angel's to one of his own unreal (angelic) conceptions of human nature, indicate their role as complementary agents of dehumanization. Both betray Tess in a world of paradisal lushness, though the resemblance should not blind one to the essential differences between Trantridge and Talbothays. Both feed her with fruit (v, xxx). Both are associated in action and commentary with fire; Alec in its red, murky aspect and Angel with its radiance—the fire of hell and heaven.

There are other parallels stressed by radiation outwards from the central crisis of Tess's confession. The fertility of her experience at Talbothays in Phase the Third, rising to its climax of hope in her engagement to Clare, is balanced in Phase Five by the sterility at Flintcombe Ash, which touches the bottom of despair at Alec's return. Her reintegration into natural rhythms in Phase Two is offset by her increasing subjection to mechanical rhythms in Phase Six, and pointed up by the repetition of the word 'past' at the end of each phase. The final swallowing up of the particular aim in the general doom in Phase the Seventh is an ironical development of

236

John Durbeyfield's claim to definition by family in Phase the First.

Such parallels suggest a rich layer of archetypal myth directing the course of Tess's life. Hardy's rich poetic and narrative resources combine to bring out the deeper meaning of the novel by imaginative description of the way characters move and speak and relate to their environment. The central events are described in Darwinian terms of struggle and adaptation, extinction and renewal of the species. But the discovery of Tess's ancestry initiates all the myths about the meaning of being human; myths that are explored in the rest of the novel through an intricate network of poetic cross-references. It may be dismissed as top dressing, but a responsiveness to poetic overtones in the first chapters reveals why Hardy placed the d'Urberville theme in a key position.

'Sir John d'Urberville—that's who I am,' declares shiftless peasant Jack Durbeyfield. His prostrate position 'upon the bank among the daisies' suggests the effigies in the d'Urberville vault. The attempt of insecure man, no longer able to give himself meaning by reference to a creator with a holy plan, to define himself through the name and fame of his human pedigree, becomes an ironical definition through death. 'I've—got—a—gr't—family—vault—at—Kingsbere—and—knighted-forefathers-in-lead-coffins-there!' Ancestry becomes a metaphor for all the impersonal forces which swallow up individual effort and lethargy alike in the final and inclusive impersonality of death.

Hardy's poetic and dramatic presentation of the various layers of Tess's past prepares us to view her in the double aspect indicated by the title. The lyrical meditation that begins Chapter II, on the 'fertile and sheltered tract of country' where Tess was born gives way to a shot, nearer in space and time but still distanced, of the transformed fertility rite that connected primitive man to the cycle of nature. Jack Durbeyfield's mock-heroic progress, with its absurd hero chanting his meaningless identification with things that are dead, provides an ironical backdrop to this 'local Cerealia'—an inheritance older than the d'Urbervilles that once gave religious and social definition, if a violent one, to man in the mass—and draws attention to Tess taking part. The colour combination which picks her out—'She wore a red ribbon in her hair, and was the only one of the white company who could boast of such a pronounced adornment'—persistently links her with a complex of passion, guilt, sacrifice, and purity. Here it associates her with the noble white hart killed violently in the forest, the first of the hunting images that run through the book as types of Tess's fate. As we move to close-up in the present moment, Tess comes before us not only as herself, but also as a product of the same nonhuman forces that produced landscape, ritual and heredity. On the outskirts of the scene stands Angel Clare, urban invader of the unconscious harmony with his disease of modern thought and 'creeds which futilely attempt to check what wisdom would be content to regulate', watching a primitive try at regulation. The dramatic composition is masterly.

The need for wisdom to regulate is made clear in Chapter III, where the picture of Tess's inheritance is completed. Joan Durbeyfield, fixed forever at the cradle and the washtub, opposes 'the muck and muddle of rearing children' to the memory Tess brings with her of an ordered ritual that once gave religious significance to fertility. Tess, as a budding woman, is cast for the role of child-bearer too. But the dramatic juxtaposition questions the value of the primitive, unaware fertility of shiftless Marlott for modern conditions of self-conscious responsibility.

The dramatic and poetic vision that links Tess to her inheritance as animal, woman, and human being has already suggested the three fundamental and interconnecting myths that she will be lived by. They are the fertility scapegoat, Paradise Lost, and that twentieth century response to the 'ache of modernism', the exile. Marlott and Trantridge, sheltered and languorous, smaller in scale than the Valley of the Great Dairies where Tess reaches maturity, present the first of these, the world of fertility myth, or primal harmony before the birth of consciousness. (Richard Beckman, in 'A Character Typology for Hardy's Novels', *English Literary History*, xxx, 1963, suggests that the pattern of moods built up in the novels parallels the pattern of evolution in 'Before Life and After'——Nescience—Consciousness—Nescience.)

'They followed the road with a sensation that they were soaring along in a supporting medium, possessed of original and profound thoughts, themselves and surrounding nature forming an organism of which all the parts harmoniously and joyously interpenetrated each other. They were as sublime as the moon and stars above them, and the moon and stars were as ardent as they.'

The figures in this world take on the Dionysian attributes of vegetation gods:

'Of the rushing couples there could barely be discerned more than the high lights—the indistinctness shaping them to satyrs clasping nymphs—a multiplicity of Pans whirling a multiplicity of Syrinxes; Lotis attempting to elude Priapus, and always failing . . .'

and it is on this night of traditional licence that Tess is seduced. But Hardy's poetic presentation casts doubt on the meaning of fertility myth for modern man. The elements of the 'supporting medium' which contribute to the harmony of all the parts—moonlight, candlelight, pollen dust (the first of the many pollen images that link Tess with fertility throughout the book), fog, and 'the spirit of wine' lend it a nightmare quality, and distance it as an illusion of the irresponsible. Tess becomes aware of the need for a more advanced harmony, which will not affront the dignity of a self-conscious human being by ignoring the dissonance of personal pain, when the inharmonious accident to Prince proves the universe's 'serene dissociation from these two wisps of human life'. The birds, who 'shook themselves in the hedges, arose, and twittered' as usual, and the incongruous beauty of spilt blood in the sunrise suggest a duplicity in the cosmos too complex for communal fertility ritual to cope with.

Nevertheless, the sexual guilt of causing life subconsciously demands a scapegoat whose purity will carry off the sins of the world. Tess's role as victim is stressed in those scenes where the symbolic overtones of red and white set up rich dissonances of pain and purity, guilt and innocence, life and death, the paradox of living. The red is often the red of real blood. Prince's blood glares against the paleness of dawn, the lane, and Tess's white features as she tries to stop the hole with her hand. The violent colour contrast, the crimson stain Tess receives as the result of her effort, the suggestion of sexual guilt in the blood ('Princely' but worn-out like the d'Urbervilles) that pours from a hole pierced by the phallic spike on a dark night, foreshadow her seduction and doom of murder and sacrifice. Such foreshortenings of reality, as Morrell points out in *Thomas Hardy: The Will and the Way*, are not necessarily images of what *must* happen, but of what *may* happen if steps are not taken to avert disaster. Tess's association with blood is often neutral, or at least ambivalent. Another dawn scene, when she humanely kills the bleeding pheasants, reveals to her not only her own predicament in the cosmos as a creature 'brought into being by artificial means' in order to be killed, but also her superior freedom as a human being not to hurry to her destiny. The nest she had made for herself under the boughs recalls the nest of leaves Alec made for her in The Chase but the plight of the pheasants restores her to human nature from the animal nature Alec's act implied: 'I be not mangled, and I be not bleeding, and I have two hands to feed and clothe me.' As she stands hesitant at the door of Emminster Vicarage,

'a piece of bloodstained paper, caught up from some meat-buyer's dustheap, beat up and down the road without the gate; too flimsy to rest, too heavy to fly away; and a few straws kept it company.'

The blood-stained paper and straw, here literally a floating omen, is transmuted by her crucial loss of courage at Emminster into a fixed image of the fate she has helped to release. When she strikes Alec on the rick with a gauntlet, 'the blood began dropping from his mouth upon the straw', and Tess, 'with the hopeless defiance of the sparrow's gaze before its captor twists its neck', accepts the domination of her impersonal role. 'Once victim, always victim—that's the law!'

Even Hardy's figurative description of Alec, when Tess first meets him, as 'one who stood fair to be the blood-red ray in the spectrum of her young life' modulates before long through the forced strawberries and early roses he has given her to another blood omen in the thorn that pricks her chin. The suspicion that he has been decking a sacrificial victim, in this region 'wherein Druidical mistletoe was still found on aged oaks' (a phrase recalled when Tess confesses to an impulse of suicide under Angel's ironical gift of mistletoe over the wedding bed) is strengthened when Joan washes her daughter's hair (a fertility symbol) for the second visit to Trantridge, and

'put upon her the white frock that Tess had worn at the club-walking, the airy fulness of which, supplementing her enlarged *coiffure*, imparted to her developing figure an amplitude which belied her age, and might cause her to be estimated as a woman when she was not much more than a child.'

She is wearing the same white dress when she is seduced.

Descriptions of natural phenomena, used so variously in Hardy's work, combine with colour symbolism to define Tess's role as ritual victim. The sun-god, who demanded blood to perpetuate his life-giving powers, is much in evidence. Hardy's accuracy in conveying the effect of sunlight at different times of the day and year make these effects a poetic correlative to Tess's acceptance of her role. At Wellbridge Manor, just before she confesses, the low afternoon winter sunlight 'stretched across to her skirt, where it made a spot like a paint-mark set upon her'. The stain sets up reverberations not only of Prince's blood, which splashed her 'from face to skirt', but also of the text-painter who embodied her conventional sense of guilt in red letters, 'THY, DAMNATION, SLUMBERETH, NOT'. At Flintcombe Ash, where the red threshing machine drives Tess with the impersonality of immutable law, 'a wrathful shine' from the March sunset dyes the tired faces of the enslaved threshers with 'a coppery light', giving to the human features the look of ritual masks that marked the men who surrounded Tess on the Stone of Sacrifice at sunrise, 'their faces and hands as if they were silvered, the remainder of their figures dark'. Even the benevolent morning sun of the Marlott harvest, 'a golden-haired, beaming, mild-eyed, God-like creature', throws 'stripes like red-hot pokers' on cottage furniture and intensifies the ruddy hue of the 'revolving Maltese cross' on the reaping machine, reminding us that sun worship had its sacrificial aspect. At all times Tess is linked intimately to the natural world from which her consciousness isolates her. Hardy's double vision presents her both as an extension of nature moved by forces beyond her control—most obviously in the Talbothays idyll, where her sexuality blossoms with the maturing season—and as a subjective being whose moral awareness pushes her beyond the world of fertility myth to the world of knowledge gained and Paradise lost.

One world can be seen modulating into the other in Chapter XIV. The Marlott harvest shows the highest achievement possible to a way of life still closely linked to fertility ritual. It is a good life. All the details contribute to a picture of natural harmony: the youthful sun-god, taking a personal interest in the ritual, the reaping machine which starts with a non-mechanical ticking 'like the love-making of the grasshopper', and the horses who pull it, made as much a part of the sun-directed pattern by their glistening brasses as the men by their twinkling trouser buttons. The women too are 'part and parcel of outdoor nature', timing their dance-like movements to the unhurried pace of machine and horses. Once again, as in Chapter II, Tess is seen first as an integral part of landscape and ritual; as one of the field-women, who has 'somehow lost her own margin, imbibed the essence of her surrounding, and assimilated herself with it'. As Hardy describes the 'clock-like monotony' of Tess's work in great detail, the tense changes to the eternal present (a common feature of Hardy's style when describing the unchanging rhythms of country labour) and the rhythm of binding controls the rise and fall of the sentences. The quiet rhythms, soft consonants and subtle vowel progressions are halted abruptly by the hardness of the last word as Hardy draws attention to the girl's bare arm: '. . . and as the day wears on its feminine smoothness becomes scarified by the stubble, and bleeds.' The abrupt halt serves to remind us of Tess's connection, by now well-established through colour imagery, with the motif of sacrifice. The undertones are strengthened by the red 'Maltese cross' to which Hardy draws attention and the ritual encirclement of small animals, which tallies closely with Frazer's description in *The Golden Bough* of the killing of the corn spirit/vegetation god/scapegoat at harvest. But even this does not destroy the harmony. It is distanced by time, '. . . the doom that awaited them later in the day', and by the ritual pattern of their death, that abstracts individuality from participants in the dance. The choreography is continued by the children carrying the baby, who 'rose above the stubbly convexity of the hill' to repeat the earlier movement pattern of the reaper and horses. Feeding the baby adds another feminine rhythm to the eternal ritual. The baby, the friendliness of the rustics, the unhurried rhythm of work and repose where nature, animal, man and machine work together in unforced harmony, build up a vision of a world where primal rightness has not yet taken the tinct of wrong.

The good life, doing what it must, with no hope, no despair, no human awareness or choice of action, has its own dignity. But certain elements in the scene—the moonlight progress, the sense of oneness with nature—throw the mind back to the drunken revel at Chaseborough, and the two scenes held in balance with Hardy's comment on Tess's subjective sensations demonstrate the falseness of a philosophy of harmony for the modern thinking and feeling human being, who has emerged from innocence to awareness of alienation. 'The familiar surroundings had not darkened because of her grief, nor sickened because of her pain.'

There is something in Tess at war with nature which she needs the qualities denoted by Angel's name to bring out. Communal fertility ritual cannot cope with a personal 'misery which transcended that of the child's simple loss'. Her concern for the baby's individual soul belongs to the kind of Christianity practised, if not preached, by Angel's parents. Her passage thus from 'simple girl to complex woman' is embodied in a striking visual image in the second half of the chapter, the baptism of her baby, which carries overtones still sounding from the harvest ritual. The modulation begins in the paragraph that joins the two parts. The picture of Tess taking part in the traditional ride home on the harvest wagon, at one with her ballad-singing companions and the rhythms of life and death denoted by harvest and balladry, is lit by

'a broad tarnished moon that had risen from the ground to the east-wards, its face resembling the outworn gold-leaf halo of some worm-eaten Tuscan saint.'

The worm-eaten saint superimposed on the symbol of fertility/purity prepares both for Tess's growth towards a more advanced kind of religion and for the deadness of its outer forms. The eye moves from the moonlit and sunlit communal ritual to the solitary candlelit figure of Tess performing a sacred rite of the Christian church. 'The ecstasy of faith almost apotheosized her.' The priest-like white nightgown, the basin and jug and other properties of this 'act of approximation' are made divine and meaningful not by any virtue in the rite of baptism itself, but by the value of the individual human being that stands at the centre of Christ's religion.

'The children gazed up at her with more and more reverence, and no longer had a will for questioning. She did not look like Sissy to them now, but as a being large, towering, and awful—a divine personage with whom they had nothing in common.'

The sign of the cross that marks the baby baptizes Tess as a suffering human being. Conception in sorrow, toil for daily bread, frailty, freedom of will and awareness of human alienation are to define the new-created woman in place of nobility human and divine and innocence lost. Her 'desires are limited to man and his humble yet formidable love' (*The Plague*)—the basic human rights to live, love, work and be happy. She also takes with her to Tal-bothays an inheritance of vital animal instincts with which human values must come to terms. These are constantly present in Hardy's minutely detailed evocations of the maturing summer in the fertile Valley of the Great Dairies, where growth is felt as an active sexual

243

force that affects vegetation, animals, maids and men alike. The details that denote the observant naturalist are selected by the poet to evoke simultaneously the mystery of the 'great passionate pulse of existence' that orders the movement of the natural world, and a solid sense of everyday reality.

'Rays from the sunrise drew forth the buds and stretched them into long stalks, lifted up sap in noiseless streams, opened petals, and sucked out scents in invisible jets and breathings.'

'During the day the animals obsequiously followed the shadow of the smallest tree as it moved round the stem with the diurnal roll; and when the milkers came they could hardly stand still for the flies.'

'On the gray moisture of the grass were marks where the cows had lain through the night—dark-green islands of dry herbage the size of their carcases, in the general sea of dew. From each island proceeded a serpentine trail, by which the cow had rambled away to feed after getting up, at the end of which trail they found her; the snoring puff from her nostrils, when she recognized them, making an intenser little fog of her own amid the prevailing one.'

The sense of reality is vital to the novel. It is the reality of the physical world in which a human being without God finds meaning and definition. Tess's response to it takes the obvious form of response through a lover. Angel and Tess are constantly seen as an image of the highest fulfilment in the human pair not divorced from the natural setting that is their present meaning and past history.

'The sun was so near the ground, and the sward so flat, that the shadows of Clare and Tess would stretch a quarter of a mile ahead of them, like two long fingers pointing afar to where the green alluvial reaches abutted against the sloping sides of the vale.'

Talbothays stands fair to become Paradise regained. It is a fully human paradise, that does not exclude moral awareness and un-merited personal suffering. It provides constant reminders of the doom of death and the shortness of life: butterflies trapped in the milkmaids' gauze skirts, 'another year's instalment of flowers, leaves, nightingales, thrushes, finches, and such ephemeral creatures',

'wooden posts rubbed to a glossy smoothness by the flanks of infinite cows and calves of bygone years, now passed to an oblivion almost in-conceivable in its profundity.'

Work is transformed from God's curse to a harmony with country rhythms and one of the factors in the growth of love, for every emotional crisis happens during the course of the dairy chores. The three milkmaids, suffering as individuals from a gratuitous passion which reduces each to 'portion of one organism called sex' accept their pain with dignity and generosity. Sex itself is not evil at Talbothays: only thinking makes it so. Tess's spiritual quality of purity is rooted in her vital sexual nature. Talbothays gives hope of reconciliation between the natural harmony of a pre-conscious state and a respect for the conscious human self.

Angel Clare is seen as the 'god-like' Adam to Tess's Eve. With his modern consciousness, advanced views and vaunted respect for the variegated Hodge, he has qualities of spiritual delicacy that could benefit an untutored Paradise. But the poetic undercurrents flowing through his encounters with Tess suggest that his angelic qualities have some kinship with the snake that deceived her in the earlier unconscious Eden. The snake is still there, in the form of her sex. 'She was yawning, and he saw the red interior of her mouth as if it had been a snake's.' It was a moment 'when the most spiritual beauty bespeaks itself flesh'. The unweeded garden where Tess 'undulated upon the thin notes of the second-hand harp' looks back to the sinister lushness of Marlott. Her inability to leave the spot, 'like a fascinated bird' looks forward to her bird-like submission to her sexual master Alec on the rick. The distortion of reality produced by Angel's music on her subjective consciousness—

'The floating pollen seemed to be his notes made visible, and the dampness of the garden the weeping of the garden's sensibility. Though near nightfall, the rank-smelling weed-flowers glowed as if they would not close for intentness, and the waves of colour mixed with the waves of sound . . .'

—the confusion of senses and distances, the pollen, the sense of exaltation—'Tess was conscious of neither time nor space'—even the rhythm of the sentences, echo the self-deception of the Trantridge revellers. Yearning for absolute harmony is the other side of the coin of sexual attraction.

Hardy's double stress on the objective reality of the garden, full of attractive but foul-smelling weeds and sticky blights that stain Tess as she is drawn towards the angelic music (played, as Hardy is careful to point out, on a *second-hand* harp and with poor execution) and its subjective beauty when filtered through Tess's unweeded emotions, point the dangers as well as the advantages of the angelic power to transform the physical world into the spiritual. Tess's comment, after confessing her fears of life, 'But *you*, sir, can raise up dreams with your music, and drive all such horrid fancies away!' marks the kind of deceiver Angel will be in this new conscious garden of Eden. The sham d'Urberville raised hopes of definition by human pedigree; the sham angel appeals to the human yearning for the absolute, which leads likewise to death. But ideal dreams persist. Angel is introduced into the story by a typically idealistic remark on William Dewey's deception of the bull with the Nativity hymn, which caricatures Angel's attempts to impose his superhuman vision on the living physical world. In a godless world human beings depend on each other for definition. But Angel betrays the humanness of Tess by his distorted perception. To him she 'was no longer the milkmaid, but a visionary essence of woman'—Artemis, Demeter, Eve, a goddess. His preference of essence to existence adds a modern Existentialist slant to Hardy's version of the Paradise myth.

Angel's replacement of the living Tess by a lifeless image is realized in a closely-woven poetic texture. It links together the various manifestations of automatic impulsion which drive Tess to her death when she leaves Talbothays. This can be seen clearly in Chapter xx, where the identification with Adam and Eve is explicit. The chapter is built on tension between physical reality and distorted perception of it which is central to the novel.

'Whilst all the landscape was in neutral shade his companion's face, which was the focus of his eyes, rising above the mist stratum, seemed to have a sort of phosphorescence upon it. She looked ghostly, as if she were merely a soul at large. In reality her face, without appearing to do so, had caught the cold gleam of day from the north-east; his own face, though he did not think of it, wore the same aspect to her.'

The strange poetic effects of light and mist are just as natural, and just as neutral, as the physical solidity of the cows. It is the self-deceiving mind of Angel that takes appearance for reality. Hardy stresses the 'preternatural' 'non-human' quality of those early morning hours, yet 'it was then . . . that [Tess] impressed him most deeply', not as a human being who craved warmth but as 'a visionary essence of woman'. The 'dignified largeness both of disposition and physique' which 'Tess seemed to Clare to exhibit' compels comparison not only with the physical 'luxuriance of aspect' that rivets Alec's eyes, but also with the baptism of the baby, where the divinity of this being, 'large, towering, and awful' is created by what Angel forgets—the imperfect human being at the centre of the ritual. The 'minute diamonds of moisture' that temporarily give Tess a 'strange and ethereal beauty' look back to 'the miniature candle-flame inverted in her eye-pupils', in the baptism scene, which 'shone like a diamond', and forward to the brilliants which help Angel to create another Tess. The unreal essence of fine lady he has created, dramatically embodied in the debased d'Urberville portraits 'builded into the wall' like his fixed definition of purity, moves him to turn from the living woman.

'Sinister design lurked in the woman's features, a concentrated purpose of revenge on the other sex—so it seemed to him then. The Caroline bodice of the portrait was low—precisely as Tess's had been when he tucked it in to show the necklace; and again he experienced the distressing sensation of a resemblance between them.'

The fog in Chapter xx, and the remoteness imposed on human figures by effects of light and distorted subjective perception, carry echoes of the confused, unreflective life of Marlott and Trantridge, which add overtones of the subhuman to this scene of superhuman harmony with nature.

'At these non-human hours they could get quite close to the water-fowl. Herons came, with a great bold noise as of opening doors and shutters, out of the boughs of a plantation which they frequented at the side of the mead; or, if already on the spot, hardily maintained their standing in the water as the pair walked by, watching them by moving their heads round in a slow, horizontal, passionless wheel, like the turn of puppets by clockwork.'

Like the heron that Mrs Yeobright watches as she lies near death on Egdon Heath, these herons, with their 'noise as of opening doors and shutters', suggest the freedom of the absolute. The mechanical similes that describe their movements fuse the unreflecting animal life with that other mode of automatic impulsion, machinery, to imply the mechanical nature of the universe that crushes the vital qualities of Tess's nature after Angel's rejection of her personal self for a 'passionless' 'non-human' image of purity.

Careful attention to the details of such scenes where Angel is a chief actor reveals his archetypal role as human agent of the impersonal powers which, once released, will destroy Tess's life. In Chapter xx the poetic force comes from the accumulation of lyrical details: in the sleepwalking scene, from dramatic details which form a poetic image. This scene, like the Stonehenge episode, has been criticized for its theatricality. But they are theatrical for a purpose. The staginess reinforces Hardy's Aeschylean image of Tess as 'sport' for the President of the Immortals. Tess at Stonehenge and Angel in the sleepwalking episode are playing roles assigned to them by their buried selves. Psychology bears witness to the theatrical nature of the subconscious. Movement, gesture, speech, positioning, and props of the scene grow rings of evocation. The rigid stone coffin of an abbot in which Tess's living body is placed suggests the logical end of absolute aspirations, and the destructive force of the ascetic image which will hound Tess to the Stone of Sacrifice. To Angel, the human Tess is 'Dead! Dead! Dead!' and his unconscious actions are eloquent of the repressed sexual guilt and fear of the powers of life that demand a sacrifice to purity. The precariousness of their position on the plank, Tess's trust and impassivity, and her failure to follow up her chance to take control, are all dramatic correlatives of the poetic under-pattern which drives Tess from Paradise a second time.

Tess's expulsion from the human Paradise thrusts her into the modern myth of the lonely, rootless exile from meaning. Talbothays has given her human awareness, meaning through love, and roots in the natural rhythms of life and work in a simple traditional community. Hardy's poetic treatment of Tess's new relationship to her surroundings after Angel's betrayal—the betrayal of god-in-man—shows what Camus calls 'this divorce between man and his life, the actor and his setting' which constitutes the feeling of absurdity. The divorce begins immediately after Tess's confession. 'All material objects around announced their irresponsibility with terrible iteration.' Angel's absolute mode of perceiving is revealed as inadequate. The physical world that took its meaning from human emotion now exists only as a lumpish, alien factor in the elemental struggle to survive and endure.

Flintcombe Ash brings sharply to the senses the bleak sterility of life without illusions, without love, without God, without a future goal or anything that gives a reason for living to the human being, irrelevant and abandoned on the surface of the earth in a wintry death-marked universe that does not add up. A patient accumulation of the manifestations of rain, wind and snow and their physical effects on Tess and Marian builds up a feeling of the obliteration of human identity by the 'achromatic chaos of things'. Tess's mutilation of her distinctive beauty is reflected in the huge, high swede field, over which the two girls crawl like flies: 'it was a complexion without features, as if a face, from chin to brow, should be only an expanse of skin.' Once again she is part of the landscape. But the arrival of apocalyptic Northern birds, 'gaunt spectral creatures with tragical eyes' but no memory of the cataclysmic horrors they had witnessed, gives the lie to the impression that she is 'a thing scarcely percipient, almost inorganic'. The human consciousness that has brought Tess pain and exile has also brought her knowledge and memories of the Talbothays paradise which define her as a human being against the levelling flintiness of trivial existence.

Flintcombe Ash also provides the modern false gods which step into the void created by lack of roots in heaven and earth. The threshing should be compared in every detail with the Marlott reaping as processes that are respectively meaningless and meaningful. The dawn of the cold March morning is 'inexpressive' in contrast to the August sunrise which gave definition to men, horses and furnishings. The personal sun-god has been replaced by the impersonal 'engine which was to act as the *primum mobile* of this little world': the horses and local driver who understood every stage of the reaping ritual, by an itinerant Northern engineer, described less as a person than as a mechanical function, who 'had nothing to do with preparatory labour' and remained isolated from the agricultural scene. His engagement on another farm the following day forces the breakneck pace of the work; a sad reminder of the unhurried rhythm of the Marlott harvest. The friendly rick which gave Tess shelter as she ate her lunch and fed her baby in harmonious companionship has been transformed into a threatening abstract 'trapezoidal' shape which exposes her to Alec's attentions. The thresher is a soulless 'red tyrant' that gears all the workers to its insatiable demands and drives Tess by its incessant throbbing to a state of puppet-like action independent of will. The dominance of the mechanical image over the vital qualities of life suggests that the patterned ritual dance which gave harmonious meaning to life and death has been replaced by the order of immutable law which, like the engineer, does not require process to have purpose.

'His fire was waiting incandescent, his steam was at high pressure, in a few seconds he could make the long strap move at an invisible velocity.

Beyond its extent the environment might be corn, straw, or chaos; it was all the same to him.'

The details that evoke a mechanistic universe include all the impersonal forces that abstract meaning from a human being unprotected by providential design, ritual pattern, or love. One of them is time. The accelerated motion of the machine that dominates Tess, reinforced by Alec's renewed attentions, warns that time will not stand still. Nothing but her submission to conventional judgements stands in the way of another visit to Emminster; yet still Tess fails to stamp a meaningful pattern on the flow of time by decisive action. The pathos of Tess practising Angel's favourite ballads against his return should not hide Hardy's comment: 'Tess was so wrapt up in this *fanciful dream* [my italics] that she seemed not to know how the season was advancing.' Time in the shape of heredity controls her actions in the prophetic blow she deals to Alec with a gauntlet. Time combines with another false god of the void, economic interest, to rob the human being of significance. Hardy's metaphysical meaning, as usual, comes out of a physical situation. The dominance of machinery in late nineteenth-century Wessex was one of the factors which exiled man from work rooted in nature, and defined him by the profit motive and the production schedule. The homelessness of Tess's family ties the metaphysical sense of exile from meaning to concrete economic pressures which drive man unresting over the earth with no place to go.

The logical end of all depersonalizing forces is the d'Urberville vaults where Tess, in terms of the hunt metaphor, is run to earth. The reproachful gleam of the unloaded furniture, and the spoliation of the d'Urberville tombs, build up a powerful picture of a world dead to human values. It is completed when the sham d'Urberville rises from the 'mere stone reproduction' on the oldest altar tomb, to challenge the 'hollow echo from below' with the false values that too often define the modern exile in a universe shaped by death—money and sex uncontrolled by meaningful ritual. The scene looks back to the stone coffin in which Angel places a Tess who is dead to him in her human aspect, and forward to the Stone of Sacrifice.

Alec's role as devil of negation in an absurd universe (his loud clothes, diabolical disguises, and sudden manifestations call to mind the negating devils of Dostoievsky and Thomas Mann) is defined by his poetic connection with the threshing. He turns up at the rat-hunt which is done not by harvesters engaged in the ritual dance of life and death as at Marlott, but by 'men unconnected with the threshing' as a casual sport, 'amid the barking of dogs, masculine shouts, feminine screams, oaths, stampings, and confusion as of Pandemonium'. The Plutonic engineer foreshadows Alec's satanic association with fire and smoke on the Marlott allotment, where they isolate him in a *pas de deux* with Tess. The 'red tyrant' recalls the colour through which he is linked to Tess's fate: his red house, just as alien to the landscape, 'built for enjoyment pure and simple', where strawberries, roses, fowls and Tess are forced out of the order of nature for pleasure. His element is chaos. Tess kills him, and takes responsibility (like Camus' Meuersault), to assert human purpose against the temptations of purposeless process. The murder, while it aligns Tess with inherited automatic tendencies which direct the cosmic process towards death (a *Daily Chronicle* review of Galton's *Hereditary Genius* in 1892 called heredity 'the scientific equation of the theological dogma of original sin'), paradoxically restores to her life an order she has chosen; to live and love with an intensity sharpened by knowledge of the imminent death sentence she had pronounced on herself.

After Alec's murder, Tess and Angel re-live with the poetic intensity of a drowning man a telescoped and accelerated version of Tess's life, which points her archetypal role by blending motifs from all three myths. Tess's lonely journeys over the surface of Wessex have defined her archetypal exile from harmony. Since leaving Talbothays all her journeying, with the significant exception of the abortive trip to Emminster, has pointed in the direction of Stonehenge. In a universe shaped by death, it is the only journey to end in fulfilment. The realization that 'to stay, or make a move—it came to much the same' (Camus: *The Outsider*) when all effort ends in death adds a dissonant undermelody to the paradisal interlude in the New Forest with an Angel fallen to human virtues—'Tenderness was absolutely dominant in Clare at last.' The lush woodland which recalls the richness of Talbothays and the barren Salisbury plain which recalls the Flintcombe Ash period flank the belated fulfilment of the wedding night in a mansion whose furnishings recall Wellbridge Manor. The fulfilment is as childlike, as 'temporary and unforefending' as their plans of escape. Ironical echoes of the earlier innocence at Marlott —seclusion, the dream-like atmosphere, the sense of suspended time—hint at the impossibility of Paradise for two responsible living human beings. 'Within was affection, union, error forgiven: outside was the inexorable.' Tess and Angel can only achieve absolute harmony by 'ignoring that there was a corpse'.

Tess's fate acknowledges the power of death, which allows no-one to remain unsoiled.

'. . . we can't stir a finger in this world without the risk of bringing death to somebody . . . each of us has the plague within him; no one, no one on earth, is free from it . . . What's natural is the microbe. All the rest—health, integrity, purity (if you like)—is a product of the human will, of a vigilance that must never falter.'

(Camus: *The Plague*)

Tess, in spite of her vigilance, collaborates at times with the power of death—with her desire for oblivion, her submission to impersonal forces and concepts through her love for Angel, her relapses to waiting on Providence when her responsible consciousness tells her that there is no Providence to wait on. Stonehenge and Winton-cester, with their symbols of an order based on death defined blackly against the empty sky, provide a fitting end to this modern myth about the maintenance of human identity against the void. Hardy gives full weight to the impersonal agents of that order. Yet while his cosmos robs the human individual of meaning, his poetry puts it back again.

The poetic vision gives supreme importance to Tess's inner, unique experience of the world through her sensations and emotions; unusually detailed for Hardy. She is also defined by the poetry of her work. Even the harsh work at Flintcombe Ash borrows poetic beauty from the transformations of frost and snow and the tragic evocations of the Northern birds who share and universalize Tess's will to live. The differing kinds of work take their special rhythm from the rhythms of her life, sensitively realized in narrative and speech structure. The rhythms of Tal-bothays, slow and contemplative or simple and passionate, reflecting her sweep to maturity with its hesitations, crises, reprieves and rallies, build up a very different emotional response from the monotonous, consonantal rhythm of mechanical work at Flint-combe Ash, or the deadness of shocked existence, detail after dragging detail in flat bald sentences, at Wellbridge Manor. Hardy's dialogue is not always inspired: perhaps even Angel would hardly have met the greatest crisis of his life with 'My God—how can forgiveness meet such a grotesque—prestidigitation as that!'—

but Tess's stupefied simplicity in the quarrel, her bare statements of truth—'It is in your own mind what you are angry at, Angel; it is not in me'—catch the intimate cadences of a noble and passionate woman. Her qualities even infect the rougher speech of her companions. Izz Huett's 'She would have laid down her life for 'ee. I could do no more', and 'Her mind can no more be heaved from that one place where it do bide than a stooded wagon from the hole he's in' have the noble ballad simplicity of Tess's personal rhythms. This personal rhythm is set frequently against the dance-like rhythm of scenes where human beings become part of an automatic process—the harvest, the garlic picking, the threshing. Yet the personal rhythm prevails in an overwhelming sense of Tess's beauty of character.

Tess dies, but the meaning of her life, and of the whole book, lies in her vibrant humanity, her woman's power of suffering, renewal, and compassion, which has restored Angel to his rightful nature as Man, conscious of guilt and imperfection. One could not wish to be angel or animal while Tess exists in her human love, passion, beauty, trust, forgiveness, pity, sensitivity, responsibility, endurance, dignity, integrity, and spiritual light. To accept her mortality and the terrible beauty of the earth, to discover the absurdity of immutable law that makes of her fineness a death-trap, and yet to oppose her will against the universe as she found it and make moral choice that it is better to do this than that, is to answer the question of 'The Blinded Bird', 'Who is divine?'

XII

Jude the Obscure:
A Novel of Affirmation

Jude the Obscure begins with a farewell. Phillotson's farewell to Marygreen as he sets off for Christminster starts a novel that was Hardy's farewell to novel-writing, to his lyrical evocation of nature, to the comic relief of the Wessex chorus (even in so subdued a form as Dairyman Crick's stories in *Tess*), to the traditional beliefs and securities of unreflective rural life, and to the nineteenth century. *Jude* initiates the modern novel with its ambitious working-class hero and its neurotic heroine; city life in the back streets; the problems of adaptation to a rapidly changing world; of commercial and material values; of sexual and social maladjustment of the 'abnormal' variation from the species. It foreshadows the modern themes of failure, frustration, and futility, disharmony, isolation, rootlessness, and absurdity as inescapable conditions of life. It charts rebellion against orthodox labels which inhibit spontaneity and personal growth. It probes the existentialist's terrible freedom and the burden of unlocalized guilt; the search for self-definition, self-knowledge, self-sufficiency, and purpose without significance, gods, homeland, religious myths, or absolute values. It stresses the importance and self-destructive exclusiveness of personal relationships; the value of doubt and fluidity; the intellectual overdevelopment that endangers the primary appetites for life; the ascendancy of the death-wish; the absurd and tragic predicament of human beings developed to a high degree of sensitivity in an insentient universe bearing all things away; the primacy of suffering. Jude Fawley differs from most anti-heroes, to his credit, in knowing what he wants to escape from and where he wants to go to, in holding fast to his ideal Christminster, and in refusing to demean his integrity in order to survive, Lucky Jim fashion, in the real defective world. But the line of descent is there.

Hardy's style and structure, too, have moved nearer to the modern psychological novel, without losing his traditional characteristics. His penetration into unconscious motives enabled him to embody the impulse to self-destruction, long before Freud, as self-punishment for the guilt of aspiring personal being. It can be seen at work in Jude's compulsion to degrade himself by drink, and in Sue's reversals of feeling, unnecessary housework (VI–IX), and sudden explosions of suppressed feminine desires. The psychology of evasion finds expression in Jude's half-acknowledged self-deceptions. When attracted by Arabella, 'he kept his impassioned doings a secret almost from himself'. His articulated desire to find in Sue 'a companion in Anglican worship, a tender friend', soon betrays its sexual origin; and the false logic which convinces him that he should meet Arabella instead of studying the Greek Testament is betrayed by Hardy's comment that 'foreseeing such an event he had already arrayed himself in his best clothes'. Occasionally Hardy makes use of the limited viewpoint to throw another light on a relationship that is too close to be balanced: Sue and Jude at the Great Wessex Show are seen through Arabella's vulgar but shrewd gaze. But the modern psychological subtlety contributes to the old Hardeian pattern of basic archetypes playing out a ritual of human destiny. The contrasts of style and structure reflect the discordances of modern life moving between a dead world and a world waiting to be born. The range moves from the realism of Jude's sexual relations to Sue and Arabella, and the pig-killing, to the grotesque symbolism of Little Father Time's triple murder. Epic grandeur and ironic low comedy combine in the familiar arraignment of the fundamental injustice of conscious being.

Nevertheless, *Jude* differs from the earlier novels in that its deeper reality lies less in the action than in the flow of perceptions, feelings and thoughts which make up an Ibsenite discussion drama of the inner life. The mental process by which Jude arrives at the decision to meet Arabella is a case in point. Dialogue, in a novel that embodies so much of the advanced argument of the day, takes on symbolic and cumulative importance. Hardy's touch is not always certain when he presents the play of intellectual minds, and Sue's criticism that Jude is 'too sermony' could be applied to much of the speech. But his touch is sure when human passion informs diction and rhythm, as in the last meeting of Sue and Jude, and in speeches (really monologues, true to the novel's theme of isolation) whose differing contexts dramatize the stages of Jude's career.

The revealing action, gesture, and symbol still have their place.

But a novel which rejects the old concepts of rational order and stable character looks forward in some respects to the more fluid conception which admits a sequence of external events in time to be meaningless and the human psyche to be a battleground of baffling contradictory impulses. The significance of the plot relies less on a chain of related actions than on a series of situations, created from inner tensions, which lead to 'moments of vision'— the poetic technique of later writers such as Virginia Woolf and James Joyce.

In spite of its bleakness, sexual frankness, social concern, and prosaic realism, *Jude the Obscure* is as poetic a novel as its predecessors. Its kind of poetry looks back to the epic, defiant poetry of the Book of Job and forward to the grey modern note of expected pain. The poetic strain blends several elements. Though Hardy's characteristic poetry of nature and man rooted in nature's seasonal rhythms cannot play a large part in an epic of rootlessness, the poetry of buildings and ancient cities stresses the essential themes of change and loneliness. The novel's serious concern with the ultimates of man's fate—loneliness, loss, frustration, failure, death—makes its subject as inherently poetic as the Bible or Greek tragedy. Basic myths are felt moving behind this modern pilgrim's progress to define the archetypal psychic impulses that link Jude to earlier epics of man's relation to destiny. The seeker for knowledge to expand the limited human horizon recalls Faust. His relationship to Sue takes him into the region of legend dominated by La Belle Dame sans Merci, the enchanted maiden immured between heaven and earth (Sue's inaccessibility is stressed by the windows which separate her from Jude), and the fatal mermaid sexually attractive but impossible to mate, correlative to the fear of life that yearns for absolute existence. The most prominent mythic echoes come from the Bible and Greek literature. Jude's consistent heroic prototypes are the defiant, suffering Job, Tantalus and Sisyphus—the hero who provided Camus with an image for modern man's doom of futile effort. Jude's fate is likened to the curse on the houses of Atreus and Jeroboam. These resonances from two great shaping cultures help to define the Hebraic and Hellenic attitudes, self-denial and self-assertion, to the modern predicament.

Jude's name and appearance (curly black beard and hair) help to identify him with Jewish hero-myth as well as with St Jude, patron saint of craftsmen and impossible things. The references to

256

Samson and Delilah in portrait (i–vii) and metaphor (vi–vii) are an obvious comment on Jude's relationship with Arabella and his fight against the Philistines. Norman Holland, Jr., in an article ' "Jude the Obscure": Hardy's Symbolic Indictment of Christianity' (*Nineteenth Century Fiction*, ix, 1954), finds a denial of the relevance of Christianity in the reverberations of Jewish and pagan myth. The Jewish image pattern identifies Jude with the Judaic character, combining sensuality with aspiration, Sue with the Virgin mother as well as pagan deities, Arabella the pig-breeder's daughter with the unclean animal of the Jews (and Phillotson, by implication), and Little Father Time with Christ. Mr Holland's interpretation sees Jude as the potentially Christian Jew of the Old Testament and Sue as the potentially Christian pagan; and Little Father Time's function to enact a substitute Crucifixion for the 'poor Christ' Jude has become, to point the futility of atonement in a spiritual waste land. But it seems to be less of a substitution than a parody. Father Time is introduced as 'an enslaved and dwarfed Divinity', recalling E. M. Forster's conception of absolute infinity as something mean and small. If he is another Christ, he is, like Camus' Meuersault, 'the only Christ we deserve'; a grotesque anti-Saviour, created to mock the absurdity of the cosmic process.

The personal movement of Jude's life, the modern Everyman caught in the violent contrasts of his own being and the changing world, gains poetic depth from its power to represent the larger mythical, historical and evolutionary rhythms of the cosmos. He is Everyman as Tess is Everywoman. Elfride defines to Smith the essential difference (blurred by Sue Bridehead, the modern intellectual woman) between masculine and feminine assertion of being: 'I am content to build happiness on any accidental basis that may lie near at hand; you are for making a world to suit your happiness' (*A Pair of Blue Eyes*). Jude's personal search for knowledge (a magic formula that would invest life with meaning) and a place in life takes its rise in the post-Darwinian climate of insecurity and doubt. The end of his search is a bitter contrast to the beginning. Orthodox images of scholarship and religion crumble before the true religious scholar, whose first duty as a thinker, according to Hardy's admired thinker John Stuart Mill, was 'to follow his intellect to whatever conclusions it may lead'. The Biblical and Classical counterpoint to Jude's life raises the question of the place of intellect in any Holy Plan. 'Thou shalt not' of Old Testament letter is too negative and too external a creed to control those who live by their intellects and those strong inner impulses of love recognized by the spirit of the New Testament. The conflict is imaged in the two parts of *Christ/minster*.

The search for meaning in knowledge leads to knowledge of futility. 'The yearning of his heart to find something to anchor on, to cling to' leads to experience of the void. Jude's arhythmic wanderings and sexual relationships trace his progress towards self-definition. His quest is the basic myth of twentieth-century man; of Gide's Oedipus and Sartre's Orestes, isolated from conventional securities and comforting myths of a Holy Plan, free, without hope, to create ethics without dogma and the terms of his own being:

'I had gushed up from the unknown; no longer any past, no longer any father's example, nothing to lean on any more; everything to be built up anew—country, forefathers—all to be invented, all to be discovered.'

(André Gide, *Oedipus*, tr. John Russell)

His progress from a desire to find fulfilment in College and Church to the simple need to live as a human being involves an examination of the earlier myths that man has lived by, in the scientific spirit advocated by contemporary advanced thinkers. The result denies their relevance to the modern predicament. The spirit that characterized pagan and Christian civilizations—'that zest for existence' and 'the view of life as a thing to be put up with', the clarity of 'Classic' and the spontaneity of 'Gothic'—is embodied in the story and character of Jude and Sue. Their failure to find a compromise between the best of Hebraism and the best of Hellenism contributes to their personal tragedy. Their inability to stand alone as human beings without myth, most strongly marked in Sue, leads only to a reversal of their pagan and Christian standpoints. The values and defects of both have been so thoroughly measured against human needs that Sue's return to religious orthodoxy and Jude's Saturnalian re-marriage to the 'substantial female animal' are felt as defilements of their humanity.

That Hardy does not for the most part rely on the highly-charged poetic imagery of the epic genre to develop this modern epic, but on bare narration and dialogue, acceptable to the prosaic modern spirit, is a measure of his achievement. The typical tension in Hardy's verse between jerky personal rhythm and rigid form is repeated in the structure of the novel. Jude's arhythmic wandering (Marygreen—Christminster—Melchester—Shaston—Aldbrickham and elsewhere—Christminster) are counterpointed and held together with hoops of steel by the poetic stylization of the plot. Hardy stresses that the plot is 'almost geometrically constructed—I ought not to say *constructed*, for, beyond a certain point, the characters necessitated it, and I simply let it come'.

'The "grimy" features of the story go to show the contrast between the ideal life a man wished to lead, and the squalid real life he was fated to lead. The throwing of the pizzle, at the supreme moment of his young dream, is to sharply initiate this contrast . . . It is, in fact, to be discovered in *everybody's* life . . .'

'Of course the book is all contrasts—or was meant to be in its original conception . . . e.g. Sue and her heathen gods set against Jude's reading the Greek Testament; Christminster academical, Christminster in the slums; Jude the saint, Jude the sinner; Sue the Pagan, Sue the saint; marriage, no marriage; &c., &c.'

(Life)

The structure of Jude's quest for meaning is marked by contrasting 'epiphanies' that define his progress from medieval to modern man. At Marygreen the pig's pizzle cutting across his abstract reflections makes him aware of his double nature. His brief marriage with Arabella brings into question the logic of social and natural law which show indifference to his finer aspirations. But the milestone to Christminster still carries his vision. At Christminster he encounters Sue Bridehead and the obstructive physical reality of his vision. His past relationship with Arabella and his growing love for Sue affect his studies and reflect the complexities of his nature. Arabella frustrates his nobler aspirations, Sue his sexual desires, and Christminster, attuned to a celibate ideal of scholarship, his complete fulfilment as a human being. Sue is closely linked with Christminster and its atmosphere of light. Her intellect promises Jude the freedom which the real Christminster denies him. But she is as ethereal as his vision of the city; emancipated, as he is not, from sexual appetites. His ideal intellectual city and his ideal intellectual woman frustrate his human impulses equally. The Christminster episode balances the vision of Part I—the ideal life frustrated by the physical—with his recognition of the incompleteness of the ideal alone. On the day he awakens from his dream, his vision embraces the reality of

Christminster from the heights and the depths. The unattainable Pisgah-panorama from Wren's theatre and the tavern where he drinks steadily and recites the creed in Latin to an uncomprehending rabble express his complex nature in a juxtaposition of the ideal and its negation (a structural concept basic to Hardy's poetry).

At ecclesiastical Melchester Jude's desire 'to do some good thing' as a humble man of God is disturbed by his developing passion for Sue and the influence of her free-ranging intellect on his beliefs. The epiphany that grows out of Part III is an awareness that 'the human was more powerful in him than the Divine'. Correlative to this recognition, the abstract ordinances of the Church on intimate relationships, when measured by the practical needs of the human being, are found wanting. Its concepts are based either on the subhuman or the superhuman: regarding sex as sin, yet recognizing animal desire as the sole grounds for marriage or divorce. It is typical of the modern novel that the moment of vision comes in an episode that seems extraneous to the main development of the novel, yet it grows out of dominant mood and theme: Jude's impulsive visit to the composer who, he discovers, is prostituting his talent to the mean bread-and-cheese question.

Shaston, that other 'city of a dream' where Sue lives in sexless marriage with Phillotson, the temporary quarters of eccentric itinerants, is the place where Jude sets up his standard as no more than a human individual. The unpremeditated kiss between him and Sue, each married to someone else, is the signal for Jude to burn his religious books so that 'in his passion for Sue he could now stand as an ordinary sinner, and not as a whited sepulchre'. It is also the signal for Sue to realize her false position as Phillotson's 'wife', and Phillotson, whose name suggests his Philistine role ('I hate such eccentricities, Sue. There's no order or regularity in your sentiments') to retreat from his legal rights into spontaneous human charity. ('I am not going to be a philosopher any longer! I only see what's under my eyes.') The vision gained at Shaston widens into universal significance through not being confined to Jude. The respect of both Jude and Phillotson (an older, more conventional reflection of Jude in the story) for Sue's sexual fastidiousness, for the special being of Sue Bridehead instead of for an abstraction 'the average woman', is a triumph for human individuality. It is inevitably qualified by a negation. The reverse side of individuality is anarchy. Part IV ends with the ironic low comedy of Phillotson's public defence of his charity, wrecked by his drop-out supporters. The major ironic contrast of the absurdity that vulgarly intrudes on the noblest human instincts marks the moments of vision at every stage of Jude's progress.

The title of Part V, 'At Aldbrickham and elsewhere', indicates the increasing rootlessness and isolation which follow on Jude's and Sue's attempt to live according to their own standards of truth. Social ostracism and their own sensitiveness to difference from the mass force them into an increasingly nomadic life. Fighting to keep their standards of spontaneity in a vacuum reduces both to a basic level of human existence. Jude's aspirations shrink to baking the staff of life. Sue submits to Jude's sexual desires to keep him from his lawful wife. Only the animal and unaspiring survive in an unimaginative world. The ideal vision appears only in flashes at temporary halting-places: the sense of bodiless oneness in the 'enchanted palace' of flowers at the Great Wessex show, and the Christminster cakes which embody Jude's ruling passion at Kennetbridge fair (significantly qualified by Little Father Time's sense that the roses are doomed to wither, and Arabella 'unceremoniously munching one of the cakes' which are made to be eaten.) Part V brings into prominence the forces that will crush individuality: Arabella (sex), Phillotson (convention) and Jude's son Little Father Time, whose name suggests the impersonal abstraction which assimilates human endeavour to general non-existence.

It is inevitable that Jude's progress to knowledge of self and the world he lives in should end at Christminster. His early vision is all that is left to him. Now not deceived by the reality, he sets against the hollow pomp, pride, and cruelty of Remembrance Day the justification for an obscure man's life. His great speech to the crowd compels comparison with his rehearsal of the creed, in a language not his own, of beliefs that did not square with his human experience. This spontaneous performance, the result of deep thought and painful living, is his climactic moment of triumph and vision. His physical stance, child on his arm, and the pregnant Sue at his side, stresses a vision of the dignity of a human being stripped to nothingness.

' "I am in a chaos of principles—groping in the dark—acting by instinct and not after example. Eight or nine years ago when I came here first, I had a neat stock of fixed opinions, but they dropped away one by one; and the further I get the less sure I am. I doubt if I have anything more for my present rule of life than following inclinations which do me and nobody else any harm, and actually give pleasure to those I love best. There, gentlemen, since you wanted to know how I was getting on, I have told you." '

The justification is followed by the climactic negation. Little Father Time's triple murder is the logical outcome of the absurdity at the heart of the cosmos that Jude's career has revealed. Jude's despairing remarriage to Arabella, gin-drunk, and Sue's prostitution, creed-drunk, to the religious and social orthodoxy which she thinks can take from her the responsibility of guilt for creating life doomed to death, are recognitions of absurdity. Jude's lonely death, murmuring Job's bitter indictment of life to the uncomprehending cheers of the Festival crowd outside, completes the sum of his knowledge. It is not an answer but a question. *'Wherefore is light given to him that is in misery, and life unto the bitter in soul?'*

Jude's inner development, geared as it is to the ferment of nineteenth-century advanced thought, runs the risk of being more of a tract than a novel. Its basic structure of contrasts could have turned it into a lifeless mechanical blueprint. But Hardy's poetic power of visualization clothes the abstract skeleton in a series of dramatic and interlocking scenes of sensuous human response to life that are not easily forgotten. The structural contrasts grow naturally from the details that evoke life in its variety as it falls in a sequence of related impressions on the mind of a sensitive child. Jude is Hardy's only detailed portrait of a child. The difference between *Jude the Obscure* and a manifesto on the marriage question can be gauged by examining the resonances of a scene, based on a personal childhood experience, which has reached us in three different forms; the poem 'Childhood among the Ferns', an early experience recorded in the *Life*, (pp. 15–16) and an incident in the novel.

> I sat one sprinkling day upon the lea,
> Where tall-stemmed ferns spread out luxuriantly,
> And nothing but those tall ferns sheltered me.
>
> The rain gained strength, and damped each lopping frond,
> Ran down their stalks beside me and beyond,
> And shaped slow-creeping rivulets as I conned,

With pride, my spray-roofed house. And though anon
Some drops pierced its green rafters, I sat on,
Making pretence I was not rained upon.

The sun then burst, and brought forth a sweet breath
From the limp ferns as they dried underneath:
I said: "I could live on here thus till death";

And queried in the green rays as I sate:
"Why should I have to grow to man's estate,
And this afar-noised World perambulate?"

'He was lying on his back in the sun, thinking how useless he was, and covered his face with his straw hat. The sun's rays streamed through the interstices of the straw, the lining having disappeared. Reflecting on his experiences of the world so far as he had got, he came to the conclusion that he did not wish to grow up . . . Yet this early evidence of that lack of social ambition which followed him through life was shown when he was in perfect health and happy circumstances.'

'Jude went out, and, feeling more than ever his existence to be an undemanded one, he lay down upon his back on a heap of litter near the pig-sty. The fog had by this time become more translucent, and the position of the sun could be seen through it. He pulled his straw hat over his face, and peered through the interstices of the plaiting at the white brightness, vaguely reflecting. Growing up brought responsibilities, he found. Events did not rhyme quite as he had thought. Nature's logic was too horrid for him to care for. That mercy towards one set of creatures was cruelty towards another sickened his sense of harmony. As you got older, and felt yourself to be at the centre of your time, and not at a point in its circumference, as you had felt when you were little, you were seized with a sort of shuddering, he perceived. All around you there seemed to be something glaring, garish, rattling, and the noises and glares hit upon the little cell called your life, and shook it, and warped it.

'If he could only prevent himself growing up! He did not want to be a man.'

The fear of adult responsibilities is common to all three. But the details vary to evoke different emotions. In poem and statement the response is nostalgic, but not potentially tragic. 'His experiences of the world' in the statement are not specified. 'Happy circumstances' and 'lack of social ambition' do not invest the incident with the significance of a protest against the conditions of being. The poem replaces the straw hat with a natural shelter of fern, a more adequate protection for the child who wants to regress, and dyes the sunlight to the fern's green shade. The fear of life, of which the poem is a correlative, is muted. The child has nothing worse to face than the discomforts of rain.

The incident as it is transmuted in the novel retains more features of the original. The less protective straw hat and Jude's prostrate position stress the defencelessness and defeat that have just been painfully brought home in Farmer Troutham's chastisement of the boy for his kindness to the birds. His wish to avoid responsibility grows out of the facts of his experience of the tragic dissonance that will destroy his life. The 'something glaring, garish, rattling', enacted in the prose that comes to a painful halt at every revolution of the child's thoughts, is an obvious correlative of his punishment with the rattle, and a prophecy of the vulgar sexual impulses that will cut across his finer aspirations. The pigsty, not present in poem or statement, defines the vulgarity more closely. It is the place to which he returns when defeated by lumpish physical conditions—the sheer plod of Classical grammar, the passion for Sue that makes him burn his religious books. It introduces the persistent pig imagery that is part of Jude's complex destiny as an animal being. Pigs are prominently featured in his courtship of Arabella, and it is the killing of a pig that hastens their parting and contributes to Jude's nurture by the insight it gives into their two opposed attitudes to nature's logic—the attitudes of adaptation and protest.

The details are not all of negative potentiality. Jude's affirming vision of Christminster exists in embryo in the 'white brightness' of the sun that reaches him through the translucent fog. It grows out of his moments of despair as a 'city of light', a 'heavenly Jerusalem' of all that is absolute and meaningful in a dissonant world. Its light is associated with various shades of fog and darkness that shift their meaning to define Jude's progress in disillusion. His early views of the distant city, an impressionistic mirage filtered through morning mist, an evening 'halo or glow-fog' of lamps and the romantic mists of his yearning mind, make the city seem deceptively near and the physical foreground chimaerically unreal and funereally dark. Night hides the unwelcoming countenances of the colleges when he gets there, and fog hangs over the city in the days of his final despair, chaos of principles, and bitter realization of the muddle that should have been a clear intellectual centre of light.

Unlike the statement and the poem, the incident in the novel cannot stand alone. It is part of a complex of interrelated affirmations and negations that define Jude as sufferer from the inharmonious 'ache of modernism' from beginning to end. His nature and destiny as Jude the obscure and superfluous are suggested from the start. He has no roots in family or village. His conflicting drives are obscure to his consciousness. He is caught up and lost in the atmosphere of change that prophetically begins the novel.

The inhabitants of Marygreen, particularly Aunt Drusilla and Widow Edlin, are relics of the old stable rural culture, free from 'the chronic melancholy which is taking hold of the civilized races with the decline of belief in a beneficent power'. But Aunt Drusilla tells tales of matrimonial misery, the old church is put to debased uses, and the old well into which Jude stares 'was probably the only relic of the local history that remained absolutely unchanged'. The well is a stable point to which Jude returns at moments of crisis and defeat in his changeful history. Its 'long circular perspective ending in a shining disk of quivering water', its natural encrustations, suggest the infinity he yearns for, and the mystery and continuity of life; a paradox which he is to seek in sexual experience. Phillotson, the schoolmaster who has inspired Jude with scholastic ambition, is now joining the movement of change, to seek a degree in Christminster.

The incident that draws attention to Jude—his offer of Aunt Drusilla's fuel-house to store Phillotson's piano—subtly defines the difference between master and pupil in terms of a spiritual force (music) that resounds thematically through the novel. Phillotson, who 'had never acquired any skill in playing', fails later to touch emotional chords in Sue which Jude reaches at this very piano (IV–i). It is a piquant irony that they are so moved by the emotional hymn whose composer had deserted music for the wine trade. The irony grows in power as Jude's inharmonious 'failures' —his passion for Sue, emancipation from Christian belief, the death of the children, and his own obscure death—are counterpointed by incongruous musical harmonies—psalm, hymn, waltz—entering his isolated consciousness from the communal life of Christminster and Melchester. Sue's feeling, after the death of their children,

'that the world resembled a stanza or melody composed in a dream; it was wonderfully excellent to the half-aroused intelligence, but hopelessly absurd at the full waking . . .'

is not intrusive philosophical comment, but an integral (though partial) summing up in a novel where music is a recurrent image of the harmony absent from the cosmos.

The scene that sickened his sense of harmony in Farmer Troutham's field is emotionally connected to Jude's feeling of disorientation after his teacher's departure. Like Flintcomb Ash, the field presents the earth as a lumpish, 'meanly utilitarian' antagonist to be reckoned with in desires that flout the morality of Nature. Yet Hardy never sees the opposition as simple. The comment of the young idealist out of love with life as it is—'How ugly it is here!'— leads to an evocation of the field in positive terms that Jude has missed, of its human associations with the eternal pursuits of men and women. It is here that Jude's first moment of vision, his 'perception of the flaw in the terrestrial scheme, by which what was good for God's birds was bad for God's gardener', is brought violently to our senses by Hardy's dramatic and poetic power.

'Troutham had seized his left hand with his own left, and swinging his slim frame round him at arm's-length, again struck Jude on the hind parts with the flat side of Jude's own rattle, till the field echoed with the blows, which were delivered once or twice at each revolution.

' "Don't 'ee, sir—please don't 'ee!" cried the whirling child, as helpless under the centrifugal tendency of his person as a hooked fish swinging to land, and beholding the hill, the rick, the plantation, the path, and the rooks going round and round him in an amazing circular race.'

Jude suffers a symbolic foreshortening of his fate, placed with no secure foothold in an alien mechanical world that whirls him round on its own inscrutable punishing purposes; his pain misinterpreted by man and ignored by God (the blows 'echoing from the brand-new church tower just behind the mist'). The effect is sharpened by the poet's concern with both the objective appearance of physical things and their subjective distortion through the eyes of the 'whirling child'; and with the selective language, which ranges from the simple vitality of the 'hooked fish swinging to land' to the abstract ponderousness of 'centrifugal tendency'— both appropriate to a dramatic image that evokes the helpless individual's painful dependence on impersonal forces.

But it is characteristic of Hardy that he does not leave the scene without resisting its negation with Jude's human tenderness. He swings from the long perspective of the child as a whirling atom at the mercy of mechanical law to a close-up of him picking his way on tiptoe among 'scores of coupled earthworms lying half their length on the surface of the damp ground' (perhaps another oblique forecast of the sexual and compassionate impulses that are going to keep him in rotatory submission to the earth)' without killing a single one'.

The whole novel is shaped by meaningful contrasts and repetitions growing organically from the physical life of the poetically-conceived scenes. The most obvious symbolic contrast of ideal and real, letter and spirit, intention and result, lies in the structural relationship of the characters. Arabella and Sue as Caliban and Ariel to Jude's Everyman can be seen on one level as a projection of conflicting inner forces. Arabella's role as agent of the assimilating earth is clear. The ethereal and aptly-named Sue Bridehead, who shares with Catherine Earnshaw a death-wish longing to get back to the life of her infancy and freedom, seems to evoke the paradisal innocence Jude has lost (a concept familiar to readers of twentieth-century French writers, who often, like Hardy, present the longing for the paradisal ideal in terms of strong family affinity). The picture Sue presents dressed in Jude's best clothes after her escape from the Training College, 'a slim and fragile being masquerading as himself on a Sunday', strikingly foreshadows Conrad's study of projection in 'The Secret Sharer'. Phillotson can be seen as projecting the alternative career of a more conventional Jude.

Yet the characters live first and foremost as vitally rounded people who suffer as human beings from the conflicting forces at work in themselves and the cosmos. Their inner contradictions are presented in sensuous terms, in scenes whose elements link across the novel to light character and theme from several angles. The psychological complexities of Sue, for example, swinging between 'pagan' and 'saint', love and fear of life, are evoked in scenes that are linked by religious 'props'. Jude's first romantic glimpses of her in a photograph—a prophetically insubstantial image—'in a broad hat with radiating folds under the brim like the rays of a halo', between two brass candlesticks on his aunt's mantelpiece, and at her 'sweet, saintly, Christian business' among the religious bric-à-brac of the Christminster shop, provides an ironic under-harmony to the shrine-image of the large white naked statues of Venus and Apollo, set between two candles on her chest of drawers,

'in odd contrast to their environment of text and martyr, and the Gothic-framed Crucifix-picture that was only discernible now as a Latin cross, the figure thereon being obscured by the shades.'

The complexity of Sue's response to her pagan gods invests every action, to contribute to the poetic mood surrounding her: her rebellious impulse to buy them, the white pipeclay that comes off on her gloves (evoking the incompleteness of her paganism), her nervous reaction to their nakedness, which leads her to wrap them in vegetation of sexual potency, her heretical reading of Gibbon and Swinburne as she sits in front of their home-made shrine. The Calvary print that is almost obscured, except for the Latin cross, by the pagan statues and darkness gains retrospective meaning from the huge solidly constructed Latin cross, brightly jewelled, that dominates the church of St Silas where Jude discovers a distraught Sue (vi–iii) who has sacrificed her free human individuality (reduced to 'a heap of black clothes') to take on the role of the martyred 'figure . . . obscured by the shades'. The changed perspective of the religious accessories in these two scenes tells us, as surely as Jamesian psychological nuances, of the reversals taking place in Sue's highly-strung mind.

The return to certain places connected with significant action is a well-tried narrative technique, which Hardy does not disdain to use in his most modern novel to mark the ironies in human progress. The white milestone to Christminster, the brown ploughed field of his punishment which Jude has to cross to reach the high vantage point of the Brown House, the Brown House itself, the ancient white Ridgeway and high road to Alfredston which intersect there, the neighbouring cottage where Jude and Arabella spend their short married life, form a cluster of associations that embody Jude's moments of intense affirmative vision and the moments of agony that are likewise permanent. Part of the poetic force is carried by Hardy's colour symbolism. The brown of the earth and the white light of absolute reality are repeated throughout the book, notably in the brown-fleshed Arabella and the pale, scintillating brightness of Sue, who is associated with the 'city of light' Jude first seeks from the top of the Brown House. The lofty ridge which gives him his first glimpse of subjective meaning stresses the related and essential loneliness of the human being, even as he lies there with Arabella, in 'the most apparent of all solitudes, that of empty surrounding space.' It is here that Jude kneels, like Tess, to adore the pagan gods of life in the ecstasy of the 'Carmen Saeculare', and here that he falls victim to Arabella's earthy wiles. The central scenes of their courtship and marriage are played out in the locality. The Brown House barn was 'the point at which he had planned to turn back' to his studies after walking out with Arabella. The consequences of his failure to do so bring the earlier scenes to mind when he repasses the scene with Sue, married to Phillotson. It is here that Arabella, also moved by a vision of the past, flings her religious tracts in the hedge when she determines to win Jude back from Sue. It is here that the hereditary doom of the Fawley family was enacted, where Jude's unhappily married parents parted and an ancestor was hanged after a marital tragedy that contained the elements of Jude's final tragedy—a dead child, a parting, madness. It is here that Jude elects to fulfil the doom of his house by committing virtual suicide after his last journey in the rain, ill and exhausted, to see Sue.

'He was by this time at the corner of the green, from which the path ran across the fields in which he had scared rooks as a boy. He turned and looked back, once, at the building which still contained Sue; and then went on, knowing that his eyes would light on that scene no more.

'There are cold spots up and down Wessex in autumn and winter weather; but the coldest of all when a north or east wind is blowing is the crest of the down by the Brown House, where the road to Alfredston crosses the old Ridgeway. Here the first winter sleets and snows fall and lie, and here the spring frost lingers last unthawed. Here in the teeth of the north-east wind and rain Jude now pursued his way, wet through, the necessary slowness of his walk from lack of his former strength being insufficient to maintain his heat. He came to the milestone, and, raining as it was, spread his blanket and lay down there to rest. Before moving on he went and felt at the back of the stone for his own carving. It was still there; but nearly obliterated by moss. He passed the spot where the gibbet of his ancestor and Sue's had stood, and descended the hill.'

The symphonic reiteration of familiar landmarks of his ecstasy and agony, the strong, rhythmic simplicity of diction and sentence structure, the evocation of a past beyond his own, the gesture of feeling the milestone for the marks of his identity and youthful hope, 'nearly obliterated by moss', even as he lies prostrate from the physical weight of the world, as he had done many years before, charges the connection of man and scene with a tragic emotion only the greatest of epic writers can command.

Christminster, of course, is the most pervasive double-edged metaphor of Jude's complexity. His architectural evocation of the city, as Dr C. J. P. Beatty has ably demonstrated in his London Ph.D. thesis, *The Part played by Architecture in the Life and Works of*

Thomas Hardy, has caught its many aspects as ideal and physical obstructiveness. Jude's 'heavenly Jerusalem' is dissected in Parts II and VI into all the earthly reality that defeats the vision: slum lodgings, seedy taverns, and above all the insuperable barrier of cold stone college walls that he can live at the back of and restore (as the religious medievalism that founded Christminster cannot be restored to direct complex modern life) but never enter as a scholar. His experience of Christminster swings between the impressionistic subjective— the romantic moonlight dream that enrols him among the saints and visionaries of the past, and conjures up the city from the architectural details revealed by the flash of a lamp and the feel of moulding under his fingers—and the daylight reality.

'What at night had been perfect and ideal was by day the more or less defective real. Cruelties, insults, had, he perceived, been inflicted on the aged erections. The condition of several moved him as he would have been moved by maimed sentient beings. They were wounded, broken, sloughing off their outer shape in the deadly struggle against years, weather, and man.'

The double face of the colleges, inhumanly obstructive and humanly suffering, links them to Jude himself. 'There in the old walls were the broken lines of the original idea; jagged curves, disdain of precision, irregularity, disarray': an architectural commentary on the broken design of his life, shattered by the inharmonious physical processes that corrupted the crumbling walls, and the power of the mean bread-and-cheese question that elbowed the poor scholar off the pavement.

It is significant in a novel that celebrates respect for individuality that the 'original idea' is conjured up, not by the total vision of a college or colleges, but by details, and that most of these details are Gothic. Hardy has declared his allegiance to Gothic principles of spontaneity in art and life. It was not until *The Magic Mountain* and *Dr Faustus* that another great artist, Thomas Mann, studied in depth the self-destructive aspect of the Gothic ideal which Hardy saw existing in tension with its vitality.

The only Classical building to have importance in the fable is Wren's circular theatre. It is from this structure that Jude awakens to a balanced sense of his limitations in his panoramic view of the promised land, and admits defeat of spontaneity in a speech that is a triumph of spontaneity. It is here that another child's vision—

Little Father Time's—comments ironically on his father's. His view of the colleges as 'gaols' and the procession of the Doctors in their 'blood-red' robes as the Judgement Day, soon to be tragically realized in his bloody judgement on superfluous life enacted on this tragic Remembrance Day which honours the dignity of man, is a correlative of man's tragic futility that has become more familiar through the 'prison' images of Kafka, Camus, and Bernard Malamud.

One could go on listing other scenes which dramatize the contrasts of the novel. Jude's moonlight dream of Christminster, interrupted by the 'real and local voice' of a policeman and the fact 'that he seemed to be catching a cold', is recalled to disturb the emotional current of his repassing the spot with Arabella in Part VI, seriously ill, defeated by Sue's orthodoxy, and too disillusioned to take exception to her judgement of his delirious rambling: 'Phantoms! There's neither living nor dead hereabouts except a damn policeman!' Jude's imaginary procession of welcoming worthies is set against the real procession and their ignorance of the obscure scholar in their midst. Meetings and partings comment ironically on each other. Jude's first encounters with Arabella and Sue forecast their meaning to his life. Sue's sensitivity about their place of meeting, her freedom from flirtatious scheming, her unpredictable mystery, are set against Arabella's lack of these qualities as she courts Jude over the pig's pizzle hanging from the bridge. The meeting near the Martyr's Cross is balanced by the parting by the children's graves, which leads Sue to a living martyrdom and Jude to his death. Phillotson's meetings and partings with Sue reflect on Jude's. His human motives for letting Sue go are more admirable, and more Jude-like, than his conventional motives for taking her back. The Aldbrickham pub where Jude takes Sue to begin their life together and where she refuses to 'live with' him in the usual sense, is shadowed by the temporary physical union he had there with Arabella, which strikes him as the worse offence.

The marriage/no-marriage theme is richly varied in a series of scenes that set the spirit against the letter: the two legal marriages and divorces set against the unlicensed marriage of the spirit; the wedding rehearsal that Sue forces on Jude which comments piquantly, together with the weddings (or sacrifices) they observe, on the ceremony they never have and the affinity they have; the concepts of honour, upheld by the officiating clergymen, which push Jude and Sue into a grotesque parody of honour and marriage;

the unhappy alliances of their family that ghost their own. The theme has vivid concrete portrayal in the repeated attempts to cast away flesh or spirit in obedience to orthodox conceptions—Jude burning his books, Sue burning her 'adulterous' nightgown to Widow Edlin's expostulation, 'Upon my life I don't call that religion!'—honestly placed in their futility by Arabella pitching her tracts into the hedge. 'I've tried that sort o' physic and have failed wi' it. I must be as I was born!'

The theme of separation is embodied in dramatic visual terms throughout the book: Arabella parading her dishevelled state in front of the cottage after her quarrel with Jude; the separate rooms that Jude and Sue occupy; Sue caressing Jude through a window or by letter, where the barrier of distance enables her to find release in tenderness from her fear of physical life; Jude dramatically marking Sue's decision to return to Phillotson: 'He went to the bed, removed one of the pair of pillows thereon, and flung it to the floor.'

Hardy's mixture of poetic styles conveys the basic contrasts and nightmare conjunctions of prosaic physical reality and the grotesque abstract Absurdity that disrupts it. Ibsen and Strindberg, Absurd Theatre, and the novels of Sartre, Camus, and Iris Murdoch, to name no more, have familiarized us with a mixture of planes of reality essential to a vision of absurdity. Hardy's symbolic presentation of Little Father Time is such a vision, not a mistake in a novel of social realism. The paradox of absurdity comes home with full force embodied in a child, when one remembers Jude's youthful hopes. Hardy places him firmly in the objective world (compare the poem 'Midnight on the Great Western') of train, passengers, ticket, and lamplight, until his lack of response to the playing kitten modulates to another more remote key. The solemn rhythms of the prose, the abstract Latinate sonority the language takes on ('He was Age masquerading as Juvenility' . . .) the child's movement ('a steady mechanical creep which had in it an impersonal quality—the movement of the wave, or of the breeze, or of the cloud') and unnerving incuriosity about details of the landscape, invest him as an expressionistic agent of the automatic cosmic process which abstracts significance from individual things.

'To him the houses, the willows, the obscure fields beyond, were apparently regarded not as brick residences, pollards, meadows; but as human dwellings in the abstract, vegetation, and the wide dark world.'

His meaningless and monstrous act, told with the swift movement of an absurd 'happening', is a poetic foreshortening of the reality that comes to all, though hidden by human hope, purpose, and reproduction. It is the logical end of modern perceptiveness and the disillusive centuries which, aware of the futile repetition of life without redemption, has turned the death-wish into a modern social problem.

Yet Little Father Time's negation does not constitute the total effect of this great and terrible vision of the human condition. Time and the suffering it brings is the modern affirmation of spiritual maturity. The naked pain felt in *Jude the Obscure* intensely affirms the value of life's potentialities. How great is the affirmation of love in the agonized gesture with which Sue denies Jude's last appeal for a new beginning:

'As he passed the end of the church she heard his coughs mingling with the rain on the windows, and in a last instinct of human affection, even now unsubdued by her fetters, she sprang up as if to go and succour him. But she knelt down again, and stopped her ears with her hands till all possible sound of him had passed away.'

Their suffering affirms the life that will evolve beyond their own. In I–ii, the manuscript defines Jude as 'the *coming* sort of man who was born to ache a good deal before the fall of the curtain upon his unnecessary life should signify that all was well with him again.' (My italics.) The tragedy of the children's death brings Jude and Sue to a recognition of their role as pioneers of a new, more sensitive stage of development. It was left to G. B. Shaw, at the end of *Back to Methuselah*, to envisage the final stage of creative evolution to which they are moving.

'After passing a million goals they press on to the goal of redemption from the flesh, to the vortex freed from matter, to the whirlpool in pure intelligence that, when the world began, was a whirlpool in pure force.'

The shape of things to come can be seen side by side with the conditions that resist a new awakening. Individuals are not universally unkind. Sue Bridehead is the most imaginatively realized type of the future. Her suffering springs from the contradictions of character that are inevitable because, as a pioneer variation from the parent species, her evolution is necessarily incomplete. The obsessive self-created ritual pattern of attracting a man, living with him in selfish sexless intimacy, rejecting him, feeling guilt, and submitting herself to punishment out of all proportion to the crime betrays her allegiance to original sin. Her vitality is ambiguous. Destructive and self-destroying without roots in sexual or social conformity, it is yet productive of Jude's maturity and self-control. In a world where Sue's sexlessness has offended more than Tess's sexuality, social conceptions that have become shop-soiled through insistence on the physical aspect—'marriage', 'to live with', 'sin', 'adultery'—become revitalized by Sue.

Hardy is not uncritical of Jude's and Sue's attempts to find self-fulfilment. Jude makes the usual mistakes in defining it. Hardy, as always, draws attention to those neutral moments when an exercise of human will could have turned things in another direction. Jude saw Arabella's meaning 'with his intellectual eye, just for a short fleeting while'. Brains, too, are natural. Jude and Sue abuse theirs by living too exclusively in a 'dreamy paradise', when, for example, marriage or removal would have dealt with the taunts of Little Father Time's schoolmates. Jude had the sense of responsibility and sexual control that could have risen above non-resistance to a law of nature. The boy's *Done because we are too menny* has point in a world where there is an overpopulation problem. The tragedy is to some extent avoidable.

Some critics have questioned whether a novel whose heroine is suffering from a special maladjustment can be defined as tragedy, which requires some responsible re-ordering of moral chaos. Both Sue and Jude begin in the belief, like traditional tragic heroes, that they can mould circumstances. Both have tragic recognitions of their failure in standards of sincerity, responsibility, and respect for individual being which they themselves have set up. Even after the horror, Jude has profited sufficiently by his suffering to see hope of a new start free of everything except fidelity to human needs and values. 'Is there anything better on earth than that we should love one another?' But Sue's inability to bear human burdens alone, which betrays her humanity and Jude's needs, is the real tragedy.

Tragedy in *Jude the Obscure* is the natural condition. One can only attain a modern harmony by trying to understand it. What remains to affirm the life and endeavour of Jude and Sue is a memory of their love, ennobled by its comparative freedom from physical grossness; their courageous assertion of Hellenic joy and meaning and human dignity against the abstractions of society and the looming dark of death; their compassion for all living creatures bound to them in a common mystery of suffering. In the event, it is Jude's qualities that affirm this epic of modern existentialist man. His astonishing resilience and adaptation to ever-narrowing limitations, without being reconciled to the present stage of evolution; his emotional impulses of affection and tenderness; his sensitivity, his ideal of Christminster's meaning which outlasts his disillusion with the place; his unflinching self-examination and devotion to sincerity, make him worthy to stand for man, 'neither commonplace, unmeaning, nor tame . . . but slighted and enduring', in an age of futility, darkness, and scepticism.

XIII

The Dynasts:
An Epic-Drama of Evolution

The Dynasts promotes a sharp divergence of opinion between Hardy's older and newer critics.

'Sensitive poet-critics like Lascelles Abercrombie and Edmund Blunden have declared *The Dynasts* a masterpiece, yet at the present moment the work seems to have few enthusiastic critics and, I would surmise, not many more readers.

(Irving Howe: *Thomas Hardy*)

Its size, resistance to classification, narrative/poetic/dramatic form, strange diction, long stretches of the blankest blank verse, Overworld choruses, account of 'human action in spite of human knowledge' (Hardy's psychology of the Unconscious), bleak philosophy of the Immanent Will, and vision of futile battle upon battle, are disconcerting if one looks for the quickfire dramatic conflicts, passionate human relationships, and nature poetry of the poems and novels. But if one differs from Howe's opinion that 'we are today not much concerned with questions of ultimate causation', Hardy's original treatment of those questions has turned 'the real, if only temporary, thought of the age' into a projection of the eternal quest for meaning that has as much validity as *The Iliad* or *War and Peace*. The difficulties of the conglomerate form become powerful aids to 'the modern expression of a modern outlook' (Preface) if *The Dynasts* is read with the kind of dramatic imagination that one would apply, not to Shakespearean or Ibsenite drama, or to a film script, but to the form of mixed media that embodies Brecht's epic drama.

It is futile to speculate whether Hardy would have limited *The Dynasts* to mental performance only (two stage productions of selected scenes were given later) if the modern film and lighting techniques which he so obviously anticipates had been available to him. Brecht had both means and vision to translate into terms of actual theatre the radical conceptions of total drama common to them both. Though Hardy had less faith than Brecht in the human control of fate, the futility of mass self-slaughter was clear to both. The heroism that war inspires can be found in both *Mother Courage* and *The Dynasts*, but the narrative comment that distances the illustrative drama strongly questions the waste of heroism.

Hardy's rejection as anachronistic of 'the importation of Divine personages from any antique Mythology as ready-made sources or channels of Causation' (Preface) forced a radical change of form which, while it looks back to models like Shelley's *Prometheus Unbound* and Goethe's *Faust*, and ironically to the *Persae* and *Oresteia* of Aeschylus, who employs human conflict to postulate cosmic order and justice, looks forward to Brecht's special definition of 'Epic' theatre.

'While the theatre of illusion is trying to re-create a spurious present, by pretending that the events of the play are actually taking place at the time of each performance, the 'epic' theatre is strictly *historical*; it constantly reminds the audience that it is merely getting a *report* of past events.'

(Martin Esslin: *Brecht: A Choice of Evils*)

The tension and unity of *The Dynasts* comes from the ironic incongruities of historical drama and Overworld report; of ancient epic and modern epic-drama. And the effects of form are poetic. A work that sensuously embodies such a central mystery as the Will could hardly be anything but a poem, of Hardy's inclusive ilk. The three Parts are framed and qualified by the unchanged, emaciated figure of a humanized Europe at beginning and end, and the visual metaphor of 'Life's impulsion by Incognizance' which is realized six times in the drama when the Pities ask for reasons for the futile suffering. The historical drama illustrates the poetic metaphor in action, and the epic comment frames the drama as a cosmic show.

Sound dramatic principles unite the three parts of the display. Part First begins with the apex of Napoleon's usurping career, his coronation at Milan, and ends with expectation delicately balanced between the disaster at Austerlitz and victory at Trafalgar, whose true measure is known only to the Overworld—'*Utter defeat, ay, France's naval death*' (vi, vii). The result of France's naval death is seen in Part Second. It draws together the diverse material of the Spanish, Prussian, and Austrian campaigns through Napoleon's dynastic plans. The birth of his son to Maria Louisa of Austria, whose marriage to Napoleon proved to be the knot which began severance from Russia, and the dearly-bought British victory at Albuera, raise dramatic expectation at the end of Part Second with the conflicting threads of birth and death, alliance and enmity, woven by the Will-web, to be unravelled in Part Third. The final Part brings into prominence the Russian thread that is to weave Napoleon's military and dynastic defeat. French defeats balance the previous French victories. French refugees from Vitoria (3, ii, iii) balance Sir John Moore's retreating army (2, iii, i). The drowning of French by Russians at the Bridge of the Beresina (3, i, x) revenges the massacre of Russians by French on the Satschan Lake (1, vi, iv). Napoleon's desertion of 'these stricken shades in a limbo of gloom' (3, i, xi) on the retreat from Moscow parallels the cosmic desertion of the forgotten army at Walcheren (2, iv, viii). Wellington's rise to prominence and control balances Napoleon's in Part Second; his grasp of reality and contingencies gains ground as Napoleon loses his sense of reality in a wild dream of reconquering Europe with 'seven hundred sabres'. Nevertheless, the final battle of Waterloo is presented as a clash of well-matched opposites. Hardy's first stage direction (vii) points the coincidence that both commanders were forty-six, and both mounted on chargers who are named in true epic tradition. In the battle itself, the helplessness of both is stressed by parallel appeals for reinforcements which neither can send. Hardy's eye for symmetry plays no small part in giving design to an epic of purposelessness.

As surprise can play little part in the structure of a narrative already known, the scenes are selected and juxtaposed to afford comment on the workings of the Immanent Will. Artistic form occasionally takes precedence over strict chronology. Villeneuve's suicide is antedated, as Hardy's note tells us (1, v, vi), 'to include it in the Act to which it essentially belongs'. This act is analysed by W. R. Rutland (*Thomas Hardy*) to show Hardy's imaginative use of history. But well-constructed as it is, Act v only shows to advantage when embedded in the whole panorama of rhythmic flux and reflux, tension and relaxation.

The scenes that make up Act i of the first Part present the wide-flung interrelationships that tie together the folk of Wessex, their Parliamentary leaders, and the people of France, in the web of the Will that is weaving a convulsion of nations. The central visual image (iv) of 'countless companies of soldiery, engaged in a drill-practice of embarking and disembarking, and of hoisting horses into the vessels and landing them again'

crystallizes the futility of rumour, debate, plan, and action, implies the theatrical nature of the preceding scenes of busy purpose, and dissolves that purpose into meaningless fragmentation, when 'the Show presently dims and becomes broken, till only its flashes and gleams are visible'. The whole tenor of the Act has prepared us to see Napoleon's assumption of the crown in Milan Cathedral as a climactic piece of role-playing staged by the Will, and the drama as a conflict between man's stage-management and the Will's.

Act II introduces the counter-check. ' "*Where, where is Nelson?*" *questions every tongue*'. The humane principles and sense of reality that motivate both Nelson and his worthy opponent, Villeneuve, in this Act, counterpoint the stagery which has so far surrounded the absent or distanced figure of Napoleon, and introduce into this dramatic conflict of Free-will and Necessity the possibility that human and humane choice can swerve the course of the Will. Napoleon's presentation in (iii) as little more than a planning brain, 'in trim for each alternative', is offset by the following scenes which present in human roundness the men and decisions that will annul his stage directions, and by the two Wessex scenes following, which place human figureheads and designs and wars in the perspective of eternal human values.

'Lard, Lard, if 'a [George III] were nabbed, it wouldn't make a deal of difference! We should have nobody to zing to, and play single-stick to, and grin at through horse-collars, that's true. And nobody to sign our few documents. But we should rub along some way, goodnow.'

The leitmotif tension of human design and human blindness to cosmic design, which welds together the scenes of Acts III and IV and culminates in Nelson's reputation, 'He's staunch. He's watching, or I am much deceived', prepares for Trafalgar as the climactic emotional correlative. Napoleon's designs for the conquest of Europe are counterpointed by the blindness of George III to Pitt's need for a Coalition, that prolongs the war and shortens Pitt's life (IV, i). The reputations of Villeneuve (III, i) and Mack (IV, vi) for far-sightedness are seen from another angle (IV, iii) as ignorance and confusion, stressed by the 'murk of evening' that

279

'obscures the prospect' of military preparations before Ulm. At Trafalgar, the confusion of smoke, noise, blood, life, and death, brought vividly to all the senses by Hardy's stage directions, is set against the purposeless ballet of attack and defence, while the viewpoint alternates between the 'Victory' and the 'Bucentaure', where the two most sensitive heroes of the drama, driven to compass each other's death by events they did not cause, are shown at the height of their concern for human flesh. Unlike the constantly diminished Napoleon, both Nelson and Villeneuve are allowed to meet a death consonant with heroic dignity, each exercising the limited choice accorded to him by the Will. The epic roll-call of ships captured and men dead or wounded, a device by which Homer gave individual dignity to his combatants, counterpoints the realistic portrayal of pain and meaningless fragmentation of men and things in war:

> arms, legs, trunks, heads,
> Bobbing with tons of timber on the waves,
> And splinters looped with entrails of the crew.

Yet the same incident, the explosion in the French ship 'Achille', provides one of Hardy's eternal touchstones; the grotesque humour of the captain's woman, 'desperate for life' swimming naked:

> Our men in charge,
> Seeing her great breasts bulging on the brine,
> Sang out, 'A mermaid 'tis, by God!'—then rowed
> And hauled her in.

The interrelated complex of death and glory, peace and war, finds its still point when, with Nelson dying, Captain Hardy's mind swings back to his native Wessex, and the local but eternal values for which men have always fought. The Guildhall scene which follows, placing the fame of Trafalgar and of Pitt's 'last large words' as accidents of time and place, Villeneuve's suicide, muted complementary to Nelson's death in action; the Wessex gossip of the thirsty sailors who 'broached the Adm'l'; and the ballad of Trafalgar which ends Act v, wind down the tension of the battle by crystallizing particular event into universal myth.

Act vi, after an act which stresses human action and values, returns to the theme of 'stark sightlessness' and futility at Austerlitz, Napoleon's countercheck to Trafalgar. The Russian conjectures (ii) introduce us to another kind of Hardeian hero, very different from the romantic, vigilant Nelson. The wisdom of the significantly one-eyed, sleeping Kutúzof, the only wisdom that could sustain the different nature of Napoleon's future campaigns, lies in accepting human ignorance.

> Such plans are—paper! Only tomorrow's light
> Reveals the true manoeuvre to my sight!

Part First ends with the death of a dispirited Pitt, realizing so soon after his acclamation as saviour in v that 'I am as though I had never been!' But as one wave falls, another prepares to rear. The brief mention of Wellesley's visit to Pitt introduces the man who is to redress the balance of Austerlitz at Waterloo.

To detail the structure Act by Act and scene by scene would take too long. The same care is shown throughout to select and juxtapose incidents which illustrate the ironies inherent in the conflict of human and unconscious design. Part Second ends, for example, with a cluster of scenes (vi, iii–vii) which question Napoleon's assertion of identity through his son (iii). Bloody Alburera melts down human order and definition (iv):

'The lines of the Buffs, the Sixty-sixth, and those of the Forty-eighth . . . in a chaos of smoke, steel, sweat, curses, and blood, are beheld melting down like wax from an erect position to confused heaps. Their forms lie rigid, or twitch and turn, as they are trampled over by the hoofs of the enemy's horse. . . .'

and turns men into grotesque faceless black-masked puppets (Hardy understood the massed anonymity of modern warfare), 'their mouths blackened by cartridge-biting', 'discharging musketry in each other's faces when so close that their complexions may be recognized'. The evocation of a cosmic masquerade is strengthened by the '*regal puppet-shows*' (v–vii). The mad King George III,

> *Mocked with the forms and feints of royalty*
> *While scarified by briery Circumstance*

poignantly evaluates human responsibility for the 'victory' of Albuera:

> He says I have won a battle? But I thought
> I was a poor afflicted captive here,

and the Prince Regent plays out the sub-comedy of his 'wives' at the Carlton House celebration, where he sits 'like a lay figure' in royal state, in the incongruous dress of a Field Marshal, at a table whose romanticized centrepiece recalls the now battle-scarred landscape of Albuera. But the last hope of the Pities—that the Will may wake and '*with knowledge use a painless hand*' stresses the increasing importance in Parts Second and Third of limited human choice and partial control of the Will.

This theme imposes unity and pattern on the flux and reflux of the Prussian and Spanish campaigns of Part Second—the mid-way neutral ground of the drama on which human action may stamp a design. Napoleon's one unselfish choice, to save the mother and not his child (2, vi, iii) and its happy outcome inspires the comment (qualified though it is by its source) from the Ironic Spirits, '*The Will Itself is slave to him.*' Between the dilemma of Fox, which appropriately opens Part Second, when he is faced with Napoleon's would-be assassin, and the last Chorus of the Pities in Part Third with its hope of human consciousness infiltrating the Will of which it forms part, lies a tissue of opportunities missed or taken, juxtaposed with the consequences of choice.

'If only' weaves through the texture of history. If only Villeneuve had been as conscienceless as his master; if only Pitt had been allowed to form a coalition; if only Fox had accepted the assassin's offer; if only Queen Louisa had married the Prince of Wales, or had met Napoleon before dynastic ambition had driven out susceptibility to women; if only Maria Louisa had been persuaded to join Napoleon after his escape from Elba; if only Grouchy's reinforcements had arrived in time—the list is endless—history might have taken a different turn. The defeat of Coruña follows a second chance to kill Napoleon (iii, ii) missed because the deserter had thrown away his firelock. Expediency, not morality, may control the Will that '*neither good nor evil knows*'. Constant readiness to adapt to the workings of chance and time has a cumulative effect on the course of the war. Chance location '*evolved the fleet of the Englishry*', but Nelson's vigilance and Wellington's modern methods of warfare kept England safe. The scenes of the Prussian defeat (2, i, iii–viii) imply criticism of Prussia's unadaptive sluggishness which, lost in romantic devotion to the warrior queen who embodied the myth of their military past,

> *takes no count of the new trends of time,*
> *Trusting ebbed glory in a present need.*

'The slow clocks of Muscovy', on the other hand, are instrumental in Napoleon's defeat because they are backed by the chance factor of the Russian winter and Napoleon's sense of his own dignity, though after Russia's belated answer to his marriage proposals Champagny points his freedom to choose: 'You might, of course, sire, give th'Archduchess up.'

Vigilant control is man's only defence against the unknown concomitants that affect the course of destiny. In two juxtaposed scenes (2, ii, ii, iii) Hardy shows that the Prince of Wales' dalliance with the ladies in an insular and phlegmatic country misses the disastrous consequences of Godoy's affair with the Spanish queen. But the Bourbon throne might have been saved by the self-control that is so conspicuously lacking when the queen visits her lover on the night his palace is wrecked by the mob. 'I could not help it—nay, I *would* not help!'

Part Third brings into prominence the man and the qualities which defeated Napoleon. The 'prim ponderosities' of Wellington's defence works outside Torrès Védras (2, vi, ii) introduce a concrete correlative of the endurance that was needed to survive the third phase of the war—

> They are Lord Wellington's select device
> And, like him, heavy, slow, laborious, sure

—fought over ground that manifests the basic hostilities facing man's endeavour; space, time, the elements, and insignificance. The square blocks of men who withstand the French charges at Waterloo 'like little red-brick castles' are a physical image of the control needed to do nothing but endure. 'They writhe to charge— or anything but stand!' Wellington's grasp of reality, and intelligent use of the limited foresight granted to men after a full look at the worst, comes into the ascendant as Napoleon retreats into paranoid fantasy and deception of his men, that finds its climax and hubris at Waterloo.

Through the third Part of *The Dynasts*, Napoleon's stage management is constantly juxtaposed with the reality that refuses to be directed. The silence that greets his entry into Moscow (i, viii) is an unnerving anti-climax to his posturing plans for the city's surrender (vii). The Act (v) that begins with Napoleon's rally— his escape from Elba—ends with the burning of his effigy at Durnover Green. The man who made Europe dance to his tune is seen as a puppet, devoid of significance:

'. . . only a mommet they've made of him, that's got neither chine nor chitlings. His innerds be only a lock of straw from Bridle's barton.'

From Hardy's dramatic shaping of the historical narrative he drew a poetic underpattern compounded of a complex of assent and dissent to traditional epic, which creates for him a modern myth. The historical drama provides much epic material for that 'Iliad of Europe' with Napoleon as 'a sort of Achilles' that was Hardy's earliest conception of *The Dynasts* (1875 to 1881). The problem of writing an epic, embodying a philosophical statement and the values of contemporary culture in an age when the writer 'can neither assume a core of beliefs common to himself and his audience nor adopt the long forms which artists have traditionally used for such statements' (Hynes: *The Pattern of Hardy's Poetry*) was solved by Hardy's ironic vision and the epic/dramatic/poetic form to which it gave birth.

The epic can show two broad and often interrelated genres: the epic of war (*The Iliad*) and the search for identity (*The Odyssey*). War is a measure of man's relationship to the controlling forces of the universe, his god-like potentialities for destruction and self-creation in the face of ever-present death. It raises urgently the metaphysical questions of the value of life, the basis of individual identity, and how far war is an inevitable part of human character and destiny. These questions arise both in Primary epic, which is defined by C. S. Lewis (*Preface to Paradise Lost*) as the *Iliad* type, where personal tragedy is set against the meaningless flux of history and no achievement is permanent; and in Secondary epic, where some event—the founding of Rome, the Fall of Man—invests history with pattern and suffering with meaning. The epic hero dramatizes the potentialities of his culture to deal with these questions.

The first conception of Napoleon as 'a sort of Achilles' compels comparison with the traditional epic hero. Achilles had a special relationship to the Absolute, having enough god-like force to challenge things as they are. Though nothing can happen beyond fate, his heroic energy reshapes the will of the gods to some extent, and wins him the right to self-determination within the pattern of fate. Napoleon, conscious of his role as Man of Destiny and '*unwavering, keen, and irresistible/As is the lightning prong*' (1, I, ii), is associated with the fire that was for Achilles the symbol of his part in the nature of godhead—complex of wrath, war, divinity, and death; irreconcilable and self-destructive to mortals.

> Great men are meteors that consume themselves
> To light the earth. This is my burnt-out hour.
> (3, VII, ix).

Napoleon's aspirations to godhead, 'to shoulder Christ from out the topmost niche/In human fame' are measured and found wanting to the needs of a godless age by the compassion of the Christian ideal he rejects, evoked in the incongruity of his definition (by the Spirit Ironic) as 'the Christ of War'. It is significant that the one act of Napoleon's which seems to reshape the Will is not of heroic self-assertion but of compassion for the mother of his child. 'Every generous, selfless action in the drama expresses resistance to the selfish, egocentric impulse of the Immanent Will' (J. O. Bailey, *Thomas Hardy and the Cosmic Mind*), and adumbrates the ultimate effect of the human mind upon the cosmic. Napoleon is the man of heroic force and '*suasive pull of personality*' who refuses the challenge to become this new kind of hero, falling back instead on an outmoded epic pattern. (There is some analogy with the Eustacia/Clym opposition.) This erstwhile champion of Liberty (1, I, vi) becomes a mechanism of the Will, and declares it responsible for his self-assertive drive to power (3, I, i) though the Spirit of the Pities challenges his determinist view: (3, I, v)

> *So he fulfils the inhuman antickings*
> *He thinks imposed upon him. . . .*

The Will, symbol of *primitive* energy, impels him into immediate channels and immediate successes. Where endurance and the later acquisition of foresight is needed, his law of the jungle does not always prevail. As he struggles towards his own conception of destiny, he becomes more and more aware that his Absolute aspirations are limited by mortal conditions—lack of heirs, his increasing fatness and drowsiness, the physical expanse of Russia to be crossed by exhausted men. The Overworld perspective evaluates this Man of Destiny as no more than an unheroic puppet of the Will, '*the brazen rod that stirs the fire/Because it must.*' Hardy's presentation of Napoleon selects those aspects which diminish his traditional courage and human feeling. He comes over as little more than a mechanism, a constantly planning will, weaving '*eternal artistries in Circumstance*'; a modern Sisyphus, whose whole being has been exerted to accomplishing nothing. But Hardy, as always, leaves open the question whether the compassionate choices he did not make in 'moments of equilibrium' would have altered his fate.

Like Homer, Hardy illuminates his conception of heroic character by comparing his Achilles with other leaders. In addition, the echoes of Homeric counterparts question the values of traditional epic. The English leaders, military and Parliamentary, contrast favourably in concern for their people with Napoleon's egotistical genius. Napoleon's Hector may be found in Nelson, the thoroughly human hero, who asserts himself bravely to defend the domestic values he cherishes from the war he abhors. His death ironically achieves the god-like status of death/glory which Napoleon desired. The Overworld debate that rises from his protracted suffering questions the ideals of heroism which bring needless pain to creatures so sensitively developed. But Hector did not carry the burden of modern self-alienated man, 'who is with himself dissatisfied' (1, II, i), which operates as a death-wish in Nelson: that was the doubtful privilege of Achilles alone. It enables Nelson to determine his mode of life and death within the narrow freedom allowed by the Will. Minor heroes bear the same modern burden; Picton, 'riding very conspicuously', and Brunswick, whose 'solemn and appalling guise' embodying his devotion to death attracted the bullet. They might have saved their lives if they had heeded warnings from the Overworld.

Sir John Moore presents another kind of modern hero. His painful death in defeat, his concern for the battle and those in it, his attachment to his sword (the traditional epic object that acquires symbolic honour and a life of its own)—'I wish it to go off the field with me'—mark him as the youthful romantic hero of the epic of chivalry. But he owes his immortality to the modern evaluation of failure as the human condition. (2, III, v)

> His was a spirit baffled but not quelled,
> And in his death there shone a stoicism
> That lent retreat the rays of victory.

The French can show their heroes of chivalry too, in Villeneuve and Ney. The nearest Homeric equivalent to Ney is the rash, romantic, constantly charging Diomedes, for whom heroic action is uncomplex—and immature. The danger of Ney's romantic appeal is embodied by the colourful trappings of his cavalry, *that would persuade us war has beauty in it*'. (3, VII, iv). But whereas

Siborne (Hardy's historical source here) admires 'the gorgeous, yet harmonious, colouring of this military spectacle', Hardy's Spirit of the Pities points to the un-epic disharmony of the tragic feeling of the modern soldiers who constitute the spectacle. The Overworld evaluates it ('the barbaric trick') and, with regret, Ney's gallantry, as outmoded and misguided.

> *Simple and single-souled lieutenant he* . . . .
> *Why should men's many-valued motions take*
> *So barbarous a groove?*

While the awareness to suffering of Nelson and Moore, caught in the trap of an ancient mechanism for which they are too highly evolved, implies a cautious hope that awareness will one day break into the Will, the hero who is best adjusted to the present is the man, not over-sensitive, who challenges things as they are by adjusting intelligently to the environment he finds himself in. The old Russian commander Kutúzov, 'bravely serving though slowly dying', embodies the qualities which defeated Napoleon on Russian soil—inaction, silence, endurance, and realization of man's ignorance and mortality. Wellington, like Ajax, gives the impression of being rooted to the earth; stubborn, blunt, not over-imaginative, impatient of irregularities, squarely enduring and defensive. His sober look at the worst and ballad-like expectation of human endurance in face of it—

> to hold out unto the last,
> As long as one man stands on one lame leg
> With one ball in his pouch!—

contrasts with Napoleon's betrayal of his troops into false optimism. His grasp of reality and intelligent deductions from fact accord with the Spirit of the Years' refusal to live beyond factual knowledge (3, VI, viii):

> The noonday sun, striking so strongly there,
> Makes mirrors of their arms. That they advance
> Their growing radiance shows. Those gleams by Marbais
> Suggest fixed bayonets.

Hardy's women are no exception to the tradition that epic women are depicted as victims of the death and division that war brings into their domestic lives. Josephine's distressful position, womanly charm, and lifelong devotion to Napoleon and even to his son make her a more attractive heroine than Maria Louisa. But Hardy's myth-making faculty presents them both as victims of the human condition rather than the opportunistic schemings of an Empire-builder. Napoleon's demand that Josephine should act in the formalities of divorce 'as if you shaped them of your own free will' is an image of the human action of the whole drama. Maria Louisa's cry of pain in childbirth, 'Why should I be tortured even if I am but a means to an end!' universalizes her situation to stand for all women travailing ceaselessly for a mysterious and seemingly futile end. Other women too take on mythopoeic dimension. Queen Louisa's dramatically silent image passes across the stage as the militant warrior-queen expected by a Prussia which has failed to keep up with the times, at odds with the feminine nature displayed in her dialogue with Napoleon. Colonel Dalbiac's Wessex wife, who rode to the charge at Salamanca behind her husband, and Mrs Prescott, who found hers 'lying dead and bloody there', take on mythical stature as the eternal price of a war that forces them out of their normal creative functions.

The likeness to Homeric heroic character stresses the differences that make *The Dynasts* a modern epic. Hardy does not celebrate the noble relationship of arms and the man. The temper of *The Dynasts*, nevertheless, is not anti-epic or anti-heroic. What it celebrates is a kind of heroism acceptable to the self-conscious modern world.

Epic action in *The Dynasts* is ineffective sound and fury. Though the battle-joy is felt by some of Hardy's heroes as by Homer's and Tolstoy's, '*driven to demonry/By the Immanent Unrecking*' (3, VII, viii), the needlessness of war as a testing ground of man's quality is strongly presented. Hardy's war is bestial and dehumanizing; the generous Homeric impulse is rare. Wellington, though moved to admiration by Ney's action, will not move to save him from ignominious death (3, VII, iv). All Hardy's resources are directed to a vision of war as futile and insignificant. No other epic of war can have so much of the major action relegated to comment. Wagram (2, IV, iii), Coruna (2, III, iii–iv) and much of Trafalgar and Waterloo are presented as running commentary, with all the misunderstandings, inaccuracies, and differences of opinion that attend a partial view. Napoleon exists, for much of the drama, as a voice heard through walls, in dictation, or in proclamations to his officers. Nothing could convey more dramatically the limits of human awareness and action. Napoleon realizes his inability to direct events at Waterloo. 'Life's curse begins, I see,/With helplessness. The reportage of epic action places man's function as observer and commentator on events he can neither control nor understand.

Another form of comment is the Dumb Show, which becomes a poetic and dramatic metaphor for the human condition of uncomprehended activity. The ceremony of Alexander's alliance with Napoleon on the river Niemen (2, I, vii) is qualified by the silence, the dwarfing perspective, the simultaneous balletic movements of the two barges, and the effect (like Cocteau's raised platform in *The Infernal Machine*) of the action in the 'gorgeous pavilion of draped woodwork' isolated in a void of water that imparts to the man-made stage 'a rhythmical movement, as if it were breathing'. The spectacle of man trying futilely to stage his own show while being moved by a more powerful current is broken by the Overworld's reminder of '*the prelude to this smooth scene*' in the lyric that begins

Snows incarnadined were thine, O Eylau, field of the wide white spaces.

The poetic incongruities contained in 'snows incarnadined', 'frozen limbs', 'blood iced hard', echoed in the musical dissonances of open vowels, sliding vowel progressions, and hard consonants, places the staginess of the Dumb Show inside the reality of suffering. The combination of Dumb Show and lyric comment expresses better than the Homeric dignity of ceremonial dialogue the futility of the alliance.

Hardy's aerial view from the Overworld, often glazed by mists and water, 'provides both an expansive perspective of vast "epic" actions, and an ironically contracting philosophical perspective of what those actions mean' (Hynes, op. cit.). It diminishes epic ritual to model theatre. After the coronation in Milan Cathedral, 'the point of view recedes, the whole fabric smalling into distance and becoming like a rare, delicately carved alabaster ornament' (a comment too on the relativity of '*the creed that these rich rites disclose*'). Napoleon himself is 'diminished to the aspect of a doll' after his declaration of war on Russia. The relegation of the endless processions to stage direction—coronation and wedding ceremonies, triumphal progresses and submissions, military retreats and advances, disorganized flights of refugees—diminishes human effort to find meaning in ritual to a confusion of human and cosmic cross-purposes. The modern film device suggested in Maria Louisa's ceremonial progress to meet her future husband (2, v, v)—

'The puny concatenation of specks being exclusively watched, the surface of the earth seems to move along in an opposite direction, and in infinite variety of hill, dale, woodland, and champaign'

—like the revolving stage under Mother Courage's wagon, proves the illusion of forward movement. The foreshortened view of messengers shuttling across the Channel (2, I, ii) exposes the ritual (stressed as ritual by the Rumours 'chanting in antiphons') of diplomatic negotiation as a ruthless game of skill in which *lives are ninepins to these bowling hands*. The simultaneous proclamations of war made by Napoleon and the Russians (3, I, i), each blaming the other and pretending to read enemy motives, are placed by a stage direction whose dramatic grouping anticipates Beckett's experiments in language and Schoenberg's in serial sound to project a closed circle of mechanical, meaningless echoes:

'When the reconnoitrers again come back to the foreground of the scene the huge array of columns is standing quite still, in circles of companies, the captain of each in the middle with a paper in his hand. He reads from it a proclamation. They quiver emotionally, like leaves stirred by a wind. NAPOLÉON and his staff reascend the hillock, and his own words as repeated to the ranks reach his ears, while he himself delivers the same address to those about him.'

Human communication merges into the meaningless sounds of nature. The sounds of celebration and agony are the same. Speech and hand-clapping become the babbling of waves. The groans of the soldiers drowning under fire in the Satschan Lake 'reach the ears of the watchers like ironical huzzas' (1, VI, iv).

All manifestations of the life process appear as equally significant or insignificant. Great armies are reduced to crawling caterpillars or cheesemites, Maria Louisa's wedding procession to 'a file of ants crawling along a strip of garden-matting', Napoleon himself to a puppet twitched by the Immanent Will and his victims to animalcula gyrating from his impetus. Naval convoys 'float on before the wind almost imperceptibly, like preened duck-feathers across a pond' (2, II, v). Soldiers 'wheel into their fighting-places . . . their arms glittering like a display of cutlery at a hill-side fair' (3, VII, i).

Much of the perspective is expressed in stage directions. The sensuous impact, diction, rhythm, and emotional force of Hardy's stage directions make them a potent poetic instrument in the creation of a modern myth. As the historical action moves from futile battle to futile battle, the mythopoeic underpattern moves in counterpoint from illusion of the human condition as purposeful action (Part First) through the flux and reflux of futility (Part Second) to acceptance of the reality of insignificant man in relationship with indifferent earth (Part Third). Jena, Trafalgar, and Austerlitz are questioned as victories for man's purpose and action by the flux and reflux of the Peninsular campaigns. The deserters in the cellar near Astorga (2, III, i) can still find meaning in the basic necessities of wine, women, and song. But their human reality and stability are threatened by the ultimate expressionistic nightmare reality of 'a straggling flock of military objects' retreating in ceaseless silent logicless flux.

'The Retreat continues. More of R O M A N A's Spanish limp along in disorder; then enters a miscellaneous group of English cavalry soldiers, some on foot, some mounted, the rearmost of the latter bestriding a shoeless foundered creature whose neck is vertebrae and mane only. While passing it falls from exhaustion; the trooper extricates himself and pistols the animal through the head. He and the rest pass on.'

The coughing sergeant who drills his crippled invalids into the role of a pursuing platoon; the dehumanized, unemotional executions of the horse and the prisoner chosen by lot, cause no disturbance in the current.

The Absurd juxtapositions of human order and cosmic disorder prepare for a response to Sir John Moore's funeral (2, III, iv) which is very different from the response accorded to Wolfe's poem. The gravediggers 'hastily digging a grave there with extemporised tools', the punctuating shots, the voice of the Chaplain intoning the Burial service that stresses the shortness of time, the ritual that expresses human attempt at ordering death, make an effect through the simultaneity of drama that resembles the rich counterpoint between modern futility and eternal order which Benjamin Britten catches in his *War Requiem* through juxtaposing Owen's war poetry with the Mass.

Trial in battle by fire and water of mortal men not equipped with Achilles' god-like force to overcome the elements, leads to a sojourn in Limbo. Walcheren (2, IV, viii) requires the 'dingy doom' of assimilation to the earth. It is the place where illusions of definition and meaning die; the home of the deceiving Jack-lantern and the illusory beauty of 'brass-hued and opalescent bubbles, compounded of many gases', and undefinable 'strange fishy smells, now warm, now cold'. The lament of its 'skeletoned men' forgotten and imprisoned to await futile, purposeless death in an island that is primitive earth, Homeric Underworld, and the modern Limbo of despair, is for meaningful action. All is diminished. The *ancient Delta* is an *ignoble sediment of loftier lands*. The doom of dissolution is enacted lyrically, in the sound of language and choice of words. The physical power of earth's insignificance to cover man's striving invests phrasing and rhythm:

> The ever wan morass, the dune, the blear
> Sandweed, and tepid pool, and putrid smell,
> Emaciate purpose to a fractious fear,
> Beckon the body to its last low cell—
> A chink no chart will tell.

The Russian campaign, accumulating resonance from the myth, finds the only meaning of life in life itself. Overworld perspective and stage direction present it as an epic struggle for bare survival in the primal indifference of nature. The point of observation, 'high amongst the clouds' (3, 1, ix) reveals the earth 'as a confused expanse merely'. The Pities' question '*Where are we? And why are we where we are?*' reverberates beyond the geographical confines of Russia. Gradually, the scene unfolds the fragmentary '*skinny growths*' that mean '*sustenance elsewhere yclept starvation*'. The archaic '*yclept*' and

> the rolling brume
> That parts, and joins, and parts again below us
> In ragged restlessness

roll back the years of racial memory so that the primitive '*object like a dun-piled caterpillar*' shuffling painfully along is no surprise. The Recording Angel's definition ('in minor plain-song') of the Grand Army in terms of the myth of God's chosen but exiled people strengthens by irony this modern myth of man's abandonment and insignificance, lost in a snowy silent monochrome, broken only by 'the incessant flogging of the wind-broken and lacerated horses'—the sounds of man's inhumanity to his fellow-sufferers that makes human life an inharmonious blot on the primitive landscape, and death a restoration of harmony as parts of the caterpillar shape drop off, 'are speedily flaked over, and remain as white pimples by the wayside'.

Groups break off to enact the ritual of primitive survival, which blends with the modern existentialist myth of men deserted by leader, God, and meaning. Only the poetically incongruous simile, 'icicles dangling from their hair that clink like glass-lustres as they walk' (xi) as they search for firewood, reminds us of the civilized existence that is men's right. The final stage direction points to the logical end of the myth, in language that stresses the sharp hostility of the environment: 'the stars come out in unusual brilliancy, Sirius and those in Orion flashing like stilettos; and the frost stiffens' as the exhausted soldiers, crouched round the fire unconscious of differences of rank, stiffen into an eternal sculpture of human suffering dehumanized by their trials of fire and ice, their dissonances harmonized in death.

> They all sit
> As they were living still, but stiff as horns;
> And even the colour has not left their cheeks,
> Whereon the tears remain in strings of ice.—
> It was a marvel they were not consumed:
> Their clothes are cindered by the fire in front,
> While at their back the frost has caked them hard.

The Dante-esque echoes define their experience as an experience of Hell.

Epic has always explored man's relationship to the natural world. The old anthropomorphic relationship gives poignant resonance to Hardy's myth of the earth, the most powerful physical fact of man's life, indifferent to his aims and sufferings, transforming his orderly patterns into preconscious human shapes which comment on the nature of warfare and prophesy his ultimate doom of reversion to unconsciousness (3, IV, i):

> 'All these dark and grey columns, converging westward by sure degrees, advance without opposition. They glide on as if by gravitation, in fluid figures, dictated by the conformation of the country, like water from a burst reservoir; mostly snake-shaped, but occasionally with batrachian and saurian outlines. In spite of the immensity of this human mechanism on its surface, the winter landscape wears an impassive look, as if nothing were happening.'

Natural descriptions in the context of *The Dynasts* are made grotesquely expressionistic of the deeper reality, woven by the tranced Will, underlying the scenic. The Overworld framework makes man's relation to his environment the objective correlative for a dream relationship, as Emma Clifford suggests ('The Impressionistic View of History in *The Dynasts*', *Modern Language Quarterly*, XXII, 1961). Together, the two dimensions of the historical drama and the Will which dreams it project Ultimate Reality where men and nature meet in a moment of vision that records a truth of suffering.

Yet the double function of earth as womb and tomb provides some effective poetic Hardeian tensions. The very similes which diminish naval or military manoeuvres to duck feathers or cutlery expand the importance of these homely appurtenances of peace. At the height of the carnage there are interludes which evoke, through the rhythms of war, the rhythms of peace and man's creative partnership with the earth which makes the fall of cities a catastrophe that is not final. As Nelson dies in unjustified pain, Captain Hardy remembers 'the red apples on my father's trees,/Just now full ripe'. It is a device Thomas Hardy could have learnt from Homer. On the eve of Waterloo (3, VI, viii)

> *Cavalry in the cornfields mire-bestrowed,*
> *With frothy horses floundering to their knees*

(Hardy is particularly sensitive to the bewildered agony of horses used in war) evoke the pastoral relationship of horses and corn to show the present conjunction as unnatural. The domestic words such as 'hamlet-roofs', 'chambers', 'household', referring to the small nesting creatures of Waterloo field to whom the mechanized butchery looms in magnified destructiveness, bring a sense of ultimate stability into the terror. Hardy's glimpses of women too, at their ordinary tasks, at fashionable balls, bearing children, comforting lovers, tending the wounded, balance the destruction with creation, like Homer's domestic similes. The incongruity of image and context is a powerful epic comment. Perhaps Hardy's most poetically incongruous and original adaptation of the Homeric domestic simile is his conception of the Immanent Will, unconsciously weaving a fabric of war and suffering '*like a knitter drowsed,/Whose fingers play in skilled unmindfulness*' (Forescene). The domestic image diminishes the First Cause to something terrible in its smallness.

The modern myth is completed and defined by the poetic power of Hardy's home-made theology. It could not end with a vision of insignificance. Though Hardy's regard for truth gave the vision full weight, the eternal questioning of events in space and time counterpoints it with a positive poetic emotion that implies the significance of human consciousness in the further evolution of the myth. The question, whether existence has meaning, is the total subject of the Dynasts, and '*the lobule of a Brain/Evolving always that it wots not of*' is its metaphor. The Overworld performs a vital dramatic function by keeping the Will present to the imagination when it is not embodied on the stage. They discuss its attributes, and though they are themselves swayed by Necessity, they dramatize transmission of impulses from the Unconscious by psychic phenomena, intuitions, and subconscious voices (1, v, vi; 2, v, viii, 2, vi, vii; 3, i, i, 3, vi, ii, 3, vi, iii, 3, vii, vi, 3, vii, ix) as 'Channels of Causation'. Though they share the super-knowledge of Homer's gods, they define their difference from the traditional 'celestial machinery' which takes a lively part in human affairs: '*Our scope is but to register and watch*' (Forescene).

However, Hardy makes good dramatic use of spectators with superior consciousness. They justify through the simultaneity that is possible to drama his choice of a semi-dramatic form.

> *We'll close up Time, as a bird its van,*
> *We'll traverse Space, as spirits can,*
> *Link pulses severed by leagues and years,*
> *Bring cradles into touch with biers;*
> *So that the far-off Consequence appears*
> *Prompt at the heel of foregone Cause.—*

Telescoped space and time bring into significant juxtaposition the battles of Salamanca in Spain and Borodino in Russia (3, i, iv). Telescoped time shows the futility of military plans when the result of a battle is foreseen before it begins (2, vi, iv) as '*red smears upon the sickly dawn*'. Premonitions of death bring foreknowledge of Quatre-Bras and Waterloo into the desperate gaiety of the ball at Brussels. The falling of Marie Antoinette's portrait forecasts division in the unnatural marriage between France and Austria. The Spirit Ironic breaks into Archduke Ferdinand's fears of capture by an upstart adventurer to note the future shape of things (1, iv, iii):

> *Note that. Five years, and legal brethren they—*
> *This feudal treasure and the upstart man!*

The rounded perspective stresses the opposition between the partial vision of men and the almost total consciousness of the Spirits.

The Overworld debates from its superior knowledge the inner meaning of the action, explains motives, interprets, narrates, summarizes, and makes transitions between scenes. The multiple function of the Spirits makes them important, not as gods, but as the latent divinity in human life that may supersede Necessity through a process of evolution. They represent different human responses, indicated by their names, to human suffering, if human beings were completely aware of their place in the cosmos. They are certainly the most 'realistic' individuals in the drama. Men are distanced and blurred into the workings of the Will.

The basic dramatic experience of conflict could be negated by the spectacle of conflict without meaning. But Hardy's meaning is the whole work. The war—a perfect correlative of futility—is placed in dramatic tension with the Overworld debate, which has its own inner drama. The Ancient Spirit of the Years, Showman and spokesman of the Will, represents things unemotionally as they are. Feelings and judgements which are pointless to his factual statement of existence, and which evolved with human consciousness, oppose him in the Spirit Ironic and the Spirit of the Pities. As part of the Will, feelings are as valid as facts. The Spirits of Irony and Pity challenge the determinism of the action with the possibility of limited free choice between impulses from the Unconscious and conscious sources of action—reason, intelligence, the consciousness of absurdity, unselfishness, compassion. The Pities independently disobeys the Will to suggest compassion to Napoleon (1, I, vi) and suicide to Villeneuve. At the Talavera brook (2, IV, v) 'the spectacle of Its instruments, set to riddle one another through, and then to drink together in peace and concord', pointed out in their different fashions by both Spirits, provokes the Spirit Sinister (evil for its own sake) into a fear that awareness of such piteous ironies 'may wake up the Unconscious Itself, and tempt It to let all the gory clock-work of the show, run down to spite me!'

The poetic development of the debate lies in the push of the Will, dramatized by its pioneers the Overworld in their capacity as 'the flower of Man's Intelligence', to become conscious. It is carried by the poetic peaks, in the Fore Scene and After Scene, at the end of each Part, and at major crises of suffering—Trafalgar, Austerlitz, Talavera, Walcheren, Albuera, Waterloo—which bring the question of purpose under urgent review. The intense poetic emotion is generated by arrangement of language and rhythm which takes us beyond the usual bounds of space and time. But the obsolete, coined, abstract, philosophical words which embody the strange dimension of the Overworld are usually in fruitful tension with some homely vivid word of emotional charge that relates the Overworld to our human experience.

The poetry of the Overworld can be justified dramatically. It speaks of ultimate concepts, but constantly translates the abstract mystery of the Will into immediate sensuous terms through imagery and precision in expressing emotion. The language of each Spirit is appropriate to his function. This includes the vulgar, Gilbertian, music-hall or doggerel terms and jaunty rhythms which have pained critics. When the Overworld expresses itself in such terms, it is to diminish the epic grandeur of Napoleon's coronation, the armistice between France and Austria (1, vi, v), the British battalions under sail for Spain (2, ii, v), the meeting of Napoleon and Maria Louisa (2, v, vi) and Napoleon's escape from Elba (3, v, i). Another idiosyncratic dissonance between form and subject is felt in their expression of the chaos, horror, futility, and obscenity of modern warfare in forms borrowed from Campbell, Southey, Byron, Scott, Browning, Swinburne, Tennyson, Barnes, ballad, hymn, and psalm, which had mellifluously, jubilantly, or jauntily sung of its glory or the peacefulness of peace.

The lyrics of the Overworld have been admired enough to be included in selections of Hardy's poetry. But they owe their power in *The Dynasts* to the context of many kinds of poetry and prose which express a world of multiple reality. The Overworld has almost a monopoly of lyrical poetry affirming individual feeling and personality. Their language is rich in metaphor which establishes relationship between points of experience, because their perspective is total and not fragmentary. The blank verse of the dynasts is flat and factual. Men have the experience but not the meaning. Nevertheless their verse is a dramatic instrument. It enacts the plodding obstructiveness of the human condition that defeats Napoleon, and creates the illusion of the characters acting out a cosmic play. The humble ranks speak in the humorous half-poetic prose of the novels. The stage directions, like the novels and poems, relate realistic and poetic, abstract and concrete, in powerful images that hold in tension the irreconcilables of the Will.

'So massive is the contest that we soon fail to individualize the combatants as beings, and can only observe them as amorphous drifts, clouds, and waves of conscious atoms, surging and rolling together; can only particularize them by race, tribe, and language. Nationalities from the uttermost parts of Asia here meet those from the Atlantic edge of Europe for the first and last time. By noon the sound becomes a loud droning, uninterrupted and breve-like, as from the pedal of an organ kept continuously down.'

(3, III, ii).

It is characteristic of Hardy's ironic double vision that the non-human 'atoms' are qualified by 'conscious', and the individual 'race, tribe, and language' levelled down in a musical image that incongruously evokes from the dissonance of the conflict the harmony that *should* reign at a meeting of nations.

The Fore Scene sets in motion the dramatic clash of style and idea that develops the opposition of conscious and unconscious will. The first and basic question, '*What of the Immanent Will and Its designs?*' develops the ambiguity of 'designs' into the dissonances of '*Eternal artistries//in Circumstance*', '*patterns, wrought//by rapt aesthetic rote*', '*listless//aim*'. The agitated speech rhythms that characterize the Pities, '*Still thus? Still thus?/Ever unconscious?*' oppose their warm impulsive human melody to the measured onomatapoeic tick of the Years' exposition of being.

> *You cannot swerve the pulsion of the Byss,*
> *Which thinking on, yet weighing not Its thought,*
> *Unchecks Its clock-like laws.*

The Years' language is full of imagery from the automatic motion of mechanical, biological, and astronomical law, miraculously defining the abstract Undefinable by negatives. It is reiterated and redefined in response to the unanswerable 'Why?' at scenes of suffering.

The leitmotif of the harmony that should reign instead of the dissonance that is, which threads the whole debate, is introduced by the Pities in the musical, dignified diction of basic truths. They would establish the rule of

> *Those, too, who love the true, the excellent,*
> *And make their daily moves a melody.*

The creative evolution theme that backs up their irrational hope is hinted in the Years' answer to the Earth's revolt against the futile interchange of Dynasts, '*when all such tedious conjuring could be shunned/By uncreation*':

> *Nay, something hidden urged*
> *The giving matter motion; and these coils*
> *Are, maybe, good as any.*

The dissonance of issues and styles, abstraction and concrete, returns at scenes of suffering, where human flesh is torn by an abstract force. The language dramatizes '*The intolerable antilogy/Of making figments feel*'. But at Trafalgar and Austerlitz the debate takes place in a context of evolutionary lyric that counterpoints the despair with a larger hope of eventual fulfilment to emerge from the 'sublime fermenting-vat'. '*O pause, till all things all their days fulfil!*' The Pities' Prayer to the 'Great Necessitator' to dull the suffering at Austerlitz leads by poetic logic to the quiet close of Part First where the Years seems to respond to the Pities to '*show ruth/At man's fag end, when his destruction's sure*' at Pitt's peaceful death. He has already shown pity for Villeneuve's suffering, and anger at the cynicism of the Spirit Sinister (1, i, vi).

Throughout Part Second, the defiance of the Pities to the Years' iteration of determinism grows stronger. They take on the lament of mortal futility at Walcheren, and after Alburera and the madness of George III they defy the Ironic Spirits' vision of empty stellar spaces, hammered home by the one rhyme, with their irrational determination to pray

> *To some Great Heart, who haply may*
> *Charm mortal miseries away.*

And at the end of Part Second, the evolving compassion which has developed from question to prayer which almost conjures a god from the emptiness, defies the Years' picture of the whole world obeying the Will, to assert faith in Its waking to consciousness.

In Part Third, the Pities batter the emotions to wake the Will. The confusion of battle and horror of pain, brought vividly to the senses, become more evident in their reporting. At Borodino they oppose the Years' vision of 'mechanized enchantment' with their report that the '*ugly horror*' has woken even Napoleon '*to all its vain uncouthness*'. The Choruses, which heighten the lyric mood of the Spirit's comments, sing not of the movements of battle but of exhausted and dying men. At Waterloo they transform the Years' Borodino vision of a '*web of rage/That permeates as one stuff the weltering whole*' to a web of suffering that includes all creatures in its fabric, in a lyric that is significantly shared by the Chorus of the Years. Waterloo, a victory for English virtues in the world of men,

299

in the larger world of human potentialities is a victory for compassion at the sufferings involved, and a possible indication that to feel such suffering and act on the feelings is the purpose of man's existence as pioneer of the Will in universal pity. Regret—always a positive emotion for Hardy—informs the Pities' report of Waterloo; for the unfulfilment of promise in crops and youths impartially crushed, and in men of fine calibre like Ney. The response of the Pities so far dominates Part Third that the Spirit of the Years picks out for observation examples of vindictiveness in men deserted by '*all wide sight and self-command*' which the Pities would foster. Earlier, the protest of the Pities at the intolerable antilogy of making figments feel (1, IV, v) has ranged the Spirit of the Ironies on his side because '*Logic's in that.*' Irony and Pity are two sides of the same coin, both trying to find human response in the Will. At Waterloo, the Ironic Spirits comment in a question and answer lyric that is emotionally inspired by the Pities' irrational faith.

> *Of Its doings if It knew,*
> *What It does It would not do!*

And it is the Spirit Ironic who asks Napoleon, '*Has all this been worthwhile?*'

The After Scene is a coda that brings back the themes of the conflict. But the conflict is musically resolved in one of Hardy's modern chords of dissonance. The Years reiterates the ceaseless urging of the Will-web weaving unconsciously in the stellar void

> *Where hideous presences churn through the dark—*
> *Monsters of magnitude without a shape,*
> *Hanging amid deep wells of nothingness*

and diminishes the horrifying abstract sublimity of the infinite with the ambiguity of '*this vast and singular confection*', defined as '*inutile all—so far as reasonings tell*'. But his saving clause indicates that the Pities have not agonized in vain. Their response picks up the dignified Latinate roll of the Years' style, but the inexorable law it illustrates is the law of evolution.

> *Thou arguest still the Inadvertent Mind.—*
> *But, even so, shall blankness be for aye?*
> *Men gained cognition with the flux of time,*
> *And wherefore not the Force informing them,*
> *When far-ranged aions past all fathoming*
> *Shall have swung by, and stand as backward years?*

From this point the Spirit of the Pities directs the course, emotion, and language of the debate as he would direct evolution. In the Pities' hymn to the Will of their dream the abstraction so long defined by the terrifying neuter 'It' and many resounding names of abstract and negative quality, is humanized as 'Thee' and the merciful and controlling God of Christian tradition evoked as an alternative possibility. But this God is not yet in being, except as an ideal in the compassionate faith of his pioneers. The Years admits to sympathy for their conception.

> *You almost charm my long philosophy*
> *Out of my strong-built thought, and bear me back*
> *To when I thanksgave thus . . .*

The vision of cosmic harmony aroused by the Pities' hymn brings back the musical imagery. The Years is moved to complete the hymn, in terms that blend the responses of Years and Pities, by assuming the role of questioner from which the Pities' maturity developed. '*To what tune danceth this Immense?*' The Pities complete the epic-drama with a prophecy of '*Consciousness the Will informing, till It fashion all things fair!*' But the concluding chord is that of the seventh. Hardy's power of poetry and vision makes *The Dynasts* a vast musical composition awaiting fulfilment of the final harmonizing chord.

XIV

Afterwards

Thomas Hardy, born in the nineteenth century and dying in the twentieth, bridges the two worlds. His Janus face may account for his appeal to young readers and writers today. The integrity of his personal search for meaning and self-supporting attitudes in an absurd world, his refusal to be comforted by ready-made formulae, myths and illusions, or to take refuge in cynicism, the unpretentious rough-hewn voice talking quietly of intense suffering and joy, speak to their own condition, while the backbone of certainties about fundamental human values which he inherited from his own century offsets the modern permissive confusion.

Though Hardy has been defined at various periods as an 'unfashionable' author, and the poetry largely neglected in favour of the novels in his unfashionable phases, it is in the field of modern verse that his influence can be detected most distinctly. Kenneth Marsden, in *The Poems of Thomas Hardy*, has listed some of the twentieth-century expectations which contributed to the neglect of his poetry by the common reader and critic. They include hostility to 'ideas' in poetry; dislike of Hardy's world-view, limited themes, and poetic persona, which had to contend with Eliot's influential theory of impersonality in poetry; the doctrine of expressive form and *vers libre* which drew attention away from the different kind of freedom expressed in Hardy's counterpoint of natural speech stress and traditional formalism; the modern impatience of anything less than a very high standard of competence throughout the whole body of a poet's works; and lastly, Hardy's reputation as an innovator, which disappointed preconceptions of a sensational revolution and bold avant-garde experiment. But whatever the prevailing critical opinion, practising poets have never ceased to pay tribute to his art and influence. They include Ezra Pound, Siegfried Sassoon, Edmund Blunden, Edward Thomas, Robert Graves, C. H. Sorley, Andrew Young, C. Day Lewis, James Reeves, W. H. Auden, Dylan Thomas, Philip Larkin, Philip Oakes, and Roger Frith.

However, it is not the kind of influence that is easy to pinpoint. One can usually pick out a disciple of Eliot or Hopkins through echoes of style, tone or theme. But even about those poets who have admitted Hardy's influence, 'no-one . . . seems willing to give details or even ask some obvious questions' (Marsden). Marsden quotes instances of imitation, pastiche and parody of Hardy's themes and style from C. H. Sorley, John Crowe Ransom, de la Mare, C. Day Lewis, William Plomer, John Betjeman and Philip Larkin. Larkin, a thoroughgoing admirer, who has confessed that

'one reader at least would not wish Hardy's *Collected Poems* a single page shorter, and regards it as many times over the best body of poetic work this century so far has to show . . .'

helps to define the nature of Hardy's influence on modern poets. His work shows Hardeian preoccupations, set down in the common language of common man, with the relationships of death, life, and love, with time and memory, with moments missed and moments of vision lighting the flat stretches of boredom and daily triviality, with the multiple interpretation of experience, with the assertion of human identity against cyclic flux, with the conflict of image and reality, with the sad agnosticism of honest disbelief, with the failure of things to bear out their promise.

> The glare of that much-mentioned brilliance, love,
>   Broke out, to show
> Its bright incipience sailing above,
> Still promising to solve, and satisfy,
> And set unchangeably in order. So
>   To pile them back, to cry,
> Was hard, without lamely admitting how
> It had not done so then, and could not now.
>   ('Love Songs in Age')

But the language and poetic persona are his own, while the themes are not peculiar to Hardy and Larkin; they have become part of common twentieth-century experience. Hardy has played a vital though unobtrusive role in educating us to an awareness of the common human predicament.

The difference between Hardy and his admirers constitutes, paradoxically, his major influence.

'It should be fairly obvious . . . that for another poet to be *seriously* influenced by Hardy is rather unlikely, because as the real Hardy, the one who is worth being influenced by, started from subject, the poet being influenced would do the same. He might well take over, or rather perceive anew, Hardy's subject matter, but since he would be attempting to render *his* perception it is not likely that he would employ Hardy's peculiarities of vocabulary.'

(Marsden: op. cit.)

His importance to modern poets and novelists was not as a maker of new traditions like Eliot, Hopkins and Joyce, but as a writer who battered the older forms into speaking with the idiosyncratic voice of his own persona, which invested traditional forms with a new originality. W. H. Auden, who claimed Hardy as his poetic father, recognised that he owed his independence to the older poet —the best tribute a son can pay to his father:

'Such unusual verse forms help the imitator to find out what he has to say: . . . in addition [he] taught me much about direct colloquial diction, all the more because his directness was in phrasing and syntax, not in imagery.'

('A Literary Transference', *Southern Review*, VI, 1940)

Hardy's integrity in saying what he had to say in his own way, against opposition and expectation, encouraged younger poets to achieve a self-supporting persona in the absence of 'the habits of the community formulated, corrected, and elevated by the continuous thought and direction of the Church' (T. S. Eliot, *After Strange Gods*).

Hardy's rejection of inherited dogmas led to a sifting and modification of inherited poetic methods which showed the way for modern poets to emancipation from the rich sensuous music of Victorian verse. Tennyson's doubts and Swinburne's attacks on the 'supreme evil, God' had not been reflected, as Hardy's reluctant agnosticism was, in a fundamental dissonance of form which recalls modern music. His original treatment of traditional forms makes them reflect the poignant tensions of modern verse. The hymn tune behind 'The Impercipient' and the *In Memoriam* stanza behind 'A Sign-Seeker' carry their own irony. Marsden has pointed out that Hardy's 'obsession with time and his wish to arrest the flux'—a modern trait—'could have encouraged a desire for strict and perhaps complicated forms', as in 'Looking Across'.

'The substance of the poem is the undeviating, inevitable, progression to Death, those close to him being taken one by one . . . The structure, however, seems to have been designed, consciously or not, to allow very little movement. The twenty-five lines contain only two rhymes! which run through and link every stanza; in addition one of the b rhymes of each stanza, the last line, is identical (the last line is, in fact, a modified refrain). No less than ten lines begin with 'and' which—so to speak—adds, without chronological progression; this is quite apart from the effect of the mere repetition of the word itself. Furthermore, of the remaining fifteen lines, four begin with the same word 'that'. Individually these points may be trivial; collectively I think that they are significant. The consciousness of Time and Death produces, in the last stanza, apparent acquiescence; the structure of the poem tells a different, contradictory story.'

The allusions to European culture which Eliot and Pound integrated into their poetry to counteract the break-up of a European tradition is anticipated, in a modest way, by Hardy's synthesis of language drawn from many levels of a native culture. The reflection of a world increasingly scientific, the determination that poetry should not be restricted to a special range of language or subject, the determination not to avoid triviality and ugliness (without, in Hardy's case, going to the opposite extreme by avoiding nobility and beauty) can all be found in Hardy's poetry. The failure of logic to explain an absurd godless world is enacted in the juxtaposition, without synthesis, of multiple and contradictory facets of experience—not a far cry from the fragmentation of 'The Waste Land', though Hardy never abandons strict form for free verse or the conscious level of statement in favour of the subconscious logic of association. ('I am very anxious not to be obscure' he explained to V. H. Collins: *Talks with Thomas Hardy at Max Gate 1920–1922.*)

Even where there has been no conscious imitation or confession of influence, Hardy's poetic response to the changing world opened the way to sincerity of response and boldness of experiment in the generations following. Even Eliot, for all his religious antipathy to Hardy's ability to live without God, touches the older poet's tragic vision in 'Dry Salvages'; and the futility, boredom, and unsensational recording of facts in Eliot's earlier poetry—'The Journey of the Magi', for example—can be paralleled in much of Hardy's poetry.

> A tedious time
> I found it, of routine, amid a folk
> Restless, contentless, and irascible.—
> ('Panthera')

Eliot's 'patient etherised upon a table' is simply a more violently realized image of Hardy's persistent poetic persona; of modern man as the bewildered helpless observer, born out of his time and place, powerless to alter the tragic predicament which he endures in alienated awareness.

While Hardy's own poems were still coming out, younger poets were experimenting in several different directions. Their aims were diverse, but had to some extent been anticipated in Hardy's varied output. Some of the Imagist tenets—'Everything can go, but this stark, bare, rocky directness of statement, this alone makes poetry today' (D. H. Lawrence): Ezra Pound's conviction that poetry should be 'austere, direct, free from emotional slither', . . . 'as much like granite as it can be, its force will lie in its truth'—and their concern for centrality of subject allied to craftsmanship, had been carried into practice since the beginning of Hardy's poetic career. A more surrealistic direction was pointed by some of the experiments in *Wheels*, a collection of poetry which appeared annually from 1916 to 1921. The poets represented expressed a general disgust with life and its mechanical motiveless malignity. Their response, though very different from Hardy's tragic affirmative joy in man and nature, took forms which *The Dynasts* and the five volumes of poetry so far published had introduced. The First Cause, minimized in the *Dynasts* by the domestic imagery of weaving and knitting, fares no better in *Wheels*, where elemental forces are described in terms of man-made products, as in Edith Sitwell's 'smooth black lacquer sea'. The soulless mechanical process that drives the action in Hardy's universe is recalled by the younger poets' geometric and mechanical metaphors, substituted (as they were not in Hardy) for metaphors from the world of nature. Though Hardy was not tempted to the extremes of expression reached by these two schools, the climate of opinion created by his anticipation of their themes and techniques encouraged interest in their experiments.

As a countryman, Hardy's greatest gift to a century which produced many Georgian 'nature' poets was to invest man's experience of his natural environment with cosmic implications. The best of his followers in this respect—D. H. Lawrence, Andrew Young, Robert Frost, Walter de la Mare, James Reeves—have been faithful to Hardy's detailed affirmative recording of the sensuous world, the sense of human solitude and alienation from the natural harmony which nevertheless commands his obedience, the acceptance of cosmic indifference, the inextricable weaving of life and death in the natural cycle, the preservation of local feeling and local word as symbols of identity against the encroachments of standardization.

Hardy's novels, no less than his poems, put into circulation themes and techniques which have become the commonplaces of twentieth-century thought. The poetic response to life which marks his prose as well as his poetry has nurtured a consciousness of the multiple and ambiguous faces of experience, the inextricable beauty and terror, which finds expression across the span of eighty years in similar terms.

'The huge pool of blood in front of her was already assuming the iridescence of coagulation; and when the sun rose a hundred prismatic hues were reflected from it.'

(*Tess of the d'Urbervilles*, 1891)

'On the fourth day the rats began to come out and die in batches . . . In the mornings the bodies were found lining the gutters, each with a gout of blood, like a red flower, on its tapering muzzle.'

(Camus, *The Plague*, 1947)

Even the sun-clouds this morning cannot manage such skirts.
Nor the woman in the ambulance
Whose red heart blooms through her coat so astoundingly—

(Sylvia Plath, 'Poppies in October',
Ariel, 1965)

I know the colour rose, and it is lovely,
but not when it ripens in a tumour;
and healing greens, leaves and grass, so springlike
in limbs that fester are not springlike.

(Dannie Abse, 'Pathology of
Colours', *A Small Desperation*, 1968)

The modern novel and drama have moved nearer to poetry in their Hardeian awareness of discordant and various experience which cannot be explained by any system. The relativity of truth and the unchronological pattern created by 'moments of vision' help to determine theme and shape of experimental novels written by the generation following Hardy; James Joyce, Virginia Woolf, E. M. Forster. Events and characterization are provisional, taking their significance from other events and characters in a web of leitmotif. All action is equally significant in the void of the Marabar caves or the perspective of *The Dynasts* which reduces marching armies and snowflakes to the same dead level. Though literature since the Second World War has made a partial return to straightforward narrative and plot, which mirrors the shift in interest away from post-Freudian free association in the subjective stream of consciousness to a web of continually changing exterior relationships through which man defines his identity, it owes its distinctive form to depiction of the incongruous worlds in which existentialist man has to create himself and his purposes. The incursion of irrational forces into the systems of order man tries to impose on the chaotic universe, one of Hardy's major themes, forms a vital source of tension in many modern novels. The rational society created in Angus Wilson's modern parable of what Hardy called 'human action in spite of human knowledge', *The Old Men at the Zoo*, is upset by animal violence. The Christian structures built up by Graham Greene's characters and the boys in William Golding's *Lord of the Flies* are knocked down by irrational and incomprehensible evil in human nature. The rationally planned ways of life in Iris Murdoch's novels, of which her titles are an image (*Under the Net*, *The Bell*, *The Sandcastle*, *A Severed Head*), are shown to be illusions when disrupted by the human passions of the planners and the inexplicable casual event. One need not look far in Hardy's work to find symbols of incomprehensible cosmic irrationality like the gipsy who shadows the disruptive love affair in *The Sandcastle*, or Felicity's unsuccessful attempt (in Dorset) to impose her will on the cosmos with an aid of a burning image of her enemy. Lucky Jim's luck is just as irrational as the bad luck of Hardy's characters, and rather less credible. The psychological evasions practised by modern fictional characters to hide their irrational behaviour is prefigured, as Morrell points out, in Hardy's stories. The self-deception of Kingsley Amis's Bowen (*I Like it Here*) who 'by an internal holding of telescope to blind eye, . . . had been keeping off what he had been up to', is no different in kind from Bathsheba's evasion of her true purpose in following Troy to Bath.

The 'doubleness in the action' which is the mark of poetic writing, and which has moulded the shape of so much modern fiction, was anticipated by Hardy in his use of symbolic leitmotifs to create a pattern of subconscious action that strains against the narrative level of conscious action. Bathsheba's sexual perception of the hollow in the ferns where she meets Troy defines the sword exercise as a desired seduction. In L. P. Hartley's *The Go-Between*, the adolescent boy's discovery of the belladonna just after meeting his friend's beautiful sister defines his subconscious perception of the ambiguous creative/destructive nature of sex, which consciously he cannot articulate. The older novelist does not depend, as Hartley does, on nothing but associative juxtaposition to make his point. Unlike the sword exercise, which marks a crisis in the relations of Troy and Bathsheba, Hartley's belladonna serves no narrative function in the plot. But a similar consciousness of multiple layers of personality begets similar methods of expression.

The sub-structure of symbolic leitmotif which reveals actions and desires obeying a different morality from conscious action has become a commonplace of modern novels. D. H. Lawrence, whose long essay on Hardy proves subjectively how much he owes to the older man, put into circulation a concept of personality and action whose springs were in the non-personal sexual force that moves Hardy's wilful characters to burst into being in defiance of conventional surface morality. The response of the two girls to the fox and the young man who kills it in Lawrence's short story *The Fox* realigns their personal relationships according to the non-personal sexual rhythms hidden underneath their conscious desires and moral values. Lawrence is Hardy's only true English successor in his feeling for the rhythms of eternity that bind the natural world to the ragged inconsequential lives of human beings; in his fear of mechanization and respect for individuality; in his power to depict the subconscious sexual tensions that motivate close relationships. Even in so autobiographical a novel as *Sons and Lovers*, the mother/son relationship recalls that of Clym and Mrs Yeobright, and Miriam tampering sensuously with the flowers as a substitute for the sexual experience she fears is sister to Sue Bridehead burying her face in the blooms at the Great Wessex Show. But though Hardy recognized the subconscious basis of much action and the consequent need for compassionate judgement of frailties, he saw no salvation in surrender to the dark gods. Though in the interests of realistic fiction he deplored the Victorian edict that 'the crash of broken commandments shall not be heard' ('Candour in English Fiction', *New Review*, January 1890) he was firm about the moral duty of authors.

'The higher passions must ever rank above the inferior—intellectual tendencies above animal, and moral above intellectual—whatever the treatment, realistic or ideal. Any system of inversion which should attach more importance to the delineation of man's appetites than to the delineation of his aspirations, affections, or humors, would condemn the old masters of imaginative creation from Aeschylus to Shakespeare.'

('The Profitable Reading of Fiction', *New York Forum*, March 1888)

The essential difference of outlook that marks Hardy off from modern authors with whom he shares so many preoccupations, explains why his *forte* is tragedy while the typical form of the modern novel is tragi-comedy. Hardy's heroes and heroines find moral assertion of the best values humanity has known, still possible in a chaos of indifference without fixed standards of value. Tess and Alec still represent the two choices open to modern man:

' "Why, you can have the religion of loving-kindness and purity at least, if you can't have—what do you call it—dogma."

' "O no! I'm a different sort of fellow from that! If there's nobody to say, 'Do this, and it will be a good thing for you after you are dead; do that, and it will be a bad thing for you,' I can't warm up. Hang it, I am not going to feel responsible for my deeds and passions if there's nobody to be responsible to; and if I were you, my dear, I wouldn't either!" '

(Chapter XLVII)

Alec's *credo* leads logically to the hedonistic standards of Alan Sillitoe's characters, or the opportunistic hero of Kingsley Amis, John Wain and John Braine whose aim is simply adjustment to the society in which he lives.

'. . . the sane man does not allow any of his roles to become abstract manifestations of general truth or guides to conduct. Existence is the only necessary condition, and the opportunistic hero plays any role he can in any world he can (the fantastic, the limited, or the deceitful) in order to get what he simply happens to want.'

(James Gindin, *Postwar British Fiction*)

Modern *homo fictus* is often a Lucky Jim who keeps a battery of faces to meet the various contingencies of his multiple and incongruous environment. Lacking a consistent essence against which to define himself, he continuously creates his life, values and purpose, and is cast by others, in a series of roles. Avoiding commitment to a role renders him powerless against circumstances (the tendency of Tess and Eustacia to let things drift has the same result). Lucky Jim's bad luck ceases when, in his new role of masterful

310

man, he seizes every opportunity, at the expense of others, to act out the role.

'More than ever he felt secure: here he was, quite able to fulfil his role, and, as with other roles, the longer you played it the better chance you had of playing it again. Doing what you wanted to do was the only training, and the only preliminary, needed for doing more of what you wanted to do.'

(Kingsley Amis: *Lucky Jim*)

The clash of roles causes tragedy in Hardy (though there is a touch of comic absurdity about Knight's and Angel's casting of Elfride and Tess as 'the pure woman') because the roles his characters assume *are* consistent 'guides to conduct'. *Tess* and *Jude* plead passionately against the inflexibility of 'abstract manifestations of general truth', but Tess and Jude nevertheless do not betray their steady ideals by assuming the faces required to adapt to society. The multiplicity of roles and values in the modern novel, the existentialist vision of man, responsible to no god, doomed to freedom of choice and commitment in an indifferent and Janus-faced world where the action by which he must define himself has no ultimate significance, invites the comic as well as the tragic perspective. Hardy comes nearest to the modern comic perspective in his less successful novels, where emotional identification with character is less intense. The comic perspective intrudes on serious or romantic matter to convey the bizarre duplicity of things and the lack of cosmic order. Even Graham Greene's Catholic universe cannot escape the absurd vision. Wilson's declaration of love to Scobie's wife, who does not return it, is made ludicrous by a nosebleed, the motherly concern of both Scobie and his wife, and the undignified prostrate position he is obliged to adopt.

'Louise struck at his cheek and missing got his nose, which began to bleed copiously. She said, "That's for calling him Ticki. Nobody's going to do that except me. You know he hates it. Here, take my handkerchief if you haven't got one of your own."
'Wilson said, "I bleed awfully easily. Do you mind if I lie on my back?" He stretched himself on the floor between the table and the meat safe, among the ants.'

(*The Heart of the Matter*)

In *The Sandcastle*, the stereotype of a passionate quarrel between husband and wife about Bill's affair with the young artist is punctured by Nan's hiccups and her undignified entry through the window when she cannot find her key. Sex, so tragically disruptive in Hardy, but even in *Jude the Obscure* tinged with the Absurd perspective when the pig's pizzle rudely dislocates Jude's sublime dream of Christminster, is the greatest incongruity of all. The attempted suicide of the would-be postulant Catherine in *The Bell* is made bizarre by Dora's ham-fisted rescue operations, the more resourceful life-saving of the 'aquatic nun' in her underclothes, and Catherine's public expression of love to the horror-stricken and homosexual Michael. The comic and multiple perspective questions the ultimate importance both of the sexual crisis and the ideals it disrupts.

The multiple perspective and singular form of *The Dynasts* anticipates much modern experimental drama. An epic action framed by various forms of narrative comment and other alienation techniques was placed firmly on the modern stage by Bertolt Brecht, author of that other great outcry against the futility of war, *Mother Courage*. Both dramatists see destiny as alterable by the action of men, so there are moments of choice for the protagonists when an alternative action is glimpsed; but both Napoleon and Mother Courage choose war. Brechtian spirits of Pity and Irony (Grusha and Azdak, and the two faces of the Good Woman) inspire the fundamental structure of *The Caucasian Chalk Circle* and *The Good Woman of Setzuan*. Brecht's use of mixed media can be paralleled in Hardy's varied presentation of his drama through realistic and non-realistic action and characters, dialogue, dumb show, changing perspectives, spectacle, poetry, prose, song. Only the quirk of Time prevented the use of film projection as the most appropriate medium for Hardy's stage directions and battle scenes. Brecht's instructions to his actors that the role should be demonstrated rather than acted, in the interests of alienation, recalls Hardy's suggestion of anti-naturalistic speech and gesture:

'In respect of such plays of poesy and dream a practicable compromise may conceivably result, taking the shape of a monotonic delivery of speeches, with dreamy conventional gestures, something in the manner traditionally maintained by the old Christmas mummers . . .'

(Preface, *The Dynasts*)

The 'automatic style—that of persons who spoke by no will of their own' of this mode of delivery has an unexpected descendant in

T. S. Eliot's use of the tranced chorus of aunts and uncles in *The Family Reunion*.

The repetitive futility of human action demonstrated in the modern anti-drama owns *Waiting for Godot* as parent and *The Dynasts* as prime fugleman of the line. The multiple representation of both showman and show, abstract reality and image, actor and role, which forms an essential part of the technique of Cocteau, Anouilh, Pirandello, and many playwrights of the Absurd Theatre, is anticipated in the structure of *The Dynasts* and the novels. The abstract reality of the Immanent Will concretely represented by the heaving brain-tissue has many descendants in symbolic stage props: Pinter's dumb waiter in the play of that name, which suggests cosmic cross-purposes as vividly as the jackaclock and gurgoyle in *Far from the Madding Crowd*; the platonic castle-model-cum-altar of the huge mysterious castle in which Albée's *Tiny Alice* is set; the gallows with corpse that opens *The Devils* with the question asked throughout the play:

MANNOURY: What's left, man? After that.
ADAM: Ah, you've something in your head.
MANNOURY: Has he? That's the point.

The seeker for good brave causes (Jimmy Porter, *Look Back in Anger*), for self-definition and evolution away from simple peasant standards which yet provide a stability and lovingkindness lost to the seeker (Beatie Bryant, *Roots*), for shelter against the terror of insecurity (Pinter's Rose, Davies, Stan); the inadequate failures who cast themselves and others in satisfying roles (*The Caretaker*, *The Brithday Party*, *The Cocktail Party*, *A Sleep of Prisoners*, *Hadrian VII*), and reject the love they need because it does not come in the romantic form they desire; all these modern archetypes are represented in Hardy's work. The problems of evil, death, and the death of God, of the mechanization of personality in a mechanical universe, inform his books as they inform every serious drama today. The unacknowledged death-wish, so dramatically expressed in the figure of Little Father Time and the trend of the later novels, drives man to assume the role of sacrificial victim or executioner (*The Devils, Saint's Day, Tiny Alice*). More rarely in an anti-heroic age suspicious of ideals and professions of faith, the dignified resistance of a human being (Sir Thomas More in *A Man for All Seasons*, Proctor in *The Crucible*, Grandier in *The Devils*) against assimilation into Absurdity and lack of meaning, recalls the integrity of Hardy's heroic characters faced with the temptation to nihilism. The realization of suffering as an essential element in the higher development of consciousness, and the meaning discovered in personal relationships which, in Peter Shaffer's plays *The Royal Hunt of the Sun* and *The Battle of Shrivings*, creates the only god there is, were also Hardy's positives against the darkness.

To find the purest inheritors of Hardy's cosmos, however, one must cross the Channel. His inscription (dated October 1904) in Jerome Kern's copy of *Jude the Obscure* pays tribute to European recognition: 'It was left to the French & Germans to discover the author's meaning, through the medium of indifferent translations.' Thomas Mann, backed by his German inheritance of logic and philosophy, metaphysics and music, found a powerful two-fold symbol in *Dr Faustus* for the evil that gave birth to two world wars, in Leverkuhn's twelve-tone method of composition and a hallucinatory devil, equated in their appeal to rational nihilism and regressive primitivism. They recall not only similar manifestations of Absurd evil in Kafka and Gide, but Hardy's Mephistophelian visitants—William Dare and Fitzpiers, both rationalist dilettantes, and Mop Ollamoor, whose 'chromatic subtleties' distort the diatonic harmonies of sleepy Stickleford, and who had nothing but 'devil's tunes in his repertory'.

In France, the nostalgia for an impossible purity, and the Existentialist vision developed since the two world wars, have produced a kind of novel and drama anticipated in Hardy's themes. Proust indicates a familiarity with Hardy's novels in Volume 10 ('The Captive', Part Two) of *Remembrance of Things Past*. The whole novel develops familiar Hardeian themes: the subjectivity of love, the impossibility of union with the reality of one's desire, life as a series of substitutions, the tendency to swing between memory and desire and desire and boredom, the incessant process of time and change, the past as both a positive and negative influence. Proust's subjective technique of presenting emotions and mental states indirectly through what a character notices was anticipated in, for example, Boldwood's distorted view of the snowy landscape and the summer glow of Talbothays that reflected Tess's love for Angel. R. Giannoni, in an article on 'Alain-Fournier et Thomas Hardy' (*Revue de Littérature Comparée*, XLII, 1968) discovers a link between the French author's reading of *Tess* in 1906 and his treatment of the theme of nostalgia for a lost homeland of paradisal purity, a theme which has occupied French writers at least since *Madame Bovary*.

> 'C'est en lisant *Tess*, par exemple, que Fournier commença à méditer sur le thème de la pureté perdue qui allait être au centre de ses preoccupations morales.'

Giannoni is careful to point out, however, that the nature of Fournier's debt to Hardy was independent. 'Alain-Fournier, lecteur enthousiaste de Thomas Hardy, ne fut ni un imitateur ni un disciple' but 'en la personne de Hardy, il trouva un guide précieux qui l'aida à voir clair en lui-même.'

The search for reunion with the pure part of one's being in Proust, Gide, Anouilh, Cocteau, often takes the form of an abnormal relationship, which includes the death wish. The closeness of Orpheus and Eurydice, the incestuous bond explicit in Gide's *Oedipus* and Cocteau's *The Infernal Machine* and implicit in the children of *Les Enfants Terribles*; the homosexual relationships of Gide's characters and his Narcissus' compulsion towards his mirror image, recall the special relationship between the cousins Jude and Sue. The purity of Hardy's characters is stained by the impurity of the cosmos of which they are part. Anouilh's pure lovers, like Hardy's Tess and Elfride, have unparadisal parents. His pure Thérèse (*La Sauvage*) succumbs finally, like Tess, to the compulsion of inherited impurity and the memory of past degradation. The contrast between sordid reality and the ideal dream, as clearly defined in *Antigone* or *La Sauvage* as in *Jude* and *Tess*, leaves only the choice of death or the deliberate assumption of a compromised role and acceptance of suffering in a fallen world.

All the characters in Romain Gary's *The Roots of Heaven* (1956), driven by the need for purity that involves a search for the source of man's sense of alienation from his roots, have an obsessive relationship with the wild elephants who become 'the very image of an immense liberty', of non-utilitarian natural splendour and individual dignity, almost extinct in a mechanistic and mechanized world. The desire of Camus' Tarrou for an impossible purity, the possibility of being a saint without God, is carried on with the recognition that all living creatures are tainted with the plague (the will to cause and suffer death in a universe whose only end and purpose is death). His refusal to collaborate willingly, his desire to maintain instead a constant vigilance against infection, is typical of the integrity of Hardy's tragic heroes and heroines. 'There are pestilences and there are victims, and it's up to us, so far as possible, not to join forces with the pestilences' (*The Plague*).

The refusal to be overawed by death into accepting the abstraction of significance from individuals placed many French writers, as Hardy had been placed, in opposition to social conventions. Gide's fight for the rights of the abnormal member of society, after recognition of his own homosexuality, continued Hardy's plea for greater tolerance. *Jude the Obscure* and *Tess of the d'Urbervilles*, as much as *The Immoralist* and *The Counterfeiters* and *Oedipus*, contain a rejection of authoritarian systems in favour of a personal morality which binds as much as it liberates, the courageous acceptance of one's desires, the difficulties of living with the new-found freedom of the godless and fatherless alien, the struggle not to slip back into a morality not one's own, the evolutionary and existentialist power of 'disponibilité'—the power of remaining unsatisfied and undefined, capable of change and growth. It is this power which Sue betrays by choosing to imprison herself in a rigid religious convention.

The integrity of the Hardeian response to an absurd universe is nowhere more apparent than in the work of Sartre and Camus, who brought the concepts of Absurdity and Existentialism into common consciousness on both sides of the Channel. All three writers are concerned with the practical problem of how to live in chaos. Caligula's collaboration with Absurdity, consequent on his discovery that 'men die; and they are not happy' (Camus, *Caligula*) like the collaboration of Alec, Troy, Eustacia, Fitzpiers, and Little Father Time, is rejected by his creator. Freedom for Sartre's Orestes, Camus' Clamance, Hardy's Tess, Jude, and Sue—the limited freedom of the prisoner condemned to death, and until then answerable to no authority but his own—brings a heavy burden of unatonable guilt and responsbility for all that lives and suffers.

The full look at the worst which these three authors steadily sustained brings recognition—the true tragic recognition—of both acceptance and revolt as man's destiny.

' ". . . since the order of the world is shaped by death, mightn't it be better for God if we refuse to believe in Him, and struggle with all our might against death, without raising our eyes towards the heaven where He sits in silence?" '

asks the doctor in *The Plague*. 'Fighting against creation as he found it' is the privilege and penalty of being human. Anguish and exile from paradisal harmony—'that sensation of a void within which never left us, that irrational longing to hark back to the past', realized in Hardy's concrete portrayal of a vanishing Wessex, are the marks of modern self-consciousness. Resistance involves an ordering of one's life. Existentialist man, unable to be defined by 'essences' or stereotypes of human nature (and how often the stereotyped conception causes tragedy in Hardy!) creates himself by commitment to purpose and action. His life is therefore a series of choices. A rash choice, such as Henchard's decision to make an early marriage, forges fetters that close round his fate. On the other hand, Hardy's pattern of reprieves, rallies, and re-choices shows the characters engaging in the constant process of re-defining and re-interpreting the past, and in some cases gaining partial control over the future, in a new context which proves how the first choice has changed the chooser. Morrell points out that the list of those who make, unmake, and then remake their original choice includes Fitzpiers, Grace, Angel, Eustacia, Wildeve, Pierston, Marcia, Sue, Jude, Farfrae, and Bob Loveday. Hardy's most typical tragic hero or heroine is one who fails to stand firmly by the chosen commitment. Henchard allows misunderstanding to develop at Elizabeth-Jane's wedding; Tess drifts into her mother's outmoded morality of waiting on Providence. Nevertheless Tess's constant ideal of purity makes her more than the existentialist sum of her acts.

The meaning of an author's work lives after him. Hardy has created, not a host of imitators and disciples, but an individual awareness of and thoughtful response to the human predicament that defines his spiritual successors. One cannot say with certainty whether Camus, that most upright and compassionate champion of human individuality against the abstractions of Absurdity, was influenced by reading Hardy. But he was born conscious of Hardy's universe. The values of physical life, love, friendship, emotion, happiness, goodness, clear-sightedness, daily work, heroism, personal integrity, and the love of life that is found on the other side of despair, which Camus opposes in *The Plague* to the 'nights and days filled always, everywhere, with the eternal cry of human pain'; the value of pain itself to develop sympathy with a common suffering, maintain their power across half a century of permissiveness, cynicism, and the savagery of two world wars because Hardy taught us to recognize them as the eternal truths to live by. The end of *The Plague*, reaffirming that trust in men slighted and enduring but nobler than the unconscious cosmos which crushes them, might stand as a tribute from the younger writer to his spiritual father; one of those who, 'while unable to be saints but refusing to bow down to pestilences, strive their utmost to be healers'; whose works, like his own, bore witness

'in favour of those plague-stricken people; so that some memorial of the injustice and outrage done them might endure; [and stated] quite simply what we learn in a time of pestilence: that there are more things to admire in men than to despise.'

Bibliography

I. THOMAS HARDY

References are taken from the definitive Wessex edition of Hardy's works published by Macmillan in 24 vols between 1912 and 1931. First publication dates in magazine and book form are also given. Further bibliographical information may be found in R. L. Purdy's invaluable *Thomas Hardy, A Bibliographical Study* (Oxford), 1954.

1. NOVELS

The Poor Man and the Lady. Written 1868; unpublished.

Desperate Remedies. London 1871. Wessex edn. London 1912.

Under the Greenwood Tree, or the Mellstock Quire. London 1872. Wessex edn. London 1912.

A Pair of Blue Eyes, serialized *Tinsley's Magazine,* Sept. 1872–July 1873. London 1873. Wessex edn. London 1912.

Far from the Madding Crowd, serialized *Cornhill Magazine,* Jan–Dec. 1874. London 1874. Wessex edn. London 1912.

The Hand of Ethelberta, A Comedy in Chapters, serialized *Cornhill Magazine,* July 1875–May 1876. London 1876. Wessex edn. London 1912.

The Return of the Native, serialized *Belgravia,* Jan–Dec. 1878. London 1878. Wessex edn. London 1912.

The Trumpet-Major, serialized *Good Words,* Jan–Dec. 1880. London 1880. Wessex edn. London 1912.

A Laodicean, A Story of Today, serialized *Harper's New Monthly Magazine* (European edn.), Dec. 1880–Dec. 1881. New York and London, 1881. Wessex edn. London 1912.

Two on a Tower, serialized *Atlantic Monthly* (Boston), May–Dec. 1882, simultaneously in London. London 1882. Wessex edn. London 1912.

The Mayor of Casterbridge, The Life and Death of a Man of Character, serialized *Graphic,* Jan–May 1886. London 1886. Wessex end. London 1912.

The Woodlanders, serialized *Macmillan's Magazine,* May 1886–Apr. 1887. London and New York 1887. Wessex edn. London 1912.

Tess of the d'Urbervilles, A Pure Woman Faithfully Presented, serialized *Graphic,* July–Dec. 1891. London 1891. Wessex edn. London 1912.

Jude the Obscure, serialized *Harper's New Monthly Magazine* Dec. 1894–Nov. 1895, simultaneously in New York and London. London 1896. Wessex edn. London 1912.

The Well-Beloved, A Sketch of a Temperament, serialized as *The Pursuit of the*

Well-Beloved in *The Illustrated London News*, Oct.–Dec. 1892. London 1897. Wessex edn. London 1912.

2. SHORT STORIES

'An Indiscretion in the life of an Heiress', *New Quarterly Magazine*, July 1878, simultaneously *Harper's Weekly*. London (privately printed) 1934. *Wessex Tales*, London and New York, 1888. Wessex edn. London 1912. Contents in 1888: 'The Three Strangers' (*Longman's Magazine*, March 1883); 'The Withered Arm', (*Blackwood's Edinburgh Magazine*, Jan. 1888); 'Fellow-Townsmen' (*New Quarterly Magazine*, Apr. 1880): 'Interlopers at the Knap', (*The English Illustrated Magazine*, May 1884); 'The Distracted Preacher' (as 'The Distracted Young Preacher', *New Quarterly Magazine*, April 1879). 'An Imaginative Woman' (*Pall Mall Magazine*, April 1894) added to the Osgood, McIlvaine edn. of *Wessex Tales* 1896. In Wessex edn. 1912, 'An Imaginative Woman' was removed to *Life's Little Ironies*, and 'A Tradition of Eighteen Hundred and Four' and 'The Melancholy Hussar' transferred from *Life's Little Ironies* to *Wessex Tales*.

A Group of Noble Dames, London 1891. Wessex edn. London 1912. Contents: 'The First Countess of Wessex' (*Harper's New Monthly Magazine*, Dec. 1889); 'Barbara of the House of Grebe', 'The Marchioness of Stonehenge', 'Lady Mottisfont', 'The Lady Icenway', 'Squire Petrick's Lady', 'Anna Lady Baxby' (*Graphic*, Christmas Number, 1890); 'The Lady Penelope' (*Longman's Magazine*, Jan. 1890); 'The Duchess of Hamptonshire' (as 'The Impulsive Lady of Croome Castle', *Light*, Apr. 1878); 'The Honourable Laura' (as 'Benighted Travellers', *Bolton Weekly Journal*, Dec. 1881).

Life's Little Ironies, London 1894. Wessex edn. London 1912. Contents in 1894: 'The Son's Veto' (*The Illustrated London News*, Christmas Number 1891); 'For Conscience' Sake' (as 'For Conscience Sake', *Fortnightly Review*, March 1891); 'A Tragedy of Two Ambitions', (*The Universal Review*, Dec. 1888); 'On the Western Circuit' (*The English Illustrated Magazine*, Dec. 1891); 'To Please His Wife' (*Black and White*, June 1891); 'The Melancholy Hussar of the German Legion' (as 'The Melancholy Hussar' in the *Bristol Times and Mirror*, Jan. 1890); 'The Fiddler of the Reels' (*Scribner's Magazine*, New York, May 1893); 'A Tradition of Eighteen Hundred and Four' (as 'A Legend of the Year Eighteen Hundred and Four', *Harper's Christmas*, Dec. 1882); 'A Few Crusted Characters' (as 'Wessex Folk', *Harper's New Monthly Magazine*, American and European editions, March–June 1891. In Wessex edn. 1912, 'An Imaginative Woman' was transferred from *Wessex Tales*, and 'A Tradition of Eighteen Hundred and Four' and 'The Melancholy Hussar of the German Legion' removed to *Wessex Tales*.

A Changed Man and Other Tales. London 1913. Wessex edn. London 1914. Contents: 'A Changed Man' (The Sphere, Apr. 1900); 'The Waiting Supper' (Murray's Magazine, Jan-Feb. 1888, and Harper's Weekly (America) Dec.-Jan. 1887–8); 'Alicia's Diary' (*The Manchester Weekly Times*, Oct. 1887): 'The Grave by the Handpost' (*St. James's Budget*, Christmas Number 1897); 'Enter a Dragoon' (*Harper's Monthly Magazine*, New York, Dec. 1900); 'A Tryst at an

Ancient Earthwork' (as 'Ancient Earthworks and What Two Enthusiastic Scientists Found Therein', *Detroit Post*, March 1885; and as 'Ancient Earthworks at Casterbridge', *English Illustrated Magazine*, Dec. 1893); 'What the Shepherd Saw' (*The Illustrated London News*, Christmas Number 1881); 'A Committee Man of "The Terror"' (*The Illustrated London News*, Christmas Number 1896); 'Master John Horseleigh, Knight' (*The Illustrated London News*, Summer Number 1893); 'The Duke's Reappearance' (*The Saturday Review*, Christmas Supplement, 1896); 'A Mere Interlude', *The Bolton Weekly Journal*, Oct. 1885); 'The Romantic Adventures of a Milkmaid' (*Graphic*, Summer Number 1883).

3. POETRY

Wessex Poems and Other Verses. London 1898. Wessex edn., *Wessex Poems, Poems of the Past and the Present*, London 1912.

Poems of the Past and the Present. London 1902 [1901] Wessex edn., *Wessex Poems, Poems of the Past and the Present*, London 1912.

Time's Laughingstocks and Other Verses. London 1909. Wessex edn., *The Dynasts*, Part Third, *Time's Laughingstocks*, London 1913.

Satires of Circumstance, Lyrics and Reveries, London 1914. Wessex edn., *Satires of Circumstance, Moments of Vision*, London 1919.

Moments of Vision and Miscellaneous Verses. London 1917.

Late Lyrics and Earlier with Many Other Verses. London 1922. Wessex edn., *Late Lyrics and Earlier, The Famous Tragedy of the Queen of Cornwall*, London 1926.

Human Shows, Far Phantasies, Songs, and Trifles, London 1925. Wessex edn., *Human Shows, Winter Words*, London 1931.

Winter Words, in Various Moods and Metres. London 1928. Wessex edn., *Human Shows, Winter Words*, London 1931.

My references have been taken from *Collected Poems*, London 1930.

4. DRAMA

The Dynasts, A Drama of the Napoleonic Wars, in Three Parts, Nineteen Acts, and One Hundred and Thirty Scenes. Part First, London 1903 [1904]. Part Second, London 1905 [1906]; Part Third, London 1908. Wessex edn., *The Dynasts*, Parts First and Second, London 1913; Part Third, & *Time's Laughingstocks*, London 1913. *The Famous Tragedy of the Queen of Cornwall at Tintagel in Lyonnesse*, London, 1923; Wessex edn., *Late Lyrics and Earlier, The Famous Tragedy of the Queen of Cornwall*, London 1926.

5. ARTICLES, ETC.

'How I built myself a House' (Chambers's Journal, Mar. 1885).

'The Dorsetshire Labourer' (Longman's Magazine, July 1883).

The Dorset Farm Labourer, Past and Present. Dorchester 1884.

'The Rev. William Barnes, B.D.' (*The Athenaeum*, Oct 1886)

'The Profitable Reading of Fiction' (*The Forum*, New York, Mar. 1888).

'Candour in English Fiction' (*New Review*, Vol. ii, No. 8, 1890).

'Why I Don't Write Plays' (*The Pall Mall Gazette*, Aug. 1892).

Selected Poems of William Barnes, ed. with Preface and gloss, London 1908.

Further information may be found in Purdy, *op. cit.*, and Harold Orel (ed.) *Thomas Hardy's Personal Writings*, London & Melbourne, 1967.

II. REFERENCE AND CRITICISM

1. BIBLIOGRAPHY

R. L. Purdy, *Thomas Hardy, A Bibliographical Study*, Oxford 1954.

C. J. Weber, *The First Hundred Years of Thomas Hardy: a Centenary Bibliography of Hardiana*, New York 1965.

2. BIOGRAPHY AND CRITICAL BIOGRAPHY

F. E. Hardy, *The Life of Thomas Hardy, 1840–1928* (the official biography), London 1962.

William Archer, *Real Conversations*, London 1904.

C. J. P. Beatty (ed.), *The Architectural Notebook of Thomas Hardy* (in facsimile), Dorchester 1966.

C. J. P. Beatty, *The Part Played by Architecture in the Life and Work of Thomas Hardy, with particular reference to the novels* (unpublished Ph.D. Thesis, University of London 1963).

Edmund Blunden, *Thomas Hardy*, London 1941.

V. H. Collins, *Talks with Thomas Hardy at Max Gate, 1920–1922*, London 1928.

Evelyn Hardy, *Thomas Hardy: A Critical Biography*, London 1954.

Evelyn Hardy, & R. Gittings, *Some Recollections by Emma Hardy together with Some Relevant Poems by Thomas Hardy*, London 1961.

C. J. Weber (ed.), *The Letters of Thomas Hardy*, Waterville, Maine 1954.

C. J. Weber, *Hardy of Wessex: his Life and Literary Career* (Revised edn.), New York and London 1965.

3. CRITICISM

1. GENERAL

The following list is limited to books and articles which find reflection in the present work. Many other works were consulted *en route* which may have been unconsciously absorbed without acknowledgement. Some may have missed acknowledgement in the text through the author's concern for uninterrupted flow and brevity. Gaps are inevitable unless the length of the Bibliography is going to challenge the length of the book.

L. Abercrombie, *Thomas Hardy: a Critical Study*, London 1919.

Douglas Brown, *Thomas Hardy* (2nd edn.), London 1961.

R. C. Carpenter, *Thomas Hardy*, New York 1964.

David Cecil, *Hardy the Novelist*, London 1943.

M. E. Chase, *Thomas Hardy from Serial to Novel*, Minneapolis 1927.

Samuel C. Chew, *Thomas Hardy, Poet and Novelist*, Bryn Mawr and New York 1921.

H. H. Child, *Thomas Hardy*, London 1916.

H. C. Duffin, *Thomas Hardy: a study of the Wessex Novels, the Poems, and The Dynasts* (3rd edn. revised), Manchester 1937.

P. d'Exideuil (tr. F. W. Crosse), *The Human Pair in the Work of Thomas Hardy*, London 1930.

Ruth A. Firor, *Folkways in Thomas Hardy*, Philadelphia 1931.

H. B. Grimsditch, *Character and Environment in the Novels of Thomas Hardy*, New York 1962.

ed. A. J. Guerard, *Hardy: a Collection of Critical Essays by various authors*, Engle-wood Cliffs, N.J. 1963.

A. J. Guerard, *Thomas Hardy: the Novels and Stories*, Cambridge, Mass. 1949.

A. D. Hawkins, *Thomas Hardy*, London 1950.

Irving Howe, *Thomas Hardy*, London 1968.

H. A. T. Johnson, *Thomas Hardy*, London 1968.

L. D. Johnson, *The Art of Thomas Hardy* (revised), London 1968.

ed. Laurence Lerner and John Holmstrom, *Thomas Hardy and his readers: a selection of contemporary reviews*, London 1968.

R. C. R. Morrell, *Thomas Hardy: the Will and the Way*, Kuala Lumpur 1965.

Arthur McDowall, *Thomas Hardy: a Critical Study*, London 1931.

A. E. Newton, *Thomas Hardy, Novelist or Poet?* Philadelphia, privately printed, 1929.

F. B. Pinion, *A Hardy Companion: a guide to the Works of Thomas Hardy and their Background*, London 1968.

W. R. Rutland, *Thomas Hardy: a study of his Writings and their Background*, Oxford 1938.

Hildegard Schill, *The Criticism of Thomas Hardy's Novels in England from 1871–1958* (unpublished Ph.D. thesis, University of London, 1963).

H. C. Webster, *On a Darkling Plain; the Art and Thought of Thomas Hardy*, Chicago and Cambridge, 1947.

George Wing, *Hardy*, Edinburgh and London, 1963.

SHORT STUDIES, ARTICLES, PAMPHLETS, ETC.

Carol Reed Anderson, 'Time, Space, and Perspective in Thomas Hardy': *Nineteenth Century Fiction*, IX, 1954–5.

J. O. Bailey, 'Hardy's "Mephistophelian Visitants"': P.M.L.A., LXI, 1946.

J. O. Bailey, 'Hardy's Visions of the Self': *Studies in Philology*, LVI, 1959.

Jacques Barzun, 'Truth and Poetry in Thomas Hardy': *Southern Review* (Hardy Centennial Issue), VI, 1940.

Richard Beckman, 'A Character Typology for Hardy's Novels': *E.L.H.* (Journal of English Literary History), XXX, 1963.

R. C. Carpenter, 'Hardy's "Gurgoyles"': *Modern Fiction Studies* (Hardy Special Number), VI, 1960.

F. Chapman, 'Revaluations (IV): Hardy the Novelist': *Scrutiny*, III, 1934.

Donald Davidson, 'The Traditional Basis of Thomas Hardy's Fiction': *Southern Review* (Hardy Centennial Issue), VI, 1940.

Bonamy Dobree, in *The Lamp and the Lute* (2nd edn.), London 1964.

T. S. Eliot, in *After Strange Gods*, London 1934.

Havelock Ellis, 'Thomas Hardy's Novels': *Westminster Review*, n.s., LXIII, 1883.

Eugene Goodheart, 'Thomas Hardy and the Lyrical Novel': *Nineteenth Century Fiction*, XII, 1957–8.

Ian Gregor, 'What Kind of Fiction did Hardy Write?': *Essays in Criticism*, XVI, 1966.

Barbara Hardy, in *The Appropriate Form*, London 1964.

L. J. Henkin, in *Darwinism in the English Novel 1860–1910*: N.Y. 1963.

Philip Larkin, 'Wanted: Good Hardy Critic': *Critical Quarterly*, VIII, 1966.

D. J. de Laura, '"The Ache of Modernism" in Hardy's Later Novels': *ELH*, XXXIV, 1967.

D. H. Lawrence, ed. E. D. McDonald, 'Study of Thomas Hardy', in *Phoenix; the Posthumous Papers of D. H. Lawrence*, New York 1950.

Gilbert Neiman, 'Thomas Hardy, Existentialist': *Twentieth Century Literature*, I, 1956.

Katharine Anne Porter, 'Notes on a Criticism of Thomas Hardy': *Southern Review* (Hardy Centennial Issue), VI, 1940.

Mary C. Richards, 'Thomas Hardy's Ironic Vision': *Nineteenth Century Fiction*, III, 1948–59, and IV, 1949–50.

James F. Scott, 'Thomas Hardy's Use of the Gothic: An Examination of Five Representative Works'; *Nineteenth Century Fiction*, XVII, 1962–3.

Alastair Smart, 'Pictorial Imagery in the Novels of Thomas Hardy': *Review of English Studies*, XII, n.s. 1961.

T. R. Spivey, 'Thomas Hardy's Tragic Hero': *Nineteenth Century Fiction*, IX, 1954.

J. I. M. Stewart, 'The Integrity of Hardy': *English Studies*, I, 1948.

Virginia Woolf, 'The Novels of Thomas Hardy', in *The Common Reader* (Second Series), London 1935.

Morton Dauwen Zabel, 'Hardy in Defense of his Art: The Aesthetic of Incongruity': *Southern Review* (Hardy Centennial Issue), VI, 1940.

Maurice Beebe, Bonnie Culotta, and Erin Marcus, 'Criticism of Thomas Hardy: A Selected Checklist': *Modern Fiction Studies* (Hardy Special Number), VI, 1960.

2. POETRY

E. C. Hickson, *The Versification of Thomas Hardy*, Philadelphia 1931.

Samuel L. Hynes, *The Pattern of Hardy's Poetry*, Chapel Hill and London 1961.

Kenneth Marsden, *The Poems of Thomas Hardy: a Critical Introduction*, London 1969.

J. G. Southworth, *The Poetry of Thomas Hardy* (2nd edn.), New York 1966.

SHORT STUDIES, ARTICLES, PAMPHLETS, ETC.

W. H. Auden, 'A Literary Transference': *Southern Review* (Hardy Centennial Issue), VI, 1940.

Howard Baker, 'Hardy's Poetic Certitude': *Southern Review* (Hardy Centennial Issue), VI, 1940.

J. E. Barton, *The Poetry of Thomas Hardy*, Guernsey 1969.

R. P. Blackmur, 'The Shorter Poems of Thomas Hardy': *Southern Review* (Hardy Centennial Issue), VI, 1940.

C. M. Bowra, *The Lyrical Poetry of Thomas Hardy* (Byron Foundation Lecture), Nottingham 1946.

G. Bullough, in *The Trend of Modern Poetry* (2nd edn.), Edinburgh and London 1941.

G. R. Elliott, 'Spectral Etching in the Poetry of Thomas Hardy': *P.M.L.A.*, XLIII, 1928.

ed. P. N. Furbank, in Introduction, *Selected Poems of Thomas Hardy* (Macmillan's English Classics), London and New York 1967.

A. J. Guerard, 'The Illusion of Simplicity: The Shorter Poems of Thomas Hardy': *Sewanee Review*, LXXII, 1964.

F. R. Leavis, 'Hardy the Poet': *Southern Review* (Hardy Centennial Issue), VI, 1940.

F. R. Leavis, in *New Bearings in English Poetry*, London 1950.

F. R. Leavis, 'Reality and Sincerity: Notes in the Analysis of Poetry': *Scrutiny*, XIX, 1952.

C. Day Lewis, 'The Lyrical Poetry of Thomas Hardy': *Proceedings of the British Academy*, XXXVII, 1951.

David Perkins, 'Hardy and the Poetry of Isolation': *ELH*, XXVII, 1959.

John Crowe Ransom, 'Honey and Gall': *Southern Review* (Hardy Centennial Issue), VI, 1940.

Delmore Schwartz, 'Poetry and Belief in Thomas Hardy': *Southern Review* (Hardy Centennial Issue) VI, 1940.

Lionel Stevenson, in *Darwin among the Poets*, New York 1963.

Allen Tate, 'Hardy's Philosophic Metaphors': *Southern Review* (Hardy Centennial Issue), VI, 1940.

John Wain, 'The Poetry of Thomas Hardy': *Critical Quarterly*, VIII, 1966.

G. M. Young, in Introduction, *Selected Poems of Thomas Hardy*, London 1940.

3. SPECIFIC WORKS

THE DYNASTS

J. O. Bailey, *Thomas Hardy and the Cosmic Mind*: a *New Reading of the Dynasts*, Chapel Hill, N. Carolina 1956.

Ernest Brennecke, *Thomas Hardy's Universe: A Study of a Poet's Mind*, London 1924.

A. Chakravarty, *The Dynasts and the Post-War Age in Poetry*, Oxford 1938.

Harold Orel, *Thomas Hardy's Epic-Drama: A Study of 'The Dynasts'* (2nd printing), Kansas 1963.

W. F. Wright, *The Shaping of 'The Dynasts': a Study in Thomas Hardy*, Lincoln-Nebraska 1967.

SHORT STUDIES, ARTICLES, PAMPHLETS, ETC.

Richard Church, 'Thomas Hardy as revealed in *The Dynasts*': *Etudes Anglaises*, VII, 1954.

Emma Clifford, 'The Impressionistic View of History in *The Dynasts*': *Modern Language Quarterly*, XXII, 1961.

Emma Clifford, 'Thomas Hardy and the Historians': *Studies in Philology*, LVI, 1959.

Bonamy Dobrée, 'The Dynasts': *Southern Review* (Hardy Centennial Issue), VI, 1940.

Barker Fairley, 'Notes on the Form of *The Dynasts*': *P.M.L.A.*, XXXIV, 1919.

NOVELS: SHORT STUDIES, ARTICLES, PAMPHLETS, ETC.

DESPERATE REMEDIES

Laurence O. Jones, '*Desperate Remedies* and the Victorian Sensation Novel': *Nineteenth Century Fiction*, XX 1965–6.

UNDER THE GREENWOOD TREE

N. T. Carrington, *Notes on Under the Greenwood Tree* ('Brodies' Notes on Chosen English Texts), Bath, undated.

Harold E. Toliver, 'The Dance under the Greenwood Tree. Hardy's Bucolics': *Nineteenth Century Fiction*, XVII, 1962–3.

FAR FROM THE MADDING CROWD

Howard Babb, 'Setting and Theme in *Far from the Madding Crowd*': *E.L.H.*, xxx, 1963.

I. L. Baker, *Notes on Far from the Madding Crowd* (Brodie's Notes on Chosen English Texts): Bath, undated.

R. C. Carpenter, 'The Mirror and the Sword: Imagery in *Far from the Madding Crowd*': *Nineteenth Century Fiction*, xviii, 1963–4.

Ralph Elliot, Hardy: *Far from the Madding Crowd* (Macmillan Critical Commentaries), London 1966.

THE RETURN OF THE NATIVE

M. L. Anderson, 'Hardy's Debt to Webster in *The Return of the Native*': *Modern Language Notes*, liv, 1939.

Louis Crompton, 'The Sunburnt God: Ritual and Tragic Myth in *The Return of the Native*': *Boston University Studies in English*, iv, 1960.

Leonard W. Deen, 'Heroism and Pathos in Hardy's *Return of the Native*', *Nineteenth Century Fiction*, xv, 1960–1.

John Hagan, 'A Note on the Significance of Diggory Venn': *Nineteenth Century Fiction*, xvi, 1961–2.

M. A. Goldberg, 'Hardy's Double-Visioned Universe': *Essays in Criticism*, vii, 1957.

John Paterson, *The Making of The Return of the Native*, Berkeley and Los Angeles, 1960.

John Paterson 'The "Poetics" of "The Return of the Native"': *Modern Fiction Studies* (Hardy Special Number), vi, 1960.

John Paterson, '*The Return of the Native* as Anti-Christian Document': *Nineteenth Century Fiction*, xiv, 1959–60.

Morse Peckham, 'Darwinism and Darwinisticism': *Victorian Studies*, iii, 1959.

R. W. Stallman, 'Hardy's Hour-Glass Novel': *Sewanee Review*, lv, 1947.

THE MAYOR OF CASTERBRIDGE

James R. Baker, 'Thematic Ambiguity in *The Mayor of Casterbridge*': *Twentieth Century Literature*, i, 1955.

Howard O. Brogan, '"Visible Essences" in *The Mayor of Casterbridge*': *E.L.H.*, xvii, 1950.

Douglas Brown, *Thomas Hardy: The Mayor of Casterbridge* (Studies in English Literature), London 1964.

N. T. Carrington, *Notes on The Mayor of Casterbridge* (Brodie's Notes on Chosen English Texts), Bath, undated.

D. A. Dike, 'A Modern Oedipus: *The Mayor of Casterbridge*': *Essays in Criticism*, ii, 1952.

Robert. B. Heilman, 'Hardy's *Mayor*: Notes on Style': *Nineteenth Century Fiction*, xviii, 1963–4.

F. R. Karl, '"The Mayor of Casterbridge": A New Fiction Defined': *Modern Fiction Studies* (Hardy Special Number), vi, 1960.

Robert Kiely, 'Vision and Viewpoint in *The Mayor of Casterbridge*': *Nineteenth Century Fiction*, xxiii, 1968–9.

John Paterson, '*The Mayor of Casterbridge* as Tragedy': *Victorian Studies*, iii, 1959.

F. B. Pinion, *Hardy: The Mayor of Casterbridge* (Macmillan Critical Commentaries), London, 1966.

Robert C. Schweik, 'Character and Fate in Hardy's *Mayor of Casterbridge*': Nineteenth Century Fiction, XXI, 1866–7.

G. G. Urwin, *The Mayor of Casterbridge* (Notes on English Literature), Oxford 1964.

THE WOODLANDERS

Robert Y. Drake Jr. '"The Woodlanders" as Traditional Pastoral': *Modern Fiction Studies* (Hardy Special Number), VI, 1960.

William J. Matchett, '*The Woodlanders*, or Realism in Sheep's Clothing': *Nineteenth Century Fiction*, IX, 1954–5.

TESS OF THE D'URBERVILLES

Allan Brick, 'Paradise and Consciousness in Hardy's *Tess*': *Nineteenth Century Fiction*, XVIII, 1962–3.

N. T. Carrington, *Notes on Tess of the D'Urbervilles* (Brodie's Notes on Chosen English Texts), Bath, undated.

Langdon Elsbree, '*Tess* and the Local Cerealia': *Philological Quarterly*, XL, 1961.

Elliot B. Gose, Jr., 'Psychic Evolution: Darwinism and Initiation in *Tess of the d'Urbervilles*': *Nineteenth Century Fiction*, XVIII, 1963–4.

Arnold Kettle, in *An Introduction to the English Novel*, Vol. II, London, 1953.

JUDE THE OBSCURE

Havelock Ellis, 'Concerning *Jude the Obscure*': *Savoy*, III, 1896.

Robert B. Heilman, 'Hardy's Sue Bridehead': *Nineteenth Century Fiction*, XX, 1966.

Norman Holland, Jr., '*Jude the Obscure*: Hardy's Symbolic Indictment of Christianity': *Nineteenth Century Fiction*, IX, 1954–5.

William J. Hyde, 'Theoretic and Practical Unconventionality in *Jude the Obscure*': *Nineteenth Century Fiction*, XX, 1965–6.

F. P. W. McDowell, 'Hardy's "Seeming or Personal Impressions": the Symbolical Use of Image and Contrast in "Jude the Obscure"': *Modern Fiction Studies* (Hardy Special Number), VI, 1960.

Arthur Mizener, '*Jude the Obscure* as a Tragedy': *Southern Review* (Hardy Centennial Issue), VI, 1940.

SHORT STORIES

James. L. Roberts, 'Legend and Symbol in Hardy's "The Three Strangers"': *Nineteenth Century Fiction*, XVII, 1962–3.

Index

Abercrombie, Lascelles, 8, 16–17, 143, 276
Abse, Dannie, 307
'Absolute Explains, The', 26, 44
'Abt Vogler' (Browning), 106, 107
'"According to the Mighty Working"', 32–3
Aeschylus, 16, 277
'After a Journey', 96, 102, 103
After Strange Gods (Eliot), 20, 304
'After the Last Breath', 54
'Afterwards', 64
'Agnosto Theo', 25, 26, 37, 38
'Ah, Are you Digging on my Grave?', 72, 122, 133
Alain-Fournier, *see* Fournier, Alain-
'Alain-Fournier et Thomas Hardy' (Giannoni), 314–15
'Alarm, The', 131–2
Albee, Edward, 313
Albuera (*The Dynasts*), 278, 281, 282, 296, 299
Aldclyffe, Miss (*Desperate Remedies*), 138, 153–4
'Alicia's Diary', 147
Amis, Kingsley, 308, 310, 311
'An August Midnight', 65
'Ancient Earthworks and What The Enthusiastic Scientists Found Therein', *see* 'Tryst at an Ancient Earthwork, A'
'Ancient Earthworks at Casterbridge', *see* 'Tryst at an Ancient Earthwork, A'
'And There was a Great Calm', 75–6
'Andrew Barton', 130
Angel (*Tess of the d'Urbervilles*), *see* Clare, Angel
'Announcement, The', 54–5
Anouilh, Jean, 313, 315
Appropriate Form, The (Barbara Hardy), 12
Arabella (*Jude the Obscure*), 12, 23, 255, 257, 259, 261, 262, 264, 267, 268, 269, 271, 272, 274
Archer, William, 133
'Aristodemus the Messenian', 144

Arnold, Matthew, 20, 81, 82, 84, 85, 89, 92, 217
'At a Lunar Eclipse', 149
'At a Watering-Place', 112–13
'At Castle Boterel', 89, 90, 96, 101
'At Day-Close in November', 55, 66
'At Rushy-Pond', 70
'At Shag's Heath', 106, 124, 134, 135
'At Tea', 111, 112
'At the Altar-Rail', 112
'At the Draper's', 111
'At the Piano', 104
'At the Railway Station, Upway', 144
'At Waking', 78
'At Wynyard's Gap', 114
Auden, W. H., 21, 102, 302, 304
Austerlitz (*The Dynasts*), 277, 280, 281, 291, 296, 299

'Babylon', 131
'Backward Spring, A', 65
Bailey, J. O., 17, 285
Balladry, Hardy's debt to, 119–21, 130, 138–40, 147, 154, 158, 297
Baptista, *see* Trewthen, Baptista
'Barbara of the House of Grebe', 145–6, 150
Barnes, William, 52, 297
Barton, J. E., 20
Bathsheba (*Far from the Madding Crowd*), 18, 19–20, 21, 22, 158, 159, 160, 161, 162, 164, 170, 171, 172, 174, 175, 176, 308, 309; character study, 165–7; relationship with Troy, 166–7, 168–9
'Battle of Otterburn, The', 130
Beatty, Dr C. J. P., 8, 151, 183, 206, 269–70
Beckett, Samuel, 16, 55, 290, 313
Beckman, Richard, 238
'Bedridden Peasant, The', 25, 26, 39, 41
'Beeny Cliff', 93
'Before and After Summer', 68
'Before Life and After', 25, 26, 37, 43, 44–5, 47

Bell, The (Murdoch), 308, 312
Benson, A. C., 87
'Best Times', 103
Bethell, S. L., 159
Betjeman, John, 303
'Beyond the Last Lamp', 10, 105
Biography of Hardy, 8, 69; Hardy's marriage to Emma, 81–104
'Bird-Catcher's Boy, The', 132, 133
'Birds at Winter Nightfall', 55
'Blinded Bird, The', 73, 253
Blunden, Edmund, 8, 118–19, 276, 302
Boldwood, Farmer (*Far From the Madding Crowd*), 21, 22, 120, 141, 158–76, 314; character study, 170–2
'Bonnie Annie', 117
Braine, John, 310
Brecht, Bertold, 276–7, 312
Brecht: A Choice of Evils (Esslin), 277
Bridehead, Sue (*Jude the Obscure*), 13, 15, 19, 22, 23, 255–74, 309, 315, 316, 317
Britten, Benjamin, 46, 53, 291
'Broken Appointment, A', 24, 55, 74–5
Brontë, Charlotte, 12
Brontë, Emily, 93, 95, 139–40, 143, 200
Brooke, Rupert, 76
Brown, Douglas, 9, 158, 181
Browning, Robert, 34, 96, 115, 125, 129, 297; comparisons with Hardy, 106–11, 125, 129
'Burghers, The', 122, 124, 129
'Burning the Holly', 133
'By Her Aunt's Grave', 112
'By the Earth's Corpse', 26
Byron, Lord, 297

Campbell, Roy, 297
Camus, Albert, 18, 20, 31, 72, 79, 80, 114, 184, 200, 243, 248, 251, 252, 256, 257, 271, 272, 307, 315, 316–18
'Candour in English Fiction', 309
Carpenter, Richard, 9, 186
Casterbridge; comparison with Dickens' Coketown, 206–7; description of, 205–8
'Catching Ballet of the Wedding Clothes, The', 134
Cecil, David, 8, 137–8, 140, 141, 143, 149, 153
'Channel Firing', 135
'Chapel-Organist, The', 106
'Character Typology for Hardy's Novels, A' (Beckman), 238
Characterization, 17–18; Virginia Woolf's view of Hardy's, 10, 21
Charmond, Felice (*The Woodlanders*), 17,

216, 218, 219, 220, 223, 225, 227, 230
Chaucer, Geoffrey, 148
Chekhov, Anton, 144
Chesterton, G. K.   34
'Chevy Chase', 139
'Childhood Among the Ferns', 10, 262–3
'Children and Sir Nameless, The', 119
'Choir-Master's Burial, The', 134
'Circular, A', 103
Clare, Angel (*Tess of the d'Urbervilles*), 12, 19, 22, 143, 151, 172, 186, 233–53, 311, 314, 317; compared with Alec, 236
Clifford, Emma, 294
Clym (*The Return of the Native*), *see* Yeo-bright, Clym
Cockerell, Sir Sydney, 93
Cocteau, Jean, 289, 313, 315
Coincidence, Hardy's use of, 12, 17, 72, 139, 160
Collected Poems, 25, 69, 303
Collins, V. H., 305
Common Reader, The (Woolf), 10, 12, 18, 20, 21
'Commonplace Day, A' 55–7
'Confessional, The' (Browning), 129; compared with Hardy's 'At Shag's Heath', 125
Conrad, Joseph, 200, 267
'Contretemps, The', 130
'Convergence of the Twain, The', 25, 33–4, 75
Cornwall, Hardy's life in, 87, 90, 93, 95, 96, 98, 102
Creedle, Robert (*The Woodlanders*), 220, 226, 230, 231
Crompton, Louis, 186
'Crow and Pie', 234
'Curate's Kindness, The', 106
'Curtains Now are Drawn, The', 103, 104

Dalton, R. F., 8
'Dame of Athelhall, The', 130
'Dance at the Phoenix, The', 123
Dare, William (*A Laodicean*), 138, 152, 153, 314
'Dark-Eyed Gentleman, The', 121, 122
'Darkling Thrush, The', 55, 65, 105
Darwin, Charles, 43
Davidson, Donald, 138
Day, Fancy (*Under the Greenwood Tree*), 154, 156–7, 158
'Days to Recollect', 104
de Stancey (*A Laodicean*), 13, 153
de la Mare, Walter, 303, 306
Deacon, Lois, 8

'Dead and the Living One, The', 133, 135
'Dead "Wessex" the Dog to the Household', 79
Death of Tragedy, The (Steiner), 16, 103
Desperate Remedies, 13, 23, 138, 152, 153–4
Devils, The (Whiting), 213, 313
Dewy, Dick (*Under the Greenwood Tree*), 155, 156–7, 158
Dickens, Charles, 206–7
Dike, D. A., 196, 208
'Distracted Preacher, The', 148
Dobrée, Bonamy, 14, 15, 16
Dr Faustus (Mann), 153, 221, 270, 314
Donne, John, 96
'Doom and She', 26, 28
Dostoievsky, Fyodor, 200, 201, 250
'Dream Question, A', 25, 26, 27
'Drinking Song', 43, 44
'Drizzling Easter Morning A', 41
'Drummer Hodge,' 76
'Duchess of Hamptonshire, The', 147
'Duel, The', 130
d'Urberville, Alec (*Tess of the d'Urbervilles*), 234, 235, 236, 240, 245, 247, 249, 250, 251, 310, 316; compared with Angel, 236
Durbeyfield, Joan (*Tess of the d'Urbervilles*), 238, 240
Durbeyfield, John (*Tess of the d'Urbervilles*), 237, 246
'During Wind and Rain', 58, 71–2
Dynasts, The, 8, 9, 14, 16, 23, 35, 113, 114, 115, 130, 276–301, 306, 312, 313

Edlin, Widow (*Jude the Obscure*), 265, 272
'Edward', 117, 122, 123, 139
Egdon Heath (*The Return of the Native*), description of, 177–80,
Elfride (*A Pair of Blue Eyes*), 13, 150, 151, 257, 311, 315
Eliot, George, 168–9
Eliot, T. S., 20, 47–8, 52, 69, 137, 152, 159, 190, 302, 304, 305, 306, 312–13
Elizabeth-Jane (*The Mayor of Casterbridge*), 18, 22, 197–214, 317
'Elopement, The', 130
'Enter a Dragoon', 147
Esslin, Martin, 277
Ethelberta (*The Hand of Ethelberta*), 13, 138, 151–2
Eustacia (*The Return of the Native*), see Vye, Eustacia

'Face at the Casement, The', 108
'Fallow Deer at the Lonely House, The', 59

Fanny (*Far From the Madding Crowd*), see Robin, Fanny
Far From the Madding Crowd, 8, 13, 18, 19–20, 21, 22, 120, 137, 138, 139, 140–1, 142, 158–76, 177, 308, 309, 313, 314, 316; action linked to seasons, 161; film of, 166
Farfrae, Donald (*The Mayor of Casterbridge*), 8, 19, 22, 139, 196–214, 317
Faust (Goethe), 49, 277
Fawley, Jude (*Jude the Obscure*), 12, 13, 14, 15, 19, 22, 141, 254–75, 311, 312, 315, 316, 317
'Fellow-Townsmen', 147
Few Crusted Characters, A, 148
'Fiddler of the Reels, The', 145, 154, 221
'Figure in the Scene, The', 71
Fitzpiers (*The Woodlanders*), 12, 216–32, 314, 316, 317; relationship with Grace, 23, 221–2, 226
'Five Students, The', 71–2
'Flirt's Tragedy, The', 130, 133
Folklore, Hardy's debt to, 138–9, 144, 148, 153, 154, 217
'For Conscience' Sake', 147
'For Life I had never Cared Greatly', 60
Forster, E. M., 90, 91, 257, 307
Fournier, Alain-, 314–15
Fray, Henery (*Far From the Madding Crowd*), 18, 176
Frazer, Sir James, G., 242
'Friends Beyond', 135
Frith, Roger, 302
Frost, Robert, 306

Galton, Sir Francis, 251
Garland, Anne (*The Trumpet Major*), 154, 155, 158
Gary, Romain, 315
George III (*The Dynasts*), 279, 281, 299
Giannoni, R., 314–15
Gide, André, 200, 258, 314, 315, 316
Giles (*The Woodlanders*), see Winterborne, Giles
Gindin, James, 310
'God-Forgotten', 25, 26, 39–40
'God's Education', 38
'God's Funeral', 41, 43
Goethe, Johann Wolfgang von, 49, 277
'Going, The', 96, 97–8, 106
Golden Bough, The (Frazer), 242
Golding, William, 308
Grace (*The Woodlanders*), see Melbury, Grace
Granite and Rainbow (Woolf), 11–12

Graves, Robert, 302
Graye, Cytherea (*Desperate Remedies*), 23, 138, 153–4
'Great Things', 59–60
Greene, Graham, 308, 311
Group of Noble Dames, A, 148
Guérard, A. J., 7–8, 9

Hagan, John, 192
Hand of Ethelberta, The, 13, 138, 151–2
'Hap', 16, 25, 26, 28–9, 31–2, 43
Hardy, Barbara, 12
Hardy, Captain (*The Dynasts*), 280, 288, 294
Hardy, Emma, 81–104
Hardy, F. E., *see Life of Thomas Hardy, The*
Hardy the Novelist (Cecil), 137–8
'Hardy's Hour-Glass Novel' (Stallman), 181
'Hardy's Visions of the Self' (Bailey), 17
Hartley, L. P., 309
'Harvest Supper, The', 133
'Haste to the Wedding', 83
'Haunter, The', 86
'He Abjures Love', 78
'He Prefers her Earthly', 104
'He Resolves to Say no More', 59
'He Revisits his First School', 77
'He Wonders about Himself', 39, 195
'Heiress and Architect', 122
Hemingway, Ernest, 68
Henchard, Michael (*The Mayor of Casterbridge*), 8, 13, 14, 15, 18, 19, 22, 120, 130, 138, 139, 196–215, 317
Henchard, Susan (*The Mayor of Casterbridge*), 197, 198, 199, 202, 203, 208, 210–11, 214
'Her Death and After', 122, 127, 129
'Her Dilemma', 115
'Her Immortality', 133
'Her Second Husband Hears her Story', 129, 130
Herbert, George, 35
'Heredity', 78, 149
'His Country', 76
'History of the Hardcomes, The', 22
Holland, Norman, Jr, 257
'Homecoming, The', 23, 124, 125, 126
Homer, 276, 280, 284, 286, 288, 294
Hopkins, Gerard Manley, 303, 304
'How Long, How Long?', 47
Howe, Irving, 276
'Husband's View, The', 122
Hynes, Samuel, 9, 33, 34, 284, 289

'I Am the One', 59
'I Found Her out There', 94, 96, 98
'I Look into my Glass', 78, 79
'I Watched a Blackbird', 65
Ibsen, Henrik, 85, 120, 134, 139, 147, 150, 272, 276
Iliad, The (Homer), 276, 284
'Imaginative Woman, An', 134
'Impassioned Prose' (Woolf), 11–12
'Impercipient, The', 37, 41, 304
'Impressionistic View of History in *The Dynasts*, The' (Clifford), 294
'Impulsive Lady of Croome Castle, The', *see* 'Duchess of Hamptonshire, The'
'In a Wood', 10
'In Church', 111, 112, 113
'*In Memoriam*' (Tennyson), 81, 82, 87, 89, 304
'In Sherborne Abbey', 118, 130
'In Tenebris II', 8
'In the Cemetery', 111, 112, 113
'In the Days of Crinoline', 130
'In the Moonlight', 111–12
'In the Nuptial Chamber', 111, 112
'In the Restaurant', 111
'In the Room of the Bride-Elect', 112
'In the Servants' Quarters', 123
'In the Study', 111
'In the Vaulted Way', 70
'In Vision I Roamed', 149
Infernal Machine, The (Cocteau), 289, 315
'Interlopers at the Knap', 147
'It Never Looks Like Summer', 103

'John and Jane', 121, 122
John Gabriel Borkman, 114
Johnson, Lionel, 8, 143
Jopp (*The Mayor of Casterbridge*), 199, 208, 213
Josephine (*The Dynasts*), 287–8
Joyce, James, 143, 256, 304, 307
Jude (*Jude the Obscure*), *see* Fawley, Jude
Jude the Obscure, 9, 10, 12, 13, 14, 15, 22, 23, 26, 85, 137, 138, 141, 224, 232, 254–75, 309, 311, 312, 314, 315, 316, 317
'*Jude the Obscure*: Hardy's Symbolic Indictment of Christianity' (Holland), 257
Juvenal, 96

Kafka, Franz, 271, 314
'Karshish, the Arab Physician' (Browning), 109–10
Keats, John, 45, 73

Knight (*A Pair of Blue Eyes*), 150, 151, 152, 186, 311
'Known Had I', 68, 103
Krutch, Joseph Wood, 103
Kutúzov (*The Dynasts*), 281, 287

'Laboratory, The' (Browning), 107, 129
'Lacking Sense, The', 25, 26, 34, 35, 38
'Lady from the Sea, The' (Ibsen), 134, 147
'Lady Icenway, The', 147
'Lady Penelope, The', 147
'Lament', 93, 103
Lamp and the Lute, The (Dobrée), 14, 15, 16
Laodicean, A, 13, 19, 152–3
Larkin, Philip, 302, 303
'Last Words to a Dumb Friend', 79–80
Late Lyrics and Earlier, 25
Lawrence, D. H., 153, 306, 309
'Leipzig', 130, 131
'Let Me Enjoy', 59–60
Lewes, G. H., 49
Lewis, C. Day, 48, 302, 303
Lewis, C. S., 284
'Life and Death at Sunrise', 49–52, 53, 55, 144
Life of Thomas Hardy, The (F. E. Hardy), 11, 13, 14, 15, 21, 30–1, 38, 45, 48, 67, 102, 105, 115, 198–9, 216, 217, 259, 262, 263
'Light Snow-Fall After Frost, A', 10, 67–8
'Literary Transference, A' (Auden), 304
'Logs on the Hearth', 56
'Looking Across', 72, 304
'Lost Pyx, The', 134
Love; death of, in poems, 70–1; Hardy's definition of, 19–20; musical expression of, 21–2
Lucetta (*The Mayor of Casterbridge*), *see* Templeman, Lucetta
'Lyrical Poetry of Thomas Hardy, The' (Lewis), 48

McDowall, Arthur, 8
Malamud, Bernard, 271
'Man He Killed, The', 75–6
Mann, Thomas, 153, 221, 250, 270, 314
Manston, Aeneas (*Desperate Remedies*), 138, 153–4
'Marchioness of Stonehenge, The', 144, 147
Marriage, Hardy's to Emma, 81–104
Marsden, Kenneth, 9, 13, 302, 303–4
Marty (*The Woodlanders*), *see* South, Marty
'Mary Hamilton', 117

'Master Hugues of Saxe-Gotha' (Browning), 106, 107
'Master John Horseleigh, Knight', 148,
Mayor of Casterbridge, The, 8, 12, 13, 14, 15, 18, 19, 22, 120, 130, 137, 138, 139, 150, 196–215, 317
Melbury, Grace (*The Woodlanders*), 8, 15, 17, 23, 139, 218, 219, 220, 226, 231, 232, 317; primitive side of her nature, 22; relationship with Fitzpiers, 221–2, 226; relationship with Giles, 223–4, 225–9
Melbury, Mr (*The Woodlanders*), 19, 22, 216, 218, 219, 220, 222, 226, 230, 231
Melville, Herman, 200
Meredith, George, 85–7, 88
Metre, 31, 33, 36, 52, 83, 130
Meynell, Viola, 30
Middlemarch (Eliot), 168–9
'Midnight on the Great Western', 10, 106, 272
'Military Appointment, A', 125
Mill, John Stuart, 8, 9, 87, 257
Milton, John, 28, 38
'Mismet', 72
'Mock Wife, The', 130
Modern Love (Meredith), 85–7
'Modern Oepidus, A: *The Mayor of Casterbridge*' (Dike), 196
'Molly Gone', 58, 71–2
Moore, Sir John (*The Dynasts*), 278, 286, 287, 291
Morrell, R. C. R., 9, 239, 308, 317
'Moth Signal, The', 126, 130
Mother Courage (Brecht), 277, 312
'Mother Mourns, The', 25, 26, 38
'Mound, The', 70
Murdoch, Iris, 272, 308, 311–12
'Musical Box, The', 68
'My Boy Billy', 124
'My Cicely', 127–8
'My Last Duchess' (Browning), 107, 129
Myth of Sisyphus, The (Camus), 31, 114

Napoleon (*The Dynasts*), 277–90, 296, 297, 300, 312
'Nature's Questioning', 25, 26, 36–7, 38, 95
'Near Lanivet', 103
Negative particle, Hardy's use of, 30, 73
Nelson, Lord (*The Dynasts*), 279–82, 286, 287, 294
'Nettles, The', 120
'Neutral Tones', 70
'New Year's Eve', 38

'Newcomer's Wife, The', 127

Newson (*The Mayor of Casterbridge*), 12, 197, 198, 199, 208, 210

Ney, Marshal (*The Dynasts*), 286, 287, 288, 300

Nietzsche, Friedrich, 15

'Noble Lady's Tale, The', 130

'Nobody Comes', 55, 73–4

Norcombe Hill (*Far From the Madding Crowd*), 162–3, 164

'Note on the Significance of Diggory Venn, A' (Hagan), 192

'Novels of Thomas Hardy, The' (Woolf), 10, 12, 18, 20, 21

Nunsuch, Johnny (*The Return of the Native*), 183, 191, 193

Oak, Gabriel (*Far From the Madding Crowd*), 8, 18, 19, 20, 22, 138, 158–63, 166, 167, 169, 170, 171, 174, 175, 176; character study, 164–5, 174

Oakes, Philip, 302

Oepidus (Gide), 258, 315, 316

Old age, comparison of Hardy with Yeats, 77–9

'Old Workman, The', 120

'On a Heath', 70

'On Martock Moor', 124

'On Sturminster Footbridge', 65

'On the Death-Bed', 113, 130

'On the Doorstep', 103

'On the Western Circuit', 146

'Once at Swanage', 104

'One who Married above Him', 130

Osborne, John, 313

'Outside the Window', 112

Outsider, The (Camus), 184, 251

'Over the Coffin', 112, 113

'Overlooking the River Stour', 64–5, 68, 103

Owen, Wilfred, 75, 291

'Oxen, The', 41

Pair of Blue Eyes, A, 13, 138, 150–1, 152, 186, 257, 311, 315

'Panthera', 109, 110, 305

'Paphian Ball, The', 134

Part Played by Architecture in the Life and Works of Thomas Hardy, The (Beatty), 151, 206, 269–70

Patmore, Coventry, 150

Pattern of Hardy's Poetry, The (Hynes), 9, 33, 284, 289

Paula (*A Laodicean*), 13, 19, 152, 153

'Peasant's Confession, The', 105

'Pedigree, The', 13, 149

'Phantom Horsewoman, The', 93, 101

Phillotson (*Jude the Obscure*), 22, 254, 257, 260, 261, 265, 267, 269, 271, 272

'Philosophical Fantasy, A', 26, 44, 45

Philosophy; Hardy's philosophic view of the universe, 25

'Photograph, The', 56, 59

'Pictorial Imagery in the Novels of Thomas Hardy' (Smart), 23

'Pine Planters, The', 10

'Pink Frock, The', 108

Pinter, Harold, 313

Pirandello, Luigi, 313

Pitt, William (*The Dynasts*), 279, 280, 281, 282

'Pity of It, The', 76

'Place on the Map, The', 70

'Places', 93, 95

Plague, The, (Camus) 20, 22, 79, 243, 252, 307, 316–18

'Plaint to Man, A', 38, 39, 41–3

Plath, Sylvia, 307

Plomer, William, 303

Plot; domination of, 144; importance of, 16, 17; improbable devices of, 144; regularity of, 18

Poems of the Past and the Present, 25, 39, 106

Poems of Thomas Hardy, The: A Critical Introduction (Marsden), 9, 302, 303–4

Poetry; 'application of ideas to life' in, 26–7; dramatic, 10, 105–36; elegiac, 10, 71–2, 79, 81–104; Hardy as poetic novelist, 11; Hardy's influence on modern poets, 302–7; Hardy's view of his, 25, 45, 106; Hardy's views on lyrical, 53; narrative, 10, 105–36; philosophical, 10, 25–48; prosed, 10; reasons for neglect of Hardy's, 302; Ruskin's definition of lyrical, 53; tragedy in, 16; war, 75–7, 105, 130–2

'Poetry of Thomas Hardy, The' (Barton), 20

'Poor Man and a Lady, A', 130

Pope, Alexander, 96

'Porphyria's Lover', 108

Postwar British Fiction (Gindin), 310

Pound, Ezra, 302, 305, 306

'Practical Woman, A', 121, 122

'Profitable Reading of Fiction, The', 310

'Prospect, The', 103

'Proud Songsters', 10, 66

Proust, Marcel, 66, 69, 314, 315

Providence and Mr Hardy (Deacon), 8

Purdy, R. L., 319, 321

333

'Pursuit of the Well-Beloved, The', *see* 'Well-Beloved, The'
'Puzzled Game-Birds, The', 10, 13

'Rain on a Grave', 93, 103
'Rake-Hell Muses', 108
Ransom, John Crowe, 303
Reeves, James, 302, 306
'Reluctant Confession', 134
'Reminder, The', 59
'Respectable Burgher, The, on "The Higher Criticism"', 43
Return of the Native, The, 8, 13, 15, 19, 21, 22, 23, 39, 120, 126, 137, 139, 141, 142, 143, 149, 177–95, 196, 285, 309, 310, 316, 317
'Revisitation, The', 110, 128–9, 139
Rhythms; natural, 17, 18; natural speech, 52, 55
'Riddle, A', 103
Rimbaud, Arthur, 153
Ritual, 139, 158, 175, 200; fertility rites, 22, 183, 236, 241–3
Robin, Fanny (*Far From the Madding Crowd*), 18, 139, 140–1, 142, 158, 159, 160, 161, 162, 168, 170; character study, 172–4
'Romantic Adventures of a Milkmaid, The', 145
'Rose-Ann', 120
'Ruined Maid, The', 121, 122
Ruskin, John, definition of lyrical poetry, 53
Rustics, function of, 174–6
Rutland, W. R., 8, 278

'Sacrilege, The', 124, 125, 126, 134
'St Launce's Revisited', 101, 102
Saint's Day (Whiting), 313
'San Sebastian', 110, 134
Sandcastle, The (Murdoch), 308, 311–12
Sartre, Jean-Paul, 258, 272, 316
Sassoon, Siegfried, 302
'Satin Shoes, The', 123–4
'Satires of Circumstance in Fifteen Glimpses', 82, 111, 120, 144
Satschan Lake (*The Dynasts*), 278, 290
Savage, The, 315
Scansion, 30–1
Schubert, 96
Scott, Sir Walter, 297
'Second Night, The', 133
'Seen by the Waits', 121
Select Poems of William Barnes, 52–3
'Self-Unseeing, The', 71

'Shadow on the Stone, The', 104
Shaffer, Peter, 313, 314
Shakespeare, William, 14, 150, 175, 276
Shaw, G. B., 273
'She did not turn', 55
'She Opened the Door', 104
'Sheep-Boy, The', 53, 65–6
Shelley, Percy Bysshe, 73, 277
'Shut Out that Moon', 58, 64
'Sick Battle-God, The', 115
'Sign-Seeker, A', 62–3, 83, 304
Sillitoe, Alan, 310
Sitwell, Edith, 306
Skimmity ride (*The Mayor of Casterbridge*), 13, 22, 198, 201, 210
Sleep of Prisoners, The, 313
'Sleep-Worker, The', 34–5, 37
'Slow Nature, The', 109
Smart, Alastair, 23
'Snow in the Suburbs', 65
Social reform, 23
'Soldier, The' (Brooke), comparison with 'Drummer Hodge', 76
'Son's Veto, The', 147
Sophocles, 14
Sorley, C. H., 302, 303
'Souls of the Slain, The', 76–7
'Sound in the Night, A', 122, 123, 127, 134
South, John (*The Woodlanders*), 17, 138, 221, 222–3
South, Marty (*The Woodlanders*), 23, 142, 219, 220, 221, 222, 229, 231–2
Southey, Robert, 297
Southworth, J. G., 9
'Spell of the Rose, The', 88, 101
Spencer, Herbert, 9
'Statue of Liberty, The', 122
Steiner, George, 16, 103
Stephen, Leslie, 38, 85
Strindberg, August, 272
'Subalterns, The', 25, 26, 36
Sue (*Jude the Obscure*), *see* Bridehead, Sue
'Sunburnt God, The: Ritual and Tragic Myth in *The Return of the Native*' (Crompton), 186
'Sunday Morning Tragedy, A', 110, 120, 124, 139
Supernatural, 17, 57, 132–5, 139, 140, 200
'Surview', 56
'Sweet William's Ghost', 133
Swinburne, Algernon, 297, 304

Talks with Thomas Hardy at Max Gate 1920–1922 (Collins), 305

Tamsin (*The Return of the Native*), *see* Yeobright, Tamsin

Templeman, Lucetta (*The Mayor of Casterbridge*), 13, 197–202, 208, 211–12, 213

'Temporary the All, The', 68

Tennyson, Alfred, 81, 82, 84, 85, 87, 89, 103, 107, 297, 304

Tess (*Tess of the d'Urbervilles*), 12–13, 15, 19, 20, 22, 141, 142, 150, 233–53, 257, 310, 311, 314, 315, 316, 317; association with blood, 239–40; role as ritual victim, 239–43

Tess of the d'Urbervilles, 9, 10, 12, 13, 15, 19, 20, 22, 23, 26, 121, 137, 139, 141, 142, 143, 146, 150, 151, 172, 174, 186, 224, 226, 232, 233–53, 254, 257, 307, 310, 311, 314–15, 316, 317; chapter on rural migration to towns, 23

'Tess's Lament', 10

Thomas, Dylan, 302

Thomas, Edward, 302

Thomas Hardy (Blunden), 118–19

Thomas Hardy (Brown), 158, 181

Thomas Hardy (Carpenter), 186

Thomas Hardy (Howe), 276

Thomas Hardy: A Critical Study (Abercrombie), 17, 143

Thomas Hardy: A Study of His Writings and Their Background (Rutland), 278

Thomas Hardy and the Cosmic Mind (Bailey), 285

Thomas Hardy: The Will and the Way (Morrell), 239

Thomas Hardy: The Novels and Stories (Guérard), 7

'Thomas Hardy's Alleged Son' (Dalton), 8

'Thoughts at Midnight', 73

'Thoughts of Phena', 78

'Three Ravens, The', 117

'Three Strangers, The', 144

'Throwing a Tree', 65, 66

'Thyrsis' (Arnold), 81, 82, 92

'Time There Was, A', 45–7

Time's Laughingstocks, 106

Tippett, Michael, 96, 145

'To an Unborn Pauper Child', 60, 61–2, 73, 106

'To C.F.H. on Her Christening Day', 60–1

'To Meet, or Otherwise', 73–4

Tolstoy, Leo, 276

'Tower, The' (Yeats), 78–9

'Tradition and the Individual Talent' (Eliot), 47–8

'Traditional Basis of Thomas Hardy's Fiction, The' (Davidson), 138

Trafalgar (*The Dynasts*), 277, 279, 280, 288, 291, 296, 299

'Trampwoman's Tragedy, A', 123, 124, 125, 129, 134

'Transformations', 13, 66

Transformations in nature, 65–8

Trewthen, Baptista, 144, 147, 148

Tristan und Isolde (Wagner), 85, 94

Troy, Sergeant (*Far From the Madding Crowd*), 18, 19, 21, 158–65, 171–6, 308, 309, 316; character study, 167–70; relationship with Bathsheba, 166–7, 168–9

Trumpet Major, The, 137, 154, 155–6, 158

'Tryst at an Ancient Earthwork, A', 143

Turner, Joseph M. W., 53

'Turnip Hoer, The', 130

Two on a Tower, 149

'Two Wives, The', 130

'Two Years' Idyll, A', 104

'Unborn, The', 60, 61

Under the Greenwood Tree, 23, 137, 154–5 156–7, 158

'Under the Waterfall', 69

'Unkindly May, An', 53, 65

'Unquiet Grave', 122, 133

'Upbraiding, An', 103

'Valenciennes', 131, 132

Vaughan, Henry, 33

Venn, Diggory (*The Return of the Native*), 8, 177, 179, 182, 183, 184, 191, 192–4

Verdi, 21

Villeneuve (*The Dynasts*), 278, 279, 280, 282, 286, 296, 299

'Voice, The', 13, 81–5, 96, 98, 99

'Voices from Things Growing in a Churchyard', 66

Vye, Eustacia (*The Return of the Native*), 15, 19, 21, 23, 126, 139, 177, 180–6, 191–4, 285, 310, 316, 317; character study, 188–90; her dream, 189–90

Wagner, 85, 94

Wain, John, 310

'Waiting Supper, The', 147

Walcheren (*The Dynasts*), 278, 291, 296, 299

'Walk, The', 88–9

Waterloo (*The Dynasts*), 278, 281, 283, 288, 289, 294, 295, 296, 299, 300

'We Sat at the Window', 103

Well-Beloved, The, 149–50
Wellington (*The Dynasts*), 278, 282, 283, 287, 288
Wesker, Arnold, 313
'Wessex Folk', *see* 'Few Crusted Characters, A'
Wessex Poems, 95
'What the Shepherd Saw', 147, 148
Wheels, 306
'When I Set Out for Lyonnesse', 53, 104
'Where the Picnic Was', 96, 102
'Whipper-In, The', 130
'Whitewashed Wall, The', 116–17
Whiting, John, 213
Whittle, Abel (*The Mayor of Casterbridge*), 204, 208, 214
'Who's in the Next Room?', 58
'Wife and Another, A', 122
Wildeve (*The Return of the Native*), 22, 126, 177, 180–4, 189, 191, 192, 193, 194, 317
Wilson, Angus, 308
'Wind's Prophecy, The', 104
Winter Words, 25, 321; setting by Britten, 53
Winterborne, Giles (*The Woodlanders*), 8, 12, 15, 22, 218–23, 226, 231, 232; death of, 15, 142, 217, 219, 227, 228–9, 230, 231; relationship with Grace, 223–4, 225–9
'Withered Arm, The', 145

'Woman in the Rye, The', 116–17
'Woman's Fancy, A', 130
'Wood Fire, The', 109, 110
Woodlanders, The, 8, 9, 10, 12, 13, 15, 17, 19, 22, 23, 137, 138, 139, 142, 149, 216–32, 314, 316, 317
Woolf, Leonard, 47
Woolf, Virginia, 10, 11–12, 18, 20, 21, 137, 143, 256, 307
Wordsworth, William, 45, 50, 69, 81
'Workbox, The', 122, 123
Wuthering Heights (Brontë), 93, 95, 137, 140, 200

'Year's Awakening, The', 65
Yeats, W. B., 11, 24, 77–9, 87; poetry about old age, 77–9
'Yell' ham-Wood's Story', 25, 29
Yeobright, Clym (*The Return of the Native*), 15, 19, 21, 23, 139, 141, 177–93, 285, 309; blindness, 182, 185–7
Yeobright, Mrs (*The Return of the Native*), 13, 19, 23, 139, 142, 177, 180, 181, 182, 183, 184, 190–1, 194, 309
Yeobright, Tamsin (*The Return of the Native*), 22, 180, 182, 183, 184, 191–2,
'You were the Sort That Men Forget', 55
Young, Andrew, 302, 306
'Your Last Drive', 86, 103

Fanaroff and Martin's
Neonatal-Perinatal Medicine

Fanaroff and Martin's Neonatal-Perinatal Medicine

Diseases of the Fetus and Infant

8th EDITION

Richard J. Martin, MBBS, FRACP

Professor of Pediatrics, Reproductive Biology, and Physiology and Biophysics
Case Western Reserve University School of Medicine
Director, Division of Neonatology
Rainbow Babies and Chidren's Hospital
Cleveland, Ohio

Avroy A. Fanaroff, MD, FRCP (Edinburgh), FRCPCH

Professor and Chair, Department of Pediatrics
Gertrude Lee Chandler Tucker Professor
Professor of Neonatology in Reproductive Biology
Case Western Reserve University School of Medicine
Physician in Chief
Eliza Henry Barnes Chair in Neonatology
Rainbow Babies and Children's Hospital
Cleveland, Ohio

Michele C. Walsh, MD, MS

Professor of Pediatrics
Case Western Reserve University School of Medicine
Medical Director, Neonatal Intensive Care Unit
Rainbow Babies and Children's Hospital
Cleveland, Ohio

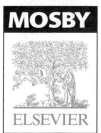

MOSBY

ELSEVIER

MOSBY
ELSEVIER

1600 John F. Kennedy Blvd.
Ste 1800
Philadelphia, PA 19103-2899

Fanaroff and Martin's Neonatal-Perinatal Medicine   ISBN-13 978-0-323-02966-7
ISBN-10 0-323-02966-3

Copyright © 2006, 2002, 1997, 1992, 1987, 1983, 1977, 1973 by Mosby, Inc.

Notice

Knowledge and best practice in this field are constantly changing. As new research and experience broaden our knowledge, changes in practice, treatment and drug therapy may become necessary or appropriate. Readers are advised to check the most current information provided (i) on procedures featured or (ii) by the manufacturer of each product to be administered, to verify the recommended dose or formula, the method and duration of administration, and contraindications. It is the responsibility of the practitioner, relying on their own experience and knowledge of the patient, to make diagnoses, to determine dosages and the best treatment for each individual patient, and to take all appropriate safety precautions. To the fullest extent of the law, neither the Publisher nor the Editors assumes any liability for any injury and/or damage to persons or property arising out of or related to any use of the material contained in this book.

The Publisher

Library of Congress Cataloging-in-Publication Data

Fanaroff and Martin's neonatal-perinatal medicine: diseases of the fetus and infant/
  [edited by] Richard J. Martin, Avroy A. Fanaroff, Michele C. Walsh.
    p. cm
  Previous ed. published with title: Neonatal-perinatal medicine.
  Includes bibliographical references and index.
  ISBN 0-323-02966-3
    1. Infants (Newborn)—Diseases. 2. Fetus—Diseases. I. Title: Neonatal-perinatal medicine. II. Fanaroff, Avroy A. III. Martin, Richard J. (Richard John) IV. Walsh, Michele C. V. Neonatal-perinatal medicine.

  RJ254.N456 2006
  618.92'01–dc22   2005047980

Acquisitions Editor: Todd Hummel
Developmental Editor: Jennifer Shreiner
Publishing Services Manager: Frank Polizzano
Project Manager: Joan Nikelsky
Design Direction: Karen O'Keefe Owens

Printed in the United States of America

Last digit is the print number: 9   8   7   6   5   4   3   2   1

To our spouses
Patricia, Roslyn, and Larry

the Martin children
Scott and Sonya,
the Fanaroff children and grandchildren
Jonathan, Amanda, Jodi, and Peter, Austin, and Morgan,
and the Walsh children
Sean and Ryan

with love, admiration, and deep appreciation
for their continued support and inspiration

Contributors

Veronica H. Accornero, PhD
Assistant Professor, Department of Pediatrics,
University of Miami Miller School of Medicine,
Miami, Florida
Infants of Substance-Abusing Mothers

Heidelise Als, PhD
Associate Professor in Psychiatry (Psychology),
Harvard Medical School; Director, Neurobehavioral
Infant and Child Study Laboratory, and Senior
Associate in Psychology, Department of Psychiatry,
Children's Hospital Boston, Boston, Massachusetts
Neurobehavioral Development of the Preterm Infant

Jacob V. Aranda, MD, PhD, FRCPC
Professor, Departments of Pediatrics and Pharmacology
and Pharmaceutical Sciences, Wayne State University
School of Medicine and College of Pharmacy and
Allied Health; Chief, Division of Clinical Pharmacology
and Toxicology, and Attending Neonatologist,
Children's Hospital of Michigan, Detroit, Michigan
Pharmacologic Intervention (Part One)

James E. Arnold, MD
Julius W. McCall Professor and Chair, Department of
Otolaryngology—Head and Neck Surgery, and
Professor of Pediatrics, Case School of Medicine;
Pediatric Otolaryngologist, Rainbow Babies and
Children's Hospital, Cleveland, Ohio
*Hearing Loss in the Newborn Infant; The Respiratory
System (Part Six)*

Sundeep Arora, MBBS, MD
Fellow, Pediatric Gastroenterology, Hepatology, and
Nutrition, Rainbow Babies and Children's Hospital,
Cleveland, Ohio
The Gastrointestinal Tract (Part Two)

Jill E. Baley, MD
Professor of Pediatrics, Case School of Medicine;
Medical Director, Neonatal Transitional Care Unit,
Rainbow Babies and Children's Hospital, Cleveland,
Ohio
*The Immune System (Part Four); Schedule for
Immunization of Preterm Infants (Appendix C)*

Eduardo H. Bancalari, MD
Professor of Pediatrics and Director, Division of
Newborn Medicine, University of Miami Miller School
of Medicine; Chief, Newborn Service, Jackson
Memorial Hospital, Miami, Florida
The Respiratory System (Part Seven)

Emmalee S. Bandstra, MD
Professor of Pediatrics and Obstetrics and Gynecology,
University of Miami Miller School of Medicine;
Attending Neonatologist, Jackson Memorial Medical
Center, Miami, Florida
Infants of Substance-Abusing Mothers

Françoise Baylis, PhD
Professor, Department of Bioethics, Dalhousie
University Faculty of Medicine, Halifax, Nova Scotia,
Canada
Ethics in Perinatal and Neonatal Medicine

Cynthia F. Bearer, MD, PhD
Associate Professor, Departments of Pediatrics and
Neurosciences, Case School of Medicine; Director of
Medical Education, Mary Ann Swetland Center for
Environmental Health; Director, Neonatology
Fellowship Training Program, Rainbow Babies and
Children's Hospital, Cleveland, Ohio
Occupational and Environmental Risks to the Fetus

A. Resai Bengur, MD
Associate Professor of Pediatrics, Case School of
Medicine, Cleveland, Ohio
The Cardiovascular System (Parts Three and Seven)

Isaac Blickstein, MD
Professor, Department of Obstetrics and Gynecology,
Hadassah School of Medicine Hebrew University,
Jerusalem; Senior Physician, Department of Obstetrics
and Gynecology, Kaplan Medical Center, Rehovot,
Israel; Chairman, The Working Group on Multiple
Pregnancy, The International Society for Twin Studies
*Fetal Effects of Autoimmune Disease; Obstetric
Management of Multiple Gestation; Postterm
Pregnancy*

Ronald S. Bloom, MD
Professor and Vice-Chairman, Department of
Pediatrics, University of Utah School of Medicine,
Salt Lake City, Utah
*Delivery Room Resuscitation of the Newborn (Parts
One and Four)*

Jeffrey L. Blumer, PhD, MD
Professor, Departments of Pediatrics and
Pharmacology, Case School of Medicine; Chief,
Pediatric Pharmacology and Critical Care, Department
of Pediatrics, Rainbow Babies and Children's Hospital,
Cleveland, Ohio
*Pharmacologic Intervention (Part Two); Therapeutic
Agents (Appendix A)*

Samantha C. Butler, PhD
Research Associate in Psychiatry (Psychology),
Harvard Medicine School and Children's Hospital
Boston, Boston, Massachusetts
Neurobehavioral Development of the Preterm Infant

Michael S. Caplan, MD
Professor of Pediatrics, Northwestern University
Feinberg School of Medicine, Chicago; Chairman,
Department of Pediatrics, Evanston Northwestern
Healthcare, Evanston, Illinois
The Gastrointestinal Tract (Part Five)

Waldemar A. Carlo, MD
Edwin M. Dixon Professor of Pediatrics and Director,
Division of Neonatology, University of Alabama at
Birmingham School of Medicine; Director of NICU,
Children's Hospital of Alabama; Director of Nurseries,
University Hospital, Birmingham, Alabama
The Respiratory System (Parts Two and Four)

Suzanne B. Cassidy, MD
Professor of Pediatrics, University of California, Irvine,
School of Medicine, Irvine; Staff Physician, Department
of Pediatrics, University of California, Irvine, Medical
Center, Orange, California
Congenital Anomalies

Gisela Chelimsky, MD
Assistant Professor of Pediatrics, Case School of
Medicine; Attending Physician, Rainbow Babies and
Children's Hospital, Cleveland, Ohio
The Gastrointestinal Tract (Part Two)

Walter J. Chwals, MD
Professor of Surgery and Pediatrics, Department of
Surgery, Case School of Medicine; Pediatric Surgeon,
Rainbow Babies and Children's Hospital, Cleveland,
Ohio
*The Gastrointestinal Tract (Parts One, Three, and
Four)*

Alan R. Cohen, MD, FACS, FAAP
Reinberger Chair in Pediatric Neurological Surgery and
Professor of Neurological Surgery and Pediatrics,
Case School of Medicine; Surgeon-in-Chief and Chief
of Pediatric Neurological Surgery, Rainbow Babies and
Children's Hospital, Cleveland, Ohio
The Central Nervous System (Parts Seven and Eight)

Daniel R. Cooperman, MD
Professor of Orthopedic Surgery, Case School of
Medicine; Attending Surgeon, University Hospitals of
Cleveland and MetroHealth Medical Center, Cleveland,
Ohio
Neonatal Orthopedics

Timothy M. Crombleholme, MD
Professor of Surgery, Pediatrics, and Obstetrics and
Gynecology, University of Cincinnati College of
Medicine; Richard and Geralyn Azizkhan Chair in
Pediatric Surgery, Division of Pediatric General,
Thoracic, and Fetal Surgery, and Director, Center for
Molecular Fetal Therapy, Cincinnati Children's Hospital
Medical Center; Director, Fetal Care Center of
Cincinnati, Cincinnati Children's Good Samaritan, and
University Hospital, Cincinnati, Ohio
Surgical Treatment of the Fetus

William T. Dahms, MD
Professor of Pediatrics, Case School of Medicine; Staff,
Division of Pediatric Endocrinology, Rainbow Babies
and Children's Hospital, Cleveland, Ohio
Metabolic and Endocrine Disorders (Part Four)

Ira D. Davis, MD, MS
Associate Professor, Department of Pediatrics, Case
School of Medicine; Division Chief, Pediatric
Nephrology, Rainbow Babies and Children's Hospital,
Cleveland
*Fluid, Electrolyte, and Acid-Base Homeostasis;
The Kidney and Urinary Tract*

Mario De Curtis, MD
Professor of Neonatology,
Dipartimento di Scienze Ginecologiche, Perinatologia
e Puericultura, University of Rome Faculty of
Medicine; Director, Neonatology Unit, Patologia
Neonatale e Terapia Intensiva Dipartimento di Scienze
Ginecologiche, Perinatologia e Puericultura,
Azienda Policlinico Umberto I, Rome, Italy
Metabolic and Endocrine Disorders (Part Two)

Katherine MacRae Dell, MD
Assistant Professor, Department of Pediatrics, Case
School of Medicine; Attending Pediatric Nephrologist,
Rainbow Babies and Children's Hospital, Cleveland,
Ohio
*Fluid, Electrolyte, and Acid-Base Homeostasis;
The Kidney and Urinary Tract*

Scott C. Denne, MD
Professor of Pediatrics, Indiana University School of Medicine; Attending Neonatologist, James Whitcomb Riley Hospital for Children, Indianapolis, Indiana
Nutrition and Metabolism in the High-Risk Neonate (Parts One and Two)

Patricia M. DePompei, RN, MSN
Director, Pediatric Network and Critical Care Services, Pediatric Administration, Rainbow Babies and Children's Hospital, Cleveland, Ohio
Care of the Mother, Father, and Infant

Glenn H. DeSandre, MD
Clinical Instructor, Department of Pediatrics, Division of Neonatology, Stanford University School of Medicine, Stanford; Attending Neonatologist, Department of Pediatrics, Division of Neonatology, Santa Clara Valley Medical Center, San Jose, California
Neonatal Jaundice and Liver Disease

Linda de Vries, MD
Professor of Neonatal Neurology, Department of Neonatology, University of Utrecht Faculty of Medicine; Attending Physician, Wilhelmina Children's Hospital, Utrecht, The Netherlands
The Central Nervous System (Parts Three and Four)

Juliann M. Di Fiore, BSEE
Research Engineer, Department of Medicine, Case School of Medicine; Research Engineer, Department of Pediatrics, Division of Neonatology, Rainbow Babies and Children's Hospital, Cleveland, Ohio
The Respiratory System (Part Two)

Morven S. Edwards, MD
Professor of Pediatrics, Baylor College of Medicine; Active Staff, Department of Pediatrics, Texas Children's Hospital and Ben Taub General Hospital, Houston, Texas
The Immune System (Parts Two and Three)

Francine Erenberg, MD
Assistant Professor of Pediatrics, Case School of Medicine; Active Staff, Department of Pediatric Cardiology, Rainbow Babies and Children's Hospital, Cleveland, Ohio
The Cardiovascular System (Parts Three and Six)

Judith A. Ernst, DMSc, RD
Associate Professor of Nutrition and Dietetics, School of Health and Rehabilitation Sciences, Indiana University, Indianapolis, Indiana
Nutrition and Metabolism in the High-Risk Neonate (Part One)

Avroy A. Fanaroff, MD, FRCP (Edinburgh) FRCPCH
Professor and Chair, Department of Pediatrics, Gertrude Lee Chandler Tucker Professor, Professor of Neonatology in Reproductive Biology, Case School of Medicine; Physician in Chief, Eliza Henry Barnes Chair in Neonatology, Rainbow Babies and Children's Hospital, Cleveland, Ohio
Epidemiology and Perinatal Services; The Respiratory System (Parts Three through Five)

Jonathan M. Fanaroff, MD, JD
Assistant Professor of Pediatrics, Case School of Medicine; Attending Neonatologist and Associate Director, Rainbow Center for Pediatric Ethics, Rainbow Babies and Children's Hospital, Cleveland, Ohio
Legal Issues in Neonatal-Perinatal Medicine

Orna Flidel-Rimon, MD
Lecturer, Department of Pediatrics, Hadassah School of Medicine, Hebrew University, Jerusalem; Attending Neonatologist, Kaplan Medical Center, Rehovot, Israel
Postterm Pregnancy

Smadar Friedman, MD
Department of Pediatrics, Hadassah School of Medicine, Hebrew University, Jerusalem; Attending Neonatologist, Kaplan Medical Center, Rehovot, Israel
Fetal Effects of Autoimmune Disease

Susan E. Gerber, MD, MPH
Assistant Professor, Department of Obstetrics and Gynecology, Division of Maternal-Fetal Medicine, Northwestern University Feinberg School of Medicine; Attending Physician, Department of Obstetrics and Gynecology, Division of Maternal-Fetal Medicine, Northwestern Memorial Hospital, Chicago, Illinois
Estimation of Fetal Well-Being (Part One)

Robert L. Goldenberg, MD
Charles E. Flowers Professor, Department of Obstetrics and Gynocology, University of Alabama at Birmingham School of Medicine, Birmingham, Alabama
Obstetric Management of Prematurity

Bernard Gonik, MD
Professor and Fann Skere Chair of Perinatal Medicine, Department of Obstetrics and Gynecology, Wayne State University School of Medicine, Detroit, Michigan
Perinatal Infections

Jeffrey B. Gould, MD, MPH
Robert L. Hess Professor in Pediatrics and Director, Perinatal Epidemiology and Health Outcomes Research Unit, Department of Pediatrics, Division of Neonatal and Developmental Medicine, Stanford University School of Medicine, Stanford; Attending Neonatologist, Lucile Packard Children's Hospital at Stanford, Palo Alto, California
The Field of Neonatal-Perinatal Medicine (Part One)

Anne Greenough, MD, FRCP
Professor of Neonatology and Clinical Respiratory
Physiology, Department of Child Health, King's
College, London, United Kingdom
*Delivery Room Resuscitation of the Newborn (Part
Two)*

Pierre Gressens, MD, PhD
Consultant, Pediatric Neurology, and Chief,
INSERM U 676, Hôpital Robert Debre, Paris, France
The Central Nervous System (Parts One and Two)

Daniel H. Gruenstein, MD
Assistant Professor of Pediatrics, Case School of
Medicine; Active Staff, Department of Pediatric
Cardiology, Rainbow Babies and Children's Hospital,
Cleveland, Ohio
The Cardiovascular System (Part Five)

Andrée Gruslin, MD, FRCS
Associate Professor, Division of Maternal-Fetal
Medicine, Department of Obstetrics and Gynecology,
University of Ottawa Faculty of Medicine; Program
Director, Maternal-Fetal Medicine, The Ottawa
Hospital, Ottawa, Ontario, Canada
Erythroblastosis Fetalis

Balaji K. Gupta, MD
Clinical Assistant Professor, Department of
Ophthalmology and Visual Sciences, University of
Chicago Pritzker School of Medicine, Chicago, Illinois
The Eye (Parts One and Two)

Maureen Hack, MB, ChB
Professor of Pediatrics, Case School of Medicine;
Director, High Risk Follow-up Program, Rainbow
Babies and Children's Hospital, Cleveland, Ohio
Follow-up for High-Risk Neonates

Barbara F. Hales, PhD
Professor of Pharmacology and Therapeutics, McGill
University Faculty of Medicine, Montreal, Quebec,
Canada
Pharmacologic Intervention (Part One)

Nancy Anderson Hamming, MD
Assistant Professor, Department of Ophthalmology;
Section Head, Pediatric Ophthalmology, Rush Medical
College, Chicago, Illinois
The Eye (Parts One and Two)

Jonathan Hellmann, MBBCh, FCP(SA), FRCPC
Professor of Pediatrics, University of Toronto Faculty
of Medicine; Clinical Director, Neonatal Intensive Care
Unit, Department of Pediatrics, Hospital for Sick
Children, Toronto, Ontario, Canada
Ethics in Perinatal and Neonatal Medicine

Susan R. Hintz, MD
Assistant Professor, Department of Pediatrics, Division
of Neonatal and Developmental Medicine, Stanford
University School of Medicine, Stanford; Attending
Neonatologist, Lucile Packard Children's Hospital at
Stanford, Palo Alto, California
*Biomedical Engineering Aspects of Neonatal
Monitoring*

Steven B. Hoath, MD
Professor of Pediatrics, University of Cincinnati College
of Medicine; Medical Director, Skin Sciences Institute,
Cincinnati Children's Hospital Medical Center,
Cincinnati, Ohio
Physical Environment (Part Two); The Skin

Jeffrey D. Horbar, MD
Professor of Pediatrics, University of Vermont College
of Medicine; Chief Executive and Scientific Officer,
Vermont Oxford Network, Burlington, Vermont
The Field of Neonatal-Perinatal Medicine (Part One)

McCallum R. Hoyt, MD, MBA
Medical Director for Perioperative Services, Central
Maine Medical Center, Lewiston, Maine
Anesthesia for Labor and Delivery

Louanne Hudgins, MD
Professor and Director of Perinatal Genetics,
Department of Pediatrics, Stanford University School
of Medicine, Stanford, California
Congenital Anomalies

Petra S. Hüppi, MD
Professor of Pediatrics, University of Geneva Faculty
of Medicine; Director, Child Development Unit,
Department of Pediatrics, Children's Hospital, Geneva,
Switzerland; Visiting Scientist, Department of
Neurology, Harvard Medical School, Boston,
Massachusetts
The Central Nervous System (Parts One and Two)

Alan H. Jobe, MD, PhD
Professor of Pediatrics, University of Cincinnati College
of Medicine; Neonatologist, Cincinnati Children's
Hospital Medical Center, Cincinnati, Ohio
The Respiratory System (Part One)

Nancy E. Judge, MD, FACOG
Associate Professor, Department of Reproductive
Biology, Case School of Medicine; Director,
MacDonald Imaging Center, Department of Obstetrics
and Gynecology, University Hospitals of Cleveland,
Cleveland, Ohio
Perinatal Ultrasound

Satish C. Kalhan, MBBS, FRCP, DCH
Professor of Pediatrics, Case School of Medicine; Director, Schwartz Center for Metabolism and Nutrition, and Staff Neonatologist, MetroHealth Medical Center, Cleveland, Ohio
Metabolic and Endocrine Disorders (Part One)

Reuben Kapur, PhD
Assistant Professor of Pediatrics, Molecular Biology, and Biochemistry, Indiana University School of Medicine, Indianapolis, Indiana
The Immune System (Part One)

Kathleen A. Kennedy, MD, MPH
Professor of Pediatrics, University of Texas Medical School of Houston, Houston, Texas
The Field of Neonatal-Perinatal Medicine (Part Two)

John H. Kennell, MD
Professor of Pediatrics Emeritus, Department of Pediatrics, Case School of Medicine; Attending Physician, Division of Behavioral Pediatrics, Rainbow Babies and Children's Hospital, Cleveland, Ohio
Care of the Mother, Father, and Infant

Marshall H. Klaus, MD
Professor of Pediatrics, University of California, San Francisco, School of Medicine, San Francisco, California
Care of the Mother, Father, and Infant

Robert M. Kliegman, MD
Professor and Chair, Department of Pediatrics, Medical College of Wisconsin; Pediatrician in Chief and Muma Family Chair in Pediatrics, Children's Hospital of Wisconsin; Executive Vice President, Children's Research Institute, Milwaukee, Wisconsin
Intrauterine Growth Restriction

Catherine A. Leitch, PhD
Research Associate Professor, Department of Pediatrics, Indiana University School of Medicine, Indianapolis, Indiana
Nutrition and Metabolism in the High-Risk Infant (Parts One and Two)

James A. Lemons, MD
Hugh McK. Landon Professor of Pediatrics and Director, Section of Neonatal-Perinatal Medicine, Department of Pediatrics, Indiana University School of Medicine, Indianapolis, Indiana
Nutrition and Metabolism in the High-Risk Infant (Part One)

Pamela K. Lemons, MSN, CNNP
Adjunct Clinical Professor, School of Nursing, Indiana University; Nurse Practitioner, Developmental Pediatrics, James Whitcomb Riley Hospital for Children, Indianapolis, Indiana
Nutrition and Metabolism in the High-Risk Infant (Part One)

Malcolm Levene, MD, FMedSc
Professor of Pediatrics and Obstetrics and Gynecology, Leeds University School of Medicine; Consultant Neonatologist, Pediatrics and Child Health, Leeds University School of Medicine, Leeds, United Kingdom
The Central Nervous System (Part Four)

Carol Andrea Lindsay, MD
Perinatologist, Department of Obstetrics and Gynecology, Ohio Permanente Medical Group, Cleveland, Ohio
Pregnancy Complicated by Diabetes Mellitus

Tom Lissauer, MB, BChir, FRCPCH
Consultant Neonatologist, St. Mary's Hospital, London, United Kingdom
Physical Examination of the Newborn

Timothy E. Lotze, MD
Assistant Professor, Department of Pediatrics, Baylor College of Medicine; Section of Child Neurology, Texas Children's Hospital, Houston, Texas
The Central Nervous System (Part Six)

Lori Luchtman-Jones, MD
Assistant Professor of Pediatrics, Washington University School of Medicine; Attending Physician, Department of Pediatrics, and Medical Director, Core Laboratory–Hematology, St. Louis Children's Hospital, St. Louis, Missouri
The Blood and Hematopoietic System

David K. Magnuson, MD, FACS, FAAP
Assistant Professor, Department of Surgery, Case School of Medicine; Chief, Division of Pediatric Surgery, Rainbow Babies and Children's Hospital, Cleveland, Ohio
The Gastrointestinal Tract (Parts One, Three, and Four)

Henry H. Mangurten, MD
Professor of Pediatrics and Acting Chairman, Department of Pediatrics, Rosalind Franklin University of Medicine and Science/The Chicago Medical School, North Chicago; Chairman, Department of Pediatrics, Lutheran General Children's Hospital, Park Ridge, Illinois
Birth Injuries

Richard J. Martin, MBBS, FRACP
Professor of Pediatrics, Reproductive Biology, and
Physiology and Biophysics, Case School of Medicine;
Director, Division of Neonatology, Rainbow Babies
and Children's Hospital, Cleveland, Ohio
The Respiratory System (Parts Three through Five)

Geoffrey Miller, MA, MB, MPhil, MD, FRCP, FRACP
Professor of Pediatrics and Neurology, Yale University
School of Medicine; Clinical Director, Child Neurology
Service, Yale–New Haven Children's Hospital,
New Haven, Connecticut
The Central Nervous System (Part Six)

Marilyn T. Miller, MD
Professor of Ophthalmology, Department of
Ophthalmology and Visual Sciences, University of
Illinois at Chicago College of Medicine; Interim
Director, Pediatric Ophthalmology and Adult
Strabismus, University of Illinois Medical Center,
Chicago, Illinois
The Eye (Parts One and Two)

Martha J. Miller, MD, PhD
Associate Professor of Pediatrics, Department of
Pediatrics, Case School of Medicine; Attending
Neonatologist, Rainbow Babies and Children's
Hospital, Cleveland, Ohio
The Respiratory System (Part Five)

Anthony Milner, MD, FRCP, FRCPCH, DCH
Emeritus Professor of Neonatology, Department of
Child Health, Guy's, King's, and St. Thomas' School of
Medicine, King's College, London, United Kingdom
*Delivery Room Resuscitation of the Newborn
(Part Two)*

Thomas R. Moore, MD
Professor and Chairman, Department of Reproductive
Medicine, University of California, San Diego, School
of Medicine, Staff Physician, UCSD Medical Center,
San Diego, California
*Erythroblastosis Fetalis; Amniotic Fluid and
Nonimmune Hydrops Fetalis*

Stuart C. Morrison, MB, ChB, FRCP
Staff Radiologist, Cleveland Clinic Foundation,
Cleveland, Ohio
Perinatal Ultrasound

Anil Narang, MD
Professor of Pediatrics (Neonatology), Department of
Pediatrics, Postgraduate Institute of Medical Education
and Research; Head, Department of Pediatrics,
Advanced Pediatric Centre, Chandigarh, India
Neonatology in Developing Countries

Vivek Narendran, MD, MRCP(UK), FAAP
Associate Professor, Division of Neonatology,
Department of Pediatrics, University of Cincinnati
College of Medicine; Staff, Division of Neonatology,
Department of Pediatrics, Cincinnati Children's
Hospital and Medical Center; Associate Director,
Neonatal Intensive Care Unit, University Hospital,
Cincinnati, Ohio
The Skin

Mary L. Nock, MD
Assistant Professor, Department of Pediatrics, Case
School of Medicine; Attending Neonatologist, Rainbow
Babies and Children's Hospital, Cleveland, Ohio
*Therapeutic Agents (Appendix A); Tables of Normal
Values (Appendix B)*

Mark R. Palmert, MD, PhD
Assistant Professor, Departments of Pediatrics and
Genetics, Case School of Medicine; Staff, Division of
Pediatric Endocrinology and Metabolism, Rainbow
Babies and Children's Hospital, Cleveland, Ohio
Metabolic and Endocrine Disorders (Part Four)

Barbara V. Parilla, MD
Associate Professor, Department of Obstetrics and
Gynecology, University of Illinois at Chicago College
of Medicine, Chicago; Attending Physician, Section of
Maternal Fetal Medicine, Lutheran General Hospital,
Park Ridge, Illinois
Estimation of Fetal Well-Being (Part Two)

Prabhu S. Parimi, MD, FAAP
Associate Professor of Pediatrics, Case School of
Medicine; Neonatologist, Department of Pediatrics,
MetroHealth Medical Center, Cleveland, Ohio
Metabolic and Endocrine Disorders (Part One)

Robert L. Parry, MD
Assistant Professor of Surgery and Pediatrics,
Department of Surgery, Case School of Medicine;
Pediatric Surgeon, Rainbow Babies and Children's
Hospital, Cleveland
The Gastrointestinal Tract (Parts One, Three, and Four)

Kousiki Patra, MD
Assistant Professor, Department of Pediatrics, Case
School of Medicine; Attending Neonatologist, Rainbow
Babies and Children's Hospital, Cleveland, Ohio
Tables of Normal Values (Appendix B)

Dale L. Phelps, MD
Professor, Departments of Pediatrics and
Ophthalmology, University of Rochester School of
Medicine and Dentistry, Rochester, New York
The Eye (Part Three)

M. Kathleen Philbin, RN, PhD
Associate Professor, Department of Pediatrics, UMDNJ
Robert Wood Johnson Medical School, Camden, New
Jersey; Adjunct Associate Professor, School of Nursing,
University of Pennsylvania, Philadelphia, Pennsylvania;
Director, Infant Development, The Children's Regional
Hospital at Cooper University Hospital, Camden,
New Jersey
Physical Environment (Part Two)

Brenda B. Poindexter, MD
Assistant Professor of Clinical Pediatrics, Indiana
University School of Medicine; Attending
Neonatologist, James Whitcomb Riley Hospital for
Children, Indianapolis, Indiana
*Nutrition and Metabolism in the High-Risk Infant
(Parts One and Two)*

Richard A. Polin, MD
Professor of Pediatrics, Columbia University College of
Physicians and Surgeons; Director, Division of
Neonatology, Morgan Stanley Children's Hospital of
New York–Presbyterian, New York, New York
The Immune System (Part One)

Tonse N. K. Raju, MD, DCH
Program Scientist and Medical Officer, Pregnancy and
Perinatology Branch, Center for Developmental
Biology and Perinatal Medicine, National Institute of
Child Health and Human Development, National
Institutes of Health, Bethesda, Maryland
*From Infant Hatcheries to Intensive Care: Some
Highlights of the Century of Neonatal Medicine*

Patrick S. Ramsey, MD, MSPH
Assistant Professor, Department of Obstetrics and
Gynecology/Maternal-Fetal Medicine, University of
Alabama at Birmingham School of Medicine; Assistant
Professor, Department of Epidemiology International
Health, University of Alabama at Birmingham School
of Public Health; Attending, University of Alabama at
Birmingham University Hospital, Birmingham,
Alabama
Obstetric Management of Prematurity

Raymond W. Redline, MD
Professor, Departments of Pathology and Reproductive
Biology, Case School of Medicine, Cleveland, Ohio;
Pediatric and Perinatal Pathologist, Department of
Pathology, University Hospitals of Cleveland,
Cleveland, Ohio
Placental Pathology

Michael D. Reed, MD
Professor of Pediatrics, Case School of Medicine;
Director, Division of Pediatric Clinical Pharmacology
and Toxicology, Department of Pediatrics, Rainbow
Babies and Children's Hospital, Cleveland, Ohio
Pharmacologic Intervention

Jacques Rigo, MD, PhD
Professor of Neonatology and Pediatrics Nutrition,
Department of Pediatrics, Division of Neonatology,
University of Liège Faculty of Medicine; Head,
Department of Pediatrics and Division of Neonatology,
CHR Citadelle, Liège, Belgium
Metabolic and Endocrine Disorders (Part Two)

Ricardo J. Rodriguez, MD, FAAP
Associate Professor of Pediatrics, Case School of
Medicine; Attending Neonatologist, Rainbow Babies
and Children's Hospital, Cleveland, Ohio
The Respiratory System (Part Three)

Susan R. Rose, MD
Professor of Pediatric Endocrinology, University of
Cincinnati College of Medicine; Staff, Department of
Pediatric Endocrinology, Cincinnati Children's Hospital
Medical Center, Cincinnati, Ohio
Metabolic and Endocrine Disorders (Part Three)

Ola Didrik Saugstad, MD, PhD, FRCPE
Professor, Department of Pediatric Research, University
of Oslo Faculty of Medicine; Consultant, Department
of Pediatrics, Rikshospitalet University Hospital, Oslo,
Norway
Delivery Room Resuscitation of the Newborn (Part Three)

Benoist Schaal, PhD
Director, Centre des Sciences du Goût (Smell and
Taste Center), Centre National de la Recherche
Scientifique, University of Burgundy, Dijon, France
Physical Environment (Part Two)

Katherine S. Schaefer, PhD
Assistant Professor of Biology, Randolph-Macon
Woman's College, Lynchburg, Virginia
The Cardiovascular System (Part One)

Mark S. Scher, MD
Professor of Pediatrics and Neurology, Case School of
Medicine; Division Chief, Pediatric Neurology, and
Director, Pediatric Sleep, Epilepsy and Fetal Neonatal
Neurology Programs, Department of Pediatrics, Rainbow
Babies and Children's Hospital, Cleveland, Ohio
The Central Nervous System (Part Five)

Alan L. Schwartz, PhD, MD
Harriet B. Spoehrer Professor and Chairman,
Department of Pediatrics, Washington University
School of Medicine; Pediatrician-in-Chief, St. Louis
Children's Hospital, St. Louis, Missouri
The Blood and Hematopoietic System

Stuart Schwartz, PhD
Professor, Departments of Human Genetics, Medicine
and Pathology, University of Chicago Pritzker School
of Medicine, Chicago, Illinois
*Genetic Aspects of Perinatal Disease and Prenatal
Diagnosis*

Gunnar Sedin, MD, PhD
Professor, Department of Women's and Children's
Health, Uppsala University Faculty of Medicine;
Senior Neonatologist, Uppsala University Children's
Hospital, Uppsala, Sweden
Physical Environment (Part One)

Dinesh M. Shah, MD
Professor of Obstetrics and Gynecology, University of
Wisconsin Medical School, Madison; Staff Physician,
Department of Obstetrics and Gynecology, Meriter
Hospital, Madison, Wisconsin
Hypertensive Disorders of Pregnancy

Eric S. Shinwell, MD
Associate Professor, Department of Neonatology,
Hadassah Medical School, Hebrew University,
Jerusalem; Director, Department of Neonatology,
Kaplan Medical Center, Rehovot, Israel
Obstetric Management of Multiple Gestation

Eric Sibley, MD, PhD
Assistant Professor, Department of Pediatrics, Division
of Pediatric Gastroenterology, Stanford University
School of Medicine, Stanford, California
Neonatal Jaundice and Liver Disease

John C. Sinclair, MD
Emeritus Professor of Pediatrics and Clinical
Epidemiology and Biostatistics, McMaster University
Faculty of Medicine, Hamilton, Ontario, Canada
The Field of Neonatal-Perinatal Medicine (Part Two)

Carlos J. Sivit, MD
Professor of Radiology and Pediatrics, Case School of
Medicine; Director, Division of Pediatric Radiology,
Rainbow Babies and Children's Hospital, Cleveland,
Ohio
Diagnostic Imaging

Ernest S. Siwik, MD
Assistant Professor of Pediatrics, Case School of
Medicine; Director, Pediatric Cardiac Catheterization
Laboratory, Rainbow Babies and Children's Hospital,
Cleveland, Ohio
The Cardiovascular System (Part Nine)

Robert C. Sprecher, MD, FAAP, FACS
Assistant Professor of Otolaryngology, Case School of
Medicine; Chief, Division of Pediatric Otolaryngology,
Rainbow Babies and Children's Hospital, Cleveland,
Ohio
*Hearing Loss in the Newborn Infant; The Respiratory
System (Part Six)*

David K. Stevenson, MD
Harold K. Faber Professor of Pediatrics and Senior
Associate Dean for Academic Affairs, Department of
Pediatrics, Division of Neonatal and Developmental
Medicine, Stanford University School of Medicine,
Stanford; Director, Charles B. and Ann L. Johnson
Center for Pregnancy and Newborn Services, and
Chief, Division of Neonatal and Developmental
Medicine, Lucile Packard Children's Hospital at
Stanford, Palo Alto, California
*Biomedical Engineering Aspects of Neonatal
Monitoring; Neonatal Jaundice and Liver Disease*

Eileen K. Stork, MD
Professor of Pediatrics, Case School of Medicine;
Director, ECMO Center, Department of Pediatrics,
Rainbow Babies and Children's Hospital, Cleveland,
Ohio
The Respiratory System (Part Eight)

John E. Stork, MD
Assistant Professor, Departments of Anesthesiology
and Pediatrics, Case School of Medicine; Chief,
Pediatric Cardiac Anesthesia, Department of
Anesthesiology, Rainbow Babies and Children's
Hospital, Cleveland, Ohio
Anesthesia in the Neonate

George H. Thompson, MD
Professor of Orthopedic Surgery and Pediatrics, Case
School of Medicine; Director, Pediatric Orthopedics,
Rainbow Babies and Children's Hospital, Cleveland,
Ohio
Neonatal Orthopedics

Philip Toltzis, MD
Associate Professor, Department of Pediatrics,
Case School of Medicine; Attending Physician,
Department of Pediatrics, Rainbow Babies and
Children's Hospital, Cleveland, Ohio
The Immune System (Part Four)

Robert Turbow, MD, JD
Adjunct Professor, Department of Biology,
California Polytechnic State University, San Luis
Obispo, California; Attending Neonatologist,
Phoenix Children's Hospital, Phoenix, Arizona;
Chief Executive Officer, Patient Patents, Inc,
San Luis Obispo, California
Legal Issues in Neonatal-Perinatal Medicine

Jon E. Tyson, MD, MPH
Professor of Pediatrics, Obstetrics, Internal Medicine,
and Epidemiology, Department of Pediatrics, Division
of Neonatal-Perinatal Medicine, University of Texas
Health Science Center Medical School at Houston,
Houston, Texas
The Field of Neonatal-Perinatal Medicine (Part Two)

George F. Van Hare, MD
Professor of Pediatrics, Stanford University School of Medicine, Stanford; Director, Pediatric Arrhythmia Center at UCSF at Stanford, Lucile Packard Children's Hospital at Stanford, Palo Alto, and UCSF Children's Hospital, San Francisco, California
The Cardiovascular System (Part Eight)

Maximo Vento, PhD, MD
Associate Professor of Pediatrics, University Miguel Hernandez Faculty of Medicine, Alicante; Staff Neonatologist, Hospital Materno-Infantil La Fe, Valencia, Spain
Delivery Room Resuscitation of the Newborn (Part Three)

Dharmapuri Vidyasagar, MD, MSc, FAAP, FCCM, DHC (Poznan Medical Academy)
Professor of Pediatrics and Obstetrics and Gynecology, Department of Pediatrics, University of Illinois at Chicago College of Medicine; Director of Neonatology, Department of Pediatrics, University of Illinois Medical Center, Chicago, Illinois
Neonatology in Developing Countries

Beth A. Vogt, MD
Associate Professor of Pediatrics, Case School of Medicine; Pediatric Nephrologist, Rainbow Babies and Children's Hospital, Cleveland, Ohio
The Kidney and Urinary Tract

Michele C. Walsh, MD, MS
Professor of Pediatrics, Case School of Medicine; Medical Director, Neonatal Intensive Care Unit, Rainbow Babies and Children's Hospital, Cleveland, Ohio
Epidemiology and Perinatal Services; Physical Environment (Part Three); The Central Nervous System (Part Eight)

Michiko Watanabe, PhD
Associate Professor, Departments of Pediatrics, Genetics, and Anatomy, Case School of Medicine; Staff, Division of Pediatric Cardiology, Rainbow Babies and Children's Hospital, Cleveland, Ohio
The Cardiovascular System (Part One)

Robert D. White, MD
Clinical Assistant Professor, Department of Pediatrics, Indiana University School of Medicine, South Bend; Adjunct Professor, Department of Psychology, University of Notre Dame, Notre Dame; Director, Regional Newborn Program, Memorial Hospital, South Bend, Indiana
Physical Environment (Parts Two and Three)

David B. Wilson, MD, PhD
Associate Professor, Department of Pediatrics, Washington University School of Medicine; Attending Physician, St Louis Children's Hospital, St. Louis, Missouri
The Blood and Hematopoietic System

Deanne E. Wilson-Costello, MD
Associate Professor of Pediatrics, Case School of Medicine; Co-director, High Risk Follow-up Clinic, Department of Pediatrics, Rainbow Babies and Children's Hospital, Cleveland, Ohio
Follow-up for High-Risk Neonates

Richard B. Wolf, DO, FACOG
Clinical Instructor in Obstetrics-Gynecology, Department of Reproductive Medicine, University of California, San Diego, School of Medicine, Attending Perinatologist, Department of Reproductive Medicine, UCSD, Medical Center, San Diego, California
Amniotic Fluid and Nonimmune Hydrops Fetalis

Ronald J. Wong, MD
Research Associate, Department of Pediatrics, Stanford University School of Medicine, Stanford; Department of Pediatrics, Lucile Packard Children's Hospital at Stanford, Palo Alto, California
Biomedical Engineering Aspects of Neonatal Monitoring; Neonatal Jaundice and Liver Disease

Mervin C. Yoder, MD
Richard and Pauline Klingler Professor of Pediatrics and Professor of Biochemistry, Department of Pediatrics, Indiana University School of Medicine; Attending Neonatologist, James Whitcomb Riley Hospital for Children, Indianapolis, Indiana
The Immune System (Part One)

Mark H. Yudin, MD, MSc
Assistant Professor, University of Toronto Faculty of Medicine; Attending Physician and Deputy Chief, Department of Obstetrics and Gynecology, Toronto, Ontario, Canada
Perinatal Infections

Kenneth G. Zahka, MD
Professor of Pediatrics, Case School of Medicine; Pediatric Cardiologist, Rainbow Babies and Children's Hospital, Cleveland Ohio
The Cardiovascular System (Parts Two through Seven and Nine)

Arthur B. Zinn, MD, PhD
Associate Professor, Departments of Genetics and Pediatrics, Case School of Medicine; Center for Human Genetics, University Hospitals of Cleveland, Cleveland, Ohio
Inborn Errors of Metabolism

Preface

The foundation for successful outcomes in neonatal-perinatal medicine has been the ability to apply knowledge of the fundamental pathophysiology of the various neonatal disorders to safe interventions. Molecular, biologic, and technologic advances have facilitated the diagnosis, monitoring, and therapy of these complex disorders. Advances at the bench have been transformed to the bedside, and survival statistics reveal steady improvements. Nonetheless, although the survival rates may give reason to rejoice, the high early morbidity and persistent neurodevelopmental problems remain cause for concern. Such problems include chronic lung disease, nosocomial infections, necrotizing enterocolitis, hypoxic-ischemic encephalopathy, cerebral palsy, and the inability to sustain the intrauterine rate of growth when the infants are born prematurely. These problems need to be addressed, in addition to the complex birth defects and genetic disorders that now loom as major problems in the neonatal intensive care unit.

With the combination of print and electronic journals, the effort to stay current in a single subspecialty remains a daunting task. Indeed, presenting the current status of the field of neonatal-perinatal medicine, even in a two-volume textbook, has become extremely challenging. It is a tribute to the contributors to *Neonatal-Perinatal Medicine* that they continue to do so as concisely as they do, because many sections are worthy of an individual textbook. We are profoundly grateful to both our loyal and our new contributors, who give so freely of their time and knowledge.

For the eighth edition, in addition to completely reorganizing and rewriting a significant number of chapters, our authors have attempted to consolidate the evidence and include the results of the Cochrane Database, meta-analyses, and large multicenter, randomized clinical trials. When appropriate, guidelines and committee statements have been included or referenced. With the technologic shrinking of the globe, we were highly privileged to draw on the expertise of a number of our colleagues from Europe, Israel, and India, to broaden the perspective of the book. We have introduced new sections on the medicolegal aspects of neonatal-perinatal medicine, and on the challenges of introducing advances in our field to the developing world, where almost 99% of the annual 4 million worldwide neonatal deaths occur.

This book would not exist without the remarkable clinical and intellectual environment that constitutes Rainbow Babies and Children's Hospital in Cleveland. On a daily basis, we gain knowledge from our faculty colleagues and fellows, and wisdom from our nursing staff, who are so committed to their young patients. Once again, we have been blessed with an in-house editor, Bonnie Siner, to whom we cannot adequately express our thanks. She is the glue behind the binding in the book and has worked tirelessly with Elsevier staff members to bring this project to fruition. Elsevier has once again provided the resources to accomplish this mammoth task.

Richard J. Martin
MBBS, FRACP

Avroy A. Fanaroff
MD, FRCP (Edinburgh), FRCPCH

Michele C. Walsh
MD, MS

Contents

Color insert follows Contents in Volume One.

VOLUME ONE

I   The Field of Neonatal-Perinatal Medicine

1. **From Infant Hatcheries to Intensive Care: Some Highlights of the Century of Neonatal Medicine** 3
   Tonse N. K. Raju

2. **Epidemiology and Perinatal Services** 19

   Part 1
   Epidemiology 19
   Michele C. Walsh
   Avroy A. Fanaroff

   Part 2
   Perinatal Services 26
   Michele C. Walsh
   Avroy A. Fanaroff

3. **Ethics in Perinatal and Neonatal Medicine** 35
   Jonathan Hellmann
   Françoise Baylis

4. **Legal Issues in Neonatal-Perinatal Medicine** 47
   Robert Turbow
   Jonathan M. Fanaroff

5. **The Field of Neonatal-Perinatal Medicine** 63

   Part 1
   Evaluating and Improving the Quality and Safety of Neonatal Intensive Medicine 63
   Jeffrey D. Horbar
   Jeffrey B. Gould

   Part 2
   Practicing Evidence-Based Neonatal-Perinatal Medicine 79
   John C. Sinclair
   Kathleen A. Kennedy
   Jon E. Tyson

6. **Neonatology in Developing Countries** 87
   Dharmapuri Vidyasagar
   Anil Narang

II   The Fetus

7. **Genetic Aspects of Perinatal Disease and Prenatal Diagnosis** 113
   Stuart Schwartz

8. **Perinatal Ultrasound** 141
   Nancy E. Judge
   Stuart C. Morrison

9. **Estimation of Fetal Well-Being** 167

   Part 1
   Antepartum Fetal Surveillance 167
   Susan E. Gerber

   Part 2
   Evaluation of the Intrapartum Fetus 172
   Barbara V. Parilla

10. **Pharmacologic Intervention** 183

    Part 1
    Developmental Pharmacology 183
    Michael D. Reed
    Jacob V. Aranda
    Barbara F. Hales

    Part 2
    Pharmacologic Treatment of the Fetus 202
    Michael D. Reed
    Jeffrey L. Blumer

11. Surgical Treatment of the Fetus 231
    Timothy M. Crombleholme

12. Occupational and Environmental Risks
    to the Fetus 255
    Cynthia F. Bearer

III Pregnancy Disorders and Their Impact on the Fetus

13. Intrauterine Growth Restriction 271
    Robert M. Kliegman

14. Hypertensive Disorders of Pregnancy . . . 307
    Dinesh M. Shah

15. Pregnancy Complicated by Diabetes
    Mellitus 321
    Carol Andrea Lindsay

16. Obstetric Management of Prematurity . . . 331
    Patrick S. Ramsey
    Robert L. Goldenberg

17. Fetal Effects of Autoimmune Disease 367
    Isaac Blickstein
    Smadar Friedman

18. Obstetric Management of Multiple
    Gestation 375
    Isaac Blickstein
    Eric S. Shinwell

19. Postterm Pregnancy 383
    Isaac Blickstein
    Orna Flidel-Rimon

20. Erythroblastosis Fetalis 389
    Andrée Gruslin
    Thomas R. Moore

21. Amniotic Fluid and Nonimmune Hydrops
    Fetalis 409
    Richard B. Wolf
    Thomas R. Moore

22. Perinatal Infections 429
    Mark H. Yudin
    Bernard Gonik

23. Placental Pathology 455
    Raymond W. Redline

IV The Delivery Room

24. Anesthesia for Labor and Delivery 467
    McCallum R. Hoyt

25. Delivery Room Resuscitation of the
    Newborn 483

    #### Part 1
    Overview and Initial Management 483
    Ronald S. Bloom

    #### Part 2
    Role of Positive Pressure Ventilation in
    Neonatal Resuscitation 491
    Anthony Milner
    Anne Greenough

    #### Part 3
    Oxygen Therapy 498
    Maximo Vento
    Ola Didrik Saugstad

    #### Part 4
    Chest Compression, Medications, and
    Special Problems 501
    Ronald S. Bloom

26. Physical Examination of the
    Newborn 513
    Tom Lissauer

27. Birth Injuries 529
    Henry H. Mangurten

28. Congenital Anomalies 561
    Louanne Hudgins
    Suzanne B. Cassidy

V Provisions for Neonatal Care

29. Physical Environment 585

    #### Part 1
    The Thermal Environment of the
    Newborn Infant 585
    Gunnar Sedin

    #### Part 2
    The Sensory Environment of the
    Intensive Care Nursery 597
    M. Kathleen Philbin
    Robert D. White
    Benoist Schaal
    Steven B. Hoath

    #### Part 3
    Design Considerations 603
    Michele C. Walsh
    Robert D. White

30. Biomedical Engineering Aspects of
    Neonatal Monitoring 609
    Susan R. Hintz
    Ronald J. Wong
    David K. Stevenson

31. Anesthesia in the Neonate 627
    John E. Stork

32. Care of the Mother, Father,
    and Infant 645
    Marshall H. Klaus
    John H. Kennell
    Patricia M. DePompei

33. Nutrition and Metabolism in the High-Risk Neonate 661

Part 1
Enteral Nutrition 661
Scott C. Denne
Brenda B. Poindexter
Catherine A. Leitch
Judith A. Ernst
Pamela K. Lemons
James A. Lemons

Part 2
Parenteral Nutrition 679
Brenda B. Poindexter
Catherine A. Leitch
Scott C. Denne

34. Fluid, Electrolyte, and Acid-Base Homeostasis 695

Part 1
Fluid and Electrolyte Management 695
Katherine MacRae Dell
Ira D. Davis

Part 2
Acid-Base Management 703
Katherine MacRae Dell
Ira D. Davis

35. Diagnostic Imaging 713
Carlos J. Sivit

36. Infants of Substance-Abusing Mothers . . . 733
Emmalee S. Bandstra
Veronica H. Accorneo

VOLUME TWO

VI Development and Disorders of Organ Systems

37. The Immune System 761

Part 1
Developmental Immunology 761
Reuben Kapur
Richard A. Polin
Mervin C. Yoder

Part 2
Postnatal Bacterial Infections 791
Morven S. Edwards

Part 3
Fungal and Protozoal Infections 830
Morven S. Edwards

Part 4
Viral Infections 840
Jill E. Baley
Philip Toltzis

38. The Central Nervous System 883

Part 1
Normal and Abnormal Brain Development 883
Pierre Gressens
Petra S. Hüppi

Part 2
White Matter Injury 909
Petra S. Hüppi
Pierre Gressens

Part 3
Intracranial Hemorrhage and Vascular Lesions 924
Linda de Vries

Part 4
Hypoxic-Ischemic Encephalopathy 938
Malcolm Levene
Linda de Vries
1. Pathophysiology 938
2. Assessment Tools 944
3. Management 949

Part 5
Seizures in Neonates 956
Mark S. Scher

Part 6
Hypotonia and Neuromuscular Disease 976
Timothy E. Lotze
Geoffrey Miller

Part 7
Disorders in Head Size and Shape 989
Alan R. Cohen

Part 8
Myelomeningocele 1014
Alan R. Cohen
Michele C. Walsh

39. Follow-up for High-Risk Neonates 1035
Deanne E. Wilson-Costello
Maureen Hack

40. Hearing Loss in the Newborn Infant ... 1045
James E. Arnold
Robert C. Sprecher

41. Neurobehavioral Development of the Preterm Infant 1051
Heidelise Als
Samantha C. Butler

42. The Respiratory System 1069

Part 1

Lung Development and Maturation 1069
Alan H. Jobe

Part 2

Assessment of Pulmonary Function 1087
Waldemar A. Carlo
Juliann M. DiFiore

Part 3

Respiratory Distress Syndrome and Its Management 1097
Ricardo J. Rodriguez
Richard J. Martin
Avroy A. Fanaroff

Part 4

Assisted Ventilation and Complications of Respiratory Distress 1108
Waldemar A. Carlo
Richard J. Martin
Avroy A. Fanaroff

Part 5

Repiratory Disorders in Preterm and Term Infants 1122
Martha J. Miller
Avroy A. Fanaroff
Richard J. Martin

Part 6

Upper Airway Lesions 1146
Robert C. Sprecher
James E. Arnold

Part 7

Bronchopulmonary Dysplasia and Neonatal Chronic Lung Disease 1155
Eduardo H. Bancalari

Part 8

Therapy for Cardiorespiratory Failure 1168
Eileen K. Stork

43. The Cardiovascular System 1195

Part 1

Cardiac Embryology 1195
Michiko Watanabe
Katherine S. Schaefer

Part 2

Causes and Associations 1202
Kenneth G. Zahka

Part 3

Fetal Cardiac Physiology and Fetal Cardiovascular Assessment 1205
Francine Erenberg
A. Resai Bengur
Kenneth G. Zahka

Part 4

Principles of Neonatal Cardiovascular Hemodynamics 1211
Kenneth G. Zahka

Part 5

Approach to the Neonate with Cardiovascular Disease 1215
Kenneth G. Zahka
Daniel H. Gruenstein

Part 6

Congenital Defects 1222
Kenneth G. Zahka
Francine Erenberg

Part 7

Cardiovascular Problems of the Neonate 1242
Kenneth G. Zahka
A. Resai Bengur

Part 8

Neonatal Arrhythmias 1252
George F. Van Hare

Part 9

Principles of Medical and Surgical Management 1265
Kenneth G. Zahka
Ernest S. Siwik

44. The Blood and Hematopoietic System 1287

Part 1

Hematologic Problems in the Fetus and Neonate 1287
Lori Luchtman-Jones
Alan L. Schwartz
David B. Wilson

Part 2

Blood Component Therapy for the Neonate 1344
Lori Luchtman-Jones
Alan L. Schwartz
David B. Wilson

45. The Gastrointestinal Tract 1357

Part 1

Development and Basic Physiology of the Neonatal Gastrointestinal Tract 1357
David K. Magnuson
Robert L. Parry
Walter J. Chwals

Part 2

Disorders of Digestion 1363
Sundeep Arora
Gisela Chelimsky

Part 3

Selected Thoracic Gastrointestinal Anomalies 1373
David K. Magnuson
Robert L. Parry
Walter J. Chwals

Part 4

Selected Abdominal Gastrointestinal Anomalies 1381
David K. Magnuson
Robert L. Parry
Walter J. Chwals

Part 5

Neonatal Necrotizing Enterocolitis 1403
Michael S. Caplan

46. Neonatal Jaundice and Liver Disease 1419
Ronald J. Wong
Glenn H. DeSandre
Eric Sibley
David K. Stevenson

47. Metabolic and Endocrine Disorders 1467

Part 1

Disorders of Carbohydrate Metabolism 1467
Satish C. Kalhan
Prabhu S. Parimi

Part 2

Disorders of Calcium, Phosphorus, and Magnesium Metabolism 1491
Jacques Rigo
Mario De Curtis

Part 3

Thyroid Disorders 1523
Susan R. Rose

Part 4

Abnormalities of Sexual Differentiation 1550
Mark R. Palmert
William T. Dahms

48. Inborn Errors of Metabolism 1597
Arthur B. Zinn

49. The Kidney and Urinary Tract 1659
Beth A. Vogt
Katherine MacRae Dell
Ira D. Davis

50. The Skin 1685
Vivek Narendran
Steven B. Hoath

51. The Eye 1721

Part 1

Diagnosis and Evaluation 1721
Balaji K. Gupta
Nancy Anderson Hamming
Marilyn T. Miller

Part 2

Neonatal Eye Disease 1726
Balaji K. Gupta
Nancy Anderson Hamming
Marilyn T. Miller

Part 3

Retinopathy of Prematurity 1747
Dale L. Phelps

52. Neonatal Orthopedics 1755

Part 1

Musculoskeletal Disorders 1755
Daniel R. Cooperman
George H. Thompson

Part 2

Bone and Joint Infections 1762
Daniel R. Cooperman
George H. Thompson

Part 3

Congenital Abnormalities of the Upper and Lower Extremities and Spine 1767
Daniel R. Cooperman
George H. Thompson

Appendices

A. Therapeutic Agents 1787
Mary L. Nock
Jeffrey L. Blumer

B. Tables of Normal Values 1795
Mary L. Nock
Kousiki Patra

C. Schedule for Immunization of Preterm Infants 1819
Jill E. Baley

Index i

FIGURE 6-8. D. Infants are weighed using a color-coded spring balance. Color codes obviate reading the exact weight by the TBAs. Weight indicator in red zone is VLBW, in yellow is LBW, in green indicates normal weight baby. Risk assessment is based on color code.

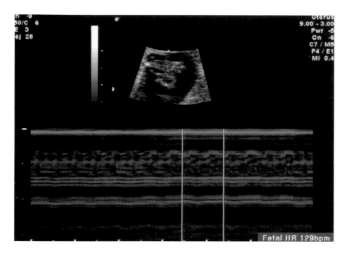

FIGURE 8-2. Transvaginal M-mode embryonic heart rate at 6⁴/₇ weeks of gestation. *Upper view:* embryo with cursor across thorax. *Lower view:* M-mode display of wall movements during two cardiac cycles (between vertical lines).

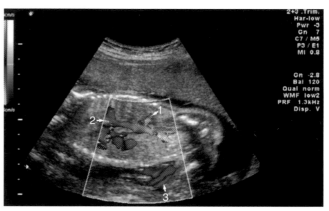

FIGURE 8-5. Color Doppler demonstration of left renal artery (*arrow #1*, red signal) arising from descending aorta (*arrow #2*, blue signal). Umbilical cord (*arrow #3*, blue signal) is also shown.

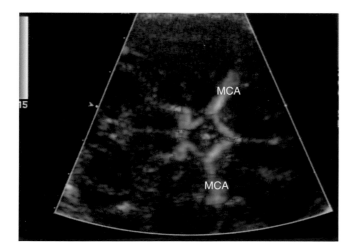

FIGURE 8-7. Power Doppler image showing the circle of Willis and both middle cerebral arteries (MCA).

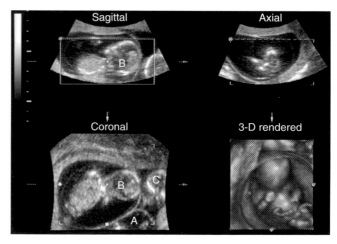

FIGURE 8-8. Triplets at 13 weeks of gestation (A, B, C) in three perpendicular planes (sagittal, axial, coronal). Three-dimensional surface rendering of fetus B is shown in the lower (R) panel.

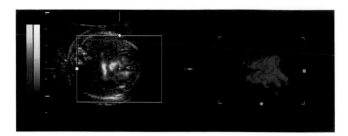

FIGURE 8-9. Spatiotemporal imaging of normal four-chamber heart at 18 weeks. Transverse chest with four-chamber view *(left panel)*, cardiac apex facing right, and rendered three dimensionally *(right panel)*, cardiac apex facing left.

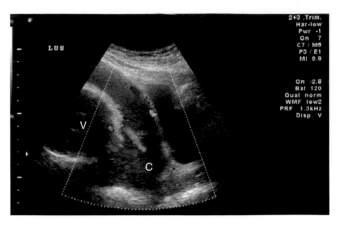

FIGURE 8-19. Vasa praevia by color Doppler. The vessels (blue) branch out within the membranes lying between the fetal vertex (V) and the cervix (C).

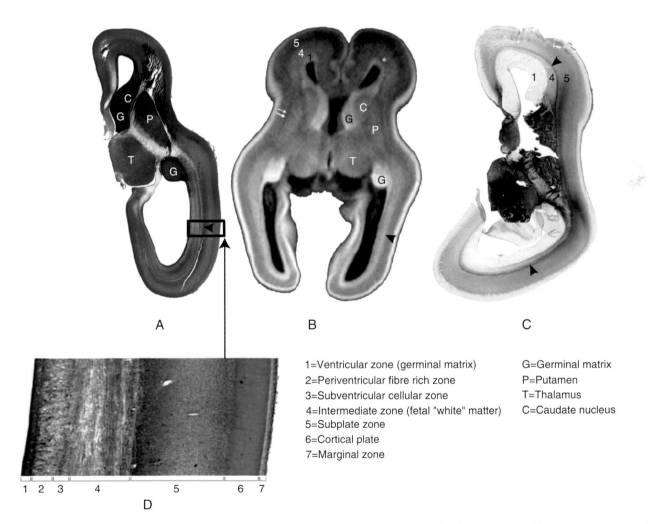

1=Ventricular zone (germinal matrix)
2=Periventricular fibre rich zone
3=Subventricular cellular zone
4=Intermediate zone (fetal "white" matter)
5=Subplate zone
6=Cortical plate
7=Marginal zone

G=Germinal matrix
P=Putamen
T=Thalamus
C=Caudate nucleus

FIGURE 38-9. The cerebral wall displays five laminar compartments of varying magnetic resonance imaging (MRI) signal intensity (**B**), which partly correspond to laminar compartments delineated on Nissl-stained (**A**) and histochemical (**C**) sections. Starting from the ventricular surface, these laminar compartments are as follows (**D**): (1) The ventricular zone (germinal matrix) of high MRI signal intensity, which corresponds to the highly cellular ventricular zone in Nissl-stained sections and, therefore is numbered 1; (2) the periventricular zone of low MRI signal intensity, which largely corresponds to the periventricular fiber-rich zone; (3, 4) the intermediate zone of moderate MRI signal intensity, which encompasses both the subventricular cellular zone and the fetal white matter; (5) the subplate zone of low MRI signal intensity, which closely corresponds to the compartment marked with 5 in Nissl-stained (**D**) and acetylcholinesterase-stained (**C**) sections; therefore it is also marked with 5 on MRI (**B**); (6, 7) the cortical plate of high MRI signal intensity, which closely corresponds to the compartment marked 6 on Nissl-stained sections (6 in **D**) but on MRI cannot be separated from the marginal zone (7 in **D**); therefore, it is always seen on MRI as a band of high signal intensity situated above the subplate zone. (From Kostovic I et al: Laminar organization of the human fetal cerebrum revealed by histochemical markers and magnetic resonance imaging. Cereb Cortex 12:536, 2002, by permission of Oxford University Press.)

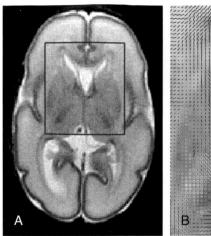
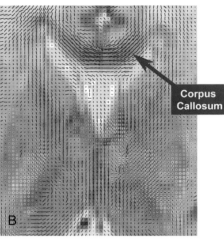

FIGURE 38-11. A, Anatomic axial T2-weighted magnetic resonance image. **B,** Diffusion tensor vector maps for the regions indicated by the red box in **A,** showing non-myelinated interhemispheric fiber connections in the corpus callosum at 28 weeks' gestational age. In B, the blue lines represent the in-plane fibers; the out-of-plane fibers are shown in colored dots ranging from green to red. (From Hüppi PS et al: Microstructural development of human newborn cerebral white matter assessed in vivo by diffusion tensor MRI. Pediatr Res 44:584, 1998, with permission.)

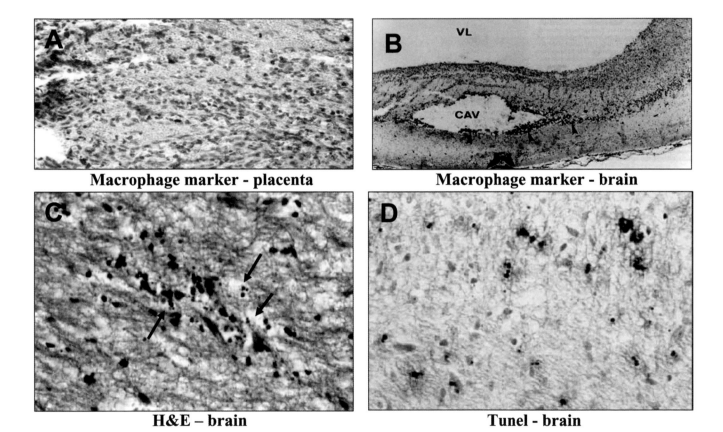

Macrophage marker – placenta

Macrophage marker – brain

H&E – brain

Tunel – brain

FIGURE 38-36. Intrauterine infection with *Escherichia coli* in pregnant rabbits induces a combination of placental and brain abnormalities. **A,** Macrophage activation is observed in all placentas. The numerous red cells correspond to activated macrophages labeled with a specific antigen. **B,** Focal cystic periventricular white matter lesions with macrophage activation is detected in some fetuses. Brown cells identified by *arrowheads* correspond to activated macrophages/microglia labeled with a specific antigen. CAV, cystic lesion; VL, lateral ventricle. **C, D,** Diffuse white matter cell death without detectable inflammatory response is observed in all fetuses on hematoxylin and eosin (H&E)-stained sections. **C,** *Arrows* point to examples of apoptotic nuclei in the periventricular white matter and on Tunel (a marker of fragmented DNA and of accompanying cell death) stained sections. **D,** Purple blue nuclei correspond to diffusely distributed dying white matter cells. (Reprinted from Developmental Brain Research, Vol. 145, Debillion T et al, p 39, Copyright 2003, with permission from Elsevier)

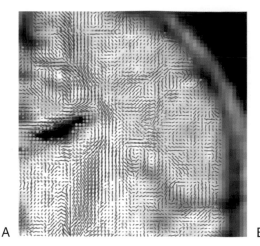 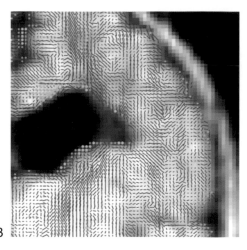

A   B

FIGURE 38-46. Diffusion vector maps overlaid on coronal diffusion-weighted images for a premature infant at term with no white matter injury (**A**) and a premature infant at term with perinatal white matter injury (**B**). The posterior limb of the internal capsule (I.C.) in **A** shows more homologous directed vectors that are longer and more densely packed than in the internal capsule of **B**. Anteroposterior-oriented white matter fibers in the area of the superior longitudinal fasciculus (SLF; yellow and green dots, with yellow representing higher anisotropy than green) in **A** indicate the presence of fiber bundles that are missing or are less prominent in **B**. The only discrete anteroposterior fiber bundles that definitely are present in **B** are the cingulate bundle (C.B.). Fibers of the corona radiata appear less well organized in **B** than **A**. Loss of axons in the central white matter and the posterior limb as outlined previously will result in neuromotor disturbances. (Modified from Hüppi PS, Murphy B, Maier SE, et al: Microstructural brain development after perinatal cerebral white matter injury assessed by diffusion tensor magnetic resonance imaging. Pediatrics 107:455–460, 2001. [© 2001, American Academy of Pediatrics])

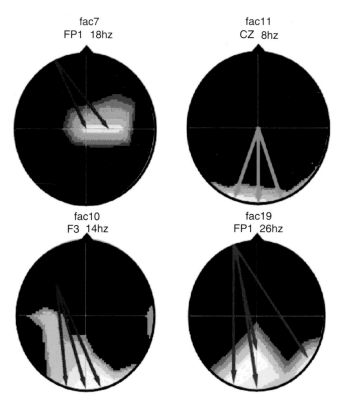

FIGURE 41-5. Electroencephalographic coherence measures at 2 weeks' corrected age, control versus experimental group infants. Four heads, each corresponding to a utilized coherence factor, top view, scalp left to image left. Each shows the maximal loadings (correlations) of original coherence variables on the indicated factor. An index electrode and frequency are printed above each head. Colored regions indicate location, magnitude, and sign (red, positive; blue, negative) of maximally loading coherences on the factor. *Arrows* also illustrate coherence variables; however, arrow color compensates for signs of factor loadings on subsequent statistically derived canonical variates, thus illustrating how original coherence variables differ between experimental (red increased, green decreased) and control infants. (Reproduced with permission from Als H et al: Early experience alters brain function and structure. Pediatrics 113:847-857, 2004, Copyright © 2004 by the AAP.)

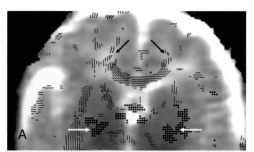

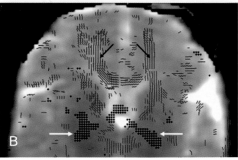

FIGURE 41-6. Comparison of control and experimental group infants, at 2 weeks' corrected age, with magnetic resonance imaging and diffusion tensor imaging. Examples of diffusion tensor maps from identical axial slices through the frontal lobes of a representative control (**A**) and an experimental group (**B**) infant obtained at 2 weeks' corrected age. In each example, the principal eigenvectors (shown in *red and black*) overlie the apparent diffusion coefficient (ADC) map to show anisotropy in white matter. The *red lines* denote eigenvectors located within the plane of the image, and the *black dots* indicate eigenvectors oriented mostly perpendicular to the image plane. Note the greater anisotropy of white matter found in the experimental infant (**B**) as compared with the control infant (**A**), at the posterior limbs of the internal capsule (*white arrows* in **A** and **B**) and the frontal white matter adjacent to the corpus callosum (*black arrows* in **A** and **B**). The greater anisotropy found in the experimental infant (**B**) suggests more advanced white matter development in these regions than is found in the control infant (**A**). (Reproduced with permission from Als H et al: Early experience alters brain function and structure. Pediatrics 113:847-857, 2004, Copyright © 2004 by the AAP.)

The Field of Neonatal-Perinatal Medicine

From Infant Hatcheries to Intensive Care: Some Highlights of the Century of Neonatal Medicine

Tonse N. K. Raju

We trust we have been forgiven for coining the words, "neonatology" and "neonatologist." We do not recall ever having seen them in print. The one designates the art and science of diagnosis and treatment of disorders of the newborn infant, the other the physician whose primary concern lies in the specialty. . . . We are not advocating now that a new subspecialty be lopped from pediatrics . . . yet such a subdivision . . . [has] as much merit as does pediatric hematology.

A. J. SCHAFFER, 1960[71]

The American Board of Pediatrics offered the first examination in the subspecialty of *neonatal-perinatal medicine* in 1975. Through November 2003, the board had certified 4136 men and women as neonatologists—practitioners of a discipline that had no formal name 45 years ago. The 1950 *Index Medicus* listed 218 annual publications under the *Infant, Newborn* subject heading. In 1967, the number had increased to 6365, and in 2003, to 7678.[59] Dr. Schaffer need not have apologized for his visionary understatement—the specialty and the physicians he christened proved him immensely prophetic. Although it was not "lopped" from pediatrics, this *final frontier* (another Schaffer term) carved a niche of its own, bridging obstetrics with pediatrics and intensive care with primary care.

The formal birth of neonatology may appear to be recent, but its roots extend into the 19th century, when systematic and organized care began for groups of premature infants. This chapter traces the origins and growth of modern perinatal and neonatal medicine, with a brief perspective on its promises and failures. The reader may consult scholarly monographs and review articles on specific topics for in-depth analyses.*

PERINATAL PIONEERS

Many scientists played key roles in developing the basic concepts in neonatal-perinatal medicine that helped

*References 6, 7, 22, 24, 61, 73, 77.

rationalize the evolving clinical care and that inspired further research. For the sake of brevity, only a few are shown in Figure 1-1.

Medicinal chemistry (later called biochemistry) and classical physiology gained popularity and acceptance toward the end of the 19th century, leading to studies on biochemical and physiologic problems in the fetus and the newborn. Sir Joseph Barcroft[8,34] and Jeffery Dawes in England (gas exchange and nutritional transfer across the placenta and oxygen carrying in fetal and adult hemoglobin); Arvo Ylppö in Finland (neonatal nutrition, jaundice, and thermoregulation); John Lind in Sweden (circulatory physiology); and Clement Smith[75] (fetal and neonatal respiratory physiology), Joseph DeLee[26,27] (who founded the first lying-in hospital in Chicago and who researched incubators and high-risk obstetrics), Richard Day (temperature regulation, retinopathy of prematurity, and jaundice), Harry Gordon[38] (nutrition), and others in the United States made numerous basic contributions and trained scores of scientists from around the world. Dr. Clement Smith once said, "If you were interested in babies and liked Boston, I was the only wheel in town!"[60] Table 1-1 highlights some of the milestones in perinatal medicine.

HIGH-RISK FETUS AND PERINATAL OBSTETRICS

Because so many deaths occurred during early infancy, many cultures adopted remarkably innovative methods

FIGURE 1-1. Some pioneers in perinatal and neonatal physiology and medicine. **A,** Joseph Barcroft; **B,** Arvo Ylppö; **C,** John Lind; **D,** William Liley; **E,** Joseph DeLee; **F,** Richard Day; **G,** Clement Smith; **H,** Harry Gordon. (**A,** From Barcroft J: Research on Pre-natal Life, vol 1. Oxford, Blackwell Scientific, 1977, courtesy of Blackwell Scientific; **B-D, F-H,** from Smith GF, Vidyasagar D [eds]: Historical Review and Recent Advances in Neonatal and Perinatal Medicine, vol 1, Neonatal Medicine. Evansville, Ind, Ross Publication, 1984, pp ix, xix, xxii, xvi, xii, xiv, respectively, courtesy of Mead Johnson Nutritional; **E,** courtesy of Mrs. Nancy DeLee Frank, Chicago, Ill.)

to deal with these tragedies. According to a Jewish tradition, full, yearlong mourning is not required for infants who die before 30 days of age.[40] In some Asian ethnic groups, infant-naming ceremonies are held only after several months, until which time the baby is simply called *it*. In India, the first infant who survives after the death of a previous newborn sibling is often given an odd or coarse-sounding name, to prevent evil spirits from repeating their deeds. In her book on the history of the Middle Ages, Barbara Tuchman notes that infants were seldom depicted in medieval artworks.[83] When they *were* shown (e.g., the infant Jesus), women in the pictures looked away from the infant, ostensibly conveying a sense of respect, but in fact suggesting fearful aloofness.

Since antiquity, the care of pregnant women has been the purview of midwives, grandmothers, and experienced female elders in the community. Wet nurses helped when mothers were unavailable or unwilling to nurse their infants. Little or no assistance was generally needed for normal or uncomplicated labor and delivery. For complicated deliveries, however, male doctors were summoned, but they could do little, for many of them lacked expertise or interest in treating women. Disasters were therefore common, rendering labor and delivery the most dreaded period in the lives of pregnant women.[43] As recently as the early 1900s, *accidents of*

childbirth—unexpected intrapartum complications—accounted for 50% to 70% of all maternal deaths in England and Wales.[17,56] Because the immediate concern during most high-risk deliveries was saving the mother, sick newborn infants were naturally ignored, and their death rates remained very high.

Rarely, however, happy outcomes did occur. In one of the oldest works of art depicting labor and delivery (Fig. 1-2A), a bearded man and his assistant are standing behind a woman in labor, holding devices remarkably similar to the modern obstetric forceps. The midwife has delivered an evidently live infant. In Figure 1-2B, three infants from a set of quadruplets, nicely swaddled, have been placed on the mother, as the unwrapped fourth infant is being handed to her for nursing. A divine figure in the background is blessing the newcomers.

Cesarean sections were seldom carried out on living women before the 13th century. Even subsequently, the procedure was performed only as a final act of desperation. Contrary to popular belief, Julius Caesar's birth was not likely by cesarean section. Because Caesar's mother was alive during his reign, historians believe that she probably delivered him vaginally. The term probably originated from *lex caesarea,* in turn from *lex regia,* the "royal law" prohibiting burial of corpses of pregnant women without removal of their fetuses.[11,89] The procedure allowed for baptism (or a

TABLE 1-1. Some Milestones in Perinatal Medicine

CATEGORY	YEAR(S)	DESCRIPTION
Antenatal aspects	1752	Queen Charlotte's Hospital, the world's first maternity hospital, is founded in London.[57]
	1915-1924	Dame Janet Campbell introduces outlines of regular prenatal visits, which become a standard.
	1923-1925	Estrogen and progesterone are discovered.
	1928	First pregnancy test is described, in which women's urine is shown to cause changes in mouse ovaries.
Fetal assessment	1543	Vesalius observes fetal breathing movements in pigs.
	1634	Ambroise Paré teaches that absence of movement suggests a dead fetus.
	1819, 1821	René Laënnec introduces the stethoscope in 1819, and his friend Kergaradec shows that fetal heart sounds can be heard using it.
	1866	Forceps are recommended when there is "weakening of the fetal heart rate."
	1903	Einthoven publishes his work on the electrocardiogram.
	1906	The first recording of fetal heart tracings is taken.
	1908	The term *fetal distress* is introduced.
	1948-1953	There are developments in the external tocodynamometer.
	1953	Virginia Apgar describes her scoring system.[3]
	1957-1963	Systematic studies are conducted on fetal heart rate monitoring.
	1970	Dawes reports studies on breathing movement in fetal lambs.
	1980	Fetal Doppler studies begin.
	1981	Nelson and Ellenberg report that Apgar scores are poor predictors of neurologic outcome.
Labor and delivery	ca. 1000-500 BC	In Ayurveda, the ancient Hindu medical system, doctors describe obstetric instruments.
	98-138	Soranus develops the birthing stool and other instruments.
	1500s	There are isolated reports of cesarean sections on living women.
	1610	The first intentional cesarean section is documented.
	1700s	The Chamberlen forceps are kept as a family secret for three generations.
	1921	The lower-segment cesarean section is reported.
	1953	The modern vacuum extractor is introduced.
Fetal physiology	1900-1950	Sir Joseph Barcroft, Dawes, Lind, Liley, and others study physiologic principles of placental gas exchange and fetal circulation.

See references 2, 41, 43, 61, and 77 for primary citations.

similar blessing) if the child was alive, or burial otherwise. Infants surviving the ordeal of cesarean birth were assumed to possess special powers, as supposedly did Shakespeare's Macduff, "not of a woman born" but of a corpse, thus able to slay Macbeth.[54]

Soranus of Ephesus (38-138 AD) influenced obstetric practice for 1600 years as did no other physician from antiquity. His *Gynecology,* perhaps the first formal textbook of perinatal medicine, was rediscovered in 1870 and translated into English in 1956.[82] In it are superb chapters on podalic version, obstructed labor, multiple gestations, fetal malformations, and other maternal and fetal disorders. In an age of magic and the occult, Soranus insisted that midwives be educated and free from superstitions, and he forbade wet nurses from drinking alcohol lest it render the infant "excessively sleepy." The chapter "How to Recognize the Newborn That Is Worth Rearing" may be one of the earliest accounts on the viability of sick newborn infants—a topic of great concern even today.

MIDWIVES AND PERINATAL CARE

In spite of an occasional caricaturing (Fig. 1-3), the midwife bore the burden of the obstetric care of the entire community for thousands of years. Men disliked obstetrics and women shied away from male doctors because of modesty. Good midwives were therefore always in great demand, and many of them held important social and political positions in European courts.[43,61,86]

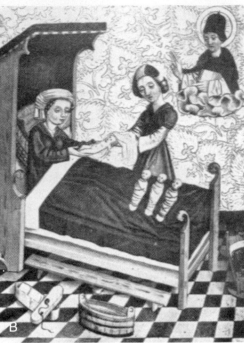

FIGURE 1-2. High-risk deliveries. **A,** A marble relief of uncertain date depicting a high-risk delivery. The physician and his assistant in the background are holding devices similar to the modern obstetric forceps. A midwife has just helped deliver a live infant while two people are looking through the window. **B,** Delivery of quadruplets. (From Graham H: Eternal Eve: The History of Gynecology and Obstetrics. New York, Doubleday, 1951, pp 68, 172.)

FIGURE 1-3. On call. *A Midwife Going to a Labour,* caricature by Thomas Rowlandson, 1811. (Courtesy of The British Museum, London.)

The emergence of man-midwives (Fig. 1-4) in England had a major effect on high-risk obstetric practice. Peter Chamberlen the Elder (1575-1628) is usually credited for inventing the modern obstetric forceps.[43,61,63] However, for 150 years, the instrument remained a trade secret through three generations in his family. By then, others had developed similar devices, and patients had been associating good obstetric outcomes with male doctors—a key factor in transforming midwifery to a male-dominated craft.[43] Some historians also argue that the shift from female midwifery to male midwifery was the result of a culmination of changing social values and gender relationships that led women to make voluntary choices about their bodies.[86] Today's high rates of home deliveries and increasing roles for female midwives are interesting reversals of trends seen in the late 18th century—albeit originating from women's personal choices and subtle pressures from the health insurance industries.

NEONATAL RESUSCITATION: TALES OF HEROISM AND DESPERATION

Popular artworks and centuries-old medical writings provide accounts of the miraculous revival of apparently dead adults and children.[66] These are tales of successes, for the failures were buried. Attempts to "stimulate" and revive apparently dead newborn infants included

FIGURE 1-4. Man-midwife. (Courtesy of Clements C. Fry Print Collections, Harvey Cushing/John Hay Whitney Medical Library, Yale University, New Haven, Conn.)

FIGURE 1-5. Virginia Apgar, U.S. postage stamp. (Courtesy of the United States Postal Service.)

such practices as beating, shaking, yelling, fumigating, dipping in ice-cold water, and dilating and blowing smoke into the rectum.[25,30,66] Oxygen administration through an orogastric tube to revive asphyxiated infants persisted well into the mid-1950s, when James and Apgar showed conclusively that the therapy was useless.[1,52]

APGAR AND THE LANGUAGE OF ASPHYXIA

Few scientists this century influenced the course of neonatal resuscitation like Dr. Virginia Apgar (1909-1974). A surgeon, she chose obstetric anesthesia as a career, and her scoring system inaugurated the modern era of assessing infants at birth on the basis of simple clinical examination.[3] Right or wrong, the Apgar score became the language of asphyxia. Whereas "giving the Apgar" often became a ritual, its profound effect was on formalizing the process of "seeing" and assessing infants at birth and communicating the findings in a consistent way. This process led to the formal steps of resuscitation at birth based on the score. Few people know that it was also Dr. Apgar who introduced umbilical artery catheterization.[16] A woman of enormous energy, talent, and compassion, Apgar was honored with her depiction on a 1994 U.S. postage stamp (Fig. 1-5).

FOUNDLING ASYLUMS AND INFANT CARE

In its early days, the Roman Empire faced a trend of decreasing population growth. The emperors taxed bachelors and rewarded married couples to encourage procreation.[76] In 315 AD, Emperor Constantine, hoping to encourage the raising of orphans and to curb infanticide, decreed that all "foundlings" would become slaves of those raising them. Similar humanitarian efforts by kings and the Council of the Roman Church led to the institutionalization of infant care by establishing *foundling asylums* for abandoned infants,[76] also called *hospitals for the innocent*—the world's first children's hospitals. Parents of unwanted infants "dropped off" their babies into a revolving receptacle at the door of such asylums, rang the doorbell, and disappeared into the night (Fig. 1-6). Such accounts are poignant reminders of the contemporary problem of child abandonment. Many states such as Alabama, Minnesota, and Texas have now begun programs to save "dumpster babies," abandoned newborn infants. Other states are planning to implement similar programs.[69]

Founded with altruistic motives, foundling asylums adopted pragmatic techniques for fundraising. In 18th-century France, lotteries were held and souvenirs were sold. In May 1749, George Frederick Handel gave a concert to support London's Hospital for the Maintenance and Education of Exposed and Deserted Young Children. The final item of the program was the playing of "The Foundling Hymn."[76]

SAVING BABIES TO MAN THE ARMY

Around the period of the French Revolution, the infant mortality rate in France was appallingly high, exceeding

FIGURE 1-6. Foundling homes. **A,** *Le Tour*—Revolving receptacle. Mother ringing a bell to notify those within that she is leaving her baby in the foundling home (watercolor by Herman Vogel, France, 1889). **B,** *Remorce* ("Remorse")—Parents after placing their infant in a foundling home (engraving and etching by Alberto Maso Gilli, France, 1875). (**A** and **B,** Courtesy of the Museum of the History of Medicine, Academy of Medicine, Toronto, Ontario, Canada; from Spaulding M, Welch P: Nurturing Yesterday's Child: A Portrayal of the Drake Collection of Pediatric History. Philadelphia, BC Decker, 1991, p 110 and p 119, respectively.)

50%. In 1789, the Revolutionary Council enacted a remarkable decree, proclaiming that working-class parents "have a right to the nation's succors at all times."[76] The postrevolutionary zeal regarding equality and fraternity stimulated such reforms, heralding an idealistic welfare state. In that era in France began the notion of collecting valid statistics on children, creating the world's first national databases.[76]

By the late 1800s, however, France faced a problem similar to that of ancient Rome—a negative population growth. The birthrate had declined and infant mortality remained high, alarming the military brass that was deeply engaged in battles with Prussia. Calling for remedial action, commissions were set up to study "depopulation," and programs were implemented to improve maternal and neonatal care.[6,7,22,24,76] Young parents were exhorted to uphold their patriotism and bear more children to "man the future French Armies." It is the irony of our times that such noble actions as saving babies were motivated by such brutal needs as enhancing military might.

AN INGENIOUS CONTRIVANCE, THE *COUVEUSE,* AND PREMATURE STATIONS

A popular story of the origin of modern incubator technology is that on seeing the poultry section during a casual visit to the Paris zoo in 1878, Stéphane Tarnier (1828-1897), a renowned obstetrician, conceived the idea of "incubators" similar to the "brooding hen" or *couveuse.*[6,7,22,24] He then asked M. Odile Martin, an instrument maker, to construct similar equipment for use with babies. With a "thermo-syphon" method to heat the outside with an alcohol lamp, Martin devised a sufficiently ventilated, one-cubic-meter, double-walled metal cage, spacious enough to hold two premature babies. The first *couveuses* were installed at the Paris Maternity Hospital in 1880. Tarnier documented dramatic improvements in the survival of premature infants.

Perhaps Tarnier knew of other incubators before his famous visit to the zoo.[7] Yet, it is Tarnier, and Pierre Budin (1846-1907) and Alfred Auvard, two of his students and associates, that we credit for institutionalizing care of premature babies. By using several incubators side by side, they developed the concept of caring for groups of premature infants in geographically identified units in their hospital.[6,7,80] Budin and Auvard also improved the original *couveuse* by replacing its walls with glass and using simpler methods for heating it. Their combined efforts had a major influence on the evolution of incubator technology during the first half of the 20th century in Europe and the United States (Fig. 1-7 and Table 1-2).

In 1884, Tarnier made another major invention. He developed a small, flexible rubber tube, introducing it through the mouth and extending it into the stomach of premature infants, so that milk could be dripped

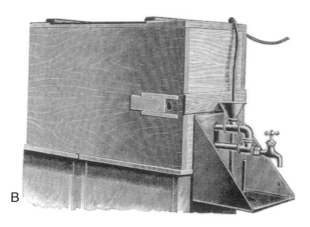

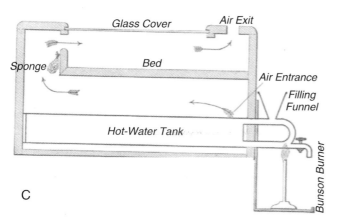

FIGURE 1-7. Early incubators. Rotch incubator (**A**), circa 1893. Holt incubator (**B**) and schematics of the Holt incubator (**C**). (**A,** From Cone TE Jr: History of American Pediatrics. Boston, Little Brown, 1979, pp 57 and 58, courtesy of Little Brown; **B** and **C,** from Holt LE: The Diseases of Infants and Children. New York, Appleton, 1897, pp 12 and 13, courtesy of Appleton.)

directly into the stomach. He called this method of nutritional support the *gavage feeding*. A large number of premature infants had been surviving by then, enabling implementation of gavage feeding into clinical

practice immediately; the two Tarnier innovations soon gave impressive results.[15,21] Tarnier also made a bold recommendation that the legal definition of viability should be 180 days of gestation; this was opposed by contemporary obstetricians.[7]

THE INCUBATORS ON THE ROAD AND PREMATURE BABY SHOWS

In the late 1890s, a bizarre set of episodes led to an era of "premature baby side shows"—a clever, if dubious, undertaking that lasted nearly 50 years.[6,7,73,80] About 15 years into using incubators in Paris, Budin had gained an international reputation as an expert on premature infants. According to a later account by one Dr. Martin Couney (a Budin associate of doubtful medical credentials), Budin had felt a need to popularize the French technology abroad and show the world the value of "conserving" premature infants. It seems that Budin asked Couney to organize a special pavilion for exhibiting incubators at the 1896 Berlin Exposition. (There is some doubt about the accuracy of this account.[7]) To add a sense of drama, Couney brought six premature infants from Rudolph Virchow's maternity unit in Berlin and exhibited the infants inside the six incubators he had brought from Paris. Couney coined a catchy phrase for the show—*kinderbrutanstalt* or *child hatchery*—igniting the imagination of a public that was thirsty for sensational scientific breakthroughs.

The premature baby exhibit was an astounding success. Comic songs and gags were constructed in its honor; at one German mark per visit, the child hatchery outdrew the Congo village, sky riders, and Tyrolean yodelers. Thousands delighted in seeing the marvel of human infants being incubated inside heated cages, similar to chicks in hatcheries. Fortunately for Budin, all six premature infants survived, probably because he had chosen "healthy-looking" babies, who had survived for at least 5 days.

Spurred by the Berlin success, Couney convinced Budin to continue such exhibitions and took the incubators to Great Britain's 1897 Victorian Era Exhibition. However, things were not so simple in Britain, for there he met with British pride: No self-respecting Londoner would let *his* premature infant be placed inside a *French* incubator! Thus, Couney requested that Budin provide him with babies, and Budin complied. "A bunch of Parisian premature infants" were transported across the English Channel in wash baskets warmed with hot-water bottles and pillows and exhibited in London's Fair.[6,7,73]

On May 29, 1897, an editorial in the *Lancet* welcomed the incubator show.[36] Concern was expressed, however, that a majority of the public might not benefit from the incubator technology, because the middle class was "not poor enough to go to the hospital, nor rich enough to purchase" the incubators. The journal proposed establishing large "incubator stations" similar to fire stations, from which the incubators could be

TABLE 1-2. The Evolution of Incubators

YEAR(S)	DEVELOPER/PRODUCT	COMMENTS
1835, ca. 1850	George von Ruehl (1769-1846)	A physician to Czarina Feodorovna, wife of Czar Paul I, Ruehl develops the first known incubator for the Imperial Foundling Hospital in St. Petersburg. About 40 of these "warming tubs" are installed in the Moscow Foundling Hospital in 1850.
1857	Jean-Louis-Paul Denucé (1824-1889)	The first *published* account of introducing an incubator is a 400-word report by Denucé. This is a "double-walled" cradle.
1880-1883	Stéphane Tarnier (1828-1897)	The Tarnier incubator is developed by M. Odile Martin, installed in 1880 at the Port-Royal Maternité.
1884	Carl Credé (1819-1892)	Credé reports the results of 647 infants treated over 20 years using an incubator similar to that of Denucé.
1887	John Bartlett	Bartlett reads a paper on a "warming-crib" based on Tarnier's concept, but uses a "thermo-syphon."
1893	Pierre Budin (1846-1907)	Budin popularizes the Tarnier incubator and establishes the world's first "special care unit for premature infants" at Maternité and Clinique Tarnier in Paris.
1893	Thomas Morgan Rotch (1849-1914)	The first American incubator with a built-in scale, wheels, and fresh-air delivery system is developed; the equipment is very expensive and elaborate.
1897	The Holt Incubator	A simplified version of the Rotch incubator is developed. In this double-walled wooden box, hot water circulates between the walls.
1897-1920s	Edward Brown, John Lyons, Joseph DeLee, Frank Allin	Many modifications are made to the early incubators by American and European physicians. These are called baby-tents, baby boxes, warming beds, and other names.
1922	Julius Hess	Hess introduces his famous incubator with an electric heating system. For transportation, he develops special boxes that can be plugged into the cigarette lighters in Chicago's taxicabs.
1930-1950s	Large-scale commercial incubators	There is worldwide distribution of Air Shields and other commercial ventilators.
1970-1980	Modern incubators	Transport incubators with built-in ventilators and monitoring equipment are developed—mobile intensive care units.

See references 6, 7, 22-24, 73, and 74 for primary citations.

loaned to the needy families. Thus, the origin of the phrase *premature infant station* has its roots in the pages of the *Lancet*.

Within 8 months of the show at Earl Court, the incubator craze was all over Britain, prompting another *Lancet* editorial.[37] This time it complained about "copycat exhibitions" organized by "all sorts of showmen . . . just as they might have exhibited marionettes, fat women, or other such catch-penny monstrosity." In many of the shows, the infants in incubators had to breathe cigar smoke and the exhaled air from thousands of visitors. Often, obnoxious odors emanated from the live leopards kept in cages next to the baby incubators to provide a dramatic contrast. Fraud was common. Some show owners brought term infants, claiming that the infants were growing, premature babies. An indignant *Lancet* asked, "Is it in keeping with the dignity of science that incubators and living babies should be exhibited amidst the aunt-sallies, merry-go-rounds, five-legged mules, wild animals, clowns, and penny peep-shows, along with the glare and noise of a vulgar fair?"

Within a year of gaining popularity at Earl Court, Couney set sail to New York, and in 1898 he organized the first U.S. incubator show at the Omaha Trans-Mississippi Exposition. Having made the United States his home by 1903, Couney began the saga of premature baby shows that lasted for nearly 40 years. He took the shows to state fairs, traveling circuses, and science expositions all over the United States (Fig. 1-8). He also established a permanent annual exhibit at New York's Coney Island.

Academic physicians were uncomfortable with making a spectacle of babies—but they grudgingly recognized the value of publicity and accepted those benefits. It is estimated that about 80,000 "Couney babies" were raised in all of the Couney exhibits. The last of the baby shows was held during the 1939-1940 season—at its site in Atlantic City there now stands a Holiday Inn. A bronze plaque has been placed on the wall next to the entrance to the hotel, commemorating the Couney shows.[73]

In the early 1920s in Chicago, Dr. Julius Hess and his nurse Ms. Evelyn Lundeen (Fig. 1-9) developed an incubator built on the concept of a double-walled metallic "cage," with warm water circulating between the walls. Hess used electricity for heating, and he

FIGURE 1-8. Incubator baby shows. **A,** People lined up to see the Infant Incubator Show, Buffalo, New York. **B,** Interior of an incubator baby show, Buffalo, New York. (**A** and **B,** From Silverman WA: Incubator-baby side shows. Pediatrics 64:127, 1979, courtesy of the American Academy of Pediatrics, 1979.)

FIGURE 1-9. Hess and Lundeen medallions at the Michael Reese Hospital, Chicago. (Photo courtesy of Tonse N. K. Raju.)

devised a system to administer free-flow oxygen. Figure 1-10 shows the Hess incubator when it was on display for 2 years at the Spertus Museum in Chicago. One of the two extant Hess incubators known to this author is now at the Museum of Surgical History in Chicago. The other is in the Smithsonian Institute but not currently on display.

In May 1922, Hess founded the first premature infant station in the United States at Sarah Morris Children's Hospital (of the Michael Reese Medical Center) in Chicago. With meticulous attention to environmental control and aseptic practices, and a regimental approach to feeding schedules using the "hands-free" method of caring, Hess and Lundeen achieved spectacular survival rates.[47,67] Hess made Couney's acquaintance in 1922; the particulars of their relationship are not clear, but Hess respected Couney for his contributions to popularizing infant care. In fact, Hess and Ms. Lundeen

FIGURE 1-10. One of two known Hess incubators, on display at the Spertus Museum in Chicago. (The incubator belongs to the International Museum of Surgical Sciences, Chicago, Ill.)

baby shows were similar to traveling moon rock exhibits, which exploited the popularity of man's landing on the moon and helped increase NASA's annual budgets.

SUPPORTIVE CARE AND OXYGEN THERAPY

In a single-page note in 1891, Bonnaire referred to Dr. Tarnier's use of oxygen in treating "debilitated" premature infants 2 years earlier[14]—this was the first published reference to the administration of supplemental oxygen in premature infants for a purpose other than resuscitation. However, the use of oxygen in premature infants did not become routine until the 1920s. Initially, a mixture of oxygen and carbon dioxide—instead of oxygen alone—was employed to treat asphyxia-induced narcosis. It was argued that oxygen relieved hypoxia, whereas carbon dioxide stimulated the respiratory center[80]; however, oxygen alone was reserved for "pure asphyxia" (whatever that meant). Only after mobile oxygen tanks became available for general use by the mid-1940s did the use of oxygen during delivery become possible on a routine basis.[51,53,74]

The success of incubator care brought new and unexpected challenges.[68] Innovative methods had to be developed to feed the increasing number of premature infants who were surviving for longer periods than ever before. Their growth needed to be monitored, and illnesses related to prematurity, such as sepsis, apnea, anemia, jaundice, and respiratory distress, had to be studied and treated. Of all of these, providing ventilatory assistance became the most urgent necessity.

helped Couney organize an exhibition at the 1933-1934 Chicago World's Fair, which was also a great hit.[67]

What of incubators in general and baby shows in particular in today's context? That the incubators were able to save babies who would otherwise die became a powerful symbol of the might of the machine. In that heroic age of mechanical revolution, this notion was all too appealing to the public and to professionals, leading to a euphoric hope that any and all human problems could be solved by machines. Such tunnel vision is quite prevalent even in today's neonatal intensive care units (NICUs). Thus, the incubator stands as the most enduring symbol of the spectacular success of modern intensive care as well as (paradoxically) its glaring failures.

The baby incubator shows of the past, on the other hand, also evoke hauntingly familiar contemporary themes. Today's news media's clamoring for stories of medical breakthroughs and the public's voyeuristic curiosity about such intensely personal events as the birth of quintuplets or sextuplets are similar to the spectacle of premature baby exhibitions. The shows are also symbolic of the difficulty in preserving a delicate balance between information and education and public awareness and sensationalism. Traveling

VENTILATORY CARE: "EXTENDED RESUSCITATION"

The first mechanical instrument used for intermittent positive pressure ventilation in newborn infants was *aerophore pulmonaire,* a simple device developed by French obstetrician Dr. Gairal.[65,66] It was a rubber bulb attached to a J-shaped tube. By placing the bent end of the tube into the infant's upper airway, one could pump air into the lungs. Holt recommended its use for resuscitation in his influential 1897 book.[48]

Before starting mechanical ventilation, however, one needed to *cannulate* the airways, a task nearly impossible without a laryngoscope and an endotracheal tube. James Blundell (1790-1878), a Scottish obstetrician, was the first to use a mechanical device for tracheal intubation in living newborn infants.[13,32] Introducing two fingers of his left hand over the infant's tongue, he would feel the epiglottis and then guide a silver pipe into the trachea with his right hand. His *tracheal pipe* had a blunt distal end and two side holes. By blowing air into the tube about 30 times a minute until the heartbeat began, Blundell saved hundreds of infants with birth asphyxia, as well as those with laryngeal

FIGURE 1-11. The Man-Can, circa 1873 to 1875. A hand-held negative-pressure ventilatory device for which a patent was applied in 1876. (From DeBono E: Eureka: How and When the Greatest Inventions Were Made: An Illustrated History of Inventions from the Wheel to the Computer. New York, Holt, Rinehart and Winston, 1974, p 159.)

diphtheria. His method of tracheal intubation is practiced in many countries even today.[85]

In the late 19th century, a wide array of instruments evolved to provide longer periods of augmented or extended ventilation for those infants who had been resuscitated in the labor room. Most of the early instruments, however, were designed for use in adults and were used later in newborns and infants, particularly to treat paralytic polio and laryngeal diphtheria.[45,78,79]

The *iron lung* (or "man-can") was one of the earliest mechanical ventilatory devices (Fig. 1-11), and a U.S. patent was issued for it in 1876.[42] In other ventilatory equipment, varying methods for rhythmic inflation and deflation of the lungs were used for prolonged ventilation.* Among those, the Fell-O'Dwyer apparatus used a unique foot-operated bellows system connected to an implement similar to the aerophore bulb.[25,65,66]

Between 1930 and 1950 there were sporadic but important reports of prolonged assisted ventilation provided to the newborn.[62,78,79] Only since the late 1950s through the 1960s, however, did more NICUs begin providing such ventilatory assistance regularly (Table 1-3), and not until the early 1970s, when continuous positive pressure was incorporated into ventilatory devices, did ventilatory care become predictably successful.[44,58,62,78]

SUPPORTIVE CARE: INTRAVENOUS FLUID AND BLOOD TRANSFUSIONS

When it comes to intravenous therapy, our legacy is one of bloodletting, not of transfusing. Blundel (of intubation fame) also made a major contribution to transfusion science. Having believed that "only human blood should be employed for humans," he developed instruments, syringes, and funnels for this purpose. In

1818, Blundel carried out the first direct transfusion from a healthy donor into a recipient; 5 of his first 10 patients survived.

Human-to-human transfusions gradually became accepted, but the 19th-century doctor was puzzled about unexpected disasters among blood transfusion recipients. It took 15 more years after Karl Landsteiner's discovery of blood groups in 1901 for the general acceptance and understanding of the scientific basis for blood group incompatibility.[87]

Adult transfusions were rare, but newborn transfusions were rarer still. On March 8, 1908, a 4-day-old term infant who had hemorrhagic disease of the newborn made history. "As the child's skin became waxen white and mucous membranes without color, it was decided to attempt transfusion of blood obtained from the infant's father," wrote Dr. Samuel Lambert from New York.[55] Surgeon Alexis Carrel from Rockefeller University Hospital performed an end-to-end anastomosis of the right popliteal vein of the baby with the left radial artery of the father. No anesthetic was given to either patient. "The amount of blood transfused could not be measured, but enough blood was allowed to flow into the baby to change her color from pale transparent whiteness to brilliant red . . . [and] as soon as the wound was sutured, the infant fed ravenously and immediately went to sleep," according to Dr. Lambert. Incidentally, Carrel was the first surgeon to develop innovative methods of suturing blood vessels—a contribution for which he received the 1912 Nobel Prize.

Despite Lambert's dramatic report, direct father-to-infant transfusion did not become routine. Because of unexpected reactions among the recipients, blood transfusions continued to be risky, in spite of proper matching of the donors' blood for major blood types. The mystery was understood only after the discovery of Rh subtypes by Landsteiner and Wiener in 1940.[87,90]

The discovery of the Rh blood types and the conquest of erythroblastosis fetalis remain rare phenomena in science—that of an orderly progression of accumulating knowledge leading to the near eradication of a disease. First came the clinical descriptions of erythroblastosis, and then evolved its treatment, followed by efforts to prevent it. These stages are superbly told in monographs and review articles.[28,29,87,90]

TOOLS AND SUPPLIES FOR NICUs

It is perhaps impossible for today's generation to realize how hard it was to perform such simple and mundane chores as the collection of blood or insertion of catheters. For intravenous therapy in children, one needed ultra-small needles, pumps, and tubing, but none were available until the 1930s. In 1912, Blackfan (1883-1941) developed an ingenious suction device for blood collection.[9] Parenteral fluid therapy was laborious, performed through venous cutdowns or subcutaneous routes. Well into the early 1970s, only a handful of laboratories in Chicago performed blood gas analyses, for which they required up to 5 mL of arterial blood samples.

References 12, 19, 20, 30, 39, 45, 46, 49, 79.

TABLE 1-3. Ventilatory Care, Respiratory Disorders, and Intensive Care

CATEGORY	APPROXIMATE TIME SPAN	PROCEDURES AND TECHNIQUES
Resuscitation and oxygen	From antiquity to early 1970s	Mouth-to-mouth breathing (although it fell from favor in the late 18th century because many influential physicians declared it a "vulgar method" of revival)
	1878	Tarnier uses oxygen in debilitated premature babies.
	1900-1930s	The Schultz, Sylvester, and Laborde methods of resuscitation involve various forms of swinging babies, traction of the tongue, and compression of the chest, respectively.
	1930-1960s	O_2 administration to the oral cavity through a rubber catheter
	1930s-1940s	Tight-fitting tracheal tube and direct tracheal O_2 administration
	1913-1920s	Byrd-Dew method: immersion in warm water, with alternate flexing and extending of the pelvis to help the "lungs open"
	1850-1930s	Dilatation of the rectum
	1930-1950s	Inhalation of O_2 and 7% CO_2 mixture (for morphine-induced narcosis)
	1940-1950s	Positive-pressure air-lock (Bloxsom method)
	1940 to late 1950s	The concept that "air in the digestive tract is good for survival" is promoted; administration of O_2 to the stomach
	1950 to late 1960s	Hyperbaric oxygen in Vickers pressure chamber
	1950-1960s	Mouth-to-mouth or mouth-to-endotracheal tube breathing
Assisted ventilation	1930s-1980s	Alexander Graham Bell develops a negative-pressure jacket.
	1930-1950	Negative-pressure ventilators and iron lungs, used rarely in infants
	1960s	Positive-pressure respirators used for prolonged ventilatory support
	1971	Continuous positive airway pressure introduced for use in newborns
	1973	Intermittent mandatory ventilator
	1970-1980s	High-frequency ventilators; continuous monitoring of pulmonary function
Surfactant	1903	Hochheim reports "hyaline membranes" noted in the lungs of infants with respiratory distress syndrome (RDS).
	1940-1950s	Clinical descriptions and pathology studied.
	1955-1956	Pattle discovers surfactant in pulmonary edema foam and lung extracts.
	1959	Avery and Mead demonstrate absence of surfactant in infants with hyaline membrane disease.[4]
	1971	Gluck introduces the lecithin-to-sphingomyelin ratio.
	1973	Liggins suggests that antenatal steroid helps mature the pulmonary surfactant system.
	1980	First effective clinical trial of postnatal surfactant therapy (bovine, Fujiwara)
	1989-1991	Commercial surfactants become available.
	1995	Widespread antenatal steroid leads to drops in rates for RDS and improves survival rates for infants with a birth weight below 1000 g, heralding a new era of epidemics of bronchopulmonary dysplasia and retinopathy of prematurity.
Border of viability debates	2005	Improved survival rates for infants between 22 and 26 weeks' gestations raise questions about the definition of border or viability, and ethics of intensive care for such infants. Debates and dilemma continue.

See references 5, 18, 25, 46, 49, 58, 61, and 88 for primary citations.

Often, the intraperitoneal route was used to infuse fluids, and the sagittal sinus or the anterior fontanelle was punctured to draw blood from newborn infants.[10,91] In 1923, Sidbury introduced umbilical venous catheterization for neonatal blood transfusions,[72] and in the 1950s Diamond and colleagues began using this route for exchange transfusions.[28,29] Only in 1951 were indwelling polyethylene tubes introduced for gastric feeding.[70]

PEDIATRIC SURGERY—NOT FOR RABBITS ANYMORE

As the trend of specialization among surgical subspecialties became popular, the generalist surgeons resisted the change. Dr. Edward Churchill, a famous surgeon, once remarked that his surgical residents at Massachusetts General Hospital "were quite proficient at operating on rabbits" and, therefore, there was no need for a subspecialty in pediatric surgery.[35] Despite those objections, Harvard Medical School founded the first department of pediatric surgery in 1941 and named William E. Ladd as its chair. Ladd and his pupils (among others) went on to show that pediatric and neonatal surgery was not the same as operating on rabbits.

NEONATOLOGY EDUCATION AND RESEARCH

Of all the advances in the 20th century, none has made a greater impact than the publication and dissemination of scientific information through journals and books. Duncan has compiled an impressive list of classic papers in neonatal and perinatal medicine.[31] The impact of current computer technology, the Internet, and the electronic age on neonatal education remains to be assessed.

GLOBAL NEONATAL CARE

By the middle of the 20th century, scores of neonatal units were built using the Hess model in a number of European countries (Fig. 1-12), including the United Kingdom.[33,61] During the final decades of the 20th century, Asian countries developed indigenous means of improving neonatal resuscitation and intensive care of sick newborn infants. The collective impact of these international initiatives on global neonatal care has yet to be assessed.[84]

THE SHAPE OF FUTURE NICUs AND SOME REMAINING PROBLEMS

Although today's NICU is a technologic marvel, conceptually it remains a miniaturized version of the adult

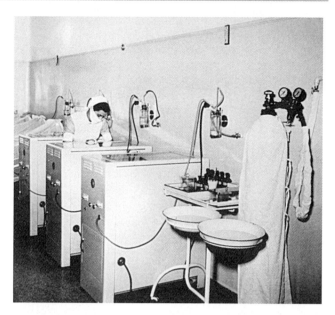

FIGURE 1-12. The first preterm infant unit in Athens, Greece, using incubators with oxygen flowing into them (circa 1947). (Courtesy of John Sofatzis, MD, Athens, Greece.)

intensive care unit (ICU). Interest in environmental influences on brain growth may change the shape of future NICUs. The Neonatal Individualized Developmental Care and Assessment Program (NIDCAP)[2] promises to transform the noisy, technical, and impersonal intensive care environment into a baby-friendly unit. Several ultramodern NICUs have now been built on the concepts of environmental care. Such "kind and gentle" NICUs may be what Tarnier, Budin, Hess, and others conceived of some 100 years ago.

Despite incredible advances in the care of premature infants, today's scientists are facing many unresolved issues: limits of viability, cost of care, quality of life for intensive care "graduates," and an ever-increasing battle against opportunistic, nosocomial microorganisms. Furthermore, one of the major concerns remains the definition of border of viability and the ethics of providing intensive or palliative care for infants born between 22 and 25 weeks' gestation.

These and similar concerns also vexed the early pioneers of our subspecialty. Future historians may assess this century of neonatal medicine with the same sense of surprised wonder and awe that we now feel when remembering the days of infant hatcheries and baby incubator shows.

SOME FAMOUS HIGH-RISK INFANTS

Shakespeare's King Henry VI offers one of the most poignant musings on the burdens of disability and the difficult birth (owing to footling presentation) of his brother, Duke of Gloucester, who later became Richard III. Henry says to the Duke,[54] who was supposedly born premature (not confirmed by other historians), "Thy mother felt more than a mother's pain, yet brought forth less than a mother's hope." King Richard himself in a different Shakespeare play bemoans his misfortune.[54] "Deformed, unfinish'd, sent before my times/ Into this breathing world scarce half made up."

Did King Richard suffer from hemiplegic cerebral palsy as a consequence of prematurity? We cannot be sure. The list of leaders, celebrities, and famous persons supposed to have been regarded as being at high risk at birth (Table 1-4), however, is impressive,[64] although the authenticity of those stories is difficult to confirm

TABLE 1-4. Ominous Beginnings for Some Famous Personalities

CATEGORY	NAME	DESCRIPTION*
Religious	Moses	Jewish tradition holds that Moses was born "6 months and 1 day" after he was conceived; thus, he could be hidden for 3 months from Pharoah's soldiers who were looking to find and kill the liberator of Jews.[50,60]
Historical personalities and characters	Duke of Gloucester (later Richard III) (1452-1485)	Footling presentation, possibly premature; might have had cerebral palsy (hemiplegia?)[54]
	Macduff (Scottish nobleman in Shakespeare's *Macbeth*)	Delivered by cesarean section after his mother's death, thus "not of a woman born" but of a corpse[54]
Artists and writers	Jonathan Swift (1667-1745)	Mentioned by Cone[24]
	Licetus Fortunio (1577-1657)	"A fetus no more than five and one-half inches" at birth. His father, a doctor, raised him in an oven, "similar to chicken hatching method used in Egypt."[81] The boy becomes scholar, writing 80 books.
	Pablo Picasso (1881-1973)	Left on the table as a stillbirth; his uncle, Don Salvador, a doctor, resuscitated him.
	Voltaire (1694-1778)	Premature and asphyxiated, the "puny little boy" was not expected to live and was hurriedly baptized; he was raised in the attic to keep him warm.
	Samuel Johnson (1709-1784)	A huge baby, he was "strangely inert" at birth, required slapping and shaking. With persuasion, he made a few whimpers and lived.
	Johann Wolfgang von Goethe (1749-1823)	After 3 days of labor, his mother delivered him; he was "lifeless and miserable" and thought to be stillborn at birth.
	Anna Pavlova (1882-1931)	Famous Russian ballerina, "a premature, so puny and weak," she was wrapped in cotton wool for 3 months.
	Thomas Hardy (1840-1928)	He was thrown aside as dead at birth. "A good slapping" from the midwife revived him.
	Sidney Poitier (born 1927)	Being 3 months premature, he was so small that his father "could place him in a shoebox." His grandmother said that despite prematurity, he would "walk with the kings." He did, when he became Bahamian ambassador to Japan in the 1990s.†
Scientists	Johannes Kepler (1571-1630)	German astronomer: a "seven-month" baby; estimated IQ, 161
	Christopher Wren (1632-1723)	Mentioned by Cone[24]
	Isaac Newton (1642-1727)	Thought to be "as good as dead" at birth. He was such a "tiny mite" that he could be placed in a quart mug.
Politicians	Franklin D. Roosevelt (1882-1945)	Weighed 10 pounds at birth, but was "blue and limp with a death like respiratory standstill" from too much chloroform given to his mother, Sara Roosevelt.
	Winston Churchill (1874-1965)	His early birth "upset the ball." Later a duchess remarked that the baby had such a lusty "earth-shaking" cry as she had ever heard. Recent historians doubt his premature birth.

*The biographical notes are derived mostly from anecdotal statements of historians or family members or are from later recollection by the characters themselves; thus, we cannot be certain of the scientific validity of these stories.
†Quoted by Sidney Poitier in the television show "Biography," CNN, Spring 2000.

because most of them were derived from anecdotal statements.

ACKNOWLEDGMENTS

I sincerely thank Kristine M. McCulloch, MD, for helping during the preparation of the manuscript, and I thank all of the copyright holders for permission to reproduce the illustrations used in this chapter.

REFERENCES

1. Akerrén Y, Fürstenberg N: Gastrointestinal administration of oxygen in treatment of asphyxia in the newborn. J Obstet Gynaecol Br Emp 57:705, 1950.
2. Als H et al: Individualized developmental care for the very low-birth-weight preterm infant: Medical and neurofunctional effects. JAMA 272:853, 1994.
3. Apgar V: A proposal for a new method of evaluation of the newborn infant. Anesth Analg 32:260, 1953.
4. Avery ME, Mead J: Surface properties in relation to atelectasis and hyaline membrane disease. Am J Dis Child 97:517, 1959.
5. Avery ME: Surfactant deficiency in hyaline membrane disease: The story of discovery. Am J Respir Crit Care Med 161:1074, 2000.
6. Baker JP: The incubator controversy: Pediatricians and the origins of premature infant technology in the United States, 1890-1910. Pediatrics 87:654, 1991.
7. Baker JP: The Machine in the Nursery: Incubator Technology and the Origins of Newborn Intensive Care. Baltimore, Johns Hopkins University Press, 1996.
8. Barcroft J: Research on Pre-natal Life, vol 1. Oxford, Blackwell Scientific, 1977.
9. Blackfan KD: Apparatus for collecting infant's blood for Wassermann reaction. Am J Dis Child 4:33, 1912.
10. Blackfan KD, Maxcy KF: The intraperitoneal injection of saline solution. Am J Dis Child 15:19, 1918.
11. Blumfeld-Kusinski R: Not of a Woman Born: Representation of Childbirth in Medieval and Renaissance Culture. Ithaca, NY, Cornell University Press, 1990.
12. Bloxsom A: Resuscitation of the newborn infant: Use of positive pressure oxygen-air lock. J Pediatr 37:311, 1950.
13. Blundell J: Principles and Practice of Obstetrics. London, E. Cox, 1834, p 246.
14. Bonnaire E: Inhalations of oxygen in the newborn. Arch Pediatr 8:769, 1891.
15. Budin P, Maloney WJ (translator): The Nursling: The Feeding and Hygiene of Premature and Full-Term Infants. London, Caxton, 1907.
16. Butterfield LJ: Virginia Apgar, MD, MPhH. Neonatal Netw 13:81, 1994.
17. Campbell DJ et al: High maternal mortality in certain areas: Reports on public health and medical subjects. London, Ministry of Health and Department of Health Publications, No. 68, 1932.
18. Clements JA, Avery ME: Lung surfactant and neonatal respiratory distress syndrome. Am J Respir Crit Care Med 157:S59, 1998.
19. Comroe JH Jr: Retrospectroscope: Man-cans. Am Rev Resp Dis 116:945, 1977.
20. Comroe JH Jr: Man-cans (conclusion). Am Rev Resp Dis 116:1011, 1977.
21. Cone TE Jr: 200 Years of Feeding Infants in America. Columbus, Ohio, Ross Laboratories, 1976.
22. Cone TE Jr: History of American Pediatrics. Boston, Little Brown, 1979, p 57.
23. Cone TE Jr: The first published report of an incubator for use in the care of the premature infants (1857). Am J Dis Child 135:658, 1981.
24. Cone TE Jr: Perspective in neonatology. In Smith GF, Vidyasagar D (eds): Historical Review and Recent Advances in Neonatal and Perinatal Medicine, vol 1, Neonatal Medicine, Evansville, Ind, Ross Publication, 1984, p 9.
25. DeBard ML: The history of cardiopulmonary resuscitation. Ann Emerg Med 9:273, 1980.
26. DeLee J: A Brief History of the Chicago Lying-In Hospital. Chicago, Alumni Association Lying-In Hospital and Dispensary Souvenir, 1895, p 1931.
27. DeLee JB: Infant incubation, with the presentation of a new incubator and a description of the system at the Chicago Lying-in Hospital. Chicago Medical Recorder 22:22, 1902.
28. Diamond LK et al: Erythroblastosis fetalis and its association with universal edema of the fetus, icterus gravis neonatorum, and anemia of the newborn. J Pediatr 1:269, 1932.
29. Diamond LK et al: Erythroblastosis fetalis. VII: Treatment with exchange transfusion. N Engl J Med 244:39, 1951.
30. Donald I, Lord J: Augmented respiration: Studies in atelectasis neonatorum. Lancet 1:9, 1953.
31. Duncan RG: "Neonatology on the Web." Available at www.neonatology.org.
32. Dunn PM: Dr. James Blundell (1790-1878) and neonatal resuscitation. Arch Dis Child Fetal Neonatal Ed 64:494, 1988.
33. Dunn PM: The development of newborn care in the UK since 1930. J Perinatol 18:471, 1998.
34. Dunn PM: Sir Joseph Barcroft of Cambridge (1872-1947) and prenatal research. Arch Dis Child Fetal Neonatal Ed 82:F75, 2000.
35. Easterbrook G: Surgeon Koop. Knoxville, Tenn, Whittle Direct Books, 1991.
36. Editorial. The Victorian Era exhibition at Earl's Court. Lancet 2:161, 1897.
37. Editorial. The danger of making a public show of incubator for babies. Lancet 1:390, 1898.
38. Gartner LM: Dr. Harry Gordon. In Smith GF, Vidyasagar D (eds): Historical Review and Recent Advances in Neonatal and Perinatal Medicine, vol 1, Neonatal Medicine, Evansville, Ind, Ross Publication, 1984, p xiv.
39. Gilmartin ME: Body ventilators: Equipment and techniques. Respir Care Clin North Am 2:195, 1996.
40. Ginzberg L: The Legend of the Jews. II: Bible Times and Characters from Joseph to the Exodus. (Translated from the German manuscript by Henrietta Szold.) Philadelphia, Jewish Publication Society of America, 1989, p 262.
41. Goodlin R: History of fetal monitoring. Am J Obstet Gynecol 133:323, 1979.
42. Gould D: Iron lung. In DeBono (ed): Eureka! An Illustrated History of Invention from the Wheel to the Computer. New York, Holt, Rinehart and Winston, 1974, p 160.
43. Graham H: Eternal Eve: The History of Gynecology and Obstetrics. Garden City, NY, Doubleday, 1951.
44. Gregory GA et al: Treatment of idiopathic respiratory distress syndrome with continuous positive pressure. N Engl J Med 284:1333, 1971.
45. Henderson AR: Resuscitation experiments and breathing apparatus of Alexander Graham Bell. Chest 62:311, 1972.

A note on the references: Citations are restricted to secondary sources and scholarly reviews; interested readers can find the original references in many of these secondary references.

46. Henderson Y: The inhalation method of resuscitation from asphyxia of the newborn. Am J Obst Gynecol 21:542, 1931.

47. Hess JH: Premature and Congenitally Diseased Infants. Philadelphia, Lea & Febiger, 1922.

48. Holt LE: The Diseases of Infants and Children. New York, Appleton, 1897, p 12.

49. Hutchison JH et al: Controlled trials of hyperbaric oxygen and tracheal intubation in asphyxia neonatorum. Lancet 1:935, 1966.

50. Isaiah AB, Sharfman B: The Pentateuch and Rashi's Commentary: A Linear Translation into English. Exodus. New York, S. S. & R., 1960, p 9.

51. Jacobson RM, Feinstein AR: Oxygen as a cause of blindness in premature infants: "Autopsy" of a decade of errors in clinical epidemiologic research. J Clin Epidemiol 11:1265, 1992.

52. James LS et al: Intragastric oxygen and resuscitation of the newborn. Acta Pediatr 52:245, 1963.

53. James LS, Lanman JT: History of oxygen therapy and retrolental fibroplasia. Pediatrics 57(Suppl):59, 1976.

54. Kail AC: The Medical Mind of Shakespeare. Balgowhas, Australia, Williams & Wilkins, 1986, p 101.

55. Lambert SW: Melaena neonatorum with report of a case cured by transfusion. Med Rec 73:885, 1908.

56. Loudon I: Deaths in childbed from the 18th century to 1935. Med Hist 30:1, 1986.

57. Morton LT, Moore RJ: A Chronology of the Diseases & Related Sciences. Aldershot, UK, Scolar Press, 1997, p 84.

58. Murphy D et al: The Drinker respirator treatment of the immediate asphyxia of the newborn: With a report of 350 cases. Am J Obstet Gynecol 21:528, 1931.

59. National Library of Medicine: Available at http://igm.nlm.nih.gov.

60. Nelson NM: An appreciation of Clement Smith. In Smith GF, Vidyasagar D (eds): Historical Review and Recent Advances in Neonatal and Perinatal Medicine. Vol 1: Neonatal Medicine. Evansville, Ind, Ross Publication, 1984, p xii.

61. O'Dowd MJ, Phillipp AE: The History of Obstetrics and Gynecology. New York, Parthenon, 1994.

62. Papadopoulos MD, Swyer PR: Assisted ventilation in terminal hyaline membrane disease. Arch Dis Child 39:481, 1964.

63. Radcliffe W: The Secret Instrument. London, William Heinemann Medical Books, 1947.

64. Raju TNK: Some famous "high-risk" newborn babies. In Smith GF, Vidyasagar D (eds): Historical Review and Recent Advances in Neonatal and Perinatal Medicine, vol 2, Perinatal Medicine. Evansville, Ind, Ross Publication, 1984, p 187.

65. Raju TNK: The principles of life: Highlights from the history of pulmonary physiology. In Donn SM (ed): Neonatal and Pediatric Pulmonary Graphics: Principles and Clinical Applications. Armonk, NY, Futura, 1998, p 3.

66. Raju TNK: The history of neonatal respiration: Tales of heroism and desperation. Clin Perinatol 1999; 26:629.

67. Rambar AC: Julius Hess, MD. In Smith GF, Vidyasagar D (eds): Historical Review and Recent Advances in Neonatal and Perinatal Medicine, vol 2, Perinatal Medicine. Evansville, Ind, Ross Publication, 1984, p 161.

68. Ransom SW: The care of premature and feeble infants. Pediatrics 9:322, 1890.

69. Roche T: A refuge for throwaways: The spate of "Dumpster babies" stirs a movement to provide a safe space for unwanted newborns. Time 155:50, 2000.

70. Royce S et al: Indwelling polyethylene nasogastric tube for feeding premature infants. Pediatrics 8:79, 1951.

71. Schaffer AJ: Diseases of the Newborn. Philadelphia, Saunders, 1960, p 1.

72. Sidbury JB: Transfusion through the umbilical vein in hemorrhage of the newborn. Am J Dis Child 25:290, 1923.

73. Silverman WA: Incubator-baby side shows. Pediatrics 64:127, 1979.

74. Silverman WA: Retrolental Fibroplasia: A Modern Parable. New York, Grune & Stratton, 1980.

75. Smith CA: Physiology of the Newborn Infant. Springfield, Charles C. Thomas, 1945.

76. Spaulding M, Welch P: Nurturing Yesterday's Child: A Portrayal of the Drake Collection of Pediatric History. Philadelphia, BC Decker, 1991, p 110.

77. Speert H: Obstetrics and Gynecology in America: A History. Baltimore, Waverly Press, 1980.

78. Stalhman MT: Assisted ventilation in newborn infants. In Smith GF, Vidyasagar D (eds): Historical Review and Recent Advances in Neonatal and Perinatal Medicine, vol 2, Perinatal Medicine. Evansville, Ind, Ross Publication, 1984, p 21.

79. Stern L et al: Negative pressure artificial respiration: Use in treatment of respiratory failure of the newborn. Can Med Assoc J 102:595, 1970.

80. Stern L: Thermoregulation in the newborn: Historical, physiological, and clinical considerations. In Smith GF, Vidyasagar D (eds): Historical Review and Recent Advances in Neonatal and Perinatal Medicine, vol 1, Neonatal Medicine. Evansville, Ind, Ross Publication, 1984, p 35.

81. Sterne L: The Life and Opinions of Tristram Shandy, Gentleman. New York, Penguin, 1997, p 231.

82. Tempkin O: On the care of the newborn. In Soranus' Gynecology. Baltimore, Johns Hopkins Press, 1956, p 79.

83. Tuchman BU: A Distant Mirror: The Calamitous 14th Century. New York, Ballantine Books, 1978, p 49.

84. Vidyasagar D et al: Evolution of neonatal and pediatric critical care in India. Crit Care Clin 13:331, 1997.

85. Wijesundera CD: Digital intubation of the trachea. Ceylon Med J 35:81, 1990.

86. Wilson A: The Making of Man-midwifery: Childbearing in England 1660-1770. Cambridge, Mass, Harvard University Press, 1995, p 1.

87. Winthrobe MM: Blood: Pure and Eloquent. New York, McGraw-Hill, 1981.

88. Wrigley M, Nandi P: The Sparklet carbon dioxide resuscitator. Anaesthesia 49:148, 1994.

89. Young JH: Caesarean Section: The History and Development of the Operation from Earliest Times. London, HK Lewis, 1994.

90. Zimerman DA: Rh. New York, MacMillan, 1973.

91. Zimmerman JJ, Strauss RH: History and current application of intravenous therapy in children. Pediatr Emerg Care 5:120, 1989.

CHAPTER 2

Epidemiology and Perinatal Services

Michele C. Walsh and Avroy A. Fanaroff

PART 1

Epidemiology

Michele C. Walsh and Avroy A. Fanaroff

OVERVIEW

The neonatal-perinatal period is a time when the mother and fetus experience a period of rapid growth and development. At birth, the fetus makes an abrupt transition from the protective environment of the uterus to the outside world; the newly born baby must undergo extreme physiologic changes to survive this transition. Therefore, it is not surprising that the highest risk of infant death occurs during the first 24 hours after birth. Increased rates of mortality and morbidity continue during the *neonatal period*, from birth to the 28th day of life.

Mortality and morbidity rates are high early in life because the fetus and infant are vulnerable to numerous metabolic, genetic, physiologic, social, economic, and environmental injuries. These factors influence the gestation, delivery, and neonatal period and have a major impact on the health of the fetus and infant.

The high incidence of mortality and morbidity during the *perinatal period*, which starts at the 28th week of pregnancy and extends to the 28th day after birth, makes it important to identify, as early as possible, the mothers, fetuses, and infants who are at greatest risk. Of equal importance is the need to lower the risk of morbidity, especially for handicapping conditions such as mental retardation. There is increasing evidence that early recognition of women with high-risk pregnancies, and of high-risk infants, followed by appropriate prenatal, intrapartum, and postpartum care, can reduce the incidence of handicapping conditions and will reduce the incidence of infant mortality.[2,9,10]

Death of an infant is a source of anguish and grief to the parents and relatives. Those infants who survive with disabilities and disease must endure personal suffering and may be a continuing source of pain, anguish, and loss of resources for their parents and society. They may also impose a biologic burden on future generations by increasing the frequency of maladaptive genes in the population. In addition to the human tragedy, the fiscal impact of these problems on our society is estimated to be in the billions of dollars each year.[4]

Infants who are born before term gestation have the greatest risk of dying during infancy and of morbidity during childhood.[5,6] Infants with a *low birthweight* (LBW, less than 2500 g), are 40 times more likely to die than infants with normal birthweight, and infants with a *very low birthweight* (VLBW, less than 1500 g) are 200 times more likely to die. Infants with LBW are at a much higher risk of being born with cerebral palsy, mental retardation, and other sensory and cognitive impairments, compared with infants of normal birthweight. Surviving infants with LBW also have an increased incidence of disability for a broad range of conditions, including various neurodevelopmental handicaps, respiratory illness, and injuries acquired as a result of neonatal intensive care. Moreover, these infants often have a diminished ability to adapt socially, psychologically, and physically to an increasingly complex environment. The risk factors for high-risk pregnancies that are often associated with LBW are listed in Box 2-1.

It is becoming evident that important antecedents of many adult diseases, such as coronary artery disease, chronic renal and liver disease, and obesity, may have roots in early childhood, which implies that there may be very early opportunities for the prevention of adult chronic diseases. Further improvement in longevity and decreased morbidity are likely to result from a better understanding of the origins of adult disease in fetal life and infancy and from the prevention and early treatment of these diseases.

HIGH-RISK INFANTS

To decrease infant morbidity and mortality, pregnant women and infants at high risk should be identified as early as possible. Most high-risk infants can be

BOX 2-1. Factors Associated With High-Risk Pregnancy

Economic
Poverty
Unemployment
No health insurance; insufficient health insurance
Poor access to prenatal care

Cultural-Behavioral
Low educational status
Poor health care attitudes
No or inadequate prenatal care
Cigarette, alcohol, drug abuse
Age <16 or >35 years
Unmarried
Short interpregnancy interval
Lack of support group (husband, family, religion)
Stress (physical, psychological)
African-American race
Abusive partner

Biologic-Genetic
Previous LBW infant
Low maternal weight at her birth
Low weight for height
Poor weight gain during pregnancy
Short stature
Poor nutrition
Inbreeding (autosomal recessive?)
Intergenerational effects
Hereditary diseases (inborn error of metabolism)

Reproductive
Previous cesarean section
Previous infertility
Prolonged gestation
Prolonged labor
Previous infant with cerebral palsy, mental retardation, birth trauma, congenital anomalies
Abnormal lie (breech)
Abruption
Multiple gestation
Premature rupture of membranes
Infections (systemic, amniotic, extra-amniotic, cervical)
Preeclampsia or eclampsia
Uterine bleeding (abruptio placentae, placenta previa)
Parity (0 or more than 5)
Uterine or cervical anomalies
Fetal disease
Abnormal fetal growth
Idiopathic premature labor
Iatrogenic prematurity
High or low levels of maternal serum α-fetoprotein

Medical
Diabetes mellitus
Hypertension
Congenital heart disease
Autoimmune disease
Sickle cell anemia
TORCH infection
Intercurrent surgery or trauma
Sexually transmitted diseases
Maternal hypercoagulable states

LBW, low birthweight; TORCH, toxoplasmosis, other agents, rubella, cytomegalovirus, herpes simplex.
From Stoll JB, Kliegman RM: Section 1: Noninfectious disorders. In Behrman RE et al (eds): Nelson Textbook of Pediatrics, 16th ed. Philadelphia, WB Saunders, 2000, p 461.

identified before birth (see Box 2-1). Others are identified in the delivery room by abnormal growth status, small size for gestational age (weight less than 3% for gestational age) or large size for gestational age (weight greater than 90% for gestational age), or congenital malformation. Examination of a fresh placenta, cord, and membranes can alert the physician to a newborn infant at high risk.

Infant Mortality

Infant mortality is a critical measure of the health and welfare of a population.[1] In 2002, 4.01 million infants were born in the United States, and 27,600 died before reaching age 1 year, resulting in an *infant mortality rate* of 6.9 deaths per thousand live births. Rates of infant death in the United States have been dropping steadily for at least 30 years and reached an all-time low in 2002 (Fig. 2-1).[1] Despite the constant improvement in national infant mortality rates, the United States ranks only 25th in the world in infant mortality, well behind

Sweden, Japan, Singapore, and Hong Kong.[1] Paradoxically, the birthweight-specific mortality in the United States is relatively low. That is, at each birthweight level, the infant mortality in the United States is very low. This low rate of birthweight-specific mortality is due to advances in neonatal care systems; the majority of extremely tiny infants who weigh as little as 750 g at birth are now surviving.[8]

Most notable in the United States is the large disparity between African-American and white infant mortality. The mortality rate for African-American infants is more than double that for white infants (Fig. 2-2). In recent years, this ethnic and racial disparity has widened because the rate of decline in infant mortality has been higher among white infants than among African-American infants. Approximately half of all infant deaths were due to one of the four leading causes of infant death in 2001: congenital anomalies, short gestation and low birthweight, sudden infant death syndrome, and maternal complications of pregnancy.[1,3] Of the four leading causes of infant deaths,

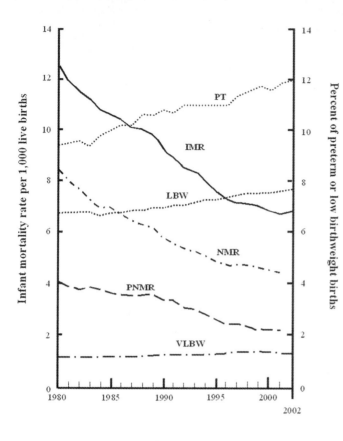

FIGURE 2-1. Infant (IMR), neonatal (NMR), and postneonatal (PNMR) mortality rates are shown annually from 1980 to 2002 in the United States. Total preterm (PT) births, low birthweight (LBW) births, and very low birthweight (VLBW) births are also shown. IMR has declined more than 40% since 1980. NMR declined more rapidly during the 1980s, whereas PNMR declined more rapidly during the 1990s. (From Arias E et al: Annual summary of vital statistics—2002. Pediatrics 112:1215, 2003.)

African-American infants are much more likely to die from being born too soon or too small and from maternal complications of pregnancy.

Infant deaths are divided into two categories according to age: *neonatal* (deaths of infants younger than 28 days) and *postneonatal* (deaths of infants between the ages of 28 days and 1 year). A decline in infant mortality rates was observed for both neonatal deaths (4.8 per 1000) and postneonatal deaths (2.4 per 1000).[5] Infant mortality numbers have declined by more than 40% since 1980. Neonatal death rates declined more steeply in the 1980s, and postneonatal death rates declined more steeply in the 1990s.[5] Neonatal deaths are generally attributable to factors that occur during pregnancy, such as congenital malformations, low birth rate, maternal toxic exposures (smoking or other forms of drug abuse), and lack of appropriate medical care.[7] In contrast, postneonatal deaths are generally associated with the infant's environmental circumstances, such as poverty, which often results in inadequate food, housing, sanitation, and medical care.

The decline in neonatal deaths among infants with LBW in the 1990s may be because of increased survival in neonatal intensive care units, healthier babies with LBW, or both.[5,6,8] It is estimated that two thirds of the decline in severity-adjusted mortality was due to increased survival in neonatal intensive care and that one third was due to healthier babies with LBW. Increased survival in neonatal intensive care is attributed to the more aggressive use of respiratory and cardiovascular treatments. The improved health of infants with LBW is attributed to improvements in obstetric and delivery room care.

Generally, for any given gestational age, the lower the infant birthweight, the higher the neonatal mortality; and for any given birthweight, the younger the gestational age, the higher the neonatal mortality. Infant death rates drop steeply with increasing infant birthweight. The lowest risk of infant death occurs among

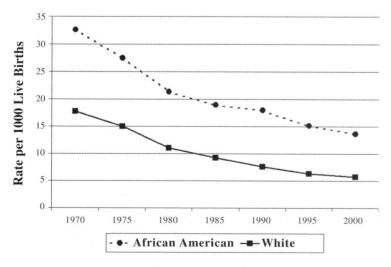

FIGURE 2-2. Infant mortality rates by race, 1970 to 1999. (From Hoyert DL et al: Deaths: Final data for 1999. Natl Vital Stat Rep 49:1, 2001.)

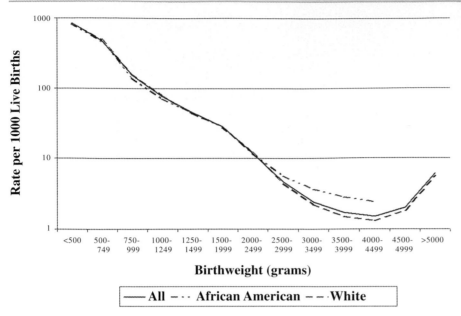

FIGURE 2-3. Infant mortality rates by birth-weight, United States, 2000 linked infant birth-death data set. (From Mathews TJ et al: Infant mortality statistics from the 2000 period linked birth/infant death data set. Natl Vital Stat Rep 50:1, 2002.)

infants with birthweights of 3000 to 4000 g, and risk increases slightly for infants over 4000 g (Fig. 2-3) and for those whose gestational age is older than 42 weeks.[5] Infants who survive past the first 28 days of life have a vastly better prognosis.

Infant Morbidity

PRETERM, LOW BIRTHWEIGHT, AND SMALL FOR GESTATIONAL AGE INFANTS

Live-born infants born before 37 completed weeks of gestation (less than 259 days after the date of the mother's last menstrual period) are defined as *preterm.* Measures of live-born infant size include *low birthweight* (infants weighing less than 2500 g) and two subgroups of LBW, *moderately low birthweight* (infants weighing between 1500 and 2499 g) and *very low birthweight* (infants weighing less than 1500 g). Other measures take into consideration both gestational age and weight, such as *small for gestational age* (SGA), defined as live-born infants weighing less than the 10th percentile for gestational age; *appropriate for gestational age,* defined as infants weighing between the 10th and the 90th percentiles for gestational age; and *large for gestational age,* defined as infants weighing more than the 90th percentile for gestational age.

The health of a baby with LBW is directly related to its gestational age. An 1800-g infant born at term is very different from an 1800-g infant born at 32 weeks. An 1800-g infant born at term is defined as LBW and SGA, but an 1800-g infant born at 32 weeks is defined as LBW, preterm, and appropriate for gestational age. Two 1800-g infants of unequal gestational ages would obviously require very different care (see Chapter 13).

In the United States today, infants with LBW account for a relatively greater proportion of infant deaths than in the past. Early in the 20th century, two thirds of infant deaths occurred in the postneonatal period,

primarily from infectious diseases. However, by 1950, 7.5% of live-born infants weighed less than 2500 g, and two thirds of all infant deaths occurred in the neonatal period. The causes of these deaths were related to antenatal and intrapartum events, such as birth injury, asphyxia, congenital malformations, and "immaturity." Advances in the development of perinatal care in the 1950s and 1960s came as a result of the awareness of the increased morbidity in surviving infants with LBW coupled with a greater understanding of fetal and infant nutrition, pharmacology, and pathophysiology. The infant mortality rate decreased 47% from 1965 to 1980, primarily because of the increased survival of high-risk infants with LBW. Regionalization of neonatal intensive care has brought perinatal intensive care to most families in need and has contributed significantly to the increase in the fraction of infants with LBW and VLBW who are cared for in tertiary centers. Decreased rates of neonatal mortality also were observed after the introduction of regionalized care[6] (see Part 2).

At the beginning of the 1980s, despite their increased survival rates, infants with LBW still accounted for two thirds of the neonatal deaths, and infants with VLBW accounted for half. Surviving infants with LBW also remained three times as likely as infants of normal birthweight to have adverse neurologic sequelae. The risk of adverse sequelae increases with decreasing birthweight. Lower respiratory tract problems, particularly infections, are more common, as are complications of neonatal care.

National rates of LBW have been essentially stable for the past four decades. The seemingly contradictory decline in infant mortality without parallel declines in LBW or preterm birth is due to the increasing survival of infants with LBW, not to prevention of LBW and preterm birth. Improvements in neonatal intensive care and in new therapies such as surfactant have resulted in measurable decreases in infant mortality and morbidity.

A slight unexplained increase in LBW was observed among African-American infants in the late 1980s. The risk of having a baby with LBW is increased among African-American women, women who smoke during pregnancy, unmarried women, women with low educational attainment, women who have no or inadequate prenatal care, and women who have had a previous infant with LBW (see Box 2-1).

There is a substantial and persistent difference between African-American and white infants in the risk of LBW and preterm delivery. African-American women are twice as likely to have a baby with LBW than white women and 2.6 times more likely than Chinese-American women. The higher LBW rate among African-American women has been observed for more than 20 years. African-American infants are more likely to die of preventable causes than are white infants. In addition, African-American infants have significantly higher rates of mortality for every cause of infant death except congenital anomalies and sudden infant death syndrome.

Decades of research about the disparities in LBW rates and infant mortality between African-American and white infants have not been able to explain the racial disparities in birth outcomes. Scientists have studied the impact of education, maternal age, vaginal infection, exposure to cigarette smoke, use of alcohol, stress, socioeconomic status, and many other risk factors. None of these factors explain the racial disparities in death or LBW rates. Compounding the widening gap between African-American and white rates of LBW is the increasing number of women at high risk in the population. Increases during the 1980s in AIDS, poverty, use of illicit drugs such as crack cocaine, syphilis, and births to unmarried women are additional factors that are associated with further increases in infant mortality and LBW.

Conditions that make the uterus unable to retain the fetus, interference with the course of pregnancy, premature separation of the placenta, or a stimulus to produce uterine contractions before term are generally associated with preterm infants with an appropriate weight for gestational age. Medical conditions that interfere with the circulation and efficiency of the placenta, the development or growth of the fetus, or the general health and nutrition of the mother are associated with infants who are small for gestational age.

DISEASE IN LOW-BIRTHWEIGHT INFANTS
Despite a substantial overlap, the incidence of certain neonatal risks varies with birthweight, gestational age, and birthweight for gestational age. Problems of major clinical significance associated with preterm birth include respiratory distress (hyaline membrane disease, pulmonary hemorrhage, transient tachypnea, congenital pneumonia, pneumothorax, bronchopulmonary dysplasia), recurrent apnea, hypoglycemia, hypocalcemia, hyperbilirubinemia, anemia, edema, cerebral anoxia, circulatory instability, hypothermia, bacterial sepsis, and disseminated intravascular coagulopathies. In addition, preterm infants often have a weak or uncoordinated ability to feed and a prolonged failure to gain weight.

Infants who are SGA are a heterogeneous population, even when those with congenital anomalies and infections are excluded. They tend to have problems related more to their gestational age than to their birthweight. Preterm infants who are SGA have a lower incidence of respiratory distress syndrome than is expected for their birthweight. Problems encountered in infants who are SGA include perinatal asphyxia, hypoglycemia, hypothermia, meconium aspiration, necrotizing enterocolitis, polycythemia, and illnesses related to congenital anomalies, syndromes, or infections. The prognosis depends in part on the cause of their growth retardation (see Chapter 13). Head circumference that is less than the 10th percentile at birth, and abnormal results from a newborn neurologic examination are associated with poor growth, later microcephaly, and neurologic deficits.

Hemorrhage is frequent and often severe in infants with LBW. Subcutaneous ecchymosis and subependymal and intraventricular hemorrhage are frequent. Contributing causes may be increased capillary fragility (including arterial and venous networks in friable periventricular germinal tissue) and increased vascular pressure. Sudden shock during the first few days of life often is due to massive intraventricular hemorrhage, which occurs predominantly in very small preterm infants. Less-severe degrees of hemorrhage may be associated with lethargy, seizures, apnea, and an acute fall in hematocrit level. Pulmonary hemorrhage has a similar pattern of increased incidence and high mortality in preterm infants.

Respiratory distress syndrome is most frequent and mortality is highest in infants of shortest gestation; incidence and mortality fall progressively with increasing gestational age (see Chapter 42, Part 3).

There is a higher *congenital malformation rate* in preterm infants with LBW and in term infants who are SGA than in term infants of normal birthweight. Those with the slowest intrauterine growth rates have the highest incidence of malformations. The incidence of *patent ductus arteriosus* is much higher in infants with LBW and in those whose gestational age is less than 34 weeks than among larger or older infants (see Chapter 43).

Hypoglycemia may occur in 15% of preterm infants and in up to 65% of infants who are SGA. Hyperglycemia is common in extremely small infants who receive high concentrations of glucose or who develop sepsis (see Chapter 47, Part 1). Recurrent apnea, necrotizing enterocolitis, and retinopathy of prematurity occur most commonly in infants with VLBW and in those with shorter gestations.

FUTURE PROGRESS

Prevention of Infant Mortality and Low Birthweight

Although we do not know all the precise causes of infant mortality and LBW, prevention efforts can make substantial progress toward decreasing infant mortality and LBW.[9,10] In the United States, much of the progress in reducing infant mortality has been a result of improvements in neonatal and perinatal care. As evidenced by the stable rates of LBW and preterm birth in the United States, there has been little or no progress to date in preventing LBW or preterm birth. However, things can be done to prevent LBW. If smoking during pregnancy was eliminated, the infant mortality rate would decrease by 10% and the LBW rate would decrease by 25%. Decreasing the incidence of unplanned pregnancies, decreasing the abuse of alcohol and illicit drugs, increasing enrollment in the Special Supplemental Food Program for Women, Infants, and Children (WIC), and providing prenatal care in a comprehensive and coordinated manner also could reduce infant mortality and LBW.[3,10]

Preventing pediatric mortality and morbidity associated with LBW requires a broad range of activities that involve the family, health care professionals, and community groups. These activities include identifying prepregnancy risks; counseling for risk reduction; implementing school health programs; increasing early, high-quality prenatal care services; expanding the content of prenatal care to meet the variable needs of individual women and selected high-risk groups, and developing, implementing, and supporting a long-term public information program with a few well-chosen messages targeted at LBW risks (e.g., smoking cessation).

Fetal Development, Physiology, and Biochemistry

Improvements in our understanding of and ability to measure embryonic and fetal physiologic and biochemical homeostasis are likely to advance the practice of neonatal-perinatal medicine. In addition, as we increase our appreciation of the mechanisms controlling labor, the protective circulatory adjustments of the fetus to hypoxia, and our understanding of pharmacology, we can develop new means to successfully detect high-risk pregnancies, treat the fetus, and prevent preterm labor.

Investigation of the cellular and molecular levels of development and pharmacology of the uterus, placenta, and fetus may be critical to understanding the mechanisms that control labor. Such an understanding would enable us to decrease the incidence of preterm infants or those with LBW. Prenatal diagnosis and biochemical and ultrasonic fetal monitoring may be only the first steps toward the development of future treatments. These future treatments may include hybridization of cells in the early blastocyst or embryo to correct inborn errors of metabolism, stimulation of embryogenesis of organs, gene therapy, acceleration of organ maturation, and pharmacologic interventions to ameliorate hypoxic injury to the central nervous system.

Legal and Ethical Issues

Advances in the field of neonatal-perinatal medicine have focused attention on a number of legal and ethical issues. There is continuing concern about life-and-death decision making in neonatal intensive care units. New and complex societal relationships among the physician, patient, family, and nursing staff exist in these units, and this development has had an enormous impact on the process of making medical decisions. As a result of regionalization, we now have nearly universal access to care in neonatal intensive care units, and this broad access has brought these ethical issues into a sharper and more demanding focus.[6]

Specific criteria must now be formulated for making decisions that previously were made on the basis of access to the health system, which was strongly influenced by the economic position of a family. For example, should a 500-g infant with a poor prognosis for intact survival be accepted to a neonatal intensive care unit when it means one cannot accept a 2000-g infant who is at high risk but has a good prognosis if he or she survives, just because the referring physician in the case of the 500-g infant calls first or because the infant is born in the same hospital where the intensive care unit is located?

Ironically, but not surprisingly, as the technology of care increases in these units, the difficult choices for the physician are not the technical medical decisions but rather the matters of judgment that require evaluating the complex human interests of the relatives, their friends and advisors, the staff, and the various consequences for the people involved. These decisions have always been the most challenging and demanding ones for physicians because they cannot be delegated to others. The new elements are the frequency and complexity of these judgments in regional neonatal intensive care centers (see Chapters 3 and 4).

Quality of Care

Whatever decision-making process is used to improve the quality of care, certain principles are important but often not easy to apply. The fundamental responsibility of all concerned is to do no harm or, at least, no harm without a reasonable expectation of a compensating benefit for the patient. A corollary principle is that there must be continuous, scientific evaluation of the care provided and of proposed innovations. Clinicians should not initiate or continue activities that on balance do harm to the well-being of a newborn infant. The definition of *well-being* is a major problem, because the varying ethical values, religious commitments, and life experiences of all those who care for and about the infants, as well as legal restraints, must be taken into consideration. In general, the minimum elements of well-being include a life prolonged beyond infancy, without excruciating pain and with the potential of participating in human experience to at least a minimal degree (see Chapter 5).

Awareness of these considerations has contributed to the impetus for further clinical specialization within pediatrics and obstetrics and gynecology, resulting in the formation of a field of clinical medicine for the fetus and neonatal infant called *neonatal-perinatal medicine*.

This field has already expanded to encompass the developing embryo before and after organ formation and to encompass older infants whose immaturity or disease process makes them best cared for in neonatal intensive care centers.

ACKNOWLEDGMENTS

We wish to acknowledge the work of Pat Shiono and Richard Behrman, previous authors of this section. Segments of the prior edition are retained without alteration.

PART 2

Perinatal Services

Michele C. Walsh and Avroy A. Fanaroff

HISTORICAL PERSPECTIVE

Before 1940, perinatal care services were delivered in the United States, Canada, and Europe without any particular organization. Most of the care was provided by an individual physician or midwife. In many areas the majority of the deliveries occurred in the home. Larger urban areas often had a number of maternity hospitals, usually serving as teaching hospitals, with home delivery services and neighborhood clinics serving a geographic area.

During the 1940s and early 1950s a number of cities in the United States developed centers for the care of premature infants. Many European countries, particularly the Netherlands and the Scandinavian countries, developed systems of care for perinatal patients based on the development of primary prenatal care clinics staffed largely by midwives, with district and regional hospitals for the care of mothers with complications.

From 1964 to 1968 studies were undertaken in Massachusetts, Wisconsin, and Arizona to analyze the causes of neonatal mortality and morbidity.[17,22] These studies suggested that expert care of high-risk neonates could reduce infant mortality rates. In 1976, the March of Dimes Committee on Perinatal Health developed recommendations based on this research that supported a network of perinatal care providers that supplied care to a geographic region. The report, entitled "Toward Improving the Outcome of Pregnancy" (TIOP), spurred many states to regionalize care.[49]

By the end of the 1980s, 26 states had regionalized perinatal care, and studies documenting a shift in deliveries from Level I to Level II and Level III centers emerged, together with data documenting reductions in neonatal mortality. Despite these data, in the early 1990s, state by state, the regionalized systems were weakened as factors put pressure on the system (Table 2-1).

In 1993, the March of Dimes convened the second TIOP conference and re-examined the theory supporting regionalization.[21] The conference participants concluded that, even in the 1990s, regionalization continued to be the best option for reducing perinatal morbidity.

PRINCIPLES OF REGIONAL CARE

General principles form the basis for the development of regional health care services for perinatal patients.[12] These include organization by geographic region, accountability for outcomes, and one standard of quality across care sites.

A region denotes a geographic area or population with definable care needs. The regional center and the network of related institutions are accountable for the overall perinatal health care for the region. Data on mortality and morbidity, frequency of problems, and quality of care are assessed for the entire population in the area. The availability and quality of care in any given institution become the responsibility of all the institutions, including the perinatal center.

Regionalization is based on the premise that there should be a single standard of quality across sites of care. Every mother and infant should have equal access to all the components of a functioning perinatal system (Table 2-2).

TABLE 2-1. Factors Threatening Regionalized Perinatal Care

PHYSICIAN RELATED	INSTITUTION RELATED
Oversupply and maldistribution of physicians	Use of high-tech procedures as a marketing tool
Desire to perform all services for which they were trained, regardless of level of care designated	Desire to perform all services to allow contractual arrangements with provider
Lack of incentive to improve care at other hospitals and potential decrease in patient referrals	Lack of incentive to improve care at other hospitals and potential decrease in patient referrals
Fear of loss of patients	Institutional ego
Failure to recognize problems deserving of referral	

Modified from Institute of Medicine: Prenatal Care: Reaching Mothers, Reaching Infants. Washington, DC, National Academy Press, 1988.

TABLE 2-2. Definitions of Care at Perinatal Centers

SERVICE	BASIC	SPECIALTY	SUBSPECIALTY
Care Provided			
Basic inpatient care for women and newborns without complications	×	×	×
High-risk pregnancies with moderate complications		×	×
Neonatal intensive care including ventilation			×
Inpatient care for critically ill neonates			×
Follow-up medical care of NICU grads			×
Follow-up developmental assessment			×
Consultation and referral arrangements			×
Transport service			×
Personnel			
Physician and nursing staff to care for uncomplicated pregnancy	×	×	×
Obstetrician		×	×
Pediatrician		×	×
Obstetric anesthesia			×
Neonatologist			×
Perinatal social worker			×
Genetic counselor			×
Pediatric subspecialists			×
Pediatric Surgery, Subspecialties, and Support Services			
Laboratories to assess fetal well-being and maturity		×	×
Level III ultrasound capability			×
Laboratories with microspecimen capability		×	×
Blood gases available on a 24-hour basis			×

NICU, neonatal intensive care unit.
From March of Dimes Birth Defects Foundation: Toward Improving the Outcome of Pregnancy: The 1990s and Beyond. White Plains, NY, March of Dimes, 1993.

Institutions operating within a region differ in their ability to provide perinatal care. Each institution is expected to deliver high-quality care up to the level of its capability. When care requirements exceed the institution's capability, the patient is referred to the closest facility that has the required capability.

Sixty to eighty percent of problems associated with increased risk for the mother, fetus, or newborn are detectable sufficiently in advance of the crisis to permit either the appropriate care resources to be made available locally or to transfer the patient to where appropriate resources are available.[30] Even under ideal circumstances, some patients must move from one facility to another during the course of care. Thus, institutions within a region must be effectively linked to permit ease of patient movement. Subspecialty centers are charged with outreach education to expand the care of basic and specialty units in their region.

Regionalization permits optimal use of both facilities and personnel. With a regional perinatal center, sufficient numbers of high-risk mothers and neonates are concentrated in a single location to economically justify the staffing and equipment necessary to meet care needs.[62] In addition, personnel who have frequent opportunities to use their skills are able to maintain and enhance these skills. Institutions with smaller numbers of high-risk patients avoid the expense of developing services that are infrequently used. The health care needs of the perinatal patient require a close working relationship among the various disciplines involved in preventing fragmentation and gaps in care.

CURRENT RECOMMENDATIONS ON ORGANIZATION

Countries with better perinatal mortality and morbidity statistics have universal primary care for all pregnant women and have established mechanisms for referring mothers and infants from primary care institutions to district hospitals when needed. They have placed less emphasis on tertiary care because of the relatively low demand for such services. In contrast, the perinatal health services of the United States and Canada place great emphasis on the specialized hospital services for the perinatal patient, but the primary care services available to the mother during her pregnancy are disorganized and inconsistent. The number of perinatal patients requiring intensive in-hospital care is inversely related to the quality and availability of primary services as well as to the general health status of the mother before pregnancy.

An organized system for perinatal care begins with a well-integrated ambulatory care system that emphasizes early risk assessment. The prenatal care may be delivered by basic providers (family practice physicians or nurse practitioners), specialty providers (obstetricians and experienced family practitioners), or subspecialty providers (maternal-fetal medicine specialists) as appropriate to the level of risk. As the woman's risk status changes during pregnancy, so may the level of care needed. No care system is effective if it is not used. TIOP II emphasized that "early and continuous prenatal care is an important and effective means to improve the outcome of pregnancy."[21] However, in the 1980s, virtually no progress was made in increasing the number of women receiving early prenatal care, and the number of women receiving late or no care increased. Therefore, more work needs to be done to better understand the barriers to prenatal care.

The Institute of Medicine described the following six barriers to adequate prenatal care: financial problems, inadequate capacity in care systems used by low-income women, services that are difficult to navigate (unfriendly), lack of awareness and acceptance of unintended pregnancy, personal beliefs about prenatal care, and social isolation.[16,35] TIOP II proposed solutions to ameliorate each of these barriers (Table 2-3).[21]

An organized system for providing care to the pregnant woman and her baby consists of the following types of facilities: physicians' offices and clinics, basic perinatal facilities, specialty perinatal facilities, subspecialty perinatal facilities, regional perinatal centers,

and specialized units such as children's hospitals and cardiac centers.

Physicians' Offices and Clinics

The basic units for care during pregnancy as well as for care of the mother and infant after delivery are physicians' offices and general clinics. These units must be able to obtain a complete health history, careful physical assessment of the mother or infant, systematic risk assessment (using one of the available risk-scoring systems), and laboratory resources for determining hematocrit or hemoglobin concentration and urinalysis.

Basic Perinatal Facilities (Level I)

Basic perinatal facilities are those designed primarily for the care of maternal and neonatal patients who have no complications. Because complications can arise in previously uncomplicated cases, basic units must have the resources to provide competent emergency services when the need arises. The necessary services for a basic perinatal facility are shown in Table 2-2 and include a normal newborn nursery. Capabilities for different levels of neonatal care are summarized in Table 2-4.

Specialty Perinatal Facilities (Level II)

Specialty perinatal facilities are hospitals that have larger maternity and newborn services. These hospitals are located in urban and suburban areas serving larger communities. In addition to providing a full range of maternal and newborn services for perinatal patients who have no complications, they provide services for some of the obstetric and neonatal patients who have one or more complications. The range of obstetric and neonatal complications an institution can treat depends on its resources. The services available in specialty

TABLE 2-3. Reducing Barriers To Prenatal Care Through System Change

BARRIERS	RELATED COPH RECOMMENDATIONS
Financing	Health care coverage for all pregnant women Mechanisms to ensure adequate provider payment
Capacity	More efficient use of existing providers Improved linkages between public and private as well as ambulatory and inpatient providers
Lack of user-friendly services	Matching provider capabilities and expertise to individual need and risks Risk assessment to identify medical, personal, and cultural barriers
Unintended pregnancy	Reproductive awareness among all women Greater emphasis on preconception and interconception care, including family planning
Personal beliefs and attitudes	Health promotion and health education for all children Reproductive awareness among all women
Social isolation	Outreach programs

COPH, Committee on Perinatal Health.
From March of Dimes Birth Defects Foundation: Toward Improving the Outcome of Pregnancy: The 1990s and Beyond. White Plains, NY, March of Dimes, 1993.

TABLE 2-4. Proposed Uniform Definitions for Capabilities Associated with the Highest Level of Neonatal Care within an Institution

Level I Neonatal Care (Basic)
Well-newborn nursery: has the capabilities to
Provide neonatal resuscitation at every delivery
Evaluate and provide postnatal care to healthy newborn infants
Stabilize and provide care for infants born at 35 to 37 weeks' gestation who remain physiologically stable
Stabilize newborn infants who are ill and those born at <35 weeks' gestation until transfer to a facility that can provide the appropriate level of neonatal care

Level II Neonatal Care (Specialty)
Special care nursery: level II units are subdivided into 2 categories on the basis of their ability to provide assisted ventilation including continuous positive airway pressure
Level IIA: has the capabilities to
Resuscitate and stabilize preterm and/or ill infants before transfer to a facility at which newborn intensive care is provided
Provide care for infants born at >32 weeks' gestation and weighing ≥1500 g (1) who have physiologic immaturity such as apnea of prematurity, inability to maintain body temperature, or inability to take oral feedings or (2) who are moderately ill with problems that are anticipated to resolve rapidly and are not anticipated to need subspecialty services on an urgent basis
Provide care for infants who are convalescing after intensive care
Level IIB has the capabilities of a level IIA nursery and the additional capability to provide mechanical ventilation for brief durations (<24 hours) or continuous positive airway pressure

Level III (Subspecialty) NICU
Level III NICUs are subdivided into 3 categories
Level IIIA: has the capabilities to
Provide comprehensive care for infants born at >28 weeks' gestation and weighing >1000 g
Provide sustained life support limited to conventional mechanical ventilation
Perform minor surgical procedures such as placement of central venous catheter or inguinal hernia repair
Level IIIB NICU: has the capabilities to provide
Comprehensive care for extremely low birthweight infants (≤1000 g and ≤28 weeks' gestation)
Advanced respiratory support such as high-frequency ventilation and inhaled nitric oxide for as long as required
Prompt and on-site access to a full range of pediatric medical subspecialists
Advanced imaging, with interpretation on an urgent basis, including computed tomography, magnetic resonance imaging, and echocardiography
Pediatric surgical specialists and pediatric anesthesiologists on site or at a closely related institution to perform major surgery such as ligation of patent ductus arteriosus and repair of abdominal wall defects, necrotizing enterocolitis with bowel perforation, tracheoesophageal fistula and/or esophageal atresia, and myelomeningocele
Level IIIC NICU: has the capabilities of a level IIIB NICU and also is located within an institution that has the capability to provide ECMO and surgical repair of complex congenital cardiac malformations that require cardiopulmonary bypass

From Stark AR, Couto J, American Academy of Pediatrics Committee on Fetus and Newborn: Levels of Neonatal Care. Pediatrics 114:1341, 2004.

units are presented in Table 2-2 and include both a normal newborn nursery and a transitional-care nursery. Care of high-risk neonates should be provided by appropriately qualified physicians. A board-certified pediatrician with special interest, experience, and in some situations subspecialty certification in neonatal-perinatal medicine should be chief of the neonatal care services.

Subspecialty Perinatal Facilities (Level III)

In addition to the resources and capabilities of a specialty unit, subspecialty facilities can provide a full range of maternal complications and newborn intensive care. The neonatal intensive care unit must have a full range of services for the neonate, with the possible exception of an occasional infant with congenital heart disease or other complex congenital anomaly who

requires a specialized unit. The services offered by subspecialty facilities are listed in Table 2-2 and include intensive care for mother and infant. The director of a subspecialty unit should be a full-time, board-certified pediatrician with subspecialty certification in neonatal-perinatal medicine.

Regional Perinatal Center

A regional perinatal center is a subspecialty facility that also is responsible for coordinating and managing special services, including transportation, that are needed for the region. In areas where there is only one subspecialty facility, the facility is expected to function as the regional perinatal center. In areas where there is more than one unit with subspecialty capabilities, one of the units would serve as the regional perinatal center. The regional perinatal center must offer outpatient and inpatient consultation and diagnostic services for basic and specialty facilities within the region, including ultrasonography, laboratory analysis of amniotic fluid, assessment of gestational age, genetic studies, and other studies of fetal health. It also should provide specialized nursing services and consultation in nutrition, social services, respiratory therapy, and laboratory and radiology services. The center is responsible for carrying on an active outreach education program for the institutions, health professionals, and public within the region.

A regional perinatal center has unique personnel needs. It should be directed by a full-time physician with extensive training and experience in perinatal medicine as well as administration. There also should be a director of obstetric services and a director of neonatal services. The director of obstetric services should be a full-time physician with training and experience in fetal-maternal medicine, including maternal intensive care. The director of neonatal services should be a full-time neonatologist with training and experience in neonatal care, including newborn intensive care. The perinatal nursing services should be directed by a clinical nurse specialist with advanced experience in maternal and neonatal nursing and in administration. The center also may require a full-time director of the outreach education program to coordinate the active participation of physicians in obstetrics and newborn care, nurses in obstetrics and newborn care, nutritionists, social workers, and other specialized personnel. The obstetrics and newborn care units, including the newborn intensive care unit, should have clinical nurse specialists in obstetrics and neonatal care responsible for organizing the nursing program and coordinating the patient-care needs.

It is important to estimate the number of pregnant women who could need specialized obstetric and neonatal services within the area of a given regional perinatal center. The percentage of pregnancies at increased risk may vary from 10% for general populations, such as an entire state or country, to more than 90% in some urban hospitals. In an Ontario perinatal study, 32% of pregnancies had some increased risk factor that resulted in 60% of the neonatal problems. In the Nova Scotia Fetal Risk Project, 11% of 9483 patients accounted for 50% of the stillbirths and 75% of the neonatal deaths.

The number of neonatal intensive care beds and neonatal intensive care days needed for a given population are most influenced by the frequency of premature birth and low birthweight. There are great differences in these frequencies among countries and among populations within a country. Infants with LBW account for less than 5% of the births in the Scandinavian countries and 6% to 9% of infants in some states in the United States; in some institutions the percentage may run as high as 15% to 20%.[45]

Swyer and associates calculated a need for neonatal intensive care beds at 0.7 beds per 1000 live births on the basis of a 7% LBW rate.[57] Transitional or intermediate and convalescent bed needs were approximately 4 per 1000 live births. The Wisconsin Perinatal Care Program predicted a need for 12 intensive care beds for 6000 live births (7% LBW rate). Data from Utah indicate a need for 2 beds per 1000 annual live births in special care facilities. The estimated breakdown was 0.5 level I beds, 0.5 level II beds, and 1 level III bed per 1000 annual live births.[37] Field and colleagues, in the United Kingdom, reported that the demand for neonatal intensive care was 1.1 beds per 1000 deliveries.[26] This was a minimum estimate, and factors such as increased survival of extremely immature infants would increase the demand for beds.

REGIONALIZATION

Impact on Neonatal Morbidity and Mortality

Paneth and associates analyzed all singleton births and deaths with known birthweight and gestational age in New York City from 1976 through 1978.[44] Mortality rates for full-term, appropriately grown infants were not influenced by the hospital of birth. However, preterm and LBW infants were at a 24% higher risk of death if birth occurred at either a level I or level II unit. These small infants constituted only a small percentage of the births but accounted for 70% of the deaths.[53]

Fanaroff's group compared the outcomes of neonates delivered between 24 and 28 weeks at National Institute of Child Health and Human Development network level III units with neonates of similar gestational age who were transported to the centers after birth.[24] Outborn infants had significantly more respiratory distress syndrome (88% versus 81%), more grade III or IV intraventricular hemorrhages (24% versus 17%; odds ratio [OR] 1.61, 1.12 to 2.16), and greater mortality (32% versus 22%; OR 1.63, 1.15 to 2.30).

Yeast and colleagues compared neonatal mortality in two 5-year periods (1982 to 1986 versus 1990 to 1994) in Missouri. They found that in both periods the relative risk of neonatal mortality in level II centers was 2.28 compared with level III centers and that no substantial improvement had occurred in those 10 years.[61] Similar data have been reported from California and North Carolina.[14,20,46] Thus, there are compelling reasons for preterm deliveries to occur at tertiary centers.

Services

MATERNAL AND NEONATAL TRANSPORT SERVICES

It is estimated that antenatal maternal transfer is not possible in up to 50% of high-risk pregnancies. In these situations neonatal transport must be performed by specially trained teams skilled in adequate stabilization before, and effective management during, transport. Hood and associates have documented a 60% greater mortality rate when neonates were transferred by an untrained versus a trained neonatal transport team.[34] Hypothermia and acidosis, in particular, were more common after transfer by an untrained team. National groups nave recommended standards for personnel configuration, training, and accreditation.[60] The transport team from the referral hospital also serves an important educational function and can influence and improve methods of stabilization at the referring center, which in turn may influence mortality statistics (see Chapter 5).

In many areas, limited regional perinatal resources have hampered referrals and required the referring physician to make multiple calls until an available bed can be located. Central telephone operator systems have partially alleviated this problem. A computer-based coordination of telecommunications has been developed in North Carolina. The system, which is linked to the state's nine tertiary centers and provides updates every 2 hours on neonatal and maternal bed availability, appears cost-effective.[15]

An effective means of managing overcrowding at the perinatal referral center is to encourage reverse transport of previously ill neonates to levels I and II nurseries for intermediate care.[36] Transfer can include not only babies with resolved acute medical problems but also those with chronic problems such as bronchopulmonary dysplasia. However, the tertiary center must be familiar with the capabilities, facilities, and resources of the hospitals to which reverse transport is occurring so that quality of care can be ensured. This evaluation can be combined with an outreach education program. Apart from the obvious cost-effectiveness of reverse transport, it can encourage family bonding and greater involvement of the pediatrician who will be offering continuing care to the infant.

The outcome of infants transported back from tertiary centers to community hospitals (level II units staffed by skilled personnel) was compared with that of infants convalescing in the tertiary center. Lynch and colleagues documented that the transported infants received appropriate care, were less likely to need readmission to the intensive care unit (7% versus 14%), and required fewer transfusions.[40] Major new health problems developed in 27% of the patients during convalescence. However, the overall complication rate was lower for the reverse transfers. The current medical economic climate is mandating that tertiary units establish criteria for reverse transfer, and many health maintenance organizations (HMOs) and preferred provider organizations are demanding early reverse transport. Tertiary units are obliged to ensure that there are appropriately trained personnel and adequate facilities at their community hospitals so as not to compromise the medical needs or care of the neonates requiring reverse transfer.

OTHER SERVICES

An effective public health nursing system is essential for effective perinatal care. Home visits during pregnancy and after birth provide a dimension of care not met by physicians' offices or community hospitals. Perinatal centers must also develop close working relationships with regional blood banks and state or regional laboratories that provide special diagnostic services to meet the needs of the perinatal patient.

Problems

One of the most common disorders of regionalization is centralization in place of regionalization. This is the end product of a regional center that operates with no outreach education program or other mechanisms for continuing the development and improvement of services in the other hospitals of the region. With such a system, the central hospital continues to receive the referrals of high-risk mothers or high-risk neonates but makes no effort to help the referring hospital develop programs for preventing the problems. This may be particularly true in university medical centers, where outreach education and service are not considered a regular academic or hospital activity. This problem improved with increased use of reverse transports.[19] However, this progress is threatened because some third-party and government payers will not reimburse the expense of the reverse transport, even when the result is to relocate care to a less-expensive institution.

A second common disorder of regionalization is unnecessary duplication of units.[32,54] This includes the unnecessary duplication of both basic and specialty units within rural or urban areas and competing subspecialty units, particularly in urban areas. The duplication results in difficulties in recruiting and maintaining the necessary personnel for such care units as well as an increased cost per patient for such care. Such duplication invariably is a result of competing institutions and competing medical staffs, who view maternal intensive care and neonatal intensive care units as important to their business, income, or institutional image.

Some regional centers are staffed with inadequate or inappropriately trained personnel. In the past a common problem was the staffing of infant intensive care nurseries with inadequately supervised resident staff as the primary responsible physicians, particularly during night hours and weekends. However, since the mid-1990s the data indicate that from 23% to 75% of subspecialty centers have increasingly moved to 24-hour in-house specialty coverage by attending neonatologists of centers.[23,54] An equally serious problem of medical supervision is seen in those intensive care units that operate with no full-time staff. The coverage and time commitment available from busy pediatric general practitioners do not permit the attention necessary for intensive care or the development of expertise.

Inadequate or inappropriate staffing also is often manifested in the use of licensed practical nurses by hospitals in place of experienced professional nurses in the care of high-risk mothers and high-risk neonates. This is usually done as a cost-saving measure with inadequate understanding of the value of experienced professional nurses in providing high-risk perinatal care. There is likewise a reluctance to use clinical nurse specialists and nurse clinicians because of the cost and lack of understanding of their role in patient care.

In most regions some institutions and physicians consistently fail to appropriately use the resources of a regional center when the care of the patient clearly indicates such a need. The hospitals that make least use of the center may be located closest to the center. Fear of loss of patients, physician ego, and failure to recognize problems promptly were the major inhibitors to appropriate use of perinatal center resources in the past. In the 1990s the HMOs emerged and directed the referral of patients along contractual rather than regional lines.[18,31,32,42] This increased the number of VLBW infants born outside regional centers. Some states, such as North Carolina and Alaska, did not see this trend toward deregionalization.[14,29]

Gerber and coworkers demonstrated a reversal of the trend toward births of VLBW infants outside subspecialty centers in Washington State in the late 1990s despite the growth of managed care organizations.[28] In fact, in some areas of Washington increased managed care penetration was actually associated with increased rates of delivery at subspecialty centers.[48] The authors speculated that HMOs recognize the cost savings associated with decreased morbidity resulting from care in a subspecialty center and changed contracting procedures to capture these savings. Data support the cost savings engendered from care by academic neonatologists in a subspecialty center.[11]

Is Regionalization of Perinatal Care Needed?

In the 1970s a spirit of cooperation drove the development of regionalized systems. The realities of health care reform, competition, and cost constraints have dimmed that spirit. More hospitals are merging and forming networks that then jointly contract with payers to supply complete health services to a population of "covered lives." These forces lead every network to wish to provide all levels of service in a given area so that covered lives stay within that system. This leads to duplication of services that runs counter to the principles of regionalization.[51]

The availability of a large supply of highly trained neonatologists, together with financial incentives, led to the creation of new levels of care termed *level IIB, level II plus,* or *community NICUs.*[43,56] The development of these centers shifted the location of high-risk births away from Level III centers to community NICUs in California and other states.[33]

Gould and coworkers evaluated the impact of this deregionalization on neonatal mortality and documented that by 1997 regional NICUs lost 5.2% of California's live births.[31] However, only 20% of the reduction occurred because of a shift of deliveries to community NICUs. Eighty percent of the shift was to Level I and Level II (intermediate) NICUs. Neonatal mortality was similar at the regional NICUs and community NICUs but remained elevated at intermediate NICUs (Odds Ratio 1.54), self-designated intermediate NICUs that were not certified by the state (OR 1.33), and primary care units (1.56).

Cifuentes, also working with health statistics from California, similarly identified a mortality disadvantage for VLBW neonates at Level II NICUs and identified an

impact of average daily census: centers with a census less than 15 had increased mortality.[20] Horbar and colleagues have been unable to confirm this association in the Vermont Oxford Network.[52]

Financial Impact

The facilities within a regional network, including a regional perinatal center, financially depend on a combination of patient revenue and public support to care for neonatal patients. With carefully coordinated use of resources and facilities, the cost of care can be contained.[27,38,39,62] It is essential that health insurance programs provide adequate coverage for obstetric and neonatal conditions and that charges reflect the cost of delivering the services.

Medical assistance and other forms of payment, as well as direct support of state and county hospitals, must be adequate for the care needs. There must be adequate nursing staff, physician coverage, equipment, and supplies to achieve an acceptable quality of care. The reimbursement schemes should provide for patient transfer between institutions without multiplication of deductibles or major financial hardship to the patient. The cost of emergency transport of high-risk maternal and newborn patients should be covered. Financial incentives should promote, rather than discourage, the use of resources appropriate to patient-care needs.

Diagnostic-related grouping has been implemented as the basis for federal reimbursement, and other third-party payers have followed suit. The limited initial database used to determine the reimbursement level did not take into account many variables that influence length of stay, particularly at a tertiary center.[13,39,47] If the guidelines are not modified, major tertiary centers will be at a distinct financial disadvantage, particularly when providing care for extremely complicated problems and infants with LBW. The system could also discourage transport of infants from both primary and specialty units if the referring hospitals perceive financial gain; hence, the quality of care may be compromised.

MEASUREMENTS OF EFFECTIVENESS OF CARE ORGANIZATION

When the effectiveness of any care system as well as its individual components is measured, it is essential to analyze data for the entire region. A hospital can show dramatic changes in mortality or morbidity statistics in the course of a single year, not as a result of improvement of care but as a result of movement of patients with particular problems to another institution. If the geographic boundaries of a region are well designed, there will be limited patient movement from region to region. This permits consistent year-to-year evaluation of the care within the region.

Maternal mortality has declined to the point that it is no longer a satisfactory index of quality of care in developed countries. Fetal and neonatal mortality are still reasonable indicators of perinatal care.[25] In evaluating a region, the data must link the hospital in which the death is recorded with the institution and the community in which the birth occurred or the care was initiated. Fetal and neonatal mortalities should also be divided by weight groups. The weight groups should be in 500-g increments or less, beginning with 500 g. If possible, the gestational age distribution and cause of death for the fetal or neonatal deaths should be established.

Sex and transport status (maternal or neonatal) have been shown to affect mortality.[24,55] Such practices make it possible to identify those areas or institutions within a region in which there are major problems with care. Any comparison of mortality is most useful if a risk adjustment tool is applied, such as the Clinical Risk Index for Babies (CRIB) or Score for Neonatal Acute Physiology (SNAP) (see Chapter 5).[50,58] Such scores correct for the inherent bias of subspecialty centers that receive only the sickest neonates and therefore experience the highest mortality.

When maternal, fetal, or neonatal mortality or morbidity rates are used, certain other information is necessary to permit useful interpretation. For maternal mortalities, it is essential to separate the maternal deaths that occurred during or as a result of pregnancy associated with other maternal disease, such as severe cardiac disease or malignancy, from those deaths associated primarily with the pregnancy. This requires analysis of each death and assignment to preventable or unpreventable categories. For evaluation of neonatal programs and regionalization, the frequency of 1-minute Apgar scores of 3 or under and 5-minute Apgar scores of 5 or under should be recorded. Also helpful in assessing effectiveness of care are the frequency of sepsis, traumatic delivery, respiratory distress syndrome, and neurologic problems; the number of intensive care days; and the number of patient transfers from community institutions to institutions of greater care capability.

All high-risk mothers and neonates should have systematic follow-up care. Those infants with a birthweight of less than 1500 g are at high risk for developmental, neurologic, or learning problems and should be followed into school age with careful neurologic and educational testing (see Chapter 39).[41,59] The incidence of child abuse and failure to thrive may also reflect parenting disorders having antecedents in the perinatal period.

FUTURE CONSIDERATIONS

Centers for newborn care have expanded at the specialty (level II) institutions with large delivery services so that many have developed capabilities similar to those at subspecialty centers. In many geographic areas the subspecialty and specialty units compete; in others the two centers work hand in hand. In all communities

it is essential that mutually productive relationships be re-established between the academic and community hospitals.

A majority of board-certified neonatologists in the United States now practice outside the traditional academic settings. These personnel needs are being met by the university-based training programs. However, with fewer training programs accredited and more trainees completing a third fellowship year, it is conceivable that in the near future there will not be enough trained neonatologists to staff the ever-expanding specialty units. At present, the major strategies are to provide cost-effective medical care, to comply with regulations that dictate standards required for reimbursement and, above all, to prevent low birthweight and prematurity.

REFERENCES

Part 1

1. Arias E et al: Annual summary of vital statistics—2002. Pediatrics 112:1215, 2003.
2. Hoyert DL, Smith BL, Arias E, Murphy SL: Deaths: Final data for 1999. National vital statistics reports vol 49 no 8. Hyattsville, Maryland: National Center for Health Statistics, 2001.
3. Institute of Medicine: Prenatal Care: Reaching Mothers, Reaching Infants. Washington, DC. National Academy Press, 1985.
4. Lewit GM, et al: The financial cost of low birthweight. Future Child 5:35, 1995.
5. Mathews TJ et al: Infant mortality statistics from the 2000 period linked birth/infant death data set. Natl Vital Stat Rep 50:1, 2002.
6. McCormick MC, Richardson DK: Access to neonatal intensive care. Future Child 5:162, 1995.
7. National Commission to Prevent Infant Mortality: Troubling Trends: The Health of America's Next Generation. Washington, DC, National Commission to Prevent Infant Mortality, 1990.
8. Richardson DK et al: Declining severity adjusted mortality: Evidence of improving neonatal intensive care. Pediatrics 102:893, 1998.
9. Shiono PH, Behrman RE: Low birthweight: Analysis and recommendations. Future Child 5:4, 1995.
10. US Department of Health and Human Services: Caring for our Future: The Content of Prenatal Care. Washington, DC: US Department of Health and Human Services, Public Health Service, Panel on the Content of Prenatal Care, 1988.

Part 2

11. Adams JM, Moreno J, Reynolds K, et al: Resource utilization among neonatologists in a university children's hospital. Pediatrics 99(6):E2, 1997.
12. Aubrey RH et al: High-risk obstetrics: I. Perinatal outcome in relation to a broadened approach to obstetrical care for patients at special risk. Am J Obstet Gynecol 105:241, 1969.
13. Beeby PJ: How well do diagnosis-related groups perform in the case of extremely low birthweight neonates? J Paediatr Child Helath 39(8):602, 2003.
14. Bode MM et al: Perinatal regionalization and neonatal mortality in North Carolina, 1968-1994. Am J Obstet Gynecol 184:1302, 2001.

15. Bostick JS et al: A minicomputer-based perinatal/neonatal telecommunications network. Pediatrics 71:272, 1983.

16. Brown SS et al: Barriers to access to prenatal care. In Kotch JB et al (eds): A Pound of Prevention: The Case for Universal Maternity Care in the United States. Washington, DC, American Public Health Association, 1992.

17. Callon HF: Regionalizing perinatal care in Wisconsin. Nurs Clin North Am 10:263, 1975.

18. Campbell MK et al: Is perinatal care in southwestern Ontario regionalized? Can Med Assoc J 144:305, 1991.

19. Chiu T et al: University neonatal centers and level II centers capability: The Jacksonville experience. J Fla Med Assoc 79:464, 1992.

20. Cifuentes J, Bronstein J, Phibbs CS, et al: Mortality in low birth weight infants according to level of neonatal care at hospital of birth. Pediatrics 109(5):745, 2002.

21. Committee on Perinatal Health: Toward Improving the Outcomes of Pregnancy: The 1990s and Beyond. White Plains, NY, March of Dimes, 1993.

22. Committee on Perinatal Welfare: Report on perinatal and infant mortality in Massachusetts, 1967 and 1968. Boston, Massachusetts Medical Society, 1971.

23. Denson SE et al: Twenty-four hour in-house coverage for NICUs in academic centers: Who, how and why? J Perinatol 10:257, 1990.

24. Fanaroff AA et al: Very-low-birth-weight outcomes of the National Institute of Child Health and Human Development Neonatal Research Network, May 1991 through December 1992. Am J Obstet Gynecol 173:1423, 1995.

25. Fanaroff AA et al: The NICHD neonatal research network: Changes in practice and outcomes during the first 15 years. Semin Perinatol 27:281, 2003.

26. Field DS et al: The demand for neonatal intensive care. BMJ 299:1305, 1989.

27. Friedman B et al: The use of expensive health technologies in the era of managed care: The remarkable case of neonatal intensive care. J Health Polit Policy Law 27:441, 2002.

28. Gerber SE et al: Managed care and perinatal regionalization in Washington State. Obstet Gynecol 98:139, 2001.

29. Gessner BD, Muth PT: Perinatal care regionalization and low birthweight infant mortality rates in Alaska. Am J Obstet Gynecol 185:623, 2001.

30. Goodwin JW et al: Antepartum identification of the fetus at risk. Can Med Assoc J 101:458, 1969.

31. Gould JB et al: Expansion of community-based perinatal care in California. J Perinatol 22:630, 2002.

32. Hein HA: Regionalization of perinatal health care: A lesson learned but lost. J Perinatol 19(Part 1):584, 1999.

33. Hernandez JA et al: Impact of infants born at the threshold of viability on the neonatal mortality rate in Colorado. J Perinatol 1:21, 2000.

34. Hood JL et al: Effectiveness of the neonatal transport team. Crit Care Med 11:419, 1983.

35. Institute of Medicine: Prenatal Care: Reaching Mothers, Reaching Infants. Washington, DC, National Academy Press, 1988.

36. Jung AL, Bose CL: Back transport of neonates: Improved efficiency of tertiary nursery bed utilization. Pediatrics 71:918, 1983.

37. Jung AL, Streeter NS: Total population estimate of newborn special-care bed needs. Pediatrics 75:993, 1985.

38. Kitchen WH et al, and the Victorian Infant Collaborative Study Group: The cost of improving the outcome for infants of birthweight 500-999 g in Victoria. J Paediatr Child Health 29:56, 1993.

39. Lagoe TJ et al: Impact of selected diagnosis-related groups on regional neonatal care. Pediatrics 77:627, 1993.

40. Lynch T et al: Neonatal back transport: Clinical outcomes. Pediatrics 82:845, 1998.

41. McCormick MC et al: The health and developmental status of very-low-birth-weight children at school age. JAMA 267:2204, 1992.

42. Mehta S et al: Differential markers for regionalization. J Perinatol 20:366, 2000.

43. Merenstein CB et al: Personnel in neonatal pediatrics: Assessment of numbers and distribution. Pediatrics 76:454, 1985.

44. Paneth N et al: The choice of place of delivery. Effect of hospital level on mortality in all singleton births in New York City. Am J Dis Child 141:60, 1987.

45. Paneth NS: The problem of low birthweight. Future Child 5:19, 1995.

46. Phibbs CS et al: The effects of patient volume and level of care at the hospital of birth on neonatal mortality. JAMA 276:1054, 1996.

47. Poland RL et al: Analysis of the effects of applying federal diagnosis-related grouping (DRG) guidelines to a population of high-risk newborn infants. Pediatrics 76:104, 1985.

48. Powell SL, Holt VL, Hickok DE, et al: Recent changes in delivery site of low-birth-weight infants in Washington: Impact on birth weight-specific mortality. Am J Obstet Gynecol 173(5):1585, 1995.

49. Report of the Committee on Perinatal Health of the American Medical Association, American College of Obstetricians and Gynecologists, American Academy of Pediatrics, and American Academy of Family Physicians: Toward Improving the Outcome of Pregnancy. New York, March of Dimes National foundation, 1975.

50. Richardson DK et al: Score for Neonatal Acute Physiology: A physiologic severity index for neonatal intensive care. Pediatrics 91:617, 1993.

51. Richardson DK et al: Perinatal regionalization versus hospital competition: The Hartford example. Pediatrics 96:417, 1995.

52. Rogowski JA et al: Indirect vs direct hospital quality indicators for very low-birth-weight infants. JAMA 291:202, 2004.

53. Roth J, et al: Changes in survival patterns of VLBW infants from 1980 to 1993. Arch Pediatr Adolesc Med 149:1311, 1995.

54. Schwartz RM, Kellogg R, Muri JH: Specialty newborn care: Trends and issues. J Perinatol 20:520, 2000.

55. Stevenson DK et al: Very low birthweight outcomes of the National Institute of Child Health and Human Development Neonatal Research Network, January 1993 through December 1994. Am J Obstet Gynecol 179:1632, 1998.

56. Stoddard JJ, Cull WL, Jewett EA, et al: Providing pediatric subspecialty care: A workforce analysis. AAP Committee on Pediatric Workforce Subcommittee on subspecialty Workforce. Pediatrics 106:1325, 2000.

57. Swyer PR et al (eds): Regional Services in Reproductive Medicine. Toronto, Joint Committee of the Society of Obstetricians and Gynaecologists of Canada and the Canadian Paediatric Society, 1973.

58. Tarnow-Mordi W et al: The CRIB (Clinical Risk Index for Babies) score: A tool for assessing initial neonatal risk and comparing performance of NICUs. Lancet 342:193, 1993.

59. Taylor HG et al: Middle-school-age outcomes in children with very low birthweight. Child Dev 71:1495, 2000.

60. Woodward GA et al: The state of pediatric interfacility transport: Consensus of the second National Pediatric and Neonatal Interfacility Transport Medicine Leadership Conference. Pediatr Emerg Care 18:38, 2002.

61. Yeast JD et al: Changing patterns in regionalization of perinatal care and the impact on neonatal mortality. Am J Obstet Gynecol 178:131, 1998.

62. Zupancic JA et al: Economics of prematurity in the era of managed care. Clin Perinatol 27:483, 2000.

3

Ethics in Perinatal and Neonatal Medicine

Jonathan Hellmann and Françoise Baylis

Medical ethics involves the systematic, reasoned evaluation and justification of the "right" action in pursuit of human good or well-being in the context of medical practice. It involves a critical examination of the concepts and assumptions underlying medical and moral decision making, and it may also include a critical evaluation of the kind of person a physician should be.[43]

This chapter explores the complexity of moral problem solving in perinatal and neonatal medicine. First, key terms and concepts are briefly described. This is followed by a short commentary on the importance of contextual factors. Next, there is a critical analysis of moral problems that arise during the antenatal period, at the time of delivery, or in the immediate postnatal period. In the antenatal period, the focus is on the management of multi-fetal pregnancies, refusal of treatment during pregnancy, and fetal therapy. At the time of delivery, the focus is on decision making at the margins of viability. In the neonatal period, the discussion centers on the ethics of withholding and withdrawing life-sustaining medical treatment, brain death and organ donation, and palliative care. This chapter also includes a section on ethical decision making that begins with a discussion of effective and respectful communication and then describes a collaborative framework for consensual decision making and guidelines for conflict resolution in the neonatal intensive care unit (NICU). The chapter ends with a brief summary of physicians' ethical responsibilities in perinatal and neonatal care.

KEY TERMS AND CONCEPTS

Moral problems abound in perinatal and neonatal medicine: a pregnant patient refuses offers of treatment for substance abuse; a couple asks to terminate their pregnancy following a routine prenatal ultrasound that identifies a minor fetal anomaly that is amenable to treatment; the parents of an infant with an extremely low birthweight insist on continuing intensive care treatment against the medical team's recommendation. In the clinical setting, these types of problems are frequently experienced as moral dilemmas, moral uncertainty, or moral distress.[27]

A *moral dilemma* is faced when the physician believes there is an obligation to pursue two (or more) conflicting courses of action. As only one of these courses of action can be pursued, the physician has to make a value-based choice that will compromise one of these moral obligations. A classic example of a moral dilemma in health care is a conflict between action required by the principle of autonomy and action required by the principle of beneficence.

Moral uncertainty typically arises when the presenting issue is unclear. For example, parents whose fetus has a major congenital anomaly are presented with the options of termination of pregnancy or postnatal surgery. They are unwilling to end the pregnancy but are underinsured and cannot afford the surgery. They are then informed about a clinical trial for in utero surgery, the cost of which would be absorbed by the institution. In this situation, the physician might experience some uneasiness about the research intervention being more likely to attract those without adequate health insurance, and might remain unclear about the principles and values that are in conflict.

Moral distress, the third type of moral problem, arises when the decision maker is certain about the morally right thing to do, but the perceived right course of action is precluded for any number of reasons, including institutional or financial constraints or a lack of decision-making authority. For example, when the parents of a newborn infant with an extremely poor prognosis insist on continued aggressive treatment that the physician believes is not in the infant's best interests, the physician may experience moral distress. Neonatal nurses who have intense hands-on contact with newborn infants may feel powerless because treatment decisions are made by others, and they too may experience moral distress.[21]

Autonomy grounds the right of competent patients to make their own health care choices. A person who makes an autonomous choice acts intentionally, with understanding, and without external controlling influences.[5]

Beneficence grounds the obligation of others to promote the best interests of patients who are not able to make autonomous health care choices. This principle is frequently understood as an obligation to pursue the course of action with the most favorable benefit-to-harm ratio.[5] In neonatal medicine, parents and physicians have a prima facie obligation to promote the best interests of the patient. Difficulties can arise, however, when parents and physicians have different understandings of what constitutes a benefit or a harm, and different understandings of what is in the patient's best interests. In perinatal medicine, the issue is more complicated still, because of conflicting views about when the developing fetus becomes a patient.

To say that a particular choice is in the *best interests of the newborn* is to assert that, all things considered, this choice will maximize benefits and minimize harms. In more technical terms, *best interests* is shorthand for the following statement: On balance, taking into consideration both the nature and probability of occurrence of the benefits and harms of various courses of action, the proposed course of action has the most favorable benefit-to-harm ratio. But benefits and harms are subjective terms, so who decides, and on what basis, what constitutes a benefit and what constitutes a harm? This procedural question is of pivotal importance because benefits and harms lie in the eyes of the beholder (e.g., the parents, the physician, or the nurse).

Parents have the moral and legal authority and responsibility to make health care decisions in the best interests of their children. At times, however, parental views on what is in the best interests of their children may conflict with the views of health care professionals. Consider, for example, a situation involving parents who believe in the sanctity of life. Their perception of the benefits and harms of aggressive intervention may be quite different from those of a physician who places greater value on quality of life and relief of suffering. Can physicians authoritatively assert that their values are better than those of the parents and thus should be the ones that inform the assessment of the best interests of the newborn? Physicians may better understand the medical facts and doubtless have more expertise and experience in dealing with sick newborn infants, but this medical expertise does not necessarily confer moral expertise.

Although the current wisdom is that the child's best interests must be pursued (even, at times, to the exclusion of family interests), some question this narrow perspective.[19,20] They argue that it is legitimate for both physicians and parents to consider *family interests* in making health care decisions for a sick family member. The concept of family-centered care has become firmly entrenched in neonatal intensive care, and family interests are generally incorporated into health care decisions for a sick newborn infant because of the recognition that family interests do matter.[19]

A sound *patient-physician relationship* is a sine qua non of good medicine. It is within this relationship that patients and physicians exercise their humanity, understanding, and respect for the values of others. A key issue in perinatal medicine is whether there are two patients in one body (the pregnant woman and the fetus) or whether there is only one patient, namely the pregnant woman. The issue is complicated and perspectives vary considerably depending on the view about the moral status of the developing fetus. However, it is clear that decision making rests with the

pregnant woman, and communication and conversation is between her (and her partner) and the physician. The ideal model for this patient-physician relationship is the deliberative model as described by Emmanuel and Emmanuel.[15] In this model, physicians not only help the patient with values clarification but also strive to make their reasoning transparent for the patient to appreciate the many factors that inform the professional recommendation. Two facts, in particular, argue strongly for this mode of interaction: the diminishing acceptance of medical paternalism by patients who want to be part of the decision-making process, and the better outcomes that result from consensual decision making.

In neonatal medicine, the patient is a newborn, unable to participate in a patient-physician relationship. The physician's relationship is thus with the parents (or legal guardians) of the newborn, who are legally and morally responsible for making health care decisions on behalf of the child. The state confers this responsibility on parents for several reasons, including recognition of the parents' moral authority and the belief that parents normally act to promote their children's best interests. The optimal *parent-physician relationship* mirrors the deliberative model of the patient-physician relationship. Within this model, it is reasonable to expect parents to identify their values and treatment preferences, and to expect physicians to provide parents with accurate and timely information (with as much medical certainty as possible) and a professional recommendation.[4] In conversation with the physician, parents may be invited to reexamine their values and treatment preferences, which, on reflection, they may either affirm or alter. On the basis of the available medical information and an understanding of the parents' values and preferences, the physician explains the reasons for the professional recommendation. The goal, through dialogue and negotiation, is to reach a harmonious decision that respects parental authority and promotes the best interests of the newborn.

Many health care providers deal with ethical problems by appealing to the principles of autonomy, beneficence, nonmaleficence, and justice. Although reference to these principles may serve as a useful checklist of moral concerns, appealing to principles can be of limited value when the problem involves a conflict of principles. In some cases, this approach may not do justice to the nature or complexity of the moral problem. In North American medicine, for example, there is a strong emphasis on individual autonomy and informed choice, sometimes to the apparent exclusion of other important values such as social or distributive justice. This chapter does not prescribe adherence to any particular *ethical theory*. There is congruence, however, with the views of Pellegrino as regards the importance of a morally correct relationship between society, its medical professionals, and the patients they serve.[43] Pellegrino describes three timeless, universal, and irrefutably true characteristics of the practice of medicine: first, the *fact of illness* and the vulnerability it creates; second, the *act of the profession* (the use of medical skills for the benefit of the patient); and third, the *act of medicine itself*—that which physicians and patients actually do together in the clinical encounter characterized by mutual intentionality. These three elements are very well illustrated in both perinatology and neonatology, where the vulnerability of anxious pregnant patients, sick infants, and their parents are manifest, where the competence and moral discretion of health professionals are utilized for the benefit of patients and parents, and where the act of the profession is carried out in a patient-parent-physician relationship characterized by mutual trust and pursuit of the patient's good.

CONTEXT

The context in which perinatal and neonatal care is provided has a definite impact on the delivery of such care. High expectations of continuous technological progress are reinforced by the ever-increasing availability of therapeutic options. (However, some expectations regarding medical capabilities are unrealistic, particularly in contexts where financial resources are limited.) In addition, care usually takes place in large institutions where there may be great moral distance between patients, parents, and members of the health care team: interactions between patient, parent, and physician increasingly take place within a medical system of multiple caregivers functioning in multi-tiered teams. This increases the risk of fragmented care and possible confusion regarding lines of responsibility. With the shift in health care from the 'personal to the technological,' however, there has been no diminution in the expectation that patients and families will be provided with personalized, ethically and culturally sensitive, compassionate care.

Cultural, Spiritual, and Religious Diversity

Culture encompasses the broad range of beliefs, values, attitudes, patterns of meaning, and behaviors that define a specific group of people; these aspects of culture are learned and shared, and although they are perpetuated by members of the cultural group, they can change over time.[14] In a pluralistic society, patients, parents, and physicians are unlikely to share the same values, cultural systems, personal histories, and experiences. At times of stress, when life-and-death decisions have to be made, differences in values and beliefs may emerge that present health care providers with significant challenges.

A first challenge is to recognize, understand, and respect the cultural, spiritual, and religious views and values of patients and families. This is critically important, as misperceptions caused by a lack of cultural and spiritual or religious sensitivity can lead to inappropriate or poor clinical outcomes. A second challenge for health care providers involves the limits of tolerance—where to draw the line, for example, between accepting established patterns of decision making between couples or

within families when these patterns contrast markedly with the prevailing cultural norm of shared responsibility for decision making. A third challenge arises because not only are patients, parents, and physicians products of their own respective cultures but their interactions take place within a further culture—that of medicine itself—with its *own* values, assumptions, and understanding of what should be done.

The health care team should avoid constructing patients' and parents' interests narrowly and should recognize that these interests are shaped by particular social, cultural, and other contexts.[13,14] At the same time, it is important not to stereotype members of specific social, cultural, or religious groups. These affiliations, though important, may not be predictive of people's beliefs and values. The health care team should regard each patient and each family as unique and listen carefully to their cultural, religious, or spiritual views and values.

When attentiveness to the views and values of families is difficult because of a language barrier, professional interpreters should be used. This is advisable for three reasons: it ensures that the parents' views are available to the health care team, it removes the burden on family members or friends for the transfer of information, and it limits the potential for miscommunication. In certain situations, a cultural interpreter can not only facilitate language comprehension but also provide useful information about cultural norms and traditions that are unfamiliar to the health care team. Access to high-quality interpretation services is an essential component of ethically and culturally sensitive care.

SPECIFIC MORAL PROBLEMS

The Antenatal Period

MULTI-FETUS PREGNANCIES

Since the mid-1970s, the incidence of multiple births in developed countries has increased significantly. Although some of this increase results from a rise in spontaneous multiple births, the major shift is due to the use of assisted reproductive technologies (e.g., ovulation induction, in vitro fertilization followed by multiple embryo transfer).[6] Advances in prenatal and neonatal care have helped to reduce mortality from multi-fetus pregnancies, but there has been little reduction in the morbidity associated with extreme prematurity. As well, there are serious consequences for women with multiple gestations, including increased risk of miscarriage, complications during pregnancy, preterm labor, cesarean delivery, and, after birth, stress, depression, and exhaustion. Therefore, recent professional guidelines and legislation in a number of jurisdictions have sought to mandate the diligent use of fertility drugs, to limit the number of embryos transferred per cycle, and to generally encourage improved patient management.

Pregnant women and couples with a multi-fetus pregnancy have three options. The pregnancy can be maintained and carefully monitored, the pregnancy can be terminated, or there can be an attempt to reduce the number of fetuses. In the latter instance, the goal has generally been to reduce a higher-order pregnancy to a twin pregnancy, but increasingly there are requests to reduce a twin pregnancy to a singleton. Whereas the case is compelling for fetal reduction with high-order multiples to reduce morbidity for the pregnant woman and the surviving fetuses, the case is much less compelling when the reduction is not done for medical benefit but is motivated by personal preference. Because the pregnant woman could choose to terminate the pregnancy, some view the option of fetal reduction with pregnancy preservation as the preferable option.

REFUSAL OF TREATMENT DURING PREGNANCY

When a pregnant woman acts in such a way as to potentially create a serious risk of harm for her developing fetus, some argue that state intervention is morally justified in an effort to promote fetal health and well-being. Others maintain that such intervention not only violates the pregnant woman's autonomy, integrity, and privacy but also undermines the principle of reproductive freedom.[16]

Those who advocate state intervention consider the principle of reproductive freedom to be morally unsound: whatever rights a pregnant woman may have to direct the course of her pregnancy, they do not include the right to harm the fetus. This perspective ignores the fetus's contested moral status: the fetus-to-be-born, unlike the child or the pregnant woman, is not uniformly recognized as a person with full moral standing. Second, it suggests that the pregnant woman intentionally seeks to harm her fetus, which is generally false.

Other participants in this debate readily acknowledge that the fetus does not have the same rights as a person and that the pregnant woman may not intend to harm her fetus. They maintain, however, that the woman has obligations to the fetus that include care. In choosing to continue her pregnancy, the woman is said to have incurred an obligation to do what is necessary (within reasonable limits) to ensure that the fetus is born healthy.[37] If she violates this obligation, the state is entitled or obliged to intervene to protect the fetus. This argument, however, misunderstands the context in which women continue their pregnancy and ignores the overlapping interests of the fetus and the pregnant woman. The relationship between the pregnant woman and her fetus is falsely characterized as adversarial—the woman is cast in the role of aggressor with the fetus in the role of innocent victim—when in fact the situation is far more complex.

Significantly, professional bodies have commonly resolved the moral dilemma between the pregnant woman's autonomy and the fetus's well-being in favor of respecting the principle of autonomy. In 1987, the American College of Obstetricians and Gynecologists stipulated, "Every reasonable effort should be made to protect the fetus, but the pregnant woman's autonomy should be respected. . . . The use of courts to resolve these conflicts is almost never warranted."[1] Similarly, the Society of Obstetricians and Gynecologists of Canada Ethics Committee "opposes involuntary intervention in the lives of pregnant women. . . . The primary objective of physicians who work with pregnant women should be to promote women's health and well-being while respecting their autonomy."[46]

Many reasons explain the prevailing ethical view of not condoning state intervention in the lives of pregnant women. First, there is the principled commitment to respect personal autonomy. Second, there is the belief that state intervention harms the pregnant woman without any benefit necessarily accruing to her fetus (e.g., when the court intervenes after fetal harm has occurred). Third is the pragmatic concern that a policy of state intervention may discourage the women whose fetuses are most at risk from seeking appropriate care, for fear of being prosecuted.[2,36] Fourth, there are concerns about oppression and gender discrimination. State intervention is disproportionately oppressive toward poor and minority women. It also typically ignores paternal actions that are hazardous to the fetus.[34] Fifth, state intervention in pregnancy is an intrusion into the lives of pregnant women in excess of anything that would be tolerated to protect nonfetal lives.[16]

For these compelling reasons, caring, compassionate health care providers confronted with a refusal of treatment during pregnancy are well advised to educate and attempt to persuade, but never to coerce pregnant women.

FETAL THERAPY

Prenatal diagnosis frequently confirms a healthy pregnancy and a healthy fetus. On occasion, however, the fetus is diagnosed with a serious genetic disorder or a major congenital anomaly. In some instances, the diagnosis leads to a decision to terminate the pregnancy. In other instances, the woman seeks treatment for her developing fetus, thereby, according to some, conferring on her fetus the status of patient.[37] Others insist that there is only one patient in the maternal-fetal dyad—the woman. In this view, "practitioners need to avoid the tendency to consider fetuses as distinct patients and instead need to emphasize the fact that there is one patient: the pregnant woman."[35] Underlying this second view is an emphasis on the fact that treatment aimed at benefiting the fetus must be provided through the pregnant woman, often with potential harm to her.

When there is a well-established therapy that clearly benefits the fetus with no (or negligible) risk of harm to the pregnant woman, treating the developing fetus is relatively noncontroversial. More typically, however, there are complicated trade-offs. Consider, for example, fetal surgery. Generally, the surgery entails the risk of medical harm for the pregnant woman with no medical benefits, although there may be psychosocial benefits. But are these benefits sufficient to outweigh the potential harms associated with abdominal surgery, or the relatively remote risk, for example, of uterine rupture during future pregnancies? In contrast, the fetus may benefit directly from the surgery, but there is the risk of increased morbidity and mortality as a consequence of the surgery, or, more commonly, as a consequence of premature delivery precipitated by the surgery. Balancing these potential harms and benefits for both the pregnant woman and the fetus is challenging. It is important to consider the nature of the fetal disorder and its natural history, whether the disorder is life threatening, whether there are alternatives to surgical intervention, and whether the surgery is experimental or a standard of care (i.e., "what a reasonably prudent physician would do in the same or similar circumstances").[3] Consider, for example, the recent experience with fetal surgical correction of myelomeningocele that is aimed at preventing mobility impairment and incontinence. Serious questions have been raised about the ethics of this surgery, because it appears that postnatal management achieves similar benefits for the newborn, without the surgical risks to the pregnant woman.[35]

The final decision to consent to or to refuse surgery rests with the pregnant woman, who will look at the total harm-to-benefit ratio for herself and her fetus. It is important to recognize, however, that her autonomy may nonetheless be compromised. When the pregnant woman is potentially vulnerable to the influence of others, including her partner, family members, and friends, the physician should endeavor to protect her from inordinate pressure. As well, to minimize the risk of exploitation, it has been suggested that when a pregnant woman is desperate to save her fetus and thus is vulnerable to the lure of unproven claims of success, health care providers should temper their enthusiasm for nonroutine care and research.[8]

The Delivery Room

THE MARGINS OF VIABILITY

Viability is typically defined in purely physiologic terms as the point at which life can be maintained ex utero. With advances in medical technology, neonatology teams have developed the capacity to maintain physiologic signs of life at extremely low gestational ages, with survival possible after a gestation as short as 22 weeks (although in less than 4% of live births reported).[24] Use of a physiologic definition of viability might suggest that every neonate born at 23 weeks should be given an opportunity for extrauterine life and should be actively supported. In sharp contrast, other definitions of viability do not focus exclusively on the likelihood of survival but rather include quality-of-life considerations—where there is an explicit value judgment regarding the degree of morbidity that is acceptable. Viability so understood might suggest that full support should be provided only at a gestational age at which a "good enough" quality of life is foreseen (e.g., ≥25 weeks).

In clinical practice, there is no universally accepted definition of a viable fetus. However, guidelines from professional societies in several countries have defined gestational age ranges at which the benefit-to-burden ratio of aggressive obstetrical or neonatal care is questionable.[33] The gray area is essentially between 23 and 25 weeks of gestation.

Decision making at the margins of viability is both complex and challenging. First, it is important to have the best data available, on the basis of which parents and physicians can engage in informed decision making.[32] The data need to be current, based on gestational age rather than birthweight, and specific to the unit in which the patient is being cared for (or the geographic region, where appropriate). The data need to include survival statistics as well as information about the quality of that survival, with quantitative as well as qualitative outcome measures (functional abilities, learning, behavior, impact on family). Differences in data collection methods, study populations, and outcome measures have confounded physicians and parents, however, and sometimes have led to different interpretations of the data.

Second, the meaning of the data needs to be carefully contextualized for parents. Fully informing parents requires more than simple disclosure of the potential benefits and harms associated with possible outcomes for, as Cole suggests, there is a tendency for parents to "use hope and denial to interpret the limits imposed by statistics."[12] It is critically important, therefore, to explore with parents the meaning of the data, and their preferences in relation to the data. To say that there is a 50% chance of mortality with a 50% chance of major morbidity at a specific gestational age may have vastly different meaning to parents and physicians. In addition, parents' views can differ widely. For example, some may regard 20% as a fair chance, whereas others may regard 80% as not enough of a guarantee.[18] Ideally, interpretation of the data needs to be carefully undertaken, with time available for parents to absorb the information, ask questions, seek opinions, and discuss options. In the absence of such conversations, the newborn's medical characteristics at the time of birth become the dominant factor in neonatologists' resuscitation decisions in the delivery room, with social issues and other family concerns bearing less weight.

The third and most difficult issue concerns the moral weight given to parents' views for delivery room decisions. Leuthner described how two different models of best interests have been used in published statements on decisions regarding resuscitation of the extremely premature infant.[31] The models give different moral weight to the preferences of the participants in the decision-making process. With the "expertise" model, the best-outcome data are used in directive counseling in pursuit of the physician's judgment of the best possible outcome. The second model of best interests is one in which decisions are "negotiated." Parental input is maximized and the decision attends to the moral values of both the physician and the parents. Some argue that the use of the directive approach is preferable at the lower gestational ages (e.g., ≤23 weeks), whereas use of the negotiated approach is preferable with increasing gestational age (e.g., ≥25 weeks).

It is a great challenge for parents and the medical team to find meaning in the decisions these morally uncertain situations demand. Greisen suggests, "Even a short and difficult life can be meaningful when the parents love the child they waited for and when the life-supporting measures are carefully chosen from the range of options—from warmth only, through oxygen and continuous positive airway pressure to the panoply of intensive care, using analgesia and comforting measures as integral parts of care—to fit the child's and family's need.[18] It is a particular challenge for physicians to find meaning for themselves when faced with the capacity to utilize technology but where the projected outcome suggests that that is not a responsible use of such technology.

The Postnatal Period

WITHHOLDING OR WITHDRAWING LIFE-SUSTAINING MEDICAL TREATMENT

Recent studies confirm that the majority of deaths in the NICU occur as a result of decisions to limit or forgo life-sustaining medical treatment (LSMT).[30,38,50] This practice relates predominantly to the increased number of infants with extremely low birthweight who are resuscitated and given trials of intensive early management. As well, changes in social attitudes and a greater appreciation of the burdens of intensive care in survivors, together with a greater expression of parental authority in decision making, may explain the reasons for discontinuation of LSMT in the NICU.

Withholding LSMT involves a choice to omit a form of treatment that is not considered beneficial; *withdrawal,* on the other hand, involves a choice to remove treatment that has not achieved its beneficial intent. From a moral perspective, there is no difference in terms of the praiseworthiness or blameworthiness of either action. If it is morally right (or wrong) to withhold treatment deemed to be ineffective, it is equally right (or wrong) to withdraw this same treatment once started, should it later become clear that the treatment is ineffective.

Dealing with Medical Uncertainty

There is often considerable prognostic uncertainty when an infant's birthweight is extremely low or in the presence of chromosomal or multiple congenital anomaly syndromes. Typically, physicians deal with this uncertainty by using one or more of three decision-making strategies: a *statistical* approach, a *wait-until-certainty* approach, or an *individualized prognostic* approach.[44]

With a statistical approach, decisions are made on the basis of a statistical analysis of the outcomes of infants with extremely low birthweight or gestational age, or with severe chromosomal or congenital anomaly disorders. At times, concerns about resource allocation may be factored into the decision-making process. The primary objective with this approach is to avoid enhancing the survival of severely impaired infants, even if this means that some potentially viable infants do not survive.

The wait-until-certainty approach to decision making begins with treatment for almost every infant with any chance of survival. The possibility of withdrawal or discontinuation of LSMT is considered only when severe, adverse medical findings become unequivocally evident. An obvious problem with this strategy is that frequently, even with the passage of time, uncertainty remains. The issue is thus not certainty per se but rather the degree of certainty required by physicians and parents to facilitate end-of-life decision making. Another significant problem with this approach is that it denies the ethical complexity of situations by failing to address the moral as well as medical uncertainty. The wait-until-certainty approach establishes a momentum in favor of continuing treatment and risks alienating parents (and other members of the health care team) from the decision-making process by relegating them to the role of bystanders.

With the individualized prognostic strategy, treatment is initiated for all infants who have a reasonable chance of survival. Decision making solely on the basis of biomedical factors is avoided, and the ongoing moral responsibility of the decision makers is emphasized in an effort to involve parents and family members in navigating the ensuing prognostic uncertainty. This approach avoids the extremes of either withholding treatment from all infants who fall below a minimum threshold or treating all infants until the outcome is absolutely certain.[29]

Criteria for Decisions to Withhold or Withdraw LSMT

Decisions to withhold or withdraw LSMT generally focus on claims about the futility of continuing medical treatment. It is difficult to know what follows from such claims, however, as there is considerable debate and diversity of opinion as to the meaning of *futility*.[22,48] In some instances, continuing care is deemed futile because death is inevitable; in other instances, continuing care is considered futile because death is likely but not certain; and in the event of survival, an extremely poor quality of life is inevitable.

In addition to debate about the meaning of the term *futility,* arguments have emerged about the authority of the physician to determine when an intervention is futile. Some contend that this is a medical decision to be made by the physician alone, whereas others believe that the decision is clearly value-laden and that patients or family members should be involved in this determination.

When futility is determined solely on the basis of medical or physiologic factors (a rare occurrence unless death is imminent), unilateral decision making by the physician based on sound medical knowledge and expertise may be appropriate. When subjective elements form part of the determination, however, the physician has no unique claim to moral expertise. As Frader and Watchko observe, attempts by physicians to "truncate and trump medical decisions through futility claims . . . do not seem to be the best way to return to a trusted position in the doctor-patient-family relationship."[17]

Instead of attempting to finesse decision making about withholding or withdrawing LSMT using references to futility, physicians should clearly state their reasons for considering this course of action. Possible reasons include the inevitability of death (situations in which it is clear that the infant will not survive to discharge from intensive care), the low probability of successful treatment (situations where treatment is likely to be ineffective—for example, surgical correction of a major cardiac abnormality in an extremely premature infant), or a poor quality of life after treatment (situations in which the infant is likely to survive with limited cognitive or relational capacity, mobility, or self-awareness, or a life of continued pain and suffering). The first two of these three reasons are most commonly cited as reasons for withholding or withdrawing LSMT. Although there is some hesitancy to use quality-of-life considerations in end-of-life decision making, poor quality of life can be a valid reason for considering forgoing or withdrawing LSMT. In view of the subjective nature of quality-of-life considerations, however, they must be explored from the perspectives of the various legitimate decision makers. In the study by Wall and Partridge, 23% of deaths resulting from a decision to withhold or withdraw LSMT included quality-of-life considerations.[50]

Use of Analgesic Agents at the Time of Withdrawing LSMT

Although it is difficult to determine whether infants perceive pain at the time of impending death, use of drugs to relieve pain and discomfort may be provided as comfort care. This can be justified not only by concern about potential pain at the time of discontinuing life support but also by concern about future pain and suffering in the event that the infant survives. Partridge and Wall have shown that in most cases of withholding or withdrawing life support from critically ill infants, neonatologists provided opioid analgesia to these infants at the end of life, despite the potential respiratory depression of these agents.[42] The *intent* of the action—to alleviate pain and promote comfort—distinguishes the use of analgesics from the use of paralyzing agents, whose intent is to *ensure* death. The introduction of neuromuscular blocking agents at the time of withdrawal of life-sustaining medical treatment is considered ethically inappropriate, as is any form of active euthanasia.[45,49]

Withdrawal of Hydration and Nutrition

In some instances, after other invasive forms of life-sustaining treatment have been withdrawn, the withdrawal of hydration and nutrition may be considered. This can be morally troubling and create great stress for caregivers who view the withdrawal of hydration and nutrition as withholding basic comfort care—care they consider morally obligatory and symbolic of their relationship with the most vulnerable and dependent members of society. The practice may be defensible, however, when an infant with a hopeless prognosis cannot be fed orally, and feeding via other routes is perceived to be burdensome life-sustaining technological support.[9,41] In practice, withdrawal of hydration or nutrition is rarely undertaken and generally would be considered only at the specific request of parents.[39] Implementation of a decision to withdraw hydration and nutrition requires intensive attention to the child's comfort. As well, support of the family and members of the health care team is essential.

BRAIN DEATH AND ORGAN DONATION

Brain death is well defined for older age groups and has been accepted in North America for over 20 years as the threshold criterion for the removal of organs from heart-beating donors (without violating the dead donor rule). However, the diagnosis of brain death, particularly in infants less than 7 days of age is difficult and is, in fact, very rarely made. A number of clinical issues limit the usefulness of the concept in this patient population: the difficulty of establishing the exact cause of the coma, the clinical assessment of brain death (particularly the determination and reliability of the absence of brainstem reflexes), and the uncertainty regarding the validity of adjunctive laboratory tests.

Aside from the clinical difficulties in diagnosing neonatal brain death, there are concerns that the process for determining brain death for the purpose of solid organ procurement may affect parental decision making and patient management. Introducing parents to the concept of brain death moves the conversation from a discussion of the inevitability of death or a predicted poor quality of life to a discussion about the criteria for whole brain silence and its confirmation. A possible negative consequence of this shift in conversation is that parents may mistakenly believe that withdrawal of LSMT should be undertaken only when electrocerebral silence is confirmed. This could result in an infant being kept alive longer than might otherwise be the case, solely to determine if the criteria for brain death can be met. This raises the potential for the infant's condition to change during the evaluation period, so that an infant with severe hypoxic-ischemic encephalopathy, for example, who would have succumbed after withdrawal of LSMT, may survive in a severely compromised state (once the window of maximal cerebral edema and respiratory depression has passed). Even if both parents and care givers may wish to salvage some good from a tragic neonatal death, extreme caution should be exercised in discussions with grieving parents about brain death and potential organ donation.

PALLIATIVE CARE

Palliative care typically involves a team approach to the prevention and relief of physical, psychological, social, and spiritual suffering for the dying infant and the family.[10] The goal is to reduce pain and suffering and to manage the expected death in a humane way. Palliative care is less well established in neonatal care than it is in adult patient care. In part, this is because NICU practices tend to focus almost exclusively on curing illness and prolonging life. Relieving suffering, providing comfort care, and ensuring a "good death" tend to be considered only after life-prolonging treatment has proven to be ineffectual and burdensome, and death appears imminent.

Reasons for the slow adoption of palliative care in the NICU include the uncertainty surrounding the determination of a terminal prognosis, difficulty in moving away from an interventionist approach when therapeutic options still seem possible, a sense of personal defeat in acknowledging an inability to cure, a tendency to compartmentalize medical care into specialist teams with different agendas, a lack of formal training in palliative care, and an underappreciation of the benefits of palliative care. These many and varied reasons do not justify failure to consider palliative care as a legitimate treatment option when it is clear that cure is no longer possible, and that an interventionist approach does not serve the child's (or family's) best interests.

Well-developed protocols that outline the delivery of palliative care for newborns are available, and every NICU should have one.[10] The protocol should ensure continuity of care for the newborn; practical, emotional, and spiritual support for the parents; family-centered decision making; symptom management and comfort care for the infant; and organizational, emotional, and spiritual support for intensive care clinicians.[11]

ETHICAL DECISION MAKING

Ethical decision making requires effective and respectful communication based on mutual trust. When this background condition is satisfied, pregnant women and parents are better able to make informed decisions, trusting in the information provided by physicians and other members of the health care team.

Effective and Respectful Communication

Pregnant patients and parents require complete and truthful information about the diagnosis and prognosis, the available treatment options (including the option of no treatment), the benefits and harms associated with each option, and the limits of available technology. Sometimes this is relatively easy information to provide. As medicine advances, however, patients, parents, and physicians must sometimes struggle with difficult decisions that are often at the limits of medical knowledge where there is considerable complexity and uncertainty. The manner in which medical uncertainty is (or is not) communicated is extremely important and will certainly influence decision making.

The timing of any communication with pregnant patients and parents is also of crucial importance. Ideally, their readiness to receive information and their coping resources should be ascertained, so that appropriate information is shared with consideration of their acculturation to the medical setting. In acute situations, however, time is limited. If an urgent decision is required, the physician needs to move the relationship rapidly from one of strangers to one in which moral issues can be discussed openly. In these situations, it is important that physicians recognize the vulnerability of pregnant patients and parents. For example, in the immediate postpartum period, when there may be shock

and grief (and possibly denial), it may be extremely difficult for parents to carefully weigh all of the relevant considerations, particularly if there is prognostic uncertainty. The problem for the physician is that although effective communication is not something that can be rushed, the urgent context in which the interaction takes place exerts its own demands.

The manner in which important information is communicated to pregnant patients and to the parents of sick newborn infants influences their understanding of the situation, their ability to discuss moral issues and values openly, and their ability to participate effectively in the decision-making process. Information communicated in an honest and respectful manner is likely to foster trust. Information that is confusing, incomplete, evasive, or conveyed in a hurried or dismissive way is unlikely to do so. *Transparent communication* emphasizes the physician's reasoning, builds an understanding of the illness, and tempers unrealistic expectations.[28] The goal is to provide patients and parents with sufficient understanding of the relevant facts so that they can meaningfully participate in the decision-making process, even when the relevant facts are largely technical. Physicians need to share with patients and parents their thought processes regarding patient management, using language and terms that are easily understood. If there is a language barrier, high-quality, culturally sensitive translation and interpretation services should be sought.

Responsibility for communication must be clearly defined and not fragmented. The differences in responsibility between conveying day-to-day information and conveying information about severe diagnoses and the prognostic significance of specific findings must be clearly understood by all the members of the health care team. In addition, fragmentation is a risk in both perinatal and neonatal medicine, where care is provided by many individuals with expertise in different fields. Although the responsibilities of each discipline are generally known, in certain situations boundaries may be difficult to define and patterns of communication may be affected. Ideally, the responsible physician is able to integrate all of the important information and maintain a consistent pattern of communication with patients and parents.

A Collaborative Framework for Consensual Decision Making

A procedurally defined, collaborative framework for ethical decision making should facilitate the management and resolution of ethical problems in a consistent and compassionate manner. The following procedural framework is suggested:

1. *Create an optimal environment for discussion.* It is important to create a quiet and uninterrupted environment in which ethical issues and values can be thoroughly explored, despite demands on the time and energy of parents and staff.

2. *Establish that the presenting issue is indeed an ethical problem,* one in which moral values

conflict or moral uncertainty exists. Ethical deliberation is often complicated by communication problems and psychological issues. These need to be disentangled from the ethical issues.

3. *Identify the rightful decision makers.* A number of individuals may legitimately be involved in the decision-making process, including, at least, the patient or the parents, the physician with primary responsibility, and other members of the health care team directly involved in that patient's care. More generally, those who bear the greatest burden of care and conscience, those with special knowledge, and those health care professionals with the most continuous, committed, and trusting relationship with the patient or parents should be involved in the decision making.[40]

4. *Establish the relevant facts.* Good ethics begins with good facts. Medical facts include the diagnosis, the prognosis (and the estimated certainty of outcomes), past experience on the unit, relevant institutional policies, and relevant professional guidelines. Nonmedical facts include information about family relationships, language barriers, cultural and religious beliefs, and past experiences with the health care system. It is also important to ascertain the pregnant woman's or parents' understanding of the medical facts, their expectations of the technology involved, the quality of communication between the parents themselves, and the degree of trust in physicians and the medical system. The willingness of the physician to discuss personal views and beliefs may enhance the gathering of such information.

5. *Explore the options.* This entails an explicit discussion of treatment options and their known potential short- and long-term consequences. For physicians, a troubling element at this stage is whether to describe *all* possible options or only those they consider beneficial. Different physicians perceive their obligations differently. Physicians who feel morally obliged to inform the pregnant woman or parents of all possible options should not hesitate, at the same time, to offer a professional recommendation on the course of action considered most appropriate.[4]

6. *Develop consensus.* Consensus implies that no individual has unilateral responsibility for the decision. All decision makers must be in agreement with the plan of action proposed at the time, even though, on occasion, agreement may be a temporizing measure. Open, honest discussion of the goals and consequences of treatment allows patients, parents, physicians, and other legitimate decision makers to carefully consider a range of professional and personal beliefs, values and preferences, and to then meaningfully explore reasoned arguments for and against various options. This process holds the promise of harmonious, consensual decision making.

7. *Implement the decision.* Once a consensual decision has been reached, additional issues may need to be addressed with patients and parents to ensure effective implementation. For example, when the decision is made to withhold or withdraw LSMT in the NICU, there should be an open discussion about the manner of death, the option for parents to be present or not, the performance of religious rituals, and the anticipated grieving process.

Following a structured decision-making process, such as the one outlined here, helps to ensure that appropriate views and preferences are made explicit. This promotes harmonious decision making, as all of the participants in the process may come to understand the reasons and values underlying a particular choice.

When Consensus Cannot Be Reached in the NICU

In most instances, participants in the decision-making process can arrive at a morally sound decision regarding the best course of action in a particular situation. Attempts at consensual decision making, however, are sometimes unsuccessful and may result in a degree of conflict and intractability. Occasionally, this conflict is between parents who disagree with each other regarding what is in the best interests of their newborn. More frequently, however, the conflict is between the parents of a newborn and the health care providers who have different perceptions of the child's best interests.

The following guidelines are proposed to promote continuing negotiation and resolution of conflict in the NICU:

1. *Allow time for further clinical observation.* In the specific case of parental objections to forgoing treatment that the physician believes is not beneficial, it may be unrealistic to expect agreement from the parents the first time this option is raised. Prudence suggests moving as fast as the slowest member of the decision-making group, provided that the infant is not thereby further compromised.

2. *Ensure full parental comprehension of the medical information.* Early expressions of treatment preference by parents, such as "do everything possible," need to be carefully examined. There is a tendency for busy medical teams to reduce parental expressions into simple one-line statements and not to explore their meaning. Such statements may be an expression of parental love or an expression of frustration with the medical team, and not really an informed choice about what is in the best interests of the newborn. In addition, in view of parents' potential denial of the severity of their infant's condition, it is important to check parents

understanding again and again.[23] If it appears that inconsistent information has been provided to parents by different individuals or teams, it may be advisable to convene a formal interdisciplinary case conference to explicate these differing viewpoints.

3. *Continue to discuss, explore, and possibly challenge the underlying reasons for the differences in choice.* It is important for health care providers to try to understand the parents' views, beliefs, and preferences. Physicians must recognize that the parents' beliefs and values are informed by ethnic and cultural traditions, customs, and institutions and that these influences may be significantly divergent from their own.[13] It is equally appropriate and professionally incumbent on physicians to challenge views that they perceive to be not in the child's best interests.

4. *Continue to negotiate toward consensus.* Parents may have great difficulty in making an unassisted decision; the burden and potential guilt of decision making experienced by parents is often immense and underappreciated by the medical team. The consensual nature of a joint decision-making process and the shared burden of the decision must be reinforced. In addition, it must be recognized that there may be medically imposed obstacles to achieving consensus: frequent changes in the responsible physician from one neonatologist to the next, the failure of each physician to establish a therapeutic alliance with the parents, the persistence of communication barriers between the physician and the parents, or the development of a contest of wills between the physician and parents as to who will sway the other. All these factors need to be considered in negotiating with parents toward consensus.

5. *Broaden the parents' moral community.* Identifying the locus of decision-making authority within each family's moral community may involve the inclusion of additional family members, grandparents, significant others, and religious or spiritual advisors in parent meetings.

6. *Share the attending physician's moral load by actively seeking opinions from colleagues.* Although the physician responsible for the case bears the final responsibility for the approach taken with the parents, for both personal as well as legal reasons, it is important to establish that the physician is supported by a responsible body of medical opinion.

7. *Involve a bioethicist or ethics consultation team, as appropriate.* There may be benefit in involving an institutional ethics committee with experience in case consultation and review, a clinical ethics consultation team, or a clinical ethicist (depending on the available resources). Most hospital ethics committees include experts in medicine, nursing, philosophy, law, religion, and social services. The functions of these committees vary widely, but some are particularly skilled at case consultation. In a few institutions, the ethics committee as a whole reviews relevant cases. More commonly, however, a smaller subcommittee, an infant care review team, or an individual ethics consultant undertakes this responsibility. The hope is that a multidisciplinary team approach will ensure consideration of all relevant concerns, and that this, in turn, will help with the elucidation of the ethical issues. However, team members may disagree among themselves, and some members may dominate others. Also, in some instances, the ethics committee or consultation team may not be qualified to deal with the subject matter, or it may be overly concerned with the institutional impact of a decision rather than with the specifics of the case. Experience suggests that consultation with individual bioethicists and smaller ethics consultation teams may be of greater benefit to decision makers than the practice of 'ethics by committee.'

8. *Consider transferring responsibility of care for the infant to another, accepting physician.* When differences of opinion remain and the degree of physician moral compromise is significant, it may be advisable to involve another staff member with whom the parents have formed a therapeutic alliance.

Despite these efforts, the moral problem may not be amenable to consensual resolution. Rational people of good will may hold views that are irreconcilable. Individuals involved in a failed attempt at deriving consensus may experience what Webster and Baylis term *moral residue*—"that which each of us carries with us from those times in our lives when in the face of moral distress we have seriously compromised ourselves or allowed ourselves to be compromised."[51]

Until consensus can be achieved, withdrawal of LSMT should not be undertaken. On rare occasions, physicians seek authority to make unilateral decisions via institutional or legal redress. Burt suggests that clinicians seeking such unilateral authority for withdrawal, even in the most extreme circumstances, should understand this course of action not only as a clinical failure but also as unjustified in principle.[7]

The Courts

When a pregnant woman or the parents dissent from the medical recommendations, and ethical conflict appears intractable, an institutional decision may be made to involve the courts. This course of action is generally unsatisfactory: it increases the anguish for patients and families, it destroys the patient-parent-physician relationship, it creates (or increases) conflict between members of the health care team and invariably results in a significant drain on staff time and morale, and it can be extremely costly and time consuming for all parties involved. Furthermore, use of the judicial system can be very damaging for the institution's reputation. Ideally, institutional policies developed by the hospital ethics committee and staff should be in place to minimize the need for judicial intervention.

A FINAL WORD: THE PHYSICIAN'S ETHICAL RESPONSIBILITIES

The physician's responsibility to the competent pregnant patient is well defined and well established—to respect the patient's wishes regarding treatment even when this may be contrary to fetal best interests.[25,26,47] So too, the physician's responsibility to the neonatal patient is well defined and well established—a right and good action within the best-interests standard of judgment. In the broadest terms, these responsibilities are best discharged in the context of a constructive and mutually respectful relationship that clearly recognizes that patient and family values and beliefs are integral to the decision-making process. Physicians' responsibilities include the necessity of challenging views that they consider contrary to the patient's best interests. Furthermore, in the context of team medicine, the attending physician is responsible for developing and maintaining positive relationships with all members of the health care team to better promote open discussion of moral problems with pregnant patients and parents of newborn children. The physician also has an obligation to foster the ethical experience and education of the interdisciplinary team, as well as that of junior staff and trainees.

By setting a standard of ethical responsibility for the care of pregnant women and fetuses, as well as newborns and families, physicians working in perinatal and neonatal care send a message to society that will promote public confidence and trust in their professional practice. The perinatal high-risk unit or NICU team should be more than a group of physicians, nurses, and many other professionals working in an isolated area of the hospital trying to master new technology and break new ground. Ideally, it should be an open, analytic, self-critical, and responsive group providing ethically responsible care to pregnant women, newborn infants, and their families.

REFERENCES

1. American College of Obstetricians and Gynecologists, Committee on Ethics: Patient choice: Maternal-fetal conflict. Washington DC, American College of Obstetricians and Gynecologists, 1987, Committee Opinion No. 55.
2. American Medical Association, Board of Trustees: Legal interventions during pregnancy: Court-ordered medical treatment and legal penalties for potentially harmful behavior by pregnant women. JAMA 264:2663, 1990.
3. Annas G: Standard of Care: The Law of American Bioethics. New York, Oxford University Press, 1993.
4. Baylis F, Downie J: Professional recommendations: Disclosing facts and values. J Med Ethics 27:20, 2001.
5. Beauchamp TL, Childress JF: Principles of Biomedical Ethics. New York, Oxford University Press, 2001.
6. Bergh T et al: Deliveries and children born after in-vitro fertilisation in Sweden 1982-95: A retrospective cohort study. Lancet 354:1579, 1999.
7. Burt RA: Resolving disputes between clinicians and family about "futility" of treatment. Semin Perinatol 27:495, 2003.
8. Caniano D, Baylis F: Ethical considerations in prenatal surgical consultation. Pediatr Surg Int 15:303, 1999.
9. Carter BS, Leuthner SR: The ethics of withholding/withdrawing nutrition in the newborn. Semin Perinatol 27:480, 2003.
10. Catlin A, Carter B: Creation of a neonatal end of life palliative care protocol. J Perinatol 22:184, 2002.
11. Clarke EB et al: Quality indicators for end-of life care in the intensive care unit. Crit Care Med 31:2255, 2003.
12. Cole FS: Extremely preterm birth: Defining the limits of hope. N Engl J Med 343:429, 2000.
13. Elliott C: Where ethics comes from and what to do about it. Hastings Cent Rep 22:28, 1992.
14. Ells C: Culture, ethics, and pediatric surgery. Semin Pediatr Surg 10:186, 2001.
15. Emanuel EJ, Emanuel LL: Four models of the physician-patient relationship. JAMA 267:2221, 1992.
16. Flagler E et al: Bioethics for clinicians. XII: Ethical dilemmas that arise in the care of pregnant women: Rethinking "maternal-fetal conflicts." Can Med Assoc J 156:1729, 1997.
17. Frader JE, Watchko J: Futility issues in pediatrics. In Zucker MB, Zucker HD (eds): Medical Futility. Cambridge, UK, Cambridge University Press, 1997.
18. Greisen G: Meaningful care for babies born after 22, 23 or 24 weeks. Acta Paediatr 93:153, 2004.
19. Hardart GE, Truog RD: Attitudes and preferences of intensivists regarding the role of family interests in medical decision making for incompetent patients. Crit Care Med 31:1895, 2003.
20. Hardwig J: What about the family? Hastings Cent Rep 20:5, 1990.
21. Hefferman P, Heilig S: Giving "moral distress" a voice: Ethical concerns among neonatal intensive care unit personnel. Camb Q Healthc Ethics 8:173, 1999.
22. Helft P et al: The rise and fall of the futility movement. N Engl J Med 343:293, 2000.
23. Howe EG: Helping infants by seeing the invisible. J Clin Ethics 12:191, 2001.
24. Hussain N, Rosenkrantz TS: Ethical considerations in the management of infants born at extremely low gestational age. Semin Perinatol 27:458, 2003.
25. In re A.C., 573 A 2d 1235 (DC Ct. App 1990).
26. In re Baby Boy Doe, 632 NE 2d 326 (Ill App 1 Dist 1994).
27. Jameton A: Nursing Practice: The Ethical Issues. Englewood Cliffs, NJ, Prentice-Hall, 1984.
28. King NM: Transparency in neonatal intensive care. Hastings Cent Rep 22:18, 1992.
29. Kinlaw K: The changing nature of neonatal ethics in practice. Clin Perinatol 23:417, 1996.
30. Kollee LAA et al: End-of-life decisions in neonates. Semin Perinatol 23:234, 1999.
31. Leuthner SR: Decisions regarding resuscitation of the extremely premature infant and models of best interest. J Perinatol 21:193, 2001.
32. Levene M: Is intensive care for immature babies justified? Acta Paediatr 93:149, 2004.
33. Lorenz JM: Management decisions in extremely premature infants. Semin Neonatol 8:475, 2003.
34. Losco J, Shublak M: Paternal-fetal conflict: An examination

of paternal responsibilities to the fetus. Politics Life Sciences 13:63, 1994.

35. Lyerly AD, Mahowald MB: Maternal-fetal surgery for treatment of myelomeningocele. Clin Perinatol 30:155, 2003.

36. Mahowald MB: Women and Children in Health Care: An Unequal Majority. New York, Oxford University Press, 1993.

37. McCullough LB, Chervenak FA: Ethics in Obstetrics and Gynecology. New York, Oxford University Press, 1994.

38. McHugh-Strong CM, Sanders MR: Experience with newborn intensive care deaths in a tertiary setting. Am J Perinatol 17:27, 2000.

39. Miraie ED, Mahowald MB: Withholding nutrition from seriously ill newborn infants: A parent's perspective. J Pediatr 113:262, 1988.

40. Mitchell C: Care of severely impaired infant raises ethical issues. Am Nurse 16:9, 1984.

41. Nelson LJ et al: Forgoing medically provided nutrition and hydration in pediatric patients. J Law Med Ethics 23:33, 1995.

42. Partridge JC, Wall SN: Analgesia for dying infants whose life support is withdrawn or withheld. Pediatrics 99:76, 1997.

43. Pellegrino E: The Philosophical Foundation of Medicine: Essays by Dr. Edmund Pellegrino. In Bulger RJ, McGovern JP, eds: Physician and Philosopher. Charlottesville, Va, Carden Jennings, 2001.

44. Rhoden NK: Treating Baby Doe: The ethics of uncertainty. Hastings Cent Rep 16:34, 1986.

45. Royal College of Paediatrics and Child Health: Withholding and Withdrawing Life-Saving Treatment in Children: A Framework for Practice. London, Royal College of Paediatrics and Child Health, 1997.

46. Society of Obstetricians and Gynaecologists of Canada (SOGC): SOGC Clinical Practice Guidelines, Policy Statement No. 67: Involuntary intervention in the lives of pregnant women. J Soc Obstet Gynaecol Can 19:1200, 1997.

47. *St. George's Healthcare NHS Trust v. SR,* 3 ALL ER 673 (1998).

48. Truog RD et al: The problem with futility. N Engl J Med 326:1560, 1992.

49. Truog RD et al: Pharmacologic paralysis and withdrawal of mechanical ventilation at the end of life. N Engl J Med 342:508, 2000.

50. Wall SN, Partridge JC: Death in the intensive care nursery: Physician practice of withdrawing and withholding life support. Pediatrics 99:64, 1997.

51. Webster G, Baylis F: Moral residue. In Rubin S, Zoloth L (eds): Margin of Error: The Ethics of Mistakes in the Practice of Medicine. Hagerstown, Md, University Publishing Group, 2000, p 217.

4

Legal Issues in Neonatal-Perinatal Medicine

Robert Turbow and Jonathan M. Fanaroff

Clinicians often experience trepidation when interacting with the legal system. The unfamiliar concepts and vocabulary coupled with the seemingly unpredictable nature of legal decision making can create an environment of confusion and apprehension. For a variety of reasons, these concerns are particularly acute for neonatal-perinatal practitioners.

There can be tremendous clinical and ethical uncertainty surrounding the decision to resuscitate an extremely premature baby. Neonatologists are often asked to attend deliveries for premature infants at the limits of viability. Must the physician honor the parents' requests? What if the parents request that their extremely premature infant not be resuscitated? What are the roles and duties of the perinatologist, the neonatologist, and the hospital administration? These questions are not obscure or theoretical. A recently overturned $60,000,000 verdict[32] accentuates the importance of a clinician's familiarity with the laws that affect clinical practice. In these cases, the legal system can seem capricious and arbitrary. When the stakes are so high, and there is a lack of applicable case law, it is understandable that clinicians are left in a quandary.

During residency and fellowship training, as well as after training is completed, clinicians interact with the legal system. This may be in the form of a contract with a new employer, a lease for office space, or as a defendant in a medical malpractice suit. This chapter focuses on recent legal developments in perinatal-neonatal medicine that can affect the daily professional lives of those who work in high-risk maternal units, delivery rooms, and neonatal intensive care units (NICUs). Several complex issues are addressed. What are the legal rights of a pregnant woman who requires medication that is known to be dangerous to her fetus? What are the legal ramifications of a neonatologist disregarding a parent's request to forgo delivery room resuscitation? What are a physician's liabilities when providing phone supervision of an ambulance transfer of a critically ill patient?

Practicing clinicians must understand their rights, duties, and liabilities as physicians. They must understand the legal relationship that they have with their employers, the hospital, their referring doctors, consultants, and the neonatal nurse practitioners (NNPs) and physician assistants (PAs) they supervise.

This chapter should also assist the clinician in understanding the terms and concepts of medical law. A certain baseline vocabulary is necessary to adequately discuss the relevant issues. Throughout the chapter, terms and definitions will be introduced. When appropriate, the reader will be referred to additional sources for further reading. Additionally, certain landmark cases will be discussed. This chapter provides legal background so the clinician will have a more complete understanding of the legal principles, cases, and statutes that affect the daily practice of perinatal-neonatal medicine.

Disclaimer

The authors of this chapter have attempted to provide a background or framework of law for the purpose of educating clinicians. Nothing contained in this chapter should be viewed as substantive legal advice. This chapter does not create an attorney-client relationship between the authors and any readers.

Laws generally vary from state to state. Federal laws may represent a separate body of rules that can affect a given practitioner.

Legal cases often hinge on very specific facts. Courts and juries make determinations based on the facts of a given case. Even slight variation in circumstances can result in a completely different legal outcome. A practitioner should never assume that his or her situation is identical to the parties in another situation. Seasoned practitioners recognize that not all 27-week gestation babies with respiratory distress syndrome have identical courses. Likewise, each legal situation has its own nuances that can determine a distinctive outcome. Courts expend considerable effort to distinguish the facts when comparing one case to another.

The authors neither advocate for nor reject the judicial decisions and legislative actions described in this chapter. Readers are hereby informed that they should become familiar with the current laws that affect practice in their state. Readers are further advised that if they have specific questions, they should always consult with a qualified attorney.

GENERAL LEGAL PRINCIPLES

Legislative Law and Case Law

Those unfamiliar with our legal system may have difficulty understanding the distinction between case law and statutes. In general, a significant portion of U.S. law is based on the common law. These laws have roots in English law from the last few hundred years. In many ways, the common law provides the foundation for the U.S. perspective on contracts, property, torts, criminal law, evidence, and many other legal disciplines.

The common law was created by judges who were generally evaluating disputes between parties. More recently, extremely well known cases such as *Brown v Board of Education*[17] or *Roe v Wade*[53] are examples of judicial decisions that became U.S. law. These were cases that involved defined parties. The U.S. Supreme Court made a determination, and the law was established.

In addition, many laws are created by elected legislative bodies, such as the U.S. Congress or a state legislature. Often, court opinions state that it is not the role of the judiciary to redefine or change the definition of laws that were created by a legislative body; rather, the legislature is generally responsible for changing the law.

The case of *Vo v Superior Court*[64] is illustrative. This Arizona case involved a woman who was shot in the head during a drive-by shooting on the freeway. The woman and her 23-week fetus died as a result of the shooting. The prosecutor subsequently charged Nghia Hugh Vo with two counts of murder. The Arizona Court of Appeals considered the propriety and legality of charging Vo with two counts of murder. The court stated that when the legislature created the murder statutes, they did not intend to include a fetus in the definition of a person or human being. The court concluded that the unlawful killing of a fetus could not be murder. Then the court stated that if the legislature intended to include a fetus in the definition of a person, it was the responsibility of the legislature to change the homicide statute. Shortly after the *Vo* opinion, the Arizona legislature amended the manslaughter statute to include the intentional or reckless killing of an "unborn child at any stage of its development by any physical injury to the mother of such child which would be murder if the death of the mother had occurred."[10]

The *Vo* case serves as an example of the dynamic balance between the two branches of government that create law. In this case, the judges stated that it was the responsibility of the legislature to change the definition of manslaughter. The legislature responded to this case by expanding the definition of manslaughter to include unlawful killing of a fetus. Although the *Vo* case has also been included in the acrimonious debate of fetal rights, it is presented here to elucidate the concept of legislative law as opposed to judicial law.

State Law and Federal Law

Another area of potential confusion is the differences between state laws and federal laws. In general, clinicians find themselves in state court subjected to state laws. There are significant restrictions that keep most cases out of federal court. For example, a civil rights case, a dispute involving the Americans with Disabilities Act (ADA), or a malpractice case that occurred at a military hospital are three examples of cases that could be adjudicated in federal court. Unless a case meets narrow criteria to qualify for federal adjudication, most legal disputes involving perinatal or neonatal practitioners are tried in state court.

How do laws in one state affect clinical practice in another state? Practitioners may wonder how a Michigan court decision will affect a practitioner in Ohio or Nevada. As a general rule, state court decisions are binding only in that state. If the Texas Supreme Court has ruled on an issue, then the courts' findings are viewed as state law in Texas, and the legislatures and courts of California, North Carolina, or Wyoming are not necessarily bound by the Texas court ruling. A state court's ruling could be persuasive in other states, but the conclusions of one state court are not generally viewed as binding on courts in other states.

This concept of one state's laws affecting another state also holds true for laws passed by state legislatures. If the California legislature passes a law concerning access to prenatal care, the law will have essentially no effect on the citizens of Connecticut or Virginia. Issues such as the definition of "live birth" are treated differently by different state governments. Clinicians are strongly urged to check their applicable state laws before relying on case law or statutes cited in this chapter.

General Structure of the Federal and State Court Systems

Several of the cases cited in this chapter mention the holdings of various state and federal appellate courts, and several U.S. Supreme Court decisions are also discussed. How does a case get to an appellate court or to the U.S. Supreme Court? A variety of rules determine which court will hear a dispute and which appellate court has the jurisdiction to review the decisions of the lower courts. Most of the cases covered in this chapter would be adjudicated in the state court system. The general hierarchies of the federal and state court systems are depicted in Figure 4-1.

SUPERVISION OF OTHERS

Theories of Liability for Attending Physicians

Attending neonatologists carry substantial responsibility. In general, they bear ultimate medical responsibility for

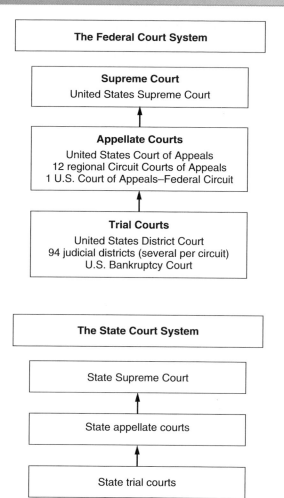

FIGURE 4-1. Hierarchy of the federal and state court systems.

the neonates under their care. Practically speaking, it is impossible for one physician to provide all of the care for a sick newborn. Depending on the clinical setting, nurses, neonatal nurse practitioners, respiratory therapists, social workers, residents, fellows, consultants, and many others all contribute greatly to patient care. The exact demarcation of responsibility and liability borne by attending physicians for these alternate providers is often difficult to determine.

In holding attending physicians liable for the acts of others, courts tend to rely upon three different theories of liability. An early theory of attending liability was known as the "captain of the ship doctrine." Physicians, particularly surgeons, were assumed to be much like naval captains and have complete control over the operating room (the "ship") and all the medical personnel (the "crew") within. With this control came responsibility for all negligent actions performed by anyone under the surgeon's "command."[15] Fortunately, most courts now recognize the increasing complexity of health care provision and have rejected the captain of the ship doctrine as "an antiquated doctrine that fails

to reflect the emergence of hospitals as modern health care facilities."[42]

Respondeat superior is a more accepted doctrine of physician liability for negligence of others under his or her control. *Respondeat superior* literally means "let the master answer." Thus because an attending physician has a right of control over an NNP or resident, the negligence of that provider is imputed to the attending physician in certain circumstances. For example, under *Respondeat Superior*, the attending would be responsible if a resident negligently places umbilical lines or an endotracheal tube. However, the attending would not necessarily be liable, under *Respondeat Superior,* if a bedside nurse was negligent in the observation or reporting of a significant intravenous infiltrate. Under the earlier "Captain of the Ship" doctrine, the attending may very well have been deemed to be responsible for the IV infiltrate.

The attending physician can also be held liable for providing "negligent supervision." For those supervisees under his or her charge, the attending physician is responsible for providing adequate training and supervision. Furthermore, the attending physician must be readily available and promptly respond to requests for assistance. This was underscored in a 2004 obstetrical malpractice case in which the attending anesthesiologist was not immediately available for an emergency cesarean section, and the fetus allegedly suffered as a result. The case was settled for $35,000,000.[11,50]

Finally, in many cases, an attending physician becomes liable for the actions of supervisees by the creation of a doctor-patient relationship that flows from the patient through the supervisee to the attending. In a recent case in New York a patient was seen by a nurse practitioner (NP) in an emergency department, and the NP misdiagnosed the condition. The attending physician discussed the patient with the NP and signed the chart but did not personally examine or speak with the patient. The court, interpreting New York's law regarding nurse practitioners, held that "the ultimate responsibility for diagnosis and treatment rests with the physician."[51]

Physician Assistants

Many NICUs now employ physician assistants. A PA is a health care professional who may practice medicine only with physician supervision. A certified physician assistant (PA-C) is a PA who has completed training and passed a national certification exam. PAs' scope of practice is governed by state law and varies from state to state. In many states PAs are authorized to prescribe medications. PAs can contribute greatly to the care of neonates. It is important, however, for physicians to determine the scope of practice for PAs in their individual state for two reasons. First, there is increased potential malpractice liability for the supervising physician when PAs exceed their scope of practice. Second, physicians may risk loss of their license if they are "found to have condoned the unauthorized practice of medicine by a nurse or other health care professional for whose conduct [they are] responsible."[12]

Advanced Practice Neonatal Nurses

In recent years there has been a rapid increase in the number of advanced practice neonatal nurses (APNNs) in the United States. An APNN is a registered nurse who has completed a master's degree in advanced nursing practice and, in most cases, has passed a national certifying exam. APNNs have played an invaluable role in improving health care for neonates in a wide variety of settings ranging from urban academic centers to small rural hospitals. Under certain circumstances, however, there has also been additional liability for the physician.

In the field of neonatology there are generally two recognized types of APNNs: one is a clinical nurse specialist (CNS), and the other is a neonatal nurse practitioner (NNP). The CNS is a registered nurse with a master's degree who has expertise in neonatal nursing. The NNP is a registered nurse with experience in neonatal nursing (many have completed a master's degree) and additional clinical training in the management of newborns. NNPs are allowed to assess, diagnose, and treat "independently," although generally they work under the supervision of a physician.

The licensure and scope of practice of APNNs vary considerably from state to state. Furthermore, each institution must have policies and procedures for granting privileges for APNNs. The American Academy of Pediatrics Policy Statement on Advanced Practice in Neonatal Nursing released in June 2003 recommends the following:

- A neonatologist should supervise an APNN in the NICU.

- The APNN should collaborate and consult with other health care professionals.

- The APNN should be certified by a nationally recognized organization and should maintain that certification.

- The APNN should participate in continuing education.

- The APNN should comply with hospital policy regarding credentialing and recredentialing.[9]

One critical issue concerning APNNs is the liability of the supervising physician. In some states, NNPs are licensed to practice independently and thus require no supervision under the law. If an NNP is hired by a hospital as an independent contractor with his or her own privileges, then the physician does not employ the NNP. In these situations, when the NNP and physician are interacting in the management of a baby, the physician is acting the same as when consulting with any other provider, with similar liability.

In the majority of instances, however, and in almost all NICU environments, APNNs are not hired as independent contractors but rather as employees of the physician or hospital. In these cases, the employer is vicariously liable for the acts of the employee. The NNP is often supervised by an attending neonatologist who bears ultimate responsibility for the patient as discussed earlier.

MALPRACTICE

Medical malpractice litigation can be contentious and acrimonious. It is a pervasive issue that appears with great regularity in the popular press. Many books have been dedicated to the subject of medical malpractice.[24,13] In the 2004 State of the Union Address, President Bush spoke of the need to reform the current medical malpractice system.[41] This section is largely limited to a discussion of malpractice in perinatal-neonatal medicine (Box 4-1).

Malpractice is part of a broader area of law known as *torts*. Tort law largely deals with the duties and responsibilities that persons have toward one another. Torts are generally divided into two groups: intentional torts and unintentional torts. For example, defamation, invasion of privacy, civil battery, and professional malpractice are all torts, but only malpractice is a type of unintentional tort.

BOX 4-1. Common Malpractice Suits in Neonatology

Delivery Room Management or Resuscitation

Poor Neurologic Outcome
Cerebral palsy: neonatologist named as codefendant with obstetrician-perinatologist
Asphyxia: plaintiff alleges some component of injury occurred postnatally

Line Complications
Vascular accidents related to central venous lines
Loss of fingers or toes associated with central lines
Thrombus and complications from thrombus

Delay in Diagnosis or Treatment
Poor blood gases, prolonged hypotension (see also poor neurologic outcome)
Delay in antibiotic administration
Congenital hip dislocation
Congenital heart disease

Transport Team (Registered Nurse and Respiratory Technologist)
Medications or care provided by transport team (e.g., excessive heparin given)
Sterling v. Johns Hopkins[1] (pregnant woman dies after transport)

Failure to Adequately Monitor
Blood sugar
Blood oxygen: either hypoxia (brain damage) or hyperoxia (ROP)
Seizure

Negligence means that a person's behavior has deviated from a standard of "due care."[26] Malpractice is considered a specific type of negligence. By some interpretations, malpractice is also considered a type of breach of contract with the patient, so the defendant is technically being accused of committing a tort and violating contract law.

Lawyers, accountants, physicians, and other professionals are held to a certain level of conduct. If one's professional conduct is substandard, and a client, customer, or patient is harmed by this substandard conduct, then a plaintiff may attempt to show that the practitioner has committed malpractice. To win a malpractice case the plaintiff must demonstrate four critical elements: duty, breach, causation, and damages.

Duty

"The duty of care owed to an individual, for purposes of a claim of medical malpractice, is based primarily on the existence of the physician-patient relationship."[57] To proceed with a negligence case, the plaintiff must demonstrate that the defendant had a duty to the plaintiff. This has been described as a "threshold issue." Does the defendant owe a duty to the injured party? If there is no duty, then no claim of negligence can be sustained.

For example, if a neonatologist has privileges only at hospital A and the physician is called and refuses to attend a high-risk delivery at hospital B, the physician likely would have no professional relationship with the pregnant woman or her baby at hospital B. The neonatologist cannot breach his or her duty if no duty to the defendant exists. This concept of duty is separate from the moral or ethical obligation to provide care. A doctor cannot be liable to a patient if there is no legal duty. Likewise, if NNP Smith is on call for the evening and NNP Jones has left town with his family for a scheduled vacation, it will be difficult for an injured plaintiff to demonstrate that NNP Jones had a duty to attend a high-risk delivery while he was out of town.

Does a physician caring for a pregnant woman have a duty to the newborn even after the baby is born and being cared for by another physician? In *Nold v Binyon*,[47] a woman tested positive for hepatitis B. Her newborn did not receive hepatitis B immune globulin (HGIB) or the hepatitis B vaccine, and the baby subsequently became a chronic carrier for hepatitis B. The trial court ruled, and the Kansas Supreme Court agreed, that the delivering doctor had a duty to inform the woman of her hepatitis B status. The Supreme Court stated, "a physician who has a doctor-patient relationship with a pregnant woman who intends to carry her fetus to term and deliver a healthy baby also has a doctor-patient relationship with the fetus."

SUPERVISING OTHERS

As discussed earlier, neonatologists are often asked to supervise the care provided by others. This supervisory role generally establishes a physician-patient relationship with any patient who is cared for by the supervised NNP or PA. In these cases, the physician has a duty to the patient even if the supervised NNP is providing all of the bedside care.

TELEPHONE ADVICE

Is "duty" established when one physician consults with another over the phone? Telephone advice and transport present an interesting legal challenge. On many transports, the responsible physician at the receiving facility is not physically present with the transport team. However, the receiving physician often begins to offer clinical advice when first contact is initiated by the referring facility. In general, this can be a situation of shared duty. Both the referring physician and the receiving physician may have a duty to the patient. However, the receiving physician may have no duty to the patient if the receiving physician is acting more in the role of a consultant.

In *Sterling v Johns Hopkins*,[57] a woman was admitted at approximately 32 to 33 weeks' gestation to a hospital and she developed severe preeclampsia and suspected HELLP (*h*emolysis, *e*levated *l*iver enzymes, *l*ow *p*latelets) syndrome. The treating physician called the emergency transport service to arrange transport to Johns Hopkins because the receiving hospital had an NICU that could potentially care for a premature infant. The receiving physician spoke with the referring physician on the telephone. The woman became unresponsive during the transport. She suffered an intracranial bleed and later died.

The husband sued the receiving hospital alleging negligent advice given over the phone. The court determined that there was no physician-patient relationship between the receiving physician and the pregnant woman. Because the receiving physician was acting more in the role of a consultant and the referring physician was free to make his own management decisions, the court ruled that the receiving doctor did not have a duty to the pregnant woman. "Where the treating physician exercises his or her own independent judgment in determining whether to accept or reject [a consultant's] advice, . . . the consultative physician should not be regarded as a joint provider of medical services with respect to the patient."[28] In this case, the court determined that the treating physician maintained decision-making power, and that the physician at the receiving facility was acting more as a consultant than comanaging the patient. The court determined that no duty existed between the receiving facility and the patient.

PRENATAL CONSULTATION

Prenatal consultations might or might not give rise to a duty between the neonatologist and the pregnant woman and her child. Among the determining factors, courts seem to evaluate the formality of the consultation and the presence or absence of contact between the parties. In *Hill v Kokosky*,[33] an obstetrician informally consulted with a neonatologist. The plaintiff had been admitted to the hospital at 22 weeks' gestation with a diagnosis of incompetent cervix. The two physicians informally discussed the case over the telephone. The obstetrician discussed the case in the abstract, and the neonatologist tended to agree with the obstetrician's management. There was no referral or formal consultation. From the record, it appeared that the neonatologist did not review the chart, speak with the mother, or even know the mother's name. The baby was born two weeks later and developed severe cerebral palsy.

In her malpractice action against the neonatologist, the mother maintained that the neonatologist gave substandard advice concerning birthing options, and that this substandard advice contributed to her child's injuries. Given the facts, the court concluded that no physician-patient relationship existed between the neonatologist and the family. It is important to understand why the court ruled for the defendant in this case. Casual telephone advice was given to a colleague. The neonatologist did not know the name of the patient and never spoke with her. The court concluded that the neonatologist did not prescribe a course of treatment but rather gave recommendations that could be accepted or rejected by the obstetrician.

In contrast to this case, if a neonatologist is formally consulted and speaks with a family and makes recommendations concerning management, then there may very well be a duty to the mother and her infant. Judicial decisions also seem to hinge on whether or not a consulting physician is recommending a specific course of therapy or merely making suggestions that the original physician can either follow or ignore.

In general, however, it is not difficult for a plaintiff to establish that a clinician had a duty to the patient. Usually, the physician has provided care to the patient and the plaintiff easily establishes that the duty requirement has been met. Especially, in the case of hospital-based physicians, such as neonatologists, the element of "duty" is generally established.

Breach

STANDARD OF CARE

What is the duty that is owed? The duty is to provide reasonable care under the circumstances. While generalists are held to a standard of "same or similar community," specialists and subspecialists, such as neonatologists, NNPs, and perinatologists, are generally held to the higher national standard of care.[48] Accordingly, an expert witness from a different state can testify about the national standard of care for a neonatologist. In these cases, the neonatologist's care is not being compared to the care provided in a similar community; the care is evaluated in light of national standards.

In many malpractice suits involving obstetricians, perinatologists, and neonatologists, considerable emphasis is placed on this element. Often the defense vigorously maintains that "the doctor did nothing wrong." The defense often takes the position that there has been an unfortunate outcome but the defendant practiced within the standard of care. If the defense can prove that the physician acted within the standard of care, then the plaintiff cannot successfully maintain a malpractice action.

A typical case is a brachial plexus injury following birth. In *Knapp v Northeastern Ohio Obstetricians,*[40] a mother alleged that her child's brachial plexus injury was the result of excessive traction applied by the obstetrician. The trial court found, and the appellate court affirmed, that the evidence did not support the mother's allegations. The court concluded that the obstetrician had not breached the standard of care.

Malpractice cases concerning retinopathy of prematurity (ROP) are another relatively common negligence case involving newborns. In *Brownsville Pediatric Associates v Reyes,*[18] a pediatrician was found liable for substandard ventilator management. The expert witness testified that the child's resulting brain damage and ROP were related to hyperventilation and hyperoxia, respectively. The plaintiff was awarded $8,000,000, and the defendant's appeal was denied.

Another ROP case[30] dealt with the responsibility of the neonatologist, the pediatricians, the pediatric ophthalmologist, and the parents when 29-week-gestation twins missed their follow-up appointments for ROP evaluation. The twins became legally blind. In this case, the neonatologist apparently provided all necessary referrals and documentation, and she was not named in the resulting suit.

THE ROLE OF THE EXPERT WITNESS

In tort proceedings other than medical malpractice, a person with common knowledge generally knows and understands "due care." If someone is walking down the street with closed eyes and bumps into someone else and injures the other person, a lay juror does not need an expert witness. The lay juror understands that one should not walk down the street with closed eyes because someone else could be injured as a result. In medical malpractice cases, however, the lay juror generally does *not* have a grasp of "reasonable care under the circumstances." This is one of the roles of the expert witness. To serve as an expert witness, a person must have specific knowledge and training that qualifies him or her to serve in this capacity. The Rhode Island statute,[52] for example, states that "only those persons who by knowledge, skill, experience, training, or education qualify as experts in the field of the alleged malpractice."

If a fetal monitoring strip shows severe, repetitive, late decelerations, should the obstetrician perform a cesarean section? It is the role of the expert witnesses to educate the jury so that the jurors have a grasp of what is (and is not) reasonable care under the circumstances. Both sides (plaintiff and defendant) usually hire their own expert witnesses. The plaintiff's expert generally maintains that the physician practiced outside of the standard of care. The defense expert maintains just the opposite. After the expert witnesses are examined and cross-examined, it is up to the jury (or arbitrators) to decide whether or not the clinician committed a breach in the standard of care.

Expert witness testimony is often required in perinatal-neonatal malpractice cases. For example, expert witnesses were used in the 2000 Pennsylvania case

Sonlin v Abington Memorial Hospital.[55] In this case, a premature infant girl who was born at approximately 34 weeks' gestation had an umbilical line. The infant developed vascular compromise in her left leg. This resulted in a thrombus that required amputation of the extremity. The plaintiff maintained that the neonatologist did not recognize the thrombus and therefore he did not institute corrective action in a timely fashion.

One can see that expert witnesses would have to explain to a jury why umbilical lines are placed, how long they are left in place, the potential complications from indwelling arterial catheters, and so on. In this case, an expert would have to explain the effect of prematurity on lung development and the subsequent necessity for monitoring blood oxygen levels. Basically, the expert must explain the standard of care, the indications for the procedures, and the potential complications.

In the Louisiana case *Hubbard v State,*[34] a full-term newborn was admitted with meconium aspiration and hypoglycemia. A peripheral intravenous infusion of $D_{10}W$ was ordered. After a change was made in the intravenous fluid, it was noted that the baby's hand became red and swollen and the baby became lethargic. His blood sugar was 450 mg/dL. Because of an error, the baby had received $D_{50}W$ instead of the $D_{10}W$ that was ordered. The infant sustained third-degree burns that left permanent disfigurement of the hand, and a CT scan showed a "possible venous thrombosis of the transverse and sagittal sinus." By the time this case reached the Louisiana Appellate Court, the child was almost 8 years old. In the interim, the child had been found to have Russell-Silver syndrome. The expert witnesses were extensively questioned about whether or not the dehydration and possible venous thrombosis contributed to his observed mental delays.

These cases represent a potential breach in the standard of care. Mistakes were made, infants were harmed, and the families attempted to hold the caregivers responsible for the damages that occurred. In both of these cases, expert witnesses were needed to assist in delineating the standard of care for the legal decision makers.

RES IPSA LOQUITUR

Res ipsa loquitur is a legal doctrine that means "the thing speaks for itself." Common medical examples of this doctrine include the retained surgical sponge, removal of the wrong kidney, or operation on the wrong patient. These three examples are factually simple. A juror's common knowledge will guide him or her to a reasonable conclusion. In practical terms, *res ipsa loquitur* generally means that the plaintiff does not need an expert to demonstrate that there was a deviation in the standard of care.

The doctrine means that certain things don't just happen. Historically, the *res ipsa loquitur* doctrine can be traced to an English case[19] from 1863 in which a passerby was injured when a barrel fell from a window. The doctrine was developed to explain that barrels do not fall out of windows unless someone has acted negligently.

A 2003 case from New York relied on the *res ipsa loquitur* doctrine. In *Rosales-Rosario v Brookdale,*[54] a woman was hospitalized to give birth. An epidural line was placed, and she was partially anesthetized. It was subsequently noted that she had sustained a burn to her leg. She had no idea how she sustained the injury. Her leg possibly was burned by an examination light, but because of her anesthetized state, she did not recall how the injury took place. She relied on the doctrine of *res ipsa loquitur.* The trial court dismissed the case, but the appellate court reversed the lower court's decision. The appellate court stated the rule of *res ipsa loquitur:* "To rely on the doctrine of *res ipsa loquitur,* a plaintiff must submit sufficient proof that: (1) the injury is of a kind that does not occur in the absence of someone's negligence; (2) the injury is caused by an agency or instrumentality within the exclusive control of the defendants; and (3) the injury is not due to any voluntary action on the part of the injured plaintiff."[54]

In the *Rosales-Rosario* case, the court concluded that leg burns do not just occur, so the first element of res ipsa was satisfied. Additionally, the physicians and hospital personnel were in exclusive control of all equipment in the delivery room, including the examination light. Finally, the patient did not engage in a voluntary act that resulted in her injuries.

Demonstrating *res ipsa loquitur* means that the plaintiff has overcome the burden for breach. The plaintiff still has the burden of demonstrating the other elements of the tort suit, but the deviation in standard of care can be proved if the court accepts the doctrine of *res ipsa loquitur.*

Causation

Of the four essential elements of a tort suit, *causation* is perhaps the most challenging to understand. Regardless of whether the dispute is malpractice or another civil complaint, causation is not always intuitive. In brief, the defendant's breach must be the *cause* of the plaintiff's injury; mere correlation is insufficient. The plaintiff must demonstrate a reasonable inference that the deviation in care resulted in the injury. Stated differently, assuming the plaintiff has suffered an injury, did the deviation in standard of care cause this injury? Once again, expert testimony is often required to answer these questions. Did the obstetrician's decision to allow a vaginal birth in the face of severe decelerations result in the newborn's neurologic damage? Did the neonatologist's "delay" in her decision to perform a double-volume exchange transfusion result in kernicterus that would have otherwise been avoided?

In many malpractice cases, the issue of causation can be extremely complex. However, causation can be particularly perplexing in the context of a perinatal-neonatal medical malpractice case. In the *Hubbard* case,[34] multiple expert witnesses disputed whether or not the severe dehydration contributed to the child's mental delay. What is the impact of the diagnosis of Russell-Silver syndrome? Was this the cause of the mental delay? The child had also had at least two documented falls during early development. Did the head injuries, which led to evaluation in an emergency department, cause the findings?

This case elucidates the particular challenge of causation. Certainly, board-certified neonatologists and pediatric neurologists could have well-substantiated yet differing opinions on the etiology of this child's mental deficits. How is a jury to rule on this complex issue? As in essentially all medical malpractice cases, expert witnesses must testify on the issue of causation. The concepts are usually too specialized for a nonexpert juror. Absent the testimony of an expert witness, a juror's common knowledge is often inadequate to decide the issue of causation.

Damages

The final element that a plaintiff must demonstrate is *damages*. For plaintiffs to recover any type of award, they must demonstrate that they were harmed. Either they experienced pain and suffering or a loss of some kind, such as loss of wages or loss of consortium. In some cases, damages are presumed. For example, if a surgeon leaves a surgical sponge in the patient, then the patient will require an additional surgery to remove the sponge. In this case, the patient will be able to demonstrate that the second surgery led to discomfort, time away from home, time away from work, lost wages, and so forth.

To understand the concept of damages, one should be familiar with the common distinction between economic and noneconomic damages. Economic damages include medical expense, cost of burial, lost earnings, loss of employment, and so on. These damages are often less complicated to calculate. Alternatively, some plaintiffs claim noneconomic damages, which are more subjective and related to nonmonetary losses. Among other claims, noneconomic damages can include pain and suffering, emotional distress, mental anguish, or destruction of parent-child relationship.

Many state legislatures have attempted to cap awards for pain and suffering or for wrongful death. For example, the California legislature[20] has placed a $250,000 cap on noneconomic damages. This generally means that any litigation involving the death of a newborn has a maximum award of $250,000. If older patients die, their estate can seek damages for lost wages, lost consortium, or other losses. However, the award for wrongful death of a newborn is essentially capped in California. Additionally, several state legislatures have placed caps on other noneconomic damages such as pain and suffering. For example, in Louisiana the Malpractice Liability for State Services Act (MLSSA) has capped state hospitals' liability at $500,000 for "pain and suffering."[43]

A great deal of tort reform litigation deals with the issue of damages. Specifically, some state legislatures have attempted to limit large jury awards by placing these caps on noneconomic damages. These disputes generally do not involve issues such as lost wages, hospitalization, or loss of property. Perceived excesses of some jury awards coupled with rising malpractice rates will likely fuel the national debate concerning caps on noneconomic damages.

If a negligent act is committed, and someone is harmed, damages are usually limited to compensatory awards. Punitive damages are awarded if the defendant is found to have committed a particularly egregious act. These damages are rarely awarded in medical malpractice cases. However, if a doctor were to alter a chart or make another attempt to change the medical record, a jury may award punitive, or punishment, damages. Thus, "spoliation of evidence" can lead to punitive damages.

Burden of Proof

How does a plaintiff win a case? Generally, each element must be proved by a preponderance of the data. This is also called the "51% test." The attorneys often frame their questions in terms of "is it more likely than not." Whether the attorneys are questioning expert witnesses or making statements to the jury, they often refer to the burden of proof. In general, this burden is on the plaintiff. The plaintiff must show that the defendant had a duty, that the duty was breached, that the plaintiff sustained damages, and that the breach was the legal cause of the damages. The plaintiff must prove each of these elements by a preponderance of the data.

Burden of proof can be contrasted with the common criminal standard of proof known as "beyond a reasonable doubt." In criminal cases, the state must demonstrate the defendant's guilt beyond a reasonable doubt. Another standard that may be familiar to readers is the "clear and convincing" standard. This standard is sometimes used in cases involving the withdrawal of care when the patient cannot communicate his or her wishes.[35] In civil cases, and particularly in malpractice cases, the standard is generally a preponderance of the data.

Protected (Nondiscoverable) Proceedings

Many hospitals have committees that review the care provided at that institution. Although the precise operations of these committees might differ, committees generally review cases that have had an untoward or unexpected result. In some institutions, all deaths are reviewed. Many state legislatures have provided protection for the proceedings from these committee meetings. For example, the Georgia statute specifically shields the specified proceedings from being used by a plaintiff in a medical malpractice case.[27] This is an issue of public policy. It is believed that care will be improved if caregivers can discuss challenging cases openly in a protected environment.

Clinicians must recognize that these proceedings do not limit the plaintiff's ability to bring suit against the doctors or the institution. A meritorious plaintiff can still subpoena hospital records and successfully bring suit against the caregiver. However, the protected proceedings will not be available as evidence in the case.

The proceedings, from a legal standpoint, are "non-discoverable." Before a physician discusses a case with an untoward outcome at a medical staff proceeding, the physician might wish to confirm that the proceedings of that meeting are nondiscoverable.

Other Tort Actions

In the context of neonatal-perinatal medicine, there are two unique causes of action. These actions are *wrongful life* and *wrongful birth*. There are distinctions between the two, and these causes of actions are not allowed in some states.

WRONGFUL BIRTH

Wrongful birth cases are brought by parents who have given birth. The cause of action is maintained on behalf of the parents. The parents contend that the child should never have been born, and they seek recovery based on the birth. These cases are often seen after the failure of a sterilization procedure or after a physician has assured a patient that he or she is not fertile. The parents generally seek economic damages related to the cost incurred in raising the child.

WRONGFUL LIFE

Wrongful life cases are maintained on behalf of a newborn. The plaintiff usually maintains there was negligence in the diagnosis or treatment of the mother and that the child should not have been born. In essence, the parent is claiming that the child would be better off if the child had not been born. Historically, these cases tended to be brought on behalf of newborns with severe congenital anomalies. A family maintains that an obstetrician or ultrasonographer missed certain important findings. Furthermore, the family claims that they would have terminated the pregnancy if they had known the child's diagnosis.

Ethically and philosophically, this tort raises many more questions. What is the value of human life? Can a person actually sustain a cause of action simply because that life exists? Would any person actually be better off if he or she had not been born?[29] As ill-equipped as many clinicians are to deal with these questions, the courts are at an even greater disadvantage. Courts tend to rely on facts and evidence. How does one compare a damaged existence to no existence at all?

Courts have grappled with this issue. Some courts have stated that there is sanctity in an impaired existence, but that this sanctity does not preclude a child's recovery for wrongful birth.[59] Courts have said that there is an almost insurmountable challenge in attempting to compare what judicial opinions characterize as the "utter void of nonexistence" with an impaired existence; however, some states do allow recovery.

WRONGFUL DEATH

This action is seen in other civil suits as well as in medical malpractice cases. If a person dies as the result of another's negligence, the estate may pursue a wrongful death claim. For example, if a pregnant woman is involved in a car crash and she miscarries as a result, the woman can sue for wrongful death of her fetus.

Although wrongful death claims can be part of other negligence suits, the claim is fairly common in malpractice actions. Although some states allow for the wrongful death of a fetus, other states only recognize this claim after a live birth.[14] A recent case in Connecticut appeared to allow for a wrongful death if the fetus is viable.[25] Other states allow recovery for the wrongful death of a fetus of any gestation.[23]

Strategies for Avoiding Tort Litigation

Physicians maintain a vested interest in avoiding malpractice litigation. When untoward medical complications arise, physicians may experience deep empathy for the patient as well as personal feelings of doubt or inadequacy. Besides the mental anguish that one can experience as a result of being named as a defendant in a malpractice case, these proceedings are often time-consuming and expensive. Rather than choosing a different career, physicians can adopt certain personal guidelines to minimize their chances of being named in a malpractice suit (Box 4-2).

Clinicians should make all necessary efforts to stay current in their discipline. Attending conferences and reading journals and textbooks will assist physicians in their clinical practice. As recently as the mid- to late 1990s, dexamethasone was widely used to wean premature babies with chronic lung disease from ventilators. Because of long-term neurologic concerns, this therapy is now normally reserved for only the sickest babies. A neonatologist who does not keep up with current practices could be administering a medication or offering a form of therapy well after its use has been widely abandoned or curtailed.

NICUs are often part of a regional system of perinatal-neonatal services. Small and large community NICUs can therefore maintain professional ties with one another and with larger medical centers. These ties allow professional interchange of ideas and recent developments. Clinicians would be wise to view their professional development as an ongoing process.

A clinician who is faced with a rare or particularly challenging case can consider calling a colleague. Attending physicians often maintain contact with their

---

BOX 4-2. Strategies to Avoid Tort Litigation

Stay current by reading journals and textbooks and by attending continuing medical education conferences
Maintain professional ties with a large medical center
When facing a difficult situation, consider consulting with a colleague
Maintain open communication with parents and families
Practice timely documentation of procedures, communication, complications, persons present
Document telephone advice
Be aware of state laws that affect your practice

former trainees. These contacts with former mentors can provide great benefit for one's patients. Perhaps a former attending physician can shed some light on a difficult situation. At large academic centers, attending physicians generally make it a point to regularly discuss the most difficult clinical cases at fetal boards, morning report, grand rounds, or other venues. By phoning a colleague, a community-based neonatologist can maintain a similar professional network.

In addition to maintaining good communication with colleagues, few issues are more vital than optimal communication with parents. It is not always easy to maintain good communication with parents, but the implications of poor communication are generally unacceptable. If parents believe a clinician is hiding something from them, they often become frustrated and angry. Parents are already dealing with having a sick infant in the NICU. If they feel mistrust, then the physician's relationship with a family can quickly deteriorate. A suboptimal relationship with the family of a sick newborn can be a harbinger of a pending malpractice suit.

Besides optimal communication, the clinician's other major defense to a tort suit is documentation. Entries in the chart should be punctual, legible, and accurate. If circumstances necessitate that a late entry be made, then this should be clearly documented as such. If a particularly important event has taken place, whether it be a complication with the infant or a comprehensive family conference, it should be documented in the chart. With respect to family conferences, it is important to document who was present and what was discussed.

One area where clinicians often fail to document is the advice that they give over the phone. Because this can be time consuming and logistically difficult, some physicians open themselves to liability by giving advice and failing to document that advice. Referring doctors or parents may ignore a physician's advice. In these situations, documentation of the phone discussion can save a tremendous amount of money, time, and frustration at a later date.

Finally, clinicians should be aware of state laws that affect their practice. This chapter presents cases and statutes from several states. Which ones affect a particular physician's practice? Many issues, such as resuscitation of extremely premature infants or accreditation of NICUs, are largely controlled by state law. Physicians should know the laws that affect their practice.

Conclusions

In general, a plaintiff must demonstrate that all four elements (duty, breach, causation, and damages) are present. Demonstrating only that the doctor made a decision outside an acceptable standard of care is insufficient. Likewise, a patient cannot sustain a cause of action simply because of suffering harm. The physician may have no duty to the patient, or the damages suffered may have no relation to the alleged breach in the standard of care. Of the four elements, breach and causation are the main elements that are commonly disputed in a malpractice case. The plaintiffs argue that the doctor's care deviated from an acceptable standard and that this deviation harmed the patient. The defendant maintains that the care was acceptable and any damages were not the result of faulty care (or decision making) by the defendant.

LIVE BIRTH

As the fetus descends through the birth canal and emerges as a living infant, many critical transitions take place. Readers of this textbook are familiar with the physiologic adaptations that accompany a live birth. In a legal sense, the fetus generally acquires full personhood when there has been a declaration of a live birth. Prior to birth, the cases cited earlier determine the fetus's legal status. Although the rules differ from state to state, there is fairly consistent interpretation that at the moment of live birth, the infant has all of the associated rights, privileges, and consequences of personhood in civil and criminal matters.[58]

It would seem intuitive how to define "live birth." Each state has a definition for "live birth," and there is considerable overlap in these definitions, but some states have placed additional clarification in the statutory language.

The Utah statute states that live birth "means the birth of a child who shows evidence of life after it is entirely outside of the mother."[63] This can be contrasted with the Alabama statute, which states, "When used with regard to a human being, [live birth] means that the human being was completely expelled or extracted from his or her mother and after such separation, breathed or showed evidence of any of the following: beating of the heart, pulsation of the umbilical cord, definite movement of voluntary muscles, or any brainwave activity."[7]

A common thread in the states' statutes is to include some physiologic sign of life, whether it is a beating heart, pulsation of the umbilical cord, spontaneous respiratory activity, or spontaneous movement. Beyond these findings, some states further clarify that an infant is considered to be alive whether or not the placenta is still attached and that an infant of any gestation can be a live birth.[45] Some statutes[22] specifically differentiate between heartbeats and "transient cardiac contractions." There is also an effort to distinguish breathing from "fleeting respiratory efforts or gasps."

The Arkansas[8] statute appears to contemplate all of these variables. It states that "live birth means the complete expulsion or extraction from its mother of a product of human conception, irrespective of the duration of pregnancy, which, after the expulsion or extraction, breathes or shows any other evidence of life such as beating of the heart, pulsation of the umbilical cord, or definite movement of voluntary muscles, whether or not the umbilical cord has been cut or the placenta is attached. Heartbeats shall be distinguished from transient cardiac contractions; respirations shall be distinguished from fleeting respiratory efforts or gasps." Additional language is added to the Maine statute, which specifically states that "each product of such a birth is considered live born and fully recognized as a human person under Maine law."[44]

In the context of criminal law, the American Law Reporter (ALR) proposes a different test for "life." This is known as a showing of a "separate and independent existence."[5] For purposes of homicide, a newborn is considered to have been born alive if it ever showed a separate and independent existence from its mother.

HANDICAPPED NEWBORNS

Federal and state governments have created protections for the most vulnerable members of society. This section deals largely with federal issues, but the states have also adopted guidelines to protect the handicapped. Persons with disabilities are protected by the Americans with Disabilities Act (ADA).[2] Furthermore, all children are protected by child abuse and child neglect statutes. The government, in general, places a high emphasis on protecting the lives of fragile chidren. Parents can lose custody of their children if they violate laws related to abuse or neglect, and they can be incarcerated for criminal endangerment[46] if their behavior is particularly egregious.

With the growing expertise in prenatal diagnosis, it is increasingly rare that the family and the health care team are surprised by the birth of a baby with congenital anomalies. Maternal serum markers, prenatal ultrasound, amniocentesis, prenatal percutaneous umbilical blood sampling (PUBS), and other procedures provide the practitioner with a considerable armamentarium to diagnose anomalies. In the case of "lethal" anomalies, this advance notice gives the family time to consider how they wish to proceed. There is often ample opportunity for the practitioners and the family to discuss the diagnosis, the implications of the diagnosis, and the care options. In the cases of lethal anomalies, care options selected by the parents may include comfort care only, aggressive resuscitation, or any level of care in between.

Federal law prohibits discrimination on the basis of handicap. Under this law, nourishment and medically beneficial treatment (as determined with respect for reasonable medical judgments) should not be withheld from handicapped infants solely on the basis of their present or anticipated mental or physical impairments.[2] These regulations encourage facilities that receive federal funds to establish infant review committees.

Baby Doe

Handicapped newborns, and the care that they receive, became a mainstream issue in the 1980s. The controversy created by the Baby Doe case still governs many decisions made by neonatologists. Baby Doe lived for less than 1 week, but the legacy remains more than 20 years later.

Most neonatal-perinatal practitioners are familiar with the basic facts of Baby Doe.[36] The infant was born with Down syndrome in Bloomington, Indiana, on April 9, 1982. As is the case with many infants with this disorder, the infant had a gastrointestinal (GI) tract atresia. Practitioners recognize that GI atresias are usually surgically correctable. Duodenal atresia is more common in Down syndrome, but Baby Doe had esophageal atresia. Because of the atresia, the infant could not be fed. Baby Doe's parents elected to forgo surgery. After discussions with the family, food and water were not provided, and the infant died at 6 days of age.

Down syndrome is not considered a lethal anomaly. Had Baby Doe not had Down syndrome, deferring surgery would not have been considered an acceptable option. Because Baby Doe did not have lethal anomalies, it was assumed that medical and surgical care were withheld because of the mental deficits associated with Down syndrome. A hospital nurse had heard about the baby who was being "starved," and she filed a complaint. This resulted in a judicial opinion that stated that the courts should not interfere in these matters. Higher courts[56] refused to hear the case. Baby Doe died while a stay was being sought in the U.S. Supreme Court.[16] The U.S. Supreme Court[39] later refused to hear the case.

The decision to forgo care was largely viewed as unacceptable. Advocates for the handicapped were particularly concerned about this case. They proposed that Baby Doe had been discriminated against on the basis of the infant's handicap, and therefore there had been a violation of Section 504 of the Rehabilitation Act of 1973.[1]

For a variety of reasons, the Baby Doe case was a landmark decision. In the three years following Baby Doe's death, the executive, the legislative, and the judicial branches of the federal government became involved. Additionally, the American Medical Association, the American Academy of Pediatrics, the American College of Obstetrics and Gynecology, and other professional organizations also became involved. The Reagan administration's position was that all handicapped newborns must be treated aggressively unless the care is obviously futile. Furthermore, they felt that physicians should be liable for neglect and discrimination if they did not comply with these rules.

The Reagan administration attempted to force hospitals to treat all severely handicapped newborns, regardless of the parents' wishes. Thus, the Department of Health and Human Services (HHS) promulgated "Baby Doe regulations" that required federally funded hospitals to post certain rules[4] in the hospital. Notices were to be prominently posted in delivery wards, maternity wards, pediatric wards, and each nursery. These signs encouraged concerned parties to call the HHS toll-free number to report suspected cases of discriminatory withholding of care from handicapped newborns. The rules also encourage the creation of infant care review committees to assist in decision making for difficult cases. Most of these regulations were ultimately disallowed by the courts.

Although infant care review committees are encouraged, the courts have ruled that parents, in conjunction with their physicians, should have the right to make health care decisions for their handicapped children. When the U.S. Supreme court decided against hearing the Baby Doe case,[39] the matter was only deferred for a few years, until the Baby Jane Doe case.

Baby Jane Doe

In 1983, the year after Baby Doe died, a child was born in New York with meningomyelocele, hydrocephalus, microcephaly, bilateral upper extremity spasticity, a prolapsed rectum, and a malformed brain stem. She has been immortalized in the neonatal literature as "Baby Jane Doe."[60-62] Her parents were presented with two options to treat the meningomyelocele: primary skin healing or surgical repair. The parents refused consent for surgical repair of the defect and for the placement of a shunt for hydrocephalus. Instead, the parents requested that the baby be treated with antibiotics and nutritional support.

An attorney who was not related to the family thought that the parents' request was an inappropriate medical decision. This attorney requested that the trial court appoint an independent guardian for the child so that consent could be given to perform the surgeries. The trial court granted the attorney's request, but the appellate court overturned that decision the following day. The appellate court found that the parents had chosen an acceptable medical option and had acted in the best interest of their child.

While this issue was being dealt with in the state court system, HHS received a complaint from a "private citizen." This complaint stated that Baby Jane Doe was being discriminated against because of her handicap. HHS referred the case to Child Protective Services, which concluded that there was no cause for state intervention. During this time, HHS also made repeated requests of the hospital to produce the infant's medical records. The hospital refused on the grounds that the parents had not consented to release the records. The federal government sought to compel access to the medical chart.

The government filed a suit in federal district court under section 504 of the 1973 Rehabilitation Act.[3] The courts found that the hospital had not violated any of the pertinent statutes because they were willing to perform the surgery if the parents would consent. Baby Jane Doe did not have surgery not because of her handicap but rather because the parents had not consented to the procedures.

As the case proceeded through the federal court system, various judges asserted that the baby was not being discriminated against on the basis of her handicap. Ultimately, the case reached the U.S. Supreme Court.[16] The U.S. Supreme Court took the opportunity to review the Baby Doe case, the Baby Doe regulations, the care of handicapped newborns, the role of the federal and state government in these cases, the rights of parents, and the rights and duties of caregivers.

The court found that there was no violation of Section 504, because the withholding of treatment was secondary to lack of parental consent, not due to discriminatory withholding based on the infant's handicap. Among other conclusions, the U.S. Supreme Court found that the parents had made reasonable decisions that were consistent with the best interests of their child. The court found no discrimination. The court also stated, "A hospital's withholding of treatment when no parental consent has been given cannot violate §504, for without the consent of the parents or a surrogate decision maker the infant is neither 'otherwise qualified' for treatment nor has he been denied care 'solely by reason of his handicap.' Indeed, it would almost certainly be a tort as a matter of state law to operate on an infant without parental consent." The final sentence of this quotation raises interesting questions in light of the *Miller* case,[32] which is discussed later.

Baby K

Baby K was found prenatally to have anencephaly.[37] Her mother declined termination of the pregnancy, and the baby was delivered by cesarean section on October 13, 1992. The baby was initially placed on mechanical ventilation so that the diagnosis could be confirmed. Following confirmation of the diagnosis, the caregivers approached the baby's mother to request permission to withdraw the ventilator. Based on the mother's religious beliefs that all life is sacred and must be protected, she insisted that the ventilator support be continued.

When the baby was 9 days of age the hospital ethics committee met with the physicians and concluded that the care was futile. Attempts to transfer the baby to another facility were not successful, and the baby was eventually transferred to an extended care facility. Baby K required three subsequent hospitalizations secondary to respiratory distress. Each time, the mother insisted that the baby be reintubated. The caregivers and the baby's father felt that the treatment was futile and inappropriate.

The hospital sought a federal court ruling that would allow them to withhold the ventilator from Baby K in the future. The hospital sought a declaratory judgment that by withholding the ventilator that they would not violate the Emergency Medical Treatment and Active Labor Act (EMTALA), the state Child Abuse Amendments, the state Malpractice Act, or ADA. The court ruled (and the 4th Circuit of the United States Court of Appeals[38] upheld) that the hospital was not entitled to such a declaration. In fact, the court reasoned that the baby's anencephaly qualified her as "handicapped" and "disabled" for the purposes of ADA. Because of procedural concerns and federal and state issues, the court did not rule on the topics of malpractice or child abuse.

In the court's interpretation of EMTALA, they reasoned that because "stabilization" included establishing and securing an airway, the refusal to intubate Baby K would be a violation of EMTALA. Because Baby K was handicapped and disabled, and the hospital received federal funds (e.g., Medicare payments), then the hospital could not deny the requests of Baby K's mother.

The EMTALA legislation was initially intended to prevent hospitals from "dumping" nonpaying patients to other facilities. In this case, the hospital was not contending that the issue was payment for the treatment. However, the court found that EMTALA applied, and Baby K must be intubated and ventilated as long as that was the mother's wish. The court stated that "absent finding of neglect or abuse, parents retain plenary authority to seek medical care for their children, even when the decision might impinge on a liberty interest of the child."

The 4th Circuit of the United States Court of Appeals stated that it was beyond their judicial limits to address the moral and ethical implications of providing emergency care to anencephalic infants. They stated that Congress did not want a case-by-case analysis but rather desired that hospitals and physicians provide stabilizing care to all patients who present with an emergency condition.

Conclusions

The preceding cases present the challenges faced when damaged newborns receive a level of care that is viewed to be inappropriate by some observers. If a child has "lethal" anomalies or a "terminal" condition, the courts have been fairly consistent in their judgment that the parents are the primary decision makers concerning the level of care.

In the Baby Doe case, the baby did not have a lethal underlying condition. Therefore, treatment would not have been "futile," and, in retrospect, many observers felt that the decision to forgo surgery was not "reasonable." The resulting national outcry was a measure of people's dissatisfaction with the decision made by the physicians and the parents.

In contrast, Baby Jane Doe had a course of therapy that was selected by her parents. While it was not the most aggressive course of treatment, some experts (at the time) believed that allowing the skin to grow over the meningomyelocele was an acceptable option. Other experts take issue with this course of therapy. However, the court ruled that the parents selected an acceptable treatment option for their daughter.

In the Baby K case, the child had what is largely viewed as a "lethal" anomaly. Despite the heartfelt objections of the physicians and staff, the courts ruled that care could not be withheld simply because the caregivers considered it to be morally and ethically inappropriate.

Can these three cases be reconciled? In the Baby Doe case, the parents made decisions that could be viewed as neglect. Baby Doe did not receive life-saving surgery because he was handicapped. It would appear that such withholding of treatment would currently be viewed as illegal. Baby Jane Doe's parents made a choice that the court ruled was a reasonable one. Therefore, there was no discriminatory withholding of

care. In Baby K's case, the courts supported a parental decision to ventilate a child with no cerebral cortex, a decision that many clinicians find untenable. If conclusions can be drawn, they would seem to indicate that the courts support parents' interests as long as decisions are not being made solely on the basis of handicap. Furthermore, the personal morals and ethics of the caregivers are fundamentally irrelevant in the legal context of parental decision making. If the parents' decisions are reasonable and there is no evidence of neglect, then parents seem to have substantial decision-making power.

PROVIDING CARE AGAINST PARENTS' WISHES

One of the most challenging aspects of neonatology is caring for the extremely premature infant. A substantial portion of this textbook addresses the medical issues involved in caring for these infants. While the care of the extremely premature neonate largely defines the parameters of the specialty, it also creates many of the legal and ethical quandaries for caregivers and families. These tiny persons existing on the cusp of viability have the same legal rights as all citizens. They are entitled to equal protection, due process, and all other constitutionally guaranteed rights and privileges of the citizens of the United States. By virtue of a heartbeat or spontaneous respiratory effort, the extremely premature infant is transformed into a "person." As mentioned in the earlier discussion of live birth, in many states, the gestational age and whether the placenta is attached are legally irrelevant.

The pending delivery of a 23-week-gestation fetus generally carries a wide variety of concerns. What are the family's wishes? Will the resuscitation go smoothly? Will the equipment all function properly? How will the infant respond to the resuscitation? Will stabilization be difficult? Will the baby require significant ventilator support, volume boluses, or an infusion of catecholamines?

More recently, the overriding concern is whether the infant must be resuscitated if it appears to be previable. What if the parents request no resuscitation? Are the caregivers liable if they overrule the parents and proceed with resuscitation of a 23-week-gestation infant? What if the parents request no resuscitation for a 24- or 25-week infant?

This extraordinarily difficult situation is exacerbated by a lack of statutory and case law. Furthermore, the existing case law seems to conflict with itself. This section addresses the unique challenge associated with the delivery of extremely premature infants. To gain optimal insight into this convoluted area of law, the reader should review the material on perinatal issues (maternal-fetal conflict), live birth, informed consent, and limiting care. The reader should have a grasp of the Cruzan[21] decision and the associated liberty interest in keeping one's body free from unwanted medical intervention. Likewise, one must appreciate that courts have found that parents generally have the right to refuse certain unwanted medical intervention for their children as long as this refusal is not neglect or abuse. Without a familiarity with the rules governing informed consent, the reader will lack the necessary foundation to appreciate the following discussion.

The Miller Case

In 1990, Karla Miller went into preterm labor at approximately 23 weeks' gestation.[31] Mrs. Miller had an "infection" that apparently was serious enough to threaten her life and (according to her obstetricians' testimony) also precluded a therapeutic termination of the pregnancy. After the neonatologist explained the grim prognosis for infants born at this gestation, Mark and Karla Miller requested that the baby not receive heroic measures. Initially, the caregivers agreed to honor the parent's wishes. However, subsequent meetings took place with the physicians and the hospital administration. It was decided that state law and hospital policy necessitated that the baby be resuscitated if she weighed more than 500 grams. This was explained to the parents, who once again requested that the baby not be resuscitated.

Sidney Miller was born later that night, several hours after Mrs. Miller had been admitted to the hospital. The infant was resuscitated, and she survives with severe impairment. The parents sued on several grounds. Among other allegations, they asserted that Sidney was treated without their consent, that the hospital was liable for having a policy necessitating resuscitation at a weight greater than 500 grams despite the absence of parental consent, and that the hospital was liable for not having a policy that would prevent such treatment without the parents' consent. The hospital maintained that the parents had no right to refuse life-saving intervention.

The jury awarded the family approximately $60,000,000. The appellate court overturned this verdict. In their analysis, the appellate court stated that this was a situation of the emergency exception to the informed consent rule. The court also relied on the Advanced Directives Act.[6] This act protects caregivers and hospitals who withhold care from terminally ill patients. The court reasoned that because Sidney Miller's condition did not fit the definition of terminal, then the parents had no right to refuse life-saving therapy. The court stated that parents have a right to determine health care decisions for their children, this is not an absolute right, and the state also has an interest in the health of children. "Having recognized, as a general rule, that parents have no right to refuse urgently-needed life-sustaining medical treatment to their non-terminally ill children, a compelling argument can be made to carve out an exception for infants born so prematurely and in such poor condition that sustaining their life, even if medically possible, cannot be justified."[31] The appellate court concluded that perhaps the legislature should address the issue of defining "terminal" with respect

to some premature babies who are born so small and so sick.

A dissenting judge on the appellate court felt that the parents' course of action was lawful. This judge supported his opinion by quoting the U.S. Supreme Court's decision in the Baby Jane Doe case.[16] This dissenting judge stated that no emergency existed. Therefore, the emergency exception to the informed consent rule was not available to the caregivers. According to the dissent, it was the caregivers' delay and indecision that led to the urgency.

Thirteen years after Sidney Miller was born, the Texas Supreme Court ruled on the case. This Court found that the hospital was not liable for resuscitating the baby.[32] While the Texas Supreme Court analyzed the case differently than the appellate court had, the decision was the same: the hospital had no liability. The high court reasoned that because it was impossible to predict how sick the infant would be at birth, the emergency did not exist until after Sidney was born. Therefore, the physician could not evaluate the situation until after the baby was born.

The Messenger Case

Gregory Messenger and Traci Messenger were faced with a situation similar to the Miller family's. Traci Messenger went into labor at 26 weeks.[49] Gregory Messenger is a physician (dermatologist). After discussing their options with their caregivers, the Messengers requested that the baby not be resuscitated. The request was not honored. The baby was resuscitated and brought to the NICU. Dr. Messenger went into the NICU, extubated his son, and placed him in Traci Messenger's arms. The baby died shortly thereafter. The neonatologist listed the cause of death as "homicide." Approximately one year later, Dr. Messenger was acquitted of manslaughter. Among other conclusions, the jury felt that Dr. Messenger was acting in the "best interest"[65] of his son.

The Messenger case was a criminal trial with a higher standard of proof. Dr. Messenger was acquitted of a crime. He removed his own extremely premature son from a ventilator, and he was found to be not guilty of intentional killing.

Conclusions

The Miller case was one decision made in one state. The decision was made by the Texas Supreme Court, so the decision is the current law only in Texas. The court's decision in the Miller case may or may not have any effect in any other state. Currently, if one practices in Texas, then *Miller v HCA* controls one's practice. Clinicians should be familiar with the facts and the judicial conclusions in this case. It appears that clinicians and hospitals in Texas will *not* be liable for resuscitating 23-week-gestation infants against the parents' wishes. Despite a parent's clear request to forgo resuscitation, a lapse of several hours between the time of the request and the time of birth, and no effort on the part of the clinicians or the hospital to transfer care to another provider, the court found no liability. Unless the U.S. Supreme Court ultimately rules on *Miller v HCA* or the Texas legislature passes contrary statutes, this case is binding in Texas.

In the Baby Jane Doe case, the U.S. Supreme Court did comment on decision making being taken away from parents. In defending the hospital's decision to honor the request of Baby Jane Doe's parents, the U.S. Supreme Court stated, "it would almost certainly be a tort as a matter of state law to operate on an infant without parental consent."

What of the remainder of the country? Perhaps some courts in other states would follow the trial court or the appellate court dissent in Miller. The trial court in Miller allowed a $60,000,000 verdict. The dissent in the appellate court quoted the U.S. Supreme Court decision in Baby Jane Doe, to question the propriety of imposing upon parents the consequences of resuscitation of 23-week-gestation babies.

The Texas Supreme Court decided that parents have no right to refuse resuscitation of their extremely premature infants. They relied heavily on their interpretation that the emergency did not exist until Sidney Miller was born. Therefore, the hospital and caregivers would basically always be protected by the emergency exception to the informed consent rule.

How does one reconcile Miller and Messenger? It is intellectually dissatisfying to conclude that the major difference between these two cases is that they were adjudicated in two different states. Surely, the inherent conflict between the two cases must have more substantial legal underpinnings than a simple difference in jurisdiction. Clearly, the fact that the Messenger case was a criminal trial with a higher burden of proof on the prosecution has some effect on the legal comparisons. Still, the inherent inconsistencies exist. In the Miller case, an extremely premature infant is resuscitated against the parent's wishes, and the hospital has no liability. In the Messenger case, an extremely premature infant is resuscitated against the parent's wishes, and the father has no criminal liability for disconnecting the ventilator with the intent to hasten the infant's death. If the baby was lawfully being cared for, then how could the father be acquitted of manslaughter? If caring for the baby against the parent's wishes was not lawful, then why did the Miller court find for the hospital?

These cases leave in question the exact legal status of the extremely premature infant. The baby is "alive" by statute. In some jurisdictions, the infant can recover for wrongful life. In some jurisdictions, a wrongful life claim will be denied because the parents have no right to refuse the care. In some jurisdictions, there is no criminal liability for a parent who overrules the doctors and takes matters into his or her own hands.

So what should a clinician do when called to the birth of a previable or periviable newborn? One should understand the issues, understand the rights of the newborn, understand the rights and the duties of the parents, and understand one's own rights and duties. Box 4-3 provides some general lessons from existing

BOX 4-3. When Parents and Caregivers Disagree on the Care of Critically Ill Newborns: Lessons from Existing Case Law

Parents Request Full Supportive Care and Caregivers Disagree
General rule: provide full supportive care
Anencephaly: Baby K case likely controls (federal case)

Parents Want No Resuscitation and Caregivers Disagree
Miller (Texas): no liability for caregivers
Messenger (Michigan): no criminal liability for father who disconnects the ventilator

Parents and Caregivers Agree to Forgo Aggressive Treatment
Possibly covered by Baby Jane Doe case: parents have right to make reasonable choice
Baby Doe case: cannot make decision solely based on present or future handicap

case law concerning situations in which parents and caregivers disagree on the care of critically ill newborns.

What would happen if Sidney Miller had been born in a state other than Texas? Did state politics play a role in this case? Is it a coincidence that Gregory Messenger was acquitted in Michigan? These are not trivial questions, but they are unanswerable given the current case law on this issue. To the family of Sidney Miller, the Supreme Court of Texas determined that the child and the family should recover nothing.

SUMMARY

There are a variety of difficulties for a physician facing a legal issue. Physicians are often unfamiliar with the legal process, and the new terminology can be daunting. As compared to science, legal results can appear to be unpredictable. In law, there are no double-blind, randomized, controlled trials. Additionally, legal events often elicit strong emotions. With respect to malpractice, families may have suffered tremendous losses, and juries can award tens of millions of dollars.

In general, practicing strong clinical medicine requires the clinician to stay current in the specialty, to maintain excellent communication with families and the hospital staff, to consistently strive to make ethical decisions, and to never knowingly violate the law.

Veteran neonatologists know the value of good documentation and effective communication with colleagues, staff, and families. However, many other nuances exist. Practitioners benefit from understanding the elements of a tort suit, recognizing the importance of informed consent, and knowing the law concerning the care of handicapped newborns, anencephalic infants, and extremely premature infants. With respect to extremely premature newborns, it is particularly difficult to discern clear legal principles from the variety of court decisions in this arena. This issue speaks to the importance of knowing the law in the state in which one practices.

Although the law may appear to be arbitrary, there are substantial underlying principles that courts and legislatures have honored for hundreds of years. Fundamentally, the legal system is not unpredictable. It can be daunting to a physician, but the process can be demystified. If one is experiencing a significant health problem, one seeks out medical advice. Likewise, the legal profession can provide meaningful insight to a physician who is in need of counsel.

REFERENCES

1. 29 USCA §794.
2. 45 CFR §84.55.
3. 45 CFR §84.61 (1985).
4. 48 Fed Reg 9630.
5. 65 ALR3d 413 (1975).
6. Advance Directives Act, VTCA Health & Safety Code §§166.002(13), 166.031, 166.035.
7. Ala Code 1975 §§26-21-2, 26-22-2 (2001).
8. Alaska Stat §18.50.950 (2001).
9. American Academy of Pediatrics Committee on Fetus and Newborn: Advanced practice in neonatal nursing. Pediatrics 111:1453, 2003.
10. Ariz Rev Stat §13-1103 (A)(5) (West 1989 & Supp 1998).
11. Arkebauer v Lojeski, No. 99 L 005157D (Ill 2004).
12. Becker S: Health Care Law: A Practical Guide, 6th ed. New York, NY, LexisNexis Matthew Bender, 1999, §17.02.
13. Bhat VN: Medical Malpractice: A Comprehensive Analysis. Westport, Conn, Auburn House, 2001.
14. Bolin v Wingert, 764 NE2d 201 (Ind 2002).
15. Boumil M et al: Medical Liability, 2nd ed. St. Paul, Minn, Thompson West Publishers, 2003, p 186.
16. Bowen v American Hospital Association, 476 US 610 (1986).
17. Brown v Board of Education, 74 SCt 686, (1954).
18. Brownsville Pediatric Associates v Reyes, 68 SW3d 184 (Tex App 2002).
19. Byrne v Boadle, 2 H&C 722, 159 EngRep 299 (Court of Exchequer 1863).
20. Cal Civil Code §3333.2
21. Cruzan v Director, MDH, 497 US 261 (1990).
22. Del Stat tit 16 §3101.
23. Farley v Sartin, 466 SE2d 522,528 (WVa, 1995).
24. Fish R, et al: Malpractice: Managing Your Defense. Oradell, New Jersey, Medical Economics, 1985.
25. Florence v Plainfield, 849A.2d7 (Conn, Sup Ct, Jan. 16, 2004.)
26. Franklin M, Robert R: Standard of care. In Franklin MA, Rabin RL (eds):Tort Law and Alternatives: Cases and Materials, 6th ed. Westbury, New York, Foundation Press, 1996, citing US v Carroll Towing Co, 159 F2d 169 (1947).
27. Ga Code Ann, §31-7-130.
28. Gilinsky v Indelicato, 894 FSupp 86 (1995).
29. Greco v United States, 111 Nev 405, 893 P2d 345 (1995).
30. Gross v Burt, 149 SW3d 213 (Tex. App, 2004).
31. HCA Inc v Miller ex rel Miller, 36 SW3d 187 (2000).
32. HCA Inc v Miller ex rel Miller, 118 SW3d 758 (Tex 2003).
33. Hill by Burton v Kokosky, 463 NW2d 265 (Mich App, 1990).
34. Hubbard v State 852 So2d 1097 (La App 4th Circ, 2003).
35. In re Fiori 673 A2d 905 (1996).
36. In re Infant Doe, No. GU8204-004A (Ind Ct App Apr. 12, 1982).
37. In the Matter of Baby K, 832 FSupp1022 (EDVa 1993).
38. In the Matter of Baby K, 16 F3d 590 (4th Cir 1994).
39. Infant Doe v. Bloomington Hospital, 464 US 961, 104 SCt 394 (1983).
40. Knapp v Northeastern Ohio Obstetricians, Ohio App 11 Dist (2003).
41. Kemper V: Bush calls for free-market fixes to the medical system. Los Angeles Times, January 21, 2004: A22.
42. Lewis v Physicians Insurance Co of Wisconsin, 243 Wis2d 648 (2001).
43. La Rev Stat Ann §40:1299.39.
44. Maine Rev Stat Ann tit 22, §1596.
45. Mo Rev Stat §193.015
46. Mo Rev Stat §568.045 (VAMS 2003).
47. Nold v Binyon, 31 P3d 274 (2001).
48. O'Neil v Great Plains Women's Clinic, 759 F2d 787 (1985).
49. People of the State of Michigan v Gregory Messenger, Ingham County Circuit Court, Lansing, Mich, Docket 94-67694FH, February 2, 1995.
50. Quinn K: Husband-wife lawyers OK $35 million for newborn's injuries. Chicago Daily Law Bulletin, February 20, 2004: 1.
51. Quirk v Zuckerman, 196 Misc 2d 496 (NY, 2003).
52. RI Gen Laws §9-19-41.
53. Roe v Wade, 93 SCt 705 (Tex, 1973).
54. Rosario v Brookdale University Hospital, 767 NYS2d 122 (2003).
55. Sonlin v Abington Memorial Hospital 748A2d 213 (2000).
56. State ex rel Infant Doe v Baker, No. 482 §140, May 27, 1982.
57. Sterling v Johns Hopkins Hospital, 802 A2d 440, 2002.
58. Turbow R: Legal issues in newborn intensive care. In Sanbar SS, Firestone MH (eds): Legal Medicine, 6th ed. Philadelphia, Mosby, 2004.
59. Turpin v Sortini, 32 Cal3d 220, 643 P2d 954 (1982).
60. United States v University Hospital, 575 FSupp 607,610 (1983).
61. Weber v Stony Brook Hospital, 95 AD2d 587.
62. Weber v Stony Brook Hospital, 60 NY2d 208.
63. Utah Code Ann §26-2-2.
64. Vo v Superior Court, 172 Ariz 195,198, 836 P2d 408,411 (App 1992).
65. Walters S: Life-Sustaining Medical Decisions Involving Children: Father Knows Best, 15 Thomas Cooley Law Review, 115:143, 1998.

5 The Field of Neonatal-Perinatal Medicine

PART 1

Evaluating and Improving the Quality and Safety of Neonatal Intensive Care

Jeffrey D. Horbar and Jeffrey B. Gould

*T*he nation's health care system lacks . . . the capabilities to ensure that services are safe, effective, patient-centered, timely, efficient and equitable. . . . Between the health care we have and the care we could have lies not just a gap but a chasm.[12]

More people die in a given year as a result of medical errors than from motor vehicle accidents, breast cancer, or AIDS.[48]

Systematic evaluation of the quality, safety, and efficiency of clinical care has become an integral part of medical practice. Physicians, hospitals, and large health care organizations are under increasing pressure to monitor, report, and continuously improve the quality, safety, and cost-effectiveness of their services. Public release of hospital performance data and report cards are becoming increasingly common.[52] Relman has described this as the "era of assessment and accountability."[68] In this new era, health professionals in neonatology must learn how to evaluate themselves and learn how they will be evaluated by others, including policy makers, hospital administrators, regulators, payers, and the families that they serve.

Evaluation is not an end in itself. Health professionals must learn how to use available information to continuously improve the quality and safety of medical care.

In this chapter, we review the ways information can be collected, evaluated, and applied to improve the quality and safety of medical care for newborn infants and their families. We discuss the available sources of such data for neonatology and describe how these data can be used to evaluate and improve the processes, outcomes, and costs of medical care for newborn infants. We begin by focusing on the case that improvement is necessary in neonatology.

THE CASE FOR IMPROVEMENT

The Institute of Medicine of the National Academy of Sciences has issued two landmark reports: *Crossing the*

Quality Chasm: A New Health System for the 21st Century, and *To Err is Human: Building a Safer Healthcare System.* These reports present a clear and compelling challenge to all health care professionals.[12,48] We must improve the quality and safety of the medical care for the patients and families that we serve.

Despite overwhelming evidence that deficiencies in quality and safety are widespread throughout the American health care system, many health care professionals in neonatology may feel that these problems do not apply to our clinical specialty. This is not the case. In neonatology, as in other clinical fields, there are substantial opportunities for improving the quality and safety of medical care.

First, infants receiving neonatal intensive care remain at high risk for mortality and acute as well as long-term morbidity. Although mortality rates for high-risk preterm infants declined steadily over the past several decades, this trend appears to have now reached a plateau.[37] Furthermore, extremely premature infants who do survive are at high risk of neurodevelopmental and sensory disabilities as well as educational disadvantages in young adulthood.[28]

Second, there is dramatic variation among neonatal intensive care units in the processes and outcomes of care. This variation cannot be explained by differences in case mix, suggesting that it is at least in part due to differences in the quality of care.[90] Nosocomial infection provides a striking example.[10] The 299 units participating in the Vermont Oxford Network database from 2000 to 2002 reported that 20% of the more than 77,000 very low birth weight infants had a nosocomial bacterial infection during their hospitalization.[33] The 30 units with the lowest rates had rates from 0% to 9%; the 30 units with the highest rates had rates ranging from 32% to 54%. This dramatic variation could not be explained by case mix or NICU type, indicating a significant opportunity for improvement.

Third, inappropriate care—defined as underuse, overuse, and misuse of interventions[24]—is common in neonatal intensive care. Examples include the underuse of hand hygiene by NICU personnel,[9] the overuse of antibiotics, and the misuse of medications because of medical errors.

Medical errors occur frequently in the neonatal intensive care unit, leading to adverse events. A study at two Boston hospitals has documented that errors in the process of ordering, dispensing, or monitoring medications occurred for more than 90% of the infants cared for in the NICU.[47] Using a voluntary, anonymous, Internet-based error-reporting system established by the Vermont Oxford Network, Suresh and colleagues have documented a broad range of errors and near errors at 54 neonatal intensive care units.[85] Only about half of the reported events involved medications; the remainder involved a wide variety of errors in multiple domains of care.

These observations are consistent with the findings of the Institute of Medicine reports. We have many opportunities to improve the quality and safety of neonatal intensive care.

Data for Improvement

It is essential that quality improvement be data driven. As a first step to quality improvement, data are used to determine one's baseline performance relative to a set of standards or peer-derived benchmarks. As one begins to implement changes, data are used to track improvement. Data regarding neonatal patients are available from a variety of sources (Box 5-1).

There are two potential sources of data: primary and secondary databases. Primary databases are designed specifically for evaluating neonatal care; secondary databases were originally designed for other purposes.[24]

Examples of secondary datasets that have been used to evaluate quality of care are the hospital discharge database and files that link birth certificates and death certificates. Although these secondary databases were not designed for evaluating perinatal care, they contain data elements that have made it possible to examine risk-adjusted perinatal complication rates,[20] cesarean delivery,[22] neonatal morbidity and mortality rates,[62] and neonatal readmission rates.[16]

Primary databases are specifically created to address perinatal issues. There are two basic approaches to primary database design. One approach attempts to create a virtual patient. This approach is exhaustive because it contains a detailed description of all aspects of a patient's hospital stay that would be included in the medical record. The advantage of the virtual approach is that it allows detailed and broad-based analyses that even include factors whose importance will be identified

---

BOX 5-1. Data Sources for Evaluating Neonatal Care

Vital Statistics
Federal and state data
Birth certificates
Death certificates
Hospital information systems
Clinical information systems
Administrative information systems
Decision support systems

Claims Data
Medicaid
Other insurers

Neonatal Databases
Locally designed databases
Commercial databases

National and International Neonatal Networks
Australian and New Zealand Neonatal Network
British Association of Perinatal Medicine
Canadian NICU Network
EuroNeoNet
Indian Neonatal Forum Network
International Neonatal Network
Ireland-Northern Ireland Network
Israel Neonatal Network
Japanese Neonatal Network
National Collaborative Perinatal Neonatal Network of Greater Beirut
NICHD Neonatal Research Network
SEN1500 (Spain)
Swiss Neonatal Network
Vermont Oxford Network

NICHD, National Institute of Child Health and Human Development; NICU, neonatal intensive care unit.

---

only in the future. The disadvantage is that multiple-item primary data collection, entry, and quality control are resource intensive.

In the future, as clinical medicine moves to the electronic medical record and as the various electronic repositories of medical information (e.g., laboratory, consultant, imaging, outpatient, resource use, and costs) are integrated,[54] it will be possible to construct a multidimensional virtual patient based entirely upon routinely collected secondary data. Today, the minimal dataset is a practical and popular approach to collecting primary perinatal data.

Minimal Dataset

The minimal dataset approach begins with the notion of creating an information base. An information base is founded on the premise that information is data that promotes action by informing decision-making and quality-improvement efforts.[91] Therefore, the first task in constructing a minimal database is to determine the areas of decision making and quality improvement to be addressed and the information needed to address these specific issues. Only data that are needed to inform these issues qualify for inclusion in a minimal database.

Achieving the appropriate granularity—that is, the proper balance between detail and simplicity—is difficult but crucial. It involves making tradeoffs between the depth and breadth of the information to be collected and the costs of collecting the data. These costs are not trivial. As more and more emphasis is placed on documenting and improving outcomes, data abstraction, entry, and analysis have become essential components of clinical care. Unfortunately, administrative budgets often fall short of what is required to adequately support these activities.

Regardless of how many data elements are included in a database, the elements must be clearly defined. Database users should have access to standardized definitions in a printed manual of operations to facilitate both the coding and the interpretation of data. Access to standardized definitions is particularly important with regard to diagnostic information. Because physicians and nurses rarely use precise definitions in their daily notes, the medical record might not provide a reliable source of clinical information. The importance of uniform definitions cannot be overstated. Without them, valid comparisons and inferences cannot be made from a database. A few well-defined data items are far more valuable than an extensive list of poorly defined items.

There are currently three methods for transferring these items to a database. The most efficient technique is to download information that has already been collected via an electronic medical record. Although this will doubtless be the standard method in the future, it is still in the early stages of development.

The second and most commonly used method is the paper form. Data are abstracted from the medical record to the paper form, which is sent to the data center and either scanned or hand entered into a master database. Paper forms, which are used to record data, must be simple and easy to use. But even the clearest of paper forms have the major disadvantage of quality-control lag. That is, to identify an error on the form (omission of an item, an out-of-range entry, or a logically inconsistent value) one must first expend the effort to enter the form into the database and run an error check. Having found the error, one must then communicate back with the NICU. The NICU then has to request the record from the medical records repository, reabstract the data item, and send back the correction, which is then used to update and correct the initial error. This lag in quality control results in a detection-correction process that requires a great deal of effort by the NICU and the data center.

To avoid this labor-intensive process there has been a recent movement toward on-site computer-based data entry systems using local or Web-based data entry interfaces. The great advantage of these systems is that they detect errors in completeness, range, and consistency as the data are being abstracted and entered. When the data entry program detects an error, it requests a valid value and does not allow data entry to proceed until it receives the correct value. The result is a clean record at the point of data entry that avoids the costly offsite error detection and correction cycles. However even with this system it is important to use methods to minimize data entry errors, such as visual verification.[34]

Creating a clean dataset is only the first step in using data to inform quality improvement. To be effective agents for change, reports generated from the data must be available in a timely manner. Data that are too old cannot reliably inform decision making. Because of the lengthy hospitalization of the very premature infant, it is often useful to enter data at the end of the first 28 days as well as at discharge. This strategy facilitates the timely analysis of neonatal outcomes.

The format in which data reports are produced and distributed is evolving from the yearly paper report to more flexible electronic media such as the CD and the confidential Internet-based report (www.cpqcc.org). Advantages of electronic media reports are the ease of performing local secondary data analysis as well as the ability to easily incorporate the report's tables and figures into local customized presentations. The presentation of a hospital's data compared with the other NICUs in a network plays an important role in motivating quality-improvement activities.[93]

DATABASE ELEMENTS

When designing a primary database or deciding which variables to extract from a secondary database, it is useful to consider the type of variables to be collected. Clinical databases consist of a series of records, each record containing data on an individual patient. A perinatal database contains four types of data: identifiers, processes, outcomes, and risk adjusters. Although we usually think of identifiers as normative (e.g., name, Social Security number, case record number), identifiers can also be virtual. A virtual identifier is a combination of characteristics such as date of birth, race, residential zip code, and birth weight that are unique to a specific infant.

Although one might favor normative identifiers, it is not uncommon for an infant's name to be changed during the first several months of life, and Social Security numbers are not always assigned to infants. Because virtual identifiers consist of a constellation of factors that are constant (for example birth date, sex, birth weight, mother's age) and tend to be unique to a specific person, they are extremely powerful, and it is possible to effectively link birth, death, and discharge data sets using virtual identifiers.[31] The Health Insurance Portability and Accountability Act of 1996 (HIPAA) has required increasing attention to the use of personal identifiers in patient databases.[49]

Processes

Having identified the patient, it is important to record certain processes of care. In a minimal dataset, only processes that have been strongly linked to the quality of outcomes should be included. The goal of using process analysis for quality improvement is to detect the underuse of processes that have been demonstrated to improve outcomes, such as the use of antenatal steroids in mothers threatening premature delivery. Process analysis can also detect the overuse of processes that have been demonstrated to be detrimental, such as the use of postnatal steroids.

In contrast to the minimal dataset, the virtual patient approach attempts to capture all activities and the diagnoses they address. Detailed electronic medical record, billing, and cost-accounting systems can be used to create a virtual patient based on secondary data. Such databases, developed as components of administrative hospital information systems, are relatively new to pediatrics and neonatology. Because these databases were designed primarily for financial analysis, coding of clinical data and procedures might not be accurate. Another drawback is that physician procedures often are not included in hospital billing systems. To be effective for evaluating clinical care, cost-accounting datasets must be customized to the local environment. This process requires clinical input and provides the neonatologist with an opportunity to build in appropriate safeguards to more accurately reflect clinical status and procedures.

Administrative information systems promise important possibilities for the future, but today primary neonatal databases offer the best approach to recording what doctors and nurses do for their patients. As a primary database, the minimal dataset can be readily expanded to collect more detailed information on the processes of care. For example one can incorporate the Neonatal Therapeutic Intervention Scoring System (NTISS) to obtain a measure of neonatal therapeutic intensity.[27] This score, based on a modification of the adult Therapeutic Intervention Scoring System (TISS),[15] assigns 1 to 4 points for each of 62 intensive care therapies in 8 categories (respiratory, cardiovascular, drug therapy, monitoring, metabolic/nutrition, transfusion, procedural, vascular access). Data for the score are abstracted from the medical record. The NTISS score is highly correlated with markers of illness severity and a measure of nursing acuity, and it is predictive of NICU length of stay and total hospital charges for survivors. If scores such as NTISS can be simplified and validated in a large number of NICUs, they will be valuable tools for measuring the scope and intensity of therapeutic interventions.

Ideally, the data items needed for measuring therapeutic intensity should be available in either the primary or secondary datasets already being collected. Future neonatal database systems should attempt to incorporate measures of therapeutic intensity so that chart review will not be necessary for collecting the required data items. Patients inherently differ in the therapeutic intensity that they require, so a perinatal service's outcomes must always be measured within the context of its case mix.

Outcomes
Outcomes are the third constituent of the perinatal database and are essential to assessing quality of care.

Pragmatically, outcomes are negative events such as death and morbidity, and quality is inferred on the basis of a lower than expected negative event rate. It is important to record a wide spectrum of outcomes, but for an outcome to serve as an effective quality indicator, there must be strong evidence that variations in process or structure can decrease its incidence. Nosocomial infection is an important quality indicator because it is a significant source of morbidity, and incorporating certain processes of patient care (such as hand hygiene and intravenous line care) has been shown to reduce its incidence.[86]

Characterizing the incidence of outcomes at an individual NICU and across a network of NICUs plays several key roles in the quality improvement cycle. It allows one to identify problem outcomes on the basis of their high incidence. It also allows one to assess the extent of the variability in outcome across a network of reporting NICUs and identify NICUs in which the incidence of the problem is lower than expected or higher than expected. NICUs with lower adverse outcomes can be assessed to identify factors and practices that have promoted the superior outcomes, with the goal of transferring these benchmark approaches to those units with high adverse outcomes. Finally, the database can be used longitudinally to track the extent to which quality improvement efforts have been effective. In addition to the rate of adverse events (e.g., death, pneumothorax, chronic lung disease), indicators of resource use such as number of days on the ventilator and length of stay are easily captured in a database and are considered important indicators of quality, especially by payers.

ADJUSTING FOR DIFFERENCES IN CASE MIX
In the previous discussion we touched upon expectation and the concept of an expected rate of negative outcomes. Expectation is pivotal to the notion of quality because quality can be defined as the ratio of observed to expected outcome.[24] In the context of clinical medicine, expected outcome includes the extent of risk features and comorbidities that are not under the control of the clinician. Does hospital A with an observed neonatal mortality rate (NMR) of 5 provide better care than hospital B with an observed NMR of 10? Without knowing the *expected* rate of mortality at these two hospitals it is impossible to assess their relative quality of care. For example, hospital B might be a regional center whose expected NMR is much higher than the observed rate of 10. Hospital A could be a primary care hospital whose observed NMR of 5 is much higher than its expected NMR.

A key challenge to quality assessment is how to control for differences in case mix so as to fairly and accurately estimate their expected morbidity and mortality rates. To estimate expected rate, we use *risk adjusters,* the fourth type of variable contained in a perinatal database. Risk adjusters have two essential requirements. They must predict adverse outcome and they must not be under the control of the entity being evaluated. Birth weight, gestational age, plurality, intrauterine growth, birth defects, and sex are risk factors that are commonly used as risk adjusters to control for institutional differences in case mix in order to make fair comparisons across NICUs.[24,72] They are highly predictive of morbidity and mortality and are not under the control of the clinician. Mode of delivery and antenatal steroid use are also important predictors of mortality.[94] Although not under the control of the neonatologist, they are under the control of the obstetrician. If neonatal mortality is used to compare the quality of care across NICUs, one can include these two factors in the risk adjustment. However, if the goal is to use neonatal mortality to compare the quality of care across perinatal services, these factors cannot be included because they are under the control of the obstetrician.

The documented outcomes of an individual NICU must always be considered in the context of the severity and complexity of that NICU's case mix, using an appropriate analytic approach to measure and adjust for differences in risk. A simple approach is to compare outcomes for relatively homogeneous categories of patients, such as individual diagnostic related groups (DRGs), discharge categories, or birth weight groupings. The outcomes and interventions for infants at a given NICU in a particular category are then compared with those for infants in that category at all other NICUs in the network.

This approach has been used by both the Healthy People 2010 report and the ACOG guidelines for assessing overuse of cesarean delivery.[1,87] The recommendation is to compare cesarean rates in a defined section of a hospital's population: primiparas with full-term, singleton infants in the vertex position. Although this subset of women may seem homogeneous, across hospitals this subset may have marked differences in the distribution of significant risk factors. For example, a recent study by Gould's group demonstrated that even when a stratum was restricted to women without a previous cesarean delivery, in active labor at term, with a singleton infant and no evidence of maternal complications or neonatal anomalies, significant differences in maternal age, parity, and ethnicity were identified across the study hospitals. After further adjustment for these differences the results changed, demonstrating the importance of a multivariate approach even within a seemingly homogeneous stratum.[22]

More-sophisticated multivariate methods can be used to adjust for differences in case mix, illness severity, and patient risk.[30,71,72] Williams and associates pioneered this type of approach to assess the objective outcomes of fetal, neonatal, perinatal, postneonatal, and infant mortality in all California hospitals.[92] The analysis used secondary data from linked birth and death certificates and was based on all births to California residents. The basic paradigm is that to make valid interpretations of the observed mortality rate, one must account for the components that affect its variability: risk, chance, and quality of care.

The *risk* component reflects differences in observed outcome that solely are due to differences in case mix. Williams considered the primary risk factors to be birth weight, race, ethnicity, sex, and plurality, because these factors have been shown to be important predictors of neonatal mortality and are available from birth and death certificates. His strategy employs indirect standardization. Using all California births, the mortality rate for each combination of the four risk factors is calculated, producing a risk matrix of 190 cells. Each cell represents the average statewide mortality for an infant with that set of characteristics. In 2001 for example, neonates weighing 500 to 750 g born to white, non-Hispanic single women have a state-wide NMR of 389.5 per 1000.[62] For a given hospital, the overall observed mortality is compared with an expected mortality calculated by applying the overall California mortality rates to each of the hospital's neonates and summing the results.

Gould's group revised this calculation using the Poisson statistic to account for the chance component in evaluating the significance between a hospital's observed and expected mortality rates.[62] A hospital with poor performance would have a higher observed mortality rate than would be expected on the basis of its birth weight, race, ethnicity, sex, and plurality case mix. Although the use of the risk matrix approach is technically sound, techniques based on regression analysis allow greater flexibility with respect to the number and types of variables and a more precise understanding of the characteristics of the adjustment model.

Regression techniques make it possible to adjust for a wider variety of risk factors that are not under the control of the neonatologist. A mortality prediction model based on variables measured before NICU admission that are routine components of a minimal neonatal database was developed by the Vermont Oxford Network and has been used in routine annual reporting to members since 1991. The logistic regression model on which the predictions are now based includes terms for gestational age (birth weight had been used in some years), gestational age squared, race (African American, Hispanic, white, other), sex, location of birth (inborn or outborn), multiple birth (yes or no), 1-minute Apgar score, size for gestational age (lowest 10th percentile, highest 10th percentile), major birth defect (yes or no, added in 1994), severity (added in 2001), and mode of delivery (vaginal or cesarean). The model is recalibrated each year.

A similar approach that takes into account gestational age (linear and quadratic terms), small for gestational age, birth defects, multiple gestation, 5-minute Apgar score, race/ethnicity, sex, transfer status, and prenatal care is used by the California Perinatal Quality Control Collaborative (CPQCC) to assess morbidity and mortality.[11] Using this approach, the expected number of deaths (or adverse outcomes) at each NICU can be determined based on the characteristics of infants treated at that NICU. The ratio of the observed number of deaths (or adverse outcomes) to the expected number of deaths (or adverse outcomes), called the *standardized mortality (or morbidity) ratio* (SMR), can then be calculated.

An SMR value of greater than 1 indicates that an NICU has more deaths than would be expected based

FIGURE 5-1. Standardized neonatal mortality ratios (SMRs) and 95% confidence intervals for 407 NICUs participating in the Vermont Oxford Network in 2002. The SMR is the ratio of observed-to-predicted deaths for infants weighing 501 to 1500 g. Predicted deaths are calculated using a logistic regression equation that includes terms for gestational age, gestational age squared, race (African American, Hispanic, white, other), sex, location of birth (inborn or outborn), multiple birth (yes or no), 1-minute Apgar score, size for gestational age (<10th percentile, >10th percentile), major birth defect (yes or no and severity), and mode of delivery (vaginal or cesarean). (Courtesy of the Vermont Oxford Network, Burlington, Vermont.)

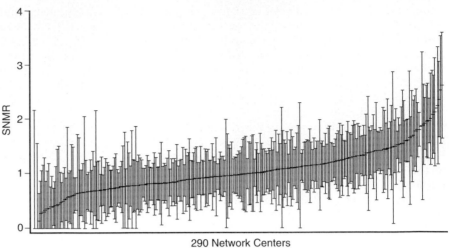

290 Network Centers
Vertical bar represents 95% confidence interval

on the characteristics of infants treated there, whereas an SMR value of less than 1 indicates that an NICU has fewer deaths than expected. The SMRs and their 95% confidence intervals for 407 NICUs participating in the Vermont Oxford Network during 2002 are shown in Figure 5-1. The data points are plotted in order of increasing SMR. It is apparent that the point estimates of the SMR vary substantially among the NICUs, with some values being less than 1 and others being greater than 1. The 95% confidence intervals are very wide because of the relatively small number of infants who are treated at each individual NICU in a given year.

Because the statistical power to detect quality of care outliers using multivariate risk-adjustment methods based on a single year may be low, it is very useful to also perform the analysis on data combined from several years.[62] Even employing very accurate predictive models and combining several years of data might not be able to overcome the problem of a small sample size in some NICUs.[35] In this case, multivariate risk models may be useful for identifying individual infants who died despite having a low predicted probability of death. The medical records of such infants can then be chosen for detailed review and audit.

Recognizing that risk adjustments based on infant characteristics are imperfect, there is value in reporting comparative performance data stratified by the type of NICU. The Vermont Oxford Network provides such stratified comparisons to its members. The Perinatal Section of the American Academy of Pediatrics is developing an NICU classification system that will be useful for this purpose. In addition to reporting standardized ratios of observed to predicted rates for mortality, the Vermont Oxford Network and the CPQCC provide their members with similar data for a range of important morbidities, with the goal of using these data to identify opportunities for improvement.

Although multivariate prediction models that are based on admission variables perform well for infants with very low birth weights for whom gestational age

or birth weight is highly predictive of mortality, physiologic measures of disease severity may be necessary to achieve similar predictive performance for larger, more mature infants. In addition to stratification and multivariate modeling based upon patient characteristics that are present before therapy is initiated, it is also possible to perform case mix adjustment based upon comparable severity of illness. Severity of illness scores for both adult and pediatric intensive care patients have been developed and validated.[30,66] These scores, based on multivariate modeling techniques, can be used to adjust for case mix differences among intensive care units when comparing patient outcomes.

Similar physiology-based severity scores have been developed for use in neonatal intensive care.[71] The Clinical Risk Index for Babies (CRIB) was developed by the International Neonatal Network under the leadership of W. O. Tarnow-Mordi to predict mortality risk for infants with birth weight less than 1500 g or gestational age younger than 31 weeks.[45,61] The score has been recalibrated with data from 1998 to 1999, using the variables sex, birth weight, gestational age, temperature on admission, and maximum base excess during the first hour. The potential for early treatment bias has been reduced by obtaining measurements in the first hour after admission. The CRIB score correlates with mortality risk or the risk for major cerebral abnormality on cranial ultrasound with a ROC area under the curve of 0.82. A major strength of the CRIB II score is its simplicity; a limitation is that it was designed specifically for infants younger than 32 gestational weeks.[61]

The Score for Neonatal Acute Physiology (SNAP), developed by Richardson and coworkers, is a physiology-based illness severity score originally based on measurements of 26 routine clinical tests and vital signs.[73,74] Birth weight and SNAP are independent predictors of mortality. An additive score that is based on birth weight, 5-minute Apgar score, size for gestational age, and SNAP, called the SNAP-PE (SNAP-Perinatal Extension), has been shown to be superior to either birth weight or SNAP alone.[70] The more recent version of the score, SNAP II, uses only six laboratory and clinical parameters (lowest mean blood pressure, lowest temperature, lowest pH level, lowest Pao_2-to-Fio_2 ratio, urine output, and seizures), collected during the first 12 hours after admission and has been shown to be compatible with SNAP I, is valid for infants of all birth weights, and takes only 5 minutes to collect.[75] A study of more than 10,000 infants at 58 sites in the Vermont Oxford Network showed that the current performance of SNAP II and SNAP-PE II is similar to that observed in the original validation report, and addition of congenital anomalies as defined by the Vermont Oxford Network to SNAP-PE II significantly improves discrimination to a level consistent with the Vermont Oxford Network risk-adjustment algorithm described earlier.[95]

The CRIB score and the SNAP score are potentially useful for comparing mortality rates and other outcomes at different NICUs. The limited number of data elements required for both CRIB II and SNAP II makes them compatible with a minimal data set approach.

One drawback of both scores is their use of variables which are measured during the first 1 to 12 hours after NICU admission. This raises two potential problems. The first problem relates to the 1- to 12-hour period of observation. The authors state that the longer the period of observation, "the more contaminated it becomes with the effects of successful (or unsuccessful) treatment and thus no longer reflects admission severity."[72] Because their values may be influenced by treatments provided after admission, these illness-severity scores are not truly independent of the effectiveness or quality of care. The second problem is that the observed severity of illness in the first hours of life may differ from the observed severity of illness in the very same infant in the first 6 hours following transfer and admission to another unit. Further studies will be required to determine the extent to which these potential problems limit the usefulness of CRIB II and SNAP II for adjusting case mix.

Further research is required to identify the best models for predicting neonatal risk and to determine their precision in identifying individual cases or institutions with poor quality of care.[60] However, even without a firm foundation in research, risk-adjusted comparisons of NICUs will become more common. The public release of risk-adjusted comparisons of mortality rates for U.S. hospitals by the Centers for Medicare and Medicaid Services and the publication of hospital-specific and surgeon-specific mortality rates for cardiovascular surgery by the New York State Department of Health[58] are two examples of this phenomenon. An example in the field of perinatology is the Pacific Business Group on Health's publication of risk-adjusted primary cesarean section rates for California hospitals (www.healthscope.org). This analysis is unique in that technical oversight was provided by neonatologists, perinatologists, and researchers who are members of the CPQCC.

The public release of comparative performance data and the use of such data for contracting and performance-based reimbursement will become increasingly common

over the next few years. The Leapfrog Group, a consortium of Fortune 500 companies, now provides hospital-specific performance data to the public on the Internet. NICU ratings are currently based on average daily census and antenatal steroid use.[52] Neonatologists must understand the strengths and weak-nesses of different methods for making risk-adjusted comparisons of neonatal outcomes as they attempt to assist the public in understanding these data and to use the data themselves to monitor, evaluate, and improve the quality of care that they provide.

Secondary Data

Although secondary data have been briefly described, thus far the discussion has focused on primary data, that is, data specifically collected to address perinatal issues. Secondary data are data collected for other purposes that can also be used to assess and improve perinatal care. Secondary data sources that are frequently used are the birth certificate, the hospital discharge abstract, and hospital billing data.

The major advantage of using secondary data is that someone else maintains the data system. The major disadvantages are that the secondary data sources might not have all of the necessary data items, the definitions might not be appropriate or the same as those used in other NICUs, and that the accuracy might not be adequate. For example, demographic information, prenatal care, mode of delivery, and birth weight tend to be fairly reliable on birth certificates.[25] However, the presence of congenital anomalies, an important item because of the high degree of complexity and mortality in this group, is markedly underreported on both birth certificates and death certificates.[32,40,83] A recent review describes both the advantages and disadvantages of using vital records for quality improvement.[25]

Linked birth and death certificate files are an important source of population-based studies of factors that affect perinatal outcomes. These studies span a wide range of areas (e.g., the effect of the increase in multiple births on infant mortality,[7] factors associated with the birth of infants with very low birth weight [VLBW] at non-NICU hospitals,[23] and quality assessment of perinatal regionalization[17]). However, to maximize the potential usefulness of vital records, clinicians must become actively involved in ensuring their uniformity of definition, accuracy, and completeness.

The hospital discharge abstract can be a useful data source for evaluating neonatal care.[41,81] The U.S. Department of Health and Human Services mandates that a uniform hospital discharge data set (UHDDS), which includes 14 core data items, be submitted for each acute patient whose care is paid for by Medicare or Medicaid. The most widely used format for these submissions is the Uniform Bill, introduced in 1992 (UB-92).[75,81] UB-92 contains data items for patient identification, insurance coverage, total charges, and entries for up to five diagnostic and three procedural codes. These codes are assigned based on the International Classification of Diseases, Ninth Revision, Clinical Modification (ICD-9-

CM).[57] UB-92 is required for hospitals submitting claims to Medicare, Medicaid, Blue Cross, and other commercial insurers. Although hospitals are not required to submit UB-92 for all neonates, most hospitals do complete this form. The Uniform Bill can provide useful information on procedures, diagnoses, and charges. The major advantage of this data source is its widespread use at a large number of institutions and its ready availability as a computer dataset at many hospitals.

There are several weaknesses, however, that must be considered. The Uniform Bill was designed for reimbursement, not for monitoring institutional performance or for clinical research. As a result, distortions in the data may result from attempts by hospitals to code diagnostic and procedural data with the goal of maximizing reimbursement.[19] Significant errors in diagnostic coding may occur. Studies of the reliability of hospital discharge abstracts have found that the principal diagnosis identified in the discharge abstract agrees with the actual diagnosis based on chart review only 65% of the time.[43]

The accuracy of coding for neonatal conditions has not been studied in detail. However, neonatal discharge abstracts tend to contain less reliable data on race than do birth certificates. Another problem with hospital discharge abstract data is the absence of birth weight as a data item. It is not included on UB-92. Because of the powerful predictive relationship of birth weight to both resource use and neonatal outcomes, recommendations to revise the UHDDS to include birth weight have been made.[41] This addition would greatly increase the value of discharge abstract data for the care of newborns.

It is also possible to use linkage strategies to enhance the usefulness of secondary data sources for quality improvement. Highly successful links can be established without using personal data such as names, hospital numbers, or Social Security numbers; instead, links can employ virtual identifiers such as postal code of residence, clinical factors, and demographic factors. California's Office of State Health Planning and Development sponsored a project to link the state-linked infant birth and death file with a modification of the UB-92 file.[31] This database allows one to select outcomes from the ICD-9-CM and procedure codes available on the discharge billing file and adjust these outcomes based on the birth weight and clinical, demographic, and socioeconomic information from the birth certificate. Further links to this database have included the mother's discharge file for the current pregnancy as well as all infant readmission discharge files during the first year of life.

Examples of population-based studies using this linked database include the relationship between discharge timing after birth and infant readmission,[16] shoulder dystocia, risk factors and neonatal outcomes,[20] and neonatal outcomes in childbearing beyond the age of 40.[21] In a project sponsored by the Pacific Business Group on Health with the technical oversight of the CPQCC, this database was used to perform a risk-adjusted analysis of primary cesarean section rates in California hospitals (www.healthscope.org). The technical details of the analysis are available at the CPQCC website (www.CPQCC.org).

Diagnosis Related Groups

Diagnosis related groups are another example of secondary data used to evaluate perinatal care. Defining case mix so as to be able to compare outcomes and resource use across institutions is of great importance to payers. DRG systems are classification schemes that use data that are routinely available in hospital discharge abstracts to group patients into relatively homogeneous categories. Outcomes and resource use are compared for similar DRGs across institutions. Because of the widespread use of DRGs, it is important for neonatologists to be familiar with these systems.

Ideally, each DRG category should contain patients who are clinically similar, whose care requires the same resource intensity, and who are at similar risk for adverse events, mortality, and morbidity. These systems, which were originally developed to guide prospective payment to hospitals, are used increasingly to classify patients for risk stratification in analyses of outcomes and costs.

Several alternative DRG classification systems have been developed (Table 5-1). They are updated periodically and exist in different versions. Individual DRGs are grouped into major diagnostic categories that contain related DRGs. The following discussion is limited to the DRGs in Major Diagnostic Category 15, which includes normal newborns and neonates with conditions originating in the perinatal period.

The Centers for Medicare and Medicaid Services DRG system (CMS DRG), which is used by Medicare, includes only seven DRG categories for neonates (Table 5-2). The CMS DRG categories are heterogeneous, explaining approximately 28% of the variation in costs and length of stay for neonates.[55] Because of the limitations of the CMS DRG system,[63,65] alternatives have been developed.

The first version of the Pediatric Modified DRG (PM-DRG) system, developed by the National Association of Children's Hospitals and Related Institutions (NACHRI) in the late 1980s, explained 46% of the variation in the costs of caring for neonates. The New York State Health Department and several other states adopted the All Patient DRG (AP-DRG) system in the late 1980s, which includes most, but not all, of the categories in the PM-DRGs. The AP-DRG version 21.0, released in January 2004, includes 24 categories for newborns and (with breakouts for multiple major problems) a total of 34 categories. This AP-DRG system explains approximately 55% of the variation in costs for neonates.[55]

The All Patient Refined DRG (APR-DRG) system was originally developed in the early 1990s by 3M Health Information Systems and the NACHRI. The APR-DRG version 20.0, released in Spring 2003, includes 28 base neonatal categories (Table 5-3). These categories are further divided into four subclasses for severity of illness (minor, moderate, major, and extreme), resulting in a total of 112 categories. The assignment to the 4 subclasses is made from an 18-step algorithm that considers the interaction of multiple secondary diagnoses and is

TABLE 5-1. Alternative Diagnosis Related Group Classification Systems

DRG SYSTEM	DEVELOPER	USERS
CMS DRG (formerly known as HCFA DRG)	Medicare	Medicare and some Medicaid programs
PM-DRG	NACHRI	No longer maintained
AP-DRG	New York State	New York and some other states
CHAMPUS DRG	Department of Defense	CHAMPUS
R-DRG	HCFA	
APR-DRG	3M Health Information Systems and NACHRI	State health departments and health data commissions

AP, all patient; APR, all patient refined; CHAMPUS, Civilian Health and Medical Program of the Uniformed Services; DRG, diagnosis related group; CMS, Centers for Medicare and Medicaid Services; HCFA, Health Care Financing Administration; NACHRI, National Association of Children's Hospitals and Related Institutions; PM, pediatric modified; R, refined.
From John Muldoon, National Association of Children's Hospitals and Related Institutions, March 2004.

TABLE 5-2. Centers For Medicare and Medicaid Services Diagnosis Related Group (CMS DRG) Categories, Version 21.0*

NUMBER	CATEGORY
385	Neonate, died or transferred to another acute facility
386	Neonate, extreme immaturity or respiratory distress syndrome
387	Prematurity with major problems
388	Prematurity without major problems
389	Full-term neonate with major problems
390	Neonates with other significant problems
391	Normal newborn

*Version 21.0 CMS DRGs were released October 2003.
From John Muldoon, National Association of Children's Hospitals and Related Institutions, March 2004.

specific to each APR-DRG category. There is also a separate set of assignments to four subclasses for risk of mortality, because some diagnoses have similar implications for intensity of care but different implications for likelihood of dying. This version of the APR-DRG system explains approximately 63% of the variation in cost for neonates.[55]

In an earlier study, Muldoon compared the structural and statistical performance of the major DRG systems for neonates.[56] He concluded that Medicare DRG categories are the least developed structurally and yield the poorest overall statistical performance and that the AP-DRG categories are intermediate in performance, rating somewhere between the Medicare DRG system and the APR-DRG system.

A difficulty with analyses based on DRGs is the validity of the ICD-9-CM diagnostic codes from which they are derived. In evaluations of charts coded by medical records personnel, error rates for some adult[14] and neonatal[82] diagnoses and procedures are as high as

20% to 40%. The practice of upcoding for the purpose of obtaining higher reimbursements has been cited as a potential source of these errors.[50] Even detailed classification schemes such as the newer DRG systems might not provide the case mix adjustment that is possible using multivariate models derived from primary perinatal data. However, because they are readily available, DRGs are often used to assess costs of care relative to case-mix severity across NICUs.

COSTS AND RESOURCES

It is important for neonatologists to understand that they will be under increasing pressure to justify and reduce the costs of neonatal care. Neonatal intensive care is one of the most expensive types of hospital care,[69,75,80] and it has come under increasing scrutiny by both public and private insurers seeking to contain health care costs. Insurers seek to compare treatment costs across institutions to determine whether costs at a given institution are excessively high.

Meaningful comparisons of neonatal intensive care treatment costs across institutions are difficult to make. Most insurers have access to data from only a small set of hospitals, whose case mix may vary considerably. If case-mix adjustments are made at all, they are typically based on the Medicare DRGs. However, the Medicare DRGs contain only seven categories for newborn infants and explain only 28% of variation in costs. Thus, the Medicare DRGs do not provide a good method for adjusting for case mix. This fact underscores the need for information systems that use alternative DRG systems to collect more detailed information on clinical aspects of care for infants treated in the NICU.

Comparisons of treatment costs across institutions are not straightforward, even in the absence of case mix differences. Because of the wide variation in pricing policies across hospitals, comparisons of charged amounts may be misleading. To compare treatment costs across institutions, costs must be computed. Data from hospital billing systems or UB-92s are typically

TABLE 5-3. All Patient Diagnosis Related Group (APR-DRG) Categories, Version 21.0*

NUMBER	CATEGORY
602	Neonate, birth weight <750 g, discharged alive
603	Neonate, birth weight <750 g, died
604	Neonate, birth weight 750-999 g, discharged alive
605	Neonate, birth weight 750-999 g, died
606	Neonate, birth weight 1000-1499 g, with significant operating room procedure, discharged alive
607	Neonate, birth weight 1000-1499 g, without significant operating room procedure, discharged alive
608	Neonate, birth weight 1000-1499 g, died
609	Neonate, birth weight 1500-1999 g, with significant operating room procedure, with multiple major problems
610	Neonate, birth weight 1500-1999 g, with significant operating room procedure, without multiple major problems
611	Neonate, birth weight 1500-1999 g, without significant operating room procedure, with multiple major problems
612	Neonate, birth weight 1500-1999 g, without significant operating room procedure, with major problem
613	Neonate, birth weight 1500-1999 g, without significant operating room procedure, with minor problem
614	Neonate, birth weight 1500-1999 g, without significant operating room procedure, with other problem
615	Neonate, birth weight 2000-2499 g, with significant operating room procedure, with multiple major problems
616	Neonate, birth weight 2000-2499 g, with significant operating room procedure, without multiple major problems
617	Neonate, birth weight 2000-2499 g, without significant operating room procedure, with multiple major problems
618	Neonate, birth weight 2000-2499 g, without significant operating room procedure, with major problem
619	Neonate, birth weight 2000-2499 g, without significant operating room procedure, with minor problem
620	Neonate, birth weight 2000-2499 g, without significant operating room procedure, with normal newborn diagnosis
621	Neonate, birth weight 2000-2499 g, without significant operating room procedure, with other problem
622	Neonate, birth weight >2499 g, with significant operating room procedure, with multiple major problems
623	Neonate, birth weight >2499 g, with significant operating room procedure, without multiple major problems
624	Neonate, birth weight >2499 g, with minor abdominal procedure
626	Neonate, birth weight >2499 g, without significant operating room procedure, with multiple major problems
627	Neonate, birth weight >2499 g, without significant operating room procedure, with major problem
628	Neonate, birth weight >2499 g, without significant operating room procedure, with minor problem
629	Neonate, birth weight >2499 g, without significant operating room procedure, with normal newborn diagnosis
630	Neonate, birth weight >2499 g, without significant operating room procedure, with other problem
635	Neonatal aftercare for weight gain
637	Neonate, died within one day of birth, born here
638	Neonate, died within one day of birth, not born here
639	Neonate, transferred <5 days old, born here
640	Neonate, transferred <5 days old, not born here
641	Neonate, birth weight >2499g, with extracorporeal membrane oxygenation

*V21.0 AP-DRGs were released in January 2004.
From John Muldoon, National Association of Children's Hospitals and Related Institutions, March 2004.

used to generate measures of treatment costs. These data contain information on charges for hospital services, which are converted to costs using information on the internal pricing structure of hospital services.

Standard methods exist for such conversions.[75,76] Calculating conversions based on detailed hospital bills can be a daunting task because of the volume of services (tens of thousands) that must be converted. Conversions based on the Uniform Bill forms are more easily performed because of the aggregation of charges on them. Cost conversion methodologies must allocate both direct and indirect costs to each hospital service. Direct costs, such as the cost of a prescription medication, are relatively easy to identify. However, decisions about how to allocate indirect costs, which include facility costs and services such as administrative salaries, security services, laundry, housekeeping, and individual services, are more difficult to make.

There are many ways to make these assignments. How indirect costs are allocated has a major effect on the ultimate calculated costs.[4] If costs at different institutions are to be compared, it is crucial that these assignments be made in a uniform manner.[75]

Computerized hospital discharge abstracts can be used to create hospital-specific reports that address perinatal care and its costs.[81] The nonprofit National Perinatal Information Center (Providence, RI) uses data from UB-92 supplemented with birth weight submitted by more than 50 participating hospitals with approximately 180,000 yearly births to create detailed reports that document and compare hospital performance and costs.[81]

Average length of stay (ALOS) is often used as a proxy for cost. In making ALOS comparisons, it is essential to adjust for differences in case mix. The Vermont Oxford Network has developed multivariate risk models for predicting length of stay that are used in routine reporting to members. As with mortality, there is substantial variation among the network hospitals even after adjusting for case mix, with adjusted total length of stay for surviving infants 501 g to 1500 g ranging from less than 40 days at some institutions to more than 75 days at others.[38]

Documenting comparative outcomes in the context of comparative costs is extremely important to managed care organizations with respect to selecting cost-effective hospitals and negotiating reimbursement rates. However, valid comparisons across institutions are difficult to make. The financial modules of generic hospital information systems are intended for application in all clinical areas of a hospital; therefore, these systems have broad appeal to hospital managers and yet may not have the granularity, clinical precision, or reporting flexibility to meet the needs of the perinatal unit.

Neonatologists must become familiar with the management tools in use at their hospitals. They must understand their analytic shortcomings and their interpretation, because decisions regarding resource allocations within hospitals increasingly will be based on these tools.

Role of Networks

Quality improvement activities for any given hospital are greatly facilitated by participating in a network. The networks facilitate valid comparisons by standardizing data definition and collection standards. Their reports allow confidential risk-adjusted comparisons to peer institutions, and the networks provide important resources for organized data-driven improvement activities.

Several NICU networks have been formed to evaluate the effectiveness and efficiency of neonatal intensive care and facilitate the use of data for quality improvement (Box 5-1). Examples include the Australian and New Zealand Neonatal Network, the Canadian NICU Network (www.caneonet.org/nicu.html), the Indian Neonatal Forum Network, the International Neonatal Network,[44] the National Institute of Child Health and Human Development (NICHD) Neonatal Research Network,[29,53] Pediatrix,[8] and the Vermont Oxford Network.[38,39]

The NICHD Neonatal Research Network is a group of 16 academic NICUs whose government-funded activities include randomized trials and observational studies. Participants in the network are chosen based on competitive application to the NICHD. The NICHD Neonatal Research Network maintains a database for infants with birth weights of 401 g to 1500 g who were treated at participating NICUs. Uniform definitions for data items and attention to maintenance of data quality make the NICHD Neonatal Research Network database a valuable resource for neonatologists. The published reports from the database can be used by other NICUs for comparison. An example of the type of data produced by the NICHD Neonatal Network is shown in Table 5-4. The validity of making comparisons with these data depends on the definitions of data items used by an individual NICU and the similarity of their patient populations to those treated at NICUs in the NICHD Network.

The Vermont Oxford Network is a collaborative network of neonatologists and other health care professionals, representing nearly 500 institutions from North America and around the world (www.vtoxford.org). Membership is voluntary and open to all who are interested. The nonprofit network is supported by membership fees, research grants, and contracts. The primary philosophy of the Vermont Oxford Network is to improve the quality, safety, and efficiency of medical care for newborn infants and their families through a coordinated program of research, education, and quality improvement projects. In support of all three aspects of this program, the network maintains a database for infants with birth weights of 401 g to 1500 g who were born at participating centers or admitted to them within 28 days of birth. Members of the Vermont Oxford Network complete brief data forms using standardized definitions.[89] Strict attention is paid to maintenance of data quality.[34] The database provides core data for network clinical trials, is used for observational studies and outcomes research, and generates reports for members that compare their performance with that of other NICUs in the network. These reports are produced quarterly and are intended for use in local quality management efforts.

In 2002, the Vermont Oxford Network database enrolled more than 33,000 infants weighing 401 g to 1500 g from 408 NICUs; in the 13-year period from 1990 to 2002, more than 213,000 infants were enrolled in the database. A major advantage of participating in a network database is that comparisons among NICUs based on uniform definitions are then possible. Members of the Vermont Oxford Network receive standardized reports that document their performance, track changes over time, and compare the individual NICU with the network as a whole and with a group of similar institutions. Data that provide comparisons with overall network reference rates as well as identification of trends over time are available to all NICUs participating in the Vermont Oxford Network database.

TABLE 5-4. Birthweight-Specific Survival and Selected Neonatal Morbidity among Survivors Born in the NICHD Neonatal Research Network Between 1/1/95 and 12/31/96*

SURVIVORS	501–750 g (n = 1002)	751-1000 g (n = 1084)	1001–1250 g (n = 1053)	1251–1500 g (n = 1299)	501-1500 g (n = 4438)
Total	540 (53.9)	935 (86.3)	992 (94.2)	1257 (96.8)	3724 (83.9)
Survived without morbidity	199 (36.9)	540 (57.8)	766 (77.2)	1132 (90.1)	2637 (70.8)
Survived with morbidity	341 (63.1)	395 (42.2)	226 (22.8)	125 (9.9)	1087 (29.2)
CLD[†]	189 (35.0)	245 (26.2)	121 (12.2)	71 (5.6)	626 (16.8)
Severe ICH[‡]	33 (6.1)	47 (5.0)	46 (4.6)	22 (1.8)	148 (4.0)
NEC[§]	22 (4.1)	30 (3.2)	32 (3.2)	23 (1.8)	107 (2.9)
CLD/Severe ICH	56 (10.4)	39 (4.2)	19 (1.9)	6 (0.5)	120 (3.2)
CLD/NEC	25 (4.6)	26 (2.8)	6 (0.6)	3 (0.2)	60 (1.6)
NEC/Severe ICH	9 (1.7)	5 (0.5)	2 (0.2)	0 (0.0)	16 (0.4)
CLD/Severe ICH/NEC	7 (1.3)	3 (0.3)	0 (0.0)	0 (0.0)	10 (0.3)

*Data expressed as number of infants with percentages in parentheses.
†Chronic lung disease defined as O_2 at 36 weeks' postmenstrual age.
‡Grade III-IV intraventricular hemorrhage.
§Necrotizing enterocolitis (Bell's classification stage ≥2).
NICHD, National Institute of Child Health and Human Development.
Courtesy of Linda L. Wright, MD, National Institute of Child Health and Human Development Neonatal Research Network, November 1999.

A limitation of the databases maintained by the NICHD and the Vermont Oxford Network is that historically they have been limited to infants with birth weights of 1500 g or less. The Vermont Oxford Network has now expanded data collection and reporting to include infants weighing more than 1500 g.

In addition to national and international networks, several statewide efforts in the United States are focused on monitoring and improving newborn care. For example, New York is in the process of implementing the Statewide Perinatal Data System (SPDS), which will consist of a core birth certificate, birth log, and modules for neonates and mothers who are at high risk. Data will be entered via the Internet. It will allow online performance of basic analyses and will serve numerous reporting needs, including those of vital records, birth logs, newborn screening, and immunization registry. The system will provide outcomes data for hospitals, integrated health care systems, and perinatal regions for use in quality-improvement efforts.[2]

Another example is the California Perinatal Quality Care Collaborative, a statewide outgrowth of an initiative proposed by the California Association of Neonatologists (CAN) and supported by the David and Lucile Packard Foundation; the California Department of Health Services, Maternal and Child Health Branch; and California Children's Services. The collaborative exists to improve the health of pregnant women, infants, and children by collecting high-quality information on perinatal outcomes and resource use and using these data for performance improvement and benchmarking processes in perinatal care and NICUs throughout California.

The CPQCC forms a public and private alliance of stakeholders, including the Maternal and Child Health Branch, California Children's Services, and the Office of Vital Records (all within the California Department of Health Services); the Office of Statewide Health Planning and Development; the Hospital Council; Regional Perinatal Programs of California; the Health Insurance Plan of California; the American College of Obstetricians and Gynecologists; the California Association of Neonatologists; the Pacific Business Group on Health; the David and Lucile Packard Foundation; and the Vermont Oxford Network. The collaborative has three goals: to provide a timely analysis of perinatal care, outcomes, and resource use based on a uniform statewide database; to provide mechanisms for benchmarking and continuous quality improvement (CQI); and to serve as a model for other states.

The Vermont Oxford Network has provided major input to the development of the CPQCC database and CQI activities. The Vermont Oxford Network database for infants weighing less than 1500 g has provided the foundation for the CPQCC database. In 2000, this was expanded to include a subset of the sickest infants weighing more than 1500 g. The large-baby data are processed by the CPQCC data center, and confidential Web-based small-baby and big-baby reports have been developed for inborn infants, outborn infants, and infants readmitted to an NICU during the first 28 days of life (www.cpqcc.org). In the future, the database will be expanded to include individual state birth certificate and death certificate data (which are now used to audit the completeness of CPQCC hospital data submission) and hospital discharge summary data. Currently there are 93 member hospitals with NICUs admitting nearly 70% of California's newborn infants who require critical care. Timely high-quality data fuel the project, but the major purpose of the CPQCC is to improve the quality of care.

Work of Quality Improvement

In the previous sections strategies have been presented for collecting and evaluating data using primary and secondary databases, the importance of risk adjustment in being able to compare outcomes and processes across institutions, and the advantages of being part of a network. In this section we will discuss strategies for translating data into action, the work of quality improvement.

To address quality of care requires the ability to specify outcomes. Outcomes may be objective or subjective. Typically, objective outcomes consist of mortality, morbidity, and long-term neurodevelopmental status. The most important morbidities to record are those that could be influenced by the quality of care, for example, nosocomial infection. In some cases, we presume that certain morbidities can be minimized by optimal care, although the specifics of what constitutes optimal care have not been defined. Conversely, it is clear that suboptimal practices can increase morbidity. For example, excessive ventilation can lead to pneumothorax or bronchopulmonary dysplasia, fluid overload can increase the risk for patent ductus arteriosus, and inadequate maintenance of thermal environment and suboptimal nutritional practices can result in prolonged hospitalization because of poor weight gain.[8] In addition to the traditional clinical outcomes, subjective outcomes, such as parent satisfaction and quality of life, will become increasingly important measures of the quality of neonatal care.[13,78,79]

Specifying and measuring the practices and outcomes of care are only the starting point for improvement. The information must be analyzed, synthesized, and presented so that opportunities for improvement can be identified and the results of improvement efforts can be monitored and evaluated. However, information and performance feedback alone cannot cause the profound changes in care processes and in the behavior of caregivers that are necessary to improve the quality of medical care. These will occur only when all members of the care team have the knowledge, skills, motivation, and organizational support required to make continuous quality improvement an integral and ongoing component of their work.

Multidisciplinary collaborative quality improvement has been applied successfully in a number of health care settings.[64] The management of quality in the field of health care has borrowed heavily from the techniques of quality management science in use in general industry. Berwick has pioneered the application of these techniques to medical care and applied them to a number of clinical problems in the Breakthrough Series of the Institute for Health Care Improvement.[5,6,42] O'Connor has shown that multidisciplinary collaborative

improvement based on feedback of performance data, quality improvement training, and collaborative learning through site visiting can reduce mortality for cardiovascular surgery.[59] Many health care organizations are now using these general methods to improve the quality of medical practice. The CPQCC and the Vermont Oxford Network provide two examples of how quality improvement is being applied to neonatal care.

The CPQCC has established a permanent subcommittee, the Perinatal Quality Improvement Panel, made up of neonatologists, perinatologists, perinatal nurses, state and hospital representatives, and health outcomes researchers with experience in quality improvement and outcomes measurement. The panel reviews the statewide data and recommends quality improvement objectives, provides models for performance improvement, and assists providers in transforming data into information that can help to improve care.[93]

The panel has directed the completion of CPQCCs first CQI cycle on antenatal steroid administration. The program was structured to improve the performance of all hospitals, and it endeavored to assist all participating hospitals in meeting established goals at the conclusion of the CQI cycle. The results achieved by the participating NICUs demonstrated substantial improvements and were publicly released on the Pacific Business Group on Health Web site (www.healthscope.org). The second topic selected for a network-wide CQI cycle with public release is nosocomial infection.

In addition to these formal public release cycles, CPQCC has conducted educational programs and workshops and has developed toolkits to facilitate CQI for several important areas. Five quality improvement toolkits are available for download on the CPQCC Web site, www.cpqcc.org. These include Antenatal Corticosteroid Administration, Improving Initial Lung Function: Surfactant and Other Means, Nosocomial Infection Prevention: Neonatal Perspectives, Practices and Priorities, Reducing Postnatal Steroid Administration, and Nutritional Support of the Very Low Birth Weight (VLBW) Infant. With more than 800 downloads in the first quarter of 2004, CPQCC is proving to be a popular source of quality improvement information for providers in California, the United States, and abroad.

The Vermont Oxford Network has been working since the early 1990s to adapt collaborative quality improvement methods and apply them to neonatal intensive care.[36,38,39] The network's initial collaborative improvement project, known as the NIC/Q Project, involved multidisciplinary teams from 10 institutions. Teams consisting of neonatologists, neonatal nurses, administrators, allied professionals, and quality improvement coaches from the institutions worked closely together to set common improvement goals, to identify potentially better practices for achieving those goals, and to implement the practices in their own NICUs.

The clinical improvement goals included reductions in nosocomial infection and chronic lung disease for infants of very low birth weight; resource-related goals included reductions in length of stay and more appropriate use of blood gas testing and x-ray procedures.

The teams received training in quality improvement from a professional quality-improvement trainer and held discussions in a series of facilitated large group and small focus group meetings and conference calls.

The potentially better practices were identified based on review and evaluation of the evidence in the literature, detailed analysis of the processes of care, and site visits to other participating institutions and benchmark units with superior performance outside the project. The Vermont Oxford Network database was used to provide performance feedback to participants and to monitor the results.

The preliminary results of the project demonstrated significant reductions in nosocomial infections (six institutions) and chronic lung disease (four institutions) in the subgroups that focused on those goals, both when compared with themselves over time, and when compared with a comparison group of 66 nonparticipating units that were members of the Vermont Oxford Network during the same period.[36] In addition, the costs of care for infants of very low birth weight at the 10 NIC/Q sites decreased over the course of the project. This project demonstrated the potential for a multifaceted intervention of training in evidence-based collaborative quality improvement, feedback of performance data, and site visiting to improve the quality of neonatal intensive care.

As a result of this initial experience, the Vermont Oxford Network organized an expanded evidence-based Quality Improvement Collaborative for Neonatology, NIC/Q 2000.[38] This collaborative, composed of multidisciplinary teams from 34 member institutions, applied four key improvement habits to a broad range of clinical, operational, and organizational improvement goals.[64] As in the original NIC/Q project, participants received training in quality improvement; worked together closely in facilitated large group meetings, focus groups, and conference calls; and used data from the Vermont Oxford Network database for feedback to monitor performance.

The Vermont Oxford Network has now concluded its third intensive improvement collaborative, NIC/Q 2002. This collaborative, composed of multidisciplinary teams from 48 institutions, worked on a broad range of quality and safety topics including pain and sedation, high-risk perinatal care, discharge planning, nurse staffing for quality and retention, organizational culture for safety, and a range of clinical improvement topics.

The Network is now beginning its NIC/Q2005 collaborative involving multidisciplinary teams from over 50 hospitals. The Vermont Oxford Network has created an Internet site for its members, www.nicq.org, to serve as the archive for NICU improvement knowledge and tools developed in the NICQ improvement collaboratives.

Internet-based Improvement Collaboratives

In addition to the intensive face-to-face improvement collaboratives just described, the Vermont Oxford Network has also conducted a series of Internet-based improvement collaboratives called iNICQ. The iNICQ collaboratives have addressed topics in quality and safety. The current iNICQ collaborative, including multidisciplinary teams from 65 NICUs around the world, is focused on reducing nosocomial infection. As a result of the NICQ and iNICQ collaboratives, more than 125 multidisciplinary teams from NICUs around the world have participated in formal collaborative efforts to improve the quality and safety of neonatal intensive care. The National Initiative for Children's Healthcare Quality (NICHQ), in partnership with the Vermont Oxford Network, is now conducting an Internet improvement collaborative for multidisciplinary teams working in the normal newborn nursery. This collaborative, Great Beginnings, will build on the lessons learned in the iNICQ collaboratives to promote a healthy and safe start for all newborns.

Four Key Habits for Improvement

The four key habits for improvement were synthesized by Paul Plsek based on his work with the Vermont Oxford Network improvement collaboratives and now serve as foundation for the NIC/Q and iNICQ collaboratives (Figure 5-2).[64]

The first is the *habit for change*. Change is difficult both for people and for organizations, yet without change, there cannot be improvement. Participants in NIC/Q and iNICQ collaboratives are taught to use a simple model for change developed by Langley, Nolan, and colleagues.[51] The model is based on three questions: What are we trying to improve? (measurable improvement goal); How will we know that a change is an improvement? (measurement); and What changes can we make that will lead to improvement? (better practices). Multidisciplinary NICU teams answer these questions and test their proposed changes in a series of plan-do-study-act (PDSA) cycles within their institution.

FIGURE 5-2. The four key habits for clinical improvement are applied by participants in the Vermont Oxford Network NIC/Q Evidence-Based Quality Improvement Collaborative for Neonatology to identify and implement better clinical, operational, and organizational practices for the care of newborn infants and their families. (Courtesy of the Vermont Oxford Network, Burlington, Vermont.)

The focus is on rapid trial and learning cycles with measurable improvement goals. Improvements are applied to a broad range of clinical, operational, and organizational domains of performance.

The second key habit is the *habit for evidence-based practice*. Participants learn to evaluate the strength and quality of the evidence for different practices and to apply the principles of evidence-based medicine in their daily practice.[77,84]

The third key habit is the *habit for collaborative learning*. This process involves collaboration among the disciplines and specialties within an institution and among multidisciplinary teams from different institutions.

The fourth key habit is the *habit for systems thinking*. This habit requires participants to see neonatal intensive care as a multifaceted process linking many people and organizational subsystems. NICUs are complex adaptive systems. By analyzing these systems and understanding the structures, patterns, and processes of care, it is possible to redesign them to be more effective and efficient. Furthermore, monitoring the implementation of and adherence to evidence-based processes of care within an institution provides a powerful method for quality improvement that in many instances is quicker, more practical, and more efficient than monitoring outcomes alone.

The participants in the NIC/Q and iNICQ collaboratives contribute the results of their learning to a growing archive of improvement knowledge maintained by the Vermont Oxford Network. This archive is being organized into an Internet site (www.nicq.org) that will provide the neonatal community with unique resources and tools for collaborative evidence-based quality improvement.

Patient Safety

The report *To Err is Human* has focused national attention on the problem of medical errors and patient safety.[48] There is widespread agreement that medical errors and the adverse events they cause represent a serious challenge to the health care system.

We are just beginning to learn about the frequency and types of medical errors that occur in the NICU. Kaushal and colleagues in a study of medication errors in hospitalized children, found that in the NICU more than 90% of infants were subjected to a medication error.[47] It has been suggested that the use of modern information technology and computerized physician order entry will reduce the frequency of medication errors and mitigate their effects.[3] The integration of enhanced information technology in the NICU requires study.

Nonmedication errors are also frequent in the NICU. Using data from an anonymous, voluntary, Internet-based error-reporting system established by the Vermont Oxford Network, Suresh and colleagues documented a broad range of errors and near errors in NICU patients.[85] Based on more than 1200 error reports from 54 NICUs over a 17-month period, the most frequent event categories were wrong medication, dose, schedule, or

infusion rate (including nutritional agents and blood products, 47%); error in administration or method of using a treatment (14%); patient misidentification (11%); other system failure (9%); error or delay in diagnosis (7%); and error in the performance of an operation, procedure, or test (4%). The most frequent contributory factors were failure to follow policy or protocol (47%), inattention (27%), communication problem (22%), error in charting or documentation (13%), distraction (12%), inexperience (10%), labeling error (10%), and poor teamwork (9%). Serious patient harm was reported in 2% and minor harm in 25% of events. A selected list of events is shown in Box 5-2.

The Center for Patient Safety in Neonatal Intensive Care, funded by the Agency for Healthcare Research and Quality, has been established to conduct research in NICU patient safety. Preliminary studies by center investigators have categorized the wide range of NICU errors,[85] reported the value of random safety audits built into daily NICU rounds,[88] documented the risks of patient misidentification in the NICU,[26] and explored the family perspective on NICU errors using the Internet tool for families www.howsyourbaby.com.[18] Future research will evaluate strategies to prevent and mitigate medical errors in the NICU

James Reason has pointed out that human error can be viewed in two ways.[67] The "person approach" focuses on individuals, blaming them for their mistakes, whereas the "systems approach" focuses on the conditions in which people work, concentrating on building safeguards into the system to prevent errors and mitigate their effects. Reason suggests that high-reliability organizations with low accident rates such as naval aircraft carriers, nuclear power plants, and air traffic control centers are successful because of a culture of safety that replaces individual blame with a system designed

BOX 5-2. Examples of Medical Errors Reported to Nicq.org

Chest tube inserted on wrong side
Human milk infused intravenously
CT scan with IV contrast on wrong infant
Positive HIV test result recorded as negative
Misplaced catheter causing liver injury
Dislodged catheter causing blood loss
Penis burn from hot Mogen clamp
Full day's IV fluids infused in 2 hours
Bili blanket wrong side up
Ultrasound exam on wrong twin
Phototherapy without eye shields
Human milk given to wrong infant
$100 \times$ dose of insulin; $10 \times$ dose of pancuronium bromide
Ligation of carotid artery rather than jugular vein
Infusion pump occlusion undetected for 24 hours

Note: Nicq.org is an Internet site maintained by the Vermont Oxford Network. Medical errors were reported voluntarily and anonymously by health professionals from 54 NICUs. These errors represent a selection from among nearly 2000 errors that have been reported as of June 2004. CT, computed tomography; HIV, human immunodeficiency virus; IV, intravenous; NICU, neonatal intensive care unit.

to be robust in the face of the unavoidable human and operational hazards. Health care organizations must now move from the person approach to the systems approach to achieve high reliability in medical care.

The Joint Commission for Accreditation of Healthcare Organizations (JCAHO) is now focusing on patient

BOX 5-3. JCAHO National Patient Safety Goals for 2004

Improve the Accuracy of Patient Identification

Use at least two patient identifiers (neither to be the patient's room number) whenever taking blood samples or administering medications or blood products.

Prior to the start of any surgical or invasive procedure, conduct a final verification process, such as a "time out," to confirm the correct patient, procedure and site, using active—not passive—communication techniques.

Improve the Effectiveness of Communication among Caregivers

Implement a process for taking verbal or telephone orders or critical test results that requires a verification read-back of the complete order or test result by the person receiving the order or test result.

Standardize the abbreviations, acronyms and symbols used throughout the organization, including a list of abbreviations, acronyms and symbols *not* to use.

Improve the Safety of Using High-Alert Medications

Remove concentrated electrolytes (including, but not limited to, potassium chloride, potassium phosphate, and sodium chloride >0.9%) from patient care units.

Standardize and limit the number of drug concentrations available in the organization.

Eliminate Wrong-Site, Wrong-Patient, Wrong-Procedure Surgery

Create and use a preoperative verification process, such as a checklist, to confirm that appropriate documents (e.g., medical records, imaging studies) are available.

Implement a process to mark the surgical site and involve the patient in the marking process.

Improve the Safety of Using Infusion Pumps

Ensure free-flow protection on all general-use and PCA (patient controlled analgesia) intravenous infusion pumps used in the organization.

Improve the Effectiveness of Clinical Alarm Systems

Implement regular preventive maintenance and testing of alarm systems.

Ensure that alarms are activated with appropriate settings and are sufficiently audible with respect to distances and competing noise within the unit.

Reduce the Risk of Nosocomial Infections

Comply with current CDC hand hygiene guidelines.

Manage as sentinel events all identified cases of unanticipated death or major permanent loss of function associated with a nosocomial infection.

safety in its hospital audits and has issued a series of National Patient Safety Goals (Box 5-3).[46] It will be important for NICU teams to apply the "four key habits" to address these safety goals in the unique setting of the NICU and to develop methods for identifying and monitoring errors.

Of course, safety is not really separate from the overall issue of quality of care. A culture of safety is an essential characteristic of the high-quality NICU. Although errors can never be totally eliminated, we must design the safest systems possible for the patients and families for whom we provide care.

CONCLUSION

The recognition that there is widespread variation among physicians and hospitals in clinical practice and patient outcomes and the growing pressure to increase the quality, safety, and cost-effectiveness of medical care have resulted in unprecedented interest in assessing, evaluating, and improving medical practice. If health professionals are to function successfully in this environment, they must understand how to evaluate their own performance and how their performance will be evaluated by others. These evaluations require accurate and reliable information.

Most importantly, neonatologists and other health care professionals must learn how to use the information to improve the quality and safety of the medical care they provide. In this part of the chapter we reviewed some of the available data sources and discussed a number of issues related to using them for improvement. Although neonatologists should not be expected to become experts in databases and evaluation methods, they do need to develop a basic understanding that will allow them to work effectively with other professionals in the changing health care environment.

In this "era of assessment and accountability," we must all develop the knowledge, skills, and motivation necessary to assume leadership roles in multidisciplinary collaborative quality improvement within our institutions, in larger health care organizations, and across regions. Only then can the potential benefits of modern databases and information systems be translated into better medical care for newborn infants and their families.

ACKNOWLEDGMENTS

We thank Mr. John Muldoon of the National Association of Children's Hospitals and Related Institutions, Jeannette Rogowski, PhD, of the University of Medicine and Dentistry of New Jersey, and Linda L. Wright, MD, of the National Institute of Child Health and Human Development Neonatal Research Network for providing information used in sections of this chapter.

Dr. Horbar's work in preparing this chapter was funded in part by a grant from the Agency for Healthcare Research and Quality (Center for Patient Safety in Neonatal Intensive Care, J Horbar, PI, P20 HS 11583) and by a grant from the Centers for Disease

Control and Prevention (Improving Health Care of Prematurely Born Children Through the Reduction of Medical Errors, J Horbar, PI, Program Announcement 02057)

PART 2

Practicing Evidence-Based Neonatal-Perinatal Medicine

John C. Sinclair, Kathleen A. Kennedy, and Jon E. Tyson

This discussion focuses on five key processes in practicing evidence-based neonatal-perinatal medicine: asking a focused clinical question; searching MEDLINE, the Cochrane Library, and other sources for high-quality evidence (both primary reports and systematic reviews); critically appraising the retrieved evidence for its validity; extracting the data; and applying the results to patient care. The role of the Cochrane Collaboration in the preparation, dissemination, and timely updating of systematic reviews of evidence from randomized clinical trials is highlighted. Strategies for promoting evidence-based clinical practice are presented.

Evidence-based medicine has been described as "the conscientious, explicit, and judicious use of current best evidence in making decisions about the care of individual patients."[124] The practice of evidence-based medicine requires efficient access to the best available evidence that is applicable to the clinical problem.

It is essential, however, to make two disclaimers. First, not every clinical decision can be based on strong evidence, because such evidence might not exist. Regarding a general internal medicine inpatient service in England, Ellis and coworkers estimated that principal treatments prescribed for patients' primary diagnoses were based on strong evidence from randomized, controlled trials (RCTs) in about 50% of cases; treatment was based on convincing non-RCT evidence in about 30% of cases; and there was no substantial evidence available in about 20% of cases.[105] In a similar study in the neonatal intensive care unit (NICU) at McMaster University Medical Centre, there was strong evidence from RCTs to support the choice of the principal prescribed treatment in 34% of cases.[99] These findings were based on surveys in institutions emphasizing the practice of evidence-based medicine, and no attempt was made to identify the proportion of all treatments prescribed that were based on strong evidence. The proportion would undoubtedly be substantially lower than 50% in these and other institutions. Indeed, many widely used therapies have not been well evaluated with respect to either effectiveness or safety.[96]

Second, evidence provides a necessary but not sufficient ground for clinical decisions. Clinical expertise is no less important under the evidence-based approach; indeed, an accurate history, physical examination, and clinical diagnosis are critical to a properly directed search for evidence that is directly applicable to the patient's problem. In addition, for some treatment decisions, it is essential to consider the values and preferences of parents with respect to the probable clinical outcomes of the treatments being considered for their baby.

ASKING A FOCUSED CLINICAL QUESTION

A focused clinical question should contain the following elements:

- the patients of interest
- the treatment or exposure of interest
- the nature of any comparisons to be made
- the primary outcome of interest and other important outcomes

The exact form of a focused clinical question depends on whether the question concerns treatment or prevention, etiology, diagnosis, or prognosis.[77,109] For questions concerning treatment or prevention, a focused question has the following form: In [patient, problem, or risk factor] does [treatment A] compared with [control or treatment B] reduce [adverse outcome(s)]?

For example: In women carrying babies of 24 to 34 weeks' gestation who are threatening to deliver, does corticosteroid (dexamethasone or betamethasone) compared with no treatment reduce the incidence of respiratory distress syndrome (RDS) in their babies? Another example: In babies of 24 to 30 weeks' gestational age, does prophylactic surfactant, given immediately at birth in the delivery room, compared with selective use of surfactant in those who develop moderate or severe RDS, reduce neonatal death or chronic lung disease?

Armed with a focused clinical question based on an accurate delineation of the clinical problem, the treatment alternatives being considered, and the important clinical outcomes, you can now target your search for valid evidence that is applicable to the problem.

FINDING EVIDENCE

Sources of Evidence

Clinical evidence that is relevant to problems in neonatal-perinatal medicine is appearing at an accelerating rate and can be found in a vast number of journals, books, conference proceedings, and other sources. Many published reports provide only weak evidence because strong research designs were not used. Evidence is constantly changing as new evidence becomes available. The challenge for the busy clinician, then, is to be able to detect evidence that is valid, up-to-date, and applicable to the clinical problem using strategies that are comprehensive and yet efficient. These strategies may be directed to retrieving both primary reports and reviews.

Recent review articles might seem like an efficient source of best available evidence. However, because most reviews do not use explicit review methods, there is a special need for the efficient retrieval of *systematic* reviews (discussed later). Although textbooks can provide valid evidence that is based on systematic methods of review, very few textbooks (except those that focus on evidence-based practice[101,106,120,127]) require contributors to use explicit and systematic methods when reviewing evidence and making treatment recommendations. Moreover, there tends to be a long time gap between the appearance of new evidence and its impact on therapeutic recommendations found in textbooks.[97] Thus, in neonatal-perinatal medicine and other fields in which new evidence is rapidly accumulating, it is especially important to be able to access systematic reviews that are frequently updated.

Efficient Strategies for Searching for Evidence

PRIMARY REPORTS

Primary reports that are relevant to neonatal-perinatal medicine are published in a large number of journals. Most of these journals are indexed in MEDLINE, but additional reports may appear in journals indexed in other computerized databases, including CINAHL and EMBASE. If you have access to the Internet, you can now search MEDLINE for clinical evidence using PubMed; you can also access other databases maintained by the National Library of Medicine (NLM). PubMed can be accessed at www.ncbi.nlm.nih.gov/pubmed; a list of other databases supported by the NLM can be found at www.nlm.nih.gov/databases.

To define the topic of your search, use Medical Subject Headings (MeSH terms), text words, or a combination, combining them appropriately in a Boolean search with AND or OR (your medical librarian can quickly teach you the logic of this). Help is also available online in the PubMed tutorial. You may choose to include search terms for the patient population, the intervention, the comparison, the outcome of interest, or all of these.

Often you will find that a MEDLINE search based only on topic descriptors yields a long list of reports that you do not have time to scan or, certainly, to read. The busy clinician needs to prune this potentially cumbersome list by incorporating into the search a strategy for limiting the retrieval to reports that are likely to be of high methodological quality and, therefore, more likely to provide valid evidence. Such a strategy includes using methodological filters that have

TABLE 5-5. Searching Medline for Sound Clinical Studies Using Methodological Filters

TYPE OF QUESTION	CRITERION STANDARD FOR METHODOLOGIC QUALITY
Treatment/ prevention	Random or quasi-random allocation of participants to treatment and control groups
Etiology	Formal control group using random or quasi-random allocation; nonrandomized concurrent controls; cohort analytic study with matching or statistical adjustment; or case control study
Diagnosis	Provision of sufficient data to calculate the sensitivity and specificity of the test, or likelihood ratios
Prognosis	A cohort of subjects who, at baseline, have the disease of interest but not the outcome of interest

Table derived from Haynes RB, et al: Developing optimal search strategies for detecting clinically sound studies in MEDLINE. J Amer Med Inform Assoc 1:447, 1994.

been validated against hand-searching[112] to detect articles that, depending on the type of focused question posed, have the methodology quality attributes shown in Table 5-5. These methodological filters are used together with your topic descriptors (through the use of AND), so that only articles that are both on topic in clinical terms and satisfy the methodological criteria are retrieved.

Furthermore, by choosing different methodological filters, you can maximize either the sensitivity (for comprehensiveness) or specificity (for fewest methodological false-positive results) of your search. To do this, use PubMed's Clinical Queries page (click on Clinical Queries on the PubMed page or access directly at www.ncbi.nlm.nih.gov/entrez/query/static/clinical.htm); then select Clinical Queries using Research Methodology Filters. You will be asked to click on the category type of the question you are asking (therapy, diagnosis, etiology, or prognosis) and on whether you want the methodological filters to emphasize sensitivity or specificity. If, for example, you are reviewing a topic and want to be comprehensive in your retrieval of sound clinical studies, you would click on "sensitivity." If you have limited time and want urgent access to perhaps only one or two reports that are likely to be methodologically sound, you would click on "specificity."

REVIEWS

Systematic reviews[100,129] are distinguished from other types of reviews by the rigor of the review methods. The objectives and methods are explicitly planned a priori, and they are documented in the review. A review without a methods section is unlikely to be a systematic review.

Systematic reviews of the results of randomized controlled trials attempt to identify all trials that have tested a defined therapy against an alternative in a defined population. Trials are included or excluded from the review on the basis of methodologic rigor (without consideration of the trial results). If the populations and the contrasting interventions are similar, the results may be summarized quantitatively by calculating a typical effect based on the results of all eligible trials. This latter step, called a meta-analysis, increases the precision of the estimates of treatment effect. A meta-analysis, however, is not a necessary part of a systematic review; indeed, if there is clinical or statistical heterogeneity across trials, it may be inappropriate to calculate a typical effect. Systematic reviews can be found in MEDLINE by limiting the publication type to "Meta-Analysis" or by using PubMed's Clinical Queries page (select Systematic Reviews).

For example: You wish to find a systematic review, with meta-analysis, of studies of women with threatened preterm delivery that assesses the effect of antenatal corticosteroids on the incidence of respiratory distress syndrome in their babies. Using PubMed, enter your search terms: corticosteroid AND respiratory distress syndrome. Limit your search by publication type to meta-analysis. Alternatively, you could enter your topic descriptors into the Systematic Reviews section of the Clinical Queries page.

Cochrane Systematic Reviews

The Cochrane Collaboration is an international organization that prepares, maintains, and disseminates up-to-date systematic reviews of health care interventions. The reviews are prepared by members of collaborative review groups, including the Pregnancy and Childbirth Review Group and the Neonatal Review Group. The reviews are published electronically in The Cochrane Library,[102] which is published every 3 months and allows the reviews to be updated as new evidence appears. The reviews prepared by the Neonatal Review Group can also be found at a Web site maintained by the National Institute of Child Health and Human Development (www.nichd.nih.gov/cochraneneonatal/cochrane.cfm). Cochrane reviews are indexed in Medline so they can also be identified using PubMed searches (using the topic descriptor alone or limiting the search by using the topic descriptor AND Cochrane). A description of these reviews has been recently published.[130]

CRITICALLY APPRAISING EVIDENCE FOR ITS VALIDITY

The fundamental goal of clinical research is to obtain an unbiased answer to the question posed. Bias leads to an answer that is systematically different from the truth. Guides to assessing the validity of clinical research in the realms of therapy, etiology, diagnosis, prognosis, and reviews are available.[110,111,113,115,116,122] A simple distillation of the major methodological issues to be considered is provided in Box 5-4. More comprehensive

---

BOX 5-4. Readers' Guides for Appraising the Validity of Clinical Studies

Therapy

Was the assignment of patients to treatments randomized?

Was randomization concealed (so that decision to enroll patient could not be influenced by knowledge of planned group assignment)?

Were all patients who entered the trial accounted for and attributed at its conclusion?

Were outcomes assessed "blindly," without knowledge of treatment group?

When possible, were patients and caretakers blind to treatment?

Etiology

Were there clearly defined comparison groups, similar with respect to important determinants of outcome, other than the one of interest?

Were the outcomes and exposures measured in the same way in the groups being compared?

Was follow-up sufficiently long and complete?

Is the temporal relationship correct?

Diagnosis

Was there an independent, blind comparison with a criterion standard?

Did the patient sample include the kinds of patients to whom the diagnostic test will be applied in practice?

Were the test results prevented from influencing the decision to perform the criterion standard (workup bias avoided)?

Can the test be replicated on the basis of the method reported?

Prognosis

Was there a representative, well-defined sample of patients at a uniform point in the course of the disease (inception cohort)?

Was follow-up sufficiently long and complete?

Were objective and unbiased outcome criteria used?

Was there adjustment for important prognostic factors?

Criteria from references 110, 113, 115, and 116.

---

guides, with specific applicability to therapeutic studies in neonatal-perinatal medicine, have been published.[123,134]

Most studies on treatment or prevention use designs that can be classified into one of four categories, listed in order of increasing methodologic rigor:

- case series without controls
- nonrandomized studies using historical controls
- nonrandomized studies using concurrent controls
- randomized, controlled trials

The randomized trial is the strongest design for evaluating the effect of treatment. It offers maximum protection against selection bias that can invalidate comparisons between groups of patients. The allocation process should be truly random (not quasi-random, e.g., alternate) and blinded so that it is impervious to tampering or code breaking. In addition, follow-up should be complete, with all randomized patients being accounted for in the primary analysis, and outcome measurements should be made by observers who are blinded to the treatment allocation. When feasible, blinding of the caretakers, the patient, and the patient's family to the treatment allocation should be accomplished. When reading reports of therapeutic studies, you should scan the "Methods" section to assess validity using these criteria.

EXTRACTING THE DATA AND EXPRESSING THE EFFECT OF TREATMENT

Table 5-6 displays the structure of a typical study that assesses the effectiveness of a treatment. There are two exposure groups (labeled *treated* or *control*) and two possible outcome categories (labeled *event* or *no event*). An event is a categorical adverse outcome such as occurrence of disease, adverse neurodevelopmental outcome, treatment side effect, or death. The effect of treatment is given by comparing the event rate in the treated and control groups, which can be accomplished using either relative or absolute treatment effect estimators.

The relative risk (RR), [a/(a + b)]/[c/(c + d)] indicates the relative, but not absolute, size of reduction in the event rate. The complement of the relative risk (1-RR) is the relative risk reduction (RRR). Thus, a relative risk of 0.75 represents a 25% RRR. The risk difference (RD) or absolute risk reduction (ARR), [c/(c + d)] − [a/(a + b)], indicates the absolute magnitude of reduction in risk. For example, a risk difference of 0.05 represents an absolute 5-percentage-point reduction of the event rate in the treated group.

The reciprocal of the risk difference (1/RD) indicates the number of patients who must be treated to expect to prevent the event in one patient. In the example, 20 patients (1/0.05) need to be treated to prevent the event in 1. The number needed to treat (NNT) is particularly relevant when deciding whether to use a treatment that is effective but causes important clinical side effects or results in an important increase in economic costs. The patient's expected event rate in the absence of treatment may be a critical determinant of this decision. When outcome data are reported on a continuous scale (e.g., blood pressure measured in mm Hg), a different measure of effect, the mean difference, is computed.

APPLYING THE RESULTS TO PATIENT CARE

The results of randomized trials of therapy indicate the likely effects of the therapy, beneficial and adverse, on important clinical outcomes. However, these effects are average effects in the patients who are entered in the trials, and they may or may not accurately predict the net benefit to be expected in specific subgroups or in individual patients.[104,107] This problem becomes especially important when a treatment has been shown to produce both benefits and harm. Often, patients at high risk of the primary outcome are more likely than those at low risk to be the ones who actually benefit from an effective therapy. However, patients at high risk and those at low risk who receive a treatment are exposed to the adverse side effects of that treatment; thus, the balance between likely benefits and harm will shift. This problem is compounded because individual patients may place different values on the relative importance of benefits and harm caused by treatment.

In deciding whether to use an effective therapy in the individual patient, particularly when that therapy results in important clinical side effects, one must consider the relative likelihood that the therapy will actually prevent the adverse target event, or cause adverse side effects, in that individual patient. One way of approaching this is to determine whether the report of the relevant trial, or systematic review of trials, described the size of risk reduction for the primary outcome, and risk increases for any side effects caused, according to patient subgroups defined by patient characteristics at entry. If so, it may be possible to derive a relative likelihood of being helped or harmed from the subgroup most similar to your patient. More often, however, either RRR across subgroups is not clearly different or you cannot judge this because data by subgroups are not presented or the groups are too small for meaningful comparisons.

Assuming that RRR is constant across the range of baseline risk, you can calculate a patient-specific absolute risk reduction (ARR) using the formula ARR = RRR × PEER, where PEER is your patient's expected event rate in the absence of treatment. In neonatal-perinatal medicine, such information may often be available from estimates of risk based on gestational age, birth weight, and postnatal age. Using this approach,

TABLE 5-6. Structure of a Study to Assess the Effect of a Treatment and Measures of Treatment Effect

	Outcome	
	EVENT	NO EVENT
EXPOSURE		
Treated	a	b
Control	c	d
TREATMENT EFFECT MEASURES		
Relative risk (RR)	a/(a+b) ÷ c/(c+d)	
Relative risk reduction (RRR)	1 − RR	
Odds ratio	ad/bc	
Risk difference (RD)	c/(c+d) − a/(a+b)	
Number needed to treat (NNT)	1/RD	

ARR (and its inverse, NNT) will be shown to vary with PEER: In patients at high risk, ARR will be high and NNT will be low, whereas in patients at low risk, the reverse will be true.[108,111,128]

An example of this form of analysis is shown in Figure 5-3. A systematic review of randomized trials of antenatal corticosteroid for the prevention of RDS in mothers who threaten to deliver prematurely showed that this therapy was effective in reducing the incidence of RDS, with an RRR of 41%.[103] RRR was fairly constant across subgroups based on gestational age. Because the expected risk for RDS is high at short gestation but decreases markedly with increasing gestation, NNT to prevent one case of RDS is low when gestation is less than 30 weeks, but it rises sharply after 34 weeks. Although the trials did not demonstrate short-term toxic effects, few of them undertook the assessment of long-term effects. Given the uncertain balance at gestation periods beyond 34 weeks between the small likelihood of short-term benefits and the undocumented but not well-studied possibility of long-term risks, the National Institutes of Health (NIH) Consensus Conference on prenatal corticosteroids recommended that women carrying babies of 34 weeks' gestation or less who threaten to deliver prematurely be considered candidates for steroid treatment (see Chapter 42).[121] Other examples and a more detailed discussion of how to balance the risks and benefits in prescribing therapies for individual patients are provided elsewhere.[132]

PROMOTING EVIDENCE-BASED CLINICAL PRACTICE

The evidence-based practice paradigm places responsibility on the physician to develop and maintain the skills needed to efficiently find relevant evidence, critically appraise it for its validity, and apply it to the clinical problem. The development of these skills should begin in undergraduate medical education, and there is evidence that teaching critical appraisal skills can be incorporated successfully into clinical clerkships.[98] A useful tool for acquiring these skills and enabling evidence-based care is the critically appraised topic,[126] which comprises asking a focused question about a patient, finding and appraising relevant articles quickly, and synthesizing the evidence into a one- or two-page summary.

Attainment of the required skills by individual practitioners, however, poses a challenge. A survey of English general practitioners[119] revealed that although they were favorably disposed to the concept of evidence-based clinical practice, they believed they lacked the necessary knowledge and skills to carry it forward. For example, only 16% had formal training in searching for evidence, and only about 33% believed they had sufficient understanding of key terms, such as *relative risk* and *number needed to treat*, that they could explain them to others. Most believed that the best way to promote evidence-based practice was the introduction of evidence-based practice guidelines or protocols.[131]

The preparation and dissemination of practice guidelines or consensus recommendations, however, does not ensure their use in practice. Several strategies aimed at promoting change of behavior among clinicians have been tested, and some have been found successful. Two of these strategies—introducing guidelines through opinion leaders and providing audit and feedback—were included in an intervention package designed to encourage the use of antenatal corticosteroids in eligible women, in accordance with the NIH Consensus recommendations.[121] In a randomized trial in which this package was compared with a control intervention consisting of the usual dissemination of recommendations, the evidence-based use of antenatal corticosteroids was found to be increased in the experimental group.[117,118] Thus, randomized trials are being employed not just to test the effectiveness of new therapies but also to evaluate competing strategies for promoting the use of evidence in clinical practice.[118,131]

There is also a need for the further development of practical methods for measuring the importance or value that patients, caregivers, and the lay public attach to clinical outcomes.[133] In neonatal-perinatal decision making, these values are usually sought from the parents, by using informal and unsystematic approaches. More formal and systematic methods for measuring

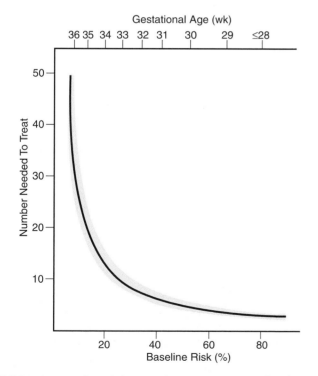

FIGURE 5-3. Number of fetuses who must be treated (NNT) with antenatal corticosteroid to prevent one case of respiratory distress syndrome (RDS), as a function of baseline risk. The NNT is derived from the typical relative risk reduction (RRR) of 41% calculated from the data of the trials included in the systematic review of Crowley.[103] The shaded zone indicates the 95% confidence interval. As the gestational age increases, baseline risk for RDS decreases and for NNT increases.

preferences,[114] including rating scales and the standard gamble, were used by teenage survivors of extremely low birth weight and their parents in a study of the quality of life of the adolescents.[125] Such methods for rating health outcomes could be used increasingly in the future to assess the importance that parents attach to the probable outcomes of neonatal-perinatal treatment alternatives and, thus, to help guide evidence-based decision making for individual patients or patients in specific risk categories.[132]

REFERENCES

Part 1

1. American College of Obstetricians and Gynecologists: Evaluation of Cesarean Delivery. Washington, DC, American College of Obstetricians and Gynecologists, 2000.
2. Applegate M: Personal communication, 2000.
3. Bates DW, Gawande AA: Improving safety with information technology. N Engl J Med 348:2526, 2003.
4. Berman JH et al: The Financial Management of Hospitals. 8th ed. Chicago, Health Administration Press, 1994.
5. Berwick DM: A user's manual for the IOM's "Quality Chasm" report. Health Aff (Millwood) 21:80, 2002.
6. Berwick DM: Improvement, trust, and the healthcare workforce. Qual Saf Health Care 12:448, 2003.
7. Blondel B et al: The impact of the increasing number of multiple births on the rates of preterm birth and low birthweight: An international study. Am J Public Health 92:1323, 2002.
8. Bloom BT et al: Improving growth of very low birth weight infants in the first 28 days. Pediatrics 112:8, 2003.
9. Boyce JM, Pitt D: Guidelines for hand hygiene in health-care settings. Recommendations of the healthcare infection control practices advisory committee and the HICPAC/SHEA/APIC/IDSA hand hygiene task force. MMWR Morb Mortal Weekly Rep 51:1, 2002.
10. Brodie SB et al: Occurrence of nosocomial bloodstream infections in six neonatal intensive care units. Pediatr Infect Dis J 19:56, 2000.
11. California Perinatal Quality Care Collaborative: http://www.cpqcc.org.
12. Committee on Quality of Health Care in America: Crossing the Quality Chasm: A New Health System for the 21st Century. Washington, DC, National Academy Press, 2001.
13. Conner J, Nelson EC: Neonatal intensive care: Satisfaction measured from a parent's perspective. Pediatrics 103(1 Suppl E):336, 1999.
14. Corn RF: Quality control of hospital discharge data. Med Care 18:416, 1980.
15. Cullen DJ et al: Therapeutic intervention scoring system: A method for quantitative comparison of patient care. Crit Care Med 2:57, 1974.
16. Danielsen B et al: Newborn discharge timing and read-missions: California, 1992-1995. Pediatrics 106:31, 2000.
17. Dooley SL et al: Quality assessment of perinatal regionalization by multivariate analysis: Illinois, 1991-1993. Obstet Gynecol 89:193, 1997.
18. Edwards W et al: Parents' perspectives on errors in neonatal intensive care. Pediatr Res 55:435A, 2004.
19. Gardner E: UB-82 forms offer wealth of information, misinformation. Mod Healthc 20:18, 1990.
20. Gilbert WM et al: Associated factors in 1611 cases of brachial plexus injury. Obstet Gynecol 93:536, 1999.
21. Gilbert WM et al: Childbearing beyond age 40: Pregnancy outcome in 24,032 cases. Obstet Gynecol 93:9, 1999.
22. Gould JB et al: Cesarean rates and neonatal morbidity in a low-risk population. Obstet Gynecol 104:11, 2004.
23. Gould JB et al: Very low birth weight births at non-NICU hospitals: The role of sociodemographic, perinatal, and geographic factors. J Perinatol 19:197, 1999.
24. Gould JB: Quality improvement in perinatal medicine: Assessing the quality of perinatal care. NeoReviews 5:e33, 2004.
25. Gould JB: Vital records for quality improvement. Pediatrics 103:278, 1999.
26. Gray JE et al: Patient mis-identification in the neonatal intensive care unit (NICU): Qualification of risk. Pediatr Res 55:519A, 2004.
27. Gray JE et al: Neonatal therapeutic intervention scoring system: A therapy-based severity-of-illness index. Pediatrics 90:561, 1992.
28. Hack M et al: Outcomes in young adulthood for very-low-birth-weight infants. N Engl J Med 346:149, 2002.
29. Hack M et al: Very-low-birth-weight outcomes of the National Institute of Child Health and Human Development Neonatal Network, November 1989 to October 1990. Am J Obstet Gynecol 172:457, 1995.
30. Hadorn DC et al: Assessing the Performance of Mortality Prediction Models. Santa Monica, Calif, RAND, 1993.
31. Herrchen B et al: Vital statistics linked birth/infant death and hospital discharge record linkage for epidemiological studies. Comput Biomed Res 30:290, 1997.
32. Hexter AC: Comments: On "rates" of birth defects. Teratology 41:473, 1990.
33. Horbar JD, Carpenter J: Nosocomial infection in very low birth weight infants: We can do better! Pediatr Res 55:404A, 2004.
34. Horbar JD, Leahy KA: An assessment of data quality in the Vermont-Oxford Trials Network database. Control Clin Trials 16:51, 1995.
35. Horbar JD: Birthweight-adjusted mortality rates for assessing the effectiveness of neonatal intensive care. Med Decis Making 12:259, 1992.
36. Horbar JD et al: Collaborative quality improvement for neonatal intensive care. Pediatrics 107:14, 2001.
37. Horbar JD et al: Trends in mortality and morbidity for very low birth weight infants, 1991-1999. Pediatrics 110:143, 2002.
38. Horbar JD: The Vermont Oxford Network: Evidence-based quality improvement for neonatology. Pediatrics 103(1 Suppl E):350, 1999.
39. Horbar JD: The Vermont-Oxford Neonatal Network: Integrating research and clinical practice to improve the quality of medical care. Semin Perinatol 19:124, 1995.
40. Hudome SM et al: Contribution of genetic disorders to neonatal mortality in a regional intensive care setting. Am J Perinatol 11:100, 1994.
41. Iezzoni LI: Data sources and implications: Administrative databases. In Iezzoni LI (ed): Risk Adjustment for Measuring Health Care Outcomes. Ann Arbor, Mich, Health Administrator Press, 1994, p 119.
42. Institute for Healthcare Improvement: http://www.ihi.org/ihi.
43. Institute of Medicine: Reliability of Hospital Discharge Abstracts. Washington, DC, National Academy of Sciences, 1977.
44. International Neonatal Network, Scottish Neonatal Consultants, Nurses Collaborative Study Group: Risk adjusted and population based studies of the outcome

for high risk infants in Scotland and Australia. Arch Dis Child Fetal Neonatal Ed 82:F118, 2000.

45. International Neonatal Network: The CRIB (Clinical Risk Index for Babies) score: A tool for assessing initial neonatal risk and comparing performance of neonatal intensive care units. Lancet 342:193, 1993.

46. Joint Commission on Accreditation of Healthcare Organizations: http://www.jcaho.org.

47. Kaushal R et al: Medication errors and adverse drug events in pediatric inpatients. JAMA 285:2114, 2001.

48. Kohn LT et al, and the Committee on Quality of Health Care in America: To Err is Human: Building a Safer Health Care System. Washington, DC, National Academy Press, 2000.

49. Kulynych J, Korn D: The effect of the new federal medical-privacy rule on research. N Engl J Med 346:201, 2002.

50. Lagnado L: Hospitals profit by upcoding illness. Wall Street Journal, April 27, 1997, B1.

51. Langley GJ et al: The Improvement Guide: A Practice Approach to Enhancing Organizational Performance. San Francisco, Jossey-Bass, 1996.

52. Leapfrog Group: Available at: www.leapfroggroup.org.

53. Lemons JA et al, and the NICHD Neonatal Research Network: Very low birth weight outcomes of the National Institute of Child Health and Human Development Neonatal Research Network, January 1995 through December 1996. Pediatrics 107:E1, 2001.

54. Lyman JA et al: Mapping from a clinical data warehouse to the HL7 reference information model. Proceedings of the AMIA Symposium, 2003:920.

55. Muldoon JH: personal communication, May 2004.

56. Muldoon JH: Structure and performance of different DRG classification systems for neonatal medicine. Pediatrics (1 Suppl E)103:302, 1999.

57. National Center for Health Statistics: International Classification of Diseases: Clinical Modifications 4th edition. Los Angeles, Practice Management Information Corporation, 1995.

58. New York State Department of Health: Cardiac Surgery in New York State. Albany, New York State Dept of Health, 1993.

59. O'Connor GT et al, and the Northern New England Cardiovascular Disease Study Group: A regional intervention to improve the hospital mortality associated with coronary artery bypass graft surgery. JAMA 275:841, 1996.

60. Park RE et al: Explaining variations in hospital death rates. Randomness, severity of illness, quality of care. JAMA 264:484, 1990.

61. Parry G et al: CRIB II: An update of the clinical risk index for babies score. Lancet 361:1789, 2003.

62. Perinatal Profiles Project: California Perinatal Profiles. Berkeley, University of California School of Public Health, 2004.

63. Phibbs CS et al: Alternative to diagnosis-related groups for newborn intensive care. Pediatrics 78:829, 1986.

64. Plsek P: Quality improvement methods in neonatal and perinatal medicine. Pediatrics 103(1 Suppl E):203. 1999.

65. Poland RL et al: Analysis of the effects of applying federal diagnosis-related grouping (DRG) guidelines to a population of high-risk newborn infants. Pediatrics 76:104, 1985.

66. Pollack MM et al: Accurate prediction of the outcome of pediatric intensive care. A new quantitative method. N Engl J Med 316:134, 1987.

67. Reason J: Human error: Models and management. BMJ 320:768, 2000.

68. Relman AS: Assessment and accountability: The third revolution in medical care. N Engl J Med 319:1220, 1988.

69. Richardson DK et al: A critical review of cost reduction in neonatal intensive care. I. The structure of costs. J Perinatol 21:107, 2001.

70. Richardson DK et al: Birth weight and illness severity: Independent predictors of neonatal mortality. Pediatrics 91:969, 1993.

71. Richardson DK et al: Measuring illness severity in neonatal intensive care. J Intensive Care Med 9:20, 1994.

72. Richardson DK et al: Risk adjustment for quality improvement. Pediatrics 103(1 Suppl E):255. 1999.

73. Richardson DK et al: Score for Neonatal Acute Physiology: A physiologic severity index for neonatal intensive care. Pediatrics 91:617, 1993.

74. Richardson DK et al: SNAP-II and SNAPPE-II: Simplified newborn illness severity and mortality risk scores. J Pediatr 138:92, 2001.

75. Rogowski JA: Measuring the cost of neonatal and perinatal care. Pediatrics 103(1 Suppl E):329, 1999.

76. Rogowski JR, Byrne DJ: Comparison of alternative weight recalibration methods for diagnosis-related groups. Health Care Finance Rev 12:87, 1990.

77. Sackett DL et al: Evidence-Based Medicine. How to Practice and Teach EBM, 2nd ed. London, Churchill Livingstone, 2000.

78. Saigal S et al: Parental perspectives of the health status and health-related quality of life of teen-aged children who were extremely low birth weight and term controls. Pediatrics 105:569, 2000.

79. Saigal S: Perception of health status and quality of life of extremely low-birth weight survivors. The consumer, the provider, and the child. Clin Perinatol 27:403, 2000.

80. St John EB et al: Cost of neonatal care according to gestational age at birth and survival status. Am J Obstet Gynecol 182:170, 2000.

81. Schwartz RM et al: Administrative data for quality improvement. Pediatrics 103(1 Suppl E):291, 1999.

82. Slagle TA, Le HA: Database information: Fact or fiction [abstract]. Pediatr Res 29:266A, 1991.

83. Snell LM et al: Reliability of birth certificate reporting of congenital anomalies. Am J Perinatol 9:219, 1992.

84. Soll RF, Andruscavage L: The principles and practice of evidence based neonatology. Pediatrics 103(1 Suppl E): 215, 1999.

85. Suresh G et al: Voluntary anonymous reporting of medical errors for neonatal intensive care. Pediatrics 113:1609, 2004.

86. Toolkit Group of the Perinatal Quality Improvement Panel: Nosocomial Neonatal Infection Toolkit. Palo Alto, California Perinatal Quality Care Collaborative, 2004. available at: http://www.cpqcc.org/NIToolkit.html.

87. US Department of Health and Human Services: Healthy People 2010. Washington, DC, US Government Printing Office, 2000.

88. Ursprung R et al: Random audits for patient safety in the NICU. Pediatr Res 55:435A, 2004.

89. Vermont Oxford Network: Vermont Oxford Network Database Manual of Operations for Infants Born in 2004 (Release 8.0). Burlington, Vermont Oxford Network, 2003.

90. Vohr BR et al: Center differences and outcomes of extremely low birth weight infants. Pediatrics 113:781, 2004.

91. Weed LL: Knowledge Coupling: New Premises and Tools for Medical Care and Education. New York, Springer-Verlag, 1991.

92. Williams RL: Measuring the effectiveness of perinatal medical care. Med Care 17:95, 1979.

93. Wirtschafter DD, Powers RJ: Organizing regional perinatal quality improvement: Global considerations and local implementation. NeoReviews 5:e50, 2004.

94. Wright LL et al: Evidence from multicenter networks on the current use and effectiveness of antenatal corticosteroids in low birth weight infants. Am J Obstet Gynecol 173:263, 1995.

95. Zupancic JAF et al: VON SNAP pilot project. Performance of the revised score for neonatal acute physiology in the Vermont Oxford Network. Pediatr Res 55:521A, 2004.

Part 2

96. Ambalavanan N, Whyte RK: The mismatch between evidence and practice. Common therapies in search of evidence. Clin Perinatol 30:305, 2003.

97. Antman EM et al: A comparison of results of meta-analyses of randomized control trials and recommendations of clinical experts. JAMA 268:240, 1992.

98. Bennett KJ, et al: A controlled trial of teaching critical appraisal of the clinical literature to medical students. JAMA 257:2451, 1987.

99. Cairns PA et al: Is neonatal care evidence-based [abstract]? Pediatr Res 43:168A, 1998.

100. Chalmers I, Altman DG (eds): Systematic Reviews. London, BMJ Publishing Group, 1995.

101. Chalmers I et al: Effective Care in Pregnancy and Childbirth. Oxford, Oxford University Press, 1989.

102. Cochrane Library: Available at: http://www3.inter science.wiley.com/cgi-bin/mrwhome/106568753/HOME.

103. Crowley P: Antenatal corticosteroid therapy: A meta-analysis of the randomized trials. Am J Obstet Gynecol 173:322, 1995.

104. Dans AL et al: Users' guides to the medical literature. XIV. How to decide on the applicability of clinical trial results to your patient. JAMA 279:545, 1998.

105. Ellis J et al: In-patient general medicine is evidence-based. Lancet 346:407, 1995.

106. Enkin M et al: A Guide to Effective Care in Pregnancy and Childbirth, 3rd ed. Oxford, Oxford University Press, 2000.

107. Glasziou P et al: Applying the results of trials and systematic reviews to individual patients. ACP J Club 129:A15, 1998.

108. Glasziou P, Irwig LM: An evidence based approach to individualizing treatment. Br Med J 311: 1356, 1995.

109. Guyatt G, Rennie D: Users' Guide to the Medical Literature. A manual for evidence-based clinical practice. Chicago, AMA Press, 2002.

110. Guyatt GH et al: Users' guides to the medical literature. II. How to use an article about therapy or prevention. A. Are the results of the study valid? JAMA 270:2598, 1993.

111. Guyatt GH et al: Users' guides to the medical literature. IX. A method for grading health care recommendations. JAMA 274:1800, 1995.

112. Haynes RB et al. Developing optimal search strategies for detecting clinically sound studies in MEDLINE. J Amer Med Inform Assoc 1:447, 1994.

113. Jaeschke R et al: Users' guides to the medical literature. III. How to use an article about a diagnostic test. A. Are the results of the study valid? JAMA 271:389, 1994.

114. Kaplan RM et al: Methods for assessing relative importance in preference based outcome measures. Qual Life Res 2:467, 1993.

115. Laupacis A et al: Users' guides to the medical literature. V. How to use an article about prognosis. JAMA 272:234, 1994.

116. Levine M et al: Users' guides to the medical literature. IV. How to use an article about harm. JAMA 271:1615, 1994.

117. Leviton LC et al: Methods to encourage the use of antenatal corticosteroid therapy for fetal maturation: A randomized controlled trial. JAMA 281:46, 1999.

118. Leviton LC, Orleans CT: Promoting the uptake of evidence in clinical practice: A prescription for action. Clin Perinatol 30: 403, 2003

119. McColl A et al: General practitioners' perceptions of the route to evidence-based medicine: A questionnaire survey. BMJ 316:361, 1998.

120. Moyer VA, Elliott EJ: Evidence-Based Pediatrics and Child Health, London, BMJ Books, 2004.

121. NIH Consensus Development Panel: Effect of corticosteroids for fetal maturation on perinatal outcomes. JAMA 273:413, 1995.

122. Oxman AD et al: Users' guides to the medical literature. VI. How to use an overview. JAMA 272:1367, 1994.

123. Reisch JS et al: Aid to the evaluation of therapeutic studies. Pediatrics 84:815, 1989.

124. Sackett DL et al: Evidence-based medicine: What it is and what it isn't. BMJ 312:71, 1996.

125. Saigal S et al: Self-perceived health status and health-related quality of life of extremely low-birth-weight infants at adolescence. JAMA 276:453, 1996.

126. Sauve S et al: The critically appraised topic: A practical approach to learning critical appraisal. Annals of the Royal College of Physicians and Surgeons of Canada 28:396, 1995.

127. Sinclair JC, Bracken MB: Effective Care of the Newborn Infant. Oxford, Oxford University Press, 1992.

128. Sinclair JC et al. When should an effective treatment be used? Derivation of the threshold number needed to treat and the minimum event rate for treatment. J Clin Epidemiol 54: 253, 2001.

129. Sinclair JC et al: Introduction to neonatal systematic reviews. Pediatrics 100:892, 1997.

130. Sinclair JC et al: Cochrane neonatal systematic reviews: A survey of the evidence for neonatal therapies. Clin Perinatol 30:285, 2003.

131. Sinclair JC: Evidence-based therapy in neonatology: Distilling the evidence and applying it in practice. Acta Paediatr 93: 1146-1152, 2004.

132. Sinclair JC: Weighing risks and benefits in treating the individual patient. Clin Perinatol 30:251, 2003.

133. Straus SE, McAlister FA: Evidence-based medicine: Past, present, and future. Annals of the Royal College of Physicians and Surgeons of Canada 32:260, 1999.

134. Tyson JE, et al: An evaluation of the quality of therapeutic studies in perinatal medicine. J Pediatr 102:10, 1983.

6

Perinatal and Neonatal Care in Developing Countries

Dharmapuri Vidyasagar and Anil Narang

Recognizing the importance of human health as a global issue, the World Bank initiated the Global Burden of Disease Study.[16] This study indicates that perinatal conditions, including infant mortality, form a significant portion (39%) of the global burden of disease. Developing countries are the major contributors to global perinatal mortality. In fact, it is one of the top ten leading causes of death in developing countries. These findings underscore the importance of improving perinatal and neonatal care in these countries. This chapter provides an overview of global perinatal problems and discusses some of the strategies to address the issues of global health.

GLOBAL BURDEN OF MATERNAL DEATHS

It is estimated that over 600,000 women die annually from causes related to pregnancy and childbirth.[51] Asia and Africa have the highest numbers of maternal deaths. There are 4000 maternal deaths in developed countries. It is estimated that 25% of maternal deaths result from hemorrhage, 15% from sepsis, 13% from abortion, 12% from hypertensive disorders of pregnancy, and 8% from obstructed labor. About 20% die from diseases that are aggravated by pregnancy (i.e., malnutrition, iron deficiency anemia, heart disease, and tuberculosis). Large numbers of women also suffer and die from human immunodeficiency virus/acquired immunodeficiency syndrome (HIV/AIDS). Unfortunately, approximately 50 million more women are known to suffer from other significant complications of pregnancy. Maternal death adds another dimension to the survival of the child. The likelihood of the death of a surviving child after maternal death is 5 times that of a child with a surviving mother. It is estimated that over 50% of the deaths related to pregnancy and childbirth can be prevented using simple, well accepted interventions.

GLOBAL BURDEN OF NEONATAL DEATHS

Figure 6-1A and B shows the number of annual births and deaths in the world by region. Of the 129 million annual births, 60% are born in Asia, 22% in Africa, 9% in Latin America, and 6% in Europe. Only 3% are born in North America.[36] Despite improvements in the reduction of infant mortality around the world, neonatal mortality continues to be a major concern. Infant mortality before reaching one year (IMR) comprises neonatal (death at less than 28 days, NMR) and post-neonatal (28 days to 1 year, PNMR) deaths. Globally, of the 129 million infants born annually, 4 million die during the neonatal period and 8 million die before reaching one year of age. Regrettably, most of the global burden of the infant mortality rate (IMR) comes from the least developed and developing countries. Ninety percent of births globally are in developing countries (e.g., those of Africa and Asia; Mexico; South America); 98% of all neonatal deaths occur in developing countries but only 10% in the developed world.[51] Moreover, the contribution of the burden of disease from neonatal deaths is enormous in terms of the loss of life. In Asia and Africa combined there is an estimated loss of 70 million years of life annually.[16]

Neonatal deaths constitute 60% of the infant mortality and 40% of the mortality for those under 5 years of age. The IMR in developing countries in 1960 was 171 per 1000 live births, which dropped to 109 per 1000 live births in 1996—a reduction of only 40% compared with 90% in developed countries.[54] The average neonatal mortality rate (NMR) in developing countries is 34 per 1000 live births, compared with 5 per 1000 live births in the developed world. The decline in global NMR has been much slower than that in the mortality rate after the neonatal period. Between 1983 and 1989 the NMR fell by only 11%, while the mortality rate after the neonatal period fell by 45%[49]; over a 25-year period (between 1972 and 1998) the NMR declined by

Annual global births

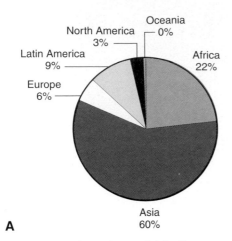

A

Annual neonatal deaths

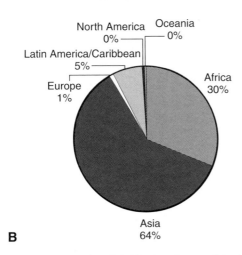

B

FIGURE 6-1. **A** and **B,** Global burden of neonatal deaths.

36%, while the mortality rate after the neonatal period declined by 63%. Neonatal health clearly remains a major global issue.

ALMA-ATA DECLARATION AND OTHER GLOBAL HEALTH INITIATIVES

Due to the concerns of high infant mortality, various global interventions have been proposed and implemented by world organizations over the past 3 decades (Table 6-1). The Alma-Ata Declaration of 1978[11] by the World Health Organization (WHO) and the United Nations Children's Fund (formerly the United Nations International Children's Emergency Fund [UNICEF]) set a goal to achieve "Health for All by the Year 2000." The declaration included a goal for the reduction of maternal and infant mortality through primary care. In 1987, the International Conference on Safe Motherhood drew attention to high maternal mortality rates (MMRs)

in developing countries and encouraged policymakers to develop new strategies to reduce maternal mortality. This action led to the worldwide program of "Safe Motherhood," placing an emphasis on antenatal care. A similar resolution, the "Bamako Initiative," was instituted at the annual meeting of the African Ministries of Health in 1987. The objective was the achievement of universal maternal child health coverage at the periphery by the year 2000. In 1988, the Task Force for Child Survival set objectives for a reduction in the MMR and IMR.[43] One of these objectives was a worldwide reduction in mortality of at least half, or by 50 to 70 per 1000 live births, whichever can be achieved first, for children 5 years of age and under. Another one was the reduction of MMRs worldwide by at least half.

In 1994, WHO developed the Mother-Baby Package to help further reduce the MMR and NMR. Recognizing that the MMR remained high, in 1999 WHO re-emphasized the need for an acceleration of national and international efforts to decrease the MMR and perinatal mortality rate through the Safe Motherhood program. At the 48th World Assembly of WHO, the concept of integrated management of childhood illness was adopted to improve the well-being of the whole child under 5 years of age. It included an emphasis on the improved care of the newborn. In 2002, the Millennium Development Goals for health were pledged by participating countries to ensure a two-thirds reduction of child mortality by the year 2015.[44] Although there have been some noticeable reductions in the mortality rates for infants and children five years of age and under, during the last few decades the goal of reducing MMRs and NMRs in developing countries remains elusive.

REGIONAL PERSPECTIVES

Over the past 4 decades the trends in global mortality show an overall decrease in the IMR. However, there are wide variations among different regions of the world (Fig. 6-2).[45] In the 1960s the IMR was the lowest in industrialized western countries (33 per 1000), which dropped to as low as 5 per 1000 by the year 2000, a reduction of 85%. On the other hand, sub-Saharan Africa had the highest IMR (157 per 1000) in 1960 and has experienced the least reduction (only 32%) among all the regions of the world during the same 40 years. Some other regions, such as South Asia, the Middle East/North Africa, and Latin America/the Caribbean, have experienced 53%, 70%, and 74% decreases, respectively. However, the IMR continues to remain significantly high: 70 per 1000 in South Asia, 45 per 1000 in the Middle East, and 27 per 1000 in Latin America. Selected countries with high IMRs from each region are reviewed below.

Asia

The Asia-Oceania region has half of the world's live births and two-thirds of the world's neonatal deaths.[59]

TABLE 6-1. Global Initiatives to Decrease Child and Maternal Mortality

INITIATIVE	ORGANIZATION	YEAR AND OCCASION	GOALS
Declaration of Alma-Ata	WHO, UNICEF	Sept 1978—USSR—International conference on primary health care	Health for all by 2000
Safe Motherhood Initiative	WHO, UNICEF, UNFPA, World Bank, and others	1987—Nairobi—International safe motherhood conference	Reduce maternal mortality to half the present rate by 2000
Bamako Initiative	UNICEF, WHO	Sept 1987—Bamako, Mali—Annual meeting of African ministers of health	Achieve universal maternal and child health coverage at the peripheral level by the year 2000 Revitalize peripheral public health systems Supply basic drugs Establish revolving funds Involve communities in health care
Task Force for Child Survival	WHO, UNICEF, World Bank, UNDP, and Rockefeller Foundation	March 1998—Talloires, France—Protecting the world's children—an agenda for the 1990s	Global eradication of polio Virtual elimination of neonatal tetanus 90% reduction in cases of measles and 95% reduction in its fatalities 25% reduction in fatalities due to ARI Reduction of IMR and MMR by half or 50-70/1000, whichever is greater Reduction of MMR by at least half
Mother-Baby Package	WHO	Sept 1994—International conference on population and development, Cairo	Reduce maternal mortality to half of the 1990 levels by 2000 Reduce perinatal and neonatal mortality from 1990 levels by 30%–40% and improve newborn health
Making Pregnancy Safer	WHO	1999	As a component of the Safe Motherhood Initiative, to accelerate the reduction of high maternal and perinatal mortality and morbidity by refocusing WHO strategies in the national and international health sectors
The Millennium Developmental Goal	WHO	2000	Reduce child mortality Reduce by two thirds the mortality rate for children under 5 between 1990 and 2015

ARI, acute respiratory infection; IMR, infant mortality rate; MMR, maternal mortality rate; UNDP, United Nations Development Program; UNFPA, United Nations Fund for Population Activities; UNICEF, United Nations Children's Fund (formerly United Nations International Children's Emergency Fund; WHO, World Health Organization.

In the 1970s neonatal mortality was on average 34 per 1000 which in the 1990s had fallen to 22 per 1000. The proportion of infant deaths that are neonatal is between 45% and 65%. Sixty percent of all neonatal deaths and 68% of the world's burden of perinatal deaths occur in Asia, with the highest burden in South Asia. The 38 million annual births in South Asia represent 27% of the world's total number of births. The 2 million neonatal deaths in South Asia represent a disproportionately high 40% of the world's total number, with India contributing an estimated 1.2 million neonatal deaths per year, representing almost 30% of the global burden of neonatal deaths, the highest for any single country.

India

India has made significant progress in reducing IMR during the last several decades (Fig. 6-3). The IMR dropped from 146 per 1000 live births in 1951 to 72 per 1000 in 1998, a reduction of approximately 50%. The current IMR is 60 per 1000 and the NMR 46 per 1000.[27] The major causes of death include low birthweight (LBW), birth asphyxia, sepsis, and hypothermia. Sixty-six percent of births take place at home and 34% at primary health care centers or the higher levels of hospitals. The data from India[26] show that only 40% of the total number of deliveries are attended by

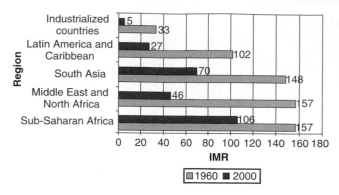

FIGURE 6-2. Comparison of the infant mortality rates (IMR) in 1960 and 2000 by world regions.

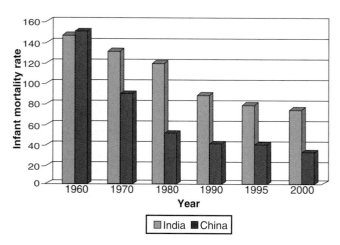

FIGURE 6-3. The infant mortality rates for India and China for the years indicated.

to the high overall literacy (95%) and very high female literacy (80%) in these two states compared with those of other states in the country. In view of the high NMR, India has launched a national program to provide essential newborn care at the grass roots level. These efforts are being vigorously implemented across the country.

China

Infant mortality in China has been decreasing steadily over the last several decades (see Fig. 6-3).[45,50] The IMR in China dropped from 150 per 1000 in 1960 to 32 per 1000 in 2000, a reduction of 80%. The major causes of the NMR are birth asphyxia, hypothermia, and sepsis. LBW is not a major contributor to the NMR or IMR in China. Maternal Child Health Services follows the traditional I/II/III levels of care. It is reported that home deliveries are rapidly decreasing, almost to none in some counties. In order to decrease NMR further, programs are being initiated to decrease home delivery and implement statewide neonatal resuscitation training and a neonatal transport system. At least one or two modern, well equipped neonatal intensive care units (NICUs) are being established in each province. The NMR of China in 2002 was 21 per 1000—9.7 per 1000 in cities and 23.2 per 1000 in rural areas.

Comparison of India and China

India and China are the most populated countries that contribute to a large proportion of global births as well as neonatal and infant deaths. However, there are distinct differences in the trends of IMR between the two countries. IMR was substantially high in both countries in 1960 (IMR of 150). However, the drop in IMR during the last 40 years has been more dramatic in China than India (see Fig. 6-3).[45] The differences between the two countries can be explained on the basis of the differences in the poverty level, literacy rate, and health expenditure. Table 6-2 shows data from China, India, and Sri Lanka. India has almost 2.5 times more poverty than China and almost 6 times more than that of Sri Lanka.[20] The literacy rate of India is also low, with Sri Lanka having the highest rate and India the lowest. There are vast differences in health expenditure among the three countries, with India spending the least and

trained personnel, although these numbers are steadily improving. Forty-four percent of mothers have three or more antenatal checkups, 67% receive two doses of tetanus toxoid, and 58% receive iron and folic acid supplementation during pregnancy. Within India, variations in IMR are found among different states. The states of Kerala and Goa enjoy the lowest rates in spite of the lack of access to modern high-tech neonatal and perinatal care. The low IMRs in these states is related

TABLE 6-2. Health Expenditure Compared with Poverty Levels in India and China

INDICATOR	% POPULATION INCOME <$1/DAY	MMR	IMR	HEALTH EXPENDITURE, % GDP	% PUBLIC HEALTH EXPENDITURE TO TOTAL HEALTH EXPENDITURE
India	44	437	70	5.2	17.3
China	18	115	31	2.7	24.9
Sri Lanka	7	30	16	3	45.4

IMR, infant mortality rate; MMR, maternal mortality rate.
From http://education.vsnl.com/healthpolicy/Draft 2001 National Health Policy.

Sri Lanka the most. The IMR of India is 2 times that of China and 4.5 times that of Sri Lanka. These observations show the impact of poverty, the literacy rate, and health expenditure of the country on IMR.

Africa

In sub-Saharan Africa more than 50% of infant deaths occur in the neonatal period, primarily from premature birth, asphyxia, and infectious diseases.[32] Sub-Saharan Africa has shown slower progress in reducing neonatal mortality. In the 1970s the average neonatal mortality was 44 per 1000 and by the 1990s had dropped to only 39 per 1000. The current average IMR in Africa (i.e., for the year 2000) is 77 per 1000 live births, down from 130 per 1000 live births in 1975.

In their examination of the global decline in child mortality during the second half of the 20th century, Ahmad and colleagues[2] stated that the region with the poorest performance was Africa. They noted that the average decline in child mortality in Africa was 42%, compared with a decline of 60% to 72% in other regions over the same period. In addition, more than half of the countries in Africa experienced a decline of less than 20% in child mortality, some experienced only 0% to 10% reductions, and some actually experienced an increase, probably due to the HIV/AIDS epidemic.

Latin America

Recent data show that there are wide variations in IMR patterns among the South American countries (Fig. 6-4).[45] The average NMR was 34 per 1000 in the 1970s and in the 1990s had fallen to 22 per 1000. The proportion of neonatal deaths varies between 50% and 70%. In Brazil

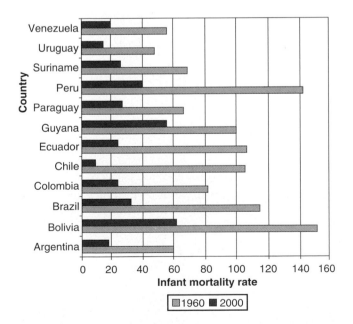

FIGURE 6-4. The infant mortality rates for South American countries in 1960 and 2000.

infant mortality declined by 39.8% between 1985 and 1997, but over the same period the proportion of infant mortality comprising neonatal deaths increased by 27.6%. These variations reflect the changing economic demography. During the last decade infant mortality showed a consistent decrease, especially in the post-neonatal period, in Latin American countries. It seems that as infant mortality declines, the proportion of deaths occurring in the neonatal period tends to increase. In order to reduce neonatal mortality, more rigorous interventions and advances in perinatal technology are required. The use of surfactants in the treatment of preterm infants with respiratory distress syndrome shows a different impact on mortality in Latin America than it does in developed countries. Neonatal mortality was reduced by up to 70% in the first 2 days of life, but many neonates died of infection and necrotizing enterocolitis; therefore, the final reduction in neonatal mortality was 20% after surfactant therapy.[8]

Countries Dependent on Oil and Other Natural Resources

Resource-rich countries depend on oil and minerals, which constitute a sizable portion of their economy. The oil- and mineral-rich countries form a unique group because of their wide disparities of wealth and health.[7] Countries in this group are mostly in the Middle East, Africa, and Latin America. Unfortunately, most of them, in spite of high per capita gross national products, do not do well in terms of health status. They have high IMRs and high mortality rates for children 5 years of age and under, low life expectancy, and poor literacy. Although the overall IMR has dropped from 200 per 1000 in the 1950s to 50 per 1000 in 2000, in some countries the IMRs are far higher than those for countries in Latin America and East Asia.[33] From various analyses it appears that oil wealth breeds poor health.[41] This disparity is aptly referred to as "The Oil Curse."[7]

CAUSES OF NEONATAL MORTALITY

There are biologic and nonbiologic causes that influence neonatal mortality. Although biologic factors such as maternal and neonatal medical problems are well known causes of a high IMR, nonbiologic factors such as socioeconomic conditions, maternal literacy, poverty levels, and gender equity are equally important. They directly or indirectly affect the health access and health care of the mother and the baby. Some of these important factors are discussed below.

Nonbiologic Factors Influencing Neonatal and Infant Mortality Rates

Nonbiologic factors play a pivotal role in the NMRs and IMRs of developing countries. The ones influencing the IMR include social, economic, and environmental factors. The status of women, literacy, and women's health policies also play an important role. In India, while

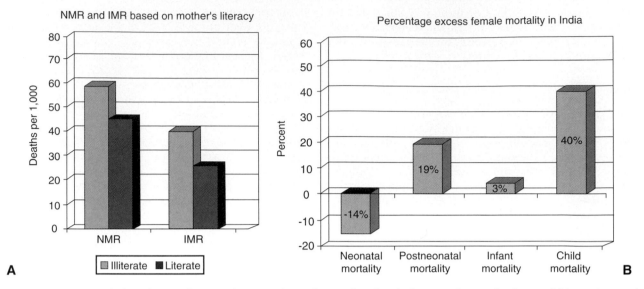

A

B

FIGURE 6-5. A and **B,** Nonbiologic factors influencing the neonatal mortality rate (NMR) and infant mortality rate (IMR). CMR, child mortality rate (age <5 years).

overall literacy itself is low, female literacy (ages 6 and above) is 56%, compared with 31% in males. The IMR is higher in women who are not literate (Fig. 6-5A). In India the states of Kerala and Goa enjoy the lowest IMR (15 per 1000). The IMR and female mortality rate for children 5 years of age and under exceed those for the male child (Fig. 6-5B). These findings reflect severe gender bias practices beyond the neonatal period. Gender discrimination is not unique to a particular region of the world. Grave concerns have been expressed regarding this problem in South American countries.[28] It was found that gender-biased discrimination begins to manifest itself early in life, leading to poorer nutrition and health in girls than boys. Other nonbiologic factors include housing, access to potable water, and access to a toilet (Fig. 6-6). The NMR and IMR are obviously higher among populations who do not have access to a flush or pit toilet. Similarly, the lack of access to piped (i.e., running) water has an adverse effect on the IMR.

THE OIL CURSE

Extensive analyses by economists and policymakers[41] have shown that excessive dependence on revenue derived primarily from the mineral and oil resources of a country correlate with poor health indexes. Among the 25 countries that are the richest in oil and mineral resources, it has been found that an increase in mineral and/or oil dependency is associated with an increase in mortality for children under five years of age. Resource-dependent countries spend less money on health care. In general, they rank low on the human development index (HDI), have low literacy, and have high malnutrition rates. The major causes of these inequalities are ascribed to the lack of strong political and economic institutions in these countries. For those countries that

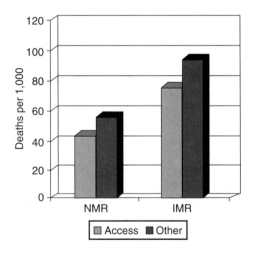

FIGURE 6-6. The neonatal mortality rate (NMR), infant mortality rate (IMR), based on access to flush and pit toilets.

have strong political and economic institutions (Botswana, Norway, Kuwait), the health indexes are better.[7]

EFFECTS OF CULTURAL BELIEFS

Care during pregnancy, childbirth, and the neonatal period worldwide are greatly influenced by regional, religious, ethnic, and cultural beliefs. Some of these practices may be helpful or harmless; however, some of them may be harmful. Educational programs should focus on the harmful effects of traditional practices. Because of the recent increasing migration of different ethnic groups to the western world, practicing neonatologists should develop awareness and cultural sensitivity to better serve their patients. Understanding cultural beliefs and their impact on the care of the mother and baby are critical to the development of programs to reduce the MMR or IMR. Practicing neonatologists should be familiar with the cultural practices of the people they serve.[37]

Biologic Causes of NMR

The major causes of neonatal death include birth asphyxia, sepsis, pneumonia, and prematurity (Fig. 6-7).[36] Most neonatal deaths are preventable. WHO estimates that 40% to 60% of neonatal deaths are preventable. The major factors contributing to the NMR are discussed below.

BIRTH ASPHYXIA

In developing countries an estimated 4 to 9 million infants per year experience birth asphyxia, and only about 1 to 2 million are resuscitated successfully.[58] There are 1 million neonatal deaths resulting from birth asphyxia each year, which contributes to 20% to 40% of all neonatal deaths. Many factors contribute to the high incidence of birth asphyxia in developing countries.[52] They include the poor health of pregnant women, higher prevalence of pregnancy and labor complications, inadequate care during labor and delivery, and high rates of prematurity. The lack of proper resuscitation is another major factor contributing to asphyxia-related deaths. In addition, there is a severe shortage of skilled personnel and equipment.

In recent years, great strides have been made to decrease the number of deaths from birth asphyxia. A number of countries have initiated training programs to improve resuscitation skills at the grass roots level. In addition to the earlier efforts of WHO and UNICEF, the Neonatal Resuscitation Program (NRP), developed by the American Academy of Pediatrics and American Heart Association, has been adopted in its full or modified form by over 72 countries worldwide, including India and China (see Chapter 25). In India the NRP has become a standard skill-training module for the last 15 years.[48] A significant reduction in deaths related to birth asphyxia after NRP training was reported in a study in India.[13,14] China recently declared NRP to be a national priority.[50] It is expected that NRP will have a major impact in reducing asphyxia-related deaths globally in years to come.

INFECTIONS

Of the estimated 129 million children born annually worldwide, 20% die of neonatal infection. Infections in the neonatal period account for 30% to 40% of all neonatal deaths. There are about 1.5 to 2 million deaths related to neonatal sepsis each year.[42] This figure translates to 4000 to 5000 deaths every day. The incidence of sepsis is estimated to be 5 to 6 per 1000 live births among hospitalized patients (600,000 to 750,000). Meningitis accounts for 0.7 to 1.0 per 1000 live births (88,000 to 126,000 cases per year), and acute respiratory infections account for 800,000 deaths in neonates. Among these deaths are cases of pneumonia, bronchiolitis, and laryngotracheitis; cord infections vary from 2% to 54% of live births, and case-fatality rates are as high as 15%. Neonatal tetanus is one of the preventable major acquired infections. The initial goal was to achieve a universal coverage of at least 90% of pregnant women with at least two doses of tetanus toxoid by the year 2000; unfortunately, about 400,000 cases each year are still reported, with a fatality rate of 85% in untreated cases (370,000).

HIV INFECTION (See Chapters 22 and 37)

The maternal transmission of HIV to the newborn is a major factor contributing to neonatal deaths in some countries, particularly sub-Saharan Africa. Ninety percent of the children infected with HIV in the year 2000 were in Africa. Reported transmission rates range from 25% to 48% in developing countries.[56] Foster's study[18] concluded that IMRs have increased due to HIV/AIDS, reversing earlier declines that had been occurring in many countries over the last few decades. He also cited IMRs as 20% higher in Kenya and Uganda due to the AIDS epidemic. The prevention of mother-to-child transmission can be achieved through the primary prevention of HIV infection among potential parents, the prevention of unwanted pregnancies in HIV-infected women, and the prevention of mother-to-child HIV transmission by the use of anti-retroviral drugs and safe delivery processes of HIV-infected patients. Safe infant feeding has led to a considerable reduction in mother-to-child infection. Exclusive breast feeding is recommended for the first month of life. Breast feeding should be discontinued as soon as possible. All HIV-infected women should be counseled on the risks of various infant-feeding options. Alternative feeding sources can be used when available, affordable, and sustainable.

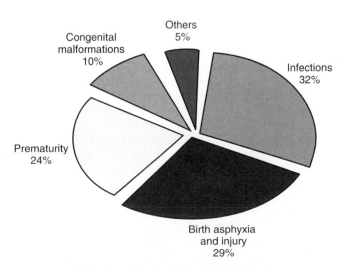

FIGURE 6-7. Direct causes of neonatal mortality.

- Others 5%
- Congenital malformations 10%
- Infections 32%
- Prematurity 24%
- Birth asphyxia and injury 29%

HYPOTHERMIA (See Chapter 29)

Neonatal hypothermia is defined as a core body temperature below 36.5°C (97.7°F). Hypothermia is more common in developing countries.[57] In Ethiopia, an 8-year study showed that 67% of high-risk infants and those with LBW were hypothermic on admission. In China, the incidence of sclerema was found to be 6.7 per 1000. In Nepal over 80% of infants became hypothermic at birth, and 50% remained hypothermic at 24 hours after birth.[21] A hypothermic baby is at an increased risk of developing health problems and dying. The causes of hypothermia in developing countries are many. A lack of understanding of the importance of keeping the infant warm due to various cultural and regional practices is a major factor. For example, giving routine baths soon after birth without prior attention to the possibility of heat loss is one typical cause of hypothermia. Worldwide efforts are being made to increase awareness of the deleterious effects of hypothermia. Kangaroo care is becoming a universal practice. It has proven to be a very inexpensive but very effective method of providing thermal protection to the newborn in the immediate neonatal period. In addition, the initiation of breast feeding provides skin-to-skin contact as well as early provision for calories. Newborn infants are also prone to heat loss during transport from home to hospital or hospital to hospital. In the absence of sophisticated and expensive incubators, simple techniques have been adopted.[9] Plastic bags and wrapping with saran wrap or aluminum foil at birth are some of the methods used by others.

LEVELS OF PERINATAL HEALTH SERVICES

Health is a governmental responsibility in developing countries. Maternal child health (MCH) programs are under the Ministries of Health. Most countries have well developed MCH services.[48,53] In general, there are three levels of MCH services according to the location and level of service provided: the subcenter, primary health center (PHC), and tertiary center or district hospital (level III). The PHCs are sometimes graded as level I or II.

Subcenters are located in rural areas and serve a population of 3000 to 5000 residents. They provide both curative and preventive services; all of them have delivery rooms. Level II PHCs serve a population of about 1,000,000 residents; they are located in rural areas. The staff typically includes a professional nurse or midwife, a health inspector, and a sanitary assistant. These centers are the "first-referral hospitals" in the rural community. Level II centers also have an operating room, basic laboratory, and delivery room. Neonatal facilities contain equipment for resuscitation. Workers in these centers are usually trained in midwifery, family planning, and prenatal care. Resuscitation at this level includes mouth to mask and bag and mask. The district hospital, a level III center, serves the local community and the region as the ultimate referral center. It provides both secondary and tertiary curative services. The district hospital is staffed with doctors and a multidisciplinary team capable of providing a range of services, including those that are curative, to the mother and child. Since 65% to 75% of the deliveries in the developing world take place in rural areas and at home, the focus of discussion here is on the services provided at home and the PHCs.

Staffing

The personnel at a district hospital consists of different specialists, nursing staff, and other support staff, whereas at level I and II PHCs the doctor is supported by an auxiliary nurse midwife (ANM), traditional birth attendants (TBAs), and community health workers (CHWs). At each health center the doctor is responsible for providing neonatal care, developing the protocols, and maintaining the quality of care. The doctors at PHCs usually have a short course of formal training in neonatal care, with special reference to levels I and II care, including the stabilization and transport of sick infants. The ANM stationed at the center is formally trained in the nursing aspects of various components of level I care. Both the ANM and doctor are available at the center for consultation and services. The PHC staff is responsible for maintaining the skills and knowledge of health care workers. Educational programs are conducted by using different modalities, including pictographs and manikins. Protocols for patient management are prepared at the center.

It is noteworthy that the majority of newborn care is provided at home by the mother and health care workers. The major role of the doctor is at the district hospital. The health care workers assume an increasing role at the subcenter, PHC, and home. The cost of care is less at the health centers than at the hospital. However, there has been an increasing trend toward "institutional deliveries" (i.e., at PHCs), with the objective of decreasing the currently high MMRs and NMRs noted with home deliveries.

Available Equipment

The facilities and services provided at the PHC are dependent on its functions for obstetric and neonatal care. Facilities for the care of some moderately sick babies may be available at some centers. The problems of maintaining the effective functioning of centers in rural areas include an uninterrupted supply of water and electricity. Each center should have an alternate back-up system in case of power failure or interruption of the supply of piped water. A refrigerator, suction machine, oxygen cylinder, flowmeter, microscope, hemoglobin meter, clock, disinfectants, soap, essential life-saving drugs, and consumables like syringes and needles are all components of the standard requirements for any PHC. At levels II and III centers, special equipment for the monitoring of vital signs such as heart rate, respiration, and oxygen saturation and special treatment devices such as ambu bags, laryngoscopes, endotracheal tubes, and oxygen hoods for oxygen administration, with a supply of at least two oxygen cylinders with flowmeters, are needed. Additional necessary equipment includes intravenous pumps and phototherapy units. The investigative facilities at levels II and III centers should include radiologic, hematologic, and bacteriologic services. Also important are simple investigative tools that include a hemoglobin meter, microscope, supporting consumables and stains, and glucometers for the screening of hypoglycemia. Facilities for the estimation of serum bilirubin are mandatory if phototherapy is provided at the center. However, the majority of subcenters, PHC, and district hospitals in developing countries are far less well equipped.

Facilities for Delivery at Home

The facilities for delivery of the baby at home have to be improvised so that the principles of Essential Care of the Newborn can be followed by the TBA, CHW, or members of the family. These preparations are made well in advance of delivery by the CHW or TBA, who follows the woman during pregnancy. The family is asked to prepare a clean area in a well lighted part of the house for delivery. They are asked to prepare clean old sheets and clothes for use at the time of delivery. The health care professional responsible for home delivery and neonatal care carries a disposable delivery kit containing a mucus extractor, basic equipment for resuscitation (resuscitation bag with neonatal mask), a clinical thermometer, and a portable spring balance for weighing the baby.

Care of the Mother and the Newborn in the Community

The Child Survival and Safe Motherhood Program[51] emphasizes the primary care of the mother and newborn through the promotion of the concepts of essential

---

BOX 6-1. Essential Components of Newborn Care*

1. Care at birth
   - Aseptic techniques at delivery time
2. Prevention and management of hypothermia
   - Ensuring maintenance of warmth for the baby
3. Resuscitation of baby not crying
   - Identification and referral of at-risk neonates
4. Physical examination of the baby and identification of risk
   - Identifying babies with low birthweight for home care
   - Identifying babies with low birthweight who need referral
5. Ensuring early and successful breast feeding and breast milk feeding by spoon
   - Ability to identify feeding problems
   - Successfully initiating breast feeding soon after birth
6. Identifying signs of illness
   - Providing essential newborn care
7. Grading severity of illness (see Table 6-5)

See text for details.

---

obstetric care and essential care of the newborn. The components of essential obstetric care include the early detection of pregnancy, at least four antenatal checkups, the identification of high-risk pregnancies, immunization against tetanus (at least 2 doses), supplementation with iron and folic acid, and provision for adequate nutrition. Various home-based models of obstetric care have been tested in different countries. Although the focus of these studies was to improve maternal outcome, they also benefit neonatal outcome. The major issues are the delayed recognition of potential problems, a delay in decision making, a delay in the transport of the mother, and a delay in receiving quality care. The components of Essential Obstetric and Newborn Care are shown in Box 6-1 and Figure 6-8. They are discussed further below.

CARE AT BIRTH

Aseptic Care at Birth

Whether the delivery takes place at home or at the health center, the same principles of cleanliness are observed. The principles of the "five cleans" are followed. Improper cord care has been responsible for neonatal tetanus. Cord cutting with a clean blade and tying with clean thread are two important procedures of newborn care. Once it is tied and cut, the cord must be cleaned, with no further bleeding. The cord must be left open without any dressing; it usually falls off by 5 to 10 days. The health care worker should examine the cord 2 to 4 hours after ligation for any bleeding and then afterwards for any discharge and redness of the skin around the base. Such infants should be treated with antibiotics. The eyes should be cleaned at birth. If a discharge is noticed, it must be treated with antibiotic ointment. With regard to skin care, the infant is immediately cleaned and dried at birth; bathing is not recommended. Various traditions of bathing should be postponed until a later age, when the child is more stable. This process must be strictly observed when there is a premature infant or one with LBW.

Management of Hypothermia

Hypothermia in the immediate newborn period is a major problem in infants delivered at home or poorly equipped community centers. The principles of the "warm chain"[57] are used to minimize heat loss soon after birth. The warm chain consists of 10 steps.

1. Keeping the place of birth (delivery room) warm
2. Immediately drying the infant
3. Keeping the infant warm during resuscitation
4. Maintaining skin-to-skin contact between the mother and baby
5. Initiating breast feeding
6. Postponing bathing and weighing

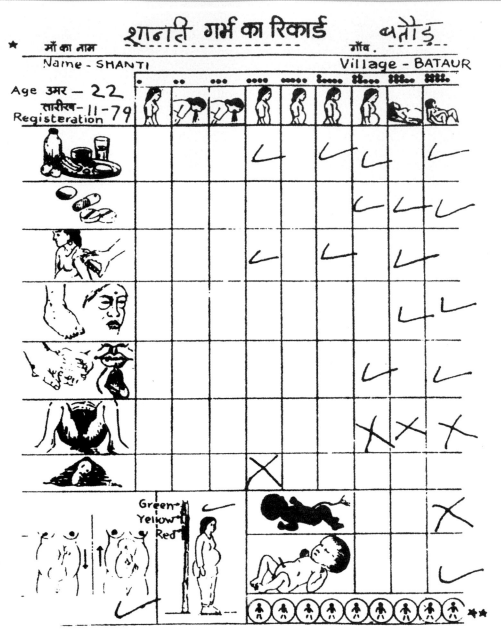

FIGURE 6-8 **A** through **I**, Essential care of the mother and newborn in a rural community. **A** and **B**, Facsimile of home-based pictorial records. These cards obviate the need for writing in words. The TBA and VHW record their negative findings with a cross (X) and positive findings with a check (√).[23] Home-based obstetrical pictorial record (A): months of pregnancy are shown in dots with corresponding clinical symptoms (e.g., hyperemesis in early pregnancy). The first column shows diet, medicines, vaccinations, and other physical findings. At the bottom, fetal assessment is depicted. Home-based infant pictorial record (B): infant growth with age is shown in lunar cycles. The signs and symptoms assessed are shown in the right columns. *Continued*

7. Providing appropriate clothing and bedding
8. Keeping the mother and baby together
9. Keeping the infant warm during transport
10. Increasing the awareness of health care workers regarding the importance of maintaining neonatal temperature

The mother with her baby is encouraged to maintain close physical contact with the infant, who is wrapped in clothing that includes a head cap and covering for hands and feet. At the health center, the ANM/nurse records axillary temperature. At home, the mother and TBA or other health worker are trained to assess the infant's temperature without a thermometer by placing the dorsum of the hand on the abdomen and feet alternately and comparing the difference (see Fig. 6-8F). The difference in warmth between the two sites may provide useful information. The kangaroo care method has been shown to have better outcomes in developing

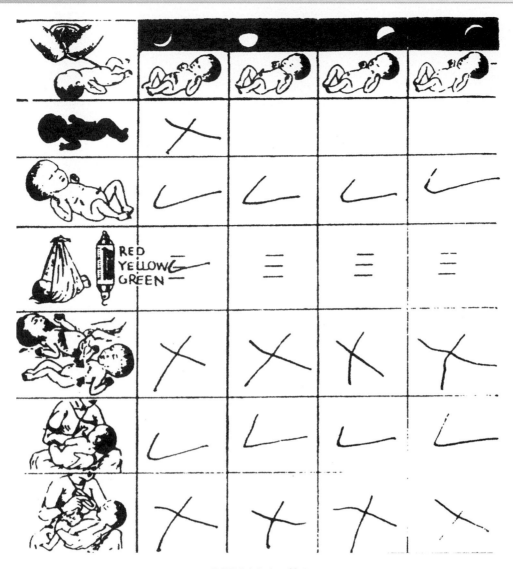

FIGURE 6-8, Cont'd B

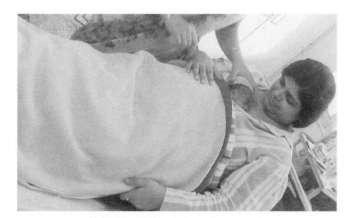

FIGURE 6-8, Cont'd C, Kangaroo care is encouraged soon after birth to keep the newborn warm. The mother holds the baby close to her body, and the baby is wrapped with a blanket.

countries. In a study in Nepal,[21] the incidence of early hypothermia in the first 2 hours after delivery was reduced by ≈50% and the incidence of late hypothermia in the first 24 hours after birth was reduced by 30% by implementing one of three interventions after delivery (kangaroo care, traditional mustard oil massage under a radiant heater, or plastic swaddling). It has been shown that 90% of the babies for whom skin-to-skin contact with their mothers was maintained reached normal temperatures, compared with only 60% of the babies in incubators. Skin-to-skin contact has been shown to have positive effects.[17] It promotes mother-infant bonding, enhances lactation, leads to stimulation of the infants, and improves the psychological state of the mother. In a study on skin-to-skin contact in preterm infants, they not only remained clinically stable but also showed more efficient gas exchange.

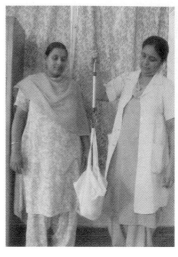

FIGURE 6-8, Cont'd D, Infants are weighed using a color-coded spring balance. Color codes obviate reading the exact weight by the TBAs. Weight indicator in red zone is VLBW, in yellow is LBW, in green indicates normal weight baby. Risk assessment is based on color code. See color insert.

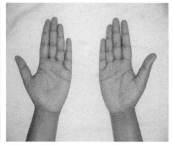

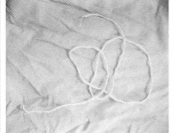
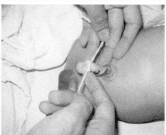

FIGURE 6-8, Cont'd E, Components of FIVE CLEANS are shown here: clean hands, clean blade, clean cloth, clean tie, clean the umbilical cord.

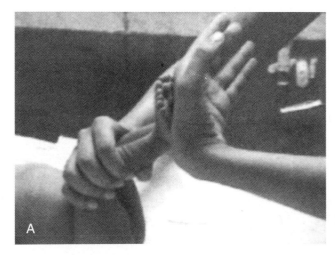
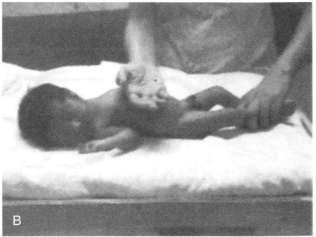

FIGURE 6-8, Cont'd F, Assessment of infant's skin temperature using the dorsum of the hand (A) with simultaneous assessment of abdominal and foot temperatures (B). See text for details.

FIGURE 6-8, Cont'd G, TBA and VHW are trained in neonatal resuscitation using a mouth-to-mask device and a manikin.

At the health center, hypothermia is better managed by using the clinical skills of assessment (e.g., touch) in addition to the basic instruments (Table 6-3). Skin-to skin contact is easy to promote and implement and is the least expensive; therefore, it should be encouraged in developing countries.

FIGURE 6-8, Cont'd H, Bathing the newborn soon after birth is discouraged using the universal sign X as shown in this poster.

Care of the Baby Not Crying at Birth

The newborn infant is kept under a warming device, the mouth and nostrils are cleaned, and the baby is dried. If the infant still does not cry, gentle tactile stimulation is given on the side. If the infant does not respond, bag and mask ventilation is initiated. Various forms of ventilation have been used: bag and mask, mouth-to-mask, and mouth-to-mouth. Self-inflating bags are commonly used. In their absence, mouth-to-mask ventilation may be carried out. The mask must form a tight seal around the chin, and the attendant should deliver a steady tidal volume 30 to 40 times/min while watching the movements of the chest wall and also observing the infant for an improvement in color and respiratory movements. Deficiencies in equipment (e.g., O_2 sources) and skilled personnel are major constraints

that hinder adequate resuscitation. Self-inflating resuscitation bags are commercially available; they are relatively inexpensive, and paramedics have been extensively trained to use them. Some of them have developed innovative ways of making masks from disposable plastic bottles. Oxygen is important in neonatal resuscitation, but it is expensive and a scarce commodity in rural areas. Clinical trials have confirmed the efficacy of room air[30,35] in neonatal resuscitation (see Chapter 25). The long-term follow-up of these infants is also favorable. Although all studies were limited to term infants, resuscitation should be carried out using room air in the absence of available O_2 for the resuscitation of the asphyxiated newborn in rural areas.

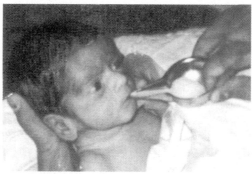

FIGURE 6-8, Cont'd I, LBW and premature infants are fed with a spoon or *a paladai,* a cup with long beak.

TABLE 6-3. Management of Hypothermia*

CATEGORY	TEMP RANGE	BY TOUCH	CLINICAL FEATURES	MANAGEMENT
Normal	36.5-37.5°C	Warm trunk/warm extremities	Normal baby	Cover adequately Keep next to mother
Cold Stress	36-36.5°C	Warm trunk/cold extremities	Extremities bluish and cold Poor weight gain if chronic cold stress	Cover adequately Warm room or bed Skin-to-skin contact Provide warmth Consult doctor
Moderate Hypothermia	32-36°C	Cold trunk/cold extremities	Poor feeding, lethargy Fast breathing	Cover adequately Skin-to-skin contact Provide warmth Transfer to hospital Reassess every 15 minutes; if no improvement provide additional heat
Severe Hypothermia	<32°C	Extremely cold trunk/cold extremities	Lethargic, poor perfusion/mottling Fast breathing, apnea Bleeding	Rapid rewarming until baby is 34°C and then slow rewarming Oxygen IV fluids (dextrose [warm]) Consult doctor and transfer to hospital

*Table shows the range of temperatures that can be detected clinically by health workers or mother by touching trunk and feet simultaneously.
IV, intravenous; Temp, temperature.

BREAST FEEDING

Exclusive breast feeding of all infants is promoted as an important part of essential newborn care. Infants delivered at an institution must be given only breast milk. To promote breast feeding worldwide, in 1991 UNICEF and WHO launched the campaign "Baby-Friendly Hospital Initiative" (BFHI).[46,55] The objective of this global initiative is to create a hospital environment that ensures breast feeding as the only means of nutrition. The principles of this program are shown in Box 6-2. Other policies that have influenced the global rates of breast feeding involve substitutes provided by the International Code of Marketing of Breast Milk. These efforts are having a major international impact. Over 14,500 hospitals around the world have been certified as "Baby Friendly." It is recognized that since some infants, particularly those with LBW or very low birthweight (VLBW), may experience difficulty in latching on to the breast, they need special techniques to receive feeding. The use of spoons or traditional feeding cups ("Paladai") (see Fig. 6-8I) in feeding premature infants in place of feeding tubes is an inexpensive way of providing the preterm or sick infant with food.

PRIMARY CARE BY "MOTHER—THE BEST NEONATOLOGIST"

It is often forgotten that the mother is the best natural and instinctive caregiver of the newborn. She is the

BOX 6-2. Ten Steps to a Baby-Friendly Hospital

1. Have a written breast-feeding policy that is routinely communicated to all health care staff.
2. Train all health care staff in the skills necessary to implement this policy.
3. Inform all pregnant women about the benefits and management of breast feeding.
4. Help mothers initiate breast feeding within 1 hour of birth.
5. Show mothers how to breastfeed and maintain lactation even if they should be separated from their infants.
6. Give newborn infants no food or drink other than breast milk unless medically indicated.
7. Practice allowing mothers and infants to remain together 24 hours a day.
8. Encourage breast feeding on demand.
9. Give no artificial teats or pacifiers to breast-feeding infants.
10. Foster the establishment of breast-feeding support groups and refer mothers to them at discharge.

best person to monitor the infant's course. Therefore, emphasis should be placed on the mother's "health education" before and during pregnancy regarding self-care and newborn care. This approach is extremely important in rural and community settings, where skilled professionals are not readily available. Besides providing information regarding her own health, the importance of folic acid and iron intake, and vaccination against tetanus, she should be given structured education regarding normal infants as well as those with LBW. They should be given skill training in reference to keeping the baby warm (kangaroo care), breast feeding, monitoring growth, and immunization. In particular, mothers should be trained to recognize the danger signs of illness. They should be encouraged to seek help from health care workers in the community when the infant manifests any one or more of these signs: poor feeding, sucking, or crying; cold to the touch; difficulty breathing; change in color; or convulsions.

HOME VISITS BY THE HEALTH CARE WORKER

A suggestive schedule for home visits is given in Table 6-4.[31] All infants delivered at home must be seen by the health care worker within 48 hours of birth. The assessment includes all the items of essential newborn care. If the infant is doing poorly or the weight is below 1500 g, the infant should be transferred to a health center. An infant whose birthweight is less than 2000 g must be given kangaroo care at home. In addition to routine care, exclusive breast feeding must be given. Infants with poor sucking and poor overall activity should be visited more frequently (once or twice a week). Those whose birthweights are over 2000 g should be visited once every 4 weeks unless they present a problem at the time of the first visit or the mothers observe any sign of illness.

After the initial stabilization, the health care worker should carefully assess each infant. The assessment is necessary in order to decide if the infant can be left in the care of the mother or needs transfer to a health center or from a level I center to a higher level of care. Workers must be trained to identify high-risk infants so that they can use simple clinical skills of observation of the infant (Table 6-5). The concept of the severity of illness and its consequences must be well understood. The grading of illness in newborn babies is based on activity, feeding behavior, color, temperature, breathing, and the presence of convulsions. After these observations

are considered, one could determine the need for care at a health center or hospital. The following manifestations are indications for such a referral: the presence of moderate to severe illness with any birthweight, mild illness in babies (1500 to 2000 g), and any weight of less than 1500 g. Any infant with a suspected major congenital malformation requiring surgery should be transferred to a district hospital. An infant who receives care at home or at a health center should be closely followed by the health care worker. The timing and frequency of visits depend on the birthweight and behavior.

ROLE OF THE TRADITIONAL BIRTH ATTENDANT AND COMMUNITY HEALTH WORKER

The lack of availability of a skilled attendant at the time of delivery is one of the major reasons for the increased number of maternal and infant deaths in developing countries. The community TBA plays an important role in attending deliveries at home.[22,29] Her focus is initially on only the mother. Later, the workers in the field find the TBA to be an important resource person to care for the newborn as well. Other workers find the CHWs to be more appropriate in providing newborn care.[4] There are differences between the two types of health care worker. TBAs are illiterate, older, and learn by tradition; therefore, it is difficult for them to change their perceptions and practices. Conversely, CHWs are younger, literate, and adaptable to new principles and practices. Although most of them are women, in some parts of the world CHWs could be men. CHWs are also known as village health workers in some regions. Their roles have been examined by a number of interesting field studies, which validate the effectiveness of the TBA or CHW in reducing NMR/IMR. These studies have been conducted in several regions of the world (Table 6-6).[22] They show that neonatal mortality can be reduced if the community-based health care workers are well trained, well equipped, and supervised. Some of the important studies are reviewed next.

TABLE 6-4. Home Visit Schedule

ACTIVITIES	BIRTHWEIGHT	TIMING	TASKS
Initial visit	All birthweights	Within 48 hours	Essential newborn care Transfer <1500-g infant
Subsequent visits	>2500 g	Once every 2 weeks	Essential newborn care Check for signs of illness
	2000-2500 g	Every week for 4 weeks	Essential newborn care Check for signs of illness
	1500-2000 g	Every week for 4 weeks	Kangaroo care Cup/spoon feeding Recognize signs of illness

TABLE 6-5. Grading Severity of Illness in a Newborn Infant

	MILD	MODERATE	SEVERE
Activity	Normal	Mild lethargy, relieved by feeding and warmth	Very lethargic, with poor response to treatment
Feeding Behavior	Poor feeding by spoon	By tube or IV for up to 3 days	By IV for more than 3 days
Color	Pink without O_2	Pink with O_2	Poor response to O_2 or signs of shock
Jaundice	Onset after 24 h, with jaundice over trunk and up to face	Onset within 24 h or jaundice up to arms and legs	Jaundice over palms and soles or baby symptomatic
Hypothermia	Body temperature 35-36.5°C	Temp 32-35°C	Temp <32°C
Breathing	Rate 60-80 breaths/min; no grunting or retractions	Rate >80 breaths/min or presence of grunting or retractions	Presence of apneic attacks or deterioration on treatment
Seizures	Only irritable	Seizure relieved with treatment	Poor response to treatment
LBW	2000-2500 g Weak sucking, color pale	1500-2000 g Weak sucking, blue, difficulty breathing, cold, or jaundiced	All <1500 g With any of the additional symptoms, follow the recommended home visit schedule in Table 6-4.

IV, intravenous; LBW, low birthweight; Temp, temperature.
Modified from Bhakoo ON, Kumar R, Singh SA: Facilities required for primary care (level-1) of newborn infants. J Neonatol 16:9, 2002.

Home-Based Antenatal Care

Home-based antenatal care can be achieved through health care workers. The health care provider at the community level is expected to identify pregnant women in the community, ascertain the risks of pregnancy, ensure vaccination against tetanus, and administer folic acid and iron. After assessing the risk factors, health care workers also develop a plan for residential or institutional delivery. They seek assistance from the PHC in these matters. The training of health care workers at the village level is critical to the success of these programs. Since the educational background of village-based TBAs varies from illiterate to minimally literate, innovative techniques such as pictograms have been used to train them. Kumar and Walia[23] showed that when a pictorial card is used, illiterate TBAs could be taught to keep useful maternal data records that help provide timely and important interventions. The cards illustrate the events of pregnancy, which the TBA can record by crossing them out with a pen. In their study of home-based medical records, they are able to provide a minimum standard of care. These cards can be modified to suit local health care needs. Similar home-based records have been used in Nigeria and other countries.[24] Extensive studies have been conducted to determine the effectiveness of home-based neonatal care provided by TBAs and/or CHWs in rural settings in India and Bangladesh. The essential components of home delivery include the preparation of a clean space, provision of clean linen, and preparation of a disposable delivery kit, which includes soap; sterilized cord ties; a clean blade; a clean, dry cloth sheet; and a gauze pad, all in one package. Health care workers are trained to observe the "five cleans" (*clean* surface, *clean* hands, *clean* cord tie, *clean* cord, and *clean* blade).

Home-Based Neonatal Care

Raina and Kumar[29] studied the impact of training TBAs in resuscitation techniques. There was a 19% reduction in perinatal mortality. Mortality was also reduced in cases where advanced techniques were used. TBAs have a significant effect on reducing asphyxia-related neonatal mortality in the community. The pioneering work of Bang and coworkers[4] in a rural setting showed that by training TBAs and CHWs to diagnose pneumonia with the use of a WHO algorithm and treating patients with a standard dose of antibiotic, the case-fatality rate for neonatal pneumonia was reduced to 0.8% compared with 23.6% among those untreated, and the IMR was 89 per 1000 compared with 121 per 1000 in the control areas. The NMR was 67.8 per 1000 compared with 97.2 per 1000 in the control areas. The addition of TBAs to their study increased the coverage, and with supervision the TBAs made few errors. Bang et al[3] conducted another double-blind study on the treatment of sepsis, showing how TBAs and CHWs are trained to diagnose sepsis by using set clinical criteria. They were instructed to treat the infant with a standard dose of antibiotics. Among those receiving antibiotics, there was a 58% reduction in NMR during the study, and the case-fatality rate from neonatal sepsis declined from 16.6% before the intervention to 2.8% after it. Similar observations have been made in studies of neonatal resuscitation given by the TBA and/or CHW.

In conclusion, TBAs and CHWs are very important in health care delivery. Although CHWs are preferable in

TABLE 6-6. Community-Based Studies on Newborn Care Interventions for Reduction of Neonatal Mortality

AUTHOR	REFERENCE	PLACE	PERIOD	HEALTH CARE PERSONNEL	REDUCTION OUTCOME OF NMR
Rahman	J Trop Pediatr 28:163, 1982	Bangladesh	1991	Health care worker TBA	NMR 38.9 NMR 23.8
Pratinidhi 6:115, 1986	World Health Forum	India	1986	CHW	NMR declined from 51.9 to 38.8 after 1 y
Greenwood	J Trop Med Hyg 93:58, 1990	Gambia	1990	TBA	33% reduction in NMR
Daga	Indian Pediatr 34:1021, 1992	India	1992	TBA, AWW, ANM	NMR reduced to 33.6 from 57.1 in preprogram period after 3 y
O'Rourke	Int J Gynaecol Obstet 48:S95, 1995	Guatemala	1995	TBA	27% reduction in PMR
Alisjahbana et al	Int J Gynaecol Obstet 48:S83, 1995	Indonesia	1995	TBA	12.6% reduction in PMR
Kumar	Prenat Neonat Med 3:225, 1998	India	1998	TBA	PMR 19% less in intervention than in control community
Bang et al	Lancet 354:1955, 1999	India	1999	TBA, CHW	NMR reduced from 62 to 25.5 in intervention compared with 59.6 in control community

ANM, auxiliary nurse midwife; AWW, Anganwadi worker; CHW, community health worker; NMR, neonatal mortality rate; PMR, perinatal mortality rate; TBA, traditional birth assistant.

certain interventions, such as sepsis treatment, TBAs have shown that when trained they are just as useful and important for effective neonatal health care. The use of both TBAs and CHWs is integral to neonatal health care in developing countries.

Health care workers can use a simple algorithm based on clinical observations of a sick neonate at home or in the community to triage a baby. Figure 6-9 shows the elements of observation and action based on certain findings. They include common functions of the infant: feeding, crying, variations in skin temperature on touching, activity, breathing pattern, and condition of the cord. They can be graded from mild to severe. Any two milder forms of distress can be treated and managed at home by the health care worker and the mother. Those infants demonstrating more severe forms of distress must be treated and transferred to level II or III health centers.

RELEVANCE OF NEWER TECHNOLOGIES IN DEVELOPING COUNTRIES

Modern technology has been a major contributor to a reduction in neonatal mortality, especially in the developed world. Technology has been very helpful in improving the survival of infants with LBW and VLBW. Incubators were one of the earliest technological advances used in the care of premature infants. Newer and improved electronic monitoring and supportive technologies for neonatal use did not appear until the middle of the 20th century. While the newer technologies greatly enhanced the care of the critically ill neonate, they proved to be very expensive, which hindered the development of NICUs in developing countries for a long time. Emphasis was therefore placed on "low technology" and "appropriate technology" that was affordable and sustainable. Many noninvasive devices developed in the 1980s to monitor vital signs are now readily available in developing countries (Table 6-7). Even though the initial cost is relatively high, the long-term benefits are many. Blood sampling and the need for a sophisticated laboratory can be avoided. Therefore, the investment is cost effective and the use of these devices simple; health care workers can be easily trained to use them.

Among monitoring devices, the oxygen saturation monitor is the single most useful one because of its simplicity in application and fast response. It provides very important real-time information on heart rate and oxygenation without having to draw blood. In skilled hands, this unit can be very effective at any level for monitoring infants in distress. The glucometer requires the use of blood from a heel stick and a chemical strip. However, the test can be performed at the bedside. It requires consumable supplies. On the other hand, the transcutaneous bilirubinometer does not require any drawing of blood. No consumable supplies are required. The noninvasive blood pressure monitor requires a one-time investment. The transillumination device may be highly useful for detecting air leaks such as a pneumothorax without the need to obtain a chest x-ray.

Management of Neonatal Sepsis by traditional birth attendants and village health workers

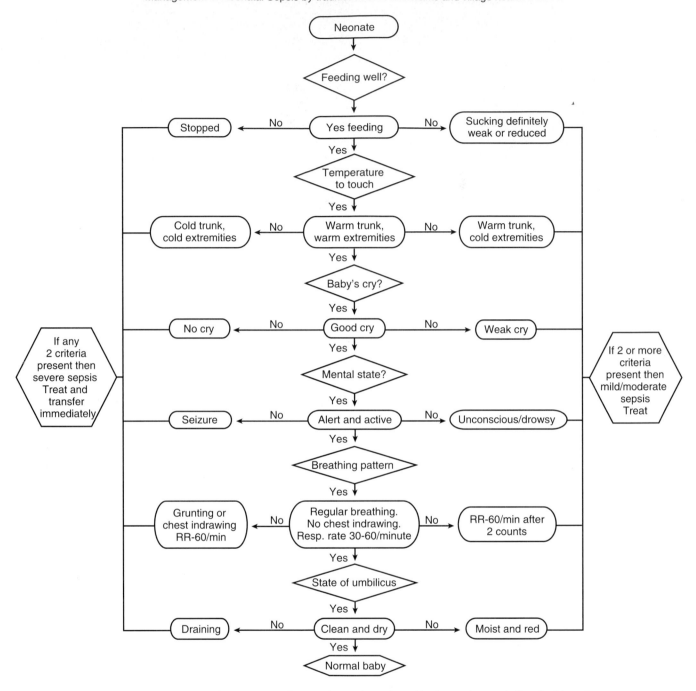

FIGURE 6-9. Assessment and management of neonatal sepsis by traditional birth attendants and village health workers.

The bag and mask is the most useful device for resuscitation, providing short-term ventilation until the patient is placed on a mechanical ventilator. The use of bag and mask or mouth-to-mask devices in neonatal resuscitation is an example of low-cost technology that has a major impact on neonatal outcome. The Neonatal Resuscitation Program, which was introduced in India in 1989,[48] has become the standard of care in the delivery room for all newborns. There is evidence that asphyxia-related deaths are decreasing[14] after the implementation of NRP in several hospitals in India.

The infant showing respiratory distress after birth or resuscitation needs closer observation. In the absence of laboratory facilities, the doctor and nursing personnel must depend on their clinical skills to recognize and manage the critically ill newborn. Clinical scoring systems may be helpful in objectively assessing and monitoring the infant, especially at levels I and II health centers.

TABLE 6-7. Bedside Diagnostic and Treatment Devices

MONITORS	ITEM DESCRIPTION	WHERE USEFUL
O_2 saturation monitor	Measures oxygenation	All levels
Noninvasive BP monitor	Measures blood pressure	All levels
Glucometer	Checks blood glucose	All levels
Bilirubinometer	Measures bilirubin levels	All levels
Bag and mask	Resuscitates patient	All levels
Nasal CPAP	Treats RDS	All levels
Fiberoptic transilluminator	Checks for pneumothorax	All levels

BP, blood pressure; CPAP, continuous positive airway pressure; RDS, respiratory distress syndrome.

The Respiratory Distress Score, which was developed by Downes and associates[15] (Table 6-8), correlates clinical features with acid-base and blood gas levels, with scores greater than 6 indicating the need for further evaluation and even assisted ventilation. This scoring system is simple because it uses the five common clinical assessments and requires no biochemical determinations. The scores correlate well with physiologic parameters. The score provides therapeutic and prognostic guidance. This scoring system can be used in primary-, secondary-, and tertiary-level health centers. Once it is found to have increasing respiratory distress, the infant is transferred to a health center of the appropriate level. Most of the levels II and III health centers may have only oxygen and no ventilator at all. Simple devices such as nasal continuous positive airway pressure (CPAP) will be very valuable in managing such infants.

Use of Nasal Continuous Positive Airway Pressure

The use of CPAP has proved to be a very simple intervention to support the infant in respiratory distress.[34] In developing countries CPAP equipment is relatively simple to use and very cost effective. A study in Oman on premature infants showed that in cases of mild to moderate disease there was significant improvement of respiratory distress syndrome (RDS) in patients in whom nasal CPAP was used.[5] At the levels II and III health centers in developing countries, which have

limited resources, this method of treating moderate RDS is very useful.

Surfactant Therapy

Premature infants who do not respond to nasal CPAP require intubation and ventilatory support. However, providing ventilatory support requires skilled nursing and support staff and laboratory facilities. The cost could be very high. Surfactant therapy is known to shorten the time needed for assisted ventilation. Despite the effectiveness of surfactant in improving the survival of premature infants with RDS, its use in developing countries was hindered by its high cost. The cost per dose exceeds the per capita annual income of many of the citizens in developing countries. In addition to its high cost, the use of surfactant therapy is impeded because of the lack of ventilatory support after surfactant administration. Nevertheless, a number of studies show that the use of surfactant could be cost effective, even in developing countries.[25] The studies of Verder and associates[47] show that surfactant therapy followed by nasal CPAP is an equally effective strategy for managing RDS in infants without the support of mechanical ventilation. Similarly, the use of surfactant in the treatment of preterm infants with respiratory distress in Latin America[8] reduced mortality by 70% during the first few days of life, although mortality at 28 days was reduced by only 20%. These studies show that endotracheal surfactant in established cases of RDS followed by nasal

TABLE 6-8. Clinical Scoring System for Respiratory Distress Syndrome

SCORE	0	1	2
Respiratory Rate (breaths/min)	60	60-80	>80 or apneic episode
Cyanosis	None	In room air	In 40% oxygen
Retractions	None	Mild	Moderate to severe
Grunting	None	Audible without a stethoscope	Audible without a stethoscope
Air Entry (crying)*	Clear	Delayed or decreased	Barely audible

*The RDS scoring system is useful at levels II and III centers that manage infants with moderate to severe respiratory distress.

CPAP can be used effectively. Those infants who continue to require endotracheal intubation and ventilation and do not respond to nasal CPAP must be transferred to a level III tertiary care unit for alternative therapy.

ESTABLISHMENT OF TERTIARY CARE UNITS IN DEVELOPING COUNTRIES

The evolution of NICUs in developing countries has been understandably slow because of the high cost and lack of skilled personnel. In India, where there were only four or five NICUs in the 1980s, there were 27 accredited level II NICUs in the 1990s.[48] The results of a national survey in 1987 and 1994/1995 showed that in 1995, an increasing number of centers became fully equipped. Newborn care facilities, particularly those able to provide assisted ventilation at level III NICUs, are steadily increasing both in China and India,[48,50] which reflects the trend in other developing countries. The evolving NICUs are having a major impact on the survival of institution-based deliveries, particularly on infants with LBW and VLBW. Those requiring assisted ventilation must be transported to NICU facilities where available. Properly organized neonatal transport systems in developing countries are nonexistent, although well organized transport systems are beginning to evolve in some rural regional hospitals. Other limiting factors include the high cost of NICU care and the availability of NICU beds. Singh and colleagues[39] in India and Bhutta and coworkers[6] in Pakistan have documented that despite limited resources, intensive care, including ventilation, can be provided in developing countries, with good short- and long-term outcomes. These emerging data clearly indicate that as the overall survival of infants with LBW and VLBW increases, there will be an increased demand for NICU facilities.

The overall cost of neonatal intensive care at the tertiary level in developing countries is still high and affordable to only a few middle and upper income groups. Bhutta and associates[6] have shown that infants with RDS can be successfully managed with ventilatory support. In their study, the overall mortality of infants with RDS treated with assisted ventilation was 39%, the average length of stay was 24.6 ± 21.1 days, and the average cost was US $1391 per survivor. However, in terms of a country's own economy, this cost amounts to multiples of the country's per capita gross national product (US $420). Surfactant therapy was not used in this group of infants. Shanmugasundaram and colleagues[38] in India have a similar cost analysis. In his study in India, Narang[25] showed that although surfactant is an expensive drug (2 to 3 times the country's per capita gross national product), its use has reduced the overall hospital stay and thereby the overall cost. Therefore, neonatologists must be aware of the economic implications for families and must inform them of the expected clinical outcome, particularly when treating extremely premature and/or critically ill infants. The real goal should be to consider preventive antenatal measures and newer treatment modalities that are less expensive, such as antenatal steroids in preterm labor, implementation of delivery room neonatal resuscitation, early use of CPAP, and surfactant therapy.

With the increase in the survival of infants receiving neonatal intensive care in developing countries, the survival of premature infants and those with VLBW is also increasing. Unfortunately, increased survival is also associated with increased morbidity (e.g., intraventricular hemorrhage, retinopathy of prematurity, chronic lung disease). Although some data regarding the prevalence of retinopathy of prematurity[1] is emerging at an institutional level, there are no data at a national level. There is an urgent need for a policy at the international level to monitor these emerging new diseases across the globe.

ETHICAL DILEMMAS

With increasing awareness of the importance of access to technology, there is an urgent need to develop NICUs in countries with economic constraints. As noted above, such trends in neonatal practices raise concerns regarding economic, social, and ethical issues. It is indeed frustrating for neonatologists in developing countries, who face the dilemma of balancing the use of available technology to save the infant with acknowledging the economic limitations of the family. Undue emphasis may be placed on saving an individual infant at a greater cost to the family. As stated by Singh,[40] in order to ensure the principle of cost effectiveness in resource-poor countries, the narrow principle of the" best interests" of the child should be replaced by the concept of a broader benefit to the family, society, and state. His point is valid and should be considered as a policy matter in resource-poor countries. However, the welfare of an individual who can afford the cost of expensive treatment cannot be denied. In her analysis of health care policy, Deaton[10] indicates that "a policy that harms no one, while making at least some people better off, is a good thing." The criterion also says that innovations are beneficial and should be encouraged. For the proponents of public health, this concept is contradictory to the principle of equality. That is, that inequality is inherently bad, and innovations that increase it should be discouraged. However, policies based on such positions result in the deaths of some people who could have lived without neglecting others. Such policies also delay the diffusion of knowledge or technology that in most cases will also benefit poor people, though with some delay. These arguments are important and interesting for policymakers at the national level.

In recent years, rapid demographic and economic transitions have been developing in different countries, particularly in India, China, and many Latin American countries. In countries such as these, while the health care policies of the national government focus on the care of the poor using public health principles, the private sector is rapidly expanding its role to cater to those who are economically more viable and can afford high-tech, high-cost, modern medicine. The same is true for neonatal care.

Pediatricians and neonatologists in developing countries must be well trained in the use of modern technology and cultivate a sensitivity to the economic implications of NICU care for families. They must provide accurate information regarding complications and the quality of life for the infant at risk. It is also important to recognize that there are no supportive therapies after discharge for the infants who subsequently manifest developmental disabilities. It is also incumbent upon institutions with NICUs to organize a developmental follow-up clinic and other support services. Families must be well informed.

STRATEGIES TO IMPROVE GLOBAL PERINATAL OUTCOME

Strategies to reduce perinatal mortality in developing countries should include both social and medical programs. At the social level, the emphasis should be on improving women's health and avoiding gender bias against the female child, which can be achieved through an increase in female literacy. A related issue is female empowerment, which can be achieved through economic self-sufficiency. Female literacy is a proxy for one or more socioeconomic variables.

Figure 6-10 shows the interaction of education, economic power, and health. Gender bias plays a role at different phases of life. It also shows how education and the economic autonomy of women engender political empowerment to overcome gender bias. There is evidence from many countries showing that a woman who has more education has fewer children, better economic status, a lower fertility rate, a lower IMR, and improved quality of life. It has been shown that even in developed countries every additional year of education for women decreases mortality rates at all ages. Education increases earning potential and income reduces mortality. Earning power provides women with economic, social, and political empowerment. In short, education is seen as a means of ensuring health. The microcredit program for women in Bangladesh has become an important model for other countries.[19] Other social programs include improving household conditions such as access to clean water and toilet facilities. Health strategies should include increasing awareness of maintaining health, improving health-seeking behavior, and improving access to health care. Finally, health care professionals should focus on both the preventive and curative aspects of care for the mother and child. The principles of essential obstetric and newborn care should be implemented so that 90% of the population in poor rural and urban areas can be served. Finally, we should take advantage of the highly developed scientific basis of clinical practice and use it at the grass roots level to prevent the most common causes of death. There are several evidence-based interventions and treatment modalities that have reduced the NMR and IMR (Table 6-9). We should make these technologies universally available, considering them more a friend than foe in achieving these health care goals. Harnessing highly developed perinatal medicine and highly sophisticated medical and Internet technology to reach the neonate has an impact on the global burden of IMR. One report[12] showed that modern Internet technology was effectively used for consultations and patient management at rural PHCs through e-mail communication with the level III health center at a medical school. It resulted in better management of mildly to moderately sick infants at PHCs and reduced neonatal transfers to the tertiary care hospitals. This approach was also found to be very cost effective.

In summary, the majority of the burden of perinatal disease is in rural communities. Therefore, policymakers should strengthen rural PHCs in accordance with the recommendations of WHO and UNICEF. They should be provided with basic equipment needs. Health care personnel should focus on the preventive and primary care of the mother and infant, adhering to the principles of essential obstetric and newborn care.

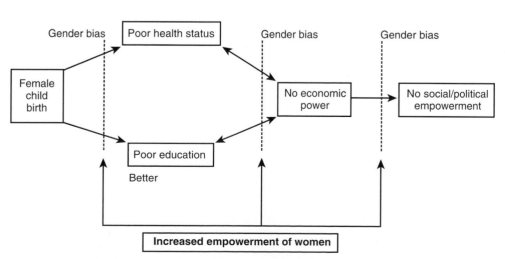

FIGURE 6-10. Interaction of education, health, and wealth.

TABLE 6-9. Strategies That Have Proved Effective in the Prevention and Treatment of Neonatal Illnesses

STRATEGY	PREVENTION	STRENGTH OF EVIDENCE FOR EFFECTIVENESS
Breast feeding	Diarrhea Pneumonia Neonatal sepsis	Strong
Management of temperature	Hypothermia	Good
Clean delivery	Neonatal sepsis Neonatal tetanus	Strong
Tetanus toxoid vaccine	Neonatal tetanus	Strong
Maternal history with antenatal steroid therapy in prematurity	Respiratory distress syndrome HMD/RDS	Strong
Antibiotics for PROM	Preterm delivery and sepsis	Good
Water, sanitation, and hygiene	Diarrhea	Strong
HIV treatment	HIV	Strong
Antibiotics	Sepsis and pneumonia	Strong
Neonatal resuscitation	Prevention of birth asphyxia	Good

HIV, human immunodeficiency virus; HMD/RDS, hyaline membrane disease/respiratory distress syndrome; PROM, premature rupture of (fetal) membranes.
Adapted from Gareth J et al: How many child deaths can we prevent this year? Lancet 362:65, 2003.

Furthermore, communication among the community (i.e., its members and/or their representatives), subcenter, PHC, and district hospital can be improved by using modern information technology. The early recognition of high-risk cases and early consultations by e-mail or telephone should be encouraged.

At the social and political levels the policymakers should direct their efforts toward eliminating gender bias and improving female literacy and economic empowerment. Public health plans should focus on providing running water, electricity, and access to pit or flush toilets.

Preventive public health programs are very cost effective in reducing the NMR and IMR.

REFERENCES

1. Agarwal R et al: Changing profile of retinopathy of prematurity. J Trop Pediatr 48:239, 2002.
2. Ahmad OB et al: The decline in child mortality: A reappraisal. Bull World Health Org 78:1175, 2000.
3. Bang AT et al: Pneumonia in neonate: Can it be managed in the community? Arch Dis Child 68:550, 1993.
4. Bang AT et al: Effect of home-based neonatal care and management of sepsis on neonatal mortality: Field trial in rural India. Lancet 355:1955, 1999.
5. Bassiouny et al: Nasal continuous positive airway pressure in the treatment of respiratory distress syndrome: An experience from a developing country. J Trop Pediatr 40:341, 1994.
6. Bhutta ZA: Is management of neonatal respiratory distress syndrome feasible in developing countries? Experience from Karachi (Pakistan). Pediatr Pulmonol 27:305, 1999.
7. Birdsall N, Subramanian A: Saving Iraq from its oil. Foreign Affairs 83:77, 2004.
8. C.L.A.P. (PAHO/WHO): Perinatal situation of Latin America and Caribbean. Available at http://www.clap.hc.edu.uy/english/c.l.a.p./sitper.htm.
9. Daga SR, Daga AS: Reduction in neonatal mortality with simple interventions. J Trop Pediatr 35:191, 1989.
10. Deaton A: Policy implications of the gradient of health and wealth. Health Affairs 21:13, 2002.
11. Declaration of Alma-Ata International Conference on Primary Health Care, Alma-Ata, USSR, September 6-12, 1978.
12. Deodhar J: Telemedicine by email: Experience in neonatal care at a primary care facility in rural India. J Telemed Telcare 8(suppl):20, 2002.
13. Deorari AK et al for the Medical College Network: Impact of education and training on neonatal resuscitation practices in 14 teaching hospitals in India. Annals Trop Pediatr 21:29, 2001.
14. Deorari AK et al: The national movement of neonatal resuscitation in India. J Trop Pediatr 46:315, 2000.
15. Downes JJ et al: Respiratory distress syndrome of the newborn: A clinical score with acid-base and blood gas correlations. Clin Pediatr 9:325, 1970.
16. Executive Summary of the Global Burden of Disease and Injury Series. Available at www.hsph.harvard.edu/organizations/bdu/GBDseries.html.
17. Fohe K et al: Skin to skin contact improves gas exchange in premature infants. J Perinatol 20:311, 2000.
18. Foster G: Africa's children and AIDS—a continent in crisis: The devastation of HIV/AIDS pandemic. AIDSLink 45:4, 1997.
19. Hassan Z: Assessing the impact of micro-credit on poverty and vulnerability in Bangladesh. Policy Research Working Paper. Developmental Economics. The World Bank, Washington, DC, USA, 1999. http://www.cgap.org.
20. http://education.vsnl.com/healthpolicy/Draft2001NationalHealthPolicy.
21. Johanson RB et al: Effects of post-delivery care on neonatal body temperature. Acta Paediatr 81:859, 1992.

22. Kumar R: Reducing neonatal mortality through primary care. J Neonatol 16:15, 2002.

23. Kumar V, Walia I: Pictorial maternal and neonatal records for illiterate traditional birth attendants. Int J Gynaecol Obstet 19:281, 1981.

24. Matthews MK et al: Training traditional birth attendants in Nigeria—the pictorial method. World Health Forum 16:409, 1995.

25. Narang A: personal communication, 2000.

26. National Family Health Survey, 2nd ed. International Institute for Population Sciences, Mumbai, India, 1998-1999.

27. Newborn health key to child survival: Present scenario, current strategies and future directions for newborn health in India. Child Health Division, Dept. of Family Welfare, Ministry of Health and Family Health, Delhi, India.

28. PAHO program on women's health and development address special needs. Available at http:www.paho.org/English/DPI/100feature10.htm.

29. Raina N, Kumar V: Management of birth asphyxia by traditional birth attendants. World Health Forum 10:243, 1989.

30. Ramji S et al: Resuscitation of asphyxic newborn infants with room air or 100% oxygen. Pediatr Res 34:809, 1993.

31. Ramji S: Training paramedics in primary newborn care: Curriculum and skills. J Neonatol 16:4, 2002.

32. Regional issues. J Perinatol 22(suppl 2):S10, 2002.

33. Roudi F: Population: Trends and Challenges in the Middle East and North Africa. Washington DC, Population Reference Bureau, 2001.

34. Sahni R, Wung JT: Continuous positive airway pressure (CPAP). Indian J Pediatr 65:265, 1998.

35. Saugstad OD: Resuscitation with room air or oxygen supplementation. Clin Perinatol 25:741, 1998.

36. Save the Children: State of the World's Newborns. Washington, DC, September 2001.

37. Shah MA (ed): Transcultural Aspects of Perinatal Health Care: A Resource Guide. Elk Grove Village, IL, National Perinatal Association and American Academy of Pediatrics, 2004.

38. Shanmugasundaram R et al: Cost of neonatal intensive care. Indian J Pediatr 65:249, 1998.

39. Singh M et al: Assisted ventilation for hyaline membrane disease. Indian J Pediatr 32:1267, 1995.

40. Singh M: Ethical and social issues in the care of the newborn. Indian J Pediatr 70:417, 2003.

41. Slack K: Policy advisor, October 2001. Available at www.oxpanamerica.org.

42. Stoll BJ: The global impact of infection. Clin Perinatol 24:1, 1997.

43. Task Force for Child Survival: Protecting the world's children: An agenda for the 1990s. Talloires, France, Tufts Univ. European Center, March 10-12, 1988.

44. UN General Assembly, 56th Session: Roadmap Towards the Implementation of the United Nations Millennium Declaration: Report of the Secretary General (UN document #A/56/326). New York, United Nations, 2001.

45. UNICEF: The state of the world's children. New York, 2004.

46. UNICEF: Baby Friend Hospital Initiative: Progress report. New York, 1999.

47. Verder H et al: Nasal continuous positive airway pressure and early surfactant therapy for RDS in newborns of <30 weeks gestation. Pediatrics 103:e24, 1999.

48. Vidyasagar D et al: Evolution of neonatal and pediatric critical care in India. Crit Care Clin 13:331, 1997.

49. Vinod KP, Meharban S: Regionalized perinatal care in developing countries. Sem Neonatol 9:117, 2004.

50. Wei KL, President of Chinese Neonatal Society: personal communication, 2004.

51. World Health Organization Maternal Health and Safe Motherhood Program: Perinatal mortality: A listing of available information. Geneva, World Health Organization, WHO/FRM/MSM/967.

52. World Health Organization: Basic newborn resuscitation: A practical guide. Geneva, World Health Organization, WHO/RHT/MSM/98.1, 1994.

53. World Health Organization: Care of mother and baby at the health center. Geneva, World Health Organization, WHO/FHE/MSM/94.2, 1994.

54. World Health Organization: Essential Newborn Care. A report of a technical working group. Geneva, World Health Organization, WHO/FRM/MSM/96.13, 1996.

55. World Health Organization: Evidence for the ten steps to successful breastfeeding. Geneva, World Health Organization, 1998.

56. World Health Organization: Prevention of mother to child transmission of HIV: Selection and use of nevirapine. Technical notes. Geneva, World Health Organization, WHO/HIV-AIDS/2001. 3. WHO RHR/01.21, 2001.

57. World Health Organization: Thermal protection of the newborn: A practical guide. Geneva, World Health Organization, WHO/RHT/MSM/97.2, 1994.

58. World Health Organization: World Health Report 1998: Life in the twenty-first century: A vision for all. Geneva, World Health Organization, 1998.

59. Yu VY: Global, regional and national perinatal and neonatal mortality. J Perinat Med 31:376, 2003.

The Fetus

Genetic Aspects of Perinatal Disease and Prenatal Diagnosis

Stuart Schwartz

Although specific genetic diseases and congenital malformations are rare occurrences, as a whole they are significant causes of perinatal mortality and morbidity. Approximately 3% of all infants are born with genetic disorders or congenital anomalies that lead to mental or physical handicaps or early death.[14] Minor malformations are found in an additional 7% to 8% of newborns (see Chapter 28). A Canadian study assessing genetic load found that approximately 12% of all individuals (from birth to age 25) suffered health problems related to recognized genetic syndromes, diseases with genetic influences, or congenital disorders, and roughly half of the congenital disorders had a genetic etiology.[4] Approximately 18.6% of the visits to a New York emergency room involved individuals (age 18 and younger) with known or suspected genetic disorders.[23]

Genetic disorders and birth defects generally fall into three major categories: chromosomal abnormalities, single gene mutations inherited primarily in a mendelian fashion, and multifactorial defects that may result from a combination of genetic and environmental factors. Projections based on the increased diagnostic accuracy of modern techniques suggest that approximately 1% of newborns have a recognizable chromosomal abnormality; earlier newborn screening studies found an incidence of about 0.56%.[17] Genetic disorders caused by single gene mutations, regardless of the mode of inheritance, were found in 0.4% of the population in the Canadian study, and the incidence of multifactorial genetic disease was approximately 10-fold higher (4.6%).[4] Unfortunately, many birth defects have no obvious or likely explanation, a situation that contributes to the mental and emotional anguish of the parents and other family members who must cope with the birth and subsequent care of an infant with a severe handicap.

CHROMOSOMAL ABNORMALITIES

With the advent of chromosome banding in 1970, it became possible to identify conclusively each chromosome on the basis of individual banding properties. Since then, the resolution with which chromosomes can be analyzed has improved. Abnormalities fall into two categories: *numerical* abnormalities, in which the modal number varies from the norm, and *structural* abnormalities, in which physical changes occur in the chromosome structure. In humans, each normal somatic cell contains 46 chromosomes *(diploid state)*. Twenty-two pairs of chromosomes, the *autosomes,* are identical in both sexes. In women, the *sex chromosomes* constitute a homologous pair, designated X *chromosomes;* men have a nonhomologous pair, the X and Y *chromosomes.*

Chromosome Structure

Each chromosome is composed of a linear molecule of DNA complexed with proteins to form chromatin. This complex becomes a highly compact structure during cell division, reducing the length of the DNA molecule approximately 10,000-fold. Each chromosome may be defined structurally on the basis of telomeres, a centromere, and a long and short arm. *Telomeres,* the tips of chromosomes, contain tandemly repeated copies of the sequence TTAGGG. The telomere is critical to maintaining the integrity and stability of the chromosome. It is also important in the replication and localization of the chromosome in the nucleus. In dividing cells, the *centromere* appears as a primary constriction; it is here that the microtubules attach to the chromosome to effect chromosome movement during cell division. The centromere is essential for proper segregation of the chromosomes in both mitosis and meiosis. The position of the centromere divides the chromosome into two arms—the *p* (or short) arm and the *q* (or long) arm.

The relative position of the centromere determines whether the chromosomes are *metacentric* (having arms of approximately equal length), *sub-metacentric* (having the centromere nearer to one end), or *acrocentric* (having a greatly shortened p arm). In humans the acrocentric chromosomes are pairs 13, 14, 15, 21, and 22. The ends of the p arms of these chromosomes contain specialized structures called *stalks* and *satellites,* which is where the ribosomal RNA (rRNA) genes and other repetitive sequences are located (Fig. 7-1).

Chromosome analysis involves production of a karyotype, in which the chromosomes are paired and placed in a roughly decreasing order according to size and with the p arms oriented upward. A standard nomenclature has been developed that allows a karyotype to be described by dividing each chromosome into regions, bands, and sub-bands. The present version of this nomenclature, the International System for (Human) Cytogenetic Nomenclature (ISCN 1995),[31] includes the incorporation of fluorescent in situ hybridization (FISH) technology, which is discussed later. A karyotype designation includes the modal chromosome number and the sex chromosome constitution, followed by standard abbreviations and band designations for abnormalities and variants. A chromosomally normal woman is denoted as 46,XX and a chromosomally normal man as 46,XY (Fig. 7-2).

Numerical Abnormalities

Abnormalities in the number of chromosomes generally arise from an anomaly in cell division (*non-disjunction*)

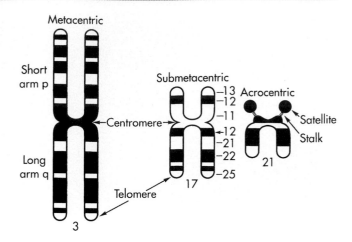

FIGURE 7-1. Human chromosome types with designated structural landmarks and diagrammatic banding representing the pattern seen with standard Giemsa staining, or G banding. The arrow on chromosome 17 points to a specific position on the chromosome that would be designated as 17q12 under the International System for (Human) Cytogenetic Nomenclature.[44]

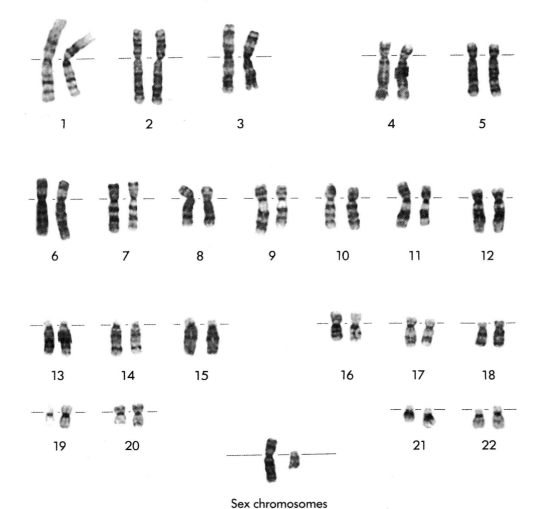

Sex chromosomes

FIGURE 7-2. G-banded normal male karyotype.

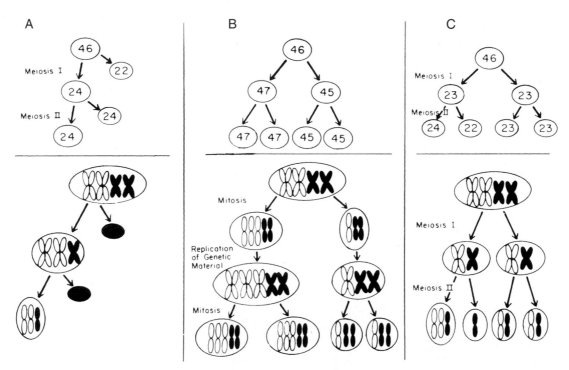

FIGURE 7-3. A, Non-disjunction in female meiosis I, resulting in an ovum with 24 chromosomes. Blackened circles represent the first and second polar bodies. **B,** Non-disjunction in mitosis demonstrating development of mosaicism, with one cell line having 45 chromosomes and the other having 47. **C,** Non-disjunction in male meiosis II, resulting in spermatozoa having 22, 23, and 24 chromosomes.

in which aberrant segregation leads to the loss or gain of one or more chromosomes by a daughter cell (Fig. 7-3). The resulting cell is called *aneuploid* because its modal number is not an exact multiple of the haploid (n) number. Non-disjunction can occur during either meiosis or mitosis, but it more commonly occurs during meiosis.[16]

In meiosis I, homologous chromosomes synapse (because DNA replication occurs before meiosis, each chromosome consists of two sister chromatids), undergo recombination, and segregate, with one homologue migrating to each daughter cell. The chromosome number has been reduced by half. Then, during meiosis II, sister chromatids separate, and one chromatid migrates to each daughter cell. The genetic content is reduced by half to the haploid state in the resulting gamete. Errors of non-disjunction in either meiosis I or meiosis II may lead to aneuploid gametes.

Fertilization of an aneuploid gamete with a normal gamete forms a conceptus with an extra *(trisomy)* or missing *(monosomy)* chromosome. Because non-disjunction can involve any chromosome, most of the resulting aneuploidies are nonviable. Almost all conceptions with autosomal monosomy and most with autosomal trisomy are spontaneously aborted. Even the viable trisomies (21, 13, and 18) are associated with a high rate of pregnancy loss. Approximately 70% of the fetuses with trisomy 21 spontaneously abort, and the pregnancy loss figures for trisomies 13 and 18 are as high as 95%.

Numerical abnormalities of the sex chromosomes form a special class. The more common sex chromosome aneuploidies are 47,XXY (Klinefelter syndrome); 47,XYY; 47,XXX; and 45,X (Turner syndrome). Unlike most sex chromosome aneuploidies, Turner syndrome is associated with a very high rate of fetal loss. It is estimated that 99% of 45,X conceptions are lost as

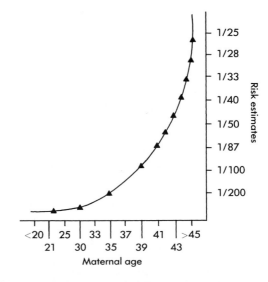

FIGURE 7-4. Risk estimates of chromosomal abnormalities in live births relative to maternal age at the time of delivery.

spontaneous abortions. Compared with the autosomal aneuploidies, the phenotypic effects of sex chromosome aneuploidies seen in living children are relatively mild. Many sex chromosome abnormalities are not apparent until puberty, and a large percentage of them (especially XYY and XXX) are underdiagnosed.

Although the fundamental causes of meiotic non-disjunction are not well understood, there is a clear association between advanced maternal age and non-disjunction (Fig. 7-4). The most common chromosomal abnormality seen in newborns, trisomy 21 (Down syndrome), has long been recognized as an increased risk in the pregnancies of older mothers. Molecular studies have demonstrated that in approximately 90% of the patients with trisomy 21, the meiotic error was maternal in origin. Most errors occurred during the first meiotic division. It is believed that the reduced frequency

of recombination between homologous chromosomes (crossing over) leads to an increase in non-disjunction. Other aneuploidies correlated with advanced maternal age include trisomy 18, trisomy 13, Klinefelter syndrome, and triple X syndrome. The principal features of the autosomal trisomies are shown in Figure 7-5.

Numerical abnormalities that involve multiples of the haploid number are found primarily in material from spontaneous abortions. *Triploidy* (modal number of 69 chromosomes) usually arises from the simultaneous fertilization of a normal ovum by two sperm *(dispermy),* yielding a conceptus with three haploid chromosome sets. Although most (99.9%) triploid fetuses spontaneously abort (seen in approximately 15% of chromosomally abnormal spontaneous abortuses), they occasionally survive to term. However, this condition is incompatible with long-term survival. *Tetraploidy*

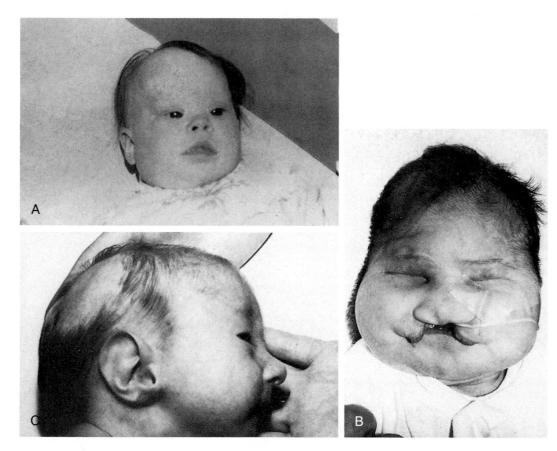

FIGURE 7-5. A, Trisomy 21. Prominent features of the syndrome noted during the neonatal period and the system or organ involved are as follows: central nervous system—abnormal neurologic examination (hypotonia); head—mild microcephaly, flat occiput, midfacial hypoplasia; eyes—Brushfield spots, epicanthal folds, upslanting palpebral fissures; mouth—protuberant tongue; ears—anomalous auricles; hands—simian crease, distal triradius, increased ulnar loops, short metacarpals and phalanges; fingers—dysplasia of midphalanx of fifth finger; cardiac—cardiac defects (approximately 40%); genitalia—hypogonadism; pelvis—hypoplasia, shallow acetabular angle; other—redundant skin at nape of neck, wide space between first and second toes. **B,** Trisomy 13. Prominent features of the syndrome noted during the neonatal period and the system or organ involved are as follows: central nervous system—severe malformations, holoprosencephaly; head—microcephaly, sloping forehead; eyes—microphthalmia, colobomata; mouth—cleft lip, cleft palate; ears—abnormal auricles, low-set ears; hands—distal triradius, simian crease; fingers—polydactyly; chest wall—thin or missing ribs; cardiac—cardiac defects (over 80%); genitalia—cryptorchidism, abnormal scrotum; pelvis—hypoplasia; other—apneic spells, seizures, persistence of fetal hemoglobin, increased nuclear projection in neutrophils. **C,** Trisomy 18. Prominent features of the syndrome noted during the neonatal period and the system or organ involved are as follows: central nervous system—malformations; head—narrow biparietal diameter, occipital prominence; eyes—short palpebral fissures; mouth—micrognathia, small mouth; ears—malformed auricles, low-set ears; hands—increased arches, hypoplastic nails; fingers—overlapping fingers; chest wall—short sternum; cardiac—cardiac defects (over 50%); genitalia—cryptorchidism; pelvis—small pelvis, limited hip abduction; other—growth deficiency, thrombocytopenia.

(modal number of 92 chromosomes) occurs in about 6% of the chromosomally abnormal spontaneous abortions and is incompatible with survival.[8]

The non-disjunction that occurs during mitosis results in *mosaicism,* which is the presence of more than one cell line in an individual. Most often, both a cytogenetically abnormal cell line and a cytogenetically normal cell line are present. Mosaicism is more often encountered in abnormalities of the sex chromosomes. For example, in Turner syndrome, approximately 15% of diagnosed patients have a normal female cell line in addition to a cell line with monosomy X. In the karyotypic designation, the cell lines in a mosaic individual are separated by a forward slash (/), and the number of cells in each is placed in brackets (e.g., mos 45,X [8]/46,XX [12]). Autosomal abnormalities such as trisomy 21 are also seen in mosaic form but usually in only 2% to 3% of the cases. In general, the phenotypic effects are similar to but less severe than those observed when there is no normal cell line present.[35] However, gross generalizations should not be made.

Because the distribution of mosaic cell lines may vary from tissue to tissue in an affected individual, the diagnosis depends on the presence and level of the abnormal cell line in the specimen sent for analysis. For example, in Pallister-Killian syndrome, tetrasomy 12p has been identified as an abnormal mosaic cell line in affected individuals {mos 46,X- [ ]/47,X-, + i(12) (p10) [ ]}. However, the diagnosis is usually made by chromosome analysis of skin fibroblasts, because peripheral blood contains predominantly chromosomally normal cells. In some cases of fetal mosaicism a chromosomally abnormal cell line appears to be confined to extraembryonic tissue (confined placental mosaicism),[32] which may be a complicating factor in prenatal diagnosis.

Structural Abnormalities

Structural abnormalities are the result of chromosome breakage that is improperly repaired. Chromosome rearrangements may maintain the diploid genetic content *(balanced),* or they may result in the loss or gain of one or more chromosome segments *(unbalanced).* Structural rearrangements may segregate within a family *(familial),* or they may arise as a new "mutation" *(de novo).*

Translocation involves the exchange of segments between two chromosomes. There are two major types of translocation—*reciprocal* and *Robertsonian.* In reciprocal translocation the breakage occurs within two chromosome arms, with exchange of the distal segments (Fig. 7-6A). The derivative chromosomes are hybrids of the involved chromosomes, containing parts of both of them. Although most balanced translocation carriers are phenotypically normal, they are at risk of producing unbalanced gametes. Meiotic segregation of the chromosomes involved in a translocation is complex and different types of segregation are possible, but there are four major patterns. Alternate segregation of a reciprocal translocation gives rise to either chromosomally normal gametes or gametes carrying the

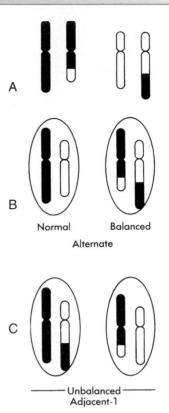

FIGURE 7-6. Reciprocal translocation. **A,** Reciprocal translocation between two nonhomologous chromosomes. In addition to the derivative chromosomes, each cell contains a normal copy of each chromosome. **B,** The meiotic products of alternate segregation. **C,** The meiotic products of adjacent-1 segregation.

balanced translocation (Fig. 7-6B). In adjacent-1 segregation the centromeres segregate appropriately (homologous centromeres to opposite poles), but the gamete receives the normal homologue of one chromosome and the derived homologue of the other chromosome (Fig. 7-6C), thus producing unbalanced gametes. In this situation, there is duplication of one translocated segment and deletion of the other.[8] Adjacent-2 segregation is similar to adjacent-1, except that the homologous centromeres go to the same pole. In 3:1 segregation, either three chromosomes segregate together or one by itself, resulting in a fetus with 45 or 47 chromosomes. The risk of abnormal segregation and a phenotypically abnormal outcome varies based on the chromosomes involved, size of the translocated pieces, and ascertainment of the translocation. The overall approximate risk is 10%, with a range of 3% to 20%.

Although a normal phenotype is seen in most individuals with a balanced translocation, there is an increased incidence of both congenital anomalies and mental retardation in translocations that are de novo. There is an approximately 8% chance of a phenotypic abnormality in de novo rearrangements detected prenatally.[47] These abnormalities may result from the effects of position, a break within a gene, a subtle deletion or duplication, or uniparental disomy.[2]

Robertsonian translocations are the most common structural abnormalities, occurring in about 1 of 1000 live births. They involve two acrocentric chromosomes and arise from exchanges within the pericentromeric region of the short arm. Most of the short-arm segments normally present on the involved chromosomes are lost as a result of these exchanges. Because the short arms of acrocentric chromosomes contain redundant genetic material, the loss of a portion of this material has no phenotypic effect. Although the translocation involving chromosomes 14 and 21 is the most common Robertsonian rearrangement, any acrocentric chromosomes can be involved, including homologous chromosomes [e.g., der (21;21) (q10;q10)]. Because a Robertsonian rearrangement is a fusion between two chromosomes, a balanced carrier has a modal number of 45 chromosomes, whereas an individual with an unbalanced karyotype has 46 chromosomes.

As in reciprocal translocations, alternate segregation of a Robertsonian translocation gives rise either to chromosomally normal gametes or to balanced gametes that carry the translocation (Fig. 7-7B). Adjacent-1 segregation leads to the duplication or deletion of an entire long arm, and most segregants are nonviable. However, if the aberrant segregant gives rise to a viable trisomy (e.g., trisomy 21), unbalanced offspring may result. For example, a woman who carries a 14/21 translocation [der (14;21) (q10;q10)] has a 10% to 15% risk of having

a child with Down syndrome who carries two normal copies of chromosome 21 in addition to the Robertsonian translocation [46,X-,der (14;21) (q10;q10),+21]. For a man carrying the same translocation, the risk is considerably lower (less than 5%). Approximately 3% of the live-born infants with Down syndrome carry an unbalanced form of the Robertsonian translocation. Half of these are inherited, so there is a significant risk of recurrence in those families. De novo cases of Down syndrome translocation carry a negligible risk of recurrence.[8]

Other types of structural abnormality include inversions, deletions, and duplications (Fig. 7-8). A chromosome inversion is the result of two breaks in a single chromosome, with the resulting interstitial segment assuming a reversed orientation during repair of the breaks. In a *pericentric* inversion, each arm of the chromosome has one breakpoint and the inverted segment contains the centromere. In a *paracentric* inversion, both breakpoints are in a single arm—either the long or the short one—and the centromere is not included in the rearrangement. Although most carriers of inversions are phenotypically normal, there is a reproductive risk. Meiotic recombination within the inverted segment may lead to the formation of an unbalanced recombinant chromosome.[8] These recombinations and the resulting unbalanced offspring are more likely to occur with carriers of pericentric rather than paracentric inversions. The recombinant chromosomes formed by both the paracentric and pericentric carriers have both deletions and duplications; however, the recombinant chromosomes from paracentric carriers are dicentric (two centromeres) or acentric (no centromere) and less likely to be viable.

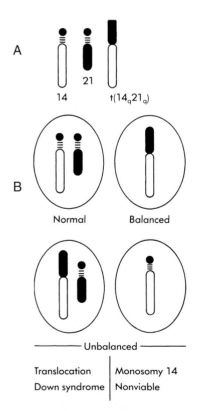

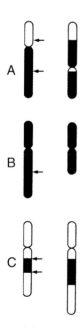

FIGURE 7-7. Robertsonian translocation. **A,** Robertsonian translocation between two acrocentric chromosomes [t(14;21)(q10;q10)]. **B,** Four of the possible segregants of a Robertsonian translocation. Only the "normal" and "balanced" products are genetically balanced.

FIGURE 7-8. Structural chromosome abnormalities. In each panel, the normal chromosome is illustrated on the left and the abnormal one on the right. Breakpoints are indicated by arrows. **A,** Pericentric inversion. **B,** Terminal deletion. **C,** Tandem duplication.

Chromosome deletions may be either terminal or interstitial. In a terminal deletion, a segment of varying size is missing from the end of a chromosome; in an interstitial deletion, two breaks occur within a single chromosome, with the loss of the central segment before repair. In either type of deletion, the genetic constitution is unbalanced and the individual is monosomic for the deleted segment. A specific subgroup of deletions—the microdeletion (or contiguous gene deletion) syndromes—has become extremely important in clinical genetics. The diagnosis of these disorders is facilitated by the use of FISH and is explained in greater detail later.

In chromosome duplications, a chromosome segment of varying size is duplicated within the chromosome. Because the homologous chromosome is normal (contains one copy of the relevant segment), an individual with a duplication is trisomic for a specific segment (i.e., he or she has three copies of the duplicated segment). In tandem duplications, the additional segment may be in the normal orientation with respect to the centromere (direct duplication) or it may be in an inverted orientation (inverted duplication).

The nature and effects of structural abnormalities can be summarized as follows. Because most of the chromosome breakage is apparently a random occurrence, the variety of potential abnormalities is infinite with respect to the breakpoints, type of rearrangement, and chromosome segments involved. Therefore, in most cases each rearrangement is unique (unless the disorder is familial). In terms of the effect on the phenotype, the critical issue is not the type of rearrangement but whether it is balanced. Most individuals with balanced rearrangements are phenotypically normal. With a de novo rearrangement that is apparently balanced, there is an 8% empirical risk that the rearrangement is associated with adverse phenotypic consequences.[47] This condition implies that a subset of rearrangements appearing to be balanced is actually unbalanced at a sub-microscopic level (presumably a sub-microscopic duplication or deletion) or may involve breakage within a gene.[2,3] More complex explanations, such as the effects of position on gene expression, may also be involved.

The vast majority of autosomal imbalances that can be detected microscopically have associated phenotypic abnormalities, including mental retardation. An imbalance that constitutes more than 4% to 5% of the haploid autosomal genome is nonviable, regardless of the chromosome segment involved. In fact, many smaller imbalances are nonviable. In general, for a given chromosome segment, trisomy is better tolerated than monosomy.[8]

Fluorescent In Situ Hybridization

The advances in DNA technology that have been applied to the field of cytogenetics have bridged the resolution gap between light microscopy and the molecular level. Using specially labeled DNA probes, we can now determine the presence or absence of specific genes or gene sequences along the length of a chromosome. Changes in DNA structure from 2 kb to 2 Mb along the length of the chromosome can be pinpointed by the process of FISH. Furthermore, this technology can be applied to interphase cells as well as to metaphase chromosomes, thus expanding the possibilities of diagnosing chromosomal abnormalities in nondividing cells.

FISH technology depends on two factors: the intrinsic ability of single-stranded DNA to bind and anneal to complementary DNA sequences and the generation of DNA probes that have been modified by incorporating biotin–deoxyuridine triphosphate or digoxigenin–uridine triphosphate in place of thymine in the probe DNA sequence and now, most commonly, DNA probes that are directly labeled with a fluorochrome. The labeled DNA probe is denatured and hybridized in the cells of interest to the native DNA, which also has been denatured to the single-stranded state. After the probe has annealed to the complementary DNA sequence (or sequences) of the cells, the newly formed DNA complex can be detected directly (or indirectly). The cell DNA probe, DNA complex is visualized by analysis with epifluorescence microscopy in which a light source with appropriate excitation wavelengths is used. Imaging may also be enhanced by using a digital imaging microscope. Using different fluorochromes tagged to two or more different DNA probes allows simultaneous visualization of multiple chromosome sites within a single cell.

DNA probes for FISH may be formulated to detect specific genes or gene sequences or to anneal to chromosome-specific centromere sequences, and many probes corresponding to specific disorders are commercially available. In addition, because of the Human Genome Project, there are bacterial artificial chromosomes available that map to essentially every area in the genome.[22,44] This process facilitates the overall examination of chromosomes with FISH by providing a detailed physical map. Other available types of probe for FISH include whole chromosome "paints" or libraries that have been derived by flow cytometry or single-cell human hybrids, region-specific probes made by microdissection, and centromere-specific probes. The usefulness of a given probe depends on the type of cytogenetic abnormality being evaluated and the type of tissue being analyzed. For example, centromeric probes from unique α-satellite DNA sequences (e.g., chromosomes 18, X and Y) have been used in conjunction with single-copy probes to detect aneuploidy in interphase cells (Fig. 7-9A). Because of the sequence similarity of centromeric α-satellite DNA of chromosomes 13 and 21, specific identification of a trisomic 13 or trisomic 21 condition in interphase cells is not possible if only a probe based on an α-satellite is used. Therefore, specific single-copy probes for these chromosomes are used.

The ability to use FISH to detect specific gene sequences that may be duplicated or deleted in specific chromosomes has greatly enhanced our ability to diagnose contiguous gene syndromes, also known as microdeletion syndromes. These syndromes are patterns

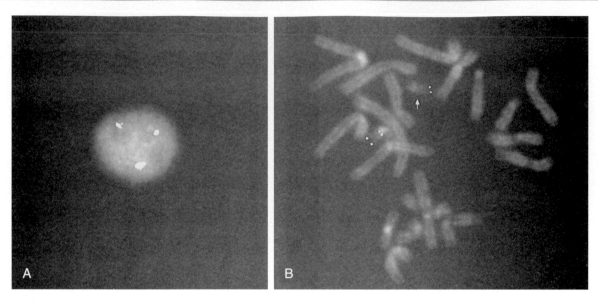

FIGURE 7-9. A, Fluorescent in situ hybridization (FISH) analysis of an interphase nucleus (with the use of a chromosome X pericentromeric α-satellite DNA probe) reveals three signals consistent with three copies of chromosome X. **B,** FISH analysis of metaphase chromosomes with the use of the DiGeorge chromosome region probe (22q11.2), reveals the absence of the DiGeorge locus on one of the two chromosomes 22, indicated by an arrow. A specific probe (22q13.3) for the telomeric region of chromosome 22 is used as a control to show hybridization to each chromosome 22.

of abnormality that arise because of the loss of a continuous segment of DNA, usually involving multiple genes. The affected individual thus has only one copy of the gene present per cell, a condition also called segmental aneusomy. Over 20 of these syndromes have been defined by the association of a region of a chromosome with characteristic physical and developmental problems. Some of the more common microdeletion syndromes and their critical chromosome regions are the association of aniridia with Wilms tumor (11p13), DiGeorge and velocardiofacial (VCF) syndromes (22q11.2), Miller-Dieker syndrome (17p13.3), and Prader-Willi and Angelman syndromes (15q11-13, which is discussed later). FISH technology allows unequivocal delineation of these syndromes by identifying a deletion at the sub-microscopic level, which can be visualized as the loss of a binding site of a region-specific probe in the cells of the affected individual. For example, in VCF and DiGeorge syndromes, only about 30% of cases can be identified by a deletion seen with high-resolution cytogenetics. With FISH techniques, almost all patients with one of these syndromes can be shown to have the deletion (see Fig. 7-9B).

Another major application of FISH is the increased ability to identify marker chromosomes, which occur in about 1 of 750 prenatal diagnoses and in about 1 of 2500 newborns. By definition, marker chromosomes are chromosome fragments that lack distinctive banding patterns, making identification by standard staining methods virtually impossible. Although many patients with marker chromosomes may be asymptomatic, identifying the source of a marker is always important for clinical management. For example, patients with a 45,X/ 46,X,+mar karyotype may be at risk for gonadoblastoma

if the origin of the marker is the Y chromosome. By using FISH techniques, it can usually be determined whether the marker is derived from an X or Y chromosome and whether the removal of streak gonads is indicated. Some studies of marker chromosomes have demonstrated that about half of the satellite markers are derived from chromosome 15, and many nonsatellite markers originate from chromosomes 15, 18, and X.[10,30] Although this information is not always clinically useful, the presence or absence of specific genes or these markers may be associated with an abnormal or normal phenotype. For example, the presence of SNRPN in a marker derived from chromosome 15 is associated with an abnormal phenotype.

Of similar diagnostic importance is the use of FISH to identify cryptic chromosomal rearrangements that might go undetected with standard banding techniques. For example, through FISH methodology, children affected with Miller-Dieker syndrome, with ostensibly normal karyotypes, have been identified as carriers of an unbalanced translocation involving 17p. This technology has been used to detect the presence of deleted material in presumably balanced translocations and the presence or absence of specific genes in cytologically visible deletions.[2,40] The greatest advance in this area has been in the use of subtelomeric probes, which are unique DNA probes within approximately 300 kb of the end of the chromosome. They are directly labeled and used as FISH probes to determine if there are detectable cryptic rearrangements (e.g., deletions, duplications) that are not seen with routine G banding. It has been estimated that 2% to 5% of the cases with no detectable G-banded abnormality may have a cryptic rearrangement ascertained by telomeric FISH analysis.[18]

Other available FISH techniques that better characterize structural abnormalities include comparative genomic hybridization (CGH), reserve painting, spectral karyotyping (SKY), and multicolor FISH (M-FISH). CGH is a technique that uses DNA from the individual (or cell line) with an abnormal karyotype.[21] The test DNA is labeled green, and a control (normal) DNA is labeled red. They are mixed and hybridized to normal chromosomes. The red:green ratio is analyzed by computer software, allowing for the detection of the gain or loss of chromosomal material from the test DNA.[21] Both SKY and M-FISH are techniques that use combinatorial or ratio-labeled probes to create a distinct "color" for each chromosome.[36,41] These probes are all applied simultaneously, and specialized computer software is used to detect the probes and pseudocolor the chromosomes. The metaphase can then be visualized and analyzed, with a distinct pseudocolor for each chromosome. In reverse painting, the unidentified chromosome is either flow-sorted away from the other chromosomes or scraped off a microscope slide. The DNA is extracted, amplified, and labeled and is then used as a probe on normal metaphases to identify the origin of the chromosomal material. Other applications of FISH technology now appear to be limited only by the development, definition, and availability of specific diagnostic probes. It is apparent that this technology continues to progress along with the delineation of the human genome, availability of more probes, and delineation of more genes. The most recent advance has been in the use of CGH with bacterial artificial chromosome arrays to identify chromosome imbalance. This technique is similar to the CGH described above, with the exception that it allows greater resolution (up to 1 MB) by using the hybridization of test DNA to bacterial artificial chromosomes arranged on a filter.[22,25,44]

SINGLE GENE DISORDERS

Human genetic disorders caused by mutations within single genes that lead to recognizable and predictable expression in the individual (phenotype) and segregate within families in generally predictable proportions are called mendelian genetic traits.[28] These disorders follow the classic laws of inheritance established by Gregor Mendel for all diploid organisms. These laws state that genes from nonhomologous chromosomes assort independently during gamete formation and pairs of genes (alleles) from homologous chromosomes segregate during gamete formation.

In humans, as in all diploid organisms, genes exist in pairs on homologous chromosomes (with the exception of the sex chromosomes in men). Thus, single gene disorders are classified on the basis of the interaction between a specific pair of alleles—the *genotype*—leading to an expressed, observable genetic effect—the *phenotype*. An individual with nonidentical alleles at any specific genetic locus is called a *heterozygote* or is said to have a *heterozygous* genotype. If the alleles at a specific genetic locus are identical, the individual

is *homozygous* for this genetic characteristic and may be called a *homozygote*. If the interaction of a single mutant allele with a normal gene leads to the expression of the disorder in the individual, the genetic disorder is expressed in the heterozygous state and is considered to be *dominant*. A *recessive* genetic disease can occur only when both alleles are mutant or homozygous. Single gene disorders are further categorized as to whether they are transmitted on the autosomes or the sex chromosomes; thus, there are four major patterns of mendelian inheritance in humans: autosomal dominant, autosomal recessive, X-linked dominant, and X-linked recessive.

For many genetic disorders in humans, the specific genetic defect is unknown, although with the sequencing of the human genome, more genes associated with disorders have been identified. In addition, there are many instances of genetic heterogeneity or different gene mutations leading to the same phenotype. A good example is retinitis pigmentosa, a disorder leading to hyperpigmentation within the retina and eventual blindness. Retinitis pigmentosa may be inherited as an autosomal dominant, autosomal recessive, or X-linked recessive disorder, or it could be due to environmental agents. When the precise biochemical or molecular basis for genetic diseases with similar phenotypes is unknown, the principal means of discriminating between heterogeneous mutations and determining the pattern of inheritance is by the analysis of the family history, or pedigree.[7,42]

Autosomal Dominant Inheritance

The example of an autosomal dominant pedigree in Figure 7-10 demonstrates the general rules for autosomal dominant inheritance.

1. There is a *vertical* pattern of transmission, with the genetic disorder appearing in each successive generation.

2. Affected individuals are equally likely to be male or female.

3. Affected children have at least one affected parent, except in cases of new mutations.

4. Affected individuals, if reproductively fit; transmit the abnormal gene to their progeny with a 50:50

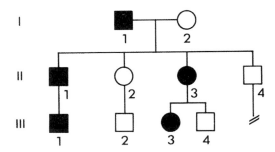

FIGURE 7-10. Example of an autosomal dominant pedigree. Note the vertical pattern of transmission. ○, female; □, male; ●, ■, affected.

probability. Within any one family, about half the children of an affected parent are normal and about half affected.

5. In addition to transmission to their daughters, affected men may transmit the gene to their sons, which is called male-to-male transmission.

6. Individuals within the family who are not affected will not transmit the gene to their progeny in most cases.

Other characteristics of autosomal dominant genetic diseases in humans are frequently noted. In the homozygous state, autosomal dominant diseases or disorders are rare and generally lethal. For example, matings between individuals with autosomal dominant achondroplastic dwarfism lead to families with approximately two thirds of the children affected and one third normal rather than three fourths affected and one fourth normal. The homozygous children with achondroplasia either do not survive to delivery or die shortly after birth. Another characteristic often associated with autosomal dominant disorders is *variable expressivity*. Not all the individuals who inherit the mutant gene are affected to the same degree. In *neurofibromatosis*, a relatively common autosomal dominant genetic disorder affecting about 1 in 3000 individuals, the range of expression may vary from mild (with minimal café-au-lait spots and few if any tumors) to severe (with numerous café-au-lait spots and massive neurofibromata covering the entire body). *Penetrance* is another concept used in the characterization of autosomal dominant diseases. Not every individual carrying the gene overtly manifests the disorder. In a "fully penetrant" disorder, any person with the dominant gene always demonstrates phenotypic expression. If the disorder has "reduced penetrance," there may be individuals within the pedigree who transmit the gene but ostensibly do not have the disease. Penetrance is often confused with variable expressivity, but penetrance is a statistical concept indicating the percentage of individuals within the pedigree at risk for the disorder (i.e., those having the mutant gene) and affected by it. Variable expressivity refers to the degree to which the gene is expressed within a single individual.

Finally, one of the problems in differentiating an autosomal dominant genetic disease from other patterns of inheritance is a new mutation. Any dominant mutation carried in the gamete at conception leads to the appearance of the dominant disorder for the first time in the kindred. For example, achondroplasia is a new mutation in approximately 80% of occurrences.[20] For the normal parents of a child with achondroplasia there is little likelihood of recurrence in future pregnancies, but for the affected child the mutation will be transmitted to 50% of his or her offspring. In many dominant genetic disorders affecting humans, there is a positive correlation between the increased rate of new mutations and paternal age. Examples include achondroplasia, Apert disease, Marfan syndrome, and progeria. This correlation is thought to reflect the accumulation

of DNA replicative errors during spermatogenesis throughout the long period of male reproductive life. The primary germ cells in the female population have a finite period of replication of approximately 22 to 26 cell divisions, as opposed to the continuous mitotic replenishment of sperm precursor cells in the male population once puberty begins.

As previously described, somatic non-disjunction can give rise to chromosomal mosaicism. Mutational mosaicism can arise as the result of postfertilization errors of replication or the repair of nucleotide sequences in somatic cells or germ cells at any stage of development. In the rare cases in which two *unaffected* parents have two or more affected offspring with a completely penetrant-dominant condition (e.g., osteogenesis imperfecta, neurofibromatosis, or achondroplasia), germline mutation mosaicism of one parent can be inferred. When there are new cases of dominant disorders in the offspring of normal parents, there are implications for genetic counseling that recurrence risks must be revised upward by a few percentage points to account for the possibility of germline mosaicism in one of the parents.[15,42]

Autosomal Recessive Inheritance

Because they occur only in the homozygous state, recessive disorders are much rarer than autosomal dominant disorders. An example of a typical autosomal recessive pedigree is shown in Figure 7-11. There are five primary features of an autosomal recessive pattern of inheritance.

1. The disorder most often occurs in siblings in a *horizontal* pattern within a generation.

2. Both male and female populations are affected.

3. Parents are usually unaffected, and affected individuals rarely have affected children.

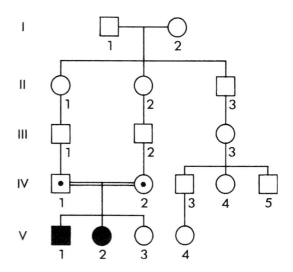

FIGURE 7-11. Example of an autosomal recessive pedigree. Note the horizontal pattern of affected individuals. ○, female; □, male; =, consanguinity; ⊙, ⊡, obligate carriers; ●, ■, affected.

4. In each subsequent pregnancy, the recurrence risk for known carriers is 1 in 4 (25%).

5. Consanguinity is often observed in the pedigrees of extremely rare recessive disorders.

For some of the known recessive genetic diseases in which the specific defective gene product has been identified, biochemical tests can confirm the absence or deficiency of that product in the affected individual. Carrier status, signified by reduced levels of the gene product, can be determined in the parents. A well-known example of such a biochemical diagnosis is found in *Tay-Sachs disease,* in which affected individuals have deficient or greatly reduced levels of hexosaminidase A in serum and lymphocytes. The carriers of this disorder can be identified by the reduced levels of hexosaminidase A activity—approximately 50% of that found in the tissues of noncarriers. As an increasing number of genetic diseases are identified at the DNA level by alterations in the nucleotides making up the gene itself rather than at the level of the gene product, more carriers will be identified by molecular analysis and an increasing number will be identified as the human genome is delineated.[9,15,42]

Sex-Linked Inheritance

Because relatively few genes associated with abnormal phenotypes have been identified on the Y chromosome in humans (see discussion later), sex-linked disorders are often considered synonymous with X-linked genetic diseases. There are proportionally more recognized genetic diseases linked to the X chromosome than to any of the autosomes, which reflects the fact that men, with only one X chromosome, are *hemizygous* for X-linked genes and therefore are affected by any mutant gene located on the X chromosome. X-linked diseases such as hemophilia A were among the earliest recognized human genetic diseases because of the differential rate of expression in the male population. Women, with two X chromosomes, may be either homozygous or heterozygous for any X-linked gene. An example of an X-linked recessive pedigree is shown in Figure 7-12. There are four features of an X-linked recessive mode of inheritance.

1. Men are more frequently affected than women.

2. Male-to-male transmission of the mutant gene is never seen.

3. The daughters of affected men are obligate carriers for the disorder.

4. Carrier mothers of X-linked disorders transmit the disorder to half of their sons; half of their daughters are carriers. Therefore, in an X-linked pedigree, all affected male members are related to one another through the female members.

An interesting association between sporadic cases of known X-linked disorders, such as hemophilia A and Lesch-Nyhan syndrome, and the age of the maternal grandfather has been observed. Just as there appears to

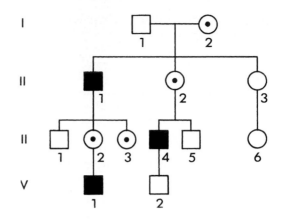

FIGURE 7-12. X-linked recessive pattern of inheritance. Note that sons of affected men are not affected. ○, female; □, male; ⊙, ⊡, obligate carriers; ●, ■, affected.

be an increase in the risk for new dominant mutations with advancing paternal age, there is an increased risk for new mutations of X-linked disorders in the sons of mothers whose fathers were older. It is speculated that a well known historical example of a new mutation—that of hemophilia A in the descendants of Queen Victoria—may be the consequence of an X-linked mutant gene inherited from her unaffected father, who was older than 50 years of age when she was born.

X-linked dominant disorders in humans are relatively rare diseases. The best described example is the resistance of rickets to vitamin D (hypophosphatemia). X-linked dominant disorders can be distinguished from X-linked recessive diseases by the following criteria (Fig. 7-13).

1. Affected women are twice as common in the pedigree as affected men. In some disorders, the mutation may be lethal in men.

2. Affected men have affected daughters but no affected sons.

3. Affected women transmit the disorder to half of their daughters and half of their sons. There is a 50% chance of having an affected child.

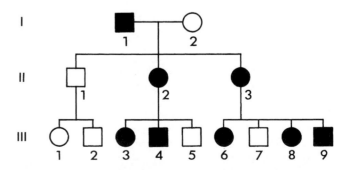

FIGURE 7-13. X-linked dominant pedigree. Approximately twice as many women as men are affected. ○, female; □, male; ●, ■, affected.

X Chromosome Inactivation in the Female Population

A unique mechanism that has evolved to regulate gene expression in mammalian females, including humans, is random inactivation of one X chromosome in the somatic tissues. Although both X chromosomes must be "turned on" for genetic transcription to occur in ovarian tissues to ensure normal oogenesis and secondary sexual development, only one entire X chromosome remains accessible for genetic transcription in somatic cells. This feature is necessary because the two X chromosomes in women must be compensated for to be equivalent to the one X chromosome in men. The hypothesis of dosage compensation was initially espoused by Mary Lyon in the 1960s. The Lyon hypothesis, which has been proved correct in most aspects, states that the following activity occurs in the somatic cells of chromosomally normal women.[26,27]

1. Only one of the two X chromosomes is transcriptionally active.

2. The inactivation of one X chromosome occurs early in embryonic life.

3. The inactivation of one X chromosome occurs randomly, and either the maternal or the paternal X chromosome in a cell is inactivated.

4. The inactivation is irreversible and clonally propagated, such that all the descendants of a given cell have the same inactivated X chromosome.

More recent studies indicate that there are some exceptions to the original Lyon hypothesis. Random X inactivation does not always occur, whether it is due to stochastic effects, mutations, or the presence of structurally abnormal X chromosomes. Not every gene is inactivated on the inactive X chromosome. It is now estimated that at least 15% of the genes on the X chromosome are not inactivated.[5] Lastly, X inactivation is not irreversible; it is reversible in the development of the germ cells.

The inactive X chromosome can be visualized in such nondividing cells as the Barr body (sex chromatin), a densely compacted, heterochromatic structure within the nucleus associated with the nuclear membrane. In dividing cells, the inactive X chromosome can be identified by special techniques that demonstrate DNA replication and the late replication pattern of the inactive X chromosome during the S phase of mitosis.[26,27]

Because only one X-linked gene is functionally active in the somatic tissues of women, a woman who is heterozygous for an X-linked disorder is a mosaic for cells expressing either the normal or abnormal gene. For this reason, carrier women themselves may manifest some signs of X-linked recessive diseases if by chance the X chromosome carrying the normal gene is inactive in most of the cells in critical tissues. For example, a woman who is a carrier of Duchenne Muscular Dystrophy (DMD) may demonstrate mild muscular weakness, and a carrier of hemophilia A may have diminished clotting activity. This variability in X chromosome expression also makes it extremely difficult to identify female carriers of X-linked recessive disorders even when the biochemical defect or marker is known (e.g., hypoxanthine guanine phosphoribosyltransferase activity in Lesch-Nyhan syndrome). The measurable levels of the X chromosome gene product in carriers may overlap with the normal range of gene products found in noncarrier women. When the mother of an affected son does not have other affected sons, brothers, or maternal uncles, it may be difficult to determine whether the X-linked disorder represents a new mutation or an inherited defect. Molecular genetic diagnostic techniques play an important role in distinguishing between these two possibilities.[9,37,42]

Y Chromosome Inheritance

As stated earlier, few genes associated with abnormal phenotypes have been identified on the Y chromosome in humans. The best examples of genes localized to the Y chromosome are those involved in dimorphic traits, sexual development, or sperm production. SRY, the testis-determining factor, is localized to the short arm of the Y chromosome. A mutation in this gene leads to a sex-reversed fetus. The DAZ gene is localized to the long arm of the Y chromosome. A mutation in this gene leads to azoospermia and infertility. There are three features of a Y-linked mode of inheritance.

1. Only the male population is affected.

2. All the sons of an affected father are affected.

3. Male-to-female transmission of the mutant gene is never seen.

Nontraditional Patterns of Inheritance

Although Mendel's laws have withstood the test of time, recent studies have revealed some remarkable exceptions. Nontraditional forms of inheritance that are not predicted by Mendel's laws have been identified. There are three major types of nontraditional inheritance: mitochondrial inheritance, imprinting, and trinucleotide repeats.

MITOCHONDRIAL INHERITANCE

As described earlier, most genes located on chromosomes within the cell nucleus follow mendelian patterns of inheritance. However, another source of DNA within mammalian cells is the circular molecule of DNA located within mitochondria and thus confined to the cell cytoplasm. Although many of the proteins controlling mitochondrial function and the respiratory enzyme complex are coded by nuclear genes, some of the mitochondrial proteins are the translation products of mitochondrial DNA. The mitochondria contain circular DNA, consisting of 16,569 bp. This DNA contains a unique genetic code that differs from the nuclear DNA. There are no introns, and the DNA sequence codes for 2 RNA genes and 22 transfer RNA (tRNA) genes.

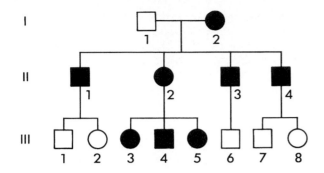

FIGURE 7-14. Mitochondrial inheritance. Note that children of affected men are not affected. ○, female; □, male; ●, ■, affected.

An example of mitochondrial inheritance is shown in Figure 7-14. There are five general rules for such inheritance.

1. Genes encoded by mitochondrial DNA follow a matrilineal inheritance. All the functional mitochondria are derived from the cytoplasm of the oocyte. At fertilization the mitochondria within the sperm head are not transferred to the ovum.

2. An affected woman passes the trait to *all* her children.

3. An affected man *never* passes the trait to his children.

4. There is significant tissue and organ variability due to *heteroplasmy* (see discussion later).

5. The phenotype may vary over time.

Because mitochondria are the cellular organelles with the key function of energy production, mitochondrial genetic diseases fundamentally affect the processes of oxidative phosphorylation. The phenotype of a specific mitochondrial genetic disorder may vary considerably, depending on both the nature of the mutation and a unique property of mitochondrial genetics known as heteroplasmy. At the time of fertilization, the cytoplasm of the human ovum contains thousands of mitochondria. In addition, each mitochondrion may contain multiple copies of DNA. Therefore, mitochondrial inheritance may involve the distribution of both mutant and normal mitochondrial DNA within the cytoplasm of cells. If a mitochondrial genetic variant is present, the ovum probably contains both normal and variant genotypes. Furthermore, as mitochondrial DNA replicates, the possibility of mitochondrial DNA mutation means that multiple copies of DNA within the single organelle may not be genetically identical. Depending on the replication and distribution patterns of the mutant mitochondria in developing tissues as well as their specific energy requirements, the clinical phenotype in mitochondrial disorders may be highly unpredictable and may change over a lifetime. A single family may have widely different manifestations of the same mitochondrial disease, and in a single individual the manifestations may change with age.

Predictably, in disorders of energy metabolism, the most affected tissues are those with the highest energy demands. Myopathy is a common expression of a mitochondrial genetic disease. External ophthalmoplegia, or paralysis of the muscles of the eye and eyelid, is found in Kearns-Sayre syndrome; cardiac arrhythmia may be a clinical feature of this syndrome as well. Hypertrophic cardiomyopathy may be another presenting feature of mitochondrial genetic disease, and disorders of the central nervous system are likely to be cardinal features. Myoclonic epilepsy with ragged red fibers is characterized by ataxia, hearing loss, and generalized dysfunction of the central nervous system as well as by myoclonic seizures. The clinical hallmark of Leber hereditary optic neuropathy is the acute or subacute onset of blindness in late childhood or adolescence resulting from isolated involvement of the optic nerve and retinal degeneration.

Because there are nuclear genes coding for the proteins, structural components, and enzymes of the mitochondria as well as mitochondrial genes, defining the particular genetic defects leading to a problem with energy metabolism can be exceedingly difficult. The diagnosis of mitochondrial disorders requires specialized investigations. DNA-based diagnostic procedures are now available for many mitochondrial diseases because the DNA sequence of the mitochondrial chromosome has been delineated, and many mutations have been detected. Therapy for individuals with mitochondrial disease is limited to an attempt to increase adenosine triphosphate production and efficiency by replacing cofactors involved in energy metabolism, involves the removal of noxious metabolites, and can be palliative.[43]

IMPRINTING

Genomic imprinting refers to the differential modification of the paternal and maternal contributions to the zygote, resulting in the differential expression of parental alleles (for some genes the paternal and maternal alleles function differently). This feature is a clear departure from typical mendelian inheritance and applies to only a small number of genes.

Pronuclear transplantation experiments in mice have revealed that the sex of the parent may reversibly affect the genetic contribution to the embryo. Mouse embryos have been conceived with both haploid chromosomal complements coming from either the mother or the father. Mouse zygotes with all *paternally* derived genes had placental development with arrested embryonic development; those with all *maternally* derived genes had embryonic development with arrested placental development. Neither embryo developed normally beyond an early stage. This phenomenon, known as genomic imprinting, leads to the concept that some genes or chromosome segments are expressed differently in the embryo, depending on whether they were inherited from the mother or the father. Human examples of genomic imprinting include *hydatidiform moles* or *complete moles*, which are placental tumors with no embryonic tissue and a genome derived from two paternal sets of haploid chromosomes. *Ovarian teratomata* are benign tumors consisting of disorganized masses of differentiated embryonic tissue but devoid of placental tissue. These teratomata contain two maternally derived sets of haploid chromosomes.[13]

As the molecular dissection of human genetic syndromes has advanced, genomic imprinting has been demonstrated to play an important role in specific syndromes. The best known examples are Prader-Willi and Angelman syndromes. Prader-Willi syndrome is characterized by hypotonia at birth, obesity and uncontrolled appetite with age, and moderate mental retardation. In most cases (70%), it is associated with a deletion of chromosome 15 [del (15) (q11-q13)]. Angelman syndrome is characterized by severe mental retardation, inappropriate laughter, and characteristic ataxic movements. It is also associated with the deletion of 15q11-q13, the same region deleted in Prader-Willi syndrome. The problem of explaining two distinct genetic conditions caused by the same cytogenetic deletion was unresolved until it was demonstrated that the deletion in Prader-Willi syndrome was always *paternally* derived and that the deletion in Angelman syndrome was *maternally* derived.[6] Infants who inherit a 15q11-q13 deletion from their fathers have Prader-Willi syndrome because a critical region on maternal chromosome 15 required for normal development is imprinted or inactivated during the normal process of maternal meiosis. The corresponding region on paternal chromosome 15, which normally must remain active in embryonic development, is lost with the paternal 15q11-q13 deletion. Infants develop Angelman syndrome because one gene from the chromosome 15 region (UBE3A) is normally paternally imprinted and inactive in certain developmental stages. Because of the maternally derived deletion, these infants do not have the corresponding complementary active maternal genetic information.[6,46]

Interestingly, only about 70% of patients with either Angelman or Prader-Willi syndrome can be demonstrated by cytogenetic analysis to have this deletion. Furthermore, molecular analyses of the chromosomes of some individuals without cytologically detectable deletions have revealed submicroscopic deletions or mutations below the level of cytogenetic resolution. These molecular studies revealed that in the cells of approximately 5% of the individuals with these disorders, a portion of the imprinting center (within 15q11-q13) is either deleted or has a mutation responsible for the disorders. In addition, in 25% to 30% of the patients with Prader-Willi syndrome and in approximately 3% of those with Angelman syndrome, *both* copies of chromosome 15 were either paternally or maternally derived and thus paternally or maternally imprinted. The critical region of the corresponding active maternal or paternal genetic component is missing in these rare individuals because they have no maternally or paternally inherited chromosome 15.[6,46] In addition, in Angelman syndrome the mutations of UBE3A, a maternally imprinted gene, account for about 8% of these cases.

It has now been recognized that the uniparental inheritance of chromosomes, or *uniparental disomy* (UPD), can be the basis for syndromes demonstrating genomic imprinting in other genetic conditions. Two categories of UPD have been defined: *isodisomy*, which is the inheritance of two identical copies of a chromosome from the same parent, and *heterodisomy*, which is the inheritance of two different copies of the same chromosome from the same parent. This is not a trivial distinction if the parent contributing the chromosome is a carrier for a recessive disorder. An individual with uniparental isodisomy for a chromosome with a gene for a recessive disease would be affected with that disorder. Several cases of cystic fibrosis (CF) in children have been determined to be caused by isodisomy of chromosome 7 from a parent who carries one mutation of the disease.

The magnitude of genetic morbidity resulting from UPD remains unknown, but its demonstration should not be surprising. As mentioned earlier, about 10% of all the clinically recognized pregnancies that end in miscarriage are trisomies, which result from disomy in one gamete. Therefore, in meiosis we would expect an approximately equal number of nullisomic and disomic gametes to arise. An apparently normal conception could result from the rescue of a nullisomic gamete by fertilization of a gamete with UPD for the missing chromosome.[6,46] Alternatively, fetuses with three of the same chromosomes could lose one of them, denoted as "trisomy rescue." If a fetus inherits two maternal chromosomes 15 and one paternal chromosome 15 and it loses the paternal chromosome, maternal UPD would result.

Not all chromosomes have been identified as having imprinted genes. For example, chromosomes 13 and 21 do not demonstrate any imprinting effects, and there are many chromosomes for which it is unknown whether an effect occurs. However, in addition to chromosome 15, UPD of several other chromosomes demonstrates a phenotypic effect. Only a small number of cases of Beckwith-Wiedemann syndrome are due to the inheritance of both copies of paternal chromosome 11. However, 50% of patients with this syndrome have an epigenetic mutation resulting in the loss of imprinting of a transcribed program (KCNQ1OT1).[46,48] Some cases of Russell-Silver syndrome are due to UPD 7, and some cases of transient neonatal diabetes are due to UPD 6. Additionally, UPD for chromosome 14 (both maternal and paternal) has been associated with developmental delay. Because of the many nonspecific phenotypic features associated with this disorder, it is often misdiagnosed. In some of these syndromes some specific genes have been implicated as being imprinted, but in several cases the causative genes are still not known.

TRINUCLEOTIDE REPEAT EXPANSIONS

A number of disorders, such as fragile X syndrome, Huntington disease, and myotonic dystrophy, have been characterized as having an underlying defect caused by the expansion of a repeated trinucleotide sequence within the relevant gene. All these disorders have an unusual and nontraditional mendelian type of inheritance. For example, although myotonic dystrophy was known to be inherited as an autosomal dominant disorder, increasing severity could be seen in successive generations. The disorder could be anticipated in affected individuals. After the analysis of the X-linked fragile X syndrome, Hagerman and colleagues postulated several findings that appeared to be a paradox, given the standard X-linked recessive disorder. These findings included two postulates: The probability of offspring with mental retardation is increased by the number of generations through which the mutation has passed, and the probability of offspring with mental retardation is higher for both the sons and daughters of affected women or women with affected sons.

The trinucleotide repeat expansion provides a rationale for this phenomenon and is discussed in greater detail later.

In addition, some of the genes involving mutations of trinucleotide repeats have been shown to be remarkably unstable because they are inherited from generation to generation. Although the inheritance pattern may be predictable, the prediction of the phenotypic expression is extremely complex in such cases. For example, there are documented cases of contraction of the CTG trinucleotide repeat numbers in myotonic dystrophy during transmission from affected parents to their children. In this particular disease, contraction is more likely to occur if the father is the affected parent.

In recent years over 16 disorders involving expansions of trinucleotide repeats (or dynamic mutations) have been reported. They can be in the coding region: 5' to the coding region or 3' to the coding region. Fragile X syndrome involves the expansion of a trinucleotide repeat in the 5' noncoding region. An expansion here is a mutation with a loss of function, leading to the deficient production of the FMR-1 protein. Huntington disease is an autosomal dominant disorder with a CAG expansion (coding for a polyglutamine tract) in the coding region of the gene. This expansion leads to a gain in function, and the phenotype is due to the production of a gene with a new deleterious function. With these expansions, the increase in severity and the age of ascertainment decrease with the expansion of the repeats. Many of these repeats will expand in successive generations, depending on the affected parent and the disorder, leading to more severely affected individuals in each generation.

DNA Diagnosis

Many genetic diseases were previously diagnosed through an assay of the gene product (protein) or through the detection of secondary effects or clinical symptoms (e.g., intestinal enzyme levels in CF or the sonographic detection of polycystic kidneys). If the genetic locus involved in a single gene defect has been at least partially characterized, the inheritance of the genetic defect can be followed at the DNA level. Because the genomic DNA is identical in every somatic cell, the diagnosis can be made using any available tissue, eliminating the need for the active expression of the gene product in the sampled tissue or at the onset of physiologic abnormalities.

DNA diagnosis relies on the detection of sequence variation among individuals. If the sequence of nucleotides from 10 unrelated individuals is analyzed, a variation in the nucleotide sequence is encountered in approximately 1 of every 200 bp of DNA. Most sequence variation is present within those stretches of nonfunctional DNA that are interspersed with genes. (A gene is defined as a transcription unit capable of expression in the form of an RNA transcript.) Although this type of sequence variation is of no consequence to the individual, it has many uses in the identification of individuals and the single gene defects they may carry. In DNA diagnosis, such DNA polymorphism can be used as a marker if it is known to be genetically linked to a disease locus.

The principle of linked markers was initially applied to disease diagnosis with the use of protein markers. An early example of this principle is myotonic dystrophy, an autosomal dominant disease that demonstrates genetic linkage to the blood group factor *secretor*. Although the two gene loci coding for these properties are functionally completely unrelated, allelic forms of the genes segregate together within a family, presumably as a result of physical linkage within the genome. More recently, these studies have used the sequence variation of nonfunctional DNA.

The use of polymorphic DNA markers that are physically linked but functionally unrelated to a disease locus is called "linkage analysis," or "indirect diagnosis." This approach is versatile because less knowledge of the disease gene is required and the pool of potentially useful markers may be quite large. (Because the polymorphic variation is random, many markers are not informative in a given family.) However, it is inherently less accurate than a direct diagnosis because the linkage pattern may be altered through genetic recombination. In addition, it is labor intensive because the linkage pattern for each family must be independently ascertained.

However, it is important to note that sequence variation (i.e., polymorphism) is still very valuable in genetics. In addition to linkage analysis, these polymorphic markers can be used for UPD studies, analysis of the origin of non disjunction, identity analysis for both forensic and twin studies, chimerism analysis in bone marrow transplantation, and cancer studies on the loss of heterozygosity.

However, with the proliferation of molecular genetic analysis and the completion of the sequencing of the human genome, the vast majority of genetic diagnoses are now performed by direct diagnosis (i.e., mutation analysis) of a given gene. Over 4000 genetic diseases have been postulated, but there are only a limited number in which the DNA sequence of at least part of a gene is available. Clinical or research DNA diagnosis is performed for over 1000 diseases, about 700 of which are clinical tests and approximately 300 are still considered only research. These numbers have been considerably increased over the past several years.

The causes of the mutations that result in genetic diseases are sequence variations within functional genes. A mutation within a gene may be innocuous (in which case it is useful as a polymorphic marker) or, by having a detrimental effect on the function of the gene product, the basis of genetic disease. When a deleterious mutation can be identified on the molecular level, genetic disease can be directly diagnosed. This approach requires knowledge of the nucleotide sequence of a disease gene. The mutations underlying genetic disease may be relatively disease specific, as in sickle cell anemia, in which most individuals have a single amino acid alteration (a single base change within codon 6 replaces glutamic acid with valine). This situation is more the exception than the rule, and in most genetic diseases the mutations are heterogeneous and may be dispersed throughout the gene sequence. CF is a prime example of a genetic disease with marked heterogeneity. Since the identification of the CF gene in 1989, the isolation and nucleotide sequencing of CF transmembrane regulator genes from patients with CF have led to the delineation of more than 1000 different mutations worldwide. Linkage analysis can be one approach for CF families with rare and undefined mutations; however, with the delineation of the gene sequence, DNA sequencing is the most frequently used. Examples of the prenatal diagnosis of CF in which both direct mutation and linkage analyses are used are shown in Figure 7-15.

APPROACH TO DIAGNOSIS

The primary methodologies used in DNA diagnosis are *Southern blot analysis* and *polymerase chain reaction* (PCR). PCR was introduced in 1986 and quickly became the state of the art in molecular diagnosis. Southern blot analysis and PCR are often used together for molecular diagnosis, but PCR has become the major diagnostic approach for most genetic disorders.

Southern blot analysis uses a class of bacterial enzymes called restriction endonucleases (Fig. 7-16). Each "restriction enzyme" has the ability to recognize a specific DNA sequence (four to eight nucleotides in length) and cut double-stranded DNA at that position. Normally, the host organism uses this ability to protect itself from invasion by foreign organisms, but in the test tube it is a powerful mechanism for manipulating DNA from any source. Because digestion by restriction enzymes is sequence specific, DNA from any individual can be cut into a discrete series of fragments. The resulting fragments are quite similar among individuals, but whenever sequence variation affects the recognition sequence of the applicable enzyme, the size of one or more restriction fragments is altered. This process is known as restriction fragment length polymorphism (RFLP). An RFLP pattern that is useful in identifying an allele is an informative one, and the RFLP patterns demonstrated to be linked on a chromosome are called *haplotypes.*

Cloned DNA probes are used to analyze the large population of the DNA fragments produced. A cloned probe is a specific, discrete fragment of DNA that has been isolated and propagated. The probe is used to visualize a small subset of the large number of fragments present in digested genomic DNA. Specifically, a probe anneals to those fragments that contain sequence homology to the probe. Artificially synthesized short segments of nucleic acids (oligonucleotides) may also be used as probes (see discussion later).

In standard Southern blot analysis, gel electrophoresis is used to fractionate the DNA fragments through an electric field on the basis of size, thus dispersing the fragments in a predictable pattern. The DNA fragments are then immobilized on a firm support (a hybridization membrane). To detect the fragments of interest, a "tagged" DNA probe is applied to the membrane. Through complementary base pairing (hybridization), the probe adheres only to the homologous fragments in the genomic DNA. Because the DNA fragments are invisible to the naked eye, a tag is necessary to see where hybridization has occurred.

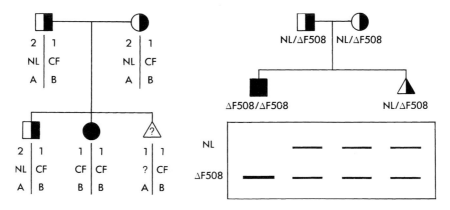

FIGURE 7-15. DNA diagnosis of cystic fibrosis. **A,** Linkage analysis with the use of two flanking DNA probes "1,2" and "A,B." The first (carrier) and second (affected) offspring have inherited the parental haplotypes. In the current pregnancy, there has been a recombination between the two probes ("1" is no longer linked to "B"); therefore, this analysis is not useful in predicting the status of the fetus. **B,** Direct diagnosis with the use of the ΔF508 mutation. Both parents are carriers of the ΔF508 mutation, and the affected offspring is homozygous for the mutation. The fetus also is a carrier. The results of polymerase chain reaction analysis are illustrated below the pedigree, where the 3-bp difference in size between the two alleles allows amplification products to be resolved by gel electrophoresis. ○, female; □, male; ●, ■, affected.

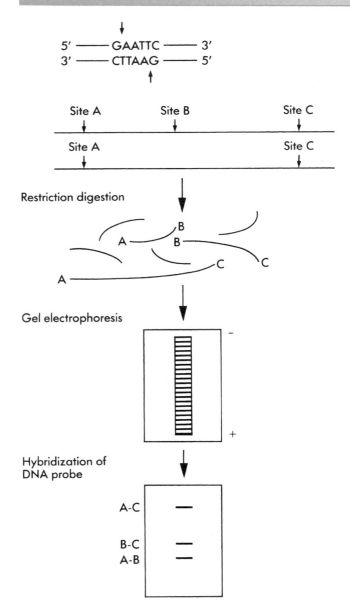

FIGURE 7-16. Restriction endonuclease digestion and Southern blot hybridization. **A,** Recognition sequence for the restriction endonuclease Eco RI. **B,** Illustration of restriction site polymorphism, where "Site B" is missing from the lower allele. **C,** DNA fragments generated by enzyme digestion of genomic DNA. **D,** Gel electrophoresis. **E,** Result of hybridization with a DNA probe homologous to region A-B-C.

Although the tag has traditionally been a radioactive compound, nonradioactive enzymatic tags are becoming increasingly useful.

The second major technological advance in DNA diagnosis has been PCR analysis (Fig. 7-17). PCR allows the physical amplification of a defined segment of DNA without the need to isolate that segment from the remainder of the genomic DNA. This method provides an efficient way of generating sufficient quantities of DNA from an individual for DNA diagnosis. Although this approach is extremely powerful, it requires at least the partial determination of the nucleotide sequence of

interest by DNA sequencing. Amplification is achieved through the use of two single-stranded oligonucleotide primers (20 to 30 nucleotides in length) that are homologous to the segment of interest and opposite in polarity with respect to the target sequence. Therefore, the primers define the boundaries of the segment of DNA to be amplified because they direct DNA synthesis across the region of interest in opposite directions.

The basic steps in the PCR process are (1) *denaturation* of the DNA in the reaction, thus converting the DNA duplex to single strands; (2) *priming* by hybridization of the oligonucleotide primers to the target sequence; and (3) *strand synthesis* with DNA polymerase, beginning at each primer and using the denatured target DNA as a template. Amplification proceeds in a manner similar to DNA replication, except that only a discrete segment of genomic DNA is involved. The efficiency of this reaction allows the routine amplification of fragments ranging from 50 to more than 2000 bp in length. The amplification products of a given target DNA are identical in length and sequence. Thus, the PCR amplification of DNA from an individual who is heterozygous for a small deletion falling within the boundaries of the target yields two discrete amplification products that correspond to the normal and deleted alleles.

Repeated rounds of amplification result in the creation of more than 1 million copies of the target sequence. This process has been automated through the use of machines designed especially for this purpose and the availability of heat-stable DNA polymerase that survives multiple rounds of temperature-driven DNA denaturation. PCR is not intrinsically a method of DNA diagnosis but an elegant, efficient way to obtain sufficient amounts of DNA for further analysis. The amplified DNA can be digested with restriction enzymes and used for Southern blot analysis (or a modification of that technique), or the amplification product can be visualized directly after gel electrophoresis in most applications, many times after cutting with an appropriate restriction enzyme.[24]

Presently, the vast majority of genetic diagnoses involve the use of PCR. However, as explained later, PCR is only a starting point for most diagnostic work. The involvement of PCR in genetic diagnosis is important for a variety of reasons.

1. Only a small amount of tissue (DNA) is needed, such as that obtained from a hair bulb or cheek swab.

2. PCR is especially effective for indirect analysis with the use of polymorphic markers.

3. Although many initial studies used PCR to amplify probes for Southern blot analysis or amplify segments for direct mutation analysis with the restriction enzyme method, most investigators use PCR to amplify segments for allele-specific oligonucleotides (ASOs) or DNA sequencing.

With DNA sequencing for an increasing number of genes and specific mutations, many diagnostic analyses

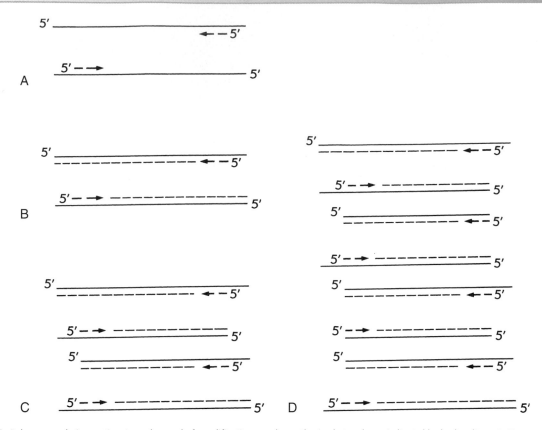

FIGURE 7-17. Polymerase chain reaction. In each round of amplification, newly synthesized strands are indicated by broken lines. **A,** Denatured DNA duplex showing hybridization of oligonucleotide primers. **B,** First-round synthesis of complementary strands, producing two DNA duplexes from the original one. **C,** Products of the second round of amplification. **D,** Products of the third round of amplification.

involve both ASO and direct DNA sequencing. ASO analysis involves the amplification of a DNA segment of the gene in question and hybridization with a specific oligonucleotide, which may contain a normal (wild-type) sequence or a mutation. The hybridization is so precise that it will not occur if there is even one base change. While this procedure was originally used as dot blot hybridization, it is now most frequently used in conjunction with DNA sequencing instru-mentation. Therefore, it can be used to detect an individual carrier of a normal and a mutant allele. Also, because of the proliferation of identified sequences and mutations, DNA sequencing is used more frequently for mutation analysis. These studies are used for many disorders, including *connexin 26* analysis for deafness, Rett syndrome, and prion diseases.

APPLICATIONS: DIAGNOSIS OF FRAGILE X SYNDROME

The utility of DNA molecular technology in the diagnosis of genetic diseases is strikingly apparent when considering the advances made in the diagnosis of fragile X syndrome. This syndrome is the most common inherited cause of mental retardation, with an incidence of approximately 1 in 1200 among the male population and 1 in 2500 among the female population. In addition to mental retardation and behavioral problems,

men affected with fragile X syndrome often have characteristic physical features, including a long face with prominent forehead and prognathia, large ears, and macro-orchidism. Affected women generally have a similar but milder phenotypic expression of facial characteristics and a developmental handicap.[11] Before the underlying genetic defect leading to fragile X syndrome was elucidated, diagnosis depended on the expression of a fragile site on the long arm of the X chromosome at Xq27.3 in cells cultured under conditions of folate deprivation. However, diagnostic accuracy was limited by the variable expression of the fragile site (generally less than 50% in affected individuals and even more unpredictable in individual carriers).

Localization and isolation of the gene causing fragile X syndrome dramatically reduced the issues related to diagnostic uncertainty. As explained above, it is one of the characterized genetic diseases (along with Huntington disease and myotonic dystrophy) that have an underlying defect caused by the expansion of a repeated trinucleotide sequence within or proximal to the relevant gene (previously discussed). These disorders show expansions in the 5′ untranslated region, in the 3′ untranslated region, and within the gene itself. The expansion increases in successive generations, leading to earlier detection and, in some cases, more severe phenotypic consequences. In fragile X syndrome, the mutation involves the expansion of the nucleotide sequence CGG, near the 5′ untranslated end of the *FMR1* gene, to more than 200 repeats in affected individuals. Normal individuals carry approximately 6 to 50 CGG repeats, whereas the premutation state ranges from 50 to 200 repeats. The normal allele range and the premutation range overlap somewhat, but most normal alleles constitute less than 50 repeats, with an average of 29 to 30. Men and women carrying a premutation are unaffected, but there is a disparate risk to their offspring. A premutation can increase to a full expansion mutation *only* after transmission through female meiosis. Therefore, a male premutation carrier can have only unaffected daughters with premutations, but they are at risk of transmitting an expanded mutation to their offspring. The larger the size of the premutation in a woman, the greater the risk of full mutation in her children.[11] In recent years some studies have shown that premutation carriers may not be clinically uninvolved, presenting with three different clinical disorders. They may present with mild cognitive/behavioral deficits, premature ovarian failure, or tremor/ataxia associated with fragile X syndrome.[12]

Expansion to the full mutation of more than 200 CGG repeats is almost always associated with methylation of the promoter region of the gene and subsequent gene inactivation. Although it is clear that gene inactivation by methylation is an important mechanism in the expression of the fragile X phenotype, the effects are not always predictable, especially in women. However, the methylation status and the size of the trinucleotide repeat of the *FMR1* gene form the basis for the accurate diagnosis of the genotype of individuals at risk of being carriers or being affected.

The techniques applicable to the molecular diagnosis of fragile X syndrome are PCR and Southern blot

analyses. Each one has intrinsic advantages and disadvantages. PCR analysis is used to amplify a fragment of DNA encompassing the repeat region. The size of the PCR-amplified DNA gives a close approximation of the number of CGG repeats in an allele of a given individual. PCR analysis is extremely accurate in sizing alleles in the normal, premutation, and borderline expansion ranges. Very large mutations involving high numbers of repeats are not as amenable to PCR amplification and may go undetected in PCR assays. In addition, rare cases of fragile X syndrome have been identified with a microdeletion in the Xq27.3 region, which precludes PCR amplification. Southern blot analysis is the tool of choice to demonstrate the presence of full mutations, and it also has the advantage of providing simultaneous assessment of the methylation status. The size of the repeat and the methylation status of the *FMR1* allele can be determined by using a methylation-sensitive restriction endonuclease that is unable to cleave methylated sites. The disadvantages of Southern blot analysis include the need for larger quantities of genomic DNA, more labor-intensive procedures, and the production of only an approximate, relative determination of allele size rather than a more precise estimate of the number of CGG repeats. An example of *FMR1* diagnosis is shown in Figure 7-18. The American College of Medical Genetics has established guidelines for appropriate referrals for the diagnostic testing of individuals and families that may be at risk for fragile X syndrome.[33]

The number of genetic diseases for which DNA diagnosis is feasible continues to grow. Early on much of the effort in the development of these capabilities focused on severe diseases of childhood, such as CF and Tay-Sachs disease. There the emphasis has been on prenatal testing for families wishing to avoid the

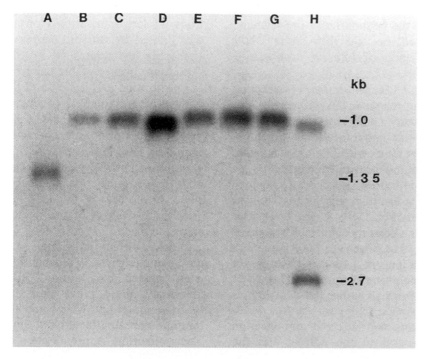

FIGURE 7-18. Molecular diagnosis of premutation carrier status in an affected female patient with fragile X syndrome and Southern blot analysis of CGG repeats in genomic DNA digested by PST-1 and hybridized with probe PX6. Lanes B through G are results from normal men with unexpanded *FMR1* alleles about 1 kb in size. Lane A is DNA from a man with an *FMR1* premutation expanded to 1.35 kb, with approximately 150 CGG repeats. Lane H is the DNA pattern from an affected woman with one normal allele of approximately 1 kb and a second allele of 2.7 kb, representing a full mutation with more than 600 CGG repeats.

birth of an affected child. DNA testing for many adult-onset diseases is either available or under development. Huntington disease is the prototype of an adult-onset disease for which presymptomatic DNA diagnosis is available, but the resulting information cannot be used to alter the course of the disease. In this situation, many at-risk individuals decline DNA testing. As the testing for more common conditions with genetic susceptibility factors becomes available, it is important to establish how the resulting information can be used and involve the patient in the decision-making process.

MULTIFACTORIAL DISORDERS

Many of the more common birth defects, such as cleft lip and palate or spina bifida, cannot be explained on the basis of a mendelian pattern of inheritance, yet a familial tendency or liability has been recognized in their occurrence. Some medical problems in adults, such as certain forms of cancer, hypertension, and diabetes mellitus, also belong to this category of increased familial risk. Although some specific forms of these disorders might be due to single gene defects (e.g., cancer), they are most often thought to result from a combination of additive genetic factors that lead to an increased liability or threshold for expression and environmental factors that trigger manifestations of the disorder in development. This combination of multiple gene liability and extrinsic environmental interaction is called *multifactorial inheritance*. Genetic traits that result from the additive effect of many genes are called *polygenic traits*. These terms are often used interchangeably in practice. Polygenic traits are generally quantitative rather than qualitative and follow a normal (gaussian) distribution in the population. Common examples are height and blood pressure.

The evidence that genetic factors are important in common diseases and birth defects is derived from epidemiologic studies that compare the frequency of disease among related individuals with that among the population at large. Some of the evidence for a genetic influence can be summarized.

1. Certain disorders occur more frequently among certain ethnic groups or those with particular racial backgrounds, such as neural tube defects in Ireland and northern India.

2. There is a higher frequency of specific birth defects among the relatives of affected individuals, and this frequency is proportional to the degree of relatedness. For example, the percentage of siblings of an individual with cleft lip with or without cleft palate who are similarly affected is 4.1% (first-degree relative), of nieces and nephews 0.8% (second-degree relative), and of first cousins 0.3% (third-degree relative).

3. The most convincing evidence of the genetic basis for multifactorial inheritance comes from twin studies. If a disorder is inherited in a mendelian fashion, there will be 100%

concordance between monozygotic twins, who are genetically identical. Dizygotic twins, who share approximately half their genes, are expected to be 50% concordant. If a trait is multifactorial with a significant genetic component, there is likely to be a high degree of concordance for identical twins (but less than 100%) and a much higher degree of concordance than that for nonidentical twins. For example, the concordance for cleft lip and palate between monozygotic twins is 40%, whereas that between dizygotic twins is only 4%—still significantly higher than between second- or third-degree relatives.

The observations with regard to multifactorial genetic traits have led to the threshold model of genetic liability. This model assumes that there is a continuous distribution of genetic risk for a specific disorder and that affected individuals fall to the extreme right of the genetic liability (Fig. 7-19). First-degree relatives who share only half of their genes also have a threshold of genetic risk that falls to the right of the general population but not as extreme as the displacement in affected individuals. As the degree of relationship to the affected individual decreases, the genetic liability for the relative begins to approach the average liability for the general population.

The prediction of recurrence risks for multifactorial genetic disorders with the use of the threshold model is based on empirical data and cannot be done specifically, as in mendelian disorders. However, there are general guidelines with regard to these disorders and recurrence risks.

1. Recurrence risks represent an average risk, and they vary among family members. The exact risk cannot be given for any specific family member,

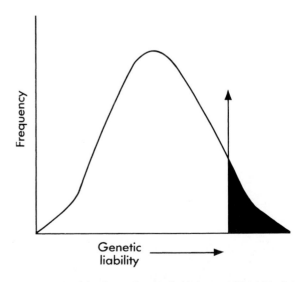

FIGURE 7-19. Model of genetic threshold for multifactorial disease. Liability for a particular trait follows a normal distribution, but abnormal classes or affected individuals exceed the threshold.

but it decreases greatly with a decrease in the degree of relationship.

2. The risk within the family increases with the number of affected family members. For example, if one sibling has cleft lip with or without cleft palate, the risk of recurrence in another sibling is 4%; if two siblings are affected, the risk rises to 10%.

3. The risk increases with the severity of the malformation or the disease. The recurrence risk for a sibling with unilateral cleft lip without cleft palate is 2.5%, but it rises to 6% if the defect is bilateral with cleft palate.

4. When a multifactorial disorder is found more often in one sex than the other, the offspring of the less affected sex are at higher risk. For example, congenital pyloric stenosis occurs five times more frequently in men than women. The threshold of genetic liability for girls is therefore higher than that for boys, and a girl who is affected is expected to have more genes or a greater genetic predilection to transmit it to her offspring. Therefore, the risk for a son of an affected woman with pyloric stenosis is 19.4%, and that for a daughter is 7.3%. Conversely, the risk for a son of an affected man is only 5.5% and for a daughter 2.4%.

One of the major difficulties in predicting and understanding recurrence risks for multifactorial genetic disorders is the role of environmental factors (see Chapter 12). The initial problem of identifying individuals with the genetic predilection is compounded by the lack of knowledge and understanding about the environmental components that trigger the developmental expression of birth defects or disease states. Current and future research on genetic diseases will focus first on the identification of genes that concomitantly create threshold susceptibility and second on the identification and alteration of the environmental conditions that may lead to expression.[45] Complex disorders such as asthma, hypertension, obesity, cancer, and heart disease are still poorly understood, but because of their greater frequency they are now increasingly studied. These studies are beginning to identify candidate genes and delineate the genetics of the disorders.[32,49] It is hoped that future elucidation of the genes involved in these disorders will lead to new treatments.

ENVIRONMENTAL DISORDERS

The environmental causes of birth defects fall into three major categories: congenital infections, drug and chemical exposures, and physical agents, such as radiation. Approximately 7% of all congenital malformations are believed to be the result of environmental factors. The degree to which an infant is affected by prenatal toxic exposure depends on two major factors: the stage of embryonic or fetal development at which the exposure occurs and, as discussed previously, the genetic susceptibility of the mother and fetus to the external toxic factor (see Chapter 12).

During the period of gametogenesis, environmental exposure to toxic agents is probably lethal to these cells. There have been no studies in which preconceptional drug use has been shown to produce a statistically significant teratogenic effect on subsequent pregnancies. It is thought that the egg may be more vulnerable as a receptacle for toxic effects because of its extensive cytoplasmic as well as nuclear contribution to early embryonic development. In contrast, the contribution of sperm is limited to nuclear genetic information.

An "all-or-nothing" effect on cells resulting from potentially lethal environmental damage to the gamete probably extends from preconception through the post-conceptional period to the time of primitive streak formation, about 3 weeks into human development. Exposure during this time most likely results in the death of the embryo rather than the survival of the fetus with major malformations.

The teratogenic effects of environmental agents are the most severe during the subsequent period of development: 4 to 9 weeks of gestation. Drugs for which a cause/effect relationship exists between exposure during this stage of gestation and major malformations include thalidomide, hydantoins, trimethadione, warfarin, aminopterin, ethanol, valproic acid, retinoic acid, and methyl mercury (resulting in Minamata disease) (see Chapter 12). Although high levels of androgens have been implicated as potentially masculinizing agents in the developing female embryo, only the effects of diethylstilbestrol on fetal development have been well documented. In contrast, birth control pills are thought to be unlikely teratogens. Infectious agents recognized as teratogens in the developing embryo include rubella, cytomegalovirus, herpes simplex virus types 1 and 2, toxoplasmosis, equine encephalitis virus, and syphilis. Varicella is considered a potential teratogen. Viral infections before 9 weeks of gestation generally result in widespread damage to multiple organ systems (see Chapters 22 and 37). Extremely high levels of radiation exposure during this period appear to have a more limited effect, that of microcephaly. After 9 weeks of gestation, the effects of teratogenic agents are more likely to be manifested as organ damage or growth disturbance than malformation. For each organ system, there is a critical period of development in which malformation may result from teratogenic interference. Table 7-1 lists the critical time frames for some of the more common congenital malformations.

Questions about teratogenic risks during pregnancy are always extremely difficult to answer. For most drugs the information about their safety or the possibility of low-level teratogenic effects has not been established in human beings, and extrapolation from animal studies may lead to erroneous conclusions (see Chapter 10). Mouse and rat embryos are relatively insensitive to thalidomide, but it is the most notorious of the recognized human teratogens and also severely affects monkey

TABLE 7-1. Time Frame for Development of Common Congenital Malformations

SITE OF MALFORMATION	MALFORMATION	TIME OF DEVELOPMENT
Face	Cleft lip	5-7 wk
	Posterior cleft palate	8-12 wk
Gastrointestinal tract	Esophageal atresia and tracheoesophageal fistula	4 wk
	Rectal atresia (with fistula)	6 wk
	Malrotation	10 wk
	Omphalocele	10 wk
	Duodenal atresia	7-8 wk
Central nervous system	Anencephaly	3-4 wk
	Meningomyelocele	4 wk
Cardiovascular system	Transposition of great vessels	5 wk
	Ventricular septal defect	5-6 wk
Genitourinary system	Agenesis of the kidney	30 d
	Extroversion of the bladder	4 wk
	Bicornuate uterus	10 wk
	Retained testis (cryptorchidism)	36-40 wk
	Hypospadias	12 wk
Limb	Aplasia of the radius	38 d
	Syndactyly	6 wk

and rabbit embryos. Furthermore, case reports of exposure in humans are difficult to interpret because of their limited number and the wide variation in timing and the amount of exposure. More information is available on the effect of radiation exposure in humans because of the studies performed on the survivors of the atomic bomb explosions in Japan and their descendants and on the survivors of the nuclear accident at Chernobyl. Exposure of 10 rad or less to the mother is considered a reasonable upper limit for defining low risk to the fetus. Only under extremely unusual circumstances would diagnostic medical x-ray exposure exceed this limit. By comparison, the level of natural background radiation varies from 80 to 1000 mrad per year, depending on location, and a single chest x-ray would result in an exposure of approximately 100 to 200 mrad.

Counseling parents about birth defects with a suspected environmental cause must be a cautious undertaking. Parental guilt generated by such a suspected association can be overwhelming, and raising this issue may lead to questions of legal liability. However, if causality by an environmental agent can be established, parents may be reassured about future pregnancies, particularly if maternal immunity to a viral agent can be demonstrated or a certain drug can be avoided. Parents should be counseled as objectively as possible about environmental toxic exposure during pregnancy, presenting the most current information about the agent and all available options, including prenatal evaluation. The parents' decision to terminate a pregnancy must be reached on the basis of an honest presentation and interpretation of risk.[39]

GENETIC EVALUATION AND COUNSELING

The evaluation plan to ascertain a possible genetic cause in an infant with congenital anomalies varies somewhat, depending on the child's age and condition. Obviously, evaluating a fetal death is more difficult than examining a living child. Nevertheless, vigorous efforts should be made to evaluate the fetus, particularly if it had had suspected genetic abnormalities. One of the most frustrating problems for health care providers and families alike in attempting to assess the genetic risks for future pregnancies is the lack of information about the nature of abnormalities and the lack of etiologic evidence for a previous pregnancy loss. Couples coping with the death of a newborn with severe anomalies may refuse an autopsy and internal examination only to find later that such information would have been helpful in defining the genetic risks for future pregnancies and for other family members. One of the roles of the genetic counselor in this situation is to provide psychological support for the couple while explaining the need for them to obtain answers that they will find valuable once their intense grief has subsided.

An organized plan for the evaluation of a fetus or child with suspected genetic disorders must always include a detailed family history, including pedigree and pregnancy history. This information provides important clues in separating genetic disorders from nongenetic causes. The minimum history should include the age, sex, and present health of all first-degree (parents and siblings) and second-degree (aunts, uncles, and grandparents) relatives. Questions about previous stillborns or spontaneous abortions should always be asked because this valuable information is rarely volunteered. Ethnic background, as well as the possibility of consanguinity, should be elicited. The pregnancy history, including any maternal disease such as diabetes or epilepsy; maternal weight gain; fetal activity in utero; a detailed description of temporary maternal illness, particularly viral infections; and drug exposure, both over the counter and prescription, should be sought.

The physical examination of the fetus or child should be as extensive and detailed as possible, with particular attention devoted to minor structural deviations (see Chapters 26 and 28). Careful measurements of body proportions and facial features should be collected for comparison with the standard measures for age and sex. Dermatoglyphic characteristics and ophthalmologic examinations may provide useful diagnostic clues. Radiologic studies, including bone films, computed tomographic scans, and sonograms, should be used extensively for the examination of possible internal malformations. Laboratory tests are essential and should include cytogenetic studies, including FISH analysis; metabolic screening to rule out inborn errors of metabolism; and DNA studies, as appropriate. In case of perinatal death, the cells should be frozen for future evaluation as different and newer tests become available. Finally, photographs as well as standard x-ray films should be taken as part of a permanent file to provide a basis for the comparison of progressive changes in the living child or to form the basis for the reevaluation of unknown disorders as new syndromes and diseases are delineated.

Although the foregoing aspects of genetic evaluation are generally attainable from a living child, it is often difficult to obtain similar evaluations of a fetus or stillborn. Unfortunately, such evaluations are not standard practice in many hospital pathology departments, and it is important to establish with the pathologist in advance the precise studies that may be informative for genetic assessment.

Counseling the parents of a child with a genetic disorder or birth defect should be tempered by the recognition of the parents' major emotional responses of anger, grief, and guilt. Because individual genetic diseases are so rare and 95% of them occur with no family history, denial, frustration, and a sense of isolation are the common reactions of parents and may impede their understanding of the nature of the disorder (see Chapter 32).

The course of genetic counseling after the birth of an affected child generally consists of two phases: first, an information-gathering stage focused on the nature of the problem and the prognosis for the child, and second, consideration of the genetic risks for future pregnancies or for other family members. If the couple anticipates future pregnancies, a major issue is whether prenatal diagnosis is possible and, if so, the diagnostic procedures available and the stage of the pregnancy. The time interval between the two phases of genetic counseling may be considerable for some couples, and emotional trauma may preclude their clear understanding of genetic issues, which is often difficult for even the most scientifically sophisticated parents. For these reasons it is important that any counseling discussions be followed up by written explanations from the geneticist, reviewing and re-emphasizing the various points of concern.[15]

PRENATAL GENETIC DIAGNOSIS

Prenatal genetic evaluations fall into two general categories: generalized screening tests to identify pregnancies at risk and specialized diagnostic tests to recognize a specific genetic risk to the fetus. Generalized screening can determine those couples with an increased risk for abnormality before the birth of an affected child. It is limited to a few genetic diseases associated with particular ethnic backgrounds, including screening for the carrier state of Tay-Sachs and Canavan diseases in individuals of Eastern European (Ashkenazi) Jewish heritage, for β-thalassemia in those of Mediterranean ancestry (Italians, Greeks, Sephardic Jews), for α-thalassemia in Chinese and Southeast Asian peoples, and for sickle cell trait and other hemoglobinopathies in blacks. As more information about the nature of common genetic diseases is learned, screening for the carrier state will undoubtedly increase. The identification of the most common mutations in CF (see previous discussion) indicates that over 95% of the carriers for this disorder in those of Northern European or Ashkenazi ancestry and at least 90% in other populations can be identified. Screening for CF is currently recommended by both the American College of Medical Genetics and the American College of Obstetricians and Gynecologists not only for those with a family history of the disorder but also for more widespread screening programs in individuals that are Caucasian or have Ashkenazi Jewish ancestry. Although this screening has not been recommended in other populations, it has been suggested that the availability of screening be discussed with all individuals.[34]

Another prenatal test that falls into the category of general screening is the determination of maternal serum α-*fetoprotein* performed at 15 to 20 weeks of gestation. This inexpensive test to measure the amount of α-fetoprotein traversing from the fetal circulation into the maternal bloodstream is unique in that both the high and low levels of α-fetoprotein correlate with an increased risk for specific birth defects.

Elevations in maternal serum α-fetoprotein identify nearly 100% of the fetuses with anencephaly, 70% to 85% with open spina bifida, and 70% with ventral wall defects as well as a diverse group of miscellaneous fetal anomalies (e.g., urogenital malformations) that affect amniotic fluid volume or fetal circulation and placental function. In addition to screening for fetal abnormalities, elevations in maternal serum α-fetoprotein are predictive of poor pregnancy outcome and complications in the third trimester, including increased risks for miscarriage, fetal death, stillbirth, prematurity, intrauterine growth restriction, and preeclampsia.

Decreased levels of α-fetoprotein interpreted in conjunction with maternal age were initially able to identify a cohort of pregnancies at an increased risk for Down syndrome—a particularly valuable association—because 80% to 85% of babies with Down syndrome are born to women younger than age 35. Trisomies 13 and 18 fetuses are also found with reduced amounts of α-fetoprotein.

When maternal age and maternal serum α-fetoprotein are used, the detection rate in women younger than 35 is approximately equal to that when only the age of women older than 35 is considered. At least two or three other maternal serum tests are currently used in conjunction with α-fetoprotein for predictive Down syndrome screening. One of them, *unconjugated estriol* (uE$_3$), is a product of fetal adrenal gland and fetal liver biosynthesis, with placental modification before entering the maternal circulation. Levels of uE$_3$ that fall below the normal range suggest an increased risk for Down syndrome, as do low levels of α-fetoprotein. However, higher than expected levels of β-*human chorionic gonadotropin* (β-hCG) in the second trimester of pregnancy correlate with Down syndrome in the fetus. α-Fetoprotein is the least sensitive discriminator in identifying Down syndrome pregnancies, with a sensitivity of about 15% to 20%, followed by uE$_3$, which detects about 25%. The most sensitive discriminator is β-hCG (40%).

The use of these three maternal serum tests in combination with maternal age has been adopted by centers throughout the United States and Europe. When the triple screen was prospectively applied to a population of women aged 35 or older, 89% of the cases of Down syndrome were identified by using a cutoff for amniocentesis of 1:200. These results led to the suggestion that universal referral for amniocentesis because of maternal age can be modified by maternal serum triple-screen testing to reduce unnecessary amniocentesis procedures and decrease the small risk of procedure-related pregnancy loss. This approach has been taken outside the United States, but referrals in the United States are still based on advanced maternal age or the screening findings.

An increasing number of laboratories are beginning to use a quadriplex marker screening with inhibin rather than only triple marker screening. Inhibin is produced mainly from the placenta and is part of the transforming growth factor-β superfamily. The addition of serum inhibin A to triple screening leads to the positive screening of 7% to 8% of the population and detection of up to 90% of all Down syndrome cases.[29] Although β-hCG is the most sensitive discriminator for identifying Down syndrome pregnancies, inhibin is almost as effective, with a detection rate of 37%.

In pregnancies with trisomy 18, the serum levels of all three common second-trimester markers are greatly diminished and inhibin is elevated. The specificity for trisomy 18 detection is the greatest with uE$_3$ measurement; both trisomy 18 and 45,X pregnancies can be detected, but trisomy 13 pregnancies are not predictably screened by triple marker analysis of maternal serum. This is one reason why maternal serum screening has not been accepted as a standard of care in the genetics and obstetrics communities in the United States, particularly in women older than age 35.

First-trimester screening has also been initiated and includes pregnancy-associated plasma protein A (PAPP-A), the free β subunit of hCG, and the ultrasonographic detection of nuchal translucency. PAPP-A is a homodimer from the placenta, and its function is unknown. In the first trimester, PAPP-A is decreased and free β-hCG increased in Down syndrome. When PAPP-A and β-hCG are combined with nuchal translucency detection, which measures skin thickness at the posterior neck, the initial studies indicate that the detection rates for Down syndrome are equal to those obtained with triple screening in the second trimester.[1] First-trimester screening can detect about 79% of Down syndrome cases, with a positive screening rate of 5%. The American College of Obstetrics and Gynecology has stated that first-trimester screening can be offered only if appropriate ultrasound training and quality monitoring programs are in place, comprehensive counseling is available, and access to diagnostic testing is available for cases with positive results.

Specialized prenatal diagnostic procedures are offered when there are known genetic risks. In contrast to the generalized screening tests, these procedures are individualized, require special techniques or training, and may involve procedure-related risk to the pregnancy. There are a number of generally accepted reasons for referral to genetic counseling and possible prenatal diagnosis.

1. Advanced maternal age, usually 35 or older at delivery

2. A previous fetus or child with a chromosomal abnormality or other major birth defect

3. A family history of a specific genetic disorder

4. One parent who is a known carrier for a chromosomal translocation or rearrangement, with abnormal reproductive consequences

5. A high or low maternal serum α-fetoprotein level or an abnormal triple/quadriplex screen

6. A maternal disease associated with congenital malformations

7. Parents who are known carriers of a specific genetic disorder

8. Environmental exposure during pregnancy to drugs, medications, infections, or other recognized environmental hazards

9. Known or suspected consanguinity

10. Abnormal prenatal ultrasonographic findings

Amniocentesis

Amniocentesis has become widely accepted as the standard method for determining whether a fetus is affected by a wide variety of chromosomal disorders, metabolic diseases, or disorders detected by DNA analysis. The desquamated fetal cells and amniocytes from the amnion provide sources of mitotically active cells that can be used for cytogenetic evaluation or to establish cultures for enzymatic determinations or DNA analysis. Amniotic fluid itself can be used for α-fetoprotein analysis, and acetylcholinesterase electrophoresis can be used to detect open neural tube defects in pregnant women with either a family history of such defects or elevations of maternal serum α-fetoprotein. Enzyme analysis and metabolite measurements of amniotic fluid have provided diagnostic information in some genetic disorders, such as defects in the urea cycle, in which abnormal levels of metabolites may be found in the amniotic fluid. DNA analysis of amniotic fluid is possible for any disorder in which a PCR-based assay is used and only small amounts of DNA are needed.

Amniocentesis is traditionally performed at 16 to 18 weeks of gestation with the use of ultrasonographic guidance. Approximately 20 to 30 mL of amniotic fluid is aspirated through a 20- to 22-gauge spinal needle into a sterile syringe. The first few milliliters of fluid are withdrawn in a separate syringe and discarded before aspiration of the sample for diagnosis. This procedure is performed to preclude the contamination of the amniotic fluid cultures with maternal skin cells, which may lead to discrepant cytogenetic analysis. At this stage of pregnancy, the amniotic fluid volume of the uterus is rapidly replenished by the active urine output of the fetal kidneys. Amniocentesis is generally successful in greater than 95% of cases, with only one needle insertion necessary if performed by an experienced physician. Similarly, the success rate for establishing cell cultures from amniotic fluid cells is expected to be greater than 99%, although there may be wide variation in the rate of growth because of variation in the number of viable cells in the sample and the types of cells obtained. Cytogenetic analysis is generally completed within 7 to 12 days of the procedure.

The risk of pregnancy loss attributed to amniocentesis is low, probably less than 1 in 200, or 0.5% above the pregnancy losses in control studies matched for maternal age. Chorioamnionitis after amniocentesis has been reported, but the actual frequency has not been documented. A reasonable estimate of risk for this particular complication is 1 in 1000 or less. Fetal injury during amniocentesis is unlikely because of the ultrasonic guidance used for needle insertion and is usually limited to superficial scars or dimpling of the skin. Spotting or leakage of amniotic fluid for several days after the procedure has been reported, a complication that occurs in about 1 of 300 to 1 of 500 cases.[30]

The major drawback to midtrimester amniocentesis for prenatal genetic diagnosis is the late gestational age when fetal abnormalities are confirmed. The option for elective termination of an affected pregnancy is complicated by the extreme psychological trauma of the loss of a fetus whose movements are already perceived and whose size makes the pregnancy loss public knowledge. In addition, there are the physical complications of undergoing the induction of labor, followed by labor and delivery itself. For this reason, there has been a move toward earlier prenatal diagnosis by means of early amniocentesis or chorionic villus sampling (CVS).

Early amniocentesis is usually offered at 12 to 15 weeks of gestation and is performed in much the same manner as the standard amniocentesis procedure. Modifications of the technique include using only a 22-gauge spinal needle and removing 1 mL of amniotic fluid per week of gestation. Ultrasound guidance is essential for the earlier amniocentesis procedure. Despite the smaller volume of the sample obtained at this stage of gestation than that in midtrimester amniocentesis, the diagnostic turnaround time for cytogenetic analysis is comparable, possibly reflecting a larger percentage of mitotically active cells per milliliter of amniotic fluid at earlier gestational ages. In general, the complication rate for pregnancy loss after early amniocentesis at 13 to 14 weeks is similar to the midtrimester risk. There is increased difficulty in obtaining fluid before 13 weeks of gestation and a greater chance of culture failure as well as a slightly increased risk of procedure-related pregnancy loss. There have been some reports of an increased risk of membrane rupture if the procedure is performed before 13 weeks of gestation. At 12 weeks the amnion and chorion may not be fused, requiring a more vigorous technique for inserting the needle to prevent membrane "tenting," which has been estimated to occur in 5% to 10% of these early amniocentesis procedures.[30]

Chorionic Villus Sampling

The earliest prenatal diagnostic procedure routinely offered is CVS, in which a biopsy of the villi of the developing placenta is obtained at 8 to 11 weeks of gestation (usually between 9 and 10 weeks) from the last menstrual period. CVS can be performed transcervically by inserting a fine plastic catheter through the vagina and cervical os and, under ultrasonographic guidance, advancing the catheter to the edge of the developing placenta, the chorion frondosum. After the catheter is in position within the placenta, the stylet is removed, and a 20-mL syringe containing a small amount of cell culture medium is attached to the catheter. The sampling is accomplished by moving the tip of the catheter back and forth while applying suction to the syringe. Samples of chorionic villi of approximately 10 to 50 mg of wet weight are obtained, an amount more than adequate for cytogenetic, biochemical, or DNA diagnostic studies.

An alternative method for CVS is the transabdominal approach, which is particularly successful if the placenta is located in an anterofundal uterine position and inaccessible by the transcervical method. The transabdominal method involves the placement of an 18- to

19-gauge spinal needle under ultrasonographic guidance through the maternal abdominal and uterine walls and into the body of the placenta in a manner similar to that for amniocentesis. A syringe containing medium is attached to the needle, which is moved vertically as suction is applied to aspirate the villi. Slightly smaller amounts and more fragmented villi are obtained by this method.[19]

The diagnostic tests that can be performed on cultured amniotic fluid cells have been adapted for use with CVS. Cytogenetic analysis can be performed directly on the cytotrophoblastic layer of the villi, which contains many cells in active mitosis, as well as on cells cultured from the villus fragments. Cytogenetic analysis is never performed on the cytotrophoblastic cells alone because these results are not always reflective of the fetus. Although the accuracy of CVS in predicting cytogenetically abnormal fetuses is roughly comparable to that of amniocentesis, there are some differences. The rate of maternal cell contamination in cultures obtained from CVS is greater than that in cultures obtained from amniocentesis. Furthermore, the amount of chromosomal mosaicism and the type of cytogenetic mosaicism found in placental tissue are much greater and more numerous, respectively, than those observed in cells of fetal origin. For this reason, about 1% of patients undergoing CVS may be offered amniocentesis to obtain fetal cells for confirmation of a CVS cytogenetic diagnosis.

The background fetal loss rate after normal first-trimester ultrasonography is approximately 2.5% to 3%. Pregnancy losses attributable to CVS range from 0.5% to 2% above the background rate, with the lowest loss rates reported by centers with the most experience with CVS. Losses after transcervical CVS may result from three main mechanisms: infection, premature rupture of membranes, and placental disruption. Infection is less problematic with transabdominal CVS, a major advantage of this approach. An additional concern with CVS is the possibility of limb abnormalities associated with the procedure. Limb reduction defects were initially reported out of London and Chicago after both transabdominal and transcervical CVS. An increased incidence of limb reduction defects after CVS was not found in the initial U.S. collaborative CVS report, and such defects have subsequently been largely limited to CVS procedures performed earlier than 66 days of gestation, involving the use of a large catheter or the recovery of a large sample size of villi, and perhaps in which the operator was inexperienced.[19] However, some studies suggest that limb reduction defects are increased in CVS procedures performed after 11 weeks.

The risks associated with CVS, though small, are greater than those associated with amniocentesis. Patients must understand that the convenience of first-trimester termination of an abnormal fetus may be outweighed by an increased risk of losing a normal pregnancy. Patients with only a small risk for genetic abnormalities, such as those associated with maternal age of 35 or older or with a history of infertility, may be reluctant to consider CVS, whereas a couple with a 25% risk for a metabolic genetic disease in their offspring would most likely consider the pregnancy loss rate associated with CVS to be a minimal concern.

Fetal Blood Sampling

The final major category of specialized prenatal testing is fetal blood sampling, also known as *percutaneous umbilical blood sampling* or cordocentesis. Percutaneous umbilical blood sampling is basically a modification of the amniocentesis procedure and is generally limited to pregnancies of more than 19 weeks of gestation. Under ultrasonographic guidance, a 20- to 22-gauge spinal needle is directed to the umbilical vein at the level of cord insertion and into the placenta (umbilical cord root). Small syringes are used to prevent excessive suction that could cause the collapse of the vein. Once blood is obtained, it is important to ascertain that the sample is fetal and not maternal. The larger diameter of fetal than maternal blood cells is the basis for determining the purity of the sample. This procedure is effectively accomplished by a Coulter cell channelyzer, which determines the frequency distributions of fetal and maternal cells based on erythrocyte volume. At later gestational ages, when the size discrepancy between fetal and maternal cells is less marked, the *Kleihauer-Betke test,* based on the tendency of adult cells to lyse in an acid solution, can be used to measure the purity of a fetal blood sample.

The major indication for fetal blood sampling is to obtain rapid cytogenetic analysis within 48 to 72 hours, usually in late gestations, when a congenital anomaly is detected close to term or close to the legal time limit for elective termination. In cases of suspected cytogenetic mosaicism found in cells from amniotic fluid, in which the abnormal cell line may be derived from the amnion rather than fetus, fetal blood sampling may provide reassurance about the cytogenetic status of the fetus. Factor VIII levels have been determined in fetal blood when the prenatal diagnosis of hemophilia A was inconclusive, and serum enzyme levels have been measured in cases of suspected inherited metabolic disease. However, in those cases in which the mutation is known, DNA studies can be easily performed on chorionic villous or amniotic fluid cells. Finally, fetal blood sampling has been used in cases of suspected congenital infection to measure immunoglobulin M levels and in instances of isoimmunization and suspected fetal anemia. Because the production of immunoglobulin M antibodies depends on gestational age and may vary with the infectious agent involved, the development of PCR for quick, direct testing of microbial DNA to confirm a fetal infection (e.g., cytomegalovirus, toxoplasmosis) has meant a return to amniocentesis as the more common diagnostic approach. Fetal blood sampling currently has a limited but specific application compared with amniocentesis, and experience tends to be restricted to major tertiary referral centers, where the procedure-related risks are generally quoted as 1% to 3%.[30]

ASSISTED REPRODUCTION

The development of in vitro fertilization and other assisted reproduction techniques, as well as advances in molecular genetics, is changing the scope of obstetrics and prenatal diagnosis. Preimplantation genetic diagnosis separates conception from pregnancy, thus offering at-risk couples an alternative to the diagnosis of the fetus and possibly the late termination of a well developed pregnancy. With the preimplantation analysis of genetic status, the cessation of development in the affected embryo is easily managed. Preimplantation diagnosis also opens up the possibility for the development and implementation of directed gene therapy to correct known genetic defects.

Assisted reproduction technologies were initially developed to treat women with obstructive tube disease but are much more broadly applied today. Hormonal manipulation produced superovulation, and the recovery of multiple follicles was made possible by ultrasonographic visualization of the stimulated ovaries. Access to ova and their polar bodies gave rise to a new source of tissue for genetic testing. With in vitro techniques and the micromanipulation of embryos in culture, blastomeres and the trophectoderm can be isolated and analyzed, with only the unaffected embryos implanted in the uterus.

Single-sperm analysis is not possible because this reproductive cell would be destroyed in the process of genetic analysis. Therefore, the first polar body represents the best opportunity for preconceptional genetic diagnosis. It is accessible through the zona pellucida and can be removed without affecting conception or later development. The analysis of the DNA of the polar body is highly appropriate for women who are carriers for autosomal recessive diseases, autosomal dominant diseases, or X-linked disorders. The chromosome in the polar body can be analyzed directly and identified as carrying the normal or mutant gene. By inference, the genetic status of the complementary chromosome in the egg can be determined.

Blastomere biopsy (one or two cells) can be performed at the eight-cell stage of the embryo. Successful pregnancies have been achieved in couples at risk for Lesch-Nyhan syndrome (X-linked), fragile X syndrome, Tay-Sachs disease, and CF with a preimplantation diagnosis of blastocysts.[38]

Technological advances in both molecular genetics and molecular cytogenetics have revolutionized the field of preimplantation genetics. The development of PCR analysis has allowed the DNA extracted from one to a few cells to be selectively expanded to an amount sufficient for genetic analysis. This DNA is amenable to most mutation detection methods, including heteroduplex analysis, single-stranded confirmation polymorphism, fluorescent PCR, and restriction digestion. However, the power of PCR to amplify small amounts of DNA represents the greatest difficulty in the technology because of several associated problems. Unintended replication of contaminating DNA, such as that of the sperm adherent to the zona pellucida, allele dropout, and reduced amplification efficiency, can all be sources of diagnostic error. Advances in FISH have also been crucial to the advancement of preimplantation genetic diagnosis. Initially used for embryo sexing in the diagnosis of X-linked traits, these studies have been enhanced by probe and technological developments. FISH is commonly performed by using multicolor analysis with nine probes (13, 14, 15, 16, 18, 21, 22, X, and Y) to diagnose the most frequent aneuploidies in both live births and spontaneous abortions. There is a 10% to 15% chance of a misdiagnosis because the testing of one cell has been shown to be problematic due to mosaicism. Both chromosome paints and subtelomeric probes have been used to study the segregation of translocations.

SUMMARY

The growing number of diagnostic procedures now available for prenatal genetic evaluation has given couples at high genetic risks, who otherwise might have forgone parenthood, the opportunity to have healthy children. Despite the criticism that prenatal genetic evaluations are nothing more than procedures to eliminate defective fetuses, studies based on interviews with couples who have high genetic reproductive risks have demonstrated a very positive effect. The availability of prenatal diagnosis has led to many more planned conceptions and births of normal children than the terminations of fetuses diagnosed as genetically abnormal. As the technology improves, it is likely that prenatal diagnoses will have even more positive effects, allowing couples to have healthy children and reducing the burden of genetic disease.

REFERENCES

1. ACOG Committee Opinion #296: First-trimester screening for fetal aneuploidy. Obstet Gynecol 104:215, 2004.
2. Astbury C et al: Detection of deletions in de novo "balanced" chromosome rearrangements: Further evidence for their role in phenotypic abnormalities. Genet Med 6:81, 2004.
3. Astbury C et al: Delineation of complex chromosomal rearrangements: Evidence for increased complexity. Hum Genet 114:448, 2004.
4. Baird PA et al: Genetic disorders in children and young adults: A population study. Am J Hum Genet 42:677, 1988.
5. Brown CJ et al: A stain upon the silence: Genes escaping X inactivation. Trends Gen 19:432, 2003.
6. Cassidy SB et al: Prader-Willi and Angelman syndromes and disorders of genomic imprinting. Rev Mol Med 77:140, 1998.
7. Emery AEH et al: Principles and Practice of Medical Genetics, 4th ed, vols 1-3. New York, Churchill Livingstone, 2002.
8. Gardner RJM et al: Chromosome Abnormalities and Genetic Counseling, 3rd ed. New York, Oxford University Press, 2003.
9. Gelehrter TD et al: Principles of Medical Genetics, 2nd ed. Baltimore, Williams & Wilkins, 1998.

10. Graf MD, Schwartz S: Molecular approaches for delineating marker chromosomes. Methods Mol Biol 204:211, 2002.

11. Hagerman RJ et al: Fragile X-Syndrome: Diagnosis, Treatment, and Research, 3rd ed. Baltimore, Johns Hopkins University Press, 2002.

12. Hagerman RJ et al: The fragile-X permutation: A maturing perspective. Am J Hum Genet 74:805, 2004.

13. Hall JG: Human diseases and genomic imprinting. Results Probl Cell Differ 25:119, 1999.

14. Hall JG: Medical genetics. Pediatr Clin North Am 39:1, 1992.

15. Harper PS: Practical Genetic Counseling, 5th ed. Oxford, Butterworth Heinemann, 1998.

16. Hassold T et al: To err (meiotically) is human: The genesis of human aneuploidy. Nat Rev 2:280, 2001.

17. Jacobs PA et al: Estimates of the frequency of chromosome abnormalities detectable using moderate levels of banding. J Med Genet 29:103, 1992.

18. Jalal SM et al: Utility of subtelomeric fluorescent DNA probes for detection of chromosome anomalies in 425 patients. Genet Med 5:28, 2003.

19. Jenkins TM et al: First trimester prenatal diagnosis: Chorionic villus sampling. Semin Perinatol 5:403, 1999.

20. Jones KL: Smith's Recognizable Patterns of Human Malformation, 5th ed. Philadelphia, WB Saunders Co, 1997.

21. Kallioniemi OP et al: Comparative genomic hybridization: A rapid new method for detecting and mapping DNA amplification in tumors. Semin Cancer Biol 1:41, 1993.

22. Krzywinski M et al: A set of BAC clones spanning the human genome. Nucleic Acids Res 32:3651, 2004.

23. Kumar P et al: Prevalence and patterns of presentation of genetic disorders in a pediatric emergency department. Mayo Clin Proc 76:777, 2001.

24. Lewin B: Genes VIII. New York, Oxford University Press, 2004.

25. Locke DP et al: BAC microarray analysis of 15q11-q13 rearrangements and the impact of segmental duplications. J Med Genet 41:175, 2004.

26. Lyon MF: Imprinting and X-chromosome inactivation. Results Probl Cell Differ 25:73, 1999.

27. Lyon MF: X-chromosome inactivation. Curr Biol 9:R235, 1999.

28. McKusick VA: Mendelian Inheritance in Man, 12th ed. Baltimore, Johns Hopkins University Press, 1998. Available online at: http://www.ncbi.nlm.nih.gov/query.fcgi?db=OMIM

29. Meeserlian GM: Recent advances in maternal serum screening for Down syndrome. Med Health R I 85:362, 2002.

30. Milunsky A: Genetic Disorders and the Fetus: Diagnosis, Prevention and Treatment, 5th ed. Baltimore, Johns Hopkins University Press, 2004.

31. Mitelman F: An International System for Human Cytogenetic Nomenclature (ISCN, 1995). S. Karger, Basel, 1995.

32. Muhle R et al: The genetics of autism. Pediatrics 113:e472, 2004.

33. Policy Statement, American College of Medical Genetics: Fragile X syndrome: Diagnostic and carrier testing. Am J Med Genet 53:380, 1994.

34. Richards CS et al: Standards and guidelines for CFTR mutation testing. Genet Med 4:379, 2002.

35. Robinson WP et al: Molecular studies of chromosomal mosaicism: Relative frequency of chromosome gain or loss and possible role of cell selection. Am J Hum Genet 56:444, 1995.

36. Schrock E et al: Spectral karyotyping refines cytogenetic diagnostics of constitutional chromosomal abnormalities. Hum Genet 3:255, 1997.

37. Scriver CR et al: The Metabolic and Molecular Bases of Inherited Disease, 8th ed. New York, McGraw-Hill, 2001.

38. Sermon K et al: Preimplantation genetic diagnosis. Lancet 363:1633, 2004.

39. Shepard TH: Catalog of Teratogenic Agents, 14th ed. Baltimore, Johns Hopkins University Press, 2004.

40. Sirko-Osadsa DA et al: Molecular refinement of karyotype: Beyond the cytogenetic band. Genet Med 1:254, 1999.

41. Speicher MR et al: Karyotyping human chromosomes by combinatorial multi-fluor FISH. Nat Genet 4:368, 1996.

42. Thompson MW et al: Genetics in Medicine, 5th ed. Philadelphia, WB Saunders Co, 1991.

43. Thornburn DR: Mitochondrial disorders: Prevalence, myths and advancers. J Inherit Metab Dis 27:349, 2004.

44. UCSC Genome Browser: Available at: http://genome.ucsc.edu/

45. Vercelli D: Genetics, epigenetics and the environment: switching, buffering, releasing. J Allergy Clin Immunol 113:381, 2004.

46. Walter J, Paulson M: Imprinting and disease. Semin Cell Dev Biol 14:101, 2003.

47. Warburton D: De novo balanced chromosome rearrangements and extra marker chromosomes identified at prenatal diagnosis: Clinical significance a distribution of breakpoints. Am J Hum Genet 5:995, 1991.

48. Weksberg R et al: Beckwith-Wiedemann syndrome demonstrates a role for epigenetic control of normal development. Hum Mol Genet 12:R61, 2003.

49. Wills-Karp M et al: Time to draw breath: Asthma-susceptibility genes are identified. Nat Rev Genet 5:376, 2004.

8 Perinatal Ultrasound

Nancy E. Judge and Stuart C. Morrison

From a current perspective it seems incredible that less than fifty years ago, obstetric practice thrived without diagnostic sonography. Beginning with cumbersome, improvised devices and progressing to today's sleek, highly engineered commercial products, ultrasound has become an integral part of prenatal care. As images have improved in quality and variety, applications that both inform and complicate clinical decision making have proliferated. The maturation of some core applications has inspired the exploration of less intuitive but no less useful relationships between ultrasound findings and fetal development, growth, and well-being.

ULTRASOUND TECHNIQUES

The first A-mode ultrasound images were *amplitude* spikes of returning echoes displayed as a function of time. These images persist in diathermy and lithotripsy and have applications for ophthalmology and otolaryngology. B-mode images vary *brightness* with signal intensity. Static images, compiled by sweeping the transducer across patients, were succeeded by real-time scanning, which is standard for prenatal studies (Fig. 8-1). Ideally, the transducer is positioned as close as possible to its target; transvaginal scans are common in gynecology and early gestation. Poor images are more common with obese individuals if tissues have limited fluid interfaces or transmit echoes poorly, e.g., scar tissue or calcifications, and when structures are badly positioned with respect to the beam.

M-mode ultrasound, used for studying cardiac chambers and valve excursions, is a linear, direct representation of the ultrasound beam reflected by *moving* edges. Interpretation requires standardized, stable views, which are hard to achieve prenatally; the de-emphasis of M-mode imaging coincided with improvements in B-mode resolution. M-mode ultrasound remains useful in arrhythmia, altered contractility, and pericardial effusion. M-mode "snapshots" are also widely available for documenting cardiac activity and rate, particularly in early gestation (Fig. 8-2).

Doppler ultrasound uses the frequency shift that occurs when the beam is reflected off moving objects to evaluate the presence, velocity, and direction of bloodflow. Pulsed, time-gated waves are used to measure flow velocity from individual vessels at angles of insonation that are between 30 and 60 degrees (Fig. 8-3).[27] Fetal and uterine vessels are narrow and tortuous, interfering with direct volume assessment; as a compensatory measure, Doppler findings are expressed as ratios (Fig. 8-4).

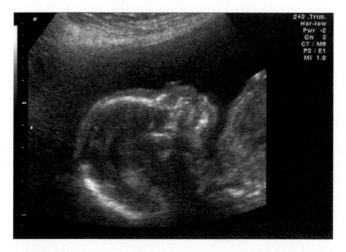

FIGURE 8-1. Transabdominal B-mode, two-dimensional scan. Profile of 18-week fetus.

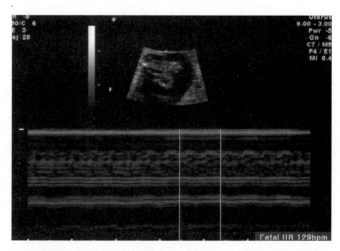

FIGURE 8-2. Transvaginal M-mode embryonic heart rate at 6⁴/₇ weeks of gestation. *Upper view:* embryo with cursor across thorax. *Lower view:* M-mode display of wall movements during two cardiac cycles (between vertical lines). See color insert.

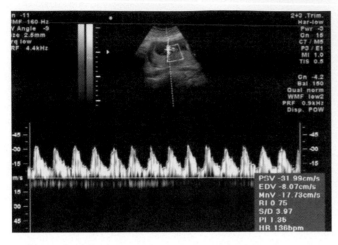

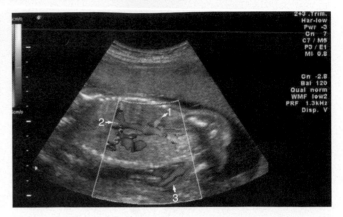

FIGURE 8-3. *Upper view:* Gated, pulsed Doppler acquisition (small, transverse, parallel lines) of umbilical artery signal from placental cord insertion site (trapezoid). *Lower view:* Doppler waveform recorded from umbilical artery (see Figure 8-4).

FIGURE 8-5. See color insert. Color Doppler demonstration of left renal artery (*arrow #1*, red signal) arising from descending aorta (*arrow #2*, blue signal). Umbilical cord (*arrow #3*, blue signal) is also shown.

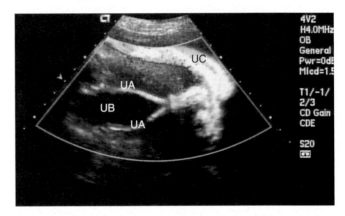

FIGURE 8-4. Schematic of Doppler arterial waveform. V, velocity; S, peak systolic velocity; D, end-diastolic velocity; S/D, peak systolic velocity/end-diastolic velocity; RI (Pourcelot ratio), (S-D)/S; PI (pulsatility index), (S-D)/Vm (mean of maximum velocities over one cycle).

FIGURE 8-6. Transverse view of fetal pelvis, umbilical cord (UC), and urinary bladder (UB), with power Doppler showing bifurcation of the umbilical arteries (UA).

Color Doppler semiquantitatively assigns direction to flow; by convention, warm colors denote movement toward the transducer, with saturation keyed to velocity. Color Doppler is used to image the heart and find vessels, often for gated, pulsed measurements (Fig. 8-5). Color Doppler energy, or power Doppler, is a format based on signal intensity; amplitude corresponds to blood cell motion. Power Doppler, effectively independent of angulation, is sensitive to very low flow. It is useful for finding and mapping vascular beds and for spotting umbilical and other vessels (Fig. 8-6). Color Doppler views of the middle cerebral artery are central to new clinical applications (Fig. 8-7).[45]

Three-dimensional ultrasound is one of the most intriguing new developments in the field. Processing and transducer developments permit the analysis of existing signals along a third axis. These new images show both surfaces and volumes from multiple perspectives. Surface rendering yields facial details

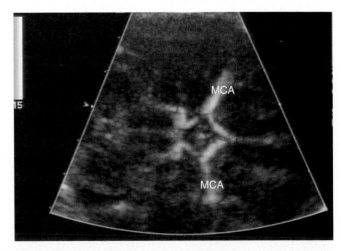

FIGURE 8-7. Power Doppler image showing the circle of Willis and both middle cerebral arteries (MCA). See color insert.

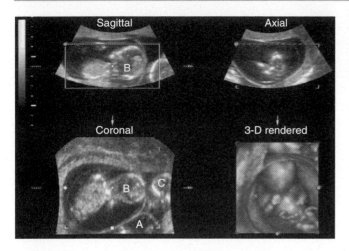

FIGURE 8-8. Triplets at 13 weeks of gestation (A, B, C) in three perpendicular planes (sagittal, axial, coronal). Three-dimensional surface rendering of fetus B is shown in the lower (R) panel. See color insert.

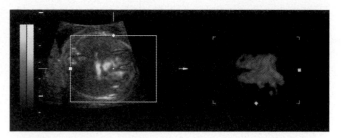

FIGURE 8-9. Spatiotemporal imaging of normal four-chamber heart at 18 weeks. Transverse chest with four-chamber view (left panel), cardiac apex facing right, and rendered three dimensionally (right panel), cardiac apex facing left. See color insert.

and small parts; multiplanar views and stratified slices have shown great potential for locating abnormalities and circumventing fetal malposition (Fig. 8-8). Three-dimensional ultrasound also aids in the measurement of volume, exploration of complex spatial relationships, and clarification of findings for patients.[9] Spatiotemporal correlation with color and power Doppler is likely to become part of the standard approach to cardiac imaging (Fig. 8-9). Software allows post hoc image manipulation; submitting studies as three-dimensional data sets may eventually become standard for remote or consultative interpretation. Repeat analysis of stored volumes by legal experts also seems an inevitable if less auspicious application. Some machines now produce dramatic, real-time, three-dimensional ("four-dimensional") views for fetal cardiology and behavior studies. The problems facing three-dimensional imaging include artifacts from acquisition times, a dependence on high-quality two-dimensional signals, nonstandard engineering, and time-intensive interpretation strategies.

BIOEFFECTS AND THE SAFETY OF ULTRASOUND

Because sonograms are obtained so frequently throughout gestation, it is reassuring that after two generations of use, there is no persuasive evidence of harm in humans. Ultrasound is not oncogenic; the preponderance of studies of neural behavior, development and growth are reassuring, although concern remains.[2] The frequencies used are inaudible but produce pressure and heat. Adverse small-mammal effects include malformations and decreased growth and litter sizes. Dangerous thermal levels do not occur with B-mode ultrasound but could result from extended Doppler use or with underlying fever. Mechanical disruption from

the cavitation of gas bubbles is unlikely in fetal tissues; provocative microbubble contrast agents are not used in pregnancy. Streaming effects, cell lysis, intracellular shearing, altered cell permeability, and abnormal chromosome function have also been reported but only under nonclinical conditions. Manufacturers originally limited scanner outputs along with penetration and resolution. Currently the settings can be adjusted for better images; minimizing the risk is now the job of the operators. Ultrasound machines display estimated temperature and disruption risks as the thermal index (TI), the ratio of the transducer output to that required to warm tissue by 1°C, and the mechanical index (MI), indicating the pulse amplitude effects of compression and decompression within tissues. The TI is further categorized as soft tissue (TIS), useful for embryos; bone (TIB); and cranium (TIC). TIB is typically used for the fetal brain and TIC for direct cranial application as well as for neonates.[1] The TI should remain below 2 and the MI below 0.3 for most studies. Thermal effects increase approximately threefold with each change from B- to M-mode through color to pulsed Doppler imaging. The American Institute of Ultrasound in Medicine currently recommends that indicated studies be performed at as low as reasonably achievable power, duration, and intensity for adequate visualization (ALARA).[2,4] Clearly excluded by this rubric are exposures for videos, three-dimensional portraits, determining fetal sex, and personal use. It seems reasonable to minimize the use of Doppler in the first trimester except for research and clear clinical need.[39]

Pregnancy ultrasounds are routine in spite of little proof of benefit in normal patients. The 1993 Routine Antenatal Diagnostic Imaging with Ultrasound Study (RADIUS) found no significant differences in outcomes for prematurity, prolonged pregnancy, anomalies, or twins with scans in low-risk patients except for predicted costs exceeding $1 billion.[23] RADIUS had a very low rate of detecting anomalies, which was ascribed to the inclusion of nonacademic sites, and very strict criteria for normalcy. It is unlikely that most patients would accept prenatal care without ultrasound, making human studies of bioeffects and effectiveness increasingly difficult to design.

ETHICAL CONSIDERATIONS

Ultrasound generates some unique ethical concerns. As a rapidly developing but decentralized technology, ultrasound challenges practitioners struggling to remain proficient in arcane skills. Large collaborative groups, benefiting from referral pools, restricted technologies, and complex statistical analyses, properly question the applicability of findings beyond their own centers. Altruism and medicolegal and economic pressures promptly push physicians to adopt the new practices in spite of good reason for caution.[3] For example, a single linear measurement of nuchal lucency, used in early aneuploidy screening, appears to require rigorous initial instruction and periodic audits to achieve and maintain uniformity (Fig. 8-10).[63] A proprietary course, incorporating graduates in the data pool, is an ingenious means of generalizing research but disturbing in its wider implications. Practitioners should be frank in discussions of their ability to provide new techniques.

Selective abortion after prenatal ultrasound identification of fetal sex (Fig. 8-11; see Fig. 8-58) has been a long-standing and unresolved international issue.[28] Compliance with the wishes of the patient, a policy of nondisclosure of fetal sex, and omission of the genital examination are current approaches that do not satisfactorily address a societal aberration.

Targeted scans can be effective for at-risk patients, but success varies according to the problem and skill of the operator. Patients and doctors may share unrealistic expectations for accuracy; equivocal results impose added burdens. Corresponding problems in low-risk women arise when major anomalies or variants linked to aneuploidy ("markers") are found during studies for dating or growth. Failing to comment on a marker may place the sonologist in legal jeopardy, yet the impact on an unprepared patient's emotional well-being from possible aneuploidy can be severe.[25] Ultrasound tests

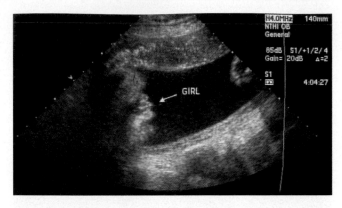

FIGURE 8-11. Transverse perineal view of 20-week female fetus showing labial folds *(arrow)*.

have a broad range of accuracy and predictive value; errors may have grave consequences not only in anatomy scans but also in predicting well-being, prematurity, and placental complications. As with any procedure, informed consent should be obtained from patients before booking an ultrasound test.[46] Ultimately, all couples should judge for themselves their tolerance for uncertainty in diagnosis and imperfection in their offspring.

APPLICATIONS OF ULTRASOUND

Genetic Screening

Genetic screening combines ultrasound and biochemical testing to enhance the detection of chromosomal abnormalities, resulting in greater scrutiny of younger patients and less frequent invasive testing for women over 35 (see Chapter 7). Unfortunately, subtly different strategies yield wide variations in sensitivity, false positive rates, and even estimates of confirmatory test risks. The diagnostic features of Down syndrome have long included endocardial cushion defects and duodenal atresia but now incorporate markers, alone or in combinations: nuchal lucency and thickness in the first and second trimesters, respectively; lateral ventricles; choroid cysts; nasal and digital ossification; long bone length; papillary muscles; bowel echogenicity; renal pyelectasis; and toe positioning, with possible future additions of ear length; hip angles; and more (see Fig. 8-10; Fig. 8-12). Components may be affected by race, build, and fetal sex; the permutations can thwart counselors attempting to provide (and patients trying to grasp) usable descriptions of the risks and benefits. A recent protocol from the United Kingdom, reporting integrated findings from first- and second-trimester testing, achieved a sensitivity of 85% at a false positive rate of 0.95%.[66] The same protocol in the United States had nearly 3% false positive rates for the same sensitivity; withholding initially abnormal findings for integration is also problematic here.[43,44]

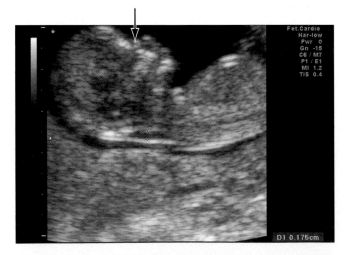

FIGURE 8-10. Nuchal lucency (calipers) and nasal bone *(arrow)* in 12-week fetus.

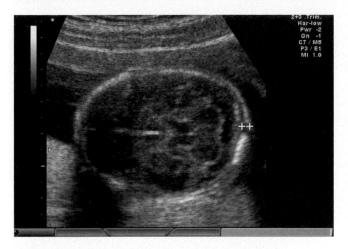

FIGURE 8-12. Normal posterior nuchal thickness (calipers) at 21 weeks.

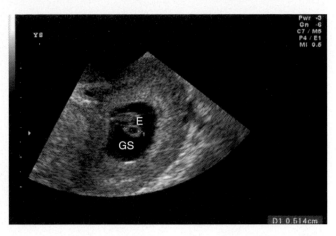

FIGURE 8-13. Gestational sac (GS), yolk sac (calipers), and embryo (E) at 6⁴/₇ weeks.

Assisted Reproduction

Ultrasound studies in infertile women describe the follicular size and number, uterine cavity, and endometrial characteristics, optimizing therapy. Scans are crucial to the timing and success of egg retrieval and embryo transfer.[22] There are more twins and higher-order multiples; the early assessment of embryos, amnionicity, and chorionicity is essential to subsequent management. Patients also risk ectopic and heterotopic pregnancies. Ultrasound rapidly identifies abnormal implantations, facilitating the medical or minimally invasive therapy and treatment of hyperstimulation. Recently, three dimensional scans, contrast, and vascular studies have been investigated for benefits to fertility care.[41,61]

First-Trimester Studies

Traditionally, first-trimester transvaginal scans exclude ectopic implantations and confirm viability by demonstrating an intrauterine "double sac," a yolk sac and embryo with cardiac activity; identifiable embryos in the salpinx are uncommon. Heterotopic pregnancy (coexisting intra- and extrauterine implantation) occurs in 1 of 4000 patients,[8] consistent with the pragmatic dictum that finding an intrauterine pregnancy excludes ectopia; however, in assisted reproduction the rate of heterotopia approaches 1%.[64] The double sac is seen transvaginally at levels of 1000 to 1500 IU (third/fourth SI) of human chorionic gonadotropin at 4 to 5¹/₂ menstrual weeks; the appearance of the yolk sac by the fifth week confirms the intrauterine site. The gestational sac diameter grows 1 mm daily in early pregnancy, and the embryonic disc should be visible at 15 mm (Fig. 8-13). The maximum embryonic length increases linearly, also by 1 mm daily; the transvaginal documentation of cardiac activity is expected just before the seventh week.[40] Embryonic heart rates increase to over 160 beats per minute by the ninth week and then decline slightly through the thirteenth week. Persistent rates below 100 beats per minute are associated with abortion, aneuploidy, and anomalies.[21] Embryonic and early fetal surveys have traditionally been cursory; however, recent investigators have achieved detailed transvaginal fetal anatomic studies at the onset of the second trimester.[13] These studies can be time intensive; in addition, midtrimester studies retain some advantages with respect to evolving abnormalities and the resolution of the heart, sacrum, and other problematic structures.[65]

Multiple Gestation

Multiple gestation presents particular challenges for ultrasound studies (see Chapter 18). Dizygotic twinning occurs in about 1% of pregnancies, varying by ethnicity and increasing with maternal age, parity, family history, and fertility treatments. Monozygotic twinning is more constant at 1 in 250 pregnancies, although it is susceptible to increases with in vitro techniques.[59] With an increase in the number of fetuses, scans also become more complex, time consuming, and error prone. Most monozygotic pairs are monochorionic, with an attrition rate of over 30% from early abortion, anomalies, and prematurity. Twin-twin transfusion syndrome is a unique complication in which unbalanced, shared perfusion may restrict growth in one twin and cause hydrops in the other. Ultrasound-guided thermal or mechanical interruption of vascular connections and, to a lesser extent, serial amniocentesis have been effective in reducing intrauterine losses and prematurity. Mono-amniotic twins face lethal cord entanglements; once this condition is confirmed by ultrasound, labor is contraindicated. The management of anomalous, discordant, or moribund co-twins differs significantly based on chorionicity, which is best determined in the first trimester; in later trimesters both the membranes and the site of their juncture at the placental surface are thicker for dizygotic twins (Fig. 8-14). Serial monitoring of multiple gestation to assess the risk for growth, well-being, and prematurity has become standard.

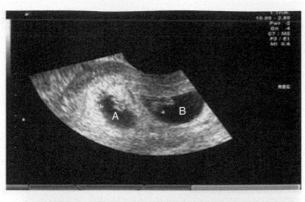

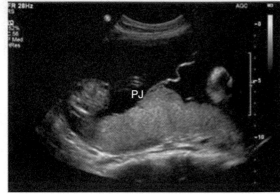

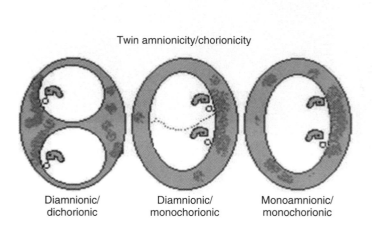

Twin amnionicity/chorionicity

Diamnionic/
dichorionic

Diamnionic/
monochorionic

Monoamnionic/
monochorionic

FIGURE 8-14. Diamnionic, dichorionic twins showing distinct first-trimester sacs (A and B) *(upper panel)*; third-trimester membranes with triangular placental juncture (PJ) *(lower panel)*.

PREGNANCY EVALUATION

More than fifty fetal structures have now been measured by ultrasound, with the results expressed as a function of gestational age. Commercial ultrasound machines come with preinstalled biometry-based dating algorithms, for example, those of Hadlock and colleagues.[31] Referenced study designs and pertinent limitations should be reviewed before applying nomograms to other populations. Biometrics is used to assess the size and development of structures with known dating; however, one of the most powerful applications of prenatal sonography is to use biometry to establish or confirm gestational age. Once accelerated or restricted growth alters fetal size, usually in the third trimester, the accuracy of ultrasound decreases. However, through 22 weeks of gestation, most normal fetal exams cluster quite closely on curves for a wide range of anatomic structures.[18] Methodological errors remain significantly fewer than those of menstrual dating until well into the third trimester.[15]

One of the first dating parameters developed was the biparietal diameter (BPD), obtained after the parietal bones have calcified during the twelfth week. BPD is measured from the outer to the inner table of the skull, perpendicular to the parietal bones and central falx cerebri, on a plane containing the cavum septum pellucidum, thalami and third ventricle, and tentorial

hiatus, in conjunction with the circumference of the bony table head circumference [HC] (Fig. 8-15). BPD and HC change slowly in the event of disturbed fetal growth; BPD can be distorted by position or compression. The abdominal circumference (AC), measured along the outer margin of the abdominal skin line at the level of the gastric bubble and the intrahepatic portion

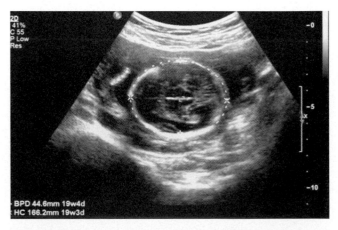

FIGURE 8-15. Transverse view of the fetal head showing measurement of biparietal diameter (BPD) (calipers) and head circumference (dotted line) at 19 weeks.

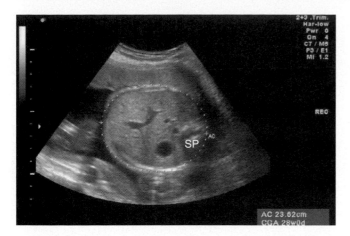

FIGURE 8-16. Transverse 28-week fetal abdomen at the proper level for measurement of circumference. Fetal spine (SP) is on the right of the image.

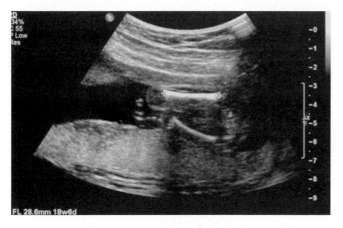

FIGURE 8-17. Femoral length (between cursors) at 19 weeks. The proximal femur is to the right of the image.

of the umbilical vein at the bifurcation of the portal veins, is the best single predictor of growth aberrations but correspondingly less helpful for dating (Fig. 8-16). Femoral length keeps the long axis of the femoral diaphysis perpendicular to the beam, measuring from the junction of the bone and cartilage of the greater trochanter to the junction of the metaphysis and distal epiphysis (Fig. 8-17).[36] Extraocular and transcerebellar diameters and humeral, clavicular, and pedal lengths are common ancillary dating parameters. A combination of femoral length and head circumference is sufficient for most evaluations.[31] Other biometric sites may be substituted when anomalies or positional limitations permit. Some additional curves have been generated for non-Caucasian ethnicity or multiple gestation but are not widely used.

Fetal Growth

Serial measurements over time represent the best assessment of fetal growth. Initially the sac and embryo grow perceptibly each day; after the second trimester, intervals of 2 to 3 weeks are more reliable. A continued challenge for sonography is simultaneously attempting to establish the age and weight percentile that lack accurate clinical dating. The AC is more sensitive to both increased glucose and decreased perfusion than the cranial measures are; the ratios of AC to the head and femur amplify the differences but have poor sensitivity and specificity. Strategies to identify small-for-date fetuses have included risk panels, Doppler measurements, amniotic fluid volume, placental appearance, and biometry. Even suboptimal efforts to find and manage the small-for-date fetus may have contributed to improved outcomes.[56] The estimation of fetal weight has been a major focus of ultrasound measurements. Critical obstetric and neonatal decisions at the extremes of viability and size often depend on calculations carried out to the nearest gram; unfortunately, the accuracy of ultrasound dating ranges from ±15%. Clinical algorithms and physician and even maternal estimates all compare well with ultrasound in estimating birthweight.

Placental Location

The location of the placenta can be confidently established by ultrasound, although low-lying placentation persists as placenta previa in only 1% to 2% of patients (Fig. 8-18). With the use of color Doppler the fetal vessels can be identified near the cervix, permitting the identification of cord presentations and vasa praevia (Fig. 8-19). Recent significant advances in placental imaging have been related to the evaluation of placental accretion, where there is a loss of the normal cleavage plane between the decidua and the placental vessels. Accretion, deeper penetration of the vessels into the myometrium (incretion), and serosal penetration (percretion) were often identified when an attempt to deliver the placenta precipitated massive hemorrhage, usually leading to hysterectomy. Placental accretion is

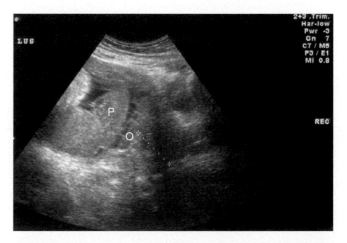

FIGURE 8-18. Placenta previa by transabdominal scan at 34 weeks. The cervix is indicated by the dotted line. The placenta (P) completely covers the internal os (O).

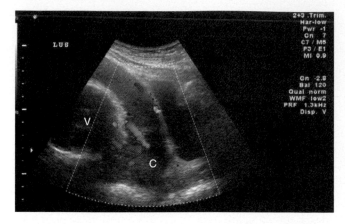

FIGURE 8-19. See color insert. Vasa praevia by color Doppler. The vessels (blue) branch out within the membranes lying between the fetal vertex (V) and the cervix (C).

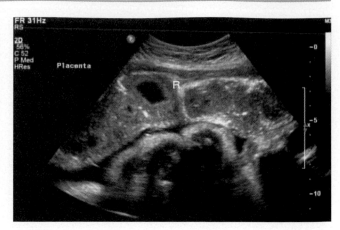

FIGURE 8-21. Grade III placenta showing characteristic hyperechoic rings (R) and echo-free centers.

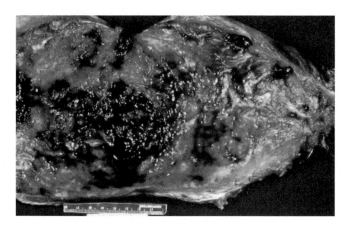

FIGURE 8-20. Gross specimen of a bivalved uterus with placenta accreta and adherent clot.

more likely in women with placenta previa and a history of cesarean section, curettage, or high parity; the frequency of accretion has increased to 1 in 2500 from 1 in 30,000, reflecting trends in the incidence of cesarean section.[48] Antenatal diagnosis demonstrating the loss of the placental margin, associated with large placental lakes and thinning of the myometrial border, permits patient education and preparation for transfusion, balloon tamponade, arterial embolization, and even expectancy and for the more traditional hysterectomy (Fig. 8-20). Sensitivity and specificity are in the range of 85%;[19,26] with additional enhancement possible with magnetic resonance imaging (MRI); rapid dissemination of the techniques is likely because of the severity of the condition. On the other hand, the diagnosis of placental abruption remains challenging; ultrasound is reported to have only 24% sensitivity for this diagnosis in the third trimester (positive predictive value of 88%), although specificity may reach 88%.[29] The chief role of imaging in this disorder is to exclude placenta previa, a cause of third-trimester bleeding of similar frequency

and gravity. Subchorionic hematomas are commonly identified by transvaginal scans early in gestation; symptomaticity and (less consistently) size and persistence have been associated with poorer outcomes.[53] During the second and third trimesters, abruptions are more difficult to visualize; acute bleeding is isoechoic with the placental tissue and can be mistaken for an unusually thick placenta. The evolution of the area of abruption over time may result in a hyperechoic infarct. Initial interest in characterizing placental appearance throughout gestation attempted to link sonographic grade to growth or maturational disturbances, with limited success.[30] The persistence of immature placentation is weakly linked to hydrops fetalis, although increased echogenicity and thickening are more common findings. A precociously mature placenta infrequently precedes growth restriction as an isolated finding (Fig. 8-21).

Amniotic Fluid Volume

The volume of amniotic fluid is initially determined by secretions from the amnion; however, by the sixteenth week of pregnancy the fetal renal production accounts for the majority (see Chapter 21). Malformations of the esophagus and upper gastrointestinal tract, inhibited fetal swallowing, aneuploidy, intermittent renal obstruction, maternal diabetes, twin-twin transfusion, some cases of dwarfism, and impending fetal hydrops are associated with severe polyhydramnios. Severe growth restriction with polyhydramnios carries a poor prognosis. Idiopathic polyhydramnios accounts for almost half of the cases; the mechanical consequences include prematurity, malposition, abruption, preeclampsia, and puerperal hemorrhage. Altered amniotic fluid volumes are often qualitatively recognized but may be confirmed by measurements of the maximum pocket size. An index adjusted for gestational age sums the vertical extent of cord-free fluid spaces in each of the four quadrants (Fig. 8-22).[55]

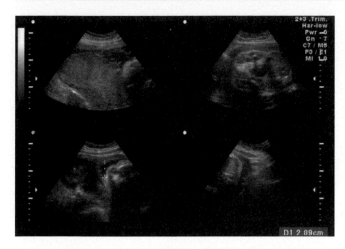

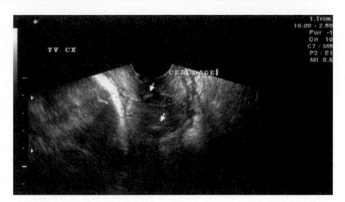

FIGURE 8-23. Measurement of transvaginal longitudinal cervix, with cross sections of MacDonald cerclage *(arrows)*.

FIGURE 8-22. Amniotic fluid index in oligohydramnios. Of the four quadrants of the uterus, a cord-free vertical pocket of fluid (between cursors) is present only in the lower left one.

Oligohydramnios may be a consequence of ruptured amniotic membranes; without amniorrhexis the fluid may be decreased by fetal adaptation to reduced placental perfusion, by functional and obstructive urogenital anomalies, and to a lesser extent by the altered status of maternal hydration. The amniotic fluid index appears to be more helpful in the identification and management of polyhydramnios; the absence of any 2 × 2-cm, cord-free pocket is better correlated with adverse outcomes in oligohydramnios. In combination with nonstress testing or with fetal movements, tone, and breathing, the measurement of amniotic fluid is often combined with nonstress testing, movement counts, and breathing for an index of fetal well being. The mechanisms of amniotic fluid dynamics, the role of fluid assessment in clinical care, and the appropriate therapies for abnormalities remain poorly understood.[58]

Cervical Length

The length of the cervix has been increasingly recognized as an important component of the routine and targeted ultrasound evaluations.[5] The length of the closed portion of the endocervical canal has a direct correlation with the duration of gestation, with 30 mm representing the lower limit of the norm. In patients already at risk for prematurity, shorter cervical lengths are strongly predictive of delivery before term; in combination with the assessment of fetal fibronectin, ultrasound can be used to identify the subgroup at the highest risk for imminent delivery.[35] Attempts to prevent prematurity through tocolysis have been largely ineffective for a number of reasons; however, delaying birth long enough for the steroid enhancement of lung maturity has proven more feasible. The early second-trimester identification of candidates for prophylactic cervical cerclage has been unsuccessful; moreover, the use of both preventive and "rescue" procedures remains controversial (Fig. 8-23).[32] The appearance of the uterus

is also amenable to ultrasound study. The congenital findings of the greatest obstetric significance are mullerian duplications and septations, occurring in roughly 0.5% of the population. Bicornuate uteri appear to be linked to irregular bleeding in early pregnancy, prematurity through alterations in cervical stroma and competency, and (rarely) losses secondary to torsion or rupture of one horn. Poorly vascularized septations are etiologically associated with abruption. Myomas have been reported to complicate up to 1.4% of pregnancies, with more frequent cesarean sections and an increased likelihood of prematurity, abruption, degeneration, and fetal malposition; less commonly seen are deformation, mechanical and functional dystocia, obstetric hemorrhage, and hysterectomy (Fig. 8-24).[37,57] Normal adnexal structures are rarely palpable after the first trimester. Ultrasound is currently the standard approach for the initial ovarian evaluation during pregnancy, although both computed tomography and MRI may be of value in difficult cases. Ovarian torsion is a rare but acute surgical complication; more frequent in the first trimester and postpartum, it usually occurs in the presence of an

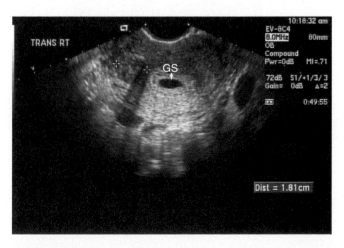

FIGURE 8-24. Early intrauterine gestational sac (GS), *(arrow)* with intramural myoma (between cursors).

ovarian cyst or other adnexal mass. The loss of Doppler flow and demonstration of the twisted vasculature or visualization of an edematous, rapidly enlarging ovary are valuable diagnostic findings that aid in the expedient recognition and treatment of this entity.[20] Adnexal masses, ranging from corpora lutea through hydrosalpinges and benign cystic teratomas, are frequently identified and expectantly managed based on reassuring ultrasound and Doppler characteristics.[11] Ultrasound is preferred for the initial evaluation of appendicitis during pregnancy; in equivocal cases a spiral computed tomogram, MRI, or exploratory surgery may be required.

In the course of an untargeted study for the evaluation of fetal size, number, placentation, and amniotic fluid, a number of fetal structures are routinely imaged in the second trimester.[5] The basic study usually includes the documentation of fetal cranial integrity; midline and lateral brain structures, including the cavum septum pellucidum and thalami; the lateral and third ventricles and choroid plexus; and posteriorly the cerebellum and posterior fossa. The measurement of the nuchal fold is often performed as part of a routine midtrimester study; abnormal thickness, though associated with a range of adverse outcomes, is infrequently identified, yielding a low positive predictive value.[62] Views confirming facial symmetry, intact nares and lips, and a normal profile and neck are routine in comprehensive studies. Fetal swallowing and respiratory movements are frequently noted. The spinal column is normally imaged in both the long-axis and coronal views. Some distinct advantages in the visualization of the facial features and spine are offered by three-dimensional imaging (Fig. 8-25). Views of the thorax, particularly those of the axis, site, and relative proportions of the cardiac and mediastinal structures with respect to the fetal lung and pulmonary

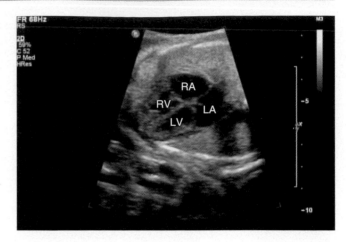

FIGURE 8-26. Transverse chest showing four-chamber heart at 29 weeks. The apex of the heart is on the left of the image. Right and left atria (RA, LA) and ventricles (RV, LV) are approximately equal in size.

vessels, can also provide indirect support for the integrity of the diaphragm. The standard evaluation of the heart has gradually expanded from the initial confirmation of the normal axis, laterality, and rate to a requisite symmetric four-chamber view, with routine efforts to document the presence of both outflows—the ductal and aortic arches (Fig. 8-26). Targeted cardiac studies can include the M-mode evaluation of rhythm, measurements of the intracardiac structures, pericardial space, Doppler identification and assessment of pulmonary veins, bloodflow across the valves and through the outflows, and documentation of the ductus arteriosus and ductus venosus, vena cava, coronary arteries, and other vessels as well as the estimation of myocardial contractility. The abdominal views confirm the closure of the ventral wall, normal situs of the liver and gastric bubble, unremarkable umbilical cord appearance, normal renal contours, bowel dimensions and echogenicity, bladder filling, and more recently the documented presence of the spleen and gallbladder (Fig. 8-27). The

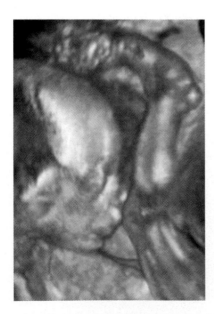

FIGURE 8-25. Three-dimensional rendering of 29-week fetus in frank breech position.

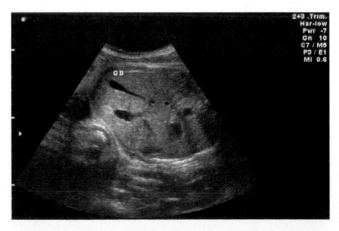

FIGURE 8-27. Transverse abdominal view of fetal gallbladder (GB).

accuracy of the assignment of fetal sex increases to over 98% halfway through the second trimester (see Figs. 8-11 and 8-58). Normal curves exist for all the long bones and fetal feet, and enhanced resolution allows the appearance of the digits to be investigated as needed.

DOPPLER ULTRASOUND

Initially hailed as a key component of prenatal imaging, Doppler ultrasound became hampered by costs, time constraints, safety concerns, and the lack of a clear benefit for normal patients. Current applications, still more frequent in research and referral centers, include measurements of uterine artery bloodflow, umbilical cord arteries, and more recently the ductus venosus and middle cerebral artery. Uterine bloodflow patterns are affected by both maternal vascular resistance and the site of placentation.[38] Abnormal patterns are predictive of growth restriction and maternal hypertensive complications. The umbilical cord arteries are readily identified by color Doppler as they bifurcate around the bladder (see Fig. 8-6). A two-vessel cord is associated with cardiac and renal anomalies, aneuploidies, and growth restriction. Abnormally high resistance to flow in umbilical arteries is predictive and characteristic of uteroplacental constraints on fetal growth and, less frequently, fetal anomalies. It is very helpful when the etiology of a size/date discrepancy is unclear; weight estimation remains a more reliable identifier for small-for-date fetuses. The persistent absence or reversal of end-diastolic flow, though uncommon, is associated with severe growth abnormality and greater perinatal morbidity and mortality. Middle cerebral artery resistance and venous patterns in the fetus are altered later in the course of compromised fetal perfusion; a paradoxical pattern in the ductus venosus appears to be useful as a premorbid finding. A management scheme combining clinical risk factors, Doppler findings, and biometry to identify the optimum time for intervention has recently been proposed.[7]

Recently, Doppler measurement of peak systolic velocity in the middle cerebral artery has been incorporated in the management of fetal anemia and isoimmunization (Fig. 8-28). Previously, maternal antibody levels dictated the need for invasive cord blood sampling or amniocentesis. The former is associated with technical obstacles, a long learning curve, fetal losses, and prematurity; the latter is less accurate and is informative only for the hemolytic sources of anemia. The peak velocities of the middle cerebral artery are negatively correlated with hemoglobin values, are noninvasive, and are relatively easy to obtain. At a cutoff of 1.5 MOM, the sensitivity for moderate to severe anemia has been reported to be 100% by several investigators, with a false positive rate of 0% to 28%. It is anticipated that noninvasive testing will replace amniocentesis and percutaneous umbilical blood sampling as the first screen for fetal anemia.[45] Color flow Doppler is essential for studying vascular structures and anomalies,

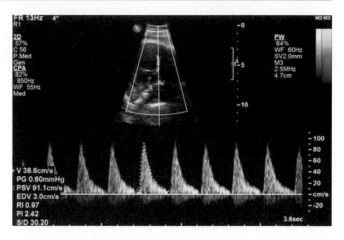

FIGURE 8-28. Peak velocity of middle cerebral artery (MCA) in Rh isoimmunization. Cursors show Doppler gate within the MCA near the circle of Willis; peak velocity is displayed in lower panel.

distinguishing between cystic and vascular lesions, confirming the absence or ectopy of organs, and evaluating cardiovascular anatomy. Recent combinations of color flow Doppler with three-dimensional scanning have provided promising glimpses of the future of vascular imaging.

PROCEDURES

Real-time ultrasound is ideally suited by virtue of its safety, economy, and convenience for the guidance of needles, cannulas, and other devices used in fetal diagnosis and therapy. The range of procedures includes egg retrieval and embryo transfers, embryonic and fetal reduction, chorionic sampling, placental and skin biopsies, amniocentesis and amnioreduction, cord blood sampling and intrauterine transfusion, aspiration of fluid accumulation in various compartments, and an adjunct to fetoscopy and vascular ablation. The effects of the intervention can be continuously monitored during and after the procedures. Determination of fetal and umbilical cord positions during delivery, versions, and immediately before transfusions, surgical interventions, and the EXIT (ex utero intrapartum treatment) procedure are also important applications.

FETAL MAGNETIC RESONANCE IMAGING

MRI can now be performed quickly, obviating the need for maternal and fetal sedation. Each image is obtained with an ultrafast sequence in under 1 second. There are no known harmful biologic effects, but large longitudinal studies are lacking. Individually tailored to specific problems or anatomic areas, MRI is not used for comprehensive screening, unlike ultrasound.[42] The large field of view, excellent soft tissue contrast, and multiple planes of construction make MRI an appealing imaging modality and can supplement the weaknesses of ultrasound in such cases as maternal obesity and oligohydramnios.

Indications for MRI have included the detection of agenesis of the corpus callosum, hypoxic/ischemic brain damage (both difficult for ultrasound), further delineation of meningomyelocele, lung volume, and liver position with congenital diaphragmatic hernia.

FETAL ANOMALIES (See Chapter 28)

Ultrasound reveals fetal malformations before birth. Many major fetal anomalies can be identified by 16 to 18 weeks of gestation or earlier. Some abnormalities do not become apparent until later in pregnancy. Indications for antenatal ultrasound examination are listed in Box 8-1.

Central Nervous System

FETAL VENTRICULOMEGALY (See Chapter 38)
Strictly speaking, hydrocephalus and ventriculomegaly are not synonymous. *Hydrocephalus* connotes raised intracranial pressure; this functional observation cannot be made by ultrasound. The lateral ventricles may be enlarged, without altered pressure, because of a developmental abnormality. Enlargement of the atrium and posterior horns of the lateral ventricles (colpocephaly)

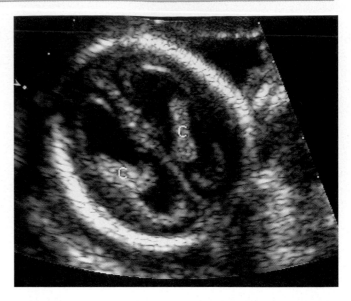

FIGURE 8-29. Ventriculomegaly. Dilated lateral cerebral ventricles with dangling choroids (C) can be seen.

often occurs in association with agenesis of the corpus callosum or type II Arnold-Chiari malformation. The lateral ventricles may also be wider as a result of brain destruction from a variety of causes, including ischemia and in utero infection by cytomegalovirus. A single measurement at the level of the atrium of the lateral ventricle is used to define *ventriculomegaly;* measurements exceeding 10 mm are considered abnormal.[16] The width of the atrium varies little during pregnancy. The normal choroid plexus position depends on gravity; on standard axial views the choroid, attached at the level of the foramen of Monro, rests on the dependent wall of the lateral ventricle. It marks the limit of the lateral ventricle even when the wall itself cannot be seen; a "dangling" choroid plexus establishes the extent and severity of ventricular enlargement (Fig. 8-29).

The clinical outcome with markedly dilated ventricles has been discouraging (Fig. 8-30). Survivors are often mentally and physically impaired. Unfortunately, it has proved impossible to define a group of fetuses with ventriculomegaly who might benefit from in utero shunting. Mild ventriculomegaly (atrial size between 10 and 15 mm) has an uncertain prognosis; the majority of infants are normal.

MENINGOMYELOCELE AND (TYPE II) CHIARI MALFORMATION
A *meningomyelocele* (Fig. 8-31) can occur in association with downward displacement of the hindbrain and with other brain anomalies. It may or may not include ventriculomegaly. Often hydrocephalus does not develop in these children until after birth. In cases of an open neural tube defect, the α-fetoprotein level is elevated in both maternal serum and amniotic fluid (see Chapter 7).

A meningomyelocele is demonstrated by ultrasound as splaying or divergence of the posterior ossification

---

BOX 8-1. Indications for Antenatal Ultrasound

Dating pregnancy
No accurate dates
Uterine size/date discrepancy
- Suspected growth restriction
- Suspected large-for-date pregnancies; rule out
  - Multiple gestation
  - Polyhydramnios
  - Macrosomia
  - Uterine abnormality (e.g., fibroid tumor)
  - Molar pregnancy

Fetal/placental localization
Confirm pregnancy
Suspected missed abortion
Suspected ectopic pregnancy
Suspected placenta previa
Before amniocentesis
Before fetal transfusion/surgery

Survey of fetal anatomy, particularly to exclude anomalies
History of malformation
Maternal age more than 35 years
Diabetic pregnancy
Polyhydramnios/oligohydramnios
Abnormal presentation
Exposure to teratogens (e.g., alcohol, retinoic acid)
Suspicious maternal serum markers

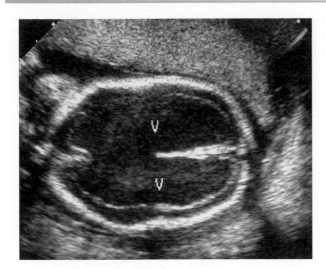

FIGURE 8-30. Severe ventriculomegaly. Dilated lateral cerebral ventricles (V) are surrounded by a small amount of brain parenchyma.

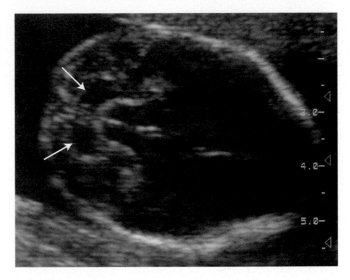

FIGURE 8-32. "Lemon" and "banana" signs. The concavity of the bony calvaria, seen to the right of the image, represents the lemon sign. Arrows mark the banana-shaped cerebellum.

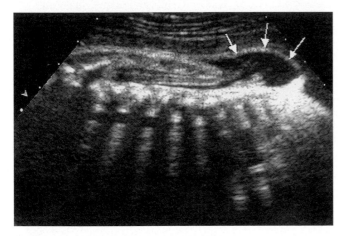

FIGURE 8-31. Meningomyelocele. Longitudinal view of a fetus shows absence of posterior bony neural arch at the lower portion of the spine. The meningomyelocele sac is shown *(arrows)*, and the spinal cord is seen in its normal position above this defect.

VENTRICULOMEGALY

The lemon sign refers to the altered appearance of the calvaria, similar in shape to a lemon, on an axial scan (Fig. 8-32).[50] The biconcave frontal bones produce the calvarial distortion. This sign is dependent on gestational age, which is demonstrated between 18 and 24 weeks and not totally specific; it is sometimes found in otherwise normal children. The banana sign refers to an abnormal position of the cerebellum, which is curled in a crescent (banana-like) around the brainstem (Fig. 8-32). Obliteration of the cisterna magna and cerebellar distortion are secondary to downward displacement of the hindbrain, which is associated with type II Arnold-Chiari malformation.

ANENCEPHALY

Anencephaly, which is the absence of the normal brain and calvaria superior to the orbits, can be detected by 10 to 14 weeks of gestation (Fig. 8-33). Associated polyhydramnios (50%) appears late in the second trimester. Maternal serum α-fetoprotein is elevated in most cases. Approximately 50% have associated anomalies, such as meningomyelocele, cleft palate, and clubfoot. Occasionally the typical appearance is altered by the presence of echogenic material superior to the orbits, identified pathologically as angiomatous stroma ("area cerebrovasculosa"). Anencephaly is considered incompatible with meaningful postnatal survival.

ENCEPHALOCELE (See Chapter 38)

The protrusion of brain tissue within a meningeal sac is usually a straightforward ultrasound diagnosis. Most encephaloceles in the western world are occipital and midline, and a distinction should be made between them and soft tissue edema or cystic hygroma of the neck. The identification of the bony calvarial defect

centers, which is best appreciated on axial views of the spine. A fluid-filled sac may be seen, and the integrity of the overlying skin can be assessed. The diagnostic sensitivity of ultrasound for the detection of meningomyeloceles is 80% to 90%. Higher sensitivities have been described by experienced sonologists with prior knowledge of elevated serum α-fetoprotein. The level of the meningomyelocele can also be ascertained by ultrasound examination, which is helpful for predicting the outcome in affected children.

The following intracranial signs are associated with a meningomyelocele: a small BPD or HC, anterior curvature of the cerebellum (the "banana" sign), concave frontal bones (the "lemon" sign), and obliteration of the cisterna magna.

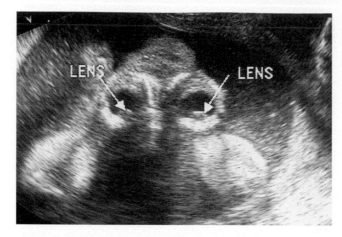

FIGURE 8-33. Anencephaly. Coronal image shows the orbits and eye lenses. Echogenic material superior to the orbits is angiomatous stroma.

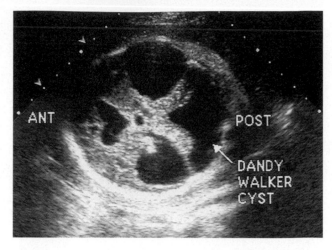

FIGURE 8-35. Dandy-Walker cyst shown in transverse scan of the brain. Note the marked splaying of the cerebellar hemispheres. ANT, anterior; POST, posterior.

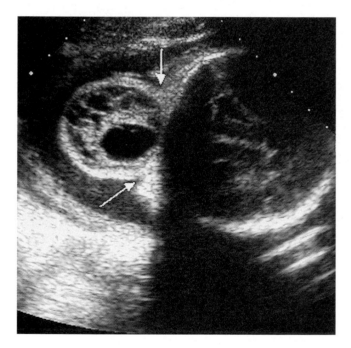

FIGURE 8-34. Occipital encephalocele. Defect in the posterior calvarium, through which the brain has herniated (*arrows*), is seen.

development of the cerebellar vermis may not be complete until that time.[12]

The Dandy-Walker variant, associated with an increased incidence of chromosomal abnormalities, consists of direct communication between the fourth ventricle and cisterna magna without posterior fossa enlargement. The inferior cerebellar vermis is only mildly hypoplastic.

CHOROID PLEXUS CYST

A *choroid plexus cyst* is identified in 1% to 2% of normal pregnancies in the second trimester and usually resolves by the early third trimester (Fig. 8-36). An association with aneuploidy, especially trisomy 18, has been reported. The management of choroid plexus cysts is

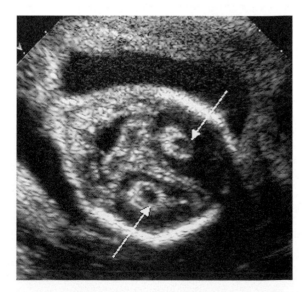

FIGURE 8-36. Choroid plexus cysts. Coronal view of the brain shows bilateral choroid plexus cysts (*arrows*).

allows a specific diagnosis (Fig. 8-34). Encephaloceles may occur in isolation or be associated with amniotic band syndrome (when off midline) and genetic syndromes such as Meckel-Gruber.

DANDY-WALKER CYST

Dandy-Walker malformation is a fluid-filled cyst of the posterior fossa with or without enlargement of the lateral ventricles (Fig. 8-35). Enlargement of the posterior fossa is always present with uplifting of the tentorium. Agenesis of the cerebellar vermis may also be recognized. The cerebellar hemispheres are rudimentary, separated by the posterior fossa cyst. Agenesis should not be diagnosed before 18 weeks because the

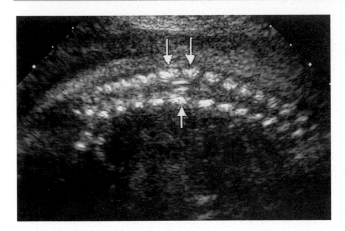

FIGURE 8-37. Coronal view through the fetal spine showing a hemivertebra. The spinal ossification center *(upper left arrow)* has no mate.

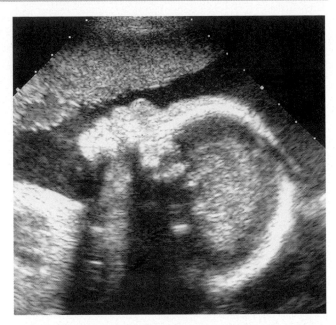

FIGURE 8-38. Sonogram demonstrates a normal forehead, nose, and jaw.

controversial; the risks for amniocentesis exceed the likelihood of abnormal results in low-risk patients, provided that a detailed examination of the fetus is otherwise normal.

Spine

Spinal anomalies demonstrable by ultrasound include congenital vertebral anomalies (Fig. 8-37) and *diastematomyelia,* which is identified as an extraposterior echogenic focus between the fetal spinal laminae.[6] This disorder is often associated with splaying of posterior spinal elements.

Sacrococcygeal teratoma is a large mass arising posteriorly from the rump of the fetus. The posterior elements of the lumbosacral spine are intact. This tumor is often associated with polyhydramnios and prematurity and more rarely with hydrops. The mass may be cystic or solid, extend into the fetal pelvis and abdomen, and rarely undergo malignant degeneration.

Head and Neck

After 14 weeks the visualization of the nose, orbits, forehead, lips, and ears is feasible. Orbits are clearly seen axially; the ocular diameters, interocular distance (defining hyper- and hypotelorism), and binocular distance are measured. The profile reveals the forehead, nose, and jaw sagittally (Fig. 8-38). The coronal view, the best for facial structures, includes the orbits (and lenses), eyelids, nose, and lips. The coronal view demonstrates facial clefting abnormalities, including the cleft lip and cleft palate, which may be central or lateral (Fig. 8-39).[52] Sagittal views should include the nasal bone; hypoplasia or its absence is used by some as a marker for Down syndrome. The complex anatomy of the fetal face is shown exquisitely by three-dimensional sonography.[34]

Cystic hygroma (lymphatic malformation) is a septate, cystic mass arising in the neck and occiput; it may extend to the remainder of the trunk (Fig. 8-40).

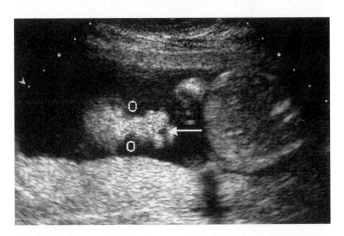

FIGURE 8-39. Coronal view of the face showing a right-sided cleft lip *(arrow).* The top of the head is to the left of the image. O, orbits.

Posterior septation of the nuchal ligament distinguishes this lesion from neural tube defects. Associated aneuploidies, including monosomy X, are common. Less frequent neck masses include anterior goiter, teratoma, and hemangioma.

Increased nuchal translucency (subcutaneous sonolucent area) is associated with trisomies 21 and 18.[67] From 11 to 13 weeks a width of 3 mm or more is a sensitive marker for aneuploidy, although technical challenges may limit its use (Fig. 8-41).[60] The cause of the transient fluid accumulation in the neck is unknown; the appearance at birth is usually normal. Nuchal lucencies in chromosomally normal fetuses have been linked to other abnormalities, including cardiac defects and skeletal dysplasias.

155

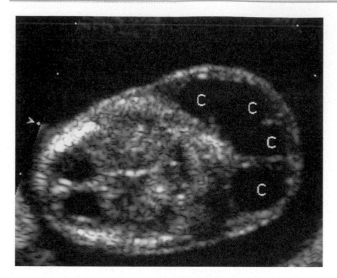

FIGURE 8-40. Transverse image through the head showing cystic hygroma. C, septate cysts.

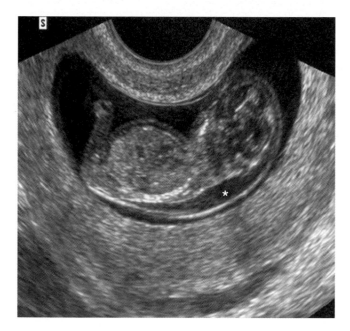

FIGURE 8-41. Increased nuchal translucency. Transvaginal ultrasound performed at 12 weeks demonstrates a sonolucent area *(asterisk)* over the posterior neck and upper thorax. (Compare with Figure 8-10.)

Heart (See Chapter 43)

Most fetal echocardiograms are obtained at 18 to 20 weeks of gestation; however, the fetal heart may be evaluated as early as 12 weeks with transvaginal ultrasound. Optimal timing is a compromise between offering a diagnosis as early as possible and adequately visualizing complex anatomy, recognizing that some lesions develop late in pregnancy. A four-chamber view of the fetal heart should be part of all obstetric ultrasound examinations (see Fig. 8-26). Abnormal four-chamber views will detect approximately 50% of all

cases of congenital heart disease in a nonselected population. Fetal arrhythmias may also be diagnosed.

Outlet views of the ventricles, linking the aorta with the left ventricle and the pulmonary artery with the right ventricle, improve the diagnostic yield[17] by permitting the identification of the transposition of the great vessels, tetralogy of Fallot, and truncus arteriosus. The sensitivity for complex cardiac lesions exceeds that for isolated septal defects. The correct diagnosis is highly dependent on operator experience.

An echogenic intracardiac focus reflects calcification of the papillary muscle tip; it is of no functional significance and is unassociated with cardiac malformations; the risks of Down syndrome are slightly increased.

Gastrointestinal Tract (See Chapter 45)

NORMAL BOWEL APPEARANCE

Physiologic bowel migration into the proximal umbilical cord occurring from 7 to 10 weeks of gestation can be seen on first-trimester scans (Fig. 8-42). It should never be mistaken for ventral abdominal wall defects.[10] The normal fetal stomach is seen transvaginally by 9 to 10 weeks of gestation as a fluid-filled structure in the upper left abdominal quadrant, changing in size as it empties and fills. The fetal small bowel usually is not distinguished early in gestation but appears as fluid-filled loops in the central abdomen by the late second trimester (Fig. 8-43). The large bowel is clearly identified by the third trimester as a hypoechoic tubular structure in the periphery of the abdomen. Meconium in the large bowel is normal in the third trimester. Occasionally, during the second trimester meconium shows increased echogenicity. This can be a normal finding, resolving by the end of the second trimester. An echogenic bowel may be a nonspecific but abnormal finding linked to poor fetal outcomes: the more echogenic the bowel, the worse the outcome. An *echogenic bowel* has been associated with aneuploidy (trisomy 21), cystic fibrosis,

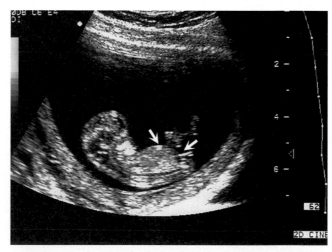

FIGURE 8-42. A 10-week fetus within its gestational sac. Physiologic midgut herniation is seen at this gestational age *(arrows)*.

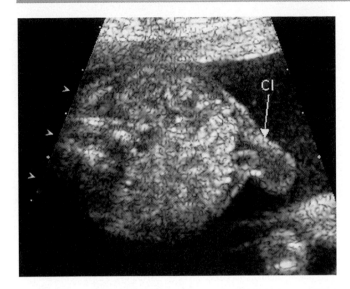

FIGURE 8-43. Cross section of the abdomen, at the level of the umbilical vein, demonstrating fluid-filled loops of normal small bowel in the abdomen. CI, cord insertion.

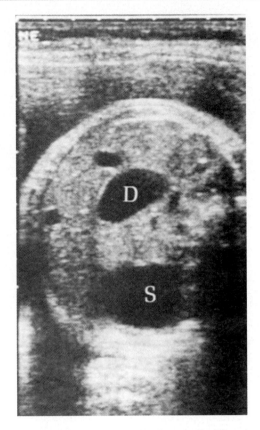

FIGURE 8-44. Duodenal atresia. Dilated stomach (S) and proximal duodenum (D) produce "double bubble" sign. Duodenal obstruction can also be caused by annular pancreas or malrotation of the bowel.

bowel atresia, congenital infections (such as cytomegalovirus), and intrauterine growth restriction.[51]

Obstruction of the gastrointestinal tract can be diagnosed by ultrasound. Blockage of the proximal alimentary canal interferes with amniotic fluid turnover, which involves swallowing and absorption by the fetus. In proximal bowel obstruction, polyhydramnios is an invariable finding (see Chapter 21).

ESOPHAGEAL ATRESIA AND TRACHEOESOPHAGEAL FISTULA

A nonvisualized fetal stomach combined with polyhydramnios should alert the examiner to the possibility of *esophageal atresia*. Unfortunately, these two signs are identified in only 40% of the cases. Nonvisualization of the stomach is not specific for esophageal atresia; a proximal esophageal pouch is almost never visualized. Polyhydramnios, which is seen in two thirds of the cases, may not develop until the third trimester. The VACTERL complex consists of *v*ertebral, *a*nal, *c*ardiovascular, *t*racheal, *e*sophageal, *r*enal, and *l*imb malformations; these systems should be scrutinized in the fetus when a *tracheoesophageal fistula* from poor gastric filling is suspected. The stomach may not fill when there is little to swallow, as in oligohydramnios, or when there are abnormalities of the neural or musculoskeletal system (e.g., Pena-Shokeir syndrome) that interfere with swallowing.

SMALL-BOWEL OBSTRUCTION

With *duodenal atresia*, a distended stomach and proximal duodenum produce a "double-bubble" sign akin to the x-ray appearance of the neonate (Fig. 8-44). The association (25%) with Down syndrome justifies genetic amniocentesis when duodenal atresia is suspected. Other etiologies include the annular pancreas, the duodenal

web, malrotation, and severe duodenal stenosis. *Ileal* and *jejunal atresia* can be diagnosed by the presence of multiple bowel loops, often exhibiting peristalsis (Fig. 8-45). More distal bowel obstruction, seen in meconium ileus, Hirschsprung disease, and anal atresia, may similarly produce dilated loops of bowel that are not usually apparent until the third trimester (Fig. 8-46). Meconium peritonitis, a sterile chemical form of the disease resulting from intrauterine bowel perforation of any cause, is identified by peritoneal calcifications and free intraperitoneal fluid on ultrasound.

ANTERIOR ABDOMINAL WALL DEFECTS

With an approximate incidence of *omphalocele* of 1 in 5000 and of gastroschisis of 1 in 10,000 live births, abdominal wall defects are among the more common neonatal abnormalities. A midline defect involving the base of the umbilical cord is characteristic of omphalocele (Fig. 8-47). A sac surrounds the herniated viscera and may also include the liver. Omphaloceles are frequently associated with other anomalies (e.g., Beckwith-Wiedemann syndrome) and aneuploidies (trisomies 13 and 18). In gastroschisis, herniated bowel loops float in the amniotic cavity without a covering membrane (Fig. 8-48). The defect is lateral to the umbilical cord insertion, typically on the right. Associated fetal abnormalities are rare.

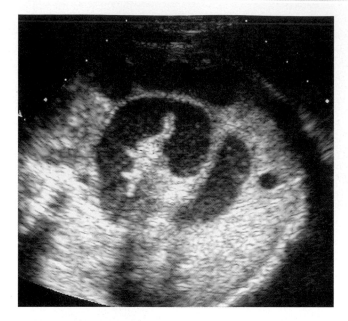

FIGURE 8-45. Ileal atresia. Transverse image of abdomen showing multiple dilated, fluid-filled loops of small bowel.

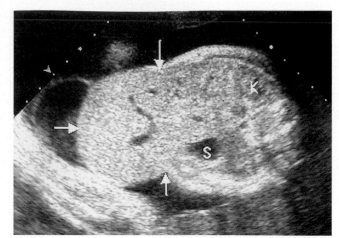

FIGURE 8-47. Omphalocele. Anterior abdominal wall defect *(arrows)* with surrounding membrane. The liver has herniated into this defect. S, stomach; K, kidney.

DIAPHRAGMATIC HERNIA

The diagnosis of *congenital diaphragmatic hernia* is made when the abdominal organs (usually the stomach and bowel) are seen in the thorax (Fig. 8-49). Fluid-filled loops of bowel may show peristalsis in the thoracic cavity. Polyhydramnios, left-sided cardiac hypo-development, and detection before 24 weeks were all predictors of poor neonatal outcome (see Chapters 11, 42, and 45).[47]

Diaphragmatic hernia shows a mass effect, with a mediastinal shift and lung compression. Unfortunately,

the extent of pulmonary hypoplasia, measured at the level of the four-chamber heart, cannot by itself predict postnatal outcome. The best current predictor is the measurement of the lung-to-head ratio. The presence of liver herniation into the chest, a poor prognostic sign, can be documented by fetal MRI (Fig. 8-50). In utero correction by tracheal PLUG (*p*lug the *l*ung *u*ntil it *g*rows) has not been shown to reduce mortality,[33] reinforcing the need for randomized trials of new medical and surgical therapies.

Gallbladder and Bile Ducts (See Chapter 46)

A choledochal cyst is a localized dilation of the biliary system, often involving the common bile duct. It is

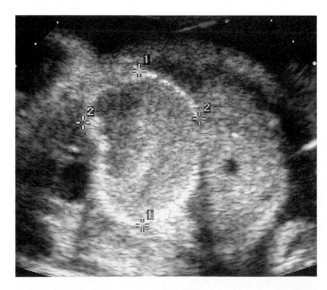

FIGURE 8-46. *Transverse image of abdomen, with meconium pseudocyst marked with cursors. This finding is associated with cystic fibrosis.*

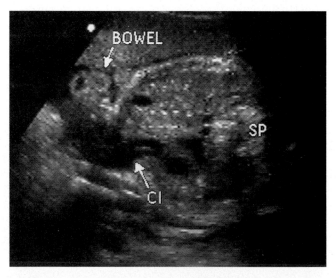

FIGURE 8-48. Gastroschisis. Transverse scan of the fetal abdomen shows loops of bowel floating freely in the amniotic cavity to the right of the cord insertion (CI). SP, spine.

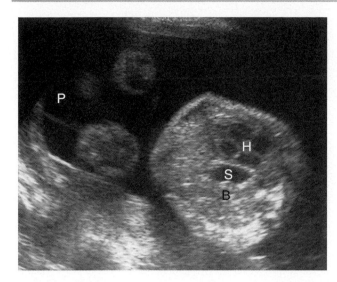

FIGURE 8-49. Diaphragmatic hernia. Transverse view of the fetal chest shows the heart (H) shifted to the right of the fetal chest by the bowel (B). The stomach bubble (S) is to the left of the heart. Polyhydramnios (P) is present.

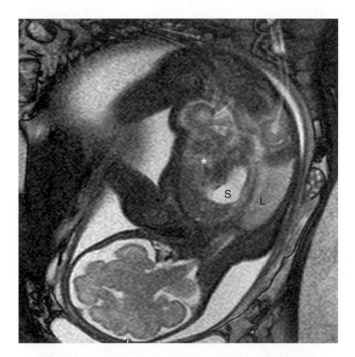

FIGURE 8-50. Magnetic resonance imaging (MRI) of diaphragmatic hernia. Note fluid-filled stomach (S) in the chest, together with collapsed loops of bowel *(asterisks)*. Contralateral lung (L), which appears normal, is identified.

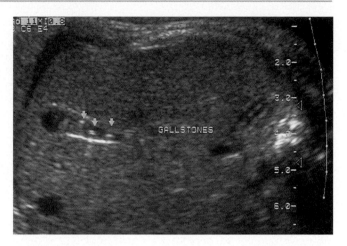

FIGURE 8-51. Transverse scan through abdomen showing gallstones *(arrows)* in the fetal gallbladder. (Compare with Figure 8-24.)

Genitourinary Tract (See Chapter 49)

The kidneys are identified lateral to the fetal spine at 12 to 14 weeks of gestation (Fig. 8-52). Normal kidney size can be plotted against gestational age; by the end of the third trimester, fat deposition creates an echogenic border, enhancing contrast for the demonstration of renal structures. The bladder is visible as early as 13 weeks of gestation. Color Doppler demonstrates the umbilical arteries on either side of the bladder (see Fig. 8-6). Normal fetal ureters are never visible by ultrasound. The fetal adrenal glands are easily identified later in pregnancy because of the relatively large cortex.

Lethal renal malfunctions such as *bilateral multicystic kidneys* or bilateral renal agenesis result in the absence of fetal urine production; oligohydramnios may not become apparent until 18 to 20 weeks of gestation. Amniotic fluid after 16 weeks is almost entirely

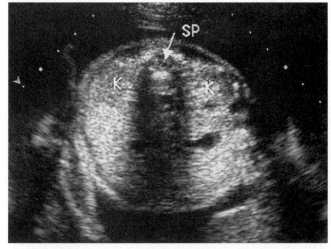

FIGURE 8-52. Transverse view of the abdomen demonstrating two normal kidneys (K). SP, spine.

seen as a fluid-filled cyst in the upper right abdominal quadrant, separate from the gallbladder.

Echogenic material (suspected gallstones) is occasionally noted in the gallbladder lumen on third-trimester scans (Fig. 8-51). Follow-up studies in neonates have shown resolution in the majority of cases; children have been reported to be asymptomatic.[14]

fetal urine. Infants born after prolonged oligohydramnios have a characteristic facial appearance, limb deformities, and pulmonary hypoplasia, called Potter syndrome (or sequence). When oligohydramnios is noted on ultrasound examination, attention should be directed to the fetal urinary tract. If the bladder is not seen at first, the patient should be rescanned at 30-minute intervals. Unfortunately, the lack of surrounding amniotic fluid in oligohydramnios obscures fetal anatomy. The inability to find the fetal bladder and kidneys in the presence of oligohydramnios is strongly suggestive of bilateral renal agenesis. The fetal adrenal glands are larger than those in the neonate and may be mistaken for the kidneys. Fetal MRI can be ideal in clarifying the identification. Care must be exercised in diagnosing unilateral renal agenesis to exclude renal ectopy with a pelvic kidney.

Mild dilation of the fetal renal pelvis is common; it is a normal feature that should not be misinterpreted as hydronephrosis. Pyelectasis is not affected by maternal hydration and has been reported to be a marker for Down syndrome. Identifying a single measurement to predict the development of obstructive uropathy after birth has proved elusive. Pathologic dilation of the upper urinary tract was previously diagnosed when the renal pelvis measured 10 mm or more in the anteroposterior dimension (Fig. 8-53). This measurement failed to identify hydronephrosis before the third trimester; a cutoff of 4 mm is now used earlier in pregnancy. Obstruction of the urinary tract produces a variable sonographic appearance, depending mainly on the timing of onset. Renal dysplasia, sometimes with cyst formation, is the consequence of early obstruction, and obstruction occurring later in gestation is more likely to result in dilation of the collecting system. The Society for Fetal Urology has proposed the following grading system.

Grade 1—Renal pelvis dilation with or without visible infundibula

Grade 2—Renal pelvis dilation with visible calices

Grade 3—Renal pelvis and dilated calices

Grade 4—Addition of renal parenchymal thinning[24]

Hydronephrosis may be unilateral, resulting from obstruction of the ureteropelvic junction, or bilateral, resulting from lower urinary tract obstruction by posterior urethral valves or urethral agenesis. A distended, often thick-walled bladder will be imaged in a male fetus with posterior valves. Hydroureters are usually present, and urinary ascites may occur. "Keyhole" dilation of the posterior urethra helps distinguish this lesion from prune-belly syndrome (Fig. 8-54).

Multicystic renal dysplasia appears as several noncommunicating cysts varying in size and lacking organization. This presentation contrasts with the findings in severe hydronephrosis, where there is an orderly arrangement of the enlarged renal pelvis surrounded by smaller calices. Dysplastic cysts can change in size, and bilateral renal anomalies (including bilateral multicystic renal dysplasia) are common (40%) in the fetus (Fig. 8-55).

Dilated ureters may be seen in ureterovesical junction obstruction (primary megaureter). Dilated ureters have also been attributed to reflux. Autosomal recessive polycystic kidney disease causes bilaterally enlarged, echogenic kidneys, which retain their reniform shape (Fig. 8-56). Many other renal anomalies have been identified prenatally, including duplicated collecting systems (Fig. 8-57) and bladder extrophy.

Distinguishing the male from the female fetus by examining the external genitalia is reliably accomplished by 16 to 20 weeks of gestation (see Fig. 8-11; Fig. 8-58). Ovarian cysts, fluid-filled or septate with fluid levels, have been found in utero; ovarian cysts are often abdominal and not easily distinguished from other abnormal cysts. Hydrometrocolpos is another cause of a fluid-filled pelvic structure in females.

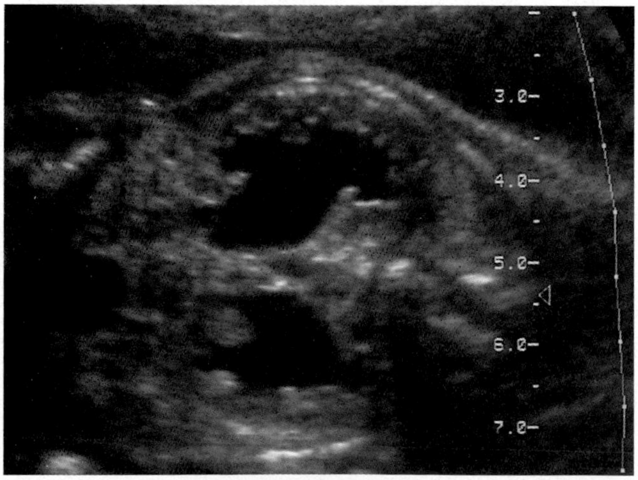

FIGURE 8-53. Coronal image showing bilateral ureteropelvic obstruction. Dilated renal pelvis with dilated calices is seen bilaterally.

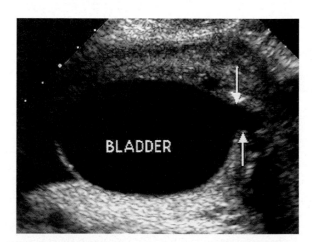

FIGURE 8-54. Posterior urethral valve. Coronal scan of the fetal pelvis shows an enlarged bladder and dilated posterior urethra. Arrows are proximal to the posterior urethral valves. Note the oligohydramnios.

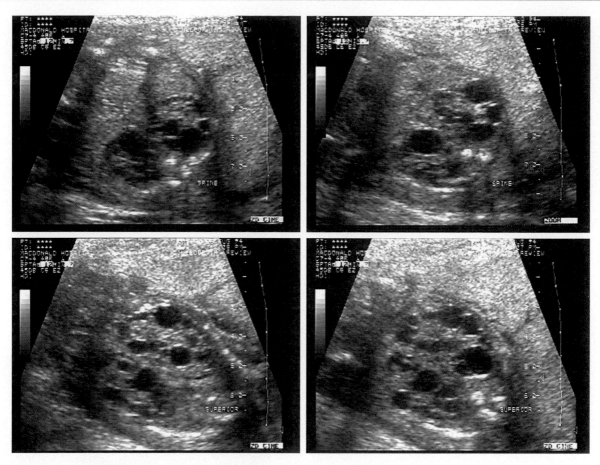

FIGURE 8-55. Multiple views of bilateral multicystic dysplastic kidneys. Note severe oligohydramnios.

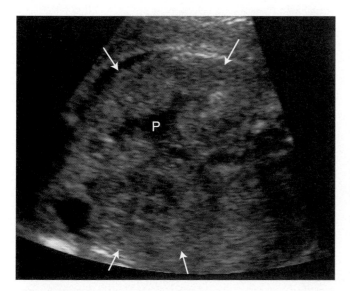

FIGURE 8-56. Polycystic kidneys. Transverse scan of the fetal abdomen shows enlarged hyperechoic kidneys filling the fetal abdomen (arrows). Oligohydramnios is present. P, renal pelvis.

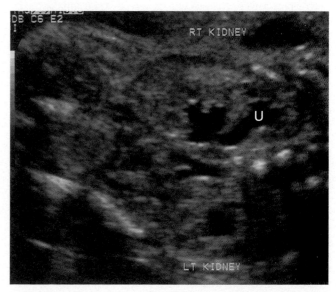

FIGURE 8-57. Coronal image through fetus showing a duplicated renal collecting system in the right (RT) kidney. LT, left kidney; U, upper pole.

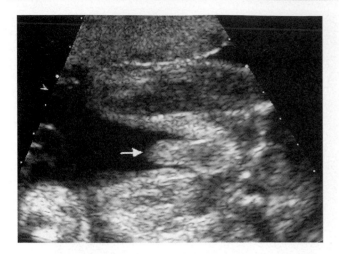

FIGURE 8-58. Male fetus. Arrow shows penis. (Compare with Figure 8-11.)

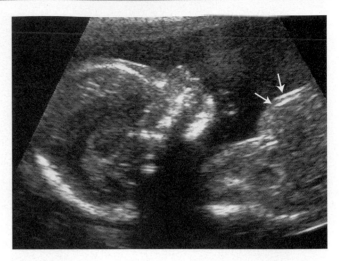

FIGURE 8-59. Thanatophoric dysplasia. Sagittal view of the fetus reveals severe deformation of the rib cage, with protrusion of the abdomen (*arrows*).

Musculoskeletal System

The examination of all four extremities and the measurement of the length of the femur are routine parts of prenatal studies. Standardized tables exist for all the long bones in the second and third trimesters. Shortening of the extremities beyond 3 SD for age is suggestive of skeletal dysplasia. Because measurements in the normal population are distributed below the 5th percentile, it is reassuring that the majority of skeletal dysplasias show dramatic reductions; an abnormal femur-to-foot ratio, usually near unity, may add additional support. The BPD will continue to reflect gestational age as long as the skull is not involved in the dysplastic syndrome.

The careful measurement of all bones in the peripheral skeleton is required in suspected cases of skeletal dysplasia, first to define the category of dysplasia and then, if possible, to make a diagnosis (see Chapters 28 and 52). Overall limb reduction is referred to as *micromelia; rhizomelia* refers to proximal (femurs and humeri), *mesomelia* to more distal (forearms and lower legs), and *acromelia* to the most distal (feet and hands) dysplasias. Fractures and curvatures should be noted as well as bone density, the skull, the ribs, and the appearance of the spine.

Pulmonary hypoplasia is a frequent cause of death in fetuses with severe skeletal dysplasia. Lung volume can be assessed on the four-chamber view of the heart. Polyhydramnios with skeletal dysplasia may also be present.

Thanatophoric dysplasia is a uniformly lethal skeletal dysplasia that can often be recognized in utero. Features are severe micromelia, curved femurs, and pulmonary hypoplasia (Fig. 8-59). One form of thanatophoric dysplasia includes a cloverleaf skull deformity. Achondrogenesis is another lethal condition with severe micromelia and a lack of vertebral ossification.

Lethal type II osteogenesis imperfecta produces short, fractured bones, often bent or curved (Fig. 8-60). Bone density is decreased, and it is best appreciated

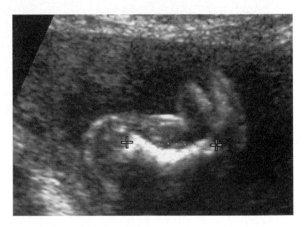

FIGURE 8-60. Osteogenesis imperfecta. Humerus with marked shortening and abnormal shape secondary to multiple fractures is indicated by cursors.

in the calvaria.[49] The lethal form of hypophosphatasia may have a similar ultrasound appearance of severe demineralization.

Heterozygous achondroplasia is the most common nonlethal skeletal dysplasia. Shortening of the femur characterizes this rhizomelic disorder. The retardation of femoral growth may not be noticeable until the third trimester, limiting the likely prenatal diagnosis to known carriers of the autosomal dominant disorder.

Other abnormalities of the musculoskeletal system include the malformation or absence (dysostosis) of various parts of the skeleton, for example, limb reduction anomalies such as radial clubhand or hemimelia (Fig. 8-61).

Pitfalls in the diagnosis of skeletal dysplasia are appreciable. A phenocopy gives a fetus the attributes of a specific syndrome, but the cause may be another factor, such as infection, another genetic abnormality,

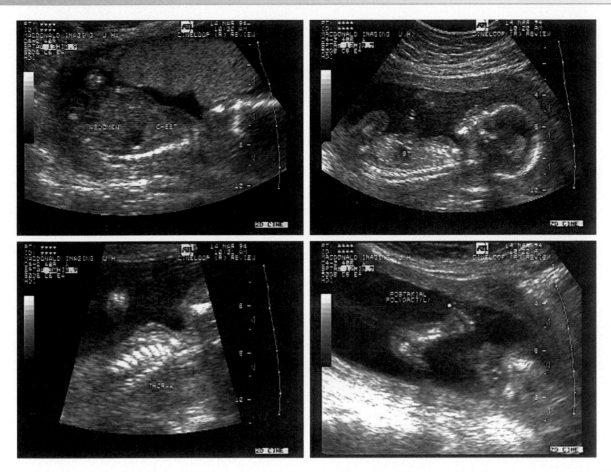

FIGURE 8-61. Fetus with short-ribbed polydactyly syndrome. Multiple images show a small chest with hypoechoic ribs, large amounts of amniotic fluid, and postaxial polydactyly.

or teratogen exposure. An example of a phenocopy is the stippling of epiphyses caused by maternal warfarin use, mimicking stippled epiphyseal skeletal dysplasia.

Two-Vessel Umbilical Cord

A *single umbilical artery* (SUA) is identified on transverse section and confirmed by color Doppler imaging at the level of the fetal bladder (Figs. 8-62 and 8-63). SUA may be associated with other congenital anomalies, prompting a careful anatomic survey; unfortunately, the reported anomalies do not display a consistent pattern. It is unclear whether isolated SUA is associated with aneuploidy, but discretion would suggest counseling and karyotyping if desired. A small size for gestational age is more common in neonates with SUA. Serial third-trimester exams can confirm fetal growth, and tests for fetal well-being may be indicated.[54]

SUMMARY

Sonography appears to be nearing maturity, with a gratifying degree of success in fulfilling its early potential. Initial limitations have yielded to advances in technology and techniques or have been more effectively addressed by other approaches, like biochemical

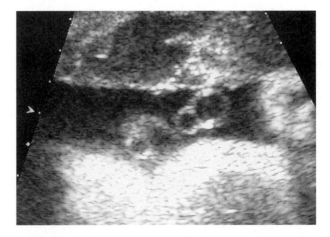

FIGURE 8-62. Two-vessel umbilical cord. A transverse scan of the umbilical cord shows the vein and a single artery.

testing or MRI. Although the unimaginably rapid pace of the last 3 decades is likely to slow, the future remains bright for further advances in quality, applications, and insights through obstetric ultrasound.

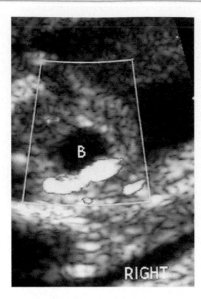

FIGURE 8-63. Two-vessel umbilical cord. Transverse scan of the fetal pelvis, at the level of the bladder (B), reveals absence of the left umbilical artery. (Compare with Figure 8-7.)

REFERENCES

1. Abbott JG: Rationale and derivation of MI and TI: A review. Ultrasound Med Biol 25:431, 1999.

2. Abramowicz JS: Ultrasound in obstetrics and gynecology: Is this hot technology too hot? J Ultrasound Med 21:1327, 2002.

3. American College of Obstetricians and Gynecologists: ACOG Committee Opinion No. 296: First-trimester screening for fetal aneuploidy. Obstet Gynecol 104:215, 2004.

4. American Institute of Ultrasound in Medicine: AIUM Practice Guideline for the Performance of an Antepartum Obstetric Ultrasound Examination. J Ultrasound Med 22:1116, 2003.

5. Anderson HF: Transabdominal and transvaginal ultrasonography of the uterine cervix during pregnancy. J Clin Ultrasound 19:77, 1991.

6. Anderson NG et al: Diastematomyelia: Diagnosis by prenatal sonography. Am J Roentgenol 163:911, 1994.

7. Baschat AA et al: Qualitative venous Doppler waveform analysis improves prediction of critical perinatal outcomes in premature growth-restricted fetus. Ultrasound Obstet Gynecol 22:240, 2003.

8. Bello G et al: Combined pregnancy: The Mount Sinai experience. Obstet Gynecol Surv 41:603, 1986.

9. Benacerraf B: Three-dimensional fetal sonography. J Ultrasound Med 21:1063, 2002.

10. Bowerman R: Sonography of fetal midgut herniation: Normal size criteria and correlation with crown-rump length. J Ultrasound Med 5:251, 1993.

11. Bromley B et al: Adnexal masses during pregnancy: Accuracy of sonographic diagnosis and outcome. J Ultrasound Med 16:447, 1997.

12. Bromley B et al: Closure of the cerebellar vermis: Evaluation with second trimester US. Radiology 193:761, 1994.

13. Bronshtein M: Fetal scanning between 18 and 22 weeks is passé. Ultrasound Obstet Gynecol 16:69, 2000.

14. Brown DL et al: Echogenic material in the fetal gallbladder: Sonographic and clinical observations. Radiology 182:73, 1992.

15. Campbell S et al: Routine ultrasound screening for the prediction of gestational age. Obstet Gynecol 65:613, 1985.

16. Cardoza JD et al: Exclusion of fetal ventriculomegaly with a single measurement: The width of the lateral ventricular atrium. Radiology 169:711, 1988.

17. Carvalho JS et al: Improving the effectiveness of routine prenatal screening for major congenital heart defects. Heart 88:387, 2002.

18. Chervenak FA et al: How accurate is fetal biometry in the assessment of fetal age? Am J Obstet Gynecol 178:678, 1998.

19. Comstock CH et al: Sonographic detection of placenta accreta in the second and third trimesters of pregnancy. Am J Obstet Gynecol 190:1135, 2004.

20. Di Salvo DN: Sonographic imaging of maternal complications of pregnancy. J Ultrasound Med 22:69, 2003.

21. Doubilet PM et al: Long-term prognosis of pregnancies complicated by slow embryonic heart rates in the early first trimester. J Ultrasound Med 18:537, 1999.

22. Ekerhovd E et al: An ultrasound-based approach to the assessment of infertility, including the evaluation of tubal patency. Best Pract Res Clin Obstet Gynaecol 18:13, 2004.

23. Ewigman BG et al: Effect of prenatal ultrasound screening on perinatal outcome. RADIUS (Routine Antenatal Diagnostic Imaging with Ultrasound Study). N Engl J Med 329:821, 1993.

24. Fernbach SK et al: Ultrasound grading of hydronephrosis: Introduction to the system used by the Society for Fetal Urology. Pediatr Radiol 23:478, 1993.

25. Filly RA et al: Routine obstetrical sonography. J Ultrasound Med 21:713, 2002.

26. Finberg HJ et al: Placenta accreta: prospective sonographic diagnosis in patients with placenta previa and prior cesarean section. J Ultrasound Med 11:333, 1992.

27. Fleischer AC: Sonography in Gynecology and Obstetrics. New York, McGraw-Hill, 2004.

28. Fletcher JC et al: Ethics in reproductive genetics. Clin Obstet Gynecol 35:763, 1992.

29. Glantz C et al: Clinical utility of sonography in the diagnosis and treatment of placental abruption. J Ultrasound Med 21:837, 2002.

30. Grannum PA et al: The ultrasonic changes in the maturing placenta and their relation to fetal pulmonic maturity. Am J Obstet Gynecol 133:915, 1979.

31. Hadlock FP et al: Estimating fetal age: Computer assisted analysis of multiple fetal growth parameters. Radiology 152:497, 1984.

32. Harger JH: Cerclage and cervical insufficiency: An evidence-based analysis. Obstet Gynecol 100:1313, 2002.

33. Harrison MR et al: A randomized trial of fetal endoscopic tracheal occlusion for severe fetal congenital diaphragmatic hernia. N Engl J Med 349:1916, 2003.

34. Hata T et al: Three dimensional sonographic visualization of the fetal face. Am J Roentgenol 170:481, 1998.

35. Iams JD et al: The length of the cervix and the risk of spontaneous delivery. N Engl J Med 334:567, 1996.

36. Jeanty P et al: Estimation of gestational age from measurements of fetal long bones. J Ultrasound Med 3:75, 1984.

37. Katz VL et al: Complications of uterine leiomyomas in pregnancy. Obstet Gynecol 73:593, 1989.

38. Kofinas AD et al: Uteroplacental Doppler flow velocity waveform indices in normal pregnancy: A statistical exercise and the development of appropriate reference values. Am J Perinatol 9:94, 1992.

39. Kurjak A: Are color and pulsed Doppler sonography safe in early pregnancy? J Perinat Med 27:423, 1999.

40. Laing FC et al: Ultrasound evaluation during the first trimester of pregnancy. In Callen PW (ed): Ultrasonography in Obstetrics and Gynecology, 4th edition. Philadelphia, WB Saunders Co, 2000.

41. LaTorre R et al: Transvaginal sonographic evaluation of endometrial polyps: a comparison with two-dimensional and three-dimensional contrast sonography. Clin Exp Obstet Gynecol 26:171, 1999.

42. Levine D: Ultrasound versus resonance imaging in fetal evaluation. Magn Res Imaging 12:25, 2001.

43. Malone FD et al: First-trimester sonographic screening for Down syndrome. Obstet Gynecol 102:1066, 2003.

44. Malone FD et al: First And Second Trimester Evaluation of Risk (FASTER) trial: Principal results of the NICHD multicenter Down Syndrome Screening Study: SMFM Abstract. Am J Obstet Gynecol 189:1, 2003.

45. Mari G et al: Noninvasive diagnosis by Doppler ultrasonography of fetal anemia due to maternal red-cell alloimmunization: Collaborative Group for Doppler Assessment of the Blood Velocity in Anemic Fetuses. N Engl J Med 342:9, 2000.

46. Marteau TM: Towards informed decisions about prenatal testing: A review. Prenat Diagn 15:1215, 1995.

47. Metkus AP et al: Sonographic predictors of survival in fetal diaphragmatic hernia. J Pediatr Surg 31:148, 1996.

48. Miller DA et al: Clinical risk factors for placenta previa-placenta accreta. Am J Obstet Gynecol 177:210, 1997.

49. Munoz C et al: Osteogenesis imperfecta type II: Prenatal sonographic diagnosis. Radiology 174:181, 1990.

50. Nicolaides KH et al: Ultrasound screening for spina bifida: Cranial and cerebellar signs. Lancet 2:72, 1986.

51. Nyberg DA et al: Echogenic fetal bowel during the second trimester: Clinical importance. Radiology 188:527, 1993.

52. Nyberg DA et al: Paranasal echogenic mass: Sonographic sign of bilateral complete cleft lip and palate before 20 menstrual weeks. Radiology 184:757, 1992.

53. Pearlstone M et al: Subchorionic hematoma: A review. Obstet Gynecol Surv 48:65, 1993.

54. Persutte WH et al: Single umbilical artery: A clinical enigma in modern prenatal diagnosis. Ultrasound Obstet Gynecol 6:216, 1995.

55. Phelan J et al: Amniotic fluid index measurements during pregnancy. J Reprod Med 32:601, 1987.

56. Resnick R: Intrauterine growth restriction. Obstet Gynecol 99:490, 2002.

57. Rice JP et al: The clinical significance of uterine leiomyomas in pregnancy. Am J Obstet Gynecol 160:1212, 1989.

58. Ross MG et al: National Institute of Child Health and Development Workshop Participants. J Matern Fetal Med 10:2, 2001.

59. Sebire NJ et al: Multiple gestation. In Nyberg, DA et al (eds): Diagnostic Imaging of Fetal Anomalies. Philadelphia, Lippincott ,Williams & Wilkins, 2003.

60. Seeds JW: Ultrasonographic screening for fetal aneuploidy. N Engl J Med 337:1689, 1997.

61. Sladkevicius P et al: Advanced ultrasound examination in the management of subfertility. Curr Opin Obstet Gynecol 12:221, 2000.

62. Smith-Bindman R et al: Second-trimester ultrasound to detect fetuses with Down syndrome: A meta-analysis. JAMA 285:1044, 2001.

63. Snijders RC et al: First trimester trisomy screening, nuchal translucency measurement training and quality assurance to correct and unify technique. Ultrasound Obstet Gynecol 19:953, 2002.

64. Tal J et al: Heterotopic pregnancy after ovulation induction and assisted reproductive technologies: A literature review from 1971 to 1993. Fertil Steril 66:1, 1996.

65. Timor-Tritsch IE: Transvaginal sonographic evaluation of fetal anatomy at 14 to 16 weeks. J Ultrasound Med 20:705, 2001.

66. Wald NJ et al: SURUSS in perspective. Br J Gynaecol 111:521, 2004.

67. Wapner R et al: First-trimester screening for trisomies 21 and 18. N Engl J Med 349:1405, 2003.

Estimation of Fetal Well-Being

PART 1

Antepartum Fetal Surveillance

Susan E. Gerber

The primary goal of antenatal fetal surveillance is the avoidance of intrauterine fetal death. Pregnant women are counseled on the importance of fetal movement, and routine prenatal care provides for routine fetal surveillance. However, in certain populations with an increased risk of fetal demise, a greater degree of fetal surveillance may be warranted. This first part of the chapter addresses the methods used to perform such surveillance and the evidence for their use.

RATIONALE FOR SURVEILLANCE

The incidence of intrauterine fetal death at 28 weeks or more of gestation was 3.3 per 1000 births in 2001 in the United States.[13] Intrauterine fetal death may result from a variety of etiologies, such as congenital malformations, fetal-maternal hemorrhage, congenital infection, isoimmunization, and antiphospholipid syndrome. In many circumstances such deaths are precipitated by sudden catastrophic events such as an abruptio placentae and cord prolapse. Such events are often unpredictable and not preventable by any form of antepartum surveillance. Women at risk for such events may not benefit from increased surveillance. For example, maternal cocaine use may increase the risk of abruptio placentae and intrauterine fetal death, but without underlying uteroplacental insufficiency or growth restriction, such an event would not be predictable.

The methods commonly used for antenatal fetal surveillance rely on fetal biophysical parameters that are sensitive to hypoxemia and acidemia, such as heart rate and movement. Blood flow in the fetoplacental circulation is responsive to these conditions as well. The surveillance tools are useful in a fetus who is at risk for hypoxemia because of chronic uteroplacental insufficiency. It is hoped that if fetal surveillance identifies a fetus in jeopardy, the physician will have an opportunity to intervene before progressive fetal hypoxemia and acidosis lead to fetal death or to the delivery of a severely compromised neonate.

INDICATIONS FOR SURVEILLANCE

Pregnancies at increased risk for intrauterine fetal demise fall into two categories: those with maternal conditions and those with pregnancy-associated conditions. Table 9-1 lists some of the conditions in which antenatal surveillance should be considered. There are a number

TABLE 9-1. Indications for Antenatal Surveillance

MATERNAL CONDITIONS	PREGNANCY-RELATED CONDITIONS
Antiphospholipid syndrome	Pregnancy-induced hypertension
Hyperthyroidism (poorly controlled)	Decreased fetal movement
Diabetes mellitus	Oligohydramnios
Cyanotic heart disease	Polyhydramnios
Systemic lupus erythematosus	Intrauterine growth restriction
Hypertensive disorders	Multiple gestations
Chronic renal disease	Post-term pregnancy
Hemoglobinopathies (hemoglobin SS, SC, or S-thalassemia)	Previous fetal demise (unexplained or recurrent risk) Isoimmunization (moderate to severe) Preterm premature rupture of membranes Unexplained third-trimester bleeding

of situations in which a population is known to have an increased risk of fetal death, but the etiology is unclear. One such population is the 1% of all pregnant women that are found to have an unexplained elevated maternal serum α-fetoprotein. Although numerous studies have confirmed the elevated risk of fetal death in this population, there is no consensus on whether antenatal surveillance reduces this risk.[32] Antenatal testing in such a population is commonly performed, but it remains controversial.

PHYSIOLOGIC BASIS FOR ANTENATAL SURVEILLANCE

In experiments involving animal and human fetuses, hypoxemia and acidosis have been shown to consistently alter fetal biophysical parameters such as heart rate, movement, breathing, and tone.[5,20,27] The fetal heart rate (FHR) is normally controlled by the fetal central nervous system (CNS) and mediated by sympathetic or parasympathetic nerve impulses originating in the fetal brainstem. Therefore, the presence of intermittent FHR accelerations associated with fetal movement is believed to be an indicator of an intact fetal autonomic nervous system. In a study of fetal blood sampling of pregnancies resulting in healthy neonates, Weiner and colleagues established a range of normal fetal venous pH measurements.[31] In this population, the lower 2.5 percentile of fetal venous pH was 7.37. Manning and associates demonstrated that fetuses without heart rate accelerations had a mean umbilical vein pH of 7.28 (±0.11), and those with abnormal movement had a mean pH of 7.16 (±0.08).[22] These and similar observations were the basis for the development of the antenatal fetal testing modalities that are currently in use.

Nonstress Test

In most institutions, the first-line assessment tool for fetal surveillance is the nonstress test (NST). Lee and coworkers first described the association between FHR accelerations and fetal movements in 1975.[14] Monitoring

for the presence or absence of both elements was proposed as a method for the evaluation of fetal well-being. The NST is performed in a nonlaboring patient (as opposed to the contraction stress test [CST], in which the patient has regular uterine contractions, either spontaneously or induced). At times a woman undergoing an NST is found to have spontaneous contractions, thereby adding the reassurance of a negative CST.

With the patient in a recumbent, tilted position, the FHR is monitored with an external transducer for up to 40 minutes. The FHR tracing is observed for the presence of accelerations above the baseline. A reactive test is one in which there are at least two accelerations that peak 15 beats per minute above the baseline and last (not necessarily at the peak) for at least 15 seconds before returning to the baseline (Fig. 9-1). The majority of NSTs are reactive within the first 20 minutes. For those that are not, possibly because of a fetal sleep cycle, an additional 20 minutes of monitoring may be needed. A non-reactive NST is one in which two such accelerations do not occur within 40 minutes or when the acceleration peaks are fewer than 15 beats per minute.

Although it is noninvasive and easy to perform, the NST is limited by a high rate of false-positive results. Normal fetuses often have periods of nonreactivity due to benign variations such as sleep cycles. Vibroacoustic stimulation may be used safely in the setting of a nonreactive NST in order to elicit FHR accelerations without compromising the sensitivity of the NST.[34] In this situation, the operator places an artificial larynx on the maternal abdomen and activates the device for 1 to 3 seconds. This technique is often useful in situations in which the FHR has normal beat-to-beat variability and no decelerations but does not demonstrate any accelerations on an NST. If the test remains non-reactive, further evaluation with a biophysical profile or CST is warranted.

Contraction Stress Test

The CST is designed to evaluate the FHR response to maternal uterine contractions. The principles that are applied to the evaluation of intrapartum FHR monitoring (see Part 2) are used here. In response to the stress

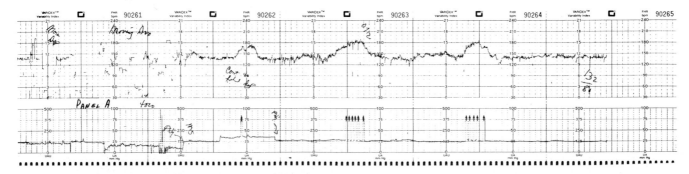

FIGURE 9-1. Reactive nonstress test, demonstrating accelerations occurring with fetal movement. Note the arrows on the contraction channel. (From Freeman R, Garite T: Fetal heart rate monitoring, Baltimore, Williams & Wilkins, 1981.)

of the contraction, a hypoxemic fetus demonstrates FHR patterns of concern such as late decelerations, indicating worsening hypoxemia or fetal compromise.

Similar to the NST, for the CST the patient is placed in a recumbent, tilted position, and the FHR is monitored with an external fetal monitor. The FHR pattern is then evaluated while the patient experiences at least three contractions lasting 40 seconds within a 10-minute period. If the patient is not contracting spontaneously, contractions may be induced with either nipple stimulation or intravenous oxytocin. If no late or significant, variable decelerations are noted on the FHR tracing, the CST is considered to be negative. If there are late decelerations after at least 50% of the contractions, the CST is positive. If late decelerations are present less than 50% of the time or if significant, variable decelerations are present, the test is considered to be equivocal. Contraindications to the performance of this test include those clinical situations in which labor would be undesirable (e.g., placenta previa or previous classic cesarean section).

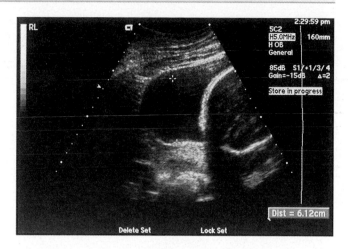

FIGURE 9-2. Ultrasound image of the maximum vertical pocket measured as part of either the biophysical profile or amniotic fluid index. Note the absence of the umbilical cord in the measured pocket.

Biophysical Profile (See Chapter 19)

The biophysical profile (BPP) was developed by Manning and associates as an alternative tool to other methods of antenatal surveillance to evaluate fetal well-being.[21] As originally described, it combines the NST with four components evaluated by ultrasonography. In a 30-minute time period, the following observations are made.

> Fetal breathing motions (one or more episodes lasting at least 30 seconds)
> Fetal movement (three or more discrete body or limb movements)
> Fetal tone (one or more episodes of active extension with return to flexion of a limb or trunk or the opening and closing of a fetal hand)
> Amniotic fluid volume (originally described as a single vertical pocket of greater than or equal to 1 cm, subsequently modified to greater than or equal to 2 cm [Fig. 9-2])
> Reactive NST

Each component is assigned a score of 2 if present and 0 if absent. A combined score of 8 or 10 is considered to be indicative of fetal well-being. A score of 6 is considered to be equivocal, and it usually merits delivery if the pregnancy is at term or repeat testing in 24 hours if the pregnancy is preterm. A score of 4 or lower is considered to be abnormal, and delivery is warranted except for extenuating circumstances. The BPP has also been analyzed with the four ultrasonographic parameters alone, and when all are present, it has been shown to have a false-negative rate similar to that with the full BPP.[19]

AMNIOTIC FLUID VOLUME ASSESSMENT

Amniotic fluid volume is commonly estimated ultrasonographically by means of one of two methods. The amniotic fluid index is calculated by measuring the maximal vertical pockets of fluid (without loops of umbilical cord) in each of the four quadrants of the maternal abdomen (see Fig. 9-2). Alternatively, the single deepest vertical pocket of fluid is measured. Decreased amniotic fluid volume, or *oligohydramnios*, is typically defined as either an amniotic fluid index of 5 cm or less or no measurable vertical pocket of fluid greater than 2 cm. Unfortunately, while both measurement techniques are equally effective in estimating amniotic fluid volume, both have relatively poor sensitivity for the detection of oligohydramnios.[16]

In most circumstances, oligohydramnios is thought to be a reflection of fetal compromise (see Chapter 21). A decrease in placental perfusion results in decreased blood flow and consequently decreased oxygen delivery to the fetus. There is also decreased renal perfusion by the preferential shunting of blood to the fetal brain. Decreased renal perfusion results in decreased fetal urine output, which leads to decreased amniotic fluid volume.

Oligohydramnios is commonly associated with post-term pregnancy, fetal growth restriction, maternal hypertension, and preeclampsia. In various clinical scenarios, oligohydramnios has been found to be associated with an increased risk of preterm delivery, low or very low birth weight, low Apgar scores, intrauterine fetal death, meconium-stained amniotic fluid, admission to a neonatal intensive care unit, and cesarean delivery for non-reassuring fetal status.[3,12,15] In the term pregnancy, oligohydramnios is considered an indication for delivery. In the preterm pregnancy immediate delivery may not be desirable, and in such cases increased surveillance is warranted. However, in the preterm fetus with oligohydramnios, delivery is indicated for non-reassuring or abnormal fetal surveillance or when there is no interval growth on ultrasound.

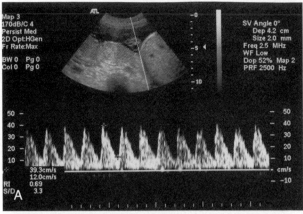

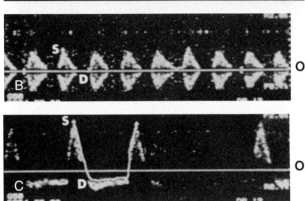

FIGURE 9-3. Composite images of three studies of fetal umbilical artery velocimetry, ranging from normal to markedly abnormal. **A,** Normal velocimetry pattern. **B,** Absent diastolic flow, indicating increased placental resistance. **C,** Reversal of diastolic flow, indicating worsening placental function. D, diastolic velocity; S, systolic velocity.

Modified Biophysical Profile

Although the NST reflects the present fetal neurologic status and oxygenation, the amniotic fluid volume is a better measure of chronic placental function. Therefore, some authors have favored the use of the modified BPP, which consists of the combination of the NST and the amniotic fluid index. In a study of 15,482 women undergoing antenatal testing, Miller and colleagues found the modified BPP to have a lower false-negative rate than the NST.[24] An abnormal result may be followed by the performance of a full BPP or a CST.

Doppler Flow Velocimetry

Ultrasonography of fetal blood flow is also used to evaluate fetal well-being antenatally. Doppler measurements of the pulsatile blood flow in the umbilical arteries directly reflect the status of the fetomaternal circulation (Fig. 9-3). A progressive decrease in placental function or blood flow is thought to manifest itself as an increased resistance to flow, which is evidenced by a diminution in the diastolic flow and eventual absence or reversal of flow during diastole in the fetal vessels. In clinical practice, commonly measured indexes include the systolic/diastolic ratio (S/D), resistance index (S-D/S), and pulsatility index (S-D/A).

Doppler flow velocimetry of the fetal umbilical artery has been studied in a number of at-risk populations. Pregnancies with suspected intrauterine growth restriction have been extensively studied, and there is evidence that the use of umbilical artery Doppler flow velocimetry as the primary testing method results in fewer antenatal tests and less intervention, with similar neonatal outcomes, than monitoring by the NST.[11] There is also evidence that abnormal umbilical artery Doppler flow velocimetry precedes FHR abnormalities by a median of 7 days.[2] A randomized, controlled trial of surveillance with NST and umbilical artery Doppler flow velocimetry in a high-risk population demonstrated a decreased incidence of cesarean delivery for fetal distress in the Doppler group but no difference in neonatal morbidity or the overall cesarean section rate.[33]

Doppler flow velocimetry has not been found to confer any benefit on a low-risk population.[1] The selective use of Doppler flow velocimetry for traditional indications within a general population also has not been shown to result in decreased maternal hospitalization or improved neonatal outcome.[28]

Doppler flow velocimetry has also been studied in other vessels, including the ductus venosus, the aortic and pulmonary outflow tracts, and the uterine artery. The fetal cerebral arteries demonstrate altered blood flow in the setting of hypoxemia. In certain pregnancies, such as those complicated by isoimmunization, the fetus is at risk for the development of severe anemia. Traditionally, the standard practice has been to evaluate such pregnancies with serial amniocentesis and/or cordocentesis to determine if a fetus is at risk for intrauterine death due to anemia. Mari described the use of Doppler velocimetry of the fetal middle cerebral artery to evaluate fetuses at risk for anemia due to maternal isoimmunization.[23] The peak systolic velocity of the middle cerebral artery is inversely correlated with fetal hemoglobin, and the measurement provides a noninvasive means of detecting an increased risk of fetal anemia (Fig. 9-4).

INTERPRETATION OF TEST RESULTS

The realistic goal of antepartum testing is to decrease the risk of intrauterine fetal demise or perinatal mortality in the tested population so that it will approach the rate for a low-risk population without an excessive or unacceptable false-positive rate that may result in unnecessary intervention. When corrected for congenital anomalies and unpredictable causes of intrauterine death, the rate of stillbirth in the tested population (after antepartum testing, with normal results) has been reported to be approximately 1.9 per 1000 for the NST, 0.3 per 1000 for the CST, 0.8 per 1000 for the BPP, and 0.8 per 1000 for the modified BPP.[1] These rates are comparable to those for the risk of fetal death in a low-risk population.

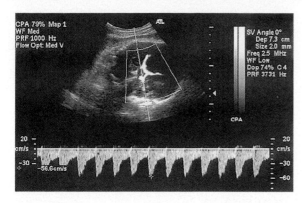

FIGURE 9-4. Ultrasound image of the fetal cerebral vasculature, with Doppler visualization of the middle cerebral artery and measurement of the peak systolic velocity. (From Dukler D et al: Noninvasive tests to predict fetal anemia: A study comparing Doppler and ultrasound parameters. Am J Obstet Gynecol 188:1310, 2003.)

The false-positive rate is more difficult to ascertain because a positive test usually results in obstetric intervention, thereby significantly decreasing the likelihood of intrauterine death. However, one study demonstrated that 90% of non-reactive NSTs are followed by a negative CST result, which is consistent with a high false-positive rate for the NST.[8] A study of CSTs in which physicians were blinded to the results found that there were no fetal late decelerations in labor, no low Apgar scores, and no significant neonatal morbidity in 61% of patients with positive tests .[30] Manning and associates reported on a cohort of 913 infants delivered after a BPP score of 6 or less.[18] Nearly 40% of those with scores of 6 demonstrated no markers of fetal compromise at delivery, as defined by fetal distress in labor, admission to the neonatal intensive care unit, a 5-minute Apgar score of 7 or less, or an umbilical cord pH of less than or equal to 7.20. However, there was a significant inverse linear association between the BPP score and these markers, and all fetuses with scores of 0 had at least one of these markers at delivery.

In a clinically stable situation, reassuring tests (a reactive NST, negative CST, and BPP of 8 or 10) are considered reliable for one week; therefore, testing is usually performed on a weekly basis. Labile conditions may merit more frequent testing, which is left to the discretion of the physician. If the indication for testing is not a persistent one (e.g., maternal perception of decreased fetal movement), there is no evidence to support the continuation of antenatal testing. In certain high-risk populations, the false-negative rate of NST may be unacceptably high. The stillbirth rate within 1 week of a reactive NST is markedly higher for patients with diabetes mellitus (14 per 1000) and fetal growth restriction (20 per 1000).[4] Similarly elevated results have been reported for patients with prolonged gestation.[25] Boehm and coworkers found that the stillbirth rate decreased from 6.1 per 1000 to 1.9 per 1000 in their high-risk population when the frequency of testing

was changed from once weekly to twice weekly.[6] For this reason, twice-weekly testing may be appropriate in select populations such as those described.

FETAL GESTATIONAL AGE AND ANTENATAL SURVEILLANCE

FHR variability and reactivity vary with gestational age. Before 28 weeks of gestation, up to 50% of all NSTs may not be reactive. From 28 to 32 weeks of gestation, approximately 15% of normal fetuses will have non-reactive NSTs.[1] While fetal breathing movements and body movements are noted to decrease before the onset of spontaneous labor,[7] the biophysical parameters that constitute the BPP score are present at early gestational ages and are therefore useful in the evaluation of a very premature fetus.

The optimal gestational age at which to begin antenatal surveillance depends on the clinical condition. In making this decision, the physician must weigh the risk of intervention at a premature gestational age against the risk of intrauterine fetal death. The American College of Obstetricians and Gynecologists recommends initiating testing at 32 to 34 weeks of gestation for most at-risk patients, with the acknowledgment that some situations may merit testing as early as 26 to 28 weeks of gestation.[1]

CLINICAL CONSIDERATIONS

It is important to remember that a large number of clinical situations not related to fetal well-being will temporarily affect the interpretation of the antenatal surveillance techniques. Maternal cigarette smoking and alcohol ingestion decrease fetal movement, breathing, and heart rate reactivity.[9,10,17] Commonly used maternal medications such as opioids and corticosteroids significantly decrease various fetal biophysical parameters, including movement, breathing, and heart rate reactivity, without compromising neonatal outcome.[26,29] Maternal medical conditions such as acute asthma exacerbation or diabetic ketoacidosis may result in non-reassuring fetal surveillance, including worrisome BPP scores. Delivery in such an unstable condition is dangerous and undesirable. Fortunately, the improvement or elimination of such conditions usually results in an improvement in fetal status. This outcome is accompanied by an improvement in antenatal testing results, and it negates the need for a premature delivery.

SUMMARY

In high-risk populations at an increased risk of perinatal mortality, antenatal fetal surveillance plays a significant role in prenatal care. Those pregnancies at risk for progressive deterioration of placental function leading to fetal hypoxemia and acidosis are the most likely to benefit from the methods currently in use. The various modalities, including NST, CST, BPP, and Doppler velocimetry, rely on fetal biophysical parameters that are significantly associated with the presence or absence of fetal hypoxemia. As all tests are associated with a rate of false-positive results, each test result should be interpreted within the clinical context presented by the patient.

PART 2

Evaluation of the Intrapartum Fetus

Barbara V. Parilla

Fetal heart rate (FHR) monitoring is currently the primary method used for the assessment of fetal well-being in the intrapartum period. Before the development of modern methods of assessment, *fetal distress* was usually diagnosed on the basis of criteria that are now considered to be faulty or erroneous. For example, meconium-stained amniotic fluid in the absence of an abnormal FHR pattern is an indication for aggressive airway management at delivery, but it is not by itself diagnostic of fetal intolerance to labor. FHR monitoring involves the evaluation of the pattern as well as the rate. It can help the physician identify and interpret changes in FHR patterns that may be associated with fetal conditions such as hypoxia, umbilical cord compression, tachycardia, and acidosis.

The ability to interpret FHR patterns and understand their correlation with the condition of the fetus allows the physician to institute maneuvers such as maternal oxygen therapy, amnioinfusion, and tocolytic therapy to improve the abnormality. In addition, the antepartum history must be considered when evaluating the intrapartum fetus. Is it a normal-sized or growth-restricted fetus? Is there oligohydramnios or are there other complications that may affect the course of labor? FHR monitoring alone should not be a substitute for informed clinical judgment.

A reassuring FHR monitoring strip is almost always associated with a nonacidotic fetus and a vigorous neonate at birth. However, non-reassuring patterns are nonspecific and cannot reliably predict whether a fetus will be well oxygenated, depressed, or acidotic. Factors other than hypoxia may lead to a non-reassuring FHR, and an abnormal pattern may neither depict the severity of the hypoxia nor predict how it will progress if labor is allowed to continue. Nevertheless, because alterations in fetal oxygenation occur during labor and because many complications can occur during this critical period, some form of FHR evaluation should be provided to all patients.

For the purposes of this chapter, the following definitions are used.

> *Hypoxemia:* Decreased oxygen content in the blood
> *Hypoxia:* Decreased level of oxygen in tissue
> *Acidemia:* Increased concentration of hydrogen ions in the blood
> *Acidosis:* Increased concentration of hydrogen ions in tissue
> *Asphyxia:* Hypoxia with metabolic acidosis

PHYSIOLOGY

The fetus is well adapted to extracting oxygen from the maternal circulation, even with the additional stress of normal labor and delivery. Transient and repetitive episodes of hypoxemia and hypoxia, even at the level of the central nervous system (CNS), are extremely common during normal labor, and they are generally well tolerated by the fetus. Furthermore, a progressive intrapartum decline in baseline fetal oxygenation and pH is virtually universal; levels of acidemia that would be ominous in an infant or adult are commonly seen in normal newborns. Only when hypoxia and the resulting metabolic acidemia reach extreme levels is the fetus at risk for long-term neurologic impairment.[42] However, alterations in the fetoplacental unit resulting from labor or intrapartum complications may subject the fetus to decreased oxygenation, leading to potential damage to any susceptible organ system or even fetal death.

Oxygen delivery is critically dependent on uterine blood flow. Uterine contractions decrease placental blood flow and result in intermittent episodes of decreased oxygen delivery. The fetus normally tolerates contractions without difficulty, but if the frequency, duration, or strength of contractions become excessive, fetal hypoxemia may result. Maternal position and the use of conduction anesthesia can also alter uterine blood flow and oxygen delivery during labor. Finally, labor may be complicated by conditions such as preeclampsia, abruptio placentae, chorioamnionitis, and other pathologic situations that can further alter blood flow and oxygen exchange within the placenta.

Some fetuses are unusually susceptible to the effects of intrapartum hypoxemia, such as those with growth restriction and those who are born prematurely. In these circumstances hypoxia tends to progress more rapidly and is more likely to cause or aggravate metabolic acidemia, which in extreme cases correlates with poor long-term neurologic outcome. In severe cases, such hypoxia can lead to death (see Chapter 38, Part 4).[35]

The fetal CNS is susceptible to hypoxia. Experimentally induced hypoxia has been associated with consistent, predictable changes in the FHR.[36] Because the FHR and its alterations are under CNS control through sympathetic and parasympathetic reflexes, alterations in the FHR can be sensitive indicators of fetal hypoxia.

GUIDELINES FOR PERFORMING FETAL HEART RATE MONITORING

The FHR may be evaluated by intermittent auscultation with a DeLee-Hillis stethoscope or a Doppler ultrasound device or by electronic monitoring. Continuous FHR and contraction monitoring may be performed externally or internally. Most external monitors use a Doppler device with computerized logic to interpret and count the Doppler signals. Internal FHR monitoring is accomplished with a fetal electrode, which is a spiral wire placed directly on the fetal scalp or other presenting part. This method records the fetal electrocardiogram. In either case, the FHR is recorded continuously on the upper portion of a paper strip, and every beat-to-beat interval is recorded as a rate. The lower portion of the strip records uterine contractions, which also may be monitored externally or internally.

Well controlled studies have shown that intermittent auscultation of the FHR is equivalent to continuous electronic monitoring in assessing fetal condition when performed at specific intervals with a 1:1 nurse-to-patient ratio.[53] The intensity of FHR monitoring used during labor should be based on risk factors, and when they are present, the FHR should be assessed according to the following guidelines.

If auscultation is used during the active phase of the first stage of labor, the FHR should be evaluated and recorded at least every 15 minutes after a uterine contraction. If continuous electronic monitoring is used, the tracing should be reviewed at least every 15 minutes.

During the second stage of labor, if auscultation is being used, the FHR should be evaluated and recorded at least every 5 minutes. When electronic monitoring is used, the FHR strip should be reviewed every 5 minutes.

The optimal frequency at which intermittent auscultation should be performed in the absence of risk factors has not been established. One method is to evaluate the FHR at least every 30 minutes in the active phase of the first stage of labor and at least every 15 minutes during the second stage of labor.

RISKS AND BENEFITS

Currently, neither the most effective method of FHR monitoring nor the specific frequency or duration of monitoring to ensure optimal perinatal outcome has been identified by a significant body of scientific evidence.

Seven randomized, controlled trials have compared continuous electronic FHR monitoring with intermittent auscultation in patients at high risk and those at low risk, and no differences in intrapartum fetal death rates were found.[52] In contrast, one controlled trial did show a significant reduction in perinatal deaths from asphyxia in the electronically monitored group.[56] It is not clear why this single study is so discordant with the others, but it does provide some promise that further studies

may yet elucidate the real value of electronic FHR monitoring.

The primary risk of electronic FHR monitoring is a potential increase in the cesarean delivery rate. This effect has been observed in both retrospective trials and the majority of prospective, randomized trials. More accurate interpretation of FHR monitoring, fetal scalp blood pH determination, and the use of scalp stimulation to elicit FHR accelerations can lead to more precise interpretation of the fetal status, which may lead to a decrease in the cesarean delivery rate.[39,40,54]

The U.S. Food and Drug Administration has approved labeling for the use of fetal pulse oximetry in patients with non-reassuring fetal heart rate patterns. A large, randomized clinical trial of fetal pulse oximetry showed a decrease in cesarean delivery for non-reassuring FHR patterns but a corresponding increase in cesarean delivery for dystocia.[44] Neonatal outcomes in the fetal pulse oximetry group were similar to those in a group with non-reassuring patterns managed without fetal pulse oximetry.[44] Other reports suggest that sustained or repetitive saturations below 30% are associated with a fall in fetal pH below 7.1 and may be indicative of neonatal problems. Further studies are needed before this technique can be considered standard practice. The one area where this technology may well hold promise is in the intrapartum management of fetuses with dysrhythmias, where FHR interpretation is problematic.

INTERPRETATION OF FETAL HEART RATE PATTERNS

The initial FHR pattern should be carefully evaluated for any abnormalities of the baseline and for the presence or absence of accelerations and decelerations. In one study, the first 30 minutes of electronic FHR monitoring identified about 50% of all fetuses that underwent cesarean delivery for a non-reassuring FHR pattern or fetal distress.[46] Although the progression of decelerations usually explains changes in the baseline later in labor, abnormalities of the baseline on admission, such as fetal tachycardia or loss of variability, may be difficult to interpret because data regarding previous changes are lacking.

Baseline Fetal Heart Rate

Rate and variability are two specific and important parameters of the baseline FHR. The baseline heart rate at term usually ranges from 120 to 160 beats per minute. The initial response of the FHR to intermittent hypoxia is deceleration, but baseline tachycardia may develop if the hypoxia is prolonged and severe. Tachycardia may also be associated with conditions other than hypoxia, such as maternal fever, intra-amniotic infection, thyroid disease, the presence of medication, and cardiac arrhythmia (Fig. 9-5). The presence of variability, or variation of successive beats in the heart rate, is a useful

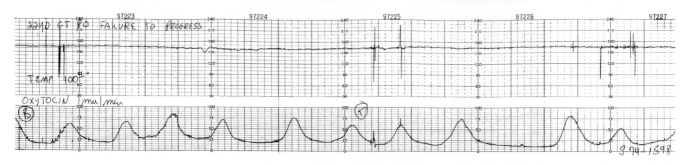

FIGURE 9-5. Fetal tachycardia. Heart rate is 165 beats per minute. This tachycardia is associated with maternal fever (note temperature). Also note the associated loss of variability. Because of the absence of associated decelerations and the presence of an explanation (fever), hypoxia is an unlikely cause. (From Freeman R, Garite T: Fetal heart rate monitoring. Baltimore, Williams & Wilkins, 1981, p 70.)

indicator of fetal CNS integrity. In the absence of maternal sedation, magnesium sulfate administration, chronic beta blocker treatment, or extreme prematurity, the decreased variability, or flattening of the FHR baseline, may serve as a barometer of the fetal response to hypoxia. Because decreased variability or flattening is presumed to be a CNS response, in most situations decelerations of the FHR precede the loss of variability, indicating the cause (Fig. 9-6).

Periodic changes in the FHR are common in labor; they occur in response to contractions or fetal movement and include accelerations and decelerations.

Accelerations

Accelerations in the FHR seem to occur the most commonly in the antepartum period, in early labor,

and in association with variable decelerations. They are almost always associated with fetal movement. The presence of accelerations in the intrapartum period is always reassuring and reflects a normal fetal pH. The absence of accelerations in the intrapartum period is not alarming as long as the baseline FHR and variability are normal (Fig. 9-7).

Decelerations

In some instances of decreased oxygenation, the FHR pattern can identify the mechanism. For instance, umbilical cord compression coincides with variable decelerations.[38] Variable decelerations are the most common decelerations seen in labor, and they are generally associated with a favorable outcome. They are defined as slowing of the FHR, with an abrupt

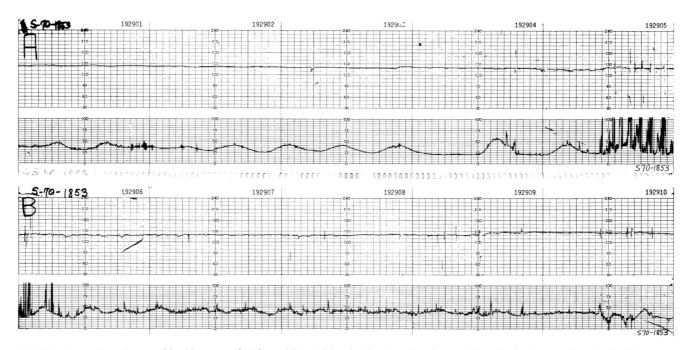

FIGURE 9-6. Complete absence of fetal heart rate (FHR) variability without decelerations. The absence of late decelerations implies that fetal hypoxemia does not currently exist. However, the absence of FHR variability for this duration suggests fetal neurologic impairment antecedent to labor. (From Freeman R, Garite T: Fetal heart rate monitoring. Baltimore, Williams & Wilkins, 1981, p 138.)

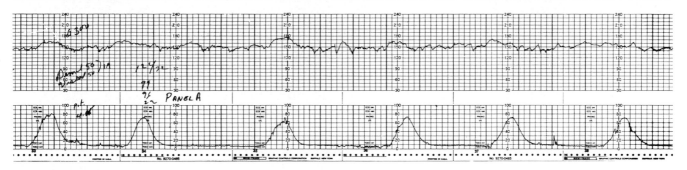

FIGURE 9-7. Normal, reassuring fetal heart rate (FHR) pattern. Note perturbations of FHR (small amplitude represents FHR variability; larger amplitude represents FHR reactivity). If seen during antepartum testing, this tracing would be interpreted as a reactive, negative contraction stress test. (From Freeman R, Garite T: Fetal heart rate monitoring. Baltimore, Williams & Wilkins, 1981, p 72.)

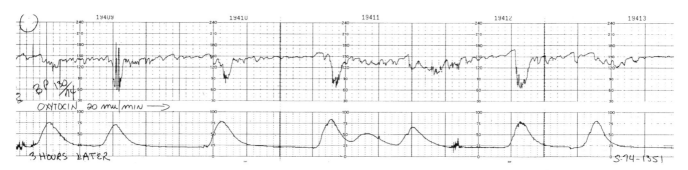

FIGURE 9-8. Mild, variable decelerations are shown. Baseline heart rate and variability are normal. Note the brief, reassuring acceleration preceding deceleration on panel 19412. (From Freeman R, Garite T: Fetal heart rate monitoring. Baltimore, Williams & Wilkins, 1981, p 78.)

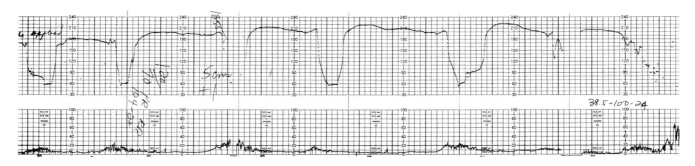

FIGURE 9-9. Severe, variable decelerations are shown, with baseline heart rate rising to 210 beats per minute and with virtually no variability. Note the prolonged fetal heart rate "overshoot" in the middle portion of the panel; it is an ominous tracing. This baby was premature, delivered by cesarean section, with Apgar scores of 1 at 1 minute and 2 at 5 minutes. (From Freeman R, Garite T: Fetal heart rate monitoring. Baltimore, Williams & Wilkins, 1981, p 80.)

onset and return, and they are frequently preceded and followed by small accelerations in the FHR. These decelerations vary in depth, duration, and shape on the tracing, but they generally coincide with the timing of the uterine contractions (Fig. 9-8). Only when variable decelerations become persistent, progressively deeper, and longer lasting are they considered to be non-reassuring. Although progression is more important than absolute parameters, persistent, variable decelerations to less than 70 beats per minute and lasting longer than 60 seconds are generally of concern, especially if they are accompanied by a change in baseline and decreased variability (Fig. 9-9). In addition, a slow return to baseline is worrisome because this reflects hypoxia persisting beyond the relaxation phase of the contraction.[9]

Late decelerations may be secondary to transient fetal hypoxia in response to the decreased placental perfusion associated with uterine contractions. Occasional or intermittent late decelerations are not uncommon during labor. These are U-shaped decelerations of gradual onset and gradual return that are usually shallow (10 to 30 beats per minute) and reach their nadir after the peak of the contraction (Fig. 9-10). When late decelerations become persistent, they are

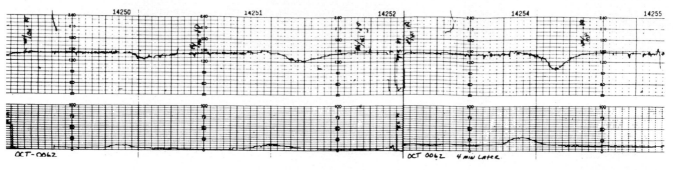

FIGURE 9-10. Late decelerations with absence of fetal heart rate (FHR) variability and reactivity. This is an ominous FHR pattern. (From Freeman R, Garite T: Fetal heart rate monitoring. Baltimore, Williams & Wilkins, 1981, p 201.)

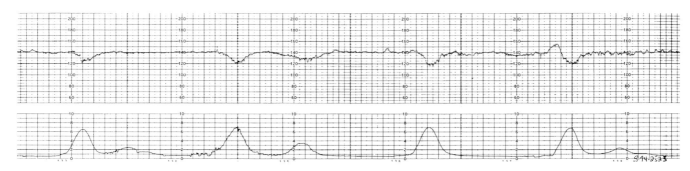

FIGURE 9-11. Early decelerations are shown with each contraction on this panel. They are uniform, mirror the contractions, and decelerate only 10 to 20 beats per minute. Fetal heart rate variability at the end of the panel is satisfactory, a reassuring sign. (From Freeman R, Garite T: Fetal heart rate monitoring. Baltimore, Williams & Wilkins, 1981, p 74.)

considered to be non-reassuring, regardless of the depth of the decelerations. Late decelerations begin as a vagal reflex and characteristically have good variability and fetal reactivity. The decelerations generally become deeper as the degree of hypoxia becomes more severe. However, as metabolic acidosis develops from tissue hypoxia, late decelerations are believed to be the result of direct myocardial depression, and their depth will not indicate the degree of hypoxia.[43]

Early decelerations are shallow and symmetric, with a pattern similar to that of late decelerations, but they reach their nadir at the same time as the peak of the contraction and therefore look like mirror images of the contractions. They are infrequently seen and are believed to be caused by fetal head compression in the active phase of labor (Fig. 9-11).

A prolonged deceleration, often incorrectly referred to as bradycardia, is an isolated, abrupt decrease in the FHR to levels below the baseline that lasts at least 60 to 90 seconds. These changes are always of concern and may be caused by any mechanism that can lead to fetal hypoxia. Clinical events associated with acute uteroplacental insufficiency are uterine rupture, maternal cardiovascular collapse, total placental abruption, maternal seizures, and titanic uterine contractions. The severity of the event causing the deceleration is usually reflected in the depth and duration of the deceleration,

as well as by the degree to which variability is lost during the deceleration. If such a deceleration is resolved, a transient fetal tachycardia and loss of variability may occur while the fetus is recovering from hypoxia (Fig. 9-12). The degree to which such decelerations are non-reassuring depends on their depth and duration, the loss of variability, the response of the fetus during the recovery period, and, most importantly, the frequency and progression of the recurrence.

A sinusoidal heart rate pattern consists of a regular oscillation of the baseline variability, resembling a sine wave. This smooth, undulating pattern, lasting at least 10 minutes, has a relatively fixed period of 3 to 5 cycles per minute and an amplitude of 5 to 15 beats per minute above and below the baseline (Fig. 9-13). This pattern may be associated with severe and chronic, as opposed to acute, fetal anemia. It has also been described after the use of alphaprodine or other medications; in such circumstances, it may not represent fetal compromise. Additionally, severe hypoxia and acidosis are occasionally manifested as a sinusoidal FHR, the reason for which is not understood. True sinusoidal patterns are quite rare. Unfortunately, small, frequent accelerations of low amplitude are easy to confuse with sinusoidal patterns. The former are benign and occur more frequently. A true sinusoidal FHR is always non-reassuring.

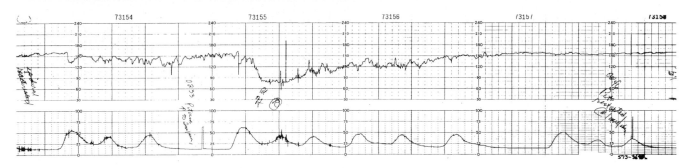

FIGURE 9-12. Prolonged deceleration associated with excessive uterine activity secondary to oxytocin hyperstimulation. A rebound tachycardia with decreased variability follows the prolonged deceleration. Oxytocin was stopped and restarted at a lower rate, and the heart rate subsequently returned to normal. (From Freeman R, Garite T: Fetal heart rate monitoring. Baltimore, Williams & Wilkins, 1981, p 85.)

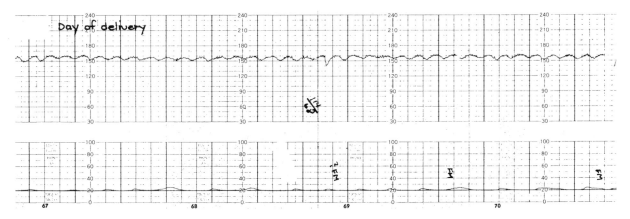

FIGURE 9-13. Sinusoidal fetal heart rate pattern with fetal hydrops from Rh (Rhesus) sensitization. (From Freeman R, Garite T: Fetal heart rate monitoring. Baltimore, Williams & Wilkins, 1981, p 166.)

EVALUATION AND MANAGEMENT OF NON-REASSURING PATTERNS

With a persistently non-reassuring FHR pattern in labor, the clinician should determine the etiology of the pattern when possible and attempt to correct it by specifically correcting the primary problem or by instituting general measures aimed at improving fetal oxygenation and placental perfusion. For example, it is not uncommon to see a prolonged deceleration or repetitive late decelerations after epidural placement secondary to splanchnic relaxation, with resulting uterine hypo-perfusion.[55] Such measures as ensuring that the woman is in the lateral recumbent position and administering an intravenous fluid bolus are helpful. If there is systemic hypotension, ephedrine administration should be considered. Excessive uterine contractions may also be responsible for decelerations (Fig. 9-14). The careful use of oxytocin is necessary to minimize uterine hyper-stimulation. If non-reassuring FHR changes occur in patients receiving oxytocin, the infusion should be decreased or discontinued. Restarting the infusion at a lower rate and increasing it in smaller increments may be better tolerated. General measures that may improve fetal oxygenation and placental perfusion should also be used. We cared for a woman with severe anemia secondary to sickle cell disease whose fetus was remote from term and had repetitive late decelerations. After maternal administration of packed red blood cells, the fetal heart rate tracing normalized.

Maternal Position

Maternal position during labor can affect uterine blood flow and placental perfusion. In the supine position, the vena cava and aortoiliac vessels are compressed by the gravid uterus. This activity results in a decrease in the return of blood to the maternal heart, leading to a reduction in cardiac output and blood pressure and therefore uterine blood flow. In the supine position, aortic compression may result in an increase in the incidence of late decelerations and a decrease in fetal scalp pH. The lateral recumbent position (either side) is the best for maximizing cardiac output and uterine blood flow. It is often associated with improvement in the FHR pattern.[41]

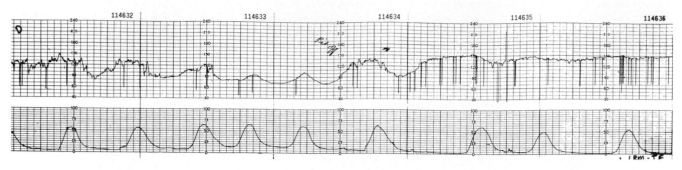

FIGURE 9-14. Late decelerations associated with uterine hyperstimulation from oxytocin. Note compensatory relative fetal tachycardia developing as recovery occurs. (From Freeman R, Garite T: Fetal heart rate monitoring. Baltimore, Williams & Wilkins, 1981, p 114.)

Oxygen Therapy

The arterial PO_2 in the fetus is normally about 25% of that in the mother. Despite this low PO_2, the fetal blood can carry a large amount of oxygen from the placenta because of the increased heart rate and the high affinity of fetal hemoglobin for oxygen. When there is evidence of a non-reassuring pattern, the administration of supplemental oxygen to the mother is thought to be useful. A significant increase in maternal oxygenation is accomplished with a tight-fitting facemask and an oxygen flow rate of 8 to 10 L/min. Although such administration results in only a small increase in fetal PO_2, animal studies have suggested that a 30% to 40% increase in fetal oxygen content may occur.[50]

Amnioinfusion

For severe variable or prolonged decelerations, a pelvic exam should be performed to rule out umbilical cord prolapse or rapid descent of the fetal head (Fig. 9-15). If no cause for such decelerations is found, one can usually conclude that umbilical cord compression is responsible. In patients with decreased amniotic fluid volume, replacement of amniotic fluid with normal saline infused through a transcervical intrauterine pressure catheter has been reported to decrease both the frequency and severity of variable decelerations.[51] Investigators have also reported a decrease in newborn respiratory complications from meconium in patients who receive amnioinfusion. This outcome presumably results from the dilutional effect of amnioinfusion and possibly from prevention of in utero fetal gasping that may occur during episodes of hypoxia caused by umbilical cord compression.[47]

Tocolytic Agents

Excessive uterine contractions accompanied by a non-reassuring FHR may require a tocolytic agent if general measures are not successful. Terbutaline and magnesium sulfate have been reported to be of value to rapidly improve the fetal condition by promoting uterine relaxation during active labor. Even in the absence of uterine hypertonia, abnormal FHR patterns occurring in response to uterine contractions may be improved by the administration of tocolytic agents. This approach is especially useful when unavoidable delays in effecting operative delivery are encountered.

EVALUATION AND MANAGEMENT OF PERSISTENT, NON-REASSURING FETAL HEART RATE PATTERNS

If the FHR pattern remains uncorrected, the decision to intervene will depend on the clinician's assessment

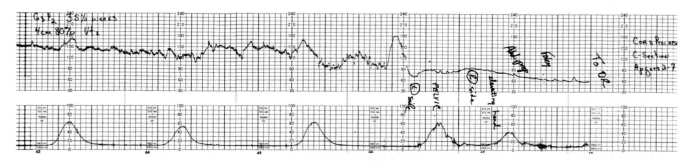

FIGURE 9-15. This patient showed a sudden and prolonged deceleration in the early active phase of labor. An immediate pelvic examination revealed cord prolapse, and a cesarean delivery was performed. (From Freeman R, Garite T: Fetal heart rate monitoring. Baltimore, Williams & Wilkins, 1981, p 83.)

of the likelihood of severe hypoxia and the possibility of metabolic acidosis, as well as the estimated time to spontaneous delivery. For the fetus with persistent, non-reassuring decelerations, normal FHR variability and the absence of tachycardia generally indicate a lack of acidosis. The presence of FHR variability should probably be confirmed with a fetal electrode in the presence of non-reassuring decelerations. Persistent late decelerations or severe variable decelerations associated with the absence of variability are always non-reassuring and generally require prompt intervention.

The presence of spontaneous accelerations of greater than 15 beats per minute and lasting at least 15 seconds almost always ensures the absence of fetal acidosis. Fetal scalp stimulation or vibroacoustic stimulation can be used to induce accelerations, which indicate the absence of acidosis.[39,54] Conversely, there is about a 50% chance of acidosis in a fetus that fails to respond to stimulation in the presence of a non-reassuring pattern.[39,54] In these fetuses, the assessment of scalp blood pH should be considered to clarify the acid-base status. Surprisingly, this technique is underused in obstetric practice.[39,45]

If the FHR pattern remains worrisome, either induced accelerations or repeat assessment of scalp blood pH is required every 20 to 30 minutes for continued reassurance. For cases in which the FHR pattern is persistently non-reassuring and acidosis is present or cannot be ruled out, the fetus should be promptly delivered by the most expedient route, whether abdominally or vaginally.

Perinatal Asphyxia and Cerebral Palsy

With the advent and liberal use of electronic FHR monitoring in the 1970s, there was great hope that intrapartum fetal death and morbidity associated with intrapartum asphyxia could be virtually eliminated. This has not been proved in several prospective, randomized, controlled trials and retrospective, controlled studies.[36,49,52]

In western industrialized countries, the rate of cerebral palsy in term infants (1 to 2 per 1000) has not changed in the past 20 years despite new neonatal and obstetric technologies. However, there continues to exist a misperception that birth asphyxia accounts for a significant proportion of infants with cerebral palsy despite the lack of evidence to support this impression. New data, discussed in a task force by the American College of Obstetricians and Gynecologists in collaboration with the American Academy of Pediatrics, confirm that intrapartum hypoxia is uncommonly the sole cause of neonatal encephalopathy or cerebral palsy.[37] Less than one fourth of infants with neonatal encephalopathy have evidence of hypoxia or ischemia at birth. Several clinical and experimental reports confirm that only severe and prolonged asphyxia is associated with an increased risk of subsequent neurologic dysfunction. It is now accepted that most neonatal encephalopathy and cerebral palsy have their origins in developmental abnormalities, metabolic abnormalities, autoimmune and

---

BOX 9-1. Criteria to Define an Acute Intrapartum Event as Sufficient to Cause Cerebral Palsy

Essential Criteria (must meet all four)
1. Evidence of a metabolic acidosis in fetal umbilical cord arterial blood obtained at delivery (pH < 7 and base deficit ≥12 mmol/L)
2. Early onset of severe or moderate neonatal encephalopathy in infants born at 34 or more weeks of gestation
3. Cerebral palsy of the spastic quadriplegic or dyskinetic type*
4. Exclusion of other identifiable etiologies, such as trauma, coagulation disorders, infectious conditions, or genetic disorders

Criteria That Collectively Suggest an Intrapartum Timing (within close proximity to labor and delivery, e.g., 0-48 hours) but Are Nonspecific to Asphyxia Insults
1. A sentinel (signal) hypoxic event occurring immediately before or during labor
2. A sudden and sustained fetal bradycardia or the absence of fetal heart rate variability in the presence of persistent, late, or variable decelerations, usually after a hypoxic sentinel event when the pattern was previously normal
3. Apgar scores of 0-3 beyond 5 minutes
4. Onset of multisystem involvement within 72 hours of birth
5. Early imaging study showing evidence of acute nonfocal cerebral abnormality

Spastic quadriplegia and, less commonly, dyskinetic cerebral palsy are the only types of cerebral palsy associated with acute hypoxic intrapartum events. Spastic quadriplegia is not specific to intrapartum hypoxia. Hemiparetic cerebral palsy, hemiplegic cerebral palsy, spastic diplegia, and ataxia are unlikely to result from acute intrapartum hypoxia. (From Nelson KB, Grether JK: Potentially asphyxiating conditions and spastic cerebral palsy in infants of normal birth weight. Am J Obstet Gynecol 179:507, 1998.) Modified from MacLennan A: A template for defining a causal relation between acute intrapartum events and cerebral palsy: International consensus statement. BMJ 319:1054, 1999. With permission from the BMJ Publishing Group.

---

coagulation defects, infection, trauma, or combinations of these factors. In assessing a possible relationship between perinatal asphyxia and neurologic deficit in an individual patient, four essential criteria are necessary, while an additional five criteria suggest intrapartum timing (Box 9-1). (This box is a modification and update of the International Cerebral Palsy Task Force Consensus Statement.[37,48])

When prolonged and severe asphyxia does occur, it is often followed by death, although many infants who survive severe birth asphyxia develop normally.[35]

SUMMARY

Because alterations in fetal oxygenation occur during labor and many complications can occur during this critical period, some form of FHR evaluation should be provided for all patients. By understanding the physiologic and pathophysiologic bases of FHR monitoring as well as its capabilities and limitations, the clinician can reduce the need for interventions.

REFERENCES

Part 1

1. American College of Obstetricians and Gynecologists: Antepartum fetal surveillance. ACOG Practice Bulletin 9. Washington, DC, ACOG, 1999.

2. Arduini D et al: The development of abnormal heart rate patterns after absent end-diastolic velocity in umbilical artery: Analysis of risk factors. Am J Obstet Gynecol 168:43, 1993.

3. Baron C et al: The impact of amniotic fluid volume assessed intrapartum on perinatal outcome. Am J Obstet Gynecol 173:167, 1995.

4. Barrett J et al: The nonstress test: An evaluation of 1,000 patients. Am J Obstet Gynecol 141:153, 1981.

5. Boddy K et al: Foetal respiratory movements, electro-cortical and cardiovascular responses to hypoxaemia and hypercapnia in sheep. J Physiol 243:599, 1974.

6. Boehm FH et al: Improved outcome of twice weekly nonstress testing. Obstet Gynecol 67:566, 1986.

7. Carmichael L et al: Fetal breathing, gross fetal body movements and maternal and fetal heart rates before spontaneous labour at term. Am J Obstet Gynecol 148:675, 1984.

8. Evertson LR et al: Antepartum fetal heart rate testing: I. Evolution of the non-stress test. Am J Obstet Gynecol 133:29, 1979.

9. Fox HE et al: Maternal ethanol ingestion and the occurrence of fetal breathing movements. Am J Obstet Gynecol 132:34, 1978.

10. Graca LM et al: Acute effects of maternal cigarette smoking on fetal heart rate and fetal body movements felt by the mother. J Perinatal Med 19:385, 1991.

11. Haley J et al: Randomised controlled trial of cardiotocography versus umbilical artery Doppler in the management of small for gestational age fetuses. Br J Obstet Gynaecol. 104:431, 1997.

12. Hsieh TT et al: Perinatal outcome of oligohydramnios without associated premature rupture of membranes and fetal anomalies. Gynecol Obstet Invest 45:232, 1998.

13. Kochanek KD, Martin JA: Supplemental analyses of recent trends in infant mortality. Hyattsville, MD, National Center for Health Statistics, 2004.

14. Lee CY et al: A study of fetal heart rate acceleration patterns. Obstet Gynecol 45:142, 1975.

15. Magann EF et al: Comparability of the amniotic fluid index and single deepest pocket measurements in clinical practice. Aust N Z J Obstet Gynaecol 43:75, 2003.

16. Magann EF et al: How well do the amniotic fluid index and single deepest pocket indices (below the 3rd and 5th and above the 95th and 97th percentiles) predict oligohydramnios and hydramnios? Am J Obstet Gynecol 190:164, 2004.

17. Manning FA, Feyerbend C: Cigarette smoking and fetal breathing movements. Br J Obstet Gynecol 83:262, 1976.

18. Manning FA et al: Fetal assessment based on fetal biophysical profile scoring: IV. An analysis of perinatal morbidity and mortality. Am J Obstet Gynecol 162:703, 1990.

19. Manning FA et al: Fetal biophysical profile scoring: Selective use of the non-stress test. Am J Obstet Gynecol 156:709, 1987.

20. Manning FA, Platt LD: Maternal hypoxemia and fetal breathing movements. Obstet Gynecol 53:758, 1979.

21. Manning FA et al: Antepartum fetal evaluation: Development of a fetal biophysical profile score. Am J Obstet Gynecol 136:787, 1980.

22. Manning FA et al. Fetal biophysical profile score: VI. Correlation with antepartum umbilical venous fetal pH. Am J Obstet Gynecol 169:755, 1993.

23. Mari G: Noninvasive diagnosis by Doppler ultrasonography of fetal anemia due to maternal red-cell alloimmunization. N Engl J Med 342:9, 2000.

24. Miller DA et al: The modified biophysical profile: Antepartum testing in the 1990s. Am J Obstet Gynecol 174:812, 1996.

25. Miyazaki F, Miyazaki B: False reactive nonstress tests in postterm pregnancies. Am J Obstet Gynccol 140:269, 1981.

26. Mulder EJ et al: Antenatal corticosteroid therapy and fetal behaviour: A randomised study of the effects of betamethasone and dexamethasone. Br J Obstet Gynecol 104:1239, 1997.

27. Murata Y et al: Fetal heart rate accelerations and late decelerations during the course of intrauterine death in chronically catheterized rhesus monkeys. Am J Obstet Gynecol 144:218, 1982.

28. Omtzigt AM et al: A randomized controlled trial on the clinical value of umbilical Doppler velocimetry in antenatal care. Am J Obstet Gynecol 170:624, 1994.

29. Smith CV et al: Influence of intravenous fentanyl on fetal biophysical parameters during labor. J Maternal-Fetal Med 5:89, 1996.

30. Staisch KJ et al: Blind oxytocin challenge test and perinatal outcome. Am J Obstet Gynecol 138:399, 1980.

31. Weiner CP et al: The effect of fetal age upon normal fetal laboratory values and venous pressure. Obstet Gynecol 79:713, 1992.

32. Wilkins-Haug L: Unexplained elevated maternal serum alpha-fetoprotein: What is the appropriate follow-up? Curr Opin Obstet Gynecol 10:469, 1998.

33. Williams KP et al: Screening for fetal well-being in a high-risk pregnant population comparing the nonstress test with umbilical artery Doppler velocimetry: A randomized controlled clinical trial. Am J Obstet Gynecol 188:1366, 2003.

34. Zimmer EZ, Divon MY: Fetal vibroacoustic stimulation. Obstet Gynecol 81:451, 1993.

Part 2

35. American College of Obstetricians and Gynecologists: Fetal and neonatal neurologic injury. Washington, DC, American College of Obstetricians and Gynecologists, 1992. ACOG Technical Bulletin 163.

36. American College of Obstetricians and Gynecologists: Fetal heart rate patterns: Monitoring, interpretation, and management. Washington, DC, American College of Obstetricians and Gynecologists, 1995. ACOG Technical Bulletin 207.

37. American College of Obstetricians and Gynecologists: Neonatal encephalopathy and cerebral palsy: Defining the pathogenesis and pathophysiology. A report by the American College of Obstetricians and Gynecologists and the American Academy of Pediatrics Task Force on Neonatal Encephalopathy and Cerebral Palsy. Washington, DC, American College of Obstetricians and Gynecologists, 2003.

38. Ball RH, Parer JT: The physiologic mechanisms of variable decelerations. Am J Obstet Gynecol 166:1683, 1992.

39. Clark SL et al: The scalp stimulation test: A clinical alternative to fetal scalp blood sampling. Am J Obstet Gynecol 148:274, 1984.

40. Clark SL, Paul RH: Intrapartum fetal surveillance: The role of fetal scalp blood sampling. Am J Obstet Gynecol 153:717, 1985.

41. Clark SL et al: Position change and central hemodynamic profile during normal third-trimester pregnancy and post partum. Am J Obstet Gynecol 164:883, 1991.

42. Fee SC et al: Severe acidosis and subsequent neurologic status. Am J Obstet Gynecol 162:802, 1990.

43. Freeman RK et al: Fetal Heart Rate Monitoring, 2nd ed. Baltimore, Williams & Wilkins, 1991.

44. Garite TJ et al: A multicenter controlled trial of fetal pulse oximetry in the intrapartum management of non-reassuring fetal heart rate patterns. Am J Obstet Gynecol 183:1049, 2000.

45. Goodwin TM et al: Elimination of fetal scalp blood sampling on a large clinical service. Obstet Gynecol 83:971, 1994.

46. Ingemarsson I et al: Admission test: A screening test for fetal distress in labor. Obstet Gynecol 68:800, 1986.

47. Macri CJ et al: Prophylactic amnioinfusion improves outcome of pregnancy complicated by thick meconium and oligohydramnios. Am J Obstet Gynecol 167:117, 1992.

48. MacLennan A: A template for defining a causal relation between acute intrapartum events and cerebral palsy: International consensus statement. BMJ 319:1054, 1999.

49. Melone PJ et al: Appropriateness of intrapartum fetal heart rate management and risk of cerebral palsy. Am J Obstet Gynecol 165:272, 1991.

50. Meschia G: Placental respiratory exchange and fetal oxygenation. In Creasy RK, Resnik R (eds): Maternal-Fetal Medicine: Principles and Practice. Philadelphia, WB Saunders Co, 1999.

51. Nageotte MP et al: Prophylactic amnioinfusion in pregnancies complicated by oligohydramnios: A prospective study. Obstet Gynecol 77:677, 1991.

52. Nelson KB et al: Uncertain value of electronic fetal monitoring in predicting cerebral palsy. N Engl J Med 334:613, 1996.

53. Shy KK et al: Effects of electronic fetal-heart-rate monitoring, as compared with periodic auscultation, on the neurologic development of premature infants. N Engl J Med 322:588, 1990.

54. Smith CV et al: Intrapartum assessment of fetal well-being: A comparison of fetal acoustic stimulation with acid base determinations. Am J Obstet Gynecol 155:726, 1986.

55. Steiger RM, Nageotte MP: Effect of uterine contractility and maternal hypotension on prolonged decelerations after bupivacaine epidural anesthesia. Am J Obstet Gynecol 163:808, 1990.

56. Vintzileos AM et al: A randomized trial of intrapartum electronic fetal heart rate monitoring versus intermittent auscultation. Obstet Gynecol 81:899, 1993.

10 Pharmacologic Intervention

PART 1

Developmental Pharmacology

Michael D. Reed, Jacob V. Aranda, and Barbara F. Hales

There are no two things under Heaven which do not have the mutual relationship of the 'self' and the 'other'. Both the 'self' and the 'other' equally desire to act for themselves, thus opposing each other as strongly as East and West. On the other hand, the 'self' and the 'other' have at the same time the mutual relationship of lips and teeth . . . therefore the action of the 'other' on its own behalf at the same time helps the 'self'. Thus, though mutually opposed, they are incapable of mutual negation.

A. J. SCHAFFER, 1960[71]

DRUGS AND THE FETUS

Exposure of the Fetus to Drugs

Although advances in prenatal diagnosis are now permitting physicians to consider the fetus the primary patient (see Part 2 of this chapter), it is often the passive recipient of drugs. Consequently, any effects of drugs on the fetus are usually undesirable. Such effects may vary from transient alterations of physiologic function(s) to irreversible structural defects. Concern has increased over the potentially harmful effects of drugs taken during pregnancy since the catastrophic teratogenic effects of thalidomide were discovered in the early 1960s.[40] This drug, thought to be harmless at the time, illustrated the totally unpredictable nature of drug toxicity in the fetus during the first trimester; thalidomide doses that induced analgesia with no demonstrable undesirable side effects in the mother produced major structural defects in the fetus.[40]

Although a number of drugs are possible teratogens in human beings, at present only a few have been positively identified as such.[36,70] In the case of abnormalities that occur quite often in the population, physicians may not be alerted to the direct causal relationship between exposure of the fetus to the drug and the resulting adverse effect(s). It has been estimated that to establish that a given drug changes the naturally occurring frequency of a congenital deformity by 1%, a sequential trial involving approximately 35,000 patients would be required. The discovery that thalidomide caused congenital malformations was made possible because this drug was widely used, induced dramatic and rare congenital defects, and had a high probability (estimated at 20% to 35%) of producing a teratogenic effect after exposure from the third to the eighth week after conception. Unfortunately, these three criteria are rarely met when one is attempting to assess the teratogenicity of other drugs. Thus, much of the data in the biomedical literature concerning the adverse effects of drugs on the fetus is circumstantial.

MATERNAL CONSUMPTION OF DRUGS

Drugs are usually administered for the symptomatic relief of benign problems in the mother, with little or no consideration given to the unintended recipient, the fetus. The magnitude of the problem can be appreciated by considering that in several studies the average number of drugs prescribed during pregnancy was about four.[15,36,71,81] When self-prescribed drugs were included in these studies, the average number taken during pregnancy increased to somewhere between 8.7 and 11. Among obstetric patients, 92% to 100% took at least one physician-prescribed drug and 65% to 80% also took self-prescribed drugs.[32] Compounding this problem for women of childbearing age is additional occupational or environmental exposure to potential teratogens (see Chapter 12). In one controlled study, a significant association was found between fetal loss and the occupational exposure of nurses to anti-neoplastic drugs.[68] The self-prescribed use of herbal medications during pregnancy and their unknown effects on the fetus further underscore the importance of determining the effectiveness and tolerability of medicines ("foods") consumed during pregnancy.

PLACENTAL TRANSFER OF DRUGS

The physiochemical properties that allow most drugs to cross cell membranes also permit their passive transport across the placenta and into the fetus. The factors involved in the placental transfer of drugs include lipid solubility and the degree of ionization, molecular weight, protein binding, affinity for specific transporters (e.g., phosphorylated [P-] glycoprotein [P_{gp}]), placental circulation, fetal circulation, placental maturation, and the metabolism of drugs.[36,78] Most of the drugs administered to the mother reach the fetus; the extent of fetal exposure to a drug administered to the mother depends on its physiochemical properties, the dose and duration of maternal treatment, and the rate of maternal drug elimination. If the drug is readily diffused, it can equilibrate between the maternal and fetal compartments very rapidly (Fig. 10-1). With fast transplacental equilibration and slow maternal elimination, the fetal pharmacokinetic profile mimics the maternal pattern after either a single dose or multiple doses. A drug that is polar or protein bound is diffused more slowly into the fetus. However, high concentrations of a drug may still accumulate in the fetal compartment if multiple doses are administered to the mother (see Fig. 10-1). In clinical practice it is best assumed that the fetus and its compartment are exposed to whatever medication the mother has consumed or is consuming during pregnancy. The clinically relevant effects, if any, require careful investigation.

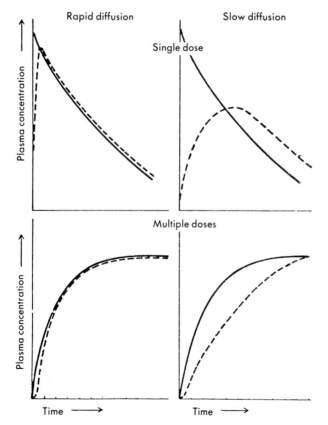

FIGURE 10-1. Schematic representation of maternal (solid line) and fetal (dotted line) plasma concentrations of drugs with time after single or multiple intravenous doses. Simple transplacental diffusion rates that are rapid (left) or slow (right) are hypothesized; it is assumed that the half-lives of the drugs diffusing rapidly or slowly are the same. (From Neims AH et al: Principles of neonatal pharmacology. In Schaffer AJ et al [eds]: Diseases of the Newborn, 4th ed. Philadelphia, WB Saunders Co, 1977.)

DRUG INGESTION BY THE FATHER

Although concern about the potential teratogenic effects of maternally ingested substances has grown in the past 30 years, the possibility that paternal drug exposure may have adverse effects on the progeny has not been of such widespread concern.[2,66] In animals there is experimental evidence of adverse effects occurring in the progeny of males that ingest certain chemicals before mating; these effects include decreased litter size and birthweights, malformations, and increased neonatal mortality. It is difficult to elucidate the mechanisms underlying this phenomenon. The drug itself may be present in semen and may cause developmental alterations after fertilization; alternatively, drug exposure may directly alter the genetic material or its packaging in spermatozoa and consequently the developmental program of the zygote.

In human beings, a variety of paternal occupational exposures have been associated with adverse outcomes in progeny; they include exposure to wood, metals, solvents, pesticides, and hydrocarbons.[58] Further research is needed to investigate the relationship between paternal drug ingestion and perinatal outcome in human beings.

Effects of Drugs on the Fetus

The adverse effects of in utero exposure to drugs can vary from reversible effects such as transient changes in clotting time and fetal breathing movements to irreversible effects such as fetal death, intrauterine growth retardation, structural malformations, and mental retardation.[70,71,81] The specific drug, the dosage, the route of administration, the timing of treatment, and the genotype of the mother and/or the fetus may be critical determinants of the effect of a drug on the fetus. The disease being treated would also appear to be an important consideration. The factors that combine to influence the outcome of drug administration include the diet and coadministration of other drugs. It is difficult to control these parameters in human beings, so the incontrovertible establishment of a drug as a teratogen in human beings requires the combination of extreme situations such as those previously outlined for thalidomide. Consequently, it has been necessary to rely heavily on animal studies to assess the teratogenic potential of drugs.[8]

The *timing* of drug exposure is frequently a critical determinant of the effect of a drug on the fetus (Fig. 10-2). The first week after fertilization is the "period of the zygote" (cleavage and gastrulation). During this time the most common adverse effect of drugs is the termination of pregnancy, which may occur before the woman even knows that she is pregnant. Exposure of the preimplantation embryo to embryotoxic drugs may retard development, perhaps by decreasing cell numbers in the blastocyst, or it may even produce malformations. The second to the eighth week of gestation is the "period of the embryo." It is mainly during this period of organogenesis that drugs produce dramatic and catastrophic structural malformations. Other adverse

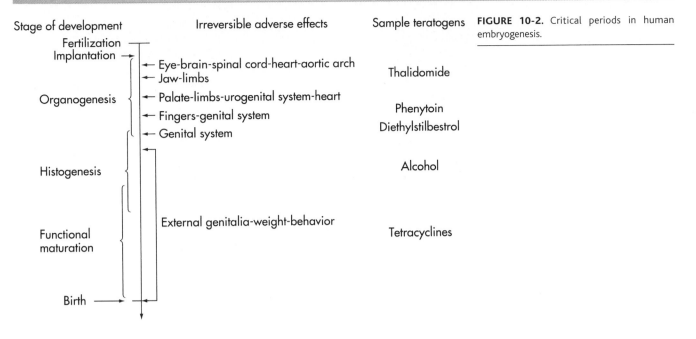

Stage of development   Irreversible adverse effects   Sample teratogens   **FIGURE 10-2.** Critical periods in human embryogenesis.

effects during this phase may include fetal waste, transplacental carcinogenesis (e.g., diethylstilbestrol), and intrauterine growth retardation. From the third to the ninth month of gestation, the "period of the fetus," the differentiation of the central nervous system and the reproductive system continues. Certain drugs given during this period have been implicated as behavioral teratogens. Some drugs may cause disproportionate growth retardation (in infants whose head growth has been spared after 30 or more weeks) or may alter the differentiation of the reproductive system or external genitalia.

The consideration of the irreversible adverse effects of drugs on development usually stops with birth. However, it is well known that sensory and other higher nervous system functions are not fully developed until well after birth. Thus, birth is not really a termination point but only another milestone in development. Little is known about the long-term or delayed adverse effects of drugs administered to the mother during labor and delivery or those given directly to the neonate. When administered postnatally, antitumor agents such as cyclophosphamide can have long-term effects on the histogenesis of the cerebellum, on growth and development, and on reproductive function.

The decision of whether to give a drug during pregnancy is difficult. Some of the information available on the potential adverse effects of pharmacologic classes of drugs is listed in Tables 10-1 and 10-2, which summarize the results of studies on the effects of in utero exposure to frequently used therapeutic agents.

SELF-ADMINISTERED NONTHERAPEUTIC AGENTS

Chronic ethanol intake during pregnancy is associated with a readily identifiable *fetal alcohol syndrome* (see Chapters 12 and 36) and has been cited as the most frequently documented cause of mental deficiency in the western world. Prenatal and postnatal growth retardation; mental deficiency; persistent microcephaly; and minor anomalies of the face, eyes, heart, joints, and genitalia have been identified.[27,31,35] The Collaborative Perinatal Study reported a mortality rate of 17% and mental retardation in 44% of the infants of alcoholic mothers.[27]

A dose-response relationship may exist between the severity of fetal alcohol syndrome and alcohol consumption by the mother. Among women who have infrequent social exposure (i.e., limited amounts) to alcohol in the first trimester, no increased risk has been demonstrated. However, among babies born to mothers who drank 1.5 ounces or more of *absolute* alcohol daily (equivalent to about four or five drinks), 63% demonstrated neurologic impairment, 16% were born prematurely, and 28% were small for their gestational age. Among the infants born to heavy drinkers, 32% had congenital and 16% major malformations.[27] Binge drinking may be more harmful than the same amount consumed over a longer period. The mechanisms by which alcohol produces teratogenic effects on the fetus are likely to include a direct toxic effect on the developing brain and the impairment of placental-fetal bloodflow.[31] Interestingly, binge alcohol consumption during early gestation by women who are not alcohol dependent appears to result in a greater degree of disinhibited behavior that might predispose the offspring to later behavioral dysfunction.[56]

It is now well established that *maternal tobacco smoking* substantially reduces the birthweight of offspring (see Chapters 12 and 13).[4,14] There is a significant dose-response relationship, and early cessation of smoking can result in birthweights similar to those of the offspring of nonsmoking mothers. The largest studies also document an increase in mortality rates resulting from abruptio placentae, placenta previa, and prematurity as

TABLE 10-1. Drugs Associated with Growth and Congenital Malformations

DRUGS	FETAL GROWTH	GROWTH RETARDATION	MENTAL RETARDATION	CENTRAL NERVOUS SYSTEM	CARDIOVASCULAR	MUSCULOSKELETAL	UROGENITAL	EYE AND EAR	THYROID
Antimicrobials									
Tetracycline						X			
Streptomycin								X	
Quinine								X	
Anti-neoplastics									
Methotrexate	X	X		X		X			
Busulfan, chlorambucil, cyclophosphamide	X	X		X		X	X	X	
Central nervous system drugs									
Cocaine				X	X				
Lithium					X				
Thalidomide						X			
Anticonvulsants									
Phenytoin		X	X			X		X	
Barbiturates			X		X	X			
Trimethadione			X		X	X	X	X	
Valproic acid		X		X		X			
Carbamazepine				X		X			
Steroid hormones									
Androgens							X		
Diethylstilbestrol							X		
Estrogen, progestins							X		
Iodine, propylthiouracil									X
Warfarin		X				X		X	
Alcohol		X	X		X	X	X	X	
Tobacco smoking	X	X							
Isotretinoin, vitamin A			X	X		X		X	

TABLE 10-2. Effects on the Fetus of In Utero Exposure to Physician- or Self-Administered Therapeutic Agents

SPECIFIC AGENT	RESULTS AND RECOMMENDATIONS
Anti-neoplastic Agents	
Antimetabolites, alkylating agents, antitumor antibiotics	As a group, these are the most potent teratogens known. It is difficult to delineate one agent because of frequent combined uses in addition to irradiation.
Antimetabolites (purine analogues, pyrimidine analogues, folic acid antagonists)	Potent teratogens; they are associated with skeletal defects.
Alkylating agents (busulfan, chlorambucil, cyclophosphamide, nitrogen mustard)	Some reports have described drug-related defects; others have reported cases with no drug-related defects.
Antimicrobial Agents	
Sulfonamides	Conflicting reports on teratogenicity; avoid use in third trimester because of theoretical risk of kernicterus.
Tetracyclines	Results in staining of dentition; avoid use in second and third trimesters and early childhood.
Penicillins Cephalosporins	These appear to be safe when administered at any phase of pregnancy.
Aminoglycosides Streptomycin, dihydrostreptomycin	Auditory nerve defects and ocular nerve damage may occur in infants after prenatal exposure.
Antitubercular agents Isoniazid	Five children with severe encephalopathies were reported after prenatal exposure; prophylactic administration of vitamin B_6 to pregnant women receiving isoniazid is often recommended.
Ethionamide, ethambutol, rifampin	No clear relationship with abnormal fetal development has been noted.
Antiparasitic agents	Quinidine has caused deafness; for others no definite teratogenicity.
Anticonvulsant Agents	Women requiring anticonvulsant therapy should be counseled before becoming pregnant as to the nature and magnitude of risk to the fetus; overall risk of having a malformed child is about 1 in 10.
Hydantoins Phenytoin	Typical fetal hydantoin syndrome with mild to moderate growth and mental deficiencies, limb anomalies, and dysmorphic facies (low nasal bridge, short nose, mild ocular hypertelorism) has been reported.
Barbiturates, deoxybarbiturates Primidone, phenobarbital, secobarbital, amobarbital	Postnatal effects are similar to those in fetal hydantoin syndrome; associated cardiovascular malformations also may occur.
Oxazoladinediones Trimethadione	Fetal trimethadione syndrome has been reported, with developmental delay, speech difficulty, V-shaped eyebrows, epicanthus, low-set ears, palatal anomaly, and irregular teeth.
Valproic acid Carbamazepine	Neural tube defects have been found. Increased neural tube defects have been found.
Psychotropic Agents	The teratogenicity of most psychotropics is not established; caution is necessary in administering them during pregnancy; neonatal withdrawal syndrome can occur when drug is taken late in pregnancy.
Thalidomide	Teratogenic to human beings when administered from the first to the eighth week of pregnancy; limb reduction anomalies.
Benzodiazepines Diazepam, chlordiazepoxide	Ingestion before parturition may cause hypotonia, apnea, and hypothermia.
Tricyclic antidepressants	Some evidence of increased malformations has been reported.
Monoamine oxidase inhibitors	Few data are available on human beings; only phenelzine is reported as embryotoxic in rats.
Lithium	May induce malformations such as Ebstein anomaly. The increased risk is probably small.
Antinauseants, Antihistamines	No evidence of association with malformation in human beings.
Non-narcotic Analgesics; Anti-inflammatory, Antipyretic Agents	Little evidence exists to associate these with malformations (see the following specific exceptions). As a group, considering their wide usage, they are not considered to be teratogenic in human beings.

Continued

TABLE 10-2. Effects on the Fetus of In Utero Exposure to Physician- or Self-Administered Therapeutic Agents—cont'd

SPECIFIC AGENT	RESULTS AND RECOMMENDATIONS
Salicylates	Concern exists regarding effects on platelet function that could cause hemorrhagic complications in a traumatic birth; possible intrauterine closure of patent ductus arteriosus, pulmonary hypertension.
p-Aminophenols Acetaminophen	No evidence of toxicity or association with malformations after therapeutic doses.
Narcotic Analgesics	These appear to be nonteratogenic in human beings; withdrawal symptoms may occur in infants or narcotic-addicted women.
Hormones and Hormone Antagonists Androgens	Increased risk of masculinization or pseudohermaphroditism in human beings has been reported.
Antiandrogens Cyproterone acetate	These are associated with abnormal sexual development in male laboratory animals; effects in human beings are unknown.
Progestins Ethisterone, norethindrone	Depending on the treatment period during pregnancy, association with equivocal or frankly masculinized external genitalia of varying degrees has been described.
Estrogens Diethylstilbestrol	These are associated with vaginal adenosis and adenocarcinoma in young women exposed in utero; in exposed men there was increased evidence of genitourinary tract disturbances but no increase in cancer incidence.
Antiestrogens Clomiphene	Multiple pregnancy has been reported.
Oral contraceptive agents	No association between first-trimester exposure and malformations.
Corticosteroids (natural and synthetic mineralocorticoids and glucocorticoids)	All are teratogens in animals, producing cleft lip and palate. Large human studies have failed to demonstrate that these agents are major teratogens.
Antithyroid agents (iodides and propylthiouracil)	These may produce neonatal goiter and tracheal obstruction; also may be associated with hypospadias, aortic atresia, and developmental retardation.
Hypoglycemic Drugs Tolbutamide, chlorpropamide	Neonatal hypoglycemia.
Insulin	Insulin is teratogenic to mice and rabbits but not to human beings
Vitamins and Iron	These are used almost universally by pregnant women, with only rare reports of associated malformations (see the following).
Vitamin A	Hypervitaminosis A appears to be teratogenic in animals, and cases of related urinary malformations have been reported in human beings.
Isotretinoin	Characteristic pattern of malformations involving craniofacial, cardiac, thymic, and central nervous system structures has been found.
Iron-containing drugs	Association with congenital malformations appears unlikely.
Diuretics	In general, these are not associated with congenital malformations.
Benzothiadiazides (Thiazides)	Thrombocytopenia, altered carbohydrate metabolism, and hyperbilirubinemia have been reported in infants exposed late in gestation.
Cardiovascular Drugs (antiarrhythmics, digitalis, glycosides)	Very few reports relate these to malformations in human beings.
Antihypertensives Angiotensin-converting enzyme inhibitors	Hypoplasia of the skull calvaria, oligohydramnios, renal failure, death, and neonatal anemia have been reported.
Propranolol	Associations with decreased uterine bloodflow and intrauterine growth retardation have been reported; bradycardia and hypoglycemia may occur in the newborn infant.
Anticoagulants Warfarin	Only warfarin has shown teratogenicity in human beings. Exposure during the first trimester has been related to chondrodysplasia punctata and nasal hypoplasia associated with radiographic stippling of the epiphyses (Conradi disease). Exposure in the third trimester is known to cause fetal or placental hemorrhage; thus, it is recommended that patients requiring anticoagulant therapy be treated with an agent that will not cross the placenta.

TABLE 10-2. Effects on the Fetus of In Utero Exposure to Physician- or Self-Administered Therapeutic Agents—cont'd

SPECIFIC AGENT	RESULTS AND RECOMMENDATIONS
Cough and Cold Medicines	
Bronchodilators, centrally acting antitussive agents, decongestants, expectorants	Of these, only the iodide expectorants have been associated with adverse effects (fetal hypothyroidism and goiter).
Sympathomimetic amines (phenylephrine, phenylpropanolamine, ephedrine, dextroamphetamine)	These have been associated with little risk to the developing fetus.

well as an increased incidence of spontaneous abortion in smoking mothers.[4,14,29]

Data concerning an association between smoking during pregnancy and congenital defects in the infant are conflicting.[29,52] There may be important functional consequences of exposure to cigarette smoke, such as decreased fetal breathing movements and increased fetal heart rate.[48,63] Several studies have reported a significant relationship between maternal smoking during pregnancy and low achievement, increased hyperactivity, and minimal cerebral dysfunction in the offspring.[29]

The exact ingredients in cigarette smoke that cause the effects are not known; nicotine, carbon dioxide, and thiocyanate have all been implicated as well as other contaminants (e.g., lead, cyanates).[14] There does not seem to be a significantly beneficial effect on the birthweight or perinatal mortality rates from reducing the nicotine and tar content or smoking filtered cigarettes. Apparently, preventing the harmful effects of tobacco on the fetus can be achieved only by the cessation of smoking. The safety of nicotine replacement therapy as one part of a coordinated smoking cessation program remains to be defined.[14,29] Animal studies involving nicotine administration to simulate transdermal patch application have shown similar negative fetal effects when associated with tobacco smoke exposure. The applicability of these findings to human beings requires study. At present, smoking cessation and the avoidance of environmental tobacco exposure are the best and safest means by which a mother can prevent the constellation of clearly linked unhealthy fetal effects associated with nicotine and tobacco smoke exposure.[29]

Although caffeine has been found to be teratogenic in high doses in animal experiments, some reports suggest little teratogenic danger to human beings. However, the administration of caffeine does alter ovine fetal respiratory activity, and the presence of caffeine in most cord plasma samples suggests that it may alter human fetal respiratory activity or even neonatal breathing patterns. Nevertheless, most authorities believe that the usual range of human exposure to caffeine from food and drink is far below any potential threshold doses that may be associated with abnormal fetal effects.[10]

The use of cocaine, or "crack," during pregnancy has been associated with reduced birthweight, premature labor, and abruptio placentae. As many as one third of cocaine-exposed babies have neurologic problems that include depression of interactive behavior and poor organizational responses to environmental stimuli.[20,28] Smoking and the excess consumption of alcohol, caffeine-containing products, and cocaine are highly correlated. The potential interaction of these influences, as well as other drug and environmental factors, is presently being systematically considered[8] and underscores the tremendous difficulty in defining specific human teratogens.

FACTORS MODIFYING THE FETAL RESPONSE TO DRUGS

Genetic Background

In addition to the drug itself, the dosage, timing during gestation, and genetic background of the individual fetus and mother all play important roles in determining susceptibility to the teratogenic effects of a drug.[21] Genetics at least partially explains the observation that within a given exposed population, some offspring will manifest an associated malformation while others do not.[45] Furthermore, under genetic control, the presence, maturity, and functional capacity of various placental transporters markedly influence fetal exposure and undoubtedly outcome.[22,78]

Experiments in mice differing at one allele have demonstrated the importance of both the maternal and fetal genotypes in determining the outcome of exposure to a toxic drug. Fraser demonstrated genetic (strain) differences in the susceptibility of inbred mice to the development of a cortisone-induced cleft palate.[21] A study of mice deficient in glucose-6-phosphate dehydrogenase (G6PD) concluded that this enzyme was important in protecting the fetus against oxidative stress; after exposure to a teratogen, the incidence of fetal death and malformations was higher in G6PD-deficient than control mice.[54] In addition, a genetic defect in arene oxide detoxification may increase the risk that women with epilepsy who are treated with phenytoin (fetal hydantoin syndrome; see Chapter 28) could have babies with major birth defects.[75] Thus, congenital malformations are under multifactorial control.

Drug-Drug Interactions

Individuals taking drugs rarely consume only one; rather, they use various combinations. Animal experiments have provided evidence that the administration of one drug can modify the teratogenicity of another. For example, the treatment of rats with phenobarbital increased the teratogenicity of the antitumor drug cyclophosphamide.[26] It is thought that pretreatment with phenobarbital induced maternal hepatic cytochrome P-450, increasing the activation of cyclophosphamide to mutagenic or teratogenic metabolites. It has been suggested that the teratogenic effects of anticonvulsants are more common in women on multiple anticonvulsant therapy because many of these agents perturb drug-metabolizing enzymes. Moreover, one would expect drugs that modulate placental P_{gp}[78] to conceivably result in an increase or decrase in the exposure of the fetal compartment to selected maternal xenobiotics (see Additional Factors That Influence Absorption below). Unfortunately, the many negative fetal perturbations that could occur as a result of the maternal consumption of concurrent medications/herbal products are unknown.

Mechanisms of Drug Toxicity in the Fetus

Various mechanisms have been postulated for the adverse effects of drugs on the fetus. They may interact with a receptor or transporter, inhibit an enzyme, degrade a membrane, or chemically damage macromolecules, including nucleic acids, proteins, and lipids. The consequences of such actions may include mutations, altered differentiation, inhibition of the biosynthesis of structural proteins (e.g., collagen), inhibition of tissue interactions, and altered morphogenetic movements caused by selective cell death (Fig. 10-3).

We now know that many chemical carcinogens (or mutagens) are *precarcinogens* (or *premutagens*) and must be metabolically activated to reactive electrophilic metabolites, or "ultimate" carcinogens, to initiate the cell damage leading to cancer.[38] Early experiments with limb bud and whole embryo culture techniques suggest that at least one teratogen, cyclophosphamide, requires activation to its ultimate teratogen.[26] There is also evidence that thalidomide, phenytoin, chlorcyclizine, and diethylstilbestrol require metabolic activation to be teratogenic.[38] The ultimate teratogen may be a reactive

intermediate of the drug or a reactive species of oxygen.[62] The mechanisms by which active metabolites produce their effects are thought to involve reactions with DNA (leading to covalent modification of DNA, causing base substitution or frame shift mutations), proteins (blocking crucial steps in cell metabolism), or structural lipids (promoting lipid peroxidation). We know that as a result of their instability, many active metabolites react with any available cell nucleophile. Thus, a combination of these mechanisms may be involved.

Such reactive electrophilic metabolites can be detoxified by conjugation with nucleophiles such as glutathione, which is catalyzed by the glutathione S-transferases. Animal experiments have revealed the presence of enzymes during development that may result in other deactivation processes, including hydration, glucuronidation, acetylation, and sulfation. Our understanding of the ontogeny of these processes is evolving.[34,45]

DETERMINATION OF ADVERSE DRUG EFFECTS IN THE FETUS

Human studies of the effects of drugs during pregnancy are often retrospective. Amniocentesis and ultrasonography can be used to screen for some birth defects, but pregnancy is already well advanced by the time these procedures can be used. An alternative, *chorionic villus sampling,* permits the detection of genetic abnormalities in the first trimester (see Chapter 7).

Epidemiologic studies can subsequently correlate a drug with a defect and thus prevent the exposure of future fetuses.[8] However, to delineate the effects of drugs, taken alone or in combination, on unidentified multiple developmental factors is difficult in human beings, even in large epidemiologic studies. The facts that preclinical testing is often done in relatively small numbers of patients and none of them are consciously pregnant underscore the importance of careful post-marketing surveillance to detect an increase in uncommon problems and specific birth defects. The international availability of teratology information services provides a new source of data for prospective epidemiologic studies with a large sample size.[18,32,70]

Data from animal models provide the initial information on the effects of drugs on the fetus. Such data permit the definitions of drug dosage and the timing (i.e., critical periods) of drug exposure during gestation under conditions in which the environment and genotype are controlled. This control has increased our understanding of the mechanisms of drug-induced teratogenicity. Rodents, specifically mice and rats, are frequently chosen as animal models because they are easy to breed and inexpensive and have short gestational periods. However, not all human teratogens are teratogens in different animal species. Thalidomide is an unfortunate example of a human teratogen that is not very teratogenic in rodents. Fortunately, almost every drug that has since been found to be teratogenic in human beings has been shown to cause similar teratogenic effects in animals, underscoring the

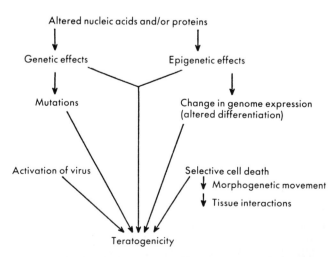

FIGURE 10-3. Potential mechanisms of drug-induced teratogenicity.

importance of multianimal species teratogen studies. Nevertheless, the lack of any teratogenic effects in early preclinical drug development must not be equated with the lack of possible human teratogenicity, underscoring the vital importance of postmarketing phase IV epidemiologic evaluations for teratogenic effects.[18]

Further study of the mechanisms of drug-induced teratogenicity may permit the development of anti-teratogens to prevent the fetotoxic effects of the drugs essential for the mother during pregnancy. A number of such compounds (e.g., nicotinamide, ascorbate, cysteine, vitamins such as folic acid) have been studied in laboratory experiments.[41] Some of these approaches may be useful in decreasing the incidence of adverse pregnancy outcomes in human beings; there is now strong evidence that adequate periconceptional maternal folic acid supplementation is associated with a reduction in the occurrence and recurrence of neural tube defects (see Chapter 10, Part 2).

New, quick, inexpensive screening tests for tera-togens need to be developed. Such tests should prefer-ably include metabolic routes of the drug similar to those in human beings. Whole embryo or organ culture techniques (limb bud, palate) are being increasingly accepted as screening systems to test for teratogens in vitro. Such systems can have drug-metabolizing enzymes incorporated (in liposomes or intact human liver parenchymal cells) to activate any preteratogen such as thalidomide or cyclophosphamide. Other studies have suggested that the inhibition of tumor cell attach-ment may be useful in the prediction of drug teratogenicity in vitro.[23]

DRUG USE, DISPOSITION, AND METABOLISM IN THE NEWBORN INFANT

At birth a term infant in North America receives at least three types of drugs: an ophthalmic antimicrobial agent, vitamin K, and an antibacterial agent for the cord. Low birthweight and sick infants in a neonatal intensive care unit additionally receive an increasing number of drugs, with the constant introduction of new drugs or old drugs with new indications in the neonatal thera-peutic armamentarium. Thus the overall xenobiotic exposure of the fetus and newborn exceeds current estimates, particularly when environmental agents (e.g., lead, methyl mercury, volatile hydrocarbons), drugs of habit (e.g., caffeine, alcohol, cocaine, opiates), and maternal therapeutic agents are taken into consideration. Because many of these agents are pharmacologically active, their effects may be significant if sufficient amounts reach the fetus or newborn. Besides the usual oral or parenteral routes, unintentional portals of drug entry include the transplacental route; inadvertent, direct fetal injection; pulmonary, dermal, or conjunctival entry; and ingestion of breast milk. The lack of aware-ness or underestimation of the degree of drug entry through these routes and of altered drug disposition

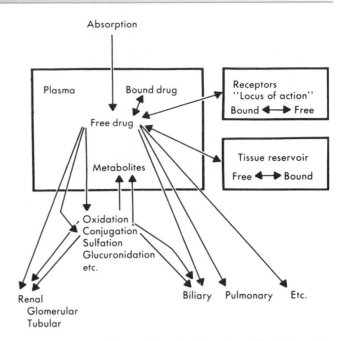

FIGURE 10-4. Interrelationships of absorption, distribution, bio-transformation, and excretion of a drug and its concentration at the receptor site.

and metabolism in the perinatal period has led to well recognized therapeutic misadventures in neonatology.[34] The prevention of toxic reactions to drugs and their rational and safe use require a thorough understanding of the various pharmacologic profiles of each drug used in the treatment of the neonate.

Figure 10-4 illustrates many of the interrelation-ships of the absorption, distribution, binding, bio-transformation, and excretion of a drug and its concentration at the locus of action.[34,69] To produce its characteristic effect, a drug must be present in sufficient concentrations at its sites of action or receptor sites. The concentration of the drug at the receptor site depends not only on the amount of drug administered but also on the interrelationships listed above and shown in Figure 10-4. Those factors that have been evaluated in the newborn infant differ substantially from those in the adult and even in the young infant beyond the neonatal period.[34]

Absorption of Drugs in the Neonate

Drug absorption is the passage of a drug from its site of administration into the circulation. In a sick neonate the intravenous route is preferred because of the ease of delivery, accuracy of dosage, possible poor periph-eral perfusion, and poor gastrointestinal function. In neonates who can tolerate gastric feedings, the oral route of drug administration is the most convenient and probably the safest. The absorption of a drug or substance through the gastrointestinal system may be defined as the net movement of a drug from the gastro-intestinal lumen into the systemic circulation draining this organ. This process entails the movement of drugs across the gastrointestinal epithelium, which behaves like a semipermeable lipid membrane and constitutes the main barrier to absorption. The various processes operating to induce the transepithelial membrane movement of drug molecules include simple diffusion through lipid membranes or aqueous pores of the membrane; filtration through aqueous channels or membrane pores; and carrier-mediated transport, such as active transport or facilitated diffusion, and vesicular transport, such as pinocytosis. Of these, the most important is the process of simple diffusion because most drugs administered orally are absorbed via this process. This is evident from the direct proportionality between the concentration of the drug in the intestine and the amount of the drug absorbed over a wide range of concentrations. Moreover, one drug does not compete with another for transfer, indicating that the process of absorption is a simple nonsaturable one.[6,34]

The rate and extent of gastrointestinal drug absorption are partly determined by the physical and chemical characteristics of the drug. Polarity, nonlipid solubility, and a large molecular size tend to decrease absorption. In contrast, nonpolarity, lipid solubility, and a small molecular size increase absorption. The degree of ionization, determined by the pK_a of the drug and the pH of the solution in which it exists, is an important determinant in drug absorption. The gastrointestinal epithelium is more permeable to the nonionized form because this portion is usually lipid soluble and favors absorption. The degree of drug ionization changes as the pH increases from the stomach through the distal portion of the gut. The slow gastric emptying time in the newborn may retard drug absorption and can limit the rate because the primary site for drug absorption is the proximal bowel, which has the greatest absorptive surface area. Conversely, a slow transit time or slow intestinal motility may facilitate the absorption of some drugs.

These physiologic processes undergo substantial changes during the neonatal period. Gastric acid production is generally low at birth, and the gastric pH is usually 6 to 8, decreasing within a few hours to pH values of 3 to 1. Acid secretion is low in the first 10 days of life; it tends to rise thereafter and approaches adult values around 6 to 8 months of age. Intestinal motility is slow in the newborn, and the transit time from the stomach to the cecum is generally prolonged relative to that in the adult. The gastric emptying time after milk feeding is considerably prolonged in the neonate and approaches adult values at age 6 to 8 months. The precise influence of milk feeding on neonatal drug bioavailability requires further evaluation.

Drug absorption requires an intact splanchnic vascular circulation. In sick neonates, especially those with hypotension, perfusion of the gut may decrease to maintain adequate perfusion of vital organs, resulting in decreased drug absorption.

Current evidence indicates that the amount of absorption of most drugs is independent of age, although the rate of absorption of certain drugs shows a nonlinear correlation with age. Data indicate that the gastrointestinal absorption of drugs is relatively slow in the neonate and undergoes maturational changes similar to those found in drug distribution, metabolism, and disposition. Although the neonatal drug absorptive deficit may influence the achievement of an optimal pharmacologic effect, it is likely that its clinical significance is minor relative to the age-related alterations in drug distribution, metabolism, and disposition.[6,34]

ADDITIONAL FACTORS THAT INFLUENCE ABSORPTION

Two additional factors from those described above that influence the rate and extent of drug absorption after oral administration include the presence and functional capacity of P_{gp} and the type and extent of bacterial flora.[6,34] P_{gp} is abundant within the human and normally found within the cellular membranes of the intestinal tract (duodenum, ileum, jejunum, colon), apical membrane of hepatocytes, and renal proximal tubular cells and on the luminal side of the capillary endothelial cells that comprise the blood brain barrier and placenta. In human beings P_{gp} is the most prominent member of the ATP binding cassette family of proteins. This protein is responsible for cellular drug efflux, translocating substances from the intracellular to the extracellular compartment. This efflux protein has an affinity for a broad range of hydrophobic substrates and effectively "pumps" xenobiotics out of cells, influencing the amount a drug may be absorbed into the systemic circulation. Depending on the functional capacity and affinity for P_{gp}, the activity of this pump influences the rate at which a drug may be cleared by the liver or kidney and influences the amount of the drug that crosses the placenta or enters the central nervous system.[78] Furthermore, the activity of this important drug transporter may be modulated by the incorporation of P_{gp} inhibitors or inducers. It is this latter occurrence that is most likely responsible for a number of clinically important drug-drug interactions. Although only limited ontogenic data exist for P_{gp}, it is probable that the variability in the characteristics of intestinal absorption for many drugs is probably a direct result of the variability of P_{gp} expression within the intestinal tract as well as the presence or absence of P_{gp} modulators. Unfortunately, the ontogeny of P_{gp} in any human organ has not been described. The importance of understanding P_{gp} ontogeny cannot be overemphasized, considering the important role that this efflux pump plays in the absorption, distribution, and clearance of many clinically important drugs.[6,78]

Finally, the colonization of the gastrointestinal tract by bacteria is another process that influences intestinal drug absorption. Intestinal flora are involved in the metabolism of bile salts and selected drugs as well as intestinal motility and varies with age, type of delivery, type of feeding, and concurrent drug therapy. Although the actual characterization of the colonization of intestinal flora relative to age is limited, data suggest that all full-term, formula-fed, vaginally delivered infants are colonized with anaerobic bacteria by 4 to 6 days of postnatal life. By 5 to 12 months of age, an adult pattern of microbial reduction products appears to be established. Unfortunately, only very limited data on the metabolic activity of the gut flora are available, underscoring our need to better understand the ontogenic and metabolic effects of this important process. In addition, the previously described drug absorption in the effects of flora ontogeny (e.g., digoxin) may represent, totally or partially, the importance of P_{gp} ontogeny.

Protein Binding of Drugs in the Neonate

The unbound or free concentration of a drug in plasma is considered to be the pharmacologically active fraction of the drug. For some drugs, including theophylline, phenytoin, phenobarbital, penicillin, and salicylates, the binding to plasma protein is decreased in the newborn compared with that in the nonpregnant adult.[6,17] This outcome suggests that a more intense pharmacologic response may be obtained in the newborn infant than the adult for the same total drug concentration. The primary drug-binding protein in human beings is albumin. The developmental changes in protein-drug binding and the postnatal age at which adult-like binding is achieved have not been defined with confidence for all drugs used in the neonatal period. The reasons underlying this deficient plasma protein binding of drugs at birth may include decreased plasma albumin concentrations, possible qualitative differences in neonatal plasma proteins, and competitive binding by many endogenous substrates, such as hormones. Hyperbilirubinemia may accentuate this competition by displacing a drug, such as phenytoin, from its albumin-binding site. This activity contrasts with the well known drug-protein binding interaction with bilirubin, in which drugs such as sulfonamides or their excipients may displace bilirubin from its binding site.

Deficient plasma protein binding is usually not considered in calculating neonatal drug dosages. However, this factor must be considered in the application of adult therapeutic plasma concentrations to the neonatal patient. Moreover, decreased protein binding influences the calculation of apparent volumes of distribution based on plasma concentrations of the total drug amount. In terms of therapeutic monitoring, drug concentrations obtained from saliva reflect those of the unbound fraction in plasma and may represent a less invasive approach to therapeutic drug monitoring, although the lack of collection methods and standards for saliva limits its clinical utility.[6]

Drug Metabolism and Disposition in the Neonate

Many drugs are lipophilic and require conversion to more water-soluble metabolites for efficient elimination from the body. These metabolic processes are traditionally categorized as either phase I or II reactions. In a phase I reaction, a more polar compound is formed through oxidation, reduction, or hydrolysis of the parent molecule. Although they are often considered part of a detoxification process, phase I metabolites may be more pharmacologically active than the parent compound. It is the reactive product of phase I metabolism that accounts for the carcinogenic and teratogenic effects of certain xenobiotics as well as organotoxic effects (e.g., acetaminophen liver toxicity). Phase II metabolism involves conjugation with endogenous substrates such as sulfate, acetate, and glucuronic acid. Drugs may be conjugated directly or made more amenable to conjugation after the introduction of a functional group by phase I metabolism (e.g., hydroxylation). It is well recognized that the neonate is deficient in many of the enzymes responsible for phases I and II drug metabolism.[6,34] Unfortunately, these deficiencies have led to a number of adverse reactions, including the "gray baby" syndrome associated with chloramphenicol and cardiac arrhythmias associated with cisapride. Recent advances in our understanding of the ontogeny of the enzymes responsible for drug metabolism can explain past cases of drug toxicity in the neonate and help prevent such events in the future.

Phase I metabolism is mediated primarily by the cytochrome P-450 enzymes. These enzymes are present in several tissues throughout the body, including the intestine, lung, kidney, and adrenal glands, but are the most highly concentrated in the liver. Numerous isoforms have been identified; the primary enzymes involved in drug metabolism are listed in Table 10-3. Considerable individuality is evident with respect to substrate specificity, polymorphic expression, and susceptibility to induction and inhibition. The general pattern of development of these enzymes is illustrated in Figure 10-5. In the fetal liver, studies have shown that CYP3A7 is by far the most significant cytochrome P-450 enzyme in terms of protein expression and activity.

CYP3A7 concentrations decline during the neonatal period; in adults the concentration is less than 20% of that for CYP3A4.[39,76] CYP3A4 is the most abundant cytochrome P-450 enzyme in adults, accounting for 30% to 40% of hepatic cytochrome P-450 and as much as 70% of the content of cytochrome P-450 in the intestine. The majority of other cytochrome P-450

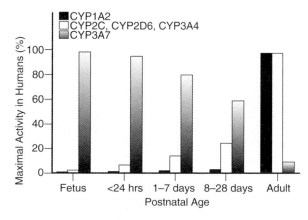

FIGURE 10-5. Maturational change in the activity of the cytochrome P-450 isoenzymes implicated in human drug metabolism. (See text for details.)

enzymes develop rapidly in the neonatal period. Whether they are triggered by the loss of a maternal repressing factor or stimulated by transcription factors intrinsic to newborns, concentrations of CYP2D6 and CYP2E1 increase within hours of birth, followed closely by the CYP2C and CYP3A4 enzymes.[34] By 1 month of age, hepatic concentrations are approximately 25% to 30% of those in adults. The notable exception is CYP1A2, which develops more slowly, reaching less than 5% of adult concentrations in the first month.[34,74] The total content of enzymes of the cytochrome P-450 3A subfamily remains relatively constant throughout the neonatal period and into adulthood because declining concentrations of CYP3A7 are matched by increasing concentrations of CYP3A4.[39] It is generally assumed that premature babies exhibit greater impairment in drug metabolism than full-term infants; this response has been documented in several studies involving drugs metabolized by a wide range of cytochrome P-450 enzymes.[9,42-44,47,53,65] It may be due to the greater degree of immaturity of these enzymes at birth, a delay of the postnatal surge in cytochrome P-450 concentration observed in full-term babies, or a combination of these two factors.

The pharmacokinetics of many drugs in neonates is consistent with the pattern of development of the cytochrome P-450 enzymes shown in Figure 10-5. Caffeine, which is administered for the treatment of neonatal apnea, exhibits an extremely prolonged half-life of several days in neonates compared with 4 to 6 hours in adults.[5,42] This result is due to the delayed development of the CYP1A2 enzyme, which is responsible for the demethylation of caffeine, the primary metabolic pathway.[25] The structurally related bronchodilator theophylline also exhibits reduced clearance and a prolonged half-life in neonates.[16] However, the effect is not as dramatic as that observed with caffeine because theophylline is partially oxidized by other cytochrome P-450 enzymes, such as CYP2E1 in addition to CYP1A2.[77] For drugs metabolized primarily by CYP2D6 or CYP2C, it seems reasonable to expect drug clearance to be low at birth but increase rapidly during the first month of life. Data on tolbutamide and phenytoin, which are substrates for CYP2C9, support this view.[9] The half-life of tolbutamide was found to decrease from 46 hours to 6 hours within the first 2 days after birth in a neonate exposed to the drug by placental transfer from the mother.[9] The clearance of drugs metabolized by CYP3A4 may be reduced less in neonates than substrates for other cytochrome P-450 enzymes if CYP3A7 is capable of contributing to the metabolic process. CYP3A4 and CYP3A7 show more than 85% amino acid sequence homology and have partially overlapping affinities for both endogenous and exogenous substrates.[57] CYP3A7 appears to play an important role in the metabolism of steroids by the fetus and is 10- to 20-fold more active than CYP3A4 in catalyzing the 16α-hydroxylation of dehydroepiandrosterone. In addition, the ratio of 6β-hydroxycortisol to cortisol in urine declines in a parallel manner with the decrease in CYP3A7 concentration in neonates, suggesting that CYP3A7 is involved in this reaction. The catalytic activity of CYP3A4 toward drugs such as midazolam, carbamazepine, and nifedipine is greater than that of CYP3A7, whereas the latter appears relatively active in metabolizing erythromycin.[57] However, even if catalytic activity is low, CYP3A7 may contribute to the overall clearance of a drug at birth due to the high concentrations present. This activity may account for the observation that the elimination of CYP3A substrates such as carbamazepine[72] and the reverse transcriptase inhibitor nevirapine[51] during the first week of life is relatively similar to that observed in adults.

The metabolism of phase II drugs is mediated by a number of different enzymes, the most important of which are N-acetyltransferase (acetylation), sulfotransferase (sulfation), and uridine 5′-diphosphate glucuronosyltransferase (UGT) (glucuronidation). Acetylation activity is polymorphically expressed in adults, with 10% to 20% of Asians and 40% to 60% of whites and African Americans being slow acetylators. Delayed development in neonates is suggested by some studies indicating that a much higher percentage (greater than 75%) of newborns and children younger than 2 years of age are phenotypically slow acetylators of caffeine and isoniazid compared with adults.[60,61] Sulfation appears to be reasonably well developed at birth relative to other pathways of drug metabolism. The proportion of a dose of acetaminophen excreted as a sulfate conjugate is higher in neonates than older children or adults.[79] Increased sulfation partially compensates for the reduced glucuronidation of acetaminophen and ritodrine in neonates.[7] Glucuronidation is an important route of metabolism for many drugs (acetaminophen, morphine, zidovudine) as well as endogenous compounds such as bilirubin.[13] Although UGT activity is generally presumed to be immature at birth, establishing a clear pattern for its development is complicated by the existence of numerous isoforms of the enzyme with broad and overlapping substrate specificity. UGT1A1, which is involved in the glucuronidation of bilirubin, is virtually absent in the fetus and develops slowly over several months after birth. A somewhat similar pattern of development exists for UGT1A6, which is responsible for the glucuronidation of acetaminophen. UGT2B7 is expressed to a greater extent in the fetus and neonate (10% to 20% of adult values) and catalyzes the formation of morphine-3-glucuronide and morphine-6-glucuronide.[13] However, morphine clearance in neonates remains well below that of older children. The UGT isoform involved in the metabolism of substrates such as zidovudine and chloramphenicol has not been clearly identified. Chloramphenicol is of particular interest, as impaired glucuronidation is the primary cause of gray baby syndrome, which is associated with the use of this drug. Similar to observations with drugs metabolized by cytochrome P-450, glucuronidation in premature infants is impaired to a greater extent than it is in full-term infants.[50,67]

Conclusions based on studies of drug metabolism in the neonate must be interpreted with caution due to the small numbers of subjects in many investigations and the potentially confounding effects of genetics and disease states on metabolism, as access to healthy babies during the first month of life is limited. Nevertheless, the available data suggest the following tentative conclusions.

1. The rate of drug metabolism is generally low at birth in full-term babies and even lower in premature infants regardless of the specific route of metabolism. Decreased clearance and a prolonged drug half-life require drug administration with longer dosing intervals.

2. Many of the enzymes responsible for metabolism exhibit significant development during the first month of life. Dosing regimens appropriate during the first few days of postnatal life may not be appropriate 3 to 4 weeks after birth because dose requirements may increase and dosing intervals decrease.

3. The development of individual drug-metabolizing enzymes varies widely among neonates and may be delayed in premature infants. Predicting clearance is difficult, and dosing regimens must be individualized for patients based on the careful observation of the patient's response and tolerance; monitoring of plasma drug concentrations may be useful for selected drugs.

Renal Excretion of Drugs

The kidneys are the most important organs for drug elimination in the newborn because the most frequently used drugs, such as antimicrobial agents and histamine-2 receptor antagonists, are excreted by way of this organ as well as the route of elimination after metabolism for most agents. Renal elimination of these drugs reflects and depends on neonatal renal function, which is characterized by a low glomerular filtration rate, low effective renal bloodflow, and low tubular function compared with that in the adult (see Chapter 49). The neonatal glomerular filtration rate is about 30% of the adult value and is greatly influenced by gestational age

at birth. Glomerular filtration is negligible and highly variable at less than 34 weeks of gestation, the rate of which is often approximately 2 to 4 mL/min per 1.73 m^2 in preterm infants.[34] The ontogeny of renal function is addressed in more detail in Chapter 49. The most rapid changes in renal function occur during the first week of life, and these events are reflected in the plasma disappearance rates of aminoglycosides, which are eliminated mainly by glomerular filtration. These age-related (gestational and postnatal) changes have been considered in the dosage regimen recommendations for drugs and other antibiotics used in the treatment of infants.[34]

Effective renal bloodflow may influence the rate at which drugs are presented to and eliminated by the kidneys. Effective renal bloodflow, as measured by para-aminohippurate (PAH) clearance, is substantially lower in infants than adults, even when PAH extraction values are correlated (i.e., PAH extraction is 60% in infants, compared with greater than 92% in adults). Available data suggest that there is low effective renal bloodflow during the first 2 days of life (34 to 99 mL/min per 1.73 m^2), which increases to 54 to 166 mL/min per 1.73 m^2 by 14 to 21 days and further increases to adult values of about 600 mL/min per 1.73 m^2 by age 1 to 2 years. These data are probably not applicable to premature infants with very low birthweights, particularly those who weigh less than 750 g at birth. It is assumed, pending definitive data, that the glomerular filtration rate and renal bloodflow in these micronates are substantially lower than those in bigger, premature infants, such as those who weigh more than 1000 g at birth. Nevertheless, renal function in these patients is highly variable and reflected in the highly variable body clearance of numerous administered drugs and underscores the need for the rigorous monitoring of drug efficacy and patient tolerability.

The pharmacokinetic behavior of drugs eliminated via the neonatal kidneys exhibits characteristics similar to those underlying hepatic bio-transformation. For instance, the half-lives of many antimicrobials, such as ampicillin (Fig. 10-6), show marked interindividual variability at birth, which narrows somewhat with advancing age. The plasma half-life also shortens progressively

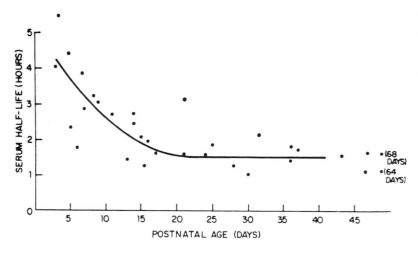

FIGURE 10-6. Postnatal changes in the serum half-life of ampicillin. (From Axline SG, et al: Clinical pharmacology of antimicrobials in premature infants: II. Ampicillin, methicillin, oxacillin, neomycin, and colistin. Pediatrics 39:97, 1967. © American Academy of Pediatrics, 1967.)

after birth, achieving adult rates of elimination within 1 month. The drug-dependent variability in the elimination process partially reflects the major renal mechanism of drug excretion. Those drugs that undergo substantial elimination by glomerular filtration (e.g., aminoglycosides) may be excreted more rapidly than those requiring substantial tubular excretion (e.g., penicillins). These differences may reflect neonatal glomerular preponderance. Studies of the pharmacokinetics of ceftazidime and famotidine have shown direct correlations between plasma drug clearance and the maturational changes in renal function.[34]

As with hepatic metabolism, the renal excretion of certain drugs may be as efficient as that in adults. For example, colistin, an antibiotic, is eliminated by neonates at rates similar to those in adults. However, as a rule, drug excretion by way of the neonatal kidneys is deficient relative to that in the adult. Pathophysiologic insults further compromise the inherent deficiency in drug elimination, complicating individual drug dosage regimens. Moreover, very small infants, who receive the most drugs in the neonatal population, exhibit the worst functional deficiency in drug elimination. Unfortunately, if drug doses are not adjusted appropriately, accumulation and toxicity may ensue. Hypoxemia further decreases the slow glomerular and tubular functions in neonates, leading to the slower renal excretion of drugs, as shown with amikacin. A linear relationship between oxygen tension and hepatic oxidation has been reported, so drugs that require hepatic biotransformation or renal excretion may be excreted much more slowly when hypoxemia is present. The determination of the plasma concentrations of drugs, coupled with appropriate caution and clinical awareness, helps ensure optimal and safe drug therapy in the neonate.

Pharmacokinetic Considerations, Dosage Guidelines, and Therapeutic Monitoring in Neonatal Drug Therapy (See Appendix A)

Knowledge of the pharmacokinetic profile of a drug allows the manipulation of the dosage to achieve and maintain a given plasma concentration. A typical plasma disappearance curve for a drug administered in the newborn period is shown in Figure 10-7. In this example, the log of the plasma concentration decreases linearly as a function of time, with a brief but fast distribution (alpha [α]) phase and a slower elimination (beta [β]) phase. This process exemplifies a two-compartment model and first-order kinetics; that is, a certain fraction (not amount) of the drug remaining in the body is eliminated with time, and after the distribution phase the plasma concentration reflects or is proportional to the concentration of the drug in other parts of the body. This model is applicable to a wide variety of drugs used in the neonatal period, although some drugs (e.g., gentamicin, diazepam, digoxin) fit a multicompartmental model. Others (e.g., ethanol, phenytoin) exhibit saturation kinetics; that is, a certain amount (not fraction) of the drug is eliminated per unit

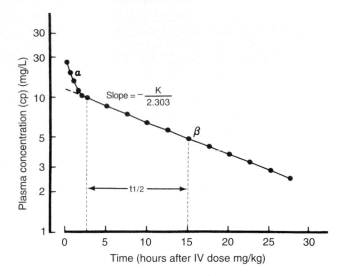

FIGURE 10-7. Representative plasma disappearance curve of a drug given intravenously and plotted semilogarithmically as a function of time. A fast distribution phase (α) is followed by a slower elimination phase (β). IV, intravenous.

of time. For newborn infants, in whom the elimination phase is extremely prolonged relative to the distribution phase, the relative contribution of the distribution phase to overall elimination and dosage computations may not be significant. Thus, the entire body may behave kinetically as though it were a single compartment (e.g., the one-compartment model).

The administration of a loading dose (in milligrams per kilogram) to quickly achieve a given plasma drug concentration depends on the rapidity with which the onset of drug action is required. For many drugs used in neonates, loading doses are generally greater than those for older children or adult subjects. This requirement of a larger loading dose in neonates reflects the differences in the amounts and distribution of body water between the neonate and older infants, children, and adults. Total body water varies inversely with age; in the young fetus it constitutes nearly 92% of the body weight, whereas in the term infant and 6-month-old infant it constitutes ≈75% and 60%, respectively, of the body weight. The prolonged half-life warrants the age-appropriate maintenance dosage given at longer intervals to prevent toxic effects or overdosage. The rapid postnatal changes in drug elimination require the adjustment of maintenance dosage rates (in milligrams per kilogram per day) with advancing postnatal age; this adjustment may also be a function of the drug used. Monitoring drug concentrations is extremely useful if the desired pharmacologic effect is not attained or if adverse reactions occur and a clear relationship has been defined between the drug's effect and the pharmacodynamic response (see below). Moreover, therapeutic drug monitoring seems prudent, especially for those drugs with a narrow therapeutic index used during a period in which there is a rapid change in drug elimination.

In the clinical setting, the therapeutic drug monitoring of anticonvulsants (phenytoin, phenobarbital, carbamazepine), antimicrobials (gentamicin, tobramycin, chloramphenicol, vancomycin), cardiac glycosides (digoxin), and methylxanthines (caffeine, theophylline) is often useful in individualizing drug therapy.[6,34] Rapid microassay techniques such as the enzyme multiplied immunoassay and high-pressure liquid chromatography require only small volumes of blood samples and are well suited for neonates. Therapeutic drug monitoring to verify the appropriateness of the drug dosing schedule is useful when (1) dose adjustments are contemplated, (2) there is the lack of a desired therapeutic effect, (3) there are adverse or toxic effects, and (4) factors modifying drug metabolism and elimination are present, such as abnormal renal and hepatic function. Because most of the drugs used in neonates exhibit first-order kinetics, the change in dose is proportional to the change in plasma drug concentration at a steady state. Thus, a plasma phenobarbital concentration of 10 mg/L at a dose of 5 mg/kg per day would be expected to increase 100% to 20 mg/L if the dose were increased 100% to 10 mg/kg per day. Conversely, a plasma phenobarbital concentration of 10 mg/L would decrease to 5 mg/L if the phenobarbital dose were decreased 50% to 2.5 mg/kg per day. These predictions are expected to occur at a steady state, in which the fraction of the drug dose eliminated from the body is usually held constant with the amount absorbed.

For many drugs used in the neonatal intensive care unit, published definitions exist for "target" plasma drug concentrations, e.g., aminoglycosides, vancomycin, and anticonvulsants. However, the sensitivity of these purported concentrations for many drugs administered to neonates, particularly antimicrobial drugs, are highly questionable. Critical analysis of the literature published over the last 3 decades attempting to correlate plasma antibiotic concentrations fails to substantiate a sensitive, direct relationship between plasma aminoglycosides or vancomycin and adverse effects. Nevertheless, these data do demonstrate that if the antibiotic plasma concentration remains within the purported target range, clinical efficacy is usually achieved. Thus, the dosing of those drugs in sick neonates should be focused on the use of defined, age-appropriate dose regimens that rely on this body of "population-based" evidence and plasma drug concentrations obtained in those patients who are not responding to therapy as expected or demonstrate adverse effects on or whose excretory organ function markedly changes during therapy.

Roles of Fetal Maturity and Advancing Postnatal Age on Neonatal Drug Dose and Dose Interval

Infants with very low ($\leq$500 to 750 g) to low (751 to 1000 g) birthweights are showing increasing numbers in many neonatal intensive care units. This phenomenon is due to several factors, including attempts to decrease the rates of perinatal death caused by fetal distress, fetal growth retardation, premature rupture of membranes,

or simply the inability to stop labor by existing tocolytic measures. The major organs for drug metabolism and excretion in these very small, premature neonates—namely the liver and kidneys—are substantially immature; therefore, the plasma clearance of drugs is exceptionally slow or diminished. This fact indicates that the total drug dose per day must be decreased and the intervals between drug doses must be much longer than those in term newborns or premature neonates with a greater degree of maturation (i.e., greater than 32 weeks of gestation). Drug doses, particularly for those agents excreted by the kidneys, are dynamically changing as functions of gestational and postnatal ages. These requirements are exemplified by two agents commonly used in the neonatal nursery—gentamicin and vancomycin. In general, the total daily dose of the drug is directly related to postconceptional age. The lower the fetal or postconceptional age, the smaller the total daily drug dose. Moreover, fetal maturity is inversely related to dose interval. Thus, the younger the gestational age, the longer the dose interval. These dose adjustments reflect the relatively deficient drug elimination of the very small, premature infants discussed above.

DRUGS AND LACTATION

Until recently, investigations of drugs and other compounds in breast milk were hampered by the very small numbers of lactating women studied and the insensitivity of drug assay methods. Much of the early literature concerns isolated case reports and a small selection of drugs.[11] With today's higher incidence of breast feeding there are more situations in which lactating women are exposed to various medications, and an increasing number of useful studies of drugs in breast milk can be expected. There are currently up to 80% of Canadian and American women who breastfeed their infants; unfortunately, as many as 50% discontinue breast feeding by 3 to 4 months after delivery. In addition to pharmaceuticals, environmental pollutants and nontherapeutic or "social" chemicals find their way into breast milk. Public awareness of these problems is high, and the clinician is often called on for counseling.

Passage of Exogenous Compounds from Maternal Blood to Milk

The presence and concentration of compounds in breast milk depend on a number of important factors, including the drug's molecular weight, degree of ionization, protein binding in blood, lipid solubility, and specific uptake by mammary tissue as well as the amount and composition of the milk. These physiochemical characteristics, which are the same as those discussed above, influence drug absorption from any site of administration. The constituents of breast milk vary relative to the postpartum period and could influence drug distribution and accumulation within breast milk, depending on the drug's physiochemical characteristics.[11] Drugs that are not absorbed after oral ingestion do not appear in milk.

Small compounds with molecular weights of less than about 200 appear freely in breast milk and are presumed to have passed through pores in the mammary alveolar cell. Large compounds such as insulin or heparin do not enter the milk. Intermediate-size compounds must penetrate the lipoprotein cell membrane by diffusion or active transport.

In general, drugs that are not ionized at blood pH traverse the alveolar cell membrane with greater ease than highly ionized compounds. Because breast milk pH is 7 or slightly less, milk may act like a trap for weak bases.

Drugs pass through the cell membrane only in their free form; thus, highly protein-bound drugs are less available for passage. Drugs or other chemicals that are very lipid soluble readily cross the alveolar cell, and because breast milk contains a considerable amount of lipid, these compounds are trapped in the milk. For the most part, drugs enter breast milk by passive diffusion. This is best described in pharmacokinetic terms as a three-compartment model, with the breast milk as a deep third compartment (Fig. 10-8). These principles also apply to drug metabolite transfer into breast milk.

A number of important variables specific for the type of drug, age, and time after delivery and/or disease influence a drug's ability to penetrate into breast milk.

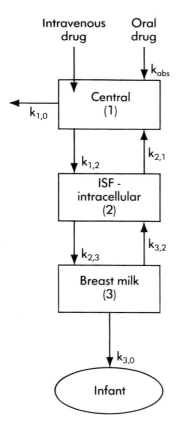

FIGURE 10-8. Three-compartment model for drug transfer into breast milk. ISF, interstitial fluid; k_{abs}, absorption rate constant; k_{xy}, rate constant for transfer from compartment x to compartment y. (Modified from Wilson JT: Determinants and consequences of drug excretion in breast milk. Drug Metab Rev 14:619, 1983.)

The interrelationships between these and other variables yet to be identified are complex, making it very difficult to predict the actual amounts of drug distribution into the milk. Although many investigators and clinicians have attempted to collapse the many important characteristics into one simple surrogate marker of drug penetration into breast milk, i.e., the ratio of milk to plasma protein (M/P ratio), this parameter is overly simplistic and often misrepresents the true nature of drug distribution into breast milk. The M/P ratio is defined as the ratio of the drug concentration in breast milk to the drug concentration in maternal plasma at a simultaneous point in time after maternal drug administration. Thus, the M/P ratio is based on the erroneous assumptions that the drug concentrations in maternal blood and milk are constant and in equilibrium at the time of sampling and that the drug's distribution characteristics in these two matrices are parallel. Although the M/P ratio is often quoted, it cannot account for many of the interdependent variables important for systemic drug distribution. Although many investigators have realized the limitations of the M/P ratio for decades and alternative mathematical models of varying complexity have been developed as M/P replacements, all of them have yet to be validated and the complexity of most limits their clinical usefulness. Based on these real and severe limitations, the M/P ratio should be used with caution, if at all, as a means of quantitating drug distribution in breast milk and infant exposure. Alternatively, we believe that the M/P ratio may be used as a simplified qualitative measure of infant exposure combined with the knowledge of a drug's physiochemical and pharmacokinetic characteristics and appropriate infant monitoring of the drug's primary and/or secondary effects.[3,11]

Delivery of Compounds to and Disposition of the Infant

The concentration of the drug in milk and the total volume of milk consumed by the infant in a known period determine the dosage delivered. Because the daily volume intake of breast milk is exceedingly variable and impractical to measure routinely, one could assume a *high average* daily consumption of milk to be about 1 L. To produce an effect, the drug in the milk must either act locally in the gut or be absorbed. Furthermore, because a drug may be concentrated in just the breast milk, the actual amount that may reach the infant's system may be below that necessary for any clinically relevant effect(s). This latter scenario seems to reflect the majority of clinical experience and explains the lack of clinically important effects in the breastfed infants of mothers receiving medication. It is possible that the milk proteins bind to certain drugs and thereby impede absorption; it is also possible that the bowel of a very young infant may permit the absorption of large molecules that are normally excluded.

The infant's disposition toward the drug in milk changes with postnatal age (see Drug Use, Disposition, and Metabolism in the Newborn Infant above). In addition, one must always be aware of the drug's potential for the displacement of bilirubin from serum albumin.

Compounds in Breast Milk

ANTICOAGULANTS

Heparin does not enter breast milk. Newer synthetic heparin has a much lower molecular weight and thus a greater potential for passage into breast milk, although heparins are unstable in gastric contents. These drugs are safe for use during breast feeding. Oral anticoagulants of the *inandione* group, as well as *bishydroxycoumarin* and *ethyl biscoumacetate,* are found in milk and have been associated with infant coagulopathies.[12] *Warfarin* must be considered the drug of choice; by virtue of its acidity and high degree of protein binding, it is undetectable in breast milk.[59]

ANTI-INFLAMMATORY AND ANALGESIC DRUGS

Acetylsalicylic acid appears to pose no danger when used occasionally. Older infants have been found to receive about 0.2% to 0.3% of a single dose of acetyl-salicylic acid administered to the mother.[19] Although detailed studies do not exist, *acetaminophen* also seems to be safe.[1]

ANTIMICROBIAL DRUGS

Fortunately, most antimicrobial agents in breast milk appear to be safe for nursing infants.[11] Selected antibiotics, particularly those with broad antimicrobial spectra, may change the infant's intestinal flora and cause diarrhea and thrush; theoretically, they could also incite hypersensitivity. The *cephalosporins* appear to be secreted in insignificant amounts in breast milk. The passage of the various *sulfonamide derivatives* is influenced by their differing degrees of ionization and protein binding; all have the potential to displace bilirubin from albumin. Nevertheless, the amounts present in breast milk combined with the actual bioavailable dose to the infant suggest that maternal sulfonamide administration is acceptable during breast feeding. The ingestion of *sulfasalazine* leads to the appearance of the metabolite sulfapyridine in breast milk; it has been estimated that the infant of a mother using this drug on a long-term basis will receive about 0.3% of the maternal dose per day. *Erythromycin,* clarithromycin, and azithromycin are present in milk in a higher concentration than that in maternal plasma. This accumulation of the macrolides and azilide in breast milk reflects the tremendous cellular tissue penetration characteristics of these drugs. Nevertheless, the actual amount an infant would receive per day from breast feeding would appear to be minimal, particularly when one considers the poor bioavailability characteristics of these agents. The *tetracyclines* in breast milk purportedly have the potential to cause dental staining, and many sources have suggested that women taking tetracyclines avoid breast feeding. Closer examination of these suggestions against breast feeding during tetracycline therapy appear to be based on theoretical grounds rather than any supporting evidence. Moreover, the bioavailability of tetracyclines under the conditions of breast feeding suggests that the maternal administration of tetracycline and its analogues is safe and without complications in infants.[11] Similarly, most authors recommend that *chloramphenicol* not be taken by lactating women, even though the drug levels in milk would not produce a dose anywhere near that associated with gray baby syndrome. The *aminoglycosides* are poorly absorbed from the infant's gastrointestinal tract. *Isoniazid* and *para-aminosalicylate* have not been associated with ill effects in nursing infants. *Metronidazole* therapy in the usual doses is not contraindicated for breast-feeding women.

The data outlined above and elsewhere[11] demonstrate the overall safety of most maternally administered antibiotics to the breastfed infant, and only in rare instances should mothers requiring antibiotic therapy be recommended to discontinue breast feeding their infant.

DRUGS AFFECTING THE CARDIOVASCULAR SYSTEM

The amount of *digoxin* present in milk depends on the maternal dose; infants whose mothers received 0.25 mg/day did not ingest enough digoxin in milk to have detectable blood levels.[46] Diuretics in general seem to be harmless, although if a nursing woman were to become dehydrated because of diuretic use, lactation would be greatly depressed. The effects of diuretics on milk composition are not clear. *Spironolactone* and its less active metabolite are secreted in breast milk, and an estimated 0.2% of the mother's daily dose is received by the infant.[64] *Chlorthalidone* and propranolol appear in small amounts in breast milk and seem safe. In contrast, the water-soluble, renally excreted β-adrenergic receptor antagonists atenolol and acebutolol should be avoided during periods of breast feeding because these agents have been shown to induce β-receptor blockade in breastfed infants.[3] *Quinidine* is secreted in breast milk at a concentration that is about 60% of that found in maternal blood, but no ill effects have been observed.[30]

DRUGS AFFECTING THE CENTRAL NERVOUS SYSTEM

Diazepam is converted in the body to the active metabolite *desmethyldiazepam,* and both are excreted in breast milk. Both of these compounds have prolonged half-lives in infants, and the long-term use of diazepam by nursing women has been associated with lethargy and weight loss in their babies. The concentration of *barbiturates* in breast milk depends on their different degrees of ionization and lipid solubility. In anticonvulsant doses they seem to be safe.[37,55] *Chlordiazepoxide* in breast milk has been linked to depression in nursing infants. *Meprobamate* should probably be avoided because the drug achieves breast milk concentrations several times greater than those in maternal plasma.

Lithium has been contraindicated during lactation because of a few case reports that described significant cardiovascular and central nervous system signs in two infants. It would appear from a closer evaluation of these cases that transplacental exposure cannot be ruled out and maternal drug interaction may have predisposed these infants to a level of lithium toxicity beyond what would have occurred from breast feeding alone. As a result, breast-feeding mothers who require lithium therapy should be permitted to continue to breastfeed, with close infant monitoring that could include the recording of blood lithium concentrations in the infant 1 to 2 weeks after initiating breast feeding.

Phenytoin is found in breast milk in concentrations of about one fifth those in maternal blood.[33] *Primidone* and *ethosuximide* both achieve breast milk levels near that of maternal blood, although significant symptoms in infants have not been noted.[33,37] *Phenobarbital* is metabolized much more slowly in neonates than adults; it is possible that the drug may accumulate in the breastfed infants of phenobarbital-treated mothers. These infants should be monitored for lethargy and poor weight gain.[1]

Antidepressants are commonly administered before conception and during postpartum. Of the older tricyclic antidepressants, most appear safe during lactation, with minimal to no infant effects. However, one of them, doxepin, should be avoided during breast feeding because maternal administration has been associated with infant sedation and unresponsiveness. Among the newer class of antidepressants, the selective serotonin reuptake inhibitors, which are the preferred agents in the treatment of most patients with depression, the greatest number of case reports describing effects in infants involves fluoxetine. This finding is not unexpected considering the pharmacologic activity and lipid solubility characteristics of fluoxetine and its primary active metabolite norfluoxetine and the slow body clearance of both compounds. Infant manifestations of fluoxetine exposure during breast feeding have usually involved gastrointestinal complaints, agitation, and lethargy, with resulting poor feeding.[3] These effects reverse on the maternal discontinuation of fluoxetine, but complete reversal may take up to 5 to 7 days due to the very slow neonatal elimination of accumulated norfluoxetine. For this reason, sertraline or paroxetine would appear to be preferable for use in breast-feeding mothers because both are cleared from the body at intermediate rates compared with fluoxetine and metabolites appear to have limited, if any, contribution to the drug's overall pharmacologic and side effect profiles.

DRUGS AFFECTING THE ENDOCRINE SYSTEM

Drugs of the *thiouracil* family, such as *methimazole, carbimazole,* and *iodides,* are contraindicated during breast feeding; they achieve a high breast milk concentration and can suppress the infant's thyroid function.[1] Revision of this dogma has been suggested, and *propylthiouracil* may be given to nursing mothers, provided that the infant's thyroid function is monitored.

Thyroxine and other thyroid hormone preparations seem to be safe; endogenous thyroid hormone, which is naturally secreted in breast milk, may mask congenital cretinism during breast feeding.[1] The long-term effects of exogenous *glucocorticoids* and their derivatives in breast milk are not known. Women receiving *prednisone* and *prednisolone* excrete very small amounts of these compounds in breast milk.

A common problem confronting health care providers is the maternal concern over the use of *oral contraceptives* during lactation. Little is known about the effects of long-term exposure to small doses of these compounds in breast milk. Contraceptives with a high concentration of estrogen and progestins depress lactation, especially if they are begun soon after parturition. If their use is imperative, it is best to start treatment about 4 weeks after delivery, ensuring that lactation is already well established, and to use the lowest dosage possible. The infants should be followed with care because there have been reports of gynecomastia and changes in the vaginal epithelium. A study of delayed effects in exposed infants is urgently needed. However, contemporary oral contraceptives contain low maternal hormone doses, and many are progestin-only products. The oral contraceptives in current clinical use are not contraindicated for mothers who are breast feeding and those that are progestin-only products should be considered the oral contraceptive preparations of choice during breast feeding.[3]

OTHER DRUGS

Cimetidine, a histamine H_2-receptor antagonist, has been reported in breast milk at concentrations 3 to 12 times greater than those in maternal blood; this drug may be actively transported into breast milk.[73] Because cimetidine and ranitidine are known to be safe and effective when used for therapy in infants, they are not contraindicated during lactation. Similarly, proton pump inhibitors (e.g., omeprazole, lansoprazole) are also used in neonates and infants and should be safe for maternal use during breast feeding because of the expected low infant exposure to these drugs.

Maternal *theophylline* ingestion has been associated with infant irritability. Extracts of *ergot* have been responsible for toxic reactions in nursing infants and should be avoided. The use of *isotopes* for diagnosis or therapy should be avoided during lactation. An acceptable level of an isotope in breast milk is not known. It has been suggested that women not nurse for 10 days after exposure to ^{131}I, 3 days after exposure to ^{99m}Tc, and 2 weeks after exposure to ^{67}Ga. If radiopharmaceuticals are required during lactation, breast feeding should be avoided while the radioactive agent is present in breast milk. In uncertain cases consultation should be obtained from a specialist in nuclear medicine.

Narcotics

Heroin, methadone, morphine, and other *opiate derivatives* have been found in breast milk and may be responsible for both addiction and withdrawal symptoms in the nursing infant if maternally consumed for prolonged periods. Most briefly used opiate analogues appear to have little clinical effect. However, those opiate derivatives with excellent oral bioavailability and slow body clearance (e.g., methadone) or active metabolites with slow body clearance (e.g., meperidine) should be avoided during breast feeding. The breast-feeding infants of mothers who receive these opiate analgesics may be more likely to manifest lethargy, poor feeding, and possibly apnea and cyanosis, underscoring the importance of administering other analogues as needed, such as morphine or fentanyl parenterally or hydrocodone or oxycodone orally. It has been suggested that women receiving methadone maintenance doses take a daily dose after the last breast feeding in the evening because the methadone levels in breast milk peak about 4 hours after the administration of the drug orally.

NONTHERAPEUTIC AGENTS IN BREAST MILK

Caffeine

One hour after the ingestion of an average cup of coffee, a peak breast milk caffeine level of about 1.5 mg/mL is obtained. Caffeine levels in breast milk are about half the corresponding maternal blood level. Although the daily amount of caffeine consumed by a nursing infant might be small, the long half-life of caffeine could cause symptoms such as wakefulness or jitteriness and might be considered in the evaluation of infants whose mothers consume large quantities of caffeine-containing products (e.g., cola, diet aids, coffee, and tea).

Ingredients of Cigarettes

The *nicotine* content of breast milk from women smoking one pack per day has been found to be about 100 to 500 parts per billion. No symptoms have been ascribed to this degree of contamination. *Thiocyanate*, which is elevated in the blood of smoking women, does not appear in elevated amounts in their breast milk.[49]

Ethanol

Ethanol, a small molecule, is freely diffused into breast milk and achieves levels equivalent to those in blood. The metabolite *acetaldehyde* does not appear in breast milk. Excessive maternal ethanol intake may depress the nursing infant's central nervous system.

ENVIRONMENTAL POLLUTANTS IN BREAST MILK
(See Chapter 12)

Lead

Lead has been found in both bovine and human milk as well as commercial infant formulas. The lead content of human milk has remained rather constant during the past 4 decades, in contrast to the levels of some other pollutants. One study found the lead level in human milk in the United States to be about 0.03 g/mL. There are no reports of signs and symptoms of lead toxicity from this source.

Mercury

Metallic or inorganic mercury poisoning in adults is usually associated with occupational exposure. There are no reports of metallic mercury poisoning from the consumption of breast milk. Organic mercury—more specifically, *methyl mercury*—has been used industrially in fungicides, pulp and paper factories, and chloralkali plants. In the late 1950s, Minamata Bay, Japan, was contaminated with industrial waste containing methyl mercury; the compound found its way into human beings through contaminated fish. There was a high incidence of neurologic abnormalities in children born in this area, probably related to in utero exposure to the chemical rather than exposure during lactation. Methyl mercury was found in breast milk at a concentration of about 5% of that in blood; the half-life for the disappearance of mercury from breast milk was estimated to be about 70 days.

Several epidemics in Iraq in the last 15 years were traceable to the contamination of grains with methyl mercury fungicides. A number of nursing infants ingested enough methyl mercury in breast milk to achieve blood levels above the toxic limit.

Pesticides

Organic pesticides are concentrated in body fat. Breast milk production, with its export of large quantities of lipid, is an efficient way for a woman to rid her body of these poisons.[80] The nursing human infant thus becomes the highest animal in the "food chain." *Dichlorodiphenyl trichloroethane* (DDT) was first identified in breast milk in 1951, and the levels have been falling slowly since its use was restricted in North America in the early 1970s. Current levels of DDT in breast milk vary geographically and are related to the agricultural use of the compound. In Canada in 1979, the average level of DDT in breast milk was 44 ng/g. A 5-kg infant ingesting 1 kg of breast milk each day would thus take in about 0.009 mg/kg per day. The recommendation of the Food and Agriculture Organization and World Health Organization for the maximum allowable intake by an adult is about 0.005 mg/kg per day. Nevertheless, there are no known harmful effects to the infant from the ingestion of breast milk contaminated to this degree.

Many other pesticides have been found in breast milk, reflecting their commercial use in a particular region or country. For instance, concentrations of *dieldrin,* which was banned in the United States after 1974, are decreasing in breast milk.

Industrial Byproducts

The extremely toxic dioxin *TCDD* (2,3,7,8-tetra-chlorodibenzo-*p*-dioxin) caused environmental contamination in Seveso, Italy, in 1976. Chloracne developed in children who were directly exposed; further effects remain to be determined. This toxin has been found in breast milk.

There has been great public interest in the *polychlorinated biphenyls* (PCBs).[24] This class of compound has had 50 years of industrial use, primarily in the manufacture of electric apparatuses (transformers, capacitors), although such use is declining. Because of the contamination of rivers and lakes by industrial effluents, PCBs have been widely distributed in freshwater fish and those animals that eat them. As with organic pesticides, PCBs remain in body fat stores and are excreted with the fat of breast milk. An epidemic of poisoning by PCBs (Yusho disease) occurred in 1968 in Japan when a commercial rice oil product was inadvertently contaminated with PCBs. The fetuses exposed in utero suffered growth retardation both antenatally and postnatally. Several infants whose only exposure was from breast milk had weakness and apathy. It is of great concern that the breast milk levels of PCBs in North America appear to be increasing. In Canada in 1979, the average PCB level in breast milk was 12 ng/g, whereas presently women who are exposed occupationally to PCBs or consume game fish from contaminated waters may have much higher levels in their breast milk.

The *polybrominated biphenyls (PBBs)* received attention as the result of an incident in Michigan in 1973 and 1974 in which several hundred pounds of PBBs, normally used as fire retardants in the plastics industry, accidentally contaminated cattle feed, resulting in the widespread intoxication of farm animals. PBBs have the usual propensity to lodge in fat tissue and persist in the body. To date no ill effects have been noted in infants exposed to PBBs through their mothers' milk. In Michigan, the surveillance of PBB in breast milk has provided an accurate picture of the contamination of the general population. This method of epidemiologic analysis of fat-soluble poisons is highly recommended because the collection of milk samples is far easier than that of adipose tissue specimens. The levels of PBB in breast milk in the contaminated areas of Michigan averaged 0.07 part per million.

CONCLUSIONS CONCERNING BREAST FEEDING AND MATERNAL DRUG THERAPY

As with the helpless fetus in utero, the nursing infant is exposed to nearly everything entering the body of its mother. The dangers, especially over the long term, are unclear. Environmental pollutants are almost impossible to avoid, and the elimination of nontherapeutic (recreational) compounds involves changing lifestyles. Drug administration is the easiest to control, but often a difficult choice must be made between maternal therapy and potential harm to the infant. The following simple guidelines should be observed.

1. A lactating woman should not receive a drug that one would be reluctant to give directly to her infant at that particular postnatal or gestational age.

2. Drug secretion into milk is so variable that one should not attempt to *treat* an infant by administering the drug to the lactating mother.

3. Milk that is donated to milk banks must be free from contamination.

4. When maternal drug administration is necessary one may attempt to minimize the dosage to the infant by withholding nursing at the time of maximum secretion of the drug into breast milk, although this maneuver is rarely necessary for the majority of maternally administered therapeutic agents.

5. Signs and symptoms in a nursing child should be correlated with maternal drug ingestion. In investigations it is very useful to measure the levels of the drug and its metabolites in the infant's body fluids rather than at isolated times in maternal blood or breast milk.

6. When therapy is necessary, it should be with single agents if possible. In the case of long-term therapy, consideration should be given to monitoring the infant's activity and growth.

PART 2

Pharmacologic Treatment of the Fetus

Michael D. Reed and Jeffrey L. Blumer

Advances in medical science and diagnostic technology have provided us with new and exciting information about the dynamic nature of life in utero (Box 10-1). We have gained insight and understanding into the structure and function of the placenta. At the same time, advances in neonatal care have led to increased survival rates for infants of low and very low birthweight. Nevertheless, the innovations in diagnostic technology are what have added most to our understanding of human development and simultaneously have created some of our greatest clinical and moral/ethical challenges.

BOX 10-1. Changes in Medical Science and Technology Leading to Fetal Therapeutics

Recognition of the structure and function of the placenta
Advances in neonatal care leading to increased survival rates
   of infants of low and very low birthweight
Amniocentesis
Fetoscopy
Fetal cell gene identification responsible for disease(s)
Chorionic villus sampling
Fetal blood sampling
Fetal surgery
Fetal echocardiography
Real-time fetal ultrasonography

BOX 10-2. Indications for Antenatal Ultrasonography

Determination of fetal viability when abortion or intrauterine fetal death is suspected

Dating pregnancy when there is a consistent discrepancy between clinical and historical data

Localization of placenta in patients with vaginal bleeding or when the fetus is in an unstable position

Evaluation of pregnancy when there is a consistent, clinically significant discrepancy between uterine size and dates at any time

Immediately before any amniocentesis

Evaluation of fetal growth

Determination of fetal number

Suspected fetal congenital malformations

Evaluation of fetal size in breech presentation

Evaluation of amniotic fluid quantity

Postdates pregnancy evaluation

Suspected hydatidiform mole and possible associated pelvic masses

As adjunct to special procedures, such as fetoscopy and intrauterine transfusion

Evaluation of pelvic mass

Assessment of fetal well-being by observation of fetal activity (e.g., the biophysical profile)

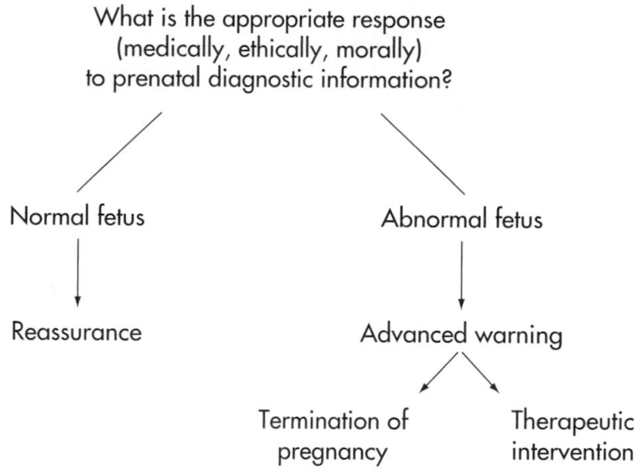

FIGURE 10-9. Dilemma confronted by parents and clinicians when presented with results of routine diagnostic evaluations of a fetus.

BOX 10-3. Approach to Management of Fetal Disorders

Selective abortion
  Anencephaly, hydranencephaly, and familial alobar holoprosencephaly
  Severe anomalies associated with chromosomal abnormalities (e.g., trisomy 13)
  Bilateral renal agenesis and infantile polycystic kidney disease
  Severe, untreatable, inherited metabolic disorders (e.g., Tay-Sachs disease)
  Lethal bone dysplasias (e.g., thanatophoric dysplasia, recessive osteogenesis imperfecta)
Diagnosis in utero; treatment after delivery at term
  Cardiac anomalies
  Esophageal, duodenal, jejunoileal, and anorectal atresias
  Meconium ileus (cystic fibrosis)
  Enteric cysts and duplications
  Small, intact omphalocele
  Small, intact meningocele; myelomeningocele; and spina bifida
  Unilateral multicystic, dysplastic kidney and hydronephrosis
  Craniofacial, extremity, and chest wall deformities
  Cystic hygroma and mesoblastic nephroma
  Small sacrococcygeal teratoma
  Benign cysts (e.g., ovarian, mesenteric, choledochal)
May require premature delivery
May require operative delivery
  Conjoined twins
  Giant omphalocele and ruptured omphalocele/gastroschisis
  Large sacrococcygeal teratoma or cystic hygroma
  Malformations requiring preterm delivery in the presence of inadequate labor or fetal distress
May require treatment in utero

Our ability to assess fetal vitality and genetic, biochemical, and physical "normality" has been greatly enhanced through the development of amniocentesis, fetoscopy, chorionic villus sampling, fetal blood sampling (cordocentesis), and real-time ultrasonography. Because ultrasonography is noninvasive, safe, and relatively less expensive than some of the other procedures and can be used serially, it is becoming a routine screening procedure (Box 10-2). Of course, one problem with the widespread use of ultrasonography is that we find things. Most of the observations made are serendipitous; however, they may reflect grave or dire consequences for the outcome of the pregnancy (see Chapter 8).

Many clinicians believe that the use of ultrasound is both good and appropriate (Fig. 10-9). If the test reveals a normal fetus, both the parents and the physician are reassured. On the other hand, if it reveals fetal abnormalities, especially those that may be identified during the first trimester of pregnancy, decisions can be made regarding further (perhaps more invasive) evaluation, special medical needs required during delivery, special-care needs required after birth, or, in extreme cases, whether to continue the pregnancy. However, these diagnostic advances have always been coupled with the idea that, as in other areas of medicine, the ability to make a diagnosis should be followed by the development of appropriate therapeutic interventions. This belief has led to an ever-expanding set of treatment options for recognized fetal disorders (Box 10-3). Moreover, the dramatic increase in our knowledge and capability to define fetal abnormalities early in the pregnancy with genetic testing[90] of amniotic

fluid will continue to evolve and permit rational family-physician decision making (see Chapter 7).

From an intriguing concept several decades ago, fetal therapy has become a reality. There are now basically three approaches to treating fetal disease, the most common one being the use of drug therapy directed toward the recognized fetal disorder. In addition, several centers have begun to perform surgical procedures on fetuses with recognized malformations (see Chapter 11). The third and most exciting of these approaches is fetal gene therapy for the correction of genetic defects ascertainable in utero.[90]

This part of the chapter focuses primarily on the use of drug therapy to ameliorate or cure fetal disorders. It initially deals with the pharmacology of the maternal-fetal-placental unit, and then some of the more common fetal therapeutic interventions are discussed in more detail.

PHARMACOLOGY OF THE MATERNAL-FETAL-PLACENTAL UNIT

Three aspects of pharmacotherapy must be considered when one is treating patients (Fig. 10-10). In general, *pharmacokinetics* includes the processes of drug absorption, distribution, metabolism, and excretion, whereas *pharmacodynamics* refers to the mechanisms of drug action and drug safety. The *pharmaceutic* aspects of drug therapy pertain to the actual formulation of the drug (e.g., tablet, liquid, suspension, capsule), including its inert ingredients. In therapeutics, if, for a given disorder and a given patient, a drug can be identified

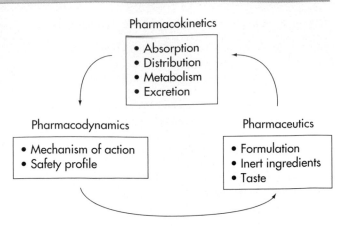

FIGURE 10-10. Determinants of effective drug therapy. Clinicians must account for all pharmacokinetic and pharmacodynamic characteristics of a drug when designing an optimum dose regimen.

that has favorable characteristics in each of these three areas, therapy will be effective.

The identification of such a drug is usually a fairly complex problem that takes into account not only all the individual differences in physiology and biochemistry that determine individual differences in drug disposition but also any impact that the pathophysiologic state imposes on these processes. In addition, differences

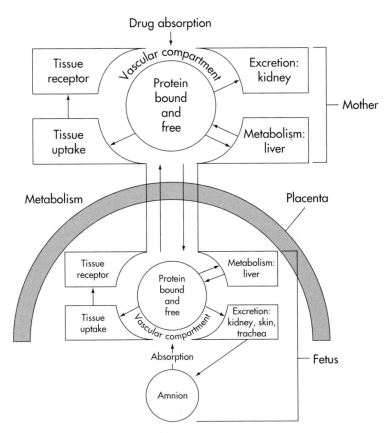

FIGURE 10-11. Drug disposition in the maternal-placental-fetal unit.

in disease severity and expression must be considered along with any changes in the disease process during therapy. This complex set of issues must be assessed each time a patient is treated.

In fetal therapy the situation is even more complex. Although direct fetal therapy by intra-amniotic drug administration is used, in most instances the drug is administered to one individual (the mother) with the intent of producing a therapeutic effect in another (the fetus). Moreover, instead of dealing with the pharmacokinetic and pharmacodynamic processes in a single individual, one must consider three pharmacokinetically and pharmacodynamically distinct but intimately interconnected compartments—the mother, the fetus, and the placenta (Fig. 10-11).[90]

Maternal Drug Disposition during Pregnancy

Pregnancy is a period of change in female physiology.[129] A number of important changes directly influence drug disposition in both the maternal and fetal environments (Table 10-3).

DRUG ABSORPTION

Among the changes seen during pregnancy that potentially affect drug disposition, the decrease in intestinal motility is prominent. This decrease in turn may reduce the rate of absorption of orally administered medications. As a result, the observed peak maternal serum drug concentration is blunted or delayed or both. For the majority of clinical situations, these effects are of little clinical consequence in the treatment of maternal disorders and would appear to be of no clinical significance relative to fetal distribution. Alterations in the absolute peak serum drug concentration and time to peak do not influence the resulting fetal drug exposure because it is the steady-state maternal drug concentration that appears to be the more important determinant of the extent of drug diffusion from the maternal to the fetal compartment, not the absolute peak serum drug concentration. For the increasing number of drugs that

TABLE 10-3. Characteristics of the Primary Cytochrome P-450 Enzymes Involved in Human Drug Metabolism

ENZYME	% OF TOTAL CYTOCHROME P-450 IN ADULT LIVER	POLYMORPHIC EXPRESSION	SELECTED SUBSTRATES	INHIBITORS	INDUCERS
CYP1A2	15-20	No	Caffeine, theophylline, R-warfarin	Ciprofloxacin, cimetidine, erythromycin, amiodarone, fluvoxamine	Broccoli, Brussels sprouts, omeprazole, tobacco smoke
CYP2C8/9	20-30 (includes CYP2C19)	1%-3% Caucasian PMs	Ibuprofen, phenytoin, S-warfarin	Sulphaphenazole, fluconazole, amiodarone, paroxetine, sertraline, trimethoprim	Rifampin
CYP2C19		3%-5% Caucasian PMs; 15%-20% Asian PMs	S-mephenytoin, omeprazole, diazepam, imipramine, phenobarbitol, indomethacin, lansoprazole		Carbamazepine, prednisone, rifampin
CYP2D6	1-5	5%-10% Caucasian PMs; 1%-3% Asian PMs	Debrisoquine, dextromethorphan, codeine, amitriptyline, imipramine, fluoxetine, propranolol, tramadol	Quinidine, haloperidol, fluoxetine, amiodarone, cimetidine	Dexamethasone, rifampin
CYP3A4/5	30-40	No	Testosterone, ethinyl-estradiol, cyclosporine, clarithromycin, carbamazepine, erythromycin, indinavir, saquinavir, ritonavir, lovastatin, midazolam, quinidine, terfenadine, nifedipine, diltiazem, verapamil	Ketoconazole, itraconazole, erythromycin, cimetidine, verapamil, diltiazem, grapefruit juice, fluconazole, amiodarone, indinavir, ritonavir, clarithromycin, voriconazole	Barbiturates, carbamazepine, glucocorticoids, phenytoin, rifampin, rifabutin

PMs, poor metabolizer.

are metabolized within the gastrointestinal tract (e.g., cyclosporine, carbamazepine, tacrolimus), this increased time within the gastrointestinal tract may lead to decreased maternal bioavailability.

Aerosolized (inhaled) medications may achieve greater absorption into the maternal systemic circulation after pulmonary exposure because of pregnancy-associated increases in minute ventilation. Similarly, maternal exposure to environmental toxins and pollutants also increases during pregnancy. On average, maternal tidal volume increases approximately 39%, with an accompanying average increase in minute ventilation of approximately 42% during pregnancy.[117] The primary determinant of drug exposure after aerosolized drug administration is minute ventilation, not the absolute dose of the medication per exposure. This fact is of the greatest significance for medications that are characterized by excellent bioavailability after inhalation (e.g., adrenergic receptor agonists [epinephrine, albuterol], dexamethasone). It is unknown whether the enhanced pulmonary exposure during pregnancy poses any real threat to the mother or the fetus. Some investigators have attempted to extrapolate the differences in exposure rates between men and women for certain environmental diseases (e.g., silicosis) based on enhanced exposure during pregnancy.[117] However, because this aspect of possibly enhanced drug exposure has not been specifically studied, its impact on fetal drug exposure remains unknown. Nevertheless, it seems prudent to closely monitor the therapeutic response and systemic effects of aerosolized medications, as well as the amount and types of environmental exposures encountered by pregnant patients.

With respect to percutaneous drug exposure or administration, the differences that occur in peripheral regional bloodflow during pregnancy are of particular interest.[117] During pregnancy the bloodflow increases about sixfold in the human hand and about twofold in the human foot, with only small increases observed in the human forearm and leg. These increases in perfusion take on added importance with the increasing number of medications administered topically as either patch formulations or ointments and creams. Although the primary determinant of dermal drug absorption is lipid solubility (stratum corneum and stratum lucidum) and water solubility (stratum granulosum, stratum spinosum, stratum basale, and the basement membrane), exposed surface area and bloodflow to the skin are also important components. Although the increases in dermal bloodflow are well documented, their impact on drug absorption has not been determined. Moreover, the specific regions that have been reported to receive greater bloodflow do not represent the more common sites for the application of patch formulations (e.g., chest, back). Thus, the possibility of enhanced systemic exposure from topically administered medications during pregnancy may be of limited clinical significance, with the exception of the direct application of medications to the hand or foot.

The overall effects of changes in intestinal motility, minute ventilation, and regional bloodflow during pregnancy remain largely unknown. It is the steady-state concentration of the drug in the maternal circulation that ultimately determines the amount of the drug available for distribution to the fetal compartment. Because steady-state concentration is more a product of drug clearance than drug absorption, these changes in maternal physiology would be predicted to have little impact on fetal drug exposure. Nevertheless, data are lacking and studies needed.

DRUG DISTRIBUTION

During pregnancy, several physiologic changes occur that may influence drug distribution (Tables 10-4 to 10-6). Maternal total body water, extracellular fluid, and plasma volumes all increase during gestation by about 32%, 36%, and 52%, respectively. These substantial changes in the sizes of various body fluid compartments occur gradually throughout pregnancy (see Table 10-5). The increase in body water is the primary reason for the observed decreases in peak drug concentrations with standard dosing. When the drug dose is kept constant in the presence of increasing body water, the drug's apparent volume of distribution increases and steady-state drug concentrations decrease. Such a decrease in steady-state concentrations markedly influences the amount of the drug available for diffusion across the placenta.

Maternal cardiac output also increases by about 40% to 50% by the middle of the second trimester, remaining

TABLE 10-4. Influence of Pregnancy on the Physiologic Aspects of Drug Disposition

PHARMACOKINETIC PARAMETER BY SYSTEM	CHANGE
Absorption	
Gastric emptying	Increased
Intestinal motility	Decreased
Pulmonary function	Increased
Cardiac output	Increased
Bloodflow to the skin	Increased
Distribution	
Plasma volume	Increased
Total body water	Increased
Plasma proteins	Decreased
Body fat	Increased
Metabolism	
Hepatic metabolism	±
Extrahepatic metabolism	±
Excretion	
Uterine bloodflow	Increased
Renal bloodflow	Increased
Glomerular filtration rate	Increased
Pulmonary function	Increased

Modified from Mattison DR et al: Physiologic adaptations to pregnancy: Impact on pharmacokinetics. In Yaffe SJ et al (eds): Pediatric Pharmacology: Therapeutic Principles in Practice. Philadelphia, WB Saunders, 1992, p 81.

TABLE 10-5. Changes in Maternal Body Composition That Can Influence the Characteristics of Maternal Drug Distribution

TIME OF GESTATION (WK)	BODY WEIGHT (KG)	BODY FAT	PLASMA VOLUME (L)	EXTRACELLULAR FLUID VOLUME (L)
0	50.0	16.5	2.50	11
10	50.6	16.8	2.75	12
20	54.0	18.6	3.00	13
30	58.5	20.0	3.60	14
40	62.5	19.8	3.75	15

Modified from Mattison DR et al: Physiologic adaptations to pregnancy: Impact on pharmacokinetics. In Yaffe SJ et al (eds): Pediatric Pharmacology: Therapeutic Principles in Practice. Philadelphia, WB Saunders, 1992, p 81.

TABLE 10-6. Human Maternal and Fetal Serum Protein Concentrations during Pregnancy

TIME OF GESTATION (WK)	SERUM ALBUMIN CONCENTRATION (MG/DL)		SERUM α_1 ACID GLYCOPROTEIN CONCENTRATION (MG/DL)	
	Maternal	Fetal	Maternal	Fetal
12-15	2.8	1.1	57	5
16-25	3.4	1.9	73	8
26-35	2.8	2.6	58	16
36-41	2.9	3.4	60	21

Modified from Hill MD et al: The significance of plasma protein binding on the fetal/maternal distribution of drugs at steady-state. Clin Pharmacokinet 14:156, 1988.

elevated until delivery.[117] This increase is the result of increases in both the heart rate (10 to 15 beats per minute) and stroke volume. Therefore, more of the drug will be presented for hepatic metabolism and renal elimination per unit of time. The increase may also result in a decrease in the duration of time that the drug resides in the villous space (see later) and is available for transfer to the fetal compartment. Furthermore, the volume of blood within the placenta increases with gestation from ≈60 mL at 10 weeks to 950 mL at term.[129]

Coincident with the changes in body water distribution and cardiac output, the amount of maternal fat increases at a relatively constant proportion to the increase in body weight (see Table 10-4). In addition, concentrations of circulating serum proteins fluctuate during gestation (see Table 10-6), resulting in changes in the free fraction of various highly protein-bound drugs.[105] Unfortunately, the overall impact of changes in body composition and the resulting changes in drug distribution on fetal drug exposure is largely unknown. The resulting interactions are complex, making predictions regarding their impact on fetal drug exposure speculative at best.

DRUG METABOLISM AND EXCRETION

There are few data to suggest any true change in the maternal rate of hepatic drug metabolism. In contrast, the renal plasma flow increases by about 30% and the glomerular filtration rate by about 50%. As a result, serum creatinine, urea, and uric acid concentrations are lower during pregnancy. These changes in renal function may also be expected to enhance the elimination of drugs primarily dependent on the kidneys for elimination from the body.

The Placenta (See Chapter 23)

After fertilization, the rapidly dividing conceptus travels down the fallopian tube toward the uterus. By the third day the mulberry-appearing conceptus divides into approximately 16 cells and enters the uterus. This stage of embryonic development, called the *morula*, consists of an inner cell mass and a surrounding layer, the outer cell mass. The inner cell mass forms the *embryo*, whereas the outer cell mass forms the *trophoblast*, which helps to form the placenta. Once in the uterus, maternal fluids penetrate the zona pellucida and accumulate within the inner cell mass between the cells. This developmental stage represents the first exposure of the conceptus to maternal fluids. Gradually, a cavity (the *blastocele*) forms, displacing the inner cell mass to one pole of the embryo. These changes signal the blastocytic stage of embryonic development. The zona pellucida disappears, allowing implantation to take place. Around the sixth day after fertilization, the trophoblastic cells lining the inner cell mass begin to penetrate the uterine mucosa, attaching the conceptus to the myometrial epithelium. Proteolytic enzymes from the uterine mucosa and the trophoblast probably work in concert to allow the implantation of the zygote. Thus, by the end of the first week after fertilization, the human zygote has passed through the morula and blastocytic stages of development and begun implantation in the uterine mucosa. Up to this point, no interface for maternal-fetal exchange has been established.[95,124]

By the second week of development, lacunae formed within the trophoblastic cell mass have fused to form interconnected lacunar networks. These lacunae function as early intervillous spaces in the placenta. Maternal blood seeps into and flows slowly throughout the lacunar system, establishing the uteroplacental circulation. Around the end of the second week, primary chorionic villi form and begin to differentiate in the placenta. Early in the third week, the mesenchyme grows into the primary chorionic villi, forming a placard of loose connective tissue. Mesenchymal cells in the villi differentiate into capillaries and form arteriovenous networks. Blood vessels from within these maturing villi become connected with the embryonic heart, later establishing the umbilical cord. By the end of the third week, embryonic blood begins to circulate through the capillaries of the chorionic villi, and by the end of the fourth week the essential elements necessary for physiologic exchange between the mother and the embryo are well established.[95,124]

From the fourth week of gestation until term, the surface area of the placenta increases dramatically to accommodate the increasing needs of the maturing fetus. In contrast, the thickness of the placental membrane decreases with advancing gestation. During late gestation, at about 32 weeks, the fetal capillaries become oriented beneath the thin layers of syncytial trophoblast. In these areas the tissue barrier separating the maternal and fetal circulations may be less than $2 \mu m$. This characteristic of the placenta, decreasing membrane thickness with advancing gestation, favors the greater transfer of drugs during late gestation (from approximately 50 to 100 μm to 2 to 5 μm at term). These areas become specialized in the transport functions of the placenta (i.e., rapid diffusion of substances) rather than the metabolic ones. By term, the placenta has only a single cell layer of fetal chorionic tissue separating the fetal capillary endothelium from the maternal blood. This separation, with its loose intercellular connections, presents little hindrance to small-molecule transfer.[95,124]

IMPORTANT DIFFERENCES BETWEEN HUMAN AND ANIMAL PLACENTAS

As described earlier, the human placenta is a network of specialized cells and tissues whose functional capacity evolves during gestation.[95,124] These dynamic processes (which most likely vary with the time during gestation), combined with the ontogeny of placental drug transporters (e.g., P_{gp}), influence the ability of drugs and other compounds to cross from the maternal to the fetal compartment. Unfortunately, the many medical, ethical, and social barriers that limit our ability to study human placental development necessitate our reliance on the studies of placental mechanics performed in various animal species to model the human system.

Although much has been learned about placental maturation and function from such studies, these data must be extrapolated to the human placenta with extreme caution. It is of the utmost importance to recognize that the cellular arrangement of the human placenta differs markedly from that of many other mammals. The differences in placental structure between human beings and other mammals influence the rate at which a compound crosses in either direction and the extent to which it does so. Thus, the placental transfer for a particular drug or substrate defined in the rat or sheep may bear very little relation to human placental function and substrate disposition.[95,124]

Studies that have compared the placental transport function and capacity for specific substrates between human beings and various animal species have revealed substantial differences.[118,124] For this reason, one should rely solely on data derived in human systems to develop possible fetal treatment strategies. Some of these differences are most likely due to the anatomic differences between the placentas of human beings and various animal species. Some of the more important differences in placental structure in species commonly studied as potential models for human development are now discussed briefly. The reader who has an in-depth interest in the embryology and structure of the placentas of various animal species is referred to more detailed discussions of this topic.[95,124]

The placenta in most mammals is classified as *chorioallantoic*. It includes a chorion vascularized by blood vessels derived from the allantois. Once vascularized, the chorion forms the placenta. In human beings, other primates, pigs, and ruminants, a chorioallantoic placenta persists throughout gestation. In contrast, many rodents and lagomorphs have two types of placenta that persist throughout gestation: the chorioallantoic placenta and the inverted yolk sac placenta. In these placentas, active transport mechanisms develop rapidly. In the human placenta the transfer of most compounds, including drugs, appears to involve simple diffusion.[124] Thus, the drug transfer mechanics described in some animal placentas may bear no real relation to the drug transfer dynamics in human placentas.

The human placenta consists of three layers of fetal tissue: the trophoblastic epithelium covering the villi, the chorionic connective tissue, and the capillary endothelium. The surface area of the villi, which represents the real area for exchange, varies according to the time of gestation. At 28 weeks the villous surface area is about 3.4 m^2, compared with about 12.6 m^2 at term.[118] Furthermore, the thickness of the placental membrane decreases with gestation, being the thinnest (about 2 cm thick) in late gestation. These changes in placental surface area and thickness during gestation enhance the ability of most drugs to diffuse across the placenta.

DRUG TRANSFER ACROSS THE PLACENTA
(See Part 1)

Despite numerous studies and exhaustive reviews[95,100,118,124,129] that focus on the processes and extent of drug transfer across the placenta, very little specific information defines the mechanisms of this transfer. This circumstance is a direct result of the difficulties inherent in studying the target population and our reliance on data obtained from the models of nonhuman systems. It is difficult to obtain not only general information relative to drug disposition at the human maternal-placental-fetal interface (i.e., to what extent an administered dose of a drug crosses the placenta) but also specific information concerning the processes involved in the drug disposition of the placenta. For example, very little is known about the rate at which the placenta metabolizes drugs or the extent to which it does so.[103]

A number of interdependent variables influence the rate and extent of drug transfer across the placenta from the maternal to the fetal compartment. Most investigators and clinicians believe that any compound found in the maternal circulation will cross the placenta and enter the fetal compartment.[100] Therefore, the fundamental questions are the rate and extent of this activity. Unfortunately, even today this information is only partially available for just a few chemical entities. Similarly, the mechanisms by which drugs are transferred across the placenta are known only for a few selected compounds. An understanding of these transport mechanisms is important for the design of fetal drug therapy.

The physical variables that will influence drug transfer across the placenta include the surface area of the exchange membrane, the thickness of the endotheliosyncytial membrane, the integrity of the maternal bloodflow and resulting hydrostatic pressure in the intervillous chambers, the blood pressure in fetal capillaries, the ontogeny of placental drug transporters, and any differences between the maternal/fetal osmotic pressures and pH. Maternal osmotic pressure is higher than that in the fetal compartment, whereas a pH difference of 0.1 to 0.15 unit exists between the fetal and maternal blood (i.e., fetal umbilical blood is −0.1 unit of pH lower than maternal blood).[95,118] Furthermore, the decreasing thickness of the placenta as term approaches facilitates further maternal-placental exchange during the later stages of gestation.

The possible modes of drug transfer across the placenta are listed in order of importance in Box 10-4. For the majority of drugs and other compounds, it is presumed that the primary mode of transfer is by simple, passive, nonionic diffusion. Simple diffusion does not require energy and is described by the Fick equation as

$$\text{Rate of diffusion} = K \cdot A\,(C_m - C_f)/d$$

where K is the diffusion constant of the drug, which is dependent on the drug's physiochemical characteristics; A is the surface area of the membrane to be traversed; C_m and C_f are the concentrations of the drug in maternal and fetal blood, respectively; and d is the thickness of the membrane to be traversed. Thus, $C_m - C_f$ represents the concentration gradient across the placenta, which is primarily regulated by the surface area (A) and thickness (d) of the placenta. In addition to these changes in the surface area and membrane thickness, one additional variable increases with increasing gestation and appears to be an important factor in placental drug transfer—uterine bloodflow, which is a factor not considered in the Fick equation. At term, uterine bloodflow is estimated to approach 150 mL/min per kilogram of newborn body weight. Depending on the physicochemical characteristics of the drug in this environment, bloodflow has an important influence on the rate and amount of drug transfer.

Important physicochemical characteristics that influence drug transfer across membranes, including the placenta, are outlined in Box 10-5. The characteristics that facilitate placental transfer include high lipid solubility, the un-ionized form under physiologic and pathophysiologic conditions, low molecular weight (<500 D), and low protein binding. Very few clinically important drugs meet all these "ideal" characteristics, which explains the high degree of variability reported in various studies of placental transfer. It appears that a classification system (based on these important physicochemical characteristics) for compounds and their ability to cross the placenta could be developed and used to guide fetal drug therapy. Unfortunately, this classificatory scheme is not possible because of the tremendous interdependence of each of these physicochemical properties in determining the characteristics of the actual transfer across the placenta.

Further confusion regarding the extent to which a particular drug or compound may traverse the placenta is propagated by uncontrolled studies that compare a

---

BOX 10-4. Mechanisms of Drug Transfer across the Human Placenta*

Simple diffusion
Facilitated transport
Active transport
Pinocytosis (phagocytosis)

*Listed in order of importance.

BOX 10-5. Physicochemical Factors That Influence the Transfer of Compounds across the Human Placenta

- Degree of lipid solubility
   Lipid soluble favored over water soluble
- Molecular weight (MW)
   MW < 100 readily crosses the placenta
   MW 600-1000 variable placental transfer
   MW > 1000 impermeable
- Bloodflow
   Drug (oxytocics) can decrease or alter rate and extent of transfer
- pH
   Un-ionized form under physiologic or pathologic conditions favors transfer
- Protein binding
   Low protein binding favors transfer across the placenta

single maternal blood concentration to an almost simultaneous concentration obtained from cord blood. Many published experiences have attempted to quantitate drug transfer as a ratio of fetal to maternal drug concentration by using these determinations at a single point in time. Such an approach to the estimation of placental drug transfer is analogous to the severely flawed milk:plasma ratio, which is used to estimate drug distribution into breast milk (see Part 1). Unfortunately, the usefulness of such assessments is often limited and must be interpreted with extreme caution. This ratio is highly dependent on a number of very important variables, including the number of maternal doses administered (i.e., first-dose compared with steady-state administration) and the time after the dose that the sample is obtained. The amniotic sac may be understood as an additional separate anatomic compartment into which a drug must be distributed. It is extremely unlikely that instantaneous distribution occurs for most of the drugs used clinically. Thus, a lag time exists for drug distribution into the amniotic sac and to the fetus, markedly shifting the concentration-time curve for the fetus to the right relative to the mother. Thus, the peak plasma concentration in the maternal circulation may occur at the trough in the fetus and conversely. It would appear that the determined absolute concentration and the interval relative to drug administration are much more important than a ratio of limited physiologic significance.

METABOLIC CAPABILITY OF THE HUMAN PLACENTA

The placenta performs many important functions that ensure homeostasis in the fetal environment. The placenta regulates the delivery of oxygen, nutrients, hormones, and other substrates from the maternal circulation to the fetus while removing metabolic end products from the fetal compartment. In addition, the human placenta is capable of synthesizing, metabolizing, and transferring a wide range of endogenous and exogenous substances. The degree to which the placenta metabolizes a drug, if at all, definitely influences the amount that is estimated to cross the placenta and the amount of active drug that reaches the fetus. Similarly, a number of efflux and influx transporters are functional within the placenta, with their functional capacity fluctuating during gestation.[127]

Many cytochrome P-450 mixed-function oxidase enzymes have been isolated from the human placenta.[103,127] Most of these enzymes appear to be located in the smooth endoplasmic reticulum and mitochondria of trophoblasts. Although each enzyme possesses its own substrate specificity, substantial overlap exists in the metabolizing capacity of these enzymes. It is clear that a number of these enzymes are also susceptible to modulation (i.e., induction or inhibition) by exogenous influences. Furthermore, P_{gp} is expressed on the maternal side of the placental-trophoblastic layer, where it mediates active efflux from the fetal compartment. This efflux is unidirectional from the fetal to maternal circulation and is probably responsible for the removal of highly lipid-soluble compounds (e.g., drugs) from the fetal compartment.[127]

Human placental microsomal enzymes are capable of bio-transforming a wide variety of chemical species. Although the number of different substrates biotransformed by enzymes located in the human placenta is large, the actual content of cytochrome P-450 enzymes in placental tissue is low. Attempts to quantitate the functional drug-metabolizing enzyme capacity of the human placenta have led to disparate results, but the activity appears to be much lower than that determined in the fetal or adult liver.[103,124] Thus, the actual contribution of placental enzyme activity to the bio-transformation of administered drugs is believed to be inconsequential and of limited clinical significance for most drugs administered either maternally or into the fetal compartment.[103,124] Nevertheless, the differential placental metabolism of certain corticosteroids (e.g., prednisolone, in contrast to betamethasone) and the resulting poor clinical outcomes reported with prednisolone in enhancing fetal lung maturation[132] suggest a potential effect of placental metabolism in certain fetal therapeutic endeavors (see Augmentation of Fetal Lung Maturation later in this part). In contrast, placental metabolism may be of greater importance relative to toxicology outcome than to the metabolism of therapeutically administered drugs. In addition to mixed-function oxidase activity, the human placenta possesses some capacity to catalyze phase II reactions. The conjugation of substances to enhance water solubility and promote excretion is a primary mechanism of in vivo drug bio-transformation.

Drug Disposition of the Fetus

In contrast to our knowledge of drug disposition in the pregnant woman and the placenta, our understanding of drug disposition in the fetus is inadequate. Contrary to the popular belief that the fetus resides in a privileged and protected environment, it is clear that it is exposed to virtually every chemical entity to which the mother is exposed. Thus, the absorption of a drug into the fetal circulation is both rapid and complete. Although most of this absorption was previously believed to occur through passive nonionic diffusion down the concentration gradients between maternal and fetal blood (which oppose each other in the placental villi), where they are separated by only a single layer of cells, a number of energy-dependent placental transporters have been characterized and are responsible for drug influx and efflux.[127] In addition, the fetus may undergo continued drug exposure after its elimination because of the recirculation of amniotic fluid through the fetal gastrointestinal tract.

Once a drug is within the fetal circulation, we have little knowledge of its fate or potential activity. It will certainly be distributed to the fetal organs in a manner similar to that observed after birth. However, it is not known whether there are any unusual fetal barriers to drug distribution analogous to those of the blood-brain barrier or the anterior chamber of the eye. In fact, it is not even known whether these barriers actually exist during fetal life.

Once a drug has reached various organs, it is not known whether it has any effect at all. It is clear that both receptor number and receptor affinity change during development. Likewise, receptor-effector coupling undergoes a programmed maturation. Thus, even though a drug may interact with specific receptors, there may be no discernible pharmacologic effect because the effector mechanisms have not yet developed.

There is no question that the mean residence time for drugs in the fetus is longer than that observed in older children and adults because of the immaturity of drug clearance mechanisms. This effect is especially true for drugs that are cleared entirely by renal excretion. The ontogeny of glomerular filtration and tubular secretion has been well studied. In contrast, for those drugs undergoing significant metabolism, there are many unknown factors. Although most hepatic metabolic pathways are less active in the fetus than the adult, this is not universally true. Moreover, in the fetus the adrenal gland has a significant complement of drug-metabolizing enzymes that, though active during fetal and neonatal life, disappear by 6 months of postnatal age.[103] Thus, the true ability of the fetus to metabolize drugs is largely unknown, but it at least partially depends on the particular drug under consideration, the gestational age of the fetus, and its drug metabolism phenotype.

As noted earlier, multiple enzyme systems are involved in xenobiotic metabolism within the body.[103] Of the phase I or oxidative enzymes, cytochrome P-450 predominates. These CYP enzymes constitute a superfamily of heme-containing monooxygenases, with a minimum of 14 *CYP* gene families appearing to exist in mammals. The *CYP1, CYP2,* and *CYP3* families are the most important in human drug metabolism, with the largest number of therapeutic agents undergoing CYP metabolism by the 3A family. Although the fetuses of many species appear to possess a very poor capacity to metabolize xenobiotics, the liver of the human fetus is relatively well developed in its capacity to metabolize various compounds, and it appears to mirror those processes performed by the placenta.[83] Nevertheless, the overall functional capacity of fetal CYP activity is very low. Furthermore, the metabolic capacity of the human fetal liver is qualitatively and quantitatively very different from the activity observed in the adult liver. The human fetal liver contains many different CYP forms (Table 10-7), although they are present in fewer numbers and less density than the adult liver. The total amount of CYP-450 in the fetal liver approximates 0.2 to 0.4 nmol/mg of microsomal protein, which represents approximately 20% to 70% of that found in the adult liver. Thus, the metabolic capacity of CYP-mediated reactions is less in the fetus than the adult.[83]

The CYPs are found in many tissues in the extrauterine organism, including the liver, adrenal gland, lung, brain, kidney, and intestine (see Table 10-7). Of these CYP forms, minimum CYP3A7 is expressed in the adult liver. Preliminary data suggest that the fetal brain may express CYP2D6 and 2E1 and that several other

TABLE 10-7. Expression of Cytochrome P-450 Forms in the Fetal Liver and the Adrenal Gland

ORGAN/GLAND*	CYP FORM
Liver†	1A, 2D6, 3A, 3A5, 3A7†
Adrenal†	1A1, 2A5, 3A,† 3A7, B1, 17
Questionable expression	2C, E1

*Primary form/isoform expressed at specific site.
†Primary site for CYP expression in the human fetus (fetal adrenal > liver containing CYP protein).

embryonic and fetal tissues may be minimally involved in xenobiotic metabolism. Although our understanding of the expression of CYP forms by the fetus is growing exponentially, the extent of our understanding of their function unfortunately remains limited. Nevertheless, the available data clearly indicate that the overall functional capacity of the fetus to effectively metabolize xenobiotics is limited.[83]

Conclusions Concerning Clinical Pharmacokinetics and the Maternal-Placental-Fetal Unit

Most of the pharmacologic agents present in the maternal circulation cross the placenta and enter the fetal circulation.[103,124,129] The myth that the placenta is a "barrier" that maintains a secure, safe environment protected from the maternal environment has long since been discounted. Thus, what is present in the maternal circulation should be considered present in the fetal circulation. The factors regulating drug transfer across the placenta (see Box 10-5) are the same as those that regulate its transfer across the biologic membranes in other parts of the body. Thus, the primary determinants of drug transfer across the placenta into the fetal compartment are the maternal steady-state drug concentration, functional capacity and specificity of transporters,[127] and integrity of the maternal and fetal circulations.

The gross physiologic changes that occur during pregnancy (see Tables 10-4 to 10-6) influence both the ultimate steady-state drug concentration achieved and the time required to achieve it. The changes that occur in maternal fluid compartment volumes, renal function (see Tables 10-4 and 10-5), and protein binding (see Table 10-6) directly influence the maternal body stores of a drug and the amount of that drug in the maternal circulation. These factors then determine the concentration gradient achieved at the maternal-placental-fetal interface and therefore the amount of the drug available for fetal transfer.

For the majority of un-ionized, lipophilic compounds, the rate-controlling process in placental transfer is placental bloodflow. Alterations in the hemodynamics of either the maternal or fetal circulation can markedly affect the placental transfer of most compounds. It seems obvious that alterations in total placental bloodflow modulate the rate and extent of drug transfer from the mother to the fetus and conversely from the fetus to the mother. Numerous physiologic and therapeutic interventions can alter the hemodynamics of both circulations. For example, uterine contractions associated with labor, preeclampsia, hypertension, the removal of amniotic fluid, and the administration of oxytocic drugs decrease placental bloodflow.

Once a drug crosses the placenta it enters the umbilical vein, flowing to the fetal liver by way of the portal circulation. Portions of this bloodflow enter the fetal liver, the remainder appearing to bypass this route and flowing through the ductus venosus. Any drug present in the blood that flows through the fetal liver is available for metabolism. In contrast, the compounds present in blood flowing through the ductus venosus bypass any initial metabolism, possibly allowing a greater amount of the unmetabolized portion of the compound to be distributed to its receptors in the fetus. The clinical significance and ontogeny of this phenomenon are unknown.

Given the truly rudimentary nature of our understanding of drug disposition and action in the maternal-placental-fetal unit, it seems prudent to perform focused animal experiments and controlled clinical trials before embarking on a generalized treatment of recognized fetal disorders. A number of influences result in a marked variation in the amount of fetal drug exposure that occurs after maternal administration (Table 10-8). However, most of our attempts at fetal therapy have been much more empirical. The remainder of this chapter describes some of these attempts.

PHARMACOLOGIC TREATMENT OF SPECIFIC FETAL DISORDERS

The successful treatment of specific pathophysiologic disorders in the fetus by administering pharmacologic agents to the mother or directly within the fetal compartment has permitted the development of therapeutic strategies to prevent or reverse a number of fetal abnormalities. Today, fetal therapy is a common practice for a number of intrauterine disorders. Some relatively common disorders that have been successfully treated with fetal therapy are listed in Table 10-9. They represent only some neonatal diseases that occur and progress in utero, which underscores the present and future importance of fetal therapy in decreasing neonatal morbidity and mortality rates.

Augmentation of Fetal Lung Maturation
(See Chapter 42, Part 1)

One of the earliest attempts to influence fetal development focused pharmacologically on lung maturation and the amelioration or prevention of neonatal respiratory distress syndrome (RDS).

The first description of the pharmacologic acceleration of fetal lung development was reported in the 1960s. This finding of corticosteroid-induced acceleration of the functional maturation of the lung was serendipitous because the primary purpose of this study was to compare the influence of mineralocorticoid and glucocorticoid effects on parturition. This early work was followed by a number of investigations involving a variety of animal models and clinical trials.[111,112,128] The exact mechanisms of the corticosteroid enhancement of lung maturation are unknown, but they appear to be primarily the result of the ability of the drug to augment structural changes in the lung parenchyma through steroid-induced enzyme induction and stimulation of protein synthesis, as well as the enhancement of surfactant synthesis. In human beings the endogenous,

TABLE 10-8. Limitations to Assuming Uniform Fetal Exposure from the Administration of a Uniform Weight-Adjusted Dose to the Mother

VARIATION EXISTS IN	DUE TO DISPARITY IN
Interindividual disposition	Maternal absorption Maternal distribution Maternal metabolism/elimination
Placental transfer	Uterine bloodflow Placental bloodflow Placental thickness and surface area Placental metabolism
Fetal tissue exposure	Fetal position/site of placentation Fetal tissue distribution Fetal metabolism/elimination

TABLE 10-9. Some Disorders in Which Fetal Therapy Has Been Attempted

DISORDER	THERAPY
Mixed carboxylase deficiency	Biotin
Methylmalonicacidemia	Vitamin B_{12}
Neural tube defects	Folate
Hypothyroidism	Thyroid hormone
Adrenogenital syndrome	Steroids
Fetal arrhythmia	Digoxin
Fetal sedation	Valium
Fetal withdrawal (prevention)	Methadone
RDS/IVH	Steroids
Idiopathic thrombocytopenic purpura	Steroids
Toxoplasmosis	Spiramycin
Group B streptococcus	Ampicillin
Syphilis	Penicillin
Tuberculosis	Antituberculotic agents
HIV	Zidovudine (AZT)

RDS, respiratory distress syndrome
IVH, intraventricular hemorrhage
HIV, human immunodeficiency virus

programmed elevation of cortisol during late gestation is very important in stimulating surfactant synthesis, alveolar septal thinning, and the reduction of the double capillary system to a single layer, all culminating in lung capacity maturation.[87,88] Furthermore, steroids also appear to influence structural changes, specific growth factors, lung fluid metabolism, antioxidant enzymes, and (importantly) the β_2-adrenergic receptor. In preterm infants, the immaturity of the hypothalamic pituitary adrenal axis may result in insufficient cortisol secretion for normal lung development, underscoring the need for maternal exogenous antenatal glucocorticoid steroid in threatened preterm labor.[111]

The effects of corticosteroid administration on lung maturation are relatively rapid, occurring within 24 hours of maternal steroid therapy, and infants exposed for 24 hours or less are reported to have up to a 50% decrease in the incidence of RDS.[128] The most dramatic effects on neonatal lung function are observed when maternally administered corticosteroid therapy is provided for approximately 1 to 7 days before delivery.

The controversy surrounding the effectiveness of corticosteroid therapy in reducing the incidence and severity of neonatal RDS has arisen from some studies that have used various corticosteroid preparations. Investigators have used cortisone, prednisone, or prednisolone rather than betamethasone or dexamethasone, both of which have been associated with clinical success. The data from these studies show clearly that the specific corticosteroid preparation used was more important than the dose administered. Ward summarized corticosteroid dosing data from various clinical studies by normalizing the total amount of steroid administered per treatment course to "cortisol equivalents."[128] It was not until the dose of hydrocortisone was raised to about 2000 cortisol equivalents that any positive effect on the incidence of RDS was observed. This dose is more than three times the effective dose in the cortisol equivalents recommended for betamethasone. Furthermore, when as much as 250 mg of methylprednisolone was administered, which is equal to approximately 1000 cortisol equivalents, no decrease in the incidence of RDS was observed. It is very clear from these data that either betamethasone or dexamethasone is the corticosteroid analogue to be used to promote fetal lung maturation.

The studies using other corticosteroid analogues, including methylprednisolone, prednisone, and prednisolone, raise questions concerning the placenta, fetal metabolism, and drug disposition dynamics within the fetal compartment as important influences precluding therapeutic success. The investigators who assessed the placental transfer of prednisone and prednisolone clearly showed that substantial amounts of prednisolone were present in the maternal circulation regardless of the formulation administered (prednisone requires in vivo conversion to the active prednisolone moiety). In contrast, very little prednisolone was measured in cord blood. The study design of these investigators appears to be adequate for an accurate assessment of this observed discrepancy. An initial bolus dose was administered and followed by a 160-minute continuous intravenous infusion of the study drugs before paired blood sampling was performed, thus approximating steady-state conditions. Only 12% of the maternal prednisolone concentration was identified in the fetal circulation. These data strongly suggest prednisolone metabolism by the placenta as the most likely explanation for the lack of clinical benefit seen with methylprednisolone, even when it is given in very high doses.

It is possible that the inactivation of prednisolone and other corticosteroid analogues (e.g., cortisone, hydrocortisone) is catalyzed by 11β-hydroxysteroid dehydrogenase, which is found in placental tissue.[106] Preparations of minced human placenta have been shown to effectively metabolize cortisol and prednisolone to their inactive metabolites, whereas only minimal metabolic activity has been observed under identical laboratory conditions with dexamethasone (1.8% metabolized) and betamethasone (7.1% metabolized). These investigators, using isolated, perfused placental cotyledons, observed more extensive metabolism of betamethasone (47%) and dexamethasone (54%), but the extent was still much lower than the 73% and 86% metabolism observed with cortisol and prednisolone, respectively. Further extending these studies, investigators have described efficient placental transfer that achieved equivalent maternal and cord blood concentrations with betamethasone and dexamethasone. Thus, the increased placental metabolism of nonhalogenated, substituted corticosteroids (e.g., cortisone, prednisolone) and the attainment of high concentrations in the fetal circulation support the importance of using either betamethasone or dexamethasone as the corticosteroid of choice for fetal therapy to enhance the maturation of fetal lung function.

The effectiveness of prenatal steroid therapy on lung development is not without possible long-term effects. As early as 1968 some studies in mice were suggestive of steroid-induced reductions in the DNA and RNA content in the brain, with enduring changes in brain cell numbers. Similar findings were described in different animal species. Published meta-analyses assessing offspring development strongly suggest that prenatal steroid administration is associated with decreased birthweight and brain growth; these findings appear to occur most often after multiple prenatal courses of glucocorticosteroid rather than after a single course. More research is clearly needed to catalogue the possible long-term effects of single- and multiple-course prenatal steroid administration. Until these data are available, multiple prenatal steroid courses should be generally avoided.[102,111] Sufficient experience and data demonstrate the superiority of steroid-induced lung effects when administered less than 24 hours before delivery, with positive therapeutic effects lasting up to at least 7 days.[111]

In conclusion, the majority of published studies in which betamethasone or dexamethasone was used as the compound of choice have demonstrated a clear reduction in the incidence of neonatal RDS compared with its incidence in those studies in which placebo was used. The results of multiple exhaustive meta-analyses that included only published studies involving randomized, blinded, placebo-controlled evaluations support this conclusion.[111] Complementing these impressive efficacy data are the long-term outcome data demonstrating little, if any, adverse, delayed effects on infant growth or development after a single treatment regimen.[102,111]

In Utero Prevention of Intracranial Hemorrhage (See Chapter 38)

Early brain injury in infants with very low birthweight remains an unfortunate and common clinical problem. The most common form of brain injury in these infants is periventricular-intraventricular hemorrhage (PIVH).[122,129] Advances in neonatal intensive care and the increasing use of prenatal corticosteroids to enhance fetal lung maturation[128] have resulted in a lowering of the incidence to less than 20% in infants with very low birthweight.[123] The importance of fetal treatment to prevent PIVH is underscored by the clear relationship between the incidence of PIVH and postnatal age. Nearly all of the PIVH observed in infants with very low birthweight is apparent within the first 4 days of life. These data clearly demonstrate the need for in utero measures to prevent PIVH rather than the use of focused therapy in early postnatal life. It is estimated that approximately 26% of the infants whose birthweight is between 50 and 750 g and 12% between 751 and 1000 g will develop severe forms of hemorrhage.[122]

Although numerous early studies, including a meta-analysis, suggested that antenatal phenobarbital is effective in decreasing the frequency and severity of intraventricular hemorrhage, more recent data strongly refute these earlier suggestions. In a well designed, randomized, placebo-controlled study involving over 600 women whose fetuses were younger than 34 weeks of gestation (range, 24 to 33 weeks), the National Institute of Child Health and Human Development Neonatal Research Network[123] clearly demonstrated that properly dosed phenobarbital administered to the mother resulted in no greater benefit over placebo in these premature infants. Important to the findings of this study was the fact that 59% and 58% of the women receiving phenobarbital and placebo, respectively, received antenatal corticosteroids, which provide protection against intraventricular hemorrhage.[123] A Cochrane review of the topic, including over 1750 women, confirmed these findings.[91]

Fetal Therapy to Prevent Maternal-Infant Transmission of Human Immunodeficiency Virus (See Chapter 22 and Chapter 37, Part 4)

Infection with the human immunodeficiency virus (HIV) (and the subsequent development of the acquired immunodeficiency syndrome [AIDS]) was one of the most important public health concerns of the 20th century and continues to be so today. Because there is no known cure for this devastating disease, infants infected in utero are committed to a short, difficult, turbulent life. For this reason, aggressive attempts have been made to identify the means of decreasing the possibility of mother-to-child transmission of HIV.

The risk of vertical transmission in the absence of maternal anti-retroviral therapy is 25% to 30%. Unfortunately, the timing of vertical HIV transmission is not well established, complicating the institution of preventive therapies. Several factors increase the risk of maternal transmission to the fetus, including a high maternal viral load, rapidly replicating viruses, maternal immunodeficiency, the prolonged rupture of membranes, and conditions that may disrupt the integrity of the placenta, such as other active, sexually transmitted diseases or chorioamnionitis.

Strategies targeting prevention or decreasing the incidence of maternally transmitted (vertical) HIV infection have been developed, and they focus on the use of zidovudine (AZT). The effectiveness of perigestational therapy is unequivocal. Maternal AZT therapy has been clearly shown to reduce vertical transmission by 67%, with evolving data suggesting that this transmission rate can be almost eliminated with more aggressive multidrug therapy.[84]

Prevention of Certain Fetal Infectious Diseases with Vaccination

It has been recognized for decades that the active immunization of newborn infants is effective in preventing subsequent infection with certain pathogens, including diphtheria, pertussis, tetanus, and poliomyelitis. However, such a therapeutic strategy is not effective in preventing the occurrence of these diseases immediately after birth[114] because such disease implies infection in utero, for which fetal immunization would be needed for successful prevention. Direct immunization of the fetus is seldom contemplated because of its known and unknown risks, but passive immunization is possible through maternal immunization. This approach to protecting the infant from infection in utero has been used successfully in the past for some infectious diseases (e.g., influenza, respiratory syncytial virus infection) and is a promising therapeutic strategy for others (Box 10-6).

The success of passive immunization of the fetus is dependent on the effectiveness of the transplacental transfer of immunoglobulins. In human beings, IgG is

---

BOX 10-6. Infectious Diseases Affecting the Newborn That May Be Preventable by In Utero Vaccination

Pertussis
Tetanus
Hepatitis B polio
Rabies
Meningococcal disease

the only immunoglobulin that crosses the intact placenta. IgA, IgD, and IgM do not cross the human placenta. Of primary importance to the passive immunization of the fetus is the fact that the IgG_1 subclass possesses the greatest affinity for the Fc receptor, affording the accumulation of this immunoglobulin in the fetus.[114] Most of this immunoglobulin crosses the placenta by simple passive diffusion, the mechanism by which many compounds cross the placenta. The extent to which IgG crosses the placenta by passive diffusion is directly proportional to the maternal IgG concentration. In addition, Fc receptor–bound IgG, which is located in the placental trophoblast membrane, is actively transported across the placenta by endocytosis. The passage of IgG across the placenta occurs at as early as 8 weeks of gestation and increases quantitatively with advancing gestation. By 17 to 20 weeks fetal IgG concentrations approach 100 mg/L. The transfer of maternal antibodies to the fetus provides protection from infection and transiently protects the neonate from a variety of infectious diseases.

On the basis of the data discussed earlier, investigators and clinicians have successfully provided passive immunization to the fetus. Some of the more important infectious diseases successfully prevented by in utero vaccination are listed in Box 10-6. This list should be considered only a temporary and partial one because research and clinical experience with passive immunization by maternal vaccination are growing rapidly. Moreover, the initial concerns regarding the use of live virus vaccines during pregnancy are also under reevaluation. The potential increased risk to the fetus of acquiring infection from maternally administered, live virus vaccine has been a major concern to investigators and clinicians for decades. Nevertheless, available data do not support this concern and have actually demonstrated the safe use of maternal vaccination with live virus preparations when needed.[114]

Extensive experience with yellow fever vaccinations in pregnant women has yielded no evidence of an increased incidence of untoward fetal effects.[114] Furthermore, current guidelines from the Centers for Disease Control and Prevention recognize the legitimate need for the maternal administration of live virus vaccines if immediate protection is necessary because of imminent exposure to yellow fever or poliomyelitis. Despite these experiential data, it is clear that more detailed research is needed on the efficacy and maternal-fetal safety of live virus vaccinations during pregnancy.

Much of the available data describing the safety of in utero vaccination has been obtained under less than optimal conditions. Outbreaks of specific, serious infectious diseases in various parts of the world have required aggressive immunization programs that have included pregnant women. Reports of outbreaks involving pertussis, tetanus, and poliomyelitis and a single case report on the use of human rabies vaccine support the efficacy and safety of in utero vaccination with specific vaccine preparations. Similarly, outbreaks of meningococcal disease in Brazil, necessitating a mass public immunization campaign that included pregnant women, yielded the important information that antibodies effectively crossed the placenta and that the titers measured in the newborn infant and the mother were much higher than those in the control subjects. These data suggest the efficacy of vaccination for the prevention of this epidemic-associated disease.

Additional investigations into the development of effective vaccine strategies against other more common infections that affect the fetus and neonate, including *Haemophilus influenzae,* group B streptococci, polyvalent pneumococcal conjugate vaccine, and measles, continue to be pursued. The roles of these and other vaccines targeting the protection of the fetus through maternal vaccination require more specific study. Nevertheless, these data demonstrate the efficacy and overall safety of maternal immunization to protect mothers and their unborn children from certain infectious diseases.[93,115]

Congenital Toxoplasmosis (See Chapters 22 and 37)

Toxoplasma gondii is an organism that is ubiquitous in nature and causes a variety of illnesses in human beings. Toxoplasmosis is one of the most common infections worldwide. The incidence varies with geographic region and an individual's level of immunocompetence. A recent resurgence in infections caused by *T. gondii* has been observed in patients with AIDS. The primary source of human infection is contact with soil or other objects contaminated with cat feces that contain sporulated cysts. A less common source of infection is the ingestion of poorly cooked meat contaminated with latent cysts. Estimates of the incidence of toxoplasmosis during pregnancy range from 3 to 6 cases per 1000 live births in high-risk countries and 1 to 2 cases per 1000 live births in low-risk countries.[116]

Fetal infection with *T. gondii* is acquired from the mother. Organisms present in the maternal circulation infect the placenta first. After a lag period, organisms are released from the placenta and infect the fetus. The placenta serves as a reservoir for these parasites, continuously seeding the fetus throughout pregnancy. The highest rate of maternal transmission to the fetus occurs when the mother acquires the disease late in gestation. In contrast, transplacental infection early in the first trimester is low, approximating 15%. This discrepancy in infection rates relative to the trimester may reflect the differences in placental membrane thickness with gestation. Overall, the risk of fetal infection because of maternal toxoplasmosis approximates 40%. The risk of fetal infection depends on a number of variables, including the severity of maternal parasitemia, the maturity of the placenta, and the competency of the maternal immune system. It appears that clinically significant congenital toxoplasmosis involves transplacentally infected fetuses younger than 26 weeks of gestation.[116] Unfortunately, the risk or presence of fetal infection does not correlate with maternal symptoms, complicating the clinical approach to these patients.

Congenital toxoplasmosis is associated with a wide variety of serious sequelae. The so-called classic triad of hydrocephalus, chorioretinitis, and intracranial calcifications is rarely observed today. Greater than 90% of congenitally infected infants are free of symptoms at birth; if untreated, the infection will progress, resulting in serious sequelae such as intracranial calcifications, chorioretinitis, hearing impairment, and developmental delay. Common early and late manifestations of congenital toxoplasmosis are shown in Box 10-7. The clinical importance of these effects argues for rapid maternal and fetal diagnosis of the disease and prompt institution of the appropriate therapy.

Complicating the decision to initiate therapy is the difficulty of making an accurate diagnosis. Maternal diagnosis is often based on evidence of recent primary infection assessed by the combination of seroconversion, a marked increase in antibody titers for several weeks, and the presence of IgM antibodies. Although the findings may be positive, the exact timing of maternal infection often cannot be determined. The diagnosis in utero involves the identification of parasites in fetal blood or amniotic fluid. When the index of suspicion is high, attempts to isolate parasites from the placenta at birth should be performed. More recently, the use of a specific polymerase chain reaction technique has facilitated a diagnostic determination.

Therapy for toxoplasmosis during pregnancy is aimed at both preventing vertical transmission and treating the infected mother and the fetus. Because of the unpredictability and insensitivity of current diagnostic methods, it is not possible to assess the efficacy of fetal prevention methods accurately; thus, most clinicians who attempt therapy during pregnancy select drug regimens that may prevent or treat maternal disease.

One of the earlier drugs used for the treatment of toxoplasmosis was the macrolide antibiotic spiramycin. It achieves high concentrations in the placenta and about 50% of maternal serum concentrations in the fetus.

The drug is used primarily in Europe, and few maternal or fetal side effects have been reported. Uncontrolled studies suggest a maternal benefit and a possible impact on vertical transmission, but they do not support any benefit of spiramycin in fetuses already infected. The differential effect of the drug relative to the fetus may merely reflect the very high concentrations achieved in the placenta compared with fetal tissue concentrations.

By far the most common drug regimen used to treat toxoplasmosis in newborns, pregnant women, and nonpregnant patients involves the combination of pyrimethamine and a sulfonamide (e.g., sulfadiazine). The combination of maternally administered spiramycin with pyrimethamine and sulfadiazine appears to provide the best treatment results for both the mother and fetus. A large study involving the placentas obtained from 223 proven cases of toxoplasmosis supports this assertion. Samples from these placentas were inoculated intraperitoneally into mice and revealed parasites in 76 of the 85 mothers (89%) who were untreated or inadequately treated, 89 of the 118 placentas (75%) obtained from the mothers who received 3 g of spiramycin for more than 15 days, and only 10 of the 20 placentas (50%) obtained from the patients who received combined spiramycin, pyrimethamine, and sulfadiazine.

Daffos and associates in France demonstrated that in 15 spiramycin-treated women with documented toxoplasmosis who chose to continue their pregnancies to term, the addition of pyrimethamine and sulfadiazine by 28 weeks of gestation resulted in 13 of 15 newborns who had no clinical evidence of disease at follow-up.[92] The two affected offspring had only mild chorioretinitis.

In conclusion, controlled data establishing treatment guidelines for toxoplasmosis infection during pregnancy are limited. If therapy is started early enough after maternal infection, spiramycin may reduce the incidence of fetal infection or possibly even prevent the transplacental transmission of parasites to the fetus. With active fetal infection, the addition of antiparasitic therapy beginning around the middle of the third trimester appears to provide effective therapy. The true efficacy of this regimen is unknown because of the large number of affected pregnancies that are electively terminated, but it appears to reduce the severity of neonatal infection and consequently neonatal morbidity and mortality rates. To date, no published data have appeared describing any teratogenic or adverse fetal effects of these drugs, which suggests their safety for use during pregnancy.

Fetal Endocrine Disorders (See Chapter 47, Parts 3 and 4)

TREATMENT OF CONGENITAL ADRENAL HYPERPLASIA

Congenital adrenal hyperplasia (CAH) is an autosomal recessive disorder that results from a deficiency of one

---

BOX 10-7. Common Manifestations of Congenital Toxoplasmosis

Early*	Late†
Mental retardation	Chorioretinitis
Convulsions	Abnormal CSF (increased protein level)
Spasticity and palsies	Anemia
Severely impaired vision	Convulsions
Hydrocephalus or microcephaly	Intracranial calcifications
Deafness	Jaundice
	Hydrocephalus
	Splenomegaly
	Lymphadenopathy
	Hepatomegaly
	Microcephaly

*Occurring early after birth and within the first 3 months of life.
†Late in the course of disease; sequelae from no or inadequate treatment, severe disease, or both.
CSF, cerebrospinal fluid.

of many different enzymes required for the synthesis of cortisol from cholesterol within the adrenal cortex. A deficiency in the 21-hydroxylase enzyme is the most common cause of CAH, occurring in approximately 1 of 140,000 live births. The CYP21AZ gene codes for the 21-hydroxylase enzyme and is located on chromosome 6p21.3.[106] Multiple large studies involving different populations have described the pattern and frequency of CYP21 mutations, allowing for informed genetic counseling regarding an infant's phenotype (i.e., the simple virilizing or salt-wasting form of CAH).[106] Virilizing CAH is much less common and is the result of 11β-hydroxylase deficiency, occurring in less than 10% of CAH cases. Both of these deficiencies are responsive to prenatal therapy.[89,119]

The normal synthetic pathway for cortisol synthesis from cholesterol is shown in Figure 10-12. Cortisol synthesis is strictly regulated by a negative feedback control loop involving two types of hormone: the pituitary adrenocorticotropic hormone and the hypothalamic corticotropin-releasing hormone. With increasing cortisol secretion, glucocorticoid receptors in the higher centers bind to cortisol, signaling a diminished need for the transcription of the adrenocorticotropic hormone and the corticotropin-releasing hormone. This action reduces the production of these hormones, which are responsible for stimulating cortisol secretion. CAH is characterized by a reduction in cortisol synthesis caused by a deficiency in 21-hydroxylase, leading to the continuous overproduction of the adrenocorticotropic hormone, adrenocortical hyperplasia, and the accumulation of 17α-hydroxyprogesterone and other precursors to 21-hydroxylase activity. These accumulated precursors are shunted into sex steroid pathways, which promote the excessive production of virilizing hormones such as testosterone and other potent androgens. The sex steroids are produced from 17-hydroxylated pregnenolone, progesterone, dehydroepiandrosterone, or androstenedione by the catalytic activity of 17,20-lyase.[119] In addition, the accumulation of the products of 3β-hydroxysteroid dehydrogenase will affect aldosterone synthesis, with a resulting effect on fluid and electrolyte homeostasis.

Thus, the mechanisms of production of these important steroids are interrelated and will be perturbed by an early defect in 21-hydroxylase activity. Depending on the extent of the enzyme deficiency and the enhanced production of sex steroids, newborn infants

with CAH may have varying anatomic anomalies. In a newborn female infant with severe virilizing CAH, it is not uncommon for the infant to have a single perineal orifice originating from a fused vagina and urethra. The clitoris is often very enlarged, with the appearance of a hypospadiac phallus. The labia majora are fused at the midline, rugose, and empty of glans. 21-Hydroxylase deficiency is the most commonly recognized cause of ambiguous genitalia in the female newborn. The extent of the deformities varies with the variability in enzyme deficiency.[119]

In contrast to newborn female infants, male infants with 21-hydroxylase or 11β-hydroxylase deficiency have no apparent genital defects, with the exception of possibly an elongated penis, and respond well to corticosteroid replacement therapy after birth.

Intrauterine therapy is needed in fetuses known to have CAH because the resulting severe physical deformities in the female infant have an impact on the parents, parent-infant bonding, family, friends, and the patient herself in later years.[119] Fetal therapy should prevent the occurrence of associated structural genital anomalies, sparing the infant and family from surgical procedures and sequelae. For more than a decade, in utero suppression of adrenal activity by the maternal administration of dexamethasone has been used for female fetuses identified to be deficient in 21-hydroxylase activity. More recently, Cerame and coworkers reported the successful treatment of a female fetus that had 11β-hydroxylase deficiency with maternally administered dexamethasone (20 μg/kg per day divided into three equal doses).[89]

For the greatest possibility of completely preventing or minimizing the CAH-associated structural anomalies in susceptible female fetuses, dexamethasone therapy should be started as soon as possible after conception. The adrenal cortex is first detected at approximately 7 weeks of gestation, with fetal steroid production beginning in the latter half of the first trimester. The complete prevention of genital virilization may require starting maternal dexamethasone before 6 weeks of gestation, at a time when the affected adrenal gland appears to be capable of secreting androgens. Obviously, the earliest suspicion that a fetus may be affected comes from genetic counseling and the genotyping of families with a history of an infant born with CAH. Ideally, genotyping should be performed before any planned pregnancies in families considered at risk

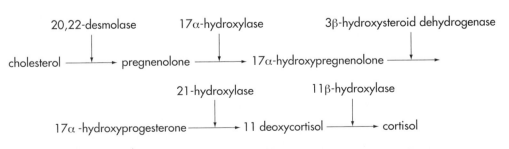

FIGURE 10-12. Normal synthetic pathway for cortisol production by the adrenal cortex.

for such a mutation. With parental consent, maternal dexamethasone therapy at 20 µg/kg per day in three equally divided doses is started as soon after conception as possible. Additional studies are then performed to assess the sex of the fetus and the presence of CAH. Chorionic villus sampling performed at approximately 9 to 10 weeks of gestation for first-trimester diagnosis or amniocentesis performed after 14 weeks of fetal age for second-trimester diagnosis can be used for the perinatal diagnosis of 21-hydroxycorticosteroid deficiency (e.g., the Medical Library Association typing of cultured fetal cells or 21B gene analysis of extracted DNA).[119] After amniocentesis, if karyotype analysis (by 12 to 14 weeks of gestation) reveals a male fetus or DNA analysis reveals an unaffected infant, dexamethasone therapy may be discontinued. If the fetus is female and later DNA analysis reveals a 21-hydroxylase or 11β-hydroxylase deficiency, dexamethasone therapy is continued to term. Unfortunately, the decision to treat must be made before a diagnosis is possible, exposing a fair number of fetuses to suprapharmacologic maternal doses of dexamethasone (≈7 of 8 unaffected fetuses).

For infants born with classic 21-hydroxylase deficiency, sodium and mineralocorticoid replacement therapy is required. The most common approach to replacing mineralocorticoid activity is with the oral administration of 9α-fluorohydrocortisone at 50 to 100 µg/day along with tailored sodium chloride supplementation.

The efficacy of maternal dexamethasone in preventing the anomalies associated with CAH is dependent on a number of factors, including early institution and proper dosing. The degree of structural deformity in the female infant will be directly related to the timing of the institution of therapy. Once the deformity has occurred, maternal dexamethasone therapy cannot reverse the deformity but may prevent its progression. Pang reported her experience with prenatal dexamethasone administration in 54 fetuses (52 with classic 21-hydroxycorticosteroid deficiency).[119] Of the newborns whose mothers received dexamethasone before 10 weeks of fetal age and continued therapy to birth, 34% had normal genitalia, 52% had mild virilized genitalia not requiring surgery, and 14% had significantly virilized genitalia requiring surgical repair. Of the experience to date, maternally administered dexamethasone throughout gestation appears to be safe and without teratogenic effects (see later).[119] Moreover, before the advent of fetal therapy, all infants with profound enzyme deficiency were severely disfigured, whereas even delayed therapy was found to decrease the degree of deformity in affected offspring. Thus, early institution of dexamethasone therapy and strict maternal compliance are essential to a good outcome. However, the initiation of maternal dexamethasone after 10 weeks of fetal age or the discontinuation of dexamethasone treatment by the late second trimester is usually associated with severe virilization.[119]

Another important variable influencing the efficacy of maternal dexamethasone therapy is drug dose. The efficacy of maternal dosing for the suppression of fetal adrenal activity can be assessed by monitoring the maternal blood or urine concentrations of the hormone estriol. This hormone accurately reflects the fetal synthesis of one of its precursor steroids, 16α-hydroxy-dehydroepiandrosterone. In mothers receiving adequate doses of dexamethasone, fetal adrenal activity is suppressed and the maternal blood and urinary concentration values of estriol are zero.

As discussed earlier, when dexamethasone therapy is used to enhance fetal lung maturation, fetal exposure appears to be both safe and effective. Obviously, the duration of maternal dexamethasone therapy for CAH is substantially longer than that for the enhancement of fetal lung maturation, subjecting the fetus to a possibly greater risk of adverse effects. The published experience to date with long-term maternal dexamethasone therapy administered throughout gestation reveals no greater incidence of fetal or neonatal adverse effects associated with dexamethasone than what is seen with more limited use at the time of preterm delivery. Early suggestions that dexamethasone therapy may be associated with a higher incidence of cleft palate have been refuted in more recent controlled evaluations. Similarly, no influence of therapy has been observed in the subsequent mental and physical development of these infants.[106,119] Furthermore, it is clear that female fetuses who do not receive effective prenatal therapy have marked differences from unaffected controls in their social and behavioral development.[85] Nevertheless, the possibility of late behavioral effects, as suggested from the administration of a prenatal steroid for data on accelerated lung maturation, may occur with the dexamethasone dosing regimens required for CAH treatment. Only careful monitoring of these patients as they mature throughout childhood will provide this data. However, the number of patients with possible or definite CAH is small, and it will require many years to acquire the experience necessary to define the true toxic profile of the regimen.

Unfortunately, clinically important adverse effects associated with dexamethasone have been observed in mothers taking the drug throughout pregnancy. All the known side effects associated with long-term corticosteroid therapy have been described in treated mothers, which include Cushing syndrome, weight gain, edema, elevations in blood pressure or blood glucose concentrations, gastric distress, and irritability. The maternal side effects of chronic dexamethasone therapy are listed in Table 10-10. The incidence and severity of these effects appear directly related to the duration of therapy. Unfortunately, no known means of reducing the development or incidence of these maternal side effects is available. Mothers receiving dexamethasone therapy should be closely monitored for the occurrence of these and other dexamethasone-associated adverse effects, and the need to discontinue maternal dexamethasone therapy should be decided on a case-by-case basis. In addition, it may be possible to reduce the incidence and severity of dexamethasone-associated maternal adverse effects by determining the true maternal dose needed to suppress fetal adrenal activity. Lower maternal doses

TABLE 10-10. Common and Potentially Adverse Effects to the Mother Associated with Dexamethasone Therapy* in the Treatment of Congenital Adrenal Hyperplasia

Excess weight gain (≥4.5-12 kg)
Cushingoid complications
Moon face, increased facial hair
Extreme striae causing permanent scarring (abdomen, hip, breasts, arms, thighs, shoulders)
Overt diabetes or diabetic OGTT
Hypertension
Extreme emotional lability
Epigastric pain
Fatigue, pedal edema
Potential risks not established
Osteoporosis
Aseptic necrosis of the hip
Predisposition to cesarean section

*Chronic therapy, first trimester to term.
OGTT, oral glucose tolerance test.
Modified from Pang S: Congenital adrenal hyperplasia. Endocrinol Metab Clin N Am 26:853, 1997.

TABLE 10-11. Causes of Congenital Hypothyroidism with Approximate Incidence

CAUSES	INCIDENCE
Thyroid dysgenesis	1:4000
Agenesis	
Dysgenesis	
Ectopia	
Thyroid dysmorphogenesis	1:30,000
TSH receptor defect	
Iodide trapping defect	
Organification defect	
Iodotyrosine deiodinase deficiency	
Thyroglobulin defect	
Transient hypothyroidism	1:40,000
Drug induced	
Maternal antibody induced	
Idiopathic	
Hypothalamic-pituitary hypothyroidism	1:70,000 to 1:100,000
Hypothalamic-pituitary anomaly	
Panhypopituitarism	
Isolated TSH deficiency	
TSH structural defect	

TSH, thyroid-stimulating hormone (thyrotropin).
Modified from Fisher DA: Fetal thyroid function: Diagnosis and management of fetal thyroid disorders. Clin Obstet Gynecol 40:16, 1997.

may decrease the severity of side effects, and the dose needed could be assessed by individual dose-response relationships focused on how much daily dexamethasone is needed to suppress maternal urinary estriol excretion, targeting a urinary concentration value of zero.

TREATMENT OF FETAL THYROID DISORDERS
(See Chapter 47, Part 3)
The fetus may demonstrate hypothyroidism, hyperthyroidism, or goiter associated with either hypothyroidism or hyperthyroidism. Concerns over thyroid dysfunction in the fetus and the possibility of the subsequent development of abnormalities in the infant have stimulated some investigators to consider in utero therapy as a way to avoid these potentially irreversible sequelae. Nevertheless, considerable controversy persists about whether fetal therapy is needed in the vast majority of cases of congenitally diagnosed thyroid disease.

The maturation and function of the thyroid gland represent a complex interplay among it, the pituitary gland, and the hypothalamus. By the 10th week of gestation, thyroid colloid, iodide uptake, and thyroid hormone synthesis have been demonstrated, and the thyrotropin-releasing hormone has been identified in hypothalamic extracts.[97] It is important to recognize that the normal ontogeny of the fetal thyroid gland occurs relatively independent of the maternal environment. The placenta appears to be freely permeable to iodide and the thyrotropin-releasing hormone, only partially permeable to the iodothyronines, and impermeable to thyrotropin. The maturation of the gland continues throughout gestation and after birth, so an adequate maternal intake of iodine is important.[106]

Of the congenital thyroid disorders, fetal hypothyroidism, as uncommon as it is, is the most frequently encountered congenital thyroid disease. The more frequent causes of fetal hypothyroidism are listed in Table 10-11.[97] The majority of these cases are caused by abnormal thyroid, pituitary, or hypothalamic embryogenesis. Because of the infrequency of the disease and the cause of the dysgenesis, active diagnostic evaluation of the fetus to assess fetal thyroid status is unusual unless an abnormal thyroid gland is observed during an ultrasonographic evaluation performed for other reasons. In the remainder of patients with congenital hypothyroidism, abnormalities in thyroid hormone synthesis and disposition, abnormal gland function, and transient effects caused by maternal antibodies or maternal antithyroid drugs are generally implicated.[97]

Most infants born with thyroid gland dysgenesis or modest goiter have no symptoms and respond promptly to postnatal thyroid replacement therapy.[97] However, fetal hypothyroidism is most likely associated with mild IQ deficits and defects in bone maturation. There appears to be an inverse relationship between the severity of maternal hypothyroidism and the cognitive development of the offspring at 8 years of age.[106] The type of fetal hypothyroidism resulting from maternal therapy with antithyroid medications (e.g., methimazole, propylthiouracil) requires diligent dosage adjustment to define the maternal requirement associated with the lowest dose to treat the maternal hyperthyroidism. Other maternally consumed therapeutic agents with antithyroid activity exerted on the fetus, including lithium, amiodarone, and iodine, must also be dosed carefully, with close monitoring. Reference values for the markers of fetal thyroid status, which are derived from measurements performed with amniotic fluid, are available and can be used to diagnose and guide the treatment of fetal thyroid disorders.[86]

Fetal hyperthyroidism with thyrotoxicosis is very uncommon but when it occurs is nearly always associated with maternal Graves disease. Increased fetal thyroid function is due to the placental transfer of maternal thyroid-stimulating IgG antibody, which stimulates fetal T_4 secretion during the later stages of gestation. If T_4 stimulation is pronounced enough and expressed for a sufficient period of time, hyperthyroidism develops in the fetus, with classic symptoms including tachycardia, growth retardation, advanced bone maturation, and goiter.[97] The most common initial manifestation of fetal hyperthyroidism is tachycardia.

Fetal goiter has been associated with tracheal compression and altered amniotic fluid volume. In addition, fetal goiter may develop because of various abnormalities in thyroid function, including defects in thyroid hormone synthesis, the maternal transfer of goitrogen, and, as described earlier, maternal autoimmune thyroid disease. Goiter may be associated with either hypothyroidism or hyperthyroidism; therefore, if the diagnosis cannot be determined from the maternal history, further investigation may require the direct determination of fetal thyroid function by performing hormone concentration studies of amniotic fluid or using cordocentesis to obtain fetal blood samples. Despite these advances in our ability to evaluate fetal thyroid status more critically, the risk to the infant of untreated congenital goiter in the euthyroid mother appears to be minimal. The success of postnatal therapy suggests that fetal therapy should be instituted only in cases of very large goiter, which may cause mechanical damage, or in situations associated with altered amniotic fluid volume.

Fetal hypothyroidism, with or without goiter, has been treated successfully with the intra-amniotic instillation of T_4. The optimum dose for the intra-amniotic instillation of T_4 is not known; the successful management of a small number of cases suggests a 250- to 500-μg dose of T_4, given intra-amniotically once or twice a week.[97,106] The quantitation of concentrations of trough hormone in the amniotic fluid may be useful in guiding the intervals for subsequent intra-amniotic dosing. In contrast, the clinically important manifestations of fetal hyperthyroidism may be the most effectively treated with the maternal administration of an antithyroid medication, either methimazole or propylthiouracil, with or without such supportive therapy as the use of propranolol. Methimazole is the preferred drug because a greater amount of it than that of propylthiouracil crosses the placenta. The increased transplacental transfer of methimazole is the primary reason that it is otherwise avoided during pregnancy. The use of propylthiouracil to treat maternal hyperthyroidism has less of an effect on the fetus. The monitoring of fetal heart rate is usually sufficient to determine the success of therapy, with the normalization of fetal heart rate occurring within 2 weeks. The maternal antithyroid drug dose is adjusted to maintain fetal heart rate at approximately 140 beats per minute.

Polyhydramnios

Amniotic fluid is the only environment of the fetus throughout gestation and provides support and protection until the time of delivery. The volume of amniotic fluid increases with gestational age, reaching a plateau at approximately 30 to 37 weeks (see Chapter 21). The total volume of amniotic fluid is highly variable but usually ranges between 500 and 1100 mL. The actual amount produced is dependent on a number of variables controlled by the dynamic interactions among the maternal-placental-fetal compartments.[110] *Polyhydramnios* refers to an excess of amniotic fluid, usually more than 2000 mL. The incidences of oligohydramnios and polyhydramnios may be observed in as many as 1% to 7% of all pregnancies. An abnormal volume of amniotic fluid is highly correlated with the risk and occurrence of fetal anomalies. The use of amniotic fluid screening as a guide to further targeted ultrasound evaluation is becoming an increasingly more common practice.[86]

The causes of polyhydramnios are many. The more important causes, listed in order of importance, are shown in Table 10-12. The overall incidence of polyhydramnios appears to range between 0.13% and 3.5% of all pregnancies. This rate remains relatively constant and independent of the method of diagnosing the disorder, although the clinical assessment of amniotic fluid volume is not always reliable. Before ultrasonography became available, polyhydramnios was diagnosed on the basis of an abnormally large uterine size for gestational age and the inability to palpate aspects of the fetus.[110] With the use of ultrasound techniques, the determination of the *amniotic fluid index* is a very useful method for diagnosis. However, the method of ultrasonography will influence the sensitivity of the amniotic fluid index; color flow Doppler imaging appears to overestimate oligohydramnios and underestimate polyhydramnios.

TABLE 10-12. Causes of Polyhydramnios

CAUSE*	% OF CASES
Idiopathic	≈60
Fetal anomalies 　Gastrointestinal 　Central nervous system 　Cardiovascular	≈19
Multiple gestation	≈7.5
Maternal diabetes	≈5
Other causes	≈8.5
*Listed in order of importance.	

The need to treat polyhydramnios is dependent on maternal symptoms. Polyhydramnios per se causes no ill effects for the fetus; the mother alone is affected. Nevertheless, it may be a manifestation of many fetal disorders, necessitating close investigation of the fetus in identified cases. The indications for maternal treatment include maternal respiratory compromise, gastrointestinal difficulties or pain, and preterm labor. The available data suggest that despite its risks, indomethacin therapy is effective in cases of idiopathic polyhydramnios, maternal gastrointestinal obstruction or diabetes, and fetal nephrogenic diabetes insipidus (e.g., those cases caused by maternal lithium therapy).

Indomethacin is a propionic acid, nonsteroidal anti-inflammatory drug that competitively inhibits the activity of cyclooxygenase, which results in decreased prostaglandin synthesis. Its precise mechanism of action in decreasing amniotic fluid volume is unknown. Most investigators believe that indomethacin influences amniotic fluid production by either impairing the production of fetal lung fluid or enhancing its reabsorption, decreasing fetal urine production, and/or increasing fluid movements across fetal membranes.[110] The preliminary data on sheep also suggest that the maternal administration of indomethacin may increase fetal respiratory movements, which in combination with increased pulmonary fluid reabsorption can lead to a decrease in amniotic fluid production. The overall effect of the drug is probably due to a combination of these events.

Many different indomethacin dosage regimens have been used. An initial regimen consisting of 25 mg PO administered every 6 hours ($\approx$1.4 to 1.5 mg/kg per day) may be effective. This dosage has been reported to decrease fetal urine production.[125] Some investigators have suggested higher doses, such as 2.2 to 3.0 mg/kg per day.[82] Maternal indomethacin doses of greater than 2 mg/kg per day do not appear to afford any greater benefit, but they are clearly associated with increased maternal and fetal drug toxicity. These adverse effects may be dose limiting, especially when constriction of the ductus arteriosus occurs. The impact of this drug-induced effect on the fetus cannot be overemphasized. For this reason, maternal indomethacin should probably not be administered after 32 weeks of gestation, and it is contraindicated after 34 weeks.[110]

With short-term indomethacin administration (i.e., 72 hours), the incidence of clinically important adverse effects on the fetus is small and does not necessitate any extraordinary patient monitoring. With longer courses of therapy, Kramer and colleagues recommend serial echocardiography to determine whether ductal constriction is present.[110] These authors obtain an initial fetal echocardiogram 24 hours after starting maternal indomethacin therapy and weekly during the treatment period. If ductal closure is noted, the administration of maternal indomethacin is reduced from 25 mg PO every 6 hours to the same dose every 8 hours. Another fetal echocardiogram is obtained in 24 hours. If tricuspid regurgitation with ductal constriction is noted, indomethacin therapy is immediately discontinued. Fetal hydrops, postnatal persistence of the fetal circulation,

and pulmonary hypertension may all be manifestations of prolonged tricuspid regurgitation with severe ductal insufficiency. The indomethacin-induced constriction of fetal ductal tissue has been described at as early as 24 weeks of gestation, and most authorities encourage close echocardiographic monitoring starting at 27 weeks.[110]

In contrast to the serious indomethacin-associated adverse effects that can occur in the fetus, maternal tolerance of therapy is generally good, rarely requiring the discontinuation of therapy. The most common maternal side effects of indomethacin therapy are gastric upset (e.g., heartburn), nausea, and headache. With the long-term administration of indomethacin, the incidences of headache, vertigo, and tinnitus appear to increase. When current indomethacin dosing recommendations have been followed, only rare instances of decreased maternal urine output and worsening maternal hypertension have been described. In addition, like all nonsteroidal anti-inflammatory drugs, indomethacin interferes reversibly with platelet function and aggregation. Thus, patients with underlying coagulation disorders should not receive the drug.

Fetal Arrhythmias (See Chapter 43)

Abnormal cardiac rhythm occurs in approximately 1% to 3% of fetuses during the third trimester. It is presumed that the number is actually larger, considering the large number of fetuses that probably have intermittent extrasystoles, which cause no symptoms and go undiagnosed. The most common means by which fetal cardiac dysrhythmias are diagnosed is through incidental observations obtained during regular clinic visits. Fetal echocardiography is the primary means by which the diagnosis of fetal dysrhythmia is confirmed and is used to determine whether other congenital cardiac abnormalities are present. Recent advances in imaging and integrated computer technology, including measurements from color flow Doppler imaging, have greatly increased the clinician's ability to diagnose and manage fetal cardiac anomalies.[109,126,129] Among the fetuses that appear to have cardiac dysrhythmia on initial evaluation, approximately 80% are found to have extrasystoles, with the remaining 20% having some type of tachyarrhythmia or bradyarrhythmia. Fortunately, most fetal cardiac dysrhythmias involve uncomplicated, nonsustained extrasystoles that do not require intervention. However, depending on the severity, many sustained tachyarrhythmias do require therapeutic intervention.

Sustained fetal tachycardia or bradycardia that remains untreated can result in a terminal form of fetal heart failure culminating in fetal hydrops (see Chapter 43 and 21). *Hydrops* refers to a group of physical findings, including anasarca, cardiac dilation, and hepatosplenomegaly. If fetal hydrops remains untreated, the perinatal mortality rate will range from 50% to 98%. This staggering mortality rate and the recognition that a major cause is fetal dysrhythmia underscore the importance of the prompt and successful treatment of sustained fetal dysrhythmias.[107,125]

Fetal tachycardia is frequently defined as a fetal heart rate persistently more than 180 to 200 beats per minute, whereas *fetal bradycardia* is a persistent heart rate of less than 100 beats per minute regardless of gestational age. The dysrhythmia should be categorized as either sustained or intermittent. *Sustained dysrhythmia* frequently describes a duration of dysrhythmia for more than 50% of the time, whereas *intermittent dysrhythmia* occurs for a shorter duration.[107] Such a characterization of the dysrhythmia (i.e., sustained or intermittent) is important in formulating a therapeutic plan. For example, it is not uniformly accepted that every fetus with intermittent or sustained tachycardia is in imminent danger of sudden death or the development of hydrops.[109] In contrast, most clinicians believe that the hydropic fetus is unlikely to spontaneously improve.

Fetuses with severe bradycardia are susceptible to the development of hydrops.[109] Complete atrioventricular block is the most frequently diagnosed sustained fetal bradycardia. This disorder appears to occur as a result of congenital heart disease or, in the fetus with normal intracardiac anatomy, as a result of maternal antibodies that cross the placenta and cause autoimmune damage to the fetal atrioventricular conduction tissue.[109]

Supraventricular tachycardia is the most common form of tachyarrhythmia; the remaining tachyarrhythmias tend to involve atrial flutter and reciprocating or atypical supraventricular tachycardia (see Chapter 43).[107,109] Although fetal dysrhythmias may be associated with any pathophysiologic perturbation of either the mother or fetus, tachyarrhythmias appear most often to represent the primary abnormalities of the heart and/or conduction, with only a small percentage of cases caused by cardiac malformations, infection, or uterine contractions. Consequently, when sustained fetal dysrhythmias are diagnosed and treatment is required, therapy usually involves the administration of an antiarrhythmic agent to the mother, with the goal of suppressing the abnormal fetal rhythm.

Extrasystoles rarely progress to tachyarrhythmia and therefore rarely require therapeutic intervention. Nevertheless, patients should be monitored serially to ensure that the extrasystoles do not degenerate into more serious rhythm disturbances. As stated above, most authorities recommend a trial of antenatal antiarrhythmic therapy for sustained fetal tachyarrhythmia. Nevertheless, the decision is complex. The options include simple serial monitoring with repeated fetal echocardiograms and sonograms to assess disease progression, maternal antiarrhythmic drug therapy, direct fetal therapy, or the premature delivery of the infant. Decisions must be made on a case-by-case basis. In contrast, fetal bradyarrhythmias do not respond to antiarrhythmic therapy because they are frequently a result of fetal abnormalities that include fetal hypothyroidism, structural anomalies of the heart, and an abnormality of the sinus node. Fetal prognosis is relative to the type of bradycardia,[113] so close monitoring is essential in order to undertake prompt delivery and postnatal therapy if fetal survival is jeopardized.[107,109,125]

The decision to treat a fetal dysrhythmia must be predicated on a thorough understanding of the natural cause of the arrhythmia and a critical evaluation of the neonatal risk associated with any treatment strategy. The literature is replete with reports of the successful management of fetal tachyarrhythmias with maternally administered antiarrhythmic drugs. The most frequently used drugs are listed in Box 10-8. Nevertheless, a review of the therapeutic outcomes of 119 published cases of supraventricular tachycardia and atrial flutter revealed that 50% of these cases failed to respond to maternally administered digoxin monotherapy.[107] Of the patients in whom therapy with digoxin initially failed, 80% of those with supraventricular tachycardia and 60% of those with AF were treated successfully with the addition of a second maternally administered antiarrhythmic agent. The presence of fetal heart failure was associated with a poor response to digoxin monotherapy. This experience has been confirmed by the series of Simpson and Sharland, who have clearly shown the negative impact that hydrops has on the fetal response to antiarrhythmic therapy (see later).[125] The increased distribution volume of digoxin in the presence of polyhydramnios and hydrops, thus reducing the likelihood of fetal efficacy, further complicates the design of a safe dosing regimen. These variables preclude a detailed assessment of the true efficacy rate of digoxin monotherapy. Nevertheless, digoxin monotherapy appears to be efficacious in a large number of cases. In nonresponders the additional antiarrhythmic drugs are often therapeutic, most notably a calcium channel antagonist.[125]

Many clinically important variables influence maternal-fetal drug therapy and outcome, including the differences in gestational age at the time of diagnosis, severity of underlying fetal cardiac dysrhythmia, presence of other maternal-fetal diseases, maternal digoxin dose, use of a maternal digoxin loading regimen on the initiation of therapy, targeted or attained steady-state maternal serum digoxin concentrations, time of determining maternal cord serum drug concentrations, and duration of monotherapy before the start of combination antiarrhythmic drug therapy.

Appropriate dosing is one question that remains in treating fetal dysrhythmias through maternal drug administration. The answer to this important question must address the complex nature of the maternal-

BOX 10-8. Antiarrhythmic Medications Used to Treat Fetal Tachyarrhythmias

Digoxin*
Propranolol
Sotalol
Flecainide*
Amiodarone
Propafenone
β-Methyldigoxin

*Most frequently used either alone or in combination.

placental-fetal unit. Nevertheless, some general principles of drug therapy may be used to guide drug administration in this context (Box 10-9). The majority of the reported experience recommends targeting traditionally accepted therapeutic serum drug concentrations in the mother (Table 10-13), presumably to provide therapeutic concentrations to the fetus. These purported "ranges of therapeutic serum antiarrhythmic drug concentration" are guidelines; they should not be interpreted as absolute. Furthermore, these concentration ranges have been assessed primarily in adult patients with various underlying cardiac diseases. Their relevance to the healthy mother and the fetus with cardiac disease is unknown. Nevertheless, they can be used as targets to guide initial maternal antiarrhythmic drug dosing so that maternal serum drug concentrations can be balanced against maternal tolerance and fetal cardiac effects. From the limited published experience, it appears that a mother with normal cardiovascular function is very tolerant of the effects of maternally circulating antiarrhythmic agents. The mother whose fetus (and who herself) has clinically significant cardiac disease is clearly a major challenge.

Maternal drug dosing should be aggressive because of the many physiologic changes that occur during pregnancy (see Tables 10-4 to 10-6) and influence

TABLE 10-13. Therapeutic Maternal Serum Antiarrhythmic Drug Concentrations

DRUG	INITIAL THERAPEUTIC MATERNAL SERUM CONCENTRATIONS*
Digoxin†	1-3 ng/mL
Procainamide	4-12 mg/L
N-Acetylprocainamide	10-30 mg/L
Quinidine	2-5 mg/L
Flecainide	0.4-1 mg/L
Amiodarone	0.5-2.5 mg/L

*Initial target maternal serum drug concentrations. Drug dose should be adjusted as needed to treat fetal arrhythmia and as tolerated by the mother.
†Must account for the presence of endogenous digoxin-like substances (see text for details).

BOX 10-9. General Principles to Guide Maternal Antiarrhythmic Drug Therapy for the Treatment of Fetal Dysrhythmias

Initiate maternal drug dosing aggressively. Use loading doses when appropriate. Repeatedly assess maternal drug pharmacokinetics when possible to account for pregnancy-associated differences in drug disposition. The mother should be hospitalized during the initiation of antiarrhythmic therapy.

Monitor mother closely for antiarrhythmic drug effects. Carefully assess mother for effects of antiarrhythmic drug: presence, severity, and tolerance. Carefully assess mother for any drug-associated adverse effects.

Monitor fetus closely for antiarrhythmic drug effects. Perform repeated assessment of fetal heart function (e.g., echocardiography, continuous external fetal heart rate monitoring). Target fetal monitoring to coincide with expected or documented maternal antiarrhythmic steady state.

Adjust maternal antiarrhythmic drug therapy as needed and tolerated. Initial doses are given to target upper limit of usual range of therapeutic serum concentration. Adjust doses upward as needed for fetal heart effect and maternal tolerance. Second antiarrhythmic agent is indicated only with maternal intolerance of maximum antiarrhythmic monotherapy. Initiate antiarrhythmic dosing of second agent as aggressively as that with first drug. Maintain dose of first drug when adding second antiarrhythmic drug.

Unsuccessful maternal antiarrhythmic drug therapy requires reassessment. Reassess patient and cardiac diagnosis. Ensure proper drug administration and patient compliance. Consider direct fetal therapy (e.g., intra-amniotic, intracord, fetal intramuscular).

maternal drug disposition. As discussed earlier, most alterations necessitate the maternal administration of doses that are higher than usual to achieve serum drug concentrations similar to those achieved in the nongravid state. If the desired therapeutic effect on the fetal heart is not realized, the dose of the antiarrhythmic drug should be increased regardless of the maternal serum concentration until the mother's intolerance limits further dose escalation or the therapeutic effect on the fetus is achieved. If maximally tolerated doses are administered without therapeutic success, the dose of the first drug should be maintained at a constant rate and a second drug added. Dosing with the second drug should be aggressively initiated, again initially targeting the upper limit of the range for the therapeutic serum concentration. For antiarrhythmic drugs without monitoring parameters for the serum drug concentration (e.g., propranolol, propafenone, sotolol), specific physiologic parameters, such as maternal heart rate and blood pressure, should be used to determine the initial doses and aggressive dose escalation (see Box 10-8).

Of the antiarrhythmic drugs available to treat fetal arrhythmias, digoxin has been used the most extensively. It is the drug of choice for the treatment of fetal tachyarrhythmias in the nonhydropic infant. Digoxin is a positive inotrope, and it increases the refractory period through the atrioventricular node. In the patient with a normal heart (e.g., the pregnant woman), digoxin therapy may cause systemic hypertension as a result of vasoconstriction, a decreased sinus rate, and a slight decrease in cardiac output. Complicating the routine monitoring of the serum digoxin concentration in both the fetus and the mother is the presence of endogenous digoxin-like immunoreactive substances. They interact with currently routinely used laboratory immunoassay methods to quantitate digoxin concentrations in biologic fluids.[107] The presence of these endogenous substances leads to a falsely elevated serum digoxin concentration. The physiologic role of these substances is not understood, and maternal and fetal concentrations vary with time. Thus, an attempt to use a single baseline determination of the concentration of endogenous digoxin-like immunoreactive substances before digoxin therapy to subtract from subsequent serum concentrations is inaccurate. Instead, blood samples must be sent for specific analysis by high-performance liquid chromatography in order to accurately account for the presence of these substances and determine only the serum digoxin concentration derived from exogenous digoxin.

The overall modest success rate in treating fetal tachyarrhythmias with digoxin monotherapy (≈50%) raises questions about the possible presence of factors that may decrease the efficacy of this drug in this setting. The presence of fetal hydrops decreases the likelihood of success with maternal digoxin mono-therapy, but the reasons are unknown. It is possible that stress and other aspects of fetal hydrops may enhance the binding of digoxin to the placenta or P_{gp}, a drug-transporting protein that is dependent on adenosine triphosphate.[94,107,127] Digoxin binding to these components markedly reduces the concentration of pharmacologically active free digoxin, possibly reducing the efficacy of drug therapy. Thus, in fetuses with severe, advanced cardiac disease; hydrops; or both, combination antiarrhythmic drug therapy should be used to achieve and maintain control of cardiac rhythm.[125]

Cardioactive drugs other than digoxin that have been used to treat fetal arrhythmias are listed in Box 10-8. In many cases, successful fetal therapy has been described in most digoxin nonresponders with the addition of one of these agents. Caution must be exercised when some of these medications are coadministered with digoxin because of known drug-drug interactions that lead to the accumulation of digoxin. The possible impact of the coadministration of some of the more important anti-arrhythmic medications with digoxin on the resulting steady-state serum digoxin concentrations is shown in Table 10-14.

In the past, procainamide was often coadministered with digoxin in digoxin-unresponsive patients. This drug combination appeared to be well tolerated by the mother and fetus and to treat fetal arrhythmia successfully in a number of cases.[107] More recent data indicate the efficacy of the calcium-channel blocking drug flecainide[107] and suggest superiority over procainamide as a second-line therapy alone or in combination with digoxin.[125] These encouraging data on flecainide suggest that diltiazem, a calcium-channel blocker with minimum cardiac depressant activity, might also be useful for the treatment of fetal tachyarrhythmias. A recent case report described the accumulation of flecainide in the fetal compartment at concentrations that exceeded those of maternal blood, underscoring the need for proper dosing strategies guided by close clinical monitoring of both the mother and the fetus.

With advances in the direct fetal administration of medications (e.g., cordocentesis, intra-amniotic drug injection, and direct fetal intramuscular or intra-peritoneal injections),[101,131] adenosine may be a reasonable drug for use in certain patients with complicated cases. Adenosine slows the sinus rate and decreases (blocks) atrioventricular nodal conduction. After bolus administration, the drug's pharmacologic effects are observed within 20 to 30 seconds and are very short-lived. The elimination half-life of adenosine is approximately 10 seconds. Although the drug has been very effective in successfully terminating supraventricular tachycardia in most of the patients who receive it, its effects are short-lived, as previously mentioned. This disorder will recur in many patients, requiring additional antiarrhythmic therapeutic maintenance. Ito and coworkers described one 28-week hydropic fetus with incessant supraventricular tachycardia who, despite the failure of maternal procainamide therapy, initially responded to direct fetal injections of adenosine on two occasions.[107] It recurred until the spontaneous delivery of the infant. Hansmann and colleagues have described success with the direct fetal administration of digoxin alone or in combination.[104] The potential need for repeated, direct fetal injections of adenosine severely limits its clinical usefulness. In those patients whose cases are difficult to manage, adenosine might be a useful adjunct for the termination of supraventricular tachycardia with longer-acting antiarrhythmics maternally administered to maintain improved fetal cardiac rhythm.[125]

Defects in Neural Tube Development and Folic Acid

Of the congenital malformations diagnosed at birth, many involve the neural tube. Although these congenital malformations may be associated with other congenital anomalies, they are often isolated defects. Surviving infants with neural tube defects consume substantial medical resources throughout their lifetimes, usually with marked life-changing consequences for their families. For these reasons, efforts have focused on determining the factors that predispose the conceptus to the development of neural tube defects so that effective preventive therapy can be developed.

TABLE 10-14. Probable Influence of Commonly Coadministered Antiarrhythmic Medications on the Steady-State Serum Digoxin Concentration*

COADMINISTERED MEDICATION	INCREASE IN TROUGH SERUM DIGOXIN CONCENTRATION*(%)
Quinidine	100-200
Amiodarone	50-100
Flecainide	10-20

*Data are presented as possible percentage increases in the steady-state trough serum digoxin concentration. The actual effect on serum digoxin concentration from these digoxin drug-drug interactions is highly variable, necessitating close monitoring.

Modified from Ito S et al: Drug therapy for fetal arrhythmias. Clin Perinatol 21:543, 1994.

Unfortunately, no specific inciting event can be identified in many infants born with neural tube defects; their spectrum is considered a complex genetic disorder reflecting the important influences of both genetics and environmental factors on causation.[91,99] Nevertheless, a considerable amount of data demonstrates the efficacy of folic acid supplementation in preventing neural tube defects in a large number of cases. Because of the timing of neural tube development, periconceptional folic acid supplementation appears to be of the utmost importance.

The neural tube begins to form from the neural plate by the third week after fertilization (see Chapter 38). The neural plate develops infolding that forms the neural groove, with neural folds on both sides. During the middle of the fourth week after fertilization, the neural folds begin to fuse, forming the neural tube. By the end of the fourth week of gestation, the closure of the neural tube is complete, with openings at the cranial (rostral neuropore) and caudal (caudal neuropore) ends. The cranial portion of the neural tube forms the brain and the caudal end develops into the spinal cord.[121] The defects arise from the failure of the neural tube to close anywhere along the tube except (most commonly) at the caudal and cranial portions. Spina bifida is caused by nonfusion of the embryonic halves of the vertebral arches, leading to a condition of diverse presentations and varying severity.

The cause of many neural tube defects is unknown. Some data suggest a possible association between the maternal use of phenytoin, carbamazepine, or valproic acid and neural tube defects. Spina bifida appears to occur in 1% to 2% of newborns whose mothers are receiving valproic acid: The frequency rates for carbamazepine-induced neural tube defects appear to be very similar to those observed with valproic acid.[96] A possible relationship between folate deficiency and the development of neural tube defects is suggested by the apparent association of poor diet, inadequate vitamin supplementation, and the use of folic acid antagonists during pregnancy with an increased risk of neural tube defects.[121] It is interesting that no known association exists between maternal folate-deficient megaloblastic anemia and an increased risk of having an infant with a neural tube abnormality.[121] The long period that is often necessary to manifest microscopic signs of megaloblastic anemia may indicate its absence in early gestation.

A number of studies have assessed the efficacy of folic acid supplementation in reducing the risk and incidence of congenital neural tube defects. Regardless of the findings, considerable controversy has ensued. The published experience strongly suggests that the periconceptional administration of folic acid substantially reduces the overall risk of congenital neural tube abnormalities as well as the risk of recurrence in a later pregnancy. A reduction in the risk of recurrence is important because the incidence of neural tube defects may be as high as 20-fold greater in women with a previous pregnancy resulting in the birth of an infant with a neural tube defect than in the general population (20 cases per 1000 live births compared with an estimated prevalence rate in the general U.S. population of 1.3 cases per 1000 live births).[121] It is important to note that any effect of periconceptional folic acid supplementation must be realized by the fourth week of gestation, at which time neural tube closure is complete. Folic acid supplementation after neural tube closure has no effect on the incidence or severity of congenital neural tube defects. In 1996, the U.S. Food and Drug Administration decided to direct the supplementation of the nation's diet with folic acid. Although altered folate use or deficiency is the compelling hypothesis for the etiology of neural tube defects, it is not the sole mechanism responsible for these pathophysiologic processes.[120] It is quite possible that the variability in the genes of the folate pathway may be the primary modifier of risk and not actually causative.[96] Free radical scavengers and/or free radical scavenging enzyme activity and the status of maternal homocysteine are also important in this regard. With an increasing understanding of the gene array associated with neural tube development and abnormality, universally effective therapy will be defined. Until that time, adequate folic acid supplementation is mandatory; however, some practitioners recommend concurrent antioxidant and trace metal supplementation.

The maternal doses of folic acid that have been used to prevent the development of neural tube defects have varied. For the most part, folic acid doses have ranged from 0.4 to 4 mg/day. The evidence supports a dose of 0.4 to 0.8 mg/day to prevent folate-susceptible abnormalities. As stated earlier, folic acid therapy must be started as soon after conception as possible, if not before (e.g., planned pregnancy), and continued for at least 4 weeks after the beginning of gestation.

ACCESS TO THE FETUS AND FETAL COMPARTMENT BY DIRECT MANIPULATION

Advances in technology have greatly expanded the opportunities to treat fetal disorders by guiding direct access to the fetus or the fetal compartment. Case reports have described successful in utero drug therapy by direct intraperitoneal injection into the amniotic fluid and by direct intramuscular and intravenous drug administration to the fetus.[104,106] Weiner and Thompson described a fetus with supraventricular tachycardia that did not respond to maternal digoxin administration but did respond to multiple intramuscular injections of the drug.[131] Similarly, Gembruch and colleagues have successfully treated supraventricular tachycardia with intravenous digoxin administration to the fetus,[101] and Hughes[106] described intra-amniotic thyroid hormone (T3) for the successful treatment of fetal hypothyroidism complicated by a goiter. Despite the foregoing and other successes, these approaches to fetal drug therapy should be considered only when maternal therapy is not possible or successful because experience with the direct fetal administration of drugs is limited.

Questions remain regarding this approach to drug administration, including drug-dosing guidelines and associated risks such as in utero infection and the precipitation of premature labor. The assessment of drug doses is extremely difficult and empirical at present. Until more experience with this mode of fetal drug therapy is acquired, the dose for an intravenous, intramuscular, or intraperitoneal injection should be based on the weight of the fetus and the volume of amniotic fluid estimated from calculations based on ultrasound and gestational age. The drug dose administered would be the same per unit of body weight that is administered to infants of similar gestational ages.

Similarly, for intra-amniotic drug administration, the volume of amniotic fluid present could be estimated by ultrasound and used as a component of a calculation of the fetal "volume of distribution," which in turn could be used to calculate the dose required to achieve a targeted fetal drug concentration. Finally, once direct fetal drug therapy is instituted, the elimination of the drug through the maternal circulation must also be considered. It may be necessary to provide some maternal drug dosing to retain an adequate drug concentration in the fetal compartment. Obviously, these approaches to fetal drug administration are only initial guidelines, and they require close fetal monitoring for efficacy and safety. The degree of accuracy achieved for targeted drug concentrations in the fetus could be assessed by direct fetal blood sampling,[130] whereas overall efficacy is determined by critical clinical assessment for the desired pharmacologic effect.

FUTURE DIRECTIONS WITH FETAL GENE THERAPY

Most inherited disorders would benefit from therapeutic intervention as early as possible in life to prevent disease expression. Ideally, prevention could be achieved with gene therapy early in pregnancy. Theoretically, such therapy, even during the last two trimesters of pregnancy, could allow the targeting of ever-expanding stem cell populations that may no longer be accessible later in life.

To date, a limited number of studies have used viral vectors to direct fetal gene incorporation. Some difficulties have been encountered in targeting specific genes to specific organs and determining the optimum time points for vector delivery. There is also concern that current strategies, which are aimed at somatic cells, provide insufficient safeguards against genelike transfection. Flake and associates described the successful treatment of a fetus with severe, combined X-linked immunodeficiency by in utero transplantation of paternal bone marrow.[98]

Thus, fetal gene therapy is an approach on the horizon, but is near. Although it appears to be poised for human trials, some important clinical and ethical issues remain to be resolved. When this technology is applied to human genetic disease, a vast new frontier in medicine will be opened. It is hoped that our technological capabilities will not exceed our ability to handle their consequences.

Major challenges persist relative to the identification of optimum vectors and routes of administration to the fetus as well as the real risks associated with the inadvertent modification of germ cell lines and/or aberrations of varying oncogenes.[90] Such a therapeutic approach could have a great impact on eradicating important genetic disorders, including cystic fibrosis, sickle cell disease, spinal cord deformities, and many other diseases encountered in pediatric practice.[90,108]

REFERENCES

Part 1

1. American Academy of Pediatrics Committee on Drugs: The transfer of drugs and other chemicals into human milk. Pediatrics 93:137, 1994.
2. Anderson BJ et al: Caffeine overdose in a premature infant: Clinical course and pharmacokinetics. Anaesth Intensive Care 27:307, 1999.
3. Anderson PO et al: Adverse drug reactions in breastfed infants: Less than imagined. Clin Pediatr (Philadelphia) 42:325, 2003.
4. Andres RL, Day MC: Perinatal complications associated with maternal tobacco use. Semin Neonatol 5:231, 2000.
5. Aranda JV et al: Pharmacokinetic profile of caffeine in the premature newborn infant with apnea. J Pediatr 94:663, 1979.
6. Blumer JL, Reed MD: Neonatal pharmacology. In Jaffe S, Aranda JV (eds): Neonatal and Pediatric Pharmacology: Therapeutic Principles in Practice, 3rd ed. Philadelphia, Lippincott, Williams, and Wilkins, 2005, p 146.
7. Brashear WT et al: Maternal and neonatal urinary excretion of sulfate and glucuronide ritodrine conjugates. Clin Pharmacol Ther 44:634, 1988.
8. Brent RL: Utilization of animal studies to determine the effects and human risks of environmental toxicants (drugs, chemicals, and physical agents). Pediatrics 113:984, 2004.
9. Christesen HB, Melander A: Prolonged elimination of tolbutamide in a premature newborn with hyperinsulinaemic hypoglycaemia. Eur J Endocrinol 138:698, 1998.
10. Christian MS, Brent RL: Teratogen update: Evaluation of the reproductive and developmental risks of caffeine. Teratology 64:51, 2001.
11. Chung AM et al: Antibiotics and breast-feeding: A critical review of the literature. Paediatr Drugs 4:817, 2002.
12. De Swiet M, Lewis PJ: Excretion of anticoagulants in human milk. N Engl J Med 297:1471, 1977.
13. De Wildt SN et al: Glucuronidation in humans: Pharmacogenetic and developmental aspects. Clin Pharmacokinet 36:439, 1999.
14. Dempsey DA, Benowitz NL: Risks and benefits of nicotine to aid smoking cessation in pregnancy. Drug Saf 24:277, 2001.
15. Doering PL, Stewart RB: The extent and character of drug consumption during pregnancy. JAMA 239:843, 1978.
16. Dothey CI et al: Maturational changes of theophylline pharmacokinetics in preterm infants. Clin Pharmacol Ther 45:461, 1989.
17. Ehrnebo M et al: Age differences in drug binding by

plasma proteins: Studies on human foetuses, neonates and adults. Eur J Clin Pharmacol 3:189, 1971.

18. Einarson A et al: How physicians perceive and utilize information from a teratogen information service: The Motherisk Program. BMC Med Educ 4:6, 2004.

19. Erickson SH, Oppenheim GL: Aspirin in breast milk. J Fam Pract 8:189, 1979.

20. Frank DA et al: Growth, development, and behavior in early childhood following prenatal cocaine exposure: A systematic review. JAMA 285:1613, 2001.

21. Fraser FC: The multifactorial/threshold concept—uses and misuses. Teratology 14:267, 1976.

22. Ganapathy V et al: Placental transporters relevant to drug distribution across the maternal-fetal interface. J Pharmacol Exp Ther 294:413, 2000.

23. Genschow E et al: The ECVAM international validation study on in vitro embryotoxicity tests: Results of the definitive phase and evaluation of prediction models. European Centre for the Validation of Alternative Methods. Altern Lab Anim 30:151, 2002.

24. Giacoia GP, Catz CS: Drugs and pollutants in breast milk. Clin Perinatol 6:181, 1979.

25. Ha HR et al: Biotransformation of caffeine by cDNA-expressed human cytochromes P-450. Eur J Clin Pharmacol 49:309, 1996.

26. Hales BF: Modification of the mutagenicity and teratogenicity of cyclophosphamide in rats with inducers of the cytochromes P-450. Teratology 24:1, 1981.

27. Hanson JW et al: The effects of moderate alcohol consumption during pregnancy on fetal growth and morphogenesis. J Pediatr 92:457, 1978.

28. Harvey JA: Cocaine effects on the developing brain: Current status. Neurosci Biobehav Rev 27:751, 2004.

29. Higgins S: Smoking in pregnancy. Curr Opin Obstet Gynecol 14:145, 2002.

30. Hill LM, Malkasian GD Jr: The use of quinidine sulfate throughout pregnancy. Obstet Gynecol 54:366, 1979.

31. Jones MW, Bass WT: Fetal alcohol syndrome. Neonatal Netw 22:63, 2003.

32. Kacew S: Effect of over-the-counter drugs on the unborn child: What is known and how should this influence prescribing? Paediatr Drugs 1:75, 1999.

33. Kaneko S et al: The levels of anticonvulsants in breast milk. Br J Clin Pharmacol 7:624, 1979.

34. Kearns GL et al: Developmental pharmacology—drug disposition, action, and therapy in infants and children. N Engl J Med 349:1157, 2003.

35. Koren G et al: Fetal alcohol spectrum disorder. CMAJ 169:1181, 2003.

36. Koren G et al: Drugs in pregnancy. N Engl J Med 338:1128, 1998.

37. Koup JR et al: Ethosuximide pharmacokinetics in a pregnant patient and her newborn. Epilepsia 19:535, 1978.

38. Kulkarni AP: Role of biotransformation in conceptal toxicity of drugs and other chemicals. Curr Pharm Des 7:833, 2001.

39. Lacroix D et al: Expression of CYP3A in the human liver—evidence that the shift between CYP3A7 and CYP3A4 occurs immediately after birth. Eur J Biochem 247:625, 1997.

40. Laffitte E, Revuz J: Thalidomide: An old drug with new clinical applications. Expert Opin Drug Saf 3:47, 2004.

41. Landauer W: Antiteratogens as analytical tools. In Persaud TVN (ed): Teratogenic Mechanisms: Advances in the Study of Birth Defects. Baltimore, University Park Press, 1979.

42. Lee TC et al: Population pharmacokinetics of intravenous caffeine in neonates with apnea of prematurity. Clin Pharmacol Ther 61:628, 1997.

43. Lee TC et al: Population pharmacokinetic modeling in very premature infants receiving midazolam during mechanical ventilation: Midazolam neonatal pharmaco-kinetics. Anesthesiology 90:451, 1999.

44. Lee TC et al: Theophylline population pharmacokinetics from routine monitoring data in very premature infants with apnoea. Br J Clin Pharmacol 41:191, 1996.

45. Leeder JS: Developmental and pediatric pharmaco-genomics. Pharmacogenomics 4:331, 2003.

46. Loughnan PM: Digoxin excretion in human breast milk. J Pediatr 92:1019, 1978.

47. Lugo RA et al: Pharmacokinetics of dexamethasone in premature neonates. Eur J Clin Pharmacol 49:477, 1996.

48. Manning FA, Feyerabend C: Cigarette smoking and fetal breathing movements. Br J Obstet Gynaecol 83:262, 1976.

49. Meberg A et al: Smoking during pregnancy—effects on the fetus and on thiocyanate levels in mother and baby. Acta Paediatr Scand 68:547, 1979.

50. Mirochnick M et al: Zidovudine pharmacokinetics in premature infants exposed to human immunodeficiency virus. Antimicrob Agents Chemother 42:808, 1998.

51. Musoke P et al: A phase I/II study of the safety and pharmacokinetics of nevirapine in HIV-1-infected pregnant Ugandan women and their neonates (HIVNET 006). AIDS 13:479, 1999.

52. Naeye RL: Relationship of cigarette smoking to congenital anomalies and perinatal death: A prospective study. Am J Pathol 90:289, 1978.

53. Nakamura H et al: Changes in urinary 6-beta-hydroxycortisol/cortisol ratio after birth in human neonates. Eur J Clin Pharmacol 53:343, 1998.

54. Nicol CJ et al: An embryoprotective role for glucose-6-phosphate dehydrogenase in developmental oxidative stress and chemical teratogenesis. FASEB J 14:111, 2000.

55. Niebyl JR et al: Carbamazepine levels in pregnancy and lactation. Obstet Gynecol 53:139, 1979.

56. Nulman I et al: Binge alcohol consumption by non-alcohol-dependent women during pregnancy affects child behaviour, but not general intellectual functioning: A prospective controlled study. Arch Women Ment Health 7:173, 2004.

57. Ohmori S et al: Differential catalytic properties in metabolism of endogenous and exogenous substrates among CYP3A enzymes expressed in COS-7 cells. Biochem Biophys Acta 1380:297, 1998.

58. Olshan A et al: Male-Mediated Developmental Toxicity. New York, Plenum, 1995.

59. Orme ML et al: May mothers given warfarin breast-feed their infants? Br Med J 1:1564, 1977.

60. Pariente-Khayat A et al: Caffeine acetylator phenotyping during maturation in infants. Pediatr Res 29:492, 1991.

61. Pariente-Khayat A et al: Isoniazid acetylation metabolic ratio during maturation in children. Clin Pharmacol Ther 62:377, 1997.

62. Parman T et al: Free radical-mediated oxidative DNA damage in the mechanism of thalidomide teratogenicity. Nat Med 5:582, 1999.

63. Phelan JP: Diminished fetal reactivity with smoking. Am J Obstet Gynecol 136:230, 1980.

64. Phelps DL, Karim Z: Spironolactone: Relationship between concentrations of dethioacetylated metabolite in human serum and milk. J Pharm Sci 66:1203, 1977.

65. Renwick AG: Toxicokinetics in infants and children in

relation to the ADI and TDI. Food Addit Contam 15(Suppl):17, 1998.

66. Rosenberg L et al: Lack of relation of oral clefts to diazepam use during pregnancy. N Engl J Med 309:1282, 1983.

67. Scott CS et al: Morphine pharmacokinetics and pain assessment in premature newborns. J Pediatr 135:423, 1999.

68. Selevan SG et al: A study of occupational exposure to antineoplastic drugs and fetal loss in nurses. N Engl J Med 313:1173, 1985.

69. Sereni F, Principi N: Developmental pharmacology. Annu Rev Pharmacol 8:453, 1968.

70. Shepard TH et al: Update on new developments in the study of human teratogens. Teratology 65:153, 2002.

71. Shillingford AJ, Weiner S: Maternal issues affecting the fetus. Clin Perinatol 28:31, 2001.

72. Singh B et al: Treatment of neonatal seizures with carbamazepine. J Child Neurol 11:378, 1996.

73. Somogyi A, Gugler R: Cimetidine excretion into breast milk. Br J Clin Pharmacol 7:627, 1979.

74. Sonnier M, Cresteil T: Delayed ontogenesis of CYP1A2 in the human liver. Eur J Biochem 251:893, 1998.

75. Strickler SM et al: Genetic predisposition to phenytoin-induced birth defects. Lancet 2:746, 1985.

76. Tateishi T et al: No ethnic difference between Caucasian and Japanese hepatic samples in the expression frequency of CYP3A5 and CYP3A7 proteins. Biochem Pharmacol 57:935, 1999.

77. Tjia JF et al: Theophylline metabolism in human liver microsomes: Inhibition studies. J Pharmacol Exp Ther 276:912, 1996.

78. Unadkat JD et al: Placental drug transporters. Curr Drug Metab 5:125, 2004.

79. Van Lingen RA et al: Pharmacokinetics and metabolism of rectally administered paracetamol in preterm neonates. Arch Dis Child Fetal Neonatal Ed 80:F59, 1999.

80. Vuori E et al: The occurrence and origin of DDT in human milk. Acta Paediatr Scand 66:761, 1977.

81. Webster WS, Freeman JA: Prescription drugs and pregnancy. Expert Opin Pharmacother 4:949, 2003.

Part 2

82. Abhyankar S, Salvi VS: Indomethacin therapy in hydramnios. J Postgrad Med 46:176, 2000.

83. Alcorn J, McNamara PJ: Ontogeny of hepatic and renal systemic clearance pathways in infants: Part I. Clin Pharmacokinet 41:959, 2002.

84. Bardeguez AD et al: Effect of cessation of zidovudine prophylaxis to reduce vertical transmission on maternal HIV disease progression and survival. J Acquir Immune Defic Syndr 32:170, 2003.

85. Berenbaum SA et al: Behavioral effects of prenatal versus postnatal androgen excess in children with 21-hydroxylase-deficient congenital adrenal hyperplasia. J Clin Endocrinol Metab 85:727, 2000.

86. Blackwell SC et al: Abnormal amniotic fluid volume as a screening test prior to targeted ultrasound. Med Sci Monit 9:MT119, 2003.

87. Bolt RJ et al: Glucocorticoids and lung development in the fetus and preterm infant. Pediatr Pulmonol 32:76, 2001.

88. Bolt RJ et al: Body composition in infants with chronic lung disease after treatment with dexamethasone. Acta Paediatr 91:815, 2002.

89. Cerame BI et al: Prenatal diagnosis and treatment of 11beta-hydroxylase deficiency congenital adrenal hyper-plasia resulting in normal female genitalia. J Clin Endocrinol Metab 84:3129, 1999.

90. Coutelle C et al: The hopes and fears of in utero gene therapy for genetic disease—a review. Placenta 24(Suppl B):S114, 2003.

91. Crowther CA, Henderson-Smart DJ: Phenobarbital prior to preterm birth for preventing neonatal periventricular haemorrhage. Cochrane Database Syst Rev 2003; CD000164.

92. Daffos F et al: Prenatal management of 746 pregnancies at risk for congenital toxoplasmosis. N Engl J Med 318:271, 1988.

93. Daly KA et al: Pneumococcal conjugate vaccines as maternal and infant immunogens: Challenges of maternal recruitment. Vaccine 21:3473, 2003.

94. Derewlany LO et al: The transport of digoxin across the perfused human placental lobule. J Pharmacol Exp Ther 256:1107, 1991.

95. Derewlany LO: Role of the placenta in perinatal pharmacology and toxicology. In Radde IC, MacLeod SM (eds): Pediatric Pharmacology and Therapeutics, 2nd ed. St. Louis, Mosby, 1993, p 405.

96. Finnell RH et al: Pathobiology and genetics of neural tube defects. Epilepsia 44(Suppl 3):14, 2003.

97. Fisher DA: Fetal thyroid function: Diagnosis and management of fetal thyroid disorders. Clin Obstet Gynecol 40:16, 1997.

98. Flake AW et al: Treatment of X-linked severe combined immunodeficiency by in utero transplantation of paternal bone marrow. N Engl J Med 335:1806, 1996.

99. Frey L, Hauser WA: Epidemiology of neural tube defects. Epilepsia 44(Suppl 3):4, 2003.

100. Garland M: Pharmacology of drug transfer across the placenta. Obstet Gynecol Clin North Am 25:21, 1998.

101. Gembruch U et al: Direct intrauterine fetal treatment of fetal tachyarrhythmia with severe hydrops fetalis by antiarrhythmic drugs. Fetal Ther 3:210, 1988.

102. Guinn DA et al: Single vs weekly courses of antenatal corticosteroids for women at risk of preterm delivery: A randomized controlled trial. JAMA 286:1581, 2001.

103. Hakkola J et al: Xenobiotic-metabolizing cytochrome P450 enzymes in the human feto-placental unit: Role in intrauterine toxicity. Crit Rev Toxicol 28:35, 1998.

104. Hansmann M et al: Fetal tachyarrhythmias: Transplacental and direct treatment of the fetus—a report of 60 cases. Ultrasound Obstet Gynecol 1:162, 1991.

105. Hill MD, Abramson FP: The significance of plasma protein binding on the fetal/maternal distribution of drugs at steady-state. Clin Pharmacokinet 14:156, 1988.

106. Hughes IA: Management of fetal endocrine disorders. Growth Horm IGF Res 13(Suppl A):S55, 2003.

107. Ito S et al: Drug therapy for fetal arrhythmias. Clin Perinatol 21:543, 1994.

108. Keswani SG, Crombleholme TM: Gene transfer to the tracheobronchial tree: Implications for fetal gene therapy for cystic fibrosis. Semin Pediatr Surg 13:44, 2004.

109. Kleinman CS, Nehgme RA: Cardiac arrhythmias in the human fetus. Pediatr Cardiol 25:234, 2004.

110. Kramer WB et al: Treatment of polyhydramnios with indomethacin. Clin Perinatol 21:615, 1994.

111. Lamer P: Current controversies surrounding the use of repeated courses of antenatal steroids. Adv Neonatal Care 2:290, 2002.

112. Liggins GC, Howie RN: A controlled trial of antepartum glucocorticoid treatment for prevention of the respiratory distress syndrome in premature infants. Pediatrics 50:515, 1972.

113. Lin MT et al: Postnatal outcome of fetal bradycardia without significant cardiac abnormalities. Am Heart J 147:540, 2004.

114. Linder N, Ohel G: In utero vaccination. Clin Perinatol 21:663, 1994.

115. Linder N et al: Placental transfer of measles antibodies: Effect of gestational age and maternal vaccination status. Vaccine 22:1509, 2004.

116. Matsui D: Prevention, diagnosis, and treatment of fetal toxoplasmosis. Clin Perinatol 21:675, 1994.

117. Mattison DR et al: Physiologic adaptations to pregnancy: Impact on pharmacokinetics. In Yaffe SJ, Aranda JV (eds): Pediatric Pharmacology: Therapeutic Principles in Practice, 2nd ed. Philadelphia, WB Saunders Co, 1992, p 81.

118. Pacifici GM, Nottoli R: Placental transfer of drugs administered to the mother. Clin Pharmacokinet 28:235, 1995.

119. Pang S: Congenital adrenal hyperplasia. Endocrinol Metab Clin North Am 26:853, 1997.

120. Pippenger CE: Pharmacology of neural tube defects. Epilepsia 44(Suppl 3):24, 2003.

121. Rieder MJ: Prevention of neural tube defects with periconceptional folic acid. Clin Perinatol 21:483, 1994.

122. Shalak L, Perlman JM: Hemorrhagic-ischemic cerebral injury in the preterm infant: Current concepts. Clin Perinatol 29:745, 2002.

123. Shankaran S et al: The effect of antenatal phenobarbital therapy on neonatal intracranial hemorrhage in preterm infants. N Engl J Med 337:466, 1997.

124. Simone C et al: Drug transfer across the placenta: Considerations in treatment and research. Clin Perinatol 21:463, 1994.

125. Simpson JM, Sharland GK: Fetal tachycardias: Management and outcome of 127 consecutive cases. Heart 79:576, 1998.

126. Sklansky M: New dimensions and directions in fetal cardiology. Curr Opin Pediatr 15:463, 2003.

127. Unadkat JD et al: Placental drug transporters. Curr Drug Metab 5:125, 2004.

128. Ward RM: Pharmacologic enhancement of fetal lung maturation. Clin Perinatol 21:523, 1994.

129. Ward RM: Pharmacological treatment of the fetus: Clinical pharmacokinetic considerations. Clin Pharmacokinet 28:343, 1995.

130. Wax JR, Blakemore KJ: Fetal blood sampling. Obstet Gynecol Clin North Am 20:533, 1993.

131. Weiner CP, Thompson MI: Direct treatment of fetal supraventricular tachycardia after failed transplacental therapy. Am J Obstet Gynecol 158:570, 1988.

132. Yang K: Placental 11 beta-hydroxysteroid dehydrogenase: Barrier to maternal glucocorticoids. Rev Reprod 2:129, 1997.

11 Surgical Treatment of the Fetus

Timothy M. Crombleholme

As prenatal diagnosis has become increasingly sophisticated and as technological advances have enhanced the range of diagnostic capabilities, invasive therapies have developed from our expanded understanding of the natural history and pathophysiology of structural anomalies. In the 1960s and 1970s, despite rapid progress in prenatal diagnosis, few invasive therapies were considered, much less employed. Once a prenatal diagnosis was made, parents had only two choices: terminating pregnancy, if prior to 24 weeks, or continuing to term. An additional option that was soon recognized was altering the delivery site so that appropriate pediatric specialists would be available immediately to treat the newborn with a congenital anomaly. As the natural history of many prenatally diagnosed anomalies became better understood, early delivery was recognized as an option to avoid ongoing damage caused by the anomaly in utero. Fortunately, today there are more alternatives. In this chapter we present a comprehensive review of the treatment options currently available for the entire spectrum of fetal diagnoses that are potentially surgically correctable. The current indications, contraindications, and outcomes for shunting procedures, fetoscopic surgery, and open fetal surgery are reviewed.

FETAL SHUNTING PROCEDURES

A new era in invasive fetal therapy began in the early 1980s when several independent groups introduced shunting procedures for hydrocephalus and hydronephrosis.[33] These first few cases represented an extension of invasive fetal therapy from simple intrauterine blood transfusion for a medical illness to the first attempts at in utero treatment of structural anomalies.

During this period, hydronephrosis and hydrocephalus were recognized more frequently with ultrasound examination. The prenatal natural history of these lesions was established by serial sonographic observation of untreated cases.[16,23,75] Fetuses with high-grade obstructive uropathy followed to term were often born with advanced hydronephrosis, type IV cystic dysplasia, and pulmonary hypoplasia, conditions that were incompatible with life. In the case of obstructive hydrocephalus, it was known that shunting in the newborn period improved neurologic outcome, and it was reasoned that decompression in utero might avert progressive brain

damage.[49] At the time, the understanding of the natural history, pathophysiology, and patient selection criteria was rudimentary and incomplete at best. However, experimental work by numerous investigators, in appropriate animal models, helped to define the pathophysiology of these lesions and establish the theoretical basis for intervention.[35]

Ventriculoamniotic Shunts

Among the most important lessons learned in invasive fetal therapy were the necessity to understand the natural history of the untreated condition and the ability to identify fetuses most likely to benefit from treatment. On the basis of the observation that postnatal shunting for hydrocephalus is beneficial, Birnholz and Frigoletto[33] reported using serial percutaneous cephalocentesis to treat hydrocephalus in utero. The results of their efforts were disappointing because the fetus had unrecognized intracranial abnormalities and Becker-type muscular dystrophy. Shortly thereafter, ventriculoamniotic shunts were developed to provide consistent ventricular decompression.[33] Although these procedures enjoyed a brief period of enthusiasm, results proved to be poor, often related to undetected central nervous system (CNS) and non-CNS anomalies, and the shunts failed to provide consistent ventricular decompression because of obstruction or migration.[18,64]

The fetus that is likely to benefit from ventriculoamniotic shunting is one with isolated progressive ventriculomegaly.[16,18,52,64] However, the incidence of associated CNS anomalies in reported series has varied from 70% to 84%, with many of these defects being undetected prenatally.[16,18,52,64] Most reports list the incidence of isolated progressive ventriculomegaly as being from 4% to 14%.[52,58] Even with improved diagnostic capabilities, identifying appropriate candidates for fetal intervention may be difficult.

If ventriculoamniotic shunting is to be reinstated, selection criteria must first be defined. These criteria would include fetuses with isolated progressive ventriculomegaly, accurate exclusion of other CNS and extra-CNS anomalies, and development of a valved shunt less likely to clog, become dislodged, or cause ventriculitis than previous versions. In fact, a completely internalized ventriculoperitoneal shunt may have advantages over percutaneous shunting because of the limitations associated with percutaneous shunting. With the increased accuracy of ultrafast fetal MRI for diagnosing CNS abnormalities, the ability to identify isolated rapidly progressive hydrocephalus is greater now than ever before.[58] It is not clear, however, that ventricular decompression, even in these highly selected fetuses, will improve the postnatal outcome in these cases.

Thoracoamniotic Shunts

Thoracoamniotic shunting is the treatment of choice for management of the fetus with symptomatic fetal *hydrothorax* (FHT) before 32 weeks of gestation (Fig. 11-1). In contrast, thoracentesis is a diagnostic maneuver performed to obtain pleural fluid for differential cell count and viral culture and to establish whether the effusion is chylous. Even repeated thoracentesis usually provides inadequate decompression of the fetal chest. There have been several reports of thoracentesis for FHT performed with either complete resolution or a good outcome despite reaccumulation. Others have had disappointing results with repeated thoracentesis for FHT, owing to rapid reaccumulation of the effusion and neonatal death from respiratory insufficiency.[62,76] Spontaneous resolution of FHT may occur in as many as 10% of cases, and resolution after thoracentesis may or may not be related to the procedure. In general, thoracentesis alone cannot provide continuous decompression of the fetal chest to allow pulmonary expansion and prevent pulmonary hypoplasia.

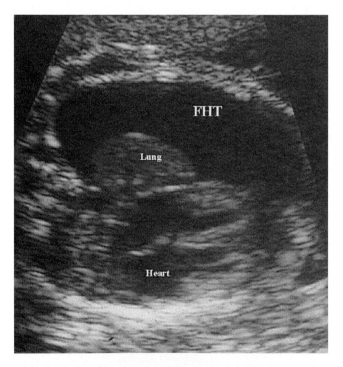

FIGURE 11-1. Fetal sonogram demonstrating larger tension fetal hydrothorax (FHT) compressing the adjacent lung and causing shift of the heart into the contralateral hemithorax. (From Shaaban AF et al: The role of ultrasonography in fetal surgery and invasive fetal procedures. Semin Roentgen 34:62, 1999.)

Thoracoamniotic shunting for FHT, first reported by Rodeck and colleagues in 1988, provides continuous decompression of the fetal chest, allowing lung expansion.[85] If instituted early enough, this procedure allows compensatory lung growth and may prevent neonatal death from pulmonary hypoplasia.

The indications for thoracoamniotic shunting are not well defined. Most authors consider the presence of FHT-induced hydrops or polyhydramnios to be an indication for shunting.[62,76,85] In addition, thoracoamniotic shunting is recommended for primary FHT with evidence of effusion under tension, even in the absence of hydrops (Fig. 11-2). Because spontaneous resolution has been observed even in severe cases of FHT, we reserve thoracoamniotic shunting for cases in which tension hydrothorax recurs after two thoracenteses.

Thoracoamniotic shunts have also been used in the treatment of *congenital cystic adenomatoid malformation* (CCAM) of the lung with a dominant cyst (see Chapter 42). Nicolaides and associates reported the first case of CCAM treated by shunt insertion in utero in 1987.[77] Decompression of a large, type I CCAM in a fetus of 20 weeks' gestation by percutaneous placement of a thoracoamniotic shunt was subsequently reported by Clark in 1987.[17] This procedure resulted in resolution of both mediastinal shift and hydrops and successful delivery at 37 weeks of gestation. Postnatally, the infant underwent uneventful resection of the CCAM. Six subsequent cases of thoracoamniotic shunting in CCAM had a good outcome in five of the six fetuses treated. Recently, Wilson and colleagues updated this single center's experience with 10 cases of thoracoamniotic shunting for CCAMs.[97] There was a 51% reduction in the CCAM volume immediately after the placement of the thoracoamniotic shunt. Seven of the 10 fetuses treated by thoracoamniotic shunt survived.

More commonly, it is the type III CCAM, in which microcystic lesions become enlarged, that results in hydrops and intrauterine fetal demise. In these later cases, open fetal surgery and resection are indicated. However, in the rare instances in which there is a single large cyst in CCAM responsible for hydrops, thoracoamniotic shunting is the treatment choice.

Vesicoamniotic Shunts

The first case of a fetus with obstructive uropathy treated in utero by vesicoamniotic shunting was reported by Golbus and associates in 1982.[36] Advances soon followed in diagnosis, technique, shunt design, and patient selection.[22,23,54,75] The procedure became widely implemented before stringent selection criteria for treatment were developed and before therapeutic efficacy of the procedure was established. The widespread use of vesicoamniotic shunts also had the effect of shifting cases away from centers studying these questions and limiting attempts to better define the role of vesicoamniotic shunting in the management of fetal obstructive uropathy. A detailed discussion of vesicoamniotic shunting appears later (see "Prenatal Treatment" under "Obstructive Uropathy").

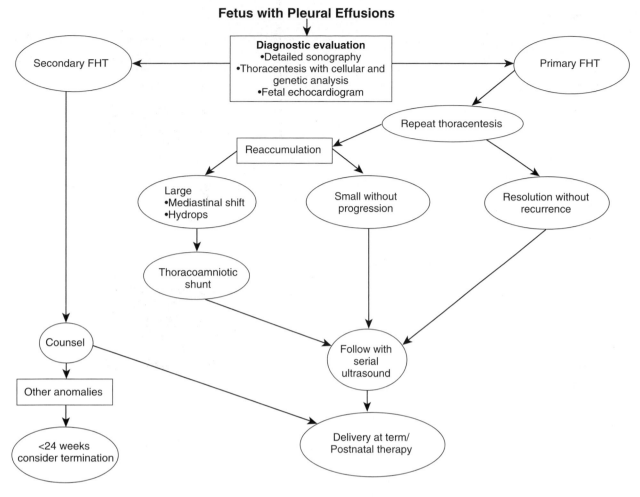

FIGURE 11-2. Proposed algorithm for the management of fetal hydrothorax.

OPEN FETAL SURGERY

Experience has demonstrated the usefulness of shunting procedures in some fetal conditions, but the limitations of the catheters have also become apparent. In addition to their problems with obstruction, dislodgment, and short functional life span, shunting procedures are not adequate for many conditions. The experience with open fetal surgery in the 1960s for the treatment of erythroblastosis fetalis was discouraging, and it was soon abandoned with the introduction of percutaneous techniques of fetal transfusion.[60] Harrison and colleagues introduced open fetal surgery for the treatment of obstructive uropathy in 1982.[41] Although the procedure (bilateral ureterostomy) was technically successful, the fetus made no urine, oligohydramnios persisted, and the infant died of pulmonary hypoplasia. Despite this initial unsuccessful result, a new era in fetal therapy was opened. Soon, successful open surgical procedures were reported in the treatment of obstructive uropathy,[23] congenital diaphragmatic hernia, cystic adenomatoid malformation,[38] and sacrococcygeal teratoma (Table 11-1).[1] An appreciation of the fetal natural history of these

conditions and the success of Harrison's group at the University of California at San Francisco encouraged groups in Philadelphia, Boston, Denver, Memphis, and Cincinnati in the United States, as well as Seoul (South Korea), Melbourne (Australia), and Paris (France), to undertake open fetal surgery. Clinical experience is still quite limited, however: it is estimated that fewer than 400 cases of open fetal surgery are performed per year worldwide.

Obstructive Uropathy

Posterior urethral valves (PUVs) are the leading cause of antenatally diagnosed lower urinary tract obstruction and are the structural genitourinary anomaly amenable to fetal therapy. PUVs are found only in the male population and have an incidence of 1 in 5000 births. The mortality rate in these patients has been reported to be as high as 63%, especially when PUV is associated with severe oligohydramnios owing to pulmonary hypoplasia (see also Chapter 49).

The natural history and outcome of antenatally diagnosed obstructive uropathy differ significantly from

TABLE 11-1. Treatable Fetal Malformations

FETAL MALFORMATION	FETAL PRESENTATION	FETAL/NEONATAL CONSEQUENCES	FETAL TREATMENT OPTIONS
Acardiac/acephalic twin (TRAP sequence)	Polyhydramnios	IUFD, hydrops, cardiac failure Multifocal leukoencephalomalacia	Fetoscopic cord ligation Fetoscopic cord coagulation
Amniotic band syndrome	Edematous limb from constricting band Umbilical cord constriction	Limb amputation Fetal death	Fetoscopic laser lysis of bands —
Aqueductal stenosis	Rapidly progressive isolated hydrocephalus	Neurologic damage	Ventriculoamniotic shunt Ventriculoperitoneal shunt
Complete heart block	Hydrops, slow heart rate	IUFD, neonatal death	Fetal epicardial pacemaker
Congenital diaphragmatic hernia (CDH)	Herniated viscera in chest	IUFD, pulmonary hypoplasia and respiratory insufficiency, neonatal death	Open fetal tracheal clip Fetoscopic tracheal clip Fetoscopic tracheal balloon
Cystic adenomatoid malformation of the lung (CCAM)	Chest mass, mediastinal shift Hydrops	Pulmonary hypoplasia, IUFD, neonatal death	Thoracoamniotic shunt (if there is dominant cyst) Fetal resection of CCAM (if it is solid tumor)
Fetal hydrothorax	Mediastinal shift, hydrops, polyhydramnios	Pulmonary hypoplasia	Thoracoamniotic shunt
Myelomeningocele (MMC)	Neural tube defect, "lemon" sign, "banana" sign	Paralysis, hindbrain herniation Hydrocephalus	Open fetal MMC repair
Neck masses (cervical teratoma, lymphangioma)	Polyhydramnios, neck mass, absent stomach bubble	Inability to ventilate due to lack of airway Anoxic brain injury, neonatal death	EXIT procedure
Ovarian cyst	Wandering cystic abdominal mass	Ovarian torsion, polyhydramnios	Cyst aspiration
Posterior urethral valves	Hydronephrosis and oligohydramnios	Renal dysplasia and renal insufficiency Pulmonary hypoplasia and respiratory insufficiency	Vesicoamniotic shunt Cystoscopic laser ablation of valves Open vesicostomy
Sacrococcygeal teratoma	High output failure Hydrops	IUFD, prematurity, tumor rupture, hydrops, hemorrhage	Open resection Radiofrequency coagulation
Twin-twin transfusion syndrome	Oligohydramnios and polyhydramnios, growth discordance	IUFD, heart failure Multifocal leukoencephalomalacia	Serial amnioreduction Microseptostomy Cord coagulation Selective laser photocoagulation

EXIT, ex utero intrapartum treatment; IUFD, intrauterine fetal death; TRAP, twin reversed arterial perfusion.

those of postnatally diagnosed obstruction. Reports of PUVs diagnosed at birth reveal a significant mortality associated with respiratory and renal insufficiency.[75] Oligohydramnios occurring before 24 weeks of gestation profoundly affects fetal lung development during the critical transition from the canalicular to the alveolar phase. Profound oligohydramnios owing to PUV is also associated with clubfoot and Potter facies, and there is a 9% incidence of chromosomal anomalies in obstructive uropathy.

PRENATAL DIAGNOSIS

The major diagnostic tool in obstructive uropathy remains antenatal ultrasonography.[51] Fetal ultrasonography may detect urinary tract anomalies at as early as 12 to 13 weeks of gestation.

The prenatal diagnosis of obstructive uropathy requires an understanding of physiologic and pathologic dilation of the urinary tract. *Hydronephrosis* is the most common pathologic finding on prenatal ultrasonography in cases of fetal obstructive uropathy. The discovery of echogenic kidneys with pronounced cystic dysplasia is an ominous finding, universally associated with a poor overall prognosis. However, with less severe pathology, distinguishing pathologic dilation of the renal pelvis (pelviectasis) from physiologic dilation is difficult, especially early in pregnancy. Transient dilation of the fetal urinary tract is a relatively common finding, occurring in 1 out of every 100 pregnancies. This frequency is far more common than that of pathologic obstruction, as found on postnatal evaluation and autopsies.

Measurements of the anteroposterior (AP) pelvic diameter and its ratio to the overall AP renal diameter have been proposed as criteria for discriminating between normal and abnormal pelvic dilation.[9] In fetuses younger than 20 weeks' gestation, the parameters of abnormal pelvic distention have not been defined. A recent prospective study correlating screening ultrasonography in fetuses at 16 to 23 weeks' gestation with postnatal outcome revealed that a pelvic diameter greater than 4 mm was 76% sensitive in identifying a pathologic obstruction.[8] Furthermore, fetuses with a urinary tract obstruction demonstrated a more rapid increase in this dilation over the remainder of gestation than did fetuses without obstruction. For fetuses older than 23 weeks' gestation, threshold values associated with pathologic fetal hydronephrosis are an AP pelvic diameter greater than 10 mm, and a ratio of the AP pelvic diameter to the AP renal diameter of greater than 0.5. The additional finding of caliectasis provides even stronger support to a pathologic etiology (Fig. 11-3A).[56] If any of these criteria are met, the patient should undergo further sonographic assessment and a full prognostic profile, including sequential taps of the fetal bladder for urinary electrolyte determination if oligohydramnios develops in a case of suspected bladder outlet obstruction.

Lower urinary tract obstruction must be distinguished from the other pathologic causes of fetal hydronephrosis. The presence of megacystis, thickened bladder wall, posterior urethral dilation, bilateral hydronephrosis, and ureterectasis characterizes the changes associated with PUV (see Fig. 11-3B) and urethral atresia in contrast to the more common ureteropelvic junction obstruction, ureterovesical obstruction, or vesicoureteral reflux. These cases of lower urinary tract obstruction lead to oligohydramnios, as urinary output is the major component of amniotic fluid after 16 weeks' gestation. In contrast, a unilateral obstruction, such as a ureteropelvic junction obstruction, does not lead to oligohydramnios, and it carries a universally favorable prognosis provided that the other kidney functions normally.[23]

Among cases of fetal urinary tract obstruction, a fetus with preserved renal function produces more hypotonic urine, whereas one with advanced renal dysfunction is a "salt waster," producing less hypotonic urine. The

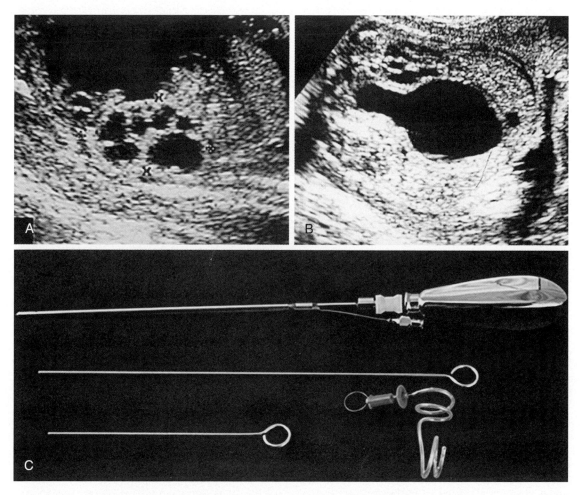

FIGURE 11-3. A, Fetal sonogram demonstrating hydronephrosis with caliceal dilation owing to posterior urethral valves. **B,** Obstructed bladder outlet demonstrating the "keyhole" sign owing to posterior urethral valves. **C,** Standard trocar and Rocket catheter for fetal shunting procedures. (From Shaaban AF et al: The role of ultrasonography in fetal surgery and invasive fetal procedures. Semin Roentgen 34:62, 1999.)

usefulness of assessing urine chemistry in fetal obstructive uropathy lies in the separation of fetuses into "good" or "poor" prognostic categories based on preservation of renal function reflected by the tonicity of the fetal urine.[22] In one study, urine samples taken from fetuses who subsequently had a good outcome revealed levels of Na^+ less than 100 mEq/L, Cl^- less than 90 mEq/L, and osmolarity less than 210 mOsm/L.[35] These values were chosen because they were two standard deviations from the mean values of fetuses with a good prognosis. Fetuses with urine chemistries beyond these values had irreversible renal damage and suffered from severe oligohydramnios and pulmonary insufficiency. The efficacy of these proposed criteria were subsequently confirmed to reflect postnatal outcome and to appropriately select fetuses for intervention.[22] In a separate study, this approach was modified to include three sequential vesicocenteses at 24-hour intervals. This regimen permits a comparative analysis of stagnant urine (first sample) with fresh urine (third sample). Fresh urine samples more accurately reflect fetal renal function, and this approach increases the predictive value of fetal urinary electrolytes.[54]

Urinary β_2-microglobulin levels have become an important adjunct in predicting the severity of renal damage. In one study, β_2-microglobulin levels below 2 mg/L were found to have as good a predictive value as urinary sodium levels below 70 mEq/L.[74] Furthermore, urinary β_2-microglobulin levels may have greater value in predicting the outcome of fetal obstructive uropathy in the absence of oligohydramnios. In one study, β_2-microglobulin levels from fetuses with evidence of obstructive uropathy but without oligohydramnios were significantly higher in those who eventually developed renal insufficiency at 1 year of age. This distinguishing feature may enable the selective antenatal treatment of fetuses with a good prognostic profile who, despite normal amniotic fluid volume, are still at risk for ongoing renal damage.

PRENATAL TREATMENT

The two goals of prenatal intervention in fetal obstructive uropathy are decompression of the obstructed fetal urinary bladder and restoration of amniotic fluid dynamics. Percutaneous vesicoamniotic shunting has been the most common technique used to accomplish these goals with minimal maternal morbidity in patients with isolated lower urinary tract obstruction and a good prognostic profile (see Fig. 11-3C).[22,35,64,74]

Because of the lack of a prospective, randomized trial, the most difficult question to address in the treatment of fetal obstructive uropathy is the efficacy of prenatal decompression. The only series that attempted to address this question, albeit in a retrospective analysis, was reported by Crombleholme and coworkers.[22] In fetuses predicted to have either good or poor prognoses by fetal urine electrolyte and ultrasound criteria, the survival rate was greater among those decompressed in utero, as opposed to those who were not decompressed. In the group of fetuses predicted to have a poor prognosis by selection criteria, 10 fetuses were treated.

Three of those fetuses were electively terminated, four neonates died from pulmonary hypoplasia or renal dysplasia, and three neonates survived. All three survivors had had restoration of normal amniotic fluid levels and had no pulmonary complications, but two subsequently developed renal failure and underwent renal transplantation. Among the 14 patients with no intervention, there were no survivors (11 terminations and three neonatal deaths from pulmonary hypoplasia).

In the group of fetuses predicted to have a good prognosis by selection criteria, nine fetuses were treated, with one elective termination (after the development of procedure-related chorioamnionitis), no deaths, and eight neonatal survivors. Of the seven patients in the good prognosis group who were not treated, five survived and two died after birth. Two of the survivors later developed renal failure.

When oligohydramnios develops during the canalicular stage of lung development (16 to 24 weeks), the fetus usually has pulmonary hypoplasia that precludes survival.[22,75] When in utero intervention for obstructive uropathy associated with oligohydramnios restores amniotic fluid volume, neonatal demise from pulmonary hypoplasia is clearly averted.[22,36] In the group of fetuses reported by Crombleholme and coworkers, there was a preponderance of oligohydramnios in the poor prognosis group (23 of 24) compared with the good prognosis group (7 of 16).[22] Despite this, fetuses from the good prognosis group seemed to survive as a direct result of fetal treatment. In the good prognosis group, six of the seven fetuses with oligohydramnios had intervention, and all six survived with normal renal function. However, the patient with oligohydramnios who was not treated died at birth of pulmonary hypoplasia. In the entire series, uncorrected oligohydramnios was associated with a 100% neonatal mortality rate. Normal or restored amniotic fluid volume was associated with a 94% survival rate.[22]

Although in utero decompression appears to prevent neonatal death from pulmonary hypoplasia, the effect of in utero decompression on renal function is less clear. The maternal morbidity of vesicoamniotic shunting has been reported to be minimal, but there has been a high incidence (14%) of associated chorioamnionitis.[22,36] These cases of chorioamnionitis occurred before routine use of prophylactic antibiotics and during a period when long-term (4 to 16 hours) bladder catheterization, rather than aspiration, was used for fetal urine sampling. In addition, there have been reports of shunt-induced abdominal wall defects with herniation of bowel through trocar stab wounds and maternal ascites from leakage of amniotic fluid into the maternal peritoneal cavity.[64]

The usefulness of vesicoamniotic shunts is limited by brief duration of decompression, risk of infection, catheter obstruction or dislodgment, fetal injury during placement, and potentially inadequate decompression of the fetal urinary tract.[22,35] These factors make vesicoamniotic shunts less appealing for long-term decompression of the urinary tract early in gestation. In addition, there is a growing appreciation that the long-term outcome of children after vesicoamniotic shunting may be complicated by renal insufficiency, bladder dysfunction, and growth problems.[32] Freedman and coworkers reported outcomes in 14 patients who survived beyond 2 years of age. Renal function was normal in only 6 (43%). Of the remaining 8 patients, 5 had renal failure requiring kidney transplantation and 3 have chronic renal insufficiency. Three of the 4 whose obstructive uropathy was due to posterior urethral valves have required bladder augmentation. In addition, growth has been a problem, with 86% below the 25th percentile and 50% below the 5th percentile. The postnatal problems after vesicoamniotic shunting, including renal failure and bladder dysfunction, have been a catalyst for the development of alternative open fetal surgical or fetoscopic techniques to treat obstructive uropathy in utero.[24,81]

Dissatisfaction with catheter decompression first led Harrison and colleagues to perform a small series of open fetal procedures for PUVs, initially bilateral ureterostomies, and, subsequently, open vesicostomy.[23,41] Open vesicostomy is certainly the most definitive compression of the urinary tract. However, there are increased maternal risks with this approach. These issues have led some investigators to pursue percutaneous fetal cystoscopy and fulguration or laser ablation of PUVs.[24,80,81] Although this technique appears to be technically feasible and may have theoretical advantages over shunting, there have been no survivors in the initial experience.

Once the diagnosis and favorable prognostic profile are confirmed, we recommend percutaneous vesicoamniotic shunting for fetal lower urinary tract obstruction. Fetoscopic cystoscopy is offered as an alternative to assess the posterior urethra to determine if the fetus is a candidate for laser ablation of valves. Those who are not candidates for laser ablation have a vesicoamniotic shunt placed. Vesicostomy is rarely employed but might be considered if vesicoamniotic shunting fails to decompress the bladder and restore amniotic fluid dynamics. Experienced ultrasound guidance is essential in vesicoamniotic shunt placement. Furthermore, serial sonography is critical to confirm sustained shunt function, good bladder drainage, decompression of the upper urinary tracts, and normalization of amniotic fluid volume.

Congenital Diaphragmatic Hernia (See also Chapter 42, Parts 5 and 8, and Chapter 45.)

Congenital diaphragmatic hernia (CDH) is most often a posterolateral defect in the left hemidiaphragm (88%) on one side, which leads to herniation of the viscera into the thorax, resulting in pulmonary hypoplasia and respiratory embarrassment. CDH occurs in approximately 1 in 2500 to 5000 live births and as frequently as 1 in 2200 prenatal ultrasound studies.[2] This discrepancy between neonates who survive birth and transport to a tertiary newborn treatment center and fetuses diagnosed by prenatal ultrasonography supports the notion of a "hidden" mortality.[2,3,40] With inclusion of cases

that never reach the treatment stage of disease, the mortality approaches 75%. Although familial cases with an autosomal-dominant inheritance have been reported, most cases of CDH are sporadic.

Associated anomalies are seen in 25% to 57% of all cases of CDH and in 95% of stillborns with CDH and include congenital heart defects, hydronephrosis, renal agenesis, intestinal atresia, extralobar sequestrations, and neurologic defects, including hydrocephalus, anencephaly, and spina bifida.[29] Chromosomal anomalies, including trisomy 21, 18, and 13, occur in association with CDH in 10% to 20% of cases that are diagnosed prenatally.

PRENATAL DIAGNOSIS
The diagnosis of CDH is often an unexpected finding on routine prenatal ultrasound examination or a scan prompted by polyhydramnios. Critical ultrasound findings include the presence of viscera in the right or the left hemithorax above the level of the inferior margin of the scapula or at the level of the four-chamber view of the heart (Fig. 11-4A).[69] The hypoechoic signal of the fluid-filled stomach, gallbladder, or bowel can be distinguished from the hyperechoic signal of the fetal lung. A small ipsilateral lung, a defect in the ipsilateral diaphragm, and a shift of the mediastinum away from the affected side are other common findings. In the case of a right-sided CDH, the liver may be the only herniated organ, and it is difficult to distinguish it from the fetal lung because of their similar echodensities. Identification of the diaphragm does not exclude the possibility of CDH because some portion of the diaphragm is usually present in CDH.

The differential diagnosis includes type I CCAM, bronchogenic cysts, neurenteric cysts, and cystic mediastinal teratoma, which may mimic the appearance of herniated bowel. Identification of abnormal upper abdominal anatomy and presence of peristalsis in herniated bowel loops helps distinguish CDH from other diagnoses. The location of the gallbladder in fetuses with CDH is helpful because it may be displaced to the midline or in the left upper quadrant or herniated into the right chest.

In most severe cases, the liver and the stomach are present in the thorax. Bowing of the portal vein or sinus venosus to the left of the midline or coursing of the portal branches to the lateral segment of the left lobe of the liver above the diaphragm, which can be seen with color flow Doppler imaging, is the best sonographic predictor of liver herniation (see Fig. 11-4B).[43] In addition, the position of the stomach (easily seen in contrast to the more echogenic fetal lung) in a posterior or midthoracic location is also associated with liver herniation. Several sonographic features have been suggested as prognostic indications in cases of CDH, including polyhydramnios, early gestation diagnosis (less than 24 weeks), stomach herniation, herniation of the left lobe of the liver, evidence of fetal cardiac ventricular disproportion before 24 weeks of gestation, and lung-to-head circumference ratios. However, no single sonographic feature of CDH has been uniformly helpful in

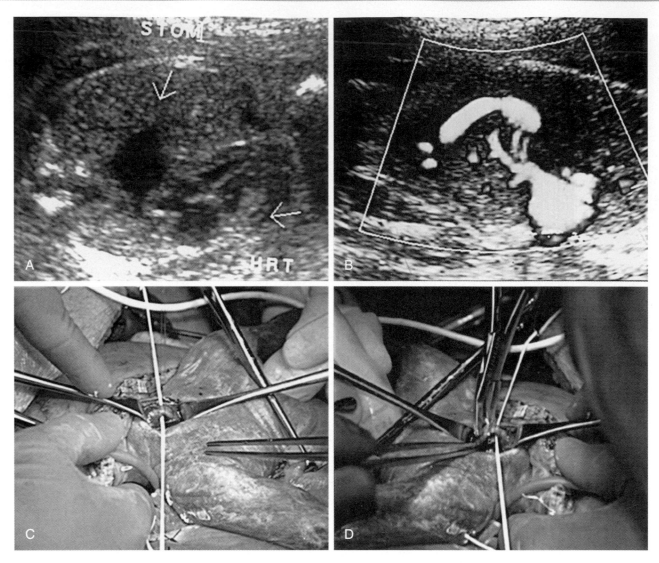

FIGURE 11-4. A, Fetal sonogram demonstrating a large congenital diaphragmatic hernia (CDH), with the stomach in the chest seen at the level of the four-chamber view of the heart. **B,** Power Doppler image demonstrating bowing of the sinus venosus toward the left in left CDH. **C,** Exposure of the fetal trachea during tracheal clip application. **D,** Application of fetal tracheal clip. (From Shaaban AF et al: The role of ultrasonography in fetal surgery and invasive fetal procedures. Semin Roentgen 34:62, 1999.)

predicting outcome. A more direct estimate of pulmonary hypoplasia that correlates with neonatal outcome is needed.

The ratio of the lung area to the head circumference (LHR) (using the two-dimensional area of the right lung measured at the level of the four-chamber view of the heart) was assessed prospectively to determine its value in predicting the postnatal outcome with conventional therapy.[69] The LHR, although still useful, has proven less reliable in predicting survival than was previously thought, especially in the most severe category. LHRs greater than 1.4 are still associated with an excellent survival rate in the 80% to 85% range, with only 25% of fetuses requiring extracorporeal membrane oxygenation (ECMO). An LHR between 1.0 and 1.4 is associated with a survival of about 75%, with 69% requiring ECMO. The largest change has been in the survival observed with

fetuses whose LHR is less than 0.9; in these cases, survival of up to 62% of fetuses can be expected but almost all survivors require ECMO. It is not known if the improved survival when the LHR is less than 1.0 reflects improved neonatal care, such as the use of gentle ventilation strategies, or if greater experience with larger numbers of patients in this category of LHR is now giving a more accurate reflection of survival.

The position of the liver in fetuses with left-sided CDH remains an important prognostic factor. In the most recent experience at Children's Hospital of Philadelphia, survival in left-sided CDH when the liver is in the abdomen was 91%, with only 24% of patients requiring ECMO. On the other hand, survival in left-sided CDH with significant herniation of the left lobe of the liver was only 51%, with 79% of patients requiring ECMO. These statistics apply, however, only to cases of

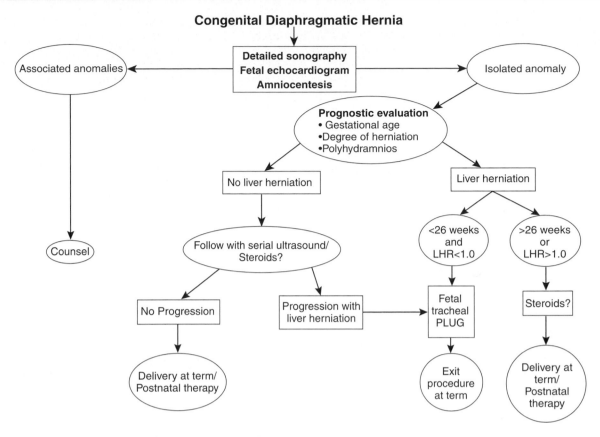

Congenital Diaphragmatic Hernia

FIGURE 11-5. Proposed algorithm for the management of fetal congenital diaphragmatic hernia.

left-sided CDH. The LHR does not apply to right-sided CDH, in which the liver is almost always herniated, and where it is not necessarily associated with a worse prognosis. In fact, in a review of the Children's Hospital of Philadelphia experience with 22 cases of prenatally and 6 cases of postnatally diagnosed right-sided CDH, Hedrick and coworkers found an overall survival rate of 70%[46] (Fig. 11-5). Among those diagnosed prenatally, there was a choice to terminate the pregnancy in four cases, and of the remaining 18, 16 survived (89%; 73% if terminations are included). Half of the patients (12 of 23, 53%) required ECMO, and among those, the survival rate was 75%. Unfortunately, none of the prognostic features that assist us in counseling parents whose fetus has a left-sided CDH apply to those whose fetus has a right-sided CDH. However, obstetrical complications including polyhydramnios, preterm labor, and premature rupture of membranes occurred in 50% of the right-sided CDH pregnancies.

PRENATAL TREATMENT

Despite the advances in neonatal care, such as high-frequency oscillatory ventilation, inhaled nitric oxide, and ECMO, the mortality rate of isolated CDH remains substantial. Out of frustration with these grim statistics, Harrison and colleagues pioneered fetal surgery for CDH.[37,40,43] Unfortunately, the survival rate after complete in utero repair was poor. These failures resulted

from herniation of the left lobe of the liver. Reduction of the liver during repair inevitably resulted in kinking of the umbilical vein, leading to fetal bradycardia and cardiac arrest. Herniation of the left lobe of the liver became an exclusion criterion for complete in utero repair of CDH. However, even if cases with left lobe herniation are excluded, the survival rate in the series by Harrison and colleagues was only 41%, which was no better than with conventional postnatal therapy at the time. A prospective trial sponsored by the National Institutes of Health (NIH) confirmed these findings; thus, there is no indication for complete repair of CDH in utero. The shortcomings of in utero repair led to the development of a new approach.

Known for decades, fetal tracheal occlusion results in accelerated fetal lung growth in animal models.[6] It was not until 1994, however, that tracheal occlusion was applied to the problem of CDH.[27] In animal models of CDH, tracheal occlusion induces lung growth, and increases alveolar surface area, alveolar number, and visceral reduction from the chest.[27] The results of these experiments were so compelling that fetal tracheal occlusion was applied in human fetuses with severe CDH. The results of open fetal surgery for a tracheal clip procedure in high-risk patients with CDH were disappointing in both the University of California at San Francisco and Children's Hospital of Philadelphia experience.[30,44] As a result of the poor outcomes with the procedure, another procedure was described using transuterine endoscopy, or FETENDO.[94] The results from the FETENDO approach in high-risk fetuses with CDH were promising, and the NIH sponsored a trial comparing fetoscopic tracheal clip application with conventional postnatal therapy. Shortly after initiation of the FETENDO trial for CDH, the University of California at San Francisco group developed a less invasive endoluminal balloon tracheal occlusion technique requiring only a single port as opposed to the five for the FETENDO approach.[39] This approach, using a detachable balloon, was incorporated into the NIH-sponsored trial. The trial was halted after enrollment and randomization of 24 fetuses because of an unexpectedly high survival rate with standard postnatal care. The Data and Safety Monitoring Board concluded that further recruitment would not result in significant differences between the groups.[42] Eight of 11 (73%) in the tracheal occlusion group and 10 of 13 (77%) in the group that received standard postnatal care survived. There are several important lessons to be learned from this trial. First, these results apply primarily to fetuses with an LHR of greater than 0.9 and less than 1.4. It remains unknown if the most severely affected fetuses (with LHR less than 0.9 and liver herniation) would do better with fetal tracheal occlusion. Second, the outstanding survival rates achieved with "standard" therapy

were obtained at a tertiary center that cares for a large number of fetuses and neonates with diaphragmatic hernia. These results may not be generalizable to centers that do not have extensive experience caring for critically ill newborns with severe pulmonary hypoplasia due to CDH.

In the most severe cases of diaphragmatic hernia, fetal intervention is still being investigated. In Belgium, Jan Deprest is offering fetoscopic balloon tracheal occlusion for patients with CDH and LHRs of less than 0.9 and herniation of the liver. An alternative fetal treatment offered for patients with high-risk CDH is the ex utero intrapartum treatment (EXIT)-to-ECMO strategy. The use of EXIT-to-ECMO was first described for the management of patients with severe CDH (liver herniation and an LHR of less than 0.9) associated with congenital heart disease.[11] This has now been applied to cases of high-risk CDH by teams at Children's Hospital Boston and at Cincinnati Children's Hospital (Fig. 11-6). Data demonstrating that this approach is superior to conventional postnatal therapy in either survival or morbidity rates are not yet available. The rationale for this approach is that by transitioning directly from placental support to ECMO support, the infant is never hypoxic, acidotic, or hypotensive and is never exposed to barotrauma from vigorous neonatal resuscitation. In addition, during venovenous ECMO, oxygenated blood

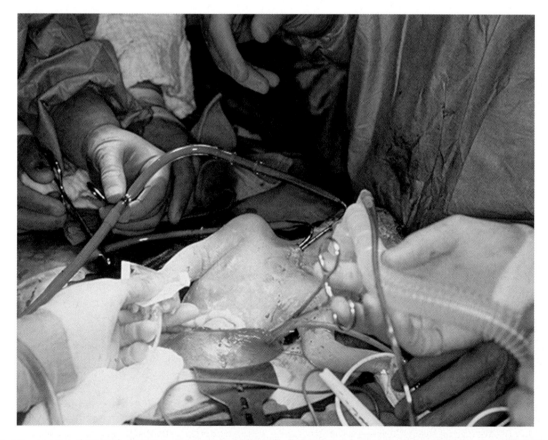

FIGURE 11-6. Intraoperative photograph during ex utero intrapartum treatment (EXIT)-to-extracorporeal membrane oxygenation (ECMO) procedure for severe CDH (ratio of the lung area to the head circumference [LHR] of 0.7, and left lobe of liver herniated into the chest) associated with tetralogy of Fallot. Note the arterial and venous cannulae are already in place.

is delivered into the right heart and the pulmonary vascular bed, which may have direct therapeutic effects. From a maternal risk standpoint, this approach does obligate the mother to surgical delivery. From the fetal standpoint, because this approach is reserved for fetuses with high-risk CDH with liver herniation and LHR less than 0.9 who would be expected to require ECMO, no additional fetal risk is incurred. Whether EXIT-to-ECMO improves survival or reduces morbidity associated with CDH is not known.

Congenital Cystic Adenomatoid Malformation (See also Chapter 42, Part 5.)

CCAM is a rare pulmonary maldevelopment that is usually restricted to one lobe of the lung. Grossly, CCAM represents a multicystic mass of pulmonary tissue with proliferation of bronchial structures.[91] These lesions may result from a failure of maturation of bronchiolar structures or focal pulmonary dysplasia arising in the fifth or sixth week of gestation. Histologic studies reveal rapid vascular and epithelial growth within the tumor.[91] Findings of accelerated cellular proliferation and decreased apoptosis within resected CCAM specimens further suggest a benign neoplastic development.

CCAM is a rare anomaly that occurs slightly more often in the male population than in the female population. These lesions are almost always unilateral (85% to 95%), but occasionally they arise bilaterally (2%). Associated anomalies include renal agenesis or dysgenesis, truncus arteriosus, tetralogy of Fallot, jejunal atresia, CDH, hydrocephalus, and skeletal anomalies. It has been suggested that approximately 6% of prenatally diagnosed cases of CCAM "resolve."[65] This may in fact be because CCAMs become isoechogenic with adjacent normal lung, rendering them sonographically invisible. In these cases, fetal MRI demonstrates the presence of the CCAM even when ultrasound cannot.

Stocker and coworkers proposed a histologic classification of CCAMs as types I through III, according to cyst size and relative number.[91] A single cyst or a small number of large cysts between 3 and 10 cm is classified as a type I CCAM, which typifies 50% of postnatal cases. Multiple small cysts make up a type II lesion, occurring in approximately 40% of postnatal cases. Type III lesions are composed of relatively homogeneous microcystic tissue.

PRENATAL DIAGNOSIS

The prenatal diagnosis of CCAM can be difficult and relies on a number of sonographic features.[65,66] Usually, a mass is identified in the fetal chest (Fig. 11-7). This mass may be solid, cystic, or both, usually without evidence of systemic arterial blood flow by color Doppler ultrasonography. If present, cysts may be solitary or multiple. With large CCAMs, mediastinal shift may occur away from the lesion, and polyhydramnios resulting from esophageal compression may be present. In the worst cases, evidence of cardiac compression and fetal hydrops may be found. Fetal hydrops is universally associated with ensuing fetal demise and relates to cardiac or caval compression from tumor expansion within the thoracic cavity.

The differential diagnosis includes CDH; cystic hygroma; bronchogenic, enteric, or pericardial cysts; neuroblastoma; bronchopulmonary sequestration; and bronchial atresia or stenosis. Large microcystic CCAMs are highly echogenic and thus are distinguished easily from neuroblastoma. The absence of peristalsis helps distinguish CCAM from herniated bowel in a patient with CDH. Using color and power Doppler imaging, the demonstration of a systemic blood supply emanating from the descending thoracic or abdominal aorta suggests the diagnosis of *bronchopulmonary sequestration* or hybrid CCAM lesion. A systemic arterial feeding vessel to an echogenic lung mass was previously considered pathognomonic of bronchopulmonary sequestration; however, Cass and associates have reported a series of "hybrid lesions," which histologically appear to be CCAMs but have a systemic arterial supply.[15] The natural history of hybrid lesions appears to be more favorable than CCAM but less favorable than bronchopulmonary sequestration.

Sonographic criteria taken from studies correlating the Stocker classification, or microcystic versus macrocytic appearance, with fetal outcome have been unreliable in predicting the development of fetal hydrops. A more consistent correlation may exist between overall volume of the lesion at presentation and the likelihood of development of fetal hydrops. Crombleholme and colleagues demonstrated in a small retrospective study that the development of hydrops correlated with the volume of the CCAM at the time of presentation.[21] In order to follow patients and correct for fetal growth, the cystic adenomatoid malformation (CAM) volume was divided by the head circumference to yield the CAM volume ratio (CVR). Based on retrospective data, a CVR of 1.6 was determined from the mean of the CVR of the group of fetuses that did not develop hydrops plus 2 standard deviations of the mean to identify 95% of fetuses who would be at low risk for the development of hydrops. Fetuses with a CVR of less than 1.6 at presentation were defined as being at low risk for hydrops, and those fetuses with a CVR of greater than 1.6 at presentation were defined as being at high risk for the development of hydrops. A prospective study conducted with 55 patients using CVRs confirmed that a CVR of less than 1.6 identified a group of fetuses at very low risk for the development of hydrops. Only one patient in this group developed hydrops and required fetal intervention. The exceptions to this rule were the CCAMs that had a dominant cyst constituting more than one third of the volume of the CCAM. These cysts can enlarge rapidly, and their prenatal natural history is distinct from that of a solid tumor, which grows more slowly. Serial measurements of CAM volumes and CVRs show that the growth of CCAMs is exponential between 20 and 25 weeks' gestation, after which the CCAM growth reaches a plateau. The mean gestational age at which this growth plateau is reached is 25 weeks of gestation, but it can range from 23 to 30 weeks. After the plateau is reached, there is a slow decrease in the

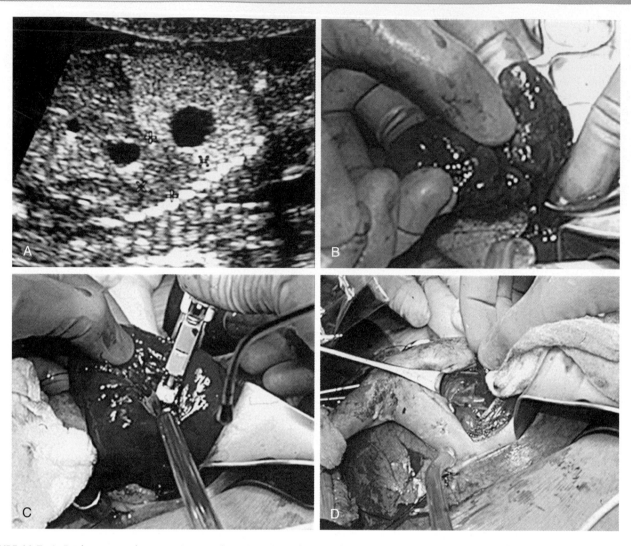

FIGURE 11-7. **A,** Fetal sonogram demonstrating an echogenic congenital cystic adenomatoid malformation of the lung (CCAM), with a single large cyst and compressed normal lung outlined by cursors posteriorly. **B,** Exposure of CCAM through fetal thoracotomy. **C,** Resection of CCAM from adjacent normal lung and hilum using surgical stapler. **D,** Fetal pleural cavity after resection of the CCAM. (From Shaaban AF et al: The role of ultrasonography in fetal surgery and invasive fetal procedures. Semin Roentgen 34:62, 1999.)

size of the CCAM. Subjectively, this may appear to be a greater decrease in the appearance of the CCAM as the fetus continues to grow around the CCAM. No fetuses followed by serial CVRs developed hydrops once they reached the growth plateau. This is an important milestone, as the fetus is usually assured of a favorable outcome once the growth plateau is reached.

PRENATAL TREATMENT

The indication for treating a fetus with a CCAM is the development of nonimmune hydrops. The form of treatment depends on the type of CCAM. Those CCAMs with a dominant cyst may respond to cyst aspiration and, if it recurs, to thoracoamniotic shunting (Fig. 11-8).

In contrast to the approach to type I CCAMs with a dominant cyst, solid type III CCAMs require open fetal surgery for resection of the CCAM. In the combined experience of Children's Hospital of Philadelphia and

University of California at San Francisco, with 26 cases of open fetal surgery to resect fetal CCAMs, the survival rate has been 61%. The survival of the fetus undergoing fetal surgery for CCAM resection is clearly influenced by fetal hemodynamic status. Many of the fetuses referred for fetal surgery for CCAMs are in advanced hydrops and are almost moribund at the time of surgery. A significant improvement in the outcome of fetal surgery has been achieved by the combination of close serial observation, allowing fetal surgery in the earliest stages of hydrops, and the use of intraoperative echocardiography. The intraoperative management of these patients has changed to include obtaining intravenous access in all patients for the administration of crystalloid or blood products to address volume status, and of inotropic agents to improve contractility. The need for either of these interventions is assessed by echocardiography to determine the adequacy of ventricular filling, the

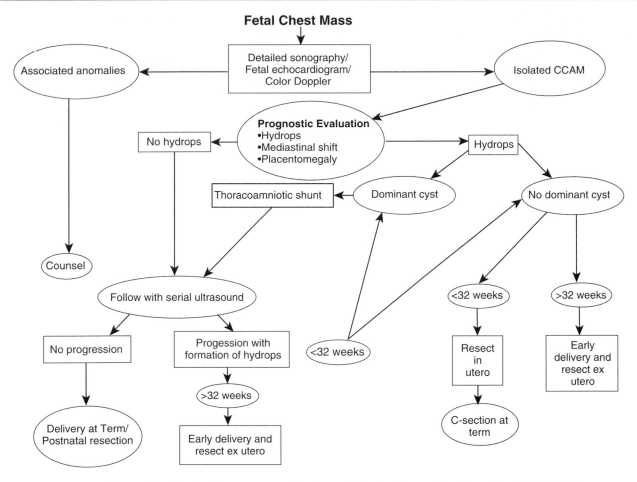

FIGURE 11-8. Proposed algorithm for the management of fetal congenital cystic adenomatoid malformation (CCAM) of the lung.

contractility of the heart, and the competence of the atrioventricular valves during the procedure. A recent retrospective study comparing the survival after fetal surgery for fetuses with conditions associated with hydrops managed before or after routine intraoperative echocardiographic monitoring found an increase from 42% before to 78% afterward.[55]

When fetal surgery is not an option, the use of maternal steroids had been reported to arrest the growth of fetal CCAMs.[93] Although the mechanism is unknown, it is thought that steroids may induce the plateau in CCAM growth to occur earlier in the gestation. Because CCAMs do plateau in growth, it is difficult without prospective data to be certain whether steroids induced the growth plateau or the plateau would have occurred anyway.[21]

Fetal surgery for CCAM is performed with maternal laparotomy with exposure of the uterus and ultrasound to determine the orientation of the fetus and the placenta to plan the hysterotomy in the upper uterine segment overlying the fetal chest. The hysterotomy is made and the fetal arm and chest are exposed, leaving the head and remainder of the body within the amniotic sac. A fetal thoracotomy exposes the lobe containing the CCAM (see Fig. 11-7). The mass is exteriorized, and any systemic feeding vessels and the pulmonary vein are

draining the CCAM are ligated. Normal adjacent lobe or lobes are preserved and dissected from the CCAM using electrocautery. The lobar hilum is divided using a surgical stapler (see Fig. 11-7). The thoracotomy is then closed. The fetus is returned to the amniotic cavity and the hysterotomy closed. Ultrasound examinations should be performed to confirm the resolution of placentomegaly and fetal hydrops, which usually takes 1 to 2 weeks. In addition, ultrasonography is helpful in assessing chorioamniotic separation or low amniotic fluid volume. Similarly, daily fetal echocardiography in the early postoperative period is needed to detect the presence of constriction of the ductus arteriosus and tricuspid regurgitation while the patient is on postoperative indomethacin therapy. Later, weekly ultrasound studies should be performed to confirm compensatory fetal lung growth. Cesarean section is planned for just before term or earlier for uncontrolled premature labor. In survivors of fetal surgery for CCAM, the outcome has been excellent, with minimal or no need for postnatal ventilatory support.

Sacrococcygeal Teratoma

A sacrococcygeal teratoma (SCT) is formed from multiple neoplastic tissues that lack organ specificity, that are foreign to the sacrococcygeal region, and that are derived from all three germ layers. SCT is thought to arise from totipotent somatic cells originating in the primitive knot (Hensen node) or caudal cell mass and, by an unknown mechanism, to escape the normal inductive influences of the surrounding normal cells. SCT is the most common tumor of the newborn, occurring in 1 in 35,000 to 40,000 live births.[31]

The American Academy of Pediatrics Surgical Section (AAPSS) classification system groups these tumors according to the relative amount of pelvic or external tumor present.[7] The importance of this classification system relates to the ease of detection and resection and, consequently, survival. Type I tumors are completely external and easily identified on prenatal ultrasound examination or at birth, leading to early referral and resection with less morbidity. In contrast, type IV tumors are completely internal and are usually recognized late, after they have undergone malignant transformation and become symptomatic. Type II has intrapelvic extension of SCT, and type III has intra-abdominal extension of SCT. Fortunately, most SCTs are type I or II.

Although the postnatal mortality of SCT is quite low and relates to development of malignant transformation, prenatal mortality from SCT is over 50% as a consequence of associated physiologic derangement or mass effect of the tumor.[31] These effects are related to a vascular "steal" phenomenon, polyhydramnios-induced preterm labor, tumor rupture, and dystocia. Depending on tumor size, rate of growth, ratio of cyst to solid composition, and probably the tissue components of the tumor, the metabolic requirements of SCT vary dramatically. Furthermore, spontaneous internal or external hemorrhage of the SCT may result from necrotic or cystic degeneration of the tumor as it outgrows its blood supply or because of minor trauma in utero. The resulting fetal anemia may initiate or exacerbate the effects of the vascular steal. Both mechanisms may indeed lead to high output failure, placentomegaly, and hydrops.

PRENATAL DIAGNOSIS

The diagnosis of SCT is usually made by obstetric ultrasonography performed as a screening procedure or to assess uterine size too large for date (polyhydramnios versus tumor enlargement). Characteristic findings are of a caudal or intrapelvic mass, which can be routinely identified during the second trimester (Fig. 11-9A,B). The sonographic appearance of a fetal SCT may be cystic, solid, or mixed, and it may demonstrate irregular echogenic patterns secondary to areas of tumor necrosis, cystic degeneration, internal hemorrhage, or calcification.[90] Other critical sonographic information includes the presence of abdominal or pelvic extension, evidence of bowel or urinary tract obstruction, assessment of the integrity of the fetal spine, and documentation of lower extremity function.

The major differential diagnosis includes myelomeningocele, meconium pseudocyst, and obstructive uropathy. Sonographically detectable features that may

exclude these other possibilities include the presence of normal kidneys, the absence of solid components and calcifications within the mass, the presence of spinal dysraphic features, and the lack of a meconium appearance to the fluid contained within the cysts. Echocardiographic and Doppler ultrasound measurements are essential after the diagnosis of a large SCT. Echocardiographic features that should be monitored serially include inferior vena cava diameter, combined ventricular output, and descending aortic flow velocity. In addition, Doppler ultrasonography is useful to detect reversal of diastolic blood flow in the umbilical arteries, which is indicative of "placental steal" by the SCT. Most importantly, signs of fetal hydrops should be sought, including pleural or pericardial effusions, ascites, skin or scalp edema, cardiomegaly, or placentomegaly. Follow-up examinations in fetuses with hemodynamically significant SCT demonstrate marked increases in combined ventricular output, descending aortic flow, and umbilical venous flow. Total placental flow increases dramatically. However, the portion of total descending aortic flow directed toward the placenta decreases as a result of steal of the descending aortic blood flow by the enlarging SCT. At least weekly, if not twice weekly, sonography and echocardiography should be performed on patients with SCT to detect the development of high output failure as early as possible.

PRENATAL TREATMENT

The published clinical experience with fetal surgery for SCT is limited to a few series of patients treated at the University of California at San Francisco and the Children's Hospital of Philadelphia.[1] Review of the patients from these centers who were followed closely with serial ultrasonography and echocardiography reveals that the success of fetal intervention relies on early aggressive therapy before the onset of advanced physiologic or physical disturbance. If fetal intervention is to be successful, then candidates must be selected with the earliest signs of high cardiac output physiology before the development of frank hydrops and severe placentomegaly. If lung maturity has been reached, treatment should be focused on cesarean section delivery for postnatal resection of the tumor. Before lung maturity, fetal surgery (see Fig. 11-9C) is an option as long as overt hydrops has not developed and there is no evidence of preterm labor.

Experience with 30 cases of prenatally diagnosed fetuses with SCT was recently reported.[1,47] The mean gestational age at diagnosis was 23 weeks, with SCT occurring in one fetus out of three sets of twins. The outcomes in this series included terminations in 4, fetal deaths in 5, neonatal deaths in 7, and 14 survivors. Of note, significant obstetrical complications occurred in 81% of the pregnancies, including polyhydramnios ($n = 7$), oligohydramnios ($n = 4$), preterm labor ($n = 13$), preeclampsia ($n = 4$), gestational diabetes ($n = 1$), HELLP (*h*emolysis, *e*levated *l*iver enzyme levels and a *l*ow *p*latelet count) syndrome ($n = 1$), and hyperemesis ($n = 1$). Fetal intervention in this series included cyst aspiration ($n = 6$), amnioreduction ($n = 3$), amnioinfusion

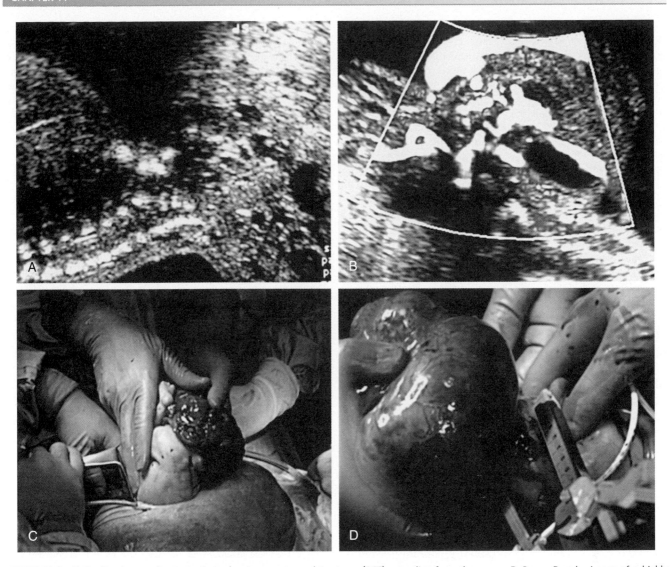

FIGURE 11-9. A, Fetal sonogram demonstrating a large sacrococcygeal teratoma (SCT) extending from the coccyx. **B,** Power Doppler image of a highly vascular SCT. **C,** Exposure of SCT during open fetal surgery for resection. **D,** Base of the SCT, including its vascular pedicle about to be divided using a surgical stapler. (From Shaaban AF et al: The role of ultrasonography in fetal surgery and invasive fetal procedures. Semin Roentgen 34:62, 1999.)

(n = 1), and open fetal surgical resection (n = 4). It is interesting that only 4 of the 15 fetuses with solid SCTs at risk for the development of placental steal, placentomegaly, and hydrops met the criteria for fetal surgery. Of the four fetuses who underwent fetal surgery, all were successfully debulked and delivered at a mean gestational age of 29 weeks' gestation (range, 27.6 to 31.7 weeks). The outcomes in these fetuses included a neonatal death due to closure of the ductus arteriosus in utero with secondary heart failure. A second child sustained in utero embolization after fetal resection with loss of the left kidney and multiple jejunal atresias. One child had chronic lung disease and another developed metastatic endodermal sinus tumor at 1 year of age.

In an effort to avoid the risk of open fetal surgery, some groups have attempted to use laser or radio-frequency ablation (RFA) or tumor embolization. The University of California at San Francisco group reported a disappointing experience with RFA used in four pre-natally diagnosed SCTs.[78] Two fetuses died secondary to hemorrhage after a significant portion of the tumor mass was ablated. The other two fetuses were delivered at 28 and at 31 weeks' gestation, with evidence of extensive perineal and gluteal necrosis. Another case report of RFA described fetal demise on postoperative day 2. Ibrahim and coworkers reported a newborn in whom RFA resulted in a large soft tissue defect, hypo-plastic hip joint, and loss of sciatic nerve function.[53,57] The uncontrolled thermal effects of RFA may preclude its safe use to treat fetal SCT because of the close proximity of the tumor to the anorectal complex, vagina, urethra, sciatic nerves, and hip joints.

As is the case with other fetal conditions that may cause hydrops and placentomegaly, SCT can precipitate the maternal "mirror" syndrome. This is an absolute contraindication to fetal surgery, and every mother considering fetal surgery in the presence of a hydropic fetus and associated placentomegaly should be screened for this syndrome. One of the earliest signs is the development in the mother of proteinuria and peripheral edema. A more ominous indication is the development of maternal hypertension.

In SCT, as in CCAM, close scrutiny must be given to the mother's postoperative fluid balance as the high output failure in the fetus resolves and placental flow improves. The situation is especially tenuous in cases of the maternal mirror syndrome. Routine postoperative echocardiographic assessment should include measurement of ventricular diameters, combined ventricular output, descending aortic flow, umbilical vein flow, and vena cava diameter. Consideration should be given to percutaneous umbilical blood sampling to check for fetal anemia and to perform fetal blood transfusion should evidence for high output failure persist. With resolution of high output failure, decreased or resolved polyhydramnios, and control of preterm labor, a cesarean delivery should be planned for as close to term as possible.

Myelomeningocele (See Chapter 38, Part 8.)

Myelomeningocele (MMC) is a protrusion of the meninges and spinal cord through a defect in the vertebral arches, muscle, and skin. MMC is associated with significant postnatal morbidity and lifelong disability and a small but significant mortality rate related to complications.

MMC is a relatively common anomaly affecting 1 in 2000 live births.[89] The disabilities associated with MMC include paraplegia, hydrocephalus, sexual dysfunction, skeletal deformities, bowel and bladder incontinence, and cognitive impairment. Although most children with MMC have normal intelligence, 15% require some form of custodial care.

Dietary folate supplementation has been shown to prevent MMC in some cases. To be effective, folate must be supplemented soon after conception, but 50% of women of childbearing age do not take supplemental folate, and most pregnancies are unplanned. In addition, it is estimated that 30% of neural tube defects are refractory to folate supplementation. For these reasons, despite folate supplementation, MMC is an anomaly that probably will continue to affect children.

Traditionally, efforts to treat MMC have focused on postnatal surgical correction to prevent infection and to improve physical disabilities that cannot be corrected or reversed. The rationale for prenatal correction of MMC is to repair the defect before neurologic damage has occurred or when there is still potential for recovery.

The neurologic damage in MMC is hypothesized to result from the initial defective spinal cord development and the damage to the exposed spinal cord caused by failure of mesodermal migration. This has been referred to as the two-hit hypothesis. Examination of the spinal cords of mid-gestation fetuses with MMC shows near-normal cord development in most cases.[71] In addition,

leg movement in fetuses with MMC has been observed at as early as 16 to 17 weeks of gestation. In contrast, most fetuses with MMC exhibit severe neurologic impairment of the lower extremities by the time of birth, suggesting that the neurologic injury may occur later in gestation.[71] This injury may occur during labor or as a result of passage through the birth canal.[63] The neurologic injury may also occur by direct abrasion of the exposed cord against the uterine wall during gestation. An additional insult to the spinal cord may be a constituent of the amniotic fluid. However, amniotic fluid at 34 weeks of gestation was found to be more toxic to rat spinal cords in an in vitro organ culture model than was amniotic fluid from earlier in gestation.

Animal models that mimic human MMC have been developed in primates,[72] rats,[49] pigs,[50] and sheep.[70] Perhaps the model that comes closest to simulating human MMC is the ovine model. In this model, laminectomy is performed at 75 days of gestation, and MMC repair is performed at 100 days of gestation. At birth, lambs that do not undergo fetal repair have MMC-like lesions, flaccid paralysis, incontinence, and absent hind limb somatosensory-evoked potentials. In contrast, lambs that do undergo repair in utero are normal.[70]

PRENATAL DIAGNOSIS
Elevation of maternal serum α-fetoprotein concentrations obtained in the first trimester of pregnancy identified 75% to 80% of pregnancies with MMC before 16 weeks of gestation.[79] Amniocentesis is performed in at-risk cases identified by screening for α-fetoprotein concentration in maternal serum and amniotic fluid. α-Fetoprotein and acetylcholinesterase elevations suggest the presence of a neural tube defect. The structural defect can be readily identified by ultrasonography by 18 to 22 weeks' gestation.[79] The presence of an MMC may also be suggested by the presence of a "lemon" sign, which is a scalloping of the frontal bones. A full anatomic survey should be performed to detect associated anomalies such as ventriculomegaly, Chiari malformation with hindbrain herniation, and clubfoot. The presence or absence and quality of leg and foot movements should be assessed, but it may be difficult to distinguish spontaneous from reflex fetal movement. Ultrafast fetal magnetic resonance imaging (MRI) provides additional anatomic detail about the MMC and the brain.

PRENATAL TREATMENT
The first attempted repair in utero of an MMC was reported in a letter by Bruner and colleagues in 1987; they used a fetoscopic technique to apply a skin graft in two fetuses. A full report of this experience revealed that four fetuses were operated on between 22 and 24 weeks' gestation.[13] There were two deaths: one from chorioamnionitis, requiring delivery 1 week postoperatively, and the second from placental abruption on the day of surgery. The two other fetuses were delivered at 28 and 35 weeks' gestation. Both fetuses required ventriculoperitoneal shunting postnatally and surgery to close the defect, and it is not clear that there

was any neurologic benefit. This fetoscopic approach has since been abandoned.

The first evidence of improved neurologic function from repair of MMC in utero was reported by Adzick and coworkers in 1998.[4] Open fetal surgical repair of a large T11-to-S1 MMC was performed at 23 weeks of gestation. Postnatally, the infant had a right clubfoot with a neurologic L4 level and a left foot with an L5 level. Postnatal MRI demonstrated resolution of the hindbrain herniation, and there was no hydrocephalus. Almost all neonates with thoracolumbar MMC are paraplegic and require ventriculoperitoneal shunting for hydrocephalus. The outcome in this case suggested the potential neurologic benefit of in utero repair of MMC. Subsequent experience in 10 cases, between 22 and 25 weeks of gestation, by this same group demonstrated by pre- and postoperative fetal MRI that closure of the MMC in utero reverses the hindbrain herniation of the Chiari malformation. In addition, only 1 of the 10 required ventriculoperitoneal shunting.[92] Bruner and colleagues reported the Vanderbilt experience at the same time, with 29 cases between 24 and 30 weeks of gestation.[14] At birth, there was evidence of hindbrain herniation in only 38% of these patients compared to 95% in a postnatal comparison group. In addition, 17 of the 29 (59%) required ventriculoperitoneal shunts, which compared favorably with a postnatal comparison group in which they were required in 91%.

The Children's Hospital of Philadelphia group has reported experience with 50 cases in which fetal MMC repair resulted in resolution of hindbrain herniation in 100% of cases by 6 weeks postoperatively as assessed by fetal MRI.[92] In addition, the postnatal shunt rate in these patients was 43%, which is lower than the predicted shunt rate of 84% based on 297 historical controls from the Children's Hospital of Philadelphia spina bifida clinic between 1993 and 2000.[84] It is important to note that there were three fetal deaths (6%) in this series. This is a substantial mortality considering MMC is not a lethal anomaly in utero. These deaths were the result of fetal arrhythmia during the procedure, caused by cord compression in one, chorioamnionitis in one, and severe prematurity in the third.

The preliminary results at three centers, Children's Hospital of Philadelphia, University of California at San Francisco, and Vanderbilt, led to an NIH-sponsored, prospective, randomized clinical trial of 200 patients comparing fetal surgery to postnatal treatment of MMC in the MOMS trial (Management of Myelomeningocele Study).[5] The selection criteria for the MOMS trial include MMC at T1 through S1 with hindbrain herniation, maternal age greater than or equal to 18 years; gestational age at randomization of 19 0/7 weeks to 25 6/7 weeks; and a normal karyotype. The exclusion criteria include being a non-U.S. resident, multifetal pregnancy, insulin-dependent pre-gestational diabetes, fetal anomaly unrelated to MMC, fetal kyphosis of greater than 30 degrees, history of incompetent cervix, placenta previa, other serious maternal medical condition, cervix less than 20 mm by ultrasound, obesity, previous spontaneous singleton delivery at less than 37 weeks' gestation,

maternal-fetal Rh isoimmunization, positive maternal human immunodeficiency virus or hepatitis B or C, no support person to stay with the mother at the center, uterine anomaly, failing psychosocial evaluation, and inability to comply with travel and follow-up protocols. The primary outcome variable of the MOMS trial is whether fetal repair of MMC at 19 to 25 weeks' gestation improves outcome measured by death or the need for ventriculoperitoneal shunting at 1 year of age. Secondary outcomes include the effect on the Chiari II malformation by neuroimaging, and neuromotor status at 12 and 30 months of age. Neonatal morbidity and need for postnatal surgical interventions will also be evaluated. In addition, the long-term psychological and reproductive consequences in mothers who undergo intrauterine repair of MMC will be compared to those in the postnatal repair group.

This trial has been enrolling patients since 2002. Although recruitment has been slower than anticipated, the trial has the advantage that there is no "back door." That is, no other center in the United States is offering this procedure while the trial is being conducted. It is hoped that the results of the MOMS trial will determine if fetal intervention can improve outcomes for children with spina bifida.[5]

The results of fetal MMC repair are difficult to evaluate, especially given the limited duration of follow-up. Although hindbrain herniation is definitely reversed, ventriculoperitoneal shunting may still be needed. With longer follow-up time, both the Philadelphia and Nashville groups have observed a progressive rise in the number of patients requiring ventriculoperitoneal shunting. Whereas some patients in the Philadelphia series appear to have significantly improved neurologic level of function, most have not, and none of the patients in the Nashville group have shown improved neurologic function. These results will need to be evaluated in prospective trials with 4- to 5-year follow-up to determine if fetal MMC repair is truly beneficial. This is especially important because of the fetal deaths after fetal MMC repair for this nonlethal lesion.

Fetal Airway Obstruction

Obstruction of the fetal airway presents a particularly difficult problem at delivery. The airway under such circumstances can be difficult to secure quickly, often necessitating emergent tracheostomy, which rarely can be performed in sufficient time to prevent anoxic brain injury or death. Cervical teratoma, lymphangioma, or intrinsic laryngeal or tracheal obstruction may compromise the fetal airway. Congenital high airway obstruction syndrome (CHAOS), resulting from tracheal or laryngeal occlusion, is relatively rare but almost always fatal.[48] CHAOS most often involves occlusion at the level of the larynx by laryngeal atresia, with laryngeal webs or severe subglottic stenosis or atresia occurring less frequently. Similarly, cervical teratoma and lymphangioma may compromise the fetal airway by compression, resulting in complete occlusion of the fetal trachea.

Dilatation of the airway distal to the obstruction results from impaired efflux of fetal lung fluid. Compensatory hypersecretion resulting from stretch of the lung tissue accelerates this process.[96] Experimental models of CHAOS have confirmed this pathophysiology.[20] If left unchecked, the rising intrathoracic pressures eventually lead to placentomegaly and fetal hydrops as a result of compromised cardiac function. These conditions can be detected prenatally, thereby facilitating a planned and controlled delivery by the EXIT procedure.

PRENATAL DIAGNOSIS

Giant fetal neck masses that occlude the airway are usually identified during routine ultrasonography. Most of these lesions are hypoechogenic cysts with a solid component present in teratomas. Intrinsic laryngeal or tracheal obstructions are more difficult to diagnose. The trachea and lungs are dilated distal to the obstruction, and the diaphragms may be flattened or everted. The tense fluid accumulation gives the lungs an echogenic appearance. As CHAOS evolves, placentomegaly, fetal ascites, and generalized hydrops may develop.[61] Absence of lung fluid efflux may be noted on color Doppler imaging of the dilated trachea during fetal breathing movements.

The frequency of associated CNS anomalies, renal anomalies, vascular anomalies, and esophageal atresia or fistula with laryngeal atresia may be as high as 50%. Fraser syndrome (cryptophthalmus, abnormal genitalia, syndactyly of the toes and fingers) has been described in association with laryngeal atresia.[88] With this association, there is an 85% incidence of major renal anomalies, including unilateral or bilateral renal agenesis or multicystic renal dysplasia. Even if the kidneys are present, they are usually echogenic and poorly functioning, resulting in oligohydramnios. Therefore, the presence of fetal airway obstruction with oligohydramnios should raise the suspicion of Fraser syndrome and its poor prognosis.

PRENATAL TREATMENT

Laryngeal and tracheal obstruction from giant neck masses carries a good overall prognosis if the airway can be secured at delivery. Similarly, in the absence of associated anomalies, fetuses with laryngeal or tracheal atresia may also do well. The EXIT procedure provides time with the fetus on placental support to secure the airway in these cases. Given proper anesthesia and uterine relaxation, sufficient uteroplacental gas exchange can be maintained for up to an hour, which permits either endoscopic or surgical control of the fetal airway without risk of fetal hypoxia.

The timing of the EXIT procedure relates to the well-being of the fetus. A fetus with airway obstruction from any cause may be followed to term (36 to 38 weeks) with serial ultrasonography, provided that there are no signs of hydrops. However, amnioreduction may be required in fetuses with neck masses associated with esophageal obstruction and severe polyhydramnios secondary to impaired swallowing. With the evolution of

fetal hydrops or uncontrollable preterm labor, the EXIT procedure should be performed expeditiously.

In performing the EXIT procedure, the hysterotomy is created away from the placenta using a uterine stapling device to prevent hemorrhage. The fetal head and upper chest are delivered. If necessary, large cystic neck masses may be decompressed to permit delivery and to partially relieve the compression on the fetal airway. Fetal oxygenation is monitored with a pulse oximeter applied to the exposed fetal hand. Also, fetal cardiac function is assessed with continuous transthoracic fetal echocardiography. Deep anesthesia is maintained by maternal inhaled desflurane in oxygen, providing uterine relaxation, fetal anesthesia, and preservation of uteroplacental gas exchange.[25,34,68]

The EXIT procedure provides time for laryngoscopy and bronchoscopy if there is significant distortion of the airway (Fig. 11-10A). In addition, tracheostomy or even partial tumor resection may be accomplished during placental support (see Fig. 11-10B). A recent report of five giant fetal neck masses confirmed the usefulness of this approach. Laryngoscopy was performed in all five

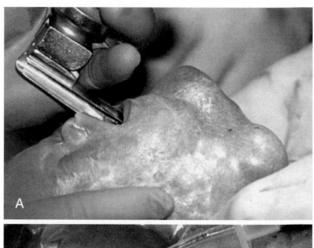

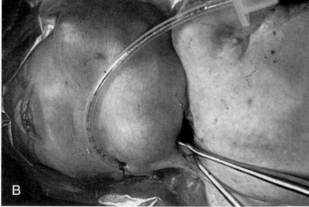

FIGURE 11-10. **A,** Direct laryngoscopy performed during ex utero intrapartum treatment (EXIT) procedure on a fetus with airway compromise owing to a giant cervical teratoma. **B,** Tracheostomy performed during the EXIT procedure, requiring tunneling of an endotracheal tube through the soft tissues of the neck because of the severe distortion of the fetal airway. (From Shaaban AF et al: The role of ultrasonography in fetal surgery and invasive fetal procedures. Semin Roentgen 34:62, 1999.)

cases, bronchoscopy in three, and tracheostomy in two. The mean time on placental support was 28 minutes (range, 8 to 54 minutes), with excellent uteroplacental gas exchange, as reflected by the results of cord blood gases.[59] The indications for the EXIT procedure have been expanded to include large chest or mediastinal masses, CDH, and emergent separation of conjoined twins

FETOSCOPIC SURGERY

Embryoscopy and fetoscopy have been used as diagnostic tools since the late 1960s. More recently, they have been used diagnostically to guide chorionic villus sampling and fetal skin and liver biopsies. Fetoscopy also has been used therapeutically in the treatment of CDH for fetal tracheal occlusion,[44] in the release of amniotic bands,[3,30] and in the treatment of twin reversed arterial perfusion (TRAP) sequence and twin-twin transfusion syndrome.[19,82] The limitations of the initial fetoscopic procedures were largely related to the primitive optics and instrumentation available at the time. The recent surge in operative laparoscopy has kindled rapid technical advances in optics and instrumentation. These advances are illustrated by a report that details the usefulness of transabdominal fetoscopy in a case of Meckel-Gruber syndrome, in which a diagnosis could not be made by ultrasound examination.

The same technological advances that have made minimally invasive videoendoscopic surgery possible in children and adults offer the potential for minimally invasive fetal surgery (see Table 11-1).[24] The small uterine puncture sites required for fetoscopic surgery, in theory, would prevent the morbidity of a large hysterotomy. Specifically, the fetoscopic approach could reduce the risks of preterm labor, hemorrhage, amniotic fluid leak, and uterine rupture and could eliminate the need for cesarean section delivery after fetal surgery.

TWIN REVERSED ARTERIAL PERFUSION SEQUENCE

TRAP sequence occurs only in the setting of a monochorionic gestation and complicates approximately 1% of monochorionic twin gestations, with an incidence of 1 in 35,000 births. In TRAP sequence, the acardiac/acephalic twin receives all of its blood supply from the normal "pump" twin. The term *reversed perfusion* is used to describe this scenario because blood enters the acardiac/acephalic twin in a retrograde manner through its umbilical artery and exits through the umbilical vein. Because of the increased demand that the abnormal circulation in TRAP sequence places on the heart of the pump twin, cardiac failure is the primary concern in TRAP sequence. If left untreated, the pump twin dies in 50% to 75% of cases. This is especially true when the acardiac/acephalic twin weighs more than 50% of the estimated weight of the pump twin.[73]

It is important to exclude a chromosomal abnormality before offering a fetoscopic procedure in TRAP sequence, because the incidence of chromosomal abnormality in the pump twin may be as high as 9%. Fifty-one percent of TRAP sequence pregnancies are complicated by polyhydramnios, and 75% are complicated by preterm labor. The difference in estimated fetal weight between the pump twin and the acardiac/acephalic twin is predictive of outcome. When the acardius-to-pump twin weight ratio exceeds 0.5, adverse pregnancy outcome is predicted in 64% of cases.[73] If this weight ratio is greater than 0.7, the adverse pregnancy outcome for the pump twin is approximately 90%.

Techniques of sectio parva (selective removal of an anomalous twin) and ultrasound-guided embolization were used in an attempt to interrupt the vascular communication between the pump twin and the acardius. These procedures have been associated with substantial morbidity and unreliable outcomes, which led to the development of fetoscopic approaches to this problem. McCurdy and associates were the first to report a case of fetoscopic cord ligation in TRAP sequence.[67] The acardiac/acephalic twin's cord was successfully ligated, but only after the pump twin's cord was ligated and then released after the error was recognized. The pump twin developed persistent bradycardia and was noted to be dead on ultrasound examination on postoperative day 1.

Quintero and colleagues reported the first successful umbilical cord ligation for TRAP sequence.[83] The procedure was performed at 19 weeks of gestation, using two percutaneous trocars and a 1.9-mm endoscope. The cord was successfully ligated, and except for some mild postoperative uterine irritability, the patient responded well. Three weeks after the procedure, the mother presented with leakage of amniotic fluid that subsequently resolved. The pregnancy continued until 36 weeks of gestation, when a healthy boy was delivered.

A number of different techniques have been used to treat TRAP sequence; among 40 cases, there was cord occlusion by embolization in 5, ligation in 15, laser photocoagulation in 10, bipolar diathermy in 7, and monopolar diathermy in 3. Intrafetal ablation has also been performed by alcohol injection in 5, monopolar diathermy in 3, interstitial laser in 4, and RFA in 13. In a review of the various techniques that have been reported to treat TRAP sequence, Tan and colleagues concluded that intrafetal radiofrequency ablation was associated with a lower rate of premature delivery, a lower rate of rupture of membranes before 32 weeks' gestation (23%, versus 58% for other techniques), and a higher rate of clinical success than cord occlusion techniques.

TWIN-TWIN TRANSFUSION SYNDROME (See also Chapters 23 and 44.)

Twin-twin transfusion syndrome (TTTS), or oligohydramnios/polyhydramnios sequence, is a rare syndrome that occurs at an estimated rate of 0.1 to 0.9 per 1000 births. This diagnosis carries an extremely poor prognosis, and it may be responsible for 15% to 17% of all perinatal deaths in twins. TTTS occurs usually in the setting of monochorionic gestations and rarely in dichorionic twins when vascular connections between the two placentas exist.

It is estimated that 85% of monochorionic placentas have anomalous vascular connections; however, only 5% to 10% have sufficient imbalance to produce TTTS. It is also believed that the number of vascular anastomoses and the types of anastomoses within a placenta determine whether TTTS develops.

The natural history of TTTS is associated with a 60% to 100% mortality for both twins in the most severe cases. The most severely affected fetuses usually present with signs of TTTS before 20 weeks' gestation. Mothers commonly present clinically after 20 weeks' gestation with an acute increase in abdominal girth, discomfort, and occasionally respiratory compromise or preterm labor. Physical examination reveals tense poly-hydramnios. However, presentation before 20 weeks' gestation is usually asymptomatic, and diagnosis is usually a serendipitous finding on routine ultrasound.

Diagnostic criteria for TTTS include monochorion-icity (chorionicity is best determined in the first trimester and is more difficult to determine in the second trimester); a marked discordance in amniotic fluid volume between the twins (thus the term *oligohydramnios/polyhydramnios sequence*); a size discordance, with the larger twin in the polyhydramniotic sac (except in TTTS presenting before 20 weeks' gestation, in which case size discordance may not be pronounced); same-sex twins; and a single placental mass.[12] The most characteristic feature is the presence of a "stuck twin," in which the larger, recipient twin has a large bladder and a polyhydramniotic sac, and the smaller, donor twin has a small bladder and is stuck against the uterine wall in an oligohydramniotic sac. A stuck twin can occur from causes other than TTTS, including premature rupture of membranes, placental insufficiency, urinary tract or other structural abnormalities, chromosomal anomalies, and infectious etiologies.

Initially, the twins present on ultrasound with a growth discrepancy between the larger, recipient twin and the growth-restricted, donor twin. It is not un-common for the donor twin to have a velamentous placental cord insertion, which may exacerbate the growth discrepancy. The volume stress on the recipient heart in TTTS often leads to cardiac changes. The recipient may develop cardiomyopathy with ventricular dysfunction that culminates in fetal hydrops. These cardiac changes include ventricular hypertrophy, tricuspid valvular insufficiency, and, in advanced cases, an akinetic right ventricle and a pulmonic valvular insufficiency or atresia.[98] Co-twin demise (usually the recipient) may occur as the fetal hydrops worsens. The surviving twin is at risk for severe neurologic injury caused by vascular resistance changes and consequent ischemic neurologic events. The surviving co-twin is

also at risk for concomitant demise in at least 4% to 10% of cases and maybe as high as 50% of cases.[28]

The several treatment options for TTTS include medical therapy, serial amnioreduction, amniotic sep-tostomy, and fetoscopic approaches. Experience with medical therapy has been anecdotal, with case reports of resolution of TTTS with either digoxin or indo-methacin therapy. These therapies have not been widely accepted or applied in patients diagnosed with TTTS.

Serial amnioreduction is one of the most commonly used and widely accepted therapies for TTTS. Its mechanism of action is unknown, but it appears to prolong gestation and to improve uteroplacental blood flow. Advocates of this therapy believe that amnio-reduction increases the survival rate when compared with the natural history of TTTS and shows survival rates comparable to those observed with laser therapy. The major criticism of amnioreduction is that it may not prevent the neurologic complications of TTTS.

Amniotic septostomy has been intentionally performed in a small number of cases.[87] Proponents of amniotic septostomy report equilibration of amniotic fluid volumes between the two fetuses that lasts for the duration of the pregnancy. Although the mechanism of amniotic septostomy is unclear, its success may be related to its effects on fetoplacental hemodynamics. Amniotic septostomy may allow amniotic fluid to cross into the stuck twin's sac, resulting in a fluid bolus as the amniotic fluid is imbibed by the fetus. It is likely that restoration of amniotic fluid volume after just one or two amnioreductions is successful because of un-intentional and unrecognized septostomy. An interesting observation is that TTTS does not seem to occur in monochorionic monoamniotic pregnancies, perhaps for the same reason that amniotic septostomy works. How-ever, as with serial amnioreduction, amniotic septostomy would not be expected to prevent the neurologic sequelae in the event of the demise of either co-twin. In addition, if too large a septostomy is created, the twins are at risk for cord entanglement. Because of this risk, a microseptostomy is created, which is only a series of needle punctures of the intertwin membrane. Saade and coworkers reported the results of a prospec-tive randomized trial comparing amnioreduction to septostomy. The survival in each group was 65%; however, no data on neurologic outcome was provided.[86]

Fetoscopic laser as a treatment for TTTS was initially described by DeLia and colleagues in 1990.[26] Experimental work in both sheep and monkey models showed the efficacy of fetoscopic laser photocoagula-tion using a neodymium:yttrium-aluminum-garnet laser before its use in the first three human cases was reported in 1990. The three women were treated at 18.5, 22, and 22.5 weeks of gestation after presenting with acute polyhydramnios. Two of the three proce-dures went uneventfully, but the third was complicated by a placental vessel perforation. The first two patients delivered at 27 and 34 weeks' gestation because of premature rupture of membranes. The third patient developed severe preeclampsia at 29 weeks' gestation, necessitating delivery. Four of the six infants survived.

A follow-up to these initial cases was published in 1995. DeLia and colleagues reported 26 patients treated by a fetoscopic laser.[26] The inclusion criteria were ultrasonographic findings consistent with TTTS, posterior placenta, gestational age younger than 25 weeks, and clinical polyhydramnios. The treated patients had a mean gestational age of 20.8 weeks (range, 18 to 24 weeks). One patient had surviving triplets, eight had surviving twins, nine had a single survivor (two neonatal and seven fetal deaths), and eight had no survivors (all had pregnancy loss within 3 weeks of the procedure). Surviving fetuses were delivered for obstetric reasons at a mean of 32.2 weeks (range, 26 to 37 weeks). Fifty-three percent (28 of 53) of fetuses survived, with 96% (27 of 28) showing normal development at a mean of 35.8 months of follow-up (range, 1 to 68 months).

A similar experience was reported by Ville and associates.[95] Forty-five women were treated at a median gestational age of 21 weeks (range, 15 to 28 weeks). The rate of fetuses surviving to delivery was also 53%. Among the survivors, the median gestational age at delivery was 35 weeks (range, 25 to 40 weeks), with a median interval between treatment and delivery of 14 weeks (range, 0 to 21 weeks). All of the survivors were developing normally at a median age of 12 months (range, 2 to 24 months).

It may be that the vessels on the chorionic plate are only part of the chorioangiopagus and that more vascular connections occur deep within the cotyledons of the placenta. Quintero and coworkers described the selective technique of fetoscopic laser photocoagulation for TTTS to address these deep communications.[82] The placental surface is fetoscopically inspected for what they term *nonparticipating vessels* and *truly participating vessels* as well as the location of the intertwin membrane. Nonparticipating vessels occur in pairs, with an artery entering a cotyledon and a vein returning to the same umbilical cord. In contrast, vessels truly participating in the TTTS are unpaired. An artery leaving the umbilical cord of the donor enters a cotyledon, but there is no vein returning to the donor umbilical cord; rather, a vein draining this cotyledon can be seen on the other side of the vascular equator heading back to the umbilical cord of the recipient fetus. It is unlikely, however, that sufficient pressure changes could be transmitted across these deep communications within the cotyledons to account for the ischemic injury seen in surviving co-twins on fetal demise. Although these deep vessels may contribute to TTTS, they are unlikely to be responsible for all of its morbidity. It is for that reason that these unpaired vessels, along with any direct artery-to-artery or vein-to-vein communications on the chorionic plate, are selectively laser photocoagulated.[82]

A report from Germany compared outcomes of selective fetoscopic laser photocoagulation with those of serial amnioreduction for TTTS.[45] Unlike the technique described by DeLia, in which all vessels crossing the intertwin membrane are photocoagulated, the selective technique selects only those vessels for coagulation that appear to connect the circulations of the twins. These connections may be artery to vein, vein to vein, artery to artery, or connections within the placenta in which a cotyledon is perfused by an artery from one twin but drains by a vein returning to the other twin. Seventy-three women were treated between 1995 and 1997 in one center by fetoscopic laser photocoagulation, and 43 patients were treated at another center between 1992 and 1996 by serial amnioreduction. Women treated by fetoscopic laser instead of serial amnioreduction had a higher proportion of pregnancies with greater than one survivor (79% versus 60%), a lower number of spontaneous intrauterine fetal deaths (3% versus 19%), a lower incidence of abnormal ultrasonographic findings in the brains of surviving neonates (6% versus 18%), and an older gestational age at the time of delivery (33.7 versus 30.7 weeks). On the basis of this information, the authors concluded that fetoscopic laser photocoagulation is a more effective treatment for TTTS than serial amnioreduction. A study of the long-term follow-up of the cohort of patients undergoing fetoscopic laser treatment from this series found that despite the low incidence of abnormalities on neonatal head ultrasound in these patients, there was a significant incidence of neurodevelopmental abnormalities.[10] The neurodevelopmental problems were severe in 11% and included cases of mental retardation, hemiplegia, and quadriplegia. Moderate neurodevelopmental problems occurred in an additional 11%.

All of the treatment strategies for TTTS discussed here have evidence from retrospective, single-center, or prospective but nonrandomized studies, suggesting that they improve survival. It is not clear, however, which therapy is best under what circumstances. In most centers in the United States, the current standard of care is serial amnioreduction. Microseptostomy is available in relatively few centers, despite the recent prospective randomized trial demonstrating efficacy equivalent to serial amnioreduction. Fetoscopic laser photocoagulation is available in only a few centers, and the lack of controlled trials has limited enthusiasm for this more invasive therapy.

At present, it is not known which therapy for TTTS is best for specific patients, for either survival or neurodevelopmental outcome. There are two ongoing prospective randomized clinical trials, the Eurofetus trial in Europe led by Yves Ville and the NIH-sponsored trial in the United Stated led by this author. Both trials compare aggressive serial amnioreduction to fetoscopic laser photocoagulation. The NIH-sponsored trial will correlate the results of serial prenatal ultrasounds, fetal echocardiographs, and fetal MRIs with treatment by blinded reviewers. In addition to the primary endpoint of recipient and donor twin survival, the NIH-sponsored trial will evaluate neonatal comorbidities and correlate neuroradiologic findings with neurodevelopmental outcomes at 18 to 22 months by evaluation at centers in the participating National Institute of Child Health and Human Development (NICHD) Neonatal Network. It is hoped that these prospective randomized clinical trials will, for the first time, address in rigorous fashion many of the questions that remain unanswered about the treatment of severe TTTS.

SUMMARY

Significant strides have been made in invasive fetal therapy. In recent years, progress seems to be accelerating, providing innovative treatment for fetuses with malformations that would otherwise be fatal. However, these pioneering efforts should not be mistaken for establishing invasive fetal therapy as the standard treatment for any condition. Although there is tremendous potential for fetal salvage in several highly lethal conditions, much experimental work remains to be done. Assessing the risk-to-benefit ratio for a mother with a fetus with a life-threatening malformation will evolve as technical advances diminish the potential risks of fetal surgery. Fetal surgery's contributions to advances in perinatal care and tocolytic management have implications far beyond the narrow sphere of fetal therapy. In the last analysis, the collateral advances that occur as a result of invasive fetal therapy may be the most important and lasting contributions of this experimental endeavor. The field of invasive fetal therapy is rapidly evolving and will undoubtedly provide new and exciting therapeutic options for the unborn patient.

REFERENCES

1. Adzick NS et al: A rapidly growing fetal teratoma. Lancet 349:538, 1997.
2. Adzick NS, Harrison MR: The unborn surgical patient. Curr Prob Obstet Gynecol Fertil 18:173, 1995.
3. Adzick NS et al: Diaphragmatic hernia in the fetus: Prenatal diagnosis and outcome in 94 cases. J Pediatr Surg 20:357, 1983.
4. Adzick NS et al: Successful fetal surgery for spina bifida. Lancet 352:1675, 1998.
5. Adzick NS, Walsh DS: Myelomeningocele: Prenatal diagnosis, pathophysiology, and management. Semin Pediatr Surg 12:168, 2003.
6. Alcorn D et al: Morphological effects of chronic tracheal ligation and drainage in the fetal lamb lung. J Anat 123:649, 1977.
7. Altman RP et al: Sacrococcygeal teratoma: American Academy of Pediatrics Surgical Section Survey—1973. J Pediatr Surg 9:389, 1974.
8. Anderson N et al: Detection of obstructive uropathy in the fetus: Predictive value of sonographic measurements of renal pelvic diameter at various gestational ages. Am J Roentgenol 164:719, 1995.
9. Arger PH et al: Routine fetal genitourinary tract screening. Radiology 156:485, 1985.
10. Banek CS et al: Long-term neurodevelopmental outcome after intrauterine laser treatment for severe twin-twin transfusion syndrome. Am J Obstet Gynecol 188:876, 2003.
11. Bouchard S et al: The EXIT procedure: Experience and outcome in 31 cases. J Pediatr Surg 37:418, 2002.
12. Brennan JN et al: Fetofetal transfusion syndrome: Prenatal ultrasonographic diagnosis. Radiology 143:535, 1982.
13. Bruner JP et al: Endoscopic coverage of fetal myelomeningocele in utero. Am J Obstet Gynecol 180:153, 1999.
14. Bruner JP et al: Fetal surgery for myelomeningocele and the incidence of shunt-dependent hydrocephalus. JAMA 282:1819, 1999.
15. Cass DL et al: Cystic lung lesions with systemic arterial blood supply: A hybrid of congenital cystic adenomatoid malformation and bronchopulmonary sequestration. J Pediatr Surg 32:986, 1997.
16. Chervenak FA et al: The management of fetal hydrocephalus. Am J Obstet Gynecol 151:933, 1985.
17. Clark SL et al: Successful fetal therapy for cystic adenomatoid malformation associated with second trimester hydrops. Am J Obstet Gynecol 157:294, 1987.
18. Clewell WH: The fetus with ventriculomegaly: Selection and treatment. In: Harrison MR et al (eds): The Unborn Patient: Prenatal Diagnosis and Treatment, 2nd ed. Philadelphia, WB Saunders, 1991, p 444.
19. Crombleholme TM: The treatment of twin-twin transfusion syndrome. Semin Pediatr Surg 12:175, 2003.
20. Crombleholme TM, Albanese CT: The fetus with airway obstruction. In Harrison MR et al (eds): The Unborn Patient: The Art and Science of Fetal Therapy. 3rd ed. Philadelphia, WB Saunders, 2001, p 357.
21. Crombleholme TM et al: Cystic adenomatoid malformation volume ratio predicts outcome in prenatally diagnosed cystic adenomatoid malformation of the lung. J Pediatr Surg 37:331, 2002.
22. Crombleholme TM et al: Fetal intervention in obstructive uropathy: Prognostic indicators and efficacy of intervention. Am J Obstet Gynecol 162:1239, 1990.
23. Crombleholme TM et al: Early experience with open fetal surgery for congenital hydronephrosis. J Pediatr Surg 23:1114, 1988.
24. Crombleholme TM, Johnson MP: Fetoscopic surgery. Clin Obstet Gynecol 46:76, 2003.
25. Crombleholme TM et al: Salvage of a fetus with congenital high airway obstruction syndrome by ex utero intrapartum treatment (EXIT) procedure. Fetal Diagn Ther 15:280, 2000.
26. DeLia JE et al: Fetoscopic laser ablation of placental vessels in severe previable twin-twin transfusion syndrome. Am J Obstet Gynecol 172:1202, 1995.
27. DiFiore JW et al: Experimental fetal tracheal ligation reverses the structural and physiological effects of pulmonary hypoplasia in congenital diaphragmatic hernia. J Pediatr Surg 29:248, 1994.
28. Eglowstein M, D'Alton ME: Single intrauterine demise in multiple gestation: Theory and management. J Matern Fetal Med 2:272, 1993.
29. Fauza DO, Wilson JM: Congenital diaphragmatic hernia and associated anomalies: Their incidence, identification, and impact on prognosis. J Pediatr Surg 29:1113, 1994.
30. Flake AW et al: The treatment of severe congenital diaphragmatic hernia by fetal tracheal occlusion: Clinical experience with fifteen cases. Am J Obstet Gynecol 183:1059, 2000.
31. Flake AW et al: Fetal sacrococcygeal teratoma. J Pediatr Surg 21:563, 1986.
32. Freedman AL et al: Long-term outcome in children after antenatal intervention for obstructive uropathies. Lancet 345:374, 1999.
33. Frigoletto FD Jr et al: Antenatal treatment of hydrocephalus by ventriculoamniotic shunting. JAMA 248:2495, 1982.
34. Gaiser RR et al: The cesarean delivery of twin gestation

under 2 minimum alveolar anesthetic concentration isoflurane: One normal and the other with a larger neck mass. Anesth Analg 88:584, 1997.

35. Glick PL et al: Management of the fetus with congenital hydronephrosis: II. Prognostic criteria and selection for treatment. J Pediatr Surg 20:376, 1984.

36. Golbus MS et al: In utero treatment of urinary tract obstruction. Am J Obstet Gynecol 142:383, 1982.

37. Harrison MR et al: Correction of congenital diaphragmatic hernia in utero: VII. A prospective trial. J Pediatr Surg 32:1637, 1997.

38. Harrison MR et al: Antenatal intervention for congenital cystic adenomatoid malformation. Lancet 336:965, 1990.

39. Harrison MR et al: Fetoscopic temporary tracheal occlusion by means of detachable balloon for congenital diaphragmatic hernia. Am J Obstet Gynecol 185:730, 2001.

40. Harrison MR et al: Congenital diaphragmatic hernia: The hidden mortality. J Pediatr Surg 13:227, 1978.

41. Harrison MR et al: Fetal surgery for congenital hydronephrosis. N Engl J Med 306:591, 1982.

42. Harrison MR et al: A randomized trial of fetal endoscopic tracheal occlusion for severe fetal congenital diaphragmatic hernia. N Engl J Med 349:1916, 2003.

43. Harrison MR et al: Correction of congenital diaphragmatic hernia in utero: V. Initial clinical experience. J Pediatr Surg 25:47, 1990.

44. Harrison MR et al: Correction of congenital diaphragmatic hernia in utero: IX. Fetuses with poor prognosis (liver herniation and low lung-to-head circumference ratio) can be saved by fetoscopic temporary occlusion. J Pediatr Surg 33:1017, 1988.

45. Hecher K et al: Endoscopic laser surgery versus serial amniocentesis in the treatment of severe twin-twin transfusion syndrome. Am J Obstet Gynecol 180:717, 1999.

46. Hedrick HL et al: Right congenital diaphragmatic hernia: Prenatal assessment and outcome. J Pediatr Surg 39:319, 2004.

47. Hedrick HL et al: Sacrococcygeal teratoma: Prenatal assessment, fetal intervention, and outcome. J Pediatr Surg 39:430, 2004.

48. Hedrick MH et al: Congenital high airway obstruction syndrome (CHAOS): A potential for perinatal intervention. J Pediatr Surg 29:271, 1994.

49. Heffez DS et al: The paralysis associated with myelomeningocele: Clinical and experimental data implicating a preventable spinal cord injury. Neurosurgery 26:987, 1990.

50. Heffez DS et al: Intrauterine repair of experimental surgically created dysraphism. Neurosurgery 32:1005, 1993.

51. Hobbins JC et al: Antenatal diagnosis of renal anomalies with ultrasound: I. Obstructive uropathy. Am J Obstet Gynecol 148:868, 1984.

52. Hudgins RJ et al: Natural history of fetal ventriculomegaly. Pediatrics 82:682, 1988.

53. Ibrahim D et al: Newborn with an open posterior hip dislocation, and sciatic nerve injury, after intrauterine radiofrequency ablation of a sacrococcygeal teratoma. J Pediatr Surg 38:248, 2003.

54. Johnson MP et al: Sequential urinalysis improves evaluation of fetal renal function in obstructive uropathy. Am J Obstet Gynecol 173:59, 1995.

55. Keswani SG et al: Impact of continuous intraoperative monitoring on outcomes in open fetal surgery. Fetal Diag Ther Vol. 20, 2005.

56. Kleiner B et al: Sonographic analysis of the fetus with ureteropelvic junction obstruction. Am J Roentgenol 148:359, 1987.

57. Lam YH et al: Thermocoagulation of fetal sacrococcygeal teratoma. Prenat Diagn 22:99, 2002.

58. Levine D et al: Central nervous system abnormalities assessed with prenatal magnetic resonance imaging. Obstet Gynecol 99:1011, 1999.

59. Liechty KW et al: Intrapartum airway management for giant fetal neck masses: The EXIT (ex utero intrapartum treatment) procedure. Am J Obstet Gynecol 177:870, 1997.

60. Liley AW: Intrauterine transfusion of foetus in haemolytic disease. Br Med J 2:1107, 1963.

61. Lim FY et al: Congenital high airway obstruction syndrome (CHAOS): Natural history and management. J Pediatr Surg 38:940, 2003.

62. Longaker MT et al: Primary fetal hydrothorax: Natural history and management. J Pediatr Surg 24:573, 1989.

63. Luthy DA et al: Cesarean section before the onset of labor and subsequent motor function in infants with myelomeningocele diagnosed antenatally. N Engl J Med 324:662, 1991.

64. Manning FA et al: Catheter shunts for fetal hydronephrosis and hydrocephalus: Report of the International Fetal Surgery Registry. N Engl J Med 315:336, 1986.

65. Mashiach R et al: Antenatal ultrasound diagnosis of congenital cystic adenomatoid malformation of the lung: Spontaneous resolution in utero. J Clin Ultrasound 21:453, 1993.

66. McCullagh M et al: Accuracy of prenatal diagnosis of congenital cystic adenomatoid malformation. Arch Dis Child 71:F111, 1994.

67. McCurdy CM et al: Ligation of the umbilical cord of an acardiac-acephalus twin with an endoscopic intrauterine technique. Obstet Gynecol 82:708, 1993.

68. McKenzie T et al: The EXIT procedure. Curr Opin Pediatr 14:453, 2002.

69. Metkus AP et al: Sonographic predictors of survival in fetal diaphragmatic hernia. J Pediatr Surg 31:148, 1996.

70. Meuli M et al: In utero surgery rescues neurological function at birth in sheep with spina bifida. Nat Med 1:342, 1995.

71. Meuli M et al: The spinal cord lesion in human fetuses with myelomeningocele: implications for fetal surgery. J Pediatr Surg 32:448, 1997.

72. Michejda M: Intrauterine treatment of spina bifida: Primate model. Z Kinderchir 39:259, 1984.

73. Moore TR et al: Perinatal outcome of forty-nine pregnancies complicated by acardiac twinning. Am J Obstet Gynecol 163:907, 1990.

74. Muller F et al: Fetal urinary biochemistry predicts postnatal renal function in children with bilateral obstructive uropathies. Obstet Gynecol 82:813, 1993.

75. Nakayama DK et al: Prognosis of posterior urethral valves presenting at birth. J Pediatr Surg 21:45, 1986.

76. Nicolaides KH, Azar GB: Thoraco-amniotic shunting. Fetal Diagn Ther 5:164, 1990.

77. Nicolaides KH et al: Chronic drainage of fetal pulmonary cyst. Lancet 1:618, 1987.

78. Paek BW et al: Radiofrequency ablation of human fetal sacrococcygeal teratoma. Am J Obstet Gynecol 184:503, 2001.

79. Platt LD et al: The California Maternal Serum alpha-Fetoprotein Screening Program: The role of ultrasonography in the detection of spina bifida. Am J Obstet Gynecol 166:1328, 1992.

80. Quintero RA et al: Percutaneous fetal cystoscopy and endoscopic fulguration of posterior urethral valves. Am J Obstet Gynecol 172:206, 1995.

81. Quintero RA et al: In-utero percutaneous cystoscopy in the management of fetal lower obstructive uropathy. Lancet 346:537, 1995.

82. Quintero RA et al: Selective photocoagulation of placental vessels in twin-twin transfusion syndrome: Evolution of a surgical technique. Obstet Gynecol Surv 53(Suppl):S97, 1998.

83. Quintero RA et al: Brief report: Umbilical-cord ligation of an acardiac twin by fetoscopy at 19 weeks of gestation. N Engl J Med 330:469, 1994.

84. Rintoule NE et al: A new look at myelomeningocele: Functional level, vertebral level, shunting, and the implications for fetal intervention. Pediatrics 109:409, 2002.

85. Rodeck CH et al: Long-term in utero drainage of fetal hydrothorax. N Engl J Med 319:1135, 1988.

86. Saade GR et al: Randomized trial of septostomy versus amnioreduction in the treatment of twin oligohydramnios polyhydramnios sequence (TOPS) [abstract]. Am J Obstet Gynecol 187:3, 2003.

87. Saade GR et al: Amniotomy: A new approach to the 'stuck twin' syndrome. Am J Obstet Gynecol 172:429, 1995.

88. Schauer GM et al: Prenatal diagnosis of Fraser syndrome at 18.5 weeks gestation, with autopsy findings at 19 weeks. Am J Med Genet 37:583, 1990.

89. Shaw GM et al: Epidemiologic characteristics of phenotypically distinct neural tube defects among 0.7 million California births, 1983-1987. Teratology 49:143, 1994.

90. Sheth S et al: Prenatal diagnosis of sacrococcygeal teratoma: Sonographic-pathologic correlation. Radiology 169:131, 1988.

91. Stocker JT et al: Congenital cystic adenomatoid malformation of the lung: Classification and morphologic spectrum. Hum Pathol 8:155, 1977.

92. Sutton LN et al: Improvement in hindbrain herniation demonstrated by serial fetal magnetic resonance imaging following fetal surgery for myelomeningocele. JAMA 282:1826, 1999.

93. Tsao K et al: Resolution of hydrops fetalis in congenital cystic adenomatoid malformation after prenatal steroids therapy. J Pediatr Surg 38:508, 2003.

94. VanderWall KJ et al: Fetal endoscopic ("Fetendo") tracheal clip. J Pediatr Surg 31:1101, 1996.

95. Ville Y et al: Preliminary experience with endoscopic laser surgery for severe twin-twin transfusion syndrome. N Engl J Med 332:224, 1995.

96. Wigglesworth JS et al: Fetal lung growth in congenital laryngeal atresia. Pediatr Pathol 7:515, 1987.

97. Wilson RD et al: Thoracoamniotic shunts: Fetal treatment of pleural effusions and congenital cystic adenomatoid malformation. Fetal Diagn Ther 19:413, 2004.

98. Zosmer N et al: Clinical and echocardiographic features of in utero cardiac dysfunction in the recipient twin in twin-to-twin transfusion syndrome. Br Heart J 72:74, 1994.

12 Occupational and Environmental Risks to the Fetus

Cynthia F. Bearer

Occupational and environmental risks to the fetus are becoming increasingly important. In 2004 women were 46.4% of the U.S. workforce (approximately 62.9 million female workers).[95] Seventy-three percent of working women are of reproductive age.[96] It is estimated that 52% of pregnant women work.[98] (This is an estimated number because no U.S. Department of Labor or Bureau of Labor Statistics figures exist to quantify the percentage of working women who give birth each year or the birth rate among employed women.) The number of births in 2000 was 4.1 million. Assuming that multiple births are negligible, approximately 2.1 million infants were born to mothers employed outside the home.

Environmental exposures are increasing as both population and economic needs continue to expand. In 1900, there were 1.25 billion people on Earth. This number doubled by 1950, then it doubled again to 5 billion by 1987. There are now more than 6 billion people on Earth, and this number may double by 2050.[94] The pressures of population growth on the environment are reflected in increasing need for land, water, food, and fuels.

With more people and increasing economic expansion come the problems of emissions and pollution from daily living, industry, commerce, and agriculture.[105] Land is overused; water, air, food, and soil are contaminated. Every human being on this planet is exposed to chemicals and other agents. The Centers for Disease Control and Prevention (CDC) is monitoring 116 environmental pollutants in human blood and urine (will increase to 149 pollutants by 2005; see http://www.cdc.gov/exposurereport/). This chapter describes the various types of exposures (nonconcurrent and concurrent with pregnancy), the unique pharmacokinetics of the fetus, and the spectrum of adverse outcomes known to be associated with occupational and environmental exposures (Fig. 12-1).

EXPOSURES NOT CONCURRENT WITH PREGNANCY

Environmental exposures that affect newborns may occur before conception. The main effect of these exposures may be on the ovum or sperm, which then leads to the development of an abnormal fetus, but a woman's exposure may result in a delayed exposure to the developing fetus by the ongoing elimination of the chemical from the mother's body. Because the initial exposure is experienced by the mother before conception, these exposures are not concurrent with the pregnancy. For some chemicals, such as the organohalogens, the fetus can be affected by both nonconcurrent and concurrent maternal exposures.

Preconceptional Effects

EXPOSURES AFFECTING THE OVUM
Ova begin to develop in early fetal life. During female fetal development the oogonia are formed by meiotic division. Before birth, all oogonia have developed into primary oocytes and have completed the prophase of the first meiotic division (Fig. 12-2).[55] At the end of prophase, the chromosomes are condensed and spindle fibers connect them to the centrioles, which have

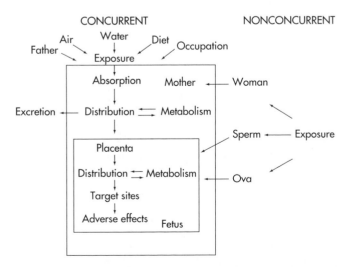

FIGURE 12-1. Maternal concurrent and nonconcurrent exposures and fetal exposure.

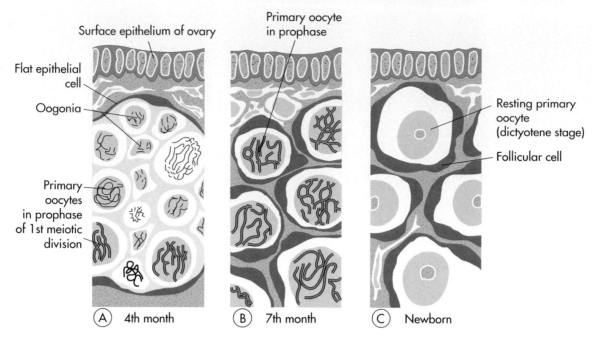

FIGURE 12-2. Segment of ovary at different stages of development. **A,** At 4 months' gestation; oogonia are grouped in clusters in the cortical part of the ovary. Some show mitosis, whereas others have already differentiated into primary oocytes and have entered prophase of first meiotic division. **B,** At 7 months' gestation; almost all oogonia are transformed into primary oocytes in prophase of first meiotic division. **C,** At birth; oogonia are absent. Each primary oocyte is surrounded by a single layer of follicular cells, forming primordial follicle. Oocytes have entered the dictyotene stage, in which they remain until just before ovulation, when they enter metaphase of first meiotic division. (From Langman J: Medical Embryology. Baltimore, Williams & Wilkins, 1975, p 11, with permission.)

reached the poles of the cell. The nuclear membrane has disappeared.[25] The oocyte remains in this state until puberty and perhaps for as long as 50 years.

The oocyte may be vulnerable to environmental exposures. This hypothesis is supported by the increasing incidence of nondisjunctional events with increasing maternal age and, therefore, with prolonged environmental exposure. Environmental exposures to the oocyte have been shown in two studies.[93] Xenobiotics (chemicals foreign to the metabolic network of the body) were measured in samples of human follicular fluid collected during oocyte harvesting for in vitro fertilization. Concentrations of representative xenobiotics from one study are shown in Table 12-1. A second study showed an association between failed fertilization and the concentration of p,p′-DDE (a metabolite of DDT) in follicular fluid.[110]

The easiest outcome to measure is loss of fertility. Loss of ova from such exposures can reduce fertility as reported in women born to mothers who smoke.[67,99] Few outcome studies on environmental exposures have been reported, however, due to the lengthy period from exposure to outcome in such transgenerational studies. The population of women who took diethylstilbestrol (DES) during pregnancy is an exception because the exposure was well documented.[39,40] Several reports on transgenerational effects from DES exposure (effects in persons whose grandmothers took DES during pregnancy [i.e., DES grandchildren]) have been made. These include increased incidence of hypospadias in grandsons (prevalence ratio of 21.3, 95% confidence interval [CI] 6.5-70.1)[49] and prematurity of DES grandsons and granddaughters.[39,49]

Paternal Effects

In contrast to effects on ova, effects on sperm can be measured relatively easily in the next generation, so there is more evidence in the literature to suggest that

TABLE 12-1. Xenobiotics in Human Follicular Fluid

CONTAMINANT	MEAN CONCENTRATION (PPB)	SEM
Lindane	1.22	0.18
Total DDT	3.37	0.44
PCBs	8.03	0.88
Hexachlorobenzene	2.59	0.24
Dieldrin	0.13	0.03
Heptachlor epoxide	0.12	0.02

DDT, dichlorodiphenyltrichloroethane; PCBs, polychlorinated biphenyls; PPB, parts per billion; SEM, standard error of the mean.
From Trapp M et al: Pollutants in human follicular fluid. Fertil Steril 42:146, 1984.

paternal exposures before conception may constitute a risk to the fetus. The sperm itself represents a vulnerable stage to the effects of mutagens; in its final form the sperm has no DNA repair mechanisms.

Cancer is not usually thought to be a result of preconceptional or prenatal exposures. New data, however, suggest that the sperm may be a vulnerable target for carcinogens. The risk of cancer in the offspring and paternal occupation (as a proxy for exposure) has been extensively studied. One recent study reported increased risk of central nervous system tumors with paternal occupational exposure to pesticides (relative risk [RR] 2.36; 95% CI, 1.27-4.39) and work as a painter (RR 2.18; 95% CI 1.26-3.78),[29] and increased risk of leukemia with paternal woodworking (RR 2.18, 95% CI 1.26-3.78).

In 1998, 48 published studies representing more than 1000 specific combinations of occupation and cancer were reviewed.[20] Important findings were that occupations and exposures of fathers were investigated much more frequently than those of mothers, and the studies have limitations related to the quality of the exposure assessment, small numbers of exposed cases, multiple comparisons, and possible bias toward the reporting of positive results. Despite these limitations, evidence was found for associations of childhood leukemia with paternal exposure to solvents and paints and with paternal employment in occupations related to motor vehicles.

The studies on the association of birth defects with paternal occupation also have been recently reviewed and found to have many of the same limitations as the studies of paternal occupation and cancer.[17] However, birth defects were repeatedly reported to be associated with men in several common occupations (janitors, painters, printers, firefighters, and those in occupations exposed to solvents or related to agriculture).

Additional evidence that paternal exposures may result in fetal abnormalities comes from observations that certain birth defects and diseases are associated with older fathers. These abnormalities include ventricular septal defects, atrial septal defects, and situs inversus.[56] The strongest association between advanced paternal age and birth defects is with achondroplasia.[81] One study found that 2% of children born to men 50 years or older will have schizophrenia.[61] The data on paternally mediated effects have been reviewed extensively.[51,59,68]

There may be several mechanisms by which paternal preconceptional exposures affect the fetus. It appears that increasing autosomal dominant mutations occur with advanced paternal age; the incidence of Apert syndrome and achondroplasia increase with paternal age. Another possible mechanism for paternally mediated effects is the impairment of a paternal gene that is necessary for the normal growth and development of the fetus. In animals and human beings, the fetus requires genes derived from both the father and the mother, a phenomenon called *genetic imprinting*. Replacement of the father's genetic material with a second copy of the mother's genetic material (uni-parental disomy), or vice versa, results in a nonviable conceptus.[35]

One example of a defect in genetic imprinting is Prader-Willi syndrome, caused by a functional mutation in paternal 15q, resulting in inactivation of the genes in that region of the chromosome. Angelman syndrome occurs if maternal 15q is affected.

Environmental factors may play a role in functional uniparental disomy and lead to paternally mediated effects on the fetus. Two studies have shown an association between paternal exposure to hydrocarbons and Prader-Willi syndrome.[15,91] In one study, approximately 50% of the fathers of patients with Prader-Willi syndrome were occupationally exposed to hydrocarbons.[15]

Another novel mechanism for preconceptional paternally mediated effects has been proposed by Yazigi and associates.[108] They found a high-affinity binding site for cocaine on sperm and postulated that sperm acted as a transporter of cocaine into the ovum.

Secondary Fetal Exposure: Maternal Body Burden

Nonconcurrent fetal exposure can result from either ongoing excretion of xenobiotics from maternal storage compartments or mobilization of contaminated compartments during pregnancy. Both adipose tissue and skeletal tissue are known storage sites for chemicals.

POLYCHLORINATED BIPHENYLS

Organohalogens are extremely stable chemicals both in the environment and in biologic systems. They bioaccumulate, becoming concentrated in tissues as they move up the food chain. Polychlorinated biphenyls (PCBs) are an example of this kind of chemical. They are ubiquitous in our environment because of their widespread use as liquid insulators for transformers and capacitors and because of their resistance to chemical and biologic breakdown. Their global distribution was first reported in 1966.[47] Their production peaked in 1970 and subsequently declined as many countries banned or limited their use.[44]

Two major human poisonings have occurred through rice oil that was contaminated with PCBs, one in Japan in 1968 (called *yusho disease*) and one in Taiwan in 1979 (called *yu-cheng disease*). In Taiwan, approximately 2000 adults had an illness characterized by hyperpigmentation, acne, and peripheral neuropathy. Of the first 39 hyperpigmented children born to poisoned women, 8 died.[43] In 1985, a cohort of 117 children born since the 1979 episode was found to have an excess of ectodermal defects and developmental delay.[78] Very few of these children were in utero during the actual poisoning episode. Their exposure to PCBs was from the elevated maternal body burden.

In a later report,[16] Taiwanese children born up to 6 years after maternal exposure were as developmentally delayed as those children born within 1 year of maternal exposure (Fig. 12-3). The developmental delay persisted in these children at all times measured. Thus, these children had significant adverse effects

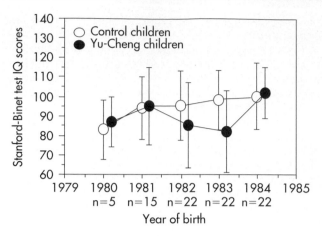

FIGURE 12-3. Stanford-Binet test IQ scores in 4-year-old children with yu-cheng and those in a control arm by year of birth. Error bars represent 1 standard deviation. Note that the contaminated rice was consumed in 1979. (From Chen Y-C et al: Cognitive development of yu-cheng ["oil disease"] children prenatally exposed to heat degraded PCBs. JAMA 268:3216, 1992.)

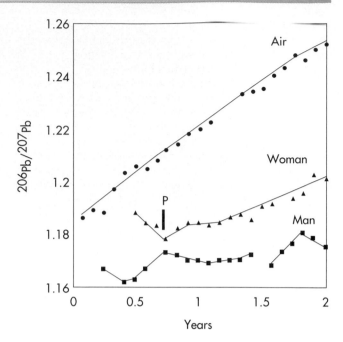

FIGURE 12-4. Isotopic ratio of airborne lead to blood lead of a man and a peripartum woman in 1974 and 1975. Declining isotopic ratio in the woman's blood before birth indicates a different source of lead from that of the man. Dietary sources of lead were the same. The only different source of lead for the woman is that coming from her skeleton during pregnancy. P, time of birth. (From Manton WI: Total contribution of airborne lead to blood lead. Br J Ind Med 42:168, 1985, p 169.)

from a maternal exposure to PCBs that occurred up to 6 years before their birth.

The cognitive defects seen in the children with yu-cheng disease are comparable to those observed in American children exposed to higher levels of background PCBs. In North Carolina, small motor deficits were observed in children up to 2 years of age who had been prenatally exposed to PCBs through maternal body burden acquired from background exposure.[30] In Michigan, short-term memory deficits were measured in 4-year-old children who had elevated cord blood levels of PCBs and whose mothers had regularly consumed sport fish contaminated with PCBs.[45] Further follow-up of these children at 11 years of age showed that those in the highest exposure group were three times more likely to have low-average IQ scores and twice as likely to be 2 years behind in reading comprehension.[46]

LEAD

The major repository for lead is bone, where the turnover rate is approximately 25 to 30 years. Chronic lead exposure results in significant accumulation of lead in the skeleton. During pregnancy, calcium turnover is greatly increased,[52] which may increase mobilization of lead stores from bone.

Lead mobilization was measured in one expectant couple by determining the isotopic ratio (IR) of lead, ^{206}Pb:^{207}Pb (Fig. 12-4).[62] The couple had initially lived in England, which has one IR for lead, and subsequently moved to Australia, which has a different IR for lead. If blood lead is primarily derived from air, then the IR of blood lead would parallel the IR prevalent in Australia. If blood lead is primarily derived from bone, then blood lead IR will not parallel that found in Australia; instead, it will be a reflection of the IR of lead absorbed in England during childhood. The man's blood lead IR paralleled that of Australia, but the woman's did not,

indicating a significant source of lead for her other than an environmental one, probably from her skeletal stores. After delivery, her blood lead IR also paralleled that prevalent in Australia.

This hypothesis has been confirmed in two larger studies: one on pregnant Latin American women living in California,[80] the other on pregnant Eastern European women living in Australia.[33] Demonstration of significant fetal exposure because of an elevated maternal body burden of lead comes from two case reports of congenitally lead-poisoned children delivered by women inadequately treated for childhood plumbism.[86,92]

MERCURY

The CDC Web site on biomonitoring shows that approximately 8% of women have body burdens of mercury already exceeding the reference dose for this toxicant and are at risk for bearing children already harmed by mercury.

MATERNAL EXPOSURES CONCURRENT WITH PREGNANCY

Exposures concurrent with pregnancy can come from many sources. Biologic markers of exposure to the fetus are being developed using meconium[3,5,103] and hair.[77]

Occupation

Several occupations have been shown to increase the risk of a poor outcome of pregnancy, and the studies showing that result have recently been reviewed.[74,85,102] Many studies are inconclusive or difficult to interpret. The strongest associations between workplace exposures and poor reproductive outcome (e.g., spontaneous abortion, miscarriage, and birth defects) have been found for lead, mercury, organic solvents, ethylene oxide, and ionizing radiation. Table 12-2 lists agents that are suspected to cause adverse pregnancy outcomes.[102]

Paraoccupation

Other important sources of exposures to the mother occur through paraoccupational routes. These exposures occur when the father or others bring or track home occupational chemicals, when the home itself is in an occupational setting, or when industrial chemicals are brought home for home use.[65]

Paraoccupational exposure occurred when a janitor in Alamogordo, New Mexico, brought home from a local seed company some grain that was intended for planting only. This grain had been treated with a fungicide containing organic mercury. The janitor used this grain to feed his hogs, one of which was subsequently slaughtered for consumption by the family. Three of nine children in the family became severely ill with organic mercury poisoning.[24,75] The mother also ate the contaminated meat during the second trimester of her pregnancy. Both maternal serum and urine had elevated levels of mercury, as did the neonate's urine, indicating placental transfer of the mercury.[22] The newborn had gross tremulous movements of his extremities, which developed into myoclonic convulsions. At 1 year of age he could not sit up, and he was blind. The mother remained free of symptoms.

Air

Air is an important source of exposure to the pregnant woman and fetus. For example, exposure of the mother to environmental tobacco smoke causes decreased birth weight,[34,38,64] an increased risk of sudden infant death syndrome (SIDS),[23,69] and a predisposition to persistent pulmonary hypertension (Fig. 12-5).[2] In addition, exposure of the mother to fumes of naphthalene has resulted in severe fetal hemolysis in the presence of glucose-6-phosphate dehydrogenase deficiency.[106]

Water

Because the embryo and fetus develop through multiple short critical periods, the quality of water consumed by a pregnant woman is a daily concern; a yearly average of contaminants is not sufficient to protect the developing fetus. Public and well water supplies can vary greatly over the course of a year.

A review of the relationship of drinking-water contaminants to adverse pregnancy outcomes illustrates the risk from exposure to byproducts of chlorinated water disinfectants.[9] These studies show a moderate association between trihalomethane exposure and babies who are small for gestational age, babies with neural tube defects, and spontaneous abortions. Excess neural tube defects, oral clefts, cardiac defects, and choanal atresia were found in studies evaluating trichloroethylene-contaminated drinking water.[9]

Diet

Diet may be an important vehicle for exposure. A tragic case occurred in Minamata Bay, Japan, where methyl mercury from an acetaldehyde-producing plant contaminated the food chain.[37] Pregnant women from a fishing village on the same bay gave birth to severely neurologically damaged infants, whereas they themselves had mild transient paresthesias or no symptoms at all.[63] The safe limit of both organic and inorganic mercury ingestion for pregnant women is the subject of much discussion and ongoing research.[60,101] The U.S. Environmental Protection Agency (EPA) has recently set the reference dose of mercury at 0.1 µg/kg/day.

PATHWAYS OF FETAL EXPOSURE

Placenta-Dependent Pathways

Two possible routes of fetal exposure to environmental hazards are placenta-dependent pathways and placenta-independent pathways (Box 12-1). For a placenta-dependent chemical to reach the fetus, it must first enter the mother's bloodstream and then cross the placenta in significant amounts. Not all environmental toxins meet these criteria; for example, asbestos and radon gas do not meet these criteria unless they have been ingested.

Three properties that enable chemicals to cross the placenta are low molecular weight, fat solubility, and resemblance to nutrients that are specifically transported. An example of a low-molecular-weight compound is carbon monoxide (CO), a constituent of environmental tobacco smoke. CO is an asphyxiant because it displaces oxygen from hemoglobin, forming carboxyhemoglobin (COHb). If enough COHb accumulates in the circulation, cellular metabolism is impaired because oxygen transport, delivery, and use are inhibited. Fetal COHb accumulates more slowly than maternal COHb, but it increases to an equilibrium approximately 10% greater than in the maternal circulation.[41,58] Thus, nonfatal CO poisoning of the mother may prove to be fatal to the fetus.[28]

Examples of fat-soluble chemicals that readily cross the placenta are ethanol and polycyclic hydrocarbons (benzo[a]pyrene, a carcinogen in environmental tobacco smoke, is a polycyclic hydrocarbon). Ethanol causes fetal alcohol syndrome (see Chapter 36). In pregnant ewes, intravenous (IV) infusion of ethanol results in identical maternal and fetal blood alcohol levels.[18] PCBs have been measured in equal concentrations in fetal and maternal blood.[12]

TABLE 12-2. Agents Associated with Adverse Female Reproductive Capacity or Developmental Effects in Human and Animal Studies*

AGENT	HUMAN OUTCOMES	STRENGTH OF ASSOCIATION IN HUMANS[†]	ANIMAL OUTCOMES	STRENGTH OF ASSOCIATION IN ANIMALS[†]
Anesthetic gases[‡]	Reduced fertility, spontaneous abortion	1, 3	Birth defects	1, 3
Arsenic	Spontaneous abortion, low birth weight	1	Birth defects, fetal loss	2
Benzo[a]pyrene	None	NA	Birth defects	1
Cadmium	None	NA	Fetal loss, birth defects	2
Carbon disulfide	Menstrual disorders, spontaneous abortion	1	Birth defects	1
Carbon monoxide	Low birth weight, fetal death (high doses)	1	Birth defects, neonatal death	2
Chlordecone	None	NA	Fetal loss	2, 3
Chloroform	None	NA	Fetal loss	1
Chloroprene	None	NA	Birth defects	2, 3
Ethylene glycol ethers	Spontaneous abortion	1	Birth defects	2
Ethylene oxide	Spontaneous abortion	1	Fetal loss	1
Formamides	None	NA	Fetal loss, birth defects	2
Inorganic mercury[‡]	Menstrual disorders, spontaneous abortion	1	Fetal loss, birth defects	1
Lead[‡]	Spontaneous abortion, prematurity, neurologic dysfunction in child	2	Birth defects, fetal loss	2
Organic mercury	CNS malformation, cerebral palsy	2	Birth defects, fetal loss	2
Physical stress	Prematurity	2	None	NA
Polybrominated biphenyls (PBBs)	None	NA	Fetal loss	2
Polychlorinated biphenyls (PCBs)	Neonatal PCB syndrome (low birth weight, hyperpigmentation, eye abnormalities)	2	Low birth weight, fetal loss	2
Radiation, ionizing	Menstrual disorders, CNS defects, skeletal and eye anomalies, mental retardation, childhood cancer	2	Fetal loss, birth defects	2
Selenium	Spontaneous abortion	3	Low birth weight, birth defects	2
Tellurium	None	NA	Birth defects	2
2,4-Dichlorophenoxyacetic acid (2,4-D)	Skeletal defects	4	Birth defects	1
2,4,5-Trichlorophenoxyacetic acid (2,4,5-T)	Skeletal defects	4	Birth defects	1
Video display terminals	Spontaneous abortion	4	Birth defects	1
Vinyl chloride[‡]	CNS defects	1	Birth defects	1, 4
Xylene	Menstrual disorders, fetal loss	1	Fetal loss, birth defects	1

*Major studies (Birnbaum LS, Tuomisto J: Non-carcinogenic effects of TCDD in animals. Food Addit Contam 17:275, 2000) of the reproductive health effects of exposure to dioxin have shown that dioxin should be added to this list.
[†]1, limited positive data; 2, strong positive data; 3, limited negative data; 4, strong negative data.
[‡]Agent may have male-mediated effects.
CNS, central nervous system; NA, not applicable because no adverse outcomes were observed.
From Welch LS et al (eds): Case studies in environmental medicine: Reproductive and developmental hazards. Washington, DC, 1993, Agency for Toxic Substances and Disease Registry, US Department of Health and Human Services.

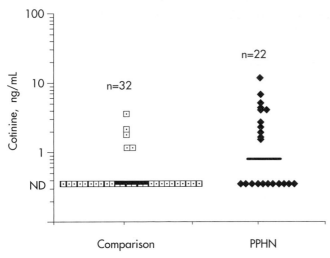

FIGURE 12-5. Distribution of cotinine concentrations of infants with persistent pulmonary hypertension of the newborn (PPHN) and a healthy comparison group after exclusion of mothers who smoke tobacco products. Mothers who smoke were identified by history of smoking or by umbilical cord cotinine concentrations greater than 13.7 ng/mL. Horizontal bars indicate medians of both groups. Medians were significantly different between the two groups (Mann-Whitney rank sum test: Z = 2.78941; *P* = .0053). (From Bearer CF et al: Maternal tobacco smoke exposure and persistent pulmonary hypertension of the newborn. Environ Health Perspect 105:202, 1997, p 205.)

BOX 12-1. Pathways of Fetal Exposure

Placenta-Dependent Pathways
Small molecular weight: carbon monoxide
Lipophilic: benzo[*a*]pyrene, ethanol
Specific transport mechanism: lead

Placenta-Independent Pathways
Ionizing radiation
Heat
Noise
Electromagnetic fields

Calcium is a nutrient that is actively transported across the placenta to provide the fetus with 100 to 140 mg/kg per day during the third trimester (see Chapter 47, Part 2).[89] It is believed that lead is transported by the calcium transporter. The fetal blood lead concentration is equivalent to the maternal blood lead concentration.[32] Recent animal studies have demonstrated that calcium supplementation may reduce the transfer of lead from prepregnancy maternal exposures to the fetus.[36]

Placenta-Independent Pathways

Placenta-independent hazards to the fetus include ionizing radiation, heat, noise, and, possibly, electromagnetic fields.

RADIATION

Ionizing radiation is a well-characterized teratogen. Much of our knowledge comes from studies of the survivors of the atomic bombs in Hiroshima and Nagasaki. Children exposed in utero at younger than 18 weeks' gestation showed a dose response of increasing microcephaly with increasing dose of radiation. The lowest observable effect occurred at a dose of 1 to 9 rad (Fig. 12-6).[7]

In comparison, the brain of a neonate undergoing cranial computed tomography with settings of 400 mA, 125 kV (peak), and a standard slice thickness of 4 mm receives a dose of 10.5 rad.[104] Because this level is close to that resulting in microcephaly, it has been recommended that computed tomography be used sparingly for premature infants, particularly when other imaging techniques are available.[21] An excess of cancer among the Japanese exposed in utero has also been reported (Fig. 12-7).[109]

Not all forms of radiation are hazardous to the fetus. Ultraviolet light does not penetrate to the fetus and does not constitute a future cancer risk.

HEAT

Heat may directly penetrate to the fetus and cause birth defects. In a study of the effects of heat on the outcome of pregnancy, 22,491 women undergoing α-fetoprotein screening were asked about their use of hot tubs, saunas, and electric blankets and whether they had experienced a fever during the first trimester.[66] The adjusted relative risk for neural tube defects with hot tub use was 2.8, with a 95% CI of 1.2 to 6.5. With exposure to two of these heat sources, the relative risk increased to 6.5.

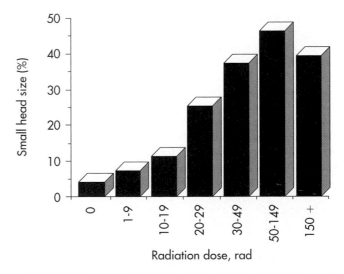

FIGURE 12-6. Percentage of Hiroshima children with head circumference 2 or more standard deviations below average, by fetal dose. Exposure occurred before 18 weeks of gestation. (From Blot WJ: Growth and development following prenatal and childhood exposure to atomic radiation. J Radiat Res [Tokyo] 16[Suppl]:82, 1975.)

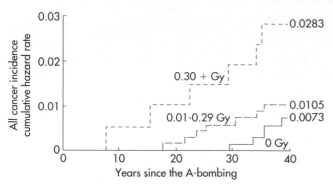

FIGURE 12-7. Cumulative hazard rate for cancer among survivors of intrauterine radiation in Hiroshima and Nagasaki, for three exposure groups through 1984. (From Yoshimoto Y et al: Risk of cancer among children exposed in utero to A-bomb radiations, 1954. Lancet 2:667, 1988.)

NOISE

Noise has a waveform that may be transmitted to the fetus (see Chapter 29, Part 2), and noise has been associated with certain birth defects, prematurity, and low birth weight.[22] In addition, noise-induced hearing loss may be evident following in utero exposure. In a study of 131 infants whose mothers worked in noisy conditions and received a noise dose of 65 to 95 LAeq.9m (dB) (a unit of noise dose calculated by an international standard and averaged over the 9 months of pregnancy), there was a threefold increase in the risk of a high-frequency hearing loss among infants whose mothers had received the highest doses of noise (Table 12-3).[54]

NEONATAL INTENSIVE CARE UNIT

A unique source of exposure to the fetus occurs if the fetus is born prematurely. Premature infants in the neonatal intensive care unit have several types of exposure in this highly artificial setting, including plasticizers,[76] noise,[6] electromagnetic fields,[1] and lead.[4] This subject has been discussed in several articles and is not reviewed here.[10]

TABLE 12-3. Comparisons of Percentages of Children with Hearing Loss at 4000 Hz (>10 dB HL) between Classes of Noise Exposure during Their Fetal Life

		Children with Hearing Loss	
INDEPENDENT VARIABLE	NO.	%	x^2 (P)
LAeq.9m (dB)			
65-75	2	5.9	
75-85	3	7.0	8.3
85-95	13	24.1	(.01)

dB HL, decibel hearing level
From Lelande NM et al: Is occupational noise exposure during pregnancy a risk factor of damage to the auditory system of the fetus? Am J Ind Med 10:427, 1986.

FETAL PHARMACOKINETICS

Fetal Distribution

The distribution of chemicals in the fetus differs from that in the adult (see Chapter 10). Because there is reduced protein binding in the fetus as a result of relative hypoproteinemia, chemicals can diffuse into tissues more readily. The blood-brain barrier is immature; therefore, chemicals can reach the brain easily. There is little or no body fat until approximately 29 weeks of gestation. Before that time, chemicals that normally accumulate in fat accumulate in other fat-containing tissues, especially the brain. An example of this redistribution is shown in Figure 12-8.[27]

DDT (an organochlorine pesticide, dichlorodiphenyltrichloroethane) was administered orally to mice at various ages that correspond to the human-brain growth spurt. The amount of radioactivity was measured in brain tissue after 24 hours and again after 7 days. There were striking differences in both the initial amount of DDT accumulated and the retention of DDT after 1 week. Twenty-day-old mice accumulated more DDT in their brains at 24 hours than mice at other ages. However, the DDT persisted longest in the animals given DDT at 10 days of age. In subsequent experiments, the mice treated at 10 days appeared to have more behavioral abnormalities than mice treated on either day 3 or day 19 of life, suggesting that the persistence of the pesticide was more important than the initial accumulation in regard to toxic effects. These results reflect the complexities of chemical distribution in the fetus as many organ systems continue to develop and mature.

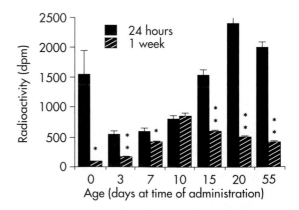

FIGURE 12-8. Radioactivity levels (in disintegrations per minute [dpm]) in mouse brain 24 hours and 1 week after oral administration of 1.48 MBq [^{14}C]DDT (dichlorodiphenyltrichloroethane) per kg of body weight. Height of bars represents mean ± standard deviation; statistical difference between 24 hours and 1 week is indicated by P < .01 (*single asterisk*) and P < .001 (*double asterisk*). (From Eriksson P: Age-dependent retention of [^{14}C]DDT in the brain of the postnatal mouse. Toxicol Lett 22:326, 1984.)

Fetal Metabolism

Chemicals are metabolized by a wide variety of enzymes, which differ among individuals both by genetic polymorphisms and by gestational age. *Ecogenetics* is the study of genetic predisposition to the toxic effects of chemicals.[38] An example of fetal ecogenetics is the susceptibility of some fetuses to the development of the fetal hydantoin syndrome with in utero exposure to phenytoin (see Chapter 10). Buehler and coworkers prospectively monitored 19 women receiving phenytoin during their pregnancy.[11] Epoxide hydrolase, an enzyme important in the metabolism of phenytoin, was measured in amniocytes from these pregnancies. Four of the samples had less than 30% of the standard activity (Fig. 12-9). All four infants corresponding to these samples had features of the fetal hydantoin syndrome; thus, their genetic background made them susceptible to an environmental exposure.

The expression of many proteins, including enzymes that metabolize xenobiotics, changes with gestational age. The developmental expression of alcohol dehydrogenase in the guinea pig is given in Figure 12-10.[14] Activity in the fetal liver is two orders of magnitude less than in the maternal liver. Even at 2 days of age, the difference in activity is still at one order of magnitude; therefore, environmental and occupational chemicals might not be cleared from the fetal compartment as rapidly as from the mother.

On the other hand, the fetus may be protected against toxic effects if the active form of a chemical is its metabolite. An example of such a chemical is acetaminophen, the most common drug used in suicide attempts during pregnancy. Acetaminophen is metabolized by the P-450 cytochrome system to hepatotoxic and nontoxic intermediates.[88] The expression of the P-450 enzymes is highly regulated both developmentally and by induction (see Chapter 10). Because many of

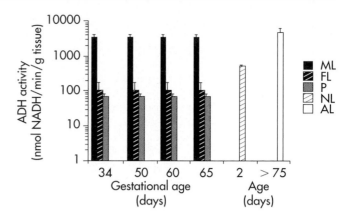

FIGURE 12-10. Activity of alcohol dehydrogenase (ADH) in guinea pig maternal liver (ML), fetal liver (FL), placenta (P), neonatal liver (NL), and adult liver (AL). Data are presented as mean ± SD (n = 6 at 34 days' gestation, n = 5 at 50 days' gestation, n = 6 at 60 days' gestation, n = 6 at 65 days' gestation, n = 5 at 2 postnatal days, and n = 8 at older than 75 postnatal days). (From Card SE et al: Ontogeny of the activity of alcohol dehydrogenase and aldehyde dehydrogenase in the liver and placenta of the guinea pig. Biochem Pharm 38:2535, 1989.)

these enzymes are poorly expressed in fetal tissues, the fetus may be protected from the effects of high doses of acetaminophen. In four case reports, the liver enzymes of neonates who were delivered on an emergency basis to overdosed women were normal or minimally elevated in the presence of severe maternal hepatotoxicity.[13,53,79,90]

SPECTRUM OF OUTCOMES

Because of the complexity of development and of developmental processes from the fertilized egg to the newborn infant, sites of action of chemicals and radiation are numerous. An intrauterine exposure to radiation or chemicals may result in a broad array of phenotypic effects. Box 12-2 lists some of the phenotypes.

Major malformations surpassed low birth weight and respiratory distress syndrome as the leading causes of infant death in 2002.[50] The rates for the top three causes of infant death per 100,000 live births were (1) congenital malformations, deformations, and chromosomal abnormalities, 140.7; (2) disorders relating to short

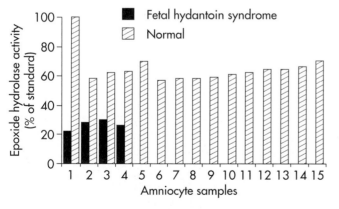

FIGURE 12-9. Epoxide hydrolase activity in amniocyte samples from 19 prospectively monitored fetuses. Samples from 4 fetuses subsequently given a diagnosis of fetal hydantoin syndrome are indicated by black bars. Samples from 15 fetuses subsequently confirmed not to have characteristic features of the syndrome are indicated by hatched bars. (From Beuhler BA et al: Prenatal prediction of risk of the fetal hydantoin syndrome. N Engl J Med 322:1570, 1990.)

BOX 12-2. Spectrum of Phenotypic Effects

Preterm birth
Growth restriction
Microcephaly
Major and minor malformations
Deformations
Metabolic dysfunction
Cognitive dysfunction
Behavioral dysfunction
Malignancy

gestation and low birth weight, not elsewhere classified, 114.4; and (3) SIDS, 50.6. All three have been associated with environmental exposures as discussed in this chapter.

Further evidence has linked the environment to birth defects. A study of 371,933 women investigated the relative risk of a child being born with a birth defect similar to the birth defect affecting the preceding sibling (Table 12-4).[57] The relative risk of a similar birth defect was 11.6 (95% CI, 9.3 to 14.0), and it dropped by more than 50% when the mother changed her living environment between the two pregnancies.

Reproductive dysfunction may also be a manifestation of occupational and environmental exposures. For example, when hamsters are exposed in utero to phenobarbital, they demonstrate altered neonatal behavior and reproductive maturation.[8] In studies of a cohort of adolescents exposed in utero to phenobarbital as part of a study to reduce postnatal hyperbilirubinemia, long-term effects, including lower testicular volume of exposed boys, were evident.[107] Dioxin and similar compounds have been shown to alter male reproductive function in wildlife.[19] Scientific debate continues over whether these observations in wildlife apply to human beings.

Permanent metabolic dysfunction has been associated with prenatal and neonatal exposure to monosodium glutamate (MSG) in animals. In female rats exposed neonatally to MSG, circulating growth hormone was reduced by 75% to 85%, and animals were mildly obese.[72] In addition, levels of a female-specific cytochrome P-450 were increased by almost 100%.[67] In male rats, neonatal exposure to MSG permanently blocked growth hormone secretion and resulted in stunted body growth, obesity, and impaired drug metabolism.[87] There

was irreversible suppression of cytochrome P-450 2C11 These effects have now been linked to increased apoptosis in the developing brains of animals exposed to glutamate.[70] As a result of these observations in animals, MSG was removed from baby foods in 1969. The effects of both phenobarbital and MSG have been called delayed teratogenic expression because the effects of the exposure are not immediately apparent at birth.

Developmental neurotoxicity deserves special mention. The development of the central nervous system requires expression of unique proteins in specific cell populations within specific critical windows of time. Injury to these populations may result in neurodevelopmental disorders, such as mental retardation, autism, dyslexia, and attention-deficit/hyperactivity disorder.

It is estimated that 3% to 8% of the 4 million children born each year in the United States are affected by a neurodevelopmental disability.[100] Some disabilities are caused by genetic aberrations (Down syndrome, fragile X syndrome), some by perinatal anoxia or meningitis, and some by exposure to drugs of abuse (ethanol, cocaine). However, the cause of most neurodevelopmental disabilities is unknown. Environmental chemicals, such as lead, PCBs, and mercury, are known developmental neurotoxins.

Of the 3000 chemicals produced or imported at over 1 million pounds a year, 43% have not received even minimal toxicologic assessment, and a mere 22% have been tested to determine whether they have the potential to cause developmental damage.[31] As of 1998, of all chemicals regulated by the EPA, only 12 have had any developmental neurotoxicity testing.[97] Thus, it remains a real possibility that neurodevelopmental disabilities arising in the newborn period are a result of in utero chemical exposure.

TABLE 12-4. Risk of Similar and Dissimilar Birth Defects in Second Infants of Mothers with an Affected First Infant

| | | Second Infant | | | | | |
| | | Similar Defect | | | Dissimilar Defect | | |
DEFECT IN FIRST INFANT	NO. AT RISK	OBSERVED	EXPECTED	RELATIVE RISK	OBSERVED	EXPECTED	RELATIVE RISK
Clubfoot	2784	100	14.7	7.3 (5.9-9.1)*	59	42.0	1.4 (1.0-1.7)†
Genital defect	1447	25	5.1	4.9 (3.2-7.3)	35	24.2	1.5 (1.0-2.0)
Limb defect	957	25	2.2	11.3 (7.2-17)	41	17.1	2.4 (1.7-3.3)
Cardiac defect	567	6	1.0	6.0 (2.2-13)	11	10.5	1.1 (0.5-1.9)
Total cleft lip	436	18	0.6	31.4 (19-52)	10	8.2	1.2 (0.6-2.2)
Isolated cleft palate	144	3	0.1	44.5 (9.0-134)	2	2.9	0.7 (0.1-2.5)
All combined‡	9192	201	26.4	7.6 (6.5-8.8)†	249	164.6	1.5 (1.3-1.7)†

*Numbers in parentheses are 95% confidence intervals for the odds ratios.
†Asymptotic confidence interval (numbers are too large for exact calculation).
‡Includes all 23 categories of isolated defects and the category of multiple defects. In addition to those listed above, the categories were anencephaly; spina bifida; hydrocephalus; other; central nervous system defects; eye defects; ear, face, or neck defects; circulatory system defect; respiratory system defect; esophageal defect; abdominal wall defects; anal defect; renal defects, axial defects; skin, hair, or nail defect; or birth defect: Down syndrome and other chromosomal syndromes.
From Lie RT et al: A population-based study of the risk of recurrence of birth defects. N Engl J Med 331:14, 1994.

CONCLUSION

In this chapter the many different sources of exposure and the timing of exposure to occupational and environmental chemicals have been described. The complexity of the maternal-fetal pharmacokinetics has been outlined, and many of the various types of outcomes have been discussed. The science of environmental medicine continues to evolve, elucidating sources of potential harm. What can one do now with the limited information available?

First, women who work have a right by law to be informed about the chemicals they work with,[73] and they have a right by law to be protected from harmful exposures. Materials safety data sheets should be available to any employee who requests them. These sheets supply information about potential reproductive effects. Personal protective gear should be available, and increased monitoring of potential exposures should be instituted. In certain instances, temporary job shifting may prevent potential exposure.

More insidious are the exposures that occur outside the workplace, which are often unknown to the person exposed. Sources of exposure include the chemicals and radiation in our environment: our water, our food, and our air. Current regulations rarely consider the unique susceptibilities and vulnerabilities of unborn children. Efforts should be made to inform the public and the legislature about these potential toxins so that safeguards to our children's health may be devised.

It is very challenging for the neonatologist confronted with a neonate who has a problem resulting from an environmental exposure to determine the cause of that problem. Confirming the etiologic agent is almost impossible and requires several steps. First, a detailed exposure history is vital. Guidelines for taking this history can be found in a monograph from the U.S. Department of Health and Human Services, Agency for Toxic Substances and Disease Registry (ATSDR), *Case Studies in Environmental Medicine: Taking an Exposure History* (see Carter et al in Additional Reading).

It is not enough to know the mother's occupation. One must ascertain exactly what she does at work, what the father does at work, what their hobbies are, what they do at home, what type of residence they have, and what type of neighborhood they live in. What is the composition of their diet? Do they smoke or use alcohol or other types of recreational drugs? Were medicines, both those prescribed and those available over the counter, used during the pregnancy? One must also be aware that taking this history has the potential for raising guilt feelings in the parents, and one must be prepared to address this issue.

Once the history of exposure has been taken, one must gauge the amount of exposure. An industrial hygienist might be able to make an estimate, but such an estimate is expensive and time consuming. For certain types of exposure, biomarkers may be confirmatory. Examples are cord blood concentrations of cotinine for prenatal exposure to the products of tobacco smoke and urinary concentrations of mercury for mercury exposure.

Second, one must ascertain whether a neonate's particular problem is known to occur with a given type of exposure. Appendices for computerized databases are listed in the ATSDR monograph, and birth defect information services are available online at http://www.otispregnancy.org/.

Third, when an association is made between an exposure and an adverse outcome, one must determine the likelihood that the exposure caused the adverse outcome. This assessment should be carried out with the help of the teratology hotline (www.otispregnancy.org) and any additional resources available (e.g., dysmorphologist, neuropsychologist). For example, methylethylketone (MEK), a commonly used solvent, has been shown to cause an increase in major malformations and intrauterine growth retardation in rats[26,82,83] and mice.[80] In addition, human epidemiologic studies have shown an association between organic solvent exposure (in human studies rarely does one find exposure to only one organic solvent) and malformations.[42,48,71] Thus, it is reasonable to conclude that the microcephaly and mental retardation observed in a child delivered to a woman exposed to MEK during her pregnancy are a result of this exposure.

More formal criteria for assessing causation have been reviewed by Scialli.[84] What the mother should do to prevent a recurrence is a complicated issue. If the exposure is job related, job discrimination may result.[73] It may be necessary for both the patient and her doctor to work with the employer to find a suitable (and legal) alternative. Sometimes simple hygienic measures, such as changing contaminated clothing at work or frequent hand washing, are the only requirements. Additional interventions may be the use of personal protective equipment and temporary job rotation to a position in which exposure does not occur.

The hotlines for teratology information are part of the Organization of Teratology Information Services (OTIS) and are listed online at www.otispregnancy.org. Case Studies in Environmental Health can be obtained from the ATSDR at www.atsdr.cdc.gov/atsdrhome.html.

ACKNOWLEDGMENTS

The author gratefully acknowledges the editorial comments by Dr. Susan Cummins, Dr. Sophie Balk, and Dr. Robert Karp.

ADDITIONAL READING

Carter W et al: Case Studies in Environmental Medicine: Taking an Exposure History. Atlanta, Agency for Toxic Substances and Disease Registry, U.S. Department of Health and Human Services, 2000. Available at: www.atsdr.cdc.gov/HEC/CSEM/exphistory/index.html.

Gehle K et al: Case Studies in Environmental Medicine: Pediatric Environmental Health. Atlanta, Agency for Toxic Substances and Disease Registry, U.S. Department of Health and Human Services, 2002. Available at: www.atsdr.cdc.gov/HEC/CSEM/pediatric/index.html.

Isaacson RL et al (eds): The Vulnerable Brain and Environmental Risks, vols 1-3. New York, Plenum Press, 1992.

Paul M (ed): Occupational and Environmental Reproductive Hazards: A Guide for Clinicians. Baltimore, Williams & Wilkins, 1993.

Persaud TVN: Environmental Causes of Human Birth Defects. Springfield, Ill, Charles C. Thomas, 1990.

Scialli AR: A Clinical Guide to Reproductive and Developmental Toxicology. Boca Raton, Fla, CRC Press, 1992.

Welch LS et al (eds): Case Studies in Environmental Medicine: Reproductive and Developmental Hazards. Atlanta, Agency for Toxic Substances and Disease Registry, U.S. Department of Health and Human Services, 1993.

REFERENCES

1. Bearer CF: Electromagnetic fields and infant incubators. Arch Environ Health 49:352, 1994.
2. Bearer CF et al: Maternal tobacco smoke exposure and persistent pulmonary hypertension of the newborn. Environ Health Perspect 105:202, 1997.
3. Bearer CF et al: Ethyl linoleate in meconium: A biomarker for prenatal ethanol exposure. Alcohol Clin Exp Res 23:487, 1999.
4. Bearer CF et al: Lead exposure from blood transfusion to premature infants. J Pediatr 137:549, 2000.
5. Bearer CF et al: Validation of a new biomarker of fetal exposure to alcohol. J Pediatr 143:463, 2003
6. Bess FH et al: Further observations on noise levels in infant incubators. Pediatrics 63:100, 1979.
7. Blot WJ: Growth and development following prenatal and childhood exposure to atomic radiation. J Radiat Res (Tokyo) 16(Suppl):82, 1975.
8. Bonner MJ: Prenatal and neonatal pharmacologic stress on early behavior and sexual maturation in the hamster. J Clin Pharmacol 34:713, 1994.
9. Bove F et al: Drinking water contaminants and adverse pregnancy outcomes: A review. Environ Health Perspect 110 (Suppl 1):61, 2002.
10. Brown AK et al: Environmental hazards in the newborn nursery. Pediatr Ann 8:698, 1979.
11. Buehler BA et al: Prenatal prediction of risk of the fetal hydantoin syndrome. N Engl J Med 322:1567, 1990.
12. Bush B et al: Polychlorobiphenyl (PCB) congeners, p,p′-DDE, and hexachlorobenzene in maternal and fetal cord blood from mothers in upstate New York. Arch Environ Contam Toxicol 13:517, 1984.
13. Byer A et al: Acetaminophen overdose in the third trimester of pregnancy. JAMA 247:3114, 1982.
14. Card SE et al: Ontogeny of the activity of alcohol dehydrogenase and aldehyde dehydrogenase in the liver and placenta of the guinea pig. Biochem Pharmacol 38:2535, 1989.
15. Cassidy SB et al: Occupational hydrocarbon exposure among fathers of Prader-Willi syndrome patients with and without deletions of 15q. Am J Hum Genet 44:806, 1989.
16. Chen Y-C et al: Cognitive development of yu-cheng ("oil disease") children prenatally exposed to heat-degraded PCBs. JAMA 268:3213, 1992.
17. Chia SE, Shi LM: A review of recent epidemiological studies on paternal occupations and birth defects. Occup Environ Med 59:149, 2002.
18. Clarke DW et al: Activity of alcohol dehydrogenase and aldehyde dehydrogenase in maternal liver, fetal liver and placenta of the near-term pregnant ewe. Dev Pharmacol Ther 12:35, 1989.
19. Colborn T et al (eds): Chemically Induced Alterations in Sexual and Functional Development: The Wildlife/Human Connection. Princeton, NJ, Princeton Scientific Publishing, 1992.
20. Colt JS, Blair A. Parental occupational exposures and risk of childhood cancer. Environ Health Perspect. 106(Suppl 3):909, 1998.
21. Committee on Environmental Health: Risk of ionizing radiation exposure to children: A subject review. Pediatrics 101:717, 1998.
22. Committee on Environmental Health: Noise: A hazard for the fetus and newborn. Pediatrics 100:724, 1997.
23. Council on Scientific Affairs, American Medical Association: Environmental tobacco smoke: Health effects and prevention policies. Arch Fam Med 3:865, 1994.
24. Curley A et al: Organic mercury identified as the cause of poisoning in humans and hogs. Science 172:65, 1971.
25. Darnell J et al: Molecular Cell Biology. New York, Scientific American Books, 1986, p 149.
26. Deacon MM et al: Embryo- and fetotoxicity of inhaled methyl ethyl ketone in rats. Toxicol Appl Pharmacol 59:620, 1981.
27. Eriksson P: Age-dependent retention of [^{14}C]DDT in the brain of the postnatal mouse. Toxicol Lett 22:323, 1984.
28. Farrow JR et al: Fetal death due to nonlethal maternal carbon monoxide poisoning. J Forensic Sci 35:1448, 1990.
29. Feychting M et al: Paternal occupational exposures and childhood cancer. Environ Health Perspect 109:193, 2001.
30. Gladen BC et al: Effects of perinatal polychlorinated biphenyls and dichlorodiphenyl dichloroethene on later development. J Pediatr 119:58, 1991.
31. Goldman LR, Koduru S: Chemicals in the environment and developmental toxicity to children: A public health and policy perspective. Environ Health Perspect 108:443, 2000.
32. Goyer RA: Transplacental transport of lead. Environ Health Perspect 89:101, 1990.
33. Gulson BL et al: Pregnancy increases mobilization of lead from maternal skeleton. J Lab Clin Med 130:51, 1997.
34. Haddow JE et al: Second-trimester serum cotinine levels in nonsmokers in relation to birth weight. Am J Obstet Gynecol 159:481, 1988.
35. Hall J: Genomic imprinting: Review and relevance to human diseases. Am J Hum Genet 46:857, 1990.
36. Han S et al: Effects of lead exposure before pregnancy and dietary calcium during pregnancy on fetal development and lead accumulation. Environ Health Perspect 108:527, 2000.
37. Harada M: Methyl mercury poisoning due to environmental contamination ("Minamata disease"). In Oehme FW (ed): Toxicity of Heavy Metals in the Environment. New York, Marcel Dekker, 1978, p 261.
38. Hauth JC et al: Passive smoking and thiocyanate concentrations in pregnant women and children. Obstet Gynecol 63:519, 1984.
39. Herbst AL et al: A comparison of pregnancy experience in DES-exposed and DES-unexposed daughters. J Reprod Med 24:62, 1980.
40. Herbst AL et al: Reproductive and gynecologic surgical experience in diethylstilbestrol-exposed daughters. Am J Obstet Gynecol 141:1019, 1981.
41. Hill EP et al: Carbon monoxide exchanges between the human fetus and mother: A mathematical model. Am J Physiol 232:H311, 1977.
42. Holmberg PC et al: Congenital defects of the central

nervous system and occupational factors during pregnancy: Case referent study. Am J Ind Med 1:167, 1980.

43. Hsu S-T et al: Discovery and epidemiology of PCB poisoning in Taiwan: A four-year follow-up. Environ Health Perspect 59:5, 1985.

44. International Agency for Research on Cancer (IARC): IARC Monographs on the Evaluation of the Carcinogenic Risk of Chemicals to Humans, Polychlorinated Biphenyls and Polybrominated Biphenyls, vol 18. Lyon, France, IARC, 1978.

45. Jacobson JL et al: Effects of in utero exposure to polychlorinated biphenyls and related contaminants on cognitive functioning in young children. J Pediatr 116:38, 1990.

46. Jacobson JL, Jacobson SW: Intellectual impairment in children exposed to polychlorinated biphenyls in utero. N Engl J Med 335:783, 1996.

47. Jensen S: A new chemical hazard. New Sci 32:612, 1966.

48. Khattak S et al: Pregnancy outcome following gestational exposure to organic solvents: A prospective controlled study. JAMA 281:1106, 1999.

49. Klip H et al: Hypospadias in sons of women exposed to diethylstilbestrol in utero: A cohort study. Lancet 359:1102, 2002.

50. Kochanek KD, Smith BL: Deaths: preliminary data for 2002. Natl Vital Stat Rep 52:1, 2004.

51. Kuhnert B, Nieschlag E: Reproductive functions of the aging male. Hum Reprod Update 10:327, 2004.

52. Kumar R et al: Vitamin D and calcium hormones in pregnancy. N Engl J Med 142:40, 1980.

53. Kurzel RB: Can acetaminophen excess result in maternal and fetal toxicity? South Med J 83:953, 1990.

54. Lalande NM et al: Is occupational noise exposure during pregnancy a risk factor of damage to the auditory system of the fetus? Am J Ind Med 10:427, 1986.

55. Langman J: Medical Embryology. Baltimore, Williams & Wilkins, 1975, p 11.

56. Lian ZH et al: Paternal age and the occurrence of birth defects. Am J Hum Genet 39:648, 1986.

57. Lie RT et al: A population-based study of the risk of recurrence of birth defects. N Engl J Med 331:1, 1994.

58. Longo LD: Carbon monoxide in the pregnant mother and fetus and its exchange across the placenta. Ann N Y Acad Sci 174:313, 1970.

59. Lowery MC et al: Male-mediated behavioral abnormalities. Mutat Res 229:213, 1990.

60. Mahaffey KR: Methylmercury: A new look at the risks. Public Health Rep 114:396, 1999.

61. Malaspina D et al: Advancing paternal age and the risk of schizophrenia. Arch Gen Psychiatry 58:361, 2001.

62. Manton WI: Total contribution of airborne lead to blood lead. Br J Ind Med 42:168, 1985.

63. Marsh DO: Dose response relationships in humans: Methyl mercury epidemics in Japan and Iraq. In Eccles CU (ed): The Toxicity of Methyl Mercury. Baltimore, Johns Hopkins University Press, 1987, p 45.

64. Mathai M et al: Passive maternal smoking and birthweight in a South Indian population. Br J Obstet Gynecol 99:342, 1992.

65. McDiarmid MA et al: Fouling one's own nest revisited. Am J Ind Med 24:1, 1993.

66. Milunsky A, et al: Maternal heat exposure and neural tube defects. JAMA 268:882, 1992.

67. Munafo M et al: Does cigarette smoking increase time to conception? J Biosoc Sci 34:65, 2002.

68. Narod SA et al: Human mutagens: Evidence from paternal exposure? Environ Mol Mutagen 11:401, 1988.

69. Nicholl JP et al: Epidemiology of babies dying at different ages from the sudden infant death syndrome. J Epidemiol Community Health 43:133, 1989.

70. Olney JW et al: Environmental agents that have the potential to trigger massive apoptotic neurodegeneration in the developing brain. Environ Health Perspect 108 (Suppl 3):383, 2000.

71. Olsen J: Risk of exposure to teratogens amongst laboratory staff and painters. Dan Med Bull 30:24, 1983.

72. Pampori NA et al: Subnormal concentrations in the feminine profile of circulating growth hormone enhance expression of female-specific CYP2C12. Biochem Pharmacol 47:1999, 1994.

73. Paul M: Occupational and Environmental Reproductive Hazards: A Guide for Clinicians. Baltimore, Williams & Wilkins, 1993, p viii.

74. Persaud TVN: Environmental Causes of Human Birth Defects. Springfield, Ill, Charles C Thomas, 1990, p 73.

75. Pierce PE et al: Alkyl mercury poisoning in humans. JAMA 220:1439, 1972.

76. Ploniart SL et al: Exposure of newborn infants to di-(2-ethylhexyl)-phthalate and 2-ethylhexanoic acid following exchange transfusion with polyvinylchloride catheters. Transfusion 33:598, 1993.

77. Pragst F et al: Illegal and therapeutic drug concentrations in hair segments—a timetable of drug exposure? Forensic Sci Rev 10:81, 1998.

78. Rogan WJ et al: Congenital poisoning by polychlorinated biphenyls and their contaminants in Taiwan. Science 241:334, 1988.

79. Rosevear SK et al: Favourable neonatal outcome following maternal paracetamol overdose and severe fetal distress: Case report. Br J Obstet Gynecol 96:491, 1989.

80. Rothenberg SJ et al: Maternal bone lead contribution to blood lead during and after pregnancy. Environ Res 82:81, 2000.

81. Rousseau F et al: Mutations in the gene encoding fibroblast growth factor receptor-3 in achondroplasia. Nature 371:252, 1994.

82. Schwetz BA: Embryo- and fetotoxicity of inhaled carbon tetrachloride, 1,1-dicloroethane and methyl ethyl ketone in rats. Toxicol Appl Pharmacol 28:452, 1974.

83. Schwetz BA et al: Developmental toxicity of inhaled methyl ethyl ketone in Swiss mice. Fundam Appl Toxicol 16:742, 1991.

84. Scialli A: A Clinical Guide to Reproductive and Developmental Toxicology. Boca Raton, Fla, CRC Press, 1992, p 257.

85. Scialli A: A Clinical Guide to Reproductive and Developmental Toxicology. Boca Raton, Fla, CRC Press, 1992, p 209.

86. Shannon M et al: Lead intoxication in infancy. Pediatrics 89:87, 1992.

87. Shapiro BH et al: Irreversible suppression of growth hormone dependent cytochrome P450 2C11 in adult rats neonatally treated with monosodium glutamate. J Pharmacol Exp Ther 265:979, 1993.

88. Snawder JE et al: Loss of CYP2E1 and CYP1A2 activity as a function of acetaminophen dose: Relation to toxicity. Biophys Res Commun 203:532, 1995.

89. Steichen JJ et al: Osteopenia and rickets of prematurity. In Polin RA, et al (eds): Fetal and Neonatal Physiology, vol 2, Philadelphia, WB Saunders, 1991, p 1767.

90. Stokes IM: Paracetamol overdose in the second trimester of pregnancy: Case report. Br J Obstet Gynecol 91:286, 1984.

91. Strakowski SM, et al: Paternal hydrocarbon exposure in Prader-Willi syndrome [letter]. Lancet 2:1458, 1987.

92. Thompson GN et al: Lead mobilization during pregnancy [letter]. Med J Australia 143:131, 1985.

93. Trapp M et al: Pollutants in human follicular fluid. Fertil Steril 42:146, 1984.

94. United Nations: Available at http://www.population connection.org/Communications/FactSheets/Demo%20Facts%202004.pdf

95. US Department of Labor, Bureau of Labor Statistics: 20 Leading Occupations of Employed Women: 2001 Annual Averages. Washington, DC: US Department of Labor; 2001. Available at: www.dol.gov/wb/wb_pubs/20lead2001.htm.

96. US Department of Labor, Bureau of Labor Statistics: http://www.bls.gov/cps/cpsa2003.pdf

97. US Environmental Protection Agency: A Retrospective Analysis of Developmental Neurotoxicity Studies, 1999. SAP Report No 99-01B.

98. Waldfogel J: Family leave coverage in the 1990s. Monthly Labor Review. October:13-20, 1999.

99. Weinberg CR et al: Reduced fecundability in women with prenatal exposure to cigarette smoking. Am J Epidemiol 129:1072, 1989.

100. Weiss B, Landrigan PJ: The developing brain and the environment: An introduction. Environ Health Perspect 108:373, 2000.

101. Weiss J et al: Human exposures to inorganic mercury. Public Health Rep 114:400, 1999.

102. Welch LS et al (eds): Case Studies in Environmental Medicine: Reproductive and Developmental Hazards. Washington DC, Agency for Toxic Substances and Disease Registry, U.S. Department of Health and Human Services, 1993.

103. Whitehall JS et al: Fetal exposure to pollutants in Townsville, Australia, detected in meconium. Pediatr Res 47:299A, 2000.

104. Wilson-Costello D et al: Radiation exposure from diagnostic radiographs in extremely low birth weight infants. Pediatrics 97:369, 1996.

105. World Resources Institute, UN Environment Programme, and UN Development Programme: Population and health. In World Resources 1988-89. New York, Oxford University Press, 1988, p 33.

106. Worley G et al: Delayed development of sensorineural hearing loss after neonatal hyperbilirubinemia: A case report with brain magnetic resonance imaging. Dev Med Child Neurol 38:271, 1996.

107. Yaffe SJ et al: Effects of prenatal treatment with phenobarbital. Dev Pharmacol Ther 15:215, 1990.

108. Yazigi RA et al: Demonstration of specific binding of cocaine to human spermatozoa. JAMA 266:1956, 1991.

109. Yoshimoto Y et al: Risk of cancer among children exposed in utero to A-bomb radiations, 1954-1980. Lancet 2:665, 1988.

110. Younglai EV et al: Levels of environmental contaminants in human follicular fluid, serum, and seminal plasma of couples undergoing in vitro fertilization. Arch Environ Contam Toxicol 43:121, 2002.

Pregnancy Disorders and Their Impact on the Fetus

13 Intrauterine Growth Restriction

Robert M. Kliegman

Fetal development is characterized by sequential patterns of tissue and organ growth, differentiation, and maturation that are influenced by the maternal environment, uteroplacental function, and the inherent genetic growth potential of the fetus. When circumstances are optimal, none of these factors has a rate-limiting effect on fetal growth and development. Thus, the healthy fetus should achieve complete functional maturity and genetically determined somatic growth, and an uncomplicated intrapartum course and a smooth neonatal cardiopulmonary and metabolic adaptation to extrauterine life can be anticipated.

However, fetal growth and development do not always occur under optimal intrauterine conditions.[70,98] Those neonates subjected to aberrant maternal, placental, or fetal circumstances that restrain intrauterine growth are a high-risk group and are traditionally categorized as having intrauterine growth restriction (IUGR). The cumulative effects of adverse environmental conditions and aberrant fetal growth threaten continued intrauterine survival; labor, delivery, and neonatal adaptation become increasingly hazardous. Similarly, postneonatal growth and development may be impaired as a result of IUGR and the subsequent problems encountered during the neonatal period. Neonates who have IUGR are a heterogenous group. Many with IUGR may in fact have poor intrauterine growth as an adaptation to a suboptimal uterine environment.

The terms *IUGR* and *small for gestational age* (SGA), although related, are not synonymous.[27,58,74,100,144] IUGR is a deviation from, or a reduction in, an expected fetal growth pattern and is caused by innate reduced growth potential or by multiple adverse effects on the fetus. IUGR is the result of any process that inhibits the normal growth potential of the fetus. Fetal growth at term may be predicted by anthropometric analysis of fetal dimensions with second-trimester ultrasonography. Deviations from the predicted weight at term may result in an infant with IUGR but may not result in an infant who is SGA. The term *SGA* describes an infant whose weight is lower than population norms or lower than a predetermined cutoff weight (e.g., −2 SD, 5%, 10%); the cause may be pathologic, as in an infant with IUGR, or nonpathologic, as in an infant who is small but healthy. Not all infants who are IUGR are SGA: for example, in comparison with siblings, ethnically derived fetal growth curves, or their own growth potential, infants'

birthweight may be less than expected despite their weight being above an arbitrary normative population growth percentile standard. A customized birthweight would take into consideration important epidemiologic variables such as parity, maternal anthropometrics, and ethnicity.[27] (See growth curves in Appendix B.)

Low birthweight as a classification includes premature infants (younger than 37 weeks), preterm infants who are SGA (younger than 37 weeks), and term (37 weeks or older) infants who are SGA. Many preterm infants are also IUGR when growth is based on fetal growth standards.[74,144] These IUGR preterm infants are at increased risk for perinatal demise and neonatal complications.

FETAL GROWTH AND BODY COMPOSITION

Through anthropomorphic measurements that include fetal weight, length (crown to heel), abdominal circumference, and head circumference as well as three-dimensional fetal ultrasonography, fetal growth standards have been determined for various reference populations from various locations.[14,35,118] Although the range of birthweight at each gestational age in these populations may vary (Table 13-1), the overall pattern of fetal growth (Fig. 13-1) is representative of these and subsequent groups. Both early and late fetal growth patterns appear to be linear, beginning at approximately 20 weeks' gestation and lasting until 38 weeks; thereafter, the rate of weight gain begins to decline. Fetal growth curves based on prematurely born infants may result in inaccurate assessment of fetal growth. Premature infants often have IUGR and thus skew the fetal growth curve to standards lower than those that would have been obtained if the fetus had not been born early. The cause of the preterm labor may also cause IUGR, or alternatively the IUGR may produce fetal distress resulting in spontaneous or elective delivery.[53] (See growth curves in Appendix B.)

Figure 13-2 demonstrates a similar linear relationship between fetal weight and gestational age. Near term, the fetal weight gain appears to decelerate; after birth, it again assumes the intrauterine rate. Fetal weight gain (grams per day) is constant during the second trimester

TABLE 13-1. Birth Weights from Six Sources

NEAREST WEEK OF GESTATION	Mean Birthweight (g ± 1 SD)					
	Denver	Baltimore	Montreal	Portland	Chapel Hill	12 U.S. Cities (Cluster Method)
28	1150 ± 259	1050 ± 310	1113 ± 150	1172 ± 344	1150 ± 272	1165 ± 109
29	1270 ± 294	1200 ± 350	1228 ± 165	1322 ± 339	1310 ± 299	1295 ± 94
30	1395 ± 341	1380 ± 370	1373 ± 175	1529 ± 474	1460 ± 340	1440 ± 115
31	1540 ± 375	1560 ± 400	1540 ± 200	1757 ± 495	1630 ± 340	1601 ± 117
32	1715 ± 416	1750 ± 410	1727 ± 225	1881 ± 437	1810 ± 381	1760 ± 128
33	1920 ± 505	1950 ± 420	1900 ± 250	2158 ± 511	2010 ± 367	1955 ± 138
34	2200 ± 539	2170 ± 430	2113 ± 280	2340 ± 552	2220 ± 395	2160 ± 202
35	2485 ± 526	2390 ± 440	2347 ± 315	2518 ± 468	2430 ± 408	2387 ± 208
36	2710 ± 519	2610 ± 440	2589 ± 350	2749 ± 490	2650 ± 408	2621 ± 274
37	2900 ± 451	2830 ± 440	2868 ± 385	2989 ± 466	2870 ± 395	2878 ± 288
38	3030 ± 451	3050 ± 450	3133 ± 400	3185 ± 450	3030 ± 395	3119 ± 302
39	3140 ± 403	3210 ± 450	3360 ± 430	3333 ± 444	3170 ± 408	3210 ± 434
40	3230 ± 396	3280 ± 450	3480 ± 460	3462 ± 456	3280 ± 422	3351 ± 448
41	3290 ± 396	3350 ± 450	3567 ± 475	3569 ± 468	3360 ± 435	3444 ± 456
42	3300 ± 423	3400 ± 460	3513 ± 480	3637 ± 482	3410 ± 449	3486 ± 463
43		3410 ± 490	3416 ± 465	3660 ± 502	3420 ± 463	3473 ± 502

From Naeye RL, Dixon JB: Distortions in fetal growth standards. Pediatr Res 12:987, 1978.

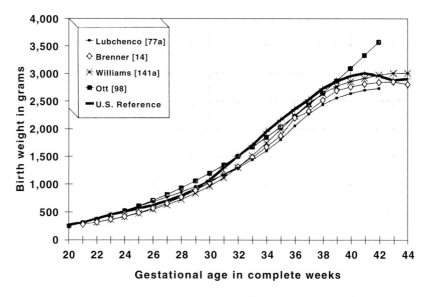

FIGURE 13-1. Fetal weight as a function of gestational age by selected references. (From Alexander GR et al: A United States national reference for fetal growth. Obstet Gynecol 87:163, 1996.)

and then accelerates during most of the third trimester, but it declines near term. During the neonatal period, the rate of gain accelerates again. This relative slowing of growth as the normal fetus approaches term may be caused by some mild restraint of fetal growth. These restraining factors may be related to uterine size or placental function. Some fetuses, however, continue to grow in utero after week 40. During the neonatal period, growth resumes and approaches the in utero rate once this restraint has been eliminated.

Although weight gain per day is maximal before term, when growth is expressed as percent increment per day, it is greatest during embryonic and early fetal development (see Fig. 13-2). In the last half of preg-

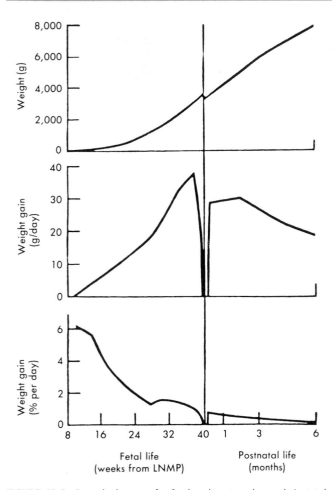

FIGURE 13-2. Smoothed curves for fetal and postnatal growth in total grams, in grams gained per day, and expressed as percent increment of body weight per day. LNMP, last normal menstrual period. (From Usher R et al: In Davis J et al [eds]: Scientific Foundations of Pediatrics. Philadelphia, WB Saunders, 1974.)

TABLE 13-2. Contribution of Organs to Body Mass during Development

TISSUE	FETUS (20-24 WK) (%)	TERM BABY (%)	ADULT (%)
Skeletal muscle	25	25	43
Skin	13	15	7
Skeleton	22	18	18
Heart	0.6	0.5	0.4
Liver	4	5	2
Kidneys	0.7	1	0.5
Brain	13	13	2

From Widdowson E: In Assali N (ed): Biology of Gestation, vol 2. New York, Academic Press, 1968.

mass.[145] Fetal muscle growth, as well as all protein synthesis in the fetus, depends on active transport of essential amino acids across the placenta. Once provided with these precursors, fetal protein synthesis is autonomous and results in the net synthesis of proteins that have amino acid patterns determined by the fetal genome. Although the building blocks may be the same, developmentally the fetal muscle has a lower fibrillar protein content, whereas the sarcoplasmic protein concentration remains unchanged as maturation proceeds. Besides those immunoglobulins (IgG), that cross the placenta, all protein present in the fetus has been synthesized de novo by fetal tissue.

Paralleling the patterns of fetal growth, the macromolecular composition of the body also undergoes sequential patterns of change. One general trend includes a decrease of total body and extracellular water content as the fetus and infant mature (Fig. 13-3 and Table 13-3). Simultaneously, there is an increment of body protein and fat content (Fig. 13-4). Whereas the increase of tissue protein is gradual during development, the increment of fetal body fat is delayed until the third trimester. Once initiated, the deposition of subcutaneous and deep body adipose tissue accelerates more rapidly than the rate of protein accumulation. Infants with IUGR have a smaller percent body fat (17% versus 23%), which is mainly a reduction of subcutaneous adipose tissue rather than intra-abdominal adipose tissue.[45]

Coinciding with the changes in the extracellular fluid space, the sodium and chloride concentrations in the fetus decline, whereas the expansion of the intracellular fluid space results in an increase in potassium concentration (see also Chapter 34, Part 1). The decline in total body sodium is less than that for chloride, because sodium is also a component of fetal bone. Calcium, phosphorus, and magnesium are nevertheless the major minerals in bone. By term, the total body calcium-to-phosphorus ratio is 1.7:1.8, with 98% of calcium, 80% of phosphorus, and 60% of magnesium deposited within the bone.

nancy, the fetus gains 85% of its birthweight. However, the nature of fetal growth differs between early and later fetal life. During the embryonic and early fetal growth period, tissues and organs increase in cell number rather than cell size (the hyperplastic phase of cell growth, when total DNA content increases in new tissues). Later phases of growth include a period when cell size also increases (protein and RNA content), along with continued enhancement of cell number (mixed hyperplastic and hypertrophic phase). In muscle and brain (especially the cerebellum), this phase of growth may continue through adolescence and the second year of life, respectively. The final stage of growth is a purely hypertrophic phase, when only cell size increases.

The contribution of each tissue to body weight changes during fetal and postnatal development is depicted in Table 13-2. Muscle represents only 25% of fetal and neonatal body weight; once full adult maturity has been achieved, it accounts for 40% of the body's

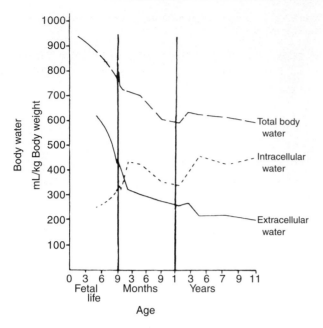

FIGURE 13-3. Developmental alterations of fluid space distribution. (From Uttley W, Habel AH: Fluid and electrolyte metabolism in the newborn infant. Clin Endocrinol Metab 5:3, 1976.)

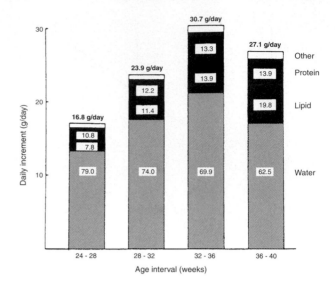

FIGURE 13-4. Composition of fetal weight gain. (From Ziegler E et al: Body composition of the reference fetus. Growth 40:329, 1976.)

TABLE 13-3. Body Composition of the Reference Fetus

GESTATIONAL AGE (WK)	BODY WEIGHT (g)	Per 100 g Body Weight				Per 100 g Fat-Free Weight							
		Water (g)	Protein (g)	Lipid (g)	Other (g)	Water (g)	Protein (g)	Ca (mg)	P (mg)	Mg (mg)	Na (mEq)	K (mEq)	Cl (mEq)
24	690	88.6	8.8	0.1	2.5	88.6	8.8	621	387	17.8	9.9	4.0	7.0
25	770	87.8	9.0	0.7	2.5	88.4	9.1	615	385	17.6	9.8	4.0	7.0
26	880	86.8	9.2	1.5	2.5	88.1	9.4	611	384	17.5	9.7	4.1	7.0
27	1010	85.7	9.4	2.4	2.5	87.8	9.7	609	383	17.4	9.5	4.1	6.9
28	1160	84.6	9.6	3.3	2.4	87.5	10.0	610	385	17.4	9.4	4.2	6.9
29	1318	83.6	9.9	4.1	2.4	87.2	10.3	613	387	17.4	9.3	4.2	6.8
30	1480	82.6	10.1	4.9	2.4	86.8	10.6	619	392	17.4	9.2	4.3	6.8
31	1650	81.7	10.3	5.6	2.4	86.5	10.9	628	398	17.6	9.1	4.3	6.7
32	1830	80.7	10.6	6.3	2.4	86.1	11.3	640	406	17.8	9.1	4.3	6.6
33	2020	79.8	10.8	6.9	2.5	85.8	11.6	656	416	18.0	9.0	4.4	6.5
34	2230	79.0	11.0	7.5	2.5	85.4	11.9	675	428	18.3	8.9	4.4	6.4
35	2450	78.1	11.2	8.1	2.6	85.0	12.2	699	443	18.6	8.9	4.5	6.3
36	2690	77.3	11.4	8.7	2.6	84.6	12.5	726	460	19.0	8.8	4.5	6.1
37	2940	76.4	11.6	9.3	2.7	84.3	12.8	758	479	19.5	8.8	4.5	6.0
38	3160	75.6	11.8	9.9	2.7	83.9	13.1	795	501	20.0	8.8	4.5	5.9
39	3330	74.8	11.9	10.5	2.8	83.6	13.3	836	525	20.5	8.7	4.6	5.8
40	3450	74.0	12.0	11.2	2.8	83.3	13.5	882	551	21.1	8.7	4.6	5.7

From Ziegler E et al: Body composition of the reference fetus. Growth 40:329, 1976.

FETAL METABOLISM

Maternal and thus fetal nutritional deprivations can adversely affect fetal growth. The fetus depends on maternal nutrient intake as well as on maternal endogenous substrate stores as precursors for fetal tissue synthesis and as fuel for fetal oxidative metabolism. The oxygen consumed by the fetus in turn provides energy to support essential fetal work, such as maintenance of transmembrane potentials and replacement of tissue components that are continuously being renewed. In addition, fetal oxygen consumption is required for net synthesis of complex macromolecules such as DNA, RNA, protein, and lipid. Each gram of protein synthesized requires the expenditure of 7.5 cal, whereas a gram of triglycerides requires 11.6 cal. Because 4.85 cal use 1 L of oxygen, net tissue synthesis represents a substantial proportion of fetal oxygen consumption, which is approximately 4 to 6 mL/kg per minute. The energy cost of neonatal growth as measured in premature infants constitutes the energy stored in tissue plus that expended for the synthesis of that tissue. Total energy cost per gram of new tissue is approximately 5.7 cal, whereas that remaining in structural or depot macromolecules represents 4.0 cal. Therefore, 1.7 cal is expended to produce 1 g of new tissue.[15] A similar relationship should occur in the third-trimester fetus, because energy requirements for growth should not change after birth.

Maternal metabolic adjustments during pregnancy are characterized by fuel and hormonal alterations that attempt to secure a continuous provision of substrates for use by the fetus. During normal periods of alimentation, sufficient substrates are presented to the uteroplacental circulation while maternal fuel stores are simultaneously enriched. During the third trimester, maternal insulin resistance and decreased insulin production may partition ingested fuels toward the fetus.[62] When fasting occurs during pregnancy, fuel mobilization is accelerated, as is evident by the rapid rise of maternal free fatty acids and ketone bodies. This accelerated mobilization of maternal adipose tissue stores is facilitated by a rapid decline of maternal insulin levels and an enhanced secretion of human placental somatomammotropin. This latter placental hormone has lipolytic activity and may also directly diminish maternal glucose oxidation. In addition, maternal glucose use is attenuated, because free fatty acids and ketones replace glucose as a fuel in maternal tissues, whereas hypoinsulinemia reduces glucose uptake in the insulin-dependent tissues of the mother. Thus, fetal glucose provision may be continued. In addition, alternate substrates mobilized during maternal fasting, such as ketones, cross the placenta and may maintain fetal oxidative metabolism. Ketones may be oxidized or serve as precursors for fetal lipid or protein synthesis. This accelerated mobilization of maternal fuels can ensure fetal growth during short periods of maternal fasting; however, prolonged periods of starvation adversely affect fetal outcome.

TABLE 13-4. Oxidizable Substrates in the Ovine Fetus*

SUBSTRATE	TOTAL OXYGEN CONSUMPTION ACCOUNTED FOR (%)
Glucose	50
Amino acids	25
Lactate	20
Acetate	5–10
Free fatty acids	Not significant
Fructose	Not significant
Glycerol	Not significant
Keto acids	Not significant

*Sheep placenta is impermeable to free fatty acids and ketones, in contrast to the placenta of other mammals, which may be permeable to these substrates.
From Milley J et al: Metabolic requirements for fetal growth. Clin Perinatol 6:365, 1979.

The substrates used to maintain fetal oxygen consumption have been most accurately determined in the ovine fetus (Table 13-4).[81,91] Glucose accounts for approximately 50% of fetal energy production in sheep when the mother is maintained in a high nutritional plane. Amino acids, in addition to functioning as precursors for fetal protein synthesis, serve as an oxidizable fuel; they may contribute to 25% of ovine fetal oxygen uptake. Taken together, lactate and acetate may supply an additional 25%. Data from human pregnancies suggest that glucose oxidation may contribute a greater proportion of fetal energy production than in the ovine fetus.

Similarly, the fetal respiratory quotient has been estimated to be close to 1.0 in other mammalian species, which suggests that carbohydrate oxidation is the predominant source for fetal oxidative metabolism. Fasting during human pregnancy may result in an alteration of substrates presented to the fetus when maternal and subsequently fetal ketone bodies increase. Although free fatty acids, especially the essential fatty acids, must cross the placenta, their role in fetal energy production and adipose tissue growth is limited, because the essential fatty acids are probably deposited in structural tissues (Fig. 13-5).[68]

In addition to the provision of substrates for fetal oxygen consumption and growth, tissue growth also depends on an appropriate fetal endocrine milieu. Among the hormones, insulin and insulin-like growth factors have been implicated as "growth hormones" of the fetus.[108,109] Because insulin does not usually cross the placenta, this growth-enhancing hormone must be of fetal origin. Insulin promotes fetal deposition of adipose and glycogen stores while potentially stimulating amino acid uptake and protein synthesis in muscle. In the absence of fetal insulin production, as in conditions such as pancreatic aplasia, transient neonatal diabetes

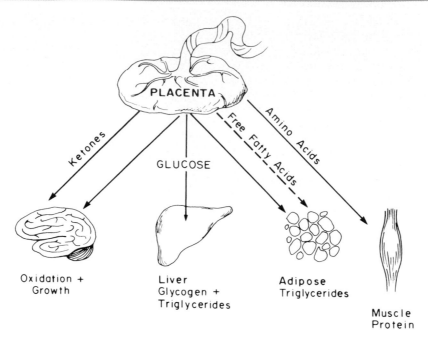

FIGURE 13-5. Placental nutrient support and disposition of substrates. (Modified from Adam PAJ: In Falner F et al: Human Growth, vol 1. New York, Plenum Press, 1978.)

mellitus, or congenital absence of the islets of Langerhans, fetal growth is severely impaired. Moreover, when the peripheral action of insulin is attenuated by diminished receptor or postreceptor events, as in leprechaunism and the Rabson-Mendenhall syndrome, fetal growth may be impaired.[57,130] Insulin resistance due to insulin receptor gene mutations without the phenotype of leprechaunism, and potentially due to mutations in the postreceptor phosphorylation products such as insulin receptor substrate-1 of the insulin receptor signal transduction pathway, may produce IUGR and postnatal growth retardation. As adults, these patients may manifest diabetes mellitus and other complications of hyperglycemia or hyperinsulinemia.[57,130]

Fetal monogenic disorders that effect fetal insulin secretion or action may produce IUGR.[47,143] Alterations of the fetal glucokinase gene, which facilitates insulin release after it senses elevated ambient glucose concentrations in the pancreas, result in IUGR when the mutation produces reduced enzyme function. Fetal weight reduction due to a loss of function mutation may be as great as 500 g. As an adult, the affected patient will manifest diabetes mellitus. If the mother also has this mutation, she probably has maturity-onset diabetes of youth and will be hyperglycemic, which may attenuate the fetal growth retardation in an affected fetus. In contrast, gain of function mutations of this pancreatic glucose-sensing enzyme enhances fetal insulin secretion and may increase fetal weight. Another genetic cause of fetal hyperinsulinism is the mutation of the sulfonylurea receptor of the potassium inward rectifier channel. Persistent activation of this channel causes fetal hyperinsulinism and enhanced fetal weight.

Pancreatic agenesis (homozygous mutation of insulin promoter factor-1) and transient neonatal diabetes (paternal isodisomy or duplication of chromosome 6q22-q33) are also associated with IUGR. The leprechaun syndrome (homozygous or compound heterozygous insulin receptor mutation) produces IUGR due to insulin resistance.

On the other hand, those neonates having prolonged periods of hyperinsulinism in utero, such as infants of diabetic mothers or infants with Beckwith-Wiedemann syndrome or persistent hyperinsulinemic hypoglycemia (nesidioblastosis), demonstrate enhanced adipose and muscle tissue mass, resulting in excessive birthweight (see also Chapter 47, Part 1). Amniotic fluid levels of C-peptide, a cleavage protein of proinsulin, vary directly with fetal growth status: C-peptide is reduced with IUGR and increased with fetal macrosomia.

Fetal growth hormone probably does not influence fetal growth, because there are few growth hormone receptors on fetal liver.[108,109] The birthweight of a panhypopituitary fetus is not very different from that of a normal fetus. Nonetheless, fetal length may be reduced in the presence of growth hormone insensitivity as a result of a growth hormone receptor deficiency.[108,109] Maternal levels of placenta-derived growth hormone are low in cases of IUGR.[22] Placental growth hormone increases maternal nutrient provision to the fetus and is thought to enhance mobilization of maternal substrates for fetal growth.

The final common pathway of growth hormone action is mediated by the generation of insulin-like growth factors. Insulin-like growth factor (IGF) type 1 is a single polypeptide encoded on chromosome 12. IGF1 messenger RNA (mRNA) and its receptor are present in many fetal cells and are not regulated by growth hormone.[104] IGF2 is also a single polypeptide and is encoded on chromosome 11. Its mRNA is much (200-fold to 600-fold) more abundant in most fetal tissues than that for IGF1. IGF1 and IGF2 are 60% homologous to each other and 40% homologous to insulin. IGF1 may be regulated by substrate availability. Its level declines in fetal models of IUGR but increases in infants who are large for gestational age. Fetal levels of IGF1 correlate best with fetal weight. IGF1 and IGF2 receptor binding initiates transmembrane signaling, which activates cell metabolism and DNA synthesis.

IGF1 and IGF2 are present in fetal plasma as early as 15 weeks of gestation. Nonetheless, plasma levels may not reflect tissue-specific action, because these proteins act as competence factors for the cell division cycle in a paracrine or an autocrine, rather than an endocrine, manner. Knockout gene models deleting the *IGF1* gene or the paternal *IGF2* gene or both demonstrate an additive reduction of fetal growth with both gene deletions. Deletion of the paternal *IGF2* gene with genomic imprinting also produces IUGR.

Partial deletion of the *IGF1* gene produces severe prenatal and postnatal growth retardation as well as sensorineural deafness and mental retardation. The IUGR is symmetric.[143] In addition, genetic variations (polymorphisms) of the *IGF1* gene are also associated with symmetric IUGR.[5,67] These children also have low circulating IGF1 levels. In adult life, low IGF1 levels are associated with diabetes mellitus and may explain in part the fetal-origins-of-adult-disease hypothesis.

IGFs are modulated by six IGF-binding proteins (IGFBPs), which usually attenuate or occasionally enhance IGF bioavailability and are subject to regulatory signals similar to those that regulate IGF protein synthesis.[56,135] Fetal IGFBP-1 serum levels are inversely related to birthweight and may restrict the availability of IGF1 to fetal tissues. In animals, overexpression of IGFBP-1 produces IUGR. Acute fetal hypoxia and possibly fetal catecholamine release reduce IGF1 levels but increase IGFBP-1 levels in the ovine fetus.[59,63] Reduced nutrient availability and lower insulin levels associated with some models of IUGR reduce fetal IGF1 levels, whereas they increase IGFBP-1 levels. Fetal IGFBP-3 serum levels usually parallel those of IGF1 and are thus increased in fetuses who are large for gestational age but reduced in fetuses with IUGR.[19,29]

Maternal nutrient availability is also regulated by IGF1. IUGR is associated with reduced maternal IGF1 levels or when IGFBP-1 is increased. In mice, increasing maternal IGF1 levels results in heavier fetal weight; in sheep, maternal IGF1 infusions result in increased fetal glucose levels and enhanced placental amino acid uptake.

Reduced function or production of the IGF1 receptor (IGF1R) is associated with IUGR. This transmembrane heterotetramer is encoded at band 15q26 and is structurally similar to the insulin receptor. Hemizygosity of the IGF1R is associated with IUGR in the ring chromosome 15 syndrome.[101]

More complex epigenetic mechanisms such as imprinting may regulate fetal growth. Abnormal expression of a normally inactive gene (loss of imprinting) is seen in Silver-Russell syndrome and transient neonatal diabetes mellitus. Silver-Russell syndrome is characterized by prenatal and postnatal growth restriction; 10% of patients have uniparental disomy of chromosome 7 (maternal). Transient neonatal diabetes manifests with IUGR and may result from overexpression of imprinted paternally expressed gene or genes at 6q24, due to paternal uniparental isodisomy of chromosome 6, paternally inherited duplication of 6q24, or a methylation (imprinting) defect.[131]

Epidermal growth factor (EGF) in the neonate mediates mitosis and development of ectodermal and mesodermal structures; in rodents, EGF mediates eye opening and tooth eruption. EGF is a single 53-amino-acid polypeptide chain derived from the prepro-EGF peptide and may play a minor role in fetal growth and development; there is no fetal EGF RNA expression. Nonetheless, EGF receptors are abundant in the fetus, autophosphorylate themselves, and phosphorylate cytoplasmic proteins. EGF receptor phosphorylation is attenuated in the placenta of women who smoke and who deliver IUGR infants.[38,40] Transforming growth factor-α, which is 40% homologous to EGF, binds to the EGF receptor, is involved in angiogenesis, and may be the fetal ligand for this receptor, which is similar to the *erbB* proto-oncogene. Fetal growth is regulated by growth factors and growth factor receptors that are similar to products of nuclear proto-oncogenes. Uncontrolled or constitutive (loss of regulated inhibition) activity of oncogenes is characteristic of malignant transformation, in contrast to the controlled and regulated activity of these proto-oncogene products (growth factors or receptors) during growth. Leprechaunism, an IUGR syndrome, in addition to having insulin resistance, also demonstrates EGF resistance because of an abnormal EGF receptor.

Leptin (from Greek *leptos,* thin) is a 16-kDa, 167-amino-acid protein discovered in 1994 as the product of the obese (ob) gene. The human leptin gene is on chromosome 7q31 and consists of more than 15,000 base pairs and three exon sites. Leptin is primarily produced in white adipose tissue but has been shown to be produced in the human placenta and gastric epithelium. It has been shown to regulate body weight through a negative feedback loop between adipose tissue and the hypothalamic satiety centers. Studies have shown that in children and adults, serum leptin concentrations correlate with body fat mass as well as body weight. There is also a gender difference that persists into adulthood—girls have higher serum leptin levels than boys. This gender difference has not been proven conclusively in the fetus and neonate.

Leptin has been detected in amniotic fluid and cord blood of the newborn and can be seen as early as at 29 weeks of gestational age.[6] Amniotic fluid leptin is derived from the mother, whereas cord blood leptin is derived from the placenta and fetal tissues.[86] Although cord blood leptin levels appear to correlate with birthweight, maternal leptin concentration is not an accurate indicator of fetal growth. There is also a correlation between cord blood leptin level and fetal fat mass. This relationship suggests that leptin may have a role in fetal growth, but this role still needs to be defined. Cord blood leptin levels have been shown to be decreased in newborns with IUGR.[9,23] This logically follows, given that increases in cord blood leptin correlate with the exponential increase in fat mass that occurs during the last trimester, and given that this fat mass is greatly reduced in fetuses or newborns with IUGR. Furthermore, in the newborn group with IUGR, there is a positive correlation between cord blood leptin levels and body mass index (which indicates fat mass) and not with body weight. The role of ghrelin in fetal growth is still under investigation.[122]

The roles of other hormones, notably corticosteroids and thyroid hormone, have not been well defined for fetal growth. Nonetheless, repeated doses of dexamethasone to the mother may reduce birthweight and possibly brain growth. Mutations that affect the metabolism of cortisol may produce IUGR. Placental 11β-hydroxysteroid dehydrogenase (11βHSD) inactivates cortisol and thus reduces cortisol exposure to the fetus. Placental 11βHSD is reduced in pregnancies complicated by IUGR and in growth-restricted female fetuses born to women with asthma.[94,115]

With thyroid hormone deficiency in the human athyrotic cretin, birthweight is not altered. These hormones, however, probably have a more significant role as regulatory signals for the initiation of maturation and differentiation in fetal tissues (see also Chapter 47, Part 3).

FETAL ORIGIN OF ADULT DISEASES

Reduced birthweight has been associated with certain adult morbidities that would not be obvious based on an understanding of IUGR and its immediate neonatal sequelae. Low birthweight in the fetus has been related to the subsequent risk of adult onset hypertension, non–insulin-dependent diabetes, stroke, obesity, and coronary artery disease. Recognized risks for adult morbidities include those infants born thin who demonstrate catch-up growth and who in later life become obese, as well as those with IUGR who are also born short.[79,80,123]

The fetal organ hypothesis states that poor maternal nutrition programs the fetus and produces reduced birthweight and subsequent adult-onset diseases.[18,25,46,139] This suggests that such programming occurs during a critical or sensitive period in early fetal life. Studies have confirmed a relationship between poor maternal diet and blood pressure in offspring. Potential programming or imprinting mechanisms include changes in cell-cell interaction, alterations in fetal angiogenesis or innervation, reduction in cell number, clonal selection of cell types (cells with poor availability of nutrients such as lipids may be selected to produce more endogenous lipids), metabolic differentiation (enzymes,

transporters, transcription factors, gene expression), and hepatocyte polyploidization (extra chromosome copies can enhance gene expression and alter metabolism). These adaptive fetal processes may be beneficial to the fetus but may permanently alter metabolism and result in adverse metabolic diseases as adults.[43,139]

Although genetic influences may have a role in postnatal and adult metabolic disorders, the fetal origin hypothesis has been demonstrated in the smaller or discordant fetus of identical twins. In addition, babies after ovum donation tend to have birthweights that correlate to the recipient mother. Furthermore, thin mothers who have poor weight gain in pregnancy have offspring with higher blood pressures than offspring of thin mothers with adequate weight gain during pregnancy. Young children or adults who were IUGR have been demonstrated to have impaired endothelial cell formation, increased carotid artery stiffness, abnormal retinal vascular morphology, and poor postnatal adaptive responses.[50,65,83,84]

Various monogenic disorders also affect birthweight (see earlier).[46,47,124,142] Fetal insulin resistance or poor insulin production may be one primary overriding problem and not just the poor maternal nutrition found in some offspring with postnatal insulin resistance.[66] The opposing hypotheses are noted in Figure 13-6.[46]

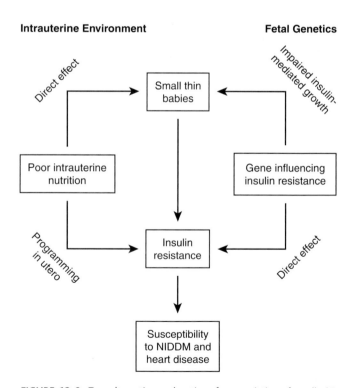

FIGURE 13-6. Two alternative explanations for association of small, thin babies with later onset of insulin resistance, non–insulin-dependent diabetes mellitus (NIDDM), and ischemic heart disease: intrauterine environment and fetal genetics. (From Hattersley AT et al: The fetal insulin hypothesis: An alternative explanation of the association of low birthweight with diabetes and vascular disease. Lancet 353:1789, 1999. Copyright 1999 by The Lancet Ltd.)

EPIDEMIOLOGY OF LOW BIRTHWEIGHT

The term *low birthweight* refers to infants born weighing less than 2500 g. The neonatal mortality rate is directly related to the low-birthweight rate in a given population. These high-risk infants are a heterogeneous group consisting of infants born preterm (less than 37 weeks) and those born at term but of reduced weight.[35,118]

IUGR is the predominant cause of low birthweight in developing areas and nations with low birthweight rates greater than 10%. Socioeconomic improvement decreases the proportion of IUGR. Between 20% and 40% of preterm infants also have decreased growth for gestational age. Although there appear to be differences in the relative incidence of IUGR and premature birth in different countries, risk factors associated with birth of an infant with low birthweight are similar (Box 13-1).

The rate of reduced weight at term gestation is probably twice as great among black infants as among white. This may be partially independent of socioeconomic factors because black infants often have lower birthweight than infants of Hispanic or Asian parents of similar socioeconomic status. The risk of low birthweight is related to the occupation not only of the child's parents but also of the grandparents. There is a strong familial aggregation of births of low birthweight in both white and black families. Provision of adequate nutrition to the future mother and other environmental factors may alter that future mother's growth and future reproductive capability. This intergenerational effect explains in part the observation that mothers of infants of low birthweight were themselves neonates of low birthweight.[31]

Although medical complications of pregnancy occur equally in all socioeconomic groups, many adverse behavioral attitudes or practices contribute to the greater low-birthweight rate among women of low socioeconomic status.

MATERNAL CONTRIBUTIONS TO ABERRANT FETAL GROWTH

Physical Environment

Certain otherwise normal mothers are prone to repeated delivery of infants who are SGA; the recurrence rate may be 25% to 50%.[72,99] Many of these women themselves were born SGA, raising the possibility of intergenerational transmission of a physical regulator of fetal growth. A proportion of these women also remain small throughout life and are identifiable by low prepregnancy weight and stature. These women may exert a restraint on fetal growth by some unknown regulator, possibly related to their own stature, previous nutritional status, endocrine environment, or uterine capacity. In breeding experiments using Shetland ponies

BOX 13-1. Overview of Risk Factors* for Low Birthweight

Demographic
- Race (black)
- Present low socioeconomic status
- Socioeconomic status of infant's grandparents

Prepregnancy
- Low weight for height
- Short stature
- Chronic medical illness
- Poor nutrition
- Low maternal weight at mother's birth
- Previous infant of low birthweight
- Uterine or cervical anomalies
- Parity (none or more than five)

Pregnancy
- Multiple gestation
- Birth order
- Anemia
- Elevated hemoglobin concentration (inadequate plasma volume expansion?)
- Fetal disease
- Preeclampsia and hypertension
- Infections
- Placental problems
- Premature rupture of membranes
- Heavy physical work
- Altitude
- Renal disease
- Assisted reproductive technology

Behavioral
- Low educational status
- Smoking
- No care or inadequate prenatal care
- Poor weight gain during pregnancy
- Alcohol abuse
- Illicit and prescription drugs
- Short interpregnancy interval (less than 6 months)
- Age (less than 16 or over 35 years)
- Unmarried
- Stress (physical and psychological)

*Many of these variables are risk factors for both intrauterine growth restriction (IUGR) and prematurity. These variables are not necessarily univariant risk factors but rather interact in a complex relationship. Only a few factors exert an independent effect. The relationship between black race and low birthweight remains a significant factor, with a twofold increase in the incidence of prematurity and IUGR when controlled for other risks. Modified from Committee to Study the Prevention of Low Birthweight: Prevention of Low Birthweight. Washington, DC, Institute of Medicine, National Academy Press, 1985.

and Shire horses, the offspring resulting from breeding a male Shire to a female Shetland was similar in birthweight to a Shetland pony, whereas the birthweight of offspring born to a male Shetland and a female Shire approached that of a Shire. The smaller Shetland female apparently exerts a growth restraint on the genetic potential derived from the larger Shire male. Similar observations are noted in humans. When ova are donated to a recipient mother, the fetal weight correlates best with that of the recipient mother.[139]

Another risk for IUGR is maternal failure to expand plasma volume during pregnancy. Such women have reduced placental weights and a hematocrit level that does not reflect an expanded plasma volume.[112]

Maternal genetic factors have a major direct effect on fetal growth. This influence depends on a transfer of maternal genes but also on the other, unexplained maternal genetic factors related in part to uteroplacental function. The observation that sisters of mothers with infants who were SGA are at higher risk of carrying fetuses who are SGA than their sisters-in-law gives further evidence of maternal genetic influences on fetal growth. The mother's genetic component to fetal growth is less than 25%.

Paternal factors have less effect on fetal growth. Paternal genes affect fetal growth directly by transfer of genetic material, which may be modified (accelerated or inhibited) by maternal factors. Paternal genotypic potential is best expressed as a function of postnatal growth. Nonetheless, paternal patterns of imprinting of genes *(IGF2)* may enhance fetal growth.

Other constraints on fetal growth may be exerted during *multiple gestations,* because fetal growth declines when the number of fetuses increases. The onset of growth retardation in multiple gestations is also related to the number of fetuses: growth restraint begins sooner with triplets than with twins (Fig. 13-7). In multiple gestations, the uterine constraint appears to occur when combined fetal size approaches 3 kg. Placental implantation site, uterine anomalies, vascular anastomoses, and nutritional factors may also interfere with growth in these pregnancies. The uterine capacity itself may also place a constraint on optimal fetal growth. Independent of the number of fetuses, the use of assisted reproductive technologies increases the risk of IUGR.[113]

Maternal Nutrition

Prepregnancy weight and pregnancy weight gain are two important independent variables that affect fetal growth.[1,54,125] Underweight mothers and those affected with malnutrition deliver infants with diminished birthweight. Weight gain during pregnancy in nonobese patients correlates significantly with fetal birthweight. Poor weight gain by as early as 16 weeks' gestation may predict low birthweight. The effect of prepregnancy weight in obese women is independent of pregnancy weight gain and offsets the frequently observed poor weight gain of these overweight women (Fig. 13-8). Infants who are SGA are unusual for obese women, whereas macrosomia is common. This may be related to large maternal nutrient stores. Calculating the pregravid body mass index (BMI),

$$BMI = \text{prepregnancy weight (kg)/height}^2 \text{ (m)} \times 100,$$

helps the clinician determine the target for pregnancy weight gain, which may reduce the risk of IUGR. A low BMI (less than 19.8) may require a pregnancy weight gain of 12.5 to 18 kg, a normal BMI (19.8 to 26) may require a weight gain of 11.5 to 16 kg, and a high BMI

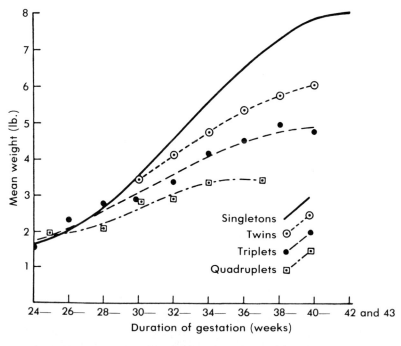

FIGURE 13-7. Birthweight-gestational age relationships in multiple gestation, denoting origin of aberrant fetal growth. (From McKeown T, Record RG: Observations on foetal growth in multiple pregnancy in man. J Endocrinol 8:386, 1952.)

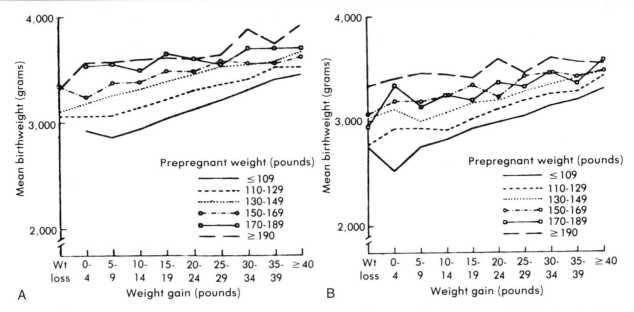

FIGURE 13-8. Effect of prepregnancy weight and weight gain during pregnancy among white women (**A**) and black women (**B**). Note the reduced birthweight at term at all levels of maternal weight variables among black women. Also note that weight gain during pregnancy has its most positive effect on birthweight among lean women. Nonetheless, prepregnancy weight among obese, usually nondiabetic, women has the greatest effect on birthweight. (From Niswander K et al: Weight gain during pregnancy and prepregnancy weight. Obstet Gynecol 33:482, 1969.)

(greater than 26 to 29) may require a weight gain of 7 to 11.5 kg, whereas obese women (BMI greater than 29) may need a weight gain of only 6 kg. Appropriate weight gain during pregnancy based on BMI may mitigate the risk of IUGR.[54]

The effects of maternal nutritional status on fetal growth are minimal during the first trimester of pregnancy. This is related to the large surfeit of nutrients presented to the relatively small, undemanding embryo and early fetus. As fetal growth accelerates, the requirements for fetal growth increase and may not be sufficiently provided by an inadequate maternal diet. Earlier attempts to limit weight gain in pregnancy with a 1200-kcal diet to prevent preeclampsia resulted in a 10-fold increase in growth retardation. In an otherwise healthy population of Dutch women experiencing a short period of famine during the Hunger Winter of 1944-1945, fetal growth was most severely affected when deprivation occurred in the third trimester.[125] Substrate deficiency during this period resulted in an overall reduction in birthweight of 300 g. Maternal weight gain and placental weight were even more drastically reduced, demonstrating preferential use of nutrients for the fetus. Poor nutrition may also reduce uterine blood flow, placental transport, and villous surface area. Observations similar to those of the Dutch experience occurred during a more severe and prolonged famine in wartime Leningrad, where birthweight was reduced by 500 g at term.

There may even be an intergenerational effect of being in utero during maternal starvation. The daughters of women who experienced starvation during the Dutch famine of 1944-1945 have an increased risk of delivering infants of low birthweight if the daughters were exposed to starvation in utero during the first or second trimester. The reduction in the next generation's birthweight is approximately 200 to 300 g.[78]

As illustrated in Figure 13-9, decreased caloric uptake below critical caloric needs may result in diminished fetal growth. Increased maternal caloric expenditure can occur two ways: excessive physical activity and greater waste of calories. The nutritional aspects of cigarette smoking may be an example of the second way. Furthermore, the diminished heat expenditure that occurs among obese women may result in caloric storage and explain in part their excessively large babies. Increased maternal storage of calories may be exemplified by the "selfish mother" hypothesis. These women may not develop the usual insulin resistance during pregnancy and may direct ingested calories toward their own tissue stores. These women have fasting hypoglycemia and/or accelerated disappearance of glucose after intravenous glucose tolerance testing. The opposite occurs among women of low socioeconomic status who receive food supplementation; their skinfold thickness decreases as fetal weight increases. Decreased transport may reflect placental defects in function, nutrient supply, or blood flow. Decreased blood flow may be caused by peripheral vascular disease or failure to expand blood volume and cardiac output, as in normal pregnancy. Fetuses with insulin resistance or decreased numbers of cells may not be able to grow despite adequate nutrient supply. Examples of fetuses with diminished cell numbers include fetuses affected by rubella embryopathy, autosomal trisomies, and other genetic causes of IUGR.

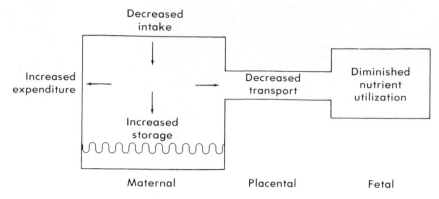

FIGURE 13-9. Interrelationship of caloric intake and expenditure and fetal nutrient availability. Multiple mechanisms can reduce nutrient availability or utilization (even in the presence of adequate fuel availability).

Attempts at improving the low-birthweight outcome in high-risk populations (characterized by having poor nutritional histories) have demonstrated a positive effect of nutritional supplementation. Additional calories, rather than protein supplementation, correlate best with enhanced fetal weight. Caloric supplements greater than 20,000 cal per pregnancy reduced the number of infants with low birthweight; every 10,000 cal supplemented above the standard diet improved fetal weight by an average of 29 g. In Gambia, supplementation during seasonal periods of food shortage resulted in a net positive caloric intake of more than 400 kcal/day. This increased fetal weight 224 g and reduced the low-birthweight rate from 28% to less than 5%. A threshold of 1500 kcal/day was observed, which augmented fetal weight when the mother was in positive caloric balance.[103] In the United States, participation in the Women, Infants, and Children (WIC) program has reduced the number of births that are SGA.[2]

Protein supplementation may even have adverse neurodevelopmental effects on the fetus. Aside from periods of famine and geographic areas where malnutrition is endemic, other conditions associated with poor maternal nutrition and suboptimal fetal growth are included in Box 13-2. Adolescent women, in particular, are at risk because of their own growth requirements in addition to those of the fetus.

Certain maternal metabolic aberrations are associated with suboptimal fetal growth. Mothers who demonstrate excessively low fasting blood glucose values and those whose blood glucose levels are not sufficiently elevated after an oral glucose tolerance test are at risk of delivering an infant who is SGA. A "selfish mother" hypothesis has been proposed to explain the poor growth of these infants (see Fig. 13-9).

Chronic Disease

Of all disease mechanisms that interfere with fetal growth, those resulting in uterine ischemia or hypoxia, or both, have the most extreme effect. Chronic maternal hypertension caused by either primary renal parenchymal disease, such as nephritis, or those conditions

extrinsic to parenchymal disorders, such as essential hypertension, significantly alters fetal growth and well-being.[37,116] This effect is related to the duration of hypertension and to the absolute elevation of the diastolic pressure and is most severe in the presence of end-organ disorders, such as retinopathy. Well-controlled hypertension, without the development of preeclampsia, may not affect fetal growth.

Pregnancy-induced hypertension is of paramount importance to perinatologists in relation to its effect on fetal growth and well-being (see also Chapter 14). This disease, which may affect uteroplacental perfusion and fetal growth long before clinical signs of edema, proteinuria, and hypertension develop, reduces uterine blood flow, as determined by Doppler flow velocity waveforms of the uterine artery. Preeclampsia is characterized by retention of the spiral arteries muscle layer, reduced perfusion of the intervillous space, necrotizing atherosis, and decreased trophoblastic invasion of the decidual spiral arteries. Such trophoblastic invasion depends on decidual laminin, fibronectin, maternal

BOX 13-2. Women with Poor Nutrition and Risk of Suboptimal Fetal Growth

- Adolescent women, especially those who are not married
- Women with low prepregnancy weights
- Women with inadequate weight gain during pregnancy
- Women who have low income or problems in purchasing food
- Women with a history of frequent conception, especially with short interpregnancy intervals
- Women with a history of giving birth to infants with low birthweight
- Women with diseases that influence nutritional status: diabetes, tuberculosis, anemia, drug addiction, alcoholism, or mental depression
- Women known to be dietary faddists or with frank pica
- Women who do heavy physical work during pregnancy

From Christakis G: Nutritional assessment in health programs. Am J Public Health 63(Suppl):57, 1973.

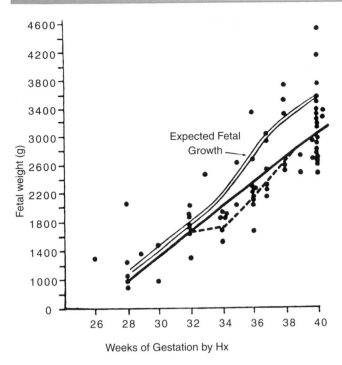

FIGURE 13-10. Fetal weight after eclampsia. *Broken line* demonstrates mean weight alteration. (From Zuspan FP: Treatment of severe preeclampsia and eclampsia. Clin Obstet Gynecol 9:954, 1966.)

cytokines, and trophoblastic integrins and proteases. Similar arterial pathologic changes may be present in idiopathic IUGR. In pregnancies complicated by eclampsia, fetal growth deviates from the expected norm from 32 weeks onward (Fig. 13-10). Treatment of hypertension in pregnancy with antihypertensive drugs may further contribute to IUGR. This is independent of the medication; with a decline of 10 mm Hg, fetal weight may be reduced 145 g.[137] Vascular insufficiency resulting from advanced maternal diabetes mellitus, especially in the presence of end-organ disease in the kidney or retina, also produces IUGR despite the presence of maternal hyperglycemia (see also Chapter 15). Women with serious autoimmune disease associated with the lupus anticoagulant are also a high-risk population for preeclampsia and IUGR (see also Chapter 17).

Another major category associated with diminished fetal weight gain is that resulting from maternal hypoxemia. Severe cyanotic congenital heart disease, such as tetralogy of Fallot or Eisenmenger complex, is the best example of this mechanism, whereas sickle cell anemia is representative of diseases that can produce local uterine hypoxia and ischemia. The maternal morbidity rate is high with cyanotic heart disease. Nutritional anemias are not usually associated with aberrant fetal growth. In sickle cell anemia, the abnormal cells may interfere with local uterine perfusion during episodes of sickling, and growth retardation is observed.[16]

A common and nonpathologic factor related to maternal hypoxia is the diminished environmental

oxygen saturation that is present at high altitudes. Infants born in the mountains of Peru demonstrate lower birthweights than do Peruvian infants born at sea level. Placental mass has hypertrophied in these newborns in an attempt to compensate for the lower circulating maternal oxygen concentration. These neonates are not born with polycythemia as a response to fetal hypoxia, as proposed for other infants who are SGA. The decline in body weight becomes manifest at an altitude of 2000 m, which corresponds to a barometric pressure of 590 mm Hg.[93]

Drugs (See also Chapters 10, 12, 28, and 36.)

The effects of maternal drug administration on the fetus are usually considered primarily in terms of teratogenicity. However, a continuum of fetal compromise may be present because many malformation syndromes are associated with diminished birthweight, whereas other agents may interfere only with fetal growth. Some drugs associated with IUGR are included in the following list*:

Amphetamines
Antimetabolites (e.g., aminopterin, busulfan, methotrexate)
Bromides
Cigarettes (possibly carbon monoxide, thiocyanate, polycyclic aromatic hydrocarbons, nicotine)
Cocaine
Ethanol (acetaldehyde)
Heroin
Hydantoin
Isotretinoin
Methadone
Methylmercury
Phencyclidine
Polychlorinated biphenyls
Propranolol
Steroids (prednisone)
Toluene
Trimethadione (Tridione)
Warfarin

Many of the typically abused drugs have been implicated as agents producing fetal growth retardation by reducing maternal appetite and by being associated with lower socioeconomic groups. However, at least for heroin, methadone, and ethanol, a cellular toxic effect acting directly on cell replication and growth appears to be involved. This is most evident in fetal alcohol syndrome: the prenatal onset of growth retardation persists during postnatal periods despite adequate food intake. A placental transfer block for specific amino acids has been observed in fetal alcohol syndrome.

The effects of cocaine on fetal growth may be multifactorial and may include uterine artery vasospasm, reduced maternal prepregnancy weight, reduced weight gain during pregnancy, and, possibly, direct

---

*References 26, 52, 73, 77, 85, 114.

fetal endocrine effects. Multidrug use, poor nutrition, and poor prenatal care are common among many drug-dependent women.

Cigarette smoking during pregnancy reduces eventual fetal birthweight, which is directly related to the number of cigarettes smoked.[77] Birthweight at term is reduced an average of 170 g if more than 10 cigarettes per day are used; smoking more than 15 per day may reduce weight by 300 g. The mechanism of fetal growth retardation is uncertain, but nicotine and subsequent catecholamine release may produce uterine vasoconstriction and fetal hypoxia. Carbon monoxide and cyanide may cause a more direct effect: after binding to hemoglobin, carbon monoxide and cyanide may diminish oxygen unloading from the mother to the fetus and from the fetus to its tissues. Nutritional supplementation does not completely eliminate the reduced fetal weight. Moreover, the effects of cigarettes may be greatest at advanced maternal age. Another mechanism producing IUGR is related to the presence of polymorphisms of the genes for glutathione *S*-transferase and CYP1A1, which are enzymes responsible for the metabolism of polycyclic aromatic hydrocarbons, arylamines and *N*-nitrosamines. Certain gene polymorphisms may reduce fetal growth by as much as 1285 g at term.[138]

Drugs such as propranolol and other beta-blocking agents and corticosteroids probably have a direct effect on the fetus, although the confounding influence of the chronic maternal illnesses for which these agents are prescribed may also contribute to IUGR.

Socioeconomic Status

Poor environmental conditions related to lower socioeconomic status have been associated with infant malnutrition of both prenatal and postnatal onset. With improvement of these conditions, birthweight is enhanced. This was extensively studied after living conditions improved in postwar Japan. The improvement in birthweight during this era occurred only in infants born during the latter part of the third trimester; nutritional and environmental effects seem greatest during this period of fetal growth.[44,129]

Many maternal factors, such as drug abuse, poor nutritional habits, and cigarette smoking, are interrelated and are covariables associated with poor socioeconomic status.[10,34,141] Factors such as adverse environmental living conditions and low levels of education are more prevalent among reproductive-age women of lower socioeconomic status. Adolescent and single-parent families and the failure to seek adequate prenatal advice are also more common. Many investigations have demonstrated that such women are at risk of having babies with IUGR. It has been suggested that if chronic maternal illness and certain behavioral characteristics are eliminated and prenatal care is available, the remaining women of lower socioeconomic status do not have a higher incidence rate of infants who are SGA. The specific behavioral characteristics more common among poor women are noted in Box 13-1.[44]

PLACENTAL DETERMINANTS

Optimal fetal growth depends on efficient function of the placenta as a nutrient supply line, a metabolic and endocrine unit, and an organ of gaseous exchange. Placental functional integrity requires additional energy production because placental oxidative metabolism may equal that of the fetus. This large energy requirement is essential for maintaining fetal growth-promoting roles, which include active transport of amino acids, synthesis of protein and steroid hormones, and support of placental maturation and growth. Placental growth parallels that of the fetus; however, toward term there is a greater decline in the rate of placental weight gain than in the rate of weight gain by the fetus. During this decline of placental weight, the fetus also exhibits a decrease in the rate of weight change, which suggests that placental function and the rate of weight gain have declined and led to reduced fetal growth. However, despite the change in the rate of placental weight gain, the placenta continues to mature. The placental villous surface area continues to increase with advancing gestational age (Fig. 13-11); simultaneously, the syncytial trophoblast layer continues to thin, and vascularization of the terminal villi continues to improve.[76] Functionally, urea clearance is enhanced toward term in the ovine placenta (Fig. 13-12), suggesting that permeability and diffusing distance improve as the placenta approaches term. Birthweight has been correlated with placental weight (Fig. 13-13) and with villous surface area (see Fig. 13-11), suggesting that macroscopic and microscopic events are related to optimal placental function.

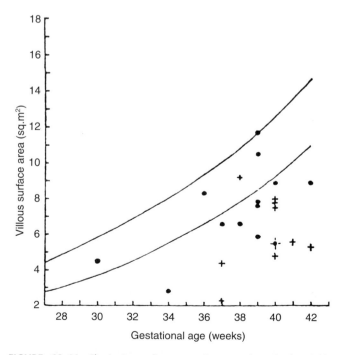

FIGURE 13-11. Chorionic surface area in normal and abnormal pregnancies. •, Maternal hypertension; +, normotensive intrauterine growth restriction. (From Aherne W et al: Quantitative aspects of placental structure. J Pathol Bacteriol 91:132, 1966.)

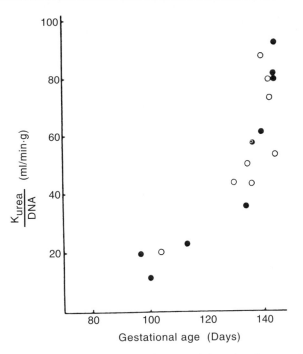

FIGURE 13-12. Urea permeability per gram of the ovine placenta with increasing gestational age. *Filled circles,* singletons; *open circles,* twins. (From Kulhanek J et al: Changes in DNA content and urea permeability of the sheep placenta. Am J Physiol 226:1257, 1974.)

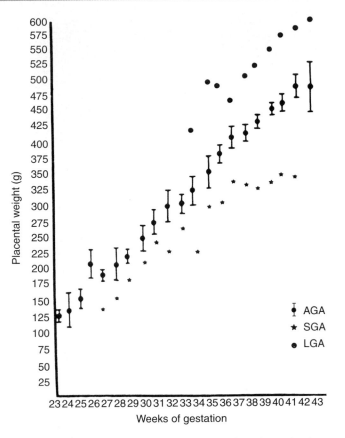

FIGURE 13-13. Relationship between placental weight and gestational age in neonates. Mean placental weight ± SEM. AGA, appropriate for gestational age; LGA, large for gestational age; SGA, small for gestational age. (From Molteni R et al: Relationship of fetal and placental weight in human beings. J Reprod Med 21:327, 1978.)

When placental insufficiency occurs, there may be a functional failure of the placenta as a respiratory or nutritive organ or both. Placental insufficiency associated with maternal nutritional deficiency has more than one effect on fetal growth. In addition to diminished fetal substrate provision, placental metabolism is altered directly, as proposed in Figure 13-9. Diminished placental growth adversely affects total nutrient transfer, whereas reduced placental production of chorionic somatomammotropin attenuates maternal mobilization of fuels to the fetus. Reduced placental energy production and protein synthesis limits active transport of amino acids and facilitative transport of glucose.

When placental insufficiency complicates maternal vascular disease such as preeclampsia, placental weight and volume also diminish. In addition, a decline in villous surface area (see Fig. 13-11) and a relative increase in nonexchanging tissue occur. At the same time, these placentas demonstrate thickening of the capillary basement membrane.

Following is a list of additional findings in placental disorders associated with diminished birthweight[20,36,106]:

Twins (implantation site)
Twins (vascular anastomoses)
Chorioangioma
Villitis (involving *t*oxoplasmosis, *o*ther [congenital syphilis and viruses], *r*ubella, *c*ytomegalovirus, and *h*erpes simplex virus [TORCH] association)
Villitis (unknown cause)
Avascular villi

Ischemic villous necrosis
Vasculitis (decidual arteritis)
Multiple infarcts
Syncytial knots
Chronic separation (abruptio placentae)
Diffuse fibrinosis
Hydatidiform change
Abnormal insertion
Single umbilical artery (?)
Fetal vessel thrombosis
Circumvallate placenta
Reduced capillarization
Reduced terminal villus branching
Elevated vascular tone
Increased glucose utilization
Confined chromosomal mosaicism (trisomy of 2, 3, 7, 8, 9, 13, 14, 15, 16, 18, 22, or X)
Reduced spiral artery recruitment

Multiple gestations may produce significant placental disorders in suboptimal sites of implantation or, more often, related to abnormal vascular anastomoses in diamniotic monochorionic twinning (Fig. 13-14). As a result of arteriovenous interconnections, one twin

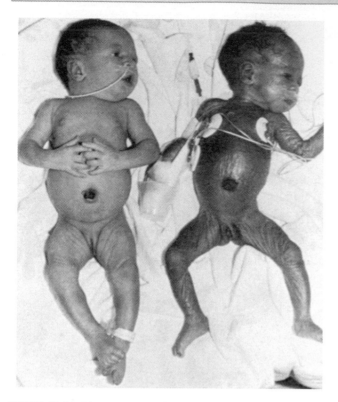

FIGURE 13-14. Diamniotic monochorionic twins, 36 weeks' gestational age, with birthweights of 1.3 and 2.0 kg.

serves as the donor and develops IUGR, losing nutrient supplies, whereas the other is the recipient and has satisfactory growth. These anastomoses may be detectable on careful gross examination of the placenta. Ablation of vascular communications in the second trimester, by fetoscopic neodymium:yttrium-aluminum-garnet laser photocoagulation, may reduce the morbidity of the twin-twin transfusion syndrome, which develops in 5% to 17% of monozygotic twins[30] (see also Chapters 18 and 23).

Other detectable potential causes related to aberrant fetal growth include chorioangiomas, large retroplacental infarcts and hemorrhages, abnormal cord insertion patterns, and (questionably) single umbilical artery. Combined reductions of uterine and umbilical blood flow have also been detected in IUGR.[64] Furthermore, increased vascular resistance has been demonstrated in these circulations (Table 13-5). In addition, reduced placental prostacyclin (a potent vasodilator) production may be present in IUGR. Increased placental vascular tone may be fixed or dynamic. The latter may be due to reduced activity of placental nitric oxide synthase or increased circulating fetal levels of angiotensin II or endothelin.

Genetic, enzymatic, and endocrine abnormalities of placental tissue may reduce fetal growth. Decreased expression of enzymes involved in redox regulation (thioredoxin, glutaredoxin) may place placental vessels at risk for endothelial cell oxidative stress and is associated with IUGR.[111] In animals, decreased expression of IGF1R and the insulin receptor produces IUGR.[105] Furthermore, genes that may regulate nutrient transfer (connexin 2b, *Esx1*) are also associated with IUGR in mice.[51]

FETAL DETERMINANTS

Optimal fetal growth depends on adequate provision of substrates, their effective placental transfer, and the inherited regulatory factors within the fetal genotype that affect nutrient utilization. In addition to substrates, oxygen must be transferred, and an appropriate hormonal milieu must be present. There must also be sufficient room within the uterus. In the absence of adverse environmental effects, the inherent growth potential of the fetus may be achieved.

TABLE 13-5. Abnormalities of Uteroplacental and Fetal Blood Flow in IUGR Pregnancies

OBSERVATION	COMMENT
50% ↓ Uteroplacental flow	[113]InCl to mother
↓ Uterine flow in malnutrition	Failure to increase cardiac output with pregnancy
↓ Placental nutrient transfer	
↑ Uterine artery systolic/diastolic waveform ratio	Suggests increased uterine artery resistance
↑ Umbilical artery velocity waveform	
↓ Fetal descending aortic pulsatile index*	Suggests increased peripheral vascular resistance
↓ Fetal descending aortic end-diastolic velocity	
↑ Fetal descending aortic resistance index	Suggests decreased cardiac output, shunting away from descending aorta to brain, and fetal distress
↓ Fetal descending aortic peak velocity	
Reversed diastolic flow	Suggests severe reduction in flow and fetal compromise
↓ Umbilical venous flow	Associated with impending fetal distress
↓ Placental prostacyclin production	May promote platelet aggregation or diminish uterine vessel dilation

*Pulsatile index = (peak velocity − end-diastolic velocity)/mean blood flow velocity.
[113]InCl, indium-113 chloride; IUGR, intrauterine growth restriction.

Genetic determinants of fetal growth are inherited from both parents, and population norms must be established to detect aberrant fetal growth. For example, the average birthweight of Cheyenne Indians is 3800 g at term, whereas that of the New Guinea Luni tribe is 2400 g. Genetic potentials are usually determinants of early fetal growth; nutritional and environmental problems should not affect the fetus until the requirements for tissue growth increase during the third trimester. Indeed, reduced first-trimester growth as determined by crown-rump length is a risk factor for IUGR. This risk is even stronger in the presence of increased maternal α-fetoprotein levels.

Approximately 20% of birthweight variability in a given population is determined by the fetal genotype; maternal hereditary and environmental factors contribute an additional 65%; the remaining contributing factors are unknown. Birth order affects fetal size: infants born to primiparous women weigh less than subsequent siblings. The second child and each additional child weigh an average of 180 g more than the firstborn. This relationship is not true for multiparous adolescent pregnancies, in which subsequent births during adolescence produce neonates with lower term weights than that of the firstborn. Male sex of the fetus is associated with greater birthweight, beginning to become predominant after 28 weeks' gestation. At term, boys weigh approximately 150 g more than girls. A male twin, in addition to affecting its own somatic growth, can also enhance the growth of its female twin. Androgenic hormonal stimulation of fetal growth or paternal imprinting of IGF2 may contribute to these observed differences. Also, a theory states that maternal-fetal antigenic (HLA, ABO) differences are responsible for this effect.[55] These antigenic differences result in enhanced placental trophoblastic invasion of the decidua, improving placental and subsequent fetal growth. As a corollary, interference with maternal immunologic function may inhibit this antigenic growth advantage and explain in part the diminished birthweights after maternal immunosuppressive therapy.

Alternately, chromosomes may carry growth-determining genes: genetic material on the Y chromosome may enhance the growth of the male fetus. Similarly, chromosomal deletions or imbalances result in diminished fetal growth. For example, Turner syndrome (XO) is associated with diminished birthweight. The converse is not true: additional X chromosomes beyond the norm are associated with reduced fetal growth. For each additional X chromosome (in excess of XX), birthweight may be reduced 300 g. Similarly, autosomal trisomies, such as Down syndrome, are also associated with abnormal fetal growth. Chromosomal aberrations often result in diminished fetal growth by interfering with cell division. An intrinsic defect in cultured fibroblasts from patients with trisomy 21 has been observed in tissue culture. Single-gene defects may also reduce fetal growth. The inborn errors most notably associated with diminished fetal weight are included in a list of factors that affect fetal growth, following these paragraphs. Many syndromes with autosomal-recessive, autosomal-dominant, polygenetic, or unknown inheritance are also associated with poor fetal growth and occasionally may produce marked IUGR (see also Chapter 28).

Monogenic disorders that affect fetal growth often impair insulin secretion or insulin action. These include reduced fetal insulin secretion by an attenuated insulin-sensing mechanism from a loss of function mutation in the pancreatic glucose-sensing enzyme glucokinase. Reduced insulin action is noted in leprechaun syndrome, which results from a mutation in the insulin receptor. IUGR has also been reported with deletion of the IGF1 gene. More complicated genetic mechanisms associated with IUGR include maternal uniparental disomy for chromosome 6, which probably unmasks an autosomal-recessive gene mutation. Paternal uniparental disomy of chromosome 6 is associated with transient neonatal diabetes and IUGR.

Abnormalities of the epigenetic process known as imprinting may result in reduced or excessive fetal growth. Epigenetic modification of genes by reversible modification of DNA by methylases and demethylases can suppress gene function (methylation) in a specific parent (maternal or paternal) of origin without altering the DNA sequence of that gene. Imprinted genes cluster in specific chromosome regions or domains. Imprinting is active in gametogenesis, with different genes being imprinted (methylated, suppressed) depending on the parent of origin. The fertilized egg then undergoes a series of DNA demethylations only to be followed by new patterns of methylations in the embryo.[97] Loss of imprinting of the IGF2 gene results in excessive fetal growth and is also noted in certain malignancies (Wilms tumor, colon, ovary).[143] The IGF2 gene, located at a highly imprinted region (11q15.5), is maternally imprinted (suppressed) but paternally expressed. The normal pattern is that only one allele is expressed (paternal). Biallelic expression predisposes to excessive growth and tumors.[96]

Beckwith-Wiedemann syndrome (BWS) is a common overgrowth syndrome that illustrates the role of imprinting in the regulation of fetal growth. BWS is a multi-genetic disorder that may be sporadic or familial; cases may also be associated with chromosomal abnormalities in the highly imprinted region at chromosome 11p15.5. Duplication of paternally derived 11p15 and paternal uniparental isodisomy of 11p are noted. Overgrowth may result from overexpression of paternally expressed genes that enhance growth or from suppression of maternally expressed genes that inhibit growth. Many sporadic cases of BWS demonstrate biallelic expression (normal is expression of the paternally derived gene only, as the maternal gene is imprinted and suppressed) of the IGF2 gene.[60,140]

Because imprinting through methylation and demethylation is quite active during gametogenesis and embryogenesis, there may be alterations in the pattern of differentially expressed genes during various assisted reproductive technologies. Indeed, children born after assisted reproductive technologies have a higher incidence of potential imprinting disorders such as BWS, Angelman syndrome, and retinoblastoma.[42]

Additional disorders due in part to imprinting errors include uniparental disomy for chromosome 7 with IUGR, 10% of Silver-Russell syndrome, and transient neonatal diabetes.[12,102,131] An imprintable gene possibly involved in Silver-Russell syndrome, *GRB10,* codes for growth-factor-receptor binding proteins that interact with the insulin and insulin-like growth factor receptors.

Infectious agents are typically sought as being responsible for early onset of IUGR. Of these, cytomegalovirus and rubella virus are the most important identifiable agents associated with marked fetal growth retardation. After maternal viremia, both agents invade the placenta, producing varying degrees of villitis, and subsequently gain access to fetal tissues. The effects of placentitis itself on fetal growth are unknown, but once congenital fetal infection has occurred, these viral agents have direct adverse effects on fetal development. Intracellular rubella virus inhibits cellular mitotic activity in addition to producing chromosomal breaks and subsequently cytolysis. In addition, this virus produces an obliterative angiopathy that further compromises cell viability. Cytomegalovirus also causes cytolysis, resulting in areas of focal tissue necrosis. These viral agents therefore reduce cell number and subsequent birthweight by simultaneously inhibiting cell division and producing cell death (see also Chapters 22 and 37).

Following are examples of factors affecting fetal growth.

A. Chromosome disorders associated with IUGR
   1. Trisomies 8, 13, 18, 21
   2. 4p Syndrome
   3. 5p Syndrome
   4. 13q, 18p, 18q syndromes
   5. Triploidy
   6. XO
   7. XXY, XXXY, XXXXY
   8. XXXXX

B. Metabolic disorders associated with diminished birthweight
   1. Agenesis of pancreas
   2. Congenital absence of islets of Langerhans
   3. Congenital lipodystrophy
   4. Galactosemia (?)
   5. Generalized gangliosidosis type I
   6. Hypophosphatasia
   7. I-cell disease
   8. Leprechaunism
   9. Maternal and fetal phenylketonuria
   10. Maternal renal insufficiency
   11. Maternal Gaucher disease
   12. Menkes syndrome
   13. Transient neonatal diabetes mellitus

C. Syndromes associated with diminished birthweight
   1. Aarskog-Scott syndrome
   2. Anencephaly
   3. Bloom syndrome
   4. Cornelia de Lange syndrome
   5. Dubovitz syndrome
   6. Dwarfism (e.g., achondrogenesis, achondroplasia)
   7. Ellis-van Creveld syndrome
   8. Familial dysautonomia
   9. Fanconi pancytopenia
   10. Hallermann-Streiff syndrome
   11. Meckel-Gruber syndrome
   12. Microcephaly
   13. Möbius syndrome
   14. Multiple congenital anomalads
   15. Osteogenesis imperfecta
   16. Potter syndrome
   17. Prader-Willi syndrome
   18. Progeria
   19. Prune-belly syndrome
   20. Radial aplasia; thrombocytopenia
   21. Robert syndrome
   22. Robinow syndrome
   23. Rubinstein-Taybi syndrome
   24. Seckel syndrome
   25. Silver syndrome
   26. Smith-Lemli-Opitz syndrome
   27. VATER (*v*ertebral defects, imperforate *a*nus, *t*racheoesophageal fistula, and *r*adial and *r*enal dysplasia) and VACTERL (*v*ertebral abnormalities, *a*nal atresia, *c*ardiac abnormalities, *t*racheoesophageal fistula, and/or *e*sophageal atresia, *r*enal agenesis and dysplasia, and *l*imb defects) syndromes
   28. Williams syndrome

D. Congenital infections associated with IUGR
   1. Rubella
   2. Cytomegalovirus
   3. Toxoplasmosis
   4. Malaria
   5. Syphilis
   6. Varicella
   7. Chagas disease

THE INFANT WITH IUGR/SGA

Definition

The infant with low birthweight (less than 2500 g) is not always premature (earlier than 37 weeks). Worldwide, more than 20 million infants are born weighing less than 2500 g. Between 30% and 40% of these infants are born at term gestation and are therefore undergrown (SGA status). Population norms need to be determined for each specific genetic group, especially those characterized by unusual inherited patterns of fetal growth. In general, these population norms established in various North American and European cities describe the usual fetal growth pattern for industrial societies and may be used as the reference norms for similar ethnic groups (see Fig. 13-1 and Table 13-1). Each curve defines either standard deviations or percentile units that include the normal variability or distribution of birthweights at each gestational age. By definition, infants less than two standard deviations or those at less than the third percentile (10th for Denver curves because of the lower birthweight at higher altitudes) are classified as SGA.

Therefore, between 2.5% and 10% of each population has SGA status. The use of population means can be misleading. Within a sibship, fetal birthweight is less variable and more consistent than that for an entire population. Compared with family members, 80% of infants with congenital rubella infection were classified as SGA, whereas only 40% were SGA when population standards were used. Fetal growth assessment must therefore be considered in the context of prior reproductive history and clinical examination of the newborn.

Infants with IUGR may or may not be SGA. Alternatively, infants who are SGA may not have been affected by growth-restricting processes that produce IUGR. Weight parameters at birth may be insensitive in determining IUGR. The ponderal index (weight divided by length cubed) or other body proportion ratios (head circumference to weight or length, femur length to abdominal circumference, head circumference to abdominal circumference) may be useful in detecting additional cases of IUGR during the fetal or neonatal period. IUGR resulting from placental insufficiency usually reduces birthweight more than length, and to a greater degree than head circumference, and it would be evident by a reduced ponderal index with a smaller, albeit relatively large (spared), head circumference. The greater the severity of IUGR, the greater is the deviation of weight, length, and (less so) head circumference from gestational age norms. Alterations of body proportion ratios may create a continuum rather than a dichotomous classification of birthweight status (appropriate for gestational age [AGA] versus SGA).

Deviations of fetal weight from a predetermined genetic potential produce IUGR with or without SGA status. Second-trimester fetal anthropometric and biometric ultrasonography can be used to predict an ideal weight, which may be modified by intrinsic and extrinsic growth-limiting factors. Any variation from the predicted weight would be considered IUGR. The growth potential realization index assesses deviations from norms of weight and of head, abdominal, and thigh circumferences. This index is applied to the infant after birth by calculating a neonatal growth assessment score that includes the deviation of each growth parameter from its related normative value for that gestational age. A neonatal growth assessment score of zero indicates ideal growth, and scores greater than 20 indicate IUGR but not necessarily SGA.

Aberrant Fetal Growth Patterns

Fetal growth retardation may have its origins early or late during fetal development. Infants who demonstrate reduced fetal growth early in gestation constitute approximately 20% of all infants who are SGA. They are symmetrically growth retarded: head circumference, weight, and length are proportionately affected to equivalent degrees. These fetuses and infants continue to grow, albeit with reduced net effect (Fig. 13-15A). In addition to inherent genetic growth constraint, other factors may produce diminished growth potential in these neonates. Congenital viral infections usually have their worst effect if infection occurs during the first

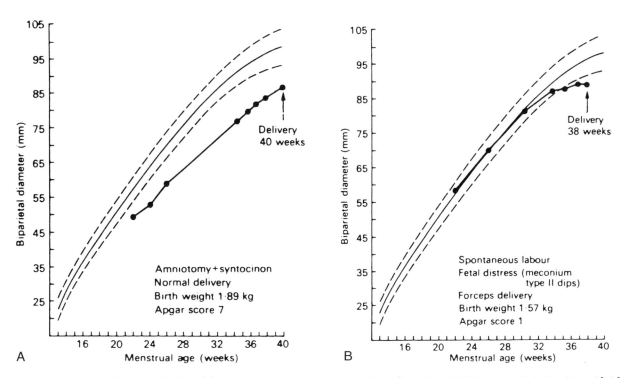

FIGURE 13-15. Low-profile (**A**) and late-flattening (**B**) patterns of intrauterine growth restriction. (From Campbell S: Fetal growth. In Beard R et al [eds]: Fetal Physiology and Medicine. Philadelphia, WB Saunders, 1976, p 271.)

trimester, when they have a significant effect on cell replication and subsequently on birthweight. Similarly, abnormal genetic factors, such as single gene deletions and chromosomal disorders, also reduce the intrauterine growth rate at an early stage of development. Very early onset of growth delay has been reported in anomalous infants of diabetic mothers. Box 13-3 lists characteristics and examples of IUGR.

Growth retardation of a later onset is usually associated with impaired uteroplacental function or nutritional deficiency during the third trimester (see Fig. 13-15B). Nutrient supplies, oxygen, and uteroplacental perfusion

BOX 13-3. Characteristics and Examples of Intrauterine Growth Restriction

Symmetric
- Early onset
- Constitutional or "normal" small
- Low profile biparietal diameter
- ? Growth potential
- Normal ponderal index
- Low risk for perinatal asphyxia
- Brain symmetry to body size, short femur
- Normal blood flow in internal carotid artery
- Proportionate abdominal circumference
- Normal maternal and fetal arterial waveform velocity
- Glycogen and fat content relative
- Low risk for hypoglycemia

Examples
- Genetic
- TORCH (*t*oxoplasmosis, *o*ther [congenital syphilis and viruses], *r*ubella, *c*ytomegalovirus, and *h*erpes simplex virus association)
- Chromosomal
- Anomalad syndromes
- Insulin-like growth factor type 1 deficiencies

Asymmetric
- Late onset
- Environmental
- Late-flattening biparietal diameter
- Growth arrest
- Low ponderal index
- ? Risk for asphyxia
- Brain sparing, normal femur length
- Redistribution to internal carotid artery bloodflow
- Decreased abdominal circumference
- ? Maternal and fetal arterial waveform velocity
- ? Glycogen and fat content
- ? Risk for hypoglycemia

Examples
- Chronic fetal distress (hypoxia)
- Preeclampsia
- Chronic hypertension
- Diabetes classes D to F
- Poor caloric intake

are in excess of their requirements during early fetal development and should not interfere with fetal growth until the growth rate exceeds the provision of substrates or oxygen or both. During the last trimester, the fetal growth rate and net tissue accretion increase markedly; if the uteroplacental supply line is compromised, IUGR will develop. The anthropometric findings among these infants demonstrate a relative sparing of head growth, whereas body weight and somatic organ growth are more seriously altered. Spleen, liver, adrenal, thymus, and adipose tissue growth is affected to the greatest extent in these newborns who are late-onset SGA (Figs. 13-16 and 13-17). The relative sparing of fetal head (brain) growth is caused by preferential perfusion of the brain with well-oxygenated blood containing adequate substrates after redistribution of the cardiac output during periods of fetal distress. Infants with IUGR resulting from unknown or nutritional causes may have successfully adapted to a "hostile" in utero environment with reduced growth. After birth, in a more favorable environment, catch-up growth ensues.

Antenatal Care

DIAGNOSIS

Antenatal diagnosis of IUGR has proved difficult. Many of these infants deliver at or beyond term without prior antenatal detection. At best, when sought with careful maternal physical examination, accurate dating, and risk-assessment analysis, only 50% of these infants may be identified by clinical examination before birth. Antenatal detection is an essential component of care for these infants because they require intensive obstetric and neonatal management to reduce their excessive perinatal morbidity and mortality rates. This poor outcome is associated with unexplained antepartum or intrapartum fetal death, neonatal asphyxia, and major neonatal adaptive problems. Neonatal risks are increased at each gestational age (Fig. 13-18).[89] Antenatal identification and intensive perinatal care of the mother, the fetus, and, later, the neonate are imperative components that result in improved outcome for these infants.

Careful measurement and recording of fundal height at each antenatal visit are a reasonable clinical screening aid in the diagnosis of IUGR. When dates are confirmed by onset of quickening, audible heart tones and accurate menstrual history, size-date discrepancy (i.e., fundal height less than or lagging behind the norm for gestational age) is suggestive of IUGR. History findings that may be components of a risk assessment score for IUGR include a history of a previous infant who was SGA, vaginal bleeding, multiple gestation, low prepregnancy weight, and poor pregnancy weight gain, as noted earlier. Chronic maternal illness and preeclampsia are also high-risk situations indicating possible IUGR.

Laboratory tests, including determination of maternal serum estriol level, placental lactogen, and various pregnancy-associated proteins, have been unreliable markers for IUGR. The diagnosis of chronic fetal distress in the absence of obvious alterations of fetal

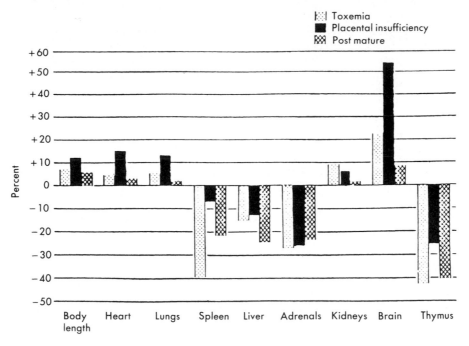

FIGURE 13-16. Deviation of organ weights after intrauterine growth restriction. (From Naeye R et al: Judgment of fetal age: 3. The pathologist's evaluation. Pediatr Clin North Am 13:849, 1966.)

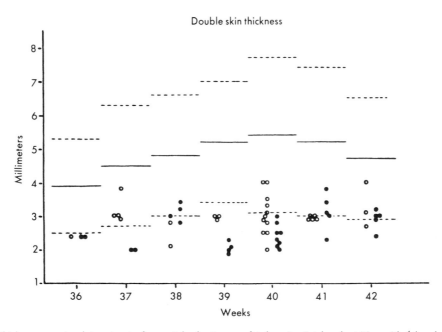

FIGURE 13-17. Skinfold thickness: a major determinant of neonatal subcutaneous fat deposits. Fetal malnutrition with *(closed circles)* and without *(open circles)* severe clinical signs of wasting. (From Usher R: Clinical and therapeutic aspects of fetal malnutrition. Pediatr Clin North Am 17:169, 1970.)

heart rate patterns is now possible with cordocentesis *(percutaneous umbilical blood sampling)*. Although not indicated for all patients with IUGR, fetal blood sampling may demonstrate hypoxia, lactic acidosis, hypoglycemia, and normoblastemia caused by chronic fetal distress. Hypoxia may precede fetal acidosis. Fetal blood sampling may also permit rapid karyotyping of the fetus with IUGR with malformations and the identification of TORCH infections through the assessment of antibody titers, culture, or DNA diagnosis of TORCH agents.

Ultrasonographic assessment of the fetus can help detect the presence of IUGR. Either used as a routine two-step process (dating/sizing in mid-second trimester; follow-up assessment at 32 to 34 weeks) or based on

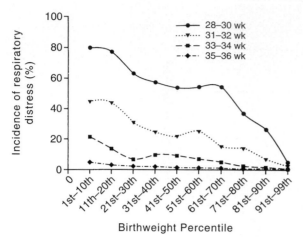

FIGURE 13-18. Incidence of respiratory distress among 12,317 preterm infants, according to birthweight percentile after stratification according to gestational age (28 to 30 weeks, 31 to 32 weeks, 33 to 34 weeks, and 35 to 36 weeks). (From McIntire DD et al: Birth weight in relation to morbidity and mortality among newborn infants. N Engl J Med 340:1234, 1999.)

variable decelerations from cord compression, and intrauterine fetal death in as many as 5% to 10% of affected fetuses. The risk of congenital anomalies with oligohydramnios increases from 1% to 9% with mild-to-severe amniotic fluid deficits; at the same time, the risk of IUGR increases from 5% to 40%. Second-trimester oligohydramnios, with elevated α-fetoprotein levels, has a particularly poor prognosis (see also Chapter 21).

The degree of oligohydramnios can be determined ultrasonographically and quantitated by means of the four-quadrant amniotic fluid index (AFI). The vertical diameters of four pockets of amniotic fluid are added to determine the amniotic fluid index. Between 26 and 38 weeks of gestation, the amniotic fluid index is 12.9 ± 4.6 cm; an index of less than 5 cm signifies severe oligohydramnios.

Morphometric analysis of fetal growth parameters includes determination of serial biparietal diameters as analyzed by absolute number and rate of change (Figs. 13-19 and 13-20, and see Fig. 13-15). Head sparing in asymmetric IUGR may make fetal measurements of the biparietal diameter less sensitive; however, truncometry—measuring the fetal abdominal circumference (in part, liver size) at the level of the umbilical vein—may add accuracy (Fig. 13-21). Using ratios of fetal growth parameters (Fig. 13-22) and adding the femur length and the fetal ponderal index may increase the sensitivity of fetal biometry.[28,107] Three-dimensional evaluation may improve the prenatal estimate of fetal size.

Doppler flow velocity waveforms, assessed in the maternal and fetal circulations, may detect increased maternal and fetal vascular resistance before the onset

risk analysis, fetal ultrasonography is the primary method for identifying fetuses with IUGR.[17,134] Ultrasonography includes real-time biometric and anthropomorphic analysis of fetal growth parameters (head circumference, biparietal diameter, abdominal circumference, femur length), detection of anomalies, and identification of oligohydramnios.[28,107] Oligohydramnios is a risk factor for congenital anomalies, severe IUGR with reduced urine production, pulmonary hypoplasia,

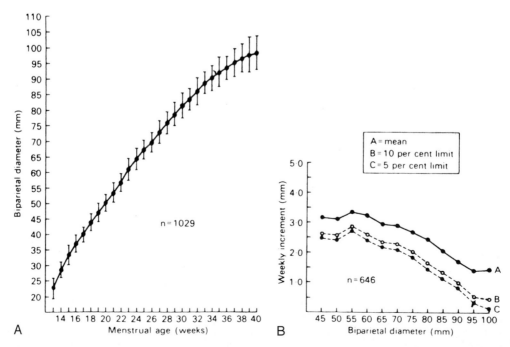

FIGURE 13-19. Absolute measurement (**A**) and rate of change (**B**) of fetal biparietal diameter. (From Campbell S: Size at Birth. Amsterdam, Elsevier Scientific, 1974.)

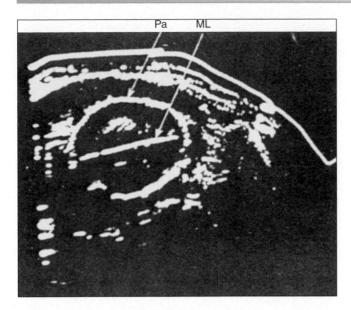

FIGURE 13-20. Sonogram demonstrating determination of the biparietal diameter. ML, midline echo; Pa, parietal bone. (From Campbell S: Fetal growth. In Beard R et al [eds]: Fetal Physiology and Medicine. Philadelphia, WB Saunders, 1976, p 271.)

of IUGR.[69,95,133,134] Maternal arcuate arterial flow may reflect trophoblastic invasion of the myometrium because increased flow may be associated with increased vascular invasion and better placental perfusion. Alternatively, decreased maternal arcuate arterial waveform velocity may demonstrate increased maternal vascular resistance and decreased uteroplacental perfusion. Uterine vessel velocimetry is less accurate than waveforms in fetal vessels in predicting IUGR and fetal hypoxia.

Chronic fetal distress with hypoxia (with or without acidosis) is associated with fetal Doppler arterial waveform velocities that indicate reduced systemic (descending aorta, umbilical artery) flow and normal or increased cerebral (middle cerebral artery) flow (head sparing).[95] The greatest risk is associated with absent or even more seriously with reversed diastolic flow in the umbilical artery.[69] Absent end-diastolic velocimetry may be stable or it may progress to reversed flow; both indicate placental insufficiency. Reversed flow greatly increases fetal risk and is usually unstable and requires consideration for delivery. If other features are otherwise normal (biophysical profile, amnionic fluid volume, reassuring cardiotocograms, minute-to-minute variation), steroids can be given and delivery temporarily delayed.

Assessment of the fetal middle cerebral artery (MCA) may show centralization in the compromised fetus, demonstrating increased flow in the MCA relative to the placenta. Preservation of MCA diastolic flow may be seen with absent or even at times reversed flow in the umbilical artery. Decreased MCA flow is associated with fetal cardiac decompensation and is an ominous sign.[82] Umbilical venous pulsation or dilation of the ductus venosus and reversed flow in the vena cava also suggests serious cardiac compromise from hypoxia or anemia. Abnormalities on the venous side of the circulation occur later than in the umbilical arteries. Nonetheless, these Doppler waveform abnormalities may precede classic signs of fetal distress, such as abnormal results on contraction stress.

ANTENATAL MANAGEMENT (See also Chapter 9.)
Once the diagnosis of IUGR is suspected and strengthened by ultrasonography, it is essential to institute appropriate maternal and fetal care and closely monitor the well-being of the fetus. With severe IUGR, maternal activity should be limited and bed rest initiated, with the mother assuming a left lateral recumbent position to ensure optimal uterine blood flow. Administration of oxygen (55% O_2 at 8 L/min) to the mother has

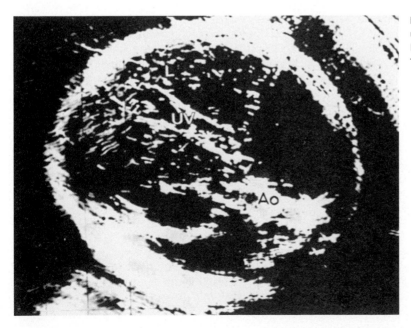

FIGURE 13-21. Truncometry at the level of fetal liver (L), umbilical vein (UV), and aorta (Ao). (From Campbell S: Size at Birth. Amsterdam, Elsevier Scientific, 1974.)

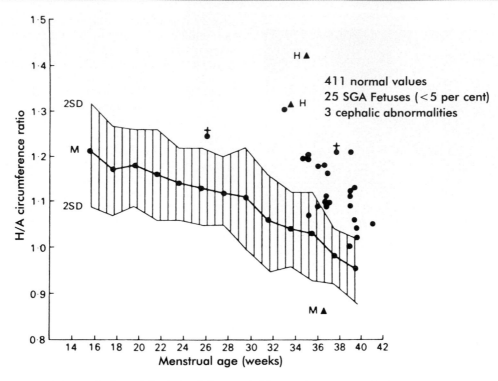

FIGURE 13-22. Assessment of aberrant fetal growth by the head-abdomen (H/A) circumference ratio. H, hydrocephalus; M, microcephalus; +, fetal demise; *filled circle*, small for gestational age (SGA); *triangle-H*, hydrocephaly; *triangle-M*, microcephaly. (From Campbell S: Fetal growth. In Beard R et al [eds]: Fetal Physiology and Medicine. Philadelphia, WB Saunders, 1976, p 271.)

resulted in improved fetal oxygenation, some growth, and normalization of fetal aortic blood flow velocity in some IUGR fetuses with chronic fetal distress.[8]

Assessment of fetal well-being should begin once the diagnosis is suspected and the fetus has approached a gestational age compatible with extrauterine survival. An inexpensive screening tool is a log of fetal activity recorded by the mother; normal activity is a reasonable sign of well-being. A specific period should be monitored, such as after a meal, and fetal activity should be recorded each day. In addition to this maternal record, a systematic approach to fetal evaluation should be performed routinely and frequently. Classically, the oxytocin challenge test (OCT) has been used to predict the potential for fetal demise or acute intrapartum death in a marginally oxygenated, compromised fetus. This test requires the intravenous administration of oxytocin, which must result in three uterine contractions within 10 minutes. Late decelerations denote relative uteroplacental insufficiency and suggest that the oxygenation of the fetus may be impaired. A positive OCT result (three late decelerations with three contractions) also suggests that the fetus may not tolerate the contractions that occur during labor. This is not a universal observation; a significant percentage of these infants may be able to withstand spontaneous or oxytocin-induced labor without the development of fetal acidosis. Fewer decelerations than those for a positive OCT result should be considered suspect, and the test should be repeated

(along with technically unsatisfactory tracings) within the next 24 to 48 hours.

Because technical and time difficulties are related to the OCT, and because contraindications exist for its use, such as a previous classic cesarean section, placenta previa, and concern about inducing premature labor, the nonstress test (NST) has been employed. This test examines fetal well-being by determining the acceleration of the fetal heart rate after spontaneous fetal movement. A healthy fetus (nonhypoxic) will respond to its own body movements with a mean acceleration of 15 beats per minute above the baseline heart rate. In addition, the frequency of fetal movements should be ascertained; at the same time, examination of beat-to-beat and long-term variability can offer additional useful information. The NST can also supplement the OCT, because fetuses with a positive OCT result but a reactive NST result and normal beat-to-beat variability are more likely to tolerate labor without untoward problems. Under stable maternal conditions and with signs of fetal well-being (negative OCT result and [or] reactive NST result), these tests may be repeated weekly.

The false-positive rate for OCT (25%) and NST (20%) is high compared with the false-negative rate for OCT (0.4 in 1000) and NST (6.8 in 1000). The rate of intrauterine fetal death is high after a positive OCT result (32%) but lower with a nonreactive NST result (12%). Therefore, the contraction stress test is more predictive of fetal death and has fewer false negative results.

However, more false positive results are obtained than with the NST.

Biophysical determinants have been used successfully to assess fetal well-being. The combined analyses of fetal breathing movements, gross body movements, fetal tone, fetal heart reactivity to movement, and qualitative amniotic fluid volume have improved the antenatal management of IUGR (Table 13-6). This biophysical profile provides a nonweighted score that can identify the fetus at risk. A biophysical profile score of 8 to 10 carries a 0.8% chance of fetal death, whereas a score of 0 predicts a fetal mortality rate of 40%. This analysis takes approximately 30 minutes and should be repeated weekly with scores of 8 to 10. If the score is less than 8, the biophysical profile should be repeated that afternoon. If the score is again less than 8, an OCT should be performed and a decision made to deliver the infant, regardless of gestational age, unless severe anomalies are determined. A low biophysical profile correlates with fetal hypoxia determined by cordocentesis. Assessment of fetal aortic flow with the pulsatile index (see Table 13-6) may also help determine optimal timing for delivery. If fetal lung maturity is present, aortic blood flow is reduced, and there is other evidence of fetal distress, the fetus may need to be delivered before term. Factors that affect the biophysical profile score include sedation, stimulants (cocaine, theophylline), indomethacin (decreases amniotic fluid), cigarette smoking (decreases fetal breathing movements), hyperglycemia (increases fetal breathing movements), and hypoglycemia (decreases all activities).

The mode of delivery is not necessarily dictated by the abnormalities recorded by biophysical or electrophysiologic surveillance of the fetus. Some patients can tolerate labor after a positive OCT result, with oxygen administration and a left lateral recumbent position. However, it would be judicious to avoid labor in those situations complicated by a nonreactive NST result, a flat baseline, absent or reversed diastolic flow, and a positive OCT result. Similarly, premature infants who are SGA, in particular those with a breech presentation and those whose mothers have a completely unfavorable cervix, should be delivered by the abdominal route. Particular attention should be given to the asymmetrically (late-flattening) growth-retarded fetus with chronic fetal distress who tolerates labor poorly and readily develops signs of acute fetal distress, compared with the symmetrically undergrown fetus and the normal fetus. Whether labor is induced or spontaneous, continuous intrapartum fetal heart rate monitoring combined with appropriate use of fetal scalp pH determinations and fetal pulse oximetry should be employed (see also Chapter 9).[41,117] If late decelerations become evident, scalp blood pH might be evaluated, and if fetal acidosis has developed, delivery should be expedited.

During labor, uterine contractions may further compromise marginal placental perfusion and fetal gas exchange. The myocardium of these fetuses may have diminished glycogen stores, a key energy source partially responsible for the fetal ability to withstand asphyxia. Because there is a high incidence of intrapartum birth asphyxia, it is essential that the delivery be coordinated with the neonatal team, which should be prepared to resuscitate a depressed or asphyxiated neonate. In addition, combined obstetric-pediatric management is indicated if meconium is present in the amniotic fluid. This event often follows periods of fetal hypoxia and stress, occurring with greatest frequency in the term or post-term neonate who is SGA. Obstetric management should include oropharyngeal suctioning immediately after delivery of the head. Immediately after birth, the neonatal team should further clear the oropharynx, and possibly also the trachea, of additional meconium (see also Chapter 42, Part 5).

Saline amnioinfusion may be beneficial in the presence of oligohydramnios and an AFI of less than

TABLE 13-6. Biophysical Profile Scoring: Technique and Interpretation*

BIOPHYSICAL VARIABLE	NORMAL (SCORE = 2)	ABNORMAL (SCORE = 0)
Fetal breathing movements	≥1 episode of ≥30 s in 30 min	Absent or no episode of ≥30 s in 30 min
Gross body movements	≥3 discrete body or limb movements in 30 min (episodes of active continuous movement considered as single movement)	≤2 episodes of body or limb movements in 30 min
Fetal tone	≥1 episode of active extension with return to flexion of fetal limb(s) or trunk (opening and closing of hand considered normal tone)	Slow extension with return to partial flexion or movement of limb in full extension or absent fetal movement
Reactive fetal heart rate	≥2 episodes of acceleration of ≥15 beats/min and of ≥15 s associated with fetal movement in 20 min	<2 episodes of acceleration of fetal heart rate or acceleration of <15 beats/min in 20 min
Qualitative amniotic fluid volume	≥1 pocket of fluid measuring ≥1 cm in two perpendicular planes	Either no pockets or a pocket of <1 cm in two perpendicular planes

*See Manning FA et al: Antepartum fetal evaluation: Development of a biophysical profile. Am J Obstet Gynecol 136:787, 1980.
Modified from Manning FA et al: Fetal assessment based on fetal biophysical profile scoring. Am J Obstet Gynecol 151:343, 1985.

5 cm.[128] Titration to an index of greater than 8 cm may lower the incidence of meconium-stained fluid, variable decelerations, end-stage bradycardia, fetal distress, and acute fetal acidosis.

APPROACH TO THE INFANT WHO IS SMALL FOR GESTATIONAL AGE

After birth, the infant who is SGA may develop significant neonatal problems (Table 13-7). In the delivery room, it is essential to ensure optimal neonatal cardiopulmonary physiologic adaptation while ensuring minimal heat loss in a warm environment. Once stabilization has been established, a careful physical examination should be performed.

When infants with obvious anomalies and syndromes and those born to mothers with severe illness or malnutrition are excluded, there still remains a heterogeneous population of infants who are SGA. These infants have a characteristic physical appearance: the heads look relatively large for their undergrown trunks and extremities, which seem wasted. The abdomen is scaphoid, misleading one to suspect a diaphragmatic hernia. The extremities have little subcutaneous tissue or fat, which is best exemplified by a reduced skinfold

TABLE 13-7. Perinatal Problems of the Small-for-Gestational-Age Neonate

PROBLEM	PATHOGENESIS	ASSESSMENT/PREVENTION/TREATMENT
Fetal death	Placental insufficiency, chronic fetal hypoxia	Biophysical profile Vessel velocimetry Cordocentesis Maternal O_2 Early delivery
Asphyxia	Acute fetal hypoxia superimposed on chronic fetal hypoxia, acidosis Placental insufficiency ↓ Cardiac glycogen stores	Antepartum and intrapartum monitoring Efficient neonatal resuscitation
Meconium aspiration pneumonia	Hypoxic stress	Pharyngeal-tracheal aspiration
Fasting hypoglycemia	↓ Hepatic glycogen ↓Gluconeogenesis ↓Counter-regulatory hormones Cold stress Asphyxia-hypoxia	Early oral or intravenous alimentation or both
Alimented hyperglycemia	"Starvation diabetes"	Glucose infusion not to exceed 8 mg/kg/min except with hypoglycemia
Polycythemia/hyperviscosity	Placental transfusion Fetal hypoxia Erythropoietin	Neonatal partial exchange transfusion
Temperature instability	Cold stress Poor fat stores Catecholamine depletion Hypoxia, hypoglycemia Reduced fasting oxygen consumption	Neutral thermal environment Early alimentation
Dysmorphology	TORCH Syndrome complexes Chromosome disorders	Disease-specific therapy or prevention
Teratogen exposure		Disease-specific therapy or prevention
Pulmonary hemorrhage (rare)	Hypothermia, polycythemia ↓ O_2/DIC	Avoid cold stress, hypoxia Endotracheal administration of epinephrine PEEP
Immunodeficiency	"Malnutrition" effect TORCH	Unknown Specific therapy if available
Decreased bone mineral density	Possible substrate deficiency or altered vitamin D metabolism	Appropriate postnatal oral calcium and vitamin D intake

DIC, disseminated intravascular coagulation; PEEP, positive end-expiratory pressure; TORCH, *toxoplasmosis, other* (e.g., congenital syphilis and viruses), *rubella, cytomegalovirus,* and *herpes* simplex virus association.

thickness (see Fig. 13-17). In addition, the skin appears to hang; it is rough, dry, and parchment-like; and it desquamates easily. Fingernails may be long, and the hands and feet of these infants tend to look too large for the rest of the body. The facial appearance suggests the look of a "wise old person," especially compared with that of premature infants (Fig. 13-23). Cranial sutures may be widened or overriding; the anterior fontanel is larger than expected, representing diminished membranous bone formation. Similarly, epiphyseal ossification at the knee (chondral bone) is also retarded. Decreased bone mineralization may also be present.[25] When meconium is passed in utero, there is often yellow-green staining of the nails, skin, and umbilical cord, which may also appear thinner than usual. Many of these infants have subclinical chronic fetal hypoxia,

which is detectable by cordocentesis or Doppler waveform velocimetry of the umbilical arteries.

Gestational age assessment of the infant who is SGA may result in misleading data when based on physical criteria alone. Vernix caseosa is frequently reduced or absent as a result of diminished skin perfusion during periods of fetal distress or because of depressed synthesis of estriol, which enhances vernix production. In the absence of this protective covering, the skin is continuously exposed to amniotic fluid and begins to desquamate after birth. Sole creases are determined in part by exposure to amniotic fluid and therefore appear more mature. Breast tissue formation also depends on peripheral blood flow and estriol levels and become markedly reduced in infants who are SGA. In addition, the female external genitalia appear less mature

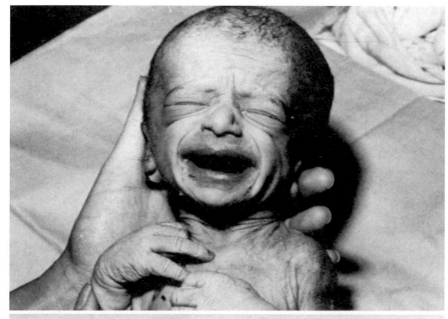

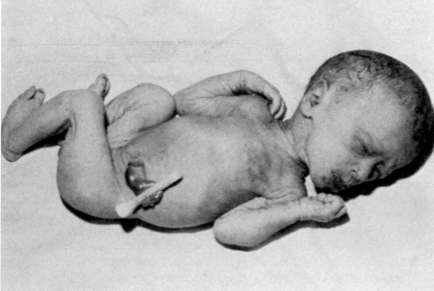

FIGURE 13-23. Term infant who is small for gestational age, demonstrating wizened facies and dry, desquamating, hanging skin. Birthweight, 1500 g.

because of the absence of the perineal adipose tissue covering the labia. Ear cartilage, as noted in bone ossification, may also be diminished.

Neurologic examination for gestational age assessment may be affected less by IUGR than the physical criteria. Infants with IUGR achieve appropriate neurologic maturity functionally. Peripheral nerve conduction velocity and visual- or auditory-evoked responses correlate well with gestational age in normal neonates and are not impaired after IUGR. These aspects of neurologic maturity are not sensitive to deprivation, and occasionally maturity may even become accelerated. Determinants of active or passive tone and posture may be reliable in infants who are SGA, assuming that infants with significant central nervous system disorders (anomalies, asphyxia) and metabolic disorders (hypoglycemia) are excluded.

Specific organ maturity occurs despite diminished somatic growth. Cerebral cortical convolutions, renal glomeruli, and alveolar maturation all relate to gestational age and are not retarded with IUGR. As a result of stress in utero, these infants may occasionally accelerate the maturity of specific organ systems, such as the lung, thus explaining the low incidence of respiratory distress syndrome in preterm neonates who are SGA.

When examined in closer detail, infants who are SGA demonstrate specific behavioral characteristics that suggest, despite electric neurologic maturity, that functional central nervous system maturity may be impaired.[7] In the absence of significant central nervous system disease, these neonates demonstrate abnormal sleep cycles and diminished muscle tone, reflexes, activity, and excitability. This hypoexcitability suggests an adverse effect on polysynaptic reflex propagation and implies that central nervous system functional maturity does not necessarily proceed independently of the intrauterine events that result in IUGR.

Once stabilized and assigned a gestational age, the neonate who is SGA should be examined in more detail to direct the diagnostic workup as detailed in the following outline:

A. History and physical examination[119]
B. Accurate growth parameters
C. Findings:
   1. Dysmorphic features suggesting:
      a. Chromosome abnormality
      b. Syndrome
      c. Drugs (fetal exposure)
   2. Blueberry-muffin rash, petechiae, hepatosplenomegaly, and ocular pathologic changes suggesting:
      a. Rubella
      b. Cytomegalovirus
      c. Other infection
   3. Neither 1 nor 2 suggests:
      a. Chronic fetal hypoxia
      b. Constitutional factors
      c. Genetic factors
      d. Nutritional factors
      e. Toxins
      f. Placenta (e.g., twins)
      g. Unknown

Dysmorphic features, "funny-looking" facies, and abnormal hands, feet, and palmar creases, in addition to gross anomalies, suggest congenital malformation syndromes, chromosomal defects, or teratogens. Ocular disorders, such as chorioretinitis, cataracts, glaucoma, and cloudy cornea, in addition to hepatosplenomegaly, jaundice, and a blueberry-muffin rash, suggest a congenital infection (see also Chapters 22 and 37). The remaining infants constitute a heterogeneous group that represents most neonates who are SGA. Multiple gestations are the most recognizable cause in this category. TORCH infections resulting in extremely low birthweight are unusual in the absence of other clinical signs of congenital infection; however, a screening determination on cord blood for IgM values and a urine culture for cytomegalovirus may be indicated. Radiographic examination of the long bones, together with ultrasonography of the head, is diagnostically useful. Careful data related to the present and past reproductive history of the mother, in addition to ongoing neonatal management and close observation, are indicated in the remaining large number of neonates who are SGA whose underlying disorders may never be determined.

NEONATAL PROBLEMS

The perinatal mortality rate among infants who have IUGR is 10 to 20 times that among infants who are AGA. Intrauterine fetal death from chronic fetal hypoxia, immediate birth asphyxia, the multisystem disorders associated with asphyxia (hypoxic-ischemic encephalopathy, persistent fetal circulation, cardiomyopathy), and lethal congenital anomalies are the main contributing factors to the high mortality rate for fetuses and neonates who have IUGR. Problems due to prematurity such as respiratory distress syndrome are also more common with IUGR (see Fig. 13-18). Neurologic and other morbidities are also more frequent in infants who have IUGR; they have a rate 5 to 10 times that of infants who are AGA. Most intrauterine fetal deaths occur between 38 and 42 weeks' gestation and can be potentially avoided by careful assessment and intervention as noted in Table 13-7.

ASPHYXIA

Perinatal asphyxia and its sequelae constitute the most significant immediate problem of infants who have IUGR. As discussed, uterine contractions may add an additional hypoxic stress on the chronically hypoxic fetus with a marginally functioning placenta. The ensuing acute fetal hypoxia, acidosis, and cerebral depression may result in fetal death or neonatal asphyxia. IUGR accounts for a large proportion of stillborn infants. Myocardial infarction, amniotic fluid aspiration, and signs of cerebral hypoxia are noted in the stillborn infants with IUGR. With repeated episodes of fetal asphyxia or persistent hypoxemia, myocardial glycogen reserves are depleted, further limiting the fetal cardiopulmonary adaptation to hypoxia. If inadequate resuscitation occurs at birth and Apgar scores are low, the combination of intrapartum and neonatal asphyxia places the infant in double jeopardy for a continuum of central nervous system insult. The sequelae of perinatal asphyxia include multiple organ system dysfunction potentially characterized by hypoxic ischemic encephalopathy, ischemic heart failure, meconium aspiration pneumonia, persistent fetal circulation, gastrointestinal perforation, and acute tubular necrosis. Concomitant with these sequelae, there may be metabolic derangements such as hypoglycemia. Hypocalcemia is partly caused by excessive phosphate release from damaged cells or acidosis; it is exacerbated by sodium bicarbonate and diminished calcium intake. Hypocalcemia does not occur more often with IUGR unless these problems are present. Meconium aspiration syndrome may complicate the clinical picture and further compromise respiratory function and oxygenation with the development of pneumonitis and pneumothorax.

NEONATAL METABOLISM

Fasting hypoglycemia develops in infants who are SGA more than in any other neonatal subgroup or category. The propensity for hypoglycemia is greatest during the first 3 days of life; however, some of these infants have ketotic hypoglycemia months later. Key to the occurrence of hypoglycemia is the diminished hepatic glycogen stores (Fig. 13-24). Glycogenolysis constitutes the predominant source of glucose for the neonate during the immediate hours after birth. Later in the day, when glycogen stores become depleted, fasting glucose production results from the incorporation of lactate and gluconeogenic amino acid precursors into glucose. Infants who are SGA demonstrate an inability to increase

blood glucose concentration after oral or intravenous administration of alanine, the key gluconeogenic amino acid.[75] Hypoglycemic infants who are SGA have elevated alanine and lactate levels, suggesting that substrate availability is not rate limiting for gluconeogenesis and that the enzymes or cofactors are not active. Hypoglycemic infants probably have reduced hepatic glucose production. Nonhypoglycemic infants who are SGA do demonstrate rates of gluconeogenesis from alanine that are equivalent to the rates seen in nonhypoglycemic neonates who are AGA.[39]

Immediately after birth, fasting infants who are SGA may have lower plasma-free fatty acid levels than normally grown infants. Fasting blood glucose levels in infants who are SGA directly correlate with free fatty acid and ketone body levels in plasma. In addition, infants who are SGA have deficient use of intravenous triglycerides. After the intravenous administration of triglyceride emulsion, infants who are SGA have high free fatty acid and triglyceride levels, but ketone body formation is attenuated.[110] This suggests that use and oxidation of free fatty acids and triglycerides are diminished in neonates who are SGA. Free fatty acid oxidation is important because it spares peripheral tissue use of glucose, whereas hepatic oxidation of free fatty acids may contribute the reducing equivalents and energy required for hepatic gluconeogenesis. Deficient provision or oxidation of fatty acids may be partly responsible for the development of fasting hypoglycemia in these infants (Fig. 13-25).

Endocrine alterations have also been implicated in the pathogenesis of hypoglycemia in infants who are SGA. Hyperinsulinemia or excessive sensitivity to insulin may be one factor.[4] Catecholamine release is deficient

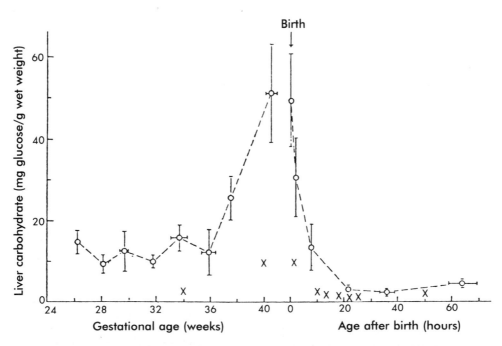

FIGURE 13-24. Fetal and neonatal hepatic glycogen content (X) in patients with intrauterine growth restriction. (From Shelly H et al: Neonatal hypoglycemia. Br Med Bull 22:34, 1966.)

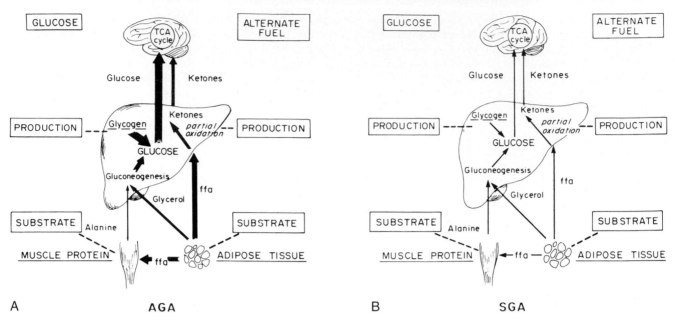

FIGURE 13-25. Postnatal glucose and fatty acid metabolic relationships in neonates who are appropriate for gestational age (AGA) (**A**) and small for gestational age (SGA) (**B**). *Arrows* reflect magnitude of flux. Infants who are SGA demonstrate both diminished glycogen stores and gluconeogenesis. In addition, they may have attenuated fatty acid oxidation. ffa, free fatty acids; TCA, tricarboxylic acid. (Modified from Adam PAJ: In Falkner F et al [eds]: Human Growth, vol 1. New York, Plenum Press, 1978.)

in these neonates during periods of hypoglycemia. Although basal glucagon levels may be elevated, exogenous administration of glucagon fails to enhance glycemia. These data suggest an abnormality of counter-regulatory hormonal mechanisms during periods of neonatal hypoglycemia in infants who are SGA.

With improved standards of care and attempts at early enteral feeding or intravenous alimentation, fasting hypoglycemia in the neonate who is SGA is a less common event. Before the start of alimentation, careful monitoring with Dextrostix reagent strips for determining blood glucose values identifies infants with asymptomatic hypoglycemia. If whole-blood glucose concentrations decline to less than 45 mg/dL during the first 3 days in term infants or preterm infants and no untoward symptoms have occurred, early feeding or glucose infusion at 4 to 8 mg/kg per minute should begin. After this initial rate, the infusion should be titrated until blood glucose values achieve normal levels. If the hypoglycemia is symptomatic, particularly when seizure activity intervenes, an intravenous mini-bolus of 10% dextrose in water at 200 mg/kg should be given, followed by an infusion as just described. Infants at greatest risk of having hypoglycemia are those who have been asphyxiated and those who appear most undergrown according to the ponderal index (Fig. 13-26).

Temperature Regulation (See also Chapter 29.)

After the birth of an infant whose gestation was complicated by uteroplacental insufficiency, the neonate's initial body temperature may be elevated. When placental function fails, the neonate's heat-eliminating capacity also becomes deficient, resulting in fetal hyperthermia. On exposure to the cold environment of the delivery room, infants who are SGA can increase their heat production (oxygen consumption) appropriately because brown adipose tissue stores are not necessarily depleted as a result of IUGR.[71] However, the infants' core temperature drops if the cold stress continues, implying that heat loss has exceeded heat production. Heat loss in these infants is partly caused by the large body surface area exposed to cold and the deficiency of an insulating layer of subcutaneous adipose tissue stores. Indeed, magnetic resonance imaging detection of reduced fetal fat stores is highly suggestive of IUGR that may result in fetal distress. Infants who are SGA therefore have a narrower neutral thermal environment than term infants but a broader one than premature neonates. In infants who are SGA, hypoglycemia or hypoxia, or both, interfere with heat production and may contribute to thermal instability. In all infants, particularly those who are SGA, a neutral thermal environment should be sought to prevent excessive heat loss and to promote appropriate postnatal weight gain.

When nursed in a neutral thermal environment, infants who are SGA demonstrate the usual decline of the respiratory quotient after birth, representing a shift toward free fatty acid oxidation. During the first 12 hours after birth, basal oxygen consumption may be diminished in neonates who are SGA. Similar observations have been recorded in utero among fetal lambs that are spontaneously SGA, suggesting in both situations that there is a deficiency of potentially oxidizable substrates. Supporting this hypothesis is the marked increment of oxygen consumption that occurs in well-

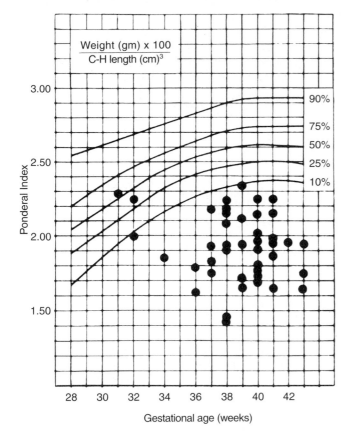

FIGURE 13-26. Relationship between ponderal index and neonatal hypoglycemia in intrauterine growth restriction. *Black circles* represent hypoglycemic infants. C-H length, crown-to-heel length. (From Jarai I et al: Body size and neonatal hypoglycemia in intrauterine growth retardation. Early Hum Dev 1:25, 1977.)

body cell number in congenitally infected infants and in those with chromosomal disorders exemplifies primordial growth retardation in these neonates.

Hyperviscosity-Polycythemia Syndrome
(See also Chapter 44.)

The plasma volume immediately after birth of infants who are SGA averages 52 mL/kg, as compared with 43 mL/kg in infants who are AGA. Once equilibrated at 12 hours of life, the plasma volume becomes equivalent in the two groups. In addition to an enhanced plasma space, the circulating red blood cell mass is expanded. Fetal hypoxia and subsequent erythropoietin synthesis induce excessive red blood cell production.[120] Alternatively, a placental-fetal transfusion during labor or periods of fetal asphyxia may result in a shift of placental blood to the fetus. Nonetheless, the elevation of the hematocrit level potentially increases blood viscosity, which interferes with vital tissue perfusion. The altered viscosity adversely affects neonatal hemodynamics and results in an abnormal cardiopulmonary and metabolic postnatal adaptation, producing hypoxia and hypoglycemia. These infants are at increased risk of having necrotizing enterocolitis. In the event that polycythemia is present (central hematocrit level greater than 65%) with such symptoms, appropriate therapy is directed at correcting hypoxia and hypoglycemia, and a partial exchange transfusion to reduce blood viscosity and to improve tissue perfusion should be considered.

Other Problems

IUGR is associated with a slower than normal production of long-chain polyunsaturated fatty acids.[132] Intestinal absorption of xylose is also attenuated. At birth, cord prealbumin and bone mineral content are low in term infants who are SGA. Thrombocytopenia, neutropenia, prolonged thrombin and partial thromboplastin times, and elevated fibrin degradation products are also problems among infants who are SGA.[90] Sudden infant death syndrome may be more common after IUGR. Inguinal hernias also typically follow preterm IUGR. Additional problems and their management are noted in Table 13-7.[24,34]

FOLLOW-UP
When infants who are SGA and have serious congenital malformations or viral infections are excluded, the remaining neonates should benefit from optimal antenatal detection, very careful management of pregnancy, and avoidance of hypoxic fetal distress. In addition, with ideal neonatal intensive care, the morbidity and mortality rates for infants who are SGA should be reduced to a minimum, and postnatal developmental handicaps should be diminished. Nonetheless, these infants continue to contribute to the excessive fetal and neonatal morbidity and mortality rates. The neonatal mortality rate is much greater than that for term neonates and for weight-matched premature neonates. The incidence of fetal death remains higher for infants who are SGA.

alimented infants who are SGA. This latter observation is also analogous to the rise of energy production after the nutritional rehabilitation of infants with marasmickwashiorkor. The increment of oxygen consumption after fetal or infantile malnutrition represents the energy cost of growth. Infants who are SGA usually have a significantly smaller postnatal weight loss because they are maturationally capable of achieving an adequate caloric intake earlier than premature neonates. Because of this enhanced caloric intake, infants who are SGA have a higher oxygen consumption than less mature neonates. Nutritional balance studies of premature infants who are SGA demonstrated an increase of fecal fat and protein loss, despite faster rates of growth compared with premature infants who are AGA. Energy storage was lower with IUGR, suggesting less fat deposition.

A subgroup of neonates who are SGA do not demonstrate an elevation of oxygen consumption after appropriate caloric intake. These infants have had lowprofile intrauterine growth and may be considered to have had "primordial" fetal growth retardation. Their growth is set and fixed at a slower rate, and their eventual growth potential is reduced. The diminished

In addition to the etiologic events that lead to the development of IUGR, these infants have additional multisystem problems that further compromise survival and future growth or development. Among these fetuses, the perinatal mortality rate is 10 times that of infants who are AGA. The incidence of intrauterine fetal death is greatest among the most severely undergrown infants. Both antepartum and intrapartum events contribute to fetal death. Lethal congenital malformations and birth asphyxia are the two leading causes of death among neonates who are SGA. Infants with very low birthweight who are SGA (less than 1500 g) are at significant risk of reduced postnatal growth and development in addition to chronic neonatal sequelae such as bronchopulmonary dysplasia or retinopathy of prematurity.

Developmental Outcome

When infants with congenital infections and severe malformations are excluded, there remains a heterogenous group of undergrown neonates. Intellectual and neurologic functions in these remaining infants depend heavily on the presence or absence of adverse perinatal events, in addition to the specific cause of IUGR.[11] Cerebral morbidity will be worsened by hypoxic-ischemic encephalopathy subsequent to birth asphyxia, and by the postnatal problems of hypoxia and hypoglycemia.[88] Therefore, the prognosis must consider all the potentially adverse perinatal circumstances in addition to IUGR.[7,61,126,127] When these perinatal problems are minimal or are avoided, the neonate who is SGA may still demonstrate cerebral developmental problems, especially in the presence of relative head growth retardation.[79,80,87] If term neonates who are AGA are used as a standard, term infants who are SGA demonstrate developmental problems when they are examined at follow-up at ages 2 and 5 years and into adult years. Even when compared with premature neonates, term infants who are SGA continue to have developmental disadvantages. Follow-up of these infants reveals little difference in intelligence quotient or neurologic sequelae; however, their school performance is poor, partly because of behavioral, visuospatial, visuomotor, and learning disorders.[121,136] Preterm infants who are SGA may have an even greater percentage of abnormal neurodevelopmental outcomes than term neonates who are SGA. Those infants who were SGA early, demonstrating decreased growth of the biparietal diameter before 26 weeks' gestation, and those with symmetric growth retardation have diminished developmental quotients in infancy. However, some follow-up observations in both term and preterm neonates who are SGA are favorable: these neonates compare well with their counterparts who are AGA. Cerebral palsy is uncommon after uncomplicated IUGR. Infants who are SGA are a heterogeneous group, and the populations investigated may vary in the severity of neurodevelopmental handicap; similarly, antenatal detection and perinatal management varies among high-risk centers. It therefore appears that these latter favorable reports may

represent the outcome after optimal obstetric management and neonatal care. Adults who were SGA tend to have a normal IQ, but they demonstrate school difficulties, and fewer become professionals. Despite this, they report to be well adjusted and socially satisfied with their lives.[126,127]

Another major determining influence on neonatal neurodevelopmental outcome in infants who are SGA is the family's socioeconomic status. Parent educational background, place of rearing, and environmental conditions all have a strong effect on outcome. Infants who are SGA born to families of higher socioeconomic status demonstrated little developmental difference on follow-up, whereas those born to poorer families had significant developmental handicaps (see also Chapter 39). In addition, neurodevelopmental outcome is favorably influenced by breastfeeding.[87,92]

Growth

Postnatal growth after IUGR depends in part on the cause of the growth retardation, the postnatal nutritional intake, and the social environment.[13,48,49] Although birthweight correlates best to maternal weight, postnatal growth is related to both maternal and paternal growth characteristics. Neonates who are SGA who

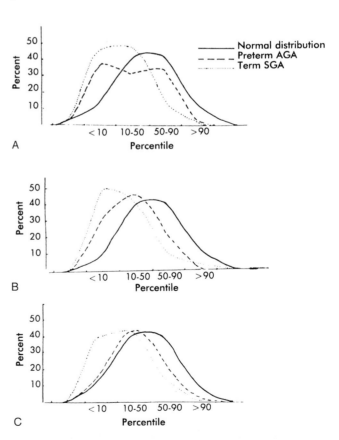

FIGURE 13-27. Eventual physical growth of small-for-gestational-age (SGA) term, appropriate-for-gestational-age (AGA) premature, and AGA term neonates at 4 years of age. **A,** Height. **B,** Weight. **C,** Head circumference. (From Lubchenco L: The High-Risk Infant. Philadelphia, WB Saunders, 1976.)

have primordial growth retardation related to congenital viral, chromosomal, or constitutional syndromes remain small throughout life. Those infants whose intrauterine growth was inhibited late in gestation because of uterine constraint, placental insufficiency, or nutritional deficits will have catch-up growth after birth and approach their inherited growth potential when provided with an optimal environment. Those infants with a low ponderal index or asymmetric growth retardation have an accelerated growth phase once adequate postnatal caloric intake has been established, which suggests release of an in utero constraining factor after birth. Catch-up growth occurs in about 90% of SGA infants; it occurs usually by 2 years of age and is most likely to occur in infants who have normal birth length despite being SGA.[3,21] Despite the catch-up period, some of these infants remain smaller than appropriately grown neonates (Fig. 13-27), especially those who had the onset of growth retardation before 26 weeks. Growth hormone therapy in higher than usual doses for primordial IUGR and for IUGR of unknown cause has produced growth acceleration.[32,33] Some infants with IUGR demonstrate abnormal postnatal growth hormone physiology, suggestive of growth hormone resistance at the receptor or IGF signal transduction pathways.

REFERENCES

1. Abrams B et al: Maternal weight gain in women with good pregnancy outcome. Obstet Gynecol 76:1, 1990.
2. Ahluwalia IB et al: The effect of WIC participation on small-for-gestational-age births: Michigan, 1992. Am J Public Health 88:1374, 1998.
3. Albertsson-Wikland K, Karlberg J: Natural growth in children born SGA with and without catch up growth. Horm Res 59:129, 2003.
4. Antunes JD et al: Childhood hypoglycemia: Differentiating hyperinsulinemic from nonhyperinsulinemic causes. J Pediatr 116:105, 1990.
5. Arends N et al: Polymorphism in the IGF-1 gene: Clinical relevance for short children born small for gestational age (SGA). J Clin Endocrinol Metab 87:2720, 2002.
6. Auwerx J et al: Leptin. Lancet 351:737, 1998.
7. Azzopardi D et al: Phosphorus metabolites and intracellular pH in the brains of normal and small for gestational age infants investigated by magnetic resonance spectroscopy. Pediatr Res 25:440, 1989.
8. Battaglia C et al: Maternal hyperoxygenation in the treatment of intrauterine growth retardation. Am J Obstet Gynecol 167:430, 1992.
9. Bazaes RA et al: Glucose and lipid metabolism in small for gestational age infants at 48 hours of age. Pediatrics 111:804, 2003.
10. Berg CJ et al: Gestational age and intrauterine growth retardation among white and black very low birthweight infants: A population-based cohort study. Paediatr Perinat Epidemiol 8:53, 1994.
11. Besson-Duvanel C et al: Long-term effects of neonatal hypoglycemia on brain growth and psychomotor development in small-for-gestational-age preterm infants. J Pediatr 134:492, 1999.
12. Blagitko N et al: Human GRB10 is imprinted and expressed from the paternal and maternal allele in a highly tissue- and isoform-specific fashion. Hum Molec Genet 9:1587, 2000.
13. Brandt I et al: Catch-up growth of head circumference of very low birth weight, small for gestational age preterm infants and mental development to adulthood. J Pediatr 142:463, 2003.
14. Brenner W et al: A standard of fetal growth for the United States of America. Am J Obstet Gynecol 126:555, 1976.
15. Brooke O et al: Energy retention, energy expenditure, and growth in healthy immature infants. Pediatr Res 13:215, 1979.
16. Brown AK et al: The influence of infant and maternal sickle cell disease on birth outcome and neonatal course. Arch Pediatr Adolesc Med 148:1156, 1994.
17. Burke G et al: Is intrauterine growth retardation with normal umbilical artery blood flow a benign condition? BMJ 300:1044, 1990.
18. Campbell DM et al: Diet in pregnancy and the offspring's blood pressure 40 years later. Br J Obstet Gynaecol 103:273, 1996.
19. Cance-Rouzaud A et al: Growth hormone, insulin-like growth factor-I and insulin-like growth factor binding protein-3 are regulated differently in small-for-gestational-age and appropriate-for-gestational-age neonates. Biol Neonate 73:347, 1998.
20. Challis DE et al: Glucose metabolism is elevated and vascular resistance and maternofetal transfer is normal in perfused placental cotyledons from severely growth-restricted fetuses. Pediatr Res 47:309, 2000.
21. Chatelain P et al: New insights into the postnatal growth of infants born idiopathic small for gestational age. J Pediatr Endocrinol Metab 14:1515, 2001.
22. Chowen JA et al: Decreased expression of placental growth hormone in intrauterine growth retardation. Pediatr Res 39:736, 1996.
23. Christou H et al: Cord blood leptin and insulin-like growth factor levels are independent predictors of fetal growth. J Clin Endocrinol Metab 86:935, 2001.
24. Chunga Vega F et al: Low bone mineral density in small for gestational age infants: Correlation with cord blood zinc concentrations. Arch Dis Child 75:F126, 1996.
25. Clark PM et al: Weight gain in pregnancy, triceps skinfold thickness, and blood pressure in offspring. Obstet Gynecol 91:103, 1998.
26. Clarren S et al: The fetal alcohol syndrome. N Engl J Med 298:1063, 1978.
27. Clausson B et al: Perinatal outcome in SGA births defined by customizes versus population-based birth-weight standards. Br J Obstet Gynaecol 108:830, 2001.
28. Combs CA et al: Sonographic estimation of fetal weight based on a model of fetal volume. Obstet Gynecol 82:365, 1993.
29. Deal C: Polymorphisms and mutations in the GH-IGF axis in very short children born SGA due to IUGR, and the implications for the patients in childhood and adult life. Horm Res 59:130, 2003.
30. DeLia JE: Fetoscopic neodymium:yag laser occlusion of placental vessels in severe twin-twin transfusion syndrome. Obstet Gynecol 75:1046, 1990.
31. Dempsey JC et al: Weight at birth and subsequent risk of preeclampsia as an adult. Am J Obstet Gynecol 189:494, 2003.
32. De Zegher F et al: Early, discontinuous, high dose growth hormone treatment to normalize height and weight of short children born small for gestational age: Results over 6 years. J Clin Endocrinol Metab 84:1558, 1999.
33. De Zegher F: Growth hormone treatment of children born small for gestation age. Horm Res 59:142, 2003.

34. Doctor BA et al: Perinatal correlates and neonatal outcomes of small for gestational age infants born at term gestation. Am J Obstet Gynecol 185:652, 2001.

35. Draper ES et al: Prediction of survival for preterm births by weight and gestational age: Retrospective population-based study. BMJ 319:1093, 1999.

36. Edwards A et al: Sexual origins of placental dysfunction. Lancet 355:203, 2000.

37. Fischer MJ et al: Kidney disease is an independent risk factor for adverse fetal and maternal outcomes in pregnancy. Am J Kidney Dis 43:415, 2004.

38. Fondacci C et al: Alterations of human placental epidermal growth factor receptor in intrauterine growth retardation. J Clin Invest 93:1149, 1994.

39. Frazer T et al: Direct measurement of gluconeogenesis from $[2,3^{13}C_2]$ alanine in the human neonate. Am J Physiol 240:615, 1981.

40. Gabriel R et al: Alteration of epidermal growth factor receptor in placental membranes of smokers: Relationship with intrauterine growth retardation. Am J Obstet Gynecol 170:1238, 1994.

41. Gorenberg DM et al: Fetal pulse oximetry: Correlation between oxygen desaturation, duration, and frequency and neonatal outcomes. Am J Obstet Gynecol 189:136, 2003.

42. Gosden R et al: Rare congenital disorders, imprinted genes, and assisted reproductive technology. Lancet 361:1975, 2003.

43. Gstaiger M et al: Control of nutrient-sensitive transcription programs by the unconventional prefoldin URI. Science 302:1208, 2003.

44. Hanke W et al: Heavy physical work during pregnancy: A risk factor for small-gestational-age babies in Poland. Am J Ind Med 36:200, 1999.

45. Harrington TAM et al: Distribution of adipose tissue in the newborn. Pediatr Res 55:437, 2004.

46. Hattersley AT et al: The fetal insulin hypothesis: An alternative explanation of the association of low birth-weight with diabetes and vascular disease. Lancet 353:1789, 1999.

47. Hattersley AT et al: Mutations in the glucokinase gene of the fetus result in reduced birth weight. Nat Genet 19:268, 1998.

48. Hediger ML et al: Growth and fatness at three to six years of age of children born small- or large-for-gestational age. Pediatrics 104:E33, 1999.

49. Hediger ML et al: Growth of infants and young children born small or large for gestational age. Arch Pediatr Adolesc Med 152:1225, 1998.

50. Hellström A et al: Abnormal retinal vascular morphology in young adults following intrauterine growth restriction. Pediatrics 113:e77, 2004.

51. Hemberger M, Cross JC: Genes governing placental development. Trends Endocrinol Metab 12:162:2001.

52. Hersh J et al: Toluene embryopathy. J Pediatr 106:922, 1985.

53. Hershkovitz R et al: Comparison study between induced and spontaneous term and preterm births of small-for-gestational age neonates. Eur J Obstet Gynecol Rep Biol 97:141, 2001.

54. Hickey CA et al: Prenatal weight gain, term birth weight, and fetal growth retardation among high-risk multiparous black and white women. Obstet Gynecol 81:529, 1993.

55. Hoff C et al: Maternal-fetal ABO/Rh antigenic relationships and human fetal development. Am J Obstet Gynecol 154:126, 1986.

56. Holmes RP et al: Maternal insulin-like growth factor binding protein-1, body mass index, and fetal growth. Arch Dis Child Fetal Neonatal Ed 82:F113, 2000.

57. Hone J et al: Homozygosity for a new mutation ($Ile^{119} \rightarrow$ Met) in the insulin receptor gene in five sibs with familial insulin resistance. J Med Genet 31:715, 1994.

58. Hooper PM: A model for fetal growth and diagnosis of intrauterine growth restriction. Statist Med 21:95, 2002.

59. Hooper SB et al: Catecholamines stimulate the synthesis and release of insulin-like growth factor binding protein-1 (IGFBP-1) by fetal sheep liver in vivo. Endocrinology 134:1104, 1994.

60. Horike S et al: Targeted disruption of the human LIT1 locus defines a putative imprinting control element playing an essential role in Beckwith-Wiedemann syndrome. Hum Molec Genet 9:2075, 2000.

61. Hutton JL et al: Differential effects of preterm birth and small gestational age on cognitive and motor development. Arch Dis Child 76:F75, 1997.

62. Ishizuka T et al: Effects of overexpression of human GLUT4 gene on maternal diabetes and fetal growth in spontaneous gestational diabetic C57BLKS/J LEPR[SUP DB/+] mice. Diabetes 48:1061, 1999.

63. Iwamoto HS et al: Effects of acute hypoxemia on insulin-like growth factors and their binding proteins in fetal sheep. Am J Physiol 263:E1151, 1992.

64. Iwata M et al: Prenatal detection of ischemic changes in the placenta of the growth-retarded fetus by Doppler flow velocimetry of the maternal uterine artery. Obstet Gynecol 82:494, 1993.

65. Jackson JA et al: Early physiological development of infants with intrauterine growth retardation. Arch Dis Child Fetal Neonatal Ed 89:F46, 2004.

66. Jaquet D et al: Combined effects of genetic and environmental factors on insulin resistance associated with reduced fetal growth. Diabetes 51:3473, 2002.

67. Johnston LB et al: Association between insulin-like growth factor I (IGF-1) polymorphisms, circulating IGF-1, and pre- and postnatal growth in two European small for gestational age populations. J Clin Endocrinol Metab 88:4805, 2003.

68. Jones JN et al: Altered cord serum lipid levels associated with small for gestational age infants. Obstet Gynecol 93:527, 1999.

69. Karsdorp VHM et al: Clinical significance of absent or reversed end-diastolic velocity waveforms in umbilical artery. Lancet 344:1664, 1994.

70. King A et al: Unexplained fetal growth retardation: What is the cause? Arch Dis Child 70:F225, 1994.

71. Kinnala A et al: Differences in respiratory metabolism during treatment of hypoglycemia in infants of diabetic mothers and small-for-gestational-age infants. Am J Perinatol 15:363, 1998.

72. Klebanoff MA et al: Second-generation consequences of small-for-dates birth. Pediatrics 84:343, 1989.

73. Kuzma JW, Sokol RJ: Maternal drinking behavior and decreased intrauterine growth. Alcohol Clin Exp Res 6:396, 1982.

74. Lackman F et al. The risks of spontaneous preterm delivery and perinatal mortality in relation to size at birth according to fetal versus neonatal growth standards. Am J Obstet Gynecol 184:946, 2001.

75. LeDune M: Response to glucagon in small for dates hypoglycemic and nonhypoglycemic newborn infants. Arch Dis Child 47:754, 1972.

76. Lee M et al: Fetal microcirculation of abnormal human placenta: Scanning electron microscopy of placental

vascular casts from small for gestational age fetus. Am J Obstet Gynecol 154:1133, 1986.

77. Lieberman E et al: Low birthweight at term and the timing of fetal exposure to maternal smoking. Am J Public Health 84:1127, 1994.

77a. Lubchenco LO, Hansman C, Dressler M, Boyd E: Intrauterine growth as estimated from liveborn birth-weight data at 24 to 42 weeks of gestation. Pediatrics 32:793, 1963.

78. Lumey LH: Decreased birthweights in infants after maternal in utero exposure to the Dutch famine of 1944-1945. Paediatr Perinat Epidemiol 6:240, 1992.

79. Lundgren EM et al: Birth characteristics and different dimensions of intellectual performance in young males: A nationwide population-based study. Acta Paediatr 92:1138, 2003.

80. Lundgren EM et al: Prediction of adult height and risk of overweight in females born small-for-gestational-age. Paediat Perintal Epidemiol 17:156, 2003.

81. Marconi AM et al: Steady state maternal-fetal leucine enrichments in normal and intrauterine growth-restricted pregnancies. Pediatr Res 46:114, 1999.

82. Maršál K: Intrauterine growth restriction. Curr Opin Obstet Gynecol 14:127, 2002.

83. Martin H et al: Impaired acetylcholine-induced vascular relaxation in low birth weight infants: implications for adult hypertension? Pediatr Res 47:457, 2000.

84. Martin H et al: Impaired endothelial function and increased carotid stiffness in 9-year-old children with low birthweight. Circulation 102:2739, 2000.

85. Mastrogiannis DS et al: Perinatal outcome after recent cocaine usage. Obstet Gynecol 76:8, 1990.

86. Masuzaki H et al: Nonadipose tissue production of leptin: Leptin as a novel placental-derived hormone in humans. Nat Med 3:1029, 1997.

87. McCowan LME et al: Perinatal predictors of neurodevelopmental outcome in small-for-gestational-age children at 18 months of age. Am J Obstet Gynecol 186:1069, 2002.

88. McDonnell M et al: Neonatal outcome after pregnancy complicated by abnormal velocity waveforms in the umbilical artery. Arch Dis Child 70:F84, 1994.

89. McIntire DD et al: Birth weight in relation to morbidity and mortality among newborn infants. N Engl J Med 340:1234, 1999.

90. Meberg A: Hematologic syndrome of growth-retarded infants. Am J Dis Child 143:1260, 1989.

91. Milley J et al: Metabolic requirements for fetal growth. Clin Perinatol 6:365, 1979.

92. Morley R et al: Neurodevelopment in children born small for gestational age: A randomized trial of nutrient-enriched versus standard formula and comparison with a reference breastfed group. Pediatrics 113:515, 2004.

93. Mortola JP et al: Birth weight and altitude: A study in Peruvian communities. J Pediatr 136:324, 2000.

94. Murphy VE et al: Maternal asthma is associated with reduced female fetal growth. Am J Respir Crit Care Med 168:1317, 2003.

95. Noordam MJ et al: Doppler colour flow imaging of fetal intracerebral arteries and umbilical artery in the small for gestational age fetus. Br J Obstet Gynaecol 101:504, 1994.

96. Ogawa O et al: Relaxation of insulin-like growth factor II gene imprinting implicated in Wilms' tumour. Nature 362:749, 1993.

97. Okano M et al: DNA methyltransferases Dnmt3a and Dnmt3b are essential for de novo methylation and mammalian development. Cell 99:247, 1999.

98. Ott WJ: Intrauterine growth retardation and preterm delivery. Am J Obstet Gynecol 168:1710, 1993.

99. Ounsted M et al: Maternal regulation of intrauterine growth. Nature 220:995, 1966.

100. Papiernik E: Fetal growth retardation: A limit for the further reduction of preterm births. Matern Child Health J 3:63, 1999.

101. Peoples R: Hemizygosity at the insulin-like growth factor I receptor (IGFIR) locus and growth failure in the ring chromosome 15 syndrome. Cytogenet Cell Genet 70:228, 1995.

102. Polychronakos C, Kukuvitis A: Parental genomic imprinting in endocrinopathies. Eur J Endocrinol 147:561, 2002.

103. Prentice A et al: Prenatal dietary supplementation of African women and birthweight. Lancet 1:489, 1983.

104. Reece EA et al: The relation between human fetal growth and fetal blood levels of insulin-like growth factors I and II: Their binding proteins and receptors. Obstet Gynecol 84:88, 1994.

105. Reid GJ et al: Placental expression of insulin-like growth factor receptor-1 and insulin receptor in the growth-restricted fetal rat. J Soc Gynecol Invest 9:210, 2002.

106. Robinson J et al: Placental control of fetal growth. Reprod Fertil Dev 7:333, 1995.

107. Robson SC et al: Ultrasonic estimation of fetal weight: Use of targeted formulas in small for gestational age fetuses. Obstet Gynecol 82:359, 1993.

108. Rosenfeld RG: Insulin-like growth factors and the basis of growth. N Engl J Med 349:2184, 2003.

109. Rosenfeld RG et al: Growth hormone (GH) insensitivity due to primary GH receptor deficiency. Endocr Rev 15:369, 1994.

110. Sabel K et al: Interrelation between fatty acid oxidation and control of gluconeogenic substrates in small for gestational age (SGA) infants with hypoglycemia and with normoglycemia. Acta Paediatr Scand 71:53, 1982.

111. Sahlin L et al: Decreased expression of thioredoxin and glutaredoxin in placentae from pregnancies with pre-eclampsia and intrauterine growth restriction. Placenta 21:603, 2000.

112. Salas SP et al: Maternal plasma volume expansion and hormonal changes in women with idiopathic fetal growth retardation. Obstet Gynecol 81:1029, 1993.

113. Schieve LA et al: Low and very low birth weight in infants conceived with use of assisted reproductive technology. N Engl J Med 346:731, 2002.

114. Seidler A et al: Maternal occupational exposure to chemical substances and the risk of infants small-for-gestational-age. Am J Ind Med 36:213, 1999.

115. Shams M et al: 11β-hydroxysteroid dehydrogenase type 2 in human pregnancy and reduced expression in intrauterine growth restriction. Hum Reprod 13:799, 1998.

116. Sibai B et al: Pregnancy outcome of intensive therapy in severe hypertension in first trimester. Obstet Gynecol 67:517, 1986.

117. Siristatidis C et al: Intrapartum surveillance of IUGR fetuses with cardiotocography and fetal pulse oximetry. Biol Neonat 83:162, 2003.

118. Smith GCS et al: First-trimester growth and the risk of low birth weight. N Engl J Med 339:1817, 1998.

119. Snijders RJM et al: Fetal growth retardation: Associated malformations and chromosomal abnormalities. Am J Obstet Gynecol 168:547, 1993.

120. Snijders RJM et al: Fetal plasma erythropoietin concentration in severe growth retardation. Am J Obstet Gynecol 168:615, 1993.

121. Sommerfelt K et al. Neuropsychologic and motor function in small-for-gestation preschoolers. Pediatr Neurol 26:186, 2002.

122. Soriano-Guillén L et al: Ghrelin levels from fetal life through early adulthood: Relationship with endocrine and metabolic and anthropometric measures. J Pediatr 144:30, 2004.

123. Soto N et al: Insulin sensitivity and secretion are related to catch-up growth in small-for-gestational age infants at age 1 year: Results from a prospective cohort. J Clin Endocrinol Metab 88:3645, 2003.

124. Spiro RP et al: Intrauterine growth retardation associated with maternal uniparental disomy for chromosome 6 unmasked by congenital adrenal hyperplasia. Pediatr Res 46:510, 1999.

125. Stein Z et al: Prenatal nutrition and birth weight: Experiments and quasi-experiments in the past decade. J Reprod Med 21:287, 1978.

126. Strauss RS: Adult functional outcome of those born small for gestational age. JAMA 283:625, 2000.

127. Strauss RS et al: Growth and development of term children born with low birth weight: Effects of genetic and environmental factors. J Pediatr 133:67, 1998.

128. Strong TH et al: Prophylactic intrapartum amnioinfusion: A randomized clinical trial. Am J Obstet Gynecol 162:1370, 1990.

129. Tafari N et al: Effects of maternal undernutrition and heavy physical work during pregnancy on birth weight. Br J Obstet Gynaecol 87:222, 1980.

130. Tamemoto H et al: Insulin resistance and growth retardation in mice lacking insulin receptor substrate-1. Nature 373:182, 1994.

131. Temple IK, Shield JPH: Transient neonatal diabetes, a disorder of imprinting. J Med Genet 39:872, 2002.

132. Uauy R et al: Long chain polyunsaturated fatty acid formation in neonates: Effect of gestational age in intrauterine growth. Pediatr Res 47:127, 2000.

133. Valcamonico A et al: Absent end-diastolic velocity in umbilical artery: Risk of neonatal morbidity and brain damage. Am J Obstet Gynecol 170:796, 1994.

134. Van Splunder P et al: Fetal atrioventricular, venous, and arterial flow velocity waveforms in the small for gestational age fetus. Pediatr Res 42:765, 1997.

135. Verhaehge J et al: IGF-I, IGF-II, IGF binding protein-1, and C-peptide in second trimester amniotic fluid are dependent on gestational age but do not predict weight as birth. Pediatr Res 46:101, 1999.

136. Villar J et al: Heterogeneous growth and mental development of intrauterine growth-retarded infants during the first 3 years of life. Pediatrics 74:783, 1984.

137. Von Dadelszen P et al: Fall in mean arterial pressure and fetal growth restriction in pregnancy hypertension: A meta-analysis. Lancet 355:87, 2000.

138. Wang X et al: Maternal cigarette smoking, metabolic gene polymorphism, and infant birth weight. JAMA 287:195, 2002.

139. Waterland RA et al: Potential mechanisms of metabolic imprinting that lead to chronic disease. Am J Clin Nutr 69:179, 1999.

140. Weksberg R et al: Beckwith-Wiedemann syndrome demonstrates a role of epigenetic control of normal development. Hum Molec genet 12:R61, 2003.

141. Wilcox A et al: Why small black infants have a lower mortality rate than small white infants: The case for population-specific standards for birth weight. J Pediatr 116:7, 1990.

141a. Williams RL: Intrauterine growth curves: Intra- and international comparisons with different ethnic groups in California. Prevent Med 4:163, 1975.

142. Woods KA et al: Intrauterine growth retardation and postnatal growth failure associated with deletion of the insulin-like growth factor I gene. N Engl J Med 335:1363, 1996.

143. Young LE et al: Epigenetic change in IGF2R is associated with fetal overgrowth after sheep embryo culture. Nat Genet 27:153, 2001.

144. Zaw W et al: The risks of adverse neonatal outcome among preterm small for gestational age infants according to neonatal versus fetal growth standards. Pediatrics 111:1273, 2003.

145. Ziegler E et al: Body composition of the reference fetus. Growth 40:329, 1976.

CHAPTER 14

Hypertensive Disorders of Pregnancy

Dinesh M. Shah

Hypertensive disorders of pregnancy are one of the most serious complications in pregnancy because of their potential to cause serious maternal and perinatal morbidity and mortality. Although a substantial number of hypertensive patients have relatively good outcome, difficulty in differentiating among various hypertensive conditions, inability to predict which patients are at highest risk, and variability in the progression of pre-eclampsia make these disorders the greatest challenge of clinical medicine in obstetrics.

CLASSIFICATION

Various systems have been used to classify hypertensive disorders of pregnancy. Some terms, such as *pregnancy-induced hypertension,* have misleading connotations about the underlying mechanism. Misleading terms reflect the lack of clear understanding about the etiologic factors and lack of a gold standard diagnostic test. The current classification was developed by the National Institutes of Health working group on hypertension in pregnancy.[49] This classification proposes that hypertensive disorders of pregnancy be divided into four categories: preeclampsia-eclampsia, gestational hypertension, chronic hypertension, and preeclampsia superimposed on chronic hypertension.

Preeclampsia-Eclampsia

Preeclampsia is new-onset hypertension with protein-uria with or without edema. Edema alone with hypertension is not reliable for diagnosis of preeclampsia because edema occurs frequently, even in normal pregnancy, and it is difficult to distinguish physiologic collection of fluid from pathologic edema. However, edema that occurs in nondependent sites, rapidly increasing edema (as evidenced by rapid weight gain of at least 2.25 kg or 5 lb per week), or persisting facial edema after the patient has been upright for several hours should be suspected as pathologic edema.

Hypertension is defined as blood pressure greater than 140/90 mm Hg or mean arterial pressure (MAP) greater than 105 mm Hg. Proteinuria is defined as protein excretion of 30 mg/dL in a random specimen (equal to 1+ on urine strips) or 300 mg in a 24-hour urine specimen.

Eclampsia is the development of convulsions or coma or both in the clinical setting of preeclampsia.

Gestational Hypertension

Gestational hypertension is hypertension occurring after the 20th week of pregnancy or during the first 24 hours postpartum without evidence of proteinuria or other signs of preeclampsia and in the absence of evidence of preexisting hypertension.

Chronic Hypertension

Chronic hypertension is hypertension diagnosed before pregnancy or before the 20th week of pregnancy. Hypertension is defined as blood pressure greater than 140/90 mm Hg. This definition may overlook isolated systolic or diastolic hypertension. Some investigators have therefore suggested use of MAP greater than 105 mm Hg as the alternate diagnostic criterion. MAP is calculated as diastolic pressure plus one-third pulse pressure (pulse pressure is systolic pressure minus diastolic pressure). Hypertension diagnosed any time during pregnancy but persisting beyond the 42nd postpartum day is also classified as chronic hypertension.

Superimposed Preeclampsia

Superimposed preeclampsia is either aggravation of hypertension or onset or increase in degree of proteinuria in a patient with a chronic hypertensive disorder. Aggravation of hypertension is an increase in systolic pressure by 30 mm Hg or diastolic pressure by 15 mm Hg.

Comment on Classification

Increases of 30 mm Hg in systolic and of 15 mm Hg in diastolic blood pressure have been shown to be unreliable criteria for diagnosis of preeclampsia. The majority of patients with an increase of this magnitude do not have a hypertensive disorder.[93]

One of the difficulties of diagnosing hypertension before the 20th week of gestation is that a patient's blood pressure is generally lower in the first half of pregnancy compared with the nonpregnant state. The lowering of blood pressure is a result of the vaso-relaxant effect of gestation, which masks hypertension in some patients before the 20th week of pregnancy. Patients with chronic hypertension have been shown to have a greater decline in their blood pressure than normal patients.[77] Diagnosis of chronic hypertension as persisting after the 42nd postpartum day is useful only for classifying patients retrospectively (e.g., for grouping patients in a study) but is not useful for clinicians in managing the index pregnancy.

PREECLAMPSIA-ECLAMPSIA

Pathophysiology

One of the most fundamental abnormalities recognized in preeclampsia-eclampsia is uteroplacental ischemia.[53] The diagnosis of uteroplacental ischemia is based on histopathologic examination of the placenta, revealing ischemic lesions[5]; study of the uterine vascular bed revealing vascular lesions called acute atherosis[100]; restriction of fetal growth secondary to reduced uteroplacental blood flow[39]; and radionuclide studies of uteroplacental perfusion demonstrating reduced clearance of radionuclide.[44] Therefore, understanding the pathogenic mechanism requires understanding uterine vascular modeling in implantation and development of the placenta and understanding the mechanisms of regulation of blood flow in the maternal uteroplacental vasculature.

UTERINE VASCULAR MODELING

Terminal uterine vessels are known as *spiral arteries.* In the process of gestational development, under the influence of sex steroids, these vessels grow in length and to some degree in diameter.[27] Trophoblastic invasion of these vessels occurs in the process of implantation and development of the placenta. Trophoblastic invasion results in complete replacement of endothelium by a layer of trophoblastic cells. Furthermore, the medial coat of the vessel, which consists of smooth muscle cells and connective tissue, is completely replaced by the invading trophoblasts.[57] At the end of this remodeling, the spiral artery is made of a thin adventitial layer internally lined by trophoblasts; it is considerably dilated in diameter and is known as the uteroplacental vessel.[12]

It has been suggested that trophoblastic invasion occurs in two phases. The first phase extends from the time of implantation until the 10th to 12th week of gestation[57]; invasive growth progresses to two-thirds depth in the decidua. The second phase extends from the 12th week to the 16th to 18th week of gestation. The vessels are remodeled up to the terminal resistance portion of the vessel into the myometrial layer. This results in a marked decrease in the resistance of the blood that flows into the uteroplacental vessels and thence into the intervillous space. Furthermore, as placentation progresses, trophoblastic invasion incorporates greater numbers of vessels, until an average of 100 decidual arteries are tapped for intervillous circulation.[12]

In patients who eventually develop preeclampsia, the invasion depth in the second-phase trophoblastic invasion might be deficient.[56] The insufficient depth allows greater numbers of decidual spiral arteries to retain the resistance portion of the vessel, which prevents adequate dilation of these vessels. More important, the contractile portion of these vessels remains intact. This has profound implications for the effect of vasomotor regulators of circulation.

VASOMOTOR REGULATION OF UTEROPLACENTAL CIRCULATION

Regulation of Uterine Blood Flow

It is now well recognized that many organs have mechanisms for regional regulation of blood flow. The uterus is similar to the kidney in its embryologic origin, anatomic vascular arrangement, and mechanisms for regulation of blood flow. Like the kidney, uteroplacental circulation produces various vasodilators and vasoconstrictors including eicosanoids,[92] endothelin,[34] nitric oxide,[42] renin,[45,73,89] and angiotensinogen.[46,73]

Various aberrations occur in these vasomotor regulators in preeclampsia. Prostaglandin production has been shown to be decreased in preeclampsia; however, such deficiency accounts for only a small degree of change in blood pressure (3 to 5 mm Hg).[22] Thromboxane is considered a counterregulatory vasoconstrictor eicosanoid to prostacyclin, and its production has been shown to be increased.[21] Viewing these two facts together, the balance of eicosanoids could be disturbed in preeclampsia.[22,96] Some investigators have suggested that endothelin levels may be increased in preeclampsia.[91] Others have shown that it is not.[72]

In experimental gravid animal models, pharmacologic interventions to decrease nitric oxide production are associated with development of systemic hypertension.[102] However, nitric oxide production by measurements of urinary metabolite has been shown not to be deficient in human preeclampsia.[17]

Role of the Renin-Angiotensin System

The renin-angiotensin system might be involved in the pathogenesis of preeclampsia.[87] The role of angiotensin II in regulating uterine blood flow directly or through alterations of eicosanoids has been suggested in experimental settings. Uterine venous angiotensin II levels are higher in the hypertensive human pregnancy.[59] More important, systemic vasculature becomes more responsive to angiotensin II in preeclampsia.[24]

In view of evidence for uteroplacental ischemia and evidence for local renin and angiotensinogen production in the uterus, it is reasonable to assume that uterine vasculature is also modified to become more sensitive to angiotensin II in human preeclampsia. This vascular maladaptation (e.g., increased responsiveness to angiotensin II and development of hypertension) was first described by Goldblatt and confirmed in renin gene overexpression models with development of hypertension.[47] This research on renin gene overexpression models with hypertension emphasizes the role of renin in the evolution of vascular maladaptation.

The change in the vasculature in renin-mediated hypertension is primarily driven by functional changes in the vasculature. Such functional changes in vasculature in renin-mediated hypertension are biochemically mediated by alterations in the cyclooxygenase pathway of arachidonic acid metabolism and increased thromboxane production,[99] protein kinase C–mediated mechanism and its effect on calcium handling by the vascular smooth muscle,[50] alterations in the Na^+-K^+ pump and cotransport,[51] and change in endothelin expression and release.[8] Initial change in vasculature in renin-mediated vasoconstriction appears to be mediated through increased sympathoadrenal activity. Many of these alterations have been described in human preeclampsia,[21,22] including increased sympathoadrenal activity.[70]

Takimoto and colleagues[90] reported the development of preeclampsia-eclampsia syndrome by crossbreeding transgenic mice, with the introduction of human renin (*REN*) and human angiotensinogen (*ANG*) genes into the mouse genome. Specifically, when male mice carrying human *REN* were mated with female mice carrying human *ANG*, preeclampsia syndrome developed, and REN overexpression was demonstrated on the fetal side of the placenta. One unique aspect of the mouse model of preeclampsia is that fetal renin from the placenta appeared to transfer to the maternal circulation much more readily than is reported in humans.[37]

In human preeclampsia, renin gene expression is increased in the decidua vera on the maternal side.[75] Circulating levels of renin have been shown to peak earlier in women who develop superimposed preeclampsia, as compared with women with chronic hypertension who do not.[2] Increased renin production from the uterus has been shown to occur in response to decreased blood flow to the uterus in experimental settings.[101] Collectively, these data suggest a role of increased renin production in the uteroplacental interphase in the pathogenic mechanism of preeclampsia.

Increased heterodimerization of angiotensin AT_1 and bradykinin B_2 receptors has been described in preeclampsia.[1] Collectively, data from these investigators support the concept that AT_1-B_2 heterodimerization mediates at least part of the increased responsiveness to angiotensin II in preeclampsia, bypassing the angiotensin II refractoriness by using the B_2 intracellular domain for the signal transduction.[1] AT_1 homodimers' susceptibility to inactivation by peroxide treatment suggests that oxidative stress of normal pregnancy confers some of the angiotensin II refractoriness, and AT_1-B_2 heterodimers' resistance to peroxide inactivation may contribute to enhanced angiotensin II responsiveness in preeclampsia.[1] The mechanism by which the AT_1-B_2 heterodimerization is induced is not yet defined.

Patients with preeclampsia develop autoantibodies against the second loop of the AT_1 receptor (AT_1-AA),[95] which might be another mechanism involved in AT_1

receptor and adrenoreceptor signaling. How an antibody against the AT_1 receptor could cause signal transduction to occur through the α_1 adrenoreceptor remains unexplained. These antibodies enhance the tissue factor (TF) expression in vitro with increased immunoreactivity for tissue factor in preeclamptic placentas.[11] These data on AT_1-AA correlate with the findings of anti-ssDNA and anti-dsDNA autoantibodies in preeclampsia,[103] suggesting an abnormal or unrestrained B-cell activation in preeclampsia, or perhaps aberrantly increased antigen presentation, or both. Collectively, these data provide evidence that in preeclampsia an autoantibody against AT_1 receptor may play a role in mediating angiotensin II responsiveness through AT_1 receptor and α_1 adrenoreceptor.

Angiotensinogen mutation with increased angiotensin II production and susceptibility to development of preeclampsia has been shown in some populations but not in others.[97] Because other biochemical aberrations that mediate vascular maladaptation are renin mediated, renin from uteroplacental interphase might have a role in initiating the pathogenesis of preeclampsia (Fig. 14-1).

In addition to development of systemic hypertension, alterations in regional organ circulation occur in sites that are normally renin-angiotensin dependent. This reduction in local blood flow could explain the spectrum of clinical manifestations of preeclampsia.

Vasomotor Implications of Vascular Modeling

The intactness of the resistance portion of the uteroplacental vessels with preserved ability for vasoconstriction should have profound implications for uteroplacental ischemia. These vessels should also become increasingly responsive to angiotensin II that is produced locally. Thus, the local renin-angiotensin system could initiate vasoconstriction-mediated ischemia and cellular injury in the uteroplacental vascular bed.

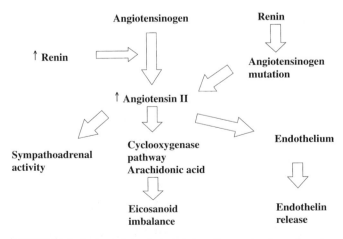

FIGURE 14-1. Renin-angiotensin system in pathogenesis of preeclampsia.

PATHOPHYSIOLOGIC BASIS OF CLINICAL MANIFESTATIONS

The renin-angiotensin system is involved in physiologic regulation of blood flow in various organs. These sites include the heart and systemic vasculature and the uterus, kidney, liver, and brain (Table 14-1). These are, therefore, also the sites for major clinical manifestations of preeclampsia-eclampsia, which emphasizes the role of *RAS* in the pathogenesis of this disorder. Clinical manifestations are described here according to the systemic or regional circulations involved. The primary mechanism at all sites is increased responsiveness to angiotensin II, leading to increased vascular resistance initially and vasoconstriction later with attendant hypoxemia and cell damage. Furthermore, when vasoconstriction and hypoxemia occur, endothelial dysfunction sets in, and free radical formation and lipid peroxidation may further accelerate the process.[68] Endothelial dysfunction can occur earlier in persons susceptible to such endothelial damage (e.g., thrombophilic conditions).[35] Other studies suggest that such persons might not be at an increased risk.[52]

Cardiovascular Manifestations

Increased sympathoadrenal activity may mediate increases in cardiac output. Increase in cardiac work demanded by increased cardiac output is generally well tolerated by young patients, but it may occasionally precipitate left ventricular failure. Decreased renal perfusion, high hydrostatic pressure due to the cardiovascular changes, and decrease in oncotic pressure due to proteinuria compounded by fluid overload may result in development of pulmonary edema.

Systemic vasculature is most frequently and fairly consistently involved with vasoconstriction, the primary manifestation being development of hypertension. Usually, both systolic and diastolic blood pressures are elevated, and hypertension is proportional to renal manifestations, especially proteinuria, at least in uncomplicated cases. Hypertension to some degree depends on increased sympathoadrenal activity, which explains the fluctuations in blood pressure and accelerations related to anxiety.

High cardiac output in the face of markedly increased peripheral vascular resistance results in traumatic intravascular hemolysis. This can cause a decreased haptoglobin level, increased free hemoglobin level, increased bilirubin levels, burr cells and schistocytes in the peripheral blood, and an increased free serum iron level.

Uterine Vasculature

Initially, high cardiac output and increased vascular resistance without change in vessel diameter may result in increased uteroplacental perfusion. Later, with a marked increase in local vasoconstriction, regional blood flow would decrease.

Uteroplacental ischemia and placental infarcts are well-recognized pathologic findings of preeclampsia-eclampsia syndrome.[53] Decreased uteroplacental blood

TABLE 14-1. Findings and Clinical Manifestations of Preeclampsia

VASCULATURE OR SYSTEM	FINDINGS	CLINICAL MANIFESTATIONS
Cardiovascular	Increased cardiac output and systemic vasoconstriction	Systemic hypertension
	Increased hydrostatic pressure	Generalized edema
	High cardiac output and hypertension	Intravascular hemolysis
Uteroplacental	Uteroplacental insufficiency	Fetal somatic growth deficiency; fetal hypoxemia and distress
	Decidual ischemia	Abruptio placentae; placental infarcts
	Decidual thrombosis	Thrombocytopenia
Renal	Decreased renal blood flow and glomerular filtration rate; endothelial damage	Proteinuria; elevated creatinine and decreased creatinine clearance; oliguria
	High AII responsiveness of tubular vasculature	Elevated uric acid
	All of the above	Renal tubular necrosis and renal failure
Cerebrovascular	Cerebral motor ischemia	Generalized grand mal seizures (eclampsia)
	High cerebral perfusion pressure with regional ischemia	Cerebral hemorrhage
	Cerebral edema	Coma
	Regional ischemia	Central blindness; loss of speech
Hepatic	Ischemia; hepatic cellular injury	Elevated liver enzymes
	Mitochondrial injury	Intracellular fatty deposit
Hematologic	Intravascular hemolysis	Schistocyte burr cells; elevated free hemoglobin and iron; decreased haptoglobin levels
	Decidual thrombosis, release of FDP	Thrombocytopenia; antiplatelet antibodies

AII, angiotensin II; FDP, fibrin degradation products.

flow explains increased frequency of somatic growth deficiency in this condition[39] (see also Chapter 13.) Severe reductions in uteroplacental blood flow can cause fetal hypoxemia, which is clinically manifested as fetal distress, hypoxemic multiorgan failure, or death. Uteroplacental interphase hypoxemia can also result in cellular injury to the decidua and injury to the vascular wall itself, with resultant small hemorrhages.

These two processes—hypoxemic cell injury and hemorrhage—sometimes cause small disruptions of placental attachment, which in turn can cause further disruption of the vascular wall as a result of the mechanics of physical separation. Disruption of the vascular wall causes bleeding in the uteroplacental interphase. This explains development of abruptio placentae. Uteroplacental interphase vessels normally have fibrin deposition, a process that can be aggravated by vasoconstriction, and further decreases in the blood flow in these vessels. These reductions in blood flow explain the decidual thrombosis and initiation of thrombocytopenia with local platelet consumption.[64] Dissemination of small fibrin degradation products from these vessels and release of tissue thromboplastin from decidual and trophoblast cell injury can cause disseminated intravascular coagulopathy.[60]

Renal Vasculature

Decreased renal blood flow and high renal perfusion pressure and associated hypoxemia can cause glomerular injury, which in turn causes proteinuria. Glomerular injury may be associated with fibrin deposits in the basal layer and swelling of endothelial cells, resulting in glomerular endotheliosis seen in renal histology.[20] A severe decrease in renal blood flow can cause oliguria, and severe vasoconstriction and hypoxemia with cellular injury might explain renal tubular necrosis seen occasionally in preeclampsia.

Excess circulating placental soluble fms-like tyrosine kinase 1 (sFlt-1), an antagonist of vascular endothelial growth factor (VEGF), has been demonstrated in preeclampsia. By reducing the circulating levels of VEGF, sFlt-1 may contribute to the endothelial dysfunction and impaired renal vasorelaxation.[33,43] This sFlt-1 is a splice variant of VEGF receptor-1 (VEGFR-1); it is produced by the placenta and has been known to enter the maternal circulation. Administration of sFlt-1 to pregnant rats induced hypertension, proteinuria, and glomerular endotheliosis.[43]

Decreased renal tubular blood flow (this vasculature is sensitive to angiotensin II) results in proximal tubular exchange of urate in favor of plasma, which explains frequent association of elevated serum uric acid as a manifestation of preeclampsia. Elevated uric acid thus more accurately reflects angiotensin II responsiveness,[19] thereby explaining the ability of elevated uric acid to predict fetal death better than systemic hypertension does.[66] Decreased glomerular filtration rate, combined with proteinuria-induced decrease in oncotic pressure and high hydrostatic pressure due to increased cardiac output, increased vascular resistance, and sodium and obligatory water retention (aldosterone effect), causes increased dependent and even generalized edema of preeclampsia.

Rare cases of diabetes insipidus of renal origin occur. Measurements of arginine vasopressin levels are generally normal, and placental aminopeptidase is responsible for rapid degradation of arginine vasopressin, resulting in functional deficit.

Hepatic Vascular Changes

Angiotensin II responsiveness of hepatic vasculature is well recognized; it has been used for selective chemotherapy for tumors by angiotensin II infusion-induced vasoconstriction of normal vasculature to protect normal liver tissue. In later phases of disease, hepatic vasoconstriction-mediated hypoxemia and cellular injury are expected to result in release of hepatic enzymes into the circulation, with elevation of liver enzymes in blood.[32] Hepatic vasculature in the subcapsular region appears particularly susceptible to injury, resulting in small hemorrhages. In combination with disseminated intravascular coagulopathy, these hemorrhages can become larger and cause major subcapsular hematomas of the liver. Tissue injury with edema of liver parenchyma and capsule and with stretching of the capsule could explain the hepatic origin of epigastric pain.

HELLP syndrome[98] is a combination of intravascular *h*emolysis, *e*levated *l*iver enzymes, and thrombocytopenia or *l*ow *p*latelets.

Acute fatty liver of pregnancy (AFLP)[31,45] is a condition with a predominantly hepatic manifestation; it is frequently associated with thrombocytopenia and frequently occurs without cardiovascular manifestations of preeclampsia. Cellular hypoxemic injury explains mitochondrial damage, disruption of fatty acid metabolism, and deposition of microvesicular fat in hepatic cells. Susceptible women (those with a carrier state of deficiency of enzymes of fatty acid metabolism and short- and long-chain fatty acid dehydrogenase) might develop AFLP.[29] AFLP occurs, in most cases, independent of preeclampsia. There appears to be some overlap in the pathophysiology of AFLP and preeclampsia with AFLP; hepatic manifestations predominate in persons with such susceptibility. Mitochondrial enzyme defects may thus occur as gene defects or be acquired through cell injury mediated by free radicals.

Central Nervous System

High cardiac output and increased vascular resistance may be associated with greater regional circulation in the brain at higher perfusion pressure.[3] However, some regions of the brain, especially in advanced stages of the disease, might have locally decreased perfusion.

Vasoconstriction and hypoxemia in the microvasculature of the brain result in cellular injury. The injury causes extracellular release of intracellular sodium, which provides the means for generating aberrant electrical impulses. The motor cortex appears to be particularly susceptible to such cellular injury, with resultant convulsions and eclampsia.[61] Vasoconstriction of different regions of the brain produces different manifestations: vasoconstriction in the frontal cortex causes frontal headache, constriction in the occipital cortex causes visual disturbances and central blindness, and constriction in the Broca area causes loss of speech. Blindness may also develop as a result of retinal detachment. Most patients who develop blindness recover completely without medical intervention. In cases of cerebral edema, coma and loss of recent memory of specific convulsive episodes occur.

Cerebrovascular accidents occur as a result of cerebral vasospasm, hypoxemia-induced vascular damage, and systolic hypertension that causes mechanical rupture or disruption of the vessel wall. Current data in developed countries suggest that almost 70% of hypertension-related maternal mortality is due to cerebrovascular accidents.[63]

Hyperreflexia has been recognized as a sign of neurologic irritability in epilepsy and is also seen before eclamptic seizures, but many women have normally active deep tendon reflexes without neurologic irritability.

Clinical Considerations

PREDISPOSING FACTORS
Several factors are associated with, or suggested to be associated with, an increased risk of preeclampsia-eclampsia:

Parity: Both eclampsia and preeclampsia are recognized to occur more frequently in the first pregnancy.[7]

Age: Relationship is described as a J-shaped curve with slightly increased incidence in young primigravidae and a more pronounced increased incidence in older primigravidae.[7]

Race: Incidence of hypertension is not increased in African Americans, contrary to a commonly held belief, although a higher incidence of proteinuria is observed.[80]

Family: In a study of women with eclampsia, their daughters had an incidence of preeclampsia of 26%, their sisters had an incidence of 37%, and their daughters-in-law had an incidence of 8%.

Genetics: Genetic predisposition has been suspected on the basis of increased familial incidence, suggesting a recessive trait possibly of maternal origin.

Diet: Most studies suggest that protein, carbohydrate, or total calorie intake does not influence the incidence of preeclampsia.

Social status: Several reports suggest that lower socioeconomic populations have a higher incidence of preeclampsia and severe preeclampsia.

Twin pregnancies: Twinning is associated with a higher incidence of preeclampsia compared with singleton gestation. Furthermore, severe preeclampsia occurs more frequently in monozygotic twinning, especially in multiparous women.

Diabetes: The incidence of preeclampsia is generally thought to be increased in diabetic pregnancies.[13]

Hydatidiform mole: The higher incidence and early onset of preeclampsia are well recognized in molar gestation[54]; these features are also observed in triploidy gestations, which usually have partial mole.[84]

Hydrops fetalis: The incidence of preeclampsia appears to be increased only in nonimmune hydrops fetalis.[71]

Polyhydramnios: Increased incidence of preeclampsia observed in association with polyhydramnios is related to causes of polyhydramnios, including multiple gestation, diabetes, and hydrops fetalis.[71]

Climate and season: Despite considerable interest and analysis, climatic and seasonal factors do not seem to contribute to the incidence of preeclampsia.

Cigarette smoking: The incidence of preeclampsia is lower in smokers compared with nonsmokers.[85] However, if preeclampsia does occur, fetal risks are greater in smokers compared with nonsmokers.

Although susceptibility to preeclampsia might be increased by maternal thrombophilic mutations, most of the data have been inconclusive and contradictory. However, a recent case control study suggests that prevalence of factor V and factor II mutations is increased in patients with preeclampsia who did not have a previous thromboembolic disorder.[4] Researchers have suggested that the thrombophilic mechanism might interact with other pathogenic factors to determine clinical features of the disease.[4]

DIFFERENTIAL DIAGNOSIS
One of the most fundamental issues faced by clinicians is differentiation of a preexisting hypertensive disorder from the development of preeclampsia. This is because preeclampsia is a progressive disorder of increasing severity, which demands intervention in the form of delivery to halt the progression of the condition. This contrasts with preexisting hypertensive disorders, which exhibit stable manifestations, allowing clinicians to prolong gestation.

This difference in clinical course of action has profound implications for prevention of interventional prematurity. Because preeclampsia is progressive, observation of the patient may reveal progression of the disorder. However, this approach is fraught with the risk of the patient's developing serious complications of preeclampsia. Therefore, such an approach is valid when the severity of suspected preeclampsia is judged to be mild or moderate and gestational age is preterm enough to justify prolongation of gestation and postponement of delivery. This philosophy should maximize perinatal outcome within the bounds of maternal safety.[76]

Preexisting essential hypertension should be suspected in the absence of proteinuria and other laboratory findings, especially if there is a family history of hypertension, and in the presence of maternal obesity. Corroborative information on mild elevations in blood pressure prior to pregnancy may be obtained by careful inquiry into all previous health care encounters by the patient, including visits for contraceptive advice.

Preexisting chronic hypertension secondary to renal disease can be readily diagnosed in patients with type 1 diabetes mellitus or known systemic lupus erythematosus. In other patients, preexisting renal disease should be suspected when proteinuria is in marked disproportion to the degree of hypertension, especially in multiparous patients[44] and whenever a patient presents with clinical manifestations of preeclampsia at preterm gestation. This is supported by renal biopsy data showing that 43% of multiparous women presenting with preeclampsia had evidence of preexisting renal parenchymal or vascular disease.[20] It is further supported by follow-up data on patients presenting with preeclampsia prior to 34 weeks' gestation, of whom almost 70% had laboratory or renal biopsy evidence of preexisting renal disease.[30]

Because most patients with chronic hypertension have essential hypertension, new-onset proteinuria in patients with essential hypertension makes it easier to diagnose superimposed preeclampsia. However, this requires that an estimation of proteinuria be obtained earlier in pregnancy by quantitative laboratory analysis (e.g., from a 24-hour urine collection). In the presence of preexisting proteinuria in chronic hypertensive disorders of renal cause, a physiologic increase in proteinuria early in the third trimester is difficult to distinguish from pathologic proteinuria due to superimposed preeclampsia. Under these circumstances, development of other laboratory abnormalities, e.g., thrombocytopenia, may assist the diagnosis. Generally, proteinuria in the severe range—5 g in 24 hours or greater—should be regarded as superimposed preeclampsia in patients with preexisting proteinuria.

Convulsions or coma not related to a hypertensive disorder can develop from neurologic causes; therefore, hypertension, proteinuria, or edema provides corroborating background. In a small number of patients, the disease process may progress so rapidly that convulsions might occur without proteinuria or before proteinuria develops.

VARIABILITY IN PROGRESSION OF PREECLAMPSIA

A well-recognized characteristic of preeclampsia is the variability in progression of the disease (Fig. 14-2). Therefore, it is necessary to establish an algorithm for each individual case in order to monitor progression.

Figure 14-2 graphically depicts various scenarios of the progression of preeclampsia, indicating that the clinician may encounter these patients at different stages of the disease process. At point A, all patients have similar degrees of severity, such as mild preeclampsia. If delivery is not undertaken because of prematurity, then the monitoring algorithm should initially consider the possibility of rapid progression. If rapid progression is not observed in 24 to 48 hours, then frequency of laboratory testing and monitoring of other parameters can be reduced until some clinical signs are detected

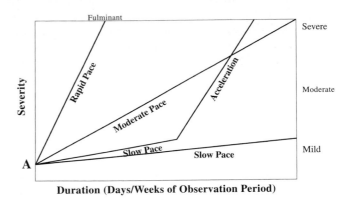

FIGURE 14-2. Four representative samples of rate of progression of the preeclamptic process, starting at point A and ending in mild, moderate, severe, or fulminant disease over a variable course of time.

that suggest acceleration of the disease process. Clinically, this can manifest as acceleration of hypertension or development of increasing facial edema along with glistening sheen, known as *toxemic facies*. When such a change is observed clinically, additional testing of laboratory parameters might be necessary to reevaluate the patient.

SEVERITY OF PREECLAMPSIA

Preeclampsia can be categorized for its severity, arbitrarily defined as mild or severe; in clinical settings it might also be reasonable to consider moderate severity. Severe preeclampsia is defined based on the following criteria[10]:

- Systolic blood pressure greater than 160 mm Hg or diastolic blood pressure greater than 110 mm Hg
- Proteinuria of 5 g or more per 24 hours (3+ or 4+ on urine dip strip examination)
- Oliguria defined as urine output of 500 mL or less in 24 hours
- Visual disturbances, particularly scotomata (black spots or flashes)
- Epigastric pain
- Cerebral symptoms, such as persistent frontal headache
- Pulmonary edema or cyanosis

Mild preeclampsia should include hypertension, systolic blood pressure 140 to 150 mm Hg, diastolic blood pressure 90 to 100 mm Hg, and proteinuria 300 to 1000 mg per 24 hours (1+ on urine dip strip). Moderate preeclampsia can be defined as systolic blood pressure 150 to 160 mm Hg, diastolic blood pressure 100 to 110 mm Hg, and proteinuria more than 1 g but less than 2.5 g per 24 hours.

PRINCIPLES OF MANAGEMENT

The goals of management of women with preeclampsia-eclampsia include prevention of maternal morbidity and mortality and reduction of perinatal morbidity and mortality. Arrest of disease progression and recovery is most effectively achieved by delivery. Many patients require hospitalization for evaluation and monitoring.

Diagnostic parameters are standard hospitalization criteria, and they have contributed to prevention of eclampsia. Clinicians must continue to pay close attention to the blood pressure profile because the mean duration from acceleration of hypertension to the time delivery is indicated is approximately 3 weeks.[76] Such acceleration of hypertension may herald the failure of uteroplacental circulation and activation of vasomotor mechanisms with progressive evolution of the disorder.

Assessment of fetal well being by fetal heart rate monitoring, nonstress test, and ultrasonic biophysical profile is used for antepartum assessment (see also Chapter 9). Continuous electronic fetal heart rate monitoring of baseline rate, beat-to-beat variability, and presence of decelerations is used in the intrapartum period for detection of fetal distress. Fetal growth evaluation by ultrasound is indicated in antepartum inpatient monitoring of preeclampsia.

Indications For Delivery

The following are indications for delivery:

- Preeclampsia of any severity at term
- Moderately severe preeclampsia near term (i.e., after 34 weeks' gestation)
- Eclampsia at any gestational age
- Rapidly progressive preeclampsia with secondary system involvement, such as thrombocytopenia and elevated liver enzymes, at any gestational age
- Clinical unequivocal evidence of fetal compromise, such as persistent nonreactive nonstress test, poor biophysical profile score, or spontaneous repetitive decelerations in fetal heart rate monitoring, at any gestational ages
- Established evidence of fetal pulmonary maturity

Intrapartum Treatment

Antihypertensives

Severe hypertension has serious cerebrovascular consequences in terms of parenchymal ischemia and hemorrhage. Decisive treatment of hypertension is indicated for hypertensive episodes. Such blood pressure criteria are generally a diastolic pressure of greater than 105 mm Hg or systolic pressure 160 mm Hg or greater.

Sublingual nifedipine and an intravenous bolus of hydralazine are the primary antihypertensives used. The results of meta-analysis of randomized, controlled trials are not robust enough to guide clinical practice, but they do not support use of hydralazine as first-line treatment of severe hypertension in pregnancy; labetalol and nifedipine show most promise, but clinical trials are needed.[40] There is no evidence of inadvertent precipitation of angina and myocardial infarction with use of sublingual nifedipine in this generally healthy young population. However, caution is indicated with use of nifedipine for older mothers (age 40 and older) when there is a family history of coronary artery disease at a young age and especially in women who are heavy smokers. Labetalol and clonidine have also been used for the same purpose (Table 14-2).

Corticosteroids

Evidence supports use of glucocorticoids safely in patients with preeclampsia for accelerating fetal pulmonary maturation.[67]

Method of Delivery

Cesarean section is best reserved for specific obstetric clinical indications. Availability of cervical ripening agents containing prostaglandins makes the success of vaginal delivery more feasible. Vaginal delivery following induction of labor remains the mainstay method for patients with preeclampsia and most cases of eclampsia because induction of labor in patients with preeclampsia may be easier than predicted by cervical findings.[104]

TABLE 14-2. Pharmacotherapy for Maternal Hypertensive Emergencies

DRUG	INITIAL DOSE	REPEAT DOSES	COMMENTS AND PRECAUTIONS
Hydralazine (bolus)	5 mg IV bolus; response time 10-15 minutes	5-10 mg every 20-30 minutes	If no response with total dose of 20 mg, consider alternatives.
Hydralazine (infusion)	40 mg in 500 mL D5/LR; begin at 15-25 mL/h	Begin at 1 mL/min, titrate against blood pressure	
Nifedipine	10 mg sublingual, response time 10 minutes with maximum effect at 30 minutes	10 mg in 30 minutes	If no response after 20 mg, consider alternatives; avoid in elderly or with family history of coronary disease, especially if smokers.
Clonidine	0.1 mg PO	0.1 mg in 30 minutes, then 0.1 mg every hour	Patient must be placed on equivalent maintenance dose tid.
Labetalol	20 mg IV bolus, response time 5-10 minutes	20 mg dose or begin infusion of 1-2 mg/min	Check cardiac functional suppression.

D5/LR, 5% dextrose in lactated Ringer solution; IV, intravenous; PO, by mouth; tid, three times a day.

Seizure Prophylaxis and Treatment of Eclampsia

Magnesium sulfate infusion for prevention of seizures is routinely recommended by most authorities in the United States. This is partly because the signs and symptoms of preeclampsia are not reliable predictors of eclampsia[83] and partly because magnesium sulfate infusion is remarkably safe prophylaxis.[61] Several other agents have been used for seizure prophylaxis, including phenytoin. However, an international randomized trial now supports use of magnesium sulfate as the agent of choice over phenytoin for such prophylaxis.[15]

Magnesium sulfate is well recognized as the treatment for preventing further seizures in patients presenting with eclampsia.[61] Magnesium sulfate can be safely used even in patients taking nifedipine (a calcium channel blocker), because there is no evidence of adverse consequences and there is no sound theoretical basis for avoiding such a combination.

The most commonly used regimen of magnesium sulfate is intravenous infusion[105] given as a 2- to 4-g bolus over 5 to 30 minutes followed by continuous infusion starting at 1 g/h and increasing up to 2 g/h to maintain therapeutic levels of 4 to 6 mEq/L. Intramuscular injection of magnesium sulfate has fallen out of favor because of pain associated with the injections and lack of precision in maintaining therapeutic levels. Close supervision of the patient's deep tendon reflexes and urine output measurements is important.

Neonatal serum magnesium concentrations are very similar to those of the mother.[61] Stone and Pritchard[86] reported that Apgar scores do not correlate with magnesium levels. Clinical observations by neonatologists suggest higher frequency of neonatal hypotonia and decreased intestinal motility in infants exposed to magnesium sulfate (see also Chapter 47, Part 2).

PREVENTION OF PREECLAMPSIA

Until all aspects of the pathogenic mechanisms are well defined, prevention of preeclampsia remains an unrealized goal. Studies of aspirin and calcium supplementation have not supported their use in either low-risk or high-risk populations.[38,79]

OUTCOME IN PREECLAMPSIA-ECLAMPSIA

Perinatal Outcome

Perinatal mortality is increased in women with preeclampsia-eclampsia.[48,83] Fortunately, the fetal death rate has decreased in recent times,[18] but perinatal morbidity due to clinically indicated interventional prematurity continues to be a major problem.[76] Major causes of perinatal morbidity and mortality are uteroplacental insufficiency, abruptio placentae,[48] and interventional prematurity.[76] Fetal death rate correlates with clinical parameters that reflect the disease process. The fetal death rate has been shown to increase with increases in both hypertension and degree of proteinuria[23] and with high uric acid levels.[66]

Perinatal morbidity is primarily a result of the need for delivery. Although prematurity remains the single most important threat to the infants of hypertensive mothers, analysis suggests that these infants might have better outcomes than preterm infants delivered spontaneously.[74] A study of neurodevelopmental outcome suggests that maternal hypertension seems to protect against cerebral palsy in preterm infants without increasing the risk of cognitive impairment independent of use of magnesium sulfate.[25] Recent improvements in perinatal mortality appear to be due to reduction in fetal but predominantly neonatal death rates.

Maternal Mortality and Morbidity

Maternal mortality is still a major risk from hypertensive disorders.[36] Marked improvements in maternal morbidity and mortality have occurred in recent times. These improvements are attributable to improvements in medical care (e.g., blood transfusion, prevention of aspiration), in methods of stabilization (e.g., reduced use of sedation) of eclamptic and severe preeclamptic patients, and expedited delivery after stabilization. Maternal mortality rates close to zero have been achieved.[83] In areas of the world where good medical care is readily available, cerebrovascular accidents remain the single most common reason for maternal mortality, accounting for 60% to 70% of all deaths due to hypertensive disorders.[63] Therefore, future decrease in maternal mortality and morbidity rates in hypertensive disorders in developed parts of the world will come from assertive and decisive treatment of severe hypertension.

Remote Prognosis

Long-term follow-up studies of eclampsia by Chesley and coworkers[6] revealed that in women with hypertension in the first pregnancy, 33% had a hypertensive disorder in any subsequent pregnancy, and 5% had a recurrence of eclampsia. Multiparous women with eclampsia had recurrence of hypertension in 50% of subsequent pregnancies.[6] Sibai and associates[81] reported a 45% recurrence of preeclampsia in women with severe preeclampsia, and they also showed that risk of such recurrence is higher in women who develop preeclampsia in the late second or early third trimester.[82] Renal biopsy data from the University of Chicago suggest that approximately 22% of primigravidae with preeclampsia have an underlying renal disorder.[20] Collectively, these data suggest that 22% to 45% of primigravid women who develop preeclampsia, severe preeclampsia, or eclampsia have essential hypertension or renal parenchymal disease, or both, as the primary cause.

It has been suggested that there is an increased risk for developing hypertension later in life in women who develop preeclampsia in their first pregnancy. However, this misconception is due to erroneously including chronic hypertensive disorders in the preeclamptic patients being studied. Long-term follow-up studies of preeclampsia-eclampsia in the first pregnancy by Chesley and coworkers[6] suggest there was no increase in the rate of hypertension. However, multiparous women do exhibit excess rates of hypertension and cardiovascular mortality, which is best explained by underlying hypertensive disorders.

OTHER HYPERTENSIVE DISORDERS

Gestational Hypertension

Gestational hypertension typically occurs in the third trimester. Recurrence of nonproteinuric hypertension of this type in 15% to 25% of the patients with hypertensive disorders suggests an underlying hypertensive disorder, especially if there is a family history of essential hypertension. Under such circumstances, and in the absence of signs and symptoms of preeclampsia, antihypertensive treatment should be considered.[55] Such antihypertensive therapy may reduce the need for hospitalization and makes outpatient monitoring and management easier. Patients managed as outpatients benefit from ambulatory blood pressure monitoring.

Antihypertensive treatment is similar to that for patients with chronic hypertension. Acceleration of hypertension or need for progressively increasing antihypertensive therapy may indicate development of superimposed preeclampsia or misdiagnosis of the condition as transient hypertension. Careful evaluation of signs and symptoms of preeclampsia before beginning antihypertensive therapy can minimize such difficulties. Patients with severe hypertension without evidence of preeclampsia might have severe hypertension due to cocaine abuse.[94] All patients with severe hypertension manifesting in an episodic manner should have a toxicology urine screen test for accurate diagnosis and appropriate treatment of hypertension and substance abuse.

Chronic Hypertension

Chronic hypertension in pregnancy is hypertension (i.e., blood pressure greater than 140/90 mm Hg) diagnosed before the 20th week of gestation or hypertension before pregnancy. Overt hypertension is easily diagnosed, but latent hypertension does not become apparent until later in pregnancy. Latent hypertension is frequently misdiagnosed as transient hypertension.

CLASSIFICATION

Hypertension in pregnancy is classified as primary, secondary, or chronic (Box 14-1). *Primary* (essential or idiopathic) hypertension is the most common type observed; *secondary* hypertension is secondary to a known cause. Causes of secondary hypertension include renal parenchymal disease and renal vascular disease, adrenal diseases, coarctation of the aorta, and thyrotoxicosis. Renal parenchymal disease is the second most common cause of chronic hypertension, other causes being rare.

A patient should be considered to be at risk of *chronic* hypertensive disease of pregnancy in the presence of one or more of the following:

- A diastolic blood pressure in a nonpregnant state or before the 20th week of gestation that consistently exceeds 80 mm Hg
- A history of hypertension

BOX 14-1. Classification of Hypertension in Pregnancy

Primary Hypertension
Essential or idiopathic hypertension, the most common type observed

Secondary Hypertension
Hypertension secondary to a known cause

Renal Disease
- Parenchymal disease (glomerulonephritis, chronic pyelonephritis, interstitial nephritis, polycystic kidney)
- Renal vascular disease

Adrenal Disease
- Cushing syndrome (cortical)
- Hyperaldosteronism (cortical)
- Pheochromocytoma (medullary)

Other
- Coarctation of aorta
- Thyrotoxicosis

Chronic Hypertension
Hypertensive disease with superimposed preeclampsia.
A patient should be considered at risk of chronic hypertensive disease of pregnancy in the presence of one or more of the following:
- Diastolic blood pressure in a nonpregnant state or before the 20th week of gestation that consistently exceeds 80 mm Hg
- History of hypertension
- History of secondary causes of hypertension (e.g., renal disease)
- Family history of hypertension
- Hypertension in a previous pregnancy
- Hypertension with oral contraceptives

- A history of secondary causes of hypertension (e.g., renal disease)
- A family history of hypertension
- Hypertension in a previous pregnancy
- Hypertension with oral contraceptives

EVALUATION OF THE PREGNANT HYPERTENSIVE PATIENT

Evaluation of the pregnant hypertensive patient includes a complete physical examination, including a funduscopic examination for severe hypertension.[14] Heart size must be evaluated if long-standing or significant hypertension is a factor. Auscultation over the renal arteries should be performed to rule out a bruit consistent with renovascular hypertension; however, a bruit is rarely first detected by obstetricians. Simultaneous palpation of the femoral and radial arteries should be performed to rule out coarctation of the aorta; again, this is rarely first detected by obstetricians.

SCREENING LABORATORY DATA

A complete urinalysis for protein and for microscopic sediment should be performed to diagnose renal disease. A 24-hour urinalysis for protein and determination of creatinine clearance should be performed to assess renal function. Serum electrolyte levels to rule out primary hyperaldosteronism should be checked only if the diagnosis is not obviously essential hypertension or renal disease.

If blood pressure elevation is episodic and reaches systolic pressures of 180 mm Hg and diastolic pressures greater than 110 mm Hg, urinary catecholamines should be measured to rule out pheochromocytoma. These patients should also have a toxicology screen.[94]

Ultrasonography of the kidneys may be considered when clinically relevant (e.g., chronic pyelonephritis) to assess renal size and pelvic dilatation if the patient did not have a diagnostic study before pregnancy. Electrocardiography and an echocardiogram can be considered depending on the severity of the hypertension.

PRECONCEPTION COUNSELING

If possible, counseling should be provided before conception to the woman who has chronic hypertension. This is important for establishing adequate control of hypertension and making changes in the antihypertensive regimen. It is important to establish baseline data and to teach self-monitoring of blood pressure. If the patient is taking diuretic medication, she should be advised that she should discontinue use of this medication before conception. An appropriate diet that curtails heavy salt use is recommended. Patients taking angiotensin-converting enzyme inhibitors should be advised to discontinue them because of serious risks of fetal defects and pregnancy loss.

MANAGEMENT DURING PREGNANCY

Bedrest is suggested to increase uterine blood flow and promote nutrition to the fetus.[88] Uterine size and compression of the inferior vena cava and aorta are factors that alter blood pressure recordings in the supine position in the third trimester. The currently recommended position for outpatient blood pressure measurement, as advocated by the American Heart Association, is the sitting position. The brachial artery blood pressure is highest when sitting, lower when lying on the back, and lowest when lying on the side.

Home Blood Pressure Monitoring

All patients with chronic hypertension benefit from self-monitoring of blood pressure. Self-monitoring reduces use of antihypertensives and need for hospitalization.[62] Self-monitored blood pressure readings tend to be lower, and they also reflect patients' blood pressure readings in their environment more accurately. It is advisable to take blood pressure measurements at least three times a day. If the patient works outside the home, blood pressures should be taken during the workweek and weekend. This identifies the effects of the environment on blood pressure.

Newer digital blood pressure monitors are easy to use and moderately inexpensive. For these reasons it is time to abandon the sphygmomanometer and stethoscope for self-monitoring. It is important to check calibration of the patient's machine in the office.

Other Considerations

Therapeutic abortion is generally not necessary or recommended, but the decision regarding whether to continue the pregnancy should be determined on an individual basis. It is essential to establish the estimated date of confinement. History, early pelvic examination, and early ultrasonography aid in this process. Ultrasonography is needed (at 3- to 6-week intervals from 24 to 28, 28 to 32, and 32 to 36 weeks) during pregnancy to detect intrauterine growth restriction, which is most likely to develop after the 30th week of gestation.

Pharmacotherapy

There is no current proof that pharmacotherapy (Table 14-3) alters fetal salvage or prevents pre-eclampsia, but it does control major accelerations of maternal blood pressure during pregnancy. This might reduce the risk of complications of severe hypertension, especially cerebrovascular accidents. Antihypertensive medication should be started when home diastolic blood pressure consistently exceeds 84 mm Hg or office blood pressure readings consistently exceed 90 mm Hg.

The current drug of choice is methyldopa (Aldomet).[65] Since the mid-1980s, beta blockers such as propranolol or atenolol have been used.[69] However, these agents increase the risk of intrauterine growth restriction and might increase fetal morbidity. Alternative drugs include calcium channel blockers,[9] clonidine, and labetalol.[28,77] An analysis of clinical trials of beta-

TABLE 14-3. Common Antihypertensive Agents for Chronic Hypertension in Pregnancy

AGENT	MECHANISM OF ACTION	DOSE
Methyldopa	Centrally acting alpha agonist	250 mg bid to 500 mg qid
Clonidine	Centrally acting alpha agonist	0.1-0.6 mg tid, rarely exceeding 0.4 mg tid
Nifedipine XL	Calcium channel blocker	30 mg XL qd to 60 mg XL bid; maximum dose 120 mg/day
Norvasc	Calcium channel blocker	5-10 mg qd
Labetalol	Beta blocker	Starting dose 100 mg bid; usual dose 200-400 mg bid; maximum dose 1600-2400 mg

bid, twice a day; qd, every day; tid, three times a day; XL, long acting.

blockers indicates that the effect of these agents on perinatal outcome is uncertain; the worrying trend to an increase in infants small for gestational age is partly dependent on one small outlying trial.[41] All drugs may cross the placenta; however, these drugs have not been shown to cause birth defects, except angiotensin converting enzyme inhibitors.[26,58]

One should avoid using two antihypertensives of the same class whenever a patient needs more than one agent to control the hypertension. This is most likely to occur for agents acting on the adrenergic system; for example, avoid combining methyldopa with labetalol. It is better to use a vasodilator such as nifedipine as a second agent. Until better evidence is available, the choice of an antihypertensive should depend on the experience and familiarity with a particular drug and on what is known about adverse maternal and fetal side-effects, with the exception of diazoxide and ketanserine, both of which are probably not good choices.[16]

Complications
Chronic hypertension is associated with a fourfold to eightfold increase in the incidence of abruptio placentae. Planned delivery at or near term may be advisable. The patient should be observed for pre-eclampsia as indicated by an increase in blood pressure and development of proteinuria. The patient should be hospitalized if preeclampsia is suspected.

ANTEPARTUM FETAL EVALUATION
Antepartum fetal evaluation includes serial ultrasound to diagnose intrauterine growth restriction. Beginning at 32 weeks of gestation, nonstress tests should be performed twice a week, and fetal movement activity counts should show at least 4 movements per hour or 3 movements in 30 minutes, indicating fetal health.

LABOR AND DELIVERY
If a decision is made to proceed to delivery and the cervix is not favorable for induction of labor, prosta-glandin may be administered vaginally. Continuous electronic fetal monitoring should be performed during labor. Regional analgesia with epidural administration is ideal, as is also the case for patients with preeclampsia. It is recommended that a pediatrician be available for evaluation of the newborn.

SUMMARY
Women who have chronic hypertension usually do well during pregnancy, although 5% to 10% have major catastrophic events. Patients with chronic hypertension may take oral contraceptives postpartum; a barrier form of contraception is an alternative. For women who have completed their childbearing, a permanent form of contraception may be desirable.

Superimposed Preeclampsia-Eclampsia

Superimposed preeclampsia-eclampsia is a condition that supervenes on a preexisting hypertensive disorder of any cause. Clinically, this is the most severe form of disease; it is associated with the most severe degree of hypertension and proteinuria. A diagnosis of super-imposed preeclampsia generally indicates a need for expedited delivery. Establishment of baseline data on renal and other functions during the prenatal course is helpful for comparison. Usually, liver function abnormality indicates superimposed preeclampsia; however, association of methyldopa with elevation of liver enzymes without development of superimposed preeclampsia is known to occur. When such a diagnosis is entertained, hospitalization is essential for evaluation, close supervision, monitoring, and delivery.

REFERENCES

1. Abdalla S et al: Increased AT_1 receptor heterodimers in preeclampsia mediate enhanced angiotensin II responsiveness. Nat Med 7:1003, 2001.
2. August P et al: Longitudinal study of the renin-angiotensin-aldosterone system in hypertensive pregnant women: Deviations related to the development of superimposed preeclampsia. Am J Obstet Gynecol 163:1612, 1990.
3. Belfort MA et al: Preeclampsia may cause both over-perfusion and underperfusion of the brain: A cerebral perfusion based model. Acta Obstet Gynecol Scand 78:586, 1999.
4. Benedetto C et al: Factor V Leiden and factor II G20210A in preeclampsia and HELLP syndrome. Acta Obstet Gynecol Scand 81:1095, 2002.
5. Brosens I, Renaer M: On the pathogenesis of placental infarcts in pre-eclampsia. J Obstet Gynaecol Br 79:794, 1972.
6. Chesley LC et al: The remote prognosis of eclamptic women. Am J Obstet Gynecol 124:446, 1976.
7. Christianson RE: Studies on blood pressure during pregnancy. Am J Obstet Gynecol 125:509, 1976.
8. Chua BH et al: Regulation of endothelin-1 mRNA by angiotensin II in rat heart endothelial cells. Biochem Biophys Acta 117:201, 1993.
9. Constantine G et al: Nifedipine as a second line antihypertensive drug in pregnancy. Br J Obstet Gynaecol 94:1136, 1987.
10. Cunningham FG, Lindheimer MD: Hypertension in pregnancy. N Engl J Med 326:927, 1992.
11. Dechend R et al: AT_1 receptor agonistic antibodies from preeclamptic patients cause vascular cells to express tissue factor. Circulation 101:2382, 2000.
12. DeWolf FD et al: Ultrastructure of the spiral arteries in the human placental bed at the end of normal pregnancy. Am J Obstet Gynecol 117:833, 1973.
13. Diamond MP et al: Complication of insulin-dependent diabetic pregnancies by preeclampsia and/or chronic hypertension: Analysis of outcome. Am J Perinatol 2:263, 1985.
14. Dimmitt SB et al: Usefulness of ophthalmoscopy in mild to moderate hypertension. Lancet 20:1103, 1989.
15. Duley L et al: Which anticonvulsant for women with eclampsia? Evidence from the collaborative eclampsia trial. Lancet 345:1455, 1995.
16. Duley L, Henderson-Smart DJ: Drugs for treatment of high blood pressure during pregnancy. Cochrane Database Systematic Reviews (4):CD001449, 2002.
17. Egerman RS et al: Neuropeptide Y and nitrite levels in preeclamptic and normotensive gravid women. Am J Obstet Gynecol 181:921, 1999.

18. Ferranzzani S et al: Proteinuria and outcome of 444 pregnancies complicated by hypertension. Am J Obstet Gynecol 162:366, 1990.

19. Ferris TF, Gorden P: Effect of angiotensin and norepinephrine upon urate clearance in man. Am J Med 44:359, 1968.

20. Fisher KA et al: Hypertension in pregnancy: Clinical-pathological correlations and remote prognosis. Medicine 60:267, 1981.

21. Fitzgerald DJ et al: Thromboxane A_2 synthesis in pregnancy-induced hypertension. Lancet 335:751, 1990.

22. Fitzgerald DJ, FitzGerald GA: Eicosanoids in the pathogenesis of preeclampsia. In Laragh JH, Brenner BM (eds): Hypertension: Pathophysiology, Diagnosis and Management, vol. 2. New York, Raven Press, 1990, p 1789.

23. Friedman EA, Neff RK: Pregnancy outcome as related to hypertension, edema and proteinuria. In Lindheimer MD et al (eds): Hypertension in Pregnancy. New York, Wiley, 1976, p 13.

24. Gant NF et al: A study of angiotensin II pressor response throughout primigravid pregnancy. J Clin Invest 51:2682, 1973.

25. Gray PH et al: Maternal hypertension and neuro-developmental outcome in very preterm infants. Arch Dis Child 79:F88, 1998.

26. Hanssens M et al: Fetal and neonatal effects of treatment with angiotensin-converting enzyme inhibitors in pregnancy. Obstet Gynecol 78:128, 1991.

27. Harris JWS, Ramsey EM: The morphology of human uteroplacental vasculature. Contrib Embryol 38:43, 1966.

28. Horvath JS et al: Clonidine hydrochloride: A safe and effective antihypertensive agent in pregnancy. Obstet Gynecol 66:634, 1985.

29. Ibdah JA et al: A fetal fatty-acid oxidation disorder as a cause of liver disease in pregnant women. N Engl J Med 340:1723, 1999.

30. Ihle BU et al: Early onset pre-eclampsia: Recognition of underlying renal disease. BMJ 294:79, 1987.

31. Kaplan MM: Acute fatty liver of pregnancy. N Engl J Med 313:367, 1985.

32. Killam AP et al: Pregnancy-induced hypertension complicated by acute liver disease and disseminated intravascular coagulation: Five case reports. Am J Obstet Gynecol 123:823, 1975.

33. Koga K et al: Elevated serum soluble vascular endothelial growth factor receptor 1 (sVEGFR-1) levels in women with preeclampsia. J Clin Endocrinol Metabol 88:2348, 2003.

34. Kubota T et al: Synthesis and release of endothelin-1 by human decidual cells. J Clin Endocrinol Metab 75:1230, 1992.

35. Kupferminc MJ: Increased frequency of genetic thrombophilia in women with complications of pregnancy. N Engl J Med 340:9, 1999.

36. Lawson HW et al: Maternal mortality related to pre-eclampsia and eclampsia in the United States 1979-1986. MMWR Morbid Mortal Wkly Rep CDC Surveill Summ 40:1, 1991.

37. Lentz T et al: Prorenin secretion from human placenta perfused in vitro. Am J Physiol 260:E876, 1991.

38. Levine RJ et al: Trial of calcium to prevent preeclampsia. N Engl J Med 337:69, 1997.

39. Lin CC, et al: Fetal outcome in hypertensive disorders of pregnancy. Am J Obstet Gynecol 142:255, 1982.

40. Magee LA et al: Hydralazine for treatment of severe hypertension in pregnancy: Meta-analysis. BMJ 327:955, 2003.

41. Magee LA, Duley L: Oral beta-blockers for mild to moderate hypertension during pregnancy. Cochrane Database Systematic Reviews (3):CD002863, 2003.

42. Matsumoto M et al: Endothelium-derived relaxation of the pregnant and nonpregnant canine uterine artery. J Reprod Med 37:529, 1992.

43. Maynard SE et al: Excess placental soluble fms-like tyrosine kinase 1 (sFlt1) may contribute to endothelial dysfunction, hypertension, and proteinuria in preeclampsia. J Clin Invest 111:649, 2003.

44. McClure Browne JC et al: The maternal placental blood flow in normotensive and hypertensive women. J Obstet Gynaecol 60:141, 1953.

45. Moise KJ, Shah DM: Acute fatty liver of pregnancy: Etiology of fetal distress and fetal wastage. Obstet Gynecol 69:482, 1987.

46. Morgan T et al: Human spiral artery renin-angiotensin system. Hypertension 32:683, 1998.

47. Mullins JJ et al: Fulminant hypertension in transgenic rats harbouring the mouse Ren-2 gene. Nature 344:541, 1990.

48. Naeye RL, Friedman EA: Causes of perinatal death associated with gestational hypertension and proteinuria. Am J Obstet Gynecol 133:8, 1979.

49. National High Blood Pressure Education Program Working Group: Report on high blood pressure during pregnancy. Am J Obstet Gynecol 163:1689, 1990.

50. O'Donnell ME: Endothelial cell sodium-potassium-chloride co-transport: Evidence of regulation by Ca^{2+} and protein kinase C. J Biol Chem 266:11559, 1991.

51. Orlov SN et al: Na^+-K^+ pump and Na^+-K^+ co-transport in cultured vascular smooth muscle cells from spontaneously hypertensive and normotensive rats: Baseline activity and regulation. J Hypertens 10:733, 1992.

52. O'Shaughnessy KM et al: Factor V Leiden and thermolabile methylenetetrahydrofolate reductase gene variants in an East Anglian preeclampsia cohort. Hypertension 33:1338, 1999.

53. Page EW: On the pathogenesis of pre-eclampsia and eclampsia [review]. J Obstet Gynaecol Br Commonw 79:883, 1972.

54. Page EW: The relation between hydatid moles, relative ischaemia of the gravid uterus and the placental origin of eclampsia. Am J Obstet Gynecol 37:291, 1939.

55. Pickles CJ et al: The fetal outcome in a randomized double-blind controlled trial of labetalol versus placebo in pregnancy-induced hypertension. Br J Obstet Gynaecol 96:38, 1989.

56. Pijnenborg R et al: Placental bed spiral arteries in the hypertensive disorders of pregnancy. Br J Obstet Gynaecol 98:648, 1991.

57. Pijnenborg R et al: Trophoblastic invasion of human decidua from 8 to 18 weeks of pregnancy. Placenta 1:3, 1980.

58. Piper JM et al: Pregnancy outcome following exposure to angiotensin-converting enzyme inhibitors. Obstet Gynecol 80:429, 1992.

59. Pipkin FB et al: The uteroplacental renin-angiotensin system in normal and hypertensive pregnancy. Contrib Nephrol 25:49, 1981.

60. Pritchard JA et al: Coagulation changes in eclampsia: Their frequency and pathogenesis. Am J Obstet Gynecol 124:855, 1976.

61. Pritchard JA Pritchard SA: Standardized treatment of 154 consecutive cases of eclampsia. Am J Obstet Gynecol 123:543, 1975.

62. Rayburn WF: Self blood pressure monitoring during pregnancy. Am J Obstet Gynecol 148:159, 1984.

63. Redman CWG: The treatment of hypertension in pregnancy. Kidney Int 18:267, 1980.

64. Redman CWG et al: Early platelet consumption in preeclampsia. BMJ 1:467, 1978.

65. Redman CWG et al: Fetal outcome in trial of anti-hypertensive treatment in pregnancy. Lancet 2:753, 1976.

66. Redman CWG et al: Plasma-urate measurements in predicting fetal death in hypertensive pregnancy. Lancet 1:1370, 1976.

67. Ricke PS et al: Use of corticosteroids in pregnancy-induced hypertension. Obstet Gynecol 48:163, 1976.

68. Roberts JM et al: Clinical and biochemical evidence of endothelial cell dysfunction in pregnancy syndrome preeclampsia. Am J Hypertens 4:700, 1991.

69. Rubin PC et al: Placebo-controlled trial of atenolol in treatment of pregnancy-associated hypertension. Lancet 1:431, 1983.

70. Schobel HP et al: Preeclampsia: A state of sympathetic overactivity. N Engl J Med 335:1480, 1996.

71. Scott JS: Pregnancy toxaemia associated with hydrops fetalis, hydatidiform mole and hydramnios. J Obstet Gynaecol 65:689, 1958.

72. Shah DM et al: Circulating endothelin-1 is not increased in severe preeclampsia. J Matern Fetal Med 1:177, 1992.

73. Shah DM et al: Definitive molecular evidence of RAS in human uterine decidual cells. Hypertension 36:159, 2000.

74. Shah DM et al: Neonatal outcome of premature infants of mothers with preeclampsia. J Perinatol 15:264, 1995.

75. Shah DM et al: Reproductive tissue renin gene expression in preeclampsia. Hypertens Pregnancy 19:341, 2000.

76. Shah DM, Reed G: Parameters associated with adverse perinatal outcome in hypertensive pregnancies. J Hum Hypertens 10:511, 1996.

77. Sibai BM et al: A comparison of no medication versus methyldopa or labetalol in chronic hypertension during pregnancy. Am J Obstet Gynecol 162:960, 1990.

78. Sibai BM et al: Pregnancy outcome in 303 cases with severe preeclampsia. Obstet Gynecol 64:319, 1984.

79. Sibai BM et al: Prevention of preeclampsia with low-dose aspirin in healthy, nulliparous pregnant women. N Engl J Med 329:1213, 1993.

80. Sibai BM et al: Risk factors for preeclampsia in healthy nulliparous women: A prospective multicenter study. Am J Obstet Gynecol 172:642, 1995.

81. Sibai BM et al: Severe preeclampsia-eclampsia in young primigravid women: Subsequent pregnancy outcome and remote prognosis. Am J Obstet Gynecol 155:1011, 1986.

82. Sibai BM et al: Severe preeclampsia in the second trimester: Recurrence risk and long-term prognosis. Am J Obstet Gynecol 165:1408, 1991.

83. Sibai BM et al: The incidence of nonpreventable eclampsia. Am J Obstet Gynecol 154:581, 1986.

84. Sorem KA, Shah DM: Advanced triploid pregnancy and preeclampsia. South Med J 88:1144, 1995.

85. Spinillo A et al: Cigarette smoking in pregnancy and risk of pre-eclampsia. J Hum Hypertens 8:771, 1994.

86. Stone SR, Pritchard JA: Effect of maternally administered magnesium sulfate on the neonate. Obstet Gynecol 35:574, 1970.

87. Symonds EM: Aetiology of preeclampsia: A review. J R Soc Med 73:871, 1980.

88. Symonds EM: Bed rest in pregnancy. Br J Obstet Gynaecol 89:593, 1982.

89. Symonds EM: Renin and reproduction. Am J Obstet Gynecol 158:754, 1988.

90. Takimoto E et al: Hypertension induced in pregnant mice by placental renin and maternal angiotensinogen. Science 274:995, 1996.

91. Taylor RN et al: Women with preeclampsia have higher plasma endothelin levels than women with normal pregnancies. J Clin Endocrinol Metab 71:1675, 1990.

92. Terragno NA et al: Prostaglandins and the regulation of uterine blood flow in pregnancy. Nature 249:57, 1974.

93. Villar MA, Sibai BM: Clinical significance of elevated mean arterial blood pressure in second trimester and threshold increase in systolic or diastolic blood pressure during third trimester. Am J Obstet Gynecol 160:419, 1989.

94. Volpe JJ: Effect of cocaine use on the fetus. N Engl J Med 327:399, 1992.

95. Wallukat G et al: Patients with preeclampsia develop agonistic autoantibodies against the angiotensin AT_1 receptor. J Clin Invest 103:945, 1999.

96. Walsh SW: Preeclampsia: An imbalance in placental prostacyclin and thromboxane production. Am J Obstet Gynecol 152:335, 1985.

97. Ward K et al: A molecular variant of angiotensinogen associated with preeclampsia. Nat Genet 4:59, 1993.

98. Weinstein L: Syndrome of haemolysis, elevated liver enzymes, and low platelet count: A severe consequence of hypertension in pregnancy. Am J Obstet Gynecol 142:159, 1982.

99. Wilcox CS et al: Thromboxane mediates renal hemodynamic response in infused angiotensin II. Kidney Int 40:1090, 1991.

100. Wolf FD et al: The ultrastructure of acute atherosis in hypertensive pregnancy. Am J Obstet Gynecol 123:164, 1975.

101. Woods LL: Role of renin-angiotensin system in hypertension during reduced uteroplacental perfusion pressure. Am J Physiol 257:204, 1989.

102. Yallampalli C, Garfield RE: Inhibition of nitric oxide synthesis in rats during pregnancy produces signs similar to those of preeclampsia. Am J Obstet Gynecol 169:1327, 1993.

103. Yamamoto T et al: Anti-ssDNA and -dsDNA antibodies in preeclampsia. Asia Oceania J Obstet Gynaecol 20:93, 1994.

104. Zuspan FP: Factors affecting delivery in preeclampsia: Condition of the cervix and uterine activity. Am J Obstet Gynecol 100:672, 1968.

105. Zuspan FP: Problems encountered in the treatment of pregnancy-induced hypertension: A point of view. Am J Obstet Gynecol 131:591, 1978.

15 Pregnancy Complicated by Diabetes Mellitus

Carol Andrea Lindsay

Diabetes mellitus is a group of metabolic diseases, all having hyperglycemia in common, that result from defects in insulin secretion, insulin action, or both.[30] Diabetes mellitus is classified in one of three ways: type 1 (insulin dependent), type 2 (non–insulin dependent), or gestational. Diabetes mellitus in pregnancy is further subdivided according to the classification of Priscilla White (Table 15-1). She reported that the prognosis for pregnancy is related to control of maternal diabetes, occurrence of congenital fetal defects, degree of maternal vascular disease, gestational age at delivery, duration of diabetes, age of onset of diabetes, and balance of the sex hormones of pregnancy.[94]

Gestational diabetes mellitus is defined as carbohydrate intolerance of variable severity with onset or first recognition during pregnancy.[64] Of the 3% to 5% of pregnancies complicated by diabetes mellitus, 80% to 90% are cases of gestational diabetes.[16,17,30] Risk factors for the development of gestational diabetes mellitus include age older than 25 years; obesity, defined as pregravid body mass index (BMI) greater than 27.3 kg/m²; family history of type 2 diabetes mellitus, particularly maternal; persistent glucosuria; sedentary lifestyle; prior gestational diabetes; hypertension; dyslipidemia and history of prior pregnancies complicated by macrosomia; congenital malformation; or stillbirth.[30,44] Ethnicity also plays a role in the risk of development of diabetes mellitus, with people of color having a higher incidence.[44] However, more than 50% of all patients who exhibit abnormal glucose tolerance lack the risk factors mentioned.[54]

PATHOPHYSIOLOGY

The pathophysiology of diabetes mellitus is complex, with hyperglycemia being a common manifestation. Type 1 diabetes mellitus primarily represents insulin deficiency that results in chronic hyperglycemia and disturbances of protein and lipid metabolism.[36] People with type 1 diabetes require insulin for survival, and in the absence of insulin, they risk developing diabetic ketoacidosis.[15] They are also at increased risk for developing micro- and macrovascular complications.[30]

Type 2 diabetes mellitus results from an imbalance between insulin sensitivity and beta cell function. This type of diabetes mellitus has an insidious onset and generally is seen in older and more obese patients,[15] although there is an alarming increase in obesity and type 2 diabetes in adolescents. In both type 2 diabetes and gestational diabetes there is decreased hepatic and peripheral insulin sensitivity and relatively decreased insulin response for the degree of hyperglycemia.[15] However, because of the decrease in insulin sensitivity, insulin response may actually be greater than in women with normal glucose tolerance.[15] As a consequence, women with type 2 diabetes may have normal or increased insulin levels.[30]

In women with normal glucose tolerance in pregnancy, more endogenous insulin is required to maintain normal glucose tolerance.[63] As a result, plasma insulin levels are greater in these women than in weight-matched nonpregnant women.[63] In lean women, maternal metabolism is adapted to allow for increased maternal fat stores early in pregnancy and increased availability of carbohydrate, lipid, and protein to the

TABLE 15-1. Modified White's Classification of Diabetes Mellitus In Pregnancy*

CLASS	DESCRIPTION
A1	Onset during pregnancy, treated with diet only
A2	Onset during pregnancy, requiring insulin therapy
B	Onset at ≥ 20 years old, <10 years' duration
C	Onset 10-19 years old, 10-19 years' duration
D	Onset <10 years old, ≥ 20 years' duration or background retinopathy
F	Any duration or age of onset with the presence of nephropathy
H	Any duration or age of onset with the presence of atherosclerotic heart disease
R	Any duration or age of onset with the presence of proliferative retinopathy
T	Any duration or age of onset with the presence of a renal transplant

*If a patient falls into two or more classes, she is assigned to the most severe class.
Adapted from White P: Pregnancy complicating diabetes. Am J Med 7:609, 1949, with permission from Excerpta Medica Inc.

fetus in late pregnancy when increased fetal growth occurs.[15]

Gestational diabetes is characterized by a 60% decrease in peripheral insulin sensitivity and the inability of the pancreas to produce adequate insulin in response to a glucose load.[1] Several hormones produced by the placenta have antagonistic effects on insulin, and in the past this was thought to lead to this decrease in insulin sensitivity.[1] These hormones may include human placental lactogen (human chorionic somatomammotropin) and progesterone.[1] However, Kirwan's group has reported that tumor necrosis factor–α (TNFα) produced by fat cells and placenta was the most significant predictor of insulin sensitivity in pregnancy.[46] As a consequence of decreased insulin sensitivity, levels of plasma glucose, free fatty acids, branched chain amino acids, and ketone bodies are elevated.[1]

SIGNS AND SYMPTOMS

Many women with gestational diabetes and type 2 diabetes are asymptomatic; however, any signs and symptoms of hyperglycemia should be evaluated, including fatigue, polyuria, polydipsia, weight loss, polyphagia, and blurred vision.[30] In the first trimester, women with type 1 diabetes may experience periods of hypoglycemia.[54] In the presence of infection, these women are at increased risk for developing ketoacidosis.

DIAGNOSIS

Screening based on risk factors has been advocated by the American Diabetes Association.[30] Screening should be performed between 24 and 28 weeks of gestation. Some advocate earlier screening in women with significant risk factors. Factors that increase a woman's risk for gestational diabetes include age older than 25 years, obesity, having a first-degree relative with diabetes mellitus, being a member of an ethnic group at high risk (Hispanic, American Indian, Asian, African American), history of abnormal glucose metabolism, history of poor obstetric outcome, history of previous gestational diabetes mellitus, and concomitant glucocorticoid therapy.[30,54,62]

Screening is generally performed with a 50-gm, 1-hour oral glucose tolerance test. The cutoff for which further testing is indicated ranges from 130 to 140 mg/dL. The sensitivity at a cutoff of 140 mg/dL is 75%, with 6% to 15% of the tests being abnormal.[1,12,15] Lowering the cutoff to 130 mg/dL enhances sensitivity but impairs specificity.[54] At 130 mg/dL the sensitivity increases to nearly 100%, but 15% to 25% of the population must undergo a diagnostic test as a result of an abnormal value.[12,15]

An abnormal screening test is followed by a 75-g or a 100-g 3-hour oral glucose tolerance test. The criterion for diagnosis of gestational diabetes is at least two abnormal values on the 3-hour glucose tolerance test. This criterion was initially set forth by O'Sullivan and Mahan.[75] Abnormal values were based on the risk that the woman would develop glucose intolerance after delivery and not based on perinatal outcome. Abnormal values were defined as two or more values greater than 2 standard deviations above the mean.[75]

In 1979, the National Diabetes Data Group revised the O'Sullivan criterion, which was based on whole blood, to reflect plasma values.[72] Carpenter and Coustan further refined the National Diabetes Data Group criteria to reflect the glucose oxidase methods by which plasma glucose is currently obtained, rather than the former Smogyi method.[11,72] These criteria are fasting blood glucose of 95 mg/dL or less, 1-hour blood glucose of 180 mg/dL or less, 2-hour blood glucose of 155 mg/dL or less, and 3-hour blood glucose of 140 mg/dL or less, with either a 75-g or a 100-g glucose load. These criteria have been recommended by the American Diabetes Association and the Fourth International Workshop Conference on Gestational Diabetes.[32,62]

Women who have one abnormal value on the oral glucose tolerance test are also at increased risk for fetal macrosomia.[55] Repeat testing at 32 to 34 weeks has been recommended in this group because 33% of these women have a positive test at that time.[73]

Glycosylated hemoglobin, although not useful for diagnosis, is useful for managing patients with type 1 or type 2 diabetes. Higher levels indicate poorer glycemic control. It should be noted that in pregnancy, erythropoiesis is increased, leading to younger red blood cells, which cause the red blood cells of pregnant women to be less glycosylated than those in nonpregnant women.[12]

Women with gestational diabetes should undergo testing for glucose intolerance in the postpartum period because of their increased risk of developing diabetes mellitus.[75] The diabetes that occurs following gestational diabetes is primarily type 2 diabetes, but in 3% to 5% of these patients, type 1 diabetes is diagnosed; this is important because women with type 2 diabetes are at increased risk for the development of hyperlipidemia and increased risk of cardiovascular disease.[62] Fifty to sixty percent of women with prior gestational diabetes develop type 2 diabetes during their lifetime.[51] Risk factors for developing an abnormal glucose tolerance test postpartum after gestational diabetes mellitus include early gestational age at the time of diagnosis (less than 24 weeks), increased fasting glucose, and obesity.

Diabetes mellitus in nonpregnant patients is defined as a glucose level of 126 mg/dL or greater after an 8- to 14-hour fast or as a 2-hour postprandial glucose level of 200 mg/dL or greater after a 75-g oral glucose tolerance test.[32,62] The diagnosis can also be made in the symptomatic patient with a random plasma glucose concentration greater than 200 mg/dL.[30]

Impaired glucose tolerance exists when the fasting plasma glucose level is 110 to 125 mg/dL or when the 2-hour value is 140 to 199 mg/dL. Impaired glucose tolerance is not a clinical diagnosis but rather a risk factor for future development of diabetes and cardiovascular disease.[30,32] If the fasting plasma glucose is less than 110 mg/dL and the 2-hour value is less than

140 mg/dL, glucose tolerance is normal, but frequent testing is recommended.[32]

MANAGEMENT OF DIABETES MELLITUS

In Pregnancy

GLUCOSE CONTROL

Glucose control is the mainstay of the management of diabetes in pregnancy, whether the diabetes is pregestational or gestational. Women can monitor their own blood glucose, with the goal being maintenance of glucose levels between 60 and 120 mg/dL.[54] Recommended regimens for glucose evaluation for women with gestational diabetes mellitus vary widely from weekly office visits to eight daily checks. Euglycemia can be achieved with self-monitoring of blood glucose (SMBG).[42] In general, SMBG is thought to be superior to monitoring that is less frequent.[15,36,62,83] One of the most frequently used protocols involves fasting blood sugar, which is checked before each meal, 2 hours after each meal, and at bedtime.[76] If nocturnal hypoglycemia is suspected, an additional capillary glucose level test at 3:00 AM can be added.[76]

Target levels of glucose in pregnancy are as follows: fasting, before meals and bedtime snack, 60 to 95 mg/dL; 1 hour after meals, 130 to 140 mg/dL; 2 hours after meals, 120 mg/dL or less; and 2:00 AM to 6:00 AM, 60 to 90 mg/dL.[15,38,54,63,76] When the mean plasma glucose values are maintained below 100 mg/dL during pregnancy, perinatal mortality is reduced to that of a control population with normal glucose tolerance.[23,43] Maintaining euglycemia may also improve the rates of several fetal or neonatal complications such as macrosomia, hyperbilirubinemia, hypocalcemia, respiratory distress syndrome, and intrauterine fetal demise (see Chapter 47, Part 1).[37,54] A reduction in maternal complications may also be seen, for example, in the reduced need for cesarean delivery.[83]

In addition to SMBG, daily urine tests for ketones are advocated.[28] Ketonuria may be a result of accelerated fat catabolism.[62] Ketonuria has been associated with lower IQ scores than expected in children of pregnancies complicated by diabetes.[19] Checking the first voided urine sample can determine if the patient has an adequate caloric intake and is taking adequate insulin.[15] Ketonuria can also be a sign that a woman with type 1 diabetes mellitus is developing diabetic ketoacidosis.

Weight Management

The amount of weight gain recommended in pregnancy is based on prepregnancy weight. In obese patients, defined as BMI greater than 29 kg/m^2, a weight gain of approximately 7 kg is recommended during pregnancy[38]; in lean patients, with BMI less than 19.8 kg/m^2, a weight gain of up to 18 kg is recommended.[62] For women with a normal BMI that is between 19.8 and 26 kg/m^2, weight gain ranging from 11 to 16 kg is recommended.[45]

Most women with gestational diabetes are 50% to 70% overweight.[57] Caloric requirements are weight based. Obese patients can be managed on diets consisting of as little as 1600 kcal per day as long as ketonuria does not develop.[54] Women with normal weight require from 2200 to 2400 kcal per day[15]; approximately 30 to 35 kcal/kg ideal body weight is recommended.[17] The amount of calories is similar to that required by the pregnant woman with normal glucose tolerance and may be less[1]; however, attention must be paid to the composition and distribution of meals. It is recommended that the patient eat three meals and one to three snacks each day.[54,76] This approach requires consumption of 10% to 15% of calories at breakfast, up to 10% as a midmorning snack, 20% to 30% at lunch, up to 10% as a midafternoon snack, 30% to 40% at dinner, and up to 10% as a bedtime snack.[41] The composition of the diet is as follows: 50% to 60% complex carbohydrates, 12% to 20% protein, 20% to 30% fat.[4,15,17,54,63]

Exercise can be used as an adjunct to diet in the management of gestational diabetes. Regular aerobic exercise and non–weight-bearing exercise have been shown to lower fasting and postprandial glucose concentrations.[10,62] In some cases, exercise can prevent the need for insulin therapy in women whose diabetes cannot be controlled by diet alone.[40]

Medication

If target glucose levels are not attained on a consistent basis with diet and exercise, insulin might be required. Patients undergoing frequent SMBG are more likely to require insulin; however, there is a significant reduction in adverse pregnancy outcomes.[37] Insulin can be given as a combination of short-acting and intermediate-acting insulin in multiple daily injections. Insulin requirements usually change throughout pregnancy, requiring frequent adjustment. Occasionally, in the woman with pregestational diabetes, the continuous subcutaneous insulin infusion pump is used. However, this method has never been demonstrated to be superior to multiple insulin injections for maintaining euglycemia.[24] The type of insulin therapy should be individualized based on a particular patient's needs. The major maternal complication of insulin therapy is hypoglycemia. Maternal hypoglycemia most frequently occurs in the context of a missed meal, decreased carbohydrate content of a meal, or increased physical activity.[3]

Previously, oral hypoglycemic agents were not used during pregnancy because of a concern for fetal hyperinsulinemia[1,15] and neonatal hypoglycemia. However, there has been growing interest in the use of oral hypoglycemic agents as an alternative to insulin therapy. There has been one randomized, controlled trial of the use of the sulfonylurea glyburide, which does not cross the placenta, after the first trimester; this trial demonstrated equal efficacy when compared with insulin in obtaining glycemic control.[58] Outcomes were similar between the two groups with respect to the rates of preeclampsia, cesarean section, macrosomia, neonatal lung complications, hypoglycemia, admission to a neonatal intensive care unit, or fetal anomalies.[58,59] Data are conflicting on the safety of the biguanide metformin in pregnancy.[58,59,82] Further study is needed before recommending widespread use of oral hypoglycemic agents in pregnant women with diabetes.

TESTING

Antepartum testing is important as it may decrease the risk of intrauterine fetal demise and neonatal mortality, especially in patients with fasting and postprandial hyperglycemia.[6] There are four main components to antenatal testing: laboratory evaluation, ultrasound, fetal movement counts, and fetal heart rate testing (see Chapter 9).

Women with diabetes have a 10-fold increased risk for babies with neural tube defects. These women should be offered maternal serum α-fetoprotein screening at 16 to 18 weeks' gestation, followed by a detailed ultrasound examination.[54] Maternal serum α-fetoprotein levels are affected by maternal race and weight and are lower in pregnancies complicated by diabetes.[15] An adjustment for this fact must be made before interpreting results.

Ultrasound assists in managing pregnancies complicated by diabetes. Because women with pregestational diabetes have an increased risk of congenital anomalies, a detailed anatomic survey at 18 to 20 weeks' gestation can be used to detect fetal malformation. There is no increased risk of karyotype abnormalities with diabetes mellitus. Echocardiography is usually performed at 20 to 22 weeks' gestation because there is a fivefold increase in the risk of cardiac malformations in the fetuses of women with diabetes mellitus. There is also an increased risk of septal hypertrophy, which is a component of an obstructive cardiomyopathy.[54] In addition, in the third trimester, ultrasound can be used to estimate fetal weight and to detect polyhydramnios.[54] Women with diabetes are at risk for fetal growth disturbances, so serial ultrasound testing in the third trimester at 4- to 6-week intervals should be considered.[54] The mother should also monitor the activity of her fetus, starting at approximately 28 weeks' gestation, by counting fetal movements.

There is fairly universal agreement that women with pregestational diabetes and gestational diabetes requiring insulin should have antenatal testing. Whether women with uncomplicated gestational diabetes managed with diet alone require antenatal testing remains controversial. There are no prospective trials evaluating the appropriate use of antenatal testing in the woman with uncomplicated gestational diabetes.

Antenatal testing or fetal heart rate monitoring commonly consists of nonstress testing. In women with pregestational diabetes or gestational diabetes requiring insulin twice weekly, nonstress testing is begun at 32 to 34 weeks of gestation. Nonstress testing is started earlier in the presence of vascular disease, poor diabetes control, hypertension, previous intrauterine fetal demise, or other pregnancy complications.[7,54,66,76,85] At 36 to 40 weeks, nonstress testing is considered in women with gestational diabetes managed with diet alone.[76] Some investigators recommend only the use of fetal movement

assessment by the mother in the woman with well-controlled gestational diabetes, that is, in the absence of hypertension, adverse obstetric history, or other risk factors.[23] The rationale for this approach is that abnormal results are unusual in this group of women.[23] Other investigators recommend weekly nonstress testing beginning at 36 weeks.[1,15]

DELIVERY

The appropriate timing of delivery for the woman with gestational diabetes has not been clearly established. In the past, women with diabetes delivered between 35 and 36 weeks of gestation, but the current recommendation is to delay elective delivery until term, when lung maturity can be ensured.

When considering the timing of delivery, one must be aware of certain goals in the management of the woman with diabetes. The main goal of management is to prevent fetal demise or fetal morbidity, such as from a traumatic birth from the macrosomic fetus at the time of delivery.[35] The woman with uncomplicated gestational diabetes need not deliver before 40 weeks unless there is a specific maternal or fetal indication.[88] This approach gives women a better chance to enter labor spontaneously, resulting in a smaller number of inductions of labor and, consequently, fewer cesarean deliveries for failed induction.[28]

After 38 weeks, delivery is considered if the patient has poor glycemic control, poor compliance, a fetus with macrosomia, vasculopathy, or history of prior fetal demise.[21] Early delivery reduces the rate of macrosomia, the incidence of traumatic births, and cesarean deliveries in women with gestational diabetes.[35]

Determination of lung maturity with lecithin-to-sphingomyelin ratios can be used when dates are uncertain or early delivery is considered. Before 38 or 39 weeks' gestation, an amniocentesis should be considered to document lung maturity.[54] Phosphatidylglycerol is the marker for pulmonary maturation. Although its presence may be delayed in women with diabetes,[54] it is a reliable predictor of lung maturity. In the presence of a positive phosphatidylglycerol result, the risk of respiratory distress syndrome is 1%. Expectant management beyond 38 weeks increases the incidence of infants who are large for gestational age; however, if the cervix is unfavorable for delivery, expectant management may be considered.[76]

In general, vaginal delivery is advocated in the woman with diabetes in the absence of other obstetric indications for cesarean section. The cesarean delivery rate remains high in women with diabetes, however, ranging from 20% to 60%.[54] Elective cesarean delivery is advocated for the woman with diabetes who has a fetus with an estimated fetal weight greater than 4000 to 4500 g.[35]

Postpartum Management

Breast feeding should be encouraged in women with diabetes mellitus; it results in increased high-density lipoprotein and decreased blood glucose levels.[49] In addition, no adverse metabolic effects of breast feeding have been found.[1] Breast feeding also is associated with a lower long-term risk of obesity and diabetes in the offspring.[62]

At the postpartum visit, follow-up testing for overt diabetes is recommended in all women who have gestational diabetes. Testing should be performed yearly thereafter because these women are at high risk for subsequent development of diabetes. The risk of subsequent development of diabetes is determined by the severity of glucose intolerance during pregnancy; that is, diabetes mellitus develops in 29% of women who required insulin but in only 7% of women managed on diet alone.[50]

Other predictors of postpartum abnormal glucose tolerance include gestational age at diagnosis of gestational diabetes and fasting glucose level at the time of the antepartum oral glucose tolerance test.[17] Increased maternal age and hyperglycemia at 2 hours during antenatal testing are also associated with an increased likelihood of abnormal glucose tolerance and overt diabetes postpartum.[1] Postpartum impaired glucose tolerance results in an 80% risk of developing diabetes within 5 years or a 16% annual incidence of diabetes.[51]

Modifiable risk factors, which can be adjusted to decrease the risk of developing diabetes postpartum, include diet, weight loss, exercise, smoking cessation, and medications that adversely affect glucose metabolism (corticosteroids, nicotinamide, high-dose thiazide diuretics).[1,62] Each 10-pound gain of weight above the initial postpartum weight doubles the risk for the development of diabetes.[51]

The recurrence rate for gestational diabetes ranges from 30% to 50%,[1,70] and the risk increases with age and postpartum weight gain.[33,70] Subsequent pregnancy after a history of prior gestational diabetes is associated with a greater chance of developing type 2 diabetes, with a relative risk of 3.34.[51]

COMPLICATIONS

Complications of pregestational diabetes that have an impact on pregnancy include hypertension, nephropathy, retinopathy, urinary tract infections such as pyelonephritis, neuropathy, and diabetic ketoacidosis.[1,23,30,76] Maternal complications of diabetes in pregnancy include hypoglycemia, pregnancy-induced hypertension, progression of diabetic retinopathy, cephalopelvic disproportion, malpresentation, cesarean section, and operative vaginal delivery.[1,76]

Adverse effects seen in the embryonic period from conception to 8 weeks include spontaneous abortions and congenital malformations.[76,78] Beyond 8 weeks, particularly in late second and early third trimester, the pregnancy is at risk for fetal hyperinsulinism, macrosomia, polyhydramnios, cardiac septal hypertrophy, chronic hypoxia, fetal growth restriction in women with hypertension or vascular disease, intrauterine fetal death, and increased perinatal mortality.[15,76,78,86,93] In the intrapartum period, one must be concerned with shoulder dystocia and neonatal trauma.

Hypertension in Pregnancy

One of the major risks of gestational diabetes mellitus is the development of hypertensive disorders. The risk is approximately two- to threefold higher in women with gestational diabetes mellitus than in women with normal glucose tolerance.[60,62,74] The incidence rate of pregnancy-induced hypertension in women with diabetes is 11.7%, ranging from 10% in women with gestational diabetes to 15.7% in women with class D, F, or R diabetes (see Table 15-1).[22] Chronic hypertension is seen in 9.6% of all women with diabetes and in up to 16.9% of women with class D, F, or R diabetes.[22] The incidence of hypertensive complications in all pregnant women with diabetes is 18%, ranging from 14.6% in women with gestational diabetes to 30.9% in women with class D, F, or R diabetes.[22]

Nephropathy

Class F diabetes includes the 5% to 10% of patients with underlying renal disease.[54] *Nephropathy* is defined as reduced creatinine clearance or proteinuria of at least 400 mg in 24 hours, measured in the first trimester, in the absence of urinary tract infection.[54,65] These patients have increased risk of preeclampsia, intrauterine growth restriction, and premature delivery.[54] As gestation progresses, nephropathy may worsen, particularly in patients with a serum creatinine concentration greater than 1.5 mg/dL.[22] Patients with nephropathy should be followed with serial 24-hour urine collections for total protein and creatinine clearance.[15] Fetal testing can begin at 28 weeks.

Retinopathy

The longer a woman has diabetes and the greater the degree of hyperglycemia, the more likely she is to develop proliferative diabetic retinopathy.[25,26] Any woman who has had diabetes for more than 5 years requires a retinal examination.[5] Pregnancy doubles the risk of progression of diabetic retinopathy.[54] Progression to proliferative retinopathy from background retinopathy or no retinal disease is rare; however, untreated proliferative retinopathy may progress to vision loss.[51] Of patients with untreated proliferative retinopathy, 86% have progression of their disease during pregnancy, whereas only 16% of patients with background retinopathy have disease progression.[26] Photocoagulation before or during pregnancy may help prevent the progression of retinal disease.[26] The course of background retinopathy for the pregnant woman is not different from that for the nonpregnant woman.[26] Women who have severe florid disc neovascularization that is unresponsive to laser therapy may be at a significant risk for visual deterioration, and termination of pregnancy should be considered.[54]

Diabetic Ketoacidosis

Diabetic ketoacidosis is a complication seen primarily in women with type 1 diabetes, but it can be seen in women with type 2 or gestational diabetes. In this condition, dehydration leads to hypovolemia and hypotension, which can result in a reduction of blood flow to the placenta.[54] The fetal mortality rate in maternal diabetic ketoacidosis can exceed 50%.[23]

Diabetic ketoacidosis is usually the result of inadequate circulating insulin.[22] It can occur at much lower circulating glucose levels in pregnant women than in nonpregnant women; in some cases glucose levels are as low as 150 to 200 mg/dL.[22] Normally, the accelerated starvation of pregnancy is characterized by increases in plasma free fatty acids, ketones, and glycerol and by decreases in maternal glucose concentrations and gluconeogenic amino acids.[15] There is an increase in plasma concentrations of glucose and insulin after a meal.[14] There is also an increased fetal-placental transfer of glucose,[54] contributing to lower fasting plasma glucose levels in late gestation. These normal physiologic changes contribute to the development of diabetic ketoacidosis at much lower glucose concentrations in the pregnant woman than in the nonpregnant woman.

Heart Disease

Class H diabetes is an infrequently seen class of diabetes in pregnancy, representing ischemic heart disease.[54] In women with a previous myocardial infarction or an infarction during pregnancy, the maternal mortality rate exceeds 50%.[54] These patients should be evaluated with an electrocardiogram. If any abnormalities are noted, an echocardiogram or a modified stress test to assess ventricular function should be performed prior to conception.[54]

Congenital Anomalies

Women with diabetes are at risk for fetal anomalies. The congenital malformation rate in infants of women with diabetes varies from 5% to 10%.[28,54,65,91] This rate represents a two- to fourfold higher rate of anomalies when compared with a control population.[53,54,63] The rate of malformation is related to glucose control during organogenesis. Congenital anomalies have become the most common cause of perinatal loss in women with pregestational diabetes,[54] accounting for 30% to 50%.[90] The perinatal mortality rate in pregnancies complicated by diabetes is less than 4%, with approximately 50% of these being due to congenital anomalies,[23,65] which makes congenital anomalies the leading cause of perinatal deaths in these pregnancies.[63]

The congenital anomaly most specific to pregnant women with diabetes mellitus is caudal dysplasia (sacral agenesis), which occurs 200 to 400 times more often in women with diabetes than in women without diabetes.[54] Although this lesion is most specific for diabetes, it is not the most frequently encountered anomaly in the pregnancies of women with diabetes mellitus, because it is so rare.[28] Neural tube defects and congenital heart defects are far more common.[23] Malformations of the central nervous system, such as anencephaly, open myelomeningocele, and holoprosencephaly, are increased 10-fold, and cardiac anomalies, such as transposition of the great vessels and ventricular septal defects, are increased fivefold.[54] Other anomalies commonly observed in women with pregestational diabetes are discussed in Chapter 47, Part 1.

Why women with diabetes are at such a high risk for congenital anomalies is uncertain. The high risk may be due to an increased supply of substrate leading to an oxidative stress on the developing fetus, which in turn generates excess free oxygen radical formation that might ultimately be teratogenic.[15,78] Tight glucose control during organogenesis reduces the rate of anomalies.[77]

Macrosomia

The rate of *macrosomia,* defined as an estimated fetal weight in the 90th percentile or higher for gestational age, is 8% to 14% in normal pregnancies and 25% to 45% in pregnancies complicated by diabetes.[9,39,48] The Pedersen hypothesis states that the increase in fetal growth is the result of increased concentrations of maternal glucose, which crosses the placenta and results in fetal hyperglycemia and subsequently hyperinsulinemia.[77] This hyperinsulinemia affects primarily insulin-sensitive tissues such as fat.[15,34]

Infants of women with gestational diabetes have increased body fat when compared with infants of women with normal glucose tolerance; this increased body fat is independent of birth weight.[18] In fetuses of women with diabetes, the liver, heart, adipose tissue, adrenal tissue, and pancreatic islet tissue are enlarged.[54,78] It is thought that the macrosomic infant of the woman with diabetes has excessive fat deposition on the shoulders and trunk. This excess fat increases the risk of shoulder dystocia when compared with infants of similar weight in women with normal glucose tolerance.[69] Increasing maternal glycemia is a risk factor for fetal macrosomia.* Normalizing glucose values decreases the risk of macrosomia but does not eliminate it.[93]

Fetuses of women with diabetes experience shoulder dystocia five times more often than fetuses of women with normal glucose tolerance, with a 23.1% incidence rate of shoulder dystocia in infants weighing 4000 to 4499 g and a 50% rate in infants weighing 4500 g or more.[2] Shoulder dystocia complicates 0.2% to 2% of deliveries in women with normal glucose tolerance,[2,56] compared with 3% to 9% of pregnancies complicated by diabetes.[29]

Most cases of shoulder dystocia in women with diabetes occur in the macrosomic infant.[21] In women without diabetes, approximately 60% of shoulder dystocia cases occur in infants weighing 4000 g or more; the comparable rate in women with diabetes is 84%.[56] Therefore, induction of labor at term for diabetic mothers of infants who are large for gestational age has been advocated by some investigators.[20] Cesarean delivery has been recommended for women with diabetes whose

---

*References 8, 37, 38, 57, 62, 83, 86.

fetuses are estimated to weigh 4000 to 4500 g, although predictions of birth weight by antenatal ultrasound or clinical examination are poor.[2,8]

Macrosomia also is associated with a number of maternal and neonatal complications. There is an increased risk of cephalopelvic disproportion and shoulder dystocia that leads to traumatic birth injury and asphyxia.[54] These risks are highest when birth weight is greater than 4 kg and is greater in infants of diabetic mothers than in infants of women without diabetes whose children have a similar birth weight.[2,15] These infants are at risk for birth trauma such as Erb palsy and clavicle fracture (see Chapter 27).[93]

Erb palsy has the potential for a long-term morbidity because the neurologic deficit can be permanent in approximately 5% to 15% of cases.[61] The rate of Erb palsy in macrosomic, vaginally delivered infants weighing 4500 g or more is 5%, compared with 0.7% in those weighing less than 4500 g.[78] Additional neonatal complications associated with shoulder dystocia include neonatal depression and a greater incidence of an Apgar score less than 7. The combination of diabetes and fetal weight of more than 4000 g is the best predictor of subsequent development of shoulder dystocia, accounting for over 50% of the incidence of shoulder dystocia.[2]

Polyhydramnios

Polyhydramnios is seen more frequently in pregnancies that are complicated by diabetes (see also Chapter 21). The reported rate ranges from 15% to 18%.[22,93] The etiology is unknown; however, possible mechanisms include fetal hyperinsulinemia or hyperglycemia, which increase the fetal osmotic load and lead to fetal polyuria, or insulin's effect on fetal kidneys, which increases sodium excretion.

Intrauterine Growth Restriction

Growth disturbances (i.e., fetuses who are too big or too small) can complicate pregnancies in women with diabetes (see also Chapter 13). Women with class A, B, or C diabetes are more likely to have macrosomic infants, but women whose pregnancies are complicated by diabetic vasculopathy have an increased incidence of intrauterine growth restriction, which is thought to be caused by reduced uterine blood flow.[54]

Hypoxia

Hyperinsulinemia has also been linked to hypoxemia in the fetus,[54] which leads to an increase in oxygen consumption and a decrease in arterial oxygen content.[13] When such a fetus becomes hypoxic, the maternal hyperglycemia accentuates the rise in lactate and the decline in pH in the fetus.[62] There is also increased erythropoietin-induced red blood cell production in response to fetal hypoxia,[7,89] resulting in polycythemia in the neonate.

Intrauterine Fetal Demise

Maternal and fetal hyperglycemia and hyperinsulinemia may lead to fetal acidemia and hypoxia[93]; therefore, the incidence of intrauterine fetal demise, which is related to glucose control, is increased in women with diabetes. In women with gestational diabetes, the stillbirth rate increases when the postprandial glucose level is greater than 120 mg/dL, which is similar to pregestational diabetes with glucose levels of 160 mg/dL or greater.[21] Patients who are poorly compliant with prenatal care are also at increased risk for fetal demise, particularly if they also have poor glucose control.[21]

Perinatal Mortality

As the fasting glucose levels rise above 105 mg/dL, the likelihood of adverse perinatal outcomes increases.[31] In pregnancies complicated by diabetes, the perinatal mortality rate has been reported to be as high as 31 to 38 per 1000.[28,88] When gestational diabetes is undiagnosed or untreated, the risk of perinatal mortality increases.[85] Hyperglycemia, defined as fasting blood sugar greater than 105 mg/dL and 2-hour postprandial blood sugar greater than 120 mg/dL, is the greatest risk factor for intrauterine or neonatal death.[54] Perinatal mortality also is influenced by the age of onset of diabetes, the duration of disease, and the presence of vasculopathy.[54] Women with gestational diabetes who are normoglycemic have a lower perinatal mortality rate.[54] Similarly, those requiring insulin are at greater risk of prenatal mortality than those whose diabetes is controlled by diet alone.[54]

OFFSPRING

In addition to the mothers, children of women with gestational diabetes are at increased risk of developing type 2 diabetes or impaired glucose tolerance.[27,62,89] Children of mothers whose pregnancies were complicated by diabetes are also at risk of becoming obese as adolescents and adults.[23,62,81,92,93] These facts may represent the influence of the metabolic abnormalities in the intrauterine environment, such as hyperglycemia, rather than genetic influences alone.[79,80]

PRECONCEPTION COUNSELING

Because women with diabetes are at significant risk for complications during pregnancy, preconception counseling is recommended.[47] It is preferable for a woman to establish normal glucose levels at least 1 year before attempting conception.[51] The glycosylated hemoglobin should be within one standard deviation of the mean,[31] which could reduce the rate of spontaneous abortions and congenital anomalies to nearly normal.[15,68]

Before conception, the patient should undergo evaluation of glucose control with measurement of hemoglobin A_{1c} (HbA_{1c}), renal function with serum creatinine,

24-hour urine for total protein and creatinine clearance, and a rubella titer.[76] Measurement of glycosylated HbA_{1c} gives retrospective insight into glycemic control. Higher first-trimester glycosylated hemoglobin is associated with a greater likelihood of anomalies.[65] Therefore, the goal is to establish good control with normal levels of hemoglobin A_{1c} before conception. After conception these laboratory studies should be repeated each trimester.

In addition to laboratory studies, patients should be evaluated for proliferative retinopathy with a retinal examination. If peripheral retinopathy is present, therapy should be instituted before conception. Because women with diabetes are at increased risk for asymptomatic bacteriuria and pyelonephritis, periodic urine cultures are necessary, with aggressive treatment of any infection. Some also advocate an electrocardiogram as a baseline study for women older than 30 years.[46,54,67] Because women with diabetes are at increased risk for neural tube defects, they should start folate supplementation, 4 mg daily, once they are trying to conceive, continuing through the first 12 weeks of gestation. This supplement may decrease the risk of neural tube defects.[71]

Because diabetes mellitus is a complex constellation of diseases with variable effects both on the mother and on her fetus, preconception counseling is recommended in order to achieve optimal maternal health prior to conception. In addition, maintenance of euglycemia before conception and throughout gestation is highly recommended to reduce the incidence of maternal, fetal, and neonatal complications.

REFERENCES

1. Abrams RS, Coustan DR: Gestational diabetes update. Clinical Diabetes 8:19, 1990.
2. Acker DB et al: Risk factors for shoulder dystocia. Obstet Gynecol 66:762, 1985.
3. American Diabetes Association: Clinical practice recommendations: American Diabetes Association 1991-1992. Diabetes Care 15:30, 1992.
4. American Diabetes Association: Medical Management of Pregnancy Complicated by Diabetes. Alexandria, Va, American Diabetes Association, 1993.
5. American Diabetes Association: Special report: Principles of nutrition and dietary recommendations for individuals with diabetes mellitus, 1979. Diabetes 28:1027, 1979.
6. American Diabetes Association: Summary and recommendations of the Second International Workshop-Conference on Gestational Diabetes Mellitus. Diabetes 34 (Suppl 2):123, 1985.
7. Barret JM et al: The non-stress test: An evaluation of 1000 patients. Am J Obstet Gynecol 141:153, 1981.
8. Benedetti TJ, Gabbe SG: Shoulder dystocia: A complication of fetal macrosomia and prolonged second stage of labor with midpelvic delivery. Obstet Gynecol 165:837, 1991.
9. Buchanan TA et al: Utility of fetal measurements in the management of gestational diabetes mellitus. Diabetes Care 21:B99, 1998.
10. Bung P et al: Exercise in gestational diabetes. An optional therapeutic approach? Diabetes 40(Suppl 2):182, 1991.
11. Carpenter MW, Coustan DR: Criteria for screening tests for gestational diabetes. Am J Obstet Gynecol 144:768, 1982.
12. Carr SR: Screening for gestational diabetes mellitus: A perspective in 1998. Diabetes Care 21:B14, 1998.
13. Carson BS et al: Effects of a sustained insulin infusion upon glucose uptake and oxygenation of the ovine fetus. Pediatr Res 14;147, 1980.
14. Catalano PM: Carbohydrate metabolism and gestational diabetes. Clin Obstet Gynecol 37:25, 1994.
15. Catalano PM et al: Diabetes Mellitus in Reproductive Endocrinology, Surgery, and Technology. Philadelphia, Lippincott-Raven, 1996.
16. Catalano PM et al: Carbohydrate metabolism during pregnancy in control subjects and women with gestational diabetes. Am J Physiol 264:E60, 1993.
17. Catalano PM et al: Incidence and risk factors associated with abnormal postpartum glucose tolerance in women with gestational diabetes. Am J Obstet Gynecol 165:914, 1991.
18. Catalano PM et al: Increased fetal adiposity: A very sensitive marker of abnormal in utero development. Am J Obstet Gynecol 189:1698, 2003.
19. Churchill JA et al: Neuropsychological deficits in children of diabetic mothers. A report from the Collaborative Study of Cerebral Palsy. Am J Obstet Gynecol 105:257, 1969.
20. Conway DL, Langer O: Elective delivery of infants with macrosomia in diabetic women: Reduced shoulder dystocia versus increased cesarean deliveries. Am J Obstet Gynecol 178:922, 1998.
21. Conway DL, Langer O: Optimal timing and mode of delivery in the gestational diabetic pregnancy. Prenat Neonat Med 3:555, 1998.
22. Cousins L: Pregnancy complications among diabetic women: Review 1965-1985. Obstet Gynecol Surv 42:140, 1987.
23. Coustan DR: Diabetes in Pregnancy in Neonatal and Perinatal Medicine. St. Louis, Mosby, 1996.
24. Coustan DR et al: A randomized clinical trial of the insulin pump versus intensive conventional therapy in diabetic pregnancies. JAMA 225:631, 1986.
25. Diabetes Control and Complications Trial Group: The effect of intensive diabetes treatment on the progression of diabetic retinopathy in insulin-dependent diabetes mellitus. The Diabetes Control and Complications Trial. Arch Ophthalmol 113:36, 1995.
26. Dibble CM et al: Effect of pregnancy on diabetic retinopathy. Obstet Gynecol 59:699, 1982.
27. Dornhorst A, Rossi M: Risk and prevention of type 2 diabetes in women with gestational diabetes. Diabetes Care 21:B43, 1998.
28. Drury MI et al: Pregnancy in the diabetic patient: Timing and mode of delivery. Obstet Gynecol 62:279, 1983.
29. Elliot JP et al: Ultrasonic prediction of fetal macrosomia in diabetic patients. Obstet Gynecol 60:159, 1982.
30. Expert Committee on the Diagnosis and Classification of Diabetes Mellitus: Report of the Expert Committee on the Diagnosis and Classification of Diabetes Mellitus. Diabetes Care 20:1183, 1997.
31. Gabbe SG: The gestational diabetes mellitus conferences: Three are history: Focus on the fourth. Diabetes Care 21:B1, 1998.
32. Gabbe SG: Unresolved issues in screening and diagnosis of gestational diabetes mellitus. Prenat Neonat Med 3:523, 1998.
33. Henry OA, Bleisher NA: Long-term implication of gestational diabetes for the mother. Baillieres Clin Obstet Gynaecol 5:461, 1991.

34. Hill DJ et al: Growth factors and the regulation of fetal growth. Diabetes Care 21:B60, 1998.

35. Hod M et al: Antepartum management protocol: Timing and mode of delivery in gestational diabetes. Diabetes Care 21:B113, 1998.

36. Hollander P: Approaches to the treatment of type 1 diabetes. Laboratory Medicine 8:522, 1990.

37. Homko CJ et al: Is self-monitoring of blood glucose necessary in the management of gestational diabetes mellitus? Diabetes Care 21:B118, 1998.

38. Jovanovic L: American Diabetes Association's Fourth International Workshop-Conference on Gestational Diabetes Mellitus: Summary and discussion. Therapeutic interventions. Diabetes Care 21:B131, 1998.

39. Jovanovic L et al: Metabolic and immunologic effects of insulin lispro in gestational diabetes. Diabetes Care 22:1422, 1999.

40. Jovanovic-Peterson L et al: Randomized trial of diet versus diet plus cardiovascular conditioning on glucose levels in gestational diabetes. Am J Obstet Gynecol 161:415, 1989.

41. Jovanovic-Peterson L ed: Medical Management of Pregnancy Complicated by Diabetes, 2nd ed. Alexandria, Va, American Diabetes Association, 1995.

42. Jovanovic L et al: Feasibility of maintaining normal glucose profiles in insulin-dependent pregnant diabetic women. Am J Med 68:105, 1980.

43. Karlsson K, Kjellmer I: The outcome of diabetic pregnancies in relation to the mother's blood sugar level. Am J Obstet Gynecol 112:213, 1972

44. King H: Epidemiology of glucose intolerance and gestational diabetes in women of childbearing age. Diabetes Care 21:B9, 1998.

45. King JC: New National Academy of Sciences guidelines for nutrition during pregnancy. Diabetes 40(Suppl 2):151, 1991.

46. Kirwan, JP et al: TNF-alpha is a predictor of insulin resistance in human pregnancy. Diabetes 51:2207, 2002.

47. Kitzmiller JL et al: Preconception management of diabetes continued through early pregnancy prevents the excess frequency of major congenital anomalies in infants of diabetic mothers. JAMA 265:731, 1991.

48. Kitzmiller JL: Macrosomia in infants of diabetic mothers: Characteristics, causes, prevention. In Jovanovic L et al (eds): Diabetes in Pregnancy: Teratology, Toxicology and Treatment. New York, Praeger, 1986.

49. Kjos SL et al: The effect of lactation on glucose and lipid metabolism in women with recent gestational diabetes. Obstet Gynecol 82:451, 1993.

50. Kjos SL et al: Hormonal choices after gestational diabetes: Subsequent pregnancy, contraception, and hormone replacement. Diabetes Care 21:B50, 1988.

51. Kjos SL et al: Postpartum screening and contraceptive use in women with gestational diabetes. Prenat Neonat Med 3:563, 1998.

52. Klein BEK et al: Effect of pregnancy on the progression of diabetic retinopathy. Diabetes Care 13:34, 1990.

53. Kucera J: Rate and type of congenital anomalies among offspring of diabetic women. J Reprod Med 7:73, 1971.

54. Landon MB, Gabbe SG: Diabetes mellitus and pregnancy. Obstet Gynecol Clin North Am 19:633, 1992.

55. Langer O et al: Management of women with one abnormal oral glucose tolerance test value reduces adverse outcome in pregnancy. Am J Obstet Gynecol 161:593, 1989.

56. Langer O et al: Shoulder dystocia: Should the fetus weighing >4000 grams be delivered by cesarean section? Am J Obstet Gynecol 165:831, 1991.

57. Langer O: Insulin and other treatment alternatives in gestational diabetes mellitus. Prenat Neonat Med 3:542, 1998.

58. Langer O: Oral hypoglycemic agents in pregnancy: Their time has come. J Matern Fetal Neonatal Med 12:376, 2002.

59. Langer O: When diet fails: Insulin and oral hypoglycemic agents as alternatives for the management of gestational diabetes mellitus. J Matern Fetal Neonatal Med 11:218, 2002.

60. Lavin J et al: Clinical experience with 107 diabetic pregnancies. Am J Obstet Gynecol 147:742, 1983.

61. Levine MG et al: Birth trauma: Incidence and predisposing factors. Obstet Gynecol 63:792, 1984.

62. Metzger BE, Coustan DR: Summary and recommendations of the Fourth International Workshop-Conference on Gestational Diabetes Mellitus. The Organizing Committee. Diabetes Care 121:B161, 1998.

63. Metzger BE, Freinkel N: Diabetes and pregnancy: Metabolic changes and management. Clinical Diabetes 8, 1990.

64. Metzger BE: Summary and recommendations of the Third International Workshop Conference on Gestational Diabetes Mellitus. Diabetes 40(Suppl 2):197, 1991.

65. Miller E et al: Elevated maternal hemoglobin A1c in early pregnancy and major congenital anomalies in infants of diabetic mothers. N Engl J Med 304:1331, 1981.

66. Miller JM, Horger EO: Antepartum heart rate testing in diabetic pregnancy. J Reprod Med 30:515, 1985.

67. Mills JL et al: Lack of relations of increased malformation rates in infants of diabetic mothers to glycemic control during organogenesis. N Engl J Med 318:671, 1988.

68. Mills J et al: Incidence of spontaneous abortion among normal and insulin-dependent diabetic women whose pregnancies were identified within 21 days of conception. N Engl J Med 319:1617, 1988.

69. Modanlou HD et al: Large-for-gestational age neonates: Anthropometric reasons for shoulder dystocia. Obstet Gynecol 60:417, 1982.

70. Moses RG: The recurrence rate of gestational diabetes in subsequent pregnancies. Diabetes Care 19:1349,1996.

71. MRC Vitamin Study Research Group: Prevention of neural tube defects: Results of the Medical Research Council Vitamin Study. Lancet 338:131, 1991.

72. National Diabetes Data Group: Classification and diagnosis of diabetes mellitus and other categories of glucose intolerance. Diabetes 28:1039, 1979.

73. Neiger R, Coustan DR: The role of repeat glucose tolerance tests in the diagnosis of gestational diabetes. Am J Obstet Gynecol 165:787, 1991.

74. Olofsson P et al: Diabetes and pregnancy: A 21 year Swedish material. Acta Obstet Gynecol Scand (Suppl 122):3, 1984.

75. O'Sullivan JB, Mahan CM: Criteria for the oral glucose tolerance test in pregnancy. Diabetes 13:278, 1964.

76. Pasui D, McFarland KF: Management of diabetes in pregnancy. Am Fam Physician 55:2731, 1997.

77. Pedersen J: The Pregnant Diabetic and Her Newborn: Problems and Management, 2nd ed. Baltimore, Williams & Wilkins, 1977.

78. Persson B, Hanson U. Neonatal morbidities in gestational diabetes mellitus. Diabetes Care 21:B79, 1998.

79. Pettitt DJ et al: Abnormal glucose tolerance during pregnancy in Pima Indian women. Long-term effects on offspring. Diabetes 40(Suppl 2):126, 1991.

80. Pettitt DJ, Knowler WC: Long-term effects of the intrauterine environment, birth weight and breast-feeding in Pima Indians. Diabetes Care 21:B138, 1998.

329

81. Phillips DIW: Birth weight and the future development of diabetes: A review of the evidence. Diabetes Care 21:B150, 1998.

82. Preece R, Jovanovic L: New and future diabetes therapies: Are they safe during pregnancy. J Matern Fetal Neonatal Med 12:365, 2002.

83. Reece EA, Homko CJ: Optimal glycemic control, fetal morbidity and monitoring protocols in gestational diabetes mellitus. Prenat Neonat Med 3:526, 1998.

84. Report of the Expert Committee on the Diagnosis and Classification of Diabetes Mellitus. Diabetes Care 20:1183, 1997.

85. Rosenn BM, Miodovnik M: Antenatal fetal testing in pregnancies complicated by gestational diabetes mellitus: Why, who and how? Prenat Neonat Med 3:550, 1998.

86. Sermer M et al: The Toronto tri-hospital gestational diabetes project. Diabetes Care 21:B33, 1998.

87. Shannon K et al: Erythropoiesis in infants of diabetic mothers. Pediatr Res 20:161, 1986.

88. Shea MA et al: Diabetes in pregnancy. Am J Obstet Gynecol 111:801, 1971.

89. Silverman BL et al: Long-term effect of the intrauterine environment: The Northwestern University Diabetes in Pregnancy Center. Diabetes Care 21(Suppl 2):B142, 1998.

90. Simpson JL et al: Diabetes in pregnancy, Northwestern University Series (1977-1981). I. Prospective study of anomalies in offspring of mothers with diabetes mellitus. Am J Obstet Gynecol 146:263, 1983.

91. Sinclair SH et al: Macular edema and pregnancy in insulin dependent diabetes. Am J Ophthalmol 97:154, 1984.

92. Slaine DR et al: Long term outlook for the offspring of the diabetic woman. In Jovanovic L (ed): Controversies in Diabetes in Pregnancy. New York, Springer-Verlag, 1988.

93. Uvena J, Catalano PM: Short- and long-term effects of gestational diabetes mellitus on the neonate. Prenat Neonat Med 3:517, 1988.

94. Weiss PA, Hoffman H: Intensified conventional insulin therapy for the pregnant diabetic patient. Obstet Gynecol 64:629, 1984.

95. White P: Pregnancy complicating diabetes. Am J Med 7:609, 1949.

CHAPTER 16

Obstetric Management of Prematurity

Patrick S. Ramsey and Robert L. Goldenberg

Preterm labor is defined as contractions with cervical change, occurring at less than 37 weeks of gestation.[118] A preterm delivery, as defined by the World Health Organization, is one that occurs at less than 37 and more than 20 gestational weeks. In the United States, the prematurity rate is approximately 9% to 12%, whereas in Europe it varies between 5% and 7%. Despite advances in obstetric care, the rate of prematurity has not changed substantially over the past 40 years and may actually have increased slightly in recent decades.[64] Prematurity remains a leading cause of neonatal morbidity and mortality worldwide, accounting for 60% to 80% of deaths of infants without congenital anomalies.[234] Recent advances have shed important insights into the pathophysiology of preterm labor and may serve as a basis for promising novel approaches to address this important clinical problem. In this chapter we will review various issues related to preterm labor and delivery, including complications, pathophysiology, risk factors, preventive strategies, and treatment.

PREMATURITY

Spontaneous preterm labor accounts for 40% to 50% of all preterm deliveries, with the remainder resulting from preterm premature rupture of membranes (25% to 40%) and obstetrically indicated preterm delivery (20% to 25%). As the risk of neonatal mortality and morbidity near term is low, great attention has been focused on early preterm birth (23 to 32 weeks' gestation).[4] Although preterm births in this gestational age group represent less than 1% to 2% of all deliveries, this group contributes to nearly 50% of long-term neurologic morbidity and to about 60% of perinatal mortality.

Survival of preterm babies is highly dependent on the gestational age at the time of the preterm birth.[106] Neonatal mortality rates have declined over recent years largely because of improved neonatal intensive care. In general, for a given gestational age, female infants demonstrate a greater rate of survival than male infants, and black neonates tend to do better than white neonates.[57] Neonatal survival dramatically improves as gestational age progresses, with over 50% surviving at 25 weeks' gestation, and over 90% by 28 to 29 weeks' gestation.[57] The gestational age-specific neonatal mortality rates are listed in Table 16-1. Similarly, neonatal survival rates increase as infant birthweight increases: 501 to 750 g, 49%; 751 to 1000 g, 85%; 1001 to 1250 g, 93%; and 1251 to 1500 g, 96%.[345] In the United States, survival rates of 20% to 30% have been noted in neonates delivered at 22 to 23 weeks' gestation; however, these premature infants are often left with long-term neurologic impairment.[137,139,234]

TABLE 16-1. Changes in Survival Rates over Time

GESTATIONAL AGE (WK)	1993*		2001-2002†	
	Survival by Gestational Age (%)	Weekly Improvement in Survival (%)	Survival by Gestational Age (%)	Weekly Improvement in Survival (%)
23	1.8	1.8	24	—
24	9.9	8.1	59	35
25	15.5	5.6	77	18
26	54.7	39.2	88	11
27	67	12.3	91	3
28	77.4	10.4	91	0

*Modified from Cooper RL et al: A multicenter study and gestational age specific mortality. Am J Obstet Gynecol 168:78, 1993.
†Modified from data obtained between 1/1/01 and 12/31/02 from the National Institute of Child Health and Human Development.

TABLE 16-2. Morbidity by Gestational Age (23-28 wk) for Infants Born in the NICHD Neonatal Research Network

Gestational Age (wk)	23	24	25	26	27	28	TOTAL
n	295	509	560	642	748	808	3562
				MORBIDITY (%)			
Respiratory Distress Syndrome*	78	82	71	63	54	45	61
Surfactant Therapy	95	90	89	84	78	67	81
Bronchopulmonary Dysplasia	34	48	47	40	28	20	35
Patent Ductus Arteriosus	55	61	52	48	36	30	44
Grade III-IV Intraventricular Hemorrhage	45	32	23	16	12	11	18
Necrotizing Enterocolitis (Proven)	12	13	9	11	10	7	10
Late-Onset Septicemia	41	48	45	37	25	23	34

*An infant was determined to have respiratory distress syndrome if each of the following was true: required oxygen at 6 hours of life, continuing to age 24 hours; demonstrated clinical features up to age 24 hours; needed respiratory support to age 24 hours; had an abnormal chest radiograph up to age 24 hours.
Modified from data obtained between 1/1/01 and 12/31/02 from the National Institute of Child Health and Human Development (NICHD).

Neonatal morbidities that result from prematurity remain a significant clinical problem. These morbidities include respiratory distress syndrome, intraventricular hemorrhage, periventricular leukomalacia, necrotizing enterocolitis, bronchopulmonary dysplasia, sepsis, patent ductus arteriosus, cerebral palsy, mental retardation, and retinopathy of prematurity. The risk for these morbidities is directly related to the delivery gestational age and birthweight. The neonatal morbidity rates that are specific to gestational age are listed in Table 16-2.[314] Use of antenatal corticosteroids (betamethasone or dexamethasone) has been shown to reduce the incidence or severity of respiratory distress syndrome, intraventricular hemorrhage, and necrotizing enterocolitis.[274] Despite these benefits, the use of antenatal corticosteroids has not been widespread until recently.

Cerebral palsy, defined as a nonprogressive motor dysfunction with origin around the time of birth, complicates approximately 2 per 1000 live births. In the majority of cases, the cerebral palsy does not have a specific identifiable etiology. Although the majority of cases of cerebral palsy occur in term infants, the relative risk for an early preterm infant developing cerebral palsy is nearly 40 times that of a term infant. Intrauterine infection has been shown to be associated with the subsequent development of periventricular leukomalacia, intraventricular hemorrhage, and cerebral palsy.[73,88,276,356] Intrauterine infection and the various inflammatory cytokines appear to substantially increase the risk of cell death, resulting in "leukomalacia" and periventricular hemorrhage, and ultimately in cerebral palsy.[208,377] Infants born at the same gestational age, but without evidence of infection, appear to have a substantially lower risk for periventricular damage and cerebral palsy. Children with extremely low birthweight (less than 1000 g) have substantially higher rates of mental retardation, cerebral palsy, and visual disabilities, as well as neurobehavioral dysfunction and poor school performance.[138,139,366] Approximately 10% of surviving newborns born weighing less than 1000 g will develop cerebral palsy. Despite the fact that more very low birthweight infants survive, the rate of cerebral palsy ranges from 13 to 90 per 1000 for survivors weighing 500 to 1500 g.[324]

PATHOGENESIS

The pathogenesis of preterm labor is not well understood.[283] It is unclear whether preterm labor represents an idiopathic activation of the normal labor process or whether it results from a different pathologic mechanism. It is becoming increasingly clear that the factors that lead to the development of preterm labor are multiple and are distinct from those that occur with term labor—hence, they represent a pathologic rather than a physiologic process. Central to all pathophysiologic pathways leading to the onset of parturition, whether term or preterm, are three main biologic events: cervical ripening, formation and expression of myometrial oxytocin receptors, and myometrial gap junction formation. Prostaglandins E_2 and $F_{2\alpha}$ (PGE_2 and $PGF_{2\alpha}$) are believed to be important factors involved in these events. The evidence is based on several findings. First, increased prostaglandin levels are present in amniotic fluid, maternal plasma, and urine during labor.[78] These prostaglandins have been shown to facilitate cervical ripening and to promote myometrial gap junction formation.[221] Further support for the important role of prostaglandins in the process of parturition comes from the observation that exogenous prostaglandins administered by various routes are effective in facilitating cervical ripening and in inducing labor at any point in gestation. Finally, the administration of prostaglandin synthetase inhibitors effectively delays the onset of parturition, arrests preterm labor, and delays abortions. From these data, it is relatively clear that the prostaglandins are an important component of the parturition process. What is less clear, however, is the mechanism by which this cascade of events, which culminates in parturition, begins. Several theories exist regarding the initiation of parturition: (1) progesterone withdrawal, (2) oxytocin initiation, and (3) premature decidual activation.

The progesterone withdrawal theory stems from a large body of work previously done with sheep. Endogenous progesterone is known to inhibit decidual prostaglandin formation and release.[1] As parturition nears, the fetal adrenal axis becomes more sensitive to adrenocorticotropic hormone, which incites an increased secretion of cortisol. Fetal cortisol then stimulates trophoblast 17α-hydroxylase activity, which decreases progesterone secretion and leads to a subsequent increase in estrogen production. This reverse in the estrogen-to-progesterone ratio results in increased prostaglandin formation.[47] Although this mechanism is well established in sheep, it does not appear to be the primary initiator of parturition in humans. First, there is a minimal decrease of progesterone levels in pregnant women prior to the onset of labor. Moreover, administration of progesterone to women in labor or in preterm labor has no inhibitory effect.[103] Withdrawal of progesterone at the cellular level as a result of the presence of binding proteins has been proposed.[336] Changes in the binding of progesterone to plasma proteins or changes in the metabolism of progesterone have also been implicated.[210] To date, these proposed mechanisms are not well supported in the literature.

The second parturition theory involves oxytocin as an initiator of labor. As term approaches, the number of myometrial oxytocin receptors increases substantially. As oxytocin is intimately related to the initiation of uterine contractions and has been shown to promote the release of prostaglandins, it is natural to suggest that it plays an important role in the initiation of labor.[102] Accepting oxytocin as the initiating agent for the onset of labor, however, is difficult for two reasons: blood levels of oxytocin do not rise before labor, and the rate of clearance of oxytocin remains constant during pregnancy.[204] It is important to note that the prostaglandin levels in amniotic fluid are lower in oxytocin-induced labor than in spontaneous labor.[293] Oxytocin probably ensures uterine contractions, prevents blood loss after labor, and plays a crucial role in lactation. The involvement of oxytocin in parturition probably represents a final common pathway.

The final and most likely theory regarding preterm parturition involves premature decidual activation. Although decidual activation may in part be mediated by the fetal-decidual paracrine system, it appears that in many cases, especially those involving early preterm labor, this activation occurs in the context of an occult upper genital tract infection (Fig. 16-1).[48,105,116] Indeed, there is a growing body of evidence that has established a strong link between upper genital tract infection and spontaneous preterm delivery.[105] Colonization or infection of the upper genital tract results in inflammation and disruption of the choriodecidual interface, initiating

a cascade of events ultimately resulting in spontaneous labor.[105] The evidence for these events is well supported by the biochemical changes that have been observed within the amniotic fluid, trophoblast, and decidua of patients with spontaneous preterm labor. Further support for this hypothesis comes from studies of mid-trimester amniotic fluid, obtained at the time of genetic amniocentesis, which demonstrate that elevated interleukin (IL)-6 levels are often associated with subsequent spontaneous abortion, fetal death, or preterm labor.[322,373] Elevated IL-6 levels most likely result from a subclinical upper genital tract infection, which is often present many weeks before the eventual onset of preterm delivery or adverse pregnancy outcome. In addition to the levels of IL-6, amniotic fluid levels of the pro-inflammatory cytokines IL-1 and tumor necrosis factor-alpha (TNFα) have been associated with intrauterine infection and preterm labor.[11,159]

Interleukin-1 and TNFα are known to be present in amniotic fluid during labor and are produced by the decidua and fetal membranes in vitro.[62] These cytokines have been shown to induce production of other cytokines in vitro, including IL-6 by the decidua and chorion, and IL-8 by the decidua, amnion, and chorion.[79,80,183,358] IL-1, IL-6, and TNFα result in stimulation of prostaglandin synthesis by amnionic, chorionic, and decidual cells in vitro.[217,251] Concentrations of prostaglandins PGE$_2$ and PGF$_{2\alpha}$ and their metabolites increase dramatically during labor.[78] The amnion and the chorion are the main sources of PGE$_2$.[250,287] The decidua too is capable of producing PGE$_2$, but it is the only source of PGF$_{2\alpha}$.[287,339] IL-8 is a granulocyte chemotactant and activator that, in turn, releases specific collagenases and elastases. These substances cause the breakdown of the cervical-chorionic-decidual extracellular matrix, leading to cervical ripening, separation of the chorion from the decidua, and possible membrane rupture.

It appears that the majority of cases of spontaneous preterm labor and delivery, especially those occurring early in gestation, are the result of occult upper genital tract infection with coincident activation of the decidua. Interestingly, an inverse relationship exists between bacterial colonization of the chorioamnion and amniotic fluid, and gestational age at delivery in women with spontaneous preterm labor.[50,148] Chorioamnion colonization is associated with nearly 80% of the very early spontaneous preterm births. In contrast, microbial colonization of the upper genital tract appears to play a much less important role in the initiation of parturition at or near term.[50,148] The strong association between microbial chorioamnion colonization and preterm birth is an important advance in our understanding of the mechanisms involved in spontaneous preterm delivery and represents a potential target for therapeutic intervention.[148]

RISK FACTORS

The identification and management of preterm labor have been directed at defining various epidemiologic,

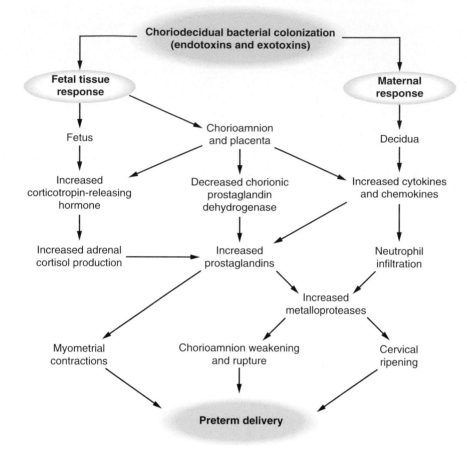

FIGURE 16-1. Pathogenesis of infection-related preterm labor and delivery. (From Goldenberg RL et al: Intrauterine infection and preterm delivery. N Engl J Med 342:1500, 2000. © 2000 Massachusetts Medical Society. All rights reserved.)

clinical, and environmental risk factors that are related to preterm labor and delivery.[113] Early identification of these risk factors may allow modification of the traditional approaches to prenatal care and ultimately may reduce the rate of preterm deliveries. In this section, we will review the major risk factors that have been associated with preterm delivery (Box 16-1).

Demographics

In the United States, race is a significant risk factor for preterm delivery. Black women have a prematurity rate of about 16% to 18%, in comparison with 7% to 9% for white women. Very low birthweight neonates (less than 1500 g) demonstrate the greatest risk of neonatal morbidity and death, and they are disproportionately represented by black neonates. Various other factors have been implicated, including maternal age. Women less than 17 years and more than 35 years old carry a higher risk of preterm delivery.[248] When similar age groups are compared by race, black women still have a higher rate of preterm deliveries. Less education and lower socioeconomic status have also been shown to be risk factors, although these are probably not independent of each other.[94] When these factors are

controlled, black women continue to have a higher rate of preterm delivery than women in other ethnic groups. The cause of preterm birth appears to differ ethnically: preterm labor is more common in white women, and preterm premature rupture of membranes is more common in black women.[241]

Various behavioral factors increase the risks. Nutritional status, either poor or excessive weight gain, seems to have an adverse effect.[372] Women with a low body mass index (less than 19.8 kg/m²) are at higher risk than other women for preterm delivery. Smoking plays a more significant role in growth restriction than it does in preterm delivery. However, women who smoke have about a 20% to 30% increase in preterm births.[338] In the United States, where it is estimated that 20% to 30% of pregnant women smoke, 10% to 20% of all preterm births can be attributed to maternal smoking. The increasing use of cocaine during pregnancy is another important behavioral factor.[220] The pathophysiology may be similar to that of smoking—that is, vasoconstriction leading to an increased rate of abruption[375] (see also Chapter 36).

Another behavioral factor is the degree of physical activity and stress during pregnancy. Several studies have evaluated the effects of employment on preterm

BOX 16-1. Risk Factors Associated with Preterm Delivery

Demographic Factors
- Age
- Race
- Socioeconomic status

Behavioral Factors
- Smoking
- Substance abuse
- Poor nutrition
- Absent or inadequate prenatal care

Maternal Medical Conditions
- Poor obstetric history
- Uterine or cervical malformations
- Myomas
- Exposure to diethylstilbestrol
- Hypertension
- Diabetes
- Other medical conditions

Current Pregnancy Complications
- Multiple gestation
- Excess or decreased amniotic fluid
- Vaginal bleeding
- Low body mass index (<19.8 kg/m^2)
- Fetal anomalies
- Abdominal surgery
- Infection (systemic or local)

TABLE 16-3. Recurrence of Spontaneous Preterm Delivery According to Prior Pregnancy Outcome

FIRST BIRTH	SECOND BIRTH	RATE OF PRETERM DELIVERY IN NEXT PREGNANCY (%)
Term	—	5
Preterm	—	15
Term	Preterm	24
Preterm	Preterm	32

Carr-Hill RA, Hall MH: The repetition of spontaneous preterm labour. Br J Obstet Gynaecol 92:921, 1985.

delivery, with results ranging from an increase in the rate of preterm deliveries, to no difference, to an actual decrease in the working group.[227,237,270] Unfortunately, none of these studies addresses the physical activity of domestic labor. Activity in the standing position does increase uterine irritability. This is probably caused by uterine compression of pelvic vessels, which results in a decreased venous return to the heart. Contractions of the uterus may relieve this compression. A Swiss study demonstrated increased uterine activity in relation to standing in two thirds of singleton pregnancies, and in all cases of twins studied.[332] Maternal stress also appears to be associated with an increased risk for preterm birth. Copper and colleagues, in a study of 2593 women assessed between 25 and 29 weeks' gestation, showed that maternal stress was significantly associated with spontaneous preterm birth.[59] What seems reasonably clear is that women who work hard physically for long hours and are under increased stress do have an increased risk of preterm birth.

Obstetric History

Obstetric history plays an important role in the occurrence of preterm labor. A history of a prior preterm delivery is one of the most significant risk factors. The recurrence risk of preterm birth in women with a prior history of preterm delivery ranges from 17% to 40% and appears to depend on the number of prior preterm deliveries. Carr-Hill and coworkers, in a study of 6572 Scottish women, demonstrated a threefold increased risk for preterm delivery in women with one prior preterm delivery (15%) as compared with women with no previous preterm delivery (5%)[46] (Table 16-3). For those women who had two previous preterm births, a sixfold (30%) increase in the risk for recurrent preterm delivery was noted. Mercer and associates reported on 1711 women who had a prior preterm delivery and noted a 2.5-fold increased risk of spontaneous preterm delivery with their next pregnancy.[246] Interestingly, the earlier the gestational age of the prior preterm delivery, the greater the risk for a subsequent spontaneous preterm delivery.

Prior second-trimester abortions, whether single or multiple, also increase the risk of preterm delivery. However, the picture is not as clear for prior first-trimester abortions, either spontaneous or induced. Several studies evaluating one first-trimester abortion reported no increased risk, and data regarding multiple first-trimester abortions are inconsistent.[52,212]

Cervical and Uterine Factors

Patients with congenital müllerian anomalies have a higher risk of preterm delivery.[153] Approximately 3% to 16% of all preterm births are associated with a uterine malformation. Heinonen and colleagues evaluated 126 patients with known uterine anomalies involving 256 pregnancies.[153] Overall, the incidence of preterm labor varied greatly depending on the type of uterine anomaly. Unicornuate, didelphic, and bicornuate abnormalities had preterm labor rates ranging from 18% to 80%, whereas the rates for a septate uterus varied from 4% to 17%, depending on whether the division was incomplete or complete.

Uterine leiomyomata have also been associated with an increased risk of preterm delivery because of an increased incidence of antepartum bleeding and preterm premature rupture of membranes (PPROM). Of the various types of myomata, submucosal and subplacental myomata appear to be most strongly associated with preterm delivery.[269]

Cervical incompetence is another important risk factor that can lead to preterm delivery. The classic clinical description of cervical incompetence included a history of painless cervical dilation occurring between 12 and 20 weeks that led to either preterm labor or PPROM. A history of a second-trimester pregnancy loss has been the cornerstone of the diagnosis of cervical incompetence. Various etiologic factors such as cone biopsies of the cervix and traumatic forceps deliveries have been identified as potential causes of cervical incompetence.

A significant factor associated with congenital causes of cervical incompetence is intrauterine exposure to diethylstilbestrol (DES). It has been estimated that between 1 and 1.5 million women were exposed in utero to DES between the late 1940s and 1971. These women have an increased risk of preterm delivery ranging from 15% to 28%, with an increased risk of spontaneous abortions of from 20% to 40%.[181,347] DES-exposed women with associated anomalies, such as T-shaped uterus, cervical incompetence, or vaginal structural anomalies, have a greater risk of preterm delivery than those who do not demonstrate changes. Because most women exposed to DES in utero are now over 35, this risk factor is now seen only rarely and is expected to disappear in the next few years.

Upper and lower genital tract structural abnormalities range from 33% to 66% in DES-exposed women.[180] Visible cervical and vaginal abnormalities occur in about 25% to 50% of these patients. These changes include transverse septa, cervical collars, hoods, cockscombs, abnormal mucus, and cervical incompetence.[347] The upper genital tract also has associated abnormalities, such as the T-shaped uterus, synechiae and diverticula, and structural alteration of the fallopian tubes.[181] DES-exposed women have an increased incidence of preterm labor and delivery in comparison with control subjects, and those with visible cervicovaginal abnormalities tend to have worse outcomes. Normal cervicovaginal anatomy in DES-exposed women does not rule out the possibility of cervical incompetence, as documented by Ludmir and coworkers.[215]

Trauma during various obstetric or gynecologic procedures can cause cervical incompetence. First-trimester dilation and curettage, if performed by an experienced operator with the preoperative use of laminaria, appears to confer minimal risk for subsequent cervical incompetence.[335] In contrast, cervical conization, performed for the diagnosis and treatment of cervical intraepithelial neoplasia by either cold knife, laser, or loop electrosurgical excision procedure, has been associated with cervical incompetence in subsequent pregnancies.[173] An extensive review of the literature by Harger showed a minimal role for these procedures in relation to cervical incompetence, with only the depth of the biopsy determining the subsequent risk.[144] Sadler and colleagues recently reported similar findings, noting that the risk for preterm birth and PPROM was directly related to the height of tissue removed from the cervix in conization.[326] Among women with the highest cone height (i.e., 1.7 cm), there was a greater than threefold increase

in the risk for PPROM compared with untreated women (adjusted odds ratio [OR], 3.6; 95% confidence interval [CI], 1.8-7.5).[326] Interestingly, these investigators noted that the risk of PPROM was significantly increased after treatment with laser conization and after loop electrosurgical excision procedures, but not after laser ablation.[326]

Distinguishing between cervical incompetence and preterm labor can at times be difficult. Several techniques have been used to diagnose cervical incompetence in nonpregnant women. These include passage of a No. 8 Hegar dilator with ease through the internal os, measurement of the pressure necessary to pull a Foley balloon catheter inflated with 1 mL of water through the internal os, and identification of an abnormal cervical canal and isthmic funnel angle by either hysterosalpingography or hysteroscopy. All these methods evaluate cervical incompetence in the nonpregnant state, making the results at best suggestive in relation to cervical function or to anatomy in the pregnant woman.[296]

Multi-Fetal Gestations

Multiple gestations carry one of the highest risks of preterm delivery. Approximately 50% of twin and nearly all of higher-multiple gestations end before 37 completed weeks. A British study reported that as the number of fetuses increases, the average duration of gestation decreases.[49] Whereas the average length of gestation for singleton pregnancies is 39 weeks, the average length of gestation is significantly shorter for twins (35 weeks), triplets (33 weeks), and quadruplets (29 weeks).[49] In a report evaluating the clinical predictors of preterm labor, multiple gestation resulted in a greater than 40-fold increase in the rate of preterm delivery as compared with control subjects with a singleton pregnancy.[152]

Bleeding

Vaginal bleeding caused by placenta previa or abruption is associated with almost as high a risk of preterm delivery as multiple gestation.[152] In a study by Heffner and colleagues, bleeding in the first or second trimester was associated with an increased risk of preterm delivery.[152] A retrospective study of 341 patients with PPROM documented a relative risk (RR) of 7.4 when antepartum bleeding occurred in more than one trimester.[146] Additionally, second-trimester bleeding, not associated with either placenta previa or abruption, has also been significantly associated with preterm birth. Ekwo and associates observed a strong association between bleeding in the second trimester and PPROM (RR, 15.1; 95% CI, 2.8-81) and preterm labor (RR, 19.7; 95% CI, 2.1-186).[86] The mechanism responsible for the development of preterm labor in the setting of vaginal bleeding appears to be related to thrombin deposition with subsequent production of prostaglandins and plasminogen activators that stimulate an array of degradative enzymes leading to destruction of the extracellular matrix.

Infection (See also Chapter 22.)

Infections of the decidua, fetal membranes, and amniotic fluid have been associated with preterm delivery[72,116,127,367] (see Fig. 16-1). Intra-amniotic infection, or chorioamnionitis, complicates 1% to 5% of term pregnancies and nearly 25% of patients with preterm delivery.[15] Heffner and colleagues demonstrated that clinical chorioamnionitis had a relative risk for preterm delivery of 48 over control subjects, representing the strongest correlation among all risk factors examined.[152] Romero and coworkers demonstrated that intraamniotic infection was present in 16.1% of 367 patients.[321] Most women initially did not manifest overt signs and symptoms of chorioamnionitis, but approximately 60% had clinical signs at some point during their pregnancies. Sixty-five percent of cases were refractory to tocolysis treatment versus 16% with negative culture results, and PPROM was more likely to occur (40% versus 3.8%).

There is a growing body of evidence establishing a strong link between occult upper genital tract infection and spontaneous preterm delivery.[105,321] Histologic chorioamnionitis has been strongly associated with prematurity and extremely low birthweight (1000 g or less).[136,157,268] Guzick and colleagues prospectively evaluated placentas from 2774 women with preterm delivery.[136] Histologic chorioamnionitis was more common in preterm than term deliveries (32.8% versus 10%). Among women with PPROM, 48.6% had histologic evidence of chorioamnionitis.

Watts and associates investigated a series of patients with preterm labor, demonstrating that positive amniotic fluid cultures were present in 19% of women with spontaneous preterm labor and intact membranes with no clinical evidence of intrauterine infection.[371] Additionally, the likelihood of a positive amniotic fluid culture in this investigation was inversely proportional to the gestational age.[371] An association between histologic chorioamnionitis and preterm delivery has also been established.[136,157,158,268] Hillier and colleagues evaluated placental microbiology and histology in women delivered prematurely as compared with those delivered at term.[157] Isolation of microorganisms from the chorioamnion of women who delivered preterm was strongly associated with histologic chorioamnionitis (OR, 7.2; 95% CI, 2.7-19.5).[157] Organisms that have been associated with histologic chorioamnionitis include *Ureaplasma, Mycoplasma, Gardnerella, Bacteroides,* and *Mobiluncus* species.[50,158,371] Further support for this hypothesis is derived from data linking the presence of pathogenic organisms in both the amniotic fluid and the chorioamnion with spontaneous labor in otherwise asymptomatic women with intact membranes.[50,148] Cassell and coworkers demonstrated the poor sensitivity of amniotic fluid cultures for identifying upper genital tract microbial colonization, noting that women were twice as likely to have microbial colonization of the chorioamnion than of the amniotic fluid.[50] Interestingly, an inverse relationship exists between colonization of the chorioamnion and amniotic fluid, and the gestational age at delivery in women with spontaneous preterm labor.[50,148] Chorioamnion colonization was associated with nearly 80% of the very early spontaneous preterm births. In contrast, microbial colonization of the upper genital tract appeared to play a much less important role in the initiation of parturition at or near term.[50,148]

Numerous theories exist regarding the underlying pathogenesis of intra-amniotic infection: (1) ascending infection from the vagina and cervix, (2) transplacental passage through hematogenous dissemination, (3) retrograde seeding from the peritoneal cavity through the fallopian tubes, and (4) iatrogenic means as a result of intrauterine procedures such as amniocentesis and chorionic villous sampling. There is some evidence to support each of these theories, but most of the evidence gives greatest credence to an ascending infection. Evidence from several sources supports this theory. Histologic chorioamnionitis is more common and severe at the site of membrane rupture than at other locations.[93] In cases of congenital pneumonia, inflammation of the chorioamniotic membrane is present, and the bacteria identified are similar to those found in the genital tract.[26]

The mechanism may start with excessive overgrowth of certain organisms within the vagina and cervical canal. These microorganisms gain access to the intrauterine cavity by infecting the decidua, the chorion, and finally the amnion, leading to the amniotic cavity itself. Therefore, bacteria are able to cross intact membranes. The fetus then becomes infected by aspirating or swallowing infected amniotic fluid or by direct contact, which may result in localized infection such as pneumonitis, otitis, or conjunctivitis. Seeding of these areas can lead, in turn, to generalized fetal sepsis. Sepsis may also result from maternal bacteremia, leading to a placental infection that is passed to the fetus through the umbilical cord.

Prostaglandins are believed to play a crucial role in the mechanism of both preterm and term labor. Stimulation of the production of these prostaglandins by intraamniotic infection may be mediated by bacterial endotoxins. Prostaglandins $PGF_{2\alpha}$ and PGE_2, as well as their metabolites, are in increased concentrations in patients with preterm labor and intraamniotic infection.[319] Bacterial products are sources of phospholipase A_2 and C and can stimulate prostaglandin production by the human amnion. Lipopolysaccharide, which is a known endotoxin in gram-negative organisms, is present in the amniotic fluid of patients with gram-negative infections and can stimulate the amnion and decidua to make prostaglandins.[315,317] However, the quantities of endotoxin required to stimulate prostaglandin production by the amnion are generally not found in the amniotic fluid of women with preterm labor and intra-amniotic infection. It is believed that these endotoxins stimulate the production of various cytokines by the host, which in turn stimulate prostaglandin production.

There is an increased presence of PGE_2 and $PGF_{2\alpha}$ in the amniotic fluid of women with intra-amniotic infection and PPROM.[316] Amniotic fluid concentrations of endotoxins are higher in women with preterm labor and PPROM than in those without labor and PPROM.[318] That 28% of patients with PPROM have positive results on amniotic fluid cultures without labor suggests that it takes more than the presence of bacteria to stimulate prostaglandin production and labor.

Various organisms have been implicated as causal agents for preterm labor and PPROM. Asymptomatic bacteruria occurs in 2% to 10% of all pregnant women, and 30% to 50% of these will have pyelonephritis if left untreated.[176] In a meta-analysis by Romero and colleagues, asymptomatic bacteruria carried a higher relative risk of subsequent premature birth than was found in control subjects (OR, 1.9).[320] Treatment of these patients lowered the risk of prematurity.

Neisseria gonorrhoeae infection is associated with prematurity. Preterm delivery was more common in those patients with positive culture results (25.2% versus 12.5%). PROM, defined here as membrane rupture anytime before labor, was higher in the positive culture group than in control subjects (26% versus 19%).

Group B streptococcus (GBS) plays a major role in neonatal morbidity and death, especially in premature infants. Reporting on genital colonization, Regan and colleagues cultured cervical specimens from 6706 pregnant women on admission to the hospital and found a prevalence of 13.4%.[308] The incidence of preterm delivery, at less than 32 weeks of gestation, was higher in colonized than noncolonized women (5.4% versus 1.26%). PROM, defined here as rupture 1 hour before the onset of contractions, was also greater in the colonized group (15.3% versus 7%). Bobitt and coworkers obtained vaginal cultures monthly beginning at 24 weeks of gestation and at the time of admission. Positive culture results were obtained in 11.3% of the patients.[35] A higher incidence of low birthweight was noted in the colonized than the noncolonized group (8.4% versus 3.4%), and the incidence of PROM was higher (5.6% versus 1.7%). Moller and colleagues collected urine culture specimens between 12 and 38 weeks of gestation and reported an overall positive culture incidence (regardless of the colony count) of 2.5%.[256$] Prematurity was more frequent in the positive culture group (20% versus 8.5%), as was PROM (35% versus 15%).

In a randomized, controlled, double-blind trial of women with a urine culture positive for GBS treated with antibiotics, Thomsen and associates reported that the treated group had a lower incidence of premature delivery than the nontreated group (5.4% versus 37.5%, respectively).[352] The occurrence of PROM was statistically significant between the two groups (53% versus 11%). These studies demonstrate that asymptomatic bacteruria with GBS is a risk factor for preterm delivery and that eradication with antibiotics decreases the risk. However, no study to date has shown that treatment of GBS genital tract colonization decreases the risk of PROM. In the Thomsen study, all patients with urinary colonization also had positive results on cervical and vaginal cultures, possibly indicating that the presence of GBS in the urine may be a marker of more severe forms of genital tract colonization.[352]

In 1996, the Centers for Disease Control and Prevention (CDC), in conjunction the American College of Obstetricians and Gynecologists and the American Academy of Pediatrics, set forth recommendations for obstetric providers to adopt either a culture-based or a risk-based approach for the prevention of GBS disease.[51] For the culture-based strategy, intrapartum antibiotic prophylaxis was offered to women identified as GBS carriers through prenatal screening cultures collected at 35 to 37 weeks' gestation and to women who developed premature onset of labor or rupture of membranes prior to 37 weeks' gestation. For the risk-based approach, which does not use cultures, intrapartum antibiotic prophylaxis is provided to women who, at the time of labor or membrane rupture, develop one or more of the following risk conditions: (1) preterm labor at less than 37 weeks' gestation, (2) preterm premature rupture of membranes at less than 37 weeks, (3) membranes ruptured for 18 hours or longer, or (4) maternal fever of 38.0°C or higher.

In 2002, after a population-based comparison of the culture-based and risk-based strategies revealed a significantly lower incidence of early-onset GBS disease among women cared for using the culture-based approach, the CDC revised the recommendations to adopt the culture-based approach for the prevention of early-onset neonatal GBS infection.[333,334] These guideline changes have subsequently been supported by the American College of Obstetricians and Gynecologists.

For women who are culture positive for GBS, intrapartum chemoprophylaxis with intravenous penicillin G (5 million units initially and then 2.5 million units every 4 hours) is recommended until delivery. Intravenous ampicillin (2 g initially, and then 1 g every 4 hours until delivery) is an acceptable alternative to penicillin G. Because of emerging resistance of GBS to macrolides, the new guidelines have been modified for women who are allergic to penicillin.[333] In penicillin-allergic women who are not at high risk for anaphylaxis, intravenous cefazolin (2 g initially, and then 1 g every 8 hours until delivery) is recommended. In penicillin-allergic women who are at high risk for anaphylaxis, clindamycin and erythromycin susceptibility testing of the GBS isolate is recommended. If the isolate is sensitive to clindamycin or erythromycin, intravenous treatment with the appropriate agent is recommended (clindamycin at 900 mg every 8 hours until delivery, or erythromycin at 500 mg every 6 hours until delivery).[333] If the GBS isolate is resistant to either agent or susceptibility is unknown, treatment with intravenous vancomycin (1 g every 12 hours until delivery) is recommended. Although these guidelines have been shown to decrease the incidence of early-onset GBS sepsis, the overall rate of early-onset neonatal sepsis caused by *Escherichia coli* has increased.[348]

Another infection reported to be associated with prematurity is *Chlamydia trachomatis*. Harrison and colleagues noted an 8% incidence of positive cultures indicating infection with *C. trachomatis* among 1365 women screened.[147] Although no differences were documented in the prematurity rate, premature rupture of membranes, both term and preterm, was more common in women with positive immunoglobulin M (IgM) titers than in those with none (41.1% versus 7.5%). Gravett and coworkers showed that a positive culture result had a significant association with preterm delivery before 34 and 37 weeks, with ORs of 4.0 and 4.7, respectively.[126] A chlamydial infection also had an elevated OR (2.7) for PPROM. Similarly, Andrews and colleagues reported that patients with chlamydia noted during pregnancy have an OR of 2.0 for spontaneous preterm birth.[12] These studies demonstrate a correlation between *C. trachomatis* infection and prematurity, especially when PPROM is the event leading to preterm birth.

Bacterial vaginosis is a common lower genital tract infection found in approximately 20% to 40% of African-American women and 10% to 15% of white women.[109] Bacterial vaginosis is a clinical syndrome characterized by a decrease in the normal vaginal lactobacilli-dominant microflora resulting in a predominance of bacteria such as *Gardnerella vaginalis, Prevotella, Bacteroides, Peptostreptococcus, Mobiluncus, Mycoplasma hominis,* and *Ureaplasma urealyticum.*[156] Characteristically, patients with symptomatic bacterial vaginosis complain of a watery, homogenous grayish discharge with a fishy amine odor.

Bacterial vaginosis has been associated with increased risk for preterm labor or delivery.[126,160,195,235] Gravett and associates showed in 1986 a relative risk of 2.7 and 2.0 for PPROM and preterm delivery, respectively, at less than 37 weeks.[126] Now, there are more than 15 studies showing an association between bacterial vaginosis and spontaneous preterm birth. Nearly 40% of early spontaneous preterm births, especially among African-American women, may be attributable to bacterial vaginosis.[97] Bacterial vaginosis seems to be associated more with early preterm birth than with late preterm birth. Additionally, two randomized clinical trials have demonstrated that treating bacterial vaginosis in patients who are at high risk for preterm delivery resulted in substantial reductions in the preterm birth rates.[149,260] An important point is that, on the basis of data now available, treatment of bacterial vaginosis appears to be effective in preventing preterm birth only in high-risk populations. Data from a study of low-risk women with bacterial vaginosis in Australia and from a National Institute of Child Health and Human Development Maternal-Fetal Medicine Units (NICHD MFMU) Network study in the United States, evaluating and treating asymptomatic women with bacterial vaginosis, failed to demonstrate a reduction in preterm delivery.[42,236]

The majority of women with bacterial vaginosis never manifest any signs or adverse outcomes related to the colonization, and it is likely that bacterial vaginosis is only a surrogate marker for a more important, presently unrecognized condition that may be the cause of the preterm birth. One compelling theory is that bacterial vaginosis is a marker for occult upper genital tract infection.[141,157,192,194] Therefore, premature births, attributed to bacterial vaginosis or prevented by its treatment, may instead be related to an associated upper genital tract infection.

Many other maternal infections/colonizations have been reported to be associated with preterm birth.[29,111,126,200,230] One of the difficult questions to answer is whether these relationships are causal or merely associations. Gonorrhea, chlamydia, *Trichomonas,* syphilis, and other genital pathogens are more frequently found in women who have a spontaneous preterm birth. However, the women affected by these infections often have other risk factors for preterm birth (e.g., low socioeconomic status, malnutrition, smoking, substance abuse, bacterial vaginosis). These confounding variables make it difficult to establish causality, as most studies have not controlled for them. In general, gonorrhea and chlamydia have been associated with a twofold increased risk for preterm delivery.[350] Similarly, trichomoniasis appears to be associated with a 1.3-fold increased risk for preterm delivery.[60] GBS has been associated with prematurity in some studies, but the majority of studies demonstrate no association.[256,308,352] Many of the other sexually transmitted diseases, such as human immunodeficiency virus, hepatitis B, and genital herpes simplex virus, have been associated with an increased risk for spontaneous preterm birth in some, but not most, studies. Syphilis is widely reported to be associated with a twofold increased risk of preterm birth, and this relationship is relatively consistent among most studies.

Other Risk Factors

A variety of other factors have been associated with an increased risk for preterm labor (see Box 16-1). Extremes in the volume of amniotic fluid, such as hydramnios or oligohydramnios, have been associated with an increased risk for preterm labor. Similarly, fetal anomalies, especially those involving multiple organ systems and central nervous system abnormalities, carry a higher risk. Maternal abdominal surgery in the late second and third trimester causes an increase in uterine activity leading to preterm delivery.[162] Maternal medical conditions, such as gestational or preexisting diabetes and hypertension (essential or pregnancy induced), are associated with a higher rate of preterm delivery; however, these preterm births are often intentional preterm deliveries because of maternal complications rather than the result of spontaneous preterm labor.[152] Asymptomatic bacteriuria is associated with an increased rate of prematurity.[320] Systemic infections, such as bacterial pneumonia, pyelonephritis and acute appendicitis, often lead to increased uterine activity, potentially leading to premature delivery.

PREDICTING PRETERM LABOR

The ultimate goal is to reduce the incidence of preterm labor and delivery. Achievement of this goal has been complicated by the fact that preterm deliveries often have multiple causes. Deliveries indicated for maternal or fetal reasons account for approximately 20% to 25% of preterm births. PPROM is associated with another 25% to 40%, and under these conditions prevention with tocolysis is generally contraindicated. Of the remaining 40% to 50% of idiopathic cases, nearly half occur beyond 34 weeks, when the use of tocolysis would be of questionable benefit. Consequently, only about 15% to 20% of patients in preterm labor are candidates for treatment.[361] This frustrating statistic has led to various attempts to identify risk factors that may predict preterm labor. Three main areas are explored in the following paragraphs: classic predictors, biochemical predictors, and ultrasound predictors.

Classic Predictors

Cervical change is the first of the classic clinical predictors. In one of the largest studies to date, Papiernik and colleagues evaluated 8303 pregnancies followed with weekly cervical examinations, to determine whether precocious cervical change was associated with preterm birth.[295] These investigators noted that, regardless of gestational age at delivery, cervical changes occurred approximately 3 to 4 weeks before delivery. After controlling for other risk factors in their study, they found that cervical dilation of more than 1 cm carried a twofold to threefold increased relative risk for preterm delivery. Unfortunately, no sensitivity or positive predictive value was reported, although the authors claimed a reduction, from about 7% to 5%, in the preterm birth rate during an 8-year period using this screening strategy.

Mortensen and coworkers evaluated cervical changes in 1300 pregnancies with examinations performed at 24, 28, and 32 weeks.[264] The population was divided into high- and low-risk groups on the basis of various factors. Cervical changes in the low-risk group were extremely poor predictors of preterm delivery, with a positive predictive value of 4%. In the high-risk group, however, the predictive value was 25% to 30%, with a sensitivity of 65%.[264]

Another potentially important clinical factor is the presence of uterine contractions. In a study involving approximately 2500 patients, in which multiple gestations, vaginal bleeding, PPROM, and hydramnios were excluded, Nageotte and colleagues evaluated uterine activity differences in patients with preterm, term, and post-term deliveries.[273] The authors demonstrated an increase in uterine activity beginning 6 weeks before delivery, regardless of gestational age at birth, and a surge in uterine activity that occurred within 72 hours of delivery in all three groups.[273] These patients, however, depended on tocodynamometry to determine this increase in frequency. When patients are instructed to self-detect an increase in uterine activity, they can identify only 15% of the contractions noted by tocodynamometry.[279] In another study, using contractions as a screening tool, Main and associates evaluated intermittent uterine monitoring in an office setting.[224] One hundred thirty-nine patients were screened for 1 hour on at least three occasions between 28 and 32 weeks of gestation; six contractions per hour during at least one occasion was used as a minimum. The test had a sensitivity of 75% and a positive predictive value

of 32%.[224] The preterm delivery rate was 11.5%, higher than would be expected. Copper and colleagues evaluated the use of tocodynamometry and cervical examination at 28 weeks' gestation in 589 nulliparous women to determine whether patients at risk for preterm delivery could be identified.[58] These investigators noted that the best predictors of spontaneous preterm birth were the presence of a soft or medium-consistency cervix and two or more contractions in 30 minutes. The risk for spontaneous preterm delivery increased from 4.2% for those patients with no contractions detected, to 18.2% for those patients having four or more contractions in 30 minutes.

Other studies have also found that although an association was noted between the reported presence of contractions and preterm delivery, monitoring contractions was not clinically useful in defining a population at especially high risk for spontaneous preterm birth.[171] Uterine activity does appear to play a role in preterm delivery, but the use of home uterine monitoring as a screening tool in most, if not all, populations is not justified because of the difficulty of identifying patients at risk and because of cost.

Beginning in the early 1980s, attempts were made to combine these various factors into a risk scoring system to determine which patients were at jeopardy for preterm delivery. Creasy and coworkers combined socioeconomic factors such as age, height, weight, previous medical history, smoking, work habits, and aspects of the current pregnancy into a risk scoring system.[63] A total of 10 points or more indicated a high risk of preterm delivery (Table 16-4). The initial study held promise, with a positive predictive value of 38%. Subsequent studies of various populations, however, had much lower positive predictive values, in the range of 18% to 22%.[223,267,290] One of the problems with the Creasy risk scoring system is the emphasis placed on a previous preterm delivery, which by itself elevates a patient into a high-risk category. Unfortunately, 50% of preterm deliveries happen in primigravidas, whose obstetric histories lower the predictive value even further. Overall, classic predictors have had limited success in predicting preterm delivery, and no well-performed study has demonstrated a reduction in preterm birth with their use.

Biochemical Predictors

The biochemical process leading to the initiation of either term or preterm labor has not been well established in human studies. Recently, however, important insights into the pathophysiology of spontaneous preterm labor have helped to identify various biochemical markers that may predict preterm delivery[119] (see Fig. 16-1).

Perhaps one of the most important and powerful biochemical markers identified to date is fetal fibronectin.[303] This glycoprotein, found in the extracellular matrix surrounding the extravillous trophoblast at the uteroplacental junction, is a prototypic example of a marker of choriodecidual disruption.[95] Typically, fetal fibronectin

TABLE 16-4. System* for Determining Risk of Spontaneous Preterm Delivery

POINTS ASSIGNED	SOCIOECONOMIC FACTORS	MEDICAL HISTORY	DAILY HABITS	ASPECTS OF CURRENT PREGNANCY
1	Two children at home Low socioeconomic status	Abortion (×1) Less than 1 yr since last birth	Works outside home	Unusual fatigue
2	Maternal age <20 yr or >40 yr Single parent	Abortions (×2)	Smokes >10 cigarettes per day	Gain of <5 kg by 32 wk
3	Very low socioeconomic status Height <150 cm Weight <45 kg	Abortions (×3)	Heavy work or stressful work that is long and tiring	Breech at 32 wk Weight loss of 2 kg Head engaged at 32 wk Febrile illness
4	Maternal age <18 yr	Pyelonephritis		Bleeding after 12 wk Effacement Dilation Uterine irritability
5		Uterine anomaly Second-trimester abortion Diethylstilbestrol exposure Cone biopsy		Placenta previa Hydramnios
10		Preterm delivery Repeated second-trimester abortion		Twins Abdominal surgical procedure

*Score is obtained by adding the number of points earned by all items that apply. The score is computed at the first visit and again at 22 to 26 weeks' gestation. A total score of greater than 10 places the patient at high risk for spontaneous preterm delivery.
Modified from Creasy RK et al: System for predicting spontaneous preterm birth. Obstet Gynecol 55:692, 1980.

is absent from cervicovaginal secretions from around the 20th week of gestation until near term. Detection of elevated cervicovaginal levels of fetal fibronectin has been shown to be strongly associated with an increased risk for preterm delivery in patients at high risk for preterm delivery.[109,110,169,213,298] Lockwood and colleagues examined the concentrations of fetal fibronectin in amniotic fluid, cervical and vaginal secretions, and maternal serum from 163 uncomplicated pregnancies with delivery at term.[213] Fetal fibronectin was detected in only 4% of cervical and 3% of vaginal secretions between 21 and 37 weeks. In 65 patients with PPROM, 93% had fetal fibronectin in amniotic fluid and in vaginal or cervical secretions. In the preterm labor group, the presence of fetal fibronectin had a sensitivity of 81% and a specificity of 82% in predicting preterm labor.[213] Three subsequent studies, by various authors, of women with symptoms[263] and of symptom-free women[214,273] have reported sensitivities in the 80% to 90% range and positive predictive values of 30% to 60%.

Goldenberg and associates demonstrated that detection of elevated cervicovaginal fetal fibronectin levels (greater than 50 ng/mL) at 24 weeks' gestation in asymptomatic women was strongly associated with subsequent spontaneous preterm delivery, with ORs of 59.2 (95% CI, 35.9-97.8) for preterm delivery before 28 weeks' gestation, 39.9 (95% CI, 25.6-62.1) for preterm delivery less than 30 weeks' gestation, and 21.2 (95% CI, 14.3-62.1) for preterm delivery less than 32 weeks' gestation.[110] Additionally, fetal fibronectin levels have been correlated with cervical length, bacterial vaginosis, IL-6, and peripartum infection.[107,109] These data clearly suggest that fetal fibronectin is one of the most potent markers for spontaneous preterm delivery identified to date. It is clear that infection of the upper genital tract with disruption of the choriodecidual interface is a feature common to many cases of preterm birth.

Measurement of estriol has recently been promoted as a potential biochemical marker that may be of use in predicting preterm delivery.[303] Estriol is a unique hormone of pregnancy produced almost entirely by the trophoblast from precursors derived from the fetal adrenal gland and liver. Initial investigations with urinary and plasma estriol attempted to use this assay as a measure of fetal well-being in utero.[21,22] Subsequent investigations, however, have failed to demonstrate a significant difference in perinatal outcome based on estriol-based management.[76,82]

Levels of estriol have been shown to rise throughout pregnancy, with a characteristic exponential increase 2 to 4 weeks prior to the spontaneous onset of labor at term.[74,238] Interestingly, patients induced at term in the absence of spontaneous labor fail to demonstrate this increase in estriol.[261] The use of salivary estriol levels to identify patients at risk for preterm delivery has been assessed.[75,240] These studies have suggested that detection of an early estriol surge may identify those patients at risk for preterm labor and delivery. Estriol appears to be a better marker for late, rather than early, spontaneous preterm birth, so the clinical utility of this biochemical marker is unclear. As with many of the other markers, no reduction in the preterm birth rate has been demonstrated with its use.

A variety of other serologic, cervical, and amniotic fluid markers have been evaluated as predictors for preterm delivery including alpha-fetoprotein, human chorionic gonadotropin, human placental lactogen, corticotropin-releasing factor, C-reactive protein, alkaline phosphatase, ferritin, placental isoferritin, progesterone, estradiol, matrix metalloproteinase, IL-6, TNFα, and granulocyte colony-stimulating factor.[100,112,114,115,302] Each of these markers has been shown to have modest correlation with spontaneous preterm delivery.

Progesterone and estradiol are potentially interesting markers, based on the theory that progesterone withdrawal may be the initiating event. An early study noted a fall in progesterone levels before the onset of term labor and abortion.[362] Subsequent investigations have measured total or free progesterone, estradiol, or the estradiol-to-progesterone ratio during term or preterm labor.[10,142] One prospective study examined both progesterone and estradiol concentrations weekly and found no correlation.[33]

Corticotropin-releasing hormone (CRH) is a placental peptide produced during the second and third trimesters. It may play a role in the initiation of parturition, and it is elevated weeks before the onset of preterm labor.[309,370,374] Wolfe and colleagues prospectively assessed 168 patients after measuring serial plasma CRH levels at 24 weeks' gestation and found that the CRH levels rose at a 25% faster rate in the preterm than the term labor group, although these results did not achieve statistical significance.[374] Tropper and coworkers demonstrated that CRH levels are significantly higher in maternal serum and umbilical cord serum in patients who delivered preterm than in controls matched for gestational age who delivered at term.[359] Berkowitz and colleagues, however, observed that CRH levels were not predictive of preterm birth or PPROM.[28] They noted, however, that CRH binding protein levels decreased at near term, suggesting that the bioavailability of CRH may increase coincident with the onset of parturition. Leung and associates furthered these observations through an evaluation of 1047 low-risk women between 15 and 20 weeks' gestation.[207] Elevated mid-trimester serum CRH levels were significantly associated with preterm delivery before 34 weeks' gestation. Using an arbitrary cutoff of 1.9 multiples of the median to predict preterm birth, elevated CRH had a sensitivity of 72.9%, a specificity of 78.4%, and a positive predictive value of 3.6% and negative predictive value of 99.6%. The use of CRH as a marker for preterm delivery holds promise, as results are elevated not only in preterm labor but also with PPROM and intrauterine infection.[81]

A variety of degradative enzymes have been characterized in relationship to the prediction of women at risk for preterm delivery. Serum collagenases are one group of these potential markers. IL-1 stimulates cervical, decidual, and other cells to produce various collagenases, resulting in breakdown of the collagen matrix of the cervix. Rajabi and colleagues measured serum levels of collagenase at various gestational ages.[300] They found that the levels remained relatively constant until the onset of labor, when an increase of 66% occurred over that of control values. In preterm deliveries, this rise was eightfold greater than control values.

In addition to the collagenases, the metalloproteinases and their inhibitors have received increasing interest in relationship to preterm labor. In particular, metalloproteinase-2 (MMP-2), MMP-9, and MMP-8 have been associated with preterm labor, especially PPROM.[16,99] Fortunato and coworkers demonstrated that elevated amniotic fluid levels of MMP-2 and MMP-9 were associated with PROM, suggesting that the metalloproteinases may play a role in degradation of the chorioamnion basement membrane, resulting in membrane weakening and rupture.[99] Athayde and colleagues further explored the association of amniotic fluid MMP-9 levels and preterm delivery, noting that MMP-9 levels were increased in patients who had preterm labor and who delivered prematurely as compared with patients with preterm contractions who delivered at term and with a control group without complications.[16] Tu and associates evaluated plasma MMP-9 levels to determine whether they predict subsequent spontaneous preterm birth.[360] Serum MMP-9 levels appeared to remain unchanged throughout pregnancy until the spontaneous onset of labor, at which time MMP-9 levels significantly increased. MMP-9 levels, however, did not increase prior to the onset of labor. Although MMP-9 levels may be a useful marker for true labor, elevated levels do not seem to be useful in predicting which patients may be at risk for developing preterm labor.

Cervical granulocyte elastase activity has also been the subject of several studies.[174,175] Granulocytes are stimulated by IL-8, which is elevated in amniotic fluid of labor patients. Granulocyte elastase is one specific granulocyte degradative enzyme that may play a role in parturition. This elastase activity is increased in both term and preterm labor, which suggests that it may be involved in cervical ripening and in degradation of fetal membranes, leading to PPROM.[174,175]

Given the association of occult upper genital tract infection with early spontaneous preterm birth, a variety of serum, amniotic fluid, and cervicovaginal inflammatory markers have also been evaluated as potential markers for the prediction of spontaneous preterm delivery. Both serum and cervical IL-6 levels have been found to be significantly elevated at 24 weeks' gestation in women with subsequent spontaneous preterm birth at less than 35 weeks' gestation.[107,271] Elevated cervical IL-6 levels are also strongly associated with elevated fetal fibronectin levels.[107] Rizzo and colleagues characterized cervical and amniotic fluid levels of several inflammatory cytokines (IL-1, IL-6, TNFα) in a series of patients with preterm labor and intact membranes.[313]

receiving only standard antenatal care without monitoring. In a study by Iams and colleagues, no difference was demonstrated between the monitored and unmonitored groups.[167] A study by Dyson and coworkers concluded that daily nursing support was more effective than home monitoring, although only in a twin subgroup.[84] A critical review of these data by McClean and colleagues suggested that this conclusion may be invalid because the same nursing team was involved in both groups.[233] One of the largest studies was conducted by Dyson and associates.[85] These investigators enrolled 2422 high-risk women, including 844 with twins, into a three-armed trial to receive weekly contact with a nurse, daily contact with a nurse, or daily contact with a nurse and a uterine contraction monitor. No significant differences were noted among the three treatment arms with respect to the rate of preterm delivery before 35 weeks, mean cervical dilation at the time of preterm labor diagnosis, or neonatal outcome. The women who received daily nurse contact and monitoring had more visits and were more frequently treated with prophylactic medications than the women who were contacted only once a week.

Although some of the earlier and smaller trials with home uterine activity monitoring demonstrated a significant decrease in preterm births among enrolled subjects,[178,262] subsequent studies have not.[34,55,84,85] Hence, it appears that home uterine activity monitoring is of no benefit in reducing the frequency of preterm birth.

TREATMENT

One of the main problems encountered when deciding on the optimal therapeutic intervention to prevent preterm delivery is the ability to accurately distinguish between preterm labor and preterm contractions. Traditionally, this distinction is made by the combination of persistent uterine contractions with change in the dilation or effacement of the cervix by digital examination. Another dilemma is in regard to the aggressiveness with which we desire to treat preterm labor. Clearly, gestational age plays an important role in this decision. Before 32 weeks' gestation, an aggressive approach seems reasonable because of the neonatal consequences of early preterm birth. However, beyond this gestational age, when neonatal morbidity and mortality rates approach those of term infants, maternal treatment becomes more controversial. Many of the therapies that will be discussed in this section have the potential for significant maternal and fetal side effects, and the risks of these adverse events may outweigh the benefits of treatment.

The therapeutic interventions implemented in the setting of preterm labor have the following purposes: (1) to prevent premature onset of contractions and labor, (2) to control contractions when they do occur and delay the time from onset of contractions to the actual time of delivery, and (3) to optimize fetal status and maturation prior to preterm delivery. In these

paragraphs, we will review many of the contemporary obstetric therapeutic strategies proposed to achieve the above goals.[118] As our clinical strategies have evolved with time, some therapies have been relinquished to the history books (e.g., ethanol tocolysis) and will not be discussed here.

Bed Rest

Bed rest represents one of the most common interventions implemented for the prevention or treatment of threatened preterm labor. Despite the common use of this recommendation, limited data exist that demonstrate significant benefit. Goldenberg and colleagues reviewed the use of bed rest for the treatment of a variety of pregnancy complications.[108] Although bed rest is prescribed for over 20% of pregnancies for a wide range of conditions, there is little evidence of effectiveness. Unfortunately, there are not conclusive, well-performed, prospective, randomized studies that have independently evaluated the potential effects for the treatment or prevention of preterm labor in singletons. No benefit to reducing preterm birth was found when bed rest was used for twin gestations.

Hydration or Sedation

One of the mainstays in the initial treatment of preterm labor is the use of oral or intravenous hydration to differentiate true preterm labor from preterm contractions before cervical change. Several theories suggest why hydration may be effective in treating preterm contractions. Hydration inhibits the release of antidiuretic hormone through the Henry-Gauer reflex. This reflex, however, has been demonstrated only in animals.[32] The second theory is based on the fact that patients with preterm labor may have hypovolemia, with plasma volumes below normal. Significant delays in delivery have been reported to occur in patients with preterm contractions whose plasma volumes are expanded with albumin.[122] Few studies have evaluated the use of hydration in a prospective manner. Pircon and coworkers conducted a prospective randomized study of 48 women with preterm contractions.[299] Twenty-eight women were randomly assigned to a hydration and bed rest group and the remaining 20 women to a control bed-rest-alone group. No differences were found in the percentage of patients whose contractions stopped with hydration and bed rest as compared with bed rest alone. In addition, patients whose contractions were stopped by either treatment remained at an increased risk of preterm delivery.[299] Guinn and colleagues reported similar findings in a prospective randomized study of 179 women with preterm contractions.[133] Patients in this investigation were randomized to observation alone, to intravenous hydration, or to a single dose of subcutaneous terbutaline. No significant differences were noted between the three groups with regard to mean days to delivery or the incidence of preterm delivery; hence, intravenous hydration appears to offer no clinical benefit.

In addition to hydration, sedation is a strategy commonly used to differentiate between true preterm labor and preterm contractions. As is true for hydration, there are limited data documenting the efficacy of sedation in this clinical setting. Helfgott and associates performed a prospective comparative study of 119 women with preterm labor who were randomly assigned to treatment with hydration and sedation or to the control treatment of bed rest alone.[154] Women in the hydration and sedation group received 500 mL of lactated Ringer's solution intravenously over 30 minutes and 8 to 12 mg of intramuscular morphine sulfate. The results from this investigation demonstrated no significant difference between hydration and sedation, and bed rest alone with regard to contraction cessation and preterm delivery.

Overall, the literature does not support the use of hydration or sedation in the initial treatment of preterm labor. In many cases, initial hydration with intravenous infusion of fluid occurs before the start of intravenous infusion of a tocolytic agent. Rehydration with a large fluid bolus may increase the risk of fluid overload and subsequent development of pulmonary edema when used in the setting of tocolytic therapy, especially with beta-sympathomimetic agents.

Progesterone

Based on the progesterone withdrawal hypothesis of parturition initiation, interest has been shown in the potential use of progesterone or similar other progestins for the treatment or prevention of preterm labor and delivery. Although progesterone or 6α-methyl-17α-hydroxyprogesterone (medroxyprogesterone) has been shown to have no beneficial inhibiting effect on acute preterm labor,[102,289] a meta-analysis of six randomized controlled trials of 17α-hydroxyprogesterone caproate to prevent preterm labor and delivery revealed a significant decrease in preterm birth (OR, 0.5; 95% CI, 0.3-0.85).[182]

Recently, the results of two randomized controlled trials have confirmed the efficacy of progesterone therapy for the prevention of preterm birth.[72,243] Da Fonseca and colleagues reported findings of a trial designed to evaluate the efficacy of progesterone vaginal suppositories for the prevention of preterm birth.[72] In this double-blind, placebo-controlled trial of 142 high-risk pregnancies, a significant reduction in the rate of preterm births at less than 37 weeks was noted among those women treated with weekly progesterone (13.8%) when compared with the placebo group (28.5%; P < .05). Preterm birth at less than 34 weeks was also significantly lower in the progesterone group (2.7%) when compared with the placebo group (18.5%; P < .05). Meis and colleagues from the NICHD MFMU Network reported similar results from a large randomized clinical trial designed to evaluate the efficacy of 17α-hydroxyprogesterone caproate for the prevention of preterm birth in high-risk women.[243] Among women receiving weekly intramuscular progesterone therapy from 16 to 36 weeks' gestation, the incidence of preterm birth at less than 37 weeks' gestation was 36.3%, compared with an incidence of 54.9% in the placebo-treatment group (RR, 0.66; 95% CI, 0.54-0.81). The incidence of preterm birth at less than 35 weeks (RR, 0.67; 95% CI, 0.48-0.93) and at less than 32 weeks (RR, 0.58; 95% CI, 0.37-0.91) was also significantly less among women treated with progesterone when compared with placebo. Although progesterone therapy is efficacious to prevent preterm birth in women at high risk for recurrent preterm birth, the mechanisms by which progesterone attenuates a woman's risk for subsequent preterm birth are largely unknown.

Cerclage

Use of cerclage is generally limited to patients with a history consistent with an incompetent cervix. A cerclage is basically a suture placed circumferentially around internal cervical os, which acts to strengthen the cervix. The cerclage can be placed either vaginally (McDonald cerclage, Shirodkar cerclage) or abdominally, depending on the cervical anatomy and obstetric history. The timing of cerclage placement is important. Elective placement has a much higher success rate and a much lower complication rate than when cerclage is attempted after cervical changes have begun to occur.[38] Generally, the optimal time for placement of a cerclage is early in the second trimester (12 to 14 weeks). By 12 weeks, the risk of spontaneous miscarriage in the first trimester is reduced and major anatomic fetal abnormalities, such as anencephaly, can be detected by ultrasound prior to cerclage placement. In patients at high risk of aneuploidy or metabolic abnormalities, chorionic villus sampling can be performed before cerclage placement. There is no consensus as to the upper limit of gestational age beyond which cerclage placement is contraindicated; however, with fetal viability beginning around the 24th week of gestation, the risk of complications related to cerclage placement may outweigh the potential benefit after this time in pregnancy.

Initial studies evaluating the efficacy of a cerclage for treatment of incompetent cervix claimed success rates of 75% to 90%.[124] The primary limitation of these early studies was that the women involved served as their own control subjects, comparing this pregnancy outcome with those of previous pregnancies. This is an important confounding variable, in that there are data to support the occurrence of a successful pregnancy after repeated mid-trimester losses.[145] Subsequently, several randomized control studies have attempted to evaluate the efficacy of cerclage in patients without a classic history of cervical incompetence. Dor and coworkers examined twin pregnancies in which 50 patients were randomly assigned to cerclage or no cerclage.[77] No statistical difference was found in gestational age at delivery or incidence of PPROM. Rush and colleagues[325] and Lazar and associates,[203] using similar study designs, evaluated 700 patients and found no statistical difference in gestational age at delivery or perinatal mortality rate between the cerclage and the control groups. In both reports, there was a higher incidence of hospitalization and treatment with tocolytic agents for patients in the cerclage group. In a meta-analysis of all three studies, Grant again showed no statistically significant differences in outcomes between the cerclage and control groups.[124] There was, however, a nonsignificant increase in preterm delivery noted in the cerclage placement group.

In one of the largest studies to date, conducted by the Royal College of Obstetricians and Gynaecologists, 1292 patients with histories of early deliveries or prior cervical surgery were randomly assigned to cerclage or no cerclage.[125] Significantly fewer deliveries occurred at less than 33 weeks in the cerclage group (13% versus 17%). There was, however, a higher incidence of puerperal pyrexia in the cerclage group.[125] Limitations of all of these studies include the ill-defined subjective enrollment criteria and the lack of statistical power to adequately address neonatal morbidity outcomes.

The advent of transvaginal cervical sonography has introduced a tool by which a woman's cervix length can be objectively assessed as a marker of risk for a subsequent preterm birth. Several prospective studies have recently been conducted using cervical length assessment and cerclage for the prevention of preterm birth.[5,23,130,355] Althuisius and colleagues reported findings from a small randomized trial comparing the efficacy of therapeutic cerclage plus bed rest to bed rest alone for the prevention of subsequent preterm birth in women with an ultrasonographically determined short cervix (less than 25 mm) prior to 27 weeks' gestation.[5] Use of cerclage in this study was associated with a significant reduction in the incidence of preterm birth at less than 34 weeks when compared with women treated with bed rest alone (0% versus 44%; $P = .002$).[5] In contrast to these findings, To and colleagues, in a large multicenter, randomized trial of cervical cerclage for women with an ultrasound-detected short cervix (less than 15 mm) at between 22 and 24 weeks' gestation, reported that the use of prophylactic Shirodkar cerclage did not significantly reduce the incidence of preterm birth at less than 33 weeks' gestation when compared with expectant management (22% versus 26%; $P = .44$).[355] A recent meta-analysis by Belej-Rak and colleagues evaluated the literature relating to the effectiveness of cervical cerclage for a sonographically detected shortened cervix.[23] Based on this systematic analysis of the six pertinent trials, the authors reported that there was no statistically significant effect of cerclage on the rates of preterm birth (less than 37, less than 34, less than 32, and less than 28 weeks).[23]

At present, cerclage remains indicated only for patients with a classic history of cervical incompetence. The evidence does not support the use of cerclage for a sonographically detected shortened short cervix.[23] An NICHD-funded, multi-center, randomized trial is under way to evaluate the efficacy of prophylactic cerclage in women with a history of a previous preterm birth and a sonographically detected shortened cervix.

Contraindications to cerclage placement include prior rupture of membranes, evidence of intrauterine infection, major fetus anomalies, active vaginal bleeding of unknown cause, and active labor. Potential morbidities associated with cerclage placement include anesthesia risk, bleeding, infection, rupture of membranes, maternal soft tissue injury, and spontaneous suture displacement. Cerclage placement does not appear to incite prostaglandin release or to initiate labor.[284] Complications associated with delivery include cervical laceration, the incidence of which ranges from 1% to 13%.[144] Rare cases of uterine rupture have been reported in patients in whom labor occurred before suture removal. Scarring of the cervix from the procedure may also contribute to an increased incidence of cesarean delivery.

Removal of the cerclage is normally accomplished at about 36 to 37 weeks of gestation unless labor ensues prior to that time. The cerclage should be removed promptly in the setting of PPROM to reduce the risk of infection, as the suture left in situ may act as a wick for ascending infections.[216]

Pessaries

Use of pessaries for the prevention of preterm birth in women at risk for preterm birth has been evaluated. Newcomer reviewed the literature detailing the use of pessaries for the prevention of preterm birth.[278] Although several prospective nonrandomized studies have suggested potential benefit of pessary use for women either at high risk for preterm birth or with a history of incompetent cervix, the majority of these investigations have been retrospective in nature and have involved limited numbers of women.[278] Only one prospective randomized trial comparing the efficacy of pessary versus cerclage for women with incompetent cervix has been reported. Forster and colleagues randomized 250 women with a presumed diagnosis of cervical incompetence to receive either cerclage or pessary treatment.[98] No significant differences were noted between the study groups with respect to delivery gestational age, infant birthweight, or neonatal morbidity. Therapy in this study, however, was not initiated until a mean gestational age of 27 weeks.[98] Additional randomized trials are currently under way to assess the therapeutic benefit of vaginal pessary use for women at risk for preterm birth.

Tocolytics

β-SYMPATHOMIMETIC AGENTS

Three types of β-adrenergic receptors exist in humans: β_1 receptors occur primarily in the heart, small intestine, and adipose tissue; β_2 receptors are found in the uterus, blood vessels, bronchioles, and liver; and β_3 receptors are predominantly found on white and brown adipocytes.[202] Stimulation of the β_2 receptors results in uterine smooth muscle relaxation. β-Sympathomimetic agents are structurally related to catecholamine and when administered in vivo these agents stimulate all β-receptors throughout the body. Although some β-sympathomimetic agents have been proposed as β_2-selective agents, stimulation of all receptor types often occurs at the dosages used pharmacologically. Such stimulation results in many of the side effects associated with the β-sympathomimetic agents. Of the β-sympathomimetic agents, the β_2-selective agents (e.g., ritodrine, terbutaline) have been the primary drugs utilized for the treatment of preterm labor.

Ritodrine

Ritodrine is the only medication approved by the U.S. Food and Drug Administration for the treatment of preterm labor. This approval resulted largely from studies done by Barden and coworkers[20] and Merkatz and colleagues,[247] which demonstrated efficacy similar to that of other tocolytic agents but with fewer side effects. In addition, pregnancy prolongation was statistically significant, with a reduction in neonatal morbidity and mortality.

Subsequent reports have not been as positive with respect to neonatal morbidity and mortality. The Canadian Preterm Labor Investigators Group conducted a prospective, randomized, placebo-controlled study of ritodrine therapy.[40] Ritodrine treatment significantly delayed delivery, however, it did not significantly modify perinatal outcomes. King and associates conducted a meta-analysis involving 16 clinical trials with a total of 890 women and demonstrated that women treated with ritodrine had significantly fewer deliveries within 24 and 48 hours of the start of therapy.[186] However, no statistically significant decrease in the incidence of respiratory distress syndrome, birthweight less than 2500 g, or perinatal death was demonstrated. These studies were completed before the use of antenatal steroid therapy became widespread.

Ritodrine can be administered either intravenously or orally. Treatment usually begins with intravenous infusion. The patient should be closely monitored for fluid balance, cardiac status, electrolytes (including potassium and glucose), and fetal monitoring. The initial infusion rate of 100 µg/min described by Barden and colleagues[20] may be too high. A study by Caritis and coworkers suggested an initial infusion of 50 µg/min with a maximal rate of 350 µg/min.[44] With cessation of uterine activity, the rate should be reduced at hourly intervals. Oral ritodrine has a rigorous dosing scheme of 10 mg every 2 hours, or 20 mg every 4 hours. The half-life is 1 to 2 hours. Plasma levels are only 27% of those obtained during intravenous infusion, which suggests that a higher dose is needed to maintain adequate plasma levels.[331] Relative contraindications include diabetes mellitus, underlying cardiac disease, use of digitalis, hyperthyroidism, severe anemia, and hypertension.

Many of the maternal side effects are the result of stimulation of beta-receptors throughout the body. These side effects include tachycardia, hypotension, tremulousness, headache, fever, apprehension, chest tightness or pain, and shortness of breath.[25] Serious maternal cardiopulmonary side effects reported with the use of ritodrine include pulmonary edema, myocardial ischemia, arrhythmia, and even maternal death. Pulmonary edema may occur in about 4% of patients receiving parenteral ritodrine. Predisposing factors associated with this complication include a multiple

gestation, positive fluid balance, blood transfusion, anemia, infection, polyhydramnios, and underlying cardiac disease. Pulmonary edema probably results from overhydration and an activation of the renin-angiotensin system, resulting in an increase in aldosterone, which causes salt and water retention. If untreated, the pulmonary edema can progress to adult respiratory distress syndrome. The associated use of corticosteroids has been implicated in the development of pulmonary edema. The two most commonly used antepartum steroids, betamethasone and dexamethasone, have minimal mineralocorticoid activity; hence, it is unlikely that these drugs contribute to this complication. Peripartum heart failure has been reported with long-term use of β-sympathomimetics.[201] Maternal mortality has been reported with intravenous ritodrine therapy and is associated with pulmonary edema or arrhythmia.[20,222] A baseline electrocardiogram should be obtained before the start of therapy, and therapy should be discontinued with a heart rate greater than 130 beats per minute or systolic blood pressure less than 90 mm Hg.

Metabolic effects of ritodrine include hypokalemia resulting from an increase in insulin and glucose concentrations, which drives potassium intracellularly and resolves within 24 hours of discontinuing therapy. Total body potassium remains unchanged. Elevated serum glucose levels are the result of an increase in cyclic adenosine monophosphate, with peak levels achieved 3 hours after initiation of treatment. Serum insulin levels also increase in response to the serum glucose elevation and as a direct effect of β_2 stimulation of the pancreas. Beta-1 stimulation results in lipolysis and mobilization of free fatty acids, acetoacetate, and beta-hydroxybutyrate.[342] In patients with diabetes, diabetic ketoacidosis may occur if blood sugar concentrations are not controlled.

Initial studies evaluating long-term exposure to β-sympathomimetics demonstrate no differences in Apgar scores, head circumference, or neurologic status in terms of developmental delay and behavioral differences.[140,166] Fetal cardiac complications have been reported. These medications readily cross the placental barrier, achieving concentrations in the fetus similar to those in maternal serum.[132] Elevation in the baseline fetal heart rate is seen, as well as a questionable increase in heart rate variability. A wide range of complications have been described, including rhythm disturbances, such as supraventricular tachycardia and atrial flutter. These usually resolve within a few days to 2 weeks after cessation of therapy.[39,155] Septal hypertrophy in the fetus and neonate has been described with maternal ritodrine treatment. The degree of hypertrophy correlates with the duration of therapy and usually resolves within 3 months of age.[285]

Other, more serious fetal complications have included hydrops fetalis, pulmonary edema, and extrauterine cardiac failure.[39] Fetal stillbirth, neonatal death, and a histologic finding of myocardial ischemia have been reported.[36,206,285] Neonatal hypoglycemia is another potential complication with β-sympathomimetics and usually develops when delivery occurs within 2 days of treatment. The hypoglycemia is transient and results from medication-induced hyperinsulinemia.[91] Neonatal periventricular-intraventricular hemorrhage may be increased with β-sympathomimetic therapy. In a retrospective study of 2827 women delivering preterm, there was a twofold increase in hemorrhage in fetuses that received betamimetics.[131] Overall, ritodrine has fallen out of favor as a primary tocolytic agent, largely as a result of these potential complications.

Terbutaline

Terbutaline is the most commonly used β₂-selective β-sympathomimetic agent. It was initially studied by Ingemarsson, who randomly assigned 30 patients with preterm labor to intravenous terbutaline therapy rather than a placebo and demonstrated an 80% success rate, in comparison with 20% for the placebo.[172] Unfortunately, as with other tocolytic agents, subsequent studies have not reported similarly high success rates.[61,164] One possible mechanism for the failure of long-term treatment with β-sympathomimetics is desensitization or downregulation of responsiveness to these agents.[27] The use of a low-dose subcutaneous infusion pump attempts to overcome this problem. Terbutaline is often administered subcutaneously in 250-μg doses every 20 to 30 minutes (four to six doses) as the first-line tocolytic agent for preterm labor. It has been effective in arresting premature labor, but not preterm birth. Lam and colleagues compared the use of the terbutaline pump with oral terbutaline therapy.[199] The average duration of therapy before breakthrough of preterm labor was 9 weeks with the pump and 2 weeks with oral administration of terbutaline. Total daily drug dosage was considerably lower (3 mg versus 30 mg/d).[199] Guinn and associates conducted a prospective, double-blind, randomized clinical trial comparing terbutaline pump maintenance therapy to placebo.[134] These investigators demonstrated no significant differences in the preterm delivery rate or neonatal outcomes between the women treated with the terbutaline pump and those treated with placebo.

Terbutaline can be administered via the oral, subcutaneous, or intravenous route. When it is administered intravenously, the protocol includes careful monitoring of the fetus, fluid balance, cardiac status, and electrolytes. The initial infusion is 5 to 10 μg/min, with the rate gradually increased every 10 to 15 minutes to a maximum of 80 μg/min.[368] Orally administered terbutaline undergoes significant first-pass metabolism in the intestinal tract, resulting in a bioavailability ranging from 10% to 15%.[286] The mean half-life of terbutaline is 3.7 hours, with increased clearance in pregnant patients.[218] The usual oral dosages range from 2.5 to 5 mg every 4 to 6 hours, titrated by patient response and maternal pulse.[43,368]

Maternal side effects and complications are similar to those stated for ritodrine. Terbutaline seems to affect the maternal heart rate less than ritodrine when administered intravenously.[43] Both oral and intravenous forms of terbutaline are more diabetogenic than ritodrine.[225,368] Subcutaneous administration of terbutaline by the pump

does not appear to increase the risk of gestational diabetes but does cause elevations in blood glucose levels in patients with diabetes.[211] Neonatal effects of maternally administered terbutaline are similar to those of ritodrine.

MAGNESIUM SULFATE

Magnesium sulfate is one of the most commonly utilized tocolytic agents. Use of magnesium sulfate as a tocolytic agent was first described by Steer and Petrie in a randomized study of 71 patients with preterm labor.[344] Patients were allocated to intravenous infusion of either magnesium or ethanol, or to a placebo of intravenous dextrose in water. The magnesium group received a 4-g bolus followed by a maintenance infusion of 2 g/h. The success rate, defined by the absence of contractions for 24 hours, was 77% for the magnesium versus 45% for ethanol and 44% for the placebo group.[344] Miller and colleagues conducted a randomized comparison of magnesium and terbutaline and demonstrated that magnesium had similar efficacy and fewer side effects than terbutaline.[249] In contrast to intravenous magnesium sulfate for tocolysis, oral magnesium therapy is not effective for the treatment of preterm labor.[231,310,312]

Magnesium affects uterine activity by decreasing the release of acetylcholine at the neuromuscular junction, resulting in decreased amplitude of motor endplate potential and, hence, decreased sensitivity. Magnesium also causes an increase in cyclic adenosine monophosphate, altering the amount of calcium pumped out of myometrial cells and possibly blocking entry of calcium into cells.

Magnesium sulfate is administered intravenously and is normally given as an initial bolus of 4 to 6 g over 30 minutes, followed by a maintenance infusion of 1 to 4 g/h. Magnesium is almost exclusively excreted by the kidneys. Approximately 75% of the infused dose of magnesium is excreted during the infusion and 90% by 24 hours.[70] Magnesium is reabsorbed at the renal level by a transport-limited mechanism; therefore, the glomerular filtration rate significantly affects excretion. Serum magnesium levels of 5 to 8 mg/dL are considered therapeutic for inhibiting myometrial activity on the basis of in vitro studies.[6] Once cessation of uterine activity is achieved, the patient is maintained at the lowest possible rate for 12 to 24 hours and then weaned off as tolerated.

Maternal side effects caused by magnesium sulfate are typically dose related. Common side effects of the use of magnesium sulfate include flushing, nausea, headache, drowsiness, and blurry vision. Constant monitoring of deep tendon reflexes and serum magnesium levels is mandatory to avoid toxicity. Diminished deep tendon reflexes occur when serum magnesium levels reach or exceed 12 mg/dL (10 mEq/L). Significant respiratory depression can occur as serum levels reach 14 to 18 mg/dL (12 to 14 mEq/L), and cardiac arrest may occur with levels greater than 18 mg/dL (15 mEq/L). In general, respiratory depression does not occur before loss of deep tendon reflexes. The toxic effects of high magnesium levels can be rapidly reversed with the infusion of 1 g of calcium gluconate.

The use of magnesium sulfate is absolutely contraindicated in patients with myasthenia gravis or heart block. It is relatively contraindicated in patients with underlying renal disease, with recent myocardial infarction, or who are receiving calcium channel blockers. Concurrent use of calcium channel blockers and magnesium sulfate can result in profound hypotension and should be avoided.[24,196] Pulmonary edema has been reported to have an incidence of approximately 1%.[89] The risk for pulmonary edema is increased in patients with multi-fetal gestations and those receiving combined tocolytic therapy. Because of the potential risk of fluid overload and the subsequent development of pulmonary edema, periodic assessment of fluid balance is essential.

Magnesium readily crosses the placenta, achieving fetal steady-state levels within hours of the start of treatment. Fetal heart rate variability is unaffected by maternal magnesium treatment.[343] No significant alterations in neurologic states or Apgar scores have been reported with mean umbilical cord concentrations of 3.6 mg/dL.[128] At a cord concentration of between 4 and 11 mg/dL, respiratory depression and motor depression have been seen. Long-term use of magnesium (greater than 7 days) has been reported to cause fetal bone loss in the proximal humerus, involving 6 of 11 fetuses in comparison with control fetuses.[163] No other studies have reported this finding to date. Serum calcium levels in the fetus and newborn are unchanged or minimally reduced.[69] In summary, overall neonatal side effects and complications with magnesium are minimal compared with β-sympathomimetic therapy.

One interesting and proposed beneficial effect of magnesium sulfate is the potential for reduced neonatal mortality and neurologic morbidity.[161,304] Three observational reports have suggested that antenatal magnesium sulfate treatment for preterm labor or preeclampsia is associated with a decreased risk for cerebral palsy in very low birthweight infants.[150,277,330] Grether and coworkers conducted a case-control study and demonstrated that magnesium sulfate tocolysis was associated with a decreased risk of mortality (adjusted OR, 0.09; 95% CI, 0.01-0.93).[129] A large prospective multicenter trial is presently ongoing to further explore the potential neonatal benefits of antenatal magnesium sulfate therapy. Schendel and colleagues further investigated the association of magnesium sulfate therapy with cerebral palsy and noted a strong inverse relationship between magnesium exposure in women and cerebral palsy in low birthweight infants.[330] Cerebral palsy was noted in only 1% (1/111) of infants exposed prenatally to magnesium sulfate, whereas the incidence was 10% (39/390) among infants not exposed to magnesium (OR, 0.11; 95% CI, 0.02-0.81).[330] These investigators demonstrated that this reduction in the incidence of cerebral palsy was not the result of an increased mortality rate among the most vulnerable neonates. In addition, magnesium exposure was associated with a reduction in mental retardation noted at age 3 to 5 years.[330]

Several randomized studies have been or are being conducted to evaluate the potential neuroprotective effects of antenatal magnesium sulfate therapy. The first of these investigations was the MagNET trial.[253] The MagNET trial was a four-group, single-center trial designed to explore the potential neuroprotective effects of antenatal magnesium on the incidence of cerebral palsy in prematurely born infants. This trial, however, was prematurely terminated because of excessive "pediatric" mortality (fetal, neonatal, or infant mortality up to 1 year) in the magnesium therapy group, and it has been the subject of considerable methodological and analytic criticism.[253] Of these deaths, one occurred in utero, four in the neonatal period, and four during the postnatal period (up to 1 year of age), and the grouping of fetal, neonatal, and infant deaths was a post hoc decision. In the "tocolytic" portion of the study, eight pediatric deaths occurred in the children of the 46 women randomized to magnesium, whereas none of the children of the 47 women randomized to other tocolytics experienced a pediatric death (RR, 15.2; 95% CI, 4.4-26).[253] Although these data raise concern about the antenatal use of magnesium sulfate, no clear magnesium-mediated mechanism for the deaths has been identified. Interestingly, the incidence of cerebral palsy was 0% (0/37) among the children exposed to magnesium sulfate as a tocolytic, whereas it was 8% (3/36) among those who were exposed to other tocolytics ($P = .11$).[252]

Crowther and colleagues recently reported findings from the Australian Collaborative Trial of Magnesium Sulphate (ACTOMgSO$_4$). In this investigation, 1062 women with gestations less than 30 weeks, whose delivery was anticipated within 24 hours, were randomized to receive either intravenous magnesium sulfate or placebo therapy. Infants were followed through 2 years of age.[68] Although the total perinatal mortality and cerebral palsy rates were similar between the treatment groups, the incidence of gross motor dysfunction was significantly lower among infants who were exposed to magnesium sulfate. Currently, a similar prospective multi-center trial (Beneficial Effects of Antenatal Magnesium [BEAM] trial) is being conducted in the United States by the NICHD MFMU Network to assess the potential of maternal magnesium sulfate therapy to prevent cerebral palsy in children of women who deliver very early preterm.

PROSTAGLANDIN SYNTHETASE INHIBITORS

As prostaglandins appear to play a pivotal role in the pathway leading to preterm labor and delivery, attempts to interrupt this cascade of events are of utmost importance. Prostaglandins are 20-carbon cyclopentane carboxylic acids derived from membrane phospholipids (primarily arachidonic acid) via the enzymatic action of phospholipase A and cyclooxygenase (prostaglandin synthetase). As a number of drugs are available that inhibit the action of prostaglandin synthetase (e.g., aspirin, ibuprofen, indomethacin, sulindac), this pathway represents a key target for pharmacologic intervention. Of these drugs, indomethacin has been the most extensively studied.

Indomethacin

Indomethacin was first used as a tocolytic agent by Zuckerman and associates, who administered it to 50 patients with preterm labor.[380] Tocolysis was achieved in 40 of the 50 patients for at least 48 hours. The first prospective, randomized, double-blind, placebo-controlled study was performed by Niebyl and colleagues.[280] In this study of 30 women with preterm labor, only 1 of 15 women in the indomethacin group failed therapy after 24 hours, in comparison with 9 of 15 women in the placebo group. Morales and co-workers compared indomethacin with ritodrine in a randomized trial and found similar efficacies at 48 hours and 7 days.[258] Maternal side effects causing discontinuation of treatment were much more common in the ritodrine group (24% versus 0%). No differences in fetal side effects were noted except for higher serum glucose levels in the ritodrine group. Similar efficacy was noted by the same authors in a comparative trial of indomethacin and magnesium sulfate.[259]

Indomethacin is usually administered orally or rectally in divided doses. A loading dose of 50 to 100 mg is followed by a total 24-hour dose not greater than 200 mg. Initial duration of therapy is 48 hours. Indomethacin blood concentrations usually peak 1 to 2 hours after administration, whereas rectal administration is associated with levels that peak slightly sooner.[7] Approximately 90% of the drug is protein bound and is excreted by the kidneys unchanged.[357] Indomethacin readily crosses the placenta, equilibrating with maternal concentrations 5 hours after administration. The half-life is approximately 15 hours in a term neonate and somewhat shorter in the preterm neonate.[31]

Most studies have limited the use of indomethacin to 24 to 48 hours' duration because of concerns regarding the development of oligohydramnios and constriction of the ductus arteriosus, which may lead to fetal pulmonary hypertension and persistent fetal circulation.[41,226,254] If longer therapy is required, close fetal monitoring is indicated, including weekly amniotic fluid indexes and ductal velocities examining for ductal constriction or closure. If the amniotic fluid volume (measured as the fluid depth in the four quadrants of the uterus) falls below 5 cm, or if the pulsatility index of the ductus arteriosus is less than 2 cm/s, discontinuation of therapy should be considered. Several long-term studies have evaluated the efficacy and safety of this drug. One study involving 31 fetuses exposed to indomethacin for an average of 44 days compared outcomes to appropriately matched control fetuses and found no statistically significant differences in outcome.[104]

Maternal contraindications to indomethacin use include peptic ulcer disease; allergies to indomethacin or related compounds; hematologic, hepatic, or renal dysfunction; and drug-induced asthma. Fetal contraindications include preexisting oligohydramnios, a

gestational age greater than 32 weeks, and congenital fetal heart disease in which the fetus is dependent on the ductus arteriosus for circulation. Major maternal side effects are minimal and infrequent. Gastrointestinal upset may occur but can be relieved by either taking the medication with meals or using an antacid.

Several fetal side effects have been reported with the use of indomethacin. It has been associated with oligohydramnios.[41,188] Fetal urine output has been shown to decrease after its administration. Within 24 hours after discontinuation of indomethacin therapy, however, urine output returns to baseline levels, indicating a role for prostaglandins in urine production.[41,188] Examining the effect on renal artery blood flow, Mari and colleagues found no change in the pulsatility index in 17 fetuses during the first 24 hours of indomethacin therapy.[229] This finding suggests that renal artery constriction and a decrease in blood flow were not responsible for the reduction in urine output. Long-term therapy for more than 7 days eventually results in the development of oligohydramnios.[189] The onset of oligohydramnios seems to vary from one patient to another and is somewhat unpredictable. Therefore, the amniotic fluid index should be followed while the patient is receiving therapy. Resolution usually occurs within 48 hours of discontinuation of treatment. Persistent anuria, neonatal death, and renal microcystic lesions have been reported with prenatal indomethacin exposure.[365] Most of these infants were exposed to doses greater than 200 mg/d for up to 36 weeks of gestation with inadequate amniotic fluid assessment.[365]

Another important potential complication is the development of ductal constriction or closure with prenatal indomethacin exposure. It is theorized that ductal constriction or closure leads to the diversion of right ventricular blood flow into the pulmonary vasculature. With time, this causes pulmonary arterial hypertrophy. After birth, relative pulmonary hypertension can cause shunting of blood through the foramen ovale and away from the lungs, resulting in persistent fetal circulation. This complication has been described with long-term indomethacin therapy but not in fetuses exposed to the drug for less than 48 hours.[30,104]

Development of ductal constriction identified by Doppler echocardiography in human fetuses was first described by Huhta and associates.[165] Moise and colleagues detected ductal constriction in 7 of 14 fetuses exposed in utero, with the change seen up to 72 hours after initiation of treatment.[254] There was no correlation with maternal drug levels, and the constrictions resolved within 24 hours after treatment was stopped. No cases of persistent fetal circulation were reported. The observed effects on ductal constriction have been shown to increase with advancing gestational age.[255] At 32 weeks' gestational age, 50% of fetuses demonstrate constriction. On the basis of these data, indomethacin therapy should be discontinued by 32 weeks at the latest.

Another reported complication is an increased risk of necrotizing enterocolitis in infants exposed to indomethacin prenatally and delivered at less than 30 weeks. Norton and coworkers performed a retrospective case-control study of 57 neonates that delivered at less than 30 weeks' gestation after recent antenatal exposure to indomethacin and compared them with 57 matched control fetuses.[282] In this study, the incidence of necrotizing enterocolitis was 29% in the indomethacin group versus 8% in the control group. Additionally, a statistically higher incidence of grade II to IV intraventricular hemorrhage and patent ductus arteriosus was noted in the indomethacin treatment group.[282] No correlations were made with regard to duration of treatment, or with the time frame of exposure to indomethacin in relationship to delivery. Although these results are of concern, indomethacin appears to be a relatively safe and effective tocolytic agent when used with the appropriate caution (less than 48 hours of therapy, less than 30 to 32 weeks' gestation).

Sulindac

Sulindac is another prostaglandin synthetase inhibitor that is closely related to indomethacin in structure and has been reported to have fewer side effects when used for tocolysis.[306] Preliminary experiences, however, indicate that oral sulindac therapy may not be very useful in the prevention of preterm birth.[45] Kramer and colleagues conducted a randomized double-blind study to evaluate the comparative effects of sulindac and terbutaline on fetal urine production and amniotic fluid volume.[193] Sulindac administration resulted in a significant decrease in fetal urine flow and amniotic fluid volume. Additionally, two fetuses developed severe ductal constriction. Thus, sulindac shares many of the fetal side effects associated with indomethacin.

Cyclooxygenase-2 Inhibitors

Both indomethacin and sulindac are nonselective cyclooxygenase (COX) inhibitors. In the setting of inflammation, cyclooxygenase-2 (COX-2) is preferentially upregulated. Given that many early cases of preterm labor and delivery are related to underlying occult infection or inflammation of the upper genital tract, specific targeting of COX-2 represents a logical target for tocolytic therapy. By specifically targeting COX-2, there is a theoretical potential for reduction of some of the untoward renal, gastrointestinal, and cardiac side effects that are relatively common with the nonselective COX inhibitors.

The emergence of several selective COX-2 inhibitors (e.g., celecoxib, nimesulide) has led to several investigations designed to evaluate the efficacy of these agents for the treatment of preterm labor.[327,328,346] Stika and colleagues reported findings from a randomized, double-blind, placebo-controlled trial of celecoxib versus indomethacin for the treatment of preterm labor.[346] In this small study of 24 women, no difference between the two agents was noted with respect to length of prolongation of pregnancy. Although a transient decrease in amniotic fluid volume was noted with both agents, mean maximal ductal flow velocity was not significantly altered in women receiving celecoxib,

whereas indomethacin therapy resulted in a significant increase in maximal ductal flow velocity.[346] Sawdy and colleagues conducted a similar small randomized double-blind, placebo-controlled study of nimesulide versus indomethacin versus sulindac for the treatment of preterm labor.[328] Similar reductions were noted between the three treatment groups with respect to amniotic fluid volume, fetal urine production, and ductal Doppler pulsatility index over the initial 48-hour treatment period.[328] To date, no large trials have been reported that have critically evaluated the therapeutic efficacy of the COX-2 inhibitors to prevent preterm birth or reduce neonatal morbidity in women presenting with preterm labor.

CALCIUM CHANNEL BLOCKERS

Calcium channel blockers are agents that antagonize or normalize excessive transmembrane calcium influx, thus controlling muscle contractility and pacemaker activity in cardiac, vascular, and uterine tissue. The majority of clinical investigations evaluating the use of calcium channel blockers for the treatment of preterm labor have utilized nifedipine. Ulmsten and associates first reported the use of nifedipine for the treatment of preterm labor in a study involving 10 patients, with resultant cessation of uterine activity for 3 days in all patients during treatment.[363] In a subsequent randomized control study, Read and colleagues reported that the nifedipine group had a significantly longer time interval from presentation to delivery than either a ritodrine or a placebo-controlled group.[307] Ferguson and coworkers demonstrated that nifedipine was as effective as ritodrine in prolonging pregnancy but had far fewer side effects causing discontinuation of therapy.[96]

Nifedipine can be administered orally or in sublingual form. It is rapidly absorbed by the gastrointestinal tract with detectable blood levels attained within 5 minutes of sublingual administration. Nifedipine readily crosses the placenta, and serum concentrations of the fetus and the mother are comparable. An initial loading dose of 20 mg orally is typically given, followed by 10 to 20 mg every 6 to 8 hours. Up to 30 mg can be administered per dose but may result in more side effects. The sublingual form is usually not used for treatment of preterm labor because it acts more rapidly than the oral form and can cause acute hypotension.

Contraindications to the use of nifedipine, or any of the calcium channel blockers, include hypotension, congestive heart failure, aortic stenosis, and preexisting peripheral edema. Concurrent use of calcium channel blockers and magnesium sulfate can result in profound hypotension and hence should be avoided. Maternal side effects from calcium channel blockers result from the potent vasodilatory effects. These side effects can include dizziness, lightheadedness, flushing, headache, and peripheral edema. The incidence of these side effects is approximately 17%, whereas severe effects resulting in the discontinuation of therapy occur in 2% to 5% of patients.[351]

Studies evaluating the fetal effects of calcium channel blocker therapy have been limited to date. One concern is the potential adverse effect calcium channel blockers may have on uteroplacental blood flow, as has been reported in animal studies.[143] Several reports have examined uteroplacental blood flow in patients receiving nifedipine.[228] These studies have demonstrated no significant adverse effects on fetal or uteroplacental blood flow during treatment.[228] Additional studies are needed to more completely evaluate the potential fetal effects of calcium channel blocker therapy. The role of the calcium channel blockers for the treatment of preterm labor remains to be defined.

OXYTOCIN ANTAGONISTS

Oxytocin antagonists have been set forth as a novel category of agents that may be useful for the treatment of preterm labor. As preterm labor may result from early gap junction formation coupled with a rise in oxytocin receptor concentration, oxytocin may be a pivotal hormone in the evolution of parturition.[17,102] Oxytocin has been shown to be intimately involved in the physiologic pathways leading to both term[379] and preterm labor.[37] While the role of oxytocin may represent the terminal event for a variety of pathophysiology pathways leading to preterm delivery, it represents an important central pathway which may be amenable to therapeutic intervention. As the primary cellular targets for oxytocin are the myometrium and decidua, oxytocin antagonists have the theoretical benefit of being highly organ specific and thus have minimal potential for adverse side effects.

Oxytocin antagonists have been shown to effectively inhibit oxytocin-induced uterine contractions in both in vitro and in vivo animal models. The initial human experience with oxytocin antagonist therapy came from several small uncontrolled studies from the late 1980s.[3,8] Akerlund and colleagues reported on a series of 13 patients who received a short-term infusion of an oxytocin antagonist, which resulted in inhibition of premature labor in all patients; however, 10 of these patients subsequently required treatment with β-agonists.[3] Similarly, Andersen and associates reported their experience with 12 patients between 27 and 33 weeks of gestation, who were treated with a competitive oxytocin receptor antagonist for 1.5 to 13 hours.[8] Of these 12 patients, nine had arrest of contractions, and the remaining three had no change in contraction frequency.

The most-studied oxytocin antagonist is atosiban. Atosiban is a nonapeptide oxytocin analogue that competitively antagonizes the oxytocin-vasopressin receptor and is capable of inhibiting oxytocin-induced uterine contractions. Atosiban is typically administered intravenously. Standard dosing recommendations are for a single initial intravenous bolus of 6.75 mg of atosiban, followed by an intravenous infusion of 300 μg/min for the first 3 hours and then 100 μg/min for up to 18 hours. Maintenance therapy can be implemented at a rate of 30 μg/min via continuous infusion.

Several prospective, randomized, blinded clinical trials have demonstrated that atosiban is effective in diminishing uterine contractions in women with threatened preterm birth without causing significant maternal, fetal, or neonatal adverse effects. Goodwin and colleagues demonstrated that a 2-hour infusion of atosiban significantly decreased contraction frequency compared with placebo.[123] Romero and coworkers, in a prospective, randomized, double-blind, placebo-controlled, multicenter investigation of 501 women with documented preterm labor, demonstrated that atosiban is significantly more effective than placebo in delaying delivery 24 hours, 48 hours, and 7 days.[323] Importantly, however, the median from start of therapy to delivery or treatment failure was not significantly different between the study groups, nor were perinatal outcomes. Moutquin and colleagues compared atosiban to ritodrine for the treatment of preterm labor.[266] In this multicenter, double-blind, randomized, controlled trial of 212 women with documented preterm labor, the investigators demonstrated that the tocolytic efficacy of atosiban was comparable to that of conventional ritodrine therapy; however, atosiban use was associated with fewer adverse side effects. Similarly, no differences were noted between the groups with respect to neonatal outcomes. The potential use of atosiban for maintenance therapy in patients with arrested preterm labor has also recently been evaluated. Valenzuela and associates reported experience from a multicenter, double-blind, placebo-controlled trial of 513 women with arrested preterm labor.[364] Median time from start of maintenance therapy to first recurrence of labor was significantly longer for women treated with atosiban (32.6 days) than for those treated with the placebo (27.6 days).

These data suggest that atosiban may be useful in delaying delivery 24 to 48 hours in the setting of preterm labor, but this delay appears to have minimal impact on neonatal outcomes. Atosiban represents a new approach to the treatment of preterm labor. Further studies are needed to more clearly elucidate the role of the oxytocin antagonists into the therapeutic armamentarium for preterm labor.

NITRIC OXIDE DONORS

Nitric oxide is a potent endogenous hormone that facilitates smooth muscle relaxation in the vasculature, the gut, and the uterus. Recently, interest has arisen about the potential use of nitric oxide donors (e.g., nitroglycerin, glycerol trinitrate) as potential tocolytic therapy. Lees and colleagues compared transdermal glycerol trinitrate to ritodrine for tocolysis in a randomized investigation of 245 women with documented preterm labor between 24 and 36 weeks' gestation.[205] These investigators found no significant differences between the women treated with glycerol trinitrate and those treated with ritodrine with respect to tocolytic effect and neonatal outcomes. Use of glycerol trinitrate, however, was associated with fewer maternal side effects.

Clavin and coworkers provided further insights into the potential use of nitric oxide donors for the treatment of preterm labor.[53] Thirty-four women in preterm labor were randomized to either tocolysis with intravenous nitroglycerine or magnesium sulfate. No difference in the tocolytic efficacy was noted between the two treatments; however, 3 of the 15 women who received nitroglycerin experienced severe hypotension.[53] Similarly, El-Sayed and colleagues evaluated 31 women with documented preterm labor prior to 35 weeks' gestation in a randomized comparison of intravenous nitroglycerin and magnesium sulfate.[90] Tocolytic failures (tocolysis administered for 12 hours or more) were significantly more common in patients treated with nitroglycerin than with women treated with magnesium sulfate. Importantly, 25% of the patients treated with nitroglycerin experienced significant hypotension that required discontinuation of treatment. Given the potential profound hemodynamic effects of these nitric oxide donors on the central and peripheral circulation, these agents should be utilized with caution in the pregnant patient. Clinical use of these agents for the treatment of preterm labor remains experimental.

Antibiotics

As previously discussed, preterm labor, especially at less than 30 weeks' gestation, has been associated with occult upper genital tract infection. Many of the bacterial species involved in this occult infection are capable of inciting an inflammatory response, which ultimately may culminate in preterm labor and delivery.[232,239] It is on this basis that antibiotics have been suggested as a potential therapy for the treatment or prevention of spontaneous preterm birth.

Elder and associates provided the first insights into the potential use of antibiotics to prevent preterm birth.[87] They demonstrated that treatment of nonbacteriuric asymptomatic pregnant patients with daily tetracycline therapy, as part of an ongoing randomized treatment study of bacteruria in pregnancy, resulted in fewer preterm births.[87] Subsequent prospective trials of antibiotics in women colonized with *Chlamydia, Ureaplasma,* and group B streptococci have shown no significant decrease in preterm birth.[92,190] However, the association of bacterial vaginosis with preterm birth has prompted renewed interest in the potential use of antibiotics to prevent preterm birth in asymptomatic women. Several prospective antibiotic trials have demonstrated that antenatal treatment of bacterial vaginosis in asymptomatic women at high risk for spontaneous preterm delivery may reduce the subsequent spontaneous preterm delivery rate.[149,260] Hauth and colleagues conducted a prospective, randomized, double-blind, placebo-controlled study of 624 women who were identified as being at risk for preterm delivery (e.g., history of previous preterm birth or prepregnancy weight of less than 50 kg).[149] These women were randomized to either metronidazole (250 mg three times a day for 7 days) and erythromycin (333 mg three times a day for 14 days), or to placebo. These investigators observed a significant reduction in the rate of preterm birth (49% versus 31%) in women with bacterial vaginosis who received antibiotic treatment; however, antibiotic treatment of women without bacterial vaginosis was associated with a significant *increase* in the rate of

preterm birth (13.4% versus 4.8%, P = .02).[149] Carey and coworkers evaluated the potential use of metronidazole to prevent preterm birth in a prospective, randomized, placebo-controlled study of 1704 low-risk asymptomatic women with bacterial vaginosis.[42] Results from this investigation revealed that treatment of asymptomatic bacterial vaginosis in low-risk women does not reduce the risk for preterm delivery or adverse perinatal outcomes. On the basis of these data, it appears that screening and treatment of bacterial vaginosis in women at high risk for preterm delivery may be an effective treatment to prevent preterm birth. Nondiscriminative screening and treatment of asymptomatic, low-risk women does not appear to offer any clear benefit.

Several recent investigations have explored the use of fetal fibronectin as a screening tool for asymptomatic women at greatest risk for early preterm birth induced by infection or inflammation, to allow for targeted antibiotic use.[14,65,120,151,303] Goldenberg and colleagues provided the initial assessment of the potential use of antibiotics for the prevention of preterm birth among women who are fetal fibronectin positive.[120] In a subgroup analysis of women enrolled in trial of antibiotic therapy for the prevention of preterm birth, 70 women with bacterial vaginosis and a positive fetal fibronectin test result were randomized to receive either two courses of metronidazole treatment or placebo.[120] In this subgroup analysis, women who received metronidazole treatment had a lower incidence of preterm birth (8%) than the placebo-controlled group (16%), but this difference did not reach statistical significance (P = .311).[120] Although not statistically significant, this trend was compelling and has led to several randomized clinical trials to evaluate the efficacy of antibiotic therapy in women with a positive fetal fibronectin test result.[14,65,151,303]

In the largest of these trials, Andrews and colleagues, as part of the NICHD MFMU Network, conducted a large, multicenter, randomized, double-blind, placebo-controlled clinical trial of antibiotics for asymptomatic women who were fetal fibronectin positive.[14] These investigators screened 16,317 women between 21 and 25 gestational weeks with cervical or vaginal swabs for fetal fibronectin. Of the screened women, 1079 (6.6%) had a positive fetal fibronectin test result (50 ng/mL or greater). Of these women, 715 consented to randomization to receive either metronidazole (250 mg orally three times per day) and erythromycin (250 mg orally four times per day) or identical placebo pills for 10 days.[83] The primary outcome for the investigation was defined as spontaneous delivery before 37 weeks' gestation. No difference was observed in incidence of spontaneous preterm birth at less than 37 weeks' (14.4% versus 12.4%, P = .43), less than 35 weeks' (6.9% versus 7.5%, P = .76), or less than 32 weeks' (4.3% versus 2.2%, P = .12) gestation between the antibiotic-treated women and the placebo-treated women. Among women with a prior spontaneous preterm delivery, however, the rate of repeat spontaneous preterm delivery at less than 37 weeks was significantly higher in the metronidazole plus erythromycin group than in the placebo group (46.7% versus 23.9%, RR, 1.95; 95% CI, 1.03-3.71; *P* = .04).[14]

These findings are consistent with those of two similar trials that evaluated the use of antibiotic therapy in asymptomatic women who were fetal fibronectin positive.[65,151] It is clear from these investigations that the use of antibiotic therapy in asymptomatic women with a positive cervical or vaginal fetal fibronectin test in the late mid-trimester does not decrease the incidence of spontaneous preterm delivery.

In contrast to these data, the use of antibiotics for the treatment of documented preterm labor has had mixed results.[187,272,281,305,349] Over 15 investigations have been reported that evaluate the efficacy of a range of antibiotic regimens (ampicillin, erythromycin, clindamycin, ceftizoxime, co-amoxiclav, ampicillin plus erythromycin, ampicillin plus sulbactam, ampicillin plus metronidazole, co-amoxiclav plus erythromycin, and mezlocillin plus erythromycin) for the prevention of spontaneous preterm birth in women presenting with preterm labor and intact membranes.[187,354] These studies have yielded inconsistent results on the benefits of antibiotic use with regard to pregnancy prolongation and short- and long-term neonatal outcome.[187,272,281,305,349] The ORACLE II trial, the largest study to date that has evaluated the efficacy of antibiotics for the prevention of preterm birth, was a multicenter, prospective, randomized study of antibiotics (erythromycin alone, co-amoxiclav alone, or both) versus placebo in 6295 women with preterm labor and intact membranes.[184] This study failed to demonstrate significant prolongation of pregnancy or a predefined composite neonatal outcome among women receiving antibiotic therapy.

King and colleagues reviewed the use of antibiotics in women with preterm labor and intact membranes in a recent Cochrane meta-analysis.[187] They concluded the following: (1) antibiotic use is associated with a significant prolongation of pregnancy (5.4 days; 95% CI, 0.9-9.8), (2) maternal infection is decreased in women receiving antibiotic treatment (OR, 0.59; 95% CI, 0.36-0.97), (3) the incidence of necrotizing enterocolitis is significantly reduced in women who received antibiotics (OR, 0.33; 95% CI, 0.13-0.88), and (4) a trend toward decreased risk of neonatal sepsis is noted among women receiving antibiotics (OR, 0.67; 95% CI, 0.42-1.07). Surprisingly, the meta-analysis demonstrated that increased perinatal mortality was significantly associated with antibiotic treatment (OR, 3.36; 95% CI, 1.21-9.32).[187] The authors concluded that although there was a prolongation in time to delivery, clear overall benefit of antibiotic treatment for preterm labor was not noted.[187]

One important use of antibiotics in the setting of preterm delivery is in relationship to PPROM. Numerous investigations have shown that the use of a variety of antibiotics in this setting can result in an increased latency period from the time of membrane rupture to the time of delivery. Mercer and coworkers reported on a large prospective randomized clinical investigation conducted through the NICHD MFMU Network and designed to more clearly address the neonatal benefits

of antenatal antibiotic use in women with PPROM.[245,246] For this investigation, 614 women with PPROM were randomized to treatment with either intravenous ampicillin (2 g every 6 hours) with erythromycin (250 mg every 6 hours) for 48 hours, followed by oral amoxicillin (250 mg every 8 hours) and erythromycin base (333 mg every 8 hours) for 5 days, or to a matched placebo treatment regimen. In addition to significantly increasing the latency period, the use of antibiotics in this investigation resulted in a significant reduction in the incidence of respiratory distress syndrome, necrotizing enterocolitis, and composite neonatal morbidity (defined as any of the following: fetal or infant death, respiratory distress, severe intraventricular hemorrhage, stage 2 or 3 necrotizing enterocolitis, or sepsis within 72 hours of birth).[246]

In contrast, Kenyon and colleagues reported that antibiotic use in the setting of PPROM did not result in a reduction in neonatal morbidity.[185] These investigators conducted a large, multicenter, multinational investigation of 4809 women with PPROM at less than 37 weeks' gestation. Women were randomized to one of four treatment regimens for 10 days: placebo, co-amoxiclav, erythromycin, or co-amoxiclav plus erythromycin. Significant prolongation of pregnancy was noted among all antibiotic treatment groups when compared with placebo therapy. The investigators, however, noted no significant difference between the four treatment groups with regard to composite neonatal morbidity (defined as neonatal death, chronic lung disease, or major cerebral abnormality on ultrasound): placebo, 15%; co-amoxiclav, 14%; erythromycin, 13%; co-amoxiclav plus erythromycin, 14%.[185]

On the basis of the available literature, the use of antibiotics in the setting of PPROM appears to result in significant prolongation of pregnancy, and in certain subsets (i.e., early PPROM at less than 32 weeks' gestation), it reduces neonatal short-term morbidity.

Corticosteroids (See also Chapter 42.)

The use of antenatal corticosteroids for the prevention of neonatal respiratory distress syndrome stems from the animal original work by Liggins and Howie in the late 1960s. They observed that gravid sheep, which had received glucocorticoids to induce preterm labor, gave birth to lambs that had accelerated fetal lung maturity and decreased respiratory problems at birth. To follow up on this interesting observation, these investigators conducted the first trial of antenatal glucocorticoid therapy in humans and found that antenatal glucocorticoid administration (12 mg of betamethasone, on two occasions 24 hours apart) resulted in a significant decrease in the incidence of respiratory distress syndrome, with an associated decrease in perinatal mortality, in newborns born before 34 weeks.[209]

Since that landmark study was published, over 15 additional prospective, randomized, controlled trials have confirmed the decrease in neonatal respiratory distress syndrome related to antenatal administration of glucocorticoids (either betamethasone or dexamethasone).

Crowley conducted a meta-analysis of 15 randomized controlled trials and confirmed that antenatal gluco corticoid therapy significantly decreased the incidence and severity of neonatal respiratory distress syndrome.[66] Neonatal mortality was also significantly reduced, as was the incidence of intraventricular hemorrhage and necrotizing enterocolitis. The optimal window for these benefits appeared to be maximal if delivery occurred more than 24 hours after starting treatment but within 7 days.

Despite these data, antenatal corticosteroids remained underutilized throughout the 1980s and early 1990s. Therefore, the National Institutes of Health (NIH) convened a Consensus Development Conference on Antenatal Steroids in 1994 to review the potential risks and benefits of antenatal corticosteroid therapy.[274] The panel concluded that sufficient data exist that demonstrate that antenatally administered corticosteroids (betamethasone or dexamethasone) significantly reduce the incidence or severity of respiratory distress syndrome, intraventricular hemorrhage, and potentially necrotizing enterocolitis.[274] The panel recommended that all fetuses between 24 and 34 weeks' gestation at risk for preterm delivery, and that are eligible for tocolytic therapy, should be considered candidates for antenatal corticosteroid treatment. Additionally, given that treatment for less than 24 hours was significantly associated with a decreased risk for respiratory distress syndrome, intraventricular hemorrhage, and mortality, the panel concluded that steroids should be administered unless delivery is imminent. For patients with PPROM, treatment was recommended at less than 30 to 32 weeks because of the high risk of intraventricular hemorrhage.

Long-term follow-up (at 3 and 6 years) of children who were exposed in utero to antenatal corticosteroid therapy has not demonstrated any adverse effect on growth, physical development, motor or cognitive skills, or school progress.[54,219] Hence, a single course of corticosteroids appears to be an efficacious and safe treatment modality to improve neonatal outcomes in patients with preterm delivery.

One unresolved issue is that related to the safety and efficacy of repeated steroid dosing. In animal studies, repeat courses of antenatal corticosteroids have been shown to have a deleterious effect on lung growth and organization, cerebral myelination, the function of the hypothalamic-pituitary-adrenal axis, fetal growth, and retinal development.[2,83,101,378] Data from retrospective and case-control studies in humans, however, have yielded inconclusive results about the short- and long-term adverse effects of repeat doses of corticosteroids.

Several recent randomized trials have evaluated the efficacy of repeated steroid dosing in women at risk for preterm delivery.[135,369] Guinn and associates reported results from a randomized, double-blind, placebo-controlled clinical trial comparing repeated weekly betamethasone administration with a single dose of betamethasone administered to pregnant women at the onset of threatened preterm delivery.[135] In this study of 502 women, these investigators noted no overall benefit

from repeated steroid dosing with regard to composite neonatal morbidity (defined as any of the following: fetal or neonatal death, bronchopulmonary dysplasia, intraventricular hemorrhage, sepsis, necrotizing enterocolitis, and periventricular leukomalacia) when compared with single-dose steroid administration (22.5% versus 28.0%, respectively; P = .16).[135] Whereas the incidence of severe respiratory distress syndrome was significantly lower among those infants in the repeated steroid dosing group (15.3%) when compared with those in the single dose group (24.1%, P = .01), the incidence of severe intraventricular hemorrhage was higher in the repeated steroid dosing group (7.6% versus 2.0%, P = .06).[135] Wapner and colleagues from the NICHD MFMU Network conducted a randomized trial of single versus weekly dosing of corticosteroids for women at less than 32 weeks' gestation who were at increased risk for spontaneous preterm birth.[369] The primary study outcome was stillbirth and neonatal death (scored together), severe respiratory distress syndrome, grade III to IV intraventricular hemorrhage, periventricular leukomalacia, or chronic lung disease. No difference was noted between the study groups with respect to the primary study outcome. An important finding of this investigation, however, was a significant reduction in birthweight among infants exposed to four or more courses of steroids.[369]

In response to concerns about repeated-dose corticosteroid use, the NIH reconvened a Consensus Development Conference in 2000 to review the available data on potential risks and benefits of repeated-dose steroid use when compared with single-dose administration.[275] On the basis of this literature review, the panel concluded that there was insufficient scientific data from randomized clinical trials regarding efficacy and safety to justify repeat courses of corticosteroids, and that repeat dosing should not be used outside the context of a randomized trial.[275]

The commonly utilized steroids for the enhancement of fetal maturity are betamethasone (12 mg intramuscularly every 24 hours, two doses) and dexamethasone (6 mg intravenously every 6 hours, four doses). These two glucocorticoids have been identified as the most efficacious as they readily cross the placental barrier to reach the fetal compartment and have long half-lives and limited mineralocorticoid activity. A recent national shortage of these corticosteroids has raised the question of whether other steroids might be suitable to enhance fetal lung maturity. Hydrocortisone (500 mg intravenously every 12 hours for four doses) may be a suitable alternative.[257]

Unresolved issues related to the use of corticosteroids include the efficacy and safety of "rescue" steroid dosing, the appropriate dosing and efficacy in multifetal pregnancies, and the potential to enhance fetal lung maturation beyond 34 weeks' gestation.

Thyrotropin-Releasing Hormone

The potential use of thyrotropin-releasing hormone (TRH) to enhance fetal pulmonary maturation was initially proposed because animal studies had demonstrated that triiodothyronine (T3) enhances surfactant synthesis. Administered prenatal TRH crosses the placental barrier and reaches the fetus, resulting in increased T3 and prolactin biosynthesis. Concurrent administration of glucocorticoid and T3 has been shown to be more effective than glucocorticoid alone to accelerate surfactant and improve lung compliance in the lamb.[329] Several studies have demonstrated enhanced fetal lung maturation with the combined use of TRH and glucocorticoids compared to the glucocorticoid treatment alone.[18,191] Ballard and colleagues conducted a prospective randomized trial of TRH and glucocorticoid versus glucocorticoid alone in gestations of less than 32 weeks.[18] When one full course of treatment was given and delivery occurred within 10 days, there was no difference in the incidence of respiratory distress syndrome in newborns weighing less than 1500 g. However, the incidence of chronic lung disease was 18% in the combined-therapy group, versus 44% with glucocorticoid therapy alone ($P < .01$), and fewer cases of chronic lung disease or death (19% versus 38%, $P < .01$) occurred with combined treatment. No short-term adverse effects were noted.

To further evaluate the potential benefit of TRH, Ballard and coworkers conducted a subsequent prospective placebo-controlled study of 996 women randomized to treatment with TRH and glucocorticoid or placebo with glucocorticoid.[19] Results from this investigation, in contrast to the findings from their original study, demonstrated that antenatal TRH and glucocorticoid offered no additional benefit with respect to neonatal morbidity and mortality when compared with glucocorticoid treatment alone. Similar findings were noted with data from the Australian ACROBAT trial, in which 1234 women were randomized to receive either TRH with corticosteroids or corticosteroids alone.[67] This study failed to demonstrate any beneficial effects from the use of TRH. In fact, the incidence of respiratory distress syndrome was actually increased in the patients who received the combined treatment. Additionally, the investigators observed that 7% of the mothers became overtly hypertensive as a result of the thyrotropin therapy. These investigators concluded that the use of TRH to augment fetal maturation appears to offer little benefit, with potential harmful maternal and neonatal effects; hence, the use of TRH cannot be recommended.

Phenobarbital and Vitamin K

Until recently, antenatal maternal treatment with phenobarbital or vitamin K was thought to reduce the incidence of intraventricular hemorrhage. This assumption was based on a series of reports of observed benefit from this therapy; however, these reports failed to control for the use of corticosteroids, which have been shown to significantly decrease the incidence of intraventricular hemorrhage.[244] In an attempt to more definitively determine the potential benefit of phenobarbital and vitamin K for the prevention of intracranial hemorrhage, Thorp and colleagues conducted a prospective, randomized, placebo-controlled study of 372 women at risk for preterm birth.[353] Patients were randomized to receive either placebo or treatment with phenobarbital and vitamin K. These investigators found no difference in the incidence of grade 3 or grade 4 intraventricular hemorrhage in newborns of less than 34 weeks' gestation between the two treatment groups. Similarly, Shankaran and associates conducted a prospective placebo-controlled clinical trial of 610 women with threatened preterm delivery.[337] Women were randomized to either treatment with antenatal phenobarbital or placebo. The results from this investigation demonstrated that antenatal phenobarbital does not decrease the risk of intracranial hemorrhage. Hence, it appears that neither phenobarbital nor vitamin K offers significant advantage for the prevention of intraventricular hemorrhage beyond that observed with antenatal corticosteroids.

SUMMARY

We have reviewed the epidemiology, pathophysiology, and the current therapeutic strategies used in the setting of preterm labor. Despite our efforts thus far, preterm labor and delivery remains a significant clinical problem globally, accounting for a substantial component of all neonatal morbidity and mortality. Although we have gained important insights into the pathophysiology of preterm labor over the past several decades, effective therapeutic interventions to decrease spontaneous preterm delivery are limited. Clearly, the development of effective screening tools to identify patients at greatest risk for spontaneous preterm delivery is important for the development of novel therapeutic strategies. As our insights into the diverse etiologies of spontaneous preterm labor evolve, these strategies may lead to a significant reduction in the incidence of spontaneous preterm delivery, with concomitant improvement in perinatal morbidity and mortality rates. Ongoing research is needed to further explore the pathophysiology of spontaneous preterm delivery and potential therapeutic approaches to deal with this important clinical problem.

REFERENCES

1. Abel MH et al: Suppression of concentration of endometrial prostaglandin in early intrauterine and ectopic pregnancy in women. J Endocrinol 85:379, 1980.
2. Aghajafari F et al: Repeated doses of antenatal corticosteroids in animals: A systematic review. Am J Obstet Gynecol 186:843, 2002.
3. Akerlund M et al: Inhibition of uterine contractions of premature labour with an oxytocin analogue: Results from a pilot study. Br J Obstet Gynaecol 94:1040, 1987.
4. Allen MC et al: The limit of viability: Neonatal outcome of infants born at 22 to 25 weeks' gestation. N Engl J Med 329:1597, 1993.
5. Althuisius SM et al: Final results of the Cervical Incompetence Prevention Randomized Cerclage Trial (CIPRACT): Therapeutic cerclage with bed rest versus bed rest alone. Am J Obstet Gynecol 185:1106, 2001.
6. Altura BM et al: Mg^{+2}-Ca^{+2} interacts in contractility of

smooth muscle: Magnesium versus organic calcium-channel blockers on myogenic tone and agonist-induced responsiveness of blood vessels. Can J Physiol Pharmacol 65:729, 1987.

7. Alvan G et al: Pharmacokinetics of indomethacin. Clin Pharmacol Ther 18:364, 1976.

8. Anderson PJ et al: Non-protein-bound estradiol and progesterone in human peripheral plasma before labor and delivery. J Endocrinol 104:7, 1985.

9. Anderson HF et al: Prediction of risk for preterm delivery by ultrasonographic measurement of cervical length. Am J Obstet Gynecol 163:859, 1990.

10. Andersen LF et al: Oxytocin receptor blockade: A new principle in the treatment of preterm labor? Am J Perinatol 6:196, 1989.

11. Andrews WW et al: Amniotic fluid interleukin-6: Correlation with upper genital tract microbial colonization and gestational age in women delivered after spontaneous labor versus indicated delivery. Am J Obstet Gynecol 173:606, 1995.

12. Andrews WW et al: The preterm prediction study: Association of mid-trimester genital chlamydia infection and subsequent spontaneous preterm birth. Am J Obstet Gynecol 176:S55, 1997.

13. Andrews WW et al: Second-trimester cervical ultrasound: Associations with increased risk for recurrent early spontaneous delivery. Obstet Gynecol 95:222, 2000.

14. Andrews WW et al for the NICHD MFMU Network: Randomized clinical trial of metronidazole plus erythromycin to prevent spontaneous preterm delivery in fetal fibronectin-positive women. Obstet Gynecol 101:847, 2003.

15. Armer TL et al: Intraamniotic infection in patients with intact membranes and preterm labor. Obstet Gynecol Surv 46:589, 1991.

16. Athayde N et al: Matrix metalloproteinases-9 in preterm and term human parturition. J Matern Fetal Med 8:213, 1999.

17. Balducci J et al: Gap junction formation in human myometrium: A key to preterm labor? Am J Obstet Gynecol 168:1609, 1993.

18. Ballard RA et al: Respiratory disease in very-low-birth weight infants after prenatal thyrotropin-releasing hormone and glucocorticoid. Lancet 339:510, 1992.

19. Ballard RA et al: Antenatal thyrotropin-releasing hormone to prevent lung disease in preterm infants. North American Thyrotropin-Releasing Hormone Group. N Engl J Med 338:493, 1998.

20. Barden TP et al: Ritodrine hydrochloride: A beta-mimetic agent for use in preterm labor: I. Pharmacology, clinical history, administration, side effects, and safety. Obstet Gynecol 56:1, 1980.

21. Bashore RA et al: Plasma unconjugated estriol values in high risk pregnancy. Am J Obstet Gynecol 128:371, 1997.

22. Beischer N et al: Urinary oestriol assay for monitoring fetoplacental function. Aust N Z J Obstet Gynaecol 31:1, 1991.

23. Belej-Rak T et al: Effectiveness of cervical cerclage for a sonographically shortened cervix: A systematic review and meta-analysis. Am J Obstet Gynecol 189:1679, 2003.

24. Ben-Ami M et al: The combination of magnesium sulphate and nifedipine: A cause of neuromuscular blockade. Br J Obstet Gynaecol 101:262, 1994.

25. Beneditti TJ: Maternal complications of parenteral beta-sympathomimetic therapy for preterm labor. Am J Obstet Gynecol 145:1, 1983.

26. Benirschke K et al: Intrauterine bacterial infection of the newborn infant. J Pediatr 54:11, 1959.

27. Berg G et al: β-Adrenergic receptors in human myometrium during pregnancy: Changes in the number of receptors after β-mimetic treatment. Am J Obstet Gynecol 151:392, 1985.

28. Berkowitz GS et al: Corticotropin-releasing factor and its binding protein: Maternal serum levels in term and preterm deliveries. Am J Obstet Gynecol 174:1477, 1996.

29. Berman SM et al: Low birth weight, prematurity and post-partum endometritis: Association with prenatal cervical Mycoplasma hominis and Chlamydia trachomatis infections. JAMA 257:189, 1987.

30. Besinger RE et al: Randomized comparative trial of indomethacin and ritodrine for the long-term treatment of premature labor. Am J Obstet Gynecol 164:981, 1991.

31. Bhat R et al: Disposition of indomethacin in preterm infants. J Pediatr 95:313, 1979.

32. Bieniarz J et al: Inhibition of uterine contractility in labor. Am J Obstet Gynecol 111:874, 1971.

33. Block BSB et al: Preterm delivery is not predicted by serial plasma estradiol and progesterone concentration measurements. Am J Obstet Gynecol 150:716, 1984.

34. Blondel B et al: Home uterine activity monitoring in France: A randomized controlled trial. Am J Obstet Gynecol 167:424, 1992.

35. Bobitt JR et al: Amniotic fluid infection as determined by transabdominal amniocentesis in patients with intact membranes in premature labor. Am J Obstet Gynecol 140:947, 1981.

36. Bohm N et al: Focal necrosis, fatty degeneration and subendocardial nuclear polyploidization in the myocardium of newborns. Eur J Pediatr 109:687, 1986.

37. Bossmar T et al: Receptors for and myometrial responses to oxytocin and vasopressin in preterm and term human pregnancy: Effects of the oxytocin antagonist atosiban. Am J Obstet Gynecol 171:1634, 1994.

38. Branch W: Operations for cervical incompetence. Clin Obstet Gynecol 29:240, 1986.

39. Brosset P et al: Cardiac complications of ritodrine in mother and baby. Lancet 1:1461, 1982.

40. Canadian Preterm Labor Investigators Group: The treatment of preterm labor with beta-adrenergic agonist ritodrine. N Engl J Med 327:308, 1992.

41. Cantor B et al: Oligohydramnios and transient neonatal anuria: A possible association with the maternal use of prostaglandin synthetase inhibitors. J Reprod Med 24:220, 1980.

42. Carey JC et al: Metronidazole to prevent preterm delivery in pregnant women with asymptomatic bacterial vaginosis. National Institute of Child Health and Human Development Network of Maternal-Fetal Medicine Units. N Engl J Med 342:534, 2000.

43. Caritis SN et al: A double-blind study comparing ritodrine and terbutaline in the treatment of preterm labor. Am J Obstet Gynecol 150:7, 1984.

44. Caritis SN et al: Pharmacokinetics of ritodrine administered intravenously: Recommendations for changes in the current regimen. Am J Obstet Gynecol 162:429, 1990.

45. Carlan SJ et al: Outpatient oral sulindac to prevent recurrence of preterm birth. Obstet Gynecol 85:769, 1995.

46. Carr-Hill RA et al: The repetition of spontaneous preterm labour. Br J Obstet Gynecol 92:921, 1985.

47. Casey ML et al: Biomolecular processes in the initiation of parturition: Decidual activation. Clin Obstet Gynecol 31:538, 1988.

48. Casey ML et al: The formation of cytokines in human decidua: The role of decidua in the initiation of both term and preterm labor [abstract]. Proceedings of the Society for Gynecological Investigation, Baltimore, 1988.

49. Caspi E et al: The outcome of pregnancy after gonadotropin therapy. Br J Obstet Gynaecol 83:967, 1976.

50. Cassell G et al: Chorioamnion colonization: Correlation with gestational age in women delivered following spontaneous labor versus indicated delivery. Am J Obstet Gynecol 168:425, 1993.

51. Centers for Disease Control and Prevention. Prevention of perinatal group B streptococcal disease: A public health perspective. MMWR Morb Mortal Wkly Rep 45(RR-7):1, 1996.

52. Chung C et al: Induced abortion and spontaneous fetal loss in subsequent pregnancies. Am J Public Health 72:548, 1982.

53. Clavin DK et al: Comparison of intravenous magnesium sulfate and nitroglycerin for preterm labor. Am J Obstet Gynecol 174:307, 1996.

54. Collaborative Group on Antenatal Steroid Therapy: Effects of antenatal dexamethasone administration in the infant: Long-term follow up. J Pediatr 104:259, 1984.

55. Collaborative Home Uterine Monitoring Study (CHUMS) Group: A multicenter randomized trial of home uterine activity monitoring. Am J Obstet Gynecol 172:253, 1995.

56. Copper RL et al: Warning symptoms, uterine contractions, and cervical examination findings in women at risk of preterm delivery. Am J Obstet Gynecol 162:748, 1990.

57. Copper RL et al: A multicenter study of preterm birth weight and gestational age specific neonatal mortality. Am J Obstet Gynecol 168:78, 1993.

58. Copper RL et al: Cervical examination and tocodynamometry at 28 weeks' gestation: Prediction of spontaneous preterm birth. Am J Obstet Gynecol 172:666, 1995.

59. Copper RL et al: The prematurity prediction study: Maternal stress is associated with spontaneous preterm birth at less than thirty-five weeks' gestation. National Institute of Child Health and Human Development Maternal-Fetal Medicine Units Network. Am J Obstet Gynecol 175:1286, 1996.

60. Cotch MF et al: Trichomonas vaginalis associated with low birth weight and preterm delivery. The Vaginal Infections and Prematurity Study Group. Sex Transm Dis 24:353, 1997.

61. Cotton DB et al: Comparison of magnesium sulfate, terbutaline, and a placebo for inhibition of preterm labor: A randomized study. J Reprod Med 29:92, 1984.

62. Cox SM et al: Accumulation of interleukin-1beta and interleukin-6 in amniotic fluid: A sequela of labour at term and preterm. Hum Reprod Update 3:517, 1997.

63. Creasy RK et al: System for predicting spontaneous preterm birth. Obstet Gynecol 55:692, 1980.

64. Creasy RK: Preterm birth prevention: Where are we? Am J Obstet Gynecol 168:1223, 1993.

65. Crenshaw S et al: Double blind placebo controlled trial (PREMET) of metronidazole to prevent early preterm delivery in high risk, fetal fibronectin positive women. J Soc Gynecol Investig 10:323A, 2003.

66. Crowley P: Prophylactic corticosteroids for preterm birth. Cochrane Database Syst Rev 2:CD000065, 2000.

67. Crowther CA et al: Australian Collaborative Trial of Antenatal Thyrotropin-Releasing Hormone (ACROBAT) for prevention of neonatal respiratory disease. Lancet 345:877, 1995.

68. Crowther CA et al: Effect of magnesium sulfate given for neuroprotection before preterm birth. JAMA 290:2669, 2003.

69. Cruikshank DP et al: Effects of magnesium sulphate treatment on perinatal calcium metabolism. Am J Obstet Gynecol 134:243, 1979.

70. Cruikshank DP et al: Urinary magnesium, calcium, and phosphate excretion during magnesium sulphate infusion. Obstet Gynecol 58:430, 1981.

71. Daikoku NH et al: Premature rupture of membranes and spontaneous preterm labor: Maternal endometritis risks. Obstet Gynecol 59:13, 1982.

72. Da Fonseca EB et al: Prophylactic administration of progesterone by vaginal suppository to reduce the incidence of spontaneous preterm birth in women at increased risk: A randomized placebo-controlled double-blind study. Am J Obstet Gynecol 188:419, 2003.

73. Dammann O et al: Maternal intrauterine infection, cytokines, and brain damage in the preterm newborn. Pediatr Res 42:1, 1996.

74. Darne J et al: Saliva oestriol, oestradiol, oestrone, and progesterone levels in pregnancy: Spontaneous labour at term is preceded by a rise in the saliva oestriol:progesterone ratio. Br J Obstet Gynaecol 94:227, 1987.

75. Darne J et al: Increased saliva oestriol to progesterone ratio before idiopathic preterm delivery: A possible predictor for preterm labour? Br Med J 294:270, 1987.

76. Dooley SL et al: Urinary estriols in diabetic pregnancy: A reappraisal. Obstet Gynecol 64:469, 1984.

77. Dor J et al: Elective cervical suture of twin pregnancies diagnosed ultrasonically in the first trimester following induced ovulation. Gynecol Obstet Invest 13:55, 1982.

78. Dray F et al: Primary prostaglandins in amniotic fluid in pregnancy and spontaneous labor. Am J Obstet Gynecol 126:13, 1976.

79. Dudley DJ et al: Biosynthesis of interleukin-6 by cultured human chorion laeve cell: Regulation by cytokines, J Clin Endocrinol Metab 75:1081, 1992.

80. Dudley DJ et al: Decidual cell biosynthesis of interleukin-6: Regulation by inflammatory cytokines. J Clin Endocrinol Metab 74:884, 1992.

81. Dudley DJ: Immunoendocrinology of preterm labor: The link between corticotropin-releasing hormone and inflammation. Am J Obstet Gynecol 180:S251, 1999.

82. Duenhoelter JH et al: An analysis of the utility of plasma immunoreactive estrogen measurements in determining delivery time of gravidas with a fetus considered at high risk. Am J Obstet Gynecol 125:889, 1976.

83. Dunlop SA et al: Repeated prenatal corticosteroids delay myelination in the ovine central nervous system. J Matern Fetal Med 6:309, 1997.

84. Dyson DC et al: Prevention of preterm birth in high-risk patients: The role of education and provider contact versus home uterine monitoring. Am J Obstet Gynecol 164:756, 1991.

85. Dyson DC et al: Monitoring women at risk for preterm labor. N Engl J Med 338:15, 1998.

86. Ekwo EE et al: Unfavorable outcome in penultimate pregnancy and premature rupture of membranes in successive pregnancy. Obstet Gynecol 80:166, 1992.

87. Elder HA et al: The natural history of asymptomatic bacteriuria during pregnancy: The effect of tetracycline on the clinical course and outcome of pregnancy. Am J Obstet Gynecol 111:441, 1971.

88. Ellenberg J et al: Birth weight and gestational age in

children with cerebral palsy or seizure disorders. Am J Dis Child 133.1044, 1979.

89. Elliot JP et al: Magnesium sulfate as a tocolytic agent. Am J Obstet Gynecol 147:277, 1983.

90. El-Sayed YY et al: Randomized comparison of intravenous nitroglycerin and magnesium sulfate for treatment of preterm labor. Obstet Gynecol 93:79, 1999.

91. Epstein MF et al: Neonatal hypoglycemia after beta-sympathomimetic tocolytic therapy. J Pediatr 94:449, 1979.

92. Eschenbach DA et al: A randomized placebo-controlled trial of erythromycin for the treatment of *Ureaplasma urealyticum* to prevent premature delivery. Am J Obstet Gynecol 164:734, 1991.

93. Evaldson GR et al: Premature rupture of the membranes and ascending infection. Br J Obstet Gynaecol 89:793, 1982.

94. Fedrick J et al: Factors associated with spontaneous preterm birth. Br J Obstet Gynaecol 83:342, 1976.

95. Feinberg FR, Kliman JH: Fetal fibronectin and preterm labor. N Engl J Med 172:134, 1992.

96. Ferguson JE II et al: A comparison of tocolysis with nifedipine or ritodrine: Analysis of efficacy and maternal, fetal, and neonatal outcome. Am J Obstet Gynecol 163:105, 1990.

97. Fiscella K: Racial disparities in preterm births: The role of urogenital infections. Public Health Rep 111:104, 1996.

98. Forster F et al: Therapy in cervical insufficiency: Cerclage or support pessary. Zentralbl Gynakol 108:230, 1986.

99. Fortunato SJ et al: MMP/TIMP imbalance in amniotic fluid during PPROM: An indirect support for endogenous pathway to membrane rupture. J Perinat Med 27:362, 1999.

100. Foulon W et al: Markers of infection and their relationship to preterm delivery. Am J Perinatol 12:208, 1995.

101. French NP et al: Repeated antenatal corticosteroids: Size at birth and subsequent development. Am J Obstet Gynecol 180:114, 1999.

102. Fuchs F et al: Treatment of threatened premature labor with large doses of progesterone. Am J Obstet Gynecol 79:173, 1960.

103. Fuchs AR et al: Oxytocin receptors and human parturition: A dual role for oxytocin in the initiation of labor. Science 215:1396, 1982.

104. Gerson A et al: Safety and efficacy of long-term tocolysis with indomethacin. Am J Perinatol 7:71, 1990.

105. Gibbs RS et al: A review of premature birth and subclinical infection. Am J Obstet Gynecol 166:1515, 1992.

106. Gilstrap LC III et al: Survival and short-term morbidity of the premature neonate. Obstet Gynecol 65:37, 1985.

107. Goepfert AR et al: The preterm prediction study: Association between cervical interleukin-6, fetal fibronectin, and spontaneous preterm birth. Am J Obstet Gynecol 176:S6, 1997.

108. Goldenberg RL et al: Bed rest in pregnancy. Obstet Gynecol 84:131, 1994.

109. Goldenberg RL et al: The preterm prediction study: Fetal fibronectin, bacterial vaginosis, and peripartum infection. Obstet Gynecol 87:656, 1996.

110. Goldenberg RL et al: The preterm prediction study: Fetal fibronectin testing and spontaneous preterm birth. Obstet Gynecol 87:643, 1996.

111. Goldenberg RL et al: Sexually transmitted diseases and adverse outcomes of pregnancy. Clin Perinatol 24:23, 1997.

112. Goldenberg RL et al: Plasma ferritin, PROM and pregnancy outcome. Am J Obstet Gynecol 179:1599, 1998.

113. Goldenberg RL et al: The prematurity prediction study: The value of new vs standard risk factors in predicting early and all spontaneous preterm births. NICHD MFMU Network. Am J Public Health 88:233, 1998.

114. Goldenberg RL et al: The preterm prediction study: Cervical lactoferrin, other markers of lower genital tract infection, and preterm birth. Am J Obstet Gynecol 182:631, 2000.

115. Goldenberg RL et al: The preterm prediction study: Granulocyte colony stimulating factor and spontaneous preterm birth. Am J Obstet Gynecol 182:625, 2000.

116. Goldenberg RL et al: Intrauterine infection and preterm delivery. N Engl J Med 342:1500, 2000.

117. Goldenberg RL et al: Toward a multiple marker test for spontaneous preterm birth (SPB). Am J Obstet Gynecol 182:S12, 2000.

118. Goldenberg RL: The management of preterm labor. N Engl J Med 100:1020, 2002.

119. Goldenberg RL et al: Biochemical markers for the prediction of preterm birth. Am J Obstet Gynecol (in press).

120. Goldenberg RL et al: Metronidazole treatment of women with a positive fetal fibronectin test result. Am J Obstet Gynecol 185:485, 2001.

121. Gomez R et al: Ultrasonographic examination of the uterine cervix is better than cervical digital examination as a predictor of the likelihood of premature delivery in patients with preterm labor and intact membranes. Am J Obstet Gynecol 171:956, 1994.

122. Goodlin RC et al: The significance and diagnosis of maternal hypovolemia. Semin Perinatol 5:163, 1981.

123. Goodwin TM et al: The effect of the oxytocin antagonist atosiban on preterm uterine activity in the human. Am J Obstet Gynecol 170:474, 1994.

124. Grant AM: Cervical cerclage: Evaluation studies. Proceedings of a Workshop on Prevention of Preterm Birth, Paris, INSERM, 1986.

125. Grant AM et al: Final report of the Medical Research Council/Royal College of Obstetricians and Gynaecologists multicentre randomized trial of cervical cerclage. Br J Obstet Gynaecol 100:516, 1993.

126. Gravett MG et al: Independent associations of bacterial vaginosis and *Chlamydia trachomatis* infections with adverse pregnancy outcome. JAMA 256:1899, 1986.

127. Gravett MG et al: Preterm labor associated with subclinical amniotic fluid infections and with bacterial vaginosis. Obstet Gynecol 67:229, 1986.

128. Green KW et al: The effects of maternally administered magnesium sulfate on the neonate. Am J Obstet Gynecol 146:29, 1983.

129. Grether JK et al: Magnesium sulfate tocolysis and risk of neonatal death. Am J Obstet Gynecol 178:1, 1998.

130. Groom KM et al: Elective cervical cerclage versus serial ultrasound surveillance of cervical length in a population at high risk for preterm delivery. Eur J Obstet Gynecol Reprod Biol 112:158, 2004.

131. Groome LJ et al: Neonatal periventricular-intraventricular hemorrhage after maternal β-sympathomimetic tocolysis. Am J Obstet Gynecol 167:873, 1992.

132. Gross TJ et al: Maternal and fetal plasma concentration of ritodrine. Obstet Gynecol 65:793, 1985.

133. Guinn DA et al: Management options in women with preterm uterine contractions: A randomized clinical trial. Am J Obstet Gynecol 177:814, 1997.

134. Guinn DA et al: Terbutaline pump maintenance therapy

for prevention of preterm delivery: A double-blind trial. Am J Obstet Gynecol 179:874, 1998.

135. Guinn DA et al: Single vs weekly courses of antenatal corticosteroids for women at risk of preterm delivery: A randomized controlled trial. JAMA 286:1581, 2001.

136. Guzick DS et al: The association of chorioamnionitis with preterm delivery. Obstet Gynecol 65:11, 1985.

137. Hack M et al: Outcomes of extremely immature infants: A perinatal dilemma. N Engl J Med 329:1649, 1993.

138. Hack M et al: School-age outcomes in children with birth weights under 750 g. N Engl J Med 331:753, 1994.

139. Hack M et al: Outcomes of children of extremely low birthweight and gestational age in the 1990's. Early Hum Dev 53:193, 1999.

140. Hadders-Algra M et al: Long-term follow-up of children prenatally exposed to ritodrine. Br J Obstet Gynaecol 93:156, 1986.

141. Hammed C et al: Silent chorioamnionitis as a cause of preterm labor refractory to tocolytic therapy. Am J Obstet Gynecol 149:726, 1984.

142. Hanssens MC et al: Sex steroid hormone concentrations in preterm labour and the outcome of treatment with ritodrine. Br J Obstet Gynaecol 85:411, 1978.

143. Harake B et al: Nifedipine: Effects on fetal and maternal hemodynamics in pregnant sheep. Am J Obstet Gynecol 157:1003, 1987.

144. Harger JH: Cervical cerclage: Patient selection, morbidity and success rates. Clin Perinatol 10:321, 1983.

145. Harger JH et al: Etiology of recurrent pregnancy losses and outcome of subsequent pregnancies. Obstet Gynecol 62:574, 1983.

146. Harger JH et al: Risk factors for preterm premature rupture of fetal membranes: A multicenter case-control study. Am J Obstet Gynecol 163:130, 1990.

147. Harrison HR et al: Cervical *Chlamydia trachomatis* and mycoplasmal infections in pregnancy: Epidemiology and outcomes. JAMA 247:1585, 1983.

148. Hauth JC et al: Infection-related risk factors predictive of spontaneous preterm labor and birth. Prenat Neonatal Med 3:86, 1998.

149. Hauth JC et al: Reduced incidence of preterm delivery with metronidazole and erythromycin in women with bacterial vaginosis. N Engl J Med 333:1732, 1995.

150. Hauth JC et al: Reduction of cerebral palsy with maternal $MgSO_4$ treatment in newborns weighing 500-1000 g. Am J Obstet Gynecol 172:419, 1995.

151. Hauth JC et al: Mid-trimester metronidazole and azithromycin did not prevent preterm birth in women at increased risk: A double-blinded trial. Am J Obstet Gynecol 185:S86, 2001.

152. Heffner LJ et al: Clinical and environmental predictors of preterm labor. Obstet Gynecol 81:750, 1993.

153. Heinonen PK et al: Reproductive performance of women with uterine anomalies. Acta Obstet Gynecol Scand 61:157, 1982.

154. Helfgott AW et al: Is hydration and sedation beneficial in the treatment of threatened preterm labor? A preliminary report. J Matern Fetal Med 3:37, 1994.

155. Hermansen MC et al: Neonatal supraventricular tachycardia following prolonged maternal ritodrine administration. Am J Obstet Gynecol 149:798, 1984.

156. Hill GB: The microbiology of bacterial vaginosis. Am J Obstet Gynecol 169:450, 1993.

157. Hillier SL et al: A case-control study of chorioamnionic infection and histologic chorioamnionitis in prematurity. N Engl J Med 319:972, 1988.

158. Hillier SL et al: Microbiologic causes and neonatal outcomes associated with chorioamnion infection. Am J Obstet Gynecol 165:955, 1991.

159. Hillier SL et al: The relationship of amniotic fluid cytokines and preterm delivery, amniotic fluid infection, histologic chorioamnionitis, and chorioamnion infection. Obstet Gynecol 81:941, 1993.

160. Hillier SL et al: Association between bacterial vaginosis and preterm delivery of a low-birth-weight infant. The Vaginal Infections and Prematurity Study Group. N Engl J Med 333:1737, 1995.

161. Hirtz DG, Nelson K: Magnesium sulfate and cerebral palsy in premature infants. Curr Opin Pediatr 10:131, 1998.

162. Holbrook RH Jr et al: Evaluation of a risk-scoring system for prediction of preterm labor. Am J Perinatol 6:62, 1989.

163. Holcomb WL et al: Magnesium tocolysis and neonatal bone abnormalities. Obstet Gynecol 78:611, 1991.

164. Howard TE et al: A double-blind randomized study of terbutaline in premature labor. Milit Med 12:4, 1982.

165. Huhta JC et al: Detection and quantitation of constriction of the fetal ductus arteriosus by Doppler echocardiography. Circulation 2:406, 1987.

166. Huisjes HJ et al: Neonatal outcome after treatment with ritodrine: A controlled study. Am J Obstet Gynecol 147:250, 1983.

167. Iams JD et al: A prospective random trial of home uterine activity monitoring in pregnancies at increased risk of preterm labor. Am J Obstet Gynecol 157:638, 1987.

168. Iams JD et al: Cervical sonography in preterm labor. Obstet Gynecol 84:40, 1994.

169. Iams JD et al: Fetal fibronectin improves the accuracy of diagnosis of preterm labor. Am J Obstet Gynecol 173:141, 1995.

170. Iams J et al: The length of the cervix and the risk of spontaneous premature delivery. N Engl J Med 334:567, 1996.

171. Iams JD et al: Prediction of preterm birth with ambulatory measurement of uterine contraction frequency. Am J Obstet Gynecol 178:S2, 1998.

172. Ingemarsson I: Effect of terbutaline on premature labor. Am J Obstet Gynecol 125:520, 1976.

173. Jones JM et al: The outcome of pregnancy after cone biopsy of the cervix: A case-control study. Br J Obstet Gynaecol 86:913, 1979.

174. Kanayama N et al: Collagen types in normal and prematurely ruptured amniotic membranes. Am J Obstet Gynecol 153:899, 1985.

175. Kanayama N et al: The relationship between granulocyte elastase like activity of cervical mucus and cervical maturation. Acta Obstet Gynecol Scand 70:29, 1991.

176. Kass EH: Bacteriuria and pyelonephritis of pregnancy. Arch Intern Med 105:194, 1960.

177. Katz M et al: Initial evaluation of an ambulatory system for home monitoring and transmission of uterine activity data. Obstet Gynecol 66:273, 1985.

178. Katz M et al: Assessment of uterine activity in ambulatory patients at high risk of preterm labor and delivery. Am J Obstet Gynecol 154:44, 1986.

179. Katz M et al: Early signs and symptoms of preterm labor. Am J Obstet Gynecol 262:230, 1990.

180. Kaufman RH et al: Genital tract anomalies associated with in utero exposure to diethylstilbestrol. Isr J Med Sci 14:347, 1978.

181. Kaufman RH et al: Upper genital tract abnormalities and pregnancy outcome in diethylstilbestrol-exposed progeny. N Engl J Med 313:1322, 1985.

182. Keirse MJ. Progestogen administration in pregnancy may prevent preterm delivery. Br J Obstet Gynaecol 97:149, 1990.

183. Kelly RW et al: Choriodecidual production of interleukin-8 and mechanism of parturition. Lancet 339:776, 1992.

184. Kenyon SL et al: Broad-spectrum antibiotics for spontaneous preterm labour: The ORACLE II randomised trial. ORACLE Collaborative Group. Lancet 357:989, 2001.

185. Kenyon SL et al: Broad-spectrum antibiotics for preterm, prelabour rupture of fetal membranes: The ORACLE I randomised trial. ORACLE Collaborative Group. Lancet 357:979, 2001.

186. King JF et al: Beta-mimetics in preterm labour: An overview of randomized, controlled trials. Br J Obstet Gynaecol 95:211, 1988.

187. King J, Flenady V: Antibiotics for preterm labour with intact membranes. Cochrane Pregnancy and Childbirth Group. Cochrane Database Syst Rev 4:CD000246, 2002.

188. Kirshon B et al: Influence of short-term indomethacin therapy on fetal urine output. Obstet Gynecol 72:51, 1988.

189. Kirshon B et al: Long-term indomethacin therapy decreases fetal urine output and results in oligohydramnios. Am J Perinatol 8:86, 1991.

190. Klebanoff MA et al: Outcome of the Vaginal Infections and Prematurity Study: Results of a clinical trial of erythromycin among pregnant women colonized with group B streptococci. Am J Obstet Gynecol 172:1540, 1995.

191. Knight DB et al: A randomized controlled trial of antepartum thyrotropin-releasing hormone and beta-methasone in the prevention of respiratory disease in preterm infants. Am J Obstet Gynecol 171:11, 1994.

192. Korn AP et al: Plasma cell endometritis in women with symptomatic bacterial vaginosis. Obstet Gynecol 85:387, 1995.

193. Kramer W et al: Randomized, double-blind study comparing sulindac to terbutaline: Fetal renal and amniotic fluid effects. Am J Obstet Gynecol 174:244, 1996.

194. Krohn MA et al: The genital flora of women with intraamniotic infection. J Infect Dis 171:1475, 1995.

195. Kurki T et al: Bacterial vaginosis in early pregnancy and pregnancy outcome. Obstet Gynecol 80:173, 1992.

196. Kurtzman JL et al: Do nifedipine and verapamil potentiate the cardiac toxicity of magnesium sulfate? Am J Perinatol 10:450, 1993.

197. Kurtzman JL et al: Transvaginal versus transperineal ultrasound: A blinded comparison in the assessment of cervical length at mid-gestation. Am J Obstet Gynecol 178:S15, 1998.

198. Kushnir O et al: Transvaginal sonographic measurement of cervical length: Evaluation of twin pregnancies. J Reprod Med 40:380, 1995.

199. Lam F et al: Use of the subcutaneous terbutaline pump for long-term tocolysis. Obstet Gynecol 72:810, 1988.

200. Lamont RF et al: The role of mycoplasmas, ureaplasmas and chlamydiae in the genital tract of women presenting in spontaneous early preterm labour. J Med Microbiol 24:253, 1987.

201. Lampert MB et al: Peripartum heart failure associated with prolonged tocolytic therapy. Am J Obstet Gynecol 168:493, 1993.

202. Lands AM et al: Differentiation of receptor systems by sympathomimetic amines. Nature 214:597, 1967.

203. Lazar P et al: Multicentered controlled trial of cervical cerclage in women at moderate risk of preterm delivery. Br J Obstet Gynaecol 91:724, 1984.

204. Leake RD et al: Pharmacokinetics of oxytocin in the human subject. Obstet Gynecol 56:701, 1980.

205. Lees CC et al: Glyceryl trinitrate and ritodrine in tocolysis: An international multicenter randomized study. GTN Preterm Labour Investigation Group. Obstet Gynecol 94:403, 1999.

206. Lenke R et al: Sudden unforeseen fetal death in a woman being treated for premature labor. J Reprod Med 29:872, 1984.

207. Leung TN et al: Elevated mid-trimester maternal corticotrophin-releasing hormone levels in pregnancies that delivered before 34 weeks. Br J Obstet Gynaecol 106:1041, 1999.

208. Leviton A et al: White matter damage in preterm newborns: An epidemiologic perspective. Early Hum Dev 24:1, 1990.

209. Liggins GC, Howie RN: A controlled trial of antepartum glucocorticoid treatment for the prevention of RDS in premature infants. Pediatrics 50:515, 1972.

210. Lin TJ et al: Metabolic clearance of progesterone in the menstrual cycle. J Clin Endocrinol Metab 35:879, 1972.

211. Lindenbaum C et al: Maternal glucose intolerance and the subcutaneous terbutaline pump. Am J Obstet Gynecol 166:925, 1992.

212. Linn S et al: The relationship between induced abortion and outcome of subsequent pregnancies. Am J Obstet Gynecol 146:136, 1983.

213. Lockwood CJ et al: Fetal fibronectin in cervical and vaginal secretions defines a patient population at high risk for preterm delivery. N Engl J Med 325:669, 1991.

214. Lockwood CJ et al: Fetal fibronectin predicts preterm deliveries in asymptomatic patients [abstract]. Am J Obstet Gynecol 168:311, 1993.

215. Ludmir J et al: A prospective study of cerclage in the DES-exposed pregnant patient [abstract]. Society of Perinatal Obstetrics, Orlando, Fla, 1987.

216. Ludmir J et al: Poor perinatal outcome associated with retained cerclage in patients with premature rupture of membranes. Obstet Gynecol 84:823, 1994.

217. Lundin-Schiller S et al: Prostaglandin production by human chorion laeve cells in response to inflammatory mediators. Placenta 12:353, 1991.

218. Lyrenas S et al: Pharmacokinetics of terbutaline during pregnancy. Eur J Clin Pharmacol 29:619, 1986.

219. MacArthur BA et al: School progress and cognitive development of 6-year-old children whose mothers were treated with betamethasone. Pediatrics 70:99, 1982.

220. MacGregor SN et al: Cocaine use during pregnancy: Adverse perinatal outcome. Am J Obstet Gynecol 157:686, 1987.

221. MacKenzie LW et al: Effects of estradiol-17beta and prostaglandins on rat myometrial gap junctions. Prostaglandins 26:925, 1983.

222. MacLennan FM et al: Fatal pulmonary oedema associated with the use of ritodrine in pregnancy: Case report. Br J Obstet Gynaecol 92:703, 1985.

223. Main DM et al: Prospective evaluation of a risk scoring system for predicting preterm delivery in black inner city women. Obstet Gynecol 69:61, 1987.

224. Main DM et al: Intermittent weekly contraction monitoring to predict preterm labor in low-risk women: A blinded study. Obstet Gynecol 72:757, 1988.

225. Main EK et al: Chronic oral terbutaline tocolytic therapy is associated with maternal glucose intolerance. Am J Obstet Gynecol 157:664, 1987.

226. Manchester D et al: Possible association between maternal indomethacin therapy and primary pulmonary

hypertension of the newborn. Am J Obstet Gynecol 126:467, 1976.

227. Marbury MC et al: Work and pregnancy. J Occup Med 26:415, 1984.

228. Mari G et al: Doppler assessment of the fetal and utero-placental circulation during nifedipine therapy for preterm labor. Am J Obstet Gynecol 161:1514, 1989.

229. Mari G et al: Doppler assessment of the renal blood flow velocity waveform during indomethacin therapy for preterm labor and polyhydramnios. Obstet Gynecol 75:199, 1990.

230. Martin DH et al: Prematurity and perinatal mortality in pregnancies complicated by maternal *Chlamydia trachomatis* infections. JAMA 247:1585, 1982.

231. Martin RW et al: Oral magnesium and the prevention of preterm labor in a high-risk group of patients. Am J Obstet Gynecol 166:144, 1992.

232. Maudsley RF et al: Placental inflammation and infection: A prospective bacteriologic and histologic study. Am J Obstet Gynecol 95:648, 1966.

233. McClean M et al: Prediction and early diagnosis of preterm labor: A critical review. Obstet Gynecol Surv 48:2091, 1993.

234. McCormick MC: The contribution of low birth weight to infant mortality and childhood morbidity. N Engl J Med 312:82, 1985.

235. McDonald HM et al: Prenatal microbiological risk factors associated with preterm birth. Br J Obstet Gynecol 99:190, 1992.

236. McDonald HM et al: Impact of metronidazole therapy on preterm birth in women with bacterial vaginosis flora (*Gardnerella vaginalis*): A randomised, placebo controlled trial. Br J Obstet Gynaecol 104:1391, 1997.

237. McDowall M et al: Employment during pregnancy and infant mortality. Population Trends 26:12, 1981.

238. McGarrigle HHG et al: Increasing saliva (free) oestriol to progesterone ratio in late pregnancy: A role for oestriol in initiating spontaneous labour in man? Br Med J 289:457, 1984.

239. McGregor JA et al: Association of cervico-vaginal infections with increased vaginal fluid phospholipase A2 activity. Am J Obstet Gynecol 167:1588, 1988.

240. McGregor JA et al: Salivary estriol as risk assessment for preterm labor: A prospective trial. Am J Obstet Gynecol 17:1337, 1995.

241. Meis PJ et al: Causes of low birthweight births in public and private patients. Am J Obstet Gynecol 156:1165, 1987.

242. Meis PJ et al: Regional program for prevention of premature birth in northwest North Carolina. Am J Obstet Gynecol 157:550, 1987.

243. Meis PJ et al: National Institute of Child Health and Human Development Maternal-Fetal Medicine Units Network. Prevention of recurrent preterm delivery by 17 alpha-hydroxyprogesterone caproate. N Engl J Med 348:2379, 2003.

244. Ment L et al: Antenatal steroids, delivery, mode and intraventricular hemorrhage in preterm infants. Am J Obstet Gynecol 172:795, 1995.

245. Mercer BM et al: Antibiotic therapy for reduction of infant morbidity after preterm premature rupture of the membranes: A randomized controlled trial. National Institute of Child Health and Human Development Maternal-Fetal Medicine Units Network. JAMA 278:989, 1997.

246. Mercer BM et al: The preterm prediction study: Effect of gestational age and cause of preterm birth on subsequent obstetric outcome. National Institute of Child Health and Human Development Maternal-Fetal Medicine Units Network. Am J Obstet Gynecol 181:1216, 1999.

247. Merkatz JR et al: Ritodrine hydrochloride: A beta-mimetic agent for use in preterm labor—II. Evidence of efficacy. Obstet Gynecol 56:7, 1980.

248. Miller HC et al: Maternal factors in the incidence of low birthweight infants among black and white mothers. Pediatr Res 12:1016, 1978.

249. Miller JM et al: A comparison of magnesium sulfate and terbutaline for the arrest of premature labor. J Reprod Med 27:348, 1982.

250. Mitchell MD et al: Specific production of prostaglandin E by human amnion in vitro. Prostaglandins 15:377, 1978.

251. Mitchell MD et al: Interleukin-6 stimulates prostaglandin production by human amnion and decidual cells. Eur J Pharmacol 192:189, 1991.

252. Mittendorf R et al: Does exposure to antenatal magnesium sulfate prevent cerebral palsy? Am J Obstet Gynecol 182:S20, 2000.

253. Mittendorf R et al: Is tocolytic magnesium sulphate associated with increased total paediatric mortality? Lancet 350:1517, 1997.

254. Moutquin JM et al: Double-blind, randomized, controlled trial of atosiban and ritodrine in the treatment of preterm labor: A multicenter effectiveness and safety study. Am J Obstet Gynecol 182:1191, 2000.

255. Moise KJ et al: Indomethacin in the treatment of premature labor: Effects on the fetal ductus arteriosus. N Engl J Med 319:327, 1988.

256. Moise KJ: Effect of advancing gestational age on the frequency of fetal ductal constriction in association with maternal indomethacin use. Am J Obstet Gynecol 168:1350, 1993.

257. Moller M et al: Rupture of fetal membranes and premature delivery associated with group B streptococci in urine of pregnant women. Lancet 2:69, 1984.

258. Moore LE, Martin JN Jr: When betamethasone and dexamethasone are unavailable: hydrocortisone. J Perinatol 21:456, 2001.

259. Morales WJ et al: Efficacy and safety of indomethacin versus ritodrine in the management of preterm labor: A randomized study. Obstet Gynecol 74:567, 1989.

260. Morales WJ et al: Efficacy and safety of indomethacin compared with magnesium sulfate in the management of preterm labor: A randomized study. Am J Obstet Gynecol 169:97, 1993.

261. Morales WJ et al: Effect of metronidazole in patients with preterm birth in preceding pregnancy and bacterial vaginosis: A placebo-controlled, double-blind study. Am J Obstet Gynecol 171:345, 1994.

262. Moran DJ et al: Lack of normal increase in saliva estriol/progesterone ratio in women with labor induced at 42 weeks' gestation. Am J Obstet Gynecol 167:1563, 1992.

263. Morrison JC et al: Prevention of preterm birth by ambulatory assessment of uterine activity: A randomized study. Am J Obstet Gynecol 156:536, 1987.

264. Morrison JC et al: Oncofetal fibronectin in patients with false labor as a predictor of preterm delivery. Am J Obstet Gynecol 168:538, 1993.

265. Mortensen OA et al: Prediction of preterm birth. Acta Obstet Gynecol Scand 66:507, 1987.

266. Mou SM et al: Multicenter randomized clinical trial of home uterine monitoring for detection of preterm labor. Am J Obstet Gynecol 165:858, 1991.

267. Mueller-Heubach E et al: Evaluation of risk scoring in a preterm birth prevention study of indigent patients. Obstet Gynecol 160:829, 1989.

268. Mueller-Heubach E et al: Histologic chorioamnionitis and preterm delivery in different patient populations. Obstet Gynecol 75:622, 1990.

269. Muran D et al: Myomas of the uterus in pregnancy: Ultrasonographic follow-up. Am J Obstet Gynecol 138:16, 1980.

270. Murphy JF et al: Employment in pregnancy: Prevalence, maternal characteristics, perinatal outcomes. Lancet 1:1163, 1984.

271. Murtha AP et al: Maternal serum interleukin-6 concentration as a marker for impending preterm delivery. Obstet Gynecol 91:161, 1998.

272. Nadisauskiene R et al: Ampicillin in the treatment of preterm labor: A randomised, placebo-controlled study. Gynecol Obstet Invest 41:89, 1996.

273. Nageotte MP et al: Quantitation of uterine activity preceding preterm, term, and postterm labor. Am J Obstet Gynecol 158:1254, 1988.

274. National Institutes of Health (NIH) Consensus Development Conference: Effect of corticosteroids for fetal maturation on perinatal outcomes. Am J Obstet Gynecol 173:246, 1995.

275. National Institutes of Health (NIH) Consensus Statement: Antenatal Corticosteroids Revisited: Repeat Courses. NIH Consensus Statement 2000. Bethesda, Md, August 17-18; 17:1-10.

276. Nelson KB et al: Antecedents of cerebral palsy: Multivariate analysis of risk. N Engl J Med 315:81, 1986.

277. Nelson KB et al: Can magnesium sulfate reduce the risk of cerebral palsy in very-low birthweight infants? Pediatrics 95:263, 1995.

278. Newcomer J: Pessaries for the treatment of incompetent cervix and premature delivery. Obstet Gynecol Surv 55:443, 2000.

279. Newman RB et al: Maternal perception of prelabor uterine activity. Obstet Gynecol 68:765, 1986.

280. Niebyl JR et al: The inhibition of premature labor with indomethacin. Am J Obstet Gynecol 136:1014, 1980.

281. Norman K et al: Ampicillin and metronidazole treatment in preterm labour: A multicentre, randomised controlled trial. Br J Obstet Gynaecol 101:404, 1994.

282. Norton ME et al: Neonatal complications after the administration of indomethacin for preterm labor. N Engl J Med 329:1602, 1993.

283. Norwitz ER et al: The control of labor. N Engl J Med 341:660, 1999.

284. Novy MJ et al: Plasma concentrations of prostaglandin F2 alpha and prostaglandin E2 metabolites after transabdominal and transvaginal cervical cerclage. Am J Obstet Gynecol 156:1543, 1987.

285. Nuchpuckdee P et al: Ventricular septal thickness and cardiac function in neonates after in utero ritodrine exposure. J Pediatr 109:687, 1986.

286. Nyberg L: Pharmacokinetic parameters of terbutaline in healthy men: An overview. Eur J Respir Dis 65(Suppl 134):149, 1984.

287. Okazaki T et al: Initiation of human parturition: XII. Biosynthesis and metabolism of prostaglandins in human fetal membranes and uterine decidua. Am J Obstet Gynecol 139:373, 1981.

288. Okitsu O et al: Early prediction of preterm delivery by transvaginal ultrasonography. Ultrasound Obstet Gynecol 2:402, 1992.

289. Ovlisen G, Iversen J: Treatment of threatened premature labor with 6α-methyl-17α-acetoxyprogesterone. Am J Obstet Gynecol 86:291, 1963.

290. Owen J et al: Evaluation of a risk scoring system as a predictor of preterm birth in an indigent population. Am J Obstet Gynecol 163:873, 1990.

291. Owen J et al: Mid-trimester endovaginal sonography in women at high risk for spontaneous preterm birth. JAMA 286:1340, 2001.

292. Owen J et al: Vaginal sonography and cervical incompetence. Am J Obstet Gynecol 188:586, 2003.

293. Padayachi T et al: Changes in amniotic fluid prostaglandins with oxytocin-induced labor. Obstet Gynecol 68:610, 1986.

294. Papiernik E et al: Prevention of preterm births: A perinatal study in Haguenau, France. Pediatrics 76:154, 1985.

295. Papiernik E et al: Precocious cervical ripening and preterm labor. Obstet Gynecol 67:238, 1986.

296. Parisi VM: Cervical incompetence and preterm labor. Clin Obstet Gynecol 31:585, 1988.

297. Parulekar SG et al: Dynamic incompetent cervix uteri. J Ultrasound Med 7:481, 1988.

298. Peaceman AM et al: Fetal fibronectin as a predictor of preterm birth in patients with symptoms: A multicenter trial. Am J Obstet Gynecol 177:13, 1997.

299. Pircon RA et al: Controlled trial of hydration and bed rest versus bed rest alone in the evaluation of preterm uterine contractions. Am J Obstet Gynecol 161:775, 1989.

300. Rajabi M et al: High levels of serum collagenase in premature labor: A potential biochemical marker. Obstet Gynecol 69:179, 1987.

301. Ramin KD et al: Ultrasound assessment of cervical length in triplet pregnancies. Am J Obstet Gynecol 180:1442, 1999.

302. Ramsey PS et al: Elevated cervical ferritin levels at 24 weeks gestation are associated with spontaneous preterm birth in asymptomatic pregnant women. J Soc Gynecol Invest 7:190A, 2000.

303. Ramsey PS, Andrews WW: Biochemical predictors of preterm labor: Fetal fibronectin and salivary estriol. Clin Perinat 30:701, 2003.

304. Ramsey PS, Rouse DJ: Magnesium sulfate as a tocolytic agent. Sem Perinatol 25:236, 2001.

305. Ramsey PS, Rouse DJ: Therapies administered to mothers at risk for preterm birth and neurodevelopmental outcome in their infants. Clin Perinatol 29:725, 2002.

306. Rasanen J et al: Fetal cardiac function and ductus arteriosus during indomethacin and sulindac therapy for threatened preterm labor: A randomized study. Am J Obstet Gynecol 172:70, 1995.

307. Read MD et al: The use of a calcium antagonist (nifedipine) to suppress preterm labour. Br J Obstet Gynaecol 93:933, 1986.

308. Regan JA et al: Premature rupture of membranes, preterm delivery, and group B streptococcal colonization of mothers. Am J Obstet Gynecol 141:184, 1981.

309. Reis FM et al: Putative role of placental corticotropin-releasing factor in the mechanisms of human parturition. J Soc Gynecol Invest 6:109, 1999.

310. Ricci JM et al: Oral tocolysis with magnesium chloride: A randomized controlled prospective clinical trial. Am J Obstet Gynecol 165:603, 1991.

311. Richey SD et al: The correlation between transperineal sonography and digital examination in the evaluation of the third-trimester cervix. Obstet Gynecol 85:745, 1995.

312. Ridgeway LE et al: A prospective randomized comparison of oral terbutaline and magnesium oxide for the

maintenance of tocolysis. Am J Obstet Gynecol 163:879, 1990.

313. Rizzo G et al: Interleukin-6 concentrations in cervical secretions identify microbial invasion of the amniotic cavity in patients with preterm labor and intact membranes. Am J Obstet Gynecol 175:812, 1996.

314. Robertson PA et al: Neonatal morbidity according to gestational age and birth weight from five tertiary centers in the United States, 1983-1986. Am J Obstet Gynecol 166:1629, 1992.

315. Romero R et al: Infection and labor: The detection of endotoxin in amniotic fluid. Am J Obstet Gynecol 157:815, 1987.

316. Romero R et al: Prostaglandin concentrations in amniotic fluid of women with intraamniotic infection and preterm labor. Am J Obstet Gynecol 157:1461, 1987.

317. Romero R et al: Endotoxin stimulates prostaglandin E2 production by human amnion. Obstet Gynecol 71:227, 1988.

318. Romero R et al: Labor and infection: II. Bacterial endotoxin in amniotic fluid and its relationship to the onset of preterm labor. Am J Obstet Gynecol 158:1044, 1988.

319. Romero R et al: Amniotic fluid concentrations of prostaglandin F2 alpha, 13,14-dihydro-15-keto-11,16 cycloprostaglandin E2 (PGEM-II) in preterm labor. Prostaglandins 37:149, 1989.

320. Romero R et al: Meta-analysis of the relationship between asymptomatic bacteriuria and preterm delivery/ birth weight. Obstet Gynecol 73:576, 1989.

321. Romero R et al: Infection and preterm labor. Clin Obstet Gynecol 31:553, 1988.

322. Romero R et al: Two thirds of spontaneous abortions/ fetal deaths after midtrimester genetic amniocentesis are the result of a pre-existing subclinical inflammatory process of the amniotic cavity. Am J Obstet Gynecol 172:261, 1995.

323. Romero R et al: An oxytocin receptor antagonist (atosiban) in the treatment of preterm labor: A randomized, double-blind, placebo-controlled trial with tocolytic rescue. Am J Obstet Gynecol 182:1173, 2000.

324. Rosen MG et al: The incidence of cerebral palsy. Am J Obstet Gynecol 167:417, 1992.

325. Rush RW et al: A randomized controlled trial of cervical cerclage in women at moderate risk of preterm delivery. Br J Obstet Gynaecol 91:731, 1984.

326. Sadler L et al: Treatment for cervical intraepithelial neoplasia and risk of preterm delivery. JAMA 291:2100, 2004.

327. Sawdy RJ et al: Experience of the use of nimesulide, a cyclo-oxygenase-2 selective prostaglandin synthesis inhibitor, in the prevention of preterm labour in 44 high-risk cases. J Obstet Gynaecol 24:226, 2004.

328. Sawdy RJ et al: A double-blind randomized study of fetal side effects during and after the short-term maternal administration of indomethacin, sulindac, and nimesulide for the treatment of preterm labor. Am J Obstet Gynecol 188:1046, 2003.

329. Schellenberg JC et al: Synergistic hormonal effects on lung maturation in sheep. Am J Physiol 65:94, 1988.

330. Schendel DE et al: Prenatal magnesium sulfate exposure and the risk of cerebral palsy on mental retardation among very-low-birthweight children age 3 to 5 years. JAMA 276:1805, 1996.

331. Schiff E et al: Currently recommended oral regimens for ritodrine tocolysis result in extremely low plasma levels. Am J Obstet Gynecol 169:1059, 1993.

332. Schneider KTM et al: Premature contractions: Are they caused by maternal standing? Acta Genet Med Gemellol (Roma) 34:175, 1985.

333. Schrag S et al: Prevention of perinatal group B streptococcal disease. Revised guidelines from CDC. MMWR Recomm Rep 51(RR-11):1, 2002.

334. Schrag SJ et al: Active Bacterial Core Surveillance Team. A population-based comparison of strategies to prevent early-onset group B streptococcal disease in neonates. N Engl J Med 347:233, 2002.

335. Schuly KF et al: Measures to prevent cervical injury during suction and curettage abortion. Lancet 1:1182, 1983.

336. Schwarz BE et al: Initiation of human parturition: V. Progesterone binding substance in fetal membranes. Obstet Gynecol 48:685, 1976.

337. Shankaran S et al: The effect of antenatal phenobarbital therapy on neonatal intracranial hemorrhage in preterm infants. N Engl J Med 337:466, 1997.

338. Shiono PH et al: Smoking and drinking during pregnancy. JAMA 255:82, 1986.

339. Skinner KA et al: Changes in the synthesis and metabolism of prostaglandin by human fetal membranes and decidua at labor. Am J Obstet Gynecol 171:141, 1984.

340. Smith CV et al: Transvaginal sonography of cervical width and length during pregnancy. J Ultrasound Med 11:465, 1992.

341. Sonek JD et al: Measurement of cervical length in pregnancy: Comparison between vaginal ultrasonography and digital examination. Obstet Gynecol 76:172, 1990.

342. Spellacy WN et al: The acute effects of ritodrine infusion on maternal metabolism: Measurements of levels of glucose, insulin, glucagon, triglycerides, cholesterol, placental lactogen, and chorionic gonadotropin. Am J Obstet Gynecol 131:637, 1978.

343. Stallworth JC et al: The effect of magnesium sulfate on fetal heart rate variability and uterine activity. Am J Obstet Gynecol 140:702, 1981.

344. Steer CM, Petrie RH: A comparison of magnesium sulfate and alcohol for the prevention of premature labor. Am J Obstet Gynecol 129:1, 1977.

345. Stevenson DK et al: Very low birth weight outcomes of the National Institute of Child Health and Human Development Neonatal Research Network, January 1993 through December 1994. Am J Obstet Gynecol 179:1632, 1998.

346. Stika CS et al: A prospective randomized safety trial of celecoxib for treatment of preterm labor. Am J Obstet Gynecol 187:653, 2002.

347. Stillman RJ: In utero exposure to diethylstilbestrol: Adverse effects on the reproductive performance in male and female offspring. Am J Obstet Gynecol 142:905, 1982.

348. Stoll BJ et al: Changes in pathogens causing early-onset sepsis in very-low-birth-weight infants. N Engl J Med 347:240, 2002.

349. Svare J et al: Ampicillin-metronidazole treatment in idiopathic preterm labour: A randomised controlled multicentre trial. Br J Obstet Gynaecol 104:892, 1997.

350. Sweet RL et al: *Chlamydia trachomatis* infection and pregnancy outcome. Am J Obstet Gynecol 156:824, 1987.

351. Talbert RL et al: Update on calcium-channel blocking agents. Clin Pharm 2:403, 1983.

352. Thomsen AC et al: Antibiotic elimination of group B streptococci in urine in prevention of preterm labour. Lancet 1:591, 1987.

353. Thorp JA et al: Combined antenatal vitamin K for preventing intracranial hemorrhage in newborns less than 34 weeks' gestation. Am J Obstet Gynecol 86:1, 1995.

354. Thorp JM Jr et al: Antibiotic therapy for the treatment of preterm labor: A review of the evidence. Am J Obstet Gynecol 186:587, 2002.

355. To MS et al: Fetal Medicine Foundation Second Trimester Screening Group. Cervical cerclage for prevention of preterm delivery in women with short cervix: Randomised controlled trial. Lancet 363:1849, 2004.

356. Torfs CP et al: Prenatal and perinatal factors in the etiology of cerebral palsy. J Pediatr 116:615, 1990.

357. Trager A et al: The pharmacokinetics of indomethacin in pregnant and parturient women and in their newborn infants. Zentralbl Gynakol 95:635, 1973.

358. Trautman MS et al: Amnion cell biosynthesis of interleukin-8: Regulation of cytokines. J Cell Physiol 153:38, 1992.

359. Tropper PJ et al: Corticotropin releasing hormone concentrations in umbilical cord blood of preterm fetuses. J Dev Physiol 18:81, 1992.

360. Tu FF et al: Prenatal plasma matrix metalloproteinases-9 levels to predict spontaneous preterm birth. Obstet Gynecol 92:446, 1998.

361. Tucker JM et al: Etiologies of preterm birth in an indigent population: Is prevention a logical expectation? Obstet Gynecol 177:343, 1991.

362. Turnbull AC et al: Significant fall in progesterone and rise in estradiol levels in human peripheral plasma before onset of labour. Lancet 11:110, 1974.

363. Ulmsten U et al: Treatment of premature labor with the calcium antagonist nifedipine. Arch Gynecol 229:1, 1980.

364. Valenzuela GJ et al: Maintenance treatment of preterm labor with the oxytocin antagonist atosiban. The Atosiban PTL-098 Study Group. Am J Obstet Gynecol 182:1184, 2000.

365. van der Heijden BJ et al: Persistent anuria, neonatal death, and renal microcystic lesions after prenatal exposure to indomethacin. Am J Obstet Gynecol 171:617, 1994.

366. Vohr BR et al: Neurodevelopmental and functional outcomes of extremely low birth weight infants in the National Institute of Child Health and Human Development Neonatal Research Network, 1993-1994. Pediatrics 105:1216, 2000.

367. Wahbeh CJ et al: Intra-amniotic bacterial colonization in premature labor. Am J Obstet Gynecol 148:739, 1984.

368. Wallace RL et al: Inhibition of premature labor by terbutaline. Obstet Gynecol 51:387, 1978.

369. Wapner R for the NICHD MFMU Network: A randomized trial of single vs weekly courses of corticosteroids. Am J Obstet Gynecol 189:S56, 2003.

370. Warren WB et al: Elevated maternal plasma corticotropin releasing hormone levels in pregnancies complicated by preterm labor. Am J Obstet Gynecol 166:1198, 1992.

371. Watts DH et al: The association of occult amniotic fluid infection with gestational age and neonatal outcome among women in preterm labor. Obstet Gynecol 79:351, 1992.

372. Wen SW et al: Intrauterine growth retardation and preterm delivery: Prenatal risk factors in an indigent population. Am J Obstet Gynecol 162:213, 1990.

373. Wenstrom KD et al: Elevated amniotic fluid interleukin-6 levels at genetic amniocentesis predict subsequent pregnancy loss. Am J Obstet Gynecol 175:830, 1996.

374. Wolfe CDA et al: The rate of rise in corticotropin releasing factor and endogenous digoxin-like immunoreactivity in normal and abnormal pregnancies. Br J Obstet Gynaecol 97:832, 1990.

375. Woods FR Jr et al: Effect of cocaine on uterine blood flow and fetal oxygenation. JAMA 157:957, 1987.

377. Yawn BP et al: Preterm birth prevention in a rural practice. JAMA 262:230, 1990.

376. Yoon BH et al: High expression of interleukin-6, interleukin-1β, and tumor necrosis factor-α in periventricular leukomalacia. Am J Obstet Gynecol 174:399, 1996.

378. Yunis KA et al: Transient hypertrophic cardiomyopathy in the newborn following multiple doses of antenatal corticosteroids. Am J Perinatol 16:17, 1999.

379. Zeeman GG et al: Oxytocin and its receptor in pregnancy and parturition: Current concepts and clinical implications. Obstet Gynecol 89:873, 1997.

380. Zuckerman H et al: Inhibition of human premature labor by indomethacin, Obstet Gynecol 44:787, 1974.

CHAPTER 17

Fetal Effects of Autoimmune Disease

Isaac Blickstein and Smadar Friedman

PLACENTAL TRANSFER: GENERAL REMARKS

The maternal-fetal interface is quite efficient in its selective exclusion of substances during the transport process from the maternal to the fetal circulation. At the same time, the placenta selectively transfers other substances, a process that is facilitated by the proximity of the respective maternal-fetal vascular systems within the placental cotyledons. Although there is no mixing of the maternal and fetal blood, the placental barrier is not absolutely impermeable and small amounts of fetal blood, including fetal cells, may access the maternal circulation, in most pregnancies through breaks in the fetal-maternal interface. When fetal blood cells are recognized as antigens by the maternal immunologic system, they may provoke an immune response and the production of immunoglobulins. This mechanism, however, occurs in only a minority of pregnancies and is the basis of incompatibility disorders (see also Chapter 20), whereby exogenous antigens, such as fetal cells or incompatible blood, sensitize the maternal immune system. The maternal antibodies, which are produced as a response to sensitization, cross the placenta and may destroy fetal cells. Generally, the mother is disease free, and the diagnosis is reached after the delivery of an affected child or by screening tests.

A second type of maternal antibody that crosses the placenta and affects the fetus may arise from sensitization of the mother's immune system by her endogenous antigens, with the resultant production of autoantibodies. The mother with autoantibodies suffers from an autoimmune disorder, and the diagnosis of the maternal disease usually precedes the diagnosis of the fetal or neonatal complication.

These generalizations describe immune processes that may affect the fetus or neonate. Although the maternal immune system may produce a wide range of immunoglobulins, only maternal antibodies of the immunoglobulin G (IgG) class (but not IgM or IgA) can cross the placental barrier. Thus, the common denominators of such disorders are the production of IgG in the maternal compartment, the transfer of IgG through the placenta, and the effects of these antibodies in the fetal compartment or neonate. This chapter discusses examples of such disorders.

FETAL THROMBOCYTOPENIA

The immunologic etiologies of fetal, and consequently neonatal, thrombocytopenia are shown in Box 17-1. The most significant pathologies are neonatal alloimmune thrombocytopenia and immune (idiopathic) thrombocytopenic purpura. Although the two conditions have some similarities, they are distinct diseases with different underlying pathogeneses (Table 17-1) (see also Chapter 44).

Immune Thrombocytopenic Purpura

Immune (or idiopathic) thrombocytopenic purpura (ITP) in adults is often a chronic disease mediated by autoantibodies directed against cell surface components (glycoproteins) of platelets (IIb/IIIa or Ib/IX). Thrombocytopenia occurs when the platelet-antibody complexes are destroyed by the reticuloendothelial system. ITP is suspected by a low platelet count, but the diagnosis is reached after exclusion of other causes of thrombocytopenia by history, physical examination, blood count, peripheral blood smear, and autoimmune profile.[7] A spuriously low platelet count should be evaluated by examining a blood smear exclude pseudo-thrombocytopenia caused by ethylenediamine tetra-acetic acid (EDTA)-dependent platelet agglutination. The normal range of platelet counts in nonpregnant women and neonates is 150,000 to 400,000/μL; however, the mean counts tend to be lower during pregnancy. The prevalence of maternal ITP is one or two cases per 1000 deliveries. The potential risk of a low platelet count for the mother is bleeding; however, the risk becomes significant only when the platelet count

BOX 17-1. Immunologic Etiology of Fetal or Neonatal Thrombocytopenia

1. Maternal production of autoantibodies
   - Immune thrombocytopenic purpura
   - Systemic lupus erythematosus
   - Drug-induced thrombocytopenia
2. Neonatal alloimmune (isoimmune) thrombocytopenia
3. ABO incompatibility

TABLE 17-1. Characteristics of Neonatal Thrombocytopenia Based on Etiology

	ALLOIMMUNE THROMBOCYTOPENIA	MATERNAL IMMUNE THROMBOCYTOPENIC PURPURA
Cause of sensitization	Antigen on fetal platelets	Autoantibodies
Maternal platelet count	Normal	Low
Fetal platelet count	Low	Variable
Fetal risk (pregnancy)	High	Low
Fetal risk (delivery)	High	Depends on platelet count
Maternal risk	None	Depends on platelet count

drops below 20,000/μL. A maternal platelet count of greater than 50,000/μL is considered to be hemostatic during vaginal or cesarean birth.

Thrombocytopenia of the fetus or newborn is caused by active transplacental transport of the antiplatelet antibodies. A low platelet count increases the risk for hemorrhage, but this seems to be more theoretical than real because intrauterine fetal hemorrhage has not been reported in patients with ITP. The concern is for the potential trauma at birth and the potential risk for cerebral hemorrhage in the neonate. This serious complication is rare, because the prevalence of fetal or neonatal ITP is about 10% that of maternal ITP, and less than half of these infants have platelet counts below 20,000/μL. In the past, obstetricians performed antepartum cordocentesis (percutaneous umbilical vein blood sampling [PUBS]) or fetal scalp blood sampling to identify the fetus with a platelet count below 50,000/μL and to deliver it by the abdominal route. The current view holds that PUBS and fetal scalp sampling are unnecessary in pregnant women without known ITP even with platelet counts as low as 40,000/μL. In general, when the maternal platelet count is greater than 50,000/μL and the fetal platelet count (or the platelet count of previous babies) is unknown, cesarean section is not indicated; a vaginal delivery is allowed and the cesarean option is reserved for obstetrical indications. If the fetal platelet count is known to be less than 20,000/μL, cesarean section is appropriate.

Treatment of ITP during pregnancy follows the guidelines published since 1996.[7,17] Pregnant patients with ITP and platelet counts greater than 50,000/μL throughout gestation, as well as those with platelet counts of 30,000 to 50,000/μL in the first or second trimester, do not routinely require treatment.[17] Treatment in the form of glucocorticoids or intravenous immune globulin (IVIG) is indicated in patients with platelet counts less than 10,000/μL, and for those with platelet counts of 10,000 to 30,000 /μL who are in their second or third trimester or are bleeding. IVIG is an appropriate initial treatment for women with platelet counts less than 10,000/μL in the third trimester, and for those with counts of 10,000 to 30,000/μL who are bleeding. When glucocorticoid and IVIG therapy have failed, splenectomy is appropriate in the second trimester in women with platelet counts less than 10,000/μL who are bleeding. Splenectomy should not be performed in asymptomatic

pregnant women with platelet counts greater than 10,000/μL.[17] Platelet transfusion is indicated for women with counts less than 10,000/μL before a planned cesarean or for those who are bleeding and expected to deliver vaginally. Prophylactic transfusions are unnecessary when the platelet count is greater than 30,000/μL and there is no bleeding. ITP does not prevent breastfeeding.

A recent retrospective study examined the morbidity of 92 obstetric patients with ITP during 119 pregnancies over an 11-year period.[27] The authors found that most of these women had thrombocytopenia during pregnancy. At delivery, 89% had platelet counts lower than 150,000/μL. For many, the pregnancy was uneventful; however, 21.5% of the women had moderate to severe bleeding. In 31.1% of the pregnancies, treatment was required to increase the platelet counts. Most deliveries (82.4%) were vaginal. Platelet counts of less than 150,000/μL were found in 25.2% of the infants, including 9% with platelet counts lower than 50,000/μL. Treatment for hemostatic impairment was necessary in 14.6% of the infants. During the study period, two fetal deaths occurred, including one caused by hemorrhage.[27]

After birth, the platelet count of newborns whose mothers have ITP-mediated thrombocytopenia may continue to drop, and careful follow-up of the thrombocytopenia should be performed during the first week of life. Ultrasound imaging of the brain seems to be indicated if the count is less than 50,000/μL, even in the absence of neurologic findings. Neonates who exhibit severe thrombocytopenia (less than 20,000/μL) should be treated with platelet transfusion and/or IVIG. Those with platelet counts of 20,000 to 50,000/μL do not necessarily require IVIG treatment; however, tight platelet count monitoring is needed. Neonates with intracranial hemorrhage or any other bleeding manifestation should be treated with combined platelet transfusion and IVIG or glucocorticoid therapy, especially if the platelet count is less than 20,000/μL.

Neonatal Alloimmune Thrombocytopenia

The pathogenesis of neonatal alloimmune (also known as isoimmune) thrombocytopenia is similar to Rh disease: The mother with antigen-negative platelets is sensitized by antigen-positive fetal platelets gaining access to the maternal circulation via breaches in the placental barrier. As a result, the mother produces anti-platelet antibodies, and these IgG antibodies cross the placenta and destroy the fetal platelets. In contrast to Rh disease, neonatal alloimmune thrombocytopenia may occur during the first pregnancy. This difference is explained by the higher immunogenicity of the platelet antigen and by the smaller size of the platelets, which may facilitate their fetomaternal transfusion. Of the several types of platelet antigens, the human platelet antigen 1a (HPA-1a) is involved in 80% to 90% of neo-natal alloimmune thrombocytopenia cases in whites, and HPA-5b is responsible for a further 5% to 15% of the cases.[16] Among people of color (e.g., Asians), HPA-1a incompatibility is a rare cause of neonatal alloimmune thrombocytopenia, and other alloantigens (e.g., HPA-4b) are implicated.[4] The fetus acquires the antigen from the father. When the father is heterozygous, 50% of the babies will be affected, whereas all babies of a homozygous father will be HPA positive.

The prevalence of neonatal alloimmune thrombo-cytopenia is 0.5 to 2 cases per 1000 deliveries. Interest-ingly, fetomaternal platelet incompatibility is much more frequent. The discrepancy is explained by the facilitating role of certain human leukocyte antigen (HLA) types that are associated with the development of neonatal alloimmune thrombocytopenia. For example, HLA-DR3 is associated with a 10- to 30-fold risk for HPA-1a antibody production.

In the usual scenario, an asymptomatic woman delivers an otherwise normal baby in an otherwise uncomplicated birth. Most neonates are asymptomatic and the thrombocytopenia is detected by a blood count performed for other perinatal causes. In some cases, the neonates present with generalized petechiae, hemor-rhage into abdominal viscera, excessive bleeding after venipuncture or circumcision, or, in extreme cases, with abnormal neurologic manifestations secondary to intra-cranial hemorrhage. The diagnosis of thrombocytopenia in the newborn should immediately lead to diagnostic measures to exclude neonatal alloimmune thrombo-cytopenia.

The diagnosis of neonatal alloimmune thrombo-cytopenia involves typing platelet antigens in the newborn and in the parents to demonstrate that the mother lacks a platelet antigen that is present on the platelets of the father and the neonate. A more sophisticated test is to establish the existence of the antiplatelet antibody in the mother's serum that is directed against a platelet antigen in the father. Testing the baby is, in general, not necessary if the father is available for testing. Older methods that measure the antibody associated with platelets lack adequate specificity, but newer enzyme-linked immunosorbent assays (ELISAs) detect specifically the antiplatelet anti-body. In antigen capture immunoassays, monoclonal antibodies directed against platelet antigens are used to individually identify various known platelet antigens, although these may be negative in maternal blood 2 to 4 weeks after delivery in up to 30% of the cases. Flow cytometry and polymerase chain reaction assays can also be used to identify the patient's platelet antigens.

Establishing the diagnosis of neonatal alloimmune thrombocytopenia has immediate importance as well as implications for future pregnancies.

MANAGEMENT OF THE NEONATE

In suspected cases of neonatal alloimmune thrombo-cytopenia, treatment should commence on the basis of the clinical diagnosis without waiting for the results of the immunologic workup. Treatment is based on transfusion of random-donor, ABO- and Rh-compatible, and HPA-1a–negative platelets (preferably with HPA-5b–negative platelets as well) in neonates with severe thrombocytopenia. This transfusion is compatible in approximately 90% of the cases of neonatal alloimmune thrombocytopenia.[4,13,28] When random-donor platelets are unavailable, washed maternal platelets can be administered. HPA-incompatible platelets should be used only if compatible ones are not available; they can be combined with IVIG treatment to achieve a transient rise in the platelet count until IVIG becomes effective.[4] High-dose IVIG, 1 g/kg per day for 2 days or 0.5 g/kg per day for 4 days, is also effective in raising the platelet count in most cases,[4] although the rise may be delayed for 1 or 2 days.[9] Corticosteroids were used in the past but are less popular since the availability of IVIG. In any case, the neonatal platelet count should be closely monitored during the first days of life.

MANAGEMENT OF A SUBSEQUENT PREGNANCY

The recurrence rate of neonatal alloimmune thrombo-cytopenia in a subsequent pregnancy is high (greater than 90%), and the risk for intracranial hemorrhage is the same or even greater than in the previous preg-nancy. The difference, however, is that in a subsequent pregnancy, the patient, as well as her caregivers, are aware of the neonatal alloimmune thrombocytopenia affecting the first child. In the absence of screening (which has very low cost-effectiveness) for the presence of antiplatelet antibodies in maternal blood, the diag-nosis is almost impossible without a history of neonatal alloimmune thrombocytopenia in a previous gestation. One exception is an incidental finding of intracranial hemorrhage during an ultrasound scan.

The risk for antenatal intracranial hemorrhage in the fetus with alloimmune thrombocytopenia is sub-stantial enough to merit intervention either by giving the mother weekly infusion of high-dose IVIG with or without corticosteroids (the preferred approach in North American centers) or by repeated in utero fetal platelet transfusions (the preferred approach in some European centers).[4] There is no way to predict which baby is going to have intracranial hemorrhage.[26] There-fore, antenatal therapy is aimed to increase the number of fetal platelets regardless of the presence of a risk factor.

Although screening procedures are not indicated to detect neonatal alloimmune thrombocytopenia, a high index of suspicion is needed in certain cases (Box 17-2). Typically, a woman presents in early pregnancy with a history of delivering a baby with neonatal alloimmune thrombocytopenia or presents with some clues to the diagnosis.[21] The first step should be assessment of the father. In the heterozygous case, the status of the baby is unknown, and direct assessment of fetal platelets via PUBS should be performed. The timing of the procedure, as well as the risk involved, is a matter of debate. Failure to treat carries the risk for intrauterine intracranial hemorrhage, which is expected to occur in as many as 30% of the cases, with 10% of affected newborns dying and 20% experiencing neurologic sequelae secondary to intracranial hemorrhage. The procedure itself, on the other hand, carries a high risk for miscarriage or fetal death. Moreover, the operator must be prepared to transfuse platelets if the results show a dangerously low platelet count. If the baby is found to be HPA positive, or if the father is homozygous for the allele, there is a choice between serial platelet transfusions and IVIG administered to the mother.[25]

Serial intrauterine platelet transfusions carry the risk of a single PUBS multiplied by the number of procedures. Because the survival of transfused thrombocytes is short, serial intrauterine transfusions means repeating the procedure every week or 10 days.[25] In a study of the fetal loss rate in neonatal alloimmune thrombocytopenia managed by serial platelet transfusions, the authors found two perinatal losses in 12 pregnancies managed by a total of 84 platelet transfusions.[25] One loss was procedure related and resulted from exsanguination despite platelet transfusion. The procedure-related fetal loss rate was 1.2% per procedure but 8.3% per pregnancy. The authors calculated a cumulative risk for serial weekly transfusions of approximately 6% per pregnancy, indicating the need to develop less invasive approaches.[25]

The invasive procedure is used less often now than previously. This may be the result of favorable outcomes related to maternal treatment with high-dose IVIG (1 g/kg per week). The beneficial effect of megadose IVIG is presumably mediated by masking the antigenic effect of fetal platelets, thus reducing the production of antiplatelet antibodies. Moreover, IVIG also stabilizes endothelial cells and reduces the incidence of intracranial hemorrhage even when the fetal platelet count remains low. It is debatable whether corticosteroids should be added to the IVIG management protocol.[20]

A recent European collaborative study of the antenatal management of neonatal alloimmune thrombocytopenia attempted to determine whether the severity of the disease in the current pregnancy could be predicted from the history of neonatal alloimmune thrombocytopenia in previous pregnancies, and to assess the effects of different types of antenatal intervention.[3] The study enrolled 56 women who had had a prior infant affected by neonatal alloimmune thrombocytopenia due to HPA-1a alloimmunization. The authors found that fetuses with a sibling history of antenatal intracranial hemorrhage or severe thrombocytopenia (a platelet count of less than 20,000/μL) had significantly lower pretreatment platelet counts than those whose siblings had less severe thrombocytopenia or postnatal intracranial hemorrhage. Maternal therapy resulted in a platelet count exceeding 50,000/μL in 67% of cases. None of the fetuses managed by serial platelet intrauterine transfusions suffered intracranial hemorrhage after treatment. However, several serious complications of PUBS arose. The results of this study suggest that the start of therapy can be stratified on the basis of the sibling history of neonatal alloimmune thrombocytopenia and support the use of maternal therapy as first-line treatment.[3]

Some patients who receive IVIG do not respond. Nonresponders, however, cannot be recognized without PUBS.[8] When PUBS is planned to assess the effectiveness of therapy, the preparation for intrauterine platelet transfusion should be similar to the procedure used when PUBS is performed to diagnose neonatal alloimmune thrombocytopenia in a case with a heterozygous father (i.e., when the risk of an affected fetus is 50%). Nonresponders may then be treated with either serial intrauterine platelet transfusions or with steroids added to IVIG. It has been suggested that such assessment of treatment is not necessary in patients who previously responded to IVIG therapy.

FETAL-NEONATAL CONSEQUENCES OF MATERNAL ANTINUCLEAR ANTIBODIES

Antinuclear antibodies (ANAs) are produced in various diseases with an immune component (Box 17-3). ANAs of the IgG and IgM types bind to nuclei or to nuclear components. Their presence is detected in the patient's serum, and they may be classified according to their subunits, each of which is related to the diagnosis of a disease. For example, anti–double-stranded DNA (anti-dsDNA) antibodies are specific for systemic lupus erythematosus. In this chapter, the maternal manifestations of these autoimmune diseases will not be discussed, but focus will be on neonatal lupus—a model of passively acquired autoimmunity—and the effects of the ANAs anti-Ro and anti-La.

Neonatal lupus is caused by transplacental passage of maternal autoantibodies. It is rare: only about 1% of babies with maternal ANAs develop neonatal lupus. The baby may present with cardiac, dermatologic, hepatic, and hematologic manifestations. In children with neonatal lupus, there is commonly involvement of

BOX 17-3. Conditions Associated with Antinuclear Antibodies

Rheumatologic Conditions
- Systemic lupus erythematosus
- Rheumatoid arthritis
- Mixed connective tissue disease
- Sjögren syndrome
- Necrotizing vasculitis

Infections
- Chronic active hepatitis
- Subacute bacterial endocarditis
- Infection with human immunodeficiency virus
- Tuberculosis

Miscellaneous Conditions
- Type I diabetes mellitus
- Multiple sclerosis
- Pulmonary fibrosis
- Silicone gel implants
- Pregnancy
- Age: older adult

Medications
- Drug-induced lupus erythematosus

only one or two organ systems. The skin lesions on the face and scalp, often in a distinctive periorbital distribution, may be present at birth but usually develop within the first few weeks of life and tend to resolve in a few weeks or months without scarring.[23] Fetal heart block typically begins during the second or third trimester of pregnancy. In some instances, this begins as first- or second-degree block and then progresses to third-degree block.[23] Complete heart block appears to be irreversible and may be combined with cardiomyopathy[23] (see also Chapter 43). Hepatobiliary complications (10% of cases) may be manifested as liver failure occurring at birth or in utero, transient conjugated hyperbilirubinemia, or transient transaminase elevations occurring in infancy.[23] Thrombocytopenia, neutropenia, or anemia occurs in about 10% of affected babies.

Mothers of children with neonatal lupus may have ANA-related connective tissue disease (such as systemic lupus erythematosus, Sjögren syndrome, undifferentiated autoimmune syndrome, or rheumatoid arthritis). The recurrence rate of neonatal lupus for a mother with anti-Ro autoantibodies, which are present in almost 95% of patients, is approximately 25%. The IgG autoantibodies are found alone or in combination, and are directed against Ro (SSA), La (SSB), and/or U1-RNA (U1-RNP) antigens, and their presence increases the risk for neonatal lupus erythematosus.

Anti-Ro and anti-La autoantibodies recognize cardiac adrenoceptors as well as muscarinic receptors, and this recognition may explain the cardiac arrhythmia associated with these ANAs. Maternal anti-Ro and anti-La antibodies and complement components are deposited in fetal heart tissues, leading to inflammation, calcification, necrosis, and fibrosis of the conducting tissue (and, in some cases, of the surrounding myocardium).[10] The postinflammation fibrotic response to injury is quite fast and, in most cases, irreversible. The process by which maternal anti-Ro or anti-La antibodies begin and propagate inflammation that leads to scarring of the atrioventricular node has not been yet defined. It has been proposed that it all begins with apoptosis of cardiocytes, resulting in translocation of Ro or La antigens and subsequent surface binding by maternal ANAs. This leads to a phagocytosis-mediated scarring process.[10]

The cardiac rhythm disorders increase the risk for fetal congestive heart failure and point to the most important intervention during pregnancy: close follow-up with echocardiography and sonography. Echocardiography can demonstrate the conduction defect and estimate the cardiac function.

About 10% of the fetuses with congenital heart block are born with hydrops fetalis and congestive heart failure, and their prognosis is poor (see also Chapter 21). Intrauterine treatment with maternal corticosteroids may decrease the pericardial effusion or improve the symptoms of heart failure, but the heart block remains. Prophylactic treatment with IVIG awaits larger clinical trials.[11] It is possible to place an intrauterine pacemaker, but success is not assured. Neonatal mortality rate in infants born with a congenital heart block ranges from 20% to 30%; however, death may occur from late pacemaker failure later in childhood. Most of the neonates born with a heart block due to neonatal lupus require pacemaker placement in the neonatal period or later in life. It appears that most children with neonatal lupus do not develop rheumatic diseases, but follow-up has been limited to late adolescence.[11]

FETAL-NEONATAL CONSEQUENCES OF MATERNAL ANTIPHOSPHOLIPID ANTIBODIES

Phospholipids (PLs) are involved in facilitating the coagulation cascade. Anti-PL antibodies (APLAs) are autoantibodies against PLs or against plasma proteins bound to PLs. The most common subgroups involved in disease states are the anticardiolipin antibodies (ACAs), the lupus anticoagulant antibodies, and the anti-β2-glycoprotein I antibodies. The hypercoagulability function of these antibodies is epitomized by the fact they cause "bleeding in the test tube but clotting in the body," referring to their involvement in pathologic clotting. The APLAs promote clotting in both arteries and veins (i.e., thrombophilia) by activation of endothelial cells, via oxidant-mediated injury to endothelium, and by modulating the regulatory function of coagulation proteins.

It is common practice to use clinical and laboratory criteria for the diagnosis of APLA syndrome. According to the Sapporo criteria, patients are required to have either vascular thrombosis (venous or arterial, including neurologic disease) or fetal loss, and to demonstrate evidence of APLA either by the detection of ACAs or by a positive test for lupus anticoagulant antibodies.[18] To differentiate between persistent autoantibody response and transient responses from other causes, APLA must be detected on at least two occasions 6 weeks apart. These classification criteria are reported to have a sensitivity of 71% and a specificity of 98%. Patients with APLA and one major clinical criterion are considered to have APLA syndrome. Primary APLA syndrome refers to the syndrome occurring outside the setting of systemic lupus erythematosus.[24]

In women with APLA, there is a high incidence of pregnancy complications. Of women with a history of recurrent miscarriage (three or more consecutive losses of pregnancy), 15% have persistently positive test results for APLA and a rate of fetal loss of 90% when no specific treatment is given during pregnancy.[18] Moreover, 25% of successful pregnancies were delivered prematurely.[18] Other potential complications of pregnancy include preeclampsia, placental insufficiency, maternal thrombosis (including stroke), and complications of treatment.[6]

The pathogenesis underlying thrombosis and fetal loss in APLA syndrome remains to be established. The potential mechanisms that have been proposed include interference with the function of the coagulation cascade leading to a procoagulant state, cellular immune mechanisms, and the presence of predisposing factors. For example, a "second hit" may be necessary for the clinical manifestation of the syndrome to occur.[18] The adverse effect of APLA syndrome on pregnancy is most likely associated with abnormal placental function.[6] Studies have shown abnormalities in the decidual spiral arteries, narrowing of the spiral arterioles, intimal thickening, acute atherosis, and fibrinoid necrosis in cases of fetal loss associated with APLA syndrome.[6] Others have found extensive placental necrosis, infarction, and thrombosis (see also Chapter 23).

Treatment options include corticosteroids, low-dose aspirin, heparin (either fractionated or unfractionated),[5] and IVIG. These were administered either as single agents or in combination to increase the live birth rates in women with APLA. Although the available studies are flawed by small sample size, varying entry criteria and treatment protocols, and lack of standardized laboratory assays, many clinicians would treat APLA patients with a combination of aspirin and heparin (fractionated or unfractionated).

There are few trials evaluating treatment of refractory APLA syndrome (recurrent pregnancy losses occur in 20% to 30% of cases in most studies). Women whose pregnancy fails on a prophylactic regimen should receive full anticoagulation therapy in the subsequent pregnancy.[6] If the treated pregnancy fails while on full anticoagulation, some physicians advise adding glucocorticoids, IVIG, or hydroxychloroquine to the anticoagulation regimen.[6]

MYASTHENIA GRAVIS

Myasthenia gravis is an autoimmune neuromuscular disease affecting twice as many women as men, and it usually affects women in their third decade of life. The symptoms include weakness and fatigue of the skeletal muscles of the face and extremities. The diagnosis, which is beyond the scope of this chapter, involves a comprehensive neurologic workup based on clinical history and signs, improvement with anticholinesterase injection (edrophonium), determination of serum anti-AChR antibody titers by radioimmunoassay, and electromyography.

In as many as 90% of patients with myasthenia gravis, autoantibodies (usually IgG) against human acetylcholine receptors (AChRs) are detected. The antibodies interfere with impulse conduction across neuromuscular junctions by decreasing the number of available AChRs there. Because myasthenia gravis typically affects women during reproductive years, the potential for exacerbation, respiratory failure, adverse drug response, crisis, and death during pregnancy are of great concern. However, myasthenia gravis has a variable and unpredictable course during pregnancy, including exacerbation, crisis, and remission. In one study, 17% of asymptomatic patients with myasthenia gravis who were not on therapy before conception had a relapse; among patients receiving therapy, myasthenia gravis symptoms improved in 39%, remained unchanged in 42%, and deteriorated in 19% of the pregnancies. Myasthenia gravis symptoms worsened after delivery in 28% of the pregnancies.[1] In another study,[14] the myasthenia gravis symptoms deteriorated in 15% of the pregnancies, and a further 16% deteriorated during the puerperium.

Therapy is based on anticholinesterase medications and plasmapheresis during a myasthenia gravis crisis. Other medications often have adverse effects on the disease, resulting in a long list of drugs that should be avoided in these patients. Plasmapheresis can be performed during pregnancy but may be associated with preterm birth. Of special concern are cesarean delivery and the hazards of anesthesia, which might prove very stressful for these patients.

Some complications of myasthenia gravis in the form of exacerbation should be anticipated during pregnancy, including anxiety and physiologic stress of pregnancy (mainly present as hypoventilation), infection, a prolonged second stage at delivery (because the patient may become exhausted and be unable to push), and the contraindication to using magnesium sulfate in patients with preeclampsia.

Neonatal risks of myasthenia gravis include neonatal myasthenia gravis, prematurity, malformation, and death. Neonatal myasthenia gravis occurs in 10% to 20% of babies born to mothers with myasthenia and is due to the transplacental transport of immunoglobulins from mother to infant. There is not a correlation between myasthenia gravis severity and neonatal myasthenia gravis, nor is there one between maternal anti-AChR antibody titers and the occurrence of neonatal myasthenia gravis. This discrepancy is partially explained in neonatal myasthenia gravis by the protective role of α-fetoprotein, which inhibits the binding of myasthenia gravis antibody to its receptor.

The infant's symptoms are generally manifested by the third day of life in the form of respiratory distress and inadequate suck, which may gradually subside over 1 to 4 weeks. Rarely, the disease becomes permanent when there is irreversible destruction of AChR by the maternal antibodies, or when there is production of antibodies by the infant. Recent analysis of data collected from the Medical Birth Registry of Norway, comparing 127 births by women with myasthenia gravis to 1.9 million births by women without myasthenia gravis, showed that women with myasthenia gravis had a higher rate of complications at delivery. In particular, the risk for preterm rupture of membranes was threefold higher in the myasthenia gravis group. Interventions during birth were also significantly increased, and the rate of cesarean section was twice that of the general population. Five children (3.9%) born to mothers with myasthenia gravis had severe anomalies, and three of them died.[19]

HERPES GESTATIONIS

Herpes gestationis (HG), also known as pemphigoid gestationis, is a rare autoimmune skin disease of pregnancy, occurring in less than 1 in about 50,000 pregnancies. Despite its name, HG has no association with the herpes virus infection. During pregnancy, IgG autoantibodies are produced against an important element in epidermal-dermal adhesion—the bullous pemphigoid antigen 2 (BPAg2, also known as BP180). It is assumed that these autoantibodies bind complement to the basement membrane of the epidermis and thus activate an immunodermatologic reaction that is responsible for the development of subepidermal vesiculae and bullae.[22]

HG is sometimes associated with other autoimmune diseases, and it seems that all these conditions have in common a relationship to HLA-B8 and HLA-DR3. Although HG most commonly manifests during the second and third trimesters, in as many as 25% of the cases it develops during the puerperium. There are reported cases of persistent HG, but usually the disease spontaneously regresses after birth.[2]

Affected women usually present with inexorable pruritus associated with erythematous urticarial patches and plaques, which are typically located around the navel. The skin lesions may progress to tense vesicles and blisters, which spread peripherally. The face, palms, soles, and mucous membranes are usually unaffected. Although the symptoms usually wane toward the end of pregnancy, peripartum exacerbations do exist. HG may recur in subsequent pregnancies, and, interestingly, it may recur with menses and oral contraception.

The diagnosis is usually reached by collaboration between the attending obstetrician and an immunodermatologist. Treatment is directed to alleviate itching and to suppress blistering. Lukewarm baths or compresses may reduce the irritation, but corticosteroids (local, intralesional, or systemic) remain the primary therapeutic means. New treatment modalities including cyclosporin, IVIG, and tetracyclines postpartum have shown promising results.[22]

HG is associated with a greater incidence of premature birth and neonates who are small for gestational age. The babies of affected mothers may rarely have transient cutaneous manifestations, which disappear along with the clearance of maternal autoantibodies.[12,15] Blistering, however, may increase the risk for superimposed infection, thermoregulatory problems, and fluid and electrolyte imbalance. The attending neonatologist should also be aware of the medications received by the mother.

SUMMARY

This chapter discussed several examples of maternal immune-mediated conditions that may directly affect the fetus or neonate. Some of these conditions are quite rare, but some may be encountered in daily practice. From the neonatal point of view, the main mechanism of disease is transplacental transfer of antibodies from the mother to the fetus and the effect of these antibodies on fetal components. The last decade has witnessed great progress in better understanding the underlying pathogenesis of most of these conditions. However, in many instances, therapy remains controversial.

REFERENCES

1. Batocchi AP et al: Course and treatment of myasthenia gravis during pregnancy. Neurology 52:447, 1999.
2. Berti S, Amato L, Coronella G et al: Persistent herpes gestationis. Skinmed 1:55, 2002.
3. Birchall JE et al, and the European Fetomaternal Alloimmune Thrombocytopenia Study Group: European collaborative study of the antenatal management of fetomaternal alloimmune thrombocytopenia. Br J Haematol 122:275, 2003.
4. Blanchette VS, Johnson J, Rand M: The management of alloimmune neonatal thrombocytopenia. Baillieres Best Pract Res Clin Haematol 13:365, 2000.
5. Blickstein D, Blickstein I: Low molecular weight heparin in perinatal medicine. In Kurjak A et al (eds): The Fetus as a Patient: The Evolving Challenge. London: Parthenon, 2002, p 261.
6. Branch DW, Khamashta MA: Antiphospholipid syndrome: Obstetric diagnosis, management, and controversies. Obstet Gynecol 101:1333, 2003.
7. British Committee for Standards in Haematology General Haematology Task Force: Guidelines for the investigation and management of idiopathic thrombocytopenic purpura in adults, children and in pregnancy. Br J Haematol 120:574, 2003.
8. Bussel JB et al: Antenatal management of alloimmune thrombocytopenia with intravenous gamma-globulin: A randomized trial of the addition of low-dose steroid

to intravenous gamma-globulin. Am J Obstet Gynecol 1/4:1414, 1996.

9. Bussel J, Kaplan C: The fetal and neonatal consequences of maternal alloimmune thrombocytopenia. Baillieres Clin Haematol 11:391, 1998.

10. Buyon JP, Clancy RM: From antibody insult to fibrosis in neonatal lupus: The heart of the matter. Arthritis Res Ther 5:266, 2003.

11. Buyon JP, Clancy RM: Neonatal lupus syndromes. Curr Opin Rheumatol 15:535, 2003.

12. Chen SH et al: Herpes gestationis in a mother and child. J Am Acad Dermatol 40:847, 1999.

13. Davoren A et al: Neonatal alloimmune thrombocytopenia in the Irish population: A discrepancy between observed and expected cases. J Clin Pathol 55:289, 2002.

14. Djelmis J et al: Myasthenia gravis in pregnancy: report on 69 cases. Eur J Obstet Gynecol Reprod Biol 104:21, 2002.

15. Erickson NI, Ellis RL: Images in clinical medicine: Neonatal rash due to herpes gestationis. N Engl J Med 347:660, 2002.

16. Forestier F, Hohlfeld P: Management of fetal and neonatal alloimmune thrombocytopenia. Biol Neonate 74:395, 1998.

17. George JN et al: Idiopathic thrombocytopenic purpura: A practice guideline developed by explicit methods for the American Society of Hematology. Blood 88:3, 1996.

18. Hanly JG: Antiphospholipid syndrome: An overview. CMAJ 168:1675, 2003.

19. Hoff JM et al: Myasthenia gravis: Consequences for pregnancy, delivery, and the newborn. Neurology 61:1362, 2003.

20. Kaplan C et al: Feto-maternal alloimmune thrombocytopenia: Antenatal therapy with IVIG and steroids: More questions than answers. European Working Group on FMAIT. Br J Haematol 100:62, 1998.

21. Kaplan C: Alloimmune thrombocytopenia of the fetus and the newborn. Blood Rev 16:69, 2002.

22. Kroumpouzos G, Cohen LM: Specific dermatoses of pregnancy: An evidence-based systematic review. Am J Obstet Gynecol 188:1083, 2003.

23. Lee LA: Neonatal lupus: Clinical features and management. Paediatr Drugs 6:71, 2004.

24. Levine JS et al: The antiphospholipid syndrome. N Engl J Med 346:752, 2002.

25. Overton TG et al: Serial aggressive platelet transfusion for fetal alloimmune thrombocytopenia: Platelet dynamics and perinatal outcome. Am J Obstet Gynecol 186:826, 2002.

26. Sosa ME: Alloimmune thrombocytopenia in the fetus: Current management theories. J Perinat Neonatal Nurs 17:181, 2003.

27. Webert KE et al: A retrospective 11-year analysis of obstetric patients with idiopathic thrombocytopenic purpura. Blood 102:4306, 2003.

28. Williamson LM et al: The natural history of fetomaternal alloimmunization to the platelet-specific antigen HPA-1a (PLA1, Zwa) as determined by antenatal screening. Blood 92:2280, 1998.

18 Obstetric Management of Multiple Pregnancies and Births

Isaac Blickstein and Eric S. Shinwell

The human female is programmed by nature to mono-ovulate, to nurture one fetus, and to take care of one neonate at a time. This natural pattern resulted in the relatively rare birth of twins (about 1 per 80 to 100 births) and in the extremely rare occurrence of high-order multiple pregnancies. The rarity of high-order multiple pregnancies can be appreciated by the quasi-mathematical Hellin-Zellany rule for twins, triplets, and quadruplets.[15] According to this rule, if the frequency of twins in a population is $1/N$, then the frequency of triplets will be $1/N^2$ and that of quadruplets $1/N^3$.

The Hellin-Zellany relationship was found to be quite accurate as long as the population remained homogenous and enjoyed natural procreation. However, quite soon it became apparent that deviations from the rule occur mainly because of racial differences in the frequency of dizygotic twinning.

This ordinary circumstance did not change until the emergence of effective treatment of infertility. Thereafter, it became clear that within an infinitely small fraction in human history, all we knew about natural multiples has been profoundly changed. Physician-made (iatrogenic) multiple pregnancies are now seen in most developed countries, with frequencies approaching 50% of twins and more than 75% of high-order multiple pregnancies. The contribution of infertility treatment can be appreciated from data of the Israel Neonatal Network. The data indicate that among infants weighing less than 1500 g, 10% of singletons were conceived by assisted reproduction compared with 60% of twins and 90% of triplets.[40]

BIOLOGY

Most human conceptions (>99.2%) emerge from a single zygote (i.e. monozygotic, [MZ]), resulting in the fertilization of a single egg by a single spermatozoon. In the remaining cases, more than one egg is ovulated and fertilized, resulting in polyzygotic conceptions (dizygotic [DZ], trizygotic, etc.). This phenomenon occurs more often in taller, older, parous, heavier, and black women. Although direct and indirect evidence point to a genetic predisposition, the exact mechanism whereby the ovary is naturally stimulated to release more than one egg per cycle is basically unknown. At the same time, however, all infertility treatments are associated with ovarian stimulation and polyovulation. The contribution of infertility treatments to polyzygotic pregnancies has become extremely significant since the 1970s.

The vast majority of MZ conceptions result in singleton birth. In only a small fraction of the cases (0.4% of all natural conceptions) the zygote splits to form an MZ twin gestation. The mechanism of zygotic splitting is unclear. It has been postulated that all forms of assisted reproduction produce a breach in the integrity of the zona pellucida—the acellular layer of the egg—resulting in herniation of the part of the early embryo through that gap and splitting of the embryo.

The frequency of MZ splitting is also increased with all methods of assisted reproduction.[16] The true incidence of zygotic splitting following assisted reproduction is unknown. In a large study of single-embryo transfers, a sixfold increase in zygotic splitting was found. The frequency was not influenced by using fresh versus frozen-thawed embryos or by performing embryo transfers during a spontaneous versus an induced cycle.[16]

Two points related to the issue of DZ and MZ twinning deserve further discussion. The first is the change of overall frequency of MZs. In a population comprising mainly spontaneous gestations, the usual quoted frequency of MZ twinning is about one third of the twin population, whereas in a population comprising a sizable proportion of iatrogenic pregnancies one should expect one MZ pregnancy in 10 to 14 twin gestations.

The second point to consider is the placental arrangement (see also Chapter 23). DZ twins have two placentas (separate or fused), each with its chorion and amnion, forming the so-called dichorionic (DC) placenta. Placentation of the MZs, however, depends on the stage of embryonic development at which the split occurs. Early splits (about one third) result in DC placentas, whereas later splits result in monochorionic (MC) placentas. Moreover, if the amnion has not yet differentiated, the MC placenta includes two amniotic sacs: the MC-diamniotic (MCDA) placenta (about two thirds of the cases). If the split occurs later than 8 days after fertilization, an MC-monoamniotic (MCMA) placenta develops. Finally, even later splits result in all varieties of conjoined twins.

When describing the multiple pregnancy, one must differentiate between zygosity and chorionicity. Because MZs with a DC placenta cannot be differentiated clinically from same-sex DZ twins (half of the DZs) who also have a DC placenta, zygosity can be determined with certainty only in the DC-unlike-sex twins (all must be DZs) and in twins with an MC placenta (all must be MZs). Simple calculation reveals that we are blind to zygosity in about 45% of the cases, and zygosity determination must be performed by DNA testing. Importantly, nothing should be said about zygosity to parents of same-sex twins with a DC placenta.

MATERNAL CONSEQUENCES

When discussing maternal complications during multiple pregnancy, two important issues should be considered. The first issue involves the significant changes in women's role in western societies witnessed after World War II. The new roles in society were facilitated by effective contraception, allowing ample time to achieve education and a career. This, in turn, resulted in increased maternal age at first delivery. However, because age and fecundity are inversely related, infertility treatment to achieve a pregnancy often becomes inevitable. Because all infertility treatments carry an increased risk of multiple gestations, the end result of these sociomedical trends is an increased age of the cohort of mothers of multiples. U.S. data clearly show that the increase in maternal age is more striking in high-order multiple pregnancies than in twins and in twins than in singletons, with a net result of multiples being more often delivered to older mothers in whom chronic disease conditions have already accumulated.[17]

The second issue involves the overwhelmed maternal homeostasis. Consider the fact that the average singleton, twin, and triplet has a similar birthweight until 28 weeks (around 1000 g). However, by 28 weeks, the mother of twins and the mother of triplets has accumulated twice and three times the fetal mass of singletons, respectively. This excess of fetal mass must come from either existing maternal resources or from supplemental energy. It is thus clear that during the third trimester all maternal systems are overwhelmed and some may be only a step away from clinical insufficiency.

Two examples vividly demonstrate the situation. The first is the increased frequency of clinically significant anemia as a result of either depleted maternal iron stores or from inadequate iron supplementation.[4] Indeed, the incidence of anemia is significantly increased among mothers of multiples. A second example relates to the increased cardiac output. It has been estimated that in the worst-case scenario (i.e., preterm labor due to infection in a multiple pregnancy) the cardiac output may exceed 10 L/min (2 to 3 times the normal value). It is therefore understandable why cardiac function so easily turns into dysfunction when additional load—in the form of beta-sympathomimetic tocolysis—is administered to a patient with multiples who experiences premature contractions.[44]

Regardless of the inherent changes in maternal physiology due to the multiple pregnancy, there are some maternal disease conditions that are more frequent in these gestations. For instance, hypertensive disorders are 2 to 3 times more frequent[42] and their most dangerous complication—eclampsia—is 6 times more frequent among mothers of multiple gestations.[28] Moreover, preeclamptic toxemia (PET) occurs earlier in multiples than in singletons and often occurs in a more severe form.[3] Because triplets and other high-order multiples were rare in the past, there were scant data related to hypertensive disorders in high-order multiple pregnancies. With the current epidemic dimensions of multiple gestations it has been shown that the risk of hypertensive disorders is plurality dependent: the risk in triplets is higher than that in twins, and the risk in twins is higher than that in singletons.[45]

Although the data are still conflicting, it seems that the frequency of gestational diabetes is also increased among mothers of multiples. Critical reading of the literature suggests that most stimulation tests to detect glucose intolerance of various degrees showed a diabetogenic effect of multiple gestations, whereas demographic analyses failed to show increased rates of gestational diabetes.[30] However, one must realize that the latter were conducted in the era before the epidemic of iatrogenic multiples and before the effect of older maternal age could be documented.[30] Sivan's group showed that the risk of gestational diabetes is plurality dependent, as is the case for hypertensive disorders.[43] The correlation of multiple gestation with hypertensive disorders and gestational diabetes seems to point, at least in a teleological way, to the increased placental size—hyperplacentosis—as a potential common denominator.

All mothers of multiples are at considerably greater risk of preterm labor and delivery. Quite often, preterm contractions with or without cervical changes necessitate tocolytic treatment. Many prophylactic measures, including progestatives, cervical sutures (cerclage), beta-sympathomimetics, bed rest, and hospitalization, were proposed to reduce the preterm birth rates (see also Chapter 16). Regrettably, all *prophylactic* measures failed to significantly reduce this common complication of multiple pregnancy. Nevertheless, expecting mothers of multiples are frequently asked to leave work and to conduct a more sedentary lifestyle.

Box 18-1 lists the most common maternal complications during multiple gestations.[23]

FETAL-NEONATAL CONSEQUENCES

Animal models, like humans, demonstrate an inverse relationship between litter size and both gestational age

BOX 18-1. Maternal Complications More Frequently Seen in Multiple Pregnancies

Hypertensive Diseases
- Preeclamptic toxemia
  - HELLP syndrome
  - Acute fatty liver
- Pregnancy-induced hypertension
- Chronic hypertension
- Eclampsia

Anemia

Gestational Diabetes Mellitus (?)

Premature Contractions and Labor
- Complications associated with tocolysis

Delivery-associated Complications
- Cesarean section
- Operative delivery
- Premature rupture of membranes
- Postpartum endometritis
- Placental abruption

HELLP, hemolysis, elevated liver enzymes, low platelets

TABLE 18-1. Categories of Structural Defects in Twins

CATEGORY	DEFECT
Malformations more common in twins than in singletons	Neural tube defects Hydrocephaly Congenital heart disease Esophageal and anorectal atresias Intersex Genitourinary tract anomalies
Malformations unique to monozygotic twins	Amniotic band syndrome TRAP sequence Conjoined twins Twin embolization syndrome
Placental malformations	Single umbilical artery Twin-twin transfusion syndrome Velamentous cord insertion
Deformations due to intrauterine crowding	Skeletal (postural) abnormalities

TRAP, twin reverse arterial perfusion.
Adapted from Blickstein I, Smith-Levitin M: Multifetal pregnancy. In Petrikovsky BM (ed) Fetal disorders: Diagnosis and management. New York, John Wiley and Sons, 1998, p 223.

and birthweight. In the human, the average gestational age at birth is around 40 weeks for singletons, 36 weeks for twins, 32 weeks for triplets, and 29 weeks for quadruplets. Although multiple pregnancies exhibit many specific complications, the consequences of prematurity are by far the most common.

Malformations

Most texts cite a twofold to threefold increased risk of malformations among multiples. However, it seems that the increased risk is primarily related to MZ twinning and that the malformation rates of DZs is similar to that of singletons.[6] The higher malformation rate among MZs is explained by the hypothesis of a common teratogen: the one that causes the split of the zygote is also responsible for the malformation.

Malformations among multiples are grouped into four types (Table 18-1).[6] The first type includes malformations that are more frequent among multiples, notably those affecting the central nervous and the cardiovascular systems. The second type involves malformations related to MZ twinning such as twin reverse arterial perfusion (TRAP) sequence and the various forms of conjoined twins. The third type relates to consequences of placental malformations, in particular the MC placenta, resulting in the twin-twin transfusion syndrome (TTTS). Finally, the fourth type involves skeletal (postural) abnormalities such as clubfoot that are caused by intrauterine fetal crowding.

Some malformations can have a major impact on the properly formed twin. For instance, in the TRAP sequence, the circulation of the severely anomalous

acardiac-acephalic twin is entirely supported by the normal (pump) twin. Sooner or later, this cardiac overload will lead to cardiac insufficiency. Another example is the case in TTTS whereby both twins are completely normal, but the anomalous transplacental shunt of blood can cause serious morbidity in both twins. The most striking example is the case of single fetal demise in MC twins, whereby the surviving fetus dies in utero soon after the death of the first twin. Alternatively, the surviving twin can be seriously damaged (see later).

In contrast to structural malformations, chromosomal anomalies are not more frequent among multiples. For example, each member of the multiple gestation has the same maternal-age-dependent risk for trisomy 21. However, by pure probability calculations, the risk for a mother that one of her twins will have trisomy 21 is greater than that of a mother of a singleton. Roughly, a 32-year-old mother of twins has the same risk of one infant with trisomy 21 as a 35-year-old mother of a singleton.[35]

Because multiples are commonly seen in older mothers and invasive cytogenetic procedures (amniocentesis or chorionic villus sampling) carry a much higher risk of pregnancy loss when performed in multiples, there is a genuine utility to biochemical maternal screening of aneuploidy to minimize the need for invasive procedures in these premium pregnancies. Regrettably, screening tests like the triple test (second trimester maternal serum hCG or free β-hCG, alpha-fetoprotein, and unconjugated estriol) have a significantly lower prediction for trisomy 21 in multiples compared with singletons.[23] A recent advance is the implementation of nuchal translucency thickness measurement in screening for aneuploidy.

Most structural anomalies can be detected by a comprehensive sonographic scan. In addition, echocardiography and Doppler velocimetry can detect structural and functional cardiovascular anomalies. This ability raises the question of reduction of the anomalous twin. In multichorionic multiples, reduction is accomplished by ultrasound-guided intracardiac injection of potassium chloride. However, because of the risk to the survivor in MC sets, highly invasive procedures are used to interrupt the umbilical circulation of the anomalous twin.

All invasive procedures (amniocentesis, chorionic villus sampling, and the reduction methods) are associated with the risk of 5% to 10% of membrane rupture and loss of the entire pregnancy. When an invasive procedure is considered during the second trimester, the risk of extremely preterm birth of the normal twin is apparent. This situation is exemplified in discordant lethal malformations. For instance, when one twin is anencephalic, the risk of reducing this twin should be weighed against the risk of endangering the normal fetus by preterm birth.

Embryonic and Fetal Demise

From the early days of sonography, it was clear that there are more twin pregnancies than twin deliveries. The early loss of one twin was eventually designated *vanishing twin syndrome* (VTS) to denote the disappearance of an embryonic structure during the first trimester.[32] Many authorities consider this spontaneous reduction the natural equivalent of intentional multifetal pregnancy (numerical) reduction. Obviously, the true frequency of VTS is unknown, as many twin pregnancies remain unnoticed unless sonography is performed at an early stage. One estimate of VTS frequency comes from iatrogenic conceptions: Spontaneous reduction of one or more gestational sacs or embryos occurred before the 12th week of gestation in 36% of twin, 53% of triplet, and 65% of quadruplet pregnancies.[27]

Single fetal death occurring beyond the first trimester is also more common in multiples. In DC twins, it is believed that the risk to the surviving twin is extremely low and present only if there is an external insult such as maternal disease. In contrast, fetal death in MC twins is a totally different story.

Historically, it was believed that some ill-defined thromboplastin-like material is transfused from the dead to the live fetus—the twin embolization syndrome. The theory was that these emboli might either cause fetal death or result in end organ damage, such as brain and kidney lesions. In the early 1990s, after meticulous postmortem examinations, the embolic theory was replaced by the ischemic theory, which postulates that blood is acutely shunted from the live twin to the low-resistance circulation of the deceased fetus, causing acute hypovolemia, ischemia, and end organ damage in the survivor. The chance of serious damage in the survivor is significant and estimated to be between 20% and 30%.

Quite often, however, the diagnosis is made some time after single fetal death, and the question arises whether prompt delivery is indicated to reduce the risk for the survivor. Recent data suggest that acute blood loss occurs just before the time of death of the surviving twin, and therefore it is unlikely that immediate delivery of the surviving twin could decrease the associated high mortality and morbidity rates.[38] It is therefore prudent to suggest conservative management in such cases, especially remote from term, and to use ultrasound and magnetic resonance imaging (MRI) to exclude brain lesions.

Twin-Twin Transfusion

One of the most interesting consequences of MC twinning is the twin-twin transfusion syndrome (see also Chapter 23). TTTS is seen mainly (or only) in the diamniotic variety.[2] The extensive literature on TTTS may lead to the erroneous impression that the syndrome is frequently seen. In fact, TTTS occurs in about 10% to 15% of MC twins, and about half are of mild severity. Nonetheless, early onset (before 20 weeks' gestation) severe TTTS, unless intensively treated, is associated with 100% mortality of both twins.

The pathology behind TTTS is transplacental arteriovenous anastomoses that lead to shunting of blood from one twin (the donor) to the other (the recipient). Since all MC placentas have inert-twin anastomoses, the syndrome probably occurs because of fewer compensating veno-venous and arterio-arterial connections. The hypovolemia of the donor is manifested by poor micturition (absent bladder and oligohydramnios on sonographic scan) and signs of growth restriction. Conversely, the hypervolemic recipient is surrounded by polyhydramnios and manifests signs of cardiac overload ranging from tricuspid regurgitation to cardiac insufficiency and hydrops fetalis.[46]

Many treatment modalities were suggested to treat TTTS (Box 18-2).[39,46] In general, TTTS means serious morbidity, but the specific outcome is related to the gestational age when TTTS occurred and to the severity of the syndrome. No single therapy has emerged as a treatment of choice with significantly better short-term results, which puts the clinician in a difficult position vis-à-vis the patient. Recent data, however, suggest that long-term outcomes are better with laser occlusion than with amnioreduction (see also Chapter 11). Nonetheless, in some instances intervention can be used to buy time (i.e., increasing gestational age to the point of viability) rather than as a true solution to the intertwin shunt.

Because we are unable to accurately predict which case is going to deteriorate over time, buying time may mean delivery of more mature twins who are in a worse or worsening condition. In addition, discordant fetal conditions remote from term pose difficult ethical questions: Waiting obviously increases the risk for fetal death and long-term morbidity for the ailing twins, whereas pregnancy termination by cesarean section exposes both twins to the risk of preterm delivery.[46] Despite these difficulties, innovations in the treatment of TTTS may lead to an expected breakthrough in the future.

BOX 18-2. Treatment Modes of Twin-to-Twin Transfusion Syndrome

Conservative Management with Careful Monitoring
- Monitoring
  - Ultrasound assessment
  - Biophysical profile
  - Doppler blood flow velocimetry
  - Fetal echocardiography
  - Cardiotocography
- Digoxin

Serial Amnioreduction

Septostomy

Fetoscopic Laser Occlusion of Placental Vessels

Selective Feticide
- Cord embolization
- Nd:YAG laser technique
- Fetoscopic cord ligation
- Bipolar coagulation

Nd:YAG, neodymium yttrium-aluminum-garnet

In the classic presentation of TTTS, the twins are discordant in size (at least 20% to 25%) and in hemoglobin levels (at least 5 g/dL). The donor is usually pale and anemic, whereas the recipient is polycythemic.[2] The donor twin might be acutely distressed, with severe anemia and hypovolemic shock necessitating transfusion or exchange of blood products, or both. The recipient occasionally requires partial dilution exchange and support for cardiac failure (see also Chapter 44).

Fetal Growth

As noted earlier, multiples grow in utero to the same extent as singletons until about 28 weeks. Thereafter, during the third trimester, growth curves of multiples show a clear decelerating trend compared with the growth curve of singletons. Not surprisingly, the limited uterine capacity to nurture multiples leads to growth aberrations (see also Chapter 13).[12]

The higher risk of delivering low birthweight (LBW) infants in a multiple birth is well known, as is the advantage for the multiparous patient. For instance, analysis of population-based data related to 12,567 liveborn twin pairs found that overall, the risk of having at least one very low birthweight (VLBW, <1500 g) infant was 1:5 among nulliparous women and 1:12 among multiparous women. The risk of having two VLBW twins among nulliparas (1:11) was double that of multiparas (1:22).[10] A similar trend and similar frequencies, but for extremely LBW (<1000 g) babies, were found in the analysis of triplets.[14]

The most common growth aberration in multiples is birthweight discordance.[19] Birthweight discordance occurs whenever there is difference in birthweights between the larger and the smaller infant of a multiple pregnancy set. When one analyzes a large series of multiples, one rarely finds that all members of the set have the same birthweight. Indeed, some variation is expected between siblings and therefore the magnitude of the difference—the degree of discordance—must be incorporated in the definition. The most common definition of discordance is the *percent* definition, whereby the birthweight disparity is calculated as a percentage of the larger infant. However, the definition does not refer to the actual size of the twins, and it can assign the same degree of discordance (e.g., 20%) to a twin pair weighing 1500 g and 1200 g and to a pair weighing 3000 g and 2400 g. The cumulative frequency[19] shows that about 75% of twins exhibit less than 15% discordance, about 20% are 15% to 25% discordant, and about 5% are more than 25% discordant.

The definition of birthweight discordance is even more complex in triplets. Clinicians usually use the same percent definition used for twins and calculate the difference between the largest and smallest triplet of each set, although this scheme ignores the middle-sized triplet and therefore the true intertriplet relationship.

Recently, a new description was developed in which the relative birthweight of the middle triplet was defined.[18] The middle triplet was defined as *symmetrical* when its birthweight was within 25% of the average birthweight of the largest and smallest triplets, as *low-skew* when a set comprised one large and two small triplets, and as *high-skew* if the set comprised one small and two large triplets. The frequencies of different types of triplet discordance did not change with gestational age, suggesting three distinct types of discordant growth in triplets that are independent of gestational age (average values: symmetrical 57%, high-skew 30%, low-skew 13%).[18]

An important related issue is the birth order of the smaller twin in a discordant set; it was a common belief that the smaller twin is usually the second-born twin. However, it has been determined that at lower levels of discordance either twin can be the smaller but the likelihood of the second-born twin being the smaller increases with increasing discordance levels.[27] At discordance levels greater than 25%, the smaller twin was 3 to 6 times more often the second born.[7]

DATA FROM MULTIPLE BIRTH DATA SETS
Population-based studies using the Israeli and the U.S. Matched Multiple Birth Data Set have reached the following conclusions.

Levels of Discordance
Data[7,9] suggest that there are three levels of discordance. In the lowest levels (probably at less than 25%), discordance seems to be related to the normal variation expected from the natural dissimilarities between siblings. In the highest level (probably greater than 35%), discordance seems to be related to the exhausted uterine environment and reflects growth restriction.

The clinical approach to both levels is generally accepted: observation or intervention for the lowest and highest degrees of discordance, respectively. However, between these levels are twins, constituting 10% of the entire twin population, who are of special interest because of the controversies involved in their clinical management (aggressive versus conservative). The benefit of discordance would therefore be an adaptive measure to promote maturity (i.e., delivery at a more advanced gestational age) by reducing the inevitable uterine overdistention, as has been shown in the group of twins within a total birthweight range of 3000 g to 5000 g.[21]

Mortality

Mortality was 11 times higher among highly discordant smaller twins (>30%) compared with nondiscordant smaller twins. Risk estimates ranged from 1.1 among 15% to 19% discordant twins to 2.0 among highly discordant twins. After accounting for the association between fetal growth and discordance, mortality risk was substantially higher among smaller and larger twins who were highly discordant (30% or more). The authors concluded that after controlling for fetal growth, smaller and larger twins affected by higher levels of birthweight discordance (>25%) remain at disproportionate risk for neonatal mortality.[24] Increasing birthweight discordance has been associated with increased risk of intrauterine death and malformation-related neonatal deaths.[26]

When it became clear that not all discordant twins have the same outcome, discordance was further classified according to the birthweight of the smaller twin. Indeed, when neonatal mortality rates were compared among three groups of discordant twins (>25%), distinguished by the birthweight of the smaller twin being in the lowest 10th percentile (62.4%), in the 10th to 50th percentile (32.9%), or above the 50th percentile (4.7%), the rate was significantly higher among pairs in which the smaller twin's birthweight was in the lowest 10th percentile (29% vs. 11.1% and 11 per 1000).[22] This difference results from the higher mortality rates among the smaller but not among the larger twins. The authors concluded that even in severely discordant twin pairs, about 40% do not comprise a growth-restricted fetus. Identification of this group is an imperative step in the management of birthweight discordance in twin gestations and in avoiding unnecessary interventions that may lead to iatrogenic prematurity.[25,31]

An important practical issue in the assessment of growth in a multiple pregnancy is whether to use singleton or twin growth curves. Because so many twins and, logically, almost all infants in high-order multiple pregnancies weigh less than singletons of the same gestational age, it seems that multiples grow differently than singletons do and therefore are frequently and erroneously defined as small for gestational age by singleton standards.[12] Before birth, sonographic assessment of individual fetal growth cannot establish a pattern of growth restriction unless repeated scans are performed and deceleration or arrest of the growth pattern is established. Moreover, despite the relative accuracy achieved by sonographic estimations of the individual fetal weight, the "plus or minus" situation that

exists for each estimation can cause quite significant under- and overestimation of the weight difference between fetuses and to low positive predictive values of discordance.[5]

As is the case with singletons, growth restriction—genuine or relative—is usually managed conservatively unless signs of fetal distress are seen. At times, however, discordant growth and discordant fetal well-being go hand in hand. When the risk for the unaffected neonates is lower than the expected risk for the affected fetus, delivery is a clear option, as would be the case at greater than 32 weeks. Clinical dilemmas may arise, however, remote from term, when a decision to save the ailing fetus may endanger the healthy fetus with potential risks of extreme preterm birth.

Fetal assessment in multiples is no different from assessment in singletons, although it is more complicated. For instance, with the availability of modern equipment, fetal heart rate is currently traced for both twins at the same time. Intrapartum dual tracing is as important as during pregnancy, and once the membranes are ruptured, the presenting twin is usually traced with a scalp electrode while the nonpresenting twin is followed with an external Doppler electrode. The fetal biophysical profile is similarly assessed individually.

DELIVERY CONSIDERATIONS

Almost 80% to 90% of twins and practically all high-order multiple pregnancies initiate spontaneous labor at less than 38 weeks' gestation. In recent years, data have suggested that at least for twins, "term" by singleton standards (i.e., 40 weeks) might be inappropriate and could carry a similar risk to postterm singletons. This concept emerged from data suggesting that neonatal mortality[36] and morbidity[34] are increased after 37 completed weeks compared with singletons, and the concept that twins should be delivered by 37 or 38 weeks comes from evidence that the fetal systems of the multiple pregnancy are mature by this date.[1,33]

There are many reasons why cesarean section could be indicated in most twins and all high-order multiple pregnancies.[8] Because twin gestations often involve maternal and fetal complications and are quite often considered "premium" pregnancies, many clinicians follow the principle "no high-risk pregnancy should end with a high-risk delivery" and deliver twins by cesarean section for many subtle reasons other than clear-cut, evidence-based indications. Thus, the decision for an abdominal birth in twins, intentionally or not, is based on qualitative variables that were not quantified by randomized trials and on quantitative variables that suggest no advantage for a cesarean delivery in the majority of cases.[8]

Vaginal birth is permitted in twins whenever the first twin is in vertex presentation. Breech delivery of the second twin or internal podalic version of a transverse-lying second twin is still permitted; however, a Canadian randomized trial was initiated in 2004 to evaluate the safety of such births. Otherwise, all pairs with a non-vertex presenting twin are likely to undergo a cesarean section. Nuances on this construct consider fetal size, discordance, prior uterine surgery, and—mainly—the experience and dexterity of the obstetrician.

When a multiple birth is expected, the main neonatal problem is logistic, rather than medical, because immediate neonatal treatment of an infant of a multiple pregnancy is not significantly different from treating a singleton, except that twins come in pairs, and triplets come in sets. In practical terms, this means more staff in the delivery suite, more cribs available in the nursery, and more stations ready in the neonatal intensive care unit (NICU). At times, delivery of several very preterm sets in a short period may occupy the entire NICU for a relatively long period. It is clear that if the availability of NICU cribs lags behind the increased production of multiples, a serious public health situation may be created.

OUTCOME

Given the much-increased risk of maternal and fetal complications during a multiple pregnancy, the overall outcome for multiples is worse compared with the outcome for singletons. For example, the increased risk of cerebral palsy among multiples is clear: 28 to 45 for triplets, 7.3 to 12.6 for twins, and 1.6 to 2.3 for singletons per 1000 survivors, indicating that the greater the number of fetuses, the greater the prevalence of cerebral palsy. Moreover, the increase in cerebral palsy with the number of fetuses seems to be exponential.[13]

However, the as yet unanswered question is: are the outcomes of multiples poorer than the outcomes of singletons matched for birthweight or gestational age? For instance, consider whether the usual prophylactic dose of corticosteroids given to singletons is enough for twins to enhance lung maturity and reduce the risk of neonatal respiratory distress.[37]

One way to estimate neonatal morbidity is to examine the influence of plurality on a cohort of infants with similar initial characteristics. Multivariate logistic regression analysis using all significant perinatal covariates of prospectively collected data from the Israel national VLBW infant database (n = 5594: 3717 singletons, 1394 twins, and 483 triplets) has shown that respiratory distress syndrome was significantly more common in twins and triplets despite increased exposure to antenatal steroids.[40] In addition, VLBW triplets were at increased risk of death. VLBW twins and triplets had no increased risk of chronic lung disease or adverse neurological findings.[40]

Another way is to examine the influence of birth order on these variables.[41] Comparisons of outcome variables by birth order of VLBW twins, after stratification by mode of delivery and gestational age, revealed that second twins had increased risk of respiratory distress syndrome, chronic lung disease, and death, but not adverse neurologic findings. Mode of delivery did not significantly influence outcome.

SUMMARY: PREVENTION VERSUS CURE

The epidemic dimensions of multiple births, and especially of high-order multiple pregnancies, became clear toward the end of the 1980s as an aftershock resulting from effective infertility treatment.[11] To amend this untoward consequence of infertility treatment, clinicians proposed to reduce the number of embryos during pregnancy.[29] Multifetal pregnancy reduction, albeit considered by many to be the ultimate paradox of medicine,[15] soon became a popular "cure" of the side effects of infertility treatment. This procedure, performed during the early second trimester via the transvaginal or transabdominal route, carries a risk of about 5% total loss. However, multifetal pregnancy reduction is certainly associated with better outcomes because fewer fetuses will expectedly do better than more fetuses. Once clinicians refined and mastered the technique, the debate about the final number became pertinent, and the current controversy is about multifetal pregnancy reduction of triplets.[20]

As always in medicine, prevention is better than cure. In terms of infertility treatment, this means transferring only one embryo in in vitro fertilization programs and canceling ovulation induction cycles when more than one ripe follicle is visualized. Obviously, such preventive measures will reduce the overall success rates, although it is debatable if a multiple pregnancy with 3 or 4 severely premature infants constitutes success.

It is evident that multiple pregnancies and births are a true challenge for all medical disciplines involved in caring for the mother and fetuses and infants. At the same time, the increase in iatrogenic multiple births may have an anti-evolution effect with as yet unknown consequences.

REFERENCES

1. Allen MC, Donohue PK: Neuromaturation of multiples. Semin Neonatol 7:211, 2002.
2. Blickstein I: The twin-twin transfusion syndrome. Obstet Gynecol 76:714, 1990.
3. Blickstein I et al: Perinatal outcome of twin pregnancies complicated with preeclampsia. Am J Perinat 9:258, 1992.
4. Blickstein I et al: Hemoglobin levels during twin versus singleton pregnancies: Parity makes the difference. J Reprod Med 40:47, 1995.
5. Blickstein I et al: Is intertwin birth weight discordance predictable? Gynecol Obstet Invest 42:105, 1996.
6. Blickstein I, Smith-Levitin M: Multifetal pregnancy. In Petrikovsky BM (ed): Fetal disorders: Diagnosis and management. New York, John Wiley and Sons, 1998, p 223.
7. Blickstein I et al: The relation between intertwin birth weight discordance and total twin birth weight. Obstet Gynecol 93:113, 1999.
8. Blickstein I: Cesarean section for all twins? J Perinatol 28:169, 2000.
9. Blickstein I et al: Adaptive growth restriction as a pattern of birth weight discordance in twin gestations. Obstet Gynecol 96:986, 2000.

10. Blickstein I et al: Risk for one or two very low birth weight twins: A population study. Obstet Gynecol 96:400, 2000.

11. Blickstein I, Keith LG. The epidemic of multiple pregnancies. Postgrad Obstet Gynecol 21:1, 2001.

12. Blickstein I: Normal and abnormal growth of multiples. Semin Neonatol 7:177, 2002.

13. Blickstein I: Cerebral palsy in multifoetal pregnancies. Dev Med Child Neurol 44:352, 2002.

14. Blickstein I et al: The odds of delivering one, two or three extremely low birth weight (<1000 g) triplet infants: A study of 3288 sets. J Perinat Med 30:359, 2002.

15. Blickstein I, Keith LG: Iatrogenic multiple pregnancy. Semin Neonatol 7:169, 2002.

16. Blickstein I et al: Zygotic splitting rates following single embryo transfers in in-vitro fertilization. New Engl J Med 348:2366, 2003.

17. Blickstein I: Motherhood at or beyond the edge of reproductive age. Int J Fertil Womens Med 48:17, 2003.

18. Blickstein I et al: A novel approach to intertriplet birth weight discordance. Am J Obstet Gynecol 188:172, 2003.

19. Blickstein I, Kalish RB: Birth weight discordance in multiple pregnancy. Twin Res 6:526, 2003.

20. Blickstein I, Keith LG: Outcome of triplets and higher order multiple pregnancies. Curr Opin Obstet Gynecol 15:113, 2003.

21. Blickstein I, Goldman RD: Intertwin birth weight discordance as a potential adaptive measure to promote gestational age. J Reprod Med 48:449, 2003.

22. Blickstein I, Keith LG: Neonatal mortality rates among growth discordant twins, classified according to the birth weight of the smaller twin. Am J Obstet Gynecol 190:170, 2004.

23. Blickstein I, Keith LG: Multi-Fetal Gestations. In Gronowski A (ed): Handbook of Clinical Laboratory Testing During Pregnancy. Totowa, NJ, Humana Press, 2004.

24. Branum AM, Schoendorf KC: The effect of birth weight discordance on twin neonatal mortality. Obstet Gynecol 101:570, 2003.

25. Cheung VY et al: Preterm discordant twins: What birth weight difference is significant? Am J Obstet Gynecol 172:955, 1995.

26. Demissie K et al: Fetal and neonatal mortality among twin gestations in the United States: The role of intrapair birth weight discordance. Obstet Gynecol 100:474, 2002.

27. Dickey RP et al: Spontaneous reduction of multiple pregnancy: Incidence and effect on outcome. Am J Obstet Gynecol 186:77, 2000.

28. Douglas KA, Redman CW: Eclampsia in the United Kingdom. BMJ 309:1395, 1994.

29. Evans MI et al: Multifetal pregnancy reduction. Baillieres Clin Obstet Gynaecol 12:147, 1998.

30. Hazan Y, Blickstein I: Diabetes and multiple pregnancies. In Hod M et al (eds): Textbook of Diabetes and Pregnancy. London, Martin Dunitz, 2003, p 502.

31. Hollier LM et al: Outcome of twin pregnancies according to intrapair birth weight differences. Obstet Gynecol 94:1006, 1999.

32. Landy HJ, Keith LG: The vanishing twin: A review. Hum Reprod Update 4:177, 1998.

33. Lewis DF et al: Respiratory morbidity in well-dated twins approaching term. What are the risks of elective delivery? Reprod Med 47:841, 2002.

34. Luke B et al: The cost of prematurity: A case-control study of twins vs singletons. Am J Public Health 86:809, 1996.

35. Meyers C et al: Aneuploidy in twin gestations: When is maternal age advanced? Obstet Gynecol 89:248, 1997.

36. Minakami H, Sato I: Reestimating date of delivery in multifetal pregnancies. JAMA 275:1432, 1996.

37. Murphy DJ et al: Cohort study of the neonatal outcome of twin pregnancies that were treated with prophylactic or rescue antenatal corticosteroids. Am J Obstet Gynecol 187:483, 2002.

38. Nicolini U et al: Fetal blood sampling immediately before and within 24 hours of death in monochorionic twin pregnancies complicated by single intrauterine death. Am J Obstet Gynecol 179:800, 1998.

39. Ropacka M et al: Treatment options for the twin-twin transfusion syndrome: A review. Twin Res 5:507, 2002.

40. Shinwell ES et al: Excess risk of mortality in very low birth weight triplets: A national, population-based study. Arch Dis Child Fetal Neonatal Ed 88:F36, 2003.

41. Shinwell ES et al: Effect of birth order on neonatal morbidity and mortality among very low birthweight twins: A population based study. Arch Dis Child Fetal Neonatal Ed 89:F145, 2004.

42. Sibai BM et al: Hypertensive disorders in twin versus singleton gestations. National Institute of Child Health and Human Development Network of Maternal-Fetal Medicine Units. Am J Obstet Gynecol 182:938, 2000.

43. Sivan E et al: Impact of fetal reduction on the incidence of gestational diabetes. Obstet Gynecol 99:91, 2002.

44. Skupski DW. Maternal complications of twin gestation. The Female Patient 6:16, 1995.

45. Skupski DW et al: Multiple gestations from in vitro fertilization: Successful implantation alone is not associated with subsequent preeclampsia. Am J Obstet Gynecol 175:1029, 1996.

46. Wee LY, Fisk NM: The twin-twin transfusion syndrome. Semin Neonatol 7:187, 2002.

19 Post-Term Pregnancy

Isaac Blickstein and Orna Flidel-Rimon

The human gestation is said to last 266 days from fertilization or 280 days from the last menstrual period (LMP). This amounts to 40 weeks of gestation—10 lunar months, or about 9.5 calendar months. In fact, as no one knows exactly how long any particular pregnancy should last, clinicians use statistical distributions of gestational ages to conclude that a given pregnancy should last between 37 and 42 completed weeks (called *term*). Using such a distribution, about 80% of babies are delivered at term, 10% are delivered before 37 completed weeks, and about 10% are delivered post-term (greater than 42 completed weeks). The American College of Obstetricians and Gynecologists was rather strict in defining *post-term*—that is, pregnancies carried beyond what is considered to be term—as any time after 42 completed weeks from the LMP.[1]

The problem in defining the end of pregnancy is that the beginning of a pregnancy is seldom known. In contrast to conceptions that follow in vitro fertilization, where the day of transferring the embryo is known, spontaneous pregnancy is associated with educated guessing, resulting in accuracies of about plus or minus 2 to 3 weeks. Ultrasound assessment, especially with earlier measurements, has increased the accuracy of pregnancy dating. Sonographic dating is now available using the crown-rump length, the biparietal diameter, and the femur length. Of these, the crown-rump length is the most accurate as it is measured as early as in the second half of the first trimester. The biparietal diameter is the most popular biometric value and is most accurate during the first half of the second trimester. The femur length is the most consistent marker for gestational age and is used from the beginning of the second trimester onward. The addition of the sonographic measurement has improved our educated guess of the gestational age and narrowed the margin of error to about plus or minus 1 week (especially when an early scan is performed). It is customary to use the known (but inaccurate) LMP whenever the calculations are within 1 week of the estimated age by early sonography. If, however, the first scan is done late in the second trimester, the sonographic accuracy is much reduced. As ultrasound assessment is not available everywhere, dating may be inferred from a series of clinical estimations (Box 19-1).

Accurate dating is important because inaccurate dating is the most common reason for a pregnancy appearing to be post-term. Inaccurate dating may be a result of late ovulation, especially in cases of infrequent menstruation, or simply because the patient cannot accurately remember the LMP. Genuine post-term gestations may rarely be associated with *anencephaly* or with *placental sulfatase deficiency*. Both of these mechanisms point to the concept of the fetal placental clock, which involves the role of corticosteroid-releasing hormone and estriol in normal parturition and delivery.[16]

This chapter will discuss the consequences and management of prolonged pregnancy.

RISKS OF POST-TERM PREGNANCY

In general, the risks of post-term pregnancy are of two types. In one type, the placenta continues to function, more or less as in the previous months, and the fetus continues to grow. This results in a large baby—the so-called macrosomic infant. McLean and colleagues studied 7000 infants with confirmed expected date of confinement (±7 days) and showed a gradual shift toward higher birthweight between 39 and 43 weeks' gestation.[15] These authors voiced their concern for fetal macrosomia rather than for intrauterine growth restriction (IUGR) in post-term pregnancy (see also Chapter 13).

The other type, which seems to be more common, occurs when the placenta's function is reduced. When this situation is prolonged, some form of placental insufficiency results. Typically, placental insufficiency is associated with a reduction in the nutrients and oxygen transferred to the fetus, leading not only to a wide range of perinatal morbidities but also to increased rates of perinatal mortality. In an attempt to quantify this rate, Divon and coworkers evaluated the National

---

BOX 19-1. Clinical Methods to Estimate Gestational Age

- Promote early prenatal care. The earlier the patient is seen, the more accurate is the estimation.
- Take a very careful menstrual history.
- If unknown, try to track the last menstrual period.
- Find out when the symptoms of pregnancy began.
- Perform a pelvic examination: dating by uterine size is better than nothing and often quite accurate. This is also true for dating by fundal height.
- Positive or negative pregnancy test results can help exclude unlikely dates.
- Look for heart tones with a simple Doppler. They appear as early as 9 to 11 weeks.

Swedish Medical Birth Registry.[8] In 181,524 singleton pregnancies with reliable dates delivered at greater than 40 weeks, the authors found a significant rise in the odds ratio for fetal death at greater than 41 weeks' gestation, but the odds ratios for neonatal mortality did not demonstrate a significant gestational age dependency. Importantly, IUGR was associated with significantly higher odds ratios for both fetal and neonatal mortality rates at every gestational age examined. This extensive study of accurately dated pregnancies documented a significant increase in fetal mortality beyond 41 weeks' gestation—an observation corroborated by many others[4]—and a significant contribution of IUGR to the perinatal mortality in these pregnancies.[8]

Another assessment of the Swedish population found that perinatal mortality was parity dependent.[10] The stillbirth rate was highest for primiparas at 38 completed weeks (2.3%), and lowest at 40 weeks (1.2%), and then it increased to 2.36% in the post-term period, but the difference compared to multiparas was significant only from 41 weeks onward.[10] Neonatal mortality was increased at 41 completed weeks for primiparas, but for multiparas it changed significantly only after 42 completed weeks. Except for the parity effect on stillbirth, this study documented the parity-independent risk of neonatal deaths after 42 completed weeks.

Macrosomia

The well-known risks of macrosomic fetuses include dystocia (i.e., difficult delivery), borderline cephalopelvic disproportion necessitating instrumental or abdominal delivery, frank cephalopelvic disproportion ending in abdominal birth, traumatic delivery (shoulder dystocia) with or without birth trauma (brachial plexus injury, fracture of the clavicle), neurologic damage, and infant death. The risk of each of these complications is related to the degree of macrosomia—that is, the larger the baby the greater is the risk. However, it is not entirely clear what the relative contributions are of prolonged pregnancy, maternal diabetes, and obesity in producing macrosomia. In cases of gestational diabetes, it is logical to assume that if there is no placental insufficiency, the fetus will be continuously influenced by the growth-promoting effect of the maternal disease (see also Chapter 15).

Management of fetal macrosomia is complicated by two factors. First, the diagnosis (clinical or sonographic) is often inaccurate; thus prediction and therefore prevention of these risks are not always possible. Second, these risks are primarily, but not exclusively, associated with vaginal birth. Thus, when the diagnosis is uncertain, preventing most of the potential complications means performing many unnecessary cesarean deliveries. For example, Rouse and colleagues calculated that in nondiabetic pregnancies, 2345 and 3695 cesarean deliveries are necessary to prevent one permanent brachial plexus injury in fetuses with antenatal estimated weights of 4000 and 4500 g, respectively.[19]

Because the medicolegal environment often fuels decision making in cases of potential macrosomia, clini-

cians may choose to induce labor in the diabetic patient before 40 completed weeks to avoid the development of macrosomia and its sequelae.[13] Alternatively, cesarean section is offered when the estimated fetal weight is greater than 4500 g, and to diabetic mothers when the estimated fetal weight is greater than 4000 to 4200 g.

Dysmaturity

The dysmaturity (postmaturity) syndrome was described almost 50 years ago.[6] It affects about 20% of post-term pregnancies.[7] It is associated with arrest of fetal growth (IUGR) and is attributed to placental insufficiency. The neonate may exhibit many of the following signs: low weight, relative absence of subcutaneous fat, wrinkling of the skin, prominent fingernails and toenails (nails appear to be long, as if the infant were 8 days old), absence of the vernix caseosa, desquamation of the skin, and yellowish-greenish discoloration of the umbilical cord, nails, and skin (Fig. 19-1). Dysmaturity was historically associated with increased perinatal mortality rate (3% to 15%), ante- and intrapartum fetal distress, increased neonatal morbidity, meconium aspiration, peripartum asphyxia, neonatal hypoglycemia, hypothermia, hyperviscosity, and polycythemia. These complications may result in developmental sequelae.

Meconium passed in utero may be aspirated either in utero or with the initial respiratory efforts of the infant, and it is not certain which occurred in infants with meconium aspiration syndrome. The current recommendation of the American Academy of Pediatrics and the American Heart Association is that if the baby is vigorous (has strong respiratory efforts, good muscle tone, and a heart rate greater than 100 beats per minute), the mouth and nose need to be cleared of secretions, and oxygen may need to be administered. If the baby is *not* vigorous, the mouth and the trachea may need to be suctioned via endotracheal intubation (see also Chapter 42, Part 5).

Obstetric management of dysmaturity and its related complications is primarily preventive. It requires close

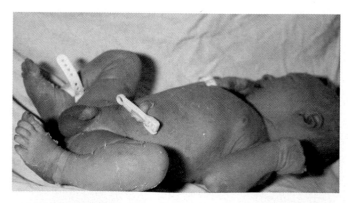

FIGURE 19-1. Infant of 42 weeks' gestation. Note the prominent nails, absence of the vernix caseosa, desquamation of the skin, and discoloration of the umbilical cord, nails, and skin.

follow-up of patients approaching post-term and the consideration of avoiding a post-term situation by inducing labor during the 40th or the 41st week of gestation.

During labor, oligohydramnios and meconium are associated with increased incidence of variable fetal heart rate decelerations. This particular type of tracing is more likely when the cord is compressed between the fetal body and the uterine wall. Some clinicians perform amnioinfusion (i.e., intra-amniotic instillation of saline) to increase the amniotic fluid volume and to dilute the meconium.

ASSESSMENT OF FETAL WELL-BEING

All methods of assessing fetal well-being are associated with good negative predictive value and relatively poor positive predictive value. It follows that most of the tests will adequately exclude signs of fetal distress. The reverse is not true, because the tests are not sensitive enough to detect all truly distressed fetuses. As a result, many fetuses with suspected fetal distress are, in fact, not distressed at all (see also Chapter 9).

Methods to assess fetal well-being include fetal heart rate monitoring without contractions (the nonstress test); fetal heart rate reaction to contractions (the oxytocin challenge test); sonographic assessment of fetal movements, tone, breathing movements, and amniotic fluid (together called the biophysical profile); and the more sophisticated Doppler velocimetry of various maternal or fetal vessels (Table 19-1).

In the past, visualization of the color of membranes via a transcervical amnioscope was used to exclude the possibility of meconium in the amniotic fluid. This procedure is no longer performed because meconium

TABLE 19-1. Methods of Assessing Fetal Well-Being

TEST	METHOD	DESCRIPTION	INTERPRETATION
Nonstress test (NST)	Cardiotocography	Fetal heart rate (FHR) tracing in the absence of uterine contractions showing FHR accelerations (≥15 beats per minute above baseline for >15 s)	Reactive (normal) NST: ≥2 FHR accelerations within 20 min, regardless of fetal movement Nonreactive NST: <2 FHR accelerations over a 40-minute period
Contraction stress test (CST)	Cardiotocography	Response of the FHR to uterine contractions (3 per 10 min), assuming that fetal oxygenation deteriorates transiently during contractions. Contractions may be spontaneous or induced by oxytocin (OCT) or nipple stimulation.	Negative (normal): no late or severe variable decelerations Positive: late decelerations after ≥50% of contractions Suspect: intermittent late decelerations or severe variable decelerations
Fetal movement	Kick counts	A perception of decreased fetal movement sometimes precedes fetal death.	>5 fetal movements per 30 min is considered reassuring.
Biophysical profile (BPP)	Cardiotocography and ultrasound	NST Fetal breathing movements Fetal movement Fetal tone Amniotic fluid volume	Normal: ≥1 episode of rhythmic fetal breathing of ≥30 s per 30 min ≥3 discrete body or limb movements per 30 min ≥1 episode of extension or flexion of a fetal limb A vertical pocket of amniotic fluid >2 cm Scoring: 0 (abnormal, absent, or insufficient), 2 (normal). Score results: >8 is normal, 6 is equivocal, and ≤4 is abnormal.
Umbilical artery Doppler velocimetry (systolic to end-diastolic [S/D] ratio)	Doppler ultrasound	Normally growing fetuses have low S/D ratios. In patients with intrauterine growth restriction, the ratio is high. Absent end diastolic or reversed flow is an ominous sign.	S/D ratio >4 is considered high.
Amniotic fluid index (AFI)	Ultrasound	Sum of 4 vertical pockets of amniotic fluid	AFI decreases with gestational age. AFI <8 cm is considered oligohydramnios.

OCT, ocytocin challenge test.

staining is no longer considered to be a reliable sign of acute fetal distress. Even the current method of assessing the nonreassuring fetal state—the amount of amniotic fluid as indicated by the amniotic fluid index (AFI)—yields equivocal results. It was found, for example, that neither the AFI nor the reduction in AFI was related to meconium staining and fetal distress.[21] In contrast, Morris and coworkers found in a large prospective study that an AFI of less than 5 cm was significantly associated with birth asphyxia, meconium aspiration, cesarean section for fetal distress in labor, cord arterial pH less than 7 at delivery, and low Apgar scores.[17] Despite the significant association with adverse outcomes, the sensitivities of AFI were as low as 28.6%, 12%, and 11.5% for major adverse outcome, fetal distress in labor, and admission to the neonatal unit, respectively.[17] Deciding the optimal management on the basis of fetal heart rate monitoring is also difficult because of the high frequency of nonreassuring patterns on electronic monitoring of normal pregnancies with normal fetal outcomes.[14]

All of these factors point to the need for a more holistic approach to the evaluation of the prolonged pregnancy. The first question is whether to avoid the potential complication by inducing delivery before 42 weeks. If the answer is yes, when should it be done? Finally, does such intervention actually reduce neonatal complications?

SHOULD WE INDUCE LABOR BEFORE 42 WEEKS?

The benefit of reducing potential fetal risks with induction of labor must be balanced against the morbidity associated with this procedure. Management of an otherwise uncomplicated pregnancy prolonged beyond the estimated date of confinement, when the woman presents with unfavorable cervical conditions, has been the subject of extensive research for more than a decade. One of the earliest studies compared two strategies for managing post-term pregnancy—immediate induction and expectant management.[18] Patients with uncomplicated pregnancies at 41 weeks' gestation were randomized to either immediate induction of labor (within 24 hours of randomization) or expectant management (nonstress test and AFI assessment twice a week). Adverse perinatal outcome (neonatal seizures, intracranial hemorrhage, the need for mechanical ventilation, or nerve injury) was similar in both groups (1.5% in the induction group versus 1% in the expectant management group). There were no fetal deaths in either group, nor were there differences in mean birthweight or the frequency of macrosomia. The cesarean delivery rate was not significantly different between the groups.[18]

The latest study is a systematic review with meta-analysis of 16 randomized controlled trials that compared induction and expectant management for uncomplicated, singleton, live pregnancies of at least 41 weeks' gestation.[20] Patients who underwent labor induction had lower cesarean delivery rates (odds ratio, 0.88; 95% confidence intervals, 0.78, 0.99). No significant differences were found in perinatal mortality rates, rates of admission to neonatal intensive care units, meconium aspiration, meconium below the cords, or abnormal Apgar scores.[20] These results lead to the conclusion that labor induction at 41 weeks' gestation for otherwise uncomplicated singleton pregnancies reduces cesarean delivery rates without compromising perinatal outcomes.[20] Clearly, implementation of such policy is expected to influence neonatal morbidity. Indeed, the new policy influenced the frequency of meconium aspiration syndrome, which decreased nearly fourfold from 1990-1992 to 1997-1998. The only change in neonatal characteristics was a 33% decrease in births at more than 41 weeks, with a reciprocal 33% increase in births at 38 to 39 weeks during 1997-1998.[23]

An equally important question is whether to induce post-term pregnancies when the woman has a favorable cervix. A recent study found that cesarean rate was not different between expectant management and immediate induction, and that 95% of the expectant group delivered within 1 week after enrollment. Maternal and fetal complications in both groups were similar, as were the mean birthweight and the frequency of macrosomia. It follows that both expectant management and immediate induction are acceptable.[5]

HOW SHOULD LABOR BE INDUCED?

When it became clear that labor induction was an acceptable choice in the management of prolonged pregnancies, the question of how labor should be induced became equally pertinent. Generally, methods of labor induction include mechanical, surgical, pharmacologic, and nonpharmacologic methods (Box 19-2). All mechanical methods share a similar mode

---

BOX 19-2. Methods of Labor Induction

Mechanical
- Intracervical balloon
- Stripping of the membranes

Surgical
- Artificial rupture of the membranes

Nonpharmacologic
- Nipple stimulation

Pharmacologic
- Oxytocin stimulation
- Prostaglandins (in various forms)
- Misoprostol
- Mifepristone

of action: local pressure, which stimulates the release of natural prostaglandins. One of the most popular mechanical methods is to use a saline-filled balloon (Foley catheter or a special balloon), which exerts mechanical pressure directly on the cervix. In some designs, it is possible to infuse extra-amniotic saline or prostaglandins. Ripening of the cervix after balloon insertion is not equivalent to the natural ripening, and the procedure often involves augmentation of labor with oxytocin.[12] Another popular mechanical means is stripping of the membranes. Stripping results in increased phospholipase A_2 activity and prostaglandin $F_{2\alpha}$ concentrations, and it causes mechanical dilation of the cervix, which, in turn, releases prostaglandins. Both nulliparas and multiparas who received weekly stripping starting at 38 weeks had significantly earlier deliveries and significantly fewer deliveries at 41 weeks or greater.[2] The combination of membrane stripping and intravaginal prostaglandin E_2 gel has been claimed to reduce post-term pregnancies and antenatal visits.[9]

The most popular surgical method is amniotomy (artificial rupture of the membranes). It is postulated that the resultant amniorrhexis (leak of amniotic fluid) is involved in increased levels of prostaglandins. However, amniotomy is more frequently successful when performed in women with a favorable cervix. Often, oxytocin should be given for augmentation of labor.

One of the nonpharmacologic methods is nipple stimulation, which increases the level of oxytocin via the nipple-posterior pituitary neurohormonal axis. Evidence is lacking to support this method as a practical method of labor induction. Nipple stimulation, however, is frequently used when there is a relative contraindication to oxytocin stimulation, such as cases of grand multiparity or trial of labor after a previous uterine surgery.

The simplest pharmacologic method of labor induction is oxytocin infusion. Myometrial receptors to oxytocin are scant during the first half of gestation but increase thereafter to 100 to 300 times the initial number. Oxytocin increases intracellular calcium levels and stimulates the contractions of myometrial smooth muscle cells. Interestingly, the number of receptors increases with contraction, leading to a positive feedback cycle that increases the efficiency of the uterine muscle. Over the years, two regimens of oxytocin stimulation—the low dose (physiologic levels) and high dose (pharmacologic levels)—were proposed. Both regimens are equally potent for labor induction. Vaginal or cervical prostaglandins (prostaglandin E_2), on the other hand, change the composition of the extracellular cervical matrix and facilitate the process of dilation. There is, however, also some effect on the myometrium, which causes uterine stimulation as well. In a recent Cochrane review of 52 studies comparing prostaglandins for cervical ripening or labor induction with placebo or no treatment, it was found that vaginal prostaglandins increase the odds for a vaginal birth within 24 hours of application.[11] Other agents, such as misoprostol (a synthetic prostaglandin E_1 analog) and mifepristone (an antiprogesterone agent) are still in experimental stages.

POST-TERM TWIN PREGNANCIES

In the usual setting, the major problem associated with twins is preterm birth (see also Chapter 18). Whereas *term* is defined by the period during pregnancy after which most pregnancies end in spontaneous labor, this period is not defined for twins. Twins are delivered about 3 weeks earlier than singletons, which has raised the question of whether term occurs earlier in twins. If this is indeed the case, many of the complications attributed to post-term singleton pregnancies are expected in twins as early as at 38 weeks' gestation. Several arguments support this view.[3]

First, the distribution of twin births by gestational age is almost identical to that of singletons but shifted toward a lower gestational age. Second, comparison between growth patterns of twins and of singletons suggests that incremental growth reaches the near-term plateau earlier in twin pregnancies, suggesting that birthweight does not significantly increase beyond 37 to 38 weeks' gestation. Third, morbidity increases beyond 37 weeks. For example, the risk of cerebral palsy in singletons and in twins decreases steadily until 36 to 37 weeks, and thereafter, the risk of cerebral palsy in singletons continues to decrease but that for twins increases once again after 37 weeks' gestation. Fourth, perinatal death rates in twins gradually decline until 37 to 38 weeks' gestation and then increase again, in a manner similar to that observed after 40 weeks' gestation in singletons. The incidence of perinatal death seen at 38 weeks' gestation in twins was similar to that seen at 43 weeks in singletons.

These lines of circumstantial evidence seem to indicate that term occurs earlier in twins. Accordingly, limiting the estimated date of delivery to 37 to 38 weeks may be appropriate. However, it should be stressed that if 38 weeks or more for twins represents post-term, it does not follow that 36 to 37 weeks is equivalent to term in singletons. Thus, twin deliveries around 36 weeks are still associated with increased morbidity compared with births at 38 weeks.[22]

SUMMARY

Management and outcomes of post-term pregnancies have improved over the past two decades. Improvement seems to be a direct result of better understanding of the associated pathology, implementation of new technologies, careful assessments of risk versus benefit of various strategies, and new methods of assessing fetal well-being and avoiding unwarranted complications. The key points in risk reduction in post-term pregnancies are as follows:

- Accurate dating is imperative. First-trimester sonographic confirmation of the LMP is essential for an accurate diagnosis of post-term pregnancies.
- A plan of management is necessary for cases presenting during the 42nd week of gestation (i.e., after 41 completed weeks). This plan should be discussed with the patient and should include

the pros and cons for each management option (e.g., expectant follow-up versus labor induction).

- If a favorable cervix is found on pelvic examination during the 42nd week, induction seems to be a logical option.

- If the cervix is unfavorable, the option of labor induction should be considered. Because induction of labor may take some time, some clinicians start the induction procedure 1 to 2 days before 42 weeks.

- If induction is not acceptable to the patient, proactive and frequent fetal assessment should be offered. Fetal size and well-being should be carefully assessed. Nonreassuring fetal conditions must be promptly treated.

- Close intrapartum surveillance is recommended. The potential need for a neonatologist during the immediate postpartum period should be anticipated.

REFERENCES

1. American College of Obstetricians and Gynecologists: Management of postterm pregnancy. ACOG Practice Patterns. Washington, DC, ACOG, 1997.
2. Berghella V et al: Stripping of membranes as a safe method to reduce prolonged pregnancies. Obstet Gynecol 87:927, 1996.
3. Blickstein I: Multiple pregnancy: Clinical targets for the next decade. Female Patient 27:26, 2002.
4. Caughey AB, Musci TJ: Complications of term pregnancies beyond 37 weeks of gestation. Obstet Gynecol 103:57, 2004.
5. Chanrachakul B, Herabutya Y: Postterm with favorable cervix: Is induction necessary? Eur J Obstet Gynecol Reprod Biol 106:154, 2003.
6. Clifford SH: Postmaturity with placental dysfunction. J Pediatr 44:1, 1954.
7. Cucco C et al: Maternal-fetal outcomes in prolonged pregnancy. Am J Obstet Gynecol 161:916, 1989.
8. Divon MY et al: Fetal and neonatal mortality in the post-term pregnancy: The impact of gestational age and fetal growth restriction. Am J Obstet Gynecol 178:726, 1998.
9. Doany W, McCarty J: Outpatient management of the uncomplicated postdate pregnancy with intravaginal prostaglandin E2 gel and membrane stripping. J Matern Fetal Med 6:71, 1997.
10. Ingemarsson I, Kallen K: Stillbirths and rate of neonatal deaths in 76,761 postterm pregnancies in Sweden, 1982-1991: A register study. Acta Obstet Gynecol Scand 76:658, 1997.
11. Kelly AJ et al: Vaginal prostaglandin (PGE2 and PGF2a) for induction of labour at term. Cochrane Database Syst Rev 2:CD003101, 2002.
12. Levy R et al: A randomised comparison of early versus late amniotomy following cervical ripening with a Foley catheter. BJOG 109:168, 2002.
13. Lurie S et al: Induction of labor at 38 to 39 weeks of gestation reduces the incidence of shoulder dystocia in gestational diabetic patients class A2. Am J Perinatol 13:293, 1996.
14. MacLennan A: A template for defining a causal relation between acute intrapartum events and cerebral palsy: International consensus statement. BMJ 319:1054, 1999.
15. McLean FH et al: Postterm infants: Too big or too small? Am J Obstet Gynecol 164:619, 1991.
16. McLean M et al: A placental clock controlling the length of human pregnancy. Nat Med 1:460, 1995.
17. Morris JM et al: The usefulness of ultrasound assessment of amniotic fluid in predicting adverse outcome in prolonged pregnancy: A prospective blinded observational study. BJOG 110:989, 2003.
18. National Institute of Child Health and Human Development Network of Maternal-Fetal Medicine Units: A clinical trial of induction of labor versus expectant management in postterm pregnancy. Am J Obstet Gynecol 170:716, 1994.
19. Rouse DJ et al: The effectiveness and costs of elective cesarean delivery for fetal macrosomia diagnosed by ultrasound. JAMA 276:1480, 1996.
20. Sanchez-Ramos L et al: Labor induction versus expectant management for postterm pregnancies: A systematic review with meta-analysis. Obstet Gynecol 101:1312, 2003.
21. Stigter RH et al: The amniotic fluid index in late pregnancy. J Matern Fetal Neonatal Med 12:291, 2002.
22. Udom-Rice I et al: Optimal gestational age for twin delivery. J Perinatol 20:231, 2000.
23. Yoder BA et al: Changing obstetric practices associated with decreasing incidence of meconium aspiration syndrome. Obstet Gynecol 99:731, 2002.

20 Erythroblastosis Fetalis

Andrée M. Gruslin and Thomas R. Moore

HISTORICAL BACKGROUND

Hippocrates initially described features of erythroblastosis fetalis in 400 BC, but the first clinical report of this disorder is attributed to a French midwife who delivered twins in 1609. The first twin was hydropic and stillborn; the second twin was severely jaundiced and later died of kernicterus.

Diamond and colleagues noted the presence of extramedullary erythropoiesis along with erythroblastosis and red blood cell hemolysis in 1932.[22] The pathophysiology underlying these findings remained unclear until 1940, when Landsteiner and associates discovered the Rh antigen. By injecting blood from *Macaca mulatta* (rhesus monkey) into guinea pigs and rabbits, they obtained red blood cell antiserum that, when injected into other rhesus monkeys, provoked red cell agglutination. Agglutination was the direct result of the presence of an antigen they called *rhesus* (Rh). Some animals have the D antigen (RhD positive) and some do not (RhD negative). In 1941, Levine and coworkers observed that if a woman who is RhD negative is exposed to erythrocytes that are RhD positive, she forms antibodies that cause red cell hemolysis.

In 1948, Wiener postulated that transplacental passage of RhD-positive fetal blood into the maternal circulation could trigger the production of antibodies against fetal cells[79] and supported an immunologic rationale for the therapeutic use of exchange transfusion in affected infants. He wrote, "It is theoretically possible that when an infant's blood is susceptible to the action of Rh antibodies, a complete exsanguination transfusion, entailing the removal of all but a small quantity of the infant's blood and its replacement by Rh negative blood . . . may serve to prevent a lethal outcome."[80] Maternal sensitization through transplacental passage of RhD-positive blood was also later confirmed by Chow in the mid 1950s.[15]

Improved understanding of the pathophysiology of erythroblastosis fetalis allowed Finn and colleagues,[26] in 1961, to propose the administration of anti-D antibodies to nonimmunized mothers immediately postpartum, which would prevent maternal antibody production by eliminating any fetal cells entering the maternal circulation. Clarke and associates studied a group of RhD-negative male volunteers who had been sensitized through previous injection of Rh-positive red cells.[16] Half of this group had also received anti-D immunoglobulin M (IgM). IgM was used (rather than immunoglobulin G [IgG]) because anti-A and anti-B were

known to be IgMs. The ineffectiveness of IgM became very obvious through the production of antibodies in a high percentage of both control and treatment subjects. Another study was initiated using IgG, whose efficacy had been previously demonstrated in vitro by Stern and associates.[72] Successful protection from isoimmunization was accomplished in 18 of 21 study subjects.[16]

Subsequently, Freda and coworkers, using whole serum, studied the efficacy of specific anti-D IgG in RhD-negative male volunteers from the Sing Sing correctional facility in Ossining, New York.[29] Ten inmates received monthly injections with RhD-positive cells for 5 months. Five subjects in the treatment group also received a dose of anti-D IgG before each RhD-positive red blood cell injection. Sensitization was prevented in all volunteers who had been cotreated with anti-D IgG, whereas four of the five control subjects produced anti-D antibodies. This result provided clear evidence of effective prophylaxis against sensitization by administration of anti-D IgG before exposure to RhD-positive red cells.

Unfortunately, one cannot know in advance if and when a mother will be exposed to RhD-positive cells and become immunized. Because it is impossible to predict maternal exposure to RhD-positive cells during pregnancy, the cotreatment form of prophylaxis would be difficult to apply clinically. Therefore, a second series of injections was conducted in a different group of 20 male inmate volunteers, to whom prophylaxis was administered about 72 hours after exposure to RhD-positive cells. However, because researchers feared that a strictly timed protocol might promote a prison break, Freda and coworkers used a variable period for postexposure injection of anti-D IgG, up to a maximum of 72 hours.[29] This injection schedule, based on prison logistics, remains the basis for the recommended schedule of anti-D administration even today. Fortunately, postexposure prophylaxis was equally successful in preventing sensitization. This work inspired subsequent British and American trials among pregnant women, which further established the safety and efficacy of anti-D IgG administration.

GENETICS OF THE Rh SYSTEM

The Rh blood group system includes antigens encoded by two genes localized on chromosome 1p36.13-1p34.3. The *RhD* gene codes for the red blood cells' D antigen (an integral membrane protein with several antigenic epitopes), and it is linked to a highly homologous region, RhCcEe. Although this system comprises more than 40 discrete antigens, only 5 of them are clinically relevant: D, C, c, E, and e. Of these, only the D antigen has no antithetical counterpart. Most blood group alleles arise through point mutations (e.g., RhE/e), but this does not appear to be the case for persons who are D negative. Indeed, in this situation, absence of the entire RhD polypeptide has been demonstrated, suggesting that gene deletion is responsible for the D-negative phenotype. The complete absence of the peptide is thought to be partly responsible for the high immunogenicity of the D antigen.

As the Rh blood group system has been more extensively studied, rare genetic variants of the D antigen have been reported, including weak D and partial D.[6,28] With the weak-D variant, it is believed that whereas the red cells display the major D epitopes, there are fewer antigen sites per cell, resulting in a weak D reaction. In general, these patients are considered Rh positive and therefore not candidates for Rh immune prophylaxis. However, the partial-D variant is found in an Rh positive person who has a significant genetic variant of the D antigen (D^{VI}) involving major epitopes; this person can therefore develop anti-D antibodies of importance as exemplified by case reports of neonatal deaths from severe anemia.[13] It might therefore be prudent to consider testing for partial D phenotype in cases of weak D where the patient is not otherwise a candidate for immune prophylaxis.

The unraveling of the molecular basis of the Rh system has led to the development of techniques that allow Rh typing for not only paternal but also fetal genotyping. Polymerase chain reaction (PCR) determination of paternal RhD status can facilitate counseling and dictate the need for intervention, because paternal heterozygosity is associated with a 50% risk of fetal RhD negativity, whereas homozygosity always produces an RhD-positive conceptus, and the fetus will therefore be affected. Furthermore, the application of this technology to fetal RhD typing using amniocytes or villi as early as the first trimester correctly identifies fetuses at risk while providing reassurance in cases where the fetus also lacks the D antigen.

PATHOPHYSIOLOGY OF RhD ISOIMMUNIZATION

Sensitization

Erythroblastosis fetalis is characterized by fetal red blood cell hemolysis that results from the presence of anti-D maternal antibodies in the fetal circulation. The isoimmunization process occurs initially because the mother, who is RhD negative, is exposed to red cells that are RhD positive. This exposure can occur after transfusion of unmatched blood, in association with parturition or abortion, or during pregnancy through asymptomatic transplacental passage of RhD-positive fetal cells. Fetomaternal transfusion has been documented in 7%, 16%, and 29% of patients in their first, second, and third trimesters, respectively. In the peripartum period, the incidence of fetomaternal hemorrhage can be as high as 50%.[17] It is essential to emphasize the potential for maternal sensitization as early as the first trimester in association with miscarriage or ectopic pregnancy. As few as 0.2 mL of fetal cells is sufficient to cause maternal anti-D sensitization.[17]

The clinician should be aware of other potential sensitizing events (Table 20-1), including elective pregnancy termination (5% risk of fetomaternal hemorrhage), amniocentesis, chorionic villus sampling, cordocentesis, external cephalic version, and even intravenous (IV) drug abuse, in which women who are Rh negative share needles with people who are Rh positive. In fact, it is in a group of IV drug abusers that Bowman and colleagues have observed the severest cases of fetal Rh disease, possibly as a consequence of repetitive maternal exposure to the RhD antigen.[12]

Maternal exposure to RhD-positive cells does not always result in sensitization. In some cases, this circumstance can be explained by the protection conferred by ABO blood group incompatibility. Under those conditions, hemolysis activated by the ABO system destroys all fetal cells present in the maternal circulation. As a result, the RhD antigen is never seen by the Rh system; therefore, no immune reaction is elicited. With ABO incompatibility, the risk of Rh isoimmunization is reduced from 16% to between 1% and 2%.

In most instances, however, exposure triggers the production of IgM, which constitutes a slow and weak response. Because of its high molecular weight, IgM does not cross the placenta and thus has no effect on the fetus. However, the second exposure to RhD leads to the production of IgG, which, because of its lower molecular weight, readily crosses the placenta and enters the fetal circulation.

Antibody transfer across the placenta occurs in two steps.[43] Initially, IgGs undergo pinocytosis into endosomes and bind to Fc receptors with a high degree of affinity. Subsequently, the IgG-Fc complex is transported in vesicles to the basolateral surface of the placenta, where the IgG is released. This process, although present early in gestation, is known to increase significantly after 22 weeks as manifested by an exponential rise in fetal IgG levels until term. This rise in fetal concentration of IgG reflects a maturation in immunoglobulin transfer. Once in the fetal circulation, IgG antibodies bind to the RhD antigens on the fetal erythrocyte membranes, and the antibody-coated fetal red cells adhere to macrophages, forming rosettes and leading ultimately to hemolysis and macrophage phagocytosis.

The underlying pathophysiology of RhD sensitization as described, however, is under the influence of other factors. Discrepancies between maternal titer and severity of fetal disease have been reported, and mothers with marked sensitization have delivered infants with mild disease. These results may be explained by the presence of inhibitory antibodies in maternal serum.

TABLE 20-1. Indications for Rh Immunoglobulin Prophylaxis

INDICATION	JUSTIFICATION	Dosage (μg)	
		FIRST TRIMESTER	SECOND OR THIRD TRIMESTER
Spontaneous abortion/IUFD	2%-3% Sensitization	50	300
Therapeutic abortion	4%-5% Sensitization	50	300
Ectopic pregnancy	2%-5% Sensitization	50	300
Chorionic villus sampling	50% FMH	50	300
Amniocentesis	10% FMH	300	300
Percutaneous umbilical blood sampling	40% FMH	300	300
Abruptio placentae/placenta previa	Variable	300	300
Antepartum vaginal bleeding	Variable	300	300
External cephalic version	Variable	N/A	300
Trauma	Variable	300	300
Pregnancy (28 weeks' gestation and ≤ 72 hr postpartum)	7%-8% Sensitization* 15% Sensitization†	N/A	300
Delivery	50% FMH	N/A	300

FMH, fetomaternal hemorrhage; IUFD, intrauterine fetal demise.
*First pregnancy.
†Second pregnancy.

More specifically, HLA-DR antibodies have been shown in vitro to inhibit monocytolytic activity against red cells, thereby preventing significant hemolysis.[67] Studies have shown that these antibodies were detected in a majority of women presenting with the clinical picture described here. These antibodies presumably would cross the placenta and inhibit destruction of fetal red cells by macrophages through the formation of a complex on the membranes of these macrophages, resulting in receptor blockage.

Characteristics of the antibody, such as subclass, concentration, and specificity, also modulate the maternal-fetal response. For instance, IgG3 appears to have a more important role than IgG1; in vitro experiments have demonstrated greater adherence as well as phagocytic and lytic activities for IgG3 than IgG1.[40] In addition, the severity of hemolysis is related to antibody concentration, and this appears to depend on maternal HLA phenotype. For example, HLA-DQB1 allele 0201 could play a particular role, given its markedly higher frequency in women with higher anti-D titers than in those with lower anti-D titers (77% versus 20%).[34] Antibody specificity against cells of erythroid lineage is also an important determinant of disease severity, as is antigen density. Indeed, for marked hemolysis to occur, the antigen must be distributed in significant amounts on fetal red cells; therefore, the maturation of expression of these antigens is important. For example, D antigen is known to be present by 4 to 6 weeks' gestation, thereby allowing hemolysis to be initiated at an early stage. By contrast, other antigens, such as A and B, are sparingly distributed on these same red cells, partly explaining the milder degrees of disease severity seen in these situations.

Hydrops Fetalis

The progressive immunologic destruction of red blood cells must be matched by fetal erythropoiesis if anemia is to be avoided. More reticulocytes and immature red cell forms appear in the circulation of affected fetuses. With an increasing IgG titer and increasing severity of hemolysis, extramedullary tissues (liver, spleen) are recruited for erythropoiesis. Erythroblastosis results in severe cases. The outcome for the fetus depends on the relative severity of antibody-mediated hemolysis versus erythropoietic capability. In the extreme, severe anemia leads to fetal hydrops and death (see also Chapter 21). This sequence of events was demonstrated by Nicolaides and associates in a group of 127 isoimmunized pregnancies at 17 to 36 weeks' gestation.[50] Moderate fetal anemia was associated with reticulocytosis, whereas markedly decreased hemoglobin concentrations (7 g/dL) were associated with erythroblastosis.

Despite efforts at increased erythropoiesis, the fetus could experience overwhelming hemolysis, which could result in profound anemia. Fortunately, through marked increases in cardiac output, the fetus typically maintains pH and partial pressure of oxygen and carbon dioxide within normal limits until a hemoglobin deficit of 7 g/dL is reached. At this point, the high concentrations of lactic acid exceed the placenta's clearance capacity, and lactic acidosis develops. A hematocrit of 15% appears to be a critical level below which compensatory mechanisms are usually insufficient, leading to the onset of hydrops.[49] Signs of hydrops include pericardial and pleural effusions, ascites, skin edema, hepatosplenomegaly, polyhydramnios, and placental thickening (Fig. 20-1A to C).

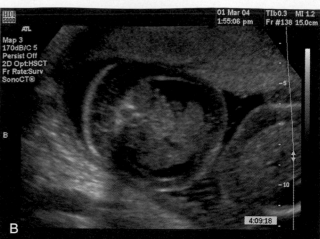

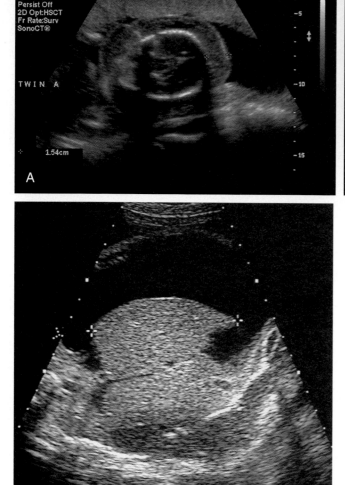

FIGURE 20-1. Ultrasonographic findings in hydrops fetalis. **A,** Cross section of fetal head. Note the presence of severe edema surrounding the skull (indicated by calipers). **B,** Cross section of fetal abdomen, showing marked ascites as well as subcutaneous edema. **C,** Transverse section of the fetal abdomen, demonstrating marked hepatomegaly (indicated by calipers) and ascites.

Although it has been reported that hydrops could develop with a hemoglobin deficit of 7 g/dL, that finding should be evaluated in the context of gestational age. This approach is supported by a report including 111 fetuses at risk for anemia.[45] A clear increase in median values of hemoglobin was noted with advancing gestational age, from 10.6 g/dL at 18 weeks to 13.8 g/dL at 40 weeks. Given these significant variations, deficits in hemoglobin must be interpreted carefully because they have different meanings at different gestational ages. Indeed, it has been suggested that the use of a hemoglobin value of less than 0.5 times the median for gestational age would appear to be more appropriate for identifying fetuses at significant risk for hydrops.

The exact pathophysiologic mechanism for hydrops is still unclear. Three mechanisms have been proposed: high-output cardiac failure, liver dysfunction, and fetal hypoxemia. Many believe that a combination of these factors is involved. It is likely that with worsening anemia, hemodynamic demands exceed cardiac reserves,

resulting in heart failure, fetal hypoxemia, and high systemic venous pressure. These conditions cause endothelial damage, followed by extravascular protein leakage, which results in accumulation of fluid in various body cavities.

This hypothesis is strongly supported by the work of Nicolaides and associates, who studied 17 isoimmunized fetuses between 18 and 25 weeks of gestation.[49] They demonstrated hypoalbuminemia in six of seven hydropic fetuses and in only two nonhydropic fetuses. More important, the albumin and total protein concentrations in the ascitic fluid were more than 50% of their corresponding plasma levels, suggesting extravascular loss through endothelial damage.

Hypoproteinemia can also result from decreased hepatic synthesis caused by erythroblasts infiltrating the liver. Crowding of hepatic structures leads to portal hypertension and hepatic ischemia. Current data also support this explanation. Nicolini and coworkers measured liver enzymes in 25 fetuses with severe Rh disease and compared the results with those of 17 fetuses in a control group.[53] Levels of aspartate aminotransferase and alanine aminotransferase were more elevated in hydropic fetuses than in Rh-sensitized nonhydropic fetuses, although an overlap was observed between hydropic and nonhydropic fetuses. The researchers also observed a positive correlation between nucleated red blood cell counts (a reflection of extramedullary erythropoiesis) and levels of aspartate aminotransferase, which suggests that liver infiltration by erythropoietic cells can cause hepatic dysfunction.

Animal models have been proposed to examine the underlying pathophysiologic mechanisms involved in fetal anemia.[3,19,47,48,54] In a fetal sheep model, anti-erythrocyte antibodies infused to a group of experimental animals induced significant anemia, more closely reflecting the natural pathophysiology of fetal Rh disease.[81] The authors confirmed several of the observations just discussed and provided evidence to support the role of this model in the design of new therapeutic approaches, such as fetal erythropoietin (EPO) supplementation. For instance, fetal Po_2 correlated with fetal hematocrit but particularly in the face of a fall of at least 25% of this red cell index. In addition, reticulocytosis, and lactate were inversely related to fetal hematocrit; the greatest change was seen with a hematocrit fall of 25%. In the first days of anemia, however, EPO values remained unchanged. This suggests that fetuses can compensate for the severity of their anemia until a critical level is reached, after which increases in cardiac output can no longer provide adequate tissue perfusion. This leads to fetal hypoxia, which then triggers an EPO response that leads to stimulation of erythropoiesis.

FIRST-TRIMESTER AND PREIMPLANTATION DIAGNOSIS

When alloimmunization is a risk factor and the father is an RhD heterozygote, fetal disease is a possibility, depending on fetal genotype. Recent advances in our understanding of the molecular genetics of the Rh system have led to new techniques that can specify the genotype very early. These techniques have made it possible to determine the fetal RhD status during the first trimester with great accuracy and, more recently, have also allowed preimplantation diagnosis, thereby completely preventing the disease through selective transfer of RhD-negative embryos.

A PCR-based technique can be used for fetal typing using amniocytes or villi, allowing diagnosis in the first trimester.[4,18,74] The validity of this approach was recently assessed, particularly in the context of potential maternal contamination.[18] In this study, PCR correctly identified RhD type in all fetuses. Identification was possible even in samples contaminated with up to 95% maternal DNA, thereby supporting the validity and accuracy of this approach.

Fisk and colleagues also used PCR in fetal RhD typing.[27] They obtained amniotic fluid from five women

and chorionic villi from one. All women were RhD negative and had partners who were heterozygous for the RhD antigen. When PCR was used to amplify DNA samples, four fetuses were shown to be Rh positive. In the two remaining fetuses, Rh negativity was correctly diagnosed. The diagnoses were confirmed serologically after delivery.

A review of 500 cases reported sensitivity of 98.7% and specificity of 100% when using PCR typing of amniotic cells.[74] PCR typing provides patients with options such as termination and aggressive early assessment and therapy and prevents further procedures in fetuses who are Rh negative. The benefits of the information obtained along with the accuracy of the methods used have greatly contributed to the use of prenatal genotyping in obstetric practice.

The clinician must, however, remember the risk of fetomaternal hemorrhage with chorionic villus sampling and amniocentesis and weigh this risk against the benefits of fetal Rh typing. To eliminate this complication, RhD fetal typing[65] is performed using cell-free fetal DNA isolated from maternal plasma.[62] Although this approach requires confirmation, results indicate a sensitivity of 100% and a specificity of 96.6% and is therefore promising. Furthermore, successful preimplantation typing using single blastomere analysis was also reported.[7] This method, based on simultaneous amplification of an RhD-specific sequence and an internal control in single cells, allowed the selective transfer of only RhD-negative embryos.

The application of these molecular methods represents one of the more important recent advances in the field of Rh disease. In the future, it will likely contribute to major reductions in unnecessary intervention and will further prevent the disease through embryo selection.

MANAGEMENT

Rh Immunoglobulin Prophylaxis

Formation of RhD antibodies in the mother can be prevented by administering Rh immune globulin, but the exact mechanism by which these antibodies are formed is not well understood. Several theories have been proposed.[41] These include an inhibition of B cells by cross-linking heterologous receptors, leading to co-inhibition. Therefore, in cases of RhD prophylaxis, antigen-specific B cells would be inhibited before an immune response is established. At current anti-D doses used for prophylaxis, most of the D antigen sites remain unoccupied.

Another potential mechanism involves the influence of anti-idiotypic antibodies. Although there is currently not a lot of evidence to support this, monovalent anti-idiotypic antibodies could deliver weak inhibitory signals to B cells, thereby contributing to a suppression in immune response. Antigen masking might also play a role in immune suppression. Indeed, it is possible that anti-D could bind to all D antigen sites on erythrocytes, making it impossible for them to interact with red cells.

However, not all antigen sites are bound by anti-D in RhD prophylaxis, and therefore this potential mechanism is unlikely to be of major importance.

The clearance and destruction of erythrocytes has been suggested as an important mechanism. In this situation, anti-D IgG in the maternal circulation binds to the fetal red cells carrying the RhD antigen. Subsequently, immunoglobulin-bound cells are lysed through complement fixation; phagocytosis by macrophages also contributes to the elimination of RhD antigenic sites. There may be an additional effect that is accomplished by trapping the IgG-coated red blood cells in the spleen and lymph nodes, in which a central suppressive effect may be achieved. As a result, further production of antibodies is suppressed, and all existing antibodies are actively destroyed. Further research is required to clearly define the mechanisms involved in RhD-immune prophylaxis, because it is likely that multiple complex interactions among erythrocytes, immune cells, and even cytokines play a role in the overall process.

Rh IgG prophylaxis is indicated in the management of all nonimmunized pregnant women who are Rh negative. Current recommendations include routine administration of IgG at 28 weeks to all pregnant women who are RhD negative and within 72 hours postpartum for those with an infant who is RhD positive. Use of the 28-week dose reduces third-trimester sensitization from 1.8% to less than 0.11%. The standard dose, 300 µg, is based on the amount of IgG that will provide protection for up to 30 mL of fetal blood (15 mL of packed fetal cells). This dose provides satisfactory prophylaxis for 99% of all term deliveries. In a few cases, a greater amount of fetal blood will enter the maternal circulation. In women at high risk, a Kleihauer-Betke smear test can be performed to quantitate the fetal blood present. For every 30 mL of fetal blood detected, an additional 300 µg of IgG can be administered. High-risk conditions include abruptio placentae, placenta previa, and manual placenta removal.

Because the half-life of Rh IgG is 21 to 30 days, the 28-week injection should be protective until term. One should then give Rh IgG to the mother of an Rh-positive infant within 72 hours of delivery, because a protective effect has been documented if the treatment is given within that period. Because this ideal interval has been determined empirically, Rh IgG still can be administered up to 13 days after exposure for partial protection. Situations mandating Rh IgG prophylaxis are summarized in Table 20-1.

The current practice of obtaining Rh IgG from pooled donors' sera raises the issue of transmission of human immunodeficiency virus (HIV) and hepatitis B and C viruses. Fortunately, it appears that the technique used (cold alcohol fractionation) destroys these viruses. Additionally, all donors are now tested for these viruses; so far, no cases of transmission of HIV or hepatitis B virus are reported to have resulted from the administration of Rh IgG. However, isolated cases of hepatitis C transmission have been reported in Europe, before universal screening of donors.[59]

To eliminate this potential risk and to ensure a continuous supply of Rh IgG, researchers are directing their efforts toward developing monoclonal anti-D antibodies.[39] Recent investigations have suggested that the use of a combination of at least IgG1 and IgG3 may be necessary to achieve protection. Thus far, trials have shown promising results. Administration of two monoclonal antibodies, BRAD-3 (IgG3) and BRAD-5 (IgG1), produced from lymphoblastoid cell lines, protected a small group of volunteers from mounting a primary anti-D response to D-positive red blood cells.[39]

The International Blood Group Reference Laboratory (Bristol) has reported on their monoclonal anti-D development program.[42] The antibody used for this large multicenter trial consisted of a blend of BRAD-3 and BRAD-5, which was administered to 95 RhD-negative subjects. This group was injected with 5 mL of RhD-positive red cells; subsequent to immunization with BRAD-3 and BRAD-5, a 95% clearance rate for RhD-positive red cells was achieved. This preparation's ability to prevent an immune response was then investigated. Results indicated only one definite failure of prophylaxis, which is less than what would have been expected from the current RhD immune prophylaxis. These data will need confirmation in a large cohort but are so far very promising.

Screening

Antenatal management of the Rh-negative pregnant woman begins with screening. The efficient identification of pregnancies in which there is a risk of Rh isoimmunization requires that all patients undergo an indirect Coombs test in the first trimester. This allows detection of RhD antibodies as well as other atypical antigens that can also cause hydrops. It is important that all women of reproductive age know their own RhD status and understand the procedures to be followed should they become pregnant.

Patients demonstrating sensitization to RhD should have their anti-D titer evaluated by a reliable laboratory because the risk of severe disease correlates roughly with the amount of IgG passing across the placenta to the fetus. Although each laboratory should set guidelines based on local experience, anti-D titers of 1:8 rarely, if ever, result in significant fetal jeopardy. In these cases, monthly maternal titer assessment is adequate follow-up. However, if the titer exceeds 1:8 or 1:16, invasive evaluation may be required.

The timing of the first amniocentesis or cordocentesis has traditionally been determined by considering the titer as well as the obstetric history. Low titers (1:8 to 1:16) in the first sensitized pregnancy can be evaluated by amniocentesis beginning at 26 to 28 weeks. However, a woman with a prior pregnancy with fetal hydrops or fetal death before 18 to 20 weeks might require cordocentesis as early as 22 weeks. In general, if titers are 1:128 or higher, the first procedure should be performed at 20 to 24 weeks' gestation.

Validation of the measurement of fetal middle cerebral artery peak systolic velocity in the assessment of fetal anemia has been performed. Results indicate that this approach can predict moderate to severe anemia with a sensitivity of 100% and a false positive rate of 12%,[45] making this measurement a useful adjunct in the overall evaluation of the at-risk fetus and helping the clinician to establish the timing of amniocentesis or cordocentesis (see Ultrasound, later).

Antenatal management of fetuses at risk for erythroblastosis fetalis has relied on the careful follow-up of anti-D titers, but discrepancies between the height of antibody titer and the severity of the fetal disease continue to occur. Therefore, several new assays improve the identification of fetuses at risk. These can be divided into quantitative and cellular (functional) assays.

QUANTITATIVE ASSAYS

Quantitative tests, using technologies such as enzyme-linked immunosorbent assay (ELISA), flow cytometry, and radioimmunoassay, attempt to measure binding of anti-D IgG to red blood cells in maternal serum. Several authors have demonstrated that quantification of antibodies, using AutoAnalyzer (Technicon Corporation, UK), appears to better distinguish affected fetuses from unaffected fetuses, although there are still difficulties in establishing a threshold beyond which severe hemolytic disease will occur. Flow cytometry, although helpful in distinguishing subclasses of antibody present, does not appear to be useful currently as a screening test.

FUNCTIONAL ASSAYS

Cellular assays aim to measure the biologic activity of antibodies by determining their ability to promote interactions between D-positive red cells and effector cells. This is achieved by sensitizing erythrocytes with maternal antibodies and subsequently incubating them with effector cells (e.g., monocytes). Interaction of these two cells in the form of binding, lysis, and phagocytosis is measured by different assays. For example, the chemiluminescence test measures the metabolic response of monocyte activation in the form of a light emission produced subsequent to respiratory bursts associated with their interaction with erythrocytes. The monocyte monolayer assay measures the adherence and phagocytosis of red cells by monocytes, and the antibody-dependent cellular cytotoxicity (ADCC) assay measures lysis of radiolabeled, coated erythrocytes.

The value of these assays has been assessed retrospectively and prospectively. The chemiluminescence test has been applied to a population of 132 sensitized pregnant women.[32] Results showed that this assay was superior to antibody quantification (AutoAnalyzer) in predicting the need for invasive testing and that a cutoff value of greater than 30% identified all cases of hemolysis. Although it would appear from the data that chemiluminescence could help to improve appropriate identification of affected infants, chemiluminescence has had a limited role in predicting unaffected infants.[83]

Studies using monocyte monolayer assays have produced controversial data. Although some have reported appropriate identification of affected fetuses in 95% of

subjects using a cutoff of 20%, others have not been able to reproduce these findings.

ADCC assays have been more extensively studied,[83] and they have been applied clinically in the Netherlands because of their ability to correctly identify unaffected infants when results remain under a given threshold. One report[56] compared the value of ADCC with standard maternal antibody titer in predicting fetal and neonatal hemolytic disease. Above a cutoff of 80% ADCC, 43% of fetuses were severely anemic, whereas below 50%, there were no cases of severe anemia. The authors suggested performing ADCC every 2 weeks in an at-risk patient and weekly if this level reaches 50%, in which case referral to tertiary care was also recommended. To further support the use of this assay, authors demonstrated that ADCC was a better predictor of fetal hemolytic anemia than maternal titers and that in their study, its use decreased the number of patients undergoing invasive testing from 84% to 49%.

Although none of these assays are in routine clinical use in North America, more data are emerging to suggest that they could contribute significantly to better identification of the fetus at risk for hemolysis, therefore directing invasive diagnosis and treatment more appropriately. Several authors have indeed suggested that these assays be incorporated into a structured approach in the evaluation of Rh isoimmunization. For instance, once sensitization has been identified using maternal titers, chemiluminescence and ADCC assays can be used to further assess the risk of fetal disease and to predict severity more accurately. The additional assays can help to prevent or delay invasive procedures or to target for early diagnosis and treat the fetus who is at greater risk. Because both approaches theoretically could improve fetal and maternal outcome, it is worthwhile to pursue a more accurate and structured approach toward proper identification of unaffected and affected fetuses.

Spectrophotometry

OPTICAL DENSITY OF AMNIOTIC FLUID

A scheme for assessing the severity of fetal hemolysis was first developed by Liley in 1961. Using spectrophotometry, the examiner measures the change in optical density at 450 nm (ΔOD 450), which reflects the concentration of bilirubin in amniotic fluid. From this change, an estimate of the fetal hemolytic process can be made. Quantification of this increase in optical density at 450 nm is obtained by connecting OD values at 375 and 525 nm and then measuring the distance between this line and the rise in OD at 450 nm (Figs. 20-2 and 20-3).

Liley collected these data initially from 101 Rh-isoimmunized pregnant women between 27 and 41 weeks of gestation. By plotting the ΔOD 450 against gestational age on semilogarithmic paper (the Liley curve), he defined three zones that correlated with disease severity. Zone 1 predicts an unaffected fetus or a minimally affected infant with a 10% risk of need for postnatal exchange transfusion. Zone 2 correlates with

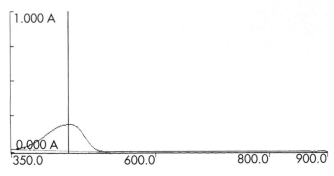

FIGURE 20-2. Change in optical density at 450 nm (ΔOD 450) measurement by spectrophotometry at 32 weeks' gestation in Rh-sensitized pregnancy.

moderate disease. Zone 3 indicates a high degree of hemolysis and is correlated with fetal or neonatal death unless delivery or transfusion is accomplished. Predictive power is improved further by dividing zone 2 into a lower zone (20% risk of exchange transfusion) and an upper zone (80% risk of exchange transfusion), for a total of four zones.

Readings falling into zone 1 or lower zone 2 indicate the test should be repeated within 2 to 4 weeks. Upper zone 2 values indicate follow-up in 1 week. For values within upper zone 2 (for earlier gestational age fetuses) or reaching zone 3, fetal blood sampling and fetal

transfusion or delivery, depending on gestational age, are recommended.

Unfortunately, since Liley's pioneering work, several problems have arisen with using this amniotic fluid density measurement to assess the degree of fetal anemia. For example, meconium or blood contamination of amniotic fluid can obscure the 450 nm reading, making determination of the peak value impossible. More importantly, the predictability of ΔOD 450 values obtained in the second trimester have been questioned. The original data obtained by Liley were from pregnancies between 27 and 41 weeks because in utero management or delivery of fetuses less than 27 weeks' gestation was not feasible in 1961. Today, however, availability of treatment options for fetuses as young as 20 to 22 weeks' gestation has required an extrapolation of the Liley zones to as early as 18 weeks' gestation. Nevertheless, simple retrograde extension of zone boundaries might not be appropriate.

To assess the validity of this extrapolation, Nicolaides compared hematocrits of umbilical cord blood obtained from 50 RhD-isoimmunized fetuses at 18 to 25 weeks' gestation and determined the peak ΔOD 450 of amniotic fluid obtained simultaneously.[51] The control group consisted of 475 amniotic fluid samples and 153 blood samples obtained from unaffected pregnancies between 16 and 36 weeks. Their results revealed a significant inaccuracy of ΔOD 450 values in predicting severity of isoimmunization between 18 and 25 weeks. In fact, no identifiable cutoff level for ΔOD 450 could discriminate

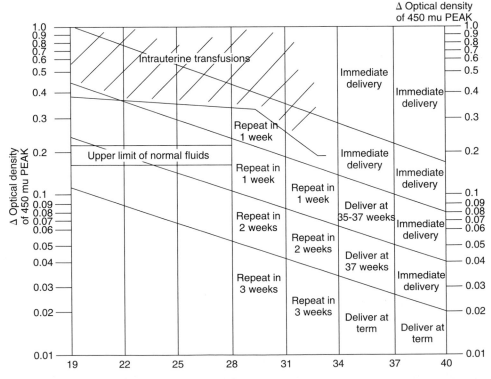

FIGURE 20-3. Modified Liley curve with improved predictability from ΔOD 450 readings in the second trimester. Gestational age is shown on the horizontal axis. ΔOD 450, change in optical density at 450 nm.

between mildly and severely affected fetuses. Fortunately, the results did confirm the accuracy of amniocentesis for predicting severe disease after 27 weeks.

The diagnostic accuracy of amniotic fluid ΔOD 450 was reassessed in a subset of 79 pregnancies with RhD alloimmunization (excluding hydrops) where amniocentesis was performed within 4 days of fetal blood sampling at a mean gestational age of 29 weeks (range, 20 to 35 weeks).[68] Using a straight extrapolation of the Liley curve, although only a weak correlation existed between fetal hemoglobin and ΔOD 450 values, authors reported a 75% accuracy in predicting severe anemia for values in zone 3. This accuracy increased to 86% when values from the upper third of zone 2 were included. The sensitivity of the ΔOD 450 values for zone 3 or upper zone 2 was 95% (CI 95%; 74,100) before and 98% (CI 98%; 89,100) after 27 weeks.

Although these results initially appear to contradict Nicolaides' findings, the difference is likely due to a difference in study populations. For instance, in Nicolaides' study, once hydropic fetuses were excluded, ΔOD 450 values in upper zone 2 carried a sensitivity of 94% in predicting a hemoglobin concentration of less than 6 g/dL. This suggests that ΔOD 450 measurements still play a role in predicting early fetal anemia from RhD alloimmunization, particularly in a nonhydropic group where values are found in upper zone 2 and zone 3. However, these results still should be interpreted with caution, particularly with values in middle and lower zone 2 and in the very preterm fetus.

Given the controversy over the usefulness of a direct extrapolation of the Liley curve, Queenan and co-workers pooled their data on amniotic fluid bilirubin concentrations obtained during genetic amniocenteses and created a new graph.[60] Their observations confirmed the predictability of this testing in the late second and third trimesters and further suggested that extrapolation to 20 weeks of gestation using flattened curves was more appropriate in identifying affected fetuses early on.

However, in a comparative study of the Queenan and Liley curves, Spinnato and colleagues questioned the performance of the Queenan curve and suggested that it frequently overestimated the risk.[70] Although some methodological questions were raised about Spinnato and colleagues' study—for example, the inclusion of patients sensitized to antigens other than D—it pointed to some potential difficulties in interpreting results obtained early in the second trimester.

MODIFIED LILEY CURVE

To avoid the inaccuracies mentioned above, use of a modified curve (see Fig. 20-3) that provides prognostic information is recommended. The four typical zones are depicted (zone 1, lower zone 2, upper zone 2, and zone 3), but from 19 to 28 weeks, an upper limit of normal ΔOD 450 values for these gestations is defined, consistent with the observation of Nicolaides and associates.[51] The curve also delineates an upper zone in which intrauterine transfusion is necessary. The improved predictability in this modified chart relies on the

flattening of the curve between 19 and 28 weeks, setting the upper limit of normal at a much lower value than would be expected if the original curve were simply extrapolated.

The findings described earlier suggest that in certain instances, fetal blood sampling rather than amniocentesis may be needed to evaluate fetal hematocrit before 27 weeks. However, the convenience of direct umbilical blood sampling must be weighed against the risks of fetomaternal hemorrhage (50% incidence)[8] and of provoking increased maternal antibody production. The risk of fetal death (1%) associated with cordocentesis[64] is, of course, much greater than that associated with amniocentesis (1 in 300). Fortunately, in these situations, Doppler evaluation of the peak systolic velocity of the fetal middle cerebral artery can be very useful in determining the need for and timing of cordocentesis (see Ultrasound, next).

Ultrasound

Rh ISOIMMUNIZATION

High-resolution ultrasound is an essential adjunct to assessment of isoimmunized pregnancies, allowing documentation of extent, progression of disease, and early detection of hydrops. Additionally, ultrasound guidance is indispensable in interventions such as fetal blood sampling and transfusion. Finally, ultrasound assessment of fetal behavior (the biophysical profile) provides important evidence of fetal well-being (see Chapter 9).

Ultrasound evaluation in cases of Rh isoimmunization requires a thorough examination of fetal anatomy, placental morphologic features, and amniotic fluid volume. The fetus should be examined for indications of hydrops (skin edema, ascites, pericardial and pleural effusion, and hepatosplenomegaly). Early signs of ascites include visualization of both sides of the bowel wall and lucent outlining of organs such as the bladder and stomach.[63] Approximately 30 mL of free peritoneal fluid is associated with this finding. With further fluid accumulation, a clear rim appears adjacent to the fetal bladder; this correlates with the presence of 50 mL of fluid. Marked ascites (100 mL) is frequently accompanied by findings of fetal skin edema and is particularly evident in the scalp, the extremities, and the abdominal wall (see Fig. 20-1).

Hepatosplenomegaly, reflecting increased extramedullary erythropoiesis, can be detected through increasing abdominal circumference measurements (see Fig. 20-1).[79] Vintzileos and colleagues proposed that liver enlargement could represent one of the earliest findings of significant fetal anemia.[77] Similarly, worsening of fetal hemolysis is associated with gradual thickening of the placenta, and a cross section greater than 4 cm thick is associated with significant anemia (Fig. 20-4).[79] Cardiomegaly also may be visible given the demands on the myocardium necessary to maintain perfusion (Fig. 20-5). Finally, a quantitative examination of amniotic fluid volume can provide important clues to early fetal anemia. Initially, subjectively increased fluid volume is seen and may be followed by polyhydramnios

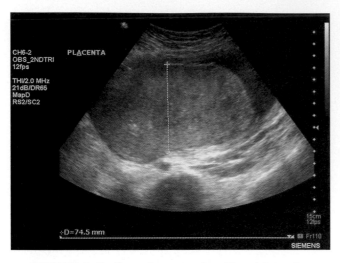

FIGURE 20-4. Significant placentomegaly at 26 weeks' gestation.

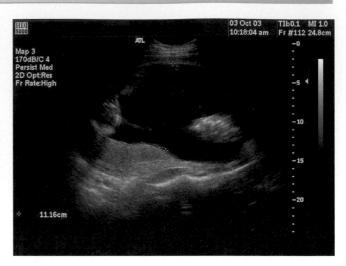

FIGURE 20-6. Sagittal view of the uterus, showing severe polyhydramnios.

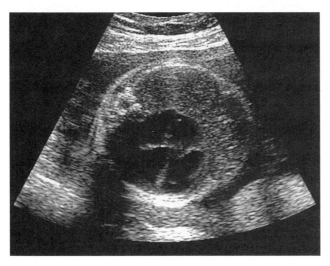

FIGURE 20-5. Transverse view of fetal thorax, demonstrating marked cardiomegaly, which reflects compensatory changes in the context of severe fetal anemia.

(Fig. 20-6). Further deterioration is later manifested by oligohydramnios, an ominous finding dictating intervention, especially when it is associated with signs of hydrops. The significance and usefulness of most markers are summarized in Table 20-2.

PREDICTION OF ANEMIA

Fetal blood sampling provides the most accurate determination of fetal hematocrit. Such invasive procedures, however, carry a significant fetal loss rate; therefore, investigators have attempted to use ultrasound to predict the degree of anemia. The course of deteriorating erythroblastosis fetalis is marked by polyhydramnios, followed by placentomegaly, hepatomegaly, ascites, and, finally, generalized fetal hydrops.

Hoping to identify one of these signs or a specific sequence of events as a predictor for the severity of anemia, Chitkara and coworkers evaluated 15 isoimmunized pregnancies with fetal blood sampling and various ultrasound parameters.[14] Their findings revealed that only frank hydrops was predictive of severe fetal anemia (hematocrit less than 15%). Nicolaides and associates[52] reported similar results from a series of 50 isoimmunized pregnancies, demonstrating poor predictive power of placental thickness and amniotic fluid volume. Reece and associates compared ultrasound and ΔOD 450 analysis of amniotic fluid in predicting neonatal complications of isoimmunization (i.e., need for exchange transfusion, organomegaly, ascites, and neonatal death).[61] Their results demonstrated consistently poor predictive power when ultrasound, ΔOD 450, or a combination of both was used.

Small studies have also correlated spleen size to severe anemia with varying success and have explained their observations of splenomegaly by the need for extramedullary hematopoiesis in cases of severe anemia. Other single findings such as the presence of pericardial effusion and measurement of fetal biventricular diameter have also been examined and found to be limited in their usefulness in part due to a poor sensitivity.[79]

Doppler flow analysis offers a noninvasive tool that can be useful in identifying the anemic fetus. The objective is to detect compensatory hemodynamic changes in the fetal circulation that would be associated with mild to moderate anemia. These changes are based on physiologic observations. As anemia progresses, fetal right and left ventricular outputs increase up to 45%, and the heart rate remains unchanged. Therefore, stroke volume must increase. Assuming that a given fetal blood vessel cross-sectional area also remains unchanged, and applying Poiseuille's law (blood velocity is directly proportional to flow) because anemia leads to decreased viscosity, increased stroke volume results in increased flow (flow being the product of velocity and cross-sectional area).[20]

With these principles in mind and with evolving experience and use of sophisticated technologies, Iskaros

TABLE 20-2. Sonographic Morphologic Markers Used to Detect Fetal Anemia in Alloimmunization

MARKER	THRESHOLD	COMMENTS
Dilated umbilical vein	>2 SD for gestational age	Not substantiated in follow-up studies
Increased placental thickness	>4 cm in width at any gestational age	Anecdotal finding; finding obscured by polyhydramnios
Double bowel sign	Visualization of both sides of the bowel	Anecdotal finding; thought to be earliest finding for fetal ascites
Pericardial effusion	Echo-poor rim of at least 2 mm detected on M-mode ultrasonography	Anecdotal finding; thought to be early sign of fetal decompensation
Biventricular outflow diameter/biparietal diameter	>95th percentile for gestational age compared with controls	Increased incidence of neonatal transfusion, prolonged NICU stay, lower neonatal hematocrit; not sensitive enough to be an independent parameter to predict neonatal anemia.
Fetal liver enlargement	>90th percentile for gestational age	Significant correlation between liver lengths and fetal hemoglobin (R = 0.79) and reticulocyte count before transfusion (R = 0.72).
Fetal splenic enlargement	>95th percentile for gestational age	All severely affected fetuses had measurements above the 95th percentile
	>2 SD above the mean for gestational age	Splenomegaly correctly predicted 44 of 47 cases (sensitivity 83%, specificity 86%). Showed accelerated growth until first transfusion.
	Splenic circumference multiples of the median for gestational age	Sensitivity 100%, false-positive 5.3% (no prior transfusions). Did not predict anemia overall. Prediction improved with severity of hemoglobin deficit. Poor predictor after transfusion.

NICU, neonatal intensive care unit; SD, standard deviation.
From Whitecar PW, Moise KJ: Sonographic methods to detect fetal anemia in red blood cell alloimmunization. Obstet Gynecol Surv 55:240, 2000.

and coworkers demonstrated in a very small prospective study that serial measurements of maximum velocity of umbilical vein flow correlated to some degree with fetal hematocrit and predicted the need for postnatal exchange transfusion in 6 of 7 cases.[37] Their data also suggested that elevation in maximum velocity of umbilical vein flow preceded hepatosplenomegaly.

A new splenic artery Doppler velocimetry index also was established and studied in a small population of sensitized pregnant women.[9] Results showed that a normal Doppler angle in the main splenic artery predicted a decreased risk of severe anemia, whereas a smaller angle reflected a rapid deceleration phase owing to the hyperdynamic fetal state caused by the anemia. Application of this Doppler index in this very small study carried a sensitivity of 100% and a false positive rate of 8.8% in the diagnosis of severe anemia in nonhydropic fetuses. However, its use is limited by the technical expertise required. The size of this study suggests a need for further evaluation.

The Collaborative Group for Doppler Assessment of the Blood Velocity in Anemic Fetuses reported their experience with the use of peak velocity measurements of the middle cerebral artery (MCA) in predicting moderate to severe anemia.[45] This vessel was selected because it has been well established that cerebral arteries respond rapidly to hypoxemia by increasing blood flow velocity in order to optimize brain perfusion. In addition, it also has been shown that as fetal hematocrit rises, peak systolic velocity (PSV) in the MCA decreases. A group of 111 fetuses at risk of anemia from maternal red cell isoimmunization were studied using these physiologic observations. Peak velocity measurements of the MCA were compared to the severity of anemia, and using a cutoff value of 1.5 times the median (because these values change with advancing gestational age), all fetuses with moderate and severe anemia were correctly identified (Fig. 20-7, Table 20-3).

Given a sensitivity of 100% in the prediction of moderate and severe anemia and a false positive value of 12%, the authors concluded that measurement of peak velocity in fetal MCAs was an accurate and noninvasive tool for identifying the fetus at risk, thereby improving the identification of those requiring invasive procedures such as transfusions. This approach has since been examined in a multicenter, intention-to-treat analysis of a group of 124 mothers and 125 fetuses with red cell alloimmunization (not exclusively to RhD).[82] The authors reported that MCA PSV predicted moderate to severe anemia with a sensitivity of 88% and specificity of 87% (negative predictive value, 98%; positive predictive value, 53%). However, this measurement had no discriminative power after 35 weeks' gestation.

In a comparison of conventional management versus management with the use of MCA Doppler in the evaluation of 28 fetuses with alloimmunization (not exclusively RhD), Pereira and coworkers reported that in this small group there was no statistically significant

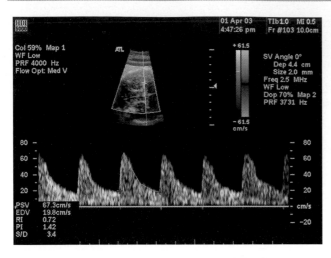

FIGURE 20-7. Measurement of peak systolic velocity (PSV) in the middle cerebral artery of an anemic fetus. As seen, PSV was 67.3 cm/s, which exceeds the 1.50 multiple of the median (MoM) for 26 weeks.

TABLE 20-3. Reference Values of Peak Systolic Velocity of Middle Cerebral Artery

GESTATIONAL AGE (WK)	Peak systolic velocity* of middle cerebral artery				
	Multiples of the Median				
	1	1.3	1.5	1.7	2
15	20	26	30	34	40
16	21	27	32	36	42
17	22	29	33	37	44
18	23	30	35	39	46
19	24	31	36	41	48
20	25	33	38	43	50
21	26	34	39	44	52
22	28	36	42	48	56
23	29	38	44	49	58
24	30	39	45	51	60
25	32	42	48	54	64
26	33	43	50	56	66
27	35	46	53	60	70
28	37	48	56	63	74
29	38	49	57	65	76
30	40	52	60	68	80
31	42	55	63	71	84
32	44	57	66	75	88
33	46	60	69	78	92
34	48	62	72	82	96
35	50	65	75	85	100
36	53	69	80	90	106
37	55	72	83	94	110
38	58	75	87	99	116
39	61	79	92	104	122
40	63	82	95	107	126

*Peak systolic velocity (cm/sec) = $e^{(2.31 + 0.046*GA)}$ where GA = gestational age.

Data from Mari G et al.: Noninvasive diagnosis by Doppler ultrasonography of fetal anemia due to maternal red-cell alloimmunization. Collaborative Group for Doppler Assessment of the Blood Velocity in Anemic Fetuses. N Engl J Med 342:9, 2000.

difference between the two managements; however, MCA Doppler might still be a better predictor of moderate to severe anemia.[57] Indeed, MCA Doppler was associated with a 50% decrease in the false positive rate compared with standard management (and would have prevented two cordocenteses), and it detected all fetuses with moderate to severe anemia, whereas the conventional approach missed one case of severe anemia.

Two other series confirmed the usefulness of MCA Doppler measurement in predicting fetal anemia in isoimmunization due to anti-D as well as to other atypical antigens.[1] Taken together these data support the use of MCA PSV as a predictor of fetal anemia in cases of red cell alloimmunization not only restricted to RhD. In addition, it is particularly helpful in determining the timing of invasive procedures. However, after an intrauterine transfusion (IUT) the characteristics of fetal blood are altered because adult red cells are smaller and less rigid and they display an increased tendency for erythrocyte aggregation. Therefore it became pertinent to examine the usefulness of MCA PSV following IUT.

It was shown that MCA PSV decreased to normal range following IUT probably as a result of an increased afterload resulting from increased blood velocity and improved fetal oxygenation.[21,71] In addition, given the altered characteristics of blood velocity, MCA PSV was found to be slightly higher for a given hemoglobin concentration after a fetus has received one transfusion. This led to a change in the established cutoff level for MCA PSV from 1.50 MoM (multiples of the median) in the fetus never transfused to 1.69 MoM in this population.[21] Widespread use of this technique could contribute to further decreasing the number of fetuses exposed to invasive diagnostic approaches, such as cordocentesis, thereby reducing fetal losses directly related to the procedure itself.

It has been estimated that incorporating MCA PSV in a monitoring program for fetal anemia from allo-immunization would prevent invasive procedures in 70% of cases.[82] Currently, MCA PSV is used by the majority of maternal-fetal medicine specialists in North America.[21] It is measured on a weekly basis until a level of 1.50 MoM is reached, at which point fetal blood sampling with possible transfusion is indicated. It is likely that as our knowledge and technology evolve, a combination of predictors will be used for assessing the at-risk fetus. This would include MCA PSV as well as other promising tools such as splenic artery Doppler PSV[10] and measurement of spleen perimeter.[33]

Suppressive Therapy

INTRAVENOUS IMMUNOGLOBULIN

Although most fetuses with severe RhD hemolytic disease are treated successfully with IUTs, some cannot be, owing to a very young gestational age or technical difficulties that make access to the umbilical vessels impossible. In those instances, an adjunct may be helpful in delaying the transfusion until it is technically possible. Maternal administration of IV immunoglobulin (IVIG) has been proposed as an adjunct because it might lead to feedback inhibition of maternal antibody synthesis, blockade of reticuloendothelial Fc receptors, or blockade of placental antibody transport.[14] So far, although IVIG's mechanism of action remains unclear, early studies are showing promising results. Indeed, maternal IVIG administration has been shown retrospectively and prospectively in small studies to be associated with improved outcomes in index pregnancies compared with previous ones and with significant delays in need for IUTs.[2,78]

Unfortunately, the cost of IVIG remains an important limiting factor and significantly restrains its use. At this time, given limited available data and financial constraints, maternal IVIG administration should remain an adjunct to intravascular transfusions or be used only in cases in which transfusions are technically impossible. However, the encouraging results provided by the early studies suggest that this therapy warrants further prospective evaluation. In the same context, case reports on the use of IVIG in combination with plasmapheresis alone[25,55] or with prednisone and azathioprine in very severe cases also point to the need to investigate an integrated approach in these very rare cases.

Fetal Transfusion

INTRAVASCULAR TRANSFUSION

One of the most significant advances in the management of erythroblastosis fetalis has been the development of fetal transfusion techniques. In 1963, Liley inadvertently punctured the fetal peritoneal cavity during an attempted amniocentesis. On that day, as stated so eloquently by his daughter, "he punctured not only the uterus and the fetal abdomen but also the conceptual barrier that the fetus was beyond the reach of treatment."[44] Indeed, he exploited this accident by successfully performing the first intraperitoneal transfusion of red cells. These cells are subsequently absorbed via the subdiaphragmatic lymphatics to reach the venous circulation. However, this process can be significantly impeded by the presence of hydrops.

In 1984, Rodeck and colleagues introduced intravascular transfusion (IVT) facilitated by fetoscopy.[63] The high rate of fetal loss with fetoscopy (10% to 12%) led to the use of ultrasound to guide access to the fetal umbilical circulation. The risk of fetal death in nonhydropic fetuses with ultrasound-guided transfusion is now approximately 2%.[25,64]

IVT involves maternal premedication with relaxants, prophylactic antibiotics, and, at times, tocolytic agents or steroids. After premedication, ultrasound is used to locate the best access site, which is usually at the umbilical insertion into the placenta. If this site cannot be used, other areas can be sampled, including the cord insertion in the fetal abdomen, a free loop of cord, or the hepatic portion of the umbilical vein. Intracardiac sampling also has been reported. Occasionally, the combination of intraperitoneal and intravascular approaches has been used in an attempt to delay the next transfusion by creating a reservoir of red cells in the peritoneal cavity.

Once the area to be sampled has been identified, the maternal abdomen is cleaned aseptically, and a 20- or 22-gauge needle is introduced through the maternal abdomen into the target vessel. Once the needle is in place, a depolarizing agent may be injected to induce fetal paralysis. A sample of fetal blood is obtained and immediately analyzed for hemoglobin, hematocrit, and blood type. The fetal source of blood can be verified by mean corpuscular volume because the fetal value is 100 to 120 μm^3 and the adult value is approximately 90 μm^3.

A hematocrit less than 30% indicates the need for transfusion because this finding represents significant anemia (a value of 30% falls within the lowest 2.5% of fetuses older than 20 weeks' gestation). Group O Rh-negative blood is used for transfusion. Many centers use irradiated blood to prevent graft-versus-host disease; however, Bowman and coworkers reported 275 survivors who had transfusions with nonirradiated blood without disease.[11]

The goal is to reach a fetal hematocrit of 40% (and up to 60% depending on the institution); the amount of blood necessary varies according to initial hematocrit and fetal weight. To minimize potential increases in fetal blood viscosity, a transfusion hematocrit of 90% is used, and post-transfusion fetal hematocrit should not exceed 55%. Although different centers use different target hematocrits, values of approximately 40% are acceptable by most, because they are more physiologic (at term, a normal fetal hematocrit is around 45%). Though there are formulas and nomograms that calculate the volume needed to obtain a reasonable hematocrit,[35] many prefer to determine the hematocrit intermittently during the transfusion and adjust the amount to be transfused.

During the IVT, an ultrasonographer observes the fetal heart rate. Also, one can easily visualize the turbulence of bloodflow within the umbilical vessel as evidence of flow continuity. During this time, an increase in umbilical venous pressure by 1.7 to 4.6 mm Hg has been documented to occur along with a 25% decrease in cardiac output.[64] This result may be explained by an increased afterload owing to the increased viscosity that causes the fetus to decrease its stroke volume and cardiac output. These parameters return gradually to their baseline; for cardiac output, this is accomplished within 24 hours. At completion of the procedure, a sample of fetal blood is obtained to determine a final hematocrit. The needle is withdrawn, and the fetal heart rate is monitored until it is reassuring.

Complications related to IVT are fairly uncommon in experienced hands. The procedure-related fetal loss

TABLE 20-4. Comparison of Transfusion Techniques

TECHNIQUE	ADVANTAGES	RISKS AND DISADVANTAGES
Intravascular transfusion	Allows determination of hematocrit Rapid correction of anemia Only procedure benefiting severely hydropic fetuses Superior survival rates compared with IPT in many studies Rapid reversal of hydrops	Cardiac overload Hemorrhage from venipuncture Fetomaternal hemorrhage (40%) Cord hematoma Rapid decline in hematocrit More difficult technique if inexperienced examiner Fetal bradycardia (8%) Fetal loss (2%) Infection Possible increased incidence of porencephalic cyst
Intraperitoneal transfusion	Technically easy procedure Very effective in absence of hydrops Long-lasting adequate hematocrit requiring fewer interventions	Low success rate in hydrops Possibility of impairment of venous return if excessive blood is transfused Slow RBC absorption Possible hepatic tear and intra-abdominal organ damage No allowance for determination of hematocrit

IPT, intraperitoneal transfusion; RBC, red blood cell.

rate is reported to be from 1% to 2%. Other risks are detailed in Table 20-4; however, the incidence of fetomaternal hemorrhage (50%) associated with IVT deserves special mention.

INTRAPERITONEAL TRANSFUSION

Intraperitoneal transfusion (IPT) was first performed in 1963 and significantly contributed to improved survival of fetuses affected by Rh disease. IPT is technically less difficult than IVT, but it is also less effective, especially in the hydropic fetus. Ultrasound is used to direct a 20-gauge needle into the fetal peritoneal cavity; a location just above the bladder is ideal. Proper placement of the needle is ascertained by injecting saline solution before the blood is transfused.

The blood volume necessary to obtain the targeted hemoglobin value must be carefully calculated to prevent excessive intraperitoneal pressure associated with overtransfusion, which can impede umbilical vein blood-flow and lead to fetal death. Bowman and coworkers reported a simple equation for IPT volume[11]:

Transfused volume = (weeks of gestation − 20) × 10 mL

In addition to the lack of direct observation of fetal hematocrit, there are other inherent difficulties with IPT.[8] Hydropic fetuses, for example, might not benefit from IPT because of compromised ability to absorb red blood cells through the lymphatic vessels. Bowman and coworkers also reported a 20% spontaneous labor rate after IPT.[4] Finally, the daily absorption of red cells in the nonhydropic fetus is limited to 10% to 12%, leading to slow recovery from severe anemia.

The IPT procedure remains useful in cases in which the caliber of the umbilical vessels does not allow placement of the needle for transfusion or when IVT is technically impossible because of the location of the cord insertion and the fetal position. Some also advocate IPT because the slower post-transfusion decline in hematocrit (compared with that of IVT) requires fewer procedures. On the basis of available data, IVT remains the procedure of choice, especially in the hydropic fetus. However, IPT should be considered in the special circumstances noted.

The timing of subsequent transfusions depends partly on the hematocrit reached at the completion of the procedure and can be assessed more accurately with MCA PSV. Grannum and associates[31] observed a daily hematocrit drop of approximately 1% and they therefore recommended an additional procedure within $1^{1}/_{2}$ to $2^{1}/_{2}$ weeks of the initial one. Bowman and co-workers reported that the average donor hemoglobin attrition rate was 0.4 g/dL per day, and they give repeated transfusions every 2 to 3 weeks.

IPT allows larger transfused volumes and generally has to be repeated less frequently in an affected pregnancy. In fact, Bowman and coworkers noted that to treat a fetus from age 21 to 34 weeks, fewer than four IPTs are typically required, compared with seven or eight IVTs. However, the clinician must exercise caution in assessing the volume of blood to be transfused, because a lower survival rate has been associated with transfusion volumes exceeding 20 mL/kg.[66]

The intraperitoneal and intravascular approaches have been helpful in increasing intervals between transfusions. Indeed, the mean daily decrease in fetal hematocrit was reported to compare favorably with the 1.14% reported with IVT.[46]

During the intervals between transfusions, serial fetal biophysical assessments are recommended, with monitoring for any evidence of deterioration, such as the development of polyhydramnios or hydrops and most of all for the assessment of MCA PSV to help determine, along with all the clinical information, the more appropriate timing of subsequent procedures.

Timing of Delivery

Disease severity and gestational age remain the most significant determinants of the timing of delivery. Usually, no fetal or maternal benefit is gained by continuing the pregnancy beyond 36 to 38 weeks; in fact, continuation can be detrimental to the fetus. In general, the last transfusion is performed at around 35 weeks, when there is a reasonable chance of pulmonary maturity and an amniocentesis to determine lung maturity can be performed. Both lecithin-to-sphingomyelin ratio and phosphatidylglycerol levels should be assessed, but results could be altered by bilirubin in the amniotic fluid. If a mature profile is obtained, delivery is preferable. Otherwise, delivery can be planned in 2 to 3 weeks.

The site of delivery also deserves mention. A fetus in the low-risk group (Liley zone 1) may be delivered in a hospital that can perform exchange transfusion, which is needed in 10% of cases. Moderately or severely affected fetuses need expert neonatal care because their presentation may be complicated by hydrops and prematurity; therefore, a tertiary care center is the location of choice for the birth of these infants.

OUTCOME

Short Term

Because of more sophisticated ultrasound technology and improved operator skills and techniques in neonatal care, perinatal survival after in utero transfusions has improved significantly. This improvement was well demonstrated in a summary of studies using direct fetal IVTs. A total of 411 fetuses were studied, and the overall survival rate was 84%.[64] The data further revealed, as suspected, that fetuses with severe anemia but no hydropic features were five times more likely to survive than those with hydrops. Indeed, the nonhydropic survival rate was 94%, but the survival rate was 74% for hydropic fetuses.

Three other series have confirmed these data. Janssens and coworkers have described 92 fetuses who underwent in utero transfusions and reported an overall survival rate of 83.7%.[25] Similarly, in a series of 43 fetuses, an overall survival rate of 81% was achieved.[30] Once again, the influence of hydrops on outcome was demonstrated through an important difference in perinatal mortality (4 out of 11 for hydropic fetuses versus 4 out of 32 for nonhydropic fetuses). An evaluation of the relative statistical value of a set of clinical parameters in determining fetal survival in a group of 86 transfused fetuses (RhD) revealed that again the best predictor of fetal loss was hydrops (OR 8.7), followed by a hemoglobin deficit of more than 6 g/dL (OR 3.2).[23]

In an attempt to further define fetal risks and outcomes following IUT, another study defined hydropic changes by their severity and correlated these with outcomes.[75] Mild hydrops was characterized by the presence of a rim of ascites with or without a pericardial effusion, whereas severe hydrops included fetuses with abundant ascites with or without pericardial effusion, pleural effusion, and skin edema. Although fetal hematocrit was not significantly different between the two groups, the survival was higher for fetuses with mild hydrops compared with those who had severe manifestations (98% versus 55%). The similarity in fetal red cell indices in these two groups might be a reflection of a lesser ability to compensate for the same degree of anemia in the fetuses with severe hydrops. In addition, survival was positively associated with a higher number of transfusions and a younger gestational age at first transfusion. Reversal of hydrops, which occurred in 65% of all fetuses, resulted in a survival rate of 98% irrespective of the severity of the hydropic changes.

Once delivered, the neonate should be examined thoroughly to establish the need for further therapy. Hyporegenerative anemia, which may complicate the postnatal course of infants with Rh isoimmunization, consists of depressed erythropoiesis with accompanying low reticulocyte counts and a low or undetectable number of erythrocytes containing fetal hemoglobin. Its etiology is unclear but at least three mechanisms have been postulated to play a role: intramedullary destruction of red blood cell precursors, bone marrow suppression from IUT, and a relative erythropoietin deficiency.[58]

The contribution of the suppressive effect of IUT has been demonstrated in the study by Janssens and coworkers,[25] where such suppression was confirmed by demonstrating a positive correlation between the number of IUTs and the number of postnatal transfusions. However, a negative correlation existed between the number of IUTs and the number of exchange transfusions, as well as the need for phototherapy, which suggests that although appropriate in utero treatment appears to optimize immediate neonatal hematologic conditions and to improve survival, it suppresses erythropoiesis.

Although this result suggests a possible role for bone marrow suppression, bone marrow aspirates from infants with classic features of hyporegenerative anemia appear to be very different from aspirates from infants with Rh isoimmunization. Indeed, the former group shows erythroid hypoplasia with an increased myeloid-to-erythroid ratio, and the latter displays erythroid hyperplasia that correlates inversely with hemoglobin, suggesting that in the isoimmunized group, other factors (e.g., anti-RhD antibodies) could be interfering with erythropoiesis.[58] Nevertheless, this hyporegenerative anemia usually resolves spontaneously by 16 weeks of age.[58] Therefore, it is important to continue surveillance of these infants for an extended period with follow-up of hematocrit and reticulocyte count. Administration of recombinant EPO appears promising in this population, but criteria have yet to be established.[58] At this time, symptomatic infants displaying poor weight gain or lethargy or asymptomatic infants with hemoglobin of 6 g/dL or less often are given transfusions.

Long Term

More data are now emerging on long-term outcomes of fetuses who received transfusions in utero. Although information is still limited and should be interpreted with caution, it appears to be reassuring. Indeed, even in those with severe disease, most infants seem to achieve normal neurologic development. This observation was well demonstrated in a series of 40 children who were followed until 62 months of age.[36] The 22 infants who were assessed between 9 and 18 months showed a normal global developmental quotient; the 11 followed until 62 months displayed normal cognitive abilities. Only one case of severe bilateral deafness and one case of right spastic hemiplegia were diagnosed. Both children were delivered by emergency cesarean section, the first because of severe hydrops at 32 weeks and the second because of fetal distress and premature rupture of membranes at 34 weeks. There was no correlation between the global development quotient and the severity of disease, including presence of hydrops and number of transfusions. This information, combined with a 4.5% incidence of major neurologic handicaps, supports the continued use of IVTs.

A larger series of 92 fetuses was recently reported with outcomes on 69 infants from 6 months to 6 years of age.[25] In this group, most children were found to have no significant general health problems, but 56% had frequent respiratory tract infections. As a result, there was a certain degree of hearing loss in five children, and three children had otherwise unexplained hearing disability. A 17% incidence of motor or speech delay was noted in those in early childhood, but for most children these conditions were resolved with physical or speech therapy. Of the 69 children tested, 64 had no neurologic abnormalities and 92.8% had normal developmental outcome. The risk of neurologic abnormality was related to the presence of perinatal asphyxia and was increased in infants with lower cord blood hemoglobin levels. A smaller series involving 36 infants treated with IUT for anti-D and anti-Kell isoimmunization reported normal neurologic outcome in all but one.[24]

Even longer-term follow-up data are available. In a study by Grab and associates, 30 children were followed for up to 6 years of age.[30] All children were able to attend regular primary school, and only two survivors displayed mild sensorineurologic disabilities. One suffered slight speech delay; the other was delivered at 29 weeks by an emergency cesarean section because of persistent bradycardia following a transfusion. The second child initially showed mild psychomotor disabilities, but further neurologic evaluations were normal at the age of 6 years. Both children were not hydropic in utero, and no cases of either moderate or severe neurologic disabilities were observed even in the presence of very severe disease and hydrops.

Although these results are encouraging, difficulties in appropriate follow-up of all children remain a problem, which is partly why the data should be interpreted carefully. Very few studies have been able to describe outcomes for all children, raising the possibility that those lost to follow-up might have had worse outcomes. However, despite this shortcoming, the available data suggest that for most infants, a normal neurodevelopmental outcome can be expected, thereby justifying aggressive treatment of fetuses with severe hemolytic disease including hydrops.

ATYPICAL ANTIGENS

Many other antigen systems are present on the surface of fetal red blood cells. After transfusion of unmatched blood, 1% to 2% of patients acquire antibodies against these *atypical antigens* and face the possibility of isoimmunization in a subsequent pregnancy. Fortunately, antibodies produced against most of these antigens are of the IgM type and are of no consequence to the fetus because they do not cross the placenta. This is also the case for anti-Le and anti-P. Other antibodies can cause mild disease for which no treatment is indicated (e.g., Fy, Jk, Lw).

However, Kell, Duffy, Diego, Kidd, MNSs, P, C, c, and E have all been associated with moderate to severe hemolytic disease. Of these, Kell antigen is probably second to RhD in its importance and strength. The Kell blood group system consists of 23 antigens encoded by a single gene on chromosome 7. The strongest immunogens of this system are K1 and K2. However, because 91% of the population is Kell negative and only 5% of those people will develop anti-Kell antibody after an incompatible transfusion, this type of isoimmunization remains relatively uncommon.[36]

Modern approaches to the management of the Kell-sensitized pregnant woman require an understanding of the pathophysiologic principles behind this entity, because this process appears to be different from RhD sensitization. For example, fetuses affected by Kell sensitization, compared with fetuses who are RhD sensitized, have a lower number of circulating reticulocytes and an inappropriately low number of normoblasts for the degree of anemia.[8] In addition, the bilirubin concentration in the amniotic fluid is lower than expected for the degree of anemia, and the antibody titer does not correlate with disease severity. These observations suggest that Kell sensitization leads to suppression of erythropoiesis. In support of this suggestion, Vaughan and colleagues have demonstrated the inhibition of Kell-positive erythroid progenitor cells by anti-Kell antibodies.[76] This inhibition was found to be dose dependent and specific for cells of erythroid lineage. A greater effect was noted on more immature erythroid cells, suggesting a differential importance for Kell antigen at specific stages of erythroid development.

This information has very important implications for the management of Kell-sensitized pregnant women. The initial approach should include paternal Kell genotyping followed by fetal genotyping (chorionic villus sampling or amniocentesis by PCR)[6,69] if the father is heterozygous. Titers are not generally reliable and hemolysis is not as important as in RhD; therefore, serial amniocentesis for ΔOD 450 measurements might not be very helpful and could even be misleading. Indeed, even low titers and low ΔOD 450 levels have been found in the presence of severe anemia. Suggested approaches consist of early ultrasound surveillance for the development of hydrops with cordocentesis at 20 to 22 weeks to evaluate the degree of anemia. The need for transfusion using this approach can then be re-evaluated every few weeks and transfusion schedules can be established as needed.

REFERENCES

1. Abdel-Fattah SA et al: Noninvasive diagnosis of anemia in hydrops fetalis with the use of middle cerebral artery Doppler velocity. Am J Obstet Gynecol 185:1411, 2001.
2. Alonso JG et al: Repeated direct fetal intravascular high dose immunoglobulin therapy for the treatment of Rh hemolytic disease. J Perinatol Med 22:415, 1994.
3. Anderson JR: The experimental production of erythroblastosis foetalis in rabbits. Br J Haematol 2:44, 1956.
4. Avent ND: Antenatal genotyping of the blood groups of the fetus. Vox Sang 74 (Suppl 12):365, 1998.
5. Avent ND, Reid ME: The Rh blood group system: A review. Blood 15:375, 2000.
6. Avent ND, Martin PGP: Kell typing by allele-specific PCR (ASP). Br J Haematol 93:728, 1996.
7. Avner R et al: Management of rhesus isoimmunization by preimplantation genetic diagnosis. Mol Hum Repro 2:60, 1996.
8. Babinszki A et al: Prognostic factors and management in pregnancies complicated with severe Kell alloimmunization experiences of the last 13 years. Am J Perinatol 15:685, 1998.
9. Bahado-Singh R et al: A new splenic artery Doppler velocimetric index for prediction of severe anemia associated with Rh alloimmunization. Am J Obstet Gynecol 181:49, 1999.
10. Bahado-Singh R et al: Splenic artery Doppler peak systolic velocity predicts severe fetal anemia in rhesus disease. Am J Gynecol 1222, 2000.
11. Bowman JM: Hemolytic disease (erythroblastosis fetalis). In Resnick R et al (eds): Maternal Fetal Medicine: Principles and Practice, 3rd ed. Philadelphia, WB Saunders, 1994, p 711.
12. Bowman J et al: Intravenous drug abuse causes Rh immunization. Vox Sang 61:96, 1991.
13. Cannon M et al: Fetal hydrops fetalis caused by anti-D in a mother with partial D. Obstet Gynecol 102(5 Pt 2):1143, 2003.
14. Chitkara U et al: The role of sonography in assessing severity of fetal anemia in Rh and Kell isoimmunized pregnancies. Obstet Gynecol 71:393, 1988.
15. Chow B: Anemia from bleeding of the fetus into the maternal circulation. Lancet 1:1213, 1954.
16. Clarke CA et al: Further experimental studies on the prevention of Rh haemolytic disease. BMJ 1:979, 1963.
17. Copel JA et al: Alloimmune disorders and pregnancy. Semin Perinatol 15:251, 1991.
18. Cotorruelo C et al: Early detection of RhD status in pregnancies at risk of hemolytic disease of the newborn. Clin Exp Med 2:77, 2002.
19. Davis LE, Hohimer AR: Hemodynamics and organ blood flow in fetal sheep subjected to chronic anemia. Am J Physiol 261:R1542, 1991.
20. Detti L et al: Doppler blood flow in obstetrics. Curr Opin Obstet Gynecol 14:587, 2002.
21. Detti L et al: Doppler ultrasound velocimetry for timing the second intrauterine transfusion in fetuses with anemia from red cell alloimmunization. Am J Obstet Gynecol 185:1048, 2001.
22. Diamond LK et al: Erythroblastosis fetalis and its association with universal edema of the fetus, icterus gravis neonatorum and anemia of the newborn. J Pediatr 1:269, 1932.
23. Farina A et al: Survival analysis of transfused fetuses affected by Rh-alloimmunization. Prenat Diagn 20:881, 2000.
24. Farrant B: Outcome of infants receiving in-utero transfusions for haemolytic disease. N Z Med J 114:400, 2001.
25. Fernandez-Jimenez MC et al: Treatment with plasmapheresis and intravenous immunoglobin in pregnancies complicated with anti-PP$_1$Pk or anti-K immunization: A report of two patients. Vox Sang 80:117, 2001.
26. Finn R et al: Experimental studies on the prevention of Rh hemolytic disease. BMJ 1:1486, 1961.
27. Fisk NM et al: Clinical utility of fetal RhD typing in alloimmunized pregnancies by means of polymerase chain reaction on amniocytes or chorionic villi. Am J Obstet Gynecol 171:50, 1994.
28. Flegel WA, Wagner FF: Molecular biology of partial D and weak D: Implications for blood bank practice. Clin Lab 48:53, 2002.
29. Freda VJ et al: Successful prevention of experimental Rh sensitization in man with an anti-Rh gamma2-globulin antibody preparation: A preliminary report. Transfusion 77:26, 1964.
30. Grab D et al: Treatment of fetal erythroblastosis by intravascular transfusions: Outcome at 6 years. Obstet Gynecol 93:165, 1999.
31. Grannum PAT et al: Prevention of Rh isoimmunization and treatment of the compromised fetus. Semin Perinatol 12:234, 1988.
32. Hadley AG et al: The ability of the chemiluminescence test to predict clinical outcome and the necessity for amniocentesis in pregnancies at risk of haemolytic disease of the newborn. Br J Obstet Gynaecol 105:231, 1998.
33. Haugen G et al: Ultrasonographic monitoring of pregnancies complicated by red blood cell alloimmunization in a cohort with mild to moderate risk according to previous obstetric outcome. Acta Obstet Gynecol Scand 81:227, 2002.
34. Hilden JO et al: HLA phenotypes and severe Rh(D) immunization. Tissue Antigens 46:313, 1995.
35. Hoogeveen M et al: A new method to determine the feto-placental volume based on dilution of fetal haemoglobin and an estimation of plasma fluid loss after intrauterine intravascular transfusion. BJOG 109:1132, 2002.
36. Hudon L et al: Long-term neurodevelopmental outcome after intrauterine transfusion for the treatment of fetal hemolytic disease. Am J Obstet Gynecol 179:858, 1998.
37. Iskaros J et al: Prospective non-invasive monitoring of pregnancies complicated by red cell alloimmunization. Ultrasound Obstet Gynecol 11:432, 1998.
38. Janssens HM et al: Outcome for children treated with fetal intravascular transfusions because of severe blood group antagonism. J Pediatr 131:373, 1997.

39. Kumpel BM: Monoclonal anti-D for prophylaxis of RhD haemolytic disease of the newborn. Tranfus Clin Biol 4:351, 1997.

40. Kumpel BM, Hadley AG: Functional interactions of red cells sensitized by IgG1 and IgG3 human monoclonal anti-D with enzyme B modified monocytes and FcR-bearing cell lines. Mol Immunol 27:247, 1990.

41. Kumpel BM, Elson CJ: Mechanism of anti-D-mediated immune suppression—a paradox awaiting resolution? Trends Immunol 22:1, 2001.

42. Kumpel BM: Monoclonal anti-D development programme. Transplant Immunology 10:199, 2002.

43. Lambin P et al: IgG1 and IgG3 anti-D in maternal serum and on the RBCs of infants suffering from HDN: Relationship with the severity of the disease. Transfusion 42:1537, 2002.

44. Liley HJ: Rescue in inner space: Management of Rh hemolytic disease [editorial]. J Pediatr 131:340, 1997.

45. Mari G: Noninvasive diagnosis by Doppler ultrasonography of fetal anemia due to maternal red-cell alloimmunization. N Engl J Med 342:9, 2000.

46. Moise KJ et al: Comparison of four types of intrauterine transfusion. Effect on fetal hematocrit. Fetal Ther 4:126, 1989.

47. Moise KJ et al: An animal model for hemolytic disease of the fetus and newborn. II. Fetal effects in New Zealand rabbits. Am J Obstet Gynecol 173:747, 1995.

48. Moise KJ et al: An animal model for hemolytic disease of the fetus or newborn in New Zealand White and New Zealand Red rabbits: Newborn effects. Am J Obstet Gynecol 179:1353, 1998.

49. Nicolaides KH et al: The relationship of fetal plasma protein concentration and hemoglobin level to the development of hydrops in rhesus isoimmunization. Am J Obstet Gynecol 152:341, 1985.

50. Nicolaides KH et al: Erythroblastosis and reticulocytosis in anemic fetuses. Am J Obstet Gynecol 159:1063, 1988.

51. Nicolaides KH et al: Have Liley charts outlived their usefulness? Am J Obstet Gynecol 155:90, 1986.

52. Nicolaides KH et al: Failure of ultrasonographic parameters to predict the severity of fetal anemia in rhesus isoimmunization. Am J Obstet Gynecol 158:920, 1988.

53. Nicolini U et al: Fetal liver dysfunction in Rh alloimmunization. Br J Obstet Gynecol 98:287, 1991.

54. Nimrod C et al: Ultrasound evaluation of tachycardia-induced hydrops in the fetal lamb. Am J Obstet Gynecol 157:655, 1987.

55. Noia G et al: Complementary therapy for severe Rh-alloimmunization. Clin Exp Obstet Gynecol 29:297, 2002.

56. Oepkes D et al: Clinical value of an antibody-dependent cell-mediated cytotoxicity assay in the management of RhD alloimmunization. Am J Obstet Gynecol 184:1015, 2001.

57. Pereira L et al: Conventional management of maternal red cell alloimmunization compared with management by Doppler assessment of middle cerebral artery peak systolic velocity. Am J Obstet Gynecol 189:1002, 2003.

58. Pessler F, Hart D: Hyporegenerative anemia associated with Rh hemolytic disease: Treatment failure of recombinant erythropoietin. J Pediatr Hematol Oncol 24:8, 2002.

59. Power JP et al: Hepatitis C viraemia in recipients of Irish intravenous anti-D immunoglobulin. Lancet 344:1166, 1994.

60. Queenan JT et al: Deviation in amniotic fluid optical density at a wavelength of 450 nm in Rh-immunized pregnancies from 14 to 40 weeks' gestation. A proposal of clinical management. Am J Obstet Gynecol 168:1370, 1993.

61. Reece EA et al: Ultrasonography versus amniotic fluid spectral analysis: Are they sensitive enough to predict neonatal complications associated with isoimmunization? Obstet Gynecol 74:357, 1989.

62. Rijnders RJP et al: Clinical applications of cell-free fetal DNA from maternal plasma. ACOG 103:157, 2004.

63. Rodeck CH et al: The management of severe rhesus iso-immunization by fetoscopic intravascular transfusion. Am J Obstet 150:769, 1984.

64. Schumacher B, Moise KJ: Fetal transfusion for red blood cell alloimmunization in pregnancy. Obstet Gynecol 88:137, 1996.

65. Sekizawa A et al: Fetal cell recycling: Diagnosis of gender and RhD genotype in the same fetal cell retrieved from maternal blood. Am J Obstet Gynecol 181:1237, 1999.

66. Selbing A et al: Intrauterine intravascular transfusions in fetal erythroblastosis: The influence of net transfusion volume on fetal survival. Acta Obstet Gynecol Scand 72:20, 1993.

67. Shepard SL et al: Inhibition of the monocyte chemiluminescent response to anti-D sensitized red cells by FcX receptor I-blocking antibodies which ameliorate the severity of haemolytic disease of the newborn. Vox Sang 70:157, 1996.

68. Sikkel E et al: Amniotic fluid ΔOD 450 values accurately predicts severe fetal anemia in D-alloimmunization. Obstet Gynecol 100:51, 2002.

69. Soohee L et al: Prenatal diagnosis of Kell blood group genotypes: KEL1 and KEL2. Am J Obstet Gynecol 175:455, 1996.

70. Spinnato JA et al: Hemolytic disease of the fetus: A comparison of the Queenan and extended Liley methods. Obstet Gynecol 92:441, 1998.

71. Stefos T et al: Correction of fetal anemia on the middle cerebral artery peak systolic velocity. Obstet Gynecol 99:211, 2002.

72. Stern K et al: Experimental isoimmunization to hemo-antigens in man. J Immunol 87:189, 1961.

73. Stockman III JA: Overview of the state of the art of Rh disease: History, current clinical management and recent progress J Ped Hem/Onc 23:554, 2001.

74. Van den Veyver LB, Moise KJ: Fetal RhD typing by polymerase chain reaction in pregnancies complicated by rhesus alloimmunization. Obstet Gynecol 88:1061, 1996.

75. Van Kamp IL et al: The severity of immune fetal hydrops is predictive of fetal outcome after intrauterine treatment. Am J Obstet Gynecol 185:668, 2001.

76. Vaughan JL et al: Inhibition of erythroid progenitor cells by anti-Kell antibodies in fetal alloimune anemia. N Engl J Med 338:798, 1998.

77. Vintzileos AM et al: Fetal liver ultrasound measurements in isoimmunized pregnancies. Obstet Gynecol 68:162, 1986.

78. Voto LS et al: High-dose gamma globulin (IVIG) following by intrauterine transfusion (IUTs) a new alternative for the treatment of severe fetal hemolytic disease. J Perinat Med 25:85, 1997.

79. Whitecar PW et al: Sonographic methods to detect fetal anemia in red blood cell alloimmunization. Obstet Gynecol Surv 55:240, 2000.

80. Wiener AS: Diagnosis of treatment of anemia of the newborn caused by occult transplacental hemorrhage. Am J Obstet Gynecol 56:717, 1948.

81. Wolf RB et al: Antibody-induced anemia in fetal sheep:

Model for hemolytic disease of the fetus and newborn. J Soc Gynecol Investig 8:224, 2001.

82. Zimmerman R et al: Longitudinal measurement of peak systolic velocity in the fetal middle cerebral artery for monitoring pregnancies complicated by red cell allo-immunisation: A prospective multicentre trial with intention-to-treat. BJOG 109:746, 2000.

83. Zupanska B et al: The ability of cellular assays to predict the necessity for cordocenteses in pregnancies at risk of haemolytic disease of the newborn. Vox Sang 80:234, 2001.

21 Amniotic Fluid and Nonimmune Hydrops Fetalis

Richard B. Wolf and Thomas R. Moore

The volume of amniotic fluid that surrounds and protects the developing embryo throughout gestation provides an indirect indicator of fetal well-being. The precise mechanisms involved in the regulation of amniotic fluid volume have not been defined. However, understanding the dynamics of amniotic fluid pathways and the normal exchange of water and solutes among the fetus, mother, and amniotic fluid aids appreciation of the physiologic basis of the clinical conditions of oligohydramnios and polyhydramnios. Nonimmune hydrops fetalis, a condition associated with fluid overload in the fetus, is also discussed in this chapter. Immune hydrops fetalis, which produces erythroblastosis fetalis, is discussed in Chapter 20.

AMNIOTIC FLUID DYNAMICS

The pathways of production and removal of amniotic fluid have long been misunderstood. It was formerly believed that the majority of amniotic fluid represented a transudate from the maternal vessels. Fetal urination was not believed to be a likely source of amniotic fluid because it was "unreasonable to suppose that nature would have an individual floating in and drinking its own excreta."[23] Modern research in amniotic fluid dynamics has defined several pathways for movement of amniotic fluid and solutes, including fetal swallowing, urination, respiratory secretion, and transport within and across the fetal membranes.

Composition

Amniotic fluid contains 98% to 99% water, but its composition changes throughout gestation. Early in pregnancy the fluid is isotonic with maternal serum, representing its probable origin as a transudate from maternal or fetal tissues.[7] As fetal skin becomes keratinized and renal function matures, amniotic fluid osmolality declines from 290 mOsm/kg in the first trimester to approximately 255 mOsm/kg near term.[7] With advancing gestation, amniotic fluid creatinine, urea, and uric acid concentrations increase progressively.

Proteins (principally albumin) are found in relatively low concentrations in late pregnancy and provide a minor source of nutrition for the developing fetus. Near term the amniotic fluid contains significant quantities of desquamated fetal skin and gastrointestinal cells, hair, vernix caseosa, and occasionally meconium.

Volume

During pregnancy, approximately 6 L of water accumulates in the gravid woman. The majority of this fluid is associated with growth of the conceptus: 2800 mL in the fetus and 400 mL in the placenta, with 700 to 800 mL of amniotic fluid.[81] The remainder of the fluid is associated with the uterus (800 mL), breasts (500 mL), and maternal blood volume expansion (850 mL).[81] Despite complex osmotic, electrostatic, and hydrostatic forces, amniotic fluid volume is highly regulated, gradually rising in the first trimester, stabilizing in the second trimester, and declining late in the third trimester while remaining within a relatively narrow range of volumes.

In a meta-analysis comprising 12 studies using the direct measurement or dye dilution technique in 705 normal pregnancies, Brace and Wolf showed that amniotic fluid volume increases steadily in early gestation and remains relatively stable between 22 and 39 weeks, averaging 750 to 800 mL at term (Fig. 21-1).[6] Amniotic fluid declines after 40 weeks by 8% per week, with the mean volume approximately 500 mL by 42 weeks. From the curve shown in the figure, it can be seen that variation from the mean is modest at the lower end (5th percentile, 300 mL) but relatively substantial at the upper end (95th percentile, 1750 mL).

Magann and colleagues subsequently evaluated the amniotic fluid volume in 144 pregnancies with the dye dilution technique[51] and found that amniotic fluid volume continues to increase throughout gestation, with a mean volume of approximately 800 mL at term. The relative accuracy of this indicator dilution technique has been validated by comparing the actual amniotic fluid volume at the time of cesarean delivery to that predicted immediately before by dye dilution,[53] with a 7% difference

FIGURE 21-1. Amniotic fluid as a function of gestational age. Dots are means for 2-week intervals. Lines represent percentiles calculated from polynomial regression. (Modified from Brace RA, Wolf EJ: Normal amniotic fluid volume changes throughout pregnancy. Am J Obstet Gynecol 161:382, 1989.)

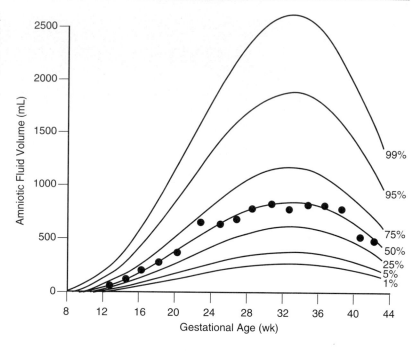

between the dye-determined and direct measurement volumes ($r = .99$, $p < .001$).

Production and Regulation

Amniotic fluid production has not been investigated fully in early gestation, but studies of amniotic fluid turnover in the second half of pregnancy show that the bulk of amniotic fluid is produced by fetal urination and removed by fetal swallowing (Fig. 21-2). A significant amount of fluid is also produced from secretions of the respiratory tract, with lesser amounts coming from nasopharyngeal secretions. Excess fluid is reabsorbed via intramembranous and transmembranous routes.[30]

Using serial ultrasound measurements of the fetal bladder every 2 to 5 minutes, Rabinowitz and associates estimated that amniotic fluid production by fetal urination increases from 120 mL per day (5 mL per hour) at 20 weeks to 1200 mL per day (50 mL per hour) at term.[75] Previous studies[99] involving less frequent observations of fetal bladder volume had shown urine production to be approximately one half of the amount calculated by Rabinowitz and colleagues. Extrapolating from more precise measurements in animal models, the true rate is probably somewhere between those values, with near-term urine flow at approximately 700 to 900 mL per day.[37] Fetal urine production is known to be decreased in pregnancies with abnormalities of placental function such as intrauterine growth restriction (IUGR).[99] However, low fetal urine output is not associated with lower Apgar scores, pH less than 7.25, or late decelerations in labor.[99] Furthermore, there appears to be no correlation between fetal weight and urine production in women with normal pregnancies.[99]

Fetal lungs secrete approximately 300 to 400 mL of fluid per day, which is driven by chloride ion exchange across the pulmonary epithelium.[7] However, the fetus swallows approximately half of this fluid before it enters the amniotic cavity.[31] Amniotic fluid is prevented from re-entering the lungs by the closed larynx, producing a net efflux of fluid.[7] Thus, the net amount of lung fluid entering into the amniotic fluid is approximately 150 to 200 mL per day.

Fetal swallowing of amniotic fluid begins as early as 8 to 11 weeks and increases with gestational age. In animal studies, swallowing accounts for removal of approximately 1000 mL per day near term, and the

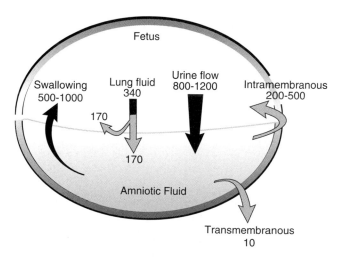

FIGURE 21-2. Pathways for daily fluid production and removal between the fetus and amniotic fluid compartments (measured in milliliters). (From Gilbert WM et al: Amniotic fluid dynamics. Fetal Med Rev 3:89, 1991. Reprinted with permission of Cambridge University Press.)

amount removed increases from 100 mL/kg per day to 500 mL/kg per day over the last third of gestation.[92] In studies of normal, near-term human fetuses, amniotic fluid ingested ranged from 210 to 840 mL per day (average, 565 mL), amounting to almost 5% to 10% of the fetal body weight.[73]

With 1200 mL per day entering the amniotic sac from the kidneys and 1000 mL per day removed by fetal swallowing, it is clear that an additional route of fluid absorption must exist to maintain volume balance. Data from animal studies suggest that the excess fluid not removed by fetal swallowing is reabsorbed into the fetal circulation via an *intramembranous pathway*.[30] In humans the intramembranous pathway is represented by the fetal vessels on the surface of the placenta. This pathway is capable of absorbing large quantities of fluid:[30] in animal studies in which the fetal esophagus was ligated, amniotic fluid returned to near-normal levels after 2 to 3 weeks. In sheep, Gilbert and Brace demonstrated rapid absorption of intra-amniotic water into the fetal circulation via fetal vessels on the surface of the placenta.[30] Other sites of potential fluid exchange, such as the nasopharyngeal mucosae and the fetal skin, are unlikely to add significantly to the overall fluid volume dynamics.[7]

CLINICAL DETERMINATION OF AMNIOTIC FLUID VOLUME

Assessment of the amniotic fluid volume is important because variation above or below normal levels is associated with increased perinatal morbidity and mortality.[11,12] The ideal method for assessing amniotic fluid volume should be reproducible and clinically efficient, as well as have a high predictive value. The techniques currently available for assessing amniotic fluid were recently reviewed by Schrimmer and Moore[80] and include subjective estimation and semiquantitative techniques: measurement of the maximum vertical pocket and the two-diameter pocket, and the amniotic fluid index. While each has been studied extensively, no technique is universally considered superior in predicting perinatal outcome. Three-dimensional ultrasound may be useful in the future as the techniques and clinical correlations are developed.

Subjective Estimation

Subjective ultrasonographic estimation of amniotic fluid volume is based on the presence or absence of echolucent pockets between the fetal limbs and the fetal trunk or uterine wall. Estimations of normal, increased, reduced, or absent fluid have been correlated with fetal outcome.[18] Pregnant women with reduced or absent amniotic fluid have an increased incidence of meconium-stained fluid, fetal acidosis, and birth asphyxia. Subjective scoring systems have been proposed,[61] but the predictive ability of subjective methods varies widely and depends on the experience of the sonographer.

Measurement of Maximum Vertical Pocket

Initial semiquantitative assessment of amniotic fluid volume provided an evaluation of the width of the amniotic fluid pocket.[54] When the widest pocket visualized was less than 1 cm, decreased amniotic fluid volume was associated with IUGR, and perinatal morbidity was increased 10-fold. However, this method was relatively insensitive in predicting poor perinatal outcome. Chamberlain and associates proposed the *maximum vertical pocket* (MVP) as more predictive of poor outcome.[11,12] They defined oligohydramnios as an MVP of less than 2 cm and polyhydramnios as an MVP of 8 cm or greater (Table 21-1).

Measurement of Amniotic Fluid Index

The *amniotic fluid index* (AFI) is currently the most widely used clinical method for determining amniotic fluid volume. The AFI is calculated as the mathematical sum of the deepest vertical pockets from each of the four quadrants of the uterus, with the maternal umbilicus as the central reference point.[69] With this technique, severe oligohydramnios is defined as an AFI of 5 cm or less and polyhydramnios as an AFI of 25 cm or more.[63,69,70] A normal AFI is illustrated in Figure 21-3.

The AFI correlates closely with actual amniotic fluid volume as determined by the dye dilution technique for normal fluid volume, although it loses its predictive value at the extreme upper and lower ends (Fig. 21-4).[17] The AFI is still superior to single MVP techniques in identifying patients with abnormal volumes of amniotic fluid.[63] Furthermore, the AFI is a relatively simple technique with good intra- and interobserver correlation.[78]

In a classic study of 791 normal pregnancies, Moore and Cayle established the mean and outer boundaries (5th and 95th percentiles, respectively) in use today for the AFI from 16 to 42 weeks of gestation.[62] Recently, Magann and associates repeated this study using 50 patients during each gestational week from 14 to

TABLE 21-1. Diagnostic Categories by Measurement of the Maximum Vertical Pocket

AMNIOTIC FLUID VOLUME	MVP VALUE	PATIENTS
Polyhydramnios	≥8.0 cm	3%
Normal	>2–<8 cm	94%
Moderate oligohydramnios	≥1–≤2 cm	2%
Severe oligohydramnios	<1 cm	1%

MVP, maximum vertical pocket.
Modified from Chamberlain PF et al: Ultrasound evaluation of amniotic fluid volume: I. The relationship of marginal and decreased amniotic fluid volumes to perinatal outcomes. Am J Obstet Gynecol 150:245, 1984.

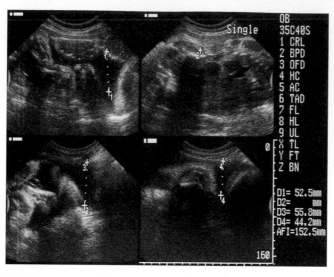

FIGURE 21-3. Normal four-quadrant amniotic fluid index totaling 153 mm.

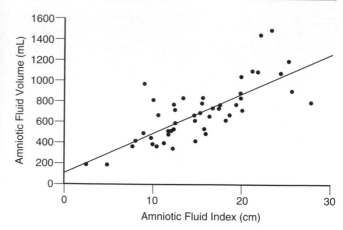

FIGURE 21-4. Correlation of amniotic fluid index to actual amniotic fluid volume determined by the dye dilution technique. (Modified from Croom CS et al: Do semiquantitative amniotic fluid indexes reflect actual volume? Am J Obstet Gynecol 167:995, 1992.)

FIGURE 21-5. Amniotic fluid index (AFI) showing four-quadrant sum of deepest vertical pockets (measured in millimeters). Gray lines indicate AFI values after Moore; black lines indicate values after Magann. Solid line indicates the median values. Upper and lower dashed lines are the 95th and 5th percentiles, respectively. (Adapted from Moore TR, Cayle JE: The amniotic fluid index in normal human pregnancy. Am J Obstet Gynecol 162:1168, 1990; Magann EF et al: The amniotic fluid index, single deepest pocket, and two-diameter pocket in normal human pregnancy. Am J Obstet Gynecol 182:1581, 2000.)

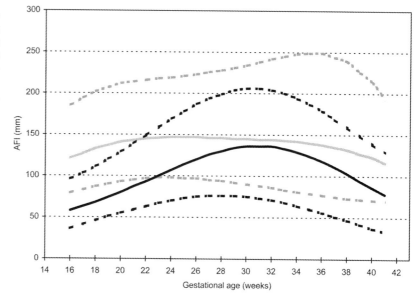

41 weeks of gestation.[52] As shown in Figure 21-5, the shape of Magann's AFI curve more closely resembles that from Brace and Wolf[6] as determined from direct amniotic fluid measurements (see Fig. 21-1), with the AFI values 1 to 2 cm less on average than Moore's.

Throughout most of the pregnancy, the mean AFI is approximately 12 to 14 cm, declining after 33 weeks. The average AFI near term is 12 cm, with the 95th percentile (polyhydramnios) being approximately 20 cm and the 5th percentile (oligohydramnios) being approximately 7 cm. Note that the maximum normal AFI is less than 25 cm. The typical limits for amniotic fluid assessment by AFI are shown in Table 21-2.

TABLE 21-2. Diagnostic Categories by Measurement of the Amniotic Fluid Index

AMNIOTIC FLUID VOLUME	AFI VALUE	PATIENTS
Polyhydramnios	≥25 cm	2%
Normal	>8–<25 cm	76%
Moderate oligohydramnios	≥5–≤8 cm	20%
Severe oligohydramnios	<5 cm	2%

AFI, amniotic fluid index.
Modified from Moore TR: Oligohydramnios. Contemp Obstet Gynecol 41:15, 1996.

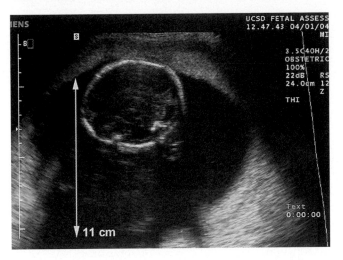

FIGURE 21-6. Appearance of "stuck twin" in twin-twin transfusion syndrome. Note that the fetus appears suspended from the anterior wall of the uterus and surrounded by a large fluid collection (polyhydramnios of second twin). The membranes surrounding this twin are not visible on ultrasound examination.

Amniotic Fluid Assessment in Multifetal Pregnancies

Assessing relative amniotic fluid volume in twins is important because oligohydramnios is a significant component of the *twin oligohydramnios-polyhydramnios sequence* (TOPS).[8] *Twin-twin transfusion*, the severe extreme of TOPS in monochorionic twin gestation, may present as a "stuck twin," in which the fetus appears to be suspended from the uterine wall, with no visible intervening membrane due to severe oligohydramnios, and surrounded by polyhydramnios of the second twin (Fig. 21-6).

Techniques for assessing amniotic fluid volume in twins and higher-order multiples include measuring the AFI of total amniotic fluid without regard to the intervening membrane, AFI for each sac, MVP of each sac, and a two-diameter pocket in each sac.[80] Magann and coworkers[52] found the two-diameter pocket superior in predicting oligohydramnios in twin gestation, although many simply regard identifying a 2 × 2 cm pocket as adequate for each fetal sac. At present, no technique for estimating amniotic fluid in twins is universally accepted, and all are relatively poor at identifying low or high amniotic fluid volumes.

ABNORMALITIES OF AMNIOTIC FLUID VOLUME

Clinical Associations with Poor Perinatal Outcome

INCREASED PERINATAL MORBIDITY AND MORTALITY

Pregnancies complicated by extremes of amniotic fluid volume are associated with increased morbidity and mortality. In a study involving 7582 high-risk obstetric referral patients, Chamberlain and associates[11,12] measured the amniotic fluid using the MVP technique. The corrected *perinatal mortality* (PNM) rate for patients with normal amniotic fluid volume was 1.97 in 1000. For patients with polyhydramnios the PNM rate was 4.12 in 1000; and for those with oligohydramnios the PNM rate increased over 50-fold to 109.4 in 1000. In the series of Shipp and colleagues,[84] only 10% of the patients with severe second trimester oligohydramnios survived. Those diagnosed in the third trimester fared better, although there was still a 15% PNM rate. Moore[61] reported that patients with anhydramnios (absent amniotic fluid) had a PNM rate of 88%, compared with 11% for those with moderate oligohydramnios. The sonographic appearance of anhydramnios is illustrated in Figure 21-7.

Jacoby and Charles[43] noted a 34% PNM rate in their series of 156 patients diagnosed with polyhydramnios at the time of delivery without the aid of ultrasound. Of those deaths, 48% were due to congenital anomalies (mostly anencephaly). In a series by Hill and coworkers, the PNM rate for polyhydramnios diagnosed before delivery was 58.8 in 1000 after correcting for lethal congenital anomalies.[39]

The perinatal morbidity associated with oligohydramnios is increased, with higher rates of meconium-stained amniotic fluid, fetal distress, and low Apgar scores.[78] IUGR (birthweight less than the 10th percentile for gestational age at delivery) also is common in pregnancies with oligohydramnios.[54] Operative intervention for fetal distress during labor is three times more likely in women with oligohydramnios than in those with normal amniotic fluid.[14] Even without IUGR or a fetal anomaly, the patient with idiopathic oligohydramnios is three times more likely to deliver preterm and 30 times

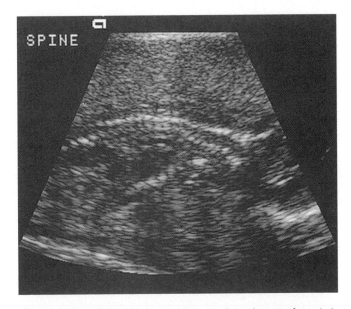

FIGURE 21-7. Anhydramnios. Note the complete absence of amniotic fluid.

more likely to be induced for fetal indications than those with normal amniotic fluid volume.[76]

Polyhydramnios increases maternal and neonatal morbidity and is associated with diabetes, congenital anomalies, and multiple gestation.[22,39] Deliveries are complicated by malpresentation in 20% of cases,[43] and cord prolapse is increased fivefold. Chromosomal abnormalities are increased 5- to 30-fold compared with patients with normal fluid volume.[22] Preterm delivery also is prevalent in those with polyhydramnios, with 18.9% of fetuses delivered before 37 weeks of gestation in one series.[55] Even after correcting for specific causes, such as diabetes and congenital anomalies, idiopathic polyhydramnios is associated with higher rates of malpresentation, macrosomia, and cesarean delivery.[68]

INCREASED CONGENITAL ANOMALIES

Congenital anomalies are present in approximately 20% of patients with polyhydramnios,[39,43] compared with 2% to 4% of all pregnancies. The most common congenital anomalies associated with polyhydramnios are those that impair fetal swallowing, such as gastrointestinal obstruction (e.g., esophageal or duodenal atresia) and intracranial anomalies (e.g., anencephaly).[21] The risk of a fetal anomaly correlates with the degree of polyhydramnios, with markedly more severe cases (MVP of greater than 16 cm) increasing the risk of an anomaly to nearly 90%.[21]

Oligohydramnios is generally associated with genitourinary tract anomalies that impair fetal urination (e.g., renal agenesis, polycystic kidneys, urinary obstruction).[65] In a series by Bastide and colleagues, the incidence of major congenital anomalies in the fetuses of women with severe oligohydramnios was approximately 13%.[4] Prolonged oligohydramnios, particularly during the critical period of fetal pulmonary development, can cause pulmonary hypoplasia.[94] Positional deformities (e.g., skeletal and facial abnormalities) also are common in chronic oligohydramnios.

UTEROPLACENTAL INSUFFICIENCY

Oligohydramnios may be indicative of poor placental function. Because placental function and maternal hydration determine fetal urinary output, oligohydramnios is frequently associated with IUGR, intrapartum asphyxia, and fetal death. In a Doppler imaging study by Cruz and coworkers, patients with oligohydramnios and intact membranes were found to have higher flow resistance in the uterine and umbilical arteries than that in patients with normal amniotic fluid volumes.[19] Nicolaides and associates noted that urine production in growth-restricted fetuses was decreased and correlated with the degree of fetal hypoxemia.[66] This is perhaps an endocrine response to intrauterine stress with increased vasopressin secretion, shunting bloodflow preferentially to the fetal heart, brain, and adrenal glands and away from the kidneys.

In post-term pregnancies, amniotic fluid volume is more predictive of fetal distress than the fetal heart rate tracing: Women with adequate amniotic fluid volume have significantly better perinatal outcomes than those without adequate amniotic fluid.[24] Oligohydramnios in post-term pregnancies is associated with a fourfold increase in cesarean deliveries, mostly for fetal distress.

Oligohydramnios

The diagnostic study and clinical management of oligohydramnios should be directed toward diagnosing lethal fetal anomalies, identifying uteroplacental insufficiency, evaluating for *premature rupture of membranes* (PROM), and correcting or alleviating remediable underlying conditions. Moderate oligohydramnios is defined as an AFI of less than 8 cm[62] or an MVP of less than 2 cm in depth[11] and severe oligohydramnios as an AFI of less than 5 cm[69] or an MVP of less than 1 cm.[11] The diagnosis of oligohydramnios should be confirmed by repeating the measurement several times, averaging the result, and comparing it with the normal values appropriate for that gestational age.

ETIOLOGY

The conditions associated with oligohydramnios are shown in Box 21-1. In a series by Shenker and colleagues, the most common cause of oligohydramnios was PROM (50%), followed by IUGR (18%) and congenital anomalies (14%).[83] Aneuploidy was seen in 4% of Shipp and coworkers' series of patients with severe oligohydramnios.[84] Genitourinary malformations associated with oligohydramnios include renal agenesis, cystic dysplasia of the kidneys, and obstructive uropathies, including posterior urethral valve syndrome. The sonographic appearance of posterior urethral valves with megacystis is shown in Figure 21-8.

Oligohydramnios can be the result of maternal ingestion of certain medications. The most significant medications are the prostaglandin synthetase inhibitors, which are used to inhibit labor, reduce polyhydramnios, and relieve pain.[46] These medications reduce the fetal glomerular filtration rate, resulting in decreased fetal urine output and oligohydramnios in up to 70% of patients. They may also decrease uteroplacental perfusion and cause the ductus arteriosus to close prematurely.[46] Although these effects are reversible, patients maintained on indomethacin for over 72 hours should be evaluated with semiweekly amniotic fluid assessments and fetal echocardiography. Angiotensin-converting enzyme (ACE) inhibitors also have been implicated in causing oligohydramnios, presumably secondary to severe fetal hypotension.[36] In addition, ACE inhibitors are associated with producing prolonged neonatal anuria, renal anomalies, ossification defects in the fetal skull, and death; therefore, they are contraindicated in pregnancy.

DIAGNOSTIC EVALUATION
Rule Out Ruptured Membranes

A sterile speculum examination should be performed on any patient suspected of having PROM. However, these examinations are often negative or equivocal, frequently making it difficult to diagnose chronic fluid leakage as the cause of low amniotic fluid. If a normal-sized fetal bladder is still observed on ultrasound with

BOX 21-1. Principal Diagnoses Associated with Oligohydramnios

Fetal
Chromosomal abnormalities
Congenital anomalies
   Genitourinary (renal agenesis, polycystic or multicystic
      dysplastic kidneys, ureteral or urethral obstruction)
Intrauterine growth restriction
Intrauterine fetal demise
Postmaturity
Rupture of membranes (occult or overt)
   Preterm
   Prolonged

Maternal
Uteroplacental insufficiency
   Autoimmune condition
      Antiphospholipid antibodies, collagen vascular disease
   Maternal hypertension
   Nephropathy
   Diabetic vasculopathy
   Maternal hypovolemia
   Preeclampsia/pregnancy-induced hypertension
Medications
   Prostaglandin synthetase inhibitors
   Angiotensin-converting enzyme inhibitors

Placental
Chronic abruption
Placental crowding in multiple gestation
Twin-twin transfusion
Placental infarction

Idiopathic

Modified from Peipert JF, Donnenfeld AE: Oligohydramnios: A review. Obstet Gynecol Surv 46:325, 1991.

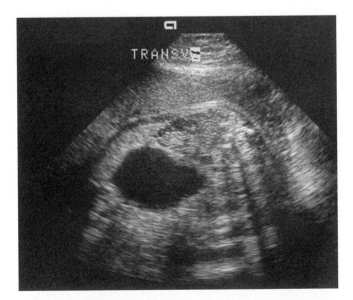

FIGURE 21-8. Posterior urethral valve syndrome. Male fetus with "keyhole" bladder on ultrasound is shown. Note the absence of amniotic fluid.

concomitant, severe oligohydramnios the likelihood of PROM is high.

Assess Fetal Anatomy

Renal and ureteral anomalies are the most common causes of severe oligohydramnios in the absence of ruptured membranes.[65] However, cardiac, skeletal, and central nervous system anomalies may coexist with primary renal anomalies. Therefore, a careful anatomic survey should be performed to rule out congenital anomalies, paying close attention to the renal parenchyma, dimensions of the renal pelvis, and morphologic features of the fetal urinary bladder. In addition, renal anomalies may be associated with aneuploidy (i.e., trisomies 21 and 18),[67,88] so evaluation for signs of aneuploidy should be included and genetic amniocentesis considered. With bilateral renal agenesis, there is virtual anhydramnios from 16 weeks onward. The identification of the absence of renal arteries on power Doppler imaging (Fig. 21-9) may be necessary to document renal agenesis because the fetal adrenal glands

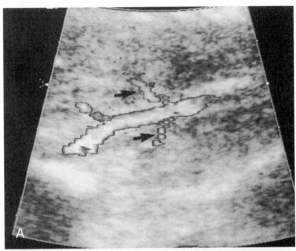

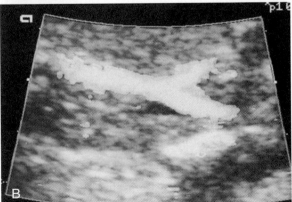

FIGURE 21-9. Bilateral renal agenesis. **A,** Doppler image of normal renal arteries *(arrows)* at 19 weeks of gestation. **B,** Power Doppler image of fetal abdominal aorta and its bifurcation at 20 weeks of gestation demonstrating the bilateral absence of renal arteries. (From Sepulveda W et al: Accuracy of prenatal diagnosis of renal agenesis with color flow imaging in severe second-trimester oligohydramnios. Am J Obstet Gynecol 173:1788, 1995.)

can become hypertrophied and resemble renal structures.[82] Conversely, polycystic renal disease and obstructive uropathy (e.g., ureteropelvic junction obstruction) may not become evident until the late second trimester. Unilateral disease rarely causes significant decreases in amniotic fluid.

Assess Fetal Growth

Oligohydramnios is known to be associated with IUGR.[54] Therefore, if PROM and congenital anomalies are excluded, IUGR resulting from uteroplacental insufficiency should be considered. Chronically poor placental function may be due to maternal autoimmune disease, hypertension, or vasculopathy. In general, asymmetric IUGR, with the fetal abdomen lagging behind the fetal head in growth, is more predictive of uteroplacental insufficiency, whereas symmetric IUGR is more likely to be due to aneuploidy or a congenital anomaly.

Doppler studies of uterine and umbilical bloodflow may reveal patterns of high resistance in patients with oligohydramnios and IUGR, confirming the diagnosis of placental insufficiency.[49] Absent or reverse diastolic flow in the umbilical arteries is associated with higher perinatal mortality.[44] Absent and reverse end-diastolic flow patterns are demonstrated in Figure 21-10.

Because the risk of fetal asphyxia and death is high in oligohydramnios with IUGR,[54] intensive fetal monitoring and hospitalization should be considered in cases diagnosed between 26 and 32 weeks of gestation. Amniocentesis to assess lung maturity should be performed after 32 weeks, and delivery should be undertaken if the lungs are mature.

Assess Fetal Pulmonary Status

Pulmonary hypoplasia, whether from renal or nonrenal etiology, is a known complication of prolonged oligohydramnios, with a PNM rate exceeding 70%.[84] The pathophysiology and antenatal diagnosis of pulmonary hypoplasia were recently reviewed.[47] The risk of developing pulmonary hypoplasia is the greatest if oligohydramnios is prolonged and occurs during the canalicular phase of alveolar proliferation, which is from 16 to 24 weeks of gestation. Hadi and associates showed that the absence of a fluid pocket of at least 2 cm between 20 and 25 weeks of gestation is predictive of impaired survival (30% survival if the pocket is less than 2 cm and 98% if the pocket is 2 cm or greater).[35] The estimated probability of developing pulmonary hypoplasia with oligohydramnios in the second trimester is illustrated in Figure 21-11. Although the precise pathophysiology of pulmonary hypoplasia is unclear, the inhibition of fetal breathing, the lack of a trophic function of amniotic fluid within the airways, and simple mechanical compression of the chest have been proposed as causes (see Chapter 42).[47]

Several techniques for the evaluation of the fetal chest to predict pulmonary hypoplasia have been proposed. Vintzileos and coworkers reviewed six ultrasonographic parameters for predicting pulmonary hypoplasia and found that the highest sensitivity (85%)

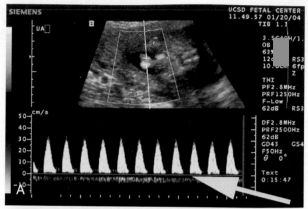
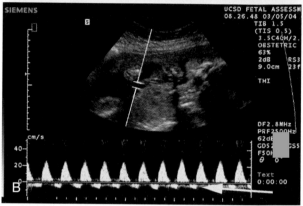

FIGURE 21-10. Doppler umbilical artery velocimetry. **A,** Absent end-diastolic flow. Note that the umbilical artery flow velocity waveform returns to zero after each fetal heartbeat (*large arrow*). **B,** Reverse end-diastolic flow. Here the waveform extends below the zero line (negative flow) between the fetal heartbeats (*small arrow*).

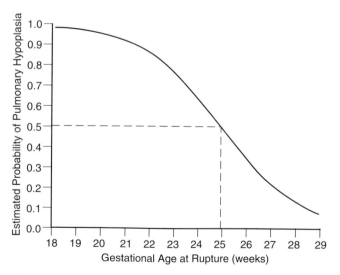

FIGURE 21-11. Estimated probability of the development of pulmonary hypoplasia by gestational age in severe oligohydramnios (less than 2 cm maximum vertical pocket). Solid line indicates probability curve. Dashed lines illustrate 50% probability at approximately 25 weeks of gestation. (From Vergani P et al: Risk factors for pulmonary hypoplasia in second-trimester premature rupture of membranes. Am J Obstet Gynecol 170:1359, 1994.)

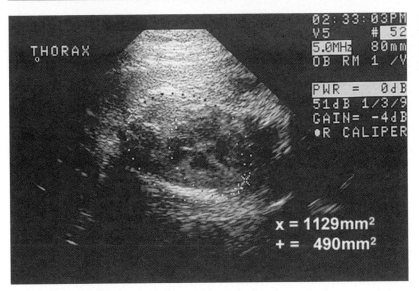

FIGURE 21-12. Decreased ratio of lung area to chest area, which is suggestive of pulmonary hypoplasia. The lung area is calculated as [(1129 − 490) ÷ 1129] × 100 = 56,6%, and it is clearly reduced.

and specificity (85%) were achieved by calculating the lung area ratio.[95]

$$\frac{(\text{Chest area} - \text{Cardiac area}) \times 100}{\text{Chest Area}}$$

The normal lung area ratio should be greater than 66% (Fig. 21-12). D'Alton and colleagues proposed using the thoracic-to-abdominal circumference ratio, with a ratio of less than 0.80 in severe oligohydramnios virtually 100% predictive of lethal pulmonary hypoplasia.[20]

DIAGNOSTIC ADJUNCTS

A precise diagnosis is necessary to guide appropriate counseling and treatment of women whose pregnancies are complicated by oligohydramnios, but decreased amniotic fluid makes ultrasonographic analysis difficult. Amnioinfusion, indigo carmine dye, and furosemide are adjuncts that have been recommended to improve diagnostic capability in oligohydramnios.

Amnioinfusion

Infusion of normal saline solution into the amniotic cavity has been used in the middle of the trimester to improve ultrasound evaluation in suspected renal agenesis. In a series by Fisk and colleagues, suspected fetal anomalies were confirmed in 90% of patients.[27] However, 13% of the etiologic diagnoses were changed as a result of information obtained at amnioinfusion. Aspiration of a small amount of the fluid instilled during amnioinfusion for chromosome analysis can be successful in obtaining a karyotype in 70% of patients.[74]

Indigo Carmine Dye

Instillation of indigo carmine dye at the time of amnioinfusion can help diagnose PROM if the dye subsequently stains a tampon placed in the vagina. However, most cases of PROM can be diagnosed clinically without this invasive procedure. Methylene blue dye has been reported to cause methemoglobinemia and hemolysis, and therefore should not be used.[58]

Furosemide Challenge

Although it was initially promising as a method of stimulating fetal bladder filling and demonstrating renal function, maternal furosemide has subsequently been found to be inconsistent in its effects. In animal studies, Chamberlain and associates showed that maternally administered furosemide failed to cross the placenta.[13] However, Gilbert and coworkers showed that furosemide injected into the amniotic sac could enter the fetal circulation via the intramembranous route.[32]

TREATMENT

The management of oligohydramnios depends on the severity of the condition, the underlying cause of the condition, and the gestational age of the patient. In general, mild oligohydramnios can be managed conservatively with frequent biophysical testing and appropriately timed delivery. Severe oligohydramnios may benefit from amnioinfusion, although cases of renal agenesis and other lethal congenital or chromosomal defects require little more than expectant management or termination of the pregnancy. The patient with PROM should be delivered if there is evidence of infection; otherwise, the patient can be treated conservatively until the fetus reaches an age of likely lung maturity (greater than 34 weeks) or has abnormal biophysical test results. Approximately 10% will reseal and can be followed thereafter with outpatient monitoring.

Women with term and post-term pregnancies who have an AFI of less than 5 cm or an MVP of less than 2 cm have a fetus at high risk of morbidity.[11] Therefore, antepartum testing in these patients should always include twice-weekly AFI evaluations. If the fluid is decreased the delivery should be considered, although management of the appropriately grown fetus with oligohydramnios is controversial. Indeed, a recent review of data from the RADIUS trial[100] concluded that isolated oligohydramnios was not associated with growth restriction or an increased number of adverse outcomes.

Maternal Hydration

Low amniotic fluid volume has been associated with decreased maternal intravascular volume. However, when Powers and Brace infused isotonic lactated Ringer's irrigation in patients with low AFIs, it did not improve the amniotic fluid volume.[72] When diluted (hypotonic), lactated Ringer's irrigation was infused, the maternal serum osmolality was lowered. This result produced an increase in fetal urine production and improved amniotic fluid volume. Oral hydration with plain water has also been shown to improve the AFIs of patients with low amniotic fluid by approximately 30%, and in patients with normal amniotic fluid the AFI improved by 16%.[45] Flack and colleagues subsequently demonstrated that hypotonic hydration improved uteroplacental perfusion, which improved amniotic fluid volume.[28] A recent comparison of techniques for maternal hydration showed that PO and IV hypotonic solutions were equally effective at increasing the AFI, with changes in amniotic fluid correlating inversely with changes in maternal osmolality.[25] These results suggest that increasing maternal fluid volume while decreasing maternal osmolality may be effective in improving oligohydramnios.

Amnioinfusion

Intrapartum infusion of saline solution into the amniotic cavity has become an accepted practice for patients with low AFIs and repetitive, variable fetal heart rate decelerations.[1] Miyazaki and Nevarez demonstrated a dramatic 12-fold reduction in fetal heart rate decelerations in their study using transcervical amnioinfusion, but the procedure did not significantly change the cesarean section rate (18.4% vs. 25.5%, $P = .55$).[59] However, in this study, the AFI was not evaluated as part of the patient's selection. Subsequently, Strong and associates used amnioinfusion in patients with oligohydramnios and achieved a significant reduction in operative delivery for fetal distress by maintaining the AFI at greater than 8 cm.[90] Meconium passage; severe, variable decelerations; and end-stage bradycardia also were reduced. Prophylactic amnioinfusion is especially effective in preterm patients with PROM.[1] Transabdominal amnioinfusion has also been used effectively as prophylaxis against fetal distress before induction of labor in patients with oligohydramnios at term. However, complications from amnioinfusion, including uterine overdistention, hypertonus, and amniotic fluid embolism, warrant using this modality with cautious, close monitoring.[4]

In severe second-trimester oligohydramnios, serial transabdominal amnioinfusion has also been advocated as a therapeutic procedure to prevent pulmonary hypoplasia and improve outcome.[27] However, in Fisk and colleagues' limited series of nine patients, only 33% of the neonates survived.[27] In Locatelli and associates' study of 49 women with PROM prior to 26 weeks, 36 underwent serial amnioinfusion.[48] They were successful in maintaining the MVP over 2 cm in 11 patients. Their perinatal outcomes were similar to those in whom amnioinfusion was unnecessary: Pulmonary hypoplasia was reduced from 62% to 10%, with no abnormal neurologic outcomes. Further study remains necessary to determine whether repeated amnioinfusion in second-trimester oligohydramnios improves neonatal outcome.

Polyhydramnios

Polyhydramnios (or hydramnios) is a condition of amniotic fluid in excess of 2000 mL at term.[6] In general, patients with polyhydramnios have a better prognosis than those with oligohydramnios,[11,12] with the clinical management directed toward diagnosing fetal anomalies, correcting underlying maternal conditions (e.g., diabetes), and reducing the amniotic fluid volume in selected circumstances. Clinically, polyhydramnios is defined as an AFI of greater than the 95th percentile for gestational age,[62] over 25 cm at any gestational age,[70] or an MVP of 8 cm or more in depth.[12] Polyhydramnios can be diagnosed at as early as 16 weeks of gestation, but it is rare before 25 weeks of gestation. Because amniotic fluid normally decreases in the late third trimester,[52,62] polyhydramnios can be present with an AFI of less than 20 cm. An example of polyhydramnios is shown in Figure 21-13. Maternal symptoms of polyhydramnios include dyspnea, edema, increased weight, and distention of the uterus. Perinatal complications include preterm labor, PROM, umbilical cord prolapse, placental abruption, malpresentation, an increased risk of operative delivery, and postpartum hemorrhage.[55,68]

ETIOLOGY

The conditions associated with polyhydramnios are shown in Box 21-2. Historically, polyhydramnios has been idiopathic in approximately 35% to 65% of cases.[5,43] However, with advances in ultrasonographic capability, the etiology can now be detected in up to 90% of the cases of moderate to severe polyhydramnios.[39] Congenital anomalies that interfere with swallowing or intestinal absorption are the most commonly associated

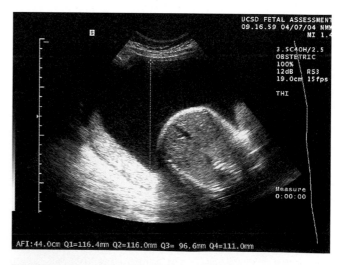

FIGURE 21-13. Polyhydramnios. The amniotic fluid index is 440 mm, and the single largest vertical pocket is greater than 80 mm.

BOX 21-2. Principal Diagnoses Associated with Polyhydramnios

Fetal
Chromosomal abnormalities
Congenital anomalies
    Gastrointestinal (duodenal or esophageal atresia,
        tracheoesophageal fistula, gastroschisis, omphalocele,
        diaphragmatic hernia)
    Craniofacial (anencephaly, holoprosencephaly, hydrocephaly,
        micrognathia, cleft palate)
    Pulmonary (cystic adenomatoid malformation, chylothorax)
    Cardiac (malformations, arrhythmias)
    Skeletal dysplasias
Fetal hydrops (immune or nonimmune)
Anemia (fetomaternal hemorrhage, parvovirus infection,
    isoimmunization, thalassemia)
Neuromuscular disorders (myotonic dystrophy)
Neoplasias (teratomas, hemangiomas)
Constitutional macrosomia

Maternal
Diabetes mellitus
    Gestational
    Adult onset (type II)

Placental
Chorioangioma
Twin-twin transfusion

Idiopathic

Adapted from Phelan JP, Martin GI: Polyhydramnios: Fetal and neonatal implications. Clin Perinatol 16:987, 1989; Hill LM et al: Polyhydramnios: Ultrasonically detected prevalence and neonatal outcome. Obstet Gynecol 69:21, 1987; Ben-Chetrit A et al: Hydramnios in the third trimester of pregnancy: A change in the distribution of accompanying anomalies as a result of early ultrasonographic prenatal diagnosis. Am J Obstet Gynecol 162:1344, 1990.

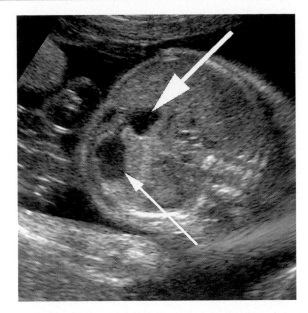

FIGURE 21-14. Duodenal atresia. Note the characteristic double bubble sign within the fetal abdomen illustrating the fluid-filled stomach *(small arrow)* and duodenum *(large arrow)* on this transverse view of the fetal abdomen.

conditions. The prevalence of congenital anomalies correlates with the severity of polyhydramnios, with a 2.6 times greater incidence of anomalies in severe polyhydramnios (75%) than in mild polyhydramnios (29%).[3] Aneuploidy is reported in 3% to 13% of the pregnancies associated with polyhydramnios.[89] The development of the Rh (Rhesus) immunoglobulin to prevent immune hydrops fetalis due to Rh isoimmunization (see Chapter 20) and improved control of diabetes in pregnancy (see Chapter 15) have decreased the incidence of polyhydramnios resulting from these conditions.

DIAGNOSTIC EVALUATION
Assess Fetal Anatomy
A detailed anatomic survey should be performed with ultrasound to search for possible congenital anomalies, paying particular attention to the gastrointestinal system for abnormalities that impair fetal swallowing and absorption of the fluid. With proximal obstruction (e.g., esophageal atresia or esophageal compression from

diaphragmatic hernia or a lung mass), the usual stomach "bubble" is absent. Distal obstruction may produce multiple cystic structures in the fetal abdomen (e.g., duodenal atresia may have a characteristic "double bubble" [Fig. 21-14]). The decreased fetal swallowing associated with anencephaly, trisomy 18, trisomy 21, muscular dystrophy, and skeletal dysplasia may result in polyhydramnios.

Ultrasound markers of aneuploidy should be viewed carefully and amniocentesis considered if any are identified.[89] Polyhydramnios combined with IUGR is particularly suspicious, with almost 40% having chromosomal aneuploidy in one series.[85] However, if the fetus is otherwise structurally normal, amniocentesis may not be warranted.

In patients with multiple gestation and polyhydramnios, twin-twin transfusion should be suspected. Vascular anastomoses can exist in monochorionic placentas, causing a donor-to-recipient flow of blood with subsequent vascular fluid overload and marked polyhydramnios in the recipient twin's sac. The donor twin is usually smaller and fluid restricted, typically appearing "stuck" (see Fig. 21-6), which can be missed during cursory ultrasound examination. Discordance in amniotic fluid volume often precedes growth disturbances in twins; therefore, serial ultrasound examinations are prudent in monozygotic twins (see Chapter 18).

Rule Out Maternal Diabetes
If the fetal abdominal circumference is significantly greater than the head circumference on ultrasound in a patient with otherwise unexplained polyhydramnios, maternal diabetes should be suspected and evaluated

with a glucose tolerance test (see Chapter 15). Polyhydramnios in diabetes is associated with increased perinatal morbidity and mortality beyond those of diabetes itself, and it is associated with poor glycemic control.[15] Polyhydramnios in maternal hyperglycemia results from osmotic diuresis in the fetus, with subsequently increased urine production. Macrosomia is also linked to polyhydramnios.

TREATMENT

If polyhydramnios is due to diabetes or erythroblastosis fetalis, the patient should be treated as outlined in Chapters 15 and 20. If nonlethal congenital anomalies are uncovered, appropriate pediatric specialists should be consulted for postnatal treatment. In patients with mild polyhydramnios (AFI of 24 to 40 cm), the perinatal outcome should be no different than that in patients with normal amniotic fluid volume if there are no chromosomal or anatomic abnormalities and the patient is not diabetic or isoimmunized.[86] However, in these patients, uterine overdistention may stimulate preterm uterine contractions, and labor may ensue. The patients should be counseled about the signs and symptoms of preterm labor and examined on a weekly or twice-weekly basis for early cervical changes. In women with severe polyhydramnios (AFI over 40 cm), amnioreduction or administration of prostaglandin inhibitors should be considered.

Amnioreduction

The removal of large volumes of excessive amniotic fluid may prolong pregnancy in patients with severe polyhydramnios. Caldeyro-Barcia and coworkers used transabdominal intrauterine pressure transducers to demonstrate that amnioreduction reduces the baseline tonus and contractility of the uterus in cases of polyhydramnios[9]; however, amniotic fluid invariably returns, making serial amnioreductions necessary for maternal dyspnea and preterm labor. In a series of 200 amnioreductions performed in 94 patients by Elliott and associates, the median volume removed was 1500 mL (range, 350 to 10,000 mL).[26] The goal is to restore a normal fluid volume (AFI less than 25 cm or MVP less than 8 cm). They reported a very low complication rate (1.5%), with delivery delayed to a median gestational age of 37 weeks. Complications of amnioreduction include labor, abruption, PROM, hypoproteinemia, and infection.

Prostaglandin Synthetase Inhibitors

Indomethacin is a potent inhibitor of prostaglandin synthesis and effective in reducing the amniotic fluid volume in over 90% of the cases of polyhydramnios.[46,60] Indomethacin reduces amniotic fluid by decreasing fetal urine production, enhancing fluid reabsorption by the fetal lungs, and increasing transmembrane absorption of excess amniotic fluid.[60] The dose is generally 25 mg PO every 6 hours but can range up to 100 mg every 4 to 8 hours, depending on the severity of polyhydramnios and clinical response.[60] Treatment should be discontinued once the fluid is reduced by one half

to one third of its original volume or when the AFI is less than 20 cm. Complications during indomethacin treatment include premature closure of the ductus arteriosus, renal complications, and necrotizing enterocolitis. Chronic ductal closure in utero can produce right-sided hypertension, fetal hydrops, and persistent pulmonary hypertension in the neonate.[93] The risk of ductal constriction is 5% at 27 weeks and increases to almost 50% by 32 weeks[93]; therefore, indomethacin treatment should be discontinued before 32 weeks to avoid iatrogenic side effects. Indomethacin treatment should be monitored with twice-weekly ultrasound amniotic fluid assessment and periodic fetal echocardiography to evaluate for ductal constriction.

Nonimmune Hydrops Fetalis

Hydrops fetalis is a condition of excess fluid accumulation in the fetus, with resulting high morbidity and mortality. In 1943, Potter distinguished *nonimmune hydrops fetalis* (NIHF) from immune hydrops fetalis in a group of hydropic neonates whose mothers were Rh positive.[71] Since then, with the development of the Rh immunoglobulin in the 1960s for the prevention of Rhesus disease (see Chapter 20), approximately 90% of the cases of hydrops fetalis are diagnosed as being due to nonimmune disease.[42,96] Improvements in ultrasound technology have allowed earlier antenatal diagnosis of conditions that would have otherwise presented as unexplained stillbirth, and those improvements have expanded our understanding of the underlying conditions that cause NIHF. The prognosis for NIHF patients remains poor, with PNM rates that range from 50% to over 90% in several series.[57,97] Maternal complications include preeclampsia (10% to 20%), malpresentation (24%), and an increased rate of cesarean delivery for fetal distress (29%).[34]

DIAGNOSIS

The antenatal diagnosis of NIHF is made by the ultrasonographic finding of fluid accumulation in the fetus or placenta in the absence of a circulating maternal antibody. Specifically, it is defined by identifying excess serous fluid in at least one space (ascites, pleural effusion, or pericardial effusion) accompanied by skin edema (greater than 5 mm thick) or in two potential spaces without the accompanying edema.[77] Ascites can be detected when a minimum of 50 mL is present in the fetal abdomen. Polyhydramnios and placental thickening (greater than 6 cm thick) also are associated with NIHF.[29] When oligohydramnios develops in patients with NIHF, it is an especially ominous finding.[29] The frequencies of ultrasonographic findings in NIHF are listed in Table 21-3. Typical sonographic findings in NIHF are shown in Figure 21-15.

PATHOPHYSIOLOGY

The basic mechanism for the formation of fetal hydrops is an imbalance of interstitial fluid production and the lymphatic return. Fluid accumulation in the fetus can result from congestive heart failure, obstructed lymphatic

TABLE 21-3. Principal Ultrasonographic Findings in Nonimmune Hydrops Fetalis

FINDINGS	PATIENTS
Ascites	85%
Scalp edema	59%
Thickened placenta	55%
Body wall edema	52%
Polyhydramnios	48%
Pleural effusion	33%
Pericardial effusion	22%

Adapted from Mahony BS et al: Severe nonimmune hydrops fetalis: Sonographic evaluation. Radiology 151:757, 1984.

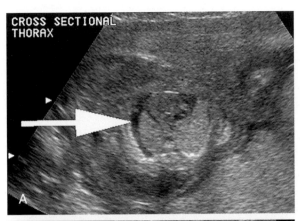

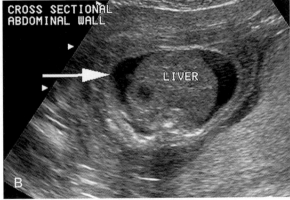

FIGURE 21-15. Classic hydrops fetalis on ultrasound. **A,** Thoracic findings. Note the pericardial effusion, bilateral pleural effusions *(large arrow)*, and skin thickening. **B,** Abdominal findings. Note the fetal ascites *(small arrow)*.

flow, or decreased plasma osmotic pressure.[40] The fetus is particularly susceptible to interstitial fluid accumulation because of its greater capillary permeability, compliant interstitial compartments, and vulnerability to venous pressure on lymphatic return. Compensatory mechanisms for maintaining homeostasis during hypoxia resulting from underlying disease include increased efficiency of oxygen extraction, redistribution of bloodflow to the brain and heart, and volume augmentation

to enhance cardiac output. Unfortunately, these mechanisms increase venous pressure and ultimately produce interstitial fluid accumulation and characteristic hydropic changes in the fetus. Increased venous pressure contributes to edema and effusion by increasing the capillary hydrostatic pressure and decreasing the lymphatic return. Furthermore, the hepatic synthesis of albumin may be impaired due to decreased hepatic perfusion and increased extramedullary hematopoiesis. Because albumin acts as the predominant oncotically active plasma protein, hypoalbuminemia increases transcapillary fluid movement at times of circulatory compromise. NIHF typically undergoes a steadily degenerative course unless the underlying cause is amenable to intrauterine therapy. Although NIHF is sometimes resolved spontaneously, cases diagnosed earlier in pregnancy have a worse prognosis than those diagnosed later in pregnancy.[41]

ETIOLOGY

The possible etiologies of NIHF are continually expanding as formerly unknown causes are being reported. An incomplete list of the conditions associated with NIHF is presented in Box 21-3.

The ventricles of the fetal heart are generally less compliant than they are later in life, so the conditions that increase preload or significantly restrict outflow ultimately lead to cardiac stress and right-sided heart failure. Therefore, whether the underlying disease causes low output failure (e.g., congenital heart block, cardiac anomalies, cardiomyopathy, or intrathoracic masses) or high output failure (e.g., vascular tumors such as chorioangioma and sacrococcygeal teratoma or vascular anastomoses in twin-twin transfusion), the result is cardiac failure and NIHF.

Anemia resulting from infection, intrinsic blood disease, or fetomaternal hemorrhage can cause NIHF. Severe anemia from infection, causing high output failure, accounted for approximately 18% of cases in one series,[91] although 5% to 10% is more typical. In the case of human parvovirus B19, the anemia is due to bone marrow suppression and aplasia; however, as the fetal immune system matures, the hydrops may become spontaneously resolved. Viral infections also can cause myocarditis and hepatitis that further worsen cardiac output and liver function. Intrinsic blood disorders such as α-thalassemia can produce severe fetal anemia. In women of Southeast Asian descent, α-thalassemia is the predominant cause of NIHF and is due to a complete absence of synthesis of the α chain of hemoglobin.[2] Anemia from fetomaternal hemorrhage (e.g., abruption, trauma, or amniocentesis) can be diagnosed by Kleihauer-Betke stain of the maternal blood or by elevated serum α-fetoprotein.

Other etiologies for NIHF include chromosomal abnormalities, intrathoracic masses, and metabolic diseases. Chromosomal anomalies frequently produce *cystic hygromas*, which are common in fetuses diagnosed with NIHF before 20 weeks. The most common chromosomal anomaly with cystic hygroma is Turner syndrome (45,XO), although trisomies 21, 18, and 13 can also

BOX 21-3. Principal Diagnoses Associated with Nonimmune Hydrops Fetalis

High Cardiac Output
Tachyarrhythmia
Twin-twin transfusion
Placental chorioangioma
Intracranial meningeal hemangioendothelioma
Truncus arteriosus
Cavernous hemangioma
Thyrotoxicosis

Fetal Anemia
β_1-Glucuronidase deficiency
Congenital leukemia
Hemoglobinopathy (e.g., α-thalassemia)
Hemolytic anemia
Hemorrhagic endovasculitis
Intracerebral hemorrhage
Massive fetomaternal hemorrhage
Methemoglobinemia
Glucose-6-phosphate dehydrogenase deficiency
Parvovirus B19

Infection
Toxoplasmosis
Rubella
Cytomegalovirus
Herpes simplex virus
Syphilis
Adenovirus

Genetic Abnormality
Trisomy 21
Trisomy 18
Trisomy 13
Turner syndrome (45,XO)
Triploidy
Noonan syndrome
XXXXY syndrome
Skeletal dysplasia

Arthrogryposis multiplex congenita
Multiple pterygium syndrome

Vascular Obstruction
Intrathoracic
Chylothorax
Cystic adenomatoid malformation
Diaphragmatic hernia
Intrapericardial teratoma
Mediastinal teratoma
Peribronchial tumor
Pleural effusion
Premature closure of the ductus arteriosus
Premature restriction of the foramen ovale
Pulmonary sequestration

Elsewhere
Absent ductus venosus
Renal vein thrombosis
Hemochromatosis
Umbilical cord torsion

Lymphatic Obstruction
Cystic hygroma
Hypomobility
Congenital myotonic dystrophy

Metabolic Disease
Gaucher disease
Gangliosidosis (GM_1)
Hurler syndrome
Tay-Sachs disease
Mucolipidosis, type 1
Niemann-Pick disease
Lysosomal storage disorders

Idiopathic

---

exhibit cystic hygroma. The cystic hygroma itself can cause hydrops by restricting lymphatic flow and increasing interstitial edema. These fetuses also often have heart defects that contribute to the formation of hydrops.[77] Intrathoracic masses (e.g., cystic adenomatoid malformation, pulmonary sequestration, and diaphragmatic hernia) restrict lymphatic flow and contribute to the formation of hydrops. Chylothorax can produce massive fetal pleural effusions that can result in pulmonary hypoplasia, carrying a 50% mortality rate if polyhydramnios accompanies the effusions.[98] Metabolic diseases (e.g., Gaucher, Tay-Sachs, gangliosidosis) may require parental testing for carrier status or direct fetal blood analysis for diagnosis.

The frequency of diagnoses associated with NIHF is shown in Table 21-4. In the past, cardiovascular malformation or arrhythmia was the most common finding, representing nearly 25% of the total cases. However, in a review of seven series reported since 1995,[*] chromosomal abnormalities were more common (present in over 25%, with cardiac abnormalities accounting for 15%). In Anandakumar and colleagues' series from Singapore,[2] anemia was present in 23%, reflecting the prevalence of α-thalassemia and Bart hemoglobinopathy in Southeast Asia. The etiology may remain undetermined before or after delivery in up to one third of the cases.[91]

DIAGNOSTIC EVALUATION

The diagnostic workup of the hydropic fetus should focus on finding the underlying cause. In general, the diagnostic workup should begin by obtaining the maternal history of hereditary or metabolic diseases, diabetes, or anemia; history of exposure to infection;

---

*References 2, 38, 41, 42, 57, 87, 91.

TABLE 21-4. Frequency of Diagnoses Associated with Nonimmune Hydrops Fetalis

STUDY, Y	ANEUPLOID	CARDIAC	SYNDROME	INFECTION	THORAX	ANEMIA	TTTS	OTHER	UNKNOWN	*n*
Sohan et al, 2001	23 (27.7)	11 (13.3)	5 (6.0)	13 (15.6)	12 (14.5)	1 (1.2)	5 (6.0)	2 (2.4)	11 (13.3)	83
Ismail et al, 2001	14 (25.5)	5 (9.1)	8 (14.5)	8 (14.5)	6 (10.9)	1 (1.8)	2 (3.6)	0	11 (20.0)	55
Heinonen et al, 2000	26 (44.8)	3 (5.2)	16 (27.6)	4 (6.9)	2 (3.4)	0	0	3 (5.2)	4 (6.9)	58
Swain et al, 1999	3 (7.5)	6 (15.0)	4 (10.0)	7 (17.5)	1 (2.5)	1 (2.5)	3 (7.5)	1 (2.5)	14 (35.0)	40
Iskaros et al, 1997	35 (77.8)	3 (6.7)	1 (2.2)	2 (4.4)	0	0	0	0	4 (8.9)	45
Anandakumar et al, 1996	10 (10.0)	23 (23.0)	9 (9.0)	2 (2.0)	5 (5.0)	23 (23.0)	3 (3.0)	1 (1.0)	24 (24.0)	100
McCoy et al, 1995	13 (15.9)	19 (23.2)	9 (11.0)	3 (3.7)	11 (13.4)	4 (4.9)	5 (6.1)	0	18 (22.0)	82
Total	124	70	52	39	37	30	18	7	86	463
Percent	(26.8)	(15.1)	(11.2)	(8.4)	(8.0)	(6.5)	(3.9)	(1.5)	(18.6)	

Numbers in parentheses indicate percent of total in individual series.
TTTS, twin-twin transfusion syndrome.
Data compiled from references 2, 38, 41, 42, 57, 87, and 91.

and use of medications. A detailed ultrasonographic fetal evaluation and maternal laboratory analysis should follow. A systematic approach is imperative with invasive fetal testing, using amniocentesis or cordocentesis to follow, based on initial maternal laboratory results. The recommended workup of a fetus with NIHF is outlined in Box 21-4.

Ultrasound

Once the diagnosis of NIHF has been made, a detailed ultrasound examination should be undertaken to determine the etiology and to better grade the prognosis. Scoring systems, which were developed to predict whether anemia is involved, may be useful for objectively assessing progress. Thereafter, serial sonographic examinations are indicated to follow the progression or improvement of disease with treatment.

The anatomy of the fetus should be carefully surveyed for structural malformation. The chest should be evaluated for mass lesions (e.g., cystic adenomatoid malformation, pulmonary sequestration, and diaphragmatic hernia) (Fig. 21-16). Echogenic areas within the fetal abdomen may indicate cystic fibrosis, viral infection, hepatic fibrosis, or polycystic kidneys. Echolucent areas may indicate bowel obstruction (e.g., duodenal atresia and volvulus). Neural tube defects and intracranial masses or defects should be ruled out. The fetal skeleton should be evaluated biometrically, and because skeletal dysplasias are associated with hydrops, bone mineralization, shape, and fractures should be noted. Fetal movement should be ascertained to assess neuromuscular disease. Progressive reduction in fetal movement is predictive of poor outcome and frequently precedes intrauterine death. The placenta and umbilical cord should be assessed for chorioangiomas, which can lead to hydrops from high output cardiac failure.

Doppler studies of bloodflow within the umbilical and middle cerebral arteries (MCAs) should be performed to detect placental resistance and fetal anemia. Elevated systolic-to-diastolic ratios indicate diminished umbilical artery diastolic bloodflow such as that seen in IUGR

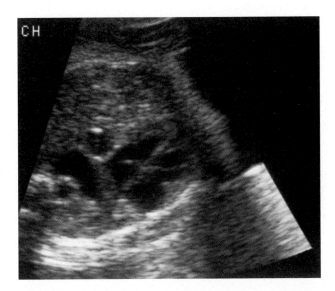

FIGURE 21-16. Diaphragmatic hernia. Transverse image at the level of the fetal heart demonstrating loops of bowel within the left side of the thorax and displacement of the heart to the right.

BOX 21-4. Antenatal Evaluation of Nonimmune Hydrops Fetalis

Maternal History
Age, parity, gestation
Hereditary or metabolic diseases, anemia
Recent infections or contacts
Medication use

Maternal Laboratory Evaluation
Complete blood cell count
Blood type, Rh, indirect Coombs antibody screen
Kleihauer-Betke stain
Syphilis, TORCH and parvovirus B19 titers
Culture for group B streptococcus, *Listeria*
Maternal triple screen
Oral glucose tolerance test
Optional as indicated
    Metabolic studies
    Hemoglobin electrophoresis
    G6PD, pyruvate kinase
    Autoimmune screen (SLE, anti-Ro and -La)

Ultrasonography
Identify anatomic abnormalities
Evaluate extent of edema and effusions
Rule out twin gestation
Doppler bloodflow assessment
    Umbilical artery
    Middle cerebral artery

Fetal Echocardiography
Evaluate cardiac malformation, arrhythmia

Amniocentesis
Karyotype
Culture or PCR for TORCH, parvovirus
Amniotic fluid α-fetoprotein
Restriction endonucleases (thalassemias)
Lecithin-sphingomyelin ratio, phosphatidyl glycerol to evaluate lung maturity

Fetal Blood Sampling
Karyotype
Complete blood cell count
Blood type; hemoglobin electrophoresis
Blood chemistries, albumin, gases
Culture or PCR for TORCH, parvovirus
Metabolic testing (Tay-Sachs, Gaucher, GM_1 gangliosidosis)

Fetal Effusion Sampling
Culture or PCR for TORCH, parvovirus
Protein content
Cell count and cytology

G6PD, glucose-6-phosphate dehydrogenase; PCR, polymerase chain reaction; SLE, systemic lupus erythematosus; TORCH, toxoplasmosis, other agents, rubella, cytomegalovirus, herpes simplex.
Modified from Swain S et al: Prenatal diagnosis and management of nonimmune hydrops fetalis. Aust N Z J Obstet Gynaecol 39:285, 1999.

fetuses. Absent or reverse diastolic flow in the umbilical arteries (see Fig. 21-10) indicates higher placental resistance and is associated with increased PNM.[44] Increased MCA peak systolic flow may indicate fetal anemia or hypoxia.[56]

Fetal Echocardiography

Because cardiac anomalies are common causes of NIHF, a complete fetal echocardiogram is necessary to rule out structural cardiac defects and evaluate cardiac rate and rhythm. Areas to be evaluated include the four-chamber view (to rule out a hypoplastic ventricle), atrioventricular septum (for septal defects), valves, and outflow tracts. Biventricular width should be measured because outer dimensions higher than the 95th percentile are associated with poor outcome.[10] Masses within the heart (e.g., teratoma, rhabdomyoma) may also be present. Cardiac arrhythmias are best evaluated using M-mode ultrasound; both tachyarrhythmias and bradyarrhythmias are implicated in NIHF. Complete fetal heart block warrants the evaluation of maternal connective tissue disease and autoimmune antibodies.

Laboratory Testing

Maternal blood testing should include blood typing and indirect Coombs antibody screening to rule out immune causes of the fetal hydrops. Congenital fetal infection is evaluated by the use of TORCH titers (*t*oxoplasmosis, *o*ther agents [congenital syphilis, parvovirus B19], *r*ubella, *c*ytomegalovirus, *h*erpes simplex). Fetal anemia is otherwise evaluated with a Kleihauer-Betke stain to evaluate fetomaternal hemorrhage and maternal hemoglobin electrophoresis if indicated by genetic and family histories. A maternal triple screen should be drawn because α-fetoprotein and human chorionic gonadotropin are often elevated in NIHF.[79] The results may give some indication of the etiology and prognosis of NIHF.

Invasive Fetal Testing

If maternal blood testing and ultrasound evaluation fail to provide a definitive cause for the NIHF, invasive testing may be necessary. Amniocentesis provides amniotic fluid samples for karyotype, viral culture, α-fetoprotein, and metabolic and enzymatic analysis. The analysis of chromosomes by fluorescent in situ hybridization can give preliminary karyotype results within days, whereas the results of the standard cell culture technique may take up to 2 weeks. Similarly, studies in which polymerase chain reaction is used to detect viral agents can give rapid results, whereas culture confirmation takes longer. In addition, lung maturity status can be evaluated to help develop plans for delivery.

If fetal anemia is suspected, cordocentesis for direct fetal blood sampling may be warranted. In addition to giving direct information on hematologic, metabolic, and chromosomal parameters, cordocentesis also provides access for intrauterine treatment. Additionally, the identification of specific immunoglobulins and isolation of viral antigens are possible. However, the risk of complications associated with cordocentesis is higher than that of amniocentesis (1% versus 0.3%), and it should be performed only by skilled individuals.

Postnatal Evaluation

If the prenatal evaluation failed to identify the etiology of the NIHF, postnatal evaluation should be undertaken (Box 21-5). Blood samples should be obtained for laboratory analysis in a manner similar to that for antenatal testing: complete blood cell count, hemoglobin electrophoresis, metabolism, chemistry, and karyotype studies. In addition, fetal blood type should be ascertained. The structural defects of the neonate should be evaluated with skeletal radiographs and ultrasound. A dysmorphology or genetic consultation also may be helpful, particularly to determine recurrence risks. In case of intrauterine or neonatal death an autopsy is recommended, with samples obtained for bacterial culture and karyotype studies. Chromosome cultures may fail in approximately one third of the cases if there is long-standing intrauterine death or prostaglandin use for terminating the pregnancy.

TREATMENT

In general terms, treatment depends on the underlying cause of NIHF and the gestational age of the fetus (Box 21-6). If the fetus is older than 34 weeks of gestation, has a mature lung profile, or is deteriorating from the effects of NIHF, delivery should be considered.

BOX 21-5. Postnatal Evaluation of Nonimmune Hydrops Fetalis

> **Laboratory Evaluation**
> Complete blood cell count
> Blood type, Rh factor
> Karyotype
> Blood chemistries, metabolic studies
> Hemoglobin electrophoresis, if indicated
>
> **Radiographic Imaging**
> Skeletal
> Ultrasonographic
> Cardiac
> Thoracic
> Abdominal
>
> **Dysmorphology Evaluation**
>
> **Autopsy**

BOX 21-6. Management of Nonimmune Hydrops Fetalis

> **Conservative Management in Hospital**
> Hospitalize the patient if
>   Fetal skin thickening
>   Pericardial effusion
>   Nonreactive nonstress test
>   Biophysical profile ≤ 6
>   Subjective decreased fetal movement
>   Gestational age below 32 to 34 weeks
> Treat underlying cause if possible
> Administer antenatal corticosteroids
> Monitor serial growth and effusion volumes
> Nonstress test and biophysical profile every 2 or 3 days
>
> **Deliver Patient**
> Gestational age over 34 weeks
> Mature fetal lung profile
> Biophysical profile persists < 6
> Maternal compromise (e.g., Mirror syndrome)

Otherwise, therapy is restricted to the treatment of anemia, cardiac arrhythmia, polyhydramnios, and pleural effusion. In the case of anemia, a single fetal transfusion often reverses the signs of hydrops, although serial transfusions may be required. Infection by parvovirus B19 is amenable to intrauterine transfusion, but neonatal stem cell transplantation may be needed for α-thalassemia. Fetomaternal hemorrhage is also treated with intrauterine transfusion. However, if the bleeding is ongoing, delivery may be required. Maternal digitalization may control tachyarrhythmias, but this procedure should be performed in consultation with a pediatric cardiologist (see Chapter 10). Amnioreduction can be performed to reduce maternal symptoms and preterm labor in excessive polyhydramnios. Pleurocentesis may decrease the incidence of pulmonary hypoplasia, which can complicate large pleural effusions. Occasionally, fetal paracentesis of marked ascites will facilitate vaginal delivery and prevent dystocia. However, the hydropic fetus may be less tolerant of hypoxic episodes that can occur in labor, so cesarean section is often used for delivery. The parents should still be fully informed about the guarded prognosis regardless of the delivery route.

Conservative Management

For patients in whom no cause can be ascertained, close observation for fetal decompensation is recommended, especially for gestations of less than 32 weeks. The patient should be hospitalized if ultrasonography demonstrates fetal edema or pericardial effusion or if antenatal testing with nonstress testing or a biophysical profile is less than reassuring. During the hospitalization, steroids should be administered to accelerate fetal lung maturity and reduce the risks of intraventricular hemorrhage. Serial ultrasound should be performed to follow growth and monitor fluid accumulation, with antepartum testing (nonstress testing and biophysical profile) continued every 2 or 3 days. During this time, continued efforts should be undertaken to ascertain the underlying etiology of the NIHF.

Fetal Surgery and Experimental Treatment
(See Chapter 11)

Occasionally, a hydropic fetus may be a candidate for in utero surgical intervention, such as the repair of a diaphragmatic hernia, congenital cystic adenomatoid malformation, or extralobar pulmonary sequestration. Urinary diversion in cases of bladder outlet obstruction also has been used, although the long-term prognosis remains poor. Paracentesis and thoracentesis have been attempted, but in Watson and Campbell's series,[97] 27% of the fetuses reaccumulated fluid within 48 hours. Goldberg and associates reported using a peritoneal shunt in a case of massive ascites of unknown etiology that improved the ascites, but the fetus died after developing other signs of NIHF.[33] Treatments with intraperitoneal injections of albumin have been attempted, with some promising results. In a series by Maeda and coworkers, 75% of the hydropic fetuses without pleural effusion who were treated with intraperitoneal albumin survived.[50] However, more than 90% of the fetuses with pleural effusion so treated died. Intravascular injection of albumin has also been attempted but without success. Shunts placed to drain pleural effusion have also been attempted, with improved survival.[64]

Delivery Indications

After 34 weeks of gestation, the best management for the hydropic fetus is delivery; indeed, between 32 and 34 weeks, few therapeutic maneuvers are likely to be of benefit compared with expert neonatal care. A mature fetal lung profile from amniocentesis or a degenerating fetal condition warrants even earlier delivery. However, the premature hydropic infant presents enormous management challenges with a high PNM rate. Therefore, the optimal timing of delivery should be discussed among the involved obstetricians, perinatologists, and neonatologists. Additional consultations with pediatric surgeons, cardiologists, and cardiothoracic surgeons may be necessary. In cases of maternal compromise from Mirror syndrome (maternal hydrops), a preeclampsia-like disease in mothers of hydropic fetuses, delivery is necessary.

PROGNOSIS

Overall, the prognosis for patients with NIHF is poor, particularly if there are known structural defects or its cause is unknown. In these circumstances the PNM rate approaches 100%. The structural cardiac defects associated with NIHF carry a PNM rate of 80% to 100%.[16] Conversely, the best prognosis is in cases of fetal arrhythmia, assuming that the arrhythmia is amenable to maternal treatment with antiarrhythmic medications.[77] For all other cases, the PNM rate may exceed 50%. Cases discovered early in pregnancy (before 24 weeks) have a worse prognosis,[57] whereas those discovered late in pregnancy may benefit from delivery and intensive neonatal care. However, most patients deliver preterm, with only 1 in 10 hydropic fetuses delivered after 37 weeks.[97] Indeed, in one large series,[40] 35% were delivered before 28 weeks of gestation and 60% between 28 and 36 weeks of gestation. Fortunately, the risk of recurrence in a subsequent pregnancy is low, although 10% of patients had recurrent hydrops in one series.[97]

SUMMARY

NIHF is a syndrome of multiple possible etiologies causing fluid overload in the fetus, with a common endpoint of high perinatal morbidity and mortality. Despite meticulous diagnostic study, up to 33% of cases remain idiopathic, even after delivery. Thoughtfully designed treatment regimens may help some fetuses, but delivery may be the only recourse in cases of a degenerating fetal condition. Therefore, antenatal testing should be directed toward identifying potentially viable fetuses, detecting lethal anomalies, and preventing maternal morbidity from unnecessary intervention.

REFERENCES

1. American College of Obstetricians and Gynecologists: Fetal Heart Rate Patterns: Monitoring, Interpretation, and Management. Washington, DC, American College of Obstetricians and Gynecologists, 1995, ACOG Technical Bulletin 207.
2. Anandakumar C et al: Management of non-immune hydrops: 8 years' experience. Ultrasound Obstet Gynecol 8:196, 1996.
3. Barkin SZ et al: Severe polyhydramnios: Incidence of anomalies. AJR Am J Roentgenol 148:155, 1987.
4. Bastide A et al: Ultrasound evaluation of amniotic fluid: Outcome of pregnancies with severe oligohydramnios. Am J Obstet Gynecol 154:895, 1986.
5. Ben-Chetrit A et al: Hydramnios in the third trimester of pregnancy: A change in the distribution of accompanying anomalies as a result of early ultrasonographic prenatal diagnosis. Am J Obstet Gynecol 162:1344, 1990.
6. Brace RA, Wolf EJ: Normal amniotic fluid volume changes throughout pregnancy. Am J Obstet Gynecol 161:382, 1989.
7. Brace RA: Physiology of amniotic fluid volume regulation. Clin Obstet Gynecol 40:280, 1997.
8. Bromley B et al: The natural history of oligohydramnios/polyhydramnios sequence in monochorionic diamniotic twins. Ultrasound Obstet Gynecol 2:317, 1992.
9. Caldeyro-Barcia R et al: Uterine contractility in polyhydramnios and the effects of withdrawal of the excess of amniotic fluid. Am J Obstet Gynecol 73:1238, 1957.
10. Carlson DE et al: Prognostic indicators of the resolution of nonimmune hydrops fetalis and survival of the fetus. Am J Obstet Gynecol 163:1785, 1990.
11. Chamberlain PF et al: Ultrasound evaluation of amniotic fluid volume: I. The relationship of marginal and decreased amniotic fluid volumes to perinatal outcome. Am J Obstet Gynecol 150:245, 1984.
12. Chamberlain PF et al: Ultrasound evaluation of amniotic fluid volume: II. The relationship of increased amniotic fluid volume to perinatal outcome. Am J Obstet Gynecol 150:250, 1984.
13. Chamberlain PF et al: Ovine fetal urine production following maternal intravenous furosemide administration. Am J Obstet Gynecol 151:815, 1985.

14. Chauhan SP et al: Perinatal outcome and amniotic fluid index in the antepartum and intrapartum periods: A meta-analysis. Am J Obstet Gynecol 181:1473, 1999.

15. Cousins L: Pregnancy complications among diabetic women: Review 1965-1985. Obstet Gynecol Surv 42:140, 1987.

16. Crawford DC et al: Prenatal detection of congenital heart disease: Factors affecting obstetric management and survival. Am J Obstet Gynecol 159:352, 1988.

17. Croom CS et al: Do semiquantitative amniotic fluid indexes reflect actual volume? Am J Obstet Gynecol 167:995, 1992.

18. Crowley P: Non quantitative estimation of amniotic fluid volume in suspected prolonged pregnancy. J Perinat Med 8:249, 1980.

19. Cruz AC et al: Continuous-wave Doppler ultrasound and decreased amniotic fluid volume in pregnant women with intact or ruptured membranes. Am J Obstet Gynecol 159:708, 1988.

20. D'Alton M et al: Serial thoracic versus abdominal circumference ratios for the prediction of pulmonary hypoplasia in premature rupture of the membranes remote from term. Am J Obstet Gynecol 166:658, 1992.

21. Damato N et al: Frequency of fetal anomalies in sonographically detected polyhydramnios. J Ultrasound Med 12:11, 1993.

22. Dashe JS et al: Hydramnios: Anomaly prevalence and sonographic detection. Obstet Gynecol 100:134, 2002.

23. DeLee JB: Physiology of pregnancy: Development of the ovum. In DeLee JB (ed): The Principles and Practice of Obstetrics. Philadelphia, WB Saunders Co, 1913, p 28.

24. Divon MY et al: Longitudinal measurement of amniotic fluid index in postterm pregnancies and its association with fetal outcome. Am J Obstet Gynecol 172:142, 1995.

25. Doi S et al: Effect of maternal hydration on oligohydramnios: A comparison of three volume expansion methods. Obstet Gynecol 92:525, 1998.

26. Elliott JP et al: Large-volume therapeutic amniocentesis in the treatment of hydramnios. Obstet Gynecol 84:1025, 1994.

27. Fisk NM et al: Diagnostic and therapeutic transabdominal amnioinfusion in oligohydramnios. Obstet Gynecol 78:270, 1991.

28. Flack NJ et al: Acute maternal hydration in third-trimester oligohydramnios: Effect on amniotic fluid volume, uteroplacental perfusion, and fetal blood flow and urine output. Am J Obstet Gynecol 173:1186, 1995.

29. Fleischer AC et al: Hydrops fetalis: Sonographic evaluation and clinical implications. Radiology 141:163, 1981.

30. Gilbert WM, Brace RA: The missing link in amniotic fluid regulation: Intramembranous absorption. Obstet Gynecol 74:748, 1989.

31. Gilbert WM et al: Amniotic fluid dynamics. Fetal Med Rev 3:89, 1991.

32. Gilbert WM et al: Potential route for fetal therapy: Intramembranous absorption of intraamniotically injected furosemide. Am J Obstet Gynecol 172:1471, 1995.

33. Goldberg JD et al: Prenatal shunting of fetal ascites in nonimmune hydrops fetalis. Am J Perinatol 3:92, 1986.

34. Graves GR, Baskett TF: Nonimmune hydrops fetalis: Antenatal diagnosis and management. Am J Obstet Gynecol 148:563, 1984.

35. Hadi HA et al: Premature rupture of the membranes between 20 and 25 weeks' gestation: Role of amniotic fluid volume in perinatal outcome. Am J Obstet Gynecol 170:1139, 1994.

36. Hanssens M et al: Fetal and neonatal effects of treatment with angiotensin-converting enzyme inhibitors in pregnancy. Obstet Gynecol 78:128, 1991.

37. Hedriana HL, Moore TR: Accuracy limits of ultrasonographic estimation of human fetal urinary flow rate. Am J Obstet Gynecol 171:989, 1994.

38. Heinonen S et al: Etiology and outcome of second trimester non-immunologic fetal hydrops. Acta Obstet Gynecol Scand 79:15, 2000.

39. Hill LM et al: Polyhydramnios: Ultrasonically detected prevalence and neonatal outcome. Obstet Gynecol 69:21, 1987.

40. Im SS et al: Nonimmunologic hydrops fetalis. Am J Obstet Gynecol 148:566, 1984.

41. Iskaros J et al: Outcome of nonimmune hydrops fetalis diagnosed during the first half of pregnancy. Obstet Gynecol 90:321, 1997.

42. Ismail KM et al: Etiology and outcome of hydrops fetalis. J Matern Fetal Med 10:175, 2001.

43. Jacoby HE, Charles D: Clinical conditions associated with hydramnios. Am J Obstet Gynecol 94:910, 1966.

44. Karsdorp VH et al: Clinical significance of absent or reversed end diastolic velocity waveforms in umbilical artery. Lancet 344:1664, 1994.

45. Kilpatrick SJ, Safford KL: Maternal hydration increases amniotic fluid index in women with normal amniotic fluid. Obstet Gynecol 81:49, 1993.

46. Kirshon B et al: Influence of short-term indomethacin therapy on fetal urine output. Obstet Gynecol 72:51, 1988.

47. Lauria MR et al: Pulmonary hypoplasia: pathogenesis, diagnosis, and antenatal prediction. Obstet Gynecol 86:466, 1995.

48. Locatelli A et al: Role of amnioinfusion in the management of premature rupture of the membranes at <26 weeks' gestation. Am J Obstet Gynecol 183:878, 2000.

49. Lombardi SJ et al: Umbilical artery velocimetry as a predictor of adverse outcome in pregnancies complicated by oligohydramnios. Obstet Gynecol 74:338, 1989.

50. Maeda H et al: Intrauterine treatment on non-immune hydrops fetalis. Early Hum Dev 29:241, 1992.

51. Magann EF et al: Amniotic fluid volume in normal singleton pregnancies. Obstet Gynecol 90:524, 1997.

52. Magann EF et al: The amniotic fluid index, single deepest pocket, and two-diameter pocket in normal human pregnancy. Am J Obstet Gynecol 182:1581, 2000.

53. Magann EF et al: Dye-dilution techniques using aminohippurate sodium: Do they accurately reflect amniotic fluid volume? J Matern Fetal Neonat Med 11:167, 2002.

54. Manning FA et al: Qualitative amniotic fluid volume determination by ultrasound: Antepartum detection of intrauterine growth retardation. Am J Obstet Gynecol 139:254, 1981.

55. Many A et al: The association between polyhydramnios and preterm delivery. Obstet Gynecol 86:389, 1995.

56. Mari G: Noninvasive diagnosis by Doppler ultrasonography of fetal anemia due to maternal red-cell alloimmunization. N Engl J Med 342:9, 2000.

57. McCoy MC et al: Non-immune hydrops after 20 weeks' gestation: Review of 10 years' experience with suggestions for management. Obstet Gynecol 85:578, 1995.

58. McEnerney JK, McEnerney LN: Unfavorable outcome after intraamniotic injection of methylene blue. Obstet Gynecol 61:35S, 1983.

59. Miyazaki FS, Nevarez F: Saline amnioinfusion for relief of repetitive variable decelerations: A prospective randomized trial. Am J Obstet Gynecol 153:301, 1985.

60. Moise KJ Jr: Polyhydramnios. Clin Obstet Gynecol 40:266, 1997.

61. Moore TR et al: The reliability and predictive value of an amniotic fluid scoring system in severe second-trimester oligohydramnios. Obstet Gynecol 73:739, 1989.

62. Moore TR, Cayle JE: The amniotic fluid index in normal human pregnancy. Am J Obstet Gynecol 162:1168, 1990.

63. Moore TR: Superiority of the four-quadrant sum over the single-deepest-pocket technique in ultrasonographic identification of abnormal amniotic fluid volumes. Am J Obstet Gynecol 163:762, 1990.

64. Negishi H et al: Outcome of non-immune hydrops fetalis and a fetus with hydrothorax and/or ascites: With some trials of intrauterine treatment. J Perinat Med 25:71, 1997.

65. Newbould MJ et al: Oligohydramnios sequence: The spectrum of renal malformations. Br J Obstet Gynecol 101:598, 1994.

66. Nicolaides KH et al: Relation of rate of urine production to oxygen tension in small-for-gestational-age fetuses. Am J Obstet Gynecol 162:387, 1990.

67. Nyberg DA et al: Age-adjusted ultrasound risk assessment for fetal Down's syndrome during the second trimester: Description of the method and analysis of 142 cases. Ultrasound Obstet Gynecol 12:8, 1998.

68. Panting-Kemp A et al: Idiopathic polyhydramnios and perinatal outcome. Am J Obstet Gynecol 181:1079, 1999.

69. Phelan JP et al: Amniotic fluid measurements during pregnancy. J Reprod Med 32:601, 1987.

70. Phelan JP, Martin GI: Polyhydramnios: Fetal and neonatal implications. Clin Perinatol 16:987, 1989.

71. Potter EL: Universal edema of the fetus unassociated with erythroblastosis. Am J Obstet Gynecol 46:130, 1943.

72. Powers DR, Brace RA: Fetal cardiovascular and fluid responses to maternal volume loading with lactated Ringer's or hypotonic solution. Am J Obstet Gynecol 165:1504, 1991.

73. Pritchard JA: Fetal swallowing and amniotic fluid volume. Obstet Gynecol 28:606, 1966.

74. Quetel TA et al: Amnioinfusion: An aid in the ultrasonographic evaluation of severe oligohydramnios in pregnancy. Am J Obstet Gynecol 167:333, 1992.

75. Rabinowitz R et al: Measurement of fetal urine production in normal pregnancy by real-time ultrasonography. Am J Obstet Gynecol 161:1264, 1989.

76. Roberts D et al: The fetal outcome in pregnancies with isolated reduced amniotic fluid volume in the third trimester. J Perinat Med 26:390, 1998.

77. Romero R et al: Nonimmune hydrops fetalis. In Romero R et al (eds): Prenatal Diagnosis of Congenital Anomalies. Norwalk, Conn, Appleton & Lange, 1988, p 414.

78. Rutherford SE et al: Four-quadrant assessment of amniotic fluid volume: Interobserver and intraobserver variation. J Reprod Med 32:587, 1987.

79. Saller DN Jr et al: The detection of non-immune hydrops through second-trimester maternal serum screening. Prenat Diagn 16:431, 1996.

80. Schrimmer DB, Moore TR: Sonographic evaluation of amniotic fluid volume. Clin Obstet Gynecol 45:1026, 2002.

81. Seitchik J: Water and electrolyte metabolism in normal pregnancy. Clin Obstet Gynecol 7:185, 1964.

82. Sepulveda W et al: Accuracy of prenatal diagnosis of renal agenesis with color flow imaging in severe second-trimester oligohydramnios. Am J Obstet Gynecol 173:1788, 1995.

83. Shenker L et al: Significance of oligohydramnios complicating pregnancy. Am J Obstet Gynecol 164:1597, 1991.

84. Shipp TD et al: Outcome of singleton pregnancies with severe oligohydramnios in the second and third trimesters. Ultrasound Obstet Gynecol 7:108, 1996.

85. Sickler GK et al: Polyhydramnios and fetal intrauterine growth restriction: Ominous combination. J Ultrasound Med 16:609, 1997.

86. Smith CV et al: Relation of mild idiopathic polyhydramnios to perinatal outcome. Obstet Gynecol 79:387, 1992.

87. Sohan K et al: Analysis of outcome in hydrops fetalis in relation to gestational age at diagnosis: Cause and treatment. Acta Obstet Gynecol Scand 80:726, 2001.

88. Sohl BD et al: Utility of minor ultrasonographic markers in the prediction of abnormal fetal karyotype at a prenatal diagnostic center. Am J Obstet Gynecol 181:898, 1999.

89. Stoll CG et al: Study of 156 cases of polyhydramnios and congenital malformations in a series of 118,265 consecutive births. Am J Obstet Gynecol 165:586, 1991.

90. Strong TH et al: Prophylactic intrapartum amnioinfusion: A randomized clinical trial. Am J Obstet Gynecol 162:1370, 1990.

91. Swain S et al: Prenatal diagnosis and management of nonimmune hydrops fetalis. Aust N Z J Obstet Gynaecol 39:285, 1999.

92. Tomada S et al: Amniotic fluid volume and fetal swallowing rate in sheep. Am J Physiol 249:R133, 1985.

93. Van den Veyver IB et al: The effect of gestational age and fetal indomethacin levels on the incidence of constriction of the fetal ductus arteriosus. Obstet Gynecol 82:500, 1993.

94. Vergani P et al: Risk factors for pulmonary hypoplasia in second-trimester premature rupture of membranes. Am J Obstet Gynecol 170:1359, 1994.

95. Vintzileos AM et al: Comparison of six different ultrasonographic methods for predicting lethal fetal pulmonary hypoplasia. Am J Obstet Gynecol 161:606, 1989.

96. Warsof SL et al: Immune and non-immune hydrops. Clin Obstet Gynecol 29:533, 1986.

97. Watson J, Campbell S: Antenatal evaluation and management in nonimmune hydrops fetalis. Obstet Gynecol 67:589, 1986.

98. Weber AM, Philipson EH: Fetal pleural effusion: A review and meta-analysis for prognostic indicators. Obstet Gynecol 79:281, 1992.

99. Wladimiroff JW, Campbell S: Fetal urine-production rates in normal and complicated pregnancy. Lancet 1:151, 1974.

100. Zhang J et al: Isolated oligohydramnios is not associated with adverse perinatal outcomes. BJOG 111:220, 2004.

22 Perinatal Infections

Mark H. Yudin and Bernard Gonik

Infection of the female urogenital tract is a common complication of pregnancy. Responsible pathogens include a vast array of viruses, bacteria, and other organisms. Infections complicating pregnancy may be the result of a single pathogen or may be polymicrobial, which commonly occurs with other genital tract infections.

Infectious complications during pregnancy are serious and lead to an increase in morbidity and mortality for both patients—the fetus and the mother. Premature rupture of the membranes, premature labor, and preterm delivery can be the result of infection. Pyelonephritis, endometritis, and sepsis are common causes of maternal morbidity. Neonatal infection, occurring at a time when the immature immunologic system is less protective, may predispose the patient to meningitis, pneumonia, sepsis, or death.

Early diagnosis and aggressive treatment of infection during pregnancy may substantially lower the associated morbidity and mortality. In this chapter the discussion focuses on common clinical disorders and specific pathogens causing infection during pregnancy.

CLINICAL DISORDERS

Urinary Tract Infection

Urinary tract infections are the most common bacterial infections in adult women and the most common medical complication of pregnancy. They may be classified as asymptomatic or symptomatic (acute cystitis or pyelonephritis).

There are many factors present during gestation that predispose pregnant women to symptomatic urinary tract infection. Among these are significant physiologic changes that increase risk. The "physiologic hydronephrosis" of pregnancy, which is the dilation of the ureters and renal pelves, results from decreased muscle tone surrounding the ureters (caused by progesterone) and the mechanical obstruction of the enlarging uterus. This condition contributes to a slower rate of passage of urine through the urinary tract. Decreased bladder muscle tone leads to increased bladder capacity and incomplete emptying. These changes predispose the patient to vesicoureteric reflux, which facilitates the ascending spread of bacteria. In addition to the physiologic changes of the urinary tract, there are physicochemical properties of urine during pregnancy that may predispose women to symptomatic urinary tract infection. Urinary pH is elevated, glycosuria is common, and excess excretion of estrogen may enhance the capability of certain bacteria to cause infection. Clinical conditions such as anemia and sickle cell trait have also been reported to predispose the patient to urinary tract bacterial colonization.

Asymptomatic bacteriuria, defined as greater than 100,000 organisms per milliliter on culture in the urine of a patient who lacks symptoms, is present in 4% to 7% of the pregnant population. Dipstick testing has been shown to be unreliable for the diagnosis of asymptomatic bacteriuria, and urine culture should be used. The prevalence of bacteriuria is related to lower socioeconomic status, sickle cell trait, and increased parity. Women with neurogenic urinary retention secondary to spinal cord injuries, diabetes mellitus, and structural abnormalities of the urinary tract are also at increased risk. Although pregnant women have about the same prevalence as nonpregnant, sexually active women of reproductive age, pregnant women are more likely to develop symptoms of acute infection. As in nonpregnant women, *Escherichia coli* is by far the most common organism (80% to 90%).[71,140] *Proteus mirabilis, Klebsiella pneumoniae,* and group B (β-hemolytic) streptococcus (GBS) are also commonly identified pathogens.

The goal of antibiotic treatment for pregnant women with asymptomatic bacteriuria is sterile urine for the remainder of the pregnancy, which is usually accomplished with a short course of a sulfonamide, ampicillin, or nitrofurantoin and monthly culture surveillance. Several recent studies have documented increasing antibiotic resistance in *E. coli*, especially to ampicillin.[71,96] However, isolates were almost uniformly susceptible to nitrofurantoin. Recurrences are common after treatment (approximately one third of the patients), and suppressive therapy with a short course of antibiotics should be instituted once the culture is again cleared.[104]

CYSTITIS IN PREGNANCY

Acute cystitis occurs in 1.3% of pregnancies. It seems to be a clinical entity separate from asymptomatic bacteriuria and acute pyelonephritis. In contrast to these two conditions, cystitis is not usually preceded by bacteriuria in the initial screening cultures, does not recur as frequently, and is not the result of fluorescent-positive, antibody-coated bacteria that suggest upper urinary tract involvement. The most common pathogen is again *E. coli,* and antibiotic treatment with ampicillin, sulfonamides, or nitrofurantoin is appropriate. The duration of therapy should be 3 days, and longer courses of medication are usually unnecessary and may contribute to the development of bacterial resistance.

ACUTE PYELONEPHRITIS IN PREGNANCY

The incidence of acute pyelonephritis during pregnancy is 1% to 2.5%, with an estimated recurrence rate of 10% to 18% during the same pregnancy. Clinical manifestations include fever and chills, costovertebral angle tenderness, nausea, vomiting, and symptoms of lower urinary tract infection, such as dysuria, frequency, and urgency. The pregnant patient may become quite ill, with severe dehydration, transient renal dysfunction, respiratory distress, and septicemia.

The microbiology of pyelonephritis is similar to that described for lower urinary tract disease in pregnancy, with *E. coli* being the most common bacteria isolated. Initial antibiotic therapy includes the use of an aminoglycoside or an advanced-generation penicillin or cephalosporin. Therapy can be tailored to the results of the urine culture when these data become available. Ampicillin-resistant *E. coli* is increasingly identified, with studies documenting resistance in almost 50% of cases.[62,145] The clinical response to treatment is usually rapid, with 85% of cases showing a decrease in temperature elevation within 48 hours. The recurrence of pyelonephritis may be as high as 60% if suppressive antimicrobial therapy is not maintained throughout the duration of the pregnancy. Renal calculi and anatomic obstruction can be responsible for the failure to respond to otherwise effective antibiotic treatment. Ultrasonography, limited-exposure intravenous pyelography, or magnetic resonance imaging may be used in the evaluation of a patient with a persistent fever or worsening symptoms.

Acute respiratory distress more frequently complicates the treatment of pyelonephritis in pregnant than nonpregnant women. Those with the highest fevers and highest maternal heart rates and those receiving concomitant tocolytic agents may be at the greatest risk.[139] However, clinical parameters do not clearly delineate the women who are at risk for this potentially fatal complication.

The effect of pyelonephritis on the outcome of pregnancy is unclear. In the preantibiotic era, untreated pyelonephritis was associated with a 20% to 50% risk of prematurity. However, antibiotic treatment significantly reduces the risk of preterm delivery. One study reporting on 107 cases of acute pyelonephritis in 103 gravidas noted no increase in prematurity or in infants of low birthweight when compared with a control group.[47] Another study documented a significant decrease in uterine contractile activity after the administration of intravenous antibiotics.[91] The recognized maternal morbidity and potential perinatal morbidity mandate the prompt and appropriate treatment of acute pyelonephritis in the pregnant patient.

Preterm Labor and Premature Rupture of Membranes

Prematurity complicates 7% to 10% of all births and is responsible for a disproportionately large percentage of perinatal morbidity and mortality. Although the various mechanisms underlying the premature rupture of membranes (PROM) and preterm labor (PTL) are imperfectly understood, there is a growing body of evidence to suggest that between 20% and 40% of preterm births (PTBs) may have intrauterine infection or inflammation as a precipitating factor.

There are many examples of this evidence suggesting an association between PTB and infection. Histologic chorioamnionitis is more common in cases of PTB, and clinical infections are observed more frequently in mothers and neonates after PTB. Several genital tract isolates are known to be associated with PTB, and 10% to 15% of amniotic fluid cultures from women with PTB are positive for infectious microorganisms. Prostaglandin and cytokine production are increased after infection and inflammation. In some clinical trials, antibiotic treatment of infections has been shown to lower the PTB rate.[53] In addition to human data, there are also data from animal trials linking infection and PTB.

PRETERM PREMATURE RUPTURE OF MEMBRANES

Premature rupture of membranes (PROM) is responsible for one third of all PTBs, accounting for 130,000 births in the United States annually.[101] Neonatal morbidity and mortality are associated with gestational age at birth. Antibiotics have been used in women with preterm PROM to attempt to prolong the time from membrane rupture to the onset of contractions and delivery and to decrease infectious morbidity.

A number of trials have been reported in which various antibiotics were studied in a randomized, prospective fashion. When taken together, several findings become important. Antibiotics administered to women with preterm PROM do prolong gestation. In addition, a decrease in the incidence of intra-amniotic infection (IAI) has been reported. A decrease in perinatal mortality is difficult to prove, although these studies suggest a trend toward fewer stillbirths and infant deaths due to sepsis. Culture-proven neonatal sepsis, respiratory distress syndrome, intraventricular hemorrhage, and pneumonia are seen less frequently when antibiotics are used in women with preterm PROM.[89,90] These benefits are more pronounced at the earlier gestational ages (less than 32 weeks of gestation). Between 32 and 36 weeks, it is less obvious that expectant management and antibiotics are as beneficial.

The optimum antibiotic regimen for the patient with preterm PROM has not yet been defined. The evidence appears to be the strongest for erythromycin with respect to both the prolongation of pregnancy and prevention of neonatal morbidity.[75,90] Initial treatment with broad-spectrum antibiotics such as ampicillin plus erythromycin or an extended-spectrum penicillin or cephalosporin is reasonable. After 48 hours, oral therapy should be continued to finish a week-long course. GBS carriers should be treated with penicillin.

ANTIBIOTICS IN PRETERM BIRTH PREVENTION

The use of antibiotics in pregnancies complicated by PTL with intact membranes has likewise been studied. In this clinical scenario, antibiotics do not seem to prolong pregnancy or decrease neonatal morbidity.[43] In other situations, antibiotics have been helpful in preventing PTB. *Neisseria gonorrhoeae* and *Chlamydia trachomatis* should be routinely screened for in pregnant women. Infection with *C. trachomatis* is an independent risk factor for PTB.[5] Treatment of both infections will decrease PROM and PTB, improve neonatal birthweight, and prevent transmission of these genital tract infections. Bacterial vaginosis is another risk factor for PTL, especially in women with a prior history of PTL or PTB. Screening for and treating bacterial vaginosis in such women have been shown to improve pregnancy outcome in some studies[81,82] but not others.[74] It is standard to screen for and treat asymptomatic bacteriuria in pregnancy, which is associated with maternal pyelonephritis and PTB. Although the treatment of maternal GBS colonization is not recommended, antibiotic treatment for group B streptococcal bacteriuria has been shown to decrease the PTB rate. While it is reasonable to treat symptomatic *Trichomonas vaginalis* infection, the screening for and treatment of asymptomatic infection are not recommended and have been shown to increase the rate of PTB.[78] Finally, recent evidence suggests that periodontal disease is a risk factor for PTL and PTB. Treatment with teeth and root scaling has been shown to decrease these risks, although the addition of antibiotics did not decrease the risks further.[72]

Intra-Amniotic Infection

Clinically evident intrauterine infection complicates 1% to 10% of pregnancies, leading to an increase in maternal morbidity and perinatal morbidity and mortality. A variety of terms have been used for this clinical entity. In this chapter, the term *intra-amniotic infection* (IAI) is used to distinguish the overt clinical infection from bacterial colonization of the amniotic fluid or histologic inflammation of the umbilical cord or placenta.

PATHOPHYSIOLOGY

Before the rupture of membranes and labor, the amniotic cavity is almost always sterile. The cervical mucus, placental membranes, and amniotic fluid provide physical and chemical barriers to bacterial invasion. However, there are several ways that bacteria can gain access to the uterine cavity, causing infection. Instrumentation such as that used during amniocentesis, percutaneous umbilical blood sampling, and intrauterine transfusion can introduce bacteria into the previously sterile environment. Viruses most commonly infect the fetus and amniotic fluid by means of a hematogenous

spread through the placenta and umbilical cord. *Listeria monocytogenes* may cause fulminant IAI by this route; however, the most likely route of infection associated with IAI is the ascending one.

Recent studies have demonstrated that IAI is a polymicrobial infection involving aerobic and anaerobic bacteria. When comparing patients in labor with clinical evidence of IAI with matched controls, Gibbs and colleagues found that the infected patients had greater numbers of more virulent organisms cultured from their amniotic fluid.[54] The infectious organisms included *Bacteroides* spp., 25%; GBS, 12%; other streptococci, 13%; *E. coli*, 10%; and other gram-negative rods. The organisms of bacterial vaginosis, namely *Gardnerella vaginalis*, *Mycoplasma hominis*, and anaerobes, have also been found in the amniotic fluid of women with IAI, suggesting that women with bacterial vaginosis may be more likely to develop IAI. Chlamydia does not seem to contribute to the incidence of IAI, and the role of *Ureaplasma urealyticum* has yet to be defined.

There is a growing body of evidence that with the microbial invasion and inflammation of the amniotic cavity, cytokines are produced. Elevated levels of interleukin-6 and interleukin-8 have been documented in the amniotic fluid, uterine tissue, and cord blood of patients with IAI.[70] It is hypothesized that these proinflammatory cytokines may contribute to the increased risk of PTB observed in women with IAI.

DIAGNOSIS

The clinical diagnosis of IAI is made in the presence of maternal fever, a foul odor of the amniotic fluid, and leukocytosis (Box 22-1), which are the three most common findings. Maternal and fetal tachycardia are variably present. Uterine tenderness and foul-smelling amniotic fluid are specific signs but are present in only a minority of cases.

The laboratory diagnosis of IAI is very nonspecific. Peripheral blood leukocytosis commonly occurs in normal labor. Maternal bacteremia occurs in only 10% of women with IAI. Positive Gram stains and bacterial colony counts of greater than 10^2/mL of amniotic fluid are associated with clinical infection. However, in unselected patients with ruptured membranes, bacteria are often demonstrated in the amniotic fluid despite the lack of clinical evidence of infection.

Clinical risk factors associated with IAI include the duration of membrane rupture, transcervical instrumentation, and digital examinations. Patients with premature PROM are more likely to experience IAI.

BOX 22-1. Clinical Diagnosis of Intra-amniotic Infection

Maternal fever
Foul-smelling amniotic fluid
Leukocytosis
Uterine tenderness
Maternal and/or fetal tachycardia

Patients with intact membranes have occasionally had IAI after undergoing amniocentesis or percutaneous umbilical blood sampling, and more frequently after placement of a cervical cerclage.

After labor is completed, the diagnosis of IAI may be made by the symptoms and signs observed in the neonate or child. Neonatal sepsis that is blood culture positive is relatively uncommon (8% to 12%), even in the presence of overt maternal IAI.[148] Most cases of early-onset neonatal sepsis begin before delivery, even if the diagnosis is not confirmed until later. The neonatal response to infection is nonspecific, and the diagnosis of sepsis immediately after delivery is difficult. The earliest signs are subtle and include changes in color, tone, activity, feeding, and poor temperature control. Late signs may include dyspnea, apnea, arrhythmias, hepatosplenomegaly, seizures, bulging fontanelle, and irritability. Signs of meningitis or pneumonia or both may follow. Evidence has been accumulating to suggest an association between IAI and neonatal cerebral palsy, although the relationship is still incompletely understood.[111,147] Overall, perinatal morbidity and mortality, particularly in the preterm infant, are increased in association with maternal IAI.

MATERNAL TREATMENT

Antibiotic therapy should be instituted on establishing the diagnosis of IAI. Immediate intrapartum treatment benefits both the mother and the neonate. Broad-spectrum, intravenously administered antibiotics (frequently ampicillin and an aminoglycoside) should be initiated. Although it is more frequently performed in the presence of IAI, cesarean section is undertaken only for obstetric indications. Clindamycin or other agents with anaerobic coverage are added to the therapeutic regimen to reduce the risk of antibiotic failure during the postoperative period if cesarean section is undertaken. The length of antibiotic therapy has been debated, and recent reports suggest that shorter courses of treatment may be adequate.[42] Complications from maternal infection are more frequent after a cesarean section than after vaginal delivery and may include endometritis (up to 30%), wound infection (3% to 5%), sepsis (2% to 4%), pelvic abscess, and septic pelvic thrombophlebitis.[148]

Bacterial Vaginosis

Bacterial vaginosis is the most common infectious cause of vaginitis in reproductive-aged women. In 1955, Gardner and Dukes[52] described the classic clinical findings of this type of vaginitis: (1) a gray-white homogeneous discharge, (2) elevated pH of vaginal discharge to more than 4.5, (3) a fishy amine odor on mixing the discharge with 10% potassium hydroxide, and (4) clue cells on wet preparation. Vaginal culture reveals a variety of organisms, including *G. vaginalis*, *Mobiluncus* spp., a wide range of anaerobic organisms, and *M. hominis*. *Lactobacillus,* normally the dominant organism in the vagina and responsible for the low vaginal pH, is absent or present only in low numbers. The prevalence of bacterial vaginosis is 10% to 30% in pregnant women, the majority of whom are asymptomatic. The most common complaint among symptomatic women is the malodorous vaginal discharge.

A number of studies have linked bacterial vaginosis with adverse pregnancy outcomes, including PTB associated with PTL or preterm PROM or both; chorioamnionitis; postpartum endomyometritis; and post-cesarean wound infections.[79,88] The exact mechanisms linking bacterial vaginosis with these adverse outcomes remain unclear, but it has been hypothesized that the association may be explained by the spread of bacteria and inflammation from the lower to the upper genital tract.[76] Some treatment trials of bacterial vaginosis in pregnancy have led to a reduction in the rate of PTB in women at high risk.[63,85,98] In other trials, women at low risk for PTB did not benefit from antibiotic treatment, and it did not lower the PTB rate.[58,74,85]

In nonpregnant women, oral or vaginal metronidazole or clindamycin can be used effectively to treat bacterial vaginosis. In pregnancy, the use of oral (systemic) therapy has been shown to reduce adverse pregnancy outcomes in women at high risk,[63,85,98] while studies evaluating the use of topical clindamycin cream have either failed to show a decrease in PTB or have showed trends toward PTL, low birthweight, or perinatal infections.[73,74,86,142] In a recent study by Yudin and co-workers, oral and vaginal metronidazole were equally efficacious in producing a therapeutic cure for bacterial vaginosis in pregnant women.[149] Metronidazole is extremely effective in the treatment of this condition in nonpregnant women. However, because of reported carcinogenicity in rodents and mutagenicity in bacteria, some clinicians have been reluctant to use this drug during the first trimester of pregnancy. A meta-analysis that reviewed the records of over 200,000 women did not find an association between metronidazole use in the first trimester of pregnancy and birth defects.[19] Ampicillin is curative only 40% to 50% of the time, whereas sulfonamides and erythromycin are not significantly more successful than placebo. Intravaginal clindamycin cream and metronidazole gel have been shown to be efficacious in limited clinical trials. Because of the potential to reduce PTB in populations at high risk, serious consideration should be given to the use of metronidazole in women with bacterial vaginosis.

VIRAL PATHOGENS

Human Immunodeficiency Virus
(See Chapter 37, Part 4.)

Our understanding of the pathogenesis and treatment of human immunodeficiency virus (HIV) has expanded greatly over recent years:

A disease that was unknown two decades ago, that was untreatable only a decade ago, and whose rate of mother-to-child transmission was immutable just 5 years ago, is now readily diagnosed, treated with increasing effectiveness, and blocked from transmission in the large majority of cases.[95]

It is imperative that clinicians keep abreast of the latest data and literature to provide the best care for the pregnant woman and her offspring. Care should be provided by a multidisciplinary team of physicians and other health care personnel who are up to date in their knowledge and are experienced and comfortable with the issues surrounding HIV in pregnancy.

EPIDEMIOLOGY

In the early 1980s, reports began to surface of opportunistic infections in homosexual men, such as *Pneumocystis carinii* pneumonia and candidiasis. It would ultimately be discovered that these individuals were infected with HIV. The ensuing epidemic caused by HIV and acquired immunodeficiency syndrome (AIDS) has led to the infection of over 50 million people worldwide, with approximately 20 million deaths. HIV infection and AIDS currently affect individuals from all walks of life and of all ages and both genders. In the United States, women represent the population segment with the greatest increase in the number of cases. The Centers for Disease Control and Prevention (CDC) reported over 100,000 cases of AIDS in women in the United States by the end of 2000, with approximately 10,000 new cases diagnosed annually. This figure represents approximately 25% of new cases diagnosed each year. A large proportion (>50%) of these women are African American. It is assumed that 107,000 to 150,000 U.S. women are currently asymptomatic HIV carriers. In 1995 HIV infection was the third leading cause of death among women aged 25 to 44 years and the leading cause of death among African American women in this age group.[95] By 2000 it was the fifth leading cause of death among people aged 25 to 44, the fourth leading cause of death among women aged 25 to 44, and the second leading cause of death among African American women aged 25 to 44.

SCREENING

The ethics and issues involved in prenatal screening have been hotly debated. Counseling regarding voluntary and confidential screening should be offered as part of routine prenatal care. The targeted (risk-based) testing of pregnant women who are perceived to be at increased risk for infection fails to identify a significant number of HIV-positive women.[8,119] As a result, universal HIV screening is advocated for all pregnant women by the American College of Obstetricians and Gynecologists. In the United States and Canada, various states and provinces use either an opt-in or opt-out approach to testing. Under the opt-in approach, women are provided pretest counseling and must specifically consent to an HIV test. Under the opt-out approach women are notified that an HIV test is one of the routine prenatal tests, and it is omitted only if she refuses. Jurisdictions using the opt-in strategy have lower testing rates than those that have adopted an opt-out approach.[30] It has also been documented that switching from an opt-in to an opt-out screening strategy results in an increased testing rate in pregnant women.[137] Pretest and post-test counseling should be offered to all women screened, and extensive social and medical support services need to be identified for those testing positive.

CLINICAL CONSIDERATIONS

HIV infection leads to progressive incompetence of the immune system, making the individual susceptible to opportunistic infections and unusual neoplasms. An HIV-infected individual with an opportunistic infection, neoplasia, dementia encephalopathy, or wasting syndrome receives the diagnosis of AIDS. This diagnosis has been expanded to include those with CD4 counts of less than 200 lymphocytes/mm^3, cervical cancer, pulmonary tuberculosis, and recurrent pneumonia.

Many clinical studies have attempted to determine both the effects of pregnancy on the course of maternal HIV-related disease and the effects of HIV infection on pregnancy outcome. Although some degree of immunosuppression may occur during pregnancy, it does not seem to alter the disease in pregnant women. The effect of pregnancy on immunologic parameters in HIV-positive women is marginal, and pregnancy does not appear to markedly influence the progression of HIV infection.

The effect of HIV infection on pregnancy outcome has been difficult to quantify. It appears that this infection is associated with an increased risk of adverse pregnancy outcomes, but the relationship is clouded by uncontrolled and confounded data. There appears to be a fourfold risk of spontaneous abortion but no increase in fetal anomalies. HIV-infected gravidas have an increased odds ratio of about 2 for growth restriction, low birthweight, and PTB. This tendency toward adverse outcomes is less obvious in developed countries. An increase in the number of stillbirths is not seen in developed countries.[14]

DIAGNOSIS AND TREATMENT

An enzyme-linked immunosorbent assay is used for the initial screening. This test relies on a colorimetric change mediated by an antigen-antibody reaction. If it is repeatedly positive, a Western blot test is performed. This test identifies antibodies against specific portions of the virus; it is positive if antibodies to p24, p31, and either gp41 or gp160 are present.

Because of the high viral turnover rate, it has become clear that early institution of multiple potent antiretroviral agents provides the best long-term control of viral replication. Monotherapy with a single agent is not recommended. Multiagent drug therapy may be started with a variety of regimens. The three main classes of drugs are the nucleoside reverse transcriptase inhibitors, the non-nucleoside reverse transcriptase inhibitors, and the protease inhibitors. In pregnancy the goals of treatment are twofold: treatment of maternal disease and prevention of vertical transmission. Treatment should be initiated in any pregnant woman with clinical, virologic, or immunologic parameters that would warrant treatment if she were not pregnant. Most authorities would argue that all pregnant women should receive antiretroviral therapy even if they do meet the criteria for treatment in nonpregnant individuals because of the proven beneficial effect on decreasing vertical transmission. All regimens in pregnancy should include zidovudine because it is the only agent that has been shown to block vertical transmission.[35] When pregnancy and HIV infection are diagnosed simultaneously, the patient may wish to complete the first trimester before undertaking potent combination therapy.[20] The appropriate use of combination therapy should drive the viral load to below the limits of detection.[97]

TRANSMISSION

Transplacental infection has been well documented. HIV has been isolated directly from the placenta, amniotic fluid, and early products of conception. HIV is also found in breast milk, and breast feeding is a documented means of late perinatal infection. Because a safe infant formula is available in the United States, the Public Health Service has recommended that infected mothers avoid breast milk feeding.[27]

Intrapartum infection of the neonate accounts for 70% to 80% of the vertical transmissions. When no efforts are made to block transmission, 25% to 30% of newborns acquire the infection; higher rates have been reported in developing countries and in symptomatic patients. The original evidence that vertical transmission could be reduced came as a result of the AIDS Clinical Trial Group (ACTG) protocol 076. This trial enrolled pregnant women who had no clinical indication for or use of antiretroviral therapy during the current pregnancy and who had CD4-positive counts of more than 200/mm³. The efficacy of zidovudine monotherapy compared with placebo was studied. The preliminary analysis of 364 births showed a 67% reduction in HIV transmission from 25.5% to 8.3%.[35] Because of this information, the trial was stopped and the Public Health Service recommended offering zidovudine to pregnant women at more than 14 weeks of gestation to lower the risk of fetal infection. ACTG protocol 185 demonstrated that similar results could also be obtained in women who had previous exposure to zidovudine or a CD4 count of less than 200/mm³. Since the publication of these trials, other studies have shown that a decrease in vertical transmission can be accomplished by using shorter courses of zidovudine[37,130,144] or nevirapine[56] and combination therapy.[36]

In addition to the use of medical therapy to reduce vertical transmission, changes in obstetric management have been evaluated. Studies have investigated reducing the number of episiotomies and use of instrumentation and minimizing the duration of the rupture of membranes to reduce the fetal exposure to the virus found in vaginal blood and secretions.

Several studies have suggested that the use of cesarean section before the onset of labor or membrane rupture would independently reduce the rate of transmission.[46,69]

This effect appears to hold up even when antiretroviral therapy was used. A meta-analysis of 15 prospective cohort studies conducted between 1982 and 1996 demonstrated a 10.4% transmission rate with elective cesarean section versus a 19.0% rate with other routes of delivery when antiretroviral agents were not used. When antiretroviral therapy was used, the rate of transmission was only 2.0% with elective cesarean section versus 7.3% with other modes of delivery.[69] However, these studies do not include information on viral load, which influences the transmission rate. Studies have shown that rates of transmission are greatly affected by viral load, and these rates are in the range of 1% with viral loads that are undetectable (<50 copies/mL).[51,68] It may be that as combination therapy is used, driving viral loads to undetectable levels, the use of elective cesarean section will add little to the reduction of neonatal infection. It also must be stressed that cesarean section is not without its own inherent risk, which may be increased in HIV-infected women. Unfortunately, trials examining the use of cesarean section in women taking potent combination therapy are not feasible because of the large numbers of patients that would be required to demonstrate a difference in transmission rates. For now, the risks of surgical morbidity versus the benefits of cesarean delivery to reduce the risk of neonatal infection will have to be weighed in each individual clinical situation.

ANTEPARTUM MANAGEMENT

Antepartum evaluation of the HIV-positive patient should include both clinical and laboratory surveillance for immune dysfunction, disease progression, and opportunistic infection. Evidence of sexually transmitted diseases, such as syphilis, gonorrhea, chlamydia, and herpes simplex virus, should be sought. Baseline serologic markers for toxoplasmosis and cytomegalovirus may be useful in documenting previous exposure and the risk of fetal infection. Immune function studies should include a complete blood cell count with differential, CD4 count, and viral load studies each trimester. A tuberculosis skin test should be included with the prenatal laboratory studies, and appropriate controls must be used to detect possible anergy. The patient should have documented prior immunization to hepatitis B, pneumococcus, and influenza or receive appropriate vaccination during pregnancy.

At present, fetal surveillance is limited to traditional studies, including ultrasonography to evaluate fetal growth and other biophysical parameters. Although fetal blood sampling might possibly identify infected fetuses, the use of this modality may increase the risk of infection and is avoided.

Further antenatal management must be individualized to the patient. Opportunistic infections should be aggressively treated. *P. carinii* pneumonia is a common AIDS-defining disease with a significant mortality rate. Cervical dysplasia and tuberculosis may also more frequently complicate the pregnancies of women infected with HIV-1.

Varicella-Zoster Virus (See Chapter 37, Part 4.)

Varicella-zoster virus (VZV) is a deoxyribonucleic acid (DNA) herpesvirus found exclusively in humans. Exposure in childhood results in chickenpox, which is one of the most communicable diseases in North America. The vast majority of cases occur in childhood, and 85% to 95% of young adults in temperate climates have developed immunity to the virus. Ten percent to 20% of adults experience a reactivation of the virus, developing the painful skin lesions of herpes zoster along one or two adjacent dermatomes, commonly called shingles.[136]

VZV is a highly contagious virus, with an incubation period of 10 to 21 days. After this time, children usually experience a 4- to 7-day period in which pruritic, erythematous vesicles cover the head, neck, and trunk. Adults constitute only 2% of the chickenpox cases but frequently have a more severe illness. They account for 25% of the mortality, which is primarily due to varicella pneumonia. Pregnant women may be at a particularly high risk of death when they develop this complication.[32]

INFECTIONS FROM VARICELLA-ZOSTER VIRUS IN PREGNANCY

Because most pregnant women acquire immunity to VZV in childhood, varicella infection is uncommon in pregnancy. The incidence of varicella in pregnancy has been estimated at 5 per 10,000, and the incidence of zoster, primarily a disease of older people, is assumed to be even less. Even when pregnant women give a negative or uncertain history of childhood varicella infection, serologic testing reveals that approximately 85% are immune to VZV.

Varicella-zoster immune globulin (VZIG) has been used in pregnant women who do not have an antibody to VZV to prevent or modify the course of the disease. VZIG is most effective if administered within 72 to 96 hours of exposure but may have benefit up to 10 days after exposure. If a pregnant woman is exposed to VZV, susceptibility should be determined as soon as possible with antibody titers. The ability of VZIG to block vertical transmission is unknown, but it may benefit the fetus by decreasing maternal viremia.

In maternal varicella, there is a wide range in the severity of illness. One of the most serious potential complications is varicella pneumonia. Women who are smokers or have greater than 100 skin lesions are at the greatest risk for this complication.[61] Although acyclovir has little effect on the course of uncomplicated varicella in adults, the early use of this antiviral agent in the treatment of varicella pneumonia has been shown to reduce mortality in pregnant patients. It appears to be safe for use in pregnancy, and an increase in birth defects has not been attributed to its use during pregnancy.

There are two manifestations of VZV infection in the fetus: fetal varicella syndrome and congenital varicella.

FETAL INFECTIONS FROM VARICELLA-ZOSTER VIRUS

The fetal varicella syndrome can result if maternal varicella occurs in the first 20 weeks of gestation. The risk of this syndrome ranges from 0% to 3%, with the highest incidence occurring when maternal infection is observed between 13 and 20 weeks of gestation.[103] Multiple systems can be involved, including dermatologic (scarring skin lesions in a dermatomal distribution), neurologic (mental retardation, seizures, cortical atrophy, brain calcifications), ophthalmologic (chorioretinitis, congenital cataracts, microphthalmia), and musculoskeletal (limb hypoplasia, muscle atrophy).[102] Low birthweight may also result. This syndrome has never been reported when maternal infection developed in the second half of pregnancy.

Fetal varicella syndrome can be diagnosed in utero when structural findings are demonstrated on ultrasonographic evaluation. When polymerase chain reaction (PCR) analysis of placental or fetal specimens is undertaken, it appears that transplacental infection occurs much more commonly (36%) than the full-blown fetal syndrome.[80]

NEONATAL INFECTIONS FROM VARICELLA-ZOSTER VIRUS

A neonate may be exposed to varicella infection in utero without developing the fetal varicella syndrome or may be infected postnatally (Table 22-1). Infants exposed to varicella infection in utero during the second half of pregnancy up to 21 days before delivery run a very minimal risk of fetal varicella syndrome; however, they may develop zoster in infancy. Infants who were exposed to varicella from 20 days to 6 days before delivery may display serologic evidence or minimal symptoms of chickenpox at birth. Because the time before delivery allows the formation and transplacental passage of maternal antibody, these infants are at little risk for severe disease. However, infants delivered to mothers who develop varicella less than 5 days before

TABLE 22-1. Maternal-Fetal Transmission of Varicella Zoster Virus

MATERNAL INFECTION	FETAL INFECTION
First trimester	Fetal varicella syndrome (rare)
Second and third trimesters up to 21 days before delivery	May develop zoster during infancy
From 20 days until 6 days before delivery	Serologic evidence or minimal symptoms of chickenpox
5 days before delivery to 2 days after delivery	17% chance of acute infection; 31% untreated case-mortality rate

delivery or up to 2 days after delivery are at much higher risk of serious sequelae because they lack the passively acquired maternal antibody. In this circumstance infants have a 17% chance of manifesting congenital varicella infection, with an untreated case-fatality rate of 31%.[80] Immediate administration of VZIG to these infants is therefore recommended after delivery. Approximately half of these infants will still develop chickenpox despite VZIG, but the disease severity will be modified. Antiviral therapy with acyclovir may also be helpful in ameliorating disease in these infants.

Birth defects have been occasionally reported in pregnancies complicated by maternal zoster. However, it is doubtful that significant viremia with zoster occurs in the presence of specific VZV antibodies and therefore unlikely that maternal zoster is responsible for an increase in fetal anomalies.[44]

PREVENTION
A live, attenuated varicella vaccine has been developed that can be administered before conception to women who are susceptible to varicella infection. Some recommend routine serologic screening on the first prenatal visit for those without a history of childhood infection.[33] When the vaccine is routinely administered in the postpartum period to those who are seronegative, this approach appears to be a cost-effective way to reduce the morbidity and mortality associated with perinatal infection.[55,134]

Rubella (See Chapter 37, Part 4.)

Rubella is a mild viral infection, is confined to the human host, and occurs worldwide. Infection during pregnancy can result in miscarriages, stillbirths, congenital malformations, or late sequelae that may appear years later. The introduction of the rubella vaccine has greatly reduced but not eliminated the neonatal morbidity associated with infection during pregnancy.[117]

EPIDEMIOLOGY AND CLINICAL MANIFESTATIONS
Before the introduction of rubella vaccination in 1969, the disease was the most common in 5- to 9-year olds, with 85% of 15- to 19-year-olds demonstrating immunity. Epidemics occurred at 6- to 9-year intervals, with major pandemics every 10 to 30 years. Maternal rubella infection early in pregnancy frequently results in fetal malformations consistent with congenital rubella syndrome. The incidence of congenital rubella syndrome in 1970 was 1.8/100,000 live births. The epidemiology of this infection has changed dramatically with the licensure of the live, attenuated rubella vaccine. An all-time low of 225 cases of rubella was reported to the CDC in 1988, a 99% decrease since 1969, the year the vaccine was introduced. Cases of congenital rubella syndrome are occasionally reported in the United States after outbreaks of rubella infection. Risk factors for infection include young age and birth in a country where vaccination is not routine (e.g., Latin America).[39] It is the goal of the CDC to eradicate the virus in the United States by the diligent use of the rubella vaccine.[110]

Rubella infection is subclinical in 30% of patients. Symptomatic disease is typically mild and occurs 14 to 21 days after infection. A mild prodrome of fever, malaise, and low-grade fever may precede the rash. The rash is macular, begins on the face and neck, proceeds downward, and disappears over 3 to 4 days. Postauricular, suboccipital, and posterior cervical lymphadenopathies are typically present. Diagnosis on clinical grounds is difficult, and serologic confirmation of a fourfold increase in antibody titers is required. Immunoglobulin M (IgM) is present for 4 weeks after the rash. Low or equivocal levels of IgM should be viewed with caution because cross-reactivity with human parvovirus IgM has been described.

MATERNAL-FETAL TRANSMISSION
Fetal infection can occur after maternal rubella viremia at any stage of pregnancy. Miller and associates prospectively evaluated 1016 women with confirmed rubella during pregnancy, 407 of whom elected to carry the fetus to term.[92] The risk of congenital infection varied from 81% with exposure in the first 12 weeks to 30% with exposure at 23 to 30 weeks and 100% if exposure occurred during the last month of pregnancy. The malformations associated with congenital rubella syndrome are dependent on gestational age. Multiple defects occur after very early exposure, and almost every fetus exposed during the first month of pregnancy develops abnormally. Cardiac defects almost always follow exposure before 10 weeks of gestation. Deafness occurs after exposure at up to 16 weeks of gestation. Congenital defects following exposure after 20 weeks are rare.[143] Reinfection can occasionally occur when a person with documented rubella immunity is re-exposed to the virus.[114] Congenital rubella syndrome has been rarely reported when reinfection occurs before 12 weeks of gestation.[110]

FETAL INFECTION
The full-blown congenital rubella syndrome includes, in a descending order of frequency, hearing loss, mental retardation, cardiac malformation, and ocular defects. Hearing loss is sensorineural and can occur along with other defects or alone in 40% of cases.[129] Mental retardation is common and frequently severe. Cardiac lesions are present in half of the infants exposed during the first 2 months of pregnancy. Patent ductus arteriosus is the most common (approximately 70%), with pulmonary artery stenosis, aortic valve stenosis, and tetralogy of Fallot also seen. Ocular abnormalities commonly include congenital cataracts, retinopathy, and microphthalmia.

Delayed manifestations of congenital rubella syndrome are also common, occurring in more than 20% of congenitally infected individuals. Insulin-dependent diabetes mellitus develops by age 35 in 20% to 40%, and thyroid disease develops in 5% of those with congenital rubella infection. Deafness and eye abnormalities not evident at birth can also develop. Progressive rubella panencephalopathy has been described in 12 males who developed progressive encephalopathy leading to death.[129]

PREVENTION

Despite recommendations for universal immunization, it is estimated that up to 20% of women of reproductive age in the United States are seronegative for rubella. The prevention of congenital rubella syndrome relies heavily on vaccinating susceptible females. The vaccine is a live, attenuated vaccine, and it is recommended that it be avoided within 3 months of conception or during pregnancy because of theoretical risks to the fetus. Although no cases of congenital rubella syndrome have been reported when the vaccine has been administered during this period, there is a small theoretical risk of congenital infection (0% to 2%).[22]

Because of the high percentage of pregnancies affected when exposed to rubella infection, counseling regarding the termination of pregnancy should be offered. Prenatal diagnosis can be made after 20 weeks of gestation when IgM is detected in fetal blood. The presence of a virus can also be detected by using reverse transcription and nested PCR in chorionic villus, amniotic fluid, or fetal blood samples.[106,138]

Herpes Simplex Virus

The herpes simplex virus (HSV) is a large, double-stranded DNA virus that infects only humans. Infections are common and can result from either of the two known serologic subtypes: HSV-1 and HSV-2. It was traditionally thought that most orolabial infections were caused by HSV-1 and that most genital infections were caused by HSV-2, but it is now accepted that either subtype can infect any site, and an increasing proportion of genital infections are attributed to HSV-1.

EPIDEMIOLOGY AND CLINICAL MANIFESTATIONS

HSV infection is one of the most common sexually transmitted infections worldwide and one of the three most prevalent sexually transmitted infections in North America. Between 70% and 80% of sexually transmitted infectious genital ulcers are caused by HSV. It is estimated that over 600,000 new HSV infections occur annually to contribute to a pool of over 50 million cases.[112] The seroprevalence of HSV infection is dependent on age, gender, sexual activity, and socioeconomic class.[48] Seroepidemiologic studies in obstetric populations show the antibody to HSV-2 to be present in 19% to 55% of the patients, depending on the population source.[48]

There are three clinically recognized types of genital infection from HSV. A primary infection is an initial infection with HSV-1 or HSV-2 but without prior exposure (antibody) to either. A nonprimary first episode refers to a first clinical episode with HSV-1 or HSV-2 in an individual with prior exposure (antibody) to the other serotype. Finally, a recurrent infection is a reactivation of a latent virus. A primary infection is typically associated with multiple painful genital lesions with associated inguinal adenopathy and systemic symptoms (fever, malaise, myalgia). Nonprimary and recurrent episodes are typically not as severe as primary episodes and tend to resolve more quickly. Recurrences are common after primary infections, and 80% to 85% of women with primary HSV will have at least one recurrence during their lifetime.[11] Because there is considerable overlap in the manifestation of HSV infections, it is often difficult to distinguish clinically between primary and recurrent disease.[64] Furthermore, 20% to 30% of the pregnant women who are seropositive for HSV have never been symptomatic.[16]

Asymptomatic shedding of the virus is not uncommon. It may occur in 3% to 16% of pregnant women and may be as high as 33% in women acquiring the infection during pregnancy.[16] It appears to be the most common after HSV-2 (rather than HSV-1) infection soon after a primary outbreak resolves and in patients with frequent recurrences. This condition may represent a potential avenue for transmission of the virus because individuals with asymptomatic shedding may be infected but have no symptoms.

Viral culture is still the gold standard for making the diagnosis of genital HSV. Recently, however, PCR techniques and type-specific serologic testing have become available and may assist in the diagnosis.[112] There are currently three antiviral agents available for the treatment of acute and recurrent genital HSV. The safety of acyclovir during pregnancy has been fairly well established, and its use is beneficial in severe or disseminated disease.[77,124] Valacyclovir, which is metabolized to acyclovir, and famciclovir are also used to treat genital HSV. The experience with these drugs in pregnancy is more limited; both are members of the class B drugs of the Food and Drug Administration.

ISSUES IN PREGNANCY

Approximately 2% of pregnant women acquire primary genital HSV during pregnancy. Although the majority of vertical transmission occurs intrapartum, the route of transmission is transplacental in approximately 5% of the cases of neonatal HSV. Primary HSV infections during the first trimester seem to increase the frequency of spontaneous abortions, stillbirths, and prematurity. Clinical features associated with congenital infection include skin vesicles or scarring, chorioretinitis, hydranencephaly, microphthalmia, and microcephaly. Infants born with suspected in utero infection may have one of three clinical presentations. Neonatal disease can be manifested as SEM (involving the *skin*, *eyes*, and *mouth*), SEM and central nervous system involvement, or disseminated disease. Most infected infants present with SEM disease, but 60% to 70% ultimately progress to central nervous system involvement or disseminated disease. Primary infection in the later trimesters does not seem to increase the risk of transplacental infection, although these mothers have a longer course of viral shedding and more numerous recurrences and are therefore more likely to expose the neonate during delivery.

The major risk of infection for the neonate is intrapartum exposure to an infected birth canal. Vaginal delivery in the presence of a primary infection results in neonatal infection approximately 50% of the time. Asymptomatic maternal infection has a 33% risk of neonatal infection. Transmission risk drops to 3% to 4% when recurrent lesions are present at vaginal delivery, and the risk of transmission drops to 0.004% in the presence of asymptomatic shedding.[124] The major risk factors for transmission during labor and delivery include primary (compared with recurrent) infection, cervical (compared with labial) viral shedding, and the use of fetal scalp electrodes.[17] Current recommendations include cesarean section before or shortly after the rupture of membranes when an active HSV lesion or prodromal symptomatology is present to minimize the neonate's viral exposure.[113] Unfortunately, this strategy does not prevent all cases of neonatal HSV because the majority of infected infants are born to mothers who have never had symptoms.

The prophylactic use of acyclovir in the last weeks of pregnancy to reduce the chance of recurrence necessitating cesarean section has been examined. It has been demonstrated that using daily acyclovir, starting at 36 weeks of gestation, decreases the incidence of both recurrent genital lesions and positive cultures at the time of labor.[125-127] In one study this treatment regimen was translated into a decrease in the number of cesarean sections performed for HSV.[125] It is still unclear whether using prophylactic antiviral medications in this way decreases asymptomatic shedding (see Chapter 37, Part 4).

Cytomegalovirus

Cytomegalovirus (CMV) is a ubiquitous virus that infects most people in their lifetime. In adults the primary infection is usually asymptomatic, although approximately 10% will experience a mononucleosis-type syndrome, with fever, fatigue, and lymphadenopathy. Reactivation of latent infection can occur, with viral shedding in cervical secretions, tears, saliva, urine, and breast milk. The virus can be transmitted to the fetus after primary or recurrent infection, and approximately 40,000 congenitally infected infants are born annually in the United States. Approximately 10% of the infected infants are noticeably affected at birth, and many more develop sequelae over the first 5 years of life.

EPIDEMIOLOGY AND CLINICAL MANIFESTATIONS
Acquisition rates of CMV vary inversely with socioeconomic status, and this is the most important determinant of seroprevalence. Seroepidemiologic studies in the United States indicate that 50% to 60% of pregnant, middle-class women have antibodies to CMV, compared with 70% to 85% of those from lower socioeconomic groups. Two percent to 2.5% of susceptible women will acquire CMV infection during pregnancy.[135] As noted above, primary infection is most often asymptomatic in healthy individuals, with a small proportion experiencing a mononucleosis-like illness.

Seroconversion from IgG-negative to IgG-positive status is the best demonstration of primary infection. A fourfold rise in IgG titers most likely represents primary infection, while a smaller rise can be seen in recurrent infection.[15] IgM develops in only 75% of those with primary infection and may persist for up to 18 months. It may also be present in 10% of those with recurrent infection.

MATERNAL-FETAL TRANSMISSION
Vertical transmission can occur after either primary or recurrent CMV infection. One percent to 2% of all infants born in the United States have documented congenital infection. Congenital CMV infection occurs in 30% to 40% of infants born to mothers experiencing primary CMV infection during pregnancy (Fig. 22-1).[135] The rate of transmission after recurrent infection is probably similar to that for primary disease, although

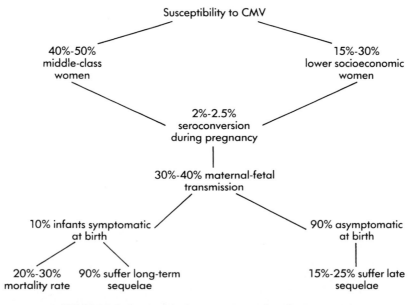

FIGURE 22-1. Maternal-fetal cytomegalovirus (CMV) transmission.

the percentage of infants symptomatic at birth (less than 1%) or developing serious sequelae (5% to 10%) is much lower.[107] The timing of maternal infection may also be critical, and it has been suggested that the risk of delivering a symptomatic infant or one who will develop sequelae is higher if maternal infection occurs during the first half of pregnancy.

FETAL AND NEONATAL INFECTION (See Chapter 37.) The diagnosis in utero of fetal CMV infection may be suggested by an abnormal ultrasound evaluation. CMV is a relatively common cause of nonimmune hydrops. Intrauterine growth restriction, microcephaly, periventricular calcification, hepatosplenomegaly, an echogenic bowel, and oligohydramnios may also be present. In utero diagnosis may also be accomplished by the identification of viral DNA obtained via amniocentesis or fetal blood sampling by using PCR techniques.

Of the infants born with CMV infection, 10% are symptomatic at birth. Infant mortality in this group is 20% to 30%, and most suffer some form of long-term, serious sequelae. Hepatosplenomegaly is the most common clinical finding. Microcephaly is also common and is frequently associated with periventricular calcifications. Optic abnormalities, intellectual impairment, and dental defects have also been reported. Sensorineural hearing loss develops in 30% of the infants symptomatic at birth.

However, most infected infants (greater than 90%) are asymptomatic at birth. It has been recently recognized that 15% to 25% of these infants may suffer late sequelae, including neurologic abnormalities, sensorineural hearing loss, and mental retardation.[135] These sequelae are much more likely to follow primary rather than recurrent maternal infection.

The prevention of congenital CMV hinges on the prevention of maternal infection by using such measures as careful hand washing, latex condoms, and avoiding contact with children's secretions. Vaccines are currently undergoing clinical trials, and an effective vaccine may one day be used as a means to prevent congenital infection. There is currently no effective treatment for congenital CMV infection, and antiviral agents such as gancyclovir are used to treat only severe infections in newborns or immunocompromised mothers.[100]

Hepatitis

Hepatitis is a common and highly contagious viral illness. Six distinct types of viral hepatitis exist, each with different implications for the pregnant woman and her fetus. Hepatitis A, B, and D will be discussed first, followed by the non-A, non-B hepatitis viruses (Hepatitis C, E, and G).

HEPATITIS A
Hepatitis A virus (HAV) is a small, nonenveloped RNA virus that is responsible for approximately 30% to 35% of the cases of acute hepatitis in the United States. Transmission usually occurs via the fecal-oral route, and outbreaks are usually due to contaminated food or water. Parenteral transmission is rare. The clinical signs of infection occur after an incubation period of 15 to 50 days and include a mild flulike illness. The acute infection is self-limiting and does not result in a chronic carrier state. Diagnosis is made by the identification of an IgM-specific antibody, which appears 30 days after exposure and persists for 6 months. Treatment is supportive, and hospitalization is reserved for those with severe illness and dehydration. Sexual and household contacts should receive intramuscular immunoglobulin and a hepatitis A vaccine. The vaccine is safe for use in pregnant women.

HAV complicates approximately 1 in 1000 pregnancies. The virus is not teratogenic, and infection does not seem to increase the risk of adverse pregnancy outcomes. The newborn infants of acutely infected women should receive immunoglobulin to decrease the risk of transmission after delivery. Breast feeding is not contraindicated.

HEPATITIS B
Of all the viruses that cause acute hepatitis, hepatitis B virus (HBV) is the one that is responsible for most of the concerns related to pregnancy. The virus is an enveloped, double-stranded DNA virus with three major structural antigens. There is an outer-envelope protein, the hepatitis B surface antigen [HbsAg] and two inner-core proteins, the hepatitis B core antigen [HbcAg] and hepatitis B e antigen [HbeAg].

Epidemiology and Clinical Manifestations
HBV accounts for 40% to 45% of the cases of acute hepatitis in the United States. There are over 300,000 new cases of HBV annually, with 12,000 to 20,000 of these becoming chronic carriers. The prevalence of the carrier state varies from a high of 5% to 15% among Alaskan Inuits and Asians to less than 0.5% of the general American population. Approximately 1 million Americans are chronic HBV carriers. Transmission can occur via the parenteral, sexual, or mother-to-child routes. The highest risk for transmission occurs in the sexual or household contacts of infected individuals. Most cases of HBV occur in homosexual or bisexual males, intravenous drug abusers, and the heterosexual partners of infected men, although no risk factors are identifiable in approximately one third of newly infected individuals. The risk of post-transfusion HBV infection dropped dramatically with the screening of blood donors.

The incubation period for acute HBV varies from 2 to 4 months, with a mean of 12 weeks. Approximately one third of healthy adults are asymptomatic; an even higher percentage of children and infants infected during the first year of life exhibit no symptoms. The symptoms of acute hepatitis in the adult include anorexia, nausea, vomiting, malaise, weakness, and abdominal pain; clinical signs include jaundice, icterus, hepatic tenderness, and weight loss. The acute course usually runs 3 to 4 weeks, but symptoms may persist for up to 6 months. After the acute infection, 80% to 85% of individuals have complete resolution (with the development

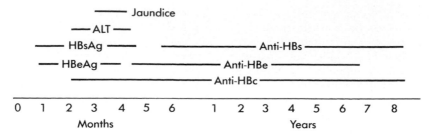

FIGURE 22-2. Clinical and serum markers of hepatitis. ALT, alanine aminotransferase; HBc, hepatitis B core (antigen); HBeAg, hepatitis B e antigen; HBsAg, hepatitis B surface antigen.

of protective anti-HBs antibodies), while 10% to 15% become chronic carriers (with the persistence of HBsAg in serum). In chronic, active infection, HBeAg may persist for years, followed by the gradual seroconversion to anti-HBe. Asymptomatic carriers are characterized by the presence of HBsAg and anti-HBc, with normal liver function tests. Fulminant hepatitis rarely occurs (in less than 1% of patients) and is characterized by acute liver failure, hepatic encephalopathy, coma, and death in 70% to 80% of cases.

The diagnosis of HBV is based on serologic markers (Fig. 22-2). HBsAg is the first marker to appear and is present 2 to 4 weeks before the onset of clinical symptoms and during the acute infection. At about the same time, HBeAg appears. This antigen disappears before clinical symptoms resolve and is usually followed by the antibody (anti-HBe). The antibody to the surface antigen (anti-HBs) appears during the convalescent period, and high titers are indicative of immunity. The core antigen (HBcAg) is not present in serum in sufficient quantities to be clinically useful. The antibody to HBcAg is typically present in the window period between the disappearance of HBsAg and the development of anti-HBs.

Maternal-Fetal Transmission

Acute HBV infection complicates 1 to 2 in 1000 pregnancies, and chronic infection is present in 5 to 15 in 1000 pregnancies. The transmission rate of the virus from mother to infant varies with the clinical setting (Table 22-2). Women infected with HBV in the first or second trimester rarely pass the infection to the neonate (up to 10%). A transplacental leak of HBV with a maternal-fetal hemorrhage may account for the unusual cases of in utero infection. Most evidence suggests that the neonate is infected at the time of labor and delivery as a consequence of exposure to contaminated blood and genital tract secretions, and there is no effect of the mode of delivery on transmission risk. Infants who are seronegative at birth convert after an incubation period of 2 to 4 months. Women who are infected in the third trimester have an increased chance (80% to 90%) of passing the virus to their infants. The most predictive marker for vertical transmission is HBeAg; when it is present, the transmission rate reaches 80% to 90%. In chronic carriers, the additional presence of anti-HBe drops the transmission rate to 10% to 20%.[9] Breast feeding is not contraindicated in chronic carriers, but appropriate immunoprophylaxis must be administered to the infant at birth (see below).[65]

Most hepatitis infections in infants are asymptomatic, although fulminant cases are occasionally reported. Most infants who are infected at birth will become chronic carriers of HBsAg. Many of these go on to have adverse sequelae, including cirrhosis; chronic, active hepatitis; and primary hepatocellular carcinoma.

Prenatal Screening and Immunization Recommendations

The recognition that immunization at birth would be 85% to 95% effective in preventing the development of the HBV chronic carrier state in the neonate has prompted prenatal HBV screening of obstetric patients. The CDC and the American College of Obstetricians and Gynecologists advocate routine universal screening of all patients at their first antepartum visit, with testing for HBsAg, and perhaps repeat screening during the third trimester for those in especially high-risk situations.[21]

The prevention of neonatal hepatitis depends on the prompt administration of immune globulin and hepatitis B vaccination. Hepatitis B immune globulin (HBIG) given at birth reduces infection rates from 94% to 75% and the chronic carrier rate from 91% to 22%. The addition of hepatitis vaccine drops the chronic carrier rate to 0% from 14%.[150] Most authorities recommend that HBIG be given within 12 hours of delivery and vaccination begin within the first week of life. In addition to those infants at risk because of the maternal infectious status, the CDC now recommends immunization of all infants, including those born to mothers who are HBsAg negative.

TABLE 22-2. Maternal-Fetal Transmission of Hepatitis B Virus

MATERNAL INFECTION	FETAL INFECTION
Acute first/second trimester	Rare
Acute third trimester	80%-90%
Chronic carrier	
HBsAg$^+$/HBeAg$^-$	10%-20%
HBsAg$^+$/HBeAg$^+$	80%-90%

HBeAg, hepatitis B e antigen; HBsAg, hepatitis B surface antigen.

The vaccination of health care workers for HBV may prevent many of the 12,000 cases of HBV infection acquired in the workplace as a result of needle stick or splash accidents. Those who have been exposed should also receive HBIG. Pregnancy is not a contraindication to vaccination or the administration of HBIG in those at risk of infection.

HEPATITIS D

Hepatitis D (HDV) is a defective RNA virus that is dependent on HBV for replication and survival. Therefore, the epidemiology of HDV is identical to that of HBV. Acute infection can occur in two forms: coinfection and superinfection. Coinfection occurs when the patient simultaneously acquires HBV and HDV; the disease tends to be mild and self-limiting, with less than 5% of cases progressing to chronic infection. Superinfection results from a chronic carrier of HBV who becomes acutely infected with HDV. It occurs in 20% to 25% of chronic HBV carriers and frequently leads to chronic, active hepatitis; cirrhosis; and portal hypertension, with an eventual mortality rate of 25%.

Pregnant patients with hepatitis D (identified by the IgM-specific antibody or antigen detection) should receive supportive care, with close monitoring of liver function. Infection of the neonate is rare and can occur only if HBV and HDV are transmitted simultaneously. Fortunately, neonatal immunoprophylaxis against HBV is almost uniformly protective against HDV as well.

HEPATITIS C

Post-transfusion hepatitis in the absence of markers for HAV and HBV was originally termed non-A, non-B hepatitis (NANBH). Now the structure of the hepatitis C virus (HCV) has been delineated, and it is understood that HCV is primarily responsible for parenterally transmitted NANBH. It is a single-stranded RNA virus. The principal risk factors for HCV transmission are blood and blood product transfusion and the use of illicit intravenous drugs. Currently, 40% to 60% of cases result from intravenous drug use. Sexual transmission is also possible, but this is probably not a major mode of transmission.

HCV is the most common chronic, blood-borne infection in the United States and is responsible for 20% to 40% of the cases of acute hepatitis and 50% of the cases of chronic hepatitis. The number of new infections each year has declined from 230,000 in the 1980s to 36,000 in 1996 as a result of careful screening of transfused blood products. However, it is estimated that 3.9 million (1.8%) Americans are infected with HCV. Deaths from HCV-related liver disease currently number 8000 to 10,000 per year; the number is very likely to climb in the next 10 to 20 years as more people reach the age when complications from chronic liver disease occur.[28]

Acute HCV infection occurs after an incubation period of 30 to 60 days, with a mean of 8 weeks; infection is asymptomatic in 75% of patients. In the other 25%, symptoms and signs may include malaise, fever, jaundice, and abdominal pain. In those with symptoms, the clinical presentation is milder than that in HAV or HBV infections. The average time for seroconversion is 8 to 9 weeks; 80% undergo seroconversion by 15 weeks and 97% by 6 months. Although fulminant infection is rare, chronic liver disease develops in 75% to 85% of patients after HCV infection. With chronic infection, there is persistence of HCV RNA and abnormal liver biochemistry. The chronic course is slow and insidious, with most patients showing no signs or symptoms of the disease for 10 to 20 years. Of those with chronic HCV infection, 20% to 25% will ultimately develop chronic, active hepatitis or liver cirrhosis. These individuals may require a liver transplant or may die of their disease. An effective vaccine is unlikely to be developed in the near future. Treatment with interferon alfa and ribavirin has been shown to decrease detectable levels of viral RNA and normalize alanine aminotransferase levels; however, more than 50% of patients experience relapse when therapy is stopped.

Issues in Pregnancy

The prevalence of HCV in pregnancy ranges from 1% to 3%. Risk factors include substance or intravenous drug abuse, multiple sexual partners, the presence of other infections (HIV, HBV), and the absence of prenatal care. However, 30% to 60% of infected pregnant women have no identifiable risk factors.[133] The overall risk of vertical transmission is approximately 5%, and its timing is unclear. Factors that are associated with transmission include HIV serostatus, HCV viral load, and acute infection in the third trimester. In HIV-negative women the risk of fetal infection is 5.2% (range, 0% to 33%), whereas in HIV-positive women the risk of transmission is 23.4% (range, 9% to 70%).[45] Women coinfected with HIV and HCV seem to have higher viral loads of both viruses than those who are infected with only one. Maternal HCV antibodies cross the placenta; therefore, newborn screening should be done by testing for HCV RNA at 6 to 12 months of age. The long-term outcome of infected neonates is not yet well understood. Most infants remain viremic and progress to chronic hepatitis. Immunoprophylaxis in the newborn has not been demonstrated to be efficacious. Cesarean section does not provide protection against maternal-fetal transmission and should be performed for routine obstetric indications only. Breast feeding appears to be safe and is not contraindicated in HCV-infected women.

HEPATITIS E

Although HCV is the primary cause of NANBH in industrialized countries, a second distinct virus, hepatitis E (HEV), is responsible for outbreaks of enterally-acquired NANBH in developing countries. Reports of infection with HEV in U.S. citizens traveling abroad and exposed to contaminated food and water have been documented.[23]

Although many cases remain subclinical, the case-fatality rate is higher (1% to 2%) than that seen with HAV (1 to 2 in 1000). Infection is self-limiting and there are no chronic carriers. Acute HEV infection during pregnancy has been associated with an increase in both maternal mortality and adverse pregnancy outcome, including preterm delivery and stillbirth. These risks are the highest if infection occurs in the second or third trimesters.

HEPATITIS G

Hepatitis G (HGV) is an RNA virus related to hepatitis C. It is more prevalent but less virulent than HCV. Diagnosis relies on the identification of viral nucleic acids with PCR techniques. HGV commonly occurs in association with HBV, HCV, and HIV infections. A chronic carrier state exists, and perinatal transmission has been documented. The prognosis for infected infants remains to be determined.[40]

Parvovirus

Parvoviruses are the smallest DNA-containing viruses that infect mammalian cells; the human B19 parvovirus is the only one found in humans. Infection results in childhood erythema infectiosum (EI), or fifth disease. Infection is usually mild or asymptomatic in the susceptible gravida. However, in rare cases it may cause nonimmune hydrops and fetal death.

EPIDEMIOLOGY

EI is primarily a disease of school children; therefore, the prevalence is age related. In children younger than the age of 5 years, prevalence is less than 5%, rising to 40% by the age of 20. Fifty percent to 60% of women of reproductive age are immune.

The primary mode of transmission is through direct contact with the respiratory secretions of viremic patients. The incubation period is 4 to 14 days. There is a seasonal variation to parvovirus infection, with outbreaks more common in the late winter and early spring. Long-term cycles of 4 to 7 years also appear to occur within communities. Although teachers and daycare workers would seem to have the highest occupational risk of acquiring the virus, by far the greatest risk of infection in susceptible individuals is exposure to one's own infected children.[141] Removing pregnant women from the workplace during seasonal case clusters does not seem to be justified.[60]

CLINICAL FEATURES

One fourth to one third of infected individuals are asymptomatic. Children typically display a reticular, malar rash that starts on the face and spreads to the trunk and limbs. This characteristic rash is responsible for the "slapped cheek" description. It may be accompanied by a headache, sore throat, and low-grade fever. Joint involvement can occur in children (8%), but acute arthritis is much more common in adults (80%). Frequently, arthralgias involving the wrists, hands, ankles, and knees are the only symptoms that the adult perceives.

Because the parvovirus replicates in and destroys the erythroid precursor cells, a limited erythroid aplasia occurs. This condition is not clinically apparent

(resulting in a 1-g drop in hemoglobin) in an otherwise healthy adult because its duration of 7 to 10 days is short compared with the 120-day half-life of red blood cells. However, it can become a serious problem for those with chronic hemolytic anemias, such as sickle cell anemia or other hemoglobinopathies, or for immunocompromised individuals who have difficulty clearing the virus.

Viral culture is quite difficult, and the diagnosis relies on serologic testing. IgM antibodies develop very rapidly, typically persisting for 2 to 3 months, though occasionally as long as 6 months. IgG antibodies develop several days after the IgM antibodies and remain positive for a lifetime, conferring lifelong immunity. Serologic testing should be considered in patients with known exposure, with symptoms (including acute arthritis), and with nonimmune hydrops. Isolated IgM positivity may mean very recent infection, but follow-up testing should demonstrate IgG seroconversion because false-positive IgM findings have been reported. A diagnosis can also be made by using nucleic acid hybridization techniques to isolate viral DNA.

FETAL INFECTION

Vertical transmission rates appear to be about 33%. There is very little evidence to suggest that the virus is teratogenic. When infection occurs before 20 weeks of gestation, the fetal loss rate appears to be about 10%. Infection with parvovirus is the cause of approximately one quarter of all cases of nonimmune hydrops, but the overall risk of hydrops after parvovirus infection is very low. Infection after 20 weeks results in hydrops or fetal death approximately 1% of the time.[84] Hydrops is usually the result of fetal aplastic anemia but may sometimes be caused by acute viral myocarditis or cardiomyopathy (see Chapter 21). Fetal anemia can be diagnosed directly through umbilical blood sampling or indirectly with Doppler ultrasonography showing the peak systolic velocity of the middle cerebral artery. Intrauterine transfusion may be beneficial to some fetuses suffering from severe anemia. Approximately 85% of the fetuses that receive a transfusion to correct their anemia will survive.[115] However, about one third of the cases of fetal hydrops will spontaneously resolve with a healthy, live-born infant. Long-term studies suggest that development in surviving neonates is normal and excess developmental delay is not seen.[93,116]

BACTERIAL AND OTHER PATHOGENS

Gonorrhea

Neisseria gonorrhoeae, a gram-negative diplococcus, is the cause of one of the most common communicable diseases in the United States. It is found most commonly in the urogenital tract but can infect the pharynx and conjunctiva; when disseminated it causes sepsis and arthritis. Pregnancy-associated complications may include PROM, prematurity, chorioamnionitis, intrauterine growth restriction, neonatal sepsis, and postpartum endometritis.

EPIDEMIOLOGY AND CLINICAL MANIFESTATIONS

It is estimated that 600,000 new gonorrhea infections occur in the United States every year, although many of these are unreported. Over 80% of the reported cases occur in individuals in the 15- to 29-year-old age group, with an ever-increasing percentage of cases occurring among adolescents in the 15- to 19-year-old group. In nonpregnant women, uncomplicated anogenital gonorrhea infects the endocervix the most frequently but can involve the urethra, Skene or Bartholin glands, or anus. Gonococcal infections in pregnant women tend to be asymptomatic. When symptoms occur, the most common are vaginal discharge and dysuria. Cervical cultures are recommended at the first prenatal visit, and repeat cultures in the third trimester for patients at high risk may be appropriate.[94]

The CDC recommendation for treatment reflects the increasing identification of penicillinase-producing *N. gonorrhoeae* species. A single dose of ceftriaxone 125 mg IM or cefixime 400 mg PO and then azithromycin 1 g PO or doxycycline 100 mg PO twice a day for 7 days have been recommended. This antibiotic regimen also frequently treats (40% to 60%) concomitant chlamydial infections.[25] During pregnancy the CDC's recommended treatments are ceftriaxone and cefixime, and these medications have recently been shown to be equally efficacious in a prospective, randomized trial.[109]

ASSOCIATION WITH ADVERSE PREGNANCY OUTCOME

Untreated maternal endocervical gonococcal infection has been associated with complications from pregnancy such as PROM, prematurity, chorioamnionitis, intrauterine growth restriction, neonatal infection, and postpartum endometritis. These associations are controversial; gonorrhea infection may simply serve as a marker for other confounding variables known to be associated with poor pregnancy outcome.

NEONATAL GONOCOCCAL OPHTHALMIA

(See Chapters 37 and 51, Part 2.)

The conjunctivitis caused by gonorrhea has been recognized since the late 1800s. The prophylactic use of silver nitrate eye drops, erythromycin, or tetracycline ointment after delivery lowered the incidence of gonococcal ophthalmia neonatorum from 10% to less than 0.5%. Gonococcal conjunctivitis usually manifests itself within 4 days of birth, with frank, purulent discharge from both eyes. If untreated, the disease can rapidly progress to corneal ulceration, resulting in scarring and blindness. Treatment should include hospitalization, frequent ophthalmic irrigation, and intravenous therapy with ceftriaxone or cefotaxime.[25] The infant should be closely evaluated for evidence of disseminated gonococcal infection. Infants born to mothers with untreated gonorrhea should be empirically treated with a single injection of ceftriaxone.[125]

Group B Streptococcal Infection

The hemolytic streptococci cause a variety of infectious diseases and remain a significant cause of perinatal morbidity and mortality. β-Hemolytic streptococci have been divided into subgroups by serotype: A, B, and D, with groups C and G usually reported simply as β-hemolytic streptococci, not groups A, B, and D. GBS is a gram-positive, encapsulated diplococcus classified as Lancefield group B. It is a facultative organism and is capable of growth in a variety of media. Definitive identification requires detection of the group B carbohydrate antigen. Before the introduction of antibiotics, group A *Streptococcus* was responsible for puerperal sepsis and 75% of maternal mortality due to infection. Today, GBS causes the majority of the cases of perinatal morbidity and mortality: sepsis, pneumonia, and meningitis in the newborn and urinary tract infection, amnionitis with PROM or PTB, and postpartum endometritis in the gravida.[121]

EPIDEMIOLOGY AND TRANSMISSION

This organism readily adheres to mucosal cells. In humans, colonization first occurs in the gastrointestinal tract, with secondary spreading to the urogenital tract. A positive urine culture indicates heavy colonization.[146] Asymptomatic vaginal colonization with GBS occurs in 8% to 28% of pregnant women. The reported prevalence of vaginal colonization varies with age (increasing with advancing age), race (highest in African Americans), geographic locale, and gravidity. It also varies with the number of cultures performed, culture media used, and sites cultured (highest from anorectal cultures and lowest from cervical cultures). The samples obtained from both the lower genital tract and the anorectum increase detection rates by 10% to 15% over the rates from either site alone. Colonization can be intermittent or transient, making vaginal culture in the middle trimester an imperfect predictor of culture status at delivery. The maximum predictive value of cultures is achieved 1 to 5 weeks before delivery.

Vertical transmission can occur in utero through either ruptured or intact membranes or during passage through an infected birth canal. The risk of transmission has been shown to range from 40% to 70%. Although approximately two thirds of the infants born to colonized mothers become asymptomatic colonized carriers themselves, only one symptomatic GBS infection occurs for every 100 colonized infants. Symptomatic infection is divided into early onset, with symptoms present at birth or shortly thereafter, and late onset, with symptoms appearing more than 7 days after delivery.[7]

Because of the discrepancy between infant carrier rates and those of actual infection, attempts have been made to determine the risk factors for neonatal infection. Several factors play a particularly important role in symptomatic GBS in the newborn, including prematurity, prolonged rupture of membranes, and intrapartum fever. There is a 10- to 15-fold increase in the risk of early-onset GBS infection in preterm infants. Boyer and Gotoff found the attack rate in infants weighing less than 2500 g to be 7.9 per 1000 as opposed to 0.6 per 1000 in term infants.[13] Additionally, the preterm infant develops more serious disease, with a mortality rate of 28% compared with the 2% mortality rate found in the term neonate. Other factors that increase the risk of neonatal GBS infection include a mother with a history of a prior GBS-infected infant and maternal GBS bacteriuria.

NEONATAL INFECTION (See Chapter 37, Part 2.)

Early-onset GBS infection results in approximately 1600 cases and 80 deaths annually in the United States.[122] By definition, early-onset GBS infection appears in the first week of life. However, the majority of infants display symptoms within the first 48 hours, and about half are symptomatic at delivery. The three major clinical presentations include septicemia (bacteremia and clinical signs of sepsis), pneumonia (present in 40%), and meningitis (present in 30%). The fulminant form presents with shock, which is complicated by respiratory distress, and frequently results in death. Neonatal mortality rates ranged from 50% to 70% during the 1970s; however, improvements in neonatal care have placed the current mortality rate in the 5% to 20% range,[128] with infants of low birthweight or who are preterm having about twice the risk of a fatal outcome.

Late-onset GBS begins more insidiously and presents between 1 and 12 weeks of life. Infection may be acquired vertically or by nosocomial or community exposure. Many (30%) of these infants develop meningitis, some with long-term sequelae. The mortality rate, like that for those with early-onset disease, has decreased over recent years to the range of 2% to 6%.

MATERNAL INFECTION

Intrapartum maternal fever is indicative of IAI, which is frequently associated with GBS infection. Histologic evidence of chorioamnionitis and funisitis was present in 81% of the patients in whom GBS colonization was associated with preterm PROM. Postpartum endometritis, characterized by high, spiking fever within 12 hours of delivery; tachycardia; chills; and tender uterine fundus, occurs 15% to 25% of the time after PROM and is even higher after cesarean section.[87] Wound infection and sepsis may follow GBS infection. The diagnosis of intrapartum IAI or postpartum infection mandates broad-spectrum antibiotic coverage for suspected polymicrobial infection.

PREVENTION OF PERINATAL DISEASE

Infection with GBS remains a problem and its prevention a controversy. Major efforts have gone into attempting to block vertical transmission by the administration of prophylactic antibiotics. Washing the vagina with an antiseptic such as chlorhexidine has not changed the disease rates. Chemoprophylaxis during pregnancy is also unsuccessful. Administering penicillin intramuscularly to all neonates immediately after delivery may decrease some of the neonatal disease but will inadequately treat and may mask symptoms in those who are the sickest in the first few hours after delivery.

Although GBS is easily eradicated from the vaginas of pregnant carriers with antibiotics, recolonization from the gastrointestinal tract frequently occurs and the patient may become GBS positive again at the time of delivery. Because of these experiences, most experts believe that intrapartum antibiotic prophylaxis is the best strategy. Deciding which laboring patients should receive prophylaxis remains controversial.

In 1996[24] the CDC issued recommendations that took into consideration the prevention strategies that had been proposed by the American Academy of Pediatrics in 1992[2] and the American College of Obstetricians and Gynecologists in 1993.[3] They suggested that either a culture-based or a risk-based strategy could be cost-effective and lower the incidence of GBS infection in the neonate.

Under the culture-based approach, there is universal screening of all pregnant women with a combined vaginal (lower vagina/introitus) and anorectal culture at 35 to 37 weeks of gestation. Cultures remote from term may not be accurate and should not be used. The culture must be placed in selective broth media. All women with a positive culture should receive intrapartum antibiotic prophylaxis. Under the risk-based approach, the antepartum cultures are not obtained, and intrapartum prophylaxis is used in women with any of the following risk factors: PTL (<37 weeks of gestation), preterm PROM (<37 weeks of gestation), prolonged rupture of membranes (≥18 hours), maternal fever during labor (≥38.0°C, or ≥100.4°F), documented GBS bacteriuria during the current pregnancy, or previous delivery of a newborn with invasive GBS disease.

In 2002, the CDC issued replacement guidelines supporting a culture-based rather than a risk-based strategy for GBS prevention.[122] These revised guidelines were based partially on the results of several studies documenting that the incidence of neonatal GBS disease is significantly lower using the culture-based approach and that a greater proportion of GBS-positive women receive intrapartum prophylaxis under the culture-based approach.[18,123] Also in 2002, the American College of Obstetricians and Gynecologists issued a document reflecting the same opinion.[4] Under the new guidelines, all women should be screened with a culture at 35 to 37 weeks of gestation. Patients that arrive in labor with no documented culture results should be managed by using the risk-based approach. Intrapartum prophylaxis should be administered by the intravenous route. Penicillin is the agent of choice, with ampicillin an acceptable alternative. There is increasing bacterial resistance to second-line agents such as clindamycin and erythromycin[41,105]; therefore, if a patient is allergic to penicillin, it must be noted when the GBS culture is sent to the laboratory so that GBS antibiotic sensitivities can be reported with the culture results. If a patient is allergic to penicillin and not at a high risk of anaphylaxis, cefazolin may be used for intrapartum prophylaxis. If a patient is allergic to penicillin and at a high risk of anaphylaxis, clindamycin or erythromycin may be used as an alternative but only if GBS culture results document susceptibility to these agents. If culture results document resistance to clindamycin or erythromycin, vancomycin should be used as an alternative.

Strategies that involve antibiotic treatment of the newborn have also been studied. Single intramuscular injections of aqueous penicillin administered to the neonate immediately after delivery will prevent gonococcal ophthalmia and reduce the incidence of GBS infection. The major drawback to this approach is that the majority of infants developing severe early-onset disease are bacteremic at birth or very shortly thereafter, and a single intramuscular dose of penicillin is ineffective and may mask early symptoms. There are guidelines on the management of asymptomatic infants born to mothers receiving intrapartum antibiotics because of GBS coloniza-tion. Management schemes range from expectant observation to a complete workup for sepsis and prophylactic administration of antibiotics (see Chapter 37).

New avenues for the prevention of neonatal GBS infections are being actively explored. The use of a maternal vaccination against a polysaccharide capsule antigen or a universal antigen of the subtypes of GBS may allow the placental transfer of antibodies that could reduce or eliminate neonatal infection. Other research is directed at the use of hyperimmune and monoclonal intravenous immune globulin (IVIG) as adjuvant therapy or prophylaxis for the extremely preterm neonate.

Syphilis (See Chapter 37, Part 2.)

Descriptions of syphilis and its many manifestations have appeared in the medical literature since the 16th century. The introduction of antibiotics 50 years ago reduced the incidence of congenital syphilis to an all-time low of 200 reported cases in 1958. However, a resurgence of primary and secondary syphilis in recent years has caused a concomitant resurgence in neonatal cases.

EPIDEMIOLOGY

From the late 1970s to the mid-1980s, the incidence of primary and secondary syphilis rose slowly. Between 1986 and 1990, the epidemiology began to shift dramatically. The incidence of reported primary and secondary cases in women rose 240%, peaking at 20.3 cases per 100,000 population in 1990. This increase of reported cases in women seems to be related to the practice of trading sex with multiple partners to acquire illicit drugs, especially crack cocaine. Because these partners are frequently anonymous, the traditional syphilis control strategy of partner notification is ineffective. Many of these women who became pregnant received little or poor prenatal care.[26] By 1997, only 3.2 cases per 100,000 population were reported.[120] The incidence of congenital infection has paralleled this rise and fall. The recent decline may reflect the renewed attention given to syphilis control programs after the epidemic of the 1980s was recognized (Fig. 22-3). In recent years, there has been an increase in the incidence of primary and secondary syphilis cases in most urban centers in the United States, with an overall increase of more than 20% in 2002.[31] However, most of these new cases have occurred in men, with the rates among women remaining fairly stable.

CLINICAL MANIFESTATIONS, DIAGNOSIS, AND TREATMENT

After exposure to *Treponema pallidum*, there is an incubation period of 10 to 90 days before the development of primary syphilis. The hallmark of this stage

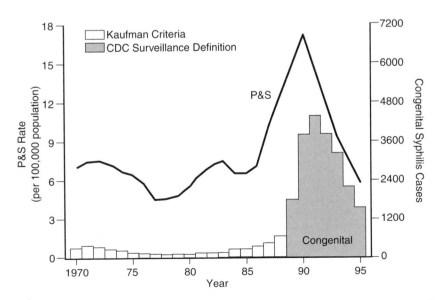

FIGURE 22-3. Congenital syphilis cases manifested in infants younger than 1 year of age and rates of primary and secondary (P&S) syphilis among women in the United States, 1970 to 1995. CDC, Centers for Disease Control and Prevention. (From the Centers for Disease Control and Prevention, Atlanta, Ga; Public Health Service, 1996.)

of infection is the painless chancre, which is usually indurated with raised borders and forms at the site of exposure. Although this manifestation is readily apparent in males, it is frequently located in the vagina or on the cervix of females and goes unnoticed. Primary syphilis is a local infection. In contrast, secondary syphilis occurs 4 to 10 weeks later and is a systemic infection, with dissemination of the organism through the bloodstream. The patient may present with a fever, generalized lymphadenopathy, or condyloma lata. The hallmark of this stage of infection is a generalized maculopapular rash involving the trunk, limbs, palms, and soles. This rash is often faint and may be missed. These symptoms and signs spontaneously resolve as the patient enters the latent stage, which may last for years. If untreated, approximately one third of these patients will go on to develop tertiary syphilis in 10 to 30 years. This stage is complicated by involvement of the central nervous and cardiovascular systems and gumma formation.[131]

Clinical diagnosis of "the great imitator" may be difficult, especially in pregnant patients. Antepartum diagnosis relies on serologic screening with nontreponemal tests such as the Venereal Disease Research Laboratory (VDRL) or the Rapid Plasma Reagin (RPR) tests. False positives occur in 1% to 2% of the tests and may be caused by recent febrile illness, subclinical autoimmune disease, or laboratory error. Reactive nontreponemal tests are confirmed by specific antibody tests such as the microhemagglutination assay for antibodies to *T. pallidum* (MHA-TP) or the fluorescent treponemal antibody-absorption (FTA-ABS) test.[67]

Syphilis is treated with penicillin. The number and route of doses depend on the stage of infection at the time of treatment.

CONGENITAL SYPHILIS (See Chapter 37, Part 2.)
Treponemes appear capable of crossing the placenta at any point in pregnancy, and infection can cause preterm delivery, stillbirth, congenital infection, nonimmune hydrops, and neonatal death. Fetal infection can also occur as a result of contact with active genital lesions during labor and delivery. Congenital syphilis causes fetal or perinatal death in 40% to 50% of the infants affected. Spontaneous abortion and stillbirth may be the results of overwhelming infection of the placenta and the resulting nonimmune hydrops. The earlier literature suggests that transmission occurs in virtually all of the infants born to mothers with primary and secondary syphilis, although only half of the infants may be symptomatic. The rate of transmission drops to 40% with early-latent (less than 2 years) and 6% to 14% with late-latent stages. Even with the appropriate antepartum diagnosis and antibiotic treatment of the mother, 11% of infants may demonstrate central nervous system involvement. The risk factors for congenital syphilis include the lack of prenatal care, substance abuse, and African-American race.

Clinical manifestations appearing in the first 2 years of life are referred to as early congenital syphilis, and those appearing later are referred to as late congenital syphilis. Early disease is associated with nonimmune

hydrops, intrauterine growth restriction, hemolytic anemia, hepatosplenomegaly, jaundice, rhinitis (sniffles), maculopapular rash, condyloma lata, bone abnormalities, ocular abnormalities, and central nervous system involvement. Bone abnormalities such as periostitis and osteochondritis of the long bone are very common. Late congenital syphilis results from untreated or incompletely treated early syphilis. Manifestations include neurologic involvement with mental retardation, eighth nerve deafness, and hydrocephalus; dental abnormalities such as Hutchinson teeth, mulberry molars, and rhagades; and bone abnormalities including a saddle nose, saber shins, and Clutton joints.

PREVENTION
The prevention of congenital syphilis requires prenatal care, antepartum screening, and appropriate antibiotic therapy. The CDC recommendations state that regardless of gestational age, infected gravidas should be immediately treated with the dose of penicillin appropriate for the stage of syphilis, as recommended for nonpregnant patients.[25] Patients with a history of penicillin allergy may be treated with penicillin after negative skin testing or penicillin desensitization. Tetracycline is not recommended during pregnancy because of adverse fetal effects. Although erythromycin may be an acceptable treatment for adults, it does not readily cross the placenta and may not treat the fetus as well as penicillin. Maternal follow-up includes monthly nontreponemal serologic testing. A rise in titers or the lack of a fourfold drop in titers over 3 months indicates a need for re-treatment. All patients should be offered counseling and testing for the HIV antibody because of the frequent association between the two infections.

As in nonpregnant patients, the treatment of the early stages of syphilis may precipitate the Jarisch-Herxheimer reaction. The typical fever, myalgia, and headache begin 2 to 4 hours after treatment and last 12 to 48 hours. Uterine contractions, decreased fetal movement, and fetal bradycardia can occur in pregnant patients. Fetal death is more likely to occur during the Jarisch-Herxheimer reaction, when the fetus is also affected.[99]

At birth the placenta and cord should be examined by dark-field microscopy for treponemes. Neonatal serum should be examined for IgM. Cerebrospinal fluid evaluation and long-bone radiography may be indicated. In the asymptomatic infant at birth, whose mother was appropriately treated and for whom close follow-up can be ensured, no antibiotic treatment may be needed. In the asymptomatic infant for whom follow-up is doubtful, a single intramuscular dose of benzathine penicillin is recommended. If the infant has active infection or neurosyphilis cannot be excluded, the CDC recommends a 10-day course of intramuscularly or intravenously administered penicillin.[25]

Listeriosis

Listeria monocytogenes is a motile, microaerophilic, gram-positive bacillus that infects primarily pregnant women, newborns, the elderly, and immunocompromised individuals. Infection with *L. monocytogenes* leads to approximately 2500 serious illnesses and 500 deaths in the United States annually. Maternal infection can lead to stillbirth and premature delivery. Neonatal infection is associated with high morbidity and mortality rates.

EPIDEMIOLOGY

L. monocytogenes is an unusual but important cause of perinatal infection. Cases may be sporadic or occur in epidemics.[34] Many types of mammals and birds harbor the organism, which is viable in manure for long periods of time. Food and dairy products have been implicated as sources of outbreaks.[29]

MATERNAL DISEASE AND TRANSMISSION

Approximately half of the women delivering infants infected with *L. monocytogenes* are asymptomatic before and during labor.[83] When symptomatic, they present with a nonspecific flulike syndrome with fever, malaise, back pain, and upper respiratory tract symptoms. Diagnosis is most accurately confirmed with blood or amniotic fluid cultures. Premature labor may accompany these findings.

Transmission is generally believed to be hematogenous, with evidence of placental infection. However, some neonates may be infected by ascending infection, even across intact membranes. It is believed that the fetus is infected first, and the amniotic fluid becomes infected by excretion of contaminated fetal urine. When listeriosis is diagnosed during pregnancy, treatment with high doses of ampicillin has been suggested.[132]

FETAL AND NEONATAL INFECTION (See Chapter 37, Part 2.)

Listeriosis septicemia may cause stillbirth or preterm delivery before viability is reached; however, it does not seem to be a cause of recurrent fetal loss. Prematurity, a birthweight of less than 2500 g, and evidence of fetal compromise are common. Like neonates with GBS infections, neonates with *L. monocytogenes* infection have either early (less than 4 hours after delivery) or late (1 to 6 weeks after delivery) manifestations. The infants presenting with early-onset disease classically have skin lesions, severe respiratory distress, hepatosplenomegaly, and laboratory evidence of sepsis. These infants are more likely to have mothers who were symptomatic before or during labor. Late-onset disease usually affects term healthy infants, with the typical symptoms of bacterial meningitis. Neonatal mortality in early-onset disease ranges from 30% to 60%.[132] In late-onset disease, neurologic sequelae such as hydrocephalus and mental retardation are common, and mortality may be as high as 40%.

Chlamydial Infection

Chlamydia trachomatis is a species of obligate intracellular bacteria. The organism depends on the invading cell for its energy supply and destroys the cell with replication. The 15 serotypes of *C. trachomatis* are responsible for three major groups of infection.

Serotypes L1, L2, and L3 cause lymphogranuloma venereum; serotypes A, B, Ba, and C cause endemic, blinding trachoma, the most common cause of blindness; and the remaining serotypes D through K are sexually transmitted agents that cause inclusion conjunctivitis, newborn pneumonia, urethritis, cervicitis, salpingitis, acute urethral syndrome, and perinatal infections.

EPIDEMIOLOGY AND CLINICAL MANIFESTATIONS

C. trachomatis is the most common bacterially sexually transmitted infection in the United States, with more than 4 million infections occurring annually. It is generally believed that 5% to 10% of sexually active women in the United States carry chlamydia in their cervix. Certain risk groups, such as young, inner-city women, especially African Americans, have a much higher prevalence. In large, prospective studies, the prevalence in pregnant women has ranged from 2% to 25%, depending on the group studied. Forty percent to 60% of women with positive gonorrhea cultures have a concomitant chlamydial infection. The anatomic site in the female genital tract that is the most frequently infected with *C. trachomatis* is the cervix. The ensuing endocervicitis may be asymptomatic or more commonly associated with a hypertrophic cervical erosion and copious mucopurulent discharge containing a high number of polymorphonuclear leukocytes. *C. trachomatis* is a common cause of tubal infertility.

Cell culture has long been the gold standard for the diagnosis of chlamydial infection. However, the most sensitive and specific tests currently available are nucleic acid amplification tests. The treatments of choice for infection with *C. trachomatis* are azithromycin and doxycycline, with erythromycin, ofloxacin, and levofloxacin as alternatives. In pregnancy the treatment options are limited. Doxycycline and ofloxacin are contraindicated, and the recommended alternatives include an erythromycin base and amoxicillin. Azithromycin in a single dose is a commonly used alternative, and it appears to have an efficacy similar to and a better side effect profile than erythromycin, although more study is still required.[1]

ASSOCIATION WITH ADVERSE PREGNANCY OUTCOME

Many studies have investigated the association between endocervical infection with *C. trachomatis* and adverse pregnancy outcomes, including prematurity, PROM, intrauterine growth restriction, and postpartum endometritis. Although some report no association of chlamydial infection with delivery before 37 weeks of gestation, others report odds ratios from 1.6 to 5.4. Berman and coworkers attempted to explain part of this discrepancy by noting a tighter association of prematurity and low birthweight with recent chlamydial infection, as demonstrated by the presence of IgM antibodies or IgG seroconversion.[12]

Antepartum treatment of chlamydia during pregnancy appears to improve pregnancy outcome, as suggested by Ryan and associates, who studied 11,544 women, 2433 (21.08%) of whom had a positive *Chlamydia*

TABLE 22-3. Association of Pregnancy Outcome and *Chlamydia trachomatis*

	CHLAMYDIA POSITIVE		CHLAMYDIA NEGATIVE	TOTAL
	UNTREATED	TREATED		
PROM	58 (5.2%)	39 (2.9%)	243 (2.7%)	340
Birthweight <2500 g	218 (19.6%)	145 (11.0%)	1068 (11.7%)	1431
Newborn survival[†]	1083 (97.6%)	1315 (99.4%)	8973 (98.5%)	11,371
Total numbers	1110	1323	9111	11,544

PROM, premature rupture of membranes.
[†]Defined as survival until hospital discharge
From Ryan GM: *Chlamydia trachomatis* infection in pregnancy and effect of treatment on outcome. Am J Obstet Gynecol 162:34, 1990.

culture on their first prenatal visit (Table 22-3).[118] Of the women with the positive cultures, 1100 were untreated and 1323 were treated with oral erythromycin or sulfamethoxazole. If untreated, culture-positive patients had a higher incidence of PROM, birthweight less than 2500 gm, and a lower incidence of newborn survival.

EFFECTS ON THE NEWBORN (See Chapter 37, Part 2.) Infants delivered vaginally to a woman with a chlamydial infection of the cervix have a 25% to 60% chance of becoming infected themselves. The manifestations of infection include conjunctivitis and pneumonia. Although it is uncommon, *C. trachomatis* has been isolated from infants delivered by elective cesarean section despite intact membranes.

Acute neonatal conjunctivitis in the newborn as a result of perinatal exposure to *C. trachomatis* has been recognized for some time. This organism is now the leading cause of neonatal conjunctivitis. Of those infants becoming infected with *C. trachomatis* after exposure during delivery, 17.5% to 46.5% will develop this conjunctivitis. When the infants of 230 culture-positive mothers received one of the three prophylactic regimens (silver nitrate, tetracycline 1%, or erythromycin 0.5%), no significant difference in the rate of chlamydial conjunctivitis was noted (20%, 11%, and 14%, respectively).[59]

Up to 20% of the infants delivered through a cervix infected with chlamydia will develop pneumonia. Infants between 4 and 11 weeks show signs of congestion and obstruction, little nasal discharge, minimal fever, tachypnea, and a prominent staccato-type cough. Chest radiograph reveals hyperinflated lungs with bilateral interstitial infiltrates. Blood gas analysis frequently shows mild or moderate hypoxia. Approximately 50% of these infants have a history of or concurrent conjunctivitis. Most infants recover quickly on oral erythromycin. Other neonatal clinical manifestations of *C. trachomatis* infection include otitis media, bronchiolitis, and perhaps gastroenteritis.

Toxoplasmosis (See Chapter 37, Part 3.)

Toxoplasma gondii is an obligate intracellular parasite with a complex life cycle occurring in three stages: the tachyzoite stage (present during acute infection), bradyzoite stage (present in tissue cysts during latent infection), and sporozoite stage (present in oocysts). Cats are the primary hosts and excrete unsporulated (noninfectious) oocysts in their feces. These cysts sporulate and become infectious in days or weeks. All other animals, including humans, are secondary hosts.

EPIDEMIOLOGY, CLINICAL MANIFESTATIONS, AND DIAGNOSIS

There are between 400 and 4000 cases of toxoplasmosis annually in the United States, and it is the third-leading infectious cause of food-borne death, after salmonella and listeria. The seroprevalence varies widely based on geography and is 20% to 50% in the United States.[6] There are three main routes of transmission: ingestion of raw or undercooked contaminated meat (the most common route in the United States), exposure to oocyst-infected cat feces, and vertical transmission. The risk factors for infection include owning cats and cleaning litter boxes, eating raw or undercooked meat, gardening, contact with soil, and travel to endemic areas. Household cats are usually not a major source of infection, but outdoor cats that hunt rodents may be.

Acute infection occurs after the ingestion of bradyzoites or sporozoites, which are then broken down by enzymes and released into the lumen of the gastrointestinal tract. From the lumen, the organisms invade endothelial cells and become tachyzoites. They are then widely disseminated to all organs (especially the central nervous system, heart, and skeletal muscle), where they form tissue cysts (bradyzoites) and persist for the life of the host. In immunocompetent adults, only 10% have symptoms of acute infection, including malaise, fever, rash, splenomegaly, and lymphadenopathy. After acute infection, permanent immunity develops.[10] Reactivation of latent disease can occur in immunocompromised individuals and often involves the central nervous system.

The diagnosis of toxoplasmosis is problematic because commercial test kits are relatively unreliable. It is recommended that positive results be confirmed in a reference laboratory. The diagnosis of acute maternal infection can be accomplished by the identification of serologic antibodies or *T. gondii* DNA by PCR. Serologic testing is the most commonly used diagnostic method, relying on the detection of IgM or the rising or high titers of IgG. A variety of tests have been used to make the diagnosis of fetal infection in utero. Ultrasound evaluation may detect dilatation of the ventricles (the most common ultrasound finding), ascites, hepatomegaly, and intracranial calcifications; however, the majority (80%) of cases will not have ultrasonographic evidence of infection.[108] Fetal blood samples for IgG and IgM and amniotic fluid for culture and mouse inoculation have been traditionally used for fetal diagnosis. However, PCR techniques performed on amniotic fluid samples alone provide a sensitivity and specificity equal to those of the older diagnostic tests, with less risk of pregnancy loss.[49]

TRANSMISSION AND NEONATAL DISEASE

The incidence of toxoplasmosis during pregnancy in the United States is approximately 1 in 1000. Intrauterine infection is possible only when the circulating tachyzoites are present to invade the placenta and then infect the fetus. Therefore, vertical transmission is limited to primary infection or reactivation in an immunocompromised host. In infection during pregnancy the organism infects the placenta, and then there is a lag period of 1 to 4 months between maternal and fetal infection. After this period, the placenta acts as a reservoir of infection and transmits viable organisms to the fetus. The risk of transmission increases with gestational age at the time of infection, such that it is from 10%-20% to 30% to 65% in the first, second, and third trimesters, respectively.[49,66] The overall risk of transmission in pregnancy is 20% to 50%. The severity of fetal disease is inversely related to gestational age at the time of infection, such that disease severity is the greatest if infection occurs in the first trimester. The vast majority of infected infants (>80% to 90%) are asymptomatic at birth. The most common clinical finding is chorioretinitis, which progresses in more than 80% of infected individuals by the age of 20.[57] Other abnormalities in the affected infant can include hydrocephaly, microcephaly, mental retardation, hepatosplenomegaly, jaundice, and lymphadenopathy.

The best information on fetal infection with *T. gondii* comes from France, where the prevalence is approximately 10 times that in the United States. There, serologic screening is compulsory. If initially seronegative, the pregnant woman is screened monthly for seroconversion. If untreated, the primarily infected gravida produces a clinically infected infant 13% to 30% of the time. The inclusion of the spontaneous abortions that may have been caused by toxoplasmosis infection would raise the transmission rate to 46%. Because of the much lower incidence of toxoplasmosis in this country, routine screening is not recommended.[6]

There are two tiers to toxoplasmosis treatment in pregnancy. For acute maternal infection and an uninfected fetus, spiramycin is used for prophylaxis. This drug prevents organisms from crossing the placenta and infecting the fetus and decreases the incidence of disease transmission. It is not available in the United States, and clarithromycin and azithromycin are alternatives.

When the fetus is infected, treatment is administered with pyrimethamine and sulfadiazine, which work synergistically, and folinic acid. This combination decreases the severity of the disease.

In France, women are now treated with spiramycin when acute infection is diagnosed. At 20 to 24 weeks, prenatal diagnosis is attempted by obtaining fetal blood through cordocentesis; amniotic fluid IgG and IgM antibody titers are performed and mice inoculated, looking for signs of infection. If the fetus appears infected, pyrimethamine and either sulfadoxine or sulfadiazine are added to the treatment regimen. Daffos and coworkers reported on 746 documented cases of maternal toxoplasmosis treated in this manner.[38] Congenital infection was demonstrated in 42 infants, 39 of whom were diagnosed antenatally. Twenty-four pregnancies were terminated and 15 were carried to term. Of the 15 fetuses with congenital toxoplasmosis, all but 2 who had chorioretinitis remained clinically well throughout follow-up. Maternal infection occurred earlier during the pregnancy in fetuses that were aborted, and almost all had ultrasonographic evidence suggestive of toxoplasmosis. Three fetuses of the remaining 702 demonstrated evidence of congenital toxoplasmosis despite negative antepartum studies: 2 with subclinical disease and 1 with meningoencephalitis and chorioretinitis. Thus, prenatal diagnosis can provide practical information for those debating pregnancy termination. It appears that the initiation of in utero therapy may reduce the severity of the disease in newborns.[50]

To prevent maternal disease, pregnant women should be advised to eat only adequately cooked meat, avoid changing cat litter or wear gloves when doing so, wear gloves when gardening, and thoroughly wash all fruits and vegetables before ingestion.

REFERENCES

1. Adair CD et al: Chlamydia in pregnancy: A randomized trial of azithromycin and erythromycin. Obstet Gynecol 91:165, 1998.
2. American Academy of Pediatrics Committee of Infectious Diseases and Committee on Fetus and Newborn: Guidelines for prevention of group B streptococcal (GBS) infection by chemoprophylaxis. Pediatrics 90:775, 1992.
3. American College of Obstetricians and Gynecologists: Group B streptococcal infections in pregnancy: ACOG's recommendations. ACOG News 37:1, 1993.
4. American College of Obstetricians and Gynecologists Committee Opinion: Prevention of early-onset group B streptococcal disease in newborns. Obstet Gynecol 100:1405, 2002.
5. Andrews WW et al: The Preterm Prediction Study: Association of second-trimester genitourinary Chlamydia infection with subsequent spontaneous preterm birth. Am J Obstet Gynecol 183:662, 2000.
6. Bader TJ et al: Prenatal screening for toxoplasmosis. Obstet Gynecol 90:457, 1997.
7. Baker CJ: Group B streptococcal infections. Clin Perinatol 24:59, 1997.
8. Barbacci M et al: Routine prenatal screening for HIV infection. Lancet 337:709, 1991.

9. Beasley RP et al: The e antigen and vertical transmission of hepatitis B surface antigen. Am J Epidemiol 105:94, 1977.

10. Beazley D, Ergerman R: Toxoplasmosis. Semin Perinatol 22:332, 1998.

11. Benedetti J et al: Recurrence rates in genital herpes after symptomatic first-episode infection. Ann Intern Med 121:847, 1994.

12. Berman SW et al: Low birth weight, prematurity and postpartum endometritis: Association with prenatal cervical *Mycoplasma hominis* and *Chlamydia trachomatis* infections. JAMA 257:1189, 1987.

13. Boyer KM, Gotoff SP: Antimicrobial prophylaxis of neonatal group B streptococcal sepsis. Clin Perinatol 15:831, 1988.

14. Brocklehurst P, French R: The association between maternal HIV infection and perinatal outcome: A systematic review of the literature and meta-analysis. Br J Obstet Gynaecol 105:836, 1998.

15. Brown H, Abernathy MP: Cytomegalovirus infection. Semin Perinatol 22:260, 1998.

16. Brown ZA et al: Genital herpes in pregnancy: Risk factors associated with recurrences and asymptomatic viral shedding. Am J Obstet Gynecol 153:24, 1985.

17. Brown ZA et al: Neonatal herpes simplex virus infection in relation to asymptomatic maternal infection at the time of labor. N Engl J Med 324:1247, 1991.

18. Brozanski BS et al: Effect of a screening-based prevention policy on prevalence of early-onset group B streptococcal sepsis. Obstet Gynecol 95:496, 2000.

19. Caro-Paton T et al: Is metronidazole teratogenic? A meta-analysis. Br J Clin Pharmacol 44:179, 1997.

20. Carpenter CCJ et al: Antiretroviral therapy for HIV infection in 1998: Updated recommendations of the International AIDS Society-USA panel. JAMA 280:78, 1998.

21. Centers for Disease Control and Prevention: Prevention of perinatal transmission of hepatitis B virus: Prenatal screening of all pregnant women for hepatitis B surface antigen. MMWR Morbid Mortal Wkly Rep 37:341, 1988.

22. Centers for Disease Control and Prevention: Measles, mumps, and rubella-vaccine use and strategies for elimination of measles, rubella, and congenital rubella syndrome and control of mumps: Recommendations of the Advisory Committee on Immunization Practices (ACIP). MMWR Morbid Mortal Wkly Rep 47(RR-8):1, 1988.

23. Centers for Disease Control and Prevention: Hepatitis E among US travelers, 1989-1992. MMWR Morbid Mortal Wkly Rep 42:1, 1993.

24. Centers for Disease Control and Prevention: Prevention of perinatal group B streptococcal disease: A public health perspective. MMWR Morbid Mortal Wkly Rep 45(RR-7):1, 1996.

25. Centers for Disease Control and Prevention: 1998 guidelines for treatment of sexually transmitted diseases. MMWR Morbid Mortal Wkly Rep 47:RR-1, 1998.

26. Centers for Disease Control and Prevention: Epidemic of congenital syphilis—Baltimore, 1996-1997. MMWR Morbid Mortal Wkly Rep 47:904, 1998.

27. Centers for Disease Control and Prevention: Public Health Service Task Force recommendations for the use of antiretroviral drugs in pregnant women infected with HIV-1 for maternal health and for reducing perinatal HIV-1 transmission in the United States. MMWR Morbid Mortal Wkly Rep 47:RR-2, 1998.

28. Centers for Disease Control and Prevention: Recommendations for prevention and control of hepatitis C virus (HCV) infection and HCV-related chronic disease. MMWR Morbid Mortal Wkly Rep 47:1, 1998.

29. Centers for Disease Control and Prevention: Update: Multistate outbreak of listeriosis—United States, 1998-1999. MMWR Morbid Mortal Wkly Rep 47:1117, 1999.

30. Centers for Disease Control and Prevention: HIV testing among pregnant women—United States and Canada, 1998-2001. MMWR Morbid Mortal Wkly Rep 51:1013, 2002.

31. Centers for Disease Control and Prevention: Primary and secondary syphilis—United States, 2002. MMWR Morbid Mortal Wkly Rep 52:1117, 2003.

32. Chandra PC et al: Successful pregnancy outcome after complicated varicella pneumonia. Obstet Gynecol 92:680, 1998.

33. Chapman SJ: Varicella in pregnancy. Semin Perinatol 22:339, 1998.

34. Cherubin CE et al: Epidemiological spectrum and current treatment of listeriosis. Rev Infect Dis 13:1108, 1991.

35. Connor EM et al: Reduction of maternal-infant transmission of human immunodeficiency virus type 1 with zidovudine treatment. N Engl J Med·331:1173, 1994.

36. Cooper ER et al: Combination antiretroviral strategies for the treatment of pregnant HIV-1-infected women and prevention of perinatal HIV-1 transmission. J AIDS 29:484, 2002.

37. Dabis F et al: Six-month efficacy, tolerance, and acceptability of a short regimen of oral zidovudine to reduce vertical transmission of HIV in breastfed children in Cote d'Ivoire and Burkina Faso: A double-blind placebo-controlled multitcentre trial. Lancet 353:786, 1999.

38. Daffos F et al: Prenatal management of 746 pregnancies at risk for congenital toxoplasmosis. N Engl J Med 318:271, 1988.

39. Danovaro-Holliday MC et al: A large rubella outbreak with spread from the workplace to the community. JAMA 284:2733, 2000.

40. Duff P: Hepatitis in pregnancy. Semin Perinatol 22:277, 1998.

41. Edwards RK et al: Intrapartum antibiotic prophylaxis 2: Positive predictive value of antenatal group B streptococci cultures and antibiotic susceptibility of clinical isolates. Obstet Gynecol 100:540, 2002.

42. Edwards RK, Duff P: Single additional dose postpartum therapy for women with chorioamnionitis. Obstet Gynecol 102(5 Pt 1):957, 2003.

43. Egarter C et al: Adjunctive antibiotic treatment in preterm labor and neonatal morbidity: A meta-analysis. Obstet Gynecol 88:303, 1996.

44. Enders G et al: Consequences of varicella and herpes zoster in pregnancy: Prospective study of 1739 cases. Lancet 343:1547, 1994.

45. Eriksen NL: Perinatal consequences of hepatitis C. Clin Obstet Gynecol 42:121, 1999.

46. European Mode of Delivery Collaboration: Elective cesarean section versus vaginal delivery in prevention of vertical HIV-1 transmission: A randomized clinical trial. Lancet 353:1035, 1999.

47. Fan YD et al: Acute pyelonephritis in pregnancy. Am J Perinatol 4:324, 1987.

48. Fleming DT et al: Herpes simplex virus type 2 in the United States, 1976 to 1994. N Engl J Med 337:1105, 1997.

49. Forestier F et al: Prenatal diagnosis of congenital toxoplasmosis by PCR: Extended experience. Prenat Diag 18:405, 1998.

50. Foulon W et al: Treatment of toxoplasmosis during pregnancy: A multicenter study of impact on fetal

transmission and children's sequelae at age 1 year. Am J Obstet Gynecol 180:410, 1999.

51. Garcia PM et al: Maternal levels of plasma human immunodeficiency virus type 1 RNA and the risk of perinatal transmission. N Engl J Med 341:394, 1999.

52. Gardner HL, Dukes CD: *Haemophilus vaginalis* vaginitis. Am J Obstet Gynecol 69:962, 1955.

53. Gibbs RS, Eschenbach DA: Use of antibiotics to prevent preterm birth. Am J Obstet Gynecol 177:375, 1997.

54. Gibbs RS et al: Quantitative bacteriology of amniotic fluid from patients with clinical intra-amniotic infection at term. J Infect Dis 145:1, 1982.

55. Glantz JC, Mushlin AI: Cost-effectiveness of routine antenatal varicella screening. Obstet Gynecol 91:519, 1998.

56. Guay LA et al: Intrapartum and neonatal single-dose nevirapine compared with zidovudine for prevention of mother-to-child transmission of HIV-1 in Kampala, Uganda: HIVNET 012 randomised trial. Lancet 354:795, 1999.

57. Guerina NG et al: Neonatal serologic screening and early treatment for congenital *Toxoplasma gondii* infection. N Engl J Med 330:1858, 1994.

58. Guise JM et al: Screening for bacterial vaginosis in pregnancy. Am J Prev Med 20(Suppl 3):62, 2001.

59. Hammerschlag MR et al: Efficacy of neonatal ocular prophylaxis for the prevention of chlamydial and gonococcal conjunctivitis. N Engl J Med 320:769, 1989.

60. Harger JH et al: Prospective evaluation of 618 pregnant women exposed to parvovirus B19: Risks and symptoms. Obstet Gynecol 91:416, 1998.

61. Harger JH et al: Risk factors and outcome of varicella-zoster virus pneumonia in pregnant women. J Infect Dis 185:422, 2002.

62. Hart A et al: Ampicillin-resistant Escherichia coli in gestational pyelonephritis: Increased occurrence and association with the colonization factor Dr adhesion. J Infect Dis 183:1526, 2001.

63. Hauth JC et al: Reduced incidence of preterm delivery with metronidazole and erythromycin in women with bacterial vaginosis. N Engl J Med 333:1732, 1995.

64. Hensleigh PA et al: Genital herpes during pregnancy: Inability to distinguish primary and recurrent lesions clinically. Obstet Gynecol 89:891, 1997.

65. Hill JB et al: Risk of hepatitis B transmission in breast-fed infants of chronic hepatitis B carriers. Obstet Gynecol 99:1049, 2002.

66. Hohfeld P et al: Fetal toxoplasmosis: Outcome of pregnancy and infant follow-up after in utero treatment. J Pediatr 115:765, 1989.

67. Hollier LM, Cox SM: Syphilis. Semin Perinatol 22:323, 1998.

68. Ioannidis JPA et al: Perinatal transmission of human immunodeficiency virus type 1 by pregnant women with RNA virus loads <1000 copies/ml. J Infect Dis 183:539, 2001.

69. The International Perinatal HIV Group: The mode of delivery and the risk of vertical transmission of human immunodeficiency virus type 1: A meta-analysis of 15 prospective cohort studies. N Engl J Med 340:977, 1999.

70. Jacobsson B et al: Microbial invasion and cytokine response in amniotic fluid in a Swedish population of women in preterm labor. Acta Obstetrica et Gyn Scand 82:120, 2003.

71. Jamie WE et al: Antimicrobial susceptibility of gram-negative uropathogens isolated from obstetric patients. Infect Dis Obstet Gynecol 10:123, 2002.

72. Jeffcoat MK et al: Periodontal disease and preterm birth: Results of a pilot intervention study. J Periodontol 74:1214, 2003.

73. Joesoef MR et al: Intravaginal clindamycin treatment for bacterial vaginosis: Effects on preterm delivery and low birth weight. Am J Obstet Gynecol 173:1527, 1995.

74. Kekki M et al: Vaginal clindamycin in preventing preterm birth and peripartal infections in asymptomatic women with bacterial vaginosis: A randomized, controlled trial. Obstet Gynecol 97(5 Pt 1):643, 2001.

75. Kenyon SL et al: Broad-spectrum antibiotics for preterm, prelabour rupture of fetal membranes: The ORACLE I randomised trial. Lancet 357:979, 2001.

76. Kimberlin DF, Andrews WW: Bacterial vaginosis: Association with adverse pregnancy outcome. Semin Perinatol 22:242, 1998.

77. Kimberlin DF et al: Pharmacokinetics of oral valacyclovir and acyclovir in late pregnancy. Am J Obstet Gynecol 179:846, 1998.

78. Klebanoff MA et al. Failure of metronidazole to prevent preterm delivery among pregnant women with asymptomatic *Trichomonas vaginalis* infection. N Engl J Med 345:487, 2001.

79. Kurki T et al: Bacterial vaginosis in early pregnancy and pregnancy outcome. Obstet Gynecol 80:173, 1992.

80. Kustermann A et al: Prenatal diagnosis of congenital varicella infection. Prenat Diag 16:71, 1996.

81. Lamont RF et al: Intravaginal clindamycin to reduce preterm birth in women with abnormal genital tract flora. Obstet Gynecol 101:516, 2003.

82. Leitich H et al: Antibiotic treatment of bacterial vaginosis in pregnancy: A meta-analysis. Am J Obstet Gynecol 188:752, 2003.

83. Lorber B: Listeriosis. Clin Infect Dis 24:1, 1997.

84. Markenson GR, Yancey MK: Parvovirus B19 infections in pregnancy. Semin Perinatol 22:309, 1998.

85. McDonald HM et al: Impact of metronidazole therapy on preterm birth in women with bacterial vaginosis flora (*Gardnerella vaginalis*): A randomized, placebo controlled trial. Br J Obstet Gynecol 104:1391, 1997.

86. McGregor JA et al: Bacterial vaginosis is associated with prematurity and vaginal fluid mucinase and sialidase: Results of a controlled trial of topical clindamycin cream. Am J Obstet Gynecol 170:1048, 1994.

87. McKenna DS, Iams JD: Group B streptococcal infections. Semin Perinatol 22:267, 1998.

88. Meis P et al: The preterm prediction study: Significance of vaginal infections. Am J Obstet Gynecol 173:1231, 1995.

89. Mercer BM: Antibiotic therapy for preterm premature rupture of membranes. Clin Obstet Gynecol 41:461, 1998.

90. Mercer B et al, for the National Institute of Child Health and Human Development Maternal Fetal Medicine Units Network: Antibiotic therapy for reduction of infant morbidity after preterm premature rupture of the membranes. JAMA 278:989, 1997.

91. Millar LK et al: Uterine contraction frequency during treatment of pyelonephritis in pregnancy and subsequent risk of preterm birth. J Perinatol Med 31:41, 2003.

92. Miller E et al: Consequences of confirmed maternal rubella at successive stages of pregnancy. Lancet 2:781, 1982.

93. Miller E et al: Immediate and long-term outcome of human parvovirus B19 infection in pregnancy. Br J Obstet Gynaecol 105:174, 1998.

94. Miller JM Jr et al: Initial and repeated screening for gonorrhea during pregnancy. Sex Trans Dis 30:728, 2003.

95. Minkoff HL: Human immunodeficiency virus infection in pregnancy. Semin Perinatol 22:293, 1998.

96. Mohammad M et al: Laboratory aspects of asymptomatic bacteriuria in pregnancy. Southeast Asian J Trop Med Public Health 33:575, 2002.

97. Montaner JS et al: Antiretroviral treatment in 1998. Lancet 352:1919, 1998.

98. Morales WJ et al: Effect of metronidazole in patients with preterm birth in preceding pregnancy and bacterial vaginosis: A placebo-controlled, double-blind study. Am J Obstet Gynecol 171:345, 1994.

99. Myles TD et al: The Jarisch-Herxheimer reaction and fetal monitoring changes in pregnant women treated for syphilis. Obstet Gynecol 92:859, 1998.

100. Nelson CT, Demmler GJ: Cytomegalovirus infection in the pregnant mother, fetus and newborn infant. Clin Perinatol 24:151, 1997.

101. Parry S, Strauss JF: Premature rupture of the fetal membranes. N Engl J Med 338:663, 1998.

102. Paryani SG, Arvin AM: Intrauterine infection with varicella-zoster virus after maternal varicella. N Engl J Med 314:1542, 1986.

103. Pastuszak AL et al: Outcome after maternal varicella infection in the first 20 weeks of pregnancy. N Engl J Med 330:901, 1994.

104. Patterson TF, Andriole VT: Detection, significance and therapy of bacteriuria in pregnancy: Update in the managed health care era. Infect Dis Clin North Am 11:593, 1997.

105. Pearlman MD et al: Frequent resistance of clinical group B streptococci isolates to clindamycin and erythromycin. Obstet Gynecol 92:258, 1998.

106. Peltola H, Leinikki P: Rubella gene sequencing as a clinician's tool. Lancet 352:1799, 1998.

107. Piper JM, Wen TS: Perinatal cytomegalovirus and toxoplasmosis: Challenges of antepartum therapy. Clin Obstet Gynecol 42:81, 1999.

108. Puder KS et al: Ultrasound characteristics of in utero infection. Infect Dis Obstet Gynecol 5:262, 1997.

109. Ramus RM et al: A randomized trial that compared oral cefixime and intramuscular ceftriaxone for the treatment of gonorrhea in pregnancy. Am J Obstet Gynecol 185:629, 2001.

110. Reef SE: Rubella and congenital rubella syndrome. Bull World Health Org 76(S2):156, 1998.

111. Riggs JW, Blanco JD: Pathophysiology, diagnosis and management of intraamniotic infection. Semin Perinatol 22:251, 1998.

112. Riley LE: Herpes simplex virus. Semin Perinatol 22:284, 1998.

113. Roberts SW et al: Genital herpes during pregnancy: No lesions, no cesarean. Obstet Gynecol 85:261, 1995.

114. Robinson J et al: Congenital rubella after anticipated maternal immunity: Two cases and a review of the literature. Pediatr Infect Dis J 13:812, 1994.

115. Rodis JF et al: Management of parvovirus infection in pregnancy and outcomes of hydrops: A survey of members of the Society of Perinatal Obstetricians. Am J Obstet Gynecol 179:985, 1998.

116. Rodis JF et al: Long-term outcome of children following maternal human parvovirus B19 infection. Obstet Gynecol 91:125, 1998.

117. Rosa C: Rubella and rubeola. Semin Perinatol 22:318, 1998.

118. Ryan GM et al: *Chlamydia trachomatis* infection in pregnancy and effect of treatment on outcome. Am J Obstet Gynecol 162:34, 1990.

119. Sampson L, King S: Evidence-based guidelines for universal counseling and offering of HIV testing in pregnancy in Canada. CMAJ 158:1449, 1998.

120. Sanchez PJ, Wendel GD: Syphilis in pregnancy. Clin Perinatol 24:71, 1997.

121. Schrag SJ et al: Group B streptococcal disease in the era of intrapartum antibiotic prophylaxis. N Engl J Med 342:15, 2000.

122. Schrag S et al: Prevention of perinatal group B streptococcal disease. Revised guidelines from CDC. MMWR Recomm Rep 51(RR-11):1, 2002.

123. Schrag S et al: A population-based comparison of strategies to prevent early-onset group B streptococcal disease in neonates. N Engl J Med 347:233, 2002.

124. Scott LL: Prevention of perinatal herpes: Prophylactic antiviral therapy. Clin Obstet Gynecol 42:134, 1999.

125. Scott LL et al: Acyclovir suppression to prevent cesarean delivery after first-episode genital herpes. Obstet Gynecol 87:69, 1996.

126. Scott LL et al: Acyclovir suppression to prevent clinical recurrences at delivery after first episode genital herpes in pregnancy: An open-label trial. Infect Dis Obstet Gynecol 9:75, 2001.

127. Scott LL et al: Acyclovir suppression to prevent recurrent genital herpes at delivery. Infect Dis Obstet Gynecol 10:71, 2002.

128. Siegel JD: Prophylaxis for neonatal group B *Streptococcus* infections. Semin Perinatol 22:33, 1998.

129. Sever JL et al: Delayed manifestation of congenital rubella. Rev Infect Dis 7(Suppl 1):S164, 1985.

130. Shaffer N et al: Short-course zidovudine for perinatal HIV-1 transmission in Bangkok, Thailand: A randomised controlled trial. Lancet 353:773, 1999.

131. Sheffield JS, Wendel GD: Syphilis in pregnancy. Clin Obstet Gynecol 42:97, 1999.

132. Silver HM: Listeriosis during pregnancy. Obstet Gynecol Surv 53:737, 1998.

133. Silverman NS et al: Hepatitis C virus in pregnancy: Seroprevalence and risk factors for infection. Am J Obstet Gynecol 169:583, 1993.

134. Smith WJ et al: Prevention of chickenpox in reproductive-age women: Cost-effectiveness of routine prenatal screening with postpartum vaccination of susceptibles. Obstet Gynecol 92:535, 1998.

135. Stango S et al: Primary cytomegalovirus infection in pregnancy: Incidence, transmission to fetus and clinical outcome. JAMA 256:1904, 1986.

136. Strauss SE et al: NIH Conference. Varicella-zoster infections: Virology, natural history, treatment and prevention. Ann Intern Med 108:221, 1988.

137. Stringer EM et al: Evaluation of a new testing policy for human immunodeficiency virus to improve screening rates. Obstet Gynecol 98:1104, 2001.

138. Tanemura M et al: Diagnosis of fetal rubella infection with reverse transcription and nested polymerase chain reaction: A study of 34 cases diagnosed in fetuses. Am J Obstet Gynecol 174:578, 1996.

139. Towers CV et al: Pulmonary injury associated with antepartum pyelonephritis: Can patients at risk be identified? Am J Obstet Gynecol 164:974, 1991.

140. Uncu Y et al: Should asymptomatic bacteriuria be screened in pregnancy? Clin Exp Obstet Gynecol 29:281, 2002.

141. Valeur-Jensen AK et al: Risk factors for parvovirus B19 infection in pregnancy. JAMA 28:1109, 1999.

142. Vermeulen GM, Bruinse HW: Prophylactic administration of clindamycin 2% vaginal cream to reduce the

incidence of spontaneous preterm birth in women with an increased recurrence risk: A randomized placebo-controlled double-blind trial. Br J Obstet Gynaecol 106:652, 1999.

143. Webster WS: Teratogen update: Congenital rubella. Teratology 58:13, 1988.

144. Wiktor SZ et al: Short-course oral zidovudine for prevention of mother-to-child transmission of HIV-1 in Abidjan, Cote d'Ivoire: A randomised trial. Lancet 353:781, 1999.

145. Wing DA et al: Limited clinical utility of blood and urine cultures in the treatment of acute pyelonephritis during pregnancy. Am J Obstet Gynecol 182:1437, 2000.

146. Wood EG, Dillon HC Jr: A prospective study of group B streptococcal bacteriuria in pregnancy. Am J Obstet Gynecol 140:515, 1981.

147. Wu YW et al: Chorioamnionitis and cerebral palsy in term and near-term infants. JAMA 290:2677, 2003.

148. Yoder PR et al: A prospective, controlled study of maternal and perinatal outcome after intra-amniotic infection at term. Am J Obstet Gynecol 145:695, 1983.

149. Yudin MH et al: Clinical and cervical cytokine response to treatment with oral or vaginal metronidazole for bacterial vaginosis during pregnancy: A randomized trial. Obstet Gynecol 102:527, 2003.

150. Zanetti AR et al: Multicenter trial on the efficacy of HBIG and vaccine in preventing perinatal hepatitis B: Final report. J Med Virol 18:327, 1986.

23 Placental Pathology

Raymond W. Redline

No evaluation of a sick neonate is complete without knowing the status of the organ that has supported the fetus through the preceding gestation—the placenta with its surrounding membranes. The placenta has two opposing functions during gestation. It is both the sole source of all metabolic fuels to the fetus and the sole protection for the fetus against noxious external influences, such as genital microorganisms, the maternal immune system, and the spatial constraints of the uterus. Therefore, it is important for the neonatologist and the obstetrician to be aware of the specific pathogenic sequences of the placental lesions that compromise these functions.

This chapter makes no attempt to comprehensively review placental pathology; the reader is referred to three general references.[13,22,54] Rather, it provides an overview of three topics: (1) the optimal use of the pathology service to obtain useful information, (2) an understanding of specific patterns of placental injury in the context of normal form and function, and (3) a clinicopathologic correlation (i.e., which lesions are seen in which clinical situations).

within 1 to 2 hours of delivery is not possible, the placentas should be immersed in 2 to 3 vol of formalin, where they can remain for an indefinite period before examination by the pathologist. An informed evaluation of the placenta requires that the pathologist be aware of the clinical situation. Some mechanism, usually a form, must be established to convey this information. A proper balance should be struck between a totally open-ended form and a tedious checklist. An example of a form that may be useful is given in Figure 23-1. Placental diagnosis requires very few special studies. Even bacterial cultures in cases of suspected chorioamnionitis rarely provide useful information beyond that which is available from placental histology and the infant's blood culture. Fungal stains of the cord and membranes may be occasionally useful for neonatal management. In selected situations a placental karyotype may be of interest. Recent data suggest that some cases of intrauterine fetal demise and idiopathic intrauterine growth restriction (IUGR) may be explained on the basis of chromosomal anomalies confined to placental tissues (confined placental mosaicism).[44,46,47,120]

OPTIMAL USE OF THE PATHOLOGIST

As just suggested, any infant requiring the care of a neonatologist should have a placental examination. Because not all placentas are submitted to pathology, every obstetric service needs to have a specific list of situations in which a placental examination is indicated. An example of such a list is provided in Box 23-1.[90] Because many sick neonates are transported from other hospitals, there should be a policy to ensure a timely placental examination. The best solution is to transport the placenta in a watertight container along with the neonate to the tertiary care center. For various reasons, the transport of the tissue specimen itself is sometimes not practical. In these cases, the slides and pathology report from the referring hospital should be requested and reviewed by the pathologist at the hospital where the neonate is to be treated. Whenever possible, the placentas should be refrigerated immediately after delivery and sent without fixative to the pathology laboratory. Specimens maintained in this fashion remain useful for as long as 7 days after delivery. When refrigeration

BOX 23-1. Indications for Placental Examination

Neonatal
Prematurity
Intrauterine growth restriction
Unexpected adverse outcome
Congenital anomalies
Suspicion of fetal infection
Fetal hydrops
Fetal hematologic abnormalities

Obstetric
Intrauterine fetal demise
Maternal disease or maternal death
Signs of maternal infection
Gestational hypertension
Oligohydramnios or polyhydramnios
Antepartum hemorrhage (acute and/or chronic)
Postpartum hemorrhage
Abnormal biophysical or biochemical monitoring
In utero therapy
Abnormal placenta noted at delivery

Sheet filled out M.D. (printed name) _____

Gestational Age (best estimate): _____

Ob Index: G____ Full Term _____ Prem ____ Ab ____ Lvg ____

Maternal History:

Baby (weight, Apgars, malformations, other):

Any specific questions about this placenta?

FIGURE 23-1. Placental data sheet used to transmit clinical history to the pathologist. Each item is widely spaced on the actual full-page form to provide sufficient space for free text.

STRUCTURE, FUNCTION, AND PATHOLOGY

Overview

At its simplest level the placenta is nothing more than a bundle of fetal vessels and surrounding connective tissue that is in turn surrounded by a continuous layer of epithelium known as the trophoblast. This fetal vascular bed sits in a pool of maternal blood called the intervillous space, which is continuously filled and drained from below by maternal uterine arteries and veins (Fig. 23-2). The same unit of structure is repeated in the membranes in an attenuated form. Early in pregnancy the fetal vasculature and maternal intervillous space involute in that portion of the gestational sac destined to become the membranes, leaving a tough shell of fetal connective tissue and the placental trophoblast in contact with the maternal uterus. Detailed knowledge of each of these anatomic compartments and their reaction patterns in abnormal pregnancies provides the basis for understanding placental pathology.

Considering the fetal circulation first, the placenta is perfused by a pair of umbilical arteries and drained by a single umbilical vein. Because there is an arterial anastomosis near the umbilical cord insertion site, the fetus is not handicapped if one of the arteries is absent or occluded. On the other hand, the vein is the sole supply of oxygenated placental blood for the fetus. It also has the thinnest wall and is the easiest of the three umbilical vessels to collapse. Large arteries and veins branching off from the umbilical vessels transmit blood through proximal stem villi to distal villous units, where gas exchange occurs. Decreased flow in these vessels leads to luminal occlusion (fibromuscular sclerosis) and involution of the distal vascular bed (avascular villi).[32] This reaction is global in the placentas from stillborn fetuses and focal in live-born infants with placental thrombi or some other cause of upstream vascular obstruction (Fig. 23-3A). Each distal villous unit consists of a central, mature, intermediate stem villus and several surrounding terminal villi. Mature, intermediate stem villi have at least one arteriole that directly regulates flow to the terminal villous capillary bed. Obliteration, stenosis, or spasm of these arterioles can have a profound impact on gas exchange.[31,35,100] Finally, terminal

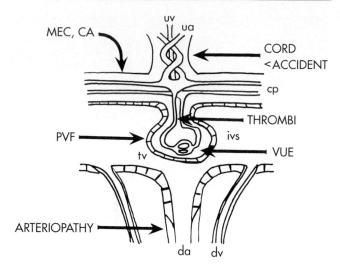

FIGURE 23-2. Schematic diagram of a functional unit in the placenta, with sites and patterns of injury indicated by arrows. Deoxygenated fetal blood enters the placenta via umbilical arteries (ua) and flows through the chorionic plate (cp) and stem villous arteries before entering terminal villi (tv). Flow into capillaries is regulated by stem villous arterioles. Postcapillary venules combine to form stem villous and chorionic plate veins, which drain into a single umbilical vein (uv) that carries oxygenated blood to the fetus. Maternal blood enters the intervillous space (ivs) via decidual arteries (da) lined with the trophoblast *(hatched lines)* and drains through unmodified decidual veins (dv). Decidual arteriopathy (ARTERIOPATHY) restricts maternal perfusion of the intervillous space. Perivillous fibrin (PVF) coats the villous trophoblast *(hatched lines)*, preventing gas exchange. Villitis of unknown etiology (VUE) expands the villous stroma, increasing the diffusion distance. A cord accident (CORD ACCIDENT) compresses the umbilical vessels, causing a global decrease in fetoplacental circulation. Meconium (MEC) and chorioamnionitis (CA) may decrease villous perfusion by damaging fetal vessels in the chorionic plate. Fetal thrombotic vasculopathy (THROMBI) similarly decreases the distal fetal vascular bed.

villi have a capillary bed that can sustain microvascular damage, leading to villous edema[77] or stromal hemorrhage,[33] or undergo reactive hyperplasia (chorangiosis) in response to hypoxia or other local stimuli.[4]

Turning to the maternal circulation, it is important to emphasize that adequate placental perfusion depends on pregnancy-related increases in maternal intravascular volume and decreases in maternal vascular tone.[75] Maternal conditions such as renal disease, essential hypertension, and collagenous-vascular disease can cause *chronic uteroplacental underperfusion* by interfering with these systemic accommodations to pregnancy. To ensure adequate perfusion of the intervillous space, the human placenta has evolved a mechanism for remodeling and enlarging uteroplacental arteries.[83,86] The placental trophoblast grows down the lumen of these vessels, invades the vascular wall, and replaces the smooth muscle layer with a noncontractile layer of fibrinoid matrix. Failure to execute this entire sequence may compromise baseline perfusion and leave uteroplacental vessels susceptible to spasm, degeneration, and rupture. These abnormalities are believed to play an important role in the pathogenesis of preeclampsia

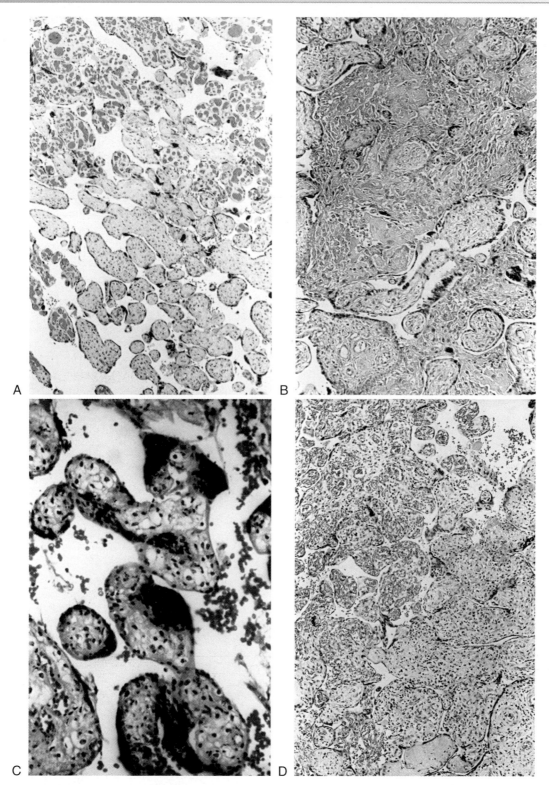

FIGURE 23-3. Histologic patterns of placental injury. **A,** Fetal thrombotic vasculopathy—avascular villi *(lower right)* due to upstream vascular occlusion. **B,** Massive perivillous fibrin deposition—fibrin with a proliferating extravillous trophoblast encases terminal villi (especially *upper left*). **C,** Chronic utero-placental underperfusion (increased syncytial knots)—aggregates of syncytiotrophoblastic nuclei gather at one pole of the villus, leading to attenuation of the remaining syncytiotrophoblastic cytoplasm, maximizing gas exchange. **D,** Villitis of unknown etiology—maternal T lymphocytes in the fetal villous stroma *(lower right)* lead to edema and fibrosis, which increase the diffusion distance between the maternal and fetal circulations.

and abruptio placentae.[19] It is also important that maternal blood contacts a nonadhesive trophoblastic cell membrane to prevent activation of the coagulation system. Another maternal disorder associated with uteroplacental underperfusion is the antiphospholipid antibody syndrome. Data indicate that the anionic phospholipid binding protein annexin-V plays an important role in preventing the assembly of active coagulation factor complexes on the trophoblast cell membrane.[87] Antiphospholipid antibodies have been shown to displace annexin-V from the cell surface, thereby accounting for preeclamptic-like pathology in affected pregnancies.

Intervening between the fetal and maternal circulations are the tissues sometimes referred to as the interhemal membrane. These tissues include the syncytiotrophoblast, the trophoblast basement membrane, and the intravillous connective tissue. One important trophoblastic reaction pattern that can reduce the diffusion distance across the interhemal membrane is syncytial knotting, an adaptive response to hypoxia (Fig. 23-3C). This elegant mechanism, which has been substantiated by in vitro organ culture studies, consists of a clustering of syncytiotrophoblastic nuclei at one pole of the villus, leading to attenuation of the cytoplasmic barrier to gas exchange around the remaining circumference.[65,114] Because the trophoblast, and especially syncytial knots, are in direct contact with maternal blood, they can be easily dislodged, as attested to by their common presence in the lungs at autopsy in cases of maternal death. Although a mechanism for villous repair and re-epithelialization exists,[80] it is inevitable that some of these traumatic events will cause villous hemorrhage and fetomaternal transfusion. Cell traffic also occurs in the opposite direction (maternofetal transfusion).[109] When maternal inflammatory cells cross the trophoblastic barrier, they may participate in an allograft-type response against fetal antigens in the villi. This process is believed to occur in *villitis of unknown etiology* (VUE), and the resulting chronic inflammation increases the diffusion distance (Fig. 23-3D).[93] Another process increasing the diffusion distance is *massive perivillous fibrin deposition* ("maternal floor infarction"), an idiopathic accumulation of trophoblast-derived extracellular matrix material that surrounds terminal villi, compromising both intervillous circulation and gas exchange (Fig. 23-3B).[67]

The final placental compartment to be discussed is the fluid-filled sac of membranes, which must rupture to allow vaginal delivery. In theory, membranes may prematurely rupture for one of two reasons: increased luminal pressure or weakening of their normal structural integrity. Increased pressure can be caused by premature contractions, cervical dilation, or polyhydramnios. Structural integrity may be compromised by trauma, inflammatory responses associated with ascending bacterial infection, or ischemic necrosis caused by premature placental separation (abruption). The amniotic fluid contained within the sac is predominantly derived from fetal urine, and its volume may in some cases reflect the fetal fluid balance.[16] Therefore, *chronic*

uteroplacental underperfusion can lead to fetal hypovolemia and oligohydramnios in the absence of membrane rupture or fetal urinary tract anomalies. Regardless of its underlying cause, oligohydramnios may lead to umbilical cord compression in the short term,[60] limb deformities in the intermediate term,[111] and failure of adequate lung growth in the long term (see Chapter 21).[118] Placental membranes can also incorporate various exogenous substances suspended in the amniotic fluid, some of which, such as meconium and bacterial products, may damage both the membranes and the underlying fetal vessel wall.[6,7,43] A third exogenous substance found in membranes is hemosiderin, which can be an indicator of chronic peripheral separation (chronic abruption).[94]

Maternal Vascular Pathology

Muscularized maternal arteries supplying the intervillous space are susceptible to stenosis, occlusion, or rupture. Stenosis leads to *chronic uteroplacental underperfusion,* which is characterized by low placental weight, increased syncytial knotting, and focal villous agglutination (microinfarction), particularly in the "watershed zones" between spiral arteries.[73,74] Total occlusion causes villous infarction.[119] Although experimental studies have shown that up to 20% to 25% of villous parenchyma can be infarcted without acute fetal compromise,[32] these studies fail to account for the impaired status of the remaining placenta in most maternal vasculopathic disorders. The rupture of maternal arteries *(acute abruption)* may occasionally be attributed to trauma but is more commonly an ischemia-reperfusion injury with a secondary rupture of the injured vascular wall. The common association of abruption with vasoactive drugs such as nicotine and especially cocaine is consistent with this pathogenesis.[2,21,76] *Chronic abruption* may also occur and presents pathologically as chronic peripheral separation, which is characterized by diffuse chorioamnionic hemosiderin deposition and placental circumvallation.[14,40,79,97] Most evidence to date suggests that chronic abruption represents venous rather than arterial hemorrhage. Because muscular arteries are incompletely remodeled in preeclampsia, maternal vascular lesions of all types are especially frequent in this disorder. However, identical lesions may be seen with idiopathic IUGR, antiphospholipid antibody syndrome, connective tissue disease, diabetes mellitus, chronic hypertension, and chronic renal disease and in patients with an underlying thrombophilic condition.*

Fetal Vascular Pathology

Fetal vessels within the umbilical cord are protected from compression by the cord matrix, a hydrated gel known as Wharton's jelly. Several processes lessen this protection: decreased hydration of the matrix, which

---

*References 1, 26, 27, 49, 50, and 117.

can occur with *chronic uteroplacental underperfusion*[55]; torsion-related kinking of the cord due to excessive coiling[23]; and insertion of the cord vessels into the membranes, which leaves them unprotected from trauma.[53] The critical parameters for deciding whether a putative cord lesion can be confirmed pathologically are thrombosis, necrosis, or hemorrhage at the proposed site of occlusion and histologic differences in the cord structures located proximal and distal to the lesion.

Large vessels in the chorionic plate and stem villi may occasionally rupture, leading to *massive subchorionic thrombosis,* a rare and often fatal lesion.[110] A more common process affecting these vessels is thrombotic occlusion *(fetal thrombotic vasculopathy).*[88,95] The factors predisposing to thrombosis are similar to those reported for thrombi in other organs: severe inflammation (villitis or chorioamnionitis), irritation (prolonged meconium exposure), stasis and irritation (chronic umbilical cord obstruction, fetal congestive heart failure), inherited predispositions to clotting (protein C and S deficiencies, maternal antiphospholipid antibodies, factor V Leiden), hyperviscosity (fetal polycythemia), and specific maternal disease states (e.g., diabetes mellitus).[3,66,93] Villi downstream from occlusive thrombi are avascular and hyalinized. Adverse sequelae of thrombotic vasculopathy include a decrease in the size of the fetal vascular bed available for gas exchange, coexistent thromboembolic disease in the fetus, and (in rare cases) fetal consumptive coagulopathy with disseminated intravascular coagulation or thrombocytopenia.

Mature, intermediate stem villous arterioles regulate placental resistance to fetal blood flow, the parameter evaluated in clinical pulsed-flow Doppler studies. These arterioles have been found to be numerically decreased in autosomal trisomies[100] and either obliterated or stenosed in patients with severe IUGR.[31,35] A large proportion of placentas with these fetal arteriolar changes also show clinical and pathologic evidence of chronic uteroplacental underperfusion.[115] It is unclear whether fetal arteriolar pathology is the cause or the result of IUGR. Placental arteriolar occlusion could cause placental hypoperfusion and growth restriction or, alternatively, might simply be the result of hypoperfusion by a sick, volume-depleted infant (see Chapter 13).

As described earlier, placental capillaries can leak fluid (villous edema) or blood (villous stromal hemorrhage), and both lesions have been shown to be associated with adverse outcomes in very premature infants.[33,77,96] The frank rupture of capillaries is the cause of placental intervillous thrombi and may be associated with hypovolemia, fetal anemia, and a compensatory increase in circulating, nucleated red blood cells.[48] Capillary rupture in some cases may be associated with massive fetomaternal hemorrhage, an important cause of fetal morbidity and mortality. The proliferation of villous capillaries (chorangiosis) is defined by a significant proportion of terminal villi having 10 or more capillary cross sections and has been associated with chronic villitis, meconium staining, diabetes, and congenital anomalies.[4]

Infection/Inflammation

Acute chorioamnionitis is caused by cervicovaginal bacteria that either overwhelm normal cervical host defense systems or gain access to the amnionic cavity after the rupture of membranes (see Chapter 22).[15,78] The inflammatory response to bacterial infection is overwhelmingly neutrophilic and generally involves the membranes and chorionic plate but not the chorionic villi. Acute chorioamnionitis is by far the most common cause of preterm labor.[41,95,102] However, few delivered infants are septic at birth, attesting to the effectiveness of the placenta as a protective barrier.

The features indicating the duration of infection in chorioamnionitis can sometimes be helpful.[99] In the initial stages (less than 6 hours), maternal neutrophils marginate in the fibrin just below the chorionic plate (early chorionitis). Later the neutrophils, predominantly maternal, infiltrate the entire chorionic plate and the full thickness of the membranes (6 to 24 hours). A concomitant fetal neutrophilic response, as manifested by transmigration across the fetal vessel walls, begins in the chorionic plate (chorionic vasculitis) and the umbilical vein (umbilical phlebitis) and are followed by the umbilical arteries (umbilical arteritis). Changes that occur later, such as fetal neutrophils in the umbilical cord stroma (perivasculitis) and necrosis of the amnion (necrotizing chorioamnionitis), suggest more than 24 hours of infection. Finally, perivascular umbilical arcs of calcific debris, glycoprotein, and neovascularization (subnecrotizing funisitis) or a chronic mononuclear component (chronic chorioamnionitis) suggests prolonged infection of days to weeks in duration.[34] Infants with subnecrotizing funisitis or chronic chorioamnionitis have often had occult membrane rupture and are at risk for pulmonary hypoplasia from secondary chronic oligohydramnios.[15,78,90] Data suggest that the fetal inflammatory response in chorioamnionitis can be deleterious and may be a risk factor for severe neonatal morbidity (bronchopulmonary dysplasia, necrotizing enterocolitis, cranial ultrasound abnormalities, and long-term neurologic impairment).[37,96] The patterns described above are typical for most bacteria. Unusual patterns that can suggest specific organisms are neutrophilic exudates involving the villi and intervillous spaces (suggestive of *Listeria monocytogenes* or *Campylobacter fetus*)[29] and microabscesses on the external surface of the umbilical cord (suggestive of *Candida albicans*).[42,85]

Chronic placentitis is caused by organisms that enter the intervillous space by means of either the maternal bloodstream or the adjacent uterus. The hallmark of chronic placentitis is destructive, diffuse villitis with fibrosis, calcification, or both.[5] Although villous inflammation is generally emphasized, these infections also involve the chorion, decidua, and other placental regions. This pattern of panplacentitis is typical of fetal infection by organisms of the TORCH group (**To**xoplasma gondii, **ru**bella virus, **c**ytomegalovirus, and **h**erpes simplex virus), *Treponema pallidum,* other herpesviruses (Epstein-Barr virus, varicella), and a host of other parasitic and protozoan infections rarely seen in the

United States. Specific histopathologic features can indicate specific etiologic agents (e.g., increased Hofbauer cells, periarteritis, and necrotizing umbilical phlebitis in syphilis[51,84,106]; villous plasma cells in cytomegalovirus[72]; stromal necrosis and calcification in herpes simplex virus [personal observation]; and umbilical cord pseudocysts in toxoplasmosis[30]).

Two other categories of neonatal infection that cannot be evaluated directly by placental pathology are transplacental and intrapartum infections. Transplacental infections spread to the fetus without affecting the placenta, presumably through breaks in the interhemal barrier (maternofetal transfusion). Important organisms in this category include human immuno-deficiency virus,[58] hepatitis B virus,[61] human parvovirus B19,[20] and the enteroviruses.[71] On the other hand, intrapartum infections are acquired by the fetus during passage down a contaminated birth canal and hence also spare the placenta. Prominent in this category are venereal pathogens such as *Neisseria gonorrhoeae, Chlamydia trachomatis,* and human papillomavirus and some pathogens associated with neonatal sepsis (e.g., group B streptococci and *Escherichia coli*).[24]

Foci of chronic villous inflammation, such as VUE, are common in term placentas (5% of all placentas), whereas chronic placentitis attributable to the organisms listed earlier is rare (1 to 2 per 100 live births).[52,105] For many years it was believed that some new organism would be discovered that could explain VUE, and indeed this may yet happen. However, certain features of VUE differ from chronic placentitis of an infectious origin. First, VUE is confined to villi and generally involves only a fraction of the villous tree. Second, the predominant cells in VUE are infiltrating T lymphocytes of a maternal origin.[39,56] Third, VUE can be a recurrent disease associated with maternal autoimmunity, whereas chronic placentitis due to infection rarely recurs because of acquired immunity.[92,107] For all of these reasons, many have argued that VUE represents a maternal antifetal immune response, a consequence of genetic differences between the mother and fetus.[56,93] The main clinical relevance of VUE is its common association with IUGR, which can be attributed to its location in the villous stroma separating the maternal and fetal circulations.[52,105]

Developmental/Structural Lesions

The members of the final group of lesions to be discussed contain gross abnormalities in placental structure. As with structural abnormalities in the infant, these placental lesions can reflect either primary maldevelopment or secondary deformations and disruptions. Uterine abnormalities such as malformations, leiomyomas, or scars from previous surgical procedures constitute a major cause of abnormal placental development. These developmental abnormalities can be separated into two groups. First are the abnormalities of lateral growth and membrane formation, in which the placenta appears to migrate away from its original implantation site to optimize its blood supply, a process that has been termed *trophotropism.*[12] Trophotropism can lead to

bilobation, accessory lobes, membranous cord insertions, and placenta previa, none of which are pathologic by themselves. However, these placental anomalies can cause problems at delivery by placing fetal vessels at risk for rupture or, in some cases, predisposing to a breech or transverse fetal presentation. The second abnormality is one of vertical growth. The uterine decidua is believed to regulate the depth of uterine implantation. Prior surgery or other uterine abnormalities can interfere with normal decidualization, leading to uncontrolled placental growth into or through the uterine wall. This pattern, known as placenta accreta or percreta, most commonly causes postpartum hemorrhage but in selected cases can lead to uterine rupture.[89]

A second set of placental structural anomalies are those associated with deformations or disruptions in the fetus. The fetal deformation sequences attributable to *amniotic bands* (amputations) or prolonged oligohydramnios (clubfoot, pulmonary hypoplasia) are potential complications of early membrane rupture.[69,118] Early membrane rupture and the subsequent oligohydramnios are associated with a placental lesion known as *amnion nodosum* (see Chapter 21).[57] Amnion nodosum consists of white membrane excrescences that are the consequence of prolonged contact between the fetal vernix and membrane amnion. Fetal disruptions are caused by in utero ischemia of either a maternal or fetal origin. Transient interruption of the maternal blood supply early in pregnancy has been correlated with limb and central nervous system anomalies.[17] Such episodes can present clinically as chronic abruption and pathologically as a *circumvallate placenta* (membranes arising inside the perimeter of the placenta, with an associated fibrin rim due to the peripheral accumulation of blood in a closed uterine environment).[14,79]

A second cause of fetal vascular disruptions is vascular anastomosis in monochorionic twins (see Chapter 18).[45] Identical twins having a single monochorionic placenta and two separate amnionic sacs (monochorionic-diamnionic) are at the highest risk. Anastomosis can cause sudden circulatory shifts at the time of delivery or, if intrinsically unbalanced, chronic twin-to-twin transfusion. Dichorionic twin placentas, whether from identical or fraternal twins, are almost never affected. Interestingly, identical twins with only one amnionic cavity (monochorionic monoamnionic) rarely have twin-to-twin transfusion but commonly have another placental complication—entangled umbilical cords—which can lead to the death of one or both twins.

Although they are present for only a short time, tumors can develop in the placenta. The most common placental tumors are chorangiomas, which are composed of proliferating fetal blood vessels (hemangiomas). Chorangiomas cause pathologic fetal conditions in two ways: by arteriovenous shunting, leading to hydrops fetalis, or by sequestering platelets, leading to disseminated intravascular coagulation.[11,13] Choriocarcinomas (malignant trophoblastic tumors) can arise from the villi of second- and third-trimester placentas and metastasize to the fetus.[10,18] The placenta can also be a metastatic site for malignant tumors of either the mother (most commonly acute myeloid leukemia, melanoma, and adenocarcinoma) or the fetus (e.g., congenital neuroblastoma).[104]

As mentioned earlier, it has recently become apparent that chromosomally normal infants do not always have chromosomally normal placentas. Placental aneuploidy or confined placental mosaicism, as this phenomenon has been called, can affect all or part of the placenta and is believed to explain some cases of idiopathic IUGR and intrauterine fetal demise.[44,46,47,120] The morphologic sequelae of this phenomenon, if any, have not yet been established. Candidate lesions include dysmorphic villi of the type described in triploidy or monosomy X[82,116] and delayed villous maturation, which has been described in the placentas of infants with congenital anomalies.[4]

CLINICAL CORRELATION

Finally, it is useful to put the various anatomic, physiologic, and pathologic reaction patterns discussed earlier in a clinical context by reviewing their involvement in a few common obstetric and neonatal disease syndromes (Box 23-2). Clearly, such generalizations may be misleading in considering individual patients, but they can be useful in considering the range of possible diagnoses and causes in a particular case.

Preterm labor is most commonly associated with pathologic evidence of *acute chorioamnionitis*.[41,59,103,108] In many cases it can be difficult to determine whether infection develops before or after the onset of labor. Because chorioamnionitis generally triggers labor relatively rapidly, the majority of cases that develop after prolonged membrane rupture likely represent secondary infection.

Most of the remaining cases of preterm birth fall into three groups: *placental abruption,* either acute or chronic; chronic maternal underperfusion, with increased syncytial knotting; and uterine structural anomalies without associated placental abnormalities (e.g., cervical incompetence).[36,74] Less commonly, preterm birth may be associated with *idiopathic chronic inflammation* (lymphoplasmacytic deciduitis, decidual perivasculitis, or eosinophilic chorionitis).[59,103,108]

IUGR may be constitutional, relating to small maternal size, malnutrition, or an anomalous fetus. When it is caused by uteroplacental disease, two clinicopathologic pictures predominate: chronic uteroplacental underperfusion, with or without associated hypertension, and VUE, generally in the absence of hypertension.[91,94] Other less frequent uteroplacental causes of IUGR are fetal thrombotic vasculopathy, chronic peripheral separation, and massive perivillous fibrin deposition ("maternal floor infarction").

Intrauterine fetal demise, particularly at or near term, is often difficult to explain pathologically. One group at increased risk is the one composed of large fetuses with histologically immature placentas, long umbilical cords, and reduced amniotic fluid.[8,60,68] A distinct subgroup in this category is the infant of a diabetic mother,

BOX 23-2. Clinicopathologic Correlation

Preterm Labor
Acute chorioamnionitis
Abruption (acute or chronic)
Chronic uteroplacental underperfusion
Idiopathic chronic uterine inflammation

Intrauterine Growth Restriction
Chronic uteroplacental underperfusion
Villitis of unknown etiology
Abruption (chronic)
Fetal thrombotic vasculopathy
Perivillous fibrin

Intrauterine Fetal Demise
Large placenta with delayed villous maturation
Massive fetomaternal hemorrhage/intervillous thrombi
Hydrops fetalis (any cause)
Multiple placental lesions

Neonatal Encephalopathy
Abruption (acute)
Umbilical cord accident
Rupture of fetal vessels

Cerebral Palsy (Preterm)
Severe villous edema
Chorionic vessel thrombi
Multiple placental lesions

Cerebral Palsy (Term)
Fetal thrombotic vasculopathy
Severe fetal chorioamnionitis
Abruption (chronic)
Multiple placental lesions

long known to be at an increased risk for stillbirth. A second common cause of stillbirth is massive fetomaternal hemorrhage, which is manifested in the placenta by intervillous thrombi and increased circulating nucleated red blood cells.[25] Fetomaternal hemorrhage and its accompanying anemia can cause congestive heart failure and hydrops fetalis. Clearly, hydrops of any cause can lead to stillbirth. Other causes of hydrops identifiable by placental examination include chronic infections such as human parvovirus B19, toxoplasmosis, and syphilis.[64] Finally, a third, smaller group of stillbirths shows evidence of more than one of the following lesions: chronic uteroplacental underperfusion, fetal thrombotic vasculopathy, VUE, and massive perivillous fibrin deposition.[28]

Neonatal encephalopathy and cerebral palsy in term infants can be related to acute birth asphyxia, chronic intermittent hypoxia, chronic uteroplacental disease, or various combinations of these problems.[63] The placental findings associated with acute asphyxia include acute abruption, umbilical cord accidents, and the *rupture of fetal vessels* (i.e., tears in the villous parenchyma or umbilical or chorionic vessels).[5,70,101] Subacute or chronic intermittent stress is often accompanied by an increase in nucleated red blood cells in the placental circulation.[112,113] The placental findings that have been associated with long-term neurologic impairment in preterm infants are severe villous edema, chorionic vessel thrombi associated with histologic chorioamnionitis, and multiple placental lesions.[96] Long-term neurologic impairment in term infants has been associated with fetal thrombotic vasculopathy and other processes affecting large fetal vessels, such as *severe fetal chorioamnionitis, meconium-associated vascular necrosis,* and *VUE with stem villous vasculitis.* Other important findings include chronic abruption and the presence of multiple placental lesions.*

SUMMARY

The placenta is the link that connects the clinical status of the neonate with underlying maternal and fetal disease processes. Careful evaluation of this organ not only provides useful diagnostic, prognostic, and therapeutic information but also enhances our overall understanding of perinatal biology. Communication among neonatologists, obstetricians, and placental pathologists brings together distinct pieces of a puzzle that none can fully solve alone. Through this process, meaningful explanations of the reasons for adverse perinatal outcomes and their chances of recurrence can be provided for concerned physicians and family members.

REFERENCES

1. Abramowsky CR et al: Decidual vasculopathy of the placenta in lupus erythematosus. N Engl J Med 303:668, 1980.
2. Acker D et al: Abruptio placentae associated with cocaine use. Am J Obstet Gynecol 146:218, 1983.
3. Alles AJ et al: The incidence of Factor V Leiden in fetal thrombotic events. Mod Pathol 10:1P, 1997.
4. Altshuler G: The placenta. In Sternberg SS (ed): Diagnostic Surgical Pathology. New York, Raven Press, 1989, p 1503.
5. Altshuler G et al: The human placental villitides: A review of chronic intrauterine infection. In Grundmann K (ed): Current Topics in Pathology. Berlin, Springer-Verlag, 1975, p 64.
6. Altshuler G et al: Meconium-induced vasocontraction: A potential cause of cerebral and other fetal hypoperfusion and of poor pregnancy outcome. J Child Neurol 4:137, 1989.
7. Altshuler G et al: Meconium-induced umbilical cord vascular necrosis and ulceration: A potential link between the placenta and poor pregnancy outcome. Obstet Gynecol 79:760, 1992.
8. Becker MJ et al: The placenta. In Becker MJ, Becker AE (eds): Pathology of Late Fetal Stillbirth. New York, Churchill Livingstone, 1989, p 3.
9. Bejar R et al: Antenatal origin of neurologic damage in newborn infants: I. Preterm infants. Am J Obstet Gynecol 159:357, 1988.
10. Belchis DA et al: Infantile choriocarcinoma: Reexamination of a potentially curable entity. Cancer 72:2028, 1993.
11. Benirschke K: Recent trends in chorangiomas, especially those of multiple and recurrent chorangiomas. Pediatr Dev Pathol 2:264, 1999.
12. Benirschke K et al: The Pathology of the Human Placenta. New York, Springer-Verlag, 1967.
13. Benirschke K et al: The Pathology of the Human Placenta, 4th ed. New York, Springer-Verlag, 2000.
14. Bey M et al: The sonographic diagnosis of circumvallate placenta. Obstet Gynecol 78:515, 1991.
15. Blanc WA: Pathology of the placenta and cord in ascending and in haematogenous infection. In Symposium on Perinatal Infections (Ciba Foundation, 1979): Perinatal Infections. New York, Excerpta Medica, 1980.
16. Brace RA: Progress toward understanding the regulation of amniotic fluid volume: Water and solute fluxes in and through the fetal membranes. Placenta 16:1, 1995.
17. Brent RL: What is the relationship between birth defects and pregnancy bleeding? Teratology 48:93, 1993.
18. Brewer JI et al: Gestational choriocarcinoma: Its origin in the placenta during seemingly normal pregnancy. Am J Surg Pathol 5:267, 1981.
19. Brosens IA et al: The role of the spiral arteries in the pathogenesis of pre-eclampsia. In Wynn R (ed): Obstetrics and Gynecology Annual. New York, Appleton-Century-Crofts, 1972, p 177.
20. Caul EO et al: Intrauterine infection with human parvovirus B19: A light and electron microscopy study. J Med Virol 24:55, 1988.
21. Chasnoff IJ et al: Cocaine use in pregnancy. N Engl J Med 313:666, 1985.
22. College of American Pathologists Conference XIX on the Examination of the Placenta: Report of the working group on indications for placental examination. Arch Pathol Lab Med 115:701, 1991.
23. Collins JC et al: Prenatal observation of umbilical cord abnormalities: A triple knot and torsion of the umbilical cord. Am J Obstet Gynecol 169:102, 1993.
24. Current concepts of infections of the fetus and newborn infant. In Remington JS, Klein JO (eds): Infectious Diseases of the Fetus and Newborn Infant, 2nd ed. Philadelphia, WB Saunders Co, 1983, p 1.
25. de Almeida V et al: Massive fetomaternal hemorrhage: Manitoba experience. Obstet Gynecol 83:323, 1994.
26. DeWolf F et al: Fetal growth retardation and the maternal arterial supply of the human placenta in the absence of sustained hypertension. Br J Obstet Gynaecol 87:678, 1980.
27. DeWolf F et al: Decidual vasculopathy and extensive placental infarction in a patient with repeated thromboembolic accidents, recurrent fetal loss, and a lupus anticoagulant. Am J Obstet Gynecol 142:829, 1982.
28. Driscoll SG: Autopsy following stillbirth: A challenge neglected. In Ryder OA et al (eds): One Medicine. Berlin, Springer-Verlag, 1984, p 20.
29. Driscoll SG et al: Congenital listeriosis: Diagnosis from placental studies. Obstet Gynecol 20:216, 1962.
30. Elliott WG: Placental toxoplasmosis: Report of a case. Am J Clin Pathol 53:413, 1970.
31. Fok RY et al: The correlation of arterial lesions with umbilical artery Doppler velocimetry in the placentas of small-for-dates pregnancies. Obstet Gynecol 75:578, 1990.
32. Fox H: Pathology of the Placenta. London, WB Saunders Co, 1978.
33. Genest D et al: Placental findings correlate with neonatal death in extremely premature infants (24-32 weeks): A study of 150 cases. Lab Invest 68:126A, 1993.

---

*References 9, 38, 62, 81, 98, and 121.

34. Gersell DJ et al: Chronic chorioamnionitis: A clinico-pathologic study of 17 cases. Int J Gynecol Pathol 10:217, 1991.

35. Giles WB et al: Fetal umbilical artery flow velocity waveforms and placental resistance: Pathological correlation. Br J Obstet Gynaecol 92:31, 1985.

36. Golan A et al: Incompetence of the uterine cervix. Obstet Gynecol Surv 44:96, 1989.

37. Gomez R et al: The fetal inflammatory response syndrome. Am J Obstet Gynecol 179:194, 1998.

38. Grafe MR: The correlation of prenatal brain damage with placental pathology. J Neuropathol Exp Neurol 53:407, 1994.

39. Greco MA et al: Phenotype of villous stromal cells in placentas with cytomegalovirus, syphilis, and nonspecific villitis. Am J Pathol 141:835, 1992.

40. Harris BA: Peripheral placental separation: A review. Obstet Gynecol Surv 43:577, 1988.

41. Hillier SL et al: A case-control study of chorioamniotic infection and histologic chorioamnionitis in prematurity. N Engl J Med 319:972, 1988.

42. Hood IC et al: The inflammatory response in candidal chorioamnionitis. Hum Pathol 14:984, 1983.

43. Hyde S et al: A model of bacterially induced umbilical vein spasm, relevant to fetal hypoperfusion. Obstet Gynecol 73:966, 1989.

44. Johnson A et al: Mosaicism in chorionic villus sampling: An association with poor perinatal outcome. Obstet Gynecol 75:573, 1990.

45. Johnson SF et al: Twin placentation and its complications. Semin Perinatol 10:9, 1986.

46. Kalousek D et al: Chromosomal mosaicism in term placentas and its association with high incidence of abnormal intrauterine development. Lab Invest 66:6P, 1991.

47. Kalousek DK et al: Chromosomal mosaicism confined to the placenta in human conceptions. Science 221:665, 1983.

48. Kaplan C et al: Identification of erythrocytes in inter-villous thrombi: A study using immunoperoxidase identification of hemoglobins. Hum Pathol 13:554, 1982.

49. Khong TY: Acute atherosis in pregnancies complicated by hypertension, small-for-gestational age infants and diabetes mellitus. Arch Pathol Lab Med 115:722, 1991.

50. Kitzmiller JL et al: Decidual arteriopathy in hypertension and diabetes in pregnancy: Immunofluorescent studies. Am J Obstet Gynecol 141:773, 1981.

51. Knowles S et al: Umbilical cord sclerosis as an indicator of congenital syphilis. J Clin Pathol 42:1157, 1989.

52. Knox WF et al: Villitis of unknown aetiology: Its incidence and significance in placentae from a British population. Placenta 5:395, 1984.

53. Kouyoumdjian A: Velamentous insertion of the umbilical cord. Obstet Gynecol 56:737, 1980.

54. Kraus FT et al: Non-Tumor Diagnostic Surgical Pathology: Placenta. Washington, DC, Armed Forces Institute of Pathology, 2004.

55. Labarrere C et al: Absence of Wharton's jelly around the umbilical cord: An unusual cause of perinatal mortality. Placenta 6:555, 1985.

56. Labarrere CA et al: Immunohistologic evidence that villitis in human normal term placentas is an immunologic lesion. Am J Obstet Gynecol 162:515, 1990.

57. Landing BH: Amnion nodosum: A lesion of the placenta associated with deficient secretion of fetal urine. Am J Obstet Gynecol 60:1339, 1950.

58. Lapointe N et al: Transplacental transmission of HTLV-III virus. N Engl J Med 312:1325, 1985.

59. Lettieri L et al: Does "idiopathic" preterm labor resulting in preterm birth exist? Am J Obstet Gynecol 168:1480, 1993.

60. Leveno KJ et al: Prolonged pregnancy: I. Observations concerning the causes of fetal distress. Am J Obstet Gynecol 150:465, 1984.

61. Lin HH et al: Transplacental leakage of HBeAg-positive maternal blood as the most likely route in causing intra-uterine infection with hepatitis B virus. J Pediatr 111:877, 1987.

62. Lipitz S et al: Midtrimester bleeding: Variables which affect the outcome of pregnancy. Gynecol Obstet Invest 32:24, 1991.

63. Low JA et al: The clinical diagnosis of asphyxia responsible for brain damage in the human fetus. Am J Obstet Gynecol 167:11, 1992.

64. Machin GA: Hydrops revisited: Literature review of 1,414 cases published in the 1980's. Am J Med Genet 34:366, 1989.

65. MacLennan AH et al: The ultrastructure of human trophoblast in spontaneous and induced hypoxia using a system of organ culture: A comparison and ultra-structural changes in preeclampsia and placental insufficiency. Br J Obstet Gynecol 72:113, 1972.

66. Manco-Johnson MJ et al: Severe neonatal protein-C deficiency: Prevalence and thrombotic risk. J Pediatr 119:793, 1991.

67. Mandsager NT et al: Maternal floor infarction of placenta: Prenatal diagnosis and clinical significance. Obstet Gynecol 83:750, 1994.

68. McLean FH et al: Postterm infants: Too big or too small? Am J Obstet Gynecol 164:619, 1991.

69. Miller ME et al: Compression-related defects from early amnion rupture: Evidence for mechanical teratogenesis. J Pediatr 98:292, 1981.

70. Miller PW et al: Dating the time interval from meconium passage to birth. Obstet Gynecol 66:459, 1985.

71. Moustofi-Zadeh M et al: Postmortem manifestations of echovirus 11 sepsis in five newborn infants. Hum Pathol 14:818, 1983.

72. Moustofi-Zadeh M et al: Placental evidence of cyto-megalovirus infection of the fetus and neonate. Arch Pathol Lab Med 108:403, 1984.

73. Naeye RL: Do placental weights have clinical significance? Hum Pathol 18:387, 1987.

74. Naeye RL: Pregnancy hypertension, placental evidences of low utero-placental blood flow and spontaneous premature delivery. Hum Pathol 20:441, 1989.

75. Naeye RL: Disorders of the Placenta, Fetus, and Neonate. St. Louis, Mosby-Year Book, 1992.

76. Naeye RL et al: Abruptio placentae and perinatal death: A prospective study. Am J Obstet Gynecol 128:740, 1977.

77. Naeye RL et al: The clinical significance of placental villous edema. Pediatrics 71:588, 1983.

78. Naeye RL et al: Antenatal infections. In Naeye RL, Tafari N (eds): Risk Factors in Pregnancy and Diseases of the Fetus and Newborn. Baltimore, Williams & Wilkins, 1983, p 77.

79. Naftolin F et al: The syndrome of chronic abruptio placentae, hydrorrhea, and circumvallate placenta. Am J Obstet Gynecol 116:347, 1973.

80. Nelson DM et al: Trophoblast interaction with fibrin matrix: Epithelialization of perivillous fibrin deposits as a mechanism for villous repair in the human placenta. Am J Pathol 136:855, 1990.

81. Nelson KB et al: Antecedents of cerebral palsy: Multi-variate analysis of risk. N Engl J Med 315:81, 1986.

82. Novak R et al: Histologic analysis of placental tissue in first trimester abortions. Pediatr Pathol 8:477, 1988.

83. Page Faulk W et al: Immunology of coagulation control in human placentae [abstract]. Am J Reprod Immunol Microbiol 16:113, 1988.

84. Qureshi F et al: Placental histopathology in syphilis. Hum Pathol 24:779, 1993.

85. Qureshi F et al: *Candida* funisitis: A clinicopathologic study of 32 cases. Pediatr Dev Pathol 1:118, 1998.

86. Ramsey EM et al: Placental Vasculature and Circulation. Philadelphia, WB Saunders Co, 1980.

87. Rand JH, Wu X-X: Antiphospholipid-mediated disruption of the annexin-V antithrombotic shield: A new mechanism for thrombosis in the antiphospholipid syndrome. Thromb Haemost 82:649, 1999.

88. Rayne SC et al: Placental thrombi and other vascular lesions: Classification, morphology, and clinical correlations. Pathol Res Pract 189:2, 1993.

89. Read JA et al: Placenta accreta: Changing clinical aspects and outcome. Obstet Gynecol 56:31, 1980.

90. Redline RW: Placenta and adnexa in late pregnancy. In Reed GB et al (eds): Diseases of the Fetus and Newborn, 2nd ed. London, Chapman & Hall Medical, 1995, p 319.

91. Redline RW: Placental pathology: The neglected link between basic disease mechanisms and untoward pregnancy outcome. Curr Opin Obstet Gynecol 7:10, 1995.

92. Redline RW et al: Clinical and pathological aspects of recurrent placental villitis. Hum Pathol 16:727, 1985.

93. Redline RW et al: Villitis of unknown etiology is associated with major infiltration of fetal tissue by maternal inflammatory cells. Am J Pathol 143:473, 1993.

94. Redline RW et al: Patterns of placental injury: Correlations with gestational age, placental weight, and clinical diagnosis. Arch Pathol Lab Med 118:698, 1994.

95. Redline RW et al: Fetal thrombotic vasculopathy: The clinical significance of extensive avascular villi. Hum Pathol 26:80, 1995.

96. Redline RW et al: Placental lesions associated with neurologic impairment and cerebral palsy in very low birth weight infants. Arch Pathol Lab Med 122:1091, 1998.

97. Redline RW, Wilson-Costello D: Chronic peripheral separation of placenta: The significance of diffuse chorioamnionic hemosiderosis. Am J Clin Pathol 111:804, 1999.

98. Redline RW, O'Riordan MA: Placental lesions associated with cerebral palsy and neurologic impairment following term birth. Arch Pathol Lab Med 124:1785, 2000.

99. Redline RW et al: Amniotic fluid infection: Nosology and reproducibility of placental reaction patterns. Pediatr Dev Pathol 6:435, 2003.

100. Rochelson B et al: A quantitative analysis of placental vasculature in the third-trimester fetus with autosomal trisomy. Obstet Gynecol 75:59, 1990.

101. Rogers BB et al: Fetal acidosis and placental pathology. Lab Invest 62:85A, 1990.

102. Romero R et al: Infection and preterm labor. Clin Obstet Gynecol 31:553, 1988.

103. Romero R et al: The preterm labor syndrome: Biochemical, cytologic, immunologic, pathologic, microbiologic, and clinical evidence that preterm labor is a heterogeneous disease. Am J Obstet Gynecol 168:288, 1993.

104. Rothman LA et al: Placental and fetal involvement by maternal malignancy: A report of rectal carcinoma and review of the literature. Am J Obstet Gynecol 116:1023, 1973.

105. Russell P: Inflammatory lesions of the human placenta. Placenta 1:227, 1980.

106. Russell P et al: Placental abnormalities of congenital syphilis. Am J Dis Child 128:160, 1974.

107. Russell P, et al: Recurrent reproductive failure due to severe villitis of unknown etiology. J Reprod Med 24:93, 1980.

108. Salafia CM et al: Placental pathologic findings in preterm birth. Am J Obstet Gynecol 165:934, 1991.

109. Seemayer TA: The graft-versus-host reaction: A pathogenetic mechanism of experimental and human disease. In Rosenberg HS et al (eds): Perspectives in Pediatric Pathology. New York, Masson, 1979, p 93.

110. Shanklin DR et al: Massive subchorial thrombohaematoma (Breus' mole). Br J Obstet Gynaecol 82:476, 1975.

111. Smith DW: Recognizable Patterns of Human Deformation. Philadelphia, WB Saunders Co, 1987.

112. Soothill PW et al: Prenatal asphyxia, hyperlacticaemia, hypoglycaemia, and erythroblastosis in growth retarded fetuses. BMJ 294:1051, 1987.

113. Thilaganathan B et al: Umbilical cord blood erythroblast count as an index of intrauterine hypoxia. Arch Dis Child 70:F192, 1994.

114. Tominaga T et al: Accommodation of the human placenta to hypoxia. Am J Obstet Gynecol 94:679, 1966.

115. Trudinger BJ et al: Flow velocity waveforms in the maternal uteroplacental and fetal umbilical placental circulations. Am J Obstet Gynecol 152:155, 1985.

116. Vanlijnschoten G et al: Intra-observer and inter-observer variation in the interpretation of histological features suggesting chromosomal abnormality in early abortion specimens. Histopathology 22:25, 1993.

117. Van Pampus MG et al: High prevalence of hemostatic abnormalities in women with a history of severe preeclampsia. Am J Obstet Gynecol 180:1146, 1999.

118. Vergani P et al: Risk factors for pulmonary hypoplasia in second-trimester premature rupture of membranes. Am J Obstet Gynecol 170:1359, 1994.

119. Wallenburg HCS et al: The pathogenesis of placental infarction: I. A morphologic study in the human placenta. Am J Obstet Gynecol 116:835, 1973.

120. Wilkins-Haug L et al: Frequency of confined placental mosaicism in pregnancies with IUGR. Am J Obstet Gynecol 166:350, 1992.

121. Williams MA et al: Adverse infant outcomes associated with first-trimester vaginal bleeding. Obstet Gynecol 78:14, 1991.

IV The Delivery Room

24 Anesthesia for Labor and Delivery

McCallum R. Hoyt

Practitioners of the analgesic techniques developed and used in obstetrics need to consider that there are two patients involved—the mother and the fetus. Therefore, the goal of any practitioner who provides analgesia to the mother is to give her what she desires or needs while minimizing the impact on the fetus. In one way the current anesthesia-provided techniques contribute to this goal because epidural and spinal dosing is reduced to achieve an analgesic state as opposed to an anesthetic one. As a result, the lower doses mean that less medication is absorbed into the maternal bloodstream, so the levels are greatly reduced and sometimes nondetectable. However, all procedures carry some risk, and they can have a fetal or neonatal effect.

Despite the proven safety and efficacy of these lower-dose neuraxial techniques, they are not available to all obstetric patients for a myriad of reasons, so many of the tried and true approaches are still commonplace in obstetric suites nationwide as well as some interesting alternative therapies. The assumption held by the proponents of alternative pain management techniques is that the pain can be controlled without any adverse effect on the neonate because medications and needles are not used. Clinical practice has not proven this assumption to be true, and the practicing neonatologist should be aware of potential problems with some of these techniques.

Research into the sensation of pain has demonstrated a very complex process that is far from being fully understood. To appreciate the complexity of providing analgesia to the laboring patient and better understand successes and expectations when doing so, a considerably abbreviated discussion of pain is in order. A clinically useful classification of pain is to define it as being visceral or somatic. Stated very simply, visceral pain originates from the viscera and is often described as cramping, dull, and steady. Somatic pain is related to nonvisceral structures and is commonly described as sharp, intermittent, and well localized. In terms of labor, the pain experienced in the first stage is predominantly visceral, with some somatic components as the uterus contracts and the cervix dilates. The second stage is more somatic in nature, with little visceral involvement. The challenge in managing labor pain is that it is a very dynamic process. It evolves over a relatively short period of time, changing not only in intensity but also from visceral to somatic pain. To add to the challenge,

not all medications are effective for all types of pain. Local anesthetics block nerve transmission and are effective where there are accessible nerves that transmit pain. In labor, the nerves transmitting the pain are well described, and most of them can be reached with a needle, making some form of nerve block with a local anesthetic a common choice. On the other hand, opioids are very effective for visceral pain but of little value for somatic pain.[36] Therefore, systemic opioids can aid a patient reasonably well during the first stage of labor but have little effect during the second stage.

While nonpharmacologic techniques do not alter the actual process of pain, they attempt to alter the person's perception and response to it, with some measured success. However, many of these approaches require preparation beforehand, and their effectiveness is subject to many variables. As a result, studies comparing Lamaze, hypnosis, and other nonpharmacologic methods to nerve blocks and medications are hard to evaluate, yet these techniques have a committed following that occasionally makes some improbable claims.

The goal of modern-day practice is to provide analgesia as the patient requests it, assuming her choice is appropriate to the labor process and conditions of the moment as determined by her obstetric provider. That may mean prepared responses to modify perception, systemic medications, nerve blocks, or any combination of these during a single labor. How and whether a mother's choice has an impact on fetal well-being and neonatal outcome is the focus. While this chapter will include a discussion of the newer anesthetic techniques as the neonatologist should understand them, it will also review some of the more established pain relief approaches as well as some of the more popular alternatives currently in vogue.

TECHNIQUES THAT MODIFY PAIN

Natural Childbirth and Other Nonpharmacologic Approaches

Many mothers consider nonpharmacologic techniques to be the safest for themselves and their babies. Although few of these alternatives provide true pain relief, most of them provide a base from which the mother can better cope with the labor and delivery process. Therefore, it is pertinent for the well-informed neonatologist to know of these techniques, especially because some of them are not as benign as presumed.

NATURAL CHILDBIRTH

Natural childbirth, as our society has come to know it, is a technique that was first defined by Ferdinand Lamaze in the 1950s and began its popular rise in the 1960s. Its premise is the use of relaxation techniques and focal points with controlled breathing during the contraction itself. The theory is that by using this technique, one can modify the sensation of and response to labor pain. The Bradley technique was developed in the 1970s and is a variant of Lamaze in which husbands are trained to be active coaches.

Several factors have come to bear on modern-day childbirth courses and the information that is provided. Couples are no longer willing to take the full 6-week training course. Instead, weekend courses are offered that try to present all the information in 2 days. This alternative makes it nearly impossible to practice and learn the pain-controlling techniques that Lamaze described. Information on pain relief options is variable, due not only to some personal biases but also very often on the instructor's knowledge of what is available at the maternity units in the area. However, there is some objective evidence that Lamaze training as originally defined is associated with β-endorphin elevations, which may help alter pain sensation.[9] The same study also found that unacceptable pain behavior was associated with the elevated levels of adrenocorticotropic hormone that occurred despite the manner of training.

A significant percentage of patients who attempt a drug-free birth eventually request some form of relief. It often comes in the form of a systemic medication, but when available, a neuraxial block such as an epidural is the request of choice. Unfortunately, mothers often view resorting to a form of analgesia, especially an epidural, as agreement failure. These labors are frequently longer and associated with higher pain scores and catch the mother feeling unprepared for the intensity of the process.[21] The more significant issue is that the mother's plan for a "natural" birth experience is based on the perception that it is a risk-free choice for her child. However, there is plenty of evidence that this perceived outcome is not always the case. Maternal and fetal Pco_2 levels are positively correlated.[2,32] If the mother does not perform the proper breathing techniques, she may actually hyperventilate during her contractions and lower her Pco_2 levels as a result. This condition would have two effects: First, hypocapnia causes uterine vasoconstriction, which reduces bloodflow to the fetus; second, the fetus also develops hypocapnia because of the maternal hypocapnia. As the fetal Pco_2 falls, the fetal oxyhemoglobin dissociation curve shifts leftward, reducing fetal oxygenation and setting the stage for hypoxia and metabolic acidosis. If metabolic acidosis develops, it has been documented to worsen during the second stage, especially if it exceeds 1 hour.[1,2,44,45] With hypoxia and a large base deficit due to metabolic acidosis, the result is a neonate who is in need of

resuscitation. Obviously this series of events does not occur in every case, but the bradycardia associated with this scenario can resemble that of a cord compression.[32] Effective analgesic techniques have been shown to improve these conditions.[1,32]

HYPNOSIS

Self-hypnosis for labor and delivery enjoys a devoted following among those for whom the process has been successful, but certainly it is a technique that not many individuals can use. It requires time for training and practice and is not a choice for those with only a weekend devoted to learning it. The process has been well described[37,52] and essentially allows the mother to enter a self-induced, trance-like state. Her partner sends her "cues" by touch that signal changes in the process. These cues have been agreed upon and practiced beforehand.

An interesting criticism of the Lamaze method comes from the proponents of hypnosis. They claim that Lamaze teaches mothers to focus on the start of a contraction in order to begin breathing.[22,68] As a result, the mother is always focusing on the initiation of pain and the length of a contraction. With hypnosis there is no need to focus on anything but the images that constitute the individual's trance, so there is no need to adjust to a contraction. Proponents claim they feel relaxed and more capable of pushing.[68]

There are no objective studies currently in the literature comparing hypnosis with other methods of pain modification; all are anecdotal reports. In addition, there are no reports on neonatal outcomes, which is unfortunate. As previously mentioned, if the breathing in the Lamaze method is improperly performed, it may have some deleterious effects on the fetus. Hypnosis does not require an alteration in breathing or an awareness of recurring pain, leaving one to wonder what impact the mother's physiologic state has on the intrauterine environment during labor and thus fetal well-being.

WATER BIRTH

The water birth movement holds that submersion for labor, delivery, or both reduces the sensation of pain. It also holds that birthing from one water environment into another is less stressful for the infant. Unfortunately for proponents, there are no substantive studies supporting this claim. Like hypnosis, almost everything in the literature is anecdotal. A Cochrane Database review article found no differences in outcome between the water birth method and other pain control methods, both pharmacologic and nonpharmacologic.[35] One of the major criticisms of water immersion and delivery methods is the potential for infection, although it has not been supported by inclusion in the literature.[7,35,46] A randomized, prospective study found no benefits in terms of fewer requests for other forms of analgesia, improved maternal outcomes, or neonatal outcomes, with one notable exception: There was a significantly higher incidence of the need for neonatal resuscitation.[7] In contrast, one retrospective review chose to exclude births in which the Apgar scores were less than 7 and then reported no adverse effects.[46] This finding points to the need to use caution when reviewing the current literature; much more work needs to be done to examine the issues associated with this form of intrapartum analgesia.

ACUPUNCTURE, SALINE INJECTIONS, AND TRANSCUTANEOUS ELECTRICAL NERVE STIMULATION

This group of techniques has often been used to address the issue of the low back pain experienced in some labors but not that of general labor pain control. In controlled trials, acupuncture has been demonstrated to be beneficial but time consuming and without consistent results.[55,65] In addition, the studies to date have been small, so more research is needed.[56] Saline injections beside the sacroiliac junctures have also been noted to have a beneficial effect on labor-induced back pain, but the studies suffer from the same issues as those concerning acupuncture (e.g., small sample size).[24,27] Transcutaneous electrical nerve stimulation involves the placement of electrodes over the affected area, in this case the sacrum. A low electrical pulse is then transmitted that modifies the sensation of pain. Again, this technique has also been shown to work well for low back pain but does not lessen the request for other analgesics, and it has worked well as an adjuvant when combined with other more conventional techniques for labor pain.[63,66] The good news is that none of these techniques appear to have any negative effect on the neonate.

Obstetric Nerve Blocks

This category of pain relief techniques comprises two nerve blocks that achieve different goals. The paracervical block provides relief for the first stage of labor pain, whereas the pudendal block is used for the delivery portion of the second stage. Both of these blocks are provided by the physician managing the labor.

PARACERVICAL BLOCKS

The purpose of the paracervical technique is to block pain transmission via the visceral afferent fibers near the dilating cervix. This objective is reached by injecting local anesthetic lateral to the cervix at the vaginal fornices. There are all sorts of small variations of the technique, and in the United States lidocaine is the local anesthetic of choice. Bupivacaine is not recommended because of its low threshold for cardiovascular toxicity.

In use since the early part of the previous century, the paracervical became a popular mode of pain control in the 1950s and 1960s. Reported to provide moderate to excellent pain relief over 75% of the time, its most common complication has been a high incidence of fetal bradycardia, up to 40%.[49] Although the bradycardia has been described to be of a short duration and usually without adverse sequelae, fetal deaths have been reported.[49] Theories to explain this adverse effect include rapid absorption of the local anesthetic by the fetus to toxic levels and even direct injection.

One study reported that the umbilical arteries, and to a smaller extent the uterine arteries feeding the placenta, constricted after anesthetic injection. The bradycardia resolved once the vessels had relaxed and approached their baseline state. However, there was no difference in the technique and thus no answer about why this phenomenon had occurred in the first place.[43]

Paracervical blocks are less commonly performed for labor pain in the United States today than they were 2 decades ago. While they are virtually unheard of in the obstetric units where neuraxial blocks are available, they are useful where neuraxial blocks are not available and are reported to have a low complication rate and a neonatal outcome no different from those of systemic opioids.[26] However, there are few well-conducted studies to adequately assess the true risks of paracervical blocks on the fetus.[49]

PUDENDAL BLOCKS

As already stated, pudendal blocks are reserved for the delivery phase of the second stage, usually with forceps and the episiotomy that follows. In this procedure a transvaginal approach is used to block the pudendal nerve by injecting 5 to 10 mL of local anesthetic at the site of the attachment of the sacrospinous ligament to the ischial spine. One significant complication is maternal intravascular injection, so aspirations are frequently performed during the procedure. Despite the avoidance of maternal injection and the typically short interval between injection and delivery, blood levels of the local anesthetic used may still be found in the neonate for up to 4 hours after delivery. However, neurobehavioral examinations have not demonstrated an impact.[42]

Systemic Medications

There are two classes of drugs commonly used during labor and delivery that fall under the scope of this segment. They are opioids for pain relief and, less often, some form of sedative to relax and reduce anxiety. A quick rule of thumb when considering the effect of these or any other medications on the fetus is whether it produces a cerebral effect on the mother, that is, it has crossed the blood-brain barrier. If the medication can cross that barrier, it can likely cross the placental barrier and reach the fetus. However, the extent to which a fetus is exposed, if ever, depends on many factors, such as the drug's pharmacokinetic properties, the dose, and the mode of delivery. The following segment will review a few of the pharmacologic principles an anesthesiologist considers as they pertain to medication choices and fetal exposure. A more complete discussion can be found in any major pharmacology text.

PHARMACOKINETICS AND THE FETUS
(See Chapter 10)
When pharmacologic properties are discussed, a medication's ionization as determined by its pH, its lipophilia, and its tendency to bind to protein are all important principles that affect whether it will leave the

maternal circulation in any significant amount. A medication that is ionized cannot cross a membrane barrier. If a drug's pH is physiologic (pKa=pH=7.4), it means that 50% of the drug is ionized and 50% non-ionized. For the purpose of discussion, local anesthetics as a class are weak bases (pKa = 7.6–9.1) so they are more ionized at the physiologic of 7.4. The ratio by which a local anesthetic is ionized as opposed to non-ionized in the circulation depends on how great a base the drug is. For instance, a local anesthetic with a pKa of 9.1 is mostly ionized, and more will stay in the maternal circulation than a local anesthetic with a pKa of 7.6. Since it is the non-ionized portion of a drug that passes to a fetus, it will reproportion itself into ionized and non-ionized forms as it enters the fetal circulation. If the fetal pH is lower than the maternal pH because of metabolic acidosis, more of the drug converts to a more ionized form and cannot return to the maternal circulation. If the maternal exposure persists, more of the drug passes from the mother to the fetus and increasing amounts accumulate in the fetal circulation. This phenomenon is called fetal ion trapping and has been associated with some of the deleterious effects produced by common medications.

Of the other pharmacokinetic properties mentioned, drugs that possess lipophilic properties as opposed to hydrophilic ones are more capable of crossing lipid-rich membranes. Most medications used in obstetrics are lipophilic but to varying degrees. For example, fentanyl and sufentanil are lipophilic opioids, but sufentanil is much more so. As a result, epidural doses of sufentanil more readily leave the epidural space and are more easily detected in the maternal circulation than fentanyl. Finally, protein binding is an important consideration. A drug that selectively binds with protein molecules remains in the maternal circulation because once bound, it becomes a bulky molecule. Only the unbound drug is free to cross a membrane and produce an effect. So in the end, it is only the unbound, non-ionized portion of a lipophilic medication that crosses the membrane barrier, be it the blood-brain barrier or the placenta, to produce an effect.

Drug metabolism is another regulator of how much or even whether a drug will exert an effect on the fetal brain. Most medications undergo extensive metabolism into inactive metabolites in the maternal circulation. As a result, very little of an effect may be found. One example of a rapidly metabolized medication is succinylcholine, a depolarizing muscle relaxant. This medication is metabolized to benign metabolites by pseudocholinesterase in the maternal plasma and has a half-life of about 90 seconds. As a result, nothing gets to the fetus. As a final note, all of the above also applies to the active metabolites of medications, so if a drug degrades to an active metabolite with properties conducive to crossing membranes, that metabolite can have fetal effects. Such is the case with normeperidine, the active metabolite of meperidine.

A useful measurement that helps estimate fetal medication exposure is the ratio of the umbilical vein to the maternal vein (UV:MV). A ratio of 1 (UV:MV = 1) means

TABLE 24-1. Placental Passage of Commonly Used Anesthetic Medications

DRUG	UMBILICAL VEIN TO MATERNAL VEIN RATIO (UV:MV)
Induction Agents	
Thiopental	1.08 (range, 0.5-1.5)
Ketamine	0.54 (range, 0.4-0.7)
Propofol	0.7
Etomidate	0.5
Nondepolarizing Neuromuscular Blocking Agents	
Pancuronium	0.19
Vecuronium	0.11
Opioids	
Morphine	0.92
Meperidine	0.81 (may exceed 1.0 after 2-3 hours)
Fentanyl	0.57
Sufentanil	Levels too low to measure in humans
Butorphanol	0.84
Nalbuphine	0.97

Adapted from Glosten B: Anesthesia for obstetrics. In Longnecker DE et al (eds): Principles and Practice of Anesthesiology, 2nd ed. St. Louis, Mosby, 1998, p 1996.

that the amounts of medication in the umbilical vein equal those in the maternal vein. A low ratio means that a small amount has crossed the placenta to reach the umbilical vein. For example, the muscle relaxants used in general anesthesia are highly ionized, hydrophilic compounds that do not cross the membrane barrier. Their UV:MV ratios tend to be on the order of 0.1. Table 24-1 lists the UV:MV ratios of some common anesthetics.

Even if the umbilical vein levels are significant, they may not be great enough to produce any significant neurobehavioral effect because two more protective barriers exist to shield the fetal brain from medication exposure. Approximately 40% to 60% of any medication entering the fetal circulation passes through the liver first and then travels through the inferior vena cava to the heart and out into the circulation. The mature or nearly mature fetal liver can metabolize most drugs, and this first pass through the liver buffers the fetal brain from exposure. Combine this with the fact that the unique fetal circulation dilutes most of the drug as it travels into the general circulation, and this dilutional effect can be quite protective of the fetal brain.

One final clinical note for the neonatologist: Not only does the dose have an impact on how much medication enters the maternal circulation for eventual fetal distribution but so does the mode of administration. Although it is obvious that intravenous administration achieves the highest maternal blood levels, all blocks and injections distribute some level of the drug to the maternal circulation *and* they differ markedly from one another.

From the greatest to the least effect on maternal blood levels, drug administration modes have the following ranking:

Intravenous > Paracervical > Epidural
> Intramuscular > Spinal

It should be noted that maternal local anesthetic levels after a spinal delivery are so low as to be clinically irrelevant.

SEDATIVES

Because the role of sedatives as they are applied in the acute labor setting is so limited today, it is rare for a neonatologist to encounter a neonate with a recent exposure. Unlike a few decades ago, the primary purpose of sedatives in modern practice is to get the parturient to rest during a prolonged latent phase or before entering active labor. Generally, hours pass between administration and delivery, so any significant drug amounts have cleared the maternal and fetal circulations and sedative effects are not clinically apparent. The classes of medications one might encounter today are benzodiazepines, barbiturates, and phenothiazines.

Benzodiazepines are the most likely class of medication to be encountered because of maternal self-administration and not from the obstetric provider. They are rarely a desirable choice because of maternal amnesia and because metabolites can remain in the system for up to 8 days. Although diazepam has teratogenic potential, this has been associated only with chronic use in the first trimester. It and other benzodiazepines have no such problems in the acute setting.

The most common barbiturate used is secobarbital (Seconal), which has been popular for decades as a sleeping aid. It has a long safety record in terms of the fetus, and although the drug crosses the placenta, it is immediately exposed to the liver and rapidly distributed to other fetal tissues. The result is that brain tissues are rarely exposed to drug levels that are high enough to have a sedative effect from a single dose.[2] It is only with repeated doses that these levels can achieve a significant effect within the fetus. However, barbiturates have a known antianalgesic effect, so administration during labor makes little sense. Another barbiturate currently in use is phenobarbital. It was previously proposed to prevent periventricular hemorrhage in the preterm infant, but this has not been substantiated.

Phenothiazines have long been used in conjunction with opioids to reduce the side effects of the opioid and produce mild sedation. Only two are used because they have minimal effects on the fetus. They are hydroxyzine (Vistaril) and promethazine (Phenergan). These medications are commonly given in conjunction with a systemic opioid such as meperidine.

OPIOIDS

The definition of an opioid is any compound, either natural or synthetic, that acts on the same receptors as and produces effects similar to those of morphine. Those compounds that stimulate all opioid receptors are known as pure agonists and include morphine, meperidine, and fentanyl. Those that act on only some of the receptors and may even block action on others are known as agonist-antagonists and include nalbuphine and butorphanol. Pure antagonists block action on all receptors and are not considered opioids but can reverse their actions. Naloxone is the most common example of this class.

Opioids do not block the transmission of pain but rather stimulate receptors to alter the perception of pain and one's response to that perception. For that reason opioids are considered incomplete analgesics. There are three known opioid receptor types and a possible fourth on which these drugs act.[36,50] The μ-receptor provides the most complete analgesia but also most of the known side effects of opioids such as pruritis, nausea and vomiting, euphoria, and gastrointestinal effects. Stimulation of this receptor can also produce marked respiratory depression. The κ-receptor mediates less intense analgesia because of what is known as a ceiling effect. The dose-response studies performed early in the investigation of medications that stimulate this receptor determined that the curve flattened at a particular dose. This flattening of the dose-response curve means that more of the drug does not produce more of an effect. This ceiling effect holds not only for analgesia but also for respiratory depression. No other side effects appear to be associated with this receptor type. Both the μ- and κ-receptors have been divided into multiple subgroups. The δ-receptor mediates the effects of the endogenous endorphins, especially as they act on the spinal cord. The final receptor, named the σ-receptor, may be responsible for some of the side effects occasionally seen with some opioids. However, the existence of this receptor is dubious. Box 24-1 lists some of the opioids commonly used in labor and their classifications.

As mentioned previously, opioids appear to have a more noticeable effect on visceral pain than somatic pain.[36] As a result, they are more effective during the first stage of labor, which tends to be visceral in nature, than the second stage, which is more somatic. Because all opioids can cross the placenta and produce an effect

---

BOX 24-1. Opioids Commonly Used during Labor

Agonists
- Natural
  - Morphine
- Semi-synthetic
  - Meperidine
- Synthetic
  - Fentanyl
  - Sufentanil
  - Alfentanil
  - Remifentanil

Agonist-Antagonists
- Nalbuphine
- Butorphanol

in the fetus, opioid use has traditionally been limited to the first stage; therefore, the opioid is metabolized from the fetus before delivery. However, not only has the selection of opioids expanded over the years but also the thoughts on how they can be delivered. Intermittent intravenous and intramuscular administrations are still the mainstay on most units, but now intravenous patient-controlled analgesia (IV-PCA) is being offered on some obstetric units. Once thought to be taboo because of the depressive effects of opioids on the neonate, current studies show that this administration technique can be provided reasonably well, but because of neonatal effects, most agree that this technique should be reserved for a time when a regional technique is either not available or contraindicated.[39]

There are several reports in the literature describing the IV-PCA technique with meperidine, fentanyl, nalbuphine, alfentanil, and remifentanil.[33,38,39,53] Those neonates whose mothers use this technique should be watched for signs of sedation, respiratory depression, and low oxygen saturation.

Opioid Pure Agonists

Opioid agonists that may be encountered on the obstetric unit are morphine, meperidine, fentanyl, sufentanil, alfentanil, and remifentanil. Morphine is the only naturally occurring agonist and, if used in labor, is used early. The reason is that not only is it more depressive than any other opioid to the neonate, but it may also depress uterine contractions, making it a questionable choice if labor is anticipated.[50]

Meperidine (Demerol) is a semisynthetic opioid with some very interesting properties. This opioid is the one that is the most commonly used systemically, and not only does it promote contractions but there is also evidence that it enhances the effacement and dilation of the cervix.[29,64] Although it crosses the placenta and the levels can be quite high, it has a less depressive effect on the neonate than morphine. The drug itself has atropine-like properties that can produce tachycardia and myocardial depression in the mother and, when injected into the epidural or spinal space, can produce a block similar to that seen with local anesthetics.[4,19,51] For this reason, there are case reports describing meperidine used in this manner in patients with a documented allergy to all forms of local anesthetics. The drug metabolizes to an active metabolite called normeperidine that can cross the placenta and accumulate in the fetus. The half-life of this metabolite is 15 to 40 hours, so its effects can be evident for some time after delivery.

When used to provide systemic analgesia, meperidine is traditionally dosed in such a way as to limit fetal exposure before delivery. The drug's duration of action is 2 to 4 hours, with a half-life of 3 to 4.5 hours. Based on that information and the fact that when given intramuscularly it takes about 45 minutes to an hour to absorb and have an effect, meperidine is not given unless delivery is expected within the hour or more than 3 hours out. Unfortunately, the estimates of delivery time are an imprecise science, and sometimes the neonate is delivered during peak exposure. However, the need for naloxone to reverse the effects is uncommon under this scenario. This drug has been used in the IV-PCA format, and protocols are published describing the administration of this drug through the first stage and even during the second stage up to delivery.[53] Although some reports state a significant incidence of depression requiring treatment,[39] others do not.[53] In any case, it would probably be best to closely observe neonates exposed to this form of analgesia.

Several commonly used opioids are analogues of meperidine. They are fentanyl, sufentanil, alfentanil, and remifentanil. Although only fentanyl and sufentanil are used for anesthetic nerve blocks, fentanyl, alfentanil and remifentanil have been used systemically in the obstetric setting. All these drugs are lipid soluble and can cross the placenta. However, they are rapidly metabolized by the first pass through the liver to inactive metabolites. Therefore, depressive effects are rare when these drugs are given as intermittent intravenous boluses.[44] (Because of its pharmacokinetic properties, remifentanil is so short acting that it can be used only in a continuous infusion mode.) In one study, fentanyl injected in an intravenous dose of 1 µg/kg was given just before cesarean section, and there were no neonatal depressive effects.[10] However, a study in Finland described the use of a special bed to noninvasively monitor the neonate for depression, and claims that those neonates exposed to intravenous fentanyl experienced more depression than those exposed to paracervical blocks.[34] However, the population was very small, and even the authors suggested that this new monitoring tool needs further evaluation.

Fentanyl has been used in the IV-PCA format,[30,48] as have alfentanil[30] and remifentanil,[20,38,67] with mild neonatal depression a common occurrence. Generally, oxygen supplementation and observation are all that is required, especially when using a medication such as remifentanil, which has such a short duration of action. However, this information underscores the limited use of this mode of administration.

One final note about the opioid agonists: All of them are associated with the suppression of fetal beat-to-beat variability, which returns as the drug exposure diminishes, suggesting a causal effect.

Opioid Agonist-Antagonists

All medications in this category stimulate the κ-receptor and thus have a ceiling effect on respiratory depression, which was described previously. This information gives providers a sense of safety. However, the ceiling effect also applies to the analgesic capabilities, making this class of drug potentially limited in its effectiveness. The two most commonly used formulations on obstetric units in this country are nalbuphine (Nubain) and butorphanol (Stadol). Both produce sedation in the mother and degrade to inactive metabolites, and although both cross the placenta, the fetal effects seem limited.[10,36] However, nalbuphine has been reported to reduce fetal beat-to-beat variability and even produce a sinusoidal pattern when used.[8,33]

It is important to note that these two medications are markedly different in how they act on the μ-receptor. Whereas butorphanol has essentially no effect on the μ-receptor, nalbuphine actively blocks it and as a result can be used in small doses in lieu of naloxone to counter the μ-recepter effects such as pruritis that are stimulated by pure opioid agonists. The danger with nalbuphine is that it can place a narcotic-addicted patient into acute withdrawal at doses commonly used for labor analgesia. It can do the same to the addicted neonate.[10,36] Therefore, caution should be exercised in using this medication if there is any indication of narcotic abuse.

A final note about systemic opioid use: Because of the sedative and respiratory depressive effects of these drugs as well as their incomplete analgesic nature, heavy intrapartum use can produce a reaction in which maternal hyperventilation during a contraction is followed by hypoventilation as the contraction recedes. This condition will produce predictable results for maternal oxygen and carbon dioxide levels as well as those of the fetus. The end result can be significant fetal acidosis that begins during the first stage and worsens during the pushing of the second stage.[1,2,31,32,45]

Opioid Antagonists

Although other antagonists exist, naloxone (Narcan) is used on obstetric units almost exclusively. This medication blocks the action of opioid on all of its receptors and is commonly used to reverse the effects of excessive amounts of opioid. Unfortunately, it has a short half-life (30 to 45 minutes), which means that repeated boluses may be necessary in some instances. Naloxone is not a benign drug and has been known to cause pulmonary edema and cardiac failure in some situations, so caution should be exercised when using it.[36] It does cross the placenta, so it will reverse any opioid effect in the fetus. As with nalbuphine, it is not a medication that should be given to a mother with a narcotic addiction. Not only will it produce withdrawal in the mother but in the addicted fetus as well.[31,36]

NEURAXIAL BLOCKS

Neuraxial blocks are procedures performed by an anesthesia provider and are more commonly known as epidurals and spinals (Box 24-2). However, within the anesthesia community the term "spinal" is often replaced by the more accurate terms of "intrathecal" and "subarachnoid." Central to the diversity of these techniques is that they can be modified to produce either an analgesic or anesthetic effect. This technical variation may seem like minutiae to many, but it defines two very different goals of the anesthesia provider. The purpose of an anesthetic is to remove all sensation; pain, temperature, touch, vibratory sense, proprioception, and motor ability. The purpose of an analgesic is to remove the sensation of pain alone, leaving all other components intact. When discussing neuraxial blocks, the endpoint sought or achieved depends on the medications

BOX 24-2. Neuraxial Blocks

- Lumbar epidural
- Patient-controlled epidural analgesia
- Intrathecal injection (spinal)
- Combined spinal-epidural

used and their doses. Logically, higher doses produce the anesthetic state. Actually, the lower the dose, the closer one can get to producing an analgesic state, although achieving a pain-free state only without any other sensory loss can be difficult. Yet this outcome is the goal in obstetric anesthesia.

Techniques

Although the basic neuraxial procedures are the epidural and intrathecal, variations include the combined spinal-epidural (CSE) and the patient-controlled epidural analgesic (PCEA). It is not the purpose of this chapter to describe these procedures in detail, but neonatologists should be aware of their most fundamental facts. A more in-depth description may be found in any anesthesia text.

LUMBAR EPIDURALS

This procedure may be performed with the patient in either the sitting or lateral position. The back is examined for the L4-5, L3-4, or L2-3 level. Once determined, the skin is prepped with the use of an antiseptic solution, and a local anesthetic such as lidocaine is injected into the tissues below. A styletted 18- or 17-gauge needle is inserted into and situated in the interspinous ligament near the ligamentum flavum. The syringe is removed and a catheter threaded through the needle for approximately 3 to 5 cm. The needle is removed over the catheter, and it is secured before a test dose followed by the intended dose is given. Although there are many variations in this procedure, this approach is common.

The epidural space is vascular as well as potential space. Therefore, possible catheter or needle complications include placement or injection into a vessel or through the dura into the cerebrospinal fluid (CSF). The needle can also be off center, with subsequent misplacement of the catheter, or the catheter can simply find its own way off center, with threading.

Once the catheter is tested and appropriately dosed, it is common to begin a continuous infusion. This technique is called the continuous epidural infusion (CEI) and has almost completely replaced the intermittent bolus technique. There are numerous drug combinations, concentrations, and infusion rates cited in the literature, but the prevalent trend today is to use diluted concentrations in an attempt to achieve an analgesic state. This also improves the safety of today's approach in that lower doses mean less chance of a deleterious effect on either the mother or fetus should the catheter migrate.

PATIENT-CONTROLLED EPIDURAL ANALGESIA

A variation of the CEI technique is the PCEA. In this procedure the patient is given the ability to bolus herself as needed. There is some debate on whether a baseline infusion is necessary, but should one be started, it is at a lower rate than that for the conventional CEI. Studies have found that when patients are given control over their epidurals, they tend to be more conservative and use approximately 35% less medication on average.

INTRATHECAL INJECTIONS (SPINALS)

The term "spinal" conveys an image of complete paralysis from the waist down. However, with today's dosing techniques, a spinal as performed for labor analgesia can preserve temperature sensation, touch, proprioception, and even mobility while providing analgesia. The approach is the same as that described for an epidural with the exception that a thinner styletted needle is used, generally in the range of 25 to 27 gauge. The stylet is not removed until a "pop" is felt as the needle passes through the dura into the CSF. Once the stylet is removed and the presence of CSF confirmed, the medication is injected and the needle removed.

Because the CSF is essentially without blood vessels, this technique is associated with the lowest maternal blood levels of all. However, the most commonly used opioids for the induction of labor analgesia are highly lipophilic and tend to travel to the μ-receptors in the central nervous system. As a result, somnolence and even respiratory depression have been reported with small doses.[14] However, there have not been any adverse neonatal effects reported as a direct result of the intrathecal narcotic. While intrathecal opioid injections have been tried as the sole labor analgesic, they are not very effective beyond the first stage nor do they usually last long enough. To resolve this issue, the following technique was adapted for use in labor.

COMBINED SPINAL-EPIDURALS

In this technique, essentially both procedures are performed but the spinal needle goes through or under the epidural needle into the dura once the epidural tip is situated in the epidural space. After the intrathecal medication is injected, the spinal needle is removed and the epidural catheter threaded into the epidural space. Then the epidural needle is removed. This procedure allows for a rapid analgesic response (the spinal) with the ability to dose and begin an infusion through the epidural catheter for longevity. Frequently, the epidural catheter is not used for dosing until the intrathecal effect has worn off.

Although this particular technique has increased in popularity, many are beginning to find that it should not be used on all parturients. There are some for whom it is better suited, such as the rapidly progressing multiparous patient who might not be offered anything otherwise. The biggest detriment is that the epidural catheter is untried in CSE; if a problem arises, there may not be time to test and dose with it. Although the CEI and PCEA have a slower onset of pain relief than CSE, they are proven modalities, with the added benefit that the epidural catheter is tried and functional should there be a sudden change in delivery plans.

Maternal Risks and Benefits

BENEFITS

Every study that compares the analgesic effect achieved with a neuraxial block with any other form of analgesic technique, whether it is pharmacologic or non-pharmacologic, documents a superior result. When done properly, these blocks allow the mother to relax and conserve her energy for the second stage of labor and become more of a participant in that process. They also prevent maternal hyperventilation in response to pain and thus all the potential sequelae associated with lower maternal P_{CO_2} levels.

Although the medications used as part of an epidural can eventually be found in the maternal circulation because of the vascularity of the epidural space, the newer techniques use lower doses, which help keep these levels to a minimum. As a result, mothers typically show very little if any systemic effect from the medications used, which also helps limit exposure to the fetus.

Several studies have demonstrated that epidurals improve both uterine and intervillous bloodflow. Two of the earliest studies documenting this result were published by Hollmen and Shnider and their respective colleagues. Hollmen and associates used intravenous radioactive markers to document improved intervillous bloodflow after an epidural. They had two epidural study groups, each using a different local anesthetic, and compared the results of those groups with a non-epidural control group.[15] They found that intervillous bloodflow actually decreased by 19% in the control group but improved by 35% and 37% in those receiving the epidurals. Shnider and coworkers examined the physiologic stress response to labor by measuring catecholamine levels before and after epidural initiation in active labor. They showed that with an epidural, norepinephrine levels drop 19% and epinephrine levels drop 56% from preblock levels.[54] These findings were significant not only because of the catecholamine effect on uterine contractions but also, more significantly, these reductions in catecholamine improved uterine bloodflow.

MATERNAL SIDE EFFECTS

Some of the commonly acknowledged side effects of neuraxial blocks are hypotension and postdural puncture headache. Hypotension is generally more common and frequently more severe after a spinal. It is also more common after an anesthetic dose than an analgesic one because the sympathectomy produced is more profound. If the hypotension is allowed to persist untreated, there are significant consequences to both the mother and fetus. However, it would be below the standard of care to not treat hypotension when it occurs. As a result, the episodes are brief and generally without any sequelae. A postdural puncture headache can be debilitating to the point of preventing the new mother from moving out of the supine position. It is the result of the dura being intentionally or unintentionally punctured during the course of the procedure, with resulting CSF leakage. The vast majority of headaches are time limited and will resolve within two weeks of the puncture if no action is taken. However, most parturients will agree to an epidural blood patch for rapid relief, with excellent results. Other irritating side effects occur because of the opioid used. They include pruritus, nausea and vomiting, sedation, and urinary retention. All are due to stimulation of the μ-receptor (opioid) and will dissipate with time. The only hazardous opioid-induced side effect is respiratory depression, and although it is rare, health care providers should always be on the alert for its signs.

MATERNAL RISKS AND POTENTIAL RISKS WITH AN IMPACT ON THE FETUS

There are many maternal risks potentially resulting from neuraxial blocks. While some are uncontested, such as epidural hematoma formation or nerve damage, others are quite fantastic, such as a reduction in the IQ of the neonate as he or she grows. For the purpose of this chapter, the following segment will consider only the maternal risks and those risks that might have a potential impact on the fetus. These risks are unintentional intrathecal or intravascular injection, longer labor, an increased incidence of operative delivery, maternal temperature elevation, and the cesarean section rate. Of those potential risks stated, some do have an effect, but it is small and of questionable clinical significance. Others are documented to no longer be a risk of neuraxial blocks but are mentioned here because the reader may not be aware of the change in their status. Such is the case with the incidence of cesarean sections.

Cesarean Sections

Over a decade ago, a study was published which claimed that epidurals increased the incidence of dystocia in primiparous patients and thus were increasing the need for cesarean sections.[62] Although there were several problems with the sentinel study, other studies were published making the same claims. These studies also suffered from the same limitation. The primary difficulty was that the patients were allowed to choose their analgesic mode or, if randomized, allowed to change to the other analgesic choice, resulting in a high crossover rate to epidurals. The dilemma was that those with difficult, protracted labors would naturally gravitate to the epidural for its superior pain relief, and investigators felt it would be unethical to deny access to it. Over time, ethically designed, randomized, controlled studies were performed and published, as were impact studies. They showed that there was no causal effect of epidurals on the cesarean section rate for dystocia.[11,12,25] It is understood now that although epidurals are associated with dysfunctional labors, they do not cause them, and dysfunctional labors increase the risk for cesarean section. When women are faced with long, painful labors, they will choose the most effective means of pain relief available, and that is often some form of neuraxial block.

Labor Prolongation

Prolongation of labor has long been blamed on neuraxial blocks. This claim is still undergoing some debate. Most recently available data indicate that neuraxial analgesia in early labor did not increase the rate of cesarean delivery, and it provided better analgesia and resulted in a shorter duration of labor than systemic analgesia.[25,69] As for second-stage prolongation, it is now generally acknowledged that there is an average increase of about 15 minutes.[11,25] There has been only one study claiming a longer second stage of approximately 1 hour.[61] The question now is whether a 15-minute increase in the length of the second stage is clinically significant. The earlier studies that looked at epidurals and their effects certainly showed that epidurals had a protective effect in that the fetal acid-base balance was better preserved. This result was not certain if the mother had not had effective analgesia. As a result of this finding, the American College of Obstetricians and Gynecologists (ACOG) changed its recommendation on time-limited pushing. The ACOG currently recommends that if an epidural is in place and there are no signs of fetal compromise, then the second stage should be allowed to continue and the patients reassessed at intervals.

Operative Vaginal Deliveries

An increased incidence in operative vaginal deliveries has also been claimed as a risk of neuraxial blockade. If the overall incidence of forceps deliveries is reviewed, there is no question that the incidence increases when an epidural is in place. However, there are many reasons to perform a forceps delivery, and the indications are not always obstetrically defined. Unfortunately, the literature rarely specifies why a forceps delivery occurs when an epidural is in place, but when the obstetric indication is documented, no increase in the use of forceps for obstetric indications is observed. A common occurrence is when an obstetrician requests that an epidural be placed rather than perform a pudendal block if he or she feels that forceps are indicated.[11,25] As a result, the birth is recorded as a forceps delivery under an epidural. Impact studies have been helpful in documenting that the presence of a new epidural service does not increase the incidence of forceps deliveries for obstetric reasons, which strongly suggests that they have no effect.[11] However, until more studies are performed where the indication for the forceps delivery is documented, it will be difficult to determine precisely what the risk is or whether one actually exists.

Maternal Temperature Elevation

Elevated maternal temperature has recently been identified as a risk and is certainly a topic of heated debate. Within the specialty of anesthesiology, this finding has been difficult to explain. It is well documented that when a patient receives an epidural anesthetic for a surgical procedure or even a cesarean section,[17] the patient's core temperature decreases. An anesthetic dose produces a significant sympathectomy that causes a general vasodilation below the level of the block, which in turn promotes increased heat loss in the immediate environment. However, studies performed in the 1990s showed that under the conditions of a low-dose analgesic epidural, maternal temperature elevates during labor after a period of very stable body temperature. Specifically, it was found that after about 5 hours, the temperature rises at about 0.07°C per hour and then stabilizes at about 39.5°C. Most of the time there were no other clinical signs of maternal infection, yet the elevated temperature was enough to trigger a sepsis workup on the neonate. The results indicated that there was no increased incidence of fetal sepsis.[11,25]

Inadvertent Injections

Inadvertent intrathecal or intravascular injections when a neuraxial block is performed can have a serious impact on the fetus. The intravascular injection of a large dose of local anesthetic can potentially cause maternal seizures, hypotension, and cardiac arrest. The acute insult to the fetus appears to be due to the maternal hypoxia that occurs during the seizure and not to the high levels of anesthetic in the maternal system, although some of it is sure to cross over. When there is a high spinal level due to improper dosing or an intrathecal injection that is not recognized, the maternal respiratory muscles become paralyzed. If this condition is not recognized and goes untreated, the maternal arrest will have obvious consequences on the fetus. Fortunately, both of these complications are exceedingly rare and very preventable with attention to good technique.

Benefits and Potential Risks for the Fetus

Most of the literature on neuraxial blockade, with its associated benefits and risks, has focused on the maternal effects. Unfortunately, many laypersons and some health care providers assume that for every negative maternal effect, there must be an associated negative fetal or neonatal effect. However, the literature does not support such a presumption. When a study is designed to examine the fetal and neonatal effects, the markers typically used are the presence or absence of base excess to determine the recent intrauterine environment, the intrapartum fetal heart rate (FHR), the Apgar scores, and a host of neuroadaptive examinations that require operator training and have varying abilities to determine any prolonged effect on the neonate from an intrapartum event or medication. For example, the popular Neurologic and Adaptive Capacity Score (NACS) may not be able to distinguish between hypoxic and drug effects in the neonate.[3] The following segment discusses the effects of neuraxial block on the fetus and neonate as defined by the aforementioned markers and concludes with a brief review on breast feeding.

ACID-BASE BALANCE

One of the most notable benefits a fetus gains from neuraxial blocks is that the mother does not hyperventilate in response to painful contractions. As mentioned previously, hyperventilation in response to painful contractions causes maternal Pco_2 levels to drop

and result in respiratory alkalosis. Because fetal levels follow maternal levels, the same respiratory alkalosis develops in the fetus, causing a leftward shift in the fetal oxyhemoglobin curve and leading to less binding of oxygen with fetal hemoglobin.[32] This sets the stage for fetal hypoxia, leading to metabolic acidosis that often worsens during a prolonged second stage. When a functioning neuraxial block is in place, these events are less likely to occur, and studies have consistently shown an improved acid-base balance when an epidural is used.[1,32,45] Neonatal base excess is believed to best reflect the intrauterine environment just before delivery, and studies comparing epidurals with systemic medications or no treatment have documented that neonatal base excess levels stay within normal limits more consistently than they do with other techniques.[25,45] Other common findings show no change in or less meconium upon delivery and equivalent or improved Apgar scores at delivery, supporting the idea of a better intrauterine environment and less stress on the fetus.[12,16,47]

FETAL HEART RATE

Reports on the effect of neuraxial blocks on FHR have been confusing. Fetal bradycardia, which occurs in approximately 10% to 12% of those in the population receiving an epidural, has been a long-recognized phenomenon. It typically begins 5 to 10 minutes after the epidural is dosed and lasts for approximately 2 to 7 minutes. It is usually significant enough to initiate intrauterine resuscitative measures during which the FHR returns to baseline and there is rarely, if ever, a need for early delivery. The Apgar scores are typically fine upon delivery.[58] This phenomenon has been described with all three commonly used local anesthetics and in all neuraxial techniques. The significance of this finding is not clear.

The other FHR effect sometimes seen in neuraxial blockade is the loss of beat-to-beat variability as a result of the opioid used. This side effect is also seen with systemic opioids and agonist-antagonist opioids.[57] When analgesic techniques are compared, FHR changes are more common with systemic medications.[10] Also, the need for naloxone is more common in those neonates whose mothers received systemic opioids during labor than in those whose mothers received neuraxial blocks containing one. Although some studies show that the neuraxial opioid effects on FHR are temporally limited, when very high doses are delivered repeatedly in the epidural space, which can occur with PCEA techniques that are opioid based, enough can cross the placenta so that the neonate may have high systemic levels and require naloxone at birth.[23] With today's dosing regimens, this result should be very atypical.

BREASTFEEDING

A frequent claim made by those opposed to the use of epidurals is that this mode of pain relief will temporarily or permanently damage the neonate's ability to breastfeed. Precisely how this occurs has never been elucidated, and those theories that have been proposed and seemed plausible have not withstood scientific scrutiny. Among the theories that have been examined is a common hypothesis that the medications used in the epidural will either cross the placenta from the maternal circulation and remain in the neonatal circulation or seep into the breast milk and affect the neonate. One study looked at the residual drug presence in the colostrum and neonate if the mother was given intravenous fentanyl (1 mg/kg) just before cesarean section. This would certainly produce more exposure to the fetus and higher maternal blood levels than epidural fentanyl. In that study, blood samples were taken from the neonate at delivery and at 2-hour intervals up to 10 hours. Colostrum samples were also collected at the same time intervals. At 10 hours there were no detectable levels in either the colostrum or the neonate, indicating that any breast-feeding difficulties would not be due to a residual drug effect.[59] Another study looked at the immediate effect on breast-feeding behaviors in those neonates whose mothers received low-dose epidurals or nothing at all, not even a local anesthetic for the episiotomy. Cord blood samples were collected for bupivacaine and fentanyl analysis, breast-feeding behaviors were documented, and an NACS evaluation was performed at 2 and 24 hours. Although they were detectable, the medication levels were low and neither the breast-feeding behaviors nor the NACS results differed between groups, indicating no medicinal effect.[41] However, some of the patients who had undergone labor without an epidural were so exhausted at the end that they were too tired to breastfeed as opposed to those who had an epidural. Other studies have not measured levels but rather have examined whether the patients who received epidurals were treated in a manner different from those mothers who did not receive them and how those policies might have an impact. In some institutions, precisely this discrepancy in nursing management was found.[13]

In summary, although there are numerous reasons why mothers and neonates do not succeed at breast feeding, the current peer-reviewed literature does not support the premise that neuraxial techniques have any effect on the abilities of the neonate to breastfeed.

DELIVERY MODES AND ANESTHETIC TECHNIQUE

When delivery is not imminent and the mother is admitted for labor, an important role for her obstetric team is to support whatever pain-relieving choices she makes as long as there is no perceived harm to her or her fetus. However, choices are not always well informed or circumstances dictate a change in labor management that conflicts with the mother's choice. For instance, the morbidly obese patient who has a difficult airway and a questionable FHR tracing should not pursue the water birth but be counseled on oxygen supplementation and placement of an epidural in anticipation of a possible emergency cesarean section.

Labor is one of the most dynamic processes in medicine, and what once proceeded routinely can change very rapidly. As a result, analgesic techniques and management plans need to be adaptable as well. Discussed below are some of the anesthetic considerations the anesthesia provider faces when a spontaneous delivery is no longer a possibility.

Operative Vaginal Delivery

There are two types of operative vaginal deliveries: the vacuum extraction and the forceps delivery. The vacuum extraction cannot be performed until the head is very low in the pelvis. The extractor is generally a pliable Silastic cup, the application of which is well tolerated by the mother. As a result, the majority of patients do not need additional analgesia even if none was used for the labor. Some local anesthetic to the perineum in anticipation of an episiotomy is all that may be required.

Forceps application and delivery generally require some level of analgesia, and often the obstetrician either requests an epidural/spinal or performs a pudendal block. There are four levels of forceps delivery described, but in today's practices the two most commonly performed are low and outlet forceps deliveries. The placement of the forceps blades is very stimulating, and it is only in a dire emergency that an obstetrician should perform such a delivery without some form of anesthesia in place. A pudendal block is a reasonable choice and can be performed by the obstetrician in less time than a spinal or epidural can be administered. However, neuraxial blocks offer more complete pain relief and, in the case of an epidural, can be extended to a higher level should the need arise. Thus, many obstetricians prefer this approach and, if time and the situation allow it, may even ask that an epidural be placed if one is not present.

Cesarean Section

Cesarean section can be performed electively, urgently, or emergently. The circumstances under which one occurs will generally dictate the form of anesthetic used. However, most anesthesiologists prefer not to use a general anesthetic because of concerns about the maternal airway and aspiration. In the general surgical population, the incidences of encountering a difficult airway are about 1 in 2300 to 3200. Unfortunately, the chance that one will encounter a difficult airway in the obstetric population is about ten times higher, an incidence quoted to be about 1 in 300.[5] Several factors contribute to this number. The changes of pregnancy itself cause edematous airways resulting from fluid accumulation.[40] Add to this the time spent in labor, especially after many Valsalva maneuvers in the second stage, and what was once a normal airway can become swollen and easily obstructed with attempts at intubation. Other changes contributing to management difficulty can include those in the pulmonary system, gastrointestinal system, and body habitus over the course of the pregnancy. These changes and the often

BOX 24-3. Absolute Contraindications to Neuraxial Blocks

- Hypotension from shock, either septic or hemorrhagic
- Infection at the site
- Thrombocytopenia or a bleeding diathesis
- Maternal refusal

emergent nature of an obstetric procedure may result in failed airway management and aspiration which contribute to obstetric mortality resulting from anesthesia. In fact, over 90% of the maternal deaths worldwide that are directly attributed to anesthesia are due to complications from airway management when performing a general anesthetic, with over 75% reported to be preventable or the result of substandard care.[60] Thus, for most anesthesia providers neuraxial anesthesia is the approach of choice whenever possible.

NEURAXIAL ANESTHESIA

In the elective or urgent situation, some form of neuraxial block is the anesthetic of choice, assuming that there are no existing contraindications (Box 24-3). If an epidural is already in place, it is an easy matter to change medications to a more concentrated, faster-onset local anesthetic. Opioids may or may not be added. Attention must still be paid to the dosing technique because moving the patient onto the operating bed may dislodge or shift the epidural catheter; therefore, test doses and aliquoted amounts are still in order. If an epidural block is not in place and the need to proceed with the cesarean section is urgent or emergent, the preferred approach in most units is to perform an intrathecal injection or possibly even a CSE. This technique gives a faster onset and limits the exposure of the fetus. It also has been shown to result in better neonatal parameters than those for general anesthetic techniques.[28]

GENERAL ANESTHESIA

The level of urgency or emergency at which a neuraxial block should either not be attempted or potentially abandoned is always a topic for debate. That decision should never be made lightly because of the issues described earlier in this section. However, there are absolute contraindications to performing a neuraxial block (see Box 24-3), and when one is present, it directs the decision making. When a general anesthetic is the choice, the question usually foremost in the neonatologist's mind at the time of delivery is what impact those medications may have on the neonate. Fortunately, the literature supports the clinical observation that under the conditions of a short incision-to-delivery time and with the current use of short-acting anesthetics, the impact is small. Those anesthetic and induction agents that are the most commonly used are discussed below.

Before the induction of a general anesthetic, the anesthesia provider will usually give the mother acid-neutralizing medications to reduce the risk of aspiration pneumonitis. Of those medications given, none have been shown to have an impact on the fetus.[10] Since it is only the induction phase and perhaps a short period of maintenance that have an impact on the fetus, the anesthetics of concern are induction agents, nitrous oxide (N_2O) and a volatile agent, a rapid-onset neuromuscular blocker such as succinylcholine, and potentially some opioids. Earlier in this chapter there was a discussion on pharmacologic properties and the presence of medications in the umbilical compared with the maternal vein (UV:MV ratio). Table 24-1 shows the UV:MV ratios of several of these drugs as a way to gauge potential crossover to the fetus.

The most common induction agents used are thiopental and ketamine, but propofol and etomidate have been used as well. All of them cross the placenta, but there is rarely an effect seen in the neonate because of the first-pass effect through the fetal liver and the dilutional effects from the circulation. Thiopental is more common and, at least in the literature, is preferred over propofol because it produces less hypotension. Ketamine is generally reserved for the hemorrhaging or volume-depleted patient because it does a better job of maintaining the hemodynamic state. Etomidate is generally reserved for patients with cardiac disease. All of these induction agents depress the maternal myocardium, but to varying degrees. As a result, intervillous bloodflow initially decreases but returns to baseline as long as maternal blood pressures are monitored and any hypotension is treated.

In order to intubate and secure the airway in the most rapid manner possible, succinylcholine is the neuromuscular agent of choice because it has the fastest onset of action. Unfortunately, it also has the shortest duration of action. It is metabolized by pseudocholinesterase to benign metabolites in the maternal plasma and has a half-life of 90 seconds. As a rule, no other neuromuscular blocking agent is needed within the time from incision to delivery, so there is no effect on the fetus. However, there are times when succinylcholine is contraindicated or delivery is delayed, so another type of neuromuscular blocking agent is required. However, this class of medications is hydrophilic and highly ionized, and so only insignificant amounts may appear in the placenta (see Table 24-1).

N_2O and a volatile agent such as isoflurane or sevoflurane are administered to maintain the anesthetic state. Although these agents pass to the fetus, they rarely have a direct effect unless the time from induction to delivery is prolonged. If more than 15 minutes pass since the induction, the concentrations of these agents in the fetus will equilibrate with the maternal levels and the neonate will be depressed at delivery. Ventilatory support for a few minutes at delivery is all that is required because these agents are expelled through the lungs. However, it is more important for the neonatologist to note that in the presence of a prolonged induction to delivery exposure or, more critically, if the uterine incision to delivery time exceeds 180 seconds, the neonate will surely be depressed because of compromised perfusion.[6]

ANCILLARY MEDICATIONS

It is not required that the mother be given sedatives or intravenous opioids before delivery, but on occasion it happens. Some patients demand some form of sedative before the cesarean section, and in those cases a small dose of midazolam (Versed) is common. A small dose does not have an impact on the neonate. At other times the neuraxial block may not be adequate for the cesarean section because either the epidural catheter is poorly positioned or insufficient time has passed for the level to rise adequately and the anesthesiologist or anesthetist may administer an opioid such as fentanyl or small doses of ketamine. These medications have already been discussed, and none have a significant effect on the neonate at the dosages commonly used.

ANESTHETIC CHOICES AND MATERNAL OBSTETRIC HISTORY

Preeclampsia

Preeclampsia is a disease unique to pregnancy that occurs because of an imbalance in the hormones produced by the placenta (see Chapter 14). Its classic triadic presentation in the mother is proteinuria, edema, and hypertension. The severe systemic involvement of this disease has several effects, not the least of which is increased systemic vascular resistance (SVR). Depending on the severity of the disease, the increased SVR can reduce the uteroplacental blood flow because of vasoconstriction and compromise the fetus. As a result, it is not unusual to see signs of fetal distress during the induction of labor in a patient with severe preeclampsia. The other clinical abnormalities associated with the disease that are particularly troublesome for the anesthesiologist are thrombocytopenia and edema. In a severely preeclamptic patient, the edema can be generalized and so severe that the tissues in the airway and around the vocal cords are involved. Clinically, the patient may literally change her speaking voice. To the attentive anesthesiologist this manifestation can be a sign that attempts at intubation will likely be difficult if not impossible. As for the thrombocytopenia, it can be so significant that a regional anesthetic is contraindicated.

In the past it was felt that because of the severe increase in SVR, any and all regional anesthetics were contraindicated because of the potential hypotension that could result from the sympathectomy produced. Of course this potential outcome would have a negative impact on uteroplacental flow. However, as newer dosing techniques were introduced, it was found that the sympathectomy achieved with an analgesic block was muted. It was also noted that epidural anesthesia onset was slow enough that the mother could be carefully fluid loaded so that circulation and blood pressure could be maintained. Finally, there were enough outcome data demonstrating that there was more risk to the mother from attempts at intubation and subsequent failure or from the marked hypertension that would result from those attempts, which might lead to intracranial bleeding, that a general anesthetic could be a higher risk option than a regional anesthetic.

For several years it was believed that only an epidural or a general anesthetic could be attempted, and not a spinal, because of the hypotension issue. However, with further studies and case reports, we now know that numerous options are acceptable as long as some aspect of the disease does not contraindicate the anesthetic choice. Over the years, more anesthesiologists have been asked to become involved early in the management of the preeclamptic patient in order for the epidural to be placed before any problems with thrombocytopenia. Should a cesarean section become necessary, the epidural can then be appropriately dosed. Spinals are reserved for those situations in which the need for a cesarean section arises before the placement of the epidural.

Given the favorable data on the measured parameters seen in the neonates of non-preeclamptic mothers, the use of regional techniques for the preeclamptic patient results in similar favorable outcomes in the neonate. Some studies have shown that even in the preeclamptic patient, intervillous bloodflow improves with a regional block as long as maternal blood pressures are maintained.[18]

Uterine Rupture

In response to the increasing pressure to reduce the cesarean section rate in the United States during the 1990s, obstetricians began to let go of the old adage "once a section, always a section." Women who had previously had a cesarean section that involved a low transverse incision during their operative delivery were now allowed a trial of labor. If successful, it was called a "vaginal birth after cesarean," or VBAC. At first the success rates seemed to be acceptable, with less risk than anticipated. However, over time it became evident that some patients were more likely to succeed than others depending on the events of the first labor. Obstetricians needed to define who should be counseled to attempt a VBAC, as success was documented to be at 60% to 70% overall. Further compounding the issues over VBAC, was the finding of scar dehiscence during labor in about 1% of these patients. Initially it was felt that women undergoing a trial of labor should not be allowed to receive an epidural because it might mask any pain associated with a uterine rupture or scar dehiscence. However, two points reversed this attitude. The first was that the most common findings of either a rupture or scar dehiscence were rarely pain or even bleeding. The most common presenting signs are a change in the FHR and contraction pattern. Secondly, with the advancing techniques in epidural analgesia, it was quickly recognized that should there be any abnormal pain response during labor, it would "break through" the low analgesic doses of the epidural. Therefore, the current practice is not to deny women undergoing a trial of labor any form of epidural analgesia but to aggressively examine them for other causes should they complain of irregular pain while under an epidural effect.

Once scar dehiscence or even a true uterine rupture is recognized, an epidural that is already in place is perfectly acceptable for the anesthesiologist to use as the anesthetic. However, it is also common practice to proceed with a general anesthetic if nothing is in place because the fetus is already in severe distress, and all attempts at this point are aimed toward delivery as fast as possible. When such an event occurs, it is probable that the depressed neonate is not suffering from adverse effects from the anesthetic, since it would be unlikely that any medication was transported. All signs and symptoms of depression would be due to the uterine rupture and the disruption of uteroplacental bloodflow.

Breech Delivery

When the cesarean section rate was not under scrutiny, it was believed that all breech deliveries should be performed abdominally to avoid the risk of hypoxia or neurologic injury in the neonate. As obstetricians felt pressure to reduce the incidence of cesarean sections, a few returned to delivering a selected form of breech position vaginally. When a woman anticipates a vaginal breech delivery, she may still receive an epidural analgesic during labor. The important point for the anesthesia provider to remember is that the preservation of her abdominal muscles is imperative so that she can maintain her ability to push. It is also very helpful to the obstetrician if the mother is comfortable enough to follow the obstetrician's directions for a controlled birth. As a result, an epidural analgesic is usually the approach of choice.

There are many potential complications from a vaginal breech delivery for the neonate because of the mechanics of the process, but problems arising from the anesthetic are rare. It is recommended that a general anesthetic or a spinal not be used in vaginal breech deliveries because the patient loses her ability to push and work with the obstetrician. However, it is still the standard in this country to deliver most breech presentations abdominally. In this situation other factors, such as the level of urgency of the section, determine the choice of anesthetic.

Fetal Distress

Fetal distress is generally an indication of some level of compromise in the intrauterine environment. Although the term is often misused, when it is truly present it signals a progressive process that produces fetal asphyxia. Unless it is corrected, it will progress to severe neurologic damage or death. The obstetric provider follows the signs of distress and makes the determination of whether labor remains a viable option for delivery or a cesarean section should be undertaken. However, between the beginning of labor and that determination, a non-reassuring fetal tracing certainly does not preclude a patient from receiving an epidural analgesic. As mentioned previously, the epidural can improve the intrauterine environment and keep the mother alert and active during her obstetric management. Certainly the maternal hyperventilation, catecholamine elevations, and potential problems due to systemic medication can have a negative intrauterine impact, further complicating the situation.

As already stated, fetal distress is a progressive problem. Most anesthesia providers would prefer to see the mother before the fetus is in severe distress and progression to a cesarean section becomes an emergency. In such a situation, many may proceed with a general anesthetic because of time constraints. However, Marx and colleagues demonstrated that even in the presence of severe fetal distress, neonatal outcomes were better, as determined by Apgar scores and base excess values, in those mothers who received a regional (local) instead of a general anesthetic.[28] This finding supports the concept that a regional anesthetic should be pursued whenever possible and underscores the need for all members of the obstetric team to communicate. However, there will be times when the only option is to proceed with the general anesthetic.

Placenta Previa

Placenta previa is the result of the placental tissue covering all or some portion of the cervical os, potentially obstructing the fetal exit. Previas are classified into three types that describe varying degrees of obstruction. The *complete* previa completely covers the os and occurs 37% of the time, and the *marginal* previa barely touches the os, occurring 46% of the time. The most diagnostically difficult one is the *partial* previa, which covers some portion of the os. The level of obstruction needs to be determined by the obstetrician near the time of labor. This type has an incidence of 27%. While the marginal previa does not prevent a vaginal delivery and the complete previa forces an abdominal delivery, the partial previa could result in either delivery mode. If the obstetrician decides that there is not enough placenta obstructing the os to prevent a vaginal birth, vaginal delivery may be the choice. However, these patients are often crossmatched and closely monitored in case of hemorrhage. As long as there is no evidence of hemorrhage, an epidural analgesic is still an appropriate choice. The dilemma arises if the patient starts to bleed. The need to proceed to a cesarean section is obvious, but there is no correct answer regarding whether to deepen the regional block or perform a general anesthetic. The briskness of the bleeding will direct much of the decision making, and the ultimate insult to the neonate.

Complete previa requires an abdominal delivery. Because this relationship is generally known in advance, an elective cesarean section under regional anesthesia is the standard. Uncontrolled bleeding is rare, and there is no increased risk to the neonate.

Placental Abruption

A placental abruption occurs when there is early separation of the placenta from the uterine wall. The separation can be complete or partial. When the abruption is not complete, the fetus should be observed for any signs of compromised bloodflow. If everything appears stable, the obstetrician may not choose to deliver immediately. However, if bleeding resumes or there is complete separation, then emergent delivery is required due to the hemorrhage. Under these conditions a regional anesthetic is contraindicated; a general one is the only choice. Because of the clinical situation, neonatal depression is due to the impact of the maternal hemorrhage and not exposure to any form of anesthetic.

REFERENCES

1. Bergmans MGM et al: Fetal and maternal transcutaneous P_{CO_2} levels during labour and the influence of epidural analgesia. Eur J Obstet Gynecol Reprod Biol 67:127, 1996.

2. Bergmans MGM et al: Fetal transcutaneous P_{CO_2} measurements during labour. Eur J Obstet Gynecol Reprod Biol 51:1, 1993.

3. Camann W, Brazelton TB: Use and abuse of neonatal neurobehavioral testing. Anesthesiology 92:3, 2000.

4. Cheun JK, Kim AR: Intrathecal meperidine as the sole agent for cesarean section. J Korean Med Sci 4:135, 1989.

5. Cormack RS, Lehan J: Difficult tracheal intubation in obstetrics. Anaesthesia 39:1105, 1984.

6. Datta S et al: Neonatal effect of prolonged anesthetic induction for cesarean section. Obstet Gynecol 58:331, 1981.

7. Eckert K et al: Immersion in water in the first stage of labor: A randomized controlled trial. Birth 28:84, 2001.

8. Feinstein SJ et al: Sinusoidal fetal heart rate pattern after administration of nalbuphine hydrochloride: A case report. Am J Obstet Gynecol 154:159, 1986.

9. Florido J et al: Plasma concentrations of beta-endorphin and adrenocorticotropic hormone in women with and without childbirth preparation. Eur J Obstet Gynecol Reprod Biol 73:121, 1997.

10. Glosten B: Anesthesia for obstetrics. In Longnecker DE et al (eds): Principles and Practice of Anesthesiology, 2nd ed. St. Louis, Mosby, 1998, p 1988.

11. Halpern SH, Leighton BL: Misconceptions about neuraxial analgesia. Anesth Clin North Am 21:59, 2003.

12. Halpern SH et al: Effect of epidural vs. parenteral opioid analgesia on the progress of labor: A meta-analysis. JAMA 280:2105, 1998.

13. Halpern SH et al: Effect of labor analgesia on breast-feeding success. Birth 26:275, 1999.

14. Hays RL, Palmer CM: Respiratory depression after intrathecal sufentanil during labor. Anesthesiology 81:511, 1994.

15. Hollmen AI et al: Effect of extradural analgesia using bupivacaine and 2-chloroprocaine on intervillous blood flow during normal labour. Br J Anaesth 54:837, 1982.

16. Impey L et al: Graphic analysis of actively managed labor: Prospective computation of labor progress in 500 consecutive nulliparous women in spontaneous labor at term. Am J Obstet Gynecol 183:438, 2000.

17. Imrie MM, Hall GM: Body temperature and anaesthesia. Br J Anaesth 64:346, 1990.

18. Jouppila P et al: Lumbar epidural analgesia to improve intervillous blood flow during labor in severe pre-eclampsia. Obstet Gynecol 59:158, 1982.

19. Kafle SK: Intrathecal meperidine for elective caesarean section: A comparison with lidocaine. Can J Anaesth 40:718, 1993.

20. Kan RE et al: Intravenous remifentanil: Placental transfer, maternal and neonatal effects. Anesthesiology 88:1467, 1998.

21. Kannan S et al: Maternal satisfaction and pain control in women electing natural childbirth. Reg Anesth Pain Med 26:468, 2001.

22. Ketterhagan D et al: Self-hypnosis: Alternative anesthesia for childbirth. MCN Am J Matern Child Nurs 27:335, 2002.

23. Kumar M, Paes B: Neonatal/perinatal case presentation. J Perinatol 23:425, 2003.

24. Labrecque M et al: A randomized controlled trial of nonpharmacologic approaches for relief of low back pain during labor. J Fam Prac 48:259, 1999.

25. Leighton BL, Halpern SH: Epidural analgesia: Effect on labor progress and maternal and neonatal outcome. Sem Perinatol 26:122, 2002.

26. Levy BT et al: Is paracervical block safe and effective? A prospective study of its association with neonatal umbilical artery pH values. J Fam Pract 48:778, 1999.

27. Martensson L, Wallin G: Labour pain treated with cutaneous injections of sterile water: A randomised controlled trial. Br J Obstet Gynecol 106:633, 1999.

28. Marx GF et al: Fetal-neonatal status following cesarean section for fetal distress. Br J Anaesth 56:1009, 1984.

29. Milwidsky A et al: Direct stimulation of urokinase, plasmin, and collagenase by meperidine: A possible mechanism for the ability of meperidine to enhance cervical effacement and dilation. Am J Perinatol 10:130, 1993.

30. Morley-Forster PK et al: A comparison of patient-controlled analgesia: Fentanyl and alfentanil for labor analgesia. Can J Anaesth 47:113, 2000.

31. Moya F et al: Influence of maternal hyperventilation on the newborn infant. Am J Obstet Gynecol 91:76, 1965.

32. Newman W et al: Fetal acid-base status. Am J Obstet Gynecol 97:43, 1967.

33. Nicolle E et al: Therapeutic monitoring of nalbuphine: Transplacental transfer and estimated pharmacokinetics in the neonate. Eur J Clin Pharmacol 49:485, 1996.

34. Nikkola EM et al: Neonatal monitoring after maternal fentanyl in labor. J Clin Monit Comput 16:597, 2000.

35. Nikodem VC: Immersion in water in pregnancy, labour and birth. Cochrane Database Syst Rev 2:CD000111, 2000.

36. Opioid agonists and antagonists. In Stoelting RK (ed): Pharmacology and Physiology in Anesthetic Practice. Philadelphia, JB Lippincott Co, 1987, p 69.

37. Oster MI: Psychological preparation for labor and delivery using hypnosis. Am J Clin Hypn 37:12, 1994.

38. Owen MD et al: Prolonged intravenous remifentanil infusion for labor analgesia. Anesth Analg 94:918, 2002.

39. Paech M: Newer techniques of labor analgesia. Anesth Clin North Am 21:1, 2003.

40. Pilkington S et al: Increase in Mallampati score during pregnancy. Br J Anaesth 74:638, 1995.

41. Radzyminski S: The effect of ultra low dose epidural analgesia on newborn breastfeeding behaviors. J Obstet Gynecol Neonatal Nurs 32:322, 2003.

42. Ranta P et al: Paracervical block—A viable alternative for labor pain relief? Acta Obstet Gynecol Scand 74:122, 1995.

43. Rasanen J, Jouppila P: Does a paracervical block with bupivacaine change vascular resistance in uterine and umbilical arteries? J Perinat Med 22:301, 1994.

44. Rayburn WF et al: Randomized comparison of meperidine and fentanyl during labor. Obstet Gynecol 74:604, 1989.

45. Reynolds F et al: Analgesia in labour and fetal acid-base balance: A meta-analysis comparing epidural with systemic opioid analgesia. Br J Obstet Gynecol 109:1344, 2002.

46. Richmond H: Women's experience of waterbirth. Pract Midwife 6:26, 2003.

47. Rojansky N et al: Effect of epidural analgesia on duration and outcome of induced labor. Int J Gynaecol Obstet 56:237, 1997.

48. Rosang OP et al: Maternal and fetal effects of intravenous patient-controlled fentanyl analgesia during labour in a thrombocytopenic parturient. Can J Anaesth 39:277, 1992.

49. Rosen M: Paracervical block for labor analgesia: A brief historical review. Am J Obstet Gynecol 186:S127, 2002.

50. Rosow CE, Dershwitz M: Pharmacology of opioid analgesic agents. In Longnecker DE et al (eds): Principles and Practice of Anesthesiology, 2nd ed. St. Louis, Mosby, 1998, p 1233.

51. Sangaslangkarn S et al: Meperidine as a spinal anesthetic agent: A comparison with lidocaine-glucose. Anesth Analg 66:235, 1987.

52. Schauble PG et al: Childbirth preparation through hypnosis: The hypnoreflexogenous protocol. Am J Clin Hypn 40:273, 1998.

53. Sharma SK et al: Cesarean delivery: A randomized trial of epidural versus patient-controlled meperidine analgesia during labor. Anesthesiology 87:487, 1997.

54. Shnider SM et al: Maternal catecholamines decrease during labor after lumbar epidural anesthesia. Am J Obstet Gynecol 147:13, 1983.

55. Skilnand E et al: Acupuncture in the management of pain in labor. Acta Obstet Gynecol Scand 81:943, 2002.

56. Smith CA et al: Complementary and alternative therapies for pain management in labour. Cochrane Database Syst Rev (2):CD003521, 2003.

57. St. Amant MS et al: The effects of epidural opioids on fetal heart rate variability when coadministered with 0.25% bupivacaine for labor analgesia. Am J Perinatol 15:351, 1998.

58. Stavrou C et al: Prolonged fetal bradycardia during epidural analgesia: Incidence, timing and significance. S Afr Med J 77:66, 1990.

59. Steer PL et al: Concentration of fentanyl in colostrum after an analgesic dose. Can J Anaesth 39:231, 1992.

60. Thomas TA: Maternal mortality. Int J Obstet Anesth 4:125, 1995.

61. Thorp JA et al: The effect of intrapartum epidural analgesia on nulliparous labor: A randomized, controlled, prospective trial. Am J Obstet Gynecol 169:851, 1993.

62. Thorp JA et al: The effect of continuous epidural analgesia on cesarean section for dystocia in nulliparous women. Am J Obstet Gynecol 161:670, 1989.

63. Tsen LC et al: Transcutaneous electrical nerve stimulation does not augment combined spinal epidural labour analgesia. Can J Anesth 47:38, 2000.

64. Uldbjerg N et al: Ripening of the human cervix related to changes in collagen, glycosaminoglycans, and collagenolytic activity. Am J Obstet Gynecol 147:662, 1983.

65. Umeh BU: Sacral acupuncture for pain relief in labour: Initial clinical experience in Nigerian women. Acupunct Electrother Res 11:147, 1986.

66. van der Spank JT et al: Pain relief in labour by transcutaneous electrical nerve stimulation (TENS). Arch Gynecol Obstet 264:131, 2000.

67. Volmanen P et al: Remifentanil in obstetric analgesia: A dose-finding study. Anesth Analg 94:913, 2002.

68. Weishaar BR: A comparison of Lamaze and hypnosis in the management of labor. Am J Clin Hypn 28:214, 1986.

69. Wong CA, Scavone BM, Peaceman AM, et al: The risk of cesarean delivery with neuraxial analgesia given early versus late in labor. N Engl J Med 352:7, 2005.

25 Delivery Room Resuscitation of the Newborn

PART 1

Overview and Initial Management

Ronald S. Bloom

In the human, the transition from fetus to neonate represents a series of rapid and dramatic physiologic changes. This transition goes smoothly most of the time; however, approximately 10% of the time the active intervention of a skilled individual or team is necessary to assist in that transition to ensure that it occurs with the least possible damage.

Although certain episodes of fetal asphyxia cannot be prevented, there are many circumstances in which, in the immediate neonatal period, a prompt and skilled resuscitation may prevent lifelong adverse sequelae. This, along with the fact that the need for intervention cannot always be predicted, has prompted the International Guidelines for Neonatal Resuscitation to state: "At least one person skilled in initiating neonatal resuscitation should be present at every delivery. An additional person capable of performing a complete resuscitation should be immediately available."[59]

Although many elements of a resuscitation sequence have been agreed on, debate and discussion regarding the process continue. Research has yet to answer many questions. For the present, guidelines such as those published by the American Academy of Pediatrics and the American Heart Association[5] as well as those of the International Liaison Committee on Resuscitation (ILCOR)[59,64] represent a middle ground for various contending views.

This chapter presents an approach to neonatal resuscitation and at the same time attempts to provide an appreciation of the more common and controversial questions and a basis for understanding conflicting views.

THE FETUS

In utero, the fetus depends on the placenta for gas exchange. Remarkably, the fetus thrives despite a Pao_2 in the range of 20 to 30 mm Hg and, in terms of fuel metabolism, is not hypoxic. The tissues receive adequate amounts of oxygen, and anaerobic metabolic pathways are not ordinarily required. Adequate oxygen delivery is accomplished with an adaptive process primarily involving the architecture of the circulatory system, the characteristics of fetal hemoglobin, and the rate of perfusion of fetal organs.

The placenta, having the lowest resistance in the circulatory system of the fetus, preferentially receives blood from the systemic circulation. Approximately 40% of the total cardiac output of the fetus flows through the placenta.[110] Blood in the umbilical artery en route to the placenta has a Po_2 of 15 to 25 mm Hg.[74] In the human, umbilical venous blood returning from the placenta to the fetus, obtained by percutaneous umbilical vein sampling, has a Po_2 as high as 55 mm Hg.[81] However, when the umbilical venous blood is mixed with venous return from the body, the result is a lower Po_2. Although the oxygen tension of the fetus is low in postnatal terms, because of fetal hemoglobin's high affinity for oxygen, the oxygen content is only mildly diminished.

When the umbilical vein enters the abdomen of the fetus, the stream splits, with slightly more than half of the blood flowing through the ductus venosus into the inferior vena cava. The remaining blood perfuses portions of the liver. The umbilical venous return entering the inferior vena cava tends to stream and does

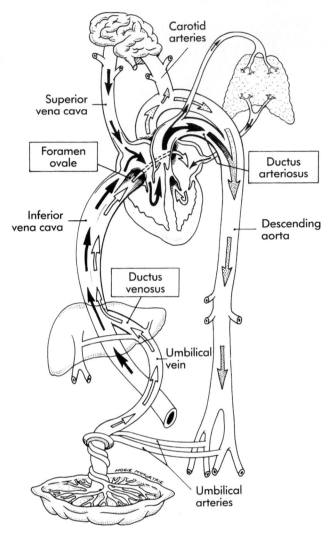

FIGURE 25-1. Fetal circulation.

not completely mix with less oxygenated blood entering the inferior vena cava from below. In the right atrium the crista dividens splits the inferior vena cava stream so that oxygenated blood from the umbilical vein flows through the foramen ovale into the left side of the heart. The less oxygenated blood returning from the body flows into the right ventricle (Fig. 25-1). (See also Chapter 43.)

In the fetus, blood flow through the lungs is diminished because of the high resistance of the fetal pulmonary circuit, the open ductus arteriosus, and the lower resistance of the systemic circuit. Approximately 87% of the right ventricular output crosses the ductus arteriosus and enters the aorta, bypassing the lungs. With little return from the pulmonary veins, oxygen in the umbilical venous blood crossing the foramen into the left atrium is only slightly diluted. Thus, the most highly oxygenated blood perfuses the head and heart through the carotid and coronary arteries before its oxygen concentration is decreased by blood entering the aorta from the ductus arteriosus.

Another adaptive mechanism keeping the tissues oxygenated is the rate of perfusion of fetal tissues. Fetal tissues are perfused with blood at a higher rate than in the adult. The increased delivery of blood compensates for the low oxygen saturation in the fetus and the higher oxygen affinity of fetal hemoglobin.

Finally, the fetus has less of an oxygen demand than the newborn. With thermoregulation unnecessary in the fetus and respiratory effort limited, two significant consumers of oxygen in the newborn are either eliminated or markedly diminished in the fetus.

The P_{CO_2} of the fetus is slightly higher than adult levels, with an umbilical venous P_{CO_2} from 35 to 45 mm Hg. Elimination of carbon dioxide from the fetus is enhanced by maternal hyperventilation during pregnancy. Because of the lower P_{CO_2} of maternal blood, a gradient is created favoring the transfer of carbon dioxide across the placenta from fetal to maternal blood.

The low fetal P_{O_2} contributes to the architecture of the fetal circulation by helping to keep the pulmonary vascular resistance high. The low P_{O_2} and prostaglandin production by the fetus also play a significant role in keeping the ductus arteriosus patent. Thus the low P_{O_2} is physiologically acceptable to the fetus. However, any compromise of fetal gas exchange or lack of effective transition at birth quickly results in asphyxia consisting of hypoxia, an elevated P_{CO_2}, and metabolic acidosis.

TRANSITION AT BIRTH

(See also Chapter 42, Part 2.)

The labor process is, to some extent, mildly asphyxiating. With each contraction, uterine blood flow decreases, with a resulting decrease in placental perfusion and a temporary impairment of transplacental gas exchange. This is accompanied by transient hypoxia and hypercapnia. The intermittent nature of labor permits the fetus to "recover" between each contraction; however, the effect is cumulative. Throughout a normal labor, the fetus undergoes a progressive reduction in P_{O_2}, some increase in P_{CO_2}, a decrease in pH, and the accumulation of a base deficit[19] (Table 25-1).

TABLE 25-1. Fetal Scalp Blood Values during Labor*

	EARLY FIRST STAGE	LATE FIRST STAGE	SECOND STAGE
pH	7.33 ± 0.03	7.32 ± 0.02	7.29 ± 0.04
P_{CO_2} (mm Hg)	44 ± 4.05	42 ± 5.1	46.3 ± 4.2
P_{O_2} (mm Hg)	21.8 ± 2.6	21.3 ± 2.1	16.5 ± 1.4
Bicarbonate (mmol/L)	20.1 ± 1.2	19.1 ± 2.1	17 ± 2
Base deficit (mmol/L)	3.9 ± 1.0	4.1 ± 2.5	6.4 ± 1.8

*Mean ± standard deviation.
From Boylan PC et al: Fetal acid-base balance. In Creasy RK et al (eds): Maternal-Fetal Medicine. Philadelphia, WB Saunders, 1989.

With birth the neonate must establish the lungs as the site of gas exchange; the circulation, which in the fetus shunted blood away from the lungs, must now fully perfuse the pulmonary vasculature. Postnatal breathing is on a continuum with in utero breathing movements that are well established but intermittent in the term fetus.[88] The events of birth stimulate peripheral and central chemoreceptors, cause tactile and thermal stimulation, and increase systemic blood pressure as a result of clamping of the cord. This combination is usually enough stimulation for the infant to pursue breathing vigorously.

Traditionally, it was thought that passage through the vaginal canal and the resulting "thoracic squeeze" resulted in clearance of a significant amount of lung fluid. We now know that during spontaneous birth with preceding labor the thoracic squeeze may have only a minor effect on clearance of lung fluid. A few days before a normal vaginal delivery, the fetal production of lung fluid slows and alveolar fluid volume decreases. The process of labor is a powerful stimulus for the clearance of lung fluid, and that transfer of fluid from the airspaces is predominantly a process of active transport into the interstitium and drainage through the pulmonary circulation, with some fluid exiting through lymphatic drainage.[60] Although started before labor and influenced by the increasing levels of endogenous catecholamines, the process accelerates immediately after birth.[15]

The first few breaths must facilitate clearance of fluid from the lungs and establish a functional residual capacity (FRC).[122] (See also Part 2 of this chapter.) The first breath of a spontaneously breathing infant has some unique characteristics. Although the peak inspiratory pressure is usually between –20 and –40 cm H_2O, the opening pressures are very low. That is, gas begins to enter the lungs at very low pressures, usually less than –5 cm H_2O pressure. Very high expiratory pressures are also generated, pressures that generally exceed the inspiratory pressure. This expiratory pressure, probably generated against a closed glottis, aids in clearing lung fluid and leads to a more even distribution of air throughout the lung. Thus, in spontaneously breathing, vaginally delivered infants, a significant FRC develops at the end of the first breath[77] (Fig. 25-2).

Expansion of the lungs is a stimulus for surfactant release,[67] which reduces alveolar surface tension, increases compliance, and helps develop a stable FRC. Simultaneously, the act of ventilation alone lowers pulmonary vascular resistance.[25] Ventilation with air leads to a fall in P_{CO_2} and a rise in pH and P_{O_2}, also causing a fall in pulmonary vascular resistance. The relationships among pH, P_{O_2}, and pulmonary vascular resistance are illustrated in Figure 25-3.[98] Clearance of lung fluid and establishment of an FRC (along with an increase in pulmonary blood flow) facilitate ventilation.

With the onset of ventilation the fetal circulatory system assumes the adult pattern. Coincident with clamping of the cord, the low-resistance placenta is removed from the systemic circuit and systemic blood pressure rises. This rise in systemic pressure, coupled

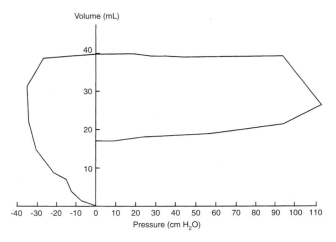

FIGURE 25-2. Typical pressure-volume loop of first breath. Air enters the lung as soon as intrathoracic pressure falls. Expiratory pressure greatly exceeds inspiratory pressure. (From Milner AD et al: Lung expansion at birth. J Pediatr 101:879, 1982.)

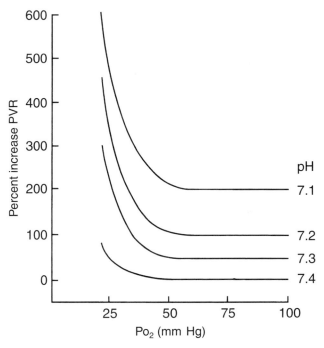

FIGURE 25-3. Pulmonary vascular resistance (PVR) in the calf. (From Rudolph AM et al: Response of the pulmonary vasculature to hypoxia and H^+ ion concentration changes. J Clin Invest 45:339, 1966.)

with the fall in pulmonary vascular resistance and in pulmonary artery pressure, decreases the right-to-left shunt through the ductus arteriosus. The increase in Pa_{O_2} further stimulates closure of the ductus arteriosus. With ductal shunting diminished, pulmonary artery blood flow increases, resulting in increased pulmonary venous return to the left atrium and increased pressure in the left atrium. Once the left atrial pressure exceeds right atrial pressure, the foramen ovale closes.[109]

An uncomplicated transition from fetal to newborn status is therefore characterized by loss of fetal lung fluid, secretion of surfactant, establishment of FRC, a fall in pulmonary vascular resistance, increased systemic pressure after removal of the low-resistance placenta from the systemic circuit, closure of two shunts (the ductus arteriosus and the foramen ovale), and an increase in pulmonary artery blood flow. In most circumstances the mild degree of asphyxia associated with labor is not enough to interfere with this process. However, the transition may be significantly altered by a variety of antepartum or intrapartum events, resulting in cardiorespiratory depression, asphyxia, or both.

CAUSES OF DEPRESSION AND ASPHYXIA

A newborn may be compromised because of problems initiated in utero with the mother, the placenta, or the fetus itself (Box 25-1). A process initiated in utero may extend into the neonatal period, preventing a normal transition. An asphyxial process also may be neonatal in origin—that is, the infant appears well until required to breathe on his or her own.

Maternal causes of fetal compromise may be related to decreased uterine blood flow, which decreases the amount of oxygen transported to the placenta. Diminished uterine blood flow may result from maternal hypotension (as a result of drugs used to treat hypertension), regional anesthesia, eclampsia, or abnormal uterine contractions. Problems with the placenta, such as infarcts, premature separation, edema, or inflammatory changes, may impair gas exchange. The fetus also may be compromised because of fetal problems related to cord compression, such as nuchal cord, prolapse, or a breech presentation with cord compression by the aftercoming head. A neonate may not breathe after delivery because of a number of problems, including drug-induced central nervous system depression, central nervous system anomalies or injury, spinal cord injury, mechanical obstruction of the airways, deformities, immaturity, pneumonia, or congenital anomalies.

Finally, there are some circumstances in which the infant may initiate breathing only to markedly diminish or stop breathing soon after birth. Examples include drug-induced depression in which the stimuli surrounding birth initially overcome the depression, diaphragmatic hernia, and spontaneous pneumothorax.

RESPONSE TO ASPHYXIA

The goal with any depressed or asphyxiated infant, whether the process is initiated in the fetal or the neonatal period, is to reverse the ongoing events as soon as possible and avoid permanent damage. An understanding of the response of the fetus or neonate to asphyxia aids in understanding the sequences of a resuscitative process.

When a fetus or neonate is subjected to asphyxia, the classic "diving" reflex takes place. This is simply

---

BOX 25-1. Factors Associated with Neonatal Depression and Asphyxia

Antepartum Risk Factors
- Maternal diabetes
- Pregnancy-induced hypertension
- Chronic hypertension
- Chronic maternal illness
- Cardiovascular
- Thyroid
- Neurologic
- Pulmonary
- Renal
- Anemia or isoimmunization
- Previous fetal or neonatal death
- Bleeding in second or third trimester
- Maternal infection
- Polyhydramnios
- Oligohydramnios
- Premature rupture of membranes
- Post-term gestation
- Multiple gestation
- Size-dates discrepancy
- Drug therapy, including:
  - Lithium carbonate
  - Magnesium
  - Adrenergic blocking drugs
- Maternal substance abuse

- Fetal malformation
- Diminished fetal activity
- No prenatal care
- Age <16 or >35 years

Intrapartum Risk Factors
- Emergency cesarean section
- Forceps or vacuum-assisted delivery
- Breech or other abnormal presentation
- Premature labor
- Precipitous labor
- Chorioamnionitis
- Prolonged rupture of membranes (>18 hours before delivery)
- Prolonged labor (>24 hours)
- Prolonged second stage of labor (>2 hours)
- Fetal bradycardia
- Nonreassuring fetal heart rate patterns
- Use of general anesthesia
- Uterine tetany
- Narcotics given to mother within 4 hours of delivery
- Meconium-stained amniotic fluid
- Prolapsed cord
- Abruptio placentae
- Placenta previa

an attempt either to accentuate or restore a fetal type of circulation. Hypoxia and acidosis increase vasoconstriction of the pulmonary vasculature[98] (see Fig. 25-3). The rise in pulmonary vascular resistance decreases pulmonary blood flow, decreasing left atrial return, which, in turn, lowers left atrial pressure. The drop in left atrial pressure increases right-to-left shunting across the foramen ovale. In the fetus, this directs the most highly oxygenated blood coming from the placenta to the left side of the heart. In the neonate, with no placenta, this shunting merely bypasses the lungs, making matters worse.

In both the fetus and the neonate, the increase in noncerebral peripheral resistance during asphyxia results in a redistribution of blood flow, with increased flow to the head and heart and decreased flow to nonvital organs. Even though the oxygen content of the blood is low, during the early stages of asphyxia the amount of oxygen brought to the head and heart is maximized by the maintenance of cardiac output and the increased flow to these organs.[78,97]

The increased peripheral resistance increases blood pressure early in the asphyxial period. The blood pressure remains at reasonable levels as long as the myocardium is able to sustain cardiac output. As the asphyxia progresses and hypoxia and acidosis worsen, the myocardium fails and both cardiac output and blood pressure fall.[36]

Superimposed on these circulatory and hemodynamic changes is a characteristic change in respiratory pattern. Initially there are gasping respirations (which may occur in utero). With continuing asphyxia, respirations cease in what is known as primary apnea. If the asphyxia is not corrected, the infant again begins to gasp irregularly and the respirations cease (secondary apnea) unless positive pressure ventilation and successful resuscitation take place[32] (Fig. 25-4).

The longer the asphyxia has gone on, the longer it will take for the onset of spontaneous ventilation to occur after positive pressure ventilation is started[1] (Fig. 25-5). Asphyxia may begin before birth, and the infant may pass through any or all of these stages of the asphyxial response in utero. It may be difficult to determine at birth how far the asphyxial episode has progressed. Thus, with any depressed infant it is essential that resuscitation be initiated without delay.

Our goal, although we recognize that it is not always attainable, is to initiate resuscitation in a timely and effective manner so that the insults of hypoxia, ischemia, hypercapnia, and acidosis are reversed before they cause permanent injury (Box 25-2).

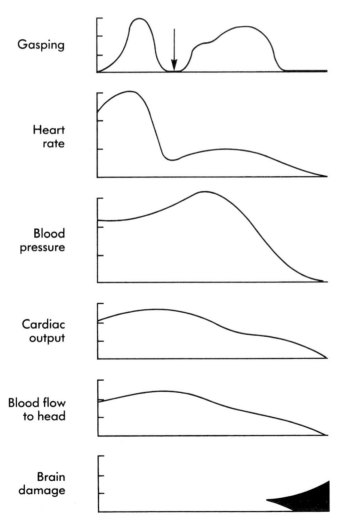

FIGURE 25-4. Schematic diagram of changes associated with asphyxia. *Arrow* indicates the point of primary apnea. (Modified from Dawes GS: Fetal and Neonatal Physiology. Chicago, Year Book Medical, 1968, p 149; and Phibbs RH: Delivery room management of the newborn. In Avery G [ed]: Neonatology, 3rd ed. Philadelphia, JB Lippincott, 1987, p 215.)

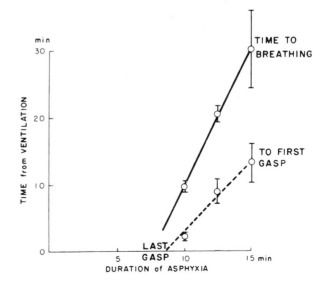

FIGURE 25-5. Time from ventilation to first gasp and to rhythmic breathing in newborn monkeys asphyxiated for 10, 12.5, and 15 minutes at 30°C. (From Adamsons K et al: Resuscitation by positive pressure ventilation and tris-hydroxymethylaminomethane of rhesus monkeys asphyxiated at birth. J Pediatr 65:807, 1964.)

BOX 25-2. Consequences of Asphyxia

Central Nervous System
- Cerebral hemorrhage
- Cerebral edema
- Hypoxic-ischemic encephalopathy
- Seizures

Lung
- Delayed onset of respiration
- Respiratory distress syndrome
- Meconium aspiration syndrome

Cardiovascular System
- Myocardial failure
- Papillary muscle necrosis
- Persistent fetal circulation

Renal System
- Cortical/tubular/medullary necrosis

Gastrointestinal Tract
- Necrotizing enterocolitis

Blood
- Disseminated intravascular coagulation

PREPARATION FOR RESUSCITATION

The key elements in preparing for resuscitation are anticipation of the problem, provision of adequate equipment, and presence of trained personnel. The chaos that, at times, occurs with resuscitation of an infant, especially an unexpected resuscitation, is primarily caused by either inadequate or unavailable equipment or staff members who are unskilled or have difficulty coordinating their activities. With some effort, both problems are avoidable.

Anticipation

A careful review of the antepartum and intrapartum history can identify a number of problems that put a mother at risk of delivering a depressed or asphyxiated infant (see Box 25-1). Identifying a high-risk situation before delivery of the infant provides time for adequate preparation. Traditionally, a cesarean section of any type has been listed as a high-risk delivery. There is now enough available information to feel confident that an uncomplicated second cesarean section carries no greater risk for the infant than a vaginal delivery.[92] Thus, only if the cesarean section involves fetal distress or other complications is there any cause for added concern. It is important to stress that we are not able to identify every infant who may need assistance. Thus,

at every delivery, equipment and personnel should be available in case of unanticipated respiratory depression.

Adequate Equipment

Whenever an infant is delivered, appropriate equipment must be close at hand and in good working order. It is not acceptable for someone to need to leave the delivery room during a resuscitation to obtain an essential piece of equipment.

Adequate Personnel

Individuals vested with the responsibility of resuscitating infants should be adequately trained, readily available, and capable of working together as a team. Having trained personnel readily available means having someone present at every delivery who has the skill required to perform a complete resuscitation, with other available staff close at hand in case they are needed. At least two, if not three, people are needed to carry out a full resuscitation. Adequate training involves more than simply going through a course and receiving a certificate of completion. The neonatal resuscitation program of the American Heart Association/American Academy of Pediatrics and similar courses are simply starting points. They do not qualify one to assume independent responsibility. Before being given independent responsibility, an individual must work under the tutelage of experienced personnel in the delivery room.

Finally, the personnel available to the delivery room should be capable of working together as a team. If staff are skilled at carrying out their responsibilities and can anticipate each other's needs, the tension inherent in any resuscitation can be reduced and the process will go much more smoothly. In those institutions in which resuscitations are not frequent events, holding mock code drills on an ongoing basis helps to maintain skills and develop coordination among staff.

ROLE OF THE APGAR SCORE

The Apgar score is a tool that can be used objectively to define the state of an infant at given times after birth, traditionally at 1 minute and 5 minutes[6] (Table 25-2). Clearly, if the 1-minute Apgar score is very low, a resuscitation is necessary and in most circumstances should have already been started by 1 minute. The Apgar score should not be used as the primary indicator for resuscitation because it is not normally assigned until 1 minute of age. As noted earlier, an asphyxial process may begin in utero and continue into the neonatal period. Thus, to minimize the chances of brain damage, one should begin resuscitation as soon as there is evidence that the infant is not able to establish ventilation sufficient to maintain an adequate heart rate. Waiting until a 1-minute Apgar score is assigned before initiating resuscitation only increases the chance of permanent damage in a severely asphyxiated infant.

TABLE 25-2. Apgar Score

SIGN	0	1	2
Heart rate	Absent	Less than 100 beats per minute	More than 100 beats per minute
Respiratory effort	Absent	Slow, irregular	Good, crying
Muscle tone	Flaccid	Some flexion of extremities	Active motion
Reflex irritability	No response	Grimace	Vigorous cry
Color	Pale	Cyanotic	Completely pink

ELEMENTS OF A RESUSCITATION

A resuscitation can be viewed as a series of elements (Box 25-3). The process is not a linear set of steps in which one marches inexorably from one point to another. Rather, it involves an evaluation of the infant's condition, a decision based on that evaluation, and action. These steps are repeated until the process is concluded. Figure 25-6 provides an overview of the resuscitation process.

BOX 25-3. Elements of a Resuscitation

- Thermal management
- Clearing the airway
- Tactile stimulation
- Establishment of ventilation
- Chest compression
- Medication

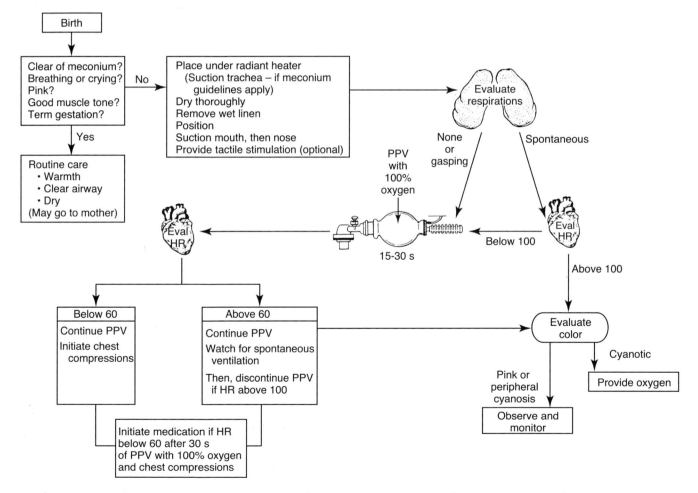

FIGURE 25-6. Overview of resuscitation in the delivery room. PPV, positive pressure ventilation. (Data from Kattwinkel J (ed): Textbook of Neonatal Resuscitation, 4th ed. Copyright American Heart Association/American Academy of Pediatrics, 2000.)

Virtually all infants undergo the initial steps. The vast majority of those requiring active resuscitation respond to positive pressure ventilation.[89] However, all infants, whether they require only the initial steps or a complete resuscitation, are entitled to a skilled and timely response, regardless of who is performing the resuscitation.

AN INITIAL QUICK OVERVIEW

Most infants are vigorous, cry upon birth, and breathe easily thereafter. There are many times when delivery room staff and the parents prefer that the infant go to the mother immediately after birth rather than be placed on a warmer and put through the "initial steps" in resuscitation. In most circumstances, a healthy and vigorous infant does not even require suctioning after delivery. With appropriate triaging and oversight many, if not most, infants can be directly given to the mother after birth without compromising the infant. It requires a rapid initial overview that will provide the information necessary to triage the infant appropriately. If the infant has not passed meconium in utero, is term, is breathing easily, is not cyanotic or pale, has good tone, and appears normal and vigorous, it may be appropriate to hand the child to the mother immediately after birth. As the mother holds the infant, it is probably a good idea to provide a light blanket to prevent rapid evaporative heat loss while covering the infant in such a way as to be able to observe the infant for signs of increasing distress. If, however, the infant has passed meconium in utero, is preterm, is not breathing easily, is cyanotic or pale, has diminished tone, or does not appear normal and vigorous, then the infant should be placed on a radiant warmer until a more thorough assessment of the infant can be done. The following steps apply to any infant who is not term, healthy, and vigorous at birth.

INITIAL STEPS

Thermal Management (See also Chapter 29.)

Delivery rooms are kept at a level of thermal comfort for the adults working in them. This leaves the neonate, with a very large surface area-to-mass ratio, susceptible to cold stress. Immediately after birth the infant should be placed in the microenvironment of a preheated radiant warmer. The infant should be thoroughly dried and the wet blankets promptly removed to avoid evaporative heat loss. These simple measures can minimize the drop in core temperature that the infant experiences at birth[75] (Fig. 25-7). Preventing excessive heat loss can become especially important with a preterm infant or an infant who is asphyxiated and hypoxic. Because hypoxia blunts the normal response to cold, a hypoxic infant undergoes a greater than normal drop in core temperature if not thermally protected.[21] Recovery from acidosis also is delayed by hypothermia.[2]

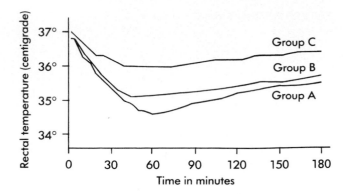

FIGURE 25-7. Mean core temperatures in three groups of infants, showing effect of drying and thermal protection immediately after birth. Group A: open crib, bathed within 1 hour; group B: open crib, no bath; group C: preheated incubator, dried immediately after birth, no bath. (From Miller DL et al: Body temperature in the immediate neonatal period: The effect of reducing thermal losses. Am J Obstet Gynecol 94:964, 1966.)

Clearing the Airway

Normally the airway is cleared with the use of a bulb syringe or a suction catheter. The mouth is suctioned first in case the infant gasps when the nose is suctioned. Care should be exercised to suction the infant gently because vigorous suctioning and stimulation of the posterior portion of the pharynx may induce bradycardia.[28] If a suction catheter is to be used, it is recommended that in the term infant the catheter be inserted no more than 5 cm from the lips and that the duration of suctioning be no more than 5 seconds.[64] The infant exposed to meconium in the amniotic fluid represents a special circumstance, to be discussed later.

Tactile Stimulation

Usually, the act of drying and suctioning the infant is enough tactile stimulation to initiate respiration. However, if the infant does not breathe after these efforts, slapping or flicking the soles of the feet or rubbing the infant's back may be enough additional stimulation to elicit regular respirations. If there is no immediate response to this additional stimulation, positive pressure ventilation should be quickly initiated. Continued tactile stimulation is not useful and may be harmful because the asphyxial process will be permitted to persist that much longer. The decisions from this point revolve around the response of the infant—primarily heart rate, respirations, and color.

Free-Flow Oxygen

Considerable discussion has surrounded the decision to use either 100% oxygen or room air in the asphyxiated infant requiring positive pressure ventilation.[16,100,108] (See Part 3 of this chapter.) However, if the infant is spontaneously breathing and the heart rate is more than 100 beats per minute, and yet the infant remains cyanotic, oxygen should be administered through a free-flow system until it can be shown that the oxygen concentration can be lowered (arterial oxygen saturation [SaO_2] greater than 85%) or that lowering the concentration makes no difference (cyanotic heart disease). A high concentration of oxygen can be obtained with an oxygen mask (with escape holes) held firmly over the face or an oxygen tube cupped in the hand. A flow-inflating bag also is capable of delivering high concentrations of oxygen. Caution should be exercised to be sure the mask is held lightly over the face to prevent positive pressure to the lungs.

It is best to heat and humidify the oxygen. During an emergency, cold, dry oxygen can be given; however, if free-flow oxygen is to be continued for any period, it should be heated and humidified and given through wide-bore tubing. An oxygen blender and oximeter are useful in determining the amount of oxygen the infant requires. This is especially pertinent to the preterm infant.

If, after suctioning and tactile stimulation, the respirations are gasping or are insufficient to sustain the heart rate at greater than 100 beats per minute, positive pressure ventilation must be initiated.

PART 2

Role of Positive Pressure Ventilation in Neonatal Resuscitation

Anthony Milner and Anne Greenough

POSITIVE PRESSURE VENTILATION

Since the early 1800s, mouth-to-mouth resuscitation and even intubation and lung inflation have been advocated for the management of the infant who fails to breathe spontaneously at birth.[39] The recognition of the need to provide a resuscitation service in the labor suite, however, was delayed until the 1960s in developed countries. Unfortunately, the need for resuscitation is greatest in communities that are most deprived and least able to afford the necessary facilities.

From the early 1990s on, there have been several national and international protocol statements providing guidance on provision of neonatal resuscitation, culminating in the recommendations of the European Resuscitation Council,[40] the Pediatric Working Group of the International Liaison Committee on Resuscitation,[64,82] and the Neonatal Resuscitation Program of the American Academy of Pediatrics and the American Heart Association.[5] These provide consensus statements drawn up by experts, but many of the recommendations are based on the experts' concept of current "best practice" rather than evidence from randomized, controlled clinical trials. The aim of this section is to examine these recommendations to identify where there is supporting evidence and which recommendations have evolved without adequate assessment.

Criteria for Providing Positive Pressure Ventilation

These are based on three observations: adequacy of respiratory activity, color, and heart rate. Regardless of the issuing body, all of the guidelines basically agree that after drying and clearing the airway, positive pressure should be initiated if the infant is apneic, has irregular or gasping respirations, has a heart rate below 100 beats per minute, or is cyanotic despite being given 100% oxygen. There are no human or animal data to support these recommendations, although in a study using tape recorders as timers, 95% of infants had commenced spontaneous breathing by 40 seconds (Tunell R, personal communication). On the other hand, it is well established that the newborn infant can survive intact after several minutes of apnea after birth; unfortunately, our techniques for identifying how much hypoxic stress the infant has suffered before delivery are very inadequate, and hence the aforementioned guideline has evolved. It will, however, inevitably result in exposing infants who would commence breathing spontaneously to unnecessary intervention.

The International Liaison Committee on Resuscitation[64] estimated that, worldwide, appropriate intervention could save 800,000 infants per year from death or disability resulting from birth asphyxia. Intervention rates vary greatly, even in populations close together. For example, two hospitals in Scotland had intubation rates of 2% and 10% of all infants.[35] Particularly low intubation rates come from Sweden. One study of 100,000 infants weighing more than 2.5 kg born in 1 year found that only 1% required any resuscitative intervention and only 0.2% intubation.[84] Of infants born after 32 weeks of gestation, after a normal labor with no asphyxial risk factors, only 0.2% required any resuscitation and 0.04% intubation.[84] A trend has developed for a reduction in the need for resuscitative intervention, probably owing to improvements in obstetric and anesthetic techniques. Allwood and colleagues found that from 1993 to 1997, the rate for all forms of ventilatory resuscitation fell from 11.0% to 8.9%, and the need for intubation from 2.4% to 1.2%.[3]

For those infants who clearly need intervention with positive pressure ventilation, the following questions must be addressed: how much pressure is needed, what is the optimal rate of ventilation, what is the optimal duration for the inspiratory times, and what is the role of end-expiratory pressure? The answers to these questions are not clear-cut; however, there are some data on which to base an approach to the practice of resuscitation. Use of supplemental O_2 is addressed in Part 3.

The first description of intermittent positive pressure ventilation (IPPV) through an endotracheal tube was by Flagg in 1928.[44] He used a side tube descending into a water column as a blow-off safety valve. He recommended that the side tube be placed so that the tip was 8 inches below the surface. This would generate inflation pressures of approximately 20 cm H_2O. It is not clear why these pressures were selected other than that they appeared to work. He recommended that the T-piece should be occluded with a thumb every 15 seconds and that carbon dioxide (at least 6%) should be added to the oxygen. The use of water columns persisted until the mid-1970s, when anxieties about transient high initial pressures due to the inertia of the water in the column[53] and the possibility of water-borne infection led to their disuse in developed countries.

When IPPV was reintroduced for the management of birth asphyxia in the late 1950s and early 1960s, a pattern of positive pressure ventilation was generally used that consists of peak pressures of 25 to 30 cm H_2O, inflation times of 0.5 to 1 second, and rates of 30 per minute. It is not clear why this pattern was adopted. Since then, there have been a number of physiologic studies of the onset of breathing in healthy neonates and the response to IPPV. Their results provide some guidance on the manner in which newborn asphyxiated infants should be resuscitated.

Measurements of Spontaneous First Breaths of Healthy Infants

Karlberg and colleagues reported that the mean intrathoracic pressure generated by infants breathing spontaneously was –30 cm H_2O (range, –3 to –72 cm H_2O); the pressure needed to expand the isolated lung from stillbirths was of a similar order.[63] Our early physiologic studies on the onset of breathing in healthy term infants also demonstrated mean negative intrathoracic pressures in the region of 30 cm H_2O.[76,104] Accurate measurement of the inflation pressures, however, depends on correct placement of the pressure measuring device in the lower third of the esophagus. If the device is too high, pressures will be under-recorded. This is the likely explanation for the very low inflation pressures (less than 10 cm H_2O) found in some of our infants and those reported by Karlberg and colleagues.

In a subsequent study, a catheter was used that incorporated two pressure transducers 2 cm apart. Inflation pressures were then accepted as accurate only when the distal transducer recorded gastric pressures, indicating that the proximal device was correctly positioned. The results showed that in healthy newborn infants, the initial inflation pressure ranges from 28 to 105 cm H_2O, with a mean of 52 and a median of 38.6 cm H_2O.[122] Healthy infants generate inflation pressures that are almost always higher than those recommended for resuscitation.

The inflation volumes generated by these pressures varied widely, ranging from 6.5 to 69 mL with a mean of 37.7 mL (approximately 10 mL/kg).[119]

Studies of Infants Requiring Intubation and Resuscitation

Studies on the efficacy of resuscitating infants using the pattern of ventilation recommended in the late 1970s, that is, inflation pressures of 25 to 30 cm H_2O at a rate of 30 per minute and with inflation times of 1 second, revealed that this resulted in inspiratory volumes in the region of 15 to 20 mL, ranging from 0 to 70 mL.[17,18] The size of the inspiratory volume was partly determined by the infants' response to the first inflation. The most common response was the development of positive intrathoracic pressures of up to 110 cm H_2O.[17,18] This inevitably limited the volume of gas entering the lung. Subsequent studies using pressure transducers in both the esophagus and stomach showed that these high positive pressures were generated by the contraction of the abdominal wall muscles (Vyas H, Milner AD, unpublished data). The second most common pattern was passive acceptance of the inflation pressure (i.e., there was no evidence on the esophageal trace that the infant was making any respiratory efforts). The third pattern was active inspiration in response to an inflation, a reflex investigated by Head and known as the Head paradoxical reflex[50]—paradoxical because this is the converse of the Hering-Breuer reflex in which lung inflation leads to apnea. This response led to the largest inspiratory volumes.

Inspection of the volume trace of the first inflation revealed that the volume had not reached a plateau, suggesting that prolonging inspiration would lead to larger inflation volumes. This is not surprising because lung fluid, which fills the lower and much of the upper respiratory tract immediately after delivery, is far more viscous than air. When initial inflation pressures of 25 to 30 cm H_2O were maintained for at least 3 seconds, inspiratory volumes in the region of 40 mL were found, very similar to the volumes achieved by the spontaneously breathing infants.[119,121,122]

An alternative approach is to use an anesthetic rebreathing bag system. In one study in which the safety blow-off valve was overridden, the bag was squeezed until chest wall movement was apparent, indicating that the lungs had been inflated.[114] This resulted in inflation pressures of 50 cm H_2O that were sustained for less than 0.5 second, and inspiratory volumes in the region of 35 mL, a pattern very similar to that generated by the spontaneously breathing infant.[121,122] Thus, adequate inflation volumes could be obtained with sustained initial inflation times at lower pressures or with short inspiratory times at higher pressures.

Formation of Functional Residual Capacity

Formation of FRC is essential for satisfactory gaseous exchange. Studies on the spontaneous onset of breathing in term infants revealed that 40 of 41 infants had formed an FRC by the end of the first breath (mean, 15.1 mL),[119] probably helped by the large positive intrathoracic

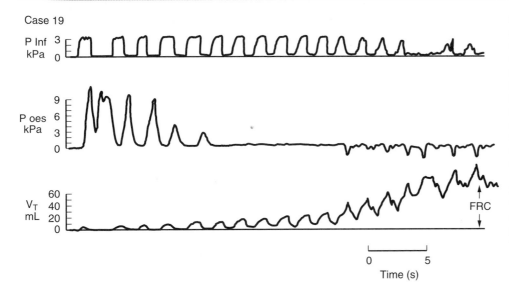

Case 19

FIGURE 25-8. Longitudinal trace shows a progressive sequential increase in tidal volume (V_T) over the initial inflations without any change in functional residual capacity (FRC). Inflation pressure (Pinf) and oesophageal pressure (Poes) are also shown. Gas was not retained in the infant's lungs until an inspiratory effort had been made, at which time the tidal volume also increased. This pattern of increasing tidal volume in response to the same inflation pressure was seen in 16 of 20 infants. (From Boon AW et al: Lung expansion, tidal exchange, and formation of the functional residual capacity during resuscitation of asphyxiated neonates. J Pediatr 195:1031, 1979.)

pressures observed during the first expiration (the first cry), which aids clearance of lung fluid. However, the combined data from two studies of infants requiring intubation and resuscitation show that only 8 of 40 such infants formed an FRC on the first breath. In seven there was a gradual formation of an FRC with subsequent inflations in the absence of respiratory efforts[17,18] (Fig. 25-8). Stimulation of the Head paradoxical reflex led to the largest and most rapid increases in FRC.

Prolonging the first inflation results in the rapid formation of FRC on the first breath. In newborns, either a square-wave inflation maintained at 30 cm H_2O for approximately 5 seconds, or a slow-rise inflation in which the pressure was increased from 0 to 30 cm H_2O over 3 to 5 seconds resulted in the establishment of an FRC on the first inflation[121] (Fig. 25-9). It is also possible to create an FRC on the first inflation by generating higher pressures, in the region of 50 cm H_2O, with brief inspiratory times[114] (Fig. 25-10).

Thus, the inflation volumes and FRCs achieved by infants commencing to breathe spontaneously can be mimicked in intubated, asphyxiated infants either by using higher inflation pressures for brief periods or standard pressures with sustained inflations. Which of these approaches is better, or indeed whether early formation of an FRC provides a useful advantage to the asphyxiated infant, have not been tested.

Preterm Infants

INFLATION PRESSURES AND VOLUMES

It is well established that preterm infants are more likely to require resuscitation at birth than term infants.[38] Although term infants appear to be relatively tolerant to the range of pressures and inflation volumes that have been used during resuscitation at birth, there are increasing anxieties that excessive lung expansion, particularly if there is inadequate surfactant, may produce lung damage and predispose to bronchopulmonary dysplasia.

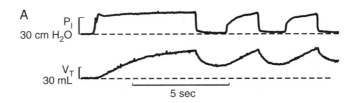

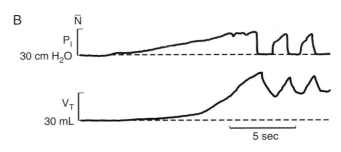

FIGURE 25-9. A, Longitudinal trace of inflation pressure (P_I) and tidal volume (V_T) showing prolonged square-wave inflation and formation of functional residual capacity (FRC). B, Longitudinal trace of pressure and tidal volume showing slow-wave inflation with formation of FRC. (From Vyas H et al: Physiologic responses to prolonged and slow-rise inflation in the resuscitation of the asphyxiated newborn infant. J Pediatr 99:6535, 1981.)

Studies of the isolated lungs of stillborn preterm infants and prematurely born, surfactant-deficient animals have demonstrated that pressures in excess of 30 cm H_2O achieve only relatively modest lung expansion and FRCs are rarely formed. As a consequence, the pattern of resuscitation recommended was that higher pressures should be used if pressures of 30 cm H_2O failed to produce chest wall movement. Studies[55,56] have shown that inflation pressures of 25 to 30 cm H_2O during the initial phases of resuscitation rarely produced inflation volumes greater than twice the anatomic dead space during the initial phases of resuscitation (i.e., effective alveolar ventilation), and that the failure

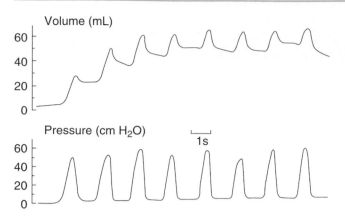

FIGURE 25-10. Resuscitation trace from an infant. Inspiration is upward on the volume trace. Note formation of functional residual capacity during first four inflations. (From Upton CJ et al: Endotracheal resuscitation of neonates using a rebreathing bag. Arch Dis Child 66:39, 1991.)

to form an FRC was significantly related to subsequent death.

In contrast, in a separate investigation, all preterm infants requiring resuscitation over a period of a year were initially exposed to inflation pressures limited to 16 cm H_2O. This pressure could be increased if there was no apparent chest wall movement. Using this protocol, no infant received inflation pressure, greater than 32 cm H_2O, with a mean of 23 cm H_2O.[54]

STUDIES ON PRETERM ANIMAL MODELS

It is now apparent that excessive volume is more important to the production of lung damage than excessive pressures. Studies on animal models have shown that the lung damage is avoided even when high inflation pressures are used when lung expansion is prevented by using banding or plaster casts[52] around the chest wall. Thus, it is excessive volume change rather than pressure that is responsible for the lung damage (i.e., volutrauma, not barotrauma). The mechanism for the damage is multifactorial. In animal models, overexpansion in the absence of sufficient surfactant can lead to physical damage to the type 1 pneumocytes,[7] an increase in microvascular protein permeability,[22] pulmonary edema,[37] and release of proinflammatory cytokines and chemokines[57] (see Chapter 42).

Resuscitation studies on immature animals have produced worrying results. Bjorklund and colleagues[13] found that six inflations of 60 cm H_2O, each lasting 5 seconds, given to preterm lambs resulted in stiffer lungs over the subsequent 4 hours and a worse appearance on lung histologic study than in controls. Five sustained lung inflations of 8, 16, and 32 mL/kg produced a dose-dependent degree of lung damage, but even the 8 mL/kg volume—rather less than the 10 mL/kg inspiratory volume of term infants breathing spontaneously—resulted in reduced lung compliance compared with nonintubated controls.[12] This pattern of lung damage was also seen if these high inflation volumes were applied immediately after the administration of surfactant,[58] but not if delayed until 15 minutes after surfactant therapy.[123]

It is not clear what inflation volume is safe for surfactant-deficient preterm infants. It may be that even limiting lung inflation to the minimum necessary to permit adequate gaseous exchange will result in damage in some very immature infants. This has led many institutions to try to avoid using IPPV if possible, instead using continuous end-expiratory pressure as the initial intervention if the infant is breathing.

Continuous Positive Airway Pressure

Continuous positive airway pressure (CPAP) was first recommended as an alternative to IPPV by Blaikley and Gibberd in 1935.[14] They advised that a loose-fitting catheter be passed into the upper trachea and connected to an oxygen–carbon dioxide mixture that was delivered at a pressure of 30 cm H_2O. They found that this generated a constant inflation pressure of approximately 15 cm H_2O in the lungs. This was maintained for "a few minutes."

Subsequently, the use of CPAP administered by nasal cannulae at the time of delivery has been explored in very immature infants.[71] A CPAP pressure of 20 to 25 cm H_2O was applied for 15 to 20 seconds, followed by a CPAP pressure of 4 to 6 cm H_2O. This was associated with a reduction in the need for intubation and IPPV from 84% to 40%, compared with historical control subjects. There was also a significant reduction in the incidence of severe intraventricular hemorrhage (from 41% to 27%), bronchopulmonary dysplasia (from 50% to 40%), and time spent in hospital (from 105 to 79 days). Others have also demonstrated that the rate of intubation is reduced if CPAP is used initially,[47,73,91] and some have even demonstrated a reduction in the rate of bronchopulmonary dysplasia.[65] This approach is undergoing further investigation in well-designed, randomized, controlled clinical trials.

Methods for Achieving Lung Inflation without Intubation

CONTINUOUS POSITIVE AIRWAY PRESSURE/ POSITIVE END-EXPIRATORY PRESSURE WITH IPPV

Devices are now available that provide CPAP to the spontaneously breathing infant (e.g., Neopuff). These devices can provide positive end-expiratory pressure during IPPV, followed by CPAP once the infant commences to breathe spontaneously. This may be of benefit because CPAP helps in the establishment of the FRC. Failure to establish an FRC during the early stages of resuscitation has been shown to be related to more severe respiratory distress syndrome and lower rates of survival.[52]

SELF-INFLATING BAGS

These depend on a flow of air or oxygen and incorporate pressure relief valves that usually function at pressures of 20 to 30 cm H_2O. Most have the facility to override this pressure relief valve when necessary. The facemask needs to be held in place over the mouth and nose with one hand; the infant's neck is slightly extended to keep the airway open. Although this technique often results in an active, spontaneously breathing infant, it is likely that the infant's response to bag-and-mask resuscitation at birth depends on stimulating the Head paradoxical reflex[50] (i.e., spontaneous inspiration in response to inflation, rather than effective ventilation).

Physiologic studies have shown that volume delivery using a self-inflating bag is poor, often little more than the anatomic dead space, particularly when the resting volume of the bag is only 250 mL.[42] The reason for this is that gas preferentially escapes through the pressure relief valve, so that peak pressures are limited and maintained only for a few hundred milliseconds. Better tidal exchange can be achieved with bag volumes of 500 mL, but performance remains poor.[42] There have been concerns that the efficacy of these devices might be limited by the upward displacement of the diaphragm resulting from gas entering and expanding the stomach. This fortunately has been shown not to be the case because gas could not subsequently be aspirated from the stomach after bag-and-mask resuscitation at birth unless pressures in excess of 55 cm H_2O were used.[120] On the neonatal unit, however, gastric distention is a common complication of bag-and-mask resuscitation. The explanation for these different findings is that during resuscitation at birth, swallowing is rarely seen, and that is the main mechanism by which air enters the stomach.[120]

T-PIECE RESUSCITATION

This method of resuscitation was first described in 1928 by Henderson[51] but did not achieve general acceptance until the late 1980s. A round facemask with two ports is used. One port receives a variable pressure, limited (up to 40 cm H_2O) supply of oxygen/air, and the other is open to ambient atmosphere, but can be occluded intermittently by a finger to produce lung inflation. A pressure monitor is incorporated in the circuit. The standard procedure is to maintain the first inflation (20 to 30 cm H_2O) for 2 to 3 seconds to facilitate lung expansion (see later) and then ventilate at rates of approximately 30 per minute, allowing 1 second for each inflation. This has been found to produce more effective tidal exchange than the bag-and-mask systems,[55,56] requires less training, and can be delivered with one hand. Commercial modifications of this technique are now available.[43]

ANESTHETIC REBREATHING BAGS

These are technically more difficult to use because the bag depends on the flow of gas for reexpansion, but provide a more versatile system that can be used to develop high pressures.[43] The bag is squeezed until the desired chest wall movement has occurred.

LARYNGEAL MASK AIRWAY

Although the use of a bag and either a mask or an endotracheal tube is the most common method of providing positive pressure ventilation, another method that may have merit is the use of a laryngeal mask airway that can be inserted blindly. A version is available for neonates weighing as little as 2.5 kg. Studies have supported the use of the laryngeal mask airway in neonatal resuscitation. However, at a pressure of approximately 23 cm, an audible air leak develops. This limits the use of the laryngeal mask airway in infants with poor compliance or in those who require higher pressures for the first or subsequent breath. The device requires less expertise than required for laryngoscopy and intubation and provides an alternative for those with limited skills.[20,46,87]

ENDOTRACHEAL INTUBATION

Insertion of an endotracheal tube is best accomplished by two people: one to insert the tube and ventilate the infant's lungs and the other to assist with the intubation and, after placement of the tube, to listen to the chest to ensure that proper placement of the tube has resulted in equal breath sounds on both sides of the chest. Tube sizes ranging from 2.0 to 4.0 Fr should be available. Although intubation can be accomplished in most preterm infants with a 2.5-Fr tube or larger, there is the occasional infant with very low birthweight (500 to 600 g or less) who may initially need a 2-Fr tube (Table 25-3). If a soft, flexible wire stylet is used, it should be secured so that it stops approximately 0.5 to 1 cm from the end of the tube. A protruding stylet can cause damage to the larynx or the trachea. If the endotracheal tube is long, it is easier to manage if it is cut to approximately 13 cm and the adapter reconnected.

The correct position of the infant for intubation is with the head slightly extended. Inexperienced people sometimes hang the head over the edge of the warmer. This hyperextends the neck, moving the trachea anteriorly and making the glottis hard to visualize. Flexion of the neck also makes the glottis hard to visualize (Fig. 25-11).

Although much has been written about the intricacies of visualizing the glottis, to a large extent this depends on recognizing the place where the blade has been initially inserted and then moving it to the proper position. In general, the blade is either not inserted far enough, is off to the side, or is inserted too far and is

TABLE 25-3. Endotracheal Tube Sizes

TUBE SIZE (mm ID)	WEIGHT (g)	GESTATIONAL AGE (wk)
2.0*	500–600 or less	25–26 or less
2.5	<1000	<28
3.0	1000–2000	28–34
3.5	2000–3000	34–38
3.5–4.0	>3000	>38

*May be needed if a size 2.5 Fr tube does not fit.
ID, internal diameter.

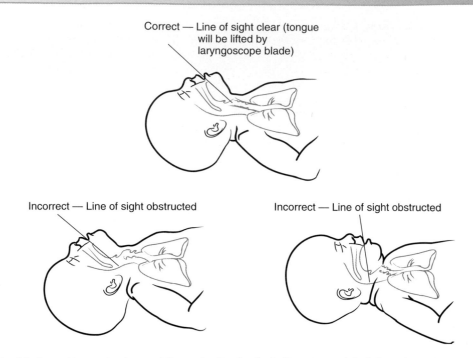

Correct — Line of sight clear (tongue
will be lifted by
laryngoscope blade)

Incorrect — Line of sight obstructed   Incorrect — Line of sight obstructed

FIGURE 25-11. Effects of flexion and hyperextension on ability to visualize the glottis. (From Kattwinkel J (ed): Textbook of Neonatal Resuscitation, 4th ed. Copyright American Heart Association/American Academy of Pediatrics, 2000. Used with permission of the American Academy of Pediatrics.)

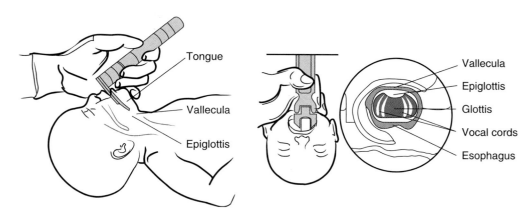

Tongue

Vallecula

Epiglottis

Vallecula
Epiglottis
Glottis
Vocal cords
Esophagus

FIGURE 25-12. Correct view of glottis in preparation for intubation. (From Kattwinkel J (ed): Textbook of Neonatal Resuscitation, 4th ed. Copyright American Heart Association/American Academy of Pediatrics, 2000. Used with permission of the American Academy of Pediatrics.)

in the esophagus. The ability to recognize the position of the blade and then move to the proper position and recognize the landmarks of the glottis facilitates an efficient intubation (Fig. 25-12). In the larger infant the blade should be inserted into the vallecula and lifted to visualize the glottis. If the vallecula is too small in the smaller premature infant, the blade should be used to lift the epiglottis. If the glottis is too far anterior, gentle pressure over the larynx will bring it into view. This pressure can be applied by either the assistant or the person performing the intubation (Fig. 25-13).

The tube should not be inserted down the center of the laryngoscope blade, which provides the line of sight, but alongside the blade. The intubator should always keep the tube in sight and insert the tube until

the vocal cord guide (black line near the tip of the endotracheal tube) is at the level of the cords. This should place the tip of the tube at a point slightly above the carina. A tip-to-lip distance can be used to check the placement of the tube. Adding 6 to the weight of the infant (in kilograms) is a reasonable estimate of the centimeter marking that should occur at the lips when the tube is properly positioned (Table 25-4).

When the tube is placed in the airway, a bag should be attached and the infant's lungs ventilated while an assistant listens to both lungs. If the tube is properly positioned, there should be bilateral and equal breath sounds, a slight rise of the chest with each ventilation, no air heard entering the stomach, and no gastric distention. Another way of checking for an in-place

Before   **After**

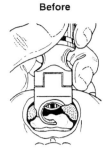 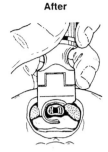

Pressure Applied by Operator   **Pressure Applied by Assistant**

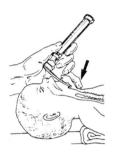 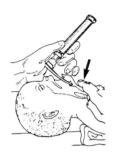

FIGURE 25-13. Downward pressure applied to larynx to help visualize the glottis. (From American Heart Association/American Academy of Pediatrics: Textbook of Neonatal Resuscitation. Dallas, American Heart Association, 1994.)

TABLE 25-5. Complications of Endotracheal Intubation

COMPLICATION	CAUSE
Hypoxia	Procedure taking too long; incorrect placement of tube
Bradycardia/apnea	Hypoxia
Vagal response	Stimulation of posterior pharynx by laryngoscope blade, endotracheal tube, or suction catheter
Pneumothorax	Overventilation of one lung caused by placement of tube in main bronchus (usually the right)
Contusions or lacerations of tongue, gums, pharynx, epiglottis, trachea, vocal cords, or esophagus	Rough handling of laryngoscope or endotracheal tube; laryngoscope blade that is too long or too short
Perforation of trachea or esophagus	Insertion of tube or stylet was too vigorous, or stylet protrudes beyond end of tube
Infection	Introduction of organisms by equipment or hands

From American Heart Association/American Academy of Pediatrics: Textbook of Neonatal Resuscitation, 4th ed. Dallas, American Heart Association, 2000.

TABLE 25-4. Endotracheal Tube Placement

WEIGHT	DEPTH OF INSERTION (cm FROM UPPER LIP)
1 kg	7*
2 kg	8
3 kg	9
4 kg	10

*Infants weighing less than 750 g may require only 6-cm insertion.
From American Heart Association/American Academy of Pediatrics: Textbook of Neonatal Resuscitation, 4th ed. Dallas, American Heart Association, 2000.

endotracheal tube is to use a carbon dioxide detector, although this may provide inaccurate results in the infant with very low birthweight.

Table 25-5 outlines some of the complications of the intubation procedure and their causes. Insertion of an endotracheal tube must be done quickly. Prolonged attempts to insert a tube simply extend the asphyxial period and increase the chance of permanent damage. If a tube has not been successfully inserted within approximately 20 seconds and the infant has bradycardia, the attempt should stop and the infant's lungs should be ventilated with a bag and mask. Another attempt at intubation can be made after a minute or so of bag-and-mask ventilation. In a severely asphyxiated infant requiring prolonged resuscitation, intubation is helpful

at some point because it is easier to use a bag and tube for a prolonged period than a bag and mask.

Table 25-6 outlines the most common problems associated with inadequate chest expansion, regardless of whether one is using a bag and mask or endotracheal

TABLE 25-6. Problems Associated with Inadequate Chest Expansion

PROBLEM	CORRECTION
Inadequate face mask seal	Reapply mask to face. Alter position of hand that holds mask.
Blocked airway	Bag and mask: Check infant's position. Suction mouth, oropharynx, and nose. Insert oral airway if indicated (Pierre Robin syndrome, macroglossia). Bag and endotracheal tube: Suction the tube.
Misplaced endotracheal tube	Remove endotracheal tube, ventilate with bag and mask, replace tube.
Inadequate pressure	Increase pressure, taking care not to overexpand the chest; may require adjusting or overriding the pop-off valve.

tube. As soon as positive pressure ventilation begins, a second person should be summoned if he or she is not already present. This second individual should auscultate the chest to ensure equal air entry bilaterally and should listen to the heart rate.

PART 3

Oxygen Therapy

Maximo Vento and Ola Saugstad

THE USE OF OXYGEN IN PERINATAL ASPHYXIA AND RESUSCITATION

Oxidative Stress: Pathophysiologic Background

Asphyxia is characterized by prolonged periods of ischemia and hypoxia, which leads to specific cellular changes affecting enzyme activities, mitochondrial function, cytoskeletal structure, membrane transport, and antioxidant defenses. All of these changes collectively predispose tissue to reoxygenation injury.[27,41,68] During hypoxia, limited oxygen availability decreases oxidative phosphorylation, resulting in a failure to resynthesize energy-rich phosphates, including adenosine 5′-triphosphate (ATP) and phosphocreatine. The membrane ATP-dependent Na^+/K^+ pump is altered, favoring the influx of Na^+, Ca^{2+}, and water into the cell, thereby producing cytotoxic edema in addition to eliciting numerous metabolic pathways that are injurious to various structural components of the cell. Furthermore, adenine nucleotide catabolism during ischemia results in the intracellular accumulation of hypoxanthine, which is subsequently converted into toxic reactive oxygen species on the reintroduction of molecular oxygen during resuscitation, provided xanthine oxidase is available.

In the endothelium, ischemia promotes expression of certain proinflammatory gene products (e.g., leukocyte adhesion molecules, cytokines) and bioactive agents (e.g., endothelin, thromboxane A_2), while repressing other "protective" gene products (e.g., prostacyclin, nitric oxide). Thus, ischemia induces a proinflammatory state that increases tissue vulnerability to further injury on reperfusion.

Reperfusion/reoxygenation of the ischemic tissues results in the formation of toxic reactive oxygen species, including superoxide anions, hydrogen peroxide (H_2O_2), hydroxyl radicals, and nitrogen reactive species, especially peroxynitrite.[33,41,68] Normally, hypoxanthine accumulated during the ischemic phase is oxidized by xanthine dehydrogenase to xanthine in those cells containing this enzyme. However, during ischemia, xanthine dehydrogenase is converted to xanthine oxidase. Xanthine oxidase uses oxygen and therefore, during ischemia, is unable to catalyze the conversion of hypoxanthine (resulting in the buildup of excess tissue levels of hypoxanthine). When oxygen is reintroduced during reperfusion, conversion of the excess hypoxanthine by xanthine oxidase results in the formation of reactive oxygen species, and in the presence of nitric oxide, in the formation of reactive nitrogen species.

Reactive oxygen species and reactive nitrogen species are potent oxidizing and reducing agents that directly damage cellular structures. They are able to peroxidize membranes, structural proteins and enzymes, and nucleic acids. In addition, they are known to be extremely important regulators of intracellular signaling pathways that modulate DNA and RNA synthesis, protein synthesis, and enzyme activation, and directly influence the cell cycle.

A vast array of enzymatic and nonenzymatic antioxidants has evolved in biologic systems to protect cellular structures against the deleterious action of free radicals.[62] Among the enzymes, the most important are superoxide dismutase, catalase, and glutathione peroxidase. The major nonenzymatic intracellular antioxidant is reduced glutathione, which is able to reduce free radicals by establishing a bond with another reduced glutathione molecule, forming oxidized glutathione and releasing one electron.

Oxidative stress in a biologic system is defined as the imbalance of pro-oxidants and antioxidants in favor of pro-oxidants.[61] Different biomarkers of oxidative stress have been used in biology and medicine. An indirect way of measuring oxidative stress is the detection of increased activity of antioxidant enzymes such as superoxide dismutase, catalase, glutathione peroxidase, or glutathione redox cycle enzymes. Another way is to measure the oxidized form of a nonenzymatic molecule such as oxidized glutathione. Thus, an increased concentration of oxidized glutathione or a decreased ratio of reduced to oxidized glutathione may indirectly reflect a pro-oxidant status.

Oxidative Stress: Differences between 100% Oxygen and Room-Air Resuscitation

In the absence of severe lung disease, or cyanotic congenital heart disease, resuscitation with 100% oxygen causes hyperoxemia ($Pao_2 \geq 100$ mm Hg). On the other hand, resuscitation with room air raises the Pao_2 to more physiologic levels, approximately 70 to 80 mm Hg. Moreover, biologic markers that are indicative of oxidative stress, such as oxidized glutathione or antioxidant enzyme activity, correlate significantly with the partial pressure of oxygen achieved in arterial blood. Thus, newborn infants resuscitated with pure oxygen have a higher degree of oxidative stress at birth than do infants resuscitated with room air.[118]

In one study, there is some evidence of oxidative stress for as long as 4 weeks postnatal age in infants resuscitated with 100% oxygen. These infants had a

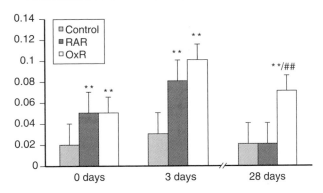

FIGURE 25-14. Ratio of oxidized glutathione to reduced glutathione in asphyxiated newly born infants resuscitated with room air (RAR) or 100% oxygen (OxR) determined at 0 day (birth), 3 days, and 28 days of life. **$P < .01$ versus control; ##$P < .01$ versus RAR.

decreased ratio of total blood reduced glutathione to oxidized glutathione and oxidized DNA bases in urine at 1 month of life. However, no such effect has been observed in infants resuscitated with room air[116] (Fig. 25-14).

Hyperoxemia has also been associated with a series of negative side effects. These include increased oxygen consumption and metabolic rate, prolonged vasoconstriction of cerebral arteries, increased activation of leukocytes and endothelial cells, and increased formation of reactive oxygen species and reactive nitrogen species.

Room Air or Pure Oxygen for Resuscitation of the Newly Born?

The traditional approach during resuscitation is to use 100% oxygen. However, in view of our increasing knowledge of oxidative stress, the question arises: what is the optimal oxygen supplementation during resuscitation of the newly born? By using the term *newly born*, a distinction is made between immediate procedures performed within minutes after birth and those performed later in newborn life. The effect of hyperoxia might well be completely different at birth than later in the neonatal period.

ANIMAL STUDIES
Animal studies have demonstrated that after a period of severe hypoxia, physiologic functions such as blood pressure and blood flow to various organs, including the brain, are restored equally efficiently with 21% and 100% oxygen. They also found that evoked potentials, as well as biochemical indicators such as base deficit and hypoxanthine, are restored efficiently using room air for resuscitation.

Some animal studies have even indicated a potential advantage in using 21% instead of 100% oxygen. For instance, a burst of oxygen radicals is produced both in the brain and the lung when the newborn is resuscitated with pure oxygen, in contrast to room air,

with which no such increase has been detected. The H_2O_2 concentration in leukocytes from the sagittal sinus increased significantly in newborn hypoxic piglets resuscitated with 100% oxygen, in contrast to those given 21% oxygen. The nitric oxide (NO) concentration in the brain also tended to become higher if pure oxygen was used compared with ambient air for resuscitation of piglets. Therefore, the stage might be set for a higher production of reactive nitrogen species and peroxynitrite if 100% oxygen is used.

Based on data obtained from resuscitation of asphyxiated newborn piglets, using a model in which asphyxia was induced by pneumothorax, a significantly better short-term neurologic outcome was found in those animals resuscitated with 21% than with 100% oxygen. In another study, brain cell membrane function was evaluated by measuring the activity of Na^+,K^+-ATPase. This membrane-bound enzyme is needed to maintain cell membrane integrity. Asphyxiated animals resuscitated with pure oxygen had an inhibition of Na^+,K^+-ATPase 2 hours after resuscitation was started, in contrast to animals given 21% oxygen, in which Na^+,K^+-ATPase activity had reached baseline at this time. There are also indications that resuscitation with 100% oxygen augments inflammatory processes more than 21% oxygen in the myocardium as well as the brain.

On the other hand, some animal studies have shown that cerebral brain microflow is reestablished faster with 100% oxygen. However, this difference almost disappears if a moderate hypercapnia is present in addition to the hypoxia, and this is the case in birth asphyxia. Hypercapnia therefore might seem to be an important factor in reestablishing brain flow after asphyxia. By contrast, in a study involving premature infants younger than 33 weeks' gestational age at 24 hours, cerebral blood flow was reduced by 20% in infants given 80% oxygen compared with those infants in whom room air was used.

Animal studies have also shown that even in severe meconium aspiration room air resuscitation is as efficient as that with 100% oxygen provided a sufficient tidal volume is given.

CLINICAL DATA
Several clinical studies have been conducted with the aim of evaluating the efficacy of resuscitation with ambient air compared with pure oxygen. To date, a total of 1750 newborn infants have been included in randomized or pseudorandomized studies aiming at investigating any differences between those resuscitated with 21% and 100% oxygen.[94,95,103,115-118]

It seems that Apgar scores are more depressed, at least at 1 minute of age, in those resuscitated with 100% compared with 21% oxygen. This is probably because those given oxygen take their first breath and cry significantly later than those given room air. Postnatal hyperoxia may also inhibit peripheral chemoreceptors and delay onset of breathing.[23] Normal, nonasphyxiated newborns delivered vaginally or by cesarean section initiate the first cry almost immediately after birth and attain a sustained pattern of respiration within the first

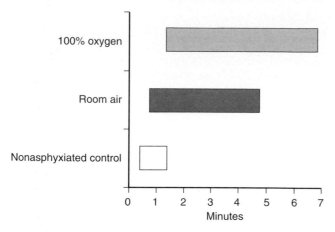

FIGURE 25-15. Time to first cry in asphyxiated newly born infants resuscitated with room air or 100% oxygen.

30 seconds of life. However, hypoxic and acidotic asphyxiated infants do not initiate breathing spontaneously and may require positive pressure ventilation. The duration of the resuscitation period directly correlates with the severity of asphyxia and the efficiency of the resuscitation procedure. In one study, the onset of respirations was a mean of 24 seconds later in those infants given 100% oxygen compared with those given room air. In another the difference was 1 minute. The time to first cry in infants resuscitated with room air ranged from 0.6 to 4.5 minutes, whereas those resuscitated with 100% oxygen took from 1.2 to 7.0 minutes to the first cry (Fig. 25-15). In another study, the duration of resuscitation until asphyxiated infants were able to sustain a spontaneous and regular pattern of breathing revealed that infants resuscitated with room air also needed less time (5.3 ± 1.5 minutes) than those resuscitated with 100% oxygen (6.8 ± 1.2 minutes) to establish a regular respiration.[118]

Meta-analysis has revealed a significant reduction of 5% in the neonatal mortality rate (odds ratio 0.58; 95% confidence interval 0.43 to 0.80) in those infants given 21% oxygen. These dramatic results raise several questions, first about the quality of the studies included and second regarding what was the cause of death in these infants. The studies represent a mixture of blinded and unblinded, multicenter and single-center studies from a number of countries. Most of the infants were recruited from so-called developing countries. But when analyzing the children from industrialized countries separately, a significant reduction of 3% in the neonatal mortality rate was still found. The causes of death can be mainly, but not exclusively, attributed to asphyxia. It is worth considering that if oxidative stress is induced in infants resuscitated with pure oxygen, this may lead to alterations of cell function and physiology that place the infant at increased risk.

In newborn infants needing intervention at birth, with an Apgar score of less than 6 at 1 minute and given room air by bag and mask, the median SaO_2 at 1 minute of age was 65%, with 10th to 90th percentiles ranging from 43% to 80%. At 3 and 5 minutes, the corresponding figures are 85% (60% to 90%) and 90% (73% to 95%). Surprisingly, those infants randomized to pure oxygen did not have higher saturations over the first 10 minutes of life.

In the only study looking at follow-up of infants resuscitated with either room air or oxygen, approximately two thirds of the infants in the Resair 2 study were followed between 18 and 24 months.[102] There were no significant differences in somatic growth or neurologic handicaps between the two groups. However, the trends, although not significant, appear to favor the group resuscitated with oxygen. Whether this is because of the impact of the increased survival of those resuscitated with room air (mortality rates: 21% oxygen versus 16% room air) or whether there are specific subgroups responsible for the trend is not known. What is clear is that the study, which was not originally designed to be a follow-up study, is underpowered to discern clinically important differences in long-term outcome.

Room Air or 100% Oxygen—Or Something Else?

An accumulating body of information raises some concerns regarding the use of pure oxygen for routine resuscitation of the newly born infant.[99,101] We believe that pure oxygen should be avoided because it has not been shown to represent an advantage and is potentially detrimental. There is also information that leads us to believe that room air, at least in most cases, is sufficient. Whether any oxygen concentration between these extremes is optimal is not known. In some centers and countries, a compromise has been reached with the recommendation to start with 30% to 40% oxygen.

Although the World Health Organization has stated that room air is sufficient for so-called basic newborn resuscitation, most guidelines at present advocate the use of 100% oxygen for resuscitation of the newly born. From a worldwide perspective on child health, the sufficiency of room air for resuscitation is an important statement because oxygen is expensive and not at hand at all deliveries around the world. It therefore is of importance that, to date, the available information indicates that room air is at least comparable with 100% oxygen in resuscitation. However, if oxygen is available it should always be at hand because a child who does not respond to room air should quickly be given oxygen supplementation. In those infants who do not respond with a normal heart rate to room air resuscitation after 90 seconds, we recommend that supplemental oxygen be used. Meanwhile, the Neonatal Resuscitation Program of the American Academy of Pediatrics/American Heart Association is reconsidering the need for their recommendation of 100% oxygen for all resuscitations.

PART 4

Chest Compression, Medications, and Special Problems

Ronald S. Bloom

Effective use of positive pressure ventilation (Part 2) and supplemental oxygen (Part 3) are key to optimal neonatal resuscitation. Although a great deal of emphasis has been placed on the implementation of chest compression and use of medications, there are some compelling data to indicate that if the issues of ventilation are managed correctly, chest compression and medication are only rarely needed. In examining 30,839 deliveries, Perlman and Risser[89] noted that with a well-trained team only 0.12% (39 of 30,839) of deliveries needed chest compressions or medication. Of equal importance, they found that in 29 of the 39 cases that progressed to chest compressions or medication, they believed that the infants received either ineffective or improper initial ventilatory support and were able to identify five infants who had malpositioning of an endotracheal tube. Along these lines, Tyson[113] wrote: "We suspect that the most common error in clinical use of epinephrine is that its use distracts the caregivers from recognizing and correcting bradycardia resulting from hypoventilation during resuscitation".

It seems clear that, with a real emphasis on the establishment of ventilation, chest compression and medication will needed in only a very few cases.

CHEST COMPRESSION

If, after effective ventilation with 100% oxygen for 30 seconds, the heart rate remains low, chest compression should be initiated to help maintain cardiac output. The heart rate at which one begins chest compression varies with the source of the recommendations. ILCOR recommends initiating chest compressions at heart rates of 60 beats per minute or less.[64] The previous recommendations of the American Heart Association/American Academy of Pediatrics started chest compressions if the heart rate is below 60 beats per minute or between 60 and 80 beats per minute and not rising. The new recommendations suggest starting chest compressions at a heart rate of 60 beats per minute or less because of the ease of teaching this value. To date, there is little evidence to suggest one number over another.

Compression of the chest should occur over the lower third of the sternum, just below an imaginary line drawn between the nipples. Care should be taken not to apply pressure to the xiphoid process at the lower end of the sternum. The sternum can be compressed by using the thumbs with the fingers encircling the chest or by placing two fingers perpendicular to the sternum (Fig. 25-16). On the basis of very limited data, it has been suggested that a greater mean arterial pressure can be obtained with the thumb method.[30,112] Regardless of which position is used, the persons providing ventilation and chest compression must position themselves so that they do not interfere with each other.

Each compression should depress the sternum approximately one third of the anterior-posterior diameter of the chest or until a palpable pulse is generated. A pulse should be palpable with each compression. Having a third person available to check the pulse is helpful. It is currently recommended that the chest be compressed 90 times a minute, with a ventilation interposed between

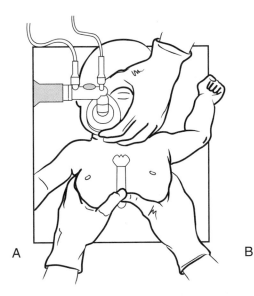

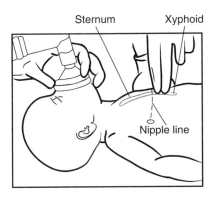

FIGURE 25-16. A, Thumb technique of chest compression. **B,** Correct finger position for chest compression. (From Kattwinkel J (ed): Textbook of Neonatal Resuscitation, 4th ed. Copyright American Heart Association/American Academy of Pediatrics, 2000. Used with permission of the American Academy of Pediatrics.)

each third compression. This provides 30 ventilations per minute. Thus, within a 2-second period, three chest compressions and a ventilation would occur.[5] Periodically, chest compression should be stopped briefly to see whether the spontaneous heart rate has risen. Once the heart rate has risen to 60 beats per minute, chest compressions can be stopped. The best way to monitor the effectiveness of chest compression is by means of arterial blood pressures obtained from a transducer attached to an umbilical artery catheter or a peripheral arterial line. These are not commonly available in delivery rooms.

An infant undergoing chest compressions may receive ventilation by either a mask or an endotracheal tube. However, a tube has advantages over a mask in these situations. A tube provides more stability and prevents gas from entering the stomach should a compression overlap with a ventilation. If a bag and mask are used, an orogastric tube must be inserted into the stomach to ensure decompression of the stomach.

It is now recommended that ventilations be interposed between compressions.[64] The reason for coordination and not simultaneous ventilation and compression is based on a reconsideration of the data supporting simultaneous ventilation and compression/cardiopulmonary resuscitation in the human adult, as well as on some laboratory evidence in infant animals.

In the adult there is clear evidence that it is not direct compression of the heart but a "thoracic pump" that plays a significant role in moving blood forward.[96] It was shown that in the adult simultaneous ventilation and compression/cardiopulmonary resuscitation increased aortic pressure and improved cerebral circulation.[26] However, further work demonstrated that although cerebral circulation increased, myocardial blood flow diminished with simultaneous ventilation and compression/cardiopulmonary resuscitation.[106] In a controlled clinical trial looking at simultaneous ventilation and compression/cardiopulmonary resuscitation versus conventional ventilation in a prehospital setting, it became clear that simultaneous ventilation and compression/cardiopulmonary resuscitation offered no advantages, and the authors concluded that simultaneous ventilation and compression/cardiopulmonary resuscitation should not be used in the clinical setting.[66] There also are some laboratory data showing no advantage to simultaneous ventilation and compression/cardiopulmonary resuscitation in the newborn piglet.[9]

In addition to the fact that simultaneous ventilation and compression offered no advantage in the adult human or the newborn piglet, there are some potential limitations to simultaneous chest compression and ventilation in the newborn. These include a compromised tidal volume; in the patient without an endotracheal tube in place, high airway pressures necessary to effect a ventilation will increase the amount of gas diverted into the stomach. A pressure monitor on the bag and mask would have limited value because it would be impossible to differentiate airway pressure associated with an adequate tidal volume from pressure associated with chest compression. Furthermore,

because ventilation is frequently administered with a self-inflating bag and mask, it would be necessary to override the pressure pop-off valve (usually set at 35 to 40 mm Hg), or the pressure generated would not be enough to deliver an adequate tidal volume.[80]

For all of these reasons, interposition of ventilation and compression is recommended: one ventilation interposed between every three compressions. Until more data are generated, a definitive statement cannot be made regarding the two-finger versus the thumb method. Regardless of the method used, if chest compressions and ventilations do not raise the heart rate above 60 beats per minute within 30 seconds of well-coordinated chest compressions and ventilation, support of the cardiovascular system with medications is indicated.

MEDICATIONS

The use of medications is required when, despite ventilation and chest compression, the infant continues to have bradycardia or when the infant is born with no detectable heartbeat. In the latter circumstance, medications are started along with ventilation and chest compression. Medications can be given through either an umbilical catheter or an endotracheal tube. If an umbilical catheter is used, it should be inserted into the umbilical vein just beneath the skin.

If the catheter is inserted too high and becomes wedged in the liver, it can be dangerous because infusing solutions into the liver may cause liver necrosis. If there is any doubt regarding the placement of the catheter, it should be reinserted to the level of the skin so that direct infusion into the liver does not occur. Table 25-7 presents an overview of the various medications, including concentration, dosage, route, and precautions.

Epinephrine

If positive pressure ventilation with 100% oxygen and chest compression are not successful in increasing the heart rate, use of medications is indicated. The first drug used should be epinephrine 1:10,000 (0.1 to 0.3 mL/kg). If necessary, the dose can be repeated every 3 to 5 minutes. Epinephrine has a beta$_1$-adrenergic effect, which stimulates the heart, but, of more importance, it also has an alpha adrenergic effect that increases noncerebral peripheral resistance. By selective vasoconstriction of peripheral vascular beds, epinephrine increased cerebral and myocardial blood flow.[10] Although in pediatric[48] and adult cases[86] larger-than-recommended doses of epinephrine have been used, there is no information indicating an advantage of larger doses in neonates. There are now data indicating that there is higher mortality and morbidity when high-dose epinephrine is used.[90] Thus, high-dose epinephrine administration is not recommended.

Epinephrine can be given intravenously or through the endotracheal tube.[69] Although there is evidence that low pulmonary blood flow associated with a resuscita-

TABLE 25-7. Medications for Neonatal Resuscitation

MEDICATION	CONCENTRATION TO ADMINISTER	PREPARATION	DOSAGE/ROUTE	WEIGHT OF INFANT/TOTAL DOSE			RATE/PRECAUTIONS
Epinephrine	1:10,000	1 mL	0.1–0.3 mL/kg IV or ET	**Weight** 1 kg 2 kg 3 kg 4 kg		**Total mL** 0.1–0.3 mL 0.2–0.6 mL 0.3–0.9 mL 0.4–1.2 mL	Give rapidly May dilute with normal saline solution to 1–2 mL if giving ET
Volume expanders	Normal saline solution Ringer lactate solution Whole blood	40 mL	10 mL/kg IV	**Weight** 1 kg 2 kg 3 kg 4 kg		**Total mL** 10 mL 20 mL 30 mL 40 mL	Give over 5–10 min
Sodium bicarbonate	0.5 mEq/mL (4.2% solution)	20 mL or two 10-mL prefilled syringes	2 mEq/kg IV	**Weight** 1 kg 2 kg 3 kg 4 kg	**Total Dose** 2 mEq 4 mEq 6 mEq 8 mEq	**Total mL** 4 mL 8 mL 12 mL 16 mL	Give *slowly*, over at least 2 min Give only if infant is being effectively ventilated
Naloxone hydrochloride	0.4 mg/mL	1 mL	0.1 mg/kg (0.25 mL/kg) IV, ET IM, SQ	**Weight** 1 kg 2 kg 3 kg 4 kg	**Total Dose** 0.1 mg 0.2 mg 0.3 mg 0.4 mg	**Total mL** 0.25 mL 0.50 mL 0.75 mL 1.00 mL	Give rapidly, IV, ET preferred. IM, SQ acceptable Do not give if mother is suspected of narcotic addiction or on methadone maintenance (may result in severe seizures)
	1.0 mg/mL	1 mL	0.1 mg/kg (0.1 mL/kg) IV, ET IM, SQ	1 kg 2 kg 3 kg 4 kg	0.1 mg 0.2 mg 0.3 mg 0.4 mg	0.1 mL 0.2 mL 0.3 mL 0.4 mL	
Dopamine				**Weight** 1-4 kg	**Total µg/kg/min** 5–20 µg/kg/min		Give as a continuous infusion, using an infusion pump Monitor heart rate and blood pressure closely

IM, intramuscular; ET, endotracheal; IV intravenous; SQ subcutaneous.

tion does not decrease plasma levels after endotracheal instillation of epinephrine,[72] there is still uncertainty as to whether the dose of epinephrine should be increased when the drug is given through the endotracheal tube.[83,93]

POTENTIAL HARMFUL EFFECTS OF EPINEPHRINE
There is an accumulating body of experimental evidence that the use of epinephrine may, in fact, lead to myocardial damage. Berg and colleagues[8] in 1994 compared standard-dose epinephrine with high-dose epinephrine and were unable to demonstrate any improvement in 24-hour survival or neurologic outcome in those adult pigs in whom high-dose epinephrine was used as part of a resuscitation. However, they did note that most animals in the simultaneous ventilation and compression/cardiopulmonary resuscitation group exhibited a hyperadrenergic state that included severe hypertension and tachycardia.

The same authors,[8a] using an asphyxial model in young pigs, were able to demonstrate not only that a hyperadrenergic state existed in those animals given simultaneous ventilation and compression/cardio-pulmonary resuscitation, but that the mortality rate was significantly higher in these animals.

In 1994, Ditchey and coworkers[34] used a beta-adrenergic blocker along with epinephrine and demonstrated that there was a reduction in myocardial damage after cardiopulmonary resuscitation. This has led to a series of studies, notably from the laboratory of Max Weil, indicating that when the beta-adrenergic effects of epinephrine are blocked, postmyocardial impairment postresuscitation is reduced. This was also true when a selective alpha agonist, such as phenylephrine, was used.[107]

Interestingly, Weil's group was also able to demonstrate the advantage of a pure alpha$_2$-adrenergic effect. They blocked the alpha$_1$-adrenergic effect on the heart along with the beta-adrenergic effect of epinephrine and were able to demonstrate an improvement in post-resuscitation cardiac and neurologic recovery. They were able to confirm this advantage by using a selective alpha$_2$-adrenergic agent, alpha-methylnorepinephrine. Postresuscitation myocardial function and survival were significantly better in animals treated with alpha-methylnorepinephrine.[105]

Thus, there is some reason to question epinephrine, with both its alpha and beta effects, as the drug of choice in resuscitation and consider the potential advantages to the use of a pure alpha$_2$-adrenergic agonist. Studies are yet to be done in the neonate.

Volume Expanders

Although an asphyxiated infant may be in shock, this is usually not caused by hypovolemia but by decreased myocardial function and decreased cardiac output. In fact, most infants who have undergone intrauterine asphyxia are not hypovolemic. In some circumstances, however, hypovolemic shock is a real possibility (Box 25-4).

It must be recognized that both asphyxia and hypovolemia can result in shock, the former as a result of decreased myocardial function and decreased cardiac output. In addition, most of the causes of hypovolemic shock result in asphyxia in the infant. Thus, most hypovolemic infants are asphyxiated, but most asphyxiated infants are not hypovolemic. The problem is in distinguishing hypovolemic shock from asphyxial shock that does not involve hypovolemia.

Because volume expanders may be detrimental in an infant who is not hypovolemic, how does one determine when they are needed? In the acute circumstance when, after adequate ventilation and oxygenation have been established, poor capillary filling persists and there is evidence or suspicion of blood loss with signs of hypovolemia, volume expanders should be given. If a pressure monitor and transducer are available in the delivery room, an umbilical arterial catheter may be used to obtain aortic blood pressure (see Appendix B, Tables of Normal Values). The use and placement of a central venous line have been debated; however, a low central venous pressure in the presence of poor capillary filling and a low aortic pressure is good evidence of hypovolemic shock and requires volume expansion.

To compound the problem in a hypovolemic infant, shock may not be evident at first in the asphyxial process. Early, there may be marked peripheral vasoconstriction, which maintains blood pressure. With an effective resuscitation, peripheral vasodilation takes place. At this point, a hypovolemic infant begins to manifest shock.

In an acute situation the volume expander of choice is normal saline. Five percent albumin has been used and previously recommended but appears to offer no advantage over normal saline. In a randomized study of infants with low birthweight with hypotension, saline was compared with 5% albumin. No differences were noted in the number of infants who went on to receive pressor support. However, those given albumin had significantly more weight gain in the first 48 hours than those given normal saline. This increase in weight may well be because albumin easily crosses capillary walls into the extravascular space, reducing the oncotic pressure difference between the vascular space and the interstitium and making fluid retention more likely.[45]

If time permits, fresh frozen plasma can be used. The best volume expander, although rarely available, is whole O-negative blood cross-matched against the mother's blood. This provides volume, oxygen-carrying capacity, and colloid.

Some have suggested that, in an emergency, blood be withdrawn from the fetal side of the placenta and infused into the infant. Although this should very rarely be necessary, if it must be done, it should be carried out in a sterile manner as soon as possible after the placenta is delivered. The syringe used to withdraw the blood should be heparinized and a filter attached to the syringe so that microclots can be filtered out before entering the syringe. Before the blood is infused into the infant, the filter should be changed and blood passed through the filter a second time during the infusion.

Infusion of volume expanders should consist of a volume of 10 mL/kg given over 5 to 10 minutes. If necessary, the infusion can be repeated. Delay in clamping of the cord is desirable in certain circumstances.

BOX 25-4. Causes of Hypovolemia

- Decreased blood return from placenta
- Cord compression resulting in venous but not arterial occlusion
- Placental separation compromising placental blood return to the fetus
- Maternal hypotension
- Loss of blood from fetal-placental circulation
- Hemorrhage from the fetal side of the placenta
- Fetal-fetal transfusion
- Incision of placenta during cesarean section

Sodium Bicarbonate

The use of sodium bicarbonate should be discouraged during the acute phase of a neonatal resuscitation in a delivery room. An asphyxiated infant may have both respiratory and metabolic acidosis. Adequate ventilation corrects the respiratory acidosis. The establishment of adequate circulation and oxygenation, along with sufficient carbohydrates for fuel, stops progression of the acidosis, results in metabolism of lactic acid, and clears the remaining acidosis. (See also Chapter 34.) There may be instances in a prolonged resuscitation when it is reasonable to use sodium bicarbonate. However, this should only be done after adequate ventilation is established.

In the absence of adequate ventilation, the administration of bicarbonate may be harmful. Bicarbonate administration results in an acute increase in carbon dioxide. The carbon dioxide crosses cell membranes quickly and lowers the pH of all major organs, including the heart and brain.[11] This can be attenuated with adequate ventilation. Therefore, before bicarbonate is administered, one must be certain that adequate ventilation is established. Another potential danger associated with the use of acute doses of bicarbonate is intracranial hemorrhage, especially in the preterm infant.[85]

If sodium bicarbonate is required, the recommended dose is 2 mEq/kg. To avoid a sudden increase in osmolality, with the risk of intracerebral hemorrhage, the concentration of bicarbonate should be 0.5 mEq/mL, infused at a rate of no more than 1 mEq/kg per minute; thus, it should take 2 minutes to infuse the entire dose. In the midst of a resuscitation this will seem like an impossibly long time.

Dopamine

There are times when the infant has suffered enough myocardial compromise that, despite resuscitative measures, poor cardiac output and hypotension remain. In these circumstances dopamine should be used. At dosages up to 10 µg/kg per minute, dopamine has both an inotropic effect as well as an alpha-adrenergic effect. At these dosages, however, the increased cardiac output antagonizes the alpha-adrenergic effect, resulting in increased cardiac output with only mild peripheral vasoconstriction. In higher doses, the alpha-adrenergic effect predominates with generalized peripheral vasoconstriction. Moreover, in low doses of up to 5 µg/kg, dopamine binds to dopaminergic receptors in the renal, mesenteric, and cerebral arteries, producing vasodilation.

Traditionally, dopamine is started at 5 µg/kg per minute and the dosage increased as necessary. However, there is some evidence that the neonate may respond to initial doses that are much smaller than those commonly recommended. If the dosage reaches 20 µg/kg per minute of dopamine without adequate response, it is unlikely that raising the dose further will make a difference.

The Drug-Depressed Infant

Respiratory depression is not uncommon if a mother has been given a narcotic analgesic within 4 hours of delivery or an inhalation anesthetic before a cesarean section. If the depression is solely related to the drug, with no overlying asphyxia, the infant usually has a good heart rate and simply needs ventilation. If the problem is caused by an inhalation anesthetic, ventilation of the infant usually removes the anesthetic from the infant's circulation. However, if the cause of the respiratory depression is due to administration of a narcotic to the mother within 4 hours of delivery, naloxone (Narcan) may be useful in antagonizing the respiratory depressant effect. The dose is 0.1 mg/kg. The preferred routes of administration of naloxone are through an endotracheal tube or an umbilical catheter. Naloxone can be given intramuscularly or subcutaneously, although when given using these routes there is a delayed onset of action because the drug needs to be absorbed from the injection site.

The duration of action of the narcotic may be longer than the duration of action of naloxone. Thus, the naloxone may wear off before the narcotic and the infant may slip back into respiratory depression. Repeated doses of naloxone may be necessary. Naloxone should never be given to an infant of a narcotic-addicted mother because the infant may have acute withdrawal symptoms, including seizures.

IMMEDIATE CARE AFTER ESTABLISHING ADEQUATE VENTILATION AND CIRCULATION

Once an infant is stabilized after resuscitation, the next steps require deliberate consideration. The future course of the infant's resuscitation is related to how well the lungs function and to the presence or absence of a good respiratory drive. Many infants improve rapidly, quickly attaining good lung compliance, adequate pulmonary blood flow, and spontaneous respiration. In these infants, resuscitative efforts can be withdrawn within a matter of minutes. Attention must be paid to the amount of assisted ventilation needed as the infant is improving. As compliance improves, there is a tendency to overventilate the infant's lungs. In addition, if 100% oxygen was needed initially, the amount of oxygen can often be lowered to avoid hyperoxygenation. The latter is especially important in the preterm infant.

Prolonged Assisted Ventilation (See also Chapter 42, Part 4.)

Some infants need a ventilator after the immediate resuscitation. In the severely asphyxiated infant, central nervous system depression may inhibit spontaneous ventilation. As pointed out earlier, the longer the asphyxial process lasts, the longer it takes for resumption of spontaneous ventilation. Most of the infants in this category also have some degree of pulmonary compromise related to the asphyxial process. Some infants with primary lung disease initially breathe spontaneously; however, these infants subsequently may need assisted ventilation to attain adequate blood gases. Whenever an infant is in need of ventilation for more than the immediate resuscitative period, evaluation of blood gases should guide the ventilatory support.

Glucose

As soon as the hypoxia is corrected, an infusion of glucose at approximately 8 mg/kg per minute should be started. Adjustment of the glucose infusion rate depends on follow-up of blood sugars. The purpose of the glucose is twofold: to provide fuel and to help eliminate the metabolic acidosis. A steady infusion of glucose provides fuel to an infant who has depleted much of his or her glycogen, especially myocardial glycogen, during the asphyxial episode. This infusion thus helps prevent the hypoglycemia that frequently accompanies asphyxia. It is important to recognize that glucose should not be started until the infant is adequately oxygenated. Anaerobic metabolism of carbohydrate leads to the formation of additional lactic acid, worsening the acidosis.

Fluids

The urine output of any infant undergoing an asphyxial episode should be carefully monitored. Oliguria is a common complication of asphyxia, and an infant can easily be overloaded with fluid. Fluid should be restricted until there is evidence of adequate urine output. The need to restrict fluid and yet give glucose emphasizes the importance of considering glucose infusion in terms of milligrams of glucose per kilogram of body weight per minute, rather than the amount of 10% glucose to be given. The concentration of infused glucose depends on how much fluid can be given to the infant. (See also Chapter 34.)

Feeding

During the asphyxial process, ischemia of the intestine occurs as a result of vasoconstriction of the mesenteric vessels. Because of the suggested relationship between ischemia of the intestine and necrotizing enterocolitis, it may be prudent to delay enteral feedings in the asphyxiated infant. (See also Chapters 33 and 45, Part 5.)

Other Problems

Other complications of asphyxia that are of concern include hypocalcemia, disseminated intravascular coagulation, seizures, cerebral edema, and intracerebral hemorrhage, as discussed elsewhere in this text.

SPECIAL PROBLEMS DURING RESUSCITATION

Meconium Aspiration (See also Chapter 42, Part 5.)

If meconium is present in the amniotic fluid, there is a chance that meconium will enter the mouth of the fetus and be aspirated into the lungs. Aspiration of meconium can result in a ball valve obstruction of the airways, causing gas trapping and pneumothorax. It can also cause a reactive inflammatory process. Because meconium-stained amniotic fluid is frequently associated with asphyxia in the newborn, the inability to effect adequate ventilation combined with the initial asphyxia may result in enough hypoxia and acidosis to maintain the increased resistance of the pulmonary vasculature and a persistence of fetal circulation.

The management of the infant born through meconium has represented a controversial area, with varying recommendations. The work of Carson and colleagues[24] in 1976 set in place a virtually universal agreement on the need to suction the hypopharynx after delivery of the head and before delivery of the shoulders. This should be done with a size 10 Fr or larger suction catheter. It is the management of the infant after birth that has generated controversy.

The hallmark study of Gregory and associates[49] in 1974, done before suctioning on the perineum was common, recommended that "all infants born through thick, particulate, or pea soup meconium should have the trachea aspirated immediately after birth." This was reinforced in a retrospective, uncontrolled study by Ting and coworkers[111] in 1975, in which vigorous infants with slight meconium were excluded. Ting and coworkers recommended immediate tracheal suction for infants born through meconium-stained amniotic fluid.

As a result of the Gregory and Ting studies and a 1977 statement by the American Academy of Pediatrics Committee on Fetus and Newborn, which said nothing about suctioning the hypopharynx on the perineum, intubation and tracheal suctioning became routine in many nurseries.

In the early and mid-1980s there were reports in the obstetrics literature that, even with "appropriate" management of the infant, meconium aspiration syndrome continued to occur.[31] In the neonatal resuscitation guidelines of 1986,[79] it was suggested that all infants with thick meconium undergo intubation and tracheal suction. No distinction was made with regard to the depressed versus the vigorous infant. In 1988, Linder and colleagues[70] published a controlled, randomized trial examining the value of endotracheal intubation and suction in *vigorous* infants. They noted that in vigorous infants the morbidity rate, including complications of intubation, was 2% greater in infants who had undergone intubation and suctioning. In 1990, Cunningham and associates[29] proposed a standard of care that reserved intubation largely for infants who were depressed and who required positive pressure ventilation.

In 1992, the American Academy of Pediatrics/American College of Obstetrics and Gynecology Guidelines for Perinatal Care[4] recommended that, in the presence of thick meconium *and* respiratory depression, the larynx be visualized, and if meconium is seen, the trachea be intubated and suctioned. It was noted that if the infant is vigorous, the indication for visualization of the cords and endotracheal suction is "less clear." In an article reporting a retrospective chart review in 1992, Wiswell and coworkers[125] argued that endotracheal intubation should not be limited to depressed infants because 54% of their study infants with meconium aspiration syndrome did not need positive pressure ventilation and were presumed vigorous at birth, including one infant with only thin meconium. Wiswell and coworkers also noted no significant adverse sequelae associated with intubation.

In 2000, a multicenter study looked at vigorous infants with a gestational age of more than 37 weeks who were born through meconium-stained amniotic fluid of any consistency. In these vigorous infants intubation and tracheal suctioning did not offer any advantage over expectant management.[124]

All depressed infants, with either thick or thin meconium, should undergo direct tracheal suctioning. However, it now appears that vigorous infants, regardless of the thickness of the meconium in the amniotic fluid, need not be handled in a special way. Although some may still recommend that the vigorous infant with thick meconium undergo endotracheal suctioning, clinical judgment should be used to determine whether the difficulty in intubation of a vigorous infant outweighs the advantages of intubation and suctioning.

If intubation is to be done and meconium removed from the trachea, the best method is to attach an adapter to the endotracheal tube so that suction can be directly applied using regulated wall suction at approximately 100 mm Hg as the tube is withdrawn. The trachea can then be reintubated and suctioned again if necessary. Because some infants with thick meconium are severely asphyxiated, it may not be possible to clear the trachea completely before beginning positive pressure ventilation. Clinical judgment determines the number of reintubations needed.

Pneumothorax (See also Chapter 42, Part 5.)

A pneumothorax is a potential problem whenever positive pressure ventilation is used. A pneumothorax should be suspected in any infant who is improving during a resuscitative effort and then suddenly decompensates. Listening to the infant, one may hear unequal breath sounds and distant heart sounds, which may be shifted from the normal position in the left side of the chest. The affected side of the chest is hyperinflated compared with the nonaffected side and has less movement during ventilation. If the pneumothorax is large enough to obstruct venous return, cardiac output falls

and the infant becomes hypotensive. When these events occur in an infant who is otherwise stable, a pneumothorax is easy to suspect. However, when a pneumothorax occurs early during resuscitation of a severely compromised infant, the signs and symptoms are not as obvious and a high index of suspicion is needed. When immediate intervention in the delivery room is needed, it may be necessary to insert a needle into the thorax before radiographic confirmation.

Diaphragmatic Hernia (See also Chapters 11; 42, Part 5; and 45, Part 4.)

An infant with a diaphragmatic hernia whose bowel suddenly fills with air as a consequence of spontaneous or mask ventilation may appear much the same as an infant with a pneumothorax.

To prevent gas from entering the intestines, one should always use an endotracheal tube when ventilating the lungs of an infant with a suspected diaphragmatic hernia. An orogastric tube should be inserted as soon as possible to remove air before it passes into the portion of intestine located in the chest. Forcing air into the intestine with bag-and-mask ventilation increases the chance of inflating intrathoracic stomach or bowel, further compromising pulmonary function.

Erythroblastosis/Hydrops (See also Chapters 20, 21, and 44.)

Successful resuscitation of an infant with hydrops demands preparation of a coordinated team with preassigned responsibilities. The team should be prepared at delivery to perform a partial (or, rarely, complete) exchange transfusion with O-negative packed cells crossmatched against the mother. In addition, they should be prepared to perform a thoracentesis, paracentesis, and complete resuscitation.

The infant with hydrops may not only be severely anemic but is likely to have ascites, a pleural effusion, and pulmonary edema. Furthermore, such infants frequently have had chronic intrauterine and intrapartum asphyxia. Because they are usually premature, respiratory distress syndrome may be an overlying confounding complication. On delivery, the infant should immediately undergo intubation because of poor lung compliance and the risk of pulmonary edema. High ventilator pressures are typically needed. If adequate ventilation cannot be attained and there is evidence of fluid in the abdomen or pleural space, consideration should be given to performing a paracentesis as well as a thoracentesis. Ultrasonography done before delivery may be helpful in determining the amount of fluid present. If the abdomen is markedly distended, the paracentesis should be performed first to relieve pressure on the diaphragm; this may need to be followed with a thoracentesis. Although most of these infants initially have a normal blood volume, after a large amount of ascitic and pleural fluid has been removed, some of this fluid may reaccumulate, lowering vascular volume. Therefore, careful attention should be paid to maintenance of intravascular volume and the prevention of shock after resuscitation.

A hematocrit obtained immediately at birth determines the need for an exchange transfusion (usually partial) in the delivery room. If the infant is extremely anemic and in need of oxygen-carrying capacity, catheters should be inserted into both the umbilical vein and artery to permit a slow isovolemic exchange with packed cells, which results in minimal impact on the already borderline hemodynamic status of the infant. These lines also can be used to monitor central venous pressure and aortic pressure to determine the volume needs of the infant. This is especially important when large amounts of fluid are removed from the thorax or abdomen.

SCREENING FOR CONGENITAL DEFECTS (See also Chapters 26 and 28.)

Two to three percent of infants are born with a congenital anomaly that requires intervention soon after birth. If undetected, some of the anomalies may result in life-threatening problems. Immediately after birth, choanal atresia or diaphragmatic hernia may result in respiratory distress. Other problems may appear later, such as aspiration caused by esophageal atresia (with esophageal fistula) or a high intestinal obstruction. A rapid screening test for congenital defects that can easily be performed by the delivery room staff can help identify many of these defects, along with others that are not life threatening but require prompt recognition and intervention.

Physical Examination

A rapid external physical examination identifies obvious abnormalities such as abnormal facies and limb, abdominal wall, or spinal column defects. A close look at the abdomen may reveal a scaphoid abdomen, which is a clue to a diaphragmatic hernia. If an umbilical vessel count reveals only two vessels, there is a possibility of other defects, especially involving the genitourinary tract.

Because infants are preferential nasal breathers, bilateral *choanal atresia* results in respiratory difficulty and requires an airway at birth (see also Chapter 42, Parts 5 and 6). Bilateral choanal atresia can be ruled out quickly if the infant is able to breathe while the mouth is held closed. Some infants with unilateral choanal obstruction appear normal until an examiner closes the mouth and then sequentially obstructs the nostrils with a finger. When the patent nostril is obstructed, such infants have difficulty breathing. Confirmation of choanal atresia results from the insertion of a soft nasogastric tube into each nostril. If an obstruction is reached within 3 to 4 cm, choanal atresia is a possibility.

An examination of the mouth identifies a cleft palate. Inserting a nasogastric tube through the mouth may help identify an *esophageal atresia* or a high intestinal obstruction. If the tube does not reach the stomach, an esophageal atresia, most often associated with a tracheoesophageal fistula, is a likely possibility. A few cubic centimeters of air forced through the tube, while listening over the stomach, confirms that the tube is in the stomach. Once the tube is in the stomach, the contents of the stomach can be suctioned. If more than 15 to 20 mL of gastric contents is obtained, the chances of a high intestinal obstruction are increased. The same tube can then be removed and gently inserted into the anal opening. Easy passage of the catheter for 3 cm into the anus makes atresia unlikely. A minute or so spent screening for congenital defects in this way may help to avert many future problems.

REFERENCES

1. Adamson K Jr et al: Resuscitation by positive pressure ventilation and tris-hydroxymethylaminomethane of rhesus monkeys asphyxiated at birth. J Pediatr 65:807, 1964.
2. Adamson SK Jr et al: The influence of thermal factors upon oxygen consumption of the newborn human Infant. J Pediatr 66:495, 1965.
3. Allwood AC et al: Changes in resuscitation practice at birth. Arch Dis Child Fetal Neonatal Ed 88:F375, 2003.
4. American Academy of Pediatrics: American Academy of Pediatrics/American College of Obstetrics and Gynecology Guidelines for Perinatal Care, 3rd ed. Elk Grove Village, Ill, American Academy of Pediatrics, 1992.
5. American Heart Association/American Academy of Pediatrics: Textbook of Neonatal Resuscitation, 4th ed. Dallas, American Heart Association, 2000.
6. Apgar V: A proposal for a new method of evaluation of the newborn infant. Curr Res Anesth Analg 32:260, 1953.
7. Auten RL et al: Volutrauma: What is it, and how do we avoid it? Clin Perinatol 28:505, 2001.
8. Berg RA et al: High-dose epinephrine results in greater early mortality after resuscitation from prolonged cardiac arrest in pigs: A prospective, randomized study. Crit Care Med 22:282, 1994.
8a. Berg RA et al: A randomized, blinded trial of high-dose epinephrine versus standard-dose epinephrine in a swine model of pediatric asphyxial cardiac arrest. Crit Care Med 24:1695, 1996.
9. Berkowitz ID et al: Blood flow during cardiopulmonary resuscitation with simultaneous compression and ventilation in infant pigs. Pediatr Res 26:558, 1989.
10. Berkowitz ID et al: Epinephrine dosage effects on cerebral and myocardial blood flow in an infant swine model of cardiopulmonary resuscitation. Anesthesiology 75:1041, 1991.
11. Bersin R: Effects of sodium bicarbonate on myocardial metabolism and circulatory function during hypoxia. In Arieff AI (ed): Hypoxia, Metabolic Acidosis, and the Circulation. Oxford, Oxford University Press, 1992.
12. Bjorklund LJ: Lung injury caused by neonatal resuscitation of immature lambs: Relation to column of lung inflation. Pediatr Res 39:362A, 1996.
13. Bjorklund LJ et al: Manual ventilation with a few large breaths at birth compromises the therapeutic effect of subsequent surfactant replacement in immature lambs. Pediatr Res 42:348, 1997.
14. Blaikley JB: Management of asphyxia neonatorum. Proc R Soc Med 49:603, 1956.

15. Bland RD: Formation of fetal lung liquid and its removal near birth. In Polin RA (ed): Fetal and Neonatal Physiology. Philadelphia, WB Saunders, 1992, p 782.

16. Bloom R et al: A consideration of neonatal resuscitation. Pediatr Clin North Am 51:669, 2004.

17. Boon AW et al: Lung expansion, tidal exchange, and formation of the functional residual capacity during resuscitation of asphyxiated neonates. J Pediatr 95:1031, 1979.

18. Boon AW et al: Physiological responses of the newborn infant to resuscitation. Arch Dis Child 54:492, 1979.

19. Boylan P: Acid-base physiology in the fetus. In Creasy RK (ed): Maternal-Fetal Medicine. Philadelphia, WB Saunders, 1989.

20. Brimacombe J, Berry A: The laryngeal mask airway: A consideration for the Neonatal Resuscitation Programme guidelines? Can J Anaesth 42:88, 1995.

21. Bruck K: Temperature regulation in the newborn infant. Biol Neonate 3:65, 1961.

22. Carlton DP et al: Lung overexpansion increases pulmonary microvascular protein permeability in lambs. J Appl Physiol 69:577, 1990.

23. Carroll JL: Developmental plasticity in respiratory control. J Appl Physiol 94:375, 2003.

24. Carson BS et al: Combined obstetric and pediatric approach to prevent meconium aspiration syndrome. Am J Obstet Gynecol 126:712, 1976.

25. Cassin S et al: The vascular resistance of the foetal and newly ventilated lung of the lamb. J Physiol (Lond) 171:61, 1964.

26. Chandra N et al: Augmentation of carotid flow during cardiopulmonary resuscitation by ventilation at high airway pressure simultaneous with chest compression. Am J Cardiol 48:1053, 1981.

27. Collard CD et al: Pathophysiology, clinical manifestations, and prevention of ischemia-reperfusion injury. Anesthesiology 94:1133, 2001.

28. Cordero L Jr et al: Neonatal bradycardia following nasopharyngeal stimulation. J Pediatr 78:441, 1971.

29. Cunningham AS et al: Tracheal suction and meconium: a proposed standard of care. J Pediatr 116:153, 1990.

30. David R: Closed chest cardiac massage in the newborn infant. Pediatrics 81:552, 1988.

31. Davis RO et al: Fatal meconium aspiration syndrome occurring despite airway management considered appropriate. Am J Obstet Gynecol 151:731, 1985.

32. Dawes GS: Birth asphyxia, resuscitation, brain damage. In Fetal and Neonatal Physiology. Chicago, Year Book Medical, 1968, p 141.

33. de Zwart LL et al: Biomarkers of free radical damage applications in experimental animals and in humans. Free Radic Biol Med 26:202, 1999.

34. Ditchey RV et al: Beta-adrenergic blockade reduces myocardial injury during experimental cardiopulmonary resuscitation. J Am Coll Cardiol 24:804, 1994.

35. Division of Information and Statistics: Hospital and Health Board Comparisons in Obstetrics 1988-1990. Scottish Health Service Common Services Agency 1992, p 57.

36. Downing SE et al: Influences of arterial oxygen tension and pH on cardiac function in the newborn lamb. Am J Physiol 211:1203, 1966.

37. Dreyfuss D et al: Role of tidal volume, FRC, and end-inspiratory volume in the development of pulmonary edema following mechanical ventilation. Am Rev Respir Dis 148:1194, 1993.

38. Dunn MS et al: Approaches to the initial respiratory management of preterm neonates. Paediatr Respir Rev 4:2, 2003.

39. Dunn PM: Dr James Blundell (1790-1878) and neonatal resuscitation. Arch Dis Child 64:494, 1989.

40. European Resuscitation Council: Part 11: Neonatal resuscitation. Resuscitation 46:401, 2000.

41. Fellman V et al: Reperfusion injury as the mechanism of brain damage after perinatal asphyxia. Pediatr Res 41:599, 1997.

42. Field D et al: Efficiency of manual resuscitators at birth. Arch Dis Child 61:300, 1986.

43. Finer NN et al: Comparison of methods of bag and mask ventilation for neonatal resuscitation. Resuscitation 49:299, 2001.

44. Flagg PJ: The treatment of asphyxia in the newborn. JAMA 91:788, 1928.

45. Fleck A et al: Increased vascular permeability: A major cause of hypoalbuminaemia in disease and injury. Lancet 1:781, 1985.

46. Gandini D et al: Neonatal resuscitation with the laryngeal mask airway in normal and low birth weight infants. Anesth Analg 89:642, 1999.

47. Gittermann MK et al: Early nasal continuous positive airway pressure treatment reduces the need for intubation in very low birth weight infants. Eur J Pediatr 156:384, 1997.

48. Goetting MG et al: High-dose epinephrine improves outcome from pediatric cardiac arrest. Ann Emerg Med 20:22, 1991.

49. Gregory GA et al: Meconium aspiration in infants: A prospective study. J Pediatr 85:848, 1974.

50. Head H: On the regulation of respiration. J Physiol 10:1, 1889.

51. Henderson Y: The prevention and treatment of asphyxia in the newborn. JAMA 90:583, 1928.

52. Hernandez LA et al: Chest wall restriction limits high airway pressure-induced lung injury in young rabbits. J Appl Physiol 66:2364, 1989.

53. Hey E et al: Safe resuscitation at birth. Lancet 2:103, 1973.

54. Hird MF et al: Inflating pressures for effective resuscitation of preterm infants. Early Hum Dev 26:69, 1991.

55. Hoskyns EW et al: Endotracheal resuscitation of preterm infants at birth. Arch Dis Child 62:663, 1987.

56. Hoskyns EW et al: A simple method of face mask resuscitation at birth. Arch Dis Child 62:376, 1987.

57. Imanaka H et al: Ventilator-induced lung injury is associated with neutrophil infiltration, macrophage activation, and TGF-beta 1 mRNA upregulation in rat lungs. Anesth Analg 92:42, 2001.

58. Ingimarsson J: Lung trauma from five moderately large manual inflations immediately after surfactant instillation in newborn immature lambs. Pediatr Res 43:286A, 1998.

59. International Guidelines for Neonatal Resuscitation: An excerpt from the Guidelines 2000 for cardiopulmonary resuscitation and emergency cardiovascular care: International Consensus on Science. Pediatrics 106, e29, 2000. Available at: www.pediatrics.org/cgi/content/full/106/3/e29.

60. Jain L: Alveolar fluid clearance in developing lungs and its role in neonatal transition. Clin Perinatol 26:585, 1999.

61. Jankov RP et al: Antioxidants as therapy in the newborn: Some words of caution. Pediatr Res 50:681, 2001.

62. Kamata H et al: Redox regulation of cellular signalling. Cell Signal 11:1, 1999.

63. Karlberg P et al: Respiratory studies in newborn infants: III. Development of mechanics of breathing during the

first week of life. A longitudinal study. Acta Paediatr Suppl 135:121, 1962.

64. Kattwinkel J et al: Resuscitation of the newly born infant: An advisory statement from the Pediatric Working Group of the International Liaison Committee on Resuscitation. Resuscitation 40:71, 1999.

65. Klerk AD et al: Nasal continuous positive airway pressure and outcomes of preterm infants. J Paediatr Child Health 37:161, 2001.

66. Krisher J et al: Comparison of pre-hospital conventional and simultaneous compression-ventilation cardiopulmonary resuscitation. Crit Care Med 17:1263, 1989.

67. Lawson EE et al: Augmentation of pulmonary surfactant secretion by lung expansion at birth. Pediatr Res 13:611, 1979.

68. Li C et al: Reactive species mechanisms of cellular hypoxia-reoxygenation injury. Am J Physiol 282:C227, 2002.

69. Lindemann R: Resuscitation of the newborn: Endotracheal administration of epinephrine. Acta Paediatr Scand 73:210, 1984.

70. Linder N et al: Need for endotracheal intubation and suction in meconium-stained neonates. J Pediatr 112:613, 1988.

71. Lindner W et al: Delivery room management of extremely low birth weight infants: Spontaneous breathing or intubation? Pediatrics 103:961, 1999.

72. Lucas VW Jr et al: Epinephrine absorption following endotracheal administration: Effects of hypoxia-induced low pulmonary blood flow. Resuscitation 27:31, 1994.

73. Lundstrom KE: Initial treatment of preterm infants: Continuous positive airway pressure or ventilation? Eur J Pediatr 155(Suppl 2):S25, 1996.

74. Meschia G: Placental respiratory gas exchange and fetal oxygenation. In Creasy RK (ed): Maternal-Fetal Medicine: Principles and Practice. Philadelphia, WB Saunders, 1989, p 303.

75. Miller DL et al: Body temperature in the immediate neonatal period: The effect of reducing thermal losses. Am J Obstet Gynecol 94:964, 1966.

76. Milner AD et al: Pressure and volume changes during the first breath of human neonates. Arch Dis Child 52:918, 1977.

77. Milner AD et al: Lung expansion at birth. J Pediatr 101:879, 1982.

78. Morin C et al: Response of the fetal circulation to stress. In Polin RA (ed): Fetal and Neonatal Physiology. Philadelphia, WB Saunders, 1992, p 620.

79. Neonatal resuscitation. In American Heart Association: Standards and guidelines for cardiopulmonary resuscitation and emergency care. JAMA 255:2969, 1986.

80. Neonatal Resuscitation Steering Committee, American Heart Association/American Academy of Pediatrics: Why change the compression and ventilation rates during CPR in neonates? Pediatrics 93:1026, 1994.

81. Nicolaides KH et al: Ultrasound-guided sampling of umbilical cord and placental blood to assess fetal wellbeing. Lancet 1:1065, 1986.

82. Niermeyer S et al: International Guidelines for Neonatal Resuscitation: An excerpt from the Guidelines 2000 for Cardiopulmonary Resuscitation and Emergency Cardiovascular Care: International Consensus on Science. Contributors and Reviewers for the Neonatal Resuscitation Guidelines. Pediatrics 106:E29, 2000.

83. Orlowski JP et al: Endotracheal epinephrine is unreliable. Resuscitation 19:103, 1990.

84. Palme-Kilander C: Methods of resuscitation in low-Apgar-score newborn infants: A national survey. Acta Paediatr 81:739, 1992.

85. Papile LA et al: Relationship of intravenous sodium bicarbonate infusions and cerebral intraventricular hemorrhage. J Pediatr 93:834, 1978.

86. Paradis NA et al: The effect of standard- and high-dose epinephrine on coronary perfusion pressure during prolonged cardiopulmonary resuscitation. JAMA 265:1139, 1991.

87. Paterson SJ et al: Neonatal resuscitation using the laryngeal mask airway. Anesthesiology 80:1248, 1994, discussion 27A.

88. Patrick J et al: Patterns of human fetal breathing during the last 10 weeks of pregnancy. Obstet Gynecol 56:24, 1980.

89. Perlman JM et al: Cardiopulmonary resuscitation in the delivery room: Associated clinical events. Arch Pediatr Adolesc Med 149:20, 1995.

90. Perondi MB et al: A comparison of high-dose and standard-dose epinephrine in children with cardiac arrest. N Engl J Med 350:1722, 2004.

91. Poets CF et al: Changes in intubation rates and outcome of very low birth weight infants: A population-based study. Pediatrics 98:24, 1996.

92. Press S et al: Cesarean delivery of full-term infants: Identification of those at high risk for requiring resuscitation. J Pediatr 106:477, 1985.

93. Quinton DN et al: Comparison of endotracheal and peripheral intravenous adrenaline in cardiac arrest: Is the endotracheal route reliable? Lancet 1:828, 1987.

94. Ramji S et al: Resuscitation of asphyxic newborn infants with room air or 100% oxygen. Pediatr Res 34:809, 1993.

95. Ramji S et al: Resuscitation of asphyxiated newborns with room air or 100% oxygen at birth: A multicentric clinical trial. Indian Pediatr 40:510, 2003.

96. Rudikoff M: Mechanisms of blood flow during cardiopulmonary "thoracic pump supported" resuscitation. Circulation 61:345, 1980.

97. Rudolph A: Fetal cardiovascular response to stress. In Wiknjosastro WH (ed): Perinatology. New York, Elsevier Science, 1988.

98. Rudolph AM et al: Response of the pulmonary vasculature to hypoxia and H^+ ion concentration changes. J Clin Invest 45:399, 1966.

99. Saugstad OD: Oxygen toxicity at birth: The pieces are put together. Pediatr Res 54:789, 2003.

100. Saugstad OD: Resuscitation of newborn infants: Do we need guidelines? Prenat Neonat Med 1:26, 1996.

101. Saugstad OD: Resuscitation with room-air or oxygen supplementation. Clin Perinatol 25:741, xi, 1998.

102. Saugstad OD et al: Resuscitation of newborn infants with 21% or 100% oxygen: Follow-up at 18 to 24 months. Pediatrics 112:296, 2003.

103. Saugstad OD et al: Resuscitation of asphyxiated newborn infants with room air or oxygen: An international controlled trial: The Resair 2 study. Pediatrics 102:e1, 1998.

104. Saunders RA et al: Pulmonary pressure/volume relationships during the last phase of delivery and the first postnatal breaths in human subjects. J Pediatr 93:667, 1978.

105. Sun S et al: Alpha-methylnorepinephrine, a selective alpha$_2$-adrenergic agonist for cardiac resuscitation. J Am Coll Cardiol 37:951, 2001.

106. Swenson RD et al: Hemodynamics in humans during conventional and experimental methods of cardiopulmonary resuscitation. Circulation 78:630, 1988.

107. Tang W et al: Epinephrine increases the severity of postresuscitation myocardial dysfunction. Circulation 92:3089, 1995.

108. Tarnow-Mordi WO: Room air or oxygen for asphyxiated babies? Lancet 352:341, 1998.

109. Teitel DF: Circulatory adjustments to postnatal life. Semin Perinatol 12:96, 1988.

110. Teitel DF: Physiologic development of the cardiovascular system in the fetus. In Polin RA (ed): Fetal and Neonatal Physiology. Philadelphia, WB Saunders, 1992, p 615.

111. Ting P et al: Tracheal suction in meconium aspiration. Am J Obstet Gynecol 122:767, 1975.

112. Todres ID et al: Methods of external cardiac massage in the newborn infant. J Pediatr 86:781, 1975.

113. Tyson JE: Immediate care of the newborn infant. In Sinclair JC, Bracken MB (eds): Effective Care of the Newborn Infant. Oxford, Oxford University Press, New York, Tokyo, 1992, p 32.

114. Upton CJ et al: Endotracheal resuscitation of neonates using a rebreathing bag. Arch Dis Child 66(1 Spec No): 39, 1991.

115. Vento M et al: Resuscitation with room air instead of 100% oxygen prevents oxidative stress in moderately asphyxiated term neonates. Pediatrics 107:642, 2001.

116. Vento M et al: Six years of experience with the use of room air for the resuscitation of asphyxiated newly born term infants. Biol Neonate 79:261, 2001.

117. Vento M et al: Hyperoxemia caused by resuscitation with pure oxygen may alter intracellular redox status by increasing oxidized glutathione in asphyxiated newly born infants. Semin Perinatol 26:406, 2002.

118. Vento M et al: Oxidative stress in asphyxiated term infants resuscitated with 100% oxygen. J Pediatr 142:240, 2003.

119. Vyas H et al: Determinants of the first inspiratory volume and functional residual capacity at birth. Pediatr Pulmonol 2:189, 1986.

120. Vyas H et al: Face mask resuscitation: Does it lead to gastric distension? Arch Dis Child 58:373, 1983.

121. Vyas H et al: Physiologic responses to prolonged and slow-rise inflation in the resuscitation of the asphyxiated newborn infant. J Pediatr 99:635, 1981.

122. Vyas H et al: Intrathoracic pressure and volume changes during the spontaneous onset of respiration in babies born by cesarean section and by vaginal delivery. J Pediatr 99:787, 1981.

123. Wada K et al: Tidal volume effects on surfactant treatment responses with the initiation of ventilation in preterm lambs. J Appl Physiol 83:1054, 1997.

124. Wiswell TE et al: Delivery room management of the apparently vigorous meconium-stained neonate: Results of the multicenter, international collaborative trial. Pediatrics 105:1, 2000.

125. Wiswell TE et al: Intratracheal suctioning, systemic infection, and the meconium aspiration syndrome. Pediatrics 89:203, 1992.

26 Physical Examination of the Newborn

Tom Lissauer

Immediately after a baby is born, all parents want to know "Is my baby all right?" A quick initial physical examination of all newborns should be performed in the delivery room to check that there are no major anomalies or birth injuries, that the newborn's tongue and body appear pink, and that breathing is normal. The whole of the newborn's body must be checked. This usually allows the clinician to reassure the parents that their infant looks well and appears normal.

Many serious congenital anomalies will have been identified prenatally, their presence anticipated, and a management plan made before delivery. If the newborn is sufficiently preterm or small for gestational age, has a significant problem diagnosed prenatally, or is unwell (e.g., with respiratory distress), the newborn must be admitted to an intermediate or intensive care nursery in accordance with hospital guidelines. If the mother had polyhydramnios, a feeding tube should be passed into the infant's stomach to exclude esophageal atresia. When the infant is born, the parents will have been informed if it is a boy or girl. If there is any doubt about the infant's gender, it is important not to guess but to inform the parents that further evaluation is required before a definite decision is made.

During the first few hours after birth, healthy newborns are usually alert and reactive and will suck at the breast. This behavior provides an initial opportunity for the mother to form a close attachment with her infant and to establish breast feeding. Medical interference during this time should be kept to a minimum.

ROUTINE EXAMINATION

Every newborn infant should have a "routine examination of the newborn."[2,22] This is a detailed examination performed by an experienced health care provider within 24 hours of birth. The objectives of the examination are listed in Box 26-1. Before approaching the mother and infant, the mother's and infant's medical and nursing records should be checked. Relevant items are listed in Box 26-2.

Introduction to the Mother

The health care provider should introduce himself or herself to the mother or preferably to both parents and explain the purpose of the examination. It is usually best at this stage to inquire if there are any problems

BOX 26-1. Objectives of Routine Examination of the Newborn

Detect congenital abnormalities not already identified at birth (e.g., congenital heart disease and developmental dysplasia of the hip).

Determine if any of the wide range of nonacute neonatal problems are present and initiate their management or reassure the parents.

Check for potential problems arising from maternal disease, familial disorders, or problems detected during pregnancy.

Provide an opportunity for the parents to discuss any questions about their infant.

Initiate health promotion for the newborn.

BOX 26-2. Mother's and Infant's Records

Items of particular relevance in the mother's and infant's medical and nursing records are

- Maternal age, occupation, and social background
- Family history
- History of maternal drug or alcohol abuse
- Details of previous pregnancies and any medical problems experienced by those children
- History of maternal disease and drugs taken during pregnancy
- Results of pregnancy screening tests (e.g., blood tests including maternal syphilis and hepatitis B surface antigen, prenatal ultrasound scans)
- Results of special diagnostic procedures (e.g., amniocentesis, chorionic villus sampling)
- Problems during labor and delivery
- Infant's condition at birth and if resuscitation was required
- Any concerns about the infant from nursing staff or parents
- The infant's birthweight
- The gestational age and if there is any uncertainty about it
- The infant's gender

with feeding and if there are any other worries about the infant. Before starting the examination, the health care professional must wash hands and ensure that the newborn can be examined in a warm, private area with good lighting.

Order of the Examination

The exact sequence in which the newborn is examined is not important. What is important is that all aspects of the newborn are examined at some stage and that the whole of the infant is observed. If the newborn is quiet, one may well take the opportunity to listen to the heart and examine the eyes directly. It is convenient to make one's general observations of the newborn's appearance, posture, and movements while undressing him or her, to then conduct the examination from head to foot, to examine the hips, and finally to pick the newborn up and turn him or her over to examine the back (Fig. 26-1). A checklist is helpful to record the findings of the examination and to ensure that nothing has been omitted.

Measurements

The infant's birthweight, gender, and gestational age should be noted. The 10th to 90th percentile for weight at 40 weeks' gestation for a male infant is 2.9 to 4.2 kg (mean 3.6 kg), and for a female infant it is 2.8 to 4 kg (mean 3.5 kg) (see Appendix). The birthweight percentile can be ascertained from the growth chart. If the infant's gestational age is uncertain, it can be determined (±2 weeks' gestational age) using a standardized scoring scheme.

The head circumference should be measured at its maximum and plotted on a growth chart to identify microcephaly or macrocephaly and to serve as a reference for future measurements. However, the measurement can change markedly in the first few days because of molding of the head during delivery. The 10th to 90th percentile is 33 to 37 cm at 40 weeks.

The infant's length (48 to 53 cm at 40 weeks) is measured routinely in the United States but not in the United Kingdom. Because the hips and lower legs need to be held extended by an assistant, the length is rarely

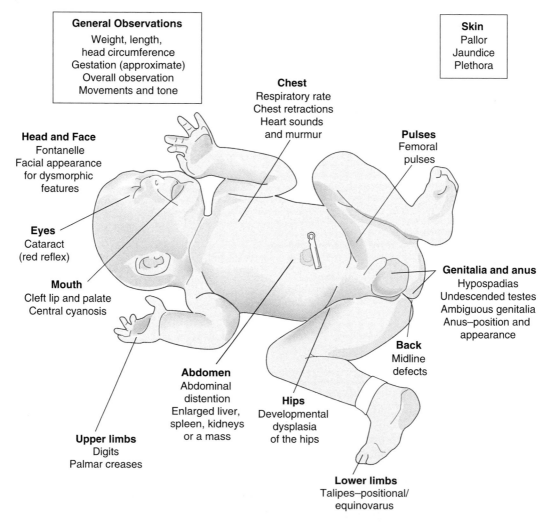

General Observations
Weight, length, head circumference
Gestation (approximate)
Overall observation
Movements and tone

Skin
Pallor
Jaundice
Plethora

Chest
Respiratory rate
Chest retractions
Heart sounds and murmur

Pulses
Femoral pulses

Head and Face
Fontanelle
Facial appearance for dysmorphic features

Eyes
Cataract (red reflex)

Mouth
Cleft lip and palate
Central cyanosis

Genitalia and anus
Hypospadias
Undescended testes
Ambiguous genitalia
Anus–position and appearance

Back
Midline defects

Abdomen
Abdominal distention
Enlarged liver, spleen, kidneys or a mass

Hips
Developmental dysplasia of the hips

Upper limbs
Digits
Palmar creases

Lower limbs
Talipes–positional/equinovarus

FIGURE 26-1. Main features of routine examination of the newborn.

measured accurately enough to identify short stature or serve as a reliable reference value when measured routinely.[22] The length of the arms and legs relative to that of the trunk is observed, although short limbs from skeletal dysplasias can be difficult to appreciate in the immediate newborn period.

General Observation of Appearance, Posture, and Movements

Much valuable information can be gleaned by simply observing the newborn. The skin of a newborn looks reddish pink. He or she may appear plethoric from polycythemia or unduly pale from anemia or shock. If polycythemia or anemia is suggested, the hemoglobin concentration or hematocrit should be checked. Jaundice within the first 24 hours of birth, unless mild, is most likely to be hemolytic and requires investigation and treatment.

Central cyanosis is best observed on the tongue. If present, it requires urgent investigation. If there is any doubt, the newborn's oxygen saturation should be checked with a pulse oximeter. Polycythemic infants sometimes appear cyanotic because they have more than 5 g of reduced hemoglobin per 100 mL of blood, even though they are adequately oxygenated.

The facial appearance is observed. If the face is abnormal, does the newborn have a syndrome? Observe the newborn's posture and tone. Is he or she moving all four limbs fully and are they held in a normal, flexed position?

Head

The fontanelle and sutures are palpated. The size of the anterior fontanelle is very variable. After delivery, the sagittal sutures are often separated and the coronal sutures are overriding. The posterior fontanelle is often open, but small. If the fontanelle is tense when the newborn is not crying, this may be from elevated intra-cranial pressure, and cranial ultrasonography should be performed. A tense fontanelle is also a late sign of meningitis.

Eyes

The eyes should be checked both by inspection and with an ophthalmoscope. The red reflex should be elicited using an ophthalmoscope. The red retinal reflex can be seen if the lens is clear but not if it is opaque from a congenital cataract or glaucoma. If the red reflex is abnormal, an ophthalmologist should be consulted urgently. Congenital cataract is the most common form of preventable childhood blindness.

Ears

The shape, size, and position of the ears are checked. Low-set ears are positioned so that the top of the pinna falls below a line drawn from the outer canthus of the eye at right angles to the face. Low-set or abnormal ears are a characteristic of a number of syndromes.

Palate

The palate must be inspected, including posteriorly, to exclude a posterior cleft palate. It should also be palpated to detect an indentation of the posterior palate from a submucous cleft or a posterior cleft palate.

Breathing

Breathing and chest wall movement are observed. The respiratory rate should be less than 60 breaths per minute without chest retraction, flaring of the alae nasi, or grunting. If the breathing is normal, it is very rare for any significant abnormalities to be detected on auscultation. If the infant has respiratory distress, further evaluation is required immediately.

Heart

The normal heart rate is 110 to 150 beats per minute in term infants but can drop to 85 beats per minute during sleep. The heart sounds should be loudest on the left side of the chest, and no murmurs should be present.

Abdomen

Observation readily reveals abdominal distention. For palpation, the infant must be relaxed. The abdomen is palpated to identify any masses. The liver is normally palpable 1 to 2 cm below the costal margin. The spleen tip and left kidney are often palpable.

Femoral Pulses

Femoral pulses are palpated when the infant is quiet. Their pulse pressure is reduced if there is coarctation of the aorta. If coarctation is suggested clinically, it can be confirmed by comparing the blood pressure in the arms and legs. The pulse pressure is increased with a patent ductus arteriosus.

Genitalia

In boys, the penis is checked for length and the position of the urethral orifice. The presence of testes in the scrotum is confirmed, especially if the scrotum is poorly developed. In girls, the clitoris and labia minora are prominent if the infant is preterm but are covered by the labia majora at full term. The position and appearance of the anus is also inspected. Passage of urine and meconium should be checked.

Extremities

The hands and arms and the feet and legs are examined to identify an abnormality, such as extra digits. Infants who were in an extended breech position in utero sometimes maintain this posture for some days after birth.

Hips

The hips are checked for developmental dysplasia of the hips (DDH). It is best left toward the end of the examination because the procedure is uncomfortable. To successfully perform this examination, the infant must lie supine on a flat, firm surface and be relaxed, because crying or kicking will result in tightening of the muscles around the hip.

The pelvis is stabilized with one hand. With the other hand the examiner's middle finger is placed over the greater trochanter and the thumb placed along the middle thigh. The Barlow test is performed to posteriorly dislocate an unstable hip that is lying in the joint (see Chapter 52, Part 3). The hip is flexed to 90 degrees and adducted, and the femoral head is gently pushed downward. If the hip can be dislocated, the femoral head will be pushed posteriorly out of the acetabulum and will move with a *clunk*.

Next, the hip is checked to see if it can be returned from a dislocated position back into the acetabulum (the Ortolani test) (see Chapter 52, Part 3). The hip is abducted and upward leverage is applied. A dislocated hip will return with a *clunk* into the acetabulum. This is best felt but can sometimes also be observed. Little force is required for these procedures; excessive force can damage the hip. During the test, clicks might be elicited but are not of long-term consequence. It should also be possible to abduct the hips fully, but limitation of abduction may be due to a dislocated hip. Other signs are asymmetry of the thigh or gluteal folds and apparent leg length shortening. Any newborn with developmental dysplasia of the hips should be checked for a neuromuscular disorder, and the spine should be examined to exclude spina bifida.

Back, Spine, and Muscle Tone

The newborn is picked up under the arms while supporting the head. A hypotonic newborn will feel as though he or she is slipping through one's hands. Most newborns support their weight with their feet. When an infant is turned prone, the infant can lift the head to the horizontal and straighten the back. Hypotonic newborns flop down like a rag doll. The whole of the back and spine are checked for midline and other defects and for any curvature of the spine.

A detailed neurologic examination is only required if an abnormality has been detected. Some pediatricians routinely perform a Moro reflex, when sudden head extension causes symmetric extension followed by flexion of all limbs. However, if normal movement of all four limbs has been observed, no further information will be elicited from this procedure. Because infants appear to find it unpleasant and parents are often alarmed and upset by it, the Moro reflex test is best omitted from the routine examination.

Most newborns are found to be normal on their routine examination. The parents should be strongly reassured that the examination was normal, and any concerns they have about their newborn should be answered fully.

CONDITIONS THAT RESOLVE SPONTANEOUSLY

A number of conditions that could be observed during the routine examination might alarm parents but resolve spontaneously.

Peripheral and Traumatic Cyanosis

Peripheral cyanosis confined to the hands and feet is common during the first day of life and is of no clinical significance.

Traumatic cyanosis is blue discoloration of the skin, often with petechiae. It can affect the presenting part in a face or breech presentation or of the head and neck if the umbilical cord was wrapped around the infant's neck. However, the tongue remains pink.

Bruising of the Head

The head can be markedly molded from having to squeeze through the birth canal. Newborns who have been in the breech position in utero often have a prominent occipital shelf. A *caput succedaneum* is bruising and edema of the presenting part of the head. It extends beyond the margins or of the skull bones. A *cephalhematoma* is caused by bleeding between the periosteum and the skull bone. It is confined within the margins of the skull sutures and usually affects the parietal bone. Bruising and abrasions after forceps deliveries, from scalp electrodes, or from fetal blood sampling are relatively common (see Chapter 27).

Swollen Eyelids

Swelling of the eyelids is common in newborns and resolves over the first few days of life. There may also be a mucoid discharge, often called a "sticky eye." When present on the first day of life, it usually resolves spontaneously. The eyelids can be cleansed with sterile water.

This must be contrasted with the erythematous, swollen eyelids with purulent eye discharge seen in conjunctivitis in the first day of life from gonococcal infection, which is extremely rare in developed countries. In the United States all infants are given eye drops as prophylaxis against gonococcal conjunctivitis.

Subconjunctival Hemorrhages

Subconjunctival hemorrhages are common. They occur during delivery and resolve in 1 to 2 weeks.

Dry, Peeling Skin

Dry skin is common, especially in post-term infants.

Capillary Hemangioma (Stork Bites)

Capillary hemangiomas are pink macules appearing on the upper eyelids, the mid forehead, and the nape of the neck from distention of dermal capillaries. Those on the eyelids and forehead fade over the first year, whereas those on the neck become covered with hair.

Neonatal Urticaria (Erythema Toxicum)

Neonatal urticaria is a common rash that usually starts on the second or third day of life. There are white pinpoint papules at the center of an erythematous base. Eosinophils are present on microscopy. The lesions migrate to different sites (see Chapter 50).

Milia

Benign white cysts may be present on the nose and cheeks from retention of keratin and sebaceous material in the pilaceous follicles.

Epstein Pearls and Cysts of the Gums

Small white pearls may be visible along the midline of the palate (Epstein pearls).

Cysts of the gums (epulis) and on the floor of the mouth (ranula) are mucus-retention cysts and do not need any treatment.

Harlequin Color Change

In harlequin color change, there is longitudinal reddening down one half of the body and a sharply demarcated blanching down the other side. This lasts for a few minutes. It is thought to be due to vasomotor instability.

Breast Enlargement

This can occur in newborns of either sex. A small amount of milk ("witch's milk") may be discharged.

Hydroceles

Hydroceles are relatively common in boys and usually resolve spontaneously.

Vaginal Discharge

There may be a white vaginal discharge or small amount of bleeding from maternal hormone withdrawal. There may also be prolapse of a ring of vaginal mucosa.

Mongolian Blue Spots

Mongolian blue spots are blue-black macular discolorations at the base of the spine or on the buttocks. They occasionally also occur on the legs and other parts of the body. They occur most often in African-American or Asian infants and fade slowly over the first few years of life. They are of no clinical significance but are occasionally misdiagnosed as bruises.

Umbilical Hernia

Umbilical hernias are common, especially in African-American infants. No treatment is indicated because they usually resolve within the first few years of life.

SIGNIFICANT ABNORMALITIES DETECTED ON ROUTINE EXAMINATION

The prevalence of the most common significant congenital abnormalities is shown in Table 26-1. Some of them will be detected prenatally, but many are first noted in the delivery room or during the routine examination of the newborn. These lesions are described briefly here but are considered in more detail elsewhere in the book.

Syndromes

Identification of abnormal facies and other abnormalities could lead one to suspect that the newborn has a syndrome. Down syndrome is by far the most common. The characteristic facies is often more difficult to recognize in the immediate neonatal period than in later life, but other abnormalities, such as the flat occiput, hypotonia, bilateral single palmar creases, and a pronounced sandal gap (an abnormal skin crease between the first two toes), are helpful additional signs. In practice, the parents usually need to be informed of the diagnosis before the results of the chromosome analysis are available.

TABLE 26-1. Prevalence of Serious Congenital Anomalies (Per 1000 Live Births)

ANOMALY	PREVALENCE
Congenital heart disease	6–8 (0.8 identified in the first day of life)
Developmental dysplasia of the hip	0.8 (about 7/1000 have an abnormal initial examination)
Talipes equinovarus	1.5
Down syndrome	1.5
Cleft lip and palate	0.8
Urogenital (hypospadias, undescended testes)	1.2
Spina bifida/anencephalopathy	0.5

Many hundreds of syndromes have been described. When the diagnosis is uncertain, a book or computer database should be consulted and advice sought from a pediatrician or clinical geneticist (see Chapter 28).

Port-Wine Stain (Nevus Flammeus)

Port-wine stains are caused by a vascular malformation of the capillaries in the dermis. They are usually present at birth. When these lesions are disfiguring, their appearance can be improved using laser therapy. Port-wine stains affecting the distribution of the trigeminal nerve may be associated with intracranial vascular anomalies (Sturge-Weber syndrome). Severe lesions on the limbs are associated with bone hypertrophy (Klippel-Trénaunay syndrome). Port-wine stains must be differentiated from strawberry nevi (cavernous hemangiomas), which are not present at birth but appear during the first month or two of life.

Brachial Plexus Lesions

Brachial plexus lesions cause lack of active movement of the affected limb; passive movement is not painful or restricted. The most common is Erb palsy from an upper root palsy (C5, C6, and sometimes C7). The arm is held internally rotated and pronated in the "waiter's tip" position. Although most brachial plexus injuries resolve, those that do not recover steadily over the first 2 months of life or that are severe should be seen by a specialist because surgical repair may be indicated. Accompanying respiratory symptoms may be secondary to damage of phrenic nerve roots (see Chapter 27).

Fracture of the Clavicle

Clavicle fractures most often occur during difficult delivery of the shoulders. A lump on the clavicle may be palpated or observed or identified because the infant keeps the arm immobile. It results from callus around a fracture and will heal without treatment.

Eye Abnormalities

On checking the eyes with an ophthalmoscope, the cornea may be opaque from a congenital cataract or enlarged and hazy from congenital glaucoma. A coloboma is a defect in the iris, resulting in a keyhole-shaped pupil. It may be associated with a defect in the retina. Newborns with these eye abnormalities should be referred immediately to an ophthalmologist.

Cleft Lip and Palate

If cleft lip and palate are recognized prenatally, the parents will be forewarned and counseled about the likely appearance and management. When diagnosed at birth, the parents will need to be reassured about the good cosmetic results after surgical repair. Before and after photographs of other children are often helpful. Assistance in establishing feeding may be required. The infant will need to be referred to a multidisciplinary craniofacial service.

Micrognathia

Micrognathia may be associated with glossoptosis and a posterior cleft palate (Pierre Robin syndrome) and may cause upper airway obstruction.

Neck Abnormalities

Redundant skin over the posterior neck, together with a flat occiput, are features of Down syndrome. A webbed neck is a feature of Turner syndrome, which may also be associated with lymphedema of the feet. A short webbed neck may indicate abnormalities of the cervical spine (Klippel-Feil syndrome). Cystic hygromas are soft, fluctuant swellings that transilluminate.

Ear Abnormalities

Malformations of the ear may be associated with hearing loss. Affected infants should have their hearing checked. Skin tags anterior to the ear and accessory auricles should be removed by a plastic surgeon. Accessory auricles are associated with an increased risk of renal anomalies.

Extra Digits

Extra digits are usually connected by a thin skin tag but can be completely attached containing bone. They should be removed by a plastic surgeon. If the digit is tied off with a silk thread, a stump of skin may remain. Polydactyly may be familial, but it can also be caused by a dysmorphic syndrome.

Heart Murmurs

Heart murmurs can be heard in about 0.6% of infants at the routine examination of the newborn.[1] Most are innocent and originate from the acute angle at the pulmonary artery bifurcation or are from a patent ductus arteriosus or tricuspid regurgitation.[5] The problem is to differentiate innocent murmurs from those caused by significant heart lesions. Clinical features may serve as a guide. Features of innocent and significant murmurs are given in Box 26-3. These clinical criteria can help residents,[17] general pediatricians[13,23] and pediatric cardiologists[37] to identify significant heart lesions.

The usefulness of electrocardiographs (ECGs) and chest radiographs in helping to distinguish innocent from significant murmurs is controversial. The neonatal ECG and chest radiograph are difficult to interpret, and these tests have been found to rarely change decisions based on the clinical examination.[37,39] Many centers have stopped performing them under these circumstances.

If a heart murmur is thought to be significant or cannot confidently be diagnosed as innocent, the infant should be referred for echocardiography directly. The management of infants with an innocent murmur

BOX 26-3. Features of a Heart Murmur in a Neonate

Features of an Innocent Murmur
- Soft (grade 1/6 or 2/6) murmur at left sternal edge
- No audible clicks
- Normal pulses
- Otherwise normal clinical examination

Features Suggesting a Murmur is Significant[29]
- Pansystolic
- Loud (≥ grade 3/6)
- Harsh quality
- Best heard in the upper left sternal edge
- Abnormal second heart sound
- Femoral pulses difficult to feel
- Other abnormality on clinical examination

depends on the availability of echocardiography. If echocardiography is readily available it can be performed directly and provides parents with a definitive diagnosis without delay. If echocardiography is not readily available, a follow-up examination should be arranged soon after discharge and the parents warned to seek medical assistance if their infant becomes symptomatic with poor feeding, labored breathing, or cyanosis.

Most innocent murmurs disappear in the first year of life, the majority in the first 3 months. However, any mention of a heart murmur can create considerable parental anxiety, which could continue for years. Attention must be paid to this to prevent parents from continuing to worry about their child's heart although the murmur has disappeared.[43]

Midline Abnormality Over the Spine or Skull

Spina bifida is often diagnosed prenatally. Affected infants must be referred to a neurosurgical service. A nevus, swelling, or tuft of hair along the spine or middle of the skull requires further evaluation because it might indicate an underlying abnormality of the vertebrae, spinal cord, or brain. Ultrasound or magnetic resonance imaging (MRI) delineates the anatomy. Sacrococcygeal pits are common and harmless, whereas a dermal sinus above the natal clefts should be investigated, because it might extend into the intraspinal space and place the infant at increased risk of meningitis.[19]

Single Umbilical Artery

Single umbilical artery occurs in about 0.3% of newborns. It is associated with an increased risk of chromosomal abnormalities and congenital malformations, particularly of the genitourinary system.[18,28] A single umbilical artery in an otherwise normal infant was associated with asymptomatic renal anomalies in 7% in one series.[8] The yield is low from ultrasound screening of the kidneys and urinary tract when this is an isolated finding,[40] and most renal abnormalities identified are transient or mild. The yield is further reduced by routine prenatal ultrasound screening for congenital anomalies. It is probably best reserved for those who also have other anomalies.

Enlarged Kidneys or Bladder

If palpation of the abdomen detects abnormally large renal masses or an enlarged bladder in a male infant, ultrasonography is required urgently to identify urinary outflow obstruction. Most cases of urinary outflow obstruction are now detected on prenatal ultrasound screening, as are other major abnormalities of the kidneys and urinary tract. Siblings of children with vesicoureteric reflux should be screened for this condition because up to 40% are also affected.[36]

Abnormalities of the Genitalia

In hypospadias the urethral meatus is in an abnormal position, usually on or adjacent to the glans penis but may be on the penile shaft or perineum. The foreskin is hooded, and chordee, causing ventral curvature of the shaft of the penis, may be present. Glanular hypospadias without chordee may not require any treatment, but more severe forms require corrective surgery, and a specialist's opinion should be sought and circumcision withheld.

If a testis is undescended, it should be rechecked at several months of age. If still undescended, referral to a pediatric surgeon or urologist is indicated. Neonatal *testicular torsion* usually occurs before birth. A pediatric surgeon should be consulted urgently, although the testis is rarely salvageable because it has usually already undergone infarction.

Talipes

Positional talipes is quite common and is caused by the position of the fetus in utero, especially if there was oligohydramnios. If the foot is held in the equinovarus position, it should be possible to fully abduct and dorsiflex the foot and ankle. If this maneuver can be performed, no treatment is required; if not, the infant is likely to have talipes equinovarus and must be referred directly to a pediatric orthopedic surgeon. Feet held in the calcaneus valgus position are usually holding the position of the feet in utero. It should be possible to dorsiflex the foot to bring its dorsal surface into contact with the anterior lower leg and to achieve normal plantar flexion. If this can be achieved, spontaneous resolution can be expected.

LIMITATIONS OF THE ROUTINE EXAMINATION

Examination of a newborn in the delivery room and at a routine examination will identify a number of problems, many of which are transient, though some are permanent and significant. However, some significant abnormalities will not be identified. Sometimes this is due to inexperience of the examiner or the difficulty of performing a satisfactory examination in an un-cooperative newborn (e.g., getting a good view of the eyes and red reflex, hearing a heart murmur, or testing for DDH). However, some significant abnormalities will not be identified because of the limitations of the examination itself.

Parents might become upset or angry when it becomes evident at a later stage that their child has a significant problem. They need to be made aware that not all abnormalities can be detected at this stage. This situation also stresses the importance of clear documentation of the routine examination for future reference. Some of the major limitations of the clinical examination are listed next.

Identification of Syndromes

Some syndromes can be difficult or impossible to identify in the immediate neonatal period but become apparent as the child grows older.

Jaundice

Jaundice usually develops after 24 hours of age, unless it is due to hemolysis. Significant jaundice can develop at several days of age even though the infant was apparently normal only 1 or 2 days earlier (see Chapter 46.)

Eye Abnormalities

Vision is better if surgery for congenital cataracts is performed before 8 weeks of age. However, in the United Kingdom only 35% of congenital cataracts are identified on the routine examination.[33] This demonstrates the difficulty in early recognition of eye abnormalities during the routine examination of the newborn. Deficiency in training of health care professionals[34] and the rarity of serious eye conditions, occurring in only 0.5 per 1000 live births, contributes to the low rate of diagnosis.

Congenital Heart Disease

Six to eight infants per 1000 live births have congenital heart disease. In a retrospective review of infants with congenital heart disease born between 1987 and 1994, 33% presented before the routine examination with symptoms or noncardiac abnormalities, 30% had an abnormal routine examination, and 37% had a normal routine examination.[42] At discharge from the hospital, a cardiac diagnosis or referral was made in 43% of infants with congenital heart disease, but a third of the remaining infants presented with symptoms or died from their cardiac condition by 6 weeks of age. This review highlights the limitations of the routine examination in identifying significant structural heart disease.

The first is that the newborn examination may be normal even when the infant has a significant or even lethal structural heart lesion. At the time of the newborn examination, the pressure in the right side of the heart is still relatively high and the ductus arteriosus may still be patent. Infants with a ventricular septal defect (the most common congenital heart lesion) or other heart lesions might not have a heart murmur at the routine examination because the pressure difference between the left and right sides of the heart will be insufficient to generate turbulent flow at this stage.

A second reason is that infants with ductus-dependent lesions can present clinically with heart failure, shock, cyanosis, or death just days or weeks after a normal routine examination. Their femoral pulses may be palpable at the initial examination because of blood flow through the ductus arteriosus.

An additional limitation is that a heart murmur may be heard but because most are innocent, those from significant heart lesions are not always identified. Prenatal diagnosis of some severe heart lesions and the increasing availability of echocardiography should reduce, but will not eliminate, failure to identify structural heart lesions before discharge from the hospital.

Developmental Dysplasia of the Hip

As a screening test, clinical examination for developmental dysplasia of the hip is problematic.[11] Ideally, all affected infants should be identified in the neonatal period, because early treatment prevents or reduces the need for surgery. In practice, a significant fraction of infants who subsequently require surgery are not identified in the neonatal period. A survey from the United Kingdom suggested that the operative rate, 0.7 per 1000 live births, has remained unchanged since screening was introduced.[21] A more recent study from South Australia found a lower operative rate, at 0.45 per 1000 births, but still only 56% of these infants were identified at the initial clinical examination.[10] However, developmental dysplasia of the hip was diagnosed in 7.7 per 1000 live births, indicating that the hips of most infants with an abnormal neonatal hip examination are normal.

An examiner might fail to identify developmental dysplasia of the hip at the initial examination because the examiner is inexperienced or because the examination is suboptimal when the infant is not relaxed. In some infants with a flat acetabular shelf, the clinical examination may be normal in the neonatal period but progresses with age.[35] Also, the irreducible dislocated hip is easily missed on examination.

The risk of DDH is increased in female infants, if there is a positive family history or breech presentation. The absolute risk of a positive result on routine examination of the newborn is shown in Table 26-2. The risk is also increased in infants with a neuromuscular disorder.

Two strategies can improve the detection rate of DDH in newborn infants. The hip examination can be performed by pediatric orthopedists, or imaging can be performed on the hips. Ultrasound will identify DDH, including a shallow acetabular shelf. However, ultrasound

TABLE 26-2. Absolute Risk for a Positive Result on Routine Examination of the Newborn Hip

NEWBORN CHARACTERISTICS	ABSOLUTE RISK OF A POSITIVE EXAMINATION PER 1000 NEWBORNS
Overall	
All newborns	11.5
Boys	4.1
Girls	19
Positive Family History	
Boys	6.4
Girls	32
Breech Presentation	
Boys	29
Girls	133

From American Academy of Pediatrics: Clinical practice guideline: Early detection of developmental dysplasia of the hip. Pediatrics 105:896, 2000.

has a high false positive rate, and it is only helpful in the first 5 months of life. Alternatively, a hip x-ray will identify DDH but only after 4 months of age. The imaging can be performed on all infants or only on high-risk infants or on those with a positive examination.

All these options have been considered in detail in the American Academy of Pediatrics guidelines on early detection of DDH.[3] They recommend that the clinical procedure be performed by a properly trained health care provider. Management of a positive or inconclusive test and of infants with a risk factor is summarized in Figure 26-2.

HEALTH PROMOTION

The routine examination is an opportunity to promote preventive health care.

Prevention of Sudden Infant Death Syndrome

All parents should be advised that infants should sleep on their backs and that overheating and parental smoking are risk factors. Attention to preventive measures has markedly reduced the incidence of sudden infant death syndrome (SIDS) in many countries.

Promotion of Breast Feeding

Mothers should be encouraged in and assisted with their breast feeding.

Hearing and Vision Screening

Children with increased risk of deafness (e.g., family history, malformations of the ear including skin tags and pits)[26] must be referred for early hearing testing. Universal hearing screening should be performed per hospital protocol. Similarly, infants at increased risk of vision loss should be referred to an ophthalmologist. The parents should be given advice about early detection of hearing and vision loss.

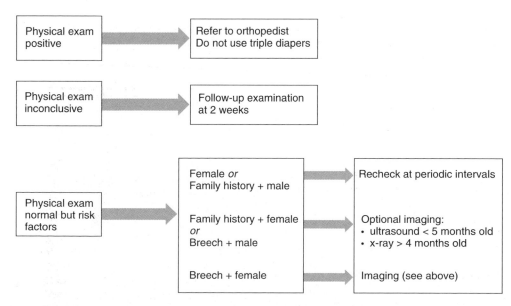

FIGURE 26-2. Management of newborn infants with physical examination that is positive for developmental dysplasia of hip, inconclusive or normal with risk factors. (Reproduced with permission from Pediatrics, Vol. 105, page 901, Copyright © 2000 by the AAP.)

Immunization

The routine examination is an opportunity to reinforce the importance of immunization.

Safe Transport

The newborn period is a good opportunity to provide advice on the need for car seats for infants.

REPEAT EXAMINATION

With shortened stay of healthy newborns in the hospital, performing a second full routine examination at discharge is of limited value in identifying additional abnormalities.[20,30] More important, the routine examination must be performed by a properly trained health care professional. For example, advanced neonatal nurse practitioners were found to be more effective than trainee pediatricians in detecting abnormalities.[27]

Criteria that must be met for the early (<48 hours) discharge of term infants have been published.[12] Before any infant is discharged, the health care provider should check that the infant has fed satisfactorily on at least 2 successive occasions, is not significantly jaundiced (or has been measured and a follow-up plan is in place), is breathing normally, and has urinated and passed stool. The clinician must also ensure that the mother is able to care adequately for her infant and that the infant is going to a suitable environment. The initial hepatitis B vaccine should have been given as indicated by the infant's risk status. Follow-up care for the infant should also be in place.

ASSESSMENT OF GESTATIONAL AGE

Formal assessment of gestational age is unnecessary for the routine newborn examination. The best guide to an infant's gestational age is an early antenatal ultrasound evaluation combined with information about the mother's last menstrual period. An evaluation of the clinical methods of assessing gestational age showed that clinical methods had 95% confidence intervals of 17 days, whereas the antenatal ultrasound had 95% confidence intervals of less than 7 days.[41] Clinical testing is most important for infants whose gestational age is unknown or discrepant with their growth.

Four methods can be employed to assess gestational age: physical criteria,[16,31] neurologic examination,[4] combined physical and neurologic examination,[6,14] and examination of the lens of the eye.[24] Physical criteria are used to establish gestational age as they progress in an orderly fashion with increasing gestation. The assessment of gestational age using neurologic criteria involves the assessment of posture, passive and active tone, reflexes, and righting reaction.[4]

Although the physical criteria can be used to establish gestational age immediately after delivery, the neurologic criteria require the infant to be in an alert, rested state, which might not occur until the second day of life. Infants who are asphyxiated at the time of delivery, who have a primary neurologic disorder, or who are affected by maternal medication cannot be assessed using neurologic criteria until they have recovered.

Gestational age can be assessed most accurately by combining the physical criteria and the neurologic assessment. Dubowitz and Dubowitz described and developed such a combined scoring system.[15] Its disadvantage is that it involves assessing 11 physical criteria and 10 neurologic findings. Although the physical criteria allow clear distinction of infants with gestational ages older than 34 weeks, neurologic criteria are essential to differentiate infants between 26 and 34 weeks because the physical changes are less evident. Ballard and her colleagues abbreviated the Dubowitz scoring system to include six neurologic and six physical criteria to shorten the time taken. The revised Ballard examination (Fig. 26-3) includes assessment for extremely premature infants.[7] Regardless of the method used, the assessment of gestational age using physical and neurologic criteria is accurate only to ±2 weeks, with a tendency toward overestimation in extremely premature infants.

NEUROLOGIC ASSESSMENT

A detailed neurological assessment is performed in infants with a neurological problem. The infant's neurologic evaluation combines elements of the standard neurologic examination and a developmental assessment of gestational age (Box 26-4). With experience, the examiner can accom-plish the evaluation with minimal or no discomfort to the infant, an important goal especially in fragile premature infants.

Level of Consciousness

Newborn infants' states of alertness at term are usually categorized[32] as:

State 1 (deep or quiet sleep): eyes closed, regular respiration, no movements

State 2 (light or rapid eye movement sleep): eyes closed, irregular respiration, no gross movements

State 3 (awake, drowsy): eyes open, no gross movements

BOX 26-4. Neurologic Evaluation

General appearance
Level of consciousness
Mechanical signs: head spine, extremities
Cranial nerves
Motor: strength, tone, movements
Deep tendon reflexes
Primitive reflexes: Moro, grasp, suck, root
Autonomic: heart rate pattern, respiratory pattern, bladder function, bowel function

NEUROMUSCULAR MATURITY

	−1	0	1	2	3	4	5
Posture							
Square window (wrist)	>90°	90°	60°	45°	30°	0°	
Arm recoil		180°	140°–180°	110°–140°	90°–110°	<90°	
Popliteal angle	180°	160°	140°	120°	100°	90°	<90°
Scarf sign							
Heel to ear							

PHYSICAL MATURITY

Skin	Sticky friable transparent	Gelatinous red, translucent	Smooth pink, visible veins	Superficial peeling and/or rash, few veins	Cracking pale areas rare veins	Parchment deep cracking no vessels	Leathery cracked wrinkled
Lanugo	None	Sparse	Abundant	Thinning	Bald areas	Mostly bald	
Plantar surface	Heel–toe 40–50 mm:−1 <40 mm:−2	>50 mm no crease	Faint red marks	Anterior transverse crease only	Creases ant. 2/3	Creases over entire sole	
Breast	Imperceptible	Barely perceptible	Flat areola no bud	Stippled areola 1–2 mm bud	Raised areola 3–4 mm bud	Full areola 5–10 mm bud	
Eye/ear	Lids fused loosely: −1 tightly: −2	Lids open pinna flat stays folded	Sl. curved pinna; soft; slow recoil	Well-curved pinna; soft but ready recoil	Formed and firm instant recoil	Thick cartilage ear stiff	
Genitals male	Scrotum flat, smooth	Scrotum empty faint rugae	Testes in upper canal rare rugae	Testes descending few rugae	Testes down good rugae	Testes pendulous deep rugae	
Genitals female	Clitoris prominent labia flat	Prominent clitoris small labia minora	Prominent clitoris enlarging minora	Majora and minora equally prominent	Majora large minora small	Majora cover clitoris and minora	

Maturity Rating

Score	Weeks
−10	20
−5	22
0	24
5	26
10	28
15	30
20	32
25	34
30	36
35	38
40	40
45	42
50	44

FIGURE 26-3. Assessment of gestational age using the revised Ballard method. (From Ballard JL et al: New Ballard Score, expanded to include extremely premature infants. J Pediatr 119:417, 1991.)

State 4 (alert): eyes open, gross movements, no crying

State 5 (crying): eyes open or closed, crying

For optimal neurological examination, a term infant should be alert and not crying (state 3). An infant who is persistently in state 1 and 2 is likely to be abnormally lethargic; if persistently in state 5, abnormally hyperexcitable. The cry may also be abnormal, e.g., high pitched from cerebral irritation, incessant from drug withdrawal.

Inspection

The physical component of the neurologic examination includes visualization and palpation of the head, spine, and extremities. The entire body is observed for visibly apparent congenital anomalies, birthmarks, or bruises. The head and spine are palpated to ascertain the presence of deformities, the position of the sutures, and the size and shape of the fontanelles. The presence of excessive head molding (caput) or cephalohematoma is determined.

The size and shape of the head provide important information regarding the occurrence of a remote or chronic insult to the fetal brain. When fetal brain growth has been compromised, head size is decreased relative to body length, and sutures might overlap. In contrast, a large head with split sutures denotes an underlying large brain, usually the consequence of congenital obstructive hydrocephalus. Postnatally, a rapidly expanding head with split sutures indicates cerebral edema, epidural or subdural hemorrhage, or acquired, progressive hydrocephalus, which may result from intraventricular hemorrhage in a premature infant.

Cranial Nerves

Despite the relative lack of interaction between the examiner and infant, the functions of essentially all of the 12 cranial nerves can be determined in the newborn infant (Table 26-3). Indeed, cranial nerve evaluations can be conducted even in premature infants near the lower limit of viability.

Cranial nerve I (olfactory) is typically not examined, given its rare involvement by a disease process and the infant's difficulty to provide an appropriate response.

Vision (cranial nerve II [optic]) is assessed both subjectively and object. Healthy full-term and older premature infants fixate on and track the examiner's face or a brightly colored (e.g., red) object presented within a foot of his or her visual field. Horizontal eye movements are more easily elicited than are vertical eye movements. Visual orientation and tracking are considered cerebral cortical functions.

The pupillary light reflex also assesses optic nerve integrity but is a subcortical function and requires an intact efferent limb, specifically the autonomic component of cranial nerve III (oculomotor). Those nerves that subserve extraocular movements include cranial nerves III, IV, and VI (oculomotor, trochlear, and abducens, respectively).

Eye movements in all directions of gaze occur spontaneously or can be induced with oculocephalic maneuvers (doll's eye reflex). The doll's eye reflex is typically elicited with the infant in the supine position by simply turning the head from one side to the other, whereupon the eyes will deviate in the opposite direction. Vertical eye movements can be ascertained by flexing or extending the head. Alternatively, the infant can be removed from the crib, suspended in the vertical plane, and rotated clockwise or counterclockwise. The eyes will deviate in the direction opposite the spin. Rotation in the axial plane induces vertical eye movements.

The eyes are observed for the presence or absence of ptosis. Unilateral or bilateral ptosis occurs as a consequence of dysfunction either of cranial nerve III, which innervates the palpebral muscle (upper eyelid only), or

TABLE 26-3. Cranial Nerve Examination

NERVE	NAME	FUNCTION	EVALUATION METHOD
I	Olfactory (and track)	Smell	Not tested
II	Optic (and retina)	Visual acuity and fields	Facies or colored object
III	Oculomotor	Extraocular movements; pupillary response, lid elevation	Observation of tracking; doll's eye reflex
IV	Trochlear	Extraocular movements	Observation of tracking; doll's eye reflex
V	Trigeminal	Mastication; facial sensation	Corneal and suck reflexes; nasal stimulation
VI	Abducens	Extraocular movements	Observation of tracking; doll's eye reflex
VII	Facial	Facial expression; taste	Nasal stimulation; corneal and sucking reflexes
VIII	Auditory	Hearing; spatial orientation	Sounds and behavioral response; doll's eye reflex
IX	Glossopharyngeal	Swallowing, vocalization	Sucking and swallowing reflex; gag reflex; quality of cry
X	Vagus	Swallowing, vocalization	Sucking and swallowing reflex; gag reflex; quality of cry
XI	Spinal accessory	Head and shoulder movement	Observation
XII	Hypoglossal	Tongue movement	Observation; atrophy; fasciculations

of ascending sympathetic nerves, which course through the neck to innervate the tarsal plates (both eyelids). Oculomotor nerve dysfunction producing ptosis is often associated with ipsilateral pupil dilation, whereas sympathetic nerve dysfunction producing ptosis is associated with ipsilateral pupil constriction (Horner syndrome).

Cranial nerve V (trigeminal) has both sensory and motor functions. Corneal and facial sensations can be tested if indicated with a wisp of cotton applied to each cornea to elicit a rapid blink or to the nares to elicit a facial grimace. The motor component of cranial nerve V subserves jaw (mandibular) opening and closure, which are best tested by observing the infant's sucking ability. A persistently open mandible suggests trigeminal motor paralysis.

Cranial nerve VII (facial) controls all superficial facial movements, including eyelid closure, and taste, which is rarely tested. Facial movements occur spontaneously and are a component of the sucking and rooting reflexes. Tickling the nares with a wisp of cotton should induce facial grimacing, whereupon either unilateral or bilateral facial paresis will become apparent.

Cranial nerve VIII subserves both hearing (auditory) and vestibular functions (see Chapter 40). Hearing is tested either subjectively or objectively, the latter by eliciting the brainstem auditory evoked response. Subjective testing at cribside is typically accomplished with the use of a bell presented to either ear, observing for increased alertness and possibly an orienting response. Initially, the sound of the bell should be of low intensity, increasing in loudness until a response is obtained. The vestibular component of cranial nerve VIII is not specifically tested other than through its interaction with brainstem pathways, which subserve reflex eye movements.

The functions of cranial nerves IX and X (glossopharyngeal and vagus, respectively) are combined to control swallowing function and vocalization. Voluntary motor functions are tested by observing the infant's sucking and swallowing abilities. In addition, the position and movement of the soft palate are observed with the aid of a tongue depressor and flashlight. The gag reflex is then tested with a tongue depressor. During the oral evaluation, cranial nerve XII (hypoglossal) function is tested by examining the tongue, noting its position, movement, and bulk. The presence of tongue fasciculations is noted, which consist of random, wormlike movements best appreciated along the lateral tongue margins and may be observed in spinal muscular atrophy. Atrophy of the tongue is observed as scalloping of its margins. Tongue fasciculations must be distinguished from tremors, the latter consisting of rhythmic movements of the structure accentuated by its protrusion during crying and are normal.

Cranial nerve XI (spinal accessory) is a pure motor nerve. It innervates the sternocleidomastoid muscle of the neck to produce either lateral or anterior flexion of the head, depending on contraction of one or both muscles. The nerve also innervates the trapezius muscle of the shoulder to produce shoulder elevation. These

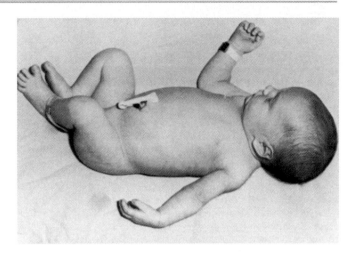

FIGURE 26-4. Full-term newborn at rest. Note that the posture of the arms and legs is slightly asymmetric. The arms are partially flexed, whereas the legs are flexed at the hips and knees.

functions typically are tested by simple observation of head and shoulder movements.

Motor Function

The motor system examination includes tests of skeletal muscle posture, tone, and movement. During the initial period of general observation, the position of the extremities is noted for flexion, extension, or neutral postures. Healthy, full-term infants typically exhibit flexion of the arms at the elbows and of the legs at the knees (Fig. 26-4). Fisting of the hands, including adduction and in-folding of the thumbs (cortical thumbs), is usual with intermittent hand opening.

Limb position and posturing are relatively symmetric, although the infant manifests spontaneous movements that are often asymmetric and jerky. Limb posture (flexion or extension) also is influenced by the position of the head. If the head is turned to one side, there is often extension of the ipsilateral arm and leg and flexion of the contralateral extremities (asymmetric tonic neck reflex). While prone, the full-term infant maintains a flexed posture of the arms and legs, with resultant elevation of the pelvis as well as hip and knee flexion.[38]

Tone is characteristic of skeletal muscle because of an intrinsic resistance to stretch that can be either active or passive. Muscle at rest resides in a state of partial relaxation, and energy is required for its full contraction. Elongation requires further muscle relaxation and concurrent contraction of the opposing or antagonistic muscle. Thus, normal muscle tone depends on a sophisticated interaction between agonistic and antagonistic muscles, which are influenced by innervating peripheral nerves (sensory and motor) as well as by the CNS. Given the strategic role played by skeletal muscle in neurologic function, it should not be surprising that alterations in muscle tone represent the clinical hallmark of a variety of neurologic disease processes.

The assessment of muscle tone includes observation of the infant's posture and movement as well as the production of an active or passive range of motion. If feasible, the infant should be suspended in the horizontal plane and the attitude and posture of the head, trunk, and extremities observed. Thereafter, the infant is held in the vertical plane to ascertain the extent and symmetry of flexor tone of the extremities. While the infant lies supine, the upper and lower extremities are extended and flexed to ascertain the presence and extent of resistance. Head control can be determined by lifting the supine infant from the surface by either the shoulders or hands.

Increased resistance to passive movement indicates hypertonicity (rigidity, spasticity), whereas reduced resistance and unrestricted movement indicate hypotonicity. In this regard, the neurologic component of the Dubowitz and Ballard scoring systems for determining gestational age largely reflects the maturation of muscle tone in premature infants. Infants who are hypertonic often exhibit an opisthotonic posture in conjunction with obligate extension when suspended in either the vertical or horizontal plane. Scissoring of the legs might be evident. In contrast, the hypotonic infant, when held in the vertical plane, tends to slide through the examiner's hands. In the horizontal plane, the infant drapes over the examiner's arms.[38]

Hypotonia should not be equated with weakness, which is a reduction in muscle strength or power, whether it is partial (paresis) or complete paralysis (paraplegia). Muscle weakness is ascertained through observation of spontaneous or sensation-induced movements of the extremities. Although muscle hypotonia and weakness often occur together, hypotonia can be seen in the absence of weakness (e.g., cerebellar dysfunction), and weakness can occur when muscle tone is normal or even increased (e.g., spastic paralysis). Indeed, hypotonia combined with weakness typically denotes an intrinsic disease of the peripheral nervous system (nerve or muscle), whereas hypotonia with a preservation of muscle strength denotes a disturbance of the brain or spinal cord.

Deep Tendon Reflexes

Deep tendon reflexes are elicited as they are for older children and adults. The limb should be positioned in partial flexion and the appropriate tendon tapped with an infant reflex hammer. The head should be maintained in the neutral position to prevent inducing an asymmetric tonic neck response, which produces asymmetric reflex activity. Typically, upper extremity deep tendon reflexes are more difficult to elicit than lower extremity reflexes. In newborn infants, the Achilles tendon is not tapped directly; the reflex is elicited by tapping a thumb positioned on the plantar surface of the partially dorsiflexed foot.

Interpretation of the results of testing deep tendon reflexes is more problematic in neonates than older children but may help to confirm an asymmetric lesion. Ankle clonus is common and usually normal in the

neonatal period. Eliciting plantar responses is not worthwhile as their interpretation is problematic.[25,38] At this age the plantar response is usually extensor.

Developmental Reflexes

The most frequently elicited primitive or developmental reflexes include the rooting, sucking, grasp, and Moro responses. These reflexes are fully developed and strong in the healthy, full-term newborn and typically disappear in the months to follow. Their persistence beyond the anticipated age of disappearance is an indicator of underlying CNS dysfunction. Other, less commonly induced primitive reflexes include the crossed extension, placing, and stepping reactions, all of which make their appearance by 36 to 38 weeks' gestational age.

Cerebral Cortical Function

Although newborn infants previously were believed to function predominantly or exclusively at a brainstem level, it has become increasingly apparent that neonates exhibit functions that involve activity of the cerebral cortex.[9] These functions include visual fixation and tracking as well as auditory alerting and localization. In addition, the phenomenon of habituation is considered a cerebral cortical function. Full-term newborns exhibit both visual and auditory habituation, which are elicited with a bright light and loud bell, respectively. The eyes are sequentially exposed to a bright light at a frequency of approximately 1 per second; the normal response is an initial strong blink followed by extinction after 3 to 5 exposures. A similar blink response occurs with repetitive auditory stimulations. Failure to respond initially to the sensory stimulation or a lack of habituation is an abnormal finding in an otherwise alert full-term newborn.

The Premature Infant

The neurologic signs in premature infants differ markedly with gestational age. In normal premature newborn infants, pupil responses to light are present, although sluggish, between 28 and 32 weeks' gestation and nonexistent before 28 weeks (see Table 26-2). Oculocephalic (doll's eye) reflexes are complete and even exaggerated in infants as immature as 24 to 25 weeks. Paradoxically, the oculovestibular (caloric) reflex is incomplete before 28 to 30 weeks, with reduced medial displacement of the eye contralateral to the ear canal stimulated with cold water (intranuclear ophthalmoplegia). Corneal and gag reflexes are present in even the small premature infant, as is facial grimacing to nasal stimulation.

The newborn's responsiveness to the environment depends not only on the state of health but also on the gestational age. Small premature infants of 25 to 30 weeks' gestation typically require intermittent arousal with external stimulation, and their waking periods are relatively short when compared with full-term infants. By 31 to 32 weeks' gestation, the premature infant

TABLE 26-4. Neurologic Maturation of the Fetus and Newborn

FUNCTION	26 WEEKS	30 WEEKS	34 WEEKS	38 WEEKS
Resting posture	Flexion of arms Flexion or extension of legs	Flexion of arms Flexion or extension of legs	Flexion of all limbs	Flexion of all limbs
Arousal	Unable to maintain	Maintain briefly	Remain awake	Remain awake
Rooting	Absent	Long latency	Present	Present
Sucking	Absent	Long latency	Weak	Vigorous
Pupillary reflex	Absent	Variable	Present	Present
Traction	No response	No response	Head lag	Mild head lag
Moro	No response	Extension; no adduction	Adduction variable	Complete
Withdrawal	Absent	Withdrawal only	Crossed extension	Crossed extension

From Fenichel GM: Neonatal Neurology, 2nd ed. New York, Churchill Livingstone, 1985.

exhibits reasonable alertness during wakeful stages. By term, the infant remains alert for prolonged periods during wakefulness and readily responds to visual, auditory, and tactile stimulation.

A notable difference in the neurologic status of the premature and full-term neonate is that of muscle tone. As indicated by the Dubowitz and Ballard scoring systems for gestational age, the more premature the infant is at birth, the greater the muscle hypotonicity is (see Fig. 26-4). The sucking and rooting reflexes do not develop until 33 to 36 weeks' gestational age. The hypotonicity is especially apparent when measuring the popliteal and heel-to-ear angles and when executing the scarf sign. The maturational changes in muscle tone must be taken into account when evaluating newborns of varying gestational ages.

At and before 28 weeks' gestational age, a premature newborn is extremely hypotonic. When held in vertical suspension, the infant does not extend the head, trunk, or extremities. The maturational change from hypotonia of the small premature infant to the predominantly flexion posture of the full-term infant is manifest first in the legs and later in the arms and head. By 34 gestational weeks, the infant lies in a froglike position while supine; the legs are flexed at the hips and knees, but the arms remain extended and relatively hypotonic.

Developmental reflexes appear at specific ages of gestation to become fully developed and strong in the healthy full-term infant (Table 26-4). The sucking and rooting reflexes do not develop until 33 to 36 weeks' gestational age. The palmar and plantar grasp responses become apparent at approximately 28 weeks and are strong by 36 weeks' gestation. The Moro reflex makes its appearance at 24 to 26 weeks' gestation and evolves through 38 weeks, at which age the entire abduction-adduction response is present.

ACKNOWLEDGMENTS

The author and editors acknowledge the contribution of Robert C. Vannucci and Jerome Y. Yager to previous editions of this chapter, portions of which remain unchanged.

REFERENCES

1. Ainsworth SB et al: Prevalence and significance of cardiac murmurs in neonates. Arch Dis Child 80:F43, 1999.
2. American Academy of Pediatrics, American College of Obstetricians and Gynecologists: Guidelines for Perinatal Care, 5th ed. Elk Grove Village, Ill, American Academy of Pediatrics, 2002.
3. American Academy of Pediatrics: Clinical practice guideline: Early detection of developmental dysplasia of the hip. Pediatrics 105:896, 2000.
4. Amiel-Tison C: Neurological evaluation of the maturity of newborn infants. Arch Dis Child 43:89, 1968.
5. Arlettaz R et al: Natural history of innocent heart murmurs in newborn babies: A controlled echocardiographic study. Arch Dis Child 78:F166, 1998.
6. Ballard JL et al: A simplified score for assessment of fetal maturation of newly born infants. J Pediatr 95:769, 1979.
7. Ballard JL et al: New Ballard Score, expanded to include extremely premature infants. J Pediatr 119:417, 1991.
8. Bourke WG et al: Isolated single umbilical artery—the case for screening. Arch Dis Child 68:600, 1993.
9. Brazelton TB: Neonatal Behavioral Assessment Scale. London, Spastics International Medical, 1973.
10. Chan A et al: Late diagnosis of congenital dislocation of the hip and the presence of a screening programme: South Australia population based study. Lancet 354:1514, 1999.
11. Clarke NMP: Diagnosing congenital dislocation of the hip. BMJ 305:435, 1992.
12. Committee on Fetus and Newborn: Policy statement: Hospital stay for healthy term newborns. Pediatrics 113:1434, 2004.
13. Du Z-D et al: Clinical and echocardiographic evaluation of neonates with heart murmurs. Acta Paediatr 86:752, 1997.
14. Dubowitz L et al: Clinical assessment of gestational age in the newborn infant. J Pediatr 77:1, 1970.
15. Dubowitz L, Dubowitz V: The Neurological Assessment of the Preterm and Full-term Newborn Infant. Clinics in Developmental Medicine, 2nd ed. London, WH Heinemann, 1999.
16. Farr V et al: The definition of some external characteristics used in the assessment of gestational age of the newborn infant. Dev Med Child Neurol 8:507, 1966.
17. Farrer KFM, Rennie JM: Neonatal murmurs: Are senior house officers good enough? Arch Dis Child 88:F147, 2003.

18. Froelich L et al: Follow up of infants with single umbilical artery. Pediatrics 52:6, 1973.

19. Gibson P et al: Lumbosacral skin markers and identification of occult spinal dysraphism in neonates. Acta Paediatr 84:208, 1995.

20. Glazener CMA et al: Neonatal examination and screening trial (NEST): A randomized, controlled, switchback trial of alternative policies for low risk infants. BMJ 318:627, 1999.

21. Godward S, Dezateux C: Surgery for congenital dislocation of the hip in the UK as a measure of outcome of screening. Lancet 351:1149, 1998.

22. Hall DMB, Elliman D: Health for All Children, 4th ed. Oxford, Oxford University Press, 2003.

23. Hansen LK et al: Initial evaluation of children with heart murmurs by the non-specialised paediatricians. Eur J Pediatr 154:15, 1995.

24. Hittner HM et al: Assessment of gestational age by examination of anterior vascular capsule of lens. J Pediatr 91:455, 1977.

25. Hogan GR et al: The plantar reflex of the newborn. N Engl J Med 285:502, 1971.

26. Kugelman A et al: Preauricular tags and pits in the newborn: The role of hearing tests. Acta Paediatr 86:170, 1997.

27. Lee TWR et al: Routine neonatal examination: Effectiveness of trainee paediatrician compared with advanced neonatal nurse practitioner Arch Dis Child 85:F100, 2001.

28. Leung AKC et al: Single umbilical artery: A report of 159 cases. Am J Dis Child 148:108, 1989.

29. McCrindle BW et al: Cardinal clinical signs in the differentiation of heart murmurs in children. Arch Pediatr Adolesc Med 150:169, 1996.

30. Moss GD et al: Routine examination in the newborn period. BMJ 302:878, 1991.

31. Parkin JM et al: Rapid assessment of gestational age at birth. Arch Dis Child 51:259, 1976.

32. Prechtl HRF: The Neurologic Examination of the Fullterm Newborn Infant, 2nd ed. London, Spastics International Medical Publications, 1977.

33. Rahi JS, Dezateux C: National cross-sectional study of detection of congenital and infantile cataract in the United Kingdom: Role of screening and surveillance. BMJ 318:362, 1999.

34. Rahi JS, Lynn R: A survey of paediatricians' practice and training in routine infant eye examination. Arch Dis Child 78:364, 1998.

35. Sanfridson J et al: Why is congenital dislocation of the hip still missed? Analysis of 96,891 infants screened in Malmo, 1956-1987. Acta Orthop Scand 62:87, 1991.

36. Scott JES et al: Screening newborn babies for familial ureteric reflux. Lancet 350:396, 1997.

37. Smythe JF et al: Initial evaluation of heart murmurs: Are laboratory tests necessary? Pediatrics 86:497, 1990.

38. Swaiman KF: Neurologic examination of the term and preterm infant. In Swaiman KF, Ashwal A (eds): Pediatric Neurology: Principles and Practice, 3rd ed. St. Louis, Mosby, 1999, p 69.

39. Temmerman AM et al: The value of the routine chest roentgenogram in the cardiological evaluation of infants and children: A prospective study. Eur J Paediatr 150:623, 1991.

40. Thummala MR et al: Isolated single umbilical artery anomaly and the risk for congenital malformations: A meta-analysis. J Pediatr Surg 33:580, 1998.

41. Wariyar U et al: Gestational assessment assessed. Arch Dis Child 77:F216, 1997.

42. Wren C et al: Presentation of congenital heart disease in infancy: Implications for routine examination. Arch Dis Child 80:F49, 1999.

43. Young PC: The morbidity of cardiac nondisease revisited. Is there lingering concern associated with an innocent murmur? Am J Dis Child 147:975, 1993.

27 Birth Injuries

Henry H. Mangurten

Birth injuries are those sustained during the birth process, which includes labor and delivery. They may be avoidable, or they may be unavoidable and occur despite skilled and competent obstetric care, as in an especially hard or prolonged labor or with an abnormal presentation. Fetal injuries related to amniocentesis and intrauterine transfusions and neonatal injuries after resuscitation procedures are not considered birth injuries. However, injuries related to the use of intrapartum monitoring of the fetal heart rate and collection of fetal scalp blood for acid-base assessment are included. Factors predisposing the infant to birth injury include macrosomia, prematurity, cephalopelvic disproportion, dystocia, prolonged labor, abnormal presentation, and certain operative deliveries, particularly vacuum extraction. The fetus may also sustain injury if the mother is involved in a motor vehicle accident, as reported by Parida and associates.[54] Although usually protected by maternal soft tissues, uterus, and amniotic fluid, the fetus may be subjected to the same acceleration-deceleration forces as the mother. This may result in full-thickness bowel injury and fulminant disseminated intravascular coagulation.[54] Thus, a thorough physical examination of the infant is critical after a maternal motor vehicle accident to identify any internal injury that may have occurred.

The significance of birth injuries may be assessed by review of mortality data. In 1981, birth injuries ranked sixth among major causes of neonatal death, resulting in 23.8 deaths per 100,000 live births.[78] During the ensuing decade, because of refinements in obstetric techniques and the increased use of cesarean deliveries over difficult vaginal deliveries, a dramatic decline occurred in birth injuries as a cause of neonatal death. Statistics for 1993 revealed a reduction to 3.7 deaths per 100,000 live births; because of the emergence of other conditions, birth injuries ranked 11th among major causes of neonatal death.[79] The most recent figures available (for 2001) identify only the 10 leading causes of infant death, with no mention of birth injuries.[4]

Despite a reduction in related mortality rates, birth injuries still represent an important source of neonatal morbidity[76] and neonatal intensive care unit admissions. Of particular concern are severe intracranial injuries after combined methods of vaginal delivery (vacuum-assisted and forceps delivery) and failed attempts at operative vaginal delivery.[64]

The clinician should consider the broad spectrum of birth injuries in the differential diagnosis of neonatal clinical disorders. Although many injuries are mild and self-limited, others are serious and potentially lethal. This chapter describes both conditions that can be managed by observation only and those that require more aggressive intervention.

INJURIES TO SOFT TISSUES

Erythema and Abrasions

Erythema and abrasions frequently occur when dystocia has occurred during labor as a result of cephalopelvic disproportion or when forceps have been used during delivery. Injuries caused by dystocia occur over the presenting part; forceps injury occurs at the site of application of the instrument. Forceps injury frequently has a linear configuration across both sides of the face, outlining the position of the forceps. The affected areas should be kept clean to minimize the risk of secondary infection. These lesions usually resolve spontaneously within several days with no specific therapy.

Petechiae

Occasionally, petechiae are present on the head, neck, upper portion of the chest, and lower portion of the back at birth after a difficult delivery; they are observed more frequently after breech deliveries.

ETIOLOGY

Petechiae are probably caused by a sudden increase in intrathoracic and venous pressures during passage of the chest through the birth canal. An infant born with the cord tightly wound around the neck may have petechiae only above the neck.

DIFFERENTIAL DIAGNOSIS

Petechiae may be a manifestation of an underlying hemorrhagic disorder. The birth history, early appearance of the petechiae, and absence of bleeding from other sites help to differentiate petechiae caused by increased tissue pressure or trauma from petechiae caused by hemorrhagic disorders (see Chapter 44). The localized distribution of the petechiae, the absence of subsequent crops of new lesions, and a normal platelet count exclude neonatal thrombocytopenia. The platelet count also may be low because of infections or disseminated intravascular coagulation. Infections may be clinically distinguished from traumatic petechiae by the presence of other signs and symptoms. Disseminated intravascular coagulation usually is associated with excessive and persistent bleeding from a variety of sites. Petechiae usually are distributed over the entire body when associated with systemic disease.

TREATMENT

If the petechiae are caused by trauma, neither corticosteroids nor heparin should be used. No specific treatment is necessary.

PROGNOSIS

Traumatic petechiae usually fade within 2 or 3 days.

Ecchymoses

Ecchymoses may occur after traumatic or breech deliveries. The incidence is increased in premature infants, especially after a rapid labor and poorly controlled delivery. When extensive, ecchymoses may reflect blood loss severe enough to cause anemia and, rarely, shock. The reabsorption of blood from an ecchymotic area may result in significant hyperbilirubinemia (Fig. 27-1).

TREATMENT

No local therapy is necessary. The rise in serum bilirubin that follows severe bruising may be decreased by the use of phototherapy (see also Chapter 46). Ecchymoses rarely result in significant anemia.

PROGNOSIS

The ecchymoses usually resolve spontaneously within 1 week.

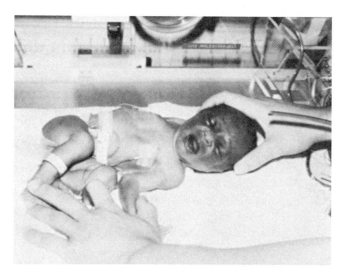

FIGURE 27-1. Marked bruising of entire face of a 1490-g female infant born vaginally after face presentation. Less severe ecchymoses were present on extremities. Despite use of phototherapy from the first day, icterus was noted on the third day and exchange transfusions were required on the fifth and sixth days.

Subcutaneous Fat Necrosis

Subcutaneous fat necrosis is characterized by well-circumscribed, indurated lesions of the skin and underlying tissue (see also Chapter 47, Part 2).

ETIOLOGY

The cause of subcutaneous fat necrosis is uncertain, although obstetric trauma is considered a possibility. Many affected infants are large and have been delivered by forceps or after a prolonged, difficult labor involving vigorous fetal manipulation. The distribution of the lesions usually is related to the site of trauma, which explains the frequent involvement of shoulders and buttocks. Other etiologic factors that have been implicated include hypothermia, local ischemia, and intrauterine asphyxia. One suggested mechanism of pathogenesis proposes that diminished in utero circulation and mechanical pressure during labor and delivery result in vascular compromise to specific areas, which eventually causes localized fat necrosis.[15] This condition has also been described in an infant whose mother used cocaine during pregnancy. The authors postulate that cocaine may be a factor because of decreased placental perfusion with subsequent hypoxemia and alteration of the maternal and fetal pituitary-adrenal axes.[12]

PATHOLOGY

Initially, histopathologic studies reveal endothelial swelling and perivascular inflammation in the subcutaneous tissues. They are followed by necrosis of fat and a dense granulomatous inflammatory infiltrate containing foreign body type giant cells with needle-shaped crystals resembling cholesterol.

CLINICAL MANIFESTATIONS

Necrotic areas usually appear between 6 and 10 days of age but may be noted as early as the second day or as late as the sixth week. They occur on the cheeks, neck, back, shoulders, arms, buttocks, thighs, and feet, with relative sparing of the chest and abdomen. The lesions vary in size from 1 to 10 cm; rarely, they may be more extensive. They are irregularly shaped, hard, plaquelike, and nonpitting (Fig. 27-2). The overlying skin may be colorless, red, or purple. The affected areas may be slightly elevated above the adjacent skin; small lesions may be easily moveable in all directions. There is no local tenderness or increase in skin temperature.

Marked symptomatic hypercalcemia may develop in infants with subcutaneous fat necrosis at 3 to 4 weeks of age; this has been characterized by vomiting, weight loss, anorexia, fever, somnolence, and irritability, with serum calcium levels as high as 16.2 mg/dL.[17,41] Improvement generally has occurred after intravenous hydration, furosemide, and hydrocortisone therapy. Investigators have suggested extrarenal production of 1,25-dihydroxyvitamin D by the granulomatous cells of fat necrosis as a possible mechanism for the hypercalcemia.[17,41]

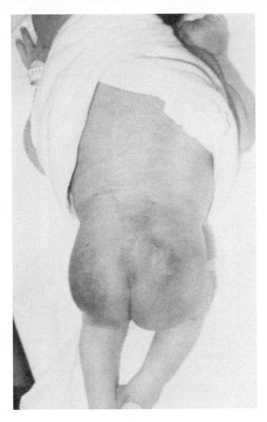

FIGURE 27-2. Subcutaneous fat necrosis in a 2900-g term infant delivered vaginally; pregnancy, labor, and delivery were completely uncomplicated. Note nodular lesion located on right buttock and surrounded by erythema (*darkened area*). (Courtesy of Dr. Rajam Ramamurthy, Cook County Hospital, Chicago.)

DIFFERENTIAL DIAGNOSIS

The differential diagnosis includes lipogranulomatosis and sclerema neonatorum, which carry a serious prognosis, and nodular nonsuppurative panniculitis, which is usually associated with fever, hepatosplenomegaly, and tender skin nodules.

TREATMENT

These lesions require only observation. Surgical excision is not indicated.

PROGNOSIS

The lesions slowly soften after 6 to 8 weeks and completely regress within several months. Occasionally, minimal residual atrophy, with or without small calcified areas, is observed. Affected infants should be followed closely during the first 6 weeks for potential development of hypercalcemia. It is important to treat this complication without delay to prevent central nervous system (CNS) and renal sequelae.[17]

Lacerations

Accidental lacerations may be inflicted with a scalpel during cesarean section. They usually occur on the scalp, buttocks, and thighs, but they may occur on any part of the body. If the wound is superficial, the edges may be held in apposition with butterfly adhesive strips. Deeper, more freely bleeding wounds should be sutured with the finest material available, preferably 7-0 nylon. Rarely, the amount of blood loss and depth of wound require suturing in the delivery room. After repair, the wound should be left uncovered unless it is in an area of potential soiling, such as the perineal area; in such locations the wound should be sprayed with protective plastic. Healing is usually rapid, and the sutures may be removed after 5 days.

INJURIES TO THE HEAD

Skull

CAPUT SUCCEDANEUM

Caput succedaneum, a frequently observed lesion, is characterized by a vaguely demarcated area of edema over that portion of the scalp that was the presenting part during a vertex delivery.

Etiology

Serum or blood or both accumulate above the periosteum in the presenting part during labor. This extravasation results from the higher pressure of the uterus or vaginal wall on those areas of the fetal head that border the caput. Thus, in a left occiput transverse presentation, the caput succedaneum occurs over the upper and posterior aspect of the right parietal bone; in a right-sided presentation it occurs over the corresponding area of the left parietal bone.

Clinical Manifestations

The soft swelling is usually a few millimeters thick and may be associated with overlying petechiae, purpura, or ecchymoses. Because of the location external to the periosteum, a caput succedaneum may extend across the midline of the skull and across suture lines. After an especially difficult labor, an extensive caput may obscure various sutures and fontanelles.

Differential Diagnosis

Occasionally, a caput succedaneum may be difficult to distinguish from a cephalhematoma, particularly when the latter occurs bilaterally. Careful palpation usually indicates whether the bleeding is external to the periosteum (a caput) or beneath the periosteum (a cephalhematoma).

Treatment

Usually no specific treatment is indicated. Rarely, a hemorrhagic caput may result in shock and require blood transfusion.

Prognosis

A caput succedaneum usually resolves within several days.

CEPHALHEMATOMA

Cephalhematoma is an infrequently seen subperiosteal collection of blood overlying a cranial bone. The incidence is 0.4% to 2.5% of live births; the frequency is higher in male infants and in infants born to primiparous mothers.

Etiology

A cephalhematoma is caused during labor or delivery by a rupture of blood vessels that traverse from skull to periosteum. Repeated buffeting of the fetal skull against the maternal pelvis during a prolonged or difficult labor and mechanical trauma caused by use of forceps in delivery have been implicated. Petrikovsky and associates[56] have described seven infants in whom cephalhematoma or caput succedaneum was identified prenatally *before* onset of labor. Occurrence of premature rupture of membranes in five of the pregnancies suggests an etiology of fetal head compression by the uterine walls, resulting from oligohydramnios subsequent to the ruptured membranes.

Clinical Manifestations

The bleeding is sharply limited by periosteal attachments to the surface of one cranial bone; there is no extension across suture lines. The bleeding usually occurs over one or both parietal bones. Less often it involves the occipital bones and, very rarely, the frontal bones. The overlying scalp is not discolored. Because subperiosteal bleeding is slow, the swelling may not be apparent for several hours or days after birth. The swelling is often larger on the second or third day, when sharply demarcated boundaries are palpable. The cephalhematoma may feel fluctuant and often is bordered by a slightly elevated ridge of organizing tissue that gives the false sensation of a central bony depression. In 1974, Zelson and coworkers[80] noted an underlying skull fracture in 5.4% of cephalhematomas. These fractures are almost always linear and nondepressed.

Radiographic Manifestations

Radiographic manifestations vary with the age of the cephalhematoma. During the first 2 weeks, bloody fluid results in a shadow of water density. At the end of the second week, bone begins to form under the elevated pericranium at the margins of the hematoma; the entire lesion is progressively overlaid with a complete shell of bone.

Differential Diagnosis

A cephalhematoma may be differentiated from caput succedaneum by (1) its sharp periosteal limitations to one bone, (2) the absence of overlying discoloration, (3) the later initial appearance of the swelling, and (4) the longer time before resolution. Cranial meningocele is differentiated from cephalhematoma by pulsations, an increase in pressure during crying, and the demonstration of a bony defect on a radiograph. An occipital cephalhematoma may be confused initially with an occipital meningocele and with cranium bifidum because all occupy the midline position.

Treatment

Therapy is not indicated for the uncomplicated cephalhematoma. Rarely, a massive cephalhematoma may result in blood loss severe enough to require transfusion. Significant hyperbilirubinemia also may result, necessitating phototherapy or other treatment of jaundice (see also Chapter 46).

The most common associated complications are skull fracture and intracranial hemorrhage. Linear fractures do not require specific therapy, but radiographs should be taken at 4 to 6 weeks to ensure closure and to exclude formation of leptomeningeal cysts; depressed fractures require immediate neurosurgical consultation. Specific treatment of blood loss or hyperbilirubinemia or both may be indicated if there has been an intracranial hemorrhage. Routine incision or aspiration of a cephalhematoma is contraindicated because of the risk of introducing infection. Rarely, bacterial infections of cephalhematomas occur, usually in association with septicemia and meningitis. Focal infection should be suspected when a sudden enlargement of a static cephalhematoma occurs during the course of a systemic infection, with a relapse of meningitis or sepsis after treatment with antibiotics, or with the development of local signs of infection over the cephalhematoma (Fig. 27-3). Diagnostic aspiration may be indicated. If a

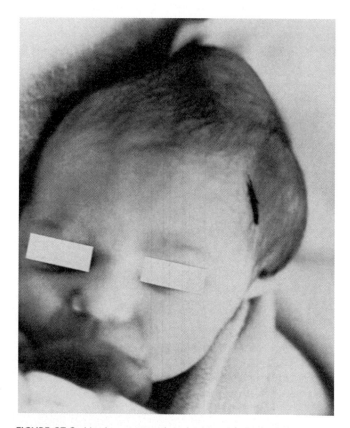

FIGURE 27-3. Massive, persistently enlarging cephalhematoma in a 13-day-old female infant delivered by midforceps after occiput-posterior presentation. Surgical drainage revealed 300 mL of yellowish material that cultured *Escherichia coli*.

local infection is present, surgical drainage and specific antibiotic therapy should be instituted. Osteomyelitis of the underlying skull may be a rare concurrent problem.[49,52] The diagnosis may be suggested by periosteal elevation and overlying soft tissue swelling on skull radiographs. Additional rare complications that may accompany an infected cephalhematoma and osteomyelitis include venous sinus thrombosis and cerebellar hemorrhage.[13] Magnetic resonance imaging (MRI) should be used to detect these two intracranial complications, whereas computed tomography (CT) is the best imaging modality to identify the permeative bone erosion and destruction of osteomyelitis.[13]

Prognosis

Most cephalhematomas are resorbed within 2 weeks to 3 months, depending on their size; most of these are resorbed by 6 weeks. In a few patients, calcium is deposited (Fig. 27-4), causing a bony swelling that may persist for several months and, rarely, up to $1^1/_2$ years.

Radiographic findings persist after the disappearance of clinical signs. The outer table remains thickened as a flat, irregular hyperostosis for several months. Widening of the space between the new shell of bone and the inner table may persist for years; the space originally occupied by the hematoma usually develops into normal diploic bone, but cystlike defects may persist at the sites of the hematoma for months or years. Rarely, a neonatal cephalhematoma may persist into adult life as a symptomless mass, the cephalhematoma deformans of Schüller.

SUBGALEAL HEMORRHAGE

Subgaleal hemorrhage (SGH) is a collection of blood in the soft tissue space between the galea aponeurotica and the periosteum of the skull (Fig. 27-5). The incidence is approximately 4 per 10,000 deliveries, with an even higher incidence after instrumental deliveries. Ng and colleagues[53] have reported an incidence of 64 per 10,000 deliveries when vacuum extraction is performed!

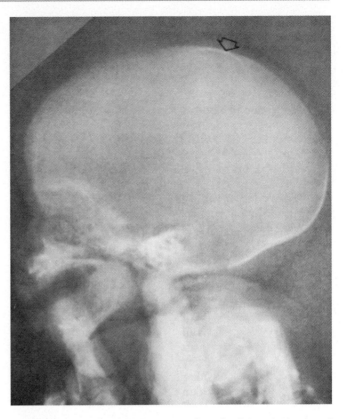

FIGURE 27-4. Calcified cephalhematoma *(arrow)* in left parietal region of 5-week-old girl. Infant weighed 1410 g at birth and was delivered rapidly because of prolapsed cord. Hard left parietal swelling was detected at 5 weeks by nurses during feeding.

Etiology

The most common predisposing factor is difficult instrumental delivery, particularly midforceps delivery and vacuum extraction.[28,57] The risk of SGH may be reduced by use of softer silicone vacuum cups instead of the original rigid metallic ones.[8] Other factors include

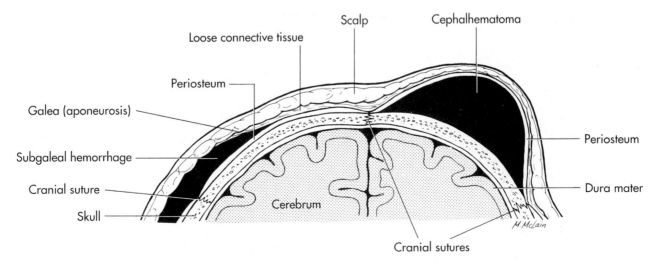

FIGURE 27-5. Subgaleal hemorrhage and cephalhematoma.

coagulopathies,[16,64] prematurity, macrosomia, fetal dystocia, and precipitous labor.[37] The loose connective tissue of the subgaleal space can accommodate as much as 260 mL of blood.[57] SGH may result from an associated skull fracture or rupture of an interosseous synchondrosis (primarily between the parietal bones), in turn causing injury to major intracrànial veins or sinuses. Another possible mechanism results from distortion of or traction on emissary veins bridging the subdural and subgaleal spaces.[28]

Clinical Manifestations

Early manifestations may be limited to pallor, hypotonia, and diffuse swelling of the scalp. The development of a fluctuating mass straddling cranial sutures, fontanelles, or both is highly suggestive of the diagnosis.[28] Because blood accumulates beneath the aponeurotic layer, ecchymotic discoloration of the scalp is a later finding.[48] This often is associated with pitting edema and progressive posterior spread toward the neck and lateral spread around the ears, frequently displacing the ears anteriorly (Fig. 27-6). Periorbital swelling and ecchymosis also are commonly observed.[57] Eventually, hypovolemic shock and signs of cerebral irritation develop. Massive lesions can cause extracranial cerebral compression, which may lead to rapid neurologic decompensation.[3] The clinician should be aware of occasional "silent presentation," in which a fluctuant mass is not apparent initially despite serial clinical examinations.[53] SGH should be considered in infants who show signs of hypoperfusion and falling hematocrit after attempted or successful vacuum delivery, even in the absence of a detectable fluctuant mass.

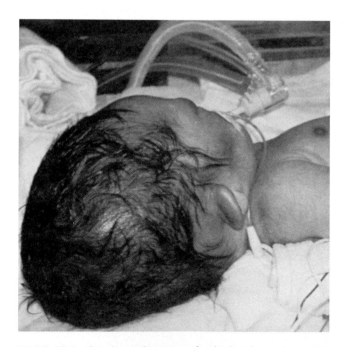

FIGURE 27-6. Clinical manifestations of subgaleal hemorrhage. Note anteriorly displaced ear.

Radiographic Manifestations

Standard radiographs of the skull may identify possible associated fractures. CT scanning may demonstrate abundant epicranial blood, parieto-occipital bone dehiscence, bone fragmentation, and posterior cerebral interhemispheric densities compatible with subarachnoid hemorrhage.[28]

Differential Diagnosis

In contrast to cephalhematoma, SGH is characterized by its more diffuse distribution, more rapid course, significant anemia, signs of CNS trauma (e.g., hypotonia, lethargy, seizures), and frequent lethal outcome.

Treatment

Prompt restoration of blood volume with fresh frozen plasma or blood is essential. If the bleeding continues, gentle compression wraps may be applied to the head; however, the value of this therapy is only anecdotal.[8] In the presence of continued deterioration, surgery may be considered as a last resort. A bicoronal incision allows for exposure of the subgaleal space. Bipolar cauterization of any bleeding points can then be accomplished, and a drain can be left in the subgaleal space. One report[3] described a successful outcome after finger disimpaction of a large clot before insertion of a drain that released an additional 200 mL of blood over 2 days.

Prognosis

Nearly 25% of infants with SGH die.[37,57] More experience with aggressive and timely surgical intervention may help to improve outcomes.

SKULL FRACTURES

Fracture of the neonatal skull is uncommon because the bones of the skull are less mineralized at birth and thus more compressible. In addition, the separation of the bones by membranous sutures usually permits enough alteration in the contour of the head to allow its passage through the birth canal without injury.

Etiology

Skull fractures usually follow a forceps delivery or a prolonged, difficult labor with repeated forceful contact of the fetal skull against the maternal symphysis pubis, sacral promontory, or ischial spine. They have also been described after a vacuum extraction delivery.[34] Most of the fractures are linear. Depressed fractures almost always result from forceps application. However, they may occur spontaneously after cesarean section[23,25] or vaginal delivery without forceps. Factors that have been implicated include pressure on the fetal skull by a maternal bony prominence (e.g., sacral promontory) or uterine fibroid, a fetal hand or foot, or the body part of a twin. Occipital bone fractures usually occur in breech deliveries as a consequence of traction on the hyperextended spine of the infant when the head is fixed in the maternal pelvis.

Clinical Manifestations

Linear fractures over the convexity of the skull frequently are accompanied by soft tissue changes and cephalhematoma. Usually the infant's behavior is normal unless there is an associated concussion or hemorrhage into the subdural or subarachnoid space. Fractures at the base of the skull with separation of the basal and squamous portions of the occipital bone almost always result in severe hemorrhage caused by disruption of the underlying venous sinuses. The infant may then exhibit shock, neurologic abnormalities, and drainage of bloody cerebrospinal fluid from the ears or nose.

Depressed fractures are visible, palpable indentations in the smooth contour of the skull, similar to dents in a Ping-Pong ball (Fig. 27-7). The infant may be entirely free of symptoms unless there is an associated intracranial injury.

Radiographic Manifestations

The diagnosis of a simple linear or fissure fracture is seldom made without radiographs in which fractures appear as lines and strips of decreased density. Depressed fractures appear as lines of increased density. On some views they are manifested by an inward buckling of bone with or without an actual break in continuity. Either type of fracture may be seen on only one view.

Differential Diagnosis

Occasionally, the fragments of a linear fracture may be widely separated and may simulate an open suture.

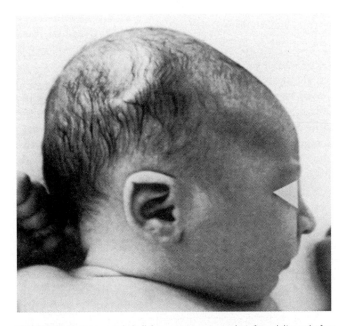

FIGURE 27-7. Depressed skull fracture in term male infant delivered after rapid (1 hour) labor. Infant was delivered by occiput-anterior presentation after rotation from occiput-posterior position.

Conversely, parietal foramina, the interparietal fontanelle, mendosal sutures, and innominate synchondroses may be mistaken for fractures. In addition, normal vascular grooves, "ripple lines" that represent soft tissue folds of the scalp, and lacunar skull may be mistaken for fractures.

Treatment

Uncomplicated linear fractures over the convexity of the skull usually do not require treatment. Fractures at the base of the skull often necessitate blood replacement for severe hemorrhage and shock in addition to other supportive measures. If cerebrospinal fluid rhinorrhea or otorrhea is present, antimicrobial coverage is indicated to prevent secondary infection of the meninges.

Small (less than 2 cm) "Ping-Pong" fractures may be observed without surgical treatment. Loeser and associates[44] reported on three infants with depressed skull fractures in whom spontaneous elevation of the fractures occurred within 1 day to $3^{1}/_{2}$ months of age. Follow-up at 1 to $2^{1}/_{2}$ years revealed normal neurologic development in all three.

Several nonsurgical methods have been described for elevation of depressed skull fractures in certain infants:

1. A thumb is placed on opposite margins of the depression and gentle, firm pressure exerted toward the middle. After several minutes of continuous pressure the area of depression gradually disappears.[62]

2. A hand breast pump is applied to the depressed area. Petroleum jelly placed on the pump edges ensures a tighter seal, and gentle suction for several minutes results in elevation of the depressed bone.[66]

3. A vacuum extractor is placed over the depression, and a negative pressure of 0.2 to 0.5 kg/cm^2 is maintained for approximately 4 minutes.[65,73]

Because these methods are technically easier and less traumatic, they may be preferable to surgical intervention in a symptom-free infant with an isolated lesion.

Comminuted or large fractures associated with neurologic signs or symptoms should be treated by immediate surgical elevation of the indented segment to prevent underlying cortical injury from pressure. Other indications for surgical elevation include manifestations of cerebrospinal fluid beneath the galea and failure to elevate the fracture by nonsurgical manipulation.

Prognosis

Simple linear fractures usually heal within several months without sequelae. Rarely, a leptomeningeal cyst may develop from an associated dural tear, and meninges or part of the brain may protrude through the fracture. The fracture line may widen rapidly within weeks, or a large defect in the skull may be noted many months later. If detected early, the cyst may be excised successfully and brain atrophy prevented. It is therefore advisable to repeat skull radiographs within 2 to 3 months to detect early widening of the fracture line. Color Doppler imaging has been demonstrated to enhance earlier diagnosis of leptomeningeal cyst during the second week of life.[77]

Basal fractures carry a poor prognosis. When separation of the basal and squamous portions of the occipital bone occurs, the outcome is almost always fatal; surviving infants have an extremely high incidence of neurologic sequelae.

The prognosis for a depressed fracture is usually good when treatment is early and adequate. When therapy is delayed, especially with a large depression, death may occur from pressure on vital areas of the brain. Because the natural history of depressed skull fractures in neonates has not been clearly elucidated, the outcome is uncertain for infants with smaller lesions managed either by simple observation or by surgery after significant delays. Despite the apparently normal outcome in the three infants reported by Loeser and associates,[44] one cannot completely exclude the possibility that subtle neurologic sequelae may develop years later.

INTRACRANIAL HEMORRHAGE
(See Chapter 38.)

Face

FACIAL NERVE PALSY
Facial nerve palsy in the neonate may follow birth injury or rarely may result from agenesis of the facial nerve nucleus. The latter condition occasionally is hereditary but usually is sporadic.

Etiology
Traumatic facial nerve palsy most often follows compression of the peripheral portion of the nerve, either near the stylomastoid foramen, through which it emerges, or where the nerve traverses the ramus of the mandible. The nerve may be compressed by forceps, especially when the fetal head has been grasped obliquely. The condition also occurs after spontaneous deliveries in which prolonged pressure was applied by the maternal sacral promontory. Less frequently, injury is sustained in utero, often in association with a mandibular deformity, by the persistent position of the fetal foot against the superior ramus of the mandible. An extremely rare cause is the pressure of a uterine tumor on the nerve.

This condition may occur rarely with a simultaneous ipsilateral brachial plexus palsy, most likely secondary to compressive forces during delivery.[20] Contributing factors include prolonged second stage of labor and midforceps delivery.

A traumatic facial nerve palsy may follow a contralateral injury to the CNS, such as a temporal bone fracture, or hemorrhage, tissue destruction, or both to

structures within the posterior fossa. This CNS injury is less frequent than peripheral nerve injury.

Clinical Manifestations
Paralysis is usually apparent on the first or second day but may be present at birth. It usually does not increase in severity unless considerable edema occurs over the area of nerve trauma. The type and distribution of paralysis are different in central facial paralysis compared with peripheral paralysis.

Central paralysis is a spastic paralysis limited to the lower half or two thirds of the contralateral side of the face. The paralyzed side is smooth and full and often appears swollen. The nasolabial fold is obliterated, and the corner of the mouth droops. When the infant cries, the mouth is drawn to the normal side, the wrinkles are deeper on the normal side, and movement of the forehead and eyelid is unaffected. Usually other manifestations of intracranial injury appear, most often a sixth cranial nerve palsy.

Peripheral paralysis is flaccid and, when complete, involves the entire side of the face. When the infant is at rest, the only sign may be a persistently open eye on the affected side, caused by paralysis of the orbicular muscle of the eye. With crying, the findings are the same as in a central facial nerve injury, with the addition of a smooth forehead on the involved side. Because the tongue is not involved, feeding is not affected.

A small branch of the nerve may be injured, with involvement of only one group of facial muscles. Paralysis is then limited to the forehead, eyelid, or mouth. Peripheral paralysis caused by nerve injury distal to the geniculate ganglion may be accompanied by a hematotympanum on the same side.

Differential Diagnosis
Central and peripheral facial nerve palsies must be distinguished from nuclear agenesis (Möbius syndrome). The latter frequently results in bilateral facial nerve palsy; the face is expressionless and immobile, suggesting muscle fibrosis. Other cranial nerve palsies and deformities of the ear, palate, tongue, mandible, and other bones may be associated with Möbius syndrome. Congenital absence or hypoplasia of the depressor muscle of the angle of the mouth also may simulate congenital facial palsy and has been associated with an increased incidence of other congenital anomalies.

Treatment
No specific therapy is indicated for most facial palsies. If the paralysis is peripheral and complete, initial treatment should be directed at protecting the cornea with an eye pad and instilling 1% methylcellulose drops every 4 hours. The functional state of the nerve should be followed closely. Falco and colleagues[24] proposed the following comprehensive approach:

1. Distinguish developmental from acquired lesions on the basis of the birth history and a detailed physical examination. Patients thought to have

developmental palsy should be examined with radiologic and electrodiagnostic studies and brainstem evoked response as appropriate.

2. Because of the expected 90% likelihood of complete spontaneous recovery, patients should be observed for 1 year before surgical intervention is considered. If recovery is suggested by physical examination or serial electromyography, observation without surgery may be delayed until the second birthday. Infants who require surgery are best treated with decompression or neuroplasty or both.

Prognosis

Most facial palsies resolve spontaneously within several days; total recovery may require several weeks or months. Electrodiagnostic testing is beneficial in predicting recovery; repeatedly normal nerve excitability indicates a good prognosis, but decreased or absent excitability early in the course suggests a poor outlook. The subsequent appearance of muscle fibrillation potentials indicates nerve degeneration. The prognosis in surgically treated infants worsens with increasing age at treatment.

FRACTURES AND DISLOCATIONS OF FACIAL BONES

Facial bone fractures may occur during passage through the birth canal, during forceps application and delivery, and during obstetric manipulation (most often the Mauriceau maneuver for delivery of the fetal head in a breech presentation). Manipulation may result in mandibular fractures and mandibular joint damage but is rarely severe enough to cause separation of the symphysis of the mandible. Fracture of the nose may result in early respiratory distress and feeding difficulties. The most frequent nasal injury is dislocation of the cartilaginous part of the septum from the vomerine groove and columella. This may result from intrauterine factors such as a uterine tumor or persistent pressure on the nose by fetal small parts or during delivery from pressure on the nose by the symphysis pubis, sacral promontory, or perineum. The presence of nasal septal dislocation may be differentiated from the more common normal variant of a misshapen nose by a simple compression test, in which the tip of the nose is compressed[18] (Fig. 27-8). In the presence of septal dislocation, the nostrils collapse and the deviated septum becomes more apparent; in the normal nose, no nasal deviation occurs with compression.

Infants who sustain nasal trauma during the birth process may demonstrate stridor and cyanosis, even in the absence of septal dislocation. Miller and coworkers[50] noted high nasal resistance in three such infants, of whom only one was found to have septal dislocation. The authors postulated the presence of edema and narrowed nasal passages from compression forces on the midface during delivery. The problem may be exaggerated by repeated nasal suctioning or transnasal

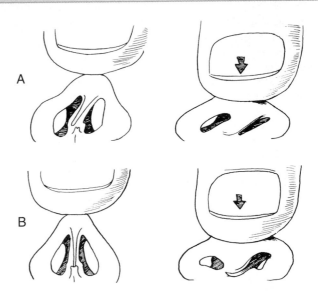

FIGURE 27-8. Result of finger compression (**A**) when nasal septum is dislocated. Normal septal relationship (**B**) results in no nasal deviation with pressure. (Modified from Daily W et al: Nasal septal dislocation in the newborn. Mo Med 74:381, 1977.)

bronchoscopy. These procedures and oral feeding should be avoided until the infant reestablishes normal nasal ventilation. Transcutaneous oxygen and carbon dioxide tensions and pulse oximetry measurements are useful in monitoring these infants.

Treatment

Fractures of the maxilla, lacrimal bones, and nose warrant immediate attention because they unite quickly, with fixation in 7 to 10 days. Nasal trauma frequently requires extensive surgery, so the pediatrician should request immediate consultation with a surgeon with expertise in nasal surgery. While waiting, the pediatrician should provide an oral airway to relieve respiratory distress. Often the surgeon can grasp the traumatized nose and elevate and remold it manually, relieving the respiratory distress. Fractures of the septal cartilage also may be reduced by simple manual remolding, but most are associated with hematomas that should be promptly incised and drained. The surgeon can visualize the deformity with an infant nasal speculum, place a septal elevator in the nose, and guide the septal cartilage into the vomerine groove; an audible and palpable click indicates return of the septum into position.[71]

Early reduction and immobilization also are advised for a displaced fracture of the mandible because rapid, firm union may occur as early as 10 to 14 days. Usually, adequate alignment can be achieved with an acrylic mandibular splint and circum-mandibular wires, which are maintained in place for 3 weeks. In more severe cases with canting of the mandibular alveolar ridge, perialveolar wires below the infraorbital rims have been used with excellent results. This procedure can prevent canted occlusion and possible facial asymmetry as the child grows, thus avoiding later extensive and costly reconstructive surgery.[59]

Prognosis

If the fracture is reduced and fixated within a few days, rapid healing without complication is the usual course. If treatment is inadequate, missed, or delayed, subsequent developmental deformities are common. Ankylosis of the mandible in the second year of life is thought to result from birth trauma to the temporomandibular joint. A young child has been described with unilateral mandibular hypoplasia, which was thought to have resulted from fibrous ankylosis caused by perinatal trauma to the condylar cartilage of the ipsilateral temporomandibular joint.[9] Other deformities may not become apparent until adolescence or young adulthood.

Eyes (See also Chapter 51.)

Mechanical trauma to various regions of the neonatal eye usually occurs during abnormal presentation, in dystocia from cephalopelvic disproportion, or as a result of inappropriate forceps placement in normal deliveries. Most of the injuries are self-limited and mild and require no specific treatment.

EYELIDS

Edema, suffusion, and ecchymoses of the eyelids are common, especially after face and brow presentations or forceps deliveries. Severely swollen lids should be forced open by an ophthalmologist for examination of the eyeball; retractors may be necessary. These findings usually resolve within a week without treatment, although an infant has been reported with totally everted upper eyelids that required suturing for 4 days before they would remain in the normal position.[61] Some believe that these injuries represent a possible cause of congenital ptosis.

A less common injury is laceration, including disruption of the lacrimal canaliculus. This has been associated with multiple upper-eyelid lacerations, including a full-thickness vertical wound lateral to the punctum and a full-thickness laceration through the lower eyelid with transection of the canaliculus after a low forceps delivery. Microsurgical repair of the lacrimal system and eyelids, including lacrimal intubation with a silicone stent, has been successful. Follow-up at 14 months revealed normal tear drainage with no amblyopia or residual deformity.[33]

An infant has been reported with superficial eyelid lacerations caused by an internal fetal monitoring spiral electrode.[43] At delivery the electrode was attached to the eyelid. Marked facial edema related to brow presentation apparently obscured the lacerations until 14 hours of age, when much of the edema had resolved. Periorbital edema was believed to have protected the infant from more serious injury to the eyelid and globe.

Lagophthalmos, the inability to close an eye, is an occasional finding thought to result from facial nerve injury by forceps pressure. It usually is unilateral. The exposed cornea should be protected by an eye pad and methylcellulose drops instilled every 4 hours. The condition usually resolves within a week.

ORBIT

Orbital hemorrhage and fracture may follow direct pressure by the apex of one forceps blade, most often in high forceps extractions. In most instances, death occurs immediately. Surviving infants demonstrate traumatic eyelid changes, disturbances of extraocular muscle movements, and exophthalmos. The presence of the latter two findings warrants immediate ophthalmologic consultation. Subsequent management also may require neurosurgical and plastic surgery consultations.

SYMPATHETIC NERVOUS SYSTEM

Horner syndrome, resulting from cervical sympathetic nerve trauma, frequently accompanies lower brachial plexus injury (see later in this chapter). The syndrome consists of miosis, partial ptosis, slight enophthalmos, and anhidrosis of the ipsilateral side of the face. Although small, the pupil reacts to light. The presence of neurologic signs indicating brachial plexus injury helps distinguish this syndrome from intracranial hemorrhage as a cause of anisocoria. Pigmentation of the ipsilateral iris is frequently delayed to several months of age; occasionally, pigmentation never occurs. Resolution of other signs of the syndrome depends on whether the injury to the nerve is transient or permanent.

SUBCONJUNCTIVAL HEMORRHAGE

Subconjunctival hemorrhage, characterized by bright red patches on the bulbar conjunctiva, is a relatively common finding in the neonate. It may be found after a difficult delivery but often is noted after easy, completely uncomplicated deliveries. This finding is considered to result from increased venous pressure in the infant's head and neck, produced by obstruction to venous return consequent to compression of the fetal thorax or abdomen by uterine contractions during labor.[40] If the infant is otherwise well, management consists of reassuring the parents. The blood is usually absorbed within 1 to 2 weeks. As the blood pigments break down and are absorbed, the color changes from bright red to orange and yellow.

EXTERNAL OCULAR MUSCLES

Injury involving the external ocular muscles may result from direct trauma to the cranial nerve (in the form of compression or surrounding hemorrhages) or from hemorrhage into the muscle sheath, with subsequent fibrosis. The sixth cranial nerve (abducens) is the most frequently injured cranial nerve because of its long intracranial course; the result is paralysis of the lateral rectus muscle. This injury may follow a tentorial laceration with extravasation of a small amount of blood around the intracranial portion of the nerve. The involvement may be mild and transient; internal strabismus noted at birth may resolve gradually within 1 to 2 months. The seventh cranial nerve may be injured simultaneously with the sixth nerve by compression with forceps. Improvement in lateral gaze of the affected eye may appear within 1 to 2 months. Alternate patching of either eye in the severely affected infant maintains visual acuity until, with time, maximum improvement has occurred. At 6 months the degree of nerve regeneration may be evaluated. Some infants subsequently require surgical repair of their strabismus.

Fourth cranial nerve (trochlear) palsy occurs infrequently. It may follow small brainstem hemorrhages with nuclear damage. The affected muscle is the superior oblique, which mainly turns the eye inferiorly and medially. This condition is difficult to identify in the newborn infant. Surgical correction may be necessary later.

Third cranial nerve (oculomotor) palsy, when complete, causes paralysis of the inferior oblique and medial, superior, and inferior rectus muscles. This results in ptosis, a dilated fixed pupil, and outward and downward deviation of the eye, with inability to adduct or elevate up and in or up and out or to depress down and out. This palsy also may occur in partial form, with or without pupillary involvement. Partial palsies may recover function spontaneously within several months, whereas complete palsies usually require surgical intervention.

OPTIC NERVE

The optic nerve may be injured directly by a fracture in the region of the optic canal or from a shearing force on the nerve, with resultant hemorrhage into the nerve sheath. The latter injury seldom is recognized because of the more apparent and severe changes in the sensorium. Occasionally, a fracture through the optic foramen results in formation of callus, which slowly compresses the nerve. A difficult forceps delivery is a frequent preceding event. If optic nerve injury is not diagnosed within several hours with prompt surgical intervention, irreversible damage is likely. The result is optic atrophy and blindness. This is characterized by a blue-white optic disc, in contrast to the grayish disc of the normal neonate. In primary optic atrophy (e.g., that caused by birth trauma), the disc margin is well defined and fine vessels are rarely present in the disc tissue. In secondary atrophy the disc margin is blurred; a central gray area and evidence of intraocular disease are present.

CORNEA

A diffuse or streaky haziness of the cornea is relatively common. This is usually caused by edema related to the birth process but also may follow use of a silver nitrate solution more concentrated than 1%. The haziness usually disappears in 7 to 10 days. When it persists, a rupture of the Descemet membrane has probably occurred, usually because of malpositioning of forceps at delivery. The consequence of a ruptured Descemet membrane is a leukoma or diffuse white opacity of the cornea. This results from interstitial damage of the substantia propria by fluids entering through the tear in the membrane. These leukomas are often permanent and, despite patching of the contralateral eye and use of glasses, are accompanied by a high incidence of amblyopia and strabismus.

A ruptured Descemet membrane has been reported after a prolonged delivery in which low forceps were used after unsuccessful attempts at vacuum extraction.[72] Because of significant corneal astigmatism at 2 months, a gas-permeable hard contact lens was applied. Patching of the contralateral eye was continued. Assessment of visual acuity at 13 months, with the use of spatial frequency sweep visual evoked potentials, demonstrated an excellent visual result.

INTRAOCULAR HEMORRHAGE

Trauma at birth may result in retinal hemorrhage, hyphema, or vitreous hemorrhage, with retinal hemorrhage the most common. The cause is most likely compression of the fetal head, resulting in venous congestion. The fetal head is compressed two to four times more forcefully than other fetal parts during the second stage of labor. Retinal hemorrhage is more common in primiparous deliveries and after forceps or vacuum extraction; it is rare after cesarean section. It may occur in normal deliveries. The most common lesion is the flame-shaped or streak hemorrhage found mainly near the disc and sparing the macula and extreme periphery; it usually disappears within 1 to 3 days (occasionally 5 days) with no residual effects. Rarely, hemorrhages may take as long as 21 days to resolve. Retinal hemorrhages may reduce the resolving power of the macula, either bilaterally to produce nystagmus or unilaterally to produce amblyopia, which may not always respond to prolonged covering of the fixing eye with improvement of the amblyopic eye.

Hyphemas and vitreous hemorrhages usually result from misplacement of forceps and often are associated with ruptures of the Descemet membrane. One infant has been described in whom a hyphema developed in one eye after spontaneous delivery.[58] The hyphema usually is clear of gross blood within 5 days; during this time the infant should be handled gently and fed frequently to minimize crying and agitation. If blood persists or secondary hemorrhage occurs, systemic administration of acetazolamide (Diamox) and surgical removal of blood may be necessary.

Vitreous hemorrhage is manifested by large vitreous floaters, blood pigment seen with the slit lamp, and an absent red reflex. The prognosis is guarded; if resolution does not occur in 6 to 12 months, surgical correction should be considered.

Ears

The proximity of ears to the site of application of forceps makes them susceptible to injury at birth. Most of the injuries are mild and self-limited, but serious injuries may occur because of slipping or misplacement of forceps (Fig. 27-9).

ABRASIONS AND ECCHYMOSES

Abrasions must be cleansed gently to minimize the risk of secondary infection. Ecchymoses, if extensive and involving other areas of the body, may result in hyperbilirubinemia.

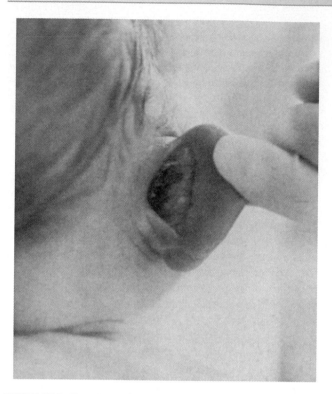

FIGURE 27-9. Extensive avulsion and laceration of auricle in term infant, resulting from forceful traction of misplaced forceps. (Courtesy of Dr. Bhagya Puppala, Lutheran General Children's Hospital, Park Ridge, Ill.)

HEMATOMAS

Hematomas of the external ear, if not treated promptly, liquefy slowly, followed by early organization and development of cauliflower ear. Wide incision and evacuation of the hematoma may be indicated.

LACERATIONS

Lacerations of the auricle may be repaired by the pediatrician if they are superficial and involve only skin. After thorough cleansing and draping, the wound edges are sutured with interrupted 6-0 or 7-0 nylon sutures, with exact edge-to-edge approximation. If the laceration involves cartilage, surgical consultation should be obtained because of the tendency toward postoperative perichondritis, which is refractory to treatment and leads to subsequent deformities. A sterile field and more meticulous presurgical preparation are essential. A contour pressure dressing is applied postoperatively.

Vocal Cord Paralysis

Unilateral or bilateral paralysis of the vocal cords is uncommon in the neonate.

ETIOLOGY

Unilateral paralysis may be a consequence of excessive traction on the head during a breech delivery or lateral traction with forceps in a cephalic presentation. The recurrent laryngeal branch of the vagus nerve in the neck is injured. The left side is involved more often because of this nerve's lower origin and longer course in the neck. Bilateral paralysis may be caused by peripheral trauma involving both recurrent laryngeal nerves, but more frequently it is caused by a CNS insult such as hypoxia or hemorrhage involving the brainstem.

CLINICAL MANIFESTATIONS

An infant with a unilateral paralysis may be completely free of symptoms when resting quietly, but crying is usually accompanied by hoarseness and mild inspiratory stridor. When associated with difficulty in feeding and clearing secretions, concurrent involvement of the 12th (hypoglossal) cranial nerve should be suspected, particularly if the tongue on the ipsilateral side does not protrude and demonstrates fasciculations. Hypoglossal paralysis also has been described in association with ipsilateral upper brachial plexus injury.[30] Affected infants demonstrate difficulty in sucking, with swelling and immobility of the affected side of the tongue. This 12th cranial neuropathy can be confirmed by concentric needle electromyography of the tongue.[29] Bilateral paralysis results in more severe respiratory symptoms. At birth the infant may have difficulty in establishing and maintaining spontaneous respiration; later, dyspnea, retractions, stridor, cyanosis, or aphonia may develop.

DIFFERENTIAL DIAGNOSIS

Unilateral paralysis of the vocal cords must be distinguished from congenital laryngeal malformations that produce neonatal stridor. A history of difficult delivery, especially involving excessive traction on the fetus, may suggest laryngeal paralysis; previously the diagnosis was confirmed only by direct laryngoscopic examination. The availability of the flexible fiberoptic laryngoscope at the bedside has facilitated earlier diagnosis without disrupting the infant's environment. Serial examinations to monitor progress also can be conducted with ease because the infant need not be transported to the operating room.

Bilateral paralysis also must be distinguished from a number of causes of respiratory distress in the neonate (see Chapter 42, Part Five); stridor should suggest the larynx as the site of disturbance. Direct or flexible fiberoptic laryngoscopy is necessary to establish the diagnosis.

TREATMENT

Infants with unilateral paralysis should be observed closely until there is evidence of improvement. Gentle handling and frequent small feedings aid in keeping the infant quiet and minimizing the risk of aspiration. Bilateral paralysis necessitates immediate tracheal intubation to establish an airway. Tracheostomy is required subsequently in most patients. Laryngoscopic examinations then should be performed at intervals to look for evidence of return of vocal cord function; early extubation may be attempted if complete return occurs within a short time.

PROGNOSIS

Unilateral paralysis usually resolves rapidly without treatment, and complete resolution occurs within 4 to 6 weeks. Glossolaryngeal paralysis or paresis due to birth injury should resolve spontaneously by 6 months of age.[29] Recognition of this subtle condition is important for two reasons. First, its self-limited course is encouraging, thus avoiding needless alarm in the parents with concern about more ominous conditions such as Werdnig-Hoffmann disease. Second, unnecessary invasive and aggressive procedures can be avoided.

The prognosis for bilateral paralysis is more variable. If untreated, a funnel deformity may develop in the lower sternal area; this may appear as early as the 15th day of life. After tracheostomy a decrease in the severity of the deformity may occur within several weeks. Some of the affected infants subsequently regain normally shaped chests; others may have residual fixed depressions, occasionally severe enough to require surgical correction. The recovery of vocal cord function varies in time and degree. Some infants may show partial recovery within a few months, with several years elapsing before complete movement of the cords is restored. Other infants who have been followed for years show no improvement. Bilateral paralysis of central origin may improve completely if it is caused by cerebral edema or hemorrhage that rapidly resolves.

INJURIES TO THE NECK, SHOULDER GIRDLE, AND CHEST

Fracture of the Clavicle (See also Chapter 52.)

The clavicle is the most frequently fractured bone during labor and delivery. Most clavicular fractures are of the greenstick type, but occasionally the fracture is complete.

ETIOLOGY

The major causes of clavicular fractures are difficult delivery of the shoulders in vertex presentations and extended arms in breech deliveries. Vigorous, forceful manipulation of the arm and shoulder usually has occurred. However, fracture of the clavicle may also occur in infants after apparently normal labor and delivery.[39,55] It has been suggested that some fetuses may be more vulnerable to spontaneous birth trauma secondary to forces of labor, maternal pelvic anatomy, and in utero fetal position.[55]

CLINICAL MANIFESTATIONS

Most often a greenstick fracture is not associated with any signs or symptoms but is first detected after the appearance of an obvious callus at 7 to 10 days of life. Thus the majority of neonatal clavicular fractures are diagnosed at discharge or at the first follow-up visit.[38] Complete fractures and some greenstick fractures may be apparent shortly after birth; movement of the arm on the affected side is decreased or absent. Deformity and, occasionally, discoloration may be visible over the fracture site with obliteration of the adjacent supraclavicular depression as a result of sternocleidomastoid muscle spasm. Passive movement of the arm elicits cries of pain from the infant. Palpation reveals tenderness, crepitus, and irregularity along the clavicle. Moro reflex on the involved side is characteristically absent. Radiographs confirm the diagnosis of fracture.

DIFFERENTIAL DIAGNOSIS

A similar clinical picture of impaired movement of an arm with an absent Moro reflex may follow fracture of the humerus or brachial palsy. The fracture is confirmed by radiographs; palsy is accompanied by additional clinical findings. Rarely an infant may present with a congenital pseudoarthrosis of the clavicle, which may be difficult to distinguish from a fracture. Pseudoarthrosis classically appears as a painless lump on the clavicle, with no associated tenderness nor limitation of mobility of the shoulder and arm. Radiography reveals disruption of the affected clavicle, with enlargement of the end of the bone. The etiology is uncertain. Recommended treatment options include observation only or surgical excision of the cartilaginous cap at approximately 4 or 5 years of age, followed by alignment of bone fragments and, if necessary, bone grafting or internal fixation.[60]

TREATMENT

Therapy is directed toward minimizing the infant's pain. The affected arm and shoulder should be immobilized with the arm abducted more than 60 degrees and the elbow flexed more than 90 degrees. A callus forms, and pain usually subsides by 7 to 10 days, when immobilization may be discontinued.

PROGNOSIS

Prognosis is excellent, with growth resulting in restoration of normal bone contour after several months.

Fracture of Ribs

Rib fractures related to labor and delivery are exceedingly rare, with a total of seven reported cases since 1977.[47]

ETIOLOGY

Risk factors are similar to those related to fracture of the clavicle, including macrosomia, a primigravida mother, shoulder dystocia, and delivery by midforceps or vacuum extraction.

CLINICAL MANIFESTATIONS

Specific clinical manifestations are often absent, making diagnosis difficult, unless a chest radiograph is obtained for other reasons, including suspected clavicular fracture (Fig. 27-10), respiratory distress, or cyanosis.

MECHANISM OF INJURY

This injury is initiated when the anterior shoulder is impacted behind the symphysis pubis, with the other

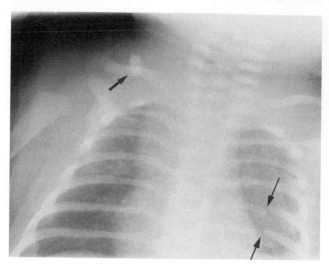

FIGURE 27-10. Chest radiograph of a 4905-g female delivered by midforceps after right shoulder dystocia. On the 11th day, a prominent mass was noted in the right midclavicular region. Radiograph reveals a right midclavicular fracture *(thick arrow)* with slight superior angulation and incidental fractures of left fifth and sixth ribs *(thin arrows)*. (From Mangurten HH et al: Incidental rib fractures in a neonate. Neonat Intensive Care 12:15, 1999.)

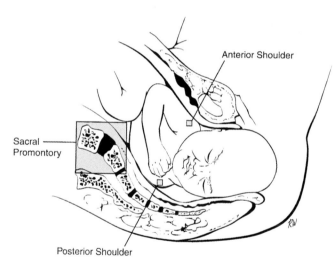

FIGURE 27-11. Diagram of fetus during delivery, illustrating impaction of anterior shoulder *(right)* behind the symphysis pubis, with left shoulder attempting to descend into posterior compartment of the pelvis. (From Mangurten HH et al: Incidental rib fractures in a neonate. Neonat Intensive Care 12:15, 1999.)

shoulder attempting to descend into the posterior compartment of the pelvis (Fig. 27-11). This results in compression forces on the fetal arms and thorax, leading to spontaneous rib fractures on the same side as the posterior shoulder (Fig. 27-12).

TREATMENT

No specific treatment is required. However, it is extremely important to document this injury immediately

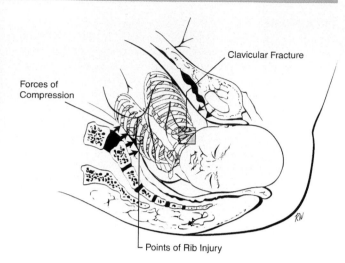

FIGURE 27-12. Diagram of fetus, illustrating compression forces on the fetal arms and thorax, which results in spontaneous fractures of right clavicle and left fifth and sixth ribs *(arrows)*. (From Mangurten HH et al: Incidental rib fractures in a neonate. Neonat Intensive Care 12:15, 1999.)

after birth to avoid later unwarranted accusation of parents or other caretakers for suspicion of child abuse.

PROGNOSIS

Prognosis is excellent, with spontaneous healing within several months.

Brachial Palsy (See also Chapter 52.)

Brachial palsy is a paralysis involving the muscles of the upper extremity that follows mechanical trauma to the spinal roots of the fifth cervical through the first thoracic nerves (the brachial plexus) during birth. Three main forms occur, depending on the site of injury: (1) Duchenne-Erb, or upper arm, paralysis, which results from injury of the fifth and sixth cervical roots and is by far the most common; (2) Klumpke, or lower arm, paralysis, which results from injury of the eighth cervical and first thoracic roots and is extremely rare; and (3) paralysis of the entire arm, which occurs slightly more often than the Klumpke type.

ETIOLOGY

Most cases of brachial palsy follow a prolonged and difficult labor culminating in a traumatic delivery. The affected infant is frequently large, relaxed, and asphyxiated and thereby vulnerable to excessive separation of bony segments, overstretching, and injury to soft tissues. Injury of the fifth and sixth cervical roots may follow a breech presentation with the arms extended over the head; excessive traction on the shoulder in the delivery of the head may result in stretching of the plexus. The same injury may follow lateral traction of the head and neck away from one of the shoulders during an attempt to deliver the shoulders in a vertex presentation. More vigorous traction of the same nature results in paralysis of the entire arm. The mechanism for isolated lower arm paralysis is uncertain; it is thought to result from stretching of lower plexus nerves under and against the coracoid process of the scapula during forceful elevation and abduction of the arm. Excessive traction on the trunk during a breech delivery may result in avulsion of the lower roots from the cervical cord. In most patients the nerve sheath is torn and the nerve fibers are compressed by the resultant hemorrhage and edema. Less often the nerves are completely ruptured and the ends severed, or the roots are avulsed from the spinal cord with injury to the spinal gray matter.

An increasing number of reports have described "no shoulder" brachial plexus palsy unrelated to excessive traction during delivery.[26,55] Some authorities have suggested an intrauterine insult *preceding* labor, such as compression by uterine tumors or maternal pelvic bony prominences.[26] One study, while confirming the well-known association of shoulder dystocia and brachial plexus injury in macrosomic infants, also identified an increased incidence of other malpresentations in low- and normal-weight infants with brachial plexus injury.[27]

CLINICAL MANIFESTATIONS

The infant with upper arm paralysis holds the affected arm in a characteristic position, reflecting involvement of the shoulder abductors and external rotators, forearm flexors and supinators, and wrist extensors. The arm is adducted and internally rotated, with extension at the elbow, pronation of the forearm, and flexion of the wrist. When the arm is passively abducted, it falls limply to the side of the body. Moro, biceps, and radial reflexes are absent on the affected side. There may be some sensory deficit on the radial aspect of the arm, but this is difficult to evaluate in the neonate. The grasp reflex is intact. Any signs of respiratory distress may indicate an accompanying ipsilateral phrenic nerve root injury (see following section).

Lower arm paralysis involves the intrinsic muscles of the hand and the long flexors of the wrist and fingers. The hand is paralyzed, and voluntary movements of the wrist cannot be made. The grasp reflex is absent; the deep tendon reflexes are intact. Sensory impairment may be demonstrated along the ulnar side of the forearm and hand. Frequently, dependent edema and cyanosis of the hand and trophic changes in the fingernails develop. After some time there may be flattening and atrophy of the intrinsic hand muscles. Usually an ipsilateral Horner syndrome (ptosis, miosis, and enophthalmos) also is present because of injury involving the cervical sympathetic fibers of the first thoracic root. Often this is associated with delayed pigmentation of the iris, sometimes of more than 1 year's duration.

When the entire arm is paralyzed, it is usually completely motionless, flaccid, and powerless, hanging limply to the side. All reflexes are absent. The sensory deficit may extend almost to the shoulder.

DIFFERENTIAL DIAGNOSIS

The presence of a flail arm in a neonate may be caused by cerebral injury or by a number of injuries about the shoulder. Cerebral injury is usually associated with other manifestations of CNS injury. A careful radiographic study of the shoulder, including an examination of the lower cervical spine, clavicle, and upper humerus, should be made to exclude tearing of the joint capsule, fracture of the clavicle, and fracture, dislocation, or upper epiphyseal detachment of the humerus. Posterior dislocation of the humeral head may be difficult to identify with standard radiographs. Torode and Donnan[75] have used CT scans to demonstrate that posterior dislocation is more common than previously believed. Hunter and coworkers[36] reported an infant in whom a posterior dislocation was uncertain with standard radiographs. Ultrasonography clearly revealed a posterior dislocation. Because posterior dislocation will complicate resolution of the palsy, ultrasonographic evaluation should be considered early in the management of these infants.

TREATMENT

The basic principle of treatment historically has been conservative, with initial emphasis on prevention of contractures while awaiting recovery of the brachial plexus. During the last decade, this approach has been replaced by a more comprehensive program that combines initial conservative management with closer follow-up and earlier decision regarding surgical intervention. This is best represented by the care plan developed by Shenaq and colleagues[70] (Fig. 27-13).

This approach is initiated with a thorough and complete physical examination that includes careful palpation of the sternocleidomastoid muscle for contracture or pseudotumor; inspection for fractures of the clavicle, humerus, or ribs; observation for abdominal asymmetry, which could indicate paralysis of the hemidiaphragm; and assessment for ocular asymmetry, which may indicate associated Horner syndrome.

Ancillary investigations, including CT or myelography and MRI, could be helpful in detecting possible avulsions. Electromyography has been unreliable in predicting extent of damage.

Some infants may demonstrate discomfort because of a painful traumatic neuritis affecting the brachial plexus. If no discomfort is apparent and other lesions as noted earlier are ruled out, early passive range-of-motion exercises, particularly involving the elbow and wrist, should be instituted. Because of shorter nursery stays, the mother should receive early demonstration and written instructions describing these exercises. She should then begin to work with the infant under the guidance of the therapy staff. Exercises include shoulder rotation, elbow flexion and extension, wrist flexion and extension, finger flexion and extension, and thumb abduction, adduction, and opposition. The infant should be reevaluated every month. If improvement in deltoid, biceps, and triceps function has not occurred by the third month of life, functional outcome without surgery is unlikely. Consequently, a decision for surgery should be made by the end of the third month, followed by primary brachial plexus exploration during the fourth month.

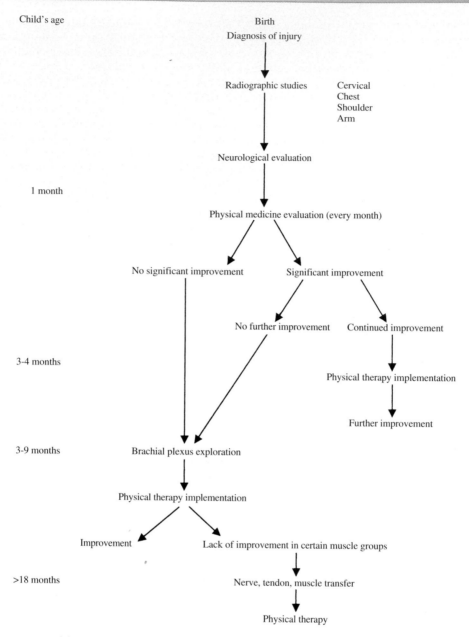

Child's age

Birth
Diagnosis of injury

Radiographic studies — Cervical / Chest / Shoulder / Arm

Neurological evaluation

1 month

Physical medicine evaluation (every month)

No significant improvement — Significant improvement

No further improvement — Continued improvement

3-4 months

Physical therapy implementation

Further improvement

3-9 months

Brachial plexus exploration

Physical therapy implementation

Improvement — Lack of improvement in certain muscle groups

>18 months

Nerve, tendon, muscle transfer

Physical therapy

FIGURE 27-13. Treatment protocol for management of obstetric brachial plexus palsy. (From Shenaq SM et al: Brachial plexus birth injuries and current management. Clin Plast Surg 25:527, 1998.)

Initial surgical intervention beyond 12 months of age at the level of the cervical root alone has resulted in disappointing outcomes. However, when infants referred at this age have been offered a combined cervical root and infraclavicular exploration with neurolysis, graph reconstruction, and nerve transfer of appropriate elements in both anatomic compartments, improved outcomes have been noted. Blaauw and Slooff[10] have reported their experience with transfer of pectoral nerves to the musculocutaneous nerve in 25 patients, 22 of whom had upper root avulsions. Seventeen patients, including one who went to surgery at 3 months of age, had excellent outcomes, five had fair outcomes, and two were considered treatment failures.

The initial surgical therapy may include a team of neurosurgeons, plastic surgeons, and physiatrists who collaborate in the exploration, evaluation, and repair of the injury. This aggressive approach has resulted in up to 90% of patients demonstrating useful function of muscle groups above the elbow. Function below the elbow has been characterized by 50% to 70% recovery because of the increased distance required for nerve regeneration.

PROGNOSIS
Continued close follow-up includes serial evaluation of shoulder, elbow, forearm, wrist, finger, and thumb function. Based on the child's progress over time, a

decision is made regarding further treatment. Physical therapy is continued until there is no further progress or the deficit is debilitating. For the infant who continues to demonstrate lack of improvement in certain muscle groups, secondary surgical reconstruction is available, with a variety of options depending on the individual deficit. In summary, the infant who does not improve spontaneously now has increased hope for recovery owing to advances in microsurgery and nerve transfer techniques.

Although most (93% to 95%) infants achieve return of function with conservative management, the remainder with persistent deficits may go on to development of long-term severe handicaps of the affected extremity. Early treatment offers significant improvement for approximately 90% of these children. Later treatment reduces this number to 50% to 70%. To avoid missing the window of opportunity for timelier and more successful treatment, infants with brachial plexus palsy should be referred to centers that have an established comprehensive program for the broad spectrum of infants with this condition.

Phrenic Nerve Paralysis (See also Chapter 42, Part 5.)

Phrenic nerve paralysis results in diaphragmatic paralysis and rarely occurs as an isolated injury in the neonate. Most injuries are unilateral and are associated with an ipsilateral upper brachial plexus palsy.

ETIOLOGY
The most common cause is a difficult breech delivery. Lateral hyperextension of the neck results in overstretching or avulsion of the third, fourth, and fifth cervical roots, which supply the phrenic nerve.

CLINICAL MANIFESTATIONS
The first sign may be recurrent episodes of cyanosis, usually accompanied by irregular and labored respirations. The respiratory excursions of the involved side of the diaphragm are largely ineffectual, and the breathing is therefore almost completely thoracic, so that no bulging of the abdomen occurs with inspiration (Fig. 27-14A and B). The thrust of the diaphragm, which often may be felt just under the costal margin on the normal side, is absent on the affected side. Dullness to percussion and diminished breath sounds are found over the affected side. In a severe injury, tachypnea, weak cry, and apneic spells may occur.

RADIOGRAPHIC MANIFESTATIONS
Radiographs taken during the first few days may show only slight elevation of the affected diaphragm, occasionally so subtle that it may be considered normal. Additional films show the more apparent elevation of the diaphragm, with displacement of the heart and mediastinum to the opposite side (Fig. 27-14C). Frequently, areas of atelectasis appear bilaterally. Early diagnosis can be confirmed by real-time ultrasonographic examination of the diaphragm, which reveals abnormal motion of the affected hemidiaphragm. This procedure provides the added advantage of availability at the bedside. Fluoroscopy should be reserved for the equivocal case. In still questionable cases, diagnosis can be further enhanced by transvenous electrical stimulation of the phrenic nerve.

DIFFERENTIAL DIAGNOSIS
Careful physical examination should allow differentiation between CNS, cardiac, and pulmonary causes of neonatal respiratory distress. The diagnosis can be confirmed by fluoroscopy and electrical stimulation of the phrenic nerve.

TREATMENT
Most infants require only nonspecific medical treatment. The infant should be positioned on the involved side, and oxygen should be administered for cyanosis or hypoxemia. Intravenous fluids may be necessary for the first few days. If the infant begins to show improvement, progressive oral or gavage feedings may be started. Antibiotics are indicated if pneumonia occurs.

Infants with more severe respiratory distress, particularly those with bilateral phrenic nerve palsy, may require assisted ventilation shortly after delivery. de Vries Reilingh and associates[21] have reviewed their experience with 23 infants who incurred phrenic nerve injury as neonates. Infants who had not recovered diaphragmatic function after 30 days of conservative treatment did not demonstrate spontaneous recovery thereafter. Accordingly, these investigators recommend limiting conservative treatment to 1 month, assuming the infant is adequately oxygenated with conventional techniques. The absence of definite improvement after 1 month is considered evidence of disruption of the phrenic nerve, thereby minimizing chances of complete spontaneous recovery. Infants in this category should be considered candidates for plication of the diaphragm early in the second month of life.

PROGNOSIS
Many infants recover spontaneously. If avulsion of the cervical nerves has occurred, spontaneous recovery is not possible, and in the absence of surgery the infant is susceptible to pneumonia in the atelectatic lung. Infants treated surgically do well, with no recurrence of pneumonia and no late pulmonary or chest wall complications.

Injury to the Sternocleidomastoid Muscle

Injury to the sternocleidomastoid muscle is designated muscular torticollis, congenital torticollis, or sternocleidomastoid fibroma. Its cause and pathologic features have been controversial.

ETIOLOGY
The birth trauma theory suggests that the muscle or fascial sheath is ruptured during a breech or difficult delivery involving hyperextension of the muscle. A hematoma develops and is subsequently invaded by

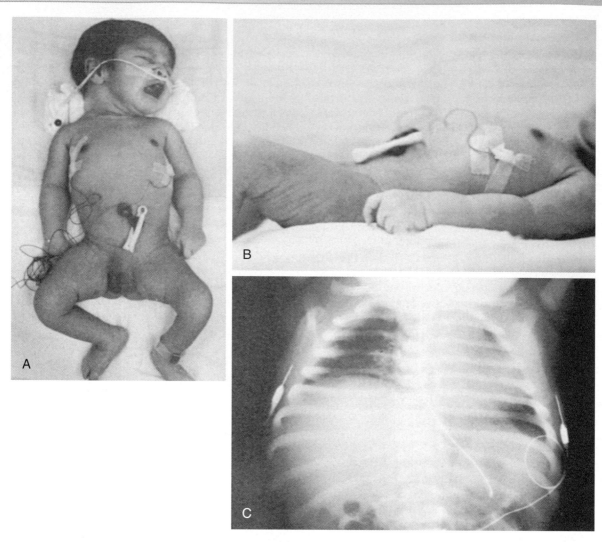

FIGURE 27-14. A, Nine-hour-old, 3190-g female infant born after difficult total breech extraction; during delivery, cervix clamped down on head, necessitating extensive tugging and pulling on both arms. Note markedly hyperexpanded chest and classic appearance of both upper extremities in Erb palsy positions. **B,** Lateral view of same infant, demonstrating increased anterior-posterior diameter of chest and close-up view of left upper extremity adducted at shoulder, extended at elbow, and pronated and flexed at wrist. **C,** Significant elevation of right hemidiaphragm to level of fifth thoracic vertebra in same infant, compatible with paralysis of right hemidiaphragm. Note significant shifting of heart and mediastinum to the left.

fibrin and fibroblasts with progressive formation of scar tissue and shortening of the muscle. The intrauterine theory postulates abnormal pressure, position, or trauma to the muscle during intrauterine life. Another theory suggests a hereditary defect in the development of the muscle. Others have noted pathologic findings resembling infectious myositis, suggesting an infection in utero or a muscle injured at delivery. Davids and coworkers,[19] using MRI in visualizing live infants and cadaver dissections and injection studies, suggest that congenital muscular torticollis results from intrauterine or perinatal compartment syndrome. According to this investigation, the sternocleidomastoid muscle compartment, defined by the external investing fascia of the neck, contains only the sternocleidomastoid muscle. In utero or intrapartum positioning of the head and neck in forward flexion, lateral bending, and rotation

can result in the ipsilateral sternocleidomastoid muscle kinking on itself. If the kinking continues for a prolonged period in utero, an ischemic injury at the site could develop, followed by subsequent edema and development of a compartment syndrome. Therefore, the mechanism of injury is localized kinking or crush, in contrast to the previously suspected mechanism of stretching or tearing (Fig. 27-15).

CLINICAL MANIFESTATIONS

A mass in the midportion of the sternocleidomastoid muscle may be evident at birth, although usually it is first noted 10 to 14 days after birth. It is 1 to 2 cm in diameter, hard, immobile, fusiform, and well circumscribed; there is no inflammation or overlying discoloration. The mass enlarges during the following 2 to 4 weeks and then gradually regresses and disappears by age 5 to 8 months.

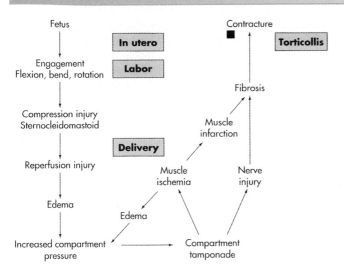

FIGURE 27-15. Algorithm illustrating the Davids study,[19] suggesting that congenital muscular torticollis results from intrauterine or perinatal compartment syndrome.

A transient torticollis produced by contracture of the involved muscle appears soon after birth. The head tilts toward the involved side, and the chin is somewhat elevated and rotated toward the opposite shoulder. The head cannot be moved passively into normal position. If the deformity persists beyond 3 or 4 years, the skull becomes foreshortened. Flattening of the frontal bone and bulging of the occipital bone occur on the involved side, whereas the contralateral frontal bone bulges and the occiput is flattened. The ipsilateral eyebrow is slanted; the clavicle and shoulder become elevated compared with the opposite normal side, and the ipsilateral mastoid process becomes more prominent. If treatment is not instituted, a lower cervical, upper thoracic scoliosis subsequently develops. Rarely, calcification develops in the affected muscles.

DIFFERENTIAL DIAGNOSIS

Careful radiographic examination should be made of the cervical spine and shoulders to rule out Sprengel deformity or Klippel-Feil syndrome, cervical myelodysplasia, and occipitalization of the atlas. In clinically equivocal cases, CT scans may differentiate classic muscular torticollis from other cervical soft tissue lesions that may cause torticollis (e.g., hemangioma, lymphangioma, and teratoma).

TREATMENT

Treatment should be instituted as early as possible. The involved muscle should be stretched to an overcorrected position by gentle, even, and persistent motion with the infant supine. The head is flexed forward and away from the affected side, and the chin is rotated toward the affected side. The mother can be instructed to repeat this maneuver several times a day. The infant also should be stimulated to turn the head spontaneously toward the affected side; the crib may

be positioned so that the infant must turn to the desired position of overcorrection in looking for window light or at a mobile or favorite rattle. During sleep the infant should be placed on the side of the torticollis; in this position, sandbags should be placed on each side of the infant's body for fixation. An alternative approach involves a helmet that is custom made for the infant. Rubber straps made of surgical drain tubing attached to the helmet are in turn fixed to the side rails of the crib at night, with appropriate adjustments made to force the infant to sleep on the prominent side of the head. This results in stretching of the shortened sternocleidomastoid muscle.

Conservative therapy should be continued for 6 months. If the deformity has not been fully corrected, surgery should be considered to prevent permanent skull and cervical spine deformities. Ultrasonography may be useful in defining the quantity of normal muscle remnant surrounding the lesion, thereby helping to determine whether the infant requires no treatment at all, conservative stretching, or surgery.[14]

Procedures that have been used include distal tenotomy, muscle lengthening, and excision of the affected muscle. All are followed by some problems. After tenotomy, contractures may recur. Lengthening is difficult because of imprecision in estimating how much elongation will be adequate for subsequent growth. Complete excision deforms the outline of the neck. Akazawa and associates[1] reported favorable results after partial resection. This was followed postoperatively with massive cotton bandaging of the neck in the neutral position for 3 weeks. Plaster casts, a brace, and physical therapy were not used. They recommend the period between 1 and 5 years of age as the optimum for surgery.

PROGNOSIS

Most infants treated conservatively show complete recovery within 2 to 3 months. If surgery is necessary and if it is performed early, the facial asymmetry will disappear almost entirely. Infants treated before their first birthday have a better outcome than those treated later, regardless of the type of treatment. Nonsurgical treatment after 1 year is rarely successful.

INJURIES TO THE SPINE AND SPINAL CORD

Birth injuries to the vertebral spine and spinal cord are rarely diagnosed. It is not certain whether the low incidence is real, reflecting improved obstetric techniques, or represents a tendency for postmortem examination to overlook spine and spinal cord lesions.

Etiology

These injuries almost always result from breech deliveries,[11] especially difficult ones in which version and extraction were used. Other predisposing factors include brow and face presentations, dystocia (especially shoulder), prematurity, primiparity, and precipitous delivery.

The injuries are usually caused by stretching of the cord. However, Hankins[32] reported an infant with lower thoracic spinal cord injury after application of maternal fundal pressure to relieve shoulder dystocia. MRI revealed focal spinal cord swelling involving T9 through T12, thought to represent ischemia or infarction due to a compressive injury. The most common mechanism responsible is probably forceful longitudinal traction on the trunk while the head is still firmly engaged in the pelvis. When combined with flexion and torsion of the vertebral axis, this becomes a more significant problem. Occasionally, a snap is felt by the obstetrician while traction is exerted. Although cesarean delivery has been recommended as optimal for infants in breech presentation with a hyperextended head, Maekawa and colleagues[46] documented spinal cord injury after cesarean section. In fact, the mother had reported weak fetal movements during the third trimester, which suggests that injury was occurring before delivery. Difficulty in delivery of the shoulders in cephalic presentations may result in a similar mechanism of injury. The spinal cord is very delicate and inelastic. Its attachments are the cauda equina below and the roots of the brachial plexus and medulla above. Because the ligaments are elastic and the muscles delicate, the infant's vertebral column may be stretched easily. In addition, the dura is more elastic in the infant than in the adult. Consequently, strong longitudinal traction may be expected to cause elongation of the spinal column and to stretch the spinal cord and its membranes. The possible result is vertebral fracture or dislocation or both and cord transection. Most often, hemorrhage and edema produce a physiologic transection. The lower cervical and upper thoracic regions are most often involved, but occasionally the entire length of the spinal canal contains a heavy accumulation of blood.

Clinical Manifestations

Affected infants may follow one of four clinical patterns. Those in the first group are either stillborn or in poor condition from birth, with respiratory depression, shock, and hypothermia. They deteriorate rapidly; death occurs within several hours, often before neurologic signs are obvious. These infants usually have a high cervical or brainstem lesion.

The second group consists of infants who at birth may appear normal or show signs similar to those of the first group; these infants die after several days. Cardiac function is usually relatively strong. Within hours or days the central type of respiratory depression that is initially present may be complicated by respiratory distress of pulmonary origin, usually pneumonia. The spinal lesion, usually in the upper or midcervical region, frequently is not recognized for several days, when flaccidity and immobility of the legs are noted. Occasionally, urinary retention may be the first symptom. Paralysis of the abdominal wall is manifested by a relaxation of the abdominal wall and bulging at the flanks when the infant is held upright. The intercostal muscles may be affected if the lesion is high enough. Sensation is absent over the lower half of the body. Deep tendon reflexes and spontaneous reflex movements are absent. The infant is constipated. The brachial plexus is involved in approximately 20% of all cases. The spinal column is usually clinically and radiographically normal.

The third group, with lesions at the seventh cervical to first thoracic vertebra or lower, comprises infants who survive for long periods, some for years. Paraplegia noted at birth may be transient. The lesion in the cord may be mild and reversible, or it may result in permanent neurologic sequelae with no return of function in the lower cord segments. The skin over the involved part of the body is dry and scaly, predisposing the infant to decubitus ulcers. Muscle atrophy, severe contractures, and bony deformities follow. Bladder distention and constant dribbling persist, and recurring urinary tract infections and pneumonia are common. Within several weeks or months this clinical picture is replaced by a stage of reflex activity, or paraplegia-in-flexion. This is characterized by return of tone and rigid flexion of the involved extremities, improvement in skin condition with healing of decubitus ulcers, and periodic mass reflex responses consisting of tonic spasms of the extremities, spontaneous micturition, and profuse sweating over the involved part of the body.

Infants in the fourth group have subtle neurologic signs of spasticity thought to represent cerebral palsy. These patients have experienced partial spinal cord injuries and occasional cerebrovascular accidents.

Differential Diagnosis

During the first few weeks of life injuries to the spinal cord may be confused with amyotonia congenita or myelodysplasia associated with spina bifida occulta[63] (see also Chapter 38). The former may be differentiated by the generalized distribution of the weakness and hypotonia and by the presence of normal sensation and sphincter control. The latter is usually associated with some cutaneous lesions over the sacral region such as dimples, angiomas, or abnormal tufts of hair; it is always associated with defects in the spinal lamina. Other conditions less often considered include transverse myelitis and spinal cord tumors, particularly in infants who demonstrate paralysis after an apparently normal labor and delivery. Cerebral hypotonia should be considered in infants who also demonstrate cranial nerve abnormalities, persistent primitive reflexes, and a dull facial appearance, contrasting to the bright, alert facies of the infant with spinal cord trauma. However, the concomitant occurrence of cerebral damage in an infant with spinal cord injury may confound the diagnosis. A final consideration is the infant with bilateral brachial plexus palsy with associated motor and sensory loss, or Horner syndrome; the demonstration of normal lower extremity function should rule out spinal cord injury.

Although somatosensory evoked potential recording has been used in establishing a diagnosis of spinal cord injury,[7] cervical responses are usually small and can be difficult to detect even in clinically normal infants; in addition, scalp potentials overlying the somatosensory cortex may be absent in normal term neonates.[42] Ultrasonography has been used to evaluate severe spinal cord injury in neonates.[5] The procedure is easily performed at the bedside with no disturbance of the patient. Initial cord edema, hematomyelia, and hemorrhage outside the cord can be assessed. MRI is the only procedure that provides a direct image of the spinal cord and clearly is the most reliable modality available to evaluate presumptive cervical spinal cord injury in the infant.[42,51] Previous limitations of ferromagnetic ventilators and monitors can now be circumvented by manual ventilation combined with nonferromagnetic monitors. Another option is the use of a nonferromagnetic ventilator.

Treatment

Treatment is supportive and usually unsatisfactory. The infant affected at birth requires basic resuscitative and supportive measures. Infants who survive present a therapeutic challenge that can be met only by the combined and interested efforts of the pediatrician, neurologist, neurosurgeon, urologist, psychiatrist, orthopedist, nurse, physical therapist, and occupational therapist.

While the infant is reasonably stable, cervical and thoracic spine radiographs should be obtained. In the rare occurrence of vertebral fracture or dislocation or both, immediate neurosurgical consultation is necessary for reduction of the deformity and relief of cord compression, followed by appropriate immobilization. Lumbar puncture in the acute period is of little practical value and may aggravate existing cord damage if the infant is excessively manipulated during the procedure. After several days, however, a persistent spinal fluid block may be demonstrated and may be an indication for exploratory laminectomy at the site of trauma. This possibility should be suspected in an infant with partial paraplegia and negative radiographs.

Prompt and meticulous attention must be given to skin, bladder, and bowel care. The position of paralyzed parts should be changed every 2 hours. Areas of anesthetic skin should be washed, dried, and gently massaged daily. Lamb's-wool covers are helpful in preventing pressure necrosis of skin. Benzoin tincture applications help protect the skin in pressure areas. A decubitus ulcer is treated by scrupulous cleansing and complete freedom from weight bearing and friction. An indwelling urethral catheter should be inserted within several hours after severe cord trauma at any level. In the smaller infant a size 3 feeding tube may be used. However, in the term infant a size 5 feeding tube can usually be inserted. Repeated instrumentation should be avoided. Cultures of urine should be obtained weekly and as clinically indicated. Antibiotic therapy should be used only in the presence of infection. After several weeks, the infant reaches the stage of paraplegia-in-flexion, and urinary retention usually is replaced by regular episodes of spontaneous voiding. The indwelling catheter may then be removed, and postvoid bladder residuals should be measured. A renal sonogram and a conventional fluoroscopically guided voiding cystourethrogram should be obtained. If there are large postvoid residuals (more than 10 to 15 mL), or if the renal sonogram or cystogram shows abnormality, urodynamic studies may be necessary. A high-pressure neurogenic bladder is treated with an anticholinergic agent such as oxybutynin chloride, 0.5 to 2.0 mg/kg per day in three or four divided doses, concurrently with clean intermittent bladder catheterization every 3 to 4 hours. Treatment of the low-pressure neurogenic bladder requires only clean intermittent catheterization.

The first infection should be treated with the appropriate antibiotic for 2 weeks. After the neonatal period this should be followed by suppressive therapy. During the first 2 months of life, this may include amoxicillin, 20 mg/kg PO in one daily dose, or ampicillin, 50 mg/kg IV daily. After 2 months, any of the following options is appropriate: trimethoprim and sulfamethoxazole (Bactrim, Septra), 2 mg/kg per day in one daily dose; nitrofurantoin (Furadantin), 1.5 to 2 mg/kg in one daily dose; or cefprozil, 15 mg/kg in one daily dose. This therapy should be continued for 6 to 12 months or longer, depending on the reversibility of the lesion. Cultures of urine should be obtained at 1 week, monthly for 3 months, and then every 3 months for 1 year or until recovery.

Fecal retention also is a common problem, especially after total cord transection. Appropriate dietary balance should aid in keeping the stools soft. Early use of glycerin suppositories at regular intervals encourages automatic defecation. Digital manipulation may be necessary to relieve fecal impaction.

Finally, physical rehabilitation should be instituted early in an attempt to minimize deformity. After several years, orthopedic procedures may still be necessary to correct contractures and bony deformities.

Prognosis

The prognosis varies with the severity of the injury. Most severe injuries result in death shortly after birth. Infants with cord compression from vertebral fractures or dislocations or both may recover with reasonable return of function if prompt neurosurgical removal of the compression is performed. Infants with mild injuries or partial transections may recover with minimal sequelae. MRI evidence of hemorrhage in the cervical spinal cord portends a poor neurologic outcome.[51] If MRI reveals extensive edema in multiple spinal cord segments without concurrent hemorrhage, complete recovery is possible.[51] Infants who exhibit complete physiologic cord transection shortly after birth without vertebral fracture or dislocation have an extremely poor outlook for recovery of function. Many die in infancy of ascending urinary tract infection and sepsis. Long-term survivors have been reported to live into their third decade. They are extremely rare, and although they may have normal intelligence and learn to walk with special appliances, these children face the late complications of pain, spasms, autonomic dysfunction, bony deformities, and genitourinary, psychiatric, and school problems.

MacKinnon and colleagues[45] have published an algorithm for predicting outcome in infants with upper cervical spinal cord injury; the algorithm is based on age at first breath and rate of recovery of breathing and limb movements in the first few weeks and months of life. For infants with rapid recovery, the prognosis was clarified by age 3 weeks. Infants who demonstrated very slow or no recovery of breathing or extremity movements by 3 months of age universally had a poor outcome. Patients with intermediate rates of recovery were thought to have an uncertain long-term prognosis at 3 months of age.

INJURIES TO INTRA-ABDOMINAL ORGANS

Although birth trauma involving intra-abdominal organs is uncommon, it frequently must be considered by the physician who cares for neonates because deterioration can be fulminant in an undetected lesion, and therapy can be very effective when a lesion is diagnosed early. Intra-abdominal trauma should be suspected in any newborn with shock and abdominal distention or pallor, anemia, and irritability without evidence of external blood loss.

Rupture of the Liver

The liver is the most frequently injured abdominal organ during the birth process. The autopsy incidence of liver injury varies from 0.9% to 9.6%.[69]

ETIOLOGY

Birth trauma is the most significant factor contributing to liver injury. The condition usually occurs in large infants, infants with hepatomegaly (e.g., infants with erythroblastosis fetalis and infants of diabetic mothers), and infants who underwent breech delivery. Manual pressure on the liver during delivery of the head in a breech presentation is probably a typical mechanism of injury. Prematurity and postmaturity also are thought to predispose the infant to this injury. Other contributing factors include asphyxia and coagulation disorders. Trauma to the liver more often results in subcapsular hematoma than actual laceration of the liver.

CLINICAL MANIFESTATIONS

The infant usually appears normal the first 1 to 3 days, but rarely for as long as 7 days. Nonspecific signs related to loss of blood into the hematoma may appear early; they include poor feeding, listlessness, pallor, jaundice, tachypnea, and tachycardia. A mass may be palpable in the right upper quadrant of the abdomen. The hematocrit and hemoglobin values may be stable early in the course, but serial determinations suggest blood loss. These manifestations are followed by sudden circulatory collapse, usually coincident with rupture of the hematoma through the capsule and extravasation of blood into the peritoneal cavity. The abdomen then may be distended, rigid, and dull to percussion, occasionally with a bluish discoloration of the overlying skin, which may extend over the scrotum in male infants. Abdominal radiographs may suggest the diagnosis by revealing liver enlargement, an abnormal course of a nasogastric tube or umbilical venous catheter, or uniform opacity of the abdomen, indicating free intraperitoneal fluid. Although paracentesis can confirm whether the latter indicates free blood in the peritoneal cavity, ultrasonography offers a noninvasive method of diagnosis.[69] Fresh intrahepatic hemorrhage appears echogenic, with possible enlargement of the involved lobe; with involution of the hemorrhage, the lesion becomes more echolucent and may disappear. CT scan of the abdomen also may assist in establishing a diagnosis of subcapsular hemorrhage without rupture.

DIFFERENTIAL DIAGNOSIS

This lesion is one of several that can result in hemoperitoneum; others include trauma to the adrenal glands, kidneys, gastrointestinal tract, and spleen. Presence of a right upper quadrant mass suggests trauma to the liver, but absence of a mass does not rule it out. Abdominal radiography, ultrasonography, and intravenous pyelography may assist in pinpointing the site of trauma, but ultimately a definitive diagnosis can be made only by laparotomy.

TREATMENT

Immediate management consists of prompt transfusion with packed red blood cells, as well as recognition and correction of any coagulation disorder. This should be followed by laparotomy with evacuation of the hematoma and repair of any laceration with sutures placed over a hemostatic agent. Any fragmented, devitalized liver tissue should be removed to prevent subsequent fatal secondary hemorrhage. Occasionally, hemostasis may be difficult to achieve at surgery. Consequently, blood transfusion and the tamponade of intra-abdominal pressure might be adequate therapy in some infants.

PROGNOSIS

In unrecognized liver trauma with formation of a subcapsular hematoma, shock and death may result if the hematoma ruptures through the capsule, reducing the pressure tamponade and resulting in new bleeding from the liver. Recognition of the possibility of liver rupture in infants with a predisposing birth history, followed by early diagnosis and prompt therapy, should improve the prognosis. Early diagnosis and correction of any existing coagulation disorder also improves the prognosis.

Rupture of the Spleen

Rupture of the spleen in the newborn occurs much less often than rupture of the liver. However, recognition of this condition is equally important because of its similar potential for fulminant shock and death if the diagnosis is delayed.

ETIOLOGY

The condition is most common in large infants, infants delivered in breech position, and infants with erythroblastosis fetalis or congenital syphilis in whom the spleen is enlarged and more friable and thereby susceptible to rupture either spontaneously or after minor trauma. An underlying clotting defect also has been implicated. Rupture of the spleen has occurred in normal-sized infants with uneventful deliveries and no underlying disease.[35]

CLINICAL MANIFESTATIONS

Clinical signs indicating blood loss and hemoperitoneum are similar to those described for hepatic rupture. The hemoglobin and hematocrit values decrease, and abdominal paracentesis may reveal free blood. Several infants have been described in whom the blood was circumscribed within the leaves of the phrenicosplenic ligament and therefore was not clinically detectable. Occasionally, a left upper quadrant mass may be palpable, and radiographs of the abdomen may show medial displacement of the gastric air bubble.

DIFFERENTIAL DIAGNOSIS

Rupture of the liver and trauma to the adrenal glands, kidneys, and gastrointestinal tract must be distinguished.

TREATMENT

Packed red blood cells should be transfused promptly, and any coexisting clotting defect should be corrected. This should be followed by immediate exploratory laparotomy. Every attempt should be made to repair and preserve the spleen to prevent the subsequent increased risk of infection.[67] Packing of the wound surface with Gel-Foam and Surgicel has been used to stop the oozing of blood.[35] The Gel-Foam and Surgicel may be removed at a follow-up laparotomy within several days, at which time the spleen may be inspected for rebleeding.

PROGNOSIS

With early recognition and emergency surgery, the survival rate should approach 100%.

Adrenal Hemorrhage

Neonatal adrenal hemorrhage is more common than previously suspected; some autopsy studies have revealed a high incidence of subclinical hemorrhage. Massive hemorrhage is much less common, and the incidence is difficult to determine because the diagnosis is often unsuspected and considered retrospectively only years later, when calcified adrenal glands are unexpectedly found on radiographs or at autopsy.

ETIOLOGY

The most likely cause is birth trauma; risk factors include macrosomia, diabetes in the mother, breech presentation, congenital syphilis, and dystocia. Placental hemorrhage, anoxia, hemorrhagic disease of the newborn, prematurity, and, more recently, neuroblastoma have been implicated. Pathologic findings vary from unilateral minute areas of bleeding to massive bilateral hemorrhage. The increased size and vascularity of the adrenal gland at birth may predispose it to hemorrhage.

CLINICAL MANIFESTATIONS

Signs vary with the degree and extent of hemorrhage. The classic findings are fever, tachypnea out of proportion to the degree of fever, yellowish pallor, cyanosis of the lips and fingertips, a mass in either flank with overlying skin discoloration, and purpura. Findings suggesting adrenal insufficiency include poor feeding, vomiting, diarrhea, obstipation, dehydration, abdominal distention, irritability, hypoglycemia, uremia, rash, listlessness, coma, convulsions, and shock.

RADIOGRAPHIC MANIFESTATIONS

Initial radiographic manifestations may be limited to widening of the retroperitoneal space with forward displacement of the stomach and duodenum or downward displacement of the intestines or kidneys. In time, calcification may appear. Typically, this is rimlike and has been observed as early as the 12th day of life. After several weeks the calcification becomes denser and retracted and assumes the configuration of the adrenal gland (Fig. 27-16). Ultrasonographic examination of the neonate is an excellent adjunctive method of diagnosis. Abdominal ultrasonography performed during the first several days may reveal a solid lesion in the location of the adrenal hemorrhage; this is thought to represent either clot fragmentation or diffuse clotted blood throughout the adrenal gland. If adrenal hemorrhage is suspected, ultrasonographic examination should be repeated at 3- to 5-day intervals. If adrenal hemorrhage has occurred, the lesion will change from a solid to a cystic appearance, coincident with liquefaction, degeneration, and lysis of the clot (Fig. 27-17).

DIFFERENTIAL DIAGNOSIS

Adrenal hemorrhage must be distinguished from other causes of abdominal hemorrhage. In addition, when a mass is palpable, the differential diagnosis must include the multiple causes of flank masses in the newborn, such as genitourinary anomaly, Wilms tumor, and neuroblastoma. If the infant is large or the delivery is traumatic or breech, an adrenal hemorrhage is most likely. Neuroblastoma may be distinguished by persistent demonstration of a solid lesion on serial ultrasonographic examinations and by increased excretion of vanillylmandelic acid and other urinary catecholamines in 85% to 90% of affected infants. Blood

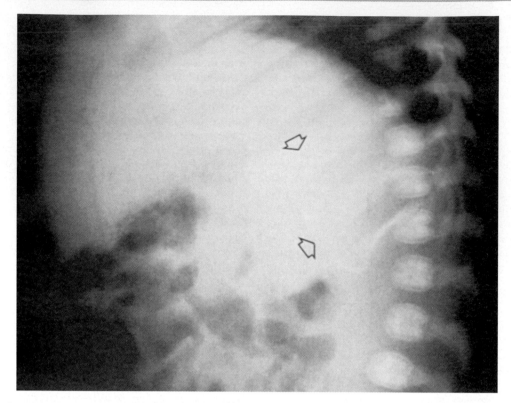

FIGURE 27-16. Lateral abdominal radiographs of a 5312-g male infant delivered vaginally, with difficulty after shoulder dystocia. At 48 hours, fever, icterus, and slow feeding were noted and a mass was palpable above the left kidney. At 31 days there was dense, retracted calcification *(arrows)* that assumed the configuration of the adrenal gland.

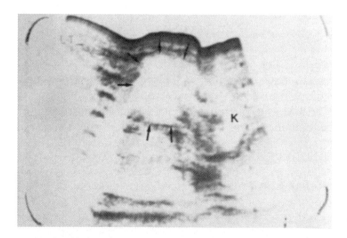

FIGURE 27-17. Sagittal gray-scale abdominal ultrasonographic examination of a 4564-g male infant whose mother had gestational diabetes. Problems included fracture of right clavicle, hyperbilirubinemia requiring three exchange transfusions, and abdominal distention with large left flank mass. Ultrasonographic examination at 14 days demonstrated fluid-filled mass *(arrows)* superior to left kidney (K), representing adrenal hemorrhage. (Courtesy of Dr. John C. McFadden, Lutheran General Children's Hospital, Park Ridge, Ill.)

pressure measurements and radiographs also may help to evaluate this possibility.

TREATMENT

Significant blood loss should be replaced with packed red blood cell transfusion. Suspicion of adrenal insufficiency may warrant the use of intravenous fluids and corticosteroids. The decision for surgical intervention is dictated by the location and degree of hemorrhage. If it appears to be retroperitoneal and limited by the perinephric fascia, some recommend blood replacement and careful observation in the hope of spontaneous control by tamponade; often this approach is successful, and surgery is not necessary. If paracentesis reveals blood or if blood loss exceeds replacement, exploratory laparotomy is indicated. Surgery may involve evacuation of hematoma, vessel ligation, and adrenalectomy with or without nephrectomy. When the hemorrhagic process extends to the peritoneal cavity, peritoneal exploration and evacuation of clots are indicated.

PROGNOSIS

Small hemorrhages are probably often asymptomatic and have no associated significant morbidity, judging from the unexpected discovery of calcified adrenal glands on abdominal radiographs taken for other reasons later in infancy and childhood. If hemoperitoneum or adrenal insufficiency or both develop, the outlook depends on the speed with which diagnosis is made and appropriate therapy instituted. Surviving infants should be followed closely after discharge from the hospital. Adrenal function should be tested with adrenocorticotropic hormone stimulation at a later date to determine whether a normal response occurs in the urinary excretion of 17-hydroxycorticosterone.

Renal Injury

Birth-related injury to the kidneys occurs rarely and less often than injury involving the liver, spleen, or adrenal gland.

ETIOLOGY

Factors that predispose an infant to any form of intra-abdominal injury also may affect the kidneys. They include macrosomia, malpresentation (especially breech), and precipitous labor or delivery or both. The potential for renal injury is enhanced by a preexisting anomaly (e.g., hydronephrosis).

CLINICAL MANIFESTATIONS

The infant may demonstrate the same signs of blood loss and hemoperitoneum noted in the other intra-abdominal lesions. More specific signs include ascites, flank mass, and gross hematuria. Radiographs may confirm the presence of ascites and flank mass. Ultrasonographic examination may further define the mass (e.g., presence of cysts) and reveal ascites and retroperitoneal hematoma. Application of a Doppler probe to the renal hilus and the region of the vessels can assist in assessing renal arterial and venous flow. In ambiguous cases, CT scanning may help to clarify ultrasonographic findings.

DIFFERENTIAL DIAGNOSIS

Other lesions that cause hematuria must be considered. They include renal tumor with hemorrhage and renal vein thrombosis with infarction.

TREATMENT

After providing supportive measures similar to those used in other intra-abdominal injuries, the clinician should consider laparotomy. Possible findings at surgery include kidney rupture or transection, renal pedicle avulsion, and kidney necrosis. Use of an intraoperative Doppler probe can determine the status of renal blood flow. If there is no flow, nephrectomy is indicated.

PROGNOSIS

Early recognition of possible renal vascular injury may lead to earlier intervention, with the potential for kidney salvage.

INJURIES TO THE EXTREMITIES

Fracture of the Humerus

After the clavicle, the humerus is the bone most often fractured during the birth process.

ETIOLOGY

The most common mechanisms responsible are difficult delivery of extended arms in breech presentations and of the shoulders in vertex presentations. Besides traction with simultaneous rotation of the arm, direct pressure on the humerus also is a factor. This may account for the occurrence of fracture of the humerus in spontaneous vertex deliveries. The fractures are usually in the diaphysis. They are often greenstick fractures, although complete fracture with overriding of the fragments occasionally occurs.

CLINICAL MANIFESTATIONS

A greenstick fracture may be overlooked until a callus is noted. A complete fracture with marked displacement of fragments presents an obvious deformity that calls attention to the injury. Often the initial manifestation of the fracture is immobility of the affected arm. Palpation reveals tenderness, crepitation, and hypermobility of the fragments. The ipsilateral Moro response is absent. Radiographs confirm the diagnosis.

DIFFERENTIAL DIAGNOSIS

The differential diagnosis includes all the previously noted lesions that cause immobility of the arm. An associated brachial plexus injury occasionally occurs.

TREATMENT

The affected arm should be immobilized in adduction for 2 to 4 weeks. This may be accomplished by maintaining the arm in a hand-on-hip position with a triangular splint and a Velpeau bandage, by strapping the arm to the chest, or by application of a cast.

PROGNOSIS

The prognosis is excellent. Healing is associated with marked formation of callus. Moderate overriding and angulation disappear with time because of the excellent remodeling power of infants. Complete union of the fracture fragments usually occurs by 3 weeks. Fair alignment and shortening of less than 1 inch indicate satisfactory closed reduction. Fractures of the long bones in infants always result in epiphyseal stimulation; the closer the fracture to the epiphyseal cartilage, the greater is the degree of subsequent overgrowth.

Fracture of the Radius

This is an extremely rare occurrence, reported only recently in a macrosomic infant born after a shoulder dystocia.[74] There was a concurrent midhumeral shaft fracture of the other arm, with lateral displacement of the distal fragment.

ETIOLOGY

This injury, because it was a spiral fracture, was thought to have resulted from rotational maneuvers attempted to alleviate the shoulder dystocia. An alternative explanation is compressive forces related to the shoulder dystocia itself—that is, the affected arm could have incurred an extreme degree of direct compression by the overlying symphysis pubis.

CLINICAL MANIFESTATIONS
Physical findings were limited to bruising of the affected forearm. However, as in any long bone fracture, if complete with displacement of fragments, additional findings may include swelling, deformity, tenderness, and crepitation.

TREATMENT
Because of the presence of bilateral fractures, casts were placed on both arms. If occurring as an isolated injury, without displacement, a radial fracture could be treated with simple immobilization.

PROGNOSIS
Radiographs at 2 weeks of age revealed a healed radial fracture and marked callus formation around the humeral fracture.

Fracture of the Femur

Although a relatively infrequent injury, fracture of the femur is by far the most common fracture of the lower extremity in the newborn.

ETIOLOGY
Fracture of the femur usually follows a breech delivery when the leg is pulled down after the breech is already partially fixed in the pelvic inlet or when the infant is improperly held by one thigh during delivery of the shoulders and arms. Femoral fracture even may occur during cesarean delivery.[2] Infants with congenital hypotonia may be more prone to this injury if their underlying disorder (e.g., severe Werdnig-Hoffmann disease) is associated with decreased muscle bulk at birth. Senanayake and associates[68] reported an infant who sustained a midtrimester fracture of the femur. No apparent maternal trauma was identified during the pregnancy. The infant was otherwise normal, with no other fractures and no evidence of skeletal dysplasia. Follow-up through age 6 years revealed normal growth, with no additional fractures. The authors were unable to identify an etiology, other than possible "unnoticed maternal trauma." It is critical to document such an occurrence to preclude inappropriate focus on the delivery process as a causation for the fracture. In addition, failure to identify and document the timing of the fracture may lead to subsequent suspicion of child abuse.

CLINICAL MANIFESTATIONS
Usually an obvious deformity of the thigh is seen (Fig. 27-18); as a rule the bone breaks transversely in the upper half or third, where it is relatively thin. Less often the injury may not be appreciated until several days after delivery, when swelling of the thigh is noted; this swelling may be caused by hemorrhage into adjacent muscle. The infant refuses to move the affected leg or cries in pain during passive movement or with

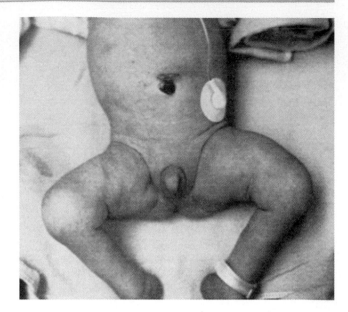

FIGURE 27-18. Fullness and obvious deformity of left thigh in 4020-g male infant with Werdnig-Hoffmann disease. Muscle wasting of both lower extremities also is apparent. Radiograph confirmed fracture of proximal third of left femur.

palpation over the fracture site. Radiographs almost always show overriding of the fracture fragments.

TREATMENT
Optimal treatment is traction-suspension of both lower extremities, even if the fracture is unilateral. The legs are immobilized in a spica cast; with Bryant traction the infant is suspended by the legs from an overhead frame, with the buttocks and lower back just raised off the mattress. The legs are extended and the thighs flexed on the abdomen. The weight of the infant's body is enough to overcome the pull of the thigh muscles and thereby reduce the deformity. The infant is maintained in this position for 3 to 4 weeks until adequate callus has formed and new bone growth has started. During the treatment period, special attention should be given to careful feeding of the infant and to protection of bandages and casts from soiling with urine and feces.

PROGNOSIS
The prognosis is excellent; complete union and restoration without shortening are expected. Extensive calcification may develop in the areas of surrounding hemorrhage but is resorbed subsequently.

Dislocations

Dislocations caused by birth trauma are rare. Often an apparent dislocation is actually a fracture displaced through an epiphyseal plate. Because the epiphyseal plate is radiolucent, a fracture occurring adjacent to an unmineralized epiphysis gives a radiographic picture simulating a dislocation of the neighboring joint. This type of injury has been termed *pseudodislocation*.[31]

Because the humeral and proximal femoral epiphyses are usually not visible on radiographs at birth, a pseudodislocation can occur at the shoulder, elbow, or hip.

Of the true dislocations, those involving the hip and knee are probably not caused by the trauma of the birth process. Most likely they are either intrauterine positional deformities or true congenital malformations. A true dislocation resulting from birth trauma is that involving the radial head. This has been associated with traumatic breech delivery. Examination reveals adduction and internal rotation of the affected arm, with pronation of the forearm; Moro response is poor, and palpation reveals lateral and posterior displacement of the radial head. This is confirmed by radiographs. With supination and extension the radial head can be reduced readily. This should be done promptly, followed by immobilization of the arm in this position in a circular cast for 2 to 3 weeks. Early recognition and treatment should result in normal growth and function of the elbow.

Bayne and associates[6] illustrated the importance of establishing an early diagnosis when they described a term infant with a swollen, tender elbow after breech delivery. Movement produced obvious pain. Radiographs at that time and again at 8 months of age were misinterpreted as normal. At 1 year an orthopedist diagnosed anteromedial dislocation. Because of several unsuccessful attempts at closed reduction, future osteotomy was required to treat this now permanent deformity.

Epiphyseal Separations

As with dislocations, epiphyseal separations are rare. They occur mostly in primiparity, dystocic deliveries, and breech presentations, especially those requiring manual extraction or version and extraction. Any delivery associated with vigorous pulling may predispose the infant to this injury. The upper femoral and humeral epiphyses are most often involved. Usually on the second day the soft tissue over the affected epiphysis develops a firm swelling with reddening, crepitus, and tenderness. Active motion is limited, and passive motion is painful. If the injury is in the upper femoral epiphysis, the infant assumes the frog-leg position with external rotation of the leg.

Early radiographs will show only soft tissue swelling, with occasional superolateral displacement of the proximal femoral metaphysis. Because the neonatal femoral capital epiphysis is not ossified, this can be interpreted mistakenly as congenital hip dislocation. However, the presence of pain and tenderness would make dislocation unlikely. Besides plain radiographs of the hips, an infant with a history and physical examination compatible with traumatic epiphysiolysis should also be studied by ultrasonography before manipulation is attempted. This examination would demonstrate a normal femoroacetabular relationship, in contrast to the abnormal findings in an infant with septic arthritis and congenital hip dislocation. In addition, in the presence of traumatic epiphysiolysis the femoral head and neck would not be continuous, in contrast to the findings of septic arthritis and congenital hip dislocation. Further differentiation between traumatic epiphysiolysis and septic arthritis can be provided by arthrocentesis; in epiphysiolysis the joint does not contain excess fluid, and what is obtained may be serosanguineous, whereas in septic arthritis, purulent fluid is obtained. After 1 to 2 weeks, extensive callus appears, confirming the nature of the injury; during the third week, subperiosteal calcification appears.

If possible, treatment should be conservative. Closed reduction and immobilization are indicated within the first few days before rapidly forming fibrous callus prevents mobilization of the epiphysis. The hip is immobilized in the frog-leg position as in congenital dislocation. Poorly immobilized fragments of the proximal or distal femur (Fig. 27-19) may require temporary fixation with a Kirschner wire (Fig. 27-20).[48] Union usually occurs within 10 to 15 days. Untreated or poorly treated epiphyseal injuries may result in subsequent growth distortion and permanent deformities such as coxa vara. Mild injuries carry a good prognosis.

Other Peripheral Nerve Injuries

In contrast to the brachial plexus and phrenic and facial nerves, other peripheral nerves are injured less often at birth and usually in association with trauma to the extremity. Radial palsy has occurred after difficult forceps extractions, both from pressure of incorrectly applied forceps and in association with fracture of the arm. Occasionally, the palsy occurs later, when the radial nerve is enmeshed within the callus of the healing fracture. Frequently, associated subcutaneous fat necrosis overlies the course of the radial nerve along the lateral aspects of the upper arm. The presence of isolated wristdrop with weakness of the wrist, finger, and thumb extensors, skin changes overlying the course of the nerve, and absence of weakness above the elbow distinguish this condition from brachial plexus injury. Palsies of the femoral and sciatic nerves have occurred after breech extractions; sciatic palsy has followed

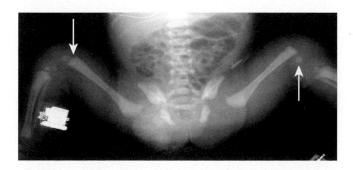

FIGURE 27-19. Radiograph of lower extremities of 4205-gm male delivered precipitously after complete breech presentation. Radiograph demonstrates displaced distal femoral physeal fracture on left (*arrow*), and nondisplaced distal femoral physeal fracture on right (*arrow*). (From Mangurten HH et al: Neonatal distal femoral physeal fracture requiring closed reduction and pinning. J Perinatol 25:216, 2005.)

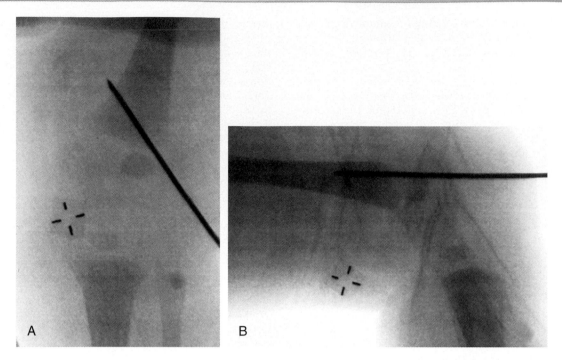

FIGURE 27-20. Because of unsuccessful attempts at closed reduction of left-sided fracture, a Kirschner wire was inserted to provide secure fixation of fracture fragments, AP view (**A**) and lateral view (**B**). (From Mangurten HH et al: Neonatal distal femoral physeal fracture requiring closed reduction and pinning. J Perinatol 25:216, 2005.)

extraction by the foot. Passive range-of-motion exercises are usually the only therapy required. Complete recovery usually occurs within several weeks or months.

TRAUMA TO THE GENITALIA

Soft tissue injuries involving the external genitalia sometimes occur, especially after breech deliveries and in large infants.

Scrotum and Labia Majora

Edema, ecchymoses, and hematomas can occur in the scrotum and labia majora, especially when they are the presenting parts in a breech presentation. Because the male newborn has a pendulous urethra that is vulnerable to compression or injury, it is possible for significant trauma to occur after a protracted labor in the breech position; the mechanism is believed to be compression of the urethra against a firm structure in the maternal bony pelvis. Rarely this may cause marked temporary hydronephrosis after delivery. The hydronephrosis usually resolves within 3 days. Because of laxity of the tissues, the degree of swelling and of discoloration occasionally is extreme enough (Fig. 27-21) to evoke considerable concern among the medical and nursing staff, especially regarding deeper involvement (e.g., periurethral hemorrhage and edema), which might hinder normal micturition. However, this has not generally been a problem, and frequently these infants void

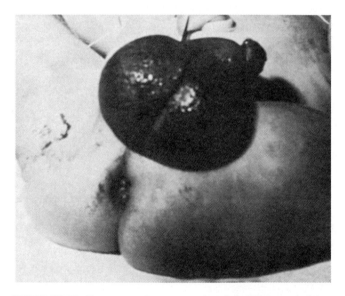

FIGURE 27-21. Hematoma of scrotum and penis in 3895-g male infant delivered vaginally after frank breech presentation. Infant voided at 22 hours and regularly thereafter. Swelling diminished appreciably within 5 hours and was gone by third day. Discoloration was greatly diminished by second day.

shortly after arriving in the nursery. Spontaneous resolution of edema occurs within 24 to 48 hours, and resolution of discoloration occurs within 4 to 5 days. Treatment is not necessary. Secondary ulceration, necrosis, or eschar formation is rare unless an associated underlying condition such as herpes simplex infection is present.

Marked scrotal hematoma may simulate testicular torsion, particularly when accompanied by a solid scrotal mass.[22] Because untreated torsion may result in loss of the testis, it is critical to distinguish the two lesions. This may be done by Doppler ultrasonography. If blood flow to the testes is clearly demonstrated, and if the testes appear symmetric in size and echotexture, torsion may essentially be ruled out.[22]

Deeper Structures

Much less often, birth trauma may involve the deeper structures of the genitalia. If the tunica vaginalis testis is injured and blood fills its cavity, a hematocele is formed. Absence of transillumination distinguishes this from a hydrocele. If the infant appears in pain, the scrotum may be elevated and cold packs applied. Spontaneous resolution is the usual course.

The testes may be injured, often in association with injury to the epididymis. Usually the involvement is bilateral. The testes may be enlarged, smoothly rounded, and insensitive. The infant may be irritable, with vomiting and poor feeding. Urologic consultation is indicated; occasionally, exploration and evacuation of blood are necessary, especially with increasing size of the testes. Severe trauma may result in atrophy or failure of the testes to grow. The occasional finding in older children of a circumscribed fibrous area within the testicular tissue is thought to represent past birth trauma to the gland.

INJURIES RELATED TO INTRAPARTUM FETAL MONITORING

Continuous monitoring of the fetal heart rate and the intermittent sampling of fetal scalp blood for determination of acid-base status often are used to monitor the fetus during labor. Thousands of patients have been monitored by these methods (see also Chapters 9 and 30). The relative infrequency of complications indicates that in experienced hands these procedures are generally safe. However, certain specific complications have occurred.

Injuries Related to Direct Fetal Heart Rate Monitoring

Direct monitoring of the fetal heart rate during labor depends on application of an electrode to the fetal scalp or other presenting part. Superficial abrasions, lacerations, and hematomas can occur rarely at the site of application of the electrode. These complications require no specific therapy beyond local treatment.

Rarely, abscesses of the scalp may follow application of scalp electrodes. These abscesses usually have been sterile and have required only local treatment. Systemic signs or symptoms require evaluation for possible septicemia.

Lauer and Rimmer[43] reported a potentially more serious complication related to use of a spiral fetal scalp electrode, as noted earlier in this chapter. At delivery the electrode was noted to be attached to the infant's eyelid, resulting in a superficial laceration. Marked surrounding edema was considered to have protected the infant from more severe injury.

Injuries Related to Fetal Scalp Blood Sampling

Fetal biochemical monitoring requires puncture of the presenting part, usually the scalp, with a 2-mm blade and the collection of blood under direct visualization in a heparinized tube. Major complications that may occur rarely are excessive bleeding and accidental breakage of the blades. The bleeding can be stopped by pressure, but on occasion this may require sutures. Rarely blood replacement may be required. It is important to obtain a detailed family history of bleeding disorders before initiation of this procedure.

The second major complication has been breakage of the blade within the fetal scalp. Removal soon after delivery has been recommended to prevent secondary infection. This has been accomplished by use of a magnet attached to a small forceps that probes the puncture site and elicits a click as the blade is attracted to the magnet. On occasion, radiographic localization followed by a small incision is necessary for withdrawal of the blade.

REFERENCES

1. Akazawa H et al: Congenital muscular torticollis: Long-term follow-up of thirty-eight partial resections of the sternocleidomastoid muscle. Arch Orthop Trauma Surg 112:205, 1993.
2. Alexander J et al: Femoral fractures at caesarean section: Case reports. Br J Obstet Gynaecol 94:273, 1987.
3. Amar AP et al: Neonatal subgaleal hematoma causing brain compression: Report of two cases and review of the literature. Neurosurgery 52:1470, 2003.
4. Arias E et al: Annual summary of vital statistics—2002. Pediatrics 112:1215, 2003.
5. Babyn PS et al: Sonographic evaluation of spinal cord birth trauma with pathologic correlation. AJR Am J Roentgenol 151:763, 1988.
6. Bayne O et al: Medial dislocation of the radial head following breech delivery: A case report and review of the literature. J Pediatr Orthop 4:485, 1984.
7. Bell HJ et al: Somatosensory evoked potentials as an adjunct to diagnosis of neonatal spinal cord injury. J Pediatr 106:298, 1985.
8. Benaron DA: Subgaleal hematoma causing hypovolemic shock during delivery after failed vacuum extraction: A case report. J Perinatol 13:228, 1993.
9. Berger SS et al: Mandibular hypoplasia secondary to perinatal trauma: Report of case. J Oral Surg 35:578, 1977.
10. Blaauw G, Slooff ACJ: Transfer of pectoral nerves to the musculocutaneous nerve in obstetric upper brachial plexus palsy. Neurosurgery 53:338, 2003.
11. Brans YW et al: Neonatal spinal cord injuries. Am J Obstet Gynecol 123:918, 1975.
12. Carraccio C et al: Subcutaneous fat necrosis of the

newborn: Link to maternal use of cocaine during pregnancy. Clin Pediatr 33:317, 1994.

13. Chan MS et al: MRI and CT findings of infected cephalhaematoma complicated by skull vault osteomyelitis, transverse venous sinus thrombosis and cerebellar haemorrhage. Pediatr Radiol 32:376, 2002.

14. Chan YL et al: Ultrasonography of congenital muscular torticollis. Pediatr Radiol 22:356, 1992.

15. Chen TH et al: Subcutaneous fat necrosis of the newborn. Arch Dermatol 117:36, 1981.

16. Cohen DL: Neonatal subgaleal hemorrhage in hemophilia. J Pediatr 93:1022, 1978.

17. Cook JS et al: Hypercalcemia in association with subcutaneous fat necrosis of the newborn: Studies of calcium-regulating hormones. Pediatrics 90:93, 1992.

18. Daily W et al: Nasal septal dislocation in the newborn. Mo Med 74:381, 1977.

19. Davids JR et al: Congenital muscular torticollis: Sequela of intrauterine or perinatal compartment syndrome. J Pediatr Orthop 13:141, 1993.

20. de Chalain TM et al: Case report: Unilateral combined facial nerve and brachial plexus palsies in a neonate following a midlevel forceps delivery. Ann Plast Surg 38:187, 1997.

21. de Vries Reilingh TS et al: Surgical treatment of diaphragmatic eventration caused by phrenic nerve injury in the newborn. J Pediatr Surg 33:602, 1998.

22. Diamond DA et al: Neonatal scrotal haematoma: Mimicker of neonatal testicular torsion. BJU Int 91:675, 2003.

23. Eisenberg D et al: Neonatal skull depression unassociated with birth trauma. AJR Am J Roentgenol 143:1063, 1984.

24. Falco NA et al: Facial nerve palsy in the newborn: Incidence and outcome. Plast Reconstr Surg 85:1, 1990.

25. Garza-Mercado R: Intrauterine depressed skull fractures of the newborn. Neurosurgery 10:694, 1982.

26. Gherman RB et al: Brachial plexus palsy: An in utero injury? Am J Obstet Gynecol 180:1303, 1999.

27. Gilbert WM et al: Associated factors in 1611 cases of brachial plexus injury. Obstet Gynecol 93:536, 1999.

28. Govaert P et al: Vacuum extraction, bone injury and neonatal subgaleal bleeding. Eur J Pediatr 151:532, 1992.

29. Greenberg SJ et al: Birth injury induced glossolaryngeal paresis. Neurology 37:533, 1987.

30. Haenggeli CA et al: Brachial plexus injury and hypoglossal paralysis. Pediatr Neurol 5:197, 1989.

31. Haliburton RA et al: Pseudodislocation: An unusual birth injury. Can J Surg 10:455, 1967.

32. Hankins GDV: Lower thoracic spinal cord injury: A severe complication of shoulder dystocia. Am J Perinatol 15:443, 1998.

33. Harris GJ: Canalicular laceration at birth. Am J Ophthalmol 105:322, 1988.

34. Hickey K, McKenna P: Skull fracture caused by vacuum extraction. Obstet Gynecol 88:671, 1996.

35. Hui CM, Tsui KY: Splenic rupture in a newborn. J Pediatr Surg 37:1, 2002.

36. Hunter JD et al: The ultrasound diagnosis of posterior shoulder dislocation associated with Erb's palsy. Pediatr Radiol 28:510, 1998.

37. Ilagan NB et al: Radiological case of the month. Arch Pediatr Adolesc Med 148:65, 1994.

38. Joseph PR et al: Clavicular fractures in neonates. Am J Dis Child 144:165, 1990.

39. Kaplan B et al: Fracture of the clavicle in the newborn following normal labor and delivery. Int J Gynecol Obstet 63:15, 1998.

40. Katzman GH: Pathophysiology of neonatal subconjunctival hemorrhage. Clin Pediatr 31:149, 1992.

41. Kruse K et al: Elevated 1,25-dihydroxyvitamin D serum concentrations in infants with subcutaneous fat necrosis. J Pediatr 122:460, 1993.

42. Lanska MJ et al: Magnetic resonance imaging in cervical cord birth injury. Pediatrics 85:760, 1990.

43. Lauer AK, Rimmer SO: Eyelid laceration in a neonate by fetal monitoring spiral electrode. Am J Ophthalmol 125:715, 1998.

44. Loeser JD et al: Management of depressed skull fracture in the newborn. J Neurosurg 44:62, 1976.

45. MacKinnon JA et al: Spinal cord injury at birth: Diagnostic and prognostic data in twenty-two patients. J Pediatr 122:431, 1993.

46. Maekawa K et al: Fetal spinal-cord injury secondary to hyperextension of the neck: No effect of cesarean section. Dev Med Child Neurol 18:229, 1976.

47. Mangurten HH et al: Incidental rib fractures in a neonate. Neonat Intensive Care 12:15, 1999.

48. Mangurten HH, Puppala B, Knuth A: Neonatal distal femoral physeal fracture requiring closed reduction and pinning. J Perinatol 25:216, 2005.

49. Miedema CJ et al: Primarily infected cephalhematoma and osteomyelitis in a newborn. Eur J Med Res 4:8, 1999.

50. Miller MJ et al: Oral breathing in response to nasal trauma in term infants. J Pediatr 111:899, 1987.

51. Mills JF et al: Upper cervical spinal cord injury in neonates: The use of magnetic resonance imaging. J Pediatr 138:105, 2001.

52. Mohon RT et al: Infected cephalhematoma and neonatal osteomyelitis of the skull. Pediatr Infect Dis J 5:253, 1986.

53. Ng PC et al: Subaponeurotic haemorrhage in the 1990s: A 3-year surveillance. Acta Paediatr 84:1065, 1995.

54. Parida SK et al: Fetal morbidity and mortality following motor vehicle accident: Two case reports. J Perinatol 19:144, 1999.

55. Peleg D et al: Fractured clavicle and Erb's palsy unrelated to birth trauma. Am J Obstet Gynecol 177:1038, 1997.

56. Petrikovsky BM et al: Cephalhematoma and caput succedaneum: Do they always occur in labor? Am J Obstet Gynecol 179:906, 1998.

57. Plauche WC: Subgaleal hematoma: A complication of instrumental delivery. JAMA 244:1597, 1980.

58. Pohjanpelto P et al: Anterior chamber hemorrhage in the newborn after spontaneous delivery: A case report. Acta Ophthalmol 57:443, 1979.

59. Priest JH: Treatment of a mandibular fracture in a neonate. J Oral Maxillofac Surg 47:77, 1989.

60. Puvabanditsin S et al: Congenital pseudoarthrosis of the clavicle. Neonat Intensive Care 14:12, 2001.

61. Rainin EA: Eversion of upper lids secondary to birth trauma. Arch Ophthalmol 94:330, 1976.

62. Raynor R et al: Nonsurgical elevation of depressed skull fracture in an infant. J Pediatr 72:262, 1968.

63. Rossitch E et al: Perinatal spinal cord injury: Clinical, radiographic and pathologic features. Pediatr Neurosurg 18:149, 1992.

64. Ryan CA et al: Vitamin K deficiency, intracranial hemorrhage, and a subgaleal hematoma: A fatal combination. Pediatr Emerg Care 8:143, 1992.

65. Saunders BS et al: Depressed skull fracture in the neonate: Report of three cases. J Neurosurg 50:512, 1979.

66. Schrager GO: Elevation of depressed skull fracture with a breast pump. J Pediatr 77:300, 1970.

67. Schullinger JN: Birth trauma. Pediatr Clin North Am 40:1351, 1993.

68. Senanayake H et al: Mid-trimester fracture of femur in a normal fetus. J Obstet Gynaecol Res 29:186, 2003.

69. Share JC et al: Unsuspected hepatic injury in the neonate: Diagnosis by ultrasonography. Pediatr Radiol 20:320, 1990.

70. Shenaq SM et al: Brachial plexus birth injuries and current management. Clin Plast Surg 25:527, 1998.

71. Silverman SH et al: Dislocation of the triangular cartilage of the nasal septum. J Pediatr 87:456, 1975.

72. Stein RM et al: Corneal birth trauma managed with a contact lens. Am J Ophthalmol 103:596, 1987.

73. Tan KL: Elevation of congenital depressed fracture of the skull by the vacuum extractor. Acta Paediatr Scand 63:562, 1974.

74. Thompson KA et al: Spiral fracture of the radius: An unusual case of shoulder dystocia-associated morbidity. Obstet Gynecol 102:36, 2003.

75. Torode I, Donnan L: Posterior dislocation of the humeral head in association with obstetric paralysis. J Pediatr Orthop 18:611, 1998.

76. Towner D et al: Effect of mode of delivery in nulliparous women on neonatal intracranial injury. N Engl J Med 341:1709, 1999.

77. Voet D et al: Leptomeningeal cyst: Early diagnosis by color Doppler imaging. Pediatr Radiol 22:417, 1992.

78. Wegman ME: Annual summary of vital statistics—1981. Pediatrics 70:835, 1982.

79. Wegman ME: Annual summary of vital statistics—1993. Pediatrics 94:792, 1994.

80. Zelson C et al: The incidence of skull fractures underlying cephalhematomas in newborn infants. J Pediatr 85:371, 1974.

28 Congenital Anomalies

Louanne Hudgins and Suzanne B. Cassidy

Congenital anomalies, whether they are isolated (single) or part of syndromes, are a common cause of medical intervention, long-term illness, and death. The neonatologist or perinatologist often is the first person to identify necessary evaluations and management and to explain the cause of the anomalies and the prognosis for the child to the parents. This chapter reviews some of the significant etiologic and epidemiologic aspects of congenital anomalies. It provides an approach to and a framework for the evaluation of the infant with congenital anomalies, with emphasis on conditions that are apparent in the delivery room. More detailed and complete differential diagnoses for each anomaly can be found in other sources.

TERMINOLOGY

It is important to distinguish between *congenital* and *genetic*, terms that are often confused. *Congenital* means present at birth, but it does not denote etiology, which may or may not be *genetic* (i.e., determined by genes). An *anomaly* is a structural defect, a deviation from the norm. A major anomaly is an anomaly that requires significant surgical or cosmetic intervention, whereas a minor anomaly has no significant surgical or cosmetic importance. Minor anomalies overlap with normal phenotypic variations and are discussed later in this chapter. It is important to classify congenital anomalies as major anomalies, minor anomalies, or normal variations, because their implications are different for both the infant and the family.

A useful approach to determining the etiology of a congenital anomaly is to consider whether it represents a malformation, deformation, or disruption.[29] A *malformation* is a primary structural defect in tissue formation, usually owing to abnormal development (morphogenesis) of the tissue for genetic or teratogenic reasons, such as a neural tube defect or a congenital heart defect. A *deformation* results from abnormal mechanical forces, often related to intrauterine constraint, acting on normally developed tissues.[9] Clubfoot and altered head shape often are due to deformation. Deformations occurring late in gestation often are reversible with removal of the force or with positioning. Breech or other abnormal positioning in utero, oligohydramnios, and uterine anomalies are the most common causes of deformations. Observation of the position of comfort of the infant combined with a careful history of fetal movement, position, and fluid volume can be very

helpful in identifying an anomaly as a deformation. A *disruption* represents interruption of development of intrinsically normal tissue, and it usually affects a body part rather than a specific organ. Vascular occlusion and amniotic bands are common causes of disruptions. Monozygotic twinning and prenatal cocaine exposure are common predisposing factors for disruptions on the basis of vascular interruption.

Disruptions and isolated deformations are usually sporadic, with negligible or low recurrence risks. Malformations, however, may predispose a fetus to deformations, such as renal agenesis (a malformation) causing oligohydramnios sequence (Potter syndrome), in which facial and limb deformations and pulmonary hypoplasia result from oligohydramnios. A neural tube defect, also a malformation, predisposes a fetus to hip dislocation and clubfoot, owing to lack of movement below the level of the lesion.

Many congenital malformations can have more than one cause, often with different possible associated anomalies and different recurrence risks. Cleft lip and palate, for example, can be isolated or can be part of dozens of different syndromes and can be multifactorial, autosomal dominant, autosomal recessive, X-linked, chromosomal, or teratogenic in etiology.[7]

If more than one anomaly is present in an individual, the clinician should consider whether it is part of a sequence, association, or syndrome, which have different implications for prognosis and recurrence risk. *Sequence* refers to a pattern of multiple anomalies derived from a single known or presumed cause. An example is the oligohydramnios sequence, often referred to as Potter syndrome, which consists of limb deformations; simple ears, a beaked nose, and infraorbital creases (Potter facies); and pulmonary hypoplasia. These features are present when there is a lack of amniotic fluid, be it secondary to chronic leakage of amniotic fluid or lack of fetal urine (renal agenesis). *Association* refers to a nonrandom occurrence of multiple malformations for which no specific or common etiology has been identified. An example is the VATER (or VACTERL) association, an acronym for a pattern of anomalies consisting of *v*ertebral abnormalities, *a*nal atresia, (*c*ardiac anomalies,) *t*racheoesophageal fistula, and *r*enal and *r*adial (*l*imb) dysplasia.[25] *Syndrome* refers to a recognized pattern of anomalies with a single, specific cause, such as Holt-Oram syndrome, in which radial dysplasia and cardiac defects occur as a consequence of an autosomal dominant gene.[12] Although the genes responsible for many previously idiopathic syndromes have been determined

TABLE 28-1. Malformations in 12,000 Consecutive Newborns

MALFORMATION	NUMBER OF NEWBORNS	TOTAL MALFORMATIONS (%)	TOTAL NEWBORNS (%)
Localized	**161**	**85.6**	**1.34**
Multifactorial inheritance	70	37.2	0.58
Mendelian inheritance	41	21.8	0.34
Unknown	50	26.6	0.42
Multiple	**27**	**14.4**	**0.22**
Chromosomal	11	5.9	0.09
Mendelian inheritance	6	3.2	0.05
Unknown	10	5.3	0.08
Totals	**188**	**100**	**1.56**

Data from Holmes LB: Inborn errors of morphogenesis: A review of localized hereditary malformations. N Engl J Med 291:763, 1974.

in the past 5 to 10 years, for many others the etiology is still unknown.

Phenotype is the observable manifestation of *genotype,* which is the genetic constitution of an individual; therefore, when one speaks of the phenotypic features, reference is being made to the observable physical features present in that individual.

EPIDEMIOLOGY AND ETIOLOGY

Major Malformations

Approximately 2% of newborn infants have a serious anomaly that has surgical or cosmetic importance (Tables 28-1[10] and 28-2[11]). This proportion is a minimum estimate because it is based only on the examination of newborn infants; additional anomalies are detected with increasing age. The etiology of malformations can be divided into broad categories: genetic (multifactorial, single gene [mendelian], or chromosomal), teratogenic, and unknown.

GENETIC
Multifactorial
The largest number (86%) of congenital malformations are isolated (i.e. not associated with other anomalies),[10] and most isolated malformations are believed to be the consequence of multifactorial inheritance, sometimes called complex inheritance. Such malformations occur when one or more genetic susceptibility factors combine with environmental factors and random developmental events. The most common and familiar birth defects fall into this category, including congenital heart defects, neural tube defects, cleft lip and palate, clubfoot, and congenital hip dysplasia. The genetic contribution to such complex disorders is being unraveled with techniques developed as a consequence of the Human Genome Project. In most cases, multiple genetic components are involved, some with large effects and some with small contributions. The nongenetic (environmental) effects have been harder to identify in most cases.

TABLE 28-2. Type and Etiology of Major Malformations in 18,155 Newborns

MALFORMATION	NUMBER
Multifactorial Inheritance	**128 (0.7%)**
Anencephaly-myelomeningocele-encephalocele	25
Cardiac anomalies	45
Cleft lip or palate	14
Clubfoot	21
Congenital hip dislocation	12
Hypospadias	8
Omphalocele	2
Bilateral renal agenesis	1
Mendelian Inheritance	**67 (0.4%)**
Autosomal dominant disorders (excluding polydactyly)	57
Autosomal recessive disorders	9
X-linked recessive disorders	1
Chromosomal Abnormalities	**27 (0.2%)**
Down syndrome	21
Trisomy 13	3
Other	3
Teratogenic Conditions	**15 (0.1%)**
Infants of diabetic mothers	14
Effects of warfarin	1
Unknown	**107 (0.6%)**
Total Number Affected	**344 (2%)**

Data from Holmes LB: Current concepts in genetics: Congenital malformations. N Engl J Med 295:204, 1976.

Single Gene (Mendelian)
Single major genes are responsible for causing 0.4% of newborns to have major malformations (see Table 28-2). The most common mode of mendelian inheritance for major malformations is autosomal dominant, with a minority of major malformations resulting from

autosomal recessive or, rarely, X-linked genes (see Table 28-2). Limb anomalies, including postaxial polydactyly, syndactyly, and brachydactyly, constitute the most prevalent major localized malformations, and they are frequently the result of a dominant gene. Any type of malformation, however, may be under the control of a single gene, including multiple anomalies arising in different structures or organ systems. Relatively little is understood about the biochemical defects underlying the production of malformations by mutant genes, although advances are being made. For example, Smith-Lemli-Opitz syndrome, characterized by genital abnormalities, syndactyly of the second and third toes, ptosis, and wide alveolar ridges, has been found to be associated with a defect in cholesterol biosynthesis.[14] Although a biochemical or molecular basis increasingly is being recognized, specific diagnosis still relies heavily on the family history and clinical evaluation.

An excellent reference for all single-gene conditions is *Mendelian Inheritance in Man*,[19] which now has an excellent on-line version called OMIM (www.ncbi.nlm.nih.gov/omim). GeneReviews, another online resource, provides a detailed description of many single-gene disorders and gives information about genetic testing availability and interpretation (www.genetest.org).

Chromosomal (See also Chapter 7.)

Approximately 0.2% of newborns have a major malformation as a result of a chromosomal disorder, amounting to 10% of all the major congenital malformations (see Table 28-2). It is important to note, however, that although approximately 0.6% of newborns have chromosomal anomalies, the abnormalities are not detectable by physical examination at birth in 66% of these infants.[13] Included among these early phenotypically undetectable chromosomal anomalies are common disorders of the sex chromosomes, such as 47,XXY, 47,XYY, and 47,XXX. The most prevalent malformation syndrome owing to an abnormal chromosomal constitution in newborns is Down syndrome, or trisomy 21, which occurs in approximately 1 in 660 births.[13] The other common trisomies are trisomy 18 and trisomy 13, each occurring in approximately 1 in 10,000 births. All three trisomies occur more frequently with increased maternal age. Other well-known chromosomal syndromes are Klinefelter syndrome (47,XXY), occurring in 1 in 1000 male births, and Turner syndrome (45,X), present in 1 in 5000 female births. Many other types of chromosomal aberrations have been identified using chromosome banding techniques, including translocations, inversions, ring chromosomes, marker chromosomes, and deletions.[26] Not all deletions are detectable by routine cytogenetic analysis, however. High resolution (prometaphase) chromosome study can identify small deletions and duplications not readily identifiable on a routine chromosome analysis. Fluorescence in situ hybridization (FISH) is a technique that uses fluorescently labeled DNA probes and chromosome metaphase spreads to identify microdeletions associated with such conditions as Williams syndrome (long arm of chromosome 7), Prader-Willi syndrome (long arm of chromosome 15), and velocardiofacial/DiGeorge syndrome (long arm of chromosome 22). FISH continues to contribute to better definitive diagnosis for conditions involving multiple congenital anomalies.[1]

TERATOGENIC (See also Chapter 12.)

A *teratogen* is anything external to the fetus that causes a structural or functional disability postnatally. Teratogens can be drugs and chemicals, altered metabolic states in the mother, infectious agents, or mechanical forces. Known teratogenic factors cause only 5% to 10% of congenital anomalies despite the ever-expanding list of potential teratogens in our increasingly chemical environment[2] (Table 28-3). Before one can attribute malformations to a teratogenic agent, there must be one anomaly, only a few specific anomalies, or a recognizable pattern of anomalies found to occur at increased incidence over the background risk in infants exposed at the appropriate developmental stage (usually 2 to 12 weeks' gestation). With only a few exceptions, teratogenic agents do not affect every exposed infant, which is probably related to genetic susceptibility factors. Dose and timing of exposure also affect teratogenic potential.

Although many drugs have teratogenic potential, several commonly used drugs are worthy of some discussion. Alcohol is thought to be the most common teratogen to which a fetus may be exposed. Chronic

TABLE 28-3. Etiology of Human Malformations

ETIOLOGY	MALFORMED LIVE BIRTHS (%)
Environmental	**10**
Maternal conditions	4
Alcoholism, diabetes, endocrinopathies, phenylketonuria, smoking, nutritional problems	
Infectious agents	3
Rubella, toxoplasmosis, syphilis, herpes simplex, cytomegalic inclusion disease, varicella, Venezuelan equine encephalitis	
Mechanical problems (deformations)	2
Amniotic band constrictions, umbilical cord constraint, disparity in uterine size and uterine contents	
Chemicals, drugs, radiation, hyperthermia	1
Genetic	**20-25**
Single gene disorders	
Chromosomal abnormalities	
Unknown	**65-70**
Polygenic/multifactorial (gene-environment interactions)	
"Spontaneous" errors of development	
Other unknowns	

Modified from Brent RL: Evaluating the alleged teratogenicity of environmental agents. Clin Perinatol 13:609, 1986.

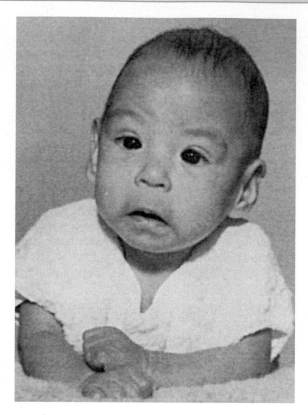

FIGURE 28-1. Fetal alcohol syndrome. Note mild ptosis, epicanthal folds, flat nasal bridge, short nose, smooth philtrum, and thin upper vermilion border. (From Dworkin PH [ed]: Pediatrics, 2nd ed. Malvern, Pa, Lea & Febiger, 1992, p 168.)

Anticonvulsants are a common category of teratogens to which a fetus is likely to be exposed. Although the medical literature is somewhat controversial, clinical geneticists, dysmorphologists, and clinical teratologists generally identify a variable but recognizable pattern of anomalies and developmental defects that occur at significantly increased frequency among fetuses exposed to all anticonvulsants used at present.[27]

Congenital anomalies also may be associated with certain infections during pregnancy. The most common and best understood infections are represented by the acronym TORCH, which stands for *t*oxoplasmosis, *o*ther agents (including syphilis), *r*ubella, *c*ytomegalovirus, and *h*erpes simplex. Although the sequelae of these infections may not be apparent until later, the clinician should consider these congenital infections in neonates with intrauterine growth retardation, microcephaly, chorioretinitis, intracranial calcification, microphthalmia, or cataracts. Confirmation of the specific diagnosis should be made by antibody studies and other evaluations such as ophthalmologic examination and imaging studies (see Chapters 22 and 37).

Mechanical forces also may be categorized as teratogens. Deformations, such as clubfoot, may be from intrauterine constraint secondary to mechanical forces such as uterine fibroids. Disruption of the amnion also may be associated with deformations and other limb anomalies.

UNKNOWN

Approximately 66% of major malformations have no recognized etiology if one includes those of presumed polygenic and multifactorial etiology.[2] It is likely that specific genetic and environmental causes of congenital anomalies will be identified in the near future. For example, folic acid has been recognized to decrease the risk of neural tube defects, thus implicating folic acid deficiency in the etiology of these anomalies.[31] Specific genes have been identified as causing the multifactorial disorder Hirschsprung disease.[24]

Anomalies in Aborted Fetuses

Spontaneously aborted fetuses have a higher incidence of malformations than do newborns[11,23] (Table 28-4), which presumably represents a natural selection process. The common major malformations present in newborns that are of presumed multifactorial inheritance, such as neural tube defects and cleft lip or palate, are also frequent in aborted fetuses and may be more severe. Other malformations, such as cloacal exstrophy, are relatively rare in newborns but are comparatively common in aborted fetuses.

In addition to these localized and single anomalies, multiple congenital anomalies commonly occur together in aborted fetuses, including well-recognized syndromes that are caused by single genes and chromosomal abnormalities[4] (Table 28-5). It is estimated that approximately half of all fetuses aborted by 20 weeks' gestation, including those whose existence was not yet known to the mothers, have a chromosomal abnormality. In

maternal alcohol use during pregnancy is associated with increased perinatal mortality and intrauterine growth restriction, as well as congenital anomalies such as cardiac defects, microcephaly, short palpebral fissures, and other anomalies (Fig. 28-1). Long-term effects include mental retardation and behavioral problems. Alcohol carries serious risks when it is used almost at any time during pregnancy in sufficient quantities because the central nervous system continues to develop throughout pregnancy. For this reason, it is recommended that women avoid alcohol, even in small amounts, throughout their pregnancy (see Chapter 36).

Some altered metabolic states in the mother also are known to have teratogenic potential. One of the most common is maternal diabetes mellitus. Infants of diabetic mothers are at increased risk for congenital heart defects, sacral dysgenesis, and central nervous system abnormalities such as holoprosencephaly.[20] In this population, there is an approximately threefold increase in congenital anomalies over those in the general population. The risk for congenital anomalies seems to be lower in offspring of diabetic mothers with better control of blood glucose, but this is not absolute, and factors other than blood glucose levels are thought to play a role in teratogenesis (see Chapter 15 and Chapter 47, Part One).

TABLE 28-4. Prevalence of Localized Malformations in Spontaneously Aborted Fetuses and Newborns (per 1000)

MALFORMATION	SPONTANEOUS ABORTIONS*			NEWBORNS†
	2-8 wk	9-18 wk	19 wk	
Anencephaly-myelomeningocele-encephalocele	31	10	116	1.4
Cleft lip/palate	3	14.5	0	0.8
Cloacal exstrophy	0	7.3	10.6	0.1
Polydactyly	0	7.3	0	0.1

*Data from Nelson T et al: Collection of human embryos and fetuses. In Hook EB et al (eds): Monitoring Birth Defects and Environment: The Problem of Surveillance. New York, Academic Press, 1971.
†Data from Holmes LB: Current concepts in genetics: Congenital malformations. N Engl J Med 295:204, 1976.

TABLE 28-5. Diagnoses in 375 Consecutive Cases of Pregnancy Loss

DIAGNOSIS	≤20 WEEKS (%)	>20 WEEKS (%)
Chromosomal abnormalities	19.4	15.7
Trisomy	54	47
Triploidy/tetraploidy	18	5.2
45,X	16	15.8
45,X mosaic	6	0
Deletion/duplication	0	15.8
Other	6	15.8
Placental abnormalities	12	5.8
Infection	7	6.6
Cord problems	7	5
Neural tube defects	6	10
Central nervous system abnormalities	1.2	5
Twins	7.4	3.3
Skeletal dysplasias	2	2.5
Recognizable syndromes	1.2	5.8
Hemoglobinopathies	0	4
Early amnion rupture sequence	3.5	5
Abdominal wall defects	1.2	0
Renal abnormalities	1.2	3.3
Cardiac abnormalities	0.7	4
Other	6.5	9
Total cases with diagnoses	76	85
Diagnoses unknown	24	15

Modified from Curry CJR: Pregnancy loss, stillbirth, and neonatal death: A guide for the pediatrician. Pediatr Clin North Am 39:157, 1992.

this context, the most common single chromosomal abnormality is 45,X, followed by triploidy. Both conditions are more common in aborted fetuses than in newborns. The trisomies, as a group, account for over 50% of all chromosomally abnormal pregnancy losses. The most frequent trisomy, accounting for almost a third of all trisomies, is trisomy 16, which does not occur in newborns.[16] Trisomy 21, the most common trisomy in newborns, occurs in less than 10% of all recognized trisomic conceptions. Unbalanced products of translocations account for 2% to 4% of all chromosomally abnormal fetuses and are three to six times more frequent in aborted fetuses than in newborns.

Minor Anomalies and Phenotypic Variants

Although major malformations often are easy to identify, minor anomalies are, by nature, more subtle and may not be appreciated unless they are specifically sought. Minor anomalies, however, are significant. They may be part of a characteristic pattern of malformations and thus may provide clues to a diagnosis. Also, their occurrence may be an indication of the presence of a more serious anomaly. In one large study of 4305 newborns, 19.6% of the 162 infants with major malformations had three or more minor anomalies.[17] A single minor anomaly, however, was associated with a major malformation in only 3.7% of cases.[17]

Minor anomalies are most frequent in areas of complex and variable features, such as the face and distal extremities[18] (Table 28-6). Among the most common features are lack of a helical fold of the pinna and complete or incomplete single transverse palmar crease patterns.[18] Typical single transverse palmar crease (simian crease) occurs in almost 3% of normal newborns, but it appears in 45% of individuals with trisomy 21.[15]

Among the most frequent phenotypic variants, those present in 4% or more of the population, are a folded-over helix of the pinna and mongolian spots in blacks and Asians[18] (Table 28-7). Before attributing medical significance to an apparent minor anomaly or phenotypic variation, it is useful to determine whether the anomaly is present in other family members or whether it is frequent in the patient's ethnic group. It is common for isolated minor anomalies such as syndactyly of the second and third toes to be familial.

Racial Differences

The prevalence of congenital malformations varies significantly among racial groups. This variation is most likely the consequence of differing genetic predispositions and variable environmental factors operating in diverse areas. Table 28-8[5,6] shows the prevalence of common major congenital malformations in white Americans, African Americans, and the Chinese. It is of interest that certain anomalies are especially common in a particular race, such as polydactyly in African Americans and hypospadias and clubfoot in white Americans. Minor malformations may show an equally

TABLE 28-6. Common Minor Malformations in Newborns (Frequency Greater Than 1:1000)

MINOR MALFORMATION	NEWBORNS (%)
Craniofacial	
Borderline micrognathia	0.32
Eye	
Inner epicanthal folds	0.42
Ear	
Lack of helical fold	3.52
Posteriorly rotated pinna	0.25
Preauricular or auricular skin tags	0.23
Small pinna	0.14
Auricular sinus	0.12
Skin	
Capillary hemangioma other than on face or posterior aspect of neck	1.06
Pigmented nevi	0.49
Mongoloid spots in white infants	0.21
Hand	
Simian creases	2.74
Bridged upper palmar creases	1.04
Bilateral combinations	0.51
Other unusual crease patterns	0.28
Clinodactyly of fifth finger	0.99
Foot	
Partial syndactyly of second and third toes	0.016
Total	**12.34**

Data from Marden PM et al: Congenital anomalies in the newborn infant, including minor variations: A study of 4142 babies by surface examination for anomalies and buccal smear for sex chromatin. J Pediatr 64:357, 1964.

TABLE 28-7. Common Phenotypic Variants

PHENOTYPIC VARIANT	NEWBORNS (%)
Craniofacial	
Flat nasal bridge	7.3
Ear	
Folded-over upper helix	43.0
Darwinian tubercle	11.0
Skin	
Capillary hemangioma on face or posterior aspect of neck	14.3
Mongolian spots in blacks and Asians	45.8
Hand	
Hyperextensibility of thumbs	12.3
Foot	
Mild calcaneovalgus	4.7
Genital	
Hydrocele	4.4

Data from Marden PM et al: Congenital anomalies in the newborn infant, including minor variations: A study of 4142 babies by surface examination for anomalies and buccal smear for sex chromatin. J Pediatr 64:357, 1964.

TABLE 28-8. Frequency of Common Congenital Malformations in Various Racial Groups (per 1000)

MALFORMATION	WHITE AMERICANS*	AFRICAN AMERICANS*	CHINESE[†]
Anencephaly-myelomeningocele-encephalocele	2.4	0.9	1.5
Cleft lip and palate	1.1	0.6	1.3
Cleft palate	0.6	0.4	
Clubfoot (talipes equinovarus)	3.9	2.3	0.1
Polydactyly	1.2	11.0	1.5
Hypospadias	2.4	1.2	0.6

*Data from Erickson JD: Racial variations in the incidence of congenital malformations. Ann Hum Genet 39:315, 1976.
[†]Data from Emanuel I et al: The incidence of congenital malformations in a Chinese population: The Taipei collaborative study. Teratology 5:159, 1972.

striking racial predisposition. Brushfield spots are common in white Americans but are rare in African Americans. Umbilical hernias, however, are common in African American infants but are relatively infrequent in white American infants. The widely varying frequencies of various traits in different races may make the determination of whether any given characteristic is considered to be a minor anomaly or a phenotypic variant strongly dependent on the race of the patient being studied. One of the best examples is mongolian spots, which occur in almost 50% of black or Asian infants but in only 0.2% of white infants.[18]

EVALUATION

Every infant with a congenital anomaly should have a thorough diagnostic evaluation; without one, accurate information about the natural history of the condition and the recurrence risk for similarly affected future children cannot be provided. For these, an accurate diagnosis and etiology are needed. In addition, parents usually are intensely interested in why the anomaly occurred, and often harbor inappropriate guilt concerning the cause.

When a child is born with one or more anomalies, a number of considerations should guide the physician in the evaluation. The most critical factors to be considered are the detailed prenatal and family history, the dysmorphic physical examination (including careful observation and measurements of individual features), and the use of appropriate diagnostic tests and evaluations, particularly if there is more than one anomaly. It is essential to identify whether the malformation is isolated or part of a constellation of anomalies. It is also essential to identify whether there are other major or minor anomalies, including perhaps inapparent internal malformations, and to recognize well-described patterns of malformations. Practice in such recognition or consultation with others who have such expertise may be required. The severity of an anomaly can sometimes be helpful in identifying whether it may be associated with other anomalies and in predicting the prognosis for the infant.

History

The evaluation of an infant with congenital anomalies begins with a detailed history. The important goal is to identify a possible genetic predisposition, environmental factor, or other clue to the cause of the anomalies. It is useful to begin with the pregnancy to document fetal movement and vigor, complications, illnesses, maternal use of any medications, or possible exposure to teratogens, as well as the timing of all complications and exposures (see Chapter 12). The extent of smoking and alcohol consumption should be determined, and every mother should be asked about illicit drug use. To identify other potentially affected family members and obtain clues to an etiology, a detailed three- to four-generation family history, charted in a concise manner in the form of a pedigree, should be constructed, using squares for male and circles for female members. Horizontal lines indicate genetic union, and vertical lines indicate genetic descent. All abortions and stillbirths should be noted. A question always should be specifically asked about possible consanguinity. A simple way to inquire is to ask if the families of the affected child's parents are related in any way. If so, then the charting should indicate the exact relationships. The presence of other relatives with congenital anomalies of any type or with growth or developmental abnormalities should be recorded along with other pertinent information, such as the maternal and paternal ages and the nature of the anomaly. Family photographs are often very useful in clarifying questions of possible unusual facial features. The pedigree should, at a minimum, include all siblings and parents of the proband as well as aunts, uncles, cousins, and grandparents. In the case of possible dominant or X-linked disorders, a more extensive pedigree may be needed.

Physical Examination (See also Chapter 26.)

The goal of the physical examination of an infant with congenital anomalies is to determine if an anomaly is isolated or to detect a recognizable pattern of malformations so that a specific etiologic determination can be made. In addition, careful attention must be directed not only to an exact description of the major anomalies but to apparent minor anomalies or variations. Distinctive physical features may become clues in identifying

the cause of multiple congenital anomalies; therefore, a detailed inspection of various features of external anatomy and measurement of them where appropriate should be performed. Normal measurements of many face and body characteristics can be found in a number of resources.[15] Objective description of anomalous features allows for appropriate use of resources or consultants. In this section, an outline of this external examination is presented by region or structure, and certain helpful points, as well as aspects of the differential diagnosis, are discussed. Greater detail in regard to examination and abnormalities of various organ systems is given in other relevant chapters in this book. The authors also refer the reader to various resources in which the anomalies and syndromes mentioned in this section are discussed at length.[8,15,30]

SKIN (See also Chapter 50.)

Normal infant skin, particularly when exposed to cold temperatures, shows a marbling pattern termed *cutis marmorata* or *livedo reticularis*. In rare instances, this pattern may be unusually prominent and familial, inherited as an autosomal dominant trait. A similar prominent pattern may occur in those with trisomy 21, hypothyroidism, or Cornelia de Lange syndrome.

A variety of lesions with altered pigmentation may provide useful clues to a diagnosis. Café-au-lait spots are characteristic of neurofibromatosis, but they also occur in other conditions and may be isolated, especially in darkly pigmented infants. Hypopigmented macules may be the earliest manifestation of tuberous sclerosis in the young infant. Multiple irregular pigmented lesions arranged in whorls are very suggestive of incontinentia pigmenti, but this disorder usually presents initially with a vesicular rash. An angiomatous patch over one side of the face may be an isolated anomaly or part of the Sturge-Weber syndrome. More than one skin hemangioma should raise suspicion of internal vascular lesions.

Generalized edema may obscure many minor anomalies, making diagnosis difficult. Turner syndrome, trisomy 21, and Noonan syndrome should be considered in newborns with generalized edema.

HAIR

The relative sparseness or prominence of body hair should be noted. Sparse hair is characteristic of an ectodermal dysplasia, but it does occur in other syndromes, such as cartilage-hair hypoplasia and oculodentodigital syndrome. Generalized hirsutism is typical of Cornelia de Lange syndrome, fetal hydantoin syndrome, and fetal alcohol syndrome, but it also may occur in those with trisomy 18. It also may be a racial (Hispanic, American Indian) or familial characteristic.

Abnormal scalp hair patterns may reflect underlying brain abnormalities. In microcephaly, there may be a lack of the normal parietal whorl, or the whorl may be displaced more centrally or posteriorly. In addition, the frontal hair may show a prominent upsweep. A low posterior hairline occurs with a short or webbed neck, as in Turner syndrome and Noonan syndrome. Punched-

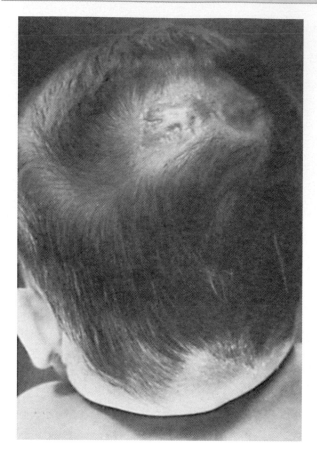

FIGURE 28-2. Scalp lesions in trisomy 13.

out scalp lesions in the parietal occipital area (aplasia cutis congenita) are typical of trisomy 13 or may be seen in isolation and may be familial (Fig. 28-2).

HEAD (See also Chapter 38, Part 7.)

The size of the head, measured by the maximum head circumference, and the sizes of the anterior and other fontanelles should be compared with those of appropriate standards. Head size varies with age, sex, and racial group and correlates with body size. Macrocephaly as an isolated anomaly often is familial and inherited in an autosomal dominant fashion; therefore, determining the head circumferences of the parents is helpful. However, macrocephaly may be a manifestation of several disorders, including hydrocephaly and various conditions affecting the skeletal system, such as achondroplasia. Microcephaly can also be familial, either autosomal dominant or recessive, but it is more commonly a manifestation of many syndromes that result in mental retardation. Large fontanelles occur in hypothyroidism; in trisomies 21, 18, and 13; and in many bone disorders, such as hypophosphatasia and cleidocranial dysostosis. A small anterior fontanelle may be a sign of failure of normal brain growth.

The normal shape of the head may vary from an increase in the anteroposterior diameter (dolichocephaly) to a decrease in this dimension (brachycephaly). Premature infants and those with trisomy 18 characteristically have dolichocephaly (Fig. 28-3), and hypotonic infants often develop dolichocephaly over time, but either type of head shape may be of familial or racial origin. Many Asian and American Indian infants, for example, have strikingly brachycephalic heads.

Premature fusion of cranial sutures (craniosynostosis) results in an abnormal configuration in head shape. Various types occur depending on the sutures involved (see Chapter 38, Part Seven). Torticollis or abnormal mechanical forces in utero can cause asymmetric head shape (plagiocephaly).

A common anomaly in head shape is frontal bossing, which is frequent in some skeletal dysplasias such as achondroplasia and in some cases of hydrocephaly.

FACE

The face is composed of a series of structures, each demonstrating considerable normal variation and providing a distinctive and unique appearance to every human being. Because examination of the face is both complex and important to establishing an etiology to anomalies, a systematic approach is necessary. It is never sufficient to describe the face merely as "funny looking" or unusual. Specific abnormalities should be analyzed and quantified, when appropriate, even though an overall gestalt impression may suggest a diagnosis in some cases. Recall that lack of resemblance to other family members is an indicator of an underlying condition.

EYES

Hypotelorism occurs when the eyes are unusually close together; *hypertelorism* occurs when the eyes are too far apart. Clinically, hypotelorism and hypertelorism are defined by the interpupillary distance, which may be estimated in a relaxed patient by measuring between the midpoints of the pupils. It is usually impossible to measure the interpupillary distance of a newborn; therefore, two other relevant and useful measurements that are easier to obtain are the inner canthal distance and the outer canthal distance. *Telecanthus* is an increase in the inner canthal distance, and it may occur in the absence of hypertelorism, such as in Waardenburg syndrome type I. There are other factors that may create an illusion of hypertelorism, such as epicanthal folds and a flat nasal bridge; therefore, a subjective impression should always be confirmed by measurement of all three distances, if possible. From the prognostic and diagnostic points of view, it is important to identify hypotelorism, because often it is associated with *holoprosencephaly*, a major malformation of the central nervous system that usually is associated with severe disturbance of brain function and early death. Holoprosencephaly can be isolated or can be part of trisomy 13 (Fig. 28-4) or occasionally other syndromes. Hypertelorism, however, occurs in a number of syndromes, such as frontonasal dysplasia, and even when it is severe, it is less likely to be related to an underlying brain malformation. Figures 28-5 and 28-6 illustrate

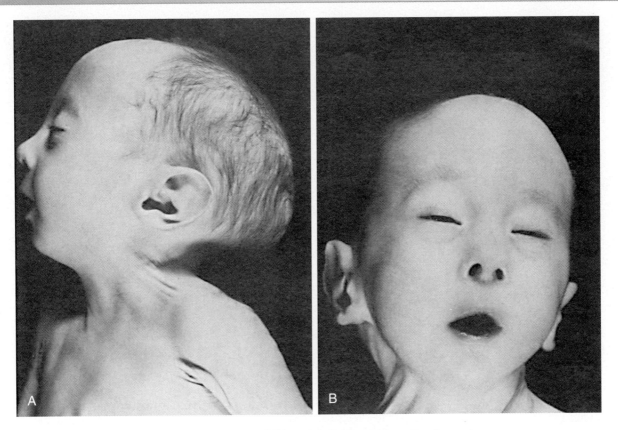

FIGURE 28-3. Trisomy 18. **A,** Note dolichocephaly. **B,** Note small mouth and anomalous ears.

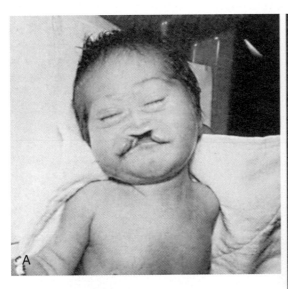

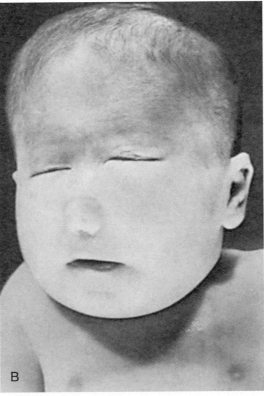

FIGURE 28-4. Trisomy 13. **A,** Note anomalous midline facial development with hypotelorism, midline cleft lip, and lack of a nose. **B,** Note hypotelorism and abnormal nose.

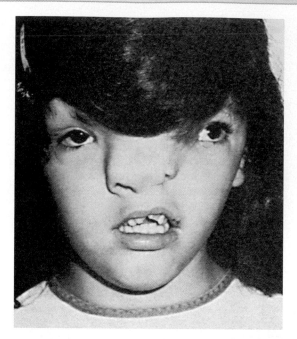

FIGURE 28-5. Frontonasal dysplasia with hypertelorism and bifid nose.

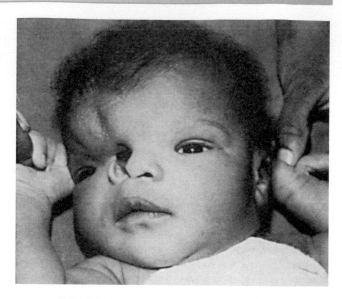

FIGURE 28-6. Frontonasal dysplasia with nasal cleft.

hypertelorism with midline facial anomalies. Comparison with familial eye distances is important.

Epicanthal folds are a feature of normal fetal development, and they may be present in normal infants. They are characteristic in trisomy 21 (Fig. 28-7A and B), but they occur in many other malformation syndromes, especially in those that include a flat nasal bridge.

Normally, an imaginary line through the inner and outer canthi should be perpendicular to the sagittal plane of the face. An upward slant to the palpebral fissure is seen in trisomy 21 (see Fig. 28-7), and a downward slant is seen in mandibulofacial dysostosis (see Fig. 28-7C). Both types of slant can be part of a number of other syndromes.

Palpebral fissure length is measured from the inner canthus to the outer canthus. Short palpebral fissures may occur in association with other ocular anomalies, such as microphthalmia, and they are characteristic of syndromes such as fetal alcohol syndrome (see Fig. 28-1) and trisomy 18 (see Fig. 28-3B).

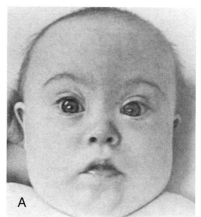

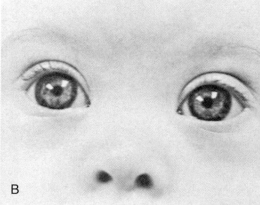

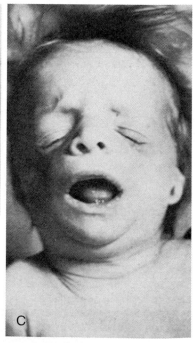

FIGURE 28-7. A, Trisomy 21. Note epicanthal folds and mongoloid slant of eyes. B, Enlargement of eyes of patient in A. Note Brushfield spots on irides. C, Mandibulofacial dysostosis (Treacher Collins syndrome) with antimongoloid slant of eyes. Note coloboma, or notch, in left eyelid.

A *coloboma* is a developmental defect in the normal continuity of a structure, and it often is used in reference to the eye. Colobomas may involve the eyelid margin, as those seen in Treacher Collins syndrome (see Fig. 28-7C), or the iris and retina, as those seen in CHARGE association (*c*oloboma, *h*eart disease, *a*tresia choanae, *r*etardation of growth development, *g*enital hypoplasia, *e*ar anomalies and/or deafness). Identification of a coloboma should lead to a formal ophthalmologic evaluation.

Synophrys, or fusion of the eyebrows in the midline, is common in hirsute infants, and it usually occurs in Cornelia de Lange syndrome. It also may be familial.

Other types of anomalies involving the internal structure of the eyes are discussed in Chapter 51.

EARS

The external ear, or pinna, commonly shows great variation, but a number of anatomic landmarks can be identified and should be described when evaluating the anomalous ear. These landmarks include the helix, antihelix, tragus, antitragus, external meatus, and lobule (Fig. 28-8). If the ears appear to be large or small, they should be measured by obtaining the maximum length of the pinna from the lobule to the superior margin of the helix. Preauricular tags or pits may be isolated or associated with other abnormalities of the pinna (Fig. 28-9).

The ears are low-set when the helix joins the head below a horizontal plane passing through the outer canthus perpendicular to the vertical axis of the head (Fig. 28-10). It is critical that this condition be assessed with the head in vertical alignment with the body, because any posterior rotation of the head can create an illusion of low-set ears. In most instances, the relative placement of the ears is more a function of head shape and jaw size than of an intrinsic anomaly of the ear.

When the vertical axis of the ear deviates more than 10 degrees from the vertical axis of the head, the ears are posteriorly rotated. This anomaly often is associated with low-set ears and represents a lag in the normal

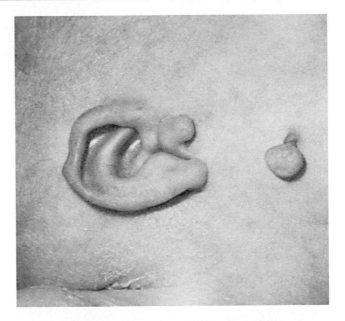

FIGURE 28-9. Preauricular tags with malformed pinna.

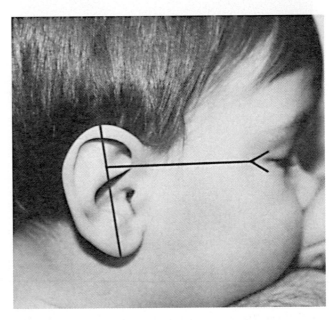

FIGURE 28-10. Normal pinna and its orientation with respect to eyes.

ascent of the ear during development (Figs. 28-11 and 28-12).

Any significant abnormality of the external ear may be an indication of additional anomalies of the middle or inner ear and may be associated with hearing loss; therefore, an early hearing assessment is indicated in such cases (see Chapter 40). Figure 28-13 illustrates a patient with hemifacial microsomia, whose findings include a severely malformed pinna and an absent ear canal. This is one condition in which an early hearing assessment is essential because hearing loss is likely.

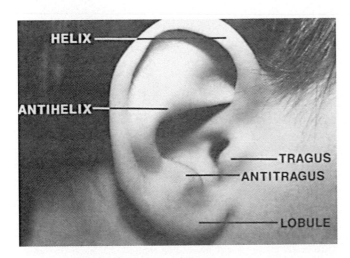

HELIX

ANTIHELIX

TRAGUS

ANTITRAGUS

LOBULE

FIGURE 28-8. Normal pinna and its landmarks.

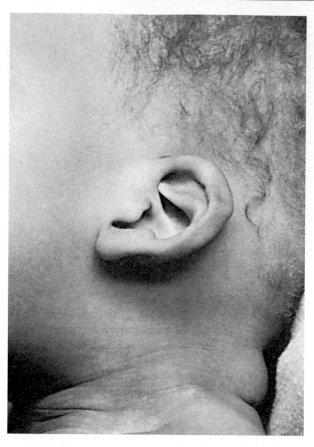

FIGURE 28-11. Abnormal pinna that is low set and posteriorly rotated in patient with Smith-Lemli-Opitz syndrome.

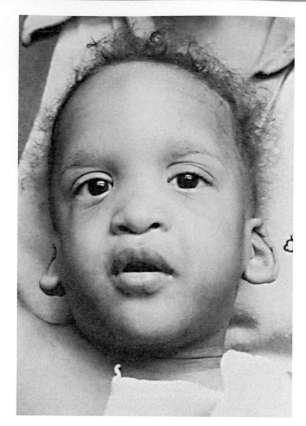

FIGURE 28-12. Facial view of patient in Figure 28-11.

NOSE

The nose, like the external ear, shows great individual variation, but certain alterations in shape are frequent in malformation syndromes involving the face. The nose may be unusually thin with hypoplastic alae nasi, as in Hallerman-Streiff syndrome, or it may be unusually broad, as in frontonasal dysplasia (see Fig. 28-5). A depressed nasal bridge with an upturned nose occurs in many skeletal dysplasias, such as achondroplasia. When the depression is severe, the nostrils may appear to be anteverted and the nose may appear to be shortened. A hypoplastic nose is often syndromic, and a nose with a single nostril is highly suggestive of holoprosencephaly (see Fig. 28-4).

MOUTH (See also Chapter 42, Part 6.)

The mouth is a complex structure with component parts that each require separate evaluation. The size and shape of the mouth may be altered. A small mouth, or microstomia, should be noted; it occurs in trisomy 18 (see Fig. 28-3). Macrostomia, a large mouth, should be noted as well; it may be present in such conditions as mandibulofacial dysostosis (see Fig. 28-7C). Severe macrostomia may result from a lateral facial cleft. The corners of the mouth may be downturned, as in Prader-Willi syndrome and other conditions with hypotonia. An

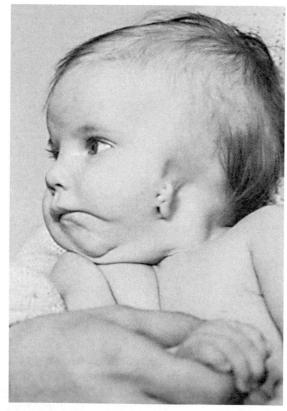

FIGURE 28-13. Hemifacial microsomia showing mandibular hypoplasia, severely malformed pinna, and absent ear canal.

asymmetric face during crying occurs with congenital deficiency in the depressor anguli oris muscle on one side, and this may be associated with other abnormalities, such as hemifacial microsomia and velocardiofacial syndrome.

Prominent, full lips occur in various syndromes, including Williams syndrome. A thin upper lip may be seen in Cornelia de Lange syndrome and in fetal alcohol syndrome (see Fig. 28-1).

A cleft upper lip is usually lateral, as in the common multifactorial cleft lip (or palate) anomaly, occurring in the position of one of the philtral ridges. The presence of pits in the lower lip associated with a cleft lip or palate, however, is suggestive of Van der Woude syndrome, which is inherited in an autosomal dominant manner. A median cleft lip is very suggestive of holoprosencephaly (see Fig. 28-4A). In fact, there are many diverse syndromes with cleft lip or palate that are important to identify because they may have other associated malformations and relatively high genetic risks of recurrence. Therefore, it is particularly important to evaluate the infant with cleft lip or palate carefully for evidence of other malformations to give accurate recurrence risk and prognostic information to the family.

Isolated cleft palate is different genetically from cleft lip. Mild forms of cleft palate are represented by submucosal clefts, pharyngeal incompetence with nasal speech (velopharyngeal insufficiency), and bifid uvula. A high arched palate may occur normally, but it is also a feature of many syndromes, especially if hypotonia or another long-standing neurologic abnormality is present. Hypertrophied alveolar ridges are apparent in the palate along the inner margin of the teeth, and they are suggestive of Smith-Lemli-Opitz syndrome (Fig. 28-14) if seen in an infant.

Macroglossia may be relative, as in the Pierre Robin malformation complex, in which the primary abnormality

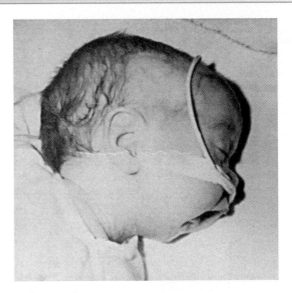

FIGURE 28-15. Micrognathia in Pierre Robin sequence.

is mandibular hypoplasia. In other cases, such as hypothyroidism, Beckwith-Wiedemann syndrome, and Down syndrome, the tongue protrudes and is enlarged. A cleft or irregular tongue or oral frenula occurs in various syndromes such as the orofaciodigital syndromes.

The lower portion of the mouth is formed by the mandible, which in young infants is relatively small. An excessively small mandible is termed *micrognathia*, which is a feature of many syndromes. It is a characteristic of the Pierre Robin sequence, which consists of the triad of micrognathia, glossoptosis, and a U-shaped cleft palate, as opposed to the common V-shaped cleft. A typical patient is shown in Figure 28-15. The Pierre Robin sequence may be part of a syndrome, such as Stickler syndrome (hereditary arthro-ophthalmopathy), and thus other anomalies and a family history must be sought. In other syndromes, the maxilla likewise may be hypoplastic, decreasing the prominence of the upper cheeks (malar hypoplasia).

NECK

The neck may be short, and limitation of rotation should raise the suspicion of fusion of cervical vertebrae, as in a Klippel-Feil anomaly. Excessive skinfolds are characteristic of Turner syndrome (Fig. 28-16), Noonan syndrome, and Down syndrome. In these examples, the excess nuchal skin often represents resolution of a cystic hygroma that was present prenatally.

CHEST

The thoracic cage may be unusually small as part of a skeletal dysplasia, such as thanatophoric dysplasia (Fig. 28-17) or Jeune asphyxiating thoracic dystrophy. The sternum itself may be unusually short, which is typical in trisomy 18, or it may be altered in shape, as is seen in pectus excavatum or pectus carinatum. The latter anomalies are commonly seen in a variety

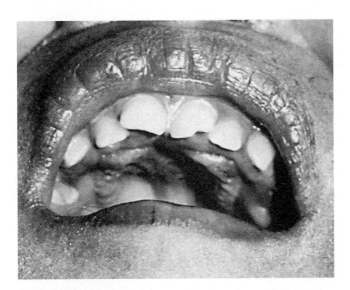

FIGURE 28-14. Prominent alveolar ridges in patient with Smith-Lemli-Opitz syndrome.

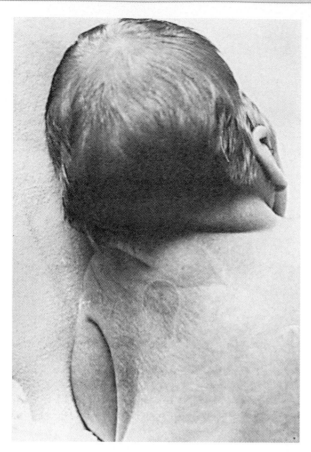

FIGURE 28-16. Excess skinfolds of the neck in patient with Turner syndrome.

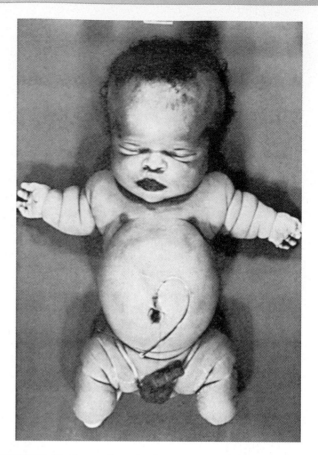

FIGURE 28-17. Thanatophoric dwarf. Note short limbs and narrow thoracic cage.

of skeletal dysplasias and connective tissue disorders (see Chapter 42, Part Five).

ABDOMEN (See also Chapter 45.)

Hypoplasia of the abdominal musculature may occur in association with intrauterine bladder outlet obstruction and other anomalies of the urogenital system. It results in a characteristic "prune-belly" appearance (see Chapter 49). An omphalocele, in which abdominal contents protrude through the umbilical opening, may be part of the Beckwith-Wiedemann syndrome (see Chapter 47, Part One) or chromosomal abnormalities such as trisomy 13. Gastroschisis, however, is usually an isolated disruption in which the abdominal contents protrude through the periumbilical abdominal wall. Anomalies of a more minor nature, such as inguinal or umbilical hernias, occur in normal infants, but they are more frequent in various syndromes, particularly in connective tissue disorders.

ANUS (See also Chapter 45.)

Imperforate anus may be isolated or may occur as the mildest expression of a caudal regression sequence, in which other anomalies such as sacral dysgenesis are seen. It is most commonly part of a constellation of anomalies, such as the VATER association. It also can be seen in a number of chromosomal abnormalities.

GENITALIA (See also Chapter 47, Part 4.)

Hypogenitalism can be seen in association with hypotonia in Prader-Willi syndrome or with low-set dysplastic ears, syndactyly of the toes, and thickened alveolar ridges in Smith-Lemli-Opitz syndrome. Genital ambiguity is associated with renal anomalies and an increased risk for Wilms tumor in Denys-Drash syndrome.

SPINE (See also Chapter 38.)

Among the most common congenital anomalies are the neural tube defects, which involve abnormalities of the central nervous system along with defects in the associated bony structures. Minor external anomalies, particularly of the lower spine, include unusual pigmentary lesions, hair tufts, dimples, and sinuses. Some of these changes, such as hair tufts and sinuses above the gluteal cleft, may be an indication of a more significant deeper anomaly and require further evaluation, such as magnetic resonance imaging.

EXTREMITIES

Extremities may be relatively long, as occur in Marfan syndrome or homocystinuria, or unusually short, as occur in a diverse group of skeletal dysplasias, the most common being achondroplasia. A simple guide to evaluating relative extremity length is to determine where the fingertips are in relation to the thighs when the upper extremities are adducted alongside the body. In the normal infant, the fingertips fall below the hip joint in the midthigh region. When the upper extremities are short, they align with the hip joint or above (see Fig. 28-17); when they are relatively long, they may reach the knees. A more precise and useful measurement is to determine the ratio of the upper segment to the lower segment. The distance from the pubis to the heel with the leg fully extended constitutes the lower segment. By subtracting the lower segment measurement from the total length, one obtains the upper segment. In normal newborns, the ratio of the upper segment to the lower segment is approximately 1.7 and decreases with age to approximately 1.0 in the adult. A high ratio suggests relative shortening of the extremities, and a low ratio implies either unusually long extremities or a foreshortened trunk, as may occur in spondyloepiphyseal dysplasia.

Paired extremities may be asymmetric in either length or overall size, suggesting either atrophy of one or hypertrophy of the other. The distinction may be difficult to make at times, although it is often evident if an extremity is unusually large or excessively small. Hypertrophy of limbs may be a manifestation of Beckwith-Wiedemann syndrome or Klippel-Trenaunay-Weber syndrome. Isolated hemiatrophy may occur with long-standing corticospinal tract damage as well, as in Russell-Silver syndrome. It is important to identify hemihypertrophy because individuals with this finding are at increased risk for intra-abdominal tumors, such as Wilms tumor, and thus require close monitoring.

Foreshortening of long bones leads to various limb abnormalities, depending on the segments involved. A number of terms have been used to describe such anomalies. *Rhizomelia* denotes proximal shortening of the limbs, such as those in achondroplasia. *Mesomelia* refers to shortening of the middle segment, and *acromelia* refers to relative shortening of the hands or feet. A shortened forearm with secondary prominence of skinfolds in a newborn with thanatophoric dysplasia is shown in Figure 28-18.

The hands and feet have epidermal ridges and creases forming a variety of configurations. Normally, there are two deep transverse palmar creases that do not completely cross the palm. In various conditions, such as trisomy 21, there may instead be a single transverse palmar crease (a simian crease). Single palmar creases may be completely transverse across the palm or may be bridged or incomplete (Fig. 28-19A and B). They may become more apparent when the palm is slightly flexed. A single phalangeal crease on the fifth finger, instead of the normal two, occurs as a consequence of a hypoplastic middle phalanx and results in clinodactyly (incurving of the digit). This is frequently seen in trisomy 21 (see Fig. 28-19C) and in a number of other conditions.

The foot also has ridge patterns. A sandal pattern of deep furrows is typical of mosaic trisomy 8 (Fig. 28-20). Figure 28-21 illustrates the increased separation of the first and second toes and a prominent interdigital furrow in trisomy 21.

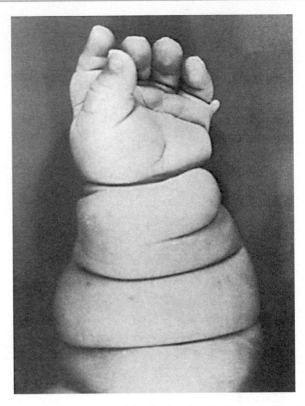

FIGURE 28-18. Forearm and hand of patient in Figure 28-17. Note rudimentary postaxial polydactyly.

Dermatoglyphics, the study of configurations of the characteristic ridge patterns of the volar surfaces of the skin, can sometimes aid in the diagnosis of the newborn with congenital anomalies. The scope of this subject is beyond that of this chapter and the reader is referred to other sources.[21]

The hands and feet may be enlarged as a result of lymphedema. This is characteristic of infants with Turner or Noonan syndrome, in which the dorsum of the hands and feet may have a puffy appearance (Fig. 28-22). Congenital lymphedema can also be an autosomal dominantly inherited condition with variable expressivity.

"Rocker-bottom feet" (Fig. 28-23) is a term used to describe a prominent heel and a loss of the normal concave longitudinal arch of the sole. This feature is common in trisomy 18 and other syndromes.

Significant anomalies of the underlying structure produce alterations in the normal form of the hands and feet. Such abnormalities may be classified into the following categories: absence deformities, polydactyly, syndactyly, brachydactyly, arachnodactyly, and contracture deformities (see Chapter 52).

Absence anomalies are of various types, and the etiology and possible associated malformations vary with the type. Congenital absence of an entire hand is termed *acheiria*, and absence of both hands and feet is *acheiropodia*. *Ectrodactyly* refers to a partial or total absence of the distal segments of a hand or foot with the proximal segments of the limbs more or less normal. All such anomalies are examples of terminal

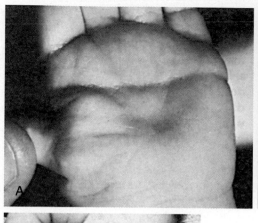

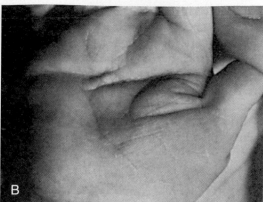

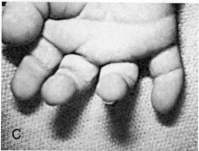

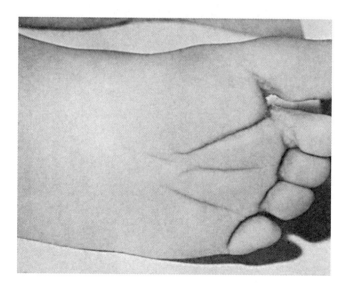

FIGURE 28-19. A, Simian crease. **B,** Incomplete bridged simian crease. **C,** Hand of patient with trisomy 21 showing simian crease, brachydactyly, and clinodactyly of fifth finger with single phalangeal crease.

FIGURE 28-20. Sandal line furrows in trisomy 8.

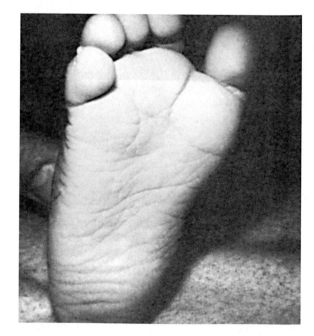

FIGURE 28-21. Trisomy 21. Note increased separation of first and second toes.

transverse defects and may occur sporadically or as part of a syndrome. The term *ectrodactyly* is frequently misused for the lobster-claw anomaly, which is best described as split hand/split foot. In this anomaly, the central rays are deficient, and there is often fusion of the remaining digits. Split hand/split foot may be seen in isolation, when it is of autosomal dominant origin, or it may be seen with other anomalies.

It is useful to determine whether the defects involve primarily the radial, or preaxial, side of the limb or the ulnar, or postaxial, side. For example, blood dyscrasias

such as Fanconi anemia and the thrombocytopenia-absent radius syndrome commonly involve radial deficiency (see Chapter 44).

Polydactyly refers to partial or complete super-numerary digits and is one of the most common limb malformations. Postaxial polydactyly is more frequent than preaxial, particularly in blacks (Fig. 28-24). As an

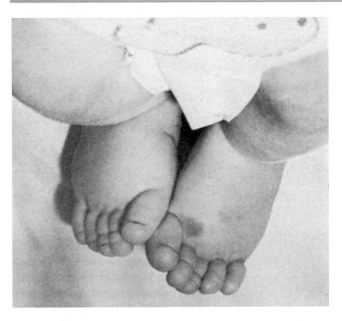

FIGURE 28-22. Dorsal edema of feet in patient with Turner syndrome.

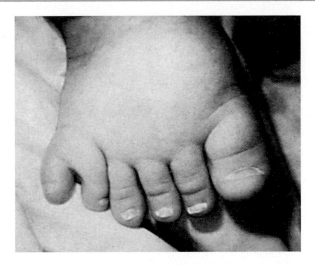

FIGURE 28-24. Postaxial polydactyly.

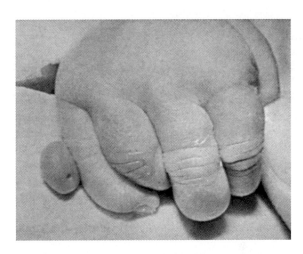

FIGURE 28-25. Postaxial polydactyly in trisomy 13.

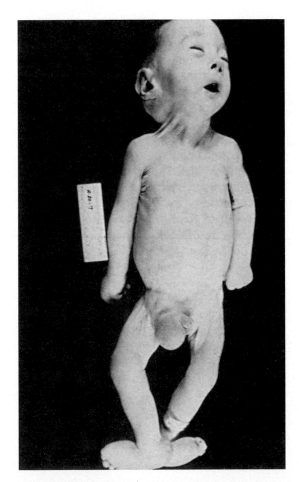

FIGURE 28-23. Trisomy 18. Note right hydrocele and rocker-bottom feet.

isolated anomaly, polydactyly may be inherited as an autosomal dominant trait. It also may be a manifestation of a multiple malformation syndrome. Postaxial polydactyly may occur in a variety of syndromes, including trisomy 13 (Fig. 28-25), chondroectodermal dysplasia, Meckel-Gruber syndrome, and Bardet-Biedl syndrome. Preaxial polydactyly is characteristic of Carpenter syndrome and Majewski short rib-polydactyly syndrome.

Syndactyly refers to fusion of digits; it is usually cutaneous, but it may involve bone. Minimal syndactyly of the second and third toes is common in normal newborns. More extensive syndactyly is shown in Figure 28-26 and can be seen in trisomy 21 and Smith-Lemli-Opitz syndrome. As an isolated anomaly, different clinical types may be distinguished, but each of them is inherited as an autosomal dominant trait with variable expressivity and incomplete penetrance. Extensive syndactyly often is part of a syndrome, and typical examples include some of the craniosynostosis conditions, such as Apert and Pfeiffer syndromes.

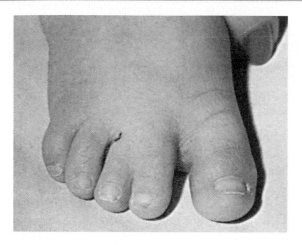

FIGURE 28-26. Syndactyly between second and third toes.

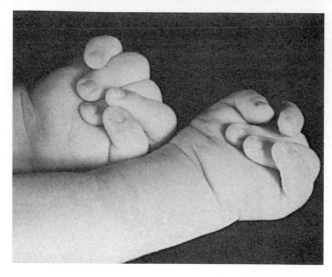

FIGURE 28-27. Trisomy 18. Note characteristic clinodactyly of second, fourth, and fifth fingers.

Brachydactyly refers to shortening of one or more digits owing to anomalous development of any of the phalanges, metacarpals, or metatarsals. Various clinical types may be distinguished, but most isolated forms of brachydactyly are inherited in an autosomal dominant fashion. Brachydactyly is also a component of numerous disorders, including skeletal dysplasias such as achondro-plasia, and syndromes such as Albright hereditary osteodystrophy and Down syndrome (see Fig. 28-19C).

Arachnodactyly refers to unusually long, spider-like digits, and it is characteristic but not invariable in Marfan syndrome and homocystinuria. The appearance of brachydactyly and arachnodactyly can be confirmed by measuring and determining the ratio of middle finger to total hand length, which is normally approximately 0.43 in the newborn.

A variety of congenital joint deformities involving the limbs may occur. *Arthrogryposis*, multiple congenital contractures, is most often sporadic and may be associated with oligohydramnios or may be the result of some underlying neuromuscular abnormality. Talipes equinovarus or calcaneovalgus deformities of the ankle are common isolated joint contractures (see Chapter 52). Contractures also may occur in numerous syndromes. Joint hypermobility is frequent in various connective tissue disorders, such as Marfan and Ehlers-Danlos syndromes, and can also be seen in a number of multiple anomaly syndromes such as Kabuki syndrome.

Clinodactyly, as discussed previously, designates an incurving of a digit, most commonly of the fifth finger. This condition is frequent in trisomy 21 and other syndromes (see Fig. 28-19C). A characteristic clinodactyly involving the fourth and fifth fingers radially and second finger in an ulnar direction occurs in trisomy 18 (Fig. 28-27) or, less often, in trisomy 13.

Camptodactyly is irreducible flexion of the digits. In the hand it usually involves the fifth finger, but it may affect other fingers as well. Isolated camptodactyly may be inherited as an autosomal dominant trait.

Camptodactyly also may be part of a syndrome such as trisomy 8, trisomy 10q, and Freeman-Sheldon syndrome.

Evaluation of the Stillborn

Evaluation of the stillborn is essential and is very similar to that of the live-born infant. There has been controversy over whether it is the responsibility of the perinatologist or the neonatologist to evaluate pregnancy loss.[32] As a result, this important function often has been inadequately performed, leaving the family with little understanding of the nature and etiology of the anomaly, the recurrence risk, and methods of preventing future occurrences. The grieving process, a natural and constant result of fetal loss, is left unaddressed and is made much more difficult without an understanding of the cause of the loss. In addition to the obvious role of the pathologist to learn as much as possible from the examination of the aborted fetus, the clinician is essential in encouraging the family to allow fetal evaluation and to allow the pathologist to conduct it. The clinician also should direct additional testing and meet with the family when the evaluation is complete to ensure that the family receives medical and genetic counseling. Given the decreasing gestational age at fetal viability, it seems reasonable to assume that before 20 weeks' gestation, responsibility of pregnancy loss evaluation rests with the perinatologist, and after this date it falls to the neonatologist. Pregnancy loss before 20 weeks occurs in at least 12% to 15% of all pregnancies[28] and in 1% to 2% of pregnancies after 20 weeks, when it is usually called stillbirth.[3,22] It is optimal for each hospital to develop a protocol for evaluating fetal loss, including which fetuses to study and which evaluations are appropriate.[3] A thorough surface examination by the clinician is useful to identify minor anomalies that may not be apparent to the pathologist as rigor mortis sets in. If indicated, a sample of blood or skin should be obtained as soon as possible under sterile conditions for chromosome analysis. Skin can be placed in viral culture media or sterile saline and sent to the laboratory for fibroblast culture. Cells from the fetal side of the placenta may grow when macerated fetal tissue may not. Examination of the stillborn and the placenta by the pathologist may identify internal anomalies that lead to a definitive diagnosis.

Diagnostic Testing and Indications

Once the history and clinical findings are noted, various laboratory studies may be indicated to aid in making an accurate diagnosis.

In a newborn with one or more obvious major malformations or with multiple minor anomalies, imaging studies are often indicated to identify other anomalies. Ultrasonography of the head and abdomen is useful to screen for major structural anomalies of the brain and kidneys. Head ultrasonography is a crude study for brain abnormalities, and if brain abnormalities are suspected, more definitive testing such as computed tomography or magnetic resonance imaging is indicated. Echocardiography also is helpful because congenital heart defects are among the most common major malformations. Detection of major anomalies involving the brain, heart, and kidneys is useful for diagnostic purposes, and it also may allow for more appropriate management and more accurate prognostication.

Routine chromosome analysis is indicated in newborns with ambiguous genitalia, two or more major anomalies, multiple minor anomalies, or growth restriction in association with anomalies. Because a routine karyotype on peripheral blood allows for better resolution than a karyotype from amniocentesis and thus will allow detection of small deletions or duplications, such a study should be performed even if a prenatal chromosome analysis had normal findings. Sometimes high resolution (prometaphase) chromosome analysis is indicated if a specific deletion is suspected or if the suspicion for a chromosome anomaly is high and no abnormality is identified on a routine study.

FISH allows for identification of microdeletions not detectable by routine cytogenetic analysis (Table 28-9). In fact, it has been shown that a significant number of neonates with conotruncal heart defects have a 22q microdeletion, so this testing is indicated in all patients with truncus arteriosus, interrupted aortic arch, and tetralogy of Fallot.

Subtelomeric probe analysis is a cytogenetic study in which a mixture of special FISH probes is used to identify small deletions or duplications involving the regions near the ends of all the chromosomes. Alterations in these regions can be missed by even high resolution chromosome analysis. Therefore, this study is indicated in those infants with multiple congenital anomalies for which there is a high suspicion for a chromosome abnormality and in whom there has been a normal result on high resolution chromosome analysis.

Molecular genetic analysis is an increasingly useful tool in diagnosing the newborn with congenital anomalies. For example, in those infants with unexplained hypotonia and contractures, DNA testing may identify an expansion in the myotonic dystrophy gene. As more disease-causing genes are identified, molecular analysis will undoubtedly become a cost-effective aid in diagnosis.

Another area of burgeoning research that is likely to result in useful diagnostic testing is that of metabolic disorders. These conditions were traditionally thought of as not being associated with congenital anomalies, but this concept is changing. A definitive diagnosis of Smith-Lemli-Opitz syndrome, which is associated with syndactyly of the second and third toes, genital abnormalities, ptosis, thick alveolar ridges, malformations of the heart, and other anomalies, can be made by obtaining a low serum cholesterol level and an elevated 7-dehydrocholesterol level. Presumably, many other conditions with congenital anomalies will be found to have a biochemical basis, which will allow for more definitive diagnoses.

The neonate with ambiguous genitalia requires a battery of tests, including chromosome analysis to determine genotypic sex, pelvic ultrasonography to identify internal genitalia, and endocrine testing (17-OH progesterone, testosterone, luteinizing hormone, follicle-stimulating hormone). It is best to defer assignment of sex until many of these tests have been performed and a urologist has evaluated the newborn. A psychologist can be very useful in helping the family deal with the uncertainty.

Ophthalmology evaluation also can be useful in diagnosing the neonate with congenital anomalies, especially if brain malformations or neurologic abnormalities are present. This evaluation also should be

TABLE 28-9. Common Microdeletion Syndromes Identifiable by Fluorescence In Situ Hybridization (FISH)

SYNDROME	CLINICAL FEATURES IN NEWBORN PERIOD	CHROMOSOMAL LOCATION
Prader-Willi syndrome	Hypotonia, hypogenitalism	15q
Velocardiofacial/DiGeorge syndrome	Conotruncal heart defects, palatal abnormalities, ear anomalies, hypocalcemia	22q
Williams syndrome	Supravalvular aortic stenosis, hypercalcemia, full lips, periorbital fullness	7q
Miller-Dieker syndrome	Lissencephaly (smooth brain)	17p

performed if small genitalia are present in a male infant (septo-optic dysplasia) or if features of the CHARGE association are present.

The value of the postmortem examination cannot be overemphasized. A thorough evaluation by an experienced pathologist can yield findings that would not be identified otherwise and that may lead to a definitive diagnosis and thus information about recurrence risk and possible prenatal testing in future pregnancies. The role of the clinician is to educate the family on the importance of such an evaluation.

Once a thorough history has been taken, a physical examination has been performed, and appropriate testing is under way, the clinician should identify those features that are most unique (Fig. 28-28). Sometimes a pattern is readily recognized, such as Down syndrome in a child with an atrioventricular canal, hypotonia, palpebral fissures that slant upward, small squared ears, and fifth finger clinodactyly. However, a review of reference texts often is required to determine whether the findings represent a previously described condition.

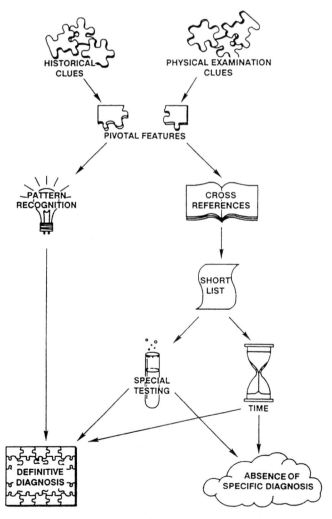

FIGURE 28-28. Diagnostic strategies: the Sherlock Holmes model. (From Aase JM: Diagnostic Dysmorphology. New York, Plenum, 1990.)

A clinical geneticist/dysmorphologist may be especially helpful at this point. Other evaluations also may be indicated (see "Diagnostic Testing and Indications," earlier).

Sometimes a diagnosis does not become apparent until later in life as the physical features change and other structural or functional abnormalities become apparent. Parents should be counseled about this possibility and that even though a diagnosis may not be apparent, the findings may very well have a genetic basis and recurrence in future pregnancies is possible.

GENETIC COUNSELING

Genetic counseling is a communication process during which families are informed about the abnormalities present in the affected individual, with medical and genetic knowledge discussed in practical language. A description of the abnormality, the natural history, associated abnormalities, and prognosis for the disorder are provided. The etiology of the abnormality (if known), whether genetic or nongenetic, is explained in such a manner that the family can understand. The family also is given reassurance that the condition in the affected individual is not the fault of any individual, and information about recurrence risk is provided.

Those family members who are at increased risk of being affected or having affected offspring, as determined by pedigree analysis and etiology, are identified, and prenatal diagnostic testing, if possible, is described, including the complications and accuracy. Assistance in reaching a decision about prenatal testing and in accessing it is offered. Genetic counselors provide supportive counseling to families, assist families in coping with a lifelong condition, and serve as patient advocates. Information about appropriate community services and family support organizations also is offered.

Genetic counseling can be given by anyone willing to take the time and to make the effort. Genetic counselors, sometimes called genetic associates, are individuals with a master's degree who have been specifically trained to understand genetic disorders and congenital anomalies and to help families with the psychological and emotional adaptation to having a family member with a serious and chronic problem. Medical geneticists are physicians (or sometimes doctors of philosophy) who have received special training in genetic counseling and in the diagnosis and management of genetic disorders and birth defects.

EDUCATIONAL RESOURCES AND SUPPORT ORGANIZATIONS

With almost universal access to the Internet, the number of education resources in the genetics arena has increased greatly. In addition to more general references for the medical community, which can be helpful to families, most individual conditions now have their own websites.

Because most congenital anomalies and genetic disorders are relatively rare, usually occurring with a frequency of 1 in 1000 or less, family support organizations have been developed to help combat the isolation and grief felt by families who have or have had an affected child. These groups usually offer support and empathy and serve as a clearinghouse for information about the disorder and its management. Often they have a newsletter for members that describes helpful coping mechanisms and keeps families updated on relevant resources and research. Many have their own website and chatroom.

Such organizations often have been started by and are usually staffed by parents of affected individuals or by affected individuals themselves. As a result, they vary greatly both in the format and content of what they offer and in the accuracy of the information they distribute. Organizations for more frequent disorders, such as Down syndrome and Prader-Willi syndrome, are usually large and professionally run; offer educational forums, such as an annual conference and lay literature; keep listings of resources locally and nationally; and may even offer grant funding for research on the disorder. Smaller organizations for less common conditions may serve primarily a social and support function. Because of this variability in the knowledge of support organizations and the resultant uncertainty concerning the accuracy of information provided, it is advisable for the physician to become familiar with an organization and its functions before referring a family.

A national organization, the Alliance of Genetic Support Groups, serves as a resource to identify whether a designated organization exists for a specific condition and also lists more general organizations. The Alliance supplies contact information and data about the organizations. It prints a directory of national genetic voluntary organizations and related resources, which it updates regularly. The Alliance can be reached by calling 1-800-336-GENE. Another group, the National Organization for Rare Disorders (NORD), functions as a clearinghouse for information on genetic disorders; it will send a summary of this information written for lay individuals for a small fee, will match families, and will make medical referrals, if appropriate. NORD can be reached at 1-800-999-NORD. Two other resources with excellent lay information about specific genetic disorders are the New York Online Access to Health Home Page (www.noah-health.org/english/illness/genetic_diseases/geneticdis.html) and the March of Dimes (www.marchofdimes.com/pnhec/4439.asp).

SUMMARY

It is the role of the neonatologist to direct the evaluation of the newborn or stillborn with congenital anomalies. Diagnostic testing and evaluations along with consultation of references and specialists in the field, such as clinical geneticists and dysmorphologists, may be helpful. The goal is to identify the etiology so that accurate information on prognosis and recurrence risk can be shared with the family.

REFERENCES

1. ACMG Test and Technology Transfer Committee: Technical and clinical assessment of fluorescence in situ hybridization: An ACMG/ASHG position statement. I. Technical Considerations. Genet Med 2/6:356, 2000.
2. Brent RL: Evaluating the alleged teratogenicity of environmental agents. Clin Perinatol 13:609, 1986.
3. Curry CJR et al: A protocol for the investigation of pregnancy loss. Clin Perinatol 17:723, 1990.
4. Curry CJR: Pregnancy loss, stillbirth, and neonatal death: A guide for the pediatrician. Pediatr Clin North Am 39:157, 1992.
5. Emanual I et al: The incidence of congenital malformations in a Chinese population: The Taipei collaborative study. Teratology 5:159, 1972.
6. Erickson JD: Racial variations in the incidence of congenital malformations. Ann Hum Genet 34:315, 1976.
7. Gorlin RJ et al: Orofacial clefting syndromes: General aspects, 4th ed. In Gorlin RJ et al (eds): Syndromes of the Head and Neck. New York, Oxford University Press, 2001, p 850.
8. Gorlin RJ et al (eds): Syndromes of the Head and Neck. New York, Oxford University Press, 2001.
9. Graham JM: Smith's Recognizable Patterns of Human Deformation, 5th ed. Philadelphia, WB Saunders, 1988.
10. Holmes LB: Inborn errors of morphogenesis: A review of localized hereditary malformations. N Engl J Med 291:763, 1974.
11. Holmes LB: Current concepts in genetics: Congenital malformations. N Engl J Med 295:204, 1976.
12. Holt M, et al: Familial heart disease with skeletal malformations. Br Heart J 22:236, 1960.
13. Hook EB: Contribution of chromosome abnormalities to human morbidity and mortality. Cytogenet Cell Genet 33:101, 1982.
14. Irons M et al: Defective cholesterol biosynthesis in Smith-Lemli-Opitz syndrome. Lancet 341:1414, 1993.
15. Jones KL (ed): Smith's Recognizable Patterns of Human Malformation, 5th ed. Philadelphia, WB Saunders, 1997.
16. Kaji T et al: Anatomic and chromosomal anomalies in 639 spontaneous abortuses. Hum Genet 55:87, 1980.
17. Leppig KA et al: Predictive value of minor anomalies: I. Association with major malformations. J Pediatr 110:530, 1987.
18. Marden PM et al: Congenital anomalies in the newborn infant, including minor variations: A study of 4142 babies by surface examination for anomalies and buccal smear for sex chromatin. J Pediatr 64:357, 1964.
19. McKusick VA et al (eds): Mendelian Inheritance in Man: A Catalog of Human Genes and Genetic Disorders. Baltimore, The Johns Hopkins University Press, 1998.
20. Mills JL: Malformations in infants of diabetic mothers. Teratology 25:385, 1982.
21. Mulvihill JJ et al: The genesis of dermatoglyphics. J Pediatr 75:579, 1969.
22. Nelson K et al: Malformations due to presumed spontaneous mutations in newborn infants. New Engl J Med 320:19, 1989.
23. Nelson T et al: Collection of human embryos and fetuses. In Hook EB et al (eds): Monitoring Birth Defects and Environment: The Problem of Surveillance. New York, Academic Press, 1971.

24. Parisi M: Hirschsprung disease overview. In GeneReviews, at GeneTests: Medical Genetics Information Resource. Copyright, University of Washington, Seattle, 1997-2004. Available at www.genetests.org. Posted July 2002.

25. Quan L et al: The VATER association. J Pediatr 82:104, 1973.

26. Schinzel A: Catalog of Unbalanced Chromosome Aberrations in Man. Berlin, Walter de Gruyter, 2001.

27. Seaver L et al: Teratology in pediatric practice. Pediatr Clin North Am 39:111, 1992.

28. Simpson JL: Genetic causes of spontaneous abortion. Contemp Obstet Gynecol 35:25, 1990.

29. Spranger J et al: Errors of morphogenesis: Concepts and terms. J Pediatr 100:160, 1982.

30. Stevenson RE et al (eds): Human Malformations and Related Anomalies. New York, Oxford University Press, 1993.

31. Werler MM et al: Periconceptional folic acid exposure and risk of occurrent neural tube defects. JAMA 269:1257, 1993.

32. Winter RM: The malformed fetus and stillbirth: Whose patient? Br J Obstet Gynaecol 90:499, 1983.

V Provisions for Neonatal Care

29 Physical Environment

PART 1

The Thermal Environment of the Newborn Infant

Gunnar Sedin

Protecting infants against excessive heat loss improves their chances for survival, reduces their bodies' need to perform heat-producing metabolic work, and eliminates the problems associated with rewarming of cold infants.

Although incubators can be traced back to ancient Egypt, where they were used for the hatching of chicken eggs, incubators used for human infant care did not exist until the late 1870s. The incubator was part of the primal technology in Professor Tarnier's method for enhancing the survival of prematurely born babies. The history of incubators is the history of neonatal medicine, which includes the bizarre but critically important use of incubators to display human infants in sideshow exhibits. Other sources provide excellent reviews of this colorful period (see also Chapter 1).

During intrauterine life, heat production by the fetus results in a fetal temperature that is about 0.5° C higher than the maternal temperature.[8] After birth, the newborn infant is exposed to air and surfaces, which have a much lower temperature than that previously experienced in utero. The skin surface at that time is covered with amniotic fluid, causing heat loss through evaporation in an environment with a low vapor pressure.[19,33] As a result, the body temperature of the infant is lowered, and the rate of this reduction is influenced by the temperature of the environmental air in the delivery room and the velocity of its flow. This gives rise to thermogenic responses that increase basal heat production,[8,11] and the skin circulation may decrease to lower the heat losses.[53]

Heat balance in newborn infants depends on the heat transfer between the infant and the environment.* This transfer is related to the temperature and humidity of the environmental air (the vapor pressure), the flow velocity of that air, the temperatures of the surfaces facing the infant (ceiling, walls of room or incubator, and bedding material), and the temperature of the surface in contact with the infant.*

After birth, the immediate interventions needed to avoid body cooling are to wipe the amniotic fluid from the skin surface to lower the loss of heat through evaporation and to cover the infant with a warm and dry towel or blanket, or both, to lessen the exposure of the infant's skin to the environment.[19,22] The infant born at term or moderately preterm can be covered with a blanket and then placed on the mother's chest,[4,5,50,60] but extremely preterm infants usually need other measures to maintain their body temperature—usually placement in an incubator or under a radiant heater,† and, if necessary, mechanical ventilation with warm and humidified gas.‡

ROUTES OF HEAT EXCHANGE

Heat exchange between the infant and its environment occurs through the skin and through the respiratory tract. The introduction of new techniques to measure the rate of evaporation from the skin§ and from the respiratory tract¶ has permitted the heat loss through evaporation to be determined.[22] It is also possible to calculate the heat loss through other modes of heat exchange, such as radiation, convection, and conduction, and to determine the heat loss per unit surface area and from the total body surface area.[44] It is also necessary to take into consideration the proportions of surface area participating in the different modes of

---

*References 7-9, 17-20, 22, 23, 38, 44.

*References 11, 19, 20, 22, 33, 44, 48.
†References 18, 20, 22, 30, 31, 51.
‡References 23, 40, 41, 45, 55, 58.
§References 17, 22, 30, 32, 43, 47, 59.
¶References 23, 24, 29, 36-39, 44, 48.

heat exchange.[19,20,22,34] In addition, the modes of heat exchange between the infant's respiratory tract and the environment can be determined.

HEAT EXCHANGE BETWEEN THE INFANT'S BODY SURFACE AND THE ENVIRONMENT

Heat exchange through evaporation, radiation, convection, and conduction can be calculated with knowledge of the transepidermal water loss, the temperature of the infant's skin (T_{skin}), the temperature of the walls facing the infant (T_{wall}), the temperature of the ambient air (T_{amb}), the temperature of the material on which the infant is placed (T_{bed}), and characteristics of the material in the infant's environment, using the equations given in the following paragraphs.[19,20]

Determination of Water Loss from the Skin

In the absence of forced convection, and if the effect of thermal diffusion is disregarded, the process of water exchange through a stationary water-permeable surface can be expressed in terms of the vapor-pressure gradient immediately adjacent to the surface.[32]

The evaporation rate (ER; g/m^2h) from the infant's skin can thus be determined by a method based on calculation of the water vapor pressure in the layer of air immediately adjacent to the skin surface.[17,32] In this zone, the relationship between the vapor pressure and the distance from the evaporating surface is linear.[32] If the gradient in this layer is known, the amount of water evaporated per unit time can be calculated.[32]

The gradient method (Evaporimeter, ServoMed AB, Varberg, Sweden) allows quick measurements of free evaporation without disturbing the infant.[17,32] Transepidermal water loss (TEWL; in g/m^2h), which is a mean value of cutaneous water loss, can be calculated according to the following equation:

$$TEWL = 0.92 \times ER_{(a,b,c)} + 1.37,$$

where $ER_{(a,b,c)}$ is the arithmetic mean of the ER measured from the chest, an interscapular area, and a buttock.[17,43,44,48]

CALCULATIONS OF HEAT EXCHANGE BETWEEN THE INFANT AND THE ENVIRONMENT

Exchange at the Surface

Heat exchange through evaporation (H_{evap}) can be calculated if TEWL is known,[17,32,43,44,48] according to the equation

$$H_{evap} = k_1 \times TEWL \ (3.6 \times 10^3)^{-1} \ (W/m^2),$$

where k_1 is the latent heat of evaporation (2.4×10^3 J/g), W is watt and 3.6×10^3 is the correction factor for time (seconds).

Heat exchange through radiation (H_{rad}) can be determined if the mean temperature of the skin (T_1;K) and the mean temperature of the surrounding walls (T_2;K = Kelvin) are known:

$$H_{rad} = S_0 \times e_1 \times e_2 \times (T_1^4 - T_2^4) \ (W/m^2),$$

where S_0 is the Stefan-Boltzmann constant (5.7×10^{-8} W/m^2K^4), e_1 is the emissivity of the skin, and e_2 is the emissivity of the surrounding walls (0.97).

Heat exchange through convection (H_{conv}) can be calculated if the mean temperature of the skin (T_1;K) and the mean temperature of the ambient air (T_3;K) are known:

$$H_{conv} = k_2 \ (T_1 - T_3) \ (W/m^2),$$

where k_2 is the convection coefficient (2.7 W/m^2K). This coefficient for convection has been used in many of the studies referred to in this chapter, but it has usually been determined in measurements on adult human skin.[44] A convection coefficient suggested as being more valid for newborn infants[59] can alternatively be used, and H_{conv} is then 48% higher.

Heat exchange through conduction (H_{cond}) can be determined if the temperature of the skin (T_{skin};K) and the temperature of the bed (T_{bed};K) are known:

$$H_{cond} = k_0 \ (T_{skin} - T_{bed}) \ (W/m^2)$$

In this equation, k_0 is a conductive heat transfer coefficient. With the thermal conductivity characteristics of most regular mattresses, the heat loss through conduction is very low.

The extent of heat exchange between the body surface area and the environment thus depends on the type of heat exchange, on the position and geometry of the body,[22,44] and on the magnitude and frequency of body movements. Because different modes of heat exchange are unequally influenced by changes in body position, the relative contribution of different modes of heat exchange might vary with time. Heat exchange is often presented per unit area of body surface exposed to the ambient air or facing the walls of the incubator.

HEAT EXCHANGE BETWEEN THE INFANT'S RESPIRATORY TRACT AND THE ENVIRONMENT

The expired air is usually more humid—that is, it has a higher water vapor pressure—than the inspired air. This implies that evaporative loss of water and heat takes place from the respiratory tract. Convective heat transfer, usually of low degree, also occurs in the respiratory tract. In research, these two processes are often considered together.[27] In the newborn, heat can also be gained through the respiratory tract if the infant inspires very warm air with a high humidity. Because of the alternating displacement of air during the respiratory cycle, convective and evaporative heat transfer in the respiratory tract is complex. When ambient air, which is cooler than the body, passes along the mucosa during inspiration, it gains heat by convection and it gains water vapor by evaporation from the mucosa. On reaching the alveoli, the air is at thermal equilibrium with the central body temperature and is saturated with water. During expiration, the expired air may become a little cooler than the body temperature before it leaves the infant.

DETERMINATION OF WATER LOSS FROM THE AIRWAY

Respiratory water loss (RWL) is usually included in measurements of total insensible water loss when these are performed with ventilated chambers, but it can be estimated separately.[26,58] Hey and Katz[26] and Sulyok and colleagues[58] found that the respiratory water loss was higher at a low ambient humidity than at a high humidity. In other studies of respiratory water loss, an open flow-through system has been used with a mass spectrometer to measure the gas concentrations.[23] Ambient air is then sucked through a specially constructed Teflon funnel attached to the infant (or the lamb), so that all expired air is collected without inclusion of evaporation from the surrounding skin.[23,36] This system provides data on respiratory water loss, oxygen consumption, and carbon dioxide production.[23,24,36-41,52]

Calculation of Heat Exchange between the Infant's Respiratory Tract and the Environment

The exchange of heat through convection in the respiratory tract, H_{conv-r}, is calculated from the air volume ventilated per unit time (V) and from the temperature difference between expired and inspired air ($T_E - T_I$) according to the following relationship:

$$H_{conv-r} = V \times \rho \times c \, (T_E - T_I) \, m^{-1} \, (W/kg),$$

where ρ is the density of the air (1 g = 0.880 L), c is the specific heat ($1 \, J \times g^{-1} \times °C^{-1}$), and m is the body weight (in kilograms).[44]

Because of the alternating inspiratory warming and expiratory cooling of the air, the convective heat exchange in the respiratory tract depends mainly on the temperature of the inspired air. In human infants nursed in incubators, there is only a very small difference between the temperatures of the inspired air and of the expired air, and convective losses are therefore very small.

Evaporative heat exchange from the airway (H_{evap-r}) depends on the difference in water content between the expired and the inspired air. This is the respiratory water loss.[23,36-41] As the formation of water vapor in the respiratory tract requires thermal energy, the amount of heat exchange by evaporation per unit time is expressed by the following equation:

$$H_{evap-r} = k_1 \times RWL \, (3.6 \times 10^3)^{-1} \, (W/kg),$$

where k_1 is the latent heat of evaporation of water (2.4×10^3 J/g), RWL is the respiratory water loss (mg/kg·min), and $(3.6 \times 10^3)^{-1}$ is the correction factor for time.

HEAT EXCHANGE IN INCUBATORS, UNDER RADIANT HEATERS, AND IN HEATED BEDS

When it was realized that a good thermal environment increases the chances of survival of newborn infants, attempts were made to provide them with a warm environment. Budin in 1900 found a higher survival rate in infants whose temperature had never been below 32° C.[9] Later studies have shown that the ambient temperature influences the survival rate and oxygen consumption in newborn infants,[11,25,26] and that a body temperature of around 37° C is appropriate for newborn infants at rest.[39] At a high ambient temperature, full-term infants start to sweat, and if they are fed cold glucose through a gastric tube, sweating is inhibited.[57]

Incubators

In a convectively heated incubator, the warm air supplied should be directed so that both the air of the incubator and the incubator walls are kept warm. If the air flow velocity is lower than 0.1 m/s, the convective heat transfer will depend on the gradient between the skin and the air temperature, and the vapor pressure gradient close to the skin surface will be maintained, avoiding an increased evaporative rate caused by increased air flow velocity.[27,34,44,59] An evaluation of environmental and climate control in incubators[52] has shown that the air flow velocities and capacity for humidification vary markedly between different types of incubators. Also, the wall temperatures vary considerably between different incubators,[52] and it is therefore necessary to determine the air flow velocities, humidity, and wall temperatures carefully before calculating heat exchange. With air flows higher than 0.2 m/s, there is a forced convection.

Radiant Heaters

A radiant warmer placed over an open bed platform provides good accessibility and visibility for the care of the newborn infant and has therefore become widely used in neonatal intensive care. Infants nursed under a radiant heater gain heat, but they may also have extensive heat losses through evaporation and convection, and also, from some surfaces, through radiation,[6,29-31,54,55] making it difficult to estimate the relative contributions of different modes of heat exchange. Because of the free movement of air above the infant's body surface, both evaporative and convective heat loss may increase as a result of a high air velocity.

Heated Beds

In the 1990s, Sarman and coworkers found that infants weighing 1000 g or more can be kept warm by placing them on a heated, water-filled mattress[42] early after birth. By covering most parts of the body except the face, direct heat exchange between the infant's skin and the environment through other modes can be almost eliminated in a large proportion of the body surface.

Preterm and term infants can maintain a normal body temperature during *skin-to-skin care* if they are placed lying naked except for a diaper on the mother's or father's chest, and are covered with the mother's clothing or a blanket.[4,5,50,60] Only the parts of the head exposed to the environmental air[4,5,60] exchange heat with the environment (see also Chapter 41).

WATER AND HEAT EXCHANGE BETWEEN THE SKIN AND THE ENVIRONMENT

In a series of studies, water evaporation from the skin surface of infants nursed in incubators has been determined by use of the gradient method* (the ServoMed Evaporimeter), and transepidermal water loss (TEWL)[17,18,21,43] and heat exchange[19,20,22] have been calculated. In these studies, the body temperature has been maintained at 36° to 37° C except when the effect of warming has been investigated, and the ambient humidity has been kept at 50% except when the effects of different humidities have been analyzed. Evaporative heat loss is usually insensible, but it might become sensible when term infants are nursed in a warm environment and start to sweat.[57] Some infants born at term and nursed in a warm environment do not begin to sweat,[57] and if they do, the sweating is preceded by an increase in skin blood flow. In preterm infants, the sweat glands are nonfunctional.[26]

Heat Exchange during the First Hours after Birth

Immediately after birth, when the infant's skin is covered with amniotic fluid, there is an enormous evaporative heat loss from the skin surface. This evaporative heat loss decreases gradually during the first hours, whether the infant is nursed in the delivery room or in an incubator[19] (Fig. 29-1, top two diagrams). Heat loss through radiation is high if the infant's skin is facing the walls of the delivery room and is much lower if it is facing the inner walls of the incubator[19] (see Fig. 29-1, middle diagrams). The heat loss through convection is lower than that through radiation but is much higher when the infant is nursed in room air (see Fig. 29-1,

lower left diagram) than when nursed in the incubator (see Fig. 29-1, lower right diagram).

Transepidermal Water Loss during the First 4 Postnatal Weeks

The transepidermal water loss from the skin surface of the newborn infant depends primarily on the gestational age at birth,[18] but it is also influenced by the postnatal age.[21] The transepidermal water loss in newborn infants is also lower in small-for-gestational-age (SGA)[43] than in appropriate-for-gestational-age (AGA) infants.[18,21,43] There is an exponential relationship between TEWL and gestational age in AGA infants when measurements are made during the first day after birth.[18] This relationship prevails over the first 4 weeks after birth, even though the difference in TEWL between the most preterm and the full-term, AGA infants gradually diminishes with increasing age. The evaporation rate and TEWL both depend on the ambient relative humidity or ambient vapor pressure.[18,43] This relationship seems to be valid for all gestational ages and also for all postnatal ages studied.[17,18,21,43,46]

Heat Exchange during the First Day after Birth

The evaporative heat exchange is directly proportional to the amount of water that evaporates from the infant's skin, and it shows the same type of relationship to gestational age as TEWL.[20,43] When infants are nursed in an ambient humidity of 50%, the evaporative heat exchange may reach 50 W/m^2 of the body surface area in the most preterm infants,[20] whereas in term infants it is close to 5 W/m^2 (Fig. 29-2). The high evaporative heat loss in very preterm infants makes it necessary to have a very high ambient temperature in the incubator to maintain a normal body temperature of 36.0° to 37.0° C in these infants. The servocontrol system of the incubator, which controls the skin temperature, regulates the temperature of the air, which also leads to changes in the temperature of the incubator walls and thereby influences the heat exchange through convection and radiation. The most preterm infants can even gain heat through these modes of heat exchange. The most preterm infants were nursed in an incubator with a relative humidity of 50% at a higher ambient vapor pressure than the more mature infants[21,43]; the heat exchange between the very preterm infants and their environment would have been even greater if comparisons had been made at equal ambient vapor pressures instead of at equal ambient humidities.

In studies of the effects of different ambient humidities, it was found that infants born at a gestational age of less than 28 weeks need a T_{amb} of around 40° C to maintain a normal body temperature at an ambient humidity of 20%, whereas full-term infants need a T_{amb} of around 34° C at this ambient humidity (Fig. 29-3). Nursing very preterm infants at a higher ambient humidity means that the lower ambient temperature can be sufficient to maintain a normal body temperature.[20]

*References 17, 18, 21, 28, 30, 32, 43.

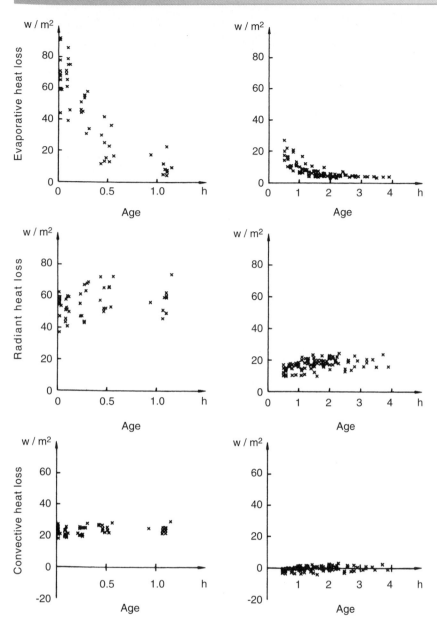

FIGURE 29-1. Heat exchange between the skin of full term infants and the environment immediately after birth and during the first 1 to 4 hours postnatally. The infants were not washed or wiped. Data presented in the left-hand scatter diagrams are based on measurements in infants initially placed at the delivery bed or at the mother's chest and later in a cot. After the measurements made at 1 and 5 minutes after birth, the infants were covered with a towel between measurements. Data in the right-hand diagrams are based on measurements in infants who were covered with a towel after birth and until they were placed in an incubator. (From Hammarlund K et al: Transepidermal water loss in newborn infants: V. Evaporation from the skin and heat exchange during the first hours of life. Acta Paediatr Scand 69:385, 1980.)

Heat Exchange at Different Ambient Humidities

Evaporative heat exchange between the skin of very preterm infants and the environment is highest at a low humidity[20] and lower at a higher ambient humidity (Fig. 29-4). In fact, heat exchange through evaporation in the most preterm infants is twice as high at 20% as at 60% ambient humidity. Other modes of heat exchange are all influenced by the ambient humidity. The sum of the different modes of heat exchange in the different gestational age groups is almost the same, but the total heat loss cannot be calculated in this way, as the proportions of the body surface area exchanging heat in different ways are not exactly known.

Heat Exchange during the First Weeks after Birth

The high evaporative losses of heat from the infant's skin that are seen in the most preterm infants during the first days after birth decrease gradually with increasing postnatal age[22] (Fig. 29-5). Heat loss through radiation is low early after birth in the most preterm infants born at 25 to 27 weeks of gestation. Heat loss from radiation is, however, the most important mode of heat exchange after the first postnatal week. In infants born at a gestational age of 28 or more weeks, the radiative heat exchange is the most important mode of heat exchange from birth, and it gradually increases with age. The heat exchange through convection is low in infants nursed

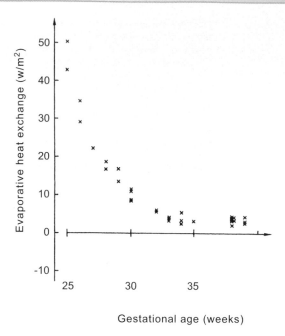

FIGURE 29-2. Heat exchange through evaporation at an ambient humidity of 50% in relationship to gestational age. Measurements were made during the first 24 hours after birth in preterm infants and during the first 30 hours in term infants. (From Hammarlund K, Sedin G: Transepidermal water loss in newborn infants: VI. Heat exchange with the environment in relation to gestational age. Acta Paediatr Scand 71:191, 1982.)

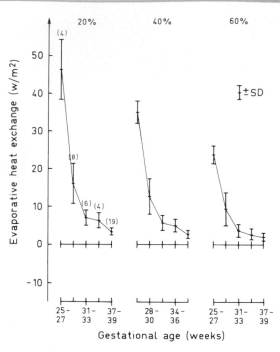

FIGURE 29-4. Heat exchange through evaporation in relationship to gestational age at relative ambient humidities of 20%, 40%, and 60%. SD, standard deviation. (From Hammarlund K, Sedin G: Transepidermal water loss in newborn infants: VI. Heat exchange with the environment in relation to gestational age. Acta Paediatr Scand 71:191, 1982.)

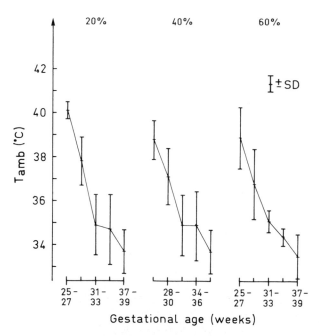

FIGURE 29-3. The relationship between gestational age and the ambient temperature needed to maintain a normal body temperature at three different humidities of 20%, 40%, and 60%. Measurements were made during the first 24 hours after delivery in preterm infants and during the first 30 hours in full term infants. (From Hammarlund K, Sedin G: Transepidermal water loss in newborn infants. VI. Heat exchange with the environment in relation to gestational age. Acta Paediatr Scand 71:191, 1982.)

in incubators. Initially, there is a gain of heat through convection in the most preterm infants early after birth.

During the first weeks after birth, the relative magnitudes of the different modes of heat exchange markedly depend on the ambient humidity (Fig. 29-6). In infants born at 25 to 27 weeks of gestation and nursed in a dry environment, evaporative heat exchange is the most important mode of heat exchange for more than 10 days after birth. At an ambient humidity of 60%, this mode of exchange is the highest only during the first 5 days. Thereafter, the radiative heat exchange is the most important mode of heat loss.[22]

The total heat exchange between the infant's skin and the environment can be calculated if the body surface area of the infant and the fractions of this area that participate in the different modes of heat exchange are known.[22,24,26] This is very difficult with available methods, especially if estimations are to be made over a longer period of time.[22] The total heat exchange is basically dependent on the metabolic rate.

Heat Exchange between the Infant's Skin and the Environment under Radiant Heaters

Several authors have considered that a lower vapor pressure in the ambient air[7] and more convective air currents under the radiant heater[6] cause an increase in evaporative water loss and heat exchange. Later

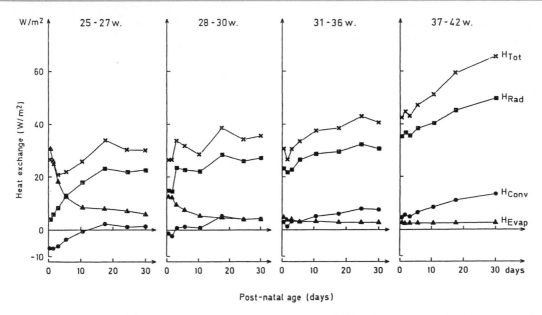

FIGURE 29-5. Heat exchange between the infant and the environment per square meter body surface area in relationship to postnatal age in different gestational age groups at an ambient humidity of 50%. (From Hammarlund K et al: Heat loss from the skin of preterm and fullterm newborn infants during the first weeks after birth. Biol Neonate 50:1, 1986.)

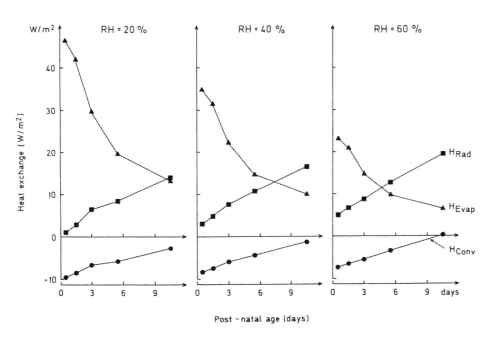

FIGURE 29-6. Heat exchange between the infant and the environment in relationship to postnatal age at relative ambient humidities (RH) of 20%, 40%, and 60% in infants born at 25 to 27 weeks of gestation. (From Hammarlund K et al: Heat loss from the skin of preterm and fullterm newborn infants during the first weeks after birth. Biol Neonate 50:1, 1986.)

determinations of the evaporation rate from the skin of term, moderately preterm, and very preterm infants, nursed in incubators with 50% ambient humidity and under a radiant heater, have shown that the evaporation rate from the skin surface of full-term infants is significantly higher under a radiant heater than in an incubator.[30] In moderately preterm infants born at 30 to 34 weeks of gestation, the evaporation rate from the skin is significantly higher at an environmental humidity of 30% than at 50%, and in very preterm infants with a gestational age of less than 30 weeks, the evaporation

rate is higher under a radiant heater than in an incubator at an environmental humidity of 50%.

A transparent heat shield positioned over the infant can lower the heat exchange (occurring through both convection and evaporation) between the infant and its environment, decrease convective air currents, and increase humidification[6] and diminish the water loss.[7,13,14] It has been suggested that a bed platform that can be used with a radiant heater or with a hood might make it easier to adapt to the mode of care that such an infant needs.[16]

Heat Exchange between the Infant's Skin and the Environment during Phototherapy

Phototherapy has been reported to increase insensible water loss in newborn infants.[6] This loss of water and heat might be caused by altered barrier properties in the skin or by increased respiratory water loss. However, other studies have indicated that in thermally stable term and preterm infants,[28] there is no increase in the evaporation rate from the skin surface during phototherapy.

Heat Exchange between the Infant's Skin and the Environment during Care on a Heated Bed

An infant on a heated bed gains heat through conduction. Some losses of water and heat from the airway take place, depending on the vapor pressure of the room air. Sarman and colleagues showed that infants weighing 1000 g or less could be kept warm when nursed on a heated water-filled mattress.[42] In a 2-week trial with infants whose birthweights were between 1300 and 1500 g, Gray and Flenady found that weight gain was lower and body temperature higher in those who were cot-nursed with warming than in those who were nursed in an incubator.[15]

Heat Exchange between the Infant's Skin and the Environment during Skin-to-Skin Care

After the introduction of skin-to-skin care for newborn infants,[60] Bauer and coworkers showed that preterm infants less than 1 week of age and with a birthweight of less than 1500 g were not exposed to cold stress during 60 minutes of such care.[4] Similarly, preterm infants born at 28 to 30 weeks of gestation and studied during the first and second week after birth increased their body temperature during 1 hour of skin-to-skin contact with no significant change in oxygen consumption.[5] More immature infants, born at 25 to 27 weeks of gestation, showed no increase in oxygen consumption but a decrease in rectal temperature during the same duration of skin-to-skin contact during the first week after birth. During the second postnatal week, the body temperature did not change in infants born at 25 to 27 weeks of gestation during skin-to-skin care.[5] It has been suggested that infants born at 25 to 27 weeks of gestation might have a very high evaporative heat loss during the first week after birth,[5] causing cold stress.[18,22]

WATER AND HEAT EXCHANGE BETWEEN THE RESPIRATORY TRACT AND THE ENVIRONMENT

Water and heat loss from the respiratory tract takes place with each expiration. Using indirect methods, it has been shown that respiratory water loss depends on the humidity of the inspired air, with lower losses occurring at a high humidity.[26,55,58] The respiratory water loss (in mg/kg·min) can be determined using a flow-through system with a mass spectrometer for measurements of gas concentrations.[23,36-41,44,48,53] In an environment with an ambient humidity of 50%, the evaporative heat loss from the airway is moderate[36]—that is, in term AGA infants, the insensible water loss from the respiratory tract (IWL_R) and that from the skin (IWL_S) are of equal magnitudes.[36] The evaporative heat loss from the respiratory tract (H_{evap-r}) and the evaporative heat loss from the skin (H_{evap-s}) are also of equal magnitudes under these conditions.

The evaporative loss of water and heat from the airway depends on the ambient humidity in both lambs[23] and infants,[36] with lower losses at a high than at a low humidity. Whereas IWL_S decreased from 9 to 2 g/kg per 24 hours in term infants when the ambient humidity was increased from 20% to 80%, the corresponding change in IWL_R was much smaller—that is, from 9 to 5 g/kg per 24 hours.[36] In infants placed in a calorimeter, Solyok and colleagues found that the respiratory heat loss was between 0.07 and 0.22 W/kg, or 3% to 10% of the total heat production from metabolism and about 40% of the insensible heat loss.[58] In term infants, respiratory water loss (RWL) and H_{evap-r} may increase during activity by up to 140% of the values at rest.[37] Data on IWL_S and IWL_R and their sum, the total insensible water loss, are shown in Table 29-1, where they are given for the hypothetical situation in which the infant spends 24 hours at the same level of activity.

During moderate heat stress, both lambs and infants can increase their RWL and H_{evap-r} without increasing their oxygen consumption and carbon dioxide production.[38-40] Exposure to radiant heat can alter the respiratory water loss in a lamb while leaving the oxygen consumption and CO_2 production unchanged. RWL is directly proportional to the rate of breathing,[38-40] which means that lambs and infants lose more water and heat

TABLE 29-1. Effect of Activity Level on Insensible Water Loss and Oxygen Consumption

ACTIVITY LEVEL	IWL_S	IWL_R	IWL_T	$\dot{V}O_2$
0	6	6	12	8
1	—	8	—	9
2	—	9	—	10
3	—	10	—	11
4	—	12	—	12
5	7	16	23	13

Insensible water loss from the skin (IWL_S) and from the respiratory tract (IWL_R) and their sum (IWL_T) in g/kg/24 h, and oxygen consumption ($\dot{V}O_2$; L/kg/24 h), in full-term, appropriate-for-gestational-age infants at different levels of activity.
From Riesenfeld T et al: Respiratory water loss in relation to activity in full term infants on their first day after birth. Acta Paediatr Scand 76:889, 1987.

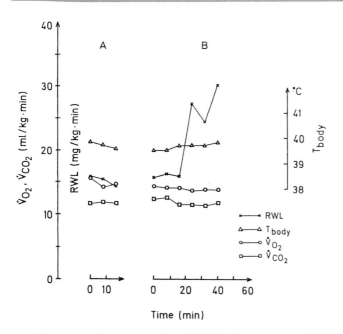

FIGURE 29-7. Respiratory water loss (RWL), body temperature (T_{body}), oxygen consumption ($\dot{V}O_2$), and CO production ($\dot{V}CO_2$) in a 6-day-old lamb before (A) and during (B) heat stress. (From Riesenfeld T et al: Influence of radiant heat stress on respiratory water loss in new-born lambs. Biol Neonate 53:290, 1988.)

when they have a high rate of breathing (Fig. 29-7). The oxygen consumption increases if the heat stress induces bodily movements with higher levels of activity.[37]

Respiratory Water and Evaporative Heat Exchange before and after Intubation

In nonintubated lambs exposed to a radiant heat source, RWL increased from 10.5 to 33.4 mg/kg per minute, while the respiratory rate increased from 54 to 161 breaths per minute and the oxygen consumption and CO_2 production were unaltered.[24] During exposure to the same heat source, intubated lambs increased their respiratory water loss from 8.1 to 18.7 mg/kg per minute

and their rate of breathing from 46 to 125 breaths per minute. In intubated lambs, both the oxygen consumption and CO_2 production increased significantly.[24]

Respiratory Water and Evaporative Heat Loss in Relation to Gestational Age

In the study by Riesenfeld and coworkers, the infants were usually asleep during the measurements.[41] RWL was found to be highest in the most preterm infants and lower in more mature infants studied in incubators with 50% ambient relative humidity and an ambient temperature that allowed the infant to maintain a normal and stable body temperature. RWL per breath (in milligrams per kilogram) was almost the same at all gestational ages, and the higher RWL values found in the most preterm infants compared with the more mature ones were thus the result of a higher rate of breathing.[41]

Respiratory Water and Evaporative Heat Exchange during Phototherapy

When term and preterm infants[29] are exposed to phototherapy in the absence of heat stress, there are no significant changes in RWL, oxygen consumption, CO_2 production, or rate of breathing[29] (Table 29-2).

Respiratory Water and Heat Exchange during Mechanical Ventilation

In clinical neonatal care with a warm and humid environment or with warm and humidified gas supplied from a respirator, heat exchange through evaporation and convection between the respiratory tract and the environment is low.[23,36,58] Infants who inspire cold air with a low water vapor pressure have high evaporative loss from the respiratory tract and also lose heat through convection. These losses may become of clinical significance, for instance during transport in a cold climate.[45]

The concept of an optimum thermal environment for newborn infants evolved during the 1960s.[1] This

TABLE 29-2. Effects of Phototherapy on Respiratory Values in Neonates

PHOTOTHERAPY STATUS	n	RWL (mg/kg/min)	$\dot{V}O_2$ (mL/kg/min)	$\dot{V}CO_2$ (mL/kg/min)	RR (breaths/min)
Before	11	4.4 ± 0.7	5.9 ± 0.9	4.0 ± 0.7	48 ± 7
12 min	11	4.4 ± 0.6	5.9 ± 1.0	3.9 ± 0.6	—
24 min	10	4.1 ± 0.8	5.5 ± 1.1	3.8 ± 0.7	—
36 min	9	4.2 ± 1.0	5.4 ± 1.0	3.6 ± 0.6	—
48 min	11	4.4 ± 0.7	5.9 ± 1.1	3.9 ± 0.7	51 ± 11
60 min	9	4.6 ± 0.9	5.9 ± 1.1	4.1 ± 0.8	—
After	9	4.8 ± 0.8	6.1 ± 0.9	4.1 ± 0.4	—

Respiratory water loss (RWL), oxygen consumption ($\dot{V}O_2$), carbon dioxide production ($\dot{V}CO_2$) (mean ± SD), and respiratory rate (RR) in full-term infants before, during, and after 60 min of phototherapy.
From Kjartansson S et al: Respiratory water loss and oxygen consumption in newborn infants during phototherapy. Acta Paediatr 81:769, 1992.

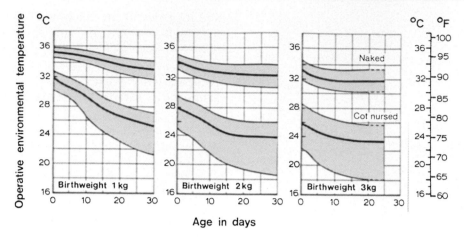

Age in days

FIGURE 29-8. The usual ranges of environmental temperatures needed to provide warmth for infants weighing 1 to 3 kg at birth in draft-free, uniform-temperature surroundings at 50% relative humidity. Upper curves represent naked infants, lower curves represent swaddled, "cot-nursed" babies. *Thick lines,* usual "optimal" temperature; *shaded area,* range within which to maintain normal temperature without increasing heat production or evaporative water loss by more than 25%. The operative environmental temperature inside a single-walled incubator is less than the internal air temperature recorded by the thermometer; the effective environmental temperature provided by the incubator can, however, be estimated by subtracting 1° C from the air temperature for each 7° C the incubator air temperature exceeds room temperature. (From Hey EN: The care of babies in incubators. In Gairdner D et al (eds): Recent Advances in Paediatrics, 4th ed. London, Churchill Livingstone, 1971.)

idealized setting, called the neutral thermal environment, is characterized as the range of environmental temperature within which the metabolic rate is at a minimum and within which temperature regulation is achieved by nonevaporative physical processes alone (Fig. 29-8). There is no reason to believe that the normal temperature of infants is different from that of adults. An infant's internal temperature within the range of 36.5° to 37.5° C (with a diurnal variation of ±0.5° C) is probably normal. Because body temperature is a measure of only the *balance* between heat production and net heat loss, a normal body temperature should not be confused with a "normal" metabolic rate.[1]

A cold-stressed infant depends primarily on mechanisms that cause chemical thermogenesis (Fig. 29-9). When an infant is stimulated by cold, norepinephrine[56] is released, inducing lipolysis in brown fat stores principally found in the interscapular, paraspinal, and perirenal areas. Because of the protein thermogenin, brown fat can decouple oxidative phosphorylation and break down fats to produce heat, without the inhibitory feedback loop of adenosine triphosphate (ATP) production. Triglycerides in the fat are broken down to fatty acids and glycerol. The fatty acids enter thermogenic metabolic paths that end in the common pool of metabolic acids. Brown fat is turned on in response to skin thermoreceptors prior to a decrease in core temperature, and shivering is initiated by a decrease in core temperature.

Glycolysis also may be stimulated during severe stress when epinephrine released from the adrenals activates glycogen stores, which may result in transient hyperglycemia.[35] Lowered blood sugars in cold-stressed infants also have been reported,[10] possibly caused by inhibition of glycolysis, by lipolysis, or by exhaustion of glycogen stores.

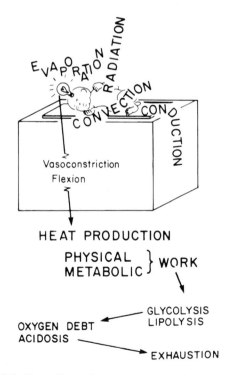

FIGURE 29-9. Homeothermy in newborns. On sensing loss of body heat, the infant minimizes heat loss from the skin and increases metabolic rate. The increase in metabolism can produce acidosis and substrate depletion.

SUMMARY

The exchange of heat between the infant's skin and the environment is influenced by the insulation provided by the skin, the permeability of the skin, and environmental factors such as the ambient temperature and humidity, air-flow velocity, and the temperature and characteristics of the incubator surfaces facing the infant. Evaporative heat loss from the skin is the major component of heat exchange in the most preterm infants early after birth, and these infants gain heat through convection and, in a very dry environment, possibly also through radiation when they are nursed in an incubator. As water loss from the skin surface of the most preterm infants decreases with postnatal age, heat loss through evaporation from the skin also decreases. Their need for a high ambient temperature also diminishes, and with the lower temperature of the incubator walls, the heat loss through radiation then increases and the heat gain by convection is changed to a low loss of heat during the first weeks after birth.

Infants nursed under a radiant heater gain heat through radiation, and as a result of the low ambient humidity, evaporative loss of water and heat may be high in very preterm infants. The loss of heat through convection greatly depends on how the infant is protected from high air velocities by arrangements made under the radiant heater, and also on the magnitude of air movements in the nursery.

In term infants nursed in incubators with an ambient humidity of 50%, the evaporative water and heat loss from the respiratory tract and from the skin are of about the same magnitude. Respiratory water and evaporative heat loss is thus low in term infants. The respiratory evaporative water loss and heat loss per breath are of about the same magnitude in calm preterm and term infants. In preterm infants, the evaporative heat losses from the skin are much more important than such heat losses from the respiratory tract. The evaporative heat loss from the airway might be considered important only in infants with high motor activity or with tachypnea, especially if they are nursed in a very dry environment. Mechanical ventilation with dry and cold air also results in a high loss of heat from the respiratory tract through evaporation and convection.

PRACTICAL CONSIDERATIONS

How to Keep a Baby Warm

THE DELIVERY ROOM

In the delivery room, a large proportion of heat loss is caused by evaporation. The skin should be dried with warm towels and evaporative losses should be limited by using plastic bags or other swaddling materials to insulate the skin from the dry room air. Polyethylene occlusive skin wrapping is an alternative to decrease heat loss after delivery.[58a] Even with the most careful drying of the newborn, it is almost impossible to dry the hair completely. To keep the head warm, it may be necessary to use caps or hooded blankets.

To keep the resuscitation of a newborn from interfering with thermal protection, the child should be placed on a preheated radiant warmer at full heater power at the start of the resuscitation. If the child requires more than 10 minutes of resuscitation, the temperature probe should be secured to the infant to control the skin temperature.

The control of heat loss must continue during the transfer of an infant from the delivery room to another care area. Even within the delivery room, the infant should remain swaddled for display to the parents. If the mother desires skin-to-skin contact with her infant, they should be swaddled together under warm blankets (see Chapter 32). In transferring a sick baby to the neonatal intensive care unit, the caretaker should be sure that the transport incubator is prewarmed and that the hot air in the transport incubator is not allowed to escape by opening the incubator widely to place the baby inside.

THE NURSERY

Swaddling may be an ancient practice, but it is not archaic. In fact, it is a simple and effective method for keeping larger babies warm who do not need to be unclothed for procedures or observation. Infants who are swaddled can be maintained in cooler ambient environments and can tolerate wider variations in environmental temperatures than infants who are naked. Nonetheless, swaddling alone does not keep small preterm infants warm at room temperature, and even term babies require additional heat if they must be exposed for observation. The alternatives when more heat is needed can be reduced to three common choices:

1. Warm the room.
2. Place the infant in a warm, enclosed incubator.
3. Place the infant under an open radiant heater.

The Warm Room

Heating a room to 36° or 37° C to keep some small and sick infants warm may distress personnel working in the nursery. These conditions also may be unfavorable for larger and healthier infants in the same area. For long-term care, heating and humidifying nurseries to appropriate temperatures is probably the least desirable method for limiting heat losses from infants, although in short-term situations such as in radiology departments, operating rooms, and treatment rooms, this method of protection can be the most applicable and effective. Ambulances used for transportation between institutions should always be warmed before initiating the transfer. Wrapping a small swaddled infant in a heated water pad controlled to a temperature of 40° C or less and adjusted with continuous measurement of skin and core temperatures can be used for brief periods when warming the room or using a radiant heater is impractical.

Convectively Heated Incubators

Convectively heated incubators create a microclimate in which to care for an individual infant. They consist of a chamber whose walls are a single or double layer of plastic, in which an infant is placed on an insulating mattress. The plastic walls of the chamber can be opened or have portholes to provide hand access to the enclosed infant. All convectively heated incubators use fans to force filtered room air at various rates of flow over relatively large heaters and, in some devices, pans that can be filled with water to increase environmental humidity. The heating of incubator air can be controlled by a feedback loop mechanism referenced to the temperature within the chamber itself or elsewhere in the air stream that heats the chamber.

Overhead (Open) Radiantly Heated Beds

The use of overhead radiant heaters to keep infants warm has become popular because they provide unimpeded access to infants receiving intensive care. Overhead radiant heaters are usually high-energy heat sources that require the use of skin servocontrol to ensure that infants do not become overheated when under their influence. The only exception to this requirement is when radiant heaters are used to protect infants for short periods immediately after birth.

Because of the known risk of causing hyperthermia when using a radiant heater, manufacturers have been improving the alarm logic in heater control designs. There also are provisions for silencing alarms. Failure to reactivate silenced alarms may expose infants under radiant heaters to a subsequent risk of severe hyperthermia; thus, the safe use of a radiant heater requires an informed awareness of the specific way that the alarms operate when the heater is used.

When comparing oxygen consumption of premature babies in incubators and radiant warmers, controlled to provide the same abdominal skin temperature, there is a slightly higher metabolic requirement in the radiant warmers. Babies nursed in the radiant warmers may also have cooler foot temperatures, which may reflect differences in the relationship between abdominal skin temperature and mean skin temperature; that is, babies nursed in radiant warmers may have a lower mean skin temperature than babies nursed in incubators if they both have the same abdominal skin temperature. A skin temperature of $36.5° \pm 0.5°$ C rather than $36.0° \pm 0.5°$ C may be needed to ensure a minimal metabolic rate in a radiant warmer. Particular infants may have a thermoneutral skin temperature at or beyond either of these extremes in either device. Errors in skin temperature measurement are more important in infants in radiant warmers because the thermal gradients between the infant's skin and various parts of the environment are much larger with a radiant warmer.

The Cold Infant

Simply stated, infants get cold when heat losses exceed heat production. Defining a specific temperature beneath which an infant can be declared to be cold is less simple. An infant with homeothermic responses may become hypermetabolic and acidotic if the body temperature cools from 37° to 36° C. Because such an infant is responding to cooling, it would be justifiable to believe that this infant with a body temperature of 36° C is cold. Assume that the same infant is now cooled

further to 35° C and then rewarmed to 36° C. The infant at this same body temperature of 36° C is no longer hypermetabolic. Is the 36° C body temperature in this warming infant still to be considered cold? Because of such dilemmas, it is better to define hypothermia using dynamic rather than static criteria. In general, an infant is cold only if the baby senses the heat loss as a stress and responds with a metabolic increase in heat production. As the normal rise in temperature that occurs because of the specific dynamic action of food is not considered to be fever, the normal drop in body temperature that occurs when an infant falls asleep should not be considered hypothermia. The use of the word *cold* implies that the condition is potentially or actually harmful. When *cold* is used as a sign of infant condition, further study is required to determine if the sign reflects a true symptom from the infant's perspective. One infant with a body temperature of 35.5° C may be hyperactive, vasoconstricted, tachypneic, tachycardic, hypermetabolic, and acidotic. Another with the same temperature may be sleeping and content. It is difficult to believe that similar meanings are contained when *cold* is applied as a description of their conditions.

Hypothermia may be a subtle sign of sepsis. An infant may not become hypermetabolic and febrile when septic because of reduced responsiveness to bacterial pyrogens. Profound sepsis that produces shock and vasodilatation can increase heat loss while suppressing an infant's normal homeothermic reactions. Such an infant, although previously able to maintain a warm body temperature in a cool environment, may get colder in the same environment. Although the lower limit of normal temperature is frequently cited as being 36 °C, individual variation beyond this value does exist.

Debates about the comparative virtues of rapid versus slow rewarming procedures notwithstanding, there is no convincing argument available to certify any method as better than another. Because rewarming some infants may induce apnea, an infant should be constantly observed and the environment carefully analyzed and controlled during the rewarming process. As a first step in rewarming, a heat-gaining environment should be produced to eliminate any further significant heat losses from the infant. In a radiant warmer, set the skin temperature to 36.5° C to produce rapid rewarming, and to 1° C above the core temperature to produce slow rewarming. The existence of a heat-gaining environment can be certified only if the infant begins to get warmer. In an incubator, simply warming the air temperature to a level that is higher than the infant's temperature is inadequate. The actual environmental temperature in a convectively heated, single-walled incubator may be 1° to 2° C less than the measured air temperature.

Evaporative losses should be minimized by raising the incubator's humidity. For small infants in radiant warmers, raise the humidity around the infant or otherwise reduce the evaporative heat loss. Radiant losses in incubators should be minimized by protecting the incubator walls from excessive cooling or by use of an inner heat shield. If evaporative and radiant losses are minimized, the absolute air temperature becomes more meaningful.

The Baby Who Is Too Hot

Most neonatal thermoregulatory studies have focused on the effects, prevention, and amelioration of hypothermia. Hyperthermia has been noted primarily as a sign of hypermetabolism when an infant is septic or otherwise stimulated. It is probably beneficial to cool an infant who has become febrile because of exposure to an overheated environment. Whether it is good to cool infants who are febrile because they are septic, or otherwise stressed by internal conditions, is less clear, although it is usually attempted.

An infant with a body temperature higher than 37.5° C is often considered to be abnormally warm. To determine whether the elevated temperature is caused by an increase in heat production, which might occur if the infant is septic, or by a decrease in heat loss, some simple presumptive clinical measures can be made.

A physiologically competent infant responds to overheating from a hot environment by incorporating heat-losing mechanisms. The infant's skin vessels dilate, the infant may appear flushed, the hands and feet are suffused and warm, and the infant assumes a spread-eagle posture. Evaporative losses increase and, although it is uncommonly observed in premature infants, active sweating may be noted in the full-term infant. If the heat stress is severe, the infant may become hyperactive and irritable. During rapid warming, the skin of the infant is warmer than the infant's core temperature.

An infant who is febrile because of an increase in endogenous heat production reflects a state of stress. The febrile infant, during the phase of rising temperature, perceives the environment to be too cold. The infant is vasoconstricted, and compared with the skin on the trunk, the extremities appear pale and blue and feel cold. Unlike the gradients expected in overheated infants, the core temperature of the hypermetabolic infant is warmer than the skin temperature. In the overheated infant, the rectal temperature may be the same as the skin temperature.

Hypothermia As Neuroprotection Against Neonatal Encephalopathy

(see Chapter 38, Part 4)

Hypothermia for neuroprotection as "rescue" therapy in neonatal encephalopathy after acute perinatal asphyxia has been shown to be safe and feasible in case series and randomized controlled trials.[2,3,12,14a,49] In these studies, the target core temperatures achieved during cooling have been reduced to a depth of 34° to 35° C, duration of cooling has extended up to 72 hours, and cooling has been achieved by either selective head cooling or whole-body cooling. Many of these studies are still in progress and the results of the first multicenter trials are encouraging. Hypothermia either alone or in conjunction with medication offers some hope as a therapy for neonatal asphyxia in term infants.

ACKNOWLEDGMENT

This chapter is based on studies supported by the Swedish Research Council (project K2003-73VX-14729-01A).

The authors and editors acknowledge the contributions of Drs. P. H. Perlstein and M. H. LeBlanc to previous editions of the chapter, from which many sections remain largely unchanged.

PART 2

The Sensory Environment of the Intensive Care Nursery

M. Kathleen Philbin, Robert D. White, Benoist Schaal, and Steven B. Hoath

The sensory environment of the traditional intensive care nursery (ICN) is largely the unplanned consequence of built environments and clinical activities that support technological care for organ systems important in the field of internal medicine.[90] At the time the first ICNs were built in the 1970s, the physical environment was regarded as a means to an end—namely, the smooth functioning of the professional staff. At that time, there was little reason to consider the effects of the sensory environment on the infant's brain. Indeed, until quite recently, the standards for ICN design mainly addressed protection from fire and infection.

Today, research shows that the sensory environment of a young organism is an important influence on the development of the sensory systems, the brain, and behavior. Work with animal models shows that sensory development is organized and progressive, with individual sensory systems having their most rapid periods of development in an invariant sequence regardless of species. The sequence is (1) skin and joints (touch, pressure, temperature, pain, movement), (2) vestibular, (3) chemical (olfaction and taste), (4) hearing, (5) vision. Different species are born or hatched at varying points in this progression, but vision always undergoes its most rapid organization after birth. The following parameters of species-typical sensory development are summarized from a review by Lickliter.[81]

1. Early development is multidimensional; no individual sensory modality or level of experience has a priority or isolated effect on developmental outcome.

2. The causal networks of sensory development are intricate and nonlinear; experience in one sensory

modality affects other modalities in ways that are not obvious.

3. Perceptual and behavioral capacities are both guided and constrained by features of the infant, as well as by features of its experiential context—the sensory environment.

4. Species-typical brain development relies on a fairly narrow range of biologically expected, moderately strong, orderly sensory stimulation.

5. Biologically atypical stimulation during early development may result in developmental delays in the stimulated sensory modality, and/or they may interfere with the development of other sensory modalities.

In this chapter, each sensory modality is presented separately for the sake of brevity and coherence. The vestibular system is not included, despite its suspected importance, because of limitations in knowledge at this time. However, such a presentation does a disservice to understanding the developmental interrelationships between the senses, the brain, and behavior.

In the future, our knowledge of the effects of the built environment and the unplanned sensory stimulation accompanying care will expand a great deal, but enough is known now to be able to base a reconsideration of the sensory environment on some degree of evidence.

ENVIRONMENTAL CONTACT WITH THE SKIN: TOUCH

Fetal Development

In contrast to all other primates, humans have sparse fur and a vast expanse of thick, interfollicular epidermis. Touch is the first sense to develop in all vertebrates and is closely linked to vestibular and proprioceptive mechanisms necessary for spatial orientation. The primacy of touch as a sensory modality overlaps pain and temperature sensation. The notion of touch is complex and multifaceted and has no simple definition. Generally, *touch* refers to contact or interaction between contiguous physical objects. Scientifically, touching implies the idea of minimal distance, and in geometry it refers especially to a line tangent to a curve. In this chapter, touch is considered in relationship to the mutual boundary shared by the developing infant and the physical environment—that is, the *actual physical interface* between the organism and the environment. It is the epidermis, an ectodermal derivative like the brain, which directly contacts the external world. Studies of the developing rat trigeminal system have demonstrated that central nervous system structures rely on peripheral inputs for normal organizational patterns to arise. The trigeminal system is particularly important for infant development and is the first general area to elicit a touch response in utero.

The ICN Environment

Over most of the body surface, it is the outermost terminally differentiated layer of the epidermis, the stratum corneum (SC), that touches the physical environment.[77] If the SC is underdeveloped, as it is in the extremely low birthweight preterm infant, evaporative water loss is high and temperature regulation impossible without external environmental support via convective incubators or radiant warming devices. Environmental disruption of the developing SC secondary to adhesive trauma or blood drawing may result in infection and pain. The surface of the SC, moreover, is highly modified by products of epidermal glandular secretions such as vernix, sweat, and sebum.[76] Bacterial colonization of the skin surface normally begins at the moment of birth. This dynamic and profuse ecosystem forms the ultimate interface mediating contact between the developing infant and the physical environment, but it is rarely considered under the concept of touch.

Touching another person is a form of physical intimacy with an important role in maternal-infant bonding, human play, and sexual development. Touch can quiet a crying infant, quell an apneic episode, or elicit a period of instability and desaturation. Touch forms a natural bridge between neurobehavioral states that can assist the infant to transition smoothly from deep sleep to wakefulness and vice versa. Unfortunately, the built environment of most existing ICNs, the traditions of caregiving, and the technical demands of care result in the preterm infant being touched by a large number of individuals, whereas close contact with the parents is quite limited.

Long-term Effects

The long-term effects of biologically unexpected touch in humans are unknown. However, there is extensive research on the long-term effects of atypical touch experience during early development in primates and other mammals. Touch is a vital component in the social and neurobehavioral development of primates.[66,75] The hormonal and behavioral sequelae of brief periods of separation from the mother have been extensively investigated in both altricial species such as neonatal rats and in precocial species such as the squirrel monkey.[66,75] The stress of separation from the mother leads to activation of the pituitary-adrenal axis, with increases in plasma cortisol levels in both infant and mother. These responses can be ameliorated by reunion and contact (and therefore touch) with the mother. The complex interaction between touch and breastfeeding deserves particular attention.

Schanberg and colleagues have shown that within hours of removing the rat pup from sensory stimulation by the mother, growth hormone release and protein synthesis are decreased, and levels of growth-promoting enzymes such as ornithine decarboxylase are diminished.[102] These biochemical responses can be restored by stroking the maternally deprived rat pups with a soft brush. In contrast, other forms of stimulation, including nutrition or kinesthetic/vestibular stimulation, are ineffective. Using a similar tactile stimulation model, Alasmi and coworkers showed that brushing the dorsal surface increased levels of circulating lactate in newborn rats, whereas the same stimulus had no effect at 1 week of age.[62] Lactate is an important and preferred metabolic substrate for the developing neonatal brain. Recent work has implicated the protein kinase C (PKC)-alpha system as an important molecular mediator of maternal touch in regulating growth hormone gene expression in infant rats.[103]

Family and Caregiver Considerations

The distinction between appropriate and inappropriate touch is nowhere more clearly seen than in the newborn intensive care unit. Infant massage has been touted as a means of promoting growth and development of the preterm infant with varying degrees of success. Skin-to-skin contact (kangaroo care) has been evaluated in a number of contexts with generally favorable outcomes. Areas such as therapeutic touch that do not involve actual physical contact with the patient are more controversial. (See Chapter 41).

Implications and Recommendations for Care

It is important to remember that nerve endings never touch the environment.[76] In the case of touch, the interface between the organism and the environment is accomplished by highly differentiated products of ectodermal origin (e.g., epidermis, SC, hair, sweat, sebum). Each sensory modality utilizes specialized ectodermal derivatives to mediate interaction between the physical environment and the central nervous system.

In practice, the "environment" may include persons as well as objects in contact with the infant. Focusing attention on those structures of the skin that actually touch the environment avoids abstraction and highlights the importance of real environmental interactions—for example, with adhesives, soaps, thermistors, and electrodes, and by bacterial colonization. This focus also highlights the complex interactions between the infant and those caregivers who touch the infant and, thus, are themselves a critical component of the physical environment. Multiple new initiatives targeting preterm infant development involve aspects of touch and environmental control. Thus, developmental care, with its emphasis on containment, position, and gentle touch, seeks to channel neurobehavioral development.[63] Exploring this controversial area of research can conjoin nursing and medicine in a useful scientific dialogue. (See Chapter 41).

Wherever possible, the choice of products that touch the skin of the infant (e.g., adhesives, lotions, heat and humidity devices) should be based on scientific evidence. Defining touch as immediate skin contact extends to the important clinical areas of hand hygiene, infant bathing, and infection control. The habitual tendency to treat the environment or skin care in general as trivial and unimportant should be avoided as illogical and unscientific.

THE CHEMOSENSORY ENVIRONMENT: TASTE AND SMELL

Fetal Development

Five distinct sensory systems contribute to what is commonly termed taste and smell. Taste buds can be seen as early as at a postconceptional age (PCA) of 10 weeks, and by about 20 weeks PCA, the receptor cells therein become accessible to stimuli.[110] In infants born prematurely, functional taste has been established at from 24 weeks to 40 weeks PCA. Responses to sweet, bitter, acid, or salty tastants show that, from about 25 weeks PCA, taste buds are connected with the central systems controlling behavioral and autonomic responses such as salivation. Like term newborns, preterm infants respond to sweet solutions with mouthing, sucking, and positive hedonic responses (i.e., facial expressions of acceptance and behavioral calming), whereas bitter, acid, and salty stimuli inhibit these responses or do not elicit them.

Nasal chemoreception or olfaction was first verified in nonhuman fetuses that are able to detect, discriminate between, and learn different odor stimuli.[100] In the human fetus, the main olfactory system can function at both peripheral and central levels from about 24 to 28 weeks PCA.[101] Indirect evidence of fetal olfaction was obtained by testing preterm infants right after birth. Before 29 weeks PCA, such infants have unpredictable orofacial and general motor responses to various odorants, but after that age, responses of detection of and discrimination between various odorants are increasingly reliable.[72,73] At the same PCA, low-intensity pleasant or unpleasant odorants elicit acceptance or avoidance responses.[70] Thus, by 29 to 32 weeks PCA, olfaction has reached a level of sensory and hedonic performance comparable to that of term newborns. The subtlety of odor processing in utero is shown when newborns are re-exposed to prenatal stimuli. Flavors from the pregnant mother's diet transferred to amniotic fluid induce appetitive responses in newborns.[99] The demonstrations that odors encoded by the fetal brain are retrievable for weeks postnatally[84] and that amniotic and lacteal fluids share a common odor profile[98] indicate that prenatal odor experience may facilitate the expression of adaptive responses in newborns.

The ICN Environment

The chemosensory experience of preterm infants in the ICN is markedly unlike that in the uterine environment or on the mother's body surface. Instead of attenuated, progressive, temporally patterned, and species-specific taste and odor cues from the mother, preterm infants are overexposed to the scents of different staff caregivers and to alien tastants and odorants. These alien stimuli are on pacifiers and in cosmetic, detergent, disinfectant, or adhesive agents applied on the infant (lotions, alcohol), on caregivers (soaped or alcohol-cleaned hands, rubber gloves), or on the incubator (cleaning agents). Preterm infants are clearly reactive to these exposures.[64] Additionally, their feeding ecology is impoverished by chemically monotonous formulas administered by means that bypass oronasal stimulation.

Long-term Effects

The specific long-term effects of prolonged exposure to biologically alien chemical stimuli during the period of biologically expected low-intensity, species-specific chemical inputs are not known. However, research suggests that odors and tastes may have lasting consequences on affective and behavioral development, and that their incorporation into care routines in the ICN is not innocuous. Infants detect, react to, and learn odors and tastes that can then modulate arousal states, provide directional cues, elicit emotional behavior, mediate recognition of significant individuals and settings, activate digestive physiology, regulate ingestive behavior, and contribute to durable alimentary and social preferences. Studies in animal and human term newborns show that perinatal experience with tastes and odors can determine enduring preferences.[84] Additionally, early selective overexposure to a single odorant can canalize the neural organization of the olfactory system and diminish a wider sensitivity. Future research should consider the enduring consequences of atypical taste and flavor experience in the ICN in relationship to alterations in sensory acuity and feeding difficulties.

Family and Caregiver Considerations

Homeostasis and behavior are benefited by bringing preterm infants out of the incubator and placing them close to the parent's body as often as possible. Close physical contact of the type provided by skin-to-skin holding exposes the infant to the soothing potency of the mother's odors, as well as eventually to her milk. Artificial odorants (e.g., perfumes) of very low intensity can also be made affectively salient through familiarization or association with mere contact or feeding. Learned biologic or artificial odorants may then be left in the incubator during periods of parental absence or used to assist infants to regain control after painful procedures.[73] Leaving a scarf or breast pad bearing the mother's scent in the infant's bed is already often practiced, but so far without formal evaluation of effects. Such practices might prompt in mothers a feeling of humane control over their infant's overly technological environment.

Implications and Recommendations for Care

The affective valence of chemosensory stimuli is highly malleable through exposure and associative learning.

But, as they are at the core of early affective integration, olfaction and taste should not be considered as indefinitely manipulable sensory modalities. Thus, access to scents and tastes from the mother—especially those that mediate perinatal continuity—should be optimized, whereas exposure to strong alien odors should be systematically minimized.

At this point of quite limited data on olfaction and taste in preterm infants, recommendations are based on what seem to be logical implications from findings of studies with term-born infants.[97] These recommendations include replacing natural carriers of the mother's scent (breast pads, scarves) daily, as odors are unstable. Any application of extraneous odors should be formulated to resemble the original reference, which is either the amniotic fluid or the mother's body, breast, or milk. Again, biologic odor mixtures are unstable and should be renewed frequently.

Re-creating the original odor ambiance of the mother is clearly a complex task. Lacking that achievement, any odorant used in the ICN should be devoid of irritative potency and delivered at very low intensity (e.g., matched with the intensity of breast milk odor), with consistency (always the same scent) and regularity (in the same temporal and functional context). Familiar odor stimuli may help promote pain control in the infant, but care should be taken not to create negative conditioning of odors. Nonfamiliar and aversive strong scents should be removed from the infant's space (e.g., alcohol or strongly scented lotions on caregivers' skin; be sure alcohol has evaporated before touching the infant or the pacifier). These cautious recommendations will no doubt evolve as data specific to the preterm infant become available.

THE ACOUSTIC ENVIRONMENT: HEARING

Fetal Development

Much of our knowledge about the acoustic environment of the fetus comes from studies of the pregnant ewe.[71] This research shows that sounds available to the developing fetus are only moderately loud and primarily in the mid-range frequencies (e.g., of speech) and lower. The mechanics of the fluid-filled fetal ear further attenuate sound, so that moderate sound levels in the uterus are reduced at the cochlea to levels that simulate a profound hearing loss. However, the closed uterine container can also amplify sounds unpredictably, and levels that are loud but tolerable externally can exceed the pain threshold at the fetal head.[61] This is particularly likely if the sound source is coupled to the mother's body (e.g., strapping a speaker to the belly, snowmobile riding, shooting, boom-box in a car, stimulation with an artificial larynx). It is not known whether repeated acoustic exposures of this type are sufficient to cause hearing loss, but individual exposures do cause abrupt changes in the flow velocity of brain blood, in behavioral state, and in gross motor activity.[61]

Moderate outside sounds, including speech, are available in the uterus but tend to be mingled with internal sounds of the mother. Loud heartbeat and vascular sounds *do not* dominate the acoustic environment as was concluded from early research. Rather, the distinct feature is the mother's voice.[71] Produced in the body and transmitted through tissue and fluid, the inflections and rhythmic patterns of the mother's voice, as well as particular features of her language, are an ongoing yet diurnally patterned stimulus to which the fetus clearly responds. A number of studies show that the human fetus detects subtle characteristics of the mother's speech.[80] Studies with human newborns shortly after term birth further reveal an active fetal learner and acute listener who can discriminate and show preferences for quite specific aspects of the mother's speech. On or near the birth day, however, term newborns do not discriminate the father's voice from that of another male, although recognition of this voice develops rapidly with exposure.

The ICN Environment

The acoustic environment of the traditional ICN is sharply dissimilar to that of the third-trimester fetus. All frequencies are available because sounds are conducted in air. Sound levels can be loud throughout the 24-hour, 7-day cycle and the ambient sound consists of myriad, loud, unpatterned signals against a loud background without circadian rhythmicity either in intensity or type of sound.[86,89] In these rooms, the most quiet 1-minute periods range between 56 and 60 dBA (decibels, A-weighted frequencies), a level at which most healthy term newborns are wakened from a light sleep. Additionally, the ambient noise either lacks or masks the mother's salient linguistic signal.

Long-term Effects

The long-term effects of acoustic conditions in ICNs, for infants and adults, are not known. The sound levels alone are not sufficient to cause hearing damage in either group but may (or may not) contribute to hearing loss for infants in conjunction with other ototoxic agents. However, recent studies suggest that continual distraction, sensory overload, and the accompanying behavioral disorganization, together with the absence of the salient, responsive mother's voice, may be associated with long-term effects on attention and auditory processing.[74]

Family and Caregiver Considerations

Noise levels of the type documented for traditional neonatal ICU (NICU) environments can affect adults' physiology, behavior, communications, and job performance.[107] Studies of the combined effects of noise, bright light, task complexity, and anxiety on attention, performance accuracy, memory, and physiology reveal a general theme of reduced performance accuracy and altered physiology as noise, anxiety, and competition from nontarget meaningful speech or signals increases. Performance in correctly understanding speech communication can deteriorate as a result of fatigue, emotional arousal, age, non-native but fluent listener or speaker, and simultaneous performance of other tasks. The addition of music is not necessarily an enhancement to performance, and individual workers tend not to be accurate judges of the effect of noise on their own performance.[67] Older adults with normal hearing may have more difficulty than younger adults in ignoring meaningful speech in the background while attending to meaningful communications directed to them.[108] This difficulty is worsened if the speech is fast. For these listeners, the recall of information in speech may be degraded even though the original speech communication was correctly perceived.[91] However, older adults in a quiet environment have shown equivalent performance to younger adults in a noisy environment.[85]

Implications and Recommendations for Care and the Built Environment

The clear implications of studies of both infant and adult responses to noise are that ICN environments must be designed and built to function quietly. New ICNs that have achieved this objective tend to include a small number of beds in each room or to provide individual rooms. These infant care rooms are protected from outside noise by full walls and closed doors with staff work areas, travel paths, and bulk storage placed outside the room.[68] Surfaces (ceilings, walls, floors) in infant rooms and areas opening onto them are covered with specialized materials that absorb sound.[88] Communication devices such as personal phones for *every* staff member ensure rapid, reliable communication and replace calling out to one another or an overhead paging system.

Permissible noise criteria for hospital nurseries have been adopted by the American Institute of Architects and a number of state regulatory agencies.[90,109] The standards presently specify hourly equivalent levels of less than 50 dBA with brief excursions to 55 dBA and no short bursts of sound above 70 dBA. Although this standard specifies levels two or three times quieter than those of traditional ICNs, it is very liberal; most adults would be roused from sleep continuously in a room operating at these criteria. Further refinements of the standard based on research with infants and adults will no doubt result in lower permissible noise levels in the future.

Skin-to-skin holding by a parent or other close relative provides the infant access to the speech patterns and language that the brain first registers and on which the infant will pattern further language development. As the ability to discriminate a signal from background sound is not mature until about 9 years of age, it is important that ambient nursery noise be very low for the parent's quiet speech to be clearly discernible. There is no credible research to support the use of tape recordings of speech or music to further the physical or mental development of preterm infants.[86] Because of infants' difficulty in discriminating the signal in a noisy environment, recorded sound at the infants' ear probably only adds to the ambient noise and overall sensory load of the ICN.

The International Organization for Standards recommends good listening conditions in work places where speech communication is part of the task.[78] These standards further recommend a 4 to 5 dB improvement in the signal-to-noise ratios for non-native speakers or listeners. Speech intelligibility tests can be conducted in existing nurseries to determine whether remediation is required to achieve good speech communication conditions. Designing to achieve specific qualities of speech communication is common in other industries for which speech communication is critical.

THE ENVIRONMENT OF LIGHT: CIRCADIAN RHYTHMICITY

Fetal Development

In utero, the fetus develops circadian rhythms similar to those of its mother for biologic functions including those related to growth hormone, norepinephrine, calcium excretion by the kidney, heart rate, and temperature.[106] Only a small amount of light reaches the eye, although studies of primates suggest that this may be enough to achieve some degree of diurnal changes. After birth, there appears to be a period of latency before the infant entrains to an external zeitgeber (or time-keeper), usually the day-night lighting cycle.[95]

The ICN Environment

The typical ICN environment provides a paucity of circadian cues to the preterm infant. Temperature is rigorously maintained at a constant level, and activity often varies little from day to night. Many ICNs in the United States do not provide cycled lighting, although the recent demonstration of the positive effects of day-night cycles is beginning to influence practice.[65,94]

Long-term Effects

Both initial[83] and recent[93,94] studies of circadian changes in lighting levels showed that the benefits to babies become more pronounced after discharge. Results are inconsistent but point to more organized or longer sleep cycles and improvements in weight gain. These benefits appear to persist for at least several months.

Family and Caregiver Considerations

The circadian physiology of caregivers in the NICU is still poorly understood. All types of night-shift workers tend to experience declines in alertness and body temperature that can be altered by brief exposure to a light stimulus sufficient to suppress melatonin. Additionally, there is concern that these workers may have an increased risk of certain forms of cancer.[104,105]

Implications and Recommendations for Care and the Built Environment

It seems likely that babies older than 28 weeks PCA may benefit from exposure to a day-night lighting cycle. It is unclear, however, whether other circadian cues such as temperature or activity should also be available to these infants and to those born at less than 28 weeks' gestation who have no zeitgeber after delivery. Babies who are nursed with skin-to-skin care for extended periods may receive some of these nonvisual cues in a form that has at least some similarities to what they received in utero.[69]

Providing a window to the outside is an important circadian stimulus for families and caregivers during the daytime. At night, a light source of at least 2500 lux situated away from direct patient care may help caregivers stay alert and comfortable.

THE ENVIRONMENT OF LIGHT: VISION

Fetal Development

The visual environment of the fetus is limited. As the retina and lens are still developing, it is possible that sig-nificant stimuli reach the rudimentary visual cortex only in rapid eye movement sleep, providing organizational but not functional input.

The ICN Environment

A premature infant's visual environment may vary from near dark (e.g., with well-fitting eye patches) to very bright. Even with closed eyelids, light transmission to the visual system is considerable in the preterm infant.[96] Oxygen consumption in the retina is decreased by exposure to light, but the impact of this on retinal and visual development is unknown.[82]

Long-term Effects

One of the most striking persistent deficits of former preterm infants is in visual discrimination tasks.[79] It is not known whether these deficits are caused by circumstances related to preterm birth itself or by aspects of the visual environment of the ICN.

Family and Caregiver Considerations

The most important aspect of the visual environment for many adults is daylight and the ability to view the world outdoors.[92] For families, the visual environment of the ICN is full of information about the hospital in general, as well as specific indications of their infant's condition and needs. For caregivers, the visual environment is the medium by which much of the assessment of patients is performed. Some aspects of giving care and recording data require bright, glare-free and shadow-free light, whereas other aspects can be performed in low light. In addition to intensity, other characteristics of light such as warmth, hue, contrast, and glare can influence the performance of essential tasks.

Implications and Recommendations for Care and the Built Environment

Prior to 28 weeks PCA, it is unlikely that external visual stimulation has benefit to the infant and could interfere with the development of other senses.[81] As it is possible that the limited development of the retina and lens may protect infants at this age from inadvertent extraneous stimuli, it seems appropriate to replicate the in utero condition with very low light levels. Efforts to protect infant sleep may also have value, as most endogenous stimuli reach the visual cortex in utero during this behavioral state. After 28 weeks PCA, circadian rhythm begins to develop and the provision of moderate levels of daytime light may support this for the preterm infant. It is unlikely that the visual cortex of the preterm infant is capable of discriminating complex forms. Therefore, it is difficult to make recommendations for the specific content of the visual environment.

Lighting and visual content needs are much different for families and caregivers than for babies, and considerable thought must be given to designing and operating the NICU visual environment. Limiting infants' visual stimulation by using incubator covers or eye patches often meets the competing needs of babies and their caregivers. Variable-intensity lighting permits low light levels when parents are in contact with the infant apart from staff tasks. Appropriate lighting and visual content of other work areas in the NICU should take into account the large body of research on adults' needs in the workplace.[95]

Babies less than 28 weeks PCA should be kept in dim light, ideally less than 10 lux (e.g., the light level of a candle-lit room). After 28 weeks, night-time lighting levels may remain in this range, with daytime levels in the range of 250 to 500 lux (e.g., that of a typical office) provided that the baby tolerates it (e.g., able to open eyes when awake and to maintain sleep).[96] All ambient lighting in the patient care area should be indirect so that babies are never in a position to look directly into a light source. Task lighting should be highly focused (framed), be rheostat controlled (variable in intensity), have a high color-rendering index (faithful to true color), and minimize glare and shadow. All lights should have individual switches and should also be connected to a master switch so they can be extinguished quickly for transillumination.

Lighting in staff work areas should also be free of glare and shadow, adjustable in intensity, and placed in such a way as to highlight important tasks and reduce extraneous, distracting stimuli. The lighting plan should discriminate between lighting for paper charting on a horizontal surface and lighting for electronic charting on a vertical screen. The lighting plan can also provide a welcoming, comforting environment for families by drawing the eye to pleasant views such as quilts, wood surfaces, or plants rather than to a jumble of technology. Whenever possible, individually controlled lighting should be provided for the family near the bedside and situated so that the infant cannot inadvertently look directly into the source.

CONCLUSION

It is apparent from the literatures of the separate sensory modalities as well as the intersensory development literature that those responsible for intensive care nurseries should, at a minimum, measure and begin to control the sensory load imposed both by the built environment and by care practices. In this effort, the infant's own responses to the nursery environment and care can guide clinicians in titrating the sensory load to an infant's particular capacity for managing it without becoming behaviorally disorganized (e.g., abrupt, large movements; back arching; crying or cry face). Systematic, skilled behavioral observations that inform the plan of daily care of the type described by Als (see Chapter 41) have been useful in this regard and show promise for improving outcomes.

It is also increasingly evident that the most salient, integrated sensory experience that nurseries can provide for infants is extended, close physical contact with parents. The Institute for Family Centered Care (www.familycenteredcare.org) can assist hospitals and their parent advisors in making the necessary adjustments to bring the parent's crucial microenvironment into the hospital consistently. At a minimum, nurseries should provide reclining chairs with foot stools, space to store belongings securely, sleep rooms, play space for visiting children, a break room with kitchen facilities, a lactation support room with visual and speech privacy, access to nourishing food, facilities for personal cleanliness, and inexpensive parking.

PART 3

Design Considerations
Michele Walsh and Robert D. White

Like other ICUs, NICUs have traditionally been designed with the needs of the caregivers in mind. Bright lights, auditory alarms, and hard surfaces that are easy to disinfect became the norm in much of the Western world. Only recently has the impact of this environment on the preterm infant begun to be explored (see Parts 1 and 2 of this chapter). Increasing recognition of the detrimental impacts of traditional ICU design on patients, family members, and caregivers has led to a reevaluation of elements once considered essential.

ADJACENCIES

In an ideal world, the NICU is located in close proximity to the labor and delivery suite. This location minimizes transport distances for the neonate whose status is critical. When such a location is not possible, some units have positioned one critical care bed within the labor and delivery area to admit and stabilize the critically ill neonate for as many hours as needed prior to transport. Other units have utilized dedicated elevators that include medical gases to permit rapid transfers when the ICU and delivery suites are located within one or two floors of each other. Any transfers should be accomplished with a battery-powered transport isolette to ensure continuous warming, and with ongoing cardio-respiratory monitoring. Transport on a portable mechanical ventilator to avoid the barotrauma of bag and mask ventilation is ideal.

The location of other critical services, such as operating rooms and radiology, must also be considered during the design process. Placement of entrances should anticipate the need to transport patients for these services.

SINGLE-PATIENT ROOMS VERSUS MULTIPLE-PATIENT ROOMS

Early in the design process, teams consider the configuration of the ICU. Some designs are driven solely by the constraints of available space and lead to multiple-patient rooms. Some designers have pioneered single-patient rooms. Table 29-3 lists some of the benefits of each design concept. Although they were once considered impractical, there is an increasing trend toward providing single-patient rooms in adult health care, pediatric intensive care, and neonatal intensive care. Families dealing with the birth of a critically ill neonate

appreciate the privacy of single-patient rooms, which also permit lighting and sound environments to be maximally individualized to the patient's needs. At the same time, single-patient rooms create logistical challenges to providing care efficiently and with similar nurse-to-patient ratios as in multiple-patient rooms, and to ensuring adequate monitoring of all patients.

DESIGNS THAT INCLUDE PARENTS AS PARTNERS IN CARE

Excellent neonatal units create space for parents, with form following function. Units that claim to welcome parents yet provide no space for extended stays at the bedside undermine their welcoming message. Parents are the constant in a child's life and must be included by providing choices for a comfortable stay at their baby's bedside day and night. Progressive units extend the parents' role to participation in teaching rounds at the baby's bedside, at the same time protecting the privacy of adjacent patients.

DESIGNS THAT SUPPORT ICU STAFF

The design of patient rooms focuses on the needs of the infant, but critical care staff have equally important needs that must be addressed. Efficient workspace with task lighting that permits handwritten and computerized charting is needed adjacent to the bedside. Increasingly, wireless communication systems are utilized to reduce environmental noise while permitting accurate and timely communication. Such system interfaces are critical to facilitating the transition of staff accustomed to multiple-patient rooms with continuous direct visualization to an ICU with single-patient rooms and limited direct visualization. The importance of support space for staff needs such as conferences with other staff and with families, respite, and storage of personal belongings cannot be overlooked.

Other key design factors are summarized in Box 29-1. The differing and sometimes competing needs of patients, families, and staff can be met with careful attention during the design process. Newer collaborations between health professionals and architects are

TABLE 29-3. Benefits of Single-Patient and Multiple-Patient Rooms

FEATURE	SINGLE-PATIENT ROOM	MULTIPLE-PATIENT ROOM
Privacy	Maximal	Easily compromised, but can be provided with built-in dividers
Light and sound	Individualized	Generally targeted to most acutely ill patient
Parental role	Easily supported	Must be actively facilitated
Staff needs	Must be provided in a separate space (zone) within the room	Generally centralized in the pod
Security	Must be addressed in design using commercial anti-abduction systems	Easily ensured with direct visualization, supplemented with commercial anti-abduction systems

BOX 29-1. Key Factors in Designing the Intensive Care Nursery

Location
- Close proximity or controlled access to delivery and transport areas
- Controlled access and egress for patient and staff safety

Space Allocation
- 120 square feet per bed, excluding sinks and aisles
- Adequate and easily accessible storage (30 square feet per bed) for supplies and equipment

Access
- 4-foot aisles in multi-bed rooms
- 8-foot aisles outside private rooms

Privacy
- Minimum of 8 feet between beds, with provisions for family privacy

Headwall
- 20 simultaneously accessible electrical outlets, divided between normal and emergency power circuits
- Three each of compressed air, oxygen, and vacuum outlets, all simultaneously accessible
- Data transmission port

Hand Hygiene
- Large sinks with hands-free controls within 20 feet of every bed
- Sinks designed to accommodate children and persons in wheelchairs
- Appropriate provision for soap, towel dispensers, and receptacles for trash and biohazardous waste

Surfaces
- Floors—easily cleanable, durable, cushioned
- Walls—easily cleanable and durable; attractive visual accents and sound-absorbent materials can be used where they can be protected from damage
- Ceilings—washable, highly sound-absorbent acoustical tile

Heating, Ventilation, Air Conditioning
- Ambient temperature 72° to 78° F
- Relative humidity 30% to 60%
- Minimum of six air exchanges per hour with appropriate filtering; two changes should be with outside air
- Exhaust vents situated to minimize drafts near patient beds
- Exhaust vents appropriately sized and constructed to minimize noise from air flow

Family Support
- Adequate and welcoming directional and informational signage
- Lounge, refreshments, restrooms, storage, library, telephones
- Overnight rooms—at least one per five patient beds
- Consultation/grieving room
- Lactation area (if sufficient privacy is not available at the bedside)
- Dedicated bedside area for infant care, work, rest

Staff Support
- Lockers, lounge, restrooms, on-call rooms
- Adequate and comfortable charting/work area at each bedside
- Clerical/work areas away from, but accessible to, each bedside
- Office/desk space for all disciplines that routinely provide care

---

just beginning to explore the beneficial health outcomes of improved design in a new field termed evidence-based design. These studies have focused on adults and have documented shortened length of stay and reduced used of analgesia when key design concepts, such as individualized lighting and access to an exterior view, are utilized. Such data are not yet available for neonatal intensive care units.

REFERENCES

Part 1

1. Adamsons K Jr et al: The influence of thermal factors upon oxygen consumption of newborn human infants. J Pediatr 66:495, 1965.
2. Azzopardi D et al: Pilot study of treatment with whole body hypothermia for neonatal encephalopathy. Pediatrics 106:684, 2000.
3. Battin M et al: Treatment of term infants with head cooling and mild systemic hypothermia (35.0° C and 34.5° C) after perinatal asphyxia. Pediatrics 111:244, 2003.
4. Bauer K et al: Body temperatures and oxygen consumption during skin-to-skin (kangaroo) care in stable preterm infants weighing less than 1500 grams. J Pediatr 130:240, 1997.
5. Bauer K et al: Effects of gestational and postnatal age on body temperature, oxygen consumption, and activity during early skin-to-skin contact between preterm infants of 25-30-week gestation and their mothers. Pediatr Res 44:247, 1998.
6. Baumgart S: Radiant energy and insensible water loss in the premature newborn infant nursed under a radiant warmer. In: Clinics in Perinatology: Fluids Balance in the Newborn Infant. Philadelphia, WB Saunders, 1982, p 483.
7. Bell EF et al: Heat balance in premature infants: Comparative effects of convectively heated incubator and radiant warmer, with and without plastic heat shield. J Pediatr 96:460, 1980.
8. Brück K: Heat production and temperature regulation. In Stave U (ed): Perinatal Physiology. New York, Plenum Medical, 1978, p 455.
9. Budin P: Le Nourrison. Paris, Dion, 1900.
10. Cornblath J, Schwartz R: Disorders of carbohydrate metabolism in infancy. In Cornblath J, Schwartz R (eds): Major Problems in Clinical Pediatrics, vol 3. Philadelphia, WB Saunders, 1966.
11. Dahm LS, James LS: Newborn temperature and calculated heat loss in the delivery room. Pediatrics 49:504, 1972.
12. Debillon T et al: Whole-body cooling after perinatal asphyxia: A pilot study in term neonates. Dev Med Child Neurol 45:17, 2003.

13. Fanaroff AA et al: Insensible water loss in low birth weight infants. Pediatrics 50:236, 1972.

14. Flenady VJ, Woodgate PG: Radiant warmers versus incubators for regulating body temperature in newborn infants. Cochrane Database Syst Rev 2:CD000435, 2003.

14a. Gluckman PD et al: Selective head cooling with mild systemic hypothermia after neonatal encephalopathy: Multicenter randomised trial. Lancet 365:663, 2005.

15. Gray PH, Flenady V: Cot-nursing versus incubator care for preterm infants. Cochrane Database Syst Rev 1:CD003062, 2003.

16. Greenspan JS et al: Thermal stability and transition studied with a hybrid warming device for neonates. J Perinatol 21:167, 2001.

17. Hammarlund K et al: Transepidermal water loss in newborn infants: I. Relation to ambient humidity and site of measurement and estimation of total transepidermal water loss. Acta Paediatr Scand 66:553, 1977.

18. Hammarlund K, Sedin G: Transepidermal water loss in newborn infants: III. Relation to gestational age. Acta Paediatr Scand 68:795, 1979.

19. Hammarlund K et al: Transepidermal water loss in newborn infants: V. Evaporation from the skin and heat exchange during the first hours of life. Acta Paediatr Scand 69:385, 1980.

20. Hammarlund K, Sedin G: Transepidermal water loss in newborn infants: VI. Heat exchange with the environment in relation to gestational age. Acta Paediatr Scand 71:191, 1982.

21. Hammarlund K et al: Transepidermal water loss in newborn infants: VIII. Relation to gestational age and post-natal age in appropriate and small for gestational age infants. Acta Paediatr Scand 72:721, 1983.

22. Hammarlund K et al: Heat loss from the skin of preterm and fullterm newborn infants during the first weeks after birth. Biol Neonate 50:1, 1986.

23. Hammarlund K et al: Measurement of respiratory water loss in newborn lambs. Acta Physiol Scand 127:61, 1986.

24. Hammarlund K et al: Endotracheal intubation influences respiratory water loss during heat stress in young lambs. J Appl Physiol 79:801, 1995.

25. Hey EN: The relation between environmental temperature and oxygen consumption in the newborn baby. J Physiol 200:589, 1969.

26. Hey EN, Katz G: Evaporative water loss in the newborn baby. J Physiol 200:605, 1969.

27. Houdas Y, Ring EFJ: Human Body Temperature: Its Measurement and Regulation. New York, Plenum Press, 1982.

28. Kjartansson S et al: Insensible water loss from the skin during phototherapy in term and preterm infants. Acta Paediatr 81:764, 1992.

29. Kjartansson S et al: Respiratory water loss and oxygen consumption in newborn infants during phototherapy. Acta Paediatr 81:769, 1992.

30. Kjartansson S et al: Water loss from the skin of term and preterm infants nursed under a radiant heater. Pediatr Res 37:233, 1995.

31. Marks KH et al: Oxygen consumption and insensible water loss in premature infants under radiant heaters. Pediatrics 66:228, 1980.

32. Nilsson G: Measurement of water exchange through skin. Med Biol Eng Comput 15:209, 1977.

33. O'Brien D et al: Effect of supersaturated atmospheres on insensible water loss in the newborn infant. Pediatrics 13:126, 1954.

34. Okken A et al: Effects of forced convection of heated air on insensible water loss and heat loss in preterm infants in incubators. J Pediatr 101:108, 1982.

35. Pribylova H et al: The effect of body temperature on the level of carbohydrate metabolites and oxygen consumption in the newborn. Pediatrics 37:743, 1966.

36. Riesenfeld T et al: Respiratory water loss in fullterm infants on their first day after birth. Acta Paediatr Scand 76:647, 1987.

37. Riesenfeld T et al: Respiratory water loss in relation to activity in fullterm infants on their first day after birth. Acta Pediatr Scand 76:889, 1987.

38. Riesenfeld T et al: Influence of radiant heat stress on respiratory water loss in new-born lambs. Biol Neonate 53:290, 1988.

39. Riesenfeld T et al: The effect of a warm environment on respiratory water loss in fullterm newborn infants on their first day after birth. Acta Pediatr Scand 79:893, 1990.

40. Riesenfeld T et al: The temperature of inspired air influences respiratory water loss in young lambs. Biol Neonate 65:326, 1994.

41. Riesenfeld T et al: Respiratory water loss in relation to gestational age in infants on their first day after birth. Acta Paediatr 84:1056, 1995.

42. Sarman I et al: Rewarming preterm infant on a heated, water filled mattress. Arch Dis Child 64:687, 1989.

43. Sedin G et al: Measurements of transepidermal water loss in newborn infants. Clin Perinatol 12:79, 1985.

44. Sedin G: Physics of neonatal heat transfer, routes of heat loss and heat gain. In Okken A, Koch J (eds): Thermo-regulation of Sick and Low Birth Weight Neonates. Berlin: Springer Verlag, 1995, p 21.

45. Sedin G: Heat loss from the respiratory tract of newborn infants ventilated during transport. XVth European Congress of Perinatal Medicine, Glasgow, p 511, 1996.

46. Sedin G: Fluid management in the extremely preterm infant. In Hansen TH, McIntosh N (eds): Current Topics in Neonatology. WB Saunders, 1996, p 50.

47. Sedin G: Transepidermal water loss in newborn infants. In Hoath S, Maibach H (eds): Neonatal Skin: Structure and Function, 2nd ed. New York, Marcel Dekker, 2003, p 253.

48. Sedin G: Physics and physiology of human neonatal incubation. In Polin R, Fox W (eds): Fetal and Neonatal Physiology. Philadelphia, WB Saunders, 2004, p 570.

49. Shankaran S et al: Whole-body hypothermia for neonatal encephalopathy: Animal observations as a basis for a randomized, controlled pilot study in term infants. Pediatrics 110:377, 2002.

50. Sinclair JC: Management of the thermal environment. In Sinclair JC, Bracken MB (eds): Effective Care of the Newborn Infant. Oxford, Oxford University Press, 1992, p 40.

51. Sjörs G et al: Thermal balance in term infants nursed in an incubator with a radiative heat source. Pediatr Res 32:631, 1992.

52. Sjörs G et al: An evaluation of environment and climate control in seven infant incubators. Biomed Instrum Technol 26:294, 1992.

53. Sjörs G et al G: Respiratory water loss and oxygen consumption in full term infants exposed to cold air on the first day after birth. Acta Pediatr 83:802, 1994.

54. Sjörs G et al: Thermal balance in term and preterm infants nursed in an incubator with a radiant heat source. Acta Paediatr 86:403, 1997.

55. Sosulski R et al: Respiratory water loss and heat balance in intubated infants receiving humidified air. J Pediatr 103:307, 1983.

56. Stern L et al: Environmental temperature, oxygen consumption and catecholamine excretion in newborn infants. Pediatrics 36:367, 1965.
57. Strömberg B et al: Transepidermal water loss in newborn infants: X. Effects of central cold-stimulation on evaporation rate and skin blood flow. Acta Paediatr Scand 72:735, 1983.
58. Sulyok E et al: Respiratory contribution to the thermal balance of the newborn infant under various ambient conditions. Pediatrics 51:641, 1973.
58a. Vohra S et al: Heat loss prevention (HELP) in the delivery room: A randomized controlled trial of polyethylene occlusive skin wrapping in very preterm infants. J Pediatr 145:750, 2004.
59. Wheldon AE: Energy balance in the newborn baby: Use of a manikin to estimate radiant and convective heat loss. Phys Med Biol 27:285, 1982.
60. Whitelaw A et al: Skin to skin contact for very low birthweight infants and their mothers. Arch Dis Child 63:1377, 1988.

Part 2

61. Abrams RM, Gerhardt KJ: The acoustic environment and physiological responses of the fetus. J Perinatol 20:S31, 2000.
62. Alasmi MM et al: Effect of tactile stimulation on serum lactate in the newborn rat. Pediatr Res 41:857, 1997.
63. Als H et al: Early experience alters brain function and structure. Pediatrics 113:846, 2004.
64. Bartocci M et al: Cerebral hemodynamic response to unpleasant odors in the preterm newborn measured by near-infrared spectroscopy. Pediatr Res 50:324, 2001.
65. Brandon DH et al: Preterm infants born at less than 31 weeks' gestation have improved growth in cycled light compared with continuous near darkness. J Pediatr 140:192, 2002.
66. Brown CC: The many facets of touch: The foundation of experience. In Johnson J (ed): Johnson & Johnson Pediatric Round Table Series, vol 10. Skillman, NJ, 1984.
67. Evans GW, Johnson D: Stress and open-office noise. J Appl Psychol 85:779, 2000.
68. Evans JB, Philbin MK: Facility and operations planning for quiet hospital nurseries. J Perinatol 20:S105, 2000.
69. Feldman R, Eidelman AI: Skin-to-skin contact (kangaroo care) accelerates autonomic and neurobehavioural maturation in preterm infants. Dev Med Child Neurol 45:274, 2003.
70. Gaugler C et al: Olfaction in premature newborns: Detection, discrimination and hedonic categorization. Biol Neonate 84:268, 2003.
71. Gerhardt RM, Abrams RM: Fetal exposures to sound and vibroacoustic stimulation. J Perinatol 20:S21, 2000.
72. Goubet N, Rattaz C, Pierrat V et al: Olfactory familiarization and discrimination in preterm and full-term newborns. Infancy 3:53, 2002.
73. Goubet N et al: Olfactory experience mediates response to pain in preterm newborns. Dev Psychobiol 42:171, 2003.
74. Gray L, Philbin MK: Effects of the newborn ICU on auditory attention and distraction. Clin Perinatol 31:243, 2004.
75. Gunzenhauser N: Advances in touch: New implications in human development. In Johnson J (ed): Johnson & Johnson Pediatric Round Table Series, vol 14. Skillman, NJ, 1990, pp. 1-192.
76. Hoath SB: Physiologic development of the skin. In Polin RA et al (eds): Fetal and Neonatal Physiology. Philadelphia, Vol 2, 3rd ed, Elsevier Saunders, 2004, pp. 597-612.
77. Hoath SB, Maibach H: Neonatal Skin: Structure and Function, 2nd ed, New York, Marcel Dekker, 2003, pp. 1-371.
78. International Organization for Standardization: ISO 9921: Ergonomics—Assessment of speech communication. International Organization for Standardization, Geneva, Switzerland, 2003, p 28.
79. Lavoie ME et al: A topographical ERP study of healthy premature 5-year-old children in the auditory and visual modalities. Electroencephalogr Clin Neurophysiol 104:228, 1997.
80. Lecanuet JP et al: Fetal discrimination of low-pitched musical notes. Dev Psychobiol 36:29, 2000.
81. Lickliter R: Atypical perinatal sensory stimulation and early perceptual development: Insights from developmental psychobiology. J Perinatol 20:S45, 2000.
82. Linsenmeier RA: Effects of light and darkness on oxygen distribution and consumption in the cat retina. J Gen Physiol 88:521, 1986.
83. Mann NP et al: Effect of night and day on preterm infants in a newborn nursery: Randomised trial. Br Med J (Clin Res Ed) 293:1265, 1986.
84. Mennella JA et al: Pre- and post-natal flavor learning by human infants. Pediatr 107:1, 2001.
85. Murphy DR et al: Comparing the effects of aging and background noise on short-term memory performance. Psychol Aging 15:323, 2000.
86. Philbin MK: The influence of auditory experience on the behavior of preterm newborns. J Perinatol 20:S77, 2000.
87. Philbin MK: Science, tradition, and revolution. Adv Neonatal Care 1:91, 2001.
88. Philbin MK: Planning the acoustic environment of a newborn intensive care unit. Clin Perinatol 31:331, 2004.
89. Philbin MK, Gray L: Changing levels of quiet in an intensive care nursery. J Perinatol 22:455, 2002.
90. Philbin MK et al: Recommended permissible noise criteria for occupied, newly constructed or renovated hospital nurseries. J Perinatol 19:559, 1999.
91. Pichora-Fuller MK et al: How young and old adults listen to and remember speech in noise. J Acoust Soc Am 97:593, 1995.
92. Rea MS (ed): The IESNA Lighting Handbook, 9th ed. New York, Illuminating Engineering Society of North America, 2000.
93. Rivkees SA et al: Newborn primate infants are entrained by low intensity lighting. Proc Natl Acad Sci USA 94:292, 1997.
94. Rivkees SA: Developing circadian rhythmicity in infants. Pediatrics 112:373, 2003.
95. Rivkees SA et al: Rest-activity patterns of premature infants are regulated by cycled lighting. Pediatrics 113:833, 2004.
96. Robinson J, Fielder AR: Light and the neonatal eye. Behav Brain Res 49:51, 1992.
97. Schaal B: From amnion to colostrum to milk: Odour bridging in early developmental transitions. In Hopkins B, Johnson S (eds): Prenatal Development of Postnatal Functions. Westport, Conn: Praeger Publishers 2005.
98. Schaal B et al: Olfaction in the fetal and premature infant: Functional status and clinical implications. Clin Perinatol 31:261, 2004.
99. Schaal B et al: Human foetuses learn odors from their pregnant mother's diet. Chem Senses 25:729, 2000.
100. Schaal B, Orgeur P: Olfaction in utero: Can the rodent model be generalized? Q J Exp Psychol 44B:245, 1992.

101. Schaal B et al: Odor sensing in the human fetus: Anatomical, functional and chemo-ecological bases. In Lecanuet JP et al (eds): Prenatal Development: A Psychobiological Perspective. Hillsdale, NJ: Lawrence Erlbaum, 1995, p 205.

102. Schanberg SM, Field TM: Sensory deprivation stress and supplemental stimulation in the rat pup and preterm human neonate. Child Dev 58:1431, 1987.

103. Schanberg SM et al: PKC alpha mediates maternal touch regulation of growth-related gene expression in infant rats. Neuropsychopharmacology 28:1026, 2003.

104. Schernhammer ES et al: Rotating night shifts and risk of breast cancer in women participating in the Nurses' Health Study. J Natl Cancer Inst 93:1563, 2001.

105. Schernhammer ES et al: Night-shift work and risk of colorectal cancer in the Nurses' Health Study. J Natl Cancer Inst 95:825, 2003.

106. Seron-Ferre M et al: The development of circadian rhythms in the fetus and neonate. Semin Perinatol 25:363, 2001.

107. Suter AH: Communication and job performance in noise: A review. American Speech-Language-Hearing Association (ASHA) Monogr 28:1, 1992.

108. Tun PA et al: Distraction by competing speech in young and older adult listeners. Psychol Aging 17:453, 2002.

109. White RD: Recommended standards for newborn ICU design: Report of the Fifth Consensus Conference on Newborn ICU Design. J Perinatol 23(Suppl 1):1, 2003.

110. Witt M, Reuter K: Scanning electron microscopical studies of developing gustatory papillae in humans. Chem Senses 22:601, 1997.

30 Biomedical Engineering Aspects of Neonatal Monitoring

Susan R. Hintz, Ronald J. Wong, and David K. Stevenson

Monitoring in the neonatal intensive care unit (NICU) has improved dramatically since the inception of neonatology as a specialty. Many devices are increasingly relied on to alert the physician to developing problems and even to direct care as technological advances make the management of infants in the NICU more complex. Although monitoring systems are diverse, they should all meet a few basic requirements. The system should be reliable, both in the sensitivity and the specificity of the information relayed by the system and in long-term equipment integrity. It should be relatively simple to operate and provide information in an easy-to-interpret manner. The system must be safe for patient use, which is especially important in the neonatal population because the sensors or probes, the portion of the system that comes in contact with the patient, must be appropriately sized and nonirritating to sensitive skin. The ideal system should be noninvasive, or at least not require invasive procedures beyond those which are routinely needed for optimal patient care. The system should provide continuous, or near-continuous, real-time information, such that personnel may respond to an event occurring at the time the information is relayed. In addition, it should be relatively small and portable. The system must be safe for personnel, and must not interfere with other vital equipment required for patient care.

To meet those requirements, a system must be engineered appropriately and dependably. Monitoring systems have afforded enormous benefits to the patient and to the clinician, and they have become such an integral part of the NICU environment that a basic understanding of the shortcomings of such equipment has been overlooked. Although the technical aspects of monitoring systems may not appear to be important when caring for patients, the clinician should be aware of the basic instrumentation and principles of each system and the system's potential limitations. This chapter reviews cardiac, respiratory, blood pressure, transcutaneous, end-tidal, and pulse oximetry monitoring.

CARDIAC MONITORING

In the modern NICU, heart rate and rhythm strip monitoring are considered to be the standard of care. This information, which may report the first warning sign of patient decompensation, is usually taken for granted. However, the electrocardiogram (EKG) is an indispensable tool that delivers vital information simply and noninvasively to the physician regarding molecular and cellular events of the heart.

Biologic Basis

Electrocardiographic recording provides a one-dimensional view of the heart, based on time-dependent electrical potential changes between two points on the body.[54] The origin of this electrical signal lies in the transmembrane potential, the result of differences in concentration of ions inside and outside the cells; in a resting cell, this electrical difference is approximately −90 mV. When a cardiac cell is activated, a cardiac action potential occurs, consisting of rapid depolarization followed by a period of repolarization (Fig. 30-1). The rapidity of the depolarization phase, the slope of repolarization, and the shape of this action potential are different depending on cardiac cell type. For instance, the initial depolarization phase in cells of the His-Purkinje system is extremely rapid, but it is much slower in nodal cells. These electrical changes in cardiac cells are the result of the opening and closing of complex ion channels in the cell membrane, first postulated by Hodgkin and Huxley in the 1950s.[49] They are now known to be regulated not only by electrical impulses, but by selective gene expression. In the normal heart, an electrical impulse arising in the sinoatrial (SA) node is propagated through the atria, then the ventricles, ending at the area around the outflow tracts. It is more difficult to explain how the spreading depolarization and repolarization of cardiac cells are translated into an EKG. The theory most often cited to explain this phenomenon is referred to as the *dipole* theory.[39]

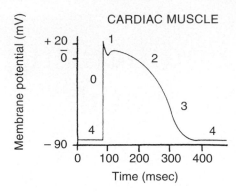

FIGURE 30-1. Cardiac action potential for a Purkinje fiber with phases 0 to 4 as marked. (From Katz AM: Physiology of the Heart, 2nd ed. New York, Raven Press, 1992.)

A dipole is an electrical source that is asymmetric with respect to charge. As discussed earlier, the outside of a myocardial cell at rest is positively charged compared with the cytosol, whereas during excitation, depolarization occurs within the cell and the outside then becomes negatively charged in comparison. The heart during excitation, when viewed from the surface, can therefore be considered a dipole because excited myocardium is negatively charged with respect to myocardium at rest. Clinical application of this principle is made possible because the heart is surrounded by tissues of the body that act as conductors for the electrical current. Therefore, the potentials generated by the dipole, in this case the heart, may be measured at the body surface by a recording electrode, or lead. From this background, a surface lead placed facing an approaching wave of excitation would record a positive potential, which is represented on the EKG as an upward deflection (Fig. 30-2). Although the dipole theory is useful for understanding how cardiac electrical activity is detectable on the body surface, it is an oversimplified explanation because the tissues surrounding the heart are inconsistent conductors and the heart is not truly a single dipole, but rather multiple dipoles.

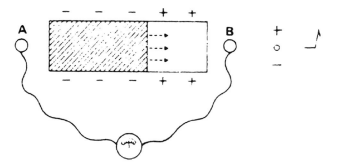

FIGURE 30-2. Wave of depolarization in a strip of myocardium after stimulation on the left side. Electrode B is facing a greater positivity than is electrode A, and thus an upward deflection is observed in the chart recorder at right. (From Katz AM: Physiology of the Heart, 2nd ed, New York, Raven Press, 1992.)

Leads and Lead Placement

It is not obvious how a lead placed on the surface of the body transmits information regarding the electrical activity of the heart. Simply stated, a lead is an electrode consisting of metal that forms the communication connection from the heart, which is a system involving electrical conduction, to the instrumentation.[21] For this process to occur, a *redox*, or reduction-oxidation reaction, must occur at the electrode surface, allowing for energy conversion, which is made possible by the reversible transfer of ions from a metal into an electrolyte solution. Theoretically, this completely reversible system describes an electrode in which the change in *equilibrium potential* is zero; however, in reality, there are several problems that can cause an electrode to operate irreversibly, at which point it is said to be *polarized*. Polarization can result in practical difficulties in using electrodes for biologic monitoring. One cause of polarization is referred to as *charge-transfer overvoltage*, which results when the transfer of ions from the metal into solution does not balance the deposition of ions on the metal surface. This imbalance is caused by differences in how much energy is required to deposit ions onto a metal surface, and can thus vary with different metal types. Another potential cause of polarization is *resistance polarization*, which describes changes in the potential of the electrode system owing to films that have accumulated, or changes in the concentration of electrolytes in the diffusion layer. These changes could be caused by the production and deposition of electrolytes or other ionic species by the body.

The type of electrode used for clinical application has been a matter of intense study and research over many years.[38] The hydrogen electrode, which is a platinized electrode bathed in an acid solution with hydrogen gas bubbled through it, is the most reproducible. It is used as the zero potential standard against which all other electrodes are measured, but clearly it is not appropriate for clinical use. In his early studies, Einthoven's approach was to immerse the arms and feet of his human subjects into buckets filled with saline, using the arms and feet as electrodes. However, of primary importance in the development of clinically useful electrodes was the investigation of metals in which electrode-electrolyte interfaces resulted in the smallest and most stable voltage potential, because this potential and its variations can be responsible for significant artifact. Researchers made a number of other observations, including that a uniform film of electrolyte-containing material on the electrode decreases this noise or artifact. For this reason, silver-silver chloride electrodes are extremely useful for noninvasive measurements in the clinical arena because they are extremely stable and the most reliable electrodes next to hydrogen electrodes. Silver-silver chloride electrodes can be prepared in a variety of forms, and they have been developed for special use in the NICU setting.

The most popular type of electrode used for EKG monitoring in the NICU is a silver-silver chloride, foil-based, recessed or floating electrode. When using this type of electrode, the metal does not come into contact with the subject directly; contact with the patient is instead made through an electrolyte solution. In the past, the metal electrodes were placed on the patient after separate application of an electrolyte paste or gel. Numerous companies now market very flexible, prewired neonatal and pediatric EKG monitoring electrodes in which cloth surrounds the small silver-silver chloride electrodes with the lead already attached to a safety socket. These types of units are backed by a sticky adhesive electrolyte gel, referred to as *hydrogel*, of which the precise composition varies with manufacturer. The hydrogel serves as both the required electrolyte interface solution and the reversible adhesive. These electrodes are usually packaged in sets of three, are relatively inexpensive, and are designed for one-time use.

Neonatal probe placement is a unique area of concern that requires special consideration. Improper lead placement is a particular problem in premature infants because the shape of the thorax yields a limited flat surface for electrode placement. In addition, the premature infant's small size markedly restricts the space available for lead placement, occasionally resulting in electrodes that are placed too close to each other or at right angles to the main P and QRS vectors. Additional problems are encountered when many noninvasive surface monitors and other equipment prevent proper placement of electrodes, leading to worrisome artifacts caused by patient movement or manipulations. Tremulousness and myoclonic seizures have been reported to simulate atrial flutter in the newborn. EKGs performed during chest percussion have been mistaken for tachyarrhythmias.[74] The most common causes of EKG artifacts are related to poor skin contact with the electrodes: (1) poor adhesiveness resulting from multiple probe replacement; (2) poor positioning on a nonflat thoracic surface, such as a bony prominence; and (3) poor contact resulting from excessive lotion or gel on the skin surface. In fact, few studies have investigated optimal EKG probe location on the neonate body surface. Lead placement for the patient in the NICU is, in practice, frequently dictated by issues such as the position of other necessary equipment or probes on a small patient. Baird and colleagues, however, did study the best positioning of leads for both respiratory and EKG signals in both term and preterm infants.[7] They found that the best EKG signal was found with one lead at the right mid-clavicular line at the level of T4 and the other at the xiphoid in term infants, whereas lead placement in a line parallel, but shifted to the left, was best in premature infants (Fig. 30-3).

Also of great importance in the consideration of EKG probe placement is the fragility of the skin of the patient, especially in the case of a premature infant. Previous reports have emphasized the possibility of skin damage with adhesive-based probes, specifically EKG probes, in premature infants. In extremely premature infants, removal of adhesive probes has been associated with stripping of the stratum corneum layer, which may be associated with increased permeability to toxic chemicals,

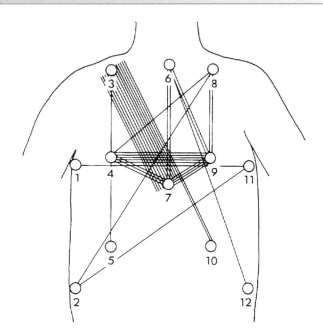

FIGURE 30-3. Optimal locations for cardiopulmonary monitoring electrodes on preterm and term infants. Electrodes between positions 3 and 7 usually have the best results.[7]

as well as serving as a site of entry for infectious agents.[45] Furthermore, transepidermal water losses (measured using an evaporimeter technique) have been shown to be extremely high in areas of the skin of preterm infants on which traditional adhesive probes were placed and then removed.[18] This water loss may result in substantial clinical complications, especially in the most premature infants whose epidermal barrier is already weak and whose water losses are significant. Other types of skin injury, such as anetoderma, have been identified in association with EKG probe placement in preterm infants and those of extremely low birth weight, and may be linked to cleansers or irritants trapped under the adhesive or to local hypoxemia.[23]

Electrocardiogram Device and Safety

Most nurseries now use computer-based cardiac monitoring systems. These systems have obvious advantages over older devices: they can store information in memory, thereby providing the opportunity for trend analysis and review; they frequently possess the capability to assess more complex EKG parameters, allowing for recognition of specific rate and rhythm disturbances; they usually have more sophisticated filtering components and therefore can reduce noise and artifact; and they allow for multiple patient parameters to be viewed on a single display with the availability of blood pressure, pulse oximetry, and other computer modules.

A typical, simplified EKG module diagram is shown in Figure 30-4. As the EKG signals pass from the patient to the monitor through the electrode leads, an input protection network provides electrical isolation, preventing electrical shock to the patient, and filters extraneous

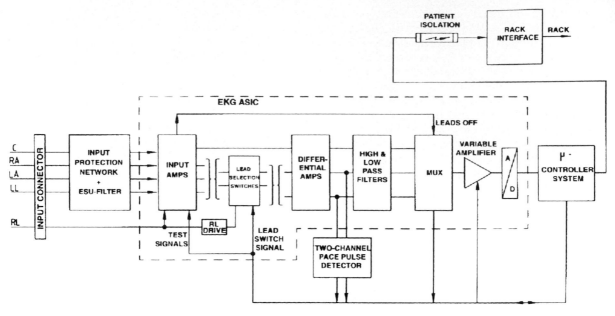

FIGURE 30-4. Block diagram of a typical electrocardiogram (EKG) module monitoring system. (Courtesy of Hewlett-Packard Corporation and Agilent Technologies, Palo Alto, Calif.)

high frequency signals from the rest of the system. The signal is next selected with respect to lead, then amplified. In many systems, the common mode signal from behind the lead selectors is used to drive the right leg amplifier to prevent interference from 60-Hz power lines, a common source of artifact. High- and low-pass filters usually are used, allowing for independent selection of diagnostic, monitoring, or filter bandwidths for each channel. Finally, an analogue-to-digital (A/D) circuit converts the signal to one that can be presented to and understood by the microprocessor. The microprocessor then routes the signal to other ancillary modules for further processing by specialized evaluation algorithms.

Troubleshooting problems with EKG monitoring should be approached in a systematic fashion. However, the most important causes of artifact are often fairly simple to correct, such as poor contact between skin and electrode or improper placement of leads. Problems with the EKG equipment, including cables and cable connections, or, less likely, internal hardware or software failure in the EKG module, also may be contributory. Finally, electrical interference from other equipment may lead to artifact (Box 30-1).

Recommendations for safe current limits for electrocardiographs have been set by the American Heart Association.[59] These recommendations address two aspects of electrical safety. First, the level of current allowable to flow through any patient-connected lead has been established at 10 μA. This recommendation is based on studies by Watson and associates,[83] which showed that the smallest current needed to produce ventricular fibrillation through an endocardial electrode in humans is 15 μA, and it was considered to be unrealistic from an engineering standpoint to establish a limit lower than 10 μA. Second, the recommended allowable chassis leakage current, or the unintentional current that flows from the electrocardiograph to ground, has been established at 100 μA. A limit of 10 μA is the optimal goal because of the small potential for the patient to contact the monitor case either directly or indirectly while being simultaneously grounded through another pathway; however, with the increasing technical complexity of monitoring systems, design challenges meeting this standard are prohibitive.

RESPIRATORY MONITORING

Respiratory assessment and monitoring are essential in the NICU. Although physical examination can provide information regarding the quality of an infant's pulmonary effort, it is a noncontinuous evaluation. Continuous monitoring is critical in the ill patient, but the quantity of information varies greatly with the method used. Surface monitoring techniques are used routinely in the NICU to monitor respiratory rate, but they are unable to provide detailed information regarding further pulmonary parameters and are often subject to artifact.

BOX 30-1. Potential Causes of Electrocardiogram Artifact

Improper electrode placement
Poor skin contact
Patient movement: hiccups, myotonic jerks, seizures, tremors
Improper lead selection
60-Hz interference
Electrical interference from other equipment or appliances
Internal electrocardiograph module hardware or software failure

---

Methods of sensing ventilation requiring tight connections with the patient's airway often provide the most data, but they are invasive and, until recently, were impractical for continuous use. It is important for all care providers to understand the benefits and limitations of the respiratory monitoring systems used in the care of their patients (also refer to Chapter 42, Part 2).

Surface and Noninvasive Monitoring

The most frequently used method of indirect monitoring in infants is *transthoracic electrical impedance*. This method measures electrical impedance changes between two electrodes on the thorax during respiration. The signal obtained could potentially be dominated by the signal generated by the polarization layer in the electrodes, so a high frequency current (greater than 25 kHz) is passed though the electrodes to minimize this possibility. By using this modulation technique, the same electrodes that are used for EKG measurement can be used for respiration detection in many devices. The impedance change caused by breathing activity is extracted from the baseline impedance of the thorax, amplified, and converted to digital form for presentation to the microprocessor. Depending on the device being used, the microprocessor then performs a number of functions, including analyzing the signal for apnea, high respiratory rate and low respiratory rate, alarm triggering, and presenting the analyzed rate for display on the monitor. Unfortunately, the change in impedance with breathing can be very small with respect to the baseline thoracic impedance. Therefore, introduction of artifact, commonly seen with improper lead placement, poor skin contact, or patient movement, is a frequent problem with this approach to respiratory monitoring. In the case of obstructive apnea, a breathing movement may be detected when no breath truly has been taken. In addition, transthoracic changes in electrical impedance are caused by other physical changes not related to respiration, and these changes also may lead to incorrect signal display or false alarms. Although impedance changes related to EKG signals are filtered out by specialized signal-processing algorithms in most microprocessor-based monitors, other changes in thoracic blood volume may result in transthoracic impedance changes. These changes may be detected, processed, and reported as a breath when no breath has been taken, or they may lead to a missed breath when one has actually occurred. Alarms may be triggered falsely as a result; conversely, no alarm may sound when an apneic event has occurred.

Inductance plethysmography is another indirect method for monitoring respiration. This technique involves the placement of a one-turn electrical wire coil around the chest and abdomen of the infant. The coil is incorporated into an elastic strap that conforms to the curvature of the infant. An electromagnetic property of each coil, known as the inductance, varies with the area outlined by the coil. This property is measured and yields signals that are proportional to the changes in area of the thorax and abdomen as the infant breathes.

This signal can be used to detect apnea and to report breath rate. Theoretically, this method could provide a signal proportional to tidal volume, thus giving an indirect estimate of this parameter.

Other Monitoring Techniques

Available for the adult patient population for many years, highly sophisticated ventilatory techniques and continuous monitoring systems are now being integrated into the NICU. With increasing interest and concern regarding the influence of differing ventilatory strategies on long-term pulmonary outcomes, coupled with significant technological advances, continuous *pneumotachography* now is frequently encountered in the NICU.

Sensors, or transducers, that have been developed to detect signals such as airflow and pressure are placed in series with the airway.[26] These signals are converted to an electrical analogue signal, then amplified and filtered. The signals are first processed by an A/D converter and then presented to the microprocessor, which further processes the data with respect to computational tasks, alarm triggering, and other factors (Fig. 30-5). The processed information is displayed on a monitor. The two basic categories of sensors most commonly used for neonatal pulmonary monitoring are *flow sensors* and *pressure sensors*.

Flow sensors are classified by how the transducer obtains information as *differential pressure type* or *thermal type*. The most common type of differential pressure sensor is one based on a fixed orifice within a tubular attachment placed in series with the airway. Pneumatic transmission lines are placed upstream and downstream of the fixed orifice, and a differential pressure is detected between them by the transducer. The flow rate can be calculated because the differential pressure signal is proportional to the square of the flow rate. Volume calculations can then be undertaken by the microprocessor.[27] Another type of differential pressure sensor is the Fleisch, or laminar flow type, in which many capillary tubes, or in some cases a screen, are between the pneumatic transmission lines. The differential pressure across these tubes is approximately

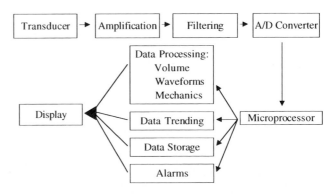

FIGURE 30-5. Simplified block diagram of a respiratory monitoring system.

linearly proportional to the flow rate. Because of the mathematical relationships used to solve for flow, the Fleisch differential pressure sensors may be more accurate over a wider range than the fixed orifice type. However, capillary tubes are more likely to have problems with moisture or secretions. Another category of flow transducer, based on the properties of heat convection, is the thermal anemometer. In these transducers, an element secured within a tube placed in line with the airway is heated continuously. As air flows past the heated wire or film, the element cools. Electrical current is delivered to the element to again attain the elevated temperature. The amount of current required is proportional, however nonlinear, to the gas flow. A second heated element is added to the system if bidirectional flow measurement is needed. These devices are accurate over a wide range, but they may be prone to difficulties stemming from particulate matter or secretions. Pressure transducers are constructed so that a thin diaphragm is flexed in response to pressure. A sensing element associated with the diaphragm then transmits the information regarding the amount of displacement sensed. The material used for the sensing element changes its electrical characteristics proportional to the strain applied. This same basic technology is used for both airway pressure transducers and esophageal pressure transducers.

An increasing number of mechanical ventilators targeted specifically for use in the neonatal population now include pulmonary function graphics monitoring capabilities (see Chapter 42, Part 2). These graphics, including pressure-volume loops, flow-volume loops, flow waves, pressure waves, and volume monitoring, may be continuously displayed on a screen intrinsic to the ventilator itself, or on a laptop computer connected to the ventilator. Trending capability over many hours is available for a variety of pulmonary function parameters in most of these newer devices. Monitoring loops and pulmonary function parameters continuously and in real time may allow the clinician quickly to detect problems such as overdistention and changes in resistance and compliance. Clinical issues leading to these problems may then be rapidly recognized and addressed, and patient response to therapy may be closely observed.

BLOOD PRESSURE MONITORING

Blood pressure monitoring of the newborn can be undertaken using a variety of methods and technologies.[58] Depending on the clinical requirements, blood pressure may be measured continuously and directly through the use of electrical transducers and catheters, or indirectly through the use of occlusive devices (cuffs) and manual or automatic methods of detecting pulsations.

Direct Monitoring

Most direct blood pressure monitoring devices used in the NICU incorporate the "catheter-type" transducer. In these devices, fluid exerts a force against a diaphragm, and the sensed deflection of the diaphragm is relayed as an electrical signal. The early versions of these instruments were relatively cumbersome, extremely expensive, and because they were reusable, had to be sterilized between each use. However, the advent of solid-state construction has allowed for smaller, less expensive, and disposable transducers.

A pressure transducer is simple in concept, but, in reality, it is a complicated system. It is well known, according to Pascal's law, that a pressure transducer will detect the same pressure as that seen at the distal tip of a fluid-filled tube (such as a catheter) as long as the two are at the same level. However, this is true only for static pressures. Because blood pressure represents a complex oscillating pattern, other factors influence the response of the catheter-transducer unit. These factors include the *mass* of all components; the *stiffness* or compliance of the "elastic" component of the transducer, which is described by the number of cubic millimeters of fluid required for the application of 100 mm Hg; and the *viscous drag*, also referred to as *damping*, which represents a retarding force that is proportional to the velocity of movement of the fluid in the transducer-catheter system. These factors are related to pressure by the following equation:

$$(M) \ d^2x/dt^2 + (R) \ dx/dt + Kx = P(t)$$

where:

M = effective mass
x = distance moved
R = viscous drag factor
K = stiffness
P(t) = pressure applied

Although seemingly complicated in this form, this relationship is simple when compared with the actual case in which the viscous drag of the fluid in the transducer must be considered separately from that of the fluid in the catheter, which in turn is influenced by resistance of the catheter. Distortions could exist in the system so that additional undulations not truly relayed at the tip of the catheter could be detected at the level of the transducer. This artificial detection could lead to a problem known as *overshoot*, which causes the transducer to read a pressure higher than that at the catheter tip. The degree to which this potential problem exists is influenced by the viscous drag or damping factor, which is proportional to the viscosity of the fluid, the square of the catheter length, and volume displacement, and is inversely proportional to the catheter diameter cubed and the square of the density of the fluid. If the damping factor is 1.0, there would be no overshoot, but the rise time would be unacceptably long. A damping factor of zero is not possible and not desirable; the amplitude of the wave at the transducer in this case would become larger and larger. In practice, systems with damping factors of approximately 0.7 are used.[21]

Clinically, it is well known that air bubbles in the system also can significantly influence the performance of the device, because air is compressible and its presence would therefore increase the volume displacement and lead to an increased damping factor and prolonged rise time. This problem may be of particular concern when, as in most cases, the same catheter is used for infusion of fluids and medications. In addition to artifact, introduced bubbles could cause significant, potentially life-threatening patient complications, especially if air is introduced to the arterial side or to the venous side in the case of central venous pressure monitoring. Distortion may be caused by movement of the catheter. Although actual pressure is the same at the catheter tip, low frequency oscillations may be produced by movement of the catheter tip in the vessel. This type of artifact often is easily detected and usually addressed simply with catheter stabilization.

Arterial and venous pressures can be measured by catheter-transducer systems. In the neonate, these measurements are usually accomplished by accessing the umbilical vessels, introducing flushed catheters into the appropriate vessels, then placing a transducer at the proximal end of the catheter. Care should be taken so that the transducer is at the level of the distal tip of the catheter. For most transducer sets, establishing a "zero" pressure reading before obtaining meaningful patient data is necessary. As with all transducers, a signal is passed through isolation before analysis by the remainder of the system. In the case of pressure monitors, mean blood pressure is calculated, which is not the simple arithmetic average of systolic and diastolic pressures, but is the area under a single pulse wave divided by the width of the pulse. Alarm systems are also incorporated into typical modular blood pressure monitors, allowing for selection and setting of systolic, diastolic, or mean pressure alarm points.

Indirect Monitoring

Indirect blood pressure monitoring is accomplished through use of an occlusive device, usually the familiar "cuff" that contains an inflatable bladder with a tube for entrance and exit of air. The cuff is placed around an extremity and is inflated to an adequately high pressure to cause occlusion of arterial flow distal to the cuff. The placement of the cuff on either the upper arm or calf, two popular sites in the preterm infant, has not been shown to result in significant differences in pressure readings in this population.[58] During the deflation of the cuff, measurements may be obtained regarding systolic and diastolic pressure levels. Selecting the proper cuff size is of great importance and cannot be overemphasized.[5] The American Heart Association recommends that a cuff width approximately 40% of the member circumference be used; using a cuff that is too narrow may result in blood pressure measurements that are falsely high because the pressure in the cuff could be high compared with the underlying tissue. In addition, the cuff should be applied snugly because a loose cuff may provide falsely high values, and it should be at the same level as the heart when making measurements. A number of cuff sizes are now available

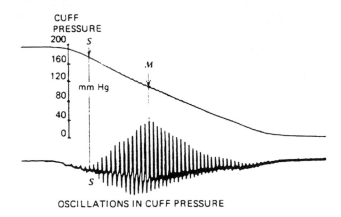

FIGURE 30-6. The oscillometric method of blood pressure monitoring. S, systolic pressure; M, mean pressure. (From Geddes LA: Cardiovascular Devices and Their Applications. New York, John Wiley & Sons, 1984. Reprinted by permission of John Wiley & Sons, Inc.)

for the neonatal population making correct size selection easier.

The most commonly taught method of indirect pressure monitoring is the *auscultatory method*, in which the examiner rapidly inflates, then slowly deflates the cuff while listening for distal Korotkoff sounds with a stethoscope. Unfortunately, this method is not useful in neonates because the frequency spectrum of arterial sounds in this age group cannot be routinely heard. The most frequently used method to assess blood pressure noninvasively in the newborn is the *oscillometric method* (Fig. 30-6). In this method, cuff pressure is raised quickly to above the systolic blood pressure. As pressure is slowly released from the cuff, the cuff pressure approaches the systolic pressure and the artery begins to pulsate; the small pulsations or oscillations are communicated to the arterial pressure sensor through the edge of the cuff. A pressure sensor also exists in these systems to monitor the true pressure of the cuff. When the cuff pressure drops below the systolic pressure, blood rushes into the artery, causing oscillations to be larger. With continued deflation, the oscillations become larger as more blood flows into the tissue until a maximum point very close to the true mean arterial pressure of oscillation is reached.[37] Oscillations continue to decrease as cuff pressure is slowly decreased.

In addition to pressure sensors, these devices have pressure pumps and deflation systems that are controlled by microprocessor technology. The oscillatory signals are extracted, then converted to a digital signal and analyzed by the microprocessor. Systolic and diastolic blood pressures are deduced through extrapolation, using attenuation rate of signal on both sides of the maximum oscillatory readings and often internal reference measurements. Each system has a slightly different algorithm, and differences in readings among devices and between the oscillometric and direct methods have been shown in the newborn population.[40,66] Many systems have timing modes that allow for frequent automatic readings, and many systems now offer multiple patient modes, allowing for selection of adult, pediatric, or neonatal parameters. Mode selection is most important in terms of cuff inflation and overpressure maximum safety limits controlled by the microprocessor.

Indirect blood pressure monitoring may be ideal in certain clinical situations in the newborn nursery, but there are important issues to consider. First, although indirect blood pressure monitoring is noninvasive, it is a noncontinuous method. In specific instances of critically ill infants, direct and continuous monitoring may be required. Second, this method is extremely sensitive to patient movement; therefore, gentle restraint often is needed to obtain a reliable reading. Finally, a full range of cuff sizes should be available to ensure accuracy of readings.

TRANSCUTANEOUS OXYGEN AND CARBON DIOXIDE MONITORING

Transcutaneous blood gas monitoring is a concept that has been considered and studied for many years.[19] After the development of clinically useful sensors in the late 1960s, patient investigations followed, focused especially on the newborn population, owing to skin permeability to gas and the need for noninvasive monitoring devices.[52] Although subsequent technical advances have made their use for long-term monitoring less widespread, these systems are still used routinely in many nurseries (refer also to Chapter 42, Part 3).

Oxygen Monitoring

Transcutaneous oxygen tension ($PtcO_2$) measurement is based on the principle of extracellular oxygen diffusion across the skin. These systems use electrodes, separated from skin and isolated from room air by an adhesive, semipermeable membrane. The oxygen from the skin reacts with the platinum/silver chloride sensor to create an electrical current proportional to the concentration of oxygen. This signal is relayed by a cable to the device, where further analysis and display functions are carried out. Because measurements are made transcutaneously, electrodes are best placed on an area of the body where the epidermis is thin and capillary network is dense. Even with this proviso, $PtcO_2$ will not approach correlation with PaO_2 unless the capillary bed is arterialized through heating; therefore, systems provide for electrode heating to 43° to 44° C before placement. These systems require calibration before each use and recalibration every 2 to 6 hours depending on the system and clinical circumstances. Studies have demonstrated a linear relationship between $PtcO_2$ measurements and PaO_2, although values may be discrepant in neonates at high or low PaO_2 levels, and accuracy differs between different instruments.[17,28]

Several factors may be associated with inaccurate $PtcO_2$ readings. The sensor must be placed on well-perfused skin, which may be exceedingly difficult with an infant suffering from septic or cardiac shock, or other conditions in which local hypoperfusion may be present. The skin site chosen also may not be maximally permeable to gas if scarring or edema is present or if the site chosen is covered with thickened skin. The sensor and device must be properly prepared, placed, and calibrated before making measurements. Air bubbles under the sensor, an insecure seal with the skin, or faulty calibration may be responsible for inaccuracies. Because of these potential problems, clinical correlation of $PtcO_2$ readings with arterial blood gases should be undertaken. $PtcO_2$ monitoring has been associated with some dermatologic complications[16,41]; therefore, care must be taken to move sensor position and inspect underlying skin frequently and to avoid placement of sensors on infants with gelatinous or fragile skin.

Carbon Dioxide Monitoring

Transcutaneous carbon dioxide ($PtcCO_2$) monitoring is possible through the use of a pH-sensitive glass electrode with a silver-silver chloride reference electrode. Carbon dioxide, which diffuses through the skin and a semipermeable membrane attaching the sensor to the skin, causes analyte pH changes that result in an electrical signal, which is relayed through a cable to a device for further analysis and display. Heating the skin is not as crucial for $PtcCO_2$ determination, but heated electrodes have been shown to provide better correlation of $PtcCO_2$ with PaO_2, although transcutaneous measurements are consistently greater than arterial values. Calibration for these systems is required, and calibration time and response time are improved when heated electrodes are used. Combined $PtcCO_2$ and $PtcO_2$ sensors now are used routinely, although some debate exists regarding the possibility that single electrodes may perform slightly better.[34] $PtcCO_2$ monitoring systems have demonstrated better sensitivity and specificity in the detection of hypercarbia than hypocarbia in term and premature infants, and different systems have slightly different levels of accuracy.[17,34,57] This form of monitoring has proven useful clinically in the continuous, noninvasive evaluation of recently extubated infants.[57] Conversely to $PtcO_2$ readings, which may be falsely low in scenarios of poor perfusion, $PtcCO_2$ will likely be falsely high. Concerns regarding sensor placement and $PtcCO_2$ system calibration are similar to those of $PtcO_2$ devices. In addition, the potential for skin injury also exists with these systems.

CAPNOGRAPHY

Another noninvasive alternative to blood gas monitoring for estimation of $PaCO_2$ is capnography. Capnography is the continuous measurement of the partial pressure of expired respiratory gases ($PetCO_2$). Although there are several possible methodologies for assessment of $PetCO_2$, infrared (IR) spectrography is the technique most frequently used because it allows for a compact and relatively inexpensive device.[11,77] Capnography is based on the principle that CO_2 molecules selectively absorb IR light at specific wavelengths (4.3 μm). The devices therefore must contain an IR light emitter or source, as well as photodetectors; IR light absorption, which is proportional to the concentration of CO_2, can thus be determined. Most of these devices use emitters that produce a continuous spectrum of IR radiation that is much broader than the narrow absorption region of CO_2, making it necessary to use an optical interference filter. Conventional capnographs usually display both $Petco_2$ (in mm Hg) and a waveform or capnogram.

There are two basic configurations for these devices: mainstream and sidestream. In mainstream systems, the sensor is placed in an airway adapter so that respiratory gases are measured directly from the patient breathing circuit. In sidestream systems, a sample of expired gas is aspirated from the patient breathing circuit into a sampling tube and analyzed by the sensor, which is remote from the circuit. There are several issues common to most devices that can affect the accuracy of measurement. Water vapor may produce erroneous measurements by condensing on the detector and absorbing infrared light, a problem that has been addressed by heating the detector to above body temperature. Moisture or secretions may also clog the airway adapter or expired gas sampling line. This potential problem has been ameliorated with vertical positioning of the sampling line, or placement of filters on the sampling line. In addition, mainstream systems cannot be used for nonintubated patients.[12,35,68]

Capnography, providing continuous and noninvasive measurements, has become an important aspect of monitoring for adult and pediatric patients. This type of monitoring has become the standard of care for patients under anesthesia in the operating room,[3] and has been used extensively in adult and pediatric intensive care environments.[1,13,72] Technical considerations have previously limited capnography use in the neonatal population. In general, the presence of lung disease influences the accuracy of capnography systems, with $Petco_2$-$Paco_2$ correlation better among those without pulmonary injury.[51] High-flow sidestream systems can produce falsely low $Petco_2$ results because of the low tidal volume and high respiratory rates of infants and the comparatively large sample cell of the device.[24,56] Mainstream devices may increase dead space and compete for tidal volume. Early studies in neonates suggested that elevations of $Paco_2$ and $Ptco_2$ could result from the presence of a mainstream device in the ventilator circuit, possibly because of a rebreathing phenomenon.[31,60]

Advances in both mainstream and sidestream technologies have made capnography more applicable for use in the NICU. Mainstream devices with significantly reduced dead space have now been developed (less than 0.5 to 1 mL). Rozycki and colleagues[71] used a mainstream device (Pryon SC-300; Pryon Corporation, Welch-Allyn, Wis.) to assess the accuracy and precision of $Petco_2$ measurements in 45 intubated preterm infants using over 400 $Petco_2$-$Paco_2$ comparison pairs. Overall,

the correlation of P_aCO_2 and $Petco_2$ was good with a correlation coefficient (r) of 0.833. This relationship was noted to be better than that reported for capillary samples compared with $Paco_2$.[76] $Petco_2$ tended to be lower than $Paco_2$ by approximately 7 mm Hg. In this study, a clinically "safe range" for $Paco_2$ of 34 to 54 mm Hg was prospectively identified by the authors; the $Petco_2$ indicated that the $Paco_2$ was within this range 91% of the time. However, the end-tidal measurements were accurate in predicting true "hypocarbia" or "hypercarbia" only 63% of the time. Thus, $Petco_2$ was not as accurate at the high or low range. The authors further found that patient ventilation index had the strongest influence on measurement bias (at least 5 mm Hg difference in $Petco_2$ and $Paco_2$ measurements), suggesting that as lung function worsens, the usefulness of $Petco_2$ monitoring may also decline. Nonetheless, within proscribed parameters, $Petco_2$ monitoring was shown to be useful for trending, and possibly helpful in alerting the clinician to potential hypocarbia or hypercarbia. Wu and colleagues[85] studied a low-volume dead space mainstream device (CO_2SMO Plus, Model 8000; Novametrix Medical Systems, Wallingford, Conn.) in 61 term and preterm patients with both respiratory and cardiac disease, assessing accuracy in 130 $Petco_2$-$Paco_2$ comparisons. Again, the authors found that $Petco_2$ slightly underestimated actual $Paco_2$ in general. Overall correlation of $Paco_2$ and $Petco_2$, however, was still strong (r = 0.818), and was similar in term and preterm infants. Although sample size was limited, and the authors did not present specific analyses at high or low ranges, the Bland-Altman plots[15] appeared to indicate that the accuracy of $Petco_2$ could be diminished during periods of true hypocarbia or hypercarbia. Mainstream capnography has also been shown to be useful in delivery room resuscitations, allowing for consistently accurate and significantly more rapid determination of tracheal and esophageal intubation than afforded by clinical examination.[69] Although in this study tracheal intubation was considered to be successful by the presence of a normal capnographic wave (Tidal Wave, Novametrix Medical Systems), disposable colorimetric devices for CO_2 detection are now widely available.

Improvements in the sidestream capnography approach have also allowed for application in the NICU. Microstream (Oridion Medical Inc., Needham, Mass.) is a technology that attempts to overcome several problems common to other sidestream systems, a few of which are particularly important for neonatal patients.[24] In contrast to other devices that use broadspectrum IR emitters, Microstream systems use a laserbased technology to generate an IR emission that matches the absorption spectrum of CO_2. The sample cell is significantly smaller than in traditional sidestream systems, and flow rate is lower, but response time has been preserved. These changes eliminate the challenges of competition for tidal volume and falsely low CO_2 readings, particularly problematic for the neonatal population. Hagerty and coworkers[44] evaluated the accuracy of this system in 20 intubated preterm and term infants, with and without pulmonary disease. As seen in other studies, Petco₂ measurements tended to underestimate Paco₂, and were less accurate among patients with primary pulmonary disease (7.4 ± 3.3 mm Hg) than without (3.0 ± 2.4 mm Hg). The authors also assessed capnograph waveform parameters and found that specific waveform predictors independently differentiated infants with pulmonary disease from those without.

Further large-scale investigations will be needed to define better, and perhaps improve the accuracy of, end-tidal monitoring systems in the neonatal population, especially at the extremes of the Paco₂ range. Similarly, the usefulness of the capnograph waveform in clinical management remains to be thoroughly studied. The impact of moderate to large endotracheal tube leaks on monitoring data also requires clarification. In summary, the benefits of rapid results and the truly noninvasive nature of capnography must be weighed against the known imprecision of Petco₂ measurements compared with actual patient Paco₂. At present, capnography may be useful in the NICU as a trending device, allowing for adjustment of ventilator support to keep Petco₂ in an optimal range. If capnography indicates hypo- or hypercapnia, a blood gas should be obtained.

PULSE OXIMETRY

Pulse oximetry has become an invaluable aspect of monitoring in the NICU. This technology is advantageous for the following reasons: it is continuous and noninvasive; it may complement other monitoring techniques; and in some cases, it can lead to a reduction in more invasive monitoring or testing. Its widespread introduction has changed the way in which medicine is practiced. In the past several years, long-term data storage has also become possible in the majority of newer pulse oximetry devices, facilitating examination of trends over time. Depending on sampling frequency and manufacturer, pulse oximeters with memory can have data storage capacities of days to weeks. The simplicity of this tool, however, may be deceptive, and the assumptions made may not be apparent. It is therefore crucial to understand the underlying principles and potential limitations of this technology.

Principles

Pulse oximetry is an optical method for estimating arterial oxygen saturation (Sao₂) by measuring the color of arterial blood at two or more wavelengths of light.[10] Hemoglobin absorbs light differently after it has bound oxygen, reflecting a change in color (Fig. 30-7). The amount of light absorbed by hemoglobin in vitro is dictated by Beer's law:

$$A = \varepsilon CL$$

where A is absorbance, ε is a constant, C is hemoglobin concentration, and L is the optical path length or the distance light has traveled through the solution. Numerous methods for estimating hemoglobin oxygen

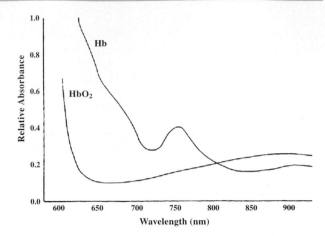

FIGURE 30-7. Relative absorption of light by hemoglobin (Hb) and oxyhemoglobin (O₂Hb). (From Benaron DA et al: Noninvasive methods for estimating *in vivo* oxygenation. Clin Pediatr 5:258, 1992.)

saturation have been developed, but most rely on measuring total absorbance at two different wavelengths, one in which there is a large difference in absorbance between deoxyhemoglobin and oxyhemoglobin and another above the isobestic point where deoxyhemoglobin and oxyhemoglobin absorbance are not different. Two equations can then be constructed and solved simultaneously, with saturation ultimately derived from the percentage of oxyhemoglobin to deoxyhemoglobin.[61] Unfortunately, the situation in vivo is highly complicated compared with that of the ideal in vitro system. There are absorbers in the body apart from hemoglobin, and light itself is reflected and scattered, making reliable calculations difficult with Beer's law alone. Early ear oximeters attempted to circumvent these complications by subtracting the light attenuated by bloodless tissue, accomplished by measuring light transmission after vigorously squeezing the pinna, from the total amount of light transmitted through the ear.[84] Hewlett-Packard (Palo Alto, Calif.) developed the first widely used oximeter, which used a broad spectrum of light, measuring absorbance at eight different wavelengths.[63] This device was highly accurate, but it was cumbersome, expensive, and unsuitable for neonates because of the large size of the ear probe (10 cm × 10 cm).

Development of modern pulse oximetry occurred after variation in earlobe absorbance was noted with each heartbeat, from a minimum during diastole to a maximum during systole.[4] During diastole, the volume of venous and arterial blood is constant, with the sum of diastolic absorbance from tissue and blood forming a baseline. During systole, tissues swell with incoming arterial blood. Subtracting the diastolic baseline from the total noted at systole yields a signal because of arterial blood (Fig. 30-8). This signal is analyzed at two wavelengths, and saturation is determined.

The instrumentation of pulse oximeters is easily understood from this background. Light transmission is accomplished by a probe placed on a well-perfused

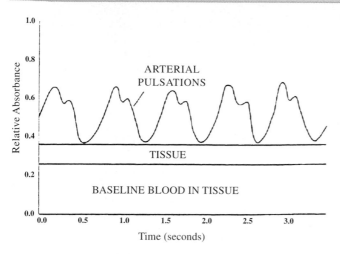

FIGURE 30-8. Influence of arterial pulsations on relative absorbance in vivo. (From Benaron DA et al: Noninvasive methods for estimating *in vivo* oxygenation. Clin Pediatr 5:258, 1992.)

capillary bed, such as a finger or toe in larger infants, or across a palm or foot in smaller infants. Adhesive-backed bandage material is used for neonatal probes. Two light-emitting diodes generate red (i.e., 660 nm) or near-IR (i.e., 940 nm) light. The light-emitting diodes are usually supplied with a chopped current at a high frequency to allow it to be distinguished from ambient light, which is accomplished in different ways by different manufacturers. A photodiode is opposite the light-emitting diodes and detects ambient light, as well as the red and near-IR light, and a current is generated that represents the intensity of light detected at each wavelength. The current then passes through an isolation network and is converted to voltage, which in turn is presented to a high pass filter that rejects ambient light. Before presentation to the microprocessor, the signal passes through an A/D converter. Depending on the pulse oximeter model or module, the microprocessor then derives the oxygen saturation value (SpO_2), a plethysmogram waveform, and a pulse value calculated from the plethysmographic signal.

Limitations

Many assumptions are made to derive an estimate of SaO_2 noninvasively, but these assumptions can lead to serious errors if they are not met (Box 30-2). Perhaps

BOX 30-2. Clinical Issues That May Affect Pulse Oximetry

Poor pulse pressure
Significant hyperoxia
Severe hypoxia
Presence of other hemoglobin forms
Electrical interference
Optical interference
Motion

the most important is the assumption of adequate pulse pressure. Because the technology of pulse oximetry depends on subtraction of a baseline absorbance from that measured at systole, pulse oximetry may be unreliable in low perfusion states. Clinically, infants in septic shock or in significant cardiac failure, those who most require oxygenation monitoring, may have unreliable or undetectable SpO_2 measurements. Low light transmission may result in a signal too weak to measure adequately. Even with optimal probe placement, this phenomenon may be observed in edematous infants. Skin pigmentation, however, does not appear to have significant effects on SpO_2 accuracy.[29] It also is crucial for neonatologists to recognize that the accuracy of pulse oximetry is approximately ±3% (when saturation is 80% to 95%)[33] and does not allow for precise estimation of PaO_2 at saturations greater than 95%.[47] Although this fact is clearly important to recognize in many clinical management scenarios, this imprecision may not be as great a factor as previously believed in the approach to preventing retinopathy of prematurity. One report[20] suggested that, among infants with very low birthweight, instituting a policy that included vigorously maintaining SpO_2 at less than 95% during the first weeks of life substantially decreased the incidence of retinopathy of prematurity grades 3-4 and the need for laser treatment. Thus, the problem of pulse oximetry imprecision at higher saturations could theoretically be avoided if SpO_2 is maintained at a lower range, which is more appropriate in this clinical scenario. Nevertheless, the potential inaccuracy of pulse oximetry should still be kept in mind, particularly when setting upper saturation limits. Inaccuracy is also inherent in the case of poorly saturated patients. In these situations, SpO_2 may be an inaccurate or insensitive reflection of actual SaO_2,[55] or it may appear clinically acceptable owing in part to the presence of high fetal hemoglobin levels in the newborn circulation, but PaO_2 may be unacceptably low. Although fetal hemoglobin does not affect oximeter accuracy itself in any clinically significant way, other hemoglobin forms, such as methemoglobin and carboxyhemoglobin, can significantly affect accuracy of the saturation reading owing to their relative absorbance at the wavelengths used by pulse oximeters.[86] Although this problem is rarely clinically relevant, it can greatly complicate and delay diagnosis if not recognized. In the presence of elevated levels of other hemoglobin forms, erroneous and falsely high SpO_2 readings occur because the pulse oximeter measures these other hemoglobin fractions as oxyhemoglobin. Consequently, the displayed SpO_2 will be higher than the true patient SaO_2. Electrical or optical interference can lead to incorrect saturation estimates by burying the absorbance signal in noise. The signal from an oximeter may be extremely small compared with other signals,[25] and it may be obscured if power sources are not shielded properly. Interference by light sources alone is usually easy to remedy by placing an opaque cover over the pulse oximeter site. Movement has also been a significant source of error or artifact in pulse oximetry, caused by the inability of conventional devices consistently to detect a pulse change and alterations in baseline patient blood volume during motion.[48] This problem can lead to substantial difficulties in optimal management during air or ground transport of critically ill infants. However, several companies have now developed relatively motion resistant devices with improved monitoring capabilities in low signal-to-noise conditions. Although each manufacturer has a different approach to overcoming motion-related interference, these "next generation" devices have reduced a potentially significant problem.

Potential Solutions

There is no doubt that pulse oximetry is a rapid, noninvasive, and generally reliable monitoring system. Many of the problems encountered in the clinical arena that affect pulse oximetry can be remedied or improved so that consistent readings can be obtained. However, the assumptions underlying conventional pulse oximetry cannot be altered, and, especially in the case of motion, solutions may be challenging.

Several companies have attempted to circumvent the problems presented by motion by designing pulse oximetry systems with complex filtering algorithms. After extensive bench-top and clinical research, Masimo Corporation (Irvine, Calif.) developed a system using a unique recessed sensor design (low noise optical probe [LNOP]), minimizing (although not eradicating) the effects of venous blood movement during motion, and a software algorithm referred to as the Discrete Saturation Transform (DST) (Fig. 30-9). In this algorithm, a noise reference is built for incoming red and IR signals for all saturations from 1% to 100%. An adaptive filter

is used to remove correlated frequencies between the noise signal and incoming red and IR signals, and the remaining output is measured and plotted for all possible saturations. If several peaks are generated, as with motion, that considered to be most consistent with arterial pulsation is reported. This algorithm is different from conventional pulse oximetry in that it calculates SpO2 without first having to reference the pulse rate. This system was studied in a rabbit model of sepsis and low perfusion and was found to be less prone to signal loss than the traditional pulse oximeter.[53] In adult volunteers in situations of motion and low perfusion, the technology was found to be superior to other traditional or advanced pulse oximeters tested.[9] Studies in the neonatal population indicate co-oximetry validation of the method, improved sensitivity and specificity, and dramatically improved reliability on transport and during extracorporeal membrane oxygenation therapy compared with traditional pulse oximetry.[36,43,46,50] Masimo has also developed additional proprietary algorithms, which work in parallel with DST, and are aimed at ensuring accuracy of output in high noise situations. Other companies also have developed signal processing algorithms and adaptive filters to attempt to address the problems encountered with motion and false alarms,[70] which are incorporated into newer oximeters including the Nellcor (Pleasanton, Calif.) N-395/N-595, Philips (U.S. headquarters: Andover, Mass.) Viridia, and Novametrix MARS (Motion Artifact Rejection System). As a direct result of these algorithms, manufacturers have integrated improved warning technologies into newer pulse oximeters. These include "Pulse Search" warning on the Nellcor N-395/N-595,

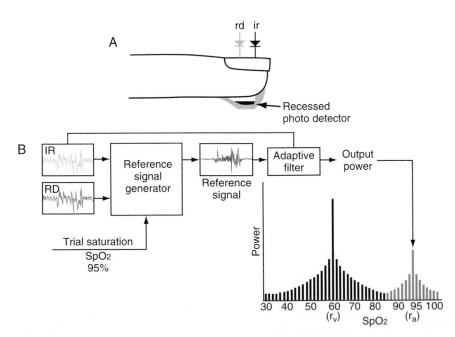

FIGURE 30-9. A, Low noise optical probe (LNOP) design. **B,** Schematic of the Discrete Saturation Transform for pulse oximetry analysis. ir, infrared; r_a, arterial optical density ratio; rd, red; r_v, venous optical density ratio. (Courtesy of Masimo Corporation, Irvine, Calif.)

and "Signal IQ" warning on Masimo devices. Data validity warning systems are meant to indicate to the clinician that the signal may be of poor quality, and therefore output may be susceptible to error. Preliminary studies in neonates have begun to assess and compare the reliability of these systems,[42,78] but larger investigations are required to determine the positive and negative predictive value of each technology.

Pulse oximetry systems with this type of technology may be more expensive than traditional pulse oximetry systems, specifically as a result of the cost of the probes or sensors. The increased cost may outweigh the potential benefits for many newborn nurseries. However, a preliminary two-center study among infants suggested that LNOP pulse oximetry probes had a useful life of 9.05 ± 4.4 days compared with 3.9 ± 2.3 days for more conventional oximetry probes.[32] In addition, much of this technology is limited to separate unit systems, and thus cannot be "retrofitted" into existing monitoring module systems. Masimo has developed partnerships and agreements with a number of other manufacturers that allow Masimo signal extraction technology to be available in the monitoring devices of other companies. The applicability of next generation pulse oximeters for routine use in newborn nurseries clearly depends on numerous factors. Nevertheless, in situations in which movement is expected, such as during ground or air transport or transport within a facility, this technology may be beneficial.

CONTINUOUS BLOOD GAS MONITORING

Intravascular sensors or ex vivo point-of-care systems for blood gas analysis offer the benefit of continuous or near-continuous measurements of pH, PaO_2, $PaCO_2$, and in some cases certain electrolytes, without patient blood loss or need to wait for results. These devices have been used and studied in the adult population for applications such as intraoperative and postoperative monitoring and have been found to provide good agreement with traditional in vitro blood gas measurements.[62,79,88] In addition, retrospective studies have revealed that these types of catheters can be used in the term and premature neonatal population with complication rates consistent with umbilical catheterization alone.[22,67] There are several types of continuous monitoring systems, and each has a slightly different theory of operation.

One such type of monitoring system, of which the Neotrend System (Diametrics Medical, Inc., St. Paul, Minn.) is representative, can report a number of parameters, including pH, $PaCO_2$, PaO_2, and temperature, owing to a sensor that is placed within a 3.7-Fr umbilical artery catheter (Fig. 30-10). The Neotrend sensor consists of three optical sensors and mirror within a 0.5-mm diameter sheath, and a thermocouple for temperature measurements. The pH sensor uses the principle that

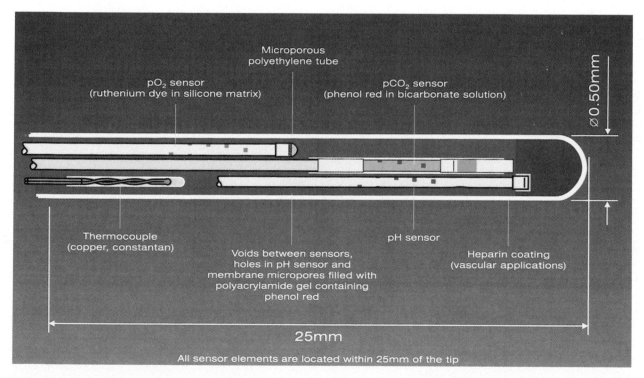

FIGURE 30-10. Cross-section through multiparameter Neotrend continuous in-line monitoring system. (Courtesy of Diametrics Medical, Inc., St. Paul, Minn.)

phenol red dye changes color reversibly in response to hydrogen ions. Hydrogen ions permeate through a microporous hollow fiber containing the dye, absorption is measured at 555 nm, and pH is calculated. The Paco$_2$ sensor uses this same principle; however, the membrane surrounding the phenol red-bicarbonate solution is surrounded by a gas-permeable, but not an ion-permeable, membrane. The Pao$_2$ sensor is based on the principle of fluorescence quenching. An oxygen-sensitive ruthenium-based dye is immobilized in a gas-permeable complex, and an excitation beam at 460 nm is transmitted. The excitation light is absorbed by the indicator dye and fluorescent light is emitted. When oxygen is present, the fluorescent light is quenched, allowing for calculation of Pao$_2$. A dedicated screen displays results continuously, and data trends are recorded for 10 minutes to 24 hours. This system has the advantage of allowing for continuous multiparameter assessment of the critically ill newborn, reducing blood sampling, and potentially reducing the chance of infection owing to multiple line access events. At present, a specifically designed, Neotrend-compatible catheter must be used in conjunction with the sensor. A one-time, 30-minute calibration is required before insertion, and an in vivo comparison blood gas analysis is required after catheter insertion. Calibration is recommended occasionally throughout the period of use. Initial studies in the neonatal population revealed bias and precision data that suggest that this type of system

could be of potential clinical benefit, although the need for traditionally obtained arterial blood gases will not be completely eliminated.[65]

Another approach to blood gas monitoring has been applied in the VIA-LVM (low volume mode) Monitor (VIA Medical Division of International Biomedical, Inc., Austin, Tex.). In this system, the monitor is a microprocessor-based instrument that integrates the functions of a volumetric infusion pump with an electrolyte and blood gas parameter measurement system (Fig. 30-11). The sensor set consists of two flow cells. The sensor set is connected to the IV cannula and contains ion selective electrodes to measure pH, Na$^+$, K$^+$, and Paco$_2$. A Clark electrode and electrical conductance technology are used to measure Pao$_2$ and hematocrit, respectively. This system is closed-looped whereby a reversible pump withdraws 1.5 mL of blood from any arterial line to the sensor set, analysis is performed, and the blood is returned to the patient followed by a 0.5-mL postsample flush from an in-line heparinized solution, which is also the calibration fluid. Results are displayed approximately 70 seconds after sampling and are also printed. The system has a 40-sample memory so that trends may be noted. An initial two-point calibration is required, after which one-point self-calibrations are performed after each sample and every 30 minutes. The sensor set may be changed every 72 hours in accordance with infection control policies. Studies in the adult population using this

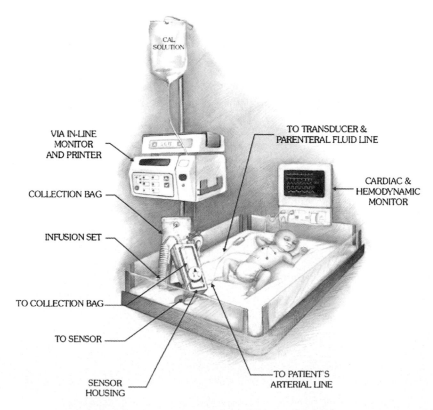

FIGURE 30-11. VIA-LVM Blood Gas and Chemistry Monitoring System. (Courtesy of VIA Medical Division of International Biomedical, Inc., Austin, Tex.)

system have reported performance criteria acceptable by the Medicare Clinical Laboratory Improvement Amendments (CLIA) proficiency standards.[6] Results from a multicenter evaluation of this system in the neonatal intensive care population[14] suggest that data obtained from this monitoring system agree with results from laboratory-based analyzers within CLIA limits.

END-TIDAL CARBON MONOXIDE MONITORING

Because the degradation of heme by the enzyme heme oxygenase leads to the formation of equimolar amounts of carbon monoxide (CO) and biliverdin, with biliverdin being immediately reduced to bilirubin, the measurement of CO in the exhaled breath of the newborn can be used as an index of heme degradation and bilirubin production in vivo (see Chapter 46). The measurement of end-tidal CO (ETCO), corrected for inhaled CO (ETCOc) is an index of the rate of bilirubin production and may aid the physician with respect to the recognition of hemolysis-associated hyperbilirubinemia, and subsequent selection of appropriate treatments or interventions.

The measurement of ETCO is a convenient, reliable, and well-studied index.[30] Measurements of ETCO have been found to correlate strongly with carboxyhemoglobin levels,[80] which can be affected by endogenous sources (e.g., hemolysis), exogenous sources (e.g., combustion engine exhaust), or both. Breath can be sampled and analyzed continuously in real time using sensitive and rapidly responding spectrophotometers based on near-IR, which are, however, expensive and often not very portable. Intermittent sampling of end-tidal breath can be performed after a 20-second breath-hold with Priestley tube-type devices.[64] Alternatively, this breath can be directly exhaled into an instrument with a quick response time for recording the peak (alveolar) CO concentration. For newborns and patients who cannot control their breathing, automatic sampling devices have been developed for measuring ETCO.[80-82,87] The CO-Stat End Tidal Breath Analyzer (Natus Medical, Inc., San Carlos, Calif.), a point-of-care device, was developed for measuring ETCOc, as well as other parameters, such as breath CO concentration uncorrected for ambient CO concentration (ETCO), ambient CO concentration (reflecting inhaled air), end-tidal CO_2, and respiratory rate.[80,82] The electronically controlled device uses two gas sensors: an IR CO_2 sensor and an electrochemical CO/hydrogen (H_2) sensor. The CO sensor first determines the average CO concentrations in breath and room air, and then calculates ETCO by an algorithm using the measured CO and CO_2 concentrations. The CO_2 sensor determines the end-tidal CO_2 concentration and quantitates respiratory rate. The device uses sidestream sampling continuously to draw a small volume of breath through a single-use, soft, clear polymer (2-mm OD) sampler consisting of a flexible, 5-Fr nasal catheter with a filter cartridge that attaches to the device.[73] A hydrogel strip ("adhesive wings") on the catheter allows proper catheter placement and insertion (5 to 6 mm into the lower edge of the nostril). The measurement is made with the subject at rest (sleeping or quiet) with minimal movement. The instrument has a range of 0 to 25 ppm (or microliters per liter) with a resolution of 0.1 ppm CO. Its accuracy is 0.3 ppm or 10% of the reading (whichever is greater) at 0 to 60 breaths per minute. It is insensitive to H_2 concentrations less than 50 ppm. However, when breath H_2 concentrations are at 50 ppm, a level that significantly interferes with ETCOc readings, breath sampling is aborted. Several studies validating its use on neonates, children, and adults have been conducted.[8,80-82]

In a large trial conducted at nine centers, Stevenson and colleagues[75] determined that a measurement of ETCOc taken at 30 ± 6 hours of age alone did not improve the predictive ability of the hours of age-specific total serum bilirubin level. However, use of the ETCOc in combination with a total serum bilirubin measurement obtained at the same time can be used to differentiate between infants with hemolysis (i.e., increased bilirubin production) and those with decreased elimination (i.e., hepatic defects in bilirubin conjugation ability). The use of ETCOc testing has been included in the 2004 revision of the American Academy of Pediatrics Clinical Practice Guideline on the Management of Hyperbilirubinemia in the Newborn Infant 35 or More Weeks of Gestation.[2] (See Chapter 46 on Neonatal Jaundice and Liver Disease.)

REFERENCES

1. Abramo TJ et al: Noninvasive capnometry monitoring for respiratory status during pediatric seizures. Crit Care Med 25:1242, 1997.
2. American Academy of Pediatrics: Clinical practice guideline on the management of hyperbilirubinemia in the newborn infant 35 or more weeks of gestation. Pediatrics 114:297, 2004.
3. American Society of Anesthesiologists: Policy Statements on Practice Parameters: Standards for basic anesthetic monitoring, 1999. Available at www/asahqorg/Standards/02html#2.
4. Aoyagi T: Improvement of the earpiece oximeter. Presented at 13th Conference of the Japanese Society of Medical Electronics and Biologic Engineering 90-91, Osaka, Japan, 1974.
5. Arafat M, Mattoo TK: Measurement of blood pressure in children: Recommendations and perceptions on cuff selection. Pediatrics 104:e30, 1999.
6. Bailey PL et al: Evaluation in volunteers of the VIA V-ABG automated bedside blood gas, chemistry, and hematocrit monitor. J Clin Monit Comput 14:339, 1998.
7. Baird TM et al: Optimal electrode location for monitoring the ECG and breathing in neonates. Pediatr Pulmonol 12:247, 1992.
8. Balaraman V et al: End-tidal carbon monoxide in newborn infants: Observations during the 1st week of life. Biol Neonate 67:182, 1995.
9. Barker SJ, Shah NK: The effects of motion on the performance of pulse oximeters in volunteers [revised publication]. Anesthesiology 86:101, 1997.
10. Benaron DA et al: Noninvasive methods for estimating in vivo oxygenation. Clin Pediatr (Phila) 31:258, 1992.

11. Bhavani-Shankar K, Kodali BS: Capnography: A comprehensive educational website. Available at www.capnography.com.

12. Bhavani-Shankar K et al: Capnometry and anaesthesia. Can J Anaesth 39:617, 1992.

13. Bhende M: Capnography in the pediatric emergency department. Pediatr Emerg Care 15:64, 1999.

14. Billman GF et al: Clinical performance of an in-line, ex vivo point-of-care monitor: A multicenter study. Clin Chem 48:2030, 2002.

15. Bland JM, Altman DG: Statistical methods for assessing agreement between two methods of clinical measurement. Lancet 1:307, 1986.

16. Boyle RJ, Oh W: Erythema following transcutaneous PO_2 monitoring. Pediatrics 65:333, 1980.

17. Carter B et al: A comparison of two transcutaneous monitors for the measurement of arterial PO_2 and PCO_2 in neonates. Anaesth Intensive Care 23:708, 1995.

18. Cartlidge PH, Rutter N: Karaya gum electrocardiographic electrodes for preterm infants. 62:1281, 1987.

19. Cassady G: Transcutaneous monitoring in the newborn infant. J Pediatr 103:837, 1983.

20. Chow LC et al: Can changes in clinical practice decrease the incidence of severe retinopathy of prematurity in very low birthweight infants? Pediatrics 111:339, 2003.

21. Cobbold RSC: Transducers for Biomedical Measurements. New York, Wiley-Interscience, 1974.

22. Cohen RS et al: Retrospective analysis of risks associated with an umbilical artery catheter system for continuous monitoring of arterial oxygen tension. J Perinatol 15:195, 1995.

23. Colditz PB et al: Anetoderma of prematurity in association with electrocardiographic electrodes. J Am Acad Dermatol 41:479, 1999.

24. Colman Y, Krauss B: Microstream capnography technology: A new approach to an old problem. J Clin Monit Comput 15:403, 1999.

25. Costarino AT et al: Falsely normal saturation reading with the pulse oximeter. Anesthesiology 67:830, 1987.

26. Donn SM et al: Rapid detection of neonatal intracranial hemorrhage by transillumination. Pediatrics 64:843, 1979.

27. Dransfield DA, Philip AG: Respiratory airflow measurement in the neonate. Clin Perinatol 12:21, 1985.

28. Duc G et al: Reliability of continuous transcutaneous PO_2 (Hellige) in respiratory distress syndrome of the newborn. Birth Defects Orig Artic Ser 15:305, 1979.

29. Emery JR: Skin pigmentation as an influence on the accuracy of pulse oximetry. J Perinatol 7:329, 1987.

30. Environmental Protection Agency: Air Quality Criteria for Carbon Monoxide. Research Triangle Park, NC, Environmental Criteria and Assessment Office, Office of Health and Environmental Assessment, Office of Research and Development, 1999, Chapter 8 (Table 8.14).

31. Epstein MF et al: Estimation of $PaCO_2$ by two noninvasive methods in the critically ill newborn infant. J Pediatr 106:282, 1985.

32. Erler T et al: Longevity of Masimo and Nellcor pulse oximeter sensors in the care of infants. J Perinatol 23:133, 2003.

33. Fanconi S: Pulse oximetry for hypoxemia: A warning to users and manufacturers. Intensive Care Med 15:540, 1989.

34. Fanconi S, Sigrist H: Transcutaneous carbon dioxide and oxygen tension in newborn infants: Reliability of a combined monitor of oxygen tension and carbon dioxide tension. J Clin Monit 4:103, 1988.

35. Fletcher R et al: Sources of error and their correction in the measurement of carbon dioxide elimination using the Siemens-Elema CO_2 Analyzer. Br J Anaesth 55:177, 1983.

36. Gangitano ES et al: Near continuous pulse oximetry during newborn ECLS. ASAIO J 45:125, 1999.

37. Geddes LA: The Direct and Indirect Measurement of Blood Pressure. Chicago, Year Book, 1970.

38. Geddes LA: Electrodes and the Measurement of Bioelectric Events. New York, Wiley-Interscience, 1972.

39. Geddes LA: Cardiovascular Devices and Their Applications. New York, Wiley-Interscience, 1984.

40. Gevers M et al: Accuracy of oscillometric blood pressure measurement in critically ill neonates with reference to the arterial pressure wave shape. Intensive Care Med 22:242, 1996.

41. Golden SM: Skin craters: A complication of transcutaneous oxygen monitoring. Pediatrics 67:514, 1981.

42. Goldstein M et al: A survey of indicators of pulse oximetry validity. Anesthesiology 99:A556, 2003.

43. Goldstein MR et al: Pulse oximetry in transport of poorly perfused babies. Pediatrics 102(Suppl 1):818, 1998.

44. Hagerty JJ et al: Accuracy of a new low-flow sidestream capnography technology in newborns: A pilot study. J Perinatol 22:219, 2002.

45. Harpin VA, Rutter N: Barrier properties of the newborn infant's skin. J Pediatr 102:419, 1983.

46. Hay WW et al: Pulse oximetry in the NICU: Conventional vs. Masimo SET. Pediatr Res 45:304A, 1999.

47. Hay WW Jr et al: Neonatal pulse oximetry: Accuracy and reliability. Pediatrics 83:717, 1989.

48. Hay WW Jr et al: Pulse oximetry in neonatal medicine. Clin Perinatol 18:441, 1991.

49. Hodgkin AL, Huxley AF: A quantitative description of membrane current and its application to conduction and excitation in nerve. J Physiol (Lond) 117:500, 1952.

50. Holmes M et al: Co-oximetry validation of a new pulse oximeter in sick newborns. Respir Care 43:860, 1998.

51. Hopper AO et al: Infrared end-tidal CO_2 measurement does not accurately predict arterial CO_2 values or end-tidal to arterial PCO_2 gradients in rabbits with lung injury. Pediatr Pulmonol 17:189, 1994.

52. Huch R et al: Transcutaneous measurement of blood PO_2 ($tcPO_2$): Method and application in perinatal medicine. J Perinat Med 1:183, 1973.

53. Hummler HD et al: Pulse oximetry during low perfusion caused by pneumonia and sepsis in rabbits. Crit Care Med 30:2501, 2002.

54. Katz AM: The Electrocardiogram, 2nd ed. New York, Raven Press, 1992, Chapter 20.

55. Kelleher JF: Pulse oximetry. J Clin Monit 5:37, 1989.

56. Kirpalani H et al: Technical and clinical aspects of capnography in neonates. J Med Eng Technol 15:154, 1991.

57. Kost GJ et al: Monitoring of transcutaneous carbon dioxide tension. Am J Clin Pathol 80:832, 1983.

58. Kunk R, McCain GC: Comparison of upper arm and calf oscillometric blood pressure measurement in preterm infants. J Perinatol 16:89, 1996.

59. Laks MM et al: Recommendations for safe current limits for electrocardiographs: A statement for healthcare professionals from the Committee on Electrocardiography, American Heart Association. Circulation 93:837, 1996.

60. McEvedy BA et al: End-tidal carbon dioxide measurements in critically ill neonates: A comparison of sidestream and mainstream capnometers. Can J Anaesth 37:322, 1990.

61. Mendelson Y: Pulse oximetry: Theory and applications for noninvasive monitoring. Clin Chem 38:1601, 1992.

62. Menzel M et al: Experiences with continuous intra-arterial blood gas monitoring: Precision and drift of a pure optode-system. Intensive Care Med 29:2180, 2003.

63. Merrick EB, Hayes TJ: Continuous, non-invasive measurements of arterial blood oxygen levels. Hewlett-Packard J 28:2, 1976.

64. Metz G et al: A simple method of measuring breath hydrogen in carbohydrate malabsorption by end-expiratory sampling. Clin Sci Mol Med 50:237, 1976.

65. Morgan C et al: Continuous neonatal blood gas monitoring using a multiparameter intra-arterial sensor. Arch Dis Child Fetal Neonatal Ed 80:F93, 1999.

66. Pichler G et al: Non-invasive oscillometric blood pressure measurement in very-low-birthweight infants: A comparison of two different monitor systems. Acta Paediatr 88:1044, 1999.

67. Pollitzer MJ et al: Continuous monitoring of arterial oxygen tension in infants: Four years of experience with an intravascular oxygen electrode. Pediatrics 66:31, 1980.

68. Raemer DB, Calalang I: Accuracy of end-tidal carbon dioxide tension analyzers. J Clin Monit 7:195, 1991.

69. Repetto JE et al: Use of capnography in the delivery room for assessment of endotracheal tube placement. J Perinatol 21:284, 2001.

70. Rheineck-Leyssius AT, Kalkman CJ: Advanced pulse oximeter signal processing technology compared to simple averaging: II. Effect on frequency of alarms in the postanesthesia care unit. J Clin Anesth 11:196, 1999.

71. Rozycki HJ et al: Mainstream end-tidal carbon dioxide monitoring in the neonatal intensive care unit. Pediatrics 101:648, 1998.

72. Saura P et al: Use of capnography to detect hypercapnic episodes during weaning from mechanical ventilation. Intensive Care Med 22:374, 1996.

73. Sheehan NJ et al: Filter unit for end tidal carbon monoxide monitor. U.S. Patent Office #5,357,971, October 25, 1994.

74. Stanger P et al: Electrocardiograph monitor artifacts in a neonatal intensive care unit. Pediatrics 60:689, 1977.

75. Stevenson DK et al: Prediction of hyperbilirubinemia in near-term and term infants. Pediatrics 108:31, 2001.

76. Strauss RG: Transfusion therapy in neonates. Am J Dis Child 145:904, 1991.

77. Tremper KK, Barker SJ: Fundamental principles of monitoring instrumentation. In Miller RD (ed): Fundamental Principles of Monitoring Instrumentation. New York, Churchill Livingstone, 1990, p 957.

78. Urschitz MS et al: Use of pulse oximetry in automated oxygen delivery to ventilated infants. Anesth Analg 94:S37, 2002.

79. Venkatesh B et al: Continuous measurement of blood gases using a combined electrochemical and spectro-photometric sensor. J Med Eng Technol 18:165, 1994.

80. Vreman HJ et al: Evaluation of a fully automated end-tidal carbon monoxide instrument for breath analysis. Clin Chem 42:50, 1996.

81. Vreman HJ et al: Semiportable electrochemical instrument for determining carbon monoxide in breath. Clin Chem 40:1927, 1994.

82. Vreman HJ et al: Validation of the Natus CO-Stat™ End Tidal Breath Analyzer in children and adults. J Clin Monit Comput 15:421, 1999.

83. Watson AB et al: Electrical thresholds for ventricular fibrillation in man. Med J Aust 1:1179, 1973.

84. Wood EH, Geraci JE: Photoelectric determination of arterial oxygen saturation in man. J Lab Clin Med 34:387, 1949.

85. Wu CH et al: Good estimation of arterial carbon dioxide by end-tidal carbon dioxide monitoring in the neonatal intensive care unit. Pediatr Pulmonol 35:292, 2003.

86. Wukitsch MW et al: Pulse oximetry: Analysis of theory, technology, and practice. J Clin Monit 4:290, 1988.

87. Yeung CY et al: Automatic end-expiratory air sampling device for breath hydrogen test in infants. Lancet 337:90, 1991.

88. Zollinger A et al: Accuracy and clinical performance of a continuous intra-arterial blood-gas monitoring system during thoracoscopic surgery. Br J Anaesth 79:47, 1997.

31 Anesthesia in the Neonate

John E. Stork

The neonatal surgical mortality rate has fallen steadily over the last 50 years.[40] Widespread availability of neonatal surgeons, technical advances in monitoring, mechanical ventilation, parenteral nutrition, antibiotics, the establishment of neonatal intensive care units (NICUs), and an advanced understanding of neonatal physiology are among cited reasons for this improvement. The development of pediatric anesthesiology as a specialty, which has resulted in perioperative management tailored to the neonate, can also be credited. At the same time, because of the advances in neonatology, the almost routine survival of infants weighing as little as 1000 g has led to new challenges for pediatric anesthesiology. Nowhere are the differences between adults and children more profound than in the neonate, particularly the premature infant. The immaturity of organ systems, homeostatic control mechanisms, and metabolic pathways are major complicating factors. Successful anesthetic management requires meticulous attention to detail, as well as a thorough understanding of neonatal physiology, pharmacology, and pathophysiology. Children anesthetized by pediatric anesthesiologists have decreased anesthesia-related morbidity compared with those cared for by nonpediatric anesthesiologists.[25] In addition to personnel, the operating room (OR) environment should be specifically adapted for neonatal care, thereby facilitating intraoperative delivery of the same degree of intensive care provided to the neonate in the NICU. Monitors, anesthesia delivery systems, mechanical ventilators, and environmental controls all need to be appropriate for use with neonates. It is also important to emphasize the *perioperative* nature of anesthetic management. Anesthesia clearly should not start and end at the door to the operative suite, and this is easily as critical in the neonate as in older children and adults. Preoperative condition and management affect intraoperative care. The postoperative period requires close monitoring and management of ventilation, fluid balance, and environment tailored to the special needs of the neonate. Assessment and control of postoperative pain requires methods and tools specific to the neonate.

Knowledge of the anatomic and physiologic differences among neonates, children, and adults is critical to careful anesthetic administration and management.

Maturity of organ systems and metabolic processes varies significantly not only between adults and neonates, but between preterm and term neonates.

ASPECTS OF NEONATAL PHYSIOLOGY AND DEVELOPMENT

Changes in cardiac and respiratory function take place at birth, and an understanding of this transition phase is a prerequisite for the pediatric anesthesiologist. (See also Chapters 42 and 43.)

The Transition Phase

Before birth, the pulmonary circulation is a high resistance circuit, the lungs receive little blood flow, and oxygenation is a placental function. At birth, approximately 35 mL of amniotic fluid are expelled from the lungs, the lungs reexpand, and respiration begins. Compliance of the lung is initially very low, and the first breath may require negative forces of 70 cm H_2O or more. With oxygenation and lung distention, pulmonary vascular resistance (PVR) decreases and pulmonary bloodflow and cardiac output increase. Increasing pulmonary flow, coupled with decreased venous return from the inferior vena cava with clamping of the placenta, lead to an increase in left atrial pressure higher than the right arterial pressure and closure of the foramen ovale. The ductus arteriosus closes somewhere between 1 and 15 hours after birth. Although PVR decreases, the pulmonary arterioles possess abundant smooth muscle, and the pulmonary vascular bed remains very reactive. In this setting, hypoxia, hypercarbia, or acidosis can cause a sudden increase in PVR and a return to a fetal circulatory pattern, a condition known as persistent fetal circulation or persistent pulmonary hypertension of the neonate. This is an acute, life-threatening condition, as shunt fraction increases to 70% to 80% and profound cyanosis results. In addition to providing adequate anesthesia, careful intraoperative attention to factors that increase PVR in the neonate is critical. (See also Chapter 43.)

Respiratory Physiology (See also Chapter 42, Part 2.)

Anesthetic agents are respiratory depressants. Central regulation of breathing is obtunded under anesthesia, with a significant decrease in the ventilatory response to increased CO_2. Lung volume and functional residual capacity (FRC) are small related to body size in the neonate compared with those of older children and adults. Alveolar ventilation per unit lung volume is very high because the neonate's metabolic rate is about twice that of an adult. Most of this alveolar ventilation is provided by a rapid respiratory rate of 35 to 40 per minute because tidal volume is limited due to the structure of the chest wall. One consequence of the small FRC and high metabolic rate in the neonate is a diminished reserve. Changes in the fraction of inspired oxygen (FIO_2) are rapidly seen as changes in PO_2, and the neonate quickly desaturates if ventilation is interrupted. This occurrence limits time for intubation, and airway management can be difficult. The high alveolar ventilation also accounts for a very rapid uptake of inhalational anesthetic agents, especially in premature infants, which can contribute to a tendency to overdose with these agents. Closing volume, which is the lung volume at which smaller airways tend to collapse, is very close to FRC in neonates. It is well known that anesthesia causes decreases in FRC.[24] In the neonate this decrease can result in airway closure at end-expiration, with resultant atelectasis, ventilation/perfusion mismatch, and increased intrapulmonary shunting. The awake infant uses laryngeal braking to provide some degree of auto-positive end-expiratory pressure (auto-PEEP) to maintain FRC, but laryngeal braking is diminished by anesthesia. In the premature neonate the immature alveoli are thick walled and saccular. Surfactant production begins at 23 to 24 weeks' gestation, but it may remain inadequate until 36 weeks. Lung volumes and compliance are therefore further decreased in the very premature infant. Whereas the lung is less compliant in the infant than in older children, the chest wall in the infant is very compliant. This combination accounts for about 75% of an increased work of breathing, with the remainder attributed to airway resistance. Because resistance to airflow is inversely proportional to the fourth power of the radius of the airway, the work of breathing is markedly increased in the small premature infant. Changes in airway resistance are common during anesthesia, often due to small endotracheal tubes and equipment factors such as inspiratory and expiratory valves in the breathing circuit. Kinking of the endotracheal tube or the presence of secretions also can adversely affect resistance. Respiratory failure from fatigue can occur easily. The low FRC, increased closing volume, and increased work, along with changes induced by anesthetics, combine to essentially require controlled positive pressure ventilation during operative procedures. Infants already being ventilated require some increase in their ventilator settings after induction of anesthesia, and infants usually require increased postoperative ventilatory support.

Tracheomalacia is common in premature infants, and if low in the airway, it may not be obviated by intubation. Bronchomalacia may result in airway collapse on expiration. Continuous positive airway pressure or PEEP increases FRC and decreases closing volume and helps to stent open the airway during anesthesia. Slower respiratory rates should be used with positive pressure ventilation to allow time for passive exhalation and to prevent air trapping. The premature lung is very susceptible to barotrauma and oxygen toxicity. Pneumothorax and interstitial emphysema may develop if high-peak inspiratory pressures are used. Airway anatomy in the infant differs from older children. The infant's head is much larger compared with body size than that of older children, although the infant's neck is short. The infant's tongue is large, but the larynx is higher and anterior, with the cords located at C4 in the infant compared with C5 or C6 in the adult. The epiglottis of the infant is soft and folded. In an adult, the larynx is cylindrical, with the narrowest point at the glottis. The neonate's larynx is conical, with the narrowest point in the subglottic area at the cricoid ring. Endotracheal tube size must be carefully considered to prevent airway trauma. Subglottic stenosis is a common complication, especially with longer-term intubation. Even modest airway edema can be serious. At the cricoid ring, as little as 1 mm of edema results in a 60% reduction in the cross-sectional area of the airway, resulting in increased airway resistance and increased work of breathing. Laryngomalacia is common in the premature infant and can result in obstruction. Periodic breathing with intermittent apneic spells is common in neonates up to 3 months of age. Small premature infants have a biphasic ventilatory response to hypoxia, with an initial increase in ventilation, followed by a progressive decrease, and apnea. The ventilatory response to CO_2 is decreased in premature infants and, as noted, is further decreased by anesthesia. Postoperative apneic spells are common in premature infants, although incidence decreases with advancing postconceptional age. These episodes can be secondary to the immature respiratory control system (central), a floppy airway (obstructive), or both (mixed or combined).

Cardiac Physiology (See also Chapter 43, Part 3.)

The transitional cardiac changes were discussed earlier. Immediately after birth, with an open ductus arteriosus, most of the cardiac output is from the left ventricle, and left ventricular end-diastolic volume is very high. Consequently, the neonatal heart functions at the high end of the Starling curve. As PVR decreases, output from the two ventricles becomes balanced at 150 to 200 mL/kg per minute. Heart rate is rapid at 130 to 160 per minute. Because end-diastolic volumes are already high, the infant heart is not able to increase stroke volume to a significant degree, and increases in cardiac output are entirely dependent on increases in heart rate. Baseline blood pressure is lower in infants than in older children, particularly in preterm infants; because cardiac output is increased, this is due to a low systemic vascular resistance. All anesthetic agents have significant effects on the cardiovascular system to varying degrees. Inhalational agents tend to be cardiovascular depressants, and they can result in decreased myocardial contractility with bradycardia and subsequent decreased cardiac output. Most anesthetic agents cause decreased autonomic tone and peripheral vasodilation, decreasing both afterload and preload. Because baroreceptor reflexes also are blunted by anesthesia, these decreases may make it impossible for the infant to compensate for preexisting volume contraction or volume losses during anesthesia. In the sick neonate, inotropic support may be necessary, and almost all infants require some degree of volume loading during anesthesia. This belief may be at odds with contemporary thoughts on respiratory management, which emphasize diuresis, and volume therapy needs to be carefully balanced to support tissue perfusion, urine output, and metabolic needs.

Fetal Hemoglobin (See also Chapter 44.)

The infant has approximately 80% fetal hemoglobin at birth. Hemoglobin F has a P50 (partial pressure of oxygen at which hemoglobin is 50% saturated) of 20 mm Hg, compared with a P50 of 27 mm Hg for hemoglobin A, which means that hemoglobin F has a higher affinity for oxygen and that the hemoglobin dissociation curve is shifted to the left. In utero, this favors transport of oxygen from the maternal to the fetal circulation. Another way to express this is that for any given oxygen saturation, the infant has a lower Po_2. Unloading of oxygen at the tissue level also is diminished, although this is compensated for by an increased hemoglobin level of approximately 17.5 g/dL at birth. The decreased unloading, however, can result in tissue hypoxia if Po_2, hemoglobin, or cardiac output decrease during surgery, with secondary development of metabolic acidosis. The hemoglobin rises slightly just after birth, then decreases progressively to a level of 9.5 to 11 g/dL by 7 to 9 weeks of life, owing to decreased red cell life span, increasing blood volume, and immature hematopoiesis. Fetal hemoglobin synthesis begins to decrease after 35 weeks' gestation, and hemoglobin F is completely replaced by hemoglobin A by 8 to 12 weeks of life, paralleling the decrease in hemoglobin and helping to maintain tissue oxygenation.

Renal Physiology (See also Chapter 49.)

Nephronogenesis is complete at 34 weeks' gestation, and the term neonate has as many nephrons as an adult, although they are immature, with a glomerular filtration rate approximately 30% of the adult's. With increasing cardiac output and decreasing renal vascular resistance, renal bloodflow and glomerular filtration rate increase rapidly over the first few weeks of life, and reach adult levels by about 1 year of life. The diminished function over the first year is actually well balanced to the infant's needs because much of the neonate's solute load is incorporated into body growth

and excretory load is smaller. Several aspects of renal physiology are pertinent to anesthesia care. First, the neonatal kidney has only limited concentrating ability, seemingly owing to a diminished osmotic gradient in the renal interstitium, whereas antidiuretic hormone secretion and activity are normal. Coupled with an increased insensible loss owing to a "thin" skin and increased ratio of surface area to volume, the limited concentrating ability of the kidney implies a tendency to become water depleted if intake or administration is not adequate. The neonatal kidney also is not able efficiently to excrete dilute urine and therefore cannot handle a large free water load. In addition, primarily owing to a short, immature proximal tubule, infants are obligate sodium wasters. There is then a tendency toward hyponatremia, especially if too much free water is administered during surgery, which can easily happen with continuous infusions from invasive pressure transducers, especially if adult transducers are used. Again, because of the lower glomerular filtration rate, the neonate also cannot handle a large sodium load and can easily develop volume overload and congestive heart failure. One final aspect concerns acid-base status: the neonatal kidney wastes small amounts of bicarbonate, owing to an immature proximal tubule; thus, infants are born with a mild proximal renal tubular acidosis, with serum bicarbonate of approximately 20 mmol/L. These changes are all greater in the preterm infant, particularly before nephronogenesis is complete at 34 weeks.

Temperature Regulation (See also Chapter 29.)

Given a large surface area, small body volume, and minimal insulation, neonates are extremely prone to heat loss. Any degree of cold stress is detrimental and increases metabolic demands in the neonate. Infants are unable to shiver effectively, and cold stress causes catecholamine release, which stimulates nonshivering thermogenesis by brown fat. The increased catechols can be detrimental, causing increased pulmonary and systemic vascular resistance, increased cardiac stress, and increased O_2 consumption. Anesthesia blunts thermoregulatory sensitivity[6] and interferes with nonshivering thermogenesis and brown fat metabolism.[14] Anesthesia also increases heat loss by inducing cutaneous vasodilation. At all times, including during transport and in the OR, the infant must be subjected to a neutral thermal environment. An overly warm environment of course can be equally detrimental. Core temperature must be carefully monitored at all times in the OR.

Carbohydrate Metabolism (See also Chapter 47, Part 1.)

Whole-body glucose demand corrected for body mass in neonates is as much as twice that in adults. Carbohydrate reserves, primarily hepatic glycogen, in the normal newborn are relatively low, and even lower in the infant with low birthweight. Hypoglycemia can readily occur if the infant is deprived of a glucose source. Even transient hypoglycemia has been associated with neurologic injury in neonates.[26] In contrast to adults, where hyperglycemia seems to potentiate brain damage during global and focal ischemia,[44] hyperglycemia in the neonate may provide some protection from ischemic damage.[13,32] In general, IV glucose (D_{10}) or IV hyperalimentation should be continued intraoperatively, especially in infants of low birthweight without adequate glycogen or fat stores. Nonetheless, hyperglycemia can also be a problem in the perioperative period. Insulin response is deficient in preterm infants, and high catecholamines owing to illness or intraoperative stress can result in hyperglycemia. Careful monitoring of serum glucose is often indicated.

TABLE 31-1. Perioperative Complications

COMPLICATION	CONTROL	FENTANYL
Frequent bradycardia	4	1
Hypotension, poor circulation	4	0
Glycosuria	1	0
Acidosis	2	0
Increased ventilatory requirements	4	1
Intraventricular hemorrhage	2	0
Total complications	17	2

From Anand KJS et al: Randomized trial of fentanyl anaesthesia in preterm babies undergoing surgery: Effects on the stress response. Lancet 1:243, 1987.

PAIN IN NEONATES (See also Chapter 41.)

Pain by its very nature is subjective and difficult to quantify and define. Assessment of pain in general has depended on self-reporting by the patient, an impossibility in the neonate. It has been suggested that the neonate's perception of pain is blunted or nonexistent. Because it was thought that anesthesia itself could induce or augment instability in the sick infant, minimal anesthesia to neonates was considered to be the safest approach. In some cases, this has included the performance of surgical procedures using only neuromuscular blockade. Nonetheless, there is clear evidence that both term and preterm neonates do experience discomfort and stress in response to painful stimuli as encountered during procedures and surgery.[10,18,47] Term and preterm neonates exhibit physiologic and hormonal responses to painful stimuli that may even be exaggerated compared with older children and adults.[2,3] A severe stress response, such as from surgery without analgesia, can result in serious complications and contribute to surgical

mortality.[4,5] This stress response is characterized by overall sympathetic stimulation, with increased catecholamine production, a hyperdynamic circulation, increased oxygen demand, insulin resistance, increased gluconeogenesis, and a catabolic state, and can be inhibited by anesthesia, as shown in Figure 31-1.[4] Blunting the stress response to pain and surgery with appropriate anesthesia may improve outcome, even in the premature neonate, as shown in Table 31-1 from a landmark study by Anand and colleagues in which fentanyl anesthesia markedly decreased the incidence of postoperative complications in a group of premature neonates.[4]

There is evidence that untreated pain experienced early in life may lead to an exaggerated response to subsequent painful episodes.[53] As an example, infants circumcised without anesthesia demonstrate exaggerated responses to later vaccination.[51] This hypersensitivity may be a consequence of painful stimuli during a particularly critical period of brain development, potentially leading to structural and functional changes in the nervous system.[47]

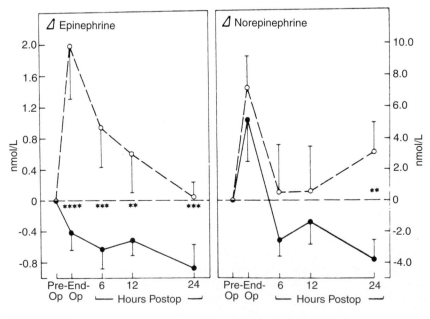

FIGURE 31-1. The change from baseline of epinephrine and norepinephrine in nanomoles per liter before surgery to the end of the operation and for the first 24 hours thereafter. The two groups reflect nitrous oxide-fentanyl anesthesia (*closed circles*) and nitrous oxide anesthesia (*open circles*). In the fentanyl-anesthetized patients, there was no increase in epinephrine or norepinephrine, not only during surgery but for the first 24 hours after surgery, indicating a significantly blunted stress response.

Pain is expressed in the neonate through both physiologic and behavioral responses, and an assessment of neonatal pain depends on a subjective evaluation of these responses by an observer. Examples of physiologic indicators are heart rate, respiratory rate, blood pressure, intracranial pressure variability, vagal tone, oxygen saturation, and autonomic effects, such as palmar sweating, pupillary dilation, and diaphoresis. Unfortunately changes in these indicators are not specific to pain, but can also occur with serious illness and nonpainful stress. Behavioral indicators include facial activity, cry, gross motor movement, and changes in behavioral state and function, such as sleeping or feeding patterns. As with physiologic indicators, these may be difficult to interpret, particularly in preterm infants or those with very low birthweight. For example, although crying can be a useful indicator, a very sick or preterm infant may not cry because of diminished energy, or obviously because of an endotracheal tube. Similarly, increased body movement may be a sign of distress, although ill infants or those with very low birthweight may become flaccid in response to painful stimuli.[47] Despite these inconsistencies, an extensive body of work makes it clear that pain can be adequately assessed in neonates, and multiple measurement tools have been designed.[19,47,48] There is increasing recognition that hospitalized neonates are subjected to significant pain and stress, and that assessment, prevention, and management of this pain is both important and of benefit.[8,37,47] Policy, position, and consensus statements from the American Academy of Pediatrics and Canadian Pediatric Society and other groups highlight the problems of pain and stress in the neonate and make recommendations for reduced exposure to pain and treatment interventions.[1,8]

PREOPERATIVE EVALUATION AND PREPARATION

The preoperative evaluation is extremely important in the neonate, and it should encompass the infant's physical condition, including any disease states, degree of transition from fetal to newborn physiology, and presence of any congenital anomalies. Particular attention should be paid to cardiorespiratory status, any required ventilatory or hemodynamic support, blood chemistries, and nutritional support. The courses of pregnancy, labor, and delivery and a full maternal history are important details. As is the case with older children, a family history of anesthetic difficulties may be important. Maternal diseases such as diabetes, systemic lupus erythematosus, and preeclampsia are clearly reflected in the neonate. Potential congenital infections, oligohydramnios, intrauterine growth restriction, and maternal drug and alcohol use are also important considerations. Gestational age, as well as birthweight and postnatal age, obviously affect anesthetic care. Birthweight does not necessarily accurately reflect maturity unless the infant is appropriate for gestational age,

defined as being within two standard deviations of the mean for the gestational age. Infants who are small for gestational age are more mature than their birthweight would indicate. Infants who are large for gestational age are often children of diabetic mothers, and they are at increased risk of hypoglycemia in the first 48 hours after birth. Newborns are characterized by birthweight as *low birthweight* (2.5 kg or less), *very low birthweight* (1.5 kg or less), and *extremely low birthweight* (less than 1000 g). *Term* is gestational age from 37 to 42 weeks; *preterm* is younger than 37 weeks; and *post-term* is older than 42 weeks. A history of birth asphyxia or neonatal resuscitation and Apgar scores are important. History should include complete details of present illness and treatment. Medications and administration times, details of vascular access, and respiratory parameters including ventilator type and settings are all critical details, especially in the sicker infants. Infants on high-frequency oscillatory ventilation may need to be switched to conventional ventilation and observed for several hours to facilitate movement to an OR. If the infant is on some other modality, such as inhaled nitric oxide or extracorporeal membrane oxygenation, arrangements may also need to be made, and transport to the OR will require more resources and assistance.

The time of the last oral feed should be ascertained, especially in elective surgery in healthier infants. Attenuation of airway reflexes with induction of anesthesia places the infant at risk of aspiration of acidic gastric contents, which can lead to serious inflammatory pneumonitis. NPO guidelines are summarized in Table 31-2,[17,42] and they are somewhat more liberal for newborns than adults. Studies suggest that a safe NPO time after a formula feed might be as short as 4 hours.[9] In part this reflects more rapid gastric emptying, although in an infant, dehydration occurs much more quickly than in an adult, and this is a concern in the infant without an IV line. As in adults, gastric emptying is delayed with stress, anxiety, and illness. Infants with diseases such as pyloric stenosis, duodenal atresia, malrotation, or other obstructive lesions are considered NPO before surgery, and they will need an IV line to maintain appropriate hydration. Despite the NPO status, there usually will be significant gastric contents, and rapid-sequence or awake intubation is required. Emptying the stomach via nasogastric drainage is not dependable and usually not adequate. Nasogastric feeds in intubated infants also should be discontinued at an appropriate time because the infant may need to be reintubated during surgery and a full stomach would increase the risk for aspiration. Physical examination includes vital signs, including temperature.

TABLE 31-2. NPO Guidelines

INTAKE	TIME
Clear liquids	2 h
Breast milk	4 h
Formula	6 h

Volume status needs to be carefully assessed because major shifts can occur easily during surgery. Many infants requiring surgery are ill. Infants with congenital anomalies often have multiple defects, which may have an impact on anesthetic care. Often a group of defects suggests a well-recognized and characterized syndrome. Some of the more common syndromes with their anesthetic implications are listed in Table 31-3, although this list is by no means complete.

Difficult intubation is a common problem in infants with congenital defects, and the airway needs to be

carefully assessed. Given the tendency for rapid desaturation in infants, difficulties with intubation can be extremely serious. In infants who are already intubated, tube size and position should be evaluated. The pressure at which a leak occurs around the tube should be documented. Nurses should be questioned about the quantity and consistency of secretions and need for frequent suctioning. The small tubes required in premature infants can easily be blocked by tenacious secretions and are easily dislodged. If there is any question about adequacy of intubation, the infant should

TABLE 31-3. Anesthetic Implications of Some Neonatal Syndromes

SYNDROME	CLINICAL MANIFESTATIONS	ANESTHETIC IMPLICATIONS
Adrenogenital syndrome	Defective cortisol synthesis Electrolyte abnormalities Virilization of girls	Supplement cortisol
Analbuminemia	Almost absent albumin	Sensitive to protein-bound drugs (thiopental, curare, bupivacaine)
Andersen syndrome	Midface hypoplasia Kyphoscoliosis	Difficult airway Impaired respiratory function
Apert syndrome	Craniosynostosis Hypertelorism Congenital heart disease possible	Difficult airway Increased ICP Cardiac evaluation, prophylactic antibiotics
Chiari malformation	Hydrocephalus Cranial nerve palsies Other CNS lesions	Aspiration precautions Vocal cord paralysis Latex allergy precautions
Arthrogryposis multiplex congenita	Contractures Restrictive pulmonary disease	Care in positioning Difficult airway Postoperative ventilation
Beckwith-Wiedemann syndrome	High birthweight Macroglossia Neonatal hypoglycemia	Difficult airway Monitor blood glucose, continuous glucose infusion, avoid boluses
CHARGE syndrome	Coloboma Heart defects Atresia choanae Retardation Genital hypoplasia Ear deformities	Bilateral choanal atresia may require oral airway Cardiac evaluation, prophylactic antibiotics
Cherubism	Intraoral masses Mandibular, maxillary tumors	Difficult airway Possible cor pulmonale
Cornelia de Lange syndrome	Micrognathia, macroglossia Upper airway obstruction Microcephaly Congenital heart disease	Difficult airway Cardiac evaluation, prophylactic antibiotics
Cretinism	Macroglossia Goiter Decreased metabolic rate Myxedema Adrenal insufficiency	Difficult airway Delayed gastric emptying Fluid and electrolyte imbalance Sensitivity to cardiac and respiratory depressants Stress steroids
Cri du chat syndrome	Abnormal larynx, odd cry Microcephaly Hypertelorism, cleft palate Cardiac abnormalities	Difficult airway Cardiac evaluation, prophylactic antibiotics
Crouzon disease	Craniosynostosis Hypertelorism	Difficult airway Increased ICP

TABLE 31-3. Anesthetic Implications of Some Neonatal Syndromes—cont'd

SYNDROME	CLINICAL MANIFESTATIONS	ANESTHETIC IMPLICATIONS
Dandy-Walker syndrome	Hydrocephalus Other CNS lesions	Increased ICP Latex allergy precautions
DiGeorge syndrome	Absent thymus, parathyroids Immunodeficiency Stridor Cardiac anomalies	Monitor calcium Exaggerated response to muscle relaxants Blood for transfusion irradiated Cardiac evaluation, prophylactic antibiotics
Down syndrome (trisomy 21)	Atlantoaxial instability Macroglossia Congenital subglottic stenosis Duodenal atresia Cardiac defects (atrioventricular canal) Mental retardation	Difficult airway, use smaller tube Care with neck manipulation Cardiac evaluation, prophylactic antibiotics
Dwarfism	Odontoid hypoplasia, atlantoaxial instability Micrognathia, cleft palate	Care with neck manipulation Cardiac evaluation, prophylactic antibiotics
Eagle-Barrett syndrome (prune-belly syndrome)	Absent abdominal musculature Renal dysplasia Pulmonary hypoplasia	Respiratory insufficiency Renal failure
Ellis-van Creveld syndrome	Ectodermal defects, short extremities Congenital heart defects Chest abnormalities Abnormal maxilla	Difficult airway Impaired respiratory function Cardiac evaluation, prophylactic antibiotics
Goldenhar syndrome	Maxillary hypoplasia, micrognathia Cleft or high arched palate Eye and ear abnormalities Hemivertebra or vertebral fusion Congenital heart defects Spina bifida	Difficult airway Cervical spine evaluation Cardiac evaluation, prophylactic antibiotics
Holoprosencephaly	Midline deformities of face, brain Dextrocardia, ventricular septal defect Incomplete rotation of colon Hepatic malfunction, hypoglycemia Mental retardation, seizures	Difficult airway Postoperative apneas Cardiac evaluation, prophylactic antibiotics
Holt-Oram syndrome (heart-hand syndrome)	Radial dysplasia Congenital heart defects	Cardiac evaluation, prophylactic antibiotics
Jeune syndrome	Chest malformations Pulmonary hypoplasia and cysts Renal disease	Respiratory insufficiency, high risk of barotrauma Renal failure
Klippel-Feil syndrome	Fusion of cervical vertebrae Congenital heart defects	Difficult intubation Cardiac evaluation, prophylactic antibiotics
Möbius syndrome	Paralysis of cranial nerves VI and VII Micrognathia Recurrent aspiration Muscle weakness	Difficult airway Aspiration precautions

Mucopolysaccharidoses (Hurler
    and Hunter syndromes)
	Macroglossia
	Hepatosplenomegaly
	Hydrocephalus
	Odontoid hypoplasia and atlantoaxial
	    subluxation
	Valvular heart disease and cardiomyopathy
		Difficult airway
		Coagulation abnormal
		Cervical spine instability
		Cardiac evaluation
		Increased ICP

Noonan syndrome	Micrognathia Webbed neck, short stature Congenital heart defects Hydronephrosis or hypoplastic kidneys	Difficult airway Cardiorespiratory evaluation Renal dysfunction

Continued

TABLE 31-3. Anesthetic Implications of Some Neonatal Syndromes—cont'd

SYNDROME	CLINICAL MANIFESTATIONS	ANESTHETIC IMPLICATIONS
Oral-facial-digital syndrome	Cleft lip and palate Mandibular, maxillary hypoplasia Hydrocephalus Polycystic kidneys Digital abnormalities	Difficult airway Increased ICP Renal dysfunction
Osteogenesis imperfecta	Blue sclera, pathologic fractures, deafness Congenital heart defects Increased metabolism and hyperpyrexia	Difficult airway Careful positioning and padding Hyperpyrexia with anesthesia (not malignant hyperpyrexia)
Pierre Robin	Micrognathia Cleft palate Glossoptosis Congenital heart defects Cor pulmonale	Difficult airway, laryngeal mask airway may be useful Cardiac evaluation, prophylactic antibiotics
Potter syndrome	Renal agenesis Low-set ears Pulmonary hypoplasia	Spontaneous pneumothorax Renal failure Respiratory insufficiency
Sturge-Weber syndrome	Vascular malformations and hemangiomas (intracranial)	Possible blood loss
Treacher Collins syndrome	Facial, pharyngeal hypoplasia Micrognathia, choanal atresia Congenital heart defects	Extremely difficult airway Cardiac evaluation, prophylactic antibiotics
Trisomy 18	Congenital heart disease common Micrognathia	Difficult airway Cardiac evaluation, prophylactic antibiotics
Turner syndrome	Micrognathia Webbed neck, short stature Congenital heart defects Renal anomalies	Difficult airway Cardiac evaluation, prophylactic antibiotics Renal insufficiency
VATER syndrome	Vertebral anomalies Imperforate anus Tracheoesophageal fistula Radial dysplasia Renal anomalies Ventricular septal defect	Cardiac evaluation, prophylactic antibiotics Tracheoesophageal fistula management
Williams syndrome	Elfin facies Infantile hypercalcemia Supravalvular aortic stenosis	Cardiac failure
Zellweger syndrome	Craniofacial dysmorphism Glaucoma Peroxisomal abnormalities in kidney and liver	Difficult airway Impaired renal drug excretion Electrolyte imbalance Abnormal coagulation

CNS, central nervous system; ICP, intracranial pressure.

be electively reintubated before surgery; emergently replacing an endotracheal tube under the drapes after beginning an operation is not a benign procedure. A complete clinical physical examination should be performed, with particular attention paid to cardiorespiratory status. Laboratory studies and x-ray films need to be reviewed, if applicable. Hemoglobin level usually should be greater than 13 g/dL to ensure adequate oxygen delivery to the tissues, given the decreased unloading at the tissue level by fetal hemoglobin.

Metabolic acidosis should be corrected, preferably by reversal of the cause of the acidosis. Electrolyte levels help to guide fluid management; hypocalcemia should be corrected. For most operations, it is important to check that blood for transfusion is available; for major procedures, fresh frozen plasma and platelets for transfusion also may be required.

There are several specific areas that should be explored by the anesthesiologist. As previously discussed, the pulmonary circulation in the neonate is hyperreactive, and in the near-term infant lung disease, asphyxia, and surgical stress can initiate episodes of pulmonary hypertension, resulting in decreased cardiac output and desaturation. Any history of such spells requires increased vigilance to avoid hypoxia, hypercarbia, and acidosis, which tend to increase pulmonary resistance. Bronchopulmonary dysplasia is a common chronic lung disease of premature infants. Infants with bronchopulmonary dysplasia are susceptible to excessive pulmonary vasoconstriction in response to hypoxia, hypothermia, or acidosis. Because of their chronic lung disease, these infants may have some degree of cor pulmonale, and decreases in myocardial function related to anesthetics may result in acute right heart failure. Other problems in bronchopulmonary dysplasia include airway hyperreactivity, increased airway secretions, electrolyte abnormalities due to diuretic therapy, and frequent tracheomalacia.[35] Congenital anomalies of the heart also must be carefully evaluated. Right-to-left shunts affect the oxygenation of the infant, but left-to-right shunts typically result in volume overload. The infant should be carefully evaluated for signs of congestive heart failure such as hepatic congestion, enlarged heart, and edema. The presence of single ventricle physiology is particularly important because the anesthesiologist needs to take great care to maintain balance between the pulmonary and systemic circulations. High inspired oxygen concentration in these infants results in pulmonary vasodilation and pulmonary overcirculation at the expense of systemic circulation, with consequent acidosis. Management may require low oxygen or room air; in some cases increased inspired carbon dioxide may be beneficial.[49] Abnormal pulses may indicate coarctation of the aorta. Antibiotic prophylaxis for endocarditis is also often important in neonates with congenital heart disease. Intrinsic arrhythmias are unusual in the neonate, although congenital heart block may occur in infants of mothers with systemic lupus erythematosus. Neurologic function also should be carefully assessed. Hemodynamic changes during surgery may affect cerebral blood flow. A history of seizures should increase the anesthesiologist's level of suspicion for intraoperative seizure if there are unexplained tachycardias or blood pressure elevations. The presence of intraventricular hemorrhage requires increased care with hemodynamic stability and is a contraindication to procedures requiring anticoagulation. A history of hydrocephalus mandates avoidance of factors that increase intracranial pressure.

TRANSPORT, MONITORING, AND OPERATING ROOM EQUIPMENT

Where to perform surgery is an important question to ask. Initially, it seems obvious—surgery is performed in the OR; however, with neonates, particularly the very premature infant, the answer is less clear-cut. Transport of the infant may be as great a risk as the surgery itself.

Great care needs to be taken to avoid cold stress. In some situations, if the surgical procedure is appropriate (e.g., patent ductus arteriosus ligation), if the surgeon is cooperative, and if a suitable locale is available, it may be preferable to perform some procedures in the NICU. Obvious basic requirements for a suitable locale include a clean area that can be closed off from traffic and adequate equipment, including lights, surgical equipment and supplies, appropriate monitors, and anesthesia equipment. In most situations however, transport to the OR is necessary.

For all but the healthiest neonates, a physician experienced in neonatal resuscitation and who has the ability to manage critically ill neonates should accompany the transport. In most situations, this person should be the anesthesiologist. Heat loss during transport must be addressed because the hospital corridors are rarely neutral thermal environments. If the infant is in an isolette, the isolette should be used for transport because heat is retained even when it is unplugged. A child on an open radiant warmer should be covered, including the head. In some institutions plastic wrap is used to retain heat and to reduce evaporative losses. Disposable chemical warmer packs are available and can be used under the infant in either an isolette or on the radiant warmer. Monitoring during transport varies depending on the condition of the infant. As a minimum, a pulse oximeter provides pulse rate and arterial oxygen saturation. In most ill neonates, the electrocardiogram and blood pressure should also be monitored, especially if the child has an indwelling arterial line. Any pumps providing infusions to the infant should have adequate battery power to operate throughout the transport, especially if vasoactive drips are running. Syringe pumps provide a very stable rate and have a long battery life, and the entire system is compact, thereby minimizing the equipment needing transport. These pumps also run accurately at a low (0.5 mL/h) rate so that concentrated infusions can be used, minimizing fluid delivered to the neonate.

The intubated infant requires hand bagging during transport. Particular care must be taken not to dislodge the endotracheal tube; small changes can result in either extubation or endobronchial intubation, particularly in the very premature infant. A self-inflating bag can be used to ventilate with room air, which may be necessary in infants with congenital heart disease and single ventricle physiology, whereas 100% oxygen can be delivered using an anesthesia bag and oxygen tank. Intermediate levels of F_{IO_2} require the use of a portable blender; for most neonates this is rarely needed during transfer. The anesthesia bag always should include a manometer because it is easy to reach pressures that can result in acute barotrauma, such as pneumothorax. A laryngoscope, endotracheal tubes, and a face mask should be taken on transport in case the endotracheal tube is dislodged. A complete round of resuscitative medications also should accompany any infant being transported to or from the NICU. Some transports require multiple personnel. Transport of infants on extracorporeal membrane oxygenation or those receiving inhaled nitric oxide is possible. With planning and an adequate number of personnel, this task can be accomplished with minimal risk to the infant.

Operating Room Equipment and Monitoring

The OR should not merely replicate NICU capabilities, it should surpass them, because the neonate will be subjected to the additional stress and destabilization of surgery. It is helpful if the room itself has adequate temperature control because it may be necessary to increase room temperature to obtain a neutral thermal environment. Before draping, radiant heat lamps can be used, although care must be taken to not place the lamps too close to the infant because overheating can occur. The operating tables for neonates should use a heating pad. For longer cases, forced-air heaters such as the Bair Hugger can be used, with a "full access" disposable air blanket that is placed under the child. Maintenance fluids, because they are given at a relatively slow rate, can usually be given at room temperature, but fluid warmers must be available for blood or faster fluid administration. Cooling is rarely necessary, but it is possible to overheat an infant if care is not taken. Temperature must be monitored (see also Chapter 29). Core temperature is the best temperature to monitor. It can be measured with a rectal, nasopharyngeal, or esophageal probe. Bladder and tympanic membrane probes are rarely used in neonates because of size. Skin temperature is a poor second choice to core measurements.

Routine monitoring requirements for neonates are shown in Table 31-4. Continuous pulse oximetry has revolutionized anesthesia, and it is a standard of care in the neonate as in the adult. In some situations, particularly with congenital heart disease or persistent pulmonary hypertension of the neonate, two pulse oximeters may be used to monitor both preductal and postductal saturations. Heart rate is monitored from both the pulse oximeter and the electrocardiogram. Disposable neonatal electrocardiogram pads are needed, both from a size standard and because they may adhere better to the vernix caseosa-covered skin of the neonate. Noninvasive blood pressure can be measured, and most available machines have neonatal cuffs and a neonatal mode, which uses a smaller air volume for cuff inflation and is accurate in the neonate.

Invasive arterial pressure measurements from an indwelling line should be routine in the majority of sicker or more premature infants. Common sites are the umbilical artery, either radial artery, and the femoral artery (as a last resort). Dorsalis pedis is rarely useful, but an axillary or posterior tibial line may be used on some occasions. The arterial line site needs to be considered in relation to the clinical condition of the neonate; for example, if a coarctation is present, a right radial line should be used. Similarly, if a right Blalock-Taussig shunt is planned, a left radial line is appropriate. Arterial lines in the neonate must be treated with the greatest delicacy. If blood is drawn from the line a small syringe should be used, and suction should never be applied, because the artery easily can go into spasm. The line always should be flushed gently, again with a syringe, and not with a pressure bag attached to the transducer. For the smaller neonates, an IV infusion pump (not a pressure bag) should be used to keep a continuous flow through the transducer, both to prevent inadvertent flushing and to limit the rate of fluid administration through the transducer (3 mL/h with the pressure bag versus 0.5 mL/h with the pump).

End-tidal CO_2 measurements also have become a standard of care, and they can be very helpful, but obtaining accurate numbers in a small neonate can be difficult. With a typical aspirating capnograph, the accuracy depends on the actual site of sampling, the type of anesthesia circuit used, and the volume of fresh gas flow through the circuit. Patient factors such as right-to-left shunt also may alter the values. The most accurate measurements are obtained using a low dead space circuit, with the sampling site in the endotracheal tube, not on the circuit. This location is accomplished by passing a small catheter into the endotracheal tube or via an endotracheal tube connector with a side port molded into it to which the capnograph sampling tubing can be attached. Blood glucose should be monitored intermittently during anesthesia; the importance of central venous pressure, urine output, and blood gases depends on the situation.

Many anesthesia machines are equipped with a relatively rudimentary, volume-limited, time-cycled ventilator, which even with a pediatric bellows is poorly suited for neonatal ventilation. Small tidal volumes are very difficult to set, and tidal volume and pressure vary tremendously depending on the fresh gas flow. In the

TABLE 31-4. Routine Monitoring Requirements

ROUTINE	OPTIONAL
Precordial or esophageal stethoscope	Central venous pressure
Pulse oximeter	Blood gases—pH, P_{CO_2}, P_{O_2}
Electrocardiogram	Urine output

Blood pressure
    Noninvasive
    Arterial line—umbilical artery
        catheter, radial, femoral
	Electrolytes

Temperature
    Core—rectal, esophageal,
        nasopharyngeal
    Skin	

End-tidal CO_2	
Peak inspiratory pressure, tidal volume, positive end-expiratory pressure	
Fraction of inspired oxygen (F_{IO_2})	
Blood glucose	

best of hands, these ventilators are impossible to use with premature neonates. Several methods have been used to get around this limitation. The simplest is to use hand ventilation throughout the case, thereby avoiding the ventilator. Although this method does allow some manual "feel" for pulmonary compliance, in many ways it limits the ability of the anesthesiologist to carry out other duties in caring for the patient. It also is very difficult to apply PEEP reproducibly when hand ventilating. A second method is to bring a NICU ventilator to the OR. Both pressure-limited, time-cycled and volume-limited ventilators are widely used to ventilate the smallest neonates. A disadvantage of pressure-limited ventilation is that tidal volume varies with changes in compliance, and care must be taken during surgery to monitor tidal volume as well as blood gases and end-tidal CO_2 to ensure adequacy of ventilation. Using a neonatal ventilator usually prevents the use of inhalation anesthetic agents, and it requires an IV anesthetic technique. As a third choice, in some centers, ventilators have been retrofitted with vaporizers to allow for the use of inhalational agents. Newer anesthesia machines incorporate significantly more sophisticated ventilators, capable of either volume-limited or pressure-limited ventilation. These ventilators can be used in pressure-limited, time-cycled mode, and they incorporate a spirometer that can measure expired tidal volumes as small as 10 mL. Fresh gas flow is uncoupled from tidal volume, and changes in flows do not affect ventilation materially. PEEP can easily be added, without the external valves used in older machines. These machines can be used routinely in infants as small as 500 g.

The circle breathing system, with inspiratory and expiratory valves and incorporating a CO_2 absorber, has become standard in adult anesthesia. A major advantage is that a semiclosed technique with very low gas flows can be used, thereby conserving anesthetic agent. Similar circle systems, appropriately sized for infants, with lower-compliance tubing and smaller bags, are commonly used in neonates. Many centers continue to use variants of the Mapleson D circuit, which has no valves and does not use an absorber, depending on higher fresh gas flows to prevent rebreathing. This circuit does have several advantages, particularly for smaller infants. The compliance of the tubing and the dead space is less; this can be critical in the smallest infants with very small tidal volumes, allowing adequate ventilation with lower pressures. In the rare situation in which the infant is allowed to breathe spontaneously, the absence of valves markedly decreases the work of breathing. The Bain circuit is a variant of the Mapleson D circuit in which the fresh gas flow passes through a tube that is concentric with the expiratory tube. This makes a compact circuit and helps to minimize heat loss.

The OR must be equipped with appropriately sized airway equipment, including Miller size 0 and 1 blades, Macintosh size 2 and 3 blades, uncuffed endotracheal tubes, and nasopharyngeal and oropharyngeal airways. An assortment of special blades should be available for difficult airway cases. The laryngeal mask airway (LMA) is a relatively new device that fits in the pharynx, covering both the glottis and the esophageal opening. A cuff seals against the walls of the pharynx. LMAs do not occlude the esophagus and may notably increase the risk of aspiration during positive pressure ventilation. LMAs are available in small sizes (1, 1½), but are not commonly used in the neonate. The LMA can be very helpful in intubating some infants with congenital anomalies, such as Pierre Robin syndrome. Essentially, the LMA is positioned and a fiberoptic bronchoscope is passed through the LMA and into the trachea. An endotracheal tube can then be passed through the LMA over the bronchoscope. The neonatal fiberoptic bronchoscope is essential for difficult airway cases. This bronchoscope is limited by extreme flexibility, and it does not have a suction channel, but it will pass through a 2.5-Fr tube.

GENERAL ANESTHESIA

Although there continues to be some interest in regional anesthesia for some specific procedures in the neonate, most infants receive general anesthesia. Successful delivery of general anesthesia in neonates requires knowledge of developmental pharmacology to predict and to understand the responses of premature infants to anesthetic drugs. Size has an effect on response to anesthetics, and developmental age has a profound impact on the dose response, distribution, and metabolism of these drugs.

Inhalational Agents

Although common in older children, inhalational anesthesia has not been extensively used in premature infants. Use of inhalational agents was thought to be extremely dangerous, and based on reports of hemodynamic instability and cardiovascular collapse, it was believed that neonates would not tolerate these drugs. In reality, these agents can be used safely, although very careful administration is required. The anesthetic effect of inhalational agents depends on the partial pressure of the anesthetic in the brain and on the potency of the agent. For several reasons, very high partial pressures of the inhalational agents in the brain develop much more rapidly in neonates than in older children and adults. First, as already discussed, the ratio of alveolar ventilation (per minute) to FRC in neonates is 5:1 compared with 1.5:1 in adults, and as a consequence, alveolar anesthetic concentration equilibrates with inspired concentration very quickly. Second, a greater fraction of the cardiac output in the neonate is distributed to the vessel-rich group and consequently the brain, and finally, the solubility of the inhaled anesthetics in blood is less in neonates than in adults.[29] Brain tissue equilibrates very quickly with the alveolar concentration of anesthetic and increases the risk of overdose in the neonate. The potency of inhalational anesthetics is expressed using the minimal alveolar concentration (MAC). The MAC is the concentration at which 50% of patients exhibit no response to stimulation

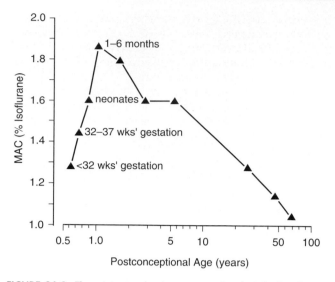

FIGURE 31-2. The minimum alveolar concentration (MAC) of isoflurane and postconceptional age on a semilogarithmic scale. (From LeDez KM: The minimum alveolar concentration [MAC] of isoflurane in preterm neonates. Anesthesiology 67:301, 1987.)

such as skin incision. MAC is related to postconceptional age and is lowest in very premature neonates, rising to a peak at a postconceptional age of approximately 1 year, then decreasing progressively from childhood through adulthood. Figure 31-2 shows this relationship for isoflurane.[28] As shown, isoflurane is more potent (lower MAC) in premature neonates than in older infants, but this MAC is not markedly different from that of adults, and difficulties using inhalational anesthetics are related more to the rapid uptake and equilibration.

Common inhalational anesthetics are halothane, isoflurane, sevoflurane, and nitrous oxide. Desflurane and enflurane are rarely used in the neonate. The inhalational anesthetics are complete anesthetics, with both analgesic and amnesic properties. In previous years, halothane probably was the most commonly used because it is minimally irritating to the airway, and it can be used for a very smooth mask induction of anesthesia. It is unfortunate that halothane was used so commonly; it is a significant myocardial depressant and sensitizes the heart to catecholamine-induced arrhythmias. Isoflurane, in contrast, is very pungent and cannot be used for mask induction, but it has less effect on cardiac output than does halothane. Systemic vascular resistance is decreased by isoflurane, and hypotension can result, especially if preload is diminished. Moderate volume loading helps to minimize any decrease in blood pressure. Isoflurane also causes cerebral vasodilation, and in the absence of hypotension, cerebral blood flow increases. In adults, isoflurane decreases cerebral metabolism and is cerebral protective. Sevoflurane has become very popular in pediatric anesthesia for mask induction. It is not irritating to the airway, and it is almost insoluble in blood, so that equilibration between brain and alveolus occurs rapidly. Thus, onset of anesthesia during mask induction is very

fast. Cardiovascular effects are more similar to those with isoflurane than with halothane. There is little published experience with sevoflurane in preterm infants, although it is certainly being used, primarily for mask inductions in healthier neonates. Sevoflurane has been associated with prolongation of the QT interval of the electrocardiogram in both adults and infants. This may be of concern because a long QT interval has been associated with sudden death. However, there have been no reports of intraoperative or postoperative complications related to sevoflurane and cardiac repolarization abnormalities, and it is uncertain if this is of any clinical concern.[15,31] Nitrous oxide is an inhalational anesthetic, but it is not in the same class as the halogenated agents. It is a weak anesthetic, with a MAC of 104% in adults, so that to reach MAC, nitrous oxide would have to be provided at hyperbaric pressures. Obviously, the need for oxygen as part of our inspired gases prevents achievement of these levels. Nitrous oxide also is almost insoluble, and onset of effect is therefore fast. Unfortunately, insolubility and the high concentration that is necessary for any meaningful effect cause nitrous oxide to enter progressively and to expand any gas-filled space in contact with the circulation, which rapidly leads to bowel distention or expansion of pneumothorax. If ventilation is interrupted for any reason, nitrous oxide also rapidly fills the alveoli, leading to dilution of the alveolar oxygen, producing a hypoxic mixture and rapid desaturation. Nitrous oxide is for these reasons best limited to adjunct use during mask induction, with a switch to an air-oxygen mixture during maintenance anesthesia.

Intravenous Agents

Intravenous agents include sodium thiopental, propofol, ketamine, various narcotics, and the benzodiazepines. Other IV agents are rarely or never used in neonates. Sodium thiopental is an ultrashort-acting barbiturate used primarily as an induction agent. There is some evidence that premature neonates are more sensitive to thiopental than are older infants, possibly because of decreased binding by serum proteins.[57] Thiopental is primarily a hypnotic, with little analgesic activity. Use is limited in smaller and sicker neonates because it has negative inotropic activity, and is a peripheral vasodilator. Hypotension is therefore common, particularly in volume-depleted patients.

Propofol is a phenol derivative supplied as an emulsion in lipid, which in older children and adults is used for induction and maintenance of anesthesia. Propofol has also been used for long-term sedation in adult and pediatric intensive care units, although there have been case reports of complications with long-term use in children, and the U.S. Food and Drug Administration has warned against such use before 16 years of age.[16,39] Recovery from the drug is rapid in adults because of redistribution and metabolism by liver and tissues. Propofol has less negative inotropic action compared with thiopental, but it is a powerful peripheral vasodilator, and hypotension is a common problem. The drug is designed as a complete anesthetic, but it does not have powerful analgesic effects, and for painful operations it should be used with narcotics. Propofol has been approved for children younger than 3 years of age, but there is little experience with the drug in premature infants.[46] One would expect a slower recovery with less fat and muscle to which to redistribute and possibly slower hepatic metabolism owing to immaturity.

Ketamine, a phencyclidine derivative, provides good hypnosis and amnesia and excellent analgesia. It is used rarely in adults and older children because it can cause a dissociative state with confusion, hallucinations, and other severe psychological side effects. Ketamine stimulates the sympathetic nervous system and therefore causes minimal respiratory and cardiovascular depression. Blood pressure may rise, and increased intracranial pressure is a concern in infants with hydrocephalus or those at risk for intraventricular hemorrhage. Ketamine can be useful in breaking hypercyanotic spells in the infant with congenital heart disease and right-to-left shunt because it both anesthetizes and increases systemic vascular resistance.

Fentanyl, a synthetic opioid, is widely used in neonatal anesthesia, and it is the most commonly used anesthetic for the premature infant. It has a wide safety margin and beneficial effects on hemodynamic stability. Fentanyl can block pulmonary hypertensive crises, and it is useful in infants with pulmonary hypertension, such as congenital diaphragmatic hernia, persistent pulmonary hypertension of the neonate, and some cardiac defects. Dosing has varied widely in the literature from as much as 50 to 60 μg/min to as low as 10 to 12.5 μg/min.[58] The pharmacokinetics of fentanyl in the early neonatal period are widely variable, depending on gestational and postnatal age and the type of surgery and medical problems of the infant.[41] Fentanyl is primarily metabolized in the liver, with only a small amount excreted unchanged by the kidneys. Clearance is lowest in the most premature infants, and it increases with gestational age and with age after birth, probably reflecting increasing hepatic maturation. Volume of distribution of fentanyl also seems to vary depending on gestational age and disease state.[41] Neonates with increased intra-abdominal pressure appear to have slower clearance of fentanyl. Slower clearance is likely due to decreased hepatic bloodflow resulting from the increased intra-abdominal pressure. Such a relationship has been demonstrated in neonatal lambs.[21,34] Given the highly variable pharmacodynamics, fentanyl dosing needs to be individualized and titrated to effect. There is a fairly wide therapeutic range, and even with high doses, hemodynamic stability is maintained. All narcotics, however, are respiratory depressants, and with higher doses of fentanyl, prolonged respiratory depression occurs, necessitating postoperative assisted ventilation.

Fentanyl in combination with a muscle relaxant has become the standard for anesthesia in the premature neonate. However, although fentanyl is a potent analgesic, it is not necessarily a complete anesthetic, and in occasional adults awareness has occurred with high-dose fentanyl alone. In the past, it was suggested that this was of minimal importance because neonates are not "aware," especially if pain was adequately treated. This belief is less well accepted today, and benzodiazepines or inhalation agents such as isoflurane are more commonly added to fentanyl anesthesia. Other synthetic narcotics, such as alfentanil and sufentanil, rarely have been used in neonates. In adults, alfentanil is less potent than is fentanyl, but it has a shorter half-life, whereas sufentanil is more potent than fentanyl. Pharmacokinetics in infants are probably similar to those of fentanyl, and there does not appear to be any significant advantage compared with fentanyl. Remifentanil is a new opioid whose duration of action is terminated by hydrolysis by tissue esterases. Consequently, remifentanil does not accumulate or have prolonged duration of action. A half-life of 4.4 minutes and a clearance of 80 mL/kg per minute have been reported in the neonate,[12] but there is very little experience with this drug.

Morphine is the principal opium alkaloid, and it is the standard against which analgesics are measured. Morphine is less potent than fentanyl, but it has a longer duration of action and is more commonly used for postoperative pain. The duration of action of morphine is increased in the premature infant. As with all narcotics, respiratory depression is a major side effect. Unlike fentanyl, morphine causes histamine release, which limits its use as an anesthetic agent.

The benzodiazepines are agents that produce sedation, anxiolysis, and amnesia, but little analgesia. As such, they are not complete anesthetic agents, although in adults they have been very useful in combination with an opioid. Experience in neonates is very limited. Midazolam is a very short-acting benzodiazepine, and it has been the most commonly used in anesthesia. Metabolism is almost entirely hepatic, and it should be expected that duration would be prolonged by immature hepatic function in the preterm neonate. Midazolam vasodilates and can cause hypotension. In high doses it can cause respiratory depression, although this is more common in conjunction with opioids. Midazolam and the longer-acting benzodiazepine lorazepam have been used for sedation in the NICU with mixed results. The Cochrane Neonatal Collaborative Review Group subjected several studies on sedation in the NICU using midazolam to a meta-analysis. In the two studies analyzed, infants treated with midazolam were more sedated (as judged by varying scoring systems) compared with infants treated with placebo. There were no differences in the incidence of intraventricular hemorrhage, pulmonary outcome, length of NICU stay, or mortality. The incidence of poor neurologic outcome was higher in the midazolam group, which at least raises questions as to the safety of midazolam infusion in these infants.[36]

Muscle relaxants are commonly used in anesthesia for neonates. They are often grouped according to mechanism of action, that is, depolarizing versus nondepolarizing, but it is more important to consider rapidity of onset and duration of action. Succinylcholine chloride is the only depolarizing agent used at present, and it remains the standard for rapid onset and rapid disappearance. As such, it is primarily used in one situation—for rapid-sequence intubation. In adults it also frequently is used when a difficult airway is feared. Given the limited reserve and rapid desaturation in infants, the difficult airway problem is probably better handled with awake intubation, so that spontaneous ventilation can be maintained. The ED_{95} (effective dose in 95% of the population receiving the dose) in neonates for succinylcholine is twice that of adults at 1.5 to 2 mg/kg. Action is terminated by metabolism by plasma pseudocholinesterase. Succinylcholine is not routinely used in children because of several rare but serious adverse reactions. In patients with myopathies or neurologic diseases, succinylcholine can cause overwhelming hyperkalemia, muscle necrosis, and cardiac arrest that is refractory to resuscitation. Bradycardia also occasionally occurs during intubation in the infant using succinylcholine. For this reason, some routinely administer atropine during a rapid-sequence intubation. Despite these reactions, succinylcholine at this point remains the choice for rapid sequence.

Nondepolarizing relaxants competitively inhibit acetylcholine at the neuromuscular junction. Pancuronium bromide is a long-acting relaxant, and it is probably the most commonly used relaxant in neonates when early extubation is not a problem. Onset occurs over several minutes, and it cannot be used for rapid sequence. Pancuronium has some vagolytic action and increases the heart rate. Vecuronium bromide is an intermediate-acting relaxant occasionally used in neonates. It has little effect on the cardiac system, although it may cause bradycardia in combination with narcotics. *Cis*-atracurium undergoes spontaneous degradation by a chemical process (Hoffman elimination), and duration is not affected by liver or kidney function. Atracurium, its parent compound, is rarely used today because it causes histamine release. Rocuronium bromide is a newer agent with a rapid onset of action that can be used in place of succinylcholine for rapid sequence. Duration of action is dose dependent, and significantly longer than succinylcholine. Rapacuronium bromide also has a fast onset, but it is a very new agent and there is no information regarding use in neonates. Most relaxants probably have a prolonged duration of action in premature neonates, and frequency of dosing should be determined using a nerve stimulator to measure response to four spaced stimuli (train-of-four response). At the completion of surgery muscle relaxation with nondepolarizing agents should be reversed with an anticholinesterase, typically neostigmine, and an anticholinergic, usually atropine in the neonate.

Induction of General Anesthesia

Most sick infants have IV access, and an IV induction can be performed. Premedication rarely is given to neonates, although some would recommend atropine before laryngoscopy and intubation. Healthier infants without IV access can undergo mask induction, typically with 50% nitrous oxide and sevoflurane, after which IV access is rapidly obtained. Infants with a full stomach, most commonly those with intra-abdominal disease, must have an IV rapid-sequence induction or an awake intubation. In rapid-sequence intubation, the infant is first preoxygenated with 100% FIO_2. Thiopental and succinylcholine, with or without atropine, are then rapidly pushed while an assistant performs the Sellick maneuver, pressure applied to the cricoid cartilage to prevent regurgitation of gastric contents. Positive pressure ventilation is not performed, and the infant is intubated expertly as soon as conditions are appropriate, usually after 45 to 90 seconds. There is little room for error with rapid sequence, and it should be performed only by individuals with significant expertise. Awake intubation with continued spontaneous ventilation is an alternative, and it may be most appropriate for infants with difficult airways, such as in Pierre Robin and Goldenhar syndromes. Minimal sedation can be given, but protective airway reflexes should not be obtunded. Once the airway is secured, induction can continue by IV or inhalational route. Management of the difficult airway requires careful planning and the availability of additional "trained hands." A pediatric fiberoptic bronchoscope and a range of special-purpose laryngoscope blades may be useful. Pediatric ear, nose, and throat consultation may also be of value. An LMA may assist with ventilation, but it does not protect the airway. The pediatric bronchoscope also can be used to intubate through the LMA.

Maintenance of Anesthesia

Maintenance of anesthesia requires monitoring as previously discussed. Temperature must be carefully controlled and adjustments in heating or cooling must be appropriately made. Fluid and metabolic requirements also must be carefully assessed throughout the course of the surgery. Fluids should be administered with an infusion pump to prevent inadvertent overload. It is usually easiest to calculate and administer maintenance fluids separately from replacement. Maintenance fluids should include glucose, unless the infant is known to be hyperglycemic. IV hyperalimentation, or a dextrose-electrolyte solution can be used, depending on the size, age, and clinical condition of the neonate. Third space losses should be initially replaced with a balanced crystalloid solution such as Ringer irrigation. Blood loss can also initially be replaced with crystalloid. Third space losses can be impressive, ranging from 2 to 15 mL/kg per hour, especially during procedures with large amounts of bowel exposed, such as for repair of gastroschisis and omphalocele. Many infants, especially if they are hypoalbuminemic, should receive some of their replacement as colloid, usually 5% albumin. In the sickest neonates, transfusion with packed red cells, fresh frozen plasma, and platelets may be required. Urine output should be followed as one sign of adequate fluid replacement.

REGIONAL ANESTHESIA

Although most neonates receive general anesthesia, a regional anesthetic is a viable option for certain procedures. Spinal and epidural (caudal) anesthesia is most common, although local infiltration or nerve block also is useful in certain specific procedures, such as circumcision, where a dorsal penile nerve block (DPNB) or penile ring block has been shown to be safe and effective.[30] Regional anesthesia is a valuable adjunct to general anesthesia, and is often very effective in reducing postoperative pain. Intercostal nerve blocks can be used for thoracotomy and flank incisions, whereas caudal anesthesia is very effective for inguinal hernia surgery. A regional technique without general anesthesia can be used in some neonates considered to be high risk, such as the infant with bronchopulmonary dysplasia. Spinal anesthesia without general anesthesia for inguinal hernia repair has been suggested as an alternative in infants at risk for postoperative apneas, although data are somewhat conflicting. Although several studies show a decrease in the incidence of apnea with spinal anesthesia,[20,55] others see no difference,[27] but the infants receiving spinal anesthesia did have higher postoperative minimum oxygen saturations and heart rates. Supplemental sedation during the spinal anesthetic does increase the incidence of apneas. Spinal anesthesia can be induced using a 25-gauge Quincke needle at the L4 or L5 level (below the cauda equina). Either tetracaine or lidocaine can be used depending on the length of procedure. Caudal anesthesia also is a useful option. The epidural space can be entered by the caudal route through the sacrococcygeal membrane. Caudal anesthesia can be given as a single injection, using a 22-gauge short-bevel needle, or a catheter can be threaded into the epidural space for continuous caudal anesthesia. With the continuous technique, the catheter can be threaded up into the epidural space, often high enough to give midthoracic anesthesia.[23] This technique seems to be well tolerated without significant hemodynamic effect. In the infant at high risk, caudal or spinal anesthesia can be used without additional sedation for appropriate procedures such as inguinal hernia repair. In this situation, simple nonpharmacologic comfort measures such as a pacifier are useful, and the technique seems to be well tolerated. More commonly, single-injection caudal anesthesia is used in combination with general anesthesia, which not only allows a "lighter" general anesthetic but is very effective for postoperative pain relief. After a caudal anesthesia with bupivacaine, most infants are free of pain immediately after inguinal hernia repair, with relief continuing for at least 3 to 4 hours. Spinal and caudal anesthesia are quite safe. The most significant but thankfully rare complication of spinal or caudal anesthesia is inadvertent intravascular injection of local anesthesia that results in seizures, arrhythmias, and cardiac arrest.

Local nerve blocks are rarely used in neonates. An exception is DPNB for *neonatal circumcision*. Safety and efficacy have been well documented, and in one prospective report of short-term complications, no significant problems were noted after DPNB in more than 7000 infants over an 8-year period.[45] Other simple methods, such as a sucrose-dipped pacifier, or a padded and physiologic restraint chair, further decrease objective signs of distress during circumcision performed with DPNB. Eutectic mixture of local anesthetic (EMLA) cream also has been used for neonatal circumcision. Although absorption of prilocaine, a component of EMLA, has the potential for causing methemoglobinemia, EMLA did not lead to measurable changes in methemoglobin levels in several studies and appears safe for both premature and term infants.[50] Care should, however, be taken. When used for circumcision, EMLA is more effective than no anesthesia, but it is not as effective as DPNB.[7,52] There are additional scattered reports of other uses for EMLA, including venous and arterial puncture, lumbar puncture, suprapubic puncture, and minor surgical procedures.[43]

RECOVERY FROM ANESTHESIA

Emergence from anesthesia in the smallest and sickest premature infants is usually a prolonged event because these neonates are not typical candidates for extubation at the conclusion of surgery; instead, they require continued intensive care in the NICU. Immaturity of drug clearance systems also prolongs recovery from the effects of most anesthetic agents in this group of infants. Transport from the OR involves the same considerations of temperature maintenance and airway management that have previously been discussed. Older and healthier infants usually can be extubated after surgery. Neuromuscular blockade should be reversed, as previously discussed. Hypothermia is a block to extubation if temperature control has not been adequate, and infants with hypothermia may need to be actively warmed. The infant should have resumed regular rhythmic respiration; to achieve this, ventilation may need to be decreased toward the end of the anesthetic to allow the P_{CO_2} to rise to mildly hypercapnic levels. Volume status must be adequate, and plasma hemoglobin should be close to normal. Flexion of the hip and contraction of the rectus abdominis muscle have been used as signs of adequate motor strength, and the infant usually begins to gag on the tube. Laryngospasm can occur on extubation, and the anesthesia personnel need to be ready to treat and reintubate if necessary.

As previously discussed, premature infants often experience periodic breathing, and there is a risk of postoperative apnea in this population. Cote and coworkers have done a meta-analysis of data from eight separate studies and have found wide variability among institutions.[11] It was clear, however, that the risk of apnea was strongly inversely related to gestational age and postconceptional age. Anemia may be a risk factor for apnea, although this is controversial. In one study the incidence of apnea was 80% in infants with hematocrits less than 30, and only 21% in those with normal hematocrits.[56] Prolonged postoperative apnea (defined as apnea longer than 15 seconds) occurs in approximately 70% of preterm infants less than 43 weeks' postconceptional age and decreases to less than 5% by postconceptional age 50 to 60 weeks.[11,33] Most episodes occur within 2 hours of anesthesia, but they may start as late as 12 hours and recur for as long as 48 hours. Caffeine has been used to reduce the risk of apnea, although it does not reduce this risk to zero.[54] A conservative approach is to avoid elective surgery and anesthesia until the former preterm infant reaches 60 weeks' postconceptional age, at which time the risk of postoperative apnea appears small.[35] If surgery cannot be delayed, it is probably prudent to admit the child after surgery and monitor the child for 12 to 24 hours after surgery or after the last apneic episode.

PAIN IN THE NEONATAL INTENSIVE CARE UNIT

The neonate in the intensive care unit is subject to frequent painful stimuli, ranging from postoperative pain to discomfort associated with intubation, suctioning, blood draws, IV access, chest tubes, and so forth. As previously suggested, historically this pain has been undertreated, if treated at all. Regional anesthesia has already been mentioned as one modality useful in the treatment of postoperative pain. Pharmacologic therapy is also commonly used. Opioids, as already described for anesthesia, can be used in appropriate dosages for moderate to severe pain. Use is sometimes limited owing to potential side effects such as respiratory depression, and development of tolerance/dependence. Nonetheless, given the analgesic potency of opioids, their minimal effect on hemodynamics, and ease of reversal of adverse effects, they are extremely useful and valuable agents. Among nonopioid analgesics, acetaminophen is most commonly used for milder pain. It can be administered orally or rectally, and is often used after circumcision. Interestingly, whereas hepatic toxicity of acetaminophen is well described in adults and older children, immaturity of hepatic enzymes may limit the development of toxic metabolites in the neonate.[47] Aspirin and nonsteroidal anti-inflammatory drugs are rarely used in neonates.

There has been increasing interest in other methods of pain management in neonates. Varied environmental and behavioral strategies have been used, including minimal stimulation, containing, swaddling or positioning, and human contact.[47] Non-nutritive sucking with a pacifier has been well studied.[38] The use of oral sucrose has also been established as effective in relieving procedural pain. The effects seem to be mediated by taste-related stimulation of endogenous opioid pathways. In experimental studies in rats, the effects are reversed by naloxone or naltrexone. The effects of sucrose and non-nutritive sucking may be additive, and are often combined. Sucrose is most effective when given just before a procedure, and is of limited duration.[22,47]

REFERENCES

1. American Academy of Pediatrics, Committee on Fetus and Newborn, Committee on Drugs, Section on Anesthesiology, Section on Surgery, Canadian Pediatric Society, Fetus and Newborn Committee: Prevention and management of pain and stress in the neonate. Pediatrics 105:454, 2000.

2. Anand KJS, Hickey PR: Pain and its effects in the human neonate and fetus. N Engl J Med 217:1321, 1987.

3. Anand KJS: Clinical importance of pain and stress in preterm neonates. Biol Neonate 73:1, 1998.

4. Anand KJS et al: Randomized trial of fentanyl anaesthesia in preterm babies undergoing surgery: Effects on the stress response. Lancet 1:243, 1987.

5. Anand KJS et al: Halothane-morphine compared with high dose sufentanil for anesthesia and postoperative analgesia in neonatal cardiac surgery. N Engl J Med 326:1, 1992.

6. Bissonnette B et al: The thermoregulatory threshold in infants and children anesthetized with isoflurane and caudal bupivacaine. Anesthesiology 73:1114, 1990.

7. Butler-O'Hara M et al: Analgesia for neonatal circumcision: A randomized controlled trial of EMLA cream versus dorsal penile nerve block. Pediatrics 101:E5, 1998.

8. Byers JF, Thornley K: Cueing into infant pain. Am J Maternal Child Nurs 29:84, 2004.

9. Cook-Sather SD et al: A liberalized fasting guideline for formula-fed infants does not increase average gastric fluid volume before elective surgery. Pediatr Anesth 96:965, 2003.

10. Coskun V, Anand KJS: Development of supraspinal pain processing. In Anand KJS et al (eds): Pain in Neonates, 2nd ed. Amsterdam, Elsevier Science, 2000, p 23.

11. Cote CJ et al: Postoperative apnea in former preterm infants after inguinal herniorrhaphy: A combined analysis. Anesthesiology 82:809, 1995.

12. Davis PJ et al: Remifentanil pharmacokinetics in neonates [abstract]. Anesth Analg 87:A1064, 1997.

13. deFerranti S et al: Intraoperative hyperglycemia during infant cardiac surgery is not associated with adverse neurodevelopmental outcomes at 1, 4, and 8 years. Anesthesiology 100:1345, 2004.

14. Dicker A et al: Halothane selectively inhibits nonshivering thermogenesis: Possible implications for thermoregulation during anesthesia of infants. Anesthesiology 82:491, 1995.

15. El-Zahaby HM: Is the prolongation of QTc interval in infants during sevoflurane anesthesia related to the speed of induction or to the duration of exposure? Egypt J Anaesth 20:53, 2004.

16. Felmet K et al: The FDA warning against prolonged sedation with propofol in children remains warranted [letter to the editor]. Pediatrics 112:1002, 2003.

17. Ferrari LR et al: Preoperative fasting practices in pediatrics. Anesthesiology 90:978, 1999.

18. Fitzgerald M: Development of the peripheral and spinal pain system. In Anand KJS et al (eds): Pain in Neonates, 2nd ed. Amsterdam, Elsevier Science, 2000, p 9.

19. Franck LS et al: Pain assessment in infants and children. Pediatr Clin North Am 47:487, 2000.

20. Frumiento C et al: Spinal anesthesia for preterm infants undergoing inguinal hernia repair. Arch Surg 135:445, 2000.

21. Gauntlett IS et al: Pharmacokinetics of fentanyl in neonatal humans and lambs: Effects of age. Anesthesiology 69:683, 1988.

22. Gibbins S et al: Efficacy and safety of sucrose for procedural pain relief in preterm and term neonates. Nurs Res 51:375, 2002.

23. Gunter JB, Eng C: Thoracic epidural anesthesia via the caudal approach in children. Anesthesiology 76:935, 1992.

24. Hatch D et al: Anaesthesia and the ventilatory system in infants and young children. Br J Anaesth 68:398, 1992.

25. Holman RS: Pediatric morbidity and mortality in anesthesia. Pediatr Clin North Am 41:239, 1994.

26. Kinnala A et al: Cerebral magnetic resonance imaging and ultrasonography findings after neonatal hypoglycemia. Pediatrics 103:724, 1999.

27. Krane EJ et al: Postoperative apnea, bradycardia and oxygen desaturation in formerly premature infants: Prospective comparison of spinal and general anesthesia. Anesth Analg 80:7, 1995.

28. LeDez KM, Lerman J: The minimum alveolar concentration of isoflurane in preterm neonates. Anesthesiology 67:301, 1987.

29. Lerman J et al: Age and the solubility of volatile anesthetics in blood. Anesthesiology 61:139, 1984.

30. Litman RS: Anesthesia and analgesia for newborn circumcision. Obstet Gynecol Surv 56:114, 2001.

31. Loeckinger A et al: Sustained prolongation of the QTc interval after anesthesia with sevoflurane in infants during the first six months of life. Anesthesiology 98:639, 2003.

32. Loepke AW, Spaeth JP: Glucose and heart surgery: Neonates are not just small adults [editorial]. Anesthesiology 100:1339, 2004.

33. Malviya S et al: Are all preterm infants younger than 60 weeks postconceptual age at risk for postanesthetic apnea? Anesthesiology 78:1076, 1993.

34. Masey SA et al: Effect of abdominal distension on central and regional hemodynamics in neonatal lambs. Pediatr Res 19:124, 1985.

35. Maxwell LG: Age-associated issues in preoperative evaluation, testing, and planning: Pediatrics. Anesthesiol Clin North Am 22:27, 2004.

36. Ng E et al: Intravenous midazolam infusion for sedation of infants in the neonatal intensive care unit [review]. Cochrane Database Syst Rev 2:CD002052, 2000.

37. Pasero C: Pain relief for neonates. A J Nurs 104:44, 2004.

38. Pinelli J, Symington A: Non-nutritive sucking in premature infants. In Sinclair JC et al (eds): Neonatal Module of the Cochrane Database of Systemic Reviews. The Cochrane Collection, Issue 4. Oxford, The Cochrane Collection, 1998.

39. Rigby-Jones AE et al: Pharmacokinetics of propofol infusions in critically ill neonates, infants, and children in an intensive care unit. Anesthesiology 97:1393, 2002.

40. Rowe MI, Rowe SA: The last 50 years of neonatal surgical management. Am J Surg 180:345, 2000.

41. Saarenmaa E et al: Gestational age and birth weight effects on plasma clearance of fentanyl in newborn infants. J Pediatr 136:767, 2000.

42. Schreiner MS: Preoperative and postoperative fasting in children. Pediatr Clin North Am 41:111, 1994.

43. Sethna N: Regional anesthesia and analgesia. Semin Perinatol 22:380, 1998.

44. Sieber FE, Traystman RJ: Special issues: Glucose and the brain. Crit Care Med 20:104, 1992.

45. Snellman LW, Stang HJ: Prospective evaluation of complications of dorsal penile nerve block for neonatal circumcision. Pediatrics 95:705, 1995.

46. Steur RJ et al: Dosage scheme for propofol in children under 3 years of age. Pediatr Anesth 14:462, 2004.

47. Stevens BJ, Franck LS: Assessment and management of pain in neonates. Paediatr Drugs 3:1174, 2001.

48. Stevens B et al: Pain assessment in the neonate. In Anand KJS et al (eds): Pain in Neonates, 2nd ed. Amsterdam, Elsevier Science, 2000, p 101.

49. Tabbutt S et al: Impact of inspired gas mixtures on preoperative infants with hypoplastic left heart syndrome during controlled ventilation. Circulation 104:I159, 2001.

50. Taddio A et al: Safety of lidocaine-prilocaine cream in the treatment of preterm neonates. J Pediatr 127:1002, 1994.

51. Taddio A et al: Effect of neonatal circumcision on pain response during vaccination in boys. Lancet 345:291, 1995.

52. Taddio A et al: Efficacy and safety of lidocaine-prilocaine cream for pain during circumcision. N Engl J Med 336:1197, 1997.

53. Taddio A et al: Conditioning and hyperalgesia in newborns exposed to repeated heel lances. JAMA 288:857, 2002.

54. Wellborn LG et al: High-dose caffeine suppresses postoperative apnea in former preterm infants. Anesthesiology 71:347, 1989.

55. Wellborn LG et al: Postoperative apnea in former preterm infants: Prospective comparison of spinal and general anesthesia. Anesthesiology 72:838, 1990.

56. Wellborn LG et al: Anemia and postoperative apnea in former preterm infants. Anesthesiology 74:1003, 1991.

57. Westrin P et al: Thiopental requirements for induction of anesthesia in neonates and infants one to six months of age. Anesthesiology 71:344, 1989.

58. Yaster M: The dose response of fentanyl in neonatal anesthesia. Anesthesiology 66:433, 1987.

CHAPTER

32 Care of the Mother, Father, and Infant

Marshall H. Klaus, John H. Kennell, and Patricia M. De Pompei

PROVISION FOR CARE

The struggles of parents of premature infants who are learning to cope with their babies provided the stimulus to explore how parents develop a close attachment to their healthy, full-term infants. Initially, research on parent-infant attachment focused mainly on the parents of full-term infants. As investigators began to study the ways in which the parent of a premature infant manages to meet the needs of the immature, sleepy, fragile baby, they noted many common adaptations and problems. In recent years, many investigators have looked closely at the complex and confusing ecology that parents encounter when the birth of a premature, sick, or malformed infant brings them into an intensive care nursery.

Research in these intensive care units is not easy or straightforward; it is frequently confounded by busy nurses and physicians, overwhelmed parents, and critically sick infants. Observations based on completed studies suggest several interventions that appear to have merit and that deserve further investigation in the traditional hospital environment. Some investigators have been refreshingly innovative and have broken down the walls of the intensive care unit to create a new and more positive environment for parents of sick infants.

To determine what triggers, fosters, or disturbs a mother's attachment to her infant, information has been gathered from clinical observations during medical care procedures; naturalistic observations of mothering; long-term, in-depth interviews of mothers; and results from closely controlled studies on the parents of full-term and premature infants. This chapter attempts to integrate this information into a general framework from which to develop some clinical recommendations.

Events that are important to the formation of a mother's attachment to her infant include the following:

A. Before pregnancy
   1. Planning the pregnancy
B. During pregnancy
   1. Confirming the pregnancy
   2. Accepting the pregnancy
   3. Becoming aware of fetal movement
   4. Perceiving the fetus as a separate individual
   5. Labor
C. Birth and after
   1. Birth
   2. Touching and smelling the baby
   3. Seeing the baby
   4. Breastfeeding the baby
   5. Caring for the baby
   6. Accepting the infant as a separate individual and welcoming the infant into the family

By observing and studying the mother in the context of these events, we can begin to describe how the parents of a normal, healthy infant build a bond with their baby.

BEFORE PREGNANCY

The literature on child development suggests that children are socialized by the powerful process of imitation or modeling. Their behavior is influenced by how they are mothered or what they observe. Long before a woman becomes a mother, she has obtained a repertoire of mothering behaviors through observation, play, and practice. She already has learned whether infants should be picked up when they cry, when and how much they are carried, and whether they should be chubby or thin. It is an interesting phenomenon that these modes of conduct, absorbed when children are very young, become unquestioned imperatives for them throughout life. Unless adults consciously and painstakingly reexamine these learned behaviors, they will probably unconsciously repeat them when they become parents.

PREGNANCY

Pregnancy appears to be a developmental crisis involving two particular adaptive tasks: the acceptance of pregnancy and the perception of the fetus as a separate individual.

Acceptance of Pregnancy

During the first stage of pregnancy, a woman must come to terms with the knowledge that she is going to be a mother. When she first realizes that she is pregnant, a mother often has mixed feelings. Many considerations, ranging from a change in her familiar patterns to more serious matters, such as economic and housing hardships or interpersonal difficulties, influence her acceptance of the pregnancy. This initial stage, as outlined by Bibring,[3] is the mother's identification of the growing fetus as an "integral part of herself."

Perception of the Fetus as a Separate Individual

The second stage of pregnancy involves a growing awareness of the baby in the uterus as a separate individual. It usually starts with the remarkably powerful event of quickening, the sensation of fetal movement. This perception occurs earlier for mothers who see their baby's movements on the screen during ultrasonography. During this period, the woman must begin to change her concept of the fetus from a being that is part of herself to a living baby who will soon be a separate individual. Bibring believes that this realization prepares the woman for birth and physical separation from her child.[3] In turn, this preparedness lays the foundation for a relationship with the child.

After quickening, a woman usually has fantasies about what the baby will be like, attributing some personality characteristics to the child and developing feelings of attachment.[3] At this time, she may further accept her pregnancy and show significant changes in attitude toward the fetus. Objectively, there usually is some outward evidence of the mother's preparation. She may purchase clothes or a crib, select a name, or rearrange her home to accommodate a baby—a human type of "nesting."

The production of a normal child is a major goal of most women, yet most pregnant women have hidden fears that the infant may be abnormal or may reveal some of their own secret inner weaknesses. Brazelton has clarified the importance of this turmoil for the subsequent development of attachment to the new infant[4]:

The prenatal interviews with normal primiparas, in a psychoanalytic interview setting, uncovered anxiety which often seemed to be of pathological proportions. The unconscious material was so loaded and distorted, so near the surface, that before delivery one felt an ominous direction for making a prediction about the woman's capacity to adjust to the role of mothering. And yet, when we saw her in action as a mother, this very anxiety and the distorted unconscious material could become a force for reorganization, for readjustment to her important new role. I began to feel that much of the prenatal anxiety and distortion of fantasy could be a healthy mechanism for bringing her out of the old homeostasis which she had achieved to a new level of adjustment. . . . I now see the shakeup in pregnancy as readying the circuits for new attachments, as preparation for the many choices which they must be ready to make in a very short critical period, as a method of freeing her circuits for a kind of sensitivity to the infant and his individual requirements which might not have been easily or otherwise available from her earlier adjustment. Thus, this very emotional turmoil of pregnancy and that in the neonatal period can be seen as a positive force for the mother's adjustment and for the possibility of providing a more individualized environment for the infant.

The caregiver's ability to help parents during this time of emotional turmoil probably has a strong influence on determining whether the pregnancy will be a positive or negative experience in the woman's life.[5]

Cohen, however, emphasizes that any stress, such as moving to a new geographic area, marital infidelity, death of a close friend or relative, previous abortions, or loss of previous children, that leaves the mother feeling unloved or unsupported or that precipitates concern for the health and survival of either her infant or herself may delay preparation for the infant and retard bond formation.[8] After the first trimester, behaviors that are a reaction to stress and suggest rejection of pregnancy include a preoccupation with physical appearance or negative self-perception, excessive emotional withdrawal or mood swings, excessive physical complaints, absence of any response to quickening, or lack of any preparatory behavior during the last trimester.

A mother's and father's behavior toward their infant is derived from a complex combination of their own genetic endowments, the infant's responses to the parents, a long history of interpersonal relationships with their own families and with each other, experiences with this or previous pregnancies, the practices and values of their cultures, their socioeconomic status, and, probably most important, the way they were raised by their own parents. The mothering or fathering behavior of each woman and man, the ability of each parent to tolerate stresses, and the needs each parent has for special attention differ greatly and depend on a mixture of these factors.

A remarkable illustration of how early caretaking of an infant, understood by the child through a complex mental process, becomes a template for the child's own parenting in later life is the case of Monica, who was born with esophageal atresia. Monica required gastrostomy feedings and was never held in anyone's arms during feeding. At 21 months of age, surgery established continuity between Monica's mouth and stomach. Systematic filming by George Engel over the next 30 years of her life showed that she repeated her own early feeding experience in every subsequent feeding situation in which she was involved.[11] As a little girl, she never held a doll in her arms; as an adolescent babysitter, she did not hold infants for whom she was responsible in her arms; and as a mother, she did not hold her own infants in her arms. She fed each of her four babies with the baby's back lying on her knees. Monica also played with her babies in the same fashion that she was played with—that is, only when they were

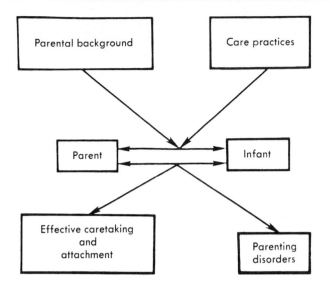

FIGURE 32-1. Major influences on parent-infant attachment and outcomes.

flat on their backs for diapering or a bath. Thus, in spite of other examples and recommendations, her own experience in infancy became the persistent model for her caretaking as a babysitter and mother.

Figure 32-1 is a schematic diagram of the major influences on parental behavior and the resulting disturbances that may arise from them. At the time the infant is conceived, some of these determinants, such as the mothering the father and mother received when they were infants, the practices of their culture, their endowments, and their relationships with their own families, are contributed by the parents. We originally believed these determinants were fixed and unchangeable. However, other investigators have argued that the influence of some of these may be changed during the crisis of birth. Other determinants relate to the hospital culture. For example, the attitudes, statements, and practices of the nurses and physicians in the hospital; whether there is early suckling and rooming-in or separation from the infant in the first days of life; the infant's temperament; and whether the infant is healthy, sick, or malformed affect the relationship. Most mothers and fathers develop warm and close attachments with their infants. However, a series of mothering disorders, ranging from mild anxiety (such as persistent concerns about a baby after a minor problem that has been completely resolved in the nursery) to the most severe manifestation (the battered child syndrome), occur with a few parents. Some problems result in part from separation and other unusual circumstances that occur in the early newborn period as a consequence of present hospital care policies.

Experiences during labor, parent-infant separation, and hospital practices during the first hours and days of life are the most easily manipulated variables in this scheme. Recent studies have partly clarified some of the steps in mother-infant attachment during this early period.

To minimize the number of unknowns for a mother while she is in the hospital, she and the father (or other supportive companion who will stay with her throughout labor and delivery) should visit the maternity unit to see where labor and delivery will take place. They should learn about delivery routines and all procedures and medication the mother will receive before, during, and after delivery. Reducing the possibility of surprise increases confidence during labor and delivery. For an adult, just as for a child entering the hospital for surgery, the more meticulously detailed every step and event is in advance, the less will be the subsequent anxiety. The less anxiety the mother experiences while delivering and becoming attached to her baby, the better will be her immediate relationship with the infant.

LABOR

Before childbirth moved from the home to the hospital, the practice in industrialized nations was for women in the community to support the mother in labor, often with the assistance of a trained or untrained midwife. In all but one of the 128 cultures studied by anthropologists, a family member or friend, usually a woman, remained with the mother during labor and delivery. Although more fathers, relatives, and friends have been allowed into labor and delivery rooms in the past 20 years, a significant number of mothers still labor and deliver in some hospitals without continuous emotional and physical support.

The clinical value of continuous emotional and physical care during childbirth by a trained woman called a doula[21] is clearly supported by the results of the 15 randomized clinical trials conducted over the past two decades. Beneficial findings are consistent across the studies despite different cultural, medical, and social practices.[21]

A meta-analysis by Scott and colleagues revealed that continuous social support during labor and delivery has a significantly more beneficial impact on childbirth outcomes than intermittent support has.[49] In six studies, the intermittent presence of a doula with mothers, when compared to the absence of any doula support, was not associated with any significantly improved outcomes. In contrast, in five studies, continuous support for mothers was significantly associated with a 36% reduction in the need for analgesia, a 71% decrease in the need for oxytocin augmentation, a 57% reduction in the use of forceps, a 45% decrease in cesarean sections, and an average shortening of the duration of labor by 98 minutes.[27,31,52] Thus, some of the original studies may have underestimated the positive effects of social support during childbirth by not requiring support to be provided continuously to experimental subjects.

The results in the study by Wolman and coworkers in South Africa revealed the favorable effects of continuous support during labor on the subsequent psychological health of the women and infants in the group of women with support from a doula.[61] At 24 hours, the mothers with a doula had significantly less anxiety than the mothers without doulas, and fewer doula-supported mothers considered the labor and delivery to have been difficult. At 6 weeks postpartum, there was a significantly greater proportion of women breastfeeding in the doula group (51% versus 29%), and feeding problems were significantly fewer in the doula group (16% versus 63%).[61]

The doula-supported mothers noted that it took an average of 2.9 days for them to develop a relationship with their baby compared with 9.8 days for the mothers without doulas. These results suggest that support during labor expedited the doula-supported mothers' readiness to bond with their babies. Using other measures, mothers in the doula group were again significantly less anxious, had scores on the depression scale that were significantly lower than those of the control group, and had higher levels of self-esteem at 6 weeks postpartum. They also felt significantly more satisfied with their partner 6 weeks after the birth (71% versus 30%) and felt their baby was better than the standard baby, more beautiful, more clever, and easier to manage, whereas the control mothers perceived that their baby was slightly less attractive than a standard infant.[61]

In a 1998 study, 413 nulliparous women in early labor were randomly assigned to receive epidural analgesia, narcotic medication, or continuous support by a doula.[34] All the babies and mothers had uneventful hospital courses. Thirty-five mothers and their babies were randomly chosen from each of the three groups for further study. There was no contact with the families until a visit to the home was made by trained and blinded observers 2 months after delivery for a 2-hour period. The interactions between mother and baby were scored on a scale of 1 to 7, with graded definitions of her physical contact, visual attention, and affectionate behaviors toward her child. The mother-infant interaction was assessed five times during the visit—for example, during a feeding and while the mother changed the baby. Inter-rater reliability was high. The mother-infant interaction scores showed significant differences between the doula-supported mothers and the group of mothers who had epidural and narcotic medication. Overall, the average mother-infant interaction scores at all five observation points for the doula and for the two nondoula groups were significantly different ($P < .001$). These scores demonstrate that providing a laboring woman with the continuous support of a doula results in a significantly more positive level of interaction with her infant 2 months after delivery.

We concur with Hodnett and colleagues that "given the clear benefits and no known risks associated with intra-partum support, every effort should be made to ensure that all laboring women receive continuous support, not only from those close to them but also from specially trained caregivers (nurses, midwives, or a doula)."[21]

A renewed interest in the first minutes, hours, and days of life has been stimulated by several provocative behavioral and physiologic observations in both mother and infant. These assessments and measurements have been made during labor, birth, and the immediate postnatal period, and at the beginning breast feedings. They provide a compelling rationale for major changes in care in the perinatal period for both mother and infant. These findings fit together to form a new way to view the mother-infant dyad.

THE FIRST HOURS AFTER BIRTH

The newborn should be thoroughly dried, except for the hands, with warm towels after birth to avoid the loss of heat, and once it is clear that the infant has good color and is active and normal (usually within 1 to 3 minutes), the baby can be given to his mother. At this time, the warm and dry infant can be placed between the mother's breasts, on her abdomen, or if she desires, next to her.

To prevent the baby from reacting to unnecessary suctioning, the resuscitation committee of the Academy of Pediatrics has recommended that since nearly 90% of newborns are vigorous term infants with clear amniotic fluid, suctioning is not required.[24] Separating the newborn from the mother to administer the initial steps in resuscitation is also not needed. Clearing of the upper airway can be accomplished by simply wiping the baby's mouth and nose (see also Chapter 25).

When newborns are kept close to their mother's body, the transition from life in the womb to existence outside the uterus is made much easier. The newborn recognizes the mother's voice and smell,[55] and her body provides warmth to just the right temperature.[7] In this way, the infant can experience sensations somewhat similar to those of the last several weeks of uterine life (Fig. 32-2).

Often, the baby's lips are placed near or on the mother's nipple immediately after birth. Some babies do start to suckle, but the majority just lick the nipple

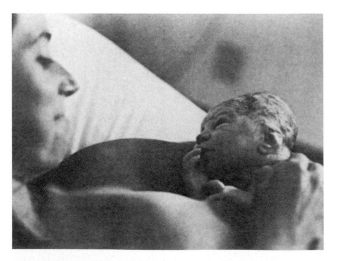

FIGURE 32-2. A mother and her infant shortly after birth. (From Klaus MH et al: Amazing Newborn. Cambridge, Mass, Perseus, 1985, p 137, with permission. Copyright Suzanne Arms Wimberley.)

or peer up at the mother. They appear to be much more interested in the mother's face, especially her eyes. They should never be forced on the breast.

One of the most exciting observations made in the modern era is the discovery that the newborn has the ability to find the mother's breast and to decide when to take the first feeding. Washing the baby's hands and the mother's breasts should be delayed so that the taste and smell of the mother's amniotic fluid is not removed. The baby uses this taste and smell to make a connection with a lipid substance on the nipple that is related to the amniotic fluid.[55]

The infant usually begins with a time of rest and quiet alertness, rarely crying and often appearing to take pleasure in looking at the mother's face. Around 30 to 40 minutes after birth (sometimes longer), the newborn begins making mouthing movements, sometimes with lip smacking, and shortly after, saliva begins to pour down the infant's chin. When placed on the mother's abdomen, babies maneuver in their own ways to reach the nipple.[45] They often use small pushups, lowering one arm first in the direction they wish to go. These efforts are interspersed with short rest periods. Sometimes babies change direction mid course. These actions take effort and time. Parents with patience find it worthwhile to wait and observe their infant's first journey.

The photos in Figure 32-3 show a newborn successfully navigating. At 10 minutes of age, the newborn first begins to move toward the left breast. Repeated mouthing and sucking of the hands and fingers is commonly observed (see Fig. 32-3A). With a series of pushups and rest periods, the infant gets to the right breast completely unassisted (see Fig. 32-3B). The infant, with lips on the areola, now begins to suckle effectively while closely observing the mother's face (see Fig. 32-3C).

This sequence is helpful to the mother as well as the baby, because the massaging and suckling of the breast induces an oxytocin surge into her bloodstream, which may help contract the uterus, expelling the placenta and closing off many blood vessels in the uterus, thus reducing bleeding. In addition, the stimulation and suckling help in the manufacture of not only prolactin in the mother but also oxytocin in the brain of both mother and the baby. Oxytocin, the "love hormone," in the dyad, probably begins to enhance their early ties together. Mother and baby appear to be well adapted for these first moments together.

To allow this first intimate encounter, injection of vitamin K, application of eye ointment, washing, and

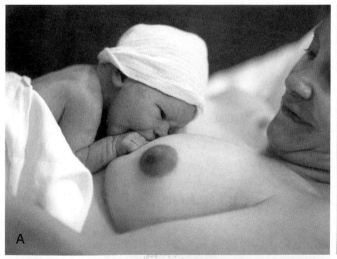

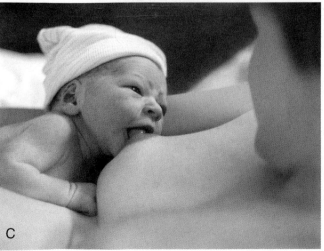

FIGURE 32-3. **A,** Infant about 15 minutes after birth, sucking on the unwashed hand and possibly looking at mother's left nipple. **B,** An arm pushup, which helps the infant to move to mother's right side. **C,** At 45 minutes of age, the infant moved to the right breast without assistance and began sucking on the areola of the breast. The infant has been looking at the mother's face for 5 to 8 minutes. (Photographed by Elaine Siegel.) (From Marshall H. Klaus, MD, and Phyllis H. Klaus, CSM, MFCC: Your Amazing Newborn. Cambridge, Mass: Perseus, 1998, pp 13, 16 & 17.)

any measuring of the infant's weight, height, and head circumference should be delayed for at least 1½ hours. Over 90% of full-term infants are normal at birth. In a few moments they can easily be evaluated to ensure that they are healthy.

The mother has an intense interest in her newborn baby's open eyes. When left alone with her infant in the first hour of life, 85% of what a mother says is related to the infant's eyes: "Please look at me" and "If you look at me, I know you love me."[29] In the first 45 minutes of life, the infant is awake and alert and in the quiet alert state.

The odor of the nipple appears to guide a newborn to the breast.[55] If the right breast is washed with soap and water, the infant will crawl to the left breast, and vice versa. If both breasts are washed, the infant will go to the breast that has been rubbed with the amniotic fluid of the mother. The special attraction of the newborn to the odor of the mother's amniotic fluid may reflect the time when the fetus swallowed the liquid in utero. It appears that amniotic fluid contains a substance that is similar to some secretion of the breast, although not the milk. Amniotic fluid on the infant's hands probably also explains part of the interest in sucking the hands and fingers seen in the photographs in Figure 32-3. This early hand-sucking behavior is markedly reduced when the infant is bathed before the initial crawl.

Many abilities enable a baby to do these tasks. Stepping reflexes help the newborn push against the mother's abdomen to propel him toward the breast. Pressure of the infant's feet on the abdomen may help the expulsion of the placenta and the reduction of uterine bleeding. The ability to move a hand in a reaching motion enables the baby to claim the nipple. Taste, smell, and vision all help the newborn detect and find the breast.[33] Muscular strength in neck, shoulders, and arms helps newborns bob their heads and do small pushups to inch forward and from side to side. It appears that our young, like other baby mammals, know how to find their mother's breast.

Swedish researchers have shown that the normal infant who is dried and placed naked on the mother's chest and then covered with a blanket maintains body temperature as well as the infant who is warmed with an elaborate, high-tech heating device, which usually separates the mother and baby. The same researchers found that when the infants have skin-to-skin contact with their mothers for 90 minutes after birth, they cry hardly at all compared with infants who were dried, wrapped in a towel, and placed in a bassinet.[7] In one study, a group of mothers did not receive pain medication, and their babies were not taken away during the first hour of life for a bath and did not receive vitamin K or application of eye ointment; 15 of 16 babies placed on their mother's abdomen were observed to make the trip on their own to their mother's breast, latch on, and begin to suckle effectively.[57] It seems likely that each of these features—the crawling ability of the infant, the decreased crying when close to the mother, and the warming capacity of the mother's chest—are

adaptive and evolved genetically to help preserve the infant's life.

Suckling of the breast by the infant stimulates the production of oxytocin in both the mother's and the infant's brain, and this oxytocin in turn stimulates the vagal motor nucleus, releasing 19 gastrointestinal hormones, including insulin, cholecystokinin, and gastrin. Five of the 19 hormones stimulate growth of the baby's and mother's intestinal villi and increase the surface area and the absorption of calories with each feeding.[39] The stimuli for this release are touch on the mother's nipple and the inside of the infant's mouth. These responses were essential for survival 10,000 years ago, before the development of modern agriculture and grain storage, when periods of famine were more common. The increased gut motility with each suckling may also help remove meconium with its large load of bilirubin.

These research findings may explain some of the underlying physiologic and behavioral processes and provide additional support for the importance of 2 of the 10 caregiving procedures that the United Nations International Children's Emergency Fund (UNICEF) is promoting as part of its Baby-Friendly Hospital Initiative to increase breast feeding, which involves early mother-infant contact, with an opportunity for the baby to suckle in the first hour, and mother-infant rooming-in throughout the hospital stay.

After the introduction of the Baby-Friendly Hospital Initiative (BFHI) in maternity units in several countries throughout the world, an unexpected observation was made. In Thailand, in a hospital in which a disturbing number of babies were abandoned by their mothers, the use of rooming-in and early contact with suckling in the first hour significantly reduced the frequency of abandonment (from 33 out of 10,000 births to 1 out of 10,000 births a year).[6] Similar observations were made in Russia, the Philippines, and Costa Rica when early contact and rooming-in were introduced. These reports are additional evidence that the first hours and days of life are a sensitive period for the human mother,[29] perhaps partly because of the special interest that a mother has shortly after birth, as she hopes her infant will look at her, and because of the infant's ability to interact in the first hour of life during the prolonged period of the quiet alert state. There is a beautiful interlocking at this early time between the mother's interest in the infant's eyes and the baby's capability for eye-to-eye interaction.

Kramer[33a] and associates answered the question about the effects of early breastfeeding and the BFHI on more than 17,000 mother-infant pairs in Belarus. The patients were randomized into two groups, traditional breastfeeding as practiced in Belarus or BFHI (all 10 steps including breastfeeding in the first hour after birth and rooming in). The BFHI group breastfed significantly more over the first year after birth than the other cohort.

A possible key to understanding what is happening physiologically in these first minutes and hours comes from investigators who noted that if the lips of the infant touch the mother's nipple in the first hour of life, a mother will decide to keep her baby in her room 100 minutes longer on the second and third day during her hospital stay than another mother who does not have contact until later.[58] This decision may be explained in part by small infusions of oxytocin (the love hormone) occurring in both the infant's and the mother's brain when breast feeding occurs. It is of interest that in sheep, dilation of the cervical os during birth releases oxytocin within the brain that, acting on receptor sites, appears to be important for the initiation of maternal behavior and for the facilitation of bonding between mother and baby.[28] In humans, there is a blood-brain barrier for oxytocin, and only small amounts reach the brain via the bloodstream. However, multiple oxytocin receptors in the brain are supplied by production in the brain. Increased levels of brain oxytocin result in slight sleepiness, calmness, a raised pain threshold, and feelings of increased love for the infant. It appears that during breast feeding, raised blood levels of oxytocin are associated with increased brain levels; women who exhibit the largest plasma oxytocin concentrations are the sleepiest.

Measurements of plasma oxytocin levels in 18 healthy women who had their babies on their chests with skin-to-skin contact immediately after birth showed significant elevations compared with the antepartum levels, and a return to antepartum levels at 60 minutes. For most women, a significant and spontaneous peak concentration was recorded about 15 minutes after delivery, with expulsion of the placenta.[41] Most mothers had several peaks of oxytocin up to 1 hour after delivery. Not only may the vigorous oxytocin release after delivery and with breast feeding help contract the uterine muscle to prevent bleeding but it also may enhance bonding of the mother to her infant.

We hypothesize that a cascade of interactions between the mother and the baby occurs during this early period, locking them together and ensuring further development of attachment. The remarkable change in maternal behavior with just the touch of the infant's lips on the mother's nipple; the effects of additional time for mother-infant contact; the reduction in abandonment with early contact, suckling, and rooming-in; and the increased maternal oxytocin levels shortly after birth in conjunction with known sensory, physiologic, immunologic, and behavioral mechanisms all contribute to the attachment of the mother to the infant. These assessments and measurements have been made during labor, birth, and the immediate postnatal period, and at the beginning breast feedings. They provide a compelling rationale for major changes in care in the perinatal period for both mother and infant. These findings fit together to form a new way to view the mother-infant dyad.

THE FIRST DAYS OF LIFE

Immediately after the birth, parents enter a unique period in which their attachment to their infant usually begins to blossom and in which events may have many effects on the family. The first feelings of love for the infant are not necessarily instantaneous with the initial contact. Many mothers have shared with us their distress and disappointment when they did not experience feelings of love for their baby in the first minutes or hours after birth. It should be reassuring for them and similar mothers to learn about two studies of normal, healthy mothers in England.

MacFarlane and associates asked 97 mothers from Oxford, "When did you first feel love for your baby?"[36] The replies were as follows: during pregnancy, 41%; at birth, 24%; first week, 27%; and after the first weeks, 8%.

In a study of two groups of primiparous mothers, 40% recalled that their predominant emotional reaction when holding their babies for the first time was indifference.[46] The same response was reported by 25% of 40 multiparous mothers. Another 40% of each group felt immediate affection. Most mothers in both groups had developed affection for their babies within the first week. The onset of this maternal affection after childbirth was more likely to be delayed if the membranes were ruptured artificially, if the labor was extremely painful, or if the mothers had been given meperidine (Demerol).

Information in closely related fields has greatly augmented our understanding of the beginning of parent-infant interactions. Detailed studies of the amazing behavioral capacities of the normal neonate in the quiet alert state have shown that the infant sees, hears,[9] imitates facial gestures, and moves in rhythm to the mother's voice in the first minutes and hour of life, resulting in a beautiful linking of the reactions of the two and a synchronized "dance" between the mother and infant.[33] The infant's appearance, coupled with this broad array of sensory and motor abilities, evokes responses from the mother and father and provides several channels of communication that are most helpful in the initiation of a series of reciprocal interactions and in the process of attachment.

With the mother's strong desire to touch and see her child, nature has provided for the immediate and essential union of the two. The alert newborn rewards the mother for her efforts by following her with his or her eyes, thus maintaining their interaction and kindling the tired mother's fascination with her baby.

Lind and coworkers in Stockholm have shown that a surprising increase in bloodflow to the breast occurs when a mother hears the cries of her infant.[35] In addition, when the infant sucks the nipple, it induces in the mother a marked increase in prolactin secretion as well as an increase in the secretion of oxytocin, which helps contract the uterus and decrease bleeding.

A SENSITIVE PERIOD

The period of labor, birth, and the following several days can probably best be defined as a sensitive period. During this perinatal period, the mother and probably the father are strongly influenced by the quality of care they themselves receive. The more appropriately and humanely the mother is cared for, the more sensitive she is 6 weeks later in the care of her own infant.

Winnicott reported a special mental state of the mother in the perinatal period that involves a greatly increased sensitivity to, and focus on, the needs of the baby.[59] He indicated that this state of "primary maternal preoccupation" starts near the end of pregnancy and continues for a few weeks after the birth of the baby. A mother needs nurturing support and a protected environment to develop and maintain this state. This special preoccupation and the openness of the mother to her baby are probably related to the bonding process. Winnicott wrote that "only if a mother is sensitized in the way I am describing, can she feel herself into her infant's place, and so meet the infant's needs." In the state of "primary maternal preoccupation,"[29] the mother is better able to sense and provide what her new infant has signaled, which is her primary task. If she senses the needs and responds to them in a sensitive and timely manner, mother and infant will establish a pattern of synchronized and mutually rewarding interactions. It is our hypothesis that as the mother-infant pair continues this dance pattern day after day, the infant will develop a secure attachment.

This heightened sensitivity might explain observations by Kaitz and colleagues.[22,23] In an innovative and well-designed series of studies, they investigated whether normal mothers were able to discriminate their own babies from other infants on the basis of smell, touch, face recognition, or cry recognition after several hours with their infants. They tested each sense separately and noted that smell was the most salient. After 5 hours of contact, nearly 100% of mothers were able to recognize the smell of their own infant. Parturient women know their infant's distinctive features after minimal exposure using olfactory and tactile cues, whereas discrimination based on sight and sound takes longer to develop. Kaitz and colleagues suggested that this order may reflect a fundamental property we share with species other than humans.

The clinical observations of Rose and associates[48] and Kennell and coworkers[26] suggested that affectional ties can be easily disturbed and may be permanently altered during the immediate postpartum period. Relatively mild conditions in the newborn (e.g., slight elevations of bilirubin levels, slow feeding, need for additional oxygen for 1 to 2 hours, and the need for incubator care in the first 24 hours for mild respiratory distress) appear to affect the relationship between mother and infant. The mother's behavior is often disturbed during the first year or more of the infant's life, even though the infant's problems are completely resolved before discharge and often within a few hours. That early events have long-lasting effects is a principle of the attachment process. A mother's anxieties about her baby in the first few days after birth, even about a problem that is easily resolved, may affect her relationship with the child long afterward. This has been described by Green and Solnit as the "vulnerable child syndrome."[20]

In the past 30 years, multiple studies have focused on whether additional time for close contact in the first minutes, hours, and days of life may alter parents' later behavior with their infant. In many biologic disciplines, these moments have been called sensitive periods. However, in most examples of a sensitive period in biology, the observations are made of the young of the species rather than of the adult.

Studies by Brazelton[5] and others have shown that if nurses spend as few as 10 minutes helping mothers discover some of their newborn infant's abilities, such as turning to the mother's voice and following the mother's face or imitation, and assisting mothers with suggestions about ways to quiet their infants, the mothers became more appropriately interactive with their infants face to face and during feedings at 3 and 4 months of age.

O'Connor and colleagues carried out a randomized trial with 277 mothers in a hospital that had a high incidence of parenting disorders.[42] One group of mothers had their infants with them for an additional 6 hours on the first and second day, but they had no early contact. The routine-care group began to see their babies at the same age but only for 20-minute feedings every 4 hours, which was the custom throughout the United States at that time. In the follow-up studies, 10 children in the routine-care group experienced parenting disorders, including child abuse, failure to thrive, abandonment, and neglect during the first 17 months of life; this compared with only two cases in the experimental group who had 12 additional hours of mother-infant contact. A similar study in North Carolina that followed 202 mothers during their infant's first year of life did not find a statistically significant difference in the frequency of parenting disorders[50]: 10 infants failed to thrive or were neglected or abused in the control group, compared with seven in the group that had extended contact. When the results of these two studies are combined in a meta-analysis ($P = .054$), it appears that simple techniques, such as allowing additional early time for the mother and infant to be together and closing the newborn nursery, may lead to a significant reduction in child abuse. However, a much larger study is necessary to confirm and validate these relatively small studies.

Evidence suggests that many of these early interactions also take place between the father and his newborn child. Parke, in particular, demonstrated that when fathers are given the opportunity to be alone with their newborns, they spend almost exactly the same amount of time as mothers do, holding, touching, and looking at them.[44]

In the triadic situation, the father tends to hold the infant nearly twice as much as the mother, vocalizes more, and touches the infant slightly more, but he smiles at the infant significantly less than the mother. The father clearly plays the more active role when both parents are present, in contrast to the cultural stereotype of the father as a passive participant. In fact, in this triadic interaction, the mother's overall interaction declines. All but one of the fathers whom Parke studied had attended labor and birth, and this could be expected to produce an unusual degree of attachment.

In an interesting and significant observation of fathers, Rödholm noted that paternal caregiving greatly increased when the father was allowed to interact and establish eye-to-eye contact with his infant for 1 hour during the first hours of life.[47] Keller and associates have reported that the group of fathers who received extended post-partum hospital contact with their infants, compared with a traditional contact group, engaged in more en face behavior and vocalization with their infants and were more involved in infant caretaking responsibilities 6 weeks after the baby's birth.[25] They also had higher self-esteem scores than did fathers in the control group.

Parke believed that the father must have an extensive early exposure to the infant in the hospital and home, where the parent-infant bond is initially formed.[44] Parke indicated that the father is much more interested in and responsive toward his infant than U.S. culture has acknowledged.

There continues to be debate on the interpretation and significance of studies of the effects that early and extended contact for mothers and fathers with their infants have on their ability to bond.[30] However, all sides agree that all parents should be offered early and extended time with their infants.[29] An extensive review of this subject can be summarized in this way. The restriction of early postnatal mother-infant interaction (which has been a common feature of the care of women giving birth in hospitals) has undesirable effects.[12] Disruption of mother-infant interaction in the immediate postnatal period may set some women on the road to breast-feeding failure and altered subsequent behavior toward their children.

Pediatricians, psychologists, and others have debated this issue, but skepticism does not constitute grounds for preserving hospital routines that lead to unwanted separation of mothers from their babies. Because such policies may actually do harm, they should be changed forthwith.

PREMATURE OR SICK INFANTS

In the years since parental visiting has been permitted in the intensive care nursery, studies have revealed that most parents continue to suffer severe emotional stress. Several researchers noted that emotional stress occurred even when parents had close contact with their infants. However, despite the anxiety, parents believed the opportunity to have this contact was helpful, and over 90% of parents interviewed were opposed to restricting their contact with their infants. Most parents thought that holding their infant made the infant feel more loved. Observers noted that when infants are transported to a neonatal intensive care unit, most parents experienced grief reactions. It is interesting that the level of their response was unrelated to the severity of the baby's problems.

From interviews and observations, researchers suggested that early parental reactions predicted how the mother would manage with her infant in the early weeks at home. Researchers found that if the mother expressed a fairly high level of anxiety, actively sought information about the condition of her baby, showed strong maternal feelings for the baby, and had strong support from the father, there usually was a favorable outcome.[36] If the mother showed a low level of anxiety and activity, her relationship with her child would probably be poor.

Minde and associates noted that the most important variables are the mother's relationship with her mother, the mother's relationship with her father, and whether the mother had a previous abortion.[38] Highly interacting mothers in the nursery visited and telephoned the nursery more frequently while the infants were hospitalized and stimulated their infants more at home. Moreover, the authors noted that mothers who touched and fondled their infants more in the nursery had infants who opened their eyes more, and they noted a correlation between the infant's eyes being open and the mother's touching, and also between gross motor stretches and the mother's smiling. Minde and coworkers could not determine to what extent the sequence of touching and eye opening reflected the primary contribution of the mother or the infant. Thus, from interviews and observations, these researchers noted that mothers who become involved, interested, and anxious about their infants have an easier time when the infant is taken home.[38]

In the past 25 years, numerous studies have revealed that if small, premature infants are touched, rocked, fondled, or cuddled daily during the stay in the nursery, they may have significantly fewer apneic periods, increased weight gain, fewer stools, and in some studies even advances in certain areas of higher central nervous system functioning that persist for a short time after discharge from the hospital.[19]

Fondling the premature infant for 5 minutes every hour for 2 weeks alters bowel motility, crying, activity, and growth. Gentle massage of preterm infants also results in less stress behavior, superior performance on the Brazelton neonatal assessment, and, more important, better performance on a developmental assessment at 8 months.[18] Several students of young premature infants, including Brazelton,[5] have perceptively noted that when some infants' visual attention is captured by an adult, the baby is so captivated by the experience that the infant may forget to breathe and even become quite blue. Until we have defined more closely the sensory needs and tolerances of these infants, it is wise to observe how the immature infant manages these exciting experiences. It is hoped that in the future, infants will be able to regulate their own environment, just as Als has adapted the environment of each infant to meet individual needs.[1a] As an example, Thoman and coworkers demonstrated that premature infants in an isolette moved and spent more time in contact with a small, breathing teddy bear than with a nonmoving teddy bear.[53] It is interesting that the infants with breathing teddy bears had a greater increase in quiet sleep 8 weeks after leaving the hospital. The long-term effects of altering the early environment of premature infants was emphasized when researchers turned the light out at night in a nursery in England for the last 2 weeks of a hospital stay for one group of infants but left it on for another group.[37] The two groups of infants appeared to be similar until 5 to 6 weeks after discharge. At 6 weeks after discharge, infants whose nursery had day and night cycles for the 2 weeks of hospital stay slept 2 hours longer per 24 hours and spent 1 hour less each day feeding, but 3 months after discharge they were 1 pound heavier than infants who did not have the light out at night.

On the basis of observations of many normal mothers and their full-term infants, Winnicott noted that what the baby observes in the caretaker's face in the early months of life helps the baby develop a concept of self.[60] He noted that some infants have mothers who do not imitate the baby, and thus the babies do not see themselves. He postulated that in these situations, the infant's own creative capacity may atrophy and they may look for other ways to get to know themselves from the environment. Winnicott's important observation was that in normal mother-infant dyads, the mother often followed or imitated the infant.

Trevarthen, using fast-film technique, confirmed these observations in mothers and infants and noted that mothers imitate their babies during spontaneous play.[54] He also noted that the mother's imitation of the infant's behavior, rather than the reverse, sustained their interaction and communication. Detailed analysis revealed that mothers were studiously imitating the infant's expression with a lag of a few tenths of a second; therefore, the infant was choosing the rhythm.

In a series of creative experimental manipulations of infant-mother face-to-face interactions, Field noted that the mother and the normal full-term infant were interacting about 70% of the time in their spontaneous play.[17] However, when the mother was asked to increase her attention-getting behavior (stimulation), her activity increased to 80% of the time, and, strikingly, the infant's gaze decreased to 50%. When the mother imitated the movements of the infant, which greatly reduced her activity, the infant's gaze time greatly increased.

When the babies were preterm infants considered to be high risk, Field noted that in the spontaneous situation, the mothers were interacting up to 90% of the time, but the infant was looking only 30% of the time.[17] If the mother was told to use attention-getting gestures, her activity increased to more than 90% of the time, and the infant's gaze decreased further. If her interactions were decreased by asking her to imitate the baby's movements, the infant's gaze increased greatly. Although generally the mother's activity was aimed at encouraging more activity or responsiveness from the premature infant, the approach appeared to be counter-productive, leading to less instead of more infant responsiveness. Thus, by three different techniques, it appears that mothers of normal infants follow or mirror their infant's behavior for significant periods.

BOX 32-1. Interventions in the Neonatal Intensive Care Unit to Enhance Developmental and Family-Centered Care

- Development of vision and philosophy of care statements in collaboration with all disciplines and family representatives
- Policies supporting parental unrestricted access to their infants
- Utilization of families in a variety of advisory roles
- Innovative family-centered facility design
- Parental presence and participation in rounds
- Parental charting in the medical record
- Preparation of community professionals to collaborate with family caregivers to provide developmentally supportive care
- Parent-to-parent support

Interventions for Parents of Premature Infants

To help parents deal with the stressful situation of having a sick or small infant, several interventions have been introduced. Some involve the parents and infants together, whereas others focus on either the parent or the infant. Various interventions to support families have been adopted by different intensive care units (Box 32-1).

INDIVIDUALIZED NURSING CARE PLANS (See also Chapter 29, Part 2, and Chapter 41.)

To reduce the disruptive effects of the nursery environment, Als and colleagues developed a method of individualized care for the premature infant that takes into account what each infant finds soothing or disruptive during a formal observation.[1] This detailed examination is performed in the first days after birth and becomes the basis of each infant's nursing care plan. Each infant's requirements for light, sound, position, and nursing are determined by this meticulous behavioral assessment. The researchers demonstrated that, when the nursing care plans are individualized to involve the behavioral and environmental needs of infants at high risk or of those who have low birthweight, the infants' outcome is remarkably altered.

In three randomized trials following the procedure of Als and colleagues, infants receiving individualized behavioral management required many fewer days on a respirator and fewer days on supplemental oxygen, their average daily waking time increased, they were discharged many days earlier, and they had a lower incidence of intraventricular hemorrhage. In addition, after discharge, their behavioral development progressed more normally, and their parents more easily developed ways of sensing their needs and responding to and interacting with them in a pleasurable fashion. Parents have an easier time adapting to premature infants who are more responsive. As the infant develops, the parents gain much by assisting with the observations and helping the nurse develop the care plan.

KANGAROO BABY CARE (See also Chapter 41.)
In South America, the United States, and Europe, mothers and fathers have found that skin-to-skin holding of the infant is uniquely helpful in developing a tie to their infant. At the first experience, the mother is usually tense, so it is best for the nurse to stay with her to answer questions and make any necessary adjustments in position and provide measures to maintain warmth such as blankets. However, most mothers discover that the experience is especially pleasurable. After the "kangaroo" contact, some mothers have mentioned timidly that they began for the first time to feel close to their baby and feel that the baby was theirs. Without prompting, one mother said that she was feeling much better because she was now doing something for her baby that no one else could do.

It is our belief that skin-to-skin care is useful in helping parents develop a closer tie to their infant. Properly detailed observations have noted that the infant's heart rate, temperature, and respiratory rate are stable with kangaroo care, and there is no increase in apnea during the daily 1- to $2\frac{1}{2}$-hour experience.[56] In kangaroo care, the premature infant has long periods of deep sleep. Brain wave patterns show two to four periods of "delta brush/hour" not seen in the incubator. Delta brush occurs with synapse formation. Additionally, significant increases in milk output and an increase in the success of lactation have been documented with skin-to-skin care.

Feldman and colleagues described a very useful and valuable study of kangaroo care in Israel with a 6-month follow-up period.[14-16] One hundred forty-six premature infants weighing between 530 to 1720 g were matched for sex, birthweight, age, and medical risk. All families were middle class. Seventy-three infants received kangaroo care (KC) and 73 were controls. At 31 to 34 weeks, the KC group received at least 1 hour per day for 2 weeks of KC, and they were studied at 37 weeks, 3 months, and 6 months of age.

At 37 weeks, KC mothers showed a significantly more positive affect, more touch, visual regard, and adaptation to infant cues, and they reported less depression and perceived the infant as less abnormal; the KC infants showed significantly more alertness, less gaze aversion, longer quiet sleep and alert wakefulness, and less time in active sleep. KC infants showed more rapid maturation of vagal tone between 32 and 37 weeks and more mature neurodevelopmental profiles with greater development of habituation and orientation.

At 3 months, mothers and fathers were more sensitive to the infants and provided a better home environment. KC infants had higher thresholds for negative emotionality and more efficient arousal modulation while attending to increasingly complex stimuli.

At 6 months, KC infants had longer duration and shorter latency to mother-infant shared attention and infant-sustained exploration in a toy session. KC mothers were more sensitive and warm in their interactions, and infants had higher scores on the Bayley Neonatal Developmental Index (KC mean, 96.39; controls mean,

91.81) and the Psychomotor Developmental Index (KC mean, 85.57; controls mean, 80.53). The authors underscore the importance of the role of early skin-to-skin contact of the mother in the maturation of the infant's physiologic, emotional, and cognitive regulatory capacities. We probably should use Kangaroo Care for every premature infant at the critical time of 31 to 34 weeks.

FAMILY-CENTERED CARE IN THE NEONATAL INTENSIVE CARE UNIT

The field of neonatal intensive care has undergone tremendous change in the past few decades. Significant scientific and concurrent technological advances have resulted in dramatic decreases in premature neonatal morbidity and mortality. The growing body of research on the psychosocial sequelae of premature birth has engendered widespread appreciation of the impact of the neonatal intensive care unit (NICU) experience on the entire family unit.

Premature birth is often an unexpected crisis, and it compounds the stressors of a normal pregnancy. Infants admitted to the NICU face significant problems that have the potential to adversely affect family functioning. Parents with infants in the NICU are confronted with several challenges, including the unexpected appearance and behavior of their infant, physical separation from their infant, difficulties in obtaining accurate information about their infant's condition, inability to protect their infant from pain, and, frequently, financial concerns.

In 1992, a group of parents knowledgeable about the NICU from personal experience were invited to meet with a group of neonatal professionals to address problems identified by the NICU parents and to explore possible solutions. "The Principles for Family-Centered Neonatal Care," a document describing the necessary elements of family-centered neonatal care, was published after the conference.[1] Many of the principles laid out in the original document can be found in national and regional organizational statements recommending care that encourages family presence and participation.[1]

The growing consumer interest in participation in the care of hospitalized loved ones, coupled with the support of administrative and clinical leaders, is paving the way for change. The experiences of many NICUs suggest that, despite the strong interest in changing care delivery, the process can be quite difficult.

Successful integration of family-centered care within the NICU requires a comprehensive approach. Family-centered care must be grounded in the vision and philosophy of the organization, supported by the physical design and environment, and adhered to daily in policies and programs consistent with the vision.

The following procedures may be considered:

- A mother and her infant should be kept near each other in the same hospital, ideally on the same floor. When the long-term significance of early mother-infant contact is kept in mind, a modification of restrictions and territorial traditions usually can be arranged.[2,29]

- If the baby does have to be moved to a hospital with an intensive care unit, the mother should be given a chance to see and touch her infant, even if the baby has respiratory distress and is in an oxygen hood or on a respirator. The house officer or the attending physician should stop in the mother's room with the transport incubator and encourage her to touch and look at her baby. A comment about the baby's strength and healthy features may be long remembered and appreciated.

- In such a transfer, the father is encouraged to use his own transportation so that he can stay in the premature unit for a few hours. This extra time allows him to get to know the nurses and physicians in the unit, to find out how the infant is being treated, and to talk with the physician about what is expected to happen to the baby in the succeeding days. He is asked to act as a link between the medical team and his family by relaying information to the baby's mother. It is suggested that he take an instant photograph, even if the infant is on a respirator, so that he can describe the baby's care in detail to the baby's mother.

- In many communities, the mother is transported from the community hospital before the delivery to the maternity division of the medical center, so she can be with her baby after the birth.

- A mother should be permitted to enter the premature nursery as soon as she is able to maneuver easily. When she makes her first visit, it is important to anticipate that she may become faint or dizzy when she looks at her infant. A stool should be nearby so that she can sit down, and a nurse stays at her side during most of the visit, describing in detail the procedures being carried out, such as respiration and heart rate monitoring, the umbilical catheter and endotracheal tube placement, feeding through the various infusion lines, and the functioning of the incubator and ventilator.

- Grandparents, siblings, and other relatives are encouraged to view the infant through the glass window of the nursery so they will begin to know and to feel attached to the infant. It is important to arrange for the grandparents and special close friends or relatives to enter the nursery and visit the baby, particularly when the baby is very ill or expected to die, so that they can provide firsthand support and understanding to the parents. Selectively allow siblings to enter the nursery if it will truly relieve (and not aggravate) a child's confusion and anxiety.

- It is necessary to find out what the mother believes is going to happen or what she has read about any problem that may have developed. Move at her pace during any discussion to ensure her understanding.

- In discussing the infant's condition by telephone with the mother who is still in the referring hospital, ask the father to stand nearby so that both can be spoken to at the same time and they can hear the same message. This group communication reduces misunderstanding and usually is helpful in assuring the mother that we are telling her the whole story.

- If the sick infant has a reasonable chance of survival, be cautiously optimistic with the parents from the beginning. No evidence has shown that the parents will be harmed by early optimism if a favorable prediction proves to be incorrect and the baby expires. Parents can almost always be prepared before the baby actually dies. If the infant lives and the physician has been pessimistic, it is more difficult for parents to become closely attached. This recommendation may be contrary to many past customs and places a heavy burden on the physician. If the infant does expire, continue to work with the mother and father and help them with their mourning reactions.

- Once the possibility that a baby has brain damage has been mentioned, the parents will not forget it. Therefore, unless convinced that the baby is damaged, do not mention the possibility of any brain damage or retardation to the parents.

- If there is a clear objective finding such as a cardiac abnormality or a specific congenital malformation, there is no reason to hide it from the parents.

- If a mother visits the nursery fewer than three times in 2 weeks, the chance of her developing a mothering disorder increases. Therefore, if her visiting pattern[13] is less than that of most other mothers, she is given extra help in adapting to the hospitalization.

- Mothers should look to nurses for guidance, support, and encouragement when they first handle the child. The nurse's guidance in showing the mother how to hold, dress, and feed the infant can be extremely valuable. Often, mothers need special reassurance and permission before they can enjoy caring for their baby. In a sense, the nurse assumes the role of the mother's own mother, teaching her the basic techniques of mothering.

- In recent years, a number of NICUs have formed groups of parents of premature babies who meet for information and emotional support. In a controlled study of a self-help group, Minde and associates reported that parents who participated in the group visited their infants in the hospital significantly more often than did parents in the control group.[38] The self-help parents also touched, talked to, and looked at their infants in the en face position more and rated themselves as more competent on infant care measures. These mothers continued to show more involvement with their babies during feedings and were more concerned about their general development 3 months after their discharge from the nursery.

INFANTS WITH CONGENITAL MALFORMATIONS

The birth of an infant with a congenital malformation presents complex challenges to the physician in charge and to the infant's family. Despite the relatively large number of infants with congenital anomalies, our understanding of how parents develop an attachment to a malformed child remains incomplete. Although previous investigators agreed that the child's birth often precipitates major family stress, relatively few have described the process of family adaptation during the infant's first year of life. A major advance was the conceptualization of parental reactions by Solnit and coworkers.[51] They emphasized that a significant aspect of adaptation is the necessity for parents to mourn the loss of the normal child they had expected. Other observers have noted the pathologic aspects of family reactions. Less attention has been given to the more adaptive aspects of parental attachments to children with malformations.

Parental reactions to the birth of a child with a congenital malformation appear to follow a predictable course. For most parents, initial shock, disbelief, and a period of intense emotional upset, including sadness, anger, and anxiety, are followed by a gradual adaptation, marked by a lessening of intense anxiety and emotional reactions (Fig. 32-4). This adaptation is characterized by an increased satisfaction with the ability to care for the baby. These stages in parental reactions are similar to those reported in other crisis situations, such as with terminally ill children. The shock, disbelief,

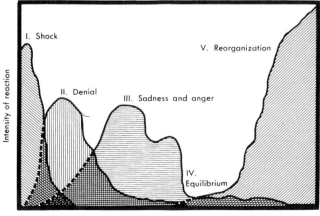

FIGURE 32-4. Hypothetical model of a normal sequence of parental reactions to the birth of a malformed infant. (Modified from Drotar D et al: The adaptation of parents to the birth of an infant with a congenital malformation: A hypothetical model. Pediatrics 56:710, 1975. Copyright American Academy of Pediatrics, 1975. Reproduced by permission of Pediatrics.)

and denial reported by many parents seem to form an understandable attempt to escape the traumatic news of the baby's malformation, so discrepant with usual parental expectations for a normal newborn.[10]

As stated, Solnit and coworkers have likened the crisis of the birth of a child with a malformation to the emotional crisis after the death of a child, in that the mother must mourn the loss of her expected, normal infant.[51] In addition, she must become attached to her living, damaged child. However, the sequence of parental reactions to the birth of a baby with a malformation differs from that after the death of a child in yet another respect. The mourning or grief work apparently does not occur in the usual manner because of the complex issues raised by continuation of the child's life and the demands of physical care. The parents' sadness, which is important initially in their relationship with their child, diminishes in most instances once the parents take over the physical care. Most parents reach a point at which they are able to care adequately for their children and cope effectively with disrupting feelings of sadness and anger. Sadly, not all parents reach the point of complete resolution, and Olshansky has described chronic sorrow that envelops the family of a mentally defective infant.[43] The mother's initiation of the relationship with her child is a major step in the reduction of anxiety and emotional upset associated with the trauma of the birth. As happens with normal children, the mother's initial experience with her infant seems to release positive feelings that aid the mother-child relationship after the stresses associated with the news of the child's anomaly and, in many instances, with the separation of mother and child in the hospital.

Interventions for Parents of Malformed Infants

To help parents deal with the situation of having an infant with a congenital malformation, the following interventions are suggested:

- The infant should be left with the mother for the first 2 or 3 days, if medically feasible. If the child is rushed to the hospital where special surgery will eventually be performed, the mother will not have enough opportunity to become attached to the infant. Even if the surgery is required immediately, as for bowel obstruction, it is best to bring the baby to the mother first, allowing her to touch and handle the infant and to point out to her how normal he or she is in all other respects.

- The mental picture of the anomaly held by parents before seeing the infant is often far more alarming than the actual problem. Any delay during which the parents suspect that a problem may exist greatly heightens their anxiety, and they may imagine the worst; therefore, the baby should be brought to both parents when they are together as soon after delivery as possible.[40]

- Arrange for the father to stay with the mother in her room on the maternity division. This opportunity to support each other, to cry and curse and talk together, is highly beneficial. Use the process of early crisis intervention, meeting several times with the parents, regardless of whether the father stays in the hospital with the mother. During these discussions, ask the mother how she is doing, how she feels her husband or partner is doing, and how the father feels about the infant. Then reverse the questions and ask the father how he is doing and how he thinks the mother is progressing. The hope is that they will think not only about their own reactions but will begin to consider each other as well.

- Parents should not be given tranquilizers. These tend to blunt their responses and slow their adaptation to the problem. A small dose of a sedative at night, however, is often helpful.

- Experience has shown that parents who initially adapt reasonably well often ask many questions and at times appear to be almost overinvolved in clinical care. In our unit, we are pleased by this and more concerned about parents who ask few questions or who appear stunned and overwhelmed by the problem.

- Many anomalies are very frustrating, not only to the parents but also to the physicians and nurses. The physician may be tempted to withdraw from the parents and their infant. The many questions asked by the parent who is trying to understand the problem can be very frustrating for the physician. The parent often appears to forget and asks the same questions repeatedly.

- Each parent may move through the process of shock, denial, anger, guilt, and adaptation at a different pace, so the two parents may not be synchronized. If they are unable to talk with each other about the baby, their relationship may be severely disrupted. It is extremely important to move at the parents' pace. Moving too quickly runs the risk of losing the parents along the way. It is essential to ask the parents how they view their infant.

SUMMARY

Because the newborn baby completely depends on the parents for survival and optimal development, it is essential to understand the process of bonding as it develops from the first moments after the child is born. Although we have only begun to understand this complex phenomenon, those responsible for the care of mothers and infants should reevaluate hospital procedures that interfere with early, sustained mother-infant contact. They should consider measures that promote a mother's contact with her infant and help her appreciate the wide range of sensory and motor responses of her neonate.

REFERENCES

1. AAP Committee on Hospital Care: Institute for Family-Centered Care. Pediatrics 112:691, 2003.
1a. Als H et al: Individualized developmental care for the very low birthweight preterm infant. JAMA 272:853, 1994.
2. Barnett CR et al: Neonatal separation: The maternal side of interactional deprivation. Pediatrics 45:197, 1970.
3. Bibring G: Some considerations of the psychological processes in pregnancy. Psychoanal Study Child 14:113, 1959.
4. Brazelton TB: Effect of maternal expectations on early infant behavior. Early Child Dev Care 2:259, 1973.
5. Brazelton TB et al: The Earliest Relationship. Reading, Mass, Addison-Wesley, 1990.
6. Buranasin B et al: The effects of rooming-in on the success of breast-feeding and the decline in abandonment of children. Asia Pac J Public Health 5:217, 1992.
7. Christenssohn K et al: Temperature, metabolic adaptation, and crying in healthy fullterm infants cared for skin to skin or in a cot. Acta Paediatr 81:488, 1992.
8. Cohen RL: Some maladaptive syndromes of pregnancy and the puerperium. Obstet Gynecol 25:562, 1966.
10. Drotar D et al: The adaptation of parents to the birth of an infant with a congenital malformation: A hypothetical model. Pediatrics 56:710, 1975.
11. Engel GL et al: Monica: Infant feeding behavior of a mother gastric fistula-fed as an infant: A 30 year longitudinal study of enduring effects. In Anthony EJ, Pollack GH (eds): Parental Influences in Health and Disease. Boston, Little, Brown, 1985, p 29.
12. Enkin M et al: A Guide to Effective Care in Pregnancy and Childbirth. Oxford, Oxford University Press, 1995, p 347.
13. Fanaroff AA et al: Follow-up of low birth-weight infants: The predictive value of maternal visiting pattern. Pediatrics 49:288, 1972.
14. Feldman R et al: A comparison of skin-to-skin (kangaroo) and traditional care: Parenting outcomes and preterm infant development. Pediatrics 110:16, 2002.
15. Feldman R et al: Skin-to-skin contact (kangaroo care) promotes self regulation in premature infants: Sleep-wake cyclicity, arousal modulation, and sustained exploration. Dev Psychol 38:194, 2002.
16. Feldman R et al: Skin-to-skin contact accelerates autonomic and neurobehavioral maturation in preterm infants. Dev Med Child Neurol 45:274, 2003.
17. Field T: Effects of early separation, interactive deficits and experimental manipulations on infant-mother face-to-face interaction. Child Dev 48:763, 1977.
18. Field T et al: Tactile kinesthetic stimulation effects on preterm neonates. Pediatrics 77:654, 1986.
19. Gottfried AW, Gaiter J (eds): Infant Stress under Intensive Care: Environmental Neonatology. Baltimore, University Park Press, 1985.
20. Green M, Solnit A: Reactions to the threatened loss of a child: A vulnerable child syndrome. Pediatrics 34:58, 1964.
21. Hodnett ED et al: Caregiver support for women during childbirth [review]. Cochrane Database Syst Rev Issue 3, 2003.
22. Kaitz M et al: Mothers' recognition of their olfactory cues. Dev Psychobiol 20:587, 1987.
23. Kaitz M et al: Postpartum women can recognize their infants by touch. Dev Psychol 23:35, 1992.
24. Kattwinkel J (ed): Textbook of Neonatal Resuscitation, 4th ed. Elk Grove Village, Ill, American Academy of Pediatrics and American Heart Association, 2000, p 1.
25. Keller WD et al: Effects of extended father-infant contact during the newborn period. Infant Behav Dev 3:337, 1985.
26. Kennell JH et al: Discussing problems in newborn babies with their parents. Pediatrics 27:832, 1960.

27. Kennell JH et al: Continuous emotional support during labor in a U.S. hospital: A randomized controlled trial. JAMA 265:2197, 1991.

28. Keverne EB et al: Maternal behavior in sheep and its neuroendocrine regulation. Acta Paediatr Scand 83:47, 1994.

29. Klaus MH et al: Bonding: Building the Foundations of Secure Attachment and Independence. Cambridge, Mass, Perseus, 1995, p 111.

30. Klaus MH et al: Maternal attachment: Importance of the first post-partum days. N Engl J Med 286:460, 1972.

31. Klaus MH et al: Effects of social support during parturition on maternal and infant morbidity. Br Med J 293:585, 1986.

32. Klaus MH et al: The Doula Book. Cambridge, Mass, Perseus, 2002.

33. Klaus MH et al: Your Amazing Newborn. Cambridge, Mass, Perseus, 1998.

33a. Kramer MS: Promotion of breastfeeding intervention (PROBIT) a randomized trial in the Republic of Belarus. JAMA 285:413, 2000.

34. Landry SH et al: The effects of doula support during labor on mother-infant interaction at 2 months [abstract]. Pediatr Res 43:13A, 1998.

35. Lind J et al: The effect of cry stimulus on the temperature of the lactating breast primipara: A thermographic study. In Morris N (ed): Psychosomatic Medicine in Obstetrics and Gynaecology. S Karger, Basel, Switzerland, 1973.

36. MacFarlane JA et al: The relationship between mother and neonate. In Kitzinger S et al (eds): The Place of Birth. New York, Oxford University Press, 1978.

37. Mann NP et al: Effect of night and day on preterm infants in a newborn nursery: A randomised trial. Br Med J 293:1265, 1986.

38. Minde K et al: Mother-child relationships in the premature nursery: An observational study. Pediatrics 61:373, 1978.

39. Moberg KU: The Oxytocin Factor: Tapping the Hormone of Calm, Love, and Healing. Cambridge, Mass, Da Capo Press, 2003.

40. National Association for Mental Health Working Party: The birth of an abnormal child: Telling the parents. Lancet 2:1075, 1971.

41. Nissen E et al: Elevation of oxytocin levels postpartum in women. Acta Obstet Gynecol Scand 74:530, 1995.

42. O'Connor S et al: Reduced incidence of parenting inadequacy following rooming-in. Pediatrics 66:176, 1980.

43. Olshansky S: Chronic sorrow: A response to having a mentally defective child. Social Casework 43:190, 1962.

44. Parke RD: Fatherhood. Cambridge, Mass, Harvard University Press, 1996.

45. Righard L et al: Effect of delivery room routines on success of first breast-feed. Lancet 336:1105, 1990.

46. Robson K et al: Delayed onset of maternal affection after childbirth. Br J Psychiatry 136:347, 1980.

47. Rödholm M: Effects of father-infant postpartum contact on their interaction 3 months after birth. Early Hum Dev 5:79, 1981.

48. Rose J et al: The evidence for a syndrome of "mothering disability" consequent to threats to the survival of neonates: A design for hypothesis testing including prevention in a prospective study. Am J Dis Child 100:776, 1960.

49. Scott KD et al: A comparison of intermittent and continuous support during labor: A meta-analysis. Am J Obstet Gynecol 180:1054, 1999.

50. Siegel E et al: Hospital and home support during infancy: Impact on maternal attachment, child abuse and neglect, and health care utilization. Pediatrics 66:183, 1980.

51. Solnit AJ et al: Mourning and the birth of a defective child. Psychoanal Study Child 16:523, 1961.

52. Sosa R et al: The effect of a supportive companion on perinatal problems, length of labor, and mother-infant interaction. N Engl J Med 303:597, 1980.

53. Thoman EB et al: Premature infants seek rhythmic stimulation, and the experience stimulates neurobehavioral development. J Dev Behav Pediatr 12:11, 1991.

54. Trevarthen C: Descriptive analysis of infant communicative behavior. In Schaffer HR (ed): Studies in Mother-Infant Interaction. New York, Academic Press, 1977.

55. Varendi H et al: Attractiveness of amniotic fluid odor: Evidence of prenatal learning? Acta Paediatrica 85:1223, 1996.

56. Whitelaw A: Kangaroo baby care: Just a nice experience or an important advance for preterm infants? Pediatrics 85:604, 1990.

57. Widström AM et al: Gastric suction in healthy infants: Effects on circulation and developing feeding behavior. Acta Paediatr Scand 76:566, 1987.

58. Widström AM et al: Short term effects of early suckling and touch of the nipple on maternal behavior. Early Hum Dev 21:153, 1990.

59. Winnicott DW: Collected Papers: Through Paediatrics to Psycho-Analysis. New York, Basic Books, 1958.

60. Winnicott DW: Playing and Reality. London, Tavistock, 1971.

61. Wolman WL et al: Postpartum depression and companionship in the clinical birth environment: A randomized, controlled study. Am J Obstet Gynecol 168:1388, 1993.

33 Nutrition and Metabolism in the High-Risk Neonate

PART 1

Enteral Nutrition

Scott C. Denne, Brenda B. Poindexter, Catherine A. Leitch, Judith A. Ernst, Pamela K. Lemons, and James A. Lemons

Evidence has been accumulating that early nutritional inadequacies have long-term consequences.[33] Providing appropriate nutritional support remains a significant challenge in premature infants, especially in infants with extremely low birthweights (less than 1000 g). Currently, nearly all such infants experience significant growth retardation during their stay in the neonatal intensive care unit.[29]

Achieving full and consistent enteral nutrition in infants with extremely low birthweights is particularly challenging, given the inherent problems of immature gut motility and function. Data about enteral feeding in this population are limited; most of the information has been obtained from larger, more mature, more stable premature infants. In addition, premature formulas and human milk fortifiers have been designed primarily for this more mature population. This chapter reviews the available evidence on enteral feeding, concentrating on high-risk infants. Recommendations regarding infants with extremely low birthweights are largely extrapolated from data obtained in larger premature infants.

There is reasonable but not universal consensus that growth and body composition in premature infants ideally should mirror that of a fetus of comparable gestational age. It must be noted that fetal growth is not uniform throughout gestation. The fetus gains approximately 5 g/d at 16 weeks of gestation, 10 g/d at 21 weeks, and 20 g/d at 29 weeks; at 37 weeks, the daily weight gain reaches a peak of 35 g.[54] The body composition changes drastically throughout gestation (Table 33-1). The percentages of body water, extracellular water, and sodium and chloride decline progressively; on the other hand, on a per kilogram basis, the fetus retains progressively more intracellular water, protein, fat, calcium, phosphorus, iron, and magnesium.

Between 24 and 40 weeks' gestation, water content declines from approximately 87% to 71%, protein rises from 8.8% to 12%, and fat from 1% to 13.1%. Glycogen represents 1% or less of body weight throughout gestation; the hepatic stores are about 10 to 18 mg/g of liver until 36 weeks of gestation, and they increase to about 50 mg/g of liver by 40 weeks.

ENERGY REQUIREMENTS AND PARTITION OF ENERGY METABOLISM IN THE ENTERALLY FED INFANT

Energy Balance

Energy balance is a delicate equilibrium between energy intake and energy loss plus storage. Energy loss is the sum of energy expenditure plus excretion of energy-containing substances in urine and feces. Positive energy balance is achieved when exogenous metabolizable energy intake is greater than energy expenditure. Growth is then possible, with the excess energy stored as new tissue, usually fat. If exogenous energy intake is less than expenditure, energy balance is negative, and body energy stores must be mobilized to meet ongoing needs. During the acute phase of disease, the primary goal is not growth but avoidance of catabolism. This is difficult for infants with very low birthweights because of their higher maintenance energy requirements, lower energy stores, and, often, reduced intake.

The estimate of caloric needs (Table 33-2) is based on the assumption that postnatal growth should

TABLE 33-1. Body Composition of Average Appropriate-for-Gestational-Age Fetus or Neonate Weighing 750, 1000, 2000, and 3500 g

	750 g	1000 g	2000 g	3500 g
Gestational age (wk)	24-25	27	33	40
Water (%/g)	87/653	85.4/854	79.8/1596	71/2485
Fat (%/g)	1/7.5	2.3/23	6.5/130	13.1/460
Glycogen (%/g)	1/7.5	1/10	1/20	1/35
Nonprotein energy (kcal)	98	248	1252	4284
Nonprotein energy (kcal/kg)*	131	248	626	1224
Minerals				
Calcium (mmol per kg/total)	140/105	145/145	170/340	210/735
Chloride (mmol per kg/total)	69/52	66/66	60/120	48/170
Copper (mg per kg/total)	3.6/2.7	3.8/3.8	4/8.1	4.1/14.3
Iron (mg per kg/total)	62/46	64/64	70/141	81/283
Magnesium (mmol per kg/total)	7.7/5.8	8/8	8.2/16.5	8.7/30
Phosphorus (mmol per kg/total)	105/80	115/115	130/260	160/560
Potassium (mmol per kg/total)	42/32	42/42	42/85	42/150
Sodium (mmol per kg/total)	95/71	90/90	82/164	79/275
Zinc (mg per kg/total)	17.7/13.3	17.6/3.8	16.9/33.8	15.3/53.6

*Assuming 4.1 kcal/g of glycogen and 9 kcal/g of fat.
Modified from Usher R and McLean F: Intrauterine growth of live-born Caucasian infants at sea level: Standards obtained from measurements in 7 dimensions of infants born between 25 and 44 weeks of gestation. J Pediatr 74:901, 1969; ESPGAN Committee on Nutrition of the Preterm Infant: Guidelines on Infant Nutrition. Acta Paediatr Scand Suppl 262:1, 1987; and Ziegler EE et al: Acta Paediatr Scand 299(Suppl):90, 1982.

TABLE 33-2. Estimated Energy Requirements for Growing, Preterm Infants

FACTOR	kcal/kg/d
Energy expenditure	
Resting metabolic rate	40-60
Activity	0-5
Thermoregulation	0-5
Synthesis/energy cost of growth	15
Energy stored	20-30
Energy excreted	15
Estimated total energy requirement	90-120

approximate the in utero growth of a normal fetus of the same postconceptional age. These needs do not take into account the increased caloric requirements of sick premature infants.

Energy Losses

Energy is lost either by excretion or by expenditure. The energy in excreta is lost mainly as fecal fat. In preterm infants receiving full enteral feeding, approximately 90% of energy intake is absorbed. This measure

of absorbed energy is remarkably consistent across many studies (90% ± 3%; range, 84% to 97%).

Usual measurements of total energy expenditure include the energy used to maintain basal metabolic rate (BMR), as well as the postprandial increase in energy expenditure (thermic effect of food- or diet-induced thermogenesis), physical activity, and energy for the synthesis of new tissue.[13,41]

BMR is the largest component of energy expenditure and includes energy requirements for basic cellular and tissue processes. In a critically ill patient, it also includes a "disease factor." Little is known about this component in neonates, but it may contribute significantly to the BMR in neonates with fever, sepsis, and chronic hypoxia. Because BMR can be measured only after overnight fasting, resting metabolic rate (RMR) has been accepted as an alternative. Absolute metabolic rate increases as the fetus grows. However, on a weight-normalized basis, the metabolic rate decreases. Thus, the RMR of preterm infants on a per kilogram basis is higher than that of term infants, and the nutritional requirements on a per kilogram basis are correspondingly greater. The energy required for thermoregulation and activity can be minimized by keeping the infant in a thermoneutral environment and limiting stimulation. For example, energy requirements for thermoregulation are negligible under thermoneutral conditions, but routine nursing procedures can increase oxygen consumption or energy expenditure by as much as 10% in stable preterm infants. Both of these components may be of considerable magnitude in a critically ill infant. The estimated RMR of infants with low birthweights, including an irreducible amount of physical activity in a thermoneutral environment, is lower immediately after birth than later, and by 2 to 3 weeks of age, approximately 50 to 60 kcal/kg per day is needed to maintain weight. Energy expenditure ranging from 40 to greater than 70 kcal/kg per day has been reported in growing infants with very low birthweights.[41] In extremely preterm (26 weeks' gestation) infants requiring mechanical ventilation at 3 to 5 weeks of age, energy expenditure rates of about 90 kcal/kg per day have been measured. Estimates of RMR for healthy, term infants range from 43 to 60 kcal/kg per day.[31]

The level of energy intake and diet composition determine the magnitude of diet-induced thermogenesis, which represents the energy required for transport, metabolism, and conversion of nutrients into stored energy. Estimates of diet-induced thermogenesis in enterally fed preterm infants vary considerably, but this component of expenditure is probably small (2 to 5 kcal/kg per day).[41]

Because neonates sleep 80% to 90% of the time, the energy expended in physical activity is a smaller component of energy expenditure in neonates than in adults. It has been estimated that activity contributes approximately 10% (range, 3% to 17%) to total energy expenditure in the neonatal period. One study[51] directly measured the energy expended in physical activity in stable preterm infants through the use of long-period respiratory calorimetry to measure total energy expenditure and a force platform to measure work output. The energy expended in physical activity was measured at 2.4 kcal/kg per day, approximately 3.5% of total energy expenditure. Although the average magnitude of this component is small, it may have a significant impact on growth in irritable infants with poor responses to nursing care and interventions.

The energy expenditure for growth includes both the energy content of the new tissue deposited (energy stored) and the energy required for the formation of that tissue (metabolic cost of growth) and is therefore largely determined by the composition of the tissue synthesized. The cost of tissue synthesis varies considerably. The cost of depositing absorbed dietary fat into adipose tissue is much less than that of synthesizing new protein. The cost of synthesizing fat from carbohydrate or protein also is considerably greater than that of simply depositing absorbed dietary fat. During growth, a mixture of fat and protein is deposited simultaneously. The total cost of growth has been estimated to be 4 to 6 kcal/g,[41] of which 1 kcal/g is oxidized for tissue synthesis.

Total energy expenditure is affected by several factors, assuming a thermoneutral environment and minimal interference from nursing procedures. Increases in metabolic rate with postnatal age are influenced primarily by energy intake and weight gain. Energy expenditure increases with increases in metabolizable energy intake, indicating increased substrate oxidation or tissue synthesis. Van Aerde[55] observed that about one fourth of each additional kilocalorie absorbed is expended. If the preterm infant is growing at the same rate as the fetus during the third trimester—that is, gaining approximately 15 g/kg per day—then about 15% of the total energy intake is used for synthesis of new tissue.

Energy Storage

Energy storage is a linear function of metabolizable intake, and the accretion rate for energy is related more to the level of metabolizable energy intake than to diet composition. Energy requirements for energy storage are difficult to predict. The increase in tissue mass during growth includes the energy stored as protein, carbohydrate (usually less than 1% of body weight), and fat. Therefore, the energy stored can be assumed to equal the sum of the cost of protein plus fat gain. The energy storage component of the energy balance equation is a function of the composition of weight gain, which in turn is a function of protein and energy intake and is likely to be quite variable. Therefore, the energy intake required to produce a specific rate of weight gain cannot be predicted without specifying the composition of that weight gain. From the point of view of energy storage, protein is a poor material, because a small quantity of energy is stored per gram of weight gain. Approximately the same amount of energy is deposited in 1 g of fat tissue as in about 8 g of lean tissue.

Most studies of enterally fed preterm infants receiving either human milk or formula report a higher rate of energy storage per gram of weight gain than that estimated for the fetus.[41] This may reflect an adaptation to extrauterine life, and if so, this model may be inappropriate for simulating rates of intrauterine energy and fat accretion. However, the effect of a large amount of weight gained as fat and the optimal rate of weight gain for these infants are presently unknown.[41]

Energy Intake

Caloric requirements for healthy neonates are based on measurements of minimal metabolic rates and on theoretical estimates of caloric needs for normal physiologic functions.[31] These studies revealed that the total daily energy requirements for full-term infants increase sharply from fetal levels during the first 48 hours of life and continue to increase at a lower rate until the end of the second week of life, reaching a value of 100 to 120 kcal/kg per day. Unlike that for full-term infants, the optimal caloric requirement for infants with very or extremely low birthweights is more difficult to define and is still to be determined for those infants and for critically ill neonates.

Preterm infants have limited total body energy stores, so providing adequate early energy resources is more crucial for preterm neonates than for full-term infants, even without considering their greater normalized rate of in utero growth. Lacking a better standard, nutritionists have adopted the concept that the in utero growth and accretion rate is ideal. Absolute weight gain increases progressively over the second half of gestation; however, the weight-normalized weight gain decreases during this period. Thus, nutritional requirements for fetal growth, when estimated from the specific weight of the fetus, are actually much higher at 24 to 28 weeks' gestation than they are at term.[13] Furthermore, actual weight gain is an underestimate of nutritional requirements, because changes in body composition during this period are not considered. The total water content of the fetus decreases from 90% at 20 weeks to 75% at term, and the size and number of cells increase during this period. Higher weight-normalized nutrient intakes are necessary to produce growth in infants with extremely low birthweights compared with older, more mature infants. Prenatal growth rate and body composition also may influence postnatal nutritional requirements. Greater weight-specific growth rates of 10th-percentile infants who are small for gestational age compared with those of 90th-percentile infants who are large for gestational age have been shown, suggesting that infants who are small for gestational age may require more nutrient intake per kilogram of body weight than larger infants.

According to the energy balance equation, the energy requirement for maintenance of existing weight and body composition is equal to energy expenditure. Individual infants vary in their activity, in their ease of achieving basal energy expenditure at thermoneutrality, and in their efficiency of nutrient absorption. Enteral intakes of 120 or 130 kcal/kg per day have been recommended, as this allows most infants with low birthweights to grow at 15 to 20 g/d—growth rates similar to those achieved in utero.[2,31] Increasing the energy intake to 140 to 150 kcal/kg per day has been shown to increase weight gain and triceps-subscapular skinfold thickness but has no effect on gain in length or head circumference or in nitrogen retention.[56] Most preterm infants achieve acceptable weight gain at these levels of energy intake. Infants who are small for gestational age or infants with diseases that increase energy requirements may need higher intakes to achieve the same growth rates. Newborn infants with growth retardation often require an increased caloric intake for growth because of both higher maintenance energy needs and higher energy costs of new tissue synthesis.

The American Academy of Pediatrics[2] and the Canadian Paediatric Society[39] have recommended an average energy intake of 105 to 130 kcal/kg per day. At present, no valid recommendations can be made with regard to the optimal energy requirements of infants with extremely low birthweights or of critically ill infants, except that their energy requirements may be higher than those of stable, growing infants with very low birthweights. On the basis of the limited available data, a target enteral energy intake of 130 to 140 kcal/kg per day may be reasonable for infants with extremely low birthweights.[13]

CARBOHYDRATE REQUIREMENTS IN THE ENTERALLY FED INFANT

Lactose is the predominant carbohydrate in human milk (6.2 to 7.2 g/dL) and supplies 40% to 50% of the caloric content. Lactose is hydrolyzed to glucose and galactose in the small intestine by β-galactosidase (lactase). Intestinal lactase activities in premature infants at 34 weeks' gestational age are approximately 30% of those of term infants.[25] Despite low lactase activities in premature infants, lactose is well tolerated by premature infants, and stable isotope data suggest efficient lactose digestion.[25] However, most premature infant formulas include glucose polymers as a significant source of carbohydrate; these glucose polymers are digested by α-glucosidases, which achieve 70% of adult activity between 26 and 34 weeks' gestation. In addition, salivary and mammary amylases may contribute to glucose polymer digestion. Glucose polymers have the advantage of increased caloric density without a rise in osmolality, and they may also enhance gastric emptying.

PROTEIN REQUIREMENTS IN THE ENTERALLY FED INFANT

The protein content and composition of human milk change throughout lactation: the concentration diminishes from about 2 g/dL at birth to about 1 g/dL for mature milk. Qualitative changes also occur during lactation, resulting in a whey-to-casein ratio of 80:20 at the beginning of lactation, changing to 55:45 in mature milk. Indeed, whereas the levels of casein, α-lactalbumin, albumin, and lysozyme remain constant, the levels of secretory immunoglobulin A and lactoferrin decrease; because these different protein fractions have different amino acid profiles, the content of the individual amino acids also is affected. Finally, about 25% of the total nitrogen in human milk is nonprotein nitrogen, the major fractions being urea and free amino acids.

Infant formula has more protein than human milk. A report by the Life Sciences Research Office (LSRO) recommends that formulas for term infants contain 1.7 to 3.4 g of protein per 100 kcal.[31] In practice, most commercially available standard term formulas in the United States contain between 2.1 and 2.4 g of protein per 100 kcal, which provides infants 2 to 2.5 g/kg per day for the first month of life. For preterm infants with birthweights between 1200 and 1800 g, the protein requirement is somewhere between 2.7 and 3.5 g/kg per day; standard preterm formulas containing between 2.5 and 3 g of protein per 100 kcal can meet those requirements if fluid intake is not restricted. Infants weighing less than 1200 g may require more protein, based on Ziegler's factorial approach. The Nutrition Committee of the Canadian Pediatric Society recommends that infants weighing less than 1000 g receive

3.5 to 4 g/kg per day of protein, although there is a paucity of clinical data supporting this recommendation.[39] However, preliminary studies suggest that higher protein intakes in infants less than 1200 g may improve growth.[14]

Casein-predominant cow's milk formulas have the same whey-to-casein ratio as cow's milk—that is, 18:82. Whey-predominant formulas are made by adding bovine whey, so that the whey-to-casein ratio becomes similar to that of human milk (60:40). Nevertheless, the protein and amino acid profile remains very different from that of human milk. Compared with human milk, whey-predominant formulas have higher levels of methionine, threonine, lysine, and branched amino acids, and casein-predominant formulas have higher levels of methionine, tyrosine, and branched amino acids.

Plasma amino acid profiles reflect protein intake and the composition of the milk proteins. In that respect, infants receiving a casein-predominant formula have higher plasma levels of tyrosine, methionine, and phenylalanine compared with infants fed human milk. Whey-predominant formulas usually produce higher concentrations of threonine. These differences in amino acid concentrations have not resulted in any apparent clinical consequences in either term or preterm infants. Currently, most commercially available formulas are whey predominant.

Protein requirements must be considered in the context of energy intake. Studies in preterm infants have documented that metabolic indexes, energy balance, and body composition of weight gain were better when feeding 115 kcal/kg per day and 3.6 g/kg per day of protein than when feeding either 115 kcal/kg per day with 2.24 g of protein or 149 kcal/kg per day with 3.5 g of protein.[26,31] Therefore, with a caloric intake of 115 to 120 kcal/kg per day, the enteral protein requirement of infants with very low birthweights is 3 to 3.6 g/kg per day. Most of these studies have been done in infants with birthweights between 1000 and 1500 g; consequently, the requirements of smaller neonates are uncertain.

Taurine is considered a conditionally essential amino acid in premature infants.[26,31] Taurine is synthesized endogenously from cysteine and is not part of structural protein. The highest concentrations are present in the retina and brain of the fetus, reaching a peak concentration at birth. Furthermore, taurine plays a role in liver function, growth, and fat absorption. Free taurine is found in human milk in higher concentrations than in maternal plasma, resulting in higher plasma and urine levels in breast-fed infants than in neonates fed unsupplemented formula. There is some evidence that taurine supplementation in infants weighing less than 1300 g allows development of more mature auditory brainstem evoked responses than in nonsupplemented infants at 37 weeks' postmenstrual age.[26,31] On the other hand, no overt disease has been identified as a result of taurine deficiency in infants. Although it is not entirely clear whether supplemental taurine is necessary, almost all term and preterm formulas contain taurine at a level similar to that in breast milk.

LIPID REQUIREMENTS IN THE ENTERALLY FED INFANT

Fat provides the major source of energy for growing preterm infants. At birth, the digestive function of premature infants is not fully developed; preterm infants have decreased gut absorption of lipids because of low levels of pancreatic lipase, bile acids, and lingual lipase.[23,24] Term and preterm infants absorb fat reasonably well because of the development of alternative mechanisms for the digestion of dietary fat. One important mechanism is intragastric lipolysis, in which lingual and gastric lipases compensate for the low pancreatic lipase concentration. By 25 weeks' gestation, lingual lipase is secreted by the serous glands of the tongue, and gastric lipase is secreted from gastric glands. The fatty acids and monoglycerides resulting from intragastric lipolysis compensate for low bile acid concentration by emulsifying lipid mixtures. Lingual lipase can also penetrate the core of the human milk lipid globule and hydrolyze the triglyceride core without disrupting the globule membrane. Human milk provides another heterogeneous group of lipases—lipoprotein lipase, bile salt–stimulated esterase, and nonactivated lipase—which continue, in the intestine, the lipolysis begun in the stomach.

Lipid digestion and absorption are also affected by the dietary fat composition. Fatty acid absorption increases with decreasing chain length and with the degree of unsaturation, meaning that medium-chain triglycerides (MCTs) with chain lengths of 6 to 12 carbons are hydrolyzed more readily than long-chain triglycerides (LCTs), and that fatty acids with more double bonds are absorbed more efficiently. In an attempt to increase the fat absorption of premature infants, the producers of commercial formulas for them have used fat that contains relatively high levels of MCTs that can be absorbed without the need for lipase or bile salts. Standard commercial formulas for healthy term infants do not contain MCTs, and human milk typically contains 8% to 12% of fat as MCTs.[23] Unlike LCTs, MCTs are readily hydrolyzed in the gut, and the released fatty acids are transported across the gut barrier without the need for bile acids. MCTs are then transported directly to the liver via the portal vein as nonesterified fatty acids. In addition, MCTs can enter mitochondria and be oxidized without the need for carnitine-mediated transport through mitochondrial membranes. However, inclusion of MCTs in infant formula remains controversial, because the available data do not support the assertion of improved fat absorption or improved growth in preterm infants.[26,31]

In human milk, fat is transported in globules consisting of a membrane composed of a polar mixture of proteins, phospholipids, triglycerides, cholesterol, glycoproteins, and enzymes surrounding a triglyceride core containing 98% of the fat in milk. The milk fat globules are among the largest structural components of milk, having a diameter of 4 μm in mature milk. The size of the globules increases with both length of lactation and length of gestation, with colostrum having smaller globules (especially in milk of women who deliver prematurely) than mature milk. As the total fat content of human milk increases postnatally, the percentage of cholesterol and phospholipids, both of which reside primarily in the milk fat globule membrane, decreases; in addition, the total phospholipid content decreases as lactation progresses. During the first weeks of lactation, preterm milk is also richer in membranous material than is term or mature milk, resulting in a higher content of cholesterol, phospholipids, and very-long-chain polyunsaturated fatty acids with chain lengths of 20 to 22 carbons (C20 to C22). These membranes act as emulsifiers that allow fat dispersion in an aqueous phase and limit lipolysis and oxidation; heat treatment or addition of fortifiers and supplements might disrupt this emulsion.

The milk fat content and nutritional value of human milk vary with time, and human milk does not always provide a complete source of nutrients for infants with very low birthweights. Its composition and energy content may vary in a pumping session and during subsequent changes throughout lactation. The total fat content of human milk at 3 days' lactation is approximately 2 g/dL; the fat content of mature milk is approximately 4 to 5 g/dL, with large individual variations possible.[8] The triglycerides of human milk are its most variable component, changing with gestational and postnatal age, time of day, duration of individual feeds, and maternal diet. Shifts in the dietary practices of a population result in changes in the fatty acid composition of human milk, because the type and amount of fat in the maternal diet affect the composition of milk fat. Maternal diets low in fat and high in carbohydrate lead to de novo synthesis of fatty acids within the mammary gland, which results in high concentrations of fatty acids of fewer than 16 carbons. Therefore, although the total amount of fat present in the milk remains in the normal range, the fat is more saturated. The protein content of breast milk decreases from about 2 to 3 g/dL in early lactation to 1 g/dL in mature milk. Although a more consistent final composition can be obtained by pooling pumped milk, even pooled breast milk cannot provide sufficient sodium, calcium, phosphorus, iron, vitamins B_2, B_6, C, D, and E, and folic acid to meet the needs of infants with very low birthweights. Studies have shown that such infants have higher rates of weight, length, and head circumference increases when fed fortified preterm human milk than those fed only mature human milk.[31]

Fatty acids represent about 85% of the triglycerides and therefore are the principal component of human milk lipids. Fatty acids in human milk are derived from the maternal diet, de novo synthesis by the mammary gland, and mobilization from fat stores. The fatty acid composition of human milk fat reflects the fatty acid composition of the maternal diet. The long-chain polyunsaturated fatty acid (LCP) compositions of the milk of women in the United States, Europe, and Africa are quite similar, with the exception of higher amounts of omega-3 (n-3) LCP in the milk of women whose diets contain a large quantity of fish. Medium-chain fatty acids (C8 to C10) do not normally account for more than 2% of the fats, even in milk from women who have delivered preterm. Arachidonic acid (C20:4n-6) is the main LCP, and eicosapentaenoic acid (C20:5n-3) is found in small quantities in human milk.[8] Docosahexaenoic acid (C22:6n-3) is the main LCP of the n-3 series.

Fatty acid composition changes with progressing lactation and with gestational age. Most striking is the higher content of C8 to C14 fatty acids and of LCPs in preterm milk as compared with term milk: the content of LCP decreases with increasing postnatal age. This may be an advantage for preterm infants, because shorter fatty acids are easier to digest, and LCPs are essential for brain and retinal development.

LCPs play an important role in the development of the infant's brain during the last trimester of pregnancy and also during the first months of life.[53] The precursor C18 fatty acids for the n-6 and n-3 LCP series are linoleic acid (C18:2n-6) and α-linolenic acid (C18:3n-3). Both are recognized as essential dietary nutrients.[31] These are further elongated and desaturated to form other fatty acids, of which arachidonic acid (AA) and docosahexaenoic acid (DHA) are essential for normal growth and development. Although the capacity for endogenous synthesis of LCP from precursor fatty acids in preterm and term infants was thought to be limited, stable isotope studies demonstrated that both term and preterm infants have the capacity to synthesize DHA and AA.[10,43] However, it remains unclear whether DHA and AA can be biosynthesized in quantities sufficient to meet the needs of these infants. In utero, LCPs are supplied to the fetus across the placenta. After birth, breast-fed infants receive sufficient preformed dietary LCP with human milk.

Although contained in human milk, until recently DHA and AA have been absent in most infant formulas. The effect of adding DHA and AA to term and preterm infant formulas has been an area of active investigation. Randomized controlled trials in term infants have shown no effect on growth.[31,49] The effect of DHA and AA supplementation on visual acuity has been measured in a number of trials using a variety of methods; inconsistent and transient changes in visual acuity have been measured. Most trials have not measured a difference of supplementation on intellectual development. The Cochrane Review of the randomized controlled trials does not support a clear benefit of DHA and AA added to the formulas,[49] and the LSRO report on infant formulas does not recommend their addition.[31] However, on the basis of the presence of DHA and AA in breast milk, the possibility of benefit, and the lack of apparent adverse effects, most formula manufacturers have made available formulas with added DHA and AA.

Multiple randomized controlled trials evaluating the addition of DHA and AA to preterm formulas have been conducted.[18,22,26,31,50] Added DHA and AA has generally resulted in positive or neutral changes in growth, although there are some reports of a negative effect. Findings of improved visual acuity have been inconsistent, but a meta-analysis suggests an overall positive effect.[42] Formula supplemented with DHA and AA has produced positive changes in neurodevelopment measured in infancy in some, but not all, studies. Studies evaluating added DHA and AA have been inconclusive, so the LSRO report assessing nutrient requirements for preterm infant formulas recommended a minimum content of zero and maximum concentrations of DHA (0.35% of total fatty acids) and AA (0.6% of total fatty acids).[31] Currently, most formula manufacturers have elected to add DHA and AA to their preterm formulas.

Cholesterol

Cholesterol is a major component of cell membranes and a precursor in the synthesis of bile acids and some hormones. It is present in human milk in concentrations ranging from 10 to 15 mg/dL, although commercial formulas contain only trace amounts of cholesterol (approximately 1 to 2 mg/dL). The high cholesterol content of breast milk relative to formula is maintained at this level regardless of maternal diet. The groups that assessed the nutrient requirements for term and preterm infant formulas did not recommend the addition of cholesterol to infant formulas because there was no convincing evidence of a beneficial short- or long-term effect of such an addition.[26,31] Furthermore, there is no evidence that added cholesterol would be equivalent to the cholesterol in a human milk globule.

Carnitine

Carnitine mediates the transport of long-chain fatty acids into mitochondria for oxidation, and the removal of short-chain fatty acids that accumulate in mitochondria. Preterm infants may be at risk for carnitine deficiency because they are heavily dependent on lipids as an energy source and because the plasma carnitine concentration in preterm infants is low because of their limited endogenous synthetic ability.[26,31] In preterm infants not receiving supplemental carnitine, plasma and tissue carnitine levels fall even in the presence of adequate precursor amino acid concentrations.[26,31] Carnitine is found in human milk and is currently added to standard term and preterm formulas in amounts somewhat higher than in human milk.

Lipid Content and Composition of Infant Formula

Recommendations for fat content and composition of term infant formulas have been outlined in the comprehensive LSRO report; a minimum fat content of 4.4 g/100 kcal (40% of total energy) and a maximum of 6.4 g/100 kcal (57% of total energy) were recommended.[31] This report also recommended a minimum of 350 mg/100 kcal of linoleic acid (about 3% of calories) and a minimum of 77 mg/100 kcal of α-linolenic acid (about 0.7% of calories).

Infants with very low birthweights are susceptible to essential fatty acid deficiency because they were deprived of fat accretion during late pregnancy and must obtain their nutritional requirements from their diet. Recent recommendations for the fat content of preterm infant formulas are similar to those for term infant formula.[31] The recommended minimum fat content for preterm infant formula is 4.4 g/100 kcal (40% of total energy) and the maximum content is 5.7 g/100 kcal (52% of total energy). The recommended amounts of linoleic and α-linoleic acids in preterm infant formulas are the same as for term infant formulas.

ORAL VITAMIN REQUIREMENTS AND SUPPLEMENTS IN THE ENTERALLY FED INFANT

Vitamins are organic compounds that are essential for metabolic reactions but are not synthesized by the body. They are therefore needed in trace amounts from enteral or parenteral sources. Higher amounts of select vitamins are required by preterm infants, because they may have greater needs for growth or because of immature metabolic or excretory function. A comprehensive review of vitamin metabolism and requirements in extremely premature infants is available.[21]

The recommended oral intakes of vitamins for infants are compared in Table 33-3. For some vitamins, the 1993 recommendations for infants with very low birthweights—a consensus of international experts and researchers—differ considerably from those of other groups.

Vitamins are classified as water soluble or fat soluble, on the basis of the biochemical structure and function of the compound. Water-soluble vitamins include the B complex vitamins and vitamin C. They serve as prosthetic groups for enzymes involved in amino acid metabolism, energy production, and nucleic acid synthesis. Needs are considered relative to dietary intake of calories and protein, as well as the rate of energy use. Water-soluble vitamins cannot be formed by precursors (with the exception of niacin from tryptophan) and do not accumulate in the body (with the exception of vitamin B_{12}). Therefore, daily intake is required to prevent deficiency. Excretion occurs in the urine and bile. Most water-soluble vitamins cross the placenta by active transport; vitamin C crosses by facilitated diffusion. Levels of water-soluble vitamins generally are higher in fetal than in maternal blood and are relatively independent of concentrations in the circulation of a nourished mother. Preterm infants and infants of undernourished mothers have lower blood levels of water-soluble vitamins at birth.[21]

Altered urinary losses resulting from renal immaturity during the first week of life predispose a preterm infant to vitamin deficiency or excess. The need for vitamin C may be greater in a preterm infant who experiences increased urinary losses and lacks p-hydroxyphenylpyruvic acid oxidase, an enzyme that catabolizes tyrosine and is stimulated by vitamin C. Transient neonatal tyrosinemia, however, has not been shown to

TABLE 33-3. Recommended Oral Intake of Vitamins for Infants

VITAMIN (AMOUNT PER 100 KCAL)	AAPCON RECOMMENDATIONS FOR PREMATURE INFANTS (2004)	CONSENSUS RECOMMENDATIONS FOR INFANTS WITH VLBW (1993)	ESPGAN-CON RECOMMENDATIONS FOR INFANTS WITH VLBW (1987)	RDA FOR INFANTS FROM BIRTH TO 6 MO (1989)
Fat Soluble				
Vitamin A (IU)	75-225	583-1250	270-450	1400
With lung disease	—	1250-2333	—	—
Vitamin D (IU)	270	125-333	800-1600 IU/d	300
Vitamin E (IU)	>1.1	5-10	0.6-10	3
Vitamin K (μg)	4	6.66-8.33	4-15	5
Water Soluble				
Vitamin B_6 (μg)	>35*	125-175	35-250	300
Vitamin B_{12} (μg)	>0.15	0.25	>0.15	0.3
Vitamin C (mg)	35	15-20	7-40	30
Biotin (μg)	>1.5	3-5	>1.5	10
Folic acid (μg)	33	21-42	>60	25
Niacin (mg)	>0.25	3-4	0.8-5	5
Pantothenate (mg)	0.3	1-1.5	>0.3	2
Riboflavin (μg)	>60	200-300	60-600	400
Thiamin (μg)	>40	150-200	20-250	300

*Assuming a vitamin B_6-to-protein ratio of 15 μg/g.

AAPCON, American Academy of Pediatrics, Committee on Nutrition; ESPGAN-CON, European Society of Paediatric Gastroenterology and Nutrition, Committee on Nutrition of the Preterm Infant; RDA, recommended dietary allowance; VLBW, very low birthweight.

From American Academy of Pediatrics, Committee on Nutrition: Pediatric Nutrition Handbook. Elk Grove Village, Ill, American Academy of Pediatrics, 2004; Tsang RC et al (eds): Nutritional Needs of the Preterm Infant: Scientific Basis and Practical Guidelines. Baltimore, Williams & Wilkins, 1993; ESPGAN Committee on Nutrition of the Preterm Infant: Guidelines on infant nutrition. Acta Paediatr Scand Suppl 262:1, 1987; Subcommittee on the Tenth Edition of the RDAs, Food and Nutrition Board, Commission of Life Sciences, National Research Council: Recommended Dietary Allowances, 10th ed. Washington, DC, National Academy Press, 1989.

be detrimental to infants. A limited riboflavin intake (less than 300 μg/100 kcal) may be necessary in the first 3 weeks of life in an infant whose birthweight was less than 750 g and who demonstrates decreased urinary excretion and increased serum levels of riboflavin.[20] The 1993 recommendation for vitamin B_6 (125 to 175 μg/100 kcal) is greater than that of the American Academy of Pediatrics (35 μg/100 kcal), reflective of the increased protein needs of infants with very low birthweights, and lower than the upper limit of recommended by the European Society of Paediatric Gastroenterology and Nutrition, Committee on Nutrition of the Preterm Infant (ESPGAN-CON) (250 μg/100 kcal), reflective of the elevated plasma concentrations (approximately six times that of cord blood) in infants receiving this amount.[20]

Fat-soluble vitamins include vitamins A, D, E, and K. These vitamins function physiologically on the conformation and function of complex molecules and membranes and are important for the development and function of highly specialized tissues. They can be built from precursors, are excreted with difficulty, and accumulate in the body, and therefore they can produce toxicity. They are not required daily, and

deficiency states develop slowly. Fat-soluble vitamins require carrier systems, usually lipoproteins, for solubility in blood, and intestinal absorption depends on fat absorption. They cross the placenta by simple or facilitated diffusion. Accumulation takes place throughout pregnancy and depends on maternal blood levels. Therefore, blood concentrations and body stores at birth are lower than normal in preterm infants and in infants of poorly nourished mothers.

The 1993 recommendation for vitamin A for preterm infants is higher than that of the American Academy of Pediatrics and ESPGAN-CON and includes increased intakes for infants with lung disease.[46] These higher intakes are considered safe and may promote regenerative healing from lung injury, possibly reducing the incidence and severity of bronchopulmonary dysplasia.

The recommendations for vitamin D for preterm infants differ significantly throughout the world, with an upper limit as high as 1600 IU/d. Multiple studies have not demonstrated any advantage of high vitamin D intakes, and 400 IU/d appears to be adequate for preterm infants, particularly those who have generous mineral intakes.[28]

Vitamin E in formula, required as 0.6 mg/g of polyunsaturated fatty acids, provides adequate amounts to prevent hemolysis of red blood cell membranes when iron intake is not excessive.[2] The recommended total intake is 3 to 4 IU/d for term infants. Recommendations are somewhat higher for preterm infants; however, pharmacologic supplementation of 100 mg/kg per day of vitamin E has not been shown to reduce the incidence or severity of retinopathy of prematurity, bronchopulmonary dysplasia, or intraventricular hemorrhage.[2]

An adequate intake of vitamin K to prevent bleeding in the first week of life when enteral intakes are low is recommended in the form of a 1-mg intramuscular injection at birth in both term and preterm neonates over 1000 g birthweight.[39] For premature infants weighing less than 1000 g, 0.3 mg is recommended.[2] Term infants can be given 2 mg orally as an alternative. Thereafter, 2 to 3 μg/kg per day or 5 to 10 μg daily is recommended in all babies.

ELECTROLYTE, MINERAL, AND TRACE ELEMENT REQUIREMENTS IN THE ENTERALLY FED INFANT

Sodium, Potassium, and Chloride (See also Chapter 34.)

From calculations based on measurements of renal function and from reported data, a sodium intake between 3 and 5 mmol/kg per day (equivalent to between 3 and 5 mEq/kg per day) is usually sufficient to allow growth in orally fed infants weighing less than 1500 g and of less than 34 weeks' gestation during the first 4 to 6 weeks of life. Sodium concentrations should generally be maintained in the 135 to 140 mEq/L range. The sodium content of human milk is low, and the plasma sodium concentration must be monitored. Supplementation of 2 to 4 mmol/kg per day as sodium chloride may be necessary. For infants who weigh less than 1000 g, sodium and other electrolytes should be measured frequently to determine their needs accurately during the first 2 weeks of life; sodium supplements of 1 to 8 mmol/kg per day are often required. Premature formulas and fortified human milk provide only 2 to 3 mmol/kg per day at full enteral intake. Between 34 and 40 weeks, the requirements fall to about 1.5 to 2.5 mmol/kg per day. Recommendations for sodium, potassium, and chloride are listed in Table 33-4.

Calcium, Phosphorus, and Magnesium (See also Chapter 47, Part 2.)

The peak of fetal accretion of minerals occurs primarily after 34 weeks' gestation, and preterm infants fed low mineral intakes develop poorly mineralized bones. The advisable intakes range from 70 to 200 mg calcium per 100 kcal, 50 to 117 mg phosphorus per 100 kcal, and 6 to 12 mg magnesium per 100 kcal (see Table 33-4). These recommended intakes are 3 to 4.5 times higher for calcium, 5 to 6 times higher for phosphorus, and 1.5 to 3 times higher for magnesium than their concentrations in human milk. Mineral concentrations have been increased in preterm formulas and human milk supplements designed for feeding premature infants in an attempt to meet requirements. Significant increases in calcium and phosphorus content may affect magnesium retention. Several studies have shown improvement of mineral retention or bone mineralization in preterm infants who receive higher calcium and phosphorus intakes than their unsupplemented peers.[26,31]

Consumption of unfortified human milk by infants with very low birthweights after hospital discharge resulted in bone mineral deficits that persisted through 52 weeks postnatally, indicating the need for additional minerals after discharge. Supplemental bioavailable calcium and phosphorus salts may be required by breast-fed, preterm infants until their weight reaches term weight (3 to 3.5 kg).[28] Soy-based formulas in former preterm infants may impair growth and aggravate osteopenia (due to inadequate calcium content).

Iron

Preterm infants are at increased risk for the development of iron deficiency anemia because they deplete their stores from birth in half the time it takes a term infant to do so (at about 2 months of age). Infants with very low birthweights or sick infants who are medically managed with frequent blood sampling lose much of the iron present in the circulating hemoglobin, which is then unavailable for erythropoiesis. The American Academy of Pediatrics, the Canadian Paediatric Society, and ESPGAN-CON agree on a recommendation of 2 to 3 mg/kg per day of dietary elemental iron, begun no later than 2 months of age in preterm infants and continued throughout the first year of life.[2,17,39] Iron intakes of 2 mg/kg per day begun at 2 weeks of age were shown to safely augment ferritin stores in infants with low birthweights without risk of vitamin E deficiency hemolytic anemia.[31] This is achieved with standard iron-containing preterm formulas at full enteral intake. Premature infants receiving human milk require iron supplementation with ferrous sulfate. Higher intakes of 3 and 4 mg/kg per day begun by 1 month of age and continued through age 12 months are suggested for infants who weighed less than 1500 and 1000 g at birth, respectively.[15]

Other Trace Elements

Trace elements contribute less than 0.01% of total body weight. They function as constituents of metalloenzymes, cofactors for metal ion activated enzymes, or components of vitamins, hormones, and proteins. The fetus accumulates stores of trace elements primarily during the last trimester of pregnancy. Therefore, the premature infant has low stores at birth and is at risk for trace mineral deficiencies if intakes are not adequate to support requirements for growth. Immature homeostatic control of trace element metabolism also increases the

TABLE 33-4. Recommended Oral Intake of Mineral and Trace Elements for Preterm Infants

MINERAL/ELEMENT (AMOUNT PER 100 KCAL)	AAPCON RECOMMENDATIONS (2004)	CONSENSUS RECOMMENDATIONS FOR INFANTS WITH VLBW (1993)	ESPGAN-CON RECOMMENDATIONS (1987)	CPS RECOMMENDATIONS (1995)
Mineral				
Calcium (mg)	175	100-192	70-140	130-200
Chloride (mEq)	—	1.7-2.5	1.6-2.5	2.1-3.3
Magnesium (mg)	—	6.6-12.5	6-12	4-8
Phosphorus (mg)	91.5	50-117	50-90	65-99
Potassium (mEq)	1.6-2.4	1.7-2.6	2.3-3.9	2.1-2.9
Sodium (mEq)	2.1-2.9	1.7-2.5	1-2.3	2.1-2.9
Iron (mg)	1.7-2.5	1.7	1.5	—
Trace Elements				
Chromium (µg)	—	0.083-0.42	—	0.043-0.082
Copper (µg)	90	100-125	90	58-100
Fluoride (µg/d)	—	—	—	—
Iodine (µg)	5	25-50	10-45	—
Manganese (µg)	>5	6.3	1.5-7.5	5
Molybdenum (µg)	—	0.25	—	—
Selenium (µg)	—	1.08-2.5	—	—
Zinc (µg)	>500	833	550-1100	420-670

AAPCON, American Academy of Pediatrics, Committee on Nutrition; CPS, Canadian Paediatric Society; ESPGAN-CON, European Society of Paediatric Gastroenterology and Nutrition, Committee on Nutrition of the Preterm Infant; VLBW, very low birthweight.
From American Academy of Pediatrics, Committee on Nutrition: Pediatric Nutrition Handbook. Elk Grove Village, Ill, American Academy of Pediatrics, 2004; Tsang RC et al (eds): Nutritional Needs of the Preterm Infant: Scientific Basis and Practical Guidelines. Baltimore, Williams & Wilkins, 1993; ESPGAN Committee on Nutrition of the Preterm Infant: Guidelines on infant nutrition. Acta Paediatr Scand Suppl 262:1, 1987; Canadian Paediatric Society Nutrition Committee: Nutrient Needs and Feeding of Premature Infants. Can Med Assoc J 152:1765, 1995.

risk of deficiency. Trace minerals established to have physiologic importance in humans include zinc, copper, selenium, manganese, chromium, molybdenum, fluoride, and iodine. The recommended oral intakes for infants are listed in Table 33-4.[2] The trace minerals that are potentially toxic in pediatric patients are lead and aluminum.

HUMAN MILK AND FORMULA

Human Milk

Human milk is the optimal food for term infants because it provides immunologic and antibacterial factors, hormones, enzymes, and opioid peptides not present in alternative infant food sources.[4] The benefits of human milk for gastrointestinal function, host defense, and possibly neurodevelopmental outcome have been well documented.[2]

There is general consensus that human milk is also the optimal primary nutritional source for premature infants. The strongest evidence of the benefit of human milk for premature infants is the reduced incidence of necrotizing enterocolitis.[44] Other benefits include

improved gastric emptying, reduced infections, and possibly better neurocognitive development.[4]

The milk from mothers of preterm infants contains more protein and electrolytes than does milk from mothers of term infants. However, these concentrations decline and approach the composition of term human milk in several weeks. Human milk does not completely meet the nutritional needs of premature infants; insufficient protein, calcium, phosphorus, sodium, zinc, vitamins, and possibly energy are provided by human milk to optimally support most premature infants. Human milk fortifiers have been developed and tested and address many of these inadequacies (Table 33-5). Premature infants fed fortified human milk may have growth rates slightly lower than those of infants fed formula, but they may also achieve earlier discharge.[44] Human milk fortifiers should be used in premature infants with birthweights less than 1500 g and should be considered in those with birthweights less than 2000 g.

Preterm Formulas

Formulas for premature infants have been developed to meet the nutritional needs of growing preterm infants and have been in use for over 20 years. However, the

TABLE 33-5. Nutrient Composition of Human Milk and Human Milk Supplements (per 100 kcal)

	Human Milk			Enfamil Human Milk Fortifier Powder 1 pkt: 25 mL Mature PTHM (Mead Johnson)	Similac Human Milk Fortifier Powder 1 pkt: 25 mL Mature PTHM (Ross Laboratories)	Similac Natural Care (SNC) Fortifier Liquid $^1/_2$ SNC + $^1/_2$ Mature PTHM (Ross Laboratories)
	Term: Mature*	Preterm: 0-2 wk†	Preterm: Mature‡			
Volume (mL)	147-161	149-150	149-150	124	124	136
Protein						
Content (g)	1.5	2.4-3.1	2.1	3.12	2.97	2.44
% energy	6	9.6-12	8.4	12.0	11.9	9.8
Whey-casein ratio	80:20	80:20	80:20	73:27	72:28	70:30
Lipid						
Content (g)	5.2	4.9-6.3	5.8	5.6	5.24	5.6
% energy	46.5	42-55	52	50	47.1	50
Source						
Medium-chain triglycerides (%)	—	—	—	3.1	2.4	25
Coconut (%)	—	—	—	—	—	10
Soybean (%)	—	—	—	—	—	15
Composition						
Saturated (%)	43	41-47	—	38-43	43-49	54-57
Monosaturated (%)	42	39-40	—	39-40	38-39	26-27
Polyunsaturated (%)	15	13-15	—	13-15	11-13	17-18
Carbohydrate						
Content (g)	11.9	8-9.8	9.9	9.52	10.41	10.29
% energy	47.7	31-38	40	38.0	41.0	41.2
Lactose (%)	100	100	100	86	82	75
Glucose polymers (%)	—	—	—	14	18	25
Minerals and Trace Elements						
Calcium (mg)	45	31-40	37	145	180	132
(mmol)	1.1	0.73-0.95	0.9	3.6	4.3	3.2
Chloride (mg)	63	76-127	82	79	114	81
(mmol)	1.8	2.1-3.6	2.3	2.3	3.3	23
Copper (μg)	58	107-111	96	134	289	181
Iodine (μg)	Variable	—	—	—	—	—
Iron (mg)	0.06	0.13-0.14	0.18	1.93	0.58	0.28
Magnesium (mg)	4.8	4.3-4.7	4.6	5.04	12.45	8.67
(mmol)	0.2	0.17-0.2	0.19	0.21	0.52	0.36
Manganese (μg)	0.65	—	1.0	13.22	11.94	7.05
Phosphorus (mg)	22.6	20-23	19	72	98	72
(mmol)	0.73	0.6-0.7	0.61	2.4	3.2	2.3
Potassium (mg)	72.5	81-93	85	95	70	109.5
(mmol)	1.86	2.1-2.4	2.2	2.4	1.79	2.8
Sodium (mg)	22.5	44-77	37	44	50	41
(mmol)	0.98	1.9-3.3	1.6	1.93	2.17	1.79
Zinc (mg)	0.38	0.61-0.69	0.51	1.3	1.7	1.1

Continued

TABLE 33-5. Nutrient Composition of Human Milk and Human Milk Supplements (per 100 kcal)—cont'd

	Term: Mature*	Human Milk Preterm: 0-2 wk[†]	Preterm: Mature[‡]	Enfamil Human Milk Fortifier Powder 1 pkt: 25 mL Mature PTHM (Mead Johnson)	Similac Human Milk Fortifier Powder 1 pkt: 25 mL Mature PTHM (Ross Laboratories)	Similac Natural Care (SNC) Fortifier Liquid 1/2 SNC + 1/2 Mature PTHM (Ross Laboratories)
Vitamins						
Fat soluble						
Vitamin A (IU)	319	413-497	581	1670	1246	949
Vitamin D (IU)	3	0.6-1.9	3.0	191	151	84
Vitamin E (IU)	0.4	0.7-12	1.6	7	5	3
Vitamin K (µg)	0.3	0.29-3	0.3	5.7	10.5	6.7
Water soluble						
Vitamin B_6 (µg)	133	9-129	22	157	279	147
Vitamin B_{12} (µg)	0.04	0.01-0.07	0.07	0.31	0.85	0.33
Vitamin C (mg)	6	6.3-7.4	16	28	44	28
Biotin (µg)	0.9	0.01-1.2	0.9	4.1	33	21
Folic acid (µg)	12	5-8.6	5	35	32	23
Niacin (mg)	0.21	0.2-0.25	0.22	3.9	4.59	2.85
Pantothenic acid (mg)	0.26	0.33	0.27	1.12	2.07	1.17
Riboflavin (µg)	50	14-79	72	332	574	373
Thiamin (µg)	30	1.4-31	31	212	313	151
Other						
Carnitine (mg)	1.04	n/a	n/a	4.33	0.9[§]	0.5[§]
Choline (mg)	13.4	10-13	10-13	8.4-10.9	8.4-10.9	10-11.5
Inositol (mg)	22.2-83.5	22	22	17.9	17.9	13.4
Taurine (mg)	6	8.6	8.6	7.2	7.2	7.7
Osmolality (mOsmol/kg H_2O)	286	290	290	350	385	280

*From Fomon SJ: Nutrition of Normal Infants. St. Louis, Mosby–Year Book, 1993, p 410; Lawrence RA: Breastfeeding: A Guide for the Medical Profession, 5th ed. St. Louis, Mosby–Year Book, 2000, p 738; Ogasa K et al: The content of free and bound inositol in human and cow's milk. J Nutr Sci Vitaminol 21:129, 1975.

[†]From Anderson DM et al: Length of gestation and nutritional composition of human milk. Am J Clin Nutr 37:810, 1983; Gross DJ et al: Nutritional composition of milk produced by mothers delivering preterm. J Pediatr 96:641, 1980; Lemons JA et al: Differences in the composition of preterm and term human milk during early lactation. Pediatr Res 16:113, 1982.

[‡]From Meeting the Special Nutrient Needs of Low-Birth-Weight and Premature Infants in the Hospital (AB100). Columbus, Ohio, Ross Products Division, Abbott Laboratories, January 1998, p 56.

[§]Value for term human milk used.

n/a, not available; PKT, packet; PTHM, preterm human milk.

design and testing of these formulas did not specifically include extremely premature (less than 1000 g) infants. Premature formulas contain a reduced amount of lactose (40% to 50%), because intestinal lactase activity may be low in premature infants. The remainder of the carbohydrate content is in the form of glucose polymers, which maintain low osmolality of the formula (300 mOsm or less with a caloric density of 80 kcal/dL). The fat blends of preterm formulas are 20% to 50% MCTs, a level that is designed to compensate for low intestinal lipase and bile salts. It is not clear that MCTs are necessary in premature infant formulas.[26,31] The protein content of preterm formulas is higher than that of term formulas (2.7 to 3 g/100 kcal), which promotes a rate of weight gain and body composition similar to the reference fetus. Premature formulas are whey predominant, which reduces the risk of lactobezoar formation and may provide a closer-to-optimal amino acid intake. Calcium and phosphorus content is also higher in preterm formulas, which results in improved mineral retention and bone mineral content. The vitamin levels of premature formulas vary, and some may require vitamin supplementation. The composition of a number of preterm formulas is shown in Table 33-6.

TABLE 33-6. Nutrient Composition of Premature Formulas and Postdischarge Formulas (Per 100 kcal)

	Premature Infant Formulas		Postdischarge Formulas	
	Similac Special Care Advance (24 cal/30 mL) (Ross)	Enfamil Premature Lipil (24 cal/30 mL) (Mead Johnson)	Similac Neosure Advance (22 cal/30 mL) (Ross)	Enfacare Lipil (22 cal/30 mL) (Mead Johnson)
Volume (mL)	123	124	134	136
Protein				
Content (g)	3.0	3.0	2.8	2.8
% energy		11	12	11 11
Whey-casein ratio	60:40	60:40	50:50	60:40
Lipid				
Content (g)	5.43	5.1	5.5	5.3
% energy		47	45	50 47
Source				
Medium-chain triglycerides (%)	50	40	25	20
Coconut (%)	20	0	30	15
Soybean (%)	30	30	45	29
Oleic (%)	0	27	0	34
Oleo (%)	0	0	0	0
Docosahexaenoic acid (DHA) (mg)	14	17	8	17
Arachidonic acid (AA) (mg)	22	34	22	34
Carbohydrate				
Content (g)	10.3	11	10.1	10.4
% energy		42	44	40 42
Lactose (%)	50	40	50	40
Glucose polymers (%)	50	60	50	60
Minerals and Trace Elements				
Calcium (mg)	180	165	105	120
(mmol)	4.5	4.1	2.6	3.0
Chloride (mg)	81	90	75	78
(mmol)	2.3	2.4	2.1	2.2
Copper (µg)	250	120	120	120
Iodine (µg)	6	25	15	15
Iron (mg)	1.8	1.8	1.8	1.8
Phosphorus (mg)	100	83	62	66
(mmol)	3.2	2.7	2.1	2.1
Potassium (mg)	129	98	142	105
(mmol)	3.3	2.6	3.6	2.7
Magnesium (µg)	12	9	9	8
(mmol)	0.5	0.28	0.37	0.33
Manganese (µg)	12	6.3	10	15
Selenium (µg)	1.8	1	2.3	2.8
Sodium (mg)	43	58	33	35
(mmol)	1.9	1	1.4	1.52
Zinc (mg)	1.5	1.5	1.2	1.25
Vitamins				
Fat soluble				
Vitamin A (IU)	1250	1250	460	450
Vitamin D (IU)	150	270	70	80
Vitamin E (IU)	4	6.3	3.6	4
Vitamin K (µg)	12		11	8

Continued

TABLE 33-6. Nutrient Composition of Premature Formulas and Postdischarge Formulas (Per 100 kcal)—cont'd

	Premature Infant Formulas		Postdischarge Formulas	
	Similac Special Care Advance (24 cal/30 mL) (Ross)	Enfamil Premature Lipil (24 cal/30 mL) (Mead Johnson)	Similac Neosure Advance (22 cal/30 mL) (Ross)	Enfacare Lipil (22 cal/30 mL) (Mead Johnson)
Vitamins (cont'd)				
Water soluble				
Vitamin B_6 (µg)	250	150	100	100
Vitamin B_{12} (µg)	0.55	0.25	0.4	0.3
Vitamin C (mg)	37	20	15	16
Biotin (µg)	37	4	9	6
Folic acid (µg)	37	40	25	26
Niacin (mg)	5	4	1.95	2.0
Pantothenic acid (mg)	1.9	1.2	0.8	0.85
Riboflavin (µg)	620	300	150	200
Thiamin (µg)	250	200	220	200
Other				
Carnitine (mg)	5.9	2.4	7.7	2
Choline (mg)	10	20	16	24
Inositol (mg)	40	44	35	30
Taurine (mg)	6.7	6	10.7	6
Osmolality (mOsmol/kg H_2O)	280	300	250	25

Specialized Formulas

Occasionally, infants do not tolerate feedings and require formulas specifically designed for conditions of malabsorption or other types of formula intolerance. These formulas are free of lactose and cow's milk protein and provide alternative sources of protein (soy, casein hydrolysates, free amino acids) and carbohydrate (sucrose, corn syrup solids, tapioca starch, cornstarch). Some provide a significant percentage of the fat as MCTs. Specialized formulas are somewhat higher in protein and mineral content but similar in vitamin composition compared with formulas designed for term babies. The vitamin and mineral contents are therefore lower compared with formulas and human milk supplements designed for preterm infants. Multivitamin and mineral supplementation of specialized formulas is generally necessary to provide the recommended intakes for premature infants. Specialized formulas have not been tested in premature infants and therefore are used only temporarily, when necessary. Alimental formulas are preferable to soy-based formulas in former preterm infants. Routine feedings for preterm infants are reinstituted as tolerated.

Preterm Discharge Formulas

It was common practice in the past to feed premature infants premature formula until discharge and then switch to term formula. However, most premature infants are discharged at far below term weight and may have ongoing and catch-up requirements that may not be met by term formulas. Three large randomized controlled trials have compared standard infant formula with a preterm infant discharge formula.[11,34,35] Preterm infant discharge formulas have a nutrient content between preterm and standard term formulas. Improvements in weight and length have been measured in preterm infants receiving the discharge formulas. One study also demonstrated increases in head circumference in preterm infants with birthweights of less than 1250 g who received the discharge formulas.[11] The use of preterm discharge formulas should be strongly considered for premature infants with birthweights of less than 1500 g for a period of 9 to 12 months. Premature infants with chronic lung disease may also benefit from enriched nutrient intakes, especially additional protein, calcium, phosphorus, and zinc.[9] The compositions of a number of preterm discharge formulas are shown in Table 33-6.

Supplementation of Infant Feedings

TERM INFANTS

Supplementation for healthy, term, breast-fed infants is usually not necessary, except for vitamin D. To prevent rickets, the American Academy of Pediatrics recommends that breast-fed infants receive 200 IU/d of vitamin D beginning during the first 2 months of life.[19]

Breast-fed infants usually require an additional iron source after 4 to 6 months of age.[2] Standard infant formulas that are iron fortified (1.8 mg iron per 100 kcal) provide adequate iron for term infants. Current recommendations are for fluoride supplementation only after 6 months of age.[2]

No vitamin supplements are necessary for term, formula-fed infants who consume at least 750 mL of infant formula daily. Term infants with chronic diseases that result in intake of formula or human milk that is less than 750 mL/d may require additional supplementation of vitamins and minerals to meet the recommended daily allowances.

Infants who experience abnormal gastrointestinal losses (persistent diarrhea or excessive ileostomy drainage) often require supplementation with zinc and electrolytes.

PRETERM INFANTS

Daily multivitamin or mineral preparations may be necessary for preterm infants once enteral feedings have been established. Preterm formulas and human milk fortifiers differ in the amounts of vitamins and minerals they contain (see Tables 33-5 and 33-6); therefore, the need for supplementation varies for infants with very low birthweights.

Preterm infants who require specialized formulas or receive standard infant formulas designed to meet the vitamin and mineral needs of term infants able to consume 750 mL/d require supplementation with vitamins and minerals to provide the recommended intakes. Multivitamin supplements that contain the equivalent of the recommended daily allowances for term infants can be given (see Table 33-3). Liquid multivitamin drops do not contain folic acid because of its lack of stability, but it can be added or given separately.

Breast-fed infants who weigh less than 3.5 kg do not consume enough human milk to acquire the recommended intakes of some vitamins and minerals. Therefore, supplementation with a multivitamin, folic acid, calcium, phosphorus, zinc, and iron may be necessary, unless one of the commercially available milk fortifiers is used.

MINIMAL ENTERAL FEEDING

The diversity of approaches to feeding preterm infants underlines the need for studies to dispel myths and find reasonable solutions to the problem of what feeding route to use, which has plagued pediatricians and neonatologists for years. Once suitable total parenteral nutrition (TPN) solutions for neonates were available, many physicians chose to use strictly parenteral nutrition in sick preterm infants because of concerns about necrotizing enterocolitis. TPN was thought to be a logical continuation of the transplacental nutrition the infants would have received in utero. However, this view discounts any role that swallowed amniotic fluid may play in nutrition and in the development of the gastrointestinal tract. In fact, by the end of the third trimester, amniotic fluid provides the fetus with the same enteral volume intake and approximately 25% of the enteral protein intake of a term breast-fed infant.[32]

Over the past 15 years, investigators have been looking at the utility of minimal enteral feedings. Minimal enteral feedings involve hypocaloric, low-volume enteral nutrition that does not contain sufficient calories to sustain somatic growth. Proposed benefits include maturation of the preterm intestine (both structurally and functionally), reduced liver dysfunction, and improved feeding tolerance. There is direct and indirect evidence of a benefit from minimal enteral feedings without an increase in the incidence of necrotizing enterocolitis.

Animal studies have been done to evaluate some of the anatomic, histologic, and enzymatic differences between enteral and parenteral feeding. Levine and coworkers compared rats receiving intravenous (IV) TPN with those receiving the same solution enterally. After 1 week, they found decreases in gut weight (22%), mucosal weight (28%), mucosal protein (35%), DNA (25%), disaccharide activity, and mucosal height in the fasted rats.[30] Other investigators confirmed these findings.[12] Thus it appears that enteral feedings may be necessary to maintain the integrity and enhance the maturation of the gastrointestinal tract.

Studies of preterm infants have evaluated gut hormone levels and the maturation of gastrointestinal motility in response to minimal enteral nutrition. Lucas and colleagues evaluated enteroglucagon, gastrin, gastric inhibitory peptide, motilin, and neurotensin in premature infants; these hormones are thought to be important in producing changes in function or growth of the gastrointestinal tract.[32] In response to small volumes of enteral feedings in these premature infants, significant elevations of all these hormones were demonstrated. Berseth and associates used low-compliance perfusion manometry to evaluate the maturation of motility and found that infants who received nutrient feedings (as opposed to sterile water) displayed significant changes in intestinal motor activity in response to feeding.[7] Furthermore, these infants achieved full enteral feedings and full nipple feedings earlier than did their counterparts who were fed sterile water.[7] Shulman and coworkers demonstrated that premature infants who received early feeding had decreased intestinal permeability and increased lactase activity at 10 days of age compared with late-fed controls.[47,48]

Supported by these animal and physiologic studies, multiple clinical trials evaluating minimal enteral feeding have been performed.[37,52] Although many of these trials were relatively small (60 patients or fewer), the more recent studies included 100 patients or more. Although study protocols varied significantly, mean birthweight was generally 1000 g and gestational age 28 weeks, and most subjects required mechanical ventilation. Early feedings were begun at about 3 days of age and consisted of human milk or formula at 12 to 24 mL/kg per day. The results of these studies were heterogeneous, but three or more studies measured a reduction in hospital stay, days to full feedings, and feeding intolerance in the early feeding group. Other benefits included improved gastrointestinal motility, increased calcium and phosphorus absorption, and reduced sepsis and sepsis evaluations. Adverse effects of early feeding were not observed in any of the studies, and the incidence of necrotizing enterocolitis, in particular, was no different between early- and late-fed premature infants. A Cochrane Review, which did not include the more recent large trials, reported that early minimal feeding produced significant reductions in number of days to full enteral feeding, total days that feedings are withheld, and days of hospital stay.[52]

In summary, the data from these studies support physiologic and clinical benefit from early minimal enteral feeding, without an increased risk of necrotizing enterocolitis. Although a large multicenter trial that more clearly evaluates early feeding may be desirable, such a trial appears unlikely. The available evidence strongly supports initiating early enteral feeding.[27]

METHODS OF FEEDING HIGH-RISK INFANTS

Gavage feeding is appropriate for infants who demonstrate an immature suck and swallowing reflex or a clinical condition that precludes nipple feeding, such as tachypnea or oral-facial anomalies. Therefore, most infants fed by gavage are younger than 34 weeks' gestational age; however, some more mature infants are unable to nipple feed.

The appropriateness of orogastric versus nasogastric versus transpyloric placement has been debated in the past, with current practice favoring orogastric tube placement. Nasal tube placement may result in partial nasal obstruction and secondary hypoventilation. Infants weighing more than 2 kg have tolerated both orogastric and nasogastric tube placement without difficulty. Placement of an anchored orogastric tube is therefore recommended in smaller infants, with transition to nasogastric intubation when the infant's weight exceeds 2 kg. Transpyloric feedings provide no improvement in energy intake or growth and carry significant risks. Transpyloric feedings should be undertaken only if standard feeding procedures have failed, and gastric feeding should be resumed as soon as possible.

The optimal rate of feeding delivery in tube-fed infants has also been a matter of controversy and may reflect regional differences as well as differences in interpretation of the scientific data. Infants appear to tolerate feedings better if rapid gastric distention is avoided. However, continuous drip feedings that deliver milk very slowly have their own potential hazards. Continuous drip feedings may be even more hazardous to infants receiving breast milk, because colonization of expressed milk is universal, and logarithmic growth of bacteria occurs in milk left at room temperature for more than 6 hours. Another disadvantage of continuous drip breast milk feedings is the potential loss of nutrient delivery (up to 34% of the expressed milk fat). Moreover, a large randomized study demonstrated increased feeding intolerance and decreased growth in premature infants fed continuously compared with those fed by bolus.[45] Although some premature infants may require continuous feedings, bolus feedings over 20 to 25 minutes are generally recommended as a first approach. Bolus feedings are usually delivered in equal volumes every 3 to 4 hours for term infants, every 3 hours for infants less than 2500 g, and every 2 to 3 hours for infants less than 1500 g. Gastric emptying may be a clinical problem but is enhanced with human milk feedings and when infants are in the prone or right-sided position. Gastric emptying is prolonged by increasing feeding density.

The substrate used to initiate feedings and the rate of advancement are controversial topics without a great deal of data. There is general consensus that given the advantages of breast milk (including tolerance), it should be the first choice and can be used undiluted. Diluting premature formulas for initial feedings is common clinical practice, but the data supporting this approach are limited. In fact, there is some evidence that undiluted formula may better promote duodenal motor responses in preterm infants.[6] The rate at which enteral feedings should be advanced in infants with very low birthweights is also unclear from available data. A number of retrospective studies suggest that rapid advancement of feedings (greater than 25 mL/kg per day) may increase the risk of necrotizing enterocolitis.[3,38] Two randomized trials compared advancing feedings at 15 to 20 mL/kg per day and 30 to 35 mL/kg per day; no difference in necrotizing enterocolitis was observed between the two groups in either study.[3,38] A recent single-center randomized controlled trial compared two approaches in premature infants: prolonged small enteral feedings (20 mL/g per day for 10 days) and advancing feedings by 20 mL/g per day.[7] A reduced incidence of necrotizing enterocolitis was measured in the group receiving prolonged small feedings. Although this study may not be definitive, a period of prolonged small feedings for preterm infants deserves some consideration.

PROGRESSION TO ORAL FEEDING

Non-nutritive sucking, though having no effect on weight gain or gastric motility, may facilitate the transition to oral feeding.[40] In particular, clinical observation of non-nutritive sucking can help the caregiver assess an infant's readiness for oral feeding. It is standard practice to offer a pacifier during tube feedings to see whether the infant demonstrates autonomic stability and attempts to suck during or between feedings. The infant initially may suck on the tongue or make feeble attempts to place the hand to the mouth, which prompts the offering of an artificial nipple. As the infant begins to suck on the pacifier, a mild baseline elevation of the heart rate generally occurs, followed by a change in the respiratory pattern. As the infant continues to suck, a rhythmic pattern of sucks interspersed with pauses (respirations) usually is established. Swallowing of oral secretions may accompany the sucking bursts and may be heard by cervical auscultation. These are reassuring signs; however, the ominous signals of tachycardia, bradycardia, and apnea indicate that the infant is not ready for oral feedings.

Positioning the infant correctly for the feeding is critical to success. The infant should be held relatively upright, rather than reclined, with care taken to support the back in straight alignment. The head should be supported in the midline, with the shoulders in forward flexion. Premature infants need help maintaining this gentle flexion posture because their movements are usually dominated by extension (a more primitive response). Bundling the infant in a receiving blanket is helpful and allows the infant to pay closer attention to the fine motor task of feeding. In healthy term infants, this feeding posture is assumed without difficulty and is the hallmark of the infant's potent hunger cue.

In the past, feedings were viewed as a procedure involving the transfer of milk from one location to another, with speed and volume the goals. Feeding might better be viewed as a process that involves the active participation of both parties, with successful feeding being redefined as autonomic stability and a feeling of satisfaction. This change in emphasis allows the infant to advance feedings with minimal risk. Routine use of pliable, high-flow-rate nipples is universally cautioned against, because they may be associated with respiratory compromise. A small volumetric container is preferable, because dead space is minimized and a vacuum more easily established. Infants should be allowed to establish their own pace for feeding and should not be prodded by jiggling the nipple or frequently changing the body position. The heart and respiratory rates must be observed closely to detect subtle changes that usually precede apnea and bradycardia.[36] Noninvasive blood gas monitoring is useful in infants who are in transition to oral feedings, but it does not replace careful observation of behavioral cues. State and motor changes are sensitive indicators of the infant's ability to integrate sucking, swallowing, and breathing and routinely are present before more obvious signs of distress.

Sucking and swallowing may be facilitated if the caregiver places a finger halfway between the infant's chin and neck, offering support to the base of the tongue. This gentle, even pressure helps the infant maintain intraoral pressure by stabilizing the jaw, thus creating effective use of the baby's musculature. Some infants also are aided by support of the cheeks, to promote a good seal around the nipple. It is vital that the feeder be aware that the infant may purposely break the seal to catch up on respiratory demands and may be attempting to increase breathing by letting air pass around the nipple. An overzealous caregiver may increase the pressure on the cheeks and tongue base as the infant attempts to breathe around the nipple, exacerbating the infant's distress until the outcome is the all too frequently seen apnea and bradycardia.

The nasogastric tube need not be removed for early feedings, because the infant can nipple feed with it in place. The feeding should be terminated promptly if cardiopulmonary compromise appears, with the remainder of the bolus given by tube. Satiety at the end of the feeding leads to a general reduction in muscle tone, with extension replacing flexion, and is often accompanied by sleep.

Establishing Lactation

The mother's milk supply is directly related to the response of prolactin and oxytocin to breast stimulation. Because a preterm infant often cannot be placed at the breast, mechanical pumping is frequently elected. The larger automatic pumps are designed to cycle 40 to 50 times per minute and require a minimum of breast manipulation. Because these models are favored by mothers and associated with the highest compliance rates, they are often recommended.[5] Double collection kits can be obtained for simultaneous pumping of both breasts, which halves the collection time and prompts increased prolactin surges, enhancing the total milk yield. Specific instructions on rental of breast pumps should be available to mothers in the nurseries where their infants are housed. Third-party reimbursement can be obtained by prescription or by submitting a letter of medical necessity, so that the cost does not interfere with the mother's desire to initiate lactation.

Emptying the breasts with the pump should be attempted 8 to 10 times daily. If a double collection kit is used, pumping takes approximately 10 minutes. Milk collected should be poured into a container large enough to hold the entire expression, and aliquots should be poured individually according to the infant's requirement. Sterile bottle liners were used in the past for this purpose, but milk is easily contaminated when the feeding is poured out. Volufeed containers may be more appropriate and can be supplied to the mother for milk storage. Banked pasteurized milk has substantial disadvantages, including a marked decrease in many nutritional components.[2] Unpasteurized donor milk is contraindicated because of the potential for transmission of infection (e.g., human immunodeficiency virus).

Freshly expressed milk can be fed to infants immediately, which is the preferred method of delivery. If milk is refrigerated, it should be discarded 24 to 48 hours after collection. Milk that is frozen should be thawed by running it under tepid water until it is room temperature. A microwave should not be used for thawing, to ensure maximum preservation of the host defenses. If the breast milk is fortified, this should be accomplished when the milk is at body temperature and just before administration. All thawed milk left over from a feeding should be discarded. Frozen milk is best stored in a refrigerator that is not self-defrosting, because the cyclic change in temperature may allow the milk lipase to partly denature the milk fat, leading to a change in milk composition.

Early Breast-Feeding Experiences

It is suggested that early skin-to-skin contact between mothers and their preterm infants is advantageous for a variety of reasons. Nearly continuous skin contact may be elected for infants in underdeveloped countries where economic constraints preclude intensive care nurseries. Infants born as young as 32 weeks' gestation have demonstrated the ability to coordinate sucking with swallowing and breathing when offered a breast feeding. These same infants, when bottle fed, showed difficulty with respiratory control and frequently demonstrated "cyanotic attacks." Noninvasive oxygen monitoring showed rapid desaturation at the onset of the feed, a response that was greater in the bottle-fed infants. The smaller infants showed the most difficulty with oxygen decline, differing from the breast-fed infants both during and after the feeding. Oral feedings are usually offered once daily, with supplementation by orogastric tube, until the infant reaches the equivalent of 34 weeks' gestation. Supplementation by bottle, if desired, can begin then.

Maternal readiness for breast feeding includes an adequate milk supply, operational let-down, projectile and nontender nipples, and the desire to commence. Enhancing the distensibility of the nipples by 1 to 2 minutes of electric pumping may encourage easier nipple latch-on. If the nipples are not a problem, it is better to let infants begin to suck non-nutritively, so that they are better prepared for the milk let-down. Reverse holds are an excellent choice for small premature infants, because the upright posture and firm, one-handed support facilitate sucking and swallowing. In this position, the mother can easily visualize the infant's mouth when he or she roots toward the nipple and can be aware of the tongue position. The mother should elicit the rooting reflex by gently stroking the perioral area with her nipple, and bring the infant forward as he or she opens the mouth and turns toward the stimulus. Touching the infant's face with anything but the nipple confuses the infant. The mother should compress the skin behind her areola, with her thumb on top of the breast and the other fingers supporting the breast from the underside. This scissors the nipple forward and makes grasping the nipple less difficult. It is advantageous to hold the nipple in this manner throughout the feeding, because the infant may not be able to maintain good position without help. The thumb should be parallel to the infant's mouth, so that the nipple and areola are evenly compressed, allowing for good filling of the lactiferous sinus when the infant drops the jaw between sucks.

The infant can be allowed to establish his or her own pace of sucking without interference. If the post-let-down flow rate is too high, the infant may let go of the nipple or let milk flow out around it. The infant should be repositioned when he or she recovers and allowed to resume the feeding. The clinician should listen for sounds of swallowing during feeding and point them out to the mother, because infant feeding noises are highly reinforcing.

First feeding experiences often involve only one breast and may be brief. A successful feeding is one that both the infant and the mother enjoy, and it should not be measured by the volume consumed. The volume will rise as the mother's and infant's performances improve over time. It is difficult to clinically assess the volume suckled at a feeding. Estimates of intake can be made by weighing the infant just before and immediately after breast feeding. In the days of mechanical scales, weighing was an unreliable assessment and very stressful to mothers. Electronic scale measurements are much more accurate, and most mothers are happy to know the infant's actual intake to ensure appropriate supplementation. The infant need not be unclothed for this procedure, because he or she can be weighed in clothes and blanket both before and after breast feeding. The weight difference in grams estimates the milliliters consumed. Mothers should be cautioned to pump on their regular schedules while the infant is being weaned to the breast, because their supply will diminish if they interrupt mechanical emptying. Routine mechanical expression can be reduced when the infant feeds vigorously, nurses from both breasts at each feeding, and is gaining weight steadily (15 to 40 g/d).

PRACTICAL APPROACH TO ENTERAL FEEDING IN THE INFANT WITH EXTREMELY LOW BIRTHWEIGHT

Many questions regarding the rationale for enteral feeding of the high-risk infant remain partly or completely unanswered. For example:

- Should intrauterine body composition and growth rates be the reasonable expectation, or even the theoretical goal, for infants with very or extremely low birthweights postnatally?
- Are specific components of human milk important in the functional maturation of the newborn infant and, in particular, the neural system?
- How quickly should enteral feeding be advanced in premature infants, and in what manner (volume and concentration)?
- How should feeding protocols be altered by specific factors (e.g., gestational age, respiratory distress, sepsis)?

It is important to develop a reasoned approach to nutritional support of the high-risk infant. Considerable flexibility must be incorporated into such guidelines.

Clearly, the relative risks insofar as they are known must be carefully weighed against benefit. When sufficient data are not available to address the relative risk versus the benefit, we must use our clinical judgment until adequate studies have been performed.

The following general guidelines represent one approach to enteral feeding of the infant with extremely low birthweight. As discussed in Part 2 of this chapter, parenteral nutrition should begin early and continue until full enteral feedings are reached; parenteral nutrition should also be reinitiated without delay when enteral feedings are interrupted.

As parenteral nutrition is being provided and advanced, minimal early enteral intake for the infant with extremely low birthweight should be strongly considered, beginning at day 2 or 3 of life. The requirement for mechanical ventilation or the presence of an umbilical arterial line should not prevent initiating minimal enteral feeding. Breast milk from the infant's mother is the preferred enteral substrate; it is usually provided undiluted and ultimately fortified with a standard breast milk fortifier when the infant has achieved full-volume feeds. If breast milk is unavailable, undiluted premature formulas can be provided; there is little support for the use of diluted formulas. Small aliquots of human milk or premature formula may be provided by the orogastric route on a regular intermittent schedule (1 to 2 mL/kg every 2 to 3 hours). Evidence suggests that such minimal intake is well tolerated and may reduce or prevent intestinal atrophy in this high-risk population.[37] Early minimal enteral intake is not intended to provide significant nutrition to the infant; rather, it is thought to serve as a priming nutrient source for the intestine, sustaining continued functional maturation postnatally.

The appropriate pathway to achieving full enteral feedings in premature newborns is an area that often generates strong opinions based on limited or incomplete data. One common approach is to advance feedings by 20 mL/kg per day if the infant tolerated the previous 24 hours of feeding; this typically results in full enteral feeding (150 mL/kg per day) in 7 to 10 days. This slow rate of advancement is based on several retrospective studies that examined the risk factors associated with necrotizing enterocolitis.[3,38] More recent data suggest that prolonging small feeding volumes for a period of time may reduce necrotizing enterocolitis.[7] Some period (5 to 10 days) of small enteral feedings (20 mL/g per day) should be considered before advancing, especially in the high-risk population of infants with extremely low birthweights. Throughout the process of advancing feeds, adjustments are made if signs and symptoms of feeding intolerance are observed (e.g., residuals, abdominal distention, blood in stools, increased respiratory distress). However, because most of these signs and symptoms are nonspecific, it often is less than clear what the optimal clinical response should be.

A number of other considerations are important for infants with extremely low birthweights as enteral feeds approach full volumes, usually 150 to 160 mL/g per day.

Existing preterm formulas were not designed for this population, and there is evidence that current formulas do not provide adequate nutrients for catch-up growth or produce acceptable growth outcomes.[16,29] Strong consideration should be given to using an increased caloric density preterm formula (27 kcal/oz) by adding both protein and nonprotein calories. Increasing the caloric and protein density can be accomplished in a variety of ways, but none of these have been tested in clinical trials. Sodium chloride supplements (2 to 4 mEq/kg per day) should also be considered for infants with extremely low birthweights on full enteral feeding to avoid the high incidence of hyponatremia. There is some evidence that sodium supplementation may improve growth as well as positively influencing developmental outcome.[1]

Although techniques for providing nutrition through peripherally or centrally placed IV catheters have enhanced our ability to support these infants nutritionally, the risks of catheter-related complications (thrombosis, infection) must be considered. Every effort should be undertaken to make a safe transition from IV to orogastric feedings, and to provide an adequate nutrient supply once full feedings are achieved. At this time, we have limited information about the safety or risk of various approaches. Nonetheless, in view of the lack of adequate data, we should avoid dogmatic approaches to the nutritional care of these infants and encourage additional clinical trials of adequate size to address these fundamental issues.

PART 2

Parenteral Nutrition

Brenda B. Poindexter, Catherine A. Leitch, and Scott C. Denne

The nutritional support of infants with extremely low birthweights, especially in early postnatal life, is almost entirely dependent on the parenteral route. In practice, the nutritional requirements of these infants are rarely met in the first 2 weeks after birth.[58] Growth failure in infants with extremely low birthweights is nearly universal,[78] but there is growing evidence that early use of parenteral nutrition may minimize losses and improve growth outcomes.[88,97] Wilson and colleagues demonstrated in infants with very low birthweights that early, aggressive parenteral nutrition combined with early enteral feeding reduced growth failure without an increased incidence of adverse clinical consequences or metabolic derangement.[99] Parenteral nutrition solutions, although still evolving, have improved markedly from the early days of use, and complications are less common. This part reviews parenteral nutrition, component by component, and provides some practical guidelines for use.

ENERGY REQUIREMENTS IN THE PARENTERALLY FED INFANT

The initial goal of parenteral nutrition is to provide sufficient energy and nitrogen to prevent catabolism and to achieve positive nitrogen balance. As discussed in Part 1 of this chapter, energy must be supplied by nutrient intake to cover two major components: energy expenditure and growth. The calories in parenteral nutrition solutions are provided primarily by carbohydrate and fat. The parenteral nutrition solution should provide sufficient amino acids for protein turnover and tissue growth.

Preterm infants have very low energy reserves because they have low amounts of body fat and low glycogen stores in the liver. Maintaining these limited energy stores requires an energy intake that approximates energy expenditure. Energy expenditure in premature infants is thought to be in the range of 50 to 60 kcal/kg per day, but it must be noted that data in ventilated infants and infants with extremely low birthweights are limited.[77] It has long been appreciated that thermal stresses can substantially increase energy expenditure: under extreme environmental conditions, energy expenditure can increase by nearly 100%.[77] Although thermal stresses can theoretically be minimized, in practice they are likely to be a significant contributor to energy expenditure. Conversely, activity contributes relatively little (3.5%) to energy expenditure in premature infants.[93]

The energy cost of growth in these infants has been estimated to be about 5 kcal/g. To achieve the equivalent of the estimated third-trimester in utero weight gain of 14 g/kg per day, theoretically an additional energy intake of about 70 kcal/kg per day is necessary. However, several studies have shown that nitrogen accretion and growth rates similar to those achieved in utero can be sustained in preterm infants with a parenteral intake of 80 kcal/kg per day if an appropriate amount of nitrogen is provided.[61,101]

A caloric intake of 50 to 60 kcal/kg per day approximates energy expenditure and therefore is a reasonable value for the maintenance requirements of premature infants for the first few days after birth. To support normal rates of growth during parenteral nutrition, 90 to 100 kcal/kg per day is required, with most of these calories supplied by lipid and glucose. Parenteral energy requirements are less than those required for enteral nutrition because there is no energy lost in the stools. It is important to point out that these recommendations are based largely on data from larger, relatively stable premature infants. Energy requirements, both for maintenance and for growth, may be higher in infants with extremely low birthweights.[60]

INTRAVENOUS CARBOHYDRATE REQUIREMENTS

Because the supply of glucose to the fetus depends solely on maternal glucose, cord clamping at the time of birth requires that a number of events occur in order to maintain glucose homeostasis in the newborn. Fetal glucose use in utero matches umbilical glucose uptake, implying that glycogenolysis and gluconeogenesis are minimal in the fetus. Several factors promote glycogen deposition in utero: blunted pancreatic B-cell regulation of insulin secretion, high insulin receptor density, and relative glucagon resistance. In late gestation, the fetus begins to prepare for the transition to postnatal life by increasing hepatic glycogen stores and brown fat deposits. Hepatic glycogen synthesis increases in response to increases in adrenal corticosteroid production, also characteristic of late gestation. At the time of delivery, glucagon levels rise, and insulin levels fall. Higher levels of plasma catecholamines, both epinephrine and norepinephrine, directly stimulate increases in hepatic glucose output. The increased levels of epinephrine and glucagon stimulate lipolysis and the activity of phosphorylase, a key enzyme in glycolysis. The increased level of glucagon also results in increased activity of phosphoenolpyruvate carboxykinase, a rate-limiting enzyme in gluconeogenesis. The newborn must be able to initiate gluconeogenesis, because glycogen stores can sustain glucose production only for several hours after birth. All of these changes together act to preserve glucose homeostasis after the infant's maternal source of glucose is removed with cord clamping. In addition, the newborn must acclimate to periods of feeding and intermittent fasting, as opposed to the constant glucose supply delivered in utero.

Rates of glucose production and use have been quantified in term and preterm infants using stable isotope methodologies. Because neural tissue makes up a greater proportion of body weight, newborns have higher rates of glucose oxidation than adults, as glucose is the primary energy substrate for the brain. The glucose production rate in term newborns is approximately 3 to 5 mg/kg per minute,[67] whereas premature infants have somewhat higher rates of basal glucose production (and use), at 7.7 to 7.9 mg/kg per minute. Both an increased ratio of brain weight to body weight and decreased fat stores probably contribute to this higher rate of glucose production in infants with extremely low birthweights.[75]

Because a preterm infant has a higher rate of basal glucose use, and because of factors such as hypothermia and respiratory distress, which also increase glucose demand, early administration of parenteral glucose is critical. Although the definition of neonatal hypoglycemia remains controversial, it seems prudent to intervene for a plasma glucose level less than 40 mg/dL, particularly in a premature infant in the first few days of life. No prospective studies have established a correlation between hypoglycemia and neurodevelopmental outcomes, particularly in infants with extremely low birthweights, nor have definitive conclusions been drawn.[64,65] (See Chapter 47, Part 1).

Infants with extremely low birthweights are even more susceptible to hyperglycemia, particularly in the first few days of life, when feedings are almost entirely parenteral. Factors such as sepsis, respiratory distress, and hypoxia may also contribute. Historically, glucose intolerance in infants with extremely low birthweights was attributed to persistent endogenous hepatic glucose production in the face of increased exogenous supply, insufficient insulin production, or tissue insensitivity to insulin. However, Hertz and colleagues demonstrated that clinically stable infants with extremely low birthweights are able to suppress endogenous glucose production when given parenteral glucose.[75] In this study, infants given a glucose infusion at a rate of 9 mg/kg per minute were able to suppress endogenous glucose production to nearly zero, demonstrating that there is no inherent immaturity in this process in extremely premature infants. From a practical standpoint, understanding rates of endogenous glucose production is important to avoid iatrogenic hyperglycemia. In infants with extremely low birthweights, a reasonable approach is to start the glucose infusion rate at 6 mg/kg per minute, gradually advancing to 10 to 12 mg/kg per minute as long as hyperglycemia does not develop.

The definition of hyperglycemia also varies, but it is generally set at a plasma level greater than 150 mg/dL (8.3 mmol/L). Each rise of 1 mmol/L (18 mg/dL) in the blood glucose concentration produces an increase in serum osmolarity of 1 mOsm/L; this can result in osmotic diuresis and subsequent dehydration with values of greater than 300 mOsm/L and has been associated with higher mortality and a higher rate of intracranial hemorrhage. Hyperglycemia is detected early through frequent glucose monitoring. Plasma glucose levels of less than 200 mg/dL usually do not require intervention. Reducing the fluid needs and insensible water loss can reduce the glucose intake. Alternatively, a lower concentration of dextrose solution can be used, although solutions that are less than 2.5% should be avoided. Sterile water can be given enterally to decrease parenteral glucose intake without compromising total fluid intake. Lipid infusions have been shown to increase plasma glucose concentrations in premature infants when given at high infusion rates. However, such high infusion rates are not routinely used in clinical practice. The mechanism most likely involves a change in glucose utilization. Although Yunis and colleagues demonstrated a statistically significant increase in plasma glucose (from 73 to 90 mg/dL) in premature infants given IV lipids,[100] it is unlikely that such an increase would be of clinical significance. Consequently, IV lipids probably contribute little to the hyperglycemia commonly seen in infants with extremely low birthweights. Discontinuing IV lipids only reduces the caloric intake and increases the risk of essential fatty acid deficiency in this particularly vulnerable population.

A continuous infusion of insulin is occasionally needed to treat hyperglycemia in infants with extremely low birthweights. Doses range from 0.05 to 0.1 U/kg per hour. Some have advocated the use of insulin to "promote growth," using insulin to facilitate tolerance of added parenteral calories. Binder and colleagues found that insulin infusions improve glucose tolerance in infants with very low birthweights and allow provision of an adequate caloric intake to hyperglycemic infants.[59] Collins and colleagues additionally concluded that infants receiving continuous insulin infusions had enhanced weight gain.[63] Using stable isotope methodology, Poindexter and colleagues measured glucose and protein kinetics in response to euglycemic hyperinsulinemia in extremely premature (26 weeks' gestation, birthweight 890 g), mechanically ventilated newborns. In response to a greater than 10-fold increase in insulin concentrations (from 7 to 79 μU/mL), protein breakdown was reduced by 20%. However, utilization of phenylalanine for protein synthesis also decreased by a similar magnitude, resulting in no net protein gain. In addition, serum lactate concentrations increased nearly threefold during the study period, with an accompanying metabolic acidosis.[84] Therefore, although this level of hyperinsulinemia was successful in reducing protein breakdown in extremely premature infants, the reduction in protein synthesis and the substantial increase in lactic acid concentrations argue against the routine use of exogenous insulin in this population. The potential anabolic effects of insulin during amino acid administration remain unclear.

INTRAVENOUS PROTEIN AND AMINO ACID REQUIREMENTS

When fetal life is interrupted by premature birth, duplicating rates of in utero protein accretion remains a difficult clinical challenge. Failure to provide adequate protein, either in quantity or in quality, can significantly impact the long-term outcome of extremely premature infants. At 26 weeks' gestation, the human fetus accretes approximately 1.8 to 2.2 g of body protein per day, with the placenta supplying about 3.5 g/kg per day of amino acids to the developing fetus. In contrast, infants with extremely low birthweights who receive glucose alone lose approximately 1.2 g/kg of protein each day they do not receive amino acids.[68] This corresponds to a daily loss of 1% to 2% of their total endogenous body protein stores (Fig. 33-1). In just a few days, the gap between what would have been protein accretion in utero and what is now postnatal protein loss widens considerably. As will be discussed in more detail later, early provision of parenteral amino acids can offset this deficit, even if total caloric intake is low.

A variety of methods have been used to quantitate protein requirements in human infants: measurement of breast milk intake and protein content, fetal accretion rate, nitrogen balance studies, serum amino acid levels, and stable isotope studies investigating the kinetics

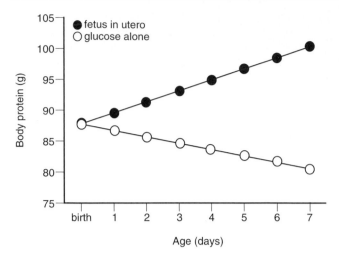

FIGURE 33-1. Change in body protein in the human fetus at approximately 26 weeks' gestation (rate of in utero gain is modified from Ziegler E et al: Body composition of the reference fetus. Growth 40:329, 1976) and theoretical loss in 26- to 27-week, 1000-g birthweight infants receiving glucose alone. (Modified from Denne SC et al: Proteolysis and phenylalanine hydroxylation in response to parenteral nutrition in extremely premature and normal newborns. J Clin Invest 97:746, 1996.)

amino acids are oxidized by the fetus, contributing significantly to fetal energy production. High rates of protein turnover are required to support protein synthesis, tissue remodeling, and growth. Analysis of fetal body composition indicates that at 28 weeks' gestation, the fetus accretes approximately 350 mg of nitrogen per kilogram per day (protein values in milligrams can be found by multiplying nitrogen values in milligrams by 6.25). At term, nitrogen accretion declines to about 150 mg/kg per day. Postnatal nitrogen loss decreases with gestational age as well, from 180 mg/kg per day at 27 to 28 weeks to 120 mg/kg per day for a full-term infant.[76] Consequently, protein requirements extrapolated from fetal nitrogen accretion rates and postnatal losses have been estimated at 2.5 to 3.5 g/kg per day for preterm infants and 1.9 to 2.5 g/kg per day for term infants. As protein losses are inversely related to gestational age, protein requirements are likely to be even higher in extremely premature infants.

Efficacy of Early Parenteral Amino Acids

Several studies have evaluated the efficacy of early parenteral amino acid administration in premature infants.[57,76,88,89,98] Using nitrogen balance techniques, each study demonstrated the ability of early parenteral amino acids to reverse the negative nitrogen balance seen in premature infants receiving glucose alone. A summary of the results obtained from studies of early amino acids is shown in Table 33-7. It is important to point out that each of these studies used a different amino acid solution. Despite these differences in the composition of the solutions used, all studies demonstrated positive nitrogen balance in infants receiving

of labeled amino acids. Clearly, the gold standard needs to be a method that safely optimizes growth and development.

Normal human fetal development is characterized by rapid rates of growth and protein accretion. In utero, the placenta supplies amino acids to the fetus far in excess of requirements for protein accretion. The excess

TABLE 33-7. Summary of Studies of Early Amino Acid Administration in Infants with Low Birthweights

STUDY (YR)	SUBJECTS	AMINO ACID SOLUTION	ENERGY INTAKE (kcal/kg/d)	Intake Nitrogen* (mg/kg/d)	Intake Amino Acids (g/kg/d)	Balance Nitrogen* (mg/kg/d)	Balance Amino Acids (g/kg/d)
Anderson et al. (1979)	27-36 wk ~1600 g	Aminosyn	60 60	0 400	0 2.5	−132 178	−0.8 1.1
Saini et al. (1989)	28 wk 1000 g	Vamin-9	36 45	0 286	0 1.8	−132 122	−0.8 0.76
van Lingen et al. (1992)	30 wk 1500 g	Aminovenous	47 48	0 368	0 2.3	−96 224	−0.6 1.4
Rivera et al. (1993)	28 wk 1000 g	Aminosyn-PF	50 50	0 250	0 1.5	−135 88[†]	−0.8 0.6
Kashyap et al. (1994)	~1000 g	TrophAmine	30 50	0 315	0 2.0	−183 114	−1.1 0.7
van Goudoever et al.(1995)	29 wk 1400 g	Primene	26 29	0 184	0 1.15	−110 10	−0.7 0.06
Thureen et al. (2003)	27 wk 950 g	Trophamine	42 49	144 432	0.9 2.7	−32 192	−0.2 1.2

*Multiply nitrogen values by 6.25 to obtain corresponding protein values in grams.
†Some of the infants in this group received cysteine supplementation and others did not. Nitrogen balance shown is that of the total group; nitrogen balance in the subgroup that received cysteine was 115 ± 41 mg/kg/d vs. 42 ± 42 mg/kg/d in the subgroup that did not receive cysteine.

early parenteral amino acids despite low total caloric intake (approximately 50 kcal/kg per day). Consequently, the initial goal of limiting catabolism and preserving endogenous protein stores can be easily accomplished if parenteral amino acids are initiated on the first day of life in infants with extremely low birthweights.

Stable isotope techniques have also been used to evaluate the effect of amino acids on protein metabolism in premature infants. In these studies, stable isotope tracers of one or more essential amino acids are used to reflect whole body protein kinetics. In addition to demonstrating positive nitrogen balance, Rivera and colleagues found that administration of amino acids (1.5 g/kg per day of Aminosyn-PF with cysteine added) beginning on the first day of life improves protein balance as a result of increased protein synthesis (as reflected by leucine kinetics).[88] Denne and colleagues demonstrated that provision of 2.5 g/kg per day of amino acids as part of a complete parenteral nutrition solution acutely reverses the negative protein balance (as reflected by phenylalanine kinetics) seen in response to glucose alone from a 1.5 g/kg per day loss to a net 0.5 g/kg per day gain.[68] Thureen and colleagues conducted a randomized trial of low (1 g/kg per day) versus high (3 g/kg per day) amino acid intake in infants with extremely low birthweights immediately after birth.[94] The higher amino acid intake produced significantly greater protein accretion, despite a modest caloric intake.

Safety is often cited as a reason to delay initiation of amino acids, particularly in the sickest, most immature infants. However, many investigators have demonstrated the safety of early provision of IV amino acids to premature infants. Normal plasma amino acid concentrations have been reported using TrophAmine.[74] Rivera and colleagues studied infants with very low birthweights given amino acids in the first days of life and found no abnormal elevations of plasma amino acids, blood urea nitrogen, or ammonia.[87] Early amino acid intake of 3 g/kg per day appears to be as safe as 1 g/kg per day, based on blood urea nitrogen and plasma aminograms as indicators of acute amino acid toxicity.[81,94] As mentioned earlier, a significant proportion of the amino acids supplied to the developing fetus are oxidized and serve as a significant energy source for the fetus. Urea production is a byproduct of amino acid oxidation. In premature infants, rates of urea production are higher than in term neonates and adults, consistent with high rates of protein turnover and oxidation. Some investigators have even suggested that azotemia might be evidence of the effective utilization of amino acids as an energy supply rather than of protein intolerance. In addition, because the secretion of insulin is thought to depend on adequate plasma concentrations of certain amino acids, such as arginine and leucine, some investigators believe that early administration of amino acids postnatally may help reduce the incidence of hyperglycemia in infants with very low birthweights.

Although the initial goal of parenteral nutrition in premature infants may be to limit catabolism and maintain endogenous protein stores, ultimately, sufficient energy and protein intake to support growth must be provided. This is true regardless of whether parenteral nutrition is used exclusively or as a bridge to full enteral feedings. The influence of nitrogen and energy intake on nitrogen retention has been evaluated by Zlotkin and colleagues. In infants who receive an adequate amount of energy to maintain growth (approximately 70 to 80 kcal/kg per day IV), nitrogen retention increases with increasing nitrogen intake.[101] Even at a protein intake as high as 4 g/kg per day, retention still increases linearly. This response is in marked contrast to that in adults, whose nitrogen retention levels off slightly above zero balance when excess dietary nitrogen is provided.

Zlotkin and colleagues studied the effect of nitrogen intake at two levels of nonprotein energy intake on nitrogen balance and weight gain in parenterally fed neonates.[101] One group of infants received 50 kcal/kg per day and a nitrogen intake of either 480 or 640 mg/kg per day, equal to 3 or 4 g/kg per day of amino acid intake, respectively. At this low caloric intake, there was no improvement in the rate of nitrogen retention or weight gain with greater nitrogen intake. At higher energy intake (80 kcal/kg per day), increasing the amino acid intake from 2 to 3 g/kg per day resulted in a significant increase in the rate of weight gain and nitrogen retention. At the higher caloric intake, providing 3 g/kg per day of amino acids resulted in weight gain (15 g/kg per day) and nitrogen accretion (approximately 300 mg/kg per day) equal to intrauterine rates. Further increasing protein intake to 4 g/kg per day at the higher caloric intake resulted in an even higher rate of nitrogen retention but no further increase in weight gain. Based on these studies, a reasonable estimate of protein requirements for growth in premature infants would be 2.5 to 3.5 g/kg per day; the requirements of infants with extremely low birthweights may be even higher.

Many conditions and interventions commonly encountered in extremely premature infants are known to increase protein requirements. Superimposed catabolic conditions such as sepsis or surgical stress increase catabolism. The use of dexamethasone is known to increase protein catabolism by increasing protein oxidation and proteolysis, resulting in decreased accretion of protein.[96]

Intravenous Amino Acid Mixtures

The first parenteral amino acid solutions used in neonates were hydrolysates of fibrin or casein. Concerns about these first-generation solutions included high concentrations of glycine, glutamate, and aspartate; the presence of unwanted peptides; and high acidity. Reports of hyperammonemia and acidosis in the early 1970s were associated with the use of these first-generation solutions in neonates. Although amino acid solutions have been significantly modified (see later), the perceived risks associated with the protein hydrolysates linger, contributing to the hesitancy of some clinicians to administer early parenteral amino acids.

The second generation of amino acid solutions consisted of crystalline amino acid mixtures (FreAmine III, Travasol, Aminosyn). The amino acid pattern of these mixtures reflects that of high-quality dietary proteins with large amounts of glycine and alanine, absence of glutamate and aspartate, and absence or poor solubility of tyrosine and cysteine.

The newest solutions include modifications of crystalline amino acids for use in pediatric patients. The currently available solutions include modifications of crystalline amino acids for use in pediatric and neonatal patients (Aminosyn-PF, Premasol, Primene, and TrophAmine; Table 33-8). Three of these solutions are commercially available in the United States and are suitable for use in neonates. TrophAmine was originally formulated to match plasma amino acid concentrations of healthy, term, breast-fed infants; Premasol is identical in composition to TrophAmine. The composition of Primene, available outside of the United States, was derived from fetal and neonatal cord blood concentrations. Both TrophAmine and Premasol supply a mixture of L-tyrosine and N-acetyltyrosine. The bioavailability of N-acetyltyrosine, however, has been questioned. Neither Aminosyn-PF nor Primene supplies a substantial amount of tyrosine. Cysteine is not supplied by most amino acid solutions because it is not stable for long periods of time in solution. However, cysteine

hydrochloride can be added during the compounding process just prior to delivery of the solution.

It is no surprise that the ideal composition of IV amino acid mixtures is unknown. Investigators disagree on the basis for determining optimal plasma amino acid levels. Some advocate using values of breast-fed infants; others suggest using cord plasma levels. The source of nonprotein energy might affect plasma amino acid levels. There is even controversy over the optimal sampling site. To optimize nutrition and growth, particularly in a premature infant, the requirements for specific amino acids need to be more precisely defined. Several amino acids are "conditionally essential" in premature infants. That is, the infant's ability to synthesize these amino acids de novo is less than functional metabolic demands. Cysteine, tyrosine, arginine, glycine, and histidine are generally considered essential amino acids for premature infants.[95]

Tyrosine is widely regarded as an essential amino acid in preterm infants, yet it is not present in appreciable amounts in currently available amino acid solutions because of its low solubility. Snyderman found lower rates of weight gain, nitrogen retention, and plasma concentrations of tyrosine in premature infants given a tyrosine-deficient diet.[91] Tyrosine is synthesized endogenously from phenylalanine by phenylalanine hydroxylase. The activity of this enzyme in premature

TABLE 33-8. Composition of Commercial Parenteral Amino Acid Solutions*

AMINO ACID	AMINOSYN-PF (ABBOTT)	PREMASOL (BAXTER)	PRIMENE (BAXTER)	TROPHAMINE (B. BRAUN)
Histidine	312	480	380	480
Isoleucine	760	820	670	820
Leucine	1200	1400	1000	1400
Lysine	677	820	1100	820
Methionine	180	340	240	340
Phenylalanine	427	480	420	480
Threonine	512	420	370	420
Tryptophan	180	200	200	200
Valine	673	780	760	780
Alanine	698	540	800	540
Arginine	1227	1200	840	1200
Proline	812	680	300	680
Serine	495	380	400	380
Taurine	70	25	60	25
Tyrosine	44	240[†]	45	240[†]
Glycine	385	360	400	360
Cysteine	—	<16	189	<16
Glutamic acid	820	500	1000	500
Aspartic acid	527	320	600	320

*Amino acid concentration in mg/dL; all amino acid mixtures shown are 10% solutions.
[†]Mixture of L-tyrosine and N-acetyltyrosine.
From the American Hospital Formulary Service: Drug information. Bethesda, Md, 2004; and Drug Product Database. Available at www.ahfsdruginformation.com.

infants was thought to be inadequate for growth and nitrogen retention without tyrosine supplements. However, stable isotope studies have demonstrated active phenylalanine hydroxylation in very premature (26 weeks) and premature (32 weeks) infants.[62,68] Therefore, in the strictest sense, tyrosine is not an essential amino acid. However, it remains unclear whether enough tyrosine can be endogenously produced from phenylalanine in premature infants to support normal rates of protein accretion. N-acetyltyrosine, although currently added to TrophAmine, is not highly bioavailable. Nonetheless, two studies provide indirect evidence that N-acetyltyrosine improves protein accretion in preterm infants.[71,73] In addition, it is unclear whether premature infants can adequately catabolize tyrosine via oxidation by the enzymes tyrosine aminotransferase and 4-hydroxyphenylpyruvate dioxygenase. Inability to catabolize tyrosine can lead to transient neonatal tyrosinemia. Further studies are needed to better define premature infants' ability to catabolize tyrosine and to determine whether an alternative source of tyrosine is needed in parenteral amino acid solutions.

Histidine is necessary for normal growth and protein synthesis in the newborn, but the exact requirement is still unclear.

The high glycine content of TPN solutions induces not only hyperglycinemia but also hyperammonemia. Solutions with a high methionine content cause hypermethioninemia, yet it is an essential sulfur-containing amino acid that may be converted into cysteine or cystine and taurine.

Cysteine also is considered an essential amino acid for preterm infants, but it is not soluble in currently available amino acid solutions. Some studies have shown that fetal liver lacks the enzymatic system to convert methionine into cysteine and that infants on a cysteine-free diet demonstrate impaired growth and low plasma cysteine levels. Other studies have shown that there is enough cystathionase in extrahepatic tissues of the fetus and preterm infant to synthesize cysteine when an adequate amount of methionine is provided. The previously mentioned study by Rivera and colleagues found improved nitrogen retention in a subgroup that received cysteine supplementation (115 ± 41 mg/kg per day, versus 42 ± 42 mg/kg per day in the subgroup that received no cysteine).[87] Stable isotope studies have also suggested improved protein retention with cysteine supplementation.[86] Cysteine hydrochloride supplements can be added to parenteral nutrition, but they can cause metabolic acidosis unless appropriately buffered with acetate. The addition of cysteine hydrochloride improves the solubility of calcium and phosphorus in parenteral nutrition solutions.

Glutamine is one of the most abundant amino acids in both plasma and human milk, yet it is not supplied by currently available amino acid solutions because it is unstable in aqueous solution. Glutamine is a major energy substrate for small-intestinal mucosa, as proven by a high glutamine uptake from the lumen and from arterial blood during the newborn period in rats. Adding glutamine to the TPN solutions of animals prevents atrophy of small-intestinal mucosa and smooth muscle, improves the gut immune function, and reduces the incidence of fatty infiltration of the liver. Several studies suggest that parenteral glutamine supplementation is of benefit in selected populations of critically ill adults. However, a large, multicenter, randomized clinical trial of parenteral glutamine supplementation conducted by the National Institute of Child Health and Human Development (NICHD) Neonatal Research Network found that parenteral glutamine supplementation did not decrease mortality or the incidence of late-onset sepsis in infants with extremely low birthweights.[85] In addition, glutamine had no effect on tolerance of enteral feeds, necrotizing enterocolitis, or growth. Although parenteral glutamine seems to be well tolerated, routine usage cannot be advocated at this time because of the lack of clinical efficacy. Future studies are needed to determine whether glutamine supplementation may have a role in select subsets of critically ill neonates.

Finally, taurine is synthesized endogenously from cysteine and is not part of structural protein. It is present in large concentrations in the retina and brain of the fetus, reaching a peak concentration at birth. When newborn nonhuman primates are fed taurine-deficient formula, growth is depressed, but this does not occur in human preterm infants despite declining plasma and urine taurine levels. Nevertheless, there is some limited evidence that taurine supplementation might influence auditory brainstem evoked responses (see also Part 1 of this chapter). Several pediatric IV amino acid solutions (TrophAmine, Primene, Aminosyn-PF) contain one to three times the amount of taurine found in breast milk; in some cases, this might lower the incidence of TPN-induced cholestasis.[69]

In summary, the importance of early amino acid administration cannot be overemphasized. Although it has been the practice of many neonatal intensive care units to delay administration of IV amino acids for several days, parenteral amino acids should probably be initiated in the first hours after birth in infants with extremely low birthweights, preferably at a dose of 3 g/kg per day. As none of the currently used amino acid solutions were designed specifically to meet the needs of extremely premature infants, future research efforts should be directed at designing a fourth generation of amino acid solutions to optimize parenteral nutrition given to these infants.

INTRAVENOUS LIPID REQUIREMENTS AND LIPID EMULSIONS

Intravenous lipids are important not only to prevent essential fatty acid deficiency but also as a significant source of nonprotein energy. Commercially available IV lipid solutions are made up of neutral triglycerides, egg yolk phospholipids to emulsify, and glycerol to adjust the tonicity. In the United States, IV lipid solutions are derived from soybean oil (Intralipid) or a combination

TABLE 33-9. Comparison of Commercial (20%) Intravenous Lipid Emulsions and Human Milk

	Intralipid (Kabi Vitrum)	Liposyn-II (Abbott)	Clinoleic (Baxter)	Human Milk
Triglycerides (g/L)	200	200	200	40
Phospholipids (g/L)	12	12	12	0.3
Glycerol (g/L)	22	25	22.5	—
Fatty acids (%)				
Palmitic acid C16:0	10	9	10.7	22
Stearic acid C18:0	3	3	3	7
Oleic acid C18:1	25	18	65	30
Linoleic acid C18:2	54	66	17	15
Linolenic acid C18:3	8	4	0.3	0.5

of soybean oil and safflower oil (Liposyn II); these solutions contain LCTs. Some lipid preparations available in Europe include MCTs (Medialipid) or a combination of olive oil and soybean oil (Clinoleic). Differences in lipid source result in slightly different fatty acid profiles. All available IV lipid products have a fatty acid profile substantially different from that of human milk (Table 33-9).

Lipid particles supplied by IV lipid solutions are similar in size to endogenously produced chylomicrons. The clearance of these lipid particles is also similar to that of chylomicrons, depending on the activity of lipoprotein lipase. In premature infants born at less than 28 weeks' gestation, lipoprotein lipase activity and triglyceride clearance are reduced. Heparin theoretically releases lipoprotein lipase from the endothelium into the circulation, but there is no evidence that this increases lipid utilization in preterm infants. In addition, increased lipoprotein lipase activity may produce high levels of free fatty acids and may be in excess of the clearance capacity of the premature infant. Consequently, the routine addition of heparin to lipid emulsions to stimulate lipolysis is not recommended on the basis of currently available evidence.

In humans, linoleic and linolenic acids cannot be endogenously synthesized and are therefore essential fatty acids. Biochemical evidence of essential fatty acid deficiency can develop in preterm infants within 72 hours. Essential fatty acid deficiency can be avoided if a minimum of 0.5 to 1.0 g/kg per day of IV lipid is provided. To meet energy requirements, additional IV lipid is required in early postnatal life.

Intravenous lipids are available as 10%, 20%, and 30% emulsions. The 20% solutions have lower phospholipid-to-triglyceride ratios and liposomal content than the 10% solutions, resulting in lower plasma triglyceride, cholesterol, and phospholipid concentrations. Consequently, 10% lipid emulsions should be avoided. A 30% solution has recently become available and may confer even more advantages, although comparative data are not available.

Carnitine facilitates transport of long-chain fatty acids through the myocardial membrane and plays an important role in their oxidation. Premature infants receiving parenteral nutrition have low carnitine levels, but the clinical significance of this remains uncertain. Meta-analysis of the studies evaluating carnitine supplementation in parenteral nutrition showed no evidence of effect on ketogenesis, lipid utilization, or weight gain. The information available is insufficient to support a recommendation for the routine supplementation with carnitine for parenterally fed neonates.

The early administration of IV lipids to preterm infants has been the subject of discussion and debate that has primarily centered on the acute metabolic effects of early IV lipids and the potential adverse effects, such as chronic lung disease, impaired oxygenation, and increased risk of kernicterus as a result of free fatty acids displacing bilirubin from albumin binding sites. Because of this displacement of bilirubin and increased risk of kernicterus, concern has been expressed about the use of IV lipids in infants with hyperbilirubinemia. In vitro studies have shown that no free bilirubin is released if the ratio of free fatty acid to serum albumin is less than 4. In vivo, free bilirubin is not generated until the molar ratio of free fatty acids to bilirubin exceeds 6. In clinical practice, ratios of free fatty acid to bilirubin greater than 6 have not been measured, and a relationship between free fatty acid concentrations and unbound bilirubin has not been documented. At present, withholding IV lipids from jaundiced premature infants does not seem warranted.

The rate of IV lipid infusion is important, and plasma lipid clearance is improved when IV lipid is given as a continuous infusion over 24 hours. Lipid infusion rates in excess of 0.25 g/kg per hour can be associated with decreases in P_{O_2}. Lipid infusion rates well under this value can be easily achieved in clinical practice if lipids are provided over 24 hours in an amount not exceeding 3 to 4 g/kg per day. This level of lipid intake is usually sufficient to supply the caloric needs of preterm infants (in combination with glucose) and is usually tolerated by premature infants. Triglyceride concentrations are most often used as an indication of lipid tolerance, and maintaining triglyceride concentrations below 150 to 200 mg/dL seems prudent.

Intravenous lipid emulsions may undergo lipid peroxidation, which may result in formation of organic free radicals and potentially initiate tissue injury. Light, especially phototherapy, may play some role in increasing lipid peroxidation in IV lipid emulsions. However, multivitamin preparations included in the IV solutions are a major contributor to a generation of peroxides, and lipid emulsions may have only a minor additive effect. Some clinicians protect IV lipid solutions from light, although the importance or efficacy of this practice is unclear.

INTRAVENOUS ELECTROLYTE, MINERAL, TRACE ELEMENT, AND VITAMIN REQUIREMENTS AND SUPPLEMENTATION

During the first week of life, sodium needs are low because of the expected free water diuresis. For extremely low birthweight infants, addition of sodium to parenteral nutrition may not be necessary until about day 3 of life. It is, however, necessary to frequently measure sodium concentrations and water balance. After the initial diuresis, 2 to 4 mEq/kg per day is usually sufficient to maintain serum sodium in the normal range, but extremely low birthweight infants sometimes require higher sodium intakes to compensate for larger renal sodium losses (see Chapter 34). Chloride requirements follow the same time course as sodium requirements and are also 2 to 4 mEq/kg per day. Once electrolytes are added to the parenteral nutrition solution, chloride intake should not be less than 1 mEq/kg per day, and all chloride should not be omitted when sodium bicarbonate or acetate is given to correct metabolic acidosis. Potassium requirements again are low on the first few days of life, and potassium should probably be omitted from parenteral solutions in extremely low birthweight infants until renal function is clearly established. Potassium intakes of 2 to 3 mEq/kg per day are usually adequate to maintain normal serum potassium concentrations.

Parenteral nutrition solutions usually require the addition of anions, either as acetate or chloride. In general, excess anions should be provided as acetate to prevent hyperchloremic metabolic acidosis. In addition, acetate can help avoid the metabolic acidosis that can occur with the administration of cysteine hydrochloride.

Supplying calcium and phosphorus in parenteral nutrition remains a significant clinical challenge because of limited solubility. It is currently not possible to supply enough calcium and phosphorus to support adequate bone mineralization in premature infants using the solutions available in the United States. Precipitation of calcium and phosphorus remains an issue. Their solubility in parenteral nutrition depends on temperature, type and concentration of amino acid, glucose concentration, pH, type of calcium salt, sequence of addition of calcium and phosphorus to the solution, the calcium-to-phosphorus ratio, and the presence of

lipid. Adding cysteine to parenteral nutrition lowers the pH, which improves calcium and phosphorus solubility. Current recommendations are to use parenteral nutrition solutions containing 50 to 60 mg/dL of elemental calcium (12.5 to 15 mmol/L) and 40 to 47 mg/dL of phosphorus (12.5 to 15 mmol/L). At typical fluid intakes (100 to 150 mL/kg per day), this will provide 50 to 90 mg/kg per day of calcium and 40 to 70 mg/kg per day of phosphorus. A calcium-to-phosphorus ratio of 1.7:1 by weight (1.3:1 by molar ratio) appears to be optimal for bone mineralization. In general, calcium and phosphorus should be added to parenteral nutrition in early postnatal life. Magnesium is also a necessary nutrient and should be supplied at 3 to 7.2 mg/kg per day. Calcium, phosphorus, and magnesium serum concentrations should be monitored frequently.

Recommendations for trace elements for term and preterm infants are primarily derived from the American Society for Clinical Nutrition guidelines from 1988 (Table 33-10). There is reasonable consensus that zinc should be included early in parenteral nutrition solutions (250 µg/kg per day for term, 400 µg/kg per day for preterm). Other trace elements are probably not needed until after the first 2 weeks of life. Zinc and copper are available in the sulfate form and can be added separately to parenteral solutions. Several pediatric trace metal solutions are available that contain zinc, copper, magnesium, and chromium in varying proportions, and these are usually administered at 0.2 mL/kg per day. When trace metal solutions are used, additional zinc is usually needed to provide the recommended intake for preterm infants. Supplementation with selenium is suggested after 2 weeks of age because preterm infants can become selenium deficient after 2 weeks of exclusive parenteral nutrition. In infants with cholestasis, copper and manganese should be discontinued, and chromium and selenium should be used with caution and in smaller amounts in the presence of renal dysfunction. At present, parenteral iron is recommended only when preterm infants are exclusively nourished by parenteral solutions for the first 2 months of life.

Only one pediatric multivitamin preparation is currently available, and it is delivered at a standard dosage of 2 mL/kg per day (maximum, 5 mL) in preterm infants and 5 mL in term infants. These dosages provide higher amounts of most of the B vitamins and lower amounts of vitamin A than is recommended (Table 33-11).

COMPLICATIONS OF PARENTERAL NUTRITION

Although myriad complications of parenteral nutrition have been reported from the early days of its use, most of these are now rare with the use of present parenteral formulations. Some of the complications (electrolyte imbalance, hypoglycemia, hyperglycemia, hypocalcemia, hypercalcemia, hypophosphatemia) can be prevented or corrected by manipulating the constituents of the

TABLE 33-10. Recommended Parenteral Intake of Trace Elements for Term and Preterm Infants

TRACE ELEMENT	TERM (μg/kg/d) ASCN (1988)	Preterm (μg/kg/d) Consensus Recommendations (1993)		
		Transitional (First 2 wk of Life)	Stable (>2 wk Old)	ASCN (1988)
Chromium*	0.20	0-0.05	0.05-0.2	0.2
Copper†	20	0-20	20	20
Iron‡	—	0-0.2	0.1-0.2	—
Fluoride§	—	—	—	—
Iodide	1	1	1	1
Manganese†	1	0-0.75	1	1
Molybdenum	0.25	0	0.25	0.25
Selenium*	2	0-1.3	1.5-2	2
Zinc‖	250	150	400	400

*Renal dysfunction can cause toxicity.

†Impaired biliary excretion can cause toxicity.

‡Recommendation is made with caution because of very limited experience with IV iron in infants and lack of a safe, acceptable IV preparation (estimated daily IV requirement is 100 μg/kg for term infants and 200 μg/kg for preterm infants).

§Because of a lack of information on the compatibility of fluoride in total parenteral nutrition (TPN) and on the contamination level of fluoride in TPN, firm recommendations cannot be made; with long-term TPN (longer than 3 mo), a dosage of 500 μg/d may be important in preterm infants, who already have a higher incidence of dental caries.

‖The only trace element recommended on day I of parenteral nutrition. If the infant requires TPN for longer than 3 mo, the dosage must be reduced to 100 μg/kg/d.

ASCN, American Society for Clinical Nutrition.

From Greene HL et al: Guidelines for the use of vitamins, trace elements, calcium, magnesium, and phosphorus in infants and children receiving total parenteral nutrition: Report of the Subcommittee on Pediatric Parenteral Nutrient Requirements from the Committee on Clinical Practice Issues of the American Society for Clinical Nutrition. AM J Clin Nutr 48:1324,1988; and Tsang RC et al (eds): Nutritional Needs of the Preterm Infant: Scientific Basis and Practical Guidelines. Baltimore, Williams & Wilkins, 1993.

infusate. The primary complications of parenteral nutrition as currently used are cholestasis and complications related to the infusion line.

Hepatic dysfunction has long been recognized as an important complication of parenteral nutrition and is manifested primarily as cholestatic jaundice. The initial lesion seen histologically is cholestasis, both intracellular and intracanalicular, followed by portal inflammation and progressing to bile duct proliferation after several weeks of TPN. With prolonged administration, portal fibrosis and ultimately cirrhosis may develop.

The precise cause of the cholestasis is unknown and most likely multifactorial. This is expected, considering that the patients at greatest risk are critically ill premature infants who are susceptible to multiple insults, such as hypoxia, hemodynamic instability, and sepsis. A higher incidence of sepsis has been reported in infants affected by cholestasis.[82] Perhaps an equally if not more important factor in the development of cholestasis is the prolonged lack of enteral nutrition; there is expanding evidence that enteral feedings, even at low caloric intakes, can reduce the incidence of cholestasis.

Early studies of parenteral nutrition suggested a possible relationship between the quantity of amino acids and hepatic dysfunction. More recent studies, using historical controls, suggest that the newer amino acid solutions may result in less cholestasis.[72] The specific role of the quantity and composition of parenteral amino acids in the cause of cholestatic jaundice in premature infants remains unclear.

An infant with TPN-associated cholestasis develops a direct hyperbilirubinemia and jaundice, although histologic changes in the liver begin occurring before this is clinically apparent. The earliest detectable biochemical marker, although not routinely measured, is an increase in serum bile acids. In addition to direct hyperbilirubinemia, another sensitive but nonspecific indicator of early cholestatic change is an elevation of γ-glutamyltranspeptidase. Elevation of hepatic transaminases (serum glutamic oxaloacetic transaminase [SGOT] and serum glutamic pyruvic transaminase [SGPT]) is a late finding. The clinical evidence of cholestasis usually resolves with discontinuation of TPN and initiation of enteral feedings. In cases of advanced liver disease and hepatic failure in infants on TPN, severe changes resulting in irreversible liver failure are thought to occur only after several months of use.

As previously noted, normal bile flow usually returns when parenteral nutrition is stopped and enteral feeding is begun. In infants with TPN-associated cholestasis who require continued parenteral nutrition, the use of hypocaloric enteral feeding in combination with parenteral nutrition may stabilize or improve hepatic function. Use of phenobarbital and ursodeoxycholic acid has been shown to be beneficial in some cholestatic states in older children and adults; however, the information on neonates is inadequate to recommend their use.

Indwelling venous catheters used to deliver TPN may also be the source of complications. Both peripheral

TABLE 33-11. Recommended Parenteral Intake of Vitamins for Term and Preterm Infants

VITAMIN	Term (Daily Dose)		Preterm (Dose/kg/d)*		
	ASCN[†] (1988)	MVI-Pediatric[†] (1 vial; 5 mL)	Consensus Recommendations[†] (1993)	ASCN[†] (1988)	MVI-Pediatric[†] (40% of vial; 2 mL/kg/d)
Fat Soluble					
Vitamin A (IU)	2300	2300	700-1500	1640	920
With lung disease	—	—	1500-2800	—	—
Vitamin D (IU)	400	400	40-160	160	160
Vitamin E (IU)	7	7	3.5 (max = 7)	2.8	2.8
Vitamin K (µg)	200	200	8-10 (300 at birth)	80[‡]	80
Water Soluble					
Vitamin B_6 (µg)	1000	1000	150-200	180	400
Vitamin B_{12} (µg)	1	1	0.3	0.3	0.4
Vitamin C (mg)	80	80	15-25	25	32
Biotin (µg)	20	20	5-8	6	8
Folic acid (µg)	140	140	56	56	56
Niacin (mg)	17	17	4-6.8	6.8	6.8
Pantothenate (mg)	5	5	1-2	2	2
Riboflavin (µg)	1400	1400	150-200	150	560
Thiamin (µg)	1200	1200	200-350	350	480

*Maximum not to exceed dosage for term infant.

[†]The consensus recommendations (1993) and the American Society for Clinical Nutrition (ASCN) recommendations (1988) are currently not achievable because no ideal IV vitamin preparation is available for preterm infants; 40% of a vial (2 mL/kg/d) of MVI-Pediatric (Armor, USA; Rorer, Canada) is the closest intake that can be achieved at this time.

[‡]This does not include the 0.5 to 1 mg of vitamin K to be given at birth, as recommended by the American Academy of Pediatrics.

From Greene HL et al: Guidelines for the use of vitamins, trace elements, calcium, magnesium, and phosphorus in infants and children receiving total parenteral nutrition: Report of the Subcommittee on Pediatric Parenteral Nutrient Requirements from the Committee on Clinical Practice Issues of the American Society for Clinical Nutrition. AM J Clin Nutr 48:1324,1988; Tsang RC et al (ed): Nutritional Needs of the Preterm Infant: Scientific Basis and Practical Guidelines. Baltimore, Williams & Wilkins, 1993.

and central venous routes have been used to deliver TPN, but central delivery allows use of more concentrated formulations. The complications associated with venous catheters are usually the result of improper insertion or placement, bacterial or fungal colonization of the catheter, or vessel irritation or thrombosis.

Peripheral venous access is usually accomplished with Teflon catheters, which may infiltrate within a short time; however, the inclusion of fat emulsion in the infusate may delay the time until infiltration.[83] Peripheral Teflon catheters also may become colonized with bacteria at a rate of over 30% when they have been in place longer than 3 days; peripheral venous catheters placed in the extremities are twice as likely to become colonized as those placed in scalp veins.[66]

Central venous catheters provide the advantage of a lower incidence of infiltration and an ability to deliver higher concentrations of infusate. However, they are not without potential disadvantages. Broviac catheters, in particular, are less than optimal for use in neonates because of the high incidence of infection and thrombosis associated with their use in this population. Long-line, small-bore catheters that can be introduced percutaneously or surgically are available for use in the neonatal population. These catheters are composed of

either silicone or polyurethane. The incidence of sepsis and thrombosis with either silicone or polyurethane lines is much lower than with the Broviac catheter. The incidence of line sepsis is not affected by whether they are placed percutaneously or surgically; however, there is a lower incidence of both infection and mechanical complication if these lines originate in a distal vein (scalp, arm, hand) rather than a proximal one. Pericardial tamponade, arguably the most serious complication, has been reported to occur with catheters made of both materials.[70] Similarly, vascular perforation, another potentially serious complication, has been reported to occur with both types of catheters. Thrombosis in these small-bore catheters can be minimized by adding heparin to the infusate in a 1:1 ratio.

Infection is probably the most frequent serious complication associated with peripheral and central catheters. Two of the most commonly implicated bacterial agents are *Staphylococcus epidermidis* and *Staphylococcus aureus*[66]; *Candida albicans* and *Malassezia furfur* (a lipophilic skin flora yeast)[79,90] are the fungal agents most often implicated (see Chapter 37). The incidence of sepsis as a complication of TPN increases as gestational age decreases and the duration of TPN increases. The predisposition to develop sepsis in these infants is probably multifactorial. As noted earlier, the incidence of sepsis increases in infants who have developed cholestasis. There is also some evidence that the infusate per se may predispose these infants to nosocomial sepsis. Coagulase-negative staphylococcal bacteremia and *M. furfur* fungemia may be associated with the use of IV lipid. In both cases, the incidence increases when lipid is added to the infusate, suggesting that the lipid may provide a rich growth medium for skin flora that have colonized indwelling catheters.

PRACTICAL APPROACH TO ADMINISTRATION OF PARENTERAL NUTRITION

As advances in neonatal care enable increasingly premature and tiny babies to survive, the need for maximizing nutritional support in this population cannot be overemphasized. In 1998, infants with extremely low birthweights (401 to 1000 g) born at centers participating in the NICHD Neonatal Research Network who survived longer than 72 hours received parenteral nutrition for an average of 27 days (1998 Generic Data Base, NICHD Neonatal Research Network). In addition, many term infants have medical and surgical disorders that preclude enteral feeding in the first several days to weeks of life. Infants who will not receive full-volume enteral feeds for more than several days are likely to benefit from parenteral nutrition.

Early provision of parenteral nutrition, particularly to an infant with extremely low birthweight, is important for a variety of reasons. Glucose solutions alone, with or without electrolyte and mineral additives, cannot prevent protein catabolism or maintain in utero rates of growth and protein accretion. In fact, infants who receive glucose alone obligatorily lose at least 1% of their endogenous nitrogen stores daily. To maximize protein accretion in a newborn infant, an appropriate balance of nonprotein substrate and amino acids must be provided. In addition, exogenous lipids are crucial both for increasing caloric intake and for preventing essential fatty acid deficiency.

Guidelines

The following practical guidelines and recommendations for administering parenteral nutrition to term and preterm infants are intended to present a reasonable approach to parenteral nutrition based on the available data.

Parenteral nutrition may be delivered by peripheral IV catheters, central venous catheters, or percutaneous central venous catheters. The decision as to which route is used should be individualized and based on an estimate of how long the infant will be unable to tolerate enteral feedings. In general, a peripheral IV is likely to be adequate to maintain nutritional stores over 1 to 2 weeks, whereas a central line will support growth when a baby is expected to require parenteral nutrition for more than 2 weeks. *Percutaneous central venous catheters* are being used with increasing frequency in the neonatal intensive care unit, because they allow delivery of a more concentrated nutrient infusate and typically can be maintained longer than a single peripheral IV line. Percutaneous central venous catheters are reasonably safe, although complications have been reported.

Glucose should be provided in the parenteral nutrition solution to maintain normal plasma glucose concentrations and to meet the demand for glucose use. As discussed earlier in this chapter, the glucose production and utilization rates in a term infant are approximately 3 to 4 mg/kg per minute, whereas a premature infant has a much greater need, 6 to 8 mg/kg per minute. Infants who weigh 1000 g or more usually tolerate a 10% glucose solution initially, whereas infants weighing less than 1000 g probably need to be started on a 5% glucose solution, given their higher total fluid requirements and predisposition for hyperglycemia.

Lipids can be started as early as the first day of life. Starting concentrations of 0.5 to 1 g/kg per day, infused over 24 hours using a 20% emulsion, should be well tolerated, even by an infant with very low birthweight. Recent studies have demonstrated the safety and efficacy of this approach. Lipid concentrations can gradually be advanced to a maximum of 3 g/kg per day while normal serum triglyceride levels are monitored and maintained.

The appropriate balance of glucose and lipid in parenteral nutrition is critical for achieving maximal nutritional benefit. In fact, nutrient and protein retention is maximal if the nonprotein caloric balance between carbohydrate and lipid is approximately 60:40.[80,92] This more closely mimics the fat content of breast milk and minimizes excess energy expenditure, which can occur if a disproportionate amount of nonprotein calories is given as glucose. Even at higher protein intakes, a parenterally fed infant with extremely low birthweight may need 80 to 90 kcal/kg per day for nonprotein energy supplies. The caloric requirements of a parenterally fed neonate are much lower than those fed enterally. It is important to realize that providing excessive calories via parenteral nutrition does not correlate with higher rates of growth. In addition, it should be emphasized that it is not difficult to provide adequate nonprotein energy, and it can be done without using highly concentrated glucose solutions (Box 33-1).

This considered, glucose concentrations of greater than 12.5% should be required only on rare occasions. In addition, glucose concentrations of greater than 10% to 12.5% should be reserved for use with central venous access.

As discussed previously, amino acids should be started as early as possible. A pediatric crystalline amino acid mixture should be used, because these mixtures are more likely to approximate plasma amino acid patterns of normal, breast-feeding, term infants. Based on available data, a minimum of 3 g/kg per day of amino acids should be initiated as soon as possible after birth to limit protein loss. This goal is readily

BOX 33-1. Calculating the Caloric Value of Parenteral Nutrition*

Example: Fluids at 140 mL/kg/d			
$D_{12.5}W$	→ 17.5 g/kg dextrose	= 60 kcal/kg	61% of total
Amino acids	→ 3 g/kg	= 12 kcal/kg	12%
20% lipid	→ 3 g/kg	= 27 kcal/kg	27%
		Total 99 kcal/kg	
Example: Fluids at 110 mL/kg/d			
$D_{12.5}W$	→ 14 g/kg dextrose	= 47 kcal/kg	55% of total
Amino acids	→ 3 g/kg	= 12 kcal/kg	14%
20% lipid	→ 3 g/kg	= 27 kcal/kg	31%
		Total 86 kcal/kg	

Dextrose = 3.4 kcal/g; protein = 4 kcal/g; lipid = 9 kcal/g.

accomplished by the availability of a neonatal stock amino acid solution. This solution, made in advance by the pharmacy, is composed of amino acids in 7.5% dextrose. When infused at a rate of 60 mL/kg per day, the solution provides 3 g/kg per day of amino acids. Consequently, infants admitted to neonatal intensive care have immediate availability of IV amino acids. Standard parenteral nutrition can be started in the next day or two, depending on the fluid and electrolyte status of the infant. The data do not support a need to advance amino acid intake slowly, as has been the past practice in many nurseries. To achieve growth, amino acid requirements may approach 4 g/kg per day, with the needs of some infants being even greater.

Electrolytes, minerals, and vitamins should also be included in the standard parenteral nutrition solution. Parenteral nutrition, once initiated, probably should be continued until enteral feedings supply approximately 100 to 110 kcal/kg per day.

Understanding the optimal means of providing nutrition to neonates is an ongoing process. As survival of premature infants continues to improve, research efforts must focus on maximizing nutritional support.

REFERENCES

Part 1

1. Al-Dahhan J et al: Effect of salt supplementation of newborn premature infants on neurodevelopmental outcome at 10-13 years of age. Arch Dis Child Fetal Neonatal Ed 86:F120, 2002.
2. American Academy of Pediatrics: Pediatric Nutrition Handbook, 5th ed. Elk Grove Village, Ill, American Academy of Pediatrics, 2004.
3. Anderson DM, Kliegman RM: The relationship of neonatal alimentation practices to the occurrence of endemic necrotizing enterocolitis. Am J Perinatol 8:62, 1991.
4. Atkinson SA: Human milk feeding of the micropremie. Clin Perinatol 27:235, 2000.
5. Auerbach KG, Walker M: When the mother of a premature infant uses a breast pump: What every NICU nurse needs to know. Neonatal Netw 13:23, 1994.
6. Baker JH, Berseth CL: Duodenal motor responses in preterm infants fed formula with varying concentrations and rates of infusion. Pediatr Res 42:618, 1997.
7. Berseth CL et al: Prolonging small feeding volumes early in life decreases the incidence of necrotizing enterocolitis in very low birth weight infants. Pediatrics 111:529, 2003.
8. Bitman J et al: Comparison of the lipid composition of breast milk from mothers of term and preterm infants. Am J Clin Nutr 38:300, 1983.
9. Brunton JA et al: Growth and body composition in infants with bronchopulmonary dysplasia up to 3 months corrected age: A randomized trial of a high-energy nutrient-enriched formula fed after hospital discharge. J Pediatr 133:340, 1998.
10. Carnielli VP et al: The very low birth weight premature infant is capable of synthesizing arachidonic and docosahexaenoic acids from linoleic and linolenic acids. Pediatr Res 40:169, 1996.
11. Carver JD et al: Growth of preterm infants fed nutrient-enriched or term formula after hospital discharge. Pediatrics 107:683, 2001.
12. Castillo RO et al: Intestinal maturation in the rat: The role of enteral nutrients. JPEN J Parenter Enteral Nutr 12:490, 1988.
13. Denne SC: Protein and energy requirements in preterm infants. Semin Neonatol 6:377, 2001.
14. Ditzenberger G et al: The effect of protein supplementation on the growth of premature infants <1500 grams. Pediatr Res 47:286A, 2000.
15. Ehrenkranz RA: In Tsang RC et al (eds): Nutritional Needs of the Preterm Infant: Scientific Basis and Practical Guidelines. Baltimore, Williams & Wilkins, 1993, p 177.
16. Embleton NE et al: Postnatal malnutrition and growth retardation: An inevitable consequence of current recommendations in preterm infants? Pediatrics 107:270, 2001.
17. European Society of Paediatric Gastroenterology and Nutrition (ESPGAN): Nutrition and feeding of preterm infants. Acta Paediatr Scand Suppl 336:1, 1987.
18. Fewtrell MS et al: Randomized, double-blind trial of long-chain polyunsaturated fatty acid supplementation with fish oil and borage oil in preterm infants. J Pediatr 144:471, 2004.
19. Gartner LM, Greer FR: Prevention of rickets and vitamin D deficiency: New guidelines for vitamin D intake. Pediatrics 111:908, 2003.

20. Greene HL et al: Water-soluble vitamins: C, B1, B2, B6, niacin, pantothenic acid, and biotin. In Tsang RC et al (eds): Nutritional Needs of the Preterm Infant: Scientific Basis and Practical Guidelines. Baltimore, Williams & Wilkins, 1993, p 121.

21. Greer FR: Vitamin metabolism and requirements in the micropremie. Clin Perinatol 27:95, 2000.

22. Innis SM et al: Docosahexaenoic acid and arachidonic acid enhance growth with no adverse effects in preterm infants fed formula. J Pediatr 140:547, 2002.

23. Jensen CL, Heird WC: Lipids with an emphasis on long-chain polyunsaturated fatty acids. Clin Perinatol 29:261, 2002.

24. Jensen RG: The lipids in human milk. Prog Lipid Res 35:53, 1996.

25. Kien CL: Digestion, absorption, and fermentation of carbohydrates in the newborn. Clin Perinatol 23:211, 1996.

26. Klein CJ: Nutrient requirements for preterm infant formulas. J Nutr 132:1395S, 2002.

27. Kliegman RM: Experimental validation of neonatal feeding practices. Pediatrics 103:492, 1999.

28. Koo WK et al: Calcium, magnesium, phosphorus, and vitamin D. In Tsang RC et al (eds): Nutritional Needs of the Preterm Infant: Scientific Basis and Practical Guidelines. Baltimore, Williams & Wilkins, 1993, p 135.

29. Lemons JA et al: Very low birth weight outcomes of the National Institute of Child Health and Human Development Neonatal Research Network, January 1995 through December 1996. NICHD Neonatal Research Network. Pediatrics 107:E1, 2001.

30. Levine GM et al: Role of oral intake in maintenance of gut mass and disaccharide activity. Gastroenterology 67:975, 1974.

31. Life Sciences Research Office Report: Assessment of nutrient requirements for infant formulas. J Nutr 128:2059S, 1998.

32. Lucas A: Minimal enteral feeding. Semin Neonatal Nutr Metab 1:2, 1993.

33. Lucas A et al: Early diet of preterm infants and development of allergic or atopic disease: Randomised prospective study. BMJ 300:837, 1990.

34. Lucas A et al: Randomised trial of nutrition for preterm infants after discharge. Arch Dis Child 67:324, 1992.

35. Lucas A et al: Randomized trial of nutrient-enriched formula versus standard formula for postdischarge preterm infants. Pediatrics 108:703, 2001.

36. Mathew OP: Breathing patterns of preterm infants during bottle feeding: Role of milk flow. J Pediatr 119:960, 1991.

37. McClure RJ: Trophic feeding of the preterm infant. Acta Paediatr Suppl 90:19, 2001.

38. McKeown RE et al: Role of delayed feeding and of feeding increments in necrotizing enterocolitis. J Pediatr 121:764, 1992.

39. Nutrition Committee, Canadian Paediatric Society: Nutrient needs and feeding of premature infants. Can Med Assoc J 152:1765, 1995.

40. Pinelli J, Symington A: Non-nutritive sucking for promoting physiologic stability and nutrition in preterm infants. Cochrane Database Syst Rev CD001071, 2000.

41. Putet G: Energy. In Tsang RC et al (eds): Nutritional Needs of the Preterm Infant: Scientific Basis and Practical Guidelines. Baltimore, Williams & Wilkins, 1993, p 15.

42. SanGiovanni JP et al: Meta-analysis of dietary essential fatty acids and long-chain polyunsaturated fatty acids as they relate to visual resolution acuity in healthy preterm infants. Pediatrics 105:1292, 2000.

43. Sauerwald TU et al: Intermediates in endogenous synthesis of C22:6 omega 3 and C20:4 omega 6 by term and preterm infants. Pediatr Res 41:183, 1997.

44. Schanler RJ et al: Feeding strategies for premature infants: Beneficial outcomes of feeding fortified human milk versus preterm formula. Pediatrics 103:1150, 1999.

45. Schanler RJ et al: Feeding strategies for premature infants: Randomized trial of gastrointestinal priming and tube-feeding method. Pediatrics 103:434, 1999.

46. Shenai JP: Vitamin A. In Tsang RC et al (eds): Nutritional Needs of the Preterm Infant: Scientific Basis and Practical Guidelines. Baltimore, Williams & Wilkins, 1993, p 87.

47. Shulman RJ et al: Early feeding, feeding tolerance, and lactase activity in preterm infants. J Pediatr 133:645, 1998.

48. Shulman RJ et al: Early feeding, antenatal gluco-corticoids, and human milk decrease intestinal permeability in preterm infants. Pediatr Res 44:519, 1998.

49. Simmer K: Long chain polyunsaturated fatty acid supplementation in infants born at term. Cochrane Database Syst Rev CD000376, 2000.

50. Simmer K, Patole S: Longchain polyunsaturated fatty acid supplementation in preterm infants. Cochrane Database Syst Rev CD000375, 2004.

51. Thureen PJ et al: Direct measurement of the energy expenditure of physical activity in preterm infants. J Appl Physiol 85:223, 1998.

52. Tyson JE, Kennedy KA: Minimal enteral nutrition for promoting feeding tolerance and preventing morbidity in parenterally fed infants. Cochrane Database Syst Rev CD000504, 2000.

53. Uauy R: Are omega-3 fatty acids required for normal eye and brain development in the human? J Pediatr Gastroenterol Nutr 11:296, 1990.

54. Usher R, McLean F: Intrauterine growth of live-born Caucasian infants at sea level: Standards obtained from measurements in 7 dimensions of infants born between 25 and 44 weeks of gestation. J Pediatr 74:901, 1969.

55. Van Aerde JEE: Acute respiratory failure and broncho-pulmonary dysplasia. In Hay WW (ed): Neonatal Nutrition and Metabolism. Chicago, Yearbook Medical, 1991, p 476.

56. Yu VY: Enteral feeding in the preterm infant. Early Hum Dev 56:89, 1999.

Part 2

57. Anderson TL et al: A controlled trial of glucose versus glucose and amino acids in premature infants. J Pediatr 94:947, 1979.

58. Berry MA et al: Factors associated with growth of extremely premature infants during initial hospitalization. Pediatrics 100:640, 1997.

59. Binder ND et al: Insulin infusion with parenteral nutrition in extremely low birth weight infants with hyperglycemia. J Pediatr 114:273, 1989.

60. Carr B: Total energy expenditure in extremely premature and term infants in early postnatal life. Pediatr Res 47:284A, 2000.

61. Chessex P et al: Effect of amino acid composition of parenteral solutions on nitrogen retention and metabolic response in very-low-birth weight infants. J Pediatr 106:111, 1985.

62. Clark SE et al: Parenteral nutrition increases leucine oxidation but not phenylalanine hydroxylation in premature infants. Pediatr Res 41:568, 1997.

63. Collins JW Jr et al: A controlled trial of insulin infusion and parenteral nutrition in extremely low birth weight infants with glucose intolerance. J Pediatr 118:921, 1991.

64. Cornblath M et al: Hypoglycemia in infancy: The need for a rational definition. A Ciba Foundation discussion meeting. Pediatrics 85:834, 1990.

65. Cornblath M, Schwartz R: Hypoglycemia in the neonate. J Pediatr Endocrinol 6:113, 1993.

66. Cronin WA et al: Intravascular catheter colonization and related bloodstream infection in critically ill neonates. Infect Control Hosp Epidemiol 11:301, 1990.

67. Denne SC, Kalhan SC: Glucose carbon recycling and oxidation in human newborns. Am J Physiol 251:E71, 1986.

68. Denne SC et al: Proteolysis and phenylalanine hydroxylation in response to parenteral nutrition in extremely premature and normal newborns. J Clin Invest 97:746, 1996.

69. Dorvil NP et al: Taurine prevents cholestasis induced by lithocholic acid sulfate in guinea pigs. Am J Clin Nutr 37:221, 1983.

70. Giacoia GP: Cardiac tamponade and hydrothorax as complications of central venous parenteral nutrition in infants. JPEN J Parenter Enteral Nutr 15:110, 1991.

71. Heird WC: New solutions for old problems with new solutions. In Cowett R et al (eds): The Micropremie: The Next Frontier. Columbus, Ohio, Ross Laboratories, 1990, p 71.

72. Heird WC et al: Amino acid mixture designed to maintain normal plasma amino acid patterns in infants and children requiring parenteral nutrition. Pediatrics 80:401, 1987.

73. Heird WC et al: Pediatric parenteral amino acid mixture in low birth weight infants. Pediatrics 81:41, 1988.

74. Helms RA et al: Comparison of a pediatric versus standard amino acid formulation in preterm neonates requiring parenteral nutrition. J Pediatr 110:466, 1987.

75. Hertz DE et al: Intravenous glucose suppresses glucose production but not proteolysis in extremely premature newborns. J Clin Invest 92:1752, 1993.

76. Kashyap S et al: Protein requirements of low birth-weight, very low birthweight, and small for gestational age infants. In Raiha N (ed): Protein Metabolism during Infancy. New York, Vevey/Raven Press, 1994, p 133.

77. Leitch CA, Denne SC: Energy expenditure in the extremely low-birth weight infant. Clin Perinatol 27:181, 2000.

78. Lemons JA et al: Very low birth weight outcomes of the National Institute of Child Health and Human Development Neonatal Research Network, January 1995 through December 1996. NICHD Neonatal Research Network. Pediatrics 107:E1, 2001.

79. Nicholls JM et al: Malassezia furfur infection in a neonate. Br J Hosp Med 49:425, 1993.

80. Nose O et al: Effect of the energy source on changes in energy expenditure, respiratory quotient, and nitrogen balance during total parenteral nutrition in children. Pediatr Res 21:538, 1987.

81. Paisley JE et al: Safety and efficacy of low versus high parenteral amino acids in extremely low birth weight neonates immediately after birth. Pediatr Res 47:293A, 2000.

82. Pereira GR et al: Hyperalimentation-induced cholestasis: Increased incidence and severity in premature infants. Am J Dis Child 135:842, 1981.

83. Phelps SJ, Cochran EB: Effect of the continuous administration of fat emulsion on the infiltration of intravenous lines in infants receiving peripheral parenteral nutrition solutions. JPEN J Parenter Enteral Nutr 13:628, 1989.

84. Poindexter BB et al: Exogenous insulin reduces proteolysis and protein synthesis in extremely low birth weight infants. J Pediatr 132:948, 1998.

85. Poindexter BB et al: Parenteral glutamine supplementation does not reduce the risk of mortality or late-onset sepsis in extremely low birth weight infants. Pediatrics 113:1209, 2004.

86. Poindexter BB et al: The effect of N-acetyl tyrosine and cysteine in parenteral nutrition on protein metabolism in extremely low birth weight neonates. Pediatr Res 47:294A, 2000.

87. Rivera A Jr et al: Plasma amino acid profiles during the first three days of life in infants with respiratory distress syndrome: Effect of parenteral amino acid supplementation. J Pediatr 115:465, 1989.

88. Rivera A Jr et al: Effect of intravenous amino acids on protein metabolism of preterm infants during the first three days of life. Pediatr Res 33:106, 1993.

89. Saini J et al: Early parenteral feeding of amino acids. Arch Dis Child 64:1362, 1989.

90. Sherertz RJ et al: Outbreak of Candida bloodstream infections associated with retrograde medication administration in a neonatal intensive care unit. J Pediatr 120:455, 1992.

91. Snyderman SE: The Protein and Amino Acid Requirements of the Premature Infant. Leiden, Netherlands, Stenfert Kroese, 1971.

92. Sosenko I et al: Effect of early initiation of intravenous lipid administration on the incidence and severity of chronic lung disease in premature infants. J Pediatr 123:975, 1993.

93. Thureen PJ et al: Direct measurement of the energy expenditure of physical activity in preterm infants. J Appl Physiol 85:223, 1998.

94. Thureen PJ et al: Effect of low versus high intravenous amino acid intake on very low birth weight infants in the early neonatal period. Pediatr Res 53:24, 2003.

95. Uauy R et al: Conditionally essential nutrients: Cysteine, taurine, tyrosine, arginine, glutamine, choline, inositol, and nucleotides. In Tsang RC et al (eds): Nutritional Needs of the Preterm Infant: Scientific Basis and Practical Guidelines. Baltimore, Williams & Wilkins, 1993, p 267.

96. van Goudoever JB et al: Effect of dexamethasone on protein metabolism in infants with bronchopulmonary dysplasia. J Pediatr 124:112, 1994.

97. van Goudoever JB et al: Immediate commencement of amino acid supplementation in preterm infants: Effect on serum amino acid concentrations and protein kinetics on the first day of life. J Pediatr 127:458, 1995.

98. van Lingen RA et al: Effects of early amino acid administration during total parenteral nutrition on protein metabolism in pre-term infants. Clin Sci (Lond) 82:199, 1992.

99. Wilson DC et al: Randomised controlled trial of an aggressive nutritional regimen in sick very low birth-weight infants. Arch Dis Child Fetal Neonatal Ed 77:F4, 1997.

100. Yunis KA et al: Glucose kinetics following administration of an intravenous fat emulsion to low-birth-weight neonates. Am J Physiol 263:E844, 1992.

101. Zlotkin SH et al: Intravenous nitrogen and energy intakes required to duplicate in utero nitrogen accretion in prematurely born human infants. J Pediatr 99:115, 1981.

34 Fluid, Electrolyte, and Acid-Base Homeostasis

PART 1

Fluid and Electrolyte Management

Katherine MacRae Dell and Ira D. Davis

Fluid and electrolyte management are crucial in caring for neonates considered high risk. Premature neonates, particularly those with low birthweight, frequently require parenteral fluids, whose quantity and composition can be highly variable. Immature neonates also have important developmental limitations in renal homeostatic mechanisms. The immature infant may be particularly susceptible to significant morbidity and mortality related to fluid and electrolyte imbalances.

This part of the chapter covers the basic renal mechanisms for maintaining fluid and electrolyte homeostasis and outlines the factors that govern fluid and electrolyte requirements for term and preterm infants. We describe methods for monitoring fluid and electrolyte balance, discuss potential complications and treatments of fluid and electrolyte imbalances, and address several specific disorders of high-risk infants that require special consideration.

BODY FLUID COMPOSITION IN THE FETUS AND THE NEWBORN

At birth, the percentage of body weight represented by water is approximately 75% in term infants and greater in premature infants (Fig. 34-1).[31] As gestational age increases, total body water and extracellular water decrease and intracellular fluid content increases. An infant born at 32 weeks' gestation has a total body water and extracellular fluid bodyweight percentage of approximately 83% and 53%, respectively.

During the first 7 to 10 days of life, all infants experience a reduction in body weight, which, in part, represents inadequate calorie intake during this period. However, this physiologic weight loss is largely the result of a reduction in the extracellular compartment of body water.[7,82-84] The precise mechanism for the postnatal contraction of the extracellular fluid compartment is unclear. However, it has been well documented that infants with low birthweight lose approximately 10% to 15% of the extracellular fluid during the first 5 days of life.[82] This phenomenon is associated with a concurrent diuretic phase resulting in negative fluid and sodium balance.[15,58]

It is important to recognize that in the first few days of life, physiologic weight loss in an infant with low birthweight represents isotonic contraction of body fluids. The contraction of the extracellular fluid space appears to be part of a normal transitional physiologic process. Perturbations of this normal transitional physiology can lead to imbalances in sodium and water homeostasis. In particular, high fluid intake resulting in a lack of extracellular fluid compartment contraction may be associated with a higher incidence of symptomatic patent ductus arteriosus[13] and necrotizing enterocolitis.[14]

SODIUM BALANCE IN THE NEWBORN

Extracellular fluid (ECF) volume, and thus plasma volume, is determined by the total sodium content of the ECF. Renal sodium handling, therefore, is crucial in maintaining sodium balance and protecting against volume depletion or overload. As with other ions that are freely filtered, the bulk of the filtered sodium is reabsorbed in the proximal tubule. Additional sodium reabsorption occurs in the loop of Henle via the sodium-potassium-2-chloride cotransporter (NKCC2), the therapeutic target of loop diuretics. In the distal convoluted tubule, sodium is further reabsorbed via the thiazide-sensitive sodium chloride cotransporter (NCCT). The major site of fine regulation of sodium reabsorption is

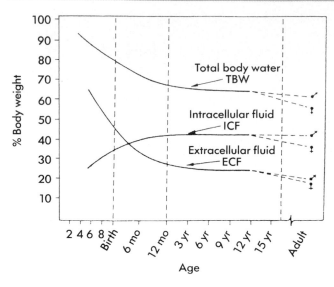

FIGURE 34-1. Change with age in total body water and its major subdivisions. (From Friis-Hansen B: Body water compartments in children: Changes during growth and related changes in body composition. Pediatrics 28:169, 1961.)

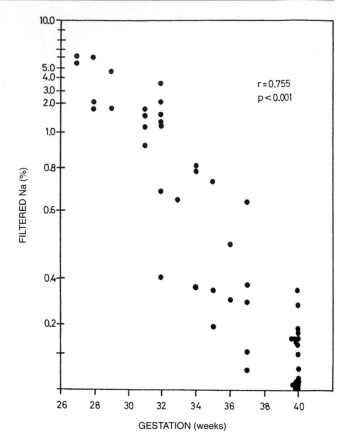

FIGURE 34-2. Scattergram demonstrating the inverse correlation between fractional sodium excretion and gestational age. (From Siegel SR et al: Renal function as a marker of human renal maturation. Acta Paediatr Scand 65:481, 1976.)

the collecting tubule, where aldosterone acts on the principal cells to promote sodium reabsorption through sodium channels located on the luminal membrane.

Renal sodium losses are inversely proportional to gestational age; the fractional excretion of sodium (FENa) is as high as 5% to 6% in infants born at 28 weeks' gestation (Fig. 34-2).[85] As a result, preterm infants younger than 35 weeks' gestation sometimes display negative sodium balance and hyponatremia during the initial 2 to 3 weeks of life because of high renal sodium losses and inefficient intestinal sodium absorption.[91]

Many mechanisms are responsible for increased urinary sodium losses in the preterm infant. The immature kidney exhibits glomerulotubular imbalance, a physiologic state in which the glomerular filtration rate (GFR) exceeds the reabsorptive capacity of the renal tubules. This is caused by a number of factors, including a preponderance of glomeruli compared with tubular structures, renal tubular immaturity, large extracellular volume, and reduced oxygen availability.[71] Decreased renal nerve activity can also contribute to increased renal sodium losses. Studies in fetal and newborn sheep demonstrate an inverse relationship between renal nerve stimulation and urine sodium excretion.[71] Decreased responsiveness to aldosterone is also characteristic of fetal and postnatal kidneys compared with adult kidneys, and it results in a decrease in sodium reabsorption.[72]

The abnormalities in sodium and water balance seen in premature infants are attenuated, to some degree, by prenatal steroid administration. Prenatal steroid treatment is associated with lower insensible water loss, decreased incidence of hypernatremia, and a lower fluid intake.[65] Diuresis and natriuresis also occur earlier

in treated infants. This beneficial effect on water and sodium balance in infants with extremely low birthweight is thought to be mediated by maturation of the renal epithelial transport systems that control fluid and electrolyte homeostasis. Specifically, prenatal glucocorticoids promote maturation of proximal tubule ion channels, including the Na^+/H^+ exchanger and the Na^+/HCO_3^- cotransporter, as well as increases in urinary flow rate and fractional excretion of sodium.[4,9]

In contrast with preterm infants, healthy term neonates have basal sodium handling similar to that of adults. Their FENa is less than 1%, although a transient increase in FENa occurs during the diuretic phase that occurs on the second and third days of life.[58]

Urinary sodium losses in preterm and term neonates may be increased in certain conditions, including hypoxia, respiratory distress, hyperbilirubinemia, acute tubular necrosis, polycythemia, increased fluid and sodium intake, and theophylline or diuretic administration.[43] Pharmacologic agents, such as dopamine, beta blockers, and angiotensin converting enzyme (ACE) inhibitors, which affect adrenergic neural pathways in the kidney and the renin-angiotensin axis, can also increase urinary sodium losses in the neonate.

WATER BALANCE IN THE NEWBORN

The Role of Antidiuretic Hormone

Water balance is primarily controlled by antidiuretic hormone (ADH), which controls water absorption in the collecting duct of the distal nephron. ADH secretion is regulated by hypothalamic osmoreceptors (which monitor serum osmolarity) and baroreceptors of the carotid sinus and left atrium (which monitor intravascular blood volume). Stimulation of ADH secretion occurs when serum osmolarity increases above 285 mOsm/kg or when effective blood volume is significantly diminished. Increases in serum osmolarity also stimulate thirst receptors in the anterior hypothalamus to promote increased water intake. Intravascular volume has a greater influence on ADH secretion than serum osmolarity. Thus, patients with hyponatremia and concomitant volume depletion are not able to suppress ADH in response to the decrease in serum osmolarity.

At baseline, when the serum osmolarity is within the normal range, the collecting duct is impermeable to water. In response to a rise in serum osmolarity, ADH produced in the hypothalamus binds to its receptor, vasopressin V2 receptor (V2R), located on the basolateral membrane of principal and inner medullary collecting duct cells.[53] Receptor activation results in elevated levels of intracellular cyclic adenosine monophosphate (cAMP). Downstream signaling pathways promote movement of vesicles containing aquaporin-2 (AQ2) water channels to the apical surface. The presence of these water channels on the watertight apical membranes renders them permeable to water. Withdrawal of ADH stimulates endocytosis of AQ2-containing vesicles, which restores the collecting duct cells to a state of water impermeability.

Renal Concentrating and Diluting Capacity

Maximal renal concentration and dilution require structural maturity, well-developed tubular transport mechanisms, and an intact hypothalamic-renal vasopressin axis.[68] In adults and older children, decreased fluid intake or increased fluid losses activate a highly efficient renal concentrating mechanism that can produce maximally concentrated urine with an osmolarity of 1500 mOsm/kg, resulting in fluid conservation. Conversely, excessive fluid intake triggers the diluting mechanism of the kidney that can produce maximally dilute urine with an osmolarity as low as 50 mOsm/kg, resulting in free water excretion.

The neonatal kidney, in contrast, has less-efficient renal concentrating and diluting capabilities, limiting the ability to adjust to fluid perturbations.[18,60] When challenged, term newborn infants can concentrate the urine to an osmolarity of 800 mOsm/kg, whereas preterm infants can concentrate to a urine osmolarity of only 600 mOsm/kg.[18]

Multiple factors limit renal concentrating capacity in the preterm infant. Structural immaturity of the renal medulla limits sodium, chloride, and urea movement to the interstitium. Preferential blood flow through the vasa recta limits generation of a medullary gradient. Diminished urea-generated osmotic gradient in the renal medulla limits production and maintenance of the countercurrent mechanisms that are essential in producing maximally concentrated urine. Finally, tubular responsiveness to vasopressin is diminished due to decreased transcription and protein synthesis of AQ2 water channels.[26,96]

Similar discrepancies are seen in the diluting capabilities of term versus preterm infants. When challenged with a water load, term infants can produce dilute urine with an osmolarity as low as 50 mOsm/kg. In contrast, the kidneys of preterm infants may be capable of diluting the urine to an osmolarity of only 70 mOsm/kg.[60,76] Although the diluting capacity of term infants approximates that of adults, term infants can still exhibit a reduced diluting capacity. Low baseline GFR and decreased activity of transporters in the early distal tubule (the diluting segment of the nephron) can both limit a neonate's diluting abilities.[87]

The diminished urinary diluting and concentrating capacities of neonates has important implications for their care. Excessive fluid restriction places newborns, particularly preterm neonates, at risk for dehydration or hypernatremia, or both. Conversely, generous fluid intake poses the risk of intravascular volume overload or hyponatremia. These facts underscore the importance of careful calculation of fluid and electrolyte requirements and close monitoring of fluid balance in high-risk neonates.

CALCULATION OF FLUID AND ELECTROLYTE REQUIREMENTS

Calculation of fluid and electrolyte requirements in the newborn is based on maintenance needs, deficits, and ongoing losses. Critical factors that determine these fluid requirements include gestational age, renal function, ambient air temperature, ventilator dependence, presence of drainage tubes, and gastrointestinal losses.

Maintenance Fluids and Electrolytes

Maintenance fluid requirements are the quantities of water needed to preserve neutral water balance in the typical preterm or term newborn. The total amount of maintenance fluid required is equal to urine production plus insensible losses. A summary of maintenance fluid requirements during the first month of life for full-term and preterm infants is listed in Table 34-1. The figures in Table 34-1 are only guidelines; they are to be used as a starting point for prescribing maintenance fluid for infants with low birthweight during the first week of life. Further adjustments must be based on the clinical

TABLE 34-1. Maintenance Fluid Requirements during the First Month of Life

BIRTH WEIGHT (g)	INSENSIBLE WATER LOSS (mL/kg/day)	Water Requirements (mL/kg/day) by Age		
		Day 1-2	Day 3-7	Day 8-30
<750	100-200	100-200 +	150-200 +	120-180
750-1000	60-70	80-150	100-150	120-180
1001-1500	30-65	60-100	80-150	120-180
>1500	15-30	60-80	100-150	120-180

Adapted from Veille JC: AGA infants in a thermoneutral environment during the first week of life. Clin Perinatol 15:863, 1988; Taeusch W, Ballard RA (eds): Schaffer and Avery's Diseases of the Newborn, 6th ed. Philadelphia, WB Saunders, 1991; Lorenz J, et al: Phases of fluid and electrolyte homeostasis in the extremely low birth weight infant. Pediatrics 96:484, 1995.

situation. In particular, close attention must be paid to the patient's volume status and assessment of factors that could increase or decrease the baseline fluid requirements if the clinician is to provide appropriate management of the infant.

Insensible Losses

Insensible water losses are primarily evaporative losses via the skin and respiratory tract. In newborn infants, one third of insensible water loss occurs through the respiratory tract, and the remaining two thirds occurs through the skin.[38] A number of physiologic, environmental, and therapeutic factors can influence insensible water loss, making it the most variable component of the maintenance fluid requirements in newborns. Table 34-2 summarizes the effect of various factors on the degree of insensible water loss in newborns. The most important variable is the maturity of the infant because there is an inverse relationship between body weight and insensible water loss in a neutral thermal environment with moderately high relative humidity.[29,94]

Transepidermal water loss contributes significantly to the increased insensible losses of the premature infant (Fig. 34-3).[35] Factors that contribute to these increased losses in preterm versus term infants include greater

water permeability through a relatively immature epithelial layer of skin, a higher ratio of surface area to bodyweight, and increased skin vascularity. Although earlier animal data suggested that prenatal glucocorticoids could decrease insensible losses in premature infants by enhancing maturation of the epidermis, more recent data in humans failed to demonstrate such an effect.[41] Infants who have conditions associated with skin breakdown, such as burns, or large skin defects, such as omphaloceles, also have increased insensible water losses.

Ambient temperature and relative humidity also play an important role in influencing insensible water losses.[10-12] A rise in ambient temperature results in increased insensible water loss. Although a decrease in ambient temperature increases energy expenditure on the basis of cold stress, it has no effect on insensible water loss. Phototherapy may increase insensible water losses by up to 50%, as well.

Relative humidity of the environment also has a significant influence on insensible water loss.[35] With ambient temperature held constant, a lower relative humidity increases water evaporation from the skin because of increased vapor pressure on the skin surface compared with the ambient vapor pressure. Alternatively, in the presence of high relative humidity, water

TABLE 34-2. Factors Affecting Insensible Water Loss in Newborn Infants

FACTOR	EFFECT ON INSENSIBLE WATER LOSS
Level of maturity	Inversely proportional to birth weight and gestational age (see Fig. 34-3)
Environmental temperature above neutral thermal zone	Increased in proportion to increment in temperature
Elevated body temperature	Increased by up to 300% at rectal temperature above 37.2°C
High ambient or inspired humidity	Reduced by 30% if ambient or respiratory vapor pressure equals skin or respiratory tract vapor pressure
Skin breakdown (e.g., burn)	Increased; magnitude depends on extent of lesion
Congenital skin defects (e.g., large omphalocele)	Increased; magnitude depends on size of defects
Radiant warmer	Increased by about 50% above values obtained in incubator setting with moderate relative humidity and neutral thermal environment
Phototherapy	Increased by up to 50%
Double-walled incubator or plastic heat shield	Reduced by 10% to 30%

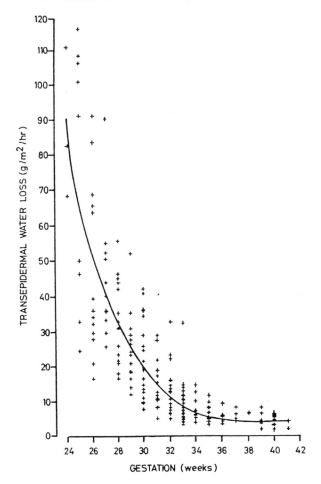

FIGURE 34-3. The effects of gestation on transepidermal water loss. Measurements were made from abdominal skin and carried out in the first few days of life. (From Hammarlund K et al: Transepidermal water loss in newborn infants. III. Relation to gestational age. Acta Paediatr Scand 68:795, 1979.)

evaporation is less. Thus, placing an infant under a radiant warmer increases insensible water loss by 50% above the values obtained in an incubator with neutral thermal environment and moderately high relative humidity.[92] In contrast, use of a double-walled incubator or plastic heat shield reduces baseline insensible water losses by 10% to 30% (see also Chapter 29).[64] Infants on mechanical ventilation, which provides a humidified oxygen delivery system, also have reduced water evaporation from the respiratory tract.

Urinary Losses

The quantity of water required for the formation of urine depends on two major factors: the degree of renal function and the renal solute load. Under normal conditions, a major determinant of renal water requirement is renal solute load. Renal solute load is derived from exogenous and endogenous sources.

During the first day or two of life, the exogenous solute load of infants with low birthweight is minimal because they usually do not receive electrolytes or protein. Because they are not usually fed enterally, however, delivery of calories by intravenous glucose-containing solutions does not meet basal energy needs. For instance, in the first day or two of life, the basal energy requirement for infants with low birthweight is approximately 50 kcal/kg body weight. If they are given 70 to 90 mL/kg per day of a 10% glucose solution, the caloric intake is 35 kcal/kg per day. The infants, therefore, must derive the remaining mandatory energy requirement from an endogenous source; in other words, they must derive energy from catabolism.

The catabolic state produces approximately 6 mOsm/kg per day of an endogenous solute load presented to the kidney. Assuming the infant can produce a maximum urinary concentration of 600 mOsm/kg, then a minimum of 10 mL/kg per day of free water is required to excrete this solute load. As the infant ages, the exogenous intake from parenteral and enteral sources increases, resulting in increased caloric intake. The exogenous solute load therefore increases, whereas catabolism decreases, resulting in a decreased endogenous solute load.

By 2 or 3 weeks of age, an infant consuming 80 to 120 kcal/kg per day has a total solute load of approximately 15 to 20 mOsm/kg per day. Assuming that the infant can produce a maximum urinary concentration of 800 mOsm/kg by this age, then 20 to 25 mL/kg per day of free water is required to excrete the solute load.

Other Fluid Losses

Water loss through the gastrointestinal tract from stool output is minimal during the first few days of life, particularly in infants with low birthweight. Once enteral feeds begin, the water loss in the stool is 5 to 10 mL/kg per day.

In a growing infant, the amount of water required for new tissue formation should be considered in calculating maintenance fluid requirements. Because infants grow at the rate of 10 to 20 g/kg per day and new tissue contains 70% water, the maintenance fluid should provide a net water balance of 10 to 15 mL/kg per day.

Electrolyte Requirements

Maintenance sodium and chloride are usually not provided during the first 1 to 2 days of life due to the relatively volume expanded state of the newborn. Similarly, potassium is not provided in parenteral fluid until urinary flow has been established and normal renal function is ensured. From postnatal days 3 to 7, maintenance sodium, potassium, and chloride requirements are approximately 1 to 2 mEq/kg per day. Beyond the first week of life, 2 to 3 mEq/kg per day or more of sodium and chloride are required to maintain the positive electrolyte balance that is necessary for the formation of new tissue. Because of high urinary sodium losses, premature infants may require up to 4 or 5 mEq/kg of sodium per day during the first few weeks of life.

Estimating Pathologic Losses and Deficit Replacement

Many clinical situations require careful estimates of ongoing pathologic losses and replacement of deficits. Commonly encountered conditions include diarrhea with dehydration, chest tube drainage, surgical wound drainage, and excessive urine losses from osmotic diuresis. The important guiding principle in managing patients with these conditions is to accurately measure the volume and composition of the pathologic losses. Electrolyte losses can then be calculated by multiplying the volume of fluid losses by the electrolyte content of the respective body fluids (Table 34-3).

Estimating replacement for pathologic fluid and electrolyte losses can be difficult, particularly in infants who accumulate fluid and electrolytes in static body fluid compartments. This phenomenon, commonly referred to as *third spacing,* occurs in several conditions including sepsis, hydrops fetalis, hypoalbuminemia, and intra-abdominal infections, as well as following abdominal or cardiac surgery. An infant with necrotizing enterocolitis, for example, often accumulates fluid in the mucosal and submucosal tissues of the small and large intestine as well as in the peritoneal cavity. Under these circumstances, large amounts of fluid, electrolytes, and protein can leak into the interstitial tissue and cannot be accurately quantified. Because fluid lost into these tissue spaces does not contribute to effective arterial blood volume and circulatory balance, these patients can appear edematous even though their intra-vascular volume is decreased. The most appropriate strategic approach to managing these infants is to replenish the extracellular fluid compartments with colloid and crystalloid.

MONITORING FLUID AND ELECTROLYTE BALANCE

Interpretation of key clinical feedback is a critical part of successful fluid and electrolyte management strategies in newborns. Fluid and electrolyte balance can be achieved by using a meticulous and organized system that obtains pertinent data and applies the physiologic principles outlined in the beginning of this chapter. A careful assessment of clinical indicators of volume status, including heart rate, blood pressure, skin turgor, capillary refill, oral mucosa integrity, and fullness of the anterior fontanelle is essential. Other pertinent data that must be monitored include body weight, fluid intake, urine and stool output, serum electrolytes, and urine osmolarity or specific gravity.

During the first few days of life, appropriate fluid and electrolyte balance is reflected by a urine output of approximately 1 to 3 mL/kg per hour, a urine specific gravity of approximately 1.008 to 1.012, and an approximate weight loss of 5% to 15% in term infants and in premature infants with very low birthweight, respectively.[84] Microsampling of serum electrolytes can be done at 8- to 24-hour intervals, depending on illness severity, gestational age, and fluid-electrolyte balance. Extracellular volume depletion is manifest by excessive weight loss, dry oral mucosa, sunken anterior fontanelle, capillary refill greater than 3 seconds, diminished skin turgor, increased heart rate, low blood pressure, elevated blood urea nitrogen, or metabolic acidosis. Serum sodium, which reflects sodium concentration but not sodium content, could be normal, decreased, or increased in states of volume depletion. Bedside monitoring of weight gain, as an indicator of volume status and growth, is essential for monitoring the adequacy of fluid and calorie intake in sick neonates. Beyond the first week of life, infants should gain approximately 20 to 30 g per day.

HYPONATREMIA AND HYPERNATREMIA

Hyponatremia

Hyponatremia, defined as a serum sodium less than 130 mmol/L, is caused by one of three general mechanisms: an inability to excrete a water load, excessive sodium losses, or inadequate sodium intake. Most commonly, sick newborns are unable to excrete a water load because a decreased effective arterial blood volume prevents the suppression of ADH secretion. Hyponatremia can also occur as the result of decreased fluid delivery to the distal nephron diluting segments. One common cause of this decreased delivery is decreased glomerular filtration rate caused by acute renal failure; another is increased proximal tubular fluid and sodium reabsorption associated with volume depletion. Defects in sodium chloride transport in the cortical and medullary ascending limb of the loop of Henle, which is essential in producing an osmotic gradient for distal water absorption via the countercurrent multiplier, also limit the diluting capacity of the nephron.

Treatment for hyponatremia varies depending on the underlying etiology. For instance, a patient with hyponatremia and volume depletion should receive increased fluids, but a patient with oliguric acute renal failure should have fluids restricted. These examples highlight the importance of assessing the neonate's volume status when determining therapy.

TABLE 34-3. Electrolyte Content of Body Fluids

FLUID SOURCE	NA (mmol/L)	K (mmol/L)	CL (mmol/L)
Stomach	20-80	5-20	100-150
Small intestine	100-140	5-15	90-120
Bile	120-140	5-15	90-120
Ileostomy	45-135	3-15	20-120
Diarrheal stool	10-90	10-80	10-110

Cl, chloride; K, potassium; Na, sodium.

Hyponatremia in the newborn can occur early during the first week of life (early onset) or in the latter half of the first month of life (late onset). The early-onset form usually reflects free water excess due to either increased maternal free water intake during labor[42] or perinatal nonosmotic release of vasopressin.[68] Nonosmotic vasopressin release is seen in conditions such as perinatal asphyxia, respiratory distress, bilateral pneumothoraces, and intraventricular hemorrhage[67] or with some medications, including morphine, barbiturates, or carbamazepine. Early-onset hyponatremia can also occur from excess free water administration in the postnatal period as well as suboptimal sodium intake in oral feeds or parenteral fluids. Sodium supplementation in premature infants (gestational age of 33 weeks or less) during the first two weeks of life was associated with improved developmental outcomes at age 10 to 13 years compared with a group of premature infants who did not receive sodium supplements.[3]

Late-onset hyponatremia is most commonly caused by negative sodium balance. Negative sodium balance can occur from either inadequate sodium intake or excessive renal losses due to a high fractional excretion of sodium, particularly in preterm infants younger than 28 weeks' gestation.[85] Retention of free water from excessive ADH release, renal failure, or edematous disorders can contribute to late-onset hyponatremia, but this is uncommon. Water restriction is necessary in treating hyponatremia related to these disorders.

THE ROLE OF ALDOSTERONE IN SODIUM AND POTASSIUM HOMEOSTASIS

Aldosterone is a steroid hormone produced in the adrenal cortex. It has a critical role in maintaining both sodium and potassium homeostasis in the kidney. It is produced in response to volume depletion, via the renin-angiotensin-aldosterone axis, or to a rise in serum potassium. Under the influence of aldosterone, apical epithelial sodium channels (ENaCs) are inserted on the luminal (urinary) surface of the collecting tubule, allowing sodium to be reabsorbed down its concentration gradient. Potassium, as the primary intracellular cation, is then excreted in return. This process is further facilitated by aldosterone-mediated increase in the activity of the basolateral Na^+,K^+,ATPase.[46,75] Aldosterone also has a role in acid-base homeostasis and promotes H^+ secretion (see Part 2, Acid-Base Management, later) via actions on the H^+ ATPase located on the luminal surface of adjacent intercalated cells. Thus, abnormalities in either production of or renal responsiveness to aldosterone can result in variable degrees of renal sodium wasting, hyperkalemia, and metabolic acidosis.

CONGENITAL ADRENAL HYPERPLASIA

There are several forms of congenital adrenal hyperplasia (CAH) (see also Chapter 47, Part 4). The most common form is complete absence of activity by 21-hydroxylase, a key enzyme in the production of aldosterone. Affected female patients have ambiguous genitalia at birth due to excess adrenal androgens. Patients typically present with severe hyponatremia, hyperkalemia, and

metabolic acidosis at 1 to 3 weeks of age as the result of a salt-losing crisis. Additional laboratory abnormalities typically seen with this disorder include elevated plasma levels of renin, adrenocorticotropic hormone (ACTH), 17-hydroxyprogesterone, progesterone, and androstenedione, as well as increased urinary 17-ketosteroids and undetectable serum cortisol levels.

Initial treatment is directed at correcting the electrolyte abnormalities. Normal saline or 3% saline should be used to correct the serum sodium to at least 125 mmol/L. Insulin at a dose of 0.1 units/kg with 0.5 g/kg of glucose should be given for serum potassium values exceeding 7 mEq/L. Transcellular shifts of potassium into cells is further facilitated by bicarbonate administration at a dose of 1 or 2 mEq/kg. Concomitant therapy to replace glucocorticoids and mineralocorticoids should be instituted to help normalize serum electrolytes and treat the underlying disease. Sodium supplements may be necessary for a prolonged period of time.

PSEUDOHYPOALDOSTERONISM

Pseudohypoaldosteronism (PHA) refers to a group of disorders characterized by apparent renal tubular unresponsiveness to aldosterone as evidenced by hyperkalemia, metabolic acidosis, and variable degrees of renal sodium wasting. PHA has two major subtypes. Type I usually manifests in infancy with hypotension, severe sodium wasting, and hyperkalemia. Type II (Gordon syndrome) typically appears in late childhood and adulthood (although rare neonatal cases are reported) with normal or increased blood pressure, metabolic acidosis, and hyperkalemia. Because hyponatremia generally does not occur with PHA type II, it is discussed in detail under Metabolic Acidosis, later.

Type I PHA can be *primary,* inherited as an autosomal recessive or autosomal dominant trait,[36] or *secondary,* as the result of tubular damage from disorders such as obstructive uropathy. Autosomal dominant type I PHA, previously designated the renal type I, is the most common type I PHA. Patients with this form usually present during early infancy with failure to thrive, weight loss, vomiting, dehydration, or shock. The history often includes polyhydramnios, reflecting excessive fetal renal salt wasting and polyuria. Sweat and salivary electrolytes are normal in this form of type I PHA. Although it is inherited in an autosomal dominant fashion, expression is variable.[69] The disorder is caused by mutations in the gene encoding the aldosterone (mineralocorticoid) receptor.[32]

Treatment involves administration of large quantities of sodium chloride, 10 to 15 mEq/kg per day. Although the defect in salt handling appears to be lifelong, serum sodium levels typically become easier to control by 1 to 2 years of age. Increased dietary sodium intake, maturation of proximal tubular transport of sodium, and improvement in the renal tubular response to mineralocorticoids all contribute to the clinical improvement over time.[78]

Autosomal recessive type I PHA, previously designated "multiple target organ defects type I PHA," is a severe, life-threatening systemic disease that affects sodium and potassium handling in the kidney, sweat glands, salivary glands, nasal mucosa, and colon.[36] Patients with this disorder usually present in the newborn period with severe salt wasting and life-threatening hyperkalemia. They also have increased sweat chloride that mimics a sign of cystic fibrosis (CF). Demonstration of an absent amiloride-sensitive nasal transepithelial voltage is a suggested method for distinguishing PHA from CF in infants with positive sweat chloride tests.[66] Rarely, patients with PHA present with respiratory distress syndrome (RDS) that is resistant to surfactant therapy.[1]

Patients with AR type I PHA have a poorer outcome compared with those who have the autosomal dominant form due to the systemic nature of the disease and complete unresponsiveness to mineralocorticoid effects in multiple organs. The disease is caused by mutations in one of three subunits of the amiloride-sensitive epithelial sodium channel (ENaC) of the principal collecting tubule cell, resulting in markedly impaired sodium reabsorption and potassium secretion.[21]

Sodium chloride supplementation alone often is not adequate to control hyperkalemia and metabolic acidosis in these patients. Dietary restriction of potassium intake and the use of rectal sodium polystyrene sulfonate resin (Kayexalate), a sodium-potassium exchange resin, is often required. Indomethacin or hydrochlorothiazide may be necessary to control the hyperkalemia and acidosis. These therapies must be continued throughout the patient's life, as type I PHA does not usually improve with age.

Secondary forms of type I PHA are also seen in the newborn period. Partial tubular insensitivity to aldosterone may be seen in patients with unilateral renal vein thrombosis, neonatal medullary necrosis, urinary tract malformations, and pyelonephritis or other tubulo-interstitial diseases. Patients with congenital obstructive uropathies, such as posterior urethral valves, sometimes exhibit aldosterone resistance, which manifests as a hyperkalemic metabolic acidosis despite relatively intact renal function.

Hypernatremia

Hypernatremia, defined as a serum sodium greater than 150 mmol/L, occurs as the result of increased insensible water losses, inadequate water intake, excess sodium administration, or increased free water losses from the urinary tract. Hypernatremia occurring in the first week of life is typically due to either the excess sodium intake that commonly occurs following resuscitation with sodium bicarbonate or high insensible losses. The latter is particularly true for infants with low birthweight.[23] Onset of hypernatremia later in the first month of life usually is due to either excess sodium supplementation or inadequate free water intake.

DIABETES INSIPIDUS

Diabetes insipidus (DI) is characterized by severe urinary water losses, reflecting an inability to produce concentrated urine. DI can occur as the result of low levels of circulating ADH (central DI) or impaired renal response to ADH (nephrogenic DI). Newborns with this disorder present with polyuria, polydipsia, chronic dehydration, irritability, poor feeding, and growth failure.

Nephrogenic DI can be inherited or can occur as the secondary result of processes that cause renal tubular damage. The most common inherited form of nephrogenic DI is caused by mutations in the gene encoding the vasopressin receptor V2R and is inherited as an X-linked recessive disease. Less commonly, autosomal recessive and autosomal dominant forms have been reported, caused by mutations in the AQ2 water channel.[54,62] Causes of secondary nephrogenic DI include congenital structural disorders such as obstructive uropathy or nephronophthisis, chronic kidney disease, hypercalcemia, or hypokalemia.

Treatment of nephrogenic DI includes feeding with a low-sodium formula to reduce solute intake and thus the obligate water loss associated with solute excretion. Thiazide diuretics, such as chlorothiazide (Diuril) at a dose of 20 to 30 mg/kg per day, are also used to reduce extracellular sodium content, which enhances sodium reabsorption in the proximal tubule and diminishes sodium and water delivery to the distal nephron. Amiloride at a dose of 0.3 mg/kg per day might also be necessary to reduce urinary potassium losses that can occur with the use of thiazide diuretics. Although prostaglandin inhibitors have been successfully used to treat nephrogenic DI, long-term use of these agents is not recommended because of gastrointestinal, hematopoietic, and renal complications.

Central DI can result from midline central nervous system malformations, anoxic encephalopathy, cerebral edema, or trauma. Although some ADH secretion may be present in central DI, levels are insufficient to promote appropriate water absorption in the distal nephron. Intranasal desmopressin acetate (DDAVP) at a dose of 5 to 30 μg per day is effective therapy for this condition.

FLUID AND ELECTROLYTE THERAPY IN COMMON NEONATAL CONDITIONS

Perinatal Asphyxia

Renal parenchymal injury from perinatal asphyxia often results in acute tubular necrosis (ATN), which is commonly accompanied by oliguria or anuria (see Chapter 49 for a more detailed discussion). In the presence of acute renal failure, fluid restriction to amounts equal to urine output plus insensible losses is critical in order to avoid volume excess. If urine volume is minimal, only insensible water losses should be replaced. In a term infant, insensible water losses are approximately 20 to 25 mL/kg per day, and stool loss is minimal. Therefore, fluid requirements during the first day of life in an anuric term infant are approximately 30 mL/kg per day. Insensible losses for an anuric premature infant can be as much as 80 mL/kg per day, depending on gestational age.

Fluid restriction is often difficult to accomplish when relatively large volumes of intravenous drugs are necessary. Parenteral nutrition with high calorie density delivered in the smallest volume possible is often necessary when fluid restriction is undertaken in order to avoid fluid overload and water intoxication. Once urine production normalizes, fluid intake can be liberalized to reflect urine output and insensible losses.

If the cause of oliguria or anuria is unclear and the infant appears to be intravascularly depleted, a test dose of 10 mL/kg body weight of normal saline can be given. During the oliguric or anuric phase of ATN, potassium should not be given because it could cause hyperkalemia. During the recovery phase of ATN, small infants can experience large urinary sodium and potassium losses, which should be calculated and replaced.[28]

In severe perinatal asphyxia, the renal parenchymal injury can be severe enough to produce renal failure lasting for several days to weeks or could be permanent in cases with cortical necrosis. In the presence of hyperkalemia, defined as a serum potassium in excess of 7 mEq/L, the cardiac rhythm of the infant should be monitored by continuous electrocardiogram to detect any cardiac arrhythmia. Treatment options for hyperkalemia include insulin given with glucose sodium polystyrene sulfonate resin (Kayexalate), sodium bicarbonate in the presence of metabolic acidosis, and peritoneal dialysis (see Chapter 49). If a significant arrhythmia is present, calcium chloride or calcium gluconate infusion is also indicated to antagonize the toxic effects of hyperkalemia on the cardiac membrane.

Symptomatic Patent Ductus Arteriosus

Patent ductus arteriosus (PDA) with left-to-right shunt and pulmonary edema is a common cause of morbidity in preterm infants, particularly those with respiratory distress syndrome in the first few days of life (see also Chapter 43). Fluid overload during this period is associated with an increased incidence of symptomatic PDA.[13] Although the precise mechanism by which fluid overload leads to an increased risk of PDA is still unclear, it could be related to the lack of isotonic contraction of body fluids in this group of infants.

To prevent symptomatic PDA, it is important to monitor fluid and electrolyte balance in infants with low birthweight to ensure that physiologic isotonic body fluid contraction does occur.[15] Although the timing of treatment for PDA, especially with respect to prophylaxis of an asymptomatic PDA, and optimal dosing regimen remain ongoing issues of debate, intravenous indomethacin remains the drug of choice for medical management of PDA.[95]

Renal insufficiency is an important potential complication of indomethacin use and is due to inhibition of vasodilating prostaglandins, which results in unopposed renal vasoconstriction. Risk factors for developing renal insufficiency following indomethacin treatment include existing renal or electrolyte abnormalities, maternal exposure to indomethacin used as a tocolytic agent, and chorioamnionitis.[40] Therefore, urine output and renal function must be monitored closely during the course of IV indomethacin therapy. The lowest possible effective doses of indomethacin should be used, and concomitant administration of other nephrotoxic agents, such as aminoglycosides, should be avoided.

Chronic Lung Disease

Infants with chronic lung disease (see also Chapter 42, Part 7) present complex challenges in fluid and electrolyte management. Because of higher basal metabolic rates[90] and increased calorie requirements, the calorie density or volume, or both, of parenteral or enteral feedings must be maximized. Care must be taken to provide optimal fluid and nutrient intake without incurring volume overload and worsening pulmonary disease.

In addition, therapies used to treat the underlying lung disease, most notably, diuretics, can have significant effects on fluid and electrolyte balance.[47] Furosemide, a potent loop diuretic, causes a marked increase in urinary sodium, potassium, and hydrogen ion excretion, leading to hypokalemic metabolic alkalosis. Chronic use of this diuretic can also enhance urinary excretion of calcium, leading to osteopenia of prematurity, urolithiasis, or nephrocalcinosis.[27,79] Furosemide should be used with caution in neonates, particularly premature infants, with acute renal failure and in those receiving concomitant aminoglycoside therapy, in order to avoid complications of ototoxicity.[37,80] Chlorothiazide, a less-potent thiazide diuretic that acts at the distal tubule, also causes a hypokalemic metabolic alkalosis. In contrast to loop diuretics, however, thiazides actually decrease urinary calcium excretion. Treatment with spironolactone, a potassium-sparing aldosterone inhibitor, can be associated with hyperkalemia.

Strategies for preventing complications of diuretic use include minimizing diuretic doses, obtaining frequent serum electrolyte measurements to detect electrolyte imbalance, monitoring urinary calcium excretion (when applicable), and supplementing with calcium to prevent osteopenia of prematurity.

PART 2

Acid-Base Management

Katherine MacRae Dell and Ira D. Davis

Acid-base management is essential to the care of high-risk neonates, especially those with low birthweight. The immature infant is particularly susceptible to significant morbidity and mortality related to acid-base imbalances. This section covers normal acid-base homeostasis in the neonate and the way these processes are influenced during the stages of nephron development. The diagnostic and therapeutic approach to acid-base disorders as well as a discussion of common acid-base disorders is also presented.

ACID-BASE HOMEOSTASIS IN THE NEONATE

Normal neonatal metabolism occurs within a tightly controlled extracellular pH ranging from 7.35 to 7.43. Normal growth and development are critically dependent on this homeostasis, which is threatened in the ill term newborn or premature infant. Maintenance of serum pH (i.e., hydrogen ion concentration) within the physiologic range requires two major processes: acute compensation and chronic compensation. Acute compensation is accomplished by rapid acid or base buffering by intracellular and extracellular buffers in response to acute decreases or increases in serum pH. Chronic compensation is accomplished by renal excretion of acid or base, including an obligate daily acid load of approximately 1 to 2 mEq/kg per day. Both renal and extrarenal homeostatic mechanisms contribute to the maintenance of acid-base balance.

Acute Compensation: Body Buffer Systems

Following an acute change in serum pH caused by losses or gains of acid or base to the body, intracellular and extracellular buffering mechanisms respond rapidly to return the serum pH to a physiologic level. In response to a decrease in plasma pH, H^+ enters the cell in exchange for K^+ by way of a H^+-K^+ exchanger. The H^+ is then buffered by intracellular buffers including hemoglobin, organic phosphates, and bone hydroxyapatite.[19] Conversely, when serum pH rises, H^+ leaves the cell in exchange for K^+. Thus, acute acidosis often results in hyperkalemia, whereas alkalosis is associated with hypokalemia.

Intracellular buffering accounts for about 47% of an acute acid load and can reach even higher levels during more prolonged episodes of acidosis. Much of this buffering capacity is in bone. In disorders characterized by chronic acidosis, bone resorption is increased and bone sodium, potassium, calcium, and carbonate are lost. These effects on bone partially explain the invariable association of growth failure, a potentially significant issue for premature infants with acidosis.[19]

The major buffering mechanism in the extracellular fluid is mediated by the carbonic anhydrase system, as reflected in the formula

$$H^+ + HCO_3^- \xrightleftharpoons{CA} H_2CO_3 \xrightleftharpoons{CA} H_2O + CO_2 \uparrow$$

where CA is carbonic anhydrase. Regulation of CO_2 excretion by the respiratory system markedly improves the efficiency of this buffering system at physiologic pH. In the presence of carbonic anhydrase, carbonic acid

(H_2CO_3) is in equilibrium with carbon dioxide (CO_2). Addition or increased production of acid results in consumption of bicarbonate (HCO_3^-) and increased H_2CO_3 and CO_2. CO_2 then crosses the blood-brain barrier, resulting in a drop in pH. This action stimulates central nervous system chemoreceptors, leading to increased respiration and resultant decreased CO_2 concentration within 12 to 24 hours. Similar respiratory compensation occurs in response to an alkali load, which leads to increased HCO_3^- concentration, resulting in hypoventilation and accumulation of CO_2.

Two formulas are particularly useful in understanding and evaluating acid-base disorders. The Henderson-Hasselbach equation expresses the relationship of pH, P_{CO_2}, and HCO_3^-:

$$pH = 6.1 + \log [HCO_3^- / (0.03 \times P_{CO_2})]$$

where 6.1 is the pKa of this equation.[77] The Winters formula[2] can be used to predict the appropriate respiratory response (decrease in P_{CO_2}) to a metabolic acidosis:

$$P_{CO_2} = (1.5 \times HCO_3^-) + 8 \pm 2$$

Respiratory compensation in response to either metabolic acidosis or alkalosis does not completely normalize the pH. For example, the Winters formula predicts that a decrease in HCO_3^- to 10 mmol/L will result in a decrease of P_{CO_2} to 21 to 25 mm Hg. By the Henderson-Hasselbach equation, the resulting serum pH is 7.22 to 7.29. This pH is markedly better than the serum pH of 7.02 that would be seen if no respiratory compensation occurred, but it is still not within the normal range. Thus, with "simple" metabolic acidosis or alkalosis, the respiratory compensation does not fully correct the serum pH. If serum pH is found to be in the normal range (or higher or lower than predicted), then a mixed acid-base disorder, with an added primary respiratory abnormality, should be considered.

Chronic Maintenance of Acid-Base Balance

Chronic maintenance of a normal serum pH depends on the balance between the production or intake of acid and base and their metabolism or excretion. Foodstuffs contain a small amount of preformed acid, but most of the daily acid load is a product of metabolism. A large portion consists of CO_2, which is carried to the lungs as bicarbonate and carbamino groups bound to hemoglobin and ultimately excreted through respiration. This preformed acid is termed *volatile acid*. Hypoventilation or hyperventilation leads to either retention or enhanced excretion of CO_2 and results in acidosis or alkalosis, respectively.

Metabolic activity also produces an obligate nonvolatile acid load of approximately 1-2 mEq/kg per day. Most of this consists of sulfuric acid, which is formed from metabolism of the sulfur-containing amino acids, methionine and cysteine. The remainder consists primarily of incompletely oxidized organic acids, phosphoric acid, and hydrochloric acid.[50,51] Successful maintenance of acid-base balance depends on renal excretion of this daily acid load.

The kidney plays an essential role in maintaining acid-base homeostasis by three major mechanisms:

- reabsorption of filtered bicarbonate and excretion of excess bicarbonate in response to metabolic alkalosis;

- excretion of the obligate daily acid load, as well as any additional acid load from pathogenic processes, such as lactic acidosis related to sepsis or bicarbonate loss due to diarrhea; and

- compensation for changes in serum pH that result from primary respiratory disorders.

Bicarbonate reabsorption occurs primarily in the proximal tubule, where 60% to 80% of the filtered bicarbonate load is reabsorbed. Bicarbonate is not reabsorbed via a specific transporter. Instead it is reabsorbed via an indirect mechanism. Bicarbonate present in the lumen is first buffered by H^+ that is secreted in exchange for sodium via a Na^+-H^+ exchanger located on the luminal membrane of proximal tubular cells (Fig. 34-4). Through the actions of carbonic anhydrase, CO_2 and H_2O are produced. CO_2 and H_2O then diffuse into the cell, where HCO_3^- is regenerated and reabsorbed across the basal cell membrane in exchange for chloride. H^+ is also regenerated, making it available once again for buffering additional filtered bicarbonate. The net effect is that for every H^+ secreted, one molecule of filtered bicarbonate is reabsorbed.

Although proximal tubule bicarbonate reabsorption is essential in preventing bicarbonate wasting, no net H^+ excretion occurs in this process. Excretion of the daily acid load is accomplished, instead, by two mechanisms: ammoniagenesis and production of titratable acids. Ammoniagenesis occurs in the proximal tubule (see Fig. 34-4) via the metabolic processing of glutamine produced in the liver. In the proximal tubule cell, glutamine is converted to ammonium (NH_4^+), which is then secreted into the lumen in exchange for Na^+. Deamination of glutamine also produces α-ketoglutarate, which buffers H^+. Through the actions of the intracellular carbonic anhydrase system, this process eventually results in the production of intracellular HCO_3^-,

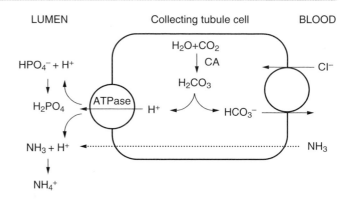

FIGURE 34-5. Distal nephron acidification mechanisms: H^+ secretion and titratable acid formation.

which can be reabsorbed across the basal membrane of the cell with Na^+. Thus, NH_4^+ secretion is the metabolic equivalent of H^+ excretion.

The remainder of acid secretion occurs in the cortical and medullary collecting tubule. H^+ is secreted into the collecting tubule against its pH gradient by H^+ ATPases located on the luminal membrane. This process is influenced by the luminal and peritubular pH, distal sodium delivery, and aldosterone. Secreted H^+ titrates filtered anions, including phosphates and sulfates, thereby producing titratable acids (Fig. 34-5). The collecting tubule also secretes ammonia from the medullary interstitium, where is it buffered by H^+ to produce NH_4^+. Both titratable acid formation and ammonia buffering require an acidic environment for protonation to occur. Thus, in addition to providing a source of H^+ for buffering, distal H^+ secretion is also important in maintaining acidic urine (pH of 4.5 to 5.0).

The net acid excretion by the kidney is equal to the sum of titratable acids plus ammonium minus any filtered bicarbonate that is not reabsorbed. During a steady state, total acid secretion equals the production of acid from diet and metabolism. In response to an acid load, ammoniagenesis can increase dramatically due to enhanced production of glutamine by the liver. Furthermore, ammoniagenesis is stimulated by hypokalemia and inhibited by hyperkalemia. Titratable acids, in contrast, are relatively fixed in their production except in instances of diabetic ketoacidosis, in which the ketone bodies themselves can form titratable acids. Alternatively, the kidney has the capacity to alter HCO_3^- reabsorption in response to changes in the filtered load of bicarbonate, further minimizing changes in pH.

DEVELOPMENTAL ASPECTS OF ACID-BASE PHYSIOLOGY

Although nephron formation is complete by 34 weeks' gestation, maturation and functional changes of the nephron continue during the first year of life. The relative immaturity of the kidney, which is more pronounced in

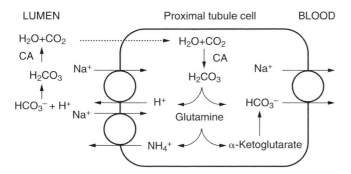

FIGURE 34-4. Bicarbonate reabsorption and ammoniagenesis in the proximal tubule.

the preterm infant, affects basal acid-base status and the response to additional acid and alkali loads.[57] During the initial 24 to 48 hours of life, acid-base balance is influenced by the degree of perinatal stress and environmental factors such as temperature and diet.[88] Between 7 and 21 days of life, neonates are in a state of mild metabolic acidosis. In some infants, blood pH drops below 7.25 or base deficit exceeds 8 mEq/L.[81]

Many factors cause metabolic acidosis in the neonate. The threshold for bicarbonate reabsorption in the proximal tubule is lower in neonates, especially premature infants, compared with that of adults, so neonates tend to waste bicarbonate at a lower blood HCO_3^- concentration (15 to 21 mEq /L). A low glomerular filtration rate (GFR), particularly in premature or stressed neonates, decreases the availability of phosphates and other buffers, thus decreasing the formation and excretion of titratable acids. Tubular immaturity results in reduced tubular secretory surface for organic acid secretion, diminished number of organic acid transport sites per unit area of renal tubular surface, and diminished energy available for organic acid transport.

Premature infants are also unable to maximally acidify their urine at birth, exhibiting a minimum urine pH of 6, in contrast with full-term neonates and adults, whose urine pH can reach 4.5. The ability of premature infants to maximally acidify their urine and to excrete an acid load correlates with gestational age. By 6 weeks of age, the capacity of premature and term infants to excrete hydrogen ions matures to permit maximal acidification.[89]

In summary, HCO_3^- conservation and net acid excretion are both diminished in neonates because of the neonatal kidney's immaturity. This is particularly true for premature infants less than 34 weeks' gestation because nephrogenesis is incomplete. These limitations not only account for decreased baseline serum bicarbonate levels but also limit the ability of the neonate to respond to additional stresses, particularly acid loading. Renal control of acid-base homeostasis does not reach adult levels of function until approximately 2 years of age.

DIAGNOSTIC APPROACH TO DISORDERS OF ACID-BASE BALANCE

In generating a differential diagnosis of an acid-base abnormality, it is helpful to ask three questions:

- What is the primary abnormality?
- What is the secondary compensation?
- Is the compensation appropriate?

The acid-base abnormality alone does not indicate if it is the primary disorder or a response to the primary disorder. For instance, a low serum bicarbonate level indicating metabolic acidosis could be due to a primary metabolic acidosis or could represent a metabolic compensation for a primary respiratory alkalosis. Conversely, an elevated serum bicarbonate could be a reflection of a primary metabolic alkalosis or a response to a primary respiratory acidosis. To distinguish the primary process from the secondary compensation, it is necessary to know the plasma pH as well as the serum bicarbonate and CO_2 levels.

In addition to simple respiratory or metabolic acid-base disorders, mixed (combined) disorders may be seen where more than one primary process is present. Mixed disorders should be considered when the expected compensation falls out of the expected range.

The nomogram presented in Figure 34-6 can aid in diagnosing simple and mixed acid-base disorders. It shows the 95% confidence limits of the expected compensatory response to a primary metabolic or respiratory acidosis or alkalosis. If the compensatory change in either P_{CO_2} or HCO_3^- falls beyond these limits (i.e., outside of the shaded region for each disorder), a combined disorder is present. For example, consider a newborn with pH 7.17, P_{CO_2} 34 mm Hg, and HCO_3^- 12 mEq/L. The acidic pH and low serum (normal neonatal value is approximately 22 mEq/L) suggest a primary metabolic acidosis. However, when the values for pH, HCO_3^-, and P_{CO_2} are plotted on the nomogram, the convergence point falls outside the range for a simple metabolic acidosis, suggesting the possibility of a superimposed respiratory acidosis.

To delineate this further, one can estimate the expected compensation (i.e., a respiratory alkalosis) based on the values presented in Table 34-4, or, alternatively, based on the Winters formula (see earlier). With a decrease in serum HCO_3^- from 22 mEq/L to 12 mEq/L, P_{CO_2} should decrease by 12.5 mmHg. Thus, the estimated compensation would result in a P_{CO_2} of 27 mm Hg. Similarly, the Winters formula predicts a compensatory P_{CO_2} of 24 to 28 mm Hg. The higher than expected P_{CO_2}, therefore, confirms the presence of a superimposed primary respiratory acidosis.

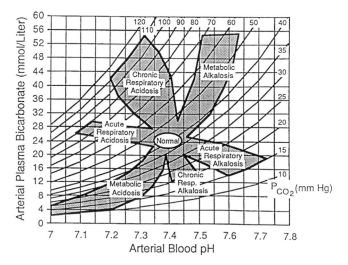

FIGURE 34-6. Acid-base map showing 95% confidence limits for compensatory responses. (From Cogan MG et al: Acid-base disorder. In Brenner BM et al: The Kidney. Philadelphia, WB Saunders, 1986, p 462.)

TABLE 34-4. Expected Compensation In Acid-Base Disorders

RESPIRATORY	ΔP_{CO_2}		ΔHCO_3^-
Acute acidosis	1 mm Hg ↑	→	↑0.1 mEq/L
Acute alkalosis	1 mm Hg ↓	→	↓ 0.25 mEq/L
Chronic acidosis	1 mm Hg ↑	→	↑0.5 mEq/L
Chronic alkalosis	1 mm Hg ↓	→	↓ 0.5 mEq/L
METABOLIC	ΔHCO_3^-		ΔP_{CO_2}
Acidosis	1.0 mEq/l ↓	→	↓ 1.25 mm Hg
Alkalosis	1.0 mEq/L ↑	→	↑0.2-0.9 mm Hg

BASIC PRINCIPLES OF THERAPY

Metabolic Acidosis

Metabolic acidosis is a common problem in the critically ill neonate. It results from either excess acid production or increased loss of base. Box 34-1 lists common causes of metabolic acidosis in the neonate.

Calculation of the anion gap allows differentiation into two groups. *Increased anion gap* metabolic acidosis can be caused by the addition of exogenous acids, such as salicylates or certain toxins. In neonates, an increased anion gap is usually due to increased production of endogenous acids, such as lactic acidosis in patients with sepsis or toxic metabolites in patients with inborn errors of metabolism. Increased anion gap metabolic acidosis is associated with a normal serum chloride. In contrast, a *normal anion gap* metabolic acidosis is due either to bicarbonate loss in the urine (proximal renal tubular acidosis) or the stool or to the inability to excrete acid due to a defect in distal nephron function (distal renal tubular acidosis). In this disorder, the serum chloride is elevated.

Correction of the underlying cause is the most important therapeutic measure in the management of metabolic acidosis. The dose of alkali required to treat metabolic acidosis in newborns ranges from 1 mEq/kg per day for mild base deficits to 5 to 8 mEq/kg per day for more severe base deficits, such as those seen in proximal renal tubular acidosis. Dialysis may be required when acid production is severe during profound states of lactic acidosis or renal failure.[63]

Administration of alkali, such as bicarbonate, has several potential adverse effects. These include volume overload, hypernatremia, decreased oxygen delivery to the brain secondary to shifts in the hemoglobin dissociation curve, increased P_{CO_2}, and a paradoxical intracellular acidosis as CO_2 diffuses into cells.[5,8,70] Bicarbonate administration should be reserved for severe acidosis, in which cardiac output could be compromised.[5,30] Aggressive alkali therapy is necessary in cases of renal tubular acidosis in order to prevent growth failure.

Metabolic Alkalosis

Metabolic alkalosis is *generated* by one of three general mechanisms: loss of acid, such as hydrochloric acid loss with vomiting; ingestion of base, such as sodium bicarbonate administration during resuscitation; or contraction of the extracellular volume, with loss of fluid containing more chloride than bicarbonate. Box 34-2 lists common causes of metabolic alkalosis in the neonate.[19]

Although the kidney usually excretes excess alkali very effectively, several conditions maintain a metabolic alkalosis once alkali is generated. Extracellular volume depletion limits bicarbonate excretion by several mechanisms. The decrease in GFR reduces the filtered load of bicarbonate, and the bicarbonate that is filtered is rapidly reabsorbed in the proximal tubule as a result of avid sodium reabsorption.

Volume depletion also stimulates release of aldosterone mediated by the renin-angiotensin system, which

---

BOX 34-1. Common Causes of Metabolic Acidosis in the Neonate

Increased Anion Gap
Lactic acidosis
    Hypoxemia, shock, sepsis
    Inborn errors of carbohydrate or pyruvate metabolism
        Pyruvate dehydrogenase deficiency
        Pyruvate carboxylase deficiency
        Mitochondrial respiratory chain defects
    Renal failure
    Ketoacidosis
        Glycogen storage disease (type I)
        Inborn errors of amino acid or organic acid metabolism

Normal Anion Gap
Bicarbonate loss: acute diarrhea, drainage from small bowel, biliary, or pancreatic tube; fistula drainage; bowel augmentation cystoplasty; ureteral diversion with bowel
Renal tubular acidosis
Mineralocorticoid deficiency
Administration of Cl⁻-containing compounds: arginine HCl, HCl, $CaCl_2$, $MgCl_2$, NH_4Cl hyperalimentation, high-protein formula
Carbonic anhydrase inhibitors
Dilution of extracellular fluid compartment

Adapted from Brewer E: Disorders of acid-base balance. Pediatr Clin North Am 37:429, 1990.

BOX 34-2. Common Causes of Metabolic Alkalosis in the Neonate

Acid loss: vomiting (e.g., pyloric stenosis), nasogastric suction
Diuretics
Chloride deficiency: chronic chloride-losing diarrhea, Bartter syndrome, low-chloride formula, loss via skin secondary to cystic fibrosis
Administration of alkali: bicarbonate, lactate, acetate, citrate

leads to an increase in distal renal tubular absorption of sodium and excretion of both hydrogen ions and potassium. Other states of hyperaldosteronism, such as excess production of endogenous mineralocorticoids or administration of exogenous steroids, lead to enhanced distal renal tubular excretion of hydrogen ion and potassium. Potassium depletion also maintains a metabolic alkalosis by stimulating renal ammoniagenesis and inhibiting movement of H^+ out of the cell. Chloride depletion or respiratory acidosis, as evidenced by an elevated PCO_2, can also maintain a metabolic alkalosis.

Therapy for metabolic alkalosis consists of correction of the underlying disorder. Alkalosis due to volume depletion typically improves with saline administration and potassium repletion. Agents such as arginine hydrochloride, ammonium hydrochloride, and dilute hydrochloric acid should be used only in rare situations because life-threatening complications can occur, such as severe acidosis or a paradoxical intracellular alkalosis.

Patients with a contraction alkalosis, which is commonly seen in infants with bronchopulmonary dysplasia, congenital heart disease, or other diseases requiring chronic diuretic therapy, typically have significant deficits of potassium and chloride. These deficits should be replaced because serum potassium levels can significantly underestimate the intracellular deficit. Limitations on the safe rate of potassium administration, which should not be infused faster than 0.5 to 1.0 mEq/kg per hour, are the result of the slow equilibration rate between the extracellular and intracellular pools of potassium. Oral and intravenous potassium supplementation may be required to correct significant total body potassium deficits.

Although the long-term complications of chronic metabolic alkalosis are unknown, prolonged pH greater than 7.6 can increase the risk for sensorineural hearing loss.[55]

Respiratory Acidosis and Alkalosis

Respiratory acidosis results from any disorder with decreased alveolar ventilation, which causes retention of CO_2. In neonates this is usually due to respiratory distress syndrome, meconium aspiration syndrome, pulmonary infections, or congenital diaphragmatic hernia (see Chapter 42). Correction of the underlying cause for respiratory acidosis is essential and frequently requires the use of assisted ventilation to increase excretion of volatile acid (CO_2). Administration of alkali to correct acidemia caused by a primary respiratory acidosis is generally not appropriate. The resultant rise in serum bicarbonate levels (and serum pH) promotes hypoventilation and a further rise in PCO_2, thereby exacerbating the respiratory acidosis. In instances where a mixed acid-base disorder is present (i.e., a primary respiratory acidosis and a primary metabolic acidosis), bicarbonate administration should be used with caution and assisted ventilation is typically required.

Respiratory alkalosis is rare in the neonate; however, it can occur during excessive assisted ventilation or during central hyperventilation due to serious central nervous system disease such as intraventricular hemorrhage. Patients with respiratory alkalosis who are dependent on ventilators are easily treated by adjusting the assisted ventilation settings. A search for underlying causes of central hyperventilation is necessary in other patients.

SPECIFIC ACID-BASE DISORDERS IN THE NEONATAL PERIOD

Renal Tubular Acidosis

Renal tubular acidosis (RTA) is a disorder characterized by a normal anion gap metabolic acidosis and is the sequela of either impaired reabsorption of bicarbonate or impaired urinary acidification or H^+ excretion.[16,20] RTA could be the result of an inherited defect in the renal handling of H^+ ion or bicarbonate.[74] Alternatively, RTA could be secondary to tubular damage from a variety of causes, such as medications or obstructive uropathy. There are three main forms of RTA, as summarized in Box 34-3: type I (distal), type II (proximal), and type IV (hyperkalemic). Each form of RTA has a distinct pathophysiology and characteristic serum and urinary laboratory findings.[24]

Type I (distal) RTA results from diminished distal H^+ secretion. Patients with distal RTA often present in the newborn period or during early infancy with lethargy, polyuria, vomiting, dehydration, and failure to thrive. Distal RTA is usually accompanied by hypokalemia, because potassium is secreted in lieu of H^+ to maintain electronegativity. Concomitant hypercalciuria and hypocitraturia predispose patients to development of nephrocalcinosis and nephrolithiasis.

Distal RTA can occur as a sporadic form, although several well-characterized inherited forms have been described. In each instance, the genetic defect results in impairment of a specific component of the distal acidification mechanisms (see Fig. 34-5). Autosomal recessive RTA with sensorineural deafness is caused by mutations in one of the subunits of the H^+-ATPase located on the luminal membrane of the collecting tubule intercalated cell.[48] Autosomal dominant RTA is caused by mutations in the chloride-bicarbonate exchanger (also known as the red cell anion exchanger) located on the basal membrane.[17]

Acquired forms of type I RTA can also occur as the result of injury to the tubules. Certain medications cause damage to the distal nephron and result in back leakage of H^+ from the lumen. Amphotericin toxicity is a classic example of this gradient-defect form of acquired distal RTA.[61] In addition, congenital lesions, most notably obstructive uropathies, can cause secondary RTA as the result of tubular damage from obstruction or infections.

Distal RTA should be suspected in any infant with urine pH greater than 6.5 in the presence of non-ion gap metabolic acidosis. Conversely, urine pH of 5.5 or less indicates that distal acidification mechanisms are intact and effectively rules out distal RTA. If the

BOX 34-3. Classification of Renal Tubular Acidosis

Type I (Distal)
Primary (autosomal dominant or recessive; sporadic)
Associated with other renal disorders
   Obstructive uropathy
   Hypercalciuria /nephrocalcinosis
Associated with acquired or other hereditary diseases
   Osteopetrosis
   Sickle cell anemia
   Hereditary elliptocytosis
   Marfan syndrome
   Primary biliary cirrhosis
   Associated with drugs or toxins (amphotericin B)

Type II (Proximal)
Primary (familial or sporadic)
Fanconi syndrome
   Primary
   Cystinosis
   Tyrosinemia
   Oculocerebral renal syndrome (Lowe syndrome)
   Hereditary fructose intolerance
   Wilson disease
   Medullary cystic disease
   Focal segmental glomerulosclerosis

Type IV (Hyperkalemic)
Pseudohypoaldosteronism
   Renal immaturity
   Obstructive uropathy
   Potassium-sparing diuretics
Chloride shunt
Hyporenin hypoaldosteronism
Cyclosporine

Adapted from Brewer E: Disorders of acid-base balance. Pediatr Clin North Am 37:429, 1990.

diagnosis is unclear, two different methods have been proposed to formally assess the distal acidification mechanisms.

Measurement of the urine-to-blood P_{CO_2} gradient can be used to assess distal tubular urinary acidification after bicarbonate loading. Following bicarbonate loading in the presence of normal distal tubular acidification, P_{CO_2} should be at least 20 mm Hg greater than the blood P_{CO_2}. With normal function, secreted hydrogen ion combines with bicarbonate to form carbonic acid and ultimately CO_2, leading to a gradient in P_{CO_2} between urine and blood. In distal RTA, this gradient is diminished due to diminished hydrogen ion secretion.[56] Alternatively, the urine anion gap ($Na^+ + K^+ − Cl^−$) indirectly assesses the amount of urine ammonium.[34] A positive value suggests a defect in urine ammonium excretion and, therefore, deficient urine acidification.[52]

Although primary distal RTA is a permanent defect, the prognosis for growth and the prevention of renal insufficiency are satisfactory when the condition is correctly treated. Therapy for distal RTA in infancy consists of administering alkali, usually in the form of an alkali-containing liquid such as Bicitra. The typical dose is 2 to 3 mEq/kg per day. Maintenance of normal blood pH and serum bicarbonate maximizes the opportunity for normal growth.

Type II (proximal) RTA is caused by a decrease in the threshold (Tmax, tubular maximum) for $HCO_3^−$ reabsorption in the proximal tubule, resulting in $HCO_3^−$ wastage. The Tmax is decreased to approximately 15 mEq/L, so reabsorption of bicarbonate does not occur until the serum levels decrease to less than this value. The loss of $HCO_3^−$ is often large because 60% to 80% of the filtered $HCO_3^−$ is normally reabsorbed in the proximal tubule. Distal urinary acidification is normal and patients can appropriately acidify the urine (pH 5.5 or less) when plasma $HCO_3^−$ levels are below 14 to 15 mEq/L. An increase in plasma $HCO_3^−$ beyond the capacity of the proximal tubule results in $HCO_3^−$ wastage and an alkaline urine pH of 7.6 or greater.

Isolated inherited forms of proximal RTA occur rarely, and they can be inherited as an autosomal recessive (with ocular abnormalities) or autosomal dominant trait.[74] More commonly, proximal RTA is a component of Fanconi syndrome, a disorder of global proximal tubule dysfunction. In addition to bicarbonate wasting, patients with Fanconi syndrome demonstrate tubular wasting of sodium, potassium, glucose, phosphorus, and amino acids. Fanconi syndrome is seen in a number of inherited metabolic disorders including Lowe syndrome, galactosemia, tyrosinemia, and hereditary fructose intolerance.[24]

Patients with proximal RTA typically require larger amounts of bicarbonate supplementation than those with distal RTA. Doses of 10 mEq/kg or more per day may be required because of excessive $HCO_3^−$ wastage.

As previously discussed, neonates display a mild degree of proximal RTA due to an altered threshold for proximal tubular $HCO_3^−$ reabsorption, with maintenance of plasma $HCO_3^−$ from 20 to 24 mEq/L in full-term neonates and 15 to 24 mEq/L in preterm infants. Over the first year of life, the Tmax for $HCO_3^−$ increases to adult levels as the proximal tubule elongates and transport function matures. Some infants demonstrate delayed maturation that results in persistent proximal RTA, which usually resolves by 5 or 6 years of age.

Type IV (hyperkalemic) RTA is characterized by impaired ammoniagenesis as the result of hyperkalemia. Hyperkalemia results from abnormalities in aldosterone production or from altered tubular sensitivity to aldosterone. Disorders associated with abnormalities in mineralocorticoid production (e.g., congenital adrenal hyperplasia) or responsiveness (i.e., inherited or acquired pseudohypoaldosteronism) were discussed earlier in this chapter. The symptoms of type IV RTA in infancy include dehydration and symptoms related to hyperkalemia. Laboratory abnormalities include nonanion gap metabolic acidosis, hyperkalemia, elevated urine sodium, and diminished urine potassium.

Therapy for type IV RTA consists of mineralocorticoid supplementation in conditions characterized by a deficiency of aldosterone. Treatment of hyperkalemia can reverse many of the abnormalities, but alkali supplementation is generally required in patients with end-organ resistance to aldosterone. The need for such supplementation seems to diminish by age 5 years, possibly because of further maturation of the kidney.

Late Metabolic Acidosis of Prematurity

In 1964, Kildeberg first used the term *late metabolic acidosis of prematurity* to describe a group of otherwise healthy premature infants between 1 and 3 weeks of age who were characterized by mild to moderate acidosis and decreased growth.[49] All infants were receiving cow's milk formula, which provided 3 to 4 grams of protein per kilogram of body weight per day.[89] Net acid excretion was increased in these infants compared with that of the normal control group. This observation suggests that the excessive protein content of cow's milk formula results in endogenous acid production beyond the excretory capacity of the premature kidney, which is limited by urinary bicarbonate losses and reduced phosphate excretion.

Kalhoff and colleagues also described an increase in renal net acid excretion in infants with low birthweight and examined the effect of bicarbonate supplementation.[44,45] When randomly assigned to control or bicarbonate therapy groups, infants in the control group who had a persistent urine pH less than 5.4 for 7 days showed a significant decrease in weight gain and a tendency to decreased nitrogen assimilation. Other studies suggest that alkali therapy might not benefit growth in this situation.[22]

Metabolic acidosis appears to be less common now, which may be explained by a lower protein intake in premature infants. When metabolic acidosis occurs, it is often self-limited and resolves with further renal maturation. Nevertheless, alkali therapy could be of benefit in a select group of infants with low birthweight who have a persistently low pH and show evidence of slow weight gain.

Gordon Syndrome

PHA type II (Gordon syndrome) is a rare disorder that usually appears in later childhood, but it has been reported in neonates.[33] Patients typically present with hypertension and laboratory tests demonstrating hyperkalemia and metabolic acidosis. PHA type II is inherited as an autosomal recessive or autosomal dominant trait. The disease is caused by mutations in the *WNK1* or *WNK4* genes, which encode serine-threonine kinases expressed in the distal nephron.[93] The hypertension and laboratory abnormalities usually correct fully with administration of thiazide diuretics.[59]

Neonatal Bartter Syndrome

In 1962, Bartter and colleagues described a syndrome characterized by hypokalemia, hypochloremic metabolic alkalosis, normal blood pressure, and hyperaldosteronism associated with hyperplasia of the juxtaglomerular complex.[6] Currently, there are three distinct variants of this syndrome, including antenatal Bartter syndrome, "classic" Bartter syndrome, and Gitelman syndrome.[25]

The antenatal variant is the most severe form and manifests in the neonatal period with dehydration, a history of polyhydramnios, and dysmorphic facies characterized by a triangular face, protruding ears, strabismus, and a drooping mouth. These patients typically have elevated urinary calcium excretion, elevated urinary prostaglandin E levels, nephrocalcinosis, and normal serum magnesium levels. This form of Bartter syndrome is inherited in an autosomal recessive pattern and is caused by mutations in genes encoding the rectifying potassium channel (ROMK) or the sodium-potassium-2-chloride cotransporter (NKCC2). Both of these transporter proteins are located in the thick ascending loop of Henle and are required for sodium and chloride reabsorption in that nephron segment.[39,86]

Treatment of the antenatal form of Bartter syndrome includes administration of indomethacin to inhibit prostaglandin production and aldosterone production, supplementation with potassium, and maintenance of adequate intravascular volume. Persistent hypokalemia and nephrocalcinosis rarely leads to chronic renal insufficiency as a result of progressive tubulointerstitial disease.[73]

REFERENCES

Part 1 and Part 2

1. Akcay A et al: Pseudohypoaldosteronism type 1 and respiratory distress syndrome. J Pediatr Endocrinol Metab 15:1557, 2002.
2. Albert MS et al: Quantitative displacement of acid-base equilibrium in metabolic acidosis. Ann Intern Med 66:312, 1967.
3. Al-Dahhan J et al: Effect of salt supplementation of newborn premature infants on neurodevelopmental outcome at 10-13 years of age. Arch Dis Child Fetal Neonatal Ed 86:F120, 2002.
4. Ali R et al: Glucocorticoids enhance the expression of the basolateral Na^+:HCO_3^- cotransporter in renal proximal tubules. Kidney Int 57:1063, 2000.
5. Ayus JC, Krothapalli RK: Effect of bicarbonate administration on cardiac function. Am J Med 87:5, 1989.
6. Bartter FC et al: Hyperplasia of the juxtaglomerular complex with hyperaldosteronism and hypokalemic alkalosis. Amer J Med 33:811, 1962.
7. Bauer K et al: Effect of intrauterine growth retardation on postnatal weight change in preterm infants. J Pediatr 123:301, 1993.
8. Baum JD, Robertson NR: Immediate effects of alkaline infusion in infants with respiratory distress syndrome. J Pediatr 87:255, 1975.
9. Baum M et al: Glucocorticoids regulate NHE-3 transcription in OKP cells. Am J Physiol 270:F164, 1996.
10. Baumgart S: Radiant energy and insensible water loss in the premature newborn infant nursed under a radiant warmer. Clin Perinatol 9:483, 1982.
11. Bell EF et al: The effects of thermal environment on heat balance and insensible water loss in low-birth-weight infants. J Pediatr 96:452, 1980.
12. Bell EF et al: Combined effect of radiant warmer and

phototherapy on insensible water loss in low-birth-weight infants. J Pediatr 94:810, 1979.

13. Bell EF et al: Effect of fluid administration on the development of symptomatic patent ductus arteriosus and congestive heart failure in premature infants. N Engl J Med 302:598, 1980.

14. Bell EF et al: High-volume fluid intake predisposes premature infants to necrotising enterocolitis. Lancet 2:90, 1979.

15. Bidiwala KS et al: Renal function correlates of postnatal diuresis in preterm infants. Pediatrics 82:50, 1988.

16. Brewer ED: Disorders of acid base balance. Pediatr Clin North Am 37:429, 1990.

17. Bruce LJ et al: Familial distal renal tubular acidosis is associated with mutations in the red cell anion exchanger (Band 3, AE1) gene. J Clin Invest 100:1693, 1997.

18. Calcagno PL et al: Studies on the renal concentrating and diluting mechanisms in the premature infant. J Clin Invest 33:91, 1954.

19. Chan JC: Acid-base disorders and the kidney. Adv Pediatr 30:401, 1983.

20. Chan JC: Renal tubular acidosis. J Pediatr 102:327, 1983.

21. Chang SS et al: Mutations in subunits of the epithelial sodium channel cause salt wasting with hyperkalaemic acidosis, pseudohypoaldosteronism type 1. Nat Genet 12:248, 1996.

22. Corbet AJ et al: Controlled trial of bicarbonate therapy in high-risk premature newborn infants. J Pediatr 91:771, 1977.

23. Costarino AT Jr et al: Sodium restriction versus daily maintenance replacement in very low birth weight premature neonates: A randomized, blind therapeutic trial. J Pediatr 120:99, 1992.

24. Dell KM, Avner ED: Tubular Function. In Behrman RE et al (eds): Nelson Textbook of Pediatrics, 17th ed. Philadelphia, Saunders, 2004, p 1758.

25. Dell KM, Guay-Woodford LM: Inherited tubular transport disorders. Semin Nephrol 19:364, 1999.

26. Devuyst O et al: Expression of aquaporins-1 and -2 during nephrogenesis and in autosomal dominant polycystic kidney disease. Am J Physiol 271:F169, 1996.

27. Downing GJ et al: Kidney function in very low birth weight infants with furosemide-related renal calcifications at ages 1 to 2 years. J Pediatr 120:599, 1992.

28. Engelke SC et al: Sodium balance in very low-birth-weight infants. J Pediatr 93:837, 1978.

29. Fanaroff AA et al: Insensible water loss in low birth weight infants. Pediatrics 50:236, 1972.

30. Fanconi S et al: Hemodynamic effects of sodium bicarbonate in critically ill neonates. Intensive Care Med 19:65, 1993.

31. Friis-Hansen B: Body water compartments in children: Changes during growth and related changes in body composition. Pediatrics 28:169, 1961.

32. Geller DS et al: Mutations in the mineralocorticoid receptor gene cause autosomal dominant pseudohypoaldosteronism type I. Nat Genet 19:279, 1998.

33. Gereda JE et al: Neonatal presentation of Gordon syndrome. J Pediatr 129:615, 1996.

34. Goldstein MB et al: The urine anion gap: A clinically useful index of ammonium excretion. Am J Med Sci 292:198, 1986.

35. Hammarlund K, Sedin G: Transepidermal water loss in newborn infants. III. Relation to gestational age. Acta Paediatr Scand 68:795, 1979.

36. Hanukoglu A: Type I pseudohypoaldosteronism includes two clinically and genetically distinct entities with either

renal or multiple target organ defects. J Clin Endocrinol Metab 73:936, 1991.

37. Henley CM, Rybak LP: Developmental ototoxicity. Otolaryngol Clin North Am 26:857, 1993.

38. Hey EN, Katz G: Evaporative water loss in the new-born baby. J Physiol 200:605, 1969.

39. International Collaborative Study Group for Bartter-like Syndromes: Mutations in the gene encoding the inwardly-rectifying renal potassium channel, ROMK, cause the antenetal variant of Bartter syndrome: Evidence for genetic heterogeneity. Hum Mol Genet 6:17, 1997.

40. Itabashi K et al: Indomethacin responsiveness of patent ductus arteriosus and renal abnormalities in preterm infants treated with indomethacin. J Pediatr 143:203, 2003.

41. Jain A et al: Influence of antenatal steroids and sex on maturation of the epidermal barrier in the preterm infant. Arch Dis Child Fetal Neonatal Ed 83:F112, 2000.

42. Johansson S et al: Perinatal water intoxication due to excessive oral intake during labour. Acta Paediatr 91:811, 2002.

43. Jose PA et al: Neonatal renal function and physiology. Curr Opin Pediatr 6:172, 1994.

44. Kalhoff H et al: Decreased growth rate of low-birth-weight infants with prolonged maximum renal acid stimulation. Acta Paediatr 82:522, 1993.

45. Kalhoff H et al: Increased renal net acid excretion in prematures below 1,600 g body weight compared with prematures and small-for-date newborns above 2,100 g on alimentation with a commercial preterm formula. Biol Neonate 66:10, 1994.

46. Kamynina E, Staub O: Concerted action of ENaC, Nedd4-2, and Sgk1 in transepithelial Na$^+$ transport. Am J Physiol Renal Physiol 283:F377, 2002.

47. Kao LC et al: Effect of oral diuretics on pulmonary mechanics in infants with chronic bronchopulmonary dysplasia: results of a double-blind crossover sequential trial. Pediatrics 74:37, 1984.

48. Karet FE et al: Mutations in the gene encoding B1 subunit of the H$^+$ ATPase cause renal tubular acidosis with sensorineural deafness. Nat Genet 21:84, 1999.

49. Kildeberg P: Disturbances of hydrogen ion balance occurring in premature infants. II. Late metabolic acidosis. Acta Paediatr 53:517, 1964.

50. Kildeberg P et al: Balance of net acid in growing infants. Endogenous and transintestinal aspects. Acta Paediatr Scand 58:321, 1969.

51. Kildeberg P, Winters RW: Balance of net acid: Concept, measurement and applications. Adv Pediatr 25:349, 1978.

52. Kim GH et al: Evaluation of urine acidification by urine anion gap and urine osmolal gap in chronic metabolic acidosis. Am J Kidney Dis 27:42, 1996.

53. Knepper MA: Molecular physiology of urinary concentrating mechanism: Regulation of aquaporin water channels by vasopressin. Am J Physiol 272:F3, 1997.

54. Knoers NV, Monnens LL: Nephrogenic diabetes insipidus. Semin Nephrol 19:344, 1999.

55. Leslie GI et al: Risk factors for sensorineural hearing loss in extremely premature infants. J Paediatr Child Health 31:312, 1995.

56. Lin JY et al: Use of the urine-to-blood carbon dioxide tension gradient as a measurement of impaired distal tubular hydrogen ion secretion among neonates. J Pediatr 126:114, 1995.

57. Lindquist B, Svenningsen NW: Acid-base homeostasis of low-birth-weight and full-term infants in early life. J Pediatr Gastroenterol Nutr 2:S99, 1983.

58. Lorenz JM et al: Phases of fluid and electrolyte homeostasis in the extremely low birth weight infant. Pediatrics 96:484, 1995.

59. Mayan H et al: Pseudohypoaldosteronism type II: Marked sensitivity to thiazides, hypercalciuria, normomagnesemia, and low bone mineral density. J Clin Endocrinol Metab 87:3248, 2002.

60. McCance RA et al: The response of infants to a large dose of water. Arch Dis Child 29:104, 1954.

61. McCurdy DK: Distal tubule affected by amphotericin B. N Engl J Med 280:220, 1969.

62. Morello JP, Bichet DG: Nephrogenic diabetes insipidus. Annu Rev Physiol 63:607, 2001.

63. Nash MA, Russo JC: Neonatal lactic acidosis and renal failure: The role of peritoneal dialysis. J Pediatr 91:101, 1977.

64. Oh W, Karecki H: Phototherapy and insensible water loss in the newborn infant. Am J Dis Child 124:230, 1972.

65. Omar SA et al: Effects of prenatal steroids on water and sodium homeostasis in extremely low birth weight neonates. Pediatrics 104:482, 1999.

66. Prince LS et al: Absence of amiloride-sensitive sodium absorption in the airway of an infant with pseudohypoaldosteronism. J Pediatr 135:786, 1999.

67. Rees L et al: Hyponatraemia in the first week of life in preterm infants. Part I. Arginine vasopressin secretion. Arch Dis Child 59:414, 1984.

68. Rees L et al: Hyponatraemia in the first week of life in preterm infants. Part II. Sodium and water balance. Arch Dis Child 59:423, 1984.

69. Riepe FG et al: Identification of a novel mutation in the human mineralocorticoid receptor gene in a German family with autosomal-dominant pseudohypoaldosteronism type 1: Further evidence for marked interindividual clinical heterogeneity. J Clin Endocrinol Metab 88:1683, 2003.

70. Ritter JM et al: Paradoxical effect of bicarbonate on cytoplasmic pH. Lancet 335:1243, 1990.

71. Robillard JE et al: Regulation of sodium metabolism and extracellular fluid volume during development. Clin Perinatol 19:15, 1992.

72. Robillard JE et al: Mechanisms regulating renal sodium excretion during development. Pediatr Nephrol 6:205, 1992.

73. Rodriguez-Soriano J: Bartter and related syndromes: The puzzle is almost solved. Pediatr Nephrol 12:315, 1998.

74. Rodriguez-Soriano J: New insights into the pathogenesis of renal tubular acidosis—from functional to molecular studies. Pediatr Nephrol 14:1121, 2000.

75. Rodriguez-Soriano J: Potassium homeostasis and its disturbances in children. Pediatr Nephrol 9:364, 1995.

76. Rodriguez-Soriano J et al: Renal handling of water and sodium in infancy and childhood: A study using clearance methods during hypotonic saline diuresis. Kidney Int 20:700, 1981.

77. Rose BD, Rennke HG: Renal pathophysiology—the essentials. Baltimore, Williams & Wilkins, 1994.

78. Rosler A: The natural history of salt-wasting disorders of adrenal and renal origin. J Clin Endocrinol Metab 59:689, 1984.

79. Ross BS et al: The pharmacologic effects of furosemide therapy in the low-birth-weight infant. J Pediatr 92:149, 1978.

80. Salamy A et al: Neonatal status and hearing loss in high-risk infants. J Pediatr 114:847, 1989.

81. Schwartz GJ et al: Late metabolic acidosis: A reassessment of the definition. J Pediatr 95:102, 1979.

82. Shaffer SG et al: Extracellular fluid volume changes in very low birth weight infants during first 2 postnatal months. J Pediatr 111:124, 1987.

83. Shaffer SG, Meade VM: Sodium balance and extracellular volume regulation in very low birth weight infants. J Pediatr 115:285, 1989.

84. Shaffer SG et al: Postnatal weight changes in low birth weight infants. Pediatrics 79:702, 1987.

85. Siegel SR, Oh W: Renal function as a marker of human fetal maturation. Acta Paediatr Scand 65:481, 1976.

86. Simon DB et al: Bartter's syndrome, hypokalaemic alkalosis with hypercalciuria, is caused by mutations in the Na-K-2Cl cotransporter NKCC2. Nat Genet 13:183, 1996.

87. Simpson J, Stephenson T: Regulation of extracellular fluid volume in neonates. Early Hum Dev 34:179, 1993.

88. Sulyok E et al: The influence of maturity on renal control of acidosis in newborn infants. Biol Neonate 21:418, 1972.

89. Svenningsen NW, Lindquist B: Postnatal development of renal hydrogen ion excretion capacity in relation to age and protein intake. Acta Paediatr Scand 63:721, 1974.

90. Weinstein MR, Oh W: Oxygen consumption in infants with bronchopulmonary dysplasia. J Pediatr 99:958, 1981.

91. Wilkins BH: Renal function in sick very low birthweight infants: 3. Sodium, potassium, and water excretion. Arch Dis Child 67:1154, 1992.

92. Williams PR, Oh W: Effects of radiant warmer on insensible water loss in newborn infants. Am J Dis Child 128:511, 1974.

93. Wilson FH et al: Human hypertension caused by mutations in WNK kinases. Science 293:1107, 2001.

94. Wu PY, Hodgman JE: Insensible water loss in preterm infants: Changes with postnatal development and non-ionizing radiant energy. Pediatrics 54:704, 1974.

95. Wyllie J: Treatment of patent ductus arteriosus. Semin Neonatol 8:425, 2003.

96. Yamamoto T et al: Expression of AQP family in rat kidneys during development and maturation. Am J Physiol 272:F198, 1997.

Imaging is instrumental in the assessment of suspected pathology in infants. It also plays an important role in monitoring indwelling lines and tubes in such patients. Therefore, an understanding of the appropriate imaging approach to common neonatal pathologic conditions is essential to maximize the value of the examination. This chapter is organized by organ system and discusses the imaging approach to common neonatal conditions. It also discusses the spectrum of imaging appearances of common neonatal abnormalities and emphasizes normal variants that may mimic disease.

CHEST

Chest radiography plays an important role in the assessment of cardiopulmonary pathology in the neonate and young infant. Respiratory distress in the newborn can stem from a variety of causes, and clinical assessment alone may not be able to differentiate them (see Chapter 42). Chest radiography is usually the initial examination of choice in the evaluation of suspected cardiopulmonary disease.

A large number of chest radiographs are obtained in many preterm infants with severe respiratory distress. As young children have greater radiosensitivity than older children and adults, there is concern regarding the potential long-term effects of low-dosage diagnostic radiation. Therefore, steps should be taken to minimize radiation exposure. These include careful beam collimation, gonadal shielding, and avoidance of repeat or unnecessary examinations.

It is also important to ensure proper patient positioning, as rotation will distort the image and make evaluation of cardiopulmonary pathology difficult. Portable chest radiographs are obtained in the anteroposterior view with the infant lying supine. The arms should be extended above the head and the thighs should be immobilized. With proper positioning, the radiograph should demonstrate symmetry of the clavicles and ribs and a midline appearance of the trachea. Additionally, extraneous objects including electrodes and leads should be removed from the field of view whenever possible, as they can obscure abnormalities on the radiograph.

Additional imaging modalities can be used to evaluate specific neonatal chest abnormalities. Sonography is useful in the assessment of diaphragmatic motion and pleural fluid. One large advantage of sonography is that it can be performed at the bedside. Computed tomography (CT) is used to evaluate parenchymal or mediastinal masses or cysts, as it allows more precise delineation of anatomic structures. Magnetic resonance imaging (MRI) is useful in the evaluation of complex congenital heart conditions and vascular rings.

Normal Chest

Familiarity with the normal appearance of the newborn chest and the spectrum of radiographic abnormalities associated with common pathologic conditions enhances the diagnostic yield of the examination. The normal lungs appear primarily radiolucent and symmetrical in volume. The pulmonary vessels are seen as branching, linear shadows that taper in size as they extend from the hilum to the lung periphery. Normal vessels decrease in size and number in the lateral one-half of lung and are not visualized in the lung periphery. The pleural space is normally empty and collapsed. It is visualized only when it contains fluid or air or is thickened. The heart borders should be distinct, and the diaphragm should be clearly outlined against the lung. The normal cardiac diameter should be less than 60% of the thoracic diameter (cardiothoracic ratio). The normal thymus is visible in most newborns. It is extremely variable in size and shape. It typically demonstrates "wavy" undulations of the lateral borders. The thymus often overlies and obscures a portion of the heart, producing the appearance of a large heart. It is composed of two asymmetric lobes and therefore often has an asymmetric appearance at chest radiography.

Respiratory Disease: Medically Treated Causes

RESPIRATORY DISTRESS SYNDROME, OR HYALINE MEMBRANE DISEASE

Respiratory distress syndrome (RDS), also referred to as hyaline membrane disease, is the most common cause of respiratory distress in the premature infant. It is the leading cause of death in premature infants. The inadequate production of surfactant because of the prematurity of type II pneumocytes leads to decreased alveolar distensibility, noncompliant lungs, and respiratory distress.

The typical radiographic appearance of RDS includes a finely granular or ground-glass pattern with diminished lung volumes. The severity of radiographic disease is quite variable and usually correlates with the severity of clinical disease. Mild radiographic disease is characterized by a finely granular pattern that allows visualization of normal vessels (Fig. 35-1), whereas severe disease results in silhouetting of the heart borders and diaphragm (Fig. 35-2). The lung volumes are usually diminished as a result of diffuse microatelectasis. Peripheral air bronchograms may be seen in the lung bases, particularly with severe disease. This finding results from air in the bronchi being visualized against a background of alveolar collapse. The distribution of disease is usually diffuse and symmetrical; however, patchy or asymmetric disease may be seen. The radiographic

changes associated with RDS are often seen immediately after birth but can also develop over the first 6 to 12 hours of life. The radiographic abnormalities related to uncomplicated RDS should resolve by the time the neonate is 3 to 4 days old.

Chest radiography can be used to help assess the effectiveness of surfactant replacement therapy in infants with RDS.[11,16] Typically, there is rapid improvement in the appearance of the lungs after surfactant administration. However, when there is a partial response, the improvement may be asymmetric or even restricted to one lung. The absence of radiographic improvement after surfactant administration is a poor prognostic sign.

Complications can result from the high distending pressures that may be required in the treatment of RDS. Alveolar rupture from overdistention results in pulmonary interstitial emphysema. The radiographic appearance of pulmonary interstitial emphysema includes distinct rounded or linear thoracic lucencies representing air in the perivascular sheath (Fig. 35-3). The abnormalities may be diffuse or focal. Focal air collections (pseudocysts) may also form in the interstitium of the lung. After alveolar rupture, air can also track along the perivascular sheath into the mediastinum or the pleural space, resulting in a pneumothorax or pneumomediastinum.

NEONATAL PNEUMONIA

Most neonatal pneumonias are of bacterial origin, including streptococci, *Staphylococcus aureus,* and *Escherichia coli.* These infections may be acquired in utero, during delivery, or after birth (see Chapter 37, Part 2). The radiographic appearance is identical to that of RDS and is characterized by diffuse ground-glass opacities of variable severity.[1,20] Focal, lobar disease is unusual in neonatal bacterial pneumonias. Peripheral

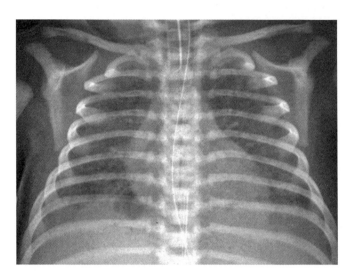

FIGURE 35-1. Mild surfactant deficiency disease. Anteroposterior chest radiograph demonstrates diffuse ground-glass opacities. Note that some normal pulmonary vessels are still visualized. Additionally, the heart borders and diaphragm are well seen.

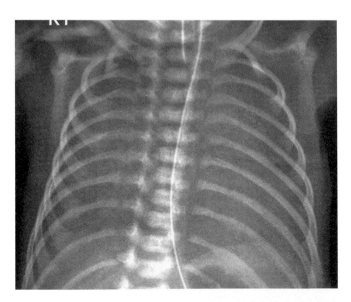

FIGURE 35-2. Severe surfactant deficiency disease. Anteroposterior chest radiograph demonstrates diffuse ground-glass opacities. Note that the heart borders and diaphragm are silhouetted.

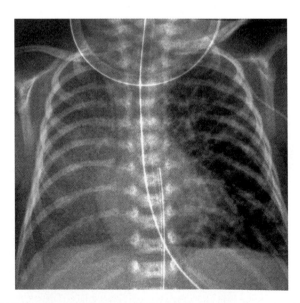

FIGURE 35-3. Pulmonary interstitial emphysema. Anteroposterior chest radiograph shows multiple rounded lucencies in the left lung secondary to interstitial emphysema.

air bronchograms may be noted. Viral pneumonias can also be seen in the newborn period. These demonstrate less specific findings at chest radiography: the radiograph may be normal or demonstrate streaky, perihilar linear markings.

TRANSIENT TACHYPNEA OF THE NEWBORN

Transient tachypnea of the newborn is also referred to as wet lung disease or retained fluid syndrome. It is associated with delivery by cesarean section, and it is felt to result from excessive retention of lung fluid after delivery. The radiograph may be normal. Radiographic abnormalities include streaky, perihilar opacities and lung overinflation. Occasionally, small pleural effusions may be seen. The radiographic changes are usually symmetric, although occasionally some asymmetry may be noted. The radiographic and clinical findings usually resolve within the first 24 to 48 hours of life.

MECONIUM ASPIRATION SYNDROME

The premature expulsion of meconium prior to birth is often related to fetal distress leading to a hypoxia-induced vagal response. It occurs more commonly in full-term or postmature infants. The aspirated meconium causes obstruction of small airways. The typical radiographic appearance of meconium aspiration includes coarse, nodular opacities, which probably represent the inspissated meconium in small airways and associated atelectasis[22] (Fig. 35-4). The distribution of disease is

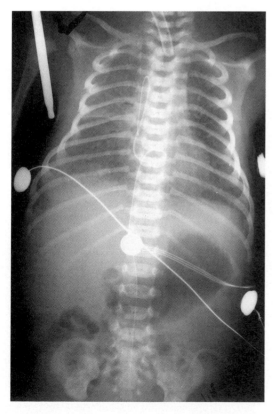

FIGURE 35-4. Meconium aspiration. Anteroposterior chest radiograph demonstrates coarse nodular opacities throughout both lung fields.

often asymmetric. Additionally, there is usually lung overinflation. The changes may be present immediately after birth or develop over the first few hours of life. Complications include pneumothorax and pneumomediastinum.

PULMONARY HEMORRHAGE

Pulmonary hemorrhage in infants may result from hypoxia-induced capillary damage and may be a manifestation of pulmonary edema. An association between pulmonary hemorrhage and surfactant therapy has been described (see also Chapter 42, Part 3). In intubated patients, the diagnosis is usually established by detecting blood in the endotracheal tube. The appearance of pulmonary hemorrhage at chest radiography is variable and nonspecific. Small amounts of hemorrhage may not be detected at chest radiography, but more extensive hemorrhages result in focal or diffuse ground-glass opacities. The latter appearance can mimic pneumonia or pulmonary edema.

CHRONIC LUNG DISEASE (BRONCHOPULMONARY DYSPLASIA)

Chronic lung disease in the premature infant who is treated with high oxygen concentrations and mechanical ventilation is labeled bronchopulmonary dysplasia.[25] It occurs most frequently after RDS, but it may also be seen in association with neonatal pneumonia, meconium aspiration, and congenital cardiac disorders. The condition results from multiple factors, including lung immaturity, high oxygen concentrations, and barotrauma. The incidence of bronchopulmonary dysplasia is increased in infants who develop pulmonary interstitial emphysema and pneumothorax.[40] The radiographic findings vary over time. Initially, the appearance is similar to that of RDS and is characterized by diffuse ground-glass opacities of variable severity. Gradually, the radiographic appearance changes and is characterized by coarse opacities that are often patchy or asymmetric in their distribution[19,41] (Fig. 35-5). Frequently, focal areas of air trapping are also noted. In severe cases, cystic areas are noted throughout the lung parenchyma; these represent emphysema. As reviewed in Chapter 42 Part 7, a more insidious development of bronchopulmonary dysplasia in the absence of prior severe RDS or barotrauma is now more frequently seen.

Respiratory Disease: Surgically Treated Causes

CONGENITAL DIAPHRAGMATIC HERNIA (See also Chapters 42 and 45.)

Congenital diaphragmatic hernia typically develops through a defect in the posterolateral foramen of Bochdalek. It results from defective fusion of the pleuroperitoneal membranes during embryologic development. Bowel and solid organs may herniate into the affected hemithorax. Congenital diaphragmatic hernia occurs more commonly on the left side. The characteristic radiographic appearance is of air-filled bowel loops in the thorax (Fig. 35-6). Initially, the bowel loops

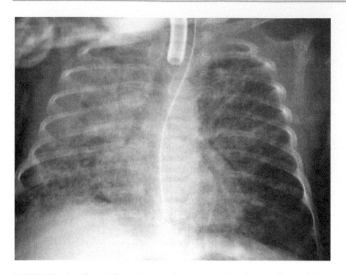

FIGURE 35-5. Chronic lung disease. Anteroposterior chest radiograph in a 4-month-old demonstrates coarse, asymmetric opacities. Note that parenchymal opacification is worse in the right lung because of areas of atelectasis, and there is air trapping in the left lung.

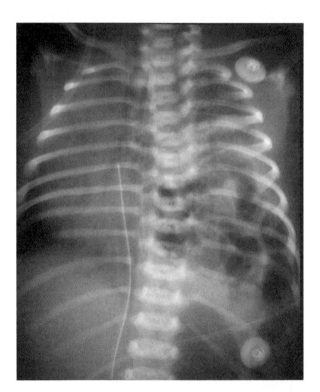

FIGURE 35-6. Congenital diaphragmatic hernia. Anteroposterior chest radiograph shows multiple bowel loops in the left hemithorax. Note the mediastinal shift from left to right.

may be fluid filled, making the diagnosis difficult. The ipsilateral lung is usually hypoplastic because the mass effect in utero affects development. There may also be hypoplasia of the contralateral lung.

CYSTIC ADENOMATOID MALFORMATION

Cystic adenomatoid malformation results from anomalous development of terminal respiratory structures, resulting in replacement of normal lung by solid or cystic elements. One lobe is involved in two thirds of cases, and two lobes are involved in one third. There are three histologic subtypes. Type I is characterized by one or more large cysts, type II contains multiple small cysts, and type III contains solid adenomatous tissue. As a result, there is a spectrum in the radiographic appearance of these lesions ranging from multiple macrocysts to a dominant cyst or solid mass[42] (Fig. 35-7). Focal emphysematous changes are often seen surrounding the lesion. CT is useful in the assessment of smaller lesions that may not be well seen by chest radiography.

CONGENITAL LOBAR OVERINFLATION (CONGENITAL LOBAR EMPHYSEMA)

Congenital lobar overinflation or emphysema (see Chapter 42) results from a focal bronchial ball-valve obstruction that results in overdistention of the distal airways within a pulmonary lobe or segment. The condition typically involves one or two lobes. There is a lobar predilection: the left upper lobe is involved most frequently, followed by the right middle lobe and the right upper lobe. Radiographically, it is characterized by a focal area of hyperlucency and increased volume[42] (Fig. 35-8). There may be compression of adjacent lung. There is usually progressive hyperinflation of the involved lobe over time. Initially after birth, there may be increased opacity within the involved lobe as a result of retained fluid. CT is useful in the precise

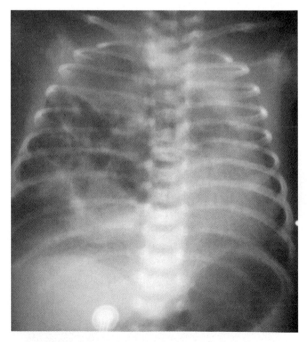

FIGURE 35-7. Cystic adenomatoid malformation. Anteroposterior chest radiograph demonstrates a multicystic mass in the right lung resulting in mediastinal shift and compression of left lung.

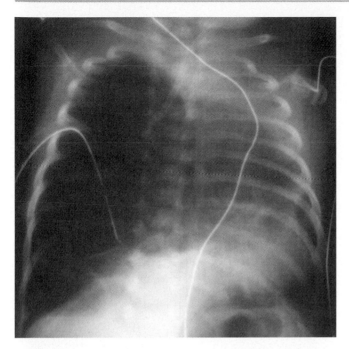

FIGURE 35-8. Congenital lobar overinflation. Anteroposterior chest radiograph shows marked overinflation of the right upper and middle lobes, resulting in displacement of mediastinal structures to the left and compression of normal left lung.

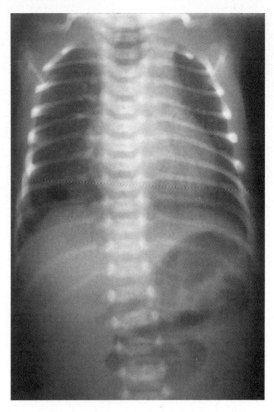

FIGURE 35-9. Tracheoesophageal fistula. Anteroposterior chest radiograph demonstrates an air-filled blind-ending esophageal pouch in the neck.

characterization of involved lobes and the degree of adjacent lung compression.

ESOPHAGEAL ATRESIA AND TRACHEOESOPHAGEAL FISTULA

The pairing of the terms *esophageal atresia* and *tracheoesophageal fistula* describes a disorder in formation and separation of the primitive foregut and esophagus. A spectrum of malformations is noted, ranging from esophageal atresia (with or without a proximal or distal tracheoesophageal fistula) to a tracheoesophageal fistula without esophageal atresia. The most common type, involving esophageal atresia with a distal tracheoesophageal fistula, accounts for over 80% of cases (see Chapter 45).

At chest radiography, a blind-ending, air-filled proximal esophageal pouch is noted[4] (Fig. 35-9). The presence of a distal fistula is supported by air in the gastrointestinal tract. Occasionally, an esophagram is performed to confirm a tracheoesophageal fistula. When an esophagram is performed in an infant with a blind-ending proximal esophageal pouch, an enteric tube is carefully placed into the proximal segment and the infant is examined in the lateral plane. A small amount of contrast (usually only 2 to 3 mL is required) is slowly injected. After confirmation that there is no proximal fistula present, the administered contrast material should be withdrawn.

Tracheoesophageal fistula is associated with multisystem abnormalities in approximately one third of cases, including vertebral, cardiac, renal, limb, and other gastrointestinal tract atresias. All infants with a tracheoesophageal atresia should undergo a renal ultrasound to evaluate possible associated renal anomalies.

HEART (See Chapter 43.)

Cardiac problems in infants are usually congenital in origin. Although radiography is an important part of the evaluation of children with suspected cardiac disease, it alone rarely leads to a specific diagnosis. Rather, its usefulness here is in the exclusion of pulmonary conditions as a cause of the respiratory distress. The clinical examination and cardiac echocardiography are the primary means of diagnosing congenital heart conditions.

Great variability in cardiac size is found in congenital heart anomalies. Typically, cardiomegaly is present in infants and neonates with large left-to-right shunts (ventricular septal defect, atrioventricular canal), Ebstein anomaly, or hypoplastic left heart syndrome, or in association with cardiomyopathy. Additionally, cardiomegaly may be transiently seen in the absence of cardiac disease in association with hypoglycemia, hypocalcemia, or severe anemia, and in infants of diabetic mothers. Enlargement of specific cardiac chambers cannot be assessed by chest radiography in infants and young children.

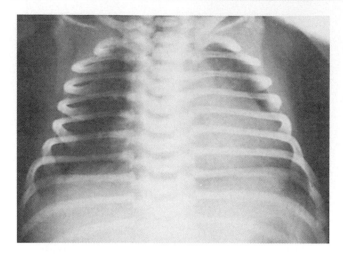

FIGURE 35-10. Persistent pulmonary hypertension. Marked enlargement of the cardiothymic silhouette and diminished caliber of the pulmonary vessels, simulating cyanotic congenital heart disease.

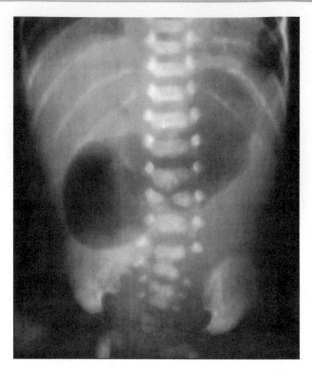

FIGURE 35-11. High intestinal obstruction. Supine abdominal radiograph in an infant with a duodenal web demonstrates a distended stomach and proximal duodenum.

In cyanotic congenital heart disease, the caliber of the pulmonary arteries is reduced, the hila appear small, and the lungs may appear more lucent. However, the distinction between normal and decreased pulmonary arterial vascularity cannot be accurately made by chest radiography. It is difficult to differentiate normal from small pulmonary vessels, as there is too much overlap in their appearance. Persistent pulmonary hypertension may mimic cyanotic congenital heart disease, both clinically and radiographically, because of cardiomegaly and pulmonary oligemia (Fig. 35-10).

Radiography is useful in diagnosing increased pulmonary arterial vascularity associated with large left-to-right shunts, including patent ductus arteriosus, ventricular septal defect, atrial septal defect, and endocardial cushion defect. Increased pulmonary arterial vascularity is seen at radiography when the ratio of left-to-right shunt is greater than 3:1. The pulmonary arterial vascularity usually appears normal with shunts of a lesser degree.

GASTROINTESTINAL TRACT

Intestinal obstruction is the most common abdominal emergency in the newborn period. Neonatal obstruction is typically characterized as high (occurring proximal to the distal ileum) or low (involving the distal ileum or colon).[9] The clinical presentations of infants with high and those with low intestinal obstruction may overlap and include abdominal distention, vomiting, and poor feeding. The vomit is often bilious. Low obstructions are often characterized by failure to pass meconium.

Abdominal radiographs are the initial imaging examination of choice to distinguish between high and low intestinal obstruction. Radiographs in infants with high intestinal obstruction typically show few dilated bowel loops (Fig. 35-11), whereas radiographs in infants with low obstruction show many dilated bowel loops (Fig. 35-12). When bowel obstruction is present, the bowel loops often become elongated and are stacked in a parallel fashion in addition to showing dilation. The distinction between high and low intestinal obstruction is important, as infants with a high obstruction may not need further imaging evaluation.[9,38] If they do require further imaging assessment, the upper gastrointestinal series is the examination of choice. Infants with a suspected low obstruction are typically evaluated with a contrast enema.[9,38]

As was discussed under "Chest," earlier, proper patient positioning is important, as rotation distorts the image and makes evaluation of abdominal pathology difficult. Portable abdominal radiographs are obtained in the anteroposterior view with the infant lying supine. With proper positioning, the radiograph should demonstrate symmetry of the lower ribs and a midline appearance of the lumbar vertebrae. Extraneous objects including electrodes and leads should be removed from the field of view whenever possible, as they can obscure abnormalities on the radiograph.

High Intestinal Obstruction

MIDGUT MALROTATION

Midgut malrotation is the most important cause of upper intestinal obstruction. Abnormal in utero rotation of the midgut results in abnormal mesenteric fixation. The lack of normal fixation of the mesentery results in a short mesenteric base that may lead to bowel twisting

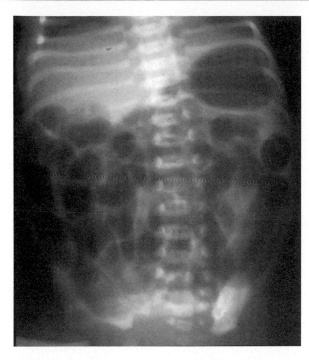

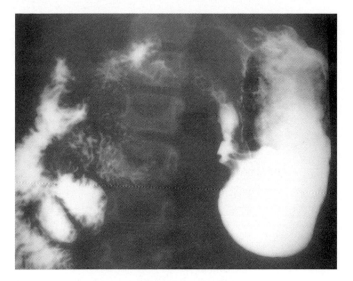

FIGURE 35-13. Midgut malrotation. Spot film from an upper gastrointestinal series shows an abnormal location of the duodenal-jejunal junction. It is located to the right of the spine and below the level of the duodenal bulb.

FIGURE 35-12. Low intestinal obstruction. Supine abdominal radiograph in an infant with midgut malrotation demonstrates multiple dilated bowel loops. No distal large bowel gas is visualized.

around the axis of the superior mesenteric artery, with resulting vascular compromise, bowel ischemia, and necrosis. Most infants with malrotation present with bilious vomiting. Nearly 40% of patients present in the first week of life.[5] Bilious vomiting in an infant should be considered a potential surgical emergency, and in the absence of another defined cause, midgut malrotation should be excluded from the diagnosis if possible.

The findings at abdominal radiography associated with midgut malrotation are variable and include duodenal obstruction (secondary to Ladd bands, which are normal peritoneal attachments) or a mid small bowel obstruction from a midgut volvulus.[5,9] The abdominal radiograph may also be normal in infants with malrotation, so a normal abdominal radiograph does not exclude the condition. The diagnostic examination of choice is the upper gastrointestinal examination, which shows an abnormal duodenal-jejunal junction (Fig. 35-13). The normal duodenal junction should be located to the left of the spine and at the same level as, or more superior to, the duodenal bulb.[9,35] If a midgut volvulus is present, a spiral or corkscrew appearance of the duodenum and jejunum is noted.

DUODENAL ATRESIA

Duodenal atresia is the most common cause of high intestinal obstruction in the newborn. It occurs more commonly than duodenal stenosis or web. Approximately 75% of cases occur proximal to the papilla of Vater and are associated with bilious vomiting. There

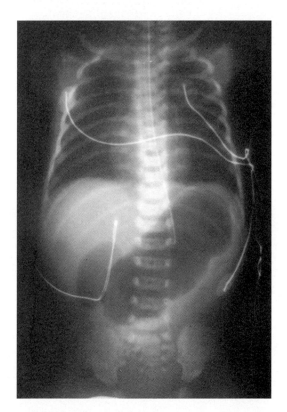

FIGURE 35-14. Duodenal atresia. Supine abdominal radiograph demonstrates a "double bubble," representing dilated stomach and duodenum.

is an association with Down syndrome and congenital heart disease.[38] Abdominal radiography typically shows gastric distention and a dilated duodenal bulb referred to as the "double bubble" (Fig. 35-14). These findings are diagnostic for duodenal atresia, and when they are present, no further study is necessary.

JEJUNAL ATRESIA

Jejunal atresia results from an ischemic injury to the developing small intestine. The injury may result from a vascular accident or a mechanical obstruction such as an in utero volvulus. A single focal area of atresia may be noted, or there may be multiple atretic segments. Abdominal radiographs typically demonstrate dilated small bowel loops that may contain air-fluid levels indicative of a mid small bowel obstruction.

Low Intestinal Obstruction

HIRSCHSPRUNG DISEASE

Hirschsprung disease is characterized by the absence of myenteric plexus ganglion cells, which results in a failure of normal colonic relaxation and subsequent obstruction. Most infants present in the first 6 weeks of life with abdominal distention, constipation, vomiting, and occasionally diarrhea. The condition is more common in male than in female infants.

Abdominal radiographic findings in Hirschsprung disease are usually nonspecific. They typically demonstrate variable dilation of small and large bowel. There is often absence of air in the rectum. Tubular filling defects that may be noted in the colon represent meconium or stool. The diagnostic examination of choice is a contrast enema. The contrast material of choice is either barium sulfate or water-soluble contrast. We prefer water-soluble contrast. A small, soft catheter should be used. If a balloon catheter is used, the balloon should not be inflated, as it may obscure pathology. The examination should start with the patient in the lateral position to better allow for demonstration of the transition zone between normal, dilated colon and contracted, aganglionic distal colon and rectum[24] (Fig. 35-15). The transition zone is located most frequently in the rectosigmoid region. The affected segment always includes rectum and a variable length of more proximal colon. There are never any skip areas. Contrast enema is diagnostic in the majority of patients. However, the examination may be normal early on if the normal segment of colon has not yet become dilated due to stool impaction. Approximately 5% of patients have total colonic aganglionosis and demonstrate a microcolon without a transition zone.[6,38]

FUNCTIONAL IMMATURITY OF THE COLON

Functional immaturity of the colon is also known as meconium plug syndrome or small left-colon syndrome. It is felt to be associated with immaturity of the myenteric plexus ganglia.[24] There is an association with maternal diabetes mellitus, eclampsia, and prematurity. Abdominal radiography shows a distal bowel obstruction with or without air-fluid levels.[24] Contrast enema shows multiple filling defects representing meconium plugs. The caliber of the colon is variable: it may be normal in its entirety or there may be a small-caliber left colon to the level of the splenic flexure with dilated proximal colon (Fig. 35-16).[14] The contrast enema is often therapeutic in these patients, helping to evacuate residual meconium.

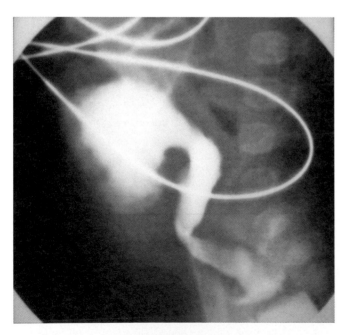

FIGURE 35-15. Hirschsprung disease. Lateral view from a contrast enema demonstrates a transition zone. The more proximal colon is dilated, whereas the caliber of the distal, aganglionic segment is normal.

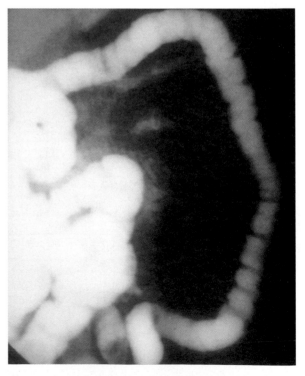

FIGURE 35-16. Small left-colon syndrome. Contrast enema demonstrates a small-caliber descending colon. Note the caliber difference between transverse and descending colon.

MECONIUM ILEUS

Meconium ileus is caused by abnormal meconium inspissation in the distal ileum. It is usually associated with cystic fibrosis.[15] The abnormal meconium produced in these infants results in a distal small bowel obstruction. Abdominal radiography demonstrates multiple dilated small bowel loops indicative of a low obstruction. A soap bubble appearance may be noted in the right side of the abdomen. Meconium ileus may be complicated by in utero perforation, resulting in meconium peritonitis. This in turn results in calcification of intraperitoneal meconium. Contrast enema should be performed in these infants. It typically demonstrates a microcolon[6] (Fig. 35-17). The contrast enema may have a therapeutic effect in some infants with meconium ileus, particularly if reflux can be achieved into the distal ileum, where much of the inspissated meconium is located.[26]

ILEAL ATRESIA

The underlying mechanism in ileal atresia is a vascular accident similar to jejunal atresia. There may be multiple atresias. Abdominal radiographs usually show a low intestinal obstruction pattern. Contrast enema demonstrates a microcolon.[6]

NECROTIZING ENTEROCOLITIS

Necrotizing enterocolitis (NEC) is seen predominantly in premature infants. It is the most common acquired gastrointestinal emergency in the neonatal intensive care unit. It appears to result from a combination of mesenteric ischemia from splanchnic vasoconstriction, thrombosis, or low perfusion states, and infection secondary to bacterial overgrowth. The most commonly involved location is the ileocecal region. Infants usually present with abdominal distention, tenderness, and feeding disturbance (see Chapter 45).

Abdominal radiography plays an important role in the diagnosis of NEC. Early findings are nonspecific and include bowel dilation and bowel wall thickening.[29] As the disease progresses, pneumatosis intestinalis is seen.[13,29,30] Pneumatosis intestinalis is considered to be specific for the diagnosis, but the findings may be transient, lasting only minutes or hours.[13] At radiography, pneumatosis appears as a "bubbly" pattern (Fig. 35-18) or a curvilinear pattern (Fig. 35-19). The bubbly pattern is difficult to differentiate from stool, but the presence of formed stool that would resemble pneumatosis is uncommon in sick premature infants. Pneumatosis is most commonly seen in the right lower quadrant. Air is also occasionally seen in the porta hepatis, where it appears as branching lucencies overlying the liver[30] (Fig. 35-20). Portal air is typically a late finding seen in advanced cases.

Once the diagnosis of NEC is established, serial imaging is usually performed to evaluate for possible bowel perforation. Most bowel perforations occur in the first 48 hours after the initial diagnosis.[39] The cross-table lateral radiograph of the abdomen is useful for assessing for possible perforation. Air collects in the most superior portion of the abdomen.

A delayed complication of NEC is bowel stricture. It represents the sequela of necrotic lesions from the bowel wall to the inner muscularis. Strictures occur in 20% to 30% of survivors who had NEC. Strictures may be single or multiple and are usually located in the colon. The most common site is the splenic flexure. A contrast enema is useful for identifying a possible

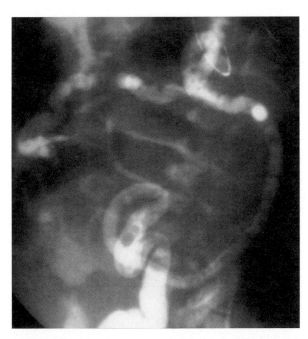

FIGURE 35-17. Meconium ileus with microcolon. Contrast enema in an infant with meconium ileus demonstrates a microcolon.

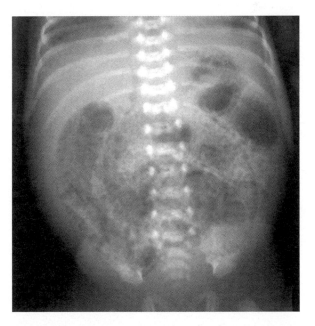

FIGURE 35-18. Necrotizing enterocolitis (NEC) with pneumatosis intestinalis. Supine abdominal radiograph in an infant with NEC demonstrates a diffuse "bubbly" appearance representing pneumatosis intestinalis.

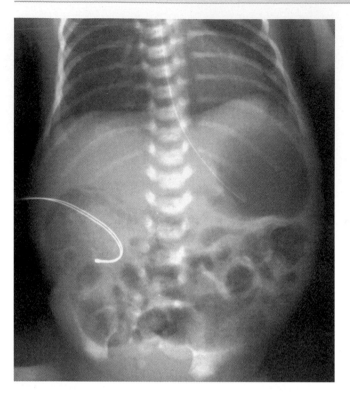

FIGURE 35-19. Necrotizing enterocolitis (NEC) with pneumatosis intestinalis. Supine abdominal radiograph in an infant with NEC demonstrates linear pneumatosis intestinalis in the right hemi-abdomen.

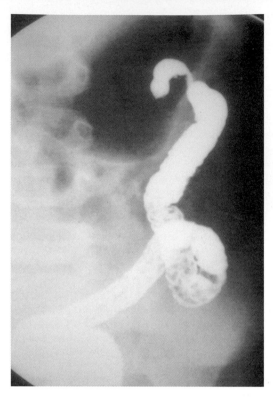

FIGURE 35-21. Colonic stricture after necrotizing enterocolitis (NEC). Image from a contrast enema examination in a 7-week-old infant demonstrates focal narrowing at the splenic flexure representing a focal stricture. The infant had been treated for NEC 4 weeks prior to this examination.

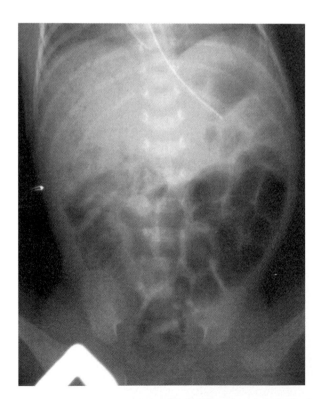

FIGURE 35-20. Necrotizing enterocolitis (NEC) with portal air. Supine abdominal radiograph in an infant with NEC demonstrates linear lucencies overlying the liver and representing portal air.

stricture. Water-soluble contrast should be utilized. A focal area of narrowing can be noted (Fig. 35-21).

HEPATOBILIARY TRACT

Sonography is the imaging examination of choice for the initial evaluation of suspected congenital or acquired hepatobiliary abnormalities in infants. Cross-sectional imaging with CT and MRI is selectively utilized in the characterization of masses.

Biliary Atresia

The underlying abnormality in biliary atresia is obliteration of the extrahepatic biliary tree and variable obliteration of portions of the intrahepatic biliary tree. Infants present with jaundice early. The clinical challenge is to differentiate biliary atresia from neonatal hepatitis. There is overlap between the two conditions and they may represent a spectrum of severity rather than distinct entities.[31] They both result in conjugated hyperbilirubinemia. The principal difference between the two entities is that there is patency of the biliary tree in infants with neonatal hepatitis (see Chapter 46).

Sonography is usually the initial imaging examination in children with neonatal jaundice. Sonography is used to exclude other causes of jaundice including

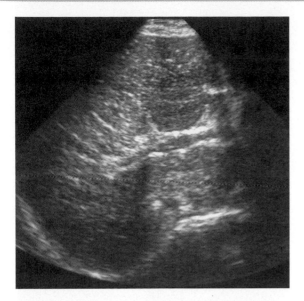

FIGURE 35-22. Triangular cord sign in biliary atresia. Transverse view through the porta hepatis in a 2-month-old infant demonstrates an echogenic linear band anterior to the portal vein, representing fibrous tissue.

FIGURE 35-23. Absence of gastrointestinal excretion of radioisotope in biliary atresia. Delayed 24-hour view after the intravenous administration of iminodiacetic acid shows good hepatic uptake and absence of gastrointestinal tract excretion.

choledochal cyst, biliary sludge, and cholelithiasis. However, in most cases of biliary atresia, the sonographic findings are nonspecific. The most specific sonographic finding is the triangular cord sign.[27,44] This echogenic linear band in the porta hepatis anterior to the portal vein (Fig. 35-22) represents the fibrous tissue in the porta hepatis. The gallbladder is not identified in approximately 80% of patients and is usually small in the remainder.[27,33,44] Hepatic parenchymal echogenicity may also be abnormal.

The hepatobiliary scan with iminodiacetic acid compounds is used for diagnosis of biliary atresia. The infant is pretreated with phenobarbital. The diagnosis is made if there is absence of gastrointestinal excretion of the administered isotope after 24 hours[37] (Fig. 35-23). Biliary atresia is associated with a variety of other abnormalities, including choledochal cyst, polysplenia, preduodenal portal vein, and azygous continuation of the inferior vena cava.[2]

Choledochal Cyst

A choledochal cyst represents cystic dilation of the extrahepatic or intrahepatic biliary tree. Among the proposed underlying etiologies are weakness of the lining of the biliary tree, obstructive cholangiopathy, and a pancreaticobiliary ductal junction anomaly. Infants with a choledochal cyst usually present with jaundice and acholic stools. The presentation may be similar to that of biliary atresia. Choledochal cysts are classified on the basis of their location, the cholangiographic morphology, and the number of intrahepatic and extrahepatic duct cysts. The most widely used classification system is by Todani and colleagues.[50]

Sonography, the initial imaging method in the evaluation of choledochal cysts, is used to evaluate the size and location of the cyst and to image the entire intrahepatic and extrahepatic biliary tree. Choledochal cysts are anechoic with a thin lining at sonography. The appearance ranges from that of a focal, rounded cyst to that of fusiform dilation of the common bile duct and possibly the extrahepatic biliary tree[28] (Fig. 35-24). The dilated segment of extrahepatic biliary tree may be eccentric relative to the adjacent ductal system.

CT is also useful in the evaluation of choledochal cysts. It is helpful in better defining the biliary origin of the cyst, particularly with large lesions. It may be difficult to determine the site of origin of large cysts by sonography. Additionally, CT can precisely delineate

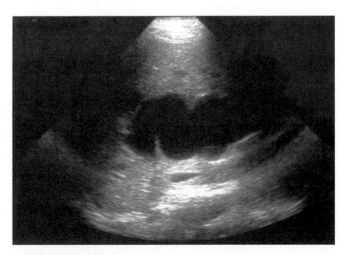

FIGURE 35-24. Choledochal cyst. Longitudinal view through the porta hepatis demonstrates cystic dilation of the biliary tree.

the relationship between the cyst, the pancreatic head, and the porta hepatis, which is useful in preoperative planning.

URINARY TRACT (See Chapter 49.)

Sonography is the imaging examination of choice for the initial evaluation of suspected urinary tract abnormalities in infants. Familiarization with the normal appearance of the neonatal kidney at sonography is important because it is different from the appearance in older children. The neonatal kidney typically demonstrates increased parenchymal echogenicity because of the relatively high number of glomeruli and the increased cellularity. Therefore, the renal parenchyma is often isoechoic or hyperechoic relative to liver and spleen. The increased parenchymal echogenicity persists until age 3 to 4 months. The neonatal kidney also demonstrates prominent, hypoechoic pyramids because of the larger medullary volume present. This finding may persist until 1 year of age and should not be confused with a dilated collecting system. Finally, the neonatal kidney demonstrates a paucity of sinus fat. Therefore, the central portion will not be echogenic. Renal sinus fat slowly accumulates during childhood.

Small amounts of fluid may be seen in the renal pelvis of infants in the absence of urinary tract pathology. It is generally accepted that fluid in the renal pelvis and an anteroposterior diameter of the renal pelvis of less than 5 mm are normal findings.[12,17] A renal pelvic diameter of 5 to 9 mm is characterized as mild pyelectasis. This finding has been reported in 6% of normal neonates,[17] it is not associated with obstructive uropathy or vesicoureteral reflux, and it has no pathologic significance. Furthermore, the findings usually resolve over the first year of life. Therefore, neonates with a renal pelvic diameter of less than 10 mm are not at increased risk for urinary tract disease and do not require further follow-up. If the renal pelvic diameter is greater than 10 mm, the infant should be evaluated for possible obstructive uropathy.

The neonatal kidney may also demonstrate increased medullary echogenicity in the first week of life[23,45] (Fig. 35-25). This increased medullary echogenicity is a result of transient tubular stasis and should not be confused with medullary nephrocalcinosis or calculi. The findings are usually diffuse and bilateral, although they may be asymmetric or focal. The increased medullary echogenicity usually resolves by 2 weeks of life and is not associated with any long-term renal dysfunction.

Obstructive Uropathy

The most common cause of urinary tract obstruction in infants is ureteropelvic junction (UPJ) obstruction. It is commonly identified initially on prenatal imaging, but infants may also present after birth with a palpable abdominal mass representing an enlarged, hydronephrotic kidney. Sonography is the initial diagnostic examination in children with suspected UPJ obstruction.

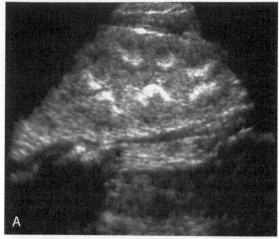
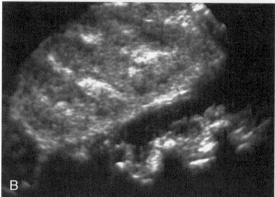

FIGURE 35-25. Transient increased medullary echogenicity of the newborn. Longitudinal views through the right (**A**) and left (**B**) kidneys in a 2-day-old infant demonstrate increased medullary echogenicity. The distribution is bilateral and symmetric. The findings had resolved by the follow-up examination 2 weeks later.

The sonographic findings include dilation of the intrarenal collecting system without ureteral dilation[8] (Fig. 35-26). The obstruction is bilateral in one fourth to one third of patients. Although the diagnosis of UPJ obstruction can be made with a high degree of certainty with sonography, renal scintigraphy is needed to quantify the degree of obstruction, and it also is used to determine renal function. The scintigraphic appearance of UPJ obstruction involves progressive increase in radionuclide activity within the renal collecting system, and delayed excretion. UPJ obstruction may be associated with vesicoureteral reflux, so the imaging evaluation of infants with the condition should include a voiding cystourethrogram (VCUG).

Posterior urethral valves are the most common cause of lower urinary tract obstruction and the leading cause of end-stage renal disease in boys. The diagnosis is also often made at prenatal imaging, but it is not unusual for the condition to be initially diagnosed after birth. Clinical findings include a palpable abdominal mass representing enlarged kidneys and/or bladder, voiding abnormalities, or symptoms related to urinary tract infection. The initial imaging examination is sonography,

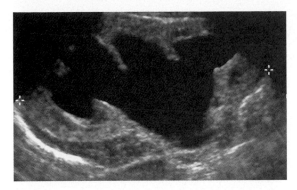

FIGURE 35-26. Ureteropelvic junction obstruction. Longitudinal view through the right kidney demonstrates marked dilation of the right intrarenal collecting system. The right ureter was not dilated.

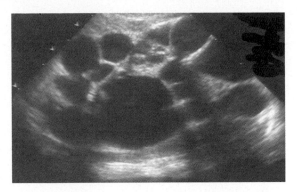

FIGURE 35-28. Multicystic dysplastic kidney. Longitudinal view through the right renal fossa demonstrates multiple cysts of varying sizes that do not communicate with each other.

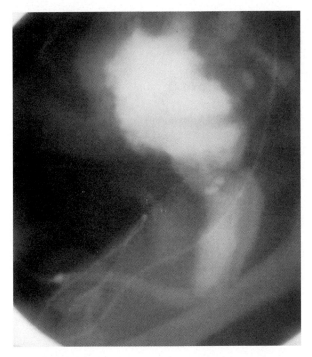

FIGURE 35-27. Posterior urethral valves. Lateral image from a voiding cystourethrogram shows a dilated posterior urethra and a normal-caliber anterior urethra.

which demonstrates bilateral hydroureteronephrosis and a dilated or thick-walled bladder.[36] The diagnosis is confirmed with a VCUG. The findings at VCUG include a dilated posterior urethra and diminution of the urethral caliber distal to the valves[36] (Fig. 35-27). There may be associated vesicoureteral reflux.

Multicystic Dysplastic Kidney

Multicystic dysplastic kidney is the result of an insult in early embryologic development that leads to pelvo-infundibular atresia. The proximal ureter, renal pelvis, and infundibula are all atretic. Subsequently, there is

cystic dilation of the collecting tubules, with formation of cystic spaces. There is no identifiable pelvocaliceal system or normal renal parenchyma. Infants with multicystic dysplastic kidney usually present with a palpable flank mass. The two most common flank masses in the newborn are of renal origin: hydronephrosis and multicystic dysplastic kidney.

Sonography is the initial examination of choice in the evaluation of a suspected abdominal mass. The sonographic criteria for diagnosing a multicystic dysplastic kidney include multiple oval or round cysts that do not communicate and absence of renal parenchyma[47] (Fig. 35-28). In most cases, there are multiple cysts, but in a small subset of instances, a single cyst is noted. The natural history of the disease on sonographic follow-up is a gradual decrease in the number and size of the cysts over several months or years as the cyst fluid resorbs.[49]

Autosomal Recessive Polycystic Kidney Disease

Autosomal recessive polycystic kidney disease is an inherited disorder characterized by nephromegaly, microscopic or macroscopic cystic dilation of the renal collecting system, and periportal hepatic fibrosis. Infants with this disease typically present with palpable abdominal masses or with renal insufficiency. The characteristic sonographic appearance includes enlarged, hyperechoic kidneys bilaterally. Renal enlargement is usually symmetrical. The cysts are typically too small to be visualized at sonography. However, the multiple interfaces associated with the cystic dilation of the renal collecting ducts result in increased renal parenchymal echogenicity.

Renal Vein Thrombosis

Renal vein thrombosis in infants is associated with hemoconcentration associated with dehydration, sepsis, and maternal diabetes mellitus. It may also be seen in association with indwelling umbilical venous catheters in infants who develop thrombi in the inferior vena cava. The clinical presentation includes a palpable mass representing an enlarged kidney, renal insufficiency, hematuria, or hypertension.

Doppler sonography is the examination of choice for the evaluation of suspected renal vein thrombosis. The sonographic findings vary depending on the extent and duration of renal venous occlusion. Sonographic findings include the presence of echogenic filling defects in the main renal vein and absence or diminution of renal venous flow surrounding the thrombus.[21] The venous outflow obstruction results in diminution of ipsilateral renal arterial flow, which in turn results in narrowing of the systolic peak and reduction or reversal of diastolic flow with an elevated resistive index in the ipsilateral renal artery.[32] Enlargement of the involved kidney with diffuse increase in parenchymal echogenicity and loss of corticomedullary differentiation is also typically seen in the acute period. Over the next several weeks, the renal parenchymal echogenicity of the involved kidney becomes heterogeneous and renal size diminishes.

Nephrocalcinosis

Nephrocalcinosis refers to the deposition of calcium in the renal parenchyma. It most commonly involves the renal pyramids and medulla, in which case it is referred to as medullary nephrocalcinosis. Hypercalciuria is an important precursor for the development of nephrocalcinosis. Most cases of medullary nephrocalcinosis in neonates are the result of furosemide therapy. Furosemide results in increased calcium excretion. It may also be seen in association with hypervitaminosis D and distal renal tubular acidosis. Most infants are asymptomatic.

Sonography demonstrates increased echogenicity in the normally sonolucent renal pyramids in patients with medullary nephrocalcinosis[48] (Fig. 35-29). Acoustic shadowing does not usually occur. Medullary nephrocalcinosis is typically seen diffusely throughout both kidneys. Sonography is usually used to monitor progression of disease or improvement. Nephrocalcinosis associated with furosemide therapy gradually resolves after the medication is stopped.

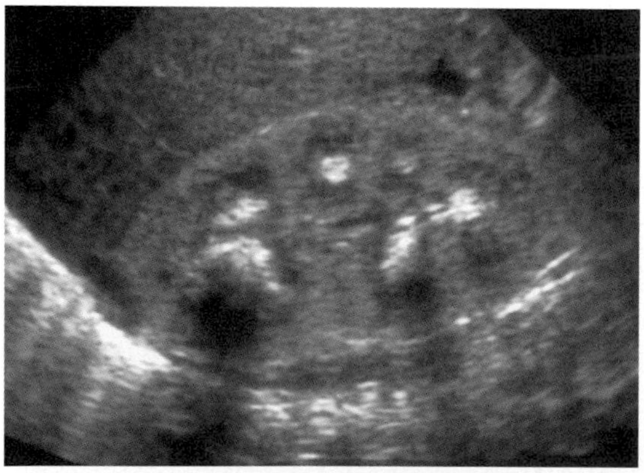

ADRENAL

Adrenal Hemorrhage

Adrenal hemorrhage is the most common cause of a neonatal adrenal mass. Right-sided hemorrhage occurs far more commonly than left-sided hemorrhage. Neonates are at increased risk for adrenal hemorrhage because of the relatively large size and increased vascularity of the gland in this age group. Conditions associated with adrenal hemorrhage include perinatal asphyxia, sepsis, coagulation disorders, hypotension, and surgery. Clinical manifestations are typically seen only when there is diffuse, bilateral gland involvement, resulting in adrenal cortical insufficiency.

Sonography is usually the initial imaging examination of choice in the evaluation of suspected adrenal hemorrhage. The sonographic appearance of adrenal hemorrhage is that of an oval or triangular solid mass of variable echotexture[18] (Fig. 35-30). There may be focal or diffuse obliteration of one or both adrenal limbs. Unilateral hemorrhage is more common than bilateral hemorrhage. Adrenal calcification may develop weeks to months after the hemorrhage. Large adrenal hemorrhages may be difficult to differentiate from tumor, particularly if calcification is already present. In such cases, serial follow-up is useful. Typically, adrenal hemorrhages are noted to gradually decrease in size over several weeks.

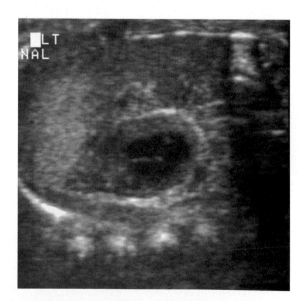

FIGURE 35-29. Medullary nephrocalcinosis. Longitudinal view through the right kidney in a 3-month-old child who had previously been treated with furosemide demonstrates increased medullary echogenicity indicative of medullary nephrocalcinosis.

FIGURE 35-30. Adrenal hematoma. Longitudinal view through the left suprarenal region demonstrates an oval left adrenal hematoma.

Neuroblastoma

Neuroblastoma is the most common adrenal neoplasm in children. It occasionally presents in the newborn period. The usual clinical presentation is that of a palpable abdominal mass. Sonography is usually the initial imaging examination of choice. A normal ultrasound is useful in excluding a mass. Approximately two thirds of abdominal neuroblastomas arise from the adrenal gland. Therefore, the most frequent sonographic appearance is that of a solid, suprarenal mass. It is typically heterogeneous in echotexture.[3] Calcifications are noted in approximately two thirds of patients. If a mass is identified at sonography, cross-sectional imaging with CT or MRI is performed for a more precise characterization of the organ of origin and for staging.

BRAIN (See Chapter 38.)

Sonography is the primary means of evaluating intracranial pathology in infants. It is performed through the anterior fontanelle with a 5- to 10-MHz sector transducer. Routine imaging is performed in the coronal and sagittal planes. The advantages of sonography are that it can be performed at the bedside, patients do not require sedation, and it is a useful modality for the evaluation of germinal matrix hemorrhage, which is the most common indication for neuroimaging in infants. However, the ability of sonography to evaluate parenchymal, subarachnoid, and subdural abnormalities is limited. CT and MRI provide accurate depiction of parenchymal, subarachnoid, and subdural disease, and they are more sensitive in the detection of germinal matrix hemorrhage than sonography.[7] Additionally, MRI provides detailed anatomic information of intracranial and extracranial vascular anatomy. A major disadvantage of both CT and MRI is that they cannot be performed portably. Additionally, MRI requires patient sedation.

Germinal Matrix Hemorrhage

Germinal matrix hemorrhage is seen primarily in premature infants. The infants at highest risk are those with a gestational age of less than 32 weeks or a birthweight of less than 1500 grams. Most hemorrhages occur by the first week of life. The site of origin for germinal matrix hemorrhage is the caudothalamic groove, an area bordered by the ventricular surface of the caudate nucleus and the thalamus. It is an extremely vascular area and, in the premature infant, composed of thin-walled blood vessels with little surrounding connective tissue. Therefore, conditions that lead to increased blood flow predispose to hemorrhage.

The classification system for germinal matrix hemorrhage was described by Papille and colleagues.[43] Their grading system is based on the presence of subependymal and intraventricular hemorrhage, ventriculomegaly, and parenchymal abnormalities. Grade 1 is

subependymal hemorrhage only; grade 2 is subependymal and intraventricular hemorrhage; grade 3 is subependymal and intraventricular hemorrhage and ventriculomegaly; and grade 4 is subependymal and intraventricular hemorrhage, ventriculomegaly, and intraparenchymal abnormalities.[43] A subsequent grading system is presented in Chapter 38, Part 3.

At sonography, a grade 1 hemorrhage appears as a subependymal echogenic mass inferolateral to the frontal horn of the lateral ventricle (Fig. 35-31). If the subependymal hemorrhage is large, it may compress the ipsilateral lateral ventricle. In grade 2 hemorrhage, blood ruptures through the ependyma and is seen within the ventricle[10] (Fig. 35-32). It may occasionally be difficult to distinguish intraventricular hemorrhage from choroid plexus. If intraventricular echogenicity is noted anterior to the foramen of Monroe, or if the choroid plexus appears asymmetrically enlarged or

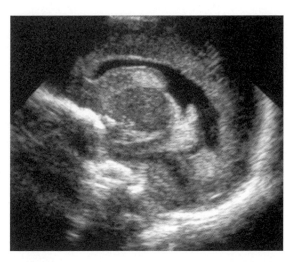

FIGURE 35-31. Grade 1 hemorrhage. Longitudinal view through the right lateral ventricle demonstrates a subependymal hemorrhage.

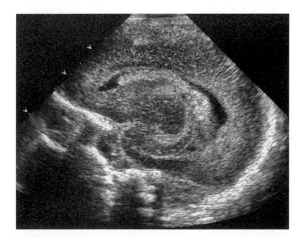

FIGURE 35-32. Grade 2 hemorrhage. Longitudinal view through the right lateral ventricle demonstrates subependymal and intraventricular hemorrhage.

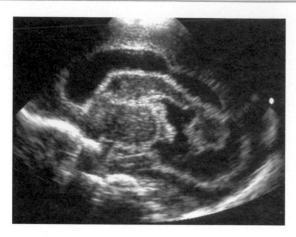

FIGURE 35-33. Grade 3 hemorrhage. Longitudinal view through the left lateral ventricle shows intraventricular hemorrhage and ventriculomegaly.

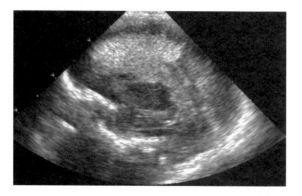

FIGURE 35-34. Grade 4 hemorrhage. Longitudinal view through the right lateral ventricle demonstrates intraventricular hemorrhage and echogenic parenchymal abnormality, representing hemorrhage and/or infarct.

irregular, it usually signifies intraventricular hemorrhage. In grade 3 hemorrhage, the intraventricular hemorrhage expands one or both ventricles, resulting in ventriculomegaly (Fig. 35-33). Grade 4 hemorrhage is characterized by echogenic periventricular abnormalities[10] (Fig. 35-34). Most of these areas represent hemorrhagic venous infarcts that result from compression of periventricular veins by the subependymal hemorrhage. The grade of the germinal matrix hemorrhage has been shown to impact neurodevelopmental outcome. The developmental outcome in infants with grades 3 and 4 hemorrhage is worse than in those with grades 1 and 2,[34] and the latter are probably not prognostic indicators.

Ventriculomegaly is a frequent consequence of intraventricular hemorrhage. It usually results from an obliterative arachnoiditis or from an intraventricular obstruction from clot or debris. The ventriculomegaly may be present initially or delayed by several weeks. Typically, the trigones and occipital horns of the lateral ventricles dilate prior to the frontal horns, and the lateral ventricles may dilate alone or to a greater degree than the third and fourth ventricles. Serial sonographic

evaluation is performed in infants with a germinal matrix hemorrhage because of the risk of developing hydrocephalus. On serial sonographic follow-up, the ventriculomegaly frequently resolves or remains static. Progressive hydrocephalus requiring shunting is seen in less than 10% of cases.

Periventricular Leukomalacia

(See Chapter 38, Part 2.)

Periventricular leukomalacia (PVL) represents infarction of deep white matter adjacent to the trigones and frontal horns of the lateral ventricles. It is frequently associated with intraventricular hemorrhage—approximately half of infants with PVL have intraventricular hemorrhage. Sonography is often normal early in the course of PVL and thus is insensitive for the early diagnosis. The earliest sonographic abnormality is increased periventricular echogenicity (Fig. 35-35). With progression of disease, cavitation occurs, resulting in parenchymal cystic areas (Fig. 35-36). These areas may communicate with the ipsilateral lateral ventricle.

CT is more sensitive than sonography for detecting the hemorrhagic component of PVL.[46] Decreased attenuation of white matter is noted at CT unless the ischemic area is accompanied by hemorrhage. The latter condition is associated with increased attenuation. MRI is the most sensitive imaging modality for the assessment of PVL.[7,46] Peritrigonal areas of hyperintensity are seen on T2-weighted images. The corpus callosum is often thinned or atrophic. Additionally, irregularity of the lateral ventricular contour and asymmetric ventricular enlargement may be noted.

Lenticulostriate Vasculopathy

Lenticulostriate vasculopathy represents mineralized deposits in arterial walls and perivascular infiltration of mononuclear cells secondary to inflammatory or

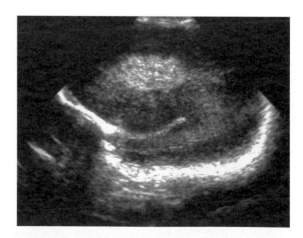

FIGURE 35-35. Periventricular leukomalacia. Longitudinal view through the right hemisphere demonstrates increased echogenicity in the frontal-parietal region.

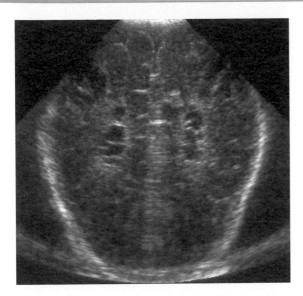

FIGURE 35-36. Periventricular leukomalacia. Coronal view through the periventricular region shows numerous parenchymal cystic areas.

necrotizing vasculitis. They are predominantly seen surrounding the lenticulostriate branches of the middle cerebral arteries. Lenticulostriate vasculopathy has been associated with various congenital infections, including syphilis, rubella, toxoplasmosis, and cytomegalovirus. It has also been associated with chromosomal abnormalities, fetal alcohol syndrome, bacterial meningitis, and perinatal asphyxia. Lenticulostriate vasculopathy is believed to represent a nonspecific response to vascular injury. The appearance at sonography is of linear or branching areas of echogenicity that may be seen in the thalami and basal ganglia (Fig. 35-37). The abnormalities are more commonly bilateral than unilateral. The initial observation of lenticulostriate vasculopathy may be in the first week of life, but more frequently it is noted at several weeks or months of age.

SKELETAL

Skeletal radiography is usually the initial imaging examination in the evaluation of suspected skeletal pathology in infants. Skeletal scintigraphy is useful in the evaluation of disseminated infection, neoplasm, or trauma. MRI is useful for the precise characterization of infection.

Intrauterine Infection (See Chapter 37.)

Intrauterine infection may result in skeletal changes. Congenital rubella and cytomegalovirus infection result in metaphyseal lesions with vertical striations that resemble a celery stalk. Congenital syphilis results in single or multifocal metaphyseal lesions representing osteomyelitis (Fig. 35-38). The metaphyseal lesions vary from radiolucent transverse metaphyseal bands to actual destruction and fragmentation of bone. Whenever the destructive changes occur bilaterally in the upper medial tibiae, the term *Wimberger sign* is applied. Associated periostitis may also be noted.

Postnatal Infection

Neonatal osteomyelitis is typically caused by staphylococci, streptococci, or *Candida*. The infection involves the metaphyses of long bones and produces focal lytic areas at radiography. Associated soft tissue edema may be noted. Skeletal radiography remains the most common mode of assessing suspected osteomyelitis. Bone scanning may be useful to characterize all of the lesions when the involvement is multifocal. CT and MRI are also useful in the detection of osteomyelitis.

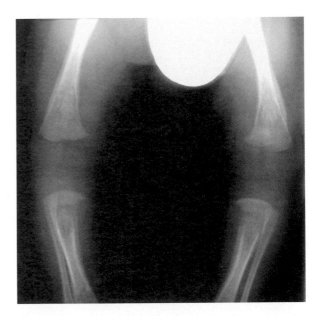

FIGURE 35-38. Congenital syphilis. Anteroposterior view of both lower extremities in a 1-week-old infant demonstrates lytic lesions in both distal femurs and proximal tibias. The lesions in the upper tibiae are characterized as Wimberger sign.

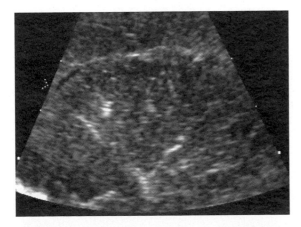

FIGURE 35-37. Lenticulostriate vasculopathy. Longitudinal view through the right thalamus demonstrates branching linear areas of echogenicity.

In infants, osteomyelitis is often seen in conjunction with septic arthritis because the metaphysis and epiphysis have contiguous blood supplies.

Rickets

Rickets occurs as a result of a relative or absolute deficiency of vitamin D, which in turn results in failure of normal mineralization of developing bone. The radiologic findings of rickets precede clinical manifestations. The radiographic abnormalities are seen in the distal metaphyses and include cupping, fraying, and irregularity. Widening of the physis and loss of definition of the epiphyses may also be noted. There is also diffuse demineralization. Because the radiographic abnormalities are seen in all of the distal metaphyses, it is not necessary to obtain radiographs of multiple joints. A single anteroposterior view of the wrist or knee is sufficient to demonstrate the abnormality (Fig. 35-39).

FUTURE DIRECTIONS

The use of diagnostic imaging in infants and neonates continues to evolve because of advances in imaging technology. Over the past decade, advancements in prenatal imaging with sonography and MRI have had a tremendous impact on the early diagnosis and treatment of many pathologic conditions affecting infants and young children. This in turn has greatly enhanced the therapeutic options available for such patients. With the continued refinement of those modalities, we will continue to see earlier and more precise diagnosis of many of these conditions. The recent introduction of multislice CT scanning has also allowed enhanced imaging in neonates by facilitating faster scan times (thus decreasing the need for sedation) and thinner imaging sections (thus allowing improved visualization of normal and abnormal anatomy in smaller patients). Advancements in duplex and color Doppler technology with the development of higher-frequency transducers and the ability to visualize lower velocities of blood flow in smaller vessels are also expanding the diagnostic capability in infants and neonates. In the future, it is likely that there will be an increasing focus on functional imaging modalities such as positron-emission tomography scanning as diagnostic imaging continues to evolve from primarily evaluating anatomy to also assessing function.

REFERENCES

1. Ablow RC et al: The radiographic features of early onset group B streptococcal neonatal sepsis. Radiology 124:771, 1977.
2. Abramson SJ et al: Biliary atresia and noncardiac polysplenic syndrome: US and surgical considerations. Radiology 163:377, 1987.
3. Amundson GM et al: Neuroblastoma: A specific sonographic tissue pattern. AJR Am J Roentgenol 148:943, 1987.
4. Berdon WE et al: Radiographic findings in esophageal atresia with proximal pouch fistula. Pediatr Radiol 3:70, 1975.
5. Berdon WE et al: Midgut malrotation and volvulus: Which films are most helpful? Radiology 96:375, 1970.
6. Berdon WE et al: Microcolon in newborn infants with intestinal obstruction. Radiology 90:878, 1978.
7. Blankenberg F et al: Sonography, CT and MR imaging: A prospective comparison of neonates with suspected intracranial ischemia and hemorrhage. AJNR Am J Neuroradiol 21:213, 2001.
8. Brown T et al: Neonatal hydronephrosis in the era of sonography. AJR Am J Roentgenol 148:959, 1987.
9. Buonomo C: Neonatal gastrointestinal emergencies. Radiol Clin North Am 35:845, 1997.
10. Carson SC et al: Value of sonography in the diagnosis of intraventricular hemorrhage and periventricular leukomalacia: A postmortem study of 35 cases. AJR Am J Roentgenol 11:677, 1990.
11. Clarke EA et al: Findings on chest radiographs after prophylactic pulmonary surfactant treatment of premature infants. AJR Am J Roentgenol 153:799, 1989.
12. Clautice-Engle T et al: Diagnosis of obstructive hydronephrosis in infants: Comparison sonograms performed 6 days and 6 weeks after birth. AJR Am J Roentgenol 164:963, 1995.
13. Daneman A et al: The radiology of neonatal necrotizing enterocolitis. Pediatr Radiol 7:70, 1978.
14. Davis WS et al: Neonatal small left colon syndrome. AJR Am J Roentgenol 120:322, 1974.
15. Del Pin CA et al: Management and survival of meconium ileus: A 30 year review. Ann Surg 215:179, 1992.
16. Dinger J et al: Radiologic changes after therapeutic use of surfactant in infants with respiratory distress syndrome. Pediatr Radiol 27:26, 1997.
17. Dremsek PA et al: Renal pyelectasis in fetuses and neonates: Diagnostic value of renal pelvis diameter in pre- and postnatal screening. AJR Am J Roentgenol 168:1017, 1997.

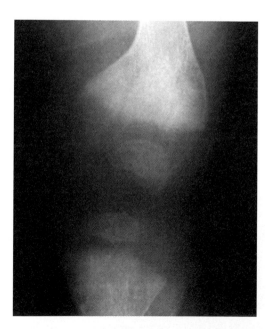

FIGURE 35-39. Rickets. Anteroposterior view of the left knee demonstrates widening, cupping, and irregularity of the left distal femoral and proximal tibial metaphyses, diagnostic of rickets.

18. Felc Z: Ultrasound in screening for neonatal adrenal hemorrhage. Am J Perinatol 12:363, 1995.

19. Griscom NT: Respiratory problems of early life now allowing survival into adulthood: concepts for radiologists. AJR Am J Roentgenol 158:1, 1992.

20. Haney PJ et al: Radiographic findings in neonatal pneumonia. AJR Am J Roentgenol 143:26, 1984.

21. Helenon O et al: Color Doppler US of renal vascular disease in native kidneys. Radiographics 15:833, 1995.

22. Hoffman RR et al: Fetal aspiration syndrome: Clinical, roentgenologic and pathologic features. AJR Am J Roentgenol 122:90, 1974.

23. Howlett DC et al: The incidence of transient renal medullary hyperechogenicity in neonatal ultrasound examination. Br J Radiol 70:140, 1997.

24. Hussain SM et al: Plain film diagnosis in meconium plug syndrome, meconium ileus and neonatal Hirschsprung's disease. Pediatr Radiol 21:556, 1991.

25. Jobe AH, Bancalari E: Bronchopulmonary dysplasia. Am J Respir Crit Care Med 163:1723, 2001.

26. Kao SCS et al: Nonoperative treatment of simple meconium ileus: A survey of the Society for Pediatric Radiology. Pediatr Radiol 25:97, 1995.

27. Kendrick APT et al: Making the diagnosis of biliary atresia using the triangular cord sign and gallbladder length. Pediatr Radiol 30:69, 2000.

28. Kim OH et al: Imaging of the choledochal cyst. Radiographics 15:69, 1995.

29. Kogutt MS: Necrotizing enterocolitis of infancy. Radiology 130:367, 1979.

30. Kosloske AM et al: Necrotizing enterocolitis: Value of radiographic findings to predict outcome. AJR Am J Roentgenol 151:771, 1988.

31. Lai M et al: Differential diagnosis of extrahepatic biliary atresia from neonatal hepatitis: A prospective study. J Pediatr 18:121, 1991.

32. Laplante S et al: Renal vein thrombosis in children: Evidence of early flow recovery with Doppler US. Radiology 189:37, 1992.

33. Lehtonen L et al: The size and contractility of the gallbladder in infants. Pediatr Radiol 22:515, 1992.

34. Levy ML et al: Outcome in preterm infants with germinal matrix hemorrhage and progressive hydrocephalus. Neurosurgery 41:1111, 1997.

35. Long FR et al: Intestinal malrotation in children: Tutorial on radiographic diagnosis in difficult cases. Radiology 198:775, 1996.

36. Macpherson RI et al: Posterior urethral valves: An update and review. Radiographics 6:753, 1986.

37. Majd M: Tc-IDA scintigraphy in the evaluation of neonatal jaundice. Radiographics 3:88, 1983.

38. McAlister WH, Kronemer KA: Emergency gastrointestinal radiology of the newborn. Radiol Clin North Am 34:819, 1996.

39. Miller SF et al: Use of ultrasound in the detection of occult perforation in neonates. J Ultrasound Med 12:531, 1993.

40. Moylan FMB et al: Alveolar rupture as an independent predictor of bronchopulmonary dysplasia. Crit Care Med 6:10, 1978.

41. Northway WH et al: Late pulmonary sequelae of bronchopulmonary dysplasia. N Engl J Med 323:1793, 1990.

42. Panicek DM et al: The continuum of pulmonary developmental anomalies. Radiographics 7:747, 1987.

43. Papille LA et al: Relationship of cerebral intraventricular hemorrhage and early childhood neurologic handicaps. J Pediatr 103:273, 1983.

44. Park WH et al: The ultrasonographic "triangular cord" couples with gallbladder images in the diagnostic prediction of biliary atresia from infantile intrahepatic cholestasis. J Pediatr Surg 34:1706, 1997.

45. Riebel TW et al: Transient renal medullary echogenicity in ultrasound studies of neonates: Is it a normal phenomenon and what are the causes? J Clin Ultrasound 21:25, 1993.

46. Rijn AM et al: Parenchymal brain injury in the preterm infant: Comparison of cranial ultrasound, MRI and neurodevelopmental outcome. Neuropediatrics 32:80, 2001.

47. Sanders RC et al: The sonographic distinction between neonatal multicystic dysplastic kidney and hydronephrosis. Radiology 151:621, 1984.

48. Shultz PK et al: Hyperechoic renal medullary pyramids in infants and children. Radiology 181:163, 1991.

49. Strife JL et al: Multicystic dysplastic kidney in children: US follow-up. Radiology 186:785, 1993.

50. Todani T et al: Congenital bile duct cysts: Classification, operative procedures, and review of thirty-seven cases including cancer arising from choledochal cyst. J Surg 134:263, 1977.

36 Infants of Substance-Abusing Mothers

Emmalee S. Bandstra and Veronica H. Accornero

THE CLINICIAN'S ROLE IN PERINATAL SUBSTANCE ABUSE

Although a multitude of legal, illegal, and diverted prescription drugs have the potential for abuse by pregnant women with deleterious effects on the developing fetus, this chapter is restricted to the current major drugs of abuse: alcohol, tobacco, marijuana, cocaine, amphetamines, and opioids. Regional differences in drug use patterns and preferences make it imperative for clinicians to work closely with other professionals in their communities and regions to develop a multilevel medical, legal, and psychosocial response. Screening by maternal self-report and toxicologic assays for substance abuse should be conducted solely for the purpose of improving patient care and not for punitive consequences.

Ideally, substance use should be terminated by women and their male sexual partner (or partners) before conception. Pregnant drug-using women should be counseled at the earliest opportunity to abstain completely from all injurious substances and to seek prenatal care. Adequate dietary intake and supplemental prenatal vitamins should be stressed. Special emphasis should be placed on serology testing for syphilis and hepatitis B and C, and on screening for human immunodeficiency virus (HIV), with pretest and post-test counseling. When deemed clinically appropriate, the following should be provided: complete blood count with differential; urine for urinalysis, culture, and sensitivity; Papanicolaou smear; gonorrhea and chlamydia tests; maternal serum α-fetoprotein screening; ultrasound screening for fetal anomalies and growth pattern; and amniocentesis with fetal karyotyping. Maternal blood pressure, electrocardiogram, and liver function tests may also be indicated.

The pregnant substance-abusing mother should be cautioned about the signs of antepartum hemorrhage, premature rupture of membranes, premature labor onset, and meconium-stained amniotic fluid, so that intervention measures can be undertaken to avert catastrophic complications. Referral to support groups and drug rehabilitation, as well as periodic random drug screens, should be incorporated into patient care plans as appropriate.

Identification of the substance-abusing mother is the first step in attempting to break the cycle of reproductive morbidity or mortality. Women entrenched in the substance-abusing lifestyle may not seek prenatal care, even when it is available, because of guilt or fear of legal reprisals, such as incarceration and child welfare proceedings. If the mother is not engaged during prenatal care, her hospitalization at the time of delivery may afford the only window of opportunity to evaluate the health and psychosocial status of both mother and infant for appropriate referrals and to provide postpartum counseling for the prevention of future drug-exposed pregnancies, sexually transmitted diseases, and HIV infection.

Current limitations of maternal self-report, selective screening criteria, and available toxicology assays preclude clinical identification of all affected infants. Physicians should become well informed about patterns of substance abuse in their community. They need to incorporate skillful interviewing techniques and appropriate toxicologic screening to identify perinatal substance abuse, know the statutory obligation to report drug-exposed infants to child protection authorities, and develop specific medical intervention strategies and viable referral patterns for substance-abusing women and their offspring.

Clinicians should also be aware of the limitations of the animal and human literature in providing definitive data on the effects of individual drugs and drug interactions. Animal studies provide an opportunity to test the teratogenicity of a single drug under controlled laboratory settings, but interspecies variations constrain our ability to generalize these findings to humans. Clinical studies provide the naturalistic environment for study of drugs of abuse, but despite concerted efforts to design and implement well-controlled studies with adequate control groups, there are numerous confounding factors that cannot be fully accounted for in study design or by statistical control.

Clinical guidelines for obstetric and neonatal screening are based on conditions shown to be associated with perinatal substance abuse, such as self-admitted alcohol or drug abuse, inadequate or no prenatal care, sexually transmitted diseases, premature onset of labor, abruptio placentae, intrauterine growth restriction, congenital malformations, and overt signs of withdrawal. However, these criteria fail to detect a large number of affected pregnancies. Self-reporting of substance abuse is unreliable because of poor maternal recall and fear of reprisals from the legal, medical, and social welfare systems. However, when biomarkers to detect remote drug use, such as in early pregnancy, are unavailable or unreliable, the only means of detecting exposure may be maternal self-report. It therefore becomes necessary to develop nonjudgmental and culturally sensitive interviewing techniques to elicit a substance abuse history. Reliance on the physical examination or the clinical condition of the infant to indicate when toxicology screening should be performed is also inadequate. Intrauterine growth restriction, microcephaly, prematurity, and congenital malformations may be associated with prenatal substance exposure, but not all affected infants present with such complications. Abnormal neurobehavioral signs and overt withdrawal signs are useful indicators, but they are not uniformly present even in narcotic-exposed infants.

Although urine toxicology screening is useful for clinical and research purposes, urinary excretion of metabolites may be detectable only for several days (e.g., benzoylecgonine) or even weeks (e.g., cannabinoids). One cannot expect to ascertain early pregnancy use or even relatively recent use if the metabolite concentration does not reach the detection threshold. Infant meconium provides a wider window of detection of gestational exposure, presumably as remote as the second trimester. Maternal and infant hair samples may provide an even wider window and some insight into time course and perhaps quantification of in utero drug exposure. However, meconium and hair assays are generally reserved for research settings and have numerous technical and interpretive limitations.

The most significant problem in interpreting clinical studies is the handling of confounding variables, such as polysubstance exposure, sexually transmitted diseases, chronic malnutrition, and cocaine binges with episodic starvation. Polysubstance exposure is common among pregnant substance-abusers, and combinations of two or more agents may be more ominous than single-agent exposure (e.g., concurrent cocaine and alcohol use). Cocaethylene, a pharmacologically active metabolite of cocaine produced in the presence of ethyl alcohol, produces enhanced euphoria and appears to result in a high prevalence of cocaine-related emergencies or death in adults. This compound has been detected in neonatal meconium and hair and may correlate with higher risk to the developing infant and child.

Similarly, it is difficult to disentangle the many social and environmental factors that accompany perinatal substance abuse. Although abuse of alcohol, tobacco, and illicit drugs crosses all races, ethnicities, and socioeconomic strata, the substance-abusing mothers who are at greatest risk are those who must also contend with poverty and its associated conditions, such as lack of food, shelter, and clothing; increased stress; poor self-esteem and poor coping skills; exposure to physical, sexual, and domestic violence; increased risk of contracting HIV, acquired immunodeficiency syndrome (AIDS), and sexually transmitted diseases; poor education, illiteracy, and joblessness; and inadequate access to culturally and linguistically appropriate health, social, legal, and addiction-treatment services.

Federally supported research and service demonstration programs and community-based initiatives throughout the nation have begun to evolve into veritable prevention and intervention networks. The most successful perinatal substance abuse programs are multidisciplinary and provide a comprehensive range of barrier-free medical, social, psychological, chemical dependency treatment, and vocational and educational services to the pregnant and postpartum mother, her infant, and her family for an extended period.

This chapter seeks to provide an overview of the drugs of interest and to emphasize specific diagnostic criteria and interventions as appropriate (e.g., the recognition of fetal alcohol syndrome or the treatment for neonatal abstinence syndrome). Recommendations regarding prevention and intervention including multidisciplinary services that should be provided for the mother and her substance-exposed infant are also provided.

ALCOHOL

Prevalence of Fetal Alcohol Syndrome

Fetal alcohol syndrome (FAS) is the leading identifiable nonhereditary cause of mental retardation and neurologic deficit in the Western world. First described over 30 years ago in separate observations by investigators in France and the United States, FAS has the following hallmarks: (1) growth retardation, (2) specific mid-facial features (short palpebral fissures, smooth indistinct philtrum, thin vermilion border of the upper lip); and (3) adverse brain effects resulting in mental retardation. Although not specifically mentioned in the FAS triad, congenital defects of other major organs have also been noted. Features consistent with FAS in humans have been reproduced in animal models of gestational ethanol exposure[160] (Fig. 36-1). Studies in mice and chicks have demonstrated that alcohol exposure at specific stages of early embryonic development leads to apoptosis of the cranial nerve crest cells destined to give rise to facial structures, perhaps due to localized retinoic acid deficiency, free radical damage, or interference with intracellular communication.[152]

According to the results obtained from the 2003 National Survey on Drug Use and Health, pregnant women aged 15 to 44 used alcohol at a rate of 9.8%, with 4.1% reporting binge drinking and 0.7 % reporting heavy drinking in the month prior to the survey.[159] These rates were significantly lower than those obtained for similarly aged nonpregnant women (53%, 23.2%, and 5.3%, respectively). Binge drinking is defined as drinking five or more drinks on the same occasion (i.e., at the same time or within a couple of hours) on at least

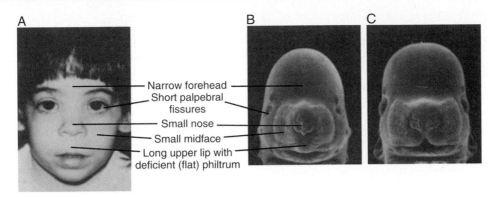

FIGURE 36-1. Similarities found in facial defects found in (**A**) humans and (**B**) mice exposed prenatally to alcohol. **C** shows a mouse fetus not exposed to alcohol. (From Smith SM: Alcohol-induced cell death in the embryo. Alcohol Health Res World 21:287, 1997.)

1 day in the past 30 days. It should be noted that the definition for heavy drinking in this survey subsumes binge drinking, in that heavy drinking is defined as the equivalent of binge drinking on each of 5 or more days in the past 30 days.[159] Current recommendations for a healthy lifestyle for women is having no more than one drink per day and for men no more than two drinks per day. Although definitions vary, for most clinical studies of prenatal alcohol exposure, more than two drinks per day exceeds what is considered moderate alcohol consumption during pregnancy,[136] and binge drinking is considered a significant separate risk factor.

Estimated from 29 prospective studies, the worldwide incidence of FAS is 0.97 cases per 1000 live births in the general obstetric population and 4.3% among heavy drinkers.[1] In the United States, the general incidence of FAS is reported to be more than 20-fold higher than in other countries (1.95 per 1000 versus 0.08 per 1000). Furthermore, low socioeconomic status (SES) is a significant risk factor. In the United States, the reported incidence of FAS among low SES groups, represented predominantly by African Americans and Native Americans, is more than 10 times higher than that of middle and upper SES, predominantly white, populations (2.29 versus 0.26 per 1000). Conditions associated with low SES (such as poor general health, increased stress, and nutritional deficiencies), a more severe pattern of alcohol ingestion, and concomitant smoking and other drug use are hypothesized to exacerbate the teratogenicity of heavy alcohol intake via mechanisms linked to hypoxia and free radical generation, leading to cell damage within the fetus. Although the risk for FAS may be relatively low even among heavy drinkers, once a woman has had one infant with FAS, her risk of having a subsequent infant with FAS may be as high as 60% to 70% if she continues to drink. Studies have shown a higher rate of offspring with FAS in women over 30 years of age, perhaps because of altered physiology or increased maternal morbidity associated with lengthy drinking histories. Obstetric consequences of heavy drinking include increased risk for spontaneous abortions, abruptio placentae, and alcohol-related birth defects, which in the most severe cases can be life threatening. In approximately 30% to 40% of infants of heavy drinkers, the cognitive and neurobehavioral deficits are milder and may occur with or without classic facial features. The original term for this less severe expression was *fetal alcohol effects* or FAE. These observations have prompted speculation that there are individual susceptibility differences in the expression of effects of alcohol in the mother and fetus, related to genetics, maternal age, serious medical conditions, and exposure to other toxicants, as well as environmental influences, including factors associated with low SES.

Fetal Alcohol Spectrum Disorders

Fetal alcohol spectrum disorders (FASD) is an umbrella term for the range of physical mental, behavioral, and learning disability effects that can occur in an individual whose mother drank alcohol during pregnancy, but FASD is not intended as a clinical diagnosis. In 1996, the Institute of Medicine published specific diagnostic criteria for FAS, partial FAS, alcohol-related birth defects (ARBD), and alcohol-related neurodevelopmental disorder (ARND) as detailed in Box 36-1.[36] The incidence of combined FAS and ARND was 9.1 of every 1000 live births in a well-studied middle-class population, born in the mid-1970s, to whom the new criteria for ARND were retrospectively applied.[143]

Despite widespread awareness of FAS, clinicians frequently fail to recognize the syndrome and its partial manifestations in the newborn period.[155] The stigmata are more easily diagnosed in the early- to mid-childhood years. The distinctive dysmorphic signs then become less pronounced as the child matures, and it is often difficult to diagnose FAS for the first time in late adolescence and adulthood without earlier photographs and medical and developmental assessments. Various techniques have been used to document facial dysmorphology for clinical and research purposes, including conventionally performed measurements with a hand-held ruler by a highly trained dysmorphologist and newer, reportedly more consistent, stereophotogrammetric methods.[122]

BOX 36-1. Diagnostic Criteria for Fetal Alcohol Syndrome (FAS) and Alcohol-Related Effects

1. FAS with Confirmed Maternal Alcohol Exposure*

A. Confirmed maternal alcohol exposure*

B. Evidence of a characteristic pattern of facial anomalies that includes features such as short palpebral fissures and abnormalities in the premaxillary zone (e.g., flat upper lip, flattened philtrum, and flat midface)

C. Evidence of growth restriction, as in at least one of the following:
- Low birthweight for gestational age
- Decelerating weight over time not due to nutrition
- Disproportional low weight to height

D. Evidence of central nervous system neurodevelopmental abnormalities, as in at least one of the following:
- Decreased cranial size at birth
- Structural brain abnormalities (e.g., microcephaly, partial or complete agenesis of the corpus callosum, cerebellar hypoplasia)
- Neurologic hard or soft signs (as age appropriate), such as impaired fine motor skills, neurosensory hearing loss, poor tandem gait, poor eye-hand coordination

2. FAS without Confirmed Maternal Alcohol Exposure

B, C, *and* D as above

3. Partial FAS with Confirmed Maternal Alcohol Exposure

A. Confirmed maternal alcohol exposure*

B. Evidence of some components of the pattern of characteristic facial anomalies
C *or* D as above *or*

E. Evidence of a complex pattern of behavior or cognitive abnormalities that are inconsistent with developmental level and cannot be explained by familial background or environment alone, such as learning difficulties; deficits in school performance; poor impulse control; problems in social perception; deficits in higher level receptive and expressive language; poor capacity for abstraction or metacognition; specific deficits in mathematical skills; or problems in memory, attention, or judgment

4. Alcohol-Related Birth Defects (ARBD)†

A. Confirmed maternal alcohol exposure,*,‡ and one or more congenital anomalies:

Cardiac
- Atrial septal defect
- Aberrant great vessels
- Ventricular septal defect
- Tetralogy of Fallot

Skeletal
- Hypoplastic nails
- Clinodactyly
- Shortened fifth digits
- Pectus excavatum and carinatum
- Radioulnar synostosis
- Klippel-Feil syndrome
- Flexion contractures
- Hemivertebrae
- Camptodactyly
- Scoliosis

Renal
- Aplastic, dysplastic, hypoplastic kidneys
- Ureteral duplications
- Hydronephrosis
- Horseshoe kidneys

Ocular
- Strabismus
- Retinal vascular anomalies
- Refractive problems

Auditory
- Conductive hearing loss
- Neurosensory hearing loss

Other
- Virtually every malformation has been described in some patient with FAS. The etiologic specificity of most of these anomalies to alcohol teratogenesis remains uncertain.

5. Alcohol-Related Neurodevelopmental Disorder (ARND)†

A. Confirmed maternal alcohol exposure*,‡ and D and/or E above

*A pattern of excessive intake characterized by substantial, regular intake or heavy episodic drinking. Evidence of this pattern may include frequent episodes of intoxication, development of tolerance or withdrawal, social problems related to drinking, legal problems related to drinking, engaging in physically hazardous behavior while drinking, or alcohol-related medical problems such as hepatic disease.

†In patients with both ARBD and ARND, both diagnoses should be rendered.

‡As further research is completed and as, or if, lower quantities or variable patterns of alcohol use are associated with ARBD or ARND, these patterns of alcohol use should be incorporated into the diagnostic criteria.

Adapted from Committee to Study Fetal Alcohol Syndrome (Stratton K, Howe CJ, Battaglia FC [eds]): Fetal Alcohol Syndrome: Diagnosis, Epidemiology, Prevention, and Treatment. Washington, DC, National Academy Press, 1996.

Central Nervous System Effects

Investigations using animal models of fetal alcohol exposure have shown significant abnormalities of midline brain development.[172] Neuropathologic studies in humans have also demonstrated significant brain anomalies associated with FAS, such as micrencephaly, anencephaly, agenesis of the corpus callosum, holoprosencephaly/arhinencephaly, cerebellar dysgenesis, and leptomeningeal glioneuronal heterotopias. Magnetic resonance imaging (MRI) findings of patients with FAS have revealed midline anomalies of the corpus callosum, cavum septi pellucidi, and cavum vergae, as well as micrencephaly, ventriculomegaly, and hypoplasia of the inferior olivary eminences.[161] Morphometric variations in the corpus callosum on MRI scans have been correlated with specific neuropsychological deficits in patients with FAS.[17] In a study of 19 nonretarded individuals with fetal alcohol exposure, only one had MRI evidence of a structural abnormality (thinned corpus callosum), but positron-emission tomography scanning showed group decreases in relative regional cerebral metabolic rates in the thalamus and basal ganglia compared with controls.[31]

Signs of acute alcohol withdrawal have been described in neonates born to mothers who received intravenous ethanol for tocolysis. The neonates, whose breath emitted the odor of alcohol for several hours after birth, exhibited hyperactivity, tremors, and seizures initially, followed by lethargy, and then a return to normal activity and responsivity.[131] Infants born to mothers who chronically ingested alcohol throughout pregnancy up until delivery may also show signs consistent with intoxication and postnatal withdrawal, such as restlessness, excessive mouthing, inconsolable crying, tremors, abnormal reflexes, and hypertonia.[35] The treatment of neonates with acute alcohol withdrawal includes the same monitoring and recommendations described in neonatal abstinence syndrome (see "Opioids," later), except that sedation rather than opioid substitution is the preferred pharmacotherapy, if needed.

Prenatal and Postnatal Growth Effects

Most studies confirm that gestational alcohol exposure is associated with deficits in infant weight, length, and head circumference at birth and during early infancy, even with control for other drugs of abuse. In the Pittsburgh Maternal Health Practices and Child Development (MHPCD) study, Day and Richardson showed a linear association between prenatal alcohol exposure and growth, with effects measured at exposure levels of less than one drink per day, thus reinforcing the potential teratogenicity of alcohol even at low levels.[45] Furthermore, prenatal alcohol exposure continued to be a significant predictor of decreased growth at age 14 years in this predominantly low-income cohort.[45] In contrast, the Seattle Longitudinal Study on Alcohol and Pregnancy showed prenatal alcohol-related deficits in birthweight, length, and head circumference that did not persist beyond infancy in a large, middle-class cohort.[142] Socioeconomic status may thus play a significant role in ameliorating long-term growth deficits in more advantaged populations.

Neurobehavioral and Developmental Effects in Infancy

Amount, timing, and pattern of gestational alcohol exposure appear to be relevant in determining the effects on the infant. Although light to moderate gestational alcohol exposure has generally shown no or few convincing effects on infant neurobehavior assessed by the Brazelton Newborn Behavioral Assessment Scale (BNBAS), a study of infants born to heavier drinkers demonstrated difficulties with habituation and arousal.[157] Another series of studies on infants exposed to alcohol throughout pregnancy, compared with controls whose mothers stopped drinking by the second trimester, had worse BNBAS scores on state control, need for

stimulation, motor tone, tremulousness, and asymmetric reflexes that were initially present and persisted over the first month.[35] Electroencephalographic studies in preterm and term infants exposed in utero to varying quantities of alcohol have suggested that the intermittent ingestion of large quantities of alcohol might be more detrimental to fetal brain development than more continuous ingestion of smaller quantities.[83] Prenatal alcohol exposure during the first trimester has also been associated with increased arousal and indeterminant sleep with decreased quiet and active sleep periods.[144] A meta-analysis of the effects of varying exposure levels (less than one drink per day, 1 to 1.99 drinks per day, and two drinks or more per day) on the Mental Development Index (MDI) of the Bayley Scales of Infant Development showed that fetal alcohol exposure was associated with a significantly lower MDI among 12- to 13-month-olds at all three exposure levels.[163]

Neuropsychological and Behavioral Effects in Childhood and Adolescence

Streissguth and colleagues first traced the natural history of FAS and FAE into adolescence and early adulthood.[156] In their initial, smaller series of 61 patients, the characteristic facial features of FAS became less distinct with maturation and the weight approached normal, but head growth and height still lagged in many of the patients. Mean IQ was 68, with a range of 20 to 105—the more severely affected being the individuals with full-blown FAS. The adolescents and adults with FAS/FAE also demonstrated elementary school level reading, spelling, and arithmetic skills and maladaptive behavior.[156] In the larger Seattle Longitudinal Study, the offspring of mothers who had an average daily ingestion of two or more drinks (1 ounce or more of absolute alcohol) demonstrated a 7-point decrement (nearly one-half a standard deviation) in IQ, after covariate adjustment, by age $7^{1}/_{2}$ years. Furthermore, learning problems were more often noted among these young school-aged children born to mothers who had reported binge drinking during pregnancy.[158]

In a review of neuropsychological findings associated with FAS/ARND, Jacobson and Jacobson highlighted specific deficits in the following: sustained attention (especially on tasks requiring active recall of information or response inhibition), focused attention, cognitive flexibility, planning, learning and memory, and socioemotional function.[84] People exposed prenatally to alcohol show impairments in performing relatively complex and novel tasks that tap executive functioning, defined as the ability to plan and guide behavior to achieve a goal in an efficient manner.[99] In a clinically referred population of adolescents and young adults with FAS/ARND, comorbid attention deficit hyperactivity disorder was found in nearly three quarters of the cases, whereas it was noted in only 36% of referrals without FAS/ARND.[23]

Animal models of prenatal alcohol exposure have demonstrated numerous sociobehavioral deficits, including sexually dimorphic changes in play, delays in induction of maternal behavior, and increased aggression in males.[97] A study showed increased aggressive and externalizing behavior in 6-year-old children exposed prenatally to as little as one alcoholic beverage per week compared with an unexposed control group.[153] As individuals with prenatal alcohol exposure, especially those with FAS, progress into later adolescence and adulthood, deficits in "real life" socioemotional functioning emerge.[97] In prenatally alcohol-exposed adolescents and young adults, impulsivity and irritable temperament, inappropriate sexual behavior, criminal activities, depression, suicidal tendencies, and difficulties in caring for children have been observed to be more frequent than in unexposed individuals. Furthermore, prenatal alcohol exposure appears to be a risk factor for developing drinking problems in young adulthood, even after controlling for other relevant covariates.[8]

Thus, numerous deficits in neuropsychological function have been observed in follow-up studies of children, adolescents, and adults exposed in utero to alcohol. Although the effects appear to represent a spectrum of teratologic impact, the outcomes are a function of the amount, timing, and pattern of toxic exposure and the environment.

Recommendations for Prevention and Intervention

The American Academy of Pediatrics (AAP) recommends abstinence from alcohol for women who are pregnant or who are planning a pregnancy, as there is no known safe amount of alcohol consumption during pregnancy.[4] However, this recommendation is not entirely without controversy, and the clinician is often faced with the unenviable task of providing a perplexing double message, especially when counseling concerned mothers who ingested light to moderate alcohol before they were aware of being pregnant. A meta-analysis of studies of moderate first-trimester alcohol consumption, defined as less than two standard drinks daily, showed no evidence for increased risk for major malformations, and the authors cautioned against women making pregnancy termination decisions based on possible misinformation about the risks of moderate alcohol consumption in the early phase of pregnancy.[136] Armstrong and Abel expressed similar concerns about eliciting a "moral panic" against all alcohol use by pregnant women while failing to envision a "moral imperative to find and help those women most at risk for adverse outcomes."[7] Summarizing a substantial body of work conducted by numerous investigators on the topic of gestational exposure to alcohol, Kalter rendered a provocative critique of the methodologies, analyses, and interpretations of the existent literature from animal models as well as human studies, especially with regard to the reported effects of low to moderate fetal alcohol exposure on offspring.[90] Considerable investigative work is needed to establish the hypothesized continuum of adverse effects of fetal alcohol exposure, at varying exposure levels and developmental stages of the organism, and to elucidate the underlying mechanisms of observed deficits in structure, function, or altered developmental trajectory of the affected offspring. These scientific reservations notwithstanding, the AAP recommendations seem prudent, especially in view of excellently designed clinical studies that show growth disturbances and ARND at relatively low levels of alcohol consumption. It is clear that FAS and its partial manifestations are irreversible lifelong conditions that are entirely preventable if a woman does not drink alcohol when she is pregnant.

Guidelines for screening and management of FAS include universal screening of pregnant women for alcohol use so that appropriate management can be provided.[4] A brief, easily administered, standardized questionnaire such as the TWEAK (Table 36-1) is applicable to nearly all obstetric settings for the identification of pregnant women at risk so that referrals can be made for further drug abuse and psychosocial assessment and treatment.[18] Because self-report may not identify all at-risk cases, further research is needed on biomarkers for detecting fetal alcohol exposure. A novel test capable of detecting fetal fatty acid ethyl esters in the meconium of newborns of heavy alcohol users may be useful for identification of infants in need of early health, developmental, and psychosocial intervention and may be useful in clinical research involving prenatal drug and alcohol exposure.[11]

TABLE 36-1. TWEAK Problem Drinking* Questionnaire

T (Tolerance)	How many drinks does it take before you begin to feel the first effects of alcohol?[†]	≥3 drinks = 2 points
W (Worried)	Have close friends or relatives worried or complained about your drinking in the past year?	Yes = 2 points
E (Eye-opener)	Do you sometimes take a drink in the morning when you first get up?	Yes = 1 point
A (Amnesia)	Has a friend or family member ever told you about things you said or did while you were drinking that you could not remember?	Yes = 1 point
K (Kut down)	Do you sometimes feel the need to cut down on your drinking?	Yes = 1 point

*Score of ≥2 or more indicates problem drinking in women.
†Standard drink is defined as 12 oz. beer, 5 oz. wine, or 1.5 oz. of spirits.
From Bradley KA et al: Alcohol screening questionnaires in women: A critical review. JAMA 280:166, 1998.

Early diagnosis, and multidisciplinary support cannot be overemphasized, given the exacting toll of FASD on the affected children and their families as well as the associated estimated economic impact for the United States ($4.0 billion annually in 1998 and $1.4 million lifetime costs of caring for an individual with FAS in 1988).[114]

The AAP recommends abstinence from alcohol preconceptionally and during pregnancy, screening of all pregnant women for alcohol usage, and referring of pregnant alcohol-abusers for assessment and treatment. Additional guidelines should focus on the following recommendations for prevention of alcohol abuse by adolescents and women of child-bearing age: education at all levels regarding the deleterious effects of alcohol on the developing fetus; provision of appropriate multidisciplinary health, neurodevelopmental, and social services to affected children and their families; fostering of federal and state legislation aimed at providing warnings and information about FAS in public places and in alcohol advertisements; and training of physicians and health professionals in FAS screening and diagnosis in affected infants and their siblings. In response, the National Center for Birth Defects and Developmental Disorders of the Centers for Disease Control and Prevention has funded medical school partners to develop regional training centers for the education and training of physicians and allied health professionals regarding screening of pregnant women for alcohol ingestion and diagnosing fetal alcohol syndrome.

TOBACCO

Prevalence and Pharmacology

Despite a large public health antismoking campaign, tobacco remains the most widely used addictive substance. According to the 2003 National Survey on Drug Use and Health, an estimated 70.8 million Americans, 29.8% of the population, reported past-month tobacco use. Approximately half of the identified individuals were classified as nicotine dependent.[159] Of the thousands of chemical constituents in tobacco, nicotine is the primary psychoactive chemical responsible for its addictive properties. Nicotine is rapidly absorbed through the lungs, permeating the brain within seconds of inhalation; it is absorbed more slowly through oral mucosa and skin. Nicotine binds to nicotinic acetylcholine receptors in the brain, stimulating the release of multiple neurotransmitters including acetylcholine, norepinephrine, gamma-aminobutyric acid (GABA), and glutamate. As with other drugs of abuse, nicotine directly stimulates dopamine release in the mesolimbic dopaminergic pathway, or the reward center, and may indirectly sustain dopamine levels in this region through actions on GABA and glutamate-containing cells.[117] A component of tobacco smoke (other than nicotine) may further increase dopamine availability in the brain by inhibiting monoamine oxidase.[63] Nicotine also acts in the periphery, stimulating release of epinephrine from the adrenal cortex, which initiates a physiologic response consistent with the flight-or-fight reaction, including increased heart rate, blood pressure, and respiration. It also suppresses insulin release, which may produce hyperglycemia and affect appetite.

Tobacco is highly addictive. Regular tobacco use produces tolerance as well as withdrawal symptoms, including irritability, headache, nausea, and craving. Tobacco remains the leading cause of preventable premature death in adults, due to cancer, chronic respiratory diseases, and cardiovascular disease, including stroke, heart attack, and certain aneurysms. Passive exposure to tobacco smoke has also proved to be a health hazard in infants, children, and adults. According to the 2004 Surgeon General's report, tobacco smoking is the cause of 440,000 deaths annually, with health care costs reaching $75 billion.

In 1992, the National Pregnancy and Health Survey performed by the National Institute on Drug Abuse (NIDA) estimated the prevalence of tobacco use during pregnancy to be 20.4%.[165] It has been well established, however, that self-report data underestimate the prevalence of prenatal tobacco exposure, as evidenced by high deception rates when biomarkers are used. Prenatal tobacco use is more prevalent in younger women and in white women compared with those of African-American or Hispanic heritage. Smoking during pregnancy is also strongly associated with lower educational attainment and income. Although pregnancy provides a powerful motivator for some women to quit smoking, data suggest that many continue throughout pregnancy, attesting to tobacco's highly addictive properties. Of smokers who abstain during pregnancy, a large number resume smoking in the months after delivery.

Fetal Effects

Prenatal tobacco use has numerous deleterious effects on the fetus. Maternal appetite suppression and poor overall nutritional status negatively impact fetal growth and development. A powerful vasoconstrictor, nicotine reduces blood flow via uterine and umbilical arteries, diminishing oxygen supply to the fetus and resulting in hypoxic and ischemic events. Compensatory hypertrophy and lesions in the placenta further restrict blood supply and decrease transplacental amino acid transfer. Increased carbon monoxide levels hinder delivery of oxygen to fetal tissue by binding with hemoglobin to form carboxyhemoglobin. Moreover, prenatal tobacco smoking is often associated with additional risk factors, including limited prenatal care, lower income status, and use of other substances of abuse.

In addition to impacting the maternal-fetal system, nicotine affects the fetus directly. Nicotine crosses the placental barrier without difficulty and is found at significantly elevated levels in amniotic fluid and fetal blood compared with maternal plasma levels. Additionally, nicotinic acetylcholine receptors are present very early in gestation and are thought to be important in normal brain development. Stimulation of these receptors during gestation may produce alteration in neuronal ontogenesis, cell differentiation and migration, and modified synaptic functioning. Slotkin reviewed evidence from animal models supporting the direct neurotoxic effect of nicotine on fetal development, independent of its hypoxic and ischemic effects.[149] In these models, prenatal nicotine exposure, even at levels that did not produce fetal growth restriction, resulted in cell damage as well as loss, presumably due to a premature signaling of the switch from cell proliferation to cell differentiation and induced apoptosis. Prenatal nicotine exposure has also been linked to an upregulation of cholinergic receptors and hypoactivity in cholinergic functioning. Because of the cholinergic interface with multiple neurotransmitter systems, diminished dopamine and norepinephrine functioning has also been observed. Additionally, in the periphery, gestational exposure to nicotine may alter the responsivity of the adrenal gland to episodes of hypoxia.

Pregnancy and Delivery Complications

Numerous pregnancy and delivery complications have been associated with maternal smoking, including perinatal death, spontaneous abortion, stillbirth, abruptio placentae, placenta previa, premature delivery, and fetal growth restriction.[33] Interestingly, smoking appears to offer some protection against preeclampsia.[24] The relationship between maternal smoking and decreased fetal growth is well established. Women who smoke during pregnancy have a significantly higher risk of delivering a small-for-gestational-age infant than nonsmokers, and infants born to smokers are significantly lighter than those of nonsmokers. The effect of maternal smoking on fetal growth appears to be dose dependent and separate from the impact on gestational age. Infant length and head circumference are also negatively impacted by prenatal tobacco exposure,[71] although some studies suggest that in utero tobacco exposure impacts weight to a greater degree. Tobacco-related decrements in fetal growth generally do not persist beyond the first few years of life.[71] In fact, there is evidence that prenatal tobacco exposure is related to higher ponderal index and increased skin-fold thickness in childhood.[166] Maternal smoking has also been shown to be a risk factor for obesity in children and adults, and this relationship remains significant even when factors such as birthweight, prematurity, breastfeeding, and diet are considered. The mechanism is unknown, although nicotine-related modifications in impulse control and endocrine function have been hypothesized.

Neonatal Complications

Prenatal tobacco exposure results in considerable infant morbidity and mortality, with increased risk of admission to a neonatal intensive care unit (NICU) because of higher rates of prematurity and intrauterine growth restriction, and once admitted, a longer stay, resulting in substantially higher neonatal costs.[3] Additionally, the risk for infant death (e.g., sudden infant death syndrome

[SIDS]) is higher in infants born to smokers than to nonsmokers.[33] Congenital malformations have not been consistently reported in tobacco-exposed infants, although an increased risk for oral clefts has been noted. Animal and human studies suggest in utero tobacco exposure alters lung development and impairs lung function independent of postnatal tobacco exposure.[72,145] As summarized by Stocks and Dezateux,[154] structural and functional changes are likely to be responsible in part for the greater incidence of respiratory difficulties (such as wheezing, respiratory infection, and poor asthma control) observed in infants and children of mothers who smoke. Anderson and Cook[6] reviewed extensive evidence from several prospective and large case-control studies supporting a dose-dependent relationship between both prenatal and postnatal tobacco smoking and SIDS. Although it is difficult to isolate the effects of prenatal and postnatal exposures, it is likely that prenatal nicotine exposure contributes uniquely to the risk for SIDS. Gestational exposure to nicotine has been shown to modify cardiorespiratory control and diminish response to hypoxic events, alter sleep-wake mechanisms resulting in prolonged periods of deep sleep, and increase the risk for respiratory infections postnatally, which may result in greater susceptibility to SIDS.

Neurobehavioral and Developmental Effects in Infancy

Maternal smoking during pregnancy negatively impacts cognitive and behavioral development.[133] Prenatal tobacco exposure has been related to neurobehavioral abnormalities in the neonatal period including increased tremulousness, diminished auditory responsiveness, and decreased auditory habituation.[67] Law and co-workers found greater autonomic excitability, hypertonicity, and stress/abstinence symptoms, as measured by the NICU Network Neurobehavioral Scale in a group of 1- to 2-day-old infants exposed primarily to tobacco. This study also documented a dose-response relationship between maternal salivary cotinine levels and stress/abstinence scores. The existence of a neonatal nicotine withdrawal syndrome has been suggested, particularly in the case of heavy tobacco exposure.

Delays in early infant development have also been reported in relationship to prenatal tobacco exposure. Prenatal tobacco exposure was found to be associated with lower verbal comprehension on the Bayley Scales of Infant Development at age 13 months after covariate adjustment.[77] In another report, tobacco-exposed infants displayed poorer verbal comprehension and auditory response on the Bayley Scales at 12 months of age. Although the prenatal tobacco effect on auditory responding remained at 24 months, prenatal tobacco-related deficits in verbal development were no longer evident once postnatal influences were considered. In one study with implications for future speech development, 8-month-old infants with moderate to heavy tobacco exposure (i.e., more than 10 cigarettes per day) were found to have double the risk of being a nonbabbler as unexposed infants.[132] Several other studies, however, have not shown tobacco-related deficits in early development.

Neuropsychological and Behavioral Effects in Childhood and Adolescence

Despite considerable literature on the topic, the long-term cognitive outcomes of children exposed prenatally to tobacco remain somewhat equivocal because of variations in study designs, outcome measures, and control of potential confounding influences. Nevertheless, certain patterns in functioning have emerged in relation to prenatal tobacco exposure. Findings from the Ottawa Prenatal Prospective Study (OPPS) suggest persistent tobacco-related deficits in cognitive functioning, primarily verbal abilities and memory, measured from early childhood through early adolescence.[70] The OPPS also found deficits in visual-spatial skills assessed when the children were 9 to 12 years old. Altered auditory responding was also observed in infancy in this cohort and continued into childhood, with the tobacco-exposed children showing poorer central auditory processing at 6 to 11 years of age and lower scores in reading, particularly involving tasks with auditory components. These findings were largely dose related and evident even after control for potential confounding influences. In another cohort, prenatal tobacco was related to poorer verbal learning and design memory at age 10 years.[38] Although some studies have reported a relationship between prenatal tobacco exposure and lower cognitive abilities, others indicate no effect on general or specific cognitive domains, particularly after adjustment for social and environmental factors.[121,133]

In utero tobacco exposure has also been shown to have a deleterious impact on behavioral and psychological outcomes. Day and colleagues reported increased externalizing problems, such as aggression and oppositional behavior, in young children exposed prenatally to tobacco.[46] Exposed children have shown greater hyperactivity and impulsivity on laboratory measures such as the Continuous Performance Task and on teacher ratings.[102,104] Higher rates of attention deficit hyperactivity disorder in relation to maternal smoking during pregnancy have been reported. Prenatal tobacco exposure has been consistently associated with greater conduct problems and substance abuse in adolescence[60] and criminal behavior and substance abuse in adulthood,[19] although the true etiologic role of prenatal tobacco in this association is unclear because of confounding influences. Maternal smoking has been linked with an increased risk for later tobacco involvement in offspring. For example, Cornelius and colleagues[37] found a 5.5-fold increased risk for early tobacco experimentation in a group of 10-year-old children exposed prenatally to tobacco, and in a separate study, Kandel and coworkers[94] reported a fourfold increased risk for persistent smoking in adolescent female offspring. These associations were evident even with statistical control for current smoking by the mother. In another prospective study, an increased risk for tobacco dependence but not marijuana dependence was found in adult offspring of mothers who smoked heavily during pregnancy.[22] Although the association between prenatal tobacco exposure and later smoking behavior may result in part from shared genetic risk, increased behavioral difficulties, and environmental factors (e.g., peer influence), animal models suggest direct biologic mechanisms involving enduring changes in the cholinergic systems and elevated testosterone levels after prenatal nicotine exposure.[2,151]

Environmental Tobacco Smoke

A significant challenge in interpreting data on the effects of prenatal tobacco exposure, particularly the long-term effects, is the issue of environmental tobacco smoke. Although it is well known that the majority of women who smoke during pregnancy continue smoking after birth, many prenatal studies have failed to adequately consider the potential impact of postnatal environmental tobacco smoke exposure on infant and child outcomes. In studies that have addressed postnatal tobacco exposure, interpretation of findings is often limited because of difficulties in measuring environmental exposure (e.g., accurately determining the hours of exposure in and out of the home; size and ventilation of living space; limits of biologic markers in terms of exposure time), accounting for additional confounding influences, and statistically separating the effects of prenatal and postnatal exposures.[55] It is, therefore, unclear in many studies whether the associated effects are attributable to maternal smoking during pregnancy or to passive tobacco exposure postnatally, or an additive effect. Overall, postnatal environmental tobacco smoke exposure is quite common in early childhood. According to the Centers for Disease Control and Prevention, between 11% and 32% of children under age 18 years are exposed to environmental smoke in their homes.[24a] Childhood exposure to environmental tobacco smoke has been strongly associated with respiratory difficulties such as wheezing, infections, and asthma complications, as well as an increased risk for SIDS.[6,154] Because brain development continues throughout childhood and adolescence, it is plausible that postnatal environmental tobacco exposure may also result in lasting neurodevelopmental complications. In one of the few studies separating the effects of postnatal environmental exposure from those of prenatal active and passive tobacco smoking, children who had postnatal environmental tobacco exposure showed poorer performance on verbal and nonverbal cognitive tasks and parent-rated hyperactivity at age 5 years than unexposed children.[56]

Prenatal environmental tobacco smoke exposure is also of concern but has been largely neglected in the literature. Data suggest that as many as 75% of non-smoking pregnant women are exposed to environmental tobacco smoke.[78] Passive exposure to tobacco smoke during pregnancy can produce fetal nicotine concentrations comparable to those achieved with light active smoking by the mother.[135] In animal models, prenatal and early neonatal environmental tobacco exposure resulted in changes in brain development similar to those seen with direct nicotine administration.[75,149] Human studies also show the impact of prenatal environmental tobacco exposure to be similar to that of active maternal smoking but to a lesser degree. A meta-analysis by Windham and colleagues[169] revealed a slightly greater risk for delivering a small-for-gestational-age infant in relation to passive tobacco exposure during pregnancy, with a pooled estimate indicating a 28-g decrement in birthweight (compared with the 150- to 200-g difference frequently observed in infants of active smokers). Additionally, Makin and coworkers[115] compared the long-term consequences of active and passive tobacco exposure during pregnancy in a group of 6- to 9-year-old children. Children who were exposed to passive tobacco smoke in utero performed more poorly on tests of general cognitive functioning, language skills, visual-spatial abilities, and parent ratings of behavior compared with unexposed children, although the deficits were not as great as those seen in children whose mother actively smoked during pregnancy.

Recommendations for Prevention and Intervention

Animal and human research studies indicate that maternal smoking during pregnancy alters fetal development and results in a number of perinatal complications with potential negative cognitive, behavioral, and physical health consequences that may persist into adulthood. Women should be counseled about the harmful effects of smoking during pregnancy and provided appropriate support for stopping as early in pregnancy as possible. Cessation of smoking early in pregnancy may diminish the impact of tobacco on fetal growth occurring mainly in the third trimester[109] and on the structure and function of emerging nicotinic cholinergic receptors important in brain development.[2] Lindley and coworkers reported that early smoking cessation can eliminate or significantly reduce tobacco's effect on birthweight and head circumference but not crown-heel length.[110] Moreover, one study has documented the long-term benefits of smoking cessation, reporting higher scores on tests of cognitive abilities for 3-year-olds whose mothers stopped smoking during pregnancy compared with those whose mothers persisted.[146] Reduction in the number of cigarettes smoked without cessation does not appear to offer major benefits with regard to birth growth parameters unless very low levels of exposure are achieved.[54] Fortunately, effective smoking cessation interventions are available for pregnant women. Brief counseling approaches adapted for use with pregnant women have yielded moderate success[124]; however, innovative and more intensive interventions may be needed to achieve higher success rates, particularly with more resistant women.[52] Although the safety and efficacy of nicotine

replacement therapy in pregnant women has not been proven, it may be a reasonable treatment option in certain circumstance (e.g., in highly addicted women, and when the potential benefits are determined to outweigh the possible negative consequences).[14]

Melvin and Gaffney[123] recently updated the best-practice model for intervening with pregnant smokers (i.e., a five-step counseling approach—ask, advise, assess, assist, and arrange). One notable recommendation is to assess and attempt to reduce exposure to second-hand smoke in smokers and nonsmokers beginning at the first prenatal visit. Interventions for reducing children's exposure to environmental tobacco smoke have overall shown positive outcomes.[98]

MARIJUANA

Prevalence and Pharmacology

Marijuana is the most widely used illegal drug in the United States, with approximately 40% of the population reporting trying it at some point. According to the 2003 National Survey on Drug Use and Health (NSDUH),[159] 14.6 million people in the United States are current marijuana users, with a third reporting frequent use during the past month. Marijuana use is most prevalent in young adults, affecting many women of childbearing age. In the 1992 National Pregnancy and Health Survey, it was estimated that 2.9% of women used marijuana during pregnancy.[165] More recent data from the 2002 and 2003 NSDUH confirm that 3.5% of pregnant women used marijuana during the last month. These self-reported estimates are most likely underestimates. Individual reports of prevalence from specific medical centers and geographic regions vary considerably, ranging from 4% to 27%, and it is clear that use of biomarkers confirms higher rates of use.

Marijuana, dried material from the hemp plant *Cannabis sativa,* is most often smoked in a cigarette or pipe, although it is highly soluble in lipids and can be administered orally with food. When smoked, it passes more rapidly into the bloodstream via the lungs, resulting in a rapid high lasting up to 3 hours. Of the more than 60 known cannabinoids in marijuana, delta-9-tetrahydrocannabinol (THC) is the primary psychoactive agent. THC binds to cannabinoid receptors (CB1) heavily concentrated in the hippocampus, cortex, cerebellum, nucleus accumbens, and basal ganglia regions of the brain, exerting influence primarily by modifying the release of several neurotransmitters. In addition to euphoria and relaxation, users experience an increase in heart rate by as much as 50% within minutes of administration; blood pres-sure may also be increased when in a seated or supine position, although hypotension sometimes occurs on standing. Other acute effects include dizziness, reduced salivation, increased appetite, impaired coordination, poor decision making, delayed responding, altered sense of time, and impaired short-term memory, concentration, and learning.

Effects of Chronic Marijuana Use in Adults

As recently summarized in a special supplement on marijuana use in the *Journal of Clinical Pharmacology*,[32] chronic marijuana use has been associated with respiratory difficulties such as bronchitis and infection, increased risk for lung, head, and neck cancers, and possible weakened immune function. Cognitive deficits, including learning and memory impairment, have been shown to persist days beyond intoxication but may be reversible with continued abstinence. Although the acute cardiovascular effects of marijuana typically dissipate with repeated use and do not cause significant problems for most healthy individuals, the long-term impact on the cardiovascular system is unclear. Depression and anxiety, as well as poor achievement and subjective reports of decreased life satisfaction, have also been associated with frequent or long-term marijuana use. Despite much debate and controversy, converging evidence from animal and human research suggests that withdrawal and dependence can occur with regular marijuana use.

Fetal and Neonatal Effects

THC crosses the placenta easily and is contained in the amniotic fluid. Because of its high lipid solubility and slow rate of elimination from the body, THC from a single administration may remain in the mother's body for weeks, with potential prolonged exposure of the infant. Cannabinoid receptors are found in the fetal brain early in gestation and are concentrated in areas similar to those in adults but at greater levels,[73] suggesting their potential importance in the development of functions such as memory, motor function, and higher-order cognitive abilities. In animal models, administration of THC (or synthetic agonists) during the prenatal and early postnatal periods produced changes in neurotransmitter systems.[61] Modification of neurotransmitters (e.g., serotonin, dopamine, and GABA) may lead to alterations in neuronal growth, maturation, or differentiation, causing structural or functional abnormalities in the fetal brain exposed to marijuana, depending on dose and timing. As the development and organization of the brain continue after birth, persistent exposure to THC through passive smoke inhalation and breast milk may further influence neonatal outcome and long-term functioning. Indirectly, regular marijuana smoking during pregnancy may reduce oxygen availability to the fetus as a result of high blood levels of carbon monoxide and impaired lung function in the mother.

Despite the potential for unfavorable outcomes in infancy and beyond, relatively little attention has been given to the short- and long-term effects of prenatal marijuana exposure on the child in comparison with other illegal drugs. In general, the impact of in utero marijuana exposure appears to be subtle, and adverse outcomes are more often associated with heavy or more frequent use. Perhaps with the exception of a higher incidence of meconium staining, significant pregnancy and delivery complications in relation to marijuana use have not been well documented.[44] In addition, research has not supported an increased risk for major physical anomalies or infant mortality associated with marijuana exposure.[69] Although prenatal marijuana exposure has been linked with shorter gestational age, most studies have not confirmed this relationship. Similarly, certain studies report lower birthweight and birth length of marijuana-exposed infants; others indicate no impact on fetal growth.[68]

Neurobehavioral and Developmental Effects

Marijuana-associated neurobehavioral abnormalities such as tremors, startle, and diminished visual response to light stimulus have been noted during the first weeks of life.[67] Additionally, exposed infants have shown sleep disturbances that persist into early childhood.[144] Prenatal marijuana exposure, on the whole, has not been linked to significant developmental delays during infancy,[69] although one study reported lower mental scores at 9 months with daily exposure during the third trimester.[139]

Reports of long-term outcomes related to prenatal marijuana exposure have emerged primarily from two large ongoing research projects, the OPPS and the MHPCD study. Data have not generally supported marijuana-related decrements in global indicators of cognitive functioning.[70] However, beginning in the pre-school period and continuing through mid-adolescence (the oldest outcomes reported in the literature), exposed children have shown deficits in specific neurocognitive domains. Lower verbal scores were found at age 3 in the MHPCD study[47] and at age 4 years in the OPPS.[69] Additionally, marijuana-associated deficits in aspects of executive functioning, including memory, visual reasoning skills, and planning, have been consistently reported, as recently summarized by Fried and Smith.[69] Moreover, marijuana-exposed children evidence attention and impulse control difficulties on continuous performance tasks and on questionnaires completed by parents and teachers. Parent and teacher reports also reveal greater hyperactivity and conduct problems,[74] and child ratings indicate higher levels of depression in exposed children compared with controls.[76] Although data are not yet published on the drug-taking behavior of children exposed prenatally to marijuana, animal research suggests that in utero marijuana exposure alters the endogenous opiate system, potentially sensitizing the offspring to the reinforcing properties of opiates and increasing vulnerability for later abuse and dependence.[129]

COCAINE

Prevalence

Few perinatal substances of abuse have engendered as much controversy as cocaine and crack cocaine.

Cocaine's propensity for causing severe toxicity, including convulsions, myocardial infarction, and death in adults, is well known. Cocaine ($C_{17}H_{21}NO_4$, benzoyl-methylecgonine), an alkaloid derived from *Erythroxylon coca* shrub leaves, is classified as a stimulant. Cocaine hydrochloride is typically snorted as a powder, but it can also be ingested orally or intravenously. Smoking of crack cocaine, an inexpensive alkaloid free-base form of nearly pure cocaine, became widespread in the 1980s, reaching epidemic proportions in many of the nation's inner cities (and thus seen in their delivery services). It was initially confined to the high-intensity, drug-trafficking areas and later spread to more remote rural areas. The 1992 NIDA National Pregnancy and Health Survey of drug use by pregnant women showed that 1.1% of them (accounting for 45,100 of U.S. births) had used cocaine during pregnancy.[165] The 2003 National Survey on Drug Use and Health showed that 0.3% of pregnant women reported some form of past-month cocaine use in contrast to 1% of nonpregnant women.[159] Regional differences exist, and cocaine use during pregnancy within some hospitals is substantially higher, as shown in investigations using systematic prenatal or postpartum interviews and bioassays.

Pharmacologic Effects

The main effects of cocaine involve the norepinephrine, dopamine, and serotonin neurotransmitter systems. Inhibition of norepinephrine reuptake leads to accumulation on the synaptic cleft and stimulation of post-synaptic norepinephrine receptors, with manifestations of tachycardia, arrhythmias, hypertension, vasoconstriction, diaphoresis, and mild tremors. Blocking of dopamine reuptake results in dopamine accumulation in the synaptic cleft and stimulation of dopamine neurotransmission, thereby causing neurochemical magnification of the pleasure response, increased alertness, enhanced sense of well-being and self-esteem, and heightened energy and sexual excitement. Ultimately, compulsive abusers experience anxiety, depression, and exhaustion, and chronic users may exhibit mood disorders, paranoid psychosis, sexual dysfunction, and addiction. Acute tolerance, rebound depression, crash, and craving are explained by regulatory changes in presynaptic and postsynaptic dopaminergic receptors after chronic cocaine use. Cocaine diminishes the need for sleep by decreasing serotonin biosynthesis as a result of decreased uptake of tryptophan.

Cocaine readily traverses the placenta and is also excreted in breast milk. Metabolism of cocaine is primarily via plasma and hepatic cholinesterases to inactive compounds, ecgonine methyl ester and benzoylecgonine, excreted renally. Demethylation of cocaine yields norcocaine, an active metabolite with a greater capacity than cocaine to inhibit norepinephrine uptake. In pregnant women, fetuses, and infants, plasma cholinesterase activity is diminished, and hence excretion may be prolonged. Individual susceptibility to cocaine's effects may be related to genetic polymorphism for the cholinesterase enzyme, and the term

placenta may also provide a degree of protection for individual fetuses by converting cocaine into less active metabolites, presumably by cholinesterase activity.

Cocaine use during pregnancy alters fetal oxygenation by reducing uterine and placental blood flow and impairing fetal oxygen transfer. Fetal tachycardia and hypertension reflect fetal hypoxemia, or increased fetal levels of cocaine or fetal catecholamines, or a combination. In animal studies, significant increases in maternal and fetal arterial pressure and decreases in uterine blood flow have been reported. In humans, maternal and fetal deaths have been linked to cocaine use, and pregnant cocaine-abusing women are at increased risk for spontaneous abortions, abruptio placentae, and premature rupture of the membranes. Transient neonatal ventricular tachycardia has been associated with maternal cocaine abuse shortly before delivery. Higher arterial blood pressure and diminished cardiac output and stroke volume have also been reported in full-term cocaine-exposed infants as compared with drug-free infants on the first postnatal day. These cardiovascular parameters are presumably affected by cocaine-associated increased norepinephrine levels.

There is no definitive dysmorphology syndrome (such as FAS) associated with prenatal cocaine exposure. In animal studies, a wide variety of congenital anomalies, including exencephaly, anophthalmia, malformed or missing lenses, cryptorchidism, hydronephrosis, grossly distended bladder, cryptorchidism, limb reduction defects, ileal atresia, and cardiovascular anomalies, have been described in response to cocaine exposure. It has been hypothesized that cocaine-induced blockage of norepinephrine uptake is responsible for placental vasoconstriction and fetal hypoxia, which produce the defects. In addition, cocaine has been determined to be teratogenic in a dose-dependent manner during late organogenesis or during the post-organogenic period in the Sprague-Dawley rat. The observed pattern of defects, principally reduction deformities of the limbs and tail and genital tubercle defects, occurred as a result of hemorrhagic necrosis, disruption, and amputation of existing and developing structures.[167] An important concept is that vulnerability to cocaine-induced structural defects may not be limited to the period of organogenesis but instead may be related to aberrations in fetal, placental, and uterine blood flow leading to fetal vascular disruption—that is, a structural defect may result from destruction of a previously formed, normal part. The structural defects described in the animal studies mirror those from human case reports and small series, especially observations from referral services such as neurology, cardiology, and nephrology/urology. However, with the possible exception of genitourinary tract malformations, systematic investigations have failed to show a discernible pattern or an increased prevalence of congenital malformations associated with gestational cocaine exposure,[13] and the vast majority of infants exposed prenatally to cocaine are born without such defects. Cocaine-induced ischemia may play a role in the development of intestinal atresia, infarction, and necrotizing enterocolitis, which has been observed in term and preterm infants prenatally exposed to cocaine.

HIV/AIDS and Sexually Transmitted Diseases

Cocaine-using women are more prone to a variety of sexually transmitted diseases both before and during pregnancy. Intravenous substance abuse by the woman or her sexual partner is a recognized HIV risk factor, but sexual promiscuity and trading of sex for cocaine or crack also increases the risk of heterosexual transmission of HIV infection and other sexually transmitted diseases in cocaine-abusing women of child-bearing age. These infections occurring in pregnancy pose additional risks to the fetus.

Prematurity

Although an increased rate of premature delivery or a shorter gestation has been reported in cocaine-using women, this finding is not consistent across studies. In one investigation, 51% of the cocaine-using women delivered prematurely; however, most of the women had no prenatal care.[29] Although the benefit of prenatal care in preterm delivery prevention in the general obstetric population has been debated, prenatal care seems to have a positive impact on the prematurity rate among substance-abusing pregnant women, especially when the mother remains drug free beyond the first trimester. Results have generally not supported a significant association between cocaine use and prematurity when the majority of the women received prenatal care. In larger samples, observed differences in gestational age between cocaine-exposed and unexposed infants, although perhaps statistically significant, have been modest (i.e., approximately 1 week).

Intrauterine and Postnatal Growth

The most frequently reported adverse consequence of prenatal cocaine exposure is intrauterine growth restriction. Studies in Long-Evans rats have shown that prenatal cocaine exposure results in dose-dependent decreases in birthweight and postnatal growth and alterations in fetal body composition, with lower levels of body fat, protein, and calcium.[30] In humans, restricted intrauterine growth may be in part the result of malnutrition and poor weight gain in the mother because of cocaine's suppression of appetite. Frank and colleagues reported that in utero cocaine exposure was associated with indicators of depressed neonatal fat stores and diminished lean body mass, even after controlling for maternal weight gain.[65] Prenatal cocaine exposure has been associated with decreased birthweight, length, or head circumference in numerous studies, although some studies indicate no cocaine-specific effects after covariate control. Richardson and coworkers found that antenatal cocaine use was negatively associated with growth regardless of prenatal care status.[140]

Cocaine-associated deficits in fetal growth do not appear to be entirely related to gestational age.[40] In a study of term infants, structural equation modeling revealed a direct impact of prenatal cocaine exposure on fetal growth as well as a partial indirect effect through gestational age, after control for potential confounders.[9] Most studies have described involvement of all three growth parameters including birthweight, length, and head circumference (i.e., so-called symmetrical growth restriction), but a more ominous paradoxical diminution of head circumference relative to somatic growth has also been described.[112] Furthermore, higher cocaine levels in maternal hair have been correlated with lower head circumferences, suggesting a dose-response effect.[10] Data on the long-term growth of cocaine-exposed children are sparse. Chasnoff and colleagues found that although exposed children caught up in terms of weight and height by age 6 years, deficits in head circumference persisted into childhood.[27] Another investigation reported that cocaine-exposed children, particularly those born to older mothers, were shorter and more likely to have clinically significant height deficits at age 7 years.[40]

Sudden Infant Death Syndrome

Like tobacco and opioids, cocaine has been hypothesized as a risk factor for SIDS. However, a meta-analysis concluded that an increased risk for SIDS could not be attributed to intrauterine cocaine exposure alone, after controlling for the confounding variable of concurrent use of other drugs.[59]

Central Nervous System Effects

Cocaine-induced alterations in cerebral blood flow have been implicated in central nervous system (CNS) hemorrhagic and ischemic lesions. Concern was raised initially by a case report of a cocaine-exposed term infant with neonatal cerebral infarction, seizures, cortical atrophy, and neurodevelopmental delay, and it was heightened by a larger series of full-term infants exposed to cocaine and/or amphetamines who were reported to have white-matter cavities, acute infarction, intraventricular hemorrhage, subarachnoid hemorrhage, and ventricular enlargement on echoencephalography.[49] A subsequent well-controlled prospective study of predominantly full-term infants, however, failed to substantiate a cocaine-associated increase in CNS structural lesions.[12] In another well-designed study of full-term infants, no group differences were noted between cocaine and comparison groups, but subependymal hemorrhages were found more frequently among infants more heavily exposed to cocaine than among unexposed infants.[66] With regard to premature infants, known to be at increased risk for intraventricular hemorrhage and periventricular leukomalacia, relatively large studies have shown no group differences in the rate of these complications between cocaine-exposed and unexposed infants.[53,170]

Cocaine adversely affects CNS development by binding with monoaminergic receptors in the fetal brain.

Animal studies have demonstrated altered neocortical development, including inappropriate placement of neurons, deficient lamination, and decreased volume, density, and total number of neocortical neurons, after prenatal administration of cocaine, and some of these abnormalities persist beyond the newborn period. Additionally, prenatal cocaine exposure has been shown to produce functional changes in the dopaminergic and serotonergic systems in offspring. Moreover, observed structural and functional alterations have been associated with neurobehavioral abnormalities in animals (e.g., attention, learning) that closely parallel findings in clinical studies.[101,108,118]

Investigations in neonatal rats exposed prenatally to cocaine have shown significant neurobehavioral deficits, including hyperactivity, abnormal sexual behavior (demasculinization) in adulthood, and significantly increased metabolic activity of the limbic, motor, and sensory system of female, but not male, rat brains. Hutchings and Dow-Edwards have provided a detailed review.[82]

In utero exposure to cocaine has been associated with neonatal electroencephalographic abnormalities,[51] clinical seizures that may extend beyond the perinatal period,[103] and aberrations in brainstem auditory evoked potential, noted in both animals and neonates exposed prenatally to cocaine.[147]

Infant and Child Development

Research on infant neurobehavioral functioning, often measured by the BNBAS, has yielded inconsistent findings related to prenatal cocaine exposure. Poorer state regulation, impaired autonomic control, irritability, poorer orientation, decreased habituation, diminished alertness, and abnormal reflexes, tone, and motor maturity have been reported among cocaine-exposed infants, although here has been little consistency across studies in the specific domains affected.[57] Such variation may be in part the result of the small sample sizes and insufficient control for confounders, or it may represent a true heterogeneity of responses among the samples. Meta-analytic results indicate reliable but modest effect sizes for the motor and abnormal reflex clusters of the BNBAS.[80] In a large cohort of full-term infants, prenatal cocaine exposure was modestly related to all BNBAS domains except abnormal reflexes, even with statistical control for other drug exposures and key infant and maternal characteristics.[126] Several controlled studies with large sample sizes detected no cocaine-associated deficits on the BNBAS at birth,[34,130,164] but two of these studies reported abnormalities in areas such as state regulation, autonomic regulation, and reflexes at 2 to 4 weeks postpartum.[34,164] Interestingly, a similar pattern was observed in a recent study with monkeys prenatally exposed to cocaine, using a version of the BNBAS adapted for nonhuman primates.[79] In another report from a large, multisite study of infants, prenatal cocaine exposure was related to lower arousal, lower regulation, and high excitability on the NICU Network Neurobehavioral Scale at 1 month of age after adjustment

for pertinent covariates.[107] Studies using other neurobehavioral measures have reported increased irritability and impaired motor functions, jitteriness, abnormal cry characteristics,[39] poorer auditory processing and habituation, and decrements in neurobehavioral indicators of CNS immaturity in cocaine-exposed newborns. A dose-response effect has been documented, with poorer neurobehavioral functioning found in infants exposed to higher or more frequent doses of cocaine prenatally.[48,58,164] Although these early neurobehavioral deficits do not appear to be related to cocaine intoxication or withdrawal symptoms, it is not yet known to what degree such abnormalities will persist beyond infancy.

Studies evaluating the effect of prenatal cocaine exposure on early development have also produced mixed results. Prenatal cocaine exposure has been associated with lower scores on the Bayley Mental Scales of Development during the infant and toddler years in some studies. Compared to unexposed children, children with gestational cocaine exposure have been more likely to score in the delayed range of functioning on the Bayley and to show a more significant decline from 6 to 24 months of age.[28,148] Jacobson and colleagues found no group differences on the Bayley at 1 year of age, but they observed poorer performance on more subtle neurobehavioral tests of visual expectancy, recognition memory, and information processing in infants exposed to heavier dosages of cocaine.[85] Similarly, studies using more specific measures of motor functioning have found cocaine-exposed infants to be at greater risk for motor dysfunction than unexposed controls. Several reports have highlighted the importance of the postnatal caregiving environment in influencing developmental outcome in cocaine-exposed children.

There are relatively few published studies with cohorts in the preschool and early-school-age years. Studies evaluating group differences between children exposed to cocaine and other drugs, children exposed to other drugs but not cocaine, and unexposed children have in general found no significant group differences in global intellectual functioning in the 3- to 6-year age range, although small sample sizes and high attrition may have influenced results. Deficits in more specialized domains, however, such as language and visual-motor and visual-spatial skills, have been reported.

Animal studies have most often associated the effects of cocaine exposure with structural and functional alterations in the monoamine system, involving norepinephrine and serotonin pathways throughout the brain and more targeted dopaminergic circuits.[118] Depletion of dopamine has been linked to long-term cocaine exposure in studies of laboratory animals and adult humans. During gestation, cocaine's effect on developing dopaminergic systems may lead to impaired neuronal differentiation in the area of the frontal lobes, systems known to play important roles in regulating attention and arousal.[119] An extensive review of the animal literature notes a consistent pattern of cocaine exposure's direct effects on dopaminergic pathways central to arousal regulation and attentional reactivity in prenatal and preweaning rats.[118] Emerging clinical data indicate that preschool- and school-aged cocaine-exposed children, when compared with nonexposed controls, exhibit impaired attentional processing as measured by omission errors on computerized continuous performance tasks, and that they evidence greater restlessness, distractibility, and noncompliance as rated by observers in a clinic setting.

As cocaine-exposed children enter late childhood and early adolescence, of particular interest is whether in utero cocaine exposure influences the child's own drug involvement. Increased self-administration of cocaine as well as alcohol has been demonstrated in adult rats after in utero cocaine exposure.[95,96]

Caveats Regarding Interpretation of Clinical Studies of Cocaine Exposure

Data regarding the adverse effects of perinatal cocaine exposure should be assessed in light of the observation by Koren and colleagues that the scientific community may be biased against the null hypothesis.[100] Early fears of devastating effects of cocaine in vast numbers of affected infants have not been substantiated by systematic prospective studies or meta-analyses. However, the reports in individual cases that show the potential for cocaine to be associated with severe anomalies or vascular disruptions should not be disregarded, as they may be indicating low-incidence lesions associated with cocaine that are expressed in certain hosts, depending on individual susceptibility factors, related to dosage or pattern of exposure, metabolism, genetics, maternal nutrition, and maternal health conditions.

Furthermore, cocaine exposure in infants is not limited to the in utero environment. Cocaine exposure via breast milk has been reported to cause intoxication in the newborn. Postnatal ingestion and passive inhalation of cocaine have also been reported to cause toxicity in young infants and toddlers and, of course, passive exposure could conceivably affect older children and adults in high-risk environments.

A systematic review concluded, on the basis of earlier studies of growth and of standardized cognitive, language, motor, and behavioral assessments through age 6 years, that "there is no convincing evidence that prenatal cocaine exposure is associated with developmental toxic effects that are different in severity, scope, or kind from the sequelae of multiple other risk factors. Many findings once thought to be specific effects of in utero cocaine exposure are correlated with other factors, including prenatal tobacco, marijuana, or alcohol, and the quality of the children's environment."[64] This conclusion served a useful purpose in discouraging the disparaging labeling of cocaine-exposed infants and young children, but larger prospective studies have begun to publish early childhood results that show converging evidence for significant, albeit relatively subtle, cocaine-associated deficits in a number of domains of neurobehavioral and neuropsychological functioning, such as growth, sustained attention, language functioning, and behavior. In many of the studies, the observed deficits appear to be statistically robust indicators of cocaine exposure, as they persist even after controlling for numerous environmental confounding variables. Furthermore, in some studies, the effects have been shown to be dose dependent, which lends credence to a teratologic effect. As pointed out by Lester and coworkers, even subtle cocaine-associated deficits may be costly in terms of increased numbers of children qualifying for special services in the school system.[106]

In summary, a great deal more evidence must be assimilated on the effects of prenatal cocaine exposure over the continuum from birth to young adulthood before drawing definitive conclusions about the teratogenicity of gestational cocaine exposure. Significant deficits in executive function may not become apparent until the child reaches late adolescence or young adulthood, as complex frontal lobe neurons complete their developmental trajectory of maturation into adulthood. Thus, "sleeper effects" of prenatal cocaine exposure may emerge later to affect real-life functionality as these children face increasing demands related to academics, social situations, and acceptance of responsibility for the well-being of themselves and others. More attention needs to be paid to gender modification of cocaine effects by addressing the potential for sex-related effects on specific outcomes, even when there are no apparent group differences in the overall sample. In reality, cocaine is seldom used as a single agent, and it has become increasingly evident that analyses should include assessment of the effects of drug-drug interactions on the outcomes of interest. Consideration of the myriad caregiving environment factors that may influence these results is also challenging but important in understanding the risk and resiliency factors and cumulative risks that predict individual and group outcomes. Such factors have been considered in the development of multidisciplinary preventions and interventions for prenatally substance-exposed infants, for their substance-abusing mothers and fathers, and for their siblings, as described by Kaltenbach and Finnegan[89] (Fig. 36-2).

AMPHETAMINES

In the western part of the hemisphere, abuse of amphetamines and methamphetamines is especially predominant, and the obstetric and neonatal complications are similar to those observed with cocaine. Amphetamine (methylphenylethylamine) is a stimulant of norepinephrine, dopamine, and serotonin release, and the clinical effects have a longer duration of action than those of cocaine. Methamphetamine (also known as meth, speed, ice, and crystal), is the N-methyl homologue of amphetamine. With better blood-brain barrier penetration than amphetamine, methamphetamine has significantly higher CNS stimulation and less peripheral nervous system and cardiovascular stimulation. Gestational methamphetamine exposure has been reported to increase the incidence of miscarriage, prematurity, intrauterine growth restriction, and placental hemorrhage. Infant feeding and sleep patterns are disturbed,

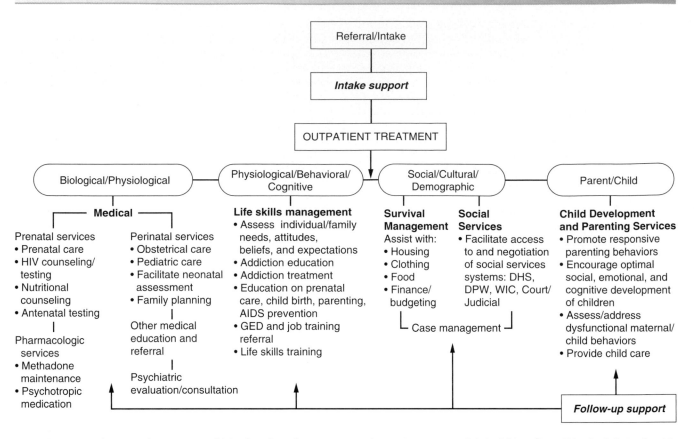

FIGURE 36-2. Family centered treatment model for drug-dependent pregnant and parenting women and their children. (From Kaltenbach K, Comfort ML: Comprehensive treatment for pregnant substance-abusing women: An enhanced model to address multiple health and human service needs. Final Report, Center for Substance Abuse Treatment, Department of Health and Human Services, Washington, DC, 1996.)

and hypertonia and tremors have been observed. Little and colleagues, in a retrospective medical record review, showed that infants exposed prenatally to methamphetamine had significantly lower birthweight, length, and head circumference than unexposed control infants.[113] No difference in congenital anomalies was noted.

MDMA (3,4-methylenedioxymethamphetamine), or "ecstasy," has become increasingly popular as a recreational drug since the late 1980s. MDMA is an indirect monoaminergic agonist that stimulates the release and inhibits the reuptake of serotonin and other neurotransmitters, thus evoking elation and pleasure, accompanied by undesirable effects of hyperactivity and hyperthermia. Subsequent monoaminergic depletion leads to depression and lethargy. Cardiac arrhythmia, acute renal failure, rhabdomyolysis, disseminated intravascular coagulation, and death have been reported in young people using MDMA and engaging in "rave" dancing at crowded clubs. Corroborated by animal studies, chronic MDMA use by adult humans has been shown to cause long-term neuropsychopharmacologic damage in terms of learning and memory, cognitive function, sleep, appetite, and loss of sexual pleasure; these effects persist even during abstinence, suggesting permanent axonal loss.

Preclinical studies in neonatal rats (postnatal days 11 to 20, correlating with the late third trimester in human brain development) show that MDMA exposure causes dose-related deficits in sequential and spatial learning and memory, but these effects are not seen with MDMA exposure at postnatal days 1 to 10 (correlating with first-trimester human brain development). This suggests that the timing of exposure plays a critical role in expression of effects.[20]

A recent study reported the characteristics of pregnant women in Toronto, Canada, who contacted the Hospital for Sick Children's Motherisk Alcohol and Substance Use Hotline and reported ecstasy use during pregnancy.[81] Compared with nonusers, MDMA users were younger and more likely to be white and single. MDMA users were also more likely to smoke cigarettes, drink alcohol, engage in binge drinking, and use other illicit drugs, to have coexisting psychiatric or emotional problems, and to have unplanned pregnancies. Thus, the typical pregnant MDMA user appears to have multiple pregnancy risk factors.[81] The United Kingdom's National Teratology Information Service collected follow-up data on 136 ecstasy-exposed pregnancies and found a significantly increased risk for congenital defects, predominantly cardiovascular and musculoskeletal anomalies, in the offspring.[120] The authors acknowledge that although the findings are clearly of interest, the study sample was quite small and had limited power to draw definitive conclusions regarding causality of the observed defects. Published reports of other neonatal and infant outcomes of gestational ecstasy exposure are not yet available, although follow-up studies have been implemented. Many of the caveats cited earlier with regard to the interpretation of findings related to prenatal cocaine exposure are applicable to the study of these stimulants.

OPIOIDS

Considerable attention has been paid in the obstetric and neonatal literature to the repercussions on the fetus from heroin use and methadone replacement. Marijuana and cocaine are the most frequently abused illicit drugs in pregnancy, and these drugs are often also used by the opioid-addicted mother. Although opioid abuse in pregnancy is less common, the impact of this class of drugs on the mother and her developing fetus can be profound and life threatening. Opioids (the term represents the family of opiates and opioids) freely cross the placenta to reach the fetus. Morphine is a naturally occurring opiate found in opium poppy. Heroin, diacetylmorphine, is a semisynthetic opioid that has morphine-like properties but is more lipophilic and crosses into the CNS more rapidly. Methadone (Dolophine), a synthetic opioid with a longer half-life than heroin, is used as an opioid substitute for treatment of heroin addiction. In addition to being highly addictive, heroin injected intravenously intensifies the risks to the mother and her fetus through potential overdose, acute bacterial endocarditis, and serious viral infections, such as hepatitis B and C, and HIV/AIDS. Heroin is also trafficked in forms that can be snorted or smoked, making the drug even more attractive to a new generation of addicts who may be wary of intravenous use, but the lifestyle and environment of many heroin addicts nonetheless facilitate contraction of sexually transmitted diseases. Prenatal risks also include extrauterine pregnancies due to salpingo-oophoritis, premature labor, premature rupture of membranes, uterine irritability, breech presentation, antepartum hemorrhage, toxemia, anemia, bacterial infections, stillbirth, and low-birthweight infants. Infants exposed prenatally to opioids have less than the expected incidence of hyaline membrane disease, presumably because of stress-induced accelerated lung maturation with an accelerated production of surfactant; this has been confirmed in animal models.[162] They also have less severe hyperbilirubinemia, which may result from induction of the glucuronyltransferase enzyme system by heroin. Thrombocytosis and increased circulating platelet aggregates have been noted in opioid-exposed neonates. Abnormal thyroid function, manifested by increased triiodothyronine and thyroxine levels, has been described in neonates of methadone-treated mothers. Mothers partaking in heroin use are subject to rapid fluctuations in opioid concentration and thus the fetus also experiences intense surges and intermittent withdrawal effects.

Neonatal Abstinence Syndrome

In humans, methadone has the advantage of a longer-lasting effect, thus lessening maternal and fetal harm compared with heroin, but methadone itself is associated with neonatal withdrawal signs, particularly at higher dosage levels. After more than 30 years of experience with methadone maintenance, methadone was endorsed by a National Institutes of Health Consensus Panel[128] as the standard of care for pregnant opioid-dependent women. Previously, the Center for Substance Abuse Treatment Consensus Panel had concluded that the "most effective dose" of maternal methadone maintenance is one that is "individually determined" and "adequate to prevent withdrawal" in the mother.[26] However, the need to determine the efficacy and safety of low versus high methadone dosing during pregnancy has provoked much controversy. Some investigators advocate maintaining pregnant women on low methadone doses to reduce or eliminate neonatal abstinence syndrome (NAS), but others have emphasized that low-dose strategies may increase maternal and fetal risk because they are related to increased maternal withdrawal signs, emergence of drug craving, and failure to curtail illicit drug use. Brown and coworkers found no differences in growth parameters at birth or withdrawal symptoms in neonates born to mothers taking less than 50 mg of methadone daily compared with neonates of mothers taking 50 mg or more daily.[21] Berghella and colleagues performed a retrospective review of 21 published studies on maternal methadone dosage (less than 80 mg versus 80 mg or more daily) and neonatal withdrawal and concluded that "the maternal methadone dose does not correlate with neonatal withdrawal; therefore maternal benefits of effective methadone dosing are not offset by neonatal harm."[15] In uncontrolled circumstances, abrupt maternal withdrawal can threaten the fetus, who also experiences withdrawal, potentially suffering hyperactivity, hypoxia, meconium passage, and in utero demise.[138] However, Dashe and coworkers found that there is a significant relationship between maternal methadone (less than 20 mg per day, 20 to 39 mg per day, and at least 40 mg per day) and neonatal abstinence scores, need for treatment of withdrawal in the infants, and duration of hospitalization.[43] Thus, these authors advocate lower dosage regimens as well as carefully monitored, gradual detoxification of pregnant opiate addicts using clonidine and relatively low dose methadone.[42] Regardless of the strategy employed, methadone maintenance during pregnancy should be monitored closely by an obstetrician experienced in such therapy in collaboration with an addiction specialist and a supportive nursing and social service team.

In utero exposure to opioids and other drugs may lead to fetal dependence and fetal and neonatal withdrawal. *Neonatal abstinence syndrome* is a term generally applied to neonatal withdrawal from heroin or methadone, but similar signs are also seen in withdrawal from other substances, such as other narcotics, alcohol, benzodiazepines, and barbiturates. Depending on the pattern of use and the timing of last use, the onset of neonatal withdrawal from narcotics generally begins in the first 2 to 3 days after birth, but it may occur at as late as 4 weeks. The clinical signs associated with NAS encompass effects in the CNS, gastrointestinal system, metabolic system, and autonomic system. Signs of abstinence occur in 60% to 80% of infants exposed to heroin or methadone. The most dramatically affected infants are extremely difficult to console; they cry incessantly in a high pitch, spend an inordinate amount of time awake, and exhibit a hyperactive Moro, hypertonicity, tremors, myoclonic jerks, hyperpyrexia, respiratory distress, vomiting, and watery stools. In the most extreme cases, approximately 2% to 11%, seizures are observed. The seizures are easily controlled with anticonvulsant therapy, but other potential etiologies, such as infections, metabolic abnormalities, CNS hemorrhage, or ischemia should be considered as well. The 1-year follow-up of infants who experience neonatal seizures due to narcotic abstinence appears to be comparable to that of opioid-exposed infants without seizures.[50]

Because many infants with mild NAS require only supportive care, the clinician's decision to treat with pharmacotherapy should be based on surveillance with serial scoring of withdrawal signs. Two scoring tools are in widespread use in clinical settings as well as research studies—the Lipsitz scale[111] and the Finnegan scale.[62] The Lipsitz scale, which includes a 0 to 3 rating of each of 11 signs; a score greater than 4 has been shown to have a 77% sensitivity for detecting significant withdrawal. The more comprehensive Finnegan scale, which was first utilized at Thomas Jefferson Hospital at the University of Pennsylvania, requires a trained observer. The most recent modification of the scale currently used in that institution is the Neonatal Abstinence Score (Fig. 36-3), which also serves to highlight the nature of the withdrawal signs. Infants should be initially scored at first appearance of NAS symptoms and then every 3 to 4 hours, based on feeding times. Pharmacotherapy is recommended when scores average 8 or higher over three scoring intervals, or 12 or higher over two scoring intervals. The goal of treatment is decreased irritability, feeding tolerance without vomiting or diarrhea, and sleeping between feedings without undue sedation. Before embarking on pharmacotherapy, however, the differential diagnosis of withdrawal in a newborn prenatally exposed to an opioid should include such conditions as hypoglycemia, hypocalcemia, hypomagnesemia, sepsis, and meningitis.

Currently available scoring systems were not designed specifically for premature infants, who have been reported to be at lower risk for neonatal abstinence syndrome, perhaps because of CNS immaturity. Pharmacotherapy for withdrawal in a sick preterm infant born to an opiate-addicted mother should be considered, however, when the infant has suggestive signs and fails to improve or thrive with conventional therapies.

Supportive care for NAS, provided alone or together with pharmacotherapy, consists of providing a quiet, dimly lit environment free from noxious stimuli, and placing the infant in a comfortable, side-lying position.[91] The latter recommendation reflects the AAP "Back to Sleep" recommendation with side-lying modification to facilitate loose but effective swaddling, which seems to have a calming effect by decreasing sensory stimulation. Neonates exposed to opiates in utero have been reported to have a higher rate of sudden infant death,[93] although this has not been uniformly supported by all investigations. Anoxia in utero may be one plausible mechanism for the observation of SIDS in opioid-exposed infants.[127]

The most frequently prescribed, and most receptor-specific, pharmacotherapy for NAS associated with opioid withdrawal is substitution therapy with morphine in the form of diluted tincture of opium (DTO), a carefully prepared and labeled 25-fold dilution of the 10 mg/mL solution to render 0.4 mg/mL of morphine equivalent, or paregoric (camphorated tincture of opium containing 0.4 mg/mL morphine equivalent). The AAP recommended dosing schedule for both of these drugs is a starting dose of 0.1 mL/kg (2 drops/kg) with feedings every 4 hours, with incremental dosage increases of 2 drops/kg every 3 to 4 hours as needed for control of withdrawal signs. After stabilization for 3 to 5 days, the dosage may be tapered gradually without altering dosing interval. Whereas paregoric was once recommended as the drug of choice for NAS,[25] the current AAP recommendation is to treat initially with the diluted tincture of opium rather than paregoric because of the latter's potentially deleterious additives such as camphor, ethanol, benzoic acid, glycerin, and isoquinolones.[5] Phenobarbital, although it has received much investigative attention in studies of infants with NAS, is not the first drug of choice for neonatal opioid withdrawal, but it is recommended for anticonvulsant therapy and for NAS induced by sedatives or hypnotics. Phenobarbital may also be administered as a second-line drug for NAS when DTO fails to alleviate withdrawal signs in a newborn born to an opiate-addicted mother. Pertinent to this discussion is a prospective, masked, placebo-controlled, trial of 20 term infants (10 per group) with NAS (Finnegan score of 8 or higher) comparing DTO alone with DTO plus phenobarbital. This study showed that the combination therapy, compared with DTO alone, resulted in less severe withdrawal, shorter mean duration of hospital stay, and reduced hospital cost. However, as the authors suggested, a larger clinical trial with long-term follow-up should be performed before combined DTO plus phenobarbital is considered optimal pharmacotherapy for NAS.[41]

Other drugs, such as parenteral morphine, methadone, clonidine, chlorpromazine, and diazepam, are not recommended at this time because of insufficient data to support their efficacy or concern regarding potential adverse effects. Naloxone is considered contraindicated in opioid-exposed neonates as it may induce acute abstinence or seizures. Methadone is excreted in small quantities in breast milk and thus, in the absence of

NEONATAL ABSTINENCE SCORE

Date: _____   Weight: _____

System	Signs & Symptoms	Score	Time (AM ... PM)	Comments
Central Nervous System Disturbances	Excessive High Pitched Cry	2		
	Continuous High Pitched Cry	3		
	Sleeps < 1 Hour After Feeding	3		
	Sleeps < 2 Hours After Feeding	2		
	Sleeps < 3 Hours After Feeding	1		
	Hyperactive Moro Reflex	2		
	Markedly Hyperactive Moro Reflex	3		
	Mild Tremors Disturbed	1		
	Moderate - Severe Tremors Disturbed	2		
	Mild Tremors Undisturbed	3		
	Moderate - Severe Tremors Undisturbed	4		
	Increased Muscle Tone	2		
	Excoriation (Specific Area)	1		
	Myoclonic Jerks	3		
	Generalized Convulsions	5		
Metabolic / Vasomotor / Respiratory Disturbances	Sweating	1		
	Fever < 101° F (37.2° - 38.2° C)	1		
	Fever ≥ 101.1° F (≥38.4° C)	2		
	Frequent Yawning (> 3 - 4 Times/Interval)	1		
	Mottling	1		
	Nasal Stuffiness	1		
	Sneezing (> 3 - 4 Times/Interval)	1		
	Nasal Flaring	2		
	Respiratory Rate - 60/min	1		
	Respiratory Rate - 60/min with Retractions	2		
Gastrointestinal Disturbances	Excessive Sucking	1		
	Poor Feeding	2		
	Regurgitation	2		
	Projectile Vomiting	3		
	Loose Stools	2		
	Watery Stools	3		
	TOTAL SCORE			
	Initials of Scorer			

FIGURE 36-3. Neonatal abstinence score used for the assessment of infants undergoing neonatal abstinence. Evaluator should check sign or symptom observed at various time intervals. Add scores for total at each evaluation. (Adapted from Finnegan LP, Kaltenbach K: The assessment and management of neonatal abstinence syndrome. In Hoekelman RA, Nelson NM [eds]: Primary Pediatric Care, 3rd ed. St. Louis, Mosby, 1992, p 1367.)

other contraindications (e.g., HIV, use of other illicit drugs) and in clinically monitored cases, breast feeding by the methadone-maintained mother may be cautiously permitted to enhance maternal-infant bonding.

While not categorized as abuse substances, there is evidence for increasingly widespread maternal use of *selective serotonin reuptake inhibitors* [SSRIs] during pregnancy.[171] These drugs are being commonly prescribed for treatment of depression and have become the treatment of choice. Although this group of SSRIs varies in such aspects as potency, pharmacokinetic effects, molecular structure, and half-life, the SSRIs act similarly by inhibiting serotonin reuptake at the presynaptic junction, leading to increased concentrations at the synaptic cleft and potentiating serotonergic neurotransmission. Thus, the fetus is exposed to increased serotonin levels during development. There is

no current evidence for major birth defects as a result of embryonic or fetal exposure. However, there is an emerging literature that prenatal SSRI exposure and possibly withdrawal may be associated with neurobehavioral effects that may include changes in behavioral state and altered autonomic reactivity. Whether this actually constitutes a neonatal abstinence syndrome remains unclear.

Fetal Growth Effects

There is general consensus that neonates born to heroin-addicted mothers have lower mean birthweight, length, and head circumference than unexposed neonates. This detrimental effect on fetal growth has also been shown in experimental animal models of prenatal heroin exposure. Women in methadone maintenance also have lower-birthweight babies than matched controls, but their babies have significantly higher birthweights than babies whose mothers use heroin and were not maintained on methadone.[92] Methadone treatment and improved obstetric attention appear to improve fetal growth, resulting in higher birthweights compared with heroin-exposed infants.

From the animal as well as human literature, however, there is no reproducible evidence that in utero opiate exposure causes congenital malformations. The most significant postnatal manifestation of in utero opiate exposure occurs when the fetus is subjected to an extrauterine environment devoid of the exogenous supply of opiates on which the fetal bodily systems have become dependent.

Central Nervous System Effects

As reviewed by Malanga and Kosofsky, gestational exposure to opioids decreases nucleic acid synthesis and protein production in fetal brain and impairs growth of neurons.[116] Rat pups exposed to morphine in utero have changes in the packing density and morphology of neurons and neuronal processes that are significantly smaller than seen with controls. Prenatal opioid exposure has been shown to decrease exploratory behavior and to increase response latency to noxious stimuli in young animals. Furthermore, gestational exposure to morphine also increases self-administration of both heroin and cocaine in adult animals. In preclinical studies in mice, Slotkin and colleagues observed that prenatal heroin exposure evokes neurochemical and behavioral deficits associated with specific interference with hippocampal cholinergic function.[150] In addition, heroin alters elements of cell signaling cascades shared by cholinergic inputs and other neurotransmitter systems. Furthermore, significant deficits in norepinephrine and dopamine turnover that were not seen in the immediate postnatal period emerged later in young adulthood, when hippocampus and cerebral cortex showed almost complete inactivation of noradrenergic and dopaminergic tonic activity. Because methadone, in contrast to heroin, does not produce enduring alterations in norepinephrine or dopamine turnover, the authors speculate that this may have favorable implications for infants born to mothers taking methadone as an opioid substitution for heroin.

Neurodevelopmental Effects

Clinical studies of infant neurodevelopmental outcome following prenatal heroin and methadone exposure are difficult to interpret because of the exposure to both agents and the difficulty with ascertaining adequate control groups and covariate control of other factors that may contribute to outcome, such as genetic factors, exposure to other teratogens, pregnancy and parturition complications, low socioeconomic status, and issues affecting the family and caregiving environment (e.g., drug and alcohol abuse by the mother or other adult household members, domestic violence, maternal HIV/

AIDS). Mothers who enter methadone maintenance programs do so because they are addicted to heroin and affected by its multiple accompanying risk factors. Furthermore, many mothers continue to supplement methadone with street heroin as well as alcohol, cigarettes, cocaine, and other drugs. Also complicating the picture is the diversity among practitioners regarding methadone dosing practices. Because heroin abuse in pregnancy is a rather low-incidence disease, the available single-site studies of heroin addiction and methadone treatment in pregnancy have tended to be relatively small, limiting statistical power and generalizability.

Nevertheless, follow-up reports shed light on the potential impact of opioid exposure on human infants and children. In a detailed review of infant and toddler outcomes, several controlled studies have shown various neurobehavioral deficits in infants exposed to methadone in utero, compared with various control groups, using the BNBAS and neurologic assessments.[57] Findings included depressed interactive behaviors; decreased visual and auditory orientation and motor maturity; significantly lower MDI at 6 and 12 months (all means in the normal range and decreasing over the first 2 years); more jerkiness, tremulousness, hypertonicity, increased arousal, and irritability, and poorer quality of cuddling; and significant mean duration of crying. In a study of videotaped feeding and play interactions, poorer interaction ratings were observed in the methadone-exposed mothers and infants.[86] In unstructured free play at 18 months, methadone-exposed children were noted to have less age-appropriate play—specifically, less time was spent in symbolic pretend play.[125]

Follow-up studies of methadone-exposed infants using the Bayley Scales of Infant Development and neurologic examinations have shown motor tone difficulties and transiently lower mean MDI and Psychomotor Development Index (PDI) scores. In one of several studies in a sample of pregnant substance abusers receiving treatment, Kaltenbach and Finnegan reported no differences between a group of methadone-exposed infants and controls on MDI at age 6 months, and the means were within normal limits for each group.[88] Rosen and Johnson described increased tone discrepancies, developmental delays and poor fine motor coordination, and lower MDI and PDI scores at 12 and 18 months in methadone-exposed infants compared with controls, but both MDI and PDI scores were in the normal range in both groups.[141] Prenatal opioid exposure was also reported to affect the special sensory organs, leading to an observed increase in otitis media, strabismus, and nystagmus.[141] Wilson and coworkers reported that infants of untreated heroin addicts had more hypertonicity than those delivered to methadone-treated heroin addicts, but the infants had similar PDI scores and both groups had means in the normal range.[168]

According to Bernstein and Hans, cumulative risk factors predict poorer outcome better than the prenatal exposure to methadone alone.[16] In an investigation comparing children who were born to heroin-dependent mothers and adopted at a very young age, with those born to heroin-dependent mothers (or fathers) but raised at home, the effect of home environment was determined to be more important than in utero exposure.[134]

Buprenorphine

Opioid addiction is an international problem, and clinicians and researchers across the globe are attempting to discover the most effective methods of prevention and treatment for this chronic, relapsing disorder. Investigations of alternative pharmacotherapeutic agents for opioid substitution are ongoing in an effort to improve treatment efficacy and diminish known side effects associated with methadone maintenance. For example, buprenorphine has received considerable attention as an opioid substitute in France since its introduction in 1996 and has become increasingly available and prescribed elsewhere in Europe and in the United States. An opioid with mixed agonist and antagonist properties, buprenorphine has a high receptor affinity and a low intrinsic activity compared with other opioids. It has fewer or no autonomic signs and symptoms of opioid withdrawal following abrupt withdrawal in adults. Similarly, it has been hypothesized that the effects of buprenorphine opioid substitution in pregnancy would be less deleterious to the mother and her fetus. Johnson and colleagues reviewed 21 published studies and found that among infants who were exposed in utero to buprenorphine (15 cohorts, 309 exposed), NAS was present in 62%, of whom 48% required treatment.[87] The authors noted that NAS associated with buprenorphine starts within 12 to 48 hours, reaches a peak at 72 to 96 hours, and lasts 120 to 168 hours, and it appears to be "similar to or less than" that seen in previous reports of in utero methadone exposure. The National Institute on Drug Abuse is initiating a multicenter controlled trial of buprenorphine versus methadone maintenance for pregnant women, to carefully examine the effects on the mothers and their offspring.

Prescription Pain Killers

Recently, a surge in drug trafficking and illicit use of prescription pain killers, specifically synthetic opioids such as oxycodone, hydrocodone, and codeine, has received attention nationally in the lay and scientific media, especially in the Appalachian and rural New England regions. As with other opioids, use of these drugs during pregnancy appears to impose risks to the mother, including maternal drug dependence, overdose, and death, as well as withdrawal symptoms in the neonate that may be severe enough to require pharmacologic intervention.[137]

REFERENCES

1. Abel EL: An update on incidence of FAS: FAS is not an equal-opportunity birth defect. Neurotoxicol Teratol 17:437, 1995.
2. Abreu-Villaca Y et al: Prenatal nicotine exposure alters the response to nicotine administration in adolescence: Effects on cholinergic systems during exposure and withdrawal. Neuropsychopharmacology 29:879, 2004.
3. Adams EK et al: Neonatal health care costs related to smoking during pregnancy. Health Econ 11:193, 2002.
4. American Academy of Pediatrics: Fetal alcohol syndrome and alcohol-related neurodevelopmental disorders. Pediatrics 106:358, 2000.
5. American Academy of Pediatrics Committee on Drugs: Neonatal drug withdrawal. Pediatrics 101:1079, 1998.
6. Anderson HR, Cook DG: Passive smoking and sudden infant death syndrome: Review of the epidemiological evidence. Thorax 52:1003, 1997.
7. Armstrong EM, Abel EL: Fetal alcohol syndrome: The origins of a moral panic. Alcohol Alcohol 35:276, 2000.
8. Baer JS et al: A 21-year longitudinal analysis of the effects of prenatal alcohol exposure on young adult drinking. Arch Gen Psychiatry 60:377, 2003.
9. Bandstra ES et al: Intrauterine growth of full-term infants: Impact of prenatal cocaine exposure. Pediatrics 108:1309, 2001.
10. Bateman DA, Chiriboga CA: Dose-response effect of cocaine on newborn head circumference. Pediatrics 106:e33, 2000.
11. Bearer CF et al: Ethyl linoleate in meconium: A biomarker for prenatal ethanol exposure. Alcohol Clin Exp Res 23:487, 1999.
12. Behnke M et al: Incidence and description of structural brain abnormalities in newborns exposed to cocaine. J Pediatr 132:291, 1998.
13. Behnke M et al: The search for congenital malformations in newborns with fetal cocaine exposure. Pediatrics 107:E74, 2001.
14. Benowitz NL, Dempsey DA: Pharmacotherapy for smoking cessation during pregnancy. Nicotine Tob Res 6:S189, 2004.
15. Berghella V et al: Maternal methadone dose and neonatal withdrawal. Am J Obstet Gynecol 189:312, 2003.
16. Bernstein VJ, Hans SL: Predicting the developmental outcome of 2-year-old children born exposed to methadone: Impact of social-environmental risk-factors. J Clin Child Psychol 23:349, 1994.
17. Bookstein FL et al: Corpus callosum shape and neuropsychological deficits in adult males with heavy fetal alcohol exposure. Neuroimage 15:233, 2002.
18. Bradley KA et al: Alcohol screening questionnaires in women: A critical review. JAMA 280:166, 1998.
19. Brennan PA et al: Relationship of maternal smoking during pregnancy with criminal arrest and hospitalization for substance abuse in male and female adult offspring. Am J Psychiatry 159:48, 2002.
20. Broening HW et al: 3,4-Methylenedioxymethamphetamine (Ecstasy)-induced learning and memory impairments depend on the age of exposure during early development. J Neurosci 21:3228, 2001.
21. Brown HL et al: Methadone maintenance in pregnancy: A reappraisal. Am J Obstet Gynecol 179:459, 1998.
22. Buka SL et al: Elevated risk of tobacco dependence among offspring of mothers who smoked during pregnancy: A 30-year prospective study. Am J Psychiatry 160:1978, 2003.
23. Burd L et al: Fetal alcohol syndrome: Neuropsychiatric phenomics. Neurotoxicol Teratol 25:697, 2003.
24. Castles A et al: Effects of smoking during pregnancy: Five meta-analyses. Am J Prev Med 16:208, 1999.

24a. Centers for Disease Control and Prevention. State-specific prevalence of cigarette smoking among adults, and children's and adolescents' exposure to environmental tobacco smoke. United States, 1996. Morbidity and Mortality Weekly Report 1997;46:1038-1043.

25. Center for Substance Abuse Treatment, Consensus Panel: Improving treatment for drug-exposed infants. DHHS Publication No. (SMA) 95-3057. Substance Abuse and Mental Health Services Administration, Rockville, Md, Treatment Improvement Protocol (TIP) Series No. 5, p 14, 1993.

26. Center for Substance Abuse Treatment, Consensus Panel: Pregnant, substance-using women. DHHS Publication No. (SMA) 02-3677. Substance Abuse and Mental Health Services Administration, Rockville, Md, Treatment Improvement Protocol (TIP) Series No. 2, 1993.

27. Chasnoff IJ et al: Prenatal exposure to cocaine and other drugs: Outcome at four to six years. Ann N Y Acad Sci 846:314, 1998.

28. Chasnoff IJ et al: Cocaine/polydrug use in pregnancy: Two-year follow-up. Pediatrics 89:284, 1992.

29. Cherukuri R et al: A cohort study of alkaloidal cocaine ("crack") in pregnancy. Obstet Gynecol 72:147, 1988.

30. Church MW et al: Effects of prenatal cocaine on hearing, vision, growth, and behavior. Ann N Y Acad Sci 846:12, 1998.

31. Clark CM et al: Structural and functional brain integrity of fetal alcohol syndrome in nonretarded cases. Pediatrics 105:1096, 2000.

32. Clinical Consequences of Marijuana (entire supplement): J Clin Pharmacol 42(Suppl 11), 2002.

33. Cnattingius S: The epidemiology of smoking during pregnancy: Smoking prevalence, maternal characteristics, and pregnancy outcomes. Nicotine Tob Res 6:S125, 2004.

34. Coles CD et al: Effects of cocaine and alcohol use in pregnancy on neonatal growth and neurobehavioral status. Neurotoxicol Teratol 14:23, 1992.

35. Coles CD et al: Neonatal ethanol withdrawal: Characteristics in clinically normal, nondysmorphic neonates. J Pediatr 105:445, 1984.

36. Committee to Study Fetal Alcohol Syndrome (Stratton K et al [eds]): Fetal Alcohol Syndrome: Diagnosis, Epidemiology, Prevention, and Treatment. Washington, DC, National Academy Press, 1996.

37. Cornelius MD et al: Prenatal tobacco exposure: Is it a risk factor for early tobacco experimentation? Nicotine Tob Res 2:45, 2000.

38. Cornelius MD et al: Prenatal tobacco effects on neuropsychological outcomes among preadolescents. J Dev Behav Ped 22:217, 2001.

39. Corwin MJ et al: Effects of in utero cocaine exposure on newborn acoustical cry characteristics. Pediatrics 89:1199, 1992.

40. Covington CY et al: Birth to age 7 growth of children prenatally exposed to drugs: A prospective cohort study. Neurotoxicol Teratol 24:489, 2002.

41. Coyle MG et al: Diluted tincture of opium (DTO) and phenobarbital versus DTO alone for neonatal opiate withdrawal in term infants. J Pediatr 140:561, 2002.

42. Dashe JS et al: Opioid detoxification in pregnancy. Obstet Gynecol 92:854, 1998.

43. Dashe JS et al: Relationship between maternal methadone dosage and neonatal withdrawal. Obstet Gynecol 100:1244, 2002.

44. Day N et al: Prenatal marijuana use and neonatal outcome. Neurotoxicol Teratol 13:329, 1991.

45. Day NL, Richardson GA: An analysis of the effects of prenatal alcohol exposure on growth: A teratologic model. Am J Med Genet 127C:28, 2004.

46. Day NL et al: Effects of prenatal tobacco exposure on preschoolers' behavior. J Dev Behav Ped 21:180, 2000.

47. Day NL et al: Effect of prenatal marijuana exposure on the cognitive development of offspring at age three. Neurotoxicol Teratol 16:169, 1994.

48. Delaney-Black et al: Prenatal cocaine and neonatal outcome: Evaluation of dose-response relationship. Pediatrics 98:735, 1996.

49. Dixon SD, Bejar R: Echoencephalographic findings in neonates associated with maternal cocaine and methamphetamine use: Incidence and clinical correlates. J Pediatr 115:770, 1989.

50. Doberczak TM et al: One-year follow-up of infants with abstinence-associated seizures. Arch Neurol 45:649, 1988.

51. Doberczak TM et al: Neonatal neurologic and electroencephalographic effects of intrauterine cocaine exposure. J Pediatr 113:354, 1988.

52. Donatelle RJ et al: Incentives in smoking cessation: Status of the field and implications for research and practice with pregnant smokers. Nicotine Tob Res 6:S163, 2004.

53. Dusick AM et al: Risk of intracranial hemorrhage and other adverse outcomes after cocaine exposure in a cohort of 323 very low birth weight infants. J Pediatr 122:438, 1993.

54. England LJ et al: Effects of smoking reduction during pregnancy on the birth weight of term infants. Am J Epidemiol 154:694, 2001.

55. Eskenazi B, Castorina R: Association of prenatal maternal or postnatal child environmental tobacco smoke exposure and neurodevelopmental and behavioral problems in children. Environ Health Perspect 107:991, 1999.

56. Eskenazi B, Trupin LS: Passive and active maternal smoking during pregnancy, as measured by serum cotinine, and postnatal smoke exposure: 2. Effect on neurodevelopment at age 5 years. Am J Epidemiol 142:S19, 1995.

57. Eyler FD, Behnke M: Early development of infants exposed to drugs prenatally. Clin Perinatol 26:107, 1999.

58. Eyler FD et al: Birth outcome from a prospective, matched study of prenatal crack/cocaine use: II. Interactive and dose effects on neurobehavioral assessment. Pediatrics 101:237, 1998.

59. Fares I et al: Intrauterine cocaine exposure and the risk for sudden infant death syndrome: A meta-analysis. J Perinatol 17:179, 1997.

60. Fergusson DM et al: Maternal smoking during pregnancy and psychiatric adjustment in late adolescence. Arch Gen Psychiatry 55:721, 1998.

61. Fernandez-Ruiz JJ et al: Role of endocannabinoids in brain development. Life Sci 65:725, 1999.

62. Finnegan LP, Kaltenbach K: The Assessment and Management of Neonatal Abstinence Syndrome. In Hoekelman RA, Nelson NM (eds): Primary Pediatric Care, 3rd ed. St. Louis, Mo: Mosby, 1992, p 1367.

63. Fowler JS et al: Neuropharmacological actions of cigarette smoke: Brain monoamine oxidase B (MAO B) inhibition. J Addict Dis 17:23, 1998.

64. Frank DA et al: Growth, development, and behavior in early childhood following prenatal cocaine exposure: A systematic review. JAMA 285:1613, 2001.

65. Frank DA et al: Neonatal body proportionality and body composition after in utero exposure to cocaine and marijuana. J Pediatr 117:622, 1990.

66. Frank DA et al: Level of in utero cocaine exposure and neonatal ultrasound findings. Pediatrics 104:1101, 1999.

67. Fried PA, Makin J: Neonatal behavioral correlates of prenatal exposure to marihuana, cigarettes and alcohol in a low risk population. Neurotoxicol Teratol 9:1, 1987.

68. Fried PA, O'Connell CM: A comparison of the effects of prenatal exposure to tobacco, alcohol, cannabis and caffeine on birth size and subsequent growth. Neurotoxicol Teratol 9:79, 1987.

69. Fried PA, Smith AM: A literature review of the consequences of prenatal marihuana exposure: An emerging theme of a deficiency in aspects of executive function. Neurotoxicol Teratol 23:1, 2001.

70. Fried PA et al: Differential effects on cognitive functioning in 9 to 12 year olds prenatally exposed to cigarettes and marihuana. Neurotoxicol Teratol 20:293, 1998.

71. Fried PA et al: Growth from birth to early adolescence in offspring prenatally exposed to cigarettes and marijuana. Neurotoxicol Teratol 21:513, 1999.

72. Gilliland FD et al: Maternal smoking during pregnancy, environmental tobacco smoke exposure and childhood lung function. Thorax 55:271, 2000.

73. Glass M et al: Cannabinoid receptors in the human brain: A detailed anatomical and quantitative autoradiographic study in the fetal, neonatal and adult human brain. Neuroscience 77:299, 1997.

74. Goldschmidt L et al: Effects of prenatal marijuana exposure on child behavior problems at age 10. Neurotoxicol Teratol 22:325, 2000.

75. Gospe SM et al: Effects of environmental tobacco smoke exposure in utero and/or postnatally on brain development. Pediatr Res 39:494, 1996.

76. Gray K, Richardson GA, Day NL: Prenatal marijuana use and child depression at age ten. Neurotoxicol Teratol 19:245, 1997.

77. Gusella JL, Fried PA: Effects of maternal social drinking and smoking on offspring at 13 months. Neurobehav Toxicol Teratol 6:13, 1984.

78. Hanke W et al: Environmental tobacco smoke exposure among pregnant women: Impact on fetal biometry at 20-24 weeks of gestation and newborn child's birth weight. Int Arch Occup Environ Health 77:47, 2004.

79. He N et al: Neurobehavioral deficits in neonatal rhesus monkeys exposed to cocaine in utero. Neurotoxicol Teratol 26:13, 2004.

80. Held JR et al: The effect of prenatal cocaine exposure on neurobehavioral outcome: A meta-analysis. Neurotoxicol Teratol 21:619, 1999.

81. Ho E et al: Characteristics of pregnant women who use ecstasy (3,4-methylenedioxymethamphetamine). Neurotoxicol Teratol 23:561, 2001.

82. Hutchings DE, Dow-Edwards D: Animal models of opiate, cocaine, and cannabis use. Clin Perinatol 18:1, 1991.

83. Ioffe S, Chernick V: Development of the EEG between 30 and 40 weeks gestation in normal and alcohol-exposed infants. Dev Med Child Neurol 30:797, 1988.

84. Jacobson JL, Jacobson SW: Effects of prenatal alcohol exposure on child development. Alcohol Res Health 26:282, 2002.

85. Jacobson SW et al: New evidence for neurobehavioral effects of in utero cocaine exposure. J Pediatr 129:581, 1996.

86. Jeremy RJ, Bernstein VJ: Dyads at risk: Methadone-maintained women and their four-month-old infants. Child Dev 55:1141, 1984.

87. Johnson RE et al: Use of buprenorphine in pregnancy: Patient management and effects on the neonate. Drug Alcohol Depend 70:S87, 2003.

88. Kaltenbach K, Finnegan LP: Prenatal and developmental outcome of infants exposed to methadone in-utero. Neurotoxicol Teratol 9:311, 1987.

89. Kaltenbach K, Finnegan L: Prevention and treatment issues for pregnant cocaine-dependent women and their infants. Ann N Y Acad Sci 846:329, 1998.

90. Kalter H: Teratology in the 20th century: Environmental causes of congenital malformations in humans and how they were established. Neurotoxicol Teratol 25:131, 2003.

91. Kandall SR: Treatment strategies for drug-exposed neonates. Clin Perinatol 26:231, 1999.

92. Kandall SR et al: Differential effects of maternal heroin and methadone use on birth weight. Pediatrics 58:681, 1976.

93. Kandall SR et al: Relationship of maternal substance abuse to subsequent sudden infant death syndrome in offspring. J Pediatr 123:120, 1993.

94. Kandel DB et al: Maternal smoking during pregnancy and smoking by adolescent daughters. Am J Public Health 84:1407, 1994.

95. Keller RW Jr et al: Enhanced cocaine self-administration in adult rats prenatally exposed to cocaine. Neurosci Lett 205:153, 1996.

96. Kelley BM, Middaugh LD: Ethanol self-administration and motor deficits in adult C57BL/6J mice exposed prenatally to cocaine. Pharmacol Biochem Behav 55:575, 1996.

97. Kelly SJ et al: Effects of prenatal alcohol exposure on social behavior in humans and other species. Neurotoxicol Teratol 22:143, 2000.

98. Klerman LV: Protecting children: Reducing their environmental tobacco smoke exposure. Nicotine Tob Res 6:S239, 2004.

99. Kodituwakku PW et al: Specific impairments in self-regulation in children exposed to alcohol prenatally. Alcohol Clin Exp Res 19:1558, 1995.

100. Koren G et al: Bias against the null hypothesis: The reproductive hazards of cocaine. Lancet 2:1440, 1989.

101. Kosofsky BE, Wilkins AS: A mouse model of trans-placental cocaine exposure: Clinical implications for exposed infants and children. Ann N Y Acad Sci 846:248, 1998.

102. Kotimaa AJ et al: Maternal smoking and hyperactivity in 8-year-old children. J Am Acad Child Adolesc Psychiatry 42:826, 2003.

103. Kramer LD et al: Neonatal cocaine-related seizures. J Child Neurol 5:60, 1990.

104. Kristjansson EA et al: Maternal smoking during pregnancy affects children's vigilance performance. Drug Alcohol Depend 24:11, 1989.

105. Law KL et al: Smoking during pregnancy and newborn neurobehavior. Pediatrics 111:1318, 2003.

106. Lester BM et al: Cocaine exposure and children: The meaning of subtle effects. Science 282:633, 1998.

107. Lester BM et al: The Maternal Lifestyle Study: Effects of substance exposure during pregnancy on neuro-developmental outcome in 1-month-old infants. Pediatrics 110:1182, 2002.

108. Lidow MS: Consequences of prenatal cocaine exposure in nonhuman primates. Dev Brain Res 147:23, 2003.

109. Lieberman E et al: Low birthweight at term and the timing of fetal exposure to maternal smoking. Am J Public Health 84:1127, 1994.

110. Lindley AA et al: Effect of continuing or stopping smoking during pregnancy on infant birth weight, crown-heel length, head circumference, ponderal index, and brain:body weight ratio. Am J Epidemiol 152:219, 2000.

111. Lipsitz PJ: A proposed narcotic withdrawal score for use with newborn infants: A pragmatic evaluation of its efficacy. Clin Pediatr 14:592, 1975.

112. Little BB, Snell LM: Brain growth among fetuses exposed to cocaine in utero: Asymmetrical growth retardation. Obstet Gynecol 77:361, 1991.

113. Little BB et al: Methamphetamine abuse during pregnancy: Outcome and fetal effects. Obstet Gynecol 72:541, 1988.

114. Lupton C et al: Cost of fetal alcohol spectrum disorders. Am J Med Genet 127C:42, 2004.

115. Makin J et al: A comparison of active and passive smoking during pregnancy: Long-term effects. Neurotoxicol Teratol 13:5, 1991.

116. Malanga CJ, Kosofsky BE: Mechanisms of action of drugs of abuse on the developing fetal brain. Clin Perinatol 26:17, 1999.

117. Mansvelder HD et al: Synaptic mechanisms underlie nicotine-induced excitability of brain reward areas. Neuron 33:905, 2002.

118. Mayes LC: Developing brain and in utero cocaine exposure: Effects on neural ontogeny. Dev Psychopathol 11:685, 1999.

119. Mayes LC et al: Regulation of arousal and attention in preschool children exposed to cocaine prenatally. Ann N Y Acad Sci 846:126, 1998.

120. McElhatton PR et al: Congenital anomalies after prenatal ecstasy exposure. Lancet 354:1441, 1999.

121. McGee R, Stanton WR: Smoking in pregnancy and child development to age 9 years. J Paediatr Child Health 30:263, 1994.

122. Meintjes EM et al: A stereo-photogrammetric method to measure the facial dysmorphology of children in the diagnosis of fetal alcohol syndrome. Med Eng Phys 24:683, 2002.

123. Melvin CL, Gaffney CA: Treating nicotine use and dependence of pregnant and parenting smokers: An update. Nicotine Tob Res 6:S107, 2004.

124. Melvin CL et al: Recommended cessation counselling for pregnant women who smoke: A review of the evidence. Tob Control 9:80, 2000.

125. Metosky P, Vondra J: Prenatal drug exposure and play and coping in toddlers: A comparison study. Infant Behav Dev 18:25, 1995.

126. Morrow CE et al: Influence of prenatal cocaine exposure on full-term infant neurobehavioral functioning. Neurotoxicol Teratol 23:533, 2001.

127. Naeye R: Hypoxia and the sudden infant death syndrome. Science 186:837, 1974.

128. National Institutes of Health: NIH Consensus Statement: Effective medical treatment of opiate addiction. Report No. 15, 1997.

129. Navarro M et al: Behavioural consequences of maternal exposure to natural cannabinoids in rats. Psychopharmacology 122:1, 1995.

130. Neuspiel DR et al: Maternal cocaine use and infant behavior. Neurotoxicol Teratol 13:229, 1991.

131. Nichols MM: Acute alcohol withdrawal syndrome in a newborn. Am J Dis Child 113:714, 1967.

132. Obel C et al: Smoking during pregnancy and babbling abilities of the 8-month-old infant. Paediatr Perinat Epidemiol 12:37, 1998.

133. Olds D: Tobacco exposure and impaired development: A review of the evidence. Mental Retardation Devel Disabil Res Rev 3:257, 1997.

134. Ornoy A et al: The developmental outcome of children born to heroin-dependent mothers, raised at home or adopted. Child Abuse Negl 20:385, 1996.

135. Ostrea EM et al: Meconium analysis to assess fetal exposure to nicotine by active and passive maternal smoking. J Pediatr 124:471, 1994.

136. Polygenis D et al: Moderate alcohol consumption during pregnancy and the incidence of fetal malformations: A meta-analysis. Neurotoxicol Teratol 20:61, 1998.

137. Rao R, Desai NS: OxyContin and neonatal abstinence syndrome. J Perinatol 22:324, 2003.

138. Rementeria J, Nunag N: Narcotic withdrawal in pregnancy: Stillbirth incidence with a case report. Am J Obstet Gynecol 116:1152, 1973.

139. Richardson GA et al: Prenatal alcohol, marijuana, and tobacco use: Infant mental and motor development. Neurotoxicol Teratol 17:479, 1995.

140. Richardson GA et al: Growth of infants prenatally exposed to cocaine/crack: Comparison of a prenatal care and a no prenatal care sample. Pediatrics 104:e18, 1999.

141. Rosen TS, Johnson HL: Children of methadone-maintained mothers: Follow-up to 18 months of age. J Pediatr 101:192, 1982.

142. Sampson PD et al: Prenatal alcohol exposure, birthweight, and measures of child size from birth to age 14 years. Am J Public Health 84:1421, 1994.

143. Sampson P et al: Incidence of alcohol-related neurodevelopmental disorder. Teratology 56:317, 1997.

144. Scher MS et al: The effects of prenatal alcohol and marijuana exposure: Disturbances in neonatal sleep cycling and arousal. Pediatr Res 24:101, 1988.

145. Sekhon HS et al: Prenatal nicotine exposure alters pulmonary function in newborn rhesus monkeys. Am J Respir Crit Care Med 164:989, 2001.

146. Sexton M et al: Prenatal exposure to tobacco: 2. Effects on cognitive functioning at age 3. Int J Epidemiol 19:72, 1990.

147. Shih L et al: Effects of maternal cocaine abuse on the neonatal auditory system. Int J Pediatr Otorhinolaryngol 15:245, 1988.

148. Singer LT et al: Cognitive and motor outcomes of cocaine-exposed infants. JAMA 287:1952, 2002.

149. Slotkin TA: Fetal nicotine or cocaine exposure: Which one is worse? J Pharmacol Exp Ther 285:931, 1998.

150. Slotkin TA et al: Heroin neuroteratogenicity: Delayed-onset deficits in catecholaminergic synaptic activity. Brain Res 984:189, 2003.

151. Smith LM et al: Prenatal nicotine increases testosterone levels in the fetus and female offspring. Nicotine Tob Res 5:369, 2003.

152. Smith SM: Alcohol-induced cell death in the embryo. Alcohol Health Res World 21:287, 1997.

153. Sood B et al: Prenatal alcohol exposure and childhood behavior at age 6 to 7 years: I. Dose-response effect. Pediatrics 108:e34, 2001.

154. Stocks J, Dezateux C: The effect of parental smoking on lung function and development during infancy. Respirology 8:266, 2003.

155. Stoler JM, Holmes LB: Under-recognition of prenatal alcohol effects in infants of known alcohol abusing women. J Pediatr 135:430, 1999.

156. Streissguth AP et al: Fetal alcohol syndrome in adolescents and adults. JAMA 265:1961, 1991.

157. Streissguth AP et al: Maternal alcohol use and neonatal

habituation assessed with the Brazelton scale. Child Dev 54:1109, 1983.

158. Streissguth AP et al: Moderate prenatal alcohol exposure: Effects on child IQ and learning problems at age $7^1/_2$ years. Alcohol Clin Exp Res 14:662, 1990.

159. Substance Abuse and Mental Health Services Administration: Results from the 2003 National Survey on Drug Use and Health: National Findings. Rockville, Md, NSDUH Series H-25, 2004.

160. Sulik K et al: Fetal alcohol syndrome: Embryogenesis in a mouse model. Science 214:936, 1981.

161. Swayze VW et al: Magnetic resonance imaging of brain anomalies in fetal alcohol syndrome. Pediatrics 99:232, 1997.

162. Taeusch HW et al: Heroin induction of lung maturation and growth retardation in fetal rabbits. J Pediatr 82:869, 1973.

163. Testa M et al: The effects of prenatal alcohol exposure on infant mental development: A meta-analytical review. Alcohol Alcohol 38:295, 2003.

164. Tronick EZ et al: Late dose-response effects of prenatal cocaine exposure on newborn neurobehavioral performance. Pediatrics 98:76, 1996.

165. U.S. Department of Health and Human Services, National Institute on Drug Abuse: National Pregnancy and Health Survey: Drug use among women delivering live births, 1992. Rockville, Md, 1996.

166. Vik T et al: Pre- and post-natal growth in children of women who smoked in pregnancy. Early Hum Dev 45:245, 1996.

167. Webster WS, Brown-Woodman PD: Cocaine as a cause of congenital malformations of vascular origin: Experimental evidence in the rat. Teratology 41:689, 1990.

168. Wilson GS et al: Follow-up of methadone treated and untreated narcotic-dependent women and their infants: Health, developmental, and social implications. J Pediatr 98:716, 1998.

169. Windham GC et al: Evidence for an association between environmental tobacco smoke exposure and birthweight: A meta-analysis and new data. Paediatr Perinat Epidemiol 13:35, 1999.

170. Wurtzel D et al: No increased risk for intracranial hemorrhage (ICH) in preterm infants exposed in utero to cocaine. Pediatr Res 23:431, 1988.

171. Zeskind PS, Stephens LE: Maternal selective serotonin reuptake inhibitor use during pregnancy and newborn neurobehavior. Pediatrics 113:368, 2004.

172. Zhou FC et al: Moderate alcohol exposure compromises neural tube midline development in prenatal brain. Dev Brain Res 144:43, 2003.

Index

Note: Page numbers followed by the letter b refer to boxed material; those followed by the letter f refer to figures, and those followed by t refer to tables.

A

ABCA3 gene, in respiratory distress syndrome, 1077, 1097

Abdomen
  birth injuries to organs of, 550–553
  examination of, 515
    for congenital anomalies, 574
  mass in, genitourinary origin of, 1665

Abdominal circumference
  in intrauterine growth restriction, 292, 294f
  perinatal ultrasonography of, 146–147, 147f

Abdominal radiography
  of duodenal atresia, 719, 719f
  of functionally immature colon, 720, 720f
  of gastrointestinal obstruction
    high, 718f–719f, 718–720
    low, 719f–722f, 720–722
  of Hirschsprung disease, 720f, 720
  of ileal atresia, 721
  of jejunal atresia, 720
  of meconium ileus, 721, 721f
  of midgut malrotation, 718–719, 719f
  of necrotizing enterocolitis, 721f, 721–722, 722f

Abdominal situs, 1242–1243

Abdominal wall defects, 1381–1385. *See also* Gastroschisis; Omphalocele.
  perinatal ultrasonography of, 157, 158f

Abducens nerve, birth injuries to, 538

Abetalipoproteinemia, 1368

ABO blood group
  compatibility of, guidelines for, 1343t
  in unconjugated hyperbilirubinemia, 1429
  incompatibility of, and reduced risk of RhD isoimmunization, 390

ABO hemolytic disease, 1298

Abortion
  prior, preterm delivery and, 335
  selective, after prenatal ultrasound, ethical issues in, 144, 144f
  spontaneous
    chromosome anomalies in, 116–117, 564–565, 565t
    congenital anomalies in, 564–565, 565t

Abrasions
  birth-related, 529
    ear injuries in, 539
  ocular, 1727

Abruptio placentae, 461
  anesthetic considerations in, 480
  bleeding caused by, in preterm delivery, 336

Abscess
  brain, macrocephaly due to, 1005
  breast, neonatal, 818

Absolute risk reduction, 82–83, 82t, 83f

Abuse, substance. *See* Substance abuse.

Accelerations, in fetal heart rate, 174, 175f

Accessory pathway reentrant tachycardia, 1254–1255, 1255f
  treatment of, 1263

Acetaminophen
  dosages of, 1787
  fetal effects of, 188t
  in breast milk, 199

Acetate anions, in parenteral nutrition, 687

Acetazolamide, dosages of, 1791

Acetoacetate, placental transport of, 1467–1468

Acetylation activity, in drug metabolism, 194

N-Acetylglutamate synthetase, deficiency of, 1651

N-Acetylprocainamide, for fetal arrhythmias, 223t, 224t

Acetylsalicylic acid, in breast milk, 199

N-Acetyltyrosine, in parenteral amino acid solutions, 684, 685

Acheiria, 575

Acheiropodia, 575

Achondroplasia, 996, 1781
  clinical manifestations of, 1781
  incidence of, paternal age and, 257
  mutation in, 122
  ultrasonography of, 162

Acid-base balance, 703–706
  developmental aspects of, 705–706
  disorders of
    diagnostic approach to, 706, 706f, 707t
    expected compensation in, 706, 707t
    specific, 708–710, 709b
    treatment of, 707b, 707–708
  maintenance of, 704–705
    buffer systems in, 704
    chronic, 703–705, 705f
    in respiratory distress syndrome, 1106
    with neuraxial blockade, 476

Acid elution test, for fetal red blood cells, in vaginal blood, 1296

Acidemia
  argininosuccinic, 1605t
  definition of, 172
  lactic. *See* Lactic acidemia.
  organic, 1638–1640, 1606t–1608t
    management of, 1639–1640
  pyroglutamic, 1638–1639

Acidosis
  definition of, 172
  in hypoxic-ischemic encephalopathy, 955
  in truncus arteriosus, 1230
  laboratory findings in, 1629t
  metabolic. *See* Metabolic acidosis.

Acidosis—cont'd
  renal tubular. *See* Renal tubular acidosis.
  respiratory, 708

Aciduria, organic, 1648
  dysmorphic features in, 1625t, 1627–1628

Acinus, development of, 1070

Acne, neonatal and infantile, 1693, 1693f

Acoustic stimuli, environmental, 600–602

Acquired immunodeficiency syndrome. *See* Human immunodeficiency virus (HIV) infection.

Acrocephalosyndactyly
  type 1 (Apert syndrome), 1011–1012, 1011f, 1011–1012, 1011f
    anesthetic implications of, 632t
    incidence of, paternal age and, 257
    ocular manifestation of, 1728
  type 3 (Saethre-Chotzen syndrome), 1013
  type 5 (Pfeiffer syndrome), 1012–1013, 1012f

Acrocyanosis, in respiratory distress syndrome, 1100

Acrodermatitis enteropathica, 1370, 1702–1703, 1703f

Acromelia, 162, 575

Acropustulosis, infantile, 1693

Actin dysfunction, neutrophil, 1317

Activated charcoal, for unconjugated hyperbilirubinemia, 1446

Activated clotting time (ACT) test, 1330

Activated partial thromboplastin time
  in evaluation of coagulation factor deficiencies, 1320
  in hemophilias, 1325–1326

Acupuncture, for back pains, during delivery, 469

Acute fatty liver of pregnancy, 311, 1615

Acute lymphocytic leukemia, 1342

Acute megakaryoblastic leukemia, in Down syndrome, 1314–1315

Acute myelogenous leukemia, 1342

Acute phase reactants, in sepsis diagnosis, 797–798

Acute tubular necrosis. *See* Renal tubular necrosis, acute.

Acyanotic congenital heart disease, 1221b, 1222, 1237–1242

Acyclovir
  dosages of, 1790
  for herpes simplex virus infection, 843
  for varicella pneumonia, 848
  for varicella-zoster virus infections, 849
  prophylactic, for herpes simplex virus infection, 438

Acyl-CoA dehydrogenase deficiency
  medium-chain, 1609t, 1648
  multiple, 1627–1628, 1639

Acyl-CoA dehydrogenase deficiency—cont'd
  short-chain, 1610t, 1648
  very-long-chain, 1610t
Acylcarnitine(s), abnormal laboratory
    findings of, 1602t–1603t
Acylcarnitine translocase deficiency, 1609t
Adenoma, persistent neonatal
    hyperinsulinemic hypoglycemia due to,
    1480–1482, 1481f
Adenosine
  dosages of, 1787
  for neonatal tachycardia, 1260t, 1261b,
    1263
Adenosine monophosphate, cyclic,
    inhibition of degradation of, 1179–1180
Adenosine triphosphate–binding cassette
    transporter (ABCA3) gene, in respiratory
    distress syndrome, 1077, 1097
Adenovirus infection, 874–875
Adhesion
  disorders of, 1315, 1316f, 1316b, 1317
  of neutrophils, 764, 765f
  of phagocytes, 767
Adrenal cortex, cortisol synthesis in, 217,
    217f
Adrenal crisis, acute, 1579
  management of, 1580–1581
Adrenal gland(s)
  congenital hyperplasia of, 1484, 1577–1584
    drug treatment of, 216–219, 219t
    electrolyte abnormalities in, treatment
      of, 701
    history in, 1559–1560
    hypertensive, 1582–1583
    in 21-hydroxylase deficiency, 1579
    lipoid, 1583–1584
    management of, 1580–1581
  fetal, in drug metabolism, 211, 211t
  insufficiency of
    bronchopulmonary dysplasia related to,
      1162
    differential diagnosis of, 1580
    in salt-losing 21-hydroxylase deficiency,
      1579
  steroid biosynthetic pathway in, 1555f
  ultrasonography of, 726–727
Adrenal hemorrhage
  birth-related, 551–553, 552f
  ultrasonography of, 726, 726f
β-Adrenergic blocking agents. See also
    Beta-blockers.
  placental transfer of, transient neonatal
    hypoglycemia due to, 1473
Adrenocorticotropic hormone
  dosages of, 1791
  in 21-hydroxylase deficiency, 1579
  unresponsiveness of, 1483–1484
Adrenogenital syndrome, anesthetic
    implications of, 632t
Adrenoleukodystrophy, X-linked, 1628
  pharmacogenetic approach to, 1654
Adult-onset disease, fetal origin hypothesis
    of, 278, 278f
Advanced practice neonatal nurses, liability
    of physicians for supervision of, 50
Africa, neonatal mortality in, 91
African Americans
  congenital anomaly prevalence in,
    565–566, 566t
  low birthweight in, 23
  mongolian blue spots in, 565, 566t, 1689b,
    1691
  neonatal mortality rates in, 20–21, 21f
  transient cutaneous lesions in, 1689b

African populations, tropical, glucose-6-
    phosphatase dehydrogenase deficiency
    in, 1429
Afterload reduction, in congenital heart
    disease, 1267
Aganglionosis, congenital intestinal, 1398
Age
  gestational. See Gestational age.
  in preeclampsia-eclampsia, 312
  maternal
    multiple gestations and, 376
    nondisjunction and, 115f, 116, 116f
    onset of carbohydrate absorption
      disorders related to, 1365, 1365t
    paternal, birth defects and, 257
    postnatal, drug dose/interval and, 197
Agenesis, of corpus callosum, 903–904
Agyria-pachygyria, 907
Aicardi syndrome, 992–993
Air, in concurrent maternal exposure, 259,
    261f
Air bubble, in pyloric atresia, 1387, 1388f
Air conduction tests, in evaluation of
    hearing, 1046
Air embolism, due to assisted ventilation,
    1131
Air leak syndromes, 1128–1133. See also
    specific type.
Airflow, measurement of, 1091–1092
Airway(s)
  anatomy of, neonatal anesthesia and, 628
  clearance of, in neonatal resuscitation,
    490
  edema of, in preeclampsia, anesthetic
    considerations in, 479
  laryngeal mask, in neonatal intubation,
    637
  obstruction of
    fetal, 247–249
      prenatal diagnosis of, 248
      prenatal treatment of, 248f, 248–249
    in apnea, 1137, 1137f
    in bronchopulmonary dysplasia, 1157,
      1158f
    neonatal, causes of, 1143–1144, 1143b
  open, in neonatal resuscitation, 951
  resistance of, in bronchopulmonary
    dysplasia, 1161–1162, 1163, 1163t,
    1164f
  upper, lesions of, 1146–1155
  water loss from, 592t, 592–594, 593t, 593f
    determination of, 587, 592
Airway pressure, mean. See Mean airway
    pressure (Paw).
Alacrima, 1733–1734
Alagille syndrome
  conjugated hyperbilirubinemia in, 1460
  heart defects associated with, 1204
Alanine aminotransferase, measurement of,
    1804t
Albinism, 1705
  ocular manifestation of, 1743
  partial, 1705–1706
Albumin
  bilirubin binding with, 1420, 1422f
    capacity of, 1435
  dosages of, 1790
  for volume expansion, in neonatal
    resuscitation, 504
  measurement of, 1804t
  plasma levels of, in preterm infant, 1804t
  salt-poor, administration of, prior to
    exchange transfusion, 1447–1448
Albuterol, dosages of, 1790

Alcohol
  cocaine abuse combined with, 734
  congenital malformations associated with,
    186t
  fetal exposure to, 734–739. See also Fetal
    alcohol syndrome.
    central nervous system effects of,
      736–737
    congenital anomalies associated with,
      563–564, 564f, 736b
    dose-response relationship in, 185
    growth effects of, 737
    neurobehavioral and developmental
      effects of, 737
    neuropsychological and behavioral
      effects of, 737–738
    prevention of, 738–739, 799
    neonatal withdrawal due to, 737
Alcohol dehydrogenase, fetal activity of,
    263, 263f
Alcohol-related birth defects, 735, 736b
Alcohol-related neurodevelopmental
    disorder, 735, 736b
Aldosterone
  mean concentrations of, 1805t
  role of, in sodium/potassium homeostasis,
    701
Alexander disease, macrencephaly
    associated with, 997
Alfentanil
  for labor pain, 472
  in neonatal anesthesia, 639
Alkali therapy
  for metabolic acidosis, 707
  for persistent pulmonary hypertension,
    1247
Alkaline phosphatase, measurement of,
    1804t
Alkalosis
  metabolic, 707b, 707–708
    laboratory findings in, 1629t
  respiratory, 708
Alkylating agents, fetal effects of, 187t
All Patient DRG system, 70–71, 72t
Allergic enteropathy, 1372
Allergic reactions, to transfusion, 1347
Alliance of Genetic Support Groups, 581
Allis sign, in developmental dysplasia of
    hip, 1774, 1775
Alloimmune (isoimmune) neutropenia, 1312
Alloimmune (isoimmune)
    thrombocytopenia, 368–370, 1338–1339,
    1340f
  neonatal management of, 369
  subsequent pregnancy management of,
    369–370, 370b
Alma Ata Declaration, for reduction of
    neonatal mortality, 88, 89t
Alopecia, in carboxylase deficiency, 1620
Alpha-fetoprotein
  elevation of, in gastroschisis, 1383
  maternal serum
    in myelomeningocele, 246
    in prenatal genetic screening, 135–136
Alveolar-arterial oxygen tension gradient
  as criterion, for extracorporeal membrane
    oxygenation, 1174–1175, 1174b
  equation for, 1090
  in bronchopulmonary dysplasia, 1163
Alveolar capillary dysplasia, 1133
Alveolar dead space, 1093
Alveolar ridge, hypertrophied, 573, 573f
Alveolar septae, development of, 1070,
    1071f

Alveolar ventilation, minute, in assisted ventilation, 1109–1110, 1110f
Alveolarization, 1072–1073, 1072b, 1072f, 1074f
Alveolus(i)
hemorrhage of, intra-alveolar, after surfactant therapy, 1104, 1104b
separation from capillaries, in bronchopulmonary dysplasia, 1158, 1159f
stability of, surfactant in, 1081, 1082f
surfactant life cycle in, 1081
type II cells in, in surfactant synthesis, 1077–1078, 1077f
Amaurosis, Leber congenital, 1743
Ambient humidity, different, heat exchange between skin and environment at, 589, 590f
Ambiguous genitalia. See Genitalia, ambiguous.
Amblyopia
classification of, 1746
treatment of, 1746
Ambulatory electrocardiography. See also Electrocardiography (ECG).
of arrhythmias, 1252
Amegakaryotic thrombocytopenia, 1340
American Academy of Pediatrics
caloric intake recommendations of, 664
Committee on Nutrition recommendations
for mineral and trace elements, 670t
for vitamin intake, 668t
guidelines of
for developmental dysplasia of hip, 521, 521f
for group B streptococcal disease prevention, 1126
respiratory syncytial virus prophylaxis recommendations of, 854, 854b
American Society for Clinical Nutrition, 687, 688t
Americans with Disabilities Act, 57
Amicar, for hemophilia A and B, 1327t
Amikacin
dosages of, 1788
for sepsis, 800, 801t, 802t
Amiloride, for nephrogenic diabetes insipidus, 702
Amino acids
analysis of, in inborn errors of metabolism, 1631–1632, 1632t
disorders of, 1604t–1605t
laboratory findings in, 1602t
essential and conditionally essential, 684
in parenteral nutrition
efficacy of early administration of, 682–683, 682t
in intravenous solutions, 683–685, 684t
quantity of, hepatic dysfunction related to, 688
safety of, 683
metabolism of, defects in, 1638
placental transport of, 1467
reference serum concentrations of, 1803t
sulfur-containing, deficiency of, in bronchopulmonary dysplasia, 1166
Aminoacidopathy, hepatic dysfunction in, 1621
γ-Aminobutyric acid, in neonatal seizures, 1617
Aminoglycosides
fetal effects of, 187t
for conjunctivitis, 811
for listeriosis, 821

Aminoglycosides—cont'd
for mastitis, 818
for meningitis, 807
for necrotizing enterocolitis, 1405
for osteomyelitis, 814, 1764
for otitis media, 810
for pneumonia, 809
for sepsis, 800
for septic arthritis, 814
for skin infections, 817
for urinary tract infections, 815, 816
in breast milk, 199
Aminophenols, fetal effects of, 188t
Aminophylline
dosages of, 1791
for bronchopulmonary dysplasia, 1165
Amiodarone
dosages of, 1787
for fetal arrhythmias, 223t, 224t
for neonatal tachycardia, 1260t, 1262b, 1264
thyroid hormone effects of, 1528
with sotalol, for neonatal tachycardia, 1262b
Amlodipine, for neonatal hypertension, 1673t
Ammonia. See also Hyperammoninemia.
blood concentration of, 1630
measurement of, 1804t
plasma levels of, 1803t
Ammoniagenesis, 705, 705f
Ammonium chloride, dosages of, 1792
Amniocentesis
in congenital cytomegalovirus infection diagnosis, 847
in erythroblastosis fetalis screening, 394
in prenatal genetic evaluation, 137
Amnioinfusion
for gastroschisis prevention, 1383
for meconium aspiration prevention, 1124
for non-reassuring fetal heart rate, 178, 178f
in intrauterine growth restriction, 295–296
in oligohydramnios, 417, 418
Amnion nodosum, 460
Amnioreduction
for nonimmune hydrops fetalis, 425
for polyhydramnios, 420
serial, for twin-twin transfusion syndrome, 250
Amniotic band syndrome
fetal deformation in, 460
fetal surgery for, 234t
limb malformations due to, 1757, 1768–1769, 1768f
Amniotic fluid
assessment of, in multiple gestations, 413, 413f
composition of, 409
DNA analysis of, 137
dynamics of, 409–411
fetal swallowing of, 410–411
gastroschisis "peel" due to, 1382–1383
infection of
intra-amniotic, 431b, 431–432, 444
preterm delivery and, 337–338
interleukins and TNF-α in, 333
leptin in, 277–278
neonatal aspiration of, 1125
odor of, breast feeding related to, 649, 650
optical density of, in erythroblastosis fetalis screening, 395–397, 396f
production of, 410f, 410–411

Amniotic fluid—cont'd
regulation of, 410–411
surfactant in
in lung maturity testing, 1085–1086
pathway of, from fetal lung, 1085, 1085f
thyroid hormones in, detection of, 1532
Amniotic fluid index
correlation of, with amniotic fluid volume, 411, 412f
in indomethacin therapy, 351
in oligohydramnios, 169
in polyhydramnios, 220, 418, 418f
in post-term neonate, 385t, 386
measurement of, 411–412, 412t, 412f
normal, 412f
Amniotic fluid volume, 409–410, 410f
abnormalities of, 413–426. See also Hydrops fetalis, nonimmune; Oligohydramnios; Polyhydramnios.
increased congenital anomalies in, 414
increased perinatal morbidity and mortality in, 413f, 413–414
uteroplacental insufficiency in, 414
assessment of, in fetal evaluation, 169, 170f
clinical determination of, 411–413
correlation of amniotic fluid index with, 411, 412f
decreased, definition of, 169
gestational age and, 409, 410f
maximum vertical pocket measurement of, 411, 411t
subjective estimation of, 411
ultrasonography of, 148–149, 149f
Amniotic sac, fluids entering, 411
Amniotic septostomy, for twin-twin transfusion syndrome, 250
Amniotomy, in labor induction, 386b, 387
Amobarbital, fetal effects of, 187t
Amoxicillin
for chlamydial infections, 447
for preterm premature rupture of membranes, 355
for urinary tract infections, in spinal cord injury, 549
Amphetamine abuse, 747–749
Amphotericin B
dosages of, 1790
for candidiasis, 832, 832t
for coccidioidomycosis, 833
for cryptococcosis, 834
Ampicillin
dosages of, 1788
for gastroenteritis, 813
for listeriosis, 821
for meningitis, 806, 807
for necrotizing enterocolitis, 1405
for otitis media, 810
for pneumonia, 809
for preterm premature rupture of membranes, 355
for sepsis, 800, 801t, 802t
for skin infections, 817
for urinary tract infections, 815
in spinal cord injury, 549
prophylactic, for sepsis, 804
Amputation, congenital, 1757, 1769
Amrinone
for afterload reduction, in congenital heart disease, 1267
inotropic effect of, 1267
Amyoplasia, 1783
Amyotonia, vs. spinal birth injuries, 548
Anaerobic infections, 819

Anal. *See* Anus.
Analbuminemia, anesthetic implications of, 632t
Analgesia
  acupuncture as, 469
  hypnosis in, 468
  in mechanical ventilation, 1116
  in withdrawal of life-sustaining treatment, 41
  natural childbirth and, 468
  nerve blocks as, 469, 641
  neuraxial blocks as. *See* Neuraxial blocks.
  neutropenia due to, 1313b
  nonpharmacologic, 467–469
  saline injections as, 469
  systemic medications as, 469–471
  transcutaneous electrical nerve stimulation as, 469
  water birth as, 468–469
Analgesics
  fetal effects of, 187t, 188t, 469–471, 470t
  opioids as, 471b, 471–473
  sedatives and, 471
  synthetic opioids as, abuse of, 753
Anatomic dead space, 1093
Andersen syndrome, anesthetic implications of, 632t
Anderson disease (chylomicron retention disease), 1368
Androgen(s)
  fetal effects of, 188t
  maternal, fetal masculinization due to, 1584–1585
Androgen-dependent target tissues, disorders of, 1575–1577
Androgen insensitivity syndromes, 1575–1577
  testicular feminization in, 1576
  incomplete, 1576–1577
Anemia
  accelerated red blood cell destruction causing, 1297–1302, 1297t, 1298t, 1300f, 1301f, 1302b
  blood loss causing, 1295–1297
  classification of, 1294t
  congenital dyserythropoietic, 1308
  definition of, 1293–1294
  Diamond-Blackfan, 1306–1307
  etiology of, 1294b
  evaluation of, 1294–1295, 1295t, 1296f
  Fanconi, 1307–1308, 1307t
    radial anomalies associated with, 1341
    vs. Diamond-Blackfan anemia, 1306
  fetal
    in hydrops fetalis, 391–393, 392f
    in nonimmune hydrops fetalis, 421, 422b
    peak systolic velocity in assessment of, 394–395
    ultrasonography in prediction of, 398–400, 400f, 400t
  fetal-fetal transfusion and, 1297. *See also* Twin-twin transfusion syndrome.
  fetal-maternal hemorrhage and, 1296–1297
  hemolytic
    causes of, 1297, 1297t
    enzymatic defects and, 1301–1302, 1302b
    erythrocyte structural defects in, 1299–1300, 1300f
    hemoglobin E and, 1304–1305
    hemoglobin S and, 1304, 1305f
    hemoglobin variants and, 1303–1305, 1304b

Anemia—*cont'd*
    hereditary elliptocytosis and, 1300, 1301f
    hereditary pyropoikilocytosis and, 1300, 1301f
    hereditary spherocytosis and, 1300, 1301f
    idiopathic, 1299
    isoimmune, 1298–1299, 1298t
    membrane lipid defects and, 1300–1301
    nonimmune, 1299–1302
    thalassemia and, 1302–1303
    unstable hemoglobins and, 1305
    vitamin E deficiency and, 1302
  in transient erythroblastopenia of childhood, 1307
  inefficient red blood cell production causing, 1305–1308
  iron-deficiency, 1305–1306
  macrocytic, 1294t
  maternal, in multiple gestations, 376
  microcytic, 1294t
  normocytic, 1294t
  of prematurity, 1306
  parvovirus-induced, 1308
  physical findings in, 1295t
  physiologic, in neonate, 1293, 1293f
  sickle cell, 1304, 1305f
  sideroblastic, 1308
  transfusions for, 1295
Anencephaly, 901, 990, 991f
  in post-term pregnancy, 383
  prevalence of, 517t
  ultrasonography of, 153, 154f
Anesthesia. *See also* Analgesia.
  for labor and delivery, 473–481
    breech presentation in, 480
    cesarean section in, 477–479
    delivery modes and techniques in, 477–479
    fetal distress and, 480
    neonatal depression due to, 505
    neuraxial blocks in. *See* Neuraxial blocks.
    operative vaginal delivery in, 477
    placenta previa in, 480
    placental abruption in, 481
    preeclampsia in, 479
    uterine rupture in, 479–480
  general
    for cesarean sections, 478
    in neonates, 637–640
  in neonates, 627–642
    Bain circuit in, 637
    carbohydrate metabolism in, 629–630
    cardiac physiology in, 628–629
    circle breathing system in, 637
    congenital anomalies and, 632, 632t–634t, 634
    fetal hemoglobin in, 629
    general anesthesia in, 637–640
      induction of, 640
      inhalational agents in, 637–638, 638f
      intravenous agents in, 638–640
    intubation in, 632, 634
      rapid-sequence, 640
    maintenance of anesthesia in, 640
    Mapleson D circuit in, 637
    monitoring requirements in, 636t, 636–637
    NPO guidelines for, 631, 631t
    operating room equipment in, 636–637
    pain perception and, 630–631, 630f, 630t
    physiology and development in, 627–630

Anesthesia—*cont'd*
    preoperative evaluation and preparation for, 631–635
    recovery from, 641–642
    regional anesthesia in, 641
    renal physiology in, 629
    respiratory physiology in, 628
    temperature regulation in, 629
    transition phase and, 627
    transport methods in, 635–636
Anesthetic gases
  in neonatal anesthesia, 637–638
  maternal exposure to, pregnancy outcome in, 260t
  minimal alveolar concentration of, 637–638, 638f
Anesthetics
  fetal exposure to, seizures associated with, 971
  placental transfer of, umbilical vein to maternal vein ratio as measure of, 470, 470t
Aneuploid, 115
ANG gene, in preeclampsia-eclampsia syndrome, 309
Angelman syndrome, genomic imprinting and, 126
Angioma, choroidal, 1729
Angiomatosis, encephalo-oculofacial, 1729
Angioplasty, balloon. *See* Balloon angioplasty.
Angiotensin-converting enzyme (ACE) inhibitors
  fetal effects of, 188t
  indications for and contraindications to, 1245
  oligohydramnios due to, 414
Angiotensin II, in uterine blood flow regulation, 308, 309f
Angiotensin type II receptor gene, in renal development, 1660t, 1661
Angiotensinogen mutation, 309, 309f
Anhydramnios, 413, 413f
Anion(s), in parenteral nutrition, 687
Anion gap
  increased, 707, 707b
  normal, 707, 707b
Aniridia, 1738
Anisocoria, 1747
Annular pancreas, 1390
Anopheles mosquitoes, 836
Anophthalmia, 1732
Anorchia, congenital, 1572
Anorectoplasty, posterior sagittal, 1401f
Anoxia, definition of, 938
Antacids, magnesium-containing, excessive administration of, 1520
Antenatal care
  barriers to, 27, 27t
  in developing countries, home-based, 102
  malpractice litigation related to, 51–52
  substance abuse identification in, 733
Antenatal ultrasonography
  indications for, 152b, 203, 203b
  of congenital heart defects, 1208–1209
  of fetal circulation, 170, 170f, 171f
  of gestational diabetes, 324
  of intrauterine growth restriction, 291–292
  of intravascular fetal transfusion, 401
  of nonimmune hydrops fetalis, 423f, 423–424
    findings in, 421t
  of renal disease, 1664, 1665b

Anterior chamber
cleavage syndromes of, 1737
examination of, 1723
hyphema of, 1727
Anti-hepatitis B surface antigen, 863, 864
Anti-inflammatory agents
fetal effects of, 187t
neutropenia due to, 1313b
Anti-La antibodies, 371
heart block due to, 1204
Anti-PL antibodies, 371
Anti-Ro antibodies, 371
heart block due to, 1204
Anti-SSA/Ro antibodies, in neonatal lupus
syndrome, 371
Anti-SSB/La antibodies, in neonatal lupus
syndrome, 371
Antiandrogens, fetal effects of, 188t
Antiarrhythmics
fetal effects of, 188t
fetal treatment with, 1210
for neonatal tachycardia, 1260t,
1261b–1262b
Antibiotics
after imperforate anus repair, 1402
associated with vitamin K deficiency, 1328
congenital malformations associated with,
186t
contraindications to, in botulism, 820
fetal effects of, 187t
for anaerobic infections, 819
for chlamydial infections, 447
for conjunctivitis, 811
for gastroenteritis, 813
for hydronephrosis, 1677
for intra-amniotic infection, 432
for listeriosis, 821
for mastitis, 818
for meningitis, 806–807
for necrotizing enterocolitis, 1405
for omphalitis, 818
for osteomyelitis, 1764
for osteomyelitis and septic arthritis, 814
for otitis media, 810
for parotitis, 818
for pneumocystis pneumonia, 838
for pneumonia, 809, 1126–1127
for premature rupture of membranes,
430–431
for preterm labor prevention, 354–355,
431
for respiratory distress syndrome, 1107
for sepsis, 799–800, 801t–803t
for septic arthritis, 1766
for skin infections, 817
for staphylococcal scalded skin syndrome,
1698
for syphilis, 824, 824t
for tuberculosis, 827, 827t
for urinary tract infections, 429, 430,
815–816
in spinal cord injury, 549
in breast milk, 199
neutropenia due to, 1313b
prophylactic
for bacterial endocarditis, 1268
for group B streptococcal infection,
444–445
in neonatal intensive care units, 829
intrapartum, for sepsis, 803–804
Antibody(ies). See also specific antibody;
Autoantibody(ies); Immunoglobulin
entries.
placental transport of, 367

Antibody-dependent cellular cytotoxicity
assay, in erythroblastosis fetalis
screening, 395
Anticardiolipin antibodies, 371
Anticoagulant proteins, congenital
deficiencies of, 1332–1333
Anticoagulants
fetal effects of, 188t
for thrombosis, 1333–1335, 1334t, 1335b,
1336b, 1337b
in extracorporeal membrane oxygenation,
1169
in hemostasis, 1321
Anticonvulsants
congenital anomalies associated with,
564
congenital malformations associated with,
186t
fetal effects of, 187t
maternal, hypocalcemia due to, 1510
neutropenia due to, 1313b
thyroid hormone effects of, 1528
Antidepressants
in breast milk, 200
neutropenia due to, 1313b
tricyclic, fetal effects of, 187t
Antidiabetic agents, placental transport of,
transient neonatal hypoglycemia due to,
1472
Antidiuretic hormone
inhibited release of, Henry-Gauer reflex
in, 345
role of, in water balance, 697
Antiepileptics
aggressive use of, 976
discontinuation of, 975
efficacy of, 974–975
for seizures, 974
Antiestrogens, fetal effects of, 188t
Antifungals
for candidiasis, 831–832, 832t, 1700
for coccidioidomycosis, 833
for cryptococcosis, 834
Antigen(s). See also specific antigen.
atypical, in erythroblastosis fetalis,
404–405
primary and secondary antibody response
to, 783, 783t
Antigen detection assays, in sepsis
diagnosis, 796
Antigen-presenting cells
in inflammatory response, 776
neonatal, 782
Antihistamines
fetal effects of, 187t
neutropenia due to, 1313b
Antihypertensives
fetal effects of, 188t
for chronic hypertension, 317t, 317–318
for preeclampsia-eclampsia, 314, 314t
indications for and contraindications to,
1245
intravenous, 1672t, 1673
oral, 1673–1674, 1673t
Antimalarials, neutropenia due to, 1313b
Antimetabolites, fetal effects of, 187t
Antinauseants, fetal effects of, 187t
Antineoplastics
congenital malformations associated with,
186t
fetal effects of, 187t
Antinuclear antibodies, maternal, fetal-
neonatal consequences of, 370–371,
371b

Antioxidants
in bronchopulmonary dysplasia
prevention, 1168
nitric oxide as, 1179
Antiparasitic agents, fetal effects of, 187t
Antiphospholipid antibodies, maternal, fetal-
neonatal consequences of, 371–372
Antiphospholipid antibody syndrome,
371–372
treatment of, 372
Antipyretic agents, fetal effects of, 187t
Antiretroviral therapy
highly active, for prevention of HIV
transmission, 857
in HIV prophylaxis, in developed
countries, 857–859
in neonates, 861
Antithrombin III, congenital deficiency of,
1332, 1333
Antithyroid agents
fetal effects of, 188t
for thyrotoxicosis, 1549
maternal ingestion of, congenital
hypothyroidism due to, 1537
neutropenia due to, 1313b
placental transfer of, 1532
α-Antitrypsin deficiency, liver disease in,
1459, 1622–1623
Antitubercular agents, fetal effects of, 187t
Antitussives, fetal effects of, 189t
Antivirals
for congenital cytomegalovirus infection,
847
for enteroviral infection, 863
for herpes simplex virus infection, 843,
1698
for varicella-zoster virus infections, 849
ophthalmic, for herpes simplex virus
infection, 843
Anuria, perinatal asphyxia and, 703
Anus
congenital anomalies of, 574
development of, 1362–1363
imperforate, 1399–1403
associated defects in, 574, 1400
diagnosis of, 1400
surgical treatment of
algorithm for, 1401f
colostomy in, 1400, 1402
definitive repair in, 1402
follow-up of, 1403
postoperative care of, 1402–1403
Aorta
coarctation of, 1234–1235
anatomy and pathophysiology of, 1234
balloon angioplasty for, 1235, 1273
clinical presentation of, 1234, 1234t
defects associated with, 1234
fetal assessment for, 1209
in transposition of great arteries, 1223
laboratory evaluation of, 1234–1235,
1235f
left heart defects in, 1234, 1237
management of, 1235
prognosis in, 1235
recurrent, balloon angioplasty for, 1274
in double-outlet right ventricle, 1231–1232
Aortic arch
double, variants of, 1250
interruption of, 1234–1235
anatomy and pathophysiology of, 1234
clinical presentation of, 1234, 1234t
defects associated with, 1234
in transposition of great arteries, 1223

Aortic arch—cont'd
    in truncus arteriosus, 1230
        laboratory evaluation of, 1234–1235,
            1235f
        management of, 1235
        prognosis in, 1235
    right
        in tetralogy of Fallot, 1225
        in truncus arteriosus, 1230
Aortic root
    dilation of, in aortic stenosis, 1232
    dimensions of, in Marfan syndrome, 1251
Aortic valve
    abnormalities of, in left heart defects, 1237
    regurgitation of, 1232
    stenosis of, 1232–1233
        balloon valvuloplasty for, 1273
Aortopulmonary window, 1241–1242
Apert syndrome (acrocephalosyndactyly,
        type 1), 1011–1012, 1011f
    anesthetic implications of, 632t
    incidence of, paternal age and, 257
    ocular manifestation of, 1728
Apgar score
    history of, 7
    in hypoxic-ischemic encephalopathy,
        955–956
    in neonatal resuscitation, 488, 489t
    low, asphyxia and, 967–968
    of preterm infant, 1062
Aplasia cutis congenita, 1713
Apnea
    caffeine for reducing risk of, 642
    due to prostaglandin E₁ therapy, 1266
    in asphyxia, 487
    in respiratory distress syndrome, 1100
    of prematurity, 1135–1141
        airway obstruction in, 1137, 1137f
        causes of, 1138–1141, 1138f
        central, 1137
        control of breathing and, 1135–1137,
            1136f
        during sleep, 1137–1138
        hypoxemia of assisted ventilation and,
            1139
        idiopathic, management of, 1139–1140
        mixed, 1137, 1138f
        respiratory patterns and, 1137–1138,
            1137f, 1138f
    postoperative, 628, 641–642
    sudden infant death associated with,
        1140–1141, 1140f
Apocrine glands, 1688
Apoptosis
    in brain development, 895–896, 896f
    in heart development, 1201–1202
    in hypoxic-ischemic encephalopathy, 943
Appearance, neonatal, physical examination
    of, 515
Appendectomy, in volvulus repair, 1395
Appropriate for gestational age. See also
        Gestational age.
    transepidermal water loss in, during first 4
        postnatal weeks, 588
    vs. small for gestational age, 289
Apt test, for neonatal gastrointestinal
    bleeding, 1325
Aqueduct of Sylvius, stenosis of
    acquired, 999
    fetal surgery for, 234t
    hydrocephalus and, 999, 999f
Arachidonic acid
    in breast milk, 666
    visual acuity related to, 666–667

Arachnodactyly, 578
Arachnoid cysts, macrocephaly due to, 1003,
    1004f
Argininemia, 1605t
Argininosuccinic acidemia, 1605t
Arhinencephalia, 902
Arias disease, unconjugated
    hyperbilirubinemia due to, 1431–1432
Arnold-Chiari malformation. See Chiari
    malformation.
Arrhythmias. See also specific arrhythmia,
        e.g., Tachycardia.
    fetal, 221–224
        assessment of, 1209, 1209f
        congestive heart failure related to, 1210
        drug treatment of, 222b, 223t, 223–224
            coadministered medications in, 224,
                224t
            guide to, 223b
        sustained, 222
        treatment of, 1210
    neonatal, 1252–1265
        ambulatory monitoring and telemetry
            in, 1252
        blood pressure measurement of in,
            1252–1253
        diagnosis of, 1252–1253
        electrocardiography of, 1252
        electrophysiologic testing in, 1252
        heart rate measurement in, 1252
Arsenic, maternal exposure to, pregnancy
    outcome in, 260t
Arterial-alveolar oxygen tension ratio, 1090
Arterial carbon dioxide tension. See Carbon
    dioxide tension (PCO₂).
Arterial ischemic stroke, 934–937,
    1331–1332. See also Stroke.
    diagnosis of, 935–936, 936f
    incidence of, 935
    prognosis of, 937
    risk factors for, 936–937
    treatment of, 1332
Arterial oxygen saturation, pulse oximetry
    and, 618, 618f
Arterial oxygen tension. See Oxygen tension
    (PO₂).
Arterial pressure monitoring, during
    anesthesia, 636
Arterial switch operation, 1269t
    for double-outlet right ventricle, 1232
    for single ventricle, 1231
    for transposition of great arteries, 1224
Arteriovenous fistula, pulmonary, 1135
Arteriovenous malformations, 1244
Artery. See named artery.
Arthritis, septic, 813–815, 1765–1766
    clinical manifestations of, 814
    diagnosis of, 814, 815f, 1765
    etiology of, 814, 1765
    imaging of, 1766
    incidence of, 813
    pathogenesis of, 814
    pathology of, 814, 1765
    prognosis in, 815
    treatment of, 814–815, 1766
Arthrogryposis multiplex congenita, 979,
    1783–1784
    anesthetic implications of, 632t
    causes of, 578
    clinical features of, 1783, 1783f
Ascites
    in hydrops fetalis, 391, 392, 392f
        ultrasonography of, 392f, 397, 398f
    meconium, 1396

Ascorbic acid. See Vitamin C.
Aseptic technique, for delivery, in
    developing countries, 95, 98f
Asia. See also Developing countries.
    neonatal mortality in, 88–89, 90f
Asians
    glucose-6-phosphatase dehydrogenase
        deficiency in, 1429
    mongolian blue spots in, 565, 566t, 1689b,
        1691
    physiologic jaundice in, 1427–1428
    transient cutaneous lesions in, 1689b
Aspartate aminotransferase, measurement of,
    1804t
Aspergillus infections, 836
Asphyxia. See also Hypoxic-ischemic insults.
    and emergence of hypoxic-ischemic
        encephalopathy. See also Hypoxic-
        ischemic encephalopathy.
    factors predicting, 967
    antepartum, 967
    definition of, 172, 938
    hypocalcemia in, 1510
    in intrauterine growth restriction, 298–299
    intrapartum, cerebral palsy due to, 179,
        179b
    low Apgar scores and, 967–968
    necrotizing enterocolitis and, 1407
    neonatal
        depression and, 486, 486b
        sensorineural hearing loss due to, 1048
    perinatal
        fluid and electrolyte therapy for,
            702–703
        neonatal mortality rate related to, 93,
            93f
        prevention of, 949–950
        resuscitation for, 950–951, 950b
        systemic management of, 951–952
    response to, 486–487, 487f, 488b
    resuscitation for. See Resuscitation,
        neonatal.
    seizures during, 966–968
    sensorineural hearing loss due to, 1048
    small for gestational age and, 296t
    transient hypoglycemia in, 1479
Asphyxiating thoracic dystrophy, 1145
Aspiration
    for joint decompression, in septic arthritis,
        1766
    of amniotic fluid, 1125
    of gastric contents
        in swallowing disorders, 1125
        NPO guidelines for prevention of,
            before anesthesia, 631, 631t
    of meconium. See Meconium entries.
    of ovarian cyst, 234t
Aspiration biopsy
    in osteomyelitis, 1763
        bone scanning after, 1764
    of synovial fluid, for septic arthritis, 1765
Asplenia syndrome
    heart defects associated with, 1243
    in single ventricle, 1231
    in total anomalous pulmonary venous
        connection, 1229
ASPM gene, in microcephaly vera, 905
Assessment of Preterm Infants' Behavior
    (APIB) scores, 1064–1065
Assisted ventilation, 1108–1122. See also
        Mechanical ventilation.
    after neonatal resuscitation, 505–506
    air embolism due to, 1131
    breathing control in, 1111

Assisted ventilation—cont'd
  carbon dioxide exchange in, 1109–1110,
    1110f
  complications of, in respiratory distress
    syndrome, 1118–1122, 1118b
  during anesthesia, 636–637
  endotracheal intubation for. See
    Endotracheal intubation.
  endotracheal tube complications in,
    1118–1119, 1119f
  extracorporeal membrane oxygenation
    and, 1172
  for meconium aspiration syndrome,
    1124–1125
  gas exchange during, 1109–1111
  history of, 12–13, 13f, 14t
  in congenital heart disease, 1265–1266
  in gastroschisis, 1383
  indications for, 1114
  infection related to, 1119
  intraventricular hemorrhage due to, 1121
  long-term outcome of, 1122
  lung injury due to
    bronchopulmonary dysplasia related to,
      1159–1163, 1167–1168
    prevention of, 1113, 1120–1121, 1120b,
      1120t
  oxygen exchange in, 1110–1111, 1110f
  oxygen therapy in, 1112
  patent ductus arteriosus and, 1121–1122
  pulmonary mechanics in, 1108–1109,
    1109f
Association, definition of, 561
Astrocytes, proliferation and differentiation
  of, 896–898, 897f
Atelectasis
  after extubation, 1117, 1119
  in respiratory distress syndrome, 1099,
    1099f
  segmental or lobar, vs. meconium
    aspiration, 808
Atenolol, for neonatal tachycardia, 1260t,
  1262b
Atherosclerosis, accelerated, after heart
  transplantation, 1270
Atlas
  development of, 1756
  occipitalization of, vs. sternocleidomastoid
    muscle injury, 547
Atomic weight, of common elements, 1817t
Atopic dermatitis, 1711
Atosiban, for preterm labor prevention, 353
Atracurium, in neonatal anesthesia, 640
Atresia. See at anatomic site.
Atrial ectopic tachycardia, 1253t, 1256
  treatment of, 1264
Atrial electrography, 1252
Atrial fibrillation, 1253t
Atrial flutter, 1253t, 1256
  treatment of, 1263
Atrial premature contractions
  fetal assessment for, 1209
  in sinus bradycardia, 1259
  treatment of, 1265
Atrial regurgitation, in endocardial cushion
  defects, 1239
Atrial septal defect, 1239
  associated with transposition of great
    arteries, 1223
  complete, in endocardial cushion defects,
    1239
  creation of. See Atrial septostomy.
  in hypoplastic left heart syndrome, 1236
  in left heart defects, 1237

Atrial septal defect—cont'd
  in total anomalous pulmonary venous
    connection, 1229
  in tricuspid atresia, 1226
  isolated, 1239
Atrial septal fusion, 1198
Atrial septostomy, 1271–1272
  balloon, 1271, 1271f
    in transposition of great arteries, 1223
  balloon angioplasty in, 1272
  blade, 1271–1272
  indications for, 1271
Atrioventricular block
  atrial flutter and, 1256
  complete, 1259
    treatment of, 1264
  second-degree, 1258–1259
Atrioventricular node reentrant tachycardia,
  1255–1256
  electrocardiographic findings in, 1253t
  reciprocating, 1254
  treatment of, 1263
Atrioventricular valves, regurgitation of, in
  congestive heart failure, 1209–1210
Atrium
  common, in endocardial cushion defects,
    1239
  tumors in, 1250
Atropine, for neonatal bradycardia, 1264
Attention deficit hyperactivity disorder
  alcohol exposure and, 737
  tobacco exposure and, 741
Audiometric testing, conventional,
  1046–1047
Auditory brainstem responses, in evaluation
  of hearing, 1046
Auditory canal, external
  atresia of, 1047
  in mechanism of hearing, 1045
Auditory nerve, assessment of, 525
Auscultation
  in blood pressure monitoring, 615
  intermittent, in fetal heart rate monitoring,
    173
Australian Collaborative Trial of Magnesium
  Sulphate (ACTOMgSO$_4$), 350
Autoantibody(ies). See also Antibody(ies).
  in preeclampsia, 309
  thyroid, measurement of, 1529–1530
Autoimmune disease. See also specific
  disease.
  fetal effects of, 367–373
Autoimmune enteropathy, 1372
Autoimmune lymphoproliferative syndrome,
  thrombocytopenia in, 1340
Autoimmune neutropenia, 1312
Automatic tachycardia, 1253, 1253t
Autonomic nervous system
  gastric innervation by, 1359
  in preterm infant, 1055, 1055t
Autonomy
  definition of, 35
  maternal, fetal rights and, 38–39
Autosomal dominant inheritance, of genetic
  disorders, 121f, 121–122
Autosomal recessive inheritance, of genetic
  disorders, 122f, 122–123
Autosomal recessive lissencephaly, with
  cerebellar hypoplasia, 908
Autosomal recessive polycystic kidney
  disease. See Polycystic kidney disease.
Autosomes, 113
Average length of stay, as proxy for cost, 73
Axis, development of, 1756

Axon(s)
  damage to, in periventricular
    leukomalacia, 912
  growth of, 891–893, 893f, 894f
  mechanisms in, 891
Azithromycin
  for chlamydial infections, 447
  for conjunctivitis, 811
  for toxoplasmosis, 449
  in breast milk, 199
Azotemia, prerenal, 1668, 1668t
AZT. See Zidovudine.
Aztreonam, for sepsis, 801t

B

B cell(s)
  activation of, 785
  antibody production and, 787, 788t
  CD molecules on, 783, 783t
  clonal anergy of, 784
  development of, 783–785, 784f, 785f
  function of, 777, 783
    tests for evaluation of, 791b
  immunoglobulin synthesis and secretion
    by, 786–787, 786f
  in breast milk, 790
  memory, 783
  phenotypic appearance of, 783
B cell receptors, 777
B-ligandin, hepatic uptake of bilirubin with,
  1421
Baby Doe case, 57–58, 61
Baby Jane Doe case, 58
Baby K case, 58–59
Bacille Calmette-Guérin vaccine, for
  tuberculosis, 828
Bacitracin, for conjunctivitis, 811
Back, examination of, 516
Bacterial endocarditis, prevention of, 1268
Bacterial flora, of gastrointestinal tract
  in neonatal drug absorption, 192–193
  necrotizing enterocolitis and, 1407
Bacterial infection(s). See also Sepsis;
    specific infection.
  anaerobic, 819
  cutaneous, 1697–1698, 1698f
  hyperbilirubinemia due to, 1430
  in osteomyelitis, 1762–1763
  in septic arthritis, 1765
  of catheters, in parenteral nutrition,
    689–690
  perinatal, 442–449
  postnatal, 791–829
  prevention of, in neonatal intensive care
    unit, 828–829
  with cephalhematoma, 532f, 532–533
Bacterial vaginosis. See Vaginosis, bacterial.
Bacteriuria, in pregnancy, 429, 431
Bag and mask ventilation, in neonatal
  resuscitation
  anesthetic rebreathing bags in, 495
  in developing countries, 99, 104, 105t
  self-inflating bags in, 494–495
Ballard examination, for gestational age
  assessment, 522, 523f
Balloon angioplasty
  for coarctation of aorta, 1235, 1273–1274
  for dilation of atrial septal puncture, 1272
Balloon atrial septostomy
  in transposition of great arteries, 1223
  technique of, 1271, 1271f

Balloon valvuloplasty
  for aortic stenosis, 1233, 1273
  for mitral stenosis, 1273
  for pulmonary atresia, 1227, 1273
  for pulmonary stenosis, 1238, 1272, 1272f
  for pulmonary valve dilation, in complex congenital heart disease, 1272–1273
Banana sign, in ventriculomegaly, 153, 153f
Bannayan-Riley-Ruvalcaba syndrome, 1709
Barbiturates
  during labor, 471
  fetal effects of, 187t
  for spasms, in tetanus neonatorum, 825
  in breast milk, 199
Barium enema, for midgut volvulus, 1394
Barlow test, for developmental dysplasia of hip, 516, 1774, 1774f
Barotrauma, bronchopulmonary dysplasia related to, 1120
Barr body, 124
Barrier nursing technique, for infection prevention, in NICU, 828–829
Barth syndrome, 1644, 1619
  hematologic anomalies in, 1620
Bartter syndrome, 710, 1680
  genetic basis of, 1662, 1662t
Basal layer, epidermal, 1686, 1686f
Basal metabolic rate, 662
Bathing of infants
  for infection prevention, 829
  postponement of, for hypothermia prevention, 95, 99f
Bayley Scales of Infant Development
  in cocaine abuse, 746
  in high-risk neonate, 1040
  in opioid abuse, 752
  in tobacco abuse, 740
  Mental Development Index of, 737, 752
  Psychomotor Development Index of, 752
Beckwith-Wiederman syndrome
  anesthetic implications of, 632t
  chromosome anomalies in, 287
  genomic imprinting and, 126
  in omphalocele, 1382
  macrencephaly associated with, 996
  major findings in, 1482b
  persistent hypoglycemia in, 1482–1483
  port-wine stain in, 1709
  renal tumors associated with, 1681
Bed
  heated, heat exchange on, 588
  radiantly heated
    heat exchange between skin and environment on, 592
    overhead (open), 596
Bed rest, for preterm labor prevention, 345
Beer's law, 618
Behavior. See also Neurobehavioral and developmental effects.
  alcohol exposure effects on, 737–738
  nonepileptic, in seizures, 962f, 960–963
  preterm infant
    assessment of, 1061–1063
      overview of, 1063–1064
    observation of, 1054–1055
  tobacco exposure effects on, 741
Behavior observation sheet, 1056f
Behavioral factors, in preterm delivery, 334–335
Behavioral language, of preterm infant, 1055t, 1055–1058, 1056f, 1058f
  in neonatal intensive care unit, 1056f, 1056–1057

Behavioral tests, in evaluation of hearing, 1046
Beneficence, definition of, 35–36
Benign external communicating hydrocephalus of infancy, 1002–1003
Benign familial seizures, genetic defects in, 973
Benign infantile mitochondrial myopathy, 1644
Benign sleep myoclonus of newborn, 960
Benzo[a]pyrene, maternal exposure to, pregnancy outcome in, 260t
Benzodiazepines
  during labor, 471
  fetal effects of, 187t
  for seizures, 974
    following hypoxic-ischemic insult, 953
  in neonatal anesthesia, 639
Benzothiadiazides
  fetal effects of, 188t
  placental transport of, transient neonatal hypoglycemia due to, 1472–1473
Beractant, dosages of, 1792
Bergmeister papilla, 1744
Bernard-Soulier syndrome, 1341–1342
Bernoulli principle, in Doppler echocardiography, 1219
Best interests of newborn, definition of, 36
Beta-blockers
  for chronic hypertension, 317–318
  for neonatal tachycardia, 1262b, 1264
  for ventricular dysfunction, 1267
Betamethasone
  for fetal lung maturation, 213
  for periventricular-intraventricular hemorrhage, 931
  for preterm labor prevention, 355, 356
Betke-Kleihauer test, for fetal red blood cells, in vaginal blood, 1296
Bicarbonate
  for metabolic acidosis, 707
  hypocalcemia due to, 1512
  in acid-base balance, 704, 705, 705f
  in neonatal resuscitation, 503t, 505
  in respiratory distress syndrome, 1106
Bickers-Adams syndrome (X-linked hydrocephalus), 999
Bile
  bilirubin excretion into, 1422–1423, 1423f
  secretion of
    ductal phase in, 1450–1451, 1452f
    hepatocellular phase in, 1450
  injury to, 1453
Bile acid biosynthesis, 1621
  defects in, hepatic dysfunction and, 1621–1622
Bile acid malabsorption, primary, 1368
Bile canaliculus, 1450, 1451f
Bile ducts
  radionuclide imaging of, 1455
  ultrasonography of, 158–159
Bile plug syndrome, 1460
Biliary atresia
  extrahepatic
    causes of, 1453
    classification of, 1458
    clinical manifestations of, 1454–1455
    conjugated hyperbilirubinemia due to, 1452–1458
    definition of, 1452–1453
    fibrous remnant of, 1453, 1454f
    hepatocytes in, 1457, 1457f
    polysplenia-heterotaxia syndrome associated with, 1454

Biliary atresia—cont'd
    treatment of, 1458
    vs. idiopathic neonatal hepatitis, 1453
  radionuclide imaging of, 723
  ultrasonography of, 722–723, 723f
Biliary system
  cysts of, 1460
  development of, 1360–1362
  extrahepatic, masses of, 1460
Bilious vomiting, 719. See also Vomiting.
  in midgut malrotation, 1394
Bilirubin
  amniotic fluid optical density related to, 395
  biochemistry of, 1419–1420, 1420f
  conjugated, 1420–1421
  conjugation of, 1421–1422, 1423f
  enterohepatic absorption of, 1423–1424, 1424f
  excretion of, 1422–1423, 1423f
  fetal, 1425
  forms of, 1420
  from heme, 1419–1420, 1420f
  hepatic uptake of, 1421
  isomerization pathways for, during phototherapy, 1440–1442, 1442f
  metabolism of, 1419–1424
  neurotoxicity of, 1436
  production of, 1420, 1421f
    increased, blood sequestration in, 1430
  synthesis of, 1420, 1421f
  total serum, measurements of, 1436–1438, 1438b, 1439f
  transport of, 1420, 1421f
    in plasma, 1420–1421, 1422f
  unconjugated, 1420
    in neonates, 1424
    solubility of, 1435
Bilirubin-albumin ratio, 1440, 1440t
Bilirubin encephalopathy, transient, 1434
Bilirubinemia. See also Hyperbilirubinemia.
  physiologic, vs. hyperbilirubinemia, 1424
Bilirubinometer, use of, in developing countries, 103
Bilirubinometry, transcutaneous, 1438–1439
Biliverdin, 1419, 1420f
Biochemical tests, for inborn errors of metabolism, 1629–1635, 1629t
  definitive diagnosis of, 1634
  specialized, 1631–1635, 1631t
Biomedical engineering aspects, of neonatal monitoring, 609–623. See also Neonatal monitoring; specific monitoring modality.
Biophysical profile
  antenatal evaluation with, 169, 169f
  in intrauterine growth restriction, 295, 295t
  in post-term neonate, 385t
  modified, 170
Biopsy
  aspiration
    in osteomyelitis, 1763
      bone scanning after, 1764
    of synovial fluid, in septic arthritis, 1765
  blastomere, in assisted reproduction, 139
  endomyocardial, cardiac catheterization in, 1275
  liver, for idiopathic neonatal hepatitis, 1456, 1456f
  myocardial, for cardiomyopathy, 1248
Biotin
  in breast milk, 672t
  in infant formula, 674t
  requirements for, 668t

Biotinidase deficiency, 1608t, 1611
  screening for, 1611
Biparietal diameter
  in intrauterine growth restriction, 292,
    292f, 293f
  perinatal ultrasonography of, 146, 146f
Birth
  body cooling after, prevention of, 585
  glucose metabolism after, 1469–1471, 1469f
  heat exchange between skin and
    environment after
    during first day, 588, 590f
    during first hours, 588, 589f
    during first weeks, 589–590, 591f
Birth attendant, traditional, in developing
  countries, 101–103, 103t
Birth certificates, in neonatal care evaluation
  database, 69
Birth defects. See Congenital anomalies.
Birth injuries, 529–557
  musculoskeletal, 1758–1762
  ocular, 1726–1727
  of chest, 541–547
  of head, 531–541
  of neck, 541–547
  of shoulder girdle, 541–547
  of soft tissues, 529–531
  of spine and spinal cord, 547–550,
    1759–1761
  traumatic, macrosomia and, 327
Birthweight
  blood pressure and, 1795f
  cerebrospinal fluid values and, 1808t
  determination of, during physical
    examination, 514
  discordance in
    levels of, 379–380
    multiple gestations and, 379
  extremely low. See Extremely low
    birthweight.
  health outcome by, at 8 years, 1036t
  hyperbilirubinemia management based
    on, guidelines for, 1450t
  low. See Low birthweight.
  male sex and, 287
  mean, 272t
  neonatal anesthesia and, 631
  neonatal mortality rates associated with,
    20–22, 21f, 22f
  neurodevelopmental outcome specific to,
    1036t
  placental insufficiency affecting, 285
  placental weight and, 284, 285f
  variability of, fetal genotype in, 287
  very low. See Very low birthweight.
Bishydroxycoumarin, in breast milk, 199
Bisphosphonate therapy, for hypercalcemia,
  1518
Bladder
  cystitis of, in pregnancy, 429–430
  development of, 1662–1663, 1663f
  enlarged, examination of, 519
  neurogenic, in spinal cord injury,
    treatment of, 549
Blade atrial septostomy, 1271–1272
Blalock-Hanlon procedure, 1269t
Blalock-Taussig shunt, 1225, 1269t
Blastocele, in embryonic development, 207
Blastomere, biopsy of, in assisted
  reproduction, 139
Blastomyces dermatitidis infection, 835
Bleeding. See Hemorrhage.
Bleeding time, prolonged, in
  thrombocytopenia, 1338

Bleeding time tests, for platelet-endothelium
  interactions, 1319
Blennorrhea, neonatal, 810
Blepharophimosis, congenital, 1730
Blindness
  cortical, 1722
  in preeclampsia-eclampsia, 312
  vs. delayed visual response, 1726
Blistering diseases, hereditary, 1700–1703
Blood
  glucose concentration in, 1470
    abnormal, 1471
  sequestration of, increased bilirubin
    production and, 1430
  whole, 1802t
Blood-brain barrier
  bilirubin passage across, 1435–1436
  fetal, transfer of chemicals across, 262,
    262f
Blood cells, packed, transfusion of, dosages
  in, 1790
Blood components
  choice of, in exchange transfusion, 1351,
    1351t, 1352b
  irradiated, indications for administration
    of, 1345b
Blood culture
  for pneumonia, 808
  for sepsis, 795
  in candidiasis, 831
  in osteomyelitis and septic arthritis, 814
Blood donation, parental, for transfusion,
  1347
Blood flow. See Circulation.
Blood gases, 1088–1091
  continuous monitoring of, 621f, 621–623,
    622f
    Neotrend system in, 621f, 621–622
    VIA-LVM system in, 622f, 622–623
  hyperoxia-hyperventilation test in,
    1090–1091
  in bronchopulmonary dysplasia, 1165
  in extracorporeal membrane oxygenation,
    1169–1170
  in inborn errors of metabolism, 1630t,
    1629–1630
  in persistent pulmonary hypertension,
    1246
  in pulmonary function assessment,
    1088–1091
  in respiratory distress syndrome,
    1101–1103
  in shunting evaluation, 1091
  mechanical ventilation effect on,
    1114–1117
    ventilator settings in, 1116, 1116t
  partial pressure of arterial carbon dioxide
    in, 1090, 1091f
  partial pressure of arterial oxygen in,
    1089–1090, 1089f
Blood loss, anemia due to, 1295–1297
Blood pressure
  and birthweight, 1795f
  diastolic, 1796f
  hemodynamics of, 1211
  high. See Hypertension.
  measurement of
    in arrhythmia, 1252–1253
    in congenital heart disease, 1216
    in neonatal intensive care units, 1244
    in renal disease, 1665
  neonatal anesthesia and, 628–629
  ranges of, in preterm infants, 1796t
  systolic, 1213, 1796f

Blood pressure monitoring, 614–616
  auscultatory method of, 615
  cuff in, 615
  direct, 614–615
  during anesthesia, 636, 636t
  home, in chronic hypertension, 317
  in developing countries, 103
  indirect, 615f, 615–616
  oscillometric method of, 615, 615f
  transducer-catheter system in, 614–615
Blood products, transfusion of, 1348–1352
Blood smears, peripheral, morphologic
  findings on, 1295t
Blood tests, for inborn errors of metabolism,
  1630t, 1631t, 1629–1630
Blood transfusion. See Transfusion.
Blood uric acid test, for inborn errors of
  metabolism, 1630
Blood vessels
  in hemostasis, 1318
  size of, 1212
Blue diaper syndrome, hypercalcemia due
  to, 1517
Blue nevus, 1705
Blue-rubber bleb nevus syndrome,
  1708–1709
"Blueberry muffin" spots, in rubella virus
  infection, 871
Body composition
  by gestational age, 661, 662t
  fetal growth and, 271–273, 272t,
    272f–274f, 273t, 274t
  maternal, in drug distribution, 207t
Body cooling, after birth, prevention of, 585.
  See also Heat exchange.
Body fluids and electrolytes. See
  Electrolyte(s); Fluid(s).
Body length, neonatal, measurement of,
  514–515
Body mass index
  pregnancy weight gain and, 323
  pregravid, 280–281
    calculation of, 280
Body surface, heat exchange between
  environment and, 586. See also Heat
  exchange.
Body temperature. See Temperature.
Bohn nodules, 1691
Bonding, parental-infant. See Parent-infant
  attachment.
Bone. See also named bone, e.g., Femur.
  aspiration biopsy of, in osteomyelitis,
    1763
  development of, 1504–1508
  growth of, factors affecting, 1505
  infections of, 1762–1767. See also
    Osteomyelitis.
  maturation of, retardation of, in
    congenital hypothyroidism, 1542
  metabolic disease of. See Osteopenia of
    prematurity.
  mineralization of
    calcium absorption in, 1494
    evaluation of, 1505–1506, 1506f,
      1507f
    factors affecting, 1505
  ontogenesis of, 1504–1505
  physiologic changes in, in postnatal
    period, 1507–1508, 1508f
  sequestrum of, in osteomyelitis, 1763
Bone conduction tests, in evaluation of
  hearing, 1046
Bone marrow, blood cell production in,
  1288

Bone mineral content
  decreased density of, in small for gestational age infant, 296t, 297
  reference values for, 1506f, 1507f
Bone mineral density, decreased, in bronchopulmonary dysplasia, 1165
Bone scanning, for osteomyelitis, 1764
Bordetella pertussis, in pneumonia, 808–809
Botulism, 819–821
  infantile, 982
Bourneville syndrome. See Tuberous sclerosis.
Bowel. See also specific part, e.g., Colon.
  echogenic, 156–157
  malrotation of, 1393–1395
    in congenital diaphragmatic hernia, 1379
    radiography of, 1394, 1394f
    treatment of, 1394–1395
    ultrasonography of, 1394
  normal, ultrasonography of, 156f, 156–157, 157f
  rotation and fixation of, 1360–1361, 1360f, 1393
Bowleg, physiologic, 1772
Brachial palsy, 542–545, 1759–1760
  causes of, 1759
  clinical manifestations of, 543
  differential diagnosis of, 543
  etiology of, 542–543
  "no shoulder," 543
  prognosis in, 544–545, 1759–1760
  treatment of, 543–544, 544f, 1760
  types of, 542
Brachial plexus, lesions of, examination of, 518
Brachycephaly, 1008–1009
  in congenital anomalies, 568, 569f
Brachydactyly, 576f, 578
Bradley technique, in natural childbirth, 468
Bradycardia
  fetal, 222
    assessment of, 1209
    congestive heart failure related to, 1210
  in apnea, 1137, 1137f
  neonatal
    mechanisms of, 1258–1259
    pacemaker implantation for, 1204
    treatment of, 1264–1265
  sinus, 1258
Brain. See also Cerebral entries; specific part.
  bilirubin entry into, 1435–1436
  development of
    abnormal, 900–909. See also specific disorder.
    alcohol effects on, 736–737
    chronology of events in, 883t
    environmental influences on, 884b, 1052f, 1052–1054, 1053f
    long-chain polyunsaturated fatty acids in, 666
    long-term, impairment of, 922–924, 922b, 924f
    marijuana effects on, 743
    mechanisms of, 883–900
    neural induction and neurulation in, 883–885, 885f
    neuronal migration in, 886–889, 887f–891f
    neuronal proliferation in, 885–886, 886f
  expansion of, skull growth determination by, 905
  fetal, maturation of, imaging of, 889, 890f–891f

Brain—cont'd
  growth, impairment of, 922–924, 922b, 924f
  heme oxygenase in, 1436
  hypoxic-ischemic damage to, 942–944. See also Hypoxic-ischemic encephalopathy.
  immature, schematic of, 889f
  large. See Macrencephaly.
  regional susceptibility of, to hypoxic-ischemic insults, 939–940
    gestational age and, 939
  small. See Micrencephaly.
  ultrasonography of, 727–729
    for congenital anomalies, 579
  vascular development in, 900
  white matter of. See White matter.
Brain abscess, macrocephaly due to, 1005
Brain death, organ donation and, 41
Brain tumor, macrocephaly due to, 1004, 1005f
Brain warts (neuronal heterotopias), 992
Brainstem, release phenomena of, seizures associated with, 964–965
Brainstem auditory evoked potentials, in hypoxic-ischemic encephalopathy, 947, 947f
Brainstem auditory evoked response, in bilirubin encephalopathy, 1434
Brazelton Neonatal Behavioral Assessment Scale, 737, 746, 1062–1063
Breach, in malpractice litigation, 52–53
Breast(s), neonatal
  abscess (mastitis) of, 818
  enlargement of, 517
Breast feeding. See also Breast milk.
  amniotic fluid odor and neonatal initiation of, 649
  Baby-Friendly Hospital Initiative for, 100, 100b, 650
  by preterm infant
    early experience with, 678
    positioning and support for, 677
  contraindications to, in HIV infection, 434
  gestational diabetes mellitus and, 324–325
  in developing countries, 100, 100b
  in methadone-maintained mothers, 751
  in parent-infant attachment, 648–651
  jaundice associated with, 1432–1433
  maternal drug therapy and, 202
  necrotizing enterocolitis and, 1406–1407
  neuraxial blockade effects on, 476–477
  progression to, from enteral nutrition, 676–678
  supplementation of
    for preterm infants, 675
    for term infants, 674–675
Breast milk. See also Formula.
  analgesics in, 199
  antibiotics in, 199
  anticoagulants in, 199
  anti-inflammatory agents in, 199
  calcium in, 1496
    absorption and retention of, 1495t
    fortifiers of, 1494
  cardiovascular drugs in, 199
  carnitine in, 667
  central nervous system drugs in, 199–200
  cholesterol in, 667
  cimetidine in, 200
  cocaine exposure via, 744, 747
  congenital lactase deficiency and, 1366
  diagnostic isotopes in, 200
  drugs in, 199–202

Breast milk—cont'd
  endocrine system drugs in, 200
  environmental pollutants in, 201–202
  ergot extracts in, 200
  exogenous compounds passed to, 197–198, 198f
    infant delivery of, 198
    infant disposition to, 198–199
  fat in, 665–666
  fatty acids in, 666
  fortifiers for, 670, 671t–672t
  frozen, 677–678
  hepatitis B transmission via, 865
  HIV transmission via, 856–857
  immunologic properties of, 788–790, 789t
  in enteral nutrition, 670, 671t–672t, 676
    adverse effects of continuous drip feeding in, 676
    for extremely low birthweight, 678–679
    necrotizing enterocolitis and, 1406–1407, 1406t
  iron in, bioavailability of, 1306
  lactobezoars due to, 1387
  lactose in, 664
  lipases in, 665
  magnesium in, 1500
    absorption and retention of, 1495t
  mechanical pumping of, 677
  narcotics in, 200–201, 750–751
  necrotizing enterocolitis and, 1406–1407, 1406t, 1409
  nontherapeutic agents in, 201
  nutrient composition of, 670, 671t–672t
  phosphorus in, 1498
    absorption and retention of, 1495t
  storage of, 677–678
  theophylline in, 200
  thyroxine in, 1533
  triiodothyronine in, 1533
Breast milk jaundice, 1433–1434
Breath testing, hydrogen. See Hydrogen breath testing.
Breathing. See also Respiration.
  control of
    chemoreceptors in, 1111, 1135–1136
    in preterm infants, 1135–1137, 1136f
    mechanoreceptors in, 1111, 1136
  during breast feeding, by preterm infant, 677
  examination of, 515
  periodic
    in preterm infants, 1137
    neonatal anesthesia and, 628
  spontaneous
    after resuscitation with oxygen, 500, 500f
    characteristics of, 485
    first breath in
      carbon dioxide tension after, 1090, 1091f
      functional residual capacity development in, 485, 485f
      measurement of, 492
      mechanisms in, 1093
      tactile stimulation of, 490
  work of
    components of, 1087, 1088f
    in pulmonary function assessment, 1095
Breech presentation
  anesthetic considerations in, 480
  developmental dysplasia of hip related to, 1774
  fetus in, ultrasonography of, 150, 150f
  knee subluxation and dislocation in, 1777

Brock procedure, 1269t
Bronchial cysts, 1134
Bronchodilators
    fetal effects of, 189t
    for bronchopulmonary dysplasia, 1165
Bronchomalacia, neonatal anesthesia and,
        628
Bronchopulmonary dysplasia, 1155–1168
    adrenal insufficiency in, 1162
    airway resistance in, 1161–1162
    anesthetic considerations in, 635
    atypical (new), 1157
    chest radiograph of, 714, 715, 716f
    clinical presentation of, 1156–1157, 1157f
    diagnostic criteria for, 1155, 1156t
    extracorporeal membrane oxygenation
        and, 1172
    fluid and electrolyte therapy for, 703
    genetic predisposition to, 1162
    in high-risk infants, 1037
    incidence of, 1155–1156, 1156f
    infection in, 1160–1161
    inflammatory reaction in, 1160–1161
    management of, 1164–1167
        bronchodilator therapy in, 1165
        corticosteroids in, 1166
        fluid management in, 1165
        infant stimulation in, 1167
        infection control in, 1166
        nutrition in, 1165–1166
        parental support in, 1167
        pulmonary vasodilators in, 1166–1167
        respiratory support in, 1164–1165
    outcome of, 1167
    oxygen toxicity in, 1160, 1160f
    patent ductus arteriosus in, 1161, 1161f
    pathogenesis of, 1158
    pathology of, 1157–1158, 1158f, 1159f
    prediction of, 1162–1163
    premature lung development and, 1158
    prevention of, 1167–1168
    α_1-proteinase inhibitor deficiency in, 1162
    pulmonary edema in, 1161
    pulmonary function in, 1163, 1163t, 1164f
    radiographic features of, 1156–1157, 1157f
    rhinovirus infection in, 873
    surfactant therapy for, 1104
    ventilation-associated lung injury in,
        1159–1163
        prevention of, 1120–1121, 1120b, 1120t
    vitamin A deficiency in, 1162
Bronchopulmonary malformations,
        congenital, 1133–1134, 1134f
Bronchoscopy
    fiberoptic, in neonatal intubation, 637
    in laryngeal examination, 1150
    rigid, of tracheoesophageal fistula, 1375,
        1375f
Bronze baby syndrome, phototherapy and,
        1445
"Bucket handle" malformation, in
        imperforate anus, 1400
Buffer systems, in acid-base balance, 704
Buffy coat examination, in sepsis diagnosis,
        795–796
Bullous ichthyosis, 1696
Bumetanide
    dosages of, 1791
    for fluid balance, in congenital heart
        disease, 1267
Buprenorphine, as opioid substitute, 753
Burden of proof, in malpractice litigation,
        54
Burns, ocular, 1727

Butorphanol
    for labor pain, 472
    umbilical vein to maternal vein ratio of,
        470t

C

C-reactive protein
    in humoral immunity, 773
    in sepsis diagnosis, 798
Cadmium, maternal exposure to, pregnancy
        outcome in, 260t
Café-au-lait macules, 1704, 1782f, 1783
Caffeine
    dosages of, 1790
    fetal effects of, 189
    for apnea, 642, 1139
    for bronchopulmonary dysplasia, 1165
    in breast milk, 201
Cajal-Retzius cells, LIS expression in, 908
Calcaneovalgus foot, 1778–1779, 1779f
    diagnosis and treatment of, 1779
    in posteromedial angulation of tibia, 1773,
        1773f
    in tibial torsion, 1772
Calcification
    in hypoxic-ischemic encephalopathy, 940
    periventricular, in cytomegalovirus
        infection, 845
Calcitonin
    effects of, 1503–1504
    fetal, 1504
    for hypercalcemia, 1518
    metabolism of, 1503
    neonatal, 1504
    secretion of
        by thyroid, 1525
        regulation of, 1504
    synthesis of, 1503
Calcitriol, serum calcium regulation by, 1492
Calcium
    absorption of, 1494–1495, 1495t
    atomic weight and valance of, 1817t
    balance of, in hyperthyroidism, 1524
    excretion of, 1495–1496, 1496f
    in breast milk, 671t, 1496
        absorption and retention of, 1495t
        fortifiers of, 1494
    in enteral nutrition, 669, 670t
    in infant formula, 673t
    in parenteral nutrition, 687
    intake of, 1496–1497
    ionized
        for asymptomatic hypocalcemia, 1513
        whole blood, 1802t
    metabolism of, 1496f
    physiology of, 1492–1497
    placental transport of, 261, 1492–1493
    serum levels of, 1509, 1492, 1493f, 1493t
        disturbances in, 1508–1518. See also
            Hypercalcemia; Hypocalcemia.
Calcium channel blockers
    contraindications to, 352
    for cor pulmonale, 1244
    for neonatal tachycardia, 1262b
    for preterm labor prevention, 352–353
Calcium chloride, dosages of, 1792
Calcium gluconate
    dosages of, 1792
    for hypocalcemia, 1513
    for hypocalcemic-induced seizures, 974
Calfactant, dosages of, 1792

California Perinatal Quality Control
        Collaborative, 67, 74–75
Caloric (oculovestibular) reflex, assessment
        of, 526
Calories
    maternal, fetal growth and, 281–282, 282f
    requirements for
        in enteral nutrition, 661–662, 662t,
            663–664
        in parenteral nutrition, 680, 690, 691b
        weight-based requirement for, in pregnant
            patients, 323
Calvaria, in ventriculomegaly, 153, 153f
Camptodactyly, 578
Camptomelic dwarfism, 1557
    SOX9 gene mutation in, 1571
Campylobacter fetus, in chorioamnionitis,
        459
Campylobacter infection, in gastroenteritis,
        812, 813
Canadian Paediatric Society, 664
Canavan disease, macrencephaly associated
        with, 997
Candida albicans
    cutaneous infection with, 1700
    in chorioamnionitis, 459
Candidiasis, 830–833
    catheter-associated, 830–831, 831b
    clinical manifestations of, 830–831, 831b
    cutaneous, 816–817, 1699–1700, 1700f
        congenital, 830, 832
    diagnosis of, 831
    disseminated, 830
    in very low birthweight infants, 830–831,
        831b
    incidence of, 830
    microbiology of, 830
    prevention of, 833
    pseudomembranous (thrush), 830
    systemic, 830–831
    treatment of, 831–833, 832t
Cannabis sativa, 742. See also Marijuana
    use.
Cantrell's pentalogy, 1381, 1381f
Capillary(ies)
    alveolar, dysplasia of, 1133
    pulmonary, development of, 1070, 1071f
    separation from alveoli, in
        bronchopulmonary dysplasia, 1158,
        1159f
Capillary hemangioma (stork bites)
    examination of, 517
    of eyelids, 1730
Capnography, 616–618
    mainstream and sidestream technology in,
        617
Captain of the ship doctrine, 49
Captopril
    dosages of, 1792
    for afterload reduction, in congenital heart
        disease, 1267
    for cardiomyopathy, 1249
    for neonatal hypertension, 1673, 1673t
Caput succedaneum
    as birth injury, 531
    examination of, 516
    vs. cephalhematoma, 532
Carbamazepine
    fetal effects of, 187t
    thyroid hormone effects of, 1528
Carbimazole, in breast milk, 200
Carbohydrate(s)
    absorption disorders of, 1365–1367, 1365t
        hypercalcemia due to, 1516

Carbohydrate(s)—cont'd
  energy stored as, 663
  in breast milk, 671t
  in infant formula, 673t
  requirements for
    in enteral nutrition, 664
    in parenteral nutrition, 680–681, 690
Carbohydrate-deficient glycoprotein
  syndrome, cardiomyopathy in, 1619
Carbohydrate metabolism
  disorders of, 1467–1491
    cataracts in, 1619
    hepatic damage in, 1622
  in thyroid, 1524
  inborn errors of, in persistent
    hypoglycemia, 1484–1485
  neonatal anesthesia and, 629–630
Carbon dioxide
  end-tidal
    in airflow measurement, 1092
    monitoring of, during anesthesia, 636
  exchange of, in assisted ventilation,
    1109–1110, 1110f
  ventilatory response to, in preterm infant,
    1135–1136, 1136f
Carbon dioxide monitoring, transcutaneous,
  616
Carbon dioxide tension (PCO_2)
  after first breath, 1090, 1091f
  changes in, chemoreceptor response to,
    1111
  in bronchopulmonary dysplasia, 1163
  in pulmonary function assessment, 1090
  mechanical ventilation effects on
    frequency rate and, 1115
    positive end-expiratory pressure in,
      1115
  reduction of, during labor, 484, 484t
  transcutaneous, 616
Carbon disulfide, maternal exposure to,
  pregnancy outcome in, 260t
Carbon monoxide
  end-tidal
    measurements of, 1439
    monitoring of, 623
  excretion of, heme degradation and, 1420
  fetal exposure to, placenta-dependent
    pathway in, 259
  maternal exposure to, pregnancy outcome
    in, 260t
Carboxyhemoglobin, 1419
  fetal exposure to, placenta-dependent
    pathway in, 259
Carboxylase deficiency, multiple, 1608t,
  1639
Carcinogens, 190
  sperm targeted by, 257
Cardiac. See also Heart entries.
Cardiac arrest, maternal, due to inadvertent
  intrathecal injections, 476
Cardiac catheterization
  hemodynamic principles and, 1211–1215
  in congenital heart disease, 1220
  in transposition of great arteries, 1223,
    1224f
  interventional, 1270–1275
    complications of, 1275
    for ablation of atrial tachycardia, 1262b,
      1264
    for angioplasty, 1273–1274
    for atrial septal defect creation,
      1271–1272
    for embolization or occlusion of blood
      vessels, 1274

Cardiac catheterization—cont'd
  for endomyocardial biopsy, 1275
  for foreign body retrieval, 1275
  for valvuloplasty, 1272–1273
  in preterm infants, 1251
  stent placement via, 1274
  transhepatic, 1274–1275
Cardiac impulse, in assessment of congenital
  heart disease, 1215–1216
Cardiac index, 1213
Cardiac monitoring, 609–612
  biologic basis of, 609–610, 610f
  computer-based, 611–612
  ECG artifacts in, 612, 612b
    causes of, 611
  ECG module in, 611–612, 612f
  leads and lead placement in, 610–611,
    611f
  safety of, 612
Cardiac outflow tract, endocardial cushion
  tissue formation and, 1200
Cardiac output
  fetal
    decreased, in intravascular transfusion,
      401
    in nonimmune hydrops fetalis, 421,
      422b
    in prediction of hemolytic anemia, 398,
      399t
    in ventricular systolic function, 1213
  maternal, in multiple gestations, 376
  preload and, 1266–1267
Cardiogenesis, scientific basis of, 1198–1202
Cardiomegaly
  disorders associated with, 1618t
  in hydrops fetalis, 397, 398f
  in inborn errors of metabolism, 1617–1619
  in infant of diabetic mother, 1475, 1476f
  radiography of, 1217f
Cardiomyopathy, 1248–1250
  congestive, 1248
  diagnosis of, 1248–1249, 1249b
  dilated, 1248, 1249b
  disorders associated with, 1618t
  fetal, 1210
  hypertrophic
    causes of, 1249b
    insulin-related, 1204
    manifestation of, 1248
  in inborn errors of metabolism,
    1617–1619
  restrictive, 1248
  tachycardia-induced, 1256
  treatment of, 1249–1250
Cardiorespiratory failure, 1168–1180
  extracorporeal membrane oxygenation
    for, 1168–1176
  nitric oxide therapy for, 1176–1180
Cardiovascular drugs
  fetal effects of, 188t
  in breast milk, 199
  in neonatal resuscitation, 502–504, 503t
  neutropenia due to, 1313b
Cardiovascular system
  congenital anomalies of. See Congenital
    heart disease.
  diagnostic imaging of, 718f
  hemodynamics of, 1211–1215
  in preeclampsia-eclampsia, 310, 310t
  in respiratory distress syndrome,
    1106–1107
  radiography of, 717–718, 718f
Cardioversion, for neonatal tachycardia,
  1262b, 1263

Carnitine
  analysis of, in inborn errors of
    metabolism, 1632
  deficiency of, primary, 988
  for acidemia, 1639
  in breast milk, 672t
  in enteral nutrition, 667
  in infant formula, 674t
  in intravenous lipid emulsions, 686
Carnitine palmitoyltransferase deficiency,
  1609t, 1648
Carnitine translocase deficiency, 1609t
Carnitine transporter deficiency, 1609t
Carotid artery, ligation of, after
  extracorporeal membrane oxygenation,
  1170
Cartilage, ossification of
  disturbances in, in congenital
    hypothyroidism, 1542
  in bone development, 1505
Cartilage-hair hypoplasia, neutropenia in,
  1311
Case law, 48
Casein
  in breast milk, 664
  in infant formula, 665
Casting
  for congenital vertical talus, 1781
  for talipes equinovarus, 1780
Catabolism, of heme, to bilirubin,
  1419–1420, 1420f
Cataracts, 1739–1743
  carbohydrate disorders and, 1619
  congenital, examination of, 520
  etiology of, 1739–1740, 1740f, 1740t
Catastrophic deterioration, associated with
  periventricular-intraventricular
  hemorrhage, 929
Catheter(s)
  candidiasis associated with, 830–831,
    831b
  for neonatal monitoring, during
    anesthesia, 636
  for parenteral nutrition
    central venous catheters in, 689
    complications of, 688–690
    guidelines for use of, 690
    peripheral Teflon catheters in, 689
  infection prevention for, 829
  umbilical
    complications of, 1102
    for blood gas assessment, in respiratory
      distress syndrome, 1102
    for cardiovascular drugs, in neonatal
      resuscitation, 502
    renal artery thromboembolism due to,
      1670, 1674
Catheterization
  cardiac. See Cardiac catheterization.
  interventional. See Cardiac catheterization,
    interventional.
  of umbilical artery
    for blood gas assessment, in respiratory
      distress syndrome, 1102
    thromboembolism related to, 1670,
      1674
  of umbilical vein
    conjugated hyperbilirubinemia
      associated with, 1461
    for cardiovascular drugs, in neonatal
      resuscitation, 502
Caudal agenesis, in infant of diabetic
  mother, 1475
Caudal anesthesia, neonatal, 641

Caudal dysplasia (sacral agenesis)
clinical manifestations of, 1771–1772
gestational diabetes mellitus and, 326
Causation, in malpractice litigation, 53–54
Cavum septum pellucidum cyst,
macrocephaly due to, 1004
Cavum vergae cyst, macrocephaly due to,
1004
CD molecules
on B cells, 783, 783t
on T cells, 779, 779t
CD3+ T cells, 780
CD4+ T cells, 779, 780
HIV infection of, 856
neonatal, 782
CD8+ T cells, 779, 780
neonatal, 782
CD11/CD18 leukocyte adhesion molecules,
764, 765f
CD14-lipopolysaccharide complexes, in
inflammatory response, 776, 777f
CD28, in T cell activation and maturation,
781
CDKN1C gene, in Beckwith-Wiederman
syndrome, 1482, 1483
Cefazolin
dosages of, 1788
prophylactic, for sepsis, 804
Cefotaxime
dosages of, 1788
for conjunctivitis, 811
for gastroenteritis, 813
for mastitis, 818
for meningitis, 807
in sepsis, 800
for otitis media, 810
for pneumonia, 809
for sepsis, 800, 801t, 802t
prophylactic, for conjunctivitis, 812
Ceftazidime
dosages of, 1788
for sepsis, 800, 801t, 802t
for skin infections, 817
Ceftriaxone
dosages of, 1788
for conjunctivitis, 811
for gastroenteritis, 813
for gonococcal conjunctivitis, 443
for sepsis, 800, 801t, 802t
prophylactic, for conjunctivitis, 812
Cell(s). *See also named cell.*
division of
anomaly in, 114–115, 115f
in heart development, 1201
responses of, to hypoxic-ischemic insults,
940
susceptibility of, to hypoxic-ischemic
insults, 939
Cell death
in heart development, 1201–1202
programmed. *See Apoptosis.*
Cellular metabolism, effect of thyroid
hormone on, 1524
Cellulitis, orbital, 1734
Centers for Disease Control and Prevention
HIV prophylaxis recommendations of,
857–858
HIV therapy recommendations of, for
neonate, 861
Centers for Medicare and Medicaid Services
DRG system, 70, 71t
Central core disease, 986
Central nervous system. *See also* Brain;
Spinal cord.

Central nervous system—*cont'd*
axonal and dendritic growth in, 891–893,
893f, 894f
bilirubin entry into, 1435–1436
development of
alcohol exposure and, 736–737
cocaine exposure and, 745–746
opioid exposure and, 752
disorders of
gestational diabetes mellitus and, 326
respiratory distress related to, 1141
seizures associated with, 969, 971, 972f
fetal
heart rate regulation by, 168
hypoxia effects on, 172
glial proliferation and differentiation in,
896–900, 897f, 898f, 899t, 900f
in preeclampsia-eclampsia, 310t, 311–312
infection of, seizures due to, 969
neuron production in, 885–886
organization of, 890–900
disorders in, 908–909
programmed cell death in, 895–896, 896f
regionalization of, 885, 885f
subplate neurons in, 890–891, 892f, 893f
synaptogenesis in, 894–895, 894f, 895f
ultrasonography of, 152–155
Central nervous system drugs
congenital malformations associated with,
186t
in breast milk, 199–200
Centromere, 113
Cephalhematoma
as birth injury, 532–533, 532f–533f
blood loss in, 1297
examination of, 516
vs. caput succedaneum, 532
vs. subgaleal hemorrhage, 534
Cephalosporins
fetal effects of, 187t
for meningitis, in sepsis, 800
for osteomyelitis, 814, 1764
for septic arthritis, 814
for skin infections, 817
in breast milk, 199
Cerclage
for preterm labor prevention, 346–347
removal of, 347
Cerebellar hemorrhage, 933–934
Cerebellar hypoplasia, autosomal recessive
lissencephaly with, 908
Cerebral artery
infarction of, 934–937. *See also* Arterial
ischemic stroke.
definition of, 934
seizures associated with, 969
middle
Doppler flow velocity of, 170, 171f
in intrauterine growth restriction, 293
peak systolic velocity assessment of,
for fetal anemia, 394–395, 399, 400f,
400t
peak velocity in, ultrasonography of,
151, 151f
Cerebral atrophy, in hypoxia-ischemia,
940–941
Cerebral cortex
developmental events in, 1052–1054
ontogenesis of, 1052, 1052f
functional assessment of, 526
Cerebral edema
in hypoxic-ischemic encephalopathy, 940,
953
respiratory distress related to, 1141

Cerebral hyperventilation, vs. transient
tachypnea, 1128
Cerebral palsy
definition of, 332
due to necrotizing enterocolitis, 1405
in high-risk neonate, 1038–1039, 1039f
in preterm infant, 332
in term infant, 461
intrapartum asphyxia and, 179, 179b
Cerebrospinal fluid
enlarged spaces for, 998–1004. *See also*
Hydrocephalus.
values for, 1808t
Cerebrospinal fluid analysis
in candidiasis, 831
in inborn errors of metabolism, 1630t,
1630–1631
in meningitis, 805–806, 805t–806t
in sepsis, 795
Cerebrovascular accident. *See* Stroke.
Cervical spinal cord, injury to, 979
Cervical spine
development of, 1756
myelodysplasia of, vs. sternocleidomastoid
muscle injury, 547
Cervix
incompetent
cerclage for, 346–347
in preterm delivery, 336
vs. preterm labor, 336
length of
transvaginal sonographic assessment of,
347
ultrasonography of, 149f, 149–151, 150f
precocious changes of, in preterm labor
prediction, 340
Cesarean section. *See also* Delivery.
anesthetic technique for, 477–479
neuraxial blockade in, 475, 478, 478b
for macrosomic infant, 384
history of, 4–5
in herpes simplex virus infection,
842–843, 843f
in HIV-infected mothers, 859
in multiple gestations, 380
vaginal birth after, anesthetic
considerations in, 479
Charcoal, activated, for unconjugated
hyperbilirubinemia, 1446
Charcot-Marie-Tooth disease, type 1, 979–980
CHARGE association
anesthetic implications of, 632t
coloboma in, 571
congenital heart disease in, 1205
in choanal atresia, 1144, 1147
in esophageal atresia/tracheoesophageal
fistula, 1373
in renal dysplasia, 1676
overlap with DiGeorge syndrome, 1144
Charge-transfer over-voltage, in polarization,
610
Chédiak-Higashi syndrome, 1317, 1706
Chelation therapy, with desferrioxamine, for
Diamond-Blackfan anemia, 1307
Chemical(s)
fat-soluble, fetal exposure to, placenta-
dependent pathway in, 259
transfer of, across fetal blood-brain
barrier, 262, 262f
Chemical burns, ocular, 1727
Chemical thermogenesis, in cold-stressed
infant, 594, 594f
Chemiluminescence test, in erythroblastosis
fetalis screening, 395

Chemokines, biology of, 775, 776t
Chemoreceptors, in breathing control, 1111, 1135–1136
Chemosensory stimuli, environmental, 599–600
Chemotaxis
　disorders of, 1317
　of neutrophils, 763f, 764–766
　of phagocytes, 767–768
Cherry-red spot, in lysosomal storage diseases, 1619
Cherubism, anesthetic implications of, 632t
Chest
　birth injuries to, 541–547
　congenital anomalies of, examination of, 573–574, 574f
　fetal, in oligohydramnios, 416–417
　normal, 713
　radiography of. See Chest radiography.
　retractions of
　　in pulmonary function assessment, 1088
　　in respiratory distress syndrome, 1100
　structural abnormalities of, respiratory distress due to, 1145, 1145f
Chest compressions, in neonatal resuscitation, 501–502, 501f, 951
Chest radiography, 713–717
　normal, 713
　of airway obstruction, 1143
　of bronchopulmonary dysplasia, 715, 716f, 1156–1157, 1157f
　of congenital diaphragmatic hernia, 715–716, 716f
　of congenital heart disease, 1217, 1217b, 1217f
　of congenital lobar emphysema, 716–717, 717f, 1134
　of cystic adenomatoid malformation, 716, 716f
　of esophageal atresia, 717, 1375, 1375f
　of heart, 717–718, 718f
　of histoplasmosis, 835
　of meconium aspiration, 1123, 1123f
　of meconium aspiration syndrome, 715, 715f
　of neonatal pneumonia, 714–715, 808
　of pneumothorax, 1129, 1129f
　of pulmonary hemorrhage, 715
　of respiratory distress syndrome, 713–714, 714f
　of total anomalous pulmonary venous connection, 1229
　of tracheoesophageal fistula, 717, 717f
　of transient tachypnea of newborn, 715, 1127
Chest tube, for pneumothorax, 1130
Chiari malformation. See also Spina bifida.
　anesthetic implications of, 632t
　hydrocephalus in, 1000–1001, 1000f
　ultrasonography of, 153, 153f
Chickenpox. See Varicella-zoster virus infections.
Chief cells, gastric, 1359
Child abandonment, 7, 8f
Child hatchery, 9
Child Health and Illness Profile, 1040
CHILD syndrome, 1694t, 1710
　cholesterol biosynthesis defects in, 1627
CHIME syndrome, 1694t
China. See also Developing countries.
　congenital anomaly prevalence in, 565–566, 566t
　neonatal mortality in, 90, 90f
　　vs. India, 90t, 90–91

Chlamydia trachomatis infection
　conjunctivitis due to, 810, 811, 1747
　epidemiology and clinical manifestations of, 447
　in pregnancy, 447–448
　　adverse outcome related to, 447–448, 448t
　in preterm delivery, 338–339
　intrapartum, 460
　neonatal effects of, 448
　pneumonia due to, 808, 1126
　screening for, for preterm labor prevention, 431
Chloral hydrate, dosages of, 1792
Chloramphenicol
　dosages of, 1788
　for sepsis, 802t
　in breast milk, 199
Chlorangiosis, definition of, 459
Chlordecone, maternal exposure to, pregnancy outcome in, 260t
Chlordiazepoxide
　fetal effects of, 187t
　in breast milk, 199
Chloride
　for pseudohypoaldosteronism, 701
　in breast milk, 671t
　in enteral nutrition, 669, 670t
　in infant formula, 673t
　　for extremely low birthweight, 679
　in parenteral nutrition, 687
　in sweat, in cystic fibrosis diagnosis, 1364
　maintenance of, 699
Chloride diarrhea, congenital, 1368–1369, 1370t
Chlorine, atomic weight and valance of, 1817t
Chloroform, maternal exposure to, pregnancy outcome in, 260t
Chloroprene, maternal exposure to, pregnancy outcome in, 260t
Chloroquine, for malaria, 836–837
Chlorothiazide
　dosages of, 1791
　for fluid balance, in congenital heart disease, 1267
　for neonatal hypertension, 1673t
　for nephrogenic diabetes insipidus, 702
Chlorpropamide
　fetal effects of, 188t
　placental transport of, transient neonatal hypoglycemia due to, 1472
Chlorthalidone, in breast milk, 199
Choanal atresia
　computed tomography of, 1144, 1144f
　congenital anomalies associated with, 1144, 1147
　diagnosis of, 1147
　physical examination of, 508
　treatment of, 1144, 1147
　unilateral vs. bilateral, 1144
Cholecystokinin, duodenal production of, 1361
Choledochal cyst
　CT scan of, 723–724
　ultrasonography of, 158–159, 723, 723f
Choledocholithiasis, 1460
Cholestasis, 1450
　due to parenteral nutrition, 688
　　prevention of, with enteral feeding, 688
Cholesterol
　biosynthesis of, defects in, 1625t, 1626–1627
　in enteral nutrition, 667

Cholesterol side-chain cleavage enzyme (20,22-desmolase) deficiency, 1583–1584
Choline
　in breast milk, 672t
　in infant formula, 674t
Chondrification, vertebral, 1756
Chondrocytes, in bone development, 1504
Chondrodysplasia, Jansen metaphyseal, 1517
Chorioallantoic placenta, 208
Chorioamnionitis
　acute, 459, 461
　after amniocentesis, 137
　decreased incidence of RDS after, 1085, 1086, 1087f
　intrapartum prophylaxis for, sepsis prevention and, 804
　preterm delivery and, 337
　severe, 462
Chorioangioma, 460
Choriocarcinoma, 460
Choriomeningitis virus, lymphocytic, 876
Chorionic villus
　sampling of
　　in fetal drug effects, 190
　　in prenatal genetic evaluation, 137–138
　surface area of, in placenta, 284, 285f
Chorioretinitis, 1743–1744
　in congenital toxoplasmosis, 838, 1743–1744
　in cytomegalovirus infection, 845, 845t, 1743
　in HIV infection, 1744
Choroid plexus
　cysts of
　　macrocephaly due to, 1003–1004
　　ultrasonography of, 154f, 154–155
　fetal, ultrasonography of, 152, 152f
Choroidal angioma, in Sturge-Weber syndrome, 1729
Christmas disease. See Hemophilia B.
Chromium
　in enteral nutrition, 670t
　in parenteral nutrition, 687, 688t
Chromosome(s)
　acrocentric, 113, 114f
　centromere of, 113, 114f
　growth-determining genes on, 287
　metacentric, 113, 114f
　monosomy, 115
　rearrangements of
　　balanced, 117
　　de novo, 117
　　familial, 117
　　unbalanced, 117
　satellites of, 113–114, 114f
　sex, 113. See also X chromosome; Y chromosome.
　　common disorders of, 563
　　numerical abnormalities of, 115–116
　stalks of, 113–114, 114f
　structure of, 113–114, 114f
　submetacentric, 113, 114f
　telomere of, 113
　translocation of
　　reciprocal, 116, 117f
　　Robertsonian, 117, 118, 118f
　trisomy, 115
Chromosome 11p deletion, ocular manifestation of, 1728
Chromosome 13q deletion, ocular manifestation of, 1728
Chromosome 22q11 deletions, heart defects associated with, 1201, 1203t, 1204

Chromosome analysis
  in ambiguous genitalia, 579
  in fluorescent in situ hybridization,
    119–121
  in intersex disorders, 1561
Chromosome anomalies, 113–121
  congenital anomalies due to, 562t, 563
  in congenital heart disease, 1202, 1203t,
    1203–1204
  in multiple gestations, 377
  in neonatal diabetes mellitus, 1490
  in nonimmune hydrops fetalis, 421–422,
    422b
  in omphalocele, 1382
  macrencephaly associated with, 997
  musculoskeletal, 1756–1757
  numerical, 114–117, 115f, 116f
    maternal age and, 115f, 116, 116f
  ocular, 1727–1728
  spontaneous abortion and, 564–565, 565t
  structural, 117f, 117–119, 118f
    deletions in, 119
    duplications in, 119
    paracentric inversion in, 118
    pericentric inversion in, 118, 118f
Chromosome deletions, 119
  diagnosis of microdeletions in, 579
Chromosome duplications, 119
Chronic benign neutropenia, 1312–1313
Chronic lung disease. See
    Bronchopulmonary dysplasia.
Chylomicron retention disease, 1368
Chylothorax, 1134–1135
  differential diagnosis of, 1135
  nonimmune hydrops fetalis due to, 422
Cigarette ingredients, transfer of, into breast
    milk, 201
Cigarette smoking. See Tobacco use.
Cimetidine
  dosages of, 1791
  in breast milk, 200
CINAHL database, 80
Circadian rhythmicity, in environment of
    light, 602
Circulation
  fetal. See Fetal circulation.
  maternal, placenta and, 456, 458
  measurement of, 1211–1212
  pulmonary. See Pulmonary circulation.
  renal blood flow in, 1663, 1663t
  separate, in cyanosis, 1221, 1221b
  uteroplacental
    abnormalities of, in intrauterine growth
      restriction pregnancies, 286, 286t
    vasomotor regulation of, in
      preeclampsia-eclampsia, 308–309
Circumcision
  bacterial endocarditis and, 1268
  dorsal penile nerve block for, 641
  eutectic mixture of local anesthetic for, 641
Cis-atracurium, in neonatal anesthesia, 640
Citrin deficiency, hepatic dysfunction in,
    1621
Citrullinemia, 1606t
Clarithromycin
  for toxoplasmosis, 449
  in breast milk, 199
Clavicular fracture, birth-related, 541, 1761
  examination of, 518
Cleft, laryngeal, 1154
Cleft lip
  examination of, 518, 573
  perinatal ultrasonography of, 155, 155f
  prevalence of, 517t

Cleft palate
  examination of, 518, 573
  isolated, 573
  perinatal ultrasonography of, 155
  prevalence of, 517t
Clindamycin
  dosages of, 1788
  for anaerobic infections, 819
  for bacterial vaginosis, 432
  for group B streptococcal infection,
    444–445
  for necrotizing enterocolitis, 1405
  for sepsis, 801t, 802t
  prophylactic, for sepsis, 804
Clinical question, focused, 79
Clinical Risk Index for Babies (CRIB), 68–69
Clinodactyly, 578, 578f
Clitoris, measurement of, 1558–1559
Clitoromegaly, 1567–1568
  causes of, 1568b
  definition of, 1567
  disorders associated with, 1558t
Cloaca
  development of, 1662–1663, 1663f
  malformation of, in imperforate anus,
    1400
    colostomy for, 1402
Clomiphene, fetal effects of, 188t
Clonic seizures, 958
  multifocal, 958
Clonidine
  for chronic hypertension, 317t
  for preeclampsia-eclampsia, 314, 314t
Clostridium botulinum, 820
  in infantile botulism, 982
Clostridium difficile, in gastroenteritis, 812
Clostridium tetani, 825
Clotting. See Coagulation.
Cloverleaf skull (kleeblattschädel), 1012
Clubfoot. See Talipes equinovarus.
Clubhand
  radial, 1767, 1768f
  ultrasonography of, 162, 163f
Coagulation
  cascade-waterfall hypothesis of, 1320,
    1320f
  disorders of
    in asphyxia, 952
    laboratory findings in, 1325, 1327t
  disseminated intravascular. See
      Disseminated intravascular
      coagulation.
  inhibitors of, reference values for,
    1324t–1235t
  intrinsic pathway of, 1320
  physiologic alterations of, 1322, 1322t,
    1323t, 1324, 1324t–1325t
  revised hypothesis of, 1321f, 1320–1321
  tests for
    in premature infant, 1323t
    in term infant, 1322t
Coagulation factors, 1320–1321, 1320f,
    1321f. See also specific factor, e.g.,
    Factor VIII.
  assays for, cord blood in, 1325
  vitamin K–dependent, 1324
Coarctation of aorta. See Aorta, coarctation
    of.
Cobb syndrome, 1709
Cocaethylene, in combined alcohol/cocaine
    abuse, 734
Cocaine abuse, 743–747
  alcohol abuse combined with, 734
  central nervous system effects of, 745–746

Cocaine abuse—cont'd
  clinical studies of, caveats regarding
    interpretation of, 747
  during pregnancy
    fetal effects of, 186t, 189
    preterm delivery and, 334
  family centered treatment model for, 747,
    748f
  HIV/sexually transmitted diseases related
    to, 745
  infant and child development effects of,
    746
  intrauterine growth restriction due to,
    283–284
  intrauterine growth restriction from, 745
  pharmacologic effects of, 744–745
  postnatal growth effect of, 745
  preterm delivery related to, 745
  prevalence of, 743–744
  sudden infant death syndrome related to,
    745
Coccidioidomycosis, 833
Cochlea, anatomy of, 1045
Cochlear implants, for hearing-impaired
    child, 1045–1046, 1049–1050
Cochrane review
  of electronic fetal monitoring controlled
    trials, 950
  systematic, 81
Codeine, abuse of, 753
Coenzyme Q₁₀, for respiratory chain defect,
    1645
COL6A1 gene, heart defects associated with,
    1203–1204
Cold infant, 596–597
  definition of, 596
Cold medicines, fetal effects of, 189t
Cold panniculitis, 1713
Collagen, in dermal development, 1688
Collagen vascular disease, maternal,
    congenital heart disease related to, 1204
Collectins, in innate immunity, 773
Collodion baby, 1695, 1695f
Coloboma
  in congenital anomalies, 570f, 571
  in microphthalmia, 1732
  of eyelids, 1729–1730, 1730f
  of iris, 1738, 1738b, 1738f
  of ocular fundus, 1743
  of optic disc, 1745
  renal, 1662, 1662t
Colon. See also Microcolon.
  development of, 1362–1363
  duplications of, 1393
  functional immaturity of, radiography of,
    720, 720f
  Hirschsprung disease of, 1398, 1399
  hypomobility of, in meconium plug
    syndrome, 1396–1397
  neonatal small left colon syndrome of,
    1396
Colony-forming unit granulocyte-
    macrophage, 762, 763
Colony-stimulating factors, 1288, 1289t
  in sepsis diagnosis, 799
Colostomy, for imperforate anus, 1400,
    1401f, 1402
Colostrum, immunologic properties of,
    788–789, 789t
Common law, 48
Communication
  channels of, in preterm infant, 1055t
  for avoiding tort litigation, 56
  in ethical decision making, 42

Communication—*cont'd*
  total, with hearing-impaired child, 1049
  transparent, 42
Community health workers
  in developing countries, 102–103, 104f.
    See also Health care personnel, in
    developing countries.
Compensatory anti-inflammatory response
  syndrome, 777
Complement system, 770–772
  activation of
    alternative pathway of, 771, 771f
      amplification loop of, 771
    classic pathway of, 770–771, 771f
  in neonatal period, 771–772, 772t
Complete heart block. *See* Heart block,
  complete.
Compliance, pulmonary, 1093–1094
  calculation of, 1094, 1094f, 1095, 1108
  dynamic, 1094, 1095
  in bronchopulmonary dysplasia, 1163,
    1163t, 1164f
  in respiratory distress syndrome, 1108
  lungs in, 1094
  specific, 1094
  static, 1094, 1096
  surfactant therapy and, 1105
Computed tomography (CT)
  of choledochal cyst, 723–724
  of congenital heart disease, 1219–1220
  of esophageal duplication, 1378, 1378f
  of hypoxic-ischemic encephalopathy, 948
Conductance, pulmonary, 1094
Conduction, heat exchange through,
  calculation of, 586
Conductive hearing loss, 1045. *See also*
  Hearing loss.
Congenital adrenal hyperplasia. *See* Adrenal
  gland(s), congenital hyperplasia of.
Congenital anomalies, 561–581. *See also*
  specific anomaly.
  alcohol-related, 563–564, 564f, 736b
  anesthetic implications of, 632, 632t–634t,
    634
  associated with gestational diabetes
    mellitus, 326
  associations in, 561
  cardiac. *See* Congenital heart disease.
  cocaine-related, 744, 747
  common types of, 517, 517t
  cutaneous, 1713–1715
  deformations as, 561
  disruptions as, 561
  due to rubella virus, 872
  educational resources for, 580–581
  environmental causes of, 133–134, 134t
  environmental exposure and, 264, 264t
  epidemiology and etiology of, 562–566
  evaluation of, 566–580
    abdomen in, 574
    anus in, 574
    chest in, 573–574, 574f
    diagnostic testings and indications in,
      579–580, 579t, 580f
    ears in, 571, 571f–572f
    extremities in, 574–578, 575f–578f
    eyes in, 568, 569f, 570f, 570–571
    face in, 568
    genitalia in, 574
    hair in, 567–568, 568f
    head in, 568, 569f
    history in, 567
    mouth in, 572–573, 573f
    neck in, 573, 574f

Congenital anomalies—*cont'd*
    nose in, 572
    physical examination in, 567–578
    skin in, 567
    spine in, 574
    stillborn infant and, 574–578, 575f–578f
  examination of, 517t, 517–519
  gastrointestinal. *See* Gastrointestinal tract,
    anomaly(ies) of.
  genetic counseling for, 580
  identification of, in neonate, 520
  in aborted fetuses, 564–565, 565t
  in congenital herpes simplex infection,
    841
  in infant of diabetic mother, 1474–1475,
    1476f
  in low birthweight infants, 23
  malformations in. *See* Malformations.
  minor, 565, 566t
  musculoskeletal. *See* Musculoskeletal
    system, congenital anomaly(ies) of.
  ocular, 1727–1729
  of lower extremities, 1772–1781
  of upper extremities, 1767–1770
  oral and oropharyngeal, 569f, 570f,
    572–573, 573f
  parent-infant attachment affected by, 657f,
    657–658
  paternal occupation and, 257
  preterm labor and delivery associated
    with, 339
  pulmonary, 1133–1135
  racial differences in, 565–566, 566t
  screening for, 508
  sequences as, 561
  spinal, 1770–1772
  support organizations for, 580–581
  terminology related to, 561–562
Congenital diaphragmatic hernia. *See*
  Diaphragmatic hernia, congenital.
Congenital disorders of glycosylation
  dysmorphic features in, 1625–1626
  testing for, 1633
Congenital erythropoietic porphyria
  jaundice in, 1429–1430
  phototherapy and, 1445
Congenital heart disease
  acyanotic, with no or mild respiratory
    distress, 1221b, 1222, 1237–1242
  anesthetic considerations in, 635
  aortic arch interruption as, 1234–1235
  aortic stenosis as, 1232–1233
  aortopulmonary window as, 1241–1242
  atrial septal defect as, 1239
  causes of, 1202–1205
  CHARGE association and, 1204
  chromosome defects in, 1202, 1203t,
    1203–1204
  coarctation of aorta as, 1234–1235
  cyanotic
    classification of, 1221–1222, 1221b
    complete mixing in, 1221b, 1222,
      1228–1231
    extracorporeal membrane oxygenation
      and, 1171
    poor mixing in, 1221, 1221b,
      1222–1224
    radiography of, 718, 718f
    restricted pulmonary blood flow in,
      1221–1222, 1221b, 1224–1228
    systemic hypoperfusion and CHF in,
      1221b, 1222, 1232–1237
    variable physiology in, 1231–1232
  diagnosis of, 1215–1220

Congenital heart disease—*cont'd*
  blood pressure measurement in, 1216
  cardiac catheterization in, 1219
  computed tomography in, 1219–1220
  echocardiography in, 1218–1219
  electrocardiography of, 1218
  hyperoxic test in, 1216–1217
  magnetic resonance imaging in,
    1219–1220
  physical examination in, 1215–1216,
    1215b
  pulse oximetry in, 1216
  radiography in, 1217, 1217b, 1217f
  diagnostic groups of, 1220–1222, 1221b
  double-outlet right ventricle as, 1231–1232
  duodenal atresia associated with, 1391
  Ebstein anomaly as, 1228
  echocardiography of, 1218–1219
    cardiac imaging in, 1218–1219, 1218b
    Doppler, 1219
    fetal, 1207–1208, 1207b
    measurement of cardiac function in,
      1219, 1219t, 1220b, 1220t
  endocardial cushion defect as, 1239
  environmental toxins in, 1204
  examination of, 520
  extracorporeal membrane oxygenation
    and, 1171–1172
  fetal
    outcome of, 1210
    risk factors for, 1207b
    treatment of, 1210
  fetal assessment for, 1207–1210
    indications for, 1207–1208, 1207b
    methods of, 1208
    recognition of abnormalities in,
      1208–1210
    timing of, 1208
  fetal circulation in, 1205–1206
  genetic influences in, 1204
  hypoplastic left heart syndrome as. *See*
    Hypoplastic left heart syndrome.
  in preterm infants, 1251–1252
  in rubella virus infection, 872
  in Turner syndrome, 1569
  management of, 1265–1275
    afterload in, 1267
    bacterial endocarditis prevention in,
      1268
    blood oxygenation in, 1266
    contractility in, 1267–1268
    for cyanotic spells, 1268, 1268b
    heart rate maintenance in, 1266
    heart transplantation in, 1269–1270
    interventional catheterization in,
      1270–1275
    oxygen and ventilation in, 1265–1266
    preload in, 1266–1267
    prostaglandin E_1 therapy in, 1266
    surgical, 1268, 1269t
  maternal diseases and, 1204
  multiple left heart defects in, 1237
  murmurs in. *See* Heart murmurs.
  patent ductus arteriosus as. *See* Patent
    ductus arteriosus.
  physiology of, 1205–1207
  presentation of, 1215
  prevalence of, 517t
  pulmonary atresia as, 1227–1228
  pulmonary stenosis as, 1238
  pulmonary vascular bed in, 1206–1207
  racial differences in, 1204
  sex influences in, 1204
  single gene defects in, 1204

Congenital heart disease—cont'd
  single ventricle as, 1231
  tetralogy of Fallot as, 1224–1226
  total anomalous pulmonary venous
    connection as, 1228–1229
  transition to extrauterine circulation in,
    1206
  transposition of great arteries as,
    1222–1223
  tricuspid atresia as, 1226–1227
  truncus arteriosus as, 1229–1231
  ultrasonography of, 156
  VACTERL association and, 1204
  ventricular septal defect as. See Ventricular
    septal defect.
Congestive heart failure (CHF), fetal
  arrhythmias in, 1210
  assessment of, 1209–1210
  causes of, 1209–1210
Conjunctiva
  examination of, 1722–1723
  pigmentation of, 1738
Conjunctivitis, 810–812
  chemical, 810, 1747
  chlamydial, 448, 810, 1747
  clinical manifestations of, 810–811
  complications of, 810–811
  diagnosis of, 811
  etiology of, 555, 810
  gonococcal, 810–812
    clinical manifestations of, 443, 810–811
    prevention of, 811–812
    treatment of, 811, 1747
    vs. swollen eyelids, 516
  incidence of, 810
  nongonococcal bacterial, 1747
  pathogenesis of, 810
  prevention of, 811–812
  treatment of, 555, 811
Connexin 26 gene, in sensorineural hearing
  loss, 1048–1049
Conradi-Hünermann syndrome, 1694t
  cholesterol biosynthesis defects in, 1627
Consciousness level, assessment of, 522, 524
Conservative therapy, for nonimmune
  hydrops fetalis, 425b, 425–426
Constipation, after imperforate anus repair,
  1402
Constriction band syndrome. See Amniotic
  band syndrome.
Contact dermatitis, 1710
Continuous blood gas monitoring, 621f,
  621–623, 622f
Continuous positive airway pressure (CPAP)
  after extubation, 1117
  as alternative to positive pressure
    ventilation, 494
  delivery methods for, 1112
  for apnea, 1139
  for respiratory distress syndrome, 1112
    in developing countries, 105
  in ventilator weaning, 1116
  patent airway establishment by, 1148
  respiratory rate and, 1111
Contraceptives, oral
  fetal effects of, 188t
  in breast milk, 200
Contraction stress testing
  in fetal evaluation, 168–169
    post-term, 385t
  in intrauterine growth restriction, 294–295
Contractures, in congenital anomalies, 578
Convection, heat exchange through,
  calculation of, 586

Convectively heated incubators, 595–596
Conversion tables
  for metric units, 1817t
  for Standard International Units,
    1814t–1816t
Convulsions, in ischemic stroke, 935
Coombs test
  for anemia, 1294
  indirect, in erythroblastosis fetalis
    screening, 394
Copper
  in breast milk, 671t
  in enteral nutrition, 670t
  in infant formula, 673t
  in parenteral nutrition, 687, 688t
  serum concentration of, 1802t
Cor pulmonale, 1243–1244
Cord. See Umbilical cord entries.
Cordocentesis
  in erythroblastosis fetalis screening, 394
  in fetal platelet count assessment, 368
  in intrauterine growth restriction
    diagnosis, 291
  in prenatal genetic evaluation, 138
Cornea
  abrasions of, 1727
  birth injury to, 539, 1727
  cloudy, 1737
  dimensions of, 1737
  dystrophy of, 1737
  enlarged, 1732
  examination of, 1723
  in anterior chamber cleavage syndromes,
    1737
  in lysosomal storage diseases, 20, 1619
  manifestations of systemic disease in,
    1737
  ulceration of, in conjunctivitis, 811
Cornelia de Lange syndrome
  anesthetic implications of, 632t
  ocular manifestation of, 1728
Cornification, disorders of, 1693–1696, 1694t
Corpus callosum
  agenesis of, 903–904, 992, 993f
  alcohol-related abnormalities of, 736–737
Cortical blindness, 1722
Corticosteroids
  before extubation, 1117
  effectiveness of, on fetal lung maturation,
    213
  fetal effects of, 188t
  for alloimmune (isoimmune)
    thrombocytopenia, 369, 1339
  for bronchopulmonary dysplasia, 1166
    complications of, 1166
  for hypoxic-ischemic encephalopathy, 953
  for induction of lung maturation, 1086,
    1098–1099
  for periventricular-intraventricular
    hemorrhage, 931
  for preeclampsia-eclampsia, 314
  for preterm labor prevention, 355–356
    long-term follow-up in, 356
  for subglottic hemangioma, 1153–1154
  surfactant therapy combined with, 1099
Corticotropin-releasing hormone, in preterm
  labor prediction, 342
Cortisol
  deficiency of
    in persistent hypoglycemia, 1483–1484
    salt-losing 21-hydroxylase deficiency
      and, 1579
  for fetal lung maturation, 213
  for 21-hydroxylase deficiency, 1580

Cortisol—cont'd
  serum, reference ranges for, 1805t
  synthesis of, in adrenal cortex, 217, 217f
Cost, of neonatal intensive care, 71–73
Cough medicines, fetal effects of, 189t
Court systems, structure of, 48, 49f
Couveuse, 8–9, 9f. See also Incubators.
Coxsackievirus infections. See also
    Enterovirus infections.
  congenital anomalies due to, 862
Crack cocaine, 744. See also Cocaine abuse.
Cradle cap, 1711
Cranial nerves. See also specific nerve, e.g.,
    Facial nerve.
  assessment of, 524t, 524–525
  birth injuries to, external ocular muscle
    injuries in, 538–539
Craniofacial anomalies. See under Face.
Craniofacial dysostosis. See Crouzon disease.
Craniofacial syndrome, 1011f, 1012f,
    1010–1013
Craniorachischisis totalis, 901
Craniosynostosis, 994–995, 1006–1013
  bilateral coronal, 1008–1009, 1009f
  classification of, 1006
  etiopathogenesis of, 1007
  in congenital anomalies, 568
  metopic, 1010, 1010f
  nonsyndromic, 1007–1010
  ocular manifestation of, 1728
  sagittal, 1007–1008, 1008f
  syndromic, 1010–1013
  unilateral coronal, 1008, 1009f
Creatinine, serum, 1803t
  in renal function assessment, 1666
  normal values for, 1663t
Creatinine clearance, 1803t
Cretinism. See also Hypothyroidism,
    congenital.
  anesthetic implications of, 632t
Cri du chat syndrome, anesthetic
  implications of, 632t
Crigler-Najjar syndrome, unconjugated
  hyperbilirubinemia in, 1431–1432
Cromolyn sodium, for bronchopulmonary
  dysplasia, 1165
Crouzon disease, 1010–1011, 1011f
  anesthetic implications of, 632t
  ocular manifestation of, 1728
  oropharyngeal airway obstruction in,
    1148, 1148f
Cryoprecipitate, transfusion of, 1350–1351
Cryotherapy, for retinopathy of prematurity,
    1751
Cryptococcosis, 834
Cryptophthalmia, 1732
Cryptorchidism, 1566–1567
  complications of, 1567
  in X-linked ichthyosis, 1696
  treatment of, 1567
  true, 1567
  X-linked thrombocytopenia with, 1341
Cuff, blood pressure, 615
Culture, medical ethics affected by, 37
Cutis laxa, 1713
Cutis marmorata, 567
Cyanosis
  central, 1215
  in congenital heart disease. See Congenital
    heart disease, cyanotic.
  in Ebstein anomaly, 1228
  in pulmonary function assessment, 1088
  in respiratory distress syndrome, 1100
  peripheral, 516, 1215

Cyanosis—cont'd
  physical signs of, 1215, 1215b
  "spells" of, treatment of, 1268, 1268b
  traumatic, 516
Cyclic neutropenia, 1311
Cyclooxygenase-2 (COX-2) inhibitors, for
    preterm labor prevention, 352
CYP21 gene, in 21-hydroxylase deficiency,
    1581
Cyproterone acetate, fetal effects of, 188t
Cyst(s). See also Pseudocyst(s).
  biliary, 1460
  bronchial, 1134
  choledochal
    CT scan of, 723–724
    ultrasonography of, 158–159, 723, 723f
  choroid plexus cyst, ultrasonography of,
      154f, 154–155
  congenital tracheobronchial, 1134
  Dandy-Walker, ultrasonography of, 154, 154f
  dermoid
    intranasal, 1148
    lingual, 1149, 1149f
    of eyelids, 1731
    orbital, 1735
  gingival (epulis), 517
  in esophageal duplication, 1378, 1378f
  in microphthalmia, 1732, 1733f
  intracranial, macrocephaly due to,
      1003–1004, 1004f
  laryngeal, 1152, 1152f
  lingual, 1149, 1149f
  nasolacrimal duct, 1147
  ovarian
    aspiration of, 234t
    ultrasonography of, 150
  thyroglossal duct, 1149
Cystathionine β-synthase deficiency, in
    neonatal period, 1612
Cysteine, in parenteral nutrition, 684, 684t,
    685, 687
Cystic adenomatoid malformation
  chest radiograph of, 716, 716f
  congenital, 241–243
    algorithm in management of, 243f
    differential diagnosis of, 241
    fetal surgery for, 234t
    manifestation of, 1134
    prenatal diagnosis of, 241–242, 242f
    prenatal treatment of, 242–243, 243f
    thoracoamniotic shunts for, 232
    ultrasonography of, 241, 242f
  in nonimmune hydrops fetalis, 422, 423
Cystic duplications, gastrointestinal, 1393
Cystic fibrosis, 1363–1364
  clinical features of, 1364
  diagnosis of, 1364
    prenatal, 1364
  DNA diagnosis of, 128, 128f
  genetics of, 1363, 1395
  incidence of, 1363
  management of, 1364
  meconium ileus in, 1364, 1395
  molecular pathogenesis of, 1363–1364
  vs. pseudohypoaldosteronism, 702
Cystic hygroma
  airway obstruction due to, 1143
  definition of, 1710
  in nonimmune hydrops fetalis, 421–422
  perinatal ultrasonography of, 155, 156f
Cystitis, in pregnancy, 429–430
Cystourethrography, voiding
  in renal function assessment, 1667
  of posterior urethral valves, 724–725, 725f

Cytochrome-b₅, in methemoglobinemia, 1308
Cytochrome c oxidase deficiency, hepatic
    dysfunction in, 1622
Cytochrome P-450 enzymes
  expression of, in fetal liver and adrenal
      gland, 211, 211t
  in drug metabolism, 193f, 193–194
    characteristics of, 205t
  placental, 210
Cytokine(s), 773–777. See also specific
    cytokine, e.g., Interleukin entries.
  activity of, after hypoxic-ischemic insult,
      943
  biology of, 774–775
  in sepsis diagnosis, 798
  in T cell function, 781–782
  inflammatory
    alveolar development affected by, 1073
    bronchopulmonary dysplasia related to,
        1161
    in necrotizing enterocolitis, 1408–1409,
        1409f
    in neonatal sepsis, 775–777, 777f, 778t
    in preterm labor prediction, 342–343
    in white matter damage, 915–916, 916f
  production of, by T helper cells, 781
  therapeutic, for neutropenia, 1313–1314
Cytokine receptor signaling, in T cell
    development, 780–781
Cytomegalic inclusion disease, 844–845
Cytomegalovirus infection, 438–439
  after heart transplantation, 1270
  clinical manifestations of, 438
    vs. toxoplasmosis, 839f
  congenital
    asymptomatic, 439, 844, 844t
    chorioretinitis in, 845, 845t, 1743
    clinical findings in, 845, 845t
    diagnosis of, 846–847
    outcome of, 845, 846t
    prevention of, 439, 847
    sequelae of, 845, 845t, 846f
    symptomatic, 439, 844–846
    treatment of, 847
  cutaneous, 1699t
  epidemiology of, 438, 843
  in sensorineural hearing loss, 1048
  maternal manifestation of, 844
  perinatal, 846
  transfusion-transmitted, 1345–1346
  transmission of, 438f, 438–439, 843–844

D

D antigen, 1429
  anti-D immunoprophylaxis for, 393–394
  anti-D monoclonal antibodies against, 394
  in Rh system, 389
D-dimer test, for disseminated intravascular
    coagulation, 1329–1330
Dacryocystitis, 1733
Dactylitis (hand-foot syndrome), 1304
Damages, in malpractice litigation, 54
Damping, in blood pressure monitoring, 614
Damus-Kaye-Stansel operation, 1231, 1269t
Danazol, maternal ingestion of, fetal
    masculinization due to, 1584–1585
Dandy-Walker syndrome
  abnormalities in, 904, 904f
  anesthetic implications of, 633t
  hydrocephalus in, 999–1000, 1000f
  ultrasonography of, 154, 154f
Dane particle, of hepatitis B, 863

Databases, for evaluation of neonatal
    intensive care. See Neonatal intensive
    care, quality of.
DAZ gene, 124
De Morsier syndrome (septo-optic
    dysplasia), 992, 1745
Dead space, 1093
Deafness. See Hearing loss.
Death
  brain, organ donation and, 41
  cell
    in heart development, 1201–1202
    programmed. See Apoptosis.
  fetal. See Fetal death.
  rate of. See Maternal mortality; Neonatal
      mortality; Perinatal mortality.
  sudden infant. See Sudden infant death
      syndrome.
  wrongful, tort actions related to, 55
Death certificates, in neonatal care
    evaluation database, 69
Debrancher enzyme deficiency, 989
Decelerations, in fetal heart rate, 174–176,
    175f–177f
  early, 176, 176f
  late, 175–176, 176f
  prolonged, 176, 177f
  variable, 174–175, 175f
Decidua, premature activation of, in
    initiation of labor, 333
Decision making. See Ethics, decision
    making in.
Decompression
  in utero, for obstructive uropathy, 236
  of joint, in septic arthritis, 1766
Decongestants, fetal effects of, 189t
Deep tendon reflexes, assessment of, 526
Deformations
  definition of, 561
  etiology of, 563t, 564
Degenerative disorders, macrencephaly
    associated with, 997
Degranulation, disorders of, 1317
Deiodinase, in thyroxine mono-
    deiodination, 1526
Dejerine-Sottas syndrome, 979–980
Delivery. See also Labor.
  analgesia for. See Analgesia.
  anesthesia for. See Anesthesia.
  by cesarean section. See Cesarean section.
  forceps. See Forceps.
  high-risk, history of, 3–5, 6f
  in chronic hypertension, 318
  in developing countries
    aseptic technique in, 95, 98f
    home delivery facilities in, 95
  in intrauterine growth restriction, 295
  in multiple gestations, considerations for,
      380–381
  in preeclampsia-eclampsia
    indications for, 314
    method of, 314
  indications for, in nonimmune hydrops
      fetalis, 426
  maternal mortality in, in early 1900s, 4
  natural child birth in, 468
  nerve blocks for, 469
  operative vaginal
    anesthetic technique for, 477
    neuraxial blockade in, 475
  preterm. See Preterm delivery.
  timing of
    for gastroschisis and omphalocele, 1383
    gestational diabetes mellitus and, 324

Delivery—*cont'd*
  tobacco effects on, 740
  vacuum extraction
    anesthetic technique for, 477
    birth injuries due to, 533
    skull fractures due to, 534
    subgaleal hemorrhage due to, 533
Delivery room
  genital examination in, 1556–1557, 1557b
  heat loss prevention in, 595
Dendrites, growth of, 891–893, 893f, 894f
Dental anomalies, in ectodermal dysplasia,
    1714
Denver Test of Infant Development II, for
    high-risk neonate, 1040
Denys-Drash syndrome, 1681
  WT1 gene mutation in, 1571
Deoxybarbiturates, fetal effects of, 187t
Deoxyribonucleic acid. *See* DNA *entries.*
Depression, neonatal
  asphyxia and, 486, 486b
  due to analgesia, 505
  meconium aspiration related to, 1123
  with neuromuscular disease, 1142
  with spinal cord injury, 1141
Dermatan sulfate, dermal, 1689
Dermatitis
  atopic, 1711
  irritant contact, 1710
  seborrheic, 1710–1711, 1711f
Dermatoglyphics, 575
Dermatoses, subcutaneous and infiltrative,
    1711–1713
Dermis. *See also* Skin *entries.*
  development of, 1688–1689
Dermoid cysts
  intranasal, 1148
  lingual, 1149, 1149f
  of eyelids, 1731
  orbital, 1735
Descemet membrane
  birth injury to, 1727
  rupture of, at birth, 539
Desferrioxamine, chelation therapy with, for
    Diamond-Blackfan anemia, 1307
Desmethyldiazepam, in breast milk, 199
17,20-Desmolase deficiency, 1575
20,22-Desmolase deficiency, 1583–1584
Desmosterolosis, cholesterol biosynthesis
    defects in, 1627
Desquamation
  dysmaturity and, 1693
  hanging skin in, 297
  physiologic, 1693
Developing countries
  cytomegalovirus infection in, 843
  delivery in
    aseptic technique in, 95, 98f
    home facilities for, 95
    maternal mortality in, 87
    neonatal care in, 95–99
      antenatal home-based care in, 102
      assessment of infant in, 101, 102t
      breast feeding in, 100, 100b
      components of, 95, 95b, 96f–99f
      home-based care in, 102–103, 104f
      home visits by health care workers in,
        101, 101t, 102t
      hypothermia management in, 95–97,
        97f–99f, 99, 100t
      maternal education and, 100–101
      modern technology in, 103–106, 105t
      nasal continuous positive airway
        pressure in, 105

Developing countries—*cont'd*
    resuscitation in, 99, 99f, 500
    strategies for improving outcome of,
      107f, 107–108, 108t
    surfactant therapy in, 105–106
    traditional birth attendant and
      community health worker in,
      101–103, 103t
  neonatal intensive care units in
    development of, 106
    ethical dilemmas in use of, 106–107
  neonatal mortality in
    by geographic region, 88–91, 90f, 90t,
      91f
    causes of, 91–94, 92f, 93f
    global burden of, 87–88, 88f
    global interventions for reducing, 88,
      89f
    in oil- and mineral-dependent
      countries, 91, 92
    strategies for reducing, 107f, 107–108,
      108t
  perinatal health services in, 94–95
    equipment for, 94–95
    staffing for, 94
Development
  after intravascular transfusion, 404
  infant stimulation for, in
    bronchopulmonary dysplasia, 1167
Developmental care model, for preterm
    infant, 1057–1058, 1058f
Developmental immunology, 761–791
Developmental reflexes, assessment of, 526
Dexamethasone
  adverse effects of, 218–219, 219t
  dosages of, 1792
  for congenital adrenal hyperplasia,
    217–218
  intrauterine therapy with, 217
  for fetal lung maturation, 213
  for preterm labor prevention, 355, 356
Dextrocardia, 1242
Dextrose solution, for hypoglycemia, 974
Diabetes insipidus
  hypernatremia and, 702
  nephrogenic, 1662, 1662t
Diabetes mellitus
  gestational, 321–328
    antepartum testing for, 324
    complications of, 325–327
    congenital anomalies associated with,
      326
    congenital heart disease related to, 1204
    definition of, 321
    diagnosis of, 322–323
    hypoxia in, 327
    intrauterine fetal demise in, 327
    intrauterine growth restriction in, 327
    macrosomia in, 326–327
    management of, 323–325
      glucose control in, 323
      medical, 323–324
      postpartum, 324–325
      weight control in, 323
    nephropathy in, 325
    offspring of mothers with, 327
    pathophysiology of, 321–322
    perinatal mortality rate in, 327
    polyhydramnios in, 327
    retinopathy in, 325
    screening for, 322
    signs and symptoms of, 322
    timing of delivery in, 324
    White's classification of, 321t

Diabetes mellitus—*cont'd*
  in nonpregnant patients, definition of, 322
  in preeclampsia-eclampsia, 312
  insulin-dependent (type 1), 321
  maternal
    congenital anomalies associated with,
      564
    hypocalcemia in, 1510
    hypomagnesemia in, 1518–1519
    indications for delivery of infant and,
      1476–1477
    infants and, 1473–1478. *See also* Infant
      of diabetic mother.
    management of, 1475–1477
    vs. polyhydramnios, 419–420
  neonatal, 1490–1491, 1490f
    management of, 1491
  non–insulin-dependent (type 2), 321
  preconception counseling in, 327–328
  risk of, after gestational diabetes, 325
Diabetic ketoacidosis, gestational diabetes
    mellitus and, 325–326
Diagnosis related groups, in neonatal care
    evaluation database, 70–71, 71t, 72t
Dialysis, for acute renal failure, indications
    for, 1669–1670
Diamond-Blackfan anemia, 1306–1307
  vs. Fanconi anemia, 1306
Diamond duodenostomy, for duodenal web,
    1392
Diaphragm
  congenital eventration of, 1146
  disorders of, respiratory distress
    associated with, 1145–1146, 1146f
  paradoxical motion of, 1146
Diaphragmatic hernia
  congenital
    algorithm for management of, 239f
    chest radiograph of, 715–716, 716f
    differential diagnosis of, 237
    extracorporeal membrane oxygenation
      in, 1169f, 1172–1173
    fetal surgery for, 234t, 237–241, 1172
    foramen of Bochdalek defect in, 1378
    foramen of Morgagni defect in, 1378
    gastrointestinal effects of, 1378–1379
    in nonimmune hydrops fetalis, 422,
      423, 423f
    left-sided, 1131, 1132f
      position of liver in, 238–239
    neonatal resuscitation and, 507
    postnatal management of, 1132,
      1172–1173
    prenatal diagnosis of, 237–239, 238f
    prenatal treatment of, 239–241, 240f
    prognosis in, 1172
    pulmonary hypoplasia in, 1074,
      1131–1132
    surfactant therapy in, 1173
    ultrasonography of, 158, 159f, 237–238,
      238f
Diarrhea, 1368–1372
  congenital chloride, 1368–1369, 1370t
  congenital sodium, 1369–1370, 1370t
  in acrodermatitis enteropathica, 1370, 1703
  in autoimmune enteropathy, 1372
  in carbohydrate absorption disorders,
    1365
  in congenital lactase deficiency, 1366
  in glucose-galactose malabsorption, 1367
  in inborn errors of metabolism, 1619
  in maltase-glucoamylase deficiency, 1366
  in microvillus inclusion disease,
    1371–1372

Diarrhea—cont'd
  in short bowel syndrome, 1370–1371
  in sucrase-isomaltase deficiency,
    congenital, 1366
  in tufting enteropathy, 1372
  osmotic, 1368
  secretory, 1368
    hormonally mediated, 1370
Diastematomyelia
  in congenital scoliosis, 1771
  perinatal ultrasonography of, 155
  spinal defects associated with, 1758
Diastolic function, 1214
  echocardiographic measurement of, 1219,
    1220b
Diazepam
  fetal effects of, 187t
  for seizures, 974
  for spasms, in tetanus neonatorum, 825
  in breast milk, 199
Diazoxide
  dosages of, 1791
  for hypoglycemia, 1487
  for neonatal hypertension, 1672t
Dichlorodiphenyl trichloroethane (DDT)
  fetal exposure to, 262
  in breast milk, 201
2,4-Dichlorophenoxyacetic acid, maternal
  exposure to, pregnancy outcome in,
  260t
Dieldrin, in breast milk, 201
Diet. See also Nutrition.
  concurrent maternal exposure and, 259
  preeclampsia-eclampsia and, 312
Dietary galactose restriction, for
  galactosemia, 1611
Diethylstilbestrol (DES)
  exposure to, cervical incompetence
    associated with, 336
  fetal effects of, 188t
  transgenerational effects of, 256
DiGeorge syndrome, 968
  anesthetic implications of, 633t
  gene abnormalities in, 1201
    chromosome 22q11 deletions in, 1201
  heart defects associated with, 1203t
  overlap with CHARGE association, 1144
  single gene defects in, 1204
Digestive disorders, 1363–1372. See also
  Gastrointestinal tract, digestive
  disorder(s) of.
Digitalis, fetal effects of, 188t
Digits. See Finger(s); Thumb; Toe(s).
Digoxin
  dosages of, 1788
  for cardiomyopathy, 1249
  for congestive heart failure, 1267
  for fetal arrhythmias, 223t, 223–224, 1210
  for neonatal tachycardia, 1260t, 1261b,
    1263, 1264
  in breast milk, 199
Digoxin immune Fab, dosages of, 1789
Dihydrostreptomycin, fetal effects of, 187t
Dihydrotestosterone, in genitalia
  differentiation, 1555f, 1556
Dilation therapy, after imperforate anus
  repair, 1402
Diluted tincture of opium, for neonatal
  abstinence syndrome, 750
Diodes, light-emitting, in pulse oximetry, 619
Dioxin, in breast milk, 201
Diploid state, 113
Dipole, 610
Dipole theory, in cardiac monitoring, 609

Directed-donor blood programs, 1347
Disability(ies). See also specific disability.
  neonatal, legal issues related to, 57–59, 61
  severe, at age 2 years, suggested criteria
    for, 1036, 1037b
Disaccharidase deficiencies, 1365–1367
Discordance, birthweight, in multiple
  gestations, 379–380
Dislocation(s)
  birth-related, 554–555
  of knee, 1777–1778, 1778f
Disomy, uniparental, 126
Dispermy, 116
Disruptions, definition of, 561
Disseminated intravascular coagulation
  diagnosis of, 1329–1330
  treatment of, 1330
  vascular malformations associated with,
    1329
  with herpes simplex virus infection, 842
Distichiasis, 1722, 1731
Diuretics
  fetal effects of, 188t
  for bronchopulmonary dysplasia, 1165
  for cardiomyopathy, 1249
  for fluid balance, in congenital heart
    disease, 1267
  for nephrogenic diabetes insipidus, 702
  for pulmonary edema, 1244
  loop, nephrocalcinosis related to, 1674
  neutropenia due to, 1313b
  placental transport of, transient neonatal
    hypoglycemia due to, 1472–1473
Diving reflex, in asphyxia, 486–487
DKC1 gene, in Hoyeraal-Hreidarsson
  syndrome, 1311
DM1 gene, in myotonic dystrophy, 984
DM2 gene, in myotonic dystrophy, 984
DNA
  denaturation and strand synthesis of, in
    polymerase chain reaction, 129
  errors of replication of, 122
  mitochondrial, 124–125
  mitochondrial-encoded, in respiratory
    chain defects, 1619, 1641t, 1643, 1644
  nuclear-encoded, in respiratory chain
    defects, 1619, 1641t, 1643, 1644
DNA analysis
  of amniotic fluid, 137
  technical advances in, 139
DNA markers, in diagnosis of genetic
  disorders, 127–132
  applications of, 130–132, 131f
  approach to, 128f, 128–130, 129f
DNA probe, for fluorescent in situ
  hybridization, 119, 120f
DNA sequencing
  for genetic mutations, 129–130
  in fascioscapulohumeral muscular
    dystrophy, 985
Dobutamine
  dosages of, 1787
  for afterload reduction, in congenital heart
    disease, 1267
  inotropic effect of, 1267
Docosahexaenoic acid
  in breast milk, 666
  visual acuity related to, 666–667
Documentation. See Medical records.
Dolichocephaly, 1007
  in congenital anomalies, 568, 569f
Doll's eye reflex
  in optic nerve assessment, 524
  in preterm infant, 526

Donlan syndrome, 1365
Dopamine
  dosages of, 1787
  in neonatal resuscitation, 503t, 505
  inotropic effect of, 1267
Doppler flow velocimetry
  fetal evaluation with, 170f, 170, 171f
  for fetal anemia, 398
    middle cerebral artery peak systolic
      velocity in, 394–395, 399, 400f, 400t
    splenic artery velocimetry index in, 399
Doppler flow velocity waveforms, in
  intrauterine growth restriction, 292–293,
  293f
Doppler ultrasonography, perinatal, 151, 151f
Dorsal penile nerve block, for circumcision,
  641
Double bubble sign, in duodenal atresia,
  719, 719f, 1391, 1391f
Double cortex syndrome, 908
Double-outlet right ventricle, 1231–1232
Down syndrome. See Trisomy 21 (Down
  syndrome).
Doxycycline, for chlamydial infections, 447
Drug(s). See also named drug or drug
  group.
  absorption of
    in neonate, 191–193
      factors influencing, 192–193
    in pregnancy, 205–206
  abuse of. See Substance abuse.
  aerosolized, maternal absorption of, 206
  discontinuation of, in seizure therapy, 975
  disposition of
    fetal, 210–211, 211t
    maternal, 205t, 205–207
    neonatal, 193f, 193–195
  distribution of
    fetal, 262, 262f
    maternal, 206t, 206–207, 207t
  dosage of, in neonate, 196
    role of maturity and postnatal age and,
      197
  effectiveness of, determinants of, 204, 204f
  fetal exposure to, 183–191
    adverse effects in, 184–185, 186t,
      187t–189t, 189–191
      determination of, 190–191
    during delivery, 469–471, 470t
    factors modifying, 189–190
    heart defects associated with, 1204
    ingestion by father and, 184
    maternal consumption and, 183
    mechanisms of toxicity in, 190, 190f
    nontherapeutic agents and, 185, 189
    placental transfer in, 183–184, 184f
    renal defects associated with, 1664
    timing of, 184–185, 185f
  illicit. See also Substance abuse.
    in maternal-placental-fetal unit, 189
    intrauterine growth restriction due to,
      283–284
  in breast milk, 199–202
  in neonate, 191f, 191–197
  interactions among, 189–190
  intrauterine growth restriction form,
    283–284
  lactation and, 197–202. See also Breast
    milk.
  maternal consumption of, 183
    breast-feeding and, 202
  metabolism of
    cytochrome P-450 enzyme
      characteristics in, 205t

Drug(s)—cont'd
  fetal, 263, 263f, 470
    maternal, 207
    neonatal, 193f, 193–195
  monitoring of, in neonate, 197
  neutropenia due to, 1312, 1313b
  paternal ingestion of, 184
  percutaneous, maternal absorption of,
    206
  pharmacokinetics of
    in fetus, 469–471, 470t
    in neonate, 194, 196, 196f
  placental transfer of, 183–184, 184f, 209b,
    209–210
    umbilical vein to maternal vein ratio as
      measure of, 470, 470t
  plasma disappearance of, in neonate, 196,
    196f
  protein binding of, in neonate, 193
  renal excretion of
    maternal, 207
    neonatal, 195f, 195–196
  toxicity of, mechanisms of, 190, 190f
  withdrawal from, seizures and, 971
Dry eye, 1733–1734
DSS gene, duplication of, 1571–1572
Dual energy x-ray absorptiometry, of bone
  mineralization, 1505
Dubowitz Neurological Assessment of
  Preterm and Full-Term Infant, 1063
Duchenne-Erb palsy, 542
Duchenne muscular dystrophy, 985
  genetics of, 124
Ductus arteriosus
  absence of, 1240
  patent. See Patent ductus arteriosus.
  premature closure of, fetal assessment of,
    1210
  right-to-left shunting through, in persistent
    pulmonary hypertension, 1246
Duhamel procedure, for Hirschsprung
  disease, 1399
Duodenal atresia, 1390–1392
  congenital anomalies associated with,
    1391–1392
  in polyhydramnios, 419, 419f
  radiography of, 719, 719f, 1391, 1391f
  treatment of, 1392
  types of, 1390, 1391f
  ultrasonography of, 157, 157f, 1391
  vs. malrotation or volvulus, 1391
Duodenostomy, diamond, for duodenal
  web, 1392
Duodenum
  development of, 1360–1362
  duplications of, 1393
  rotation and fixation of, 1360–1361,
    1360f
  villi in, 1361
  web of, surgical treatment of, 1392
Duplication(s)
  chromosomal, 119
  esophageal, 1378, 1378f
  gastrointestinal, 1392–1393, 1392f, 1393f
  limb bud insult in, 1757
Duty, legal concept of, 51–52
Dwarfism, 996
  anesthetic implications of, 633t
  camptomelic, 1557
    SOX9 gene mutation in, 1571
  thanatophoric. See Thanatophoric
    dysplasia.
Dysalbuminemic hyperthyroxinemia,
  familial, 1550

Dysautonomia, familial (Riley-Day
    syndrome)
  criteria for, 980
  ocular manifestation of, 1734
Dyserythropoiesis, X-linked
    thrombocytopenia with, 1341
Dyserythropoietic anemia, congenital, 1308
Dysfibrinogenemia, 1333
Dyshormonogenesis, familial, 1536–1537
Dyskeratosis congenita, neutropenia in,
  1311
Dyskinesia, neonatal, without electrographic
  seizures, 961, 963
Dysmature infant, desquamation of, 1696
Dysmaturity syndrome, 384f, 384–385
Dysmorphic syndromes
  cholesterol biosynthesis and, 1625t,
    1626–1627
  congenital disorders of glycosylation and,
    1625–1626
  inborn errors of metabolism causing,
    1624–1629
  large-molecule metabolism defects and,
    1624–1626, 1625t
  lysosomal storage diseases and, 1625t,
    1626
  peroxisomal disorders and, 1625t, 1628
  small for gestational age infant and, 296t,
    298
  small-molecule metabolism defects and,
    1625t, 1626–1629
  vitamin K metabolism and, 1628–1629
Dysplasia syndrome, in infant of diabetic
  mother, 1475
Dystonia, neonatal, without electrographic
  seizures, 961, 963

E

Eagle-Barrett syndrome
  anesthetic implications of, 633t
  in hydronephrosis, 1678, 1678f
Ear(s). See also specific part, e.g., Auditory
    canal.
  anatomic landmarks of, 571, 571f
  birth injuries to, 539–540, 540f
  congenital anomalies of
    examination of, 571, 571f–572f
    phenotypic variants as, 565, 566t
  developmental anomalies of, 1047–1048
  embryology of, 1047
  examination of, 515, 518
  function of, 1045
  normal orientation of, 571, 571f
  preauricular tags of, 571, 571f
Early Neonatal Neurobehavioral Scale
    (ENNS), 1063
Ebstein anomaly
  defects associated with, 1228
  fetal congestive heart failure and, 1209
Ecchymoses, birth-related, 530, 530f
  ear injuries in, 539
Eccrine sweat glands
  development of, 1687–1688
  obstruction of, miliaria related to, 1692
Echocardiography
  cardiac imaging in, 1218–1219, 1218b
  Doppler
    blood flow estimation by, 1212
    continuous-wave, 1219
    of congenital heart disease, 1208, 1219
    pulsed, 1219

Echocardiography—cont'd
  Doppler color flow, of vascular rings,
    1250–1251
  fetal
    for congenital heart disease, 1207–1208,
      1207b
    methods in, 1208
    timing of, 1208
  of arrhythmias, 1209, 1209f
  of aortic arch interruption, 1234, 1235f
  of aortic stenosis, 1233, 1233f
  of cardiac function, 1219, 1219t, 1220b,
    1220t
  of coarctation of aorta, 1234, 1235f
  of congenital heart disease, 579,
    1218–1219
    cardiac imaging in, 1218–1219, 1218b
    Doppler, 1219
    fetal, 1207–1208, 1207b
    measurement of cardiac function in,
      1219, 1219t, 1220b, 1220t
  of cor pulmonale, 1243
  of diastolic function, 1214
  of hypoplastic left heart syndrome, 1236,
    1236f
  of nonimmune hydrops fetalis, 424
  of patent ductus arteriosus, 1240, 1241f
  of persistent pulmonary hypertension,
    1247
  of pulmonary atresia, 1227
  of pulmonary stenosis, 1238
  of tetralogy of Fallot, 1225, 1225f
  of total anomalous pulmonary venous
    connection, 1229, 1229f
  of tricuspid atresia, 1226, 1226f
  of truncus arteriosus, 1230
  of ventricular septal defect, 1239
  transesophageal, bacterial endocarditis
    and, 1268
Echovirus infection. See Enterovirus
  infections.
Eclampsia, 307. See also Preeclampsia-
    eclampsia.
  fetal weight after, 283, 283f
  seizures and, hyperreflexia in, 312
  treatment of, 315
Ecogenetics, 263
Ecstasy (3,4-methylenedioxymeth-
    amphetamine), 748–749
Ectodermal dysplasia, 1714
  hypohidrotic, 1711, 1714
Ectrodactyly, 575, 576
Ectropion, congenital, 1731
Edema. See also Lymphedema.
  cerebral
    in hypoxic-ischemic encephalopathy,
      940, 953
    respiratory distress related to, 1141
  eyelid, examination of, 516
  in hydrops fetalis, 391
    ultrasonography of, 392f, 397, 398f
  of airway, in preeclampsia, anesthetic
    considerations in, 479
  of hands and feet, in Turner and Noonan
    syndromes, 575, 577f
  of vocal cords, after extubation, 1119
  pulmonary
    bronchopulmonary dysplasia related to,
      1161
    in cor pulmonale, diuretics for, 1244
    radiography of, 1217, 1217b, 1217f
  villous, 459
Edward syndrome. See Trisomy 18 (Edward
  syndrome).

Efivirenz, in HIV prophylaxis, teratogenicity of, 848
Ehlers-Danlos syndrome, 1713–1714, 1713f
Eicosanoid imbalance, in preeclampsia, 309, 309f
Einthoven's approach, in cardiac monitoring, 610
Ejection fraction, 1213
Elastance, 1094
Elastase 1, fecal, in cystic fibrosis diagnosis, 1364
Elastic fibers, dermal, 1688
Elastin gene mutations, in Williams syndrome, 1195
Elbow, congenital anomalies of, 1767
Electric shock, phototherapy and, 1445
Electrocardiography (ECG)
    ambulatory, of arrhythmias, 1252
    esophageal, of arrhythmias, 1252
    heart rate measurement by, 1252
    monitoring with, 609–612, 610f–612f, 612b
    of accessory pathway reentrant tachycardia, 1255, 1255f
    of aortic stenosis, 1233
    of arrhythmias, 1252
    of atrioventricular node reentrant tachycardia, 1255–1256
    of congenital heart disease, 1218, 1218b
    of Ebstein anomaly, 1228
    of endocardial cushion defects, 1239
    of junctional ectopic tachycardia, 1257, 1257f
    of pulmonary atresia, 1227
    of tricuspid atresia, 1226
    of truncus arteriosus, 1230
    of ventricular tachycardia, 1257, 1258f
Electroclinical uncoupling, in neonatal seizures, 963
Electrodes
    in cardiac monitoring, 610–611
    in fetal blood scalp sampling
        herpes simplex transmission related to, 841
        sepsis associated with, 793
Electroencephalography (EEG)
    of brain integrity, 944–947, 944f–946f
    of seizures, 959f–962f, 963, 964f, 965–966, 966f
Electrography, atrial, 1252
Electrolyte(s). See also specific electrolyte.
    balance of, monitoring of, 700
    in enteral nutrition, 669, 670t
    in fetal lung fluid, 1074
    in parenteral nutrition, 687
    maintenance of, 697–698
    malabsorption of, diarrhea due to, 1368–1370, 1369f
    management of, 695–703
    replacement of, 700, 700t
        in bronchopulmonary dysplasia, 703
        in patent ductus arteriosus, 703
        in perinatal asphyxia, 702–703
        in respiratory distress syndrome, 1105–1106
    requirements for, calculation of, 697–700
    serum values for, 1801t
Electrolyte gel, for electrodes, 611
Electronic fetal monitoring, controlled trials of, Cochrane Review of, 950
Elements
    common, atomic weight and valance of, 1817t
    trace. See Trace elements.

Elliptocytosis
    forms of, 1430
    hereditary, 1300, 1301f
Ellis–van Creveld syndrome
    anesthetic implications of, 633t
    heart defects associated with, 1203t
EMBASE database, 80
Embolization
    coil, for cor pulmonale, 1244
    of arteriovenous malformations, 1244
    transcatheter technique of, 1274
    ultrasound-guided, for twin reversed arterial perfusion sequence, 249
Embryo, 207
Embryogenesis, critical periods in, timing of drug exposure and, 184–185, 185f
Emesis. See Vomiting.
Emphysema
    congenital lobar, 1133–1134, 1134f
        chest radiograph of, 716–717, 717f
    in bronchopulmonary dysplasia, 1157, 1158f
    pulmonary interstitial, chest radiograph of, 714, 714f
Empyema, subdural, macrocephaly due to, 1005
Enalapril, dosages of, 1793
Enalaprilat, for neonatal hypertension, 1672t
Encephalitis
    measles, 852
    with herpes simplex virus infection, 842
Encephalo-oculofacial angiomatosis, 1729
Encephalocele, 901, 901f
    proptosis due to, 1736
    ultrasonography of, 153–154, 154f
Encephalomyelitis, congenital, 909–910. See also Leukomalacia, periventricular.
Encephalopathy
    early myoclonic, 973
    hypoxic-ischemic, 938–956. See also Hypoxic-ischemic encephalopathy.
    in term infant, 461
    neonatal, hypothermia as neuroprotection against, 597
    postasphyxial, 967
    transient, unconjugated hyperbilirubinemia due to, 1434
End-expiratory pressure. See Positive end-expiratory pressure (PEEP).
End-inspiratory occlusion, in pulmonary function assessment, 1095, 1096f
End-tidal carbon dioxide
    in airflow measurement, 1092
    monitoring of, during anesthesia, 636
End-tidal carbon monoxide
    measurements of, 1439
    monitoring of, 623
Endocardial cushion tissue
    defect of, 1239
    formation of, 1200
Endocarditis, bacterial, prevention of, 1268
Endocrine system
    disorders of
        fetal, treatment of, 216–220
        in persistent hypoglycemia, 1483–1484
    drugs affecting, breast-milk transfer of, 200
Endomyocardial biopsy, transcatheter, 1275
Endophthalmitis, in candidiasis, 831
Endothelial cells
    activation of, 1318–1319
    fibrinolytic activities of, 1319
Endothelial-leukocyte adhesion molecules, 1318

Endothelin type 1, 1245
Endothelium, platelet aggregation on, 1319–1320, 1319f
Endothelium-derived relaxing factor, 1177. See also Nitric oxide.
Endotoxin, intra-amniotic, lung maturation induction by, 1086, 1087f
Endotracheal intubation. See also Extubation.
    complications of, 497–498, 497t
        tracheal lesions in, 1118–1119, 1119f
    equipment for, 637
    for meconium removal, 1124
    for surfactant therapy, 1104
    for tracheal meconium suctioning, 507
    glottis visualization for, 495–496, 496f, 497f
    history of, 12–13
    hyperventilation with, for cyanotic spells, 1268
    in neonatal resuscitation, 495–498
    injury due to, 1154–1155, 1154f
    neonatal, resuscitation and, 951
    placement of, 496–497, 497t
    positioning of infant in, 495, 496f
    preoperative, 632, 634
    rapid-sequence intubation in, 640
    respiratory physiology and, 628
    subglottic stenosis due to, 1154–1155, 1154f
    transportation of patient and, 635
    tube sizes for, 495, 495t, 1113, 1113t
Enema
    contrast, for meconium plug syndrome, 1397
    Gastrografin, for meconium ileus, 1396
Energy
    balance of, 661–662, 662t
    expenditure of, 661–662, 662t, 680
    intake of, 663–664
    requirements for
        in enteral nutrition, 661–664
        in parenteral nutrition, 680
    storage of, 663
Enteral nutrition, 661–679. See also Nutrition; Parenteral nutrition.
    breast milk in, 670, 671t–672t, 676
    carbohydrate requirements in, 664
    cholestasis prevention or reduction by, 688
    delay of, after neonatal resuscitation, 506
    electrolytes in, 669, 670t
    energy requirements in, 661–664, 662t
    for bronchopulmonary dysplasia, 1165
    for necrotizing enterocolitis
        breast milk and, 1406–1407, 1406t
        minimal enteral feeding in, 675, 679
        rapid advancement of feedings in, 676
    for osteopenia of prematurity, 1522
    for short bowel syndrome, 1371
    formulas in
        preterm, 670, 672, 673t–674t
        preterm discharge, 673t–674t, 674
        specialized, 674
    in gastroschisis repair, 1384
    lipid requirements in, 665–667
    methods of, in high-risk infants, 676
    minimal, 675–676
        combined with parenteral nutrition, 688
    nasogastric tube for, 676
    of extremely low birthweight infant, practical approach to, 678–679
    orogastric tube for, 676
    progression to oral feeding, 676–678
    protein requirements in, 664–665

Enteral nutrition—*cont'd*
  trace elements in, 669–670, 670t
  vitamin requirements and supplements in, 667–669, 668t
Enteric nervous system
  abnormality of, in hypertrophic pyloric stenosis, 1389–1390
  gastric innervation by, 1359
Enterocolitis
  in Hirschsprung disease, 1398–1399
  necrotizing. *See* Necrotizing enterocolitis.
Enteroendocrine cells, 1359
Enterohepatic circulation, bilirubin absorption in, 1423–1424, 1424f
Enteropathy
  allergic, 1372
  autoimmune, 1370, 1372
  infectious, 1372
  tufting, 1372
Enteropeptidase deficiency, primary intestinal, 1367
Enterovirus infections, 861–863
  cutaneous, 1699t
  diagnosis of, 862
  during pregnancy, 862
  epidemiology and transmission of, 861–862
  neonatal, 862
  therapy and prevention of, 863
Entropion, 1722
  congenital, 1731
Environment
  influences of
    on brain development, 1052f, 1052–1054, 1053f
    on infant skin conditions, 1716, 1716f
    on neuronal migration, 908, 909f
  of intensive care nursery
    sensory, 597–603
      circadian rhythmicity in, 602
      hearing in, 600–602
      taste and smell in, 599–600
      touch in, 598–599
      vision in, 602–603
    thermal, 585–597. *See also* Heat exchange.
  pollutants of, in breast milk, 201–202
Environmental exposures, 255–265
  concurrent maternal, 255, 258–259, 260t, 261f
  cutaneous effects of, 1715b, 1716, 1716f
  fetal
    congenital anomalies due to, 133–134, 134t
    drug distribution in, 262, 262f
    drug metabolism in, 263, 263f
    heart defects associated with, 1204
    outcome of, 263b, 263–264, 264t
    pathways of, 259, 261–262
    pharmacokinetics of, 262f, 262–263, 263f
    placenta-dependent pathways of, 259, 261, 261b
    placenta-independent pathways of, 261b, 261f, 261–262, 262t, 262f
    secondary, 257–258, 258f
    to heat, 261
    to neonatal intensive care unit, 262
    to noise, 262, 262t
    to radiation, 261, 261f, 262f
  gastroschisis related to, 1382
  nonconcurrent maternal, 255f, 255–258
    body burden in, 257–258
      lead and, 258, 258f
      mercury and, 258

Environmental exposures—*cont'd*
    polychlorinated biphenyls and, 257–258, 258f
    ovum affected by, 255–256, 256t, 256f
    paternal effects of, 256–257
    preconceptual effects of, 255–256
Enzyme(s). *See also specific enzyme.*
  in drug metabolism, 193f, 193–195
  inherited defects of, hemolytic anemia and, 1301–1302, 1302b
  liver, elevated, in asphyxia, 951
  replacement, for inborn errors of metabolism, 1653
Epiblepharon, 1722, 1731
Epicanthal folds, in congenital anomalies, 570, 570f
Epicanthus, 1730
Epicanthus inversus, 1730
Epicardium, development of, 1201
Epidemiology, 19–25. *See also* Maternal mortality; Neonatal mortality; Perinatal mortality.
Epidermal growth factor, in fetal growth, 277
Epidermal nevi, 1710
Epidermis. *See also* Skin *entries.*
  barrier repair strategies for, 1716, 1716b
  development of, 1686–1688, 1686f, 1687f
Epidermolysis bullosa, 1700–1702
  Dowling-Meara subtype of, 1700, 1701t
  dystrophic subtype of, 1701, 1701t
  junctional subtype of, 1700–1701, 1701t, 1702f
  management strategies for, 1702, 1703b
  scarring subtype of, 1701–1702, 1701t
  subtypes of, 1700, 1701t
Epidermolytic hyperkeratosis, 1696
Epidermophyton infections, 835
Epididymis, birth injuries to, 557
Epidural anesthesia
  combined with spinal anesthesia, 474
  lumbar, 473
    continuous infusion in, 473
    patient-controlled, 474
Epiglottis
  anatomy of, 1150, 1150f
  bifid or absent, 1151, 1152f
  position of, 1150
Epiglottoplasty, for laryngomalacia, 1151, 1151f
Epignathi, intranasal, 1148
Epileptic syndromes, 971, 973. *See also* Seizures.
Epinephrine
  administration of, in neonatal resuscitation, 951
  deficiency of, in persistent hypoglycemia, 1484
  dosages of, 1787
  for hypoglycemia, 1487
  in neonatal resuscitation, 502–504, 503t
  inotropic effect of, 1267
  potential adverse effects of, 503–504
Epiphora, causes of, 1733
Epiphyseal cartilage, ossification disturbances of, in congenital hypothyroidism, 1542
Epiphyseal separations, birth-related, 555, 555f, 556f
Epithelial-mesenchymal transformation, in endocardial development, 1200
Epithelial sodium channel (ENaC), in clearance of fetal lung fluid, 1075
Epithelium, pulmonary, differentiation of, 1070–1072

Epoetin alfa, dosages of, 1790
Epoprostenol
  aerosolized, for persistent pulmonary hypertension, 1174, 1180
  endothelial cell production of, 1318
  for persistent pulmonary hypertension, 1180, 1248
Epoxide hydrolase, fetal levels of, 263, 263f
Epstein-Barr virus, 849–850
Epstein pearls
  examination of, 517
  incidence of, 1689b
  vs. milia, 1691
Erb palsy, in macrosomia, 327
Erb point, 1759
erbB proto-oncogene, 277
Ergot extracts, in breast milk, 200
Erythema, birth-related, 529
Erythema infectiosum, 869
Erythema toxicum
  clinical characteristics of, 1692
  examination of, 517
  incidence of, 1689b
Erythroblastosis fetalis, 389–405
  anemia prediction in, 398–400, 400f, 400t
  atypical antigens in, 404–405
  fetal transfusion for, 401–402
    fetal blood characteristics after, 400
    intraperitoneal, 402
    intravascular, 401–402, 402t
  genetics of Rh system in, 389–390
  historical background of, 13, 389
  management of, 393–403
  maternal Rh immunoglobulin prophylaxis for, 393–394
  neonatal resuscitation and, 507–508
  outcome of, 403–404
  preimplantation and first-trimester diagnosis of, 393
  RhD isoimmunization in
    hydrops fetalis in, 391–393, 392f
    pathophysiology of, 390–393
    sensitization in, 390–391, 391t
    ultrasonography of, 397–398, 398f, 399t
  screening for, 394–395
  spectrophotometry for, 395–397, 396f
  suppressive therapy for, 401
  timing of delivery in, 403
  transient hypoglycemia in, 1479–1480
  ultrasonography for, 397–400, 398f, 399t
Erythrocyte sedimentation rate, in sepsis diagnosis, 798
Erythrocytes. *See* Red blood cell(s).
Erythrocytosis. *See* Polycythemia.
Erythroderma, congenital ichthyosiform, 1696
Erythromycin
  dosages of, 1788
  for chlamydial infections, 447
  for conjunctivitis, 811
  for gastroenteritis, 813
  for group B streptococcal infection, 444–445
  for pneumonia, 809, 1127
  for premature rupture of membranes, 430–431
  for preterm labor prevention, 354
  for preterm premature rupture of membranes, 355
  for sepsis, 801t, 802t
  in breast milk, 199
  prophylactic, for sepsis, 804

Erythropoietic porphyria, 1714
  congenital
    jaundice in, 1429–1430
    phototherapy and, 1445
Erythropoietin, 1289t
  for anemia of prematurity, 1306
  levels of, during infancy, 1293, 1293t
  recombinant human, for respiratory
    distress syndrome, 1107
Escherichia coli
  antibiotic resistance of, 429, 430
  enteropathogenic, in gastroenteritis, 812
  in intrapartum infection, 460
  in sepsis, 792, 792t
  in white matter infections, 915, 915f
  K₁ strain of, in meningitis, 804
Esmolol, for neonatal hypertension, 1672t
Esophageal atresia, 1373–1377
  chest radiograph of, 717
  clinical presentation of, 1374
  defects associated with, 1373, 1375
  diagnosis of, 1374–1375, 1374f, 1375f
  gastroesophageal reflux in, 1377
  imperforate anus associated with, 1400
  incidence of, 1373
  lower esophageal sphincter dysfunction
    in, 1377
  pathogenesis of, 1373–1374
  physical examination of, 508
  respiratory support in, 1375
  surgical treatment of, 1375–1377
    anastomotic complications of, 1376,
      1377f
    functional disturbances after, 1376–1377
    gap length and, 1377, 1377f
    outcome of, 1377, 1378t
    postoperative care of, 1376
    upper pouch syndrome and, 1376, 1377f
  ultrasonography of, 157
Esophageal sphincter
  lower
    dysfunction of, in esophageal atresia/
      tracheoesophageal fistula, 1377
    in gastroesophageal reflux, 1379
    physiology of, 1379
  upper, 1358
Esophagus
  development of, 1357–1358
  duplications of, 1378, 1378f
  pressure in, measurement of, 1093
Esotropia, 1745
  infantile, 1745–1746
Estradiol, in preterm labor prediction, 342
Estriol
  in preterm labor prediction, 341–342
  unconjugated, screening for Down
    syndrome with, 136
Estrogens, fetal effects of, 188t
Ethambutol
  fetal effects of, 187t
  for tuberculosis, 827t
Ethamsylate, for periventricular-
  intraventricular hemorrhage, 932–933
Ethanol. *See also* Alcohol.
  in breast milk, 201
Ethical considerations, in perinatal
  ultrasonography, 144, 144f
Ethics, 35–45
  context of, 35–37
  cultural, spiritual, and religious diversity
    affecting, 37
  decision making in, 42–44
    collaborative framework for, 42–43
    communication in, 42

Ethics—*cont'd*
    criteria for, 24
    lack of consensus and, 43–44
    legal action and, 44–45
    medical uncertainty and, 40
  in antenatal period, 37–39
  in delivery room situations, 39–40
  in postnatal period, 40–42
  key terms and concepts in, 35–37
  of fetal therapy, 38–39
  of fetal viability, 39–40
  of multi-fetus pregnancy reductions, 37–38
  of neonatal intensive care, in developing
    countries, 106–107
  of organ donation, 41
  of palliative care, 41–42
  of refusal of treatment, 38
  of withholding or withdrawal of life-
    sustaining treatment, 40–41
    for handicapped neonates, 57–59
  of wrongful life cases, 55
  physician's responsibility in, 45
  theory of, 36–37
Ethionamide, fetal effects of, 187t
Ethisterone, fetal effects of, 188t
Ethosuximide, in breast milk, 200
Ethyl biscoumacetate, in breast milk, 199
Ethylene glycol, maternal exposure to,
    pregnancy outcome in, 260t
Ethylene oxide, maternal exposure to,
    pregnancy outcome in, 260t
Etomidate, as anesthetic induction agent, 478
European Society of Paediatric
    Gastroenterology and Nutrition
    Committee on Nutrition of the Preterm
    Infant, 668, 668t, 670t
Eustachian tube, embryology of, 1047
Eutectic mixture of local anesthetic (EMLA),
    for neonatal circumcision, 641
Euthyroid sick syndrome, 1544–1545
Evaporation
  heat exchange through
    at different ambient humidities, 589,
      590f, 591f
    calculation of, 586
  water and heat loss through
    before and after intubation, 593
    during phototherapy, 593, 593t
Evidence-based practice, 79–84
  application of, 82–83, 83f
  Cochrane systematic reviews in, 81
  critical appraisal in, 81–82, 81b
  focused clinical questions in, 79
  in developing countries, for reduction of
    neonatal mortality, 107, 108t
  primary reports in, 80, 80t
  promotion of, 83–84
  reviews in, 80–81
  search strategies for finding evidence in,
    80–81
  sources of evidence in, 79–80
  treatment effectiveness assessment in, 82,
    82t
Exchange transfusion. *See* Transfusion,
    exchange.
Excitotoxicity, of white matter lesions,
    915–916, 916f
Exercise(s). *See also* Physical activity.
  in management of gestational diabetes,
    323
  range-of-motion, for deformational
    plagiocephaly, 1014
EXIT procedure, for fetal airway obstruction,
    248f, 248–249

EXIT-to-ECMO, for congenital diaphragmatic
    hernia, 240f, 240–241
Exopthalmos
  hyperthyroid, 1736
  in orbital tumors, 1734, 1735
Exotropia, 1745
Expectorants, fetal effects of, 189t
Expert witness, in malpractice litigation,
    52–53
Expiratory flow, measurement of, 1096
Expiratory time, in assisted ventilation,
    1108–1109, 1109f
External auditory canal
  atresia of, 1047
  in mechanism of hearing, 1045
External ear
  anatomy of, 1045
  deformities of, 1047–1048
  embryology of, 1047
Extracorporeal membrane oxygenation
    (ECMO), 1168–1176
  basic technique of, 1169–1170
  coagulation defects and, 1330, 1331t
  cost analysis of, 1176
  disorders treated with, 1168–1169, 1169f
  for congenital diaphragmatic hernia, 239
  future considerations in, 1176
  in total anomalous pulmonary venous
    connection, 1229
  indications for, 1168
  infants on, transfusions for, 1352
  outcome of, 1175–1176
  patient selection for, 1170–1174, 1171b
    absence of complex congenital heart
      disease in, 1171–1172
    assisted ventilation duration in, 1172
    failure of medical therapy in, 1173–1174
    gestational age in, 1171
    normal cranial ultrasound in, 1171
    reversible lung disease in, 1172–1173
  personnel requirements in, 1170
  referral for, 1174–1175, 1174b
  venoarterial bypass in, 1169
  venovenous, 1170
Extrasystole, fetal, 222
Extremely low birthweight. *See also* Low
    birthweight; Very low birthweight.
  enteral feeding of, practical approach to,
    678–679
  hyperglycemia in, 681
  hypocalcemia in, 1510
  school-age outcome of, 1041
Extremity(ies). *See also specific part, e.g.,*
    Foot (feet); Hand(s).
  birth injuries to, 553–556
  congenital anomalies of
    classification of, 1757
    constriction band syndrome in, 1757,
      1768–1769, 1768f
    duplication in, 1757
    examination of, 574–578, 575f–578f
    generalized skeletal abnormalities in,
      1757
    of lower extremities, 1772–1781
    of upper extremities, 1767–1770
    overgrowth in, 1757
    part differentiation failure in, 1757
    part formation failure in, 1757
    single gene (mendelian) inheritance in,
      563
    undergrowth in, 1757
  disorders of, due to in utero positioning,
    1758
  embryology of, 1755

Extremity(ies)—cont'd
  examination of, 515
  hemihypertrophy of, 575
  hypertrophy of, 575
  length of, evaluation of, 574–575
  lower
    congenital anomalies of, 1772–1781
    examination of, meningomyeloceles and, 1015t
    torsional and angular deformities of, 1772–1773
  motor system of, assessment of, 525–526
  paired, asymmetry of, 575
  shortened bones in, 575
  thanatophoric dysplasia of, 574f, 575, 575f
  upper, congenital anomalies of, 1767–1770
Extubation
  accidental, 1118
  after esophageal atresia/tracheoesophageal fistula repair, 1376
  continuous positive airway pressure in, 1116, 1164
  intermittent mandatory ventilation with, 1116–1117
  of neonates, 641
Eye(s), 1721–1752. See also specific part, e.g., Cornea.
  birth injuries to, 538–539, 1726–1727
  burns of, chemical and thermal, 1727
  congenital anomalies of, 1727–1729
    chromosome syndromes in, 1727–1728
    craniofacial, 1728–1729
    diagnostic evaluation of, 579–580
    examination of, 518, 520, 568, 570–571, 569f, 570f
    in congenital herpes simplex infection, 841
    in inborn errors of metabolism, 1619
    in rubella virus infection, 872
    minor, 566t
    phenotypic variants of, 566t
  congenital glaucoma of, 1736–1737, 1737b, 1737f
  corneal abnormalities in, 1737
  dilation of, in fundus examination, 1723
  disorders of
    in juvenile xanthogranuloma, 1711
    in Sturge-Weber syndrome, 1709
  dry, 1733–1734
  effect of phototherapy on, 1444
  examination of
    comprehensive, 1721–1724, 1722f
    ophthalmologic consultation after, 1726
    routine, 515
    screening exam in, 1721, 1721b
  fixation of, 1724
  globe abnormalities of, 1732
  growth of, 1724
  infections of, 1747
  iris abnormalities in, 1738–1739
  large, 1732, 1733f
  leukokoria in, 1739–1743
  measurements of, 1724, 1724t
  neurologic assessment of, 524–525
  neuromuscular abnormalities of, 1745–1747
  normal findings in, 1724–1726, 1724t, 1725f
    in preterm infant, 1726, 1726f
  retinal abnormalities in. See Retina entries.
  rotational reflexes of, 1724–1725, 1725f
  saccadic movement of, 1725

Eye(s)—cont'd
  scleral abnormalities in, 1737–1738
  substance abuse effects on, 1747
  trauma to, 1726–1727
    treatment of, 1727
  watery, 1733
  wide separation of, in Apert syndrome, 1012
Eye contact
  captivation of preterm infant by, 653
  in parent-infant attachment, 648f, 649f, 650, 653
Eyebrows
  abnormalities of, 1731
  synophrys of, 571
Eyelashes
  congenital ectropion and entropion of, 1731
  examination of, 1722
  hypertrichosis of, 1731
Eyelids
  birth injuries to, 538
  coloboma of, 1729–1730, 1730f
  congenital blepharophimosis of, 1730, 1730f
  cryptophthalmia and, 1732
  epicanthus of, 1730, 1730f
  examination of, 1722
  lacerations of, 1727
  normal measurements of, 1724, 1724t
  ptosis of, 1731–1732, 1731f
  swollen, examination of, 516
  tumors of, 1730–1731

F

Face
  birth injuries to, 536–538
    bone fractures and dislocations in, 537f, 537–538
  congenital anomalies of
    examination of, 568–573
    ocular, 1728–1729
  in small for gestational age infant, 297, 297f
  minor anomalies and phenotypic variants of, 565, 566t
  toxemic, in preeclampsia-eclampsia, 313
Facial diplegia, in neuromuscular disorders, 977
Facial features, in congenital hypothyroidism, 1541f, 1540–1541
Facial nerve
  assessment of, 525
  birth injuries to, 538–539
  palsy of, birth-related, 536–537
Factor V Leiden, 1333
  in ischemic stroke, 937
Factor VII, deficiency of, 1320
Factor VIIa–tissue factor complex inhibitor, in coagulation, 1320
Factor VIII
  deficiency of, 1320. See also Hemophilia A.
  and evaluation for von Willebrand disease, 1326
  elevation of, 1333
  recombinant, for hemophilia A, 1326, 1327t
Factor IX
  deficiency of, 1320. See also Hemophilia B.
  for hemophilia B, 1327t

Factor XI, deficiency of, 1326
Factor XIII, deficiency of, 1321
Fallopian tubes, development of, 1553
Fallot's tetralogy. See Tetralogy of Fallot.
Family. See also Parent(s).
  discussion with, regarding intersex disorders, 1557
  in preeclampsia-eclampsia, 312
Family interests, in ethics, 36
Fanconi anemia, 1307–1308, 1307t
  radial anomalies associated with, 1341
  vs. Diamond-Blackfan anemia, 1306
Fanconi syndrome, 1767
  renal, disorders causing, 1637, 1637t
Farber disease, macular abnormalities in, 1744, 1744t
Fascioscapulohumeral muscular dystrophy, 985
Fat
  dietary. See Lipid(s).
  energy stored as, 663
  in body composition, during gestation, 661, 662t
Fat necrosis, subcutaneous, 1516, 1712–1713
  at birth, 530–531, 531f
Fathers. See also Parent(s); Parent-infant attachment.
  behavior of, toward infant, 646
  in early perinatal period, 652–653
  drug ingestion by, 184
Fatty acids
  free
    in fetal metabolism, 275, 276f
    in small for gestational age infant, 299, 300f
  in breast milk, 666
  in parenteral nutrition, for prevention of oxygen toxicity, 1165–1166
  long-chain polyunsaturated, 666
  oxidation of
    cardiomyopathy in, 1618t, 1618–1619
    defects in
      hepatic dysfunction in, 1622
      hypoglycemia and, 1609t–1610t, 1648–1649
    inherited disorder of, 1612–1613
  placental transport of, 1467
Febrile infant, 597
Febrile nonhemolytic reactions, to transfusion, 1347
Fecal elastase 1, in cystic fibrosis diagnosis, 1364
Fecal incontinence, after imperforate anus repair, 1402
Feces. See Stool.
Federal and state laws, 48
Feeding
  difficulties with, in congenital hypothyroidism, 1540
  gavage. See Gavage feeding.
Feeding cup (paladai), for preterm infants, in developing countries, 99f, 100
Feet. See Foot (feet).
Females, X chromosome inactivation in, 124
Femoral pulses, examination of, 515
Femur
  birth-related fracture of, 554, 554f, 1762
  length of, ultrasonography of, 147, 147f
  proximal focal deficiency of, 1776–1777, 1777f
Fentanyl
  blunting of stress response by, 630, 630f, 630t
  dosages of, 1787

Fentanyl—*cont'd*
  for cyanotic spells, 1268
  for labor pain, 472
  in neonatal anesthesia, 639
  pharmacokinetics of, 639
  umbilical vein to maternal vein ratio of,
    470t
Ferric chloride test, for inborn errors of
  metabolism, 1630
Ferritin, in very low birthweight infants, 1811t
Ferrous sulfate. *See also* Iron.
  dosages of, 1792
  for iron deficiency, 1306
Fetal alcohol effects (FAE), 735
Fetal alcohol spectrum disorders, 735, 736b
Fetal alcohol syndrome, 185. *See also*
    Alcohol, fetal exposure to.
  clinical features of, 734, 735f
  congenital anomalies associated with,
    563–564, 564f
  diagnostic criteria for, 735, 736b
  guidelines for screening and management
    of, 738–739
  prevalence of, 734–735
  prevention of, 738–739, 738t
  vs. fetal alcohol effects, 735
Fetal blood sampling
  from scalp
    birth injuries related to, 557
    electrodes in
      herpes simplex transmission related
        to, 841
      sepsis associated with, 793
    gas exchange values in, during labor,
      484, 484t
    in platelet count assessment, 368
  in prenatal genetic evaluation, 138
Fetal chest, in oligohydramnios, 416–417
Fetal circulation
  abnormalities of, in intrauterine growth
    restriction pregnancies, 281, 286t
  ductal constriction in, indomethacin
    associated with, 351
  fluid reabsorption into, via
    intramembranous pathway, 411
  gas exchange via, 483–484, 484f
  persistent. *See* Pulmonary hypertension,
    persistent.
  physiology of, 1205–1206
  placenta and, 456, 457f
  transition of, to extrauterine circulation,
    1206
  ultrasonography of, 170, 170f, 171f
Fetal death
  after amniocentesis, 137
  after chorionic villus sampling, 138
  evaluation of stillborn in, for congenital
    anomalies, 578–579
  gestational diabetes mellitus and, 327
  in antiphospholipid antibody syndrome,
    372
  in multiple gestations, 378
  incidence of, 167
  near term, 461
  small for gestational age and, 296t
Fetal distress, 172
  anesthetic considerations in, 480
  in intrauterine growth restriction, 293
  meconium aspiration in, 1122
Fetal-fetal transfusion. *See* Twin-twin
    transfusion syndrome.
Fetal growth
  aberrant patterns of, 289f, 289–290, 290b,
    291f

Fetal growth—*cont'd*
  maternal contributions to, 279–284,
    280f–283f
  as function of gestational age, 271–272,
    272f, 273f
  body composition and, 271–273, 272t,
    272f–274f, 273t, 274t, 661, 662t
  body fat and protein in, 273, 274f
  chronic disease affecting, 282–283, 283f
  cigarette smoking affecting, 284
  cocaine abuse affecting, 283–284
  fetal determinants of, 286–288
  fluid space distribution in, 273, 274f
  genetic determinants of, 287–288
  growth-determining genes in, 287
  high altitude affecting, 283
  hormones in, 275–278, 1468
  in eclampsia, 283, 283f
  in multiple gestations, 280f, 379–380
    constraints on, 280, 280f
  in oligohydramnios, 416, 416f
  insulin in, 275–276
  leptin in, 277–278
  maternal drugs affecting, 283–284
  maternal genetic factors in, 280
  maternal nutrition and, 280–282, 281f,
    282b, 282f
  opioids affecting, 751–752
  organ mass in, 273, 273t
  parallel patterns in, 273, 274t, 274f
  paternal genetic factors in, 280
  physical environment in, 279–280, 280f
  placental determinants of, 284–286,
    284f–287f, 286t
  resting metabolism in, 662
  socioeconomics affecting, 284
  suboptimal, risk of, 282b
  ultrasonography of, 147
Fetal heart rate
  accelerations in, 174, 175f
  baseline, 173–174, 174f
  central nervous system regulation of,
    168
  complete absence of, 174, 174f
  decelerations in
    early, 176, 176f
    late, 175–176, 176f
    prolonged, 176, 177f
    variable, 174–175, 175f
  neuraxial blockade effects on, 476
  non-reassuring
    amnioinfusion for, 178, 178f
    maternal position and, 177
    oxygen therapy for, 178
    persistent, 178–179
    tocolytic agents for, 178
  sinusoidal, 176, 177f
Fetal heart rate monitoring
  accelerations in, 174, 175f
  baseline rate in, 173–174, 174f
  birth injuries related to, 557
  decelerations in, 174–176, 175f–177f
  guidelines for, 173
  in asphyxia, 179
  in cerebral palsy, 179, 179b
  in gestational diabetes, 324
  in intravascular fetal transfusion, 401
  intrapartum, birth injuries related to,
    557
  non-reassuring patterns in
    evaluation and management of,
      177–178, 178f
    persistent, evaluation and management
      of, 178–179

Fetal heart rate monitoring—*cont'd*
  reassuring patterns in, interpretation of,
    173–176
  risks and benefits of, 173
Fetal-maternal hemorrhage, anemia due to,
  1296–1297
Fetal membranes, premature rupture of. *See*
  Premature rupture of membranes.
Fetal origin hypothesis, of adult-onset
  disease, 278, 278f
Fetal swallowing
  impaired, 414
  of amniotic fluid, 410–411
Fetal thrombotic vasculopathy, 459
Fetal weight
  after eclampsia, 283, 283f
  composition of, 271–273, 274f
  gestational age and, 271–272, 272f, 273f
  gestational diabetes and, 326–327
  muscle in, 273
  organs in, 273, 273t
  reference, 274t
Fetal well-being, assessment of, 167–179
  amniotic fluid in, 169, 170f
  biophysical profile in, 169, 169f
    modified, 170
  clinical considerations in, 171
  contraction stress test in, 168–169
  Doppler flow velocimetry in, 170, 170f,
    171f
  gestational age in, 171
  heart rate in. *See* Fetal heart rate.
  heart rate monitoring and. *See* Fetal heart
    rate monitoring.
  in chronic hypertension, 318
  in intrauterine growth restriction, 294
  in post-term pregnancy, 385t, 385–386
  in preeclampsia, 315
  indications for surveillance in, 167t,
    167–168
  interpretation of test results in, 170–171
  nonstress test in, 168, 168f
  physiologic basis for, 168–170
  physiology and, 172
  rationale for surveillance in, 167
FETENDO procedure, for congenital
  diaphragmatic hernia, 240
Fetomaternal hemorrhage, 461
  due to intravascular fetal transfusion, 402,
    402t
Fetoscopic laser therapy, for twin-twin
  transfusion syndrome, 250–251
Fetoscopic surgery, 249
Fetus
  abdominal circumference of, 146–147,
    147f
  abortion of. *See* Abortion.
  access to, technology advances in,
    225–226
  airway obstruction in, 247–249, 248f
  alcohol effects on. *See* Alcohol, fetal
    exposure to.
  anatomy of, first-trimester studies of, 145,
    145f
  anomalies of. *See also specific anomaly,*
    e.g., Ventriculomegaly.
    ultrasonography of, 152b, 152–163
  arrhythmias in, 221–224. *See also*
    Arrhythmias, fetal.
  bilirubin in, 1425
  biparietal diameter of, 146, 146f
  calcitonin function in, 1504
  cardiovascular assessment of, 1207–1210
  circadian rhythms of, 602

Fetus—cont'd
  congenital adrenal hyperplasia in,
      treatment of, 217f, 217–219, 219t
  cytomegalovirus infection of, 439
  disorders of. See also specific disorder.
    endocrine, 216–219, 219t
    gene therapy for, 226
    pharmacologic treatment for, 202–204,
        212t, 212–225
      access in, 225–226
      approach to, 203f, 203b, 203–204
      science and technology advances in,
          202b
    surgical treatment for, 231–252
      fetoscopic, 249
      open, 233–249, 234t
        for congenital cystic adenomatoid
            malformation, 242f, 243f
        for congenital diaphragmatic
            hernia, 238f–240f
        for fetal airway obstruction, 248f
        for obstructive uropathy, 233–237
        for sacrococcygeal teratoma, 245f
      shunting procedures in, 231–232,
          232f, 233f
  drug disposition in, 210–211, 211t
  drug exposure of, 183–191. See also
      Substance abuse.
    adverse effects in, 184–185, 185f, 186t,
        187t–189t, 189–191
    determination of, 190–191
    factors modifying, 189–190
    ingestion by father and, 184
    maternal consumption and, 183
    mechanisms of toxicity in, 190, 190f
    nontherapeutic agents and, 185, 189
    placental transfer in, 183–184, 184f
    timing of, 184–185, 185f
  effects of autoimmune disease on,
      367–373
  environmental exposures surrounding. See
      Environmental exposures, fetal.
  femur length in, 147, 47f
  gas exchange in, 483–484, 484f
  glucose metabolism in, 1468–1469, 1469f
  goiter in, 219–220
  growth of. See Fetal growth.
  head circumference of, 146
  hearing in, 600–601
  heat production by, 585
  herpes simplex virus infection of, 437–438
  HIV infection of
    antepartum management of, 434
    prevention of, 214, 434
  hyperthyroidism in, 220
  hypothyroidism in, treatment of, 219t,
      219–220
  in breech position, ultrasonography of,
      150, 150f
  inborn errors of metabolism affecting,
      1615–1616
  infection of, prevention of, 214–215, 215b
  interventional catheterization of, 1275
  intracranial hemorrhage in, prevention of,
      214
  invasive testing of, for nonimmune
      hydrops fetalis, 424–425
  listeriosis of, 447
  lung development in. See Lung(s),
      development of.
  lung maturation in, augmentation for,
      212–214
  malformations of, in multiple gestations,
      377t, 377–378

Fetus—cont'd
  metabolism of, 275–278
    free fatty acids in, 275, 276f
    maternal adjustments in, 275
    oxidative substances in, 275, 275t
  movements of, in post-term pregnancy,
      385t
  neural tube defects in, 224–225
  neuraxial blockade effects on, 475,
      476–477
  notion of touch in, 598
  olfaction in, 599
  parathyroid function in, 1501
  parvovirus infection of, 442
  perception of, as separate individual,
      646–647, 647f
  pharmacokinetics in, 469–471, 470t
  pharmacologic therapies for, 202–204, 212t
    approach to, 203f, 203b
  polyhydramnios in, 220t, 220–221
  pulmonary status in, assessment of, 416f,
      416–417, 417f
  RhD typing of, 393
  rights of, vs. maternal autonomy, 38–39
  sex determination of, ultrasonography in,
      160, 162f
  sex of, birthweight and, 287
  shunting procedures in, 231–232, 232f,
      233f
  taste buds of, 599
  thoracoamniotic shunts in, 232, 232f, 233f
  thyroid disorders in, 219–220, 220t
  tobacco effects on. See Tobacco use.
  touch in, 598
  toxoplasmosis in, 215–216, 216b, 449
  treatment of, ethical issues in, 38–39
  vaccination of, 214–215, 215b
  varicella-zoster virus infection of, 435
  ventriculoamniotic shunts in, 231–232
  ventriculomegaly in, ultrasonography of,
      152, 152f, 153f
  vesicoamniotic shunts in, 232
  viability of, ethical issues in, 39–40
  vision in, 602
  vitamin D function in, 1502
  well-being of, estimation of. See Fetal
      well-being.
FGER2 gene, mutations of, 1010, 1011
Fibrin, massive perivillous deposition of, 458
Fibrinogen, in sepsis diagnosis, 798
Fibrinolysis
  inherited abnormalities of, 1333
  physiologic alterations of, 1322, 1322t,
      1323t, 1324, 1324t–1325t
Fibrinolytic system, 1321–1322, 1322f
Fibrinolytic therapy, for thrombosis, 1336,
      1337b
Fibroblast growth factor receptors, defects
      in, craniosynostosis due to, 1007
Fibroblasts, dermal, 1688
Fibroma, myocardial, 1250, 1250f
Fibronectin
  for sepsis prevention and treatment, 801
  in immune response, 773
  in sepsis diagnosis, 798
  structure and function of, 772
Fibronectin positive women
  antibiotics for, 354–355
  in preterm labor prediction, 340–341
Fibrosarcoma, congenital, 1343
Fibula, congenital angular deformities of,
      1772–1773, 1773f
Fick equation, 209
  in blood flow measurement, 1211

Fifth disease, 869, 1308
Finegan scale, for neonatal abstinence
      syndrome, 750
Finger(s), congenital anomalies of,
      1769–1770
  amputations as, 1769
  examination of, 518, 575–578, 576f–578f
Finger spelling, for hearing-impaired child,
      1049
Fistula
  perineal, in imperforate anus, 1399, 1400,
      1402
  rectourethral, 1400
  rectovestibular, 1400
  right ventricle–pulmonary artery, in
      pulmonary atresia, 1227
  tracheoesophageal. See
      Tracheoesophageal fistula.
Flecainide
  for fetal arrhythmias, 223t, 224, 224t
  for neonatal tachycardia, 1260t, 1262b,
      1263, 1264
Fleisch differential pressure sensors, in
      respiratory monitoring, 613–614
Flora, bacterial. See Bacterial flora.
Flow rate, in mechanical ventilation, 1116
Flow sensors, in respiratory monitoring, 613
Fluconazole
  dosages of, 1790
  for candidiasis, 833
  for coccidioidomycosis, 833
Flucytosine
  dosages of, 1790
  for candidiasis, 832, 832t
  for cryptococcosis, 834
Fludrocortisone acetate, for 21-hydroxylase
      deficiency, 1580
Fluid(s). See also Water.
  body composition of, 695, 696f
    by gestational age, 661, 662t
  electrolyte content of, 700, 700t
  for bronchopulmonary dysplasia, 703
  for cyanotic spells, 1268
  for jejunoileal atresia, 1397–1398
  for patent ductus arteriosus, 703
  for perinatal asphyxia, 702–703
  for preterm labor prevention, 345
  insensible losses of, 698–699
  lung, fetal, 1074–1075, 1075f
  maintenance of, 697–698, 698t
    in neonatal anesthesia, 640
    in neonatal resuscitation, 506
    in respiratory distress syndrome,
        1105–1106
  management of, 695–703
    in bronchopulmonary dysplasia, 1165
    maternal, for oligohydramnios, 418
  requirements for, calculation of, 697–700
  restriction of, in acute renal failure, 1669
  withdrawal of, ethical issues in, 41
Fluid balance
  in congenital heart disease, 1266–1267
    postoperative, 1267
  in neonatal anesthesia, 629
  in neonate, 697
    phototherapy and, 1444–1445
  monitoring of, 700
Fluorescent in situ hybridization (FISH),
      119–121
  applications of, 119–121, 563
  DNA probes for, 119, 120f
  for chromosome microdeletions, 579
Fluorescent treponemal antibody absorption
      test, 824

Fluoride, in enteral nutrition, 670t
Fluoroscopy
    of laryngomalacia, 1151
    of upper airway, 1151
Fluoxetine, in breast milk, 200
FMR1 gene, in fragile X syndrome, 131
Folic acid
    for neural tube defect prevention, 225
    for toxoplasmosis, 449
    in breast milk, 672t
    in infant formula, 674t
    maternal doses of, 225
    requirements for, 668t
    supplemental, for myelomeningocele, 246
Folinic acid–responsive seizures, 1616
Follicle-stimulating hormone, serum levels
    of, 1805t
Fontan procedure
    for hypoplastic left heart syndrome, 1237
    for pulmonary atresia, 1227
    for single ventricle, 1231
    for tricuspid atresia, 1227
    modified, 1269t
Fontanelle(s)
    examination of, 515
    large, in congenital anomalies, 568
Foot (feet)
    calcaneovalgus, 1778–1779, 1779f
        diagnosis and treatment of, 1779
        in posteromedial angulation of tibia,
            1773, 1773f
        in tibial torsion, 1772
    congenital anomalies of. See also Talipes
        equinovarus.
        absence anomaly in, 575
        examination of, 575–578, 576f–578f
        sandal line furrows in, 575, 576f
        vertical talus in, 1780–1781, 1780f,
            1781f
    lymphedema of, in Turner and Noonan
        syndromes, 575, 577f
    metatarsus adductus of, 1778, 1778f
    minor anomalies and phenotypic variants
        of, 566t
    rocker-bottom, 575, 577f, 1780, 1780f,
        1781f
    tibial torsion effects on, 1772
Foramen ovale, 1198, 1206
    right-to-left atrial shunting through, 1246
Forced-choice preferential looking, 1724
Forceps
    anesthetic technique for delivery with,
        477
    birth injuries due to, 529
        ocular, 1727
        skull fractures due to, 534
        subgaleal hemorrhage due to, 533
    history of, 4, 6, 6f
Forearm, congenital anomalies of,
    1767–1769
Foreign bodies
    cardiac, catheter retrieval of, 1275
    ocular or orbital, 1727
Formamides, maternal exposure to,
    pregnancy outcome in, 260t
Formula. See also Breast milk; Enteral
    nutrition.
    calcium, phosphorus, and magnesium in,
        absorption and retention of, 1495t
    carnitine in, 667
    casein-predominant cow's milk type of,
        665
    cholesterol in, 667
    for extremely low birthweight infant, 679

Formula—cont'd
    for preterm infant, 670, 672, 673t–674t
        discharge formulas for, 674, 673t–674t
    iron-fortified, 1306
    lactobezoars due to, 1387
    lipid content and composition of, 667
    protein content of, 664–665
    specialized, 674
N-formyl-methionyl-leucine-phenylalanine
    (FMLP), in neutrophil chemotaxis, 765
Foundling asylums, 7, 8f
Fractures, birth-related
    clavicular, 518, 541, 1761
    facial, 537f, 537–538
    femoral, 554, 554f, 1762
    humeral, 553, 1761–1762, 1762f
    of long bones, 1761–1762, 1762f
    of ribs, 541–542, 542f
    of skull, 534–536, 535f
    radial, 553–554
Fragile X syndrome
    DNA diagnosis of, 130–132, 131f
    macrencephaly associated with, 997
    trinucleotide repeat expansions in,
        126–127
Fraser syndrome
    with laryngeal atresia, 248
    WT1 gene mutation in, 1571
Free fatty acids. See Fatty acids, free.
Free radicals
    bronchopulmonary dysplasia related to,
        1160
    formation of
        in brain, 943
        in hypoxia-ischemia, 498
Frequency rate, in mechanical ventilation,
    1115
Fresh frozen plasma
    for protein C deficiency, 1333
    for protein S deficiency, 1332–1333
    transfusion of, 1350
        dosages in, 1790
Frontal bossing, in congenital anomalies,
    568
Frontonasal dysplasia, 570f, 572
Fructose-1,6-diphosphatase deficiency,
    1484–1485, 1647–1648
Fructose intolerance
    hereditary, 1484, 1485
        hepatocellular disease associated with,
            1622
    in persistent hypoglycemia, 1484–1485
Fukuyama muscular dystrophy, 984
Functional assays, in erythroblastosis fetalis
    screening, 395
Functional residual capacity
    after first breath, 485, 485f
    anesthesia and, 628
    decrease of, during sleep, 1138
    formation of, 492–493, 493f–494f
    in bronchopulmonary dysplasia, 1163,
        1163t, 1164f
    in respiratory distress syndrome, surfactant
        therapy for improving, 1083
    measurement of, 1092
    mechanoreceptor response to, 1111
Fundoplication, for gastroesophageal reflux,
    1380
Fundus
    height of, in intrauterine growth
        restriction, 290
    ocular
        coloboma of, 1743
        examination of, 1723

Fungal infection(s). See also specific
        infection, e.g., Candidiasis.
    of catheters, in parenteral nutrition,
        689–690
    postnatal, 830–836
Funisitis, subnecrotizing, 459
Furosemide
    dosages of, 1791
    for bronchopulmonary dysplasia, 1165
    for fluid balance, in congenital heart
        disease, 1267
    for neonatal hypertension, 1673t
    treatment with
        bronchopulmonary dysplasia due to,
            703
        hypocalcemia due to, 1512
Furosemide challenge, in oligohydramnios,
    417
Futility of treatment, ethics of, 40–41

G

G phase, of mitotic cycle, 886, 886f
Gag reflex, testing of, 525
Galactose-1-phosphate uridyltransferase
    (GALT) deficiency, 1611
Galactosemia, 1610t
    cataract associated with, 1740
    hepatocellular disease associated with,
        1622
    screening for, 1611
Galeazzi sign, in developmental dysplasia of
    hip, 1774, 1775
Gallbladder
    anomalies of, ultrasonography of, 159,
        159f
    ultrasonography of, 150, 150f
Gallstones, ultrasonography of, 159, 159f
Gametogenesis, environmental exposure to
    toxins during, 133
Gamma-globulin, intravenous, for
    alloimmune (isoimmune)
    thrombocytopenia, 1339
Ganciclovir
    dosages of, 1790
    for congenital cytomegalovirus infection,
        847
Gangliosidosis, 1624
    macrencephaly associated with, 998
Gas exchange
    in assisted ventilation, 1109–1111
    in fetal circulation, 483–484, 484f
Gastric. See also Stomach.
Gastric acid
    blockade of, in esophageal atresia/
        tracheoesophageal fistula, 1375
    functions of, 1360
Gastric emptying, delayed, after
    fundoplication, 1380
Gastric lipase, 665
Gastric pacemaker, 1360
Gastric volvulus, 1385–1386, 1386f
    mesentericoaxial, 1385
    organoaxial, 1385
    surgical management of, 1386
Gastroenteritis, due to rotavirus, 868
Gastroesophageal reflux, 1379–1380
    diagnosis of, 1379–1380
    in bronchopulmonary dysplasia, 1166
    in congenital diaphragmatic hernia, 1379
    in esophageal atresia/tracheoesophageal
        fistula, 1377

Gastroesophageal reflux—*cont'd*
  lower esophageal sphincter physiology in, 1379
  Nissen fundoplication for, 1380
  treatment of, 1380
Gastrografin enema, for meconium ileus, 1396
Gastrointestinal hormones, stimulation of, by oxytocin release, 650
Gastrointestinal tract, 1357–1410. *See also specific organ.*
  absorption function of, neonatal drugs and, 191–192
  anomaly(ies) of, 1373–1380
    abdominal wall defects as, 1381–1385, 1381f–1384f
    anorectal anomalies as, 1399–1403
    congenital diaphragmatic hernia as. *See* Diaphragmatic hernia, congenital.
    duodenal atresia and stenosis as, 1390–1392, 1391f
    esophageal atresia as, 1373–1377
    esophageal duplications as, 1378, 1378f
    gastric perforation as, 1387
    gastric volvulus as, 1385–1386, 1386f
    gastroesophageal reflux as, 1379–1380
    gastrointestinal duplications as, 1392–1393, 1392f, 1393f
    Hirschsprung disease as, 1398–1399
    hypertrophic pyloric stenosis as, 1388–1390, 1389f, 1390f
    in inborn errors of metabolism, 1619
    jejunoileal atresia and stenosis as, 1397–1398, 1398f
    malrotation and midgut volvulus as, 1393–1395, 1394f
    meconium syndromes as, 1395–1397
    microgastria as, 1386, 1386f
    perinatal ultrasonography of, 156–158
    pyloric atresia as, 1387–1388, 1388f
    tracheoesophageal fistula as, 1373–1377
  bacterial flora in
    in neonatal drug absorption, 192–193
    necrotizing enterocolitis and, 1407
  bleeding of, Apt test for, 1325
  development of, 1357. *See also under specific organs.*
    in preterm infants, minimal enteral feeding for, 675
  digestive disorder(s) of, 1363–1372
    carbohydrate absorption disorder as, 1365–1367, 1365t
    diarrhea as. *See* Diarrhea.
    electrolyte absorption disorders as, 1368–1369, 1370t
    fat absorption disorders as, 1368
    pancreatic insufficiency as, 1363–1365
    protein absorption disorders as, 1367–1368
  high obstruction of, radiography, 718f–719f, 718–720
  ischemic, necrotizing enterocolitis related to, 1407
  low obstruction of, radiography of, 719f–722f, 720–722
  necrotizing enterocolitis of. *See* Necrotizing enterocolitis.
  rotation of, 1360–1361, 1360f
  villous architecture disorder in, 1371–1372
  water loss through, 699
Gastropexy, anterior, for gastric volvulus, 1386
Gastroschisis, 1381–1385
  intestinal atresia with, 1385
  pathogenesis of, 1381, 1381f, 1382

Gastroschisis—*cont'd*
  "peel" in, 1382, 1382f
    due to amniotic fluid exposure, 1382–1383
    gastrointestinal dysfunction due to, 1383
  prognosis in, 1385
  respiratory support for, 1383
  surgical management of, 1383–1384
    nutritional support during, 1384
    prosthetic "silo" in, 1384, 1384f
  temporary coverage of, 1383
  timing of delivery with, 1383
  toxic exposure in, 1382
  ultrasonography of, 157, 158f, 1383
Gastrostomy, Stamm-type, for gastric volvulus, 1386
GAT1 gene, in transient myeloproliferative disorder, 1315
GATA4 protein, in cardiogenesis, 1198
Gaucher disease, 1694t
  hepatosplenomegaly in, 1623
Gavage feeding
  for high-risk infants, 676
  history of, 8–9
  in botulism, 820
GB virus type C, 867–868
Gender
  anomalies associated with. *See* Intersex disorder(s).
  assignment of
    in 21-hydroxylase deficiency, 1581
    to intersex neonate, 1562, 1564
  congenital heart disease and, 1205
  fetal, birthweight and, 287
  neonatal mortality rates related to, sex discrimination in, 92
Gene(s). *See also specific gene.*
  growth-determining, 287
  in CNS regionalization, 885, 885f
  in holoprosencephaly, 903
  in preeclampsia-eclampsia syndrome, 309
  influencing gonadal development, 284, 1551, 1551f
  mutations of, in renal disease, 1661–1662, 1662t
  mouse models of, 1660–1661, 1660t
  of Rh system, 389–390
  polymorphism of, 284
Gene therapy
  fetal, 226
  for inborn errors of metabolism, 1653–1654
  in congenital heart disease prevention, 1202
Genetic analysis, modular, for chromosome microdeletions, 579
Genetic background, in fetal response to drugs, 189
Genetic counseling, 134–135
  for congenital anomalies, 580
  for intersex disorders, 1564
  referral for, 136
Genetic disorders, 113–121. *See also* Chromosome anomalies.
  autosomal dominant inheritance of, 121f, 121–122
  autosomal recessive inheritance of, 122f, 122–123
  DNA diagnosis of, 127–132, 128f
    applications of, 130–132, 131f
    approach to, 128f, 128–130, 129f
  DNA sequencing and, 129–130
  dominant, 121

Genetic disorders—*cont'd*
  environmental, 133–134, 134t
  imprinting in, 125–126
  in cystic fibrosis, 1363–1364
  mitochondrial inheritance of, 124–125, 125f
  multifactorial, 132f, 132–133
    congenital anomalies due to, 562, 562t
  musculoskeletal anomalies due to, 1756–1757
  nontraditional inheritance patterns in, 124–127
  polymerase chain reaction in, 128, 129, 130f
  recessive, 121
  sex-linked inheritance of, 123, 123f
  single, 121–132
    congenital anomalies due to, 562t, 562–563
  Southern blot analysis of, 128f, 128–129
  trinucleotide repeat expansions in, 126–127
  X chromosome inactivation in, 124
  X-linked dominant inheritance of, 123, 123f
  X-linked recessive inheritance of, 123, 123f
  Y chromosome inheritance of, 124
Genetic evaluation, 134–135
  prenatal, 135–138
    amniocentesis in, 137
    chorionic villus sampling in, 137–138
    fetal blood sampling in, 138
    screening tests in, 135–136
Genetic predisposition
  to congenital heart disease, 1205
  to preeclampsia-eclampsia, 312
Genetic screening
  application of perinatal ultrasonography in, 144, 145f
  for inborn errors of metabolism, 1634
  tests used in, 135–136
Genetic traits, polygenic, 132
Genital ducts, development of, 1553–1554
Genitalia
  abnormalities of, examination of, 519, 574
  ambiguous. *See also* Intersex disorder(s).
    chromosome analysis for, 579
    definition of, 1557
    early testicular regression with, 1572
    family and professional discussions regarding, 1557
    gender assignment in, 1562, 1564
    surgical correction of, 1564
  birth trauma to, 556f, 556–557
  examination of, 515
  external
    development of, 1554, 1554f
    dysgenesis of, 1585f, 1585
    female, masculinization of, 1577, 1577f
  perinatal ultrasonography of, 160, 162f
Genitography, of intersex disorders, 1562
Genitourinary tract
  anomalies of
    in congenital scoliosis, 1770
    in imperforate anus, 1400
    perinatal ultrasonography of, 159–160, 159f–162f
Genome, human, in congenital heart disease prevention, 1202
Genomic imprinting, 125–126, 257
  abnormal, 287
Genotype, 121
  definition of, 562
  fetal, birthweight variability with, 287

Gentamicin
dosages of, 1789
for meningitis, 807
for sepsis, 800, 801t, 802t
Genu varum, 1772
Germ cell(s), in sex differentiation, 1552, 1553t
Germ cell tumors, 1344
Germinal matrix
blood supply to, 925
hemorrhage in, 925. *See also*
Periventricular-intraventricular hemorrhage.
ultrasonography of, 727f, 727–728, 728f
hypoxia-ischemia of, 929
Gestation
body composition during, 661, 662t
duration of, endocervical length and, 149
human, length of, 383
multiple. *See* Multiple gestations.
Gestational age
amniotic fluid volume and, 409, 410f
appropriate for
transepidermal water loss in, during first 4 postnatal weeks, 588
vs. small for gestational age, 289
as risk factor, for respiratory distress syndrome, 1097, 1098f
assessment of
in small for gestational age infant, 297–298
methods for, 522, 523f
EMCO therapy and, 1171
estimation of, 383b
fetal evaluation and, 171
fetal viability related to, ethical issues in, 39–40
fetal weight and, 271–272, 272f, 273f
first stools by, 1797f
fractional excretion of sodium and, 696, 696f
hypotonicity associated with, 527, 527t
in hypoxic-ischemic encephalopathy, 939
large for, definition of, 22
mean neutrophil counts and, 1813f
morbidity by, 332, 332t
necrotizing enterocolitis correlated with, 1403
neonatal anesthesia and, 631
retinopathy of prematurity related to, 1748, 1748f
rubella virus infection and, 871
school-age outcome and, 1041
small for. *See* Small for gestational age.
water and evaporative heat loss and, 593
Gestational sac, ultrasonography of, 149, 149f
Gestures, use of, for hearing-impaired child, 1049
Giant melanocytic congenital nevi, 1704–1705, 1704f
Gilbert syndrome, unconjugated hyperbilirubinemia in, 1431
Gingival cysts (epulis), 517
Gitelman syndrome, 1680
Glanzmann thrombasthenia, 1341
Glaucoma, congenital, 1736–1737, 1737b, 1737f
Glenn procedure, 1269t
bidirectional, 1269t
for hypoplastic left heart syndrome, 1236–1237
for pulmonary atresia, 1227
for single ventricle, 1231
for tricuspid atresia, 1227

Glial cells
proliferation and differentiation of, 896–900, 897f, 898f, 900f, 899t
response of, to hypoxic-ischemic insult, 940
Glial-derived neurotrophic growth factor (GDNF), in renal development, 1660t, 1661
Glioma
intranasal, 1147–1148
of optic nerve, 1736
Globe abnormalities, 1732
Globin gene, expression of, in hematopoiesis, 1290–1291, 1291f
Glomerular filtration rate
estimation of, formula for, 1666
in developing kidney, 1663t, 1664
in neonate, 696
Glossopharyngeal nerve, assessment of, 525
Glucagon
deficiency of, in persistent hypoglycemia, 1484
for hypoglycemia, 1487
Glucocorticoids
alveolar development affected by, 1073
deficiency of, familial isolated, 1483
for hypercalcemia, 1518
for hypoglycemia, 1488
for idiopathic thrombocytopenic purpura, 368
in breast milk, 200
mean concentrations of, 1805t
Glucometer, use of, in developing countries, 103
Gluconeogenesis
defects of, 1647–1648
neonatal, 680
Glucose
blood levels of, 1470
abnormal, 1471
hepatic output of, 1470
homeostasis of, islets of Langerhans in, 1361–1362
impaired tolerance to
in pregnancy, 322–323
postpartum, 325
in neonatal resuscitation, 506
in parenteral nutrition, 680, 690
infusion of, prior to hypoxic-ischemic insult, 952
intrapartum administration of, 1472
intravenous infusions of, for hypoglycemia, 1486–1487, 1486f
measurement of, 1470–1471
placental transport of, 1467
plasma levels of, after birth, 1469, 1469f, 1470
preconception levels of, 327
self-monitoring of, in pregnancy, 323
target levels of, in pregnancy, 323
transport of, defects in, 1485
Glucose-6-phosphatase dehydrogenase deficiency, jaundice in, 1429
Glucose-galactose malabsorption, 1367
Glucose metabolism
after birth, 1469–1471, 1469f
fetal, 1468–1469, 1469f
in small for gestational age infant, 299, 300f
Glucose tolerance test, for gestational diabetes mellitus, 322
Glucose transporter type 1 deficiency, 1616
β-Glucuronidase deficiency, 1623–1624

Glutamate
neurotoxicity of, in white matter damage, 915–916, 916f
toxicity of, hypoxic-ischemic insult and, 942–943
Glutamine, in parenteral amino acid solutions, 684t, 685
Glutaric acidemia, 1606t
Glycerol
in intravenous lipid emulsions, 686t
placental transport of, 1468
Glycerol trinitrate, for preterm labor prevention, 353–354
Glycine
for acidemia, 1639
in parenteral amino acid solutions, 684t, 685
Glycogen, fetal
hepatic synthesis of, 680
in body composition, 661, 662t
in intrauterine growth restriction, 299, 299f
Glycogen metabolism, disorders of, 988
Glycogen storage disease
cardiomegaly in, 1617
hepatic dysfunction in, 1623
in hypoglycemia, 1647
type II (Pompe disease), 989
type III (debrancher enzyme deficiency), 989
type IV (McArdle disease), 989
type VII (phosphofructokinase deficiency), 989
Glycolysis, stimulation of, during stress, 594
Glycosaminoglycans, dermal, 1689
Glycosides, fetal effects of, 188t
Glycosuria, 1667–1668
inherited renal, 1667–1668
isolated, 1667
Glycosylated hemoglobin, gestational diabetes mellitus and, 322
Glycosylation, congenital disorders of
dysmorphic features in, 1625–1626
testing for, 1633
Goiter, 1547–1548
airway obstruction due to, 1143
fetal, 220
in congenital hypothyroidism, 1541
in Pendred syndrome, 1536
iodine-induced, 1532, 1532f
maternal antithyroid drug ingestion causing, 220
treatment of, 1546
Goitrogens, maternal ingestion of, congenital hypothyroidism due to, 1537
Goldenhar syndrome, 1729
anesthetic implications of, 633t
Gonad(s). *See also* Ovary(ies); Testis (testes).
bipotential, 1552, 1552f
descent of
examination of, 1557–1558
mechanism of, 1567
development of, 1552–1553, 1552f, 1553t
genetic control of, 1551, 1551f
differentiation of, disorders of, 1568–1574
fetal, endocrine function in, 1554–1555, 1555f
impalpable, 1558t
palpable, 1558t
small, 1558t, 1558
steroid biosynthetic pathway in, 1555f
streak, 1551
surgical removal of, 1564
Gonadal agenesis, XY, 1572

Gonadal dysgenesis, 1568–1571
  mixed, 1571
  X chromosome abnormalities in,
       1568–1570, 1570b, 1570f
    XX, 1570
    XY, 1570–1571
    XYp, 1570
  Y chromosome abnormalities in, 1570
Gonadectomy, for streak gonad, 1551
Gonorrhea
  conjunctivitis due to. See Conjunctivitis,
       gonococcal.
  epidemiology and clinical manifestations
       of, 443
  in pregnancy, 442–443
    adverse outcome related to, 443
  in preterm delivery, 338
  intrapartum, 460
  neonatal, 443
  screening for, for preterm labor
       prevention, 431
Gordon syndrome, 701, 710
Gore-Tex graft, 1225, 1269t
Goreham disease, 1709
Graft-versus-host disease, transfusion-
       transmitted, 1344–1345, 1345b
Graham-Rosenblith scales, of preterm infant
       behavior, 1062
Graham scale, of preterm infant behavior,
       1062
Granulocyte(s), transfusion of, 1350
Granulocyte colony-stimulating factor,
       1289t
  for neutropenia, 1313–1314
  in sepsis diagnosis, 799
  in sepsis therapy, 803
Granulocyte colony-stimulating hormone, in
       preterm labor prediction, 343
Granulocyte elastase, in preterm labor
       prediction, 342
Granulocyte-macrophage colony-stimulating
       factor, 1289t
  as progenitor cell for neutrophils, 762
  for neutropenia, 1313–1314
  in sepsis therapy, 803
  total pool of, in neonate, 763
Granulomatous disease, chronic, 1317
  classification of, 1318t
  clinical presentation of, 1316b
Graves disease
  in thyrotoxicosis, 1458
  thyrotropin-binding inhibiting
       immunoglobulins in, 1529–1530
Great arteries, transposition of
  D-transposition in, 1222–1223, 1224f
  L-transposition in, 1242
Greeks, physiologic jaundice in, 1427
Group B streptococcal infections. See under
       Streptococcal infections.
Growth
  disorders of, macrencephaly associated
       with, 996
  effect of thyroid hormone on, 1524–1525,
       1525f
  energy expenditure in, 663, 680
  energy requirements for, 664
  fetal. See Fetal growth.
  intrauterine restriction of. See Intrauterine
       growth restriction.
  of high-risk neonate, 1037–1038, 1038f
  postnatal
    alcohol exposure and, 737
    cocaine exposure and, 745
    prenatal, alcohol exposure and, 737

Growth chart
  extrauterine, 1799f
  for preterm infant, 1800f
  intrauterine, 1798f
Growth factors. See also specific growth
       factor, e.g., Mast cell growth factor.
  hematopoietic, 1288–1289, 1289t
  in lung development, 1069
Growth hormone
  for hypoglycemia, 1488
  serum levels of, 1805t
Growth plates, in bone development,
       1505
Grunting
  in pulmonary function assessment, 1088
  in respiratory distress syndrome, 1100
Guanosine monophosphate, cyclic
  inhibition of degradation of, 1179–1180
  synthesis of, 1177, 1177f
Günther disease, 1714

H

H19 gene, in Beckwith-Wiederman
       syndrome, 1482, 1483
Haemophilus influenzae
  cutaneous infection due to, 1698
  in sepsis, 792
  joint infections due to, 1766
Hair
  anomalies of, in inborn errors of
       metabolism, 1619
  assays of, for substance abuse, 734
  examination of, for congenital anomalies,
       567
  growth of, sex differences in, 1687
Hair cells, cochlear, sound stimulation of,
       1045
Hair follicle, growth phases of, 1687
Hallermann-Streiff syndrome, 572, 1729
Halothane, in neonatal anesthesia, 638
Hamartoma, cardiac, 1250
"Hamstring" test, in developmental dysplasia
       of hip, 1775
Hand(s)
  congenital anomalies of
    absence anomaly of, 575
    creases in, 575, 576f
    examination of, 575–578, 576f–578f
    of fingers and thumbs, 1769–1770,
       1769f, 1770f
    gigantism of, 1769–1770
    lymphedema of, in Turner and Noonan
       syndromes, 575, 577f
    minor anomalies and phenotypic variants
       of, 566t
Hand-foot syndrome (dactylitis), 1304
Handwashing, for infection prevention, in
       NICU, 828–829
Haplotypes, 128
Harlequin color change
  clinical characteristics of, 1691–1692
  examination of, 517
Harlequin ichthyosis, 1694t, 1695
Hasselbach equation, 704
Head. See also Skull.
  anomalies of
    examination of, 568, 569f
    spinal defects and, 1758
    ultrasonography of, 154f, 155, 155f
  birth injuries to, 531–541
  bruising of, examination of, 516

Head—cont'd
  circumference of
    in fetus, ultrasonography of, 146, 146f
    measurement of, 989
      during physical examination, 514
    examination of, 515, 524, 989
    large, 995–1005. See also Macrocephaly.
    shape of, 989
      abnormal, 1006–1014, 1007t
      causes of, 1006b
    size of, disorders of, 989–1005
    small, 904–906, 989–995. See also
       Microcephaly.
      evaluation and treatment of, 995
    subnormal, in small for gestational age
       infant, 1038
Head-abdomen circumference ratio, in
       intrauterine growth restriction, 292, 294f
Head paradoxical reflex
  functional residual capacity and, 493
  in assisted ventilation, 1111
  in preterm infants, 1136
  in response to inflation, 492
Headache, postdural puncture, in neuraxial
       blocks, 474–475
Health care personnel
  for extracorporeal membrane
       oxygenation, 1170
  for neonatal resuscitation, 488
  in developing countries
    at district hospitals, 94
    home visits by, 101, 101t, 102t
    traditional birth attendant and
       community health worker role in,
       101–103, 103t
  liability of attending physician for, 48–50
  malpractice litigation and, 51
  staffing needs in regionalized perinatal
       care services, 26t, 29, 30
Health promotion, during neonatal physical
       examination, 521–522
Hearing
  assessment of, 525
  evaluation of, 1046–1047
  in acoustic environment, 600–602
  mechanism of, 1045–1046
  screening tests for, of high-risk neonate,
       1040
  surgical restoration of, 1047
  tobacco exposure and altered auditory
       processing, 741
Hearing aid, 1047
  placement of, 1049
Hearing loss
  assessment of, in congenital anomalies,
       571
  cochlear implants for, 1045–1046,
       1049–1050
  conductive, 1045
  developmental anomalies and, 1047–1048
  fetal noise exposure and, 262, 262t
  habilitation for, 1049–1050
  infectious organisms causing, 1048
  mainstreaming of children with, 1049
  neonatal, 1045–1050
  risk factors for, 1048b
  screening for, 521
  sensorineural, 1045, 1048–1049
    in rubella virus infection, 872
    with cytomegalovirus infection, 844,
       845, 845t
  sign language for, 1049
  significant adverse effects of, 1045
  total communication for, 1049

Heart. *See also* Cardiac; Cardio- *entries*.
  chambers of. *See also* Atrial *entries;*
    Atrium; Ventricle(s); Ventricular
    entries.
    anomalies of, 717
    blood flow in, 1212
  conduction system of, development of,
    1201
  contractility of, pharmacologic
    management of, 1267–1268
  development of, 1195–1202
    cell division and cell death in,
      1201–1202
    cell lineage in, 1198, 1199f
    endocardial cushion tissue formation in,
      1200
    formation of primary axes in, 1198,
      1199f
    human genome study and, 1202
    looping abnormalities in, 1200
    major transitions in, 1196, 1197f
    neural crest contribution to, 1200–1201
    segment specification in, 1200
    septation in, 1200–1202
    therapeutic interventions for, 1202
    timetable of events in, 1196, 1196t
    transcription factors in, 1198–1199,
      1199f
    tubular morphogenesis in, 1198–1200
  embryology of, 1195–1202
  examination of, 515
  foreign bodies in, catheter retrieval of,
    1275
  four-chamber, ultrasonography of, 150,
    150f
  malformations of, transient hypoglycemia
    and, 1480
  malposition of, 1242–1243
  physiology of
    fetal, 1205–1207
    neonatal anesthesia and, 628–629
  primordia of, 1196
  size of, radiographic assessment of, 1217,
    1217f
  transplantation of
    complications of, 1270
    for hypoplastic left heart syndrome,
      1269–1270
    rejection of, 1270
  tumors of, 1250, 1250f
  wall stress of, 1213–1214
  wall thickness of, 1212
Heart block
  complete
    fetal assessment for, 1209
    fetal surgery for, 234t
  fetal, due to anti-Ro or anti-La antibodies,
    1204
  in neonatal lupus erythematosus, 1715
Heart disease
  congenital. *See* Congenital heart disease.
  gestational diabetes mellitus and, 326
Heart failure, congestive
  fetal
    arrhythmias in, 1210
    assessment of, 1209–1210
    causes of, 1209–1210
    inotropic agents for, 1267
    systemic hypoperfusion with, in cyanosis,
      1221b, 1222, 1232–1237
Heart murmurs
  examination of, 518–519, 519b
  in acyanotic defects, 1237–1238
  in aortic stenosis, 1232–1233

Heart murmurs—*cont'd*
  in coarctation of aorta and aortic arch
    interruption, 1234
  in congenital heart disease, 1216
  in endocardial cushion defects, 1239
  in hypoplastic left heart syndrome, 1236
  in patent ductus arteriosus, 1240
  in persistent pulmonary hypertension,
    1246
  in pulmonary atresia, 1227
  in pulmonary stenosis, 1238
  in tetralogy of Fallot, 1225
  in tricuspid atresia, 1226
  in truncus arteriosus, 1230
  in ventricular septal defect, 1238
  normal, 1237–1238
Heart rate
  developmental factors affecting,
    1214–1215
  fetal. *See* Fetal heart rate; Fetal heart rate
    monitoring.
  in myocardial performance, 1266
  measurement of, in arrhythmia diagnosis,
    1252
  monitoring of, during anesthesia, 636
Heart sounds, in congenital heart disease,
  1216
Heart valves. *See named valve, e.g.,* Aortic
  valve.
Heat
  fetal exposure to, placenta-independent
    pathway in, 261
  intolerance of, in ectodermal dysplasia,
    1714
Heat exchange
  between infant's body surface and
    environment, 586
  between infant's respiratory tract and
    environment, 586–587, 592t, 592–594,
    593t, 594f
    calculation of, 587
  between infant's skin and environment,
    588–592
    at different ambient humidities, 589, 590f
    during care on radiant bed, 592
    during first day after birth, 588, 590f
    during first hours after birth, 588, 589f
    during first weeks after birth, 589–590,
      591f
    during phototherapy, 592
    during skin-to-skin care, 592
    under radiant heaters, 590–591
  conductive, 586
  convective, 586
  evaporative, 586. *See also* Evaporation.
  in heated beds, 588
  in incubators, 587
  in radiant heaters, 587–588
  routes of, 585–586
  through radiation, 586
Heat loss. *See also* Hypothermia.
  prevention of
    during surgery, 636
    during transportation of patient, 635
    in neonatal resuscitation, 490, 490f
Heated beds, heat exchange in, 588
Heel stick technique, of hypothyroidism
  screening, 1538
Heinz body, 1305
  formation of, 1430
Helix-loop-helix proteins, in cardiogenesis,
  1198
Hellin-Zellany rule, for multiple gestations,
  375

HELLP syndrome, 311, 1615
Helmets, skull-molding, for deformational
  plagiocephaly, 1014
Hemangioma, 1707–1708
  airway obstruction due to, 1143
  capillary (stork bites)
    examination of, 517
    of eyelids, 1730
  cervicofacial, 1708
  clinical manifestations of, 1706, 1707,
    1707t, 1708f
  in Kasabach-Merritt syndrome, 1430
  myocardial, 1250
  of eyelids, 1730
  orbital, 1735
  periorbital, 1708
  subglottic, 1153–1154, 1154f
  vs. vascular malformations, 1707t
Hematocrit
  in erythroblastosis fetalis, as indicator for
    transfusion, 401
  in very low birthweight infants, 1810t
  interval between cord delivery and
    clamping and, 1291, 1293
  maintenance of, in congenital heart
    disease, 1265–1266
Hematologic system, anomalies of, in inborn
  errors of metabolism, 1620
Hematoma
  of ear, birth-related, 539
  orbital, 1735
  scrotal, birth-related, 556f, 556–557
  subdural, macrocephaly due to, 1005,
    1006f
Hematopoiesis
  anatomic and functional shifts in,
    1287–1288
  fetal, 762
Hematopoietic growth factors, 762,
  1288–1289, 1289t
Hematopoietic stem cells, 762, 1287–1288,
  1288f
Hematopoietic system, development of,
  1287–1289
Hematuria, 1667
Heme, catabolism of, to bilirubin,
  1419–1420, 1420f
Heme oxygenase
  in brain, 1436
  microsomal, 1419, 1420f
Hemifacial atrophy of Romberg,
  heterochromia associated with, 1739
Hemifacial microsomia, 571, 572f
  ocular abnormalities in, 1729
Hemimegalencephaly, 906
Hemimelia, ultrasonography of, 162, 163f
Hemivertebra, perinatal ultrasonography of,
  155, 155f
Hemodialysis, for acute renal failure, 1670
Hemodynamics, 1211–1215
  blood flow measurement in, 1211–1212
  chamber and vessel size in, 1212
  intracardiac shunting and, 1212
  myocardial performance and, 1212–1215
  pressure, flow, and resistance in, 1211
  wall thickness and, 1212
Hemofiltration, continuous venovenous, 1670
Hemoglobin
  expression of, during development, 1290,
    1290t
  fetal
    dissociation curve of, 1089
    neonatal anesthesia and, 629
    oxygen affinity of, 484

Hemoglobin—*cont'd*
glycosylated, gestational diabetes mellitus and, 322
in very low birthweight infants, 1810t
increased, in hydrops fetalis, 392
neonatal, 1293, 1293f
oxygen-carrying component of, 1419
synthesis of, in red blood cell production, 1293
unstable, 1305
variants of, 1303–1305, 1304b
Hemoglobin A, 1290, 1291
Hemoglobin E, 1304–1305
Hemoglobin F, 1290, 1291
Hemoglobin H disease, 1303
Hemoglobin S, heterozygotes for, 1304
Hemoglobin SS disease, 1304, 1305f
Hemoglobin switching, 1290–1291, 1291f
Hemoglobinuria, 1667
Hemolytic anemia. *See* Anemia, hemolytic.
Hemolytic disease. *See also* Anemia, hemolytic.
ABO, 1298
minor blood group, 1298
natural history of, 1299
Rh, 1298, 1298t
Hemolytic reactions, to transfusion, 1347
Hemophilia(s), 1325–1326
Hemophilia A, 1325–1326
genetics of, 123
treatment of, 1326, 1327t
Hemophilia B, 1325–1326
treatment of, 1326, 1327t
Hemophilia C, 1326
Hemorrhage
adrenal
birth-related, 551–553, 552f
ultrasonography of, 726, 726f
anemia due to, 1297
cerebellar, 933–934
fetomaternal, 461, 1296–1297
due to intravascular fetal transfusion, 402, 402t
gastrointestinal
Apt test for, 1325
due to duplication cyst, 1393
germinal matrix, 925
ultrasonography of, 727f, 727–728, 728f
in low birthweight infant, 23
intracranial. *See* Periventricular-intraventricular hemorrhage.
intraocular, birth-related, 539
parenchymal, 926–927, 927f, 928f
periventricular-intraventricular. *See* Periventricular-intraventricular hemorrhage.
pulmonary. *See* Pulmonary hemorrhage.
retinal, 539, 1727
severe, conjugated hyperbilirubinemia associated with, 1461
subarachnoid, 933
subconjunctival
birth-related, 538
examination of, 516
subdural, 933
subgaleal
birth-related, 533–534, 533f–534f
vs. cephalhematoma, 534
umbilical cord, 1296
vaginal, in preterm delivery, 336
vitreous, birth-related, 539
Hemorrhagic disease of newborn, 1328–1329
Hemorrhagic disorder, vs. petechiae, 529

Hemostasis, 1318–1342
anticoagulant strategies in, 1321
blood vessels in, 1318
coagulation and fibrinolysis in, physiologic alterations of, 1322, 1322t, 1323t, 1324, 1324t–1325t
coagulation factors in, 1320–1321, 1320f, 1321f
components of, 1318–1324
defects in, 1324
acquired, 1328–1330
congenital, 1325–1328
fibrinolytic system in, 1321–1322, 1322f
laboratory tests for, 1324–1325, 1326f, 1327t
platelets in, 1318, 1319
regulation of, 1337–1338
proteins in, 1321
thrombocytopenia and, 1338–1342. *See also* Thrombocytopenia.
thrombotic disorders in, 1330–1337. *See also* Thrombosis.
von Willebrand factor in, 1318, 1319–1320, 1319f
Henry-Gauer reflex, 345
Hepadnaviruses, 863
Heparin
for extracorporeal membrane oxygenation, 1330
for thrombosis, 1334, 1335b, 1336, 1336b
in breast milk, 199
in extracorporeal membrane oxygenation, 1169
intracranial hemorrhage associated with, 1171
lipoprotein lipase stimulation by, 686
Hepatic. *See also* Liver *entries.*
Hepatic ducts, diseases involving, 1451–1452
Hepatic veins, catheterization of, for interventional procedures, 1274–1275
Hepatitis
conjugated hyperbilirubinemia due to, 1452–1458, 1454f, 1456f, 1457f
idiopathic neonatal
biopsy of, 1456, 1456f
causes of, 1453
clinical manifestations of, 1454–1455, 1455b
conjugated hyperbilirubinemia due to, 1452–1458
treatment of, 1457–1458
definition of, 1452
hepatic metabolic disease and, 1459–1460
histopathology of, 1455–1456
incidence of, 1454
infectious causes of, 1458–1459
sepsis and, 1459
treatment of, 1457–1458
vs. extrahepatic biliary atresia, 1453
Hepatitis A, 439, 863
transfusion-transmitted, 1346
Hepatitis B, 439–441, 863–866
clinical manifestations of, 439–440, 440f, 864
epidemiology of, 439
immunization for, 440–441, 865–866
maternal-fetal transmission of, 440, 440t
with Rh IgG prophylaxis, 394
perinatal transmission of, 864–865
prenatal screening for, 440
transfusion-transmitted, 1346
Hepatitis B core antigen (HBcAg), 863

Hepatitis B immunoglobulin (HBIG), 440, 865, 866
Hepatitis B surface antigen (HBsAg), 863
antibody to, 863
maternal transmission of, 1458–1459
Hepatitis C
in pregnancy, 441
perinatal, 866–867
transfusion-transmitted, 1346
transmission of, 441, 866
in Rh IgG prophylaxis, 394
vertical transmission of, 1459
Hepatitis D, 441, 867
Hepatitis E, 441–442, 867
Hepatitis G, 442
and GB virus type C, 867–868
transfusion-transmitted, 1346
Hepatobiliary tract, ultrasonography of, 722–724, 723f
Hepatocellular carcinoma, in hepatitis B, 864
Hepatocellular injury, hyperbilirubinemia due to, 1450
Hepatocytes
bile canaliculus and, 1450, 1451f
in extrahepatic biliary atresia, 1457, 1457f
Hepatomegaly
in congenital heart disease, 1216
in hydrops fetalis, ultrasonography of, 392f, 397, 399t
in inborn errors of metabolism, 1623–1624, 1623t
in syphilis, 822
Hepatosplenomegaly, in hydrops fetalis
anemia associated with, 398, 399t
ultrasonography of, 397, 399t
Hereditary elliptocytosis, 1300, 1301f
Hereditary fructose intolerance, 1484, 1485
hepatocellular disease associated with, 1622
Hereditary motor and sensory neuropathy, 979–980
Hereditary pyropoikilocytosis, 1300, 1301f
Hereditary sensory and autonomic neuropathy, 980, 980b
Hereditary spherocytosis, 1300, 1301f
Heredity, in sensorineural hearing loss, 1048
Hering-Breuer reflex
apnea and, 492, 1136, 1137
in assisted ventilation, 1111
Hermaphroditism, true, 1573–1574, 1573f
definition of, 1573
Hernia
diaphragmatic
congenital. *See* Diaphragmatic hernia, congenital.
hiatal, after fundoplication, 1380
inguinal, disorders associated with, 1558t
umbilical, examination of, 517
Heroin
central nervous system effects of, 752–753
fetal effects of, 749, 751–752
in breast milk, 200
neonatal abstinence syndrome related to, 749–751, 751f
self-administration of, in adults with fetal exposure to, 752
Herpes gestationis, 373
Herpes simplex virus infection, 437–438, 840–843
clinical manifestations of, 437
congenital, 841
cutaneous, 1698, 1699t
diagnosis of, 842

Herpes simplex virus infection—cont'd
  disseminated, 842
  encephalitis with, 842
  epidemiology of, 437, 840–841
  genital, 437, 840–841
  in sensorineural hearing loss, 1048
  neonatal, 841–842
  of skin, eye, and mouth, 842
  survival rate in, 843, 843f
  transmission of, 437–438, 840–841
  treatment and prevention of, 842–843,
      843f
Heterochromia, 1738–1739
  defects associated with, 1739
  on physical examination, 1723
Heterodisomy, 126
Heteroplasmy, 125
Heterotopia
  in assisted reproduction, 145
  neuronal (brain warts), 992
Heterozygote, 121
  detection of, in 21-hydroxylase deficiency,
      1582
Hexachlorophene soap, bathing of infants
      with, 829
Hexokinase deficiency, jaundice due to, 1429
Hiatal hernia, after fundoplication, 1380
High altitude, fetal growth affected by, 283
High frequency ventilation, 1117–1118
  flow interrupters in, 1117
  jet ventilation in, 1117, 1118
  oscillatory, 1117–1118
High-risk neonate, 19–23, 1035–1042. See
      also Neonatal mortality.
  developmental testing of, 1039–1040
  early intervention in, 1041–1042
  epidemiology of, 19–23, 20b
  factors related to, 19, 20b
  famous high-risk infants, 15–17, 16t
  feeding methods for, 676. See also Enteral
      nutrition.
  follow-up for, timing of, 1039
  functional outcome in, 1040–1041
  health outcome in, 1040
  history of perinatal obstetrics and, 3–5, 6f
  medical problems of, 1036–1038
  neurodevelopmental dysfunction in,
      1035b, 1035–1036, 1036t, 1037b,
      1037f
  neurodevelopmental outcome in,
      1038–1041
  neurologic sequelae in, 1038–1039, 1039f
  neurologic testing of, 1039–1040, 1040b
  physical growth of, 1037–1038, 1038f
  school-age outcome in, 1041, 1041f
  transient neurologic problems in, 1038
Hip
  developmental dysplasia of, 1773–1776
    diagnosis of, 1774–1775, 1775f
    examination for, 516, 520–521, 521f
    imaging of, 1775, 1775f
    pathology and etiology of, 1773–1774
    prevalence of, 517t
    risk of, 520, 521t
    treatment of, 1775–1776, 1776f
  dislocation of, examination for, 516
  examination of, 516
Hirschsprung disease, 1398–1399
  enterocolitis associated with, 1398–1399
  heterochromia associated with, 1739
  radiography of, 720, 720f
  surgical treatment of, 1399
Histidine, in parenteral amino acid
      solutions, 684t, 685

Histiocytosis, 1342
  Langerhans cell, 1712
  orbital, 1736
Histoplasmosis, 834–835
History of neonatal-perinatal medicine. See
      Neonatal-perinatal medicine.
Holoprosencephaly, 902–903, 903f, 991, 992f
  alobar, 902, 991
  anesthetic implications of, 633t
  causes of, 903
  etiologies of, 884b
  genes associated with, 903
  hypotelorism associated with, 568
  in trisomy 13, 568, 569f
  lobar, 991
  semilobar, 902, 903f, 991, 992f
  single nostril in, 569f, 572
Holt-Oram syndrome
  anesthetic implications of, 633t
  heart defects associated with, 1203t
  in radial hypoplasia, 1767
  single gene defects in, 1204
Home delivery, in developing countries
  aseptic technique in, 95, 98f
  home delivery facilities in, 95
Home uterine activity monitoring, in
      prevention of preterm delivery, 344–345
Home visits, in developing countries
  antenatal care in, 102
  by health care personnel, 101, 101t, 102t
  neonatal care in, 102–103, 104f
  traditional birth attendant and community
      health worker role in, 101–103, 103t
Homeobox genes, in cardiogenesis, 1198,
      1200
Homocystinuria, 1604t
  pyridoxine-responsive forms of, 1612
  screening for, 1611–1612
Homozygote, 121
Hormones. See also specific hormone.
  fetal
    effects of, 188t
    in growth, 275–278, 1468
    in sex differentiation, 1554–1556, 1555f,
        1556f
    regulation of, 1500–1504
Horner syndrome
  birth-related, 538
  congenital, heterochromia associated with,
      1739
Hospital discharge abstract, in neonatal care
      evaluation database, 69–70, 73
Hoyeraal-Hreidarsson syndrome, 1311
HPA-1a (PI^{A1}) antigen, in alloimmune
      (isoimmune) thrombocytopenia, 1338
HPA-1a (PI^{A2}) antigen, in alloimmune
      (isoimmune) thrombocytopenia, 1338
Huebner artery, 925
Human chorionic gonadotropin
  for cryptorchidism, 1567
  testicular unresponsiveness to, 1574–1575
β-Human chorionic gonadotropin screening,
      for Down syndrome, 136
Human chorionic gonadotropin stimulation
      test, for intersex disorders, 1562
Human genome, in congenital heart disease
      prevention, 1202
Human herpesvirus types 6 and 7, 850
Human immunodeficiency virus (HIV)
      infection, 432–434, 855–861
  antepartum management of, 434
  care of mothers and infants with
    in developed countries, 857–859
    in developing countries, 859–860

Human immunodeficiency virus (HIV)
      infection—cont'd
  chorioretinitis in, 1744
  clinical considerations in, 433
  cutaneous manifestation of, 1699t
  diagnosis and treatment of, 433–434
  epidemiology of, 433
  maternal-fetal transmission of
    in Rh IgG prophylaxis, 394
    prevention of, 214, 434, 857–860
  neonatal
    clinical manifestations of, 860
    diagnosis and care of, 860–861
    mortality rate in, 93, 93f
    prognosis in, 861
    viral load in, 856
  pathogenesis of, 856–857
  screening for, 433
  transfusion-transmitted, 1346
  transmission of
    in breast milk, 856–857
    in cocaine abusers, 745
Human leukocyte antigen (HLA) complex
  in alloimmune (isoimmune)
      thrombocytopenia, 369
  in 21-hydroxylase deficiency, 1581
Human leukocyte antigen-DR antibody, in
      RhD sensitization, 391
Human metapneumovirus, 855
Human milk. See Breast milk.
Human papillomavirus infection, 875–876
Human platelet antigen, in alloimmune
      (isoimmune) thrombocytopenia, 369
Human T-cell lymphotropic virus (HTLV),
      transfusion-transmission of, 1346
Humerus
  birth-related fracture of, 553, 1761–1762,
      1762f
  head of, dislocation of, vs. brachial palsy,
      543
Humidity
  different ambient, heat exchange between
      skin and environment at, 589, 590,
      590f, 591f
  role of, in insensible water loss, 698–699
Huntington disease
  DNA diagnosis of, 132
  trinucleotide repeat expansions in,
      126–127
Hyaline membrane disease. See Respiratory
      distress syndrome.
Hyaloid artery, persistence of, 1744
  in preterm infants, 1726, 1726f
Hyaluronic acid, dermal, 1689
Hydantoins, fetal effects of, 187t
Hydatidiform mole
  genomic imprinting in, 125
  in preeclampsia-eclampsia, 312
Hydralazine
  dosages of, 1793
  for neonatal hypertension, 1672t
  for preeclampsia-eclampsia, 314, 314t
Hydramnios. See Polyhydramnios.
Hydranencephaly, 1003, 1003f, 1004f
Hydration. See Fluid(s).
Hydroceles, examination of, 517
Hydrocephalus
  advanced cases of, 998–999, 999f
  aqueductal stenosis and, 999, 999f
  cerebrospinal fluid space enlargement in,
      998–1004
  Chiari II malformation and, 1000–1001,
      1000f
  classification of, 998

Hydrocephalus—cont'd
  clinical presentation of, 998
  communicating, 998
    in meningitis, 805, 1002
  Dandy-Walker malformation and,
    999–1000, 1000f
  etiology of, 999–1004
  external, 1002–1003, 1002f
  noncommunicating, 998
    in meningitis, 805
  posthemorrhagic, 1001–1002, 1000f, 1002f
    treatment of, 1002
  postinfectious, 1002
  vs. ventriculomegaly, 152, 1001–1002
  X-linked (Bickers-Adams syndrome), 999
Hydrocephalus ex vacuo, 805
Hydrocephaly, external, 906
Hydrochloric acid, secretion of, 1360
Hydrocodone, abuse of, 753
Hydrocortisone
  dosages of, 1791
  for fetal lung maturation, 213
  for preterm labor prevention, 356
  for thyrotoxicosis, 1549
Hydrogel, for electrodes, 611
Hydrogen breath testing
  carbohydrate-specific, 1365
  in congenital sucrase-isomaltase
    deficiency, 1366
Hydrogen peroxide, in microbicidal activity,
  of neutrophils, 766
Hydronephrosis, 160, 1676–1678
  Eagle-Barrett syndrome in, 1678, 1678f
  imperforate anus associated with, 1400
  in obstructive uropathy, 234, 235f
  physiologic, 1677
  posterior urethral valves in, 1678
  postnatal management of, 1677
  prenatal management of, 1677, 1677t
  ultrasonography of, 160, 160f, 1676, 1676f
  ureteropelvic junction obstruction in, 1677
  ureterovesical junction obstruction in,
    1677–1678
  vesicoureteral reflux in, 1678
Hydrops fetalis, 391–393, 1303
  classic, ultrasound studies of, 421f
  clinical signs of, 391, 461
    ultrasonography of, 392f, 397, 398f
  in preeclampsia-eclampsia, 312
  mortality associated with, 221
  neonatal resuscitation and, 507–508
  nonimmune, 420–426, 424
    antenatal diagnosis of, 420, 421t, 421f
    antenatal evaluation of, 424b
    antiarrhythmic therapy and, 1210
    cardiovascular dysfunction in,
      1209–1210, 1209b
    conservative management of, 425b,
      425–426
    diagnoses associated with
      frequency of, 423t
      principle, 422t
    diagnostic evaluation of, 422–425, 424b
    due to parvovirus B19 infection, 869
    echocardiography of, 424
    etiology of, 421–422, 422b, 423t
    fetal surgery for, 426
    indications for delivery in, 426
    invasive fetal testing for, 424–425
    pathophysiology of, 420–421
    postnatal evaluation of, 425, 425b
    prognosis of, 426
    treatment of, 425–426
      experimental, 426

Hydrops fetalis—cont'd
  ultrasonography of, 423f, 423–424
    findings in, 421t
  parvovirus infection and, 1308
  pathophysiology of, 392–393
  reversal of, after intravascular transfusion,
    403
Hydrosyringomyelia, in Chiari malformation,
  1000
Hydrothorax
  algorithm for management of, 233f
  thoracoamniotic shunt for, 232, 232f, 234t
3-Hydroxy-3-methylglutaric aciduria, 1606t
3-Hydroxyacyl-CoA dehydrogenase
  deficiency, long-chain, 1609t
  in HELLP syndrome, 1615
β-Hydroxybutyrate, placental transport of,
  1467–1468
3-Hydroxyisobutyryl-CoA deacylase
  deficiency, 1627
21-Hydroxylase
  absence of activity by, in congenital
    adrenal hyperplasia, 701
  deficiency of, 1578–1582
    cortisol levels in, 1579
    diagnosis of, 1579–1580
      prenatal, 1581, 1582f
    gender assignment in, 1581
    genetics of, 1581
    heterozygote detection in, 1582
    neonatal screening for, 1582
    pathology of, 1579
    pathophysiology of, 1578f
    salt-losing, 1579
    simple virilizing, 1578, 1578f
    treatment of, 1580–1581
      in utero, 1581
11β-Hydroxylase deficiency, 1582–1583
17α-Hydroxylase deficiency, 1584
17-Hydroxyprogesterone, serum levels of,
  1806t
17β-Hydroxysteroid dehydrogenase, 1575
3β-Hydroxysteroid dehydrogenase
  deficiency, 1583
Hydroxyzine (Vistaril), with opioids, during
  labor, 471
Hygroma, cystic, 1710
  airway obstruction due to, 1143
  in nonimmune hydrops fetalis, 421–422
  perinatal ultrasonography of, 155, 156f
Hyperammonemia, 1649–1651
  differential diagnosis of, 1649–1650,
    1650f
  genetic disorders associated with, 1649b
  laboratory findings in, 1629t
  other causes of, 1651
  recognition of, 1630
  transient, 1650
  urea cycle defects and, 1650–1651
Hyperbilirubinemia
  classification of, 1436
  conjugated, 1423, 1450–1461, 1451f, 1452f
    Alagille syndrome and, 1460
    bile plug syndrome and, 1460
    biliary cystic disease and, 1460
    biliary masses and, 1460
    causes of, 34–43
      infectious, 1458–1459
      miscellaneous, 1460–1461
    choledocholithiasis and, 1460
    diseases manifested as, 1452, 1453b
    extrahepatic biliary atresia and,
      1452–1458
      treatment of, 1458

Hyperbilirubinemia—cont'd
    idiopathic neonatal hepatitis and,
      1452–1458
    in cystic fibrosis, 1364
    laboratory tests for, 1455b, 1455–1456
    maternal, 1425
    mechanical obstruction and, 1460
    metabolic disease and, 1459–1460
    sepsis and, 1459
    total parenteral nutrition–injury and,
      1460
    Zellweger syndrome and, 1461
  in sensorineural hearing loss, 1048
  risk factors for, 1438, 1438b, 1439f
  unconjugated
    activated charcoal for, 1446
    causes of, 1428–1434
      conjugation disorders as, 1431–1433
      enterohepatic circulation disorders as,
        1432–1434
      excretion disorders as, 1432
      hepatic uptake disorders as, 1431
      miscellaneous disorders as, 1434
      production disorders as, 1428–1431,
        1428b
    Crigler-Najjar syndrome and
      type I, 1431
      type II, 1431–1432
    diagnosis of, 1436–1440, 1437t
    erythrocyte enzymatic defects and,
      1429–1430
    erythrocyte structural defects and, 1430
    exchange transfusion for, 1446–1448,
      1447f, 1448b
    frequent milk feedings for, 1446
    genetic effects of, 1427–1428
    hypothyroidism and, 1432
    in hypertrophic pyloric stenosis, 1389
    in postterm infant, 1427
    in preterm infant, 1426–1427, 1427f
    in term infant, 1425–1426, 1426f
    increased production of bilirubin and,
      1430
    infection and, 1430
    intravenous immunoglobulins for, 1446
    isoimmunization and, 370, 1428–1429
    kernicterus and, 1434–1436
    laboratory studies of, 1437t, 1437–1438
    Lucey-Driscoll syndrome and, 1432
    metalloporphyrins for, 1446
    neonatal, 1425–1428
    nonpathologic, 1424–1428
    pathologic, 1428–1450
    pharmacologic therapy for, 1445–1446
    phenobarbital for, 1445–1446
    phototherapy for, 1440–1445
    polycythemia and, 1430–1431
    pyloric stenosis and, 1432
    red blood cell destruction and, 1430
    sequelae of, 1434–1436
    sequestration and, 1430
    transient encephalopathy and, 1434
    treatment of, 1440–1450, 1441b
      guidelines in, 1448–1450, 1448f,
        1449f, 1450t
    vs. physiologic bilirubinemia, 1424
Hypercalcemia, 1514–1518
  blue diaper syndrome and, 1517
  carbohydrate malabsorption and, 1516
  causes of, 1514b
  clinical manifestations of, 1517
  definition of, 1514
  diagnostic steps for, 1515b
  familial hypocalciuric, 1515

Hypercalcemia—cont'd
  hyperparathyroidism and
    primary, 1515–1516
    secondary, 1515
  hypothyroidism and, 1517
  idiopathic infantile, 1516
  in subcutaneous fat necrosis, 1712–1713
  Jansen metaphyseal chondrodysplasia
    and, 1517
  renal tubular acidosis and, 1516
  severe infantile hypophosphatasia and,
    1516–1517
  subcutaneous fat necrosis and, 1516
  treatment of, 1517–1518
  tumor-related, 1517
  Williams syndrome and, 1516
Hypercalcinuria, hypomagnesemia with,
  1519
Hypercapnia
  in bronchopulmonary dysplasia, 1163
  in gas exchange impairment, 1110
  permissive
    for lung damage prevention, 1121
    in mechanical ventilation, 1113
      for bronchopulmonary dysplasia,
        1164
      for congenital diaphragmatic hernia,
        1173
Hyperextension, of knee, 1777–1778, 1778f
Hyperglycemia, 1489–1490
  definition of, 327
  in extremely low birthweight infant, 681
    parenteral nutrition and, 681
  in small for gestational age infant, 296t
  neonatal anesthesia and, 630
Hyperglycinemia, nonketotic, 1604t
  neonatal response to, 1617
Hyperimmune globulin, for sepsis, 801
Hyperinsulinemia, fetal, 327
Hyperinsulinism, in persistent hypoglycemia,
  1480–1482, 1481f
Hyperkalemia, in respiratory distress
  syndrome, 1106
Hyperkeratosis, epidermolytic, 1696
Hypermagnesemia, 1520, 1520b
  in meconium plug syndrome, 1396
  secondary to magnesium sulfate
    administration, 981–982
Hypernatremia, 702
  diabetes insipidus and, 702
  in respiratory distress syndrome, 1106
  seizures and, 969
Hyperoxia-hyperventilation test, 1090–1091
Hyperoxic test, in congenital heart disease,
  1216–1217
Hyperparathyroidism
  definition of, 1515
  primary, 1515–1516
  secondary, 1515
  severe, 1515–1516
Hyperphenylalaninemia
  screening for, 1614
  treatment of, 1613–1614
Hyperpigmentation
  diffuse, 1704
  exposure to polychlorinated biphenyls
    and, 257
  localized, 1704–1705
  postinflammatory, 1705
Hyperreflexia, 961
  in eclamptic seizures, 312
Hypertelorism
  definition of, 568, 1724
  in facial anomalies, 568, 570f

Hypertelorism—cont'd
  ocular, 1729
    in Apert syndrome, 1012
  orbital, 1734
Hypertension, 1244–1245
  chronic, 307, 316–318
    antepartum fetal evaluation in, 318
    classification of, 316, 316b
    complications of, 318
    evaluation of, 316
    home blood pressure monitoring of, 317
    laboratory tests for, 317
    management of, 317–318
    preconception counseling in, 317
    preexisting, 313
    primary, 316, 316b
    secondary, 316, 316b
    with superimposed preeclampsia-
      eclampsia, 318
  definition of, 307
  diagnosis of, 1244–1245
  differential diagnosis of, 1245, 1245t
  essential, preexisting, 312–313
  gestational, 282–283, 283f, 307–318
    classification of, 307–308
  gestational diabetes mellitus and, 325
  in renal disease, 1665
  neonatal, 1670–1674
    causes of, 1670, 1671t
    clinical presentation of, 1671
    definition of, 1670, 1671f–1673f
    evaluation of, 1671–1672
    treatment of, 1672–1674, 1672t, 1673t
  pulmonary. See Pulmonary hypertension.
  renin-mediated, 309
  renovascular, 1670, 1671t, 1674
  treatment of, 1245
Hyperthermia
  in infant, 597
  radiant bed use and, 596
Hyperthyroidism
  exopthalmos in, 1736
  fetal, 220
  thyrotropin-binding inhibiting
    immunoglobulins in, 1529–1530
Hyperthyrotropinemia, transient, 1544
Hyperthyroxinemia, familial
  dysalbuminemic, 1550
Hypertonia, assessment of, 526
Hypertrichosis, 1731
Hypertrichosis lanuginosa, 1731
Hyperventilation
  cerebral, vs. transient tachypnea, 1128
  for cyanotic spells, 1268
  for persistent pulmonary hypertension,
    1247
Hyperviscosity, transient hypoglycemia in,
  1479
Hyperviscosity-polycythemia syndrome, in
  small for gestational age infant, 296t,
  301
Hyperviscosity syndrome, 1309
Hyphema, due to birth injury, 539
Hypnotics, neutropenia due to, 1313b
Hypobetalipoproteinemia, 1368
Hypocalcemia, 1508–1514
  asphyxia and, 1510
  asymptomatic, 1513
  causes of, 1509b
  clinical manifestations of, 1512–1513
  definitions of, 1508
  diagnostic steps for, 1509b
  early, 1509–1510, 1509b
    treatment of, 1513

Hypocalcemia—cont'd
  hypomagnesemia and, 1511
  hypoparathyroidism and, 1511–1512
  in infant of diabetic mother, 1475
  in preterm infants, 1510
  in term infants, 1509–1510
  late, 1510–1512, 1509b
    treatment of, 1513–1514
  maternal anticonvulsants and, 1510
  osteopetrosis and, 1512
  phosphate loading and, 1510–1511
  phototherapy causing, 1512
  prevention of, 1514
  secondary, hypomagnesemia with, 1519
  seizures due to, 968
    definition of, 968
  symptomatic, 1513
  therapies causing, 1512
  treatment of, 1513–1514
  vitamin D disorder causing, 1512
Hypocalciuric hypercalcemia, familial, 1515
Hypocapnia, in natural childbirth, 468
Hypocortisolemia, in adrenal insufficiency,
  1579
Hypofusion insults, to white matter, 913–914
Hypoglossal nerve
  assessment of, 525
  birth injury to, vocal cord paralysis related
    to, 540
Hypoglycemia, 1471–1489, 1645–1649
  clinical manifestations of, 1471–1472,
    1471b
  definition of, 968, 1471
  diazoxide in, 1487
  differential diagnosis of, 1646–1647, 1647f
  fasting, in small for gestational age infant,
    296t, 299–300, 300f, 301f
  fatty acid oxidation disorders and,
    1648–1649
  gluconeogenesis defects and, 1647–1648
  glycogen storage disease in, 1647
  hypoxic-ischemic insult and, 952
  in infant of diabetic mother, 1475
  in meconium plug syndrome, 1397
  laboratory findings in, 1629t
  management of, 1485–1488
    diazoxide in, 1487
    epinephrine in, 1487
    glucagon in, 1487
    glucocorticoids in, 1488
    growth hormone in, 1488
    intravenous glucose infusions in,
      1486–1487, 1486f
    pancreatectomy in, 1488
    somatostatin in, 1487
  metabolic defects associated with, 1646t
  neonatal anesthesia and, 629–630
  organic aciduria and, 1648
  persistent (recurrent), 1480–1485
    causes of, 1472b
    cortisol deficiency and, 1483–1484
    endocrine disorders and, 1483–1484
    epinephrine deficiency and, 1484
    fructose intolerance and, 1484–1485
    glucagon deficiency and, 1484
    hyperinsulinemic, 1480–1482, 1481f
    in Beckwith-Wiederman syndrome,
      1482–1483, 1482b
    inborn errors of carbohydrate
      metabolism and, 1484–1485
    neurohypoglycemia
      (hypoglycorrhachia) and, 1485
    pituitary insufficiency and, 1483
  prognosis of, 1488–1489

Hypoglycemia—cont'd
    seizures due to, 968
    transient
        birth asphyxia and, 1479
        causes of, 1472b
        congenital cardiac malformations and, 1480
        erythroblastosis fetalis and, 1479–1480
        failure to adapt and, 1478
        hyperviscosity and, 1479
        hypothermia and, 1479
        iatrogenic causes of, 1480
        idiopathic, 1478
        infant of diabetic mother and, 1473–1478, 1473b
        infection and, 1479
        intrapartum glucose administration and, 1472
        intrauterine growth restrictions and, 1478–1479
        maternal diabetes treatment and, 1472–1473
        maternal metabolic changes causing, 1472–1478
        neonatal problems and, 1478–1480
        small for gestational age and, 1478–1479
Hypoglycemic agents
    fetal effects of, 188t
    for gestational diabetes mellitus, 323–324
    neutropenia due to, 1313b
Hypoglycorrhachia, defective glucose transport and, 1485
Hypohidrotic ectodermal dysplasia, 1711, 1714
Hypomagnesemia, 1518–1520
    clinical manifestations of, 1519
    etiology of, 1520b
    hypocalcemia and, 1511
    hypoparathyroidism and, 1519
    in infant of diabetic mother, 1475
    intrauterine growth restriction and, 1519
    maternal diabetes and, 1518–1519
    transient, 1511
    treatment of, 1519–1520
Hypomelanosis of Ito, 1706
Hyponatremia, 700–702
    congenital adrenal hyperplasia and, 701
    definition of, 700
    in respiratory distress syndrome, 1106
    late-onset, 701
    pseudohypoaldosteronism and, 701–702
    seizures and, 968
    treatment of, 700
Hypoparathyroidism
    hypocalcemia in, 1511–1512
    hypomagnesemia and, 1519
    secondary, maternal disease and, 1511
    vitamin D for, 1513–1514
Hypoperfusion, and congestive heart failure, with mild or no cyanosis, 1222, 1221b
Hypophosphatasia, severe infantile, hypercalcemia due to, 1516–1517
Hypopigmentation disorders, 1705–1706
Hypoplastic left heart syndrome, 1235–1237
    anatomy and pathophysiology of, 1235
    clinical presentation of, 1235–1236
    conjugated hyperbilirubinemia associated with, 1461
    defects associated with, 1235
    heart transplantation for, 1269–1270
    laboratory evaluation of, 1236, 1236f
    management of, 1236–1237
    prognosis in, 1237

Hypoproteinemia, in hydrops fetalis, 392–393
Hypospadias, 1565–1566
    associated with maternal progestins, 1566f, 1577
    differential diagnosis of, 1565, 1566f
    disorders associated with, 1558t
    examination of, 519
    prevalence of, 517t
    severe, 1565, 1565f
    surgical repair of, 1566
Hypotelorism
    definition of, 568
    in congenital anomalies, 568, 569f, 570f
Hypotension
    associated with hypoxic-ischemic insult, 951
    in renal disease, 1665
    in respiratory distress syndrome, 1106
    maternal
        due to inadvertent intrathecal injections, 476
        in neuraxial blocks, 474
Hypothalamic-pituitary axis
    development of, 1533t
    in thyroid hormone secretion control, 1526–1527
Hypothalamus, in thyrotropin-releasing hormone secretion, 1527
Hypothermia
    as neuroprotection against neonatal encephalopathy, 597
    in infant, 596–597
    management of
        during transportation of patient, 635
        in developing countries, 95–97, 97f–99f, 99, 100t
        in neonatal anesthesia, 629
    neonatal mortality rate related to, in developing countries, 94
    therapeutic, for hypoxic-ischemic encephalopathy, 954–955
    transient hypoglycemia in, 1479
Hypothyroidism
    central, 1537–1538
    congenital, 1535–1543
        causes of, 219t
        central hypothyroidism and, 1537–1538
        clinical manifestations of, 1540–1541, 1541f
        defective embryogenesis in, 1536
        differential diagnosis of, 1545
        etiology of, 1535–1536
        facial features of, 1541f, 1540–1541
        familial dyshormonogenesis in, 1536–1537
        feeding difficulties in, 1540
        female incidence of, 1538
        goiters in, 1541
        hypercalcemia due to, 1517
        in Down syndrome, 1538
        iodide trapping in, 1536
        iodine deficiency in, 1537
        laboratory manifestations of, 1541–1542
        lingual thyroid tissue in, 1541, 1541f
        maternal ingestion of goitrogens in, 1537
        ocular manifestation of, 1728
        ossification disturbances in, 1542
        pathogenesis of, 1535–1536
        prognosis of, 1547
        retardation of bone maturation in, 1542
        scanning results in, interpretation of, 1542–1543

Hypothyroidism—cont'd
    screening for, 1538, 1539t–1540t, 1540–1543
        International Studies in, 1539t–1540t
    sodium-L-thyroxine for, 1545–1546
    sporadic, 1535
    thyroid hormone metabolic errors and, 1536–1537
    thyroid-stimulating hormone resistance in, 1537
    thyroxine replacement therapy for, 1546
    treatment of, 1545–1547
    TSH surge test for, 1531
    unconjugated hyperbilirubinemia due to, 1432
    fetal, 219–220
        drug treatment of, 220
    primary, transient neonatal, 1543–1544
    secondary, 1537–1538
    tertiary, 1537
    thyrotropin-binding inhibiting immunoglobulins in, 1529
Hypothyroxinemia, transient, 1544
Hypotonia
    assessment of, 516, 526
    diagnosis of, 966
    in congenital myasthenic syndromes, 980
    in hereditary neuropathies, 980
    in myotonic dystrophy, 985
    in preterm infant, 527, 527t
    in spinal muscular atrophy, 979
    muscle tone in, 976–977
    neuromuscular disease and, 976–989
Hypoventilation
    hypercapnia due to, 1110
    hypoxemia due to, 1111
Hypoxanthine, formation or reactive oxygen species and, 498
Hypoxemia
    biphasic response to, in preterm infants, 1136
    causes of, 1111
    definition of, 172
    due to shunting, 1090
    in assisted ventilation, vs. apnea, 1139
    in bronchopulmonary dysplasia, 1163
    in intrauterine growth restriction, 283
    in persistent pulmonary hypertension, 1246
    intestinal response to, necrotizing enterocolitis related to, 1407
    permissive
        for lung damage prevention, 1121
        in mechanical ventilation, 1113
Hypoxia
    definition of, 172, 938
    gestational diabetes mellitus and, 327
    in cyanotic spells, prevention of, 1268
Hypoxia-ischemia, free radical formation in, 498
Hypoxic-ischemic encephalopathy, 938–956
    perinatal
        acidosis in, 955
        Apgar scores in, 955–956
        apoptosis in, 943
        brainstem auditory evoked potentials in, 947, 947f
        calcification in, 940
        cellular responses to, 940
        cellular susceptibility to, 939
        cerebral edema in, 940, 953
        cerebral susceptibility to, 939–940
            gestational age in, 939
        chronic lesions in, 940–941

Hypoxic-ischemic encephalopathy—*cont'd*
clinical staging of, 938t
condition at birth in, 955–956
corticosteroids for, 953
CT scan of, 948
cytokines in, 943
definitions of, 938
free iron in, 943
free radical formation in, 943
glial cell response to, 940
glucose for, 952
glutamate injury in, 942–943
hypotension in, 951
management of, 949–956
brain-oriented, 952–953
neuroprotective strategies in, 954–955
primary prevention in, 949–950
prognosis in, 955–956, 955b, 956t
resuscitation in, 950–951, 950b
systemic, 951–952
microglial cell response to, 940
MR imaging of, 948–949, 948f, 949f
neuroimaging of, 948–949, 948f, 949f
neuropathology of, 940–941
neurophysiology of, 944f–946f, 944–949
nitric oxide toxicity in, 943
pathophysiology of, 938, 942–944
positron emission tomography of, 949
preconditioning to, 941–942
prognosis of, 956, 956b
seizures in, 952–953
management of, 953
somatosensory evoked potentials in, 948
studies of, 943–944
systemic adaptation to, 941–942, 941b, 942f
therapeutic hypothermia for, 954–955
type of insult in, 940
ultrasonography of, 948
visual evoked potentials in, 947–948
watershed injury in, 939
Hypoxic-ischemic insults
acute, 942
causes of, 941b
physiologic responses to, 941, 942f
systemic adaptation to, 941–942
to germinal matrix, 929
to white matter, 913–914, 914f
types of, 940

I

Ibuprofen, for closure of patent ductus arteriosus, 1241
Ichthyosiform erythroderma, congenital, 1696
Ichthyosis, 1693–1696, 1694t
bullous, 1696
collodion baby as, 1695, 1695f
harlequin, 1694t, 1695
lamellar, 1694t, 1696
X-linked, 1694t, 1695–1696
Idiopathic infantile hypercalcemia, 1516
IGF1 gene, 277
deletion of, in intrauterine growth restriction, 287
IGF2 gene, 277
in Beckwith-Wiedemann syndrome, 1482, 1483
loss of imprinting of, fetal growth and, 287

Ileal atresia
radiography of, 721
ultrasonography of, 157, 158f
Ileus, meconium. *See* Meconium ileus.
Illicit drugs. *See also* Substance abuse.
in maternal-placental-fetal unit, 189
intrauterine growth restriction due to, 283–284
Imaging. *See specific modality, e.g.,* Ultrasonography.
Immune response, primary and secondary, 783, 783t
Immune system
development of, 761–791
immaturity of
and predisposition to infection, 793, 794t
necrotizing enterocolitis and, 1408
Immune thrombocytopenic purpura, 367–368
treatment of, 368
Immunity
acquired, 777–790
B cells in, 783–788
T cells in, 779–783
evaluation for defective mechanisms in, 790–791, 791b, 791t
hematopoiesis in, 762
innate, 762–777. *See also specific components.*
cellular components of, 762–770
humoral components of, 770–777
passive, 788–790
placental transport of antibodies in, 788
via human breast milk, 788–790, 789t
Immunizations. *See also* Vaccine(s).
schedule for, in preterm infants, 1819–1820
Immunodeficiency
HIV. *See* Human immunodeficiency virus (HIV) infection.
in small for gestational age infant, 296t
severe combined
natural killer cell g-c chain mutation in, 770
X-linked, defective T cell development in, 780–781
Immunoglobulin(s)
classes of, 786
constant regions of, 786
for hepatitis B, 440
for rubella virus infection, 872
hepatitis B, 440, 865, 866
human botulinum, 820
in breast milk, 788–790, 789t
intravenous
for alloimmune (isoimmune) thrombocytopenia, 369, 370, 1339
for enterovirus prophylaxis, 863
for idiopathic thrombocytopenic purpura, 368
for infection prevention, in neonatal intensive care units, 829
for sepsis, 800–801
for unconjugated hyperbilirubinemia, 1446
maternal, for erythroblastosis fetalis prevention, 401
placental transfer of, 788
plasma concnetrations of, 1809t
production of, in fetus and neonate, 787, 788t
Rh, prophylaxis with
in management of erythroblastosis fetalis, 393–394

Immunoglobulin(s)—*cont'd*
indications for, 390, 391t
structure and function of, 786–787, 786f, 787t
surface, B cell production of, 783
variable (Fab) regions of, 786
varicella-zoster, 848, 849
Immunoglobulin A
chemical characteristics and biology of, 787, 787t
in breast milk, 788, 789
production of, in fetus and neonate, 787, 788t
secretory, 787
in breast milk, 788
values for, 1809t
Immunoglobulin D, chemical characteristics and biology of, 787, 787t
Immunoglobulin E, chemical characteristics and biology of, 787, 787t
Immunoglobulin G
chemical characteristics and biology of, 787, 787t
in breast milk, 789
in myasthenia gravis, 372–373
in Rh isoimmunization prophylaxis, 394
in RhD sensitization, 390
intravenous
for enterovirus prophylaxis, 863
maternal, for erythroblastosis fetalis prevention, 401
placental transfer of, 214–215, 367, 788
production of, in fetus and neonate, 787, 788t
structure of, 786, 786f
values for, 1809t
Immunoglobulin G-Fc complex, in RhD sensitization, 390
Immunoglobulin M
chemical characteristics and biology of, 787, 787t
human monoclonal, for sepsis, 801
in breast milk, 789
in RhD sensitization, 390
production of, in fetus and neonate, 787, 788t
values for, 1809t
Immunoreceptor tyrosine-based activation motif (ITAM), natural killer cell receptor function and, 769
Immunotherapy, for sepsis, 800–801, 803
Impedance monitoring, in airflow measurement, 1092
Imperforate anus. *See* Anus, imperforate.
Imprinting, genomic, 125–126, 257
abnormal, 287
Improvement of care. *See* Neonatal intensive care, quality of.
In vitro fertilization, genetic evaluation in, 139
Inborn errors of metabolism, 1597–1654. *See also* Metabolism, inborn errors of; *specific disorder.*
Incontinence, fecal, after imperforate anus repair, 1402
Incontinentia pigmenti, 1702
epilepsy associated with, 973
Incontinentia pigmenti achromians (hypomelanosis of Ito), 1706
Incubators
convectively heated, 595–596
development of, Hess and Lundeen in, 10–12, 11f
exhibition of premature babies in, 9–12, 11f, 12f

Incubators—cont'd
  heat exchange in, 587
  history of, 8–9, 9f, 10t, 585
India. See also Developing countries.
  neonatal mortality in, 89–90, 90f
    vs. China, 90t, 90–91
Indigo carmine dye infusion, in
    oligohydramnios, 417
Indomethacin
  administration of, 351
  dosages of, 1793
  fetal side effects of, 351
  for closure of patent ductus arteriosus,
    1106–1107, 1241
  for intraventricular hemorrhage
    prevention, 1121
  for periventricular-intraventricular
    hemorrhage, 932
  for polyhydramnios, 221, 420
  for preterm labor prevention, 351–352
  renal insufficiency due to, 703
Inductance plethysmography, 613
Industrial byproducts, in breast milk,
    201–202
Infant formula. See Formula.
Infant mortality. See Neonatal mortality.
Infant of diabetic mother, 1473–1478
  clinical manifestations of, 1474–1475
  congenital anomalies in, 1474–1475, 1476f
  hypocalcemia in, 1475
  hypoglycemia in, 1475
  hypomagnesemia in, 1475
  indications for delivery of, 1476–1477
  macrosomia in, 1474, 1475f
  maternal management in, 1475–1477
  morbidity in, 1473b
  prognosis of, 1477–1478
  rigorously managed, outcome of, 1474t
  septal hypertrophy and cardiomegaly in,
    1476f, 1475
Infantile epileptic encephalopathy, early
    (Ohtahara syndrome), 973
Infantum subitum, 850
Infarction, of cerebral artery, 934–937. See
    also Arterial ischemic stroke.
  definition of, 934
  seizures associated with, 969
Infection(s). See also Sepsis; specific
    infection, e.g., Meningitis.
  after heart transplantation, 1270
  after mechanical ventilation, 1119
  antepartum/postpartum, neonatal seizures
    associated with, 969
  bacterial. See Bacterial infection(s).
  bronchopulmonary dysplasia related to,
    1160–1161
  congenital anomalies associated with,
    563t, 564
  disorders causing susceptibility to, 790,
    791t
  evaluation of defective host defense
    mechanism in, 790–791, 791b, 791t
  fungal. See Fungal infection(s).
  in utero vaccination against, 214–215,
    215b
  intra-amniotic, 431b, 431–432
    lung maturation induction by, 1086,
      1087f
  intrauterine
    in preterm infant, 333, 334f
    premature rupture of membranes due
      to, 430–431
    radiography of, 729, 729f
  neonatal mortality rate related to, 93, 93f

Infection(s)—cont'd
  neutropenia following, 1312
  neutrophilia due to, 1315
  of bone and joints, 1762–1767
  of catheters, in parenteral nutrition,
    689–690
  of white matter, 914–915
    Escherichia coli in, 915, 915f
  placental, 459–460
  postnatal, radiography of, 729–730
  preterm delivery and, 337–339
  prevention of, in bronchopulmonary
    dysplasia, 1166
  protozoal, 836–840
  transfusion-transmitted, 1345–1346, 1345b
  transient hypoglycemia in, 1479
  unconjugated hyperbilirubinemia due to,
    1430
  viral. See Viral infection(s).
Infertility treatment, multiple gestations in,
    381. See also Multiple gestations.
Inflammation. See also Cytokine(s),
    inflammatory.
  bronchopulmonary dysplasia related to,
    1160–1161
  cutaneous, 1710–1711
  in sepsis, 775–777, 777f, 778t
  lung maturation induced by, 1085
  necrotizing enterocolitis related to,
    1408–1409, 1409f
  placental, 459–460
Influenza A and B viruses, 870–871
Ingestion, disorders of, 1317
Inguinal hernia, disorders associated with,
    1558t
Inhalational agents. See Anesthetic gases.
Inhibin, screening for trisomies with, 136
Injury. See Trauma; specific injury.
Inner ear
  congenital malformations of, 1048
  embryology of, 1047
  otoacoustic emissions within, 1045
Inositol
  in breast milk, 672t
  in infant formula, 674t
Inspiratory/expiratory time
  in assisted ventilation, 1108–1109, 1109f
  in mechanical ventilation, 1115
  ratio of, in mechanical ventilation, 1115
Inspired oxygen concentration (FiO$_2$)
  in carbon dioxide responsiveness of
    preterm infants, 1136, 1136f
  in mechanical ventilation, 1115–1116
  oxygen delivery method and, 1112
Insulin
  decreased sensitivity to, in gestational
    diabetes mellitus, 322
  dosages of, 1791
  fetal effects of, 188t
  for gestational diabetes mellitus, 323
  for growth promotion, in extremely low
    birthweight infant, 681
  for neonatal diabetes mellitus, 1491
  in fetal growth, 1468, 275–276
  neonatal hypertrophic cardiomyopathy
    related to, 1204
Insulin-like growth factor receptor, reduced
    function of, in intrauterine growth
    restriction, 277
Insulin-like growth factor–binding proteins,
    277
α8-Integrin, in renal development, 1660t,
    1661
Integument. See Skin.

Intelligence quotient (IQ) scores
  fetal alcohol exposure and, 737
  in children with yu-cheng disease, 258f
  in congenital cytomegalovirus infection,
    845, 845t
  in EMCO-treated children, 1175–1176
  in high-risk neonate, 1039
  polychlorinated biphenyls and, 258
Intensive care nursery. See also Neonatal
    intensive care unit (NICU).
  physical environment of, 585–605
    design considerations in, 603–605
    sensory, 597–603
      circadian rhythmicity in, 602
      hearing in, 601
      taste and smell in, 599–600
      touch in, 598
      vision in, 602
    thermal, 585–597. See also Heat
      exchange.
Intercellular adhesion molecules, in
    neutrophil adhesion, 764, 765f
Interferon-γ
  biology and functions of, 774–775, 775b
  in T cell function, in neonates, 782
  production and response to, in neonate,
    768
Interleukin-1, 1289t
  biology of, 774
  in preterm labor, 333
  in preterm labor prediction, 342
Interleukin-2, 1289t
  in T cell function, 781
    in neonates, 782
Interleukin-3, 1289t
Interleukin-4, 1289t
  in T cell function, 781
Interleukin-6, 1289t
  biology of, 774
  in preterm labor, 333
  in preterm labor prediction, 342–343
  in sepsis diagnosis, 798–799
Interleukin-7, 1289t
  in T cell function, 781
Interleukin-8, 1289t
Interleukin-9, in white matter damage,
    916–917
Interleukin-10, 1289t
  biology of, 774
  in T cell function, 782
  necrotizing enterocolitis and, 1409
Interleukin-11, 1289t
Interleukin-12, 1289t
  biology of, 774–775
Interleukin-15, in natural killer cell
    development, 769
Intermittent mandatory ventilation
  advantages of, 1113
  in ventilator weaning, 1116–1117
  synchronized, 1114
Intermittent positive pressure ventilation,
    history of, 12
International Classification of Diseases,
    Ninth Revision, Clinical Modification
    (ICD-9-CM), 69–70, 71
International Studies of Thyroid Screening,
    1539t–1540t
Intersex disorder(s)
  ambiguous genitalia in, definition of, 1557
  biochemistry of, 1561, 1562f
  chromosome analysis in, 1561
  clitoris size in, 1558–1559
  diagnosis of, 1560–1562, 1561b
    refining, 1562

Intersex disorder(s)—cont'd
 differential diagnosis of, 1563f
 dysmorphology associated with, 1559
 examination of, in delivery room,
  1556–1557, 1557b
 family discussion about, 1557
 gender assignment in, 1562, 1564
 genetic counseling for, 1564
 genitography of, 1562
 gonadal descent in, 1557–1558
 history of, 1559–1560
 human chorionic gonadotropin
  stimulation test of, 1562
 labioscrotal development in, 1559
 management of, 1564
 penis size in, 1558, 1559f, 1560f
 physical examination of, 1557–1560,
  1558t
 presentation of, 1557
 presenting problems in, 1565–1568
 professional discussion about, 1557
 ultrasonography of, 1561–1562
 urethral opening in, 1559
 vaginal opening in, 1559
Intestinal absorption. See also Malabsorption.
 of calcium, 1494–1495, 1495t
 of magnesium, 1499
 of phosphorus, 1497
Intestinal enteropeptidase deficiency,
  primary, 1367
Intestinal ischemia, necrotizing enterocolitis
  related to, 1407
Intra-abdominal organs, birth injuries to,
  550–553
Intra-alveolar hemorrhage, after surfactant
  therapy, 1104
Intra-amniotic infection
 diagnosis of, 431b, 431–432
 group B streptococcus in, 444
 pathophysiology of, 431b, 431–432
 preterm delivery and, 337–338
 treatment of, 432
Intracardiac focus, echogenic, 16
Intracranial hemorrhage. See Periventricular-
  intraventricular hemorrhage.
Intranasal tumors, 1147–1148
Intraocular hemorrhage, due to birth injury,
  539
Intrathecal injection (spinal), 474
Intrauterine growth restriction, 271–303,
  302f
 aberrant fetal growth patterns in, 289f,
  289–290, 291f
 antenatal diagnosis of, 290–298, 292f–294f
  biparietal diameter in, 292, 292f, 293f
  Doppler flow velocity waveforms in,
   292–293, 293f
  fetal distress in, 293
  fundal height in, 290
  head-abdomen circumference ratio in,
   292, 294f
  laboratory tests in, 290–291
  middle cerebral artery assessment in,
   293
  truncometry in, 292, 293f
  ultrasonography in, 291–292
 antenatal management of, 293–296
  amnioinfusion in, 295–296
  biophysical profile in, 295, 295t
  contraction stress test in, 294–295
  fetal evaluation in, 294
  in labor and delivery, 295
  nonstress test in, 294
  oxytocin challenge test in, 294

Intrauterine growth restriction—cont'd
 asphyxia in, 298–299
 characteristics of, 290b
 chromosome disorders associated with,
  288
 congenital infections associated with, 288
 developmental outcome in, 302
 drugs associated with, 186t, 189, 283–284
 epidemiology of, 279, 279b
 fetal determinants of, 286–288
 gestational diabetes mellitus and, 327
 growth hormone levels in, 275–276, 1805t
 hypomagnesemia and, 1519
 hypoxemia in, 283
 IGF1 gene deletion in, 287
 in cocaine abuse, 745
 in post-term pregnancy, 384
 insulin metabolism and, 276–277
 leptin levels in, 278
 limiting maternal weight gain and,
  281–282
 low birthweight in, 278, 279, 279b
 oligohydramnios in, 292, 416
 pancreatic agenesis in, 276
 perinatal mortality rate in, 298
 placental determinants of, 284–286,
  284f–286f, 286t
 ponderal index in, 289
 postnatal growth after, 302f, 302–303
 pregnancy-induced hypertension and,
  282–283, 283f
 risk factors for, 279–280
 synonyms for, 271
 transient hypoglycemia in, 1478–1479
 uteroplacental circulation in, 286, 286t
 very low birthweight in, 1037
 vs. small for gestational age, 271, 289
Intravenous agents, in neonatal anesthesia,
  638–640
Intravenous therapy
 history of, 13, 15
 of immune globulin. See
  Immunoglobulin(s), intravenous.
Intraventricular hemorrhage. See
  Periventricular-intraventricular
  hemorrhage.
Intubation
 endotracheal. See Endotracheal intubation.
 water and evaporative heat exchange
  before and after, 593
Invasive fetal testing, for nonimmune
  hydrops fetalis, 424–425
Iodides
 fetal effects of, 188t
 in breast milk, 200
 trapping of, in congenital hypothyroidism,
  1536
Iodine
 congenital malformations associated with,
  186t
 deficiency of
  congenital hypothyroidism due to, 1537
  thyroid disorders associated with,
   1531–1532, 1532f
 in breast milk, 671t
 in enteral nutrition, 670t
 in infant formula, 673t
 metabolism of, in thyroid hormone
  synthesis, 1525
 placental transfer of, 1532
 recommended intake of, during
  pregnancy, 1537
IPEX syndrome, in autoimmune
  enteropathy, 1372

IQ. See Intelligence quotient (IQ) scores.
Iris
 abnormalities of, 1738–1739
 coloboma of, 1738, 1738b, 1738f
 examination of, 1723
 unusual coloration of, 1738–1739
Iron
 for breast-fed term infants, 675
 free, increased, after hypoxic-ischemic
  insult, 943
 in breast milk, 671t
  bioavailability of, 1306
 in enteral nutrition, 669, 670t
 in infant formula, 673t
 in very low birthweight infant, 1811t
 recommended daily supplements of, for
  infants, 1305–1306
 serum, in very low birthweight infants,
  1811t
Iron-containing drugs, fetal effects of, 188t
Iron-deficiency anemia, 1305–1306
Iron dextran, dosages of, 1792
Iron lung (man-can), 13, 13f
Irritant contact dermatitis, 1710
Ischemia, definition of, 938
Ischemia-reperfusion injury, in necrotizing
  enterocolitis, 1408
Ischemic stroke, arterial, 934–937,
  1331–1332. See also Stroke, arterial
  ischemic.
Islets of Langerhans, 1361–1362
Isobutyric acidemia, 1607t
Isodisomy, 126
Isoflurane, minimal alveolar concentration
  of, 638, 638f
Isoimmunization, unconjugated
  hyperbilirubinemia due to, 370,
  1428–1429
 for idiopathic thrombocytopenic purpura,
  368
Isoniazid
 fetal effects of, 187t
 for tuberculosis, 827, 827t
 in breast milk, 199
Isoproterenol
 dosages of, 1787
 for neonatal bradycardia, 1264
 inotropic effect of, 1267
Isotopes, diagnostic, in breast milk, 200
Isotretinoin
 congenital malformations associated with,
  186t
 fetal effects of, 188t
Isovaleric acidemia, 1607t
Ito, hypomelanosis of, 1706
Itraconazole, for candidiasis, 833

J
Jagged1 gene, mutations of, in Alagille
  syndrome, 1460
Jansen metaphyseal chondrodysplasia,
  hypercalcemia due to, 1517
Jarisch-Herxheimer reaction, after syphilis
  treatment, 825
Jatene procedure, 1224, 1269t
Jaundice, 1419–1461
 breast-feeding and, 1432–1433
 breast milk, 1433–1434
 cholestatic, due to parenteral nutrition,
  688
 examination of, 520

Jaundice—cont'd
  physiologic
    genetic effects of, 1427–1428
    in ethnic populations, 1427–1428
    in post-term infant, 1427
    in preterm infant, 1426–1427, 1427f
Jaw-winking phenomenon, 1731–1732
Jejunal atresia
  radiography of, 720
  ultrasonography of, 157
Jejunoileal atresia
  apple-peel deformity in, 1397
  classification of, 1397
  pathogenesis of, 1397
  treatment of, 1397–1398, 1398f
Jeune asphyxiating thoracic dystrophy, 573
  anesthetic implications of, 633t
  pancreatic insufficiency in, 1365
Johanson-Blizzard syndrome, 1365
Joint Commission for Accreditation of
    Healthcare Organizations, 78, 78t
Jugular vein
  ligation of, after extracorporeal membrane
    oxygenation, 1170
  reconstruction of, after extracorporeal
    membrane oxygenation, 1170
Junctional ectopic tachycardia, 1253t, 1257
  treatment of, 1264
Junctional reciprocating tachycardia,
    permanent form of, 1253t, 1255
  treatment of, 1264
Juvenile myelomonocytic leukemia, 1342
Juvenile-onset recurrent respiratory
    papillomatosis, 875–876
Juvenile xanthogranuloma, 1711–1712

K

Kangaroo care. See also Skin-to-skin contact.
  for prevention of hypothermia, 96–97,
    97f
  in parent-infant attachment, 655
Kartagener syndrome, heart defects
    associated with, 1203t
Karyotype, 114, 114f
Kasabach-Merritt syndrome
  associated with disseminated intravascular
    coagulation, 1329
  blood loss in, 1297
  hemangiomas in, 1430, 1708
  thrombocytopenia and, 1340
Kasai procedure, for extrahepatic biliary
    atresia, 1453, 1454f, 1457
Kaufman test, for high-risk neonate, 1040
Kayexalate, dosages of, 1789
Kearns-Sayre syndrome, 1645
Kell antigen, sensitization to, 404–405
Keratinocytes, in epidermal development,
    1686
Keratoconjunctivitis, due to adenovirus
    infections, 875
Kernicterus
  definition of, 1434
  due to intravenous lipid emulsions, 686
  phases of, 1434–1435
  unconjugated hyperbilirubinemia due to,
    1434–1436
Ketamine
  in maternal anesthesia, 478
  in neonatal anesthesia, 639
Ketoacidosis, diabetic, gestational diabetes
    mellitus and, 325–326

Ketogenesis, defects of, metabolic acidosis
    in, 1638
Ketolysis, defects of, metabolic acidosis in,
    1637
Ketone body metabolism, defects in, 1638
Ketonuria
  gestational diabetes mellitus and, 323
  laboratory findings in, 1629t
Ketosis, laboratory findings in, 1629t
17-Ketosteroid reductase, 1575
β-Ketothiolase deficiency, 1607t, 1637
KID syndrome, 1694t
Kidney(s). See also Nephro- entries; Renal
    entries.
  birth injuries to, 553
  blood flow in
    in preeclampsia-eclampsia, 310t, 311
    normal, 1663, 1663t
  concentrating and diluting capacity of,
    1663t, 1664
    water balance in, 697
  congenital malformations of, 1675–1678,
    1675t
    defects associated with, 1665–1666, 1666f
    gene mutations in, 1661–1662, 1662t
  development of, 1659–1662, 1660f
    gene/protein mutations and, 1660–1661,
    1660t
  failure of. See Renal failure, acute.
  function of
    assessment of, 1666
    normal values for, 1663t
  fungus balls in, 831
  magnesium handling by, inherited
    disorders and, 1519
  multicystic dysplastic, 1676, 1676f. See
    also Polycystic kidney disease.
    defects associated with, 1676
    perinatal ultrasonography of, 159–160,
    161f
    ultrasonography of, 725, 725f
  neonatal
    enlarged, examination of, 519
    ultrasonography of, 724, 724f
  physiology of, 1663–1664, 1664t
    neonatal anesthesia and, 629
  polycystic. See Polycystic kidney disease.
  role of, in acid-base homeostasis, 705
  tumors of, 1680–1681
  ultrasonography of, 159, 159f
Kinky-hair disease, 1619
Kit ligand, 1288, 1289t
Kleeblattschädel (cloverleaf skull), 1012
Kleihauer-Betke test, 138
Klinefelter syndrome (47,XXY syndrome),
    115
  clinical manifestations of, 1572
  heart defects associated with, 1203t
  macrencephaly associated with, 997
  prevalence of, 563
  variant forms of, 1572
Klippel-Feil syndrome
  anesthetic implications of, 633t
  cervical vertebrae fusion in, 573, 1758
  vs. sternocleidomastoid muscle injury, 547
Klippel-Trénaunay-Weber syndrome, 1709
Klumpke palsy, 542
Knee, hyperextension, subluxation, and
    dislocation of, 1777–1778, 1778f
Kostmann syndrome, neutropenia in,
    1310–1311
Krabbe disease, 1624
Krebs cycle, defects of, 1642–1643
Kyphosis, congenital, 1771

L

L
Labetalol
  for chronic hypertension, 317t
  for preeclampsia-eclampsia, 314, 314t
  intravenous, for neonatal hypertension,
    1672t
  oral, for neonatal hypertension, 1673t
Labia majora, birth trauma to, 556
Labial fusion, posterior, disorders associated
    with, 1558t
Labioscrotal development, in intersex
    disorders, 1559
Labor. See also Delivery; Preterm labor.
  asphyxia in, 484, 484t
  chronic hypertension and, 318
  doulas in, maternal-infant attachment
    related to, 647–648
  induction of, in post-term pregnancy, 386
    methods of, 386b, 386–387
  initiation of, theories in, 333
  intrauterine growth restriction and, 295
  maternal position during, non-reassuring
    fetal heart rate and, 177
  preterm. See Preterm labor.
  prolongation of, due to neuraxial
    blockade, 475
Lacerations
  birth-related, 531
  of ear, 539
  ocular, 1727
Lacrimal glands
  abnormalities of, 1733–1734
  absent secretion of, congenital, 1734
Lactase deficiency, congenital, 1366
Lactate
  analysis of, in inborn errors of
    metabolism, 1632–1633
  placental transport of, 1468
Lactation. See also Breast milk.
  drugs and, 197–202
  establishment of, by mechanical pumping,
    677
Lactic acidemia, 1640–1645
  algorithm approach to, 1640f
  differential diagnosis of, 1640–1641, 1641t
  Krebs cycle defects and, 1642–1643
  primary, 1641–1645
  pyruvate dehydrogenase deficiency and,
    1642
  respiratory chain defects and, 1643–1645,
    1643t
Lactobezoars, 1387
Lactoferrin
  in breast milk, 790
  in humoral immunity, 773
Lactose, tolerance of, in preterm infants, 664
Ladd's bands, division of, in volvulus repair,
    1395
LAMA2 gene, in muscular dystrophy, 983
Lamaze technique, in natural childbirth, 468
Lamellar bodies
  pulmonary, development of, 1070–1071
  surfactant synthesis and, 1078, 1081
Lamellar ichthyosis, 1694t, 1696
Langerhans cell(s), in epidermal
    development, 1686, 1687
Langerhans cell histiocytosis, 1712
Language
  behavioral, of preterm infant, 1055t,
    1055–1058, 1056f, 1058f
  sign, controversy concerning, 1049
Lanugo, 1687
  persistence of, 1731

Large for gestational age. *See also* Gestational age.
  definition of, 22
Large intestine. *See* Colon; Rectum.
Large-molecule metabolism, defects of, 1624–1626, 1625t
Larsen disease, 1777, 1778
Laryngeal atresia, Fraser syndrome with, 248
Laryngeal cleft, 1154
Laryngeal mask airway
  in neonatal intubation, 637
  in neonatal resuscitation, 495
Laryngeal web, 1153
Laryngomalacia
  evaluation and treatment of, 1151, 1151f
  neonatal anesthesia and, 628
Laryngoscopy
  during EXIT procedure, 248f, 248–249
  in laryngeal examination, 1150
Larynx
  anatomy of, 1149–1150, 1150f
  cysts of, 1152, 1152f
  developmental anomalies of, airway obstruction due to, 1143, 1143b
  examination of, 1150–1151
  lesions of, 1149–1155
    congenital vs. acquired, 1151
  papillomas of, 875
Laser therapy
  fetoscopic, for twin-twin transfusion syndrome, 250–251
  for retinopathy of prematurity, 1751
Latin Americans
  neonatal mortality in, 91, 91f
  transient cutaneous lesions in, 1689b
Lead
  fetal exposure to, 258, 258f
  in breast milk, 201
  isotopic ratio of, 258
  maternal exposure to, pregnancy outcome in, 260t
Lead(s), placement of, in cardiac monitoring, 611, 611f
Leber congenital amaurosis, 1743
Lecithin-to-sphingomyelin ratio
  in lung maturation testing, 1084, 1084f
  in lung maturity, 324
LEFTY genes, in hemimegalencephaly, 906
Legal issues, 47–62
  court systems and, 48, 49f
  disclaimer about, 47
  general principles of, 48
  handicapped newborn treatment and, 57–59
  Hill v Kokosky case, 51–52
  in ethical decision making, 44–45
  legislative law and case law in, 48
  live birth laws and, 56–57
  malpractice as, 50–56
  maternal autonomy vs. fetal rights in, 38
  resuscitation against parents' wishes as, 59–61
  state law vs. federal law in, 48
  Sterling v Johns Hopkins case, 51
  substance abuse reporting requirements, 733
  supervision by physicians in, 48–50
  Vo v Superior Court case, 48
Legislative law, 48
Leiden factor, 1333
  mutation of, in ischemic stroke, 937
Leigh syndrome, 1619, 1644
  hepatic dysfunction in, 1622
Leiner disease, 1711

Leiomyoma, uterine, preterm delivery associated with, 335
Lemon sign
  in myelomeningocele, 246
  in ventriculomegaly, 153, 153f
Lens
  examination of, 1723
  subluxed, 1741, 1741f
Lenticulostriate vasculopathy, ultrasonography of, 728–729, 729f
Leprechaunism, 276
Leptin, 277
  in amniotic fluid, 277–278
Lethal infantile mitochondrial disease, 1644
Leukemia
  acute lymphocytic, 1342
  acute megakaryoblastic, in Down syndrome, 1314–1315
  acute myelogenous, 1342
  congenital, 1342
  juvenile myelomonocytic, 1342
Leukemoid reaction, 1314
Leukocyte adhesion deficiency
  type I, 1315, 1316f, 1316b
  type II, 1315, 1317
Leukocyte count, in sepsis diagnosis, 796–797, 796t, 797b, 797t
Leukocytes, polymorphonuclear, in neonates, 1310t
Leukoencephalopathy, perinatal telencephalic, 911
Leukokoria, 1739–1743
Leukomalacia
  intrauterine infection and, 332
  periventricular, 910–912
    neuropathology of
      axonal damage in, 912
      macroscopic, 910, 910f, 911f
      microglial activity in, 911–912
      microscopic, 910–911
      subplate damage in, 912, 912f
      vulnerability of oligodendroglia precursors in, 911
    ultrasonography of, 728, 728f, 729f, 917–918, 917f, 918b, 921f
Levofloxacin, for chlamydial infections, 447
Levothyroxine, dosages of, 1791
Leydig cells
  hypoplasia of, 1574–1575
  in sex differentiation, 1553, 1553t, 1554
Liability of physicians, for supervision of others, 48–50
Lidocaine
  dosages of, 1788
  for neonatal tachycardia, 1260t, 1263
  for seizures following hypoxic-ischemic insult, 953
  with mexiletine, for neonatal tachycardia, 1262b
Life-sustaining medical treatment, withholding or withdrawal of, criteria for, 40–41
Light, environment of, 602–603
Light-emitting diodes
  in phototherapy, 1444
  in pulse oximetry, 619
Liley curve, 395–397, 396f
Limbs. *See* Extremity(ies).
Lingual lipase, 665
Lingual thyroid tissue, in congenital hypothyroidism, 1541, 1541f
Linoleic acid, in intravenous lipid emulsions, 686, 686t

Linolenic acid, in intravenous lipid emulsions, 686, 686t
Lip, cleft. *See* Cleft lip.
Lip reading, for hearing-impaired child, 1049
Lipase
  gastric, 665
  lingual, 665
Lipid(s)
  absorption disorders of, 1368
  in breast milk, 665–666, 671t, 686t
  in enteral nutrition, 665–667
  in infant formula, 667, 673t
  in parenteral nutrition
    adverse effects of, 686–687
    for prevention of oxygen toxicity, 1165–1166
    intravenous lipid emulsions in, 685–687, 687t, 690
  metabolism of, effect of thyroid hormone on, 1524
  peroxidation of, in intravenous lipid emulsions, 686–687
Lipid membrane, defects of, 1300–1301
Lipogranulomatosis, vs. subcutaneous fat necrosis, 531
Lipopolysaccharide-CD14 complexes, in inflammatory response, 776, 777f
Liposome, dosages of, 1790
Lipsitz scale, for neonatal abstinence syndrome, 750
Liquid ventilation, 1118
  in ECMO-dependent newborns, 1176
LIS1 gene, in Miller-Dieker syndrome, 908, 907
Lisch nodules, 1731
Lissencephaly, 992, 993f
  autosomal recessive, 908
  bicortical, 908
  type I, 907–908, 907f
Listeria, associated with neonatal hepatitis, 1458
Listeria monocytogenes
  in chorioamnionitis, 459
  IVb serotype of, in meningitis, 804
Listeriosis
  cutaneous, 1698
  in intra-amniotic infection, 431
  in pregnancy, 446–447
  neonatal, 821–822
Lithium
  fetal effects of, 187t
  in breast milk, 199–200
Live birth, legal definitions and statutes on, 56–57
Livedo reticularis, 567
Liver. *See also* Hepatic; Hepatitis; Hepato- *entries.*
  abnormal function of
    disorders associated with, 1620t
    due to parenteral nutrition, 688
    laboratory findings in, 1629t
  acute fatty, of pregnancy, 311, 1615
  bilirubin uptake by, 1421
  fetal, in drug metabolism, 211, 211t
  hematopoiesis in, 1287
  histopathologic examination of, in conjugated hyperbilirubinemia, 1455–1456
  inborn errors of metabolism affecting, 1620–1623, 1620t
  rupture of, birth-related, 550
  vascular changes in, in preeclampsia-eclampsia, 310t, 311

Liver biopsy, for idiopathic neonatal hepatitis, 1456, 1456f
Liver disease, 1419–1461. *See also specific disorder.*
  coagulation factor effects of, 1329
  metabolic, conjugated hyperbilirubinemia due to, 1459–1460
Liver enzymes, elevated, in asphyxia, 951
Liver failure, in hepatitis B infection, 864
Liver function tests, 1804t
Liver transplantation, for biliary atresia, 1458
Lobectomy, for pulmonary interstitial emphysema, 1131
Lobster claw anomaly, 576
Long-chain-3-hydroxyacyl-CoA dehydrogenase deficiency, 1609t
  in HELLP syndrome, 1615
Long QT syndrome, torsades de pointes in, 1257, 1258f
Lorazepam
  dosages of, 1792
  in neonatal anesthesia, 639
Low birthweight. *See also* Extremely low birthweight; Very low birthweight.
  adult diseases and, 278, 278f
  as classification, 271
  definition of, 19
  epidemiology of, 279, 279b
  high-risk pregnancy associated with, 19, 20b
  hyperglycemia in, 1489–1490
  hypocalcemia in, 1510
  in multiple gestations, 379
  intrauterine growth restriction and, 278, 279, 279b
  metabolic disorders associated with, 288
  morbidity associated with, 22–23
  mortality associated with, 21
  prevention of, 23–24
  rates of, 22–23
  respiratory distress syndrome related to, 1097, 1098f
  resting metabolism in, 663
  risk factors for, 279–280
  sepsis incidence in, 793
  syndromes associated with, 288
Low noise optical probe, in pulse oximetry, 620, 620f
Lower extremity. *See also* Foot (feet).
  congenital anomalies of, 1772–1781
  examination of, meningomyeloceles and, 1015t
  torsional and angular deformities of, 1772–1773
Lucey-Driscoll syndrome, unconjugated hyperbilirubinemia due to, 1432
Lugol solution, for thyrotoxicosis, 1549
Lumbosacral agenesis, 1772
Lung(s). *See also* Pulmonary *entries;* Respiratory *entries.*
  agenesis of, 1131
  chronic disease of. *See* Bronchopulmonary dysplasia.
  compliance of. *See* Compliance, pulmonary.
  cystic anomalies of, 1134. *See also* Cystic adenomatoid malformation.
  development of, 1069–1073
    air-blood barrier in, 1070
    alveolarization in, 1072–1073, 1072b, 1072f, 1074f
    canalicular stage of, 1070–1072, 1071f
    embryologic, 1069–1070, 1070f
    epithelial differentiation in, 1070–1072

Lung(s)—*cont'd*
    fetal lung fluid in, 1074–1075, 1075f
    history of research on, 1069
    hypoplasia in. *See* Pulmonary hypoplasia.
    lethal disorders of, 1133–1135
    pseudoglandular stage of, 1070, 1071f
    saccular stage of, 1072–1073, 1072b, 1072f, 1074f
    surfactant in. *See* Surfactant.
    vascular development in, 1070
  fetal, maturation of, pharmacologic acceleration of, 212–214
  fetal fluid in
    clearance of
      during labor, 485
      perinatal, 1075
    composition of, 1074–1075, 1075f
    flow of, 1074–1075
    surfactant secretion and, 1085
  hypoplasia of. *See* Pulmonary hypoplasia.
  inflation and ventilation of, in neonatal resuscitation, 951
  inflation/deflation of,
    inspiratory/expiratory time constants in, 1108–1109, 1109f
  inflation pressure in
    equilibration of, 1108, 1108f
    in positive pressure ventilation, 492–495
    in preterm infants, 493–494
    in spontaneous first breath, 492
    measurement of, 1093
  injury to
    in assisted ventilation
      bronchopulmonary dysplasia due to, 1120
      prevention of, 1113, 1120–1121, 1120b, 1120t
    in positive pressure ventilation, 494
    peak inspiratory pressure and, 1114
    transfusion-related, 1347
  maturation of
    early spontaneous, 1085
    history of research on, 1069
    in gestational diabetes, 324
    incomplete, bronchopulmonary dysplasia related to, 1158
    induced, 1085–1086, 1087f
    inflammatory response in, 1085
    lecithin-to-sphingomyelin ratio in, 1084, 1084f
    pharmacologic acceleration of, 1098–1099
    surfactant appearance in, 1083–1085, 1084f, 1085b
    testing of, 1083–1086
  perforation of, with chest tube insertion, 1130, 1130f
  sequestration of
    congenital, 1134
    in nonimmune hydrops fetalis, 422, 423
  surfactant in. *See* Surfactant.
  volume of. *See* Lung volume.
Lung area ratio
  calculation of, 417
  decreased, 417, 417f
Lung function. *See* Pulmonary function.
Lung volume
  anesthesia and, 628
  functional residual capacity as. *See* Functional residual capacity.
  measurement of, 1092–1093
  surfactant therapy and, 1105

Lupus erythematosus, neonatal, 1715
Lupus syndrome, neonatal, maternal antinuclear antibodies and, 370–371
Luteinizing hormone
  serum levels of, 1805t
  testicular unresponsiveness to, 1574–1575
Lymphangiectasia, congenital pulmonary, 1135
Lymphangioma(s)
  cutaneous manifestation of, 1709–1710, 1710f
  deep, 1709
  of eyelids, 1730–1731
  orbital, 1735
  simple, 1709
Lymphangioma circumscriptum, 1709, 1710f
Lymphatic malformations, 1149
Lymphedema. *See also* Edema.
  Milroy primary congenital, 1709
  of hands and feet, in Turner and Noonan syndromes, 575, 577f
Lymphocyte(s), 777, 779
  B. *See* B cell(s).
  T. *See* T cell(s).
Lymphocytic choriomeningitis virus, 876
Lymphohistiocytosis, 1342–1343
Lyon hypothesis, of chromatically normal females, 124
Lysinuric protein intolerance, 1367–1368
Lysosomal storage disease
  cardiomyopathy in, 1617–1618
  dysmorphic features of, 1625t, 1626
  hepatomegaly in, 1623–1624, 1623t
  tests for, 1633
Lysozyme, synthesis of, by milk macrophage, 790

M

M phase, of mitotic cycle, 886, 886f
Macewen sign, in hydrocephalus, 998
Macrencephaly, 995–998
  chromosome disorders associated with, 997
  degenerative disorders associated with, 997
  familial, 1002–1003
  growth disorders associated with, 996
  isolated, 995–996
  metabolic disorders associated with, 998
  neurocutaneous syndromes associated with, 996–997, 997f
Macrocephaly, 906, 995–1005
  abscess causing, 1005
  benign familial, 1002–1003
  congenital
    causes of, 996b
    disorders associated with, 568
    intracranial cysts causing, 1003–1004, 1004f
  enlargement of cerebrospinal fluid in, 998–1004. *See also* Hydrocephalus.
  large brain causing, 995–998. *See also* Macrencephaly.
  trauma causing, 1005, 1006f
  tumors causing, 1004, 1005f
  vascular lesions causing, 1004–1005
Macrocornea, 1732
Macrodactyly, of fingers, 1769–1770
Macroglossia, in Pierre Robin sequence, 573
Macrophage(s)
  brain, 899–900
  in breast milk, 790
  in inflammatory response, 776, 777f

Macrophage colony-stimulating factor, 1289t
Macrosomia
  definition of, 326
  gestational diabetes mellitus and, 326–327
  in infant of diabetic mother, 1474, 1475f
  in post-term pregnancy, 384
Macrostomia, 570f, 572
Macula
  abnormalities of, 1744, 1744t
  examination of, 1723
Macular stain (salmon patch), 1689b, 1691, 1691f
Macules
  café-au-lait, 1704, 1782f, 1783
  characteristics of, 1690t
  white, in tuberous sclerosis, 1706
Maffucci syndrome, 1709
Magnesium
  absorption of, 1499
  atomic weight and valance of, 1817t
  excessive administration of, 1520
  excretion of, 1499–1500
  in breast milk, 671t, 1500
    absorption and retention of, 1495t
  in enteral nutrition, 669, 670t
  in infant formula, 673t
  in parenteral nutrition, 687
  intake of, 1500
  placental transport of, 1499
  serum levels of, 1499
    disturbances of. See Hypermagnesemia; Hypomagnesemia.
Magnesium sulfate
  antenatal, neuroprotective effects of, 350
  beneficial effect of, 350
  contraindications to, 350
  for hypocalcemia, 1513
  for hypomagnesemia, 1519
  for persistent pulmonary hypertension, 1247
  for preterm labor prevention, 349–350
  for seizures, 974
    in preeclampsia-eclampsia, 315
  maternal treatment with, 1520
Magnesium wasting syndrome
  dominant, 1519
  recessive, 1519
MagNET trial, 350
Magnetic resonance imaging (MRI)
  of congenital heart disease, 1219–1220
  of fetus, 151–152
  of hypoxic-ischemic encephalopathy, 948–949, 948f, 949f
  of spinal cord injury, 549
  of white matter injury
    conventional T1- and T2-weighted, 918–919, 918f–920f
    diffusion-weighted, 919, 921f–923f
Magnetic resonance spectroscopy (MRS), of white matter injury, 921–922
Magnetocardiography, fetal, 1207
Major histocompatibility complex, natural killer cell function and, 769
Malabsorption
  in short bowel syndrome, 1370–1371
  of bile acids, 1368
  of carbohydrates, 1516, 1365–1367, 1365t
  of electrolytes, 1368–1369, 1370t
  of fat, 1368
  of protein, 1367–1368
Malaria, 836–837
Malassezia furfur infection, 835

Malformations. *See also* Congenital anomalies.
  bronchopulmonary, 1133–1134, 1134f
  definition of, 561
  in aborted fetuses, 564–565, 565t
  lymphatic, 1149
  major
    chromosome anomalies in, 562t, 563
    epidemiology of, 562, 562t
    etiology of, 562–564, 562t, 563t
    multifactorial inheritance in, 562, 562t
    single gene (mendelian) inheritance in, 562–563, 562t
    teratogenic, 562t, 563t, 563–564, 564f
  minor, 565, 566t
  of extremities, 1757
  of renal and urinary tracts, 1675–1678, 1675t
  phenotypic variants as, 565, 566t
  racial differences in, 565–566, 566t
Malpractice, 50–56
  breach and, 52–53
  burden of proof in, 54
  causation in, 53–54
  common neonatology suits in, 50, 50b
  damages in, 54
  duty in, 51–52
  expert witnesses and, 52–53
  prenatal consultation and, 51
  protected (nondiscoverable) proceedings in, 54–55
  res ipsa loquitur doctrine and, 53
  standard of care and, 52
  strategies for avoiding, 55b, 55–56
  supervision of others and, 48–50, 51
  telephone advice and, 51
  wrongful birth, wrongful life, and wrongful death actions in, 55
Malrotation
  midgut. See Midgut malrotation.
  of bowel. See Bowel, malrotation of.
Maltase-glucoamylase deficiency, 1366–1367
Mandibulofacial dysostosis, 570f, 572
Manganese
  in breast milk, 671t
  in enteral nutrition, 670t
  in infant formula, 673t
  in parenteral nutrition, 688t
Mannose-binding lectin, 773
Maple syrup urine disease, 1604t
  screening for, 1612
March of Dimes, 581
Marcus Gunn pupil, 1722
Marfan syndrome
  diagnosis of, 1251
  heart defects associated with, 1203t
  neonatal, 1251
  single gene defects in, 1204
Marijuana use, 742–743
  adult effects of, 743
  fetal and neonatal effects of, 743
  neurobehavioral and developmental effects of, 743
  prevalence and pharmacology of, 742
Mass spectrometry–based screening tests, for inborn errors of metabolism, 1604t–1610t
Mast cell growth factor, 1288, 1289t
Mastitis, neonatal, 818
Mastocytosis, 1712
Mastoid process, embryology of, 1047
Maternal-infant attachment. *See* Parent-infant attachment.

Maternal mortality
  in developing countries, 87
  in early 1900s, 4
  in preeclampsia-eclampsia, 315
  regionalized care impact on, 32
Maternal-placental-fetal unit
  alcohol consumption/transfer in, 185
  caffeine consumption/transfer in, 189
  clinical pharmacokinetics in, 211–212, 212t
  drug absorption in, 23–24
  drug consumption/transfer in, 183–184, 184f
    illicit, 189
  drug disposition in, 205t, 205–207
  drug distribution in, 204f, 206t, 206–207, 207t
  drug metabolism and excretion in, 207
  pharmacology of, 204–212
  smoking and, 185, 189
Maternal serum alpha-fetoprotein
  in myelomeningocele, 246
  in prenatal genetic screening, 135–136
Maximum vertical pocket, measurement of, 411, 411t
McArdle disease, 989
McCune-Albright syndrome, 1704
McGovern nipple, 1148
MCPH1 gene, in microcephaly vera, 905
MDMA (3,4-methylenedioxymethamphetamine), abuse of, 748–749
Mead-Whittenberger technique, in pulmonary function assessment, 1095
Mean airway pressure (Paw)
  calculation of, 1110
  in oxygen exchange, 1090, 1110–1111
  mechanical ventilation effects on frequency in, 1115
    inspiratory/expiratory time ratio in, 1115
  ventilator settings and, 1110, 1110f
Measles (rubeola), 851–852
Mechanical methods, of labor induction, 386b, 387
Mechanical obstructions, conjugated hyperbilirubinemia due to, 1460
Mechanical stimulation program, for osteopenia of prematurity, 1522–1523
Mechanical ventilation, 1113–1117.
  See also Assisted ventilation.
  alveolar development affected by, 1072–1073, 1073f, 1074f
  blood gas effects of, 1114–1117
  endotracheal intubation for. *See* Endotracheal intubation.
  flow rate in, 1116
  for bronchopulmonary dysplasia, 1164
  frequency of, 1115
    alveolar ventilation and, 1109–1110, 1110f
  high-frequency, 1117–1118
    for bronchopulmonary dysplasia prevention, 1168
    for pulmonary interstitial emphysema, 1131
    in esophageal atresia/tracheoesophageal fistula, 1375
  in extracorporeal membrane oxygenation, 1169, 1170
  in gastroschisis repair, 1384
  inspiratory and expiratory times in, 1115
  inspiratory to expiratory time ratio in, 1115

Mechanical ventilation—*cont'd*
  inspired oxygen concentration in,
    1115–1116
  intermittent mandatory, 1113
    synchronized, 1114
  paralysis in, 1116
  patient-initiated, 1114
  patient-triggered, 1114
  peak inspiratory pressure in, 1114
  physiotherapy in, 1117
  positive end-expiratory pressure in,
    1114–1115
  positive-pressure. *See* Positive pressure
    ventilation.
  pressure-controlled, 1114
  pressure-regulated volume-controlled,
    1114
  pressure support, 1114
  pressure ventilators in, 1113
  proportional assist, 1114
  pulmonary function graphics monitoring
    capabilities in, 614
  sedation in, 1116
  suctioning in, 1117
  volume-assured pressure support, 1114
  volume guarantee, 1114
  volume ventilators in, 1113
  water and heat exchange during, 593–594,
    594f
  weaning from, 1116–1117, 1116t
    in bronchopulmonary dysplasia, 1164
Mechanoreceptors, in breathing control,
  1111, 1136
Meckel-Gruber syndrome, heart defects
  associated with, 1203t
Meconium, drug metabolites in, 734
Meconium ascites, 1396
Meconium aspiration
  prevention of, in neonatal resuscitation,
    506–507
  vs. segmental or lobar atelectasis, 808
Meconium aspiration pneumonia, in small
  for gestational age infant, 296t
Meconium aspiration syndrome, 1122–1125
  chest radiograph of, 715, 715f
  clinical features of, 1123–1124, 1123f
  in post-term pregnancy, 384
  incidence of, 1124
  management of, 1124–1125
  pathophysiology of, 1122–1123, 1123f
  prevention of, 1124, 1124b
  vs. pneumonia, 1124
Meconium ileus, 1395–1396
  complicated, 1395, 1396
  in cystic fibrosis, 1364, 1395
  radiography of, 721, 721f, 1395–1396
  simple, 1395, 1396
  treatment of, 1396
Meconium peritonitis, 1396
Meconium plug syndrome, 720, 1396–1397
  in cystic fibrosis, 1364
Meconium pseudocyst, 1396
  ultrasonography of, 157, 158f
Mediastinal masses, 1135
Medical errors, in neonatal intensive care
  units, 64, 77, 77t
Medical personnel. *See* Health care
  personnel.
Medical records
  documentation in, for avoiding tort
    litigation, 56
  in physical examination, of neonate, 513,
    513b
  protected (nondiscoverable), 54–55

Mediterranean populations, glucose-6-
  phosphatase dehydrogenase deficiency
  in, 1429
Medium-chain acyl-CoA dehydrogenase
  deficiency, 1609t, 1648
MEDLINE database, 80
Mefloquine, for malaria, 837
Megalencephaly, 906
Megalocephaly. *See* Macrocephaly.
Megalocornea, 1732, 1737
Megalophthalmia, 1732
Meiosis, 115, 115f
Melanin, 1687
Melanocytes, in epidermal development,
  1686, 1687
Melanocytic nevi, congenital, 1704
Melanosis
  congenital ocular, 1738
  oculodermal, 1738
  transient neonatal pustular, 1692, 1692f
Memory deficits, short-term, polychlorinated
  biphenyls and, 258
Mendelian inheritance
  congenital anomalies due to, 562t, 562–563
  musculoskeletal anomalies due to, 1756
Mendel's laws, exceptions to, 124–127
Meningitis, 804–807
  clinical manifestations of, 805
  diagnosis of, 805–806, 805t, 806t
  due to lymphocytic choriomeningitis
    virus, 876
  etiology of, 804
  in communicating hydrocephalus, 1002
  in sepsis, antibiotic therapy for, 800
  incidence of, 804
  pathogenesis of, 804
  pathology of, 804–805
  prognosis in, 807
  sensorineural hearing loss due to, 1049
  treatment of, 806–807
Meningocele, 1014
  proptosis due to, 1736
Meningoencephalitis, 807
Meningomyelocele, ultrasonography of,
  152–153, 153f
Menkes disease, 1619
Meperidine
  for labor pain, 472
  umbilical vein to maternal vein ratio of,
    470t
Meprobamate, in breast milk, 199
Mercury
  EPA reference dose of, 259
  fetal exposure to, 258
  in breast milk, 201
Merkel cells, in epidermal development,
  1686
Merkel corpuscles, 1689
Meropenem, dosages of, 1789
Merosin
  deficiency of, clinical presentation of, 983
  in congenital muscular dystrophy, 982
Mesocardia, 1242
Mesomelia, 162, 575
Messenger case, of neonatal resuscitation,
  60, 61
Metabolic acidosis, 707, 707b, 1635–1640
  differential diagnosis of, 1635–1637, 1636f
  in respiratory distress syndrome, 1106
  ketogenesis defects and, 1638
  ketolysis defects and, 1637
  of prematurity, 710
  renal tubular defects and, 1637–1638,
    1637t

Metabolic alkalosis, 707b, 707–708
  laboratory findings in, 1629t
Metabolic rate
  basal, 662
  resting, 662–663
Metabolism
  bilirubin, 1419–1424
  branched-chain amino acid, defects in,
    1638
  carbohydrate. *See* Carbohydrate
    metabolism.
  disorders of
    glycogen, 988
    macrencephaly associated with, 998
    seizures due to, 968–969
  drug
    cytochrome P-450 enzyme
      characteristics in, 205t
    in neonate, 193f, 193–195
  fetal, 275t, 275–278, 276f
  glucose. *See* Glucose metabolism.
  in small for gestational age infant,
    299–300, 299f–301f
  inborn errors of, 1597–1654. *See also*
    specific disorder.
    abnormal laboratory findings in,
      1602t–1603t
    approaches to, 1635–1651
    amino acid analysis in, 1631–1632,
      1632t
    biochemical diagnosis of, 1634
    biochemical testing in, 1629–1635,
      1629t
      specialized, 1631–1635, 1631t
    blood studies in, 1630t, 1629–1630
    cardiomegaly in, 1617–1619, 1618t
    cardiomyopathy in, 1617–1619, 1618t
    carnitine analysis in, 1632
    cerebrospinal fluid studies in, 1630t,
      1630–1631
    clinical phenotypes in, 1614–1629,
      1614t
    differential diagnosis of, 1614t
    dysmorphic syndromes in, 1624–1629
    gastrointestinal anomalies in, 1619
    genetic testing in, 1634
    glycosylation disorder testing in, 1633
    hair anomalies in, 1619–1620
    hematologic anomalies in, 1620
    hepatic dysfunction in, 1620–1623,
      1620t
    hepatomegaly in, 1623–1624, 1623t
    high risk for, 1599
    in sick newborn infant, 1616–1617
    laboratory phenotypes in, 1629–1651
    lactate analysis in, 1632–1633
    large-molecule, 1624–1626, 1625t
    lysosomal storage disorder testing in,
      1633
    misconceptions about, 1597–1599
    not detected by screening, 1616–1617
    ocular anomalies in, 1619
    odors in, 1624, 1624t
    organic acid analysis in, 1633, 1633b
    pathogenesis of, 1652, 1652f
    peroxisomal disorder testing in,
      1633–1634
    postmortem evaluation of, 1634–1635
    prenatal onset of, 1615–1616
    prospective approach to, 1597,
      1599–1614
    pyruvate analysis in, 1632–1633
    reactive approach to, 1597
    screening programs for, 1599–1601

Metabolism—*cont'd*
  effect of, 1603, 1611
    handling results of, 1601, 1603
    mass spectrometry–based,
      1604t–1610t
    principles of, 1599–1600
    specific disorders and, 1600–1601,
      1602t–1603t, 1604t–1610t, 1611–1614
    techniques in, 1600
  seizures and, 971
  sepsis in, 1624
  skin anomalies in, 1619–1620
  small-molecule, 1626–1629
  splenomegaly in, 1623–1624, 1623t
  treatment of, 1651–1654
    genetic manipulation in, 1653–1654
    metabolite manipulation in, 1652,
      1652t
    overview in, 1651–1652, 1652f
    protein manipulation in, 1652–1653,
      1653t
  urine studies in, 1630, 1630t
  iodine, in thyroid hormone synthesis,
    1525
  ketone body, defects in, 1638
  lipid, effect of thyroid hormone on, 1524
  maternal changes in, transient
    hypoglycemia due to, 1472–1478
  vitamin K, 1628–1629
Metabolite therapy, for inborn errors of
  metabolism, 1652, 1652t
Metalloporphyrins, for unconjugated
  hyperbilirubinemia, 1446
Metalloproteinases, in preterm labor
  prediction, 342
Metanephric blastema, 1659, 1661f
Metaphysis, infection of, 1762
Metapneumovirus, human, 855
Metatarsus adductus
  developmental dysplasia of hip related to,
    1774
  diagnosis and treatment of, 1778, 1778f
Methadone
  combined with other drugs, 752
  dosages of, 1787
  in breast milk, 200, 750–751
  low vs. high dose of, in pregnancy, 749
  neonatal abstinence syndrome related to,
    749–751
Methamphetamine abuse, 747–748
Methemoglobinemia, 1308–1309
  with nitric oxide therapy, 1178
Methimazole
  for fetal hyperthyroidism, 220
  in breast milk, 200
Methionine, in parenteral amino acid
  solutions, 684t, 685
2-Methyl-3-hydroxybutyric acidemia, 1607t
N-Methyl-D-aspartate receptors, in white
  matter lesions, 915–916, 916f
2-Methylbutyric acidemia, 1607t
3-Methylcrotonylglycinuria, 1607t
Methyldopa, for chronic hypertension, 317,
  317t
Methylene blue, for methemoglobinemia,
  1309
3,4-Methylenedioxymethamphetamine
  (MDMA), abuse of, 748–749
Methylmalonic acidemia, 1608t
Methylphenylethylamine, abuse of, 747
Methylprednisolone
  for alloimmune (isoimmune)
    thrombocytopenia, 1339
  for fetal lung maturation, 213

Methylxanthines
  for apnea, 1139
  for bronchopulmonary dysplasia, 1165
  in ventilator weaning, 1117
Metoclopramide, dosages of, 1791
Metolazone, for fluid balance, in congenital
    heart disease, 1267
Metric units, conversion tables for, 1817t
Metronidazole
  for anaerobic infections, 819
  for bacterial vaginosis, 432
  for preterm labor prevention, 354
  for sepsis, 801t
  for tetanus neonatorum, 825
  in breast milk, 199
Mevalonate kinase, deficiency of, 1627
Mexiletine
  and lidocaine, for neonatal tachycardia,
    1262b
  for neonatal tachycardia, 1260t
Mezlocillin, for sepsis, 801t
Micrencephaly
  definition of, 989
  subgroups of, 993–994
Micrencephaly vera, 993–994
  radial midbrain and, 905–906, 905f
Microbicidal activity
  of neutrophils, 766–777
  of phagocytes, 768
Microbrain, radial, 993–994
Microcephaly, 904–906
  biochemical disorders associiated with, 993
  causes of, 990b
  congenital infections and, 993, 995f
  definition of, 904, 989
  genetic defects in, 990
  in congenital anomalies, 568
  in rubella virus infection, 872
  migrational anomalies in, 992–993,
    992f–994f
  neurulation and cleavage anomalies in,
    990–991, 991f, 992f
  primary, 989, 990–994, 991f
  primary genetic congenital, 905
  radial microbrain and, 993–994
  secondary, 989, 994, 995f
  small brain causing. *See* Micrencephaly.
  with simplified gyral pattern, 906
Microcolon. *See also* Colon.
  in jejunoileal atresia, 1397
  in meconium ileus, 1395, 1396
Microgastria, 1386, 1386f
Microglia, activity of, in periventricular
    leukomalacia, 911–912
  differentiation of, 899–900
Microglial cells, response of, to hypoxic-
    ischemic insult, 940
Micrognathia
  examination of, 518
  in Pierre Robin sequence, 573, 573f
Microhemagglutination assay, for
    Treponema pallidum antibody, 824
Microlissencephaly, 906
Micromelia, 162
Micropenis, 1566
  definition of, 1558
  disorders associated with, 1558t
  measurement of, 1558, 1559f
Microphthalmia, 1732
  with associated large cyst, 1732, 1733f
Microsomia, hemifacial, 571, 572f
  ocular abnormalities in, 1729
Microspherocytes, in ABO hemolytic
    disease, 1298

Microsporum infections, 835
Microstomia, 569f, 572
Microtia, 1047
Microvillus, intestinal, 1362
Microvillus inclusion disease, 1371–1372
Midazolam
  before delivery, 479
  dosages of, 1792
  in neonatal anesthesia, 639
Midbrain, radial, micrencephaly vera and,
    905–906, 905f
Middle cerebral artery. *See* Cerebral artery,
    middle.
Middle ear
  embryology of, 1047
  ossicles of, 1045
Midgut malrotation, 1393–1395
  radiography of, 718–719, 719f, 1394,
    1394f
  treatment of, 1394–1395
  ultrasonography of, 1394
  vs. duodenal atresia, 1391
Midwives, 5–6, 6f, 7f
Mifepristone, in labor induction, 386b,
    387
Migrating motor complex, gastric, 1360
Milia
  examination of, 517
  incidence of, 1689b
Miliaria, 1689b, 1692–1693
Milk
  human. *See* Breast milk.
  lactobezoars due to, 1387
Milk feedings, frequent, for unconjugated
    hyperbilirubinemia, 1446
Milk to plasma protein (M/P) ratio, 198
Miller case, of neonatal resuscitation, 60–61,
    61b
Miller-Dieker syndrome, 907, 907f
Milrinone
  dosages of, 1787
  for afterload reduction, in congenital heart
    disease, 1267
  inotropic effect of, 1267
Milroy primary congenital lymphedema,
    1709
Mineralization
  bone
    calcium absorption in, 1494
    evaluation of, 1505–1506, 1506f,
      1507f
    factors affecting, 1505
Mineralocorticoids
  for 21-hydroxylase deficiency, 1580
  mean concentrations of, 1805t
Minerals. *See also specific mineral.*
  in body composition, during gestation,
    661, 662t
  supplemental, monitoring of, 1522
  trace. *See* Trace elements.
Minute ventilation, in assisted ventilation,
    1109–1110, 1110f
Miosis, 1747
Misoprostol, in labor induction, 386b, 387
Mitochondrial depletion syndrome, hepatic
    dysfunction in, 1622
Mitochondrial dysfunction, due to
    zidovudine prophylaxis, 858
Mitochondrial inheritance, of genetic
    disorders, 124–125, 125f
Mitochondrial myopathy, 987–988
  benign infantile, 1644
Mitosis, nondisjunction during, 117
Mitotic cycle, phases of, 886, 886f

Mitral valve
  abnormalities of, in left heart defects, 1237
  stenosis of, balloon valvuloplasty for, 1273
Mixed gonadal dysgenesis, 1571
Möbius syndrome
  anesthetic implications of, 633t
  vs. facial nerve palsy, 536
Mole
  cutaneous. *See* Nevus.
  hydatidiform. *See* Hydatidiform mole.
Molybdenum, in enteral nutrition, 670t
Mongolian blue spots
  clinical characteristics of, 1691
  examination of, 517
  frequency of, 565, 566t
  incidence of, 1689b, 1691
Monitoring. *See* Neonatal monitoring.
Monoamine oxidase (MAO) inhibitors, fetal effects of, 187t
Monocyte(s)
  deactivation of, 777
  immunoparalysis of, 777
Monocyte monolayer assays, in erythroblastosis fetalis screening, 395
Mononuclear phagocytes. *See* Phagocytes.
Monosodium glutamate, fetal exposure to, metabolic dysfunction due to, 264
Monosomy, 115
Moral dilemma, definition of, 35
Moral distress, 35
Moral residue, 44
Moral uncertainty, 35
Morbidity. *See* Neonatal morbidity; Perinatal morbidity.
Moro reflex
  assessment of, 516, 526
  in preterm infant, 527, 527t
Morphine
  dosages of, 1787
  for cyanotic spells, 1268
  for labor pain, 472
  in breast milk, 200
  in neonatal anesthesia, 639
  intramuscular administration of, in preterm labor prevention, 346
  umbilical vein to maternal vein ratio of, 470t
Mortality. *See* Fetal death; Maternal mortality; Neonatal mortality; Perinatal mortality.
Morula, in embryonic development, 207
Mosaicism, 117
  mutational, 122
  X chromosome, 1569
    forms of, 1568
Mothers
  attachment to infant. *See* Parent-infant attachment.
  substance abuse by. *See* Substance abuse.
Motor nervous system, in preterm infant, 1055, 1055t
Motor system, assessment of, 525f, 525–526
Mourning, by parents of malformed infants, 657
Mouth. *See* Oral cavity.
Movements, neonatal, physical examination of, 515
mRNS, in fetal cells, 277
MTM1 gene, in myotubular myopathy, 987
MTZ therapy, for thyrotoxicosis, 1549
Mucopolysaccharidosis
  anesthetic implications of, 633t
  macular abnormalities in, 1744, 1744t

Mucosal hypertrophy, airway obstruction due to, 1148
Mucosal injury, necrotizing enterocolitis related to, 1408, 1409f
Müllerian duct
  differentiation of, 1553–1554
  dysgenesis of, 1585–1586
Müllerian duct syndrome, persistent, 1574
Müllerian inhibiting substance
  deficiencies of, 1574
  in sex differentiation, 1555–1556, 1556f
Multi-minicore myopathy, 986–987
Multicystic dysplastic kidney, 1676, 1676f. *See also* Polycystic kidney disease.
  defects associated with, 1676
  perinatal ultrasonography of, 159–160, 161f
  ultrasonography of, 725, 725f
Multifactorial disorders, 132f, 132–133
Multifactorial inheritance, 132
  congenital anomalies due to, 562, 562t
Multifetal pregnancy reduction, 381
Multifocal clonic seizures, 958
Multiple acyl-CoA dehydrogenase, deficiency of, 1627–1628, 1639
Multiple carboxylase deficiency, 1608t, 1639
Multiple gestations. *See also* Twin *entries*.
  amniotic fluid assessment in, 413, 413f
  biology in, 375–376
  delivery considerations in, 380–381
  discordance in, 379–380
  embryonic/fetal demise in, 378
  ethical issues in, 37–38
  fetal growth in, 379–380
    constraints on, 280, 280f
  fetal mortality in, 380
  fetal-neonatal consequences of, 376–380
  Hellin-Zellany rule for, 375
  in preterm delivery, 336
  maternal complications of, 377b
  maternal consequences of, 376, 377b
  multifetal pregnancy reduction in, 381
  obstetric management of, 375–381
  outcome of, 381
  placental insufficiency in, 285–286, 286f
  post-term, 387
  preeclamptic toxemia in, 376
  "stuck twin," in twin-twin transfusion syndrome, 250, 413, 413f
  twin-twin transfusion in, 378–379, 379b
    polyhydramnios and, 419
  ultrasonography of, 145, 146f
Multiple left heart defects, 1237
Mumps, 818, 851
Murmurs. *See* Heart murmurs.
Muscle. *See also named muscle.*
  in fetal weight, 273
Muscle-eye-brain disease, 984
Muscle relaxants, in neonatal anesthesia, 639–640
Muscle tone. *See also* Hypertonia; Hypotonia.
  examination of, 516
  in hypotonia, 976–977. *See also* Hypotonia.
  neurologic examination of, 525f, 525–526
  in preterm infant, 527, 527t
Muscular atrophy, spinal, 978–979, 979f
Muscular dystrophy
  congenital, 982–984, 982f, 982b, 983f
  facioscapulohumeral, 985
  Fukuyama-type, 984
  merosin-deficient, 982, 983

Muscular dystrophy—*cont'd*
  Xp21-linked dystrophin-deficient (Duchenne type), 985
  genetics of, 124
Musculoskeletal system
  bone and joint infections in, 1762–1767
  congenital anomaly(ies) of, 1756–1758, 1767–1784
    arthrogryposis multiplex congenita as, 1783–1784, 1783f
    generalized, 1757
    genetics of, 1756–1757
    in utero positioning and, 1758
    limb malformation in, 1757
    neurofibromatosis as, 1782f, 1783
    of lower extremities, 1772–1781
    of upper extremities, 1767–1770
    osteogenesis imperfecta as, 1782–1783, 1782f
    skeletal dysplasia as, 1781–1782
    spinal, 1757–1758, 1770–1772
    teratogenic, 1756
  embryology of, 1755–1756
  perinatal ultrasonography of, 162f, 162–163, 163f
  trauma to, 1758–1762
Mustard procedure, 1223, 1269t
Mutagens, 190
Mutations, genetic
  DNA sequencing for, 129–130
  dominant, 122
Myasthenia gravis, 372–373
  acquired, 980–981
  autoimmune, 980
  congenital, 1142
  during pregnancy, 372
  neonatal, 1142
  ptosis associated with, 1732
  respiratory distress related to, 1142
  transient, 981
Myasthenic syndromes, congenital, 981, 981b
  respiratory distress related to, 1142–1143
Mycobacterium bovis, 826
Mycobacterium tuberculosis, 826
Mydriasis, 1747
Myelin, 1053
  tubular, in surfactant, 1081
Myelination
  imaging characteristics of, 898–899, 900f
  of optic nerve fibers, 1744
  oligodendrocytes in, 898–899, 898f
  sequence of, 899t
Myelitis, transverse, vs. spinal birth injuries, 548
Myeloblasts, as neutrophil precursor, 762
Myelomeningocele, 902f, 901–902
  clinical expression of, 1015, 1015t
  fetal surgery for, 234t, 246–247
  pathogenesis of, 1014–1015
  prenatal diagnosis of, 246
  prenatal treatment of, 246–247
  treatment of, 1015
  types of, 1014–1015
Myeloperoxidase, deficiency of, 1317–1318
Myelopoiesis, 1309
Myeloproliferative disorder, transient
  GAT1 mutations in, 1315
  in Down syndrome, 1314–1315
Myeloschisis, 901
Myenteric muscle contractions, 1362
Myocardial biopsy, for cardiomyopathy, 1248

Myocardial contractility
    impaired, after hypoxic-ischemic insult,
        951
    pharmacologic management of,
        1267–1268
Myocardial dysfunction
    fetal, assessment of, 1210
    in respiratory distress syndrome, 1106
Myocarditis, due to adenovirus infections,
    875
Myocardium
    ejection fraction of, 1213
    performance of, developmental aspects
        of, 1212–1215
    relaxation of, diastolic compliance
        affected by, 1214
    shortening fraction of, 1213
    structure of, developmental changes in,
        1213
    tumors of, 1250, 1250f
Myoclonic encephalopathy, early, 973
Myoclonic seizures, 960, 961f
Myoclonus, neonatal
    benign sleep, 960
    without electrographic seizures, 961, 962f
Myocyte, 1213
Myofibrils, 1213
Myofibromatosis, 1343
Myoglobinuria, 1667
Myoma, ultrasonography of, 149, 149f
Myopathy(ies)
    central core disease and, 986
    congenital, 986–987
    mitochondrial, 987–988
        benign infantile, 1644
    multi-minicore, 986–987
    myotubular, 987, 987f
    nemaline, 986, 986f
Myotonic dystrophy
    congenital, 984–985
        respiratory distress related to, 1143
    trinucleotide repeat expansions in,
        126–127
Myotubular myopathy, 987, 987f

N

Nafcillin
    for mastitis, 818
    for necrotizing enterocolitis, 1405
    for omphalitis, 818
    for osteomyelitis and septic arthritis, 814
    for sepsis, 801t, 802t
    for skin infections, 817
Nalbuphine
    for labor pain, 472
    umbilical vein to maternal vein ratio of,
        470t
Naloxone
    administration of, in neonatal
        resuscitation, 951
    contraindications to, in neonatal
        abstinence syndrome, 750
    dosages of, 1790
    for drug-depressed infant, in neonatal
        resuscitation, 503t, 505
    precautions for use of, during labor and
        delivery, 473
Narcotics. See Opioids.
Nasal. See also Nose.
Nasal flaring, in pulmonary function
    assessment, 1088

Nasal septum, dislocation of, birth-related,
    537, 537f
Nasogastric tube(s), in enteral nutrition,
    676
Nasolacrimal duct
    blockage of, conjunctivitis due to, 1747
    cysts of, 1147
    infection of, 1733
National Institute of Child Health and
    Human Development (NICHD)
    Neonatal Research Network, 73, 74t
National Organization for Rare Disorders
    (NORD), 581
Natural child birth, 468
Natural killer cells
    function of
        in neonates, 770
        transcription factors in, 769–770
    g-c chain mutation of, 770
    phenotypic and functional characteristics
        of, 768–769
    production and differentiation of, 769
    subsets of, 768–769
NEB gene, in nemaline myopathy, 986
Neck
    anomalies of
        congenital, examination of, 518, 573,
            574f
        spinal defects and, 1758
        ultrasonography of, 155, 155f
    birth injuries to, 541–547
    masses in
        fetal airway obstruction due to, 248
        fetal surgery for, 234t
Necrosis
    avascular, in developmental dysplasia of
        hip, 1776
    of subcutaneous fat, at birth, 530–531,
        531f
Necrotizing enterocolitis, 1403–1410
    bacterial colonization in, 1407
    classification of, 1403–1404, 1405t
    clinical features of, 1403–1406
    diagnosis of, 1403–1404, 1404f
    enteral nutrition and
        breast milk in, 1406–1407, 1406t
        minimal enteral feeding in, 675, 679
        rapid advancement of feedings in, 676
    epidemiology of, 1403
    in asphyxia, 952
    indomethacin associated with, 351–352
    intestinal ischemia in, 1407
    mucosal injury and inadequate host
        defense in, 1407–1408, 1409f
    outcome of, 1405–1406
    pathology of, 1406
    pathophysiology of, 1406–1409
    prematurity and, 1406
    presentation of, 1403
    prevention of, 1409
    radiography of, 721f, 721–722, 722f
    treatment of, 1404–1405
Necrotizing fasciitis, in omphalitis, 818
Necrotizing tracheobronchitis, due to
    mechanical ventilation, 1119
Negligence, definition of, 51
Negligent supervision, 49
Neisseria gonorrhoeae infection. See
    Gonorrhea.
Nemaline myopathy, 986, 986f
Neomycin
    for conjunctivitis, 811
    for sepsis, 803t
Neonatal Abstinence Score, 750, 751f

Neonatal abstinence syndrome, 749–751
    clinical signs of, 750
    methadone and, 749–750
    treatment of, 750
Neonatal care. See also Neonatal-perinatal
        medicine; Perinatal care services.
    global, development of, 15, 15f
    in developing countries. See Developing
        countries.
    intensive. See Neonatal intensive care,
        quality of; Neonatal intensive care
        unit (NICU).
    parents' attitude toward, 646–647
Neonatal Individualized Developmental Care
    and Assessment Program (NIDCAP), 15
Neonatal intensive care, quality of, 63–79
    databases for evaluation of
        adjusting for case mix differences in,
            66–69, 68f
        administrative information system data
            in, 66
        data elements in, 65–66
        diagnosis related group data in, 70–71,
            71t, 72t
        identifiers for, 65
        minimal dataset in, 64–65
        NTISS score in, 66
        outcome data in, 66–69
        primary data collection for, 64b, 64–70
        processes of care in, 65–66
        risk adjusters in, 66–67
        risk assessment models for, 67–69, 68f
        risk component in, 67
        secondary data collection for, 69–70
        virtual patient approach to, 66
    ethical considerations in, 24–25
    improvement of
        case for, 63–71
        cost information for, 71–73
        costs and resources in, 71–78
        Internet-based collaboratives for, 76
        key habits for, 76–77, 77f
        networks of NICUs and, 73–75, 74t
        patient safety and, 77b, 77–78, 78b
        work of translating data into action for,
            75–76
    in regional perinatal care centers, 31–32
    neonatal well-being and, 24–25
    standards for, in regional care, 25, 26t
Neonatal intensive care unit (NICU). See
        also Intensive care nursery.
    behavioral language of preterm infant in,
        1056f, 1056–1057
    blood pressure monitoring in, 614–616,
        615f
    capnography in, 616–618
    cardiac monitoring in, 609–612, 610f–612f,
        612b
    characteristics of, 1051–1052
    continuous blood gas monitoring in, 621f,
        621–623, 622f
    design considerations of, 603–605
        adjacencies in, 604
        ICU staff support in, 604–605, 605b
        parents as partners in care and, 604
        single-patient rooms vs. multiple-patient
            rooms in, 604, 604t
    end-tidal carbon monoxide monitoring in,
        623
    environment for preterm infant in,
        653–654
    environmental exposure in, 262
    estimating need for beds in, 29
    family-centered care in, 655–657

Neonatal intensive care unit (NICU)—cont'd
  fetal exposure to, placenta-independent
      pathway in, 262
  future of, 15
  history of, tools and supplies in, 13, 15
  improvement of care in. See Neonatal
      intensive care, quality of.
  in developing countries, 106
      ethical issues related to, 106–107
  individualized nursing care in, 654
  infection prevention in, 828–829
      antibiotic prophylaxis in, 829
      barrier nursing technique in, 828–829
      bathing of infants in, 829
      immunoglobulins in, 829
      resuscitation and ventilatory equipment
          care in, 829
      umbilicus care in, 829
  interventions for parents in, 654, 654b
  medical errors in, 64, 77, 77t
  networks of, role in evaluation of care in,
      73–75, 74t
  neurobehavioral development of preterm
      infant in, 1058–1061, 1059f–1061f
  pain management in, 642
  pulse oximetry in, 618f–620f, 618–621, 619b
  respiratory monitoring in, 612–614, 613f
  transcutaneous carbon dioxide monitoring
      in, 616
  transcutaneous oxygen monitoring in, 616
Neonatal Intensive Care Unit
      Neurobehavioral Scale (NNNS), 1064
Neonatal lupus syndrome, maternal
      antinuclear antibodies and, 370–371
Neonatal monitoring. See also specific
      monitoring modality.
  biomedical engineering aspects of,
      609–623
  blood gas, continuous, 621f, 621–623, 622f
  blood pressure, 614–616, 615f
  capnographic, 616–618
  cardiac, 609–612, 610f–612f, 612b
  during surgery, 636–637, 636t
  end-tidal carbon monoxide, 623
  pulse oximetry, 618f–620f, 618–621, 619b
  respiratory, 612–614, 613f
  transcutaneous carbon dioxide, 616
  transcutaneous oxygen, 616
Neonatal morbidity
  diseases associated with low birthweight
      infants, 23
  idiopathic thrombocytopenic purpura and,
      368
  in infant of diabetic mother, 1473b
  in preterm and low birthweight infants,
      22–23
  prematurity and, 332, 332t
  regionalized care impact on, 29
  tobacco exposure and, 740
Neonatal mortality
  after resuscitation with oxygen, 500
  categories of, 21
  causes of, 91–94
      biologic factors in, 93, 93f
      nonbiologic factors in, 91–92, 92f
  cultural beliefs and, 3–4, 92–93
  French Revolution and, 7–8
  in adenovirus infections, 875
  in developing countries
      by geographic area, 87, 88f, 88–91, 90f,
          90t, 91f
      causes of, 91–94, 92f, 93f
      strategies for reducing
          global initiatives for, 88, 89t

Neonatal mortality—cont'd
      home-based care in, 102–103, 104t
      socioeconomic and evidence-based
          interventions in, 107f, 107–108,
          108t
  personal and cultural burden of, 19
  prevention of
      evidence-based interventions in,
          107–108, 108t
      global initiatives for, 88, 89t
      risk factor reduction in, 23–24
      socioeconomic factors in, 107, 107f
  rates of
      by birthweight, 20–22, 21f, 22f
      by race, 20–21, 21f
      global burden of, 87–88, 88f
      risk models for, 66–69, 68f
  regionalized care impact on, 29, 31, 32
  risk factors associated with, 19–20, 20b
  standardized mortality ratio calculation of,
      67–68, 68f
  tobacco exposure and, 740
Neonatal-perinatal medicine. See also
      Perinatal care services.
  ethics in. See Ethics.
  evidence-based practice of, 79–84
  history of, 3–17
      Apgar scoring system and, 7
      education and research in, 15
      foundling asylums in, 7, 8f
      global neonatal care in, 15, 15f
      high-risk fetus and delivery in, 3–5, 6f
      incubators and premature baby exhibits
          in, 8–12, 9f, 10t, 11f, 12f
      intravenous fluid and blood transfusion
          in, 13
      midwives in, 5–6, 6f, 7f
      milestones in, 5t
      neonatal intensive care units in, 13 15
      oxygen therapy in, 12, 14t
      pioneers in, 3, 4f, 5t
      resuscitation in, 6–7, 14t
      supportive care in, 12–13
      surgery in, 15
      ventilatory care in, 12–13, 13f, 14t
      war manpower and, 7–8
  legal issues in. See Legal issues.
Neonatal period, definition of, 19
Neonatal resuscitation. See Resuscitation,
      neonatal.
Neonatal Therapeutic Intervention Scoring
      System (NTISS), 66
Neonate
  anesthesia for. See Anesthesia, in
      neonates.
  at high risk for metabolic disorders, 1599
      screening programs for, 1599–1601
  bacterial infections of. See Bacterial
      infection(s).
  cerebrospinal fluid values in, 1808t
  complement system of, 771–772, 772t
  cytokine biology and role in, 773–777
  depression of
      asphyxia and, 486, 486b
      due to analgesia, 505
  disabled, legal issues related to, 57–59
  drug therapy for, 191f, 191–197
      absorption in, 191–193
      dosages in, 196
          role of maturity and postnatal age
              and, 197
      metabolism and disposition in, 193f,
          193–195
      monitoring of, 197

Neonate—cont'd
      pharmacokinetics considerations in,
          196, 196f
      protein binding in, 193
      renal excretion and, 195f, 195–196
  extremely-low-birthweight. See Extremely
      low birthweight.
  follicle-stimulating hormone values in,
      1805t
  fungal infections of, 830–836. See also
      specific infection.
  hearing loss in, 1045–1050. See also
      Hearing loss.
  high-risk. See High-risk neonate.
  intersex, gender assignment in, 1562, 1564
  jaundice in, 1419–1461
  large for gestational age, 22
  life-sustaining treatment in, withholding
      of, ethics of, 40–41
  low-birthweight. See Low birthweight.
  luteinizing hormone values in, 1805t
  maternal attachment to. See Parent-infant
      attachment.
  natural killer cell function in, 770
  parental attachment to. See Parent-infant
      attachment.
  physical examination of. See Physical
      examination, neonatal.
  platelet count in, maternal idiopathic
      thrombocytopenic purpura and, 368
  premature. See Preterm infant.
  protozoal infections of, 836–840
  resuscitation of. See Resuscitation,
      neonatal.
  self-concept development in, maternal
      role in, 654
  sepsis of. See Sepsis.
  serum ammonia concentration standards
      for, 1803t
  serum electrolyte values in, 1801t
  serum testosterone in, 1805t
  sick, inborn errors of metabolism in,
      1616–1617
  small for gestational age. See Small for
      gestational age.
  sodium balance in, 695–696, 696f
  T cell function in, 782
  term. See Term infant.
  thermal environment of, 585–597. See also
      Heat exchange.
      practical considerations in, 595–597
  tobacco effects on, 740. See also Tobacco
      use.
  transient familial hyperbilirubinemia in,
      1432
  unconjugated hyperbilirubinemia in,
      1425–1428
  very-low-birthweight. See Very low
      birthweight.
  viral infections of, 432–442, 840–876
Neoplasms. See Tumor(s); specific neoplasm.
Neotrend blood gas continuous monitoring
      system, 621f, 621–622
Nephrocalcinosis
  hypomagnesemia with, 1519
  in preterm infant, 1518
  neonatal, 1674
  ultrasonography of, 726, 726f
Nephroma
  congenital mesoblastic, 1680–1681
  multilocular cystic, 1681
Nephropathy
  in gestational diabetes mellitus, 325
  uric acid, in acute tubular necrosis, 1668

Nephrotic syndrome, congenital, 1678–1679
  Finnish type, 1661–1662, 1662t, 1679, 1679f
  treatment of, 1679
Nerve blocks
  dorsal penile, 641
  intercostal, 641
  paracervical, 469
  pudendal, 469
Nesidioblastosis, persistent neonatal hyperinsulinemic hypoglycemia due to, 1480–1482, 1481f
Netherton syndrome, 1694t
Neuhauser sign, in cystic fibrosis, 1364
Neural crest cells
  enteric ganglion cells derived from, 1362
  in cardiogenesis, 1200–1201
Neural induction, 883–885, 885f
Neural tube
  closure of, 884–885
  defects of
    folic acid supplementation for, 225
    vertebral anomalies associated with, 1758
Neuraxial blocks, 473–477
  combined spinal-epidurals as, 474
  contraindications to, 478, 478b
  fetal benefits and risks in, 475, 476–477
  for operative vaginal deliveries, 475
  in cesarean sections, 475, 478, 478b
  inadvertent injections in, 476
  intrathecal injections (spinals) as, 474
  labor prolongation due to, 475
  lumbar epidurals as, 473
    patient-controlled, 474
  maternal risks and benefits of, 474–476
  maternal temperature elevation related to, 475–476
Neurobehavioral and developmental effects. See also Neuropsychological and behavioral effects.
  of alcohol exposure, 737
  of bronchopulmonary dysplasia, 1167
  of cocaine exposure, 745–746
  of extracorporeal membrane oxygenation, 1175–1176
  of marijuana exposure, 743
  of opioid exposure, 752–753
  of tobacco exposure, 740–741
Neurobehavioral Assessment of Preterm Infant (NAPI), 1063–1064
Neurobehavioral development, of preterm infant, 1051–1067. See also Preterm infant, neurobehavioral development of.
Neuroblastoma, 1343, 1343t
  ultrasonography of, 727
  vs. adrenal hemorrhage, 551
Neurocutaneous syndromes, macrencephaly associated with, 996–997, 997f
Neuroectodermal tumor, macrocephaly due to, 1004, 1005f
Neuroendocrine cells, 1359
Neuroepithelial cysts, macrocephaly due to, 1003
Neuroepithelial tumor, macrocephaly due to, 1004, 1005f
Neurofibromatosis
  bone disorders in, 1783
  café-au-lait macules in, 1704, 1782f, 1783
  genetics of, 122
  juvenile xanthogranuloma in, 1712
  plexiform, 1731
    of eyelid and orbit, 1731, 1736

Neurofibromatosis—cont'd
  type 1, macrencephaly associated with, 996–997
Neurohypoglycemia, defective glucose transport and, 1485
Neuroimaging. See specific imaging modality.
Neurologic and Adaptive Capacity Score (NACS), 1063
Neurologic assessment, 522b, 522–527
  consciousness level in, 522, 524
  inspection in, 524
  of cerebral cortical function, 526
  of cranial nerves, 524t, 524–525
  of deep tendon reflexes, 526
  of developmental reflexes, 526
  of motor function, 525f, 525–526
  of premature infant, 526–527, 527t
Neurologic sequelae
  after fetal intravascular transfusion, 404
  in high-risk neonate
    major, 1038–1039, 1039f
    transient, 1038
Neuromuscular abnormalities, ocular, 1745–1747
Neuromuscular blocking agents, in mechanical ventilation, 1116
Neuromuscular disease
  diagnosis of, 977
  hypotonia and, 976–989
  metabolic, 987–989
  neonatal, 978, 978b
  respiratory distress related to, 1142–1143
Neuromuscular junction, disorders of, 980–982, 981b
Neurons
  maturation of, 1053
  migration of, 887–889, 887f–891f
    disorders of, 906–908, 992–993, 992f–994f
    effects of environmental factors on, 908, 909f
    trajectories in, 888, 888f
  myelination of, 1053
  organization of, 1053
  proliferation of, 885–886, 886f
    abnormalities in, 904–906
  subplate, 890–891, 892f, 893f
    damage to, in periventricular leukomalacia, 912, 912f
    in brain development, 1054
Neuropathy
  motor and sensory, hereditary, 979–980
  sensory and autonomic, hereditary, 980, 980b
Neuropeptides, reduction of, in hypertrophic pyloric stenosis, 1389
Neuroprotective strategies, for hypoxic-ischemic encephalopathy, 954–955
Neuropsychological and behavioral effects
  of alcohol exposure, 737–738
  of rubella virus infection, 872
  of tobacco exposure, 741
Neurotoxicity, of bilirubin, 1436
Neurulation, 884
  in microcephaly, 990–991, 991f, 992f
  steps in, 884–885, 885f
Neutropenia, 1310–1315
  alloimmune (isoimmune), 1312
  autoimmune, 1312
  chronic benign, 1312–1313
  cyclic, 1311
  definition of, 763, 1309
  drug-induced, 1312, 1313b

Neutropenia—cont'd
  idiopathic, in very low birthweight infants, 1312
  in cartilage-hair hypoplasia, 1311
  in dyskeratosis congenita, 1311
  in reticular dysgenesis, 1311–1312
  in sepsis, 1312
  in Shwachman-Diamond syndrome, 1311
  persistent, in overwhelming sepsis, 763
  postinfectious, 1312
  severe congenital (Kostmann syndrome), 1310–1311
  therapeutic cytokines for, 1313–1314
Neutrophil(s), 762–767
  adhesion of, 764, 765f
  chemotaxis of, 763f, 764–766
  circulating pool of, 1310, 1310t
  dysfunctional actin polymerization in, 1317
  functions of, 763–764, 763f
  in breast milk, 789
  microbial activity of, 766–777
  phagocytosis by, 766, 766f
  production and circulation of, 762–763
  transfusion of, in sepsis, 1312
  values for, 1813t
Neutrophil count
  absolute, 1309
  absolute total immature, 796–797, 796t
  clinical factors affecting, 796, 797b, 797t
  immature to total (I:T) ratio in, 796, 797
  in chronic benign neutropenia, 1312–1313
  in newborn, 1309–1310, 1310t
  peripheral blood, 1310
  total, reference ranges for, 1811f–1813f
Neutrophilia, 1314–1315
  definition of, 1309
Nevirapine, in HIV prophylaxis, 858, 860
Nevus
  blue, 1705
  blue-rubber bleb syndrome, 1708–1709
  epidermal, 1710
  melanocytic congenital, 1704
    giant, 1704–1705, 1704f
  sebaceous, 1710
Nevus achromicus, 1706
Nevus anemicus, 1706
Nevus flammeus. See Port-wine stain (nevus flammeus).
New York Online Access to Health home page, 581
Newborn Individualized Care and Assessment Program (NIDCAP), 1058–1061, 1060f, 1061f
  effectiveness of, 1058–1059, 1059f
NF1 gene, in juvenile myelomonocytic leukemia, 1342
Niacin
  in breast milk, 672t
  in infant formula, 674t
  requirements for, 668t
Nicotine
  dependence on, 739
  in breast milk, 201
  neonatal withdrawal from, 740
Niemann-Pick disease
  hepatic dysfunction in, 1623
  hepatosplenomegaly in, 1623
  macular abnormalities in, 1744, 1744t
Nifedipine
  for bronchopulmonary dysplasia, 1166
  for chronic hypertension, 317t
  for preeclampsia-eclampsia, 314, 314t
  for preterm labor prevention, 352

Nipple odor, in initiation of breast feeding, 650

Nipple stimulation, in labor induction, 387, 386b

Nissen fundoplication, for gastroesophageal reflux, 1380

Nitric oxide
    dosages of, 1793
    increased production of, with pure oxygen therapy, 499
    inhaled, 1176–1180
        animal and human studies of, 1177–1180
        follow-up studies of, 1179
        for bronchopulmonary dysplasia, 1166–1167
        for persistent pulmonary hypertension, 1247–1248
        for respiratory distress syndrome, 1107
        future considerations in, 1179–1180
        in preterm infants, 1178–1179
        in term infants, 1178
        toxicity of, 1178
        physiology and pharmacology of, 1177, 1177f
    toxicity of, 943

Nitric oxide donors, for preterm labor prevention, 353–354

Nitric oxide synthase
    absence of, in hypertrophic pyloric stenosis, 1389
    forms of, 1177, 1177f

Nitrogen
    balance of, in parenteral nutrition, 682–683
    fetal accretion of, 682

Nitrogen dioxide, toxicity of, 1178

Nitroglycerin, for preterm labor prevention, 353–354

Nitroprusside. See Sodium nitroprusside.

Nitrous oxide
    as anesthetic induction agent, 478
    in neonatal anesthesia, 638

NKX2.5 gene, heart defects associated with, 1198, 1204

Noise
    fetal exposure to, placenta-independent pathway in, 262, 262t
    neonatal exposure to, hearing loss associated with, 1049

Noise criteria, permissible, for hospital nurseries, 601

Nonepileptic behaviors, in seizures, 962f, 960–963

Nonhemolytic reactions, to transfusion, febrile, 1347

Nonimmune hydrops fetalis, 420–426. See Hydrops fetalis, nonimmune.

Nonketotic hyperglycinemia, 1604t
    neonatal response to, 1617

Nonstress testing
    in fetal evaluation, 168, 168f
        post-term, 385t
    in gestational diabetes mellitus, 324
    in intrauterine growth restriction, 294

Nontherapeutic agents, in breast milk, 201

Nontraditional inheritance patterns, in genetic disorders, 124–127

Noonan syndrome
    anesthetic implications of, 633t
    excessive skinfolds in, 573
    heart defects associated with, 1203t
    lymphedema of hands and feet in, 575, 577f

Norethindrone, fetal effects of, 188t

Norrie disease, 1743

Norvasc, for chronic hypertension, 317t

Norwood procedure, 1269t
    for aortic stenosis, 1233
    for hypoplastic left heart syndrome, 1236–1237
    for single ventricle, 1231

Nose. See also Nasal entries.
    congenital anomalies of, 569f, 570f, 572
    fracture of, birth-related, 537
    hypoplastic, 572
    lesions of, 1147–1148
    mucosal hypertrophy in, 1148
    obstruction of, causes of, 1143, 1143b
    tumors of, 1147–1148

Notochord, in musculoskeletal development, 1755

Nuchal translucency, increased
    perinatal ultrasonography of, 155, 156f
    trisomies associated with, 155

Nuclear factor κB, mutations of, defective natural killer cell function due to, 769

Nurse practitioners, liability of physicians for supervision of, 50

Nursery. See also Intensive care nursery.
    genital examination in, 1556–1557, 1557b
    heat loss prevention in, 595–596

Nutrients, placental transport of, 1467–1468, 1468f

Nutrition. See also Breast feeding; Diet; Formula.
    botulism and, 820
    enteral. See Enteral nutrition.
    for bronchopulmonary dysplasia, 1165
    for preterm infants, supplementation of, 675
    for term infants, supplementation of, 674–675
    gavage feeding in, 8–9, 676
    maternal
        fetal growth and, 280–282, 281f, 282b, 282f
        preterm delivery and, 334
    neonatal, in developing countries, 99f, 100, 100b
    parenteral. See Parenteral nutrition.
    withdrawal of, ethical issues in, 41

Nystagmus, 1746
    jerk, 1746
    optokinetic, 1724
    pendular, 1746
        associated with cataracts, 1740–1741

Nystatin
    dosages of, 1790
    for candidiasis, 831–832

O

Obesity
    body mass index and, 323
    definition of, 321, 323
    pregnancy weight gain and, 280–281, 281f

Obstetric history, in preterm delivery, 335, 335t

Obstructive uropathy. See Uropathy, obstructive.

Occipitofrontal circumference, measurement of, 989

Occupational exposure, 255–265
    concurrent with pregnancy, 258–259, 260t
    fetal, pathways of, 259, 261–262
    not concurrent with pregnancy, 255–258

Octreotide
    dosages of, 1791
    for hypoglycemia, 1487
        in nesidioblastosis-adenoma spectrum, 1482

Ocular muscles, external, birth injuries to, 538–539

Ocular rotational reflexes, 1724–1725, 1725f

Oculocephalic (doll's eye) reflex
    in optic nerve assessment, 524
    in preterm infant, 526

Oculomandibulofacial dyscephalia (Hallermann-Streiff syndrome), 1729

Oculomotor nerve
    birth-related palsy of, 539
    dysfunction of, ptosis due to, 525

Oculovestibular (caloric) reflex, 526

Odontoid process, 1756

Odors, in inborn errors of metabolism, 1624, 1624t

Offspring, of mothers with gestational diabetes mellitus, 327

Ofloxacin, for chlamydial infections, 447

Ohtahara syndrome, 973

Oil-based economy, neonatal mortality rates associated with, 91, 92

Oleic acid, in intravenous lipid emulsions, 686t

Olfactory nerve, assessment of, 524

Oligodendrocytes
    immature, vulnerability of, in periventricular leukomalacia, 911
    in myelination, 898–899, 898f, 899t, 900f

Oligohydramnios, 414–418
    ACE inhibitors causing, 414
    amnioinfusion in, 417, 418
    amniotic fluid index in, 149, 149f, 169
    amniotic fluid volume in, 414
    conditions associated with, 169
    congenital anomalies associated with, 414, 1133
    diagnosis of, 414–417
        adjuncts to, 417
    etiology of, 414, 415f, 415b
    fetal chest in, 416–417
    fetal growth in, 416, 416f
    furosemide challenge in, 417
    in hydrops fetalis, 398, 398f
    in intrauterine growth restriction, 292, 416
    indigo carmine dye infusion in, 417
    long-term indomethacin therapy and, 351
    maternal hydration for, 418
    maximum vertical pocket in, 411t
    perinatal morbidity associated with, 413–414
    posterior urethral valve syndrome in, 414, 415f
    pulmonary hypoplasia in, 416, 416f, 417f, 1073–1074, 1132–1133
    renal anomalies in, 415f, 415–416, 1132–1133
    treatment of, 417–418
    uteroplacental insufficiency in, 414
    vs. premature rupture of membranes, 414–415
    with obstructive uropathy, 236

Oligohydramnios/polyhydramnios sequence, 250
    twin, 413

Oligohydramnios sequence, 561

Oligosaccharidoses, 1623t, 1624

Oliguria
    management of, 951
    perinatal asphyxia and, 703

Omphalitis, 817–818
Omphalocele, 1381–1385
  associated anomalies in, 1382
  giant, 1382, 1382f
  pathogenesis of, 1381, 1381f
  prognosis in, 1385
  surgical management of, 1385
  timing of delivery with, 1383
  ultrasonography of, 157, 158f
Ontogenesis, 1504–1505
  of cerebral cortex, developmental events
    in, 1052, 1052f
Ophthalmia neonatorum. See Conjunctivitis.
Ophthalmologic testing, of high-risk
  neonate, 1040
Ophthalmoscope, 1723
Opioids
  abuse of, 749–753
    buprenorphine as substitute in, 753
    central nervous system effects of, 752
    fetal growth effects of, 751–752
    neonatal abstinence syndrome due to,
      749–751, 751f
    neurodevelopmental effects of,
      752–753
    prescription pain killers in, 753
  agonist-antagonist type of, 471t, 472–473
  antagonist type of, 473
  during labor, 471b, 471–473, 479
  in breast milk, 200–201, 750–751
  in neonatal intensive care, 642
  intravenous patient-controlled, 472
  pure agonist type of, 471t, 472
  receptors for, 471
  umbilical vein to maternal vein ratio of,
    470t
  with phenothiazines, during labor, 471
Opium, diluted tincture of, for neonatal
  abstinence syndrome, 750
Opsonins, serum, 770
Optic disc
  abnormalities of, 1744–1745
  atrophy of, 1745
  coloboma of, 1745
  conus or congenital crescent of,
    1744–1745
  examination of, 1723
  pit of, 1745
Optic nerve
  assessment of, 524
  birth injury to, 539
  glioma of, 1736
  hypoplasia of, 1745
  retinoblastoma extension along, 1742
Optokinetic nystagmus, 1724
ORACLE II trial, 355
Oral cavity
  congenital anomalies of, 569f, 570f,
    572–573, 573f
  lesions of, respiratory distress related to,
    1148–1149, 1148f
Oral contraceptives
  fetal effects of, 188t
  in breast milk, 200
Oral-facial-digital syndrome, anesthetic
  implications of, 634t
Orbit(s)
  abnormalities of, 1734, 1734b
  birth injuries to, 538
  cellulitis of, 1734
  examination of, 1722
  hematoma of, 1735
  tumors of, 1734–1736
Orchipexy, for cryptorchidism, 1567

Organ donation, and withdrawal of life-
  sustaining treatment, 41
Organ transplantation. See Transplantation.
Organic acidemia, 1638–1640, 1606t–1608t
  management of, 1639–1640
Organic acids
  analysis of, in inborn errors of
    metabolism, 1633, 1633b
  disorders of, 1606t–1608t
Organic aciduria, 1648
  dysmorphic features in, 1625t, 1627–1628
Organic pesticides. See also Pesticides.
  in breast milk, 201
Ornithine transcarbamylase, deficiency of,
  1651
Orofacial malformations, terminal transverse
  defects with, 1729
Orogastric tube(s), in enteral nutrition, 676
Oropharyngeal lesions, 1148–1149, 1148f
Orthopedics, 1755–1784
  bone and joint infections in, 1762–1767
  congenital abnormalities in, 1767–1784
  musculoskeletal disorders in, 1755–1762
Ortolani test, for developmental dysplasia of
  hip, 1774, 1775f
Oscillometric method, of blood pressure
  monitoring, 615, 615f
Osmolality
  of breast milk, 672t
  of infant formula, 674t
Ossification
  in bone development, 1505
  of cartilage, 1505
    disturbances in, in congenital
      hypothyroidism, 1542
  vertebral, 1756
Osteoblasts, in bone development, 1505
Osteogenesis imperfecta, 1782–1783
  anesthetic implications of, 634t
  blue discoloration of sclera in, 1738
  classification of, 1782
  clinical manifestations of, 1782, 1782f
  lethal type II, perinatal ultrasonography
    of, 162, 162f
  treatment of, 1782–1783
Osteomyelitis, 813–815, 1762–1765
  clinical manifestations of, 814
  diagnosis of, 814, 815f, 1763
  etiology of, 814
  imaging of, 1763–1764, 1764f
  incidence of, 813
  neonatal, ultrasonography of, 729–730
  pathogenesis and pathology of, 814,
    1762–1763
  prognosis in, 815
  treatment of, 814–815, 1764–1765
Osteopenia of prematurity, 1521–1523. See
  also Rickets.
  biochemical features of, 1521
  diagnosis of, 1521
  enteral nutrition for, 1522
  etiology of, 1521
  hormonal features of, 1521
  mechanical stimulation program for,
    1522–1523
  mineral supplementation for, 1522
  outcome of, 1523
  parenteral nutrition for, 1522
  prevention of, 1521–1522
  radiologic features of, 1521
Osteopetrosis, infantile, 1512
Ostomy
  for meconium ileus treatment, 1396
  leveling, for Hirschsprung disease, 1399

Otitis media, 809–810
Otoacoustic emissions, in evaluation of
  hearing, 1046
Ovalocytosis, forms of, 1430
Ovary(ies)
  cyst of
    aspiration of, 234t
    ultrasonography of, 150
  development of, 256f
  differentiation of, 1553, 1553t
    genetic control in, 1551, 1551f
  in true hermaphroditism, 1573
  teratoma of, genomic imprinting in,
    125–126
Overinflation, congenital lobar, chest
  radiograph of, 716–717, 717f
Overshoot, in blood pressure monitoring,
  614
Ovum, environmental exposures affecting,
  255–256, 256t, 256f
Oxacillin
  dosages of, 1789
  for sepsis, 802t
  for skin infections, 817
Oxazolidinediones, fetal effects of, 187t
Oxidation, of fatty acids. See Fatty acids,
  oxidation of.
Oxidative stress
  pathophysiology of, 498
  resuscitation with room air vs. oxygen in,
    498–499, 499f
17-Oxidoreductase deficiency, 1575
Oxycodone, abuse of, 753
Oxygen
  exchange of, in assisted ventilation,
    1110–1111, 1110f
  transcutaneous monitoring of, 616
Oxygen concentration, inspired. See Inspired
  oxygen concentration (FiO$_2$).
Oxygen consumption
  fetal, 275, 275t, 275–276
  insensible water loss and, effect of activity
    on, 592t
  measurement of, 1211–1212
Oxygen content, calculation of, 1089, 1211
Oxygen dissociation curve, 1089, 1089f,
  1290, 1290f
Oxygen saturation
  assessment of, in mechanical ventilation,
    1114
  in bronchopulmonary dysplasia, 1165
  in persistent pulmonary hypertension,
    1246
  in single ventricle, 1231
  measurement of, 1211
    in extracorporeal membrane
      oxygenation, 1169
    monitors for, in developing countries,
      103
  variation in, shunt detection using, 1212
Oxygen tension (PO$_2$)
  alveolar-arterial gradient of, 1090
  arterial-alveolar ratio of, 1090
  fetal, 484
  in extracorporeal membrane oxygenation,
    1170
  in persistent pulmonary hypertension,
    1246
  in umbilical artery blood, 483
  measurement of, 1089–1090, 1089f
  reduction of, during labor, 484, 484t
  transcutaneous, 616
  ventilation-perfusion ratio and,
    1089–1090

Oxygen therapy
  for bronchopulmonary dysplasia, 1164
  for congenital heart disease, 1265–1266
  for non-reassuring fetal heart rate, 178
  history of, 12, 14t
  in neonatal resuscitation, 498–501
    21% vs. 100% oxygen in, 499
    free-flow oxygen in, 490–491
    room air vs. oxygen in, 499–500, 500f
  in respiratory distress syndrome, 1112
  oxidative stress related to, 498–499, 499f
  retinopathy of prematurity related to,
    1748–1749
Oxygen toxicity, bronchopulmonary
  dysplasia related to, 1160, 1160f
Oxygenation
  and lung damage prevention, 1121
  fetal, 483–484, 1206
  in congenital heart disease, 1265–1266
  intrapartum, uterine blood flow and, 172
  mean airway pressure effects on,
    1110–1111
  surfactant therapy and, 1105
Oxygenation index, 1090
  as criterion, for extracorporeal membrane
    oxygenation, 1174, 1174b, 1175
Oxygenation ratio, 1090
Oxytocin, released by breast feeding
  gastrointestinal hormones stimulated by,
    650
  maternal-infant attachment related to, 649,
    650, 651
Oxytocin antagonists, for preterm labor
  prevention, 353
Oxytocin challenge test
  in intrauterine growth restriction, 294
  in post-term neonate, 294
Oxytocin infusion, in initiation of labor, 333,
  386b, 387

P

P wave
  in accessory pathway reentrant
    tachycardia, 1255, 1255f
  in atrial ectopic tachycardia, 1256
  in atrioventricular node reentrant
    tachycardia, 1255–1256
  in sinus tachycardia, 1254
  in ventricular premature contractions, 1259
Pacemaker
  for neonatal bradycardia, 1204, 1264–1265
  for neonatal tachycardia, 1264
  gastric, 1360
Pacing
  esophageal, for neonatal tachycardia,
    1262b, 1263
  transvenous
    for neonatal bradycardia, 1264
    for neonatal tachycardia, 1262b
Packed blood cells, transfusion of, dosages
  in, 1790
Pain
  management of. See Analgesia;
    Anesthesia.
  neonatal
    indicators of, 631
    stress response to, anesthesia for, 630,
      630f, 630t
Palate
  cleft. See Cleft palate.
  examination of, 515

Palivizumab, for respiratory syncytial virus
    infection, 854–855
  in infants with bronchopulmonary
    dysplasia, 1167
Palliative care, 41–42
Pallister-Killian syndrome, 117
Palmar creases, 575, 576f
Palmitic acid, in intravenous lipid emulsions,
    686t
Palpebral fissure, in congenital anomalies,
    570, 570f
Palsy. See specific type, e.g., Cerebral palsy.
Pamidronate, for hypercalcemia, 1518
Pancreas
  acinar cells of, 1361
  annular, 1390
  development of, 1360–1362
  functions of, 1361–1362
  lesions of, neonatal diabetes mellitus due
    to, 1491
Pancreatectomy, for hypoglycemia, 1488
  in nesidioblastosis-adenoma spectrum,
    1481
Pancreatic agenesis, in intrauterine growth
    restriction, 276
Pancreatic insufficiency disorders, 1363–1365
  cystic fibrosis as, 1363–1364
  Johanson-Blizzard syndrome as, 1365
  Shwachman-Diamond syndrome as,
    1364–1365
Pancreatitis, due to gastrointestinal
    duplications, 1392, 1393
Pancuronium
  dosages of, 1792
  in neonatal anesthesia, 640
Pancytopenia, laboratory findings in, 1629t
Panniculitis, cold-induced, 1713
Pantothenic acid
  in breast milk, 672t
  in infant formula, 674t
  requirements for, 668t
Paper spot technique, in hypothyroidism
    screening, 1538
Papillomavirus, human, 875–876
Para-aminosalicylate, in breast milk, 199
Paracervical nerve blocks, 469
Parainfluenza virus infections, 850–851
Paramyxovirus infections, 850–855
Paraoccupational routes, in concurrent
    maternal exposure, 259
Parasympathetic nervous system
  gastric innervation by, 1359
  skin innervation by, 1689
Parathormone-releasing protein, fetal
    calcium regulation by, 1492–1493
Parathyroid gland, development of, defects
    in, 1511
Parathyroid hormone
  effects of, on mineral metabolism, 1500
  fetal, 1501
  in fetal calcium regulation, 1492–1493
  in phosphorus excretion, 1498
  molecular defects of, 1511
  neonatal, 1501
  reference values for, 1501–1502, 1501t
  regulation of, 1500–1502
  secretion of
    calcium regulation in, 1500–1501
    defective regulation in, 1511–1512
Parent(s)
  attitude of, toward neonatal care, 646–647
  best interests of child and, 36
  communication with, in ethical decision
    making, 43–44

Parent(s)—cont'd
  fetal viability and delivery decisions by, 39
  moral and legal authority of, 36
  of children with bronchopulmonary
    dysplasia, support for, 1167
Parent-infant attachment, 645–658
  acceptance of pregnancy in, 646
  after birth, 648–651, 648f–649f
  before pregnancy, 645
  congenital malformations and, 657f,
    657–658
  during pregnancy, 645–647, 647f
  formation of, 645
  in perinatal period, 651–653
  labor and, 647–648
  mothering disorders in, 647
  perception of fetus in, 646–647, 647f
  to premature or sick infants, 653–657
    family-centered care and, 655–657
    individualized nursing care plan for, 654
    interventions for, 654, 654b
    kangaroo care and, 655
    mild neonatal disorders and, 652
    with bronchopulmonary dysplasia, 1167
Parent-physician relationship, 36
Parenteral nutrition, 679–691. See also
    Enteral nutrition; Nutrition.
  amino acids in
    efficacy of early administration of,
      682–683, 682t
    guidelines for use of, 690–691
    intravenous solutions of, 683–685, 684t
    safety of, 683
  caloric requirements in, 680, 690, 691b
  carbohydrate requirements in, 680–681
  catheters for, 688–690
  complications of, 687–690
  electrolytes in, 687
  energy requirements in, 680
  for bronchopulmonary dysplasia,
    1165–1166
  for microvillus inclusion disease, 1372
  for osteopenia of prematurity, 1522
  for respiratory distress syndrome, 1105
  for short bowel syndrome, 1371
  guidelines for administration of, 690–691,
    691b
  in gastroschisis repair, 1384
  lipid emulsions in, 685–687
    adverse effects of, 686–687
    fatty acid profile of, 686, 686t
    rate of infusion of, 686
  minerals in, 687
  protein requirements in, 681–685, 682f
  total, conjugated hyperbilirubinemia and,
    1460
  trace elements in, 687, 688t
  vitamins in, 687, 689t
Parietal cells, development of, 1359
Paris-Trousseau syndrome, 1341
Parity, in preeclampsia-eclampsia, 312
Parotitis, 818, 851
Paroxetine, in breast milk, 200
Partial thromboplastin time, measurement
    of, 1804t
Parvovirus B19, 1308
Parvovirus infection, 442, 868–870
  clinical features of, 442
  clinical manifestations of, 869
  diagnosis of, 870
  epidemiology of, 442
  fetal, 442, 869–870
  in pregnancy, 442
  isolation of patient with, 870

Pascal's law, 614
Passive immunity, 788–790
 placental transport of antibodies in, 788
 via human breast milk, 788–790, 789t
Patau syndrome. *See* Trisomy 13 (Patau syndrome).
Patent ductus arteriosus, 1239–1241
 anatomy and pathophysiology of, 1239–1240
 assisted ventilation and, 1121–1122
 bronchopulmonary dysplasia related to, 1161, 1162f
 clinical presentation of, 1240
 defects associated with, 1240
 fluid and electrolyte therapy for, 703
 in low birthweight infant, 23
 in respiratory distress syndrome
  fluid therapy affects on, 1105–1106
  treatment of, 1106–1107
 in rubella virus infection, 872
 in total anomalous pulmonary venous connection, 1229
 indomethacin for closure of, 1106–1107, 1241
 laboratory evaluation of, 1240
 maintenance of
  in aortic arch interruption, 1235
  in aortic stenosis, 1232
  in coarctation of aorta, 1234, 1235
  in congenital heart disease, 1266
  in pulmonary atresia, 1227
  in transposition of great arteries, 1223
  stent placement for, 1274
 management of, 1240–1241
 masking of heart abnormalities by, 520
 prognosis of, 1240–1241
 pulmonary hemorrhage associated with, 1104, 1127
 spontaneous closure of, 1240–1241
 transcatheter embolization of, 1274
Pathologist, 455, 455b, 456f
Patient-physician relationship
 ethical decision making and, 36
 parent-physician relationship in, 36
Patient safety
 in neonatal intensive care units, 77–78
 JCAHO goals for, 78, 78t
Pavlik harness
 for developmental dysplasia of hip, 1776, 1776f
 for proximal femoral fractures, 1762
Peak inspiratory pressure
 bronchopulmonary dysplasia related to, 1159–1163
 in carbon dioxide exchange, 1109
 in mechanical ventilation, 1114
  for prevention of lung damage, 1120b, 1121
Pearson syndrome, 1365, 1645
 hematologic anomalies in, 1620
Pemphigoid gestationis, 373
Pendred syndrome, goiter in, 1536
Penetrance, in autosomal dominant diseases, 122
Penicillin
 fetal effects of, 187t
 for anaerobic infections, 819
 for conjunctivitis, 811
 for group B streptococcal infection, 444–445
 for skin infections, 817
 penicillinase-resistant
  for osteomyelitis, 1764
  for septic arthritis, 1766

Penicillin—*cont'd*
 for staphylococcal scalded skin syndrome, 1698
 prophylactic
  for group B streptococcal disease prevention, 1126
  for sepsis, 804
Penicillin G
 dosages of, 1789
 for sepsis, 801t, 803t
 for skin infections, 817
 for syphilis, 824, 824t
 for tetanus neonatorum, 825
Penile nerve block, dorsal, for circumcision, 641
Penis
 measurement of, 1558, 1559f, 1560f
 small, management of, 1564
Pentalogy of Cantrell, 1381, 1381f
Pentamidine isethionate, for pneumocystis pneumonia, 837–838
Percutaneous umbilical blood sampling. *See* Umbilical cord blood, samples of.
Pericardial effusion
 causes of, 1251
 diagnosis of, 1251
 in hydrops fetalis, anemia associated with, 398, 399t
Pericardial tamponade, due to venous catheters, 689
Periderm, 1686, 1686f
Perinatal care services, 25–32. *See also* Neonatal-perinatal medicine.
 basic facilities for, 26t, 27, 28t
 future considerations in, 32
 historical perspective on, 25
 organization of, 26–29, 27t
 physicians' offices in, 27
 regionalized, 25–31
  centers for, 28–29
  centralization and deregionalization in, 31
  effectiveness of, 31–32
  estimating need for, 29
  factors threatening, 25, 25t
  financial impact of, 31
  morbidity and mortality effects of, 29
  outreach education program and, 30
  principles of, 25–26, 26t
  problems in, 30–31
  quality standards in, 25, 26t
  services of, 29–30
  staffing needs in, 26t, 29, 30
  TIOP report and, 25, 27
  transport services in, 29–30
 specialty facilities for, 26t, 27–28, 28t
 subspecialty facilities for, 26t, 28, 28t
Perinatal medicine. *See* Neonatal-perinatal medicine.
Perinatal morbidity
 amniotic fluid volume abnormalities and, 413–414
 in preeclampsia-eclampsia, 315
Perinatal mortality
 after intravascular transfusion, for erythroblastosis fetalis, 403
 amniotic fluid volume abnormalities and, 413, 413f
 hydrops fetalis and, 221
 in discordant twins, 380
 in gestational diabetes mellitus, 327
 in intrauterine growth restriction, 298
 in preeclampsia-eclampsia, 315
Perinatal period, definition of, 19

Perinatal ultrasonography, 141–164, 151–152
 A-mode images in, 141
 applications of, 144–145
  in assisted reproduction, 145
  in first-trimester studies, 145, 145f
  in genetic screening, 144, 145f
  in multiple gestations, 145, 146f
 B-mode images in, 141, 141f
 bioeffects of, 143
 Doppler, 151, 151f
  color, 142, 142f
  waveforms in, 141, 142f
 ethical considerations in, 144, 144f
 in pregnancy evaluation, 146–151
 M-mode images in, 141, 141f
 of abdominal circumference, 146–147, 147f
 of abdominal wall defects, 157, 158f
 of amniotic fluid volume, 148–149, 149f
 of anencephaly, 153, 154f
 of bile ducts, 158–159
 of biparietal diameter, 146, 146f
 of bowel, 156f, 156–157, 157f
 of cardiac anomalies, 156
 of central nervous system, 152–155
 of cervical length, 149f, 149–151, 150f
 of Chiari malformation, 153, 153f
 of choroid plexus cyst, 154f, 154–155
 of Dandy-Walker cyst, 154, 154f
 of diaphragmatic hernia, 158, 159f
 of encephalocele, 153–154, 154f
 of esophageal atresia, 157
 of femoral length, 147, 147f
 of fetal anomalies, 152b, 152–163
 of fetal breech position, 150, 150f
 of fetal growth, 147
 of gallbladder, 150, 150f
 of gallbladder anomalies, 159, 159f
 of gastrointestinal tract anomalies, 156–158
 of genitalia, 160, 162f
 of genitourinary tract, 159–160, 159f–162f
 of head anomalies, 154f, 155, 155f
 of head circumference, 146, 146f
 of heart, 150, 150f
 of hydronephrosis, 160, 160f, 1676, 1676f
 of hypoxic-ischemic encephalopathy, 948
 of kidneys, 159, 159f
 of meningomyelocele, 152–153, 153f
 of multicystic kidneys, 159–160, 161f
 of multiple gestations, 145, 146f
 of musculoskeletal system, 162f, 162–163, 163f
 of myomas, 149, 149f
 of neck anomalies, 155, 155f
 of placenta accreta, 147–148, 148f
 of placenta previa, 147, 147f
 of placental location, 147f, 147–148, 148f
 of small-bowel obstruction, 157, 157f, 158f
 of spinal anomalies, 155, 155f
 of tracheoesophageal fistula, 157
 of two-vessel umbilical cord, 163, 163f, 164f
 of ureteropelvic junction obstruction, 160, 160f
 of vasa praevia, 147, 148f
 of ventriculomegaly, 152, 152f, 153f
 procedures suited to, 151
 safety of, 143
 techniques in, 141–143, 142f–143f
 three-dimensional, 142–143, 143f
Perineal fistula, in imperforate anus, 1399, 1400, 1402

Peripheral nerves, birth injuries to, 555–556
Peripheral perfusion, in congenital heart disease, 1216
Peristalsis, esophageal, 1358
Peritoneal dialysis, for acute renal failure, 1669–1670
Peritonitis
  fibroadhesive, 1396
  meconium, 1396
Periventricular heterotopia, X-linked, 906–907, 906f
Periventricular-intraventricular hemorrhage, 924–934
  anesthetic considerations in, 635
  assisted ventilation and, 1121
  asymptomatic, 929
  at germinal matrix, 925
  betamethasone for, 931
  catastrophic deterioration associated with, 929
  corticosteroids for, 931
  diagnosis of, 929–930, 929t, 930f
  ethamsylate for, 932–933
  fetal
    alloimmune (isoimmune) thrombocytopenia and, 369
    in utero prevention of, 214
    intrauterine infection and, 332
  grading system for, 929t
  hydrocephalus following, 1001–1002, 1001f, 1002f
  incidence of, 925
  indomethacin for, 932
  into parenchyma, 926–927, 927f, 928f
  into ventricles, 925–926, 927f
  neurodevelopmental outcome in, 931, 932f
  neuropathology of, 925–927, 926f
  pathogenesis of, 927–929
    cardiovascular factors in, 929
    intrapartum factors in, 928
    neonatal factors in, 929
    prenatal factors in, 927–928
  phenobarbital for, 931
  pneumothorax associated with, 1129
  posthemorrhagic ventricular dilation in, 925, 930
  prevention of, 931–933
  reduced incidence of, corticosteroids in, 1098
  respiratory distress related to, 1141
  ritodrine for, 931–932
  saltatory syndrome in, 929
  seizures associated with, 969
  steroids for, 931
  timing of, 925
  treatment of, 930–931
  ultrasonography of, 926f–928f, 929, 930f
  vitamin E for, 932–933
  vitamin K for, 932
  with cephalhematoma, 532
  with extracorporeal membrane oxygenation, 1171
Periventricular lesions, affecting white matter. See Leukomalacia, periventricular.
Perivillous fibrin deposition, massive, 458
Peroxisomal disorders, 988–989
  dysmorphic features of, 1625t, 1628
  tests for, 1633–1634
Persistent pulmonary hypertension of newborn. See Pulmonary hypertension, persistent.
Personnel. See Health care personnel.

Pessaries, for preterm labor prevention, 347
Pesticides
  fetal exposure to, 262, 262f
  in breast milk, 201
  paternal exposure to, 257
Petechiae, at birth, 529–530
Peutz-Jeghers syndrome, 1705
Pfeiffer syndrome (acrocephalosyndactyly, type 5), 1012–1013, 1012f
P_{gp}, in neonatal drug absorption, 192
pH
  during labor, 484, 484t
  in acid-base balance, 704
  level of, in persistent pulmonary hypertension, 1247
PHACES syndrome, cervicofacial hemangiomas in, 1708
Phagocytes, 1309–1318. See also Neutrophil(s).
  abnormalities of, 1310–1315
  activation of, by Toll-like receptors, 763–764
  adhesion disorders of, 1315–1317
  adhesion of, 767
  chemotaxis of, 767–768
    disorders of, 1317
  function of, 767–768, 1309
    extrinsic defects in, 1313b, 1312–1314
      causing neutrophilia, 1315
    intrinsic defects in, 1310–1312
      causing neutrophilia, 1314–1315
  ingestion and degranulation disorders of, 1317
  kinetics of, 1310, 1310t
  microbicidal activity of, 768
  number of, 1309–1310, 1310t
  oxidative killing disorders of, 1316b, 1317–1318, 1318t
  phagocytosis by, 768
  physiology of, 1309–1310
  production and differentiation of, 767
Phagocytosis
  by neutrophils, 766, 766f
  by phagocytes, 768
Pharmacokinetics
  clinical, in maternal-placental-fetal unit, 211–212, 212t
  fetal, 262f, 262–263, 263f, 469–471, 470t
  in neonatal drug therapy, 194, 196, 196f
Phenobarbital
  dosages of, 1789
  during labor, 471
  fetal effects of, 187t
  for cholestasis, 688
  for Crigler-Najjar syndrome type II, 1432
  for neonatal abstinence syndrome, 750
  for periventricular-intraventricular hemorrhage, 931
  for preterm labor prevention, 357
  for seizures, 974
    following hypoxic-ischemic insult, 953
  for unconjugated hyperbilirubinemia, 1445–1446
  in breast milk, 200
  plasma concentration of, dosage change in, 196
  thyroid hormone effects of, 1528
Phenobarbitone, for seizures following hypoxic-ischemic insult, 953
Phenothiazines
  neutropenia due to, 1313b
  with opioids, during labor, 471
Phenotype, 121, 562
Phenotypic variants, 565, 566t

Phenylalanine, in parenteral amino acid solutions, 684–685, 684t
Phenylephrine
  for cyanotic spells, 1268
  for neonatal tachycardia, 1260t
Phenylketonuria, 1604t
  congenital heart disease and, 1204
  cutaneous manifestation of, 1706
  maternal, affecting fetus, 1615
  screening for, 1613–1614
  variant, 1613
Phenytoin
  dosages of, 1789
  fetal effects of, 187t
  for seizures, 974
    following hypoxic-ischemic insult, 953
  in breast milk, 200
Phlebitis, umbilical, 459
Phosphatidylcholine
  in surfactant, 1075, 1076f
  surfactant pool size and, 1079, 1079f
Phosphatidylglycerol
  as predictor of lung maturity, 324, 1084
  in surfactant, 1075
Phosphatidylinositol, as predictor of lung maturity, 1084
Phosphodiesterase inhibitors, of cGMP and cAMP degradation, 1180
Phosphofructokinase deficiency, 989
Phospholipids
  in coagulation cascade, 371
  in intravenous lipid emulsions, 686t
  in surfactant, 1075, 1076f
  surfactant pool size and, 1079, 1080
Phosphorus
  absorption of, 1497
  atomic weight and valance of, 1817t
  elevated, hypocalcemia due to, 1510–1511
  excretion of, 1497–1498, 1498f
  in breast milk, 671t, 1498
    absorption and retention of, 1495t
  in enteral nutrition, 669, 670t
  in infant formula, 673t
  in parenteral nutrition, 687
  intake of, 1498–1499
  metabolism of, 1496f
  physiology of, 1497–1499
  placental transport of, 1497
  serum levels of, 1497
Photodiode, in pulse oximetry, 619
Photosensitivity
  in erythropoietic porphyria, 1714
  in neonatal lupus erythematosus, 1715
Phototherapy
  blue light–emitting diodes in, 1444
  complications of, 1444–1445
  effective, 1443
  effects of, on respiratory values, 593t
  for unconjugated hyperbilirubinemia, 1440–1445
  guidelines for, 1449f
  heat exchange between skin and environment during, 592
  home-centered, advantages of, 1444
  hypocalcemia due to, 1512
  light emission spectra in, 1442–1443, 1443f
  management of newborn readmitted for, 1441b
  mechanism of action of, 1440–1442, 1441f, 1442f
  standard lamps in, 1443–1444
  surface area exposed in, 1444
  technique of, 1442–1444, 1443f

Phototherapy—cont'd
  water and evaporative heat exchange
    during, 593
Phrenic nerve palsy
  birth-related, 545, 546f
  respiratory distress associated with,
    1145–1146, 1146f
Physical activity. See also Exercise(s).
  during pregnancy, preterm delivery and,
    334–335
  energy expenditure in, 663
Physical environment
  for fetal growth, 279–280, 280f
  of intensive care nursery, 585–605
    design considerations in, 603–605
    sensory, 597–603
      circadian rhythmicity in, 602
      hearing in, 600–602
      taste and smell in, 599–600
      touch in, 598–599
      vision in, 602–603
    thermal, 585–597. See also Heat
      exchange; Water loss.
Physical examination
  for congenital anomalies, 567–578
  for congenital heart disease, 1215–1216,
    1215b
  neonatal, 513–527
    for health promotion, 521–522
    for spontaneously-resolving conditions,
      516–517
    gestational age assessment in, 522, 523f
    introduction of examiner to mother in,
      513–514
    limitations of, 519–521
    measurements in, 514–515
    neurologic assessment in, 522b,
      522–527, 524t, 525f, 527t
    order of examination in, 514, 514b
    repeat of, 522
    routine examination in, 513b, 513–516
    significant abnormalities detected in,
      517t, 517–519
Physical stress, maternal exposure to,
  pregnancy outcome in, 260t
Physician
  ethical responsibilities of, 45
  liability of, for supervision of others,
    48–50
Physician assistants, liability of physicians
  for supervision of, 49–50
Physiologic dead space, 1093
Physiotherapy, in mechanical ventilation,
  1117
Physis, infection of, 1762
Pial arteriovenous malformations, 1244
Pierre Robin sequence
  airway obstruction in, 1144
  anesthetic implications of, 634t
  anomalies associated with, 573
  macroglossia in, 573
  micrognathia in, 573, 573f
  ocular abnormalities in, 1729
Pigmentary abnormalities, 1691, 1704–1706
Pigmented lesions, retinal, 1743
Pinna. See also Ear(s).
  embryology of, 1047
  in mechanism of hearing, 1045
Piperacillin/tazobactam, dosages of, 1789
Pituitary gland
  insufficiency of, in persistent
    hypoglycemia, 1483
  thyroid-stimulating hormone deficiency in,
    1538

Pityrosporum orbiculare, 835
Placenta
  antithyroid drug transfer across, 1532
  calcium transport across, 261,
    1492–1493
  chorioallantoic, 208
  circumvallate, 460
  cytochrome P-450 enzymes in, 210
  development of, 207–208
  drug transfer across, 183–184, 184f, 209b,
    209–210
    umbilical vein to maternal vein ratio as
      measure of, 470, 470t
  examination of, indications for, 455b,
    455
  fetal blood transfer across, 367
  fetal tissue layers of, 208
  functional unit of, 456, 456f
  human vs. animal, 208
  IgG transfer across, 214–215, 788
  in fetal growth, 284–286, 284f–287f, 286t
  infection of, 459–460
  inflammation of, 459–460
  insufficiency of
    diminished birth weight associated
      with, 285
    in post-term pregnancy, 383–384
    multiple gestations producing, 285–286,
      286f
  iodine transfer across, 1532
  lesions of, developmental/structural,
    460–461
  location of, ultrasonography of, 147f,
    147–148, 148f
  magnesium transport across, 1499
  maternal antibody transfer across, 367
  metabolic capability of, 210
  monochorionic, in twin-twin transfusion
    syndrome, 250
  nutrient transport across, 1467–1468,
    1468f
  pathology of, 455–462
    clinical correlation in, 461b, 461–462
    data sheet for, 456f
  phosphorus transport across, 1497
  structure and function of, 456, 457f, 458
  sulfatase deficiency of, in post-term
    pregnancy, 383
  thickening of, in hydrops fetalis, 397,
    398f, 399t
  thyroxine iodine transfer across, 1531
  tumors of, 460–461
  urea clearance in, 284, 285f
  vascular injury to, 456, 457f
    fetal, 458–459
    maternal, 458
  villous infarction in, 456, 458
  villous surface area of, 284, 285f
  weight of, birthweight and, 261
Placenta accreta, ultrasonography of,
  147–148, 148f
Placenta previa
  anesthetic considerations in, 480
  bleeding caused by, in preterm delivery,
    336
  ultrasonography of, 147, 147f
Placental abruption, 461
  anesthetic considerations in, 480
  vaginal bleeding caused by, preterm
    delivery and, 336
Placental data sheet, 455, 456f
Placentitis, chronic, 459
Placentomegaly, in hydrops fetalis, 397,
  398f, 399t

Plagiocephaly
  anterior, 1008
  deformational
    diagnosis of, 1013–1014, 1013f
    treatment of, 1014
  posterior, 1013
Plasma
  bilirubin transport in, 1420–1421, 1422f
  fresh-frozen
    for protein C deficiency, 1333
    for protein S deficiency, 1332–1333
    transfusion of, 1350
      dosages in, 1790
  glucose concentration in, after birth, 1469,
    1469f, 1470
Plasma renin activity, mean concentrations
  of, 1805t
Plasmapheresis, hypocalcemia due to, 1512
Plasminogen activator inhibitors, 1321,
  1322f
Platelet(s)
  destruction of, thrombocytopenia due to,
    1338–1339
  conditions associated with, 1340
  endothelial adhesion of, 1319–1320, 1319f
  function of, qualitative defects in,
    1341–1342
  in hemostasis, 1318, 1319
  in very low birthweight infants, 1814t
  production of, regulation of, 1337–1338
  transfusion of
    component definition in, 1350
    dosages in, 1790
    for alloimmune (isoimmune)
      thrombocytopenia, 369, 1339
      intrauterine, 370
    for Glanzmann thrombasthenia, 1341
    indications for, 1349
    pretransfusion testing in, 1349–1350
  underproduction of, thrombocytopenia
    due to, 1340–1341
Platelet-activating factor
  biology of, 775
  in necrotizing enterocolitis, 1409
Platelet count
  in maternal idiopathic thrombocytopenic
    purpura, 368
  normal circulating, 1338
Pleconaril, for enteroviral infection, 863
Plethysmography
  inductance, 613
  respiratory inductance, in vital capacity
    measurement, 1093
Pleural effusion, vs. chylothorax, 1135
Pleurocentesis, for nonimmune hydrops
  fetalis, 425
Pluripotent hematopoietic stem cells, 762
Plus disease, in retinopathy of prematurity,
  1748, 1749, 1750f
Pneumatosis intestinalis, in necrotizing
  enterocolitis, 1403, 1404f
Pneumocystis jiroveci (formerly
  Pneumocystis carinii), 837
Pneumocystis pneumonia
  clinical manifestations of, 837
  diagnosis and treatment of, 837–838
  incidence of, 837
  neonatal, 860
    prophylaxis for, 861
  pathology and pathogenesis of, 837
Pneumomediastinum
  in meconium aspiration syndrome, 1123
  management of, 1130
  radiography of, 1128, 1129

Pneumonia, 807–809, 1125–1127
   after mechanical ventilation, 1119
   chest radiograph of, 808
   chlamydial, 448
   clinical course of, 1126–1127
   clinical manifestations of, 808
   cytomegaloviral, after heart
      transplantation, 1270
   diagnosis of, 808–809
   etiology of, 807, 1125–1126
   incidence of, 807
   measles, 851
   meconium aspiration
      in small for gestational age infant,
         296t
      vs. bacterial pneumonia, 1124
   neonatal, chest radiograph of, 714–715
   pathogenesis and pathology of, 807–808
   pneumocystis, 837–838, 860, 861
   prognosis in, 809
   treatment of, 809
   varicella, 848
   viral, 1126
Pneumopericardium, 1128, 1129, 1129f
   vs. pericardial effusion, 1251
Pneumoperitoneum
   differential diagnosis of, 1128–1129
   in gastric perforation, 1387
Pneumotachography, 613
Pneumotachometer, for airflow
   measurement, 1091–1092
Pneumothorax, 1128–1130
   clinical features of, 1128–1129
   diagnosis of, 1129, 1129f
   in meconium aspiration syndrome, 1123
   in neonatal resuscitation, 507
   in pulmonary hypoplasia, 1129
   incidence of, 1128
   management of, 1130, 1130f
   pathophysiology of, 1128
Point-of-care test, in extracorporeal
   membrane oxygenation, 1311t, 1330
Polarization
   charge-transfer over-voltage, 610
   resistance, 610
Poliovirus infection. See Enterovirus
   infections.
Pollutants, environmental, in breast milk,
   201–202
Polybrominated biphenyls (PBBs)
   in breast milk, 202
   maternal exposure to, pregnancy outcome
      in, 260t
Polychlorinated biphenyls (PCBs)
   fetal exposure to, 257–258, 258f
   in breast milk, 201–202
   maternal exposure to, pregnancy outcome
      in, 260t
   poisoning by, 202
Polycystic kidney disease. See also
   Multicystic dysplastic kidney.
   autosomal dominant, 1680
   autosomal recessive, 1679–1680
      gene mutations in, 1662, 1662t, 1679
      histopathology of, 1679, 1680f
      management of, 1679–1680
      ultrasonography of, 725
Polycythemia, 1309
   in small for gestational age infant, 296t
   unconjugated hyperbilirubinemia due to,
      1430–1431
Polydactyly
   examination of, 518, 576–577, 577f
   fetal, ultrasonography of, 162, 163f

Polydactyly—cont'd
   of fingers, 1769, 1770f
   of toes, 1781
Polygenic traits, 132
Polyhydramnios, 418–420
   amnioreduction for, 420
   amniotic fluid index in, 220, 418, 418f
   causes of, 220t, 220–221
   congenital anomalies associated with, 414
   diagnosis of, 419f, 419–420
   drug treatment of, 221
   duodenal atresia in, 419, 419f
   etiology of, 418–419, 419b
   fetal anatomy in, 419, 419f
   in gestational diabetes mellitus, 327
   in hydrops fetalis, 397, 398f
   in preeclampsia-eclampsia, 312
   jejunoileal atresia associated with, 1397
   maximum vertical pocket in, 411t
   perinatal morbidity associated with, 414
   perinatal mortality associated with, 413
   prostaglandin synthetase inhibitors for,
      420
   treatment of, 420
   vs. maternal diabetes, 419–420
Polymerase chain reaction
   for Treponema pallidum detection, 824
   in genetic disease diagnosis, 128, 129, 130f
      basic steps in, 129
   in RhD typing, 393
   of fragile X syndrome, 131
Polymicrogyria, 992, 993f
Polymorphonuclear leukocytes. See also
   Leukocyte entries.
   in neonates, 1310t
Polymorphonuclear neutrophils. See
   Neutrophil(s).
Polymyxin, for conjunctivitis, 811
Polysplenia, interrupted inferior vena cava
   associated with, 1243
Polysplenia-heterotaxia syndrome, biliary
   atresia associated with, 1454
Polysyndactyly, in Apert syndrome, 1012
Pompe disease, 988
POMT1 gene, in Walker-Warburg syndrome,
   984
Ponderal index
   in intrauterine growth restriction, 289
   relationship between neonatal
      hypoglycemia and, 300, 301f
Poractant alfa, dosages of, 1792
Porphyria
   congenital, 1714
   congenital erythropoietic
      jaundice in, 1429–1430
      phototherapy and, 1445
   erythropoietic, 1714
   transient, 1714–1715
Port-wine stain (nevus flammeus)
   anomalies associated with, 1709
   clinical manifestations of, 1709
   examination of, 518
   in Klippel-Trénaunay-Weber syndrome,
      1709
   in Sturge-Weber syndrome, 1709
Positive end-expiratory pressure (PEEP)
   auto-PEEP, laryngeal braking in
      maintenance of, 628
   in carbon dioxide exchange, 1109
   in mechanical ventilation, 1114–1115
      for prevention of lung damage, 1120b,
         1121
   with positive pressure ventilation, in
      neonatal resuscitation, 494

Positive pressure ventilation. See also
      Continuous positive airway pressure
      (CPAP).
   in neonatal anesthesia, 628
   in neonatal resuscitation, 491–495
      anesthetic rebreathing bags in, 495
      continuous positive airway pressure
         and, 494
      criteria for provision of, 491–492
      excessive volume in, 494
      FRC formation and, 492–493, 493f–494f
      history of, 492
      inflation pressures in, in preterm
         infants, 493–494
      laryngeal airway mask in, 495
      positive end-expiratory pressure with,
         494
      self-inflating bags in, 494–495
      studies of infants requiring, 492
      T-piece resuscitation in, 495
   intermittent, history of, 12
Positron emission tomography (PET), of
   hypoxic-ischemic encephalopathy, 949
Post-term infant
   physiologic jaundice in, 1427
   time of first void and stool in, 1797t
Postdural puncture headaches, in neuraxial
   blocks, 474–475
Postmaturity (dysmaturity) syndrome, 384f,
   384–385
Postmortem, inborn errors of metabolism
   evaluation at, 1634–1635
Postneonatal mortality, 21
Postpartum period, gestational diabetes
   mellitus in
   glucose intolerance testing and, 322
   management of, 324–325
Posture, neonatal, physical examination of,
   515
Potassium
   atomic weight and valance of, 1817t
   in breast milk, 671t
   in enteral nutrition, 669, 670t
   in infant formula, 673t
   in metabolic alkalosis, 708
   in parenteral nutrition, 687
   in respiratory distress syndrome, 1106
Potassium channel blockers, for neonatal
   tachycardia, 1262b
Potassium homeostasis, role of aldosterone
   in, 701
Potter sequence
   anesthetic implications of, 634t
   congenital renal disease associated with,
      1665–1666, 1666f
Potts procedure, 1269t
Prader-Willi syndrome, genomic imprinting
   in, 126, 257
Precarcinogens, 190
Preconception counseling
   in chronic hypertension, 317
   in diabetes mellitus, 327–328
Prednisolone
   for fetal lung maturation, 213
   in breast milk, 200
Prednisone
   for Diamond-Blackfan anemia, 1307
   for hypercalcemia, 1518
   in breast milk, 200
Preeclampsia, 307
   anesthetic considerations in, 479
   mild, 313
   moderate, 313
   prevention of, 315

Preeclampsia—*cont'd*
  severe, 313
  superimposed, 307
Preeclampsia-eclampsia, 307, 308–315
  cardiovascular manifestations of, 310, 310t
  central nervous system in, 310t, 311–312
  clinical considerations in, 312–314
  clinical manifestations of,
    pathophysiologic basis of, 310t,
    310–312
  delivery in
    indications for, 314
    method of, 314
  differential diagnosis of, 312–313
  hepatic vascular changes in, 310t, 311
  intrapartum treatment of, 314, 314t
  management of, 313–314
  maternal mortality and morbidity in, 315
  outcome in, 315
  pathophysiology of, 308–312
  predisposing factors in, 312
  prevention of, 315
  prognosis of, 315
  progression of, variability in, 313, 313f
  renal vasculature in, 310t, 311
  renin-angiotensin system in, 308–309, 309f
  seizure treatment in, 315
  severity of, 313
  spiral arteries in, trophoblastic invasion
    of, 308
  superimposed, 318
  uterine blood flow in, regulation of, 308
  uterine vascular modeling in, 308
    vasomotor implications of, 309
  uterine vasculature in, 310t, 310–311
  uteroplacental circulation in, vasomotor
    regulation of, 308–309
Preeclamptic toxemia, in multiple gestations,
  376
Preferential looking, forced-choice, 1724
Pregnancy
  acute fatty liver of, 311, 1615
  alcohol consumption in, 185. *See also*
    Alcohol, fetal exposure to.
  body weight changes in, in drug
    distribution, 207t
  caffeine consumption in, 189
  chlamydial infections in, 447–448, 448t
  complicated by diabetes mellitus,
    321–328. *See also* Diabetes mellitus,
    gestational.
  daily vitamin D supplements during, 1502,
    1512
  diabetes mellitus in. *See* Diabetes mellitus,
    maternal.
  drug absorption in, 205–206
  drug distribution in, 206t, 206–207, 207t
  drug metabolism in, 207
  drug use in. *See also* Fetus, drug exposure
    of; Substance abuse.
    potential adverse effects of, 185, 186t,
    187t–189t
    timing of, 184–185, 185f
  enterovirus infection in, 862
  environmental exposures concurrent with,
    258–259
  ethical issues in, 37–39
  evaluation of, perinatal ultrasonography
    in, 146–151
  fetal death in. *See* Fetal death.
  first-trimester of
    maternal nutritional status in, 281
    perinatal ultrasonographic studies in,
    145, 145f

Pregnancy—*cont'd*
  HIV infection in. *See also* Human
    immunodeficiency virus (HIV)
    infection.
    vertical transmission of, prevention of,
    214
  hypertensive disorders of, 307–318. *See
    also* Hypertension; Preeclampsia-
    eclampsia.
  immune thrombocytopenic purpura in,
    367–368
    treatment of, 368
  infections during, 429–449
  maternal acceptance of, 646
  maternal autonomy vs. fetal rights in, 37
  maternal-infant attachment in, 645–647
  maternal metabolic adjustments during,
    275
  multifetal, reduction of, in multiple
    gestation, 381
  myasthenia gravis during, 372–373
  nontherapeutic agents in, self-
    administration of, 185, 189
  parent-infant attachment and. *See* Parent-
    infant attachment.
  parvovirus infection in, 442, 869
  post-term, 383–388
    dysmaturity in, 384f, 384–385
    fetal well-being in, 385t, 385–386
    induction of labor in, 386
      methods of, 386b, 386–387
    macrosomia in, 384
    risks of, 383–385
      reduction of, 387–388
    twins and, 387
  recommended iodine intake during, 1537
  rubeola in, 852
  serum protein concentrations during, in
    drug distribution, 207t
  smoking in, 185, 189
  state intervention in, 38
  substance abuse in. *See* Substance abuse.
  teratogenic risks during, 133–134
  tobacco effects on, 740. *See also* Tobacco
    use.
  toxoplasmosis in, 215–216, 216b, 838–840
  urinary tract infections in, 429–432
  use of cocaine or "crack" in, 189
  varicella-zoster virus infections in,
    435–436, 848
  weight gain in
    fetal growth and, 280–282, 281f, 282b,
    282f
    limiting, 281–282
    vs. prepregnancy weight, 280, 281f
Preload, in cardiac output, 1266–1267
Premature contractions
  atrial
    fetal assessment for, 1209
    in sinus bradycardia, 1259
  supraventricular, 1259
  treatment of, 1265
  ventricular, 1259
Premature decidual activation, in initiation
  of labor, 333
Premature rupture of membranes
  bacterial infections associated with,
    338–339
  preterm
    antibiotics for, 355, 431
    group B streptococcus in, 444
    preterm delivery and, 336
    preterm labor associated with, 430–431
    vs. oligohydramnios, 414–415

Prematurity, anemia of, 1306
Premutagens, 190
Prenatal care. *See* Antenatal care.
Prepregnancy weight, fetal growth and, 280,
  281f
Prerenal azotemia, 1668, 1668t
Pressure, in cardiovascular hemodynamics,
  1211
Pressure sensors, in respiratory monitoring,
  613–614
Preterm delivery. *See also* Delivery.
  definition of, 331
  ethical issues in, 39–40
  fetal viability and, 39–40
  in cocaine abuse, 745
  prevention of, 344–345
    in bronchopulmonary dysplasia, 1167
  risk factor(s) for, 333–339, 335b
    bleeding as, 336
    cervical changes as, 336
    demographics as, 334–335, 335b
    infection as, 337–339
    multiple gestation as, 336
    obstetric history as, 335, 335t
    uterine changes as, 335–336
  spontaneous
    determining risk of, 341t
    recurrence of, 335t
Preterm infant
  Apgar score of, 1062
  autonomic nervous system in, 1055, 1055t
  behavioral assessment of, 1062,
    1064–1066, 1066f
  behavioral language of, 1055t, 1055–1058,
    1056f, 1058f
    in neonatal intensive care unit, 1056f,
    1056–1057
  behavioral observation of, 1054–1055
    in neonatal intensive care unit, 1056f,
    1058–1061, 1059f–1061f
  blood pressure ranges in, 1796t
  brain in, interaction between environment
    and, 1052f, 1052–1054, 1053f
  cerebral palsy in, 332
  congenital heart disease in, 1251–1252
  developmental care model for, 1057–1058,
    1058f
  diseases associated with, 23
  energy expenditure in, 661–663, 662t
  enteral nutrition of. *See* Enteral nutrition.
  formula for, 670, 672, 673t–674t
  growth charts for, 1800f
  hypocalcemia in, 1510
  immaturity of vitamin D activation
    pathway in, 1503
  immunization schedule for, 1819
    with birthweights of less than 2000
      grams, 1820
    with birthweights of more than 2000
      grams, 1819
  immunoglobulin concentrations in, 1809t
  incubators for. *See* Incubators.
  metabolic acidosis of, 710
  morbidity associated with, 22–23
  motor nervous system in, 1055, 1055t
  nephrocalcinosis in, 1518
  neurobehavioral development of,
    1051–1067
    assessment of, 1061–1063
      overview in, 1063–1064
    framework in, 1051–1052
    interaction between brain and
      environment in, 1052f, 1052–1054,
      1053f

Preterm infant—cont'd
language in, 1055t, 1055–1058, 1056f, 1058f
observation of, 1054–1055
neurologic assessment of, 526–527, 527t, 1062
ocular findings in, 1726, 1726f
parental attachment to, 653–657
parenteral nutrition of. *See* Parenteral nutrition.
parents of, well-being of, 1057
physiologic jaundice in, 1426–1427, 1427f
plasma 17-hydroxyprogesterone in, 1806t
plasma albumin in, 1804t
plasma ammonia levels in, 1803t
plasma immunoglobulin in, 1809t
respiratory disorders of, 1122–1146. *See also specific disorder.*
respiratory distress in, 292f
resting metabolism in, 662
self-regulatory competence of, 1057
sepsis incidence in, 793
serum cortisol ranges in, 1805t
serum electrolyte values in, 1801t
skin characteristics in, 1715–1716
state system in, 1055, 1055t
survival of, 331, 331t
time of first void and stool in, 1797t
total protein in, 1804t
unconjugated hyperbilirubinemia in, 1426–1427, 1427f
viability of, border of, definition of, 15
whole blood ionized calcium in, 1802t
zinc and copper concentrations in, 1802t
Preterm labor. *See also* Labor.
definition of, 331
in multiple gestations, 376
morbidity associated with, 332, 332t
onset of
genital tract infection in, 333, 334f, 337
oxytocin in, 333
progesterone withdrawal in, 333
prostaglandins in, 332–333
pathogenesis of, 332–333, 334f
prediction of, 339–344
biochemical predictors in, 340–343
classic predictors in, 340, 341t
ultrasound predictors in, 343–344
premature rupture of membranes and, 430–431
prevention of, antibiotics for, 431
progesterone for, 346
risk factors for, 333–339, 335b
spontaneous, 331
treatment of, 345–357
antibiotics in, 354–355
bed rest in, 345
calcium channel blockers in, 352–353
cerclage in, 346–347
corticosteroids in, 355–356
COX-2 inhibitors in, 352
hydration in, 345
indomethacin in, 351–352
magnesium sulfate in, 349–350
nitric oxide donors in, 353–354
oxytocin antagonists in, 353
pessaries in, 347
phenobarbital in, 357
prostaglandin synthetase inhibitors in, 350–352
purpose of, 345
ritodrine in, 348–349
sedation in, 346
sulindac in, 352

Preterm labor—cont'd
β-sympathomimetic agents in, 347–349
terbutaline in, 349
thyrotropin-releasing hormone in, 356–357
tocolytic agents in, 347–354
vitamin K in, 357
vs. cervical incompetence, 336
Primaquine, for malaria, 836
Primidone
fetal effects of, 187t
in breast milk, 200
Procainamide
for fetal arrhythmias, 223t, 224
for neonatal tachycardia, 1260t, 1261b, 1263
with quinidine, for neonatal tachycardia, 1262b
Professional discussion, regarding intersex disorders, 1557
Progesterone, in preterm labor prediction, 342
Progesterone withdrawal theory, in initiation of labor, 333
Progestins
fetal effects of, 188t
maternal ingestion of
fetal masculinization due to, 1584–1585
hypospadias associated with, 1566f, 1577
Programmed cell death
in brain development, 895–896, 896f
in hypoxic-ischemic encephalopathy, 943
Progressive epileptic syndromes, 971, 973. *See also* Seizures.
Promethazine, with opioids, during labor, 471
Propafenone, for neonatal tachycardia, 1262b, 1264
Propionic acidemia, 1608t
Propofol, in neonatal anesthesia, 638–639
Propranolol
fetal effects of, 188t
for cyanotic spells, 1268
for neonatal hypertension, 1673t
for neonatal tachycardia, 1260t, 1262b, 1263
Proptosis
due to congenital deformities, 1736
in orbital cellulitis, 1734
in orbital histiocytosis, 1736
in orbital tumors, 1734, 1735
Propylthiouracil
congenital malformations associated with, 186t
fetal effects of, 188t
for thyrotoxicosis, 1549
in breast milk, 200
Prostacyclin. *See* Epoprostenol.
Prostaglandin(s)
in initiation of labor, 386b, 387
in preeclampsia, 308
in preterm labor and delivery, 332, 337–338
Prostaglandin E₁
apnea due to, 1266
dosages of, 1793
for establishing ductal patency
in congenital heart disease, 1266
in transposition of great arteries, 1223
long-term therapy with, in preterm infants, 1251
Prostaglandin E₂, in intra-amniotic infection, 337–338

Prostaglandin F₂ₐ, in intra-amniotic infection, 337–338
Prostaglandin synthetase inhibitors
for polyhydramnios, 420
for preterm labor prevention, 350–352
Protamine, dosages of, 1790
Protein(s). *See also specific protein.*
allergic enteropathy due to, 1372
anticoagulant, congenital deficiencies of, 1332–1333
energy stored as, 663
in body composition, during gestation, 661, 662t
in breast milk, 664, 671t
in hemostasis, 1321
in infant formula, 664–665, 673t
loss of, in extremely low birthweight infant, 681, 682f
malabsorption of, 1367–1368
manipulation of, for inborn errors of metabolism, 1652–1653, 1653t
metabolism of, effect of thyroid hormone on, 1524
parathormone-releasing, fetal calcium regulation by, 1492–1493
pharmacologic binding of, in neonate, 193
requirements for
in enteral nutrition, 664–665
in parenteral nutrition, 681–682, 682f
serum gestational, in drug distribution, 207t
total, in preterm infant, 1804t
vitamin K–dependent, 1324
Protein C, congenital deficiency of, 1332–1333
Protein S, congenital deficiency of, 1332
treatment of, 1332–1333
α₁-Proteinase inhibitor deficiency, in bronchopulmonary dysplasia, 1162
Proteinuria
definition of, 307
in kidney disease, 1667
Proteus syndrome, 1710
Prothrombin 20210A allele, thrombosis due to, 1333
Prothrombin time
in evaluation of coagulation factor deficiencies, 1320
measurement of, 1804t
prolonged, in hemophilia A and B, 1325
Protozoal infections, 836–840
Prune belly syndrome
anesthetic implications of, 633t
in hydronephrosis, 1678, 1678f
Pseudocyst(s). *See also* Cyst(s).
chest radiograph of, 714
meconium, ultrasonography of, 157, 158f
Pseudodislocation, birth-related, 554–555
Pseudohermaphroditism
female, 1577–1586, 1577f
male, 1574–1577
Pseudohypoaldosteronism
hyponatremia and, 701–702
type I, 701
type II (Gordon syndrome), 701, 710
vs. cystic fibrosis, 702
Pseudomonas infection
cutaneous, 1698
in gastroenteritis, 813
Pseudoptosis, 1732
Pseudostrabismus, 1746
Psychotic agents, fetal effects of, 187t

Ptosis, 1731–1732
  causes of, 1732
  congenital, 1731, 1731f
  examination for, 524–525
  in orbital histiocytosis, 1736
PTPN11 gene, in juvenile myelomonocytic
    leukemia, 1342
PubMed database, 80
Pudendal nerve blocks, 469
Pulmonary. See also Lung(s).
Pulmonary agenesis, 1131
Pulmonary arteriovenous fistula, 1135
Pulmonary artery
  banding of, for single ventricle therapy,
    1231
  in double-outlet right ventricle, 1231–1232
  pressure of, echocardiographic
    measurement of, 1219, 1220t
  stenosis of
    in truncus arteriosus, 1230
    peripheral, 1237–1238
      balloon angioplasty for, 1273–1274
Pulmonary artery sling, 1251
Pulmonary atresia
  balloon valvuloplasty for, 1273
  with intact ventricular septum and
    pulmonary stenosis, 1227–1228
Pulmonary circulation
  increased, cyanotic mixing lesions in,
    1221b, 1222, 1228–1231
  radiography in assessment of, 1217, 1217f
  restricted, cyanotic defects in, 1221–1222,
    1221b, 1224–1228
Pulmonary edema
  bronchopulmonary dysplasia related to,
    1161
  in cor pulmonale, diuretics for, 1244
  radiography of, 1217, 1217b, 1217f
Pulmonary function, 1087–1097
  airflow measurements in, 1091–1092
  assessment of, 1087–1097
  blood gas measurement in. See Blood
    gases.
  clinical techniques in measurement of,
    1095–1097
    end-inspiratory occlusion in, 1095,
      1096f
    expiratory volume clamping in, 1096
    Mead-Whittenberger technique in,
      1094f, 1095
    multiple-interruption occlusion
      technique in, 1096
    tidal flow-volume loops in, 1095, 1095f
  compliance in, 1093–1094, 1094f
  cyanosis in, 1088
  during assisted ventilation, 1108–1109,
    1108f, 1109f
  grunting in, 1088
  in bronchopulmonary dysplasia, 1163,
    1163t, 1164f, 1167
  lung volume in, 1092–1093, 1092f
  nasal flaring in, 1088
  physiologic measurements in, 1091–1097
  pressures in, 1093
  resistance in, 1094
  respiratory rate in, 1087, 1088f
  retractions in, 1088
  shunting evaluation in, 1091
  time constant in, 1094–1095
    calculation of, 1096
  work of breathing in, 1095
Pulmonary hemorrhage
  after surfactant therapy, 1104, 1104b
  causes of, 1127

Pulmonary hemorrhage—cont'd
  chest radiograph of, 715
  in small for gestational age infant, 296t
Pulmonary hypertension
  echocardiographic measurement of, 1219,
    1220t
  persistent, 1245–1248
    anesthetic considerations in, 627, 635
    diagnosis of, 1246–1247
    etiology of, 1245–1246, 1246f
    extracorporeal membrane oxygenation
      in, 1174–1175, 1174b
    hyperoxia-hyperventilation test of,
      1090–1091
    in congenital diaphragmatic hernia, 1132
    lethal lung development disorders
      presenting as, 1133–1135
    nitric oxide therapy in, 1177–1180
    prostacyclin therapy in, 1174, 1180
    radiography of, 718, 718f
    seizures associated with, 969, 970f
    sildenafil therapy for, 1180
    treatment of, 1247–1248, 1247t
  pulmonary vascular maturation and,
    1206–1207
Pulmonary hypoplasia, 1073–1074
  bilateral, 1132
  classification of, 1131, 1131b
  clinical associations of, 1073–1074, 1074b
  clinical course of, 1131
  congenital diaphragmatic hernia and,
    1131–1132, 1132f
  extracorporeal membrane oxygenation in,
    1172
  in oligohydramnios, 416, 416f, 417f,
    1073–1074, 1132–1133
  intraventricular hemorrhage associated
    with, 1129
  pathophysiology of, 1131, 1131b
  pneumothorax in, 1129
  secondary, 1073, 1074b
Pulmonary interstitial emphysema, 1130–1131
  chest radiograph of, 714, 714f
  forms of, 1130–1131
  management of, 1131
Pulmonary irritant reflexes, 1137
Pulmonary lymphangiectasia, congenital,
  1135
Pulmonary sequestration. See Lung(s),
  sequestration of.
Pulmonary status, fetal, assessment of, 416f,
  416–417, 417f
Pulmonary stretch receptors, in respiratory
  timing, 1136
Pulmonary valve
  absence of, in tetralogy of Fallot, 1225
  stenosis of
    anatomy and pathophysiology of, 1238
    balloon dilation of, in complex
      congenital heart disease, 1272–1273
    balloon valvuloplasty for, 1272, 1272f
    clinical presentation of, 1238
    defects associated with, 1238
    in double-outlet right ventricle, 1232
    laboratory evaluation of, 1238
    management of, 1238
    prognosis in, 1238
    vs. tetralogy of Fallot, 1238
Pulmonary vascular resistance
  afterload management and, 1267
  anesthetic considerations in, 627
  decrease of
    after first breath, 485, 485f
    at birth, 1206

Pulmonary vascular resistance—cont'd
  in pathophysiology of congenital heart
    disease, 1206–1207
  persistent pulmonary hypertension related
    to, 1246
Pulmonary vein
  fetal assessment of, 1208–1209
  stenosis of, balloon angioplasty for, 1274
Pulmonary venous connection, total
  anomalous, 1228–1229, 1229f
Pulse(es), assessment of
  in coarctation of aorta and aortic arch
    interruption, 1234, 1234t
  in congenital heart disease, 1216
Pulse oximetry, 618–621
  clinical issues affecting, 619b
  continuous, during surgery, 636
  fetal, USDA approval of, 173
  in aortic stenosis, 1233
  in bronchopulmonary dysplasia, 1165
  in congenital heart disease, 1216
  in respiratory distress syndrome,
    1102–1103
  in truncus arteriosus, 1230
  instrumentation for, 618–619
  limitations of, 619b, 619–620
    potential solutions to, 620f, 620–621
  low noise optical probe in, 620, 620f
  principles of, 618f, 618–619, 619f
Pupil(s)
  abnormalities of, 1746–1747
  absent response to light, in preterm
    infants, 1726
  examination of, 1722
  Marcus Gunn, 1722
  white, 1739–1743
    examination of, 1739, 1739f
    in cataract, 1739–1741, 1740f, 1740t
    in Norrie disease, 1743
    in persistent hyperplastic primary
      vitreous, 1742
    in retinal dysplasia, 1742–1743
    in retinoblastoma, 1741–1742, 1741f
    in subluxed lens, 1741, 1741f
Pupillary light reflex, in optic nerve
  assessment, 524
Pupillary membrane, persistent, 1738
Purified protein derivative (PPD) skin test,
  827
Purkinje fibers, cardiac action potential for,
  609, 610f
Pustular melanosis, transient neonatal, 1692,
  1692f
Pyelonephritis, acute, in pregnancy, 430
Pyknocytosis, infantile, 1430
Pyloric atresia, 1387–1388, 1388f
  "windsock" web in, 1387, 1388
Pyloric stenosis
  hypertrophic, 1388–1390, 1389f–1390f
    etiology and pathophysiology of,
      1388–1389
    laparoscopic pyloromyotomy for,
      1389–1390, 1390f
    ultrasonography of, 1389, 1389f
    unconjugated hyperbilirubinemia due to,
      1432
Pyloromyotomy, laparoscopic, for
  hypertrophic pyloric stenosis,
  1389–1390, 1390f
Pyoderma, staphylococcal, 1697
Pyrazinamide, for tuberculosis, 827, 827t
Pyridoxine. See Vitamin B$_6$.
Pyridoxine-responsive seizures, 1617
Pyriform aperture, stenosis of, 1147

Pyrimethamine with sulfadiazine, for congenital toxoplasmosis, 216, 449, 839
Pyropoikilocytosis, hereditary, 1300, 1301f
Pyruvate, analysis of, in inborn errors of metabolism, 1632–1633
Pyruvate carboxylase, deficiency of, 1648
Pyruvate dehydrogenase, deficiency of, 1642
Pyruvate kinase, deficiency of, jaundice due to, 1429

Q

QRS complex
  in accessory pathway reentrant tachycardia, 1255
  in junctional ectopic tachycardia, 1257
  in ventricular premature contractions, 1259
  in ventricular tachycardia, 1257
QRS tachycardia
  narrow, 1261
  wide, 1261, 1263
Quadruplets, Hellin-Zellany rule for, 375
Quality of neonatal intensive care. See Neonatal intensive care, quality of.
Quantitative assays, in erythroblastosis fetalis screening, 395
Questionnaire for Identifying Children with Chronic Conditions, 1041
Quinidine
  for fetal arrhythmias, 223t, 224t
  for malaria, 836–837
  for neonatal tachycardia, 1260t, 1261b
  in breast milk, 199
  with procainamide, for neonatal tachycardia, 1262b
Quinine, for malaria, 836–837

R

Rabson-Mendenhall syndrome, 276
Race. See also specific racial group.
  congenital anomaly prevalence and, 565–566, 566t
  congenital heart disease and, 1205
  in preeclampsia-eclampsia, 312
  in preterm delivery, 334–335, 335b
  low birthweight in, 23
  neonatal mortality rates and, 20–21, 21f
Radial nerve palsy, birth-related, 555
Radiant bed
  heat exchange between skin and environment during care on, 592
  overhead (open), 596
Radiant heaters, heat exchange under, 587–588
  between skin and environment, 590–591
Radiation
  heat exchange through, calculation of, 586
  ionizing
    fetal exposure to, placenta-independent pathway in, 261, 261f, 262f
    maternal exposure to, pregnancy outcome in, 260t
Radiofrequency ablation, for sacrococcygeal teratoma, 245
Radiography
  of cardiovascular system, 717–718, 718f
  of cephalhematoma, 532

Radiography—cont'd
  of chest, 713–717. See also Chest radiography.
  of congenital vertical talus, 1781, 1781f
  of developmental dysplasia of hip, 1775, 1775f
  of diaphragmatic paralysis, 545
  of duodenal atresia, 719, 719f, 1391, 1391f
  of gastrointestinal tract, 718–722. See also Abdominal radiography; Upper gastrointestinal radiography.
  of humeral fracture, 1761, 1762f
  of intrauterine infection, 729, 729f
  of knee hyperextension and subluxation, 1777, 1777f
  of meconium ileus, 1395–1396
  of metatarsus adductus, 1778
  of necrotizing enterocolitis, 1403, 1404f
  of osteomyelitis, 814, 815f, 1763–1764, 1764f
  of postnatal infection, 729–730
  of renal function, 1667
  of respiratory distress syndrome, 1101, 1101f
  of rickets, 730, 730f
  of septic arthritis, 1766, 1766f
  of skeleton, 729–730
  of skull fractures, 535
  of spine, 1756
  of subgaleal hemorrhage, 534
  of talipes equinovarus, 1780
Radionuclide imaging
  of biliary atresia, 723, 723f
  of congenital hypothyroidism, interpretation of results of, 1542–1543
  of extrahepatic bile ducts, 1455
  of osteomyelitis, 1764
  of osteomyelitis and septic arthritis, 814
  of renal function, 1667
  of thyroid disorders, 1530
Radioulnar synostosis, congenital, 1767
Radius
  fracture of, birth-related, 553–554
  hypoplasia of, 1767–1768, 1768f
Range-of-motion exercises, for deformational plagiocephaly, 1014
Ranitidine, dosages of, 1791
Rapacuronium bromide, in neonatal anesthesia, 640
Rapid plasma reagin test, for syphilis, 823–824
Rash
  in carboxylase deficiency, 1620
  maculopapular, 816
Rastelli procedure, 1269t
Reactive oxygen species
  formation of, in hypoxia-ischemia, 498
  in microbicidal activity, of neutrophils, 766
Receptor-ligand interactions, in neutrophil adhesion, 764, 765f
Reciprocal translocation, of chromosomes, 116, 117f
Recombinant tissue plasminogen activator, for thrombosis, 1334t
Rectourethral fistula, 1400
Rectovestibular fistula, 1400
Rectum
  cystic duplications of, 1393
  development of, 1362–1363
Red blood cell(s)
  bone marrow production of, 1288
  destruction of, 1428
    conditions associated with, 1428b

Red blood cell(s)—cont'd
  disorder(s) of, 1293–1309
    anemia as, 1293–1295, 1294b, 1295t, 1296f
      due to accelerated red blood cell destruction, 1297–1302, 1297t, 1298t, 1300f, 1301f, 1302b
      due to blood loss, 1295–1297
      due to inefficient red blood cell production, 1305–1308
      hemoglobin variants as, 1303–1305, 1304b
      methemoglobinemia as, 1308–1309
      polycythemia as, 1309
      thalassemias as, 1302–1303
    enzymatic defects of, unconjugated hyperbilirubinemia due to, 1429–1430
  function of, 1290, 1290f, 1290t
  hepatic production of, 1287
  indices for, during prenatal and postnatal development, 1291, 1292t, 1293, 1293f
  life span of, 1420
  lysis of, 1419
  parameters for, in very low birthweight infants, 1810t
  reference values for
    during first 12 weeks of life, 1292t
    on first postnatal day, 1292t
  structural defects of, 1299–1300, 1300f
    unconjugated hyperbilirubinemia due to, 1430
  transfusion of
    autologous, 1347–1348
    cell preparation for, 1349
    for adrenal hemorrhage, 552
    for liver rupture, 550
    for splenic rupture, 550
    indications for, 1348, 1348b
    pretransfusion testing in, 1343t, 1348–1349
  yolk sac production of, 1287
Red reflex, on physical examination, 515, 1721
  of pupil, 1722
  of white pupil, 1739, 1739f
5α-Reductase deficiency, 1575, 1576f
Reduction-oxidation (redox) reaction, in cardiac monitoring, 610
Reentrant tachycardia, 1253, 1253t, 1254
Reflex. See specific reflex, e.g., Hering-Breuer reflex.
Refsum disease, 1628
Refusal of treatment, maternal autonomy vs. fetal rights in, 38
Relative risk, 82
Relative risk reduction, 82
Religion, medical ethics affected by, 37
Remifentanil
  for labor pain, 472
  in neonatal anesthesia, 639
REN gene, in preeclampsia-eclampsia syndrome, 309
Renal. See also Kidney(s).
Renal agenesis, 1675–1676
  in congenital scoliosis, 1770
  in oligohydramnios, 415f, 415–416
  pulmonary hypoplasia in, 1132–1133
Renal artery, thromboembolism of, 1670, 1674
Renal disease, 1664–1667
  glycosuria in, 1667
  hematuria in, 1667
  history in, 1664–1665, 1665b

Renal disease—*cont'd*
  inherited, 1675t, 1678–1680
    gene mutations in, 1661–1662, 1662t
  laboratory evaluation in, 1666
  physical examination in, 1665–1666, 1666f
  polycystic. *See* Polycystic kidney disease.
  proteinuria in, 1667
  radiographic evaluation of, 1667
  renal function assessment in, 1666
  urinalysis in assessment of, 1666
Renal dysplasia, 1676
  defects associated with, 1676
  grading of, 160
  multicystic. *See* Multicystic dyplastic
    kidney.
Renal excretion
  of calcium, 1495–1496, 1496f
  of drugs
    maternal, 207
    neonatal, 195f, 195–196
  of magnesium, 1499–1500
  of phosphorus, 1497–1498, 1498f
Renal failure, acute, 1668–1670
  causes of, 1668, 1668t
  evaluation of, 1669
  in asphyxia, 951
  intrinsic, 1668
  medical management of, 1669
  obstructive, 1668–1669
  prerenal azotemia in, 1668, 1668t
  prognosis in, 1670
  renal replacement therapy for, 1669–1670,
    1670t
Renal insufficiency, indomethacin causing,
  703
Renal replacement therapy, 1670t, 1669–1670
  continuous, 1670
  indications for, 1669, 1669t
Renal solute load, water requirements in,
  699
Renal tubular acidosis, 708–710
  causes of, 1680
  classification of, 709b, 1680
  distal, 708–709, 709b
  hypercalcemia due to, 1516
  hyperkalemic, 709, 709b
  neonatal anesthesia and, 629
  proximal, 709, 709b
Renal tubular necrosis, acute
  hematuria in, 1667
  in intrinsic renal failure, 1668
  perinatal asphyxia and, 702
Renal tubules
  acidification mechanisms in, 705, 705f
  defects of
    hypomagnesemia in, 1519
    laboratory findings in, 1629t
    metabolic acidosis in, 1637–1638, 1637t
Renal vein thrombosis, 1331, 1674–1675
  treatment of, 1675
  ultrasonography of, 725–726, 1675
Renin-angiotensin system, role of, in
  preeclampsia, 308–309, 309f
Renin gene expression, in preeclampsia, 309
Reperfusion/reoxygenation, formation of
  reactive oxygen species in, 498
Reproduction, assisted
  application of perinatal ultrasonography
    in, 145
  genetic evaluation in, 139
Reproductive system. *See also* Genitourinary
  tract; *specific part.*
  dysfunction of, fetal environmental
    exposure and, 264

Reptilase time assay, for vitamin K
  deficiency, 1328
Res ipsa loquitur doctrine, 53
Resistance
  in cardiovascular hemodynamics, 1211
  pulmonary, 1094
    calculation of, 1108
Resistance polarization, in cardiac
  monitoring, 610
Respiration. *See also* Breathing.
  control of. *See* Breathing, control of.
  in asphyxia, 487, 487f
  monitoring of, 612–614
    surface and noninvasive, 613
    techniques in, 613f, 613–614
  patterns of, in premature infants,
    1137–1138, 1137f, 1138f
Respiratory acidosis, 708
  in respiratory distress syndrome, 1106
Respiratory alkalosis, 708
  laboratory findings in, 1629t
Respiratory chain complexes, defects of
  cardiomyopathy in, 1618t, 1618–1619
  clinical patterns in, 1643–1644
  hepatocellular disease associated with,
    1622
  lactic acidemia and, 1643–1645, 1643t
Respiratory distress
  airway obstruction in, 1143–1144, 1143b
  choanal atresia in, 1144, 1144f, 1147
  diaphragmatic disorders in, 1145–1146,
    1146f
  due to vascular rings, 1250
  extrapulmonary causes of, 1141–1146,
    1141b
    central nervous system disorders in,
      1141
    neuromuscular disease in, 1142–1143
    spinal cord injury in, 1141–1142
  in congenital heart disease, examination
    of, 1215
  in developing countries, 104–105, 105t
    clinical scoring system for, 105, 105t
    nasal continuous positive airway
      pressure for, 105
  in preterm infants, 292f
  laryngeal lesions in, 1149–1155, 1150f
  nasal and nasopharyngeal lesions in,
    1147–1148
  oral and oropharyngeal lesions in,
    1148–1149, 1148f
  Pierre Robin syndrome in, 1144
  rib cage abnormalities in, 1144–1145, 1145f
  transient tachypnea in, 1127
  with pyelonephritis, 430
Respiratory distress syndrome (RDS),
  1097–1107
  apnea in, 1138–1139, 1138f
  assisted ventilation in. *See also* Assisted
    ventilation.
    complications of, 1118–1122, 1118b
    pulmonary mechanics in, 1108–1109
  blood gas assessment in, 1101–1103
    arterial sampling in, 1102
    pulse oximetry in, 1102–1103
  chest radiograph of, 713–714, 714f
  clinical features of, 1099–1101
  coagulation defects in, 1330
  continuous positive airway pressure for,
    1112–1113
  cyanosis in, 1088, 1100
  germinal matrix-intraventricular
    hemorrhage in, 929
  grunting in, 1088, 1100

Respiratory distress syndrome (RDS)—*cont'd*
  in low birthweight infant, 23
  incidence of, 1097, 1098f
  nasal flaring in, 1088
  oxygen therapy for, 1112
  pathophysiology of, 1099, 1099f, 1100f
  prevention of, induced lung maturation
    in, 1085–1086, 1087f, 1098–1099
  pulmonary mechanics in, 1108–1109,
    1108f, 1109f
  radiographic findings in, 1101, 1101f
  retractions in, 1088, 1100
  risk factors for, 1097, 1098f
  surfactant pool size and, 1078–1079, 1078f
  surfactant protein B deficiency in,
    1076–1077
  surfactant therapy for, 1103–1105, 1104b
    functional residual capacity increased
      by, 1083
    in developing countries, 105–106
    lung damage prevention with, 1121
    prophylactic approach to, 1103–1104
  treatment of, 1101–1107
    acid-base therapy in, 1106
    antibiotics in, 1107
    blood transfusion in, 1107
    cardiovascular management in,
      1106–1107
    fluid, electrolytes, and nutrition in,
      1105–1106
    surfactant therapy in, 1103–1105. *See
      also* Respiratory distress syndrome,
      surfactant therapy for.
    thermoregulation in, 1105
Respiratory inductance plethysmography, in
  vital capacity measurement, 1093
Respiratory insufficiency of prematurity,
  1097
Respiratory quotient, fetal, 275
Respiratory rate, 1087, 1088f
  in respiratory distress syndrome, 1100
Respiratory syncytial virus immune globulin,
  853–854, 855
Respiratory syncytial virus infection, 852–855
  clinical manifestations of, 853
  prevention of, 853–855, 854b
    in bronchopulmonary dysplasia, 1167
  transmission of, 853
  treatment of, 853
Respiratory syndrome, severe acute, 873–874
Respiratory tract, 1069–1180. *See also* Lung
  entries; Pulmonary *entries.*
  disorders of, in preterm and term infants,
    1122–1146. *See also specific disorder.*
  physiology of, anesthesia and, 628
  upper airway lesions in, 1146–1155
  water/heat exchange between
    environment and, 586–587, 592–594.
    See also Heat exchange; Water loss.
Respondeat superior doctrine, 49
Resuscitation, neonatal, 483–508
  against parents' wishes, 59–61
  airway clearance in, 490
  anesthetic rebreathing bags in, 495
  anticipation of, 488
  Apgar score and, 488, 489t
  at birth, conditions requiring, 950b
  birth transition and, 484–486, 484t, 485f
  chest compressions in, 501–502, 501f
  congenital anomaly screening in, 508
  continuous positive airway pressure in,
    494
    with positive end-expiratory pressure,
      494

Resuscitation, neonatal—cont'd
diaphragmatic hernia and, 507
dopamine in, 503t, 505
drug-depressed infant in, 505
drugs in, 502–505, 503t
elements of, 489–490, 489b, 489f
endotracheal intubation for, 495–498,
495t, 496f–497f, 497t
epinephrine in, 502–504, 503t
equipment for, 488
erythroblastosis fetalis in, 507–508
ethical issues in, fetal viability and, 39
feeding in, 506
fluids in, 506
for asphyxia, 950–951
glucose in, 506
history of, 6–7, 14t
hydrops fetalis in, 507–508
immediate care for stabilized infant in,
505–506
in developing countries
methods of, 99, 99f, 104, 105t
Neonatal Resuscitation Program in, 93,
104
initial steps in, 490–491
laryngeal mask airway in, 495
legal considerations in, 59–61
Messenger case in, 60, 61
Miller case in, 60–61, 61b
meconium aspiration and, 506–507
oxygen therapy in, 498–501
free-flow oxygen in, 490–491
room air vs. oxygen in, 499–500, 500f
personnel for, 488
pneumothorax in, 507
positive pressure ventilation in, 491–495
preparation for, 488
prolonged assisted ventilation in, 505–506
self-inflating bags in, 494–495
sequence of steps in, 951
sodium bicarbonate in, 503t, 505
T-piece resuscitation in, 495
tactile stimulation in, 490
thermal management in, 490, 490f
volume expanders in, 503t, 504, 504b
Reticular dysgenesis, neutropenia in,
1311–1312
Reticulocyte(s), corrected, in very low
birthweight infants, 1810t
Reticulocyte count, in cord blood, 1293
Retina
abnormalities of, 1743–1745
hereditary, 1743
dysplasia of, 1742–1743
examination of, 1723
fold of, 1743
hemorrhage of
due to birth injury, 539
in shaken baby syndrome, 1727
infectious diseases of, 1743–1744
pigmented lesions of, 1743
vessels of, examination of, 1723
Retinitis, in candidiasis, 831
Retinitis pigmentosa, genetics of, 121
Retinoblastoma
diagnosis of, 1742
secondary malignancies in, 1742
treatment and prognosis of, 1742
white pupil in, 1741–1742, 1741f
Retinoic acid, cardiac abnormalities related
to, 1200
Retinopathy
familial exudative vitreoretinopathy as,
1751

Retinopathy—cont'd
in gestational diabetes mellitus, 325
rubella, 1740
Retinopathy of prematurity, 1747–1752
classification of, 1749, 1750f
clinical course of, 1749–1750
differential diagnosis of, 1750–1751
examination schedule for, 1751–1752,
1751b
incidence of, 1748, 1748f
pathogenesis of, 1748–1749, 1749f
plus disease in, 1748, 1749, 1750f
prethreshold disease in, 1748
threshold disease in, 1748
treatment of, 1751
Retinoschisis, 1743
Retractions, of chest wall
in pulmonary function assessment, 1088
in respiratory distress syndrome, 1100
Retrolental fibroplasia. See Retinopathy of
prematurity.
Retroviral infections, transfusion-transmitted,
1346
Rh blood group
D antigen of, 389
discovery of, 13
genetics of, 389–390
Rh-compatible blood components,
guidelines for, 1343t
Rh disease, 1298, 1298t
neutrophilia due to, 1315
Rh immunoglobulin prophylaxis
in management of erythroblastosis fetalis,
393–394
indications for, 390, 391t
Rh isoimmunization
hydrops fetalis in, 391–393, 392f
pathophysiology of, 390–393
sensitization in, 390–391, 391t
ultrasonography of, 397–398, 398f, 399t
Rhabdomyoma, cardiac, 1250
Rhabdomyosarcoma, 1343–1344
orbital, 1735–1736, 1736f
RhD gene, 389–390
RhD typing, fetal, 393
Rhinovirus infection, 873
Rhizomelia, 162, 575
Rhizomelic chondrodysplasia punctata, 1628
Rhizomelic dysplasia, cholesterol
biosynthesis defects in, 1627
Rib cage abnormalities, respiratory distress
due to, 1144–1145, 1145f
Rib fractures, birth-related, 541–542, 542f
Riboflavin
in breast milk, 672t
in infant formula, 674t
requirements for, 668, 668t
Ribonucleic acid, messenger, in fetal cells,
277
Rickets. See also Osteopenia of prematurity.
hypocalcemia with, vitamin D for, 1513
in bronchopulmonary dysplasia, 1165
radiography of, 730, 730f
Rifampin
fetal effects of, 187t
for tuberculosis, 827, 827t
Riley-Day syndrome (familial dysautonomia)
criteria for, 980
ocular manifestation of, 1734
Risk, relative, 82
Risk reduction
absolute, 82–83, 82t, 83f
relative, 82, 82t
Risus sardonicus, in tetanus neonatorum, 825

Ritodrine
administration of, 348
for periventricular-intraventricular
hemorrhage, 931–932
for preterm labor prevention, 348–349
metabolic effects of, 348
RNA, messenger, in fetal cells, 277
Roberts syndrome, 1709
Robertsonian translocation, of
chromosomes, 117, 118, 118f
Rocker-bottom foot, 575, 577f, 1780, 1780f,
1781f
Rocuronium bromide, in neonatal
anesthesia, 640
Rombam-Hasharon syndrome, 1315, 1317
Rooting reflex
elicitation of, by mother, 678
in preterm infant, 527, 527t
on physical examination, 526
Roseola, 850
Rotational reflexes, ocular, 1724–1725, 1725f
Rotavirus infection, 868
Routine Antenatal Diagnostic Imaging with
Ultrasound Study (RADIUS), 143
RPS19 gene, in Diamond-Blackfan anemia,
1306–1307
Rubella syndrome, congenital, 436, 871–872
cataract related to, 1740, 1740f
retinopathy related to, 1740
Rubella virus infection, 436–437, 871–873
clinical manifestations of, 436
vs. toxoplasmosis, 839f
cutaneous manifestations of, 1699t
diagnosis of, 872
epidemiology of, 436, 871
in sensorineural hearing loss, 1048
maternal-fetal transmission of, 436, 871
prevention of, 437, 872–873
treatment of, 872–873
Rubeola (measles), 851–852
Russell-Silver syndrome, genomic imprinting
and, 126, 288

S

S phase, of mitotic cycle, 886, 886f
Sacral agenesis (caudal dysplasia)
clinical manifestations of, 1771–1772
gestational diabetes mellitus and, 326
Sacrococcygeal teratoma. See Teratoma,
sacrococcygeal.
Saethre-Chotzen syndrome
(acrocephalosyndactyly, type 3), 1013
Salicylates, fetal effects of, 188t
Saline
for volume expansion, in neonatal
resuscitation, 503t, 504
injection of, for back pains, during
delivery, 469
Salmon patch, 1689b, 1691, 1691f
Salmonella infection, in gastroenteritis,
812–813
Saltatory syndrome, in periventricular-
intraventricular hemorrhage, 929
Sandoff disease, macrencephaly associated
with, 998
Scaling disorders of skin, 1693–1696, 1694t
Scalp
congenital anomalies of, 567–568, 568f
fetal, blood sampling from. See Fetal
blood sampling, from scalp.
Scaphocephaly, 1007

Schizencephaly, open-lip, 992, 992f
School-age child, with hearing loss, mainstreaming of, 1049
Sciatic nerve, palsy of, birth-related, 555
Scintigraphy. *See* Radionuclide imaging.
Sclera
  abnormalities of, 1737–1738
  blue discoloration of, in osteogenesis imperfecta, 1738
  examination of, 1723
  pigmentation of, 1738
Sclerema neonatorum, 1712–1713
  vs. subcutaneous fat necrosis, 531
Sclerosis, tuberous. *See* Tuberous sclerosis.
Scoliosis
  congenital, 1770–1771, 1771f
  idiopathic infantile, 1770
Score for Neonatal Acute Physiology (SNAP I and SNAP II), 68–69
  Perinatal Extension (SNAP-PE), 68–69
Screening tests. *See under* Metabolism, inborn errors of, screening programs for; *specific test.*
Scrotum, birth trauma to, 556f, 556–557
Search strategy, for evidence-based medicine, 80–81, 80t
Sebaceous glands
  development of, 1688
  hyperplasia of, 1689, 1689b, 1691, 1691f
Sebaceous nevus, 1710
Seborrheic dermatitis, 1710–1711, 1711f
Secobarbital
  during labor, 471
  fetal effects of, 187t
Secretin, duodenal production of, 1361
Sectio parva, for twin reversed arterial perfusion sequence, 249
Sedation
  for preterm labor prevention, 346
  in mechanical ventilation, 1116
Sedatives, neutropenia due to, 1313b
Seizures, 956–976
  anesthetic considerations in, 635
  classification of, 957, 958b
  clonic, 958
  consequences of, 975–976
  diagnosis of, 957–966
    algorithm in, 973–974
    brainstem release phenomena in, 964–965
    clinical criteria in, 957–960, 957b, 958b
    electroclinical dissociation in, 965
    electroencephalographic pattern abnormalities in, 965–966, 966f
    electrographic criteria in, 963–964
    nonepileptic behaviors in, 960–963, 962f
    subtle activity in, 957–958, 959f
  dilemmas regarding, 957b
  drug withdrawal and, 971
  duration and topography of, 963–964, 964f
  eclamptic, hyperreflexia in, 312
  epileptic syndromes and, 971, 973
  etiologies of, 966–973
  folinic acid–responsive, 1616
  following hypoxic-ischemic insult, 952–953
    management of, 953
  in ischemic stroke, 937
  in neonatal abstinence syndrome, 750
  in preeclampsia-eclampsia, prophylaxis for, 315
  inborn errors of metabolism and, 971

Seizures—*cont'd*
  incidence of, 965
  infection and, 969
  long-term outcome for, 947
  maternal, due to inadvertent intrathecal injections, 476
  metabolic derangements and, 968–969
  multifocal clonic, 958
  myoclonic, 960, 961f
  prognosis of, 976
  pyridoxine-responsive, 1617
  recognition of, caveats concerning, 957b
  repetitive/prolonged, consequences of, 957
  subcortical, 965
  tonic, 958, 960, 960f
  treatment of, 974
    drug use discontinuation in, 975
    efficacy of, 974–975
Selectin counter-receptors, in neutrophil adhesion, 764, 765f
Selective serotonin reuptake inhibitors, abuse of, 751
Selenium
  in enteral nutrition, 670t
  in infant formula, 673t
  in parenteral nutrition, 687, 688t
  ionizing, maternal exposure to, pregnancy outcome in, 260t
  maternal exposure to, pregnancy outcome in, 260t
Selenoprotein N gene, in muscular dystrophy, 983
Self-regulatory competence, of preterm infant, 1057
Selfish mother hypothesis, 281–282, 282f
Seminiferous tubule dysgenesis, 1572–1573
Senning procedure, 1223, 1269t
Sensorineural hearing loss, 1045, 1048–1049. *See also* Hearing loss.
Sensory environment, of intensive care nursery, 597–603
Sepsis, 791–804. *See also* Infection(s).
  apnea in, 1139
  clinical manifestations of, 794–795
  cutaneous manifestation of, 1697
  diagnosis of, 794–795
    acute-phase reactants in, 797–798
    antigen detection assays in, 796
    buffy coat examination in, 795–796
    C-reactive protein in, 797–798
    cultures in, 795
    cytokines in, 798–799
    erythrocyte sedimentation rate in, 798
    fibrinogen in, 798
    fibronectin in, 798
    leukocyte counts in, 796–797, 796t, 797b, 797t
    screening panels in, 799, 799t
  differential diagnosis of, 795
  due to parenteral nutrition catheter infections, 689–690
  early onset, 791–792, 792t
  hepatitis in, 1459
  in inborn errors of metabolism, 1624
  incidence of, 791–792
  inflammatory cytokine response to, 775–777, 777f, 778t
  late onset, 792, 792t
  microbiology of, 792–793, 792t
  mortality in, 792
  neutropenia in, 1312
  pathology of, 794
  persistent neutropenia in, 763

Sepsis—*cont'd*
  prevention of, 803–804
  risk factors for, 793–794
    maternal, 793
    neonatal, 793, 794t
    peripartum, 793
  symptoms and signs of, 794
  transmission of, 793
  treatment of, 799–804
    empirical antimicrobial therapy in, 799–800, 801t–803t
    immunotherapy in, 800–801, 803
    supportive therapy in, 800
  very-late onset, 792, 792t
Sepsis neonatorum, 791
Septal defects. *See* Atrial septal defect; Ventricular septal defect.
Septic arthritis. *See* Arthritis, septic.
Septo-optic dysplasia (de Morsier syndrome), 992, 1745
Septostomy
  amniotic, for twin-twin transfusion syndrome, 250
  atrial. *See* Atrial septostomy.
  balloon. *See* Balloon septostomy.
Sequence, definition of, 561
Sequestration, pulmonary, 1134
Serial amnioreduction, for twin-twin transfusion syndrome, 250
Serotonergic neurons, alteration of, sudden infant death related to, 1141
Serotonin, fetal exposure to, with SSRI abuse, 751
Sertoli cells, in sex differentiation, 1553, 1553t, 1554
Sertraline, in breast milk, 200
"Setting sun" sign, in hydrocephalus, 999
Severe acute respiratory syndrome, 873–874
Severe combined immunodeficiency (SCID)
  natural killer cell g-c chain mutation in, 770
  X-linked, defective T cell development in, 780–781
Sevoflurane, in neonatal anesthesia, 638
Sex. *See* Gender.
Sex chromatin, 124
Sex chromosomes, 113. *See also* X chromosome; Y chromosome.
  common disorders of, 563
  numerical abnormalities of, 115–116
Sex-linked inheritance, of genetic disorders, 123, 123f
Sexual differentiation
  abnormalities of, 1568–1586
    androgen-dependent target tissues in, 1575–1577
    congenital adrenal hyperplasia in, 1577–1584
    external genital primordia dysgenesis in, 1585, 1585f
    female pseudohermaphroditism in, 1577–1586
    gonadal differentiation disorders in, 1568–1574
    gonadal dysgenesis in, 1568–1571, 1569b, 1569f
    inborn errors of testosterone biosynthesis in, 1575
    male pseudohermaphroditism in, 1574–1577
    maternally derived androgenic substances in, 1584–1585
    maternally derived progestins in, 1577
    müllerian dysgenesis in, 1585–1586

Sexual differentiation—*cont'd*
  müllerian inhibiting substance
    deficiencies in, 1574
  testicular dysgenesis in, 1571–1573
  testicular hormone synthesis disorders
    in, 1574–1577
  testicular unresponsiveness to human
    chorionic gonadotropin and
    luteinizing hormone in, 1574–1575
  true hermaphroditism in, 1573–1574,
    1573f
  vaginal dysgenesis in, 1585–1586
  fetal, 1552b
    embryology in, 1552–1554
    endocrinology in, 1552–1554
    external genitalia development in, 1554,
      1554f,
    genital duct development in, 1553–1554
    gonadal development in, 1552–1553,
      1552f, 1553t
    genetic control of, 1551, 1551f
    gonadal endocrine function in,
      1554–1555, 1555f
    hormonal control in, 1554–1556, 1555f,
      1556f
    müllerian inhibiting substance in,
      1555–1556, 1556f
    normal, 1550–1556
    SRY gene in, 1551
    testosterone in, 1555–1556
    X-linked genes in, 1551f, 1551
    Y chromosome in, 1551
SH3BGR gene, heart defects associated with,
  1204
Shaken baby syndrome, retinal hemorrhage
  in, 1727
SHH gene, in holoprosencephaly, 903, 991
Shigella infection, in gastroenteritis, 812,
  813
Shock, electric, phototherapy and, 1445
Short bowel syndrome, 1370–1371
  due to necrotizing enterocolitis, 1405
Short-chain acyl-CoA dehydrogenase
  deficiency, 1610t, 1648
Shortening fraction, myocardial, 1213
Shoulder
  birth injuries to, 541–547
  congenital anomalies of, 1767
Shoulder dystocia, fetal, gestational diabetes
  and, 326–327
Shunt (shunting)
  balloon dilation for maintenance of, 1274
  evaluation of, 1091
  fetal, 231–232
    thoracoamniotic, 232, 232f
    ventriculoamniotic, 231–232
    vesicoamniotic, 232
  fixed right-to-left, 1216
  for congenital heart disease, 1269t
  for single ventricle, 1231
  for tetralogy of Fallot, 1225
  for tricuspid atresia, 1227
  hyperoxia-hyperventilation test of,
    1090–1091
  hyperoxic test of, 1216–1217
  hypoxemia due to, 1090, 1111
  in persistent pulmonary hypertension,
    1246
  in transposition of great arteries, 1223
  location of, by oxygen saturation level,
    1212
  pulmonary hemorrhage due to, 1127
  ventriculoperitoneal, for hydrocephalus,
    1002

Shwachman-Diamond syndrome, 1364–1365
  neutropenia in, 1311
Sickle cell anemia, 1304, 1305f
Sickle cell disease, 1304, 1305f
Sickle cell trait, 1304
Sideroblastic anemia, 1308
Sign language, for hearing-impaired child,
  1049
Sildenafil, for persistent pulmonary
  hypertension, 1180
Silver nitrate
  chemical conjunctivitis due to, 810, 1747
  for conjunctivitis prevention, 811
Silver-silver chloride electrodes, in cardiac
  monitoring, 610–611
Single ventricle. *See also* Ventricle(s),
    cardiac.
  anesthetic considerations in, 635
  forms of, 1231
  in total anomalous pulmonary venous
    connection, 1229
  surgical treatment of, 1231
Sinovenous thrombosis, 934, 935f
Sinus bradycardia, 1258
Sinus exit block, 1259
Sinus tachycardia, 1253t, 1254
Sinusoidal fetal heart rate, 176, 177f
Situs, abdominal, 1242–1243
Situs ambiguous, 1242
Situs inversus, 1242, 1243
Situs solitus, 1242, 1243
Sjögren-Larsson syndrome, 1694t
Skeleton. *See also* Musculoskeletal system.
  appendicular, growth of, 1504–1505
  appendicular and axial, development of,
    1756
  axial, growth of, 1504–1505
  dysplasias of, 1781–1782
  radiography of, 729f, 729–730, 730f
Skin, 1685–1716, 1690t
  anomalies of, in inborn errors of
    metabolism, 1620
  appendages of, development of,
    1687–1688
  blood and lymphatic vessel development
    in, 1689
  candidiasis of, 1699–1700, 1700f
  care of, 1685, 1685b, 1715–1716, 1715b,
    1716b, 1716f
  congenital disorders of, 1713–1715
  cornification disorders of, 1693–1696,
    1694t
  dry or peeling, 517
  environmental contact with, 598–599
  epidermal nevus of, 1710
  examination of
    for congenital anomalies, 567
    neonatal, 517
  harlequin color change of, 517
    examination of, 517
  heat exchange between environment and,
    588–592. *See also* Heat exchange.
    at different ambient humidities, 589,
      590f
    during care on radiant bed, 592
    during first day after birth, 588, 590f
    during first hours after birth, 588, 589f
    during first weeks after birth, 589–590,
      591f
    during phototherapy, 592
    during skin-to-skin care, 592
    under radiant heaters, 590–591
  hemangiomas and vascular malformations
    of, 1706–1710

Skin—*cont'd*
  hereditary blistering diseases of, 1700–1703
  in small for gestational age infant, 297,
    297f
  infections of, 816–817
    bacterial and yeast, 1697–1698, 1698f
    herpes simplex virus, 842
    viral, 1698, 1699, 1699t
  inflammatory diseases of, 1710–1711
  innervation of, 1689
  minor anomalies and phenotypic variants
    of, 566t
  physiological functions of, 1685, 1685b
  pigmentary abnormalities of, 1704–1706
  scaling disorders of, 1693–1696, 1694t
  structural biology of, 1686–1689, 1686f,
    1687f
  subcutaneous and infiltrative dermatoses
    of, 1711–1713
  transient lesions of, 1689–1693, 1689b,
    1690t
  vesicobullous eruptions of, 1697–1703
  water loss from. *See also* Water loss.
    determination of, 586
    during first 4 postnatal weeks, 588
Skin-to-skin care
  heat exchange between skin and
    environment during, 592
  maintenance of normal temperature
    during, 588
Skin-to-skin contact. *See also* Kangaroo care.
  breast feeding initiation and, 678
  in maternal-infant attachment, 648, 650,
    655
Skull
  birth injuries to, 531–536
  cloverleaf (kleeblattschädel), 1012
  fractures of
    birth-related, 534–536, 535f
    with cephalhematoma, 532
  growth of, brain expansion determining,
    905
  midline abnormality over, examination of,
    519
  sutures of, premature closing of. *See*
    Craniosynostosis.
Skull-molding helmets, for deformational
  plagiocephaly, 1014
SLC25A19 gene, in microcephaly vera,
  905–906
Sleep, apnea during, 1137–1138. *See also*
  Apnea.
Small for gestational age. *See also*
  Gestational age.
  approach to, 296–298, 297f
  definition of, 22, 288–290
  desquamation and, hanging skin in, 297,
    297f
  diseases associated with, 23
  facial appearance in, 297, 297f
  fasting hypoglycemia in, 296t, 299f,
    299–300, 300f, 301f
  follow-up for, 301–302
  gestational age assessment in, 297–298
  growth in, 302f, 302–303
  hyperviscosity-polycythemia syndrome in,
    296t, 301
  intergenerational transmission of, 279
  metabolism in, 299–300, 299f–301f
  perinatal problems associated with, 296t
  subnormal head size in, 1038, 1038f
  temperature regulation in, 296t, 300–301
  transepidermal water loss in, during first 4
    postnatal weeks, 296–298, 297f, 588

Small for gestational age—cont'd
  transient hypoglycemia in, 1478–1479
  vernix caseosa in, 297
  vs. intrauterine growth restriction, 271, 289
Small intestine. See also specific part e.g.,
    Duodenal entries; Duodenum.
  development of, 1362
  diversion of, for meconium ileus
      treatment, 1396
  duplications of, 1393, 1393f
  obstruction of, ultrasonography of, 157,
      157f, 158f
  transplantation of
    for microvillus inclusion disease, 1371,
        1372
    for short bowel syndrome, 1371
Small left-colon syndrome, 720, 720f
Small-molecule metabolism, defects of,
    1625t, 1626–1629
Smell, in chemosensory environment,
    599–600
Smith-Lemli-Opitz syndrome
  abnormal pinna in, 572f
  cholesterol biosynthesis defects in,
      1626–1627
  diagnosis of, 579
  heart defects associated with, 1203t
  hypertrophied alveolar ridges in, 573,
      573f
  single gene (mendelian) disorders in, 563
  syndactyly in, 577, 578f
SMN gene, in spinal muscular atrophy, 979
Smoking. See Tobacco use.
Soap-bubble appearance, in meconium
    ileus, 1395
Soave procedure, for Hirschsprung disease,
    1399
Social status, in preeclampsia-eclampsia, 312
Socioeconomic status, in developing
    countries, neonatal mortality related to,
    107f, 107–108
Sodium
  atomic weight and valance of, 1817t
  disorders of. See Hypernatremia;
      Hyponatremia.
  fractional excretion of, 1803t
    gestational age and, 696, 696f
    in acute renal failure, 1669
  in breast milk, 671t
  in enteral nutrition, 669, 670t
  in infant formula, 673t
  in parenteral nutrition, 687
  maintenance of, 699
    in respiratory distress syndrome, 1106
  urinary losses of, in neonate, 696
Sodium balance, in neonate, 695–696, 696f
Sodium bicarbonate. See Bicarbonate.
Sodium channel(s), epithelial, 701
Sodium channel blockers, for neonatal
    tachycardia, 1261b–1262b
Sodium chloride. See Chloride.
Sodium diarrhea, congenital, 1369–1370,
    1370t
Sodium homeostasis, role of aldosterone in,
    701
Sodium nitroprusside
  dosages of, 1793
  for afterload reduction, in congenital heart
      disease, 1267
  for neonatal hypertension, 1672t
Soft tissues, birth injuries to, 529–531
Somatosensory evoked potentials
  in hypoxic-ischemic encephalopathy, 948
  in spinal cord injury, 549

Somatostatin, for hypoglycemia, 1487
  in nesidioblastosis-adenoma spectrum,
      1481–1482
Somite, in spinal development, 1755, 1756
Sonography. See Ultrasonography.
Sotalol
  dosages of, 1788
  for neonatal tachycardia, 1260t, 1262b,
      1263, 1264
  with amiodarone, for neonatal
      tachycardia, 1262b
Sotos syndrome, 996
Sound amplification, for hearing-impaired
    child, 1049
Sound vibrations, transmission of, 1045
Southern blot analysis
  in genetic disease diagnosis, 128f,
      128–129
  of fragile X syndrome, 131
SOX9 gene, mutation of, 1571
Spasmus mutans, 1746
Spasticity, in high-risk neonate, 1038–1039,
    1039
Special care unit. See also Neonatal intensive
    care unit (NICU).
  characteristics of, 1051–1052
Spectrophotometry, in erythroblastosis fetalis
    screening, 395–397
Sperm, environmental exposures affecting,
    256–257
Spherocytosis, 1430
  hereditary, 1300
Sphingolipidosis, macular abnormalities in,
    1744, 1744t
Spina bifida, 225. See also Chiari
    malformation.
  prevalence of, 517t
Spina bifida occulta, 1015
  myelodysplasia with, vs. spinal birth
      injuries, 548
Spinal accessory nerve, assessment of, 525
Spinal anesthesia
  maternal
    combined with epidural anesthesia, 474
    intrathecal injection as, 474
  neonatal, 641
Spinal cord
  defects of, vertebral anomalies associated
      with, 1758
  injury to
    at neck, 979
    birth, 547–550
    respiratory distress related to,
        1141–1142
  tethered, 1015
    in imperforate anus, 1400
  tumors of, vs. birth injuries, 548
Spinal dysraphism, occult, 902
Spinal muscular atrophy, 978–979, 979f
  SMN gene in, 979
  type I, 978
    respiratory distress related to, 1142
Spine
  anomalies of
    examination of, 574
    ultrasonography of, 155, 155f
  congenital anomalies of, 1770–1772
    embryologic errors in, 1757–1758
  embryology of, 1755–1756
  examination of, 516
  injury to, 1759
    birth, 547–550
  midline abnormality over, examination of,
      519

Spiral arteries, in preeclampsia-eclampsia,
    trophoblastic invasion of, 308
Spiramycin
  for congenital toxoplasmosis, 216
  prophylactic, for toxoplasmosis, 449
Spirituality, medical ethics affected by, 37
Spironolactone
  dosages of, 1791
  in breast milk, 199
Spleen, rupture of, birth-related, 551
Splenectomy, for idiopathic
    thrombocytopenic purpura, 368
Splenic artery, Doppler velocimetry index
    of, in hemolytic anemia, 399
Splenomegaly
  in hydrops fetalis
    anemia associated with, 398, 399t
    ultrasonography of, 397, 399t
  in inborn errors of metabolism,
      1623–1624, 1623t
Sprengel deformity, 1767
  vs. sternocleidomastoid muscle injury,
      547
Sri Lanka, neonatal mortality in, 90t, 90–91
SRY gene, in fetal gonadal development,
    1551, 1551f
Staff. See Health care personnel.
Stamm-type gastrostomy, for gastric
    volvulus, 1386
Standard International Units, conversion
    tables for, 1814t–1816t
Standard of care, in malpractice litigation, 52
Staphylococcal infection, after mechanical
    ventilation, 1119
Staphylococcal scalded skin syndrome,
    1697–1698, 1698f
  vs. staphylococcal pyoderma, 1697
Staphylococcus aureus
  in atopic dermatitis, 811
  in conjunctivitis, 811
  in sepsis, 792, 792t
  in skin infections, 816
  in staphylococcal scalded skin syndrome,
      1697–1698, 1698f
  pyoderma due to, 1697
Staphyloma, 1738
State and federal laws, 48
Status marmoratus, in hypoxic-ischemic
    encephalopathy, 941
Status verrucosus deformans, 889
Stearic acid, in intravenous lipid emulsions,
    686t
Steel factor, 1288, 1289t
Stem cell(s)
  hematopoietic, 762, 1287–1288, 1288f
    transplantation of, for dyskeratosis
        congenita, 1311
  in congenital heart disease prevention,
      1202
  pluripotent, 762
Stem cell factor, 1288, 1289t
Stenosis. See at anatomic site.
Sternocleidomastoid muscle
  abnormalities of, torticollis due to, 1760,
      1761
  birth injury to, 545–547, 547f
Steroid(s). See also Corticosteroids;
    Glucocorticoids; specific steroid.
  biosynthetic pathway of, in adrenal and
      gonadal tissues, 1555f
  congenital malformations associated with,
      186t
  effectiveness of, on fetal lung maturation,
      213–214

Steroid(s)—cont'd
  for periventricular-intraventricular
      hemorrhage, 931
  maternal, 1483
Steroid sulfatase deficiency, in X-linked
    ichthyosis, 1695, 1696
Stillborn. See Fetal death.
Stimulation program, mechanical, for
    osteopenia of prematurity, 1522–1523
Stomach. See also Gastric entries.
  development of, 1358–1360
  duplications of, 1392, 1392f
  functional zones of, 1359–1360
  lactobezoars of, 1387
  migrating motor complex in, 1360
  perforation of, 1387
  secretory function of, 1360
  small-volume of (microgastria), 1386, 1386f
  volvulus of, 1385–1386, 1386f
Stool
  acholic, 1453
  culture of, in gastroenteritis, 813
  first, 1797t
    for gestational age, 1797f
  retention/impaction of, after spinal cord
      injury, 549
  water loss through, 699
Storage diseases. See Glycogen storage
    disease; Lysosomal storage disease.
Strabismus, 1745–1746
Stratum corneum, 1686, 1686f, 1687
  in preterm infant, 1716
Streak gonad, 1551
  surgical removal of, 1564
Streptococcal infections
  Group A, cutaneous, 1698
  Group B, 443–445
    cutaneous, 1698
    epidemiology and transmission of,
        443–444
    in preterm delivery, 338
    in sepsis, 792, 792t, 793
    maternal infection with, 444, 793
    neonatal infection with, 444
    pneumonia due to, 1125–1126
    prevention of, 444–445, 1126
    III serotype of, in meningitis, 804
Streptokinase, for thrombosis, 1336
Streptomycin
  fetal effects of, 187t
  for sepsis, 803t
  for tuberculosis, 827t
Stress
  during pregnancy, preterm delivery and,
      334–335
  glycolysis stimulation during, 594
  neutrophilia due to, 1315
  physical, maternal exposure to, pregnancy
      outcome in, 260t
Stress response, neonatal, anesthesia for
    blunting, 630, 630f, 630t
Stress tests. See Contraction stress testing;
    Nonstress testing.
Stridor
  level of obstruction identified by, 1150
  with laryngeal cysts, 1152
  with laryngeal web, 1153
  with laryngomalacia, 1151
  with subglottic hemangioma, 1153
  with vocal cord paralysis, 540, 1152
Stroke
  arterial ischemic, 934–937, 1331–1332
    diagnosis of, 935–936, 936f
    incidence of, 935

Stroke—cont'd
    prognosis of, 937
    risk factors for, 936–937
    treatment of, 1332
  in preeclampsia-eclampsia, 312
  seizures due to, 969, 970f
Stroke volume, ventricular, 1213
Sturge-Weber syndrome
  anesthetic implications of, 634t
  cutaneous manifestation of, 1709
  macrencephaly associated with, 997
  ocular abnormalities in, 1729
Subarachnoid hemorrhage, 933
Subchorionic thrombosis, massive, 459
Subconjunctival hemorrhage
  birth-related, 538
  examination of, 516
Subcortical seizures, 965
Subcutaneous fat necrosis, at birth, 530–531,
    531f
Subdural empyema, macrocephaly due to,
    1005
Subdural hematoma, macrocephaly due to,
    1005, 1006f
Subdural hemorrhage, 933
Subgaleal hemorrhage
  birth-related, 533–534, 533f–534f
  vs. cephalhematoma, 534
Subglottis
  anatomy of, 1150, 1150f
  hemangioma of, 1153–1154, 1154f
  stenosis of
    congenital, 1153
    due to endotracheal intubation,
        1154–1155, 1154f
    due to mechanical ventilation, 1119
    in laryngomalacia, 1151
    with bifid or absent epiglottis, 1151
Subluxation, of knee, 1777–1778, 1778f
Substance abuse
  alcohol in. See Alcohol.
  amphetamines in, 747–749
  clinician's role in identification of,
      733–734
  cocaine in. See Cocaine abuse.
  guidelines for screening of, 733–734
  heart defects associated with, 1204
  marijuana in, 742–743
  ocular effects of, 1747
  opioids in, 749–753. See also Opioids,
      abuse of.
  reporting requirements for, 733
  risk factors for, 734
  self-reporting of, 734
  tobacco in, 739–742
Subtelomeric probe analysis, for
    chromosome microdeletions, 579
Succinylcholine
  as anesthetic induction agent, 478
  in neonatal anesthesia, 639–640
Sucking
  non-nutritive
    for pain relief, 642
    in progression from enteral to oral
        feeding, 676–677
  of hand, in initiation of breast feeding,
      649f, 650
Sucking reflex
  assessment of, 525, 526
  in preterm infant, 527, 527t
Suckling, in parent-infant attachment, 5f,
    648–651
Sucrase-isomaltase deficiency, congenital,
    1365–1366

Sucrose, oral, for pain relief, 642
Suctioning
  for meconium aspiration, 506–507, 1124
  in mechanical ventilation, 1117
  of newborn
    avoidance of, 648
    bradycardia due to, 490
  pulmonary hemorrhage due to, 1127
Sudden infant death syndrome
  apnea associated with, 1140–1141, 1140f
  cocaine exposure and, 745
  enteroviral infection and, 862
  prevention of, 521
    Back to Sleep program in, 1140, 1140f
  tobacco exposure and, 740
Sufentanil
  for labor pain, 472
  in neonatal anesthesia, 639
  umbilical vein to maternal vein ratio of,
      470t
Sulfadiazine, with pyrimethamine, for
    congenital toxoplasmosis, 216
Sulfasalazine, in breast milk, 199
Sulfatase deficiency, placental, in post-term
    pregnancy, 383
Sulfation activity, in drug metabolism, 194
Sulfite oxidase deficiency, 1617
Sulfonamides
  fetal effects of, 187t
  for sepsis, 803t
  in breast milk, 199
Sulfonylurea glyburide, for gestational
    diabetes mellitus, 323
Sulindac, for preterm labor prevention, 352
Superoxide, in microbicidal activity, of
    neutrophils, 766
Supraglottis, anatomy of, 1150, 1150f
Supraventricular premature contractions,
    1259, 1265
Supraventricular tachycardia, paroxysmal,
    vs. sinus tachycardia, 1254
Surfactant. See also specific surfactant
    protein.
  alveolar life cycle of, 1081
  composition of, 1075–1077, 1076f, 1076t
  deficiency of
    chest radiograph of, 714, 714f
    in respiratory distress syndrome,
        1076–1077, 1097, 1099
  genetic abnormalities of, 1077
  metabolism of, 1075–1081
  pathway of, from lung to amniotic fluid,
      1085, 1085f
  pool size of, 1078–1081
    after corticosteroid therapy, 1086
    rate of increase of, 1078–1079,
        1078f–1080f
  recycling of, 1080–1081
  synthesis and secretion of, 1077–1078, 1077f
  therapy with
    corticosteroid combined with, 1099
    for bronchopulmonary dysplasia
        prevention, 1168
    for congenital diaphragmatic hernia,
        1173
    for meconium aspiration syndrome,
        1125
    for persistent pulmonary hypertension,
        1247
    for preterm lung, 1081–1083
      alveolar stability in, 1081, 1082f
      improved function with, 1080
      pressure-volume relationships in,
          1081, 1083, 1083f

Surfactant—cont'd
for respiratory distress syndrome, 1103–1105, 1104b
functional residual capacity increased by, 1083
in developing countries, 105–106
lung damage prevention with, 1121
prophylactic approach to, 1103–1104
history of, 14t
lack of surfactant proteins A and D in, 1105
natural vs. synthetic preparations in, 1103
Surfactant protein(s), recycling of, in preterm lung, 1080–1081
Surfactant protein A
as collectin protein, 773
function of, 1076
lack of, in synthetic surfactant, 1105
Surfactant protein B
deficiency of, in respiratory distress syndrome, 1076–1077
function of, 1076
mortality due to, 1133
Surfactant protein C
deficiency of, 1097
function of, 1077
Surfactant protein D
as collectin protein, 773
function of, 1077
lack of, in synthetic surfactant, 1105
Surgery. See also under disorder; specific procedure.
fetal, 231–252
fetoscopic, 249
open, 233–249, 234t
shunting procedures in, 231–232, 232f, 233f
for congenital heart disease, 1268, 1269t
for posterior plagiocephaly, 1014
history of, 15
Swaddling, heat loss prevention by, 595
Swallowing
assessment of, 525
disorders of
aspiration syndromes associated with, 1125
in apnea, 1137
fetal
impaired, 414
of amniotic fluid, 410–411
Sweat glands, eccrine
development of, 1687–1688
obstruction of, miliaria related to, 1692
Sweating
decreased, in ectodermal dysplasia, 1714
thermal vs. emotional, 1687–1688
Swelling. See Edema.
Swenson procedure, for Hirschsprung disease, 1399
Sympathetic nervous system
birth injuries to, 538
gastric innervation by, 1359
skin innervation by, 1689
β-Sympathomimetic agents. See also specific agent.
fetal complications of, 348–349
fetal effects of, 189t
for preterm labor prevention, 347–349
long-term exposure to, 348
placental transfer of, transient neonatal hypoglycemia due to, 1473
Synaptogenesis, 894–895, 894f, 895f
Synchondrosis, 1756

Syndactyly
examination of, 577, 578f
of fingers, 1769, 1769f
of toes, 1781
Syndrome, definition of, 561
Synophrys, in congenital anomalies, 571
Synovial fluid, culture of, in osteomyelitis and septic arthritis, 814
Syphilis
clinical manifestations of, 445–446
congenital, 822–825
clinical manifestations of, 446, 822–823, 822b, 823b, 823f
cutaneous manifestations of, 1698
diagnosis of, 823–824
early, 822, 822b
follow-up for, 825
incidence of, 822
late, 823, 823b
maculopapular rash in, 816
microbiology of, 822
pathogenesis and pathology of, 822
prevention of, 446, 825
radiography of, 729, 729f
treatment of, 824–825, 824t
diagnosis and treatment of, 445–446
during pregnancy, 445–446
epidemiology of, 445, 445f
Systolic function. See Ventricle(s), cardiac, systolic function of.

T

T cell(s), 779–783
activation and maturation of, 781
CD molecules on, 779, 779t. See also CD T-cell entries.
development of, 779–780, 780f
cytokine receptor signaling in, 780–781
function of, 777
cytokine role in, 781–782
tests for evaluation of, 791b
in breast milk, 790
subpopulations of, 779
T cell receptors, 777, 779, 781
T-helper cells (Th1, Th2), 779
naive, differentiation of, 781, 782
T-piece resuscitation, 495
Tachycardia
accessory pathway reentrant, 1254–1255, 1255f
treatment of, 1263
antidromic, 1255
atrial ectopic, 1253t, 1256
treatment of, 1264
atrial fibrillation in, 1253t
atrial flutter in, 1253t, 1256
treatment of, 1263
atrial reentry, 1253t
atrioventricular node reentrant, 1253t, 1254, 1255–1256
treatment of, 1263
automatic, 1253, 1253t
fetal, 173, 174f, 222
assessment of, 1209
congestive heart failure related to, 1210
treatment of, 1210
junctional ectopic, 1253t, 1257
treatment of, 1264
junctional reciprocating, permanent form of, 1253t, 1255
treatment of, 1264

Tachycardia—cont'd
narrow QRS, treatment of, 1261
neonatal
antiarrhythmic agents for, 1260t
classification of, 1261
management of, 1259–1264
mechanisms of, 1253–1254, 1253t
severity assessment in, 1259–1261, 1260t
treatment of, 1261, 1261b–1262b, 1263–1264
orthodromic, 1254, 1255
reentrant, 1253, 1253t, 1254
sinoatrial reentry, 1253t
sinus, 1253t, 1254
supraventricular paroxysmal, vs. sinus tachycardia, 1254
ventricular, 1257, 1258f
treatment of, 1264
wide QRS, treatment of, 1261, 1263
Tachypnea, transient, 1127–1128
Talipes, examination of, 519
Talipes equinovarus, 1779–1780, 1780f
diagnosis and treatment of, 1780
examination of, 519, 578
multifactorial genetic conditions in, 1757
prevalence of, 517t
Talus, congenital vertical, 1780–1781, 1780f, 1781f
Taste, in chemosensory environment, 599–600
Taurine
in breast milk, 672t
in infant formula, 674t
in parenteral amino acid solutions, 684t, 685
Taussig-Bing malformation, in double-outlet right ventricle, 1232
Tay-Sachs disease
autosomal recessive inheritance in, 123
macrencephaly associated with, 998
macular abnormalities in, 1744, 1744t
TBX5 gene, in Holt-Oram syndrome, 1204
Tearing
excess (epiphora), 1733
reflex, 1733
Technetium phosphate scan, of osteomyelitis and septic arthritis, 814
Telecanthus, definition of, 568, 1724
Telencephalic leukoencephalopathy, perinatal, 911
Telephone advice
documenting, 56
malpractice litigation related to, 51
Tellurium, maternal exposure to, pregnancy outcome in, 260t
Telomere, 113
Temperature
after birth, 490, 490f
ambient, role of, in insensible water loss, 698
in sepsis, 795
maternal, elevation of, due to neuraxial blockade, 475–476
monitoring of, during surgery, 636, 636t
regulation of. See also Heat exchange; Heat loss.
in neonatal anesthesia, 629
in neonatal resuscitation, 490, 490f
in respiratory distress syndrome, 1105
small for gestational age and, 296t, 300–301
Tendon reflexes, deep, assessment of, 526

Teratogen(s)
  cocaine as, 744
  congenital anomalies due to, 562t, 563t,
    563–564
  efivirenz as, 848
  exposure to, of small for gestational age
    infant, 296t
  musculoskeletal abnormalities due to, 1756
  renal defects associated with, 1664
Teratogenicity, drug-induced
  congenital anomalies and, 133–134
  genetic background in, 189
  mechanisms of, 190, 190f, 191
Teratoid tumors, 1148
Teratoma, 1344
  classification of, 1148
  intranasal, 1148
  orbital, 1735
  ovarian, genomic imprinting in, 125–126
  pericardial, 1250
  sacrococcygeal, 1344
    differential diagnosis of, 244
    fetal surgery for, 234t, 243–246
    perinatal ultrasonography, 155
    prenatal diagnosis of, 244, 245f
    prenatal treatment of, 244–246
    ultrasonography of, 244, 245f
  true, 1148
Terbutaline, for preterm labor prevention,
    349
Term infant
  amino acid concentration standards in,
    1803t
  cerebral palsy in, 461
  cerebrospinal fluid values in, 1808t
  cord blood of, hematologic values for,
    1810t
  definition of, 631
  discharge from hospital, criteria for, 522
  encephalopathy in, 461
  neutrophil values in, 1813t
  outcome of, factors affecting, 1035b
  plasma 17-hydroxyprogesterone in, 1806t
  serum electrolyte values in, 1801t
  time of first void and stool in, 1797t
  unconjugated hyperbilirubinemia in,
    1425–1426, 1426f
  whole blood ionized calcium in, 1802t
Terminal care
  analgesia in, 41
  organ donation and, 41
  palliative care in, 41–42
  withholding of life-sustaining treatment in,
    40–41
Terminal transverse defects, with orofacial
  malformations, 1729
Testicular dysgenesis, 1571–1573
Testicular feminization syndrome, 1576
  incomplete, 1576–1577
Testicular hormone synthesis, disorders of,
    1574–1577
Testicular torsion, examination of, 519
Testis (testes)
  birth injuries to, 557
  differentiation of, 1553, 1553t
    SRY gene in, 1551, 1551f
  in true hermaphroditism, 1573
  maldescent of. See Cryptorchidism.
  regression syndromes of, 1572–1573
  rudimentary, 1572
  small, 1572
  undescended
    examination of, 519
    prevalence of, 517t

Testis (testes)—cont'd
  unresponsiveness of
    to human chorionic gonadotropin,
      1574–1575
    to luteinizing hormone, 1574–1575
Testosterone
  biosynthesis of, inborn errors of, 1575
  fetal production of, 1554–1555, 1555f
  for small penis growth, 1564
  in sex differentiation, 1555–1556
  serum ranges of, 1805t
Tetanospasmin, 825
Tetanus neonatorum, 825–826
Tethered spinal cord, 1015
  in imperforate anus, 1400
Tetracycline
  fetal effects of, 187t
  for sepsis, contraindications to, 803t
  in breast milk, 199
Tetralogy of Fallot, 1224–1226
  anatomy and pathophysiology of,
    1224–1225
  balloon dilation of pulmonary valve in,
    1272–1273
  clinical presentation of, 1225
  defects associated with, 1225
  laboratory evaluation in, 1225
  management of, 1225–1226
  prognosis in, 1225–1226
  vs. pulmonary stenosis, 1238
Tetraploidy, 116–117
Thal fundoplication, 1380
α-Thalassemia, 1303
β-Thalassemias, 1303
Thalassemias, 1302–1303
Thalidomide, fetal effects of, 187t
Thanatophoric dysplasia
  examination of, 573, 574f
  extremities in, 575, 575f
  perinatal ultrasonography of, 162, 162f
  respiratory distress associated with,
    1145
Theophylline. See also Methylxanthines.
  dosages of, 1791
  for apnea, 1139
  in breast milk, 200
Thermal burns, ocular, 1727
Thermal environment, of neonate, 585–597.
    See also Heat exchange; Water loss.
  neutral, 593–594, 594f
  practical considerations in, 595–597
Thermal index, in ultrasonography, 143
Thermistor, in airflow measurement, 1092
Thermogenesis, chemical, in cold-stressed
    infant, 594, 594f
Thiamin
  in breast milk, 672t
  in infant formula, 674t
  requirements for, 668t
Thiazides, for nephrogenic diabetes
    insipidus, 702
Thimerosal, in vaccines, 866
Thiocyanate, in breast milk, 201
Thiopental
  in maternal anesthesia, 478
  in neonatal anesthesia, 638
Thiouracil, in breast milk, 200
Third spacing phenomenon, in pathologic
    fluid and electrolyte losses, 700
Thoracic dystrophy, asphyxiating, 1145
Thoracic gas volume, 1092–1093
Thoracic gastrointestinal anomalies,
    1373–1380
Thoracoamniotic shunts, 232, 232f

Thoracotomy, fetal, for cystic adenomatoid
    malformation, 243
Thrombasthenia, Glanzmann, 1341
Thrombocytopenia, 1338–1342
  alloimmune (isoimmune), 368–370,
    1338–1339, 1340f
    neonatal management of, 369
    subsequent pregnancy management in,
      369–370, 370b
  amegakaryotic, 1340
  fetal-neonatal, 367–370
    immunologic etiologies of, 367b, 368t
  immune, maternal, 1339–1340
  neonatal
    in cytomegalovirus infection, 844
    maternal immune thrombocytopenia
      causing, 1339–1340
    vs. petechiae, 529
  platelet destruction causing, 1338–1339
    conditions associated with, 1340
  platelet underproduction causing,
    1340–1341, 1340f
  prolonged bleeding time in, 1338
  X-linked, 1341
Thrombocytopenia with absent radii (TAR)
    syndrome, 1340–1341, 1340f, 1767
  heart defects associated with, 1203t
Thrombocytopenic purpura, immune
    (idiopathic), 367–368
  treatment of, 368
Thrombopoietin, 1289t
  for thrombosis, 1337–1338
Thrombosis, 1330–1337
  acquired defects resulting in, 1330–1332
  anticoagulants for, 1333–1335, 1334t,
    1335b, 1336b, 1337b
  catheter-related, 689, 1102
  congenital anticoagulant protein
    deficiencies and, 1332–1333
  dysfibrinogenemia and, 1333
  factor V Leiden and, 1333
  factor VIII elevation and, 1333
  fibrinolysis abnormalities and, 1333
  fibrinolytic therapy for, 1336, 1337b
  in antiphospholipid antibody syndrome,
    372
  prothrombin 20210A allele and, 1333
  renal arterial, hypertension due to, 1670,
    1674
  renal vein, 1331, 1674–1675
    treatment of, 1675
    ultrasonography of, 725–726, 1675
  sinovenous, 934, 935f
  subchorionic, massive, 459
  thrombopoietin for, 1337–1338
  treatment of, 1333–1337
  venous
    catheter-related, 1331
    causes of, 1332
    risk factors for, 1332, 1332t
Thrombotic vasculopathy, fetal, 459
Thrombus
  formation of, 1332
  long-term effects of, 1331
Thrush, 830, 1699, 1700
Thumb, congenital anomalies of, 1769
Thymus
  dysfunction of, in HIV infection, 856
  T cell development in, 779–780, 780f
Thyroglobulin
  iodination of, 1525
  measurement of, 1530
  serum, 1807t
Thyroglossal duct cyst, 1149

Thyroid-binding globulin
  deficiency of, 1538
  measurement of, 1529
  serum concentration of, 1807t
  serum values for, 1534t
Thyroid gland
  calcitonin secretion by, 1525
  calcium balance in, 1524
  carbohydrate metabolism in, 1524
  cellular metabolism in, 1524
  disorders of, 1523–1550. *See also specific
      disorder, e.g.,* Goiter.
    autoantibodies in, 1529–1530
    diagnosis of, 1527–1531
    fetal, 219t, 219–220
    free thyroid hormone levels in,
        1528–1529
    imaging of, 1530
    inherited, 1533t
    laboratory tests for, 1527, 1527b
    reverse triiodothyronine in, 1528
    thyroglobulin in, 1530
    thyroid hormone–binding proteins in,
        1529
    thyroid-stimulating hormone surge test
        in, 1531
    thyrotropin in, 1529
    thyrotropin-releasing hormone in,
        1530–1531
    thyroxine in, 1527–1528
    transient, 1543–1545
    triiodothyronine in, 1528
  embryogenesis of, 1531, 1533t
    defective, 1536
  function of, 1523
    fetal-maternal relationship in,
        1531–1535, 1532f, 1535t, 1534t
    hyperactivity in, 1532–1533, 1535t
    regulation of, 1526–1527
  iodine uptake by, 1525
  lingual tissue of, in congenital
      hypothyroidism, 1541, 1541f
  lipid metabolism in, 1524
  liver function and, 1524
  neurologic effects of, 1523–1524
  protein metabolism in, 1524
  vitamin D and, 1524
  water balance in, 1524
Thyroid hormone(s). *See also specific
    hormone.*
  abbreviations for, 1523b
  circulating concentration of
    drug effects on, 1528
    in thyroid disorders, 1527, 1527b
  congenital deficiency of, 1523–1524
  effect of, on growth and development,
      1524–1525, 1525f
  in amniotic fluid, detection of, 1532
  physiologic action of, 1523–1525
  resistance to, in congenital
      hypothyroidism, 1537
  secretion of, control of, 1526–1527
  serum values for, 1534t
  synthesis, release, transport, and
      utilization of, 1525–1526
Thyroid hormone–binding proteins,
    measurement of, 1529
Thyroid-stimulating hormone
  circulation of, circadian variation in, 1527
  deficiency of, pituitary, 1538
  fetal serum levels of, 1532
  in euthyroid sick syndrome, 1545
  in pituitary hypothyroidism, 1538
  in thyroid regulation, 1526–1527

Thyroid-stimulating hormone—*cont'd*
  in transient hyperthyrotropinemia, 1544
  postnatal surge of, 1533
  resistance to, in congenital
      hypothyroidism, 1537
  secretion of, 1526–1527
  serum, maternal, 1807f
  serum concentration of, 1807t
Thyroid-stimulating hormone surge test, 1531
Thyroperoxidase enzyme, deficiency of, in
    iodide oxidation, 1536
Thyrotoxicosis
  clinical manifestations of, 1548
  diagnosis of, 1548–1549
  etiology of, 1548
  fetal hypothyroidism with, 220
  pathogenesis of, 1548
  prognosis of, 1549
  treatment of, 1549
Thyrotropin
  measurement of, 1529
  normal range for, 1535t
  serum values for, 1534t
Thyrotropin-releasing hormone
  for lung maturation induction, 1086, 1098
  for preterm labor prevention, 356–357
  in thyroid regulation, 1526–1527
  measurement of, 1530–1531
  secretion of, hypothalamus in, 1527
Thyroxine (T$_4$)
  for fetal hypothyroidism, 220
  free, 1528–1529
    serum concentration of, 1807t
    serum values for, 1534t
  genetic errors of, 1536
  in breast milk, 200, 1533
  in congenital hypothyroidism, 1538
  in euthyroid sick syndrome, 1545
  in transient hyperthyrotropinemia, 1544
  in transient neonatal hypothyroidism,
      1543
  measurement of, 1527–1528
  mono-deiodination of, 1526
  normal range for, 1535t
  placental transport of, 1531
  secretion of, 1526
  serum concentration of, 1807t
  serum levels of, 1534t
    fetal, 1532
    maternal, 1806f
  synthesis of, 1526
Thyroxine-binding globulin
  decreased, 1550
  increased, 1550
  normal range for, 1535t
Thyroxine-binding proteins, 1526
  abnormalities of, 1550
  fetal serum levels of, 1532
Tibia
  congenital angular deformities of,
      1772–1773
  proximal metaphysis of, syphilis effects
      on, 822, 823f
  torsion of, 1772
Ticarcillin, for sepsis, 801t, 803t
Ticarcillin/clavulanate, dosages of, 1789
Tidal volume
  in carbon dioxide exchange, 1109
  lung damage due to, in assisted
      ventilation
    bronchopulmonary dysplasia related to,
        1160
    prevention of, 1113, 1120–1121, 1120b
  measurement of, 1093

Time constant, of respiratory system,
    1094–1095
  calculation of, 1095–1096
  in assisted ventilation, 1108–1109, 1108f,
      1109f
Tinea capitis, 835
Tinea corporis, 835
Tinea versicolor, 835
TINMAN gene, in cardiogenesis, 1198
Tissue factor pathway inhibitor, in
    coagulation, 1320
Tissue plasminogen activator, 1321, 1322f
  dosages of, 1789
  recombinant, for thrombosis, 1334t,
      1336
TNNT1 gene, in nemaline myopathy, 986
Tobacco use, 739–742
  congenital malformations associated with,
      186t
  environmental smoke exposure in,
      741–742
  fetal effects of, 185, 189, 739–740
  in preeclampsia-eclampsia, 312
  interventions for, 742
  intrauterine growth restriction due to, 284
  neonatal complications of, 740
  neurobehavioral and developmental
      effects of, 740–741
  neuropsychological and behavioral effects
      of, 741
  passive smoke exposure in, 739, 741–742
  pharmacology of nicotine and, 739
  pregnancy and delivery complications of,
      740
  preterm delivery and, 334
  prevalence of, 739
  prevention of, 742
Tobramycin
  dosages of, 1789
  for sepsis, 800, 801t, 803t
Tocolytic agents. *See also specific agent.*
  for non-reassuring fetal heart rate, 178
  for preterm labor prevention, 347–354
Toe(s), congenital anomalies of, 1781
  examination of, 576–578, 576f–578f
Tolbutamide
  fetal effects of, 188t
  placental transport of, transient neonatal
      hypoglycemia due to, 1472
Toll-like receptors
  activation of phagocytes by, 763–764
  in inflammatory response, 776, 778t
Tongue
  cysts of, 1149, 1149f
  fasciculations of, 525
    vs. tremors, 525
  neurologic examination of, 525
Tonic seizures, 958, 960, 960f
TORCH infection
  congenital, 993, 995f
    anomalies associated with, 564
  of placenta, 459
  seizures associated with, 969
Torsades de pointes, in long QT syndrome,
    1257, 1258f
Torsion
  testicular, 519
  tibial, 1772
Tort law. *See also* Malpractice.
  definition of, 50
  strategies for avoiding litigation, 55b,
      55–56
  wrongful birth, wrongful life, and
      wrongful death torts, 55

Torticollis
  muscular, 1760–1761, 1760f
    developmental dysplasia of hip related
      to, 1774
  plagiocephaly due to, 568
Total anomalous pulmonary venous
  connection, 1228–1229, 1229f
Touch, in environmental contact with skin,
  598–599
Toupet fundoplication, 1380
Toxemia, preeclamptic, in multiple
  gestations, 376
Toxemic facies, in preeclampsia-eclampsia,
  313
Toxicity
  drug-induced, in fetus, 190, 190f
  nitrogen dioxide, 1178
  oxygen, bronchopulmonary dysplasia
    related to, 1160, 1160f
Toxins, environmental exposure to. *See also*
  Environmental exposures.
  cutaneous effects of, 1716, 1716f
  during gametogenesis, 133
Toxoplasma gondii, 215, 838
  associated with neonatal hepatitis, 1458
Toxoplasmosis
  congenital, 215–216, 448–449, 838–840,
    993, 995f
    chorioretinitis in, 838, 1743–1744
    clinical manifestations of, 838–839, 839f
      compared with rubella and CMV
        infection, 839f
    diagnosis of, 448–449, 839
    epidemiology and clinical
      manifestations of, 448
    fetal drug therapy for, 216
    incidence of, 838
    manifestations of, 216b
    microbiology of, 838
    prognosis in, 839–840
    transmission and pathogenesis of, 449,
      838
    treatment of, 449, 839
  in pregnancy, 448–449, 838–840
  in sensorineural hearing loss, 1048
TPM genes, in nemaline myopathy, 986
Trace elements. *See also* Minerals.
  in breast milk, 671t
  in enteral nutrition, 669–670, 670t
  in infant formula, 673t
  in parenteral nutrition, 687, 688t
Trachea
  developmental anomalies of, airway
    obstruction due to, 1143, 1143b
  fetal, occlusion of, in congenital
    diaphragmatic hernia, 239
  injury to, from assisted ventilation,
    1118–1119, 1119f
Tracheal intubation. *See* Endotracheal
  intubation.
Tracheobronchial tree, cystic anomalies of,
  1134
Tracheobronchitis, necrotizing, due to
  mechanical ventilation, 1119
Tracheoesophageal fistula, 1373–1377
  chest radiograph of, 717, 717f
  clinical presentation of, 1374
  defects associated with, 1373, 1375
  diagnosis of, 1374–1375, 1374f, 1375f
  incidence of, 1373
  pathogenesis of, 1373–1374
  recurrence of, postoperative, 1376
  respiratory support in, 1375
  surgical treatment of, 1375–1377

Tracheoesophageal fistula—*cont'd*
  complications of, 1376–1377, 1377f
  outcome of, 1377, 1378t
  upper pouch syndrome and, 1376,
    1377f
  ultrasonography of, 157
Tracheomalacia, neonatal anesthesia and,
  628
Tracheostomy
  during EXIT procedure, 248f, 248–249
  for bifid or absent epiglottis, 1151
  for laryngomalacia, 1151
  for subglottic hemangioma, 1154
  for upper airway obstruction, 1148
  for vocal cord paralysis, 1153
Transcatheter ablation, for atrial tachycardia,
  1262b, 1264
Transcription factors
  in heart development, 1198–1199, 1199f
  in lung development, 1069
  in natural killer cell development and
    function, 769–770
Transcutaneous carbon dioxide monitoring,
  616
Transcutaneous electrical nerve stimulation,
  for back pains, during delivery, 469
Transcutaneous oxygen monitoring, 616
Transducer-catheter system, of blood
  pressure monitoring, 614–615
Transferrin, saturation of, in very low
  birthweight infants, 1811t
Transfusion, 1344–1352
  acute hemolytic reactions to, 1347
  allergic reactions to, 1347
  autologous red cell, 1347–1348
  cytomegalovirus infection caused by,
    1345–1346
  delayed reactions to, 1347
  exchange
    administration of salt-poor albumin
      prior to, 1447–1448
    bilirubin-albumin ratio as determinant
      of, 1440, 1440t
    choice of blood components in, 1351,
      1351t
    complications of, 1448b
    for anemia, 1295
    for unconjugated hyperbilirubinemia,
      1446–1448
    guidelines for, 1447f
    indications for, 1351
    partial, 1352
    potential complications of, 1351, 1352b
    volume calculation in, 1352
  febrile nonhemolytic reactions to, 1347
  fetal, for erythroblastosis fetalis, 401–402,
    402t
  for adrenal hemorrhage, 552
  for congenital heart disease, 1266
  for infants on ECMO, 1352
  for liver rupture, 550
  for respiratory distress syndrome, 1107
  for splenic rupture, 551
  for volume expansion, in neonatal
    resuscitation, 504
  graft-versus-host disease caused by,
    1344–1345, 1345b
  hepatitis caused by, 1346
  history of, 13
  hypocalcemia due to, 1512
  infections caused by, 1345–1346, 1345b
  intrauterine, for nonimmune hydrops
    fetalis, 425
  of blood products, 1348–1352

Transfusion—*cont'd*
  of cryoprecipitate, 1350–1351
  of fresh frozen plasma, 1350
  of granulocytes, 1350
  of neutrophils, in sepsis, 1312
  of platelets
    component definition in, 1350
    for alloimmune (isoimmune)
      thrombocytopenia, 369, 1339
      intrauterine, 370
    for Glanzmann thrombasthenia, 1341
    indications for, 1349
    pretransfusion testing in, 1349–1350
  of red blood cells
    autologous, 1347–1348
    cell preparation for, 1349
    for adrenal hemorrhage, 552
    for liver rupture, 550
    for splenic rupture, 550
    indications for, 1348, 1348b
    pretransfusion testing in, 1343t,
      1348–1349
  parental blood donation for, 1347
  reactions to, 1346–1347
  retroviral infections caused by, 1346
  risks of, 1344–1346
  twin-twin. *See* Twin-twin transfusion
    syndrome.
Transient erythroblastopenia of childhood,
  1307
Transient tachypnea of newborn,
  1127–1128
  chest radiograph of, 715
Transillumination device, use of, in
  developing countries, 103, 105t
Transillumination of chest, for
  pneumothorax, 1129
Transition circulation, anesthetic
  considerations in, 627
Translocation
  reciprocal, 117, 117f
  Robertson, 117, 118, 118f
Transplantation
  for inborn errors of metabolism, 1653,
    1653t
  heart, 1269–1270
  hematopoietic stem cell, for dyskeratosis
    congenita, 1311
  liver, for biliary atresia, 1458
  small intestine, 1371, 1372
Transportation of patients
  in neonatal surgery, 635–636
  in regionalized care, 29–30
    reverse transfer and, 30
  malpractice litigation related to, 51
Transposition of great arteries
  D-transposition in, 1222–1223, 1224f
  L-transposition in, 1242
Transthoracic electrical impedance, 613
Transthyretin, increased, 1550
Trauma. *See also at anatomic site; specific
  trauma, e.g.,* Fractures.
  birth. *See* Birth injuries.
  cervical incompetence due to, 336
  macrocephaly due to, 1005, 1006f
  vascular
    to placenta, 456, 457f
      fetal, 458–459
      maternal, 458
      venous catheters causing, 689
Treacher Collins syndrome
  anesthetic implications of, 634t
  coloboma in, 570f, 571
Treatment, refusal of, 38

Tremors, neonatal, 960
Treponema pallidum
  associated with neonatal hepatitis, 459
  in placentitis, 459
  in sensorineural hearing loss, 1048
  in syphilis. *See* Syphilis.
Treponemal serologic tests, 824
Triangular cord sign, in biliary atresia, 723, 723f
Trichiasis, 1722
2,4,5-Trichlorophenoxyacetic acid, maternal exposure to, pregnancy outcome in, 260t
Trichomonas infections, premature labor related to, 431
Trichophyton infections, 835
Trichosporon infections, 836
Trichothiodystrophy, 1694t
Tricuspid valve
  atresia of, 1226–1227, 1226f
  regurgitation of, in persistent pulmonary hypertension, 1246
Tricyclic antidepressants, fetal effects of, 187t
Trigeminal nerve, assessment of, 525
Triglycerides
  in breast milk, 666
  in intravenous lipid emulsions, 686, 686t
  long-chain, 665
  medium-chain, 665
Trigonocephaly, 1010, 1010f
Triiodothyronine (T$_3$)
  free, 1528–1529
    serum values for, 1534t
  in breast milk, 1533
  in euthyroid sick syndrome, 1544–1545
  in transient neonatal hypothyroidism, 1543
  measurement of, 1528
  normal range for, 1535t
  reverse, 1528
    fetal serum levels of, 1532
  secretion of, 1526
  serum concentration of, 1807t
  serum protein binding of, 1526
  serum values for, 1534t
  synthesis of, 1526
Trimethadione, fetal effects of, 187t
Trimethoprim with sulfamethoxazole
  for gastroenteritis, 813
  for pneumocystis pneumonia, 838
  for urinary tract infections, in spinal cord injury, 549
Trinucleotide repeat expansions, in genetic disorders, 126–127
Triplets, Hellin-Zellany rule for, 375
Triploidy, 116
Trisomy(ies), 115
  autosomal, 116, 117f
  common types of, 563, 565
  increased nuchal translucency associated with, 155
Trisomy 8, sandal line furrows in, 575, 576f
Trisomy 13 (Patau syndrome)
  heart defects associated with, 1203, 1203t
  holoprosencephaly in, 568, 569f
  ocular manifestation of, 1727
  postaxial polydactyly in, 577, 577f
  prevalence of, 563
  scalp lesions in, 568, 568f
Trisomy 16, occurrence of, 563
Trisomy 18 (Edward syndrome)
  anesthetic implications of, 634t
  dolicocephaly in, 568, 569f

Trisomy 18 (Edward syndrome)—*cont'd*
  heart defects associated with, 1203, 1203t
  ocular manifestation of, 1727–1728
  prevalence of, 563
  rocker-bottom feet in, 577f
Trisomy 21 (Down syndrome)
  anesthetic implications of, 633t
  duodenal atresia associated with, 1391
  endocardial cushion defects in, 1239
  epicanthal folds in, 570, 570f
  excessive skinfolds in, 573
  features of, 116, 116f
  heart defects associated with, 1203, 1203t
  imperforate anus in, 1399–1400
  in congenital hypothyroidism, 1538
  interdigital furrow in, 575, 576f
  leukemoid reaction in, 1314–1315
  ocular manifestation of, 1728
  palmar and phalangeal creases in, 575, 576f
  palpebral fissure in, 570, 570f
  prenatal screening for, 136
  prevalence of, 517, 517t, 563, 565
  risk of, in multiple gestations, 377
  syndactyly in, 577, 578f
Trochlear nerve, palsy of, birth-related, 539
Trophoblast, in embryonic development, 207
Trophotropism, placental, 460
Truncometry, in intrauterine growth restriction diagnosis, 292, 293f
Truncus arteriosus
  anatomy and pathophysiology of, 1229–1230
  clinical presentation of, 1230
  defects associated with, 1230
  laboratory evaluation of, 1230
  management of, 1230–1231
  prognosis in, 1230–1231
Trypsinogen deficiency, primary, 1367
Tuberculin-sensitive mothers
  management of infants of, 827–828, 828t
  transfer of immunity in breast milk of, 790
Tuberculosis
  clinical manifestations of, 826–827
  diagnosis of, 827
  incidence of, 826
  microbiology of, 826
  pathogenesis and pathology of, 826, 826t
  perinatal transmission of, 826, 826t
  treatment of, 827, 827t
    for asymptomatic infants of PPD-positive mothers, 827–828, 828t
Tuberous sclerosis
  café-au-lait macules in, 1704
  epilepsy associated with, 973
  macrencephaly associated with, 997, 997f
  white macules in, 1706
Tubular heart, 1198–1200
Tubular myelin, in surfactant, 1081
Tubular necrosis, acute. *See* Renal tubular necrosis, acute.
Tufting enteropathy, 1372
Tumor(s). *See also specific tumor.*
  cardiac, 1250, 1250f
  eyelid, 1730–1731
  intranasal, 1147–1148
  neonatal, 1342–1344
  orbital, 1734–1736
  placental, 460–461
  renal, 1680–1681
  risk of development of, in Y-positive gonadal dysgenesis, 1564, 1570

Tumor(s)—*cont'd*
  vasoactive intestinal polypeptide-secreting, 1370
Tumor necrosis factor-α
  as predictor of insulin sensitivity, in pregnancy, 322
  as predictor of preterm labor, 342
  biology of, 775
  in amniotic fluid, during labor, 333
Tumor necrosis factor-β, biology of, 775
Turner syndrome (45,XO syndrome), 115–116
  anesthetic implications of, 634t
  excessive skinfolds in, 573, 574f
  fetal growth in, 287
  gonadal dysgenesis in, 1568–1570, 1569b, 1569f
  heart defects associated with, 1203t
  lymphedema of hands and feet in, 575, 577f
  nonimmune hydrops fetalis due to, 421
  ocular manifestation of, 1728
  prevalence of, 563
Twin(s). *See also* Multiple gestations.
  assessment of amniotic fluid volume in, 413, 413f
  birthweight discordance in, 379–380
    mortality and, 380
  diamniotic monochorionic, placental insufficiency in, 285–286, 286f
  dizygotic, 145, 375
  growth discrepancy of, in twin-twin transfusion syndrome, 250
  Hellin-Zellany rule for, 375
  monozygotic, 145, 375
  post-term, 387
  preeclampsia-eclampsia and, 312
  structural defects in, 376t
  vascular anastomosis in, 460
Twin oligohydramnios-polyhydramnios sequence (TOPS), 413
Twin reversed arterial perfusion sequence, 377, 377t
  surgical treatment of, 234t, 249
Twin-twin transfusion syndrome, 145
  amniotic septostomy for, 250
  diagnosis of, 250
  fetoscopic laser therapy for, 250–251
  in multiple gestations, 377, 378–379
    pathology of, 378
    treatment of, 378, 379t
  incidence of, 1297
  natural history of, 250
  serial amnioreduction for, 250
  surgical treatment of, 234t, 249–252
Tympanic membrane, in mechanism of hearing, 1045
Tympanometry, in evaluation of hearing, 1047
Tyrosinase deficiency, in albinism, 1705
Tyrosine, in parenteral amino acid solutions, 684–685, 684t
Tyrosinemia, 1605t
  hepatic dysfunction in, 1621

U

UFD1 gene, in neural crest cell abnormalities, 1201
UGT activity, in drug metabolism, 194
UGT1A1 gene, mutations of, 1432
Ulegyria, in hypoxic-ischemic encephalopathy, 941

Ultrasonography
antenatal. *See* Antenatal ultrasonography.
of adrenal glands, 726–727
of adrenal hemorrhage, 726, 726f
of autosomal recessive polycystic kidney
disease, 725
of biliary atresia, 722–723, 723f
of brain, 727–729
of choledochal cyst, 723, 723f
of congenital heart defects, 1208
of developmental dysplasia of hip, 1775
of duodenal atresia, 157, 157f, 1391
of germinal matrix hemorrhage, 727f,
727–728, 728f
of hepatobiliary tract, 722–724, 723f
of hypertrophic pyloric stenosis, 1389,
1389f
of intersex disorders, 1561–1562
of intraventricular hemorrhage, 926f–928f,
930f
of lenticulostriate vasculopathy, 728–729,
729f
of midgut volvulus, 1394
of multicystic dysplastic kidney, 725, 725f
of neonatal kidney, 724, 724f
of neonatal osteomyelitis, 729–730
of nephrocalcinosis, 726, 726f
of neuroblastoma, 727
of obstructive uropathy, 724–725, 725f
of periventricular-intraventricular
hemorrhage, 929, 930f
of periventricular leukomalacia, 728, 728f,
729f
of renal vein thrombosis, 725–726, 1675
of Rh isoimmunization, 397–398, 398f,
399t
prediction of anemia in, 398–400, 400f,
400t
of spinal cord injury, 549
of urinary tract, 724–726
of white matter injury, 917–918, 917f,
918b
perinatal. *See* Perinatal ultrasonography.
transvaginal
in assessment of cervix length, 347
in preterm labor prediction, 343–344
Umbilical artery
catheterization of
for blood gas assessment, in respiratory
distress syndrome, 1102
thromboembolism related to, 1670,
1674
Doppler flow velocimetry of, 170, 170f
in fetus, 416f
in post-term neonate, 385t
in fetal circulation, 483, 484f
single, 163, 163f
examination of, 519
Umbilical cord
delivery and clamping of, interval
between, hematocrit values and,
1291, 1293
hemorrhage from, 1296
ligation of, for twin reversed arterial
perfusion sequence, 249
two-vessel, perinatal ultrasonography of,
163, 163f, 164f
Umbilical cord blood
hematologic values for, 1810t
samples of
autologous collection of, 1347–1348
conjugated hyperbilirubinemia in,
1428
for coagulation factor assays, 1325

Umbilical cord blood—*cont'd*
in intrauterine growth restriction
diagnosis, 291
in prenatal genetic evaluation, 138
reticulocyte count in, 1293
Umbilical hernia, examination of, 517
Umbilical vein
blood samples from, in fetal platelet
count assessment, 368
catheterization of
conjugated hyperbilirubinemia
associated with, 1461
for cardiovascular drugs, in neonatal
resuscitation, 502
flow velocity of, in prediction of
hemolytic anemia, 399
in fetal circulation, 483–484, 484f
plasma glucose concentration in, 1469
Umbilical vein to maternal vein ratio, as
measure of placental drug transfer, 470,
470t, 478
Umbilicus
infection prevention in, 829
inflammation of, 817–818
Uncertainty, and withholding of life-
sustaining treatment, 40
Uniform Bill (UB 92), in neonatal care
evaluation database, 69–70, 72
Uniparental disomy, 126
United Children's Fund, 88, 89t
Upper airway lesions, 1146–1155
Upper extremity. *See also* Hand(s).
congenital anomalies of, 1767–1770
Upper gastrointestinal radiography
of gastric volvulus, 1386, 1386f
of microgastria, 1386, 1386f
of midgut volvulus, 1394, 1394f
of pyloric atresia, 1386–1387, 1388f
Urea clearance, in placenta, 284, 285f
Urea cycle
defects of, 1605t–1606t
hepatic dysfunction in, 1621
hyperammonemia and, 1650–1651
disorders of, laboratory findings in,
1602t
Ureteropelvic junction obstruction
in hydronephrosis, 1677
ultrasonography of, 160, 160f, 724–725,
725f
Ureterovesical junction obstruction, in
hydronephrosis, 1677–1678
Ureters
dilated, 161f
duplicated, 160, 161f
Urethra
birth injury to, 556
development of, 1662–1663, 1663f
opening of, examination of, 1559
Urethral valves, posterior
fetal surgery for, 234t
in hydronephrosis, 1678
obstructive uropathy and, 233–234
ultrasonography of, 160, 160f
voiding cystourethrography of, 724–725,
725f
Uric acid test, for inborn errors of
metabolism, 1630
Uridine diphosphoglucuronate
glucuronosyltranferase
activity of, 1425–1426, 1426f
in bilirubin conjugation, 1422, 1423f
Urinalysis
in congenital cytomegalovirus infection,
846

Urinalysis—*cont'd*
in evaluation of hypertensive pregnant
patient, 317
in renal disease, 1666
Urinary bladder. *See* Bladder.
Urinary tract. *See also specific part.*
congenital malformations of, 1675–1678,
1675t
development of, 1659–1664
infection of
during pregnancy, 429–432
in spinal cord injury, treatment of, 549
neonatal, 815–816
ultrasonography of, 724–726
Urination, delay of, in renal function
assessment, 1666
Urine
blood in, 1667
chemistry of, in fetal obstructive uropathy,
235–236
concentration and dilution of, in
developing kidney, 1663t, 1664
culture of, for sepsis, 795
fetal output of, in amniotic fluid
regulation, 410
formation of, water in, 699
glucose in, 1667–1668
heme-containing compounds in, in renal
disease, 1666
osmolality of, in developing kidney,
1663t, 1664
protein in, 1667
specific gravity of, in renal disease, 1666
toxicologic testing of, for drugs, 734
Urine tests, for inborn errors of metabolism,
1630, 1630t, 1631t
Urokinase
dosages of, 1789
for thrombosis, 1334t, 1336
Uropathy, obstructive, 233–237
hydronephrosis in, 234, 235f
oligohydramnios with, 236
prenatal diagnosis of, 234–236, 235f
prenatal treatment of, 236–237
ultrasonography of, 235, 235f, 724–725,
725f
urine chemistry in, 235–236
Ursodeoxycholic acid, for cholestasis, 688
Urticaria, neonatal. *See* Erythema toxicum.
Urticaria pigmentosa, 1712
Usher syndrome, hearing loss associated
with, 1049
Uterine cervix. *See* Cervix.
Uteroplacental circulation
abnormalities of, in intrauterine growth
restriction pregnancies, 286, 286t
vasomotor regulation of, in preeclampsia-
eclampsia, 308–309
Uteroplacental insufficiency,
oligohydramnios and, 414
Uteroplacental underperfusion, chronic, 456,
458
Uterus
abnormalities of, in preterm delivery,
335–336
activity of
home monitoring of, 344–345
in preterm labor prediction, 340
blood flow in
in preeclampsia-eclampsia, 310t,
310–311
regulation of, 308
fetal positioning in, musculoskeletal
abnormalities due to, 1758

Uterus—*cont'd*
  rupture of
    anesthetic considerations in, 479–480
    in vaginal delivery, after cesarean
      section, 479

V

Vaccine(s)
  Bacille Calmette-Guérin, 828
  for hepatitis B, 440–441, 865–866
  for measles, 852
  for rubella virus infection, 872–873
  in utero, in prevention of fetal infections,
    214–215, 215b
  thimerosal in, 866
VACTERL association
  anomalies in, 561
  congenital heart disease in, 1205
  in esophageal atresia/tracheoesophageal
    fistula, 1373
    Adriamycin-treated rat model of, 1374
    evaluation of, 1375
  in multicystic dysplastic kidney, 1676
  in omphalocele, 1382
  in renal agenesis, 1675
  in renal dysplasia, 1676
VACTERL complex, 157
Vagal maneuvers
  for neonatal tachycardia, 1261b,
    1263–1264
  for supraventricular tachycardia, 1254
Vagina
  development of, 1554
  opening of, examination of, 1559
Vaginal discharge, neonatal, examination of,
  517
Vaginal dysgenesis, 1585–1586
Vaginal hemorrhage, in preterm delivery,
  336
Vaginosis, bacterial
  as risk factor, for preterm labor, 431
  during pregnancy, 432
  in preterm delivery, 339
Vagus nerve
  assessment of, 525
  birth injury to, vocal cord paralysis related
    to, 540
Valproic acid, fetal effects of, 187t
Valvotomy
  for aortic stenosis, 1233
  for pulmonary atresia, 1227
  for pulmonary stenosis, 1238
Valvuloplasty, balloon. *See* Balloon
  valvuloplasty.
Vancomycin
  dosages of, 1789
  for mastitis, 818
  for meningitis, 807
  for necrotizing enterocolitis, 1405
  for omphalitis, 818
  for osteomyelitis and septic arthritis, 814
  for sepsis, 800, 801t, 803t
  for urinary tract infections, 816
Vanishing testes syndrome, 1572
Vanishing twin syndrome, 378
Varicella-zoster immune globulin, 848, 849
Varicella-zoster virus infections, 435–436,
  847–849
  clinical manifestations of, 848
  congenital syndrome of, 848
  cutaneous, 1699, 1699t

Varicella-zoster virus infections—*cont'd*
  diagnosis of, 849
  epidemiology and transmission of,
    847–848
  fetal, 435
  in pregnancy, 435–436, 848
  neonatal, 435–436, 435t
  perinatal, 848–849
  prevention of, 436, 849
  treatment of, 849
Vasa praevia, ultrasonography of, 147, 148f
Vascular endothelial growth factor
  in preeclampsia-eclampsia, 311
  in retinopathy of prematurity, 1751
Vascular injury
  to placenta, 456, 457f
    fetal, 458–459
    maternal, 458
  venous catheters causing, 689
Vascular malformations, 1706, 1707t,
  1708–1709
Vascular necrosis, meconium-associated, 462
Vascular resistance
  intestinal, 1407
  pulmonary. *See* Pulmonary vascular
    resistance.
  systemic
    afterload management and, 1267
    in preeclampsia, anesthetic
      considerations in, 479
Vascular rings, 1250–1251
Vascular system, development of, in brain,
  900
Vasculopathy, thrombotic, fetal, 459
Vasoactive intestinal polypeptide
  (VIP)–secreting tumors, secretory
  diarrhea due to, 1370
Vasodilators. *See also* Nitric oxide.
  for afterload reduction, in congenital heart
    disease, 1267
  for bronchopulmonary dysplasia,
    1166–1167
VATER association
  anesthetic implications of, 634t
  anomalies in, 561
  imperforate anus in, 574
  spinal defects in, 1758
Vater-Pacini corpuscles, 1689
Vecuronium
  dosages of, 1792
  in neonatal anesthesia, 640
Vein of Galen, malformation of, 1244
  macrocephaly due to, 1004–1005
Velocardiofacial syndrome, single gene
  defects in, 1204
Velocity of circumferential fiber shortening,
  ventricular, 1213
Vena cava
  abnormalities of, fetal assessment of, 1208
  inferior, interrupted (absent hepatic
    segment of), 1243
Venereal Disease Research Laboratory
  (VDRL) test, for syphilis, 824
Venous thrombosis
  catheter-related, 1331
  causes of, 1332
  risk factors for, 1332, 1332t
Ventilation
  assisted. *See* Assisted ventilation.
  continuous positive airway pressure. *See*
    Continuous positive airway pressure
    (CPAP).
  during chest compressions, 502
  liquid, 1118

Ventilation—*cont'd*
  mechanical. *See* Mechanical ventilation.
  positive pressure. *See* Positive pressure
    ventilation.
Ventilation-perfusion (V/Q) ratio
  in arterial oxygen tension, 1089–1090
  mismatch of
    hypercapnia due to, 1110
    hypoxemia due to, 1111
    in bronchopulmonary dysplasia, 1163
Ventilators, on anesthesia machines,
  636–637
Ventricle(s)
  cardiac
    compliance of, 1214
    diastolic function of, 1214
      echocardiographic measurement of,
        1219, 1220b
      hypertrophy of, electrocardiography of,
        1218
    hypoplasia of, fetal assessment of, 1208
    premature contractions of, fetal
      assessment for, 1209
    right
      cor pulmonale and, 1243
      double-outlet, 1231–1232
    septal defect of. *See* Ventricular septal
      defect.
    septation of, 1198
    single, 1229, 1231
      anesthetic considerations in, 635
      surgical treatment of, 1231
    systolic function of, 1213–1214
      echocardiographic measurement of,
        1219, 1219t
      ejection fraction in, 1213
      peak developed pressure in, 1213
      regional wall motion in, 1214
      shortening fraction in, 1213
      stroke volume and cardiac output in,
        1213
      velocity of circumferential fiber
        shortening in, 1213
      wall stress in, 1213–1214
    wall thickness of, 1212
  cerebral
    fourth, cystic transformation of,
      999–1000, 1000f
    hemorrhage into, 925–926, 927f
    posthemorrhagic dilation of, 925, 930
    ultrasonography of, 152, 153f
Ventricular premature contractions, 1259
  treatment of, 1265
Ventricular septal defect, 1238–1239
  anatomy and pathophysiology of, 1238
  clinical presentation of, 1238–1239
  defects associated with, 1238
  fetal assessment of, 1208
  hemodynamics of, 1212
  in double-outlet right ventricle, 1232
  in left heart defects, 1237
  in transposition of great arteries, 1223
  laboratory evaluation of, 1239
  management of, 1239
  prognosis in, 1239
Ventricular septal hypertrophy, in infant of
  diabetic mother, 1475
Ventricular tachycardia, 1257, 1258f
  treatment of, 1264
Ventriculoamniotic shunts, 231–232
Ventriculomegaly
  definition of, 152
  lemon and banana signs in, 153, 153f
  posthemorrhagic, 1001, 1001f

Ventriculomegaly—*cont'd*
  ultrasonography of, 152, 152f, 153f, 728
  vs. hydrocephalus, 152, 1001–1002
Ventriculoperitoneal shunts, for
    hydrocephalus, 1002
Verapamil, for neonatal tachycardia, 1262b
Vermont Oxford Network
  neonatal care data compiled by, 73–74
  NIC/Q and iNICQ collaboratives of, 76, 77f
  prediction of length of stay, 73
  quality improvement methods of, 75–76
  standardized mortality ratio calculation of,
    67–68, 68f
Vernix caseosa
  biology of, 1688
  in small for gestational age infant, 297
Vertebrae
  anomalies of
    perinatal ultrasonography of, 155, 155f
    spinal anomalies associated with, 1758
  cervical, 1756
  missing, in imperforate anus, 1400
Vertebral body, development of, 1756
Very-long-chain acyl-CoA dehydrogenase
    deficiency, 1610t
Very low birthweight. *See also* Extremely
    low birthweight; Low birthweight.
  candidiasis in, 830–831, 831b
  definition of, 19
  hypocalcemia in, 1510
  idiopathic neutropenia and, 1312
  in multiple gestations, 379
    outcome in, 381
  iron parameters in, 1811t
  neutrophil reference ranges in, 1812f
  outcome of
    factors affecting, 1035b
    school-age, 1041, 1041f
  physiologic skeletal changes in, 1508,
    1508f
  platelet parameters in, 1814t
  sepsis in, 792–793, 792t
  white blood cell parameters in, 1814t
Vesicoamniotic shunts, 232
  for obstructive uropathy, 236–237
Vesicobullous eruptions, 1697–1703
Vesicostomy, open, for obstructive uropathy,
    237
Vesicoureteral reflux, in hydronephrosis,
    1678
VIA-LVM blood gas monitoring system, 622f,
    622–623
Video display terminals, maternal exposure
    to, pregnancy outcome in, 260t
Villitis, 459
  of unknown etiology, 458, 460
Villus
  atrophy of
    in autoimmune enteropathy, 1372
    in microvillus inclusion disease, 1371
  chorionic. *See* Chorionic villus.
  duodenal, 1361
  intestinal, 1362
Vinyl chlorides, maternal exposure to,
    pregnancy outcome in, 260t
Viral infection(s). *See also specific infection.*
  cutaneous, 1698–1699, 1699f
  natural killer cells in control of, 769
  perinatal, 432–442, 840–876
Virchow's triad, in thrombus formation, 1332
Virilization, 21-hydroxylase deficiency and,
    1578, 1578f
Virucidal wash, for HIV transmission
    prevention, 860

Viscous drag, in blood pressure monitoring,
    614
Vision
  in environment of light, 602–603
  screening of, in neonate, 521
Visual acuity
  docosahexaenoic acid and arachidonic
    acid supplementation in, 666–667
  neonatal, assessment of, 1724
Visual evoked potentials, 1724
  in hypoxic-ischemic encephalopathy,
    947–948
Vital capacity, measurement of, 1093
Vitamin(s)
  fat-soluble, 668
  fetal effects of, 188t
  for acidemia, 1639
  for inborn errors of metabolism,
    1652–1653
  for respiratory chain defect, 1645
  in breast milk, 672t
  in enteral nutrition, 667–669, 668t
  in infant formula, 673t–674t
  in parenteral nutrition, 687, 689t
  supplemental
    for preterm infants, 675
    for term infants, 674–675
  water-soluble, 667–668
Vitamin A
  congenital malformations associated with,
    186t
  deficiency of, in bronchopulmonary
    dysplasia, 1162, 1166
  dosages of, 1792
  fetal effects of, 188t
  in breast milk, 672t
  in bronchopulmonary dysplasia
    prevention, 1121
  in infant formula, 673t
  requirements for, 668, 668t
Vitamin B
  in breast milk, 672t
  in infant formula, 674t
  requirements for, 668, 668t
Vitamin B_1, for respiratory chain defect, 1645
Vitamin B_2, for respiratory chain defect, 1645
Vitamin B_6
  deficiency of, seizures associated with,
    971
  for seizures, 974
Vitamin C
  for methemoglobinemia, 1309
  for respiratory chain defect, 1645
  in breast milk, 672t
  in infant formula, 674t
  requirements for, 667, 668t
Vitamin D
  activation pathway of, immaturity of, 1503
  daily supplements of, during pregnancy,
    1502, 1512
  deficiency of. *See* Rickets.
  disorders of, hypocalcemia due to, 1512
  effects of, in calcium and phosphorus
    homeostasis, 1502
  fetal, 1502
  for breast-fed term infants, 674–675
  for hypocalcemia, with rickets, 1513
  for hypoparathyroidism, 1513–1514
  in breast milk, 672t
  in infant formula, 673t
  metabolism of, 1502
  neonatal, 1502–1503, 1503f
  reference values for, 1503
  requirements for, 668, 668t

Vitamin D—*cont'd*
  role of
    in calcium transport, 1494
    in fetal physiology, 1493
  secretion of, regulation of, 1502
  synthesis of, 1502
Vitamin D_2, dosages of, 1792
Vitamin E
  deficiency of, hemolytic anemia in, 1302
  for periventricular-intraventricular
    hemorrhage, 932–933
  in breast milk, 672t
  in infant formula, 674t
  requirements for, 668t, 669
Vitamin K
  deficiency of
    antibiotics associated with, 1328
    coagulation effects of, 1324
    in hemorrhagic disease of newborn,
      1328
  for periventricular-intraventricular
    hemorrhage, 932
  in breast milk, 672t
  in infant formula, 674t
  requirements for, 668t, 669
Vitamin K epoxide reductase deficiency,
    dysmorphic features in, 1628–1629
Vitamin K_1
  dosages of, 1792
  for hemorrhagic disease of newborn, 1329
Vitamin K_3, for respiratory chain defect, 1645
Vitreoretinopathy, familial exudative, 1748
Vitreous
  hemorrhage of, due to birth injury, 539
  persistent hyperplastic primary, 1742
Vocal cords
  edema of, after extubation, 1119
  paralysis of
    birth-related, 540–541
    evaluation and treatment of, 1152–1153
Voiding, first, 1797t
Voiding cystourethrography, of posterior
    urethral valves, 724–725, 725f
Volatile acid, 704
Volume expanders, in neonatal resuscitation,
    503t, 504, 504b
Volutrauma, 1120
Volvulus
  gastric, 1385–1386, 1386f
  intestinal, vs. duodenal atresia, 1391
  midgut, 1393–1395
    radiography of, 1394, 1394f
    treatment of, 1394–1395
    ultrasonography of, 1394
    vs. duodenal atresia, 1391
Vomiting
  bilious, 719
    in midgut malrotation, 1394
  in gastrointestinal duplications, 1392
Von Gierke disease, 1647. *See also* Glycogen
    storage disease.
Von Willebrand disease, 1326–1327
  evaluation for, factor VIII deficiency and,
    1326
Von Willebrand factor, in hemostasis, 1318,
    1319–1320, 1319f

W

Waardenburg syndrome
  heterochromia associated with, 1739
  ocular manifestation of, 1706, 1729

WAGR syndrome, 1681
  WT1 gene mutation in, 1571
Waldhausen procedure, 1269t
Walker-Warburg syndrome, 984
Warfarin
  congenital malformations associated with,
    186t
  fetal effects of, 188t
  for thrombosis, 1335
  in breast milk, 199
Warm room, for heat loss prevention, 595
Water. *See also* Fluid(s).
  accumulation of, in gravid woman, 409
  as percentage of body weight, 695, 696f
  balance of
    in neonate, 697
    thyroid gland and, 1524
  in concurrent maternal exposure, 259
Water birth technique, 468–469
Water loss, 698t, 698–699, 699f
  from respiratory tract, 592t, 592–594, 593t,
    593f, 594f
    determination of, 587, 592
  from skin
    determination of, 586
    during first 4 postnatal weeks, 588
    in preterm infant, 1716
    humidity in, 698–699
  in congenital sodium diarrhea, 1369–1370
  in microvillus inclusion disease, 1371
  insensible
    during phototherapy, 1445
    oxygen consumption and, 592t
  temperature in, 698
  urinary, 699
Watershed injury, in hypoxic-ischemia, 939
Waterstone shunt, 1269t
Watery eye, 1733
Weaning, from mechanical ventilation,
    1116–1117, 1116t
  in bronchopulmonary dysplasia, 1164
Wechsler Intelligence Scale for Children-
    Revised (WISC-R), 1066, 1066f
  for high-risk neonate, 1040
Weight. *See* Birthweight; Extremely low
    birthweight; Fetal weight; Low
    birthweight; Very low birthweight.
Weight control, gestational diabetes mellitus
    and, 323
Weight gain
  in pregnancy
    fetal growth and, 280–282, 281f, 282b,
      282f
    limiting, 281–282
    prepregnancy vs. pregnancy, 280, 281f
Well-being, fetal. *See* Fetal well-being.
Werdnig-Hoffmann disease, 978
  respiratory distress related to, 1142
West Nile virus infection, 874
Wharton's jelly, 458
Whey-to-casein ratio
  in breast milk, 664
  in infant formula, 665
White Americans
  congenital anomaly prevalence in,
    565–566, 566t
  transient cutaneous lesions in, 1689b
White blood cells, in very low birthweight
    infants, 1814t
White macules, in tuberous sclerosis, 1706
White matter
  combined insults to, 917
  development of, 892–893, 893f–894f
    impairment in, 922–924, 922b, 924f

White matter—*cont'd*
  excitotoxicity and oxidative stress of,
    915–916, 916f
  hypofusion insults to, 913–914
  hypoxic-ischemic lesions of, 913–914, 914f
  infection/inflammation of, 914–915, 915f
  injury to
    long-term deficits associated with,
      922–924, 922b, 924f
    MR imaging of
      conventional T1- and T2-weighted,
        918–919, 918f–920f
      diffusion-weighted, 919, 921f–923f
    MR spectroscopy of, 921–922
    pathogenesis in, 912–917, 913f
    ultrasonography of, 917–918, 917f, 918b
  neuropathology of, 909–912
    axonal damage in, 912
    macroscopic, 910, 910f, 911f
    microglial activity in, 911–912
    microscopic, 910–911
    subplate damage in, 912, 912f
    vulnerability of oligodendroglia
      precursors in, 911
White pupil. *See* Pupil(s), white.
White's classification, of gestational diabetes
    mellitus, 321t
Williams syndrome
  anesthetic implications of, 634t
  elastin gene mutations in, 1195
  heart defects associated with, 1203t
  hypercalcemia and, 1516
  single gene defects in, 1204
Wilms' tumor, 1681
Wilms' tumor suppressor (*WT1*) gene
  in renal development, 1660–1661, 1660t
  mutation and deletion of, 1571
Wimberger sign, 729, 822, 823f
"Windsock" web, in pyloric atresia, 1387,
    1388
Winters formula, for buffering systems, 704
Wiskott-Aldrich syndrome, 1340
  vs. autoimmune enteropathy, 1372
Withholding or withdrawal of life-sustaining
    treatment
  ethical considerations in, 40–41
  legal considerations in, 57–59
Wolff-Parkinson-White syndrome
  accessory pathway reentrant tachycardia
    in, 1254–1255, 1255f
  reciprocating atrioventricular reentrant
    tachycardia in, 1254
Wolffian ducts, differentiation of, 1553
Wolman disease, hepatomegaly in, 1623
Work of breathing. *See* Breathing, work of.
World Health Organization, 88, 89t, 500
World Health Organization classification, of
    health and functional outcome, in high-
    risk neonates, 1040
Wrist, congenital anomalies of, 1767–1769
Wrongful birth, 55
Wrongful death, 55
Wrongful life, 55

X

X chromosome, 113
  abnormalities of, 1568–1570, 1569b, 1569f
  genetic disorders linked to, 124
  inactivation of, 124
  mosaicism of, 1569
    forms of, 1568

X-linked adrenoleukodystrophy, 1628
  pharmacogenetic approach to, 1654
X-linked adrenoleukodystrophy–related
    protein, 1654
X-linked dominant inheritance, of genetic
    disorders, 123, 123f
X-linked genes, in sex differentiation, 1551,
    1551f
X-linked ichthyosis, 1694t, 1695–1696
X-linked periventricular heterotopia,
    906–907, 906f
X-linked recessive inheritance, of genetic
    disorders, 123, 123f
X-linked severe combined
    immunodeficiency (X-SCID), defective
    T cell development in, 780–781
X-linked thrombocytopenia, 1341
Xanthine oxidase, in oxidative stress, 498
Xanthine therapy. *See also*
    Methylxanthines.
  for apnea, 1139
  hypocalcemia due to, 1512
Xanthogranuloma, juvenile, 1711–1712
Xenobiotics, 256
  in follicular fluid, 256t
Xeroderma pigmentosum, 1705
45,XO syndrome. *See* Turner syndrome
    (45,XO syndrome).
XX gonadal dysgenesis, 1570
XX male, 1572–1573
47,XXY syndrome. *See* Klinefelter syndrome
    (47,XXY syndrome).
XY gonadal agenesis, 1572
XY gonadal dysgenesis, 1570–1571
  SOX9 gene mutation in, 1571
XY neonate, with small phallus, gender
    assignment in, 1562, 1564
Xylene, maternal exposure to, pregnancy
    outcome in, 260t

Y

Y chromosome, 113
  abnormalities of, 1570–1571
  genetic disorders linked to, 124
    differential diagnosis of, 1563f
  in sex differentiation, 1551
Yacoub procedure, for transposition of great
    arteries, 1224
Yolk sac
  hematopoiesis in, 1290–1291, 1287
  in first-trimester studies, 145, 145f
Yp gonadal dysgenesis, 1570
Yu-cheng disease, 257
Yusho disease, 202, 257

Z

Zellweger syndrome, 908, 994f
  anesthetic implications of, 634t
  conjugated hyperbilirubinemia in, 1461
  dysmorphic features in, 1628
Zidovudine
  for HIV prophylaxis
    CDC recommendations on, 857–858
    in developed countries, 857–859
    in developing countries, 859
    short course of, 859
  in prevention of vertical HIV transmission,
    214, 434

Zidovudine—*cont'd*
  with lamivudine, for HIV prophylaxis, 858, 859, 860
Zinc
  deficiency of, in acrodermatitis enteropathica, 1370, 1702–1703, 1703f

Zinc—*cont'd*
  in breast milk, 671t
  in enteral nutrition, 670t
  in infant formula, 673t
  in parenteral nutrition, 687, 688t, 1703
  serum concentration of, 1802t

Zinc finger proteins, in cardiogenesis, 1198
Zona pellucida, in embryonic development, 207
Zygodactyly, 1781